PSYCHOLOGY

Pearson

At Pearson, we have a simple mission: to help people make more of their lives through learning.

We combine innovative learning technology with trusted content and educational expertise to provide engaging and effective learning experiences that serve people wherever and whenever they are learning.

From classroom to boardroom, our curriculum materials, digital learning tools and testing programmes help to educate millions of people worldwide – more than any other private enterprise.

Every day our work helps learning flourish, and wherever learning flourishes, so do people.

To learn more, please visit us at **www.pearson.com/uk**

SIXTH EDITION

PSYCHOLOGY

G. NEIL MARTIN
Regent's University London, UK

NEIL R. CARLSON
University of Massachusetts, USA

Pearson

Harlow, England • London • New York • Boston • San Francisco • Toronto • Sydney • Dubai • Singapore • Hong Kong
Tokyo • Seoul • Taipei • New Delhi • Cape Town • São Paulo • Mexico City • Madrid • Amsterdam • Munich • Paris • Milan

PEARSON EDUCATION LIMITED
KAO Two
KAO Park
Harlow CM17 9NA
United Kingdom
Tel: +44 (0)1279 623623
Web: www.pearson.com/uk

First published in 2000 (print)
Second edition published in 2004 (print)
Third edition published in 2007 (print)
Fourth edition published in 2010 (print)
Fifth edition published in 2013 (print and electronic)
Sixth edition published in 2019 (print and electronic)

© Pearson Education Limited 2000, 2004, 2007, 2010 (print)
© Pearson Education Limited 2013, 2019 (print and electronic)

ISBN: 978-1-292-09058-0 (print)
        978-1-292-09063-4 (PDF)
        978-1-292-20199-3 (ePub)

British Library Cataloguing-in-Publication Data
A catalogue record for the print edition is available from the British Library

Library of Congress Cataloging-in-Publication Data
Names: Martin, G. Neil, author. | Carlson, Neil R., 1942-author. | Buskist,
   William, author.
Title: Psychology / G. Neil Martin, Regent's University London, UK, Neil R.
   Carlson, University of Massachusetts, USA, William Buskist, Auburn
   University, USA.
Description: Sixth Edition. | New York : Pearson, [2019] | Revised edition of
   the authors' Psychology, 2013.
Identifiers: LCCN 2017050948 | ISBN 9781292090580 (print) | ISBN 9781292090634
   (pdf) | ISBN 9781292201993 (epub)
Subjects: LCSH: Psychology.
Classification: LCC BF121 .M374 2018 | DDC 150–dc23

LC record available at https://lccn.loc.gov/2017050948

10 9 8 7 6 5 4 3 2 1
23 22 21 20 19

Front cover image © Andrzej Wojcicki/Science Photo Library/Getty Images

Print edition typeset in 9.75/12pt Sabon MT Pro by SPi-Global
Printed in Italy by L.E.G.O. S.p.A. Lavis (TN)

NOTE THAT ANY PAGE CROSS REFERENCES REFER TO THE PRINT EDITION

Brief contents

Contents

Preface to the sixth edition

Welcome to the sixth edition of *Psychology*. The previous edition of the textbook was published way back in 2013, and then it was a different world: the idea of Donald Trump as US President was as fanciful and bizarre as the idea of the UK voting to leave the European Union. And then the UK voted to leave the European Union. The UK got its second female Prime Minister, and the revision of the biggest diagnostic manual for diagnosing mental illness was published. In 2013, Psychology was dealing with the challenges and difficulties of being a behavioural science in the way that Psychology always has done, and then it encountered a self-inflicted crisis: the replication crisis. This was the finding that some very well-known, novel and famous studies in psychology could not be repeated with the same results. It was a very different world back then.

But some things do not change. Psychology is as exciting and as vibrant as ever. Even the replication crisis – which is not genuinely a crisis – is evidence that Psychology, of all the sciences, is putting its house in order and making sure that the findings it produces are genuine, valid and can be found in study after study. (Pharmacology and Biomedical sciences are still struggling with their issues.)

Psychology is the scientific study of why and how humans (and animals) behave in the way that they do. Being a science, it approaches the understanding of behaviour in a specific way. Everyone has an opinion on psychology and on what motivates people and what brings people to react and behave in the way that they do. We are all quasi-psychologists, in a way. Trained psychologists, however, attempt to understand behaviour through careful experimentation and empirical observation. They do this because it is the best method of gaining useful and reliable information about behaviour and the causes of behaviour. This book, the sixth edition of *Psychology*, introduces you to the scientific approach to understanding human behaviour and each chapter reviews the current state of knowledge about behaviour – from intelligence and emotion to child development and prejudice – based on sound scientific study.

Of all the reasons you are reading this book, the most likely is because it was recommended on your psychology course or because you spotted it in the library or bookshop and thought that it would enhance your understanding of people's behaviour. As a student of psychology, you are studying the most fascinating and complex subject matter in science – human behaviour. You study not just how individuals develop language, perceive visual images, reason, feel, respond to others and learn, but also the biological bases of these behaviours. You will learn about the various methods that psychologists adopt when studying behaviour and how people evolved to do the things that they do (although scientists do have disagreements over the best method of study to adopt – the one certain fact you will learn in psychology is that no finding is ever 'cut and dried', there is always discussion and controversy).

Psychology is one of the most popular degree courses in Europe and in North America – it is one of the top three degree subjects in the UK, based on student applications to study. Over 54,000 students study psychology at undergraduate level in the UK alone. The subject matter is intrinsically interesting and its study allows students to develop what are called, in education jargon, 'transferable skills' – intelligent use of IT, writing laboratory reports, critical thinking, oral, presentational and written skills, statistical analysis, statistical software package expertise, project design, effective communication . . . all of these, in addition to understanding human behaviour such as how children learn to read, why we perceive in the way that we do, how we influence others, how the brain works, how we reason and so on.

The sixth edition – pedagogical features

The sixth edition of *Psychology* is designed to give you a flavour of what modern psychology is about. It describes every major field of psychology and includes up-to-date information and clear evaluation of controversial findings, theories and models in psychology.

It addresses the issue of replication throughout and in each chapter you will encounter a reference to the importance of repeating the study which has produced an unusual finding so that this unusual finding can be tested and we can determine whether it is valid and real.

One of the best ways to learn about psychology is to keep abreast of new developments in the field. As a beginning student, you clearly need to know and understand the basics, but you also need to know how those basic findings are being modified and challenged. This edition contains over 1,000 new references, reflecting the extensive nature of the updated content and its emphasis on presenting you with up-to-date information from the psychology research literature (it also reflects how prolific psychologists are).

This edition, like the previous five, has several features to help you understand the applications and controversies in psychology and to make you think more deeply about psychological issues and psychological research. Here's a brief summary:

An international perspective

Every chapter has a section headed 'An International Perspective', which allows you to see how psychology is, and has been, studied across nations and cultures. An important issue in psychological research is whether findings are universal or specific to a group being studied. If you find that someone behaves in a particular way in one group in one culture or country, would a similar person behave in the same way, under the same conditions in another culture or country? This section provides an international perspective on topics such as happiness, personality, brain research, memory, cannabis use, infidelity, language and brain activation, prejudice, eating disorders, mental illness and many others.

Cutting edge

The Cutting Edge sections review a recent study or series of studies that are novel, important or make a really significant contribution to our knowledge and understanding of psychology. Some of the new Cutting Edge sections in this edition include: the effect of social networks on pain perception; is neuroimaging stressful?; what we know and don't know about sexual orientation; how much do people know about memory?; does listening to sexually degrading lyrics lead to endorsement of sexual stereotypes?; do we underestimate people's likelihood of complying?; can multimedia stories help children's literacy?; are we getting brighter? and so on. There are 64 new Cutting Edge sections in this edition.

Controversies in psychological science

Each chapter contains at least one section which focuses on a controversy in psychological science. The best advice I was given by one of my tutors as an undergraduate was, 'question everything'. By this, he did not mean criticising studies or theories for the sake of it. He meant that psychology was a live, constantly evolving science which, like all sciences, progresses by contradiction: somebody reports a finding; another refines this finding by showing that it applies only to certain contexts, people, conditions and so on. Most introductory texts can appear biblical: unquestionable towers of knowledge. But, although a great deal of fact is presented in this text, it also shows you how facts can be interpreted in different ways.

The sections that deal with this explicitly are the Controversies in Psychological Science (CPS) sections, which are made up of three parts. The first part (the issue) outlines the controversy; the second part (the evidence) describes and evaluates the data that give rise to the controversy; finally, the third part (conclusion) briefly suggests what we can conclude from the evidence available. One aim of the Controversies in Psychological Science sections is to engage you in critical thinking by presenting you with a controversial topic, theme or idea in psychology and then taking you through evidence for and against a topic, theme or idea. Some of these controversies include: Does our language influence our visual perception? Is psychology common sense? Does the weather influence mood and thinking? Can neuroimaging methods detect deception? Are there universally attractive body types? Can the brain create new neurons? Do learning styles exist? Oxytocin and trustworthiness. Does brain training work in healthy individuals? Do Davids and Denices die sooner? And so on. The material covered in the Controversies sections will give you a hint of the liveliness of debate surrounding some issues in psychology and could form the basis of discussion with your fellow students or with colleagues in tutorials or seminars.

Psychology in action

Research in psychology is aimed at exploring, defining and predicting the causes of behaviour. Some of it is also aimed at using such research in an applied, practical setting. The Psychology in Action (PiA) sections review the evidence for the application of psychological principles to a 'real-life' issue: for example, using closed-circuit television (CCTV) to identify criminals; jury decision-making; understanding bullying; should you smile during an interview?; getting a good night's sleep; what will make you a better student?; does speed reading work? and so on. Chapter 18 on mental disorders is almost a whole PiA section in itself because it describes the study and treatment of mental illness. These sections aim to show you how principles from psychology can be used to help us to understand why we behave in the way that we do.

What you should be able to do after reading the chapter

At the beginning of each chapter there is a brief description about what you should be able to do after reading it. This section provides you with a set of goals that you should try to achieve during the course of reading the chapter. The items in these sections are, in essence, your learning objectives.

Questions to think about

The beginning of each chapter also presents you with a series of questions to think about. The Questions to Think About feature has been designed to help you ask questions about your knowledge of psychology and to probe what you have learned from the topic you have read. There are further questions for you to think about embedded throughout each chapter.

Chapter reviews

At the end of each chapter there is a summary of the information that has gone before. The summary has been bullet-pointed to make it easy to read and understand.

Glossary

Important terms that are defined in the text and which appear in bold also appear, alphabetically, in glossary at the end of the book.

Suggestions for further reading

As an intelligent reader of an introductory textbook you will be hungry for more psychological knowledge after having tasted this starter. The suggestions for further reading are designed to satisfy your appetite. All the recommended readings come with comments and these should help you to decide on what further reading is best for you. Some of the reading is quite advanced; other readings are less demanding. You should try to consult at least a few of these per chapter because the further reading will lead you into more detailed description and discussion of psychological topics.

I really hope that you will learn a lot about psychology from the sixth edition of *Psychology*. I also hope that you enjoy what you learn and that the book will take you to places you had not thought of exploring. If you like what you have read, let me know. One of the joys of writing, teaching and researching is obtaining feedback about the work that you produce. Write to me, G. Neil Martin, at School of Psychotherapy and Psychology, Regent's University London, Regent's Park, London, N1, or email me at: neil.martin@regents.ac.uk You can also tweet me at @ThatNeilMartin

G. Neil Martin, FRSA
London, 2017

Guided tour

Each chapter begins with an overview of what the chapter will cover and some questions to think about, to help you reflect on the key issues in the topic.

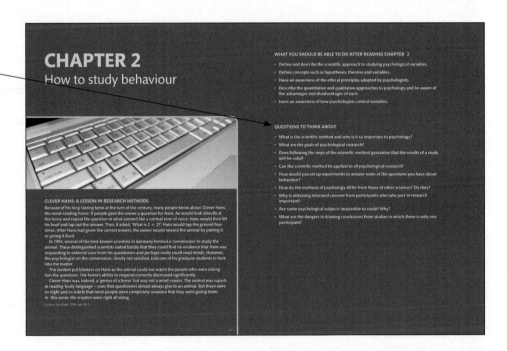

CHAPTER 2
How to study behaviour

CLEVER HANS: A LESSON IN RESEARCH METHODS

Because of his long-lasting fame at the turn of the century, many people know about 'Clever Hans', the mind-reading horse. If people gave the owner a question for Hans, he would look directly at the horse and repeat the question in what seemed like a normal tone of voice. Hans would then lift his hoof and tap out the answer. Thus, if asked, 'What is 2 + 2?', Hans would tap the ground four times. After Hans had given the correct answer, the owner would reward the animal by patting it or giving it food.

In 1904, several of the best-known scientists in Germany formed a 'commission' to study the animal. These distinguished scientists stated boldly that they could find no evidence that Hans was responding to external cues from his questioners and perhaps really could read minds. However, the psychologist on the commission, clearly not satisfied, told one of his graduate students to look into the matter.

The student put blinkers on Hans so the animal could not watch the people who were asking him the questions. The number of times Hans responded correctly decreased significantly.

Clever Hans was, indeed, a 'genius of a horse' but was not a mind-reader. The animal was superb at reading 'body language' – cues that questioners almost always give to an animal. But these were so slight and so subtle that most people were completely unaware that they were giving them. In this sense, the sceptics were right all along.

Source: Fernham, 1996, pp. 83-5.

WHAT YOU SHOULD BE ABLE TO DO AFTER READING CHAPTER 2

• Define and describe the scientific approach to studying psychological variables.
• Define concepts such as hypotheses, theories and variables.
• Have an awareness of the ethical principles adopted by psychologists.
• Describe the quantitative and qualitative approaches to psychology and be aware of the advantages and disadvantages of each.
• Have an awareness of how psychologists control variables.

QUESTIONS TO THINK ABOUT

• What is the scientific method and why is it so important to psychology?
• What are the goals of psychological research?
• Does following the steps of the scientific method guarantee that the results of a study will be valid?
• Can the scientific method be applied to all psychological research?
• How would you set up experiments to answer some of the questions you have about behaviour?
• How do the methods of psychology differ from those of other sciences? Do they?
• Why is obtaining informed consent from participants who take part in research important?
• Are some psychological subjects impossible to study? Why?
• What are the dangers in drawing conclusions from studies in which there is only one participant?

Psychology in action uses fascinating, real life examples to show how psychology is applied in the real world.

Cutting edge introduces you to some of the most interesting new subjects of study in contemporary psychology.

WHAT IS DRUG ADDICTION? | **153**

Psychology in action: The psychological consequences of taking ecstasy

In their list of the most dangerous, illegal, major psychosocial drugs – those taken recreationally to induce pleasure, euphoria or relaxation – Nutt et al. (2007) judged heroin and cocaine to be the most harmful and the ones which produced the most pleasure. Ecstasy was listed 18th (of 20). Some have pointed out that this is an unusual position for ecstasy to occupy – but the position is partly attributable to the fact that many other drugs can be injected and are, therefore, more dangerous (Parrott, 2013). The judgement that ecstasy was less pleasurable than cigarettes, which it was in this study, has also been questioned (Parrott, 2013).

Ecstasy – or 3, 4-methylenedioxymethamphetamine (MDMA) – is a so-called CNS stimulant, behaviourally similar to amphetamine and methamphetamine. Unlike those two drugs, MDMA's primary site of action is at serotonin receptors where it reverses the process of serotonin reuptake. The consequence of this is that it leaves more serotonin available in the synaptic cleft. In his review of ecstasy, Parrott (2013) noted that its use as a recreational drug emerged towards the mid-1980s. Surveys suggest that it may be the third most popular recreational drug after cannabis and cocaine. Very few people take MDMA, however, compared to other drugs – the European Monitoring Centre for Drugs and Drug Addiction (2010) found that 8.6 per cent of adults had used ecstasy. Its usage among clubbers, however, is high – some (dated) surveys suggest it is over 90 per cent (Winstock et al., 2001).

According to Parrott (2013), the first empirical study of MDMA (conducted in 100 students at a Californian University) found that common symptoms of taking the drug were teeth clenching, increased heart rate and positive mood. There is also heightened blood pressure, faster breathing, overheating, cortisol secretion, and impaired serotonin system functioning

(Benningfield and Cowan, 2013). All of these are amplified by the clubbing environment, where symptoms are accompanied by dehydration and sweating. Taking the drug can also be, perhaps paradoxically, accompanied by hypothermia – probably because the drug disrupts the body's ability to regulate temperature, and users respond to colder environments abnormally. Deaths following ecstasy are more common than deaths following amphetamine, and a common cause is organ failure (Schifano et al., 2010).

Psychologically, ecstasy has some profound and, superficially, contradictory effects. For example, although it is associated with positive mood and greater sense of intimacy (Bedi et al., 2010), research has also shown that it can intensify negative mood and induce anxiety, depending on the user's expectations and the context of the drug taking (Kirkpatrick et al., 2012). Both mood changes can occur in the same individual. According to Parrott, the drug is unusual because it is one of the few recreational drugs people give up voluntarily – the positive effects of the drug wane over time.

The cognitive effects of taking the drug are varied – some studies report impairments in the ability to retain and retrieve memory over short periods, others find that the impairment occur over much longer periods (Parrott, 2013). Users seem to have particular difficulty with planning exercises such as the Tower of London (which you will find more about in Chapter 11) but report few cognitive deficits other than this and some other executive functions. Response time and attention are unaffected. The effects may be user-dependent. Heavier users have been found to show impairments on some cognitive tests, such as visuospatial memory (Halpern et al., 2011; Murphy et al., 2012).

drug-seeking and the drug-seeking becomes compulsive and persistent and maladaptive (DSM-V). Ersche et al. (2013) noted that the United Nations estimates that drug use affects one in every 200 people. Many people – psychologists, health professionals and lay people – believe that 'true' addiction is caused by the unpleasant physiological effects that occur when an addict tries to stop taking the drug.

When people develop tolerance to a drug, they show decreased sensitivity following an continued use; the drug user must take larger and larger amounts of the drug in order for it to be effective. Once a person has taken an opiate regularly enough to develop tolerance, that person will suffer withdrawal symptoms if they stop taking the drug. Withdrawal symptoms are primarily the opposite of the effects of the drug itself. Heroin produces constipation; withdrawal from it produces nausea, cramping and diarrhoea. Heroin produces relaxation; withdrawal from it produces agitation.

Most investigators believe that the withdrawal symptoms are produced by the body's attempt to compensate for the unusual condition of heroin intoxication. That is, most systems of the body, including those controlled by the brain, are regulated so that they stay at an optimal value. When a drug artificially changes these systems for a prolonged time, homeostatic mechanisms begin to produce the opposite reaction, which partially compensates for the disturbance from the optimal value. These compensatory mechanisms account for the fact that more and more heroin must be taken in order to achieve the effects that were produced when the person first started taking the drug. They also account for the symptoms of withdrawal: when the person stops taking the drug, the compensatory mechanisms make themselves felt, unopposed by the action of the drug.

Heroin addiction has provided such a striking example of drug dependence that some authorities have concluded that

---

TECHNIQUES IN PSYCHOLOGY AND NEUROSCIENCE | **131**

Cutting edge: Are brain scanners stressful?

Having your brain imaged is not a straightforward or normal process. You're normally asked not to eat or drink, you're asked to remove metal objects from your body, just in case you find the environment too claustrophobic. In the case of MRI, there is also a loud hammering noise accompanying each scan.

It should not be too surprising, then, if this context were to affect people's mood and behaviour. What is surprising is that few studies have taken this into account. Muehlhan et al. (2013) asked 37 young adults who had never undergone a brain scan before to come in for an fMRI experiment on response time. Before being scanned, they entered a lab and were provided with brief training on a simple visual target detection task. They then took part in a structural scan for 10 mins and a functional scan for 15 minutes. Saliva

samples were taken before entering the scanner, after the structural scan and after the functional scan. The samples measured sympathetic nervous activity (described later in the chapter) via salivary alpha amylase (sAA).

Levels of sAA increased twice – once just before scanning and once at the end of the scan. The first increase correlated with a decrease in frontal and cortical activation. The increase persisted until the first part of the experiment, then declined before peaking again at the end, a pattern that mirrors heart rate during scanning (Chapman et al., 2010). The increase in sAA was not seen in all participants, but was seen in 65 per cent of them. Other research shows that 30–40 per cent of patients about to undergo scanning feel anxious (Katz et al., 1994) and that the initial distress decreases over 12 minutes (Lueken et al., 2012). These data suggest that it would be wise to help participants acclimatise to the experimental environment in the first 10 minutes of a neuroimaging study and to take the structural, rather than the functional scan, first.

found that there was a great degree of flexibility in the experimental designs used which can maximise the chances of obtaining a positive finding (Type 1 errors). Eklund et al. (2016) found that three of the software packages used by fMRI research could inflate the number of false positives reported. They claim that up to 40,000 fMRI studies could be affected. This number is probably an exaggeration but the study highlights on-going challenges faced by scientists when using this technique.

The appeal of neuroimaging has been described as seductive. Images are immediate, (obviously) visual and allow us to see something that was previously unattainable: a pictorial, anatomically correct representation of the living brain. And, as humans, we are very swayed by visual seduction. McCabe and Castel (2008) asked people to judge the degree of scientific reasoning in three articles about cognitive neuroscience. The articles were accompanied by either bar graphs, brain scans or no image. Despite there being no difference between the content of the articles, the piece accompanied by a brain map was judged to be more scientific.

These images, say McCabe and Castel, 'provide a physical basis for abstract cognitive processes, appealing to people's affinity for reductionistic explanations for cognitive phenomena' (p. 343). People find neuroscience explanations for behaviour to be much more plausible than non-neuroscience explanations (Weisberg et al., 2008, 2015; Minahan and Siedlecki, 2016) but whether images are actually more persuasive than scientific verbal descriptions is not clear: some studies find no difference (Schweitzer et al., 2011; Fernandez-Duque et al. (2015), for example, found that irrelevant neuroscientific

explanations accompanying descriptions of psychological phenomena were regarded as being of higher quality than social science explanations or explanations from the hard sciences. The presence of an fMRI image had no effect, suggesting that the allure is generated by the discipline, rather than the discipline's visual output. People's ability to think analytically did not protect against the bias – analytic thinkers were just as likely to judge the neuroscience explanations as being of good quality.

One study found that when participants were presented with descriptions of diagnoses made of politicians from parties they either did or not support, they were more likely to evaluate evidence most favourably if it included MRI scans than cognitive evaluations (Munro and Munro, 2014). Not one participant who received the MRI diagnosis considered it to be unreliable (even though the more accurate way of diagnosing dementia is via neuropsychological assessment rather than MRI). It may be the reductionistic nature of the evidence which may create the degree of persuasion. One study of undergraduates and members of the public found that across many sciences, reductionist (but irrelevant) good and bad explanations for findings were regarded more positively, as more persuasive and as more plausible (Hopkins et al., 2016). This study also found that participants rated neuroscience as being more rigorous, difficult and prestigious than chemistry, biology and physics, which may explain why this branch of psychology holds a particular 'allure'. However, neuroscience is not always persuasive. When human resources professionals, psychology student and business students, evaluated applicants' (fictional) personality tests which were accompanied by

Controversies in psychological science examine recent reports and beliefs about psychological findings to help develop your skills in critical analysis.

To be a psychologist it's vital to understand the conceptual and historical issues that shape the field. An international perspective allows you to explore global differences in psychological research, attitudes, policies and methods.

The extensive chapter review enables you to consolidate what you've just learnt and provides a great tool to help you revise.

At the end of each chapter there are suggestions for further reading for further sources of information. these allow you to broaden your understanding of the topic and provide a great starting point for your own research.

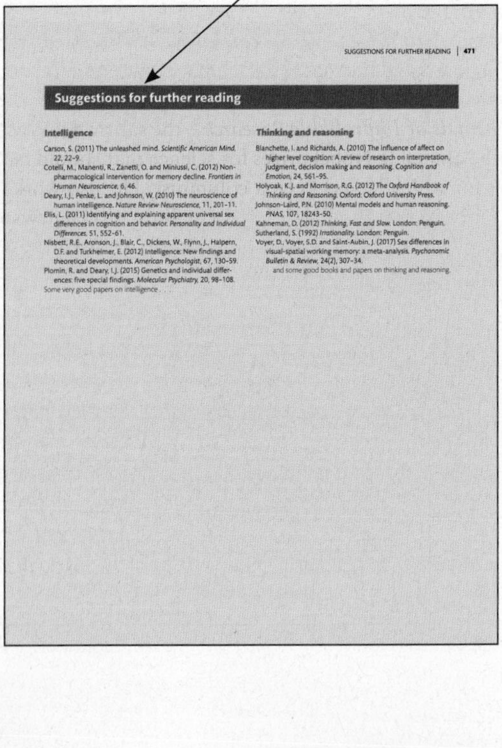

Controversies in psychological science: Well, are you 'lovin' it'? The evidence for subliminal perception

The issue

One of the quirkier yet controversial claims made in the psychology literature is that people can be influenced in the way they behave by subliminal means – that is, without awareness that they are being influenced. Normally, such influence is created by exposing participants to images or words for very brief, sub-threshold (subliminal) periods and then observing whether they behave in a way which suggests that these stimuli have had an effect. In 1957, for example, an American market researcher claimed to have increased the sales of Coca Cola and popcorn in a cinema by flashing the messages 'Drink Coca Cola' and 'Eat popcorn' on screen. There was no actual evidence that such behaviour change had occurred, however, and no study was ever published (Karremans et al., 2006). So, is there any evidence that **subliminal perception** affects behaviour?

The evidence

We know that the availability of images implicitly affects people's behaviour. People exposed to pictures of an exclusive restaurant behave with better manners when later engaged in an eating task (Aarts and Dijsterhuis, 2003); people who cast votes in school are more likely to pledge financial support for projects initiated by the school (Berger et al., 2008); and, famously, people primed with the Apple logo performed more creatively at a later task than did those primed with the IBM logo (Fitzsimons et al., 2008). People who are primed with jackpot symbols repeatedly flashed for 30 ms before playing a slot machine, bet more and are more confident in their last spin (Gibson and Zielaskowski, 2013). However, this effect was only found if betting immediately followed the prime; it wasn't found if the prime preceded the betting by 5 minutes.

People primed with images of fast food engage in more time-saving behaviour, presumably because the stimuli activate subconsciously concepts or schema of speed and time-saving (Zhong and DeVoe, 2010). In this study, people completed a lexical decision-task primed with six images of fast food restaurants. They then read a 320 word description of Toronto. The reading speed of the participants was faster if they had been primed with the fast food image.

In a second experiment, they examined the effect of fast food restaurant priming on preference for time-saving products. They asked 91 undergraduates to recall a time they spent in a fast food restaurant (or the last time they went shopping – the control condition) and then asked them to rate the desirability of various household products. Those who remembered the fast food restaurant, preferred more time-saving products.

Finally, participants were asked to judge the aesthetic appeal of either two fast food logos or the logos of two inexpensive dinners and were then asked to indicate their preference for saving (i.e. would they like $3 today or X amount of dollars in a week's time; there were various amounts increasing from $3). The participants exposed to the fast food symbols were more likely to accept a small payment on the day than wait for a larger payment. Exposure to brand logos (e.g. Macdonalds) can influence later behaviour even when five seconds passes between the subliminal presentation and the behaviour (Muscarella et al., 2013).

Karremans et al. (2006), in a review of the ostensibly subliminal effects of marketing stimuli, observe that self-help tapes which claim to improve self-esteem, memory and promote weight loss by embedding subliminal messages in the recording have been unsuccessful. One study found that when participants were subliminally primed with the words 'Coca cola' and 'thirsty', they reported an increase in how thirsty they felt (Cooper and Cooper, 2002). Karremans et al. (2006) found that priming participants with the name of a drink (Lipton's tea) influenced people's decision to drink this particular brand, but only if participants were thirsty.

This finding was replicated and extended by Bermeitinger et al. (2009). Participants played a computer game and subliminally presented the logo of a brand of dextrose pills during the game. The participants' desire to ingest these pills and their tiredness was measured. The results mirrored those for tea: participants in the subliminal condition were more likely to ingest the pills but only if they were tired. In Mack and Rock's experiments, participants were asked to indicate which of the two arms of a visually presented cross was longer. At the fourth trial, an unexpected object was presented at the same time as the cross and participants were asked whether they were aware of this object appearing. The next trials followed, with participants being told that an unexpected object might appear, and a final trial explicitly asked participants to look for an unexpected object. Around 75 per cent of participants did not recognise the appearance of an object when they were not directed to be aware of it, or had their attention directly drawn to it. Twenty-five per cent of participants failed to do this under the other (divided/full attention) conditions.

Conclusion

These experiments suggest that if subliminal perception is to work, the stimulus needs to be relevant to the participant's psychological or physiological state. The presentation of a stimulus alone will not lead to a person being influenced by it.

Memory – An international perspective

There seem to be real differences in the content of the autobiographical memories of people from different cultures. European Americans tend to recall their own roles in events and the feelings those events generated, whereas Asian Americans tend to recall details of social/group activities (Wang, 2004; Wang and Ross, 2005). One explanation for this is that American culture – at the most general level – is highly individualistic and emphasises and rewards autonomy and self-drive, whereas Asian cultures emphasise interdependence and the importance of social interaction/dependence.

To test this hypothesis, Wang (2008) asked Asian Americans to focus either on their American or their Asian background prior to recalling autobiographical memories. Those primed by the American condition recalled memories that were more self-focused and less social than were those whose Asian-ness had been primed. Participants who were not primed either way recalled the two types of content about equally.

Ji et al. (2009) hypothesised that Eastern cultures would make greater use of past information to make judgements about behaviour – presumably, because this provides more context in the same way that the background of a scene gives more context to the object in it. In an experiment where Canadian and Chinese participants were asked to read a description of a theft and then look at behaviours that had occurred near to the crime or at some time from it, Chinese participants placed more emphasis on distant events, considering them more relevant. They also recalled more detail about past events accurately than did the Canadians.

---

episode (Schacter, 1987; Cleermans, 1993). It is sometimes referred to as being synonymous with procedural memory, the memory for knowing how to do things (like riding a bike, operating a computer keyboard or playing a musical instrument) – we acquire memory via performance without consciously encoding that information. There is some question, however, over whether implicit and procedural memory are truly synonymous. Procedural memory implies that some conscious effort has been made towards learning a skill such as riding a bike or playing a musical instrument; implicit memory would assume that skills were learned without such conscious effort, which seems highly unlikely. Also, there seems to be little procedural input to performing a stem-completion task (described below), which taps implicit memory. There continues to be debate about the number of memory systems, and whether these memory systems are separate or different forms of the same system.

The acquisition of specific behaviours and skills is probably the most important form of implicit memory. Driving a car, turning the pages of a book, playing a musical instrument, dancing, throwing and catching a ball, sliding a chair backwards as we get up from the dinner table – all these skills involve coordination of movements with sensory information received from the environment and from our own moving body parts. We do not need to be able to describe these activities in order to perform them. We may not be aware of all the movements involved while we are performing them. Implicit memory may have evolved earlier than explicit memory.

Originally, the term implicit learning derived from studies of artificial grammar learning (see Chapter 10) where participants had to deduce a set of grammatical rules governing the construction of sentences comprising non-words (so that the participants are not influenced by semantic knowledge conveyed by the words). Participants were able to work out a set of rules but were unable to describe these rules – they made educated guesses based on stimuli they had previously seen. They had implicitly learned the rules (Reber, 2013).

A good example of learning without awareness is provided by an experiment conducted by Graf and Mandler (1984). These investigators showed people a list of six-letter words and had some of them engage in a task that involved elaborative processing: they were to think about each word and to decide how much they liked it. Other people were given a task that involved processing superficial features: they were asked to look at the words and decide whether they contained particular letters. Later, their explicit and implicit memories for the words were assessed. In both cases the basic task was the same, but the instructions to the subjects were different. People were shown the first three letters of each word. For example, if one of the words had been 'define', they would have been shown a card on which was printed 'def' (this is called a word-stem completion task). Several different six-letter words besides define begin with the letters 'def', such as 'deface', 'defame', 'defeat', 'defect', 'defend', 'defied' and 'deform', so there are several possible responses. The experimenters assessed explicit memory by asking people to try to remember the words they had seen previously, using the first three letters as a hint. They assessed implicit memory by asking the people to say the first word that came to mind that started with the three letters on the card.

Deliberate processing (shallow or deep processing) had a striking effect on the explicit memory task but not on the implicit memory task. When people used the three letters as cues for deliberate retrieval, they were much more successful if they had thought about whether they liked the word than if they simply paid attention to the occurrence of particular letters. However, when people simply said the first word that

---

Chapter review

Sensory memory

- Memory is the process of encoding, storing and retrieving information. It exists in three forms: sensory, short-term/working and long-term. The characteristics of each differ, which suggests that they differ physiologically as well.
- Sensory memory provides temporary storage of information until the newly perceived information can be stored in short-term memory.
- Information in sensory memory lasts for only a short time. When a visual stimulus is presented in a brief flash, all of the information is available for a short time (iconic memory). If the viewer's attention is directed to one line of information within a few hundred milliseconds of the flash, then the information can be transferred into short-term memory. Echoic memory – sensory memory for sound – appears to operate similarly.

Short-term and working memory

- Short-term memory and working memory contain a representation of information that has just been perceived, such as a person's name or telephone number. Although the capacity of short-term memory is limited, we can rehearse the information as long as we choose, thus increasing the likelihood that we will remember it indefinitely.
- Information in short-term memory is encoded according to previously learned rules. Information in long-term memory determines the nature of the encoding.
- Working memory is different from short-term memory in that it allows the short-term storage and manipulation as opposed to simple storage of material in memory.
- Working memory comprises a phonological loop – a store of phonetic, verbal information – a visuospatial scratchpad – a store of spatial information and memories for movement – and a central executive responsible for supervising and updating the content of working memory.
- Short-term memory lasts for about 20 seconds and has a capacity of about seven items. We often simplify large amounts of information by organising it into 'chunks' of information, which can then be more easily rehearsed and remembered.
- When presented with a list of items, we tend to remember the items at the beginning of the list (the primacy effect) and at the end of the list (the recency effect) better than items in the middle of the list.

- The primacy effect occurs presumably because we have a greater opportunity to rehearse items early in the list and thus store them in long-term memory. The recency effect occurs because we can retrieve items at the end of the list from short-term memory.
- The existence of acoustical errors (rather than visual ones) in the task of remembering visually presented letters suggests that information is represented phonologically in short-term memory.
- Loss of information from short-term memory appears to be primarily a result of displacement; new information pushes out old information. However, a small amount of simple decay may also occur.

Learning and encoding in long-term memory

- Long-term memory refers to the very long-term retention of information and appears to consist of physical changes in the brain – probably within the sensory and motor association cortex.
- Consolidation of memories is likely caused by rehearsal of information, which sustains particular neural activities and leads to permanent structural changes in the brain. Short-term memories probably involve neural activity (which can be prolonged by rehearsal), whereas long-term memories probably involve permanent structural changes.
- Elaboration is important to learning. Maintenance rehearsal, or simple rote repetition, is usually less effective than elaborative rehearsal, which involves deeper, more meaningful processing.
- Encoding specificity states that the way in which material is stored depends on how the material is retrieved. The most durable and useful memories are encoded in ways that are meaningful.
- Some psychologists have argued that shallow processing is a less effective way of encoding information than is deep processing (levels of processing, therefore, determine the success of retrieval). Critics, however, point out that shallow processing sometimes produces very durable memories, and the distinction between shallow and deep has proved to be impossible to define explicitly.
- Mnemonic systems are strategies used to enhance memory and usually employ information that is already contained in long-term memory and visual imagery.

Suggestions for further reading

Intelligence

Carson, S. (2011) The unleashed mind. *Scientific American Mind*, 22, 22–9.
Coteli, M., Manenti, R., Zanetti, O. and Miniussi, C. (2012) Non-pharmacological intervention for memory decline. *Frontiers in Human Neuroscience*, 6, 46.
Deary, I.J., Penke, L. and Johnson, W. (2010) The neuroscience of human intelligence. *Nature Review Neuroscience*, 11, 201–11.
Ellis, L. (2011) Identifying and explaining apparent universal sex differences in cognition and behavior. *Personality and Individual Differences*, 51, 552–61.
Nisbett, R.E., Aronson, J., Blair, C., Dickens, W., Flynn, J., Halpern, D.F. and Turkheimer, E. (2012) Intelligence: New findings and theoretical developments. *American Psychologist*, 67, 130–59.
Plomin, R. and Deary, I.J. (2015) Genetics and individual differences: five special findings. *Molecular Psychiatry*, 20, 98–108.
Some very good papers on intelligence.

Thinking and reasoning

Blanchette, I. and Richards, A. (2010) The influence of affect on higher level cognition: A review of research on interpretation, judgment, decision making and reasoning. *Cognition and Emotion*, 24, 561–95.
Holyoak, K.J. and Morrison, R.G. (2012) *The Oxford Handbook of Thinking and Reasoning*. Oxford: Oxford University Press.
Johnson-Laird, P.N. (2010) Mental models and human reasoning. *PNAS*, 107, 18243–50.
Kahneman, D. (2012) *Thinking, Fast and Slow*. London: Penguin.
Sutherland, S. (1992) *Irrationality*. London: Penguin.
Voyer, D., Voyer, S.D. and Saint-Aubin, J. (2017) Sex differences in visual-spatial working memory: a meta-analysis. *Psychonomic Bulletin & Review*, 24(2), 307–34.
and some good books and papers on thinking and reasoning.

The authors

Dr G. Neil Martin is Professor of Psychology and Head of Psychology at Regent's University London, UK. He is a Life Fellow of the Royal Society of Arts. He was educated in Wales, Scotland and England, and graduated with a first-class Master of Arts degree in psychology from the University of Aberdeen, where he won the annual Henry Prize for outstanding undergraduate achievement in psychology. He completed his PhD on psychophysiology and olfactory perception at the University of Warwick, England.

He is the author of *Psychology – A Beginner's Guide* (Oneworld, 2008), also available as a audiobook; *The Neuropsychology of Smell and Taste* (2013, Psychology Press); *Human Neuropsychology,* the first European textbook in the field (Pearson Education, 1998, 2006) now available in Polish, Greek, Italian and Arabic; *Essential Biological Psychology* (Hodder Arnold, 2003); *Study Guide – Psychology,* with Nicky Brunswick (Pearson Education, 2005); and the 6th and 7th international editions of *Psychology,* with Neil Carlson and colleagues from the US and Canada (Allyn & Bacon, 2006, 2009). With Nicky Brunswick, he wrote the first European online course in introductory psychology (Pearson Education, 2001, 2003), now in its third edition (Pearson Education, 2006). He is the author of over 150 articles on psychology, contributed the neuroanatomy of food flavour entry in the *Oxford Companion to Food (3rd edition),* and acts as consultant to industry, business and the media on the psychology of olfaction and humour. He has been an editorial board member of *The Psychologist* and the *Annals of Improbable Research* – the satirical journal which awards the annual Ig Nobel prizes for science that should never be repeated – for which he has been a columnist. He also works as a freelance journalist; his first article for a major national newspaper was entitled 'More than 20 things you needed to know about the nose'.

Dr Neil R. Carlson is Professor of Psychology at the University of Massachusetts, USA. He studied as an undergraduate and postgraduate at the University of Illinois. He wrote his first textbook, *Physiology of Behavior,* while on sabbatical leave at the University of Victoria in British Columbia. He was the first Allyn & Bacon author to submit a book manuscript on a computer disk. A few years ago he began to collaborate with Jay Alexander, an artist who works as a laboratory technician at the University of Massachusetts. They prepare all the artwork for Professor Carlson's books.

Dr William Buskist is Professor of Psychology at Auburn University, USA, where he regularly teaches the introductory psychology and the teaching of psychology courses. He has directed Auburn's psychology research laboratories. He also teaches seminars and workshops for undergraduates who are preparing for graduate study in psychology. He graduated from Brigham Young University in 1981 with a PhD in experimental psychology. Although most of his research has been in the area of human social behaviour, particularly competitive behaviours, Dr Buskist's research now largely focuses on issues in the teaching of psychology.

Dr Michael Hogg is Professor of Social Psychology at Claremont Graduate University, USA and co-author of the chapters on social psychology. He is a Fellow of the Society for the Psychological Study of Social Issues, the Society for Personality and Social Psychology and the Academy of the Social Sciences in Australia. He was the foundation director of the Centre for the Study of Group Processes at the University of Queensland, and in 2004 he was a British Academy Visiting Professor at Birmingham University. Educated at Bristol Grammar School and the University of Birmingham, he received his PhD in 1983 from Bristol University, and has held teaching posts at Bristol University, Macquarie University, the University of Melbourne, the University of Queensland and Princeton University, and visiting appointments at the University of California, Los Angeles; the University of California, Santa Cruz; the University of California, Santa Barbara; City University, Hong Kong; and the University of Kent, UK.

Michael Hogg's research on group processes, intergroup relations, social identity and self-conception is closely associated with the development of social identity theory. He has published over 200 scientific books, chapters and articles on these topics.

With Graham Vaughan he is the author of *Social Psychology –* one of the leading introductory social psychology texts in Europe and the UK, it was first published in 1995 and is now in its fifth edition. A former associate editor of the *Journal of Experimental Social Psychology,* Michael Hogg serves on the editorial board of most of the main social psychology journals, and is foundation co-editor with Dominic Abrams of the journal *Group Processes and Intergroup Relations,* and senior consultant editor for the *Sage Social Psychology Program.* This current research focuses on leadership, deviance, uncertainty reduction, extremism and sub-group relations. Michael Hogg lives in Los Angeles, but spends substantial time each year in the UK, and in Brisbane, Australia.

Dr Dominic Abrams is Professor of Social Psychology, Director of the Centre for the Study of Group Processes at the University of Kent, Canterbury, UK, and co-author of the chapters on social psychology. He is a Chartered Psychologist, Fellow of the Society for the Psychological Study of Social Issues, and of the Academy of Social Sciences. Following his undergraduate degree at Manchester University and a Masters degree at the London School of Economics and Political Sciences, he received his PhD in 1984 from the University of Kent, and held teaching posts at the universities of Bristol and Dundee before returning to Kent in 1989. He has held visiting appointments at the universities of Melbourne, Queensland and Urbana-Champaign, Illinois.

This research on intergroup relations and the self-concept has concentrated on social identity, and spans childhood to old age, and groups defined by gender, ethnicity, language, faith, sexuality and disability. He has been associate editor for the *British Journal of Social Psychology,* and special issue editor for the *Journal of Community and Applied Psychology* and the *International Journal of Behavioral Development.* He is foundation editor, with Michael Hogg, of *Group Processes and Intergroup Relations,* and serves on the editorial boards of *Journal of Personality and Social Psychology* and the *European Review of Social Psychology.* He has recently been chair of the British Psychological Society Research Board, and now chairs the Joint Committee for Psychology in Higher Education in the UK. His current research focuses on the social psychology of social inclusion and exclusion, societal indices of prejudice, the development of group understanding and the role of intergroup contact in prejudice reduction.

Acknowledgements

In the course of writing and revising six editions of *Psychology*, I have had the good fortune to call on the expertise and detailed knowledge of a number of people and they are mentioned below. Their contribution has been enormous and people have willingly given of their time and expertise.

In addition, there are one or two people in particular I would like to thank for contributing to this edition of *Psychology*. From Twitter, thanks for all the fun, advice, tips and pointers to new and interesting research, to: Stuart Ritchie (@sjritchie), Dorothy Bishop (@deevybee), Rolf Zwaan (@rolfzwaan), Keith Laws (@keith_Laws), Hal Pashler (@HPashler), Michael Kane (@Kane_WMC_Lab), Marc Abrahams (@marcabrahams), Ben Goldacre, (@badscience), Matt Wall (@m_wall), Micah Allen (@neuroconscience), Neurobolllocks (@neurobollocks), Nick Brown (@steamtraen), Matthew Hankins (@mc_hankins), R-Index (@R_index), Ken Gilhooly (@kengilhooly), Ed Yong (@edyong209), Ivan Oransky (@IvanOransky) and Gavin Buckingham (@DrGBuckingham). If you're interested in psychology and science generally, you should all follow them all. They are all brilliant.

For distraction, and laughs, a huge thank you to the following who distracted me more than was reasonable when writing this book: Maureen Johnson (@maureenjohnson; we'll always have mindology), Louis Barfe (@AlanKelloggs), David Quantick (@quantick), Keri (@mutablejoe), Sanjeev Kohli (@govindajeggy), Rhodri Marden (@rhodri), Ben Dunnell (@bendunnell), Cameron Yarde (@CameronYardeJnr), Matt Owen (@MJowen174), Zorro P Freely (@Banalyst), Thundercock (@fatherwoland), Alan Stoob (@nazihunteralan), Jeremy Duns (@JeremyDuns), Simon Blackwell (@simonblackwell) and Charlie Oughton (@DrCOughton). You should all, etc. They're all brilliant, too. Occasionally, rude.

From Pearson, the people without whom this book would not be possible: my editor at Pearson, Janey Webb, my previous editor at Pearson, Natalia Jaszczuk, Melanie Carter, Sindhuja Vadlamani, Jayanandan and Lou Atwood.

Finally, on a personal note, thank you to Niki, Nicky, Pat, Sharon, Jayne, Marmoset, John Nuttall and my team at Regent's and, finally, my special Marmoset. Correct me if I'm wrong!

From the first and second editions

From Pearson Education, I would like to thank (in chronological order), Christina Wipf-Perry who originally suggested the idea of a European adaptation and who has continued to take an interest in this blossoming pedagogy; Tim Pitts, for his unfailing philosophical outlook; Sue Phillips, development editor for the first edition; Liz Tarrant, production editor for the first edition; Jane Powell, who commissioned the first set of research updates for the website; Matthew Smith, an author's editor; and John Yates, the very tall and charming publisher who helped to launch the first edition. Finally, I would like to thank my editors and publishers: Ruth Haggerty, Louise Lakey, Karen Mclaren and the incomparable Morten Fuglevand. The second edition was written as *Fame Academy* reached its denouement. I would like to thank the inmates, especially Ainslie and David, for many hours of terpsichorean entertainment.

From the third edition

Thanks, as ever, go to the indomitable Morten Fuglevand who was the guiding hand in this, and other, projects. His influence was enormous. Thanks, too, to Janey Webb for carrying on the Psychology torch, getting the third edition into shape and for assorted treats; Sarah Wild (for all the sterling help with figure queries); Stephen Jeffrey and Nada Jolic (for all the help with MyLab); Robert Chaundy and Jonathon Price for the punctilious copy-editing and proofing; Sarah Busby, Geoff Chatterton, Georgina Clark-Mazo, Nicola Shortt, Alun Swift, Maggie Wells and the UK and AU marketing teams for all their hard work.

From the fourth edition

Janey Webb for all her help, support and encouragement during the third transmogrification; Catherine Morissey, redoubtable production-editor-in-waiting; Tim Parker, Barbara Massam, Rose James, Jane Ashley, Leo Stanley and John Matthews for all their hard work on the book and MyPsychLab; Beth Rix and Robert Chaundy for their help on the Research and Study Guide for the third edition; all of the reps at Pearson for their indefatigable drive and tenacity; and Dame Marjorie Scardino, for the coffee, the chat and the honour of discussing the project with her; the staff at Coffee Bean and Costa in High Barnet for providing the space where the bulk of the research for the fourth edition was written up and the first draft revised; and Niki for her 'how are yous?', her love of leteeoos and her patience.

From the fifth edition

From Twitter: Stuart Richie, Dean Burnett, Suzi Gage, Heather Doran, Neurobonkers, Skeptics in the Pub, Jon Sutton and Matt Wall, for all their blog and website recommendations for MyPsychLab.

Thanks, as ever, go to the terrific team at Pearson including Janey Webb, Jane Lawes, Catherine Yates, Neha Sharma, Tim Parker, Jonathon Price, Helen MacFadyen, Jane Ashley and all the reps and marketing staff who helped shaped the new edition of the book. More locally, I would like to thank Paul Assoul and 'the family' at Coffee Bean, High Barnet and the staff at Costa High Barnet for providing what turned out to be a second office as this edition was being revised. Finally, my thanks as always to my louloudi, Niki.

Reviewers and advisors for the first, second, third, fourth and fifth editions

Thanks to the following for all their feedback, advice and help on the first, second, third and fourth editions of the book:

Dave Alcock	University of Bristol
Bruce Arnow	Stanford University
Jane Barnet	Middlesex University
John H.W. Barrett	University of Bristol
Sarah Beck	University of Birmingham
Rob Bell	Queen's University Belfast
Joe Boden	University of Plymouth
Glynis Breakwell	University of Surrey
Vicki Bruce	Edinburgh University
Brian Brunswick	
Nicola Brunswick	Middlesex University
Mark Burgess	Oxford Brookes University
Andrew Calder	University of Cambridge
David Carey	University of Aberdeen
Julia Cogan	
Gillian Cohen	Open University
Martin Conway	University of Durham
Neil Cooper	University of East Anglia
Mats Danielsson	Lulea University of Technology
Alyson Davis	Surrey University
Sergia Della Sala	University of Edinburgh
Jan Deregowski	University of Aberdeen
Kate Eames	Coventry University
Eddie Edgerton	University of the West of Scotland
Paul Emmelkamp	Amsterdam University
Ann Erling	Gothenburg University
Anthony Esgate	University of Westminster
Ian Fairholm	Bath University
Nigel Foreman	Middlesex University
Nollaig Frost	Middlesex University
Adrian Furnham	University College London
Peter Garrard	Institute of Cognitive Neuroscience, UCL
Ken Gilhooly	Hertfordshire University
Nitin Gogtay	Child Psychiatry Branch, NIMH
Caroline Green	University of Aberdeen
Ruth Green	Staffordshire University
Kerry Greer	Mary Immaculate, Limerick
Sheila Hale	
Peter Halligan	University of Cardiff
Usneeral B. Hamaker	University of Amsterdam
Trevor Harley	University of Dundee
Eilis Hennessy	University College Dublin
Ronald Henss	University of Saarland
Philip A. Higham	University of Southampton
Kenneth Hugdahl	University of Bergen
Dai Jones	University of Glamorgan

Fay Julal	Southampton Solent University
Gail Kinman	University of Bedfordshire
Paul Kinnear	University of Edinburgh
Shirley Koh	Student
Winek Koisor	Pearson Education
Virginia Lam	University of East London
Scott Lilienfeld	Emory University
Robert Logie	University of Aberdeen
Monicque M. Lorist	University of Groningen, The Netherlands
Geoff Lowe	University of Hull
Bjorn Lyxell	Linkoping University
Neil Macrae	University of Aberdeen
George Maher	University of Lincoln
Caroline Mansfield	Oxford Brookes University
Mark McDaniel	University of New Mexico
Maggie McGonigle	University of Edinburgh
Aidan Moran	University College Dublin
Peter Morris	University of Lancaster
David Moxon	Peterborough Regional College
Tom Nugent	Child Psychiatry Branch, NIMH
Rory O'Connor	University of Strathclyde
Michael Oddy	Brain Injury Rehabilitation Trust
Paddy O'Donnell	University of Glasgow
Adrian Parker	Gothenburg University
Andy Peart	Blackwell
John Pickering	University of Warwick
Arne Poulsen	University of Roskilde
Jan Pryor	Wellington University
Qazi Rahman	Queen Mary University, London
Sandra Read	University of Bedfordshire
Andries F. Sanders	Vrije University
Tony Shelton	Liverpool John Moores University
Kevin Silber	University of Derby
Dean Keith Simonton	University of California, Davis
Ian Stewart	Galway University
Students from the University of Edinburgh and Southampton Solent University	
Michele Surbey	James Cook University
Frode Svartdal	University of Tromsø
Jaqui Taylor	Bournemouth University
Kevin Thomas	Trinity College Dublin
Jimmie Thomson	University of Strathclyde
Zazie Todd	University of Leeds
Andy Tolmie	University of Strathclyde
Margit Torneus	Umea University
Andy Tramo	Harvard University
John Turner	University of East London
Lorenzo Vigentini	Edinburgh University
Jamie Ward	University of Sussex
Erik Wastlund	Karlstad University
Claire Wells	
Brian Young	University of Exeter

Publisher's acknowledgements

Cartoons

Cartoon on page 252 from TCB-137777.jpg Tom Cheney / The Cartoon Bank "It's a rather interesting phenomenon. Every time I press this lever, that post-graduate student breathes a sigh of relief." Image ID: 23939

Figures

Figure 1.1 from Baker, M. (2015). First results from psychology's largest reproducibility test. Nature [online] (30/04/2015). Available at http://www.nature.com/news/firstresults-from-psychology-s-largest-reproducibility-test-1.17433 [Accessed: 15/08/18]; Figure 1.2 (a)-(d) from Schorr, A. and Saari, S. (Eds.) (1995) *Psychology in Europe*. Reproduced with permission © 1995, Hogrefe & Huber Publishers; Figure.1.4 from Feinberg, T.E. and Farah M.J. (1997). *Behavioral Neurology and Neuropsychology*. © The McGraw-Hill Companies; Figure 1.5(a) from Damasio, H., Grabowski, T., Frank, R., Galaburda, A.M. and Damasio, A.R. (1994). The Return of Phineas Gage: Clues about the brain from a famous patient. *Science*, 264: 1102–05. Department of Neurology and Image Analysis Facility, University of Iowa; Figure 1.5(b) from *An Odd Kind of Fame* (Macmillan), MIT: Bradford; Figure on page 60 from Spurious Correlations [online] http://www.tylervigen.com/spurious-correlations, [Accessed on 15/08/2018]; Figures 2.2(a) & (b) from Sternberg, Daniel A. *The largest human cognitive performance dataset reveals insights into the effects of lifestyle factors and aging*. Frontiers; Figure 3.1 from Evolution, Creationism, Intelligent Design. Gallup [online] http://news.gallup.com/poll/21814/evolution-creationism-intelligent-design.aspx [Accessed: 15/08/2018]; Figure 3.2 adapted from Lewin, R. (1984). *Human Evolution: An illustrated introduction*. Blackwell Scientific Publications, Inc; Figures 3.3(a)-(c) adapted from Dicke, U. and Roth, G. (2008) Animal Intelligence and the Evolution of the Human Mind (Intelligence evolved), *Scientific American Mind*, August; Figure 3.4 from *Portfolio review: Human Genetics 1990–2009*, Wellcome Trust (2010) Fig.2, p.11, Data: Thomson Reuters 2009; Analysis: Evidence, Thomson Reuters (Scientific UK); © The Wellcome Trust www.wellcome.ac.uk, licensed under Creative Commons Attribution 2.0 UK.; Figure 3.6(a)-(c) adapted from Klug, W.S. and Cummings, M.R. (1986), *Concepts of Genetics (2nd edn)*. *Glenview, IL: Scott, Foresman,* Scott, Foresman © 1986 Scott, Foresman & Co. Reprinted by permission of Addison Wesley Educational Publishers, Inc.; Figure 3.7 from Durante. K.M., Li, N.P. and Haselton, M.G. (2008). Changes in women's choice of dress across the ovulatory cycle: Naturalistic and laboratory task-based evidence. *Personality and Social Psychology Bulletin*, 34(11), pp.1451–1460, Copyright © 2008 by Sage Publications. Reprinted by Permission of SAGE Publications; Figure 3.8 from Comninos,

A.N., et al. (2017). Kisspeptin modulates sexual and emotional brain processing in humans. *The Journal of Clinical Investigation*, 127, 709; Figure 3.9 from D.P. Schmitt. (2004). Patterns and universals of mate poaching across 53 nations: The effects of sex, culture and personality on romantically attracting another person's partner, *Journal of Personality and Social Psychology*, 86(4), Fig.2, pp.560–584. Reprinted with permission of the APA; Figure 4.1 from Stereological estimation of total cell numbers in the human cerebral and cerebellar cortex, 8, 1–8, *Frontiers in Human Neuroscience*; Figure 4.16 from Walloe, S., Pakkenberg, B. and Fabricius, K. (2014). Coping with severe memory impairment, *Neuropsychological Rehabilitation*, 14(5), pp.481–94 by permission of the publisher and the authors; Figure 4.18 from Stelzer, J., Lohmann, G., Mueller, K., Buschmann, T. and Turner, R. (2014). Deficient approaches to human neuroimaging. *Frontiers in Human Neuroscience*. 8, 1–16; Figure on page 128 Courtesy of The Wellcome Trust; Figure 4.19(b) Courtesy of Dr J. McA. Jones, Good Samaritan Hospital, Portland, Oregon, USA; Figure 4.21 from Martin, G.N. (2006). *Human Neuropsychology*, 2nd ed., Prentice Hall Fig. 4.27, p.36; Figures 4.25(a) & (b) from Carlson, N.R. (1988). *Physiology of Behavior*, 6th ed., Allyn & Bacon p. 235, © Allyn & Bacon. Reproduced with permission; Figure 4.28 from Cell Press; Figure 4.32 from Pinel, J. (1997). *Biopsychology*, 3rd ed., Allyn and Bacon Copyright © 1997. Reprinted and electronically reproduced by permission of Pearson Education, Inc., Upper Saddle River, New Jersey; Figures 4.33(a) & (b) from Pabba, M. (2013). Evolutionary development of the amygdaloid complex. *Frontiers in Neuroanatomy*. 7, 1–4; Figure 4.38 from Vollenweider, F.X. and Kometer, M. (2010). The neurobiology of psychedelic drugs: implications for the treatment of mood disorders. *Nature Reviews Neuroscience* 11(9), 642–51; Figure 5.12 adapted from Dowling, J.E. and Boycott, B.B. (1966). Organization of the primate retina: electron microscopy, *Proceedings of the Royal Society of London, Series B*, 166, pp.80–111. Copyright © 1966, The Royal Society; Figure 5.17 from Brash, S., Maranto, G., Murphy, W. and Walker, B. (1990). American Optical Corporation; Figure 5.18 from *How Things Work: The brain*, Time-Life Books © 1990 Time-Life Books; Figure 5.21 from Beatty, J. *Principles of Behavioral Neuroscience* Madison, WI: Wm C. Brown Communications, Inc. Reprinted with permission; Figure 5.22 from Goldstein, E.B. (2007). *Sensation and Perception* (7th edn). Belmont, CA: Thompson; Figure 5.23 from Payne, D.G. and Wenger, M. (1998). *Cognitive Psychology*, Houghton Mifflin Companyp.75, © 1998 Houghton Mifflin Company. Used with permission; Figure 5.25 from Network Science and the Effects of Music Preference on Functional Brain Connectivity: From Beethoven to Eminem - https://www.nature.com/articles/srep06130; Figure 5.26 & 5.27 from Goldstein, E.B. (2007). *Sensation and Perception*, 7th ed. Thompson; Figure 5.28 from Pinel, P.J. (2003). *Biopsychology*, 5th Ed., Allyn & Bacon Copyright © 1993. Reprinted and electronically reproduced by permission of

Pearson Education, Inc., Upper Saddle River, New Jersey; Figure 5.30 from Whitfield, P. and Stoddart, M. (1985). *Hearing, taste and smell: pathways of perception*. Torstar Books p.87; Figure 5.32 from Yeshurun, Y., & Sobel, N. (2010). An odor is not worth a thousand words: From multidimensional odors to unidimensional odor objects. *Annual Review of Psychology*, 61, pp.219–241 Figure 5.34 from Goldstein, E. (2007). *Sensation and Perception*, 7th ed. Wadsworth Fig 15.4, p.331; Figure 5.36 & 5.37 from Simons, L., Elman, I. and Borsook, D. (2013). *Psychological Processing in Chronic Pain: A Neural Systems Approach* © 2013 Elsevier Ltd; Figure 6.1b & 6.1c from Moss, O. [online] http://ollymoss.com [Accessed: 15/08/2018]; Figure 6.9 from Neisser, U. (1967). *Cognitive Psychology*. Appleton-Century-Crofts; Figure 6.11 Adapted from Neisser, J. (1964). Visual search. *Scientific American Mind*, 210, 94–102; Figures 6.12, 6.13 adapted from Biederman, I. (1990). Higher-level vision, *An Invitation to Cognitive Science. Vol. 2: Visual Cognition and Action*, Figure 2.4, Figure 2.9, © 1990 Massachusetts Institute of Technology, by permission of The MIT Press; Figure 6.15 adapted from D. A. Norman, D.A., Rumelhart D.E. & the LRN Research Group. (1975). *Explorations in cognition*, W. H. Freeman pp. 279–307, Reproduced by permission of Professor Donald Norman and Professor Steve Palmer; Figure 6.16 from Palmer, S.E. (1975), The effects of contextual scenes on the identification of objects, *Memory and Cognition*, 3, pp.519–526 Reprinted by permission of the Psychonomic Society, Inc.; Figure 6.17 adapted from Rumelhart, D.E., McClelland, J.L. and the PDP Research Group (Eds.). (1986), *Parallel Distributed Processing, vol. 1: Foundations*, MIT Press (c) 1986 the Massachusetts Institute of Technology; published by the MIT Press, Cambridge, MA.; Figures 6.20, 6.25 adapted from Matlin, M.W. and Foley, H.J. (1992); *Sensation and Perception*, 3rd ed., Allyn & Bacon; Figure 6.30 from Gilbert, A.L. et al. (2006). Whorf hypothesis is supported in the right visual field but not the left. Proceeding of the National Academy of Science. 103, 489–94; Figure 6.38 from Barragan-Jason, G., Lachat, F. and Barbeau, E.J. (2012). How fast is famous face recognition? Perception Science. *Frontiers in Psychology*; Figure 6.40 from Humphreys and Riddoch (1987). *To See or Not to See*. Andover, Psychology Press, reprinted by permission of Cengage/Thomson Learning; Figure 6.44 from Plate 6.2 from Martin, G.N., (2006). Human Neuropsychology, 2nd edn, Pearson/Prentice Hall. Image kindly provided by Dr Olaf Blanke; Figure 6.19 from Barton, J.J.S. and Corrow, S.L. (2016). *Recognizing and identifying people: A neuropsychological review*, Vol. 75, February 2016, pp.132–150, Cortex. Copyright © 2015 Elsevier Ltd. All rights reserved; Figure 6.45 from Chatterjee, A. (2005). A madness to the methods of cognitive neuroscience? 17, 6, 847–9, *Journal of Cognitive Neuroscience*. © By the Massachusetts Institute of Technology; Figure 7.4 adapted from Hill W.F. (1997). *Learning: A survey of psychological interpretation*, 7th ed., Allyn & Bacon pp.70–78, Copyright © 2002. Reprinted and electronically reproduced by permission of Pearson Education, Inc., Upper Saddle River, New Jersey; Figure 7.5 adapted from Hill W.F. (1997). *Learning: A survey of psychological interpretation*, 7th ed., Allyn & Bacon Copyright © 2002. Reprinted and electronically reproduced by permission of Pearson Education, Inc., Upper Saddle River, New Jersey; Figure 7.9 from Kornmeier, J., Spitzer, M. and Sosic-Vasic, Z. (2014). *Very similar spacing-effect patterns in very different learning/ practice domains*, 9, 1–11, PLoS ONE; Figure 8.2 adapted from Sperling, G. (1960). The information available in brief visual presentations, *Psychological Monographs*, 74, pp.1–29 Adapted with permission of the APA; Figure 8.4 adapted from Logie, R. (1995). *Visual Spatial Working Memory*, Psychology Press p.127; Figures 8.6(a) & (b) adapted from Shepard, R.N. and Metzler, J. (1971). Mental rotation of three-dimensional objects, *Science*, 171, pp.701–703. © 1971 The American Association for the Advancement of Science; Figure 8.7 adapted from Peterson, L.M. and Peterson, J.M. (1959). Short-term retention of individual verbal items, *Journal of Experimental Psychology*, 58, pp.193–198, Adapted with permission of the APA; Figure 8.8 adapted from Waugh, N.C. and Norman, D.A. (1965). Primary memory, *Psychological Review*, 72, pp.89–104, Adapted with permission of the APA; Figure 8.11 based on data from Graf, P. and Mandler, G. (1984). Activation makes words more accessible, but not necessarily more retrievable. *Journal of Verbal Learning and Verbal Behavior* 23, 553–68; Figure 8.13 Adapted from Ruger, H.A. and Bussenius, C.E., (trans.). (1885/1913). Ebbinghaus, h., Memory: A contribution to experimental psychology. Teacher's college Press, Columbia University, New York; Figure 8.14 from Schmolck, H., Buffalo, E.A. and Squire L.R. (2000). Memory distortions develop over time: Recollections of the O.J. Simpson trial verdict after 15 and 32 months, *Psychological Science*, 11(1), pp. 39–45; Figure 8.15 adapted from Bahrick, H.P. (1984). Semantic memory content in permastore: Fifty years of Spanish learned in school. *Journal of Experimental Psychology: General*, 113, p. 1–29. Adapted with permission of the APA; Figure 8.17 & 8.18 based on data from Loftus, E.F. and Palmer, J.C. (1974). Reconstruction of automobile destruction: An example of the interaction between language and memory, *Journal of Verbal Learning and Verbal Behavior*, 13, 585–89; Figure 8.24 from Dobbins, I.G. & Wagner, A.D. (2005). Domain-general and domain-sensitive prefrontal mechanisms for recollecting events and detecting novelty, *Cerebral Cortex*, 15, 1768-1778; Figure 8.20 from Morris, R.G.M. et al. (1982). Place navigation impaired in rats with hippocampal lesions, *Nature*, 182(297), pp. 681–683; Figure 8.21 from Recalling routes around London: Activation of the right hippocampus in taxi drivers, *Journal of Neuroscience*, 17, p. 7103, Society for Neuroscience; Figure 8.22 from Maguire, E.A., Frackowiak, R.S.J. and Frith, C.D. (1977). Recalling routes around London: Activation of the right hippocampus in taxi drivers, *Journal of Neuroscience*, 17, p. 7103; Figure 9.4(a) & (b) from Strayer, D.L. & Johnston W.A. (2001). Driven to distraction: Dual-task studies of simulated driving and conversing on a cellular telephone, *Psychological Science*, 12(6), pp.462–6; Figure 9.6(a) & (b) from Martin, G.N.(2006). *Human Neuropsychology*, 2nd ed. Prentice Hall, Fig. 4.6; Figure 9.7 from Derbyshire et al (2014); Figure 9.8 from Horne, J.A. (1989). *Why We Sleep: The functions of sleep in humans and other mammals*, Oxford University Press © 1988 Oxford University Press, reprinted by permission; Figure 9.9 from Kanazawa, S. and Perina, K (2009). Why night owls are more intelligent, *Personality and individual differences*, Vol. 47 (7), pp. 685–690; Figure 9.10 & 9.11 from Stickgold, R. and Walker, M.P. (2007). Sleep-dependent memory consolidation and reconsolidation, *Sleep Medicine* 8(4), Fig.2, pp.331–43 Copyright (2007), with permission from Elsevier; Figure 9.12 from Nielsen, T. and Powell, R.A. (2015). Dreams of the rarebit Fiend: food and diet as instigators of bizarre and disturbing dreams. *Frontiers in Psychology*, 6, 47, 1–15; Figure 10.1 from Payne, D.G. and Wenger, M.J., Cognitive Psychology. (1998). New York: Houghton Mifflin, Copyright © 1998 by Houghton Mifflin Company; Figure 10.2 from Campbell, L. (1999). *Historical Linguistics: An Introduction*, MIT Press; Figure 10.3 from Payne, D.G. and Wenger, M.J. (1998). *Cognitive Psychology*, Houghton Mifflin,

Copyright © 1998 by Houghton Mifflin Company; Fig. 6.1, p.190, © 1999 Massachusetts Institute of Technology, by permission of The MIT Press and Edinburgh University Press, www.euppublishing.com; Figure 10.3 from Bouckaert, R.(2012). Mapping the Origins and Expansion of the Indo-European Language Family, *Science*, Vol. 337 no. 6097, pp. 957–960. Readers may view, browse, and/or download material for temporary copying purposes only, provided these uses are for noncommercial personal purposes. Except as provided by law, this material may not be further reproduced, distributed, transmitted, modified, adapted, performed, displayed, published, or sold in whole or in part, without prior written permission from the publisher.; Figure 10.5(a) & (b) from Just, M.A. and Carpenter, P.A., (1987), *The Psychology of Reading and Language Comprehension* Allyn & Bacon Copyright © 1987. Reprinted and electronically reproduced by permission of Pearson Education, Inc., Upper Saddle River, New Jersey; Figure 10.6 from Waxman, S.R. and Booth, A.E. Principles that are invoked in the acquisition of words, but not facts. *Cognition*, 2000, 77, B33–B43. © 2000, with permission from Elsevier; Figure 10.9 from Siok, W.T., Niu, Z., Jin, Z., Perfetti, C.A. and Tan, L.H. (2008). A structural–functional basis for dyslexia in the cortex of Chinese readers. *Proceedings of the National Academy of Sciences*, 105 (14), 5561–6; Figure 10.11 from Cattell, R.B., Krug, S.E., Barton, K. (1973). Florida International University; Figure 11.1 from *Technical Supplement for the Culture Fair Intelligence Tests, Scales 2 and 3*, Institute for Personality and Ability Testing, by permission of Hogrefe Ltd. © 2008 Hogrefe Ltd., Oxford, www.hogrefe.co.uk. All rights reserved. Figure 11.4 from Kalichman, S.C. (1989). The effects of sex and context on paper and pencil spatial task performance, *Journal of General Psychology*, 116(2), pp.133–9; Figure 11.5 from Terman, L.M. and Merrill, M.A. (1960). *Stanford–Binet Intelligence Scale*, Houghton-Mifflin, Used with Permission of PRO-ED, Inc.; Figure 11.8 from Blair, C., Gamson, D., Thorne, S. and Baker, D. (2005). Rising mean IQ: Cognitive demand of mathematics education for young children, population exposure to formal schooling and the neurobiology of the prefrontal cortex, *Intelligence*, 33(1), Fig.1, p.94 Figure 11.9 from Pietschnig, J. and Voracek, M. (2015) One century of global IQ gains: a formal meta-analysis of the Flynn effect (1909-2013) *Perspectives on Psychological Science*, 10, 282–30; Figure 11.11 from Salthouse, T.A. (2009). When does age-related cognitive decline begin? *Neurobiology of Aging*, 30, Fig.2, pp.507–14, Copyright (2009), with permission from Elsevier; Figure 11.13(b) from Plate 11.3 from Martin, G.N. (2006). Human Neuropsychology, 2nd ed. Pearson/ Prentice Hall; Figures 11.12 a & 11.12b from Beatty, J. (1995). *Principles of Behavioral Neuroscience*. Brown & Benchmark; Figure 11.14 from Leow, A.D., Yanovsky, I., Parikshak, N. et al. (2009). Alzheimer's Disease Neuroimaging Initiative: A one-year follow-up study using tensor-based morphometry correlating degenerative rates, biomarkers and cognition. *NeuroImage*, 45, 645–55, figure 1; Figure 11.15 from Storandt, M. (2008). Cognitive Deficits in the Early Stages of Alzheimer's Disease, *Current Directions in Psychological Science*, 17(3), Fig. 1, p.198, copyright © 2008 by Association for Psychological Science. Reprinted by Permission of SAGE Publication; Figure 11.16 from Schwindt, G.C. and Black, S.E. (2009). Functional imaging studies of episodic memory in Alzheimer's disease: a quantitative meta-analysis, *NeuroImage*, 45, Fig, 2&3, pp.181–190; Figure 11.17 adapted from and reprinted with the permission of the journal and authors https://www.ncbi.nlm.nih.gov/pubmed/19004525; Figure 11.18 from Hadi Hosseini. S. M., Kramer, J.H.and Kesler, S.R. (2014). Neural correlates of cognitive intervention in persons at risk

of developing Alzheimer's disease. *Frontiers in Ageing Neuroscience*. (26 August 2014); Figure 11.20 from Solso, R.L. (1988). *Cognitive Psychology*, 2nd ed., Allyn & Bacon, Copyright © 1988. Reprinted and electronically reproduced by permission of Pearson Education, Inc., Upper Saddle River, New Jersey; Figure 11.24 from Pinel, P.J. (1997). *Biopsychology*, 3rd ed., Allyn and Bacon, Copyright © 1997. Reprinted and electronically reproduced by permission of Pearson Education, Inc., Upper Saddle River, New Jersey; Figure 12.3 from Cowan, W.M. (1979). The Development of the brain, *Scientific American*, 241, pp.106–17 with permission of Nelson H. Prentiss; Figures 12.4(a) & (b) from Dubois, J., Dehaene-Lanbertz, G., Kulikova, S., Poupon, C., Huppi, P.S. and Hertz-Pannier, L. (2014). The early development of brain white matter: A review of imaging studies in foetuses, newborns and infants. *Neuroscience*, 276, 48–71; Figure 12.5 adapted from Cohen, L.B. and Salapatek, P. (eds). (1975). *Infant Perception: From sensation to cognition*. Academic Press; Figure 12.6 adapted from Haith,M.M. and Campos, J.J. (eds). (1986). *Handbook of Child Psychology. Vol. 2: Infancy and developmental psychobiology*, 4th ed. John Wiley & Sons, Inc, Copyright © 1983, this material is used by permission of John Wiley & Sons, Inc.; Figure 12.8 from Current Directions in Psychological Science 2016, Vol. 25(2) 135–140 © The Author(s) 2016 Reprints and permissions: sagepub. com/journalsPermissions.nav DOI: 10.1177/0963721416631955 cdps. sagepub.com; Figure 12.9 after Watson, J.S. and Ramey, C.T. (1972). Reactions to responsive contingent stimulation in early infancy, *Merrill–Palmer Quarterly*, 18, pp.219–27; Figure 12.10 from Lefrancois, G.R. (1983). *Of Children: An introduction to child development*. Wadsworth. With permission of Guy Lefrancois; Figure 12.11 from Byom, L.J., and Mutlu, B. (2013). Theory of mind: mechanisms, methods, and new directions. *Frontiers in Human Neuroscience*. (08 August 2013); Figure 12.12 from Journal of Personality and Social Psychology; Figure 12.13 from National Center on Health Statistics (2006) Health, United States, 2006; Figure 12.14 from Thoughts for Today, British Medical Journal, 2005, Vol. 331, p. 1550, unnumbered figure (24–31 December 2005) with permission from the BMJPublishing Group Figure 13.3(a) & (b) from Rolls, B.J., Rolls E.T. and Rowe E.A. (1982). How sensory properties of foods affect human feeding behaviour, *Physiology and Behaviour*, 29(3), pp.409–17; Figure 13.4 from How to Determine BMI in Adults. Shape Up [online]; Figure 13.5 from McGuire, T. et al. (1999). What predicts weight regain in a group of successful weight losers? *Journal of Consulting and Clinical Psychology*, 67(2), pp.177–85, Copyright © 1999 by the American Psychological Association, reprinted with permission; Figure 13.7 from Kaye, W. (2008). Neurobiology of anorexia and bulimia nervosa, *Physiology and Behaviour*, 94(1), pp.121–135 Copyright (2008), with permission from Elsevier; Figure 13.11 from Heini Saarimäki, *Discrete Neural Signatures of Basic Emotions*. © 2017 Oxford University Press; Figures 13.14 from Damasio, H. et al. (1994). The return of Phineas Gage: Clues about the brain from a famous patient, *Science*, 246(5162), 1102-05. Department of Neurology and Image Analysis Facility, University of Iowa; Figure 13.15 from Ekman, P. (2003). *Emotions Revealed*. Weidenfeld & Nicholson Figure 13.16 from Schellenberg, E.G. and von Scheve, C. (2012) Emotional cues in American popular music: Five decades of the top 40. *Psychology of Aesthetics, Creativity and the Arts*, 6, 196–203; Figure 13.18 from Strack, F., Stepper, S. and Martin, L.L. (1988). Inhibiting and facilitating conditions of the human smile, *Journal of Personality and Social Psychology*, 54, pp.1768–77, © Fritz Strack. Reproduced with permission; Figure 13.9

from Bolmont, M., Cacioppo, J.T. and Cacioppo, S. (2014) Love is in the gaze: an eye-tracking study of love and sexual desire. *Psychological Science*, 25, 1748–56; Figure 14.2 from *16PF® Fifth Edition Administrator's Manual*, Copyright © 1993 by the Institute for Personality and Ability Testing, Inc., Champaign, Illinois, USA. All rights reserved. Reproduced with permission. '16PF' is a registered trademark of IPAT Inc. IPAT is a wholly owned subsidiary of OPP Ltd.; Figure 14.3 from Eysenck, H.J. (1973). *The Inequality of Man*, Temple Smith; Figure 14.4 from Martin, G.N. (2006). *Human Neuropsychology*, 2nd ed. Prentice Hall, Plate 10.1; Figures 14.5(a)-(e) from Rentfrow, P.J., Jokela, M. and Lamb, M.E. (2015) Regional personality differences in Great Britain. PLoS ONE, 10, e0122245; Figure 14.6(a)-(c) from Schwartz, H.A. (2013) Personality, gender, and age in the language of social media: the open-vocabulary approach. PLoS ONE, 8, e73791; Figure 15.1 from Fiske, S. (2012) Managing ambivalent prejudices: Smart-but-cold and warmbut-dumb stereotypes. Annals AAPSS, 639, 33–48; Figure 15.2 from Goldstein, N.J., Cialdini, R.B., & Griskevicius, V. (2008). A room with a viewpoint: using social norms to motivate environmental conservation in hotels, *Journal of Consumer Research*, 35, pp.472–482; Figure 15.5 after Festinger, L. and Carlsmith, J.M. (1959). Cognitive consequences of forced compliance, *Journal of Abnormal and Social Psychology*, 58, pp.203–10; Figure 16.1 after Rittle, R.H. (1981). Changes in helping behaviour: Self versus situational perceptions as mediators of the foot-in-the-door technique, *Personality and Social Psychology Bulletin*, 7, pp.431–37; Figure 16.2 from Baron, R.A. and Byrne, D. (1997). *Social Psychology: Understanding human interaction*, 8th ed., Allyn & Bacon, Copyright © 1997. Reprinted and electronically reproduced by permission of Pearson Education, Inc., Upper Saddle River, New Jersey; Figure 16.3 from Asch, S.E. (1951). Effects of group pressure upon the modification and dis-tortion of judgment. In H. Guetzkow (ed.) Groups, Leadership, and Men. Pittsburgh, PA: Carnegie; Figure 16.4 after Abrams, D., Marques, J.M., Brown, N.J. and Henson, M. (2000). Pro-norm and anti-norm deviance within and between groups, *Journal of Personality and Social Psychology*, 78, p.911; Figure 16.5 after Gaertner, L., Sedikides, C. and Graetz, K. (1999). In search of self-definition: Motivational primacy of the individual self, motivational primacy of the collective self, or collective primacy?, *Journal of Personality and Social Psychology*, 76, p.13; Figure 16.8 after Monteith, M.J., Ashburn-Nardo, L., Voils, C.I. and Czopp, A.M. (2002). Putting the brakes on prejudice: On the development and operation of cues for control, *Journal of Personality and Social Psychology*, 83, pp.1029–50; Figure 16.9 after Darley, J.M. and Latané, B. (1968). Bystander intervention in emergencies: Diffusion of responsibility, *Journal of Personality and Social Psychology*, 8, pp.377–83; Figure 16.10 after Saegert, S.C., Swap, W. and Zajonc, R.B. (1973). Exposure, context, and interpersonal attraction, *Journal of Personality and Social Psychology*, 25, pp.234–42; Figure 17.1 from Benzenal, M., Judge, K. and Whitehead, M. (eds). (1995). *Tackling Inequalities in Health: An agenda for action*, King's Fund p.23, © 1995 King's Fund. Reprinted by permission; Figure 17.2 from *World Health Statistics* World Health Organization (2007) p.13, © World Health Organization 2007, 978-92-4-068211-5; Figure 17.4 from World Health Organization Map Production: Health Statistics and Information Systems (HSI). World Health Organization; Figure 17.8(a) & (b) from Kiecolt-Glaser, J.K., et al. (1995). Slowing of wound-healing by psychological stress, *The Lancet*, 346, pp.1194–96, © 1995 The Lancet Limited; Figure 17.11 from Tice, D.M. and Baumeister, R.F. (1997). Longitudinal study of procrastination, performance, stress and health: The costs and benefits of dawdling, *Psychological Science*, 8(6), pp.454–8; Figure 17.10(a) & (b) from James, J.B. and Spiro, A. (2007). The impact of work on the psychological health and well-being of older Americans, *Annual Review of Gerontology and Geriatrics*, 26, pp.153–74, Annual review of gerontology & geriatrics by SPRINGER PUBLISHING COMPANY. Reproduced with permission of SPRINGER PUBLISHING COMPANY in the format Republish in a book via Copyright Clearance Center.; Figure 18.1 from Simons, L., Igor Elman, I. and Borsook, D. *Psychological Processing in Chronic Pain: A Neural Systems Approach*. American Psychiatric Association; Figure 18.3 from (Freeman, W. (1949). Transorbital leucotomy: the deep frontal cut, *Proceedings of the Royal Society of Medicine*, 42 (supplement), pp.8–12; Figure 18.4a from Atlas, Wager. How Is Pain Influenced by Cognition? Neuroimaging Weighs In. *Perspectives on Psychological Science*, 8(1) 91 –97; Figure 18.4b (a) & (b) from Jubb, J. and Bensing, J.M. (2013). The sweetest pill to swallow: how patient neurobiology can be harnessed to maximise placebo effects. *Neuroscience & Biobehavioral Reviews*, 37(10), 2709–20; Figure 18.5 from Bruhl, A.B., Delsignore, A., Komossa, K. and Weidt, S. (2014). Neuroimaging in social anxiety disorder – A meta-analytic review resulting in a new neurofunctional model. *Neuroscience and Biobehavioural Reviews*, 47, 260–80; Figure 18.7 from Muhlberger, A., et al (2001). Repeated exposure of flight phobics to flights in virtual reality, *Behaviour Research and Therapy*, 39, pp.1033–1050; Figure 18.8 from Pascual et al;Figure 18.12 from N Drevets, W.C. (2011). euroimaging and neuropathological studies of depression: Implications for the cognitive-emotional features of mood disorders, *Current Opinion in Neurobiology*, 11, pp.240–49; Figure 18.13 and 18.14 from World Health Organization: 2014.

Tables

Table 1.3a and 1.3b from Whelan, C.W., Wagstaff, G. and Wheatcroft, J.M. (2015) Subjective Cues to Deception/Honesty in a High Stakes Situation: An Exploratory Approach, *The Journal of Psychology*, 149:5, 517–534; Table 1.4 adapted from Norenzayan, A., & Heine, S. J. (2005). Psychological universals: What are they and how can we know? *Psychological Bulletin*, 135, pp.763–784, Adapted with permission of the APA; Table 1.5 from Diener, E., Oishi, S. and Park, J-Y. (2014). An incomplete list of eminent psychologists of the modern era. *Archives of Scientific Psychology*, 2, 20–32; Table 2.1 from Wilkinson, S. and Kitzinger, C. (2008). Conversation analysis. In C. Willig and W. Stainton-Rogers (eds) *The Sage Handbook of Qualitative Research in Psychology*. London: Sage Publications; Table 5.3 from Ayabe-Kanamura, S., Schicker, I., Laska, M., Hudson, R., Distel, H., Kobayakawa, T. and Saito, S. (1998). Differences in perception of everyday odors: a Japanese–German cross-cultural study. *Chemical Senses*, 23, 31–8; Table 8.1 from Bartlett, F.C. (1932). *Remembering: A Study in Experimental and Social Psychology*, Cambridge University Press, p. 67; Table 8.2 from von Stumm, S., Chamorro-Premuzic, T. and Furnham, A. (2008). Decomposing self-estimates of intelligence: Structure and sex differences across 12 nations. *British Journal of Psychology*, 100(Pt 2):429–42; Tables 8.3 (a) & (b) from Simmons, D.J. and Chabris, C.F. (2011). What people believe about how memory works: A representative survey of the US population? PLoS ONE, 6, 1–7; Table 10.2 adapted from Fromkin, V.A. (1997). Speech production, in J. Berko Gleason and N.B. Ratner (eds) Psycholinguistics. Fort Worth: Holt, Rinehart and Winston

(Wadsworth1997 edition); Table 10.4 from Berko Gleason, J. (1997). *The Development of Language*, 4th ed., Allyn & Bacon, Copyright © 1997. Reprinted and electronically reproduced by permission of Pearson Education, Inc., Upper Saddle River, New Jersey; Table 10.5 adapted from Clark, H.H. and Clark, E.V. (1977). *Psychology and Language: An introduction to psycholinguistics*, Harcourt Publishers Ltd, © 1977, reprinted with permission of H.H. Clark & E.V. Clark; Table 10.6 adapted from Clark, H.H. and Clark, E.V. (1977). *Psychology and Language: An introduction to psycholinguistics*, Harcourt College Publishers, Table 13.2;

Table 10.7(a) & (b) from Morrison, D.F. (1990). *Human Neuropsychology*, 2nd ed., Prentice Hall (Martin, G.N. 2006); Table 11.1 adapted from *Multivariate Statistical Methods*, 3rd ed., McGraw-Hill; Table 11.2 adapted from Horn, J.L. (1968). Organization of abilities and the development of intelligence, *Psychological Review*, 75(3), p.249), © 1968 by the American Psychological Association. Adapted by permission; Table 13.2 adapted from Elfenbein, H.A. and Ambady, N. (2003). Universals in cultural differences in recognising emotions, *Current Directions in Psychological Science*, 12(5), pp.159–164; Table 13.3 from Stuss, D.T., Gow, C.A. and Hetherington, C.R. (1992). 'No longer Gage': Frontal lobe dysfunction and emotional changes, *Journal of Consulting and Clinical Psychology*, 60(3), pp.349–59, Copyright © 1992 by the American Psychological Association, adapted with permission; Table 13.4 after Hornak, J., Rolls, E.T. and Wade, D. (1996). Face and voice expression identification in patients with emotional and behavioural changes following ventral frontal lobe damage, *Neuropsychologia*, 34(4), pp.247–61, Copyright (1996), with permission from Elsevier; Table 15.4 after Weigel, R., Vernon, D.T.A. and Tognacci, L.N. (1974). Specificity of the attitude as a determinant of attitude–behavior congruence, *Journal of Personality and Social Psychology*, 30, pp.724–8; Table 16.1 from Reicher, S.D., Haslam. S.A. and Smith, J.R. (2012) Working toward the experimenter: reconceptualising obedience within the Milgram paradigm as identification-based followership. *Perspectives on Psychological Science*, 7, 315–24; Table 16.2 after Sternberg, R.J. (1988). The Triangle of Love. New York: Basic Books; Table 17.1 adapted from Quitting timeline, http://smokefree.nhs.uk/why-quit/timeline/, © Crown Copyright 2012 © Department of Health, Contains public sector information licensed under the Open Government Licence (OGL) v1.0.http://www.nationalarchives.gov.uk/doc/open-government-licence/open-government; Table 17.2 based on Palfai and Jankiewicz, 1991, and data from the National Institute for Alcohol Abuse and Alcoholism Clearinghouse for Alcohol Information, 1982; Table 18.2 from Lilienfeld, S.O., Ritschel, L.A., Lynn, S.J., Cautin, R.L. and Latzman, R.D. (2014). Why ineffective psychotherapies appear to work. *Perspectives on Psychological Science*, 9, 355–87; Table 18.5 from Rapoport, J.L. (1989). The biology of obsessions and compulsions, *Scientific American*, 260(3), p.63; Table 18.6 adapted from Carson, R.C., et al. (1996). *Abnormal Psychology and Modern Life*, 10th ed., Allyn & Bacon, Copyright © 1996. Reprinted and electronically reproduced by permission of Pearson Education, Inc., Upper Saddle River, New Jersey

Text

Extract on page 2 from Eysenck, H.J. (1957). *Sense and Nonsense in Psychology*, Pelican; Extract on page 42 from Furnham, A. (1996). *All in the Mind: The essence of mind*, Whurr pp.83–85; Extract on page 50 from Forer, B.R. (1949). The fallacy of personal validation: A classroom demonstration of gullibility, *Journal of Abnormal and Social Psychology*, 44 (1): 118–123. American Psychological Association; Quote on page 70 from Darwin, F. (1887). *Charles Darwin's Autobiography*, Reprinted in 1950 by Henry Schuman, New York; Extract on page 98 from Barash, D. (1982). Sociobiology and Behavior, Hodder & Stoughton, London; Quote on page 102 from Sample, I. *Mind-reading program translates brain activity into words*, The Guardian News and Media Limited (31/01/2012); Newspaper front cover story on page 133 from Guardian News and Media Ltd; Extract on page 249 taken from Babkin, B.P. (1949). Pavlov: A biography. Chicago, IL: University of Chicago Press; Extract on page 391–393 from Hale, S. (2002) The Man Who Lost His Language. London: Penguin; Extract on page 414 taken from The Guardian News and Media Limited. Extract on page 530 taken from Clarke, D. (2017). '*Visibly unhappy' Brie Larson and the amateur body linguists*. The Irish Times. (04/03/2017); Extract on page 742 from Fisher, C. Ask Carrie Fisher: I'm bipolar – how do you feel at peace with mental illness? The Guardian News and Media Limited (30/11/2016);

Photo Credits

(Key: b-below; c-centre; l-left; r-right; t-top)

Abby Johnston: John Reardon 118tr (Figure 4.15b); **Alamy Stock Photo:** 587, dpa picture alliance archive 34bl, Image Source Salsa 586, Laperruque 300tl, Richard Levine 549tl, Trinity Mirror/Mirrorpix 119, Anton Oparin 549cl, Photo 12 295; **Bridgeman Images:** 463, Head of Hypnos, or Sleep, 1st-2nd Century AD, copy of a Hellenistic original, found at Civitella d'Arno, Italy (broze), Roman/British Museum, London, UK/Bridgeman Images 335; **Corbis Images:** York Post/Corbis Sygma 344; **DK Images:** Andy Crawford 484tl & 484tc; **Paul Ekman Group, LLC:** 558, 562t; **Eye Vine Ltd:** Adam Nadel 506; **Getty Images:** Daniel Berehulak/Getty Images News 465, Bettmann 25, 26, 29bl, 31, 384; Walter Bird/Stringer/Hulton Archive 396cr, Vince Bucci/Getty Images Entertainment 636t, Peter Dench 544tl, Owen Franken/Corbis Documentary 130, Neil Harding 474, Frazer Harrison/Getty Images Entertainment 396tl, Chris Hellier/Corbis Historical 22; Jodi Hilton/Stringer/Getty Images News 33tl; Duane Howell/Denver Post 525, Robbie Jack/Corbis Entertainment 16bl, Chris Jackson/Getty Images Entertainment 396tr, Joe Klamar/AFP 477, Peter Macdiarmid/Getty Images News 446tr, 678, Colin McPherson/Corbis Entertainment 799bl, Lawrence Manning/Corbis 105tr, Ben Martin/Archive Photos 155, Larry Mulvehill/Science Source 127tr (Figure 4.19a), Popperfoto 51, SIE Productions/Corbis 90r, Rebecca Sapp/WireImage 467br, Stephen Shugerman/Getty Images Entertainment 396cl, Jeffrey Ufberg/WireImage 636b, Simon Wilkinson/The Image Bank/ 90l; **Bruce Goldstein:** 180cl; **Guardian News and Media Ltd:** Fabio De Paola 235tr; **S. Hale (2002) The Man Who Lost His Language, London, Penguin.:** 392; **Harvard Medical School:** Betty G. Martindale 108B (Figure 4.4); **Robert McCrae:** 32; Metropolitan Police Authority 216; **Douglas G. Mollerstuen:** Courtesy of Douglas G. Mollerstuen, New England Medical Center 172tl.**Olly Moss:** 203bl & 203r; **News International Syndication:** The Sun 752; **North Wind Picture Archives:** 71; **Pearson Education, Inc:** Pearson Education/Prentice Hall 129bl; **Press Association Images:** AP/EMPICS 300tr, Christophe Ena/AP/EMPICS 688, PA photos / Empics 799br, PA 387tl; **Reuters:** Rick Wilking 669tl; **Science Photo Library Ltd:** 150l (Figure 4.34), 566 (Figure 13.13, Professor Peter Cull 108T

(Figure 4.3), BSIP, Astier 118tl (Figure 4.15a), A. Barrington Brown/ Science Photo Library 77br, Scott Camazine / Photo Researchers, Inc. 129tl, Aaron Haupt 126br, Dr Andrejs Liepins 729, Claus Lunan/ Bonnier Publications 565 (Figure 13.12), Will & Deni McIntyre 624, Alfred Pasieka 444 (Figure 11.13a), Tissuepix 140cl, University of Durham/Simon Fraser 135 (Figure 4.23); **Shutterstock**: W. Disney / Everett / Rex Features 309tr, Granger 33BR, Granger/REX 672, Ken McKay/ITV/REX 16br, Olga Miltsova 215cr, Orion/Kobal/REX 786, REX 448cr, 467bl, Startraks Photo/REX 346, Summit Entertainment/ Kobal/REX 309tl; **Ross Parry Agency**: 544cl; **Dr. J. Sholtis, The Rockefeller University**: © 1995 Amgen Inc 546; **Daniel Simons**: Reproduced with kind permission Perception 1999, vol. 28, pages 1059–74, Simons D.J., Chabris C.F., "Gorillas in our midst sustained in attentional blindness for dynamic events" 330; **Stock Montage, Inc**: 23 (Figure 1.3); **SuperStock**: Louie Psihoyos 188br, Louie Psihoyos/Science Faction 192, J. Silver 169; **Barbara Tversky**: 34tr; **The Drs. Nicholas and Dorothy Cummings Center for the History of Psychology. The University of Akron**: 29br; **Woodfin, Camp & Associates, Inc.**: Loren McIntyre 755 (Figure 18.2); **World Memory Sports Council www.worldmemorychampionships.com**: 283.

PSYCHOLOGY

CHAPTER 1
The science of psychology

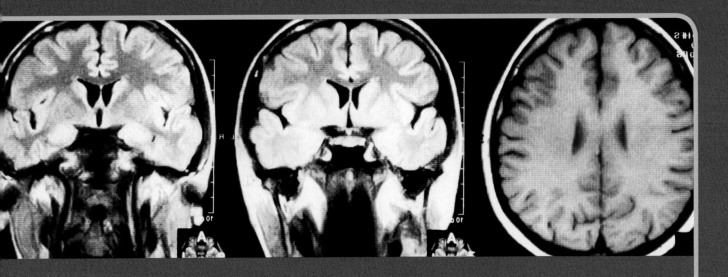

It appears to be an almost universal belief that anyone is competent to discuss psychological problems, whether he or she has taken the trouble to study the subject or not, and that while everybody's opinion is of equal value, that of the professional psychologist must be excluded at all costs because he might spoil the fun by producing some facts which would completely upset the speculation and the wonderful dream castles so laboriously constructed by the layman.

Source: Eysenck, 1957, p. 13.

WHAT YOU SHOULD BE ABLE TO DO AFTER READING CHAPTER 1

- Define psychology and trace the history of the discipline.

- Be aware of the different approaches psychologists take to study behaviour.

- Describe and distinguish between the branches of psychology.

- Understand what is meant by the 'common-sense' approach to answering questions about psychology and outline its flaws.

- Describe and understand historical developments in psychology such as structuralism, behaviourism and the cognitive revolution.

- Be aware of how psychology developed in Europe and across the world.

QUESTIONS TO THINK ABOUT

- How would you define psychology and describe its subject matter? Once you have finished reading Chapter 1, see whether your view has changed.

- What types of behaviour do you think a psychologist studies?

- Are there any behaviours that a psychologist cannot or should not study?

- What do you think psychologists mean when they say they adopt the 'scientific approach'?

- Why is this approach so important?

- Should psychological research always be carried out to help people?

- Are there different types of psychologist? If so, what are they and why?

- Do you think that much of what we know from psychology is 'common sense'? Why?

- Are some psychological phenomena universal, that is, they appear across nations and cultures?

- How does psychology differ from other disciplines, such as biology, sociology and physics? Which discipline/subjects do you think it is closest to and why?

What is psychology?

If you asked this question of several people, you would probably receive several, very different answers. In fact, if you asked this question of several psychologists, then you would still not receive complete agreement on the answer. Psychologists engage in research, teaching, counselling and psychotherapy; they advise industry and government about personnel matters, the design of products, advertising, marketing and legislation; they devise and administer tests of personality, achievement and ability. And yet psychology is a relatively new discipline; the first modern scientific psychology laboratory was established in 1878 and the first person ever to call himself a psychologist was still alive in 1920. In some European universities, the discipline of psychology was known as 'mental philosophy' – not psychology – even as late as the beginning of the twentieth century.

Psychologists study a wide variety of phenomena, including physiological processes within the nervous system, genetics, environmental events, personality characteristics, human development, mental abilities, health and social interactions. Because of this diversity, it is rare for a person to be described simply as a psychologist; instead, a psychologist is defined by the sub-area in which they work. For example, an individual who measures and treats psychological disorders is called a clinical psychologist; one who studies child development is called a developmental psychologist; a person who explores the relationship between physiology and behaviour might call themselves a neuropsychologist (if they study the effect of brain damage on behaviour) or a biopsychologist/physiological psychologist/psychobiologist (if they study the brain and other bodily processes, such as heart rate). Modern psychology has so many branches that it is impossible to demonstrate expertise in all of these areas. Consequently, and by necessity, psychologists have a highly detailed knowledge of sub-areas of the discipline and the most common are listed in Table 1.1.

Table 1.1 The major branches of psychology

Branch	Subject of study
Psychobiology/Biological psychology	Biological basis of behaviour
Psychophysiology	Psychophysiological responses such as heart rate, galvanic skin response and brain electrical activity
Neuropsychology	Relationship between brain activity/structure and function
Comparative psychology	Behaviour of species in terms of evolution and adaptation
Ethology	Animal behaviour in natural environments
Sociobiology	Social behaviour in terms of biological inheritance and evolution
Behaviour genetics	Degree of influence of genetics and environment on psychological factors
Cognitive psychology	Mental processes and complex behaviour
Cognitive neuroscience	Brain's involvement in mental processes
Developmental psychology	Physical, cognitive, social and emotional development from birth to senescence
Social psychology	Individuals' and groups' behaviour
Individual differences	Temperament and characteristics of individuals and their effects on behaviour
Cross-cultural psychology	Impact of culture on behaviour
Cultural psychology	Variability of behaviour within cultures
Forensic and criminological psychology	Behaviour in the context of crime and the law
Clinical psychology	Causes and treatment of mental disorder and problems of adjustment
Health psychology	Impact of lifestyle and stress on health and illness
Educational psychology	Social, cognitive and emotional development of children in the context of schooling
Consumer psychology	Motivation, perception and cognition in consumers
Organisational or occupational psychology	Behaviour of groups and individuals in the workplace
Ergonomics	Ways in which humans and machines work together
Sport and exercise psychology	The effects of psychological variables on sport and exercise performance, and vice versa

Psychology defined

Psychology is the scientific study of behaviour. The word 'psychology' comes from two Greek words, *psukhe*, meaning 'breath' or 'soul', and *logos*, meaning 'word' or 'reason'. The modern meaning of psycho- is 'mind' and the modern meaning of -logy is 'science'; thus, the word 'psychology' literally means 'the science of the mind'. Early in the development of psychology, people conceived of the mind as an independent, free-floating spirit. Later, they described it as a characteristic of a functioning brain whose ultimate function was to control behaviour. Thus, the focus turned from the mind, which cannot be directly observed, to behaviour, which can. And because the brain is the organ that both contains the mind and controls behaviour, psychology very soon incorporated the study of the brain.

The study of physical events such as brain activity has made some psychologists question whether the word 'mind' has any meaning in the study of behaviour. One view holds that the 'mind' is a metaphor for what the brain does and because it is a metaphor it should not be treated as if it actually existed. In his famous book *The Concept of Mind*, the philosopher Gilbert Ryle described this as the 'ghost in the machine' (Ryle, 1949). One might, for example, determine that the personality trait of extroversion exists and people will fall on different points along a dimension from not very extrovert to very extrovert. But does this mean that this trait really exists? Or is it a label used to make us understand a complex phenomenon in a simpler way? This is called the problem of **reification** in psychology: the assumption that an event or phenomenon is concrete and exists in reality because it is given a name.

The approach adopted by modern psychology is scientific, that is, it adopts the principles and procedures of science to help answer the questions it asks. Psychologists adopt this approach because it is the most effective way of determining 'truth' and 'falsity'; the scientific method, they argue, incorporates fewer biases and greater rigour than do other methods. Of course, not all approaches in psychology have this rigorous scientific leaning: early theories of personality, for example, did not rely on the scientific method (these are described in Chapter 14) and a minority of psychologists adopt methods that are not considered to be part of the scientific approach: qualitative approaches to human behaviour, for example (reviewed in Chapter 2).

There is sometimes great resistance to the scientific approach – people will often prefer to rely on personal experience and prejudice rather than evidence achieved through studying hundreds or thousands of individuals, especially if there is disagreement between what is found via this method and what people believe. This is the idea running through Hans Eysenck's quote at the beginning of the chapter. Beliefs such as vaccines cause autism, tobacco is good for you, human-made climate change doesn't exist and others are some of the more recent, egregious examples (Lewandowsky and Oberauer, 2016). The consequence of some of these beliefs are harmless; others – such as the failure to provide the measles, mumps and rubella (MMR) vaccine for children because of the incorrect belief that they cause autism – are harmful and demonstrably so. This is why evidence is important. Each person is entitled to a belief. But only evidence can be used to determine fact. General education, interestingly, may not offset the tendency to believe in issues where the scientific evidence is either supportive or negative. For example, people's political complexion can influence how they think about issues. Greater education in Democrats, for example, is associated with increased acceptance of climate change but with less acceptance in Republicans. Trust in vaccinations shows a similar pattern – better educated Democrats are more likely to trust the scientific evidence, whereas better educated Republicans are less likely to.

How much of a science is psychology?

Psychology is a young science and the discipline has tried hard to earn and demonstrate its scientific spurs. Chemistry, physics or biology seem to have no such problems: their history is testament to their status as a science. People still judge equipment associated with natural sciences to be more 'scientific' than they do equipment used by psychologists, and they rate topics studied with natural science equipment to also be more 'scientific' (and important) than the same topics using measures used by psychologists (Krull and Silvera, 2013). This study shows that, although the crucial feature of science is the method, people make judgements about the scientific status of a discipline based on its equipment and the subjects it studies.

Simonton (2004) compared the scientific status of psychology with that of physics, chemistry, sociology and biology, using a number of characteristics that typified a general science. These included the number of theories and laws mentioned in introductory textbooks (the higher the ratio of theory to law, the 'softer' – i.e. less scientific – the discipline is); the discipline's publication rate (the more frequent the publications, the more scientific the discipline is); appearance of graphs in journal papers (the 'harder' the discipline, the greater the number of graphs); the number of times publications were referred to by other academics; and how peers evaluated their colleagues. Simonton also looked at other measures of scientific standing such as 'lecture disfluency' (the number of pause words such as 'uh', 'er' and 'um': these are more common in less formal, structured and factual disciplines); and perceived difficulty of the discipline.

Not surprisingly, Simonton found that the natural sciences were judged to be more 'scientific' than were the social sciences. Psychology, however, fell right on the mean – at the junction between natural and social sciences, and was much closer to biology than to sociology. The biggest gap in scores was found between psychology and sociology, suggesting that the discipline is closer to its natural science cousins than its social science acquaintances.

A gap also separated chemistry and biology, suggesting that the sciences might be grouped according to three clusters: the physical sciences (chemistry and physics), life sciences (biology and psychology) and social science (sociology). A recent study asked physicists and psychologists to agree or disagree with various statements about the status of their disciplines including (e.g. 'My discipline is scientific', 'my discipline has a strong theoretical foundation', and so on) (Howell *et al.*, 2014). While scores on some statements were similar, there were a number of statistically significant differences in the responses of the two groups: Physicists were more likely to agree that their discipline was a science, that it had a strong theoretical basis, that it had a strong empirical foundation and that colleagues in their discipline agreed on what the subject's most important findings were. Psychologists were more likely to agree that they wished their discipline was more scientific.

They might also wish that this view was held by their students. For example, in one study, undergraduate psychology students and psychology instructors from the US were asked to agree or disagree with various statements made about the scientific standing of their discipline (Holmes, 2014). There was a large difference between them. Instructors were more likely to agree that the discipline was a science and were less interested than the students in practitioner activities. The students were much more interested in the practical, practitioner side of psychology (e.g. clinical psychology, educational psychology, counselling), than its scientific side.

Psychology majors expressed great disagreement with their tutors – they were much less likely to endorse the view that psychology was a science or that scientific enquiry was important to understand psychological issues than were their tutors. What was particularly revealing about this study was that students with practitioner interests in psychology at the beginning of their introductory-level laboratory course were five times more likely to leave their major than were students with little or moderate interest in the practice of psychology. This confirms what tutors anecdotally know: students have misperceptions about the discipline and sometimes enter Psychology at university level thinking it can solve their problems, or thinking its primary focus is on helping people and providing practical solutions to problems. Of course, it does those things but the core purpose of the psychology degree is to introduce students to the scientific method and its application to psychology, and to introduce students to the various branches of the discipline and their methods, theories and findings. Many students are unaware of these branches

or don't associate them with psychology (e.g. statistics and research methods, or biological psychology).

Simonton concluded his study with an interesting observation. He argued that psychology's position in this hierarchy does not really reflect its scientific approach but its subject matter: because the subject matter of psychology can be viewed as not directly controllable or manipulable it may be perceived erroneously, despite its adoption of the scientific method, as neither scientific fish nor fowl.

For the moment, however, consider the value of the scientific approach in psychology. Imagine that you were allowed to answer any psychological question that you might want to ask: What is the effect of language deprivation on language development, say, or the effect of personality on the stability of romantic relationships, or the effect of noise on examination revision? How would you set about answering these questions? What approach do you think would be the best? And how would you ensure that the outcome of your experiment is determined only by those factors you studied and not by any others? These are the types of problem that psychologists face when they design and conduct studies.

Sometimes, the results of scientific studies are denounced as 'common sense': that they were so obvious as to be not worth the bother of setting up an experiment. The view, however, is generally ill-informed because, as you will discover throughout this book, psychological research frequently contradicts common-sense views. As Hans Eysenck noted in this chapter's opening quote, most people believe that they are experts in human behaviour. And to some extent we are all lay scientists, of a kind, although generally unreliable ones. Lilienfeld (2011) has pointed out: people also overestimate their understanding of how toilets, zippers and sewing machines work. And humans are slightly more complicated than a lavatory.

We are also likely to discount scientific explanations for phenomena, especially if they contradict our views of these phenomena. Munro (2010), for example, presented undergraduates with scientific research which either discounted their view of homosexuality or supported it. If the evidence was not to the participants' liking, then they were more dismissive of the scientific method. This attitude then carried over into another study in which the same participants were asked to make a judgement about whether science could assist in making decisions about the retention of the death penalty. Those whose views had been challenged by science in the previous study were less likely to find science helpful in making decisions about other, unrelated topics . You'll learn more about the processes which determine attitude formation in Chapters 15 and 16.

Controversies in psychological science: Replication

The issue

What a time to be alive. If you read certain journals, news media and websites and listen to certain researchers, you might be vaguely aware that psychology is undergoing a crisis. But why? And what is the cause of the crisis? At the heart of the problem is this: replication failure.

Replication refers to the process whereby a study is repeated in a way that is as close to the original as possible with the prediction that the same results will be produced as those found in the original study. A direct replication will match the original study almost identically (but the participants will differ, the building will differ, the experimenter will differ, etc. – but these are sources of variance which should be negligible if an effect is strong). A 'conceptual' replication will reproduce the conditions of the original experiment only loosely – various parts of the methodology might differ, for example, or there may be the addition of different types of group. What has made news in psychology recently is that psychologists have been unable to replicate some well-known effects and findings in the discipline. That is, they have not been able to find the same results as earlier studies whose findings were thought to be robust and reliable (Pashler and Harris, 2012; Pashler and Wagenmakers, 2012; Laws, 2013; APS, 2015). Many of these studies led to theories and many citations and became classic in the field

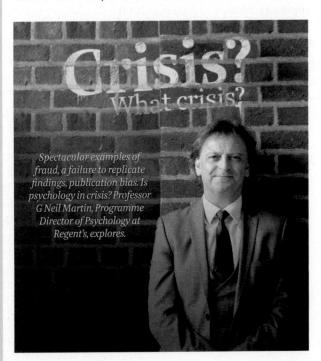

Spectacular examples of fraud, a failure to replicate findings, publication bias. Is psychology in crisis? Professor G Neil Martin, Programme Director of Psychology at Regent's, explores.

being widely cited in textbooks, including this one. There have, of course, been notable replication successes. Phenomena in cognitive psychology hold up particularly strongly (Zwaan et al., 2017) Some of the more notable recent replication failures are summarised in Table 1.2.

The problem is not specific to psychology – only 11 per cent of 53 landmark preclinical cancer trials have been found to replicate (Begley and Ellis, 2012) with 35 per cent of pharmacology studies replicating (Prinz et al., 2011). Of the 49 most widely cited papers in medicine, only 44 per cent were replicated (Ioannidis, 2005). Sixty per cent of 55 studies failed to replicate in finance (Hubbard and Vetter, 1991), 40 per cent in advertising and 46 per cent in accounting, management, finance, economics and marketing (Hubbard and Vetter, 1996). The situation is somewhat better in education (Makel and Plucker, 2014), human factors (Jones et al., 2010) and forecasting (Evanschitzky and Armstrong, 2010).

In psychology, priming research involving social factors has been particularly susceptible to non-replication (Earp and Trafimow, 2015). In priming research, participants' behaviour is influenced by exposure to stimuli of which they are not consciously aware or which influences them in a way in which they were not aware. For example, presenting someone with words related to being a professor might lead to participants performing well on a later IQ test (because their schema of a professor has been activated).

Klein et al. (2014) found that in 13 replication attempts of classic and contemporary findings using 36 samples comprising 6,344 participants, 10 were successful, one was weakly replicated and two sets of findings were not. Both failures to replicate involved social priming. The latest last set of replication attempts, however, found that of 100 experiments published in journals from the year 2008, fewer than half were successfully replicated (Open Science Collaboration, 2015), as you can see in Figure 1.1.

These, and similar results, suggest that some research may be susceptible to Questionable Research Practice (QRP) which leads to positive findings that may ultimately be nothing more than well-camouflaged Type 1 errors (Simmons et al., 2011; John et al., 2012; Makel, 2014). In statistics and psychology a Type 1 error is one where your statistical analysis yields a result – say, a difference between two groups – that has an extremely low probability of being found by chance but is actually false (the opposite is a Type 2 error where a statistical test suggests that there is no difference between two groups or conditions when there actually is).

▷

Controversies in psychological science: *Continued*

Table 1.2 Some recent failures to replicate well-known findings In psychology

Finding	Author/s	Author/s of failed replication
Exposure to high achievement words leads to better cognitive task performance	Bargh et al (2001)	Harris et al (2013)
Exposure to honesty-related words makes people disclose alcohol-related behaviour	Rasinski et al (2005)	Pashler et al (2013)
People who wrote about secrets estimated hills to be steeper	Slepian et al (2012)	LeBel & Wilbur (2013)
Using imagery to reduce prejudice	Birtel & Crisp (2014)	McDonald et al (2014)
Priming with religion affects hand grip endurance	McCullough et al (2012)	Hone & McCullough (2015)
Priming with 'elderly'-related words makes people walk like old people	Bargh et al (1986)	Shanks et al (2013)
Priming with words about professors makes people work harder	Dijksterhuis & van Knippenberg (1998)	Doyen et al (2012)
Evidence of precognition	Bem (2011)	Ritchie et al (2012)
We feel psychologically closer to people who are physically close to us	Bash & Shalev (2012)	Donellan et al (2015)
People holding a pen between their teeth rate cartoons as funnier	Strack et al (1988)	Wagenmakers et al (2016)
Priming moral purity leads to cleaning-related thoughts/behaviours	Zhong & Liljenquist's (2006)	Earp et al (2014)
Stereotype threat during maths tests in women	Spencer et al (1999)	Ganley et al (2013)
Power posing	Carney et al (2010)	Ranehill et al (2015)
Reminders of money alter people's political views	Vohs et al (2006)	Rohrer et al (2015)
Avoidant individuals will respond to social warmth with intimacy	MacDonald & Borsook (2010)	Philipp-Muller & MacDonald (2016)

John *et al.* (2012) found that more than 50 per cent of the 2,000 psychologists they asked wished to extend their study until a sufficient sample was recruited which produced a statistically significant result. Forty per cent had reported selectively publishing studies that produced significant results. Both are examples of p-hacking, the publication of a statistically significant finding or set of findings which are, to all intents and purposes, Type I errors. Type 1 errors are spurious findings – a study may show a statistically significant difference between two groups, for example, but this difference is spurious because it is based on problems with data collection, the method or data analysis.

P-hacked publications arise from studies with small samples and power, which are selective in the samples they recruit and retain, which engage in post-hoc data analysis selection, and which may exclude negative results, conditions, experiments and even participants. Simmons *et al.* (2011), for example, have demonstrated how easily a surprising and logically derived finding or phenomenon can turn out to be utterly bogus because of the methodological and statistical design and analysis decisions made by the experimenter. In their study, they were able to demonstrate that people who listened to a song about getting older made people feel younger. In the following table, they report (in bold) what was included in the

▷

Controversies in psychological science: *Continued*

Did replication match original study's results?

NO: 61   **YES: 39**

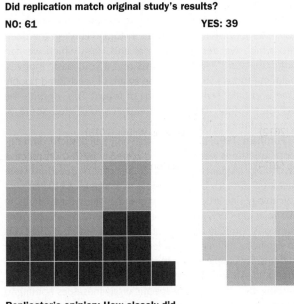

Replicator's opinion: How closely did findings resemble the original study:

- Virtually identical
- Extremely similar
- Very similar
- Moderately similar
- Somewhat similar
- Slightly similar
- Not at all similar

Figure 1.1 The degree of successful replication found in the Open Science Collaboration (2015) study.

Source: http://www.nature.com/news/first-results-from-psychology-s-largest-reproducibility-test-1.17433

original report and what was excluded from the written-up report (in grey).

It shows how excluding data and being flexible with your data analysis can lead to false positives. For example, they included some in their study but did and include others – the greater the number of factors (or variables) in your study, the easier it will be to find a significant result. You have an approximately 1 in 20 chance of finding a significant result regardless of whether that result is genuine. 'It is unacceptably easy', they conclude, 'to publish "statistically significant" evidence consistent with any hypothesis'. And reporting dramatic single effects like these reflects another problem: publication bias. This refers to journals' tendency to publish only results which are positive and statistically significant and a reluctance to publish negative results.

Why has some research in psychology been so difficult to replicate? One reason might be that the original result was not robust or valid in the first place. In statistics, this is called a false positive – claiming a result or finding exists when it doesn't. Journals have been criticised for publishing and prioritising novel, creative, significant results and for not publishing negative results or direct replications. This is called a publication bias – publishing only positive results. The result of this is that non-supporting research does not get published and that positive, but spurious, results are embedded in the literature in perpetuity. Martin and Clarke found that of 1,551 psychology journals, only 3 per cent accepted replications. Many journals emphasised the importance of new and original research in their acceptance criteria.

Table 3. Study 2: Original Report (in Bolded Text) by Simmons et al (2011) and the Requirement-Compliant Report (With Addition of Gray Text) which includes a full description of what the study did and the materials used.

Using the same method as in Study I, we asked 34 University of Pennsylvania undergraduates to listen only **to either "When I'm Sixty-Four" by The Beatles or "Kalimba"** or "Hot Potato" by the Wiggles. We conducted our analyses after every session of approximately 10 participants; we did not decide in advance when to terminate data collection. **Then, in an ostensibly unrelated task, they indicated** only **their birth date (mm/dd/yyyy) and** how old they felt, how much they would enjoy eating at a diner, the square root of 100, their agreement with "computers are complicated machines," **their father's age,** their mother's age, whether they would take advantage of an early-bird special, their political orientation, which of four Canadian quarterbacks they believed won an award, how often they refer to the past as "the good old days," and their gender. **We used father's age to control for variation in baseline age across participants.**

An ANCOVA revealed the predicted effect: According to their birth dates, people were nearly a year-and-a-half younger after listening to "When I'm Sixty-Four" (adjusted $M = 20.1$ years) rather than to "Kalimba" (adjusted $M = 21.5$ years), $F(1, 17) = 4.92$, $p = .040$. Without controlling for father's age, the age difference was smaller and did not reach significance ($Ms = 20.3$ and 21.2, respectively), $F(1, 18) = 1.01$, $p = .33$.

Controversies in psychological science: Is psychology common sense?

Take a look at the following questions on some familiar psychological topics. How many can you answer correctly?

1 Patients with schizophrenia suffer from a split personality. Is this: (a) true most of the time; (b) true some of the time; (c) true none of the time; (d) true only when the individual is undergoing psychotherapy?

2 Under hypnosis, a person will, if asked by a hypnotist: (a) recall past life events with a high degree of accuracy; (b) perform physical feats of strength not possible out of hypnosis; (c) do (a) and (b); (d) do neither (a) nor (b)?

3 The learning principles applied to birds and fish also apply to: (a) humans; (b) cockroaches; (c) both (a) and (b); (d) neither (a) nor (b)?

4 Are physically attractive people: (a) more likely to be stable than physically unattractive people; (b) equal in psychological stability; (c) likely to be less psychologically stable; (d) likely to be much more unstable?

How well did you do? These four questions featured in the 10 questions first-year psychology undergraduates who completed a 38-item questionnaire about psychological knowledge found difficult to answer (Martin et al., 1997). In fact, when the responses from first – and final-year psychology, engineering, sociology, English and business studies students were analysed, no one group scored more than 50 per cent correct. Perhaps not surprisingly, psychologists answered more questions correctly than the other students, with sociologists following close behind. But why should psychology (and other) students perform so badly on a test of psychological knowledge?

The answer lies in the fact that the questionnaire was not really a test of psychological knowledge but of common-sense attitudes towards psychological research. Common-sense mistakes are those committed when a person chooses what they think is the obvious answer but this answer is incorrect. Some writers have suggested that 'a great many of psychology's basic principles are self-evident' (Houston, 1983), and that 'much of what psychology textbooks purport to teach undergraduates about research findings in the area may already be known to them through common, informal experiences' (Barnett, 1986). Houston reported that although introductory psychology students answered 15 out of 21 questions about 'memory and learning' correctly, a collection of 50 individuals found in a city park on a Friday afternoon scored an average of 16.

Is the common-sense view of psychological research justified?

Not quite. Since the late 1970s, a number of studies have examined individuals' false beliefs about psychology, and students' beliefs in particular. Over 76 per cent of first-year psychology students thought the following statements were true: 'Memory can be likened to a storage chest in the brain into which we deposit material and from which we can withdraw later', 'Personality tests reveal your basic motives, including those you may not be aware of', and 'Blind people have unusually sensitive organs of touch'. This, despite the fact that course materials directly contradicted some of these statements (Vaughan, 1977).

Furnham (1992, 1993) found that only half of such 'common-sense' questions were answered correctly by 250 prospective psychology students, and only 20 per cent of questions were answered correctly by half or more of a sample of 110 first-year psychology, fine arts, biochemistry and engineering students. In Martin et al.'s (1997) study, final-year students answered more questions correctly than did first-year students, but there was no significant difference between first-and final-year psychology students. This suggests that misperceptions are slowly dispelled after students undergo the process of higher education and learning, but that studying specific disciplines does nothing to dispel these myths effectively. This is just one explanation.

More recent studies suggest that students continue to express misperceptions about psychology. Gardner and Brown (2012), for example, asked 137 students from US universities to judge a series of true or false statements about 11 branches of psychology. Most of the students responded that they considered the statements to be partly true or partly false. More people were likely to hold misperceptions about psychological treatment, memory, intelligence, learning and the brain. Note, however, that this study used a five-point scale on which participants made their responses – from completely false to completely true. The maximum average score for the 11 branches was 3.1. Furnham and Hughes (2014) also found that the majority of their 829 participants (267 of whom were students) held common misconceptions about psychology. The students performed better than the general population but not by much.

Another study found a better than predicted result for psychology undergraduates – and postgraduates (Hughes et al., 2015). In their test of 30 misconceptions – which contrasts with Furnham and Hughes's 249 – most students and graduates rejected the misconceptions. Thirty-five per cent of undergraduates, however, agreed with misperceptions as did 32 per cent of Masters students. Doctoral students performed better than Masters or undergraduate students – only 24 per cent agreed. In a second study, the researchers replicated the same result in a sample of 557 students, finding that graduates rejected more myths and affirmed fewer.

What, then, is 'common' about 'common sense'? Some have likened common sense to fantastical thinking. This describes ways of reasoning about the world that violate known scientific principles (Woolley, 1997). For example, the beliefs that women can control breast cancer by positive thinking (Taylor, 1983), that

▶

Controversies in psychological science: *Continued*

walking under a ladder brings bad luck and that touching wood brings good luck (Blum and Blum, 1974) violate known physical laws, but people still believe in doing such things. People often draw erroneous conclusions about psychological knowledge because they rely on small sets of data, sometimes a very small set of data (such as a story in a newspaper or the behaviour of a friend).

As you work through your psychology course and through this book, discovering new and sometimes complicated ways of analysing and understanding human behaviour, you will realise that many of the beliefs and perceptions you held about certain aspects of psychology are false or only half right. Of course, no science is truly infallible and there are different ways of approaching psychological problems (and perhaps, sometimes, some problems are insoluble or we have no good method of studying them satisfactorily). Psychology, however, attempts to adopt the best of scientific approaches to understanding potentially the most unmanageable of subject matter: behaviour. And, for those of you who were wondering, the answers to the questions at the start of the box are c, d, c and a.

Explaining behaviour

The ultimate goals of research in psychology are to understand, predict and change human behaviour: to explain why people do what they do. Different kinds of psychologists are interested in different kinds of behaviour and different levels of explanation. How do psychologists 'explain' behaviour?

First, they must describe it accurately and comprehensively. We must become familiar with the things that people (or other animals) do. We must learn how to categorise and measure behaviour so that we can be sure that different psychologists in different places are observing the same phenomena. Next, we must discover the causes of the behaviour we observe – those events responsible for its occurrence. If we can discover the events that caused the behaviour to occur, we have 'explained' it. Events that cause other events (including behaviour) to occur are called **causal events** or **determinants**.

For example, one psychologist might be interested in visual perception and another might be interested in romantic attraction. Even when they are interested in the same behaviour, different psychologists might study different levels of analysis. Some look inside the organism in a literal sense, seeking physiological causes, such as the activity of nerve cells or the secretions of glands. Others look inside the organism in a metaphorical sense, explaining behaviour in terms of hypothetical mental states, such as anger, fear, curiosity or love. Still others look only for events in the environment (including things that other people do) that cause behaviours to occur.

Established and emerging fields of psychology

Throughout this book you will encounter many types of psychologist and many types of psychology. As you have already seen, very few individuals call themselves psychologists, rather they describe themselves by their specialism – cognitive psychologist, developmental psychologist, social psychologist and so on. Before describing and defining each branch of psychology, however, it is important to distinguish between three general terms: psychology, **psychiatry** and **psychoanalysis.** A psychologist normally holds a university degree in a behaviour-related discipline (such as psychology, zoology, cognitive science) and usually possesses a higher research degree (a PhD or doctorate) if they are teaching or a researcher.

Those not researching but working in applied settings such as hospitals or schools may have other, different qualifications that enable them to practise in those environments. Psychiatrists are physicians who have specialised in the causes and treatment of mental disorder. They are medically qualified (unlike psychologists, who nonetheless do study medical problems and undertake biological research) and have the ability to prescribe medication (which psychologists do not). Much of the work done by psychologists in psychiatric settings is similar to that of the psychiatrist, implementing psychological interventions for patients with mental illness. Psychoanalysts are specific types of counsellor who attempt to understand mental disorder by reference to the workings of the unconscious. There is no formal academic qualification necessary to become a psychoanalyst and, as the definition implies, they deal with a limited range of behaviour.

Most research psychologists are employed by colleges or universities, by private organisations or by government. Research psychologists differ from one another in two principal ways: in the types of behaviour they investigate and in the causal events they analyse. That is, they explain different types of behaviour, and they explain them in terms of different types of cause. For example, two psychologists might both be interested in memory, but they might attempt to explain memory in terms of different causal events – one may focus on physiological events (such as the activation of the brain during memory retrieval) whereas the other may focus on environmental events (such as the effect of noise level on task performance). Professional societies such as the American Psychological Association and the British Psychological Society have numerous subdivisions representing members with an interest in a specific aspect of psychology. This section outlines some of the major branches or subdivisions of psychology. A summary of these can be found in Table 1.1.

Psychobiology/biological psychology is the study of the biological basis of behaviour (Martin, 2003). Other terms for the same branch include physiological psychology and biopsychology. It investigates the causal events in an organism's physiology, especially in the nervous system and its interaction with glands that secrete hormones. Psychobiologists study almost all behavioural phenomena that can be observed in non-human animals, including learning, memory, sensory processes, emotional behaviour, motivation, sexual behaviour and sleep, using a variety of techniques (see Chapter 4).

Psychophysiology is the measurement of people's physiological reactions, such as heart rate, blood pressure, electrical resistance of the skin, muscle tension and electrical activity of the brain (Andreassi, 2007). These measurements provide an indication of a person's degree of arousal or relaxation. Most psychophysiologists investigate phenomena such as sensory and perceptual responses, sleep, stress, thinking, reasoning and emotion.

Neuropsychology and **neuroscience** examine the relationship between the brain and **spinal cord,** and behaviour (Martin, 2006). Neuropsychology helps to explain the role these structures play in movement, vision, hearing, tasting, sleeping, smelling and touching as well as emotion, thinking, language and object recognition and perception, and others. Neuropsychologists normally (but not always) study patients who have suffered injury to the brain – through accident, disease or surgery – which disrupts functions such as speech production or comprehension, object recognition, visual or auditory perception and so on. **Clinical neuropsychology** involves the study of the effect of brain injury on behaviour and function.

Modern neuropsychology also uses brain imaging techniques such as positron emission tomography (PET), functional magnetic resonance imaging (fMRI), near infrared spectroscopy (NIFRS) and others, to monitor the activity of processes in the brain as some psychological task is performed. This approach combines two approaches in psychology: neuroscience and cognitive psychology (see below). Because of this, the area of study is sometimes described as **cognitive neuroscience** (Gazzaniga, 1995) or behavioural neuroscience. A new development in this area has been the study of the psychobiological processes involved in social behaviour, a sub-branch called social neuroscience. Social neuroscientists examine the role of the brain in behaviours such as empathy, turn-taking, seeing things from another person's point of view, social interaction, political outlook and so on. We look at the work of cognitive/behavioural/social neuroscientists in more detail throughout this text (see in particular Chapter 4).

Comparative psychology is the study of the behaviour of members of a variety of species in an attempt to explain behaviour in terms of evolutionary adaptation to the environment. Comparative psychologists study behavioural phenomena similar to those studied by physiological psychologists. They are more likely than most other psychologists to study inherited behavioural patterns, such as courting and mating, predation and aggression, defensive behaviours and parental behaviours.

Closely tied to comparative psychology is **ethology,** the study of the biological basis of behaviour in the context of the evolution of development and function. Ethologists usually make their observations based on studies of animal behaviour in natural conditions and investigate topics such as instinct, social and sexual behaviour and cooperation. A sub-discipline of ethology is **sociobiology** which attempts to explain social behaviour in terms of biological inheritance and evolution. Ethology and sociobiology are described in more detail in Chapter 3. Evolutionary psychology studies 'human behaviour as the product of evolved psychological mechanisms that depend on internal and environmental input for their development, activation, and expression in manifest behaviour' (Confer *et al.*, 2010, p. 110) (see Chapter 3). Although the basis of evolutionary psychology is found in the work of Charles Darwin (described in Chapter 3 and briefly below), as a sub-discipline it is relatively young having developed in the past 15 years.

Behaviour genetics is the branch of psychology that studies the role of genetics in behaviour (Plomin, 2008). The genes we inherit from our parents include a blueprint for the construction of a human brain. Each blueprint is a little different, which means that no two brains are exactly alike. Therefore, no two people will act exactly alike, even in an identical situation. Behaviour geneticists study the role of genetics in behaviour by examining similarities in physical and behavioural characteristics of blood relatives, whose genes are more similar than those of unrelated individuals. They also perform breeding experiments with laboratory animals to see what aspects of behaviour can be transmitted to an animal's offspring. Behavioural geneticists study the degree to which genetics are responsible for specific behaviours such as cognitive ability. The work of behavioural geneticists is described in Chapter 3 and discussed in the context of intelligence research and personality in Chapters 11 and 14.

Cognitive psychology is the study of mental processes and complex behaviours such as perception, attention, learning, memory, concept formation and problem-solving. Explanations in cognitive psychology involve characteristics of inferred mental processes, such as imagery, attention and mechanisms of language. Most cognitive psychologists do not study physiological mechanisms, but recently some have begun applying neuroimaging methods to studying cognitive function. A branch of cognitive psychology called **cognitive science** involves the modelling of human function using computer simulation or 'neural networks'. We briefly examine the contribution of such computer simulations to our understanding of behaviour in Chapters 7 and 10.

Developmental psychology is the study of physical, cognitive, emotional and social development, especially of children (Berk, 2009) but, more broadly, of humans from foetus to old age (these psychologists are sometimes called lifespan developmental psychologists). Some developmental psychologists study the effects of old age on behaviour and the body (a field called gerontology). Most developmental psychologists restrict their study to a particular period of development, such as infancy, adolescence or old age. This field is described and illustrated in more detail in Chapter 12. The development of children's language is described in Chapter 10, and the effects of old age on cognition in Chapter 11.

Social psychology is the study of the effects of people on people. Social psychologists explore phenomena such as self-perception and the perception of others, cause-and-effect relations in human interactions, attitudes and opinions, interpersonal relationships, group dynamics and emotional behaviours, including aggression and sexual attraction (Hogg and Vaughan, 2007). Chapters 15 and 16 explore some of the core issues and themes in social psychology. An example of how we interpret the social behaviour of others is considered in the Psychology in action section below.

Cross-cultural psychology is the study of the impact of culture on behaviour. The ancestors of people of different racial and

Psychology in action: How to detect a liar?

Take a look at this list of behaviours. Which do you think you a liar would show and why?

- Averting gaze
- Unnatural posture
- Posture change
- Scratching/touching parts of the body
- Playing with hair or objects
- Placing the hand over the mouth
- Placing the hand over the eyes

According to a standard manual of police interviewing, all of these features are characteristic of a liar (Inbau et al., 1986). A study of participants in 75 countries found that 'averting gaze' was described as the best tell-tale sign of lying (Global Deception Research Team, 2006).

Unfortunately, despite the manual's exhortations and the international guesswork, none of these behaviours is actually reliably associated with deception.

Studies of police officers and students report lying detection rates of between 40 and 60 per cent – a result no better than expected by chance (Vrij, 2000; Vrij and Mann, 2001). Police officers and people who use the polygraph technique – the so-called lie detector – generally do no better than students (Ekman and O'Sullivan, 1991). The exception to this generally ignominious performance seems to be Secret Service agents (Ekman et al., 1999). We can usually tell the difference between truth and falsity with 50 per cent accuracy (Bond and DePaulo, 2006).

You might imagine that the best lie detectors are those who routinely lie in order to get out of trouble, and you'd be right. Researchers from the University of Gothenburg, Sweden (Hartwig et al., 2004) found that criminals were significantly better than students at detecting liars – although the criminals also detected fewer truth-tellers – possibly because they are naturally suspicious (they are used to being lied to, whether in prison or in the context of their relationships with others) or because they themselves are practised liars (and, therefore, expert at detecting like-minded dissemblers). There is evidence that the more people practice lying, the better they get at it

(no surprise there, perhaps) but that if people are trained to tell the truth, they find lying harder (van Bockstaele et al., 2012). A review of studies of training in deception detection found that there was a small to medium effect of training on accurate detection (Hauch et al., 2016). Training that focused on verbal content was a better predictor of lie detection than was nonverbal information, which is consistent with other research. The same research group also found that lying was predictable from specific linguistic cues and behaviours: liars expressed more negative emotion, distanced themselves more from events, used fewer sensory and perceptual words and referred less to cognitive processes (Hauch et al., 2015).

There are also some age differences in lie-detection: people are better at telling that older people (70 year olds) are lying than they are young people (20 year olds) and older people are worse than young people at detecting deception (Ruffman et al., 2012). Also, some people are surprisingly good at detecting lying – people with aphasia, for example. There are different types of aphasia, a language disorder produced by brain injury, but one study of 10 people who had damage to the left side of the brain and severe problems in comprehending spoken sentences, were more accurate than an unimpaired group at detecting emotional liars (Etcoff et al., 2000). They were particularly good at identifying changes in facial expression and voice pitch.

A study of male offenders from a medium security Canadian prison, and a group of undergraduates, asked participants to recall four emotional events from their lives (Porter et al., 2008) but lie about two of them. The researchers measured the number of illustrators (the use of hands to signify something), self-manipulations (touching/scratching the hand, head or body), frequency of head movement and number of smiles and laughs. Verbal indicators included the number of words spoken per minute, filled pauses ('umms' and 'ahs'), self-references and pauses that were longer than two seconds. Illustrators were higher when lying than when telling the truth in both groups. Offenders, however, used more self-manipulations when lying compared with non-offenders. ▶

Psychology in action: *Continued*

Of course, these deception studies are fairly artificial. Interviewing suspects, the police would argue, gives you much more information on which to base a judgement. So, does it? Studies have shown that people who observe such interviews are better at discriminating between truth-tellers and liars than are the interviewers themselves (Buller *et al.*, 1991; Granhag and Stromwall, 2001). Interviewers also showed evidence of truth bias – the tendency to declare that someone was saying the truth when they were not.

People tend to focus on different behavioural cues when deciding on whether a person is telling the truth or lying, with people relying on verbal cues when judging the truthfulness of a story and on non-verbal cues when the story is deceptive (Anderson *et al.*, 1999). One review has suggested that the behaviours people claim to use when they detect lying are inaccurate, but the behaviours they actually use as cues show some overlap with objective clues (Hartwig and Bond, 2011).

Table 1.3a Characteristics of deceptive and honest appealers in Wheelan et al's studies Swap around 1.3a and 1.3b

Deceptive appealers	Honest appealers
Fake emotion	Genuine sadness
Fake emotion (11)	Genuine sadness (8)
Fake facial expression (4)	Facial expressions (4)
Putting on a performance (6)	Sad eyes (5)
Pretending to cry (6)	Desperation/urgency (4)
High vocal pitch (15)	
No emotional variation (4)	
Lack of emotion	Genuine/heartfelt
Lack of emotion (6)	Genuine/heartfelt (7)
Painless recall (7)	No prepared speech (5)
Calm/calculated (9)	Positive emotion expressed toward relative (6)
Lack of emotion in voice (4)	Smile appropriate to speech content (2)
Emotionally cold (7)	Genuine behaviors (3)
Lack of facial expression (4)	Credible eye contact (6)
Brutal language/detail (3)	
Distancing	Containing emotion
Impersonal (7)	Containing emotion (15)
Focus on others (9)	Calmness appropriate to speech content (9)
First person pronouns (2)	Trying to be sensible (8)
Equivocation (3)	Hopeful of finding missing relative (2)
Irrelevant/generic statements (2)	Avoiding brutal language/detail (2)
Not focused on relative (8)	
Lists (7)	
Gaze aversion (8)	
Implausibility	Sympathetic personal reaction
Nonsensical (9)	Feel the appealers' pain (3)
Making assumptions (2)	Feel sorry for the appealer (7)
Lack of hope of finding missing relative alive (7)	Normal (3)
Indication of dispute (2)	Behaving as expected (4)
Defensive (3)	
Fear/nervousness (9)	
Negative personal reaction	
Dislike for the appealer (6)	
Creepy (2)	
Behaving unnaturally (3)	
No sympathy for the appealer (6)	

Psychology in action: *Continued*

Table 1.3b Features of lying and honesty in Wheelan et al's studies

Cues to deception

Fake emotion

Fake facial expression

Putting on a performance

Behaving unnaturally

Creepy

Dislike for the appealer

No sympathy for appealer

Cues to honesty

Sad eyes

Genuinely sad

Genuine/heartfelt appeal

Urgency

Plausible

Normal

Personal & expressive voice

Voice quivering with emotion

Feel the appealer's pain

Feel sorry for the appealer

So, what are the most reliable indices of lying? Is there a 'Pinocchio's nose'? Two of the most fairly reliable indicators appear to be a high-pitched voice and a decrease in hand movements. But the way in which people are asked to identify lying is also important. For example, people are less accurate detectors when asked, 'Is this person lying?' than when asked 'Does the person x sincerely like the person y?' (Vrij, 2001). When people are questioned indirectly they tend to focus on those behavioural cues that have been found to predict deception, such as decreased hand movement, rather than those that do not (Vrij, 2001).

Two recent studies, however, have attempted to meet the criticism that most studies of lie-detection involve very artificial laboratory situations, by highlighting some real cues to deception that people emit in realistic situations. Whelan and her colleagues (Whelan, 2014a; Whelan *et al.*, 2014b) asked three groups of individuals in one of their studies to watch the real police murder appeals made by members of the public. Half of the appealers were later discovered to be liars (and murderers). Participants were asked to comment on which

behaviours they used to make their decision. Whelan *et al.* found that 17 cues were able to distinguish between appealers who were honest and those who were lying. These are listed in Tables 1.3a and b.

The finding that faked facial expressions and sad eyes were a cue to dishonesty is consistent with another study which found that appealers who were liars were more likely to express surprise with the upper part of their face, whereas honest appealers were more likely to show upper face expressions of sadness (ten Brinke and Porter, 2012). The surprise response was thought to be a misguided attempt at sadness in the liars. A study using similar stimuli but with 70 UK police officers and 37 students found that although the officers detected deception more accurately (72 per cent), the students were comparable (68 per cent). In a study of 44 studies where software had been used to detect deception, Hauch *et al.* (2014) found that (1) lies were shorter, less elaborate and less complex than true stories, (2) liars expressed more negative emotion in language (especially, anger), (3) liars expressed more of a mix of positive and negative emotions, (4) liars

▶

Psychology in action: *Continued*

distanced themselves more from the lied event more than did honest people and they used fewer first-person expressions and (5) people who tell the truth refer more to cognitive processes than do liars (they refer to their autobiographical memories more and to how they retrieved memories).

In short, there is probably no one way, nor one set of ways, of determining whether someone is telling the truth or not. The demands of the situation in which people lie can change, their motivation for doing so can vary, and the person's personality is important.

ethnic groups lived in different environments which presented them with different problems and opportunities for solving those problems. Different cultures have, therefore, developed different strategies for adapting to their environments. These strategies show themselves in laws, customs, myths, religious beliefs and ethical principles as well as in thinking, health beliefs and approaches to problem-solving. A slightly different name – **cultural psychology** – is given to the study of variations within cultures (not necessarily across cultures). Throughout the book, you will find a section entitled, '. . . An international perspective', which takes a topic in psychology and examines how it has been studied cross-culturally, for example, Are personality traits, recognition of emotion, memory, mental illness and so on culture-specific?

Forensic and **criminological psychology** applies psychological knowledge to the understanding, prediction and nature of crime and behaviour related to crime. There is a distinction between criminological and forensic psychology. Forensic psychologists can be commissioned by courts to prepare reports on the fitness of a defendant to stand trial, on the general psychological state of the defendant, on aspects of psychological research (such as post-traumatic stress disorders), on the behaviour of children involved in custody disputes and so on. Criminological psychology refers to the

application of psychological principles to the criminal justice system. The terms, however, are often used interchangeably.

Clinical psychology is probably the field most closely identified with applied psychology and psychology in general and aims 'to reduce psychological distress and to enhance and promote psychological well-being' (BPS Division of Clinical Psychology, 2010). It is an applied branch of psychology because clinical psychologists do not work in the laboratory under well-controlled experimental conditions but out in the field (usually clinic or hospital), applying the knowledge gained from practice and research. Clinical psychologists

Alastair Campbell and Ruby Wax, two tireless campaigners for the public undertstanding of mental illness.

Source: Robbie Jack/Corbis Entertainment/Getty Images (l); Ken McKay/ITV/REX/Shutterstock (r)

address problems caused by mental illnesses (see Chapter 18), and mental illness is one of the most widely misunderstood illnesses and the most peculiarly reported. It is also one of the most stigmatised – people feel embarrassed about mental illness and others may respond to sufferers unsympathetically because they do not understand the disorder. Hence, public figures such as the former UK government Director of Communications, Alastair Campbell, the comedian, Ruby Wax, and the actor and writer, Stephen Fry, have made their illnesses known and have promoted their public understanding.

Whether such promotion and the emphasis on illness succeeds in making the stigma less strident, however, is unclear. When Read and Harre (2001) asked psychology students questions such as "would you be happy being romantically involved with someone who has spent time in a psychiatric hospital," those who were more likely to believe in biological/genetic causes of mental disorder were more likely to avoid mentally ill people and regard the mentally ill as unpredictable and dangerous. This finding was replicated in a study in which people saw a man hallucinating and expressing delusions – when his behaviour was given a biological or genetic explanation, people were more likely to regard him as dangerous and unpredictable (Walker and Read, 2002).

An analysis of the portrayal of mental illness in a week's worth of children's programmes on two television stations in New Zealand found that over 45 per cent contained reference to mental illness and most of these were: 'crazy', 'mad' and 'losing your mind', although 'mad' and 'crazy' were interchangeably used to mean 'angry' (Wilson *et al.*, 2000). Other terms included 'driven bananas', 'wacko', 'nuts', 'loony', 'cuckoo' and 'freak'. Mental illness was frequently portrayed as reflecting a loss of control. Characters at the receiving end of these epithets were routinely and invariably seen as negative, as objects of amusement or derision or as objects of fear. The characters were either comical or villainous. Psychologists have identified views such as these and proposed ways of changing them (see Chapter 18).

Health psychology is the study of the ways in which behaviour and lifestyle can affect health and illness (Sarafino and Smith 2014). For example, smoking is associated with a number of illnesses and is a risk factor for serious illness and death. Health psychologists study what makes people initiate and maintain such unhealthy behaviour and can help devise strategies to reduce it. Health psychologists are employed in a variety of settings including hospitals, government, universities and private practice (see Chapter 17).

Educational psychology is another branch of applied psychology. Educational psychologists assess the behavioural problems of children at school and suggest ways in which these problems may be remedied. For example, the educational psychologist might identify a child's early inability to read (dyslexia) and suggest a means by which this may be overcome through special training. The educational psychologist might also deal with all aspects relevant to a child's schooling such as learning, social relations, assessment, disruptive behaviour, substance abuse, bullying and parental neglect.

Consumer psychology is the study of the motivation, perception, learning, cognition and purchasing behaviour of individuals in the marketplace and their use of products once they reach the home. Some consumer psychologists take a marketer's perspective, some take a consumer's perspective, and some adopt a neutral perspective, especially if they work at a university.

Organisational or **occupational psychology** is one of the largest and oldest fields of applied psychology and involves the study of the ways in which individuals and groups perform and behave in the workplace (Huczynski and Buchanan, 2010). Early organisational psychologists concentrated on industrial work processes (such as the most efficient way to shovel coal), but organisational psychologists now spend more effort analysing modern plants and offices. Most are employed by large companies and organisations.

A related branch, **ergonomics** or **human factors psychology,** focuses mainly on the ways in which people and machines work together. They study machines ranging from cockpits to computers, from robots to MP3/4 players, from transportation vehicles for the disabled to telephones. If the machine is well designed, the task can be much easier, more enjoyable and safer. Ergonomists help designers and engineers to design better machines; because of this, the terms ergonomics and engineering psychology are sometimes used interchangeably.

Sport and **exercise psychology** applies psychological principles to the area of sport. It also involves the study of the effects of sport and exercise on mood, cognition, well-being and physiology. This area is examined in more detail in Chapter 17.

Psychology: a European perspective

Psychology is one of the most popular degree courses in Europe. Around 54,000 students were studying Psychology in the UK in 2016. Modern psychology has its origins in Europe: the first psychological laboratory was established in Europe and some of the first designated university degrees in psychology were established there. Research in North America and Europe accounts for the majority of psychological studies published in the world (Eysenck, 2001) and there continues to be debate over whether these two fairly large 'geographical' areas adopt genuinely different approaches to the study of psychological processes (Martin, 2001).

Psychology as a discipline occupies a different status in different European countries and each country has established its own degrees and societies at different times, for historical or political reasons. Almost all countries have a professional organisation which regulates the activity of psychologists or provides psychological training or licensing of psychologists.

Cutting edge: How not to use the internet

In any of your psychology classes, you are likely to have access to a computer – whether your laptop, tablet or college/University's computer. And you might think that this is an advantage – you have access to a machine, you can write up notes efficiently, and you can check the internet for information as you listen to your lecturer.

But your internet use during class, especially if it is not related to your academic work, can have serious consequences for your performance. It could make you a worse student (Ravizza et al., 2016). Ravizza et al. monitored internet use during class in 84 students (from 127 who volunteered) and examined the relationship between this use and academic performance. The 84 students selected were those who came to class and checked into a proxy server during more than half of the 15 sessions they attended. Logging in attempts were quite high – the group did this an average of 12.7 times. The researchers examined whether the students used the internet for academic or non-academic use.

Those who accessed the internet for non-academic reasons were more likely to perform poorly at the end-of-term exam, and this finding was not accounted for by interest in the class, motivation to succeed or intelligence. Searching the internet for academic reasons was not associated with any benefit to exam performance. More interestingly still, when the researchers asked students whether they thought their internet use would be disruptive to their studies, those who judged that it would be, performed worse in the exam. Those who said that internet use would have a 'slightly disruptive effect' performed worse than any group. This was the group that used the internet the most. This suggests that self-awareness of the disruption caused by internet use in class is related to academic performance.

The study suggests that to use technology for learning, you need to use it in the right way and in the right context. You'll read about a similar effect in Chapter 7 in a study where students learned better by writing notes directly during a lecture, rather than writing notes on a pre-downloaded Powerpoint slides (Mueller and Oppenheimer, 2014).

The first such association in Denmark was founded in 1929 (the Psychotechnical Institute in Copenhagen) and what we would now call educational psychology formed the basis of the professional training it provided: the job of the institute was to select apprentices for the printing trade (Foltveld, 1995). The Netherlands' first psychological laboratory was founded in 1892 at Gröningen, Denmark's in 1944 at the University of Copenhagen and Finland's in 1921 by Eino Kaila at the University of Turku (Saari, 1995). Coincidentally, 1921 was also the year in which the Netherlands passed a Higher Education Act allowing philosophy students to specialise in psychology.

The British Psychological Society (BPS) was formed in 1901, with laboratories established at the University of Cambridge and University College London in 1897, closely followed by the establishment of laboratories in Aberdeen, Edinburgh and Glasgow (Lunt, 1995). Sweden's professional association was founded in 1955 (Sveriges Psykologforbund), with the Netherlands' pre-dating that in 1938 (Nederlandsch Instituut van Practizeerende Psychologen, or NIPP). Portugal is one of the younger psychology nations – the first students of psychology graduated in 1982 (Pereira, 1995). Because of the history of the country, psychology was not acknowledged as a university subject in Portugal until after the democratic revolution of 1974.

Psychology – An international perspective

Behind almost all research endeavours in psychology is a common aim: to discover a psychological universal. According to Norenzayan and Heine (2005), **psychological universals** are 'core mental attributes shared by humans everywhere'. That is, they are conclusions from psychological research that can be generalised across groups – ways of reasoning, thinking, making decisions, interpreting why people behave in the way that they do, recognising emotions and so on, are all examples of core mental attributes. A sound case for a psychological universal can be made if a phenomenon exists in a large variety of different cultures.

However, some differences may be more obvious in some groups than others – men and women, for example, the young and the old, the mentally ill and the mentally healthy and so on. At this level of analysis, we cannot say that people in general behave in a particular way, but that a specific group of people behave in a particular way. Nowhere is this more relevant than when considering the role of culture in psychological studies. A variety of behaviours is absent or are limited in a variety of cultures and nations and a new field of research has begun called geographical psychology which investigates geographical variation in the ways of thinking, feeling and

▶

Psychology: *Continued*

Table 1.4 Behaviours/concepts reported to vary across cultures, or which may be more or less evident in certain cultures. Unfamiliar terms are defined in the chapters referred to in brackets

- Memory for and categorisation of colours (see Chapter 6)
- Spatial reasoning (see Chapter 8)
- Autobiographical memory (see Chapter 8)
- Perception of the environment
- Appreciation of art
- Some types of category-based inductive reasoning (see Chapter 11)
- Some perceptual illusions
- Some ways of approaching reasoning
- Aspects of numerical reasoning
- Risk preferences in decision-making (see Chapter 11)
- Self-concept (see Chapters 15 and 16)
- Similarity-attraction effect (see Chapters 15 and 16)
- Approach-avoidance motivation (see Chapter 13)
- The fundamental attribution error (see Chapters 15 and 16)
- Predilection for aggression

- Feelings of control, dominance or subordination
- High subjective well-being and positive affect
- Communication style
- Prevalence of major depression
- Prevalence of eating disorders (see Chapter 13)
- Mental illness (see Chapter 18)
- Noun bias in language learning (see Chapter 10)
- Moral reasoning
- Prevalence of different attachment style (see Chapter 12)
- Disruptive behaviour in adolescence
- Personality types (see Chapter 14)
- Response bias (see Chapter 2)
- Recognition of emotion
- Perception of happiness
- Body shape preference

Source: Adapted from Norenzayan and Heine, 2005.

behaving (Rentfrow and Jokela, 2016). You'll find some of the fruits of this research in some of the later chapters.

Some research, for example, has highlighted significant differences between Western and Asian cultures in the types of autobiographical memory they recall, the parts of a landscape and photograph they focus on, and the way in which they draw and take a photograph (Varnum *et al.*, 2010). Table 1.4 summarises some of these differences.

Varnum *et al.* have noted that cultures can differ according to their social orientation so that some are independent and analytical and others are interdependent and holistic. Independent cultures emphasise the importance of self-direction, autonomy, the enhancement of self at the expense of others and they are self-expressive; interdependent cultures believe in being connected with others, working and living harmoniously and enhancement of the self at the expense of others is absent. The most common examples of such cultures are Western and East Asian, respectively, although these are very large categories and there will be considerable variation within them, let alone between them.

Northern Italians, for example, appear to be more independent than Southern Italians (Martella and Maass, 2000), are more analytic and categorise objects more taxonomically (Knight and Nisbett, 2007). Villages in the Black Sea region of Turkey also differ according to the type of economic activity they engage in. So, fishermen and farmers categorised objects

more thematically and perceived scenes more contextually than did herders (Uskul *et al.*, 2008). People who move home and move often are more likely to show a personal than a collective sense of identity (Oishi, 2010).

Some countries appear to bridge the two types of approach. Russians, for example, appear to be more interdependent than are Germans (Naumov, 1996) and they reason and visually perceive stimuli more holistically (looking at the whole and the context, rather than a part of a scene, say). Croats show a similar pattern of behaviour to Russians (Varnum *et al.*, 2008).

One way of demonstrating a psychological universal is to examine a behaviour in three or more cultures, two of which are very different, with a third falling between them, and see how each differs from, or is similar to, the other. The best way, however, is to examine a variety of cultures, as Daly and Wilson (1988) did. Their research examined sex differences in the international rates of homicide and found that men were more likely to kill men than women were to kill women across all cultures. Debate then ensues as to why this universal should be (and that debate is often heated, as most in psychology are).

In the book, examples of universals (and exceptions) are highlighted in the sections: '. . . An international perspective'. These will help you put the findings you read about in cultural or international context. They should also help demonstrate that, although studies sometimes report findings as being absolute and generalisable to populations in general, sometimes these findings are not.

Cutting edge: Which cities produce the 'best' psychology research?

Based on how many times researchers' publications were cited by other researchers, Bornmmann *et al.* (2012) were able to map which cities in the world produced the publications with the greatest impact in 2007. The researchers examined the top 10 per cent of journal articles (those that were most widely cited in psychology) from 2007 to 2011. They were able to use the citation data collected from those papers published in 2007 and see how often and how widely the publications were cited by researchers from 218 different cities across the world – from the UK to Australia. Papers had to have received at least 16 citations to be considered highly cited.

London was the city with the greatest number of highly cited papers with Oxford, Cambridge, Amsterdam and Nijmegen (in The Netherlands) following behind. Highly cited articles were also found in Berlin, Bremen, Dublin, Louvain, Mannheim, Munster, Leipzig, Oulu, Stockholm and Utrecht. When the researchers examined data from the US, the east coast produced the greatest number. The only other non-UK and non-US cites to have a large proportion of highly cited studies were Sydney and Parkville in Australia and Kaohsiung in Taiwan.

Psychological training and status of psychology in Europe

The types of career that psychology graduates pursue are similar across most European countries. Most psychologists are employed in the public sector, with the majority of those working in the clinical, educational or organisational fields. Training for psychologists varies between countries and controversy surrounds the licensing or the legalisation of the profession. For example, psychologists in almost all countries wish for formal statutory regulation of the profession (the medical and legal professions are regulated). In Denmark, the title of psychologist was legally protected in 1993 so that no one could call themselves a psychologist unless they had received specified training. In Greece, a law was passed in 1979 licensing psychologists to practise (Georgas, 1995). These enlightened views have not extended to some other countries, however, despite the attempts of professional organisations in lobbying their legislators. Finland and the UK have faced obstacles in legalising the profession.

The BPS has its own regulatory system so that applied psychologists need to undergo an approved route of training (e.g. to go on to practise as forensic, clinical, educational, health psychologists) before they are recognised as qualified professional psychologists by the Society. Most of these individuals choose to register themselves as Chartered Psychologists – a person using the services of a psychologist designated chartered can, therefore, be assured that the person is a recognised professional psychologist.

European views of psychology and psychologists

Non-psychologists' views of what psychology is and what psychologists do are encouragingly positive and generally accurate although their knowledge of psychological research (as you saw earlier) is flawed. Table 1.5 shows you the responses of an Austrian sample to the question, 'What do you expect a psychologist to do?', and to the sentence, 'Psychologists can . . . ' (Friedlmayer and Rossler, 1995).

Table 1.5 Austrian views of psychologists (based on a sample of 300 respondents)

Statement/question	%
'Psychologists can . . . '	
See through other people	68
Help other people to change	72
Help others to help themselves	90
Exert influence through reports	57
Release people from mental suffering	62
Listen patiently	88
Direct the attention of social policy-makers	53
Handle children well	55
Cause harm by making mistaken diagnoses	68
Make people happier	54

Table 1.5 *(Continued)*

Statement/question	%
'What do you expect a psychologist to do?'	
Talk	97
Test	90
File a report	85
Treatment/therapy	91
Train children	46
Proposing interventions	86
Negotiate conflicts	65
Give guidance and advice	94
Solve problems	44

Source: Based on FriedImayer, S. and Rossler, E., Professional identity and public image of Austrian psychologists. Reproduced with permission from *Psychology in Europe* by A. Schorr and S. Saari (eds), ISBN 0-88937-155-5, © Hogrefe & Huber Publishers, Seattle, Toronto, Göttingen, Bern.

A Finnish study which asked adults to rate which of a number of professions was more knowledgeable about human nature found that 53 per cent believed doctors were more knowledgeable, with psychologists following behind in second place (29 per cent) (Montin, 1995). A Norwegian study, however, found the opposite: 49 per cent chose psychologists and 23 per cent chose doctors (Christiansen, 1986). Figures 1.2a–d give some of the other illuminating responses to the other questions asked in the Finnish survey. These not only reveal how people receive or obtain their information about psychology but also show that the discipline is still shrouded in some mystery – 49 per cent declare knowing only 'a little' about psychology. Mercifully, 75 per cent of respondents disagreed that psychologists could read minds.

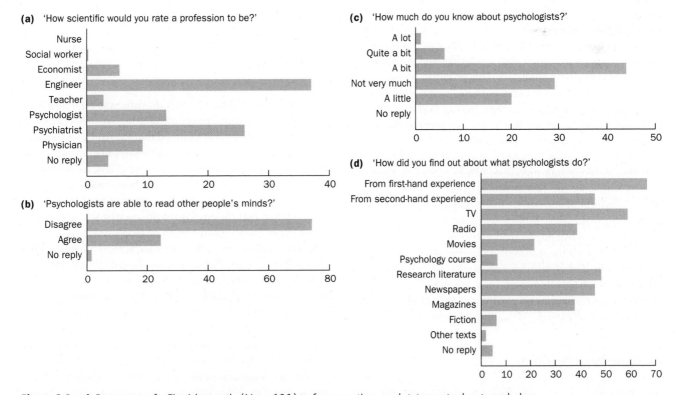

Figure 1.2a–d Responses of a Finnish sample ($N = 601$) to four questions and statements about psychology.

Source: Montin, S. The public image of psychologists in Finland. Reproduced with permission from *Psychology in Europe* by A. Schorr and S. Saari (eds), I SBN 0-88937-155-5, © 1995, Hogrefe & Huber Publishers, Seattle, Toronto, Göttingen, Bern.

Psychology: the development of a science

Although philosophers have been concerned with psychological issues for centuries, the science of psychology is comparatively young. To understand how this science came into being, it is useful to trace its roots back through philosophy and the natural sciences. These disciplines originally provided the methods we use to study human behaviour and took many centuries to develop.

Philosophical roots of psychology

Animism

Each of us is conscious of our own existence. Furthermore, we are aware of this consciousness. Although we often find ourselves doing things that we had not planned to do (or had planned not to do), by and large we feel that we are in control of our behaviour. That is, we have the impression that our conscious mind controls our behaviour. We consider alternatives, make plans and then act. We get our bodies moving; we engage in behaviour.

Earlier in human history, philosophers attributed a life-giving animus, or spirit, to anything that seemed to move or grow independently. Because they believed that the movements of their own bodies were controlled by their minds or spirits, they inferred that the sun, moon, wind, tides and other moving entities were similarly animated. This primitive philosophy is called animism (from the Latin *animare*, 'to quicken, enliven, endow with breath or soul'). Even gravity was explained in animistic terms: rocks fell to the ground because the spirits within them wanted to be reunited with Mother Earth.

Obviously, animism is now of historical interest only. But note that different interpretations can be placed on the same events. Surely, we are just as prone to subjective interpretations of natural phenomena, albeit more sophisticated ones, as our ancestors were. In fact, when we try to explain why people do what they do, we tend to attribute at least some of their behaviour to the action of a motivating spirit – namely, a will. In our daily lives, this explanation of behaviour may often suit our needs. However, on a scientific level, we need to base our explanations on phenomena that can be observed and measured objectively. We cannot objectively and directly observe 'will'.

Dualism: René Descartes

Although the history of Western philosophy properly begins with the Ancient Greeks, a French philosopher and mathematician, René Descartes (1596–1650), is regarded as the

RENÉ DESCARTES
Né à La Haye en 1596.

René Descartes (1596–1650).
Source: Chris Hellier/Corbis Historical/Getty Images

father of modern philosophy. He advocated a sober, impersonal investigation of natural phenomena using sensory experience and human reasoning. He assumed that the world was a purely mechanical entity that, having once been set in motion by God, ran its course without divine interference. Thus, to understand the world, one had only to understand how it was constructed. This stance challenged the established authority of the Church, which believed that the purpose of philosophy was to reconcile human experiences with the truth of God's revelations.

To Descartes, animals were mechanical devices; their behaviour was controlled by environmental stimuli. His view of the human body was much the same: it was a machine. Thus, Descartes was able to describe some movements as automatic and involuntary. For example, the application of a hot object to a finger would cause an almost immediate withdrawal of the arm away from the source of stimulation. Reactions like this did not require participation of the mind; they occurred automatically. Descartes called these actions reflexes (from the Latin *reflectere*, 'to bend back upon itself'). A stimulus registered by the senses produces a reaction that would be entirely physical and beyond voluntary control.

Figure 1.3 Descartes's diagram of a withdrawal reflex.
Source: Stock Montage, Inc.

There would be no intention or will to produce this physical reaction. Consider the well-known reflex of sensing the heat of a flame, as seen in Figure 1.3. The body recoils from flame in an involuntary way: we do not intentionally move away from the flame but our body reflexively puts in place a chain of muscle contractions which make us withdraw. The term 'reflex' is still in use today, but, of course, we explain the operation of a reflex differently (see Chapter 4).

What set humans apart from the rest of the world, according to Descartes, was their possession of a mind. This was a uniquely human attribute and was not subject to the laws of the universe. Thus, Descartes was a proponent of dualism, the belief that all reality can be divided into two distinct entities: mind and matter (this is often referred to as Cartesian dualism). He distinguished between 'extended things', or physical bodies, and 'thinking things', or minds. Physical bodies, he believed, do not think, and minds are not made of ordinary matter.

Although Descartes was not the first to propose dualism, his thinking differed from that of his predecessors in one important way: he was the first to suggest that a link exists between the human mind and its purely physical housing. Although later philosophers pointed out that this theoretical link actually contradicted his belief in dualism – the proposal of an interaction between mind and matter – **interactionism**, was absolutely vital to the development of the science of psychology.

From the time of Plato onwards, philosophers had argued that the mind and the body were different entities. They also suggested that the mind could influence the body but the body could not influence the mind, a little like a puppet and puppeteer with the mind pulling the strings of the body. Not all philosophers adopted this view, however. To some, such as Spinoza (1632–1677), both mental events (thinking) and physical events (such as occupying space) were characteristic of one and the same thing, in the same way that an undulating line can be described as convex or concave – it cannot be described as exclusively one thing or another (this is called **double-aspect theory**).

Descartes hypothesised that this interaction between mind and body took place in the pineal body, a small organ situated at the top of the **brain stem**, buried beneath the large cerebral hemispheres of the brain. When the mind decided to perform an action, it tilted the pineal body in a particular direction, causing fluid to flow from the brain into the proper set of **nerves**. This flow of fluid caused the appropriate muscles to inflate and move.

How did Descartes come up with this mechanical concept of the body's movements? Western Europe in the seventeenth century was the scene of great advances in the sciences. This was the century, for example, in which William Harvey discovered that blood circulated around the body. It was not just the practical application of science that impressed Europeans, however, it was the beauty, imagination and fun of it as well. Craftsmen constructed many elaborate mechanical toys and devices during this period. The young Descartes was greatly impressed by the moving statues in the Royal Gardens (Jaynes, 1970) and these devices served as models for Descartes as he theorised about how the body worked. He conceived of the muscles as balloons. They became inflated when a fluid passed through the nerves that connected them to the brain and spinal cord, just as water flowed through pipes to activate the statues. This inflation was the basis of the muscular contraction that causes us to move.

Descartes's influence on the development of psychology was considerable. He proposed the revolutionary idea that the mind and the body were mutually interacting and suggested a method of studying 'the mind' which was based on reasoning and not metaphysical analysis. Descartes's notion of interactionism gave rise to two very influential but very different schools of thought in psychology at the end of the nineteenth and the beginning of the twentieth centuries: introspectionism and behaviourism. We consider these later in the chapter.

Empiricism: John Locke and David Hume

A prevalent belief in the seventeenth century was that ideas were innately present in our minds from birth. The English philosopher John Locke (1632–1704) rejected this belief. Instead, he proposed that all knowledge must come through experience: it is empirically derived. Descartes's rationalism – pursuit of truth through reason – was replaced by **empiricism** – pursuit of truth through observation and experience (in Greek, *empeiria* means experience). His model of the mind was a tablet of soft clay, a tabula rasa, smooth at birth and ready to accept the writings of experience imprinted upon it. Locke believed that our knowledge of complex experiences was nothing more than links between simple, primary sensations: simple ideas combined to form complex ones.

This idea was developed further by the Scottish philosopher David Hume (1711–76). In his book *A Treatise of Human Nature* (1739), Hume argued that the study of human nature could best be undertaken through experience and observation. Whereas Locke wrote of ideas, Hume wrote of perceptions which were composed of impressions and ideas. Impressions were what we would consider sensations – seeing print on a paper or hearing a loud bang; ideas were the less vivid recollection of such sense experiences. Impressions, according to Hume, were the most important perceptions because these were derived directly from observation. Any ideas based on content which was not derived empirically were not valuable and not trustworthy. Hume, therefore, espoused what is known as **positivism** – the school of thought which argues that all meaningful ideas can be reduced to observable material.

Perhaps Hume's greatest contribution to psychology was the **doctrine of the association of ideas**. In *An Inquiry Concerning Human Understanding* (1748), Hume argued that there were various types of connection or association between ideas. This was not itself a new idea. Aristotle had proposed the notion that two stimuli if paired frequently enough would result in the presentation of one event stimulating thoughts of the other. Hume suggested three specific types of association: resemblance (when we look at someone's photograph, for example, this triggers off thoughts about that person), contiguity (thoughts of an object or event will trigger thoughts related to those objects and events), and cause and effect (the idea that actions have identifiable causes). These associations were the 'cement' that helped bind the universe, and all complex human experiences were based on simple ideas derived from impressions. The most important of these associations was cause and effect, and Hume developed this theme by describing behaviour in terms of custom and habit. An act which produces an effect and which makes a repetition of that act likely is a habit or custom. Think of a simple behaviour such as switching on a light. Your knowledge that switching a light on will illuminate a room leads to the habitual pressing the switch if you need light. These notions of habit and causality became very important in the twentieth century with the development of behaviourism and the work of the Swiss developmental psychologist Jean Piaget (1896–1980) (see Chapter 12).

Idealism: Bishop Berkeley

In contrast to the empiricists, the Irish bishop, philosopher and mathematician George Berkeley (1685–1753) believed that our knowledge of events in the world did not come simply from direct experience. Instead, Berkeley (who gave his name to the famous university in California) argued that this knowledge is the result of inferences based on the accumulation of past experiences derived through the senses. In other words, we must learn how to perceive. For example, our visual perception of depth involves several elementary sensations, such as observing the relative movements of objects as we move our head and the convergence of our eyes (turning inward towards each other or away) as we focus on near or distant objects. Although our knowledge of visual depth seems to be immediate and direct, it is actually a secondary, complex response constructed from a number of simple elements. The aspect of Berkeley's philosophy which argues that all ideas come from the senses (*esse est percipi*) is called **idealism**.

Materialism: James Mill

With the work of the Scottish philosopher James Mill (1773–1836), the pendulum took its full swing from animism (physical matter animated by spirits) to materialism (mind composed entirely of matter). **Materialism** is the belief that reality can be known only through an understanding of the physical world, of which the mind is a part. Mill worked on the assumption that humans and animals were fundamentally the same. Both humans and animals were thoroughly physical in their make-up and were completely subject to the physical laws of the universe. He agreed in essence with Descartes's approach to understanding the human body but rejected the concept of an immaterial mind. Mind, to Mill, was as passive as the body. It responded to the environment in precisely the same way. The mind, like the body, was a machine.

In the nineteenth century, the philosophy of the past began to make way for experimentation. In the latter part of the century, a part of Germany gave birth to modern psychology as we know it. Its midwife was Wilhelm Wundt.

Modern psychology: from the Leipzig laboratory to the cognitive revolution

Wilhelm Wundt (1832–1920) was the first person to call himself a psychologist and he shared the conviction of other German scientists that all aspects of nature, including the human mind, could be studied scientifically, an approach summarised in his book *Principles of Physiological Psychology*, the first textbook in psychology.

Wundt's approach was experimental in nature and his and his colleagues' work was conducted at the Leipzig laboratory, 200 km south of Berlin. Over 100 studies were conducted in the first 20 years of the laboratory's life. Initially, these were studies of the psychological and psychophysiological aspects of vision (seeing), audition (hearing) and somatosensation (feeling and touching). Later work focused on reaction time and the process involved in perceiving and then responding to a stimulus. Wundt also explored the nature of attention and emotional feeling as well as word association.

The fact that Germany was the birthplace of psychology had as much to do with social, political and economic influences as with the abilities of its scientists and scholars. The academic tradition in Germany emphasised a scientific approach to a large number of subject areas, such as history, phonetics, archaeology, aesthetics and literature. Thus, in contrast to French and British scholars, who adopted the more traditional, philosophical approach to the study of the human mind, German scholars were open to the possibility that the human mind could be studied scientifically. Experimental physiology, one of the most important roots of experimental psychology, was well established there. Eventually, Wundt's influence began to extend to other parts of Europe (especially the UK) and to the US.

Wilhelm Wundt (1832–1920).
Source: Bettmann/Getty Images.

Structuralism: Wilhelm Wundt

Wundt defined psychology as the 'science of immediate experience', and his approach was called structuralism, the first proper school of thought to emerge in the history of psychology. Its subject matter was the structure of the mind, built from the elements of consciousness, such as ideas and sensations. These elements could be constructed into a table of elements similar to the periodic table of elements. Structuralism's raw material was supplied by trained observers who described their own experiences under well-controlled conditions. The observers were taught to engage in introspection (literally, 'looking within'), the use of which was governed by strict rules. Introspectionists observed stimuli and described their experiences. It was intensive training: they had to produce approximately 10,000 introspective observations before their data were considered valid (Boring, 1953).

Wundt's aims were threefold: to analyse the contents of conscious experience, to determine how the elements of consciousness are connected and to devise a law which would explain such connections. Wundt and his associates, Edward Tichener (1867–1927) and Gustav Fechner (1801–87), made inferences about the nature of mental processes by seeing how changes in the stimuli caused changes in the verbal reports of their trained observers.

Wundt was particularly interested in the problem that had intrigued Berkeley: how did basic sensory information give rise to complex perceptions? His **doctrine of apperception** attempted to account for the fact that when we perceive, this perception is of a whole object and not separate elements of it. We see wholes, according to Wundt, because of the process of creative synthesis (or law of psychic resultants): a process which combines or synthesises elements to form a whole. Again, this process is very similar to a process in chemistry in which individual chemical elements when combined will form a new, wholly different entity. The whole would not be equivalent to the sum of its parts. Much of Wundt's work, however, aimed to break down and analyse the contents of the mind rather than determine how they are combined.

Wundt's method did not survive the test of time; structuralism died out in the early twentieth century. The major problem with his approach was the difficulty encountered by observers in reporting the raw data of sensation, data unmodified by experience. Although introspectionism aimed to establish well-controlled experimental conditions which would lead to reliable introspective observations, there was often little agreement between observers about their introspections. The method was also criticised for its reliance on retrospection; the recollection of an experience was frequently elicited some time after the experience itself had occurred and was, therefore, subject to error. In addition, attention began to shift from study of the human mind to the study of observable human behaviour. Behaviourism provided a devastating and critical alternative to introspectionism (see below).

Although structuralism has been supplanted, Wundt's contribution must be acknowledged. He was responsible for establishing psychology as a recognised, experimental science that was separate from philosophy. He used methods which involved observation and experimentation and trained a great number of psychologists, many of whom established their own schools and continued the evolution of the new discipline.

Memory: Hermann Ebbinghaus

Most of the pioneers of psychology founded schools, groups of people having a common belief in a particular theory and methodology. The exception to this trend was Hermann Ebbinghaus (1850–1909). In 1876, after receiving his PhD in philosophy but still unattached to an academic institution, Ebbinghaus came across a second-hand copy of a book by Gustav Fechner describing a mathematical approach to the measurement of human sensation. Intrigued by Fechner's research, Ebbinghaus decided to attempt to measure human memory: the processes of learning and forgetting.

Working alone, Ebbinghaus devised methods to measure memory and the speed with which forgetting occurred. He realised that he could not compare the learning and forgetting of two prose passages or two poems because some passages would undoubtedly be easier to learn than others. Therefore, he devised a relatively uniform set of materials – nonsense syllables, such as 'juz', 'bul' and 'gof'. He printed the syllables on cards and read through a set of them, with the rate of presentation controlled by the ticking of a watch. After reading the set, he paused a fixed amount of time, then read the cards again. He recorded the number of times he had to read the cards to be able to recite them without error. He measured forgetting by trying to recite the nonsense syllables on a later occasion – minutes, hours or days later. The number of syllables he remembered was an index of the percentage of memory that had been retained.

Ebbinghaus's approach to memory was entirely empirical; he devised no theory of why learning occurs and was interested only in gathering facts through careful, systematic observation. However, despite the lack of theory, his work made important contributions to the development of the science of psychology. He introduced the principle of eliminating **variable errors** by making observations repeatedly on different occasions (using different lists each time) and calculating the average of these observations. Variable errors include errors caused by random differences in the subject's mood or alertness or by uncontrollable changes in the environment. He constructed graphs of the rate at which the memorised lists of nonsense syllables were forgotten, which provided a way to measure mental contents across time. Ebbinghaus's research provided a model of systematic, rigorous experimental procedures that modern psychologists still emulate (see Chapter 8).

Functionalism: William James and James Angell

After structuralism, the next major trend in psychology was **functionalism** which began in the US and was, in large part, a protest against the structuralism of Wundt. Structuralists were interested in what they called the components of consciousness (ideas and sensations); functionalists were more interested in the process of conscious activity (perceiving and learning). Functionalism grew from the new perspective on nature provided by Charles Darwin and his followers. Proponents of functionalism stressed the biological significance (the purpose, or function) of natural processes, including behaviours. The emphasis was on overt, observable behaviours, not on private mental events.

The most important psychologist to embrace functionalism was William James (1842–1910), brother of novelist Henry. As James said, 'My thinking is first, last, and always for the sake of my doing.' That is, thinking was not an end in itself; its

William James (1842–1910).
Source: Bettmann/Getty Images.

function was to produce useful behaviours. Although James was a champion of experimental psychology, he did not appear to enjoy doing research, instead spending most of his time reading, thinking, teaching and writing during his tenure as professor of philosophy (later, professor of psychology) at Harvard University.

Unlike structuralism, functionalism was not supplanted; instead, its major tenets were absorbed by its successor, behaviourism. One of the last of the functionalists, James Angell (1869–1949), described its basic principles.

- Functional psychology is the study of mental operations and not mental structures. It is not enough to compile a catalogue of what the mind does; one must try to understand what the mind accomplishes by doing this.
- Mental processes are not studied as isolated and independent events but as part of the biological activity of the organism. These processes are aspects of the organism's adaptation to the environment and are a product of its evolutionary history. For example, the fact that we are conscious implies that consciousness has adaptive value for our species.
- Functional psychology studies the relation between the environment and the response of the organism to the environment. There is no meaningful distinction between mind and body, they are part of the same entity.

Evolution and heritability: Charles Darwin and Francis Galton

While Wundt was developing the experimental basis of psychology in Leipzig, another thinker – not a psychologist – was on the verge of making one of the most important contributions to the understanding of behaviour. Charles Darwin (1809–82) proposed the theory of evolution in his book *On the Origin of Species by Means of Natural Selection*, published in 1859. His work, more than that of any other person, revolutionised biology. The concept of natural selection showed how the consequences of an animal's characteristics affect its ability to survive. Instead of simply identifying, describing and naming species, biologists began now to look at the adaptive significance of the ways in which species differed.

Darwin's theory suggested that behaviours, like other biological characteristics, could best be explained by understanding their role in the adaptation of an organism (a human or other animal) to its environment. Thus, behaviour has a biological context. Darwin assembled evidence that behaviours, like body parts, could be inherited. In *The Expression of the Emotions in Man and Animals*, published in 1873, he proposed that the facial gestures that animals make in expressing emotions were descended from movements that previously had other functions. New areas of exploration were opened for psychologists by the ideas that an evolutionary continuity existed among the various species of animals and that behaviours, like parts of the body, had evolutionary histories. Darwin's notion of natural selection has had great impact on the way in which we view the genetic determinants of behaviour (see Chapter 3).

One of the first psychologists to study the influence of genetics on human behaviour was Sir Francis Galton (1822–1911), Darwin's first cousin. Galton was a polymath who made many other contributions to the field of science: he constructed the first weather maps of the British Isles, discovered and named the weather phenomenon known as anticyclone, invented the term 'correlation' (which describes the statistical relationships between two variables or factors), developed the technique of fingerprinting, founded the discipline of psychometrics, which applies statistical principles to the measurement of **individual differences** and the construction of psychological tests, and established the Anthropometric Laboratory in London in 1884, the birthplace of intelligence testing.

Galton was interested in discovering whether people's physical features correlated with each other and whether such correlations occurred for psychological features such as sensory capacity, reaction time, intellect and eminence. In fact, Galton did find that features such as height, arm length and weight were highly and positively correlated and argued from this that if one part of the body's dimensions were known then one could construct the rest of the body to scale.

Importantly, Galton was the first to provide statistical evidence for the heritability of psychological variables. In his study of eminent men, published in his book Hereditary Genius (Galton, 1869), Galton found that 31 per cent of illustrious men had eminent fathers and 48 per cent of these men had eminent sons. Of course, by today's standards, this study has several methodological shortcomings, not least of which is the collection of data from eminent men only (to make a valid comparison, you would also need to look at non-eminent men and their offspring). There is also the argument that eminence may not have been inherited but had been determined by the environment in which these men were raised (issues discussed in detail in Chapters 3 and 11).

However, Galton remains an important figure in the history of psychology. His greatest contribution is the establishment of the study of individual differences as a scientific enterprise.

Psychodynamic theory: Sigmund Freud

While psychology was developing as a fledgling science, Sigmund Freud (1856–1939) was formulating a theory of human behaviour that would greatly affect psychology and psychiatry (not necessarily for the good) and radically influence intellectual thinking of all kinds. Freud began his career as a neurologist, so his work was originally firmly rooted in biology. He soon became interested in behavioural and emotional problems and began formulating his psychodynamic theory of personality, which would evolve over his long career. Although his approach was based on observation of patients and not on scientific experiments, he remained convinced that the biological basis of his theory would eventually be established.

Freud and his theory are discussed in detail in Chapter 14 (Personality), but he is mentioned here to mark his place in the history of psychology. Freud's theory of the mind included structures, but his structuralism was quite different from Wundt's. He devised his concepts of ego, superego, id and other mental structures through talking with his patients, not through laboratory experiments. His hypothetical mental operations included many that were unconscious and hence not available to introspection. And unlike Wundt, Freud emphasised function; his mental structures served biological drives and instincts and reflected our animal nature.

For better or worse Freud's name is the one most closely allied to psychology in the mind of the public. In one study of eminent psychologists, as measured by citations in journals, introductory textbooks and nominations from self-selecting members of the American Psychological Society via an email survey, Freud was the most widely cited author in the discipline (Hagbloom *et al.*, 2002). Second and third place were taken by Jean Piaget and Hans J. Eysenck. In the most recent survey of this kind, Diener *et al.* (2014) ranked 348 'eminent' psychologists according to the total citations to their work, the number of pages devoted to them in textbooks, the number of professional awards they received, their most successful article in terms of citations, and their h-index. The h-index provides a metric of how widely cited a scientist in the context of the total number of articles he or she has produced. For example, if Paul Ekman has a h-index of 87, he has published 87 articles each of which has been cited 87 times. The top 30, based on this system to determining eminence, is presented in Table 1.6.

Behaviourism: Edward Thorndike and Ivan Pavlov

The next major trend in psychology, behaviourism, followed directly from functionalism. It went further in its rejection of the special nature of mental events, denying that unobservable

Table 1.6 Extremely Eminent Psychologists (top 30), according to Diener et al (2014)

Rank	Name	Awards	Text pages	Total citations	h-index	Highest cited article
1	BANDURA, Albert	2	40	218,219	144	33,888
2	PIAGET, Jean	2	39	152,723	148	8,056
3	KAHNEMAN, Daniel	2	23	152,529	107	24,780
4	LAZARUS, Richard	2	25	96,379	101	24,110
5	SELIGMAN, Martin	2	47	67,789	97	7,691
6	SKINNER, B. F.	2	43	66,603	83	9,162
7	CHOMSKY, Noam	2	11	191,030	123	19,447
8	TAYLOR, Shelley	2	40	50,243	88	8,675
9	TVERSKY, Amos	2	13	134,651	96	24,295
10	DIENER, Ed	2	22	67,882	110	6,853
11	SIMON, Herbert	2	6	191,431	147	16,045
12	ROGERS, Carl	2	27	56,980	78	8,462
13	SQUIRE, Larry	2	24	54,809	114	3,508
14	ANDERSON, John	2	12	72,008	98	9,004
15	EKMAN, Paul	2	24	59,121	87	3,000
16	TULVING, Endel	2	22	46,137	88	4,195
17	ALLPORT, Gordon	2	15	50,316	67	15,083
18	BOWLBY, John	2	8	72,122	81	23,681
19	NISBETT, Richard	2	20	42,852	76	6,955
20	CAMPBELL, Donald	2	8	84,135	85	14,036
21	MILLER, George	2	11	53,526	73	15,711
22	FISKE, Susan	2	16	37,054	79	8,671
23	DAVIDSON, Richard	2	22	45,549	107	1,395
24	MCEWEN, Bruce	2	6	91,872	153	3,371
25	MISCHEL Walter	2	20	31,288	73	4,341
26	FESTINGER, Leon	2	10	49,677	54	21,077
27	MCCLELLAND, David	2	7	57,493	68	21,422
28	ARONSON, Elliot	2	31	22,720	67	2,054
29	POSNER, Michael	2	7	65,649	105	5,042
30	BAUMEISTER, Roy	1	36	55,303	108	5,685

and unverifiable mental events were properly the subject matter of psychology. Behaviourists believed that because psychology is the study of observable behaviours, mental events – which cannot be observed – are outside the realm of psychology. Behaviourism is thus the study of the relation between people's environments and their behaviour; what occurs within their heads is irrelevant.

One of the first behaviourists was Edward Thorndike (1874–1949), an American psychologist who studied the behaviour of animals. He noticed that some events, usually those that one would expect to be pleasant, seemed to 'stamp in' a response that had just occurred. Noxious events seemed to 'stamp out' the response, or make it less likely to recur. We now call these processes reinforcement and punishment (see Chapter 7). Thorndike defined the law of effect as follows:

Any act which in a given situation produces satisfaction becomes associated with that situation, so that when the situation recurs the act is more likely than before to recur also. Conversely, any act which in a given situation produces discomfort becomes disassociated from that situation, so that when the situation recurs the act is less likely than before to recur. (Source: Thorndike, 1905, p. 203.)

The **law of effect** is in the functionalist tradition. It observes that the consequences of a behaviour act back upon the organism, affecting the likelihood that the behaviour that just occurred will occur again. An organism does something, and the consequences of this action make that action more likely. This process is very similar to the principle of natural selection. Just as organisms that successfully adapt to their environments are more likely to survive and breed, behaviours that cause useful outcomes are more likely to recur.

Although Thorndike insisted that the subject matter of psychology was behaviour, his explanations contained mentalistic terms. For example, in his law of effect he spoke of 'satisfaction', which is certainly not a phenomenon that can be directly observed. Later behaviourists threw out terms like 'satisfaction' and 'discomfort' and replaced them with more objective terms that reflected the behaviour of the organism rather than any feelings it might have.

Another major figure in the development of behaviourism was not a psychologist but a physiologist: Ivan Pavlov (1849–1936), a Russian who studied the physiology of digestion (for which he later received a Nobel Prize). In the course of studying the stimuli that produce salivation, he discovered that hungry dogs would salivate at the sight of the attendant who brought in their dishes of food. Pavlov found that a dog could be trained to salivate at completely arbitrary stimuli, such as the sound of a bell, if the stimulus was quickly followed by the delivery of a bit of food into the animal's mouth.

Pavlov's discovery had profound significance for psychology. He showed that through experience an animal could learn to make a response to a stimulus that had never caused this response before. This ability, in turn, might explain how organisms learn cause-and-effect relations in the environment. In contrast, Thorndike's law of effect suggested an explanation for the adaptability of an individual's behaviour to its particular environment. So, from Thorndike's and Pavlov's studies two important behavioural principles had been discovered.

Behaviourism: John B. Watson

Behaviourism as a formal school of psychology began with the publication of a book by John B. Watson (1878–1958), *Psychology from the Standpoint of a Behaviorist* (Watson, 1919). Watson was a charismatic professor of psychology at the Johns Hopkins University in the USA, a popular teacher and writer, the founding editor of the *Journal of Experimental Psychology*, and was a very convincing advocate of behaviourism. Even after leaving Johns Hopkins under mysterious circumstances and embarking on a highly successful career in advertising, he continued to lecture and write magazine articles about psychology.

According to Watson, psychology was a natural science whose domain was restricted to observable events: the behaviour of organisms. Watson's behaviourism can be best summed up by his definition published in an article entitled, 'Psychology as the behaviorist views it' (Watson, 1913):

> Psychology as the behaviorist views it is a purely objective experimental branch of natural science. Its theoretical goal is the prediction and control of behavior. Introspectionism forms no essential part of its methods, nor is the scientific value of its data dependent upon the readiness with which they lend themselves to interpretation in terms of consciousness. The behaviorist, in his efforts to get a unitary scheme of animal response, recognises no dividing line between man and brute.

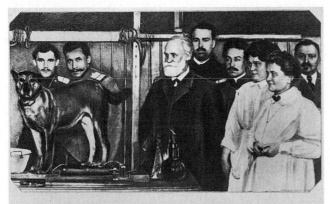

И. П. Павлов наблюдает за подопытной собакой (1911 год)

Ivan Pavlov (1849–1936) in his laboratory with some of his collaborators. His research revealed valuable, though unsought, information about the principles of learning.
Source: Bettmann/Getty Images.

John B. Watson (1878–1958).
Source: Archives of the History of American Psychology.

Watson believed that the elements of consciousness studied by structuralists were too subjective to lend themselves to scientific investigation. He defined psychology as the objective study of behaviour and the stimuli which produce such behaviour. The important feature of behaviourism was its reliance only on observable behaviour. Even thinking was reduced to a form of behaviour – talking to oneself. Watson described visually observable behaviour as 'explicit behaviour' and those behaviours which could not be directly observed but potentially observed as 'implicit behaviour'. For example, we cannot see the body's cells transmitting electrical signals but we can observe such behaviour by using the correct electrical recording equipment.

Another important feature, tied to observation, was that the brain had very little to do with what was directly observed. What was important to Watson was the concept of stimulus and response, an idea suggested by Descartes and explicitly described by Pavlov. Watson argued that, given the correct stimuli, the organism could learn to behave (give responses) in a specific way (in the same way that Pavlov's dogs had 'learned' to associate the bell with the appearance of food). Watson, however, famously went further. In his book *Behaviorism* (1930), he argued:

> Give me a dozen healthy infants, well-formed, and my own specified world to bring them up in and I'll guarantee to take any one at random and train him to become any type of specialist I might select – doctor, lawyer, artist, merchant-chief and, yes, even beggar-man and thief, regardless of his talents, penchants, tendencies, abilities, vocations and race of his ancestors.

Evidence for this ambition came from his study of the 11-month-old Albert B – the first human being to be conditioned to fear an object in a laboratory (see Chapter 7). Many of Watson's ideas, such as the notion that reflexes can be conditioned, have been incorporated into the mainstream of psychology, although the central tenet that all behaviour that is studied must be observable has not. After Watson, a new form of behaviourism emerged which took Watson's ideas and developed them further. This new form became known as neo-behaviourism or radical behaviourism.

Radical behaviourism: Edward Tolman and Clark Leonard Hull

The period 1930–1960 saw a tremendous surge not only in the description of the ways in which organisms behaved but also in the explanations for why they behaved in the way they did. This surge was generated largely by the work of a group of

American psychologists, Edward Tolman (1886–1959), Clark Leonard Hull (1884–1952) and B.F. Skinner (1904–90). Each had a different view on how behaviour occurred but all used animal experiments and the procedures of learning experiments to support their theories. Hull, for example, in his book *Principles of Behavior* proposed a highly detailed mathematical model of behaviour based on his conditioning work with rats (Hull, 1943). The basic feature of Hull's model was that all human (and any organism's) behaviour evolves through interaction with the environment. However, this interaction occurs within a wider frame of reference – the biological adaptation of the organism to the environment. The variable intervening between environment and organism was **drive** – a bodily need arising from deprivation or desire or another motivational spur. Although one of the more widely cited psychologists of his day, Hull has not made a lasting impact on psychology largely because his extremely detailed mathematical analyses were based on few experiments, the results of which were generalised well beyond the scope of the experimental context.

Tolman suggested that it was important not only to observe the stimulus and response but to take into account intervening variables. To Tolman, these intervening variables were cognitions and demands, and Tolman's theory became known as **purposive behaviourism**, so-called because all behaviour was goal-directed and had a purpose. Tolman's work did not bequeath any major principles or laws, however, although interest in his work continues (Reid and Staddon, 1998). You will find out more about Hull's and Tolman's approaches in Chapter 7.

Radical behaviourism: Burrhus Frederic Skinner

The bequest of a major framework of thinking in psychology was left to B.F. Skinner (1904–90), one of the most influential psychologists of the twentieth century whose entry into psychology's history was serendipitous. He originally wanted to be a writer, and later published novels in which he applied his research ideas. Skinner's work gave birth to the technology of teaching machines (which have since been replaced by computers), the use of behaviour modification in instruction of the mentally retarded, and the use of behaviour therapy to treat mental disorders.

Skinner's work focused on the idea of reinforcement and was based largely on observation of behaviour in pigeons. He found that a certain set of stimulus conditions (such as a box, hunger, food in sight) would elicit certain behaviours (strutting, random pecking). If the animal behaved in a certain way to obtain food then the food became the reinforcing stimulus or the reinforcer – a stimulus which increases the probability that behaviour will occur again. Using his observations of pigeons' behaviour, Skinner found that the pigeons could be trained to behave in a specific way when responding to specific signals

B.F. Skinner (1904–90).
Source: Bettmann/Getty Images.

from their environment. For example, the pigeon would learn that it would receive food only if it pecked a food-dispensing lever a certain number of times; instead of randomly pecking at this lever it would then peck only the number of times necessary.

This form of learning, instrumental or operant learning, was of three types: positive reinforcement (e.g. the attention or approval given to a child from a teacher); punishment – a negative stimulus which is presented when a behaviour occurs (e.g. a rat receiving an electric shock whenever it presses a lever); and negative reinforcement – which reduces the likelihood of negative stimulation (e.g. a rat pressing a lever to avoid electric shock).

Reinforcement could also occur according to scheduling. For example, fixed-interval reinforcement involved a reinforcer that was given only after a set time; fixed-ratio reinforcement involved a reinforcer that was given only after a predetermined number of responses. Examples of fixed-interval reinforcement include receiving a wage at the end of the week or a salary at the end of the month; an example of fixed-ratio reinforcement would be the delivery of payment after, say, a certain number of items had been produced in a factory or after a specific number of products had been sold. Chapter 7 takes up these ideas.

Unlike Tolman and Hull, however, Skinner did not propose any intervening variables. To him, the behaving person or pigeon or rat was an 'empty organism'. He argued that humans were machines which behaved in lawful and predictable ways and his system was almost entirely descriptive with little in the way of theory emerging from it. In addition to his scientific work, Skinner published a novel, Walden Two, in which he described the way in which radical behaviourism could operate (Skinner, 1948).

Psychologists, including modern behaviourists, have moved away from the strict behaviourism of Watson and Skinner; mental processes such as imagery and attention are again considered to be proper subject matter for scientific investigation. But Watson's emphasis on objectivity in psychological research remains. Even those modern psychologists who most vehemently protest against what they see as the narrowness of behaviourism use the same principles of objectivity to guide their research.

Genetic epistemology: Jean Piaget

While American approaches to psychology were dominated by the new behaviourism, a different approach to the study of cognitive function was being pursued in Europe. The Swiss psychologist Jean Piaget (1896–1980) became interested in the question of human knowledge and how we begin to acquire knowledge. He believed that answers to such questions could be obtained by empirical, scientific research and he would measure the development of the acquisition of knowledge in children by presenting them with intellectual tasks at various stages of their lives (in fact, Piaget had worked with Theophile Simon, the collaborator of the man who designed the first IQ test, Alfred Binet). Piaget termed his approach to psychology as **genetic epistemology**: the study of the origin of knowledge in child development.

Apart from Piaget's focus on the acquisition of knowledge in groups of individuals, another difference between his European approach and that of his American counterparts was the lack of interest in the applied nature of research. Questions regarding the possibility of improving or accelerating children's learning did not interest Piaget, nor did it interest other European researchers (Leahey, 2003). Although his work made little impact on psychology at the time, the subsequent circulation of his work – with translations of his books – led to a considerable interest in his research (Smith, 1996), so much so, that few psychologists have dominated the study of child development in the way that Piaget has. Piaget's contribution to our understanding of child cognition is assessed in Chapter 12.

Gestalt psychology: Max Wertheimer

The structuralism of Wilhelm Wundt was not the only German influence on the development of psychology. In 1911, a German psychologist, Max Wertheimer (1880–1943), bought a toy that presented a series of pictures in rapid succession. Each picture was slightly different from the one that preceded it, and the resulting impression was that of continuous motion, like a film. Wundt and his followers insisted that if we want to understand the nature of human consciousness we must analyse it – divide it into its individual elements. But Wertheimer and his colleagues realised that the perception of a motion picture was not that of a series of individual still pictures. Instead, viewers saw continuity in time and space. They saw objects that retained their identity as they moved from place to place. Asking people to study these pictures one at a time and to describe what they saw (the structuralist approach) would never explain the phenomenon of the motion picture.

Wertheimer and his colleagues attempted to discover the organisation of cognitive processes, not their elements. They called their approach **Gestalt psychology**. Gestalt is a German word that roughly translates into 'unified form' or 'overall shape'. Gestalt psychologists insisted that perceptions resulted from patterns of interactions among many elements – patterns that could exist across both space and time. For example, a simple melody consists of a pattern of different notes, played one at a time. If the melody is played in different keys, so that the individual notes are different, people can still recognise it. Clearly, they recognise the relations the notes have to each other, not just the notes themselves.

Although the Gestalt school of psychology no longer exists, its insistence that elements of an experience interact – that the whole is not simply the sum of its parts – has had a profound influence on the development of modern psychology. Gestalt psychology did not disappear because of some inherent fatal flaw in its philosophy or methodology. Instead, many of its approaches and ideas were incorporated into other areas of psychology. Gestalt psychology is discussed in more detail in Chapter 6.

Humanistic psychology

Humanistic psychology developed during the 1950s and 1960s as a reaction against both behaviourism and psychoanalysis. Although psychoanalysis certainly dealt with mental phenomena that could not be measured objectively, it saw people as products of their environment and of innate, unconscious forces. Humanistic psychologists insist that human nature goes beyond environmental influences, and that conscious processes, not unconscious ones, are what psychologists should study. In addition, they note that psychoanalysis seems preoccupied with mental disturbance, ignoring positive phenomena such as happiness, satisfaction, love and kindness. **Humanistic psychology** is an approach to the study of human behaviour that emphasises human experience, choice and creativity, self-realisation and positive growth.

It emphasises the positive sides of human nature and the potential we all share for personal growth. In general, humanistic psychologists do not believe that we will understand human consciousness and behaviour through scientific research. Thus, the humanistic approach has not had a significant influence on psychology as a science. Its greatest impact has been on the development of methods of psychotherapy based on a positive and optimistic view of human potential.

Individual differences: Gordon Allport, Raymond Cattell, Hans Eysenck, Walter Mischel, Paul Costa and Robert McCrae

As the humanist movement was in full swing – or as swinging as it could manage – experimental psychologists had turned their attention to the scientific measurement of another important facet of behaviour: personality. This attention took the form of a search for universal **personality traits** – enduring personal characteristics which form a continuum along which we all fall. The earliest of these theorists was Gordon Allport (1897–1967) who, using dictionary terms as his starting point, suggested that personality comprised between three and 16 personality traits. Allport's scheme formed the basis for the model devised by Raymond Cattell (1905–98). He collected data from interviews and various questionnaires, and concluded that personality comprised 16 traits.

Robert R. McCrae.
Source: Robert McCrae.

Elizabeth Loftus.
Source: Jodi Hilton/Stringer/Getty Images News/Getty Images.

many significant figures to mention, but some of the most prominent that contributed significant new data and models which helped us understand social behaviour include Leon Festinger, Albert Bandura, Stanley Milgram, Philip Zimbardo, Elliot Aronson, Robert Zajonc, Richard Nisbett and Edward Jones. All Americans or working in the USA, these psychologists demonstrated how we could hold two seemingly contradictory views (Festinger), how **deindividuation** could strip us of our humanity (Zimbardo), how observation of others makes us imitate them (Bandura), how we become obedient to authority (Milgram), how we interpret the causes of our own behaviour differently from how we interpret that of others (Nisbett, Jones), among other things. You'll find descriptions of their research and the impact this has had on our understanding of social behaviour in Chapters 15 and 16.

A more parsimonious account, based on a statistical technique called factor analysis, was proposed by Hans J. Eysenck (1916–97). Eysenck's model was, until recently, one of the most widely accepted views of personality traits. He proposed that personality comprised three dimensions – neuroticism–stability, extraversion–intraversion and psychoticism–normality – all of which had a biological basis, and that each of us scores somewhere along all three dimensions. Meanwhile, influential American psychologists such as Walter Mischel (b. 1930) argued that traits did not exist and that, when we behave, we are reacting to changes in our environment or situation (this approach is called situationism): that we may respond in a consistent way lulls us into thinking that we possess something called 'personality', characterised by a number of traits. The debate continues, but the situationists seem to be fighting a lost battle.

Considerable research supported Eysenck's model, but this was usurped in the 1980s by the Five Factor Model of personality, now most closely identified with the personality questionnaire developed by Paul T. Costa and Robert R. McCrae. The Big Five model is now the most widely accepted view of personality and argues that our personality comprises five traits which we possess to varying degrees: agreeableness, conscientiousness, extraversion, neuroticism and openness to experience. You'll find more information on all of these approaches in Chapter 14.

The development of social psychology

In the middle of the twentieth century there also appeared a phenomenal body of research explaining how we view and influence other individuals. Here, there are too

---

Public Announcement

WE WILL PAY YOU $4.00 FOR ONE HOUR OF YOUR TIME

Persons Needed for a Study of Memory

•We will pay five hundred New Haven men to help us complete a scientific study of memory and learning. The study is being done at Yale University.

•Each person who participates will be paid $4.00 (plus 50c carfare) for approximately 1 hour's time. We need you for only one hour: there are no further obligations. You may choose the time you would like to come (evenings, weekdays, or weekends).

•No special training, education, or experience is needed. We want:

Factory workers	Businessmen	Construction workers
City employees	Clerks	Salespeople
Laborers	Professional people	White-collar workers
Barbers	Telephone workers	Others

All persons must be between the ages of 20 and 50. High school and college students cannot be used.

•If you meet these qualifications, fill out the coupon below and mail it now to Professor Stanley Milgram, Department of Psychology, Yale University, New Haven. You will be notified later of the specific time and place of the study. We reserve the right to decline any application.

•You will be paid $4.00 (plus 50c carfare) as soon as you arrive at the laboratory.

- -

TO:
PROF. STANLEY MILGRAM, DEPARTMENT OF PSYCHOLOGY, YALE UNIVERSITY, NEW HAVEN, CONN. I want to take part in this study of memory and learning. I am between the ages of 20 and 50. I will be paid $4.00 (plus 50c carfare) if I participate.

NAME (Please Print). . . . .

ADDRESS . . . .

TELEPHONE NO. . . . . Best time to call you . . . .

AGE. . . . . OCCUPATION. . . . . SEX. . . . . .
CAN YOU COME:

WEEKDAYS . . . . EVENINGS . . . . . . WEEKENDS. . . . .

A photograph of Milgram's famous obedience to authority experiment, described in more detail in Chapter 16.
Source: Granger/Shutterstock.

The cognitive revolution: beyond behaviourism

The emphasis on behaviourism in the first half of the twentieth century restricted the subject matter of psychology to observable behaviours. For many years, concepts such as consciousness were considered to be outside the domain of psychology. As one psychologist put it, 'psychology, having first bargained away its soul and then gone out of its mind, seems now . . . to have lost all consciousness' (Burt, 1962, p. 229).

In the decades that followed, many psychologists protested against the restrictions of behaviourism and turned to the study of consciousness, feelings, memory, imagery and other private events (although behaviourism was still a potent force and continues to run through much of today's experimental psychology like marble). Much of cognitive psychology uses an approach called **information processing** – information received through the senses is 'processed' by various systems in the brain. Some systems store the information in the form of memory, and other systems control behaviour. Some systems operate automatically and unconsciously, while others are conscious and require effort on the part of the individual. Because the information-processing approach was first devised to describe the operations of complex physical systems such as computers, the modern model of the human brain is, for most cognitive psychologists, the computer. Another model (neural networks) is now being used as an alternative to the computer (see Chapter 7).

Amos Tversky.
Source: Barbara Tversky.

Daniel Kahneman.
Source: dpa picture alliance archive / Alamy Stock Photo.

Although cognitive psychologists study mental structures and operations, they have not gone back to the introspective methods that structuralists such as Wundt employed. Instead, they use experimental methods, under controlled conditions, to test hypotheses and discover facts about how we think and remember. Cognitive psychologists such as Donald Broadbent, Stanley Schachter, Neal Miller, Don McClelland, Alan Baddeley, Ulric Neisser, Allan Paivio, Stephen Kosslyn, Endel Tulving, Elizabeth Loftus, Daniel Kahneman and Amos Tversky (the last two won the Nobel Prize for economics in 2002) discovered new and important data about how we learn to learn, remember and reason. You'll find their research in Chapters 8 and 11 but also throughout the text.

The biological revolution

Before modern science, let alone modern neuroscience, there were two prevailing views about which aspect of biology governed our behaviour. There was the cardiocentric view, espoused by Ancient Greeks such as Aristotle, which argued that the heart was at the, well, heart of human behaviour and initiated and guided our emotions and our sensations. The cephalocentric view held that the brain was responsible for behaviour, a view held by pre-Socratic thinkers such as the Ancient Greek physicians, Alchmaeon of Croton (thought to be the first person to use dissection as an investigation method) and Galen of Pergamon (29–213 CE). Galen is particularly important to psychology because he was the first person known to undertake experiments on the nervous system and made a number of other discoveries about the brain.

For example, he identified nine of the cranial nerves in our head, distinguished between nerves responsible for sensation and those responsible for movement, and discovered that the spinal cord extended from the back of the brain. He described the anatomy of the brain – which were based on dissections of oxen brains or those of Barbary apes. He, apparently, disliked operating on monkeys because of their facial expressions when he did so (Gross, 2012).

Galen provided one of the more striking demonstrations of the superiority of the cephalocentric view when he gave a public demonstration in front of Roman espousers of the cardiocentric view. He showed that cutting the laryngeal nerves – one of the cranial nerves you will find more about in Chapter 4 – stopped the squealing of a pig. As vocalisation was thought to reflect cognitive processing of language, the demonstration showed that this processing occurred in the brain.

The neuron doctrine and neurotransmission

Biology has always been closely tied to psychology and as psychology began to flourish in the eighteenth century, it was against a backdrop of some quite staggering discoveries in the physical sciences. For example, Descartes's hydraulic model of muscular movement was shown to be incorrect by Luigi Galvani (1737–98), an Italian physiologist who discovered that muscles could be made to contract by applying an electrical current directly to them or to the nerves that were attached to them. The muscles themselves contained the energy needed for them to contract. They did not have to be inflated by pressurised fluid. This discovery is the source of a modern-day technique for helping people recover from serious, paralysing illnesses and injury: the use of brain electrical activity to control objects such as a computer cursor or a prosthetic limb.

Perhaps the single most important discovery in neuroscience was made by Camilio Golgi (1843–1926) and Santiago Ramon y Cajal in the nineteenth century. Golgi had developed a method for creating dyes which were able to stain certain tissues and parts of tissues in the body, particularly the brain. What Cajal was able to do was use the staining techniques that Golgi had developed to discover that the brain comprised nerve cells – neurons. This became known as the neuron doctrine – the notion that the nervous system comprised discrete and separable cells.

Remarking on how he first viewed Golgi's most important staining technique (a silver staining method which allowed cells to be seen whole), Cajal wrote: 'Against a clear background stood black threadlets, some slender and smooth, some thick and thorny. All was sharp as a sketch with Chinese ink on transparent Japanese paper . . . Dumfounded, I could not take my eye from the microscope'.

Using the technique, he confirmed Golgi's finding that each nerve cell featured an extension called an axon (and only one axon – see Chapter 4) but was also able to demonstrate that neurons were discrete and separate. He proposed although he was not the first that another process extending from the nerve cell, the dendrite, carried information to cells and that the axon carried this information away (the 'Law of Dynamic Polarization'). This is precisely what those two processes do. Cajal and Golgi shared a Nobel Prize for their work in 1906 although in their respective speeches they both argued against each other's theories about how the nervous system worked (Gross, 2012).

The person to name the space between neurons was the British scientist, Charles Sherrington (1857–1952). The name he used was 'synapse' a name that is used throughout neuroscience today. It was believed that signals were sent along a nerve cells electrically – the signal was an electrical impulse – but a suggestion had been made that a different process occurred at the synapse and that some chemical interaction occurred. Thomas Elliot (1877–1961), who first showed that there was a division between the sympathetic and parasympathetic nervous systems (see Chapter 4), had suggested that the chemical, adrenaline, could be released from nerve cells at the gap between two cells when the first cell was stimulated. The person to record this release from cells was Otto Loewi. Loewi found that stimulating one of a frog's cranial nerves (the vagus) produced a chemical that slowed the frog's heart. Stimulating another nerve produced a chemical which increased the speed of the frog's heart. The chemicals were acetylcholine and adrenaline, respectively, two of the most important chemical substances in the brain (neurotransmitters). He jointly won the Nobel Prize in 1936 for his discovery.

Brain damage and behaviour: Paul Broca and Carl Wernicke

As discoveries in physiology and anatomy continued, another medical endeavour was making itself felt slowly throughout the later end of the nineteenth century: the study of the effect of brain injury on behaviour. In 1861, Paul Broca (1824–80), a French surgeon, reported the results of an autopsy on the brain of a man who had suffered a stroke several years ago. The stroke (damage to the brain caused, in this case, by a blood clot) had caused the man to lose the ability to speak. The patient, whose real name was Leborgne, was called Tan because this was the only word he uttered. He did not survive long at the hospital and Broca discovered that the stroke had damaged part of the brain on the left side near the front, as

Figure 1.4 shows (although Marc Dax and others had reported similar findings earlier that century). Broca suggested that this region of the brain was a centre for speech – this part is now called Broca's area.

Broca's work was followed, independently, by that of Carl Wernicke (1848–1905), who noted that damage to an adjacent part of the brain impaired his patient's ability to comprehend speech but left speech production relatively intact. The language disorders produced by damage to the brain are described in Chapter 10.

Studying the effects of accidental brain damage on function has allowed neuroscientists to predict which regions of the brain may be involved in specific functions. A famous example of brain damage leading to speculation about the function of a brain region is that of Phineas Gage. Gage was an American railroad construction supervisor who, in the mid-nineteenth century, had an accident at work in which an iron rod shot through his face, through the front part of his brain and straight out of the top of his head. A reconstructed image of the trajectory of the rod through his skull can be seen in Figure 1.5a. Figure 1.5b is the only existing image of Gage (with the rod tastefully superimposed).

Whereas before the injury, Gage had been a hard-working and conscientious individual, after the injury he became boorish, unpleasant and unreliable. The part of the brain damaged seemed to be responsible for inhibiting inappropriate behaviour. We now know that patients with damage to this part of the brain have difficulty in inhibiting such behaviour (there is more on this phenomenon in Chapter 13).

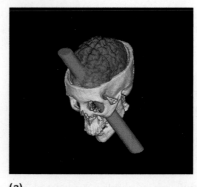 

(a)   **(b)**

Figure 1.5 On a September afternoon in 1848, an unusual accident befell a young American railroad worker called Phineas Gage. An iron rod shot through his head as a result of an uncontrolled explosion at work. Almost 150 years later, Hannah Damasio and her colleagues at the University of Iowa took the medical reports of Gage's injury and plotted the course of the rod, using modern computer technology. **(a)** Shows one of the images of the rod's trajectory. **(b)** Shows a depiction of Gage himself.

Source: (a) From H. Damasio, T. Grabowski, R. Frank, A.M. Galaburda and A.R. Damasio, The return of Phineas Gage: Clues about the brain from a famous patient. *Science*, 1994, 264: 1102–05. Department of Neurology and Image Analysis Facility, University of Iowa. (b) From Macmillan, *An odd kind of fame* MIT: Bradford.

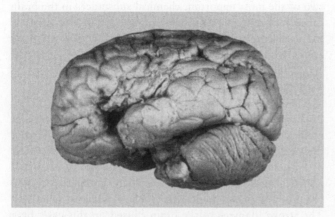

Figure 1.4 A photograph of Tan's brain. Note the egg-shaped cavity – this was thought to be responsible for his inability to speak fluently.

Source: T.E. Feinberg and M.J. Farah (1997) *Behavioral Neurology and Neuropsychology.* © The McGraw-Hill Companies.

Localisation of function: Gustav Fritsch and Eduard Hitzig and Franz Gall and Johann Spurzheim

In 1870, the German physiologists Gustav Fritsch and Eduard Hitzig discovered that applying a small electrical shock to different parts of the cerebral cortex caused movements of different parts of the body. In fact, the body appeared to be 'mapped' on the surface of the brain, so that the feet, hands, fingers and so on, had a part of the brain dedicated to them.

Originally, this work was conducted on dogs on Frau Hitzig's dressing table (because they had no available laboratory space). Platinum wires delivered brief electric currents to the brain which resulted in a 'Zuckung' or spasm/twitch (Gross, 2012). These humble conditions gave rise to the first experiment in **localisation of function** in the brain – the ability to ascribe a particular function to a part of the brain, the goal of neuropsychology. They found that the stimulation led to movement on the other ('contralateral') side, led to movement only when stimulation was in the anterior part of the brain (which is where our motor cortex is located), and that stimulation of specific regions activated different muscles. They later discovered that damaging the part of the brain that was stimulated reduced the motor activity seen during stimulation.

Fritsch later went on to develop some unusual views on White superiority. Hitzig later applied their technique to a human head and observed that stimulation caused eye movements. Fritsch and Hitzig's findings were subsequently replicated by a Scottish doctor, David Ferrier. Together, their findings corroborated the notion that the brain contained a 'topographic map' whereby certain areas of the brain were responsible for specific motor actions.

No less elaborate, but ultimately doomed, was the attempt at localising function by Franz Gall (1758–1828) and Johann Spurzheim (1776–1832). Their anatomical personology – or as it is commonly known, phrenology – suggested that if we were very adept at a function, the part of the brain responsible would be overactive. This overactivity caused an indentation in the skull and so a person's ability could be determined by palpating the head (there were thought to be 37 such functions in the brain, according to Gall and Spurzheim). If a person was mathematically gifted, therefore, the part responsible for this would be active and cause a bump in the skull, which the experimenter could palpate. This hypothesis was beautifully testable and it was not long before the edifice came crashing down when a person identified as a mathematically gifted genius transpired to be a mentally retarded criminal.

Gall had drawn conclusions based on some unusual observations – the part of the brain responsible for destructiveness was derived from an examination of a medical student who 'was so fond of torturing animals that he became a surgeon', and from the skull of a dog which really enjoyed meat (Gross, 2012). Gall and Spurzheim's system, however, was an attempt at localising function in the brain. Although Gall is best known for this, he also made more worthwhile contributions to neuroscience, such as identifying the importance of the left front part of the brain to speech, a finding which Broca acknowledged.

Speed and magnitude of nerve impulses: Hermann von Helmholtz and Ernst Weber

A different and yet essentially physical approach to studying behaviour was seen in the work of the German physicist and physiologist Hermann von Helmholtz (1821–94), who did much to demonstrate that mental phenomena could be explained by physiological means. This extremely productive scientist made contributions to both physics and physiology. He actively disassociated himself from natural philosophy, from which many assumptions about the nature of the mind had been derived. Helmholtz advocated a purely scientific approach, with conclusions based on objective investigation and precise measurement.

Until his time, scientists believed that the transmission of impulses through nerves was as fast as the speed of electricity in wires; under this assumption, transmission would be virtually instantaneous, considering the small distances that impulses have to travel within the human body. Helmholtz successfully measured the speed of the nerve impulse and found that it was only about 90 feet per second, which is considerably slower than the speed of electricity in wires. This finding suggested to later researchers that the nerve impulse is more complex than a simple electrical current passing through a wire, which is indeed true.

Helmholtz also attempted to measure the speed of a person's reaction to a physical stimulus, but he abandoned this attempt because there was too much variability from person to person. However, this variability interested scientists who followed him; they tried to explain the reason for individual differences in behaviour. Because both the velocity of nerve impulses and a person's reactions to stimuli could be measured, researchers theorised that mental events themselves could be the subject of scientific investigation. Possibly, if the proper techniques could be developed, one could investigate what went on within the human brain. Thus, Helmholtz's research was important in setting the stage for the science of psychology.

A contemporary of von Helmholtz's, Ernst Weber (1795–1878), began work that led to the development of a method for measuring the magnitude of human sensations. Weber, an anatomist and physiologist, found that people's ability to tell the difference between two similar stimuli – such as the brightness of two lights, the heaviness of two objects or the loudness of two tones – followed orderly laws. This regularity suggested to Weber and his followers that the study of perceptual phenomena could be as scientific as that of physics or biology. The study of the relation between the physical characteristics of a stimulus and the perceptions they produce is a field called psychophysics or the physics of the mind (see Chapter 6).

Cognitive neuroscience: the future of the biology of the 'mind'?

The cognitive revolution did not lead to a renewed interest in biology. But the extraordinary advances in neurobiology in the late twentieth century have revolutionised psychology. Neurobiologists (biologists who study the nervous system) and scientists and engineers in allied fields have developed ways to study the brain that were unthinkable just a few decades ago. We can study fine details of nerve cells, discover their interconnections, analyse the chemicals they use to communicate with each other, produce drugs that block the action of these chemicals or mimic their effects.

More importantly, using neuroimaging techniques such as fMRI, MRI, PET, NIRS, MEG and various other technological abbreviations, we can see the internal structure of a living human brain, and measure the activity of different processes of the brain – in regions as small as a few cubic millimetres – while people are thinking, feeling, perceiving, comprehending and moving (Martin, 2006; Raichle, 2008). The first neuroimaging study of language was published in 1988 and involved listening to or reading aloud nouns (Petersen *et al.*, 1988).

A recent development has been the study of the connectome – brain networks or hubs that involve dense, reciprocal connections and which may be functionally important to other brain regions because of these connections (Crossley *et al.*, 2014). These hubs tend to receive more blood flow, glucose and oxygen than other brain areas. A new, novel and innovative research endeavour is seeking to use brain activity to predict behaviour (Berkman and Falk, 2013). You'll find out more about this in Chapter 4 and 13 which considers the use of neuroimaging in lie detection and the use of EEG to predict emotional expression. For example, Falk *et al.* (2012) exposed smokers to three real different smoking cessations campaigns in the US and used fMRI to record their brain activation. The study found that increased activation in a part of the front of the brain (the medial prefrontal region) predicted the success of the campaign in the general population. That is, the most successful of the three campaigns –measured by the number of phone calls a helpline received – was associated with the greatest activation in this area.

The combination of cognitive psychology and neuroscience – cognitive neuroscience – provides a different way of studying behaviour and describing its causes. Currently, the endeavours in cognitive neuroscience are, because of the nature of the techniques used, directed towards studying basic, yet essential, behaviour such as rudimentary reading, recognising emotion, remembering and speaking. But this is changing and studies are now using neuroimaging to study how people converse, make moral decisions, appreciate television programmes, react to a lover's face and voice and even understand magic tricks.

However, these techniques (and the ways in which data from using these techniques are analysed) are not unproblematic. They have been criticised for being imprecise, for not recording activation from nerve cells (they don't), for providing indirect measures of neuronal activation (true), for using statistical software which may inflate the chances of finding a positive result, as well as providing experimental conditions which lack ecological validity (lying down in a scanner with a helmet on your head). You'll find a review of these issues and a description of some studies using these techniques in Chapter 4.

Conceptual and historical issues in psychology

As this chapter has shown you, understanding a discipline's past can help you better understand its present and its future. Understanding a discipline's past shows you the stages – usually chaotic, not linear or orderly – that psychology has gone through to reach the status it has attained today and the body of knowledge it has accrued. The shifts in approach and subject matter across its history will be reflected in its future shifts. But these shifts will be gradual. The danger in highlighting stages in history, as is done here, is that they are seen as discrete and self-contained. They are only discrete and self-contained because the prism of historical retrospection makes them so and we can reflect back, soberly, on some of the momentous conceptual and experimental changes that psychology underwent. We are currently amidst an extraordinary boom in neuroimaging work. In 50 years' time, all of this work may seem quaintly obsolete. We don't know.

Historical milestones are one thing. Conceptual issues are another. The trends and schools described here arose when researchers operated in a different world and context to that in which we operate today. Much – if not most – research conducted in universities is funded by government, and government has priorities. Will these priorities see a shift in the types of topics psychologists study in the future?

On a grander scale, conceptual issues can be virtually synonymous with philosophical issues. For example, the question 'Is the scientific method the best method for establishing truth?' is a philosophical, rather than a psychological question, because it doesn't have an absolute answer. When we have answers to questions, philosophy is dead. In the chapters that follow you should be able to see how research arose and in what context – how some of the work in social psychology emerged from real-life events, such as the apparent reluctance to assist a person crying for help, or a soldier saying he was only obeying orders, for example. Or how cross-cultural research on facial expression led to a theory of emotion. Or how research on race differences in IQ became controversial. Or how we classify and diagnose mental illness. Or how sociobiology, according to some views, reduces human beings to self-interested savages.

So far, you have seen how psychology is a discipline that comprises a number of different branches. This survey of the history of psychology reveals a number of methodological approaches to the study of behaviour. The next chapter describes in more detail how psychologists study behaviour. You will also discover the dominant methodological approach to answering questions about psychology.

Chapter review

What is psychology?

- Psychology is the science of behaviour, and psychologists study a large variety of behaviours in humans and other animals.
- Psychology has many major branches:

  - Psychobiology – the study of the biological basis of behaviour.
  - Psychophysiology – the study of people's physiological reactions, such as changes in heart rate and muscle tension.
  - Neuropsychology – the study of the relationship between central nervous system activity and structure and function.
  - Comparative psychology – the study of the evolution of behaviour by comparing the behavioural capacities of various species of animals.
  - Ethology – the study of the biological bases of behaviour through observation of animals in natural environments.
  - Sociobiology – the interpretation of human and animal behaviour in terms of evolution and biological inheritance.
  - Behaviour genetics – the study of the degree of influence exerted by heredity and environment on behaviour.
  - Cognitive psychology – the study of complex human behaviours such as cognition, memory and attention.
  - Cognitive neuroscience – the study of the role of the human and animal brain in behaviour.
  - Developmental psychology – the study of the development of behaviour throughout the lifespan.
  - Social psychology – the study of the effects of people on the behaviour of other people.
  - Individual differences – the study of the effects of specific characteristics or traits on behaviour.
  - Cross-cultural psychology – the study of the impact of culture on behaviour.
  - Forensic and criminological psychology – the study of the ways in which psychological knowledge can be applied in criminal and legal settings.
  - Clinical psychology – the study and treatment of mental disorders and problems of adjustment.
  - Health psychology – the study of the ways in which lifestyle and behaviour affect illness and health.
  - Educational psychology – the assessment of the cognitive, social and emotional development of children in the school environment.
  - Consumer psychology – the study of what motivates people to consume and how consumers' perceptions are formed.
  - Organisational or occupational psychology – the study of the behaviour of individuals and groups in the workplace.
  - Ergonomics – the design of machines and workplace environments to enhance work performance.

The development of psychology as a science

- Psychology has its modern roots in the thinking of the French philosopher and mathematician René Descartes who argued that the mind and the body were two separate entities which interacted (dualism).
- The mid-nineteenth century gave rise to materialism and empiricism. Materialism maintained that the mind was made of matter; thus all natural phenomena, including human behaviour, could be explained in terms of physical entities: the interaction of matter and energy. Empiricism emphasised that all knowledge was acquired by means of sensory experience; no knowledge was innate. The concept of empiricism was developed by the philosophers John Locke and David Hume.

Modern psychology

- The first laboratory of experimental psychology was established in Leipzig in 1879 by Wilhelm Wundt.
- Wundt and his colleagues' work gave rise to structuralism: the idea that the mind was made up of components which could be broken apart and studied. The method of studying these components was introspection – the observation and recall of experience.
- At about the same time, Ebbinghaus contributed important methods for objectively measuring learning and forgetting.

- Darwin's ground-breaking theory of evolution, or theory of natural selection, argued that traits necessary for survival would be inherited and that only those adaptively useful traits would survive.
- Francis Galton founded the scientific study of individual differences in human behaviour and suggested that certain psychological characteristics could be inherited.
- Functionalism, which grew out of Darwin's theory of evolution, was concerned with the processes of consciousness such as perceiving and learning. Its major advocates were William James and James Angell.
- Functionalism gave rise to behaviourism, founded by John Watson, which still dominates the way we do research. The subject matter of behaviourism is observable behaviour; according to the behaviourists, mental events – because they were unobservable – should play no part in scientific psychology. Behaviourism developed a radical strain in the 1950s which viewed the organism's behaviour strictly in terms of stimulus and response.

- Humanistic psychology is concerned with the special nature of humanity and emphasises human experience, choice and creativity, and the potential for personal growth.
- The cognitive revolution arose from the belief that behaviourism's emphasis on observable behaviour missed some of the complexity of human cognition and behaviour. The cognitive revolution saw a rekindling of interest in phenomena such as memory, thinking, creativity, imagination and so on, and human behaviour was interpreted in terms of information processing.
- The biological revolution in psychology manifested itself in the increased interest of psychologists in all fields – not just physiological psychology – in the role of biological factors in behaviour. This has given rise to cognitive neuroscience in which the disciplines of neuropsychology and cognitive psychology have combined and used neuroimaging methods to create a greater understanding of the role of the brain in thinking, feeling and perceiving, specifically to localise function in the brain.

Suggestions for further reading

The history of psychology

Crivellato, E. and Ribatti, D. (2007) Soul, mind, brain: Greek philosophy and the birth of neuroscience. *Brain Research Bulletin*, 71, 327–36.

Hock, R. (2014) *Forty Studies that Changed Psychology* (7th edn). Harlow: Pearson Education.

Leahey, T.H. (2012) *A History of Psychology* (7th edn). Englewood Cliffs, NJ: Prentice Hall International.

Several sources describe the history of psychology, including its philosophical and biological roots, and these are some very good introductions.

Concepts and controversies in psychology

Aczel, B., Palfi, B., Szollosi, A., Kovacs, M., Szaszi, B., Szecsi, P., ... & Wagenmakers, E. J. (2018). Quantifying Support for the Null Hypothesis in Psychology: An Empirical Investigation. Advances in Methods and Practices in Psychological Science, in press.

Furnham, A. and Tsvirikos, D. (2016) *All in the Mind* (3rd edn). London: Whurr Publishers.

Gelman, A., & Loken, E. (2014). The statistical crisis in science. *American Scientist*, 102(6), 460–465.

Hawkins, R. X., Smith, E. N., Au, C., Arias, J. M., Catapano, R., Hermann, E., ... & Salehi, S. (2018). Improving the replicability of psychological science through pedagogy. *Advances in Methods and Practices in Psychological Science*, 2515245917740427.

Leek, J. (2017). Five ways to fix statistics. *Nature*, 551, 557–559.

Leek, J. T., & Peng, R. D. (2015). Statistics: P values are just the tip of the iceberg. *Nature*, 520(7549), 612.

Lilienfeld, S.O. (2011) Public skepticism of psychology. *American Psychologist*, 67, 111–29.

Motulsky, H. J. (2015). Common misconceptions about data analysis and statistics. *British journal of pharmacology*, 172(8), 2126–2132.

O'Donnell, M., Nelson, L. D., Ackermann, E., Aczel, B., Akhtar, A., Aldrovandi, S., ... & Balatekin, N. (2018). Registered replication report: Dijksterhuis and van Knippenberg (1998). *Perspectives on Psychological Science*, 1745691618755704.

Rolls, G. (2014) *Classic Case Studies in Psychology* (3rd edn). London: Routledge. https://rolfzwaan.blogspot.co.uk

Zwaan, R.A., Etz, A., Lucas, R.E., & Donnellan, M.B. (in press). Making replication mainstream. Behavioural and Brain Sciences.

Excellent introductions to some controversial issues and major concepts in psychology. Zwaan et al's paper is currently the best review of the replication crisis and how to solve it

Influential psychologists

Brockman, J. (2016) *The Mind: Leading Scientists Explore the Brain, Memory, Personality and Happiness.* London: Harper Perennial.

Cohen, D. (2014) *Psychologists on Psychology.* London: Routledge.

Fancher, R.E. and Rutherford, R. (2016) *Pioneers of Psychology* (5th edn). New York: W.W. Norton.

Kimble, G.A., Wertheimer, M. and White, C.L. (2014) *Portraits of Pioneers in Psychology.* London: Psychology Press.

Cohen's book contains an excellent set of interviews with some of the leading psychologists of the time. The books by Brockman, Kimble *et al.* and Fancher contain biographical sketches of the major scientists who have contributed to psychology and so provide a good potted introduction to the personalities (and themes, ideas and developments) in psychology.

Specific topics

Special issue of *Journal of Applied Psychology: Centennial Special Issue*, 2017, vol. 102.

Motyl, M., Demos, A.P., Carsel, T.S., Hanson, B.E., Melton, Z.J., Mueller, A.B. . . . and Yantis, C. (2017) The State of Social and Personality Science: *Rotten to the Core*, Not so Bad, Getting Better, or Getting Worse? *Journal of Personality and Social Psychology*, 113(1):34–58.

ten Brinke, L., Vohs, K.D. and Carney, D.R. (2016) Can ordinary people detect deception after all? *Trends in Cognitive Sciences*, 20(8), 579–88.

CHAPTER 2
How to study behaviour

CLEVER HANS: A LESSON IN RESEARCH METHODS

Because of his long-lasting fame at the turn of the century, many people know about 'Clever Hans', the mind-reading horse. If people gave the owner a question for Hans, he would look directly at the horse and repeat the question in what seemed like a normal tone of voice. Hans would then lift his hoof and tap out the answer. Thus, if asked, 'What is 2 + 2?', Hans would tap the ground four times. After Hans had given the correct answer, the owner would reward the animal by patting it or giving it food.

In 1904, several of the best-known scientists in Germany formed a 'commission' to study the animal. These distinguished scientists stated boldly that they could find no evidence that Hans was responding to external cues from his questioners and perhaps really could read minds. However, the psychologist on the commission, clearly not satisfied, told one of his graduate students to look into the matter.

The student put blinkers on Hans so the animal could not watch the people who were asking him the questions. The horse's ability to respond correctly decreased significantly.

Clever Hans was, indeed, a 'genius of a horse' but was not a mind-reader. The animal was superb at reading 'body language' – cues that questioners almost always give to an animal. But these were so slight and so subtle that most people were completely unaware that they were giving them. In this sense, the sceptics were right all along.

Source: Furnham, 1996, pp. 83–5.

WHAT YOU SHOULD BE ABLE TO DO AFTER READING CHAPTER 2

- Define and describe the scientific approach to studying psychological variables.

- Define concepts such as hypotheses, theories and variables.

- Have an awareness of the ethical principles adopted by psychologists.

- Describe the quantitative and qualitative approaches to psychology and be aware of the advantages and disadvantages of each.

- Have an awareness of how psychologists control variables.

QUESTIONS TO THINK ABOUT

- What is the scientific method and why is it so important to psychology?

- What are the goals of psychological research?

- Does following the steps of the scientific method guarantee that the results of a study will be valid?

- Can the scientific method be applied to all psychological research?

- How would you set up experiments to answer some of the questions you have about behaviour?

- How do the methods of psychology differ from those of other sciences? Do they?

- Why is obtaining informed consent from participants who take part in research important?

- Are some psychological subjects impossible to study? Why?

- What are the dangers in drawing conclusions from studies in which there is only one participant?

The process of discovery in psychology: the scientific method

The goal of psychological research is to discover, describe, explain and change the causes of behaviour. To do this, psychologists need to describe behaviours and the events that are responsible for their occurrence in a language that is both precise enough to be understood by others and general enough to apply to a wide variety of situations. This language takes the form of explanations, which are general statements about the events that cause phenomena to occur (see Chapter 1). The nature of these general statements will become clear as we see how psychologists use the scientific method.

There are three major scientific approaches to research. Naturalistic observations – observations of people or animals in their natural environment – are the least formal and are constrained by the fewest rules. Naturalistic observations provide the foundations of the biological and social sciences. Charles Darwin's observation and classification of animals, plants and fossils during his voyage around the world provided him with the raw material for his theory of evolution (see Chapter 3). Jean Piaget collected much of his early data by observing his own children. Correlational studies are observational in nature, but they involve more formal measurement – of environmental events, of individuals' physical and social characteristics, and of their behaviour. Experiments go beyond mere measurement. A psychologist performing an experiment makes things happen and observes the results. As you will see, only an experiment can positively identify cause-and-effect relations.

The scientific method consists of a set of rules that dictates the general procedure a scientist must follow in their research. These rules are not arbitrary; they are based on logic. The following five steps summarise the rules of the scientific method that apply to experiments, the most rigorous form of scientific research. As we will see later, many of these rules also apply to observational studies. Some new terms introduced here without definition will be described in detail later in this chapter.

Stages in experimentation

1 Identify the problem and formulate hypothetical cause-and-effect relations among variables. This step involves identifying variables (particular behaviours and environmental and physiological events) and describing the relations among them in general terms. Consider the hypothesis that positive mood increases creativity. This statement describes a relation between two variables – mood and creativity – and states that an increase in one causes an increase in the other.

2 Design the experiment. Experiments involve the manipulation of factors called independent variables and the observation of dependent variables (these are defined in detail later in the chapter). For example, if we wanted to test the hypothesis that positive mood (independent variable) increases creativity (dependent variable), each variable would have to be operationally defined. The independent variable must be controlled so that only it, and no other variable, is responsible for any changes in the dependent variable.

3 Conduct the experiment. The researcher must organise the material needed to perform the experiment, train the people who will conduct the research, recruit volunteers whose behaviour will be observed, assign each of these volunteers to a treatment group or a control group and arrange the setting for the experiment. The experiment is performed and the observations are recorded.

4 Evaluate the hypothesis by examining the data from the study. Do the results support the hypothesis, or do they suggest that it is wrong? This step often involves mathematical procedures used to determine whether the relationship between two variables is statistically significant, that is, not due to chance.

5 Communicate the results. (See next section.)

Following these simple steps decreases the chances that we will be misled by our observations and come to incorrect conclusions from our research. The approach of formulating hypotheses and then setting up experiments to test them is sometimes known as hypothetico-deductive. People have a tendency to accept some types of evidence even though the rules of logic indicate that they should not (see Chapters 1 and 11). This tendency usually serves us well in our daily lives, but it can lead us to draw the wrong conclusions when we try to understand the true causes of natural phenomena, including our own behaviour. The same tendency results in the making of common-sense mistakes when predicting the outcome of psychological research (see Chapter 1).

Communicating the results of scientific research

Once psychologists have learned something about the causes of a behaviour from an experiment or observational study, they must tell others about their findings. When a piece of research is complete, it is written up in the form of a journal article and sent to an academic, peer-reviewed scientific journal. The paper will be critically evaluated, usually anonymously, by two or three of the author's peers who will have expertise in the topic written about.

The scientific method insists that scientists report the details of their research so that other investigators can repeat, or replicate, the study. Replication is one of the great strengths of science; it ensures that erroneous results and incorrect conclusions are weeded out. When scientists publish a study, they know that if the findings are important enough, their colleagues will try to replicate it (perhaps with some variation) to be sure that the results were not just a statistical fluke, specific to the sample studied or the methods used, or the result of some unsuspected errors in the design or execution of the study.

The types of article that scientists will write fall broadly into four categories. There are empirical papers that report the conduct and results of an experiment. Most scientific journals publish papers of this kind (such as *Nature, Journal of Personality and Social Psychology Bulletin, British Journal of Psychology*, etc.) and most follow a format. They will invariably comprise sections and these sections will include a title, an abstract, an introduction, the method, the results, a discussion, references and an appendix. There are deviations from this format: *Science* and the *Journal of Cognitive Neuroscience*, to name only two, do not adopt this structure (the study's methods are reported either at the end of the paper or on the journal's website). But, by and large, papers follow this structure:

- **Title (and affiliations)**. The title describes the general thrust of the article. It is normally followed by the full names of all authors normally with their affiliation (who they work for/ on behalf of, e.g. 'School of Psychotherapy and Psychology, Regent's University London, UK').
- **Abstract**. This is usually a 150 to 200-word paragraph that summarises ('abstracts' the information from) the article. It has a statement of intent, a brief description of the study and results and a general conclusion. Some abstracts have a different format and are sectioned in the same way as the paper: research suggests that this is a more informative way of summarising a paper.
- **Introduction**. This is the first of the four major sections and reviews the literature pertaining to the subject of the paper and presents a set of hypotheses derived from theory which the study aims to test.
- **Method**. This section describes what the experimenters did and who took part. Conventionally, this is divided into these subsections: participants, apparatus/materials and procedure. Under participants, all of the important information about the study's sample is included: age, sex, race, education and any other variable that the study is interested in. The apparatus/ materials section includes details of any specialist technology or materials used. The procedure section describes what the experimenters did. Anyone reading this section should be able to conduct an identical experiment – facilities and time willing – on the basis of reading this section.
- **Results**. This section reports the results of the study. At this stage of your degree, reading the results section of a paper can seem like reading a foreign language because it is replete with seemingly impenetrable statistics.
- **Discussion**. The final major section, the discussion, discusses the results found and their implications for the field. It interprets findings in light of theory and previously published data and suggests future avenues of enquiry.

- **References**. This section lists, usually in alphabetical order, all the studies cited in the text. Any study cited in the text must appear here and every item in the reference list should have been cited.
- **Appendix (optional)**. Sometimes papers include appendices providing additional information such as word lists or questionnaires.

In addition to journals that publish the results of experiments, there are also those that publish methodological papers reporting a new technique, questionnaire, procedure or new piece of equipment for use in psychological research. Thirdly, there are journals for theoretical papers that formulate a new theory arising from reviewed data. The journal *Psychological Review* is devoted to articles of this kind, for example. Finally, there are review papers that synthesise a number of articles on a given topic. *Psychological Bulletin* and *Current Directions in Psychological Science* publish papers exclusively of this kind and are good journals for providing up-to-date reviews in psychology.

Most journals in psychology, however, tend to focus on the sub-areas of psychology. *The European Journal of Social Psychology, Memory and Cognition, Journal of Applied Psychology, Neuropsychologia, Child Development, Personality and Individual Differences, Health Psychology, Emotion* and so on, are examples of this kind. Some journals publish even more specialised research (e.g. *Social Neuroscience, Laterality*).

Constructing a hypothesis

A hypothesis is the starting point of any study. It is an idea, phrased as a general statement, that a scientist wishes to test through scientific research. In the original Greek, hypothesis means 'suggestion', and the word still conveys the same meaning. When scientists form a hypothesis, they are simply suggesting that a relation exists among various phenomena (like the one that might exist between increased positive mood and increased risk-taking). Thus, a hypothesis is a tentative statement about a cause-and-effect relation between two or more events. Productive and creative scientists formulate new hypotheses by thinking about the implications of studies that they have performed or that have been performed by others.

At other times, however, researchers may not know exactly what they expect to find. Such research endeavours are called 'fishing expeditions'. In the same way that an angler may not know whether they will catch a trout or an old car seat, the researcher does not know whether they will find result X or result Y. An example of such research would be the measurement of people's attitudes towards a particular subject such as the usefulness of animal experimentation or alternative medicine. In such cases, an experimenter would not be able to make an absolute prediction based on hypothetico-deductive reasoning (unless, e.g. they compared attitudes among two groups such as vegans and meat-eaters, or users of conventional medicine and users of homoeopathic remedies).

Psychology in action: Communicating psychology

The media are voracious beasts. Newspapers, television, radio, social media and websites all have space to occupy and air to fill, often with few resources. Psychology's asset, but also its Achilles heel, is that its subject matter is something which most people think they know something about (human behaviour) and produces data that are fascinating and stimulate human interest. The BPS's Press Office has a media database of over 1,000 members, and receives around 350 queries a month. But how accurately is psychological and other research presented in the media and is this portrayal – skewed or otherwise – important?

First, let's start with the source of the research. Simply because a paper is published in a science journal does not mean that its method or results are unassailable. At the extreme end, journals can publish data that turn out to be fraudulent. In 2005, the journal *Nature* found that 0.3 per cent of the 3,247 scientists who participated in their confidential study claimed to have published bogus data and 6 per cent admitted failing to publish data that contradicted their own theoretical positions. In the same year, *Science*, one of the two premier general science journals in the world, withdrew a paper by the Korean scientist Hwang Wo-suk because the stem cell lines he had created (and wrote about in Science) did not exist.

Another scandal broke in 2004 when the *Journal of Reproductive Medicine* published a physics-defying article on the effect of prayer on in vitro fertilisation which was generally agreed to be flawed and possibly fabricated. The author was later convicted of criminal fraud. In 2009, an anaesthesiologist was found to have made up most of the data in his 10-year publishing career, and, at the time of writing, editors are being requested to withdraw 21 of his papers. This man researched the nature of pain management after operations – not a frivolous topic of little consequence. Even more seriously, flawed research claiming a link between the MMR vaccine and autism – and the enormously tendentious publicity this generated in 2002–2003 – has caused completely avoidable harm to children, given the dramatic increase in measles and mumps following this hoo-hah.

Psychology is not immune. There continues to be debate over whether the British psychologist, Cyril Burt, invented his data concerning twins and intelligence. Michael LaCour published some astonishing findings showing that if LGBT political canvassers talked about their sexuality openly when campaigning, those they canvassed were more likely to support same-sex marriage (LaCour and Green, 2014). However, the study was published in *Science* and attracted much publicity. The data were discovered to have irregularities (although a study by an independent group did find a similar effect in 2016; Broockman and Kalla, 2016). And, of course, there is psychology's bete noir, the social psychologist Diederik Stapel, who

has had (as of September 2016) 58 of his papers retracted for misconduct and data fabrication (www.retractionwatch.com).

Interestingly, there may be a way of discriminating fraudulent papers from non-fraudulent ones. Markowitz and Hancock (2015) evaluated the words used in 253 publications which had been retracted because the data were fraudulent and compared the language used with 253 papers that had not been retracted and 62 papers which had been retracted but for other reasons (ethical violations). The fraudulent papers were significantly more likely to use linguistic obfuscation (they were not clear), less likely to be readable and include more jargon. The papers which obfuscated were also the ones more likely to have the greatest number of references.

Outright fraud aside, reviewers can normally agree on the really bad studies. But there is more disagreement about the average-to-good ones. Science progresses by contradiction, and new articles develop ideas generated by previous publications or take into account variables that the previous studies had not. Although there are checks in place to weed out 'bad' research, it is common to see a lot of it published. And much published research is positive research – it reports significant findings. This is called publication bias – the tendency to publish findings that are positive rather than negative (there are many reasons for publication bias – from wanting to publish something new and original, to career advancement and journal prestige and reputation).

This is why you should adopt an inquisitive but informed approach when reading research papers: do not be afraid to question an aspect of procedure or an analysis of logical thinking if you think it is wrong or misguided. You might be right.

Although some of the stories you see reported or hear broadcast are well researched, balanced and informed, it is generally the case that most are not. Journals are intended primarily for other scientists. Journals, however, are also consulted by medical or science (or non-specialist) journalists interested in writing about innovative psychological breakthroughs. Conferences at which psychologists present the results of their studies are also extensively reported by specialist reporters in the media and some psychological societies have effective press offices which proactively publicise society conference papers.

However, never take any report you read in a newspaper or magazine or see or hear on the television or radio of a published study at face value. The American Psychological Association was so concerned about the misperceptions of the discipline (by politicians principally) that it published a document entitled 'Self-defense for the psychological scientist' in 2006. If you read the articles on the excellent website www.badscience.net, you will see why: journalists sometimes try to make a study more exciting than it is and make wild claims about the results that the researchers would never dream of doing.

▶

Psychology in action: *Continued*

According to Goldacre (2008), 'Science stories generally fall into one of three categories: the wacky stories, the 'breakthrough' stories, and the scare stories. Each undermines and distorts science in its own idiosyncratic way' (p. 208). Stories with headlines such as – and these are genuine – 'Infidelity is genetic', 'Electricity allergy real', 'Scans that spot killer babies' and 'In future, all men will have big willies' reflect a tenuous relationship with the data (if the data exist) they claim to report. Similarly, newspaper articles claiming to report the mathematical formula for (and, again, all of these are real) the perfect way to eat ice cream (A × Tp × Tm/Pt × At × V × LT × SP × W/Tt = 3d20, if you're interested), the best sitcom, the best way to boil an egg, the best joke, the most depressing day of the year are all bogus – they are not based on any real research or any real science. Most are commissioned by companies keen to harness the solid appeal of science to market their products.

The journalist Nick Davies, in his book *Flat Earth News*, describes the stories that boast none of the good features of journalism as 'churnalism': the writers parrot what is given to them by PR agencies or wire services, often unedited (Davies, 2008). In one survey, 80 per cent of British broadsheet news stories were 'wholly, mainly or partially' based on 'material provided by news agencies and the PR industry'. This is not a trivial issue because most of us will have our first encounter with new studies, not from a studious acquaintance with Google Scholar or Science Direct, but from magazines, newspapers, television or radio. We rely on journalists – the conduit between us and the research – to present findings lucidly, accurately, interestingly and not to oversimplify the data or misrepresent it. And the media has influence, through selecting what it exposes. After Kylie Minogue's well-documented cancer, the *Medical Journal of Australia* reported a 40 per cent increase in mammogram bookings; in 2009, in the UK, stories reporting the terminal cancer of a female reality TV contestant appeared to coincide with an increase in cervical cancer checks. More self-servingly, the American Association for the Advancement of Science found that a mention of a researcher's study in the *New York Times* increased the number of times his or her paper was referred to by other colleagues in their papers (this is an important indicator of impact in the science world). Television and radio exposure increased this still further.

One new field that gets both journalists and readers excited is neuroimaging. And the fact that you can illustrate a story involving the brain's role in behaviour with a screen – and print-friendly brain scan makes the research even more appealing. But neuroimaging technology, and its data analysis, is complex and the studies using it very detailed in their method. Sometimes the details are sacrificed for a headline. Hence, stories screaming: 'Scary or sensational? A machine that can look into the mind' (genuine). Chapter 4 will take a further look at the lure of neuroimaging and the way it makes research more persuasive than do words.

Creating a theory

A theory, a set of statements designed to explain a set of phenomena, is an elaborate form of hypothesis. In fact, a theory can be a way of organising a system of related hypotheses to explain some larger aspect of nature. A good theory fuels the creation of new hypotheses. More accurately, a good scientist, contemplating a good theory, thinks of more good hypotheses to test. For example, Albert Einstein's theory of relativity states that time, matter and energy are interdependent. Changes in any one will produce changes in the others. The hypotheses suggested by this theory revolutionised science; the field of nuclear physics rests largely on experiments arising from Einstein's theory.

A good theory is one that generates testable hypotheses – hypotheses that can potentially be supported or proved wrong by scientific research. Some theories are so general or so abstract that they do not produce testable hypotheses and hence cannot be subjected to scientific rigour. The framework for most psychological research is larger in scope than a hypothesis but smaller in scope than a fully fledged theory. For example, the frustration–aggression hypothesis in social psychology suggests that people (or other animals) tend to become aggressive when they do not achieve a goal that they have been accustomed to achieving. This hypothesis makes a prediction that might fit many different situations. Indeed, many experiments have been performed to test this hypothesis under different conditions.

Even though the frameworks that most psychologists construct fall short of constituting theories, they serve a similar function by stimulating researchers to think about old problems in new ways and by showing how findings that did not appear to be related to each other can be explained by a single concept. One theory of emotional experience, for example, suggests that increases or decreases in the left and right front part of the brain are associated with positive and negative emotions, reflecting a tendency to 'withdraw' or 'approach' a stimulus (Davidson and Sutton, 1995). Such a theory can be used to test a number of hypotheses such as, 'depressed individuals will show less left frontal brain activity', and research on frontal lobe activation and emotion has resulted in a modification of thinking on the relationship between the two (Peterson and Harmon-Jones, 2009) (see Chapter 13).

Quantitative research methods: designing an experiment

Although naturalistic observations enable a psychologist to classify behaviours into categories and provide hypothetical explanations for these behaviours, only an experiment can determine whether these explanations are correct. This approach is known as **quantitative research** because behaviours are reduced to quantities or can at least be seen as quantifiable. Personality or visuospatial ability may be quantified by a score on a questionnaire, for example, or the ability to react correctly and quickly on a reaction time task may be quantified by the number of correct decisions and the speed of responding.

There are various types of experiment that we can design. We could conduct an experiment in which we looked at the effect of sleep deprivation on mental arithmetic ability; one group might be deprived of sleep for 24 hours, another for 36 hours and another would be allowed to sleep normally. In a more elaborate study, we could use neuroimaging techniques to monitor changes in brain activation at each stage. In the neuroimaging study this would be the control group because it is unaffected by the features of the experiment that we are interested in looking at and can, therefore, be used as a comparison group. The others are called **experimental groups**. Because the individuals in one group are not the same people as the ones in another group, the design of the experiment is called **independent groups** or **between-groups.**

A slightly different experiment might involve people performing different levels of the same experiment. For example, we may be interested in finding out if people recognise real English words more quickly than they do pseudowords (words which follow the same rules of English but have no meaning) or non-words (words which do not follow the rules of English). This is called a lexical decision task. Here, every individual would respond to each type of word (but might be quicker responding to some types of word than others). Because each individual is exposed to the same condition of the experiment (each type of word), the design is called **repeated measures** or **within-groups.** As each participant acts as his or her control (i.e. completes each condition in the experiment), there is less variability in the data (such as sex, age and personality differences or the ability to respond quickly to visual stimuli or the tendency to think better in the morning than in the afternoon, etc.).

Independent groups designs are advantageous when you do not want to expose the same individuals to the same conditions. For example, if we wanted to compare the effect of fat, carbohydrate and protein intake on people's ability to react quickly to visual stimuli (because we hypothesised that certain foods made you drowsy), there would be disadvantages to having them all eat each different type of food (to begin with, if they were tested on different days, they may get better on the reaction time tasks because of practice; secondly, because different food is presented on each occasion, they may become

suspicious). An independent groups design would help to eliminate these problems. Such designs are useful to medicine and the study of treatment for mental illness (see Chapter 18). A mentally ill group would take treatment A, another group treatment B, another group a placebo (we will come on to this later) and a final group would receive no treatment. If treatment A is successful, there should be a difference in outcome between this group and others in the study.

Imagine that you were a researcher who was interested in discovering whether people's cognitive ability declined with age. You take five groups of adults: 20–30-year-olds, 31–40-year-olds, 41–50-year-olds, 51–60-year-olds and the over-61-year-olds. You administer a series of tests that measure a range of cognitive abilities such as verbal and visuospatial ability. You find that whereas most of the over-61 group perform more poorly at most of the tests than do the other groups, they do better at some of the verbal tests such as vocabulary. What do you conclude from this study? If you conclude that verbal ability does not decline as rapidly as other abilities with age, you would be wrong. Can you think why? (The answer appears in Chapter 11.) Using the same example, what would be the theory and what would be the hypothesis in this experiment? What would be the independent and dependent variables?

In a laboratory experiment, the experimenter has control over most of the variables that they think will affect the outcome of the experiment. For example, we could design an experiment in which the effect of ambient noise on work performance was measured. We could expose individuals to specific noises at specific levels at specific times while they completed specific tasks and questionnaires assessing mood. Alternatively, we could set up a **field experiment** in which participants would be observed under fairly 'natural' conditions. For example, we might compare the effects of different office lighting conditions, or the weather, on individuals' mood and productivity.

The important feature of naturalistic observations is that the observer remains in the background and does not interfere with the people (or animals) being observed. In some cases, psychologists do interfere with a situation in a natural setting. For example, some experiments designed (see Chapters 15 and 16) to discover what factors determine whether bystanders come to the aid of people who have been hurt or who are in distress. An 'accident' is staged, and the behaviour of passers-by is surreptitiously observed. Although studies such as these take place outside the laboratory – at job sites or on the street – they are experiments, not naturalistic observations. Such experiments might be called quasi-field studies.

Variables: what is studied and measured

Variables are things that have a particular value but which can vary. Scientists either measure or manipulate the values of variables. Manipulate literally means 'to handle' (from *manus*, 'hand'). Psychologists use the word 'manipulate' to refer to setting the value of a variable for experimental purposes. The results of this manipulation determine whether the hypothesis is true or false. Direct manipulation of an independent variable, for example, would involve placing individuals into different treatment groups, such as drug A, drug B, a placebo and no drug. Indirect manipulation would involve differentiating individuals with different personality types. For example, we might be interested in whether individuals low, medium or high in trait anxiety (the degree of anxiety they habitually feel) selectively attend to anxiety-related stimuli (such as pictures of snakes, spiders, blood and so on).

Or we might look at the effect of positive mood on risk-taking. We would assemble four groups of volunteers to serve as participants. We manipulate mood by having participants watch a comedy film (which would put participants in a positive mood), an unpleasant film (which would put participants in a negative mood) or a neutral film (which would not be expected to influence participants' mood negatively or positively). We would have a fourth group which would watch no film (the control group). We would then examine the effect of this measure (mood) on risk-taking, such as the amount spent gambling at roulette (taking care, of course, to ensure that our 'manipulation' worked).

This experiment examines the effect of one variable on another. Here, the variable that we manipulate (mood) is called the **independent variable**. We could also have a second independent variable, such as the sex of the gambler (Do men or women gamble more? Would we have a good reason for hypothesising a sex difference?). The variable that we measure (risk-taking) is the dependent variable. An easy way to keep the names of these variables straight is to remember that a hypothesis describes how the value of a **dependent variable** depends on the value of an independent variable. Our hypothesis proposes that increased gambling depends on the individual's level of mood. Suppose that you were interested in studying the effects of sleep deprivation on learning ability. Which of these two variables would be the independent variable and which would be the dependent variable? How might you define these variables operationally? You can see the relationship between the two variables illustrated in Figure 2.1.

Although one of the first steps in psychological investigation involves naming and classifying behaviours, we must be careful to avoid committing the **nominal fallacy** or reification. The nominal fallacy refers to the erroneous belief that one has explained an event simply by naming it (*nomen* means 'name'). Classifying a behaviour does not explain it; classifying only prepares us to examine and discover events that cause a behaviour. For example, suppose that we see a man frown and shout at other people without provocation, criticise their work when really it is acceptable and generally act unpleasantly towards everyone around him. Someone says, 'He's really angry today.' Does this statement explain his behaviour?

It does not; it only describes the behaviour. To say that he is angry suggests that an internal state is responsible for his behaviour – that anger is causing his behaviour. But all we have observed is his behaviour, not his internal state. Even if he is experiencing feelings of anger, these feelings still do not explain his behaviour. What we really need to know is what events made him act the way he did. Perhaps he has a painful toothache. Perhaps he had just learned that he was passed over for a promotion. Perhaps he had a terrible fight with his wife. Perhaps he had just read a book that advised him to be more assertive. Events like these are causes of both the behaviour and the feelings. Unless they are discovered, we cannot say that we have explained his behaviour. The task of a psychologist is to determine which of the many events that occurred before a particular behaviour caused that behaviour to happen.

Operational definitions

This translation of generalities into specific operations is called an **operational definition**: independent variables and dependent variables are defined in terms of the operations an experimenter performs to set their values or to measure them. In our proposed experiment on mood and gambling, for example, the operational definition of the independent and dependent variables might be:

- Independent variable: change in mood was induced by watching pleasant, neutral or unpleasant video films.
- Dependent variable: the amount of money spent betting on the outcome of a roulette wheel when the probability of winning was high and when it was low.

There are many ways to translate a general concept into a set of operations. We might decide to adopt a different measure of mood, such as having participants complete a mental arithmetic task and inform them that they did well or badly (regardless of how they actually performed). This might also be expected to increase or decrease mood. We might choose a different measure of risk-taking such as asking participants to make decisions about a hypothetical risky treatment for a disease that a person has (hypothetically) developed. Which operational definition of mood and risk-taking do you think is correct? Is there only one correct definition in this case? What these questions address is the issue of validity.

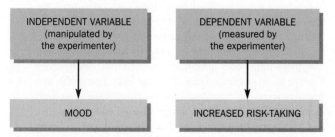

Figure 2.1 Independent and dependent variables described in the mood and risk-taking experiment.

Validity

The validity of an operational definition refers to how appropriate it is – how accurately it represents the variable whose value has been manipulated or measured. You'll sometimes find the term 'ecological validity' being used in this context: this refers to the degree to which the experimental context accurately presents that which the experimenter wants to reproduce. If you set up an experiment to monitor how much people laughed at a comedy, for example, and also measured their brain electrical activity and heart rate, which means attaching wires with electrodes to the head, fingers and chest, would this accurately represent the context in which a person would normally laugh at a comedy programme? The experience could be reasonably said to lack ecological validity.

The issue of validity is illustrated, famously, by the Barnum effect. The Psychology in action box tells you more.

Control of independent variables

If a scientist performs an experiment and finds that manipulating the value of the independent variable changes the dependent variable, the scientist can conclude that there is a cause-and-effect relation between the variables. That is, changes in the value of the independent variable cause changes in the value of the dependent variable.

In designing an experiment, the experimenter must manipulate the value of the independent variable and only the independent variable. For example, if we want to determine whether noise has an effect on people's reading speed, we must choose our source of noise carefully. If we use the sound from a television set to supply the noise and find that it slows people's reading speed, we cannot conclude that the effect was caused purely by noise. We might have selected an interesting programme, thus distracting the participants' attention from the material they were reading. If we want to do this experiment properly, we should use noise that is neutral and not a source of interest by itself, for example, noise like the 'sssh' sound that is heard when an FM radio is tuned between stations.

In this example, we intended to test the effects of an independent variable (noise) on a dependent variable (reading speed). By using a television to provide the noise, we were inadvertently testing the effects of other variables besides noise on reading speed. We introduced unwanted variables in addition to the independent variable.

Psychology in action: The Barnum effect

Research has shown that highly intelligent readers, who are attracted to the boxed off sections of introductory psychology textbooks (that is you), have a particular set of personality characteristics.

They are:

... the type of person who has a tendency to be critical of yourself. You have a great need for other people to like and admire you but you pride yourself on being an independent thinker and do not accept others' statements without satisfactory proof. You have a great deal of unused capacity which you have not turned to your advantage. While you have some personality weaknesses, you are generally able to compensate for them. You prefer a certain amount of change and variety and become dissatisfied when hemmed in by restrictions and limitations.

Does this description accurately reflect your own personality? It probably does, but more than that, it probably applies to the majority of the population. These are universally valid statements which refer to nothing specific but to general feelings and beliefs that could apply to almost everyone. The belief that vague personality descriptions accurately reflect personality is called the **Barnum effect** (Meehl, 1956), named after Phineas T. Barnum, the great American circus showman, who declared that there was a 'sucker born every minute' and believed that his entertainments provided 'a little something for everybody'. The Barnum effect is seen clearly when individuals accept that 'generalized, vague, bogus descriptions of themselves which have high base-rate occurrence in the general population' are correct (Furnham and Schofield, 1987).

The phenomenon has a long history in psychology and a less honourable one among proponents of pseudoscience and pseudotherapy. Any clairvoyant or fortune-teller will make cunning use of the Barnum effect to dupe credulous punters. This is not surprising: people have been found to be more accepting of generalised feedback than actual, factual feedback (Merrens and Richards, 1970). A study of 68 personnel managers in the 1950s highlights the way in which we can accept the most vague statements about our personality as reflecting reality. Stagner (1958) administered personality tests to these managers and gave them 13 bogus statements that were assumed to represent actual feedback about their personality from the tests (e.g. 'You have a great need to people to admire or like you' and 'You have a tendency to be critical of yourself.').

When asked to rate how strongly the participants agreed with these statements, almost all indicated that they believed them to some extent and one-third regarded their profile as a 'good' reflection of their character. For some statements such as, 'You prefer a certain amount of change and variety ... ' and 'While you have some personality weaknesses ... ', over 80 per cent of participants expressed agreement with them.

▶

Psychology in action: *Continued*

The circus showman, P.T. Barnum, who gave his name to the Barnum effect.

Source: Popperfoto/Getty Images.

In an ingenious spin on the Barnum phenomenon, Furnham (1994) set up an experiment in which undergraduates gave samples of their hair to an experimenter. A week later the participants were given a 'trichological analysis' – 24 bland statements regarding their health based on the hair sample – that was totally bogus. Most students thought that these randomly applied statements were very accurate.

What does research on the Barnum effect tell us? First, it shows us that most individuals are inclined to accept bland feedback about themselves. Secondly, it shows us that the validity of a test involves more than intuitively 'knowing' that a test measures something. Most individuals – unless they knew about the Barnum effect – would have regarded the statements at the beginning of this section as true and might have accepted the statement that intelligent but sceptical readers are drawn to boxed-off areas of textbooks. This statement is, of course, nonsense. Thirdly, and perhaps most importantly, the Barnum effect shows us that we should always adopt a sceptical and questioning approach to statements made about human behaviour – even to this last statement.

Schwartz (1999) cites a study showing that when respondents were asked to determine the causes of mass murder reported in newspapers, those who did so on notepaper headed 'Institute of Personality' cited more reasons related to personality, whereas those doing so on notepaper headed 'Institute of Social Science' gave more context-social related reasons for the crime. This example shows that even small details in the conduct of research can influence respondents' answers and thus affect validity.

Confounding and counterbalancing

One of the meanings of the word 'confound' is to fail to distinguish. If an experimenter inadvertently introduces one or more unwanted independent variables, they cannot distinguish the effects of any one of them on the dependent variable. That is, the effects of the variables will be confounded and this is called the **confounding of variables**. It is often difficult to be sure that independent variables are not confounded. We must be certain that when we manipulate the independent variable that variable only, and no other variable, is affected.

One method of addressing confounding variables is called **counterbalancing**, which means to 'weigh evenly'. Imagine that an experimenter decided to investigate the effect of a memory-enhancing drug on people's ability to remember concrete and abstract nouns. An experiment is designed in which three groups of people – one taking the drug, another

taking a harmless pill and a control group which takes nothing – complete a word recognition experiment. For all groups, the concrete words are presented in the first part of the experiment and the abstract words are presented in the second half. To the experimenter's surprise, although the drug group's performance is better than the others', all groups have more difficulty in remembering the abstract nouns. Does this finding mean that individuals find abstract nouns less memorable?

The answer is that, on the basis of the design of the experiment, we cannot know. Because the abstract words always appeared in the second half of the experiment, it is possible that the groups simply felt more tired towards the end of the experiment and that their fatigue influenced their recognition scores; they may even have become more bored towards the end of the experiment. Perhaps, having been used to memorising concrete nouns, the shift to a different type of word interfered with the individuals' memory strategy. A solution would be to counterbalance the presentation of the types of word so that some individuals received the abstract nouns first followed by the concrete nouns, whereas others received the concrete nouns first. If the original results were attributable to tiredness or fatigue then the same decrease in recall should be seen in the second half of the experiment. If individuals continue to recall abstract nouns less frequently than concrete nouns, then the result is not due to the effects of the confounding variables of tiredness and fatigue.

Having carefully designed a study, we must then decide how best to conduct it. This brings us to step 3 of the scientific method: performing the experiment. We must decide what participants will be used, what instructions will be given, and what equipment and materials will be used. We must ensure that the data collected will be accurate.

Reliability

If the procedure described by an operational definition gives consistent results under consistent conditions, the procedure is said to have high **reliability**. For example, measurements of people's height and weight are extremely reliable. Measurements of their academic aptitude (by means of standard, commercial tests) are also reliable, but less so.

Achieving reliability is usually much easier than achieving validity. Reliability is mostly a result of care and diligence on the part of researchers in the planning and execution of their studies. Alert, careful experimenters can control most of the extraneous factors that might affect the reliability of their measurements. Conditions throughout the experiment should always be as consistent as possible. For example, the same instructions should be given to each person who participates in the experiment, all mechanical devices should be in good repair, and all assistants hired by the experimenter should be well trained in performing their tasks. Sources of distraction should be kept to a minimum.

Another issue that affects reliability is the degree of subjectivity involved in making a measurement. In the experiment described above – the investigation of the effects of mood on creativity – our definition of mood was objective; even a non-expert could follow our procedure and obtain the same results. But researchers often attempt to study variables whose measurement is subjective, that is, it requires practical judgement and expertise. For example, suppose that a psychologist wants to count the number of friendly interactions that a child makes with other children in a group. This measurement requires someone to watch the child and count the number of times a friendly interaction occurs. But it is difficult to be absolutely specific about what constitutes a friendly interaction and what does not. What if the child looks at another child and their gazes meet? One observer may say that the look conveyed interest in what the other child was doing and so should be scored as a friendly interaction. Another observer may disagree.

One solution to this problem is to try to specify as precisely as possible the criteria to be used for defining an interaction as friendly in order to make the measurement as objective as possible. Then, two or more people should watch the child's behaviour and score it independently, that is, neither person should be aware of the other person's ratings. If their ratings agree, we can say that the scoring system has high inter-rater reliability. If they disagree, inter-rater reliability is low, and there is no point in continuing the study. Instead, the rating system should be refined and the raters should be trained to apply it consistently. Any investigator who performs a study that requires some degree of skill and judgement in measuring the dependent variables must do what is necessary to produce high inter-rater reliability.

There are other ways in which a researcher can test the reliability of their data. For example, say that we wanted to examine whether an individual's responses on a personality questionnaire were reliable. One method of determining this might be to divide the questionnaire and compare the responses of the participant in each of the two sections of the questionnaire. If there is strong agreement between scores from each half, the questionnaire results are said to be reliable. This is called **split-half reliability** because the measure (the personality questionnaire) is split and responses to the two split parts compared.

Nation-level studies – An international perspective

Two studies that were published in the journal *Psychological Science* claimed to have found some interesting differences between nations. One looked at 'meaning in life' in poor and wealthy nations (Oishi and Diener, 2014); one looked at environmental concerns expressed by countries across the world (Herschfield *et al.*, 2013).

The first of these examined data from a Gallup poll of 132 nations in 2007 and found that although life satisfaction was higher in wealthy nations, meaning in life was higher in poorer nations. The index of meaning in life was the suicide rate in these countries. Poorer countries had a lower suicide rate. The second study argued that the age of a country would predict its attitude to environmental matters. That is, the older the country, the more into the future its citizens would look and the more aware, and concerned about, the environment they would be. It then correlated the start date of

▶

Nation-level studies – *Continued*

131 countries with citizens' scores on a measure of environmental awareness/concern developed by Yale University. There was a positive correlation between the age of a country and its environmental performance even when taking into account GDP and the country's government.

Or was there? In a commentary on both of these studies, Kuppens and Pollet (2014) highlight some important problems with both of these studies which leads them to conclude that the studies' findings are not reliable. They point out that one of the studies did not take into account that countries near each other are similar (and so there are better ways of analysing the data) and that nation-level data are unreliable. They argue that Herschfield *et al.*'s data points are not independent because countries near each other have developed in similar ways with similar histories. They re-analysed the data from this study and found that, rather than clustering by country, the data for the environment questionnaire clustered around *regions*. And when regions were correlated with questionnaire scores, the correlation disappeared. They also divided the countries into regions based on two, independent sets of criteria and found the same result.

They take Oishi and Diener to task for presenting data with poor reliability, although they really criticise the study's validity. For example, Kuppens and Pollet rightly argue that the way in which suicide is reported (and underreported) varies greatly around the world and even within the same region. There is also the question of whether suicide rate is really a proxy for lack of 'meaning in life'. The authors also question the use of the sub-scales (Environmental Health and Ecosystem Vitality) in Herschfield *et al.*'s study – the two are negatively correlated despite being created to measure environmental performance. In the study, they are combined and the scores weighted. Kuppens and Pollet found that if you separated out the scales, age correlated with ecosystem vitality but not with environmental health (EV). When region, rather than country, was used as the other variable, the effect of 'country' on EV reduced.

Kuppens and Pollet say there is also a conceptual error in these studies. These studies use theories based on individuals to draw conclusions about nations. Kuppens and Pollet note that correlations between religiosity and life satisfaction are the opposite at the individual level, to what they are at the nation level. The correlation between suicide rate and national wealth is also the opposite of what is found at the neighbourhood level where low socioeconomic status is associated with depression and suicide. Kuppens and Pollet's article is interesting because it methodically and critically assesses two studies published in a prominent journal which report findings from some very large samples and draw conclusions which, on closer inspection, may not be correct.

Selecting participants

So far, we have dealt with what we, as researchers, would do – what hypothesis we would test, how we would design the experiment and how we would obtain valid and reliable measurements. Now let us turn to the people who will participate in our experiment: our participants. How do we choose them? How do we assign them to the experimental or control group? These decisions must be carefully considered because, just as independent variables can be confounded, so can variables that are inherent in participants whose behaviour is being observed.

When we carry out an experiment or a correlational study, we probably assume that our participants are representative of the larger population. In fact, a representative group of participants is usually referred to as a sample of the larger population. If we study the behaviour of a group of 5-year-old children, we want to make conclusions about 5-year-olds in general. We want to be able to generalise our specific results to the population as a whole – to conclude that the results tell us something about human nature in general, not simply about our participants.

All psychological experiments use samples – human or animal – and researchers usually know the type of sample they need. If they are testing the efficacy of a drug or the effectiveness of a type of rehabilitation following brain injury, for example, they include samples with specific characteristics. Most psychological researchers, however, recruit opportunity samples: people willing to give up their time and participate in research. But how representative are these opportunity samples?

As a psychology student, you will inevitably be asked to participate in a psychology experiment. This may be part of your research methods or other course; or it may be an experiment run by your tutor or department. In fact, if you look at the method sections of scientific articles published in psychology, you will find that the majority of these reports recruit participants just like you: psychology students. This is a source of concern for some psychologists because the findings from such a group may not be representative of the behaviour of other sections of the population. Psychology's participants have been described as WEIRD: Western, Educated, Industrialised, Rich and Democratic, that is the least representative populations. The geographical location of the study or the assumed nationality of the participants may be disproportional, and limit the generalisability of a study's findings. Quinones-Vidal *et al.* (2004), for example, found that of all the papers published in the leading journal of its kind, *Journal of Personality and Social Psychology*, 92 per cent came from the US and Canada and 99 per cent from Western countries.

A study of papers published in the *British Journal of Social Psychology* and the *British Journal of Psychology* in 1995 and 1996 found that only 29 per cent of them recruited non-student adults and 15.9 per cent were set in a real-life environment (Banyard and Hunt, 2000). Twenty-eight per cent were based in a laboratory and 26.2 per cent were conducted in other parts of a university such as a lecture hall. Pressure to participate was evident in 58 per cent of the studies (students would take part to obtain course credit or because experiments were a course requirement). Ethnicity was only considered in one study.

The study highlights some important points to remember when reading and explaining the findings of research (although this analysis was based on two journals published in two years). The authors do not disagree that students can make suitable samples but they query how representative this sample is. In another study, Case and Smith (2000) found that of 2,536 articles from 14 applied psychology journals over a five-year period, only 40 per cent indicated the ethnicity of the participant. In the articles that did include details of ethnicity, there was an over-representation of African Americans and an under-representation of Hispanic Americans (compared with the actual number of Hispanic people in the population). When you read primary sources in psychology, therefore, take

some time to study the sample used and think of why the authors chose this sample.

When recruited, participants must be carefully assigned to the various groups used in an experiment and the usual and best way to do this is by random assignment. Typically, the assignment is made by computer or by consulting a list of random numbers. We can expect people to have different abilities, personality traits and other characteristics that may affect the outcome of the experiment, but if people are randomly assigned to the experimental conditions, these differences should – according to the principle of random sampling – be equally distributed across the groups. A protocol whereby participants are genuinely randomly assigned to either an experimental group or a control group is called a randomised control trial. Participants have an equal probability of being assigned to the experimental or non-experimental group thereby eliminating a possible source of bias – experimenter bias or participant bias.

Whatever the randomisation, however, there may be variables which intercede between the independent variable and the dependent variable. For example, Nicholls *et al.* (2014) investigated whether student's participation in University research was influenced by variables such as motivation and sustained attention. Participants who take part early in a term, for example, have been found to have different personalities and performance characteristics than do those who take part later in the term. The researchers measured internal and external motivation and sustained attention in 80 students who participated in research for course credit or for money, early and late in the term. The sustained attention of both groups was similar early in the term, but that of the course-credit group was worse later on. The course-credit group also showed a decline in intrinsic motivation, a decline not seen in the paid group.

Cutting edge: Psychology's new recruitment drive

There have been attempts to move away from the reliance on convenience samples (such as students) for psychological research. The internet is one method of securing very large, seemingly random samples of participants, and software such as Surveymonkey and Qualtrics is used to run on-line experiments/surveys and to collect data in psychology because it is easy to administer and the potential number of participants

who can be recruited is large. A questionnaire study using these methods, for example, can recruit many 100s of participants compared to a questionnaire physically distributed in a University or college. There are also specific sites which pay participants a small fee for taking part in on-line experiments - Amazon's Mechanical Turk (MTurk) for example (Crump *et al.*, 2013). MTurk has been used to collect data

▶

Cutting edge: *Continued*

using a variety of tests and measures, including reaction time and decision-making and experiments requiring participants to sustain attention and follow complex instructions. Other online data acquisition platforms are Crowdflower and Prolific Academic – some research suggests that participants on these sites are more naive and less dishonest than those on MTurk but that data on Crowdlower were less likely to replicate well-known findings, compared with data obtained via MTurk and Prolific Academic (Peer *et al.*, 2017).

Lumosity is another web-based platform which consists of a plethora of cognitive tests which people can complete and receive feedback on (Sternberg *et al.*, 2013). In 2013, it had 36,140,947 users from 231 different countries, who had completed on-line tests over six million times. Lumosity makes its data available via the website http://hcp.lumosity.com.

Sternberg *et al.* (2013) illustrate one use of Lumosity data. They examined the relationship between lifestyle and cognitive performance. They took data from over 127,000 participants who had completed three cognitive ability tasks and correlated performance with the amount that participants reported sleeping, and alcohol consumption. The tasks included speeded mental arithmetic and tests of memory.

They found that performance on the three tasks examined was better in participants who reported sleeping for seven hours a night, a finding that has also been reported in other studies (e.g. Ferrie *et al.*, 2011). Three or more alcoholic drinks a day were associated with poorer performance. One or two drinks a day correlated with better performance. Figures 2.2a and b illustrate the findings of the study.

(a)

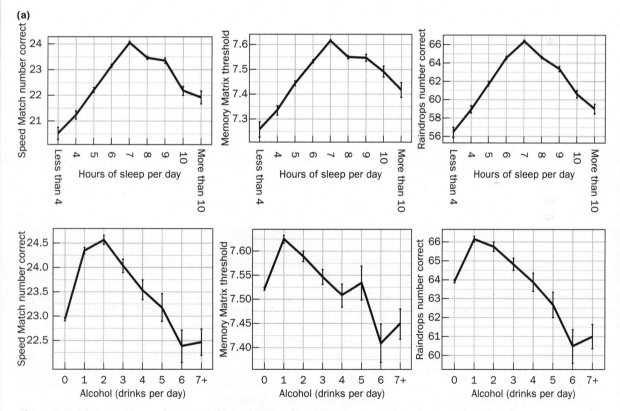

Figure 2.2a The cognitive performance of 10s of 1000s of participants recruited via the Lumosity research programme and show the effect of time of day and alcohol consumption on performance.

Cutting edge: *Continued*

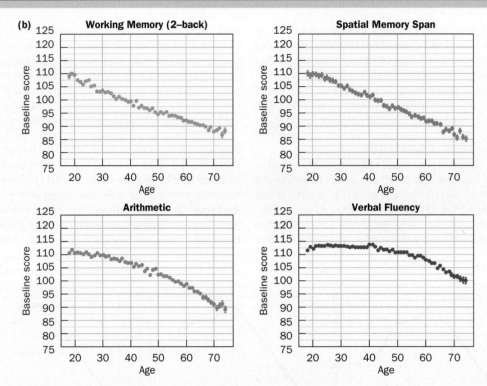

Figure 2.2b This figure shows the effect of age on four types of cognitive performance.

Response bias – An international perspective

Response bias – responding to a questionnaire in a way that is not genuine or honest but in an irrelevant way such as always responding 'yes' to a series of questions – is an important concept in research methods because it can skew results and tell researchers something which is not very meaningful. A Dutch study of six European countries found that response bias can vary by cultures.

Researchers used existing data from a multinational marketing survey to examine response bias in participants from Greece, Italy, Spain, France, Germany and the UK (Van Herk *et al.*, 2005). They found that unlike participants from north-western European countries, those from Mediterranean countries showed an abnormally high tendency to agree than disagree with answers (acquiescence), and a greater likelihood to choose extreme response categories (e.g. selecting 1 or 5 on a 5-point scale). Greek participants, in particular, significantly exhibited these response biases. Spain and Italy scored higher on these two biases than did the UK, France and Germany. The British were the least acquiescent.

The authors suggest that such differences might reflect the different types of cultures in these countries: collectivistic versus individualistic. The more individualistic the societies were, the less acquiescent they seemed.

Participants' expectations

Participants in a psychology experiment are not passive participants whose behaviour is controlled solely by the independent variables manipulated by the experimenter. They know that they are being observed, and this knowledge is certain to affect their behaviour. This is sometimes known as the Hawthorne effect and derived, ostensibly, from a phenomenon that occurred in the Hawthorne Works of the Western Electric Company in Chicago in the 1902s and 1930s.

The plant managers hypothesised that increasing the lighting conditions would increase productivity and this is what happened: the workers were aware of the manipulation and worked harder (Adair, 1984). The Hawthorne effect is written about in many textbooks and is regarded as a reliable phenomenon. However, the original studies were never published and the name given to the effect provided in a book published in 1953 (Chiesa and Hobbs, 2008). We do know that people will behave as if a hypothesis is true if they discover the hypothesis. For example, Young *et al.* (2007) found that people who were given questionnaires on motion sickness to complete before they were exposed to virtual reality displays and told these displays might induce motion sickness reported more motion sickness than those who did not complete such questionnaires.

Because a study is being conducted by a psychologist, some participants are unlikely to take what they say at face value and will look for motives hidden behind an apparently simple task. Actually, most experiments are not deceptive at all; they are what they appear to be and 'deceptive' studies often do not always succeed in fooling the participants. Experimenters must always remember that their participants do not merely react to the independent variable in a simple-minded way. These considerations are especially important in social psychology experiments (see Chapters 15 and 16). In some of these studies, the experimenter or the experimenter's assistants act out roles deliberately designed to provide a particular kind of social situation to which the participants are exposed. Obviously, the participants' interpretation of these situations affects their behaviour.

Single-blind experiments

If a participant's behaviour could be affected by their knowledge of the independent variable, two methods can circumvent this problem: single- and double-blind experiments. For example, suppose that we want to study the effects of a stimulant drug, such as amphetamine, on a person's ability to perform a task that requires fine manual dexterity. We will administer the drug to one group of participants and leave another group untreated. We will count how many times each participant can thread a needle in a 10-minute period (our operational definition of fine manual dexterity). We will then see whether taking the drug had any effect on the number of needle threadings.

But the mere administration of a drug may have effects on behaviour, independent of its pharmacological effects. The behaviour of participants who know that they have just taken amphetamine is very likely to be affected by this knowledge as well as by the drug circulating in their bloodstream. To solve this problem, we should give pills to the members of both groups. People in one group will receive amphetamine, and those in the other group will receive an inert pill – a placebo, from the Latin *placere*, 'to please'. A physician sometimes gives a placebo to anxious patients to placate them. Participants will not be told which pill they receive. By using this improved experimental procedure called a **single-blind study**, we can infer that any observed differences in needle-threading ability of the two groups were produced solely by the pharmacological effects of amphetamine. The placebo effect is a strong one – brain imaging studies have found that when people are given a placebo 'treatment' for pain, there is a reduction in the activation of brain areas involved in actual pain experience (Wager *et al.*, 2004). A placebo can be just as effective as antidepressants in treating minor depression (Barbui *et al.*, 2011).

Double-blind experiments

In a single-blind experiment, only the participants are kept ignorant of their assignment to a particular experimental group; the experimenter knows which treatment each participant receives. Now let us look at an example in which it is important to keep both the experimenter and the participants in the dark. Suppose we believe that if patients with mental disorders take a particular drug, they will be more willing to engage in conversation. The drug is given to some patients and a placebo is administered to others. We talk with all the patients afterwards and rate the quality of the conversation. But 'quality of conversation' is a difficult dependent variable to measure, and the rating is therefore likely to be subjective. The fact that the experimenters know which patients received the drug means that we may tend to give higher ratings to the quality of conversation with those patients.

The solution to this problem is simple. Just as the patients should not know whether they are receiving a drug or a placebo, neither should the experimenter. That is, we should carry out a double-blind study. Someone else should administer the pill, or the experimenter should be given a set of identical-looking pills in coded containers so that both experimenter and patient are unaware of the nature of the contents. Now the ratings cannot be affected by any preconceived ideas the experimenter may have. The double-blind procedure does not apply only to experiments that use drugs as the independent variable. Suppose that the experiment just described attempted to evaluate the effects of a particular kind of psychotherapy, not a drug, on the willingness of a patient to talk. If the same person does both the psychotherapy and the rating, that person might tend to see the results in a light that is most favourable to their own expectations. In this case, then, one person should perform the psychotherapy and another person should evaluate the quality of conversation with the patients. The evaluator will not know whether a particular patient has just received psychotherapy or is a member of the control (untreated) group.

The expectations of experimenters can influence results in studies with laboratory animals as much as in studies with human participants. Rosenthal and Fode (1963) demonstrated the influence of expectations by having students to train rats to learn the way through a maze. They told half the students that they had 'stupid' rats and the other half that they had 'smart' rats. In fact, there were no differences in the animals' abilities. However, an analysis of the results indicated that the 'smart' animals learned faster than the 'stupid' ones. The students' expectations clearly affected their rats' performances. Presumably, the students who had 'smart' rats took better care of them, which affected the animals' performances.

Psychology in action: Horses for courses

Now that you've read about some of the most important steps in applying the scientific method, we can bring these together to help understand the phenomenon described in the opening vignette – the case of Clever Hans.

Advances in ways of thinking and reasoning can come from some unusual directions. A little-known maths teacher from Berlin, for example. Few people know his name (although they certainly might know his horse, especially if they're a psychology student). He indirectly provided generations of science students and science courses with a series of perfect examples of how not to evaluate evidence critically.

His name was Wilhelm von Osten, and his horse was Clever Hans, the equine genius described in the opening vignette. There is an excellent summary of the story of Clever Hans, written by Heinzen *et al.* (2015) and based on their book, *The Horse That Won't Go Away*, Their account is described here.

Hans was unusual. He became quite famous because of his ostensible ability to carry out complex – for a horse– mathematical operations. Van Osten would stand to the horse's side, behind its right eye, and ask the horse to count the number of windows in buildings, to calculate square roots and factors, to add 2/5 to 1/2 (the horse would tap out the numerator with its hoof, and then tap out the denominator) and so on. And the horse would do this, accurately. It could also seemingly remember the faces of people it had encountered, and their names. A spectacular feat for a horse.

But, of course, with Clever Hans all was not what it seemed and people began to cast some doubt on the actual ability of this staggering, mind-reading horse. Von Osten became so agitated by accusations of fraud that he asked the Berlin Board of Education to come and observe the horse and his methods. The group assigned to do this included a circus manager, a vet and a psychologist. The psychologist was Professor Carl Stumpf and he and his student, Oskar Pfungst, became very important actors in this drama.

How did the horse do it? One clue was in the horse's feeding. von Osten kept Hans hungry. When the horse tapped its hoof, his owner would reward it with food. And this is what the horse learned: whenever it would tap its foot, it would receive food. But how would it know when to stop tapping? von Osten would lean forward when it rewarded the horse. This was the horse's physical cue to stop. The horse was no mathematical prodigy: it used the physical cues it saw to receive a reward of food.

Pfungst set up a series of well-designed studies to test Hans's cognitive ability and to eliminate non-cognitive cues. For example, in one study the questioner and the horse could see cards with numbers on or only the horse could see. In the first condition, Hans was right almost 100 per cent of the time, tapping out the number on the card. In the second, Hans was wrong almost all of the time. In 49 tests where only Hans could see the card – and, therefore, was unable to exploit intentional or unintentional physical cues – it gave the correct response only 8 per cent of the time. A similar pattern was found when the questioner read aloud a mathematical puzzle.

▶

Psychology in action: *Continued*

To determine which physical cue the horse was using – and to rule out an explanation which involved telepathy – Pfungst placed blinkers on the horse to prevent it from seeing. When this was done, Hans tapped out correct answers only 6 per cent of the time. When the blinkers were off, the success rate was 89 per cent. The inaccuracy was greater when the correct answer was one – because the horse did not know which tap would be the last tap. Pfungst also observed that whenever he leaned forward with his notebook, Hans would begin tapping, a behaviour that became explicable given the studies the young psychologist had conducted. In one study, Hans was required to count to a particular number. Pfungst would remain bent over during the task. Every time

he did this, the horse would exceed the number required until he straightened up.

He also noticed that people would jerk their head upward when Hans had reached the correct number – a signal to the horse to stop. Pfungst even tested this hypothesis and put himself in the position of the horse. He was not as good as Hans but he was able to make correct responses 73 per cent of the time by observing the movement of his questioners (350 tests with 12 questioners).

Clever Hans is a good example of logic, reasoning and the scientific method being put into practice to provide rational explanations for seemingly irrational phenomena. This is why you'll find this horse mentioned in several of your courses.

Correlational studies

To be certain that a cause-and-effect relation exists, we must perform an experiment in which we manipulate the independent variable and measure its effects on the dependent variable. But there are some variables, especially participant variables, which a psychologist cannot manipulate. For example, a person's sex, genetic history, income, social class, family environment and personality are obviously not under the psychologist's control. Nevertheless, these variables are important and interesting because they often affect people's behaviour. Because they cannot be manipulated, they cannot be investigated in an experiment. A different method must, therefore, be used to study them: a correlational study.

The basic principle of a correlational study is simple: for each member of a group of people we measure two or more variables as they are found to exist, and we determine whether the variables are related by using a statistical procedure called correlation. Correlational studies are often done to investigate the effects of personality variables on behaviour. For example, we may ask whether shyness is related to daydreaming. Our hypothesis is that shy people tend to daydream more than people who are less shy. We decide how to assess a person's shyness and the amount of daydreaming that they engage in each day, and we then take the measure of these two variables for a group of people. If shy people tend to daydream more (or less) than people who are not shy, we can conclude that the variables are related but one does not cause another (it may, of course, but this finding does not demonstrate any causality).

This is an important point because if a researcher finds a correlation between two variables, this does not confirm than

one has a causal effect on the other. A famous study published in 2012 found a correlation between chocolate consumption and the number of Nobel Prize winners in a country (Messerli, 2012). This sparked much media interest but the data were ultimately correlational: there was no causal link between the two variables. Eating chocolate does not convert you into a Nobel-Prize-winning luminary. Similar correlations have been reported for the quality of sound in a language and the amount of marital sex speakers had (Ember and Ember, 2007).

There is a famous graph which shows a significant, positive correlation between the incidence of autism and the consumption of organic food. This relationship, like those above, is an example of a spurious correlation – it does not show that one caused the other. The website www.tylervigen.com features many more of these amusing, spurious, positive but statistically significant correlations including: (1) the number of people who drowned by falling into a swimming pool, and the number of films featuring Nick Cage, (2) divorce rates in Maine, and the US per capita consumption of margarine and (3) the number of people who die by becoming entangled in bedsheets, and the total revenue from skiing facilities. A recent study of correlations between various variables and traffic accidents found that the number of acacia trees correlated with a greater number of traffic accidents leading to death and the number of countries with tonal languages (Roberts and Winters, 2013).

Can anything be done to reduce some of the uncertainty inherent in correlational studies? The answer is yes. When attempting to study the effects of a variable that cannot be altered (such as sex, age, socio-economic status or personality

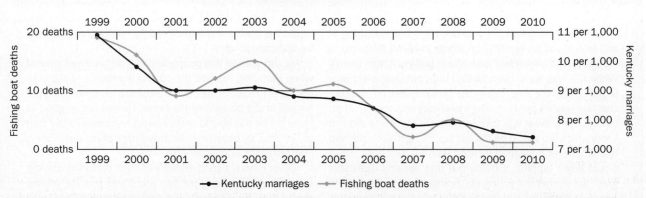

People who drowned after falling out of a fishing boat
correlates with
Marriage rate in Kentucky

Here is a very good example of a spurious correlation. There is no causal relationship between these two variables. Married fishermen and women in Kentucky are no less safe than other fishermen and women

Source: http://www.tylervigen.com/spurious-correlations.

characteristics), we can use a procedure called **matching**. Rather than selecting participants randomly, we match the participants in each of the groups on all of the relevant variables except the one being studied such as age, sex, personality, etc.

If, after following this matching procedure, there is still a correlation (between daydreaming and shyness), we can be more confident that the relation is one of cause and effect and that the differences between the two variables are not caused by a third variable. The limitation of the matching procedure is that we may not know all the variables that should be held constant. If, unknown to us, the two groups are not matched on an important variable, then the results will be misleading. In any case, even the matching procedure does not permit us to decide which variable is the cause and which is the effect; we still do not know whether shyness causes daydreaming or daydreaming causes shyness.

Single-case studies

Not all investigations in psychology use groups of participants. **Single-case study research** explores the behaviour of individuals, and for some phenomena this method is very effective. Single-case study research can involve either experiments or correlational studies. Ebbinghaus's studies of memory, for example, were based on studies of individuals (usually, Ebbinghaus himself). Similarly, much of B.F. Skinner's work was based on small numbers of participants (largely pigeons).

In a single-case study, psychologists can take advantage of events that have occurred outside their control and the most common of these are found in the field of neuropsychology. Patient HJA, for example, had sustained damage to specific regions of his brain and had difficulty in recognising objects

and would spend up to six hours making painstaking drawings of objects which he would be unable to name (Humphreys and Riddoch, 1987a, b). By conducting single-case studies of patients like HJA, psychologists can explore the unique behavioural consequences of unusual events or actions that the patient has suffered and which cannot be arranged experimentally (psychologists cannot go about deliberately damaging the brains of their participants).

Criticism of this approach, however, is that there is frequently no way of knowing for certain how an individual behaved before the accident; there is no control over the degree and type of injury sustained; and there is the possibility that personal characteristics (such as medication use, sex, age, socio-economic status, IQ) might affect performance (Martin, 2006).

Advantages of the approach, however, are that by continuously studying a participant over an extended period, we can be sure that the sample of behaviour that is measured is representative of the participant's typical behaviour. It also allows us to see the natural variability in the participant's behaviour – marked changes in behaviour that are not attributable to experimental manipulation. Participants are their own controls, thereby reducing the individual difference that could account for differences between (and within) large groups.

Meta-analysis

Imagine you're reading a study in a journal and it finds that University students are much more likely to be happier and well-balanced than are non-students when they reach their 30s. You're probably delighted to hear this news, perhaps nodding to yourself and congratulating yourself on the wisdom of having invested in 3–4 years of high-quality higher education. But then you come across another journal which has published a similar study. This time, the authors of that paper do not report this effect – graduates are no more or less happy than are non-graduates. Which is correct?

Contradictory findings like this occur all the time in psychology. It is a feature of science and it's expected. It would be highly unusual if it did not happen. But to try and make sense of a finding and to determine whether it is reliable or simply an epiphenomenon – an artefact of the way the researchers conducted their study or a fluke created by their particular sample – psychologists use a method of analysis called **meta-analysis**. In meta-analysis, researchers conduct a comprehensive literature review and pool together the studies that address a specific question with specific outcomes. They then use the statistics from those studies and see how strong a finding or effect is across all studies. You'll see the word meta-analysis used throughout this book: it is a very good method of determining what is real from what is noise in psychological data.

By pooling together, you eliminate rogue or outlying results because if most of your studies show an effect, this effect will become clear in the analysis. It is like removing noise from your data. Meta-analysis is an invaluable tool for any scientist because it can reveal an actual pattern or a reliable, consistent finding in the literature. It normally does this by referring to effect size. An effect size doesn't just tell you there is a difference between two groups, it tells you the size of the difference, and this is normally the most important statistical feature of a result.

Qualitative analysis

The majority of research undertaken in psychology is empirical and quantitative. Another approach relies less on these types of data. Some researchers suggest that the richness of human experience is better measured by paying close attention to the ways in which people use words and express feelings and arguments, and by allowing individuals to explore ideas in discussion. Themes and ideas can then be interpreted from transcripts of these discussions. This approach is called qualitative analysis and is concerned with 'meanings, context and a holistic approach to material' (Hayes, 1997). It is more popular in European research centres than in North America. The BPS's Qualitative Methods Section was formed in 2006, for example, but a proposal for a new Division of Qualitative Inquiry was rejected by the American Psychological Association in 2008.

The approach is called phenomenological because the experience, reactions and feelings of the individual are considered to be of paramount importance. It places great emphasis on people's use of language, especially the ways in which people accounted for their behaviour, thoughts and feelings: to understand real psychology meant analysing real talk (Foster and Parker, 1995). This talk is, itself, 'action'; we use words to convey some action (blame, sorrow, anger, etc.) and this type of data and approach has been used to study various topics such as the impact of a child's serious illness on the family (Hopia et al., 2005), how dietary regimes are viewed in people with type 2 diabetes (Peel et al., 2005) and how doctor and patient interact with each other (McCabe et al., 2002).

The emphasis in the qualitative approach is not on quantifying data (in many cases this is actively discouraged) but in exploring the quality of data in depth. Another important distinction between qualitative and quantitative analysis is that the former views the researcher as being central to the analysis and the process of data collection: they may participate in or facilitate discussion and will analyse the data obtained from their research. The interpretation of the data is also undertaken by the researcher/interviewer. Data collection usually takes the form of structured and semi-structured interviews.

Structured and semi-structured interviews

The **structured interview** is conducted along predefined and predetermined lines with little scope for deviation from a script. The experimenter decides what they want to explore, with little variation between interviews. Many structured interviews may comprise an interviewer reading questions from a questionnaire and soliciting responses from an interviewee.

Sometimes, however, it may be interesting and informative to explore interviewees' responses more deeply while keeping to some overall plan or structure. Semi-structured interviews provide such a possibility. The **semi-structured interview** allows the establishment of rapport with the interviewee by placing less emphasis on the order of questions, where the interviewer is free to develop themes and issues raised by the interviewee and where open-ended questions are used. For example, whereas a structured interview might ask 'Do you think that racism is caused by a, b, c or d?' and a semi-structured interview might ask 'What do you think are the causes of racism?'. It is suggested that funnelling is a useful approach to semi-structured interviews: the interviewer elicits a general opinion and then probes more specific issues relating to this general view.

The semi-structured interview has proved to be useful to some qualitative analysts. Others, however, would argue that even a semi-structured format is too restrictive and that in order to elicit and understand genuine thoughts and feelings, you must allow discussion to occur freely (Hammersley, 2008). Such an approach is taken by discourse analysis.

Some qualitative research methods

Discourse analysis is a method which was developed in the mid-1980s to identify thoughts, feelings and themes from transcripts of data derived from conversations involving two or more individuals. Discourse analysis examines what people do with conversation and writing (Potter and Wetherell, 1995) and places importance on the use of language and what people mean when they express themselves verbally (Billig, 1997). Such speech acts could be complicated and would require careful analysis in order to discover what was meant. Discourse analysis does not assume that attitudes are stable; in fact, it assumes that 'giving views' is relatively unstable and that a person can give one view to one person and a contrary view to another: context, therefore, is important to the interpretation of attitude. A teenage girl's attitudes towards social issues might be expressed differently to a parent and to a member of her peer group, for example (Billig, 1997).

As the name suggests, **conversation analysis** (CA) involves the analysis of the content and use of conversation. The assumption behind CA is that talk is action and that it is structurally organised. The focus is less on the content of the talk but on what people do with it – complaining, complementing, news-telling, turn-taking, and so on (Wilkinson and Kitzinger, 2008). Data are collected in 'naturalistic' environments – the researcher is not present and the participant is audio – or video-recorded. These data take the form of transcripts, complete with inbreaths, sound stretches, pauses and other example of oral punctuation. An example of how CA has been used to analyse how people use talk is seen in Table 2.1.

This is a transcript of an exchange between two friends, Belle and Fanny, one of whom (Belle) has some bad news to break. Take a look at this exchange before reading on. Did you notice something unusual in the conversation? Although it was Belle who had bad news to break, it was Fanny who 'announced' the news. CA has revealed that we often do this – the recipient of bad news tends to be the one who raises the matter of bad news, whether it is a cancelled trip or a medical diagnosis (Drew, 1984; Maynard, 1992). In another example of the use of CA, Clayman and Heritage (2002) analysed 4,000 questions asked by journalists in US Presidential Conferences from 1950 to 2000, and found that the questions became less deferential and more combative over time.

Unlike discourse analysis, grounded theory actively attempts to develop theory from information obtained from transcripts of conversations. Theorising is made possible by painstaking line-by-line coding of transcripts, by memo-taking and by constructing categories (themes/patterns) from responses. The theory is therefore grounded in what the respondents have had to say. An example of the approach would be the exploration of the loss of self/the expression of self in patients who have suffered traumatic brain injury (Nochi, 1998).

Limitations of qualitative analysis

Qualitative analysis, although not widely used, has been applied to several areas of psychology where analysis has explored issues such as attitudes to death, racism, the monarchy, sexual identity, chronic illness, work relationships and so

Table 2.1 The format in which conversation is transcribed in conversation analysis. The first extract shows you a conversation between two friends, one of whom had bad news to break. The second is an exchange between a doctor and a patient which, again, involves the breaking of unwelcome news.

```
Extract 1
(DA: 2 : 10. from Schegloff (1988: 443)
The audio file for this data extract can be accessed at:
<http://www.sscnet.ucla.edu/soc/faculty/schegloff/
RealSoundFiles/Servo-Mechanism/page443.ram>}
01    Bel: ... I, I-I had something
02    (.) terrible t'tell you.=
03    =So {uh:}
04 Fan:   {How t}errible {is it.}
05 Bel: {.hhhhh}
06    (.)
07 Bel: Uh: en worse it could be:.
08    0.7)
09 Fan: W'y'mean 1da?
10    (.)
11    missing line from photocopy
12 Fan: Wud she do die:?=
13 Bel: = Mm:hm.
Extract 2
(8.013), from Maynard (1992: 337-8)
01 Dr: What do you see? as- as his
02    (0.5) difficulty.
03    (1.2)
04 Mo: Mainly his uhm: (1.2) the
05    fact that he doesn't
06    understand everything.
07    (0.6) and also the fact
08    that his speech (0.7) is
09    very hard to understand
10    what he's saying (0.3)
11    lot{s of ti}me
12 Dr: { right }
13    (0.2)
14 Dr: Do you have any ideas wh:y it
15 is: are you: d}o yo}u?h
16 Mo: { No }
17    (2.1)
18 Dr: .h okay I (0.2) you know I
19    think we basically (.) in
20    some ways agree with you:
21    (0.6) .hh insofar as we think
22    that (0.3) Dan's main problem
23    (0.4) .h you know does:
24    involves you know language.
26 Mo: Mm hmm
27    (0.3)
28 Dr: you know both (0.2) you know
29    his- (0.4) being able to
30    understand you know what is
31    said to him (0.4) .h and
32    also certainly also to be
33    able to express:: (1.3) you
34    know his uh his thoughts
35    (1.1)
36 Dr: .hh uh:m (0.6) .hhh in
37    general his development...
```

Source: Wilkinson, S. and Kitzinger, C. (2008) Conversation analysis. In C. Willig and W. Stainton-Rogers (eds) *The Sage Handbook of Qualitative Research in Psychology*. London: Sage.

on. Currently, qualitative analysis has had little impact outside these areas because of several perceived shortcomings. The most obvious, and difficult to reject, is that the process of qualitative analysis is subjective: the selection, analysis and interpretation of the material are made by the analyst. This introduces an element of bias into the study which could cloud an 'objective' analysis of the data. This argument is difficult to challenge effectively, although Hayes (1997) has suggested a 'half-way house' solution whereby a theory determined prior to the study may be used to guide later analysis. In this way, the study has a pre-stated focus and direction but it also allows for unpredicted insights.

Hammersley (1992) has identified several examples of the perceived differences between qualitative and quantitative analysis. For example, it is assumed that the types of data analysed by the two methods are totally different; the environments in which studies take place are different; one focuses on meaning (qualitative), the other on behaviour; quantitative methods adopt natural science as a model whereas qualitative analysis rejects it; one is inductive, the other deductive; one seeks patterns, the other seeks laws and so on. Hayes (1997) has given an excellent account of how this dichotomy may be more imagined than real. For example, she argues that qualitative researchers do sometimes use measures of quantity and that quantitative methods are often applied in naturalistic settings. Qualitative analysts do use CA to study behaviour as well as meaning. Furthermore, the rejection of the natural science model assumes that all of the natural sciences adopt the same experimental approach. Of course, they do not. Hayes, therefore, argues that the dichotomy between the two types of research methods is not as great as it would appear. If you were to set up a study in which you wanted to explore people's attitudes to animal experimentation, say, which approach – qualitative or quantitative – would you think is best?

Ethics

Because psychologists study living participants, they must obey ethical rules as well as scientific rules. Great care is needed in the treatment of human participants because we can hurt people in very subtle ways. The rules that govern psychologists' conduct during experiments have been set by governments, institutions or professional societies and all psychologists engaged in research must abide by them.

Research with human participants

In Europe, North America and elsewhere, research undertaken by hospitals and universities will have been vetted by an ethics committee, which decides on whether the proposed research meets the institution's ethical criteria regarding the welfare of human and animal participants in scientific research. Various professional societies such as the BPS (2014) and APA (2017) issue guidelines for the treatment of humans and animals participating in research. In some countries, data may also fall within the remit of a Data Protection Act which, in its most general form, allows an individual access to any information held electronically about them and, in research, allows the participant control over the use of such material.

In general terms, a psychologist must treat participants with respect and must have taken all conceivable and practicable precautions to ensure that participants are not harmed. Threats to health, well-being, values and dignity should be eliminated.

The BPS lists a number of recommendations that its members should follow (British Psychological Society, 2009). These recommendations fall into the general categories of consent, deception, debriefing, withdrawal, confidentiality and protection of participants.

Informed consent

An important part of any procedure designed to ensure the proper treatment of participants is informed consent. When possible, a psychologist should always inform the participant of the nature of the experiment and, having been told the detail of this research, the participant – if willing – will consent to take part. This represents informed consent. Of course, it is not always possible to secure informed consent because divulging all aspects of the experiment will influence the decisions, thoughts, feelings and behaviours of the participant. This is considered in more detail in the section on deception.

Usually, the potential participant reads a written statement prepared by the researcher. This discloses aspects of the research that might affect a person's willingness to participate in the study. The informed consent statement constitutes a contract between participant and researcher and is normally signed by both of them.

If participants are children, informed consent should be obtained from parents or guardians. The issue of child participation in research is an interesting one because a child begins to grasp concepts and understand abstract ideas at certain periods in its development (see Chapter 12). This is the principal reason why parents or guardians consent to their children's participation on their behalf. A study from the University of Texas suggests that this is sensible because children often do not understand the purpose of an experiment or may not understand what confidentiality of a person's data means (Hurley and Underwood, 2002). Although the children understand some aspects better than others, they may continue to extend their trust to the experimenter.

As with healthy, normally developing child participants, if a child or an adult participant is mentally ill, is unable to communicate or is mentally retarded, then a parent, healthcare worker or guardian should be informed and consent obtained from disinterested independent advisers.

If a researcher is undertaking observational research then the privacy and psychological well-being of the participant must be accounted for. Unless consent to being observed is obtained, participants should normally be observed only under conditions where they would expect to be observed by strangers.

Deception

Psychologists are advised never to withhold information or mislead participants if an individual is likely to be uneasy when eventually told the purpose of the experiment. Sometimes, however, withholding information or using misleading information is necessary for good scientific reasons (think back to an earlier section describing the effects of knowing the hypothesis of an experiment). When this occurs, it must be undertaken after obtaining the sound advice and approval of an ethics committee and colleagues.

Debriefing

When participants take part in an experiment, the experimenter is obliged to disclose to the participant the real and actual nature of the experiment and to answer any questions that the participant may ask about the experiment. This is called **debriefing**.

Withdrawal

If a participant feels that they have been unfairly misled or improperly treated, the participant has the absolute right to withdraw from the experiment. In fact, it should be made clear to all participants from the outset of the experiment that they are free to withdraw at any time, for whatever reason.

Confidentiality

Laws of the land notwithstanding, information and data provided by the participant in research are confidential. If data are published then those of individuals should not be identifiable, unless consent has been obtained.

Protection of participants

Tied to the recommendations concerning consent and deception are those governing the protection of the participant, which are very similar. Psychologists have a primary responsibility to their participants to avoid harm (physical or mental) and if harm is identified, to remove it.

Controversies in psychological science: When is it right to deceive participants in psychological studies?

The issue

In June 2014, the journal *Proceedings of the National Academy of Sciences* published a very interesting paper that had the tell-tale hallmarks of the modern psychological study: emotion, contagion, news, social networks, and Facebook. The authors, Kramer *et al.* (2014), two of whom were affiliated to an American University, attempted to manipulate the behaviour of Facebook users by altering the type of emotion expressed in posts available in a user's NewsFeeds, including the posts of 'Friends'. They sought to explore whether the behaviour of people exposed to certain emotional content would be influenced in a way consistent with the content.

To do this they reduced the positive tone and content of friends' posts and NewsFeed posts to examine whether exposure to less happy emotional content would lead to fewer positive/more negative posts and so on. And this is what they found: people exposed to fewer positive posts, posted fewer positive posts themselves and were less expressive in the days following the manipulation. It was an almost perfect illustration of emotional contagion. Almost 700,000 participants took part (689,003).

Or, at least, they were studied. They were not aware that they were part of an experiment, were not aware that their NewsFeed content was being manipulated and they gave no explicit consent to be exposed to this manipulation. The first author of the study was an employee of Facebook and part of its research team. Was any of this right or ethical?

The evidence

On the basis of prima facie evidence, the answer was: yes. At least, this is how the authors of the study viewed the issue of consent. They argued that their participants had provided

▶

Controversies in psychological science: *Continued*

implicit and explicit consent for the following reason: when users sign up with the Facebook service, they agree to the site's Data Use Policy. This states that a user's data can be tracked, monitored and influenced. The research was conducted by Facebook Inc 'for internal purposes'. Therefore, they argued, the participants had already provided their consent to take part.

Others might disagree with this interpretation of consent. In the US, the US Department of Health and Human Services Policy for the Protection of Human Research Subjects (the Common Rule) considers that the obtaining of informed consent from participants and permitting participants to withdraw are both examples of good practice when conducting research with humans. In the US, every bona fide research university will have an Institutional Review Board which assesses applications for ethical approval. In the UK, and elsewhere, we might have Ethics Committees. Cornell University, the institution which employed the two academic authors, had such a system but its Board 'determined that the project did not fall under Cornell's Human Research Protection Program'. The journal to which the authors submitted the paper did have a policy of requesting adherence to the Common Rule but the paper was deemed publishable despite the research not complying with the Rule. The journal has since published an expression of concern and correction', but has not retracted the paper (Verma, 2014). 'It is ... a matter of concern,' the editor-in-chief writes, 'that the collection of the data by Facebook may have involved practices that were not fully consistent with the principles of obtaining informed consent and allowing participants to opt out' (p. 10779).

Given what you now know, or might already know, of the study, do you think the journal – a very prominent science journal – was right to publish the study? Is implicit consent sufficient for research of this type to be conducted? Or should participants be fully informed before they can give consent? Many psychologists might agree that they should – in order to secure informed consent, participants must be informed. Without such information, the participant will not be fully informed of what they will be expected to do.

But is the situation this clear-cut? What if your research involved deception and you did not want your participants to be aware of this deception because it might influence your participants' behaviour, bias them in some way? Would it be right to withhold this information?

Conclusion

The answer is: it depends. It depends on the study, the review panel/board, the professional rules that govern the conduct of scientists such as psychologists (the APA and the BPS have Guidelines on Ethics), and the way in which the information is provided to participants at the point of obtaining consent. It may be possible, for example, to inform participants implicitly that there may be some conditions they are exposed to but not others without explicitly stating what those conditions are. Do you agree?

Chapter review

The scientific method in psychology

- The scientific method allows us to determine the causes of natural phenomena.
- There are three basic forms of scientific research: naturalistic observations, experiments and correlational studies.
- Hypotheses are statements or predictions made on the basis of naturalistic observations, previous experiments or from formal theories.
- Psychologists might conduct experiments in which groups are independent of each other, the individuals in one group are not the same as those in the other (independent groups design); or experiments in which the same individuals take part in all conditions of the experiment (repeated measures design).
- An independent variable is an event, factor or action that is manipulated by the experimenter; the dependent variable is the quantity measured in an experiment (and is hypothesised to be influenced by the independent variable). To perform an experiment, a scientist alters the value of the independent variable and measures changes in the dependent variable.

- A psychologist must specify the particular operations that they will perform to manipulate the independent variable and to measure the dependent variable.
- Operational definitions are a necessary part of the procedure by which a hypothesis is tested; they can also eliminate confusion by giving concrete form to the hypothesis, making its meaning absolutely clear to other scientists.
- Validity is the degree to which an operational definition produces a particular value of an independent variable or measures the value of a dependent variable.
- Reliability refers to the consistency and precision of an operational definition.
- Researchers achieve high reliability by carefully controlling the conditions of their studies and by ensuring that procedures are followed correctly. Measurement involving subjectivity requires researchers to seek high inter-rater-reliability.
- When designing an experiment, experimenters ensure that they control extraneous variables that may confound their results. If an extra variable is inadvertently manipulated and if this extra variable has an effect on the dependent variable, then the results of the experiment will be invalid. Confounding of subject variables can be caused by improperly assigning participants to groups or by treatments that cause some participants to leave the experiment.
- If knowledge of the experimental condition could alter the participants' behaviour, the experiment should be conducted with a single-blind procedure (where the participant is unaware of the condition they are in). If that knowledge might also alter the experimenter's assessment of the participants' behaviour, a double-blind procedure should be used (where the participant and experimenter are unaware of the condition that the participant is in).

- Correlational studies involve assessing relations among variables that the researcher cannot readily manipulate, such as personality characteristics, age and sex. The investigator attempts to hold these variables constant by matching members in each of the groups on all relevant variables except for the one being studied. Correlational studies cannot determine which variable is the cause and which is the effect.
- Single-subject research consists of the detailed observation of individual participants under different conditions. Case studies involve careful observations of the behaviour of specific people, such as those with psychological or neurological disorders.
- A meta-analysis is a statistical review of all studies on a particular topic and which meet specific inclusion criteria; the aim is to examine whether findings are consistent across multiple, different studies.
- Qualitative analysis involves the examination of individuals' expression of ideas, thoughts and feelings and is usually based on transcripts of discussion between individuals or between the experimenter and an individual/individuals.

Ethics

- Because psychologists study living organisms, they must follow ethical principles in the treatment of their participants. Professional societies run by and for psychologists develop ethical guidelines that require informed consent, confidentiality and a post-experiment debriefing.
- Participants may withdraw their consent to participate at any time before or during an experiment without any penalty. If deception is necessary, the experimenter must be certain that the participants will not be harmed psychologically or physically and that their dignity will be maintained.

Suggestions for further reading

Research methods: general reading

There are many books about research methods, design and analysis available. Some of them you probably would not want to read – they aren't the most riveting reads – but they serve a purpose in explaining how to do things. The best of research methods

books, however, manage to engage you in the process of finding out how people behave. Some of these include the following:

Bausell, R.B. (2012) *Conducting Meaningful Experiments: 40 steps to becoming a scientist.* London: Sage.

Robson, C. (2015) *Real World Research* (4th edn). Oxford: Blackwell.

Bausell's short book is a very well-written, straightforward account of what you need to know and to do in order to become a scientist. It is laid out in the form of principles (40 of them) which the author describes, explains and illustrates. Robson's excellent, well-written book delivers a comprehensive account of how to conduct 'difficult' research (i.e. out of the laboratory).

Critical thinking

Gabennesch, H. (2006) Critical thinking: What is it good for? *Skeptical Inquirer*, 30, 2, 36–41.

Martin, G.N. (2009) *Research and Study Update for Psychology* (3rd edn). Harlow: Pearson Education.

Matthies, B. (2005) The psychologist, the philosopher, and the librarian: The information-literacy version of CRITIC. *Skeptical Inquirer*, May/June, 49–52.

Meltzoff, J. (1998) *Critical Thinking about Research: Psychology and Related Fields*. Washington, DC: American Psychological Association.

Motulsky, H. J. (2015). Common misconceptions about data analysis and statistics. *British Journal of Pharmacology*, 172(8), 2126–2132.

Reinhart, A. (2015) *Statistics Gone Wrong*. San Fransisco: No Starch Press.

Meltzoff's is an extraordinary book because instead of analysing real research articles for quality, the author has composed several fictitious ones to highlight flaws in the ways in which studies are conducted, analysed and reported. The first half of the book is an excellent introduction to research methods; the second half consists of the research articles with a critical analysis of each. Superb for helping you develop critical thinking skills. The papers by Matthies and Gabennesch give some sound advice on critical thinking, as does the Martin title.

Qualitative research

Smith, J.A. (2015) *Qualitative Psychology* (3rd edn). London: Sage.

Willig, C. and Stainton-Rogers, W. (2017) *The Sage Handbook of Qualitative Research in Psychology* (2nd edn). London: Sage.

Two relatively accessible texts on qualitative analysis.

Ethical issues in psychological testing

American Psychological Association (2017). Ethical principles of psychologists and code of conduct. Washington: APA (available online)

British Psychological Society (2014). Code of Human Research Ethics. Leicester: BPS. (available online)

Flick, C. (2016). Informed consent and the Facebook emotional manipulation study. *Research Ethics*, 12, 14–28.

Francis, R.D. (2009) *Ethics for Psychologists* (2nd edn). Oxford: Wiley-Blackwell.

CHAPTER 3
Evolution, genetics and behaviour

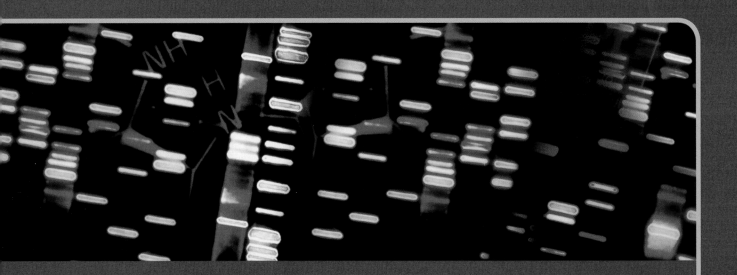

HOW MANY GENES ARE 'INVOLVED' IN INTELLIGENCE? AND WHAT DOES THIS QUESTION MEAN?

A study by the Universities of Edinburgh, Harvard and Southampton investigated the relationship between a person's DNA and their intellectual ability. The research looked at 248,000 people across the world, using a technique called Genome Wide Association. It was the largest study of genes and intelligence ever conducted and was published in March 2018.

It identified 538 genes associated with intelligence. 'We know that environments and genes both contribute to the differences we observe in people's intelligence', said Professor Ian Deary, of Edinburgh University. 'This study adds to what we know about which genes influence intelligence, and suggests that health and intelligence are related in part because some of the same genes influence them'.

Source: https://www.nature.com/articles/s41380-017-0001-5

WHAT YOU SHOULD BE ABLE TO DO AFTER READING CHAPTER 3

- Describe Darwin's theory of evolution.
- Outline the principles of genetic inheritance.
- Evaluate the contribution of genetics to psychology.
- Describe and evaluate sociobiology and evolutionary psychology's contribution to our understanding of behaviour.
- Discuss some of the reasons why we are sexually attracted to certain body types.
- Describe the psychological and evolutionary significance of altruism.

QUESTIONS TO THINK ABOUT

- What do you think is meant by the term 'evolution of behaviour'?
- When did the modern human being evolve?
- What are the implications of the theory of evolution for psychology?
- How do you think the process of evolution could explain modern behaviour such as romantic attraction, jealousy, language and marriage?
- Are we attracted to certain body types? If so, why? And is this preference universal?
- What do we mean when we say that a characteristic is heritable?
- Which has the more important effect on behaviour – genes or the environment? Or is the question not worth asking?
- Can any behaviour be studied at the genetic level?
- Why are we more altruistic to some people than others?

The development of evolutionary theory

From my early youth I have had the strongest desire to understand and explain whatever I observed, that is, to group all facts under some general laws ... Therefore, my success as a man of science, whatever this may have amounted to, has been determined, as far as I can judge, by complex and diversified mental qualities and conditions. Of these, the most important have been – the love of science – unbounded patience in long reflecting over any subject – industry in observing and collecting facts – and a fair share of invention and common sense. With such moderate abilities as I possess, it is truly surprising that I should have influenced to a considerable extent the belief of scientific men on some important points.
(*Source*: Darwin, 1887, pp. 67–71.)

These fairly humble words were written by a man who has influenced the course of scientific thought more than any other individual since Copernicus (who, in 1543, proposed that the sun, not the earth, was at the centre of the universe). Charles Darwin argued that, over time, organisms originate and become adapted to their environments by biological means. This concept is referred to as **biological evolution** – changes that take place in the genetic and physical characteristics of a population or group of organisms over time – and it stands as the primary explanation of the origin of life. The bicentenary of Darwin's birth was marked in 2009, together with the 150th anniversary of the publication of one of the most important books published in the past 300 years – *On the Origin of Species by Means of Natural Selection*. In this book, Darwin distilled his theory of evolution.

There is evidence of life on earth a billion years after the formation of the earth 4.5 billion years ago (Eiler, 2007) and the human race has existed, in various forms, for over 10 million years. This time-span has seen a tremendous change in our physical appearance, our biology and our behaviour. Our brains have developed, our societies have become more sophisticated, our intelligence has increased, our ability to communicate has improved and we have developed language systems. These processes illustrate the ways in which we have evolved and evolutionary theory seeks to explain why we have evolved in the way that we have. Why do birds have wings, giraffes have long necks, humans have bigger brains than other higher primates? How do changes in organic structure occur and how does this happen? The answers to questions such as these have important implications for the topics discussed in other chapters in this book: intelligence, personality, social interaction, the use of language, the perception and expression of emotion, sex, hunger, mental disorder and so on.

Although it has its roots in biology, Darwin's work transcends biology and has influenced all the natural sciences, especially psychology (Dewsbury, 2009). In fact, Darwin himself had some aspirations for the young science. He wrote in 1859:

In the distant future, I see open fields for more important researches. Psychology will be based on a new foundation, that of the necessary acquirement of each mental power and capacity by gradation. Much light will be thrown on the origin of man and his history.

Since the 1970s, some psychologists have become increasingly aware of the various ways in which biology can influence behaviour. As you will see later in the chapter, many behavioural differences among organisms, both within and across species, correspond to genetic and other biological differences. Understanding these differences and their evolution allows psychologists to understand behaviour in terms of its possible origins and **adaptive significance** – its effectiveness in aiding the organism to adapt to changing environmental conditions.

Psychologists might research how past environmental conditions favoured gregariousness over a more solitary existence as a means of organising human culture and how the immediate environment influenced day-to-day sociability. They are interested in understanding both **ultimate causes** (from the Latin *ultimatus*, 'to come to an end') of behaviour – events and conditions that, over successive generations, have slowly shaped the behaviour of our species – and **proximate causes** (from the Latin *proximus*, 'near'), namely immediate environmental variables that affect behaviour.

By understanding how adaptive behaviour developed through the long-term process of evolution, psychologists are able to gain a more thorough understanding of our ability to adjust to changes in our immediate environment. To understand the present, we must understand the past – the history of the individual and the history of our species. We behave as we do because we are members of the human species – an ultimate cause – and because we have learned to act in special ways – a proximate cause. Both biology and environment contribute to our personal development.

Relatively recently, a field of psychology has emerged, **evolutionary psychology** (Tooby and Cosmides, 1989; Buss, 1995), which attempts to describe and explain how an organism's evolutionary history contributes to the behaviour patterns and cognitive strategies it uses for reproduction and survival during its lifetime. Evolutionary psychology's contribution to our understanding of human behaviour is assessed later in the chapter. First, however, we describe Darwin's theory of evolution. An understanding of this complex theory will help shed light on how behaviour has been interpreted, by some psychologists, in terms of evolution.

In the beginning: the voyage of the *Beagle*

The story of how Charles Darwin developed his theory illustrates the mix of hard work, intellect and good fortune that often makes scientific discovery possible. In fact, Darwin's work is an excellent example of how observation and experimentation can lead to scientific breakthroughs.

After receiving a degree in theology from the University of Cambridge, England, in 1831, Darwin met a Captain Robert FitzRoy who was looking for someone to serve as an unpaid naturalist and travelling companion during a five-year voyage on board HMS *Beagle*. The *Beagle's* mission was to explore and survey the coast of South America and to make longitudinal measurements worldwide.

During the voyage, Darwin observed the flora and fauna of South America, Australia, South Africa and the islands of the Pacific, South Atlantic and Indian Oceans. He collected creatures and objects of every sort: marine animals, reptiles, amphibians, land mammals, birds, insects, plants, rocks, minerals, fossils and seashells. These specimens, which were sent back to England at various stages of the trip, were later examined by naturalists from all over Europe.

Darwin did not form his theory of evolution while at sea. Although he was impressed by the tremendous amount of diversity among seemingly related animals, he believed in creationism, the view that all living things were designed by God and are non-evolving (Gould, 1985).

Charles Darwin (1809–82).
Source: Northwind Photo Library.

The Origin of Species

On his return home to England in 1836, Darwin continued to marvel at the many ways animals and plants adapt to their environments. He sifted through his collections, often discussing his findings and ideas with other scientists. He carefully reviewed the work of earlier naturalists who had developed their own theories on evolution. Darwin was not the first person to propose a theory of evolution, but he was the first to amass considerable evidence in its favour. He became interested in artificial selection, a procedure in which particular animals are mated to produce offspring that possess desirable characteristics. For example, if a farmer wished to develop cattle that yielded the largest steaks, then they would examine the available breeding stock and permit only the 'beefiest' ones to reproduce. If this process is repeated over many generations of animals, the cattle should become beefier. In other words, in artificial selection, people select which animals will breed and which will not based on specific, desirable characteristics of the animals.

As he pondered on whether there might be a natural process corresponding to the role that humans play in artificial selection, Darwin's views on evolution began slowly to change. He believed that 'selection was the keystone of man's success in making useful races of animals and plants. But how selection could be applied to organisms living in a state of nature remained for some time a mystery to me' (Darwin, 1887, p. 53).

A year-and-a-half later, on reading Malthus's *Population*, Darwin proposed that because the 'struggle for existence' continued in plants and animals, then favourable variations would be preserved and unfavourable ones would die out. The result of such 'selection' would be the development of new species (Darwin, 1887).

This proposal contains the idea of natural selection: within any given population, some members of a species will produce more offspring than will others. Any animal that possesses a characteristic that helps it to survive or adapt to changes in its environment is likely to live longer and to produce more offspring than are animals that do not have this characteristic.

Darwin was well aware of the significance of his discovery but did not publish his theory until 20 years later, taking great pains to develop a clear, coherent and accurate case for his theory.

Darwin might have been even slower in publishing his theory had it not been for an intriguing coincidence. In 1858, he received a manuscript from the Welshman, Alfred Russell Wallace, another naturalist, outlining a theory of natural selection identical to his own. Darwin's colleagues suggested that he and Wallace make a joint presentation of their separate works before a learned society – the Linnean Society – so that each might lay equal claim to the theory of natural selection. This was done, and a year later Darwin published his 'abstract', which we know today as *The Origin of Species*. The book sold out on its first day of publication and has been selling steadily ever since. And although theories of evolution had existed before Darwin, he was the first to offer a systematic explanation for how evolution worked.

Darwin's theory of evolution

Two concepts are central to Darwin's theory of evolution: adaptation and natural selection. Adaptation refers to the ability of generations of species to adapt effectively to changes in the environment. Natural selection refers to the process whereby some variations in species will be transferred from one generation to the next but others will not. The zoologist, Richard Dawkins, has likened the process of natural selection to a sieve because it leaves out what is unimportant (Dawkins, 1996).

Darwin's theory has four basic premises.

1 The world's animal and plant communities are dynamic, not static: they change over time with new forms originating and others becoming extinct.

2 The evolutionary process is gradual and continuous. New species arise through slow and steady environmental changes that gradually modify each species to its surroundings. When sudden and dramatic changes occur in the environment, a species' ability to adapt is usually challenged. Some species adapt and live; others become extinct.

3 All organisms are descended from an original and common ancestor. Over time, the process of natural selection has created different species, each specifically adapted to its ecological niche.

4 Natural selection not only causes changes within populations during changing environmental conditions but also acts to maintain the status quo under relatively constant environmental conditions.

Natural selection

The essence of Malthus's essay, which Darwin was reading when the idea of natural selection first occurred to him, was that the earth's food supply grows more slowly than populations of living things. The resulting scarcity of food produces competition among animals, with the less fit individuals losing the struggle for life. For example, wolves that are agile are better able to capture prey than are slower packmates. Fast wolves will therefore tend to outlive and out-reproduce slower wolves. If a wolf's tendency to run fast is a genetically controlled trait, it will be passed on to its offspring. These offspring will be more likely to catch prey and will therefore live longer and have more opportunities to reproduce.

The ability of an individual to produce offspring defines that individual's **reproductive success** – the number of viable offspring it produces relative to the number of viable offspring produced by other members of the same species. Contrary to popular interpretation, 'survival of the fittest' does not always mean survival of the most physically fit or of the strongest. The evolutionary 'bottom line' is not physical strength but reproductive success. Physical strength is only one factor that might contribute to such success. In humans, for example, good looks, charm and intelligence play an important role in an individual's ability to attract a mate and reproduce. What is more, natural selection is not 'intentional'. Giraffes did not grow long necks in order to eat leaves from trees, but those with longer necks who were able to reach the leaves successfully reproduced while the others died out.

Two aspects of natural selection – variation and competition – are the critical factors that determine whether any particular animal and its offspring will enjoy reproductive success.

Variation

Variation includes differences among members of a species, such as physical characteristics (size, strength or physiology) and behavioural characteristics (intelligence or sociability). What factors are responsible for these sorts of variation?

First, an individual organism's genetic make-up – or its **genotype** – differs from that of all other individuals (except in the case of identical twins). As a result of these genetic differences, an individual organism's physical characteristics and behaviour, or its **phenotype,** also differs from that of every other individual.

Every individual's phenotype is produced by the interaction of its genotype with the environment. In essence, the genotype determines how much the environment can influence an organism's development and behaviour. For instance, identical twins have exactly the same genotype. If they are separated at birth and one twin has a better diet than the other, their phenotypes will be different: the better-fed twin is likely to be taller and stronger. However, regardless of diet, neither twin will ever become extremely tall or very muscular if they do not possess the genes for tallness and muscularity. Likewise, neither twin will realise their full potential for tallness and muscularity if they do not eat a nourishing diet. In this example, both the genotype (the genes related to tallness and muscularity) and a favourable environment (a well-balanced, nourishing diet) must be present for either twin to reach their full growth potential.

Phenotypes and the genotypes responsible for them may or may not be selected, depending on the particular advantage they confer. In a study that investigated the relationship between rainfall, food supply and finch population on one island, Grant (1986) discovered that the amount of rainfall and the size of the food supply directly affected the mortality of finches having certain kinds of beak. During droughts, small seeds became scarce. As a result, the finches having small, thin beaks died at a higher rate than finches having bigger, thicker beaks. During the next few years, the number of finches having bigger, thicker beaks increased – just as the principle of natural selection would predict. During times of plentiful rain, small seeds became abundant, and the number of finches having small, thin beaks became more plentiful in subsequent years.

Grant's study makes two important points. First, although evolution occurs over the long run, natural selection can produce important changes in the short run – in the space of only a few years. Secondly, phenotypic variation, in this case differences in beak size, can produce important selective advantages that affect survival. Imagine if all the finches had small, thin beaks: during the drought, most, if not all, of these finches might have died. None would be left to reproduce and these finches would have become extinct on this island. Fortunately, there was phenotypic variation in beak size among the finches, and because phenotypic variation is caused by genetic variation (different genotypes give rise to different phenotypes), some finches – those having large, thick beaks – had an advantage. Their food supply (the larger seeds) was relatively unaffected by the drought, enabling them to out-survive and out-reproduce the finches with small, thin beaks.

On the basis of this evidence, one might reasonably assume that all finches should have developed large, thick beaks. However, when rain is plentiful and small seeds are abundant, birds with small, thin beaks find it easier to feed. Under these environmental conditions, these birds have a phenotypic (and genotypic) advantage.

Competition

The second aspect of natural selection is **competition**. Individuals of a given species share a similar environment. Because of this, competition within a species for food, mates and territory is inevitable. Every fish captured and eaten by one bald eagle is a fish that cannot be captured and eaten by another bald eagle. If one bald eagle finds a suitable mate, then there is one fewer potential mates for other bald eagles and so on.

Competition also occurs between species when members of different species vie for similar ecological resources, such as food and territory. Competition for other resources indirectly influences reproductive success because the ability to find and court a suitable mate depends on the ability to stake out and defend a territory having an adequate food supply. The probability of a yellow-headed blackbird finding a mate and successfully rearing a family depends not only on its success in competing against other yellow-headed blackbirds, but also on its success in competing against red-winged blackbirds.

Natural selection works because the members of any species have different phenotypes. Because these phenotypes are caused by different genotypes, successful individuals will pass on their genes to the next generation. Over time, competition for food and other resources will allow only the best-adapted phenotypes (and their corresponding genotypes) to survive, thereby producing evolutionary change. This is what the theory would predict.

Knowledge and acceptance of evolution

How widespread do you think the acceptance of the theory of evolution is? In the US, it is law that science and religion are taught separately and that banning the teaching of evolution is unconstitutional (Scott and Matzke, 2007). In 2007, the Council of Europe's Parliamentary Assembly passed a resolution recommending that member states do not teach creationism as if it were the equivalent of science. One survey of over 1,000 students at a large American university, however, found that 25 per cent reported that their biology teacher had taught them creationism and 20 per cent were taught neither biology nor creationism (Moore, 2007). Creationism – the rejection of the theory of evolution in favour of the belief that the world was originated by a Creator – has gained some momentum in the USA, although recent legal rulings suggest that evolution is fighting back. Creationism's new incarnation is Intelligent Design but, to all intents and purposes, the terms are synonymous. The fierce and often acrimonious debate that exists between scientists and intelligent design advocates – see Dawkins's excoriating *The God Delusion* (2007) – could probably make a Controversies in Psychological Science section in itself.

Since the early 1980s, American adults at various time intervals have been asked if the following statement is true or false: 'Human beings, as we know them, developed from earlier species of animals'. Figure 3.1 illustrates how people have answered this question from 1982 to 2015.

Miller *et al.* found that over 20 years the percentage of Americans agreeing with the statement fell from 45 per cent to 40 per cent. Those who completely rejected the statement also fell from 48 per cent to 39 per cent. Those who were unsure jumped from 7 per cent in 1985 to 21 per cent in 2005. In later surveys, respondents were given the option of responding in a different way. They were asked whether the statement was definitely true, probably true, probably false, definitely false or don't know. A third of Americans considered the statement to be false and only 14 per cent regarded it as definitely true. European and Japanese respondents were more likely to accept the statement as true. In fact, the only country which was more sceptical than the US was Turkey. Eighty per cent of Iceland, Denmark, Sweden and France agreed; 78 per cent of the Japanese did. In European countries, the percentage absolutely disagreeing ranged from 7 per cent (Denmark, France, UK) to 15 per cent (the Netherlands).

The trends for belief in the evolution of humans don't make happy reading for rationalists. Figure 3.1 shows three lines on a graph plotting, from 1992 to 2015, how people's beliefs of evolution have, well, evolved (Gallup, 2015). The belief that God created humans has been the dominant belief for over 30 years. The least believed was the idea that humans evolved with no input from God.

Those who strongly believed in God, who prayed often and held pro-life beliefs were the most rejecting of the statement.

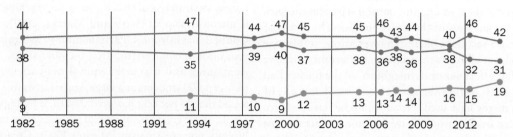

Figure 3.1 How people's beliefs about evolution have changed from 1982 to 2015.

source: http://www.gallup.com/poll/21814/evolution-creationism-intelligent-design.aspx

All of these were more common in the US. Miller *et al.* explains the geographic disparity by suggesting that biblical fundamentalism – Genesis is to be read literally – is greater in the US, whereas in Europe, Genesis is regarded as being more of a metaphor. A third of US respondents also agreed that half of the genes of mice and humans are identical and 38 per cent believed that we have half in common with chimps (as you'll see later, the percentage we share is a lot higher). Even if respondents disagreed with evolution, you might expect them to have a reasonable knowledge of the building blocks of life. Fewer than half of Americans surveyed were able to provide a passable definition of DNA.

Human evolution

Reconstruction of human evolution is a difficult job, something akin to assembling a giant jigsaw puzzle whose pieces have been scattered throughout the world. Some of the pieces may have been lost for ever; others have become damaged beyond recognition; and those few that are found force continual reinterpretation of how the other pieces might fit the puzzle. Another way in which we can date our remains is via carbon dating. Animals breathe a form of (naturally occurring) radioactive carbon called C14. When an animal dies, this carbon decays but at a constant rate. By examining the content of the carbon in the fossil or surrounding material, therefore, we can estimate the date of its existence. One problem here is that the amount of carbon found can be influenced by the amount in the air at the time.

We can also analyse the changes in DNA between similar fossils – the less the change in DNA, the closer the two fossils are in time. But the best we can do is make an educated guess about the evolution and lifestyles of our ancestors.

Many biologists and natural historians of Darwin's time believed that natural selection applied to all animals, including humans. Others insisted that although natural selection applied to other animals, it did not apply to humans. However, through study of the fossil record and recent developments in genetic research, we now know that our species is related genetically to other mammals. The gorilla and the chimpanzee are our closest living relatives, and together we appear to have descended from a common ancestor. You may have heard it said that we share 99 per cent of our genes with chimps. In fact, what we share is DNA involved in the production of proteins. Ninety-nine per cent of our DNA in this regard is identical (King and Wilson, 1975). Why, then, are we not exactly hirsute, whooping, tyre-swinging, banana-eaters? The reason is that 98 per cent of the human genome is not involved in the production of proteins. The remainder is involved in the timing of production and how much is produced (these are called regulatory genes – there is a more detailed description of genetics later in the chapter). It is this percentage which causes the great difference between the species (Demuth *et al.,* 2006). Humans also have multiple copies of genes that chimps do not (Pennisi, 2006). Therefore, while we have proteins in common, it is the way in which these proteins are organised which determines the differences between us.

Our dependence on information from fossil remains and other archaeological artefacts is problematic. As Byrne (1995) has colourfully pointed out, much of what we conclude about our ancestors' behaviour from archaeological findings is speculative; some is sensible speculation but it is speculation nonetheless. There is no way of empirically or conclusively demonstrating that artefacts were used in the way in which we suggest or that they indicate a specific way of living or behaving. In this sense, **paleoanthropology** – the study of human behaviour using information from fossil remains – is more like detective work than scientific work. 'The reality', Byrne argues, 'is that we will never know with confidence the answers to many of the most important questions we would like to ask about what happened in the past five million years' (1995, p. 6).

With this caveat in mind, the general pattern of evolution is thought to occur something like this. Our evolution from a common ancestor appears to have begun in Africa about two to four million years ago (Clark, 1993).

The earliest humans have been labelled *Homo habilis* (literally 'handy man'). *Homo habilis* was small (only about 1.3 m tall and about 40 kg in weight), but was bipedal (able to walk upright on two feet). Compared with its predecessor – a species called *Australopithecus* (apes from the South) – *Homo habilis* had a larger brain and more powerful hands. The strong hands were well suited to making simple stone tools; hence the name 'handy man'. A natural selection interpretation of such adaptively significant traits would argue that these early humans adapted to the environment in terms of creating shelter against the elements, catching and preparing food, and making weapons for self-defence.

Homo habilis was succeeded, about 400,000 years later, by *Homo erectus* (upright man). *Homo erectus* had a much larger brain and stood more erect than *Homo habilis* and had a more complex lifestyle. *Homo erectus* was the first of our ancestors to establish regular base camps, which probably served as centres for social activities, including the preparation and eating of food. We cannot be absolutely sure that these interpretations are the correct ones, however. *Homo erectus* created more efficient and stronger tools than did *Homo habilis,* successfully hunted big game, and discovered and used fire. Fire enabled these early humans to cook food, remain warm in cold weather and protect themselves from predators. *Homo erectus*'s use of fire, coupled with its apparent social nature and its ability to hunt and/or scavenge big game, permitted it to explore and settle new environments, including Europe, Asia, America and other parts of Africa (Spoor *et al.*, 2007).

The earliest known *Homo sapiens* (intelligent man) appears to have arisen about 500,000 years ago. The best known of the early *Homo sapiens, Homo sapiens neanderthalensis* (so-called Neanderthals, named after the German valley in which the fossils were discovered), lived throughout Europe and Central Asia between approximately 300,000 and 35,000 years ago. Neanderthals constructed small huts from bones and animal skins and sometimes burned bones as fuel. They were skilled big game hunters, tool makers and clothiers, and they had cultural rituals for burying their dead. In one Neanderthal burial site unearthed in France, a small boy was found positioned on his left side with a small pillow of flints under his head and an axe positioned by his right hand. Similar Neanderthal burial sites have been discovered, suggesting that these humans possessed cultural traditions not previously found in the prehistoric record.

Informed speculation suggests that Neanderthals and modern humans (*Homo sapiens sapiens*) overlapped each other, although the origin of *Homo sapiens sapiens* is unclear. It seems to have arisen between 200,000 and 100,000 years ago. The Neanderthals became extinct around 25,000 years ago, with last evidence of their existence found in Gibraltar (Finlayson *et al.*, 2006). What is clear, though, is that the *Homo sapiens sapiens* line has survived to flourish in all parts of the world, despite the presence of hostile climate, terrain and predators. Figure 3.2 charts the suspected

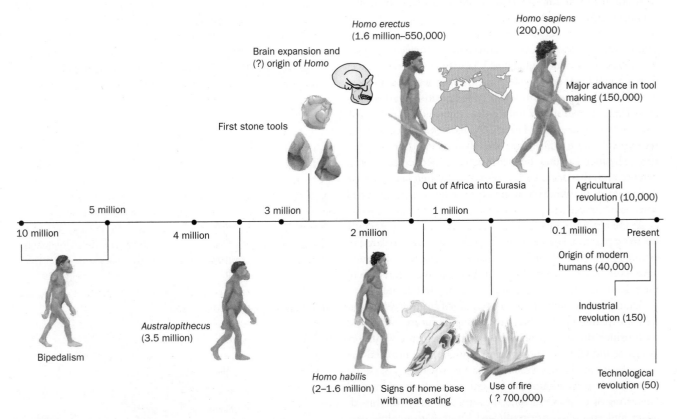

Figure 3.2 Major milestones in human evolution. The ability to walk upright freed the hands for tool use and other manipulative skills. Increased brain size accompanied increased intelligence. These two adaptations combined probably contributed significantly to all other major adaptations in human evolution.

Source: Adapted from Lewin, R., *Human Evolution: An illustrated introduction*. Cambridge, MA: Blackwell Scientific Publications, Inc., 1984.

development of *Homo sapiens sapiens*. Some theorists have suggested that the variety of species is greater nearer the equator (Hillebrand, 2004) and that tropical environments create a museum and a cradle for species to flourish (McKenna and Farrell, 2006).

Natural selection and human evolution

The apparent success of the human species in adapting to a variety of ecological niches stems from the fact that natural selection has favoured two important human characteristics: **bipedalism**, the ability to move about the environment on two feet, and **encephalisation**, increased brain size. The ability to walk upright, which appears to have evolved in our early hominid ancestors over 4 million years ago (Boaz, 1993; Ruff *et al.*, 1997), may have arisen from the need to stand on branches to reach food on other branches above (Thorpe *et al.*, 2007). Bipedalism allowed not only greater mobility, but also freed the hands for grabbing, holding and throwing objects. The ability to grasp objects, in combination with an expanding capacity for learning and remembering new skills provided by a larger brain, led to advances in tool making, food gathering, hunting and escaping predators (Eccles, 1989).

Early hominids had a brain volume of 650 cm³ (and they were about 155 cm tall). Current humans have a brain size of 1,500 cm³ and are, on average, 175 cm tall. It used to be thought that there was a relationship between body size and brain volume. However, the relationship is between relative size and brain volume and Figure 3.3a–c shows the differences in brain and body size between various species. The increase in our brain relative to our size is called **positive brain allometry**. This began around 2 million years ago and has increased, more or less, since – from 450 cm³ (*Homo habilis*) to 1,000 cm³ (*Homo erectus*) to 1,350 cm³ 100,000 years ago (*Homo sapiens*). The increase may be attributable to better diet, better defence and, therefore, better survival. Children began to live longer, thus enabling the brain to be more fully developed when they conceived.

As the brain became larger, more of its volume – especially the front part which is the most recently evolved – appeared to become devoted to thinking, reasoning, decision-making and other complex cognitive, 'higher' functions. We will return to the role of this part of the brain in thinking in Chapter 11.

Another important ability that emerged from encephalisation was planning: the ability to anticipate future events and to consider the effects of these events on an individual or group of individuals. Such planning might have involved the organisation of hunts, the institution of social customs and events (such as weddings and funerals), and the planting and harvesting of crops. Over time, the interaction between bipedalism and encephalisation allowed humans to exploit new environments and establish well-organised communities.

Advances in tool making and hunting, combined with the use of fire for cooking, protection and warmth, were adaptive: they helped humans to live longer. The increased lifespan of humans may have aided the gradual accumulation of wisdom as the older members of early human communities began to share their knowledge with younger members through language. Although the fossil record cannot tell us when language first developed, we assume that those who were able to communicate with others through language had a distinct advantage over those who could not.

Language originated and subsequently evolved because of its immensely adaptive significance (Pinker, 1994). As Skinner (1986) noted, language not only provided a simple means of warning others of danger, but also provided a means

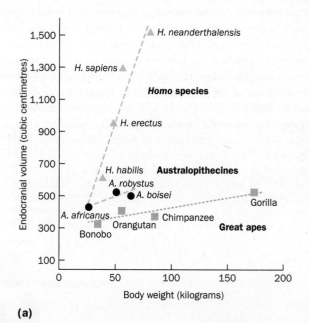

(a)

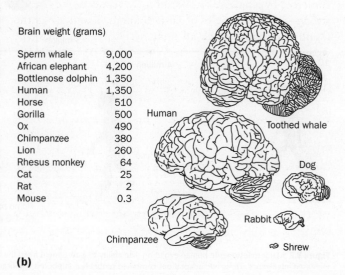

Brain weight (grams)	
Sperm whale	9,000
African elephant	4,200
Bottlenose dolphin	1,350
Human	1,350
Horse	510
Gorilla	500
Ox	490
Chimpanzee	380
Lion	260
Rhesus monkey	64
Cat	25
Rat	2
Mouse	0.3

(b)

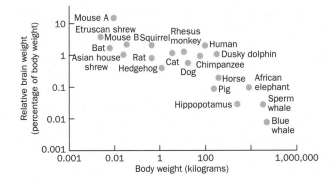

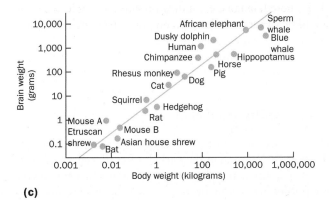

(c)

Figure 3.3 These three figures show the relationship between brain size and body weight in our human ancestors and nonhuman primates **(a)**; the weight of various species brains **(b)**; and the relationship between body weight and brain size in a variety of different species **(c)**.

Source: Dicke, U. and Roth, G. (2008). Intelligence evolved. *Scientific American Mind.*

of communicating important information to others, such as the location of a good hunting spot or instructions on how to craft a tool. Perhaps the most important advantage conferred by language was its ability to reinforce the already strong social tendencies of early humans. Language is the foundation upon which all human cultures are built (see Chapter 10).

Heredity and genetics

Darwin's work unveiled the process of natural selection and created new frontiers for exploration and experimentation. One of the most important of these frontiers is genetics, the study of 'the structure and function of genes and the way in which genes are passed from one generation to the next' (Russell, 1992, p. 2). Genetics, then, also involves the study of how the genetic make-up of an organism influences its physical and behavioural characteristics. Related to genetics are the

principles of heredity, the sum of the traits and tendencies inherited from a person's parents and other biological ancestors. Although Darwin had built a strong case for natural selection, he could not explain a key tenet of his theory – inheritance. He knew that individual differences occurred within a given species and that those differences were subject to natural selection. But he did not know how adaptations were passed from parent to offspring.

Six years after *The Origin of Species* was published, Gregor Mendel, an Austrian monk who conducted experimental cross-breeding studies with pea plants, uncovered the basic principles of heredity. Mendel demonstrated conclusively how height, flower colour, seed shape and other traits of pea plants could be transmitted from one generation to the next. His work has since been applied to studying heredity in thousands of plants and animals.

The basic principles of genetics

Genes are segments of genetic material called DNA (deoxyribonucleic acid) – strands of sugar and phosphate that are connected by nucleotide molecules of adenine, thymine, guanine and cytosine. Each pairs up with another, but guanine always pairs with cytosine and adenine with thymine. These pairs form steps in a spiral staircase called a double helix. That is, the DNA is configured like a twisted ladder: the sugar and phosphate form the sides and the four nucleotides form the rungs.

The Brit, Francis Crick, and the American, John Watson, who cracked the DNA code and were rewarded with a Nobel Prize in 1962, jointly with Marcus Williams.

Source: A. Barrington Brown/Science Photo Library Ltd.

The particular sequence of these nucleotide molecules directs the synthesis of protein molecules that regulate the biological and physical development of the body and its organs. Some protein molecules regulate cell development and others regulate the chemical interactions that occur within cells. Three billion pairs of these proteins form our genetic code (Plomin, 2008).

Protein synthesis

Genes can only influence our development and behaviour through protein synthesis. Proteins are strings of amino acids arranged in a chain. Each sequence of nucleotides (adenine, thymine, guanine and cytosine) specifies a particular amino acid. Adenine pairs with thymine; cytosine with guanine. In a sense, genes are 'recipes' consisting of different nucleotide sequences. In this case, the recipe is for combining the proteins necessary to create and develop physiological structures and for behaviour – how those structures might function in response to environmental stimulation.

Strictly speaking, however, there are no genes for behaviour, only for the physical structures and physiological processes that are related to behaviour. For example, when we refer to a gene for schizophrenia (a mental disorder characterised by irrational thinking, delusions, hallucinations and perceptual distortions), we are really referring to a gene that contains instructions for synthesising particular proteins, which, in turn, are responsible for the development of specific physiological processes that are sensitive to certain stressful environmental conditions (we may even be wrong in specifying just one gene – there may be more than one).

Genes also direct the synthesis of **enzymes**, proteins which govern the processes that occur within every cell in the body, and thus control each cell's structure and function. In 2003, the Human Genome Project was completed and this mapped the sequence of approximately 3 billion pairs of molecules that make up the rungs of DNA. It found 25,000 genes in each human cell and it is these genes which make us what we are. The human genome is around five feet in length and 50 trillionth of an inch wide. It was an outstanding achievement, but what is left to do is probably very much harder: trying to associate genes with behaviour and expression in a consistent and reliable way. In the past 25 years there has been an enormous surge in the number of human genetic studies, as Figure 3.4 shows. How does the genotype manifest itself into the phenotype? How do these genes enable organs to be developed and to function (and specific organs at that)?

Chromosomes and meiosis

Genes are located on **chromosomes**, the rod-like structures made of DNA found in the nucleus of every cell. In essence, genes are particular regions of chromosomes that contain the recipes for particular proteins. Each set of chromosomes contains a different sequence of genes. We inherit 23 individual chromosomes from each of our parents, giving us 23 pairs – 46 individual chromosomes – in most cells of the body. One pair of chromosomes, the **sex chromosomes**, contains the instructions for the development of male or female sex characteristics – those characteristics that distinguish males from females.

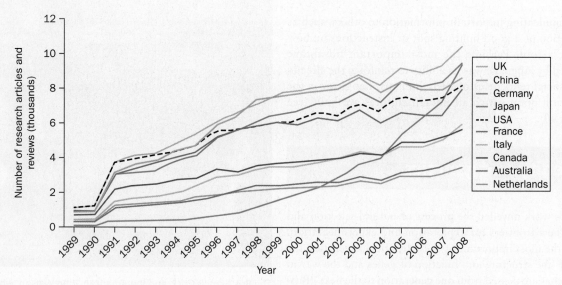

Figure 3.4 The number of papers published on human genetics between 1989 and 2008, by country. These are the top 10 producers of genetics research.
Source: The Wellcome Trust.

Sexual reproduction involves the union of a sperm, which carries genetic instructions from the male, with an ovum (egg), which carries genetic instructions from the female. Sperms and ova differ from the other bodily cells in at least two important ways. First, new bodily cells are created by simple division of existing cells. Secondly, all 23 pairs of chromosomes divide in two, making copies of themselves.

The copies pull apart, and the cell splits into two cells, each having a complete set of 23 pairs of chromosomes. Sperms and ova are formed by a special form of cell division called **meiosis.** The 23 pairs of chromosomes break apart into two groups, with one member of each pair joining one of the groups. The cell splits into two cells, each of which contains 23 individual chromosomes. The assignment of the members of each pair of chromosomes to a particular group is a random process; thus, a single individual can produce 223 (8,388,608) different ova or sperms.

Although brothers and sisters may resemble each other, they are not exact copies. Because the union of a particular sperm with an ovum is apparently random, a couple can produce 8,388,608 × 8,388,608, or 70,368,774,177,664 different children. Only identical twins are genetically identical. Identical twins occur when a fertilised ovum divides, giving rise to two identical individuals. Fraternal twins are no more similar than any two siblings. They occur when a woman produces two ova, both of which are fertilised (by different sperms).

Sex is determined by the twenty-third pair of chromosomes: the sex chromosomes. There are two different kinds of sex chromosomes, X chromosomes and Y chromosomes. Females have a pair of X chromosomes (XX); males have one of each type (XY). Because women's cells contain only X chromosomes, each of their ova contains a single X chromosome (along with 22 other single chromosomes). Because men's cells contain both an X chromosome and a Y chromosome, half of the sperm they produce contain an X chromosome and half contain a Y chromosome. Thus, the sex of a couple's offspring depends on which type of sperm fertilises the ovum. A Y-bearing sperm produces a boy, and an X-bearing sperm produces a girl. Figure 3.5 shows the human chromosomes (although see Chapter 13 for a description of new developments in the field of developmental genetics).

Dominant and recessive alleles

Each pair of chromosomes contains pairs of genes: one gene in each pair is contributed by each parent. Individual genes in each pair can be identical or different. Alternative forms

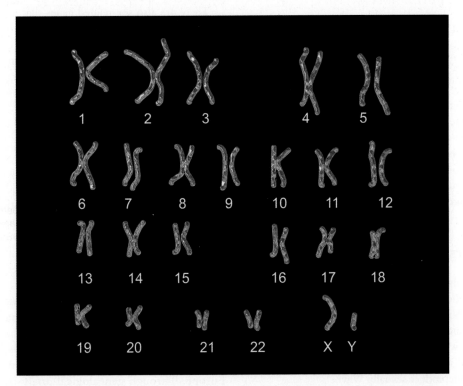

Figure 3.5 Human chromosomes: the presence of a Y chromosome indicates that this sample came from a male. A sample from a female would include two X chromosomes.

Source: Kateryna Kon/Shutterstock.

of genes are called **alleles** (from the Greek *allos,* 'other'). Consider eye colour, for example. The pigment found in the iris of the eye is produced by a particular gene. If parents each contribute the same allele for eye colour to their child, the gene combination is called homozygous (from the Greek *homo,* 'same', and *zygon,* 'yolk'). However, if the parents contribute different alleles, the gene combination is said to be heterozygous (from the Greek *hetero,* 'different').

Heterozygous gene combinations produce phenotypes controlled by the dominant allele – the allele that has a more powerful influence on the expression of the trait. The allele for brown eyes is dominant. When a child inherits the allele for brown eye colour from one parent and the allele for blue eye colour from the other parent, the child will have brown eyes. Brown eye colour is said to be a dominant trait. The blue eye colour controlled by the recessive allele – the allele that has a weaker effect on the expression of a trait – is not expressed. Only if both of a child's alleles for eye colour are of the blue type will the child have blue eyes. Thus, having blue eyes is said to be a recessive trait. Inheritance of two alleles for brown eyes will, of course, result in brown eyes. You can see this in Figure 3.6.

Other eye colours, such as hazel or black, are produced by the effects of other genes, which influence the dominant brown allele to code for more (black) or less (hazel) pigment in the iris.

It is important to remember that the genetic contributions to our personal development and behaviour are extremely complex. One reason for this complexity is that protein synthesis is often under polygenic control, that is, it is influenced by many pairs of genes, not just a single pair. The inheritance of behaviour is even more complicated, because different environments influence the expression of polygenic traits. Consider, for example, the ability to run. Running speed for any individual is the joint product of genetic factors that produce proteins for muscle, bone, blood, oxygen metabolism and motor coordination (to name but a few) and environmental factors such as exercise patterns, age, nutrition, accidents and so on.

Genetic diversity

No two individuals, except identical twins, are genetically identical. Such genetic diversity is a characteristic of all species that reproduce sexually. Some organisms, however, reproduce asexually, such as yeast and fungi. Nurseries often reproduce plants and trees through grafting, which is an asexual process. But when we examine the world around us, we find that the overwhelming majority of species reproduce sexually. Why?

One answer is that sexual reproduction increases a species' ability to adapt to environmental changes. Sexual reproduction leads to genetic diversity, and genetically diverse species have a better chance of adapting to a changing environment. When the environment changes, some members of a genetically diverse species may have genes that enable them to survive in the new environment. These genes manufacture proteins that give rise to physical structures, physiological processes, and, ultimately, adaptively significant behaviour that can withstand particular changes in the environment.

Influences of sex on heredity

An individual's sex plays a crucial role in influencing the expression of certain traits. A good example is haemophilia, an increased tendency to bleed seriously from even minor injuries. The blood of people who do not have haemophilia will begin to clot in the first few minutes after they sustain a cut. In contrast, the blood of people who have haemophilia may not do so for 30 minutes or even several hours. Haemophilia is caused by a recessive gene on the X chromosome that fails to produce a protein necessary for normal blood clotting. Because females have two X chromosomes, they can carry an allele for haemophilia but still have normal blood clotting if the other allele is normal. Males, however, have only a single X chromosome, which they receive from their mothers. If the gene for blood clotting carried on this chromosome is faulty, they develop haemophilia.

There are also sex-related genes that express themselves in both sexes, although the phenotype appears more frequently in one sex than in the other. These genes are called sex-influenced genes. For example, pattern baldness (thin hair across the top of the head) develops in men if they inherit either or both alleles for baldness, but this trait is not seen in women, even when they inherit both alleles.

Mutations and chromosomal aberrations

Changes in genetic material are caused by **mutations** or **chromosomal aberrations**. Mutations are accidental alterations in the DNA code within a single gene. Mutations are the original source of genetic diversity. Although most mutations have harmful effects, some may produce characteristics that are beneficial in certain environments. Mutations can be either spontaneous, occurring naturally, or the result of human-made factors such as high-energy radiation.

Haemophilia provides one of the most famous examples of mutation. Although haemophilia has appeared many times in human history, no other case of haemophilia has had as far-reaching effects as the spontaneous mutation that was passed among the royal families of nineteenth-century Europe. Through genealogical analysis, researchers have discovered that this particular mutant gene arose with Queen Victoria (1819–1901). She was the first in her family line to bear affected children – two female carriers and an afflicted son. The tradition that dictates that nobility marry only

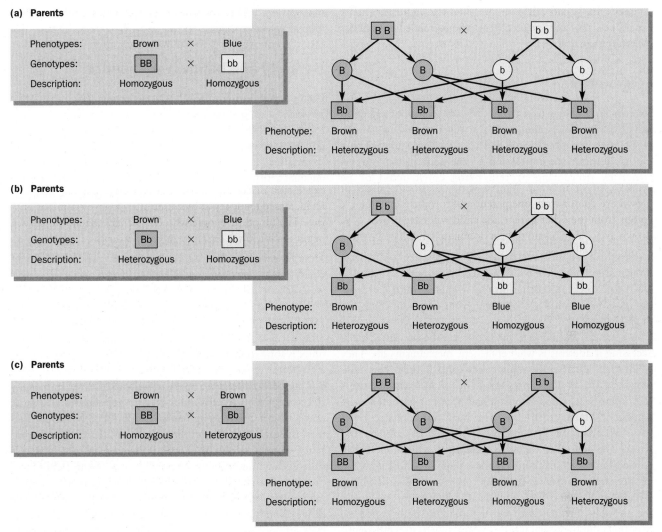

Figure 3.6 Patterns of inheritance for eye colour. **(a)** If one parent is homozygous for the dominant eye colour (BB), and the other parent is homozygous for the recessive eye colour (bb), then all their children will be heterozygous for eye colour (Bb) and will have brown eyes. **(b)** If one parent is heterozygous (Bb), and the other parent is homozygous recessive (bb), then their children will have a 50 per cent chance of being heterozygous (brown eyes) and a 50 per cent chance of being homozygous recessive (blue eyes). **(c)** If one parent is homozygous dominant (BB), and the other parent is heterozygous (Bb), then their children will have a 50 per cent chance of being homozygous for the dominant eye colour (BB) and will have brown eyes, and a 50 per cent chance of being heterozygous (Bb) for the trait and will have brown eyes.

Source: Based on Klug, W.S. and Cummings, M.R., *Concepts of Genetics* (2nd edn). Glenview, IL : Scott, Foresman, 1986. © 1986 Scott, Foresman & Co. Reprinted by permission of Addison Wesley Educational Publishers, Inc.

other nobility caused the mutant gene to spread rapidly throughout the royal families.

The second type of genetic change, chromosomal aberration, involves either changes in parts of chromosomes or a change in the total number of chromosomes. An example of a disorder caused by a chromosomal aberration – in this case, a partial deletion of the genetic material in chromosome 5 – is the **cri-du-chat syndrome**. Infants who have this syndrome have gastrointestinal and cardiac problems, are severely mentally retarded and make crying sounds resembling a cat's mewing (hence its name, 'cry of the cat'). In general, the syndrome's severity appears to be directly related to the amount of genetic material that is missing. Psychologists and developmental disability specialists have discovered that early special education training permits many individuals having this syndrome to learn self-care and communication skills. This fact highlights an important point about genetics and behaviour: even behaviour that has a genetic basis can often be modified through training or experience (Day and Sweatt, 2011), a notion called **epigenetics** (Masterpasqua, 2009).

Epigenetics

External events such as trauma, drug abuse, lack of affection can affect the functioning of DNA. When these happen, the DNA does not alter, but is coated with molecules. These molecules alter the expression of the gene in two ways – either by preventing protein being constructed or by accelerating it. As you saw earlier, protein is essential to maintain the body and the brain. In the body, there is selective gene expression – each cell in the body may have the same gene but different cells use different types of gene. It does this via a molecule called ribonucleic acid (RNA), an intermediate molecule which is used by proteins attached to DNA to convert into other proteins. This is why a cell from the lung, for example, is different from one from the brain or the heart.

A gene can be silenced; molecules can be prevented from accessing it and this is what epigenetic mechanisms do. They either facilitate or block access to the genes in cells. This, consequently, affects gene expression. In one experiment, the stress response of rats whose mothers had licked or groomed them consistently for up to 10 days after birth was compared with those who had not. The first group showed less anxiety and stress. The gene that allows the release of a hormone called corticosterone was examined in these pups and those who had not been licked had fewer corticosterone receptors in their brain (Weaver *et al.*, 2004). One proposed mechanism for this is that the hormone interacts with a structure in the brain called the hypothalamus to prevent it from overreacting to stressful events.

Another protein, brain-derived neurotrophic factor (BDNF), which is important for the growth, integrity and functioning of cells, is lower in women with depression and it has been suggested that distressing events or experiences can alter the DNA that encodes this protein. In one experiment, 'bully' mice and smaller, normal mice were placed in a cage together for five minutes and then separated by a mesh for 10 days (Berton *et al.*, 2006). As you might predict, the smaller mice showed the typical stress reaction – they would become submissive and anxious. However, when their brains were examined for levels of BDNF, these were lower in the bullied mice. More importantly, the molecule known to affect the expression of this protein was found in one region of the mice's brains. This molecule had shut off the BDNF protein. A course of antidepressants raised the levels of BDNF.

Similar to these genes are 'knockout genes', which work in a similar way. The animal is exposed to radiation which damages a gene. This inserts nucleotides in the gene which prevent it from expressing itself, hence, the gene has been 'knocked out'. When the gene which encodes for spatial learning had been knocked out in rats, their ability to learn to swim to a platform that was not visible underneath a pool of water was impaired (Nakazawa *et al.*, 2003).

Heredity and behaviour genetics

Each of us is born into a different environment and each of us possesses a unique combination of genetic instructions. As a result, we differ from one another. Consider your fellow undergraduates, for example. They come in different sizes and shapes, they vary in personality and intelligence, and they possess unequal artistic and athletic abilities. To what extent are these sorts of differences attributable to heredity or to the environment? If all your classmates had been reared in identical environments, any differences between them would necessarily be due to genetics. Conversely, if all your classmates had come from the same fertilised egg but were subsequently raised in different environments, any differences in their personal characteristics would necessarily be due only to the environment.

Heritability is a statistical term that refers to the amount of variability in a trait in a given population that is due to genetic differences among the individuals in that population. Heritability is sometimes confused with inheritance, the tendency of a given trait to be passed from parent to individual offspring. But heritability does not apply to individuals, it pertains only to the variation of a trait in a specific population. The more that a trait in a given population is influenced by genetic factors, the greater its heritability. The scientific study of heritability – of the effects of genetic influences on behaviour – is called behaviour genetics. As noted by one of this field's most prolific researchers, Robert Plomin, behaviour genetics is intimately involved with providing an explanation of why people differ (Plomin, 2008). As we will see below, behaviour geneticists attempt to account for the roles that both the heredity and the environment play in individual differences in a wide variety of physical and mental abilities.

Behavioural genetics has begun to contribute to our biological understanding of a variety of psychological variables, including types of memory, the developmental disorders autism and developmental dyslexia, personality, ageing and emotional recognition and expression, although there is currently no agreement on the precise genes necessary for the phenotypes to be expressed (Bevilacqua and Goldman, 2011; Geschwind, 2011; Harris and Deary, 2011; Munafo and Flint, 2011; Papassotiropoulos and de Quervain, 2011; Hyde *et al.*, 2016; Robinson *et al.*, 2016). For example, twin studies (see below) suggest that the heritability for the ability to recall past experiences and their spatial and temporal context – a form of memory called episodic memory (described in Chapter 8) – is between 30 and 60 per cent. Variants of genes though to be implicated in memory include *HTR2A* and *BDNF* (de Quervain *et al.*, 2003), but others include *COMT, GRM3, PRNP, CHREAMTA, APOE, PDYN* and *CPEB3* (Papassotiropoulos and de Quervain, 2011) and *KIBRA* and *CLSTN2* (Papassotiropoulos *et al.*, 2006). *KIBRA* may be associated with the conscious recall of material and *BDNF*, which has received considerable attention, with learning that is dependent on the hippocampus, a structure which you will read about in the next chapter and in Chapter 8, and which is essential for the formation of new memories.

One particular gene, the *APOE E4* allele, appears to be important to cognitive decline and the possible development of dementia associated with Alzheimer's disease (see Chapter 11) although, again, the picture is mixed and is discussed in that chapter (Harris and Deary, 2011).

Studying genetic influences

Although farmers and animal breeders had experimented with artificial selection for thousands of years, only within the past 150 years has the relation between heredity and behaviour been formally studied in the laboratory. Mendel's careful analysis of genetic influences on specific characteristics gave us the first good clue that traits were actually heritable. Galton (1869) stimulated further interest in this field with his studies showing that intelligence tends to run in families (see Chapter 1): if parents are intelligent then, in general, so are their children. The search for genetic bases of behaviour has been active ever since. In fact, the search to understand the relative contributions of heredity and environment to human behaviour is among the most heavily researched areas in psychology.

Artificial selection in animals

Any heritable trait can be selected in a breeding programme. The heritability of many traits in animals, such as aggression, docility, preference for alcohol, running speed and mating behaviours, can be studied by means of artificial selection.

Consider, for example, Tryon's (1940) study of maze learning in rats. Tryon wished to determine whether genetic variables influenced learning. He began his study with a large sample of genetically diverse rats. He trained them to learn a maze and recorded the number of errors each rat made in the process. He then selected two groups of rats – those that learned the fastest (bright) and those that learned the slowest (dull). He mated 'bright' rats with other 'bright' rats and 'dull' rats with other 'dull' rats. To ensure that the rats were not somehow learning the maze from their mothers, he 'adopted out' some of the pups: some of the bright pups were reared by dull mothers and some of the dull pups were reared by bright mothers. He found that parenting made little difference in his results, so this factor can be discounted.

Tryon continued this sequence of having rats learn the maze and selectively breeding the best with the best (bright) and the worst with the worst (dull) over many generations. Soon, the maze performance of each group was completely different. He concluded that maze learning in rats could be manipulated through artificial selection.

Later studies showed that Tryon's results were limited by the standard laboratory cage environment in which rats lived when they were not running the maze. For example, Cooper and Zubek (1958) demonstrated that differences in maze ability were virtually eliminated when bright and dull strains of rats were reared in either enriched environments designed to stimulate learning (cages containing geometric objects, such as tunnels, ramps and blocks) or impoverished environments designed to inhibit learning (cages containing only food and water dishes).

However, Cooper and Zubek's rats that were reared in the standard laboratory cage performed similarly to Tryon's rats: the bright rats outperformed the dull rats. Thus, changing the environmental conditions in which the rats lived had an important result – reducing the effects of genetic differences

Cutting edge: Genetics and legal decision-making

Since the publication of studies demonstrating a link between the gene responsible for the enzyme MAOA, and aggression, lawyers and their clients have shown an interest in this argument as one which might excuse culpability. The evidence for the link, however, is not consistent. Some studies have found that if a person has a history of childhood abuse and the allele associated with a reduction in MAOA, they are likely to be convicted of violent crime (Appelbaum and Scurich, 2014). Twin studies have found that heritability explains between 37 and 57 per cent of five aggressive behaviours and 67 per cent of antisocial behaviour (Yeh *et al.*, 2010; Tuvblad *et al.*, 2011).

To examine what effect these issues – genetic causes of violence – would have on jurors' decision-making, Appelbaum and Scurich (2014) presented 250 US participants with a vignette describing an impulsive murder. The sample was divided into four groups. Groups were told that the defendant (i) had suffered childhood abuse, (ii) was genetically predisposed to violent crime, (iii) had suffered childhood abuse or (iv) was simply impulsive. They were asked to determine what crime was committed (1st or 2nd degree murder, 1st or 2nd degree manslaughter) and what sentence to pass. Knowledge of genetic susceptibility did not affect the classification of the crime. However, defendants described has having a history or abuse, or history of abuse and genetic susceptibility were more likely to receive longer prison sentences. They also generated most fear in the participants.

The study suggests that although having a genetic disposition does not mean that a defendant will be convicted of a more serious crime, their sentences might be longer.

between the bright and dull rats. This finding makes good sense when you consider the fact that genes are not expressed in the absence of an environment.

Tryon's research demonstrated that over successive generations a trait can be made to become more or less likely in a given population, but we do not know precisely why. We do not know whether genes related to learning or genes related to other traits were selected. Tryon's rats may have been neither especially bright nor especially dull. Perhaps each of these strains differed in its capacity to be motivated by the food reward that awaited it at the end of the maze.

Can gene manipulation ever occur in humans? Experiments involving the cloning of sheep illustrate the power of molecular genetics in radically altering nature's forms. Gene mapping may help us to understand how specific DNA sequences can influence physiological processes that affect behaviour, emotion, remembering and thinking and play a crucial role in identifying specific genes involved in psychological disorders (Plomin and DeFries, 1998). Some of these issues are discussed in the chapters on memory, intelligence and mental disorders (Chapters 8, 11 and 18).

Twin studies

There are two barriers to studying the effects of heredity on behavioural traits in humans. First, ethical considerations prevent psychologists and geneticists from manipulating people's genetic history or restricting the type of environment in which they are reared. For example, we cannot artificially breed people to learn the extent to which shyness, extraversion or any other personality characteristics are inherited or deprive the offspring of intelligent people of a good education to see if their intelligence will be affected. Secondly, in most cases, the enormous variability in human environments effectively masks any correlation that might exist between genetics and trait expression.

Psychologists have been able to circumvent these barriers by taking advantage of an important quirk of nature – multiple births. Recall that identical twins, also called **monozygotic (MZ) twins**, arise from a single fertilised ovum, called a zygote, that splits into two genetically identical cells. Fraternal or dizygotic (DZ) twins develop from the separate fertilisation of two ova. DZ twins are no more alike genetically than any two siblings. Because MZ twins are genetically identical, they should be more similar to one another in terms of their psychological characteristics (such as personality or intelligence) than either DZ twins or non-twin siblings.

Concordance research examines the degree of similarity in traits expressed between twins. Twins are concordant for a trait if both of them express it or if neither does, and they are discordant if only one expresses it. If concordance rates (which can range from 0 to 100 per cent) of any given trait are substantially higher for MZ twins than for DZ twins, heredity is likely involved in the expression of that trait.

When we observe a trait exhibiting a high concordance for MZ twins but a low one for DZ twins, we can conclude that the trait may be strongly affected by genetics. This is especially true for a trait such as blood type, which has a heritability of 100 per cent. If the concordance rates are similar, the effect of heredity is low. Some research has extended this difference to psychological variables such as intelligence, attitudes and personality.

For example, pairs of identical twins have been found to hold more similar views on subjects such as religion, crime, punishment and so on than do pairs of DZ twins (Eaves et al., 1989), have fibres connecting parts of the brain that are more similar in volume (Jahanshad et al., 2010) and show greater asymmetry in the fibres connecting the front and the back of the brain. In a study of 195 pairs of MZ twins and 141 pairs of DZ twins, Olson et al. (2001) found that identical twins were more likely to share similar attitudes on 26 of 30 attitude items than were DZ twins. Does this suggest that there are genes for such attitudes?

This is highly unlikely. Instead, the authors suggest that there may be more general traits of factors which reflect specific attitudes. For example, when they took personality into account, they found that the trait of sociability was highly associated with five of the six attitude factors, perhaps suggesting that sociability may be the underlying 'cause' of such attitudes and which may be the heritable factor. Participants' attitudes towards leadership correlated with self-reported physical attractiveness, sociability and aggressiveness, but interpreting this relationship is difficult. Perhaps very attractive, sociable or aggressive people achieve leadership more easily and readily than do their less attractive, less sociable and less aggressive counterparts and that attitudes to leadership became more positive as a consequence. Conversely, participants may have been favourable towards leadership and made themselves more attractive, sociable or aggressive in order to achieve the status of leader.

Genome-Wide Association Studies

In the past 15 years, a new way of studying the genetic basis of life and behaviour has been developed. Previously, researchers had conducted inheritance studies in which genetic linkages in families were examined and common or complex disorders were studied. Many of these studies were difficult to replicate. A newer technique has allowed the investigation of the whole genome for associations between genetic variants and a trait.

For example, researchers can search for a single nucleotide polymorphism (SNP) that is associated with a trait such as an illness (or, more controversially, a behavioural trait such as intelligence). A polymorphism is a genetic variation in a population. A sample might be divided into phenotypes – people with a specific illness and those without. If alleles are present in the genome of one sample that is not found in another, then these alleles are thought to be 'associated' with the phenotype (the illness). This type of study is called a Genome-Wide Association Study (GWAS).

The first GWAS study was published in 2005 and investigated 96 patients with age-related macular degeneration (Klein *et al.*, 2005). The study found two SNPs associated with altered frequencies of alleles. Around 4,000 SNPs have now been identified. One study of 4,000 people with one of seven illnesses, and a comparison, control group of 3,000 individuals, identified 24 independent SNPs – one in bipolar disorder, one in cardio vascular disease, nine in Crohn's, three in rheumatoid arthritis, seven in type 1 diabetes and three in type 2 (Wellcome Trust Case Control Consortium, 2007). Nineteen variants have been found for brain structure (Strike *et al.*, 2015). But the technique does have its limitations. For example, if a group of researchers is examining the whole genome for specific SNPs associated with one group/trait and not another, the likelihood of committing a Type 1 error is large. To overcome this, researchers set a very conservative p value (this is 0.0000005). Researchers also use a statistical technique called an odds ratio which represents the odds that a person with a disease has a particular allele. If the frequency of an allele is increased in the sample with a disease, the odds ratio is said to be greater than 1. Very few associations have an odds ratio of greater than three.

Other potential confounds in GWAS studies are sex, age and ethnic background. Each of these can influence the results of a study. The use of GWAS in studies of intelligence is considered in Chapter 11.

Sociobiology and evolutionary psychology

Sociobiology has been defined as 'the systematic study of the biological basis of all social behaviour' (Wilson, 1975). It represents the synthesis of research findings regarding social behaviour from many other fields of science, including those from evolutionary psychology, anthropology and behaviour genetics. Evolutionary psychology and behaviour genetics are more specific fields than sociobiology in the sense that both are concerned with phenomena such as intelligence and cognition, in addition to social behaviour.

Sociobiologists are especially interested in understanding the evolutionary roots of our modern-day social actions. More often than not, sociobiologists study the evolutionary bases of social behaviour in non-human animals and then extrapolate from those species to humans (Barash, 1982). Sociobiology represents an interface between the biological sciences and

psychology. However, not all psychologists are convinced of the sociobiologists' claims, arguing that sociobiology is too simplistic and that its emphasis on genetics inadequately explains the complexities of human behaviour.

Reproductive strategies and the biological basis of parenting

Perhaps the most important social behaviours related to survival are those related to mating and parenting. According to Puts (2010), around 75 per cent of the papers published in the journals *Evolution, Hormones and Behaviour* and *Human Nature* between 1997 and 2007 were on mate choice. A focal point of sociobiological research and theory has been understanding more about the different kinds of social organisation that result from particular **reproductive strategies** – systems of mating and rearing offspring.

We assume that most Western sexual relationships are monogamous: the mating of one female and one male. If mating is successful, the individuals share in the raising of the child or children. But **monogamy** is just one of several reproductive strategies sexual creatures employ in mating and rearing of offspring (Barash, 1982). Three other major classes of reproductive strategy are also possible:

- **Polygyny:** one male mates with more than one female.
- **Polyandry:** one female mates with more than one male.
- **Polygynandry:** several females mate with several males.

According to Trivers (1972), these four reproductive strategies evolved because of important sex differences in the resources that parents invest in conceiving and rearing their offspring. Parental investment is the time, physical effort and risks to life involved in procreation and in the feeding, nurturing and protecting of offspring. According to sociobiologists, parental investment is a critical factor in mate selection. An individual who is willing and able to make a greater investment is generally more sought after as a mate and is often more selective or discriminating when selecting a mate (Trivers, 1972). Given that a human female will gestate for nine months, she should be highly selective about choosing a mate. On the basis of Trivers's theory, it is possible to predict that women will express an (evolved) preference for men who have high status and will divorce those who do not contribute the expected resources or who divert them to other women and children (Buss, 1995).

In some species, that reproduce through sex competition for mates leads to **sexual selection** – selection for traits specific to sex, such as body size or ornamentation or particular patterns of behaviour. For example, in some animals, such as buffalo, females select mates based on the male's ability to survive the skirmishes of the rutting (mating) season. In general, the larger and more aggressive males win these battles and gain access to more females and enjoy greater reproductive success.

This competition is assisted by the physical differences between men and women. For example, if fat is factored out, men are 40 per cent heavier and have 60 per cent more muscle than women, have 80 per cent greater arm muscle, 50 per cent lower body mass muscle (Lassek and Gaulin, 2008, 2009), and 90 per cent upper body strength. Their sprint times are 22 per cent faster, and they can leap 45 per cent higher; the average man is stronger than 99 per cent of women (Lassek and Gaulin, 2009). Men are also more likely to be aggressive, as are boys – they attack more, hit more and restrain more. These factors, together with masculine features such as beards and deep voices, are important factors in mate choice and contribute to contest competition – a way in which men can eliminate (metaphorically) other men who compete for female attention. It is women who normally express choice for mates and so men vie for female attention using whatever means they believe will be successful and this means removing opposition. Therefore, men compete for sexual attention and women select based on so-called gene quality (which is what fitness, strength, masculinity are thought to convey).

Men prefer women with faces that are gracile – not lined, hirsute or masculine, and who have minimal body hair and high voices (Rilling *et al.*, 2009). These features all signify youthfulness and, therefore, reproductivity. They also prefer a particular waist to hip ratio, as you will see later. It is interesting to note that no other primate has the fat distribution of women – on the breasts and hips (Pond and Mattacks, 1987).

Evolution, however, has led to the development of a male brain that can go beyond mere punch-ups and Tom Jones impersonations: men also use humour, music, poetry and other creative vehicles to attract a mate and these factors are considered important to women in a long-term relationship (Gangestad *et al.*, 2007; Prokosch *et al.*, 2009). Laughter is used as a signal of social dominance – if low and high status individuals are left to talk among themselves and their laughter is measured, dominant and submissive laughter is found, depending on the status of the individual (Oveis *et al.*, 2016). High-status people were dominant and disinhibited laughers whereas low-status laughers were inhibited. Low-status individuals were more likely to shift their type of laughter across contexts. Men also tend to prefer to hear jokes by other men when other men's voice pitch is lower (Cowan *et al.*, 2015). Men also prefer low-pitched men as friends if they report high levels of self-reported dominance.

Polygyny is by far the most common reproductive strategy among humans. Eighty-four per cent of human societies practise polygyny or allow men who are either wealthy or powerful to practise it (Badcock, 1991). Monogamy is the next most popular reproductive strategy, with about 15 per cent of all human cultures practising it. Polyandry and polygynandry are both rare: combined, these two reproductive strategies dominate in fewer than 1 per cent of all human cultures.

Polygyny: high female and low male parental investment

In many species, the female makes the greater parental investment. According to evolutionary biological theory, whether one is an ova producer or a sperm producer defines the nature of one's parental investment.

Among most mammals (including humans), the costs associated with reproduction are higher for females than for males. First, females have fewer opportunities than males to reproduce. Generally, females produce only one ovum or a few ova periodically, whereas males produce vast quantities of sperm over substantially shorter time intervals. Secondly, females carry the fertilised ovum in their bodies during a long gestation period, continuously diverting a major portion of their own metabolic resources to nourish the rapidly growing foetus. Females also assume all the risks that accompany pregnancy and childbirth, including physical discomfort and possible death. The male's contributions to reproduction are, at a minimum, the sperm and the time needed for intercourse. Thirdly, after the offspring is born, females may continue to devote some of their metabolic resources to the infant by nursing it. Just as important, they usually devote more time and physical energy than males to caring for the newborn.

In addition, a female can only bear a certain number of offspring in a lifetime, regardless of the number of males with whom she mates. In contrast, a male is limited in his reproductive success only by the number of females he can impregnate. For example, consider the differences between females and males in our species. If a woman became pregnant once a year for ten years, she might possibly conceive ten children – only a fraction of the number of children that a man is capable of fathering over the same interval. If a man impregnated a different woman every month for ten years, he could have fathered 120 children. This example is hardly an exaggeration. According to the *Guinness Book of World Records,* the largest number of live births to one woman is 69 (she had several multiple births). In contrast, King Ismail of Morocco is reported to have fathered 1,056 children.

In many polygynous species, intense competition for the opportunity to mate occurs among males. The competition almost always involves some sort of physical confrontation or display: that is, males fight among themselves for the opportunity to display or mate. Usually, the larger, stronger and more aggressive male wins, which means that only he will mate with the available females in the vicinity. If one of the smaller, weaker males attempts to mate with a female, he is generally chased away by the victorious male.

Because females in polygynous species invest so heavily in their offspring, they are – according to sociobiologists – usually highly selective of their mates, choosing to mate only with those males who possess specific attributes, such as physical size, strength and aggressiveness. Such selectivity makes adaptive sense for both the female and her progeny.

Physical attractiveness

There is evidence that some aspects of our physical appearance are preferred more than others. Some studies find that body mass index (BMI) is important, especially when full-frontal images are judged; others suggest that shape is more important if a figure is seen in profile.

Tovee and Cornelissen (2001) found that BMI, not **waist-to-hip ratio** (WHR), was the best predictor of attractiveness for figures seen from the front or in profile. Both men and women gave similar ratings, thus supporting the second hypothesis, and both sexes preferred the figures with the lowest WHR (a curvaceous figure). This suggests that BMI and WHR may reflect different aspects of female health and fitness. BMI may reflect general fitness and fertility whereas WHR is a 'more specific cue to fertility and pubertal status' although the authors acknowledge that this cue has its limitations. The WHR of anorexic and healthy women is similar, for example, although the anorexic group (which is amenorrheic, i.e. not menstruating) is not fertile whereas the healthy group is.

There is an analogous preference for low waist-to-chest ratio (WCR) in men (Maisey *et al.*, 1999). Unlike men, who prefer a certain body size, women prefer a certain shape. This is the 'inverted triangle' (narrow waist, broad shoulders). The researchers suggest that if the desirable WHR in women signifies health and reproductive potential, then a desirable WCR in men signifies physical strength.

Men's weight, however, can influence people's judgement of their personality. Wade *et al.* (2007) found that thinner men were rated as more socially desirable than overweight men. Thin men and men of normal weight also received higher ratings for friendliness, trustworthiness, intelligence and mate potential.

Bodies are often covered and we may not be able to perceive their exact shape. Faces, however, are almost always exposed and offer an immediate source of information about physical attractiveness. People with attractive faces are rated as healthier, sexier, more attractive and more fertile regardless of WHR (Furnham *et al.*, 2001). The evidence is contrary to what we would expect from the 'first pass filter' theory of mate selection. This refers to the notion that WHR is the first feature we focus on to determine our attraction to a partner; if it is acceptable, we then focus on other features and behaviours to further refine our choice.

People also find facial symmetry (where the left and right sides are almost totally symmetrical) attractive and healthy. Men with more symmetrical bodies have been reported to display more direct, sexual, competitive tactics when trying to win their date (Simpson *et al.*, 1999) and symmetrical movers are judged to be significantly better dancers than are asymmetrical ones (Brown *et al.*, 2005).

Of course, physical beauty is stereotypically (and self-evidently) skin-deep. A study by Swami *et al.* (2007) asked participants to rate line drawings of women which varied in body weight, WHR and personality (extravert, introvert). Extraverted 'women' were judged to be more attractive and sociable than introverted ones, indicating that non-physical features are also an important determinant of attractiveness. Women rate several characteristics as being more important in a partner than did men (Furnham, 2009). These included intelligence, stability, conscientiousness, height, education, social skills and compatibility in terms of politics and religion. For men, physical appearance was more important than it was for women. Men and women were more likely to like a mate who shared similar personality characteristics such as extraversion and conscientiousness.

The perils of being beautiful

Is there a disadvantage to being very attractive? Research suggests that there is. If female students are asked to judge the suitability of an attractive, average and unattractive man as a long-term partner in a lonely heart advertisement implying high, medium or low socio-economic status (SES), who do you think the women chose? If you said high-status, attractive men, you'd be wrong. If you'd said attractive men of medium status, you'd be right. Why? According to the authors (Chu *et al.*, 2007) the women regarded attractive, high-status men as pursuing a mating strategy (simply put, they were after sex), rather than a parenting strategy (wanting to settle down). High-status, attractive men would be far more likely to be the recipient of other women's attention (and, therefore, be at greatest risk of yielding to this attention). Women – well, UK undergraduates – it seems, don't want Mr Perfect, just Mr Almost Perfect.

Physically attractive men have also been found to increase financial risk-taking in other men (Chan, 2015). The reasoning behind this is that a man who is in competition with a more physically attractive man will attempt to increase his desirability by gambling more money with a view to gaining more money.

Women might also settle for Mr Average. In one study, women engaged in speed-dating were asked how important they thought a man's physical attractiveness and earning prospects were (Eastwick and Finkel, 2008). When asked to consider an ideal partner, these features were considered important. However, this preference did not predict their mate choice at the dating evening, neither did it predict their choice of real-life partners when the researchers contacted them after the study.

One theory of attractiveness (the topic of romantic attraction is considered further in Chapter 16) suggests that we choose a mate who is similar in attractiveness to ourselves (even if we prefer busty blondes or six-packed hunks). This is called the matching phenomenon (Walster *et al.*, 1966), but no model can explain this satisfactorily – is it because we are more anxious or insecure, or fear rejection or have low self-esteem? Some social psychologists argue that we view others through our own egotistical lens. 'The self provides the frame of reference from which all else is observed', state Combs and Snygg (1959). 'People are not really fat unless they are fatter than we'. This would suggest that our ratings of others' physical attractiveness is affected by our assessment of our own physical attractiveness (whether this view is shared by others or not).

Montoya (2008) found that participants' ratings of another person's attractiveness decreased with the increasing, objective, physical attractiveness of the rater. People rating themselves moderate in attractiveness paired themselves with people they thought were attractive. There is support for his finding. One study found that people rated their partners as being significantly more attractive than themselves – there was no difference between men or women (Swami *et al.*, 2009). People are also more likely to administer surveys to their peers if they have been paired with an attractive than unattractive individual and are more likely to administer surveys to older people if they are paired with unattractive people (Winegard *et al.*, 2013).

In terms of long-term satisfaction with their partners, the research regarding frequency of sex and relationship satisfaction is inconsistent but a recent three-year study of newlyweds found that there was a significant relationship between sex frequency and partner evaluations but not relationship satisfaction (Hicks *et al.*, 2016).

Monogamy: shared, but not always equal, parental investment

Around 3 per cent of the relationships in mammals are monogamous. Monogamy has evolved in those species whose environments have favoured the contributions of both parents to the survival and reproductive success of their offspring. In other words, under some conditions, two individuals sharing parental duties enjoy more reproductive success than does one individual who must do it all alone.

Although both parents in monogamous species share offspring-rearing duties, each parent may not make an equal contribution towards that end. Like females in polygynous species, females in monogamous species generally have greater parental investment in the offspring, for many of the same reasons: the limited opportunity for mating relative to that for males, pregnancy and its accompanying risks, providing milk to the newborns, and the time and energy spent in caring for them. As a result, very few monogamous species, including our own, are exclusively monogamous. In fact, there is a strong tendency in most monogamous species towards patterns of reproductive behaviour and parental investment that resemble those of polygynous species. For example, in monogamous species, females tend to be more careful than males in selecting a mate, and males tend to be more sexually promiscuous than females (Badcock, 1991).

Monogamy and hormones

Some scientists have hypothesised that monogamy may be attributable to chemicals called hormones, described in detail in the next chapter (Young *et al.*, 1998). These are generated by a region in the brain which sends signals to organs of the body to react in a certain way. The proposed relationship between hormones and monogamy has been based on studies

---

Cutting edge: Beards, high heels, lipstick, cash, cads and dancing – some influences on attraction

Recent studies from evolutionary psychology have suggested a number of physical and psychological features that people find more attractive than others in a partner. These are many and varied and include...

... beards

A study in which men and women rated the attractiveness, health, masculinity and ostensible parenting skills of men with no beard, stubble, heavy stubble or full beard found that women judged the heavily stubbled men to be more attractive but men found the heavily stubbed and fully bearded men the most attractive (Dixson and Brooks, 2013).

A full beard was regarded as signifying health and parenting ability. The greater the beard, the more masculine the rating, especially ratings given by women during the most fertile part of their cycle.

... high heels

They're not the best for your posture, but women are much more likely to wear high heels and wear them for a particular purpose: to increase sexual attraction and allure. To investigate whether the gait of a women in high-heels was rated as more feminine and attractive, Morris *et al.* (2013) used point-light technology to map out the walks of women who wore flat

Cutting edge: *Continued*

shoes or high heels. These points of light were separated from every other physical characteristic of the person. All the participant could see was moving points of light. The light points representing the woman wearing high-heels were judged to be significantly more attractive than those representing flat shoes. Femininity was also judged to be higher – stride length increased and as did the tilt and rotation of the hips.

... lipstick

Is there any relationship between economic good (or bad) fortune and tendency to spend on items to make us attractive? Hill *et al.* (2012) found that over 20 years, unemployment was associated with less spending on furniture, electronics and leisure/hobby items but also with more spending on cosmetics and clothes. In a series of studies to test whether this relationship stood in an experimental context, the researchers found that exposure to cues about recession was associated with a reduced tendency to spend on items unrelated to appearance (e.g. furniture), but a robust tendency to spend on cosmetics, especially lipstick. How do the researchers explain this? They suggest that in hard times, when there are fewer men with physical resources, women attempt to maximise their chances of attracting a resourceful partner by investing in cosmetics. They found this lipstick effect regardless of the women's SES and especially in those who wanted to attract a partner.

But how important is money to a partner? Jonason *et al.* (2012), in a series of three studies of 668 participants, found that men and women preferred a partner who was financially solvent and had earned their living. Women were particularly more interested in a partner who had earned their money rather than achieved it through inheritance or a windfall. Men were less concerned with how a woman earned her money in the short-term.

... dancing

Women do find men who are good dancers to be more attractive than are men who are bad dancers, and they also receive more visual attention (Weege *et al.*, 2012). Hendrie *et al.* (2009) conducted a study of 'sexual displays' in nightclubs. They monitored the behaviour of patrons to Majestyk nightclub in Leeds and noted that 80 per cent of those entering were without a partner and 'so were potentially sexually available'. There was a 50 per cent increase in the number of couples leaving than entering. Inside, 80 per cent of the approaches to dance were made by men towards women. Twenty percent wore tight-fitting clothes, and 40 per cent revealed parts of their body dancing '... in a sexually suggestive manner' These women attracted 49 per cent of all approaches by men.

... cads and dealbreakers

Durante *et al.* (2012) were interested in answering the question: what makes women attractive to highly unsuitable men – those who were charming and dominant but were not remotely interested in a long-term relationship? They found that ovulating women perceived attractive and charismatic men, but not nice and reliable men, as desirable and as more committed and even as better potential fathers. These women also regarded these men as being potentially good fathers to their own children, but not to the children of other women. The effect was particularly strong in women who had experienced early onset of puberty. The study suggests that what we had regarded as the costs of unsuitable suitors are not regarded as costs by women during ovulation.

A sybaritic and lubricious lifestyle is not usually regarded as a good predictor of long-term commitment but, according to Jonason *et al.* (2015), few studies have investigated directly what you might call dealbreakers (what to avoid in a potential partner) rather than dealmakers (what we find desirable). In a set of six studies involving 6,500 participants, the researchers found that such dealbreakers included undesirable personality traits, unhealthy sexual and romantic relationships, and dubious friendships. These were considered to be far more important when considering long-term relationships in men and women and more important to women in short-term relationships. People who were highly desirable (personally, physically, financially) were more likely to have more dealbreakers when considering a relationship. People who were less restrictive about their sexual behaviour, had fewer.

Men and women respond to strangers in different ways, especially if the strangers are responsive. Birnbaum *et al.* (2014) found that men regarded women who were responsive to be more feminine than those who did not respond. Men also found those women to be more sexually arousing (and more attractive and more likely to be seen as a potential partner). It does make you think twice about speaking to someone on the bus.

of a type of rodent, the vole. Researchers have found that two types of vole show very different patterns of mating: the prairie vole is largely monogamous, forming lasting partnerships; the montane vole, however, is promiscuous and not a particularly social species. The male montane vole is not parental and does not form a bond with its partner; the female montane vole abandons its offspring around two to three weeks after birth (Young *et al.*, 1998).

Psychology in action: The universality of attractive body types

In the developed world, physically attractive women are considered to be those with a low WHR. This ratio is achieved because more fat is deposited on the buttocks and hips than the waist; this, in turn, is the result of women having higher levels of oestrogen than testosterone (Singh, 1995). This apparent universal preference for women with low WHR would seem to bolster the sociobiologist's argument that mates are selected for their health and fitness. But is such a preference genuinely universal?

Yu and Shepard (1998) compared the body shape preferences of American men and men from the Matsigenka people in south-east Peru. The Matsigenka's culture is basically agrarian: they engage in slash and burn agriculture and supplement this food production with game and fruit gathered using traditional tools. None had been exposed to Western civilisation (no television, film, newspapers and so on). Whereas the Western sample predictably preferred those females with low WHR, the Matsigenka men preferred overweight females

and those with high WHR, rating these as the more attractive, healthy and more desirable as a spouse. In a similar study, Frank Marlowe and Adam Wetsman, two American anthropologists, found that whereas American men in their study preferred a low WHR and especially liked the intermediate image showing a WHR of 0.7, Hazda men, a group of hunter-gatherers who inhabit mixed savannah woodland in Tanzania, preferred a higher WHR (Marlowe and Wetsman, 2001).

British and Malaysian participants, however, are less enamoured of WHR (Swami and Tovee, 2005a). The researchers asked 682 participants to rate the photographs of real women. The study found that those who lived in urban areas preferred lower BMIs than did those living in the country, perhaps reflecting the greater exposure of urbanites to slimmer women. People who lived in urban areas also preferred men with low WCR (BMI or WHR were not good predictors) (Swami and Tovee, 2005b). In rural areas, however, BMI was the primary predictor of attractiveness. Urban raters preferred a men

Source: Simon Wilkinson/The Image Bank/Getty Images.

Source: SIE Productions/Corbis/Getty Images.

Psychology in action: *Continued*

with an 'inverted triangle' shaped torso, whereas rural raters preferred heavier men with a less triangular shape. Swami and colleagues have also reported an interaction between WHR and breast size. South African men preferred high-WHR black figures with large breasts and high-WHR white figures with small breasts, whereas white British men and British Africans preferred high-WHR black figures with small breasts and high-WHR white figures with large breasts (Swami *et al.*, 2009).

A cross-cultural study of WHR preference in participants from Africa, Indonesia, Samoa and New Zealand has confirmed the universal trend: participants rated women low in WHR as being more attractive (even when BMI was controlled for) (Singh *et al.*, 2010). One study has even extended this preference to the blind. Researchers from the USA and the Netherlands asked 19 men who had been blind since birth to rate their preference for the body shape of mannequins whose WHR could be manipulated (Karremans *et al.*, 2010). The men did this by touch. They preferred figures with a low WHR. When sighted men performed the same task, the same effect was found but the preference was stronger.

Finally, one of the largest studies of its kind examined female body preferences of 7,434 respondents from 26 countries, grouped into 10 regions drawn from North America, South America, Western Europe, Eastern Europe, Scandinavia, Oceania (Australia, New Zealand), Southeast Asia, East Asia,

South and West Asia and Africa (Swami *et al.*, 2010). Respondents from Eastern Europe, Scandinavia and Western Europe preferred heavier figures. There were significant differences between rural and urban sites in Malaysia and South Africa. The ideal body weight was heavier in societies that were less socially and economically developed.

Apart from East Asian men, other men chose a heavier figure as their preferred shape than did women, thereby highlighting a disparity about what women perceive as the ideal body shape preferred by men and men's own actual preference. 'Such misinterpretation of men's standards of bodily attractiveness on the part of women', Swami *et al.* conclude, 'may be near universal in contexts of high SES' (p. 320). One reason for the disparity may be that the media to which men are exposed feature curvier women whereas women's media idealise the thin.

American women expressed greater body dissatisfaction than women from any other region. At another level, individuals of low SES in Malaysia and South Africa also expressed low levels of body satisfaction. A correlation was found between exposure to Western media and preference for a thinner body type.

While a low WHR is considered the more appealing body shape in a large part of the world, even when controlling for weight, there are specific cultures and nations – although not many – which express a different preference.

Two key hormones have been identified that could underpin these behaviours: oxytocin (OT) and vasopressin (AVP). In prairie voles, vaginal–cervical copulation leads to an increase in the release of OT. This release may promote intense mating in females but has little effect on males. AVP, however, does affect male prairie voles. Administering this hormone in these male voles leads to a preference for an exclusive partner, aggression towards strangers and an increase in paternal care (Young *et al.*, 1998). In the montane male vole, the effect of the hormones is not aggression but self-grooming. The receptor distribution for these hormones in the brain of the prairie vole is similar to that in other monogamous types of vole; conversely, the distribution of receptors in montane voles is similar to other promiscuous vole types.

Some research has found that when people are exposed to oxytocin, their caring behaviour, parental bonding and trust increase. For example, intranasal administration of the chemical has been found to increase maintained eye contact during relationship conflict resolution (Ditzen *et al.*, 2009), sensitivity to others' feelings (Hurleman *et al.*, 2010), generosity (Barraza and Zak, 2009) and result in judgements of faces presented on a computer monitor to be more trustworthy and friendly, compared with those who did not

receive the hormone (Theodoridou *et al.*, 2009). A meta-analysis of brain imaging studies of the effect of oxytocin on social and emotional processing found greater activation in the left insula during these types of processing which might suggest that the effect of oxytocin is modulated via this brain region (Wigton *et al.*, 2014).

However, recent research has begun to cast doubt on the reliability and validity of some of the behavioural findings and two lines of evidence has contributed to the controversy: an analysis of the composition of the chemical used in these studies, and the results of studies reporting a failure to replicate positive findings. The CiPS section below considers the evidence.

Infidelity

For various evolutionary reasons, evolutionary psychologists suggest that men and women respond differently to different types of infidelity. Heterosexual men, for example, are more likely to show jealousy in response to sexual infidelity (a partner having sex with another man), whereas heterosexual women are more likely to show jealousy in response to emotional infidelity (a partner having a very deep, loving, yet non-sexual, relationship with another woman). A study in which male and female undergraduates were asked whether they would forgive the two types of infidelity in their partner conformed to the expected pattern and found that men were less likely to forgive sexual than emotional infidelity whereas women showed the opposite pattern (Shackelford *et al.*, 2002). Men were also more likely to terminate a relationship if their partner committed sexual infidelity.

Harris (2002) asked participants whether they would be more upset if they found out that their partner was trying

Controversies in psychological science: Does women's preference for different types of men change across the menstrual cycle?

The issue

A large number of studies has claimed that women's preference for certain types of men changes depending on the stage of the menstrual cycle. The first half of the cycle is called the follicular stage and starts with menstruation where levels of the hormones oestrogen and progesterone are low. These levels rise until the second half of the cycle is reached, the luteal stage (you'll find more on these hormones in Chapter 13). In two well-known, and landmark studies, Penton-Voak *et al.* (1999) and Penton-Voak and Perrett (2000) found that women in the most fertile part of their cycle were significantly more likely to prefer a masculine and symmetrical face than were women in their least fertile part. A meta-analysis by Gildersleeve *et al.* (2014) concludes that there are significant and reliable changes in preference for men across the menstrual cycle. But is the evidence really that clear?

The evidence

Gangestad *et al.* (2004) found that women during the high-fertility portion of their menstrual cycle were more attracted to men who showed social presence (composure, having an athletic presence, maintaining eye contact, lack of self-deprecation, lack of downward gaze and 'lack of nice-guy self-presentation') and 'intrasexual competitiveness' – behaviours that derogated competitors, lacked laughter and were directly sexually competitive. This preference only emerged when women wished for short-term rather than long-term relationships, suggesting that a man's demeanour can significantly alter perceived attractiveness by women high in fertility, but that this attraction may be short-lived.

One explanation for these and similar findings is that during the fertile phase of the cycle, women are more likely to seek a sexual partner (and, potentially, a father for their child) who shows evidence of 'genetic benefits' (strength, assertiveness, etc.). This explanation is based on limited experimental data, however, and more direct behaviour – such as the interaction between men and women – has not been studied.

Although very masculine male faces are judged to be dominant, their owners are less likely to be judged suitable as a long-term partner by women than are owners of less masculine faces (Boothroyd *et al.*, 2007). Women at their most fertile preferred more symmetrical faces but this preference was found only when the women were seeking a short-term partner or if the women already had a partner (Little *et al.*, 2007), replicating Gangestad *et al.*'s finding. The results suggest that this facial feature may maximise

mating by encouraging short-term relationships. Symmetrical faces are usually judged to be more attractive than asymmetrical ones and there is evidence that facial symmetry in men and women is associated with perceived healthiness (Rhodes *et al.*, 2007) and self-reported extraversion (Pound *et al.*, 2007).

Haselton *et al.* (2007) asked men and women to judge the attractiveness of partnered women who were in the luteal or follicular stage of their cycle. More women in the follicular stage were judged as 'trying to look more attractive'. The closer the women were to ovulation (when the photograph was taken), the more likely the photograph was chosen as attractive. These women were judged to wear more fashionable clothes, nicer clothes and show more upper body skin. In another study, women were asked to report to a laboratory on high – or low-fertility days (confirmed by a hormone test) and to pose for photographs and draw an outfit that they would prefer to wear that evening (Durante *et al.*, 2008). They were more likely to sketch sexier and more revealing outfits during the high-fertility period – as Figure 3.7 shows. The more sexually experienced the woman, the skimpier the outfit. Single women drew more revealing outfits than those who had partners but the more satisfied the women were with their partners, the more revealing the outfit they drew (suggesting that they were confident to express their sexuality in the context of a secure relationship).

As the most fertile part of a woman's cycle occurs in the middle and lasts a few days near ovulation, it may be important to maximise sexual behaviour (and attract a mate) during this period. Does this period influence men's behaviour towards women? And, if so, why might this be? Miller and Maner (2011a) set up three experiments in which men's responses to women appeared to be influenced by the woman's point in her cycle. In one experiment, they found that men who smelled a T-shirt of an ovulating woman were more likely to think about sex-related words than when smelling a T-shirt when the woman was at another part of her cycle. In a second experiment, the researchers found that men who were highly sensitive to odour and asked to indicate how emotional a woman whose T-shirt they smelled was, they were more likely to show enhanced judgements of the women's degree of arousal. In a final study, they paired men with a confederate who was highly fertile (or not) and observed the social interaction and the risk-taking (performance on a game of blackjack) that followed. Men exposed to the fertile confederate were more likely to mimic the behaviour of the confederate and to engage in riskier behaviour, as measured by the gambling task.

Despite findings such as these, there are some serious and generic problems with these studies and many of these issues and

Controversies in psychological science: *Continued*

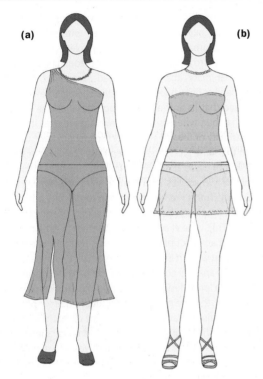

Figure 3.7 Example of an outfit illustration drawn by the same participant at low fertility **(a)** and high fertility **(b)**.

Source: Durante. K.M., Li, N.P. and Haselton, M.G. (2008) Changes in women's choice of dress across the ovulatory cycle: Naturalistic and laboratory taskbased evidence. *Personality and Social Psychology Bulletin* 34 (11), 1451–60.

criticisms were raised by Harris *et al.* (2013). For example, not all studies find an effect of menstrual cycle on women's preference for men and one meta-analysis has found no increased preference for masculinity in men when women were at different points on the cycle (Wood *et al.*, 2014). Harris *et al.* note that there is great inconsistency in the way that studies calculate fertile and non-fertile days, and these differences could influence the results. Some studies use forward calculation – ovulation is calculated by counting from the first day of the cycle. Others use backward counting – the days are counted backwards from the actual day of the next period. Their analysis finds that the approach varies – the recommendation by those purporting to find a cycle difference in male preference that backward counting is the best method is often violated by the same group. There is also inconsistency in the calculation of the number of days considered as fertile.

Harris *et al.* also point out that significant effects, when they occur, are attributable to moderators. These moderators are usually some sub-sample of the group (the effect does not occur for the group or condition as a whole, only one type of group or part of a condition, e.g. a masculine preference is found for women wanting short-term relationships not long-term ones). They take Penton-Voak *et al.* to task for finding in one study that attraction changed across the menstrual cycle and in a second that the effect was found when a woman judged the man's suitability for a short-term relationship but not a long-term relationship. They took the authors to task because this moderator isn't considered in a number of Penton-Voak *et al.*'s subsequent papers. Relationship status is considered in some studies but not in others, despite some authors discovering that relationship status is an important variable.

Conclusion

These objections render any conclusion about the reliability of the make mate preference finding literature a challenge. One meta-analysis finds a relationship, another does not. Currently, we can't conclude with any certainty that a woman's preference for more masculine men is more common during the fertile period.

In a paper in press, Jones et al conducted a longitudinal study of women's preference for men's faces and examined the relationship between this preference and women's hormone status. They found that women preferred masculine to feminine faces -especially when the women rated men's attractivess for short-term relationships- but that there was no relationship between hormone status and preference for masculine faces. The study included 584 women.

different sexual positions with another person or if their partner was falling in love with another. Some 196 participants, with a **mean** age of 37, were recruited via newspaper advertisements and flyers. Harris was also interested in whether responses would be similar in homosexual and heterosexual men and women and so recruited roughly equal numbers of each. Participants were asked if they had been 'cheated' on, whether they focused on the emotional or sexual consequences of the cheating and whether the relationship ended as a result.

As predicted by evolutionary psychology, heterosexual men were more likely to find sexual infidelity more upsetting than they would emotional infidelity when responding to the forced-choice question. The reverse pattern was found for women. When participants recalled actual examples of infidelity, however, no sex differences were found. Regardless of sexual orientation, both men and women were more likely to focus on a partner's emotional than sexual infidelity as the source of distress. No relationship was found between participants' responses to hypothetical and actual infidelity.

People who are married to disagreeable, undependable and emotionally unstable partners are less satisfied with their marriage (Shackelford and Buss, 2000). Low agreeableness, low emotional stability and low conscientiousness in women is associated with low marital satisfaction in men. Disagreeable, emotionally unstable men are also more likely to abuse their

Controversies in psychological science: Oxytocin and trustworthiness

The issue

In 2005, Kosfeld *et al.* published an intriguing finding in the journal, *Nature*. They were interested in trust, and oxytocin's effect of trust, and set up an experiment to determine whether people exposed to the hormone were more likely to find someone else trustworthy. In their experiment, participants played a Trust Game in which they were investors who transferred money to another person (a trustee) who might help triple the investment but who may or may not return all of the money to the investor. People who received intranasal oxytocin were more likely to trust the trustee than were those who received a placebo (a sham, inert chemical).

Does inhaling oxytocin really increase our sense of trustworthiness in others?

The evidence

A variant of Kosfeld *et al.*'s study found a similar result: people who had been betrayed by one individual were more likely to retain their trust in others if they had received oxytocin compared with those who had not (Baumgartner *et al.*, 2008). Both of these studies involved some financial element and so the effects may be specific to trustworthiness concerning material goods. Partly addressing this issue, Mikolajczak *et al.* (2010) found the same effect of oxytocin but in an experiment where people had to keep information confidential. In their study, participants were asked to complete a questionnaire with very personal and intimate detail about themselves (e.g. their sexual preferences) and then insert it in an envelope which would be passed to someone else. They were given the option of closing the envelope and sealing it with tape (or not). Trustful people did not seal nor close.

Since then oxytocin has been found to enhance social support, empathy and affiliation but also increase envy and gloating, conformity and defensiveness towards people who are not like us (Bethlehem *et al.*, 2014). Chen *et al.* (2014) found that heterosexual German men who received intranasal oxytocin liked 'strong'-looking men more than did men who received a placebo. Oxytocin had no effect on the ratings of a 'weak'-looking man (although the visual stimuli in this experiment were not equivalent – see figure one in their paper which did not seem to control for posture). Oxytocin was found to influence activation in various brain regions – specifically increase it – when autistic adolescents (mainly boys) were making social judgements (Gordon *et al.*,

2013). However, this study had no control group. Other studies suggested that oxytocin was associated with ascribing more meaning to inanimate objects and that people receiving oxytocin were more likely to include photographs of touching objects (animate and inanimate) in an album (Peled-Avron *et al.*, 2016). Various explanations have been cited for the chemical's effect – some have argued that its anti-anxiety properties increase pro-social, pliant behaviour, whereas others have argued that it increases social sensitivity or reward sensitivity (Bethlehem *et al.*, 2014).

When the same group tried to replicate Kosfeld *et al.*'s finding, they could not (Lane *et al.*, 2015). In fact, they failed to replicate the effect in two studies with sample sizes very similar to their original study. This is not an uncommon result: Two other studies have failed to replicate Kosfeld *et al.*'s findings (Klackl *et al.*, 2013; Yao *et al.*, 2014). Lane *et al.* suggest a number of reasons for their failure to find an effect of oxytocin including that the effect does not exist or that when it is seen, it is very small (Walum *et al.*, 2015). Walum *et al.*'s analysis concludes, on the basis of the analysis of statistical data provided by all behavioural studies of oxytocin administration, that the majority of positive findings reports in the literature are false. A review of the role of oxytocin in trust also concludes that the finding that intranasal administration increases trust is inconsistent and is not replicated well (Nave *et al.*, 2015). It also concludes that there have been serious errors in the way that oxytocin is measured.

The last finding is consistent with others reviews demonstrating that the way in which oxytocin is administered in these studies flawed (McCullough *et al.*, 2013; Leng and Ludwig, 2015) and that the doses of the hormone used in behavioural studies are insufficient to deliver enough oxytocin to the brain. In addition, they suggest that oxytocin may even have the opposite effect to trust, citing a study in which betrayed women who received oxytocin showed less trust (Yao *et al.*, 2014).

Conclusion

What began as a promising field of inquiry very quickly turned into a quagmire of disappointment. The overall evidence for the effect of oxytocin on behaviours such as trust is not strong. But what the studies of the past five years have demonstrated is the value and importance of replication, as you saw in Chapter 1. A positive and very dramatic effect can be genuine: but it will only be demonstrably genuine if others perform the same study and find the same results.

wives than their agreeable, emotionally stable counterparts. Furthermore, mate-guarding tactics such as threatening infidelity, threatening to punish infidelity and emotional manipulation (i.e. the factors which inflict costs on a relationship) are associated with lower marital satisfaction in the people at the receiving end of these tactics.

What makes a person poach or steal another's partner? One study found that 84 per cent of undergraduates reported that attempts had been made to poach them from their partners (Schmitt and Buss, 2001). Of those who were romantically linked (just over 55 per cent), 20 per cent of men and 28 per cent of women stated that their partners had been poached from

Cutting edge: Kisspeptin and sexual arousal

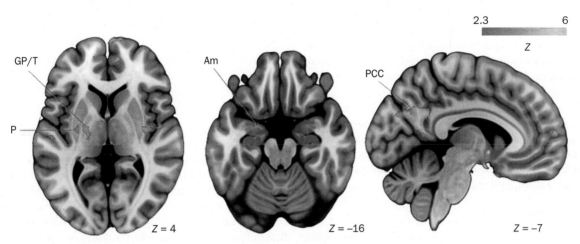

Figure 3.8 These fMRI images show the effect of kisspeptin on brain activation when participants watched sexual images. GP = globus pallidus; Am = amygdala; PCC = posterior cingulate cortex.

While the research investigating the effect of oxytocin continues, a new study suggests that another hormone called kisspeptin may be involved in sexual arousal. Kisspeptin is a recently discovered reproductive hormone which has been found in the limbic system of rodents and humans. Comninos *et al.* (2017) examined the effect of intravenous kisspeptin on sexual arousal in 29 healthy heterosexual men. First, they found increases in kisspeptin following administration which confirmed that its levels were higher following administration. Second, when the men who had received kisspeptin saw sexual images, there was an increase in activation in the limbic system, especially in the anterior and posterior cingulate and left amygdala. The greater the activation in the limbic system during kisspeptin administration, the less likely the men were to be averse to sex. Similar limbic system increases were found when the men saw images of couples bonding in a non-sexual way. Kisspeptin was not associated with increases in the limbic system when the men saw happy, neutral or fearful-themed images. The study is based on the responses of 29 men. It would be useful to replicate this in a larger sample and one that includes women. You can see the changes illustrated in Figure 3.8.

someone else. In terms of personality, agreeable and conscientious people were least likely to be mate poachers, a finding that is found internationally (Schmitt, 2004).

Those who did not regard relationships as exclusive and described themselves as having erotophilic tendencies – a constant desire to satisfy sexual needs – were more likely to poach. These individuals also scored high on sexual attractiveness: it appears that the poacher may have to be sexy, as well as adulterous. Extraverts were more likely than introverts to be recipients of poaching attempts. Those who rated themselves as sexually attractive, as not relationship exclusive and as emotionally investing (loving) were those who were most likely to be poached.

Physical attractiveness was more important for men than it was for women. Women, conversely, were more likely to view resource acquisition as a benefit of poaching, especially in short-term relationships. Because men value physical attractiveness in women, women pay greater attention to using physical characteristics as cues to attraction. Women, on the other hand, placed greater value on resources. Men, consequently, emphasised cues that indicate that they were resource-laden (such as having expensive clothes, cars, jewellery and so on). For women, a strategy aimed at making themselves more attractive by disparaging the partner of the person they wanted to poach was not as effective as one based on enhancing their own physical attractiveness.

As predicted, men were found to be more successful than women at poaching when they displayed resources and were more effective at using humour as a poaching cue than were women in the short and long term. Women employed a tactic that was significantly more effective when used by them than by men: boosting the partner's ego.

Davies and Shackelford (2015, 2017) found, in a study of undergraduates, that participants were more likely to be poached if the poacher was wealthier and more attractive than the partner whom they were dating, living with or were married to. The more committed to the relationship the person was, the more attractive and wealthier the poacher had to be. Another study found that people who were more likely to enjoy short-term relationships also had lower levels of sexual disgust (Al-Shawa *et al.*, 2015).

Mate-poaching might have neural correlates. Ueda *et al.* (2016) asked 33 Japanese men to look at photographs of attractive women who had a partner, attractive women who didn't have a partner, unattractive women who had a partner and unattractive women who did not have a partner. A neuro-imaging technique recorded brain activation while participants made judgments about how likely they were to want a romantic relationship with the woman.

Men were more likely to want a romantic relationship with an attractive woman than an unattractive one (no surprise there) – and this decision was associated with activity in a part of the brain known as the ventral striatum. They also found the women with a partner to be romantically less desirable and this decision was associated with activation in the parietal lobe. Men who showed greatest activation in the tip of the front part of the brain called the orbitofrontal cortex (OFC) were more likely to indicate that they would like to engage in a romantic relationship with a woman who had a partner. The

researchers conclude that 'the OFC is a critical region that reflects individual differences in mate poaching, with those showing higher OFC activity assigning increased value to a female with a partner.' (p. 7). In 33 Japanese men, of course.

Jealousy

Jealousy has been defined as 'when individuals perceive a threat to their relationship because of an actual or imagined rival' (Massar and Buunk, 2010, p. 634). Although romantic jealousy seems more common in men than women, the sexes may also differ in what they become jealous about. Men are more likely to be jealous, angry and upset about sexual infidelity, whereas women are more likely to be upset by emotional infidelity, such as their partner engaging in a warm and fulfilling friendship with another woman (Sagarin *et al.*, 2012). Sex differences in jealousy have been reported worldwide and in countries such as Germany, Korea, The Netherlands, Japan, Brazil, Romania, the UK, the US, Norway, Spain and others (Buss, 2013).

Infidelity – An international perspective

Evolutionary psychologists argue that the nature and degree of mate poaching/poachers should be similar across cultures but with some provisos. Studies show that men are more likely than women to engage in short-term mate poaching and so we might expect this finding across cultures.

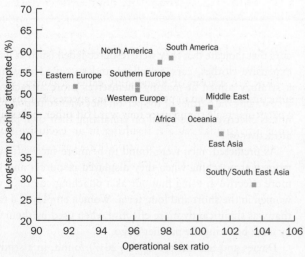

Figure 3.9 The degree of mate-poaching across nations and cultures. Europeans and Americans seem especially keen on it.

Source: D.P. Schmitt, Patterns and universals of mate poaching across 53 nations: The effects of sex, culture and personality on romantically attracting another person's partner, *Journal of Personality and Social Psychology*, 2004, 86 (4), 560–84, Figure 2.

In a study of 16,954 individuals from 53 nations, divided into 10 world regions (North America, South America, Western Europe, Eastern Europe, Southern Europe, the Middle East, Africa, Oceania, South/Southeast Asia and East Asia) mate poaching overall was very common – 70 per cent reported that they had been the object of a poaching attempt (Schmitt *et al.*, 2004). Eighty per cent of poaching attempts were apparently successful with 10 per cent of such attempts leading to a long-term relationship. Mate poaching was most common in Southern Europe, South America and Western Europe and was least common in Africa, South/Southeast Asia and East Asia, a finding that is consistent with the prediction regarding demanding environments. The number of attempts at mate poaching by members of various cultures can be seen in Figure 3.9.

Men were more vigorous mate poachers than were women, with 60 per cent of men reporting that they had attempted to mate poach and 40 per cent of women reporting so. In cultures where men and women were regarded as equals, this sex difference was smaller.

In keeping with previous studies discussed in this chapter, the personality measures showed that poachers were extraverted, disagreeable, unconscientious, slightly narcissistic and (no surprise here) unfaithful. The poached were likely to be extraverted, open, attractive and disagreeable. Both groups were likely to be highly sexual.

Of course, most of the study's participants were young undergraduates and the authors note that mate poaching may be more common in this younger group than it would be in an older sample.

Some researchers have suggested that these differences might have a neural basis. Takahashi *et al.* (2006), for example, asked men and women to think about jealousy-arousing sentences such as 'My girlfriend stayed in a double-bed room in a hotel with her ex-boyfriend' and 'My girlfriend had her underwear taken off by another man' (sexual jealousy items) or 'My girlfriend wrote a love letter to another man' and 'My girlfriend gave gorgeous birthday presents to her ex-boyfriend' (emotional jealousy items) as well as neutral statements about their partner. The groups did not differ significantly in terms of the types of infidelity they felt jealous about – both sexes became equally jealous under both conditions (emotional or sexual infidelity). However, brain activation did differ by sex.

Men showed greater activation in the amygdala during sexual jealousy and in the hypothalamus during emotional infidelity. These are structures involved in sexuality and reproduction, among other functions. Women showed greater activation in the posterior superior temporal sulcus (STS), an area the authors suggest is implicated in 'the detection of others' intention or violation of social norms'.

Is it easy to induce jealousy? Massar and Buunk (2010) exposed 40 young women to photographs of attractive or unattractive women for 60 ms. They then asked them to rate how jealous they felt when told to imagine placing themselves in a scenario designed to elicit jealousy (a rival being introduced to their partner). The researchers found that women who were exposed to attractive women reported significantly more jealousy than did those exposed to the unattractive ones, suggesting that jealousy may be primed or elicited unconsciously.

Promiscuity

Promiscuity – the tendency to engage in sexual activity with multiple partners (not necessarily at the same time) – has been associated with specific personality types. Sensation-seekers, for example, have more partners than low sensation-seekers; and the unconscientious, extravert, the less agreeable and more antagonistic similarly report having more sexual partners than the conscientious, the less extravert and the more agreeable/less antagonistic. In a study of 105 young men and 105 young women, people who were dominant had significantly more sexual partners than did those who were less so (Markey and Markey, 2007). Curiously, people who were personally warm were also more likely to have had more sexual partners than the less warm.

A related study examined whether men who engaged in unrestricted sexual activity – engaging in transient sexual relations – perceived women's attractiveness differently from men who were more restricted (Swami *et al.*, 2008). Men self-described as restricted or unrestricted rated the attractiveness of drawings of women who differed according to BMI and WHR. The men, regardless of type, used BMI rather than WHR as the basis of their judgement but unrestricted men found women with lower BMI to be more attractive and healthy than did restricted men. The unrestricted men also preferred women with a low WHR.

Polyandry: high male and low female parental investment

Polyandry is a rare reproductive strategy among humans and non-existent in other mammals. It is more prevalent among species that lay eggs. Once the eggs are laid, then either the male or the female may take care of them, although in many instances the male makes the greater investment of time and effort.

An example of polyandry in humans is found among some of the people who live in remote Himalayan villages. These people are extremely poor and live in a harsh environment, which makes their primary livelihood, farming, difficult. In order to prevent the dissolution of family farms through marriage, families that have more than one son limit the number of marriages to only one per generation – several brothers may share the same wife. A female tends to marry more than one man (most often brothers) to guarantee that she will be adequately supported. In other words, the male's primary investment – the farm, which is the source of food and some income for the family – is guarded jealously through polyandry.

Polygynandry: group parental investment

Many primates, such as chimpanzees, live in colonies in which few or no barriers are placed on which female mates with which male. In other words, the colonies are promiscuous – during periods of mating, intercourse is frequent and indiscriminate. What is the advantage of such a reproductive strategy?

The primary advantage seems to be the cooperation of males and females in the colony with respect to rearing offspring. Because the males in the colony are not sure which offspring belong to them, it is in their best interest to help rear and protect all the offspring and defend their mothers. The unity in the colony and the lack of aggression among the males contributes directly to the general welfare of all colony members. Females and males have access to many mates, and the offspring are well cared for.

However, a form of monogamy called a consortship is sometimes observed in polygynandrous species. For instance, a particular male chimpanzee may ward off other male suitors from a particular female, resulting in an exclusive sexual union. If successful, he is guaranteed the certainty of which offspring are his, albeit at some cost. There is a chance that he could be seriously injured in protecting his mate from other males, and therefore he becomes less useful as a parental investor in his offspring or those of the colony.

Altruism and kin selection

A particularly interesting and important social behaviour in terms of evolution is **altruism,** the unselfish concern of one individual for the welfare of another. Examples of altruistic behaviour abound and its most extreme form is when one person risks their life to save the life of another. Examples of altruism are also common throughout the animal kingdom.

The honey bee, for example, sacrifices its life on behalf of its hivemates by stinging an intruder. Here, the altruist's chances of survival and reproductive success are lowered while those of the other individuals are raised.

Sociobiologists seek out ultimate causes, especially the consequences of natural selection, to explain altruism. They assert that natural selection has favoured the evolution of organisms that show altruistic tendencies. However, there is an important problem here. On the surface, altruism poses an enigma to evolutionary theory. Recall that according to natural selection only phenotypes that enhance one's reproductive success are favoured. How could altruistic behaviour have evolved given that, by definition, it is less adaptive than selfish or competitive behaviour?

The geneticist William D. Hamilton (1964, 1970) suggested an answer to this question in a series of mathematical papers. Hamilton's ideas stemmed from examining natural selection from the perspective of the gene instead of from the perspective of the whole, living organism. He argued that natural selection does not favour mere reproductive success but rather **inclusive fitness**, or the reproductive success of those individuals who share many of the same genes. Altruistic acts are generally aimed at close relatives such as parents, siblings, grandparents and grandchildren. The closer the family relation is, the more likely the genetic similarity among the individuals involved. Such biological favouritism towards relatives is called **kin selection** (Maynard Smith, 1964).

The message here is clear: under the proper circumstances, individuals behave altruistically towards others with whom they share a genetic history, with the willingness to do so decreasing as the relative becomes more distant. In this view, altruism is not necessarily a conscious act but rather an act driven by a biological prompt that has been favoured by natural selection. Natural selection would favour this kind of altruism simply because organisms who share genes also help each other to survive.

Parenting is a special case of kin selection and an important contributor to one's survival and reproductive success. In the short run, parents' altruistic actions promote the continued survival of their offspring. In the long run, these actions increase the likelihood that the offspring, too, will become parents and that their genes will survive in successive generations. Such cycles continue according to biological schedule, generation after generation. In the words of sociobiologist, David Barash:

It is obvious why genes for parenting have been selected: all living things are the offspring of parents who themselves were [the offspring of] parents! It is a guaranteed, unbroken line stretching back into time. [Genes] that inclined their bearers to be less successful parents left fewer copies of themselves than did those [genes] that were more successful.

(Source: Barash, 1982, pp. 69–70.)

What is at stake is not the survival of individual organisms but the survival of the genes carried by those organisms. Genes allow organisms to maximise their inclusive fitness through altruistic behaviour directed at other organisms sharing the same genes (Dawkins, 1986). Inclusive fitness refers to the idea that reproduction and natural selection occurs because an individual's success is measured through the production of offspring. You carry copies of genes that have been in your family line for thousands of years. When the opportunity presents itself, you will most likely carry on the tradition – reproducing and thus projecting your biological endowment into yet another generation. But you did not reach sexual maturity on your own; the concern for your welfare by your parents, brothers, sisters, grandparents and perhaps an aunt or uncle has contributed to your chances of being reproductively successful. Genes not projected into the next generation simply disappear.

Another variable may mediate altruism, however: emotional closeness. Emotional closeness is defined as having a sense of concern and caring for another and enjoying a comforting, emotional relationship with them. One study asked participants to rate how willing they would be to behave altruistically towards members of their family when the family member could live or die, and when helping would be at a cost to the participant (Korchmaros and Kenny, 2001). Participants also indicated how emotionally close they were to these family members.

People were more likely to help family members with whom they shared a close relationship, regardless of the genetic closeness of the relationship, than with those with whom they shared a less close relationship. The findings suggest that emotional closeness may be a mediating cause of altruistic behaviour.

Evidence from step-relations' behaviour supports the idea of inclusive fitness. It has been reported, for example, that a disproportionate number of children in stepfamilies suffer physical harm, especially assault (Daly and Wilson, 1988). Child battering is more common in stepfamilies, as is the incidence of child abuse (Daly and Wilson, 1996). This evidence, the sociobiologists argue, supports the notion than non-genetic relatives are not disposed to invest resources in offspring that are genetically unrelated.

There is also evidence to suggest that cohabitation is a greater risk factor for spousal murder than is marriage. Canadian research published at the beginning of the 1990s suggested that women in cohabiting relationships were more likely than married women to be murdered by their partner (Wilson *et al.*, 1993, 1995). Data from specific US cities show the same pattern (e.g. Wilbanks, 1984). According to the Wilson *et al.* studies, women in their early twenties were at greater risk of homicide if they were married; for cohabiting women, women in their mid-thirties to forties were at greatest risk. A national study of over 400,000 US homicides committed between 1976 and 1994 found that women in cohabiting relationships were nine times more likely than married women to be murdered by their partner (Shackelford, 2001). The risk for married women decreased as they became older. Middle-aged women, however, were at greatest risk if they were in a cohabiting relationship. Young men were more likely to murder their wives whereas middle-aged men were more likely to murder their cohabiting partners.

One explanation for these findings is that men may tend to feel significantly and abnormally proprietorial about their partners, especially about their partner's sexuality. A man in a cohabiting relationship is more insecure than is a married man because the possibility of either partner leaving the relationship is more likely and is easier to do. The cohabiting man may, therefore, go to more extreme lengths to prevent his partner from leaving him than would a married man because cohabiting relationships are more likely to break down than are marriages. There is some evidence in support of this interpretation. Daly and Wilson (1988), for example, cite their partner data showing that men who kill their partners are more likely to do so because they suspect that their partner has been unfaithful or may be about to terminate their relationship.

Reciprocal altruism

Kin selection explains altruism towards relatives, but what about altruism directed towards non-relatives? According to Trivers (1971), this kind of altruism, called **reciprocal altruism**, exists because humans (and other organisms) can function more effectively if they work together. Human groups are hierarchical and cooperative (Buss, 1995), whether at the level of the family, canoe club or workplace. There is also evidence that kindness, dependability, emotional stability and intelligence (all traits one would associate with altruism) are the most valued personality characteristics in potential mates (Buss, 1995). Cooperation between groups is a fundamental survival strategy (Brewer and Caporael, 1990), and is seen in many higher primates (Byrne, 1995). For example, in order to win a mate from a dominant male savannah baboon, a male will engage the help of another baboon who will distract the dominant male and enter into a fight with him. This leaves the other, non-dominant male free to mate with the female. The altruism is reciprocal because the favour will be reciprocated by the successfully paired male in the future (Haufstater, cited in Byrne, 1995).

Sociobiology and evolutionary psychology as an explanation for human behaviour

So far in this chapter you have seen that sociobiologists attempt to explain social behaviour by reference to natural selection and genetic inheritance but it has been at the centre of a fierce scientific controversy ever since E.O. Wilson published *Sociobiology: The new synthesis* in 1975, the official birth date of the discipline. Wilson's *On Human Nature* (1978), which extended sociobiological theory to human affairs, ignited even more criticism. Most of the criticism focuses on the extension of the theory to human behaviour. Two issues which have caused greatest controversy are inclusive fitness and the mechanisms of adaptation.

Recall that inclusive fitness theory argues that reproduction and natural selection occur because an individual's reproductive success is measured through the production of offspring. Those characteristics which help promote the transmission of genes (either directly or indirectly) will be naturally selected, akin to Dawkins's sieve mentioned at the beginning of the chapter. Sociobiologists see humans as 'fitness maximisers', or 'fitness strivers' (Alexander, 1979), constantly applying the mechanisms for maximising inclusive fitness. The evolutionary psychologists, however, call this the 'sociobiological fallacy' (Buss, 1991, 1995) because it confuses the theory of origins of mechanisms with the theory of the nature of mechanisms. As Buss argues, if humans were 'fitness maximising blobs', why are men not queuing up at sperm banks to donate their sperm? Why do some couples forgo reproduction? We have developed a preference for fatty foods but this is known to be detrimental to us. If we know this food is unhealthy, why do we eat it? More to the point, we can look at individuals or their behaviour and easily find maximising fitness reasons for this behaviour. The inclusive fitness theory, therefore, cannot account for natural selection and, because of its breadth (one can interpret almost any behaviour in terms of maximising fitness), is virtually limitless in its application.

Instead of seeing humans as fitness maximisers, evolutionary psychologists see humans as 'adaptation executors' or 'mechanism activators' (Tooby and Cosmides, 1990). That is, humans apply evolved solutions to adaptive problems (Buss, 1995). These solutions are domain-specific. That is, the types of solution one would need to reach to select a mate are different from those one needs to obtain food or to parent children. Adaptive problems are large, complex and varied; the success of individuals in solving these problems depends on sex, species, age, context and individual circumstances (Buss *et al.*, 1998). Sociobiology, however, seems to ignore this psychological level of interpretation and goes from evolution straight to patterns of social organisation.

The most intense criticism of sociobiology is political, not scientific. Opponents argue that sociobiology sanctions the superiority of one group over another, be it a race, a gender or a political organisation. After all, they argue, if one group of individuals is genetically superior to another, then there are 'natural' grounds for justifying the 'survival of the fittest' and one group's unethical and immoral domination of another. An example is Hitler's quest for world domination in the name of Aryan superiority. Sociobiologists flatly deny such allegations and argue that it is the critics and not they who have confused the term 'natural' with the terms 'good' and 'superior'. Are political objections to sociobiology scientifically acceptable ones? Do you think that psychologists should be concerned with political objections to their findings or theories?

Evolutionary psychology is also aware of its limitations. Confer *et al.* (2010), for example, note that certain behaviours, such as those which limit reproductive success, are difficult to explain within the context of evolutionary psychology. Homosexuality – which does not increase an individual's reproductive success – and suicide are 'inexplicable on the basis of current evolutionary accounts' (p. 122). Another, more obvious limitation, is that we do not have the evidence required which would allow us to provide a full account of human nature – in short, we are hopelessly ill-informed about our evolution and our past and the specific pressures we encountered during evolution. The best we can do is make an educated guess, based on the techniques described in the earlier section. Confer *et al.* also note that explaining cultural and individual differences is problematic for the discipline and that is has been more effective at explaining species-typical and sex-differentiated behaviour. For example, although women are better than men at spatial location memory, the discipline cannot account for why there is so much variability in this ability in women.

Chapter review

Natural selection and evolution

- Understanding behaviour requires that psychologists learn more about both proximate causes of behaviour – how animals adapt to environmental changes through learning – and ultimate causes of behaviour – historical events and conditions in the evolution of a species that have shaped its behaviour.
- Darwin's voyage on the *Beagle* and his subsequent thinking and research in artificial selection led him to develop the idea of biological evolution, which explains how genetic and physical changes occur in groups of animals over time.
- The primary element of biological evolution is natural selection: the tendency of some members of a species to produce more offspring than other members do. Members of a species vary genetically; some possess specific traits to a greater or lesser extent than other individuals do. If any of these traits gives an animal a competitive advantage over other members of the species then that animal is also more likely to have greater reproductive success. Its offspring will then carry its genes into future generations.
- Two important adaptations during the course of human evolution are bipedalism – the ability to walk upright – and encephalisation – an increase in brain size. The combination of these two factors allowed early humans to explore and settle new environments and led to advances in tool making, hunting, food gathering and self-defence.
- Encephalisation appears to have been associated with language development. The study of the evolution of our species suggests the nature of the circumstances under which adaptive behaviour first emerged and those circumstances that have been important for its continued expression to the present time.

Heredity and genetics

- The instructions for the synthesis of protein molecules, which oversee the development of the body and all of its processes, are contained in genes. Genes are found on chromosomes, which consist of DNA and are found in every cell.
- Humans inherit 23 individual chromosomes, each of which contains thousands of genes, from each parent. This means that our genetic blueprint represents a recombination of the genetic instructions that our parents inherited from their parents.
- Such recombination makes for tremendous genetic diversity. Genetically diverse species have a better chance of adapting to a changing environment than do genetically non-diverse species because some members of the species may have genes that enable them to survive in a new environment.
- The expression of a gene depends on several factors, including its interaction with other genes (polygenic traits), the sex of the individual carrying the particular gene and the environmental conditions under which that individual lives. Changes in genetic material caused by mutations or chromosomal aberrations lead to changes in the expression of a particular gene. For example, haemophilia, an increased tendency to bleed from even minor injuries, is the result of a mutation.
- Behaviour genetics is the study of how genes influence behaviour. Psychologists and other scientists use artificial selection studies of animals, twin studies, and adoption studies to investigate the possible relationship between genes and behaviour in humans.

Sociobiology and evolutionary psychology

- The discovery of the biological basis for social behaviour is the primary goal of sociobiology. Sociobiologists have been especially interested in studying social behaviour related to reproduction and the rearing of offspring.
- Evolutionary psychology is a relatively new sub-field of psychology devoted to the study of how evolution and genetic variables influence adaptive behaviour.
- Different reproductive strategies are believed to have evolved because of sex differences in the resources that parents invest in procreative and child-rearing activities. These resources include the time, physical efforts and risks to life involved in procreation and in the feeding, nurturing and protection of offspring.

- A low waist-to-hip ratio appears to be preferred by Western heterosexual men; a waist-to-chest ratio that emphasises narrow hips and broad shoulders is preferred by Western heterosexual women. In some cultures, however, there is a preference for heavier, larger women. One reason for this is that these cultures may not have been exposed to the Western ideals of physical beauty, those which emphasise the curvaceousness of women.
- Recent research suggests that facial attractiveness may be a more important determinant of mate selection than is waist-to-hip ratio.
- Men and women experience different types of jealousy and these feelings appear to be mirrored in different degrees of brain activation: men are more threatened by sexual infidelity whereas women are more threatened by emotional infidelity (a male partner having a very close, non-sexual relationship with a woman).
- Polygynous and monogamous strategies tend to require greater female investment, polyandrous strategies tend to require greater male investment, and polygynandrous strategies tend to require investment on the part of members of a large group, such as a colony of chimpanzees.

- Altruism is difficult to explain by appealing to natural selection. Altruistic behaviour generally involves one organism risking its life for others with whom it shares some genes (kin selection) or who are likely subsequently to be in a position to return the favour (reciprocal altruism).
- Inclusive fitness theory argues that reproduction and natural selection occur because individuals' reproductive success is measured through the production of their and their kin's offspring. Those characteristics which help promote the transmission of genes (either directly or indirectly) will be naturally selected.
- Sociobiology has been criticised on the grounds that natural selection is no longer a factor in human evolution, that research on animal social behaviour is not relevant to understanding human social behaviour, that environmental factors play a greater role in shaping human behaviour than genetic factors, and that sociobiology is simply a way to justify the superiority of one group over another. Sociobiologists reply that natural selection has shaped and continues to shape the evolution of culture, that findings from animal research can be generalised to humans, that genes and environment interact to determine behaviour, and, finally, that sociobiology is an attempt to understand human behaviour, not to justify it.

Suggestions for further reading

Evolution: Popular accounts

Brown, A. (2000) *The Darwin Wars*. London: Simon and Schuster.
Darwin, C. (1859) *The Origin of Species by Means of Natural Selection*. London: Murray.
Dawkins, R. (2009) *The Greatest Show on Earth: The Evidence for Evolution*. London: Bantam Press.
Dunbar, R. (2016). *Human Evolution: our brains and behaviour*. USA: OUP
Some good introductions to evolutionary theory.

Evolutionary psychology

Burke, D. (2014) Why isn't everyone an evolutionary psychologist? *Frontiers in Psychology*, 5, 1–8.
Buss, D.M. (2014) *Evolutionary Psychology: The new science of mind* (5th edn). Boston, MA: Allyn and Bacon.
Eastwick, P.W. (2016). The emerging integration of close relationships research and evolutionary psychology. *Current Directions in Psychological Science*, 25(3), 183–90.
Jonason, P.K. and Schmitt, D.P. (2016) Quantifying common criticisms of evolutionary psychology. *Evolutionary Psychological Science*, 2(3), 177–88.

Jones, B.C. et al (in press). No compelling evidence that preferences for facial masculinity track changes in women's hormonal status. *Psychological Science*.
Lewis, D.M.G., Al-Shawaf, L., Conroy-Beam, D., Asao, K. and Buss, D. M. (2017) Evolutionary psychology: A how-to guide. *American Psychologist*, 72(4), 353–73.

Behavioural genetics

Grabitz, C. R., Button, K. S., Munafò, M. R., Newbury, D. F., Pernet, C. R., Thompson, P. A., & Bishop, D. V. (2017). Logical and methodological issues affecting genetic studies of humans reported in top neuroscience journals. *Journal of Cognitive Neuroscience*, in press.
Plomin, R., DeFries, J.C., Knopik, V.S. and Neiderhiser, J.M. (2016) Top 10 replicated findings from behavioral genetics. *Perspectives on Psychological Science*, 11(1), 3–23.
Polderman, T. J., Benyamin, B., De Leeuw, C. A., Sullivan, P. F., Van Bochoven, A., Visscher, P. M. and Posthuma, D. (2015) Meta-analysis of the heritability of human traits based on fifty years of twin studies. *Nature genetics*, 47(7), 702–09.
Premack, D. (2010) Why humans are unique: Three theories. *Perspectives in Psychological Science*, 5, 22–32.
Vonk, J. and Shackelford, T.K. (2012) *The Oxford Handbook of Comparative Evolutionary Psychology*. Oxford: Oxford University Press.
Some good introductions to sociobiology and evolutionary psychology.

CHAPTER 4
Psychobiology and neuroscience

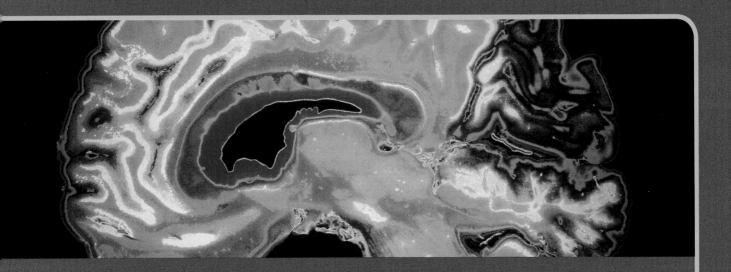

MIND READING PROGRAM TRANSLATES BRAIN ACTIVITY INTO WORDS

Ian Sample

Scientists have picked up fragments of people's thoughts by decoding the brain activity caused by words that they hear.

Experiments on 15 patients in the US showed that a computer could decipher their brain activity and play back words they heard, though at times the words were difficult to recognise.

'This is exciting in terms of the basic science of how the brain decodes what we hear', says Robert Knight, a senior member of the team at the University of Berkeley, California.

The prospect of reading minds has led to ethical concerns that the technology could be used covertly or to interrogate criminals and terrorists.

Knight said that this is in the realm of science fiction. 'To reproduce what we did, you would have to open up someone's skull and they would have to cooperate'.

Source: *The Guardian*, 31 January 2012.

WHAT YOU SHOULD BE ABLE TO DO AFTER READING CHAPTER 4

- Describe the major parts and functions of the nervous system and its principal components.

- Describe the parts of a nerve cell and how it functions and understand how nerve cells communicate with each other.

- Describe how various techniques are used in neuroscience and psychobiology to study behaviour, from lesioning to heart rate recording to neuroimaging.

- Describe the lobes and major structures of the brain and their role in behaviour.

- Be aware of the effects of drugs on behaviour and how they act on the brain to produce these behaviours.

- Be able to understand some of the psychobiological causes and correlates of behaviour.

QUESTIONS TO THINK ABOUT

- Are two human brains exactly alike?

- Do psychological functions such as language, memory or visual perception reside in specific parts of the brain?

- Do different sides of the brain undertake different functions? If they do, what purpose would this serve?

- What do you think scientists mean by 'nature v. nurture' explanations? Is this concept a sensible one?

- How can we measure the brain and body's responses to external and internal stimuli?

- Is any chemical that has an effect on our body and brain 'a drug'?

- Why do certain drugs have different effects on our behaviour?

- If a person needs a drug to function efficiently, in what way could he or she be said to be 'abusing' it?

Psychobiology and neuroscience

In 2013, the European Commission invested $1.3 billion in the Human Brain Project, a pan-European research collaboration designed to map the functions of the human brain. In the same year, President Obama launched the Brain Research through Advancing Innovative Neurotechnologies (BRAIN) initiative – another, multidisciplinary attempt to better understand the brain by mapping its functions and connections at the cell and region level, using existing technologies and new ones. In late 2016, the US government launched the International Brain Initiative designed to bring together brain mapping researchers in order to determine whether their studies use consistent methods and produce consistent results, and to encourage the sharing of data and of brain-mapping tools and techniques. There doesn't seem to be a better time to be a neuroscientist or psychobiologist.

Psychobiology is the study of the role of physiology and anatomy in the regulation and execution of behaviour – the topics studied can range from the role of hormones in sexual reproduction, the effect of glucose deprivation on hunger, the relationship between hormone secretion and stress, the effect of relaxing music on heart rate, or the activation of the brain while a person is engaged in making decisions. Neuroscience is a similar discipline but limits itself to the study of the brain, the spinal cord and components and processes within these two structures. Together these parts are known as the **central nervous system** (**CNS**), so called because not only do they occupy the central position of the body but they are also the most important part of the nervous system for maintaining and producing behaviour.

Neuroscientists attempt to understand and predict behaviour by studying the brain's structure and function and the discipline has its origins in the writing and study of the Ancient Greeks (and earlier). Neuroscientists have studied a variety of behaviours – almost every behaviour you can imagine has been studied by neuroscientists in some ways – but there are still some unsolved problems and issues. Table 4.1 describes some of the remaining problems (and some problems that may never be solved), as described by the neuroscientist Adolphs (2015).

Recent years have seen a surge in the use of the prefix 'neuro' or 'neuroscience' to behaviours or fields of study, for example, neuroeconomics, educational neuroscience (Martin, 2016). The use of the prefix adds heft, gravitas and prestige to areas – you'll see later that neuroscientific explanations for behaviour are perceived as more convincing and persuasive than are cognitive ones – and to try and discover and demonstrate physical correlates or predictors of actual behaviour. Many of these areas and studies, however, add little to our understanding of behaviour and many of the claims they make are either inaccurate or exaggerated (e.g. brain training, discussed in Chapter 8).

In the past 20 years, there has also been an eruption in studies using neuroimaging methods – techniques that allow the computerised visualisation of the structure of the brain or the function of parts of the brain. We will come back to these later in the chapter as their use has become increasingly controversial over the past five years.

Table 4.1 The unsolved problems of neuroscience

Problems that are solved, or soon will be:

I	How do single neurons compute?
II	What is the connectome of a small nervous system, like that of *Caenorhabitis elegans* (300 neurons)?
III	How can we image a live brain of 100,000 neurons at cellular and millisecond resolution?
IV	How does sensory transduction work?

Problems that we should be able to solve in the next 50 years:

V	How do circuits of neurons compute?
VI	What is the complete connectome of the mouse brain (70,000,000 neurons)?
VII	How can we image a live mouse brain at cellular and millisecond resolution?
VIII	What causes psychiatric and neurological illness?
IX	How do learning and memory work?
X	Why do we sleep and dream?
XI	How do we make decisions?
XII	How does the brain represent abstract ideas?

Problems that we should be able to solve, but who knows when:

XIII	How does the mouse brain compute?
XIV	What is the complete connectome of the human brain (80,000,000,000 neurons)?
XV	How can we image a live human brain at cellular and millisecond resolution?
XVI	How could we cure psychiatric and neurological diseases?
XVII	How could we make everybody's brain function best?

Problems we may never solve:

XVIII	How does the human brain compute?
XIX	How can cognition be so flexible and generative?
XX	How and why does conscious experience arise?

Mela-questions:

XXI	What counts as an explanation of how the brain works? (and Which disciplines would be needed to provide it?)

The nervous system: the brain and its components

The brain looks like a lump of porridge and has the consistency of blancmange. This organ, weighing an average 1,400 g in an adult human, is the most important part of the body but it was not always considered to be. Aristotle, for example, believed that the heart was more important to behaviour. It contains an estimated 10 to 100 billion nerve cells and about as many supporting cells, which take care of important support and 'housekeeping' functions. The brain contains many different types of nerve cell which differ in shape, size and the kinds of chemicals they produce. There seem to be differences between men and women – men's brains are approximately 150 g heavier and the number of neurons in women has been estimated to be 19 × 10 to the power of 9, and in men: 23 × 10 to the power of 9 (Walloe *et al.*, 2014) (see Figure 4.1). The density of neurons (brain cells) does not seem to differ significantly between the sexes but sex and age determine the total number of neurons. We lose around 9 per cent of our neutrons from 18 to 93 years old – around 85,000 a day.

Nerve cells of the brain are organised in modules – clusters of nerve cells that communicate with each other – but individual modules do not stand alone. They are connected to other neural circuits, receiving information from some of them, processing this information and sending the results on to other modules. In his famous book *The Modularity of Mind*, the philosopher Fodor (1983) argues that particular modules have particular functions – just as the transistors, resistors and capacitors in a computer chip do – and are relatively independent of each other. Although this idea – **modularity** – is still controversial, the evidence broadly supports some degree of modularity in the brain. The aim of psychobiology and neuroscience is to understand how individual nerve cells work, how they connect with each other to form modules, and just what these modules do.

The central nervous system

The brain has two primary functions: the control of behaviour and the regulation of the body's physiological processes. The brain cannot act alone – it needs to receive information from the body's sense receptors and it must be connected with the muscles and glands of the body if it is to

Superficially, two brains look almost exactly alike. Closer inspection does reveal differences between them and morphological analysis reveals further actual differences in brain cell size and number and the connections between brain cells. This brain looks no different from an ordinary brain. It belonged to Charles Babbage, the inventor of the device which gave us the modern computer.

Source: Lawrence Manning/Corbis/Getty Images

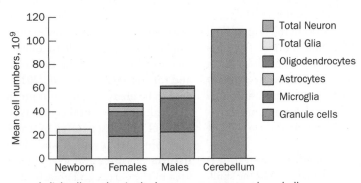

Figure 4.1 Mean total neuron and glial cell number in the human neocortex and cerebellum.

Cutting edge: Are sex differences in the brain actually size differences?

In 1994, Ringo *et al.* published an intriguing hypothesis. They argued that connections between brain regions in larger brains would not make sense as the delay in relaying messages across large areas would make the organ inefficient. They suggested, instead, that larger brains might have stronger, and more extensive connections *within* one side of the brain, and that smaller brains would have greater connections *between* the two sides of the brain.

Hanggi *et al.* (2014) measured intra (within) and intra (between) connectivity in the brains of 69 young men and 69 young women. They found that connections within one side of the brain were much stronger in larger brains than in smaller ones; there was also an increase in connectivity between the sides of the brain in the larger samples, but this was not significant. They suggest that these differences in connections are based on brain size rather than the owner's sex.

Men have larger brains than do women, a finding also replicated in Hanggi *et al.'s* study. When the researchers analysed connectivity based on sex, they found that men showed greater intra-connectivity, whereas women showed greater inter-connectivity (although the increase was not statistically significant). However, when they matched men and women for brain size, these differences disappeared. This does suggest that the differences in connectivity are due more to brain size than sex.

affect behaviour and physiological processes. The spinal cord is a long, thin collection of nerve cells attached to the base of the brain and running the length of the spinal column (see Figure 4.2). It contains circuits of nerve cells that control some simple reflexes, such as automatically pulling away from a painfully hot object. The CNS communicates with the rest of the body through the nerves – bundles of fibres that transmit information in and out of the CNS. The nerves, which are attached to the spinal cord and to the base of the brain, make up the peripheral nervous system.

The human brain has three major parts: the brain stem, the cerebellum and the cerebral hemispheres. Figure 4.3 shows photographs of the side (a), cross-section (b), top (c) and bottom/underneath (d) of the human cerebral hemispheres. The lower part of the cerebellum and brain stem projects beneath the cerebral hemisphere (see the bottom left of Figure 4.3a and d); the upper part is normally hidden. If the human brain is removed from the skull, it looks as if it has a handle or stem. The brain stem is one of the most primitive regions of the brain, and its functions are correspondingly basic – primarily control of physiological functions and automatic behaviours such as swallowing and breathing. The brains of some animals, such as amphibians, consist primarily of a brain stem and a simple cerebellum.

The two **cerebral hemispheres** constitute the largest, and most recently developed, part of the human brain. The cerebellum, attached to the back of the brain stem, looks like a miniature version of the cerebral hemispheres. Its primary function is to control and coordinate movements, although recent research has highlighted its role in language and thinking, too. The cerebellum in cross-section is on the top right of Figure 4.3b.

Because the CNS is vital to an organism's survival, it is exceptionally well protected. The brain is encased by the skull, and the spinal cord runs through the middle of a column of hollow bones known as **vertebrae.** Both the brain and the spinal cord are enclosed by a three-layered set of membranes called the **meninges** (*meninges* is the plural of *meninx*, the Greek word for 'membrane'; meningitis is an inflammation of the meninges). The brain and spinal cord do not come into direct contact with the bones of the skull and **vertebrae.** Instead, they float in a clear liquid called **cerebrospinal fluid (CSF).** This liquid fills the space between two of the meninges, thus providing a liquid cushion surrounding the brain and spinal cord and protecting them from being bruised by the bones that encase them.

The surface of the cerebral hemispheres is covered by the **cerebral cortex** (the word cortex means 'bark' or 'rind'). The cerebral cortex consists of a thin layer of tissue approximately 3 mm thick. It is often referred to as grey matter because of its appearance. It contains billions of nerve cells and is the structure where perceptions take place, memories are stored and plans are formulated and executed. The nerve cells in the cerebral cortex are connected to other parts of the brain by a layer of nerve fibres called the white matter because of the shiny white appearance of the substance that coats and insulates them. Figure 4.4 shows a slice of the brain. As you can see, the grey matter and white matter are distinctly different. According to a recent study, the brain can be divided into at least 180 areas per hemisphere based on the architecture of these areas, connections between areas and function (Glasser *et al.*, 2016). Of these, 87 are considered to be areas that had not previously been identified.

The human cerebral cortex is wrinkled in appearance; it is full of bulges separated by grooves. The bulges are called **gyri** (singular 'gyrus'), and the large grooves are called **fissures.** Fissures and gyri expand the amount of surface area of the cortex and greatly increase the number of nerve

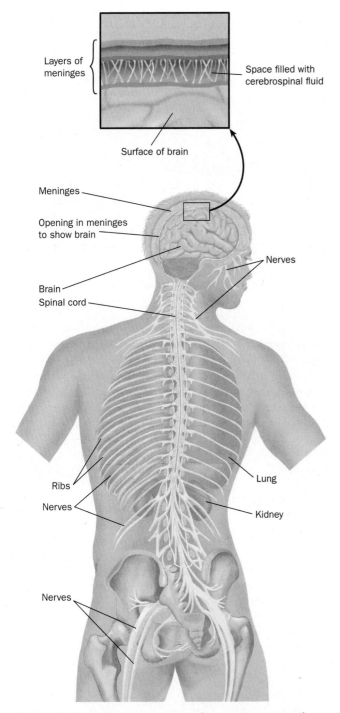

Figure 4.2 The central nervous system (brain and spinal cord) and the peripheral nervous system (cranial nerves and spinal nerves).

cells it can contain. Animals with the largest and most complex brains, including humans and the higher primates, have the most wrinkled brains and, thus, the largest cerebral cortices.

The peripheral nervous system

The peripheral nervous system consists of the nerves that connect the CNS with sense organs, muscles and glands. Nerves carry both incoming and outgoing information. The sense organs detect changes in the environment and send signals through the nerves to the CNS. The brain sends signals through the nerves to the muscles (causing behaviour) and the glands (producing adjustments in internal physiological processes).

Nerves are bundles of many thousands of individual fibres, all wrapped in a tough, protective membrane. Nerve fibres transmit messages through the nerve, from a sense organ to the brain or from the brain to a muscle or gland.

As you saw earlier, some nerves are attached to the spinal cord and others are attached directly to the brain. The spinal nerves, attached to the spinal cord, serve all of the body below the neck, conveying sensory information from the body and carrying messages to muscles and glands. The 12 pairs of **cranial nerves**, attached to the brain, serve primarily muscles and sense receptors in the neck and head. For example, when you taste food, the sensory information gets from your tongue to your brain through one set of cranial nerves. Other sets of cranial nerves bring sensory information to the brain from the eyes, ears and nose. When you chew food, the command to chew reaches your jaw muscles through another set of cranial nerves. Still other cranial nerves control the eye muscles, the tongue, the neck muscles and the muscles we use for speech.

Cells of the nervous system

Neurons, or nerve cells, are the elements of the nervous system that bring sensory information to the brain, store memories, reach decisions and control the activity of the muscles. They are assisted in their task by another kind of cell: the glia. **Glia** (or **glial cells**) get their name from the Greek word for glue and 90 per cent of cells in the brain are glial cells. They were first described in 1856 by the German anatomist, Rudolf Virchow. At one time, scientists thought that glia simply held neurons – the important elements of the nervous system – in place. They do not, however, literally stick neurons together but they do provide important physical support to neurons and providing other forms of mechanical support. Some types of glial cells, such as astrocytes (the most common type) act on damage to neurons, regulate blood flow to cells and remove toxins (Opendak and Gould, 2015). Other types are immune cells which clear up debris is the brain (microglia) (Schafe *et al.*, 2013). Others (oligodendroglia) form protective insulating sheaths (myelin) around nerve fibres. The number of glial cells is higher in men than in women, around 28 per cent higher (Walloe *et al.*, 2014).

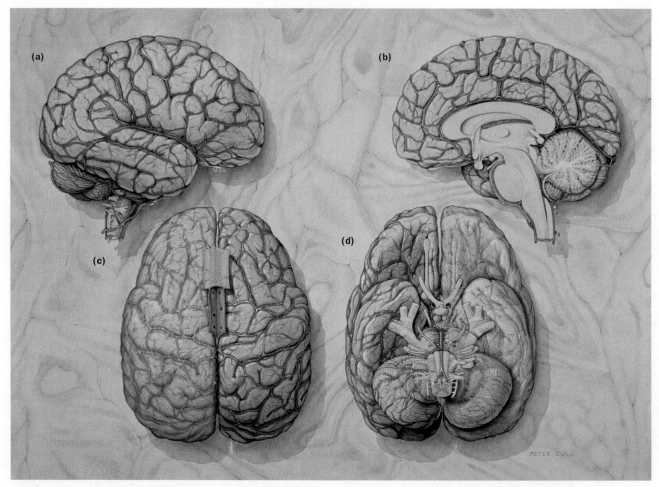

Figure 4.3 The external features of the brain from four angles: **(a)** the side (sagittal), **(b)** top, **(c)** cross-section (lateral) **(d)** bottom/ underneath.

Source: Professor Peter Cull/Science Photo Library Ltd.

When brains are of equal size, however, this difference disappears. Like neurons, glial cells decline with age – there is an approximate, 27 per cent loss.

Research suggests that glial cells may play a more important part in brain development than was originally thought. For example, one study has shown that glial cells may determine the number of junctions between neurons – called synapses – generated in the brain (Ullian *et al.*, 2001). This finding followed an experiment by researchers from the same laboratory which found that synapses of neurons grown with a certain type of glial cell were 10 times more active than those grown without. The mere proximity of glial cells to neurons made the neurons more responsive. In their most recent experiment, neurons that were exposed to glial cells formed seven times as many synapses as those that were not exposed. This is important because it indicates that glial cells have a much greater role to play in the formation of synapses in the CNS than had previously been thought. The next step is to identify how the glial cells produce this increase.

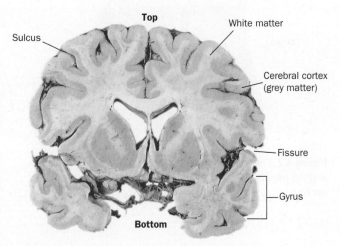

Figure 4.4 A coronal slice of a human brain showing fissures and gyri, the layer of cerebral cortex that follows these convolutions and the white and grey matter.

Source: Harvard Medical School/Betty G. Martindale.

Brain research – An international perspective

In the 1990s, scientists celebrated what became known as the Decade of the Brain, George W. Bush's initiative, supported by Congress, to help us unlock some of the brain's secrets – to help us understand what it is and why it works. That decade is over, but now there are new, and much bigger initiatives being taken across the globe to study and research the brain, and methods of establishing its structure and function.

For example, the US's Brain Research through Advancing Innovative Neurotechniques (BRAIN) was announced in 2013 by Barak Obama to 'deepen understanding of the inner workings of the human mind and to improve how we treat, prevent and cure disorders of the brain' (Martin *et al.*, 2016). It plans to do this by creating and developing new technologies, by creating the ability to observe brain function in real-time, by studying how the brain processes information and by investigating how it operates to produce behaviour. (see www.braininitiative.org). Around $1.36 billion has been committed by government and federal agencies, and private organisations, to fund these aims.

Across the Atlantic, the European Commission's Human Brain Project has been established to meet similar aims using teams from across the EU (Amunts *et al.*, 2016). The 10-year project aims to understand the structure and function of the brain by funding research into genes, cells, imaging, technology and behaviour and the connection between philosophy and neuroscience. It has recruited scientists from a dozen disciplines in 177 institutions in 19 countries. It has four sub-projects, including a plan to map the organisation of the mouse brain, the organisation of the human brain, a proposal to study the relationship between the brain and behaviour (e.g. how we recognise objects, how we encode and retrieve episodic memory) and how robotic and computer models might assist this, and a proposal to develop theories of neuroscience which might guide future experimentation.

In China, a similar 15-year plan (2016–2030) has been established to conduct basic neuroscience research, discover ways of diagnosis or intervention in brain-related impairment and to develop new technologies (Poo *et al.*, 2016). In 2016, Australia established the Australian Brain Alliance to co-ordinate brain research across the country (ABS Steering Committee, 2016) in order to study how to restore the brain to a healthy state if it is unhealthy, to understand the neural basis of behaviour and to develop new computing technologies. The Canada Brain Fund, established in 2011, was set up to meet similar aims (Jabalpurwala, 2016). Japan's initiative is more specific – the study of the marmoset brain. The small primate is being studied as a model for human function and recovery of function, via the Brain/MINDS initiative (Okano *et al.*, 2016).

If the 90s were the decade of the brain, then the current period in our scientific history is probably the apogee of brain research. The next 5–10 years should produce the first, exciting, replicable findings from these initiatives.

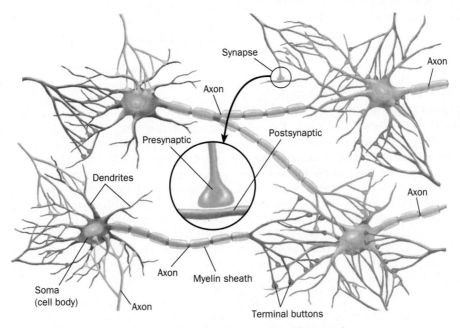

Figure 4.5 The principal parts of a neuron and its connections with other neurons (synapses).

The four principal parts of a neuron are shown in Figure 4.5.

1 The **soma,** or cell body, is the largest part of the neuron and contains the mechanisms that control the metabolism and maintenance of the cell. The soma also receives messages from other neurons.

2 The **dendrites,** the tree-like growths attached to the soma, function principally to receive messages from other neurons (dendron means 'tree'). They transmit the information they receive down their 'trunks' to the soma.

3 The nerve fibre, or **axon,** carries messages away from the soma towards the cells with which the neuron communicates. These messages, called action potentials, consist of brief changes in the electrical charge of the axon. For convenience, an action potential is usually referred to as the firing of an axon. Many axons, especially long ones, are insulated with a substance called myelin which is white and gives some parts of the brain its whiteish appearance. The principal function of myelin is to insulate axons from each other and thus to prevent the scrambling of messages. It also increases the speed of the action potential. The immune systems of people who have multiple sclerosis attack a protein in the myelin sheath of axons, stripping it away. Although most of the axons survive this assault, they can no longer function normally, and so, depending on where the damage occurs, people who have multiple sclerosis suffer from various sensory and motor impairments.

4 The **terminal buttons** are located at the ends of the 'twigs' that branch off the ends of axons. Terminal buttons secrete a chemical called a transmitter substance whenever an action potential travels down the axon, that is, whenever the axon fires. These chemicals are called neurotransmitters. The transmitter substance affects the activity of the other cells with which the neuron communicates. Thus, the message is conveyed chemically from one neuron to another. Most drugs that affect the nervous system and hence alter a person's behaviour do so by affecting the chemical transmission of messages between cells.

Controversies in psychological science: Can the brain create new neurons?

The issue

Almost two decades ago, the idea that the brain could create new neurons was viewed as the Holy Grail of neuroscience. The thinking was that we are born with all the neural hardware we will have (and much of this will be jettisoned within the first year of life) and that the generation of new cells was an impossibility.

The evidence

This changed with the discovery by Joseph Altman in the 1950s that new neurons in some parts of the brain – specifically, the hippocampus and the olfactory bulb of rats – could be created. The term for the creation of new neurons is neurogenesis. The type of neuron generated is a granule cell and these cells are found primarily in a specific part of the brain called the dendate gyrus of the hippocampus (Snyder and Cameron, 2012). You'll discover more about this structure later on in the chapter. The first demonstration of neurogenesis in humans came in 2009 following the development of a new technique which used a chemical called BrdU and made it easier to count cells in the brain (Eriksson et al., 2008). The creation of these cells is seen in many mammals, including humans and their production can be altered by environmental factors, such as stressors and even physical activity such as running or walking (Leuner and Gould, 2010; Schoenfeld and Gould, 2012; Spalding et al., 2013). Some of the factors which have been associated with new cell growth are listed in Table 4.2. This idea that the creation of new cells can result from an environmental intervention is an example of neuroplasticity – the notion that the structure of the brain can be altered by behavioural and environmental factors (Opendak and Gould, 2015).

Experiments have shown that mild types of stressor can enhance neurogenesis but that unpredictable, chronic and intense periods of stress produced, for example, by sleep deprivation or electric shock, can inhibit it (Snyder et al., 2009; Lucassen et al., 2010). Some studies have found that parenting in non-humans mammals can reduce neurogenesis (Leuner et al., 2010), probably because, despite being rewarding, looking after offspring is very stressful. One mechanism which may underpin this reduction is the inhibition of progenitor cells. That is, the cells that lead to the creation of new neurons are impaired by the experience of stress (Schoenfeld and Gould, 2012). The ultimate cause of this inhibition is likely to be the production of glucocorticoids, stress-chemicals which are released when an organism experiences stress (there is more on glucocorticoids in Chapter 17).

Controversies in psychological science: *Continued*

Table 4.2 The effect of positive and negative stimuli on neuroplasticity in the hippocampus and on anxiety and cognitive performance. Blue boxes = positive effects of stimuli; pink boxes = negative effects of stimuli; green = no effect; cross-hatched = no data available

	Stimulus	Adult neurogenesis	Cognitive performance	Anxiety-like behavior	References
Negative	Stress				5,8,82,83
	High fat diet/obesity				84,85
Positive	Physical exercise				18,19,21,22,39
	Sexual experience				36,86,87
	Enriched environment (EE)				89,90
	Intracranial self-stimulation				91,92
Mixed	Parenting				34,35,88,93
	Stress + physical exercise				74,75,94
	Stress + sexual experience				76,95
	Stress + EE				96,97

TRENDS in Cognitive Sciences

Glucocorticoids exert a number of negative effects on behaviour if their release is prolonged – people's immune system works ineffectively, for example, or their memory and ability to navigate their way around an environment becomes impaired (Conrad, 2008). Stress also exerts effects on the shape and size of some elements of existing neurons – the complexity of dendrites is reduced, for example, as is the number of spines on dendrites and the number of synapses in the hippocampus (McEwen *et al.*, 2012).

The opposite response – a behaviour leading to neurogenesis – has been found in animals when they engage in physical activity such as exercise or sex and even when they live in an enriched environment or are administered cocaine (Opendak and Gould, 2015). For example, in non-humans such as rodents, running on a treadmill or a wheel has been associated with increased number of neurons in the hippocampus (Vivar and Van Praag, 2013) although there is evidence that if the running is done alone or the physical exercise is very intense then neurogenesis does not happen (Opendak and Gould, 2015). Whether such effects can be produced in humans – where the rewarding nature of the running depends on individual differences and our motivation – is not known.

Whether new cells are function-specific or just add to the pool of neurons that can be recruited to perform a range of behaviours is also unknown. In their review, Opendak and Gould (2015) noted that when new cells are created as a result of spatial navigation learning, these cells are more responsive when they are exposed to spatial cues than other types of cue, suggesting that they may have a degree of specificity. The type of function that cells have also seems to be determined by where the cells are created.

For example, the dorsal part of the dendate gyrus – where the new cells exclusively appear – is involved in the processing of spatial data, whereas the ventral part is involved in anxiety and stress responses. Reducing neurons in the dorsal part has led to impaired ability of an organism to engage in learning (specifically, classical conditioning which you read about in chapter one and is described in more detail in Chapter 7), whereas deleting cells in the ventral part has been found to reduce the effects of anti-anxiety drugs (Wu and Hen, 2014). This evidence, at the moment however, is tentative and requires replication. Stress and sexual experience appear to affect the production of cells in the ventral part more than the dorsal part and there seem to be fewer new cells in the ventral part (Hawley *et al.*, 2012; Snyder *et al.*, 2012).

Controversies in psychological science: *Continued*

The other important question is: why are these new cells produced in the first place? According to Opendak and Gould (2015), the hippocampus's ability to generate new cells which can be altered by environmental factors 'strongly suggests that new neurons are a substrate for sculpting the brain to produce behaviours that are adaptive for the organism' (p. 6). They go on to argue that the reduction of neurogenesis can also be an advantage because the stress which creates this leads to increased anxiety and reduced exploration, which might help survival. It is an intellectual leap, but it is one explanation. There is also some evidence to suggest that once the cells are created they do not simply survive, they have to be used. For example, it is not enough for an animal to be trained for the cells to continue, the animal has

to learn. If it learns, the new cells are more likely to survive (Shors, 2014).

Conclusion

The evidence suggests that, contrary to the views held even 20 years ago, the brain – or a specific part of it, the hippocampus – can generate new neurons and that these neurons can be stimulated by activity such as exercise or sex and reduced by the experience of stress. This has been demonstrated widely in non-human mammals. Whether such neurogenesis occurs in humans, however, and to the same degree is unknown. For all kinds of ethical reasons, it is difficult to measure such outcomes in human participants.

Neurotransmitters

There are currently around 50 or so identifiable **neurotransmitters** and all are important to behaviour in some way. Some, however, play a greater role than others. The amine group of neurotransmitters, which includes dopamine, noradrenaline and serotonin (5-hydroxytryptamine), appears especially important to psychologists because they are involved in a range of behaviours – emotional expression, decision-making, response to reward, inhibiting inappropriate actions, drug-taking and many others.

A part of the brain called the nucleus accumbens, appears to be important in this respect and appears to be part of a reward system located in the front and midpart of the brain. It evaluates how salient or important events in the outside world are. It and the system it belongs to are also implicated in impulsive behaviour – the inability to delay reward and be aware of the consequences of actions, and so on (Pothuizen *et al.*, 2005) – and drug addiction (Russo *et al.*, 2010; Everitt and Robbins, 2013). Drugs which act on serotonin receptors here increase impulsivity (Pattij and Vanderschuren, 2008). Such impulsivity, according to some scientists, is linked to the initiation and maintenance of drug-seeking (Krishnan-Sarin *et al.*, 2007). There is also evidence that there is an increase in the density of the spines of dendrites in the nucleus accumbens when cocaine or heroin is administered (Shen *et al.*, 2009; Maze *et al.*, 2010).

The events to which the nucleus accumbens responds include rewarding stimuli (food, water, sex), aversive stimuli (ice, shock) and novel stimuli. Dopamine release increases here, as does the firing of dopamine receptors when an organism is rewarded with food or water (Iversen and Iversen, 2007;

Schultz, 2007). Dopamine can increase by as much as 20–100 per cent and last for up to 100 minutes (Schultz, 2007). If an organism expects a reward then there is a release of dopamine in these regions, but if an organism is completely rewarded there seems to be little dopamine activation. Dopamine is also released in freely moving organisms, which suggests that it is important for motor movement and the motivation to move. Of course, the movement disorder Parkinson's disease, discussed a little later, is treated by a dopamine precursor (called Levodopa), and excessive dopamine is thought to be implicated in some of the symptoms of schizophrenia (described in Chapter 18).

Like all the amines, dopamine receptors begin projecting from the brain stem and certain dopamine receptors terminate (end their projections) in the front part of the brain, called the **prefrontal cortex** (PFC), described below. These receptors, called D1 receptors, appear to be very important to cognitive performance and influence tasks such as our ability to store and manipulate non-verbal information over very short periods of time – a type of memory called working memory (see Chapter 8). Some people have a mutation of an allele which directly affects dopamine (by deactivating it) with the consequence that their cognitive function is impaired (Tunbridge *et al.*, 2006). Another type of dopamine receptor, D2, seems to be reduced in the striatum of drug addicts (Kalivas and Volkow, 2005).

The action potential

The message carried by the axon – the **action potential** – involves an electrical current, but it does not travel down the axon the way electricity travels through a wire. Electricity travels through a wire at hundreds of millions of metres per second. The axon transmits information at a much slower rate – less than 100 metres per second.

The membrane of an axon is electrically charged. When the axon is resting (i.e. when no action potential is occurring), the outside is charged at +70 millivolts (mV, thousandths of a volt) with respect to the inside. An action potential is an abrupt, short-lived reversal in the electrical charge of an axon. This temporary reversal begins at the end of the axon that attaches to the soma and is transmitted to the end that divides into small branches capped with terminal buttons.

The electrical charge of the axon occurs because of an unequal distribution of positively and negatively charged particles inside the axon and in the fluid that surrounds it. These particles, called ions, are produced when various substances – including ordinary table salt – are dissolved in water. Normally, ions cannot penetrate the membrane that surrounds axons. However, the axonal membrane contains special submicroscopic proteins that serve as **ion channels** or **ion transporters**. Ion channels can open or close; when they are open, a particular ion can enter or leave the axon. Ion transporters work like pumps. They use the energy resources of the cell to transport particular ions into or out of the axon, as seen in Figure 4.6.

The outside of the membrane is positively charged (and the inside is negatively charged) because the axon contains more negatively charged ions and fewer positively charged ions. When an axon is resting, its ion channels are closed, so ions cannot move into or out of the axon. An action potential is caused by the opening of some ion channels in the membrane at the end of the axon nearest to the soma. The opening of these ion channels permits positively charged sodium ions to enter, which reverses the membrane potential at that location. This reversal causes nearby ion channels to open, which produces another reversal at that point. The process continues all the way to the terminal buttons located at the other end of the axon.

Note that an action potential is a brief reversal of the membrane's electrical charge. As soon as the charge reverses, the ion channels close and another set of ion channels opens for a short time, letting positively charged potassium ions out of the axon. This outflow of positive ions restores the normal electrical charge. Thus, an action potential resembles the 'Mexican wave' that football fans often make in a stadium. People in one part of the stadium stand up, raise their arms over their heads, and sit down again. People seated next to them see that a wave is starting, so they do the same – and the wave travels around the stadium. Everyone remains at the same place, but the effect is that of something circling in the stands around the playing field. Similarly, electricity does not really travel down the length of an axon. Instead, the entry of positive ions in one location reverses the charge at that point and causes ion channels in the adjacent region to open, and so on, as seen in Figure 4.7. The ion transporters pump sodium ions out of the axon and pump potassium ions back in, restoring the normal balance.

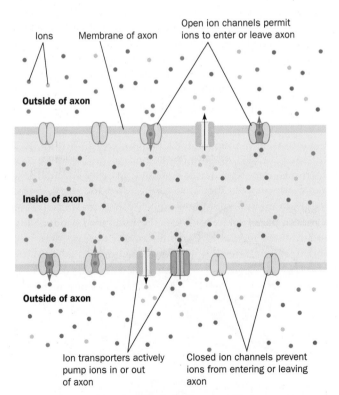

Figure 4.6 Ion channels and ion transporters. These structures regulate the number of ions found inside and outside the axon. An unequal distribution of positively and negatively charged ions is responsible for the axon's electrical charge.

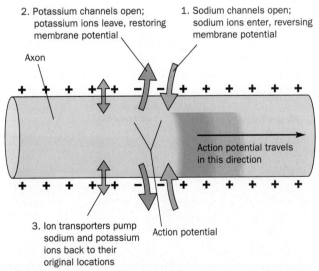

Figure 4.7 Movement of sodium and potassium ions during the action potential. Sodium ions are represented by orange arrows, potassium ions by green arrows.

Synapses

Neurons communicate with other cells by means of synapses. A **synapse** is the conjunction of a terminal button of one neuron and the membrane of another cell – neuron, muscle cell or gland cell. The terminal button belongs to the **presynaptic neuron** – the neuron that sends the message. When terminal buttons become active, they release a chemical called a transmitter substance. The neuron that receives the message (detects the transmitter substance) is called the **postsynaptic neuron.** A neuron receives messages from many terminal buttons, and in turn its terminal buttons form synapses with many other neurons. The drawing in Figure 4.8 is much simplified; thousands of terminal buttons can form synapses with a single neuron.

Figure 4.8 illustrates the relation between a motor neuron and a muscle. A **motor** neuron is one that forms synapses with a muscle and controls its contractions. When the axon of a motor neuron fires, all the muscle fibres with which it forms synapses will contract with a brief twitch. A muscle consists of thousands of individual muscle fibres. It is controlled by a large number of motor neurons, each of which forms synapses with different groups of muscle fibres. The strength of a muscular contraction, then, depends on the rate of firing of the axons that control it. If they fire at a high rate, the muscle contracts forcefully; if they fire at a low rate, the muscle contracts weakly.

Excitation and inhibition

There are broadly two types of synapse: excitatory synapses and inhibitory synapses. Excitatory synapses do just what their name implies. When the axon fires, the terminal buttons release a transmitter substance that excites the postsynaptic neurons with which they form synapses. The effect of this excitation is to make it more likely that the axons of the postsynaptic neurons will fire. Inhibitory synapses do just the opposite. When they are activated, they lower the likelihood that the axons of the postsynaptic neurons will fire.

The activity of the synapses on the dendrites and soma of the cell determines the rate at which a particular axon fires. If the excitatory synapses are the more active, then the axon will fire at a high rate. If the inhibitory synapses are the more active, then the axon will fire at a low rate or perhaps not at all, as seen in Figure 4.9.

How do molecules of transmitter substance exert their excitatory or inhibitory effect on the postsynaptic neuron? When an action potential reaches a terminal button, it causes the terminal button to release a small amount of transmitter substance into the **synaptic cleft,** a fluid-filled space between the terminal button and the membrane of the postsynaptic neuron. The transmitter substance causes reactions in the postsynaptic neuron that either excite or inhibit it. These reactions are triggered by special submicroscopic protein molecules embedded in the postsynaptic membrane called **receptor molecules** (see Figure 4.10).

A molecule of a transmitter substance attaches to a receptor molecule the way a key fits in a lock. After their release from a terminal button, molecules of transmitter substance find their way to the receptor molecules, attach to them and

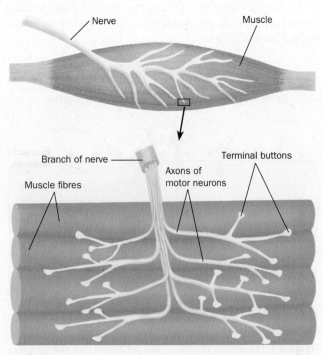

Figure 4.8 Synapses between terminal buttons of the axon of a motor neuron and a muscle.

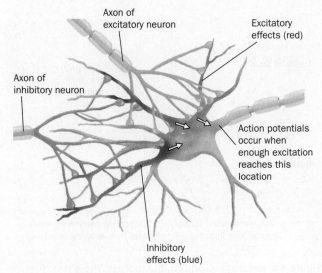

Figure 4.9 Interaction between the effects of excitatory and inhibitory synapses. The rate of firing of the axon of the neuron is controlled by these two factors.

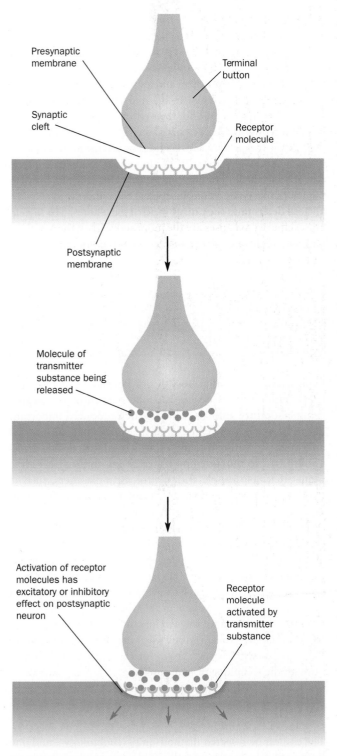

Figure 4.10 The release of a transmitter substance from a terminal button. Top: Before the arrival of an action potential. Middle: Just after the arrival of an action potential. Molecules of transmitter substance have been released. Bottom: Activation of receptor molecules. The molecules of transmitter substance diffuse across the synaptic cleft and some of them activate receptor molecules in the postsynaptic membrane.

activate them. Once they are activated, the receptor molecules produce excitatory or inhibitory effects on the postsynaptic neuron. They do so by opening ion channels. The ion channels found at excitatory synapses permit sodium ions to enter the neuron; those found at inhibitory synapses permit potassium ions to leave it (see Figure 4.11).

The excitation or inhibition produced by a synapse is short-lived; the effects soon pass away, usually in a fraction of a second. At most synapses, the effects are terminated by a process called **reuptake**. The transmitter substance is released by the terminal button and is quickly taken up again. It has, therefore, only a short time to stimulate the postsynaptic receptor molecules, as you can see from Figure 4.12. The rate at which the terminal button takes back the transmitter substance determines how prolonged the effects of the chemical on the postsynaptic neuron will be. The faster the transmitter substance is taken back, the shorter its effects will be on the postsynaptic neuron. As we will see, some drugs affect the nervous system by slowing down the rate of reuptake, thus prolonging the effects of the transmitter substance.

Neuromodulators: action at a distance

Terminal buttons excite or inhibit postsynaptic neurons by releasing transmitter substances. These chemicals travel a very short distance and affect receptor molecules located on a small patch of the postsynaptic membrane. But some neurons release chemicals that get into the general circulation of the brain and stimulate receptor molecules on many thousands of neurons, some located at a considerable distance away. The chemicals these neurons release are called **neuromodulators**, because they modulate the activity of the neurons they affect.

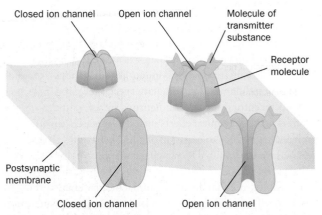

Figure 4.11 Detailed view of receptor molecules in the postsynaptic neuron. When activated by molecules of a transmitter substance, the receptor molecules allow sodium ions to enter the postsynaptic neuron, causing excitation, or allow potassium ions to leave, causing inhibition.

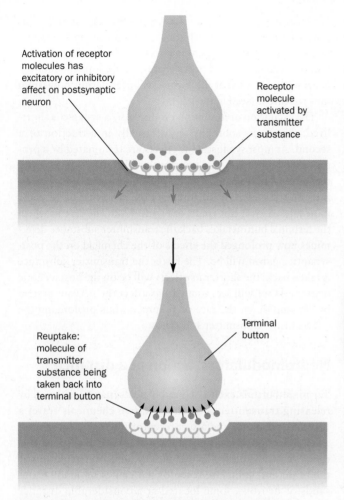

Activation of receptor molecules has excitatory or inhibitory affect on postsynaptic neuron

Receptor molecule activated by transmitter substance

Reuptake: molecule of transmitter substance being taken back into terminal button

Terminal button

Figure 4.12 Reuptake of molecules of transmitter substance.

We can think of neuromodulators as the brain's own 'drugs'. Because these chemicals diffuse widely in the brain, they can activate or inhibit many different circuits of neurons, thus exerting several behavioural and physiological effects. These effects act together to help achieve a particular goal.

The best-known neuromodulator is a category of chemicals called endorphins, or opioids ('opium-like substances'). Opioids are neuromodulators that stimulate special receptor molecules (opioid receptors) located on neurons in several parts of the brain. Their behavioural effects include decreased sensitivity to pain and a tendency to persist in ongoing behaviour. Opioids are released while an animal is engaging in important species-typical behaviours, such as mating or fighting. The behavioural effects of opioids ensure that a mating animal or an animal fighting to defend itself is less likely to be deterred by pain; thus, conception is more likely to occur and a defence is more likely to be successful.

Many years ago, people discovered that eating or smoking the sap of the opium poppy decreased their sensitivity to pain, so they began using it for this purpose. They also discovered that

the sap produced pleasurable effects: people who took it enjoyed the experience and wanted to take more. In recent times, chemists have discovered that the sap of the opium poppy contains a class of chemicals called opiates. They also learned how to extract and concentrate them and to produce synthetic versions with even greater potency. In the mid-1970s, neurobiologists learned that opiates produce their effect by stimulating special opioid receptor molecules located on neurons in the brain (Pert *et al.*, 1974). Soon after that, they discovered the brain's opioids (Terenius and Wahlström, 1975). Thus, opiates mimic the effects of a special category of neuromodulators that the brain uses to regulate some types of species-typical behaviours.

The brain produces other neuromodulators. Some help organise the body's response to stress, while others reduce anxiety and promote sleep. Some promote eating, while others help end a meal.

Techniques in psychobiology and neuroscience

Until relatively recently, most of our knowledge of the functions of the nervous system was obtained through research using laboratory animals. This research produced important discoveries about the causes and treatments of neurological and mental disorders, many of which are discussed in this book. It led to the development of drugs and surgical techniques that help people with neurological disorders, such as Parkinson's disease, and mental disorders, such as schizophrenia, depression and obsessive-compulsive disorders.

Physiological psychologists now have at their disposal a range of research methods to study the function of the brain and body that would have been impossible to imagine just a few decades ago. We have ways to identify neurons that contain particular chemicals. We have ways to take photographs of particular ions entering neurons when the appropriate ion channels open. We have ways to inactivate individual genes to see what happens to behaviour when they no longer function. We can also witness the activity of the brain as it behaves, through the technique of neuroimaging.

Lesioning

The earliest of research methods in psychobiology – and one that is still the most commonly used – involves correlating an impairment in function with damage to a specific part of the nervous system. The damage can be studied in one of two ways. For example, a neuropsychologist may examine the effects of brain damage caused by injury or disease on function, such as the effect of damage to the front part of the brain on a person's ability to create and adhere to plans.

The second way involves the investigator producing an **experimental brain lesion,** an injury to a particular part of the brain, but only in an animal's brain. Of course, neurosurgeons do lesion parts of the brain to alleviate some forms of suffering. One recent, successful treatment for the movement disorder Parkinson's disease, for example, has involved lesioning a small structure deep within the brain. A similar technique 'lesions' in another way (the procedure is called deep brain stimulation, DBS). In Parkinson's disease, a person may behave rigidly or be unable to walk properly or exhibit tremors or engage in excessive, repetitive, involuntary motor behaviour. Treatment by Levodopa (mentioned earlier) provides some respite but there are off periods when the drug does not work. DBS overstimulates parts of a collection of structures called the basal ganglia, described below. This has been found to be more successful than lesioning the parts directly (Liu *et al.,* 2008). Why lesioning and overstimulation seem to work (i.e. produce the same effect) is still a mystery. One theory is that surgery reduces the inhibitory effects of neurons in the basal ganglia and increases them in another structure, the thalamus and cortex (Liu *et al.,* 2008).

When an animal's brain is experimentally lesioned, the investigator hypothesises that this lesion might have specific consequences; they then study the effects of the lesion on the animal's behaviour. If particular behaviours are disrupted, then the reasoning suggests, the damaged part of the brain must be involved in those behaviours.

Some lesioning techniques are used in both experimental and neurosurgical work. For example, to reach the region to be lesioned, the experimenter or surgeon uses a device called a **stereotaxic apparatus** to insert a fine wire (called an electrode) into a particular location in the brain, as Figures 4.13 and 4.14 show. The term 'stereotaxic' refers to the ability to manipulate an object in three-dimensional space. The researcher passes an electrical current through the electrode, which produces heat that destroys a small portion of the brain around the tip of the electrode. After a few days, the animal recovers from the operation, and the researcher can assess its behaviour.

A stereotaxic apparatus can also be used to insert wires for recording the electrical activity of neurons in particular regions of the brain. But an electrode placed in an animal's brain can also be used to lead electrical current into the brain as well as out of it. If an electrical connector on the animal's skull is attached to an electrical stimulator, current can be sent to a portion of the animal's brain. This current activates neurons located near the tip of the electrode. The experimenter can then see how this artificial stimulation affects the animal's behaviour.

Neurosurgeons sometimes use stereotaxic apparatus to operate on humans (see Figure 4.15). Neurosurgeons can also insert electrodes into the human brain and record the electrical activity of particular regions to try to find locations that might be responsible for triggering epileptic seizures.

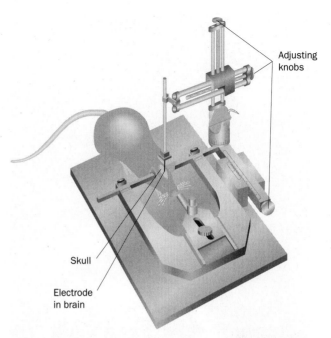

Figure 4.13 A stereotaxic apparatus, used to insert a wire into a specific portion of an animal's brain.

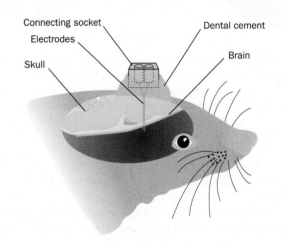

Figure 4.14 A permanently attached set of electrodes in an animal's brain and a connecting socket cemented to the skull.

Studying brain injury: clinical neuropsychology

Although we can, under very careful conditions, experimentally lesion the brains of non-humans, we cannot do this in humans, for very obvious reasons. We have, therefore, relied on studies of accidental brain injury to help us build a picture of the role of damaged brain regions in specific functional impairments.

This approach usually utilises the single-case study design (see Chapter 2). Brain injury usually results from accident or disease and, because it is more difficult to obtain information of this kind, scientists have studied a small number

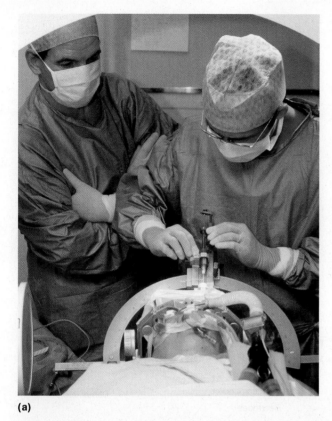

(a)

(b)

Figure 4.15 **(a)** Shows the typical stereotaxic set-up in surgery designed to reduce symptoms of Parkinson's disease. **(b)** Fergus Henderson, celebrated chef of the St John restaurant in London. Henderson suffered from Parkinson's disease until he received surgery to control the symptoms. His hands are in his pockets because he could not keep them still when this photograph was taken.
Source: (a) BSIP, Astier/Science Photo Library Ltd.; (b) © John Reardon, www.abbyjohnston.com.

of individuals intensively over a long period of time. The approach allows neuroscientists to observe how fairly local-ised brain damage can impair intellectual or emotional function.

Most human brain lesions are the result of natural causes, such as a stroke. A stroke (also known as a cerebrovascular accident, or CVA) occurs when a blood clot obstructs an artery in the brain or when a blood vessel in the brain bursts open. In the first case, the clot blocks the supply of oxygen and nutrients to a particular region and causes that region to die. In the second case, the blood that accumulates in the brain directly damages neural tissue, partly by exerting pressure on the tissue and partly through its toxic effects on cells. The most common causes of strokes are high blood pressure and high levels of **cholesterol** in the blood. We consider these fac-tors and their effect on health in Chapter 17. Lesions also occur as a result of injury to the brain by missiles or objects. Approximately 750 in every 100,000 people will experience traumatic brain injury annually (Anderson *et al.*, 2011). Men are more likely experience traumatic brain injury than are women (Moore *et al.*, 2009). Young men and boys are at a higher risk of brain injury than are girls and young women – 1.4 times higher in the under 10s and 2.2 times higher in those

between 10 and 20 years old (Thurman, 2016). The most com-mon cause of injury in the under 5s are falls; in the over 15s, it is motor vehicle accidents (Thurman, 2016).

The consequences of brain injury in such patients has given rise to a large number of neuropsychological disorders which have helped shape theories of cognitive function. These disor-ders include the inability to produce or comprehend speech (aphasia), inability to produce speech (fluent or Broca's apha-sia), inability to comprehend speech, specifically (Wernicke's aphasia), inability to recognise objects (visual agnosia), inabil-ity to follow motor commands (apraxia), reading impairment (acquired dyslexia), inability to recognise familiar faces (pro-sopagnosia), inability to attend to stimuli in one half of the visual field (spatial neglect) and a lack of awareness of visual objects, among many others (and you will read more about them in later chapters). Other impairments have no specific name but involve an inability to perform a specific function, such as recognising specific emotions in faces and voices; plac-ing events in sequence; planning; learning new material or retrieving old material from memory.

One of the most famous – if not the most famous – single-case study in neuropsychology is HM (see Chapter 8 for more details). HM underwent surgery for uncontrollable epilepsy in the late 1950s. The surgery involved removal of a part of the brain called the temporal lobe which includes a structure called the hippocampus (this has been implicated in various memory functions). After the surgery and beyond, HM exhibited a form of memory impairment called anterograde amnesia – he was unable to learn new material. The intensive study of HM led to a neurobiological theory of human memory which involved the temporal lobe and the hippocampus and the study has since been supplemented by other case studies and neuro-imaging studies of memory in healthy participants.

There have been arguments for and against the single-case study approach in neuropsychology. One argument against is that damage to a brain region does not necessarily demonstrate that this region is responsible for any function that is disrupted following injury. Other areas connected to the damaged region may be responsible for the specific function but connections to the intact areas from the lesioned area have been disrupted. There is also the need to specify exactly what function is being measured (this is a problem for psychology in general, rather than neuropsychology in particular). When we say that a region may be 'responsible' for phonological processing, what exactly is meant by phonological processing? Could the region be responsible for some other function which allows phonological processing, rather than being responsible for phonological processing itself?

There are also obvious methodological and practical problems such as the extent, variability and locus of the lesion – factors that are uncontrollable. There is also great variation in regional brain structure between individuals. Amunts *et al.* (1999), for example, found that the size of Broca's area varied enormously in a group of 10 individuals: there was a tenfold difference between participants in some cases.

When such brain injury occurs, it is also unlikely to be limited to one specific region or structure; it may extend to more than one and so conclusions drawn about the significance of findings in studies such as these need to be done circumspectly. There are other factors such as sex, personality, handedness and intellectual ability which may need to be taken into account.

The former *Top Gear* television presenter Richard Hammond, crashed his car while attempting to break the British land-speed record. His jet-powered vehicle was travelling at 314 mph when a tyre burst. Hammond was hospitalised with brain injury. Although he made a good physical recovery, he still reports periods of severe depression, emotional problems such as becoming angry or scared and not knowing how to cope with these states, and short-term memory loss, including forgetting the PINs of his credit cards.
Source: Trinity Mirror / Mirrorpix / Alamy Stock Photo.

Rehabilitation after brain injury

Rehabilitation is an 'active process whereby people who are disabled by injury or disease work together with professional staff, relatives and members of the wider community to achieve their optimum physical, psychological, social and vocational well-being' (McLellan, 1991, p. 785) and programmes have been designed for reading disorders resulting from brain injury (acquired reading disorders) (Patterson, 1994), the inability to produce or understand speech (aphasia) (Berndt and Mitchum, 1995), an inability to attend to or 'see' one half of the world (spatial neglect) (Robertson *et al.*, 1993) and memory disorders (Wilson and Powell, 1994; Glisky, 1997).

The process of helping functional recovery following brain injury is called neuropsychological rehabilitation.

A review of the content of treatment in 95 randomised control trials with 4,068 patients found that most rehabilitation programmes were created for language, visuospatial and memory function, and most patients had suffered a stroke (van Heugten *et al.*, 2012). The mean number of hours of treatment provided was 4.1 a week. If traumatic brain injury is mild, cognitive performance can be impaired after three months on tasks testing attention, memory, executive function and information processing, although other studies find no impairment (Anderson *et al.*, 2011; Dean and Sterr, 2013).

The mechanism that underpins rehabilitation is thought to be plasticity (Kolb and Gibb, 2013). According to Cramer *et al.* (2011), plasticity is 'the ability of the nervous system to respond to intrinsic or extrinsic stimuli by recognizing its structure, function and connections'. It reflects the capacity of the brain to be flexibly organised and reorganised during the early years and seems to explain why cognitive development and speech are better able to recover from a brain injury sustained in early childhood than from one sustained during adolescence or adulthood, as you'll see in Chapter 12. We know, for example, that when the brain undergoes rehabilitation after injury that the uninjured areas might take over the function of the damaged area – which is why performance is often never as completely proficient as it once was. The brain's reorganisation helps the person to undertake the impaired function.

The most common type of rehabilitation programme is **cognitive rehabilitation** (Parente and Stapleton, 1997). Here, the patient is encouraged to engage in two types of activity: (1) 'the reinforcing, strengthening or establishing of previously learned behaviour', and (2) the establishment of 'new patterns of cognitive activity or mechanisms to compensate' for the impairment (Bergqvist and Malec, 1997). It shows consistently successful results in the majority of cases of mild to severe brain injury (Ho and Bennett, 1997).

The most common form of impairment following brain injury is memory disorder. Specific problems include deficits in learning new material and in retaining other kinds of information (Wilson and Powell, 1994). Some techniques of rehabilitation used to improve memory include exercises and drills, use of external aids and the use of mnemonic strategies. The patients 'JC' and Julia Cogan are good examples of how rehabilitation strategies can work effectively in reducing problems in everyday life in individuals with severe memory impairment (Wilson, 1991, 1995; Wilson *et al.*, 1997; Oddy and Cogan, 2005). JC, for example, is a self-employed French-polisher who, during the second year at university, suffered an epileptic seizure and collapsed during a tutorial. Doctors, family and friends noted that JC showed severe loss of memory and could not remember anything 'from one minute to the next'.

JC used external aids, such as a diary or notebook, mnemonics and chaining – where tasks are broken down into smaller steps or stages and which can, for example, help patients to find their way around when planning short journeys. These benefited JC, but were developed by him into a more elaborate strategy: he has been using and refining this strategy for at least 10 years following his impairment. During the early stages, he began to use a pocketbook kept in his shirt and used a watch with an alarm that sounded every hour – he would note what he was doing in his notebook when this sounded (Wilson *et al.*, 1997). He would create weekly and daily sheets on which he would write down all appointments and lists of things to do or done. He bought a Dictaphone whose content he would transcribe at the end of every day. His aunt noted how a new watch helped him because it was

capable of 15 programmed weekly alarms and 15 one-off alarms. He would use the one-off alarms for reminding him of individual events. He would role-play some social situations to avoid the embarrassment of not being able to remember in public. He would make a log of all phone calls so that he didn't ring someone twice with the same message.

JC's success is similar to that of Julia Cogan. Cogan was a 23-year-old first-class physics graduate who was studying for a PhD in neuroimaging and oncology when she suffered brain injury (Oddy and Cogan, 2005). She made a full physical recovery but her memory was severely impaired. Her every-day problems were familiar ones; she was unable to remember what she had for breakfast, for example, and relied on the strategies she had developed so that she could lead as normal a life as possible. Like JC, she made extremely good use of her Filofax and, if she could not remember a piece of information, then she could find it quickly in her pad. The pad included extensive notes on people she had met, her travel arrangements, her recipes and so on (you can see an example in Figure 4.16). If she was asked how work was going, then she would flick to a page which described her last assignment and her next.

Julia is young, well-motivated, intelligent and very well-organised. The evidence suggests that all of these characteristics can benefit recovery following rehabilitation.

Plasticity in people without brain injury

Some studies have suggested that if the brain is trained even over a period of hours and minutes then the training will result in changes in its structure; it can even respond in this way to meditation (Holzel *et al.*, 2011; Tang *et al.*, 2012). The idea is not new in neuroscience. One of the oldest theories of learning suggests that our learning is enhanced if the connections between neurons are strengthened by repeated exposure (see Chapter 7). Repeatedly stimulating the fingertips of monkeys has been found to result in an increase in the part of the somatosensory cortex responsible for the representation of fingers (Jenkins *et al.*, 1990).

In a well-known experiment, Draganski *et al.* (2004) divided 21 men and 3 women into 2 groups: juggling-training or no-training. The jugglers were given three months to learn a three-ball cascade. MRI was used to measure brain structure before the training, when participants could juggle for 60 minutes, and after three months. Between the first and second scan, there was an increase in volume in grey matter on both sides of the middle temporal lobe (a region known as the visual motion area – hMT/V5) and a specific area, the left posterior intraparietal sulcus. This increase correlated with performance: as performance increased so did brain volume. No change was seen in jugglers. The study has received limited replication success, even from the same researchers (Boyke *et al.*, 2008; Driemeyer *et al.*, 2008) with results showing increases in area near the right V5. The increases declined after three months of the practice wasn't sustained.

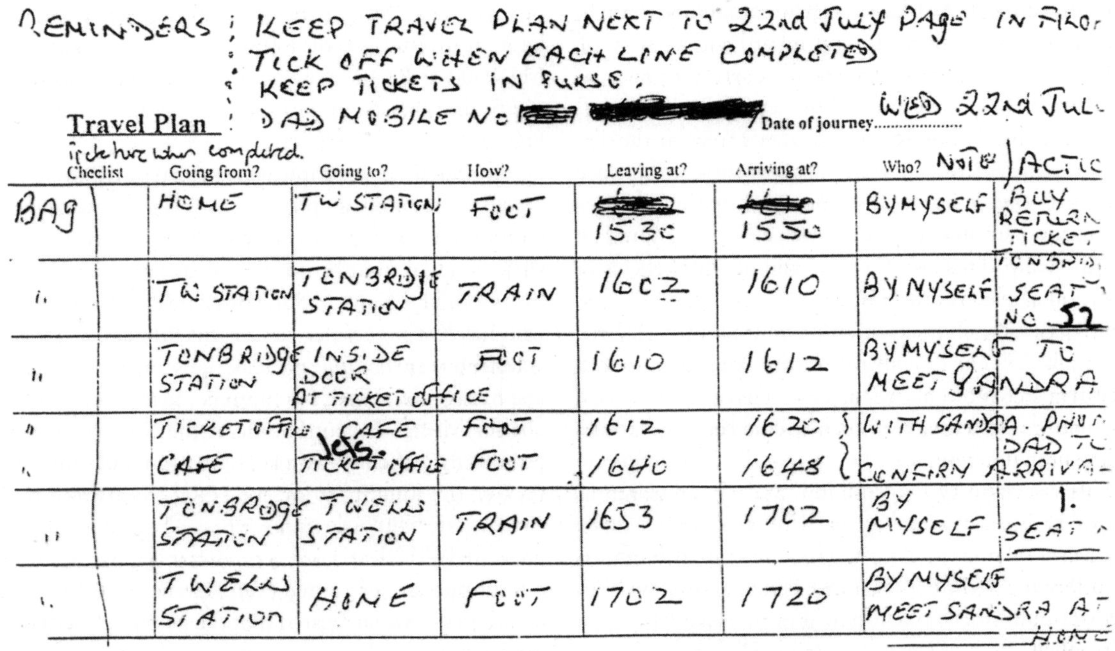

Figure 4.16 An example of the detailed timetable constructed by Julia Cogan to help her remember her travel arrangements.
Source: Figure provided by kind permission of Julia Cogan and Professor Michael Oddy.

There is evidence in support of the effects of training on brain structure. One study found that training people to undertake a complex finger sequence task across several weeks was associated with increased volume on the primary motor cortex (Karni *et al.*, 1995). White matter volume increases have been seen in people who undertook two months' worth of working memory training (Takeuchi *et al.*, 2010) and in people being taught balancing skills over six weeks (Taubert *et al.*, 2010). Scholz *et al.* (2009) found that training was associated with grey matter increases and changes in the visual cortex have been found when people spent two hours remembered colour name categories. Studies have found increases in hippocampus volume after three months of foreign language training, learning to spatially navigate, and after 12 months of aerobic exercise (Erickson *et al.*, 2011).

In their review of neuroimaging studies and plasticity in 2013, Lovden *et al.* found that 33 such studies had been published. The mechanism responsible for the structural change, if the change does happen, is unknown but candidate explanations have included: remodelling of existing neurons, neurogenesis (see the section earlier), an increase in glial cells, changes in the spines of dendrites, and changes in axonal buttons (Zatorre *et al.*, 2012; Thomas and Baker, 2013).

It seems, therefore, as if the overwhelming evidence suggests that experience and training can alter brain structure. Or does it? In their review of the literature, Thomas and Baker (2013) found that the majority of the studies they reviewed contained flaws. Four of 20 studies did not include a control group, for example. Perhaps just as important, because the error was so

common, was the failure to include a proper experimental control. Most studies divided participants into a training or control condition but did not have another condition in which participants did something similar to the experimental group but not exactly the same thing. Groups were not given different tasks so that the specific effect of training could be distinguished from the effect of just undertaking any task.

They also note another problem with these studies and that is the experimental group can differ from the control group in another way. Because they are engaged in a task for weeks, these participants may be more invested and, therefore, more motivated than are those who do nothing. Any change could be attributable to this characteristic of the sample, rather than to training. Only three studies they reviewed employed a separate training task condition although those studies showed benefits of the training. They conclude that only one study shows effects that are specific to training (Erikson *et al.*, 2011). Erikson (2013) himself has pointed out that there has also been great variation in the lengths of time people spend in training – this has ranged from three days to one year.

Psychophysiology: measuring CNS activity

When psychobiologists record brain electrical activity from deep inside it, the technique is invasive, that is, it invades the body (in this case, the brain). However, electrical activity of neurons can also be recorded from the scalp non-invasively. Both methods involve a technique called **electroencephalography**

(EEG), the recording of the brain's electrical impulses. In EEG, electrodes attached to the scalp can record the activity of groups of millions of neurons, specifically cortical pyramidal neurons (Martin, 2006; Jackson and Bolger, 2014). The number of electrodes used in brain research tends to be at the discretion of the experimenter. Some use two or three, others use a lot more (over one hundred in some cases), but in all cases researchers use a map showing where each electrode should be placed on the scalp. This avoids errors and inconsistencies in the application of electrodes.

EEG activity is seen in the form of a line-tracing or **electroencephalogram** (EEG or 'brainwave'), although some modern EEG recording machines allow the conversion of EEG data into 'brainmaps' – these are two-dimensional representations of the EEG activity. They can be coloured or in greyscale which means that areas of high and low activity can be represented by darker or lighter colours. There are different types of EEG waves – called frequencies – and these are thought to represent different psychological states. Some large, slow EEG waves, for example, are characteristic of deep sleep. One type of activity, called alpha, is the resting adult EEG; when we are engaged in thinking or making rapid movements, alpha activity changes to another type of activity called beta (Andreassi, 2007). In Chapter 9, you will see how different types of EEG brain activity occur during different stages of sleep and wakefulness.

One benefit of the EEG technique is that, as well as being non-invasive, it provides a measure of the brain's activity in real time, as it happens. We can, therefore, match the presentation of a stimulus or a task with the brain activity associated with it fairly accurately.

Sometimes, however, this electrical signal can be messy or noisy: it is difficult to distinguish between the brain's normal background activity and the activity produced by the perception of, or response to, a stimulus. The effect of perceiving a sound, for example, may be so small as to be invisible in an EEG tracing. To overcome this, psychophysiologists have devised the technique of averaging signals across trials. They can do this by **recording event-related potentials** (ERPs) (these are sometimes also called evoked potentials). These are electrical signals recorded to a repeatedly presented stimulus (or set of stimuli). Each EEG response to a stimulus is added and averaged to produce one clearer signal or evoked potential. The potentials are event-related because they are related to a specific event that is external or internal to the individual such as decision-making (internal stimulus) or perceiving a flash of light (external stimulus). The point of averaging is to make the effect of a stimulus on the EEG clearer; background noise is reduced and the effect of the stimulus becomes more obvious.

Some ERPs measure sensory responses to stimuli (this is called the N100 (or N1), so called because it appears 100 milliseconds after the onset of a stimulus), others are thought to be associated with more cognitive functions such as understanding words or being able to distinguish one type

of visual or auditory stimulus from another. These ERPs occur later, at around 300 or 400 milliseconds after stimulus onset (the P300 or P3 and N400 or N4), perhaps reflecting the time the brain takes to undertake these cognitive operations. See Figure 4.17.

The N400, for example, was the first ERP to be specifically linked with language processing and is elicited when participants read sentences in which the last word is semantically surprising or inappropriate, although linguistically legal (Kutas and Hillyard, 1980). For example, the sentence, 'A man who has lost ninety per cent of his brain is called a widower' is legal but surprising whereas the sentence, 'A man who has lost ninety per cent of his brain is called a zombie' is legal but not surprising. The amplitude of the N400 is associated with processing difficulty such that the more difficult the task, the greater the amplitude of the N400 (Kutas and Van Petten, 1994). The N400 declines when congruous sentences are presented – the last word is predictable – but not when incongruous ones are presented (Van Petten and Kutas, 1990). Some researchers have suggested that the N400 reflects a difficulty in integrating words into a sentence (Kutas *et al.*, 2000): the greater the difficulty, the larger the N400.

ERPs have been used to investigate a number of psychological functions such as decision-making, sentence comprehension, recognition memory and olfactory, visual, tactile and auditory perception amongst others. The absence of an evoked potential indicates an impairment in function or a failure to attend to stimuli. Figure 4.17 shows the difference between ERPs evoked by a decision-making task in healthy volunteers and individuals with dementia. Note the reduction in the amplitude (size) of the wave in the demented group.

Psychophysiology: measuring activity outside the CNS

Psychophysiologists can also record electrical activity in the peripheral (or autonomic) nervous system – from the heart, muscles and skin. Some of the most common techniques are EMG, ECG and GSR.

Electromyography (EMG)

The body possesses three types of muscles – skeletal, smooth and cardiac. Skeletal muscles are those such as biceps, triceps and flexor muscles of the upper arm and forearm. These are usually under voluntary control – they make up the voluntary motor system; we decide when to flex and tense our arms (such as when picking up a cup), legs (kicking a ball) or fingers (writing or typing at a keyboard). There are other muscles which are not under voluntary control. Smooth muscles are those over which we have little or no voluntary control – the constriction and dilation of blood vessels, for example. The third type of muscle is cardiac and, as the name suggests, this muscle makes up the heart and its valves. Smooth and

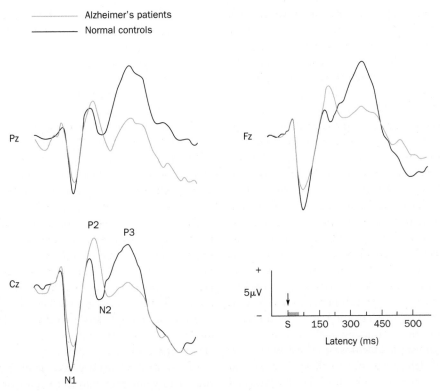

Figure 4.17 Examples of EPs measured in healthy individuals and those with Alzheimer's disease. When a participant is asked to undertake a task such as detecting the number of low tones in a series of high and low tones (where there are always fewer low tones), the ERPs illustrated here are found. The waves on the right show the brain's response to the high tones (the common ones); the N1 sensory and P2 components can be clearly seen. However, when the participant has to make a decision (discriminating between high and low tones) a late wave – the P3 – appears in response to the low tones (the rarer ones). This wave is thought to reflect the brain's decision-making processes. Note how the amplitude (height) of the P3 is lower than that seen in healthy individuals.

cardiac muscles comprise about 10 per cent of total body weight; the skeletal muscles make up around 40 per cent of this weight.

When the muscles of the body contract, they generate electrical potentials. Often, muscles contract for psychological reasons – responding to stress, emotional stimuli, pictures, sounds, faces and so on – and they sometimes contract for these reasons in ways that are undetectable to the eye. The technique used for measuring skeletal muscles' electrical activity is **electromyography** (**EMG**). EMG activity is recorded by electrodes – circular disks of around 10 mm in diameter – from the surface of the skin. The greater the muscle contraction and the closer the electrode is to the skin, the greater the electrical activity generated (in fact, EMG records activity from motor units just prior to muscle contraction). For example, imagine a simple behaviour such as gripping an object like a hammer or a handle. The harder you grip the object, the greater the electrical activity produced by musculature and this activity can be picked up as EMG activity from the recording electrode.

Imagining pleasant thoughts results in increased muscle activity in the cheek area responsible for smiling (the zygomatic muscle). A different set of muscles at the eyebrows – called corrugator muscles – are more active during the imagining of unpleasant thoughts (Schwartz *et al.*, 1980). Activity in the zygomatic muscles has also been found to increase when participants listen to stories with a sexual content rather than a non-sexual content but that corrugator activity is greater when the stories were sexual and unpleasant (Sullivan and Brender, 1986).

Electrocardiography (ECG/EKG)

Cardiac muscle activity is recorded in a similar way to that of skeletal muscle but the differences between the recordings are greater than the similarities. **Electrocardiography** (**ECG**) refers to the study of the electrical potentials generated by the working of the heart. Before understanding how biological psychologists measure heart activity, it's useful to know a little about how the heart works.

When the heart contracts, it produces an electrical current (as do all other muscular contractions). By placing electrodes near the source of the current, scientists can measure the electrical activity of the heart. The contraction of the heart is the consequence of the organ's chief function – to pump blood around the body. The heart is made up of four chambers which pump blood to the body's tissues. The two chambers at the top of the heart are the atria; the two at the bottom are the ventricles. The atria receive blood returned by the body's veins; the ventricles pump blood away from the heart via arteries (a useful way of remembering the direction in which the blood goes is to think of arteries taking blood away). When you feel – or record – your heartbeat, you are feeling or recording the contraction of the heart as it pumps blood. It beats, on average, 72 times a minute (72 bpm or beats per minute) and, therefore, about 100,000 times a day. The contraction phase of the heart's activity is called systole; the relaxation phase is called the diastole.

The activity of the heart recorded by electrodes can be seen in a typical type of electrical wave. The wave is made up of various characteristic deflections (the direction of the wave characterises various points leading to and during the contraction) – these are the P, Q, R, S and T waves. The P wave is a small deflection produced by the current generated before contraction of the atria; the QRS complex of waves is produced by what is known as depolarisation (more on this later in the chapter) prior to the contraction of the ventricles. The R wave is the largest, most prominent wave. The T wave is the next, small blip-like, deflection after the large R wave and occurs as a result of activity in the ventricles. The P–Q interval lasts about 160 milliseconds; the Q–T interval lasts around 300 milliseconds. It takes around 370 milliseconds to go from the T wave to the next contraction.

Heart rate changes can be seen in response to a number of psychological variables. The promise of financial reward for persuading others (Smith *et al.*, 1990), fear of needles (Shapiro, 1975) and playing Space Invaders (Turner *et al.*, 1983) have all been found to increase heart rate.

Electrodermal response (EDR)/galvanic skin response (GSR)

The measurement of electrical activity of the skin – **electrodermal response** (EDR) or **galvanic skin response** (GSR) – may seem to be completely irrelevant to the study of psychology. The technique, however, is surprisingly useful because skin conductance changes can be influenced by experience of positive and negative emotion, the degree of thinking that goes into the processing of information, and in perceptual awareness. In fact, a French neurologist, Charles Fere, was the first to note in 1888 that changes in a person's mood and environment could lead to changes in the electrical activity recorded from the skin.

The recording of electrodermal activity is based on the properties of skin and what skin does. Human skin has two layers – the epidermis, the outer layer which is about 1 mm thick, and the dermis, the inner layer which varies in thickness depending on the part of the body; it is thinner in the eyelids than the palms of the hands or soles of the feet, for example. The dermis contains blood vessels, hair follicles,

sensory nerves and, importantly for EDR, the secretory part of sweat glands. It is sweat which allows conductance to occur on the skin.

The body has two types of sweat glands – apocrine and eccrine. The larger of the two are the apocrine glands which are found in especially hirsute regions such as the armpits and genitals. Sweat is odourless and the odour we associate with it is the result of the reaction between sweat and bacteria on the skin. The eccrine glands are distributed widely and cover most of the skin, with some exceptions (such as lips, outer ear and glans penis, among others). Sweat glands are most numerous on the palms of the hands and soles of the feet with around one inch squared of skin having about 3,000 glands. EDR recorded from fingers and palms responds more strongly to sensory stimulation than to physical stimuli such as heat; the opposite pattern is found for EDR recorded from the forehead, neck and back of the hands which dictates the position of electrodes in EDR recording. Skin conductance increases with increased stress, arousal and cognitive activity and reduces when the organism's level of activity is low. During states of anxiety, for example, there is a great deal of sweating, especially in the palms.

One study has investigated people's psychophysiological responses while they played the part of James Bond in the game, *JB007: Nightfire* (Ravaja *et al.*, 2008). In the experiment, GSR and EMG were recorded while people either killed or wounded ne'er-do-wells, or were wounded and killed themselves. The aim was to discover the psychophysiological responses generated by different emotional and moral perspectives.

When an opponent was wounded or killed, participants' skin conductance increased but some of the muscles in the face (zygomatic, orbicularis occuli and corrugator muscles, all found around the eyes and mouth) decreased. When the protagonist was wounded or killed, there was a similar GSR increase but also an increase in two sets of facial muscles and a decrease in another set. These results suggest that the emotional consequences of attacking another or of being attacked can be characterised by subtle, facial muscle changes.

Continuing this bloody theme, Barlett *et al.* (2008) asked 65 men to play the *Mortal Kombat: Deadly Alliance* game as their heart rate was measured. The game differed in the amount of blood that was present in the game – a lot, a moderate amount, a low amount or none. Men in the high and moderate quantity conditions showed the greatest amount of heart rate and also the greatest levels of hostility. Men in the low or no-blood condition did not produce these increases. Moreover, in the high/moderate condition, the players were more likely to use their character's weapon more often.

Perhaps one of the more well-known, although poorly validated applications of GSR, has been via the polygraph, the so-called lie-detector (*poly* = many, *graphos* = writings in Greek; it is called the polygraph because different psychophysiological measurements are taken – heart rate, GSR and respiration rate). While its ability to detect actual liars is poor, GSR has been found to be a very useful technique when measuring the responses of some criminals – specifically, psychopaths – to emotional stimuli. Psychopaths are people who are utterly remorseless, superficially charming, manipulative and socially deviant. Jailed psychopaths have been found to show little GSR in response to emotional stimulation, a result that has also been found in studies of patients with damage to the front part of the brain (Blair *et al.*, 2005b). This is explored in the personality disorders section of Chapter 18.

Neuroimaging techniques

The development of machines which can be used to investigate the brain's structure and activity has revolutionised neuroscience, sometimes not entirely positively as you'll see in later sections. These techniques, more than any of the others, have provided neuroscientists with the ability to measure the function and structure of the whole, living, healthy brain in human and non-human participants. The number of papers published in **neuroimaging** has exploded in the past 30 years. Figure 4.18 shows the increase in the number of papers using a technique called functional Magnetic Resonance Imaging – more fMRI

studies have been published between 2008 and 2012 than in the whole of the 17 years before (Stelzer *et al.*, 2014).

Neuroimaging techniques allow us to create images of brain function and structure. These techniques include CT, MEG, PET, MRI and fMRI. PET and fMRI are measures of brain activity; CT and MRI are measures of brain structure. Each measures structure and function in different ways using different methods and equipment.

Measures of brain structure

Computerised tomography (CT)

Computerised tomography (CT) is a technique used to display the structure of the brain (*tomos*, meaning 'cut', describes the CT scanner's ability to produce a picture that looks like a slice of the brain). The scanner sends a narrow beam of X-rays through a person's head (see Figure 4.19a). The beam is moved around the patient's head, and a computer calculates the amount of radiation that passes through it at various points along each angle. The result is a two-dimensional image of a 'slice' of the person's head, parallel to the top of the skull.

Cutting edge: Pupil, behave

One of the most reliable physiological correlates of emotional behaviour is pupil size. Using a method called pupillometry, researchers can measure pupil dilation and constriction in response to various conditions and stimuli. For example, pupil dilation can be observed when we are aroused, are engaged in challenging cognitive tasks and decision-making, when we experience anxiety and when we process novelty (Naber *et al.*, 2013). Heterosexual men and women's pupils dilate when they watch photographs of nude women and men, respectively, although dilation is also seen for other significant visual images (mothers and babies) (Lick *et al.*, 2015). Dilation also occurs when we imagine sexual images or hear sex-related noises (Dabbs, 1997).

Two studies have shown how pupil size can depend on some unusual behaviour and might be used to predict how someone will behave. Naber *et al.* (2013), for example, asked a group of 30 young adults to play a game of 'rock, paper, scissors' against three opponents whose pupils had been filmed while they were playing the game against a computer. The group was asked to do this in one of three conditions. In one, they were asked to observe the eyes of opponents. In a second, they were told that the time of maximum pupil dilation indicated the

opponent's choice. In a third, they saw the pupil against a grey background.

In the first condition, participants' performance was at chance. In the second and third, it was above chance, suggesting that pupil size provided a clue to the behaviour of the opponent. It is a 'tell'. Pupil dilation was only a clue to performance in 60 per cent of cases. When pupil dilation was indicative of choice in 100 per cent of cases, participants performed above chance. This suggests that we do not consciously register pupil size when making decisions but if we are told to focus on it, it can influence our decisions. You can access the experiment here and try it yourself: http://www.staff.uni-marburg.de/~wetgast/rps/

And does pupil size indicate sexual interest? When asked to decide which male or female face best represented sexual arousal, participants rated those with larger and darker pupils to be the more sexually interested – and this dilation was consciously noticed in participants (Lick *et al.*, 2015). The authors conclude, 'our findings provide a context for understanding recent fashion trends, including 'baby doll' contact lenses that artificially increase the size of one's irises and pupils (www.eyecandys.com). These trends might make young women appear sexually interested to potential suitors'.

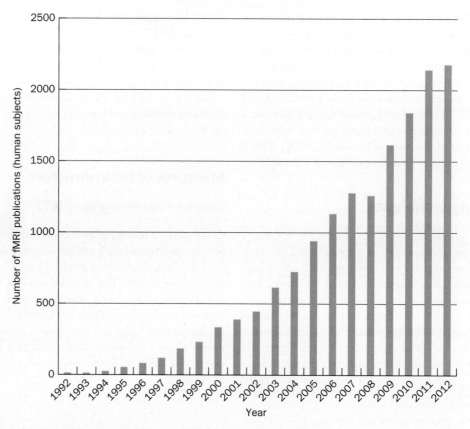

Figure 4.18 The growth in the publication of studies using fMRI from Stelzer et al (2014).

A typical recording procedure during the administration of the polygraph (right). Respiration, GSR and heart rate is recorded from various devices

Using the CT scanner, an investigator can determine the approximate location of a brain lesion in a living patient. Knowing the results of behavioural testing and the location of the brain damage, the neuropsychologist can compare them and make inferences about the normal function of the damaged brain tissue. Figure 4.19b shows CT scans of the brain of a patient with a lesion caused by a stroke.

Magnetic resonance imaging (MRI)

A **magnetic resonance imaging** (**MRI**) scanner provides more detailed images of the structure of the brain than does CT (see Figure 4.20). It does so with the use of magnetic fields and radio waves rather than with X-rays. When a magnetic field is passed over the head, reverberations are produced by hydrogen molecules. These reverberations are picked up by the scanner which can convert the activity into a structural image. This image appears in a form like that seen in Figure 4.21.

Measures of brain function

Magnetoencephalography (MEG)

A more recently developed electrophysiological technique is **magnetoencephalography** (**MEG**). Neurons can generate magnetic as well as electrical currents and these magnetic fields can be measured from the surface of the head via a machine called a superconducting quantum interference device (SQUID) which is immersed in liquid helium. The machine detects the activity of magnetic fields from a large number of neurons because the magnetic fields generated by single neurons are very weak. The subsequent recording is called the magnetoencephalograph or MEG. Unlike the EEG, MEG can be used to localise sources of activity fairly well and these sources can be plotted on a three-dimensional image of the participant's head. MEG has been used to study various functions from language to smell and taste.

Positron emission tomography (PET)

Positron emission tomography (**PET**) is an invasive measure of brain metabolism, glucose consumption and blood flow. The procedure for undergoing a PET scan goes something like this. A person is given a harmless dose of a radioactive substance (a form of glucose) which enters the brain (this is why the technique is invasive; the radioactive substance is injected into the participant's arm). The chemical accumulates in particular regions of the brain (the location depends on the specific chemical) but usually goes to active cells. PET measures brain activity by examining the amount of oxygen consumed by, or blood flow travelling to, neurons. The radioactive parts of the glucose emit positrons (hence positron emission) which are detected by a PET scanner, a large, doughnut-shaped piece of equipment which accommodates the prostrate participant's

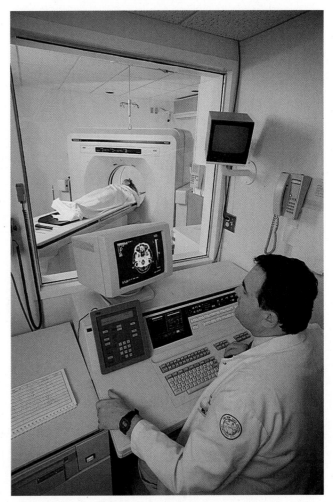

Figure 4.19 (a) A patient being placed in a computerised tomography (CT) scanner.
Source: Larry Mulvehill/Science Source/Getty Images.

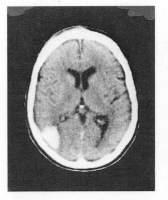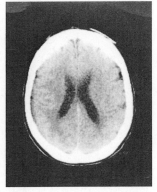

Figure 4.19 (b) A set of CT scans from a patient with a brain lesion caused by a stroke; left and right are traditionally reversed on CT scans, the brain lesion is actually in the right hemisphere.
Source: Courtesy of Dr J. McA. Jones, Good Samaritan Hospital, Portland, Oregon, USA.

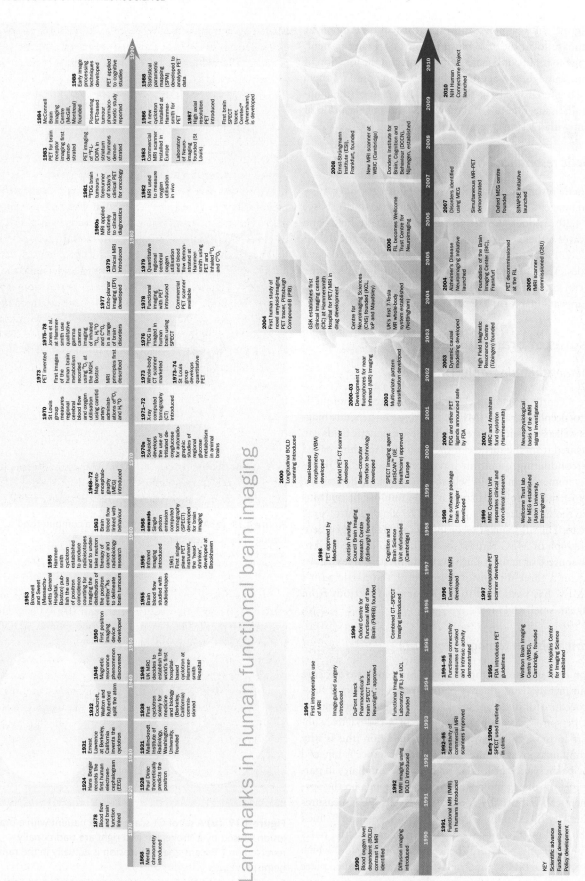

Landmarks in human functional brain imaging

The chronology of the development of neuroimaging, courtesy of The Wellcome Trust.

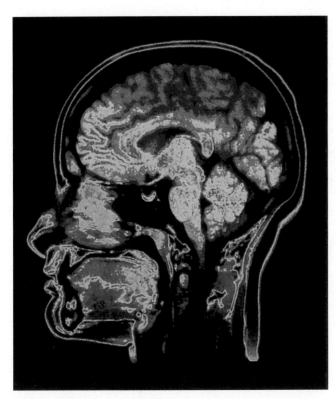

Figure 4.20 A colour-enhanced sagittal MRI scan.
Source: Scott Camazine/Photo Researchers Inc.

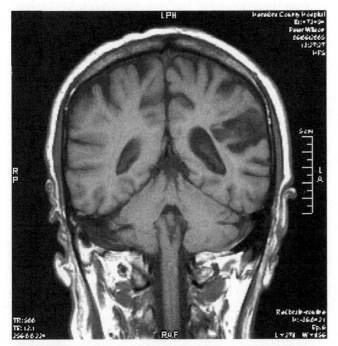

Figure 4.21 An MRI scan taken from a patient with damage to Wernicke's area, following a stroke (the right side of the image represents the left side of the brain). This slice is called 'coronal'.
Source: Figure 4.26 from *Human Neuropsychology*, 2nd edn, p. 36, Pearson/Prentice Hall (Martin, G.N., 2006).

head. This activity is then represented in the form of coloured maps. Because of the radioactivity involved, only certain participants are allowed to take part in PET research. Premenopausal women and children, for example, cannot take part, which limits the use of PET when investigating how brain function develops during the early years. See Figure 4.22.

It is difficult to overestimate the early contribution of PET research to the study of brain function, however. PET has allowed researchers to undertake investigations of the workings of the brain that were thought unrealisable 30 years ago. It is an expensive technique (the scanner's costs run into millions) but a number of PET laboratories now exist around the world and the results from these laboratories have allowed us to see whether the technique shows a consistent pattern of findings (Cabeza and Nyberg, 2000). In later chapters, you will see how PET (and fMRI) has helped us to understand the neural basis of functions such as speech perception, speech comprehension, memory, reading, attention, recognition of emotion, as well as more unconventional topics ranging from responding to the photograph of a loved one (Ortigue *et al.*, 2007), to seeing a violent act being committed (King *et al.*, 2006), to making a decision about whether to buy expensive chocolates (Knutson *et al.*, 2007) to watching a magic trick (Parris *et al.*, 2009).

Functional magnetic resonance imaging (fMRI)

It is also possible to use MRI in a functional capacity, to examine the brain's function as well as its structure. This is called **functional magnetic resonance imaging (fMRI)** and the technique is a measure of the amount of deoxygenated blood in parts of the brain (giving what is called the BOLD signal). The BOLD signals are converted into a form of visual unit called a pixel (in fMRI they are called voxels). Each image contains between 40,000 and 500,000 voxels and each voxel covers between 1 and 123 mm^3 of brain tissue (Vul *et al.*, 2009). As 1 mm^3 contains around 10–50,000 neurons, you can see that fMRI measures activity surrounding millions to hundreds of millions of neurons.

Unlike PET, which is invasive (radioactively labelled substances are introduced into the body), MRI and fMRI are non-invasive, which means that they can be used to investigate the development of function (e.g. in children). fMRI has been used to investigate similar functions to those investigated using PET: language, attention, vision, memory and so on. Both PET and MRI can be used in combination. However, while both have the advantage of good spatial resolution (you can see images and structures more precisely), they also have the disadvantage of poor temporal resolution – it is difficult to match the psychological and neural event in time precisely. The reason for this is that in PET and fMRI a number of scans are recorded and then averaged (see 'Some issues with neuroimaging' below). Scanning is also expensive – around £200 per hour per participant – and produces large amounts (gigabytes)

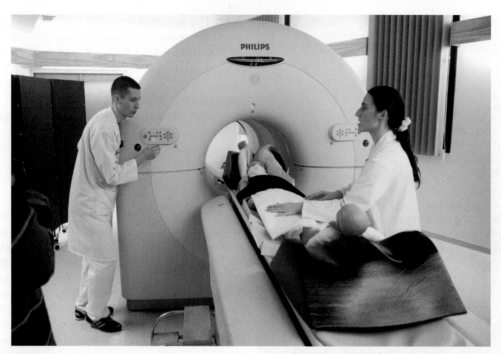

Figure 4.22 A PET scanner.
Source: Corbis/Owen Franken.

of data. The costs may be one reason why neuroimaging studies are rarely directly replicated and why the field is characterised by novelty.

fMRI has been used to understand the cerebral correlates of a variety of functions. For example, Redcay *et al.* (2010) investigated how the brain responded while a participant interacted with the experimenter via a video feed or watched a pre-recorded exchange. When the exchange was live, activation was greater in the parts of the brain known to be involved in social cognition and reward (specifically, the right temporoparietal junction, anterior cingulate cortex (AOC), amygdala and right superior temporal sulcus (STS)). When the participant was asked to follow the gaze of the experimenter – so that their attention would be drawn elsewhere – activation was seen in similar areas – the right temporoparietal TP junction and posterior STS.

Some issues with neuroimaging

Of course, neuroimaging techniques, although providing us with a new way of viewing brain activation, are not measures of actual neural functioning. Instead, they measure the processes associated with neural function – such as blood flow or oxygen and glucose consumption. They also provide data that are correlational. Researchers draw associations between the stimulus or task they present and the differences in activation in the brain they observe that are not seen at baseline. As Coltheart (2013) noted: 'we do not have any evidence showing that any particular form of brain activation is a sign that some particular

type of cognitive operation is being performed' (p. 100) (although people disagree, e.g. Mather *et al.*, 2013).

Data are not particularly time-sensitive because fMRI and PET use the technique of averaging and subtraction – several experimental scans are taken, usually in a mixed order, and then averaged to produce a scan for this condition/group. A scan is taken approximately every three seconds. The average experimental condition is subtracted from the control scan. This means that you cannot associate a scan with a specific event in time. Also, because any task will activate all of the brain to some extent, researchers focus on a region of interest (ROI) and compare activation between two tasks in this area.

Poldrack and colleagues (2008) have made a number of suggestions for researchers who use neuroimaging. These included:

- Describing the type of participants in detail
- Describing what participants were asked to do and what they did
- Describing the brain regions of interest explicitly
- Providing enough data and detail for others to replicate the study
- Reporting statistical tests to support all claims
- Accounting for the Type 1 error that can arise from multiple testing

A number of studies continues to present problems and violate these basic recommendations. For example, Carp (2012) analysed 241 fMRI studies and found that many did not report important detail of method, design and analysis. He also

Cutting edge: Are brain scanners stressful?

Having your brain imaged is not a straightforward or normal process. You're normally asked not to eat or drink, you're asked to remove metal objects from your body, you're asked to lie down and, if the technique is MRI or fMRI, you'll be asked to lie down inside a tube covering most of your body with only an alarm button for company just in case you find the environment too claustrophobic. In the case of MRI, there is also a loud hammering noise accompanying each scan.

It should not be too surprising, then, if this context were to affect people's mood and behaviour. What is surprising is that few studies have taken this into account. Muehlhan et al. (2013) asked 37 young adults who had never undergone a brain scan before to come in for an fMRI experiment on response time. Before being scanned, they entered a lab and were provided with brief training on a simple visual target detection task. They then took part in a structural scan for 10 mins and a functional scan for 15 minutes. Saliva samples were taken before entering the scanner, after the structural scan and after the functional scan. The samples measured sympathetic nervous activity (described later in the chapter) via salivary alpha amylase (sAA).

Levels of sAA increased twice – once just before scanning and once at the end of the scan. The first increase correlated with a decrease in frontal and parietal activation. The increase persisted until the first part of the experiment, then declined before peaking again at the end, a pattern that mirrors heart rate during scanning (Chapman et al., 2010). The increase in sAA was not seen in all participants, but was seen in 65 per cent of them. Other research shows that 30–40 per cent of patients about to undergo scanning feel anxious (Katz et al., 1994) and that the initial distress decreases over 12 minutes (Lucken et al., 2012). These data suggest that it would be wise to help participants acclimatise to the experimental environment in the first 10 minutes of a neuroimaging study and to take the structural, rather than the functional scan, first.

found that there was a great degree of flexibility in the experimental designs used which can maximize the chances of obtaining a positive finding (Type 1 errors). Eklund et al. (2016) found that three of the software packages used by fMRI research could inflate the number of false positives reported. They claim that up to 40,000 fMRI studies could be affected. This number is probably an exaggeration but the study highlights on-going challenges faced by scientists when using this technique.

The appeal of neuroimaging has been described as seductive. Images are immediate, (obviously) visual and allow us to see something that was previously unattainable: a pictorial, anatomically correct representation of the living brain. And, as humans, we are very swayed by visual seduction. McCabe and Castel (2008) asked people to judge the degree of scientific reasoning in three articles about cognitive neuroscience. The articles were accompanied by either bar graphs, brain scans or no image. Despite there being no difference between the content of the articles, the piece accompanied by a brain map was judged to be more scientific.

These images, say McCabe and Castel, 'provide a physical basis for abstract cognitive processes, appealing to people's affinity for reductionistic explanations for cognitive phenomena' (p. 343). People find neuroscience explanations for behaviour to be much more plausible than non-neuroscience explanations (Weisberg et al., 2008, 2015; Minahan and Siedlecki, 2016) but whether images are actually more persuasive than scientific verbal descriptions is not clear: some studies find no difference (Schweizter et al., 2011). Fernandez-Duque et al. (2015), for example, found that irrelevant neuroscientific explanations accompanying descriptions of psychological phenomena were regarded as being of higher quality than social science explanations or explanations from the hard sciences. The presence of an fMRI image had no effect, suggesting that the allure is generated by the discipline, rather than the discipline's visual output. People's ability to think analytically did not protect against the bias – analytic thinkers were just as likely to judge the neuroscience explanations as being of good quality.

One study found that when participants were presented with descriptions of diagnoses made of politicians from parties they either did or not support, they were more likely to evaluate evidence more favourably if it included MRI scans than cognitive evaluations (Munro and Munro, 2014). Not one participant who received the MRI diagnosis considered it to be unreliable (even though the more accurate way of diagnosing dementia is via neuropsychological assessment rather than MRI). It may be the reductionistic nature of the evidence which may create the degree of persuasion. One study of undergraduates and members of the public found that across many sciences, reductionist (but irrelevant) good and bad explanations for findings were regarded more positively, as more persuasive and as more plausible (Hopkins et al., 2016). This study also found that participants rated neuroscience as being more rigorous, difficult and prestigious than chemistry, biology and physics, which may explain why this branch of psychology holds a particular 'allure'. However, neuroscience is not always persuasive. When human resources professionals, psychology student and business students, evaluated applicants' (fictitious) personality tests which were accompanied by neuroscience information or not, the tests accompanied by neuroscience were rated less positively (Diekmann *et al.*, 2015).

This may seem like an interesting, if trivial, topic of investigation but it can become very significant if, for example, brain scans and other types of neurobiological evidence are used in potentially life or death circumstances: being presented in court as part of an advocate's argument in defence of his or her client, for example. Farahany (2016) reviewed the number of judicial opinions in the US that had used neuroscience (or behavioural genetics) in defence of a client. In 2012, she noted that 250 opinions involved cases where the client attributed their behaviour to their brain (dysfunction). This was double the number cited in 2007. Between 2005 and 2012, 1,585 judicial judgements considered neuroscientific evidence cited by defendants.

In a review of these 1,585 cases in the Westlaw legal database citing neurobiological evidence, Farahany found that 15 per cent of cases used brain scans as evidence, usually MRI or CT

rather than EEG or fMRI. fMRI accounted for 2 per cent of that percentage. Around 44 per cent of the cases were attempts to mitigate the defendant's sentence. One example cited in the study concerns an Arizona man and a co-worker who got drunk in a bar, left, picked up a woman walking along the road, sexually assaulted her, slit her throat and stabbed her 30 times. Convicted of murder and sentenced to death, he appealed citing neuropsychological evidence of brain damage. The court believed that had the original judge received this evidence, a less serious sentence would have been imposed. Around 20–30 per cent of appeal cases reviewed in the study succeeded on the basis of the introduction of neurobiological evidence.

Neuroimaging is now being applied to some novel areas of behaviour. One such behaviour is lying: can neuroimaging tell us anything useful about how we lie? The evidence is reviewed in a later Controversies in Psychological Science section.

Cutting edge: Using neuroimaging to understand why some people hate specific sounds

There are some people who dislike the music of Mumford and Sons, and others who dislike the sound of nails scraping down a blackboard. While emotional responses to these aversive auditory stimuli are normal, there are some responses to noise that are abnormal. Individuals with a condition called misophonia, for example, get angry of anxious if they listen to people chewing, drinking, eating or breathing. The response is extreme and makes the individual's life very unpleasant. Using fMRI, Kumar *et al.* (2016) investigated which regions of the brain might be more or less active when

misophobes listened to such noises and noises that people normally consider unpleasant (such as a baby crying, a person screaming). The noises misophobes hated were associated with significant increases blood flow to the anterior cingulate cortex. There were also abnormal connections between this area and other regions known to be involved in the regulation of emotion, including the prefrontal cortex, the amygdala and the hippocampus. Heart rate and electrodermal response was also higher in misophobes when they listened to trigger noises.

Controversies in psychological science: Can brain scanners detect deception?

The issue

If all it took to identify a liar was to examine their extending, Pinocchio-like proboscis, we would encounter a lot less deception and the police and the courts could probably take a day off. But such a Pinocchian 'tell' does not yet exist – although psychologists have tried hard to identify one (you read about the evidence in Chapter 1). However, some scientists have, controversially, tried to identify one in the brain.

The evidence

The rationale for using neuroimaging to detect deception is based on a number of assumptions: tell-tale activation may not be under conscious control – the liar may not be able to control their brain activation – and the activation may be present only when a person is lying (Sip *et al.*, 2007; Langleben, 2008; Spence, 2008).

According to Vrij (2004a, b), deception involves 'a deliberate attempt, without forewarning, to create in another a belief

▶

Controversies in psychological science: Continued

which the communicator considers to be untrue'. This definition embodies two important points: (i) a liar deliberately and purposefully intends to deceive another person and (ii) deception does not involve instructing the liar to lie – he or she will do this spontaneously.

Of the 16 peer-reviewed studies using fMRI to study deception analysed by Spence (2008), all of them implicated one particular part of the brain – the frontal lobes. The majority of the reports specifically find activation in certain areas and these are and the ventromedial prefrontal cortex (VPC), dorsolateral prefrontal cortex (DLPFC) and the ACC. For example, in studies that find these activations, researchers have asked participants to lie to the experimenter (Abe *et al.*, 2007; Sun *et al.*, 2015), asked them to lie while they had to expend effort doing something else (Vartanian *et al.*, 2013), given them two cards and asked them to lie about having one of them (Gamer *et al.*, 2007), asked them to malinger – feign a memory impairment (Lee *et al.*, 2002, 2005), or instructed them to 'steal' a watch or ring and then reward them for successfully lying about it (Kozel *et al.*, 2005), or asked them to lie about autobiographical events (Spence *et al.*, 2001; Nunez *et al.*, 2005). All activated the PFC and some activated the medial temporal gyrus. These activations were not observed when the person was telling the truth or when baseline recordings were taken.

Activation in the right amygdala, inferior frontal gyrus and left posterior cingulate cortex was found in one study when people lied (Sip *et al.*, 2013) but, more interestingly, when the liars thought that the brain scanner could detect their lying but was switched-off activation was found in the left temporal lobe and the right hippocampus when they lied (Sip *et al.*, 2013).

According to Spence *et al.* (2008), the VPC may support deceptive behaviour by suppressing a person's ability to tell the truth. Mameli *et al.* (2010) used another technique, repetitive transcranial magnetic stimulation (rTMS – see below), which involves directing an electrical current to the brain harmlessly, to study deception. Participants were tested before and after the application of a direct current or a sham current. Their response time for reacting to lies compared to no lies was longer at baseline than during the sham condition. Those receiving a current to the DLPFC showed reduced reaction time for lies which involved general knowledge.

It seems that deception can, therefore, be measured by fMRI. Or can it?

According to Sip *et al.* (2007), fMRI studies of deception are hamstrung by several methodological problems or confounds. They argue that what deception experiments primarily measure are the functions needed for lying, such as inhibiting behaviour (telling the truth), mentalising (reading others' states of mind or intentions) and relating action or behaviour to the outcome (monitoring behaviour). The authors suggest

Headlines such as these are becoming more common (but no more accurate)

Source: Guardian News and Media Ltd.: Charles O'Rear/Corbis.

that deception involves keeping track of the lies and truths being told (information management), building trust with the deceived (impression management), appreciating that the gains from lying are greater than the losses and the risks of being found out (risk management) and an intention that lying is done for some good or can be justified in some way (reputation management). All of these behaviours recruit the areas found to be active during deception.

The problem, however, is that in all fMRI experiments, the participants are instructed to lie by the experimenter. That is, they do not spontaneously lie and, furthermore, do not lie about anything significant (lying about having a playing card is in a different order to lying about running someone over in a car). These participants lack one of the key features of deception – the intention to lie – although it is possible that a person can be instructed to lie on someone's behalf (i.e. provide a false

Controversies in psychological science: Continued

alibi for a criminal). But, then again, the person is motivated to do this – it has a purpose.

The protocols also neglect the context in which lying occurs and the negative consequences of lying – a person who lies faces no punishment or no censure at all in these experiments. Again, the paradigms used can be regarded as basic and artificial.

Sip et al. have identified a number of related problems in the interpretation of fMRI studies. The first is that although a characteristic of mentalising, emotion and risk-taking is activation in a particular part of the brain, the presence of such activation does not mean that a person is lying. The second is that fMRI deception studies are based on groups – individual responses may vary greatly (depending on the seriousness of the wrongdoing and the individual's predisposition to lie or intention to lie). A third is that instructions to lie 'lift moral sanctions against lying' – there are no real consequences of lying. The fourth is that different people will have different attitudes to deception. At the extreme, think of the psychopath (described in detail in Chapter 18). A psychopath lies effortlessly and shows no empathy – he (and it is usually a he) shows reduced frontal lobe volume and

activation, not more. Psychopaths' behaviour stems from their attitude to their victim – they do not regard what they say as wrong when they lie.

Conclusion

In the US, some scientists, entrepreneurs and patent specialists are busying themselves setting up and protecting companies that they claim will use fMRI to detect deception (e.g., NoLieMRI in San Diego). However, what the studies to date have done is not so much measure deception but the cognitive processes involved in deception.

Importantly, in these studies the liar does not actually, spontaneously lie or has the intention of lying, unlike genuine deception. Future studies, therefore, need a way of allowing a person to decide whether to lie. Of course, these studies will be so tightly straitjacketed that another important element will still be missing – the belief that lying will spare some punishment or will achieve some other, very significant goal. As Sip et al. conclude, 'paradigms are still inadequate. The problems that bedevilled old techniques have not been eliminated by the new'. It seems as if there is still no room for Pinocchio's nose inside the scanner.

Modern brain stimulation: transcranial magnetic stimulation (TMS)

Despite having its origins in the nineteenth century, a relatively new, non-invasive, technique for studying localisation of function is **transcranial magnetic stimulation (TMS)**. TMS involves modulating cortical activity by passing alternating magnetic fields across the scalp (Hermann et al., 2013; Fertonani and Miniussi, in press). The consequence of exposure to these fields is that electrical currents are induced in the cortex and the excitability of the cortex is subsequently increased or decreased. In short, the magnetic pulses traverse the skull and other layers covering the brain and create depolarization in neurons, resulting in action potentials. These effects can last a few seconds or minutes to a few weeks. The technique's benefits to neuropsychology are that it can produce transient impairment or improvements in cognition non-invasively.

In practice, a metal coil is placed on a participant's scalp, as you can see in Figure 4.23. The alternating electrical current in the coil produces an alternating magnetic field at right angles to the current generated in the coil. This alternating magnetic field then passes through to the cortex and creates an electrical current in the part of the brain (around 1 to 2 cm worth) beneath the coil. The technique is apparently safe – the most likely danger, if a danger occurs, is of a seizure being

generated during repeated stimulation. Sometimes headaches can follow and slight periods of mania; scalp facial muscles might twitch. There are two types of stimulation that can be applied – anodal and cathodal. Anodal stimulation appears to enhance cortical activation (increases the likelihood of neurons firing) whereas cathodal stimulation reduces it (decreases the likelihood of neurons firing).

In TMS, the magnetic fields – or 'pulses' – can be presented either singly, in pairs a few seconds apart or in quick succession over a period of minutes. These are called single-pulse TMS, paired-pulse TMS and repetitive (r)TMS, respectively. A single pulse can be as short as 100–200 micro seconds and the effects of this one pulse will last milliseconds. Testing sessions normally last between 20 minutes and an hour. If the stimulation is high frequency (many pulses), then an increase in blood flow is observed; if stimulation is low, then excitability is reduced. Blood flow and cortical excitability are thought to be correlates in this sense although the change in blood flow may occur away from the region that is cortically excited.

Unlike neuroimaging, where activation is correlated with behaviour and may not be necessary to produce it, TMS directly stimulates brain regions and the consequences can be observed. The technique has been found to disrupt verbal working memory, verb generation, and speech.

rTMS has been used to study a variety of behaviours from pain, motor learning, memory, emotion, decision-making,

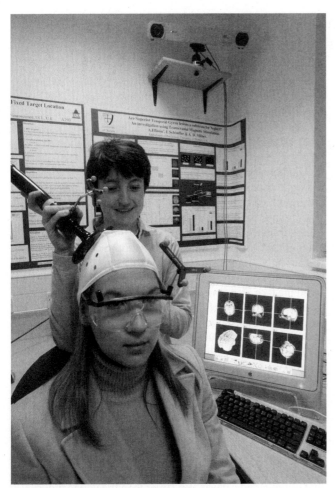

Figure 4.23 A typical rTMS procedure.
Source: University of Durham/Simon Fraser/Science Photo Library Ltd.

depressions, emotion, schizophrenia and others and its effects are more consistent for some variables (Yong-Il *et al.*, 2015). Anodal rTMS, for example, has a positive effect on a type of memory called working memory, where people have to hold material in mind and use it for some other purpose (Zaehle *et al.*, 2011; Hoy *et al.*, 2013). Motor learning has been found to be improved if participants receive anodal stimulation to the motor cortex (Foerster *et al.*, 2013).

Repetitive TMS has been used in a very novel way. Fregni *et al.* (2008) used it to stimulate a part of the front region of the brain – the DLPFC – while participants were exposed to foods such as chocolate cake, toast and sweets, or a film of foods that strongly induced craving. Participants rated how much they desired food before and after stimulation. Right-sided stimulation reduced craving after watching food whereas stimulation of the left side reduced the time that participants fixated on the food. Stimulation on both sides of the brain reduced the amount of food that people ate afterwards, compared to a sham condition (in which participants thought they were receiving brain stimulation but did not).

Other techniques

In the past few years, other functional techniques have been developed which can help understand aspects of behaviour at the neuroanatomical level. For example, the Transcranial Doppler technique measures blood flow to the right and middle cerebral arteries (these two arteries are important for language, for example, because they supply the language areas) (Somers *et al.*, 2011). The ability of this technique to localise language in a particular hemisphere of the brain is comparable to that of fMRI (Deppe *et al.*, 2000; Somers *et al.*, 2011).

One of the ways of studying the language areas in the brain that would otherwise be inaccessible is by taking advantage of surgical procedures. Patients undergoing surgery for epilepsy, for example, undergo **electrocortical stimulation mapping (ESM)** to identify the language areas that need to be avoided during their operation. Normally, this is done as described – by electrically stimulating the cortex and monitoring speech. Studies of language using this technique have found that compared to our first language, when a second language is learned, this is localised in a different region of the brain; other studies, however, find that these cortical areas overlap.

A new way of studying cortical language has been reported by Cervenka *et al.* (2011). Using a method called electrocorticography spectral mapping which can be used to study language and motor acts (it measures a frequency called gamma; a high frequency is a measure of cortical activation), the researchers studied four patients who had learned their second language (English) late in life. During the study, patients named objects they saw in both of their languages.

In three patients, the new technique identified areas activated by one language but not another. These areas were not identified using ESM. Higher gamma frequencies were observed for the second language in two of the patients, indicating a degree of effort in processing the material. Postoperative language problems (naming) were also predicted by this new technique.

Organisation of the cerebral cortex

We become aware of events in our environment by means of the five major senses: vision, audition, olfaction (smell), gustation (taste) and the somatosenses ('body' senses: touch, pain and temperature). Three areas of the cerebral cortex receive information from the sensory organs. The **primary visual cortex (V1)**, which receives visual information, is located at the back of the brain, on the inner surfaces of the cerebral hemispheres. **The primary auditory cortex,** which receives auditory information, is located on the inner surface of a deep fissure in the side of the brain. The **primary**

Cutting edge: The trouble with Einstein's brain

Few people would not be able to recognise the name Albert Einstein. Some might associate him with his theory of relativity, although few might be able to explain it. Many agree that he was a genius, although much of the mathematics contained in his work was informed by the help given by mathematicians. But the 'genius' tag is sticky and some have sought to discover whether there is something about Einstein's brain which makes it different from that of intellectually less endowed brains. It is possible to do this because Einstein's brain exists, and it has been subject to analysis at the macro (regional) and micro (cellular) level (Hines, 2014).

Einstein died on 16 April 1955 at the age of 75. Although he wished to be cremated, his pathologist, Thomas Harvey, saved his brain, the ownership of which has been the subject of considerable argument since. The first study of Einstein's brain was published 30 years after the autopsy. This found that in the four sections of the brain donated for study, there was a smaller neuron to glial cell ratio in Einstein's than in 'normal' brains (Diamond *et al.*, 1985). One part of it had more supporting cells – the left parietal area.

Hines (2014) raised a number of problems with this study including the problem that the control group was much younger than Einstein when he died. They were also likely from a lower socioeconomic group than the physicist. None of the control group had died of neurological causes, only one (of four) statistical test provided a positive result, and other measures had been excluded from analysis (such as the number of neurons and number of specific types of supporting cells). You would expect one in 20 tests to be significant by chance alone and there were 28 possible tests Diamond *et al.* could have conducted.

A second study found that the density of neurons in the right prefrontal cortex was greater in one thin slice of Einstein's brain than in the control's (Anderson and Harvey, 1996), a finding also found in some schizophrenic patients (Colombo *et al.*, 2006).

Studies of Einstein's gyri and sulci have associated features of these with his intellectual ability although drawing conclusions about intelligence based on an aged brain is questionable. Witelson *et al.* (1999) examined photographs of Einstein's brain and observed that the inferior parietal lobule was greater than in controls and that one gyrus behind the Sylvian fissure was undivided by a sulcus (Hines, 2014). They associated this with Einstein's intellectual capacity because this feature was absent in 91 controls. They also found that the parietal cortex was more symmetrical than in 'normal' brains. Others (e.g. Galaburda, 1999) challenged the observations, arguing that no such differences could be seen. The original authors countered by arguing that Galaburda was looking at a different region to the one they claim showed a difference. Such is the challenge of this sort of work.

Additional analysis on the photographs found a 'knob' in the right postcentral gyrus (Falk, 2009) which the author attributed to the scientist's violin-playing (violinists have been found to exhibit this feature). A subsequent analysis based on new photographs also found differences in the length of sulci, thickness and size of gyri and differences in the configuration of gyri. Additional findings included a 'knob' in the right frontal lobe, an enlarged left motor cortex in the face area, and a large sulcus in the right occipital lobe. The symmetry of the brain was not confirmed. The authors attribute larger areas devoted to the face and tongue to Einstein's view that thinking was muscular. But, as Hines (2014) notes, this is a post hoc explanation and so not really an explanation. Hines also makes the point that many of the explanations for Einstein's cerebral features are of this kind.

Others, using the same images as Falk *et al.*, have examined possible differences in the corpus callosum (Men *et al.*, in press). They used 10 measures and compared Einstein's brain with young and old controls. Nine of the measures showed differences – the corpus callosum was larger than that of the elderly; it was also larger than the young group in six areas. Men *et al.* suggest that this shows that Einstein's brain was more extensively connected than were normal brains although, as Hines has also pointed out, if one part of the corpus callosum is larger, then another one is likely to be too. Some researchers have found that a thicker posterior corpus callosum is correlated with high intelligence (Luders *et al.*, 2007), but that anterior regions are not. The pattern of sulci in Einstein's fusiform gyrus does appear to be statistically different from those of controls but individuals in the control group have a similar pattern to Einstein's (Weiner, 2015).

Hines also remarks that differences have been found in the white and grey matter of bilingual speakers compared with monolinguals, in areas which Falk *et al.* ascribe to Einstein's genius. Einstein was bilingual. The morphological and histological features in his brain may reflect his bilingualism, rather than his genius.

somatosensory cortex, a vertical strip near the middle of the cerebral hemispheres, receives information from the body senses. Different regions of the primary somatosensory cortex receive information from different regions of the body. In addition, the base of the somatosensory cortex, the insula, receives information concerning taste. See Figure 4.24.

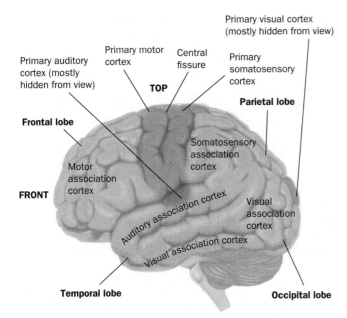

Figure 4.24 The lobes of the brain and the association areas of the cortex, together with the primary functions undertaken by these areas.

Primary sensory and motor cortex

The three regions of primary sensory cortex in each hemisphere receive information from the opposite side of the body. Thus, the primary somatosensory cortex of the left hemisphere learns what the right hand is holding, the left primary visual cortex learns what is happening towards the person's right and so on. The connections between the sensory organs and the cerebral cortex are said to be **contralateral** (contra 'opposite', lateral 'side').

The region of the cerebral cortex most directly involved in the control of movement is the **primary motor cortex (MI)**, located just in front of the primary somatosensory cortex. Neurons in different parts of the primary motor cortex are connected to muscles in different parts of the body. The connections, like those of the sensory regions of the cerebral cortex, are contralateral; the left primary motor cortex controls the right side of the body and vice versa. Thus, for example, damage to the left primary motor cortex will result in paralysis in the contralateral hand and sometimes in the left hand (Haaland and Harrington, 1989). The hand that one predominantly uses (and this usually means to write with) appears to be related to the side of the brain that is involved in speech production (we'll discuss handedness more in Chapter 10).

There is some evidence that the regions recruited during perception (visual, auditory, olfactory etc.) overlap with the regions recruited when we imagine sensory stimuli (sights, sounds, scents) (McNorgan, 2012).

Association cortex

The regions of primary sensory and motor cortex occupy only a small part of the cerebral cortex. The rest of the cerebral cortex accomplishes what is done between sensation and action: perceiving, learning and remembering, planning and acting. These processes take place in the association areas of the cerebral cortex. The central fissure provides an important dividing line between the **anterior** (front) part of the cerebral cortex and the **posterior** (back) regions. The anterior region is involved in movement-related activities, such as planning and executing behaviours. The posterior part is involved in perceiving and learning.

The cerebral cortex is divided into four areas, or lobes, named after the bones of the skull that cover them: the **frontal lobe**, **parietal lobe**, **temporal lobe** and **occipital lobe**. The brain contains two of each lobe, one in each hemisphere. The frontal lobe (the 'front') includes everything in front of the central fissure. The parietal lobe (the 'wall') is located on the side of the cerebral hemisphere, just behind the central fissure, behind the frontal lobe. The temporal lobe (the 'temple') juts forward from the base of the brain, beneath the frontal and parietal lobes. The occipital lobe (*ob* 'in back of', *caput* 'head') lies at the very back of the brain, behind the parietal and temporal lobes. The lobes and association regions of the brain can be seen in Figure 4.25a and an overview of the brain's motor functions can be seen in Figure 4.25b.

Temporal sequencing of events

Each primary sensory area of the cerebral cortex sends information to adjacent regions, called the **sensory association cortex**. Circuits of neurons in the sensory association cortex analyse the information received from the primary sensory cortex; perception takes place there, and memories are stored there. The regions of the sensory association cortex located closest to the primary sensory areas receive information from only one sensory system. For example, the region closest to the primary visual cortex analyses visual information and stores visual memories. Regions of the sensory association cortex located far from the primary sensory areas receive information from more than one sensory system; thus, they are involved in several kinds of perception and memory. These regions make it possible to integrate information from more than one sensory system. For example, we can learn the connection between the sight of a particular face and the sound of a particular voice.

Just as regions of the sensory association cortex of the posterior part of the brain are involved in perceiving and remembering, the frontal association cortex is involved in the planning and execution of movements. The anterior part of the frontal lobe – known as the PFC – contains the motor

(a)

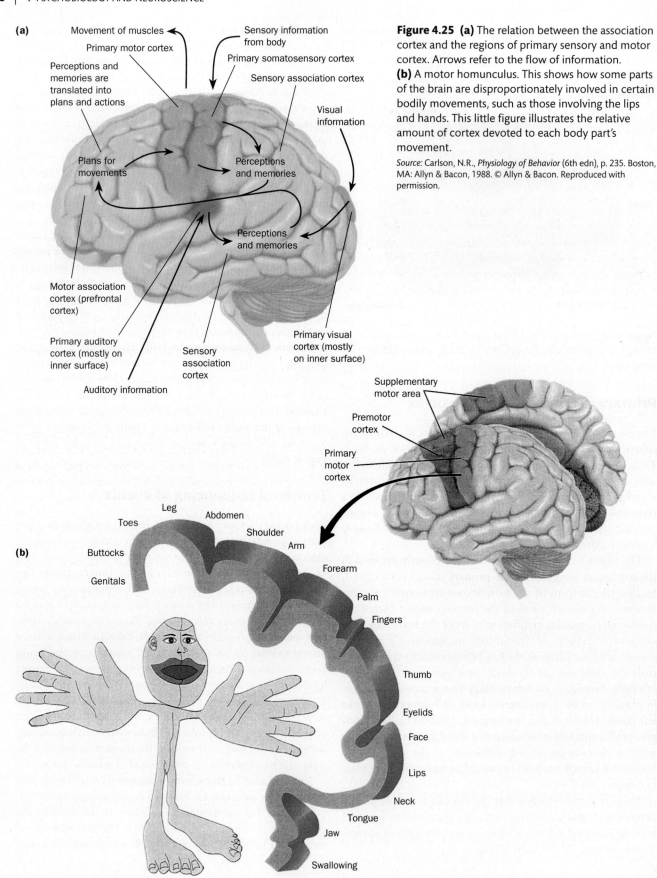

Movement of muscles

Primary motor cortex

Perceptions and memories are translated into plans and actions

Sensory information from body

Primary somatosensory cortex

Sensory association cortex

Visual information

Plans for movements

Perceptions and memories

Perceptions and memories

Motor association cortex (prefrontal cortex)

Primary auditory cortex (mostly on inner surface)

Sensory association cortex

Primary visual cortex (mostly on inner surface)

Auditory information

Figure 4.25 **(a)** The relation between the association cortex and the regions of primary sensory and motor cortex. Arrows refer to the flow of information. **(b)** A motor homunculus. This shows how some parts of the brain are disproportionately involved in certain bodily movements, such as those involving the lips and hands. This little figure illustrates the relative amount of cortex devoted to each body part's movement.

Source: Carlson, N.R., *Physiology of Behavior* (6th edn), p. 235. Boston, MA: Allyn & Bacon, 1988. © Allyn & Bacon. Reproduced with permission.

Supplementary motor area

Premotor cortex

Primary motor cortex

(b)

Leg

Toes

Abdomen

Shoulder

Arm

Buttocks

Forearm

Genitals

Palm

Fingers

Thumb

Eyelids

Face

Lips

Neck

Tongue

Jaw

Swallowing

association cortex. The **motor association cortex** controls the primary motor cortex; thus, it directly controls behaviour. Obviously, we behave in response to events happening in the world around us. Therefore, the sensory association cortex of the posterior part of the brain sends information about the environment to the motor association cortex (PFC), which translates the information into plans and actions (see Figure 4.25).

Lateralisation of function

Although the two cerebral hemispheres cooperate with each other, they do not perform identical functions. Some functions show evidence of **lateralisation**, that is, they are located primarily on one side of the brain. Another term for this is **functional hemispheric asymmetry.** The human body itself provides a number of examples of lateralisation or laterality. We have two arms, two eyes, two ears, two nostrils, two nipples, two ovaries, two testicles and so on. But even within these superficial lateralities, there are subtle asymmetries – we are more proficient with one hand than the other; one testicle descends lower than the other; one breast is larger than the other; one side of the face is not a mirror image of the other and so on.

Superficially, the brain looks symmetrical, but this physical feature belies some functional asymmetries. The left hemisphere is more involved in aspects of language such as speech production and comprehension and the appreciation of the sounds in speech than is the right hemisphere, for example. The right hemisphere is better than the left hemisphere at recognising faces, mental rotation and comprehending metaphors and it may undertake the linguistic duties of the left hemisphere when the left is damaged (see Chapter 10). These are broad, crude examples of asymmetry and there are associated regions also implicated in all these functions – the left hemisphere, for example, also plays a role in understanding metaphor.

The two cerebral hemispheres are connected by a large band of axons called the **corpus callosum,** seen in Figures 4.26a and b. It is the brain's largest collection of connective fibre, comprising 200–300 million nerve fibres. The corpus callosum connects corresponding parts of the left and right hemispheres: the left and right temporal lobes are connected, the motor areas on the left and right are connected, the left and right parietal lobes are connected, and so on (the technical term is 'homotopic'). The corpus callosum is divided into sections – from front to back, the genu, truncus, isthmus and splenium. Because of the corpus callosum, each region of the association cortex knows what is happening in the corresponding region of the opposite side of the brain. Some researchers have suggested that it plays a role in aggression because interhemispheric transfer of electrical signals is reduced in violent patients (Schutter and Harmon-Jones, 2013).

Some people have the corpus callosum surgically cut in order to alleviate the symptoms of epilepsy. So-called split-brain patients are interesting to psychologists because their two hemispheres do not appear to be able to communicate. We discuss the effects of split-brain surgery in more detail in Chapter 9 (Consciousness).

Handwriting and tool use

It's not all tablets and smartphones. Sometimes, only a pen or a pencil will do. Often, when we have no battery. Handwriting, like reading, is a learned linguistic skill requiring precision and dexterity. A recent review of the role of the brain in handwriting has identified distinct regions that allow us to do this (Planton *et al.*, 2013). They found that a network of regions in the left hemisphere showed activation when people used their hands for writing. Three were particularly involved: the left superior frontal sulcus/middle frontal gyrus, the left intraparietal sulcus and the right cerebellum. Other regions were involved in motor behaviour that was not linked to writing – areas such

Cutting edge: How do we think machines think?

You might expect yourself to respond differently to a person than a robot – you would expect one to be more expressive, engaging, in short, human. But what if you thought you were interacting with a robot but were not? Would you, and your neural substrates, behave differently?

Chaminade *et al.* (2012) asked 19 male students to take part in an interactive paper-and-scissors game and were introduced to an opponent who the participants were told was either a human agent, a 'small humanoid robot endowed with an artificial intelligence' designed to win such games, or a random number generator. Participants saw webcams displaying what they thought was the

opponent playing the game live as they competed against them. During the game, fMRI measured participants' brain activation. The actual game opponent was identical in each condition – the introduction to the opponents was a ruse.

Participants reported adopting different strategies to win against different opponents. Also, when participants thought they were competing with a human, activation in the medial prefrontal and an area bridging the temporal and parietal lobe increased. There were also differences in parietal and lateral frontal areas between the robot and generator condition and the robot and human conditions.

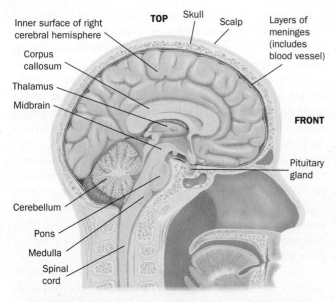

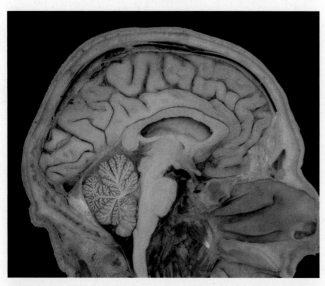

Figure 4.26 (a) A view of the brain that has been sliced through the midline (this is called a sagittal view). The corpus callosum unites the cerebral cortex of the two hemispheres. **(b)** A cross-section of a human head. You can clearly see the general structures of the brain: the neocortex, the corpus callosum, the cerebellum, the pons and the medulla.

Source: (b) Tissuepix/Science Photo Library.

as the primary motor and somatosensory cortex. A more specific study has examined which regions of the brain are implicated in the movement of toes and fingers (Lee *et al.*, 2013). This found that the primary somatosensory cortex was more active during finger than toe movements, whereas the primary motor cortex and prefrontal cortex were more active during toe movement. Some studies find that the somatosensory cortex is activated by more by knee movements than elbow or finger movements (Luft *et al.*, 2002) and by fingers than ankles (LaPointe *et al.*, 2009).

Vision: the occipital lobe

The primary business of the occipital lobe – and the lower part of the temporal lobe – is seeing. Total damage to the primary visual cortex, located in the inner surface of the posterior occipital lobe, produces cortical blindness (to distinguish it from other forms of blindness such as congenital blindness). Because the visual field is 'mapped' onto the surface of the primary visual cortex, a small lesion in the primary visual cortex produces a 'hole' in a specific part of the field of vision.

The visual association cortex is located in the rest of the occipital lobe and in the lower portion of the temporal lobe. Damage to the visual association cortex will not cause blindness. In fact, visual acuity may be very good; the person may be able to see small objects and may even be able to read. However, the person will not be able to recognise objects by sight. For example, when looking at a drawing of a clock, the person may say that they see a circle, two short lines forming an angle in the centre of a circle, and some dots spaced along the inside of the circle, but will not be able to recognise what the picture shows. On the other hand, if the person is handed a real clock, they will immediately recognise it by touch. This fact tells us that the person has not simply forgotten what clocks are. Similarly, the person may fail to recognise their spouse by sight but will be able to do so from the sound of the spouse's voice. This deficit in visual perception is called visual agnosia (a – 'without', gnosis 'knowledge') (see Chapter 6).

Audition and language: the temporal lobe

The temporal lobe contains the primary auditory cortex and the auditory association cortex. The primary auditory cortex is hidden from view on the inner surface of the upper temporal lobe. The auditory association cortex is located on the lateral surface of the upper temporal lobe. Damage to the primary auditory cortex leads to hearing losses, while damage to the auditory association cortex produces more complex deficits. Damage to the left auditory association cortex causes severe language deficits. People with such damage are no longer able to comprehend speech, presumably because they have lost the circuits of neurons that decode speech sounds. However, the deficit is more severe than that. They also lose the ability to produce meaningful speech; their speech becomes a jumble of words. Language deficits produced by brain damage are described in more detail in Chapter 10. See Figure 4.27.

Damage to the right auditory association cortex does not seriously affect speech perception or production, but it does affect the ability to recognise non-speech sounds, including patterns of tones and rhythms. The damage can also impair the ability to perceive the location of sounds in the environment. As we will see later, the right hemisphere is important in the perception of space. The contribution of the right temporal lobe to this function is to participate in perceiving the placement of sounds.

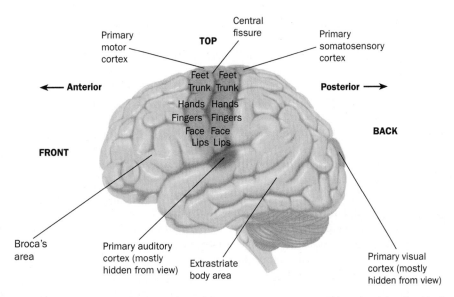

Figure 4.27 Broca's area, located just in front of the face region of the primary motor cortex. This region is involved in the control of speech.

The medial part of the temporal lobe is also known to be involved in our ability to perceive personally meaningful information. Neurons here respond to images of famous people (Quian Quiroga *et al.*, 2005) and there is also evidence that neurons respond to images of family members. Viskontas *et al.* (2009) recorded activity from 2,330 neurons while participants viewed unfamiliar faces and landscapes, familiar faces and participants' own faces. Neurons in the MLT than more likely to respond to the familiar faces than the unfamiliar stimuli.

One of the more asymmetrical regions of the brain is found in the temporal lobe – the auditory association cortex of the planum temporale in the superior temporal gyrus. This seems to be an important region because of its involvement in the phonological processing of language; it represents the region we know as Wernicke's area, an area responsible for understanding speech. Different parts of the planum temporale appear to be involved in different aspects of understanding speech. This region is larger on the left than the right. The equivalent regions on the right have been found lobe involved in the perception of music in non-experts. You'll read more about phonological processing, and this brain region, in Chapter 10.

Somatosensation and spatial perception: the parietal lobe

The primary sensory function of the parietal lobe is perception of the body. It contains the somatosensory cortex and so is responsible for the perception of touch. However, the association cortex of the parietal lobe is involved in much more than somatosensation. Damage to a particular region of the association cortex of the left parietal lobe can disrupt the ability to read or write without causing serious impairment in the ability to talk and understand the speech of other people. Damage to

another part of the parietal lobe impairs a person's ability to draw. When the left parietal lobe is damaged, the primary deficit seems to be in the person's ability to make precise hand movements; their drawing looks shaky and sloppy. In contrast, the primary deficit produced by damage to the right parietal lobe is perceptual. The person can analyse a picture into its parts but has trouble integrating these parts into a consistent whole. Thus, they have difficulty drawing a coherent picture. We will look at disorders such as these in Chapter 6.

The left parietal lobe plays an important role in our ability to keep track of the location of the moving parts of our own body, whereas the right parietal lobe helps us to keep track of the space around us. People with right parietal lobe damage usually have difficulty with spatial tasks, such as reading a map. People with left parietal lobe damage usually have difficulty identifying parts of their own bodies by name. For example, when asked to point to their elbows, they may actually point to their shoulders. There is also evidence showing that this region of the brain, together with the frontal lobe, is involved in our ability to perform mental arithmetic. This region is smaller in children with mathematical deficits when compared with children with normal maths performance (Isaacs *et al.*, 2001).

The **posterior part of the parietal cortex** (**PPC**) appears to be specialised for storing representations of motor actions (Milner, 1998). Snyder *et al.* (1997) found that some neurons in the PPC of two adult macaque monkeys were active before and during visually guided arm movements whereas others were active during eye movements. However, rather than directing attention to objects in space, the PPC seems to be responsible for the intention to move. Manipulation of body part information appears to involve the left frontal and parietal lobes whereas manipulation of numbers appears to involve the right parietal lobe (Le Clec'H *et al.*, 2000).

Thinking, doing, feeling: The frontal lobes

The frontal lobe is the largest, and most recently developed, lobe in the human brain. It contains 13 distinct anatomical areas including motor cortex and the frontal eye fields, and occupies about a third of the brain's volume. Because of its size it contains a number of regions that appear to undertake specific functions. The front part, the prefrontal cortex (PFC), for example, is involved in emotional expression, the inhibition of inappropriate behaviour, certain types of memory, creativity, navigating detours in the environment, amongst other functions. The PFC itself is not a unitary region – that is, there are regions within it which, if injured, produce different deficits. The two principal regions are the dorsolateral PFC (DLPFC) and **orbitofrontal PFC (OFC)**.

Damage can produce some unusual behaviour such as the inability to identify odour, to regulate our behavioural responses and to use cues to predict future reward or unpleasant events (Zald and Andreotti, 2010). For example, a person with PFC damage will react to events in the environment but show deficits in initiating behaviour. When asked to say or write as many words as possible or asked to describe as many uses for an object as possible, they will have great difficulty in coming up with more than a few, even though they have no problem understanding words or identifying objects by name (Eslinger and Grattan, 1993).

Damage to the primary motor cortex produces a very specific effect: paralysis of the side of the body opposite to the brain damage. If a portion of the region is damaged, then only the corresponding parts of the body will be paralysed (Passingham, 1995). The frontal eye fields are responsible for preparing the eyes for movement and for creating involuntary saccades (lateral eye movement – moving the eyes from side to side) (Vernet *et al.*, 2014). The frontal lobes can also use information received from the visual part of the brain and use and convert this information in order to co-ordinate and initiate movements (Schall, 2015).

It has been suggested that the premotor area (and a part of the parietal lobe) contains so-called **mirror neurons** (Rizzolatti and Arbib, 1998) – cells which fire when we watch someone perform an action and also fire when we execute that action. They seem to mirror the activity of neurons that are involved in 'doing'. For example, neurons in one part of this area are activated in monkeys when they make a grasping movement with their hand. However, a different set in the same region is also activated when the monkey sees another making reaching movements (Ferrari *et al.*, 2003). Some people have associated dysfunction in these mirror neurons with autism. The evidence for this is considered in Chapter 12.

Parts of the frontal lobes are involved in sophisticated cognitive and social functions such as reasoning, long-term memory retrieval (Euston *et al.*, 2012), control over attention to threat (Peers *et al.*, 2013), making decisions about whether abstract paintings are beautiful (Flexas *et al.*, 2014), deciding which actions to undertake in response to reward or perceptual cues (Domenech and Koechlin, 2015), creativity (Gonen-Yaacovi *et al.*, 2013) and inhibiting behaviour that is wrong. Chapters 11 and 15 consider the role of the frontal lobe in functions such as reasoning, social cognition and emotion.

Some areas of the frontal lobes are involved in a variety of 'higher' functions including planning, changing strategies, being aware of oneself, empathising with others, evaluating emotional stimuli, inhibiting inappropriate behaviour and behaving spontaneously – these are called executive functions because they involve executive control over our actions and which involve switching between behaviours based on changes in rules.

People with damage to the frontal lobe have difficulty changing strategies. If given a task to solve, they may solve it readily. However, if the solution is changed, they will fail to abandon the old strategy and learn a new one. The Wisconsin Card Sorting Task, for example, presents patients with packs of cards on which are printed symbols of different shape, colour or number (see Chapter 11). The experimenter decides on a sorting criterion (e.g. shape) and the patient has to detect which criterion it is by sorting the cards into piles, receiving feedback from the experimenter. When the criterion unexpectedly shifts, some patients are unable to detect this shift and carry on responding as if the previous criterion still applied. This is called **perseveration**. Not all frontal lobe patients will exhibit this behaviour (Anderson *et al.*, 1991) – only those with damage to a specific region of the frontal lobe, the dorsolateral PFC. It also appears that if general intelligence is taken into account, performance on this task is not impaired, suggesting that it is a test of intelligence rather than frontal lobe performance (Roca *et al.*, 2010).

People with damage to certain areas of the frontal lobe – the orbitofrontal cortex or OFC – may have rather bland personalities. They seem indifferent to events that would normally be expected to affect them emotionally (Stuss *et al.*, 1992). For example, they may show no signs of distress at the death of a close relative and do not show the typical physiological response to stress (see Martin, 2006, for a comprehensive description). They have little insight into their own problems and are uncritical of their performance on various tasks. The most famous case study of frontal lobe damage resulting in shifts in emotional and social behaviour is that of Phineas Gage and you read about him in Chapter 1 (his case is also discussed in Chapter 13).

In terms of daily living, the most important consequences of damage to the frontal lobe are probably lack of foresight and difficulty in planning. A person with injury to part of the frontal lobe might perform fairly well on tests of intelligence but be unable to hold down a job or organise their day (Eslinger and Damasio, 1985; Wood and Rutterford, 2004). Sequencing – the organisation of material in logical, correct or learned order – is grossly impaired in frontal patients (Sirigu *et al.*, 1995). Often, when given tasks that tap everyday activities (such as undertaking an errand or following a recipe), patients with frontal lobe damage perform poorly (Fortin *et al.*, 2003) and may engage in obsessive collecting behaviour (Anderson *et al.*, 2005). When asked to explain what a proverb means, or when asked to organise the type of activities you would expect to do if you were running a hotel, or when asked to identify social faux pas, patients with damage to the right PFC are poor at doing these (Roca *et al.*, 2010).

Patients with damage to different regions of the frontal lobe exhibit different symptoms. For example, patients such as Phineas Gage with damage to the OFC tend to exhibit impairments in social behaviour, personality and emotional expression but have relatively intact intellect. They are impulsive and don't care what others think or feel. Eslinger and Damasio's (1985) patient, EVR, is a good example. EVR, an ex-accountant who had a tumour removed from the same part of the brain injured in Phineas Gage, has superior intellect but an impaired ability to plan and organise his daily life. He performs at normal levels on tests such as the Wisconsin Card Sorting Task and he has superior IQ. However, his ability to maintain close relationships and a job and his ability to plan and organise his life are grossly impaired. Chapter 13 looks at EVR's case in greater depth.

Control of inhibition – suppressing an inappropriate response to a stimulus or event – is thought to be one of the frontal lobes' primary functions and its specific locus is considered to be the right inferior frontal cortex (Aron *et al.*, 2014). It does this via its connections with other brain regions, such as the basal ganglia and other parts of the frontal lobe, such as the dlPFC. Aron *et al.* characterise the region as a brake which either stops or pauses an individual's response and that this brake can be applied internally (self-control) or in response to an external stimulus.

One study highlighting the role of the frontal lobes in control, asked 31 smokers to view three campaigns encouraging them to give up smoking and seek a helpline. fMRI measured their brain activation (Falk *et al.*, 2012). Participants were on a cigarette-quitting programme and they were asked to judge which campaigns they thought would be most successful. The success of each campaign was measured by recording the volume of calls to the helpline. The study found that activation in the medial prefrontal cortex predicted the most successful campaign – that is, activation in this area was seen in the campaigns that turned out to be successful. The greater the activation, the greater the success of the campaign. Participants' judgement of what would be a successful campaign did not predict which campaign was successful.

Control of internal functions and automatic behaviour

The cortex consists of only the outer 3 mm of the surface of the cerebral hemispheres. There are other structures such as the brain stem, the cerebellum and the interior of the cerebral hemispheres which are important to the regulation of behaviour. The cerebellum helps the cerebral hemispheres to control movement

Cutting edge: What's the brain's most popular region?

Or, put another way, which region of the brain has attracted most interest from researchers? Curious to answer this question, Behrens *et al.* (2013) examined 7,342 brain maps published between 1985 and 2008, located at brainmap.org.

They found that top of the pops was the supplementary motor area, followed by the dorsolateral cortex. There was a 25 per cent difference in the number of papers published on the SMA and the DL cortex. Other popular regions included the frontal operculum/insula and the intraparietal sulcus, which probably reflects researchers' interests in speech and language. Figure 4.28 summarises some of the most widely studied topics and the brain area responsible for them.

What is the likelihood of having your research published in an ostensibly prestigious journal such as one with a high impact factor? (Assuming that you consider this as an index of prestige; some psychologists view it with disdain.) After the primary visual cortex, the area most likely to appear in high-impact journals was the fusiform gyrus (the human face

Figure 4.28 The most widely studied topics in neuroscience (word bubble at the bottom- the larger the word, the greater the amount of research) and the most popular areas of the brain (in red) and the least (in blue).

area), followed by the ventral and dorsal parts of the rostral medial prefrontal cortex, the anterior insula, the anterior cingulate cortex and the amygdala (all regions involved in emotion).

and to initiate some automatic movements, such as postural adjustment, on its own. The brain stem and much of the interior of the cerebral hemispheres are involved in homeostasis and control of species-typical behaviours. **Homeostasis** (from the root words *homoios* 'similar', and *stasis* 'standstill') refers to maintaining a proper balance of physiological variables such as temperature, concentration of fluids and the amount of nutrients stored within the body. **Species-typical behaviours** are the more-or-less automatic behaviours exhibited by most members of a species that are important to survival, such as eating, drinking, fighting, courting, mating and caring for offspring.

The brain stem

The brain stem contains three structures: the medulla, the pons and the midbrain. In Figure 4.29, the brain has been rotated slightly so that you can see some of the front of the brain stem, and the cerebral hemispheres are shown lightly so that the details of the brain stem can be seen. You can also see the thalamus, the hypothalamus and the pituitary gland.

The brain stem contains circuits of neurons that control functions vital to the survival of the organism in particular and of the species in general. For example, circuits of neurons in the **medulla,** the part of the brain stem closest to the spinal cord, control heart rate, blood pressure, rate of respiration, and – especially in simpler animals – crawling or swimming motions. Circuits of neurons in the **pons,** the part of the brain just above the medulla, control some of the stages of sleep, and circuits of neurons in the **midbrain** control movements used in fighting and sexual behaviour and decrease sensitivity to pain while engaged in these activities.

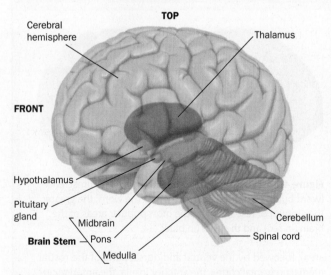

Figure 4.29 The divisions of the brain stem: the medulla, the pons and the midbrain. The thalamus, hypothalamus and pituitary gland are attached to the end of the brain stem.

The cerebellum

The cerebellum plays an important role in the control of movement but may also be involved in cognitive and emotional processing (Popa *et al.*, 2014). It receives sensory information, especially about the position of body parts, so it knows what the parts of the body are doing. It also receives information from the cortex of the frontal lobes, so it knows what movements the frontal lobes intend to accomplish. The cerebellum acts like a computer that compares the location of the body parts with the intended movements and assists the frontal lobes in executing these movements. Without the cerebellum, the frontal lobes would produce jerky, uncoordinated, inaccurate movements – which is exactly what happens when a person's cerebellum is damaged. Besides helping the frontal lobes to accomplish their tasks, the cerebellum monitors information regarding posture and balance, to keep us from falling down when we stand or walk, and produces eye movements that compensate for changes in the position of the head.

Some studies have suggested that the cerebellum may also be involved in a variety of other functions such as cognition and language (Schmahmann and Sherman, 1998). Neuroimaging studies show that various parts of the cerebellum become active during tasks involving movement and touch, language and verbal memory, spatial memory, executive function and emotional processing (Stoodley and Schmahmann, 2009). Some psychologists have also implicated the cerebellum in the reading disorder, developmental dyslexia (see Chapter 10).

Subcortical structures

The thalamus

If you stripped away the cerebral cortex and the white matter that lies under it, you would find a collection of brain structures. These are called subcortical brain structures and are some of the oldest in the brain. One of the most important is the **thalamus,** located in the heart of the cerebral hemispheres (*thalamos* is Greek for 'inner chamber'). The thalamus is divided into two parts, one in each cerebral hemisphere.

The thalamus performs two basic functions. The first, and most primitive, is similar to that of the cerebral cortex. Parts of the thalamus receive sensory information, other parts integrate the information, and still other parts assist in the control of movements through their influence on circuits of neurons in the brain stem. However, the second role of the thalamus, that of a relay station for the cortex, is even more important. As the cerebral hemispheres evolved, the cerebral cortex grew in size and its significance for behavioural functions increased. The thalamus took on the function of receiving sensory information from the sensory organs, performing some simple analyses, and passing the results on to the primary sensory cortex. In doing this, it contains a number of thalamocortical connections.

All sensory information, except olfactory information (Martin, 2013), is sent to the thalamus before it reaches the cerebral cortex. Layer four of the thalamus and the projections to it appears to be the most relevant part, although there is some evidence that other layers can be directly stimulated (Constantinople and Bruno, 2013).

The volume of the thalamus decreases with age, as do the connections between the thalamus and the frontal lobe (Hughes *et al.*, 2012). The area which shows the greatest reduction is the anterior part. Connections between the thalamus and other lobes show no significant reduction with age. The reduction in the projections from the thalamus to the frontal lobe was correlated with performance on executive function tasks: the greater the reduction, the poorer the performance, suggesting that the thalamus may be involved in functions such as attention and working memory.

The hypothalamus

Hypo – means 'less than' or 'beneath', and, as its name suggests, the hypothalamus is located below the thalamus, at the base of the brain. The hypothalamus is a small region, consisting of less than 1 cubic centimetre of tissue (smaller than a grape). Its relative importance far exceeds its relative size.

The hypothalamus, like the brain stem, participates in homeostasis and species-typical behaviours. It receives sensory information, including information from receptors inside the organs of the body; thus, it is informed about changes in the organism's physiological status. It also contains specialised sensors that monitor various characteristics of the blood that flows through the brain, such as temperature, nutrient content and amount of dissolved salts. In turn, the hypothalamus controls the **pituitary gland,** an endocrine gland attached by a stalk to the base of the hypothalamus.

Hormones are chemicals produced by endocrine glands (from the Greek *endo* – 'within', and *krinein* 'to secrete'). **Endocrine glands** secrete hormones into the blood supply, which carries them to all parts of the body. Hormones are similar to transmitter substances or neuromodulators, except that they act over much longer distances. Like transmitter substances and neuromodulators, they produce their effects by stimulating receptor molecules. These receptor molecules are located on (or in) particular cells. The presence of a hormone causes physiological reactions in these cells, which are known as **target cells**. Almost every cell of the body contains hormone receptors of one kind or other. This includes neurons; hormones that affect behaviour do so by altering the activity of particular groups of neurons in the brain. For example, the sex

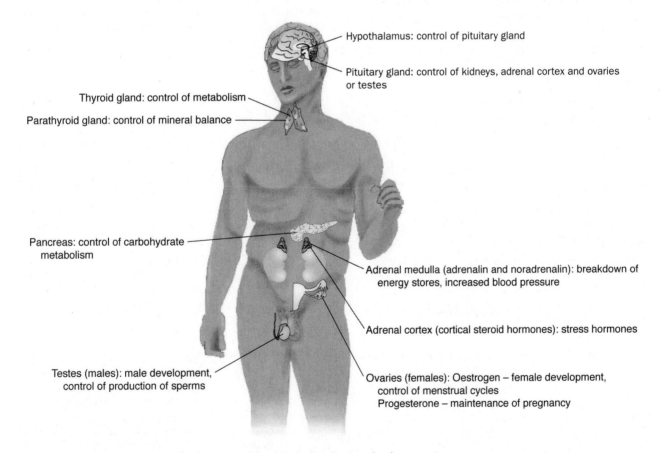

Figure 4.30 The location and primary functions of the principal endocrine glands.

hormones have important effects on behaviour and are discussed in later chapters.

The pituitary gland has been called the 'master gland' because the hormones it secretes act on target cells in other endocrine glands; thus, the pituitary gland controls the activity of other endocrine glands. By controlling the pituitary gland, the hypothalamus controls the entire endocrine system. Figure 4.30 shows some of the endocrine glands and the functions they regulate.

The hypothalamus also controls much of the activity of the **autonomic nervous system (ANS)**, which consists of nerves that control the functions of the glands and internal organs. The nerves of the ANS control activities such as sweating, shedding tears, salivating, secreting digestive juices, changing the size of blood vessels (which alters blood pressure) and secreting some hormones. The ANS has two branches. The sympathetic branch directs activities that involve the expenditure of energy. For example, activity of the sympathetic branch can increase the flow of blood to the muscles when we are about to fight someone or run away from a dangerous situation. The **parasympathetic branch** controls quiet activities, such as digestion of food. Activity of the parasympathetic

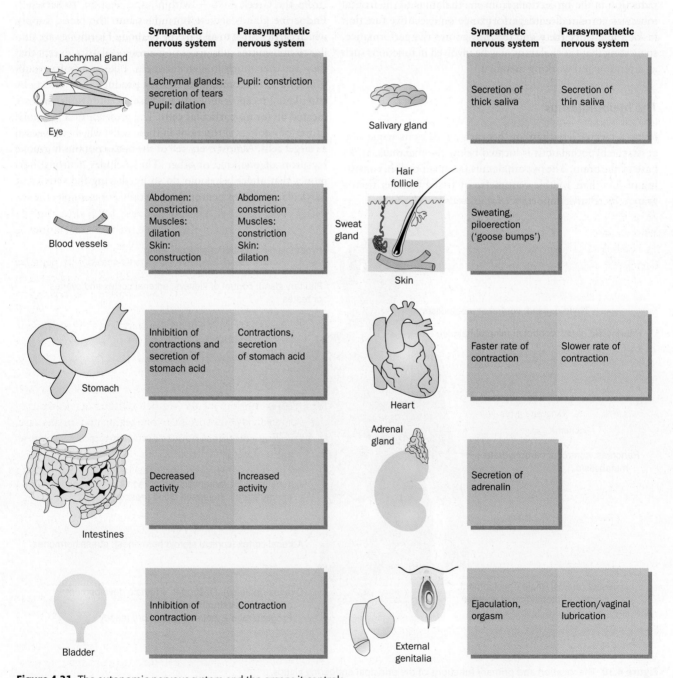

Figure 4.31 The autonomic nervous system and the organs it controls.

branch stimulates the secretion of digestive enzymes and increases the flow of blood to the digestive system, as seen in Figure 4.31.

The homeostatic functions of the hypothalamus can involve either internal physiological changes or behaviour. For example, the hypothalamus is involved in the control of body temperature. It can directly lower body temperature by causing sweating to occur, or it can raise it by causing shivering to occur. If these measures are inadequate, it can send messages to the cerebral cortex that will cause the person to engage in a learned behaviour, such as turning on an air conditioner or putting another log on the fire. Damage to the hypothalamus can cause impaired regulation of body temperature, changes in food intake, sterility and stunting of growth.

The limbic system

The **limbic system** is a set of structures located underneath the cerebral hemispheres and plays an important role in learning and in the expression of emotion. Whether it is a 'system' or just a collection of structures and regions involved in specific functions is a moot point. Originally, this part of the brain which is now described as the limbic system was termed rhinencephalon (or 'smell brain') by Paul Broca because the areas within it were thought to be involved primarily in the sense of smell.

The limbic system consists of several regions of the **limbic cortex** – the cerebral cortex located around the edge of the cerebral hemispheres where they join with the brain stem (limbus means 'border'; hence the term 'limbic system'). Besides the limbic cortex, the most important components of the limbic system are the amygdala and the hippocampus. The amygdala and the hippocampus get their names from their shapes; amygdala means 'almond' and hippocampus means 'sea horse'.

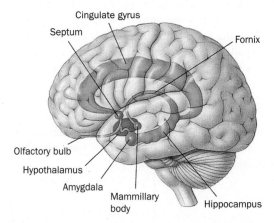

Figure 4.32 Schematic drawing illustrating the structures of the limbic system.

Source: From Pinel, J., *Biopsychology*, 3rd edn, © 1997. Published by Allyn and Bacon, Boston, MA. Copyright © by Pearson Education. By permission of the publisher.

Figure 4.32 shows a view of the limbic cortex, located on the inner surface of the cerebral hemisphere. The left hippocampus and amygdala, located in the middle of the temporal lobe, are shown projecting out into the place where the missing left hemisphere would be.

The amygdala

The **amygdala** is located in the temporal lobe and was discovered and named in the late nineteenth century. It comprises 13 different sets of neurons (nuclei) which can be categorised into different regions – the lateral, basal, central, medial and mixed nuclei (Pabba, 2013), as Figures 4.33a and b show. These nuclei receive inputs from various parts of the brain and send outputs to a variety of regions. Because of its componential nature, some have questioned whether the amygdala is a functional or structural unit (Swanson and Petrovich, 1998).

Damage to the amygdala can affect emotional behaviour, especially that caused by painful, threatening or stressful events. Some patients with amygdala injury have been found to show an inability to recognise one basic emotion, fear, in a person's voice or face (Adolphs *et al.*, 1995, 1999; Morris *et al.*, 1996) and experimental brain research in animals has confirmed that the nuclei are required for an animal to learn to be afraid (LeDoux, 1996) (see Chapter 13). If the amygdala is lesioned, an animal's ability to learn fear associations is reduced or eliminated (LeDoux and Pine, 2016).

The amygdala has normally been associated with negative emotion – such as threat or fear – but it is also implicated in positive emotion and in behaviour that can be rewarding (such as eating or seeking/having sex). People who smell pleasant odours show activation in both sides or the left side of the amygdala whereas smelling of unpleasant odours is associated with activation on the right (Patin and Pause, 2015). These activations to smell are accompanied by increases in activation in the orbitofrontal cortex, the piriform cortex and the insula (see below) thus demonstrating that activation is never specific to one region and, in this case, that smelling emotional odours activates regions known as the primary olfactory cortex.

Sergerie *et al.* (2008) found that the amygdala responded to positive and negative emotional visual stimuli and responded more strongly to faces showing emotion than to other emotional and visual stimuli. When the researchers examined the data closely, they found that the effect sizes – the strength of the phenomenon under study – were larger for studies using positive than negative stimuli.

It is worth noting, however, that neuroimaging studies of the amygdala have been criticised for the number of confounds that affects the measurement of activation. Recording a consistent pattern of activation is problematic and there is evidence to suggest that when activation is consistent, the finding is likely to be the result of activation in nearby blood vessels, especially the basal vein of Rosenthal, rather than the nuclei of the amygdala (Boubela

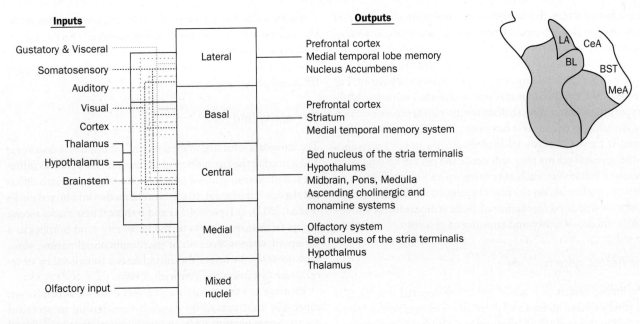

Figure 4.33 (a) The types of stimuli which influence activity in different parts of the amygdala, and the pathways leading from the amygdala to other brain areas following with stimulation. **(b)** A schematic drawing of the various parts of the amygdala.

et al., 2015). Boubela et al. suggest that 'amygdala activations' may be nothing more than signals originating in this basal vein.

Sergerie's observation is consistent with studies showing that although the neurons in the amygdala of monkeys respond to negative and positive stimuli, a greater number respond to positive than negative ones (Paton et al., 2006). These neurons also respond more quickly to the eye region of the face, one of the more emotionally revealing and meaningful features of the face. A study by Koscik and Tranel (2012) found that damage to the left side of the amygdala led to more trusting, benevolent behaviour in patients, suggesting to the authors that the structure is 'necessary for developing and expressing normal interpersonal trust'.

Because of the variety of findings reported, the role of the amygdala is probably broader than previously thought. It is more likely to be involved in monitoring the environment for signals of threat and reward or act as a memory storage device which encodes associations between events and outcomes. The role of the amygdala in emotion is taken up again in Chapter 13.

The hippocampus

The **hippocampus** (or hippocampal formation) is a collection of structures/nuclei located just behind the amygdala, and plays an important role in memory formation and spatial navigation. People with lesions of the hippocampus lose the ability to learn anything new (Milner et al., 1968; Keane et al., 1995). For them, 'yesterday' is always the time before their brain damage occurred; everything after that slips away, just as the memory of dreams often slips away from a person soon after awakening. The hippocampus and regions around it also seems to be responsible for navigating one's way around certain types of

route (Maguire et al., 1997, 1998). In healthy people the hippocampus is selectively active when we have to find our way around a route, whether it is in our mind or in virtual space.

Some have argued that the role of the structure is principally to construct scenes rather than to form memory (Maguire et al., 2015), and we return to this debate in Chapter 8 where the role of the hippocampus in memory is evaluated in more detail. There seems to be a correlation between hippocampal volume and education – the less education a person has received, the smaller the volume of the structure (volume decreases with age but it was larger in the better educated) (Noble et al., 2012).

Given that male and female brains differ in size and development – men's brains are on average 14 per cent bigger, have bigger ventricles and grow for longer during adolescence (Ruigrok et al., 2014) – researchers have sought to determine whether similar differences exist at the structural level, including the hippocampus, but the evidence for a difference is not clear. Tan et al. (2016), for example, undertook a meta-analysis of sex differences in hippocampal volume and found that although men showed larger hippocampal volume than did women, when the data were corrected for individual differences such as total brain volume, no significant difference in hippocampal volume was found between men and women.

The insula

Another structure which has been of increasing interest to psychobiologists is the **insula,** a part of the brain located inside the fold of the Sylvian fissure in the temporal lobe (and so cannot be seen from the surface). What is interesting about the insula is the range of behaviours in which it is involved; it is quite polymodal. These include auditory and language tasks (activation is found in its dorsal parts during these), upper and lower body movement (activation is seen in the posterior part), hand and eye motor control, gastric motility (ensuring that food makes its way from the stomach to anus), self-awareness, pain and temperature perception, body ownership (Mutschler *et al.*, 2009), time perception (Craig, 2009) and, particularly, taste perception (Martin, 2013).

Lesions reduce people's ability to respond emotionally to threatening visual and auditory stimuli and the region is implicated in people's ability to recognise disgust in faces and voices (Kipps *et al.*, 2007). Wilder Penfield's pioneering electrical stimulation studies of the brain found that stimulation of the insula caused gastrointestinal sensations such as nausea, chewing and swallowing, findings that have been replicated and extended to include aversion and the sensation of unpleasant taste (Krolak-Salmon *et al.*, 2003). It is also involved in language and auditory processing, as indicated in a number of neuroimaging studies, and appears to be highly active during states of anxiety and drug addiction (Jones *et al.*, 2010). The insula, like many other brain regions, does not exclusively mediate one type of function or behaviour.

The basal ganglia

One final group of subcortical structures crucial to behaviour is the **basal ganglia.** The basal ganglia is the collective name for a group of nuclei, specifically, the globus pallidus, substantia nigra, striatum (made up of the caudate nucleus and putamen) and subthalamic nucleus (see Figure 4.34).

Some of these receive inputs; some deliver output. The output nuclei, for example, send projections to the thalamus and two other subcortical regions (Utter and Basso 2008) and these influence sensory and cognitive behaviour, the movement of the head and the eyes and some aspects of locomotion and posture. (And, as you've seen, DBS in Parkinson's disease targets these nuclei.) When the nuclei become dysfunctional, they can produce Parkinson's (the dopamine neurons degenerate in the substantia nigra); the motor disorder,

Brain function – An international perspective

The past 10 years has seen a surge in studies investigating differences in brain activation between different cultural groups in response to some task or context (Rule *et al.*, 2013). Rule *et al.*, for example, note that changes have been reported in a number of brain areas, in response to perceptions of dominance, perception of foreground and background, emotional recognition and expression, memory and inferring others' mental states. When Americans and Japanese participants viewed dominant and submissive poses, the former showed activity in the head of the caudate nucleus when perceiving dominance, whereas the latter showed activity in the same area when watching the submission (Freeman *et al.*, 2009). Americans were more likely to endorse dominant values, the Japanese more likely to endorse submissive values. When earning money for family members, Latino participants were more likely to show activation in the striatum than were white participants (Telzer *et al.*, 2010).

One well-documented difference between Westerners and Easterners is that the former focus on the object at the centre of an image and largely ignore the background but the latter focus on the background and the context in which the object is displayed rather than the object (Kitayama *et al.*, 2003). You will find more about this in Chapter 6. One explanation for this finding is that Easterners see situations, objects and people as interdependent and view images holistically whereas Westerners see objects and people as context-independent and view images analytically. One fMRI study asked East Asians and Westerners to estimate the length of a line that was either within a box (which influenced judgement) or not (Hedden *et al.*, 2008). The brain activation was higher in the frontal, temporal and parietal area when making a judgement that was consistent with the group's culture. The regions were the same but they were active during different versions of the same task.

Cultural groups are better able to understand emotions expressed by their own group and this has correlates at the neural level. Amygdala activation was greater when Japanese and Caucasian participants saw fear expressed in faces from the same culture (Chiao *et al.*, 2008). Adams *et al.* (2010) found that this effect was reversed depending on where the eyes were facing in the stimulus. When the eyes looked straight at the participants, amygdala activation was greater for other-culture faces; when averted, activation was greater for same-culture faces. The degree of activation depends on the length of acculturation. For example, the response to Caucasian facial expressions of disgust is negatively correlated with the length of time non-Caucasians have lived in Caucasian culture (Derntl *et al.*, 2009). Even images of houses seem to produce culture-specific brain changes. For example, one study found that Westerners showed bilateral fusiform face area activation when passively viewing houses whereas East Asians showed right-sided activation (Goh *et al.*, 2010).

British and Chinese people show differences in brain response when they are asked to make judgements of their own or others' faces (Sui *et al.*, 2009). The British participants in this study were faster at making judgements about their own faces. However, Chinese people who thought about their mothers showed activation in a part of the brain normally activated when Westerners think about themselves, the ventro-medial prefrontal cortex (Zhu *et al.*, 2007).

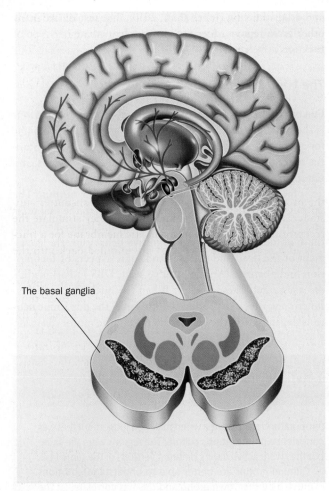

Figure 4.34 The location of the basal ganglia.
Source: Science Photo Library Ltd.

Huntington's disease where the defective gene produces degeneration in neurotransmitter-specific neurons in the striatum; extreme or convoluted posture (dystonia); Tourette's syndrome (uncontrollable blinking and facial grimacing, plus coprolalia – vigorous, unpredictable and involuntary swearing); and obsessive-compulsive disorder (described in Chapter 18), possibly because of dysfunctional loops linking the striatum with the tip of the frontal lobe.

Drugs and behaviour

Communication between neurons involves the release of transmitter substances. Neurons release many different kinds of transmitter substance, and various drugs can affect the production or release of one or more of these chemicals. Drugs can also mimic the effects of transmitter substances on receptor molecules, block these effects or interfere with the reuptake of a transmitter substance once it is released. Via these

mechanisms, a drug can alter the perceptions, thoughts and behaviours controlled by particular transmitter substances.

Drug administration can also lead to structural changes in parts of the neuron. For example, changes to the spines of dendrites, including the number and size of branches, and to cell bodies can occur in parts of the limbic system and frontal lobe (Russo *et al.*, 2010). This plasticity of dendrites in response to drugs was first described in 1997. Some drugs (e.g. morphine, cocaine, amphetamine and methylphenidate) increase the number of spines; others (opiates) decrease them. The location of the changes appears to be the nucleus accumbens, the ventral tegmental area and medial PFC. The neurons are either pyramidal and or dopaminergic.

Stimulating or inhibiting the release of transmitter substances

Some drugs stimulate certain terminal buttons to release their transmitter substance continuously, even when the axon is not firing. Other drugs prevent certain terminal buttons from releasing their transmitter substance when the axon fires. The effects of most of these drugs are more or less specific to one transmitter substance. Because different classes of neuron release different transmitter substances, these drugs affect only a selected set of neurons. An example of a stimulating drug is the venom of the black widow spider, which causes the release of a transmitter substance called acetylcholine, as illustrated by Figure 4.35. In contrast, botulinum toxin, a poison that is sometimes present in improperly canned food, prevents the release of acetylcholine. An adult will almost certainly survive the bite of a black widow spider; the symptoms are severe abdominal cramps. However, an extremely small amount of botulinum toxin – less than one-millionth of a gram – is fatal. The victim becomes paralysed and suffocates to death.

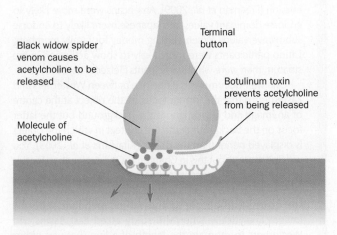

Figure 4.35 Drugs that affect the release of a neurotransmitter, acetylcholine. Black widow spider venom causes acetylcholine to be released. Botulinum toxin prevents the release of acetylcholine from the terminal buttons.

Stimulating or blocking postsynaptic receptor molecules

Transmitter substances produce their effects by stimulating postsynaptic receptor molecules, which excite or inhibit postsynaptic neurons by opening ion channels and permitting ions to enter or leave the neurons. Some drugs duplicate the effects of particular transmitter substances by directly stimulating particular kinds of receptor molecules. If we use the lock-and-key analogy to describe the effects of a transmitter substance on a receptor molecule, then a drug that stimulates receptor molecules works like a master key, turning the receptor molecules on even when the transmitter substance is not present. For example, nicotine stimulates acetylcholine receptors located on neurons in certain regions of the brain (see Figure 4.36). In low doses, this stimulation has a pleasurable (and addictive) excitatory effect; in high doses, it can cause convulsions and death.

Some drugs block receptor molecules, making them inaccessible to the transmitter substance and thus inhibiting synaptic transmission. A drug that blocks receptor molecules 'plugs up' the lock so that the key will no longer fit into it. A poison called curare, discovered by South American Indians, was used on the darts of their blowguns. This drug blocks the acetylcholine receptors that are located on muscle fibres. The curare prevents synaptic transmission in muscles. The paralysed victim is unable to breathe and consequently suffocates.

Some medically useful chemicals work by blocking receptor molecules. For example, antipsychotic drugs alleviate the symptoms of schizophrenia, a serious mental disorder, by blocking receptor molecules in the brain that are normally stimulated by a transmitter substance called dopamine. This fact has led some investigators to suggest that the symptoms of schizophrenia may be caused by malfunctions of neurons that release dopamine. We discuss antipsychotic drugs later in this chapter and in Chapter 18.

Inhibiting reuptake

The effects of most transmitter substances are kept brief by the process of reuptake. Molecules of the transmitter substance are released by a terminal button, they stimulate the receptor molecules in the postsynaptic membrane for a fraction of a second, and then they are pumped back into the terminal button. Some drugs inhibit the process of reuptake so that molecules of the transmitter substance continue to stimulate the postsynaptic receptor molecules for a long time. Therefore, inhibition of reuptake increases the effect of the transmitter substance. The excitatory effects of cocaine and amphetamine are produced by their ability to inhibit the reuptake of certain transmitter substances, including dopamine (see Figure 4.37).

Sedatives

Some drugs depress behaviour, causing relaxation, sedation or even loss of consciousness. These are called **anti-anxiety** or **anxiolytic drugs**. In most cases, the depression is caused by stimulation of a class of receptor molecules that is

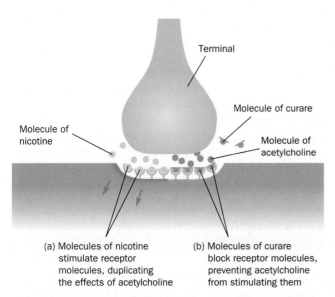

(a) Molecules of nicotine stimulate receptor molecules, duplicating the effects of acetylcholine

(b) Molecules of curare block receptor molecules, preventing acetylcholine from stimulating them

Figure 4.36 Drugs that interact with receptor molecules in the postsynaptic membrane. Nicotine directly stimulates the receptor molecules. Curare blocks receptor molecules and thus prevents acetylcholine from activating them.

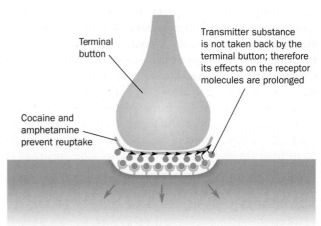

Figure 4.37 Drugs that block reuptake. Cocaine and amphetamine block the reuptake of certain transmitter substances, thus prolonging their effects on the receptor molecules in the postsynaptic membrane.

normally activated by neuromodulators produced by the brain. Barbiturates depress the brain's activity by stimulating a particular category of neuromodulator receptors. In low doses, barbiturates have a calming effect. In progressively higher doses, they produce difficulty in walking and talking, unconsciousness, coma and death. Barbiturates are abused by people who want to achieve the relaxing, calming effect of the drugs, especially to counteract the anxiety and irritability that can be produced by stimulants. They are occasionally prescribed as medication for sleep, but they are a poor choice for this purpose because they suppress dreaming and produce a particularly unrefreshing sleep. In addition, a dose of a barbiturate sufficient to induce sleep is not that much lower than a fatal dose. Ideally, the therapeutic dose of a drug is much lower than a fatal dose.

Many anti-anxiety drugs are members of a family known as the **benzodiazepines,** which include the well-known tranquilliser Valium (diazepam). These drugs, too, stimulate some sort of neuromodulator receptors located on neurons in various parts of the brain, including the amygdala. The benzodiazepines are effective in reducing anxiety and are sometimes used to treat people who are afflicted by periodic attacks of severe anxiety. In addition, some benzodiazepines serve as sleep medications. These behavioural effects suggest that they mimic the effects of neuromodulators involved in the regulation of mood and the control of sleep.

By far the most commonly used depressant drug is ethyl alcohol, the active ingredient in alcoholic beverages. This drug has effects similar to those of the barbiturates: larger and larger doses of alcohol reduce anxiety, disrupt motor coordination and then cause unconsciousness, coma and finally death. The effects of alcohol and barbiturates are additive: a moderate dose of alcohol plus a moderate dose of barbiturates can be fatal.

The primary effect of alcohol appears to be similar to that of the benzodiazepines: it stimulates some type of neuromodulator receptor. Suzdak *et al.* (1986) discovered a drug that reverses alcohol intoxication, presumably by blocking some type of neuromodulator receptor. Although the behavioural effects of alcohol may be mediated by neuromodulator receptors, alcohol has other, potentially fatal effects on all cells of the body. Alcohol destabilises the membrane of cells, interfering with their functions. Thus, a person who takes some of the anti-alcohol drug could go on to drink themselves to death without becoming drunk in the process.

Stimulants

Several categories of drugs stimulate the CNS and thus activate behaviour. Because of the effects some of these drugs have on the neural circuits involved in reinforcement (reward), they tend to be abused. Two popular stimulant drugs, amphetamine

and cocaine, have almost identical effects: they inhibit the reuptake of dopamine and thus strengthen the effectiveness of synapses that use this transmitter substance. Reinforcing stimuli – such as food for a hungry animal, water for a thirsty one or sexual contact for a sexually aroused one – exert their behavioural effects largely by increasing the activity of a circuit of dopamine-secreting neurons (see Chapter 13). Thus, amphetamine and cocaine mimic the effects of reinforcing stimuli. Free-base cocaine (crack) is particularly addictive. The drug has an immediate effect on the reuptake of dopamine and produces such a profound feeling of euphoria and pleasure that the person wants to repeat the experience again and again.

Cocaine and amphetamine, if taken in large enough doses for a few days, can produce the symptoms of the serious mental disorder paranoid schizophrenia (see Chapter 18). Heavy users of these drugs suffer from hallucinations and their thoughts become confused and difficult to control. They may come to believe that they are being attacked or plotted against. In fact, an experienced clinician cannot distinguish the drug-induced symptoms from those that occur in people who really have the psychosis. This fact has suggested to some investigators that schizophrenia may be caused by overactivity of dopamine-secreting synapses.

Opiate drugs have both excitatory and inhibitory effects on behaviour. All of these effects occur because these drugs mimic the effects of the body's own opioid neuromodulators: they stimulate opioid receptors located on neurons in various parts of the brain. The inhibitory effects include analgesia (reduced sensitivity to pain), hypothermia (lowering of body temperature) and sedation. The pain reduction is accomplished by neurons in the midbrain, the hypothermia by neurons in the hypothalamus and the sedation by neurons in the medulla. A fatal overdose of an opiate kills its victim by inhibiting the activity of circuits of neurons in the medulla that control breathing, heart rate and blood pressure. But it is the excitatory effects of opiates that induce people to abuse them. Some opioid receptors are located on dopamine-secreting neurons involved in reinforcement (reward). When a person takes an opiate such as heroin, the activity of these neurons produces feelings of euphoria and pleasure, similar to those produced by cocaine or amphetamine. These excitatory effects, and not the inhibitory ones, are responsible for addiction.

What is drug addiction?

Some drugs have very potent reinforcing effects, which lead to increased use and dependence on them. The term 'dependent' is important because there is no internationally agreed definition of 'drug addiction'. The current view of addiction is that the person undergoes a progressive loss of control over their

Psychology in action: The psychological consequences of taking ecstasy

In their list of the most dangerous, illegal, major psychosocial drugs – those taken recreationally to induce pleasure, euphoria or relaxation – Nutt *et al.* (2007) judged heroin and cocaine to be the most harmful and the ones which produced the most pleasure. Ecstasy was listed 18th (of 20). Some have pointed out that this is an unusual position for ecstasy to occupy – but the position is partly attributable to the fact that many other drugs can be injected and are, therefore, more dangerous (Parrott, 2013). The judgement that ecstasy was less pleasurable than cigarettes, which it was in this study, has also been questioned (Parrott, 2013).

Ecstasy –or 3, 4-methylendioxymethamphetamine (MDMA) – is a so-called CNS stimulant, behaviourally similar to amphetamine and methamphetamine. Unlike those two drugs, MDMA's primary site of action is at serotonin receptors where it reverses the process of serotonin reuptake. The consequence of this is that is leaves more serotonin available in the synaptic cleft. In his review of ecstasy, Parrott (2013) noted that its use as a recreational drug emerged towards the mid-1980s. Surveys suggest that it may be the third most popular recreational drug after cannabis and cocaine. Very few people take MDMA, however, compared to other drugs – the European Monitoring Centre for Drugs and Drug Addiction (2010) found that 8.6 per cent of adults had used ecstasy. Its usage among clubbers, however, is high – some (dated) surveys suggest it is over 90 per cent (Winstock *et al.*, 2001).

According to Parrott (2013), the first empirical study of MDMA (conducted in 100 students at a Californian University) found that common symptoms of taking the drug were teeth clenching, increased heart rate and positive mood. There is also heightened blood pressure, faster breathing, overheating, cortisol secretion, and impaired serotonin system functioning (Benningfield and Cowan, 2013). All of these are amplified by the clubbing environment, where symptoms are accompanied by dehydration and sweating. Taking the drug can also be, perhaps paradoxically, accompanied by hypothermia – probably because the drug disrupts the body's ability to regulate temperature, and users respond to colder environments abnormally. Deaths following ecstasy are more common than deaths following amphetamine, and a common cause is organ failure (Schifano *et al.*, 2010).

Psychologically, ecstasy has some profound and, superficially, contradictory effects. For example, although it is associated with positive mood and greater sense of intimacy (Bedi *et al.*, 2010), research has also shown that it can intensify negative mood and induce anxiety, depending on the user's expectations and the context of the drug taking (Kirkpatrick *et al.*, 2012). Both mood changes can occur in the same individual. According to Parrott, the drug is unusual because it is one of the few recreational drugs people give up voluntarily – the positive effects of the drug wane over time.

The cognitive effects of taking the drug are varied – some studies report impairments in the ability to retain and retrieve memory over short periods, others find that the impairment occur over much longer periods (Parrott, 2013). Users seem to have particular difficulty with planning exercises such as the Tower of London (which you will find more about in Chapter 11) but report few cognitive deficits other than this and some other executive functions. Response time and attention are unaffected. The effects may be user-dependent. Heavier users have been found to show impairments on some cognitive tests, such as visuospatial memory (Halpern *et al.*, 2011; Murphy *et al.*, 2012).

---

drug-seeking and the drug-seeking becomes compulsive and persistent and maladaptive (DSM-V). Ersche *et al.* (2013) noted that the United Nations estimates that drug use affects one in every 200 people. Many people – psychologists, health professionals and lay people – believe that 'true' addiction is caused by the unpleasant physiological effects that occur when an addict tries to stop taking the drug.

When people develop tolerance to a drug, they show decreased sensitivity following its continued use; the drug user must take larger and larger amounts of the drug in order for it to be effective. Once a person has taken an opiate regularly enough to develop tolerance, that person will suffer withdrawal symptoms if they stop taking the drug. Withdrawal symptoms are primarily the opposite of the effects of the drug itself. Heroin produces constipation; withdrawal from it produces nausea, cramping and diarrhoea. Heroin produces relaxation; withdrawal from it produces agitation.

Most investigators believe that the withdrawal symptoms are produced by the body's attempt to compensate for the unusual condition of heroin intoxication. That is, most systems of the body, including those controlled by the brain, are regulated so that they stay at an optimal value. When a drug artificially changes these systems for a prolonged time, homeostatic mechanisms begin to produce the opposite reaction, which partially compensates for the disturbance from the optimal value. These compensatory mechanisms account for the fact that more and more heroin must be taken in order to achieve the effects that were produced when the person first started taking the drug. They also account for the symptoms of withdrawal: when the person stops taking the drug, the compensatory mechanisms make themselves felt, unopposed by the action of the drug.

Heroin addiction has provided such a striking example of drug dependence that some authorities have concluded that 'real' addiction does not occur unless a drug causes tolerance and withdrawal. Withdrawal symptoms make it difficult for a person to stop taking heroin – they help keep the person hooked. But withdrawal symptoms do not explain why a person becomes a heroin addict in the first place; that fact is explained by the drug's reinforcing effect. Certainly, people do not start taking heroin so that they will become physically dependent on it and feel miserable when they go without it. Instead, they begin taking it because it makes them feel good.

Even though the withdrawal effects of heroin make it difficult to stop taking the drug, these effects alone are not sufficient to keep most people hooked (Baker et al., 2006). In fact, when the cost of the habit gets too high, some addicts who stop taking heroin experience 'cold turkey'. Doing so is not as painful as most people believe; withdrawal symptoms have been described as similar to a bad case of influenza – unpleasant, but survivable. Mood declines – people feel unstable, stressed, anxious and depressed (Baker et al., 2006). After a week or two, when their nervous systems adapt to the absence of the drug, these addicts recommence their habit, which now costs less to sustain. The strength of withdrawal is not related to the strength of relapse. The reason why people take – and continue to take – drugs such as heroin is that the drugs give them a pleasurable 'rush'; in other words, the drugs have a reinforcing effect on their behaviour.

The reason why they are not abused is that they do not have reinforcing effects on behaviour – they are just not any fun to take. People take drugs because they enjoy them. And the more they like them, the more excessive their drug-taking (Ahmed, 2005). Studies in rodents suggest that the greater the access to cocaine, the greater the rat's drug-seeking behaviour (Vanderschuren and Everitt, 2004). A three-month exposure to a drug led to rats being unable not to seek drugs, even when they were punished for doing so (Deroche-Gamonet et al., 2004). Rats exposed to heroin daily had lower and more stable levels of drug intake than those who were exposed to it for 24 hours (Kenny et al., 2006). As the drug-taking increases, the excitability of the reward systems, reflected in brain activation and neurotransmitter release, decreases. Therefore, more of the drug is needed to resume this level of excitability (Kenny, 2007).

Similarly, neuroimaging data from adults have shown that activation in the insula, PFC and ACC is associated with urges to take a drug, whether cigarettes, heroin, alcohol or cocaine (Naqvi and Bechara, 2008). Ultimately drugs 'work' by stimulating the release of dopamine from the brain stem tegmental area particularly the nucleus accumbens, (Naqvi and Bechara, 2008). There is significant dysfunction in the OFC in drug addiction – less activity in this area in users of cocaine and metamphetamine is correlated with a reduction in D2/3 receptors in the striatum, and grey matter volume is less in this area (Everitt and Robbins, 2013). A number of studies has

documented lack of control in inhibition tasks in participants who are cocaine users, which is consistent with dysfunctional OFC activation or structure (Everitt and Robbins, 2013).

The primary brain areas implicated in drug addiction are the prefrontal cortex, amygdala, striatum and the nucleus accumbens (Belin et al., 2013). Given the compulsive nature of drug addiction there are similarities between the brain abnormalities seen in drug addiction and those in obsessive-compulsive disorder (Everitt and Robbins, 2013). For example, in a study of the connectivity between brain regions in people with OCD and people with drug dependence, two regions in the OFC were reduced in both groups, and the degree of reduction was correlated with increased compulsion (Meunier et al., 2012). People with OCD have also been found to have reduced D2 striatal receptors (Perani et al., 2008).

Grey matter volume declines in the OFC in people with drug dependence (Ersche et al., 2013) although there is a question over the role of the drugs in this decline – do the drugs cause the reduction or does the reduction lead to the drug-taking? Ersche et al. (2012), for example, examined brain structure and the ability to regulate behaviour in 50 siblings; one of each pair met criteria for drug dependence of a stimulant drug (such as cocaine). An age – and IQ-matched control group was used as a comparison. They examined participants' ability to inhibit very well-established responses in a test called stop-signal reaction time which is thought to be subserved by the inferior frontal gyrus, the basal ganglia and the pre-SMA. These responses were as impaired in the non-drug-taking siblings as they were in the drug-taking siblings. Both pairs also showed less white matter volume than did the control group suggesting that these abnormalities 'were shared among members of the same family and may have predisposed them to drug-taking' (p. 602). The reduction in white matter correlated with the degree of stimulant use in the drug-taking group. When the researchers examined the degree of loss in the frontal lobe, they found that greater reduction in tracts near the right inferior temporal gyrus correlated with poorer performance at the inhibition task.

Cocaine users who had been taking the drug regularly and had no family history of dependence, nor any evidence of dependence, showed increased grey matter volume in the OFC, anterior cingulate and insula (Ersche et al., 2012). This study suggests that drugs do not have a uniform effect on an individual's neuroanatomy and that a person's degree of vulnerability – dependent or not dependent – may be related to the brain changes reported in the literature.

Drugs and altered states of consciousness

Throughout history, people have enjoyed changing their consciousness now and then by taking drugs, fasting, meditating or chanting. Even children enjoy spinning around and making themselves dizzy – presumably for the same reasons. Chemicals found in several different plants produce profound changes in consciousness and there are other drugs, many manufactured, that produce pleasurable sensations. Many of these are prohibited (illegal to sell and/or use) which has given rise to 'legal highs' which either act in a similar way to stimulants (examples include piperazines, mephedrone) or which synthetically mimic well-known drugs such as cannabis (Corazza *et al.*, 2013). These are sold either in specialist shops ('head shops') or via the internet. The EU identified around 57 of these drugs in 2009–10, although there are probably hundreds more.

Behaviourally, changes in consciousness are difficult to specify. Large doses of drugs such as marijuana or LSD tend to sedate laboratory animals, but the animals give no sign of having their consciousness altered. Only humans can describe the consciousness-altering effects of the drugs. Famously, Samuel Taylor Coleridge wrote Kubla Khan after a drug-taking session. In *The Doors of Perception*, Aldous Huxley described the intense vision he experienced on looking at a bowl of flowers (Jim Morrison took Huxley's title for his band's name). The experience was induced by a synthetic form of the drug mescaline (derived from cactus peyote), which has been used by shamans for centuries as religious communion.

[Plato] could never, poor fellow, have seen a bunch of flowers shining with their own inner light and all but quivering under the pressure of the significance with which they were charged; could never have perceived that what rose and iris and carnation so intensely signified was nothing more, and nothing less, than what they were – a transience that was yet eternal life, a perpetual perishing that was at the same time pure Being, a bundle of minute, unique particulars in which, by some unspeakable and yet self-evident paradox, was to be seen the divine source of all existence. I continued to look at the flowers, and in their living light I seemed to detect the qualitative equivalent of breathing – but of a breathing without returns to a starting point, with no recurrent ebbs but only a repeated flow from beauty to heightened beauty, from deeper to ever deeper meaning. (Source: Aldous Huxley (1954), *The Doors of Perception.*)

Drugs can affect consciousness in several different ways and the development of three of these drugs – LSD, psilocybin and ketamine – the effects of the last two on consciousness are illustrated in Figure 4.38.

On the advice of the novelist Aldous Huxley, Timothy Leary, then a clinical psychologist at Harvard, took his first acid trip and reported its effect. He took lysergic acid (LSD), a powerful psychotropic drug derived from a fungus (ergot) and synthesised in the laboratory in 1930.
Source: Ben Martin/Archive Photos/Getty Images.

Figure 4.38 is based on Dittrich's (1998) five states of altered consciousness scale. The scale comprises five dimensions – (1) 'oceanic boundlessness' – heightened mood, feeling at one with the environment; (2) 'anxious ego-disintegration' – disordered thought and a loss of control; (3) 'visionary restructuralisation' – visual illusions/hallucinations; (4) 'acoustic alterations' – sensitivity to sound, for example, and auditory hallucinations and (5) 'altered vigilance'. In the figure, dimension one is represented by orange, dimension two by purple and three by blue. The further away from the centre the lines are, the greater the experience of the behaviour labelled. There appears to be a correlation between the experience of some of these dimensions and brain activation. For example, people experiencing dimension one during psilocybin and ketamine administration show activation in regions of the frontal and parietal lobe but hypoactivation in regions in the limbic system, such as the amygdala (Vollenweider and Kometer, 2001).

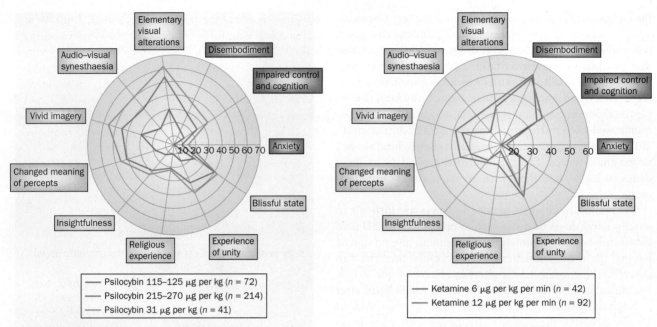

Figure 4.38 According to Dittrich, altered states of consciousness can be represented via five dimensions and other sub dimensions. This figure shows you the effect of psiocybin and ketamine on these dimensions, according to dosage. From Vollenweider & Kometer (2010).

We have the clearest understanding of one category of drugs: those that affect synapses that use a transmitter substance called serotonin. Serotonin plays an important role in the control of dreaming. Normally, we dream only when we are asleep, in a particular stage called REM sleep (because of the rapid eye movements that occur then; we'll come back to REM sleep in Chapter 9). During the rest of the day, circuits of serotonin-secreting neurons inhibit the mechanisms responsible for dreaming, thus preventing them from becoming active. Drugs such as LSD, psilocybin and dimethyltryptamine (DMT) suppress the activity of serotonin-secreting neurons, permitting dream mechanisms to become active. As a result, hallucinations occur. These hallucinations are often interesting and even awe-inspiring, but sometimes produce intense fear and anxiety. Recent research suggests that the receptors these drugs affect are quite specific – the 5-HT 2A receptor appears to be consistently implicated (Vollenweider and Kometer, 2010).

Not all hallucinogenic drugs interfere with serotonin-secreting synapses. Cocaine and amphetamine, which affect dopamine-secreting synapses, also produce hallucinations. However, the hallucinations produced by cocaine and amphetamine take some time to develop, and they are primarily auditory. LSD-induced hallucinations take place immediately and are primarily visual, as dreams are. The two types of hallucination undoubtedly occur for different reasons.

Tetrahydrocannabinol (THC), the active ingredient in marijuana, exerts its behavioural effects by stimulating THC receptors, specific neuromodulator receptors present in particular regions of the brain. THC produces analgesia and sedation, stimulates appetite, reduces nausea caused by drugs used to treat cancer, relieves asthma attacks, decreases pressure within the eyes in patients with glaucoma and reduces the symptoms of certain motor disorders. On the other hand, THC interferes with concentration and memory, alters visual and auditory perception and distorts perceptions of the passage of time (D'Souza *et al.*, 2008; Bhattacharyya *et al.*, 2010). One study found that when people who ingested a small dose of cannabis and were exposed to angry or fearful faces, less activation was seen in the amygdala although, behaviourally, participants' anxiety did not significantly reduce (Phan *et al.*, 2008). Another study found that high doses of THC significantly increased anxiety (Fusar-Poli *et al.*, 2009).

Other chemicals, such as the NMDA-antagonist, ketamine, may have antidepressant effects (Skolnick *et al.*, 2009). For example, a reduction in scores on a depression evaluation scores was found three hours after participants received a 0.5 mg dose of ketamine and lasted up to three days (Berman *et al.*, 2000; Matthew *et al.*, 2010; Aan Het Rot *et al.*, 2012). The longer-term effects of the drug, however, appear not to be as positive.

Drugs such as psilocybin and LSD may be effective treatment for obsessive-compulsive disorders (Moreno and Delgado, 1997; Moreno *et al.*, 2006). In Moreno *et al.*'s study, the effect of psilocybin was seen two hours after the administration of the drug and lasted for 24 hours.

Drug classification

In the UK, controlled substances (drugs) are classified as either A, B or C. Class A drugs are those most likely to cause harm and include LSD, heroin and cocaine. Class B drugs are considered to be not as harmful and include amphetamines, Ritalin and cannabis. In the US, cannabis is deemed a Schedule 1 substance – it has the potential to be 'abused' and has no medical use. Class C drugs include ketamine, painkillers and various other drugs that require a prescription. Cannabis or marijuana is one of the most commonly used, if not the most commonly used, prohibited drug in existence. According to one UK survey, marijuana was the most commonly experienced drug (87 per cent), followed by cocaine at 35 per cent (The Observer, 2008). The 2006 National Survey on Drug Use and Health in the US estimated that 98 million Americans over 12 years of age had tried it at least once (the figure represents 40 per cent of the population). As the International Perspective below shows, it is also commonly used by 18–25-year-olds.

The psychology of cannabis use – An international perspective

Cannabis is a drug derived from the plant genus Cannabis and comprises around 400 compounds. The most potent of these is tetrahydrocannabinol (THC), one of the 60 cannabinoids the plant contains, and a typical joint will contain between 150 and 300 mg of THC. Surveys of UK universities show that around 50–60 per cent of respondents report having used cannabis (Ashton, 2001). A study of 1,261 Australian adolescents aged between 13 and 17 years found that a quarter of the sample reported having used cannabis and this use increased with age (Rey et al., 2002).

While cannabis has been used recreationally for centuries to elevate mood, recent controversy has surrounded the use of cannabis to alleviate pain. One reason why the drug may be inappropriate is that it may have psychological consequences that could be either harmful or dangerous. Degenhardt et al. (2010) studied 1,943 Australian secondary school children from 14.9 years of age until they were 20. Adolescents who used cannabis occasionally and continued this use in early adulthood were more likely to be alcohol and tobacco-dependent and less likely to complete education after school than were non-users. Drug problems were associated with smoking cannabis at least weekly during adolescence and young adulthood.

About 50 per cent of THC in a joint of cannabis is inhaled through smoke (the amount is less when taken orally). Because THC has a half-life of seven days, it can remain vital for up to 30 days which means that traces of cannabis can be detected in the body up to a month after inhalation/ingestion. The behavioural effects of cannabis are varied. It can stimulate appetite, reduce anxiety and create psychedelic experiences. Doses of THC as low as 2.5 g in herbal cigarettes can produce a feeling of intoxication and a reduction in anxiety (Ashton, 2001). It can also produce panic attacks and paranoia. Its effects on psychomotor performance are similar to those of alcohol: behaviour becomes uncoordinated and reaction time slows. In many European countries, the second most common substance found in the bodies of drivers involved in fatal accidents or in drivers who drive poorly is cannabis. The majority of those who use cannabis show no evidence of excessive or illegal alcohol consumption. Similar performance decrements are seen in pilots (even pilots who are regular cannabis users) 24 hours after cannabis intake.

The association between cannabis use and the development of psychotic disorders, such as schizophrenia, is a controversial one. Many studies have reported that psychotic symptoms can occur but that these are short-lived; few studies have followed up such patients, however, to examine the long-term consequences of cannabis use. A study of 535 Danish patients who had been treated for cannabis-induced psychotic symptoms (Arendt et al., 2005) found that 44 per cent of cases showed schizophrenia-type symptoms. Some 77 per cent of the sample reported new psychotic symptoms. Approximately 47 per cent of the sample received a diagnosis of cannabis-induced schizophrenia a year after seeking treatment for cannabis-related psychosis.

The authors caution, however, that there was a significant delay in the majority of patients in the development of schizophrenia-type symptoms. They also note that they were unable to control for any other type of substance use during the follow-up period. Between 40 and 51 per cent of patients with schizophrenia have used cannabis (Barnett et al., 2007) and there appears to be an association between decreased grey matter and cannabis use in schizophrenia patients who are cannabis users and have had their first episode (Bangalore et al., 2008). (In psychiatry, an episode is one serious experience or appearance of a disorder.)

Cannabis use is legal in some European countries but in restricted contexts. Danish law states that cannabis is illegal but has a provision that condones possession or sale of up to 30 g of cannabis (MacCoun and Reuter, 2001). This level, set in 1976, was reduced to 5 g in 1985. Around 1,200 coffee shops sell cannabis in the Netherlands and operate according to strict guidelines (such as no advertising, no public disturbances, no sales to minors and so on).

Because of cannabis's status as an illegal drug in some European countries, especially the UK, much debate has surrounded the legitimacy of this position, with a number of doctors and patients questioning the decision to restrict or prohibit its use.

Chapter review

The brain and its components

- The brain has two major functions: to control behaviour and to regulate the body's physiological processes.
- The central nervous system (CNS) consists of the spinal cord and the three major divisions of the brain: the brain stem, the cerebellum and the cerebral hemispheres. The cerebral cortex, which covers the cerebral hemispheres, is wrinkled by fissures and gyri.
- The brain communicates with the rest of the body through the peripheral nervous system, which includes the spinal nerves and cranial nerves.
- The basic element of the nervous system is the neuron. Neurons are assisted in their tasks by glia, which provide physical support, aid in the development of the nervous system, provide neurons with chemicals they need, remove unwanted chemicals, provide myelin sheaths for axons and protect neurons from infection.
- One neuron communicates with another (or with muscle or gland cells) by means of synapses. A synapse is the junction of the terminal button of the presynaptic neuron with the membrane of the postsynaptic neuron.
- Synaptic communication is chemical; when an action potential travels down an axon, it causes a transmitter substance to be released by the terminal buttons.
- An action potential consists of a brief change in the electrical charge of the axon, produced by a brief entry of positively charged sodium ions into the axon followed by a brief exit of positively charged potassium ions.
- Ions enter the axon through ion channels, and ion transporters eventually restore the proper concentrations of ions inside and outside the cell.
- Molecules of the transmitter substance released by terminal buttons either excite or inhibit the firing of the postsynaptic neuron. The combined effects of excitatory and inhibitory synapses on a particular neuron determine the rate of firing of that neuron.
- Neuromodulators resemble transmitter substances but travel further and are dispersed more widely. They are released by terminal buttons and modulate the activity of many neurons. The best-known neuromodulators are the opioids, which are released when an animal is engaged in essential, meaningful behaviour. The opiates, extracted from the sap of the opium poppy or produced in a laboratory, stimulate the brain's opioid receptors.

Techniques for studying the brain

- Various techniques are available for neuroscientists to investigate brain function. These include experimental lesion, observing the effects of natural or accidental brain damage, recording the electrical activity of the brain or observing its structure or metabolic activity.
- Neuropsychologists study the effects of brain damage on people's behaviour, correlating their behavioural deficits with the location of their lesions.
- Neuropsychological rehabilitation refers to a programme of remediation that helps the patient regain some of the function lost through brain injury.
- Techniques used to measure activity of the peripheral nervous system or autonomic nervous system included galvanic skin response (GSR), electrocardiography (ECG) and electromyography (EMG).
- GSR is a measure of arousal indexed by electrodermal response; ECG is a measure of heart rate; EMG is a measure of muscle activity.
- Sophisticated methods of observing brain structure and activity in healthy individuals include computerised tomography (CT), positron emission tomography (PET), magnetic resonance imaging (MRI), functional magnetic resonance imaging (fMRI), magnetoencephalography (MEG) and repetitive transcranial magnetic stimulation (rTMS).
- CT and MRI are measures of brain structure; PET and fMRI are measures of brain function: activation/oxygen consumption/blood flow; MEG is a measure of brain electrical activity; rTMS involves passing a magnetic current over the head which results in temporary impairment of function.
- Psychophysiologists measure the brain's electrical activity using electroencephalography (EEG) and event-related potentials (ERP).

The cortex and its organisation

- Anatomically, the cerebral cortex is divided into four lobes: frontal, parietal, occipital and temporal.
- Functionally, the cerebral cortex is organised into five major regions: the three regions of the primary sensory cortex (visual, auditory and somatosensory), the primary motor cortex and the association cortex.
- The association cortex consists of sensory regions that are responsible for perceiving and learning and motor regions that are responsible for planning and acting.

▷

- Visual stimulation is transmitted from the eyes to the brain through the optic nerves, one of the pairs of cranial nerves. The information is sent to the primary visual cortex in the occipital lobe.
- The motor association cortex in the frontal lobe is responsible for planning activity; the primary motor cortex is responsible for initiating movement
- Somatosensory information is transmitted from the skin to the spinal cord by means of a spinal nerve. It is then sent up through the spinal cord and is relayed to the primary somatosensory cortex.
- Lateralisation refers to whether a function is localised in the left or right hemisphere. The right and left hemispheres are involved with somewhat different functions: the left is superior at reading, speech production and speech comprehension; the right hemisphere is superior for visuospatial ability and recognition of emotion.
- The two cerebral hemispheres are connected by a large bundle of axons called the corpus callosum which allows the hemispheres to transfer information to one another.
- The frontal lobe is the largest and most recently developed lobe in the brain and is involved in a variety of behaviours including smelling, tasting, inhibiting inappropriate behaviour, reasoning, action selection, executive control, attention, working memory and others.
- A region of the left frontal cortex (Broca's area) is specialised for the control of speech.
- Somatosensory information is processed by the parietal lobe, visual information by the occipital and lower temporal lobes, and auditory information by the upper temporal lobe. Other functions of the parietal lobe are related to these perceptual processes; for example, the parietal lobes are concerned with perception of space and knowledge about the body as well as mental arithmetic.

Control of internal functions and automatic behaviour

- The more primitive parts of the brain control homeostasis and species-typical behaviours. The brain stem, which consists of the medulla, the pons and the midbrain, contains neural circuits that control vital physiological functions and produce automatic movements such as those used in locomotion, fighting and sexual behaviour.
- The cerebellum assists the cerebral cortex in carrying out movements; it coordinates the control of muscles, resulting in smooth movements. It also regulates postural

adjustments and appears to play some role in cognition and reading impairment.
- The thalamus participates in the control of movement and relays sensory information to the cerebral cortex.
- The hypothalamus controls the pituitary gland, which, in turn, controls most of the endocrine glands of the body, and it also controls the internal organs through the autonomic nervous system.
- Hormones, secreted by endocrine glands, are chemicals that act on hormone receptors in target cells and produce physiological reactions in these cells. The hypothalamus can control homeostatic processes directly and automatically through its control of the pituitary gland and the autonomic nervous system, or it can cause neural circuits in the cerebral cortex to execute more complex, learned behaviour.
- The amygdala and the hippocampus are both located within the temporal lobe, specifically within the limbic system. The amygdala is involved in various cognitive and emotional processes including face perception, fear conditioning and emotional memory encoding.
- The insula is involved in several functions, including pain and temperature perception, nausea, time perception and taste.
- The hippocampus is involved in learning, scene construction and new memory formation; people with damage to this structure can recall old memories but are unable to learn anything new.

Drugs and behaviour

- Many chemicals found in nature have behavioural effects, and many more have been synthesised in the laboratory.
- Drugs can facilitate or interfere with synaptic activity. Facilitators include drugs that cause the release of a transmitter substance (such as the venom of the black widow spider); drugs that directly stimulate postsynaptic receptor molecules, thus duplicating the effects of the transmitter substance itself (such as nicotine); and drugs that inhibit the reuptake of a transmitter substance (such as amphetamine and cocaine).
- Drugs that interfere with synaptic activity include those that inhibit the release of a transmitter substance (such as botulinum toxin) and those that block receptor molecules (such as curare).
- There are several major categories of drugs that affect behaviour. Alcohol, barbiturates and tranquillisers depress the activity of the brain by stimulating various types of receptor molecule.

▷

- Amphetamine and cocaine stimulate the brain primarily by retarding the reuptake of dopamine. The opiates duplicate the effects of the brain's opioids, decreasing sensitivity to pain and producing intensely enjoyable feelings of euphoria and pleasure. LSD, psilocybin and related drugs inhibit the activity of synapses that use serotonin.
- The hallucinogenic effects of these drugs may be related to dreaming, which is controlled by circuits of serotonin-secreting neurons.
- The physiological effects of marijuana are produced by a compound called THC which stimulates receptors that are normally activated by a natural neuromodulator called anandamide.

- Psychotherapeutic drugs include those that reduce the symptoms of schizophrenia and those that relieve depression. Anti-schizophrenic drugs block dopamine receptors, and antidepressant drugs generally facilitate the action of serotonin.
- Opiates produce **tolerance and withdrawal symptoms,** which make their habitual use increasingly expensive and make quitting more difficult.
- The primary reason for addiction is the reinforcing effect, not the unpleasant symptoms produced when an addict tries to quit. Tolerance appears to be produced by homeostatic mechanisms that counteract the effects of the drug.

Suggestions for further reading

Psychobiology and neuroscience - general reading

Carlson, N.R. (2013) *Foundations of Behavioural Neuroscience* (9th edn). Boston, MA: Allyn and Bacon.

Catani, M. (2017). A little man of some importance. *Brain*, 140(11), 3055–3061.

Chance, S.A. (2014) The cortical microstructural basis of lateralised cognition: a review. *Frontiers in Psychology*, 5, 1–8.

Corballis, M.C. (2014) Left brain, right brain: Facts and fantasies. *PLoS Biology*, 12, 1. e1001767.

Domenech, P. and Koechlin, E. (2015) Executive control and decision-making in the join up prefrontal cortex. *Current Opinion in Behavioural Science*, 1, 101–16.

Frixione, E. (2017). What is in a word? Neuron: Early usage and evolution in antiquity to its long-lasting current significance. *Journal of the History of the Neurosciences*, 26, 406–24.

Genon, S., Reid, A., Langner, R., Amunts, K., & Eickhoff, S. B. (2018). How to characterize the function of a brain region. *Trends in Cognitive Sciences*, 22, 350–364.

Gross, A. (2009) The brains in brain: The coevolution of localization and its images. *Journal of the History of the Neurosciences*, 17, 380–92.

Güntürkün, O. and Ocklenburg, S. (2017) Ontogenesis of lateralization. *Neuron*, 94(2), 249–63.

Hugdahl, K. and Westerhausen, R. (2010) *The Two Halves of the Brain*. Cambridge, MA: MIT Press.

Krakauer, J. W., Ghazanfar, A. A., Gomez-Marin, A., MacIver, M. A., & Poeppel, D. (2017). Neuroscience needs behavior: correcting a reductionist bias. *Neuron*, 93(3), 480–490.

Martin, G.N. (2003) *Essential Biological Psychology*. London: Arnold.

Martin, G.N. (2006) *Human Neuropsychology* (2nd edn). Harlow: Pearson Education.

Martin, G.N. (2018). In search of the brain of Descartes. *The Psychologist*, August, 22–27.

Miller, G.A. (2010) Mistreating psychology in the decades of the brain. *Perspectives on Psychological Science*, 5, 716–43.

These are good, comprehensive introductions to the physiology of behaviour, human brain activity, structure and function and general psychobiology.

Methods

Andreassi, J.L. (2007) *Psychophysiology* (5th edn). Hillsdale, NJ: Lawrence Erlbaum Associates.

deSchotten, M.T. *et al.* (2015) From Phineas Gage and Monsieur Leborgne to H.M.: Revisiting disconnection syndromes. *Cerebral Cortex*, 25(12), 4812–27.

deWit, L., Alexander, D., Ekroll, V. and Wagemans, J. (2016) Is neuro-imaging measuring information in the brain? *Psychonomic Bulletin and Review*, 23(5), 1415–1428.

Pan, H., Epstein, J., Silbersweig, D.A. and Stern, E. (2011) New and emerging techniques for mapping brain circuitry. *Brain Research Reviews*, 67, 226–51.

Poldrack, R.A., *et al.* (2017) Scanning the horizon: Towards transparent and reproducible neuroimaging research. *Nature Reviews Neuroscience*, in press.

Stelzer, J., Lohmann, G., Mueller, K., Buschmann, T. and Turner, R. (2014) Deficient approaches to human neuroimaging. *Frontiers in Human Neuroscience*, 8, 462.

Shimamura, A.P. (2010) Bridging psychological and biological science: the good, the bad and ugly. *Perspectives on Psychological Science*, 5, 772–75.

These papers, and one book, give you an up-to-date perspective on current views of methods employed by psychobiology and neuroscience.

Drugs and behaviour

Advocat, C.D. and Comaty, J. (2014) *Julien's A Primer of Drug Action* (13th edn). San Francisco, CA: W.H. Freeman.

Broyd, S.J., van Hell, H.H., Beale, C., Yücel, M. and Solowij, N. (2016) Acute and chronic effects of cannabinoids on human cognition – a systematic review. *Biological Psychiatry*, 79(7), 557–67.

Garcia-Romeu, A., Kersgaard, B. and Addy, P.H. (2016) Clinical applications of hallucinogens: A review. *Experimental and Clinical Psychopharmacology*, 24(4), 229.

Iszáj, F., Griffiths, M.D. and Demetrovics, Z. (2016) Creativity and psychoactive substance use: A systematic review. *International Journal of Mental Health and Addiction*, 1–15.

Mackillop, J. and de Wiit, H. (2012) *The Wiley-Blackwell Handbook of Addiction Psychopharmacology*. London: Wiley Blackwell.

Some good readings on psychopharmacology Julien's book is probably the best introductory book on drugs and the biochemistry of drug use available.The psychology of cannabis use – *Continued*

CHAPTER 5
Sensation

YOUR APPOINTMENT WITH LUIGI!

You're off to have your hair cut but this is no ordinary hairdressing appointment. You have an appointment with Luigi! But where is Luigi?

Type in the following link in your browser and put your headphones on.
https://www.youtube.com/watch?v=IUDTlvagjJA

The clip illustrates an auditory illusion – in this case our ability to detect sound even though the person producing the sound is not moving (and is obviously not visible).

You can find more auditory illusions here: https://www.newscientist.com/article/dn13355-music-special-five-great-auditory-illusions/

WHAT YOU SHOULD BE ABLE TO DO AFTER READING CHAPTER 5

- Describe the difference between sensation and perception.
- Describe the processes involved in sensation, such as transduction and sensory coding.
- Describe each of the sense organs and how they function.
- Think of reasons why such senses have evolved.

QUESTIONS TO THINK ABOUT

- How many senses do we have?
- Are some senses more important to us than others?
- Which sense do we use least (or think we do) and why?
- Do the different senses function along similar lines, using similar mechanisms?
- Is the importance of a sense reflected in the amount of brain capacity needed to support it?
- Why are some animals more reliant on some senses than others?
- Are there some stimuli that we sense, even though we are not consciously aware of sensing them?
- How can we tell the difference between the sight (and sound) of a bird and a plane, or between the smell of chocolate and gas?

Sensation and behaviour

Our senses are the means by which we experience the world; everything we learn is detected by sense organs and transmitted to our brains by sensory nerves. Without sensory input, a human brain would be utterly useless; it would learn nothing, think no thoughts, have no experiences and control no behaviours.

Vision, to most people, is the most important sense modality. Through it we recognise family and friends, see their facial expressions and gestures, learn to read, perceive objects that are beyond our reach and find our way around our environment. It provides us with information about the size, shape, colour and movement of objects nearby and at a distance. Through vision, we receive some of our most powerful aesthetic experiences, in the form of art, a sexual partner and other beautiful images.

The other senses also contribute to the richness of experience. Because of the role that speech plays in human culture, audition is important for social behaviour and communication. Audition and vision provide information about distant events, as does the sense of smell, which can tell us about sources of aromatic molecules before we can see or hear that source. The other senses deal with immediate and proximal events such as the taste of our favourite food or the touch of someone we love. The body senses are closely tied to our own movements. When we feel an object, the experience is active, not passive; we move our hands over it to determine its shape, texture and temperature. And information from specialised organs in the inner ear and from receptors in the muscles and joints is generated by our own movements. This information helps us to maintain our balance as we engage in our everyday activities.

Sensory processing

Experience is conventionally divided into two classes: **sensation** and **perception**. Most psychologists define sensation as the detection of simple properties of stimuli, such as brightness, colour, warmth and sweetness. Perception is the detection of objects (both animate and inanimate), their locations, their movements and their backgrounds. According to these definitions, seeing the colour red is a sensation, but seeing a red apple is a perception. Similarly, seeing a movement is a sensation, but seeing a cricket ball coming towards us and realising that we will have to move to the left to catch it is a perception. Psychologists used to believe that perceptions depended heavily on learning whereas pure sensations involved innate, 'prewired' physiological mechanisms. However, neither behavioural nor physiological research has been able to establish a clear boundary between 'simple' sensations and 'complex' perceptions. Experience is essential to the development of some of the most elementary features of sensory systems. This is called 'functional validation' – the notion whereby the nervous system needs to be stimulated during development in order for it to develop properly.

The five conventional senses are: vision (seeing), audition (hearing), gustation (tasting), olfaction (smelling) and somatosensation (touching) but we have several more. The somatosensory system, for example, includes separate components that are able to detect touch, warmth, coolness, vibration, physical damage (pain), head tilt, head movement, limb movement, muscular contraction and various events occurring within our bodies (Kandel *et al.*, 1995). Whether we choose to call each of these components 'senses' is a matter of terminology.

Transduction

Sense organs detect the presence of environmental stimuli provided by light, sound, odour, taste or mechanical contact. This information is transmitted to the brain through neural impulses – action potentials carried by the axons in sensory nerves. The task of the sense organs is to transmit signals to the brain that are coded in such a way as to faithfully represent the events that have occurred in the environment. The task of the brain is to analyse this information and reconstruct what has occurred.

Transduction (literally, 'leading across') is the process by which the sense organs convert energy from environmental events into neural activity. Each sense organ responds to a particular form of energy given off by an environmental stimulus and translates that energy into neural firing to which the brain can respond. The means of transduction are as diverse as the kinds of stimuli we can perceive. In most senses, specialised neurons called **receptor cells** release chemical transmitter substances that stimulate other neurons, thus altering the rate of firing of their axons. In the somatosenses ('body senses'), dendrites of neurons respond directly to physical stimuli without the intervention of specialised receptor cells. However, some of these neurons do have specialised endings that enable them to respond to particular kinds of sensory information. Table 5.1 summarises the types of transduction accomplished by our sense organs.

Sensory coding

Nerves are bundles of axons which can do no more than transmit action potentials (see Chapter 4). These action potentials are fixed in size and duration; they cannot be altered. Thus, different stimuli cannot be translated into different types of action potential. Yet we can detect an enormous number of

Table 5.1 The types of transduction accomplished by the sense organs

Location of sense organ	Environmental stimuli	Energy transduced
Eye	Light	Radiant energy
Ear	Sound	Mechanical energy
Vestibular system	Tilt and rotation of head	Mechanical energy
Tongue	Taste	Recognition of molecular shape
Nose	Odour	Recognition of molecular shape
Skin, internal organs	Touch	Mechanical energy
	Temperature	Thermal energy
	Vibration	Mechanical energy
	Pain	Chemical reaction
Muscle	Stretch	Mechanical energy

different stimuli with each of our sense organs. For example, we are capable of discriminating among approximately 7.5 million different colours. We can also recognise touches to different parts of the body, and we can further discriminate the degree of pressure involved and the sharpness or bluntness, softness or hardness, and the temperature of the object touching us. We can detect over 10,000 different odours. If action potentials cannot be altered, how do the sense organs tell the brain that a red apple or a yellow lemon has been seen or that the right hand is holding a small, cold object or a large, warm one? The answer is that the information from the sense organs must be coded in the activity of axons carrying information from the sense organs to the brain.

A code is a system of symbols or signals representing information. Spoken English, written French, semaphore signals, magnetic fields on a recording tape, and the electrical zeros and ones in the memory of a computer are all examples of codes. As long as we know the rules of a code, we can convert a message from one medium to another without losing any information. Although we do not know the precise rules by which the sensory systems transmit information to the brain, we do know that they take two general forms: anatomical coding and temporal coding.

Anatomical coding

Since the early 1800s, we have known that the brain learns what is happening through the activity of specific sets of neurons. Sensory organs located in different places in the body send their information to the brain through different nerves. Because the brain has no direct information about the physical energy impinging on a given sense organ, it uses **anatomical coding** to interpret the location and type of sensory stimulus according to which incoming nerve fibres are active. For

example, if you rub your eyes, you will mechanically stimulate the light-sensitive receptors located there. This stimulation produces action potentials in the axons of the nerves that connect the eyes with the brain (the optic nerves). The visual system of the brain has no way of knowing that the light-sensitive receptors of the eyes have been activated by an unnatural stimulus. As a result, the brain acts as if the neural activity in the optic nerves was produced by light – so you see stars and flashes. Experiments performed during surgery have shown that artificial stimulation of the nerves that convey taste produces a sensation of taste, electrical stimulation of the auditory nerve produces a sensation of a buzzing noise, and so forth (Calvin and Ojemann, 1994).

Forms of anatomical coding distinguish not only between the sense modalities themselves, but also between stimuli of the same sense modality. Sensory coding for the body surface is anatomical: different nerve fibres serve different parts of the skin. Thus, we can easily discriminate between a touch on the arm and a touch on the knee. The primary somatosensory cortex contains a neural map of the skin (see Chapter 4). Receptors in the skin in different parts of the body send information to different parts of the primary somatosensory cortex. Similarly, the primary visual cortex maintains a map of the visual field.

Temporal coding

Temporal coding is the coding of information in terms of time. The simplest form of temporal code is rate. By firing at a faster or slower rate according to the intensity of a stimulus, an axon can communicate quantitative information to the brain. For example, a light touch to the skin can be encoded by a low rate of firing, and a more forceful touch by a high rate. Thus, the firing of a particular set of neurons (an anatomical code) tells where the body is being touched; the rate at which these neurons fire (a temporal code) tells how intense that touch is. As far as we know, all sensory systems use rate of firing to encode the intensity of stimulation.

Psychophysics

Psychophysics is the systematic study of the relation between the physical characteristics of stimuli and the sensations they produce (the 'physics of the mind'). To study perceptual phenomena, scientists had to find reliable ways to measure people's sensations. Two of these methods are the just-noticeable difference and the procedures of signal detection theory.

The principle of the just-noticeable difference

Ernst Weber (1795–1878), a German anatomist and physiologist, investigated the ability of humans to discriminate between various stimuli. He measured the **just-noticeable difference** (jnd) – the smallest change in the magnitude of a stimulus that a person can detect. He discovered a principle that held true for all sensory systems: the jnd is directly related to the magnitude of that stimulus. For example, when he presented subjects with two metal objects and asked them to say whether they differed in weight, the subjects reported that the two weights felt the same unless they differed by a factor of one in 40. That is, a person could just barely distinguish a 40 g weight from a 41 g weight, an 80 g weight from an 82 g weight, or a 400 g weight from a 410 g weight. Psychologically, the difference between a 40 g weight and a 41 g weight is equivalent to the difference between an 80 g weight and an 82 g weight: 1 jnd. Different senses had different ratios. For example, the ratio for detecting differences in the brightness of white light is approximately 1 in 60. These ratios are called Weber fractions.

Gustav Fechner (1801–87), another German physiologist, used Weber's concept of the just-noticeable difference to measure people's sensations. Assuming that the jnd was the basic unit of a sensory experience, he measured the absolute magnitude of a sensation in jnds. Imagine that we want to measure the strength of a person's sensation of light of a particular intensity. We seat the subject in a darkened room facing two discs of frosted glass, each having a light bulb behind it; the brightness of the light bulb is adjustable. One of the discs serves as the sample stimulus, the other as the comparison stimulus, as seen in Figure 5.1.

We start with the sample stimulus and the comparison stimulus turned off completely and increase the brightness of the comparison stimulus until our subject can just detect a difference. That value is 1 jnd. Then we set the sample stimulus to that intensity (1 jnd) and again increase the brightness of the comparison stimulus just until our subject can again tell them apart. The new value of the comparison stimulus is 2 jnds. We continue making these measurements until our stimuli are as bright as we can make them or until they become uncomfortably bright for our subject. Finally, we construct a graph indicating the strength of a sensation of brightness (in jnds) in relation to the intensity of a stimulus. See Figure 5.2.

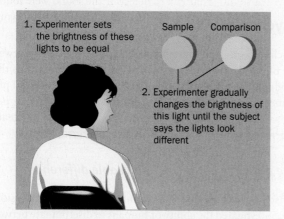

Figure 5.1 The method for determining a just-noticeable difference.

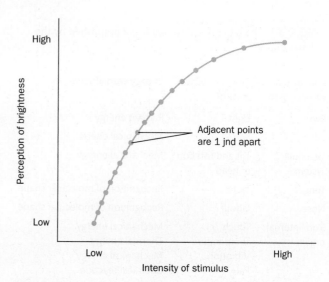

Figure 5.2 A hypothetical range of perceived brightness (in jnds) as a function of intensity.

Signal detection theory

Psychophysical methods rely heavily on the concept of a **threshold**, the line between not perceiving and perceiving. The just-noticeable difference can also be called a difference threshold, the minimum detectable difference between two stimuli. An **absolute threshold** is the minimum value of a stimulus that can be detected, that is, discriminated from no stimulus at all. Thus, the first comparison in the experiment just described – using a dark disc as the sample stimulus – measured an absolute threshold. The subsequent comparisons measured difference thresholds.

Even early psychophysicists realised that a threshold was not an absolutely fixed value. When an experimenter flashes a very dim light, a person may report seeing it on some trials but not on others. By convention, the threshold is the point at which a person detects the stimulus 50 per cent of the time. This definition is necessary because of the inherent variability of the activity in the nervous system. Even when they are not being stimulated, neurons are never absolutely still; they continue to fire. If a very weak stimulus occurs when neurons in the visual system happen to be quiet, the brain is likely to detect it. But if the neurons happen to be firing, the effects of the stimulus are likely to be lost in the 'noise'. Work such as that involved in air traffic control illustrates this point, as seen in Figure 5.3. The worker must select only the most relevant information from a background of competing information.

An alternative method of measuring a person's sensitivity to changes in physical stimuli takes account of random changes in the nervous system (Green and Swets, 1974). According to **signal detection theory**, every stimulus event requires discrimination between signal (stimulus) and noise (consisting of both background stimuli and random activity of the nervous system).

Figure 5.3 According to signal detection theory, we must discriminate between the signal, conveying information, and noise, contributed by background stimuli and random activity of our own nervous systems.

Source: J. Silver/SuperStock.

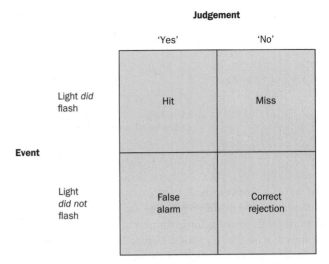

Figure 5.4 Four possibilities in judging the presence or absence of a stimulus.

An example of this might involve an individual seated in a quiet room, facing a small warning light. The experimenter informs the individual that when the light flashes, he or she hears a faint tone one second later. The person's task is to say yes or no after each flash of the warning light, according to whether or not they hear the tone. At first, the task is easy: some flashes are followed by an easily heard tone; others are followed by silence. As the experiment progresses, however, the tone gets fainter and fainter, until it is so soft that the individual has doubts about how to respond. The light flashes but did the individual really hear a tone or was it just imagined?

Response bias, as you saw in Chapter 2 is the tendency to say yes or no when unsure of detecting a stimulus and can have a considerable effect on signal detection. According to the terminology of signal detection theory, hits are saying 'yes' when the stimulus is presented; misses are saying 'no' when it is presented; correct rejections are saying 'no' when the stimulus is not presented; and false alarms are saying 'yes' when the stimulus is not presented. Hits and correct rejections are correct responses; misses and false alarms are incorrect responses. Figure 5.4 shows the relationship between these responses. If a person wants to ensure that they are correct when they say

yes (because they would feel foolish saying they have heard something that is not there), the response bias is to err in favour of making hits and avoiding false alarms, even at the risk of making misses. Alternatively, a response bias might be to err in favour of detecting all stimuli, even at the risk of making false alarms.

This response bias can seriously affect an investigator's estimate of the threshold of detection. A conservative person will appear to have a higher threshold than will someone who does not want to let a tone go by without saying yes. Therefore, signal detection theorists have developed a method of assessing people's sensitivity, regardless of their initial response bias. They deliberately manipulate the response biases and observe the results of these manipulations on the people's judgements.

The graph in Figure 5.5 is a **receiver operating characteristic (ROC) curve**, named for its original use in research at the Bell Laboratories to measure the intelligibility of speech transmitted through a telephone system. The curve shows performance when the sound is difficult to detect. If the sound were louder, so that you rarely doubted whether you heard it, you would make almost every possible hit and very few false alarms. The few misses you made would be under the low pay-off condition, when you wanted to be absolutely certain you heard the tone. The few false alarms would occur when guessing did not matter because the fine for being wrong was low or non-existent. The difference between the two curves seen in Figure 5.6 demonstrates that the louder tone is easier to detect. Detectability is measured by the relative distances of the curves from a 45-degree line.

The signal detection method is the best way to determine an individual's sensitivity to the occurrence of a particular stimulus. Note that the concept of threshold is not used. Instead, a stimulus is more or less detectable. The person decides whether a stimulus occurred, and the consequences of

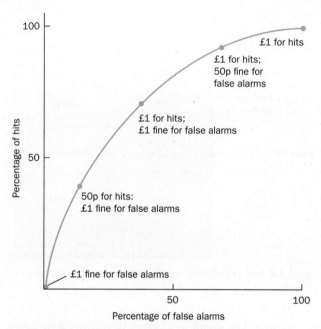

Figure 5.5 A receiver operating characteristic (ROC) curve. The percentage of hits and false alarms in judging the presence of a stimulus under several pay-off conditions.

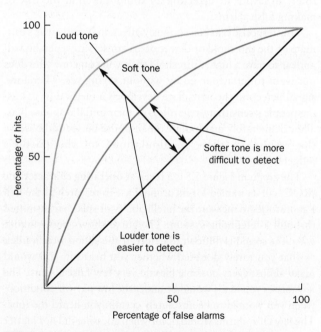

Figure 5.6 Two ROC curves, obtained by presenting a more discriminable stimulus (orange curve) and a less discriminable stimulus (red curve).

making hits or false alarms can bias this decision: for example, missing the sound of an alarm clock may be more important than missing a telephone call. Signal detection theory emphasises that sensory experience involves factors other than the activity of the sensory systems, such as motivation and prior experience. Sensitivity to a signal can be influenced by these

factors. The fact that you know that you will either be rewarded or financially penalised for making false alarms will influence the care with which you make decisions.

There is a quasi-experiment reported in the literature of factory workers complaining about the weight of large boxes that they had to shift. Carrying these heavy boxes made their backs ache. All the boxes were black. The supervisor, for reasons that you can imagine, decided to replace the black boxes with lighter-coloured ones. When the workers returned to the factory after the weekend and had to move the new boxes, they remarked on how much lighter they were than the black boxes even though the new boxes weighed the same as the old boxes. Why do you think this was?

Vision

The visual system allows us to do many activities that we take for granted: in a quick glance we can recognise what there is to see – people, objects and landscapes – in depth and full colour. Because of the dominance of visual information in our lives, it is perhaps not surprising that vision is our dominant sense.

Light

The eye is sensitive to light. Light consists of radiant energy similar to radio waves. As the radiant energy is transmitted from its source, it oscillates. Because radiant energy travels at 297,600 km/s, the waves transmitted by this antenna are approximately 3.3 m apart (297,600 km divided by 88.5 million equals approximately 3.3 m). Thus, the wavelength of the signal from the station – the distance between the waves of radiant energy – is 3.3 m (see Figure 5.7).

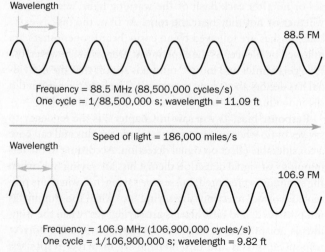

Figure 5.7 Wavelength versus vibration. Because the speed of light is constant, faster vibrations produce shorter wavelengths.

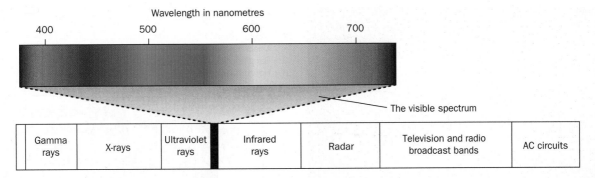

Wavelength in nanometres

| Gamma rays | X-rays | Ultraviolet rays | Infrared rays | Radar | Television and radio broadcast bands | AC circuits |

The visible spectrum

Figure 5.8 The electromagnetic spectrum.

The wavelength of visible light is much shorter, ranging from 380 to 760 nm (a nanometre, nm, is one-billionth of a metre). When viewed by a human eye, different wavelengths of visible light have different colours: for instance, 380 nm light looks violet and 760 nm light looks red.

All other radiant energy is invisible to our eyes. Ultraviolet radiation, X-rays and gamma rays have shorter wavelengths than visible light has, whereas infrared radiation, radar and radio waves have longer wavelengths. The entire range of wavelengths is known as the electromagnetic spectrum; the part our eyes can detect – the part we see as light – is referred to as the visible spectrum, as seen in Figure 5.8.

The definition of the visible spectrum is based on the human visual system. Some other species of animals would define the visible spectrum differently. Bees, for example, can see ultraviolet radiation that is invisible to us. Some plants have taken advantage of this fact and produce flowers that contain dyes that reflect ultraviolet radiation, presenting patterns that attract bees to them. Some snakes (notably, pit vipers such as the rattlesnake) have special organs that detect infrared radiation. This ability enables them to find their prey in the dark by detecting the heat emitted by small mammals in the form of infrared radiation.

The eye and its functions

The eyes are important and delicate sense organs – and they are well protected. Each eye is housed in a bony socket and can be covered by the eyelid to keep out dust and dirt. The eyelids are edged by eyelashes, which help keep foreign matter from falling into the open eye. The eyebrows prevent sweat on the forehead from dripping into the eyes. Reflex mechanisms provide additional protection: the sudden approach of an object towards the face or a touch on the surface of the eye causes automatic eyelid closure and withdrawal of the head.

Figure 5.9 shows a cross-section of a human eye. The transparent **cornea** forms a bulge at the front of the eye and admits light. The rest of the eye is coated by a tough white membrane called the **sclera** (from the Greek *skleros*, 'hard'). The **iris** consists of two bands of muscle that control the amount of light admitted into the eye. The brain controls these muscles and

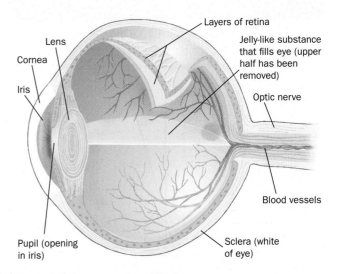

Figure 5.9 A cross-section of the human eye.

thus regulates the size of the pupil, constricting it in bright light and dilating it in dim light. The space immediately behind the cornea is filled with aqueous humour, which simply means 'watery fluid'. This fluid is constantly produced by tissue behind the cornea that filters the fluid from the blood. In place of blood vessels, the aqueous humour nourishes the cornea and other portions of the front of the eye; this fluid must circulate and be renewed (too much or a blockage leads to a disorder known as glaucoma).

The curvature of the cornea and of the lens, which lies immediately behind the iris, causes images to be focused on the inner surface of the back of the eye. Although this image is upside-down and reversed from left to right, the brain interprets this information appropriately. The shape of the cornea is fixed, but the lens is flexible; a special set of muscles can alter its shape so that the eye can obtain focused images of either nearby or distant objects. This change in the shape of the lens to adjust for distance is called **accommodation.**

The **retina**, which lines the inner surface of the back of the eye, performs the sensory functions of the eye. Embedded in the retina are over 130 million photoreceptors – specialised neurons that transduce light into neural activity. The information from the **photoreceptors** is transmitted to neurons that

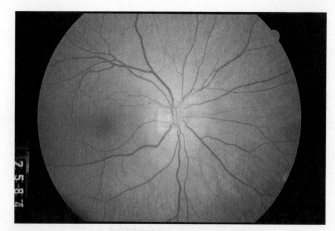

Figure 5.10 A view of the back of the eye. The photograph shows the retina, the optic disc and blood vessels.
Source: Courtesy of Douglas G. Mollerstuen, New England Medical Center.

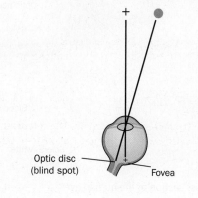

Figure 5.11 A test for the blind spot. With the left eye closed, look at the + with your right eye and move the page back and forth, towards and away from yourself. At about 20 cm, the coloured circle disappears from your vision because its image falls on your blind spot.

send axons towards one point at the back of the eye – the optic disc. All axons leave the eye at this point and join the optic nerve, which travels to the brain (see Figure 5.10).

Because there are no photoreceptors directly in front of the optic disc, this portion of the retina is blind. If you have not located your own blind spot, try the demonstration shown in Figure 5.11.

Before the seventeenth century, scientists thought that the lens sensed the presence of light. Johannes Kepler (1571–1630), the astronomer who discovered the true shape of the planets' orbits around the sun, is credited with the suggestion that the retina, not the lens, contained the receptive tissue of the eye. It remained for Christoph Scheiner (another German astronomer) to demonstrate in 1625 that the lens is simply a focusing

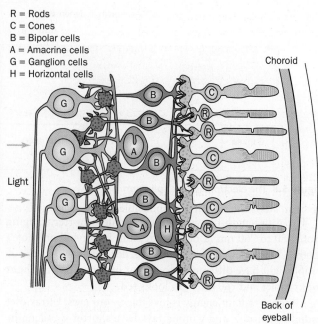

R = Rods
C = Cones
B = Bipolar cells
A = Amacrine cells
G = Ganglion cells
H = Horizontal cells

Figure 5.12 The cells of the retina.
Source: Adapted from J.E. Dowling and B.B. Boycott (1996) *Proceedings of the Royal Society of London*, 166, 80–111.

device. Scheiner obtained an ox's eye from a slaughterhouse. After carefully peeling the sclera away from the back of the eye, he was able to see an upside-down image of the world through the thin, translucent membrane that remained. As an astronomer, he was familiar with the fact that convex glass lenses could cast images, so he recognised the function of the lens of the eye.

Figure 5.12 shows a cross-section of the retina. The retina has three principal layers. Light passes successively through the ganglion cell layer (front), the bipolar cell layer (middle) and the photoreceptor layer (back). Early anatomists were surprised to find the photoreceptors in the deepest layer of the retina. As you might expect, the cells that are located above the photoreceptors are transparent.

Photoreceptors respond to light and pass the information on by means of a transmitter substance to the **bipolar cells**, the neurons with which they form synapses. Bipolar cells transmit this information to the **ganglion cells**, neurons whose axons travel across the retina and through the optic nerves. Thus, visual information passes through a three-cell chain to the brain: photoreceptor– bipolar; cell–ganglion; and cell–brain.

A single photoreceptor responds only to light that reaches its immediate vicinity, but a ganglion cell can receive information from many different photoreceptors. The retina also contains neurons that interconnect both adjacent photoreceptors and adjacent ganglion cells. The existence of this neural circuitry indicates that some kinds of information processing are performed in the retina.

The human retina contains two general types of photoreceptors: 125 million **rods** and 6 million **cones**, so called because of their shapes. Rods function mainly in dim light; they are very sensitive to light. Cones function when the level of illumination is bright enough to see things clearly. They are also responsible for colour vision. The **fovea**, a small pit in the back of the retina approximately 1 mm in diameter, contains only cones and is responsible for our most detailed vision. When we look at a point in our visual field, we move our eyes so that the image of that point falls directly on the cone-packed fovea.

Farther away from the fovea, the number of cones decreases and the number of rods increases. Up to 100 rods may converge on a single ganglion cell. A ganglion cell that receives information from so many rods is sensitive to very low levels of light. Rods are therefore responsible for our sensitivity to very dim light, but they provide poor acuity.

Colour vision

Light consists of radiant energy having wavelengths between 380 and 760 nm. Light of different wavelengths gives rise to sensations of different colours. How can we tell the difference between different wavelengths of light?

Experiments have shown that there are three types of cone in the human eye, each containing a different type of photopigment. Each type of photopigment is most sensitive to light of a particular wavelength. That is, light of a particular wavelength most readily causes a particular **photopigment** to split. Thus, different types of cone are stimulated by different wavelengths of light. Information from the three types of cone enables us to perceive colours.

The dimensions of colour

Most colours can be described in terms of three physical dimensions: wavelength, intensity and purity. Three perceptual dimensions – **hue**, **brightness** and **saturation** – corresponding to these physical dimensions describe what we see. The hue of most colours is determined by wavelength; for example, light having a wavelength of 540 nm is perceived as green. A colour's brightness is determined by the intensity, or amount of energy, of the light that is being perceived, all other factors being equal. A colour of maximum brightness dazzles us with a lot of light. A colour of minimum brightness is simply black. The third perceptual dimension of colour, saturation, is roughly equivalent to purity. A fully saturated colour consists of light of only one wavelength, for example pure red or pure blue. Desaturated colours look pastel or washed out. See Table 5.2 for a summary of the dimensions of colour.

Saturation is probably the most difficult dimension of colour to understand. White light consists of a mixture of all wavelengths of light. Although its components consist of light of all possible hues, we perceive it as being colourless. White light is completely desaturated; no single wavelength is dominant. If we begin with light of a single wavelength (a pure, completely saturated colour) and then mix in some white light,

Table 5.2 Physical and perceptual dimensions of colour

Perceptual dimension	Physical dimension	Physical characteristics
Hue	Wavelength	Frequency of oscillation of light radiation
Brightness	Intensity	Amount of energy of light radiation
Saturation	Purity	Intensity of dominant wavelength relative to total radiant energy

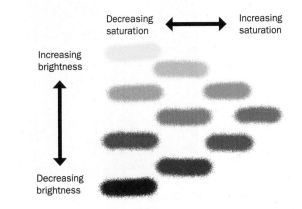

Figure 5.13 Hue, brightness and saturation. The colours shown have the same dominant wavelength (hue) but different saturation and brightness.

the result will be a less saturated colour. For example, when white light is added to red light (700 nm), the result is pink light. The dominant wavelength of 700 nm gives the colour a reddish hue, but the addition of white light to the mixture decreases the colour's saturation. In other words, pink is a less saturated version of red. Figure 5.13 illustrates how a colour having a particular dominant wavelength (hue) can vary in its brightness and saturation.

Colour mixing

Vision is a synthetic sensory modality. That is, it synthesises (puts together) rather than analyses (takes apart). When two wavelengths of light are present, we see an intermediate colour rather than the two components. In contrast, the auditory system is analytical. If a high note and a low note are played together on a piano, we hear both notes instead of a single, intermediate tone. The addition of two or more lights of different wavelengths is called **colour mixing**. Colour mixing is an additive process and is very different from paint mixing (see next paragraph). So are its results. If we pass a beam of white light through a prism, we break it into the spectrum of the different wavelengths it contains. If we recombine these colours by passing them through another prism, we obtain white light again (see Figure 5.14).

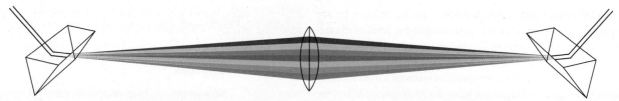

Figure 5.14 Colour mixing. White light can be split into a spectrum of colours with a prism and recombined through another prism.

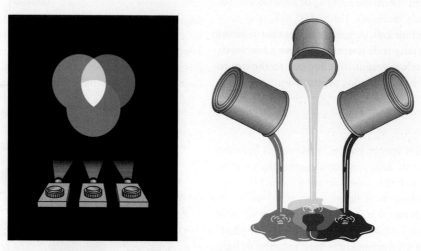

Figure 5.15 Additive colour mixing and paint mixing. When blue, red and green light of the proper intensity are all shone together, the result is white light. When red, blue and yellow paints are mixed together, the result is a dark grey.

Table 5.2 Physical and perceptual dimensions of colour

Colour mixing is not like pigment mixing – what we do when we mix paints. An object has a particular colour because it contains pigments that absorb some wavelengths of light (converting them into heat) and reflect other wavelengths. For example, the chlorophyll found in the leaves of plants absorbs less green light than light of other wavelengths. When a leaf is illuminated by white light, it reflects a high proportion of green light and appears green to us.

When we mix paints, we are subtracting colours, not adding them. Mixing two paints yields a darker result. For example, adding blue paint to yellow paint yields green paint, which certainly looks darker than yellow. But mixing two beams of light of different wavelengths always yields a brighter colour. For example, when red and green light are shone together on a piece of white paper, we see yellow. In fact, we cannot tell a pure yellow light from a synthesised one made of the proper intensities of red and green light. To our eyes, both yellows appear identical.

To reconstitute white light, we do not even have to recombine all the wavelengths in the spectrum. If we shine a blue light, a green light and a red light together on a sheet of white paper and properly adjust their intensities, the place where all three beams overlap will look perfectly white. A colour television or a computer display screen uses this system. When white appears on the screen, it actually consists of tiny dots of red, blue and green light (see Figure 5.15).

Colour-coding in the retina

In 1802, Thomas Young, a British physicist and physician, noted that the human visual system can synthesise any colour from various amounts of almost any set of three colours of different wavelengths. Young proposed a **trichromatic theory** ('three colour' theory) of colour vision. He hypothesised that the eye contains three types of colour receptor, each sensitive to a different hue, and that the brain synthesises colours by combining the information received by each type of receptor. He suggested that these receptors were sensitive to three of the colours that people perceive as 'pure': blue, green and red. Young's suggestion was incorporated into a more elaborate theory of colour vision by Hermann von Helmholtz. (We'll return to Young in the section on creativity in Chapter 11.)

Experiments in recent years have shown that the cones in the human eye do contain three types of photopigment, each of which preferentially absorbs light of a particular wavelength: 420, 530 and 560 nm. Although these wavelengths actually correspond to blue-violet, green and yellow-green, most investigators refer to these receptors as blue, green and red cones. To simplify the discussion here, we will assume that the three types of cone respond to these three pure hues. Red and green cones are present in about equal proportions. There are far fewer blue cones.

Several scientists after Young and Helmholtz devised theories that took account of the fact that people also perceive yellow as a psychologically pure hue. Late in the nineteenth century, Ewald Hering, a German physiologist, noted that the four primary hues appeared to belong to pairs of opposing colours: red/green and yellow/blue. We can imagine a bluish green or a yellowish green, or a bluish red or a yellowish red. However, we cannot imagine a greenish red or a yellowish blue. Hering originally suggested that we cannot imagine these blends because there are two types of photoreceptor, one kind responding to green and red and the other kind responding to yellow and blue.

Hering's hypothesis about the nature of photoreceptors was wrong, but his principle describes the characteristics of the information the retinal ganglion cells send to the brain. Two types of ganglion cell encode colour vision: red/green cells and yellow/blue cells. Both types of ganglion cell fire at a steady rate when they are not stimulated. If a spot of red light shines on the retina, excitation of the red cones causes the red/green ganglion cells to begin to fire at a high rate.

Negative after-images

Figure 5.16 demonstrates an interesting property of the visual system: the formation of a negative after-image. Stare at the cross in the centre of the image on the left for approximately 30 seconds. Then quickly look at the cross in the centre of the white rectangle to the right. You will have a fleeting experience of seeing the red and green colours of a radish – colours that are complementary, or opposite, to the ones on the left. Complementary items go together to make up a whole. In this context, complementary colours are those that make white (or shades of grey) when added together.

The most important cause of negative after-images is adaptation in the rate of firing of retinal ganglion cells. When ganglion cells are excited or inhibited for a prolonged period of time, they later show a rebound effect, firing faster or slower than normal. For example, the green of the radish in Figure 5.16 inhibits some red/green ganglion cells. When this region of the retina is then stimulated with the neutral-coloured light reflected off the white rectangle, the red/green ganglion cells – no longer inhibited by the green light – fire faster than normal. Thus, we see a red after-image of the radish.

Defects in colour vision

Approximately one in 12 men has some form of defective colour vision. These defects are sometimes called colour-blindness, but this term should probably be reserved for the very few people who cannot see any colour at all. Men are affected more than women because many of the genes for producing photopigments are located on the X chromosome. Because males have only one X chromosome (females have two), a defective gene there will always be expressed.

There are different types of defective colour vision. Some individuals are missing a photopigment and are called dichromats (the condition is called **dichromacy**). These people use two primary colours for matching and confuse various colours, as you will see below. Other individuals, called anomalous trichromats (**anomalous trichromacy**), have an altered – not missing – photopigment. These people account for the majority of men with colour defects although they probably do not realise they have a deficit because they may only show a slight loss of sensitivity for the reds, greens and blues, but generally good colour discrimination. Extreme cases, however, will show greater loss of sensitivity and poorer colour discrimination. In rare cases, some people may express more than three photopigments and should, theoretically, have an added dimension to their colour vision. A study of women with a phenotype expressing four photopigments found that this was the case: these people perceived more chromatic appearances than did male or female trichromats (Jameson et al., 2001).

Two of the three colour defects described below involve the red/green system. People with these defects confuse red and green. Their primary colour sensations are yellow and blue;

Figure 5.16 A negative after-image. Stare for approximately 30 seconds at the cross in the centre of the left figure; then quickly transfer your gaze to the cross in the centre of the right figure. You will see colours that are complementary to the originals.

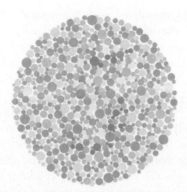

Figure 5.17 A figure commonly used to test for defective colour vision. People with red/green colour blindness will fail to see the 5.
Source: Courtesy of American Optical Corporation.

red and green both look yellowish. Figure 5.17 shows one of the figures from a commonly used test for defective colour vision. A person who confuses red and green will not be able to see the '5'.

The most serious defect, called **protanopia** (literally, 'first-colour defect'), appears to result from a lack of the photopigment for red cones. The fact that people with protanopia have relatively normal acuity suggests that they have red cones but that these cones are filled with green photopigment (Boynton, 1979). If red cones were missing, almost half of the cones would be gone from the retina, and vision would be less acute. To a protanope, red looks much darker than green, and reds and oranges generally appear very dark because the red end of the spectrum cannot be seen. Around 1 per cent of men suffer from this defect.

The second form of red/green defect, called **deuteranopia** ('second-colour defect'), appears to result from the opposite kind of substitution: green cones are filled with red photopigment. Around 8 per cent of European men and 0.5 per cent of European women have the inherited colour defect, Daltonism (protanopia and deuteranopia) (Fletcher and Voke, 1985) and there is evidence of other culture-related differences in colour vision impairment although whether such differences are due to cultural or physiological differences is unclear (Davies *et al.*, 1998). The topic of colour perception and the use of colour terms across cultures is discussed in more detail in the next chapter.

The third form of colour defect, called **tritanopia** ('third-colour defect'), involves the blue cones and is much rarer: it affects fewer than one in 10,000 people. Tritanopes see the world in greens and reds; to them, a clear blue sky is a bright green, and yellow looks pink. The faulty gene that causes tritanopia is not carried on a sex chromosome and is equally common in males and females. This defect appears to involve loss of blue cones, but because there are far fewer of these than of red and green cones to begin with, investigators have not yet determined whether the cones are missing or are filled with one of the other photopigments.

There are some individuals who claim to be able to sense colours when hearing words (and there are others who claim that tastes elicit sensations of shapes). This phenomenon is called **synaesthesia** (from the Greek *syn*, meaning 'union' and *aisthesis* meaning 'sensation'): a sensation in one modality produces an inexorable, spontaneous sensation in another (Harrison and Baron-Cohen, 1996; Simner, 2012). For example, people might involuntarily sense colours when they hear notes or tastes when they see shapes but these people regard the sensations as normal. It affects about 1 in 100,000 and cases of 'coloured hearing' were reported as early as the nineteenth century (Galton, 1883). One very famous composer, Liszt, claimed synaesthetic ability, see Figure 5.18.

Synaesthesia highlights one of the problems of studying sensation. The problem is as old as psychology and philosophy: how do we really know that the person is experiencing what they say they are experiencing? Two ways of circumventing this problem are to: (1) look for consistency of responses in an experimental group over time and compare these with control responses, and (2) compare brain activation in these two groups, working under the assumption that synaesthesia activates different areas of the brain when compared with a resting state and with a non-synaesthete control group.

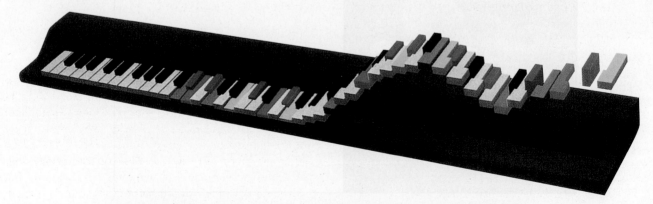

Figure 5.18 Some people claim to 'see' colours when they hear specific musical notes. The composer Liszt was one such person.
Source: Brash, S., Maranto, G., Murphy, W. and Walker, B. (1990) How Things Work: The brain. Virginia: Time-Life Books. © 1990 Time-Life Books.

Psychology in action: Seeing (and acting on) red

At the psychophysical level, red is relatively simple. It is one of the longer wavelengths of between 630 and 730 nm. It is an additive (together with blue and green) and subtractive (along with yellow and blue) primary colour. Its surprising involvement in behaviour was highlighted in a well-known paper which examined the success of contact sport winners from the 2004 Olympic Games (Hill and Barton, 2005). Contestants in the combat sports, boxing, tae kwon do, Greco-Roman wrestling and freestyle wrestling were more likely to win if they wore a red than blue outfit. Players in Euro 2004 were also more likely to win if they wore red than other colours (Attrill *et al.*, 2008), as were rugby players (Piatti *et al.*, 2012).

One study asked 42 tae kwon do referees to watch five different sparring contests in which the contestants' heads and trunks were covered in red or blue (Hagemann *et al.*, 2008). Players wearing red were awarded 13 per cent more points than were players wearing other colours. Ingeniously, the researchers then switched the colours using Photoshop and asked referees to make judgments of the same contestants. The contestants remained the same; the only variable which changed was the colour of the clothing. Those wearing red were awarded more points than those wearing blue.

When participants were asked to rate how aggressive and dominant a series of digitally manipulated images of men were, men in red were judged by men and women to be more aggressive and angrier than were men dressed in blue or grey (Wiedemann *et al.*, 2015). Only men rated the men in red as more dominant.

But the red advantage for sport is not a robust phenomenon. For example, no association between wearing red and competition success has been found in competitors in rugby (Piatti *et al.*, 2012), football (Garcia-Rubio *et al.*, 2011; Allen and Jones, 2014), or boxing (Sorokowski and Szmajke, 2009) when corrections have been made for competitor ability. One study even reported a blue advantage in judo, compared with white (Rowe *et al.*, 2005) whereas another, of 71 tournaments and which controlled for possible confounds, found no effect of blue (Dijkstra and Preenen, 2008).

Exposure to the colour red could lead to a reduction in cognitive performance because it is perceived as inhibitory (Elliot *et al.*, 2007). If red activates feelings of avoidance, people may take longer completing tests. Participants who were exposed to the colour red before a test performed less well than did those who were not. This effect was found even when participants did not express awareness of the colour and when the number was written in red ink at the top of a sheet of paper. Elliott *et al.* (2009) found that participants moved their body away from an IQ test with a red cover more often than they did one coloured grey or green.

In a review of the field, Arthur *et al.* (2016) note that when colour produces significant effects, these are typically found in experiments where the stakes are low: Materials may be unfamiliar, specific abilities are tested such as the ability to create anagrams, and the outcomes are inconsequential (Arthur *et al.*, 2016). Mehta and Zhu (2009), for example, found that priming with red led to more productive anagram formation. (However, a replication with three times the number of participants failed; Steele, 2004). When stakes are high, the experiment is knowledge-based, the content of the exercise is familiar (course material) and where the outcomes matter (getting a grade), the red effect disappears (Clary *et al.*, 2007; Meyer and Bagwell, 2012; Smajic *et al.*, 2014). Smajic *et al.* found that papers with a red cover (compared with green) had no significant effect on levels of anxiety expressed by students sitting examinations. The tests in high-stakes studies require preparation, motivation and investment, none of which are needed in low-stakes studies.

To test the effect of colour directly in a context where the outcomes were real, Arthur *et al.* accessed undergraduate outcome data where the examination papers were printed in yellow, blue, purple, red or green. In one study, they examined research methods achievement when the cover of the examination booklet was printed in red or green; in a second, they investigated any effect of the whole examination booklet printed in one colour. In both experiments, colour had no significant effect on the students' performance. So, if your exam booklet is in red, don't panic.

Audition

Vision involves the perception of objects in three dimensions, at a variety of distances, and with a multitude of colours and textures. These complex stimuli may occur at a single point in time or over an extended period. They may also involve an unchanging scene or a rapidly changing one. The other senses analyse much simpler stimuli (such as an odour or a taste) or

depend on time and stimulus change for the development of a complex perception. For example, to perceive a solid object in three dimensions by means of touch, we must manipulate it – turn it over in our hands or move our hands over its surface. The stimulus must change over time for a fully-fledged perception of form to emerge. The same is true for audition: we hear nothing meaningful in an instant.

Most people consider the sense of hearing second in importance only to vision. In some ways, it is more important. A blind person can converse and communicate with other people

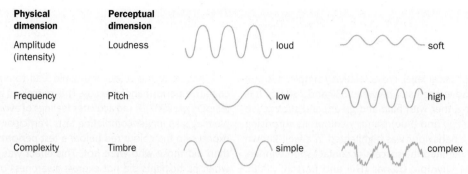

Physical dimension	Perceptual dimension		

Figure 5.19 The physical and perceptual dimensions of sound waves.

almost as well as a sighted person. Deafness is much more likely to produce social isolation. A deaf person cannot easily join in the conversation of a group of people who do not know sign language. Although our eyes can transmit much more information to the brain, our ears are used for some of our most important forms of social communication.

Sound

Sound consists of pressure changes in air. As an object vibrates, it causes the air around it to move. The surface of a vibrating object moves back and forth. As the surface moves towards you, it compresses molecules of air; as it moves away, it pulls the molecules of air farther apart. These successive waves of compression and 'rarefaction' flow away from the surface as sound. As a pressure wave arrives at your ear, it pushes your eardrum inward. The following wave of negative pressure (when the molecules are pulled farther apart) sucks your eardrum outward.

Sound waves are measured in frequency units of cycles per second called hertz (Hz). The human ear perceives vibrations between approximately 30 Hz and 20,000 Hz. Sound waves can vary in intensity and frequency. These variations produce corresponding changes in sensations of loudness and pitch. Consider a loudspeaker. Alternations in the electrical current transmitted from an amplifier cause the loudspeaker cone to move back and forth. If the cone begins vibrating more rapidly, the pitch of the sound increases. If the vibrations become more intense (that is, if the cone moves in and out over a greater distance), the loudness of the sound increases. A third perceptual dimension, timbre, corresponds to the complexity of the sound vibration. See Figure 5.19.

The ear and its functions

When people refer to the ear, they usually mean what anatomists call the pinna – the flesh-covered cartilage attached to the side of the head (**pinna** means 'wing' in Latin). But the pinna performs only a small role in audition: it helps us to determine the direction of sound. The real business of hearing is done in the inner ear (see Figure 5.20).

The eardrum is a thin, flexible membrane that vibrates back and forth in response to sound waves. It passes these vibrations, via the bones of the middle ear, to the inner ear, a 2-cm cavity which separates the outer and middle ear. The eardrum is attached to the first of three middle ear bones called the **ossicles** (literally, 'little bones'). The three ossicles are known as the malleus, incus and stapes (from Latin: hammer, anvil and stirrup) because of their shapes. These bones act together, in lever fashion, to transmit the vibrations of the eardrum to the fluid-filled structure of the inner ear that contains the receptive organ.

The part of the ear that contains the receptive organ of hearing is called the **cochlea** (kokhlos means 'snail', which also describes its shape). Uncoiled, this would reach 35 mm and 2 mm in diameter (Goldstein, 2007). It is filled with liquid and a bony chamber attached to the cochlea (the vestibule) contains two openings, the oval window and the round window. The last of the three ossicles (the stapes) presses against a membrane behind an opening in the bone surrounding the cochlea called the **oval window**, thus transmitting sound waves into the liquid inside the cochlea, where it can reach the receptive organ of hearing. The cochlea is divided along its length into three cavities by the **basilar membrane** and Reissner's membrane. The auditory receptor cells sit on the surface of

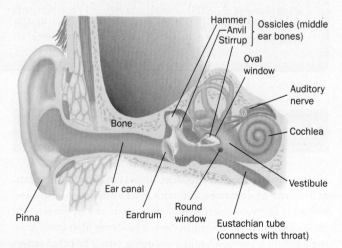

Figure 5.20 Anatomy of the auditory system.

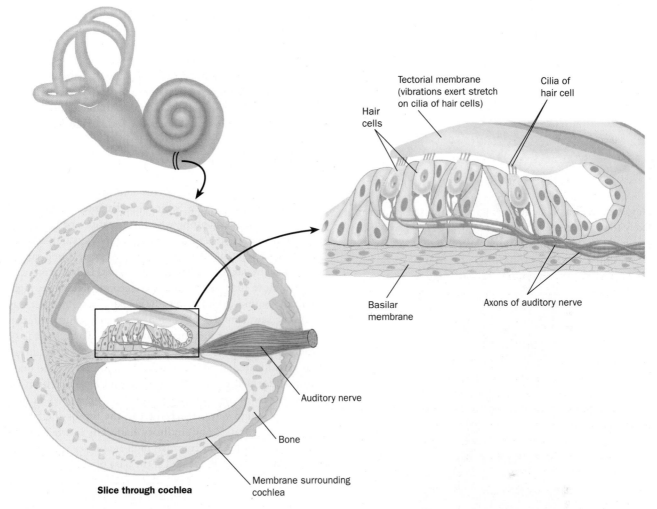

Figure 5.21 A schematic image of the cochlea.

Source: Beatty, J., *Principles of Behavioral Neuroscience*. Madison, WI: Wm C. Brown Communications, Inc. Reprinted with permission.

the basilar membrane. As the footplate of the stapes presses back and forth against the membrane behind the oval window, pressure changes in the fluid above the basilar membrane cause the basilar membrane to vibrate up and down. Because the basilar membrane varies in width and flexibility along its length, different frequencies of sound cause different parts of the basilar membrane to vibrate. High-frequency sounds cause the end near the oval window to vibrate, medium-frequency sounds cause the middle to vibrate, and low-frequency sounds cause the tip to vibrate. Figure 5.21 shows a schematic drawing and the corresponding photographic image of the cochlea.

In order for the basilar membrane to vibrate freely, the fluid in the lower chamber of the cochlea must have somewhere to go. Free space is provided by the **round window**. When the basilar membrane flexes down, the displacement of the fluid causes the membrane behind the round window to bulge out. In turn, when the basilar membrane flexes up, the membrane behind the round window bulges in.

Sounds are detected by special neurons known as **auditory hair cells,** located on the basilar membrane. Auditory hair cells transduce mechanical energy caused by the flexing of the basilar membrane into neural activity. These cells possess hair-like protrusions called cilia ('eyelashes'). The ends of the cilia are embedded in a fairly rigid shelf (the **tectorial membrane**) that hangs over the basilar membrane like a balcony. When sound vibrations cause the basilar membrane to flex back and forth, the cilia are stretched. This pull on the cilia is translated into neural activity. The threshold for hearing in humans is 100 trillionth of a metre – we can detect a sound that is as little in strength as 100 picometres. See Figure 5.22, which compares the movement of a hair cell with the equivalent necessary to move 10 mm of the Eiffel Tower.

When a mechanical force is exerted on the cilia of the auditory hair cells, the electrical charge across their membrane is altered. The change in the electrical charge causes a transmitter substance to be released at a synapse between the auditory hair cell and the dendrite of a neuron of the auditory nerve.

100 picometers

10 millimeters

Figure 5.22 Comparison of the movement of the cilia of a hair cell with the Eiffel Tower.

Source: Goldstein, E.B. (2007) *Sensation and Perception* (7th edn). Belmont, CA: Thompson.

The release of the transmitter substance excites the neuron, which transmits messages through the auditory nerve to the brain.

Detecting and localising sounds in the environment

Sounds can differ in loudness, pitch and timbre. They also have sources; they come from particular locations. The ear's ability to distinguish sounds by their timbre depends on its ability to distinguish loudness and pitch. Some common auditory stimuli and their loudness levels are presented in Figure 5.23.

Loudness and pitch

Scientists have long debated how the auditory system represents pitch on the auditory nerve. Some think that pitch is represented by axons firing in synchrony with the vibrations of the basilar membrane. However, axons cannot fire rapidly enough to represent the high pitches that we can hear. A good, young ear can distinguish frequencies of more than 20,000 Hz, but axons cannot fire more than 1,000 times per second. Therefore, high-frequency sounds, at least, must be encoded in some other way.

As we saw, sounds of different frequency cause different parts of the basilar membrane to vibrate. Thus, sounds of different frequencies stimulate different groups of auditory hair cells located along the basilar membrane. So, the brain can be informed of the pitch of a sound by the activity of different sets of axons from the auditory nerve. When low-frequency sound waves reach the ear, the top of the basilar membrane vibrates, and auditory hair cells located in this region are activated. In contrast, high-frequency sounds activate auditory hair cells located at the base of the basilar membrane, near the oval window. Therefore, the brain can tell the frequency from the set of axons which is firing.

Although different frequencies cause different regions of the basilar membrane to vibrate and therefore different axons from the auditory nerve to fire, there is also evidence that pitch information can be encoded in a different way. The basilar membrane vibrates in synchrony with the sound waves. Neurons that are stimulated by hair cells located there are able to fire in synchrony with these vibrations, thus firing at the same frequency as the sound. The brain times the intervals between these responses and thus detects the pitch. This process is an example of temporal coding.

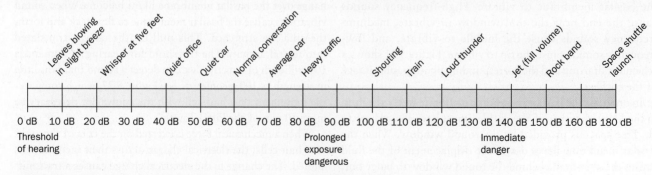

Figure 5.23 The average decibel level of some common (and uncommon) noises.

Source: Payne, D.G. and Wenger, M., *Cognitive Psychology*, 1998, p. 75. © 1998 Houghton Mifflin Company. Used with permission.

What about loudness? The axons of the cochlear nerve appear to inform the brain of the loudness of a stimulus by altering their rate of firing. More intense vibrations stimulate the auditory hair cells more intensely. This stimulation causes them to release more transmitter substance, which results in a higher rate of firing by the axons in the auditory nerve. The code is therefore similar to that used in other senses.

However, there is a problem. If they fire more frequently with sound intensity, why does that not signal a higher pitch according to the temporal code described above? Obviously, they cannot signal both loudness and pitch by the same means. The answer is that loudness is signalled by the number of auditory hair cells that are active at a given time. A louder sound excites a larger number of hair cells.

Timbre

You can easily distinguish between the sounds of a violin and a clarinet, even if they are playing tones of the same pitch and loudness. So, clearly, pitch and loudness are not the only characteristics of a sound. Sounds can vary greatly in complexity. They can start suddenly or gradually increase in loudness, be short or long, and seem thin and reedy or full and vibrant. The enormous variety of sounds that we can distinguish is in large part owing to an important characteristic of sound called **timbre**.

We can tell a clarinet from another instrument because each instrument produces sounds consisting of a unique set of simple tones called **overtones**. Their frequencies are multiples of the fundamental frequency, or the basic pitch of the sound. Timbre is the distinctive combination of overtones with the **fundamental frequency**. The fundamental frequency causes one part of the basilar membrane to vibrate, while each of the overtones causes another portion to vibrate. During a complex sound, many different portions of the basilar membrane are vibrating simultaneously. Thus, the ear analyses a complex sound. Information about the fundamental frequency and each of the overtones is sent to the brain through the auditory nerve, and the person hears a complex tone having a particular timbre. When you consider that we can listen to an orchestra and identify several instruments playing simultaneously, you can appreciate the complexity of the analysis performed by the auditory system.

Locating the source of a sound

When we hear an unexpected sound, we usually turn our heads quickly to face its source. Even newborn infants can make this response with reasonably good accuracy. And once our faces are oriented towards the source of the sound, we can detect changes in its location of as little as one degree. To do so, we make use of two qualities of sound: relative loudness and difference in arrival time.

When the source of a sound is located to the side of the head, axons in the right and left auditory nerves will fire at different times. The brain is able to detect this disparity, which causes the sound to be perceived as being off to one side. In fact, the brain can detect differences in firing times of a fraction of a millisecond (ms, one-thousandth of a second). The easiest stimuli to locate are those that produce brief clicks, which cause brief bursts of neural activity. Apparently, it is easiest for the brain to compare the arrival times of single bursts of incoming information.

Each of these cues, the difference in the loudness and the difference in the timing across the ears, allows one to discriminate between left and right. However, humans are also able to tell whether sounds come from in front or behind, above or below. This information cannot be encoded by differences across the ears. This is where the role of the pinna (mentioned above) comes to the fore. The pinna has a very distinctive shape and for humans its usefulness is far from obvious from its appearance – contrast the obvious funnel shape of a horse's ears which has plainly evolved to gather sound from a particular direction. The various ridges and folds of the human ear cause sound to interact with the surface in a process called acoustic interference. The result is that the timbre of the sound changes according to the sound direction. The importance of the pinna's corrugations in sound localisation can be demonstrated by filling up the folds with plastic material and showing that localisation becomes much poorer.

The interaction between audition and vision

The brain can also be 'persuaded' to believe that sounds can enhance the perception of visual stimuli. How senses interact is important because in real life we usually do not experience stimuli in only one sensory modality. When observers watched a single flash, which was accompanied by multiple auditory beeps, spaced 57 ms apart (Shams *et al.*, 2000), they reported having seen several flashes and not the one actually presented. Multiple flashes were consistently seen when multiple beeps were presented. When beeps were presented over 70 ms apart, however, the illusion was diminished and observers reported seeing single flashes. When a single beep was presented with multiple flashes, observers correctly reported seeing multiple flashes. The study highlights how manipulable our senses can be: in this case, simply increasing the number of presentations of stimuli in one modality (vision) while presenting single instances of a stimulus in another modality (audition) made people believe they had been presented with more stimuli in the second of these senses than they had.

A similar study explored the phenomenon whereby the introduction of a sound at the point when two identical visual targets pass 'through' each other leads people to report that they thought the two stimuli collided (Watanabe and Shimojo, 2001). Without the sound, people reported that the stimuli just seemed to stream through each other. Watanabe and Shimojo found that this collision effect could be weakened under certain conditions. For example, when identical auditory stimuli were presented 300 ms before and after the visual targets passed through each other, the collision effect did not occur. However, when the preceding and following sounds were different from the target sound, the collision effect remained. The context and the salience of the target sound, therefore, was important to preserving the effect.

The effect may exist because when two real objects collide they usually make a transient sound. The inclusion of the target noise in these experiments seemed to provide the 'missing' sound that you would expect to hear when two objects collided. But if a target noise is preceded or followed by a similar noise, it will be difficult for the viewer/listener to draw a cause-and-effect relationship between the contact of the two images and the simultaneous noise because the simultaneous noise is the same as that which preceded and followed the collision.

A novel type of sensory interaction – between taste and sound – is described in the cutting edge section below.

Audition and the temporal cortex

The cortical areas which mediate our perception of sound are located in the temporal cortex. One of the key features of the visual system is that it is organised hierarchically at the neural level. That is, sensory input is broken down and then put together to form complex stimuli in various regions of the brain. This means that different regions of neurons are responsible for processing different types of visual stimuli. A similar phenomenon has also been demonstrated for the auditory sense: tones, non-speech stimuli, meaningless speech sounds and other types of auditory stimuli have been found to generate specific areas of the cortex (as well as areas they seem to have in common).

Cutting edge: Kiki or Bouba?

Our senses interact in many interesting and unusual ways and one field in which the senses interact most interestingly is in the study of food and eating. For example, we rate foods as more flavoursome and more intense if they're the colour we expect them to be - a cake coloured a deep yellow is rated as more lemony than one not coloured lemon (duBose *et al.*, 1980); an intensely coloured orange juice is perceived as having a more intense flavour than one that is more weekly coloured despite it being the same drink (Wei *et al.*, 2012); a strawberry drink coloured red is rated as more pleasant than exactly the same drink coloured differently (Zampini *et al.*, 2008).

We hold schema about these foods - lemons are yellow; strawberries are red - and if we encounter stimuli that conflict with these schemas or are incongruent with them, this affects our perception, informs our cognitions and alters our affective response. Of course, these schemas are culture-specific. Lemons are yellow in Europe; green in Colombia.

Some recent research suggests that the type of language that we use is associated with certain types of food.

For example, before reading on, take a look at the two shapes in Figure 5.24

If you were to assign a made-up name to each, what name would you give it? Which would you call Kiki and which would you call Bouba? Look at them now before reading the next paragraph.

Would you think that a ketchup called Nodax is thicker than one called Nidax or that ice cream is creamier when called Frosch than Frisch?

If your response is consistent with other research, you described the rounded image as 'bouba' and the angular image as 'kiki'. You'd also think that Nodax was thicker and

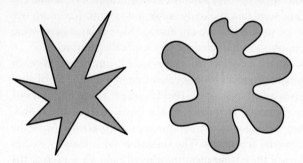

Figure 5.24 Name one of these images 'bouba' and the other 'kiki'.

Frosch was creamier. Studies have suggested that people invariably assign words such as bouba and maluma which have back vowels (such as 'o' or 'a') to rounded shapes, and words with front vowels (such as 'i' in words such as kiki) and hard velar plosives (such as 'k') to angular shapes. This also appears to be translated to foods so that soft, creamy foods are associated more with words such as bouba and maluma and with rounded shapes; and sharp, acidic, bitter, carbonated foods are associated with words such as kiki and takete and angular shapes (Gallace *et al.*, 2011; Ngo *et al.*, 2011; Spence and Gallace, 2011). However, you'll note that many of these studies report findings from the same research group. Other researchers, in other cultures, have not been able to replicate some of these findings - that carbonated drinks are associated with angular shapes and sounds, for example (Bremner *et al.*, 2013). Bremner *et al.* (2013) also found that their sample was less likely to associate bitter tastes with angular shapes/sounds.

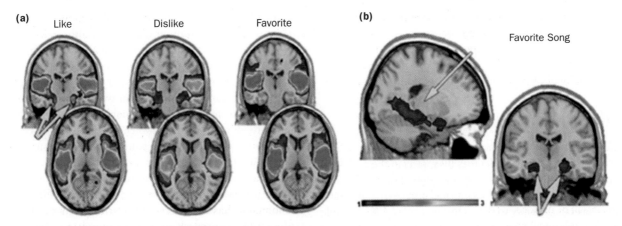

Figure 5.25 Activation in the hippocampus and auditory cortex when people listen to a favourite song and one they don't like.

In a functional magnetic resonance imaging (fMRI) study, Wessinger *et al.* (2001) presented pure tones and complex auditory stimuli to 12 healthy, right-handed men and women. They found that pure tones activated a core area – areas that surrounded Heschl's gyrus – but more complex stimuli activated areas outside this core (the pure tones did not). The authors propose that this hierarchical system of sound analysis participates in the early processing of many sounds including those for speech.

Perry *et al.* (1999) found greater right-sided activation in the temporal cortex (the primary auditory cortex) when people sang than when they passively listened to singing. This region may be responsible for the processing of complex pitches. In an ingenious experiment, Halpern and Zatorre (1999) asked people to imagine the rest of a musical excerpt (the theme to the television series Dallas) after being cued with the first few notes. When people imagined the rest of the tune, the right auditory association cortex and supplementary motor area were activated, suggesting that these regions are recruited in the imagination of meaningful complex auditory stimuli. Pantev *et al.* (1998) also found that musical training increased activation in those parts of the cortex involved in musical processing. In piano players who had played from age 12 to 28 years there was 25 per cent more activation in this region than there was in non-players.

Although there is no agreed consensus on how the terrain of the auditory cortex is divided, one view sees the auditory cortex as a region that is made up of a core (comprising the auditory cortex and nearby areas) and a parabelt (Tramo, 2001; Zatorre *et al.*, 2002), both of which contribute the hierarchical processing of sound. The core area extracts and analyses information about the pitch of tones (Zatorre *et al.*, 2002). The belt and the parabelt in the right hemisphere appear to be areas which detect changes in the duration of notes and in the patterns of music; the parabelt in both hemispheres may be involved in grouping sounds by metre (Tramo, 2001). An area beyond the auditory cortex, the frontal cortex, may be involved in organising sounds in time and keeping them 'in

mind'. When people listen to their preferred music, the default mode network is activated; it also alters the connectivity between the auditory cortex and the hippocampus which may be explained by the personal memories evoked by familiar and liked music and the emotional associations people make to it (Wilkins *et al.*, 2014), as Figure 5.25 shows.

The where and what aspects of hearing have been likened to those for sight. That is, there are two streams in the brain that allow us to locate a sound and another to identify it (Kaas and Hackett, 1999). The what, or ventral, stream is found anterior to the core of the belt and extends to the prefrontal cortex (PFC). The where, or dorsal, stream is found in posterior areas and extends to the parietal lobe. See Figure 5.26. Neurons in the anterior belt area fire more actively when responding to the pattern of sounds but weakly when trying to locate them. This neurophysiological finding is supported by research on a double dissociation in two patients with brain injury. Patient ES, for example, can recognise sounds but localises them

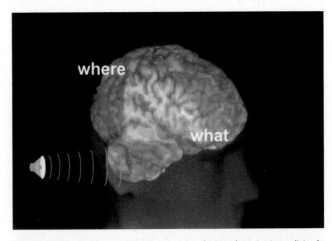

Figure 5.26 Areas associated with what (yellow) and where (blue) auditory functions, as determined by brain imaging.

Source: Goldstein, E. B. (2007) *Sensation and Perception* (7th edn). Belmont, CA: Thompson.

poorly (Clarke *et al.*, 2002), whereas another patient is poor at recognising but good at localising sound.

Given what you now know about the auditory system, how would you describe the physiological basis of listening to a favourite piece of music, from initial sensation to recognition?

Deafness

Deafness profoundly affects a person's ability to communicate with others but hearing difficulties disappear in the company of other deaf people because they can sign read; it is only in the company of people who have normal hearing that deafness hinders a person's ability to communicate (Sachs, 1989). People who are postlingually deaf – people who become deaf late in life, after they have learned oral and written language – are unlikely to learn sign language. (In this context, lingual, from the word for 'tongue', refers to the acquisition of spoken language.) Some prelingually deaf people – people who are born deaf or who become deaf during infancy – never learn sign language, primarily because they are 'mainstreamed' in community schools or attend a school for the deaf that teaches oral communication.

A recent technological development, the cochlear implant, is an electronic device surgically implanted in the inner ear that can enable deaf people to hear. Over 120,000 people have received such implants (Moore and Shannon, 2009) and the procedure is very successful (Krueger *et al.*, 2008). It is most useful for two groups: people who become deaf in adulthood and very young children who can produce speech more easily if the implant occurs before the age of five (Tye-Murray *et al.*, 1995). Putting a cochlear implant in a young child means that the child's early education will be committed to the oralist approach. Many deaf people, however, resent the implication that deafness is something that needs to be repaired, seeing themselves as different but not at all defective. In very rare cases, individuals who have damage to the auditory cortex and should, therefore, be 'cortically' deaf, appear to show evidence of hearing.

Gustation

We have two senses specialised for detecting chemicals in our environment: taste and smell. Together, they are referred to as the **chemosenses** and the process by which they sense chemicals is called **chemosensation**. The two senses are the two most important contributors to food flavour. People frequently, but erroneously, refer to food having a great taste, poor taste, and so on, but the number of actual taste qualities is small (see below). When we refer to food in this way, what we are actually referring to is flavour.

Taste, or **gustation**, is the simplest of the sense modalities. We can perceive five qualities of taste: sourness, sweetness,

saltiness, bitterness and umami (which produces a savoury sensation, like monosodium glutamate), although there are other 'secondary' taste qualities such as 'metallic' which also exist (imagine sucking a copper coin to sense this taste). Taste is not the same as flavour; the flavour of a food includes its odour, texture, temperature, shape as well as its taste: these are called head factors. You have probably noticed that the flavours of foods are diminished when you have a cold. This loss of flavour occurs not because your taste buds are ineffective (you can actually tell whether a food is sweet or salty) but because congestion with mucus makes it difficult for odour-laden air to reach your sense of smell receptors. Without their characteristic odours to serve as cues, onions taste much like apples (although apples do not make your eyes water).

Taste receptors and the sensory pathway

The purpose of the sense of taste appears to be to provide guidance or warning to the gastrointestinal system: it will reject tastes it does not like and will accept those it does. This benefits us by allowing us to avoid ingesting potentially harmful substances (most poisons, for example, tend to be very bitter).

Our ability to taste depends on the tongue, mouth and the receptors in them. The tongue has a corrugated appearance, being marked by creases and bumps. The bumps are called **papillae** (from the Latin, meaning 'nipple'). Each papilla contains a number of taste buds (in some cases as many as 200) (see Figure 5.27a-d for an illustration).

A **taste bud** is a small organ that contains a number of receptor cells, each of which is shaped rather like a segment of an orange. The cells have hair-like projections called microvilli that protrude through the pore of the taste bud into the saliva that coats the tongue and fills the trenches of the papillae. Molecules of chemicals dissolved in the saliva stimulate the receptor cells, probably by interacting with special receptors on the microvilli that are similar to the postsynaptic receptors found on other neurons. The receptor cells form synapses with dendrites of neurons that send axons to the brain through three different cranial nerves, the vagus, cranial and facial nerves. Information is sent from the nerves to the medulla, then the thalamus and then the cortex, as Figure 5.28 shows.

There are individual receptor types for some tastes and some receptors are shared by tastes. For example, receptors specialised for sweet taste have been identified – TAS1R1 and 2, for example, in 1999. TAS1R3 appears to respond to saccharin. There are many bitter receptors (Martin, 2013). We respond to bitter tastes much more quickly than we do sweet tastes and it takes us almost four times as long to identify sweet taste than salty – 845 ms vs 229 ms (Halpern, 1995). Our ability to respond to certain foods in specific ways may have a genetic basis – such as our preference for basil or coriander (Knaapila *et al.*, 2012).

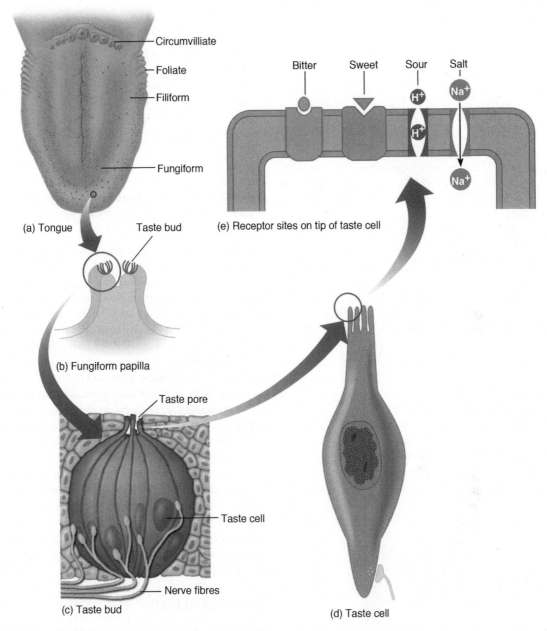

Circumvilliate
Foliate
Filiform
Fungiform

(a) Tongue

Taste bud

(b) Fungiform papilla

Taste pore

Taste cell

Nerve fibres

(c) Taste bud

Bitter Sweet Sour Salt

(e) Receptor sites on tip of taste cell

(d) Taste cell

Figure 5.27 The tongue, showing the four different types of papillae.
Source: Goldstein, E.B. (2007) *Sensation and Perception* (7th edn). Belmont, CA: Thompson.

Taste and the cortex

The cranial nerves synapse in the nucleus terminalis of the medulla. They descend and overlap here and form a gustatory nucleus. From here, projections are sent to the primary and secondary taste cortices (PTC and STC), as seen in Figure 5.29. Input from the peripheral taste apparatus is thought to enter the nucleus tractus solitarium (nucleus of the solitary tract, NST) and diverges – these two pathways become united in the insula. These two areas –the PTC and the NST are thought to have reciprocal connections. The region of the NST considered to represent sensation is thought to be rostral; the part which responds to the affective quality of taste is found near the middle (Sewards, 2004).

The insula (or insular cortex or Island of Reil) is one of the major regions of the PTC. It is divided into anterior and posterior regions by the insular sulcus. The posterior, granular portion receives greatest input from the thalamus, and parietal, occipital and temporal association cortices. The anterior portion has reciprocal connections to various regions including the anterior cingulate cortex, the ventromedial orbitofrontal cortex (OFC), the amygdala and the ventral striatum (Jones *et al.*, 2010). Stimulating the left or the right tongue with a tastant activates the right side of the

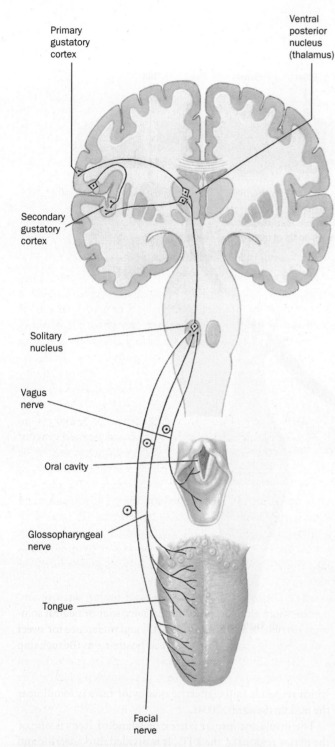

Figure 5.28 The neural pathway from tongue to brain.

Source: Pinel, P.J., *Biopsychology*, 5th edn. Published by Allyn & Bacon, Boston, MA. Copyright © Pearson Education. By permission of the publisher.

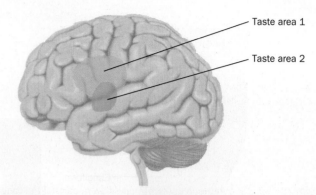

Figure 5.29 The brain seems to have two taste areas – a primary and a secondary – located near the frontal lobe.

Other brain structures, such as the amygdala, contain cells that are responsive to taste and these cells may be partly responsible for determining the hedonic quality of taste – whether the food is palatable. The amygdala forms part of an area which Small *et al.* (1997) describe as the anteromedial temporal lobe (AMTL). Patients who have had this removed or damaged report increased sensitivity to bitter tastes and an elevated ability to recognise, but not detect, citric acid. Small *et al.* (2001a) have proposed that this region may play an important role in perceiving the intensity of tastes, especially aversive taste. One reason for the increase in intensity may be that the damage to the AMTL disinhibited cells in the cortex that are sensitive to taste concentration or palatability.

In one experiment, participants who were hungry or sated were asked to taste sucrose, caffeine, saccharine and citric acid (Haase *et al.*, 2009). Hungry and sated people activated different brain regions. Hungry people showed activation in the insula, thalamus and substantia nigra. The sated participants showed less activation in the hippocampus and an area near the prefrontal lobe.

Qualities of taste

The surface of the tongue was once thought to be differentially sensitive to taste. The tip was considered most sensitive to sweet and salty substances; the sides to sour substances; and the back of the tongue, the back of the throat and the soft palate overhanging the back of the tongue to bitter substances, as Figure 5.30 illustrates.

This description, however, is largely mythical: the tongue is not this taste-specific and more than one region can detect the same sensation.

The physical properties of the molecules that we taste determine the nature of the taste sensations. Different molecules stimulate different types of receptor. For example, all substances that taste salty ionise (break into charged particles) when they dissolve. The most important salty substance is table salt – sodium chloride (NaCl). Other chlorides, such as

insula but both sides of the insula are thought to be involved in taste. The secondary taste cortex is not as well documented but appears to be principally in the OFC. This is where flavour is thought to be processed (Chapter 13).

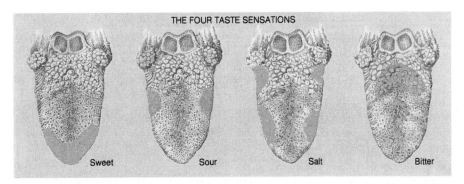

THE FOUR TASTE SENSATIONS

Sweet   Sour   Salt   Bitter

Figure 5.30 It is commonly thought that different parts of the tongue allow the experience of different tastes; the figure seen here, and in many other textbooks, is inaccurate.

Source: Whitfield, P. and Stoddart, M., *Hearing, Taste and Smell: pathways of perception*. New York: Torstar Books.

lithium or potassium chloride, and some other salts, such as bromides or sulphates, are also salty in taste, but none tastes quite as salty as sodium chloride. This finding suggests that the specific function of salt-tasting receptors is to identify sodium chloride. Sodium plays a unique role in the regulation of our body fluid. If the body's store of sodium falls, we cannot retain water and our blood volume will fall. The result can be heart failure. Loss of sodium stimulates a strong craving for the salty taste of sodium chloride.

Both bitter and sweet substances seem to consist of large, non-ionising molecules. Scientists cannot predict, merely on the basis of shape, whether a molecule will taste bitter or sweet (or neither). Some molecules (such as saccharin) stimulate both sweet and bitter receptors; they taste sweet at the front of the tongue and bitter at the back of the palate and throat. Most likely, the function of the bitterness receptor is to avoid ingesting poisons. Many plants produce alkaloids that serve to protect them against being eaten by insects or browsing animals. Some of these alkaloids are poisonous to humans, and most of them taste bitter. One study has even linked bitter taste with behavioural hostility. Participants who drank a bitter drink reported increased self-reported hostility and actual hostility towards another, whether the drinker was provoked or not (Sagioglou and Greitemeyer, 2014). In contrast, the sweetness receptor enables us to recognise the sugar content of fruits and other nutritive plant foods. When sweet-loving animals gather and eat fruit, they tend to disperse the seeds and help propagate the plant; thus, the presence of sugar in the fruit is to the plant's advantage as well.

Most sour tastes are produced by acids, in particular, by the hydrogen ion (H+) contained in acid solutions. The sourness receptor probably serves as a warning device against substances that have undergone bacterial decomposition, most of which become acidic.

People who have suffered head injury or experienced certain types of medical treatment, such as radiotherapy, sometimes experience disorders of taste. These can vary from complete loss of taste (ageusia), decreased sensitivity (hypogeusia) and distorted taste sensations, especially those for meats, eggs, fruits, coffee and carbonated drinks (dysgeusia). Patients with these symptoms, however, are rare; only around 1 per cent of patients are ageusic, for example. A common complaint among those who suffer from one of these disorders is the lack of enjoyment of food and a loss of appetite.

The development of taste preference

The development of taste preference appears to be highly malleable. For example, if a newborn is given sweetened water at 6 months of age, it will prefer sweetened water a year later; those fed normally will not show this preference for sweetened water. A similar finding is found when the newborn's diet contains additional salt (Beauchamp and Moran, 1982; Harris and Booth, 1987). This learned response is also illustrated by adults' food preferences. Our liking for foods such as lima beans, coffee, whisky and chillies, for example, grows from late childhood; children tend to find these foods too bitter (or hot in the case of chillies) to ingest.

Infants tend to consume more (and prefer) sucrose and monosodium glutamate than bitter, salty, sour or neutral solutions (Mennella and Bobowski, 2015) and preference for sweet and umami is seen in the first week postpartum (Beauchamp and Pearson, 1991). Bitter and sour tastants are rejected, even if they are dissolved with sucrose (Kaijura *et al.*, 1992). The response to salt shows a stereotypical pattern. For example, the neonate will either reject or be indifferent to NaCl but by 6 months – through to two years' of age – the infant will prefer salty food when it is presented as soup (Beauchamp and Moran, 1984; Beauchamp *et al.*, 1986), perhaps due to the maturation/activation of salt receptors. After that, however, children between 2 years 6 months and 5 years tend to reject salt solutions (Beauchamp *et al.*, 1986), unless the solution is carried in a vehicle like vegetable soup. Thus, Beauchamp and Cowart (1987) found that preference for the highest concentration of NaCl in this soup was 65 per cent in 3–6 year olds, 78 per cent in 7–10-year-olds and 13 per cent in 18–26-year-olds. Infants of mothers with morning sickness – and, therefore, prone to vomiting – show increased preference for salt intake (Crystal and Bernstein, 1998).

Supertasters

In 1931, a peculiar psychological phenomenon was observed from a chemical reaction. Some people who tasted the crystals of a thiourene called phenylthiocarbomide (PTC) found the chemical bitter, others found it tasteless (Blakeslee, 1931; Fox, 1932). This serendipitous finding hinted at the first evidence for the genetic basis of taste and for a taste quality with a unique function: one that warns us of dangerous, unpleasant or poisonous ingestants (whether rancid fat, poison, urea, etc.)

Around a third of Europeans and North Americans show heritable lack of taste sensation – a condition called specific ageusia – for PTC and its related compound, 6-n-propylthiouracil (PROP) (Guo and Reed, 2001). There is no other extensive taste polymorphism of this kind, only for bitterness, and there is evidence that the taste receptors for PROP are different from those for other bitter tastes such as quinine or urea. Around 16 per cent of people are non-tasters, 56 per cent medium tasters and 28 per cent supertasters (Bartoshuk, 1993). Supertasters judge caffeine and quinine (but not urea) to be more bitter, eat fewer vegetables, have a higher BMI (Lumeng *et al.*, 2008), dislike soy-based foods such as miso and tofu, and give higher fattiness ratings to salad dressing that is high in fat. There is growing evidence that non-tasters prefer highly fatty and fat-flavoured foods such as high-fat milk, salad dressing and fatty sweets (Hayes and Duffy, 2008). The variation in our response to bitter foods may be due to variation in the bitter receptor gene, TAS2R38.

Olfaction

Smell and taste are both near senses, or 'short distance modalities', that is, the stimuli which result in transduction of sensory signals are close to the site of transduction (the nose and mouth). This contrasts with audition and vision, which are far senses, or 'long-distance sensory modalities' (you can identify a building from 10 miles or 10 metres away, but not a smell or taste). It is a sense which we think we can do without; if asked which of the senses is least important to us or which we would be willing to relinquish if we had to, people usually nominate the sense of smell (Martin *et al.*, 2001).

Our sense of smell is more effective than a smoke detector. According to Engen (1982), we can recognise odours within zero to three seconds of encountering them, and at a distance of between one and two metres (one of the reasons why **olfaction** is more productively and creatively studied by psychologists than is gustation – see below). The Japanese Sanitation Centre noted that we (humans) can detect the

malodorous isoamyl mercaptan (a variant of which is added to odourless propane gas to make it pungent) at .77 parts per trillion (Nagata and Takeu, 1990). Cain (1977) concluded that our noses are more sensitive than a chromatograph. We can probably detect ethyl mercaptan (which is added to gas) at around one part per billion (Whisman *et al.*, 1978), the equivalent of three drops in an Olympic Swimming Pool (Yeshurun and Sobel, 2010).

People can follow a 10cm trail of chocolate essential oil in an open grass field fairly accurately while wearing a blindfold (Porter *et al.*, 2007). This study also found that both nostrils were better than one at the task but, more specifically, that the velocity of air into the right nostril was 0.45ms and in the left 0.3ms. This gives a spatial reach of 1.5–2cm in the left nostril and 1–1.5cm in the right. See Figure 5.31. There is also evidence of circadian asymmetry in sniffing. The velocity of inhalation is greater in one nostril than the other and the side changes throughout the day (Sobel *et al.*, 1999).

Our ability to name odours, however, is quite poor (around 20–50 per cent of common odours can be named) and our principal response to an odour is affective rather than linguistic or cognitive (Olofsson and Gottfried, 2015). That is, our first response to smell is whether we like it or not. Even when we do name odours, the name we give it is a referent. We say it smells 'like' something. Unsurprisingly, we are not able to identify the chemical constituents. Across the lifespan, people remember unpleasant odours better than pleasant ones (Larsson *et al.*, 2006) and these odours are detected more quickly than are pleasant odours (Boesveldt *et al.*, 2010). The likeability of faces decreases in the presence of malodour

Figure 5.31 Human's path following a scent trial, as compared to a dog's path. **(a)** Path of a dog following the scent trail of a pheasant dragged through a field (scent trail in yellow, dog's path in red). **(b)** Path of a human following a scent trail of chocolate essential oil through a field (scent trail in yellow, human's path in red).

Source: Reprinted by permission from MacMillan Publishers Ltd: *Nature Neuroscience* vol. 10. Nr 1, Jan 2007, copyright 2007 (r). Superstock: Louie Psihoyos (L).

administered at below-threshold levels (Li *et al.*, 2007). Participants exposed to an unpleasant smell are more inclined to rate strangers that are similar to themselves more positively than they would dissimilar strangers (Rotton *et al.*, 1978).

Olfaction, like audition, seems to be an analytical sense modality. That is, when humans sniff air that contains a mixture of familiar odours, we usually identify the individual components but normally not more than three or four. The molecules do not blend together and produce a single odour in the same way that lights of different wavelengths produce a single colour.

Odours interact with other senses in very peculiar ways. Djordjevic *et al.* (2004) asked participants to smell or imagine smelling the odours of either strawberry or ham as they took part in a taste detection task – the participants had to indicate at which point they detected the sweet taste of sucrose. People detected the taste of sucrose better when they smelled or imagined smelling strawberry than when they smelled/imagined smelling ham. The imagining of pleasant and unpleasant scents also activates similar brain areas to those activated during the actual inhalation of those odours (Bensafi *et al.*, 2007).

In one study, participants were presented with the odour of isovaleric acid (which has a cheesy odour) and told it was either 'body odour' or 'cheddar cheese' (de Araujo *et al.*, 2005). Participants' ratings of the odour's pleasantness under each label condition, and their brain activation, was measured. The odour was rated as significantly more unpleasant when labelled body odour than cheese, and activation in the anterior cingulate cortex (ACC) and medial OFC was greater when participants smelled clean air and the odour labelled cheese than body odour. The experiment demonstrates neatly how semantic information can influence hedonic judgement.

Odours play an important role in the lives of most mammals. Although we do not make use of olfaction in identifying one another, we do use it to avoid some dangers, such as food that has spoiled, or gas. In fact, the odour of rotting meat will trigger withdrawal – a useful response if some of the rotten meat has been swallowed. Other animals recognise friends and enemies by means of smell and use odours to attract mates and repel rivals. And the reproductive behaviour of laboratory mammals – and even the menstrual cycles of women – may be influenced by the odours emitted by other animals of the same

Odour perception – An international perspective

Perfumery is a universal art and few of us have not received or bought a gift of scent or cologne, but do all cultures and nations respond to the same smells in the same way? As you might expect, the answer is no. In general, there are cross-cultural similarities in people's responses to odour: there is a universal correlation between odour familiarity and pleasantness, for example. The more familiar a person thinks an odour is, the more likeable it is judged. A study of Japanese and German participants found that the number of memories evoked by pleasant and unpleasant odours was similar (Schleidt *et al.*, 1988). But different cultures do rate the pleasantness of some odours differently.

In one study, Haller *et al.* (1999) found that exposure to vanilla in childhood affected a German participant's food preferences later in life (Germans, at one time, received bottled milk flavoured with vanilla). When German participants were asked to rate ketchup or ketchup scented with vanilla, those who had been bottle-fed preferred the vanilla ketchup, compared with those who were breast-fed.

More directly, Doty *et al.* (1985) compared the ability of American Korean, Caucasian, African American and Japanese participants to identify odours on a brief scratch-and-sniff test called the University of Pennsylvania Smell Identification Test (the UPSIT). The Koreans were better at identification than were the Caucasians and African Americans; the last two

groups were better than the Japanese, probably because the US-validated odours were more familiar to the Westerners than to the Japanese. A study of odour detection thresholds (the lowest concentration at which a person can detect an odour) reported lower detection thresholds for Japanese ink and aniseed (Hübener *et al.*, in press).

Cultures also differ in the way they classify odour. For example, when Japanese and Sherpa people were asked to classify 20 artificial scents into perceptually similar categories, there was agreement on most but the Japanese classified some odours as 'fishy': Sherpa are not used to eating fish but the Japanese are famously fish-friendly (Ueno, 1993). Americans and French people are more likely to describe fruit odorants as sweets or flowers and flower odorants as cleaning products than are Vietnamese raters (Chrea *et al.*, 2004). Havlicek *et al.* (2008) asked a group of 717 Czech undergraduates to complete a questionnaire asking them how important the various senses were when choosing a partner and for generating sexual arousal. For women, olfactory cues were significantly more important for romance. For men, visual cues were more important. The value placed on these cues by women even extended to non-sexual domains such as choosing flowers and stimulating memory. The authors also contrast some of their findings with work conducted with North American students. Their Czech students rated body odour more positively, and

▶

Odour perception – *Continued*

Table 5.3 The odorants used in Ayabe-Kanamura *et al.* (1998), together with participants' descriptions of them

Odorants	Descriptors
Japanese	
Dried bonito flakes	dried fish
Soy sauce	soy sauce, soy
Roasted tea	Japanese tea
Dried fermented soybeans	fermented soybeans
India ink	India ink
Japanese cypress wood flakes	wood, furniture
International	
Ground coffee	coffee
Grated dark chocolate	chocolate, cacao
Chopped, roasted peanuts	peanuts
Lowenbrau	beer
Vick's Vaporub	ointment with menthol
Angel	perfume
European	
Marzipan	almond, marzipan
Blue cheese	cheese
Pernod	anise
Italian salami	salami
Sawdust of pinewood	wood, furniture
Catholic church incense	incense

placed less emphasis on visual cues, than did their trans-Atlantic counterparts.

One comprehensive study asked a sample of Japanese and German participants to rate the pleasantness and 'edibility' of three classes of odours which the authors described as 'European', 'Japanese' and 'International' (Ayabe-Kanamura *et al.*, 1998). Table 5.3 shows examples of each. Of the European odours, the Japanese sample rated the odours of church incense, anise and almond as less pleasant than did the Germans, but rated the odour of cheese and pinewood as more pleasant. Of the international odours, the German sample rated perfume to be more pleasant and the odours of beer and peanuts to be less pleasant than did the Japanese. When asked whether the substance represented by an odour was edible, the Japanese rated the Japanese food odours to be more edible than did the Germans; the Germans found anise and almond to be more edible. The odours of cheese and peanuts were rated as more edible by the Japanese than the Germans.

A coda, however. The sense of smell is notoriously duplicitous and deceitful – think of trying to put a name to a familiar or unfamiliar odour. It is difficult and is summed up by the term 'tip-of-the-nose' phenomenon. In the study above, 25 per cent of the Japanese sample thought that India ink represented an edible substance; 40 per cent of Germans thought that Vick's Vaporub did.

species, a controversial topic taken up in the Controversies in Psychological Science section.

As with taste, olfaction can present with disorders of perception and sensation. There are people who are unable to smell (anosmia), unable to detect particular smells (specific anomia), experience olfactory hallucinations (phantosmia), experience unpleasant smells that are not present (cacosmia), or have extreme sensitivity to smell (hyperosmia).

Anatomy of the olfactory system

Figure 5.32 shows the anatomy of the olfactory system. The receptor cells for the olfactory system lie in the **olfactory mucosa**, one-inch square patches of mucous membrane located on the roof of the nasal sinuses, just under the base of the brain. The receptor cells have cilia that are embedded in the olfactory mucosa. They also have axons that pass through small holes in the bone above the olfactory mucosa and form synapses with neurons in the **olfactory bulbs**. The olfactory bulbs are stalk-like structures located at the base of the brain

that contain neural circuits that perform the first analysis of olfactory information.

The primary and secondary olfactory cortex

The next stage of processing occurs after the bulbs project to the cortex, directly to what is known as the 'primary olfactory cortex' (POC). The term POC provides perhaps an overly simplistic and misleading description as it comprises various, disparate cortical regions. These are the anterior olfactory nucleus or region, the pre-piriform cortex, the lateral entorhinal cortex, the ventral tenia tecta (this is ribbon-like and covers the corpus callosum), nucleus of the lateral olfactory tract, the olfactory tubercle and the cortical nucleus of the amygdala. Various researchers will include variants of these regions – e.g. piriform cortex, entorhinal cortex – but this is a comprehensive list of the constituents of the POC.

The POC projects diffusely to what is loosely described as the secondary olfactory cortex (SOC), which includes a

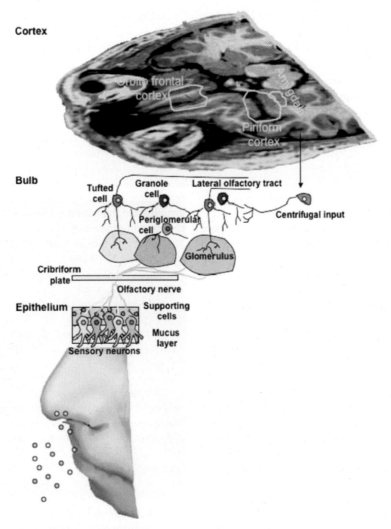

Figure 5.32 The olfactory system. The pathway of odour molecules from nares to cortex.

Source: Yeshurun, Y. and Sobel, N. (2010). An odor is not worth a thousand words: From multidimensional odors to unidimensional odor objects. *Annual Review of Psychology*, 61, 219–41.

combination of subcortical structures and cortical regions. The SOC comprises, at the subcortical level, the amygdala, the dorsomedial nucleus of the thalamus, ventral putamen, the hypothalamus, medial thalamus, nucleus basalis of Meynert, the hippocampus, the septal region, the insula, the reticular activating system, and at the cortical level, the orbitofrontal cortex. Nine of the 22 areas in the OFC receive projections from the primary olfactory cortex without synapsing in the thalamus (Mackay-Sim and Royet, 2006). There are substantial links between the OFC and insula and these two regions are consistently activated during olfactory perception (Martin, 2013).

At the cortical level, Martin (1998) found that the odours of spearmint and chocolate (but primarily chocolate) were associated with significant reductions in one type of brain activity, theta (see Chapter 9). Increases in this EEG waveband are thought to be associated with increased attention; it is plausible that the change in response to chocolate may reflect this pleasant odour's ability to distract a person's attention and make them feel relaxed.

In a novel neuroimaging experiment, Small *et al.* (1997) compared neural activation while people smelled substances, tasted them or did both (that is, perceived flavour). In some conditions, the odours and the tastes did not match. Using soy sauce, water, coffee, grapefruit and strawberry as stimuli, the experimenters found that when the odours and tastes were presented simultaneously, there was a decrease in activation at the primary taste cortex and the primary and secondary olfactory cortex. When tastes and smells did not match, increases in the amygdala were found, suggesting a role for the amygdala in the processing of novel or unpleasant stimuli. (We return to this role of the amygdala in emotion in Chapter 13.)

The interaction between odour molecule and receptor appears to be similar to that of transmitter substance and postsynaptic receptor on a neuron. That is, when a molecule of an odorous substance fits a receptor molecule located on the cilia of a receptor cell, the cell becomes excited. This excitation is passed on to the brain by the axon of the receptor cell. Thus, similar mechanisms may detect the stimuli for taste and olfaction. However, the mechanism for olfactory reception continues to be one of science's mysteries.

Unlike information from all other sensory modalities, olfactory information is not sent to the thalamus and then relayed to a specialised region of the cerebral cortex. Instead, olfactory information is sent directly to several regions of the limbic system, in particular to the amygdala and the frontal lobe.

Controversies in psychological science: Do human pheromones exist?

The issue

Some species in the animal kingdom have a terrifically efficient sense of smell. Dogs have a remarkable ability to detect and discriminate between odours, hence their use in drug-sniffing operations. The odour of vaginal copulins can arouse male monkeys. Scents which produce stereotypical responses in a receiving organism without the scent being overtly detected are called **pheromones**. A well-known example is **androstenone** (its full, chemical name is 5-alpha-16-androst-16-en-3-one), a steroid developed in the testes of pigs which has a musk-like odour and is secreted in the saliva of male pigs during mating.

The unusual feature of androstenone is that it can induce a sow to adopt the mating position when it is sprayed on her. Farmers and vets can even buy the chemical in aerosol form, Boarmate, so that the sow can be prepared for mating (Figure 5.33). (In fact, truffle hunters use sows to detect the delicacy because it contains androstenone.) Pigs are not the only species to secrete androstenone. It is also present in men's sweat glands and in the urine of men and women, although at stronger concentrations in men (Brooksbank *et al.*, 1974). Therefore, does this scent affect humans in the way it affects other mammals?

The evidence

One of the earliest studies of the pheromone effect in humans was conducted by Martha McClintock in the 1970s (McClintock, 1971). She found that 17–22-year-old women students who lived and slept in the same halls of residence reported **menstrual synchrony**. That is, their menstrual cycles began on or about the same time. The effect was unrelated to food intake, lifestyle pattern or stress. The result is difficult to explain because no mechanism that we know of can account for the finding. McClintock suggested that the mechanism might be pheromonal or mediated by an awareness of another's menstrual cycle. To explain the result, replications would be needed. If the effect was pheromonal then a controlled experiment in which menstrual cycles were deliberately manipulated would show this. This is what Russell *et al.* (1980) did.

They applied the sweaty secretions of a woman who had a history of 28-day cycles and experience of 'driving' (that is influencing) other women's cycles, on the upper lips of five women,

Figure 5.33 Farmers and veterinary surgeons sometimes spray Boarmate onto a sow to get her to adopt the mating position (Boarmate contains a variant of the pheromone, androstenone).
Source: National Geographic, September 1986; © Louie Psihoyos/Science Faction.

three times a week for four months. Six individuals wore odourless alcohol (the control group). The mean difference in cycle onset for the experimental group was three to nine days before the experiment; three to four days during driving. Controls' figures were eight days and 9.2 days, respectively. A significant difference, therefore, was found between the experimental group's cycle onset and that of controls. However, there were some important limitations to the study. The experiment was not single – or double-blind, which means (as you will recall from Chapter 2) that the experimenters knew which participant was in each condition and each participant knew the purpose of the experiment. The woman who provided the samples was also one of the experimenters.

A similar experiment found that women reported shorter menstrual cycles when compounds from the follicular (late) stage of another woman's cycle were placed on the upper lip; longer cycles were reported when receiving ovulatory compounds

Controversies in psychological science: *Continued*

(Stern and McClintock, 1998). A group from the Monell Chemical Senses Center and Chicago University also found that chemical substances collected from lactating women increased the 'sexual motivation' of other women (such as sexual desire and fantasy) (Spencer *et al.*, 2004). Women with partners experienced more sexual desire whereas women without partners experienced more sexual fantasies.

In the most ecologically valid experiment of the effect of pheromones on attraction, Black and Biron (1982) required participants to interact with a confederate of the opposite sex who wore either androstenone or a control odour. The participant was later asked to rate the confederate for attractiveness. The experimenters found no effect of these chemicals on the rated attractiveness of the confederate. People who are able to smell androstadienone appear to rate members of the opposite sex as more attractive if the smellers were men and the women were fertile (Ferdenzi *et al.*, 2016).

When brain electrical activity in response to androstenone was measured in women, the brain responded more quickly to it than it did to control odours (Lundstrom *et al.*, 2006). There may be reasons for this beyond pheromonal ones: androstenone

can be perceived as unpleasant (smelling like a gents' lavatory) by some people and as a 'chemical' smell in those who can detect it but are not repulsed by it. Both reactions could have made the brain respond to this odour more quickly. Homosexual men, like heterosexual women, show increased activation in the hypothalamus when smelling 4, 16-androstadien-3-one (Savic *et al.*, 2005). Common odours were found to activate similar areas in homosexual men and heterosexual men and women, suggesting that the response to the chemical can depend on sexual orientation more than sex.

Conclusion

There is some evidence that the organ in the brain responsible for detecting and acting on pheromones (the vomeronasal organ) may be absent in humans (Moran *et al.*, 1995). If this organ is important for sensing pheromones then humans will have difficulty sensing pheromones. Meanwhile, however, the evidence suggests that if you want to attract a member of the opposite sex, a bottle of good perfume or cologne would be a better option than would exposing your armpits, or investing in a can of Boarmate.

The dimensions of odour

Although we know that there are at least five qualities of taste and that a colour can be specified by hue, brightness and saturation, attempts at classifying odour have not been particularly successful. It seems to be a slippery sense to make sense of. One of the earliest systems, Henning's odour prism (1916), plotted different categories of odour qualities at six corners of a prism. See Figure 5.34.

Recent research in molecular biology suggests that the olfactory system uses up to 1,000 different receptor molecules, located in the membrane of the receptor cells, to detect different categories of odours (Jones and Reed, 1989; Buck and Axel, 1991; Axel, 1995). Linda Buck and Michael Axel won the Nobel Prize in 2004 for their discovery – that a family of genes was responsible for coding olfactory receptors. There are around 1,000 different receptors in mice and around 350 in humans (Buck, 2004). Presumably, the presence of molecules of a substance with a particular odour produces a particular pattern of activity in the olfactory system. That is, the molecules will strongly stimulate some receptors, weakly stimulate others, and stimulate still others not at all. This pattern of stimulation is transmitted to the brain, where it is recognised as belonging to a particular odour. Malnic *et al.* (1999) found that some odorants generated weak firing at some receptors and strong firing at others. It may be that different odorants are coded by different combinations of

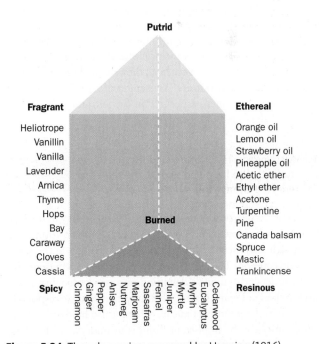

Figure 5.34 The odour prism proposed by Henning (1916).

Source: from Goldstein. *Sensation and Perception*, International Edition, 7E. (c) 2007, Wadsworth, a part of Cengage Learning, Inc. Reproduced by permission. www.cengage.com/permissions.

Cutting edge: What does weight stigma smell like?

In later chapters, especially those on social psychology, you'll read more about prejudice and how we hold (objectively unjustifiable) negative views about some groups – these groups are called stigmatised because the attributions we make to them are invariably negative. Such groups include the homeless, those in receipt of welfare, those who suffer mental illness and the overweight.

To examine how such stigma can even extend to seemingly unrelated sensory stimuli, Belsky *et al.* (2015) asked participants to view images of thin or fat people while smelling a substance (which was actually odourless). When participants were asked to rate the substance, those who were exposed to the fat images judged the scent as smelling worse than did those exposed to the thin images.

receptors so that one receptor could respond to more than one odorant. Researchers do not yet know exactly which molecules stimulate which receptors; nor do they know how the information from individual olfactory receptor cells is put together.

Sex differences

Research suggests that women are, on average, better at identifying, recognising and detecting odours than are men (Doty *et al.*, 1985) and give more positive and less negative hedonic emotional responses to some odours (Seubert *et al.*, 2009). This sex difference may have important implications for any study of the neural basis of olfactory processing. If individual differences exist at the behavioural level (e.g., detecting, recognising, identifying), then neural activation may be different in men and women when they both smell the same odours. To test this hypothesis, Yousem and his colleagues carried out an fMRI study of the brain activation of eight right-handed men and eight right-handed women as they smelled pleasant, neutral and unpleasant odours (Yousem *et al.*, 1999). Activation was greater in women, especially in the left and right frontal and perisylvian regions.

The somatosenses

The body senses, or **somatosenses**, include our ability to respond to touch, vibration, pain, warmth, coolness, limb position, muscle length and stretch, tilt of the head and changes in the speed of head rotation. The number of sense modalities represented in this list depends on one's definition of a sense modality. However, it does not really matter whether we say that we respond to warmth and coolness by means of one sense modality or two different ones; the important thing is to understand how our bodies are able to detect changes in temperature.

Many experiences require simultaneous stimulation of several different sense modalities. For example, taste and odour alone do not determine the flavour of spicy food; mild (or sometimes not-so-mild) stimulation of pain detectors in the

mouth and throat gives Mexican food its special characteristic. Sensations such as tickle and itch are apparently mixtures of varying amounts of touch and pain. Similarly, our perception of the texture and three-dimensional shape of an object that we touch involves cooperation among our senses of pressure, muscle and joint sensitivity, and motor control (to manipulate the object). If we handle an object and find that it moves smoothly in our hand, we conclude that it is slippery. If, after handling this object, our fingers subsequently slide across each other without much resistance, we perceive a feeling of oiliness. If we sense vibrations when we move our fingers over an object, it is rough. And so on. If you close your eyes as you manipulate some soft and hard, warm and cold, and smooth and rough objects, you can make yourself aware of the separate sensations that interact and give rise to a complex perception.

The skin senses

The entire surface of the human body is innervated (supplied with nerve fibres) by the dendrites of neurons that transmit somatosensory information to the brain. Cranial nerves convey information from the face and front portion of the head (including the teeth and the inside of the mouth and throat); spinal nerves convey information from the rest of the body's surface. All somatosensory information is detected by the dendrites of neurons; the system uses no separate receptor cells. However, some of these dendrites have specialised endings that modify the way they transduce energy into neural activity.

Figure 5.35 shows the sensory receptors found in hairy skin and in smooth, hairless skin (such as skin on the palms of the hands or the soles of the feet). The most common type of skin sensory receptor is the free nerve ending, which resembles the fine roots of a plant. Free nerve endings infiltrate the middle layers of both smooth and hairy skin and surround the hair follicles in hairy skin. If you bend a single hair on your forearm, you will see how sensitive the free nerve endings are.

The largest of the special receptive endings, called the **Pacinian corpuscle**, is visible to the naked eye. Pacinian corpuscles are very sensitive to touch. When they are moved, their

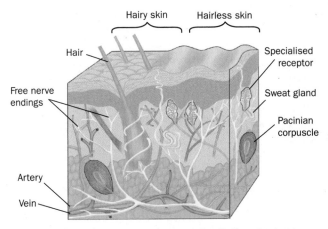

Hairy skin   Hairless skin

Hair

Free nerve
endings

Artery

Vein

Specialised
receptor

Sweat gland

Pacinian
corpuscle

Figure 5.35 Sensory receptors in hairy skin (left) and in hairless skin (right).

axons fire a brief burst of impulses. Pacinian corpuscles are thought to be the receptors that inform us about vibration. Other specialised receptors detect other sensory qualities, including warmth, coolness and pain.

Temperature

There is general agreement that different sensory endings produce the sensations of warmth and coolness. Detectors for coolness appear to be located closer to the surface of the skin. If you suddenly place your foot under a stream of rather hot water, you may feel a brief sensation of cold just before you perceive that the water is really hot. This sensation probably results from short-lived stimulation of the coolness detectors located in the upper layers of the skin.

Our temperature detectors respond best to changes in temperature. Within reasonable limits, the air temperature of our environment comes to feel 'normal'. Temporary changes in temperature are perceived as warmth or coolness. Thus, our temperature detectors adapt to the temperature of our environment. This adaptation can be easily demonstrated. If you place one hand in a pail of hot water and the other in a pail of cold water, the intensity of the sensations of heat and cold will decrease after a few minutes. If you then plunge both hands into a bucket of water that is at room temperature, it will feel hot to the cold-adapted hand and cold to the hot-adapted hand. It is mainly the change in temperature that is signalled to the brain. Of course, there are limits to the process of adaptation. Extreme heat or cold will continue to feel hot or cold, however long we experience it.

Pressure

Sensory psychologists speak of touch and pressure as two separate senses. They define touch as the sensation of very light contact of an object with the skin and pressure as the sensation produced by more forceful contact. Sensations of pressure occur only when the skin is actually moving, which means that the

pressure detectors respond only while they are being bent. Just how the motion stimulates the neurons is not known. If you rest your forearm on a table and place a small weight on your skin, you will feel the pressure at first, but eventually you will feel nothing at all, if you keep your arm still. You fail to feel the pressure not because your brain 'ignores' incoming stimulation but because your sensory endings actually cease sending impulses to your brain. Studies that have measured the very slow, very minute movements of a weight sinking down into the skin have shown that sensations of pressure cease when the movements stop. With the addition of another weight on top of the first one, movement and sensations of pressure begin again (Nafe and Wagoner, 1941). A person will feel a very heavy weight indefinitely, but the sensation is probably one of pain rather than pressure. In terms of the perception of a person's touch, we judge others' skin to be more pleasant than our own and their forearms as smoother, softer and less sticky (Guest *et al.*, 2009).

Sensitivity to subtle differences in touch and pressure varies widely across the surface of the body. The most sensitive regions are the lips and the fingertips. The most common measure of the tactile discrimination of a region of skin is the **two-point discrimination threshold**. To determine this measure, an experimenter touches a person with one or both legs of a pair of dividers and asks the person to say whether the sensation is coming from one or two points. The further apart the legs of the dividers must be before the person reports feeling two separate sensations, the lower the sensitivity of that region of skin.

Pain

Pain is a complex sensation involving not only intense sensory stimulation but also an emotional component. It has been defined as 'a highly undesirable and unpleasant sensation often associated with actual or potential tissue damage' (Advocat and Comaty, 2014). The process of sensing pain is called **nocioception** (from the Latin, *nocere* 'to injure') and the parts of the body responsible for sensing pain (the pain receptors) are called **nocioceptors**. These are found all over the body – some respond to mechanical challenge (such as a cut or extreme heat); others respond to other types of pain.

Pain is a common experience. According to a major study of pain in 46,000 participants in 16 European countries, one in five adults has suffered chronic pain (see below) several times a week for at least six months (Breivik et al, 2006). Figure 5.36. shows the effect of chronic pain on psychological and behavioural processes.

Psychologists can study either natural pain which follows disease or surgery or injury or they can study induced pain in the laboratory in healthy participant. Common methods of achieving this include the cold-pressor test, in which the participants hold their arm from the elbow down in a bath of ice-cold water; muscle ischemia in which a blood pressure-type cuff (a sphygmamanometer) is inflated around the arm causing discomfort; and exposure to extreme heat.

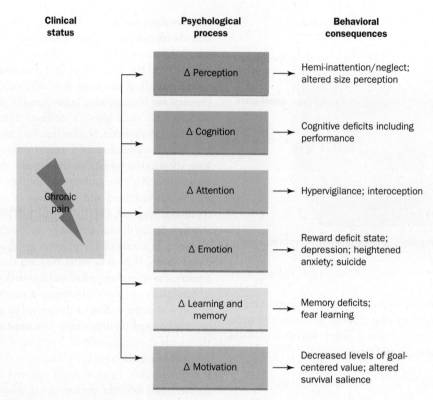

Figure 5.36 The effects of chronic pain on behaviour.

Many noxious stimuli elicit two kinds of pain: an immediate sharp, or 'bright', pain followed by a deep, dull, sometimes throbbing, pain. Some stimuli elicit only one of these two kinds of pain. For example, a pinprick will produce only the superficial 'bright' pain, whereas a hard blow from a blunt object to a large muscle will produce only the deep, dull pain. Different sets of axons mediate these two types of pain.

Pain – or the fear of pain – is one of the most effective motivators of human behaviour, especially if the onset is acute (i.e. immediate). It tells us, for example, if we have sprained an ankle, broken a bone or have an inflamed appendix or have an infected tooth which requires removal or filling. It also tells us to escape from things which can harm us – so we withdraw from a hot flame, for example. Chronic pain, however, which is continuous or intermittent for three months or more seems to serve no purpose and can lead to additional problems such as depression (Bair *et al.*, 2013; Elman *et al.*, 2013).

In addition to physical pain, some people might experience 'social' or 'psychological pain' – the feeling of being shunned and ostracised or feeling grief (whether these behaviours reflect pain in the true sense of the term is questionable). Studies have found that this type of pain is consistently associated with at least two of the brain regions involved in physical pain – the anterior and posterior cingulate cortex and the prefrontal cortex (Meerwijk *et al.*, 2013). Some researchers have argued that

different parts of the anterior cingulate are involved in different processes – the dorsal ACC is involved in emotional appraisal and expression whereas the ventral part is involved in emotional regulation (Eisenberger, 2014). However, the specific role of this/these region/s in social pain is still unclear.

Physiology of pain

One of the most important structures in the body which enables us to experience pain is the spinal cord. Sensory fibres in the spinal cord become active and this reflects our experience of pain. Our nocioceptors are connected to the spinal cord via two types of fibres – A – delta and C fibres. A fibres are small and thinly myelinated and respond to rapid pain such as a pin prick; C fibres respond to slower pain such as a dull ache, burns or nausea. These fibres enter the dorsal roots of the spinal cord and move to the dorsal horn. They synapse there and a chemical (an amino acid) called substance P is released. If the spinal cord is repeatedly stimulated in this way, the neurotransmitter glutamate is released from the dorsal horn which activates glutamate receptors and the release of N-methyl-D-aspartate (NMDA). The NMDA makes the spinal cord more responsive to pain and less responsive to pain-relieving drugs called analgesics. A schematic of the physiological responses involved in pain can be seen in Figure 5.37.

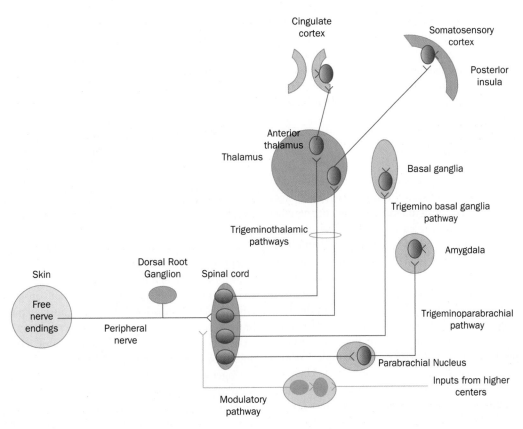

Figure 5.37 The neural pathways involved in the perception of pain.

The brain and pain

Our sensation and perception of pain, as well as the degree of attention we allocate to pain, influence our response to it. Chapter 9 will show you how attention modulates our response to the stimuli that cause us pain. All of these processes require higher-levels of cognition and there is a network of brain regions that have been shown to be active during the experience of pain. The network includes the somatosensory cortex, the anterior cingulate cortex, the thalamus, the amygdala, the cerebellum, the prefrontal cortex and the parietal cortex. Some of these regions are involved in modulating the pain response and distracting us from it.

Some researchers have sought to discover whether there is a pain signature in the brain – a pattern of activation reliably associated with the experience. In four studies, Wager *et al.* (2013) investigated the effect of pain, pain vs warmth, social pain and the effect of remifentantil (an analgesic/painkiller) on pain. They found that a pattern of activation in several areas predicted the response to pain: these included the thalamus, posterior/anterior insula, secondary somatosensory cortex, the anterior cingulate cortex and periaqueductal grey region. This signature discriminated between pain and no-pain, warmth and social pain 94 per cent, 93 per cent and 85 per cent of the time, respectively.

A recent meta-analysis sought to discover whether similar areas were activated in healthy participants experiencing experimental pain, and patients experiencing chronic pain (Jensen *et al.*, 2016). It found that similar regions were consistently activated regardless of the modality of the pain, the body part affected or the clinical experience: the right insula, the secondary sensory cortex and right ACC. The areas common to both healthy and ill patients were the thalamus, the ACC, the insula and cerebellum. Healthy people were more likely to show activation in the cingulum, thalamus and insula.

When people are given a placebo drug for their pain –an inert pill that has no pharmacological effect – people show a reduction in activation in these brain areas during pain perception (Eippert *et al.*, 2009; Atlas and Wager, 2014). The degree of reduction is related to how powerful people think the placebo is.

People's anticipation of pain has also been associated with increased activity in pain-related brain regions. For example, when people were told that an auditory cue signalled imminent high or low pain, the signal affected the subsequent brain activation. If participants thought they would experience high pain, researchers found increases in the anterior cingulate, insula and thalamus (Atlas *et al.*, 2010).

However, not all researchers have supported the idea of a pain matrix. For example, Feinstein *et al.* (2016) reported a patient, Roger, with very rare damage to the insula, anterior cingulate and amygdala. His expression and experience of pain was not just intact across a range of measures but was often hyperpathic – the pain was abnormally painful. They suggest that these regions may not be necessary for the experience of pain but may, instead, be involved in the regulation of pain. This is an interesting hypothesis, although it is based on data from one person.

Individual differences in pain

A number of individual differences can affect the response to pain and some well-studied factors include: sex, race, age, social network, ethnicity and handedness – the cutting edge section describes some recent research on the effect of social network on pain perception. One of the most consistent differences in perception is between men and women, with women reporting pain more frequently than do men (Racine *et al.*, 2012; Bartley and Fillingim, 2013). In one study women reported more pain in 10 specific body regions than did men and also reported more widespread bodily pain (Gerdle *et al.*, 2008). The incidence of pain-bearing severe illnesses –fibromyalgia, migraine, IBS, interstitial cystitis, for example – is also more common in women (Hurley and Adams, 2008). There are also differences between races in coping with pain. Black individuals, for example, have been found to experience greater pain in clinical and experimental studies but also adopt coping strategies more frequently than do white individuals (Meints *et al.*, 2016). The most common coping strategy was praying.

The internal senses

Sensory endings located in our internal organs, bones and joints, and muscles convey painful, neutral and, in some cases, pleasurable sensory information. For example, the internal senses convey the pain of arthritis, the perception of the location of our limbs, and the pleasure of a warm drink descending to our stomachs.

Muscles contain special sensory endings. One class of receptors, located at the junction between muscles and the tendons that connect them to the bones, provides information about the amount of force the muscle is exerting. These receptors protect the body by inhibiting muscular contractions when they become too forceful. During competition, some weightlifters have received injections of a local anaesthetic near the tendons of some muscles to eliminate this protective mechanism. As a result, they are able to lift even heavier weights. Unfortunately, if they use this tactic, some tendons may snap or some bones may break.

Another set of stretch detectors consists of spindle-shaped receptors distributed throughout the muscle. These receptors, appropriately called muscle spindles, inform the brain about changes in muscle length. People are not conscious of the specific information provided by the **muscle spindles**, but the brain uses the information from these receptors and from joint receptors to keep track of the location of parts of the body and to control muscular contractions.

Together these sensations are called **proprioception** – our sense of bodily position and movement – and the receptors for this sense, as the examples above show, are found in the joints of skeletons and skeletal muscles. Receptors at joints are called mechanoreceptors and these are essential for allowing us to sense the angle of a joint. There are four types of mechanoreceptors, most of which have specific functions such as responding to rapid movement of limbs or maintaining the position of limbs and so on. However, as studies of limb amputation and even hip replacements show, these receptors may take some time to adapt to changing bodily structure or function. People who have had hip replacement

---

Cutting edge: The effect of your social network on pain reduction

A 2009 study by Master *et al.* investigated whether seeing a photograph of a partner's face reduced the perception of pain in women who were in long-term relationships. Pain was applied via thermal stimulation - heating the skin (half the trials were at the threshold the woman found tolerable, half were one degree higher). Seeing a partner's face was associated with lower pain ratings than was seeing a stranger's face or seeing an object (pain was also lower when holding the partner's hand, compared with a stranger's or compared with holding an object).

The results suggested that the presence of a partner could have an analgesic or protective effect on pain, possibly due to the activation of positive mental representations. Now, a group of different researchers has suggested that the type of social network men and women have can mediate the response to pain. The team asked 152 healthy, young men and women to complete the cold-pressor test and took account of the number of friends they had. They found significant differences between men and women in the study. For example, women were more sensitive to pain when their social network contained more close relatives than non-kin, when they had known people in their network for a long time and when they reported having a lot of logistical support from their romantic partner. Men showed almost the opposite pattern - the greater logistical support they received, the less sensitive to pain they were and the fewer intimate relationships they had, the more pain they experienced.

surgery, for example, can sense limb position, but they do not sense it very well.

Unlike somatosensation, proprioceptive information seems to recruit different cortical regions so that data about tactile sensation are sent to specific areas of the somatosensory cortex and data from muscle afferents and from joints are sent to different ones. More complex proprioception and tactile sensation most probably involves posterior regions of the parietal lobes.

The vestibular senses

What we call our 'sense of balance' involves several senses, not just one. If we stand on one foot and then close our eyes, we immediately realise how important a role vision plays in balance. The **vestibular apparatus** of the inner ear provides only part of the sensory input that helps us remain upright.

The three **semicircular** canals, located in the inner ear and oriented at right angles to one another, detect changes in rotation of the head in any direction (see Figure 5.38). These canals contain a liquid. Rotation of the head makes the liquid flow, stimulating the receptor cells located in the canals.

Another set of inner ear organs, the **vestibular sacs**, contain crystals of calcium carbonate that are embedded in a gelatin-like substance attached to receptive hair cells. In one sac, the receptive tissue is on the wall; in the other, it is on the floor. When the head tilts, the weight of the calcium carbonate

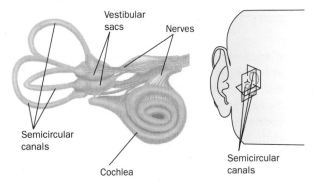

Figure 5.38 The three semicircular canals and two vestibular sacs located in the inner ear.

crystals shifts, producing different forces on the cilia of the hair cells. These forces change the activity of the hair cells, and the information is transmitted to the brain.

The vestibular sacs are very useful in maintaining an upright head position. They also participate in a reflex that enables us to see clearly even when the head is being jarred. When we walk, our eyes are jostled back and forth. The jarring of the head stimulates the vestibular sacs to cause reflex movements of the eyes that partially compensate for the head movements. People who lack this reflex because of localised brain damage must stop walking in order to see things clearly, for example to read a street sign.

Cutting edge: The vestibular sense and ballet dancers

Of ballet-dancers' many talents, and there are many, one is their ability to spin without feeling dizzy. The performance of multiple pirouettes without experiencing vertigo and suppressing the vestibulo-ocular reflex (eye movement stimulating the vestibular system when the head is moving – it is this reflex which helps stabilise an image when this happens) is a learned motor and vestibular skill. Nigmatullina et al. (2013) explored ballet dancers' perception and response to rotation and used MRI to examine whether the amount of brain tissue correlated with dancing experience. Twenty-nine experienced female ballet dancers and 20 control women were placed in a rotating chair and their vestibular responses measured. Their behaviour was then correlated with MRI recordings. In the part of the cerebellum responsible for the vestibular system, grey matter was less in the experienced dancers.

Chapter review

Sensory processing

- We experience the world through our senses. Our knowledge of the world stems from the accumulation of sensory experience and subsequent learning.
- All sensory experiences are the result of energy from events that is transduced into activity of receptors,

which are specialised neurons. Transduction causes changes in the activity of axons of sensory nerves, and these changes in activity inform the sensory mechanisms of the brain about the environmental event. The information received from the receptors is transmitted to the brain by means of two coding schemes: anatomical coding and temporal coding.

- In nineteenth-century Germany, Weber devised the concept of the just-noticeable difference (jnd), and Fechner used the jnd to measure the magnitude of sensations.
- The methods of psychophysics apply to all sensory modalities, including sight, smell, taste, hearing and touch.

Vision

- The cornea and lens of the eyes cast an image of the scene on the retina, which contains photoreceptors: rods and cones. Cones gather visual information under illuminated conditions; rods work only when the light is very dim.
- The energy from the light that reaches cones is transduced into neural activity when photons strike molecules of photopigment, splitting them into their two constituents. This event causes the cones to send information through the bipolar cells to the ganglion cells. The axons of the ganglion cells travel through the optic nerves and form synapses with neurons in the brain.
- When an image of the visual scene is cast upon the retina, each part of the image has a different colour, which can be specified in terms of its hue (dominant wavelength), brightness (intensity) and saturation (purity).
- Information about colour is encoded trichromatically by your cones; the red, green and blue cones respond in proportion to the amount of the appropriate wavelength contained in the light striking them. This information is transformed into an opponent-process coding, signalled by the firing rates of red/green and yellow/blue ganglion cells, and is transmitted to the brain.
- There are many different types of defective colour vision. Individuals missing a photopigment are called dichromats (and the condition is called dichromacy) and use two primary colours for matching and confuse various colours; anomalous trichromats (the condition is called anomalous trichromacy) have an altered – not missing – photopigment, and comprise the majority of men with colour defects; protanopia, the most serious condition, appears to result from a lack of the photopigment for red cones: red looks much darker than green, and reds and oranges generally appear very dark.
- Synaesthesia refers to the phenomenon whereby a stimulus in one modality evokes a sensation in another.

Audition

- The physical dimensions of sound – amplitude, frequency and complexity – can be translated into the perceptual dimensions of loudness, pitch and timbre for sounds ranging from 30 Hz to 20,000 Hz.
- Sound pressure waves put the process in motion by setting up vibrations in the eardrum, which are passed on to the ossicles. Vibrations of the stirrup against the membrane behind the oval window create pressure changes in the fluid within the cochlea that cause the basilar membrane to flex back and forth. This vibration causes the auditory hair cells on the basilar membrane to move relative to the tectorial membrane. The resulting pull on the cilia of the hair cells stimulates them to secrete a transmitter substance that excites neurons of the auditory nerve. This process informs the brain of the presence of a sound.
- Two different methods of detection enable the brain to recognise the pitch of a sound. Different high-frequency and medium-frequency sounds are perceived when different parts of the basilar membrane vibrate in response to these frequencies. Low-frequency vibrations are detected when the tip of the basilar membrane vibrates in synchrony with the sound, which causes some axons in the auditory nerve to fire at the same frequency.
- Low-frequency sounds are located by differences in the arrival time of the sound waves in each ear. High-frequency sounds are located by differences in intensity caused by the 'sound shadow' cast by the head.
- The auditory system will analyse sounds of complex timbre into their constituent frequencies, each of which causes a particular part of the basilar membrane to vibrate. All these functions proceed automatically.
- The temporal lobe contains the primary auditory cortex and is active during the comprehension of the phonological aspects of language tasks, and when listening to music.

Gustation and olfaction

- Gustation and olfaction refer to the senses of taste and smell, respectively, and are called chemical senses. Both are served by cells having receptors that respond selectively to various kinds of molecule.
- We can perceive sweet, salty, sour or bitter tastes and a fifth, umami (which delivers a savoury sensation). To most organisms, sweet and moderately salty substances taste pleasant, whereas sour or bitter substances taste unpleasant.
- Sweetness and saltiness receptors permit us to detect nutritious foods and sodium chloride. Sourness and bitterness receptors help us avoid substances that might be poisonous.

- Some individuals, with a particular genetic polymorphism, have an increased sensitivity to bitter tastes (supertasters).
- Olfactory information combines with information about taste to provide us with the flavour of a food present in our mouths. We can distinguish countless different odours and can recognise smells encountered in childhood. Women tend to be better detectors of odours than men.
- Unlike visual stimuli, odours do not easily blend. The detection of different odours appears to be accomplished by up to 1,000 different receptor molecules located in the membrane of the olfactory receptor cells.
- Pheromones are chemicals produced by the body which generate a stereotypical behavioural or physiological response without necessarily being detected. The evidence for human pheromones is weak, probably because humans lack the vomeronasal organ necessary to respond to such stimuli.

The somatosenses

- The somatosenses gather several different kinds of information from different parts of the body.
- The skin senses of temperature, touch and pressure, vibration and pain inform us about the nature of objects that come in contact with our skin.
- The experience of pain recruits a network of brain regions including the thalamus, insula, somatosensory cortex and anterior cingulate.
- Pacinian corpuscles in fingers can detect vibration caused by movement which helps us to determine the texture of surfaces.
- Temperature receptors detect hot and cold; free nerve endings can give rise to sensations of pain.
- Sensory receptors in muscles and joints inform the brain of the movement and location of arms and legs. This is called proprioception.
- The vestibular senses help an organism to keep balance.

Suggestions for further reading

Beauchamp, G.K. (2016) Why do we like sweet taste? A bitter tale. *Physiology and Behavior*, 164, 432–37.

de Groot, J. H., Semin, G. R., & Smeets, M. A. (2017). On the communicative function of body odors: A theoretical integration and review. *Perspectives on Psychological Science*, 12(2), 306-324.

Hatfield, G. and Allred, S. (2012) *Visual experience: Sensation, Cognition and Constancy*. Oxford: OUP.

Goldstein, E.B. and Brockmole, J. (2016) *Sensation and Perception* (10th edn). NY: Wadsworth.

Krantz, J. (2012) *Experiencing Sensation and Perception*. Harlow: Pearson Education.

Martin, G.N. (2013) *The Neuropsychology of Smell and Taste*. Hove: Psychology Press.

Mather, G. (2011) *Essentials of Sensation and Perception*. London: Routledge.

Moerel, M., DeMartino, F. and Formisano, E. (2014). An anatomical and functional topography of human auditory cortical areas. *Frontiers in Neuroscience*, 8, 1–14.

Moore, B.C.J. (2012) *An Introduction to the Psychology of Hearing*. Emerald.

Rolls, E.T. (2015) Functions of the anterior insula in taste, autonomic and related functions. *Brain and Cognition*, 110, 4–19.

Schiffman, H.R. (2012) *Sensation and Perception* (6th edn). Chichester: John Wiley.

Schnupp, J., Nelken, I. and King, A.J. (2012) *Auditory Neuroscience: Making sense of sound*. California; MIT.

Wager, T.D. and Atlas, L.Y. (2013) How is pain influenced by cognition? Neuroimaging weighs in. *Perspectives on Psychological Science*, 8, 91–7.

These are some very good, easy-to-read introductions to sensation.

CHAPTER 6
Perception

On April 15, 2013 at 2.49pm EDT, two bombs exploded near the finish line of the Boston Marathon, killing three people and injuring 246 others … initial forensic evidence indicated the explosive device was a pressure cooker packed with fragments of BBS and nails.

The FBI released images and videos of the two suspects … in part to limit the damage being done to people wrongly targeted as suspects by news and social media. Shortly after the release, the two suspects were identified as brothers by their aunt who had made a call to the FBI tip line.

It is believed that the release of their photographs provoked the brothers into further violence, fatally shooting an MIT campus officer and carjacking a Mercedes.

The investigation of the Boston Marathon bombings has been widely viewed as a failure of automated facial recognition. The technology came up empty even though [both brothers'] photos exist in official government databases.

Source: Klontz, J. C. and Jain, A. K. (2013) A case study of automated face recognition: The Boston marathon bombings suspects. *Computer*, 46(11), 91–4.

WHAT YOU SHOULD BE ABLE TO DO AFTER READING CHAPTER 6

- Define the term perception.
- Describe and understand how form, motion and space might be perceived.
- Describe the way in which the brain processes different types of visual information.
- Describe and understand the way in which we recognise faces and other categories of visual stimuli.
- Understand the consequences of brain damage on visual perception and how these help us understand how the brain normally perceives.

QUESTIONS TO THINK ABOUT

- How do we assemble sensory cues from the environment and turn them into something meaningful?
- What is it about a face that makes it recognisable?
- How can we perceive a moving object as moving?
- How can we tell a moving car from a moving bus or train?
- Do different parts of the brain mediate different types of visual perception – form, space, motion, colour – or does one system undertake it all?
- Are there stimulus-specific brain regions, ones that respond to specific categories of stimuli but not to others?
- How does brain injury affect perception?

The nature of perception

Take a look around you – around the room or out the window. What do you see as you and your eyes move around? Shapes? Figures? Background? Shadows? Areas of light and dark? Your knowledge of the objects you see and their relative location is extensive, and you have a good idea of what they will feel like, even if you have not touched them. If the lighting suddenly changes (if lamps are turned on or off or if a cloud passes in front of the sun), the amount of light reflected by the objects in the scene changes too, but your perception of the objects remains the same – you see them as having the same shape, colour and texture as before. Similarly, you do not perceive an object as increasing in size as you approach it, even though the image it casts upon your retina does get larger. Form, movement and space are the essential elements of perception.

The brain receives fragments of information from approximately 1 million axons in each of the optic nerves. It combines and organises these fragments into the perception of a scene – objects having different forms, colours and textures, residing at different locations in three-dimensional space. Even when our bodies or our eyes move, exposing the photoreceptors to entirely new patterns of visual information, our perception of the scene before us does not change. We see a stable world, not a moving one, because the brain keeps track of our own movements and those of our eyes and compensates for the constantly changing patterns of neural firing that these movements cause.

Definition of perception

Perception is the process by which we recognise what is represented by the information provided by our sense organs. This process gives unity and coherence to this input. Perception is a rapid, automatic, unconscious process; it is not a deliberate one in which we puzzle out the meaning of what we see. We do not first see an object and then perceive it; we simply perceive the object. Occasionally we do see something ambiguous and must reflect about what it might be or gather further evidence to determine what it is, but this situation is more problem-solving than perception. If we look at a scene carefully, we can describe the elementary sensations that are present, but we do not become aware of the elements before we perceive the objects and the background of which they are a part. Our awareness of the process of visual perception comes only after it is complete; we are presented with a finished product, not the details of the process.

The distinction between sensation and perception is not easy to make; in some respects, the distinction is arbitrary. Probably because of the importance we give to vision and because of the richness of the information provided by our visual system, psychologists make a more explicit distinction between visual sensation and perception than they do for any other sensory system.

Perception of form

When we look at the world, we do not see patches of colours and shades of brightness. We see things – cars, streets, people, books, trees, dogs, chairs, walls, flowers, clouds and televisions. We see where each object is located, how large it is, and whether it is moving. We recognise familiar objects and also recognise when we see something we have never seen before. The visual system is able to perceive shapes, determine distances and detect movements; it tells us what something is, where it is located, and what it is doing.

Figure and ground

Most of what we see can be classified as either object or background. Objects are things having particular shapes and particular locations in space. Backgrounds are in essence formless and serve mostly to help us judge the location of objects we see in front of them. Psychologists use the terms figure and ground to label an object and its background, respectively. The classification of an item as a figure or as a part of the background is not an intrinsic property of the item. Rather, it depends on the behaviour of the observer. If you are watching some birds fly overhead, they are figures and the blue sky and the clouds behind them are part of the background. If, instead, you are watching the clouds move, then the birds become background. If you are looking at a picture hanging on a wall, it is an object. Sometimes, we receive ambiguous clues about what is object and what is background. For example, what do you see when you look at Figures 6.1a, b and c?

One of the most important aspects of form perception is the existence of a boundary. If the visual field contains a sharp and distinct change in brightness, colour or texture, we perceive an edge. If this edge forms a continuous boundary, we will probably perceive the space enclosed by the boundary as a figure, as Figure 6.2 illustrates.

Organisation of elements: the principles of Gestalt

Most figures are defined by a boundary. But the presence of a boundary is not necessary for the perception of form. Figure 6.3 shows that when small elements are arranged in groups, we tend to perceive them as larger figures. Figure 6.4 demonstrates illusory contours – lines that do not exist. In this figure, the orientation of the pie-shaped objects and the three 45-degree segments makes us perceive two triangles, one on top of the other. The one that looks like it is superimposed on the three black circles even appears to be brighter than the background.

Figure 6.1 (a) A drawing in which figure and ground can be reversed or 'flipped'. You can see either two faces against a white background or a goblet against a dark background. This a version of the Rubin vase, based on the work of the Swiss psychologist Edgar Rubin in the 1920s. Modern variants are illustrated by figures **(b)** (Wolverine or Batman?) and **(c)** (can you see the werewolf eating Wales?), both created by artist, Olly Moss (http://ollymoss.com).

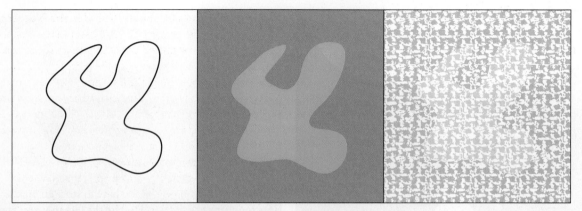

Figure 6.2 Form perception and boundaries. We immediately perceive even an unfamiliar figure when its outline is closed.

In the early twentieth century, a group of psychologists, Max Wertheimer (1880–1943), Wolfgang Kohler (1887–1967) and Kurt Koffka (1886–1941), devised a theory of perception called Gestalt psychology (see Chapter 1), Gestalt is the German word for 'form'. They maintained that the task of perception was to recognise objects in the environment according to the organisation of their elements. They argued that in perception the whole is more than the sum of its parts. Because of the characteristics of the visual system of the brain, visual perception cannot be understood simply by analysing the scene into its elements. Instead, what we see depends on the relations of these elements to one another (Wertheimer, 1912).

Elements of a visual scene can combine in various ways to produce different forms. Gestalt psychologists have observed that several principles of grouping can predict the combination of these elements. The fact that our visual system groups and combines elements is useful because we can then perceive forms even if they are fuzzy and incomplete. The real world presents us with objects partly obscured by other objects and with backgrounds that are the same colour as parts of the objects in front of them. The laws of grouping discovered by Gestalt psychologists describe the ability to distinguish a figure from its background.

The **adjacency/proximity principle** states that elements that are closest together will be perceived as belonging together (Wertheimer, 1912). Figure 6.5 demonstrates this principle. The pattern on the left looks like five vertical columns because the dots are closer to their neighbours above and below them than to those located to the right and to the left. The pattern on the right looks like five horizontal rows.

The **similarity principle** states that elements that look similar will be perceived as part of the same form. You can easily see the diamond inside the square in Figure 6.6.

Figure 6.3 Grouping. We tend to perceive a group of smaller elements as a larger figure.

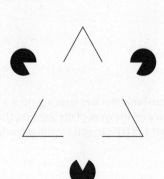

Figure 6.4 Illusory contours. Even when boundaries are not present, we can be fooled into seeing them. The triangle with its point down looks brighter than the surrounding area.

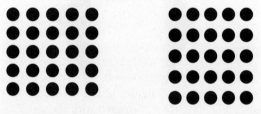

Figure 6.5 The Gestalt principle of proximity. Different spacing of the dots produces five vertical or five horizontal lines.

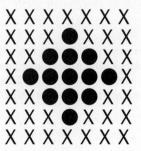

Figure 6.6 The Gestalt principle of similarity. Similar elements are perceived as belonging to the same form.

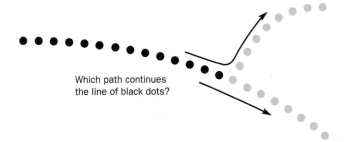

Which path continues the line of black dots?

Figure 6.7 The Gestalt principle of good continuation. It is easier to perceive a smooth continuation than an abrupt shift.

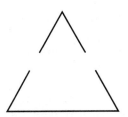

Figure 6.8 The Gestalt principle of closure. We tend to supply missing information to close a figure and separate it from its background. Lay a pencil across the gaps and see how strong the perception of a complete triangle becomes.

Good continuation is another Gestalt principle and refers to predictability or simplicity. For example, in Figure 6.7 it is simpler to perceive the line as following a smooth course than as suddenly making a sharp bend.

Often, one object partially hides another, but an incomplete image is perceived. The **law of closure** states that our visual system often supplies missing information and 'closes' the outline of an incomplete figure. For example, Figure 6.8 looks a bit like a triangle, but if you place a pencil on the page so that it covers the gaps, the figure undeniably looks like a triangle.

The final Gestalt principle of organisation relies on movement. The principle of common fate states that elements that move in the same direction will be perceived as belonging together and forming a figure. In the forest, an animal is camouflaged if its surface is covered with the same elements found in the background – spots of brown, tan and green – because its boundary is obscured. There is no basis for grouping the elements on the animal. As long as the animal is stationary, it remains well hidden. However, once it moves, the elements on its surface will move together, and the animal's form will quickly be perceived.

Models of pattern perception

Templates and prototypes

One explanation for our ability to recognise shapes of objects is that as we gain experience looking at things, we acquire templates, which are special kinds of visual memories stored by the visual system. A **template** is a type of pattern used to manufacture a series of objects (Selfridge and Neisser, 1960). When a particular pattern of visual stimulation is encountered, the visual system searches through its set of templates and compares each of them with the pattern provided by the stimulus. If it finds a match, it knows that the pattern is a familiar one. Connections between the appropriate template and memories in other parts of the brain could provide the name of the object and other information about it, such as its function, when it was seen before, and so forth.

The template model of pattern recognition has the virtue of simplicity. However, it is unlikely that it could actually work because the visual system would have to store an unreasonably large number of templates. Despite the fact that you may look at your hand and watch your fingers wiggling about, you continue to recognise the pattern as belonging to your hand. How many different templates would your visual memory have to contain just to recognise a hand? Figure 6.9 illustrates this problem using the letter A.

A more flexible model of pattern perception suggests that patterns of visual stimulation are compared with **prototypes** rather than templates. Prototypes (Greek for 'original model') are idealised patterns of a particular shape; they resemble templates but are used in a much more flexible way. The visual system does not look for exact matches between the pattern being perceived and the memories of shapes of objects but accepts a degree of disparity; for instance, it accepts the various patterns produced when we look at a particular object from different viewpoints.

Most psychologists believe that pattern recognition by the visual system does involve prototypes, at least in some form. For example, you can probably identify maple trees, fir trees and palm trees when you see them. In nature, each tree looks different from all the others, but maples resemble other maples more than they resemble firs, and so on. A reasonable assumption is that your visual system has memories of the prototypical visual patterns that represent these objects. Recognising particular types of tree, then, is a matter of finding the best fit between stimulus and prototype.

Feature detection models

Some psychologists suggest that the visual system encodes images of familiar patterns in terms of **distinctive features** – collections of important physical features that specify particular items (Selfridge, 1959). We are better at distinguishing some stimuli from others. We are better at searching for the letter A among a series of Bs than we are searching for the letter B among a series of As; we are better at finding orange-coloured objects in a series of red ones than vice versa; we find it easier to find a tilted item in a series of vertical items than finding a vertical item in a series of tilted ones. Similarly, we are better at finding a mobile object in a series of stationary ones than a stationary one in a series of mobile ones. We can detect bumps in a display of bumpy and flat surfaces better than we can the

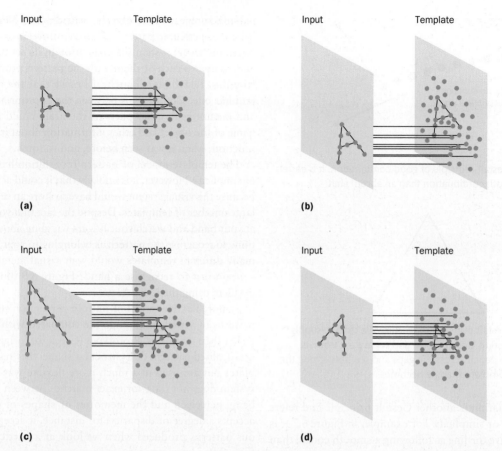

Figure 6.9 These four figures illustrate how template matching can fail. The position of the input may change **(b)**, its size may change **(c)** or its orientation may change **(d)**.

Source: Neisser, U., *Cognitive Psychology*. New York: Appleton-Century-Crofts, 1967. Reprinted with permission.

absence of bumps, and we are better at finding a single stimulus in an array of different stimuli when there are many more different stimuli. It appears, then, that some stimuli have more distinctive features than others and this enhances discrimination.

Figure 6.10 contains several examples of the letter N. Although the examples vary in size and style, recognising them is not problematic because your visual system contains a specification of the distinctive features that fit the criterion for an N: two parallel vertical lines connected by a diagonal line sloping downward from the top of the left one to the bottom of the right one.

An experiment by Neisser (1964) supports the hypothesis that perception involves analysis of distinctive features. Figure 6.11 shows one of the tasks he asked people to do. The figure shows two columns of letters. The task is to scan through them until you find the letter Z, which occurs once in each column.

You probably found the letter in the left column much faster than you did the one in the right column. Why? The letters in the left column share few features with those found in the letter Z, so the Z stands out from the others. In contrast, the letters in the right column have many features in common with the target letter, and thus the Z is 'camouflaged'.

N N **N** N *N*
N **N** **N** *N* **N**

Figure 6.10 Distinctive features. We easily recognise all of these items as the letter N.

The distinctive-features model appears to be a reasonable explanation for the perception of letters, but what about more natural stimuli, which we encounter in places other than the written page? Biederman (1987, 1990) suggests a model of pattern recognition that combines some aspects of prototypes and distinctive features. He suggests that the shapes of objects that we encounter can be constructed from a set of 36 different shapes that he refers to as geons. Figure 6.12 illustrates a few geons and some objects that can be constructed from them. Perhaps, Biederman suggests, the visual system recognises objects by identifying the particular sets and arrangements of geons that they contain.

GDOROC	IVEMXW
COQUCD	XVIWME
DUCOQG	VEMIXW
GRUDQO	WEKMVI
OCDURQ	XIMVWE
DUCGRO	IVMWEX
ODUCQG	VWEMXI
CQOGRD	IMEWXV
DUZORQ	EXMZWI
UCGROD	IEMWVX
QCUDOG	EIVXWM
RQGUDO	WXEMIV
DRGOQC	MIWVXE
OQGDRU	IMEVXW
UGCODQ	IEMWVX
ODRUCQ	IMWVEX
UDQRGC	XWMVEI
ORGCUD	IWEVXM

Figure 6.11 A letter-search task. Look for the letter Z hidden in each column.

Source: Adapted from Neisser, J., Visual search. *Scientific American Mind*, 1964, 210, 94–102.

Even if Biederman is correct that our ability to perceive categories of common objects involves recognition of geons, it seems unlikely that the geons are involved in perception of particular objects. For example, it is difficult to imagine how we could perceive faces of different people as assemblies of different sets of geons. The geon hypothesis appears to work best for the recognition of prototypes of generic categories: telephones or torches in general rather than the telephone on your desk or the torch a friend lent you.

Biederman points out that particular features of figures – cusps and joints formed by the ends of line segments – are of critical importance in recognising drawings of objects, presumably because the presence of these joints enables the viewer to recognise the constituent geons. Figure 6.13 shows two sets of degraded images of drawings of five common objects. One set, (a), shows the locations of cusps and joints; the other, (b), does not. Biederman (1990) observed that people found the items with cusps and joints much easier to recognise.

Top-down processing: the role of context

We often perceive objects under conditions that are less than optimum; the object is in a shadow, camouflaged against a similar background or obscured by fog. Nevertheless, we usually manage to recognise the item correctly. We are often helped in our endeavour by the context in which we see the object. For example, look at Figure 6.14. What do you see? Can you tell what they are? Now look at Figure 6.15. With the elements put in context it is quite easy to see what they are.

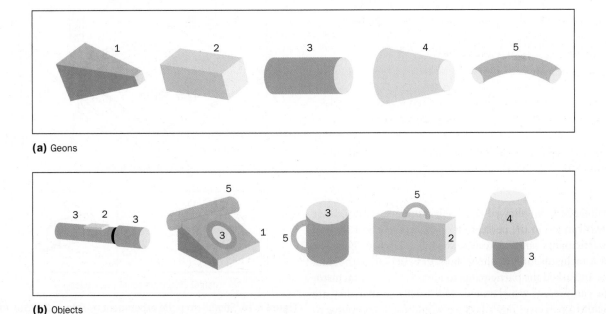

(a) Geons

(b) Objects

Figure 6.12 Geons for perception. **(a)** Several different geons. **(b)** The combination of two or three geons (indicated by the numbers) into common three-dimensional objects.

Source: Adapted from Biederman, I., Higher-level vision. In *An Invitation to Cognitive Science*. Vol. 2: Visual Cognition and Action, edited by D.N. Osherson, S.M. Kosslyn and J. Hollerbach. Cambridge, MA: MIT Press, 1990.

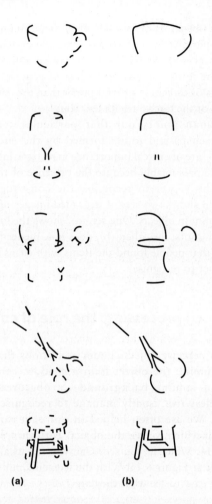

Figure 6.13 Incomplete figures. **(a)** With cusps and joints.
(b) Without cusps and joints. Which set is easier to recognise?

Source: Adapted from Biederman, I., Higher-level vision. *In An Invitation to Cognitive Science*. Vol. 2: Visual Cognition and Action, edited by D.N. Osherson, S.M. Kosslyn and J. Hollerbach. Cambridge, MA: MIT Press, 1990.

Figure 6.14 Simple elements that are difficult to recognise without a context.

Palmer (1975b) showed that even more general forms of context can aid in the perception of objects. He first showed his participants familiar scenes, such as a kitchen. Next, he used a tachistoscope to show them drawings of individual items and asked the participants to identify them. A **tachistoscope** can present visual stimuli very briefly so that they are difficult to perceive (nowadays we would use a computer to perform the same function). Sometimes, participants saw an object that was appropriate to the scene, such as a loaf of bread. At other times, they saw an inappropriate but similarly shaped object, such as a letterbox (see Figure 6.16).

Figure 6.15 An example of top-down processing. The context facilitates our recognition of the items shown in Figure 6.14.

Source: Adapted from Palmer, S.E., in *Explorations in Cognition*, D.A. Norman, D.E. Rumelhart and the LNR Research Group. San Francisco, CA: W.H. Freeman, 1975.

Palmer found that when the objects fitted the context that had been set by the scene, participants correctly identified about 84 per cent of them. But when they did not, performance fell to about 50 per cent. Performance was intermediate in the no-context control condition, under which subjects did not first see a scene. Thus, compared with the no-context control condition, an appropriate context facilitated recognition and an inappropriate one interfered with it.

The context effects demonstrated by experiments such as Palmer's are not simply examples of guessing. That is, people do not think to themselves, 'Let's see, that shape could be

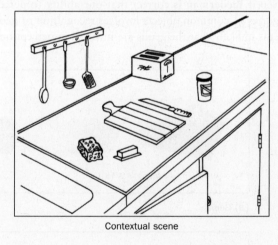

Contextual scene

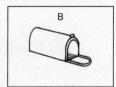

Target object (presented very briefly)

Figure 6.16 Stimuli from the experiment by Palmer (1975b). After looking at the contextual scene, participants were shown one of the stimuli below it very briefly, by means of a tachistoscope.

Source: Palmer, S.E., The effects of contextual scenes on the identification of objects. *Memory and Cognition*, 1975, 3, 519–26. Reprinted by permission of the Psychonomic Society, Inc.

either a letterbox or a loaf of bread. I saw a picture of a kitchen, so I suppose it's a loaf of bread.' The process is rapid, unconscious and automatic; thus, it belongs to the category of perception rather than to problem-solving, which is much slower and more deliberate. Somehow, seeing a kitchen scene sensitises the neural circuits responsible for the perception of loaves of bread and other items we have previously seen in that context.

Psychologists distinguish between two categories of information-processing models of pattern recognition: **bottom-up processing** and **top-down processing.** In bottom-up processing, also called data-driven processing, the perception is constructed out of the elements – the bits and pieces – of the stimulus, beginning with the image that falls on the retina. The information is processed by successive levels of the visual system until the highest levels (the 'top' of the system) are reached, and the object is perceived. Top-down processing refers to the use of contextual information – to the use of the 'big picture'. Presumably, once the kitchen scene is perceived, information is sent from the 'top' of the system down through lower levels. This information excites neural circuits responsible for perceiving those objects normally found in kitchens and inhibits others. Then, when the subject sees a drawing of a loaf of bread, information starts coming up through the successive levels of the system and finds the appropriate circuits already warmed up, so to speak.

TAE CAT
RED
SPOT
FISH

Figure 6.17 Examples of combined top-down/bottom-up processing. The effect of context enables us to perceive the letters despite the missing or ambiguous features. Note that a given letter may be perceived in more than one way, depending on the letters surrounding it.

Source: Adapted from McClelland, I.J., Rumelhart, D.E. and Hinton, G.E., in *Parallel Distributed Processing.* Vol. i: *Foundations,* edited by D.E. Rumelhart, J.L. McClelland and the PDP Research Group. © the Massachusetts Institute of Technology; published by the MIT Press, Cambridge, MA.

In most cases, perception consists of a combination of top-down and bottom-up processing. Figure 6.17 shows several examples of objects that can be recognised only by a combination of both forms of processing. Our knowledge of the configurations of letters in words provides us with the contexts that permit us to organise the flow of information from the bottom up.

Direct perception: Gibson's affordances

In the chapter so far we have considered some of the mechanisms that underlie visual perception. But is this perception a response or a process? That is, is visual perception an active or passive process? We saw in an earlier section on cross-cultural differences that context is important for visual perception. The psychologist J.J. Gibson took this notion a step further. Over a period of 35 years, Gibson proposed a theory of perception which argued that perception was direct and did not depend on cognitive processes to bring together fragmented data (Gibson, 1950, 1966, 1979). Because of this, it is considered a direct theory of perception. Originally, Gibson was interested in distinguishing between unsuccessful and successful Second World War pilots. Some of the unsuccessful pilots were unable to land accurately and seemed unable to appreciate distance. However, Gibson found that even when these pilots were given training in depth perception – which may have remedied the problem – they continued to have difficulty.

According to Gibson, 'perceiving is an act, not a response; an act of attention, not a triggered impression; an achievement, not a reflex' (Gibson, 1979). Gibson's view of perception was that classical optical science ignored the complexity of real events. For example, it would focus on the effects of trivial, basic or simple stimuli on perceptual response. Gibson abandoned the depth/space perception view of the world and, instead, suggested that our perception of surfaces was more important. Surfaces comprised ground (which we discussed earlier) and texture elements in surfaces that would be attached or detached. Attached features would include bumps and indentations in the surface, such as rocks or trees; detached features would include items such as animals (which are detached from the surface).

Given the complex world in which we live, we must be able to perceive not just simple stimuli but stimuli which mean something more to us. We must decide whether an object is throwable or graspable, whether a surface can be sat upon and so on. We ask ourselves what can this object furnish us with, what does it afford us (Gibson, 1982)? These are the meanings that the environment has and Gibson called them **affordances.** Thus, Gibson highlighted the ecological nature of perception: we do not simply perceive simple stimuli but these stimuli mean something more in a wider, more complex context. This was a radical departure in visual perception because it implied that the perception of object meaning is direct. Perception involves determining whether something is capable of being sat upon or is throwable.

However, the theory is not without its problems. Costall (1995), for example, suggests that some affordances may not be able to afford. Imagine the ground covered in frost and a frozen lake. According to Gibson, the ground afforded walking. However, although the frosty ground does, the frozen lake may not. Similarly, although we might agree with Gibson that some surfaces are graspable or supporting we might disagree quite reasonably with the notion that surfaces are edible, for example, that they afford eating. Our decision that something is edible appears to rely on more than direct perception of surfaces.

Face perception

One of the most important category of visual stimuli we process is faces. The ability to recognise and identify faces is one of the most crucial social functions we perform. It helps us form relationships with people, spot faces in a crowd and provides us with non-verbal clues to another's mental state (the role of emotion in facial expression is returned to in Chapter 13). We use faces to determine a person's trustworthiness and aggressiveness (see the Cutting Edge section below)

We identify people better on the basis of their eyes than their mouth, and both are more important than the nose (Bruce et al., 1993), even when hairstyle, make-up and facial hair are removed or minimised. A three-dimensional image of a face – such as that seen in three-quarter profile – is better recognised than is a full-frontal photograph. Upright faces are better recognised and identified than are those upside

down but there is a curious phenomenon called the 'Thatcher effect', first described by the British psychologist, Peter Thompson (1980). Take a look at the faces in Figure 6.18. They look fairly normal – you can easily identify the image as a face and, while you can see that the faces are inverted, the features appear to be in the right place, and are identifiable.

Now, turn the book upside down and look at the photographs again. It is a grotesque image, but only the eyes and the mouth have been turned around (inverted) to create this effect. This is called the Thatcher effect because Thompson created his original stimuli using the face of the British Prime Minister.

Sex of the face

We can usually discriminate between faces more quickly on the basis of their users' sex than their familiarity (Bruce et al., 1987). Men have larger noses and nasopharynxes, more prominent brows, a more sloping forehead and more deeply set eyes than do women (Enlow, 1982). Women have fuller cheeks and less facial hair, including eyebrows (Shepherd,1989). Women have smaller noses, a more depressed bridge of the nose, a shorter upper lip, and larger eyes with darker shadows, especially young women (Liggett, 1974).

When facial features are presented in isolation, eyes are the most reliable indicator of sex and the nose is the least reliable. With hair concealed, 96 per cent of participants were able to distinguish between faces based on sex (Burton et al., 1993). When individual facial features or pairs of features (such as brow and eyes, nose and mouth) were presented to participants, the features which afforded the best opportunity to make sex discriminations were (in this order): brow and

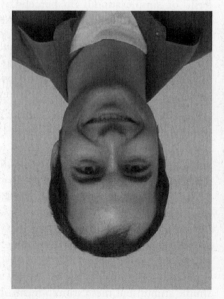

Figure 6.18 The Thatcher effect – turn the page upside down to experience the effect.

Source: Grüter, T., Grüter, M. and Carbon, C-C. Neural and genetic foundations of face recognition and prosopagnosia. *Journal of Neuropsychology* (2008), 2, 79–97, figure 3.

eyes, brow alone, eyes alone, whole jaw, chin, nose and mouth, and mouth alone (Brown and Perrett, 1993). These findings suggest that all facial features carry some information about sex (except the nose) but suggest that it is difficult to find even one or two features which distinguish absolutely between men's and women's faces.

Women and girls are better able than men or boys to recognise faces but they also remember more female faces than they do male ones (Herlitz and Loven, 2013). Women and girls are better at remembering faces of their own sex, a finding called an 'own-gender bias' – the equivalent effect is not reported in men. A similar phenomenon, and a stronger one, is seen when the race of the face matches the race of the person doing the remembering ('the own-race bias').

Distinctiveness and attractiveness

Each of us finds different faces attractive: some of us find faces friendlier than others, some meaner and others more sexually alluring. Although individual differences exist at this, what seems like, subjective level, studies have shown that some features of the face are generally regarded as more attractive than others. Psychologists in the nineteenth century were interested in what makes a face attractive and constructed composites – averages of several different images – to produce a face which they believed was attractive (Galton, 1878; Stoddard, 1886). Recent work has provided a clearer account of what makes an attractive face; it has also helped to indicate which features of the face best allow us to remember a face or which make a face distinctive.

The distinctiveness of the face – defined as the deviation from the norm – is unrelated to attractiveness (Bruce et al., 1994). Galton had hypothesised that averageness was attractiveness. That is, the more average-looking the face, the more attractive it was likely to be. This hypothesis was tested and challenged by Perrett et al. (1994), who compared the attractiveness ratings for average, attractive and highly attractive Caucasian female faces. They used special computer technology to construct an average composite of photographs of 60 female faces. The 15 faces rated as most attractive from the original 60 were then averaged. Finally, the attractiveness of this average was enhanced by 50 per cent to provide a 'highly attractive' composite.

Caucasian raters found the 'attractive' composite more attractive than the average composite and the highly attractive composite more attractive than the 'attractive' composite, thus disconfirming Galton's hypothesis. Furthermore, when similar composites were made of Japanese women, the same results were obtained: both Caucasian and Japanese raters found the enhanced composite more attractive. What distinguished an average face from an attractive one? The more attractive faces were those who had higher cheek bones, a thinner jaw and larger eyes relative to the size of the face. There was also a shorter distance between mouth and chin and between nose and mouth in the attractive faces.

Evolutionary psychologists argue that we are attracted to average faces because this behaviour evolved as a solution to attracting healthy mates – best to stick with what you know and can trust. An alternative view is that we are simply attracted to the familiar – a well-known psychological phenomenon. If this were true, we should be attracted to average-looking stimuli that are non-faces too. This is what Halberstadt and Rhodes (2000) found. They asked people to rate a selection of watches, birds and dogs for attractiveness and prototypicality (how typical they were of a category), or averageness. The researchers found that participants rated the average-looking stimuli as being the most attractive. One reason for this may be that we have a preference for averageness which 'reflects a more general preference for familiar stimuli'.

There is mixed evidence regarding the type of 'sexual' face that we like: some studies suggest that we prefer more feminised faces; others that we like masculinised ones (Johnston, 2006). The explanation for our preference for feminised faces is that they are more youthful, warm and honest; masculinised faces are colder, dominant and dishonest. Faces that are morphed to look younger are judged to be significantly more attractive (Ishi et al., 2004). We also, naturally, spend more time looking at beautiful faces than unattractive ones, but a study from a group of US researchers has found that although women spend more time looking at beautiful male and female faces than they do unattractive ones, men spend longer than women looking at beautiful female faces (Levy et al., 2008). There is also evidence to suggest that the intensity of a smile can make a relatively unattractive face less attractive (Golle et al., 2014), although this study also found that it was easier to determine whether a facial expression was happy if it belonged to an attractive face.

A directly gazing face is considered significantly more attractive than an indirectly gazing one and we are more likely to engage socially with people if they look at us directly. Strick et al. (2008) paired novel objects – pictures of unknown peppermint brands – with an attractive or unattractive face which looked straight at the participant or which averted its gaze. Objects paired with a directly gazing attractive face were more positively evaluated than were objects paired with an indirectly gazing attractive face or an unattractive face.

Theories of face perception

The mechanisms that allow us to perceive faces are considered to be different from those that allow us to perceive objects; face perception has been thought of as 'special' (Farah et al., 1998). Face perception involves a number of operations. We can perceive general characteristics such as the colour, sex and age of a face; we can perceive whether a face expresses anger, sadness or joy; we can distinguish familiar from unfamiliar faces. What model of face processing can account for these operations?

Gaze – An international perspective

The ways in which nations gaze at each other's faces seem to differ. Eye contact is longer in Canadians than it is in the Japanese, for example, and Western Europeans fixate more on the eyes and the mouth in a triangular configuration than do East Asians who are likely to gaze at the middle of the face (Senju *et al.*, 2012). Senju *et al.* (2012) asked British and Japanese adults to look at the faces of avatars which moved their mouth and also moved their eyes away from or toward the participants. The British group focused more on the mouth of the avatar than did the Japanese group who fixated on the eyes. Japanese participants were more likely to fixate their attention in the direction of the avatar's gaze, suggesting that the Japanese were more willing to conform to social norms.

Cutting edge: Trustworthy faces

We often use faces to judge the trustworthiness or dominance of their owner. Trustworthy faces are more likely to make us engage with their owners. Untrustworthy and dominant faces are responded to more slowly in reaction time tasks, and the slow response to each seems to be mediated by different brain regions (Getov *et al.*, 2014). More typical ('average') faces tend to be judged as more trustworthy than less typical faces (Sofer *et al.*, 2014). Having an untrustworthy face may even have serious consequences beyond those seen in social interaction. Wilson and Rule (2015) asked 208 volunteers on MTurk to rate the trustworthiness of the faces of 742 convicted murders from a Florida prison – half of the prisoners were on death row; half were serving life imprisonment. The untrustworthiness of the face predicted the type of prisoner – the more untrustworthy the face was perceived as being, the more likely it was that the prisoner was on death row. In a follow-up study, they examined the effect of facial untrustworthiness on the sentencing for those individuals who had been wrongly convicted and released. They found that the individuals who had been sentenced to death were perceived to have the least trustworthy face.

Bruce and Young (1986) suggested that face processing is made up of three functions: perception of facial expression, perception of familiar faces and perception of unfamiliar faces. Why does the model separate these functions? Bruce and Young reviewed extensive evidence which suggested that each of these functions is dependent on different cognitive abilities and that evidence from neuropsychology supported such a model. Current views of face processing argue that we exploit three strategies when we recognise faces. One strategy involves recognising the features of a face, a second involves recognising the relations between features in a face (configural processing) and a third suggests that we recognise the whole face (the holistic approach) (Gruter *et al.*, 2008). Configural processing works when faces are upright, but fails when they are inverted, à la the Thatcher effect. There is more on theories of face processing in a later section. Young and Bruce (2011) recently reflected on how well their model has endured. They note that the one factor they did not consider, and which should have been, was eye gaze. You can see some of the principal models of face processing summarised in Figure 6.19.

Perception of space and motion

In addition to being able to perceive the forms of objects in our environment, we are able to judge quite accurately their relative location in space and their movements. Perceiving where things are and perceiving what they are doing are obviously important functions of the visual system.

Depth perception

Depth perception requires that we perceive the distance of objects in the environment from us and from each other. We do so by means of two kinds of cues: binocular ('two-eye') and monocular ('one-eye'). Binocular cues arise from the fact that the visual fields of both eyes overlap. Only animals that have eyes on the front of the head (such as primates, cats and some birds) can obtain binocular cues. Animals that have eyes on the sides of their heads (such as rabbits and fish) can obtain only monocular cues.

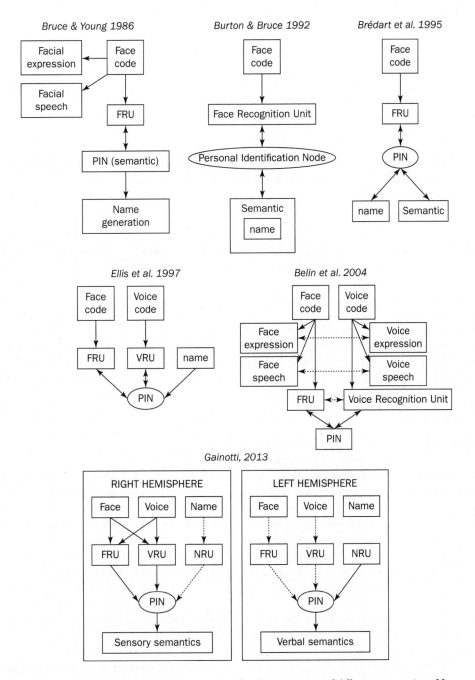

Figure 6.19 Some models of face processing and how they account for the processing of different categories of face.

One monocular cue involves movement and thus must be experienced in the natural environment or in a motion picture. The other monocular cues can be represented in a drawing or a photograph. Most of these cues were originally discovered by artists and only later studied by psychologists (Zeki, 1998). Figure 6.20 shows the most important sources of depth cues.

Binocular cues

Convergence provides an important cue about distance. The eyes make **conjugate** movements so that both look at (converge on) the same point of the visual scene. If an object is very close to your face, your eyes are turned inwards. If it is farther away, they look more nearly straight ahead. Thus, the

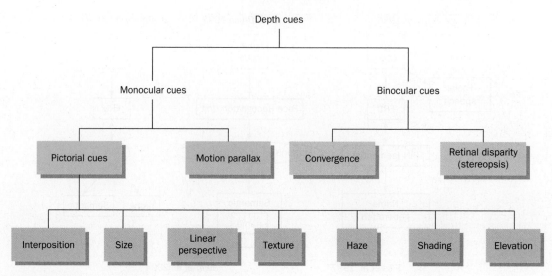

Figure 6.20 The principal monocular and binocular depth cues.

Source: From Margaret W. Matlin and Hugh H.J. Foley, *Sensation and Perception*, 3rd edn © 1992. Published by Allyn and Bacon, Boston, MA. Copyright © by Pearson Education. By permission of the publisher.

eyes can be used like range finders. The brain controls the extraocular muscles, so it knows the angle between them, which is related to the distance between the object and the eyes. Convergence is most important for perceiving the distance of objects located close to us, especially those we can reach with our hands.

Another important factor in the perception of distance is the information provided by retinal disparity ('unlikeness' or 'dissimilarity'). Hold up a finger of one hand at arm's length and then hold up a finger of the other hand midway between your nose and the distant finger. If you look at one of the fingers, you will see a double image of the other one. Whenever your eyes are pointed towards a particular point, the images of objects at different distances will fall on different portions of the retina in each eye. The amount of disparity produced by the images of an object on the two retinas provides an important clue about its distance from us.

The perception of depth resulting from retinal disparity is called stereopsis. A stereoscope is a device that shows two slightly different pictures, one for each eye. The pictures are taken by a camera equipped with two lenses, located a few inches apart, just as our eyes are. When you look through a stereoscope, you see a three-dimensional image.

Monocular cues

One of the most important sources of information about the relative distance of objects is interposition (meaning 'placed between'). If one object is placed between us and another object so that the closer object partially obscures our view of the more distant one, we can immediately perceive which object is closer to us.

Obviously, interposition works best when we are familiar with the objects and know what their shapes should look like. Just as the Gestalt law of good continuation plays a role in form perception, the principle of good form affects our perception of the relative location of objects: we perceive the object having the simpler border as being closer. Figure 6.21a can be seen either as two rectangles, located one in front of the other (Figure 6.21b), or as a rectangle nestled against an L-shaped object (Figure 6.21c). Because we tend to perceive an ambiguous drawing according to the principle of good form, we are more likely to perceive Figure 6.21a as two simple shapes – rectangles – one partly hiding the other.

Another important monocular distance cue is provided by our familiarity with the sizes of objects. For example, if a car casts a very small image on our retinas, we will perceive it as being far away. Knowing how large cars are, our visual system can automatically compute the approximate distance from the size of the retinal image.

Figure 6.22 shows two columns located at different distances. The drawing shows **linear perspective**: the tendency for parallel lines that recede from us to appear to converge at a single point. Because of perspective, we perceive the columns as being the same size even though they produce retinal images of different sizes. We also perceive the segments of the wall between the columns as rectangular, even though the image they cast on the retina does not contain any right angles.

Texture, especially the texture of the ground, provides another cue we use to perceive the distance of objects sitting on the ground. A coarser texture looks closer, and a finer texture looks more distant. The earth's atmosphere, which always contains a certain amount of haze, can also supply cues about the relative

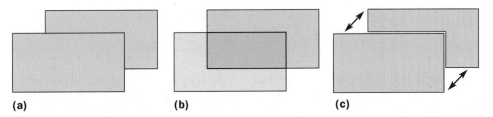

(a)   **(b)**   **(c)**

Figure 6.21 Use of the principle of good form in the perception of depth. The two objects shown in **(a)** could be two identical rectangles, one in front of the other, as shown in **(b)** or a rectangle and an L-shaped object, as shown in **(c).** The principle of good form states that we will see the ambiguous object in its simplest (best) form – in this case a rectangle. As a result, the shape to the right is perceived as being partly hidden and thus further away from us.

Figure 6.22 Principle of perspective. Perspective gives the appearance of distance and makes the two columns look similar in size.

Figure 6.23 Cues from atmospheric haze. Variation in detail, owing to haze, produces an appearance of distance.
Source: Olga Miltsova/Shutterstock.

distance of objects or parts of the landscape. Parts of the landscape that are further away become less distinct because of haze in the air. Thus, haze provides a monocular distance cue (see Figure 6.23).

The patterns of light and shadow in a scene – its **shading** – can provide us with cues about the three-dimensional shapes of objects. Although the cues that shading provides do not usually tell us much about the absolute distances of objects from us, they can tell us which parts of objects are closer and which are further away. Figure 6.24 illustrates the power of this phenomenon. Some of the circles look as if they bulge out towards us; others look as if they were hollowed out (dimpled). The only difference is the direction of the shading. Our visual system appears to interpret such stimuli as if they were illuminated from above. Thus, the top of a convex (bulging) object will be light and the bottom will be in shadow. If you turn the book upside-down, the bulges and dimples will reverse.

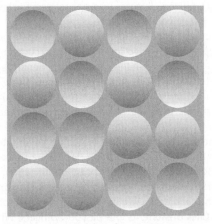

Figure 6.24 Depth cues supplied by shading. If the tops of the circles are dark, they look like depressions. If the bottoms are dark, they appear as bumps.

Psychology in action: CCTV and face recognition

In the opening vignette, you read a summary of how the two brothers who committed the Boston Marathon bombing in 2013 were caught. Photographs of the brothers were released to the public and CCTV footage of the two brothers was available. Official government organisations also had their photographs on file.

CCTV has become an ostensibly easy way to identify people committing crime. It has been estimated that around four million CCTV cameras are use in the UK alone – one for every 32 people (Kang *et al.*, 2014). In 2011, a riot in Vancouver which started as a result of the Vancouver Canucks losing the Stanley Cup, led to the police uploading 15,000 images and 3,000 videos of the riot to a website (Klontz *et al.*, 2013). This resulted in charges being brought against 221 individuals. The use of automated face recognition software in this case was considered a violation of privacy and was rejected. Such technology was used during the riots in London (and patches of the UK) when Mark Duggan was shot by police on 10 August 2011. It was not successful.

Our ability to recognise unfamiliar faces accurately is quite poor but we are very good at identifying familiar faces. Kemp *et al.* (1997) found that supermarket checkout assistants failed around 30 per cent of the time to notice that photo identification offered by customers did not depict the customer's face. The assistants were told that they were taking part in the study – even with this awareness, their recognition was poor. When the fictional photos were of someone else but looked similar to the customer, the error rate rose to 60 per cent. In another study of passport officers, 14 per cent of fraudulent photographs were not identified (White *et al.*, 2014). In a second study, the passport officers performed as badly as a group of students. They also performed no better than the general population at a face-matching task which suggests a requirement for improved training in facial recognition for some passport officers. Success was not related to the officers' length of training or experience.

Automatic Face Recognition (AFR) systems have been developed which have attempted to circumvent human error – the idea is that this software can identify faces more accurately and more quickly. However, these systems perform poorly when the images are of low-quality or the photographs they match were taken many years apart (White *et al.*, 2015a). In such situations, the software generates a list of possible matching candidates and a human makes the identification decision, a process that is also undertaken during fingerprint identification. White *et al.* (2015b) examined how well people could identify faces using the candidate selection generated by AFR software. In two studies of students and passport officers, White *et al.* asked participants to identify the target face from a list of eight faces generated by the technology.

Accuracy was no better than 50 per cent for adults' faces and 40 per cent for children's faces. There was no significant difference between students and passport officers. A group of highly trained 'facial examiners' did perform better, by around 20 per cent. Experts were better when they spent longer looking at the photographs and when faces were inverted. Such facial experts are sometimes recruited by the police. The Metropolitan Police Force, for example, recruits 'super-recognisers' whose facial recognition ability is superior to the norm – they are better at recognising familiar and unfamiliar faces and degraded and good quality images (Robertson *et al.*, 2016). The performance of normal recognisers does improve, however, when multiple, different images of the same person are viewed (White *et al.*, 2014) and

The site of the bomb placed by David Copeland. Copeland was apprehended after a colleague recognised his face from CCTV footage shown on television. Research suggests that recognition of people seen in CCTV footage is significantly more accurate if these people are familiar. If the target person is not familiar, the likelihood of false positives (making an incorrect identification) increases.

Source: Metropolitan Police Service.

Psychology in action: *Continued*

when several images of the same person are averaged together (Jones *et al.*, 2017).

The increasing use of CCTV has led to an increase in the reliance on CCTV evidence in prosecutions but the quality of these images is very variable. According to a 2009 UK Home Office and police report, around 80 per cent of CCTV images are of no practical use because they are of such poor quality. Lighting conditions, which are sometimes very poor in CCTV, affect face recognition significantly. For example, the ability to match faces (and even recognise familiar surfaces) is more accurate when lighting is from above, perhaps because it casts fewer shadows (Hill and Bruce, 1996). Our recognition of faces is not simply based on 'edge' information (contour). The shape of the face (viewpoint) and shading are also crucial in enabling us to make accurate recognition judgements.

Is recognition improved if the face is moving? Some researchers have reported that a moving image is better identified than is a static one (Knight and Johnston, 1997; Pike *et al.*, 1997). Others have found little improvement in recognition when moving and static images are compared (Christie and Bruce, 1998).

Recognition is enhanced by familiarity. Burton *et al.* (1999) took video footage of male and female university psychology lecturers caught on security cameras at the entrance to the psychology department. They then asked psychology and non-psychology students, as well as experienced police officers, to view this footage and then asked them to indicate which of the people in a set of high-quality photographs they had seen on tape. Psychology students made more correct identifications than did the non-psychology students or police officers, suggesting that previous familiarity with the target helps with recognition.

In the second experiment, the researchers looked at which specific bits of information the participants used to identify the target. They took the same video footage, but this time they either obscured the head, the body or the gait.

Participants performed quite inaccurately when gait and body were obscured but were significantly worse at identifying the target when the head was obscured. Thus the advantage of familiarity – at least, in this experiment – was due to recognition of facial features rather than the way in which people walk or their body shape. Unusual gaits or shapes may produce different results.

When people watched CCTV footage of a person and then tried to match the image in the footage with either a single snapshot or an array of snapshots, people performed the task poorly (Bruce *et al.*, 2001). However, when the participants knew the person in the footage – the targets were the participants' teachers or colleagues – they were significantly better at the task. Even in experiments where participants were made briefly familiar with the image they were exposed to, this period of familiarisation did not help the participant recognise the face.

According to Bruce *et al.* (2001), 'where a person is recognised on a CCTV image by someone familiar to them, these identifications should be taken very seriously, even if the CCTV image is of low quality'. They refer to the case of the London nail bomber, David Copeland, as an illustration of this finding. Copeland was responsible for killing three people and injuring 129 others in nail bomb explosions in three areas of London – Soho, Brick Lane and Brixton – in the spring of 1999. Copeland's final crime was committed in the Admiral Duncan pub in Soho, Central London. He left the pub at 6.05 p.m. The bomb exploded as Copeland made his way back to his hotel. Three people were killed, four required amputations and 26 suffered burns (Hopkins and Hall, 2000). Eighty minutes before the bomb was detonated Copeland's colleague had telephoned the police and told them that he thought the bomber identified on CCTV and publicised on television looked like his workmate. By that evening, police were planning a raid on Copeland's house.

Distance and location

When we are able to see the horizon, we perceive objects near it as being distant and those above or below it as being nearer to us. Thus, elevation provides an important monocular depth cue. For example, cloud B and triangle B in Figure 6.25 appear further away from us than do cloud A and triangle A.

So far, all the monocular distance cues discussed have been those that can be rendered in a drawing or captured by a camera. However, another important source of distance information depends on our own movement. Try the following demonstrations. If you focus your eyes on an object close to you

and move your head from side to side, your image of the scene moves back and forth behind the nearer object. If you focus your eyes on the background while moving your head from side to side, the image of the nearer object passes back and forth across the background. Head and body movements cause the images from the scene before us to change; the closer the object, the more it changes relative to the background. The information contained in this relative movement helps us to perceive distance.

The changes in the relative locations of the objects provide cues concerning their distance from the observer. The phenomenon is known as **motion parallax** (*parallax* comes from a Greek word meaning 'change').

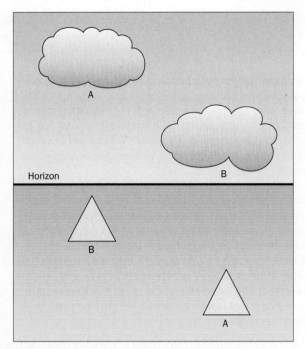

Figure 6.25 Depth cues supplied by elevation. The objects nearest the horizontal line appear furthest away from us.

Source: Adapted from Matlin, M.W. and Foley, H.J., *Sensation and Perception* (3rd edn). Boston, MA: Allyn & Bacon, 1992.

Constancies of visual perception

An important characteristic of the visual environment is that it is almost always changing as we move, as objects move, and as lighting conditions change. However, despite the changing nature of the image the visual environment casts on our retinas, our perceptions remain remarkably constant.

Visual perception across cultures

From birth onwards, we explore our environment with our eyes. The patterns of light and dark, colour and movement, produce changes in the visual system of the brain. There is evidence, however, that perception is not absolute, that it varies across cultures. Ecological variables such as those associated with geography, cultural codes and education influence perception.

The visual stimulation we receive, particularly during infancy, affects the development of our visual system. If the environment lacks certain features – certain visual patterns – then an organism might fail to recognise the significance of these features if it encounters them later in life (Blakemore and Mitchell, 1973). But this is not the only type of environment that can influence perception.

There may also be differences in the cultural codes found in pictorial representations (Russell *et al.*, 1997). Although artists have learned to represent all the monocular depth cues (except for those produced by movement) in their paintings, not all cues are represented in the traditional art of all cultures. For example, many cultures do not use linear perspective. Does the absence of particular cues in the art of a particular culture mean that people from this culture will not recognise them when they see them in paintings from another culture?

It is quite rare for a member of one culture to be totally unable to recognise a depiction as a depiction (Russell *et al.*, 1997). However, Deregowski *et al.* (1972) found that when the Me'en tribe of Ethiopia, a culture unfamiliar with pictures, were shown a series of pictures from a children's colouring book, they would smell them, listen to the pages while flexing them, examine their texture but would ignore the actual pictures. They did recognise depictions of indigenous animals, suggesting that the familiarity of a pictorial depiction is important for recognition within cultures. Familiar objects are sometimes depicted in an exaggerated way. Aboriginal depictions of the crocodile, for example, are distorted: the trunk is seen from above and the head and tail from the side (Dziurawiec and Deregowski, 1992), although this finding may be attributable to the fact that such animals are difficult to draw.

There are other geographical influences on perception. People who live in 'carpentered worlds', that is worlds in which buildings are built from long, straight pieces of material that normally join each other in right angles, are more likely to be subject to the Müller–Lyer illusion. This illusion is shown in Figure 6.26. Look at the two vertical lines and decide which is longer.

Actually, the lines are of equal length. Segall *et al.* (1966) presented the Müller–Lyer illusion (and several others) to groups of subjects from Western and non-Western cultures. Most investigators believe that the Müller–Lyer illusion is a result of our experience with the angles formed by the intersection of walls, ceilings and floors (Redding and Hawley, 1993). The angled lines can be seen as examples of linear perspective (see Figure 6.27). In fact, Segall and his colleagues did find that people from 'carpentered' cultures were more susceptible to this illusion: experience with straight lines forming right angles appeared to affect people's perception.

Although the famous Müller–Lyer illusion can be demonstrated in modalities apart from vision (Mancini *et al.*, 2010), explanations for it have been based on an understanding of the visual system. For example, people with damage to the extrastriate visual cortex in the occipital lobe are unable to perceive the illusion, fMRI data show activation of the bilateral lateral occipital cortex and the superior parietal cortex, and MEG research indicates that activation is seen at two times – once between 85 and 130 ms after the onset of the image and then again at 195–220 ms in the ventral visual pathway in the right temporal cortex, parietal and frontal cortex (Mancini *et al.*, 2011). The MEG data suggest that forming the representation

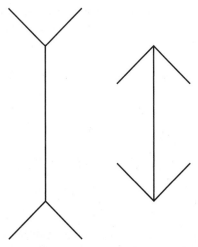

Figure 6.26 The Müller–Lyer illusion. The two vertical lines are actually equal in length, but the one on the left appears to be longer.

Figure 6.27 The impact of culture on the Müller-Lyer illusion. People from 'non-carpentered' cultures that lack rectangular corners are less likely to be susceptible to this illusion. Although the two vertical lines are actually the same height, the one on the right looks shorter.

of an object involves the lateral occipital and inferior temporal areas (Weidner *et al.*, 2010).

Mancini *et al.* (2011) used the stimulation technique, repetitive transcranial magnetic stimulation (rTMS), to examine whether these regions were involved in the Müller-Lyer illusion in the visual and haptic (somatosensory) domains. In the haptic domain, people moved their finger along a palpable version of the typical Müller-Lyer illusion but they were blindfold. Therefore, their only sensory feedback was tactile. When rTMS was applied over left and right occipito-temporal cortex, visual and haptic performance was impaired. Stimulation over the right or left superior parietal cortex did not affect the illusion.

These results suggest that the regions which allow for the processing of the illusion visually and haptically are both sides of the occipito-temporal cortex.

The size–weight illusion

As well as auditory–visual illusions, there are also visual–kinetic illusions such as the size–weight illusion (SWI). The SWI is seen when the smaller of two objects – one large, one small, both equally weighted – is perceived as heavier than the larger (Charpentier, 1891). The illusion persists even when people are told that the objects weigh the same; participants don't even have to lift the object – pushing objects produces the same illusion (Plaisier and Smeets, 2012; Buckingham, 2014). Repeated exposure to the task does not diminish the illusion.

One size–weight illusion that is manipulable involves golf balls. Ellis and Lederman (1998) found that when they made practice golf balls the same weight as normal golf balls (practice ones are lighter), golfers judged the newly adjusted practice balls to be heavier than the normal golf balls. The effect was not observed in non-golfers.

The SWI is also found when people play with dolls – people will judge the weights of female and male dolls differently but this differential judgment disappears when people close their eyes (Dijker, 2008). When told that books were important, people judged them to be physically heavier than did those who were not told this (Schneider *et al.*, 2011). Imagining having a heavy heart, in one study, was associated with judging objects as heavier than was having a light heart (Min and Choi, 2016). Finally, one study found that a cold coin placed on the forehead of a person lying down was more likely to be perceived as heavy than is a coin at room temperature – this is called the Silver Thaler illusion (Buckingham, 2014).

Why do illusions such as this occur? According to Buckingham, there are three possible explanations. One, the sensorimotor hypothesis, argues that the SWI illusion exists because of the mismatch between the assumed weight of the object we are about to hold (based on past experience) and the actual weight. We are more likely to lift large objects with a greater degree of force than smaller ones, for example. If we lift a small one, expecting it to be lighter (and it isn't), we over-estimate the weight based on this sensorimotor feedback. Feedback from participants' fingertips suggests that this is true but participants adapt this grip over time and the illusion still holds. A second, the bottom-up hypothesis, argues that participants confuse an object's density with its weight – small objects are less dense than larger ones of the same weight. A third, the top-down hypothesis, argues that prior experience determines our sensory response to the different objects. Flanagan *et al.* (2008), for example, trained participants to repeatedly lift large objects that had lower mass (so were lighter than anticipated). A group of participants who had lifted such objects 1,000 times a day, did not show the SWI suggesting the importance of prior experience.

Brightness constancy

People can judge the whiteness or greyness of an object very well, even if the level of illumination changes. If you look at a sheet of white paper either in bright sunlight or in shade, you will perceive it as being white, although the intensity of its image on your retina will vary. If you look at a sheet of grey paper in sunlight, it may in fact reflect more light to your eye than will a white paper located in the shade, but you will still see the white paper as white and the grey paper as grey. This phenomenon is known as **brightness constancy.**

Form constancy

When we approach an object or when it approaches us, we do not perceive it as getting larger. Even though the image of the object on the retina gets larger, we perceive this change as being due to a decrease in the distance between ourselves and the object. Our perception of the object's size remains relatively constant.

The unchanging perception of an object's size and shape when it moves relative to us is called **form constancy.** Psychologists also refer to size constancy, but size is simply one aspect of form. In the nineteenth century, Hermann von Helmholtz suggested that form constancy was achieved by **unconscious inference,** a mental computation of which we are unaware. We know the size and shape of a familiar object. Therefore, if the image it casts upon our retina is small, we perceive it as being far away; if the image is large, we perceive it as being close. In either case, we perceive the object itself as being the same size.

Form constancy also works for rotation. The drawing in Figure 6.28a could be either a trapezoid or a rectangle rotated away from us. However, the extra cues clearly identify the drawing in Figure 6.28b as a window, and experience tells us that windows are rectangular rather than trapezoidal; thus, we perceive it as rectangular. Obviously, this effect will not be seen in members of cultures that do

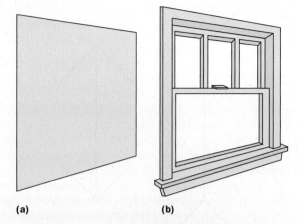

Figure 6.28 Form constancy. **(a)** This figure can be perceived as a trapezoid. **(b)** Because we recognise this figure as a window, we perceive its shape as rectangular.

not have buildings fitted with rectangular windows (or seen by people unfamiliar with the object).

The process just described works for familiar objects. However, we often see unfamiliar objects whose size we do not already know. If we are to perceive the size and shape of unfamiliar objects accurately, we must know something about their distance from us. An object that produces a large retinal image is perceived as big if it is far away and small if it is close. Figure 6.29 illustrates this phenomenon. Although the two letterboxes are exactly the same size, the one that appears to be further away looks larger. If you turn the book upside-down and look at the figure again, the appearance of depth is greatly diminished, and the two letterboxes appear to be approximately the same size.

Figure 6.29 Effect of perceived distance. Although both letterboxes are exactly the same size, the upper one looks larger because of the depth cues (perspective and texture) that surround it. If you turn the book upside-down and look at the picture, thus disrupting the depth cues, the letterboxes look the same size.

Controversies in psychological science: That dress

The issue

It started, innocently enough, one February in 2015, with a photograph of a £50 dress bought by a mother from Lancashire, England, for a daughter to attend a wedding. By the 26th February, however, it seemed that the world and its wedding congregation was talking about it. Why? The photograph of the Roman Originals dress snapped by Cecilia Bleasdale and her husband had been uploaded onto Tumblr by a friend. It caused a storm of interest because some people saw it as white and gold but others saw black and blue. How could the same dress divide opinion so dramatically and be perceived so differently by so many?

The evidence

The phenomenon highlights one of the oldest and more intractable questions in philosophy: is the same stimulus experienced by all people the same way? If I see red or blue or green, does everyone else see the same colours and, if not, should I assume that we really have no shared reality? It is a profound question and one which the dress, more prosaically but dramatically, illustrates.

Of course, we know that not all objects and their colours are seen in the same way by all people. We know this because the light which reaches our eye is a combination of wavelengths – the absolute colour of the object (which is unchanging) and the colour of the light source combine to give us a percept (a perceptual package) of what we see. Objects in natural light look different to objects in artificial light. The illumination conditions under which the photograph was taken may have explained the difference in people's perception. After all, the photograph itself was over-exposed (the background was bright) and illumination was ambiguous.

While the anecdotal response to the dress seemed overwhelming, studies supported the anecdotal response. For example, Lafer-Sousa et al. (2015) asked 1,401 participants to complete the sentence: 'this is a _____ and _____ dress' where the blanks were filled with colours. Fifty-seven per cent perceived the dress as blue/black; 30 per cent as white/gold and 11 per cent as blue/brown. A similar divide was reported by Hesslinger and Carbon (2016). Those who had seen the dress before were more likely to see blue/black or white/gold than blue/brown (Lafer-Sousa et al., 2015). Women were more likely than men to see white/gold than blue/black and the older the sample, the more common this perception became.

When participants were asked to match the colours in the dress with single colours, thereby removing any verbal/linguistic interference and difficulty, those who saw blue/black were more likely to report blue pixels as blue and those who saw white/gold, as whiter. Brown pixels were reported to be blacker by blue/black perceivers and more golden by white/gold perceivers. When the image of the dress was increased in size, the number of people reporting white/gold rose – the greater the spatial frequency, the more likely this response was. When the image was blurred, the number seeing it as white/gold dropped. Another study found that the perceived position of the light was important: blue/black perceivers were more likely to report that the source of light in the photograph came from the front (Chetverikov and Ivanchei, 2016). Perception of the illumination as coming from the front is consistent with a camera-flash which over-exposes a photograph.

Some individuals, according to Lafer-Sousa et al., perceive a cool illuminant and these people discount short wavelengths and so see white/gold. Others see warm illuminants, discount long wavelengths and see blue/black. But why? The authors suggest one answer might lie in people's chronotype – whether they are morning or evening people (Chapter 9 describes and discusses these types in more detail). If exposure influences what people see then older people and women are more likely to see white/gold because they are more likely to have a daytime chronotype – they are larks. Night owls are more likely to perceive a warmer luminant because their exposure to artificial light is greater. The evidence for this is inconsistent. Chetverikov and Ivanchei (2016), for example, found that white/gold perception was dominant in the day and afternoon but not the evening in one experiment, but in a second experiment blue/black was dominant. Interestingly, Lafer-Sousa et al also report that a high percentage of perceivers (45 per cent) switch their perception between the first and subsequent exposure to the image.

Are there differences in the way in which the brains of perceivers process these stimuli? When people who perceived the dress as one pair of colours or the other, then viewed the dress and non-dress stimuli (blocks) with the same colours, those who saw the dress in white/gold showed a greater fMRI response in the middle frontal gyrus, the inferior and superior parietal lobe, the middle temporal gyrus and the inferior frontal gyrus than they did when seeing the blocks (Schlaffke et al., 2015). There was no increased activation seen in those who perceived black/blue. Frontal and parietal regions are also found to be active when people tried to resolve the ambiguities in the stimuli described above (Vernet et al., 2014).

Conclusion

The dress is not an unusual visual illusion in psychology. So-called bistable and ambiguous stimuli such as the Necker cube and the Ruben vase highlight a similar phenomenon – as you saw earlier some people see two people or a vase (in the case of the vase) and some people see the cube as either jutting down and left, or up and right. And the dress is not the only object to have generated such sharply divided perceptions recently. 'The jacket' – an Adidas jacket on a white background – has generated very similar differences with some thinking its colours are white and blue and others thinking it is brown and black (or some other pairing).

Perception of motion

Detection of movement is one of the most primitive aspects of visual perception. This ability is seen even in animals whose visual systems do not obtain detailed images of the environment. Of course, our visual system can detect more than the mere presence of movement. We can see what is moving in our environment and can detect the direction in which it is moving.

Adaptation and long-term modification

One of the most important characteristics of all sensory systems is that they show adaptation and rebound effects. For example, when you stare at a spot of colour, the adaptation of neurons in your visual system will produce a negative after-image if you shift your gaze to a neutral background; and if you put your hand in some hot water, warm water will feel cool to that hand immediately afterwards.

Motion, like other kinds of stimuli, can give rise to adaptation and after-effects. Tootell *et al.* (1995) presented participants with a display showing a series of concentric rings moving outwards, like the ripples in a pond. When the rings suddenly stopped moving, participants had the impression of the opposite movement – that the rings were moving inwards. During this time, the experimenters scanned the participants' brains to measure their metabolic activity. The scans showed increased activity in the motion-sensitive region of the visual association cortex, which lasted as long as the illusion did. Thus, the neural circuits that give rise to this illusion appear to be located in the same region that responds to actual moving stimuli.

Interpretation of a moving retinal image

As you read this book, your eyes are continuously moving. Naturally, the eye movements cause the image on your retina to move. You can also cause the retinal image to move by holding the book close to your face, looking straight ahead and moving it back and forth. In the first case, when you were reading normally, you perceived the book as being still. In the second case, you perceived it as moving. Why does your brain interpret the movement differently in these two cases? Try another demonstration. Pick a letter on this page, stare at it and then move the book around, following the letter with your eyes. This time you will perceive the book as moving, even though the image on your retina remains stable. Thus, perception of movement requires coordination between movements of the image on the retina and those of the eyes.

Obviously, the visual system must know about eye movements in order to compensate for them in interpreting the significance of moving images on the retina. Another simple demonstration suggests the source of this information. Close your left eye and look slightly down and to the left. Gently press your finger against the outer corner of the upper eyelid of your right eye and make your right eye move a bit. The scene before you appears to be moving, even though you know better. This sensation of movement occurs because your finger – not your eye muscles – moved your eye. When your eye moves normally, perceptual mechanisms in your brain compensate for this movement. Even though the image on the retina moves, you perceive the environment as being stationary. However, if the image moves because the object itself moves or because you push your eye with your finger, you perceive movement.

In general, if two objects of different size are seen moving relative to each other, the smaller one is perceived as moving and the larger one as standing still. We perceive people at a distance moving against a stable background and flies moving against an unmoving wall. Thus, when an experimenter moves a frame that encloses a stationary dot, we tend to see the dot move, not the frame. This phenomenon is also encountered when we perceive the moon racing behind the clouds, even though we know that the clouds, not the moon, are moving.

Controversies in psychological science: How does language influence visual perception?

The issue

One of the greatest controversies in psychology (and anthropology) is whether language influences perception. Words for shades of light and colour seem to be more limited in some cultures than others. The Inuit, for example, have more than one name for various shades of snow, whereas Africans have different words for different shades of sand, presumably because these features form a crucial part of the culture's environment. The language we use to describe what we see may directly affect our perception of stimuli.

The evidence

In the mid-nineteenth century, the British statesman William Gladstone noted that Homer's Ancient Greek classics, *The Iliad* and *The Odyssey*, had no reference to blue or orange or green. The sea, in fact, was described as 'wine-dark' or violet and the

▶

Controversies in psychological science: *Continued*

sky was never described as blue; oxen were described as purple. Black was most common (170 references), followed by white (100), *eruthros*/red (13), *xanthos*/yellow (10) and violet (6). Oddly, *chloros* – which gives its name to chlorophyll – was used for non-green objects. Did the Greeks did not perceive these colours? Magnus (1880) investigated this hypothesis by gathering both linguistic and perceptual data. He sent questionnaires and colour chips to Western residents of European colonies and asked them to test the abilities of the native people to distinguish among the various colours. He assumed that language would reflect perceptual ability. If a language did not contain words to distinguish between certain colours, then the people who belonged to that culture would not be able to distinguish these colours perceptually.

Magnus was surprised to discover very few cultural differences in people's ability to perceive various colours. Linguistic differences did not appear to reflect perceptual differences. The issue emerged again in the mid-twentieth century with the principle of **linguistic relativity.** Briefly stated, this principle asserts that language used by the members of a particular culture is related to these people's thoughts and perceptions. The best-known proponent of this principle, Benjamin Whorf, stated that 'the background linguistic system ... of each language is not merely a reproducing instrument for voicing ideas but rather is itself a shaper of ideas, the program and guide for the individual's mental activity, for his analysis of impressions, for his synthesis of his mental stock-of-trade' (Whorf, 1956, p. 212). This became known as the **Sapir-Whorf hypothesis** – the idea that language can determine thought (Kay and Kempton, 1984).

Proponents of linguistic relativity suggested that colour names were cultural conventions – that members of a given culture could divide the countless combinations of hue, saturation and brightness (defined in Chapter 5) that we call colours into any number of different categories (Kay *et al.*, 1997). Each category was assigned a name, and when members of that culture looked out at the world, they perceived each of the colours they saw as belonging to one of these categories.

Two anthropologists, Berlin and Kay, examined this hypothesis in a linguistic study of a wide range of languages. They found the following eleven primary colour terms: black, white, red, yellow, green, blue, brown, purple, pink, orange and grey (Berlin and Kay, 1969; Kay, 1975; Kay *et al.*, 1991). The authors referred to these as focal colours. Not all languages used all eleven (as English does). In fact, some languages used only two: black and white (Heider, 1972). Others, such as Russian, had two words for blue (see below).

If a language contained words for three primary colours, these colours were black, white and red. If it contained words for six primary colours, these were black, white, red, yellow, green and blue. Berlin and Kay suggested that basic colour terms would be named more quickly than non-basic

colour terms, that basic terms would be more salient, that is, they would be elicited first if you asked people to name colours spontaneously, and that basic terms would be more common in written communications such as texts. In fact, people do respond more quickly to basic than they do to non-basic colour terms across a range of languages; when asked to write down a list of as many colour words in five minutes as possible and draw a line under the last words written, every minute, basic terms invariably appear at the beginning of the list (Corbett and Davies, 1997). Similarly, Heider (1971) found that both children and adults found it easier to remember a colour chip of a focal colour (such as red or blue) than one of a non-focal colour (such as turquoise or peach).

In a famous cross-cultural study, Heider (1972) studied members of the Dani culture of New Guinea. The language of the Dani people has only two basic colour terms: mili ('black') and mola ('white'). Heider assembled two sets of colour chips, one containing focal colours and the other containing non-focal colours. She taught her participants arbitrary names that she made up for the colours. Even though the participants had no words in their language for any of the colours, the group learning names for focal colours learned the names faster and remembered them better.

Categorical perception of colour refers to our ability to discriminate between two colours that seem to fall along a continuum. However, speakers of Berinmo (Papua New Guinea) and Himba do not distinguish a boundary between green and blue, which suggests that categorical perception is not universal. Roberson *et al.* (2008) tested this hypothesis in a group of native Korean – and English-speaking adults. Koreans distinguish between *yeondu* and *chorok*. The boundary between the two was described as 'green' by English speakers. Korean speakers were faster at discriminating between colours marked as a boundary in Korean but not English, but not at distinguishing between colours that fell within a colour category. The faster participants showed categorical perception only when stimuli appeared in the right visual field; slower participants showed categorical perception in both visual fields, suggesting that categorical perception may be verbally mediated by the left hemisphere.

Russian has two colour names for blue – *siniy* (dark) and *soleuboy* (light). To see whether this distinction affected perception, Winawer *et al.* (2007) asked Russian speakers to look at three squares – one at the top, two on the bottom. The task was to tell which of the two at the bottom was the same colour as the one on top (there was always one). If the top squares were dark and the odd one out light, then response time was quicker; the closer the hue of the odd one out to the other two squares, the longer the response time. But if the odd one out was two shades lighter and the upper square was dark but on the border with light, response time was shorter than if the odd one out was two shades darker. No such effect was found with English

▶

Controversies in psychological science: *Continued*

speakers suggesting that the Russians reacted to the blue shade differently.

A similar effect has been observed in English. Gilbert *et al.* (2006) had participants look at a cross in the middle of a circle made of coloured squares. One square was differently coloured to the rest. Participants were asked to indicate whether the square was to the left or right of the cross. See Figure 6.30. When the odd-one-out was very different in colour, reaction time was quick. No surprise there. However, when the odd-one-out was across the green-blue border compared to the other squares and when it was presented on the right, response time was shorter. The effect was not as pronounced on the left side.

Brain imaging research with Mandarin Chinese has also supported the Sapir–Whorf hypothesis. Tan *et al.* (2008) measured brain activation as participants saw two coloured squares and had to indicate whether they were the same or different. There were two conditions. In one, the colours were easy to name in Mandarin Chinese; in the second, the colours were just as recognisable but were hard to name. Both conditions activated identical areas in the occipital cortex and frontal gyrus. However, when the colours were easy to name activation was stronger in other regions (left posterior temporal gyrus and inferior parietal lobule, which are involved in word-finding) compared to when they were hard to name. This suggests, according to the authors, that language areas of the brain are involved in visual perception decisions.

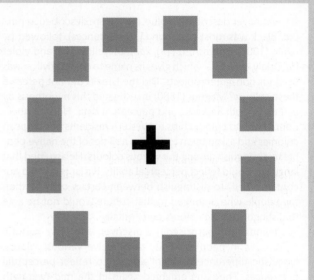

Figure 6.30 Gilbert *et al.*'s (2006) stimuli from their study demonstrating the Sapir–Whorf hypothesis even in English.

Conclusion

Colour is a difficult topic to study cross-culturally. The evidence suggests, however, that although there are cultural variations in the number of colour words used, there seems to be cross-cultural agreement on the colours considered as 'basic'.

Perception and the environment – An international perspective

There is a small amount of evidence to suggest that differences in visual perception exist between Western people and those from East Asia – Westerners tend to perceive objects more analytically and in a more focused way; East Asians are more likely to attend to the context in which objects appear (i.e. they perceive a scene 'holistically') (Choi and Nisbett, 1998; Chua *et al.*, 2005a).

In one study where American and Japanese participants were asked to describe an underwater scene, Americans were more likely to describe objects in the water but the Japanese reported 60 per cent more information about the background environment (Masuda and Nisbett, 2001). In a different scenario, Americans were also able to identify an object (a tiger) more accurately than were the Japanese when it appeared against a different background from that in which it was originally seen. Why does this focal v. context effect occur? One reason might be the types of eye movement made by different cultures.

To test this hypothesis, Chua *et al.* (2005a) asked American and Chinese participants to view scenes in which objects appeared against complex backgrounds. The eye movement of participants as they viewed the object and scene were then tracked. Compared with the Chinese, Americans focused on specific objects and more quickly. The Chinese made more **saccades** – eye movements – to the background.

The researchers suggest that this effect could partly be explained by socialisation. East Asians grow up and live in complex social networks in which paying attention to context is important (perhaps more important than focusing on individual objects or people); Westerners, however, are educated to value individuality and independence (and eye movement is, therefore, directed accordingly). This extends even to cultural products. An analysis of advertising and popular texts in Western and Asian (Korea, Japan and China)/Mexican cultures found that the latter were more individualistic and less collectivistic (Morling and Lamoreaux, 2008). ▶

Perception and the environment: *Continued*

Similar cultural effects can occur when rating facial expressions. Participants in one experiment were asked to rate the degree of emotion shown in cartoons depicting happy, sad, angry or neutral facial expressions. These faces were surrounded by other people expressing the same or different emotion (Masuda *et al.*, 2008). The surrounding stimuli influenced the ratings of Japanese participants significantly more than they did Westerners. This was evidenced by eye-tracking data. The Japanese spent more time looking at the surrounding stimuli than did the Westerners. The lack of self-absorption of Japanese participants was also seen in an experiment in which people completed a verbal fluency task – where there was an opportunity to cheat – in front of a mirror (Heine *et al.*, 2008). North Americans were more self-critical and less likely to cheat in front of the mirror; the Japanese participants were unaffected by the presence of a mirror.

Different nations and different cultures as well as groups within those nations and cultures can also produce art that can be as similar as it is different. Masuda *et al.* (2008) analysed the artistic styles in a total of 365 Western and 218 Eastern landscapes and 286 Western and 151 Eastern portrait paintings. Eastern landscape art was more likely to place the horizon higher than was Western art, which created more space for field information. For portrait paintings, the size of the models was smaller in the Eastern sample; conversely, the Western sample was less likely to include more background.

In a second study, groups of American and Taiwanese, Korean, Japanese and Chinese students were asked to draw and photograph landscapes and portraits. The use of context was greater in both types of stimuli in the Eastern sample. It was more likely to draw the horizon in a high position and draw more objects. It was also more likely to use the zoom function to minimise the size of the model in portrait photographs and make the context larger. Finally, American and East Asians students were asked to rate their preference for portrait photographs where the model and the background varied. Japanese participants were significantly less likely to prefer narrow backgrounds and larger models.

The findings are consistent with those of other studies. Miyamoto *et al.* (2006) took photographs of significant cultural institutions in the US and Japan. These included schools, post offices, hotels, etc. The institutions in Japan featured more objects and were visually more complex.

Why do these differences occur? Masuda *et al.* (2008) cite Cohen *et al.*'s insider/outsider view of how we organise information about the world (Cohen and Gunz, 2002; Cohen *et al.*, 2007). The insider is dominant in the West – this person dwells on his/her own private experiences and sees the world from his/her point of view. The outsider views the world from the point of view of an outsider looking at the self. It seems as if these roles can change. For example, people who have been exposed to Japanese scenes for a few minutes notice more context than those who are exposed to American scenes (Miyamoto *et al.*, 2006).

Does language affect our understanding of spatial relations?

You saw in the Controversies in Psychological Science section on colour and language how culture/language can influence visual perception. An even more intriguing interaction can occur when people are asked to describe directions, and more intriguing still is the community which has helped illuminate this anomaly and which is described by Detuscher (2010). The Guugu Yimithirr is a population of around 1,000 who dwell 30 miles north of Cookstown in North East Australia and have a particularly well-known claim to fame.

When Captain Cook disembarked there in 1770 and encountered a strange animal, he was told that it was a 'kanguroo'. Later explorers were baffled, however, because none of the Aborigines encountered had heard of such an animal and, by all accounts, thought they were being taught the English word for it. Fifty years later another naval explorer, Phillips King, arrived and was told that the bouncy animal was 'minnor' or 'meenuah'. What created this confusion? And which was correct? The answer came in 1971 when an anthropologist called John Haviland discovered that the Guugu Yimithirr described one type of kangaroo as gangurru. The name given by them to other types of kangaroo was a variant of what was told to King – the word meant 'meat' or 'edible animal'. They distinguished between the two types.

But the Guugu Yimithirr also have an unusual way of constructing other expressions: spatial relations. When we give directions, we do so using one of two frames of reference. If someone wants to find out where the nearest coffee shop is, you would either say 'After the newsagent, turn left and then, after the hairdresser's, turn right' or 'After the newsagent, turn west, then head north and turn north east'. The first, the one most people use, is ego-centric and the two axes of right and left depend on the orientation of the body. The second type depends on geographical coordinates (which is, objectively, more accurate but needs to be computed and is, therefore, less easy to use day-to-day).

The peculiarity of the Guugu Yimithirr is that they use this form, not the ego-centric form, to describe spatial relations.

They have no word for left, right, in front of or behind when referring to object location. Instead, they use cardinal directions – north, south, east and west. This means that any direction is given in relation to what is seen in front of them. If a person described the movement of an actor on a television programme, then the directions would depend on the position of the television (not the actor). If the television was moved, the type of direction would move. If they read a book, a character would be said to be to the west of a woman; if the book was rotated, the man would be to the north of the woman. Even memories are recalled in this way. (A similar phenomenon is seen in the Tzeltal highland tribe of South East Mexico – they describe directions in relation to downhill, uphill and across.) They do understand the concepts of left and right in English.

This form of thinking might suggest that they have a different way of constructing reality and the external world. Let's see. Take a look at the Figure 6.31 and remember the position of the objects on the table. Do that now.

Now look at Figure 6.32 and again remember the position of the objects. Do that now.

Finally, without looking at the two figures you have just seen, look at Figure 6.33 and indicate where you think the tree should go based on your memory of its position in the previous figure.

Not too difficult was it? Quite obvious, in fact. Except, to a member of the Guugu Yimithirr, there was nothing obvious about it. In fact, they would have placed the tree to the right of the doll, not the left as you did. The reason for this is that the tables in the first two figures were not in the same orientation – the second was rotated 180 degrees. They, therefore, located the tree to the south of the doll, taking into account the rotation which we ignored. The way in which they constructed and communicated spatial relations affected their memory and their decision to locate the tree. Language had affected reality.

This finding has been replicated using real tables placed in different rooms, although others have queried this finding (Li and Gleitman, 2002).

A final note about language and space. One study exploited the fact that different languages have different writing systems (Bergen and Lau, 2012). Mandarin Chinese is written left to right and top to bottom. In Taiwan, letters are written top to bottom but right to left. In Bergen and Lau's experiment Mandarin Chinese, Taiwanese and English speakers were asked to arrange the development of, for example, a frog from tadpole onwards. The stages of development were depicted on cards which the participants would arrange. The experimenters found that the English speakers plotted time from left to right, as did the majority of Mandarin Chinese speakers. The Taiwanese participants, however, were just as likely to plot time from left to right, as they were top to bottom. Some also depicted the stages going from right to left, suggesting that the way in which time is spatially represented can be influenced by writing system.

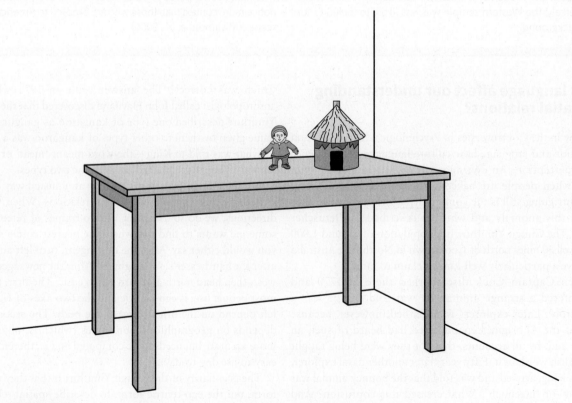

Figure 6.31

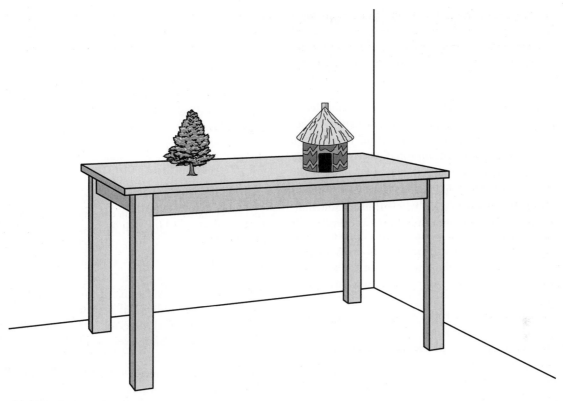

Figure 6.32

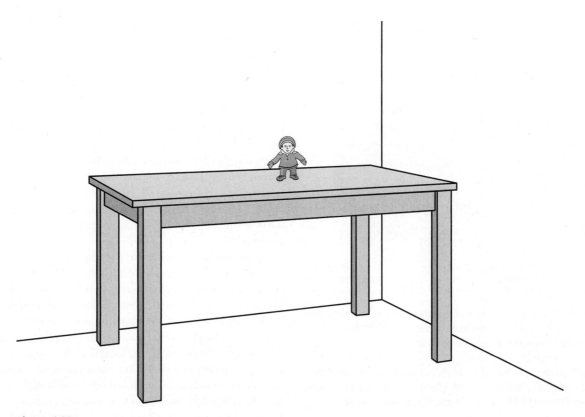

Figure 6.33

Brain mechanisms of visual perception

Although the eyes contain the photoreceptors that detect areas of different brightnesses and colours, perception takes place in the brain. The optic nerves send visual information to the thalamus, which relays the information to the primary visual cortex located in the occipital lobe at the back of the brain (see Chapters 4 and 5). In turn, neurons in the primary visual cortex send visual information to two successive levels of the visual association cortex. The first level, located in the occipital lobe, surrounds the primary visual cortex. The second level is divided into two parts, one in the middle of the parietal lobe and one in the lower part of the temporal lobe. Figure 6.34 illustrates the various regions involved in visual perception.

Visual perception by the brain is often described as a hierarchy of information processing. According to this scheme, circuits of neurons analyse particular aspects of visual information and send the results of their analysis on to another circuit, which performs further analysis. At each step in the process, successively more complex features are analysed. Eventually, the process leads to the perception of the scene and of all the objects in it. The higher levels of the perceptual process interact with memories: the viewer recognises familiar objects and learns the appearance of new, unfamiliar ones. Deprivation of the visual system or damage to it during the early years of development can have significant consequences for visual function.

The primary visual cortex

Our knowledge about the characteristics of the earliest stages of visual analysis came originally from investigations of the activity of individual neurons in the thalamus and primary visual cortex. For example, Hubel and Wiesel inserted microelectrodes – extremely fine wires having microscopically sharp points – into various regions of the visual system of cats and monkeys to detect the action potentials produced by individual neurons (Hubel and Wiesel, 1977, 1979). The signals detected by the microelectrodes are electronically amplified and sent to a recording device so that they can be studied later.

After positioning a microelectrode close to a neuron, Hubel and Wiesel presented various stimuli on a large screen in front of the anaesthetised animal. The anaesthesia makes the animal unconscious but does not prevent neurons in the visual system from responding. The researchers moved a stimulus around on the screen until they located the point where it had the largest effect on the electrical activity of the neuron. Next, they presented the animal with stimuli of various shapes in order to learn which ones produced the greatest response from the neuron.

From their experiments, Hubel and Wiesel (1977, 1979) concluded that the geography of the visual field is retained in the primary visual cortex. That is, the surface of the retina is 'mapped' on the surface of the primary visual cortex. However, this map on the brain is distorted, with the largest amount of area given to the centre of the visual field. The map is actually like a mosaic. Each piece of the mosaic (usually called a module) consists of a block of tissue, approximately 0.5 × 0.7mm in size and containing approximately 150,000 neurons.

All of the neurons within a module receive information from the same small region of the retina. The primary visual cortex contains approximately 2,500 of these modules. Because each module in the visual cortex receives information from a small region of the retina, that means that it receives information from a small region of the visual field – the scene that the eye is viewing. If you looked at the scene before you through a straw, you would see the amount of information received by an individual module. Hubel and Wiesel found that neural circuits within each module analysed various characteristics of their own particular part of the visual field, that is, of

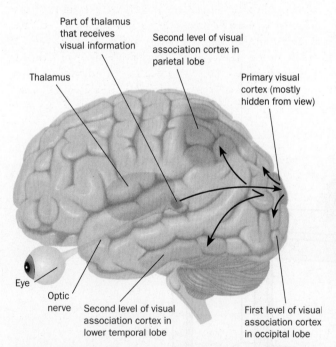

Part of thalamus that receives visual information

Second level of visual association cortex in parietal lobe

Thalamus

Primary visual cortex (mostly hidden from view)

Eye

Optic nerve

Second level of visual association cortex in lower temporal lobe

First level of visual association cortex in occipital lobe

Figure 6.34 The visual system of the brain. Arrows represent the flow of visual information. Sensory information from the eye is transmitted through the optic nerve to the thalamus, and from there it is relayed to the primary visual cortex. The results of the analysis performed there are sent to the visual association cortex of the occipital lobe (first level) and then on to that of the temporal lobe and parietal lobe (second level). At each stage, additional analysis takes place.

their **receptive field.** Some circuits detected the presence of lines passing through the region and signalled the orientation of these lines (i.e. the angle they made with respect to the horizon). Other circuits detected the thickness of these lines. Others detected movement and its direction. Still others detected colours.

Because each module in the primary visual cortex receives information about only a restricted area of the visual field, the information must be combined somehow for perception to take place. This combination takes place in the visual association cortex. Some parts of the visual cortex, such as V1, V2 and V4 respond to different aspects of colour perception (Bartolomeo *et al.*, 2013), whereas V4 and the lateral occipital cortex responds to the shape of an object (Ales *et al.*, 2013).

The visual association cortex

The first level of the visual association cortex, which surrounds the primary visual cortex, contains several subdivisions, each of which contains a map of the visual scene. Each subdivision receives information from different types of neural circuit within the modules of the primary visual cortex. One subdivision receives information about the orientation and widths of lines and edges and is involved in perception of shapes. Another subdivision receives information about movement and keeps track of the relative movements of objects (and may help compensate for movements of the eyes as we scan the scene in front of us). Yet another subdivision receives information concerning colour (Zeki, 1993; Milner, 1998). You can see these subdivisions in Figure 6.35.

The two regions of the second level of the visual association cortex put together the information gathered and processed by the various subdivisions of the first level. Information about shape, movement and colour is combined in the visual association cortex in the lower part of the temporal lobe. Three-dimensional form perception takes place here. The visual association cortex in the parietal lobe is responsible for perception of the location of objects. It integrates information from the first level of the visual association cortex with information from the motor system and the body senses about movements of the eyes, head and body.

The 'special' case of faces: evidence from neuroimaging

You saw in an earlier section, that faces are thought to be special stimuli in visual perception. Their specialness has been enhanced by evidence that there are specific brain regions that appear to respond selectively to them. For example, the perception of unfamiliar faces recruits a specific set of brain areas in the occipital and temporal lobe – these include the frontal gyrus, the inferior occipital gyrus (IOG) and the superior temporal sulcus (STS) (Natu and O'Toole, 2011), which you can see in the brain scans in Figure 6.36. There is also evidence that the amygdala responds selectively to faces and contains neurons that are thought to be particularly responsive to faces (Todorov *et al.*, 2013). One study found that there were 25 regions of the brain which responded selectively to faces and these could be reduced to three clusters based on the connections between them (Zhen *et al.*, 2013). The IOG was the key component – when the study examined the brain's response

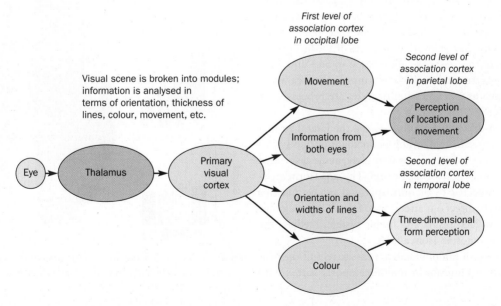

Figure 6.35 Schematic diagram of the types of analysis performed on visual information in the primary visual cortex and the various regions of the visual association cortex.

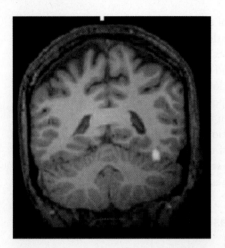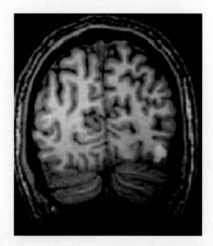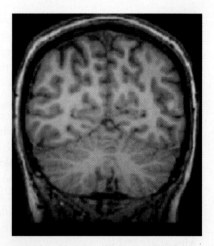

Figure 6.36 The areas involved in face processing, as illustrated by neuroimaging scans: the frontal gyrus **(a)**, the interior occipital gyrus **(b)** and the superior temporal sulcus **(c)**.

to objects, connectivity between the IOG and the rest of the brain was reduced.

Two specifically face-selective regions are the middle of the frontal gyrus, called the fusiform face area (FFA) (as seen in Figure 6.37), and the occipital face area. Neuroimaging studies have shown that the face-specific effects in the STS are not consistent and may depend on whether the stimulus is dynamic or static. If the stimulus is moving, activation here is more consistent (Fox *et al.*, 2009). There is little evidence for connectivity between these two areas – the STS and FFA – which suggests that they undertake different independent roles in face recognition (Iidaka, 2013).

Haxby *et al.* (2000) have proposed that the brain's involvement in face processing can be explained by a distributed neural model. Specifically, they suggest that first, there are core areas dedicated to face processing specifically, and these areas are the ones described above. Second, there are regions which process the invariant features of the face – such as the position of the eyes, nose, mouth and so on – and these are the fusiform gyrus and the IOG. Features of the face which can change, such as its expression or gaze, are processed by the posterior STS.

They suggest that connections between the lateral frontal gyrus and the anterior temporal lobe mediate our ability to code personal identity in a face, as well as the name associated with it and the biography of the person. The superior temporal sulcus is connected to the intra-parietal sulcus and this region allows us to direct our attention to faces. Other regions, such as the amygdala, insula and limbic system, mediate the ability to extract emotion from a face.

The recognition of famous faces appears to recruit the fusiform gyrus and the anterior or middle temporal cortex with

personally familiar faces recruiting even more areas for reasons described below. The FFA adapts fairly quickly to

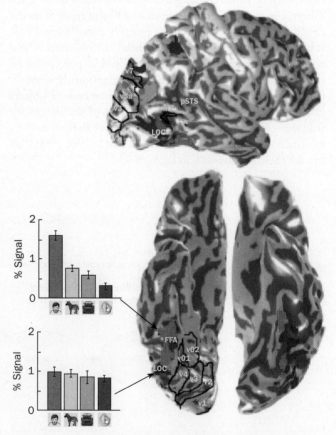

Figure 6.37 Some of the areas of the brain responding to faces and other animate and inanimate objects (Fox *et al.*, 2009).

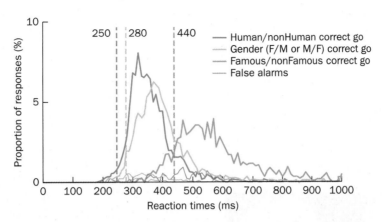

Figure 6.38 Reaction time distribution across trials. The vertical lines show minimum RTs for each condition.

repeated presentations – so activation becomes less when we see the same face over and over again. However, this activation re-starts when our viewpoint of the face changes (Andrews and Ewbank, 2004; Ewbank and Andrews, 2008).

Processing familiar faces is much more complex than processing an unfamiliar face or a famous one because the emotional and autobiographical information attributed to such a face is greater. We can normally categorise objects within 250–290 ms but our ability to recognise famous faces in a group of unknown faces takes us between 430 and 875 ms (Barragan-Jason *et al.*, 2012). When a cap is set on reaction time, only very famous faces are recognised within 600 ms. In Barragan-Jason *et al.*'s study, the minimum time required to recognise famous faces was 467 ms; that is, 180 ms more than when discriminating human faces from animals, and 160 ms slower than when distinguishing between the sex of faces. See Figure 6.38.

Gobbini and Haxby (2007) have argued that knowledge of the traits of the individual's face and the ability to evaluate the mental state of the face of a familiar person is mediated by an area called the anterior paracingulate cortex. Biographical and semantic information associated with the face is mediated by the anterior temporal cortex. Autobiographical memories associated with the face activate the precuneus and posterior cingulate cortex, with emotion mediated by the typical regions already described above.

Brain damage and visual perception

Schneider (1969) had proposed that there were two major visual system pathways: a geniculostriate pathway which was responsible for identifying stimuli and discriminating between patterns, and a retinotectal pathway which was responsible for locating objects in space. Schneider's theory has since been modified, although the idea that different brain regions are

responsible for the perception of an object's qualities and its location is valid.

Ungerleider and Mishkin (1982), for example, suggested that different parts of the brain were involved in object identification and object location: the appreciation of an object's qualities was the role of the inferior temporal cortex; the ability to locate an object was the role of the posterior parietal cortex. Primates with posterior parietal cortex lesions make consistent errors in accurately reaching out for or grasping objects although their ability to discriminate between objects is intact. Similar damage in humans also results in difficulties performing visuospatial tasks such as estimating length and distance (Von Cramon and Kerkhoff, 1993; Jeannerod *et al.*, 1994).

The parietal cortex (see Chapter 4) plays an important role in visually guiding movement and in grasping or manipulating objects (Sakata, 1997). Importantly, Ungerleider and Mishkin distinguished between a ventral and dorsal pathway or stream which projected from the primary visual cortex (PVC) to these areas. Thus, although originating in the PVC, the two pathways were independent and projected to different areas of the brain (to the occipitotemporal and the posterior half of the parietal cortex, respectively). The ventral stream was later extended to the ventrolateral and dorsolateral prefrontal cortex (ALPFC) (Kravitz *et al.*, 2011).

Goodale and Milner (1992) and Milner and Goodale (1995) developed this idea that what was important was not 'what' and 'where', but 'what' and 'how'. In Ungerleider and Mishkin's model, the ventral stream processed the 'what' component of visual perception (identification of an object) whereas the dorsal stream processed the 'where' component (the spatial location of an object). Goodale and Milner's research has focused on the 'what' and 'how' areas. The brain regions representing these streams can be seen in Figure 6.39.

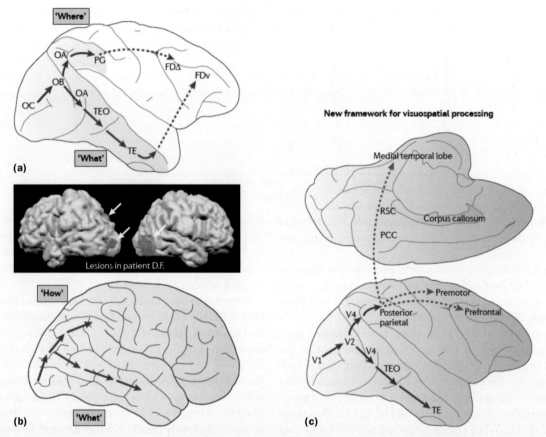

Figure 6.39 Pathways in the brain that were originally thought to mediate where a stimulus is perceived and what is **(a)** and how a stimulus is perceived **(b)** based on findings from patients such as DF (see brain scans in the middle). The two brain figures on the right **(c)** show how the ventral ('what') stream has been extended to include some of the frontal areas of the brain (Kravitz *et al.*, 2011).

Goodale and Milner have made an extensive study of DF, a woman with substantial bilateral damage to the occipital cortex (but sparing the PVC) resulting from carbon monoxide poisoning (Goodale and Milner, 1992; Milner and Goodale, 1995). DF is unable to discriminate between geometric shapes and is unable to recognise or identify objects, despite having no language or visual sensory impairment (Milner *et al.*, 1991). That is, she exhibits visual form agnosia (agnosia is described in more detail in a later section). DF is able to respond to objects. For example, she can place her hand into a slot of varying orientations or grasp blocks (Goodale *et al.*, 1991). However, when she is asked to estimate the orientation of the slot or the width of the box by verbally reporting or by gesturing, she is unable to do so. Why?

DF may be using the intact visuomotor processing system in the parietal cortex to perform the grasping and orientation tasks (Milner and Goodale, 1995; Milner, 1998). The guidance of motor behaviour relies on a primitive dorsal stream in the parietal cortex which is spared in DF. This is why the execution of her motor behaviour is accurate. When asked to indicate which of two boxes is a rectangle and which is a square, she can respond correctly when holding the boxes but less correctly when making a verbal response (Murphy *et al.*, 1996). DF would make partial movements towards one of the boxes before correcting herself. When these initial reaches were analysed, they showed the same level of accuracy as if she had verbally reported which box was which. Did DF monitor the size of her anticipatory grip before making a decision?

There is evidence that she does. When asked to look at a series of lines of varying orientation and then copy them on a separate piece of paper, DF would outline the line in the air before making a copy. When asked not to do this, her copies were still relatively accurate. She found the task easier if she imagined herself drawing the line: when she was asked to copy the line immediately – thereby preventing rehearsal from taking place – she failed (Dijkerman and Milner, 1997). DF must have generated a motor image of the lines to allow her to accomplish this task, a behaviour which would have been made possible by intact functioning of the frontal and parietal lobes.

On the basis of DF's behaviour, research from neuroimaging studies of motor movement and vision, and animal lesions to parietal and occipital areas, Milner and Goodale (1995) proposed that the dorsal stream sends information about object characteristics and orientation that is related to movement from the primary visual cortex to the parietal cortex. Damage to the ventral stream, which projects to the inferior temporal cortex, is what is responsible for DF's inability to access perceptual information. The dorsal stream is automatic, non-conscious and involves visually guided action, not spatial perception whereas the ventral stream produces the representations that are available to conscious experience. Some have argued (Kravitz *et al.*, 2011) that the dorsal stream is in fact three streams with one mediating spatial working memory (see Chapter 8), another mediating visually guided action and a third, spatial navigation. These go to the parieto-PFC, parieto-premotor cortex and parieto-medial temporal cortex, respectively. This is a challenge to the 'what' and 'how' model because Kravitz *et al.* argue that the different streams support different functions because of the cortical areas they project to.

Projections to the primary visual cortex

Two specific pathways – the parvocellular (P) and magnocellular (M) pathways – run from the retina to the cortex and terminate in different layers of the primary visual cortex (V1). Other layers of V1 project to other dorsal and ventral stream areas. Layers 2 and 3 of V1, for example, provide input to the ventral stream areas whereas layer 4B sends input to dorsal stream areas. Layer 4B also receives input from the M and P pathways and projects to areas such as V5, a region known to be involved in motion perception. Many other circuits such as this are made within the visual system but comparatively little is known about how functionally relevant such connections are or how different types of cell contribute to the circuitry. One study has shown that different types of neurons in area V1 receive different signals from the M and P pathways and forward this information to other specific cortical areas (Yabuta *et al.*, 2001). The results of the study suggest that if two types of cell project to different layers, perhaps each type carries different types of information in the cortical visual system.

Perceptual disorders

When the brain is damaged and visual perception is impaired, the patient is said to exhibit a **perceptual disorder**. There are several perceptual disorders and each is associated with damage to different parts of the visual system. It is important to note that these disorders are strictly perceptual, that is, there is no underlying impairment in sensation (patients retain visual acuity and the ability to tell light from dark and so on). The basic visual sensory system itself is, therefore, unimpaired. Three of the most important perceptual disorders are blindsight, agnosia and spatial neglect. Each is important in its own way because they demonstrate how brain damage can affect different aspects of visual perception.

Blindsight

When the primary visual cortex is damaged, a person becomes blind in some portion of the visual field. Some individuals, however, can lose substantial areas of the PVC and yet show evidence of perceiving objects despite being 'cortically blind'. This phenomenon is called **blindsight** (Weiskrantz, 1986, 1997) because although patients are unable to see properties of objects they are aware of other aspects such as movement of objects. According to Weiskrantz, blindsight is the 'visual capacity in a field defect in the absence of acknowledged awareness'. Moving objects are better detected than still ones, objects can be located if they are pointed at and they can detect movement and colour, despite being 'unable' to see the stimuli. (There are equivalent phenomena in the auditory, somatosensory and olfactory systems called deaf hearing, blindtouch and blindsmell.)

Much of the research in blindsight has been conducted with people with damage to the striate cortex (V1) and who have retained residual visual ability – they are cortically and clinically blind in the field affected by the V1 damage but they are able to make decisions in this visual field which indicates that there is some visual ability that is intact. If people do indicate an awareness of visual stimuli – the most well-known example, is showing some awareness of moving objects – they are described as having type-2 blindsight (Foley, 2014).

The earliest case of blindsight was reported at the beginning of the last century (Riddoch, 1917). Riddoch was an army medical officer who had made a study of soldiers whose primary visual cortex had been damaged by gunshot wounds. Although none of the patients could directly describe objects placed in front of them (neither shape, form nor colour), they were conscious of the movement of the objects, despite the movement being 'vague and shadowy'. This suggested to Riddoch that some residual visual ability in the PVC remained which allowed the perception of object motion but no other aspect of visual perception. Some patients need to be prompted to 'guess' (Blindsight Type 1), whereas others will report vague sensations (Blindsight Type 2) although both types claim that they cannot see anything. That the PVC is damaged led to the hypothesis that this area was responsible for conscious visual perception (Radoeva *et al.*, 2008).

Since Riddoch's study, several other cases of blindsight have been reported, notably Larry Weiskrantz's famous patient, DB (Weiskrantz, 1986). DB had undergone surgery for a brain tumour, which necessitated removal of the area of the visual cortex in the right occipital lobe. This surgery resulted in a scotoma – an area of complete blindness in the visual field. DB could indicate whether a stick was horizontal or vertical, could point to the location of an object when instructed, and could detect whether an object was present or absent. Other tasks presented greater difficulty: DB could not distinguish a triangle from a cross or a curved triangle from a normal one. The most intriguing feature of DB's behaviour, however, was a lack of awareness of the stimuli presented. According to DB, he 'couldn't see anything' when test stimuli were seen. Why could DB, and patients like DB, make perceptual decisions despite being unaware of visual stimuli?

One hypothesis suggests that perceptual tasks can be completed successfully because stray light emitted by stimuli makes its way from the intact field of vision because it reflects from surfaces outside the eye area – what is called extraocular scatter (Cowey, 2004). The stray light hypothesis, however, appears to be an unlikely explanation because DB is able to make perceptual decisions in the presence of strong ambient light which reduces the amount of stray light emitted by stimuli. More to the point, this theory does not explain how DB can still make decisions based on the spatial dimensions of objects.

An alternative hypothesis is that the ability is attributable to the degrading of normal vision, possibly due to the presence of some residual striatal cortex ('islands' of PVC cortex that are undamaged) (Wessinger *et al.*, 1999). Implicit in this hypothesis is the notion that residual abilities are not attributable to the functioning of another visual system pathway. There are 10 known pathways from the retina to the brain (Stoerig and Cowey, 1997). As you have seen, there appear to be two distinct pathways in the visual system which mediate different aspects of vision. The visual location of objects, for example, is thought to be a function of a system which includes the superior colliculus, the posterior thalamus and areas 20 and 21, whereas the analysis of visual form, pattern or colour is thought to be a function of the geniculostriate system which sends projections from the retina to the lateral geniculate nucleus, then to areas 17, 18 and 19, and then to areas 20 and 21. Blindsight could, therefore, conceivably be due to a disconnection between these two systems. Again, there are arguments against this hypothesis.

Curiously, DB, although unable to 'see' objects when presented to him, even 30 years after his deficit was first studied, appears to be aware of a visual 'after-image' after a stimulus on a monitor is switched off (Weiskrantz *et al.*, 2002). The colour and spatial structure of the stimulus can be described, a phenomenon that is correlated with increased PFC activity (Weiskrantz *et al.*, 2003). It is unclear whether this ability is due to spared striate cortex, however, because DB has surgical clips which prevent him from undergoing an MRI scan which would demarcate the preserved cortex.

Visual agnosia

Patients with posterior lesions to the left or right hemisphere sometimes have considerable difficulty in recognising objects, despite having intact sensory systems. We saw an example of this in an earlier section when we discussed the perceptual impairments seen in patient DF. This disorder is called agnosia (literally 'without knowledge'), a term coined by Sigmund Freud. Agnosia can occur in any sense (e.g. tactile agnosia refers to the inability to recognise an object by touch) but **visual agnosia** is the most common type (Farah, 1990; Farah and Ratcliff, 1994).

The existence of specific types of agnosia is a controversial topic in perception and neuropsychology. A distinction is usually made between two types of visual agnosia: associative and apperceptive. **Apperceptive agnosia** is the inability to recognise objects whereas **associative agnosia** is the inability to make meaningful associations to objects that are visually presented. Some neuropsychologists have argued that the boundaries between these two types are 'fuzzy' (DeRenzi and Lucchelli, 1993), and other sub-types of visual agnosia have been suggested (Humphreys and Riddoch, 1987a). Apperceptive agnosics have a severe impairment in the ability to copy drawings, as patient DF did. Associative agnosics, conversely, can copy accurately but are unable to identify their drawings. For example, Humphreys and Riddoch's patient, HJA, spent six hours completing an accurate drawing but was unable to identify it when he had finished. Figure 6.40 shows you an example of HJA's drawings.

There has been considerable debate concerning the specificity of visual object agnosia, that is, whether some patients are able to recognise some categories of object but not others (Newcombe *et al.*, 1994). The commonest dissociation is seen between living and non-living things. Generally, it has been found that recognition of living objects (such as animals) is less accurate in agnosic patients than is recognition of non-living objects (Warrington and Shallice, 1984; Silveri *et al.*, 1997).

Some psychologists, however, have argued that these studies do not show differences between the categories of object but between the ways in which these two different types of stimulus are presented. Parkin and Stewart (1993), for example, have suggested that it is more difficult to recognise drawings of animate than inanimate objects. An inanimate object, such as

Figure 6.40 The drawing of a building by HJA reflects great attention but he was unable to name it. The line drawings beneath are of very simple objects but HJA was unable to name them.

Source: Humphreys and Riddoch (1987). *To See or Not to See.* Andover: Psychology Press, reprinted by permission of Cengage/Thomson Learning.

Barry Wainwright, who suffers from prosopagnosia: 'If I look at a photograph of myself, I don't know it's me. I don't recognise my wife or my seven children, either, even when I'm looking right at them.'
Source: Guardian News & Media Ltd: Fabio De Paola.

a cup, is a lot less detailed than an animate object, such as a fly. The dissociation seen in agnosic patients, therefore, may be due to the complexity and/or familiarity of the perceived stimulus. Stewart *et al.* (1992) have suggested that when these artefacts are controlled for, these dissociations disappear.

Prosopagnosia

A more category-specific form of agnosia is **prosopagnosia.** Some individuals with damage to specific areas of the posterior right hemisphere (and sometimes left and right hemispheres) show an impairment in the ability to recognise familiar faces. This condition is known as prosopagnosia ('loss of knowledge for faces'). Some patients are unable to recognise famous faces (Warrington and James, 1967) or familiar people such as spouses (DeRenzi, 1986). Some people are born with an impairment in the ability to recognise faces despite intact intelligence and vision – this condition is called **developmental prosopagnosia** or congenital prosopagnosia and tends to run in families. But such cases are not unitary and clear-cut. For example, individuals may be unable to identify faces but they are able to match faces, or may be unable to do either (Susilo and Duchaine, 2013). There may also be specific features of the face which such people have difficulty in recognising or identifying – the eyes, for example.

The disorder is rare, but has unpleasant consequences for sufferers. For example, here are some comments from patients with prosopagnosia on how their condition affects them (Yardley *et al.*, 2008):

The ability to recover some ability in face recognition in acquired and developmental cases is generally poor, despite attempts at rehabilitation (Bate and Bennetts, 2014; DeGutis *et al.*, 2014). People with congenital prosopagnosia have a limited understanding of their own inabilities (Palermo *et al.*, 2017).

Much of the recent neuropsychological work on face recognition has exploited neuroimaging techniques in order to determine whether regions of the human brain respond to

'I was getting off a bus and somebody got on it and grabbed me, and I pushed them out of the way and it was only when they opened their mouth that I realized it was my own mother.'

'Sometimes if I see someone and I'm not sure if I know them I just try and keep out of their way and hope they don't see me, 'cause I don't know how to act.'

'The condition makes me less interested in the social events, the partying, the getting to know lots of people, because that just gives me a whole set of things I'll get wrong.'

'I'd try, spend three days chatting up some girl and then cut her dead in the street without knowing that I'd done it.'

faces selectively. One controversy in the area surrounds whether such selective activation is specific to faces or to some other perceptual aspect of faces. Kanwisher *et al.* (1998), for example, found that the human fusiform face area (HFFA), was significantly activated when people viewed upright and inverted greyscale faces. Inverted two-tone faces, however, were associated with significantly reduced brain activation. The results suggest that the HFFA does not respond specifically to low-level features of faces (if it did, the inverted and upright two-tone faces would have produced similar activation) but does respond to face stimuli. The authors acknowledge, however, that this may not be the only brain region specialised for face processing.

Another argument against the specificity hypothesis is that the area may respond to familiar stimuli which we are expert at identifying, rather than faces specifically. To test this hypothesis, Rhodes *et al.* (2004) set up two experiments in which people were either trained or were not trained to recognise Lepidoptera (moths and butterflies). Brain activation was monitored using fMRI while participants viewed faces and Lepidoptera. In the second experiment, experts in identifying moths and butterflies passively watched examples of the species while brain activity was recorded. In the first experiment, the FFA was more significantly activated when people watched faces than Lepidoptera, regardless of whether people had been trained to recognise examples of the species. In the second experiment, activation was greater in the FFA when the butterfly experts watched faces than Lepidoptera. There was no overlap in the areas activated by faces and moths and butterflies. The results suggest that the FFA contains neurons that allow 'individuation' of (i.e. discrimination between) faces.

Extensive testing of one individual, Edward, a 53-year old man with PhDs in theology and physics who experienced face processing difficulties in childhood, strongly suggests that the deficit in prosopagnosia is a face-specific one (Duchaine *et al.*, 2006).

Visuospatial neglect

Patients with lesions in the right posterior parietal cortex sometimes have difficulty in perceiving objects to their left (Vallar, 1998; Guariglia *et al.*, 2014). Around 50–80 per cent of patients with right hemisphere stroke are unable to attend automatically to any stimuli in left space (Halligan and Marshall, 1994; Guariglia *et al.*, 2014). This is called **visuospatial neglect** (or **unilateral spatial hemineglect**) and occurs on the side of the body that is contralateral to the side of the brain damage (the regions damaged can be seen in Figure 6.41). It is called neglect because patients can't, or show an impairment in the ability to, respond to stimuli in the visual field opposite to the area of brain injury.

Neglect for the left side is more common than right neglect (which would be caused by damage to the left hemisphere). Recent research suggests that a large number of other, subcortical structures may also result in neglect if damaged (Molenberghs *et al.*, 2011). The variety of structures involved may explain why some patients show different types of neglect depending on the medium of impairment – personal, perceptual or representational.

Problems in the perceptual domain involve ignoring visual stimuli in the left visual field; problems in the personal domain may involve not putting the left arm of a pair of glasses on the ear, or not eating what is on the left side of a plate of food or not reading the left side of a newspaper. Problems in the representational domain involve being unable to describe the left side of stimuli mentally imagined (such as remembering the location of a landmark). For this reason, psychologists administer a battery of tests, rather than one individual test (as this would not measure all types of neglect) (Guariglia *et al.*, 2014). Guariglia *et al.* suggested that differences in tests may explain the variety of degrees of reported neglect.

Spatial neglect patients show a characteristic pattern of behaviour on visuospatial tests. For example, if they are required to bisect lines of varying length, they will err to the right. If they are presented with an array of stimuli (such as small lines) and asked to mark off as many as possible, they mark off those on the right-hand side but fail to mark off those on the left, as seen in Figure 6.42.

Similarly, neglect patients, when asked to draw (or mentally imagine a scene) fail to draw or report details from the left side of the object or image (Guariglia *et al.*, 1993; Halligan and Marshall, 1994). Sometimes, patients will transfer details from the left to the right-hand side, as seen in Figure 6.43. This is called **allesthesia** or **allochiria** (Meador *et al.*, 1991).

Guariglia *et al.* (2014) found that in their study of 287 patients with right-sided brain injury, 45 per cent showed evidence of neglect based on standard test battery administration. Line bisection performance correlated with cancellation task, writing and perceptual task performance, but not with personal neglect suggesting, as other data have, that personal neglect might be a variation of – or a different disorder to – perceptual neglect.

The reasons for spatial neglect are unclear (see Halligan and Marshall, 1994, and Mozer *et al.*, 1997, for a discussion) but there are various methods for reducing the symptoms of the disorder, including optokinetic stimulation (we think our bodies rotate to the right if our field of vision is full and the stimuli move to the left and we try to compensate for this by moving to the left), neck-muscle vibration (stimulating the left neck-muscles making us think that our muscles are extended and moving to the left), caloric stimulation (inserting cold or warm water into the contralesional ear – this stimulates the vestibular nerve, creating movement

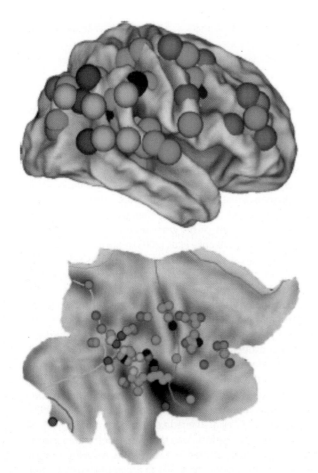

Figure 6.41 The areas of the brain damaged in spatial neglect patients.

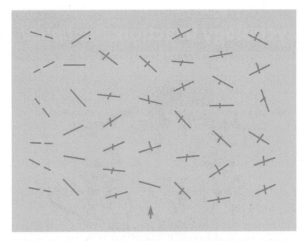

Figure 6.42 The line cancellation task. Spatial neglect patients consistently neglect one side of the display (in this example, the left side).

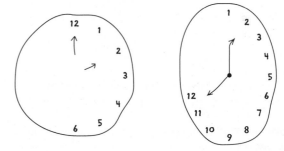

Figure 6.43 The famous clock-drawing task at which spatial neglect patients are impaired. Patients either neglect the numerals on the left side completely or bunch them up on the right.

of the eyeball), and prism adaptation (patients wear prisms that automatically shift attention to the right) (Kerkhoff and Schenk, 2012). A review of these methods used in studies from 1997 to 2012 found that only 12 randomised control trials had been published and that the prism adaptation technique was the most effective (Yang *et al.*, 2013).

Psychology in action: How does brain injury affect artists?

Losing the ability to speak, to recall information or to organise and plan everyday life efficiently are all unwelcome intruders in the world of the normally functioning. But what if the disrupted function is essential to the person's life and provides him or her with a livelihood? Beethoven composed symphonies, Evelyn Glennie plays exceptional xylophone, Stevie Wonder is an accomplished keyboardist; even James Joyce managed to produce Ulysses and *Finnegan's Wake*

despite his chronic sight loss (although this is thought to explain some of the idiosyncratic orthography). None of these, however, despite their sensory losses, sustained brain injury.

Sacks (1995) described an artist who developed an injury leaving him **achromatopsic** – the artist's world appeared 'dirty grey' and he reported being unable to imagine colours (or even being able to dream in colour). Before the accident leading to the injury, the patient painted colourful, abstract

▷

Psychology in action: *Continued*

Drawing showing left colour neglect
Arrow indicates the middle of the page.

Figure 6.44 The colour neglect seen in a drawing by Blanke *et al.*'s patient.

Source: Plate 6.2 from *Human Neuropsychology*, 2nd edn, Pearson/Prentice Hall (Martin, G.N., 2006). Image kindly provided by Dr Olaf Blanke.

creations; after the accident, the paintings became figurative and abstract. Contrast, figure and form were good as was the patient's ability to understand and describe colour but his use of colour became haphazard.

Unilateral spatial neglect has more intriguing, if predictable, consequences. Jung (1974) described four early cases of painters who developed neglect following brain injury. One, the German artist Lovis Corinth, had suffered a right hemisphere stroke. His painting changed dramatically: the contours on the left of his work disappeared and details became misplaced. Blanke *et al.* (2003) reported the case of a 71-year-old artist who could colour the right side of her paintings normally and evenly but paid minimal attention to the left. Figure 6.44 gives an example of the patient's art following injury. Neglect for colour was greater than neglect for form in the majority of the patient's paintings. Painter IK showed right neglect where entire canvasses would be created in exuberant colour but the right side lacked detail and form (Marsh and Philwin, 1987).

Perhaps the most famous example of unilateral spatial neglect is the Italian film director, Federico Fellini, whose disorder was reported by Cantagallo and Della Sala (1998). At the age of 73, Fellini suffered a stroke in the middle cerebral artery of the right parietal lobe that caused left extrapersonal spatial neglect that persisted for two months. As well as being a celebrated film director, Fellini was an accomplished cartoonist and his completion of neglect tests was peppered with his

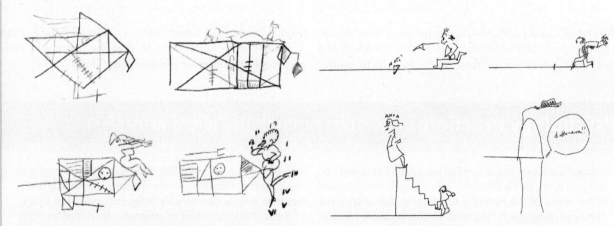

Figure 6.45 Italian film director Federico Fellini developed spatial neglect after suffering a stroke. As well as being a director, Fellini was also a talented cartoonist and he doodled comically on his psychological tests. **(a)** and **(b)** Examples of Fellini's spatial neglect test performance.

Source: Chatterjee, A. A madness to the methods of cognitive neuroscience? *Journal of Cognitive Neuroscience*, 2005, 17, 6, 847–49, © by the Massachusetts Institute of Technology.

Psychology in action: *Continued*

cartoonish embellishments. His original cartoons showed neglect of the left side. Figures 6.45a and 6.45b illustrate some of Fellini's attempts.

Fellini's neglect did not appear to be representational (he could imagine both sides of his visual field) and he was completely aware of his deficits. Unlike patients in previous reports, his increased awareness did not lead to a decrease in his neglect (Guariglia *et al.*, 1993).

As Fellini did, some artists can recover their ability to attend to the left to some extent; sometimes they will use broader strokes than normal or may be more expressive, as the painters Loring Hughes and Lovis Corinth found.

At least neglect patients can recognise their creations. Some patients with visual agnosia are unable to do this. Wapner *et al.* (1978) report the case of a 73-year-old amateur artist who developed visual agnosia following a stroke. The artist would draw extremely laboriously but failed to recognise what he drew. He could identify the general shape of the object and describe its function, and even tried to identify it from its parts, but could not put a label to it. His agnosia was perceptual, rather than conceptual, because he would sometimes describe the functions of parts of the object he drew (e.g. what a telephone was for).

Agnosic patients can sometimes imagine the objects they would like to draw. Botez *et al.* (1985), however, reported the case of a 38-year-old teacher and amateur charcoal drawer who was unable to imagine people, places or objects following dilation of one of the brain's chambers. Copying objects presented little problem but when the object was removed from sight, her drawings became simple and schematic. When she was given the name of an object to draw, she could not do this competently.

Perception seems the most likely casualty in the artist's battle with brain damage but there are some cases of impairment to other functions which led to some unusual artistic consequences. The Bulgarian artist Zlatio Boiyadjiev exhibited a natural, pictorial style prior to the development of aphasia (Zaimov *et al.*, 1969). After the aphasia, his art became bold, rich and colourful, full of striking, energetic lines and replete with bizarre imagery. Another artist with aphasia, the Polish artist RL (an Assistant Professor in Lublin), was known for highly symbolic paintings. Following aphasia, he produced very well-executed charcoal drawings, self-portraits and landscapes (Kaczmarek, 1991). No matter how hard he tried, he never did recover the symbolism of his art that existed before the aphasia.

There are number of other cases where previously unartistic individuals develop an extraordinary ability to create art after their injury (Schott, 2012) and Schott suggests that the majority of such cases where patients show fronto-temporal dementia have injury to the anterior temporal lobes. These regions may be necessary for the appearance of unexpected artistry. One other mechanism which may explain the behaviour is that a breakdown exists between connections from this region and the orbitofrontal cortex. This leads to some form of artistic disinhibition.

One case study of a former truck driver who had suffered a closed head injury and presented with a number of visuospatial and other neurological problems found that he developed an interest in drawing (Midorikawa and Kawamura, 2014). A likely lesion was found in his left temporofrontal lobe. In the first few months of rehabilitation, he would copy from photographs. Within six months, he developed a more decorative style. A few months later, he developed a 'bimorphic style', using features such as the eye.

Chapter review

Perception of form

- Perception of form requires recognition of figure and ground. The Gestalt organisational laws of proximity, similarity, good continuation and common fate describe some of the ways in which we distinguish figure from ground even when the outlines of the figures are not explicitly bounded by lines.

- One hypothesis suggests that our brain contains templates of all the shapes we can perceive. We compare a particular pattern of visual input with these templates until we find a fit. A second hypothesis suggests that our brain contains prototypes, which are more flexible than simple templates. Some psychologists believe that prototypes are collections of distinctive features (such as the two parallel lines and the connecting diagonal of the letter N).

▶

- Perception involves both bottom-up and top-down processing. Our perceptions are influenced not only by the details of the particular stimuli we see, but also by their relations to each other and our expectations. Thus, we may perceive a shape either as a loaf of bread in the kitchen or as a letterbox alongside a country road, for example.
- We can usually distinguish male and female faces on the basis of eyes, mouth and nose but rarely on the basis of single features alone.
- Lighting, form and contour significantly influence our ability to recognise faces correctly.

Perception of space and motion

- Because the size and shape of a retinal image vary with the location of an object relative to the eye, accurate form perception requires depth perception – perception of the locations of objects in space.
- Depth perception comes from binocular cues (from convergence and retinal disparity) and monocular cues (from interposition, size, linear perspective, texture, haze shading, elevation and the effects of head and body movements).
- The Sapir–Whorf hypothesis suggests that language can strongly affect the way we perceive the world although there is not much research to support it. It is possible that experience with some environmental features, such as particular geographical features or buildings composed of straight lines and right angles, has some influence on the way people perceive the world.
- We perceive the brightness of an object relative to that of objects around it; thus, objects retain a constant brightness under a variety of conditions of illumination. In addition, our perception of the relative distance of objects helps us maintain form constancy.
- Because our bodies may well be moving while we are visually following some activity in the outside world, the visual system has to make further compensations. It keeps track of the commands to the eye muscles and compensates for the direction in which the eyes are pointing.
- Movement is perceived when objects move relative to one another. In particular, a smaller object is likely to be perceived as moving across a larger one. Movement is also perceived when our eyes follow a moving object, even though its image remains on the same part of the retina and supplies important cues about an object's three-dimensional shape.
- There is evidence that language can influence the understanding and use of spatial relations. Members of the Guugu Yimithirr community, for example, described the position and relations between objects in a different way to people from the West.

Brain mechanisms of visual perception

- Visual information proceeds from the retina to the thalamus, and then to the primary visual cortex (PVC). The PVC is organised into modules, each of which receives information from a small region of the retina.
- Neural circuits within each module analyse specific information from their part of the visual field, including the orientation and width of lines, colour and movement.
- The different types of information analysed by the neural circuits in the modules of the PVC are sent to separate maps of the visual field in the first level of the visual association cortex. The information from these maps is combined in the second level of the visual association cortex: form perception in the base of the temporal lobe and spatial perception in the parietal lobe.
- The brain seems to contain visual systems which process (1) features of objects and (2) the space indication of objects. The first, the ventral stream, projects from the PVC to the inferior temporal cortex; the second, the dorsal stream, projects from the PVC to the posterior parietal cortex.
- While it was once thought that the fusiform face area was the most important brain region for face processing, fMRI research suggests that processing of different types of faces (familiar/unfamiliar; famous/not famous) depends on other brain areas.
- Visual agnosia is the inability to perceive objects accurately (apperceptive agnosia) or assign meaning to visually presented objects (associative agnosia). Prosopagnosia is the inability to identify familiar faces and results from bilateral or unilateral posterior brain damage.
- The agnosic deficits seen in patient DF may be due to an intact dorsal stream but an impaired ventral stream.
- Blindsight refers to the ability to perform visual perceptual tasks despite a lack of awareness of the perceived stimuli; it is normally associated with damage outside the primary visual cortex.
- Spatial neglect is the inability to attend to stimuli in one half of space. Patients usually neglect the left-hand side as a result of right parietotemporal cortex damage (i.e. the deficit is contralesional – occurs on the opposite side to the brain damage).

Suggestions for further reading

Barton, J.J. and Corrow, S.L. (2016) Recognizing and identifying people: a neuropsychological review. *Cortex*, 75, 132–50.

Carlin, J.D. and Calder, A.J. (2013) The neural basis of eye gaze processing. *Current Opinion in Neurobiology*, 23, 450–55.

Davies, G.M. and Young, A.W. (2017) Research on face recognition: The Aberdeen influence. *British Journal of Psychology*, in press.

Daw, N. (2012) *How Vision Works: the physiological mechanisms behind what we see*. Oxford: Oxford University Press.

Freiwald, W., Duchaine, B. and Yovel, G. (2016) Face processing systems: From neurons to real-world social perception. *Annual Review of Neuroscience*, 39, 325–46.

Goldstein, E.B. and Brockmole, J. (2016) *Sensation and Perception*. 10th edn. NY: Wadsworth.

Jones, B.C. et al (in press). No compelling evidence that preferences for facial masculinity track changes in women's hormonal status. *Psychological Science.*

Martin, G.N. (2006) *Human Neuropsychology* (2nd edn). Harlow: Prentice Hall Europe.

Mather, G. (2011) *Essentials of Sensation and Perception*. London: Routledge.

Todorov, A., Mende-Siedlecki, P. and Dotsch, R. (2013) Social judgements from face. *Current Opinion in Neurobiology*, 23, 373–80.

Young, A.W., & Burton, A.M. (2017). Recognizing faces. Current Directions in Psychological Science, 26, 212–217.

Some very good readings on visual perception and its disorders.

CHAPTER 7
Learning and behaviour

Here's a quick true or false quiz for you, before you read this chapter. Your task is to decide whether the statement is true or false. The answers are at the bottom of the page (and upside down. No peeking).

We mostly use 10 per cent of our brains.

Individual learners show preferences for the medium in which they receive information – visual, auditory, etc.

Vigorous exercise can improve mental function.

Short bouts of exercise can help the left and right hemispheres of the brain communicate better.

Individuals learn better if they receive information in their preferred learning style.

Teaching using specific learning styles is better in language learning than any other subject.

Based on Lethaby & Harries (2016).

WHAT YOU SHOULD BE ABLE TO DO AFTER READING CHAPTER 7

- Describe the concept of habituation and the phenomena of classical conditioning and operant learning.
- Understand the principles underlying classical conditioning.
- Understand the principles underlying operant conditioning.
- Describe and explain conditioned aversions.
- Apply the principles of learning theory to behaviour.
- Describe some of the factors that influence academic learning.

QUESTIONS TO THINK ABOUT

- Do different aspects of learning have different underlying principles? Is learning to ride a bike governed by different principles from those used for learning to find your way around college or university or learning a foreign language?
- Does all learning have to be intentional? Can you learn something without knowing it or without wanting to learn it?
- Is learning a process that depends on innate ability, the ability to adopt successful learning strategies or both?
- What factors do you think enhance and promote the process of learning?
- Do learning styles exist?
- What psychological factors do you think could enhance (or impair) your academic learning?

The purpose of learning

Behaviours that produce favourable consequences are repeated and become habits, but those that produce unfavourable consequences tend not to recur (Ouellette and Wood, 1998). In other words, we learn from experience. **Learning** is an adaptive process in which the tendency to perform a particular behaviour is changed by experience. As conditions change, we learn new behaviours and eliminate old ones.

This chapter considers three kinds of learning: habituation, classical conditioning and operant conditioning. All three involve cause-and-effect relations between behaviour and the environment. We learn which stimuli are trivial and which are important, and we learn to make adaptive responses and to avoid maladaptive ones. We learn to recognise those conditions under which a particular response is useful and those under which a different response is more appropriate. The types of learning described in this chapter serve as the building blocks for more complex behaviours, such as problem-solving and thinking, which we consider in later chapters.

Learning, however, cannot be truly observed in a direct sense; it can only be inferred from changes in behaviour. The influential field of behaviourism (see Chapter 1) which dominated experimental psychology in the early twentieth century demanded that only observable behaviour could be valid subject matter for psychologists. However, even the founding father of behaviourism, John B. Watson, argued that there could be two categories of observable behaviour: explicit behaviour, which is directly observable to the eye, and implicit behaviour, which could be measured by special equipment (an example would be the measurement of bodily response using psychophysiological recording equipment).

But not all changes in behaviour are caused by learning. For example, your performance in an examination or the skill with which you operate a car can be affected by your physical or mental condition, such as fatigue, fearfulness or distraction. Moreover, learning may occur without noticeable changes in observable behaviour taking place. In some cases, learning is not apparent – at least, not right away – from our observable behaviour. In other cases, we may never have the opportunity to demonstrate what we have learned. For example, although you may have received training in how to conduct an orthogonally rotated factor analysis in your computer's statistics package, you may never need to demonstrate the results of your learning again. In still other cases, you may not be sufficiently motivated to demonstrate something you have learned. For example, a tutor might pose a question in a seminar but although you know the answer, you do not say anything because you get nervous when speaking in front of others.

Learning takes place within the nervous system. Experience alters the structure and chemistry of the brain, and these changes affect the individual's subsequent behaviour. Performance is the behavioural change (or new behaviour) produced by this internal change.

Habituation

Many events may cause us to react automatically. For example, a sudden, unexpected noise causes an orienting response: we become alert and turn our heads towards the source of the sound. However, if the noise occurs repeatedly, we gradually cease to respond to it; we eventually ignore it. **Habituation**, learning not to respond to an unimportant event that occurs repeatedly, is the simplest form of learning. Even infants a few months old show evidence of habituation (see Chapter 12).

The simplest form of habituation is temporary, and is known as short-term habituation. Imagine entering a new room in an inhabited house. It is likely that you will perceive the distinctive odour of the room. Eventually, however, you begin not to notice the odour; you will have become habituated. If you return to the same house the next day, however, you will perceive that distinctive smell again but if you stay in the room for long enough, you will again become habituated.

Classical conditioning

Unlike habituation, **classical conditioning** involves learning about the conditions that predict that a significant event will occur. We acquire much of our behaviour through classical conditioning. For example, if you are hungry and smell a favourite food cooking, your mouth is likely to water. If you see someone with whom you have recently had a serious argument, you are likely to experience again some of the emotional reactions that occurred during the encounter. If you hear a song that you used to listen to with a loved one, you are likely to experience a feeling of nostalgia. If you listen to a piece of music that can be distinctly identified by nation, then people will buy more of that nation's wine. How does such classical conditioning take place?

Imagine that you have an uninflated balloon directly before you. Someone starts inflating the balloon with a pump; the balloon gets larger and larger. What are you likely to do? You will probably grimace and squint your eyes as you realise that the balloon is about to burst in your face.

Now consider how a person learns to flinch defensively at the sight of a tightly stretched balloon. Suppose that we inflate a balloon in front of a young boy who has never seen one before. The boy will turn his eyes towards the enlarging balloon, but he will not flinch. When the balloon explodes, the noise and the blast of air will cause a defensive startle reaction: he will squint, grimace, raise his shoulders and suddenly move his arms towards his body. A bursting balloon is an important stimulus, one that causes an automatic, unlearned defensive reaction.

We will probably not have to repeat the experience many times for the boy to learn to react the way we all do – flinching defensively before the balloon actually bursts. A previously neutral stimulus (the over-inflated balloon), followed by an important stimulus (the explosion that occurs when the balloon bursts), can now trigger the defensive flinching response by itself. The defensive flinching response has been classically conditioned to the sight of an over-inflated balloon. Two stimuli have become associated with each other.

Pavlov's serendipitous discovery

In December 1904, the Russian physiologist Ivan Pavlov was awarded the Nobel Prize in physiology and medicine for his work on the digestive system. Invited to Stockholm to accept the award and to deliver an acceptance speech, the 55-year-old Pavlov did not speak of his pioneering work on digestion (Babkin, 1949). Instead, his address, entitled 'The first sure steps along the path of a new investigation', focused on his more recent work involving conditional reflexes or 'involuntary' responses. Pavlov's new line of research was to take him far from the research for which he was awarded the Nobel Prize, and today he is remembered more for his work in psychology than in physiology. But it was while studying the digestive system that Pavlov stumbled on the phenomenon that was to make a lasting impact on psychology (Windholz, 1997).

Pavlov's chief ambition as a physiologist was to discover the neural mechanisms controlling glandular secretions during digestion. He measured the secretions during the course of a meal by inserting a small tube in a duct in an animal's mouth and collecting drops of saliva as they were secreted by the salivary gland. During each of the test sessions, he placed dry food powder inside the dog's mouth and then collected the saliva. All went well until the dogs became experienced subjects. After several testing sessions, the dogs began salivating before being fed, usually as soon as they saw the laboratory assistant enter the room with the food powder. What Pavlov discovered was a form of learning in which one stimulus predicts the occurrence of another. In this case, the appearance of the laboratory assistant predicted the appearance of food.

Rather than ignoring this phenomenon or treating it as a confounding variable that needed to be controlled, Pavlov designed experiments to discover exactly why the dogs were salivating before being given the opportunity to eat. He suspected that salivation might be triggered by stimuli that were initially unrelated to eating. Somehow, these neutral stimuli came to control what is normally a natural reflexive behaviour. After all, dogs do not naturally salivate when they see laboratory assistants.

To do so, he placed an inexperienced dog in a harness and occasionally gave it small amounts of food powder. Before placing the food powder in the dog's mouth, Pavlov sounded a bell, a buzzer or some other auditory stimulus. At first, the dog showed only a startle response to the sound, perking its ears and turning its head towards the sound. The dog salivated only when the food powder was placed in its mouth. But after only a dozen or so pairings of the bell and food powder, the dog began to salivate when the bell rang. Placing the food powder in the dog's mouth was no longer necessary to elicit salivation; the sound by itself was sufficient. Pavlov showed that a neutral stimulus can elicit a response similar to the original reflex when the stimulus predicts the occurrence of a significant stimulus (in this case, food powder).

This type of learning is called classical or **Pavlovian conditioning**. Pavlov demonstrated that conditioning occurred only when the food powder followed the bell within a short time. If there was a long delay between the sound and the food powder or if the sound followed the food powder, the animal never learned to salivate when it heard the sound. Thus, the sequence and timing of events are important factors in classical conditioning. Classical conditioning provides us with a way to learn cause-and-effect relations between environmental events. We are able to learn about the stimuli that warn us that an important event is about to occur. Obviously, warning stimuli must occur prior to the event about which we are being warned.

Figure 7.1 shows the basic classical conditioning procedure – the special conditions that must exist for an organism to respond to a previously neutral stimulus.

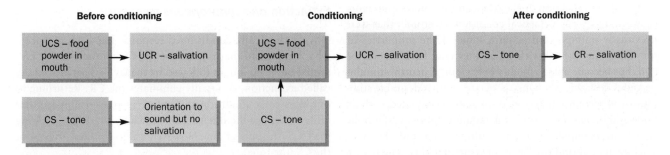

Figure 7.1 Basic components of the classical conditioning procedure. Prior to conditioning, the UCS but not the CS elicits a response (the UCR). During conditioning, the CS is presented in conjunction with the UCS. Once the conditioning is completed, the CS alone elicits a response (the CR).

A stimulus, such as food, that naturally elicits reflexive behaviour, such as salivation, is called an **unconditional stimulus (UCS)**. The reflexive behaviour itself is called the **unconditional response (UCR)**. If, for a certain dog, a bell signals food, then the bell may also come to elicit salivation through classical conditioning. Another dog may hear the sound of an electric can opener just before it is fed, in which case that sound will come to elicit salivation. A neutral stimulus paired with the UCS that eventually elicits a response is called a **conditional stimulus (CS)**. The behaviour elicited by a CS is called a **conditional response (CR)**. In the case of Pavlov's dogs, food powder was the UCS: it elicited the UCR, salivation.

At first, when Pavlov presented the sound of the bell or buzzer, the dogs did not salivate; the sound was merely a neutral stimulus, not a CS. However, with repeated pairings of the sound and the food powder, the sound became a CS, reliably eliciting the CR – salivation.

The biological significance of classical conditioning

Salivation is an innate behaviour and is adaptive because it facilitates digestion. Through natural selection, the neural circuitry that underlies salivation has become part of the genetic endowment of many species. Pavlov's experiments demonstrated that an innate reflexive behaviour, such as salivation, can be elicited by novel stimuli. Thus, a response that is naturally under the control of appropriate environmental stimuli, such as salivation caused by the presence of food in the mouth, can also come to be controlled by other kinds of stimulus.

Classical conditioning accomplishes two functions. First, the ability to learn to recognise stimuli that predict the occurrence of an important event allows the learner to make the appropriate response faster and perhaps more effectively. For example, hearing the buzz of a wasp near your head may make you duck and avoid being stung. Seeing a rival increases an animal's heart rate and the flow of blood to its muscles, makes it assume a threatening posture, and causes the release of hormones that prepare it for vigorous exercise.

The second function of classical conditioning is even more significant. Through classical conditioning, stimuli that were previously unimportant acquire some of the properties of the important stimuli with which they have been associated and thus become able to modify behaviour. A neutral stimulus becomes desirable when it is associated with a desirable stimulus or it becomes undesirable when it is associated with an undesirable one. In a sense, the stimulus takes on symbolic value. For example, we respond differently to the sight of a stack of money and to a stack of paper napkins. The reason for the special reaction to money is that money has, in the past, been associated with desirable commodities, such as food, clothing, cars, electrical equipment and so on.

Basic principles of classical conditioning

Classical conditioning involves several learning principles, including acquisition, extinction, spontaneous recovery, stimulus generalisation and discrimination.

Acquisition

In laboratory experiments, a single pairing of the CS with the UCS is not usually sufficient for learning to take place. Only with repeated CS–UCS pairings does conditional responding gradually appear. The learning phase of classical conditioning, during which the CS gradually increases in frequency or strength, is called **acquisition**.

In one study (Trapold and Spence, 1960), a tone (CS) was paired with a puff of air into the eye (UCS). The puff of air caused the participants' eyes to blink automatically (UCR). Conditioning was measured as the percentage of trials in which conditional eyeblinks (CR) occurred. Note that at the beginning of the experiment, the tone elicited very few CRs. During the first 50 trials, the percentage of CRs increased rapidly but finally stabilised.

Two factors that influence the strength of the CR are the intensity of the UCS and the timing of the CS and UCS. The intensity of the UCS can determine how quickly the CR will be acquired: more intense UCSs usually produce more rapid learning. For example, rats will learn a conditioned fear response faster if they receive higher levels of a painful stimulus (Annau and Kamin, 1961). Classical conditioning of a salivary response in dogs occurs faster when the animals are given larger amounts of food (Wagner *et al.*, 1964). Generally speaking, the more intense the UCS, the stronger the CR.

The second factor affecting the acquisition of the CR is the timing of the CS and UCS. Classical conditioning occurs fastest when the CS occurs shortly before the UCS and both stimuli end at the same time. In his experiments on salivary conditioning, Pavlov found that one half-second was the optimal delay between the onset of the CS and the onset of the UCS. With shorter or longer delays between the CS and UCS, conditioning generally was slower and weaker (see Figure 7.2).

Extinction and spontaneous recovery

Once a classically conditioned response has been acquired, what happens to that response if the CS continues to be presented but is no longer followed by the UCS? This procedure, called **extinction**, eventually eliminates the CR. Returning to our classically conditioned eyeblink response, suppose that after we reduce the intensity of the UCS, we stop presenting the UCS (the puff of air). However, we do continue to present the CS (the tone).

It is important to realise that extinction occurs only when the CS occurs but the UCS does not. For example, the eyeblink response will extinguish only if the tone is presented without

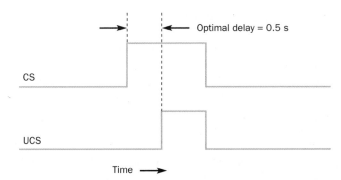

Figure 7.2 The timing of the CS and UCS in classical conditioning. The CS precedes the UCS by a brief interval of time, and both stimuli end simultaneously.

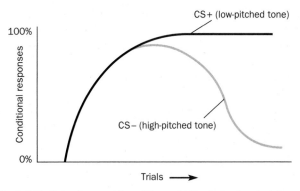

Figure 7.3 Behaviour produced through discrimination training. The CS+ is always followed by the UCS (a puff of air directed towards the eye); the CS− is always presented without the UCS.

the puff of air. If neither stimulus is presented, extinction will not occur. In other words, the subject must learn that the CS no longer predicts the occurrence of the UCS – and that cannot happen if neither stimulus is presented.

Once a CR has been extinguished, it may not disappear from the organism's behaviour permanently. Pavlov demonstrated that after responding had been extinguished, the CR would often suddenly reappear the next time the dog was placed in the experimental apparatus. Pavlov referred to the CR's reappearance after a 'time out' period as **spontaneous recovery**. He also found that if he began presenting the CS and the UCS together again, then the animals would acquire the CR very rapidly – much faster than they did in the first place.

Stimulus generalisation and discrimination

No two stimuli are exactly alike. Once a response has been conditioned to a CS, similar stimuli will also elicit that response. The more closely the other stimuli resemble the CS, the more likely they will elicit the CR. For example, Pavlov discovered that once a dog learned to salivate when it heard a bell, it would salivate when it heard a bell having a different tone or when it heard a buzzer. This phenomenon is called **generalisation:** a response produced by a particular CS will also occur when a similar CS is presented. Of course, there are limits to generalisation. A dog that learns to salivate when it hears a bell will probably not salivate when it hears a door close in the hallway.

In addition, an organism can be taught to distinguish between similar but different stimuli – a phenomenon called discrimination. Discrimination training is accomplished by using two different CSs during training. One CS is always followed by the UCS; the other CS is never followed by the UCS. For example, suppose that we regularly direct a puff of air at an animal's eye during each trial in which a low-pitched tone (CS+) is sounded, but on trials in which a high-pitched tone (CS−) is sounded, we present no air puff. At first, increased amounts of blinking will occur in response to both stimuli (generalisation). Gradually, however, fewer and fewer blinks will occur after the CS− but they will continue to be elicited

by the CS+ (see Figure 7.3). Discrimination, then, involves learning the difference between two or more stimuli. An animal learns that differences among stimuli are important – it learns when to respond to one stimulus and when not to respond to a different stimulus.

Conditional emotional responses

Many stimuli are able to arouse emotional responses, such as feelings of disgust, contempt, fear, anger, sadness, tenderness, longing or sexual desire. Many of these stimuli, such as a place, a phrase, a song or someone's voice and face, originally had no special significance. But because these stimuli were paired with other stimuli that elicited strong emotional reactions, they came, through classical conditioning, to take on emotional significance.

If you read or hear words such as 'enemy', 'ugly', 'bitter' or 'failure', you are likely to experience at least a weak negative emotional response. In contrast, the words 'gift', 'win', 'happy' and 'beauty' may elicit positive responses. These words had no effect on you before you learned what they meant. They took on their power through being paired with pleasant or unpleasant events or perhaps with descriptions of such events.

Phobias

Many people are troubled by behaviours that they wish they could stop or by thoughts and fears that bother them. Phobias are unreasonable fears of specific objects or situations, such as spiders, cars or enclosed spaces. We will look at phobias in more detail in Chapter 18. Presumably, at some time early in life, the person having the phobia was exposed to the now-feared object in conjunction with a stimulus that elicited pain or fear. For example, being stuck in a hot, overcrowded lift with a group of frightened and sweating fellow passengers might be expected to lead to a fear of lifts or perhaps even to produce a fully-fledged phobia.

Classical conditioning can occur even without direct experience with the conditional and unconditional stimuli.

For example, a child of a parent who has a snake phobia can develop the same fear simply by observing signs of fear in his or her parent. The child need not be attacked or menaced by a snake. In addition, people can develop phobias vicariously – by hearing about or reading stories that vividly describe unpleasant episodes. The imaginary episode that we picture as we hear or read a story (UCS) can provide imaginary stimuli (CSs) that lead to real conditional emotional responses (CRs).

The case of Little Albert

A famous example of an experimentally induced learned phobia is that of Little Albert. John B. Watson (you came across his work and ideas in Chapter 1) believed that behaviour had to be observable in order to be measured. He was excited by Pavlov's finding that dogs could be conditioned to respond in a specific way to a previously neutral stimulus. He and Rosalie Rayner set up the first experiment in which fear was experimentally conditioned in a human being (Watson and Rayner, 1920).

At the age of 9 months, a healthy infant called Albert B was shown to have no fear of live animals such as rats and rabbits (Albert is for ever known in textbooks as Little Albert; his real name may have been Douglas Merritte – Beck *et al.*, 2009). When a steel bar was unexpectedly struck by a claw hammer, however, he became distressed and frightened. Watson and Rayner attempted to condition fear of a previously unfeared object (a white rat) in Little Albert by pairing it with a feared stimulus (the noise of the hammer hitting the bar). They paired the rat with the noise seven times in two sessions, one week apart. When the rat was presented on its own, Albert became distressed and avoided the rat. Five days later, Albert was exposed to a number of other objects such as familiar wooden blocks, a rabbit, a dog, a sealskin coat, white cotton, the heads of Watson and two assistants, a Santa Claus mask and a packet of cotton wool. Albert showed fear of the rabbit, the dog and the sealskin coat. The initial conditioned response had generalised to some objects but not others.

Watson and Rayner's experiment is famous for two reasons. The first is that it is the earliest successful attempt at experimentally conditioning fear in a human being; the second is the number of inaccuracies reported in articles and textbooks describing the experiment (Harris, 1979). These include inaccurate information about Albert's age, the conditioned stimulus and the list of objects that Albert was believed to be frightened of after conditioning (the list includes fur pelt, a man's beard, a cat, a puppy, a glove, Albert's aunt and a teddy bear). These inaccuracies teach a valuable lesson, and that is the wisdom of consulting original sources of information. Because the study of Albert is part of psychology's history, details become distorted when information is passed down from textbook to textbook. This is a form of memory distortion described in more detail in the next chapter.

What is learned in classical conditioning?

Research shows that for classical conditioning to occur, the CS must be a reliable predictor of the UCS (Rescorla, 1991). Imagine yourself as the subject in a classical conditioning demonstration involving a tone as the CS, a puff of air into your left eye as the UCS and an eyeblink as the CR. Your psychology lecturer asks you to come to the front of the class and seats you in a comfortable chair.

Occasionally, a tone sounds for a second or two, and then a brief but strong puff of air hits your eye. The puff of air makes you blink. Soon you begin to blink during the tone, before the puff occurs. Now consider all the other stimuli in the seminar room – your tutor explaining the demonstration to the group, your colleagues' questions, squeaks from students moving in their chairs and so on. Why don't any of these sounds become CSs? Why do you blink only during the tone? After all, some of these stimuli occur at the same time as the puff of air. The answer is that among the stimuli present during the demonstration, only the tone reliably predicts the puff of air. All the other stimuli are poor forecasters of the UCS. The neutral stimulus becomes a CS only when the following conditions are satisfied:

1 The CS must regularly occur prior to the presentation of the UCS.

2 The CS does not regularly occur when the UCS is absent.

Consider another example. The smell of food is more likely to elicit feelings of anticipation and excitement about supper if you are hungry than is the smell of your mother's cologne because the smell of the food is the best predictor of a meal about to be served. Similarly, the sound of footsteps behind you as you are walking is more apt to make you afraid than the sound of a car passing by or the wind blowing in the trees because the footsteps are better predictors of being mugged or threatened with danger.

It also appears that conditioned responses are more common to novel than familiar stimuli. Pavlov had observed that a novel CS was more successfully paired with a UCS than was a familiar one. This phenomenon is known as **latent inhibition** (Lubow, 1989), and because familiar stimuli are associated less successfully with conditioning than are novel ones, this effect is called the CS **pre-exposure effect** (because participants will have already been pre-exposed to the CS). Similarly, when an organism is presented with the UCS (which may be novel) before it is used as a UCS in the experiment proper, the link between CS and UCS is weaker. This is called the UCS pre-exposure effect (Randich and LoLordo, 1979).

Why does latent inhibition occur? No one quite knows for sure, but one explanation is related to the degree of exposure to the stimulus. A familiar CS is familiar to individuals by being in the environment; because the CS is part of the environment of context then the CS becomes merged into the context of the conditioning. To use a description from signal detection theory (see Chapter 5), the signal-to-noise ratio is weak – the CS sends a weak signal because it cannot be distinguished from the context very well.

Neurobiological correlates of Pavlovian conditioning

In an experiment to determine the brain regions involved in Pavlovian fear conditioning, participants were exposed to lights that signalled the appearance of a painful electric shock (conditioned stimulus, CS) or ones that did not (Knight *et al.*, 1999). fMRI was used to monitor differences in brain activation. As training and learning progressed, the amount of neuronal activity seen during the warning CS increased in a part of the brain called the anterior cingulate, in the front of the brain. When the light and shock were not paired (i.e. they were not associated), this activation did not occur. Although the researchers suggest that this part of the brain may not be necessary for learning fear, it does facilitate the learning of fear. Another crucial structure for fear conditioning is the amygdala. You will discover more about its role in fear recognition and conditioning in Chapter 13.

After behaviourism

Pavlov's work greatly influenced his colleagues abroad, especially the pioneers of behaviourist thinking such as John B. Watson. Behaviourism was a robust and experimentally strict discipline whose principles were laid out by Watson in the first and second decades of the twentieth century. It viewed behaviour and learning in terms of stimulus and response and, as the next evolution of behaviourism described in the next section shows, reinforcement. The inner mind or introspective self-reports played no part in behaviourist thinking: these were unverifiable and held the same status as superstition to the behaviourist. Both stimulus and response could be observed and the effect of one on the other recorded. Behaviourism left a unique and historical legacy that is seen in almost all experimental work undertaken in psychology today; its effects were such that modern psychology has absorbed its principles and aims.

The torch-bearers of behaviourism, however, began to modify elements of its thinking in the mid-twentieth century and although the effects of these modifications made no significant or lasting impact on psychology by themselves, the attempts at modification did because other, more dominant approaches to studying behaviour arose from them. Two influential psychologists, whose specific work did not have a long-lasting effect on the way psychology is studied, but did bequeath a way of thinking about learning and behaviour, were Clark L. Hull (1884–1952) and Edward Chase Tolman (1886–1959).

Hull's computational approach to learning

Of all the learning theories reviewed in this chapter, Hull's is probably the most ambitious and complicated of them. In his two published books, Principles of Behaviour (1943) and A Behaviour System (1952), Hull made extremely detailed predictions about behaviour that could occur in specific situations. The books contained 153 theorems that ranged from considering how we learn to discriminate, to moving in space, to how we acquire our values, and Hull's aim was to develop a system whereby behaviour could be predicted from specified independent variables (IVs). You can quickly appreciate why the approach is seen as ambitious and complicated.

Hull organised his system by considering what Watson's behaviourism did not wish to: **intervening variables**, the variables that could modify the relationship between stimulus and response. In Hull's system, analysis of behaviour comprised four stages:

Stage 1 Analysis of the IVs from which behaviour was predicted.

Stage 2 Computing values for intervening variables.

Stage 3 Computing values at this stage, using values at stage 2.

Stage 4 Analysis of the dependent variables (DVs).

In summary, the stage process argued that knowing the values of an independent variable at stage 1 meant computing values of the intervening variables at stage 2, using these computed values to compute those at stage 3 and from this predict the outcome (or the dependent variable). Figure 7.4 summarises the main points of the system.

The number of independent variables were limitless and could range from direct stimulation (the brightness of light or

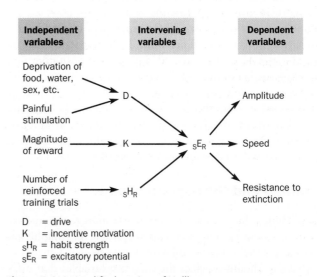

Figure 7.4 A simplified version of Hull's system.

Source: Adapted from Hill W.F., Learning: A survey of psychological interpretation, 7th edn. Published by Allyn & Bacon, Boston, MA. Copyright © 1997 by Pearson Education. By permission of the publisher.

the loudness of noise) to events that preceded the moment of study (such as degree of exercise taken or the amount of food consumed) to experiential episodes (such as the number of times a person had responded to the stimulus before). To produce a response (the DV), the IV would interact with the intervening variables at stages 3 and 4.

These intervening variables were not directly observable and were hypothetical states (you might see why Watson's behaviourism would have rejected Hull's approach). According to Hull, there were two types of intervening variable: habit strength and drive. A simple definition of each would be: habit strength is the strength of the connections that had been learned between a stimulus and a response after reinforced practice had occurred; drive is a state of activation that propels an organism to seek stimulation (a reduction in the drive would serve as a reward). (You will find out more about these concepts and their validity in Chapter 13.) A drive represents a temporary state which is produced when the body has been deprived of something it needs, such as food, water, relief from pain and so on. The greater the reward, therefore, the greater the reduction in drive: a slice of bread would not significantly reduce the drive for food, but a four-course meal might. The greater the number of times a response was followed by reinforcement, the greater the formation of habit strength and the connections between a stimulus and its response. Hull also suggested another variable, incentive motivation, which would account for the organism's response to rewards of increasing size.

As the above cursory description of the system suggests, Hull's theory was complex and followed detailed mathematical formulae. His second book contained 133 theorems which, for good measure, followed on from 17 postulates and 15 corollaries. The apparent beauty and strength of Hull's system was that one variable could be computed from another using these formulae. Where the system failed, however, was in using the values from a single experiment to predict later behaviour: this often did not work. Hull later stated that the values were meant to be regarded as illustrations rather than as fixed numbers and that, of course, values would vary across individuals. While Hull's work has not had the direct influence and impact on later theory of some other schools of learning and behaviour, it represented an ambitious and laudable attempt at pinning down behaviour to values that could be computed and used to predict later behaviour.

Tolman and the cognitive map

Like Hull, Tolman argued that there was more to the study of learning and behaviour than simply recording the stimulus and measuring the response. Tolman's view was that a theory of behaviour should consider the cognitive variables that intercede between stimulus and response: our thoughts, beliefs, attitudes, motivation to succeed and so on are all important determinants of our response to a stimulus.

Tolman's approach was called purposive behaviourism and although, like the behaviourism it followed, it concerned itself with objective and observable behaviour and the external influences that could change it, it was also concerned with the cognitive processes that guided or gave rise to that behaviour. Behaviour had a purpose; it was executed to achieve a goal, hence, purposive behaviourism.

According to Tolman, the behaviour that we engage in to achieve our goals is underpinned by our cognitions. Our cognitive processing can be measured by observing the way in which a person behaves or has experienced specific stimuli. For example, we might learn that chilli con carne tastes nicer with added ginger, cinnamon and three, rather than two, red chillies, so we make the chilli again adding these ingredients. None or any might make the chilli nicer but if none do, we experiment again either by adding or subtracting ingredients. Our experience – our cognitions – modifies our behaviour.

Tolman's most famous illustration of learning and the cognitions that lead to a response is that of reward location. If an organism finds a way of locating a reward, it may eventually find a different, more efficient method, of locating it. If you imagine yourself in a strange town centre for the first time, your first successfully navigated route to a shop may be the longest, or least efficient one. With increasing knowledge of the environment, you will eventually find the shortest, quickest route to the shop you want.

In Tolman's experiment, rats were allowed to run on a table and through an enclosed alleyway which led to various elevated pathways at the end of one of which was some food (Tolman *et al.*, 1946). When the rat had learned the location of the food, the alleyway was removed and replaced with new routes which went in different directions. Figure 7.5 shows you the difference between the two conditions.

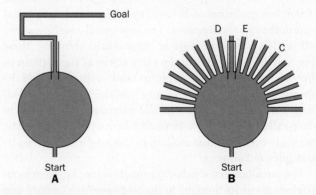

Figure 7.5 The two pathways used in Tolman's experiment. In the first, the rat takes the longer route in order to find the food. In the second, the original route is blocked and 18 new routes made available. The rats chose the tunnel marked C (that corresponding most closely to the location of the food), rather than D or E, the routes closest to that originally taken.

Source: Hill W.F., Learning: A survey of psychological interpretation, 7th edn. Published by Allyn & Bacon, Boston, MA. Copyright © 1997 by Pearson Education. By permission of the publisher.

Tolman *et al.* found that, in the second condition, the rats did not take the route they had previously learned in order to obtain the food. Instead, they took a short-cut towards the direction of the food. According to Tolman, the rat had learned a 'cognitive map' of the routes and chose the shortest one. Although this seems eminently plausible, Tolman did not seem to consider that the rat may have taken the shortest route because the smell of the food led the rodent to it.

This objection aside, Tolman's influence was important because it rejected the stiff stimulus–response (S–R) approaches of behaviourism and encouraged an emphasis on the cognitive variables that shape behaviour. The essential principles of the approach can be seen in much of modern-day experiments on transfer of learning: the principle whereby learning in one environment can be successfully transferred to a different one. Work in virtual reality technology, for example, has been able to present participants with 'virtual' versions of environments which participants can navigate and explore before encountering the actual environment, thereby assisting navigation in the real version (Wilson *et al.*, 1999).

Wilson *et al.* (1996) found that severely disabled children who explored this computer simulation were able to point successfully to objects in the real building when they later encountered it. A group of undergraduates who guessed the location of the objects, without having had the benefit of exposure to the computer simulation, performed less accurately.

Tolman died just before the beginning of what is called in psychology, 'the cognitive revolution' (see Chapter 1). However, his approach was a precursor to the cognitive revolution and prompted other disciplines, such as linguistics, to consider cognitive variables in their study. While Tolman's ideas were superseded to some extent by developments in cognitive psychology, his work could be seen as the bedrock on which cognitive psychology's general approach is based.

Operant conditioning

Habituation and classical conditioning teach us about stimuli in the environment: we learn to ignore unimportant stimuli, and we learn about those that predict the occurrence of important ones. These forms of learning deal with relations between one stimulus and another. In contrast, operant conditioning tells about the relations between environmental stimuli and our own behaviour; it is also called instrumental learning. The term 'operant' refers to the fact that an organism learns through responding – through operating on the environment. The principle behind operant conditioning is already familiar to you: when a particular action has good consequences, the action will tend to be repeated; when a particular action has bad consequences, the action will tend not to be repeated.

The law of effect

Operant conditioning was first discovered in the basement of a house in Cambridge, Massachusetts, by a 24-year-old man who would later become one of the twentieth century's most influential educational psychologists, Edward L. Thorndike. Thorndike placed a hungry cat inside a 'puzzle box'. The animal could escape and eat some food only after it operated a latch that opened the door. At first, the cat engaged in random behaviour: mewing, scratching, hissing, pacing and so on. Eventually, the cat would accidentally activate the latch and open the door. On successive trials, the animal's behaviour would become more and more efficient until it was operating the latch without hesitation. Thorndike called this process 'learning by trial and accidental success'.

Thorndike explained that the cat learned to make the correct response because only the correct response was followed by a favourable outcome: escape from the box and the opportunity to eat some food. The occurrence of the favourable outcome strengthens the response that produced it. Thorndike called this relation between a response and its consequences the law of effect.

The impact of Thorndike's discovery of the law of effect on the early development of scientific psychology would be difficult to overstate. It affected research in the study of learning in one very important way: it stimulated an enormous number of experimental studies aimed at understanding behaviour–environment interactions, a line of research that is known today as behaviour analysis. Nowhere was this effect more evident than in the work of B.F. Skinner.

Skinner and operant behaviour

Although Thorndike discovered the law of effect, Harvard psychologist Burrhus Frederic Skinner championed the laboratory study of the law of effect and advocated the application of behaviour analysis and its methods to solving human problems (Skinner, 1953, 1971; Mazur, 1994). He devised objective methods for studying behaviour, invented apparatus and methods for observing it, and created his own philosophy for interpreting it (Bolles, 1979). Moreover, he wrote several books for the general public, including a novel, Walden Two, that showed how his discoveries might be used for improving society (Skinner, 1948).

One of Skinner's most important inventions was the **operant chamber** (or Skinner box), an apparatus in which an animal's behaviour can be easily observed, manipulated and automatically recorded (as seen in Figure 7.6).

For example, an operant chamber used for rats is constructed so that a particular behaviour, such as pressing on a lever, will occasionally cause a pellet of food to be delivered. An operant chamber used for pigeons is built so that a peck at a plastic disc on the front wall will occasionally open a drawer that contains some grain. Behaviour analysts who study

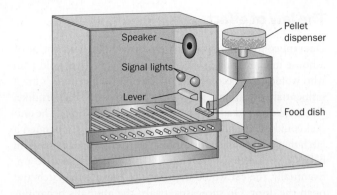

Figure 7.6 An operant chamber. (This operant chamber is used for lever pressing by rats.)

"It's a rather interesting phenomenon. Every time I press this lever, that post-graduate student breathes a sigh of relief."

human behaviour use special devices suitable to the unique characteristics of their human subjects (Baron *et al.*, 1991). In this case, instead of giving their participants some food, they give them points (as in a video game) or points exchangeable for money.

Behaviour analysts manipulate environmental events to determine their effects on response rate, the number of responses emitted during a given amount of time. Events that increase response rate are said to strengthen responding; events that decrease response rate weaken responding. To measure response rate, Skinner devised the **cumulative recorder**, a device that records each response as it occurs in time.

The invention of the operant chamber and the cumulative recorder represent clear advances over Thorndike's research methods because subjects can (1) emit responses more freely over a greater time period, and (2) be studied for longer periods of time without interference produced by the experimenter handling or otherwise interacting with them between trials.

Under highly controlled conditions such as these, behaviour analysts have been able to discover a wide range of important behavioural principles.

The three-term contingency

Behaviour does not occur in a vacuum. Sometimes a response will have certain consequences; sometimes it will not. Our daily behaviour is guided by many different kinds of discriminative stimuli – stimuli that indicate that behaviour will have certain consequences and thus sets the occasion for responding. For example, consider answering the telephone. The phone rings, you pick it up and say 'hello' into the receiver. Most of the time, someone on the other end of the line begins to speak. Have you ever picked up a telephone when it was not ringing and said, 'hello'? Doing so would be absurd, because there would be no one on the other end of the line with whom to speak. We answer the phone (make a response) only when the phone rings (the preceding event) because, in the past, someone with whom we enjoy talking has been at the other end of the line (the following event). Skinner referred formally to the relationship among these three items – the preceding event, the response and the following event – as the **three-term contingency** (see Figure 7.7).

The preceding event – the **discriminative stimulus** – sets the occasion for responding because, in the past, when that stimulus occurred, the response was followed by certain consequences. If the phone rings, we are likely to answer it because we have learned that doing so has particular (and generally favourable) consequences. The response we make – in this case, picking up the phone when the phone rings and saying 'hello' – is called an operant behaviour. The following event – the voice on the other end of the line – is the consequence of the operant behaviour.

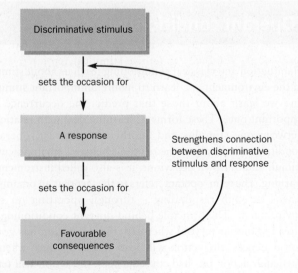

Figure 7.7 The three-term contingency.

Operant behaviour, therefore, occurs in the presence of discriminative stimuli and is followed by certain consequences. These consequences are contingent upon behaviour, that is, they are produced by that behaviour. In the presence of discriminative stimuli, a consequence will occur if and only if an operant behaviour occurs. In the absence of a discriminative stimulus, the operant behaviour will have no effect. Once an operant behaviour is established, it tends to persist whenever the discriminative stimulus occurs, even if other aspects of the environment change (Nevin, 1988; Mace *et al.*, 1990). Of course, motivational factors can affect a response. For example, you might not bother to answer the telephone if you are doing something you do not want to interrupt.

Reinforcement, punishment and extinction

Behaviour analysts study behaviour–environment interactions by manipulating the relations among components of the three-term contingency. Of the three elements, the consequence is the most frequently manipulated variable. In general, operant behaviours can be followed by five different kinds of consequence: positive reinforcement, negative reinforcement, punishment, response cost and extinction. These consequences are always defined in terms of their effect on responding.

Positive reinforcement

Positive reinforcement refers to an increase in the frequency of a response that is regularly and reliably followed by an appetitive stimulus. An appetitive stimulus is any stimulus that an organism seeks out. If an appetitive stimulus follows a response and increases the frequency of that response, we call it a positive reinforcer. For example, the opportunity to eat some food can reinforce a hungry pigeon's pecking of a plastic disc. Money or other rewards (including social rewards) can reinforce a person's behaviour. Suppose that you visit a new restaurant and really enjoy your meal. You are likely to visit the restaurant several more times because you like the food. This example illustrates positive reinforcement. Your enjoyment of the food (the appetitive stimulus) reinforces your going to the restaurant and ordering dinner (the response).

Negative reinforcement

Negative reinforcement refers to an increase in the frequency of a response that is regularly and reliably followed by the termination of an aversive stimulus. An aversive stimulus is unpleasant or painful. If an aversive stimulus is terminated (ends or is turned off) as soon as a response occurs and thus increases the frequency of that response, we call it a negative reinforcer. For example, after you have walked barefoot across a stretch of hot pavement, the termination of the painful burning sensation negatively reinforces your response of sticking your feet into a puddle of cool water.

It is important to remember that both positive and negative reinforcement increase the likelihood that a given response will occur again. However, positive reinforcement involves the occurrence of an appetitive stimulus, whereas negative reinforcement involves the termination of an aversive stimulus. Negative reinforcement is thus not the same as punishment.

Punishment

Punishment refers to a decrease in the frequency of a response that is regularly and reliably followed by an aversive stimulus. If an aversive stimulus follows a response and decreases the frequency of that response, we call it a punisher. For example, receiving a painful bite would punish the response of sticking your finger into a parrot's cage. People often attempt to punish the behaviour of their children or pets by scolding them.

Although punishment is effective in reducing or suppressing undesirable behaviour in the short term, it can also produce several negative side effects: unrestrained use of physical force (e.g. child abuse) may cause serious bodily injury. Punishment often induces fear, hostility and other undesirable emotions in people receiving punishment. It may result in retaliation against the punisher. Through punishment, organisms learn only which response not to make. Punishment does not teach the organism desirable responses.

Reinforcement and punishment are most effective in maintaining or changing behaviour when a stimulus immediately follows the behaviour. It may occur to you that many organisms, particularly humans, can tolerate a long delay between their work and the reward that they receive for it. This ability appears to contradict the principle that reinforcement must occur immediately. However, the apparent contradiction can be explained by a phenomenon called conditioned reinforcement.

Why is immediacy of reinforcement or punishment essential for learning? The answer is found by examining the function of operant conditioning: learning about the consequences of our own behaviour. Normally, causes and effects are closely related in time; you do something, and something immediately happens, good or bad. The consequences of our action teach us whether to repeat that action. Events that follow a response by a long delay were probably not caused by that response.

It is important not to confuse punishment with negative reinforcement. Punishment causes a behaviour to decrease, whereas negative reinforcement causes a behaviour to increase.

Response cost

Response cost refers to a decrease in the frequency of a response that is regularly and reliably followed by the termination of an appetitive stimulus. Response cost is a form of punishment. For example, suppose that you are enjoying a conversation with an attractive person that you have just met. You make a disparaging remark about a political party.

Your new friend's smile suddenly disappears. You quickly change the topic and never bring it up again. The behaviour (disparaging remark) is followed by the removal of an appetitive stimulus (your new friend's smile). The removal of the smile punishes the disparaging remark.

Response cost is often referred to as time-out from positive reinforcement (or simply time-out) when it is used to remove a person physically from an activity that is reinforcing to that person.

As we have just seen, there are four types of operant conditioning – two kinds of reinforcement and two kinds of punishment – caused by the occurrence or termination of appetitive or aversive stimuli. Another way to change behaviour through operant conditioning is extinction, which involves no consequence at all. See Figure 7.8.

Extinction

Extinction is a decrease in the frequency of a previously reinforced response because it is no longer followed by a reinforcer. Behaviour that is no longer reinforced decreases in frequency: it is said to extinguish. For example, a rat whose lever pressing was reinforced previously with food will eventually stop pressing the lever when food is no longer delivered. People soon learn to stop dropping money into vending machines that don't work. A young boy will stop telling his favourite 'knock-knock' joke if no one laughs at it any more.

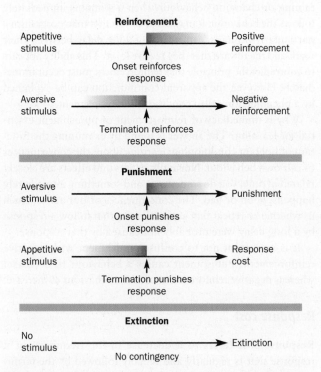

Figure 7.8 Reinforcement, punishment and extinction produced by the onset, termination or omission of appetitive or aversive stimuli. The upward-pointing arrows indicate the occurrence of a response.

Extinction is not the same as forgetting. Forgetting takes place when a behaviour is not rehearsed (or a person does not think about a particular memory) for a long time. Extinction takes place when an organism makes a response that is no longer reinforced. If the organism does not have an opportunity to make that response, it will not extinguish. For example, if you go out of town for a few weeks, you will not forget how to operate the vending machine where you often buy a bar of chocolate. However, if you put money in the machine and do not receive anything in return, your response will extinguish.

Other operant procedures and phenomena

The basic principles of reinforcement, punishment and extinction described above are used in other operant procedures to teach an organism a new response, to teach it when or when not to respond, or to teach it how to respond in a particular way.

Shaping

Most behaviour is acquired through an organism's interaction with reinforcing and punishing events in its environment. In fact, Skinner developed a technique, called **shaping**, to teach new behaviours to his subjects. Shaping involves reinforcing any behaviour that successively approximates the desired response. Imagine that we want to train a rat to press a lever when a red light is lit (the discriminative stimulus) in an operant chamber. Although the rat has used its paws to manipulate many things during its lifetime, it has never before pressed a lever in an operant chamber. And when it is first placed in the chamber, it is not likely to press the lever even once on its own.

The lever on the wall of the chamber is attached to an electrical switch that is wired to electronic control equipment or a computer. A mechanical dispenser can automatically drop pellets of food into a dish in the chamber. Thus, the delivery of a food pellet can be made dependent on the rat's pressing the lever.

Before we can shape lever pressing, we must make the rat hungry. We do so by letting the animal eat only once a day. When we know that it is hungry, we place the animal in the operant chamber and then train it to eat the food pellets as they are dispensed from the pellet dispenser. As each pellet is delivered, the dispenser makes a clicking sound. This sound is important. No matter where the rat is in the operant chamber, it can hear the sound, which indicates that the food pellet has been dispensed. Once the rat is hungry and has learned where to obtain food, we are ready to shape the desired response. We make the operation of the pellet dispenser contingent on the rat's behaviour. We start by giving the rat a food pellet for just facing in the direction of the lever. Next, we wait until the rat makes a move towards the lever. Finally, we give the rat a piece of food only if it touches the lever. Soon, our rat performs like Thorndike's cats: it makes the same response again and again.

Shaping is a formal training procedure, but something like it also occurs in the world outside the laboratory. A teacher praises poorly formed letters produced by a child who is just beginning to print. As time goes on, only more accurately drawn letters bring approval. The method of successive approximations can also be self-administered. Consider the acquisition of skills through trial and error. To begin with, you must be able to recognise the target behaviour – the behaviour displayed by a person having the appropriate skill. Your first attempts produce behaviours that vaguely resemble those of a skilled performer, and you are satisfied by the results of these attempts. In other words, the stimuli that are produced by your behaviour serve as reinforcers for that behaviour. As your skill develops, you become less satisfied with crude approximations to the final behaviour; you are satisfied only when your behaviour improves so that it more closely resembles the target behaviour. Your own criteria change as you become more skilled. Skills such as learning to draw a picture, catching a ball or making a bed are all behaviours that are acquired through shaping. After all, when a child learns these skills, they first learn behaviours that only approximate the final level of skill that they will attain. This process is perfectly analogous to the use of changing criteria in training an animal to perform a complex behaviour.

Intermittent reinforcement

So far, we have considered situations in which a reinforcing stimulus is presented after each response (or, in the case of extinction, not at all). But usually not every response is reinforced. Sometimes a kind word is ignored; sometimes it is appreciated. Not every fishing trip is rewarded with a catch, but some are, and that is enough to keep a person trying. The term **intermittent reinforcement** refers to situations in which not every occurrence of a response is reinforced.

The relation between responding and reinforcement usually follows one of two patterns: each response has a certain probability of being reinforced, or responses are reinforced after particular intervals of time have elapsed. Probability-based patterns require a variable number of responses for each reinforcer. Consider the performance of an archer shooting arrows at a target. Suppose that the archer hits the bull's-eye one-fifth of the time. On average, he will have to make five responses for every reinforcement (hitting the bull's-eye); the ratio of responding to reinforcement is five to one. The number of reinforcers the archer receives is directly proportional to the number of responses he makes. If he shoots more arrows (i.e. if his rate of responding increases), he will receive more reinforcers, assuming that he does not get tired or careless.

Behaviour analysts refer to this pattern of intermittent reinforcement as a ratio schedule of reinforcement. In the laboratory, the apparatus controlling the operant chamber may be programmed to deliver a reinforcer after every fifth response (a ratio of five to one), after every tenth, after every two hundredth or after any desired number. If the ratio is constant – for example, if a reinforcer is programmed to be delivered following every 10th response – the animal will respond rapidly, receive the reinforcer, pause a little while and then begin responding again. This type of ratio schedule is called a **fixed-ratio schedule** (specifically, a fixed-ratio 10 schedule).

If the ratio is variable, averaging a particular number of responses but varying from trial to trial, the animal will respond at a steady, rapid pace. For example, we might programme a reinforcer to be delivered, on average, after every 50 responses. This type of ratio schedule is called a **variable-ratio schedule** (specifically, a variable-ratio 50 schedule). A slot machine is sometimes programmed to deliver money on a variable-ratio schedule of reinforcement. Variable in this instance means that the person cannot predict how many responses will be needed for the next pay-off.

The second type of pattern of reinforcement involves time. A response is reinforced, but only after a particular time interval has elapsed. Imagine that you wanted to know what the weather was going to be like because your friends are due to visit, but the weather where they are is quite snowy. In order to keep abreast of the weather, you listen to the half-hourly bulletin on your local radio station. This pattern of intermittent reinforcement is called an interval schedule of reinforcement. After various intervals of time, a response will be reinforced. If the time intervals are fixed, then the animal will stop responding after each reinforcement. It learns that responses made immediately after reinforcement are never reinforced. Then it will begin responding a little while before the next reinforcer is available. This type of interval schedule is called a **fixed-interval schedule**.

If the time intervals are variable, an animal will respond at a slow, steady rate. That way, it will not waste energy on useless responses, but it will not miss any opportunities for reinforcement either. This type of interval schedule is called a **variable-interval schedule**. In a variable-interval 60-second schedule of reinforcement, a reinforcer would be delivered immediately following the first response after different time intervals had elapsed. The interval might be 30 seconds at one time, and 90 seconds at another, but, on the average, it will be 60 seconds. An animal whose behaviour is reinforced by this schedule would learn not to pause immediately after a reinforcer was delivered. Instead, it would steadily respond throughout the interval, regardless of the length of the interval.

Schedules of reinforcement are important because they show us that different reinforcement contingencies affect the pattern and rate of responding. Think about your own behaviour. How would you perform in subjects in which your grades were determined by a mid-term and a final exam, or by weekly quizzes, or by unannounced quizzes that occur at variable intervals? What kind of schedule of reinforcement is a salesperson on while waiting on potential customers?

Some people work at a slow, steady rate, but others work furiously after long periods of inactivity. Can it be that in the past their work habits were shaped by different schedules of reinforcement?

Resistance to extinction and intermittent reinforcement

A response that has been reinforced intermittently is more resistant to extinction. A response that has been continuously reinforced is much less likely to be so resistant. Baldwin and Baldwin (1998) illustrate this by citing the example of two girls who were prone to throwing temper tantrums. Connie (for it is she) received continuous reinforcement for her tantrums by her parents. Whenever she would throw a tantrum, her parents would pay her attention. Paula (for it is she), however, received only intermittent reinforcement – her parents had two other children and would only pay attention to her tantrums about once in every six episodes. This, as you now know, is a typical variable-ratio 6 method of reinforcement.

When they joined school, the teacher expressed unhappiness at the tantrums and suggested that the parents undertake a programme of extinction: they were asked to ignore all tantrums. What happened? On the first day of extinction, Connie actually experienced more tantrums (20 per cent more – Lerman and Iwata, 1995) but this dropped to zero in the next few days. Paula's behaviour, on the other hand, was less resistant to extinction. It took two to three weeks for the tantrums gradually to reduce. She continued to throw tantrums long after Connie had stopped.

Why? Well, Connie's behaviour changed because previously continuously reinforced behaviour was now not reinforced at all. Her behaviour received no reinforcement and because her tantrums did not attract the necessary attention, they stopped. They increased on the first day because Connie believed she had to produce more behaviour to receive her reinforcement. When she realised that this behaviour would not be reinforced, she stopped. Paula's behaviour, however, had previously been intermittently reinforced (every sixth tantrum) and so the new schedule had little effect on her tantrums because she had become accustomed to receiving no reinforcement for her behaviour. On the first day of the programme, therefore, she behaved as she normally would because it was pretty much like normal. Her extinction was gradual and longer than Connie's because it took a longer period to realise that reinforcement was completely absent rather than intermittent.

Generalisation and discrimination

In classical conditioning, generalisation means that stimuli resembling the CS also elicit the CR. In operant conditioning, generalisation means that stimuli resembling a discriminative stimulus also serve as discriminative stimuli for a particular response.

In operant conditioning, as in classical conditioning, generalisation can be reduced through discrimination training. In classical conditioning, discrimination means that CRs occur only in response to certain CSs and not to other, similar stimuli. In operant conditioning, discrimination means that responding occurs only when a particular discriminative stimulus is present – one that was present while responding was reinforced in the past. Responding does not occur when discriminative stimuli associated with extinction or punishment are present.

Obviously, recognising certain kinds of similarities between different categories of stimuli is a very important task in our everyday lives. When we encounter a problem to solve – for example, diagnosing a puzzling disease or improving a manufactured product – we attempt to discover elements of the situation that are similar to those we have seen in other situations and try to apply the strategies that have been successful in the past. That is, we try to generalise old solutions to new problems.

Discriminative stimuli can exert powerful control over responding because of their association with the consequences of such responding. In or out of the laboratory, we learn to behave appropriately to environmental conditions. For example, we usually talk about different things with different people. We learn that some friends do not care for sports, so we do not talk about this topic with them because we will receive few reinforcers (such as nods or smiles). Instead, we discuss topics that have interested them in the past.

Conditioned reinforcement and punishment

We have studied reinforcement mainly in terms of primary reinforcers and primary punishers. **Primary reinforcers** are biologically significant appetitive stimuli, such as food when one is hungry. **Primary punishers** are biologically significant aversive stimuli, such as those that produce pain. Behaviour can also be reinforced with a wide variety of other stimuli: money, a smile, kind words, a pat on the back, or prizes and awards. These stimuli, **called conditioned (or secondary) reinforcers**, acquire their reinforcing properties through association with primary reinforcers. Because it can be exchanged for so many different kinds of primary reinforcers in our society, money is the most common conditioned reinforcer among humans. That money is a conditioned reinforcer can be demonstrated by asking yourself whether you would continue to work if you could no longer exchange money for food, drink, shelter and other items.

Similarly, **conditioned punishers** acquire their punishing effects through association with aversive events. For example, the sight of a flashing light on top of a police car serves as a conditioned punisher to a person who is driving too fast because such a sight precedes an unpleasant set of stimuli: a lecture by a police officer and a ticket for speeding.

A stimulus becomes a conditioned reinforcer or punisher by means of classical conditioning. That is, if a neutral stimulus occurs regularly just before an appetitive or aversive stimulus, then the neutral stimulus itself becomes an appetitive or aversive stimulus. The primary reinforcer or punisher serves as the UCS because it produces the UCR – good or bad feelings. After classical conditioning takes place, these good or bad feelings are produced by the CS – the conditioned reinforcer or punisher. Once that happens, the stimulus can reinforce or punish behaviours by itself. Thus, operant conditioning often involves aspects of classical conditioning.

Conditioned reinforcement and punishment are very important. They permit an organism's behaviour to be affected by stimuli that are not biologically important in themselves but that are regularly associated with the onset or termination of biologically important stimuli. Indeed, stimuli can even become conditioned reinforcers or punishers by being associated with other conditioned reinforcers or punishers. The speeding ticket is just such an example. If an organism's behaviour could be controlled only by primary reinforcers and punishers, its behaviour would not be very flexible. The organism would never learn to perform behaviours that had only long-range benefits. Instead, its behaviour would be controlled on a moment-to-moment basis by a very limited set of stimuli. Conditioned reinforcers and punishers, such as money, grades, smiles and frowns, allow for behaviour to be altered by a wide variety of contingencies.

Conditioning of complex behaviours

The previous sections considered rather simple examples of reinforced behaviours. But people and many other animals are able to learn very complex behaviours. Consider the behaviour of a young girl learning to print letters. She sits at her school desk, producing long rows of letters. What kinds of reinforcing stimuli maintain her behaviour? Why is she devoting her time to a task that involves so much effort?

The answer is that her behaviour produces stimuli – printed letters – which serve as conditioned reinforcers. In previous class sessions, the teacher demonstrated how to print the letters and praised the girl for printing them herself. The act of printing was reinforced, and the printed letters that this act produces come to serve as conditioned reinforcers. The child prints a letter, sees that it looks close to the way it should, and her efforts are reinforced by the sight of the letter. Doing something correctly or making progress towards that goal can provide an effective reinforcer.

This fact is often overlooked by people who take a limited view of the process of reinforcement, thinking that it has to resemble the delivery of a small piece of food to an animal being taught a trick. Some people even say that because reinforcers are rarely delivered to humans immediately after they perform a behaviour, operant conditioning cannot play a major role in human learning. This assertion misses the point that, especially for humans, reinforcers can be very subtle events.

Aversive control of behaviour

Your own experience has probably taught you that punishment can be as effective as positive reinforcement in changing behaviour. Aversive control of behaviour is common in our society, from fines given to speeding motorists to the prison sentences given to criminals. Aversive control of behaviour is common for two main reasons. First, it can be highly effective in inducing behaviour change, producing nearly immediate results. A person given a fine for jumping a red light is likely, at least for a short while, to heed the sign's message. The very effectiveness of punishment as a means of behaviour change can serve as an immediate reinforcer for the person doing the punishing.

Secondly, society cannot always control the positive reinforcers that shape and maintain the behaviour of its members. However, it can and does control aversive stimuli that may be used to punish misconduct. For example, suppose that a young person's peers encourage antisocial behaviours such as theft. Society has no control over reinforcers provided by the peer group, but it can control stimuli to punish the antisocial behaviours, such as fines and imprisonment.

Escape and avoidance

Negative reinforcement teaches organisms to make responses that terminate aversive stimuli. These responses can make a stimulus cease or the organism can simply run away. In either case, psychologists call the behaviour an **escape response**: the organism endures the effects of the aversive stimulus until its behaviour terminates the stimulus. In some cases, the animal can do more than escape the aversive stimulus; it can learn to do something to prevent it occurring. This type of behaviour is known as an **avoidance response**.

Avoidance responses usually require some warning that the aversive stimulus is about to occur in order for the organism to be able to make the appropriate response soon enough. Imagine that you meet a man at a party who backs you against the wall and engages you in the most boring conversation you have ever had. In addition, his breath is so bad that you are afraid you will pass out. You finally manage to break away from him (an escape response). A few days later, you attend another party. You begin walking towards the buffet table and see the same man (discriminative stimulus) standing nearby. You decide that you will get some food later and turn away to talk with some friends at the other end of the room (an avoidance response).

As you saw earlier, phobias can be considered to be **conditioned emotional responses** – fears that are acquired through classical conditioning. But unlike most classically conditioned responses, phobias are especially resistant to extinction. If we classically condition an eyeblink response in a rabbit and then repeatedly present the CS alone, without the UCS (puff of air), the response will extinguish. However, if a person has a phobia for cockroaches, the phobia will not extinguish easily even if they encounter cockroaches and nothing bad happens. Why does the response persist?

Most psychologists believe that the answer lies in a subtle interaction between operant and classical conditioning. The sight of a cockroach makes a person with a cockroach phobia feel frightened, that is, they experience an unpleasant conditional emotional response. The person runs out of the room, leaving the cockroach behind and reducing the unpleasant feelings of fear. This reduction in an aversive stimulus reinforces the avoidance response and perpetuates the phobia.

Applications of operant conditioning to human behaviour

Instructional control

Human behaviour is influenced not only by reinforcement but also by the interactions of reinforcement with rules, that is, verbal descriptions of the relation between behaviour and reinforcement. In fact, much of our everyday behaviour involves following rules of one sort or another. Cooking from a recipe, following directions to a friend's house, and obeying the speed limit are common examples. Because rules have the potential to influence our behaviour in almost any situation, behaviour analysts are interested in learning more about how rules and reinforcement interact.

One way to investigate this interaction is to give subjects rules that are false, that is, rules that are inaccurate descriptions of the behaviour required for reinforcement (Galizio, 1979; Baron and Galizio, 1983). In such experiments, people may behave in accordance with either the rule or the reinforcement requirement. Other researchers have shown that people sometimes generate their own rules about the consequences of their behaviour (Lowe, 1979). Lowe argues that our ability to describe verbally the consequences of our behaviour explains why humans often respond differently from other animals when placed under similar reinforcement contingencies (Lowe et al., 1983). When exposed to fixed-interval schedules, animals do not respond immediately after each reinforcement. As time passes, though, responding gradually increases until the next reinforcer is delivered. Humans, on the other hand, tend to follow one of two strategies: responding very slowly or responding very rapidly. Those people who respond slowly often describe the schedule as interval-based and they respond accordingly. Those who respond rapidly usually describe the schedule as ratio-based – which it is not – and they respond accordingly. Thus, the language one uses may indeed exert some control over one's own behaviour.

Stimulus equivalence

Stimulus equivalence refers to the emergence of novel behaviour without direct reinforcement of that behaviour (Fields, 1993; Fields et al., 1995). Imagine that you were asked to learn the relationship among a group of symbols: A, B and C. Suppose further that after training without reinforcement, you discovered that A = B and A = C. How then would you respond to the following question: does B = C? You would probably reason that if A = B and A = C, then B, too, is equal to C. But notice that you were never trained or received any direct reinforcement for learning that B = C. Rather, the equivalent relationship between B and C emerged from your previous learning; hence, the term 'stimulus equivalence'.

Stimulus equivalence is an important area of research because it represents one way we learn to use and understand symbols, such as language. For example, let A represent a picture of a dog, B represent the spoken word 'dog' and C represent the printed word 'dog'. Suppose that we teach a child to point to the picture of the dog (A) and say the word 'dog' (B). In this case, the child learns that A = B and B = A. Next, suppose that we teach the child to point to the picture of the dog (A) when he sees the printed word 'dog' (C). The child learns that A = C and that C = A. What we are really interested in, though, is whether the child will have learned that the spoken word 'dog' (B) is equivalent to, or means the same thing as, the printed word 'dog' (C).

This is precisely what children learn under these circumstances, even though the equivalent relationship, B = C, has not been directly trained (Sidman and Tailby, 1982). Rather, it emerged as a consequence of the child's learning history. Understanding how stimulus equivalence develops is likely to lead to a better understanding of language development.

Does multi-tasking exist?

Multi-tasking is the 'simultaneous and/or concurrent performance of two or more tasks requiring cognitive and information processing' (Kirschner and van Merrienboer, 2013). Most of us have used the term at some point to describe, for example, our ability to complete a piece of work while emailing or listening to music or surfing the internet. The assumption is that when doing this we are multi-tasking and that we are doing it efficiently.

However, most of what we describe as multi-tasking is actually something else: task switching. Task switching is the rapid and alternate undertaking of different tasks – even when we think we are driving and using the phone, for example, we are only doing one of those things effectively; we are not engaged in both simultaneously (accidents resulting from driving and using a phone are almost as great as those observed when drinking and driving). The only circumstance in which multi-tasking is genuinely this is when a set of tasks has been so over-learned, they are automatic – such as walking and talking.

Cutting edge: Can learning chess improve cognitive ability?

It's complicated, involves concentration and recruits large amount cognitive resources. Chess is often regarded as being the sport that exemplifies the pinnacle of intellectual achievement. It's not golf, and it's certainly not darts.

In the 1970s, some researchers made some modest claims about the effect of learning chess on subsequent educational outcomes. Children who learned chess, for example, would show improved cognitive ability compared with those who did not. But these improvements then were modest and muted. In recent years, however, a number of studies has suggested that training in the game can lead to remarkable and statistically significant changes in cognitive ability, especially mathematical ability.

In his review of the field, Bart (2014) described some of this evidence. One study, for example, examined the effects of 120 hours of chess training on maths performance in African-American secondary school children living in rural Louisiana (Smith and Cage, 2000) and found that the children's maths and non-verbal ability were significantly better than a control group. A group of students in Germany who had learning disabilities and given one hour's chess training for a year, performed better at addition tasks that did those who did not learn chess (Scholz et al., 2008). A similar study of children who required special education and who were provided with 30 weeks of chess training and maths teaching or maths teaching only found that the chess group achieved better grades at the end of the year and produced better maths performance (Barrett and Fish, 2011).

Aciego et al. (2012) divided 170 6–16-year-old children into two groups: one received extracurricular instructions in chess; the other would receive instruction in other sports (such as football). The chess group out-performed the sports group on five of nine measures of intellectual ability. This is a small number of peer-reviewed studies, but why should chess training influence maths performance? Well, first, both are visuo spatial skills and it is possible that training in one will have cross-over effects to the other. Chess involves an understanding of position and the consequences of moving position, an ability to induct patterns of movement, and to evaluate quickly the consequences of making moves: many of the skills that are key to successful maths performance. These cognitive abilities are predictive of chess-playing proficiency. Second, good chess skill is associated with having good fluid reasoning, comprehension knowledge, short-term memory and processing speed (Burgoyne et al., 2016). Proficient chess-playing is also associated more with better numerical reasoning ability, than verbal or visuospatial ability (Burgoyne et al., 2016).

Cutting edge: Deliberate practice

It seems reasonable to assume that the more we practice something, the better we will become at it. Whether repeated deliberate practice does improve performance, however, depends on the domain studied. One frequently cited number is that it takes 10,000 hours of deliberate practice to become an expert – this is based on one study and this one study has been cited at least 4,200 times. Macnamara et al. (2014) in a meta-analysis of 88 studies found that deliberate practice explained 28 per cent of variance in performance for games-players, 21 per cent for music, 18 per cent for sport and 4 per cent for education (course grade was the measure). The lower percentage for the latter may be explained by the possibility that the type of deliberate practice here is less well-defined than it would be for playing the piano or playing a game. Effects of deliberate practice were stronger for activities that were very predictable (such as running). The use of objective measures of performance was associated with weaker associations between deliberate practice and performance.

Instead, we focus attention on one task at a time, switching from one to the other, applying different sets of cognitive rules as demands require. If tasks are combined and simultaneous and accompanied by interruptions, errors occur (Laxisman et al., 2007). Fox et al. (2009) found that when graduates' reading comprehension was measured after participants had been instant messaging or not while reading, test completion times and passage reading was better for the non-messaging group. The messaging group took almost twice as long to complete the tests and one and a half times as long to read a passage. Participants who are heavy media users also perform worse on tests of task-switching than do light users (Ophir et al., 2009).

Psychology in action: Drug use and abuse

Soon after Skinner outlined the principles of operant behaviour, others were quick to apply them to the study of drug action and drug-taking (Thompson and Schuster, 1968). In fact, Skinner's three-term contingency is now partly the basis of an entirely separate discipline of pharmacology known as behavioural pharmacology, the study of how drugs influence behaviour. In this field, the terms 'discriminative stimuli', 'responding' and 'consequences' translate into drugs as discriminative stimuli, the direct effects of drugs on behaviour, and the reinforcing effects of drugs, respectively. Perhaps the most interesting discovery in behavioural pharmacology is the finding that most psychoactive drugs function as reinforcers in both humans and animals.

When administered as a consequence of responding, these drugs will induce and maintain high rates of responding (Griffiths et al., 1980). There is a very high correlation between drugs that will maintain animal responding in experimental settings and those that are abused by humans (Griffiths et al., 1980). Cocaine, for example, maintains very high rates of

responding and drug consumption, to the point that food and water consumption decreases to life-threatening levels. Unlimited access to cocaine in rhesus monkeys can lead, in some cases, to death. These findings have allowed psychologists to study the abuse potential of newly available drugs in order to predict their likelihood of becoming drugs of abuse. The realisation that drugs are reinforcers has, in turn, led behavioural pharmacologists to treat cocaine dependence in people successfully by scheduling reinforcement for non-drug-taking behaviour (S.T. Higgins et al., 1994).

Just as the telephone ringing can serve as a discriminative stimulus for you answering it, the stimulus effects of drugs can also exert control over human behaviours that are reinforced by non-drug stimuli. People become more sociable under the influence of alcohol not only because the drug reduces their inhibitions, but also because people have some successful social interactions while under the drug's effects. These interactions reinforce their sociability. In fact, many laboratory studies have shown that certain drugs actually increase social responding and social reinforcement (Higgins et al., 1989).

Observation and imitation

Normally, we learn about the consequences of our own behaviour or about stimuli that directly affect us. We can also learn by a less direct method: observing the behaviour of others.

Evidence suggests that imitation does seem to be an innate tendency. Many species of birds must learn to sing the song of their species; if they are raised apart from other birds of their species, they will never sing or they will sing a peculiar song that bears little resemblance to that of normally raised birds (Marler, 1961). However, if they hear the normal song played over a loudspeaker, they will sing it properly when they become adults. They have learned the song, but clearly there were no external reinforcement contingencies; nothing in the environment reinforced their singing of the song.

Classically conditioned behaviours, as well as operantly conditioned behaviours, can be acquired through observation. For example, suppose that a young girl sees her mother show signs of fear whenever she encounters a dog. The girl herself will likely develop a fear of dogs, even if she never sees another one. In fact, Bandura and Menlove (1968) reported that children who were afraid of animals – in this case, dogs – were likely to have a parent who feared dogs, but they usually could not remember having had unpleasant direct experiences with them. We tend to imitate, and feel, the emotional responses of people we observe (see Chapter 13). The phenomenon whereby we experience a sense of reward not only by directly experiencing positive outcomes but also by

seeing people receive positive outcomes is called **vicarious reward** and the ventromedial PFC and the dorsolateral PFC is involved in this type of learning, presumably because these regions also allow us to compute value and to mentalise (Morelli et al., 2015).

Under normal circumstances, learning by observation may not require external reinforcement. In fact, there is strong evidence that imitating the behaviour of other organisms may be reinforcing in itself. However, in some cases in which the ability to imitate is absent, it can be learned through reinforcement. For example, Baer et al. (1967) studied three severely retarded children who had never been seen to imitate the behaviour of other people. When the experimenters first tried to induce the children to do what they themselves did, such as clap their hands, the children were unresponsive. Next, the experimenters tried to induce and reinforce imitative behaviour in the children. An experimenter would look at a child, say 'do this', and perform a behaviour. If the child made a similar response, then the child was immediately praised and given a piece of food. At first, the children were physically guided to make the response. If the behaviour to be imitated was clapping, then the experimenter would clap their hands, hold the child's hands and clap them together, and then praise the child and give them some food.

The procedure worked. The children learned to imitate the experimenters' behaviours. More importantly, however, the children had not simply learned to mimic a specific set of responses. They had acquired the general tendency to imitate.

When the researchers performed new behaviours and said 'do this', the children would imitate them.

Artificial intelligence

The construction of computer programs that simulate human mental functions is called artificial intelligence. The aim of such enterprises is to try to clarify the nature of mental functions. For instance, to construct a program and simulate perception and classification of certain types of pattern, the investigator must specify precisely what the task of pattern perception requires. If the program fails to recognise the patterns, then the investigator knows that something is wrong with the model or with the way it has been implemented in the program. The investigator revises the model/program, tries again, and keeps working until it finally works (or until they give up the task as being too ambitious). So far, no program is advanced enough to deal with more than a small fraction of the patterns a human can recognise.

Ideally, the task of discovering what steps are necessary in a computer program to simulate some human cognitive abilities tells the investigator the kinds of process the brain must perform. However, there is usually more than one way to accomplish a particular goal. Critics of artificial intelligence have pointed out that even if it is entirely possible to write a program that performs a task that the human brain performs – and comes up with exactly the same results – the computer may perform the task in an entirely different way. In fact, some say, given the way that computers work and what we know about the structure of the human brain, the computer program is guaranteed to work differently.

Serial computers work one step at a time and each step takes time. A complicated program will contain more steps and will take more time to execute. But we do some things extremely quickly that computers take a very long time to do. One of the best examples is visual perception. We can recognise a complex figure about as quickly as we can a simple one. For us, it takes about the same amount of time to recognise a friend's face as it does to identify a simple triangle. The same is not true at all for a serial computer. A computer must 'examine' the scene through an input device something like a television camera. Information about the brightness of each point of the picture must be converted into a number and stored in a memory location. Then the program examines each memory location, one at a time, and does calculations that determine the locations of lines, edges, textures and shapes. Finally, it tries to determine what these shapes represent. Recognising a face takes much longer than recognising a triangle.

If the brain were a serial device, its maximum speed would probably be around 10 steps per second, considering the rate at which neurons can fire (Rumelhart *et al.*, 1986). This rate is extremely slow compared with modern serial computers. Obviously, when we perceive visual images, our brain does not act like a serial device.

Parallel processing and neural networks

Instead, the brain appears to be a **parallel processor**, in which many different modules (collections of circuits of neurons) work simultaneously at different tasks. A complex task is broken down into many smaller ones, and separate modules work on each of them. Because the brain consists of many billions of neurons, it can afford to devote different clusters of neurons to different tasks (see Chapters 4 and 6). With so many things happening at the same time, the task gets done quickly.

Recently, psychologists have begun to devise models of mental functions that are based, very loosely, on the way the brain seems to be constructed. These models are called **neural networks**, and the general approach is called **connectionism**. One area of psychology where neural networks have been applied is language (see Chapter 10).

Computer simulation specialists have discovered that when they construct a network of simple elements interconnected in certain ways, the network does some surprising things. The elements have properties like those of neurons. They are connected to each other through junctions similar to synapses. Like synapses, these junctions can have either excitatory or inhibitory effects. When an element receives a critical amount of excitation, it sends a message to the elements with which it communicates, and so on. Some of the elements of a network have input lines that can receive signals from the 'outside', which could represent a sensory organ or the information received from another network. Other elements have output lines, which communicate with other networks or control muscles, producing behaviour. Thus, particular patterns of input can represent particular stimuli, and particular patterns of output can represent responses.

Investigators do not construct physical networks. Instead, they write computer programs that simulate them. The programs keep track of each element and the state of each of its inputs and outputs and calculate what would happen if a particular pattern of input is presented. Neural networks can be taught to 'recognise' particular stimuli. They are shown a particular stimulus, and their output is monitored. If the response on the output lines is incorrect, then the network is given a signal indicating the correct response. This signal causes the strength of some of the junctions to be changed, just as learning is thought to alter the strength of synapses in the brain. After several trials, the network learns to make correct responses.

If the network uses a sufficiently large number of elements, it can be trained to recognise several different patterns, producing the correct response each time one of the patterns is shown to it. In addition, it will even recognise the patterns if they are altered slightly, or if only parts of the patterns are shown. Thus, neural networks can recognise not only particular patterns but also variations on that pattern. Thus, they act as if they had learned general prototypes, not specific templates. For example, they may learn that the letter A reproduced in Times Roman font is the same as an A reproduced in Palatino font.

Learning in practice: being a student

So far, we have considered some of the important theories of learning that have made an impact on psychology and in applied contexts. Other elements of learning – such as knowledge transfer – are covered in the Chapter 8 on memory. The remainder of this chapter examines how various factors can affect academic learning and success. It explores how the use of different teaching methods can influence learning as might the type of material taught. It also considers how specific variables such as personality, learning style, group study and confidence can influence successful understanding of learned material.

Deep v. shallow learning

Perhaps the most consistently studied – and reliable – dichotomy in the psychology of learning is deep and shallow processing (or learning). In shallow learning, there is an emphasis on remembering facts, rather than on understanding them; in deep learning, there is an emphasis on knowing and understanding material, rather than on the straightforward process of remembering it.

For example, in the 1990s researchers suggested that learning could be conceptualised in five ways adapted from Hartley, 1998):

1 Learning is a means of acquiring knowledge.

2 Learning is a means of storing (remembering) information that could be used later.

3 Learning is the acquisition of facts, knowledge and methods.

4 Learning is the making sense of, or abstracting meaning from, material.

5 Learning is a process that assists the interpretation or understanding of reality.

Researchers found that those students who were classified as 'shallow' learners were most likely to adopt the first two of these learning strategies; 'deep' learners were more likely to adopt the last two. To examine whether 'depth' could be taught, Norton and Crowley (1995) studied the effect of incorporating workshops into a first-year psychology course on students' learning strategies. When the performance of those who attended all the workshops was compared with those who attended one or two or none, there was no increase in deep processing in the conscientious students. However, those who stayed with the workshops adopted a less shallow processing style as the course progressed. The results demonstrated that by encouraging students to think, to interpret and to discuss concepts and ideas – rather than asking them to learn their material by rote – this process could make them less shallow learners.

The idea was first proposed and demonstrated empirically in Sweden in the 1970s. Marton and Saljo (1976), for example, characterised deep learners as those who would agree with statements such as:

- I try to get the principal ideas.
- I try to find the main points of a chapter.

Whereas shallow learners were likely to agree with statements such as:

- I try to concentrate on remembering as much as possible.

That is, the deep learners tried to glean meaning from material whereas the shallow learners tried to remember the information. When a group of students was given a 1,400-word article on curriculum reform in Swedish universities and asked to summarise the author's main argument in one or two sentences, the results were – in light of what you now know – predictable. None of the students who were classified as shallow learners (based on their responses to a questionnaire) was able to do this; those classified as deep learners did this faultlessly.

In an article by Gibbs (1992) cited in Hartley (1998), the author lists factors which could encourage shallow processing and those which could foster deep learning. Here are some of those factors:

- Factors encouraging surface learning:
  - heavy workload;
  - excess course material;
  - reduced opportunity to study a subject in depth;
  - lack of choice in subject areas and methods of studying those subjects;
  - assessment that is threatening and anxiety-provoking.

- Factors encouraging deep learning:

  - project work;
  - learning by doing;
  - problem-based learning;
  - work that does not rely solely on remembering;
  - work that allows reflection;
  - independent learning;
  - rewarding understanding and penalising memorisation;
  - involving students in the choice of assessment method.

So, the message that seems to be clear and consistent from research is: in the contexts studied, having a 'deep' approach to study is better than one driven by a need to remember.

Controversies in psychological science: Do learning styles exist?

The issue

A mantra in education in recent years – and you may have been on the receiving end of this mantra – is that learners know how to learn best and that teaching should be delivered to fit a person's way of learning – their learning style. The content to-be-learned should match the learning style. 'Generation X', 'iGen', 'Google Generation', 'digital natives' . . . all of these terms have been created to describe a new type of learner, one who uses technology frequently, possibly efficiently, in order to discover and understand. These users – and they mean you – are surrounded by iPads, smartphones, apps, flash laptops and have become sophisticated users of technology.

Some surveys have claimed that 13–15-year-old children spend up to 15 hours using technology and media a week (Rosen, 2009), but estimates like this conflate different types of use. Two hours' worth of emailing while listening to the radio becomes eight hours of use – radio + computer + email + being online, that is, 4–2 hours for the same activity (Kirschner and van Merrienboer, 2013). We may use Google, but it does not follow that we use it effectively – research suggests that many users lack the prior knowledge or expertise to find exactly what they need on the site and whether this material is relevant (Walraven *et al.*, 2008).

That aside, is there any evidence that we do each have a distinctive learning style, a preferential way of learning which means that content and instruction should be delivered, discussed and explained via a different medium?

The evidence

One of the immediate issues we encounter when trying to answer this question is: how many learning styles are there and what are they? One widely adopted measure of learning styles is the Student Process Questionnaire (SPQ) (Biggs, 1987), a 42-item measure of a deep approach to learning (evaluating material critically; reading widely; engaging in discussion), a surface approach to learning (e.g. rote learning) and an achieving approach to learning (where the student has a strong intention to succeed and obtain high grades).

But Biggs's styles are not the only type. Coffield *et al.* (2004) identified 71 of them. There are visual and verbal styles, impulsive and reflective styles, holistic and analytic styles, amongst others (Kirschner and van Merrienboer, 2013). In learning styles studies, people are classified according to the type/group they belong to, rather than receiving a score indicating their position on a dimension. The latter would help indicate whether someone expressed more of a specific style than others (Druckman and Porter, 1991). Kirschner and van Merrienboer (2013) have identified a number of problems with this approach: the basis on which group classification is made has not been peer-reviewed; people do not fit into a categorical style because cognitive differences are gradual not nominal; the basis on which classifications are made are inadequate (the measures are poor and based on self-report); people are assigned to a group arbitrarily based on the mean/median obtained via such measures; and there are too many styles to be of any practical use in the classroom and lecture hall.

In their review of learning styles studies, Pohrer and Pashler (2012) found that only 20 studies in fields as varied as psychology, science and medicine had used the correct experimental design and most of these had produced negative results (e.g. Massa and Mayer, 2006; Cook *et al.*, 2007). Of the three studies which claimed to find evidence for learning styles, one did not include the measures on which the data were derived and only one produced a statistically significant result. In two, there were mixed results – half the tests were positive; half were negative.

What people say about how they prefer to learn is sometimes at odds with how they can best learn. An early meta-analysis found that learning preferences were not significant predictors of learning outcomes (Greene and Eaton, 2016). Massa and Mayer (2006) investigated the effect of self-reported learning style (visual, verbal) on cognitive performance and found a weak relationship between these and measures of spatial ability. Van Merrienboer (1990) examined two different methods of teaching computer programming by matching learning styles to a particular approach to teaching. One approach involved generating new code (advantaging 'impulsive' learners); the other involved studying and completing existing code (advantaging 'reflective' learners). There was a tendency for the reflective group to perform better than the impulsive group at the completion task but both groups performed better at the completion than the generation task.

Students can also be quite poor at controlling their own learning, largely because they do not know to apply strategies to do this independently (Lee *et al.*, 2010). In one study, researchers gave a group of low general ability hairdressers full control of what they decided to learn. Rather than stretch themselves, the students practiced what they liked and what they were already good at, not tasks they did not like, found difficult or were unfamiliar with. They were able to extend the types of tasks they learned with electronic prompting, regular coaching and tutor advice.

In some cases, the mode of learning might destroy learning itself – a process called mathemathantic (from the Greek, *mathema* = learning; *thatos* = death) (Clark, 1989). An assumption is made that a learning style will benefit all types of learning. However, there is no evidence for this – people with visual learning styles are no better at learning words visually versus auditorily (Constantinidou and Baker, 2002) and no better at processing verbal or pictorial information if they are self-described visualisers or verbalisers (Massa and Meyer, 2006). A study of medical students found no benefit of matching learning to sensitive/concrete and intuitive/abstract learning styles (Cook *et al.*, 2009).

▶

Controversies in psychological science: *Continued*

Conclusion

Kirschner and van Merrienboer (2013) argue that a better way of helping people to learn better is not to indulge the concept of learning styles, which has poor validity and little evidence to support it, but to tailor instruction to cognitive ability. If cognitive ability and prior learning are taken into account when instructing, this will benefit a student's learning. They cite an example from Kalyuaga *et al.* (2003). When students were divided into those with low prior knowledge or high prior knowledge, LPK students were better at learning from examples than from solving problems. HPK students showed the opposite pattern. This answers the 'why' question – why do some approaches work? rather than the 'what' question – what works? (the more superficial of the two questions).

Cheaters profiled

As a psychology student, you will probably have received a number of imprecations regarding the evils of plagiarism. This is important counsel because using someone else's words without crediting them is theft (and also not very clever). You may even have used the software, TurnItIn (TIN), which tells you the proportion of your work which overlaps significantly with published sources or sources in its archive (such as past students' essays and lab reports).

Despite the strong advice, and this software, some students continue to cheat. Is there something special about these students that distinguishes them from the honest? Williams *et al.* (2010) examined the personality characteristics of self-reported student cheaters and found that they were more likely to express the Dark Triad – Machiavelianism (being cynical, amoral and manipulative), narcissism (being arrogant, self-centred and self-enhancing) and psychopathy (having an erratic lifestyle and being manipulative, callous and antisocial), as well as being low in agreeableness and conscientiousness. When the researchers examined these traits more closely, only psychopathy was found to be a significant predictor. Those scoring high on this trait were more likely to cheat. This finding was confirmed in a naturalistic study using TIN – those who were found to plagiarise, according to the software, were more likely to show psychopathy.

There was also a relationship between cheating and poor verbal ability. Self–reported cheating was higher in men than women but this sex difference disappeared when plagiarism was measured directly via TIN.

Changes in students' views about their learning

Although the perception and understanding of material learned across a degree changes, a student's degree of academic passion changes very little across their period of study (Schellenberg and Bailis, 2015). A study from Princeton University found that the instructor's way of expressing him or herself, information about the course and an absence of criticism about the course from others was significantly related

Cutting edge: OMG, should I text in class?

The ubiquity of mobile phones and tablets now means that whereas twenty years ago, as a student, all you might have brought to classes were pens, pads and books, you can now bring a host of other electronic distractions. Some of these are thought to be put to good use – using laptops to take notes during lectures, for example (although note that the evidence suggests that talking notes with a pen and paper leads to better learning than does typing in a tablet or laptop). Mobile phones – checking updates from What's App, Facebook, Twitter and myriad other attention-seeking platforms, as well as texting – are also a common sight in classrooms.

Does using mobile phones – and texting on mobile phones specifically – impair learning in the classroom? Research on divided attention, which you'll read more about in Chapter 9, clearly suggests that it would. To test this directly, Gingerich and Lineweaver (2014) randomly assigned students to conditions in which they texted a prescribed conversation during class or did not use a phone and did not text. The students were given a quiz after the lecture which tested their knowledge and understanding of the content. In two studies, students who didn't text remembered more and understood more than did students who texted. They were also more confident in their performance. Students who texted also acknowledged that they would learn less.

to post-course evaluations in general (Babad *et al.*, 1999). The features that predicted evaluations at introductory level were not those that predicted evaluations at advanced level 4. The only consistent feature was that workload and mark leniency were weak predictors of course selection.

The features of advanced courses which were good predictors of a positive evaluation were: interesting readings, having an interesting course and instructor's knowledge and expertise. None of the personality factors – such as the lecturer's sense of humour or approachability – predicted these students' evaluations of their course. Only for the introductory students was there a (positive) relationship between the instructor's humour and the post-course evaluation.

The study appears to show that as students progress through their degree, what they value in a course changes. They become more concerned with academic substance and less with 'lighter' features such as the instructor's sense of humour. At the beginning of their education, first year students are sampling the many different things that university or college has to offer. The instructor's sense of humour and expression was important to first year students, but advanced students valued the quality of their courses and teaching, such as the content of courses and how well they were taught and prepared. The authors argue that the respondents in their sample may not be representative (because Princeton undergraduates have different course structures to those of others) but suggest that the results could be generalised to similar institutions.

A study from the University of Missouri-Columbia found that by graduation, students placed less emphasis on extrinsic factors (such as earning money, gaining popularity and how they looked) and more on intrinsic factors (valuing community, intimacy and growth) (Sheldon, 2005). The greater the shift to intrinsic values, the greater the sense of psychological well-being students felt as they progressed through college. You might find that the findings of these studies mirror your own experience as a psychology student.

Probably one of the most challenging (i.e. difficult) courses you will take in psychology will be research methods. But are there predictors of good research methods performance, beyond mathematical ability? A study from South Africa suggest that there are (Payne and Israel, 2010). They examined predictors of performance in a research design and analysis course in 80 students. Secondary school performance and age were the best predictors, but among the non-demographic characteristics were self-efficacy, help-seeking and having a reflective learning style. Those more proficient in maths were better at the course.

Personality and academic success

An analysis of 109 studies examining the relationship between psychosocial and study skill factors, grade success and student retention (how likely students are to stay on their course) has shown that there is a moderately significant relationship between remaining in college and (i) keeping academic goals, (ii) a person's capability to assess the ability to succeed academically and (iii) good academic skills. The best predictors of grade success are motivation to achieve and the student's ability to assess accurately his or her ability to succeed (Robbins *et al.*, 2004). The results seem to tally with those from the workplace where highly motivated employees and those capable of self-evaluation are those who are most successful.

However, personality may be a better predictor of academic performance than are grades or other factors. Openness to experience and agreeableness have been found to be significant predictors of academic success, but extraversion, neuroticism and conscientiousness have not (you will find a detailed description of these personality types in Chapter 14) (Farsides and Woodfield, 2003). Of all the variables studied, however, a non-personality factor – seminar attendance – was the strongest predictor of success. This said, a meta-analysis of studies exploring the relationship between personality and academic performance found that one personality variable in particular was important (Poropat, 2009). In a sample totalling over 70,000 participants from secondary and tertiary education the greatest correlation – it predicted performance better than did intelligence – was between performance and conscientiousness.

Chamorro-Premuzic *et al.* (2008) found that the personality characteristics of the lecturer interact with the students' own and these influence perceptions of teaching. Students tended to prefer lecturers with personalities similar to their own, unless lecturers were high on a trait called neuroticism. They especially preferred lecturers who were emotionally stable and conscientious.

Variations in a number of personality traits can interact with other variables to influence academic performance (Ackerman *et al.*, 2011). Caprara *et al.* (2011), for example, examined whether openness to experience and conscientiousness, as well as self-efficacy, influenced academic performance in 412 Italian children in a longitudinal study conducted from 13 to 19 years. They found that openness and self-efficacy at age 13 predicted academic performance in junior school, regardless of socioeconomic status. Grades at junior school contributed to self-efficacy beliefs at 16 and these beliefs predicted later academic success (regardless of previous grades). Conscientiousness had an indirect influence on achievement as its effect was mediated by self-efficacy.

Confidence

One variable that might mediate the relationship between learning style and academic success is confidence. A small number of studies has shown that the relationship between a person's confidence in performing well and actual performance, however, may not be that great. Studies of students have shown that those who do best are those that do not express over-generous levels of confidence: the more modestly self-assessed students performed best. Conversely, those who rate their confidence in their ability highly tend not to do as well as their self-image would predict. In one study of students from university courses in Israel, the Netherlands, Palestine, Taiwan and the US, confidence ratings were seen to be nation-dependent in some cases (Lundeberg *et al.*, 2000).

Palestinian students expressed greatest confidence in their ability (whether they were actually correct or incorrect in answering questions). Taiwan students were the least confident but were better able to discriminate between their performance when they knew they were right and when they were wrong. That is, their confidence rating was higher when they got the answer right, and lower when they got the answer wrong. Other countries such as the US, the Netherlands and Israel showed comparable performance and confidence scores. There was no significant difference between men or women in their confidence ratings and the relationship between this and performance.

There are aspects of learning that can be positively influenced by confidence, however. Participants who scored higher in conscientiousness and openness tend to be more confident about their reading and writing ability (Pulford and Sohal, 2006). Agreeableness and perfectionism predicted confidence in numeracy skills. People who expressed least confidence in speaking tended to be introvert, female, low on conscientiousness and were not especially motivated to be organised. Confidence in the ability to manage time was found in participants who were conscientious, extravert and motivated to be organised. All three personality traits predicted Grade Point Average in the first year (the greater the trait expressed, the higher the GPA).

Groupwork

Do people learn better individually or in groups? It depends on what is being learned, but evidence suggests that when people work in groups, and there is a great deal of interdependence among members, the learning outcomes are better (Tomcho and Foels, 2012). Students who preferred group work and had lower levels of anxiety about statistics, achieved a higher grade percentage at the end of their course, in one study (Gorvine and Smith, 2015).

The best way to understand a textbook

This textbook should provide you with enough basic information and further reading for you to understand important concepts, theories and findings in psychology research, to write your essays, sit your course exams or complete your course projects. But are there specific ways of reading this textbook that can maximise your learning?

According to research by Slotte and Lonka (1999), there is. They studied 226 high school students' methods of taking notes from a philosophical textbook, the content of which would be examined formally before students enrolled on a course. Half of the sample were asked to review their notes during note-taking; the other half were not given any explicit instructions. The quality and quantity of the notes was then analysed and correlated with exam performance.

They found that reviewing notes during essay writing was associated with good performance on questions that required comprehension of the text and deep, detailed knowledge. However, reviewing these notes did not help with drawing original conclusions about the text. Importantly, they note that students summarising the text in their own words with their own subheadings and structure performed better than those students who took verbatim notes or took notes in the exact order in which the material appeared in the text. This finding suggests that deeper understanding (and better performance) comes from having read and understood material in a text. The key to this is being able to express the text's ideas in your own words. If you have not done this, you haven't understood the text.

Is learning by note-taking from this book different from note-taking from a lecture? A meta-analysis suggests that the relationship between note-taking and encoding of information in a text or during a lecture is significant but modest (Kobayashi, 2005). Inexperienced students benefit more from note-taking than do experienced ones, possibly because the latter can perform successfully without substantial note-taking. Taking notes from a visual presentation was less effective than taking notes from an audio source, presumably because paying attention to the lecture together with meeting the mechanical demands of note-taking interfered with the writing.

Cutting edge: Writing skills and academic achievement

Throughout your studies, lecturers will stress upon you the importance of (i) good writing and (ii) writing regularly and often. The stress is good because writing is itself a learning skill. Some people, such as Linus Pauling, used to say that if he wanted to know about a subject, he would write a book about it. Practicing writing enhances your thinking skills, your ability to marshal an argument, your ability to select and assess material and many other advantageous cognitive skills. A large study from Chile has confirmed the relationship between writing skill and academic achievement (Preiss *et al.*, 2013).

It examined the relationship between writing skill and University success in 2,597 students. Writing skill was assessed using a two-page essay on a general subject (e.g. press freedom) that students were required to write at enrolment. Specific writing skills measured included orthography (spelling, punctuation), vocabulary, text structure (introduction, argument, conclusion), coherence, use of paragraphs,

▶

Cutting edge: *Continued*

quality of argument, presence of a thesis, counterargument and general text quality.

Even when taking into account socio-economic variables or university admissions test scores, writing skill predicted first-year university grades: the better the writing skill, the better the grade. But what was also illuminating was the finding that this relationship extended across eight semesters of learning. The researchers looked at the achievement records of 1,616 students and found that writing skill predicted academic success across the degree. Writing skill was found to be a better predictor of academic achievement across the programme than was mathematical skill. This study was based on one cohort admitted to one university in one country. Would you expect these results to generalise to other students? And why do you think writing skills were such a strong predictor of academic success?

Studying psychology – An international perspective

You might think that most psychology students study similar topics over similar periods of time across the world. In a sense, this is right but some countries teach psychology in different ways; some have only recently developed psychology degrees; some teach psychology to achieve a particular end such as training in educational psychology. How does the teaching of psychology differ across the world?

In Australia, psychology departments exist in almost all universities (in 2006 only three did not have one) (Wilson and Provost, 2006). Like those in the UK, departments in the older universities evolved from philosophy departments in the early twentieth century. Again, like the UK, the 1980s saw an expansion of Australian institutes calling themselves universities and thus offering university psychology degrees (the parallel in the UK is the transmogrification of the polytechnics into universities in the early 1990s). Like the UK, courses are accredited by a professional organisation (the Australian Psychological Society). Psychology students in Australia can study three types of psychology degrees: a three-year degree that does not prepare the student to practise psychology; a four-year degree, which does and involves the writing of a thesis and the study of ethics; and graduate degrees.

Courses are slightly different in Italy. Here, in 2006, students could study for a three-year degree, which qualifies them to practise as a 'psychological assistant' in a restricted range of areas (Prandini and McCarthy, 2006), or a five-year degree which involves an additional two years of study which qualifies the student to practise. The student then pursues a graduate programme in a specific area to specialise further. All public school teachers in Italy have to complete a postgraduate course which involves training in psychology (Prandini and McCarthy, 2006).

Surprisingly for a country that is the birthplace of modern psychology, Germany only established its first professional curriculum in psychology in 1941 (Hodapp and Langfeldt, 2006). In the 1960s, there were 18 universities offering psychology to 2,000 students taught by 31 professors. In the 1980s, there were 30 universities teaching 18,000 students. By 2006, there were around 43 universities with 450 professors teaching 32,000 students (Hodapp and Langfeldt, 2006).

Approximately 70 per cent of students are women, a figure that is echoed in the UK. German universities are changing and as of 2004, a Diplom qualification now entitles students to work in a profession related to psychology. As with all the degrees mentioned so far, the emphasis in German education is on teaching skills that will enable students to apply scientific principles to human behaviour.

The large number of departments in Germany, and other countries, isn't seen elsewhere. Greece, for example, in 2006 had four psychology departments offering two types of 'undergraduate' degree: a Ptychion (Bachelor's) degree, lasting four years, and a Master's degree (Metaptychiako Diploma) in an area such as clinical, school/educational or organisational psychology – this can last up to three years and involves internship at a relevant institution (Georgas, 2006).

The compactness of provision in Greece contrasts with Russia: 100 psychology departments have been established in the past decade (Karandashev, 2006). In 2006, students at Russian universities could study for four (Bachelor's degree) or five years (Specialist degree), in programmes regulated by the Ministry of Education (Karandashev, 2006). The four-year course trains students in general psychology; the five-year course prepares them for professional work. While Russia has divested itself of its communist shackles (partly), China has not. Psychology became an independent university discipline in China in 1960 but, following the 'Cultural Revolution' of 1966–76 and the resultant closure of all universities, psychology was attacked as pseudoscience (Zhang and Xu, 2006). Since 1980, however, psychology has clawed its way back into the university curriculum and is now one of the most popular science subjects (Zhang and Xu, 2006).

Finally, and interestingly given the politically fractious times in which we live, what of Iran? Iran was no academic late-developer: it was running courses in psychology in the 1920s. In 2006, 19 universities offered psychology courses, with the BS (Bachelor of Science) degree being awarded after four years of study (Alipour, 2006). In 2003, the Islamic Iranian parliament passed a law that granted equal status to medical and psychological counselling services.

Psychology in action: What will make you a better student?

You know the drill by now. You've lectures to attend, essays to write, lab reports to complete, papers to find, chapters in very large books to read. . . it can seem overwhelming. And when it comes to exam time with all the revision preparation that's expected and necessary, it can feel very overwhelming. Are there any steps you can take to improve your learning, any skills or techniques you could learn to make the process of learning easier and more effective?

Actually, yes, there are. And research from psychology – particularly, cognitive psychology- has helped determine which they are (Roediger and Pyc, 2012; Dunlosky et al., 2013; Dunn et al., 2013).

A number of techniques has been cited as helpful to learning: highlighting in textbooks, re-reading passages from a book or paper, testing yourself, writing, mnemonics, being asked inquisitive questions, and cramming. However, only some of these work: that is, only some show demonstrable effects on learning. And you might be surprised – and, in one case, disappointed – by what they are.

One technique that has moderate success is 'elaborative questioning/interrogation' and 'self-explanation'. That is, being prompted (or being prompted by yourself) to think about why something has happened or been found can help learning. For example, in one study undergraduates were presented with a list of sentences describing the actions of a man (e.g. 'The hungry man got into the car') (Pressley et al., 1987). One group was encouraged to ask questions about why the man behaved in this way. A second group were provided with an explanation. And third just read the sentences. They were then asked questions about the statements they had been presented with. The results were astonishing. The 'why' group was accurate 72 per cent of the time, compared with 37 per cent for the other two groups. This finding is not uncommon and extends beyond simple sentences. The same approach has been found to be successful in students who read a new chapter for a biology class and were prompted to answer questions (Smith et al., 2010).

Does underlining or highlighting work? The evidence suggests that it doesn't although the research is hampered by poor studies. Students vary in the amount of text they highlight. If the text is highlighted for students by someone else, however, they do remember those sections and adjacent sections better (Cashen and Leicht, 1970; Lorch, 1989). Highlighting is a shallow, almost automatic activity. Its success probably depends on what you highlight and what you later do with the highlighted section. For example, if you went through a text

highlighting, then took notes from the highlighted sections and only summarised the sections you needed, would it help you? (I'll let you into a little secret, this is how I – GNM – take notes in preparation for writing the editions of this book and lengthy introductions to journal papers.)

Re-reading seems to have little effect on learning, neither does the use of mnemonics (in the context of undergraduate learning).

Interleaving your work – alternating different types of work – can be beneficial, especially for mathematics performance (Dunlosky et al., 2013) but also for other types of cognitive performance. A related technique is spacing. You'll discover more about this in the next chapter, but spacing your practice is associated with better performance on a range of abilities and skills than is massed practice (cramming). It is a very old technique – Ebbinghaus used it to remember nonsense syllables (more in the next chapter) – but is reliable (Cepeda et al., 2006; Wahlheim et al., 2011). In a typical spacing exercise, you might have to learn something for five minutes every five minutes and an irrelevant activity would be introduced every five minutes, thus breaking up or chunking learning. Studies which have compared interleaving with spaced learning produce comparable results (Roher and Pashler, 2010). Some effects of spacing and interleaving on learning can be seen in Figure 7.9. Learning German–Japanese word pairs was found to be more effective, as was visual acuity, after a space of 12 hours than 24 hours (Kornmeier et al., 2014).

The best example of blocked practice/learning of course is cramming (especially for exams). There is no evidence that this works in the long-term or the short-term. As William James (1890) remarked: 'The reason why cramming is such a bad mode of study is now made clear. . . . Things learned in a few hours, on one occasion, for one purpose, cannot possibly form many associations with other things. . . . Speedy oblivion is the almost inevitable fate of all that is committed to memory in this single way' (p. 445). Think of speedy oblivion the next time you're tempted to do a bit of cramming before an exam.

And so we come to the technique that is probably the most effective way of learning, but is one that you will probably like the least. We know you will like it the least because studies of students tell us so. The method is: testing, especially frequent testing. No other technique described here is as effective nor as reliable in facilitating learning. The short conclusion is: students remember more when they're regularly

▶

Psychology in action: *Continued*

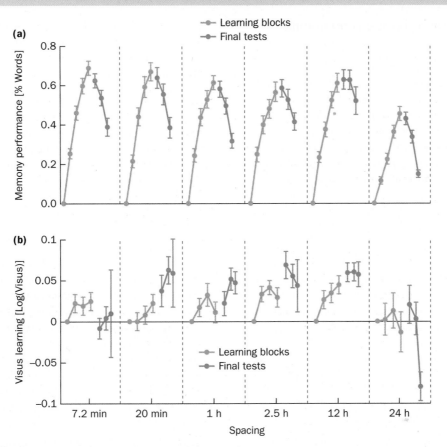

Figure 7.9 Some effects of spacing on cognitive performance and learning.

tested on material (Carpenter, 2012; Roediger and Pyc, 2012). In a typical experiment, one group is asked to learn material and is tested while a second group learns material and then re-studies it. On a subsequent test, performance of the first group is significantly better than the second's (Roediger and Karpicke, 2006; Karpicke and Grimaldi, 2012). If students are asked to read textbook chapters for an introductory psychology class or are asked to read the chapters and then this reading is tested in daily quizzes, the latter group achieve better scores when later tested about the textbook material (Batsell *et al.*, 2017).

Here's another example (Roediger and Karpicke, 2006). In one study, students are given passages to read and are told they would be tested later. One group reads the passage on four different occasions. One group reads the passage on three occasions and is then tested. One group reads the passage once and is tested three times. They then free recall (unprompted) as much of the passage as they can. Who do you think would perform better? Students in the experiment who were asked this – the same ones who took part in the actual experiment – said they thought the first group would perform best. The group that performed best was the third. There was also an interesting effect of time. If recall was measured immediately, the result was consistent with the students' prediction. However, after a week, this reversed: group one performed the worst; group three performed the best. Speedy oblivion. A good way to help you learn using this technique would be for a tutor to set you a series of quizzes, about 5–10 minutes long, regularly. You can also self-test. Use flashcards – this works, too (Wissman *et al.*, 2012).

Chapter review

Habituation and classical conditioning

- Habituation screens out stimuli that experience has shown to be unimportant. This form of learning allows organisms to respond to more important stimuli, such as those related to survival and reproduction.
- Classical conditioning occurs when a neutral stimulus occurs just before an unconditional stimulus (UCS) – one that automatically elicits a behaviour. The response that an organism makes in response to the unconditional stimulus (the UCR) is already a natural part of its behaviour; what the organism learns to do is to make it in response to a new stimulus (the conditional stimulus, or CS). When the response is made to the CS, it is called the conditional response, or CR.
- The relationship between the conditional stimulus and unconditional stimulus determines the nature of the conditional response. Acquisition of the conditional response is influenced by the intensity of the unconditional stimulus and the delay between the conditional stimulus and unconditional stimulus.
- Extinction occurs when the conditional stimulus is still presented but is no longer followed by the unconditional stimulus; the conditional response may show spontaneous recovery later, even after a delay.
- Generalisation occurs when stimuli similar to the conditional stimulus used in training elicit the conditional response.
- Discrimination involves training the organism to make a conditional response only after a particular conditional stimulus occurs.
- Classical conditioning can also establish various classes of stimuli as objects of fear (phobia) or of sexual attraction (fetishes). For classical conditioning to occur, the conditional stimulus must not only occur immediately before the unconditional stimulus, but it must also reliably predict the occurrence of the unconditional stimulus.

After behaviourism

- Hull's theory of learning reduced behaviour to numerical values; using these values Hull's system sought to predict behaviour.
- Tolman's theory of learning argued that stimulus–response models were too simplistic and suggested the concept of intervening variables – variables which mediated the relationship between a stimulus and the response to it. Tolman's research led to the coining of the term cognitive map to describe our ability to manipulate three-dimensional environments in the mind.

Operant conditioning

- The law of effect specifies a relation between behaviour and its consequences. If a stimulus that follows a response makes that response become more likely, we say that the response was reinforced. If the stimulus makes the response become less likely, we say that it was punished. The reinforcing or punishing stimulus must follow the behaviour almost immediately if it is to be effective.
- The process of operant conditioning helps adapt an organism's behaviour to its environment.
- Skinner described the relation between behaviour and environmental events as a three-term contingency: in the presence of discriminative stimuli, a consequence will occur if and only if an operant response occurs.
- A reinforcer is an appetitive stimulus that follows an operant response and causes that response to occur more frequently in the future.
- A punisher is an aversive stimulus that follows an operant response and causes it to occur less frequently in the future.
- If an aversive stimulus is terminated after a response occurs, the response is reinforced through a process called negative reinforcement. The termination of an appetitive stimulus can punish a response through a process called response cost.
- Extinction occurs when operant responses are emitted but not reinforced, which makes sense because organisms must be able to adapt their behaviour to changing environments.
- Complex responses, which are unlikely to occur spontaneously, can be shaped by the method of successive approximations.
- Various types of schedule of reinforcement have different effects on the rate and pattern of responding. When a response is reinforced intermittently, it is more resistant to extinction, probably because an intermittent reinforcement schedule resembles extinction more than a continuous reinforcement schedule does.
- Discrimination involves the detection of essential differences between stimuli or situations so that responding occurs only when appropriate.
- Generalisation is another necessary component of all forms of learning because no two stimuli, and no two responses, are precisely the same. Thus, generalisation embodies the ability to apply what is learned from one experience to similar experiences.

- The major difference between classical conditioning and operant conditioning is in the nature of the contingencies: classical conditioning involves a contingency between stimuli (CS and UCS), whereas operant conditioning involves a contingency between the organism's behaviour and an appetitive or aversive stimulus. The two types of conditioning complement each other. The pairings of neutral stimuli with appetitive and aversive stimuli (classical conditioning) determine which stimuli become conditioned reinforcers and punishers.

Conditioning of complex behaviours

- Much behaviour is under the control of aversive contingencies, which specify particular behaviours that are instrumental in either escaping or avoiding aversive stimuli.
- In conditioned flavour aversions, there is a delay between tasting a poison and getting sick; the rule that a reinforcing or punishing stimulus must immediately follow the response cannot, therefore, apply.
- We are able to acquire both operantly and classically conditioned responses through observation and imitation; we can learn to modify and combine responses learned in other contexts to solve new problems. This is referred to as insight.

- Behaviour analysts argue that behaviour is governed by external causes, such as discriminative stimuli and environmentally based reinforcers and punishers; cognitive psychologists maintain that behaviour is controlled by internal causes, such as thoughts, images, feelings and perceptions.

Factors influencing learning in an academic context

- Research has shown that various factors can influence academic learning, including personality, group study, the type of learning materials and the style of teaching.
- Students normally begin courses by adopting superficial learning styles geared towards achieving grades and covering the basics; as they progress, learning becomes deeper and more thoughtful.
- While beginning students evaluate courses based on superficial factors, such as the lecturer's sense of humour, more advanced students value the lecturer's knowledge and the quality of the learning materials more.
- The key to understanding material in textbooks is to underline the parts that you consider relevant first and then to write these parts in your own words.

Suggestions for further reading

Learning – general reading

Healy, A.F., Jones, M., Lalchandani, L. and Tack, L.A. (2017) Timing of quizzes during learning: effects on motivation and retention. *Journal of Experimental Psychology. Applied, in press.*

Malott, R.W. and Shane, T.W. (2013) *Principles of Behaviour* (7th edn). Boston, MA: Prentice Hall.

Martin, G.L. and Pear, J. (2014) *Behaviour Modification: What is it and how to do it* (10th edn). Boston, MA: Prentice Hall.

Mazur, J.E. (2017) *Learning and Behaviour.* London: Routledge.

Milenberger, R. (2015). *Behaviour Modification* (6th edn). London: Wadsworth.

Olson, M. (2012) *Introduction to the Theories of Learning* (9th edn). Boston, MA: Prentice Hall.

Terry, S. (2017) *Learning and Memory* (5th edn). Boston, MA: Allyn & Bacon.

Good, comprehensive accounts of the psychology of learning.

Learning – specific reading

Beck, H.P., Levinson, S. and Irons, G. (2009) Finding Little Albert. *American Psychologist*, 64, 605–14.

Harris, B. (1979) Whatever happened to Little Albert? *American Psychologist*, 34, 2, 151–60.

McSweeney, F.K. and Murphy, E.S. (2014). *Wiley-Blackwell Handbook of Operant and Classical Conditioning.* London: John Wiley.

Pashler, H., McDaniel, M., Rohrer, D. and Bjork, R (2009). Learning styles. *Psychological Science in the Public Interest*, 9, 105–19.

Watson, J.B. and Rayner, R. (1920) Conditioned emotional reactions. *Journal of Experimental Psychology*, 3, 1–14.

Watson and Rayner's original article on conditioned human fear is a classic of its kind – the first scientific study of conditioning of fear in a human being. Apart from its historical interest, it is also useful to read in order to avoid the mistakes highlighted in Harris's incisive review.

CHAPTER 8
Memory

THE WEAK EVIDENCE BEHIND BRAIN-TRAINING GAMES

Ed Yong, October, 2016, The Atlantic

If you repeat a specific mental task – say, memorizing a string of numbers – you'll obviously get better at it. But what if your recollection improved more generally?

This is the logic of the brain-training industry. These companies offer brief, simple video games that are meant to boost mental abilities like memory, attention and processing speed. . . . According to one set of estimates, consumers spent $715 million on these games in 2013.

And they might be wasting their money, according to a team of seven psychologists. . . . The studies, they concluded. . .provide little or no evidence that the games improve anything other than the specific tasks being trained.

WHAT YOU SHOULD BE ABLE TO DO AFTER READING CHAPTER 8

- Describe what is meant by 'memory' and describe the different types of memory process.

- Describe and understand theories of forgetting.

- Understand the term 'amnesia', be aware of different types of amnesia and understand the biological basis of the disorder.

- Distinguish between the processes of encoding and retrieval.

- Understand how memories are formed and can change over time (and how unreliable they can be).

- Be aware of the neural basis of learning and memory processes such as encoding and retrieval.

QUESTIONS TO THINK ABOUT

- What do we mean when we refer to 'memory'?

- Are there different types of memory?

- Why do we forget?

- Can memories be manipulated and, if so, how?

- Would you expect the brain mechanisms that are responsible for memory acquisition also to be responsible for retrieval? Why?

- Is memory capacity finite?

- Without memory, do we have personality?

- Is memory fixed or malleable?

- Where, in the brain, are memories stored? Can they be stored?

Memory: an introduction

Memory is the process of encoding, storing and retrieving information. **Encoding** refers to the active process of putting stimulus information into a form that can be used by our memory system. The process of maintaining information in memory is called **storage** and the active processes of locating and using information stored in memory is called **retrieval.**

When psychologists refer to the structure of memory, they are referring to two approaches to understanding memory – a literal one and a metaphorical one. Literally, memory may reflect the physiological changes that occur in the brain when an organism learns. Metaphorically, memory is viewed as a store or a process made up of systems and subsystems. These divisions may not necessarily have neurological meaning but they are useful metaphorical shorthand for describing aspects of memory. They are a way of explaining aspects of memory.

Types of memory

Research suggests that we possess at least four forms of memory: **sensory memory**, short-term memory, working memory and long-term memory (Baddeley, 1996). Sensory memory is memory in which representations of the physical features of a stimulus are stored for a very brief time, perhaps for a second or less. This form of memory is difficult to distinguish from the act of perception. The information contained in sensory memory represents the original stimulus fairly accurately and contains all or most of the information that has just been perceived. For example, sensory memory contains a brief image of a sight we have just seen or a fleeting echo of a sound we have just heard. Normally, we are not aware of sensory memory; no analysis seems to be performed on the information while it remains in this form. The function of sensory memory appears to be to hold information long enough for it to be transferred to the next form of memory, short-term memory.

Short-term memory (STM) refers to immediate memory for stimuli that have just been perceived. Its capacity is limited in terms of the number of items that it can store and of its duration. For example, most people who look at the set of numbers

1 4 9 2 3 0 7

close their eyes and recite them back, will have no trouble remembering them. If they are asked to do the same with the following set they might have a little more trouble:

7 2 5 2 3 9 1 6 5 8 4

Very few people can repeat 11 numbers. Even with practice, it is difficult to recite more than 7–9 independent pieces of information that you have seen only once. Short-term memory, therefore, has definite limits. However, there are ways to organise new information so that we can remember more than 7–9 items, but in such cases the items can no longer be considered independent.

Working memory (**WM**) is similar to short-term memory in that it involves short-term storage of information. But working memory is more than this in that it allows us to manipulate material in short-term memory. Remembering material while engaging in a different but related task, for example, illustrates working memory and you will find out more about this in a later section. If you had repeatedly recited the 11 numbers above until you had memorised them (rehearsal) you could have placed them in long-term memory. **Long-term memory** (LTM) refers to information that is represented on a permanent or near-permanent basis. Unlike short-term memory, long-term memory has no known limits and, as its name suggests, is relatively durable. If we stop thinking about something we have just perceived (e.g. something contained in short-term memory), we may not remember the information later. However, information in long-term memory need not be continuously rehearsed. We can stop thinking about it until we need the information at a future time. Some researchers have suggested that similar brain areas are activated during STM and LTM and that it is the degree of activation that differs between them (Nee and Jonides, 2013). This approach suggests that we do not necessarily have different stores for the seemingly different types of memory information, but that the types reflect different brain states. These models are called two-state models.

Other studies suggest that STM itself consists of three states (Oberauer, 2002). The first involves attention to a single item (focus of attention); the second access to additional items which are maintained for future processing (direct access region); and the third reflects passively available information from LTM. Neuroimaging data suggest that there is evidence for the three-state model. For example, Nee and Jonides (2013) found that in a study of non-verbal material, focus of attention was associated with inferior parietal cortex activation, direct access region with medial temporal lobe and hippocampus, and the left ventrolateral PFC with activated parts of LTM.

Some cognitive psychologists argue that no real distinction exists between short-term and long-term memory; instead, they see them as different phases of a continuous process. These psychologists object to the conception of memory as a series of separate units with information flowing from one to the next, as seen in Figure 8.1. Memory may be more complex than this model would have us believe, and the next sections explore the nature of sensory memory, short-term memory, working memory, long-term memory and other types of memory process.

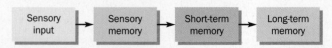

Figure 8.1 The information-processsing model of human memory.

Sensory memory

Under most circumstances, we are not aware of sensory memory. Information we have just perceived remains in sensory memory just long enough to be transferred to short-term memory. In order for us to become aware of sensory memory, information must be presented very briefly so that we can perceive its after-effects. Although we probably have a sensory memory for each sense modality, research efforts so far have focused on the two most important forms: iconic (visual) and echoic (auditory) memory.

Iconic memory

Visual sensory memory, called **iconic memory** (icon means 'image'), is a form of sensory memory that briefly holds a visual representation of a scene that has just been perceived. To study this form of memory, Sperling (1960) presented visual stimuli to people by means of a tachistoscope, an apparatus for presenting visual stimuli for extremely brief durations. Sperling flashed a set of nine letters on the screen for 50 milliseconds (ms). He then asked people to recall as many letters as they could, a method known as the whole-report procedure. On average, they could remember only four or five letters, but they insisted that they could see more. However, the image of the letters faded too fast for people to identify them all.

To determine whether the capacity of iconic memory accounted for this limitation, Sperling used a partial-report procedure. He asked people to name the letters in only one of the three horizontal rows. Depending on whether a high, middle or low tone was sounded, they were to report the letters in the top, middle or bottom line (see Figure 8.2). When the participants were warned beforehand to which line they should attend, they had no difficulty naming all three letters correctly. But then Sperling sounded the tone after he flashed the letters on the screen. The participants had to select the line from the mental image they still had: they had to retrieve the information from iconic memory. With brief delays, they recalled the requested line of letters with perfect accuracy.

For example, after seeing all nine letters flashed on the screen, they would hear the high tone, direct their attention to the top line of letters in their iconic memory, and 'read them off'. These results indicated that their iconic memory contained an image of all nine letters.

Sperling also varied the delay between flashing the nine letters on the screen and sounding the high, medium or low tone. If the delay was longer than 1 second, people could report only around 50 per cent of the letters. This result indicated that the image of the visual stimulus fades quickly from iconic memory. It also explained why participants who were asked to report all nine letters failed to report more than four or five. They had to scan their iconic memory, identify each letter and store each letter in short-term memory. This process took time, and during this time the image of the letters was fading. Although their iconic memory originally contained all nine letters, there was time to recognise and report only four or five before the mental image disappeared.

Echoic memory

Auditory sensory memory, called **echoic memory**, is a form of sensory memory for sounds that have just been perceived. It is necessary for comprehending many sounds, particularly those that constitute speech. When we hear a word pronounced, we hear individual sounds, one at a time. We cannot identify the word until we have heard all the sounds, so acoustical information must be stored temporarily until all the sounds have been received. For example, if someone says 'mallet', we may think of a kind of hammer; but if someone says 'malice', we will think of something entirely different. The first syllable we hear – 'mal' – has no meaning by itself in English, so we do not identify it as a word. However, once the last syllable is uttered, we can put the two syllables together and recognise the word. At this point, the word enters short-term memory. Echoic memory holds a representation of the initial sounds until the entire word has been heard; it seems to hold information for about four seconds (Darwin *et al.*, 1972).

Short-term memory (STM)

Short-term memory (STM) has a limited capacity, and most of the information that enters it is subsequently forgotten. Information in sensory memory enters STM, where it may be rehearsed for a while. The rehearsal process keeps the information in STM long enough for it to be transferred into long-term memory. After that, a person can stop thinking about the information; it can be recalled later, when it is needed.

This simple story is actually inaccurate. First of all, information does not simply 'enter short-term memory'. For example, most people who read the letters and put them in short-term memory have a number of strategies for achieving this.

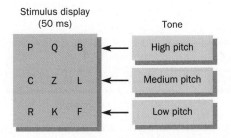

Figure 8.2 The critical features of Sperling's iconic memory study.
Source: Adapted from Sperling, G., The information available in brief visual presentations, *Psychological Monographs*, 1960, 74, 1–29.

Some would have repeated the letters to themselves or would have whispered or moved their lips. We can say the names of these letters because many years ago we learned them. But that knowledge is stored in long-term memory. Thus, when we see some letters, we retrieve information about their names from long-term memory, and then we hear ourselves rehearsing those names (out loud or silently). The five letters above contain only visual information, their names came from long-term memory, which means that the information put into short-term memory actually came from long-term memory.

P X L M R

To illustrate this, try the following experiment. Study the symbols below, then look away from the book, and try to keep them in STM.

ζ□δ ∋ □

This task is extremely difficult because few people will have learned the names of these symbols. Because of this, there is no way of recording them in short-term memory. Figure 8.3 may, therefore, be a better description of the memory process than is Figure 8.1.

Information can enter short-term memory from two directions: from sensory memory or from long-term memory. When we are asked to multiply 7 by 19, information about the request enters our short-term memory from our sensory memory. Actually performing the task, though, requires that we retrieve some information from long-term memory. What does 'multiply' mean? What is a 7 and a 19? At the moment of the request, such information is not being furnished through our senses; it is available only from long-term memory. However, that information is not recalled directly from long-term memory. It is first moved into short-term memory and then enters conscious awareness.

Psychologists have long debated the number of memory stores that we have – some view humans as having a short-term memory store and a long-term memory store (the dual-store model), whereas others argue that the distinction between these two stores is blurred and that we have one flexible memory store that deals with short-term and long-term memory retrieval (single-store model). Dual-store models were (and

are) based on a simple paradigm: participants recall items from a list; if they recall from the end of this list, these items were retrieved from STM; words recalled from the beginning of the list were retrieved from long-term memory.

Working memory

The fact that short-term memory contains both new information and information retrieved from long-term memory has led some psychologists to prefer the term 'working memory' (Baddeley and Hitch, 1974; Baddeley, 1986;). Working memory acts on material we have just perceived and allows us to manipulate this in the short-term. It allows us to keep a new telephone number 'alive' in memory long enough to dial it or allows us to perform that multiplication task mentioned in the earlier paragraph. In short, it represents our ability to remember what we have just perceived and to think about it in terms of what we already know (Baddeley, 1986; Logie, 1996). We use it to remember whether any cars are coming up the street after looking left and then right.

Originally, Baddeley and Hitch (1974) found that people were able to retain sequences of three verbal items while undertaking other tasks with no impairment to the performance of either. Retaining up to six items, however, resulted in an impairment in the concurrent task. This suggested to the authors that there was a very short-term memory system which allowed people to retain very small numbers of items while at the same time allowing them to perform other tasks. If the system is exceeded, then other processes such as mental verbal rehearsal are invoked to help retention.

A widely used test of working memory is reading span (Daneman and Carpenter, 1980). One version involves asking people to read aloud and verify the truthfulness of sentences while, at the same time, trying to remember the last word of each sentence. This task, like many others of working memory, requires a person to maintain some information in memory (storage) while simultaneously manipulating other information (processing).

Another manipulation task in working memory might involve asking the participant to recite from memory a series of five letters forwards, backwards or in alphabetical order.

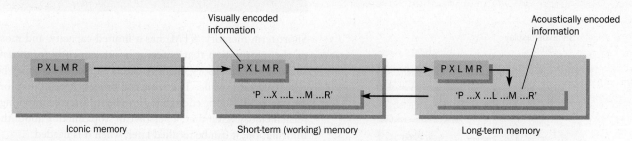

Figure 8.3 Relations between iconic memory, short-term memory and long-term memory. Letters are read, transformed into their acoustic equivalents and rehearsed as 'sounds' in the head. Information can enter short-term memory from both iconic memory and long-term memory. Visual information enters short-term memory from iconic memory, but what is already known about that information (such as names of letters) is moved from long-term memory to short-term memory.

After a delay, the participant is asked to match the number order of a given letters, according to the mental manipulation (e.g. forwards, backwards or alphabetical). So, if the letters B, M, T, E, I were presented and the participant was asked to alphabetise them, the number 4 (called a digit probe) should elicit the correct answer, M (because M is the fourth letter in the alphabetised string, B, E, I, M, T).

Although the terms 'short-term memory' and 'working memory' are sometimes used interchangeably, some psychologists make clear distinctions between them. Short-term memory has been referred to as information retained in long-term memory that is called on but not used in a sustained way. Working memory involves dual processing and actual manipulation of material in **mental space**, not simply the storage of material (Miyake, 2001). There is evidence that tests of working memory and short-term memory measure different processes (Kail and Hall, 2001).

The components of working memory

Working memory was a model devised in the 1970s and later developed extensively by the British psychologists Alan Baddeley and Graham Hitch. They regarded this type of memory as having three components which allowed us to store temporarily verbal material and visuospatial material, and to coordinate the storage of this material. The component which stores verbal material was originally called the **articulatory loop**, although this term has been superseded by the term **phonological loop** (Baddeley and Logie, 1992). The component that allows storage of visuospatial material is called the **visuospatial scratchpad** and the coordinating system is called the **central executive**. The working memory 'system' is illustrated in Figure 8.4 and is described next.

Phonological working memory

When we see a printed word, we say it out loud or silently. If it is said to ourselves, circuits of neurons that control articulation are activated. Information concerning this activity is communicated within the brain to circuits of neurons in the auditory system, and the word is 'heard'. Information is then transmitted back to the articulatory system, where the word is silently repeated. The loop continues until the person's attention turns to something else or until it is replaced with new information.

This articulatory or phonological loop allows the retention of verbal phonetic information (so it acts as a phonological store) and operates like the loop of an audiotape (hence, the name). Lists of long words are remembered more poorly than lists of short words, for example, because there is less room on the loop for lists of long words (so the words 'encyclopaedia', 'constellation' and 'antediluvian' would be more difficult to recall than would the words 'clock', 'parrot' and 'daisy'). However, because the loop also allows the rehearsal of information by **subvocal articulation** (such as subvocally rehearsing

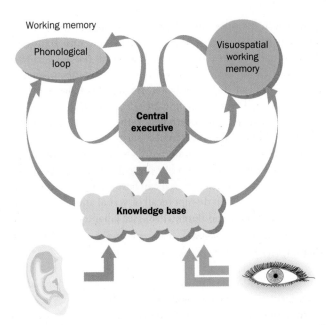

Figure 8.4 Logie's (1995) schematic drawing of the components of working memory.

Source: Adapted from Logie, R., *Visual Spatial Working Memory*, p. 127. © 1995. Reprinted by permission of Psychology Press Limited, Hove, UK.

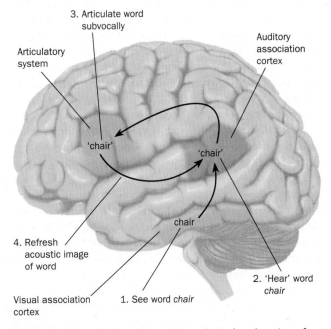

Figure 8.5 The articulatory loop. A hypothetical explanation of phonological working memory.

a telephone number), the loss of information from the phonological store can be avoided. According to Baddeley *et al.* (1975), the capacity of the phonological loop is determined by how much material the participant can rehearse in two seconds. (Figure 8.5 illustrates how the phonological loop is represented in the brain.)

However, the operation of the loop can be defective under certain circumstances. For example, Salame and Baddeley (1982) found that irrelevant speech played in the background while participants learned visually presented words interfered with the recall of these words, but the length of the words to be remembered had no significant effect on recall. However, the closer the irrelevant speech was to the words to be remembered, the greater the interference, suggesting that there was some interference in learning words while attending to the sound (or phonology) of similar ones. There is also evidence that non-speech-related material can have the same effect: even background noise can disrupt recall of verbal and arithmetical material (Banbury and Berry, 1998) (see Chapter 9).

Visuospatial working memory

Much of the information we process is non-verbal. We recognise objects, perceive their locations and find our way around our environment. We can look at objects, close our eyes and then sketch or describe them. We can do the same with things we saw in the past. The visuospatial scratchpad contains visual information either obtained from the immediate environment by means of the sense organs or retrieved from long-term memory.

An example of the ability to manipulate visual information in working memory comes from a famous experiment by Shepard and Metzler (1971). They presented people with pairs of drawings that could be perceived as three-dimensional constructions made of cubes. The participant's task was to see whether the shape on the right was identical to the one on the left; some were, and some were not. Even when the shapes were identical, the one on the right was sometimes drawn as if it had been rotated. For example, in Figure 8.6a the shape on the right has been rotated clockwise 80 degrees, but in Figure 8.6b the two shapes are different.

Shepard and Metzler found that people were accurate in judging whether the pairs of shapes were the same or different but took longer to decide when the right-hand shape was rotated. Participants formed an image of one of the drawings in their heads and rotated it until it was aligned the same way as the other one. If their rotated image coincided with the drawing, they recognised them as having the same shape. If they did not, they recognised them as being different. The data supported what the participants said – the more the shape was rotated, the longer it took for people to rotate the image of one of the shapes in working memory and compare it with the other one.

The central executive

The above elements – the phonological loop and the visuo–spatial scratchpad – do not work independently but have to be regulated and supervised, via the central executive subsystem (Baddeley, 1986). This central executive not only allocates

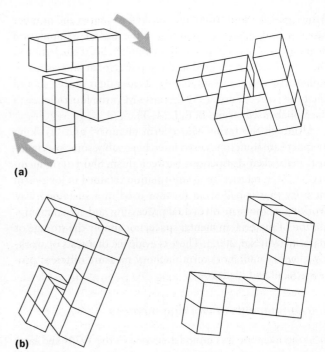

(a)

(b)

Figure 8.6 The mental rotation task. **(a)** The shape on the right is identical to the one on the left but rotated 80 degrees clockwise. **(b)** The two shapes are different.

Source: Adapted from Shepard, R.N. and Metzler, J., Mental rotation of three-dimensional objects. *Science*, 1971, 171, 701–3. © 1971. The American Association for the Advancement of Science.

mental resources to working memory tasks but also supervises the updating of what is in working memory.

How does working memory work?

Apart from allowing us to do the activities mentioned in the previous sections, working memory is also important for cognitive functions such as reading comprehension, academic ability and mathematics (Ashcraft and Kirk, 2001; Daneman and Hannon, 2001). Performance on a working memory span task involving numbers, for example, is a good predictor of spatial task performance (Kane *et al.*, 2001). Working memory performance is also a good predictor of reading comprehension or verbal ability if the working memory span tests involve verbal or numerical material (Daneman and Hannon, 2001; Hitch *et al.*, 2001; Shah and Miyake, 1996) (see Chapter 10).

According to the 'resource sharing model' of Daneman and Carpenter (the name given to it by Hitch *et al.*, 2001), a reading span task measures how flexibly we can allocate mental resources to the processing and storage of material. In practical terms, if a person is a good reader, reading sentences for their truthfulness uses up very few cognitive resources and, therefore, frees up more 'cognitive space' for other activities (in this example, storage of the last word in the sentences). If readers are poor, on the other hand, then the opposite pattern is seen and they, therefore, show poor working memory performance (Yuill and Oakhill, 1991). Working memory capacity is thought to be one factor which determines good reading comprehension ability, although this view has been challenged – some psychologists argue that working memory deficits occur with language impairment, rather than causing it (Nation and Snowling, 1998, 1999). They note that even poor readers can remember as many one-, two – or three-syllable words as good readers.

Daneman and Carpenter's view of working memory (1980) has attracted much support and has been the dominant, explanatory view of working memory. An alternative model of working memory, however, argues that it is our control of attention that leads to successful working memory performance (Engle et al., 1999). What counts is how much information can be stored, and this is determined by attention capacity. Thus, you should be able to predict people's performance on attention tasks from their working memory reading span tasks and there is some evidence to support this link.

A final alternative explanation argues that working memory depends on a person's ability to ignore irrelevant information rather than on their limited capacity to process information (Hasher and Zacks, 1988). In order to achieve this goal, there must be good inhibition of irrelevant information and a focus on only relevant material. It is a persuasive argument. Performance on working memory tasks depends on, among other factors, the ability to inhibit the interference produced by items encountered in early experimental trials (Lustig et al., 2001). It appears to be one of the keys to successful working memory performance.

Primacy and recency effects

When individuals are asked to listen to a long list of words spoken one at a time and then write down as many as they can remember (a free recall task), most participants will remember the words at the beginning and the end of the list and forget the words in between. This is called the serial position effect. The tendency to remember the words at the beginning of the list is called the **primacy effect**; the tendency to remember words at the end of the list is called the **recency effect**. Two factors may account for these effects.

The primacy effect appears to be due to the fact that words earlier in a list have the opportunity to be rehearsed more than do words in the other parts of a list. This makes good sense – the first words get rehearsed more because, at the experiment's outset, these are the only words available to rehearse. The rehearsal permits them to be stored in long-term memory. As more and more words on the list are presented, short-term memory becomes fuller so that words that appear later in the list have more competition for rehearsal time. Because the first words on the list are rehearsed the most, they are remembered better.

As Atkinson and Shiffrin (1968) point out, because the words at the end of the list were the last to be heard, they are still available in short-term memory. Thus, when you are asked to write the words on the list, the last few words are still available in short-term memory even though they did not undergo as much rehearsal as words at the beginning of the list.

A way of testing this would be to create a delay between the presentation of the last stimulus and its recall. Postman and Phillips (1965), for example, inserted a delay of 15 seconds between the last item and recall and had their participants engage in another task. The effect was to abolish the recency effect because short-term memory was occupied and was not allowed to rehearse the last items in the list. When the delay involved no intervening activity, and so short-term memory was unoccupied by another task, the recency effect remained intact (Baddeley and Hitch, 1977). However, the abolition of both recency and primacy effects seems to depend on the nature of the intervening task. If people are told to count backwards for 20 seconds after the presentation of a word list, primacy and recency effects are still shown (Tzeng, 1973). The instructions given to people are also important. If people are instructed to repeat the list in the order they heard the words, the recency effect is abolished (Tulving and Arbuckle, 1963). If they are allowed to recall the list spontaneously, the recency effect remains.

Recency (and primacy) effects extend beyond the recall of artificial word lists. They have been reported for the recall of parking positions (Pinto and Baddeley, 1991), operas attended over a quarter of a century (Sehulster, 1989), names of American presidents (Roediger and Crowder, 1976; Healy et al., 2000) and hymn verses (Maylor, 2002). Baddeley and Hitch (1977) found that when rugby players were asked to recall the teams they played, they named the most recently played teams first and with greater accuracy.

The primacy and recency effects are important because they demonstrate that memory is not a random process. Information is not just plucked from the environment and stored away randomly in the brain. Instead, the processing of information is much more orderly; it follows predictable patterns and is dependent on the contributions of rehearsal and short-term memory.

The limits of short-term and working memory

How long does information remain in short-term or working memory? The answer may lie in a classic study by Lloyd and Margaret Peterson (Peterson and Peterson, 1959). The experimenters presented participants with a stimulus composed of three consonants, such as JRG. With rehearsal, the participants easily recalled it 30 seconds later. The Petersons then made the task more challenging: they prevented participants from rehearsing. After they presented the participants with JRG, they asked them to count backwards by three from a three-digit number they gave them immediately after they had presented the set of consonants. For example, they might present participants with JRG, then say, '397'. The participants would count out loud, '397...394...391...388...385', and so on until the experimenters signalled them to recall the consonants. The accuracy of recall was determined by the length of the interval between presentation of the consonants and when recall was requested (see Figure 8.7). When rehearsal was disrupted by backward counting – which prevented individuals from rehearsing information in short-term memory – the consonants remained accessible in memory for only a few seconds. After a 15–18-second delay between the presentation of the consonants and the recall signal, recall dropped to near zero.

What, then, is the capacity of short-term memory? Miller (1956), in a famous article entitled 'The magical number seven, plus or minus two', demonstrated that people could retain, on average, seven pieces of information in their short-term memory: seven numbers, seven letters, seven words or seven tones of a particular pitch. If we can remember and think about only seven pieces of information at a time, how can we manage to write novels, design buildings or even carry on simple conversations? The answer comes in a particular form of encoding of information that Miller called chunking, a process by which information is simplified by rules which make it easily remembered once the rules are learned.

A simple demonstration illustrates this phenomenon. Read the 10 numbers printed below and see whether you have any trouble remembering them.

1 3 5 7 9 2 4 6 8 0

These numbers are easy to retain in short-term memory because we can remember a rule instead of 10 independent numbers. In this case, the rule concerns odd and even numbers.

The actual limit of short-term memory is seven chunks, not necessarily seven individual items. Thus, the total amount of information we can store in short-term memory depends on the particular rules we use to organise it.

In life outside the laboratory we are rarely required to remember a series of numbers. The rules that organise our short-term memories are much more complex than those that describe odd and even numbers. The principles of chunking can apply to more realistic learning situations. If we look at the following words:

> along got the was door crept locked slowly he until passage the he to which

and try to remember them, the task is difficult; there is too much information to store in short-term memory. If we repeat the process for the following group of words:

> He slowly crept along the passage until he got to the door, which was locked.

we would be much more successful. Once the same fifteen words are arranged in a sequence that makes sense, they are not difficult to store in short-term memory.

The capacity of short-term memory for verbal material is not measured by the number of letters, syllables or words it can retain but by how much meaning the information offers: this is working memory and long-term memory working together. The first set of words above merely contains 15 different words. However, when the items are related, we can store many more of them. We do not have to string 15 words together in a meaningless fashion but can let the image of a man creeping down a passage towards a locked door organise the new information.

Loss of information from short-term memory

The essence of short-term memory is its transience; hence, its name. Information enters from sensory memory and from long-term memory, is rehearsed, thought about, modified and then leaves. Some of the information controls ongoing behaviour and some of it causes changes in long-term memory, but ultimately, it is lost from short-term memory. What causes it to leave? The simplest possibility is that it decays, it fades away. Rehearsal allows us to refresh information indefinitely, thus preventing the decay from eliminating the information.

However, the most important cause appears to be displacement. Once short-term memory has reached its capacity, either additional information will have to be ignored or some information already in short-term memory will have to be displaced to make room for the new information.

One of the best examples of displacement of information in short-term memory comes from an experiment conducted by Waugh and Norman (1965). The people in this study heard lists of 16 digits. The last digit, accompanied by a tone,

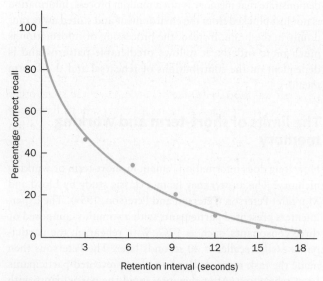

Figure 8.7 Limits of recall from working memory. Percentage correct recall of the stimulus as a function of the duration of the distractor task used in the study by Peterson and Peterson.

Source: Adapted from Peterson, L.M. and Peterson, J.M., Short-term retention of individual verbal items. *Journal of Experimental Psychology*, 1959, 58, 193-98.

was called the probe digit. When people heard it, they had to think back to the previous occurrence of the same digit and tell the experimenter the digit that followed that one.

Look at the sequence of numbers listed below. The last one, a 9, was accompanied by a tone, which told the person that it was the probe. If you examine the list, you will see that the earlier occurrence of a 9 was followed by a 4. Thus, the target, or correct, response was 4.

2 6 7 5 1 3 7 2 6 3 9 4 5 8 1 9

Notice that the 4 is separated from the second 9 by three numbers (5, 8 and 1). Waugh and Norman presented many different lists in which the location of the correct response varied. The distance between the target and the probe ranged from one to twelve items.

The study had two conditions. In one, the lists were presented rapidly, at four digits per second. In the other, they were presented slowly, at only one digit per second. The reason for this manipulation was to determine whether any effects they observed were caused by the mere passage of time rather than by displacement. They found that the more items that came between the target and the probe, the less likely it was that the target would be remembered. The critical variable seemed to be the number of items between the target and the probe, not the time that had elapsed (see Figure 8.8).

The results indicate that new information displaces old information in short-term memory. But at the longest delays (six or more intervening items), subjects performed more poorly when the items were presented slowly. Perhaps information in short-term memory does decay, but the effect is much less important than displacement.

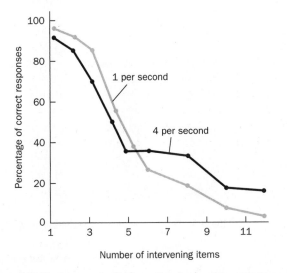

Figure 8.8 Displacement of information in short-term memory. The graph shows the percentage of correct responses as a function of intervening items presented at two different rates of time.

Source: Adapted from Waugh, N.C. and Norman, D.A., Primary memory. *Psychological* Review, 1965, 72, 89–104.

Learning and encoding in long-term memory

What allows memory to move from short-term to long-term memory? Memory involves both active and passive processes. Sometimes, we use deliberate strategies to remember something (encode the information into long-term memory), for example, rehearsing the lines of a poem or memorising famous dates for a history exam. At other times, we simply observe and remember without any apparent effort, as when we tell a friend about an interesting experience we had. And memories can be formed even without our being aware of having learned something. What factors determine whether we can eventually remember an experience?

The consolidation hypothesis

The traditional view of memory is that it consists of a two-stage process (not counting sensory memory). Information enters short-term memory from the environment, where it is stored temporarily. If the material is rehearsed long enough, it is transferred into long-term memory. This transfer of information from short-term memory into long-term memory has been called consolidation (Hebb, 1949). Through rehearsal (e.g. by means of the articulatory loop), the neural activity responding to sensory stimulation can be sustained; and if enough time passes, the activity causes structural changes in the brain. These structural changes are more or less permanent and solid (hence, the term 'consolidation'), and are responsible for long-term memory.

The **consolidation** hypothesis makes several assertions about the learning process. It asserts that short-term memory and long-term memory are physiologically different, and few investigators doubt that information that has just been perceived is stored in the brain in a different way from information that was perceived some time ago. However, some other features of the original consolidation hypothesis have been challenged. First, the hypothesis asserts that all information gets into long-term memory only after passing through short-term memory. Secondly, it asserts that the most important factor determining whether a particular piece of information reaches long-term memory is the amount of time it spends in short-term memory.

Levels of processing

Craik and Lockhart (1972) have pointed out that the act of rehearsal may effectively keep information in short-term memory but does not necessarily result in the establishment of long-term memories. They suggested that people engage in two different types of rehearsal: **maintenance rehearsal** and **elaborative** rehearsal. Maintenance rehearsal is the rote repetition of verbal information – simply repeating an item over and over. This behaviour serves to maintain the information in short-term memory but does not necessarily result in lasting changes. In contrast, when people engage in elaborative rehearsal, they think about the information and relate it to what they already know. Elaborative rehearsal involves more than new information. It involves deeper processing: forming associations, attending to the meaning of the information, thinking about that information and so on. Thus, we elaborate on new information by recollecting related information already in long-term memory. We are more likely to remember information for an examination by processing it deeply or meaningfully; simply rehearsing the material to be tested will not be effective.

Craik and Tulving (1975) gave participants a set of cards, each containing a printed sentence including a missing word, denoted by a blank line, such as 'The ___ is torn'. After reading the sentence, the participants looked at a word flashed on a screen, then pressed a button as quickly as possible to signify whether the word fitted the sentence. In this example, 'dress' will fit, but 'table' will not. The sentences varied in complexity. Some were very simple:

> She cooked the _____.
>
> The _____ is torn.

Others were complex:

> The great bird swooped down and carried off the struggling _____.
>
> The old man hobbled across the room and picked up the valuable _____.

The sentences were written so that the same word could be used for either a simple or a complex sentence: 'She cooked the chicken' or 'The great bird swooped down and carried off the struggling chicken'. All participants saw a particular word once, in either a simple or a complex sentence.

The experimenters made no mention of a memory test, so there was no reason for the participants to try to remember the words. However, after responding to the sentences, they were presented with them again and were asked to recall the words they had used. The experimenters found that the participants were twice as likely to remember a word if it had previously fitted into a sentence of medium or high complexity than if it had fitted into a simple one. These results suggest that a memory is more effectively established if the item is presented in a rich context – one that is likely to make us think about the item and imagine an action taking place.

Craik and Lockhart (1972) suggested that memory is a by-product of perceptual analysis. A central processor, analogous to the central processing unit of a computer, can analyse sensory information on several different levels. They conceived of the levels as being hierarchically arranged, from shallow (superficial) to deep (complex). A person can control the level of analysis by paying attention to different features of the stimulus. If a person focuses on the superficial sensory characteristics of a stimulus, then these features will be stored in memory. If the person focuses on the meaning of a stimulus and the ways in which it relates to other things the person already knows, then these features will be stored in memory. For example, consider the word:

> tree

This word is written in black type, the letters are lower case, the bottom of the stem of the letter 't' curves upwards to the right and so on. Craik and Lockhart referred to these characteristics as surface features and to the analysis of these features as **shallow processing**. Maintenance rehearsal is an example of shallow processing. In contrast, consider the meaning of the word 'tree'. You can think about how trees differ from other plants, what varieties of trees you have seen, what kinds of foods and what kinds of wood they provide and so on. These features refer to a word's meaning and are called semantic features. Their analysis is called **deep processing**. Elaborative rehearsal is an example of deep processing. According to Craik and Lockhart, deep processing generally leads to better retention than does surface processing (see Figure 8.9). As you saw in Chapter 7, a deep approach to learning also improves a student's performance.

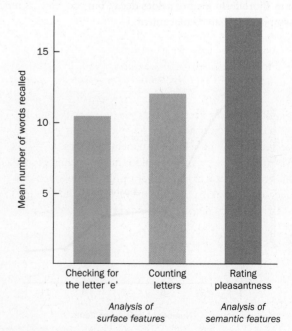

Figure 8.9 Shallow versus deep processing. Mean number of words recalled after performing tasks that required analysis of surface features or analysis of semantic features.

Source: Based on Craik, F.I.M. and Lockhart, R.S., Levels of processing: A framework for memory research. *Journal of Verbal Behavior*, 1972, 11, 671–84.

Encoding specificity

Encoding specificity refers to the principle that the way in which we encode information determines our ability to retrieve it later. For example, suppose that someone reads you a list of words that you are to recall later. The list contains the word 'beet', along with a number of terms related to music, such as 'melody', 'tune' and 'jazz'. When asked if the list contained the names of any vegetables, you may report that it did not. Because of the musical context, you encoded 'beet' as 'beat' and never thought of the tuberous vegetable while you were rehearsing the list (Flexser and Tulving, 1978). Many experiments have made the point that meaningful elaboration during encoding is helpful and probably necessary for the formation of useful memories.

Mnemonics and memory aids

When we can imagine information vividly and concretely, and when it fits into the context of what we already know, it is easy to remember later. **Mnemonic systems** (from the Greek *mnemon*, meaning 'memory'; Mnemosyne was the Greek goddess of remembrance) – special techniques or strategies consciously used to improve memory – make use of information already stored in long-term memory to make memorisation an easier task.

Mnemonic systems do not simplify information but make it more elaborate. More information is stored, not less. However, the additional information makes the material easier to recall. Mnemonic systems organise new information into a cohesive whole so that retrieval of part of the information ensures retrieval of the rest of it. Even memory champions utilise mnemonics. Sherlock Holmes, in the Mark Gatiss and Stephen Moffat rendition of the detective, has his mind palace in which he is able to organise events people and objects in order to make deductions. Simon Reinhard, who won the Extreme Memory Tournament in 2014, was able to memorise the order of a pack of playing cards in under 27 seconds and competitors at the event indicated that they used techniques – such as the ones described below – to help them remember (Putnam, 2015).

Mnemonics aren't only useful for memory champions, they can help the rest of us remember things that we find difficult to encode using normal cognitive processes. One study has recently examined the effect of using mnemonics to remember material as complex as the Australian tax code, with positive results (Smith and Shimeld, 2017).

Method of loci

In Greece before the sixth century BC, few people knew how to write, and those who did had to use cumbersome clay tablets. Consequently, oratory skills and memory for long epic poems (running for several hours) were highly prized, and some people earned their livings by using them. Because people could not carry around several hundred pounds of clay tablets, they had to keep important information in their heads. To do

World memory champion 2011 Wang Feng
Source: World Memory Sports Council, www.worldmemorychampionships.com

so, the Greeks devised the **method of loci**, a mnemonic system in which items to be remembered are mentally associated with specific physical locations (*locus* means 'place' in Latin).

To use the method of loci, would-be memory artists had to memorise the inside of a building. In Greece, they would wander through public buildings, stopping to study and memorise various locations and arranging them in order, usually starting with the door of the building. After memorising the locations, they could make the tour mentally, just as you could make a mental tour of your house to count the rooms. To learn a list of words, they would visualise each word in a particular location in the memorised building and picture the association as vividly as possible. For example, for the word 'love' they might imagine an embracing couple leaning against a particular column in a hall of the building. To recall the list, they would imagine each of the locations in sequence, 'see' each word, and say it. To store a speech, they would group the words into concepts and place a 'note' for each concept at a particular location in the sequence.

For example, if a person wanted to remember a short shopping list without writing it down and the list consists of five items: cheese, milk, eggs, soy sauce and lettuce, the person might first think of a familiar place, perhaps their house. Next, they would mentally walk through the house, visually placing different items from the list at locations – loci – in the house: a lump of cheese hanging from a coat rack, milk dripping from the kitchen tap, eggs lying in the hallway, a bottle of soy sauce on a dining chair, and a lettuce on the sofa (see Figure 8.10). Then, in the supermarket, the person mentally retraces his or her path through the house and notes what he or she has stored at the different loci.

Narrative stories

Another useful aid to memory is to place information into a **narrative**, in which items to be remembered are linked together by a story. Bower and Clark (1969) showed that even inexperienced

Figure 8.10 The method of loci. Items to be remembered are visualised in specific, well-known places.

people can use this method. The investigators asked people to try to learn 12 lists of 10 concrete nouns each. They gave some of the people the following advice (p. 181):

> A good way to learn the list of items is to make up a story relating the items to one another. Specifically, start with the first item and put it in a setting which will allow other items to be added to it. Then, add the other items to the story in the same order as the items appear. Make each story meaningful to yourself. Then, when you are asked to recall the items, you can simply go through your story and pull out the proper items in their correct order.

Here is a typical narrative, described by one of the subjects (list words are italicised):

> A *lumberjack* darted out of the forest, *skated* around a *hedge* past a colony of *ducks*. He tripped on some *furniture*, tearing his *stocking* while hastening to the pillow *where* his *mistress* lay.

People in the control group were merely asked to learn the lists and were given the same amount of time as the people in the 'narrative' group to study them. Both groups could remember a particular list equally well immediately afterwards. However,

when all the lists had been learned, recall of all 120 words was far superior in the group that had constructed narrative stories.

Not all information can be easily converted to such a form, however. For example, if you were preparing to take an examination on the information in this chapter, figuring out how to encode it into lists would probably take you more time than studying and learning it by more traditional methods.

The length of time it takes to learn mnemonics depends on the specific mnemonic. You have to remember the specific components of the technique (e.g. learning the peg images) and then practice the mnemonic until it is fairly automatic. People can memorise a mental palace in an evening, the peg method in a few minutes (Putnam, 2015).

Long-term memory: episodic and semantic memory

Long-term memory contains more than exact records of sensory information that has been perceived. It also contains information that has been transformed – organised in terms of meaning. For example, the type of information that is personally meaningful to us (such as what we had for breakfast this morning or what we were doing last night) appears to be different from the type of information that is based on general knowledge (such as knowing the capitals of the world or the order in which Shakespeare wrote his plays). These two types of memory have been termed episodic and semantic memory, respectively, and the distinction was originally made by Tulving (1972).

Episodic memory (or **autobiographical memory**) provides us with a record of our life experiences. Events stored there are autobiographical and there appears to be cross-cultural agreement on when such memories are acquired (even though cultures differ in terms of the type of memory encoded) (Conway et al., 2005). **Semantic memory** consists of conceptual information such as general knowledge; it is a long-term store of data, facts and information. Our knowledge of what psychology is, the names of the authors of this book, the components of the human sensory systems and how neuroimaging has helped localise the process of working memory should form part of your semantic memory. Semantic memories can, of course, interact with episodic ones.

The distinction between episodic and semantic memory reflects the fact that we make different uses of things we have learned: we describe things that happened to us, or talk about facts we have learned. Tulving (1983, 1984) revised his original views of the two systems, suggesting that episodic memory is a part of semantic memory, not a separate, independent system, so the debate is ongoing.

One way of determining a distinction between them would be to show that brain regions involved in one are not as involved in the other. Studies of brain injury have highlighted the involvement of the left prefrontal cortex (PFC) in the retrieval of words in response to a cue (such as another word or a letter) and the temporal lobe in object naming and the retrieval of information about an object's characteristics (Martin and Chao, 2001). The processing of semantic information appears to involve a network of regions including the left prefrontal, parietal and posterior temporal cortex. When people are allowed to generate words to visually or auditorily presented cues, the posterior temporal cortex is activated regardless of whether the words are generated from the participants' native language or from their second language (Klein et al., 1999; Tatsumi et al., 1999).

Perhaps the most controversial data supporting the notion of semantic memory concerns stimulus specificity, the notion that one region of the brain is more involved than others in the perception or retrieval of certain categories of object. Well-known examples of this, as you saw in Chapter 6, are face recognition and the naming of inanimate and animate objects (Warrington, 1975; Warrington and Shallice, 1984; Warrington and McCarthy, 1987). Warrington's patients showed evidence of a dissociation between knowledge for living and non-living things. They were able to name non-living things but had considerable difficulty in naming living things, whether the stimuli to be named were verbal or non-verbal. In a later study, Warrington and Shallice (1984) interpreted their findings by suggesting that the two types of object-naming depended on different processing mechanisms. Living things would be processed primarily according to perceptual and visual features such as their size,

colour, shape and so on, whereas non-living things would be processed according to their function.

Episodic memory across the ages

Based on a reading and understanding of the anatomical and physiological changes and reorganisation that occur in the brain during development – in childhood and old age – Shing et al. (2010) have proposed a framework to understand how we develop episodic memory across the lifespan. Episodic memory – remembering of events in time and place that the person has experienced – appears susceptible to impairment in the very young and the very old (there is very little impairment before the age of 60 years). Shing suggests that there are two interacting processes at work: (1) a strategic component, which involves the control of memory formation and retrieval, from elaboration, organising memory at encoding and evaluating the result of retrieval; and (2) an associative component, which binds together the elements of memory to form a coherent representation. They argue that children's difficulties with episodic memory stem from problems with the strategic component, which is mediated by the development of the PFC; older people's problems, however, stem from both and these are underpinned by changes in the PFC and medial temporal lobes.

Neuroimaging data have generally supported the proposition that certain brain regions are specifically activated by specific stimuli, but do not explain why. Pictures of tools have been found to generate more brain activity in the left posterior temporal cortex than do pictures of other objects and animals (Martin et al., 1996; Chao et al., 1999). An area of the brain called the fusiform gyrus, as you saw in Chapter 6, is activated during face recognition but is not as consistently or significantly activated by other types of stimuli. Other stimuli which selectively activate certain brain regions are buildings and houses (Epstein and Kanwisher, 1998).

Explicit and implicit memory

Another distinction is made between explicit and implicit memory. **Explicit memory** refers to memory for information we were aware of learning. A simple example would be our recollection of the 12 times table: this is a task that most of us were instructed to remember explicitly. Recognition and recall of material in explicit memory require active recollection of material that has been studied (McBride and Dosher, 1997). For example, we might ask participants to recall freely as many words as they can after being presented with a long list of them, or to indicate which stimuli from an array of visual stimuli were previously seen. Under these conditions, participants are explicitly instructed to recall or to recognise.

Implicit memory, however, does not appear to rely on conscious awareness. Instead, it is memory for information that is incidentally or unintentionally learned and which does not rely on the recognition or recall of any specific learning

Memory – An international perspective

There seem to be real differences in the content of the auto-biographical memories of people from different cultures. European Americans tend to recall their own roles in events and the feelings those events generated, whereas Asian Americans tend to recall details of social/group activities (Wang, 2004; Wang and Ross, 2005). One explanation for this is that American culture – at the most general level – is highly individualistic and emphasises and rewards autonomy and self-drive, whereas Asian cultures emphasise interdependence and the importance of social interaction/dependence.

To test this hypothesis, Wang (2008) asked Asian Americans to focus either on their American or their Asian background prior to recalling autobiographical memories. Those primed by the American condition recalled memories that were more self-focused and less social than were those whose Asian-ness had been primed. Participants who were not primed either way recalled the two types of content about equally.

Ji et al. (2009) hypothesised that Eastern cultures would make greater use of past information to make judgements about behaviour – presumably, because this provides more context in the same way that the background of a scene gives more context to the object in it. In an experiment where Canadian and Chinese participants were asked to read a description of a theft and then look at behaviours that had occurred near to the crime or at some time from it, Chinese participants placed more emphasis on distant events, considering them more relevant. They also recalled more detail about past events accurately than did the Canadians.

episode (Schacter, 1987; Cleermans, 1993). It is sometimes referred to as being synonymous with procedural memory, the memory for knowing how to do things (like riding a bike, operating a computer keyboard or playing a musical instrument) – we acquire memory via performance without consciously encoding that information. There is some question, however, over whether implicit and procedural memory are truly synonymous. Procedural memory implies that some conscious effort has been made towards learning a skill such as riding a bike or playing a musical instrument; implicit memory would assume that skills were learned without such conscious effort, which seems highly unlikely. Also, there seems to be little procedural input to performing a stem-completion task (described below), which taps implicit memory. There continues to be debate about the number of memory systems, and whether these memory systems are separate or different forms of the same system.

The acquisition of specific behaviours and skills is probably the most important form of implicit memory. Driving a car, turning the pages of a book, playing a musical instrument, dancing, throwing and catching a ball, sliding a chair backwards as we get up from the dinner table – all these skills involve coordination of movements with sensory information received from the environment and from our own moving body parts. We do not need to be able to describe these activities in order to perform them. We may not be aware of all the movements involved while we are performing them. Implicit memory may have evolved earlier than explicit memory.

Originally, the term implicit learning derived from studies of artificial grammar learning (see Chapter 10) where participants had to deduce a set of grammatical rules governing the construction of sentences comprising non-words (so that the participants are not influenced by semantic knowledge conveyed by the words). Participants were able to work out a set of rules but were unable to describe these rules – they made educated guesses based on stimuli they had previously seen. They had implicitly learned the rules (Reber, 2013).

A good example of learning without awareness is provided by an experiment conducted by Graf and Mandler (1984). These investigators showed people a list of six-letter words and had some of them engage in a task that involved elaborative processing: they were to think about each word and to decide how much they liked it. Other people were given a task that involved processing superficial features: they were asked to look at the words and decide whether they contained particular letters. Later, their explicit and implicit memories for the words were assessed. In both cases the basic task was the same, but the instructions to the subjects were different. People were shown the first three letters of each word. For example, if one of the words had been 'define', they would have been shown a card on which was printed 'def' (this is called a word-stem completion task). Several different six-letter words besides define begin with the letters 'def', such as 'deface', 'defame', 'defeat', 'defect', 'defend', 'defied' and 'deform', so there are several possible responses. The experimenters assessed explicit memory by asking people to try to remember the words they had seen previously, using the first three letters as a hint. They assessed implicit memory by asking the people to say the first word that came to mind that started with the three letters on the card.

Deliberate processing (shallow or deep processing) had a striking effect on the explicit memory task but not on the implicit memory task. When people used the three letters as cues for deliberate retrieval, they were much more successful if they had thought about whether they liked the word than if they simply paid attention to the occurrence of particular letters. However, when people simply said the first word that

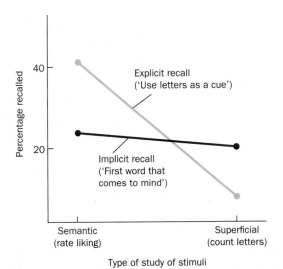

Figure 8.11 Explicit versus implicit memory. The graph shows the percentage of words recalled as a function of the type of study procedure. Deliberate processing improved performance of the explicit memory task but had little effect on the implicit memory task.

Source: Based on data from Graf, P. and Mandler, G., Activation makes words more accessible, but not necessarily more retrievable. *Journal of Verbal Learning and Verbal Behavior*, 1984, 23, 553–68.

came to mind, the way they had studied the words had little effect on the number of correct words that 'popped into their heads' (see Figure 8.11).

In one experiment, Buchner and Wippich (2000) required participants either (1) to recognise from a list of new and old words, words that had been previously seen, or (2) to complete word stems using words that had previously been seen. This last implicit task was used in a famous study of amnesics' memory and no differences were found between amnesics and controls. When the researchers analysed the reliability of these measures, the implicit measure was significantly less reliable than was the recognition measure. The study raises important questions about experiments which claim to show differences in memory performance based on implicit measures: it suggests that such differences may be due to methodological, rather than conceptual, reasons.

Are there sex differences in memory?

Evidence suggests that there are. Women's autobiographical memories have been found to be richer in detail (Andreano and Cahill, 2009) and are better-dated than are men's. Recognition memory is also better, but the question is: why? According to Heisz *et al.* (2013), it may be because women scan stimuli more during the process of encoding. They asked 40 male and 40 female undergraduates to view sixty different faces over a period of three days and tested their recognition memory for the faces on the fourth day. Eye movement was also recorded during encoding. In the study, women recognised more of the faces than did men and this

performance correlated with a greater length of time spent scanning the stimuli at encoding – women made more fixations than did men. The sex difference could be eliminated, however. When men were repeatedly exposed to the faces, their recognition memory improved.

Remembering

Remembering is an automatic process. The word 'automatic' means 'acting by itself'. But this definition implies that no special effort is involved. What is automatic is the retrieval of information from memory in response to the appropriate stimulus. What sometimes requires effort is the attempt to come up with the thoughts (the internal stimuli) that cause the information to be retrieved. In psychology experiments, retrieval can be measured in two basic ways: participants either recall material they have learned unprompted (free recall) or they are asked to identify material they had previously seen; this material is presented amongst stimuli that had not been seen (this is called a recognition memory paradigm).

The retrieval of implicit memories is automatic: when the appropriate stimulus occurs, it automatically evokes the appropriate response. Explicit memories can be retrieved automatically. Whisper your name to yourself. How did you manage to remember what your name is? How did you retrieve the information needed to move your lips in the proper sequence? Those questions cannot be answered by introspection. The information just leaps out at us when the proper question is asked (or, more generally, when the appropriate stimulus is encountered).

Reading provides a particularly compelling example of the automatic nature of memory retrieval. When an experienced reader looks at a familiar word, the name of the word occurs immediately, and so does the meaning. In fact, it is difficult to look at a word and not think of its name. Figure 8.12 contains a list of words that can be used to demonstrate a phenomenon known as the Stroop effect (Stroop, 1935; MacLeod, 1992). Look at the words in Figure 8.12 and, as quickly as you can, say the names of the colours in which the words are printed; do not read the words themselves.

Most people cannot completely ignore the words and simply name the colours; the tendency to think of the words and pronounce them is difficult to resist. The Stroop effect indicates that even when we try to suppress a well-practised memory, it tends to be retrieved automatically when the appropriate stimulus occurs.

But what about the fact that some memories seem to be difficult to recall? For most people, remembering information is effortless and smooth. It is something we do unconsciously and automatically – most of the time. Occasionally, though, our memory of a name or a place or something else fails. The experience is often frustrating because we know that the

blue blue blue green
green yellow red
yellow yellow blue
red green yellow
yellow green yellow
yellow red yellow
green blue yellow
red blue green green
blue blue green red

Figure 8.12 The Stroop effect. Name the colour in which the words are printed as quickly as you can; you will find it difficult to ignore what the words say.

information is 'in there somewhere' but we just cannot seem to get it out. This is known as the **tip-of-the-tongue phenomenon** (you encountered the olfactory analogue, the tip-of-the-nose phenomenon, in Chapter 5). It was first studied carefully during the 1960s (Brown and McNeill, 1966), and since then we have learned a great deal about it (Jones, 1989; A.S. Brown, 1991). It is a common, if not universal, experience; it can occur about once a week and increases with age; it often involves proper names and knowing the first letter of the word; and is solved during the experience about 50 per cent of the time.

The active search for stimuli that will evoke the appropriate memory, as exemplified in the tip-of-the-tongue phenomenon, has been called recollection (Baddeley, 1982). Recollection may be aided by contextual variables, including physical objects, suggestions or other verbal stimuli. These contextual variables are called **retrieval cues**. The usefulness of these retrieval cues often depends on encoding specificity. Remember from the previous section that the encoding specificity principle states that information can only be retained if it has been stored and the way in which it is retrieved depends on how it was stored. One famous example is that of encoding and retrieving material above and under water. Godden and Baddeley (1975) asked skilled scuba divers to learn lists of words either under water or on land. The divers' ability to recall the lists was later tested in either the same or a different environment. The variable of interest was where subjects learned the list: in or out of the water. When lists were learned under water, they were recalled much better under water than on land, and lists learned on land were recalled better on land than in the water. The

context in which information is learned or processed, therefore, influences our ability to recollect that information.

Reconstruction: remembering as a creative process

Much of what we recall from long-term memory may not be an accurate representation of what actually happened previously. One view of memory is that it is a plausible account of what might have happened or even of what we think should have happened. An early experiment by Bartlett drew attention to this possibility. This was Bartlett's view:

> Remembering is not the reexcitation of innumerable fixed, lifeless and fragmentary traces. It is an imaginative reconstruction, or construction, built out of the relation of our attitude towards a whole active mass of organised past reactions or experience and to a little outstanding detail which commonly appears in image or in language form. It is thus hardly ever really exact, even in the most rudimentary cases of rote recapitulation, and it is not at all important that it should be so. (Source: Bartlett, 1932, p. 213)

Bartlett had people read a story or essay or look at a picture. Then he asked them on several later occasions to retell the prose passage or to draw the picture. Each time, the people 'remembered' the original a little differently. If the original story had contained peculiar and unexpected sequences of events, people tended to retell it in a more coherent and sensible fashion, as if their memories had been revised to make the information accord more closely with their own conceptions of reality. Bartlett concluded that people remember only a few striking details of an experience and that during recall they reconstruct the missing portions in accordance with their own expectations.

Many studies have confirmed Bartlett's conclusions and have extended his findings to related phenomena. Spiro (1977, 1980) found that people will remember even a rather simple story in different ways, according to their own conceptions of reality. Two groups of people read a story about an engaged couple in which the man was opposed to having children. In one version, the woman was upset when she learned his opinion because she wanted to have children. In the other version, the woman also did not want to have children. After reading the story, people were asked to fill out some forms. While collecting the forms, the experimenter either said nothing more about the story or 'casually mentioned' that the story was actually a true one and added one of two different endings: the couple got married and have been happy ever since, or the couple broke up and never saw each other again.

Two days, three weeks or six weeks later, the participants were asked to recall the story they had read. If at least three weeks had elapsed, people who had heard an ending that contradicted the story tended to 'remember' information that resolved the conflict. For example, if they had read that the woman was upset to learn that the man did not want children but were later told that the couple was happily married, people were likely to 'recall' something that would have resolved the conflict, such as that the couple had decided to adopt a child rather than have one of their own. If people had read that the woman also did not want children but were later told that the couple broke up, then they were likely to 'remember' that there was a difficulty with one set of parents. In contrast, people who had heard an ending that was consistent with the story they had read did not remember any extra facts; they did not need them to make sense of the story. For example, if they had heard that the couple disagreed about having a child and later broke up, no new 'facts' had to be added.

People were most confident about details that had actually not occurred but had been added to make more sense of the story. Thus, a person's confidence in the accuracy of a particular memory is not necessarily a good indication of whether the event actually occurred.

However, some researchers have criticised Bartlett's findings and some have even argued that Bartlett himself drew conclusions that were not warranted (Ost and Costall, 2002). Edwards and Middleton (1987), for example, have argued that the studies reported by Bartlett – these studies reported a form of memory called serial reproduction – did not assess the normal, everyday process of remembering. For example, participants in Bartlett's experiments wrote down alone what they could remember of a story read to them (rather than being retold to them, as you might expect in most everyday contexts). Others, such as Roediger *et al.* (2000), have argued that the material to be remembered was not particularly ecologically valid. One of the stories to be recalled, *The War of the Ghosts*, was quite exotic and unusual and not like every-day prose (Wynn and Logie, 1998; Roediger *et al.*, 2000), which made connections between parts of the story difficult to form. Bartlett did use more familiar material and found that participants made the typical reconstruction of the story. Bartlett's story is reproduced in Table 8.1, together with two recalled versions. Note the differences, and types of differences, between the actual story and the remembered one.

In an experiment in which the material to be remembered was relevant, Wynn and Logie (1998) quizzed undergraduates at two-month intervals about an incident at the beginning of the academic year and asked them to recall memories from

that time. They found that memories were very resistant to change over time. However, although the study found that some distinctive memories could be accurately recalled, recent research suggests that memories can be very manipulable to the extent that false information introduced at recall can lead to this false information being incorporated into memory. The context in which memory and acquisition takes place can also influence our recall of events, as the next section shows.

Table 8.1 Two examples of *The War of the Ghosts* story. The first (a) is the original story; the second (b) is the same person's version of the story after eight days

(a) *The War of the Ghosts*

One night two young men from Egulac went down to the river to hunt seals, and while they were there it became foggy and calm. Then they heard war-cries, and they thought: 'Maybe this is a war-party.' They escaped to the shore, and hid behind a log. Now canoes came up, and they heard the noise of paddles, and saw one canoe coming up to them. There were five men in the canoe, and they said:

'What do you think? We wish to take you along. We are going up the river to make war on the people.'

One of the young men said: 'I have no arrows.'

'Arrows are in the canoe,' they said.

'I will not go along. I might be killed. My relatives do not know where I have gone. But you,' he said, turning to the other, 'may go with them.'

So one of the young men went, but the other returned home.

And the warriors went on up the river to a town on the other side of Kalama. The people came down to the water, and they began to fight, and many were killed. But presently the young man heard one of the warriors say: 'Quick, let us go home: that Indian has been hit.' Now he thought: 'Oh, they are ghosts.' He did not feel sick, but they said he had been shot.

So the canoes went back to Egulac, and the young man went ashore to his house, and made a fire. And he told everybody and said: 'Behold I accompanied the ghosts, and we went to fight. Many of our fellows were killed, and many of those who attacked us were killed. They said I was hit, and I did not feel sick.'

He told it all, and then he became quiet. When the sun rose he fell down. Something black came out of this mouth. His face became contorted. The people jumped up and cried.

He was dead.

(b) *The War of the Ghosts*

Two young men from Egulac went fishing. While thus engaged they heard a noise in the distance. 'That sounds like a war-cry,' said one, 'there is going to be some fighting.' Presently there appeared some warriors who invited them to join an expedition up the river.

Table 8.1 *Continued*

One of the young men excused himself on the ground of family ties. 'I cannot come,' he said, 'as I might get killed.' So he returned home. The other man, however, joined the party, and they proceeded on canoes up the river. While landing on the banks the enemy appeared and were running down to meet them. Soon someone was wounded, and the party discovered that they were fighting against ghosts. The young man and his companion returned to the boats, and went back to their homes.

The next morning at dawn he was describing his adventures to his friends, who had gathered round him. Suddenly something black issued from his mouth, and he fell down uttering a cry. His friends closed around him, but found that he was dead.

Source: Bartlett, F.C., *Remembering.* London: Cambridge University Press, 1932.

Why do we remember the things that we do?

According to a review of the encoding and retrieval literature by Danker and Anderson (2010), it may be because the regions of the brain that are active during encoding are reactivated, partially, when we recall or retrieve.

In their review, they found that when neutral stimuli were associated with various sensory stimuli, the presence of these 'neutral' stimuli activated sensory and emotional regions in the brain. Similarly, when people encode material in a particular way, regions associated with different encoding strategies were reactivated. 'The process of remembering an episode,' they argue, 'involves literally returning to the brain state that was present during that episode' (p. 87). Interestingly, they also cited

Controversies in psychological science: How long does memory last?

The issue

In 1885, Hermann Ebbinghaus reported the results of the first experiment to determine the duration of memory. Using himself as a participant, Ebbinghaus memorised 13 nonsense syllables such as 'dax', 'wuj', 'lep' and 'pib'. He then studied how long it took him to relearn the original list after intervals varying from a few minutes up to 31 days. Figure 8.13 shows what he found. Much of what he learned was forgotten very quickly – usually within a day or two. But even after 31 days, he could still recall some of the original information.

Ebbinghaus's research dealt with remembering nonsense syllables and began a fruitful line of enquiry for psychologists

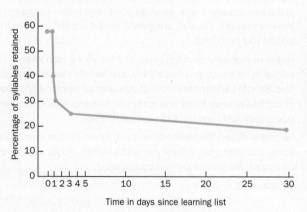

Figure 8.13 Ebbinghaus's (1885) forgetting curve.

Source: Adapted from Ebbinghaus, H., *Memory: A contribution to experimental psychology* (H.A. Ruger and C.E. Bussenius, trans.), 1885/1913. Teacher's College Press, Columbia University, New York.

interested in the length of time we can reasonably retain information before we begin to forget. For example, for how long might you remember the important experiences of your childhood? Or the information in this book? Or a well-known public event?

The evidence

Schmolck *et al.* (2000) looked at the effect of **retention interval** – the period between encoding and retrieval – on memory for the O.J. Simpson trial verdict, announced on 3 October 1995. College students were asked about how they heard the news about the verdict three days after the result, 15 months later and 32 months later. There was a significant difference between recall at 15 and at 32 months. After 15 months, about 50 per cent of recollections were accurate and only 11 per cent contained major errors; at 32 months, only 29 per cent of the recollections were accurate and 40 per cent contained major distortions. Figure 8.14 shows you how memory became distorted in these participants over time. There may be some value to this. There is neuroimaging evidence to suggest that the process of forgetting frees up regions of the brain: the forgetting of material that competes with more important information that we need to remember is associated with a decline in the activation of the PFC, for example (Kuhl *et al.*, 2007).

In a well-known study, Bahrick *et al.* (1975) investigated how much information about their classmates (such as faces or names) graduates would remember 25 years after graduation. Bahrick found that the ability to recall classmates' names and to generate a name from a photo declined over time. The longer the retention interval (RI), the greater the decline. Recognition of faces and names and the matching of names to faces,

Controversies in psychological science: *Continued*

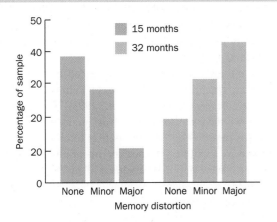

Figure 8.14 The degree of memory distortion (none, minor and major) for the O.J. Simpson trial verdict seen in Schmolck *et al.*'s study after 15 and 32 months.

Source: Schmolck, H., Buffalo, E.A. and Squire L.R., Memory distortions develop over time: Recollections of the O.J. Simpson trial verdict after 15 and 32 months. *Psychological Science*, 2000, 11(1), 39–45, reprinted by permission of Blackwell Publishers Ltd.

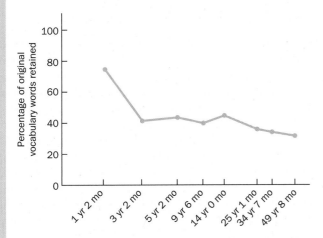

Figure 8.15 The forgetting curve for Spanish vocabulary.

Source: Adapted from Bahrick, H.P., Semantic memory content in permastore: Fifty years of Spanish learned in school. *Journal of Experimental Psychology: General*, 1984, 113, 1–29.

however, was fairly robust. Ninety per cent of responses were correct over the first 15 years (although accuracy, again, declined when the RI became longer). Bahrick (1984) also reported that retention for Spanish learned at school declined in the first six years after graduating, stabilised for the next 35 years and then declined thereafter (see Figure 8.15).

Bahrick argued that the period of stability from 6 to 35 years represents a 'permastore'; this was a store of knowledge that was resistant to forgetting and which must have been learned deeply.

An alternative interpretation, however, was suggested by Neisser (1984). He suggested that individuals have a schematic representation of a 'knowledge domain', that is, specific knowledge is not stored in a permanent way, but ways of representing that knowledge allow the retrieval of information. On the basis of this view, conceptual knowledge should be better retained (and retrieved) than would, say, straightforward facts.

Conway and co-workers (Conway *et al.*, 1991; Cohen *et al.*, 1992), measured students' retention of knowledge of cognitive psychology over 12 years (between 1978 and 1989) and found that memory declined in the first 36 months, then stabilised. However, the recall and recognition of proper names declined more rapidly than did memory for concepts. Why? If you accept Neisser's position, conceptual information should be better retained because memory is organised in such a way as to facilitate the retention of this type of information. Cohen (1990) further suggested that proper names lacked the semantic depth necessary for encoding concepts. Proper names did not need to be represented in abstract form and do not fall within a scheme of knowledge. In a follow-up study, Conway *et al.* (1992) found that coursework was a better predictor of retention than was exam performance because the learning for the former was distributed across the term whereas learning for the exam was, arguably, massed (being crammed).

Conway *et al.* (1997) found the better students seemed to 'remember' more of the answers in a multiple choice examination exam. For research methods courses, the same students 'knew' more, indicating that a **remember-to-know shift (R–K shift)** had occurred. Why, then, did better students not 'know' more after their lecture courses? One reason may be that the lecture courses contained more topics and that there was, therefore, greater variability in the types of knowledge domain to be learned (Conway *et al.*, 1997). Also, the research methods courses involved a large degree of repetition (as research methods courses do) and problem-solving is integral to the course: these factors might promote the R–K shift.

People's memory for their grades also declines with time (Bahrick *et al.*, 2008). One to 54 years after graduating, 276 participants were able to recall 3,025 of 3,967 grades. The better students made fewer errors. Of those who recalled their marks incorrectly, 81 per cent inflated the grade.

Conclusion

So, what can we conclude about long-term retention of knowledge? Non-schematic knowledge (such as the names of psychologists) declines more greatly than schematic knowledge (such as conceptual information). Better students also remember more of non-research methods psychology lecture courses and know more from research methods courses as well as recalling grades more accurately. One reason for this is that there is a shift from remembering to knowing, from episodic to semantic memory.

three studies of false memory which showed that false memory retrieval does not activate the region that is normally active during encoding.

The malleability of memory

An experiment takes place in which participants are asked to read short passages of text and then, one day later in a telephone conversation, are asked questions about the content of the text and the context in which the reading occurred. Six weeks later, they are asked the same questions and also whether they remembered answers given in their telephone conversation. This experiment by Loftus and her colleagues (see Joslyn *et al.*, 2001) found that while participants were remarkably good at remembering the correct answers they gave, they were significantly poor at remembering the questions they answered incorrectly. Perhaps the correct answers generated a positive mood or represented a more coherent memory.

This is one of several studies that indicate that our subjective beliefs about the context of content of memory can influence the recall of events. Research from social psychology and cognitive psychology shows how we can be misled into saying things or doing things we believe to be incorrect or which we are not sure about. The studies of Solomon Asch (described in Chapter 15) and Elizabeth Loftus (described below) show how malleable human behaviour can be, especially when we are faced with the pressure to conform.

Roediger *et al.* (2001) investigated whether conformity was simply a 'public' behaviour where a person wants to be seen to behave correctly and yet knows that their response is wrong, or a 'private' one, where the conversion in their belief is genuine. Studies of social psychology have shown that conformity is greater when participants make decisions in the company of others than when alone. Would the presence of another person who falsely claimed that an object had been in a room lead a participant also to claim that they remembered seeing an object in a room when no such object was present?

In one condition, a participant and a confederate watched slides of six household scenes featuring common household objects for either 15 or 60 seconds. In a collaborative recall task in which both individuals tried to recall as many objects in the scenes as they could, the confederate made occasional mistakes such as recalling items that were not in the slides. Some of these items were consistent with some of the items in the scene and other were not. After a short delay, the participant was asked to recall as many items from the scenes as they could. In a second condition, a similar experiment was carried out but no erroneous suggestions were made.

Participants in the company of those confederates who recalled objects that were not in the scenes recalled significantly more erroneous objects than did those in the control condition. This effect was magnified if people were exposed to the scenes for 15 seconds (presumably, reflecting the fact that such a short period leaves little time to monitor the scene and leads you to believe that there were objects presented that were not actually there). Participants who recalled these erroneous items were also more likely to report that they 'knew' the objects were in the scene rather than report they remembered seeing them.

Why were the participants influenced in this way? The authors interpret the results in terms of Johnson's source monitoring framework (Johnson *et al.*, 1993). This argues that because we receive information from many sources, we can recall this material but misattribute it to earlier events. The collaborative recall part of the experiment may be an example of an early event acting as a source of memory interference where more recent memories interfere with current retrieval. The more consistent the confederates' recall is with that of the event or scene, the stronger the social contagion will be; the more distinctive the recall, the less likely social contagion is to occur.

This susceptibility has significant consequences for important areas of life, especially those which can have serious repercussions, such as eyewitness testimony.

Eyewitness testimony

On 4 October 1992, an El Al plane lost its engine after take-off from Amsterdam Schiphol Airport. It returned to the airport but lost height and crashed into an 11-storey apartment building. Ten months later, Crombag *et al.* (1996) questioned 193 individuals about the crash. The event was widely reported in the news but was not actually filmed. When individuals were asked if they saw the plane hit the building, 55 per cent said that they had (they had not been present at the time of the accident); 59 per cent said that the fire started immediately on impact. In a follow-up study, 68 per cent said they had seen the crash and 67 per cent of participants said that they saw the plane hit the building horizontally (in fact, it hit the building vertically).

This experiment and those of Loftus and her colleagues (Loftus, 1997) suggest that our recollections of events may not be infallible. Loftus, for example, has reported that the kinds of questions used to elicit information after an event has been experienced can have a major effect on what people remember. Loftus's research shows that even subtle changes in a question can affect people's recollections. For example, Loftus and Palmer (1974) showed people films of car accidents and asked them to estimate vehicles' speeds when they 'contacted/hit/bumped/collided/smashed' each other. People's estimates of the vehicles' speeds were directly related to the force of the impact suggested by the verb, such as 'hit', that appeared in the question (see Figure 8.17). That is, the more expressive and dramatic the verb, the greater the

Cutting edge: Beliefs about repressed memory

In the 1990s, psychology underwent a controversy called the 'memory wars'. On one side of the war were those who believed that early memories were repressed but could be retrieved during therapy. On the other side were those who disputed the validity of repressed memories. The war was essentially won by the latter but residual belief in repressed memory continues to exist. To discover how extensive the residue was, Patihis et al. (2014) compared the beliefs about repressed memory, of various groups such as students, experimental psychologists, psychoanalysts, hypnotherapists, clinical psychology practitioners and researchers and others, with the beliefs of those surveyed in earlier studies. You can see a summary of results in Figure 8.16 and Table 8.2.

Fewer than 30 per cent of the research-oriented psychologists believed that 'traumatic memories are often repressed'. However, 60 per cent of the other groups did and the belief was particularly high amongst undergraduates (although the study does not indicate whether these students were psychology students or participants from the general undergraduate body). A similar pattern was found in response to the statement that repressed memories could be retrieved accurately in therapy – 25 per cent of the research psychologists agreed but 43 per cent of the other groups did, especially practitioners. The degree of belief correlated with scientific and critical thinking: the greater the latter, the less likely was the individual's belief in repressed memory.

Mainstream clinicians in the 2010s were more likely to be sceptical about repressed memory than were those in the 1990s. Therefore, although there are differences between the participants from these two periods in their beliefs about the existence of repressed memories, a great difference exists between the sceptical psychology and clinical psychology researchers, and clinicians and therapists.

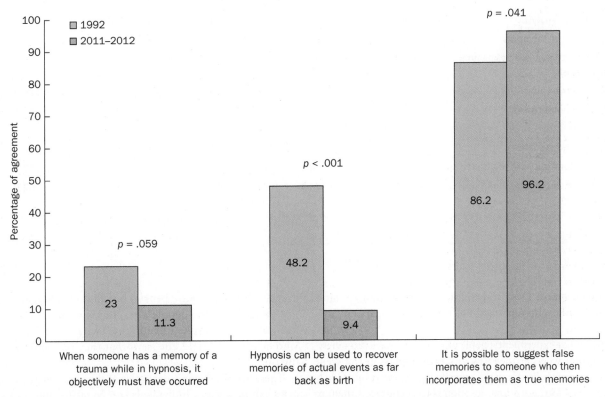

Figure 8.16 Comparision of mainstream Ph.D. psychotherapists' beliefs about hypnosis and false memories in 1992 and 2011–2012. The data for 1992, reported in Yapko (1994a), are from a Ph.D. subsample (n = 208) who were recruited from psychotherapy conventions. Our data for 2011–2012 are from board-certified psychotherapists (n = 53) who were members of the American Academy of Clinical Psychology. The p values are from two proportion z tests comparing the two groups' percentage of agreement with each of the three statements. Results for additional groups are presented in Table S2.5 in the Supplemental Material.

Cutting edge: *Continued*

Table 8.2 Percentage of participants indicating at least some agreement with key statements about repressed memory

Participant group	n	Traumatic memories are often repressed				Repressed memories can be retrieved in therapy accurately			
		Slightly agree (%)	Agree (%)	Strongly agree (%)	Total (%)	Slightly agree (%)	Agree (%)	Strongly agree (%)	Total (%)
Psychology professionals with a research or science focus									
Experimental psychologists	99	16.2	10.1	1.0	**27.3**	21.2	3.0	0.0	**24.2**
SARMAC members	70	17.1	8.6	0.0	**25.7**	14.3	2.9	0.0	**17.1**
SSCP members	62	8.1	9.7	0.0	**17.7**	8.1	1.6	0.0	**9.7**
Clinical psychologists									
Researchers	62	12.9	4.8	1.6	**19.4**	11.3	4.8	0.0	**16.1**
Practitioners	58	36.2	17.2	6.9	**60.3**	32.8	10.3	0.0	**43.1**
Psychoanalysts	81	19.8	39.5	9.9	**69.1**	28.4	16.0	2.5	**46.9**
Alternative therapists									
Neuro-linguistic programming therapists	59	18.6	49.2	22.0	**89.8**	35.6	32.2	6.8	**74.6**
Internal Family System therapists	67	20.9	38.8	20.9	**80.6**	20.9	37.3	7.5	**65.7**
Hypnotherapists	50	22.0	32.0	28.0	**82.0**	20.0	22.0	12.0	**54.0**
Others									
Undergraduates	406	34.0	34.0	9.6	**77.6**	46.8	15.8	2.0	**64.5**
General public in the United States	112	31.2	38.4	14.3	**83.9**	40.2	34.8	2.7	**77.7**
General public in the United Kingdom	112	31.2	34.8	11.6	**77.7**	48.2	17.9	1.8	**67.9**

estimated speed. Despite being one of psychology's most famous studies, no replication of the study appears on Google Scholar.

In a similar experiment, people were asked a week after viewing the film whether they saw any broken glass at the scene (there was none). People in the 'smashed' group were most likely to say yes. Thus, a leading question that encouraged them to remember the vehicles going faster also encouraged them to remember that they saw non-existent broken glass. The question appears to have modified the memory itself.

Even very subtle leading questions can affect people's recollections. Loftus and Zanni (1975) showed people short films of an accident involving several vehicles. Some people were asked, 'Did you see a broken headlight?'; others were asked, 'Did you see the broken headlight?' The particular question biased the people's responses: although the film did not show a broken headlight, twice as many people who heard the article 'the' said that they remembered seeing one.

These are not the only examples of the ways in which memories can be altered. Individuals can be misled into thinking that a 'stop' sign was a 'give way' sign (Loftus *et al.*, 1978) and that a bare-handed thief wore gloves (Zaragoza and Mitchell, 1996). This misinformation effect is much stronger in older people (Jacoby *et al.*, 2005).

Experiments such as these have important implications for eyewitness testimony in courts of law. Wells and Seelau (1995) illustrate this point with the following examples:

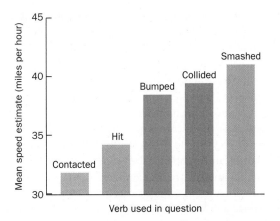

Figure 8.17 Leading questions and recall. Mean estimated speed of vehicles as recalled by people in the study of Loftus and Palmer (1974).

Source: Based on data from Loftus, E.F. and Palmer, J.C., Reconstruction of automobile destruction: An example of the interaction between language and memory. *Journal of Verbal Learning and Verbal Behavior,* 1974, 13, 585–89.

What do these famous lines have in common? 'Beam me up, Scotty', 'Me Tarzan, you Jane', 'You dirty rat', 'Play it again, Sam', 'Elementary, my dear Watson'? Their fame, yes. But none of these lines was actually said. This highlights how our memory can be very malleable.

Source: Photo 12 / Alamy Stock Photo.

In 1984, Frederick Rene Dange was identified from a set of photographs and served 10 years in a Californian prison for rape, kidnapping, robbery and murder that he did not commit. Dange was released in 1994 after a DNA test proved his innocence. In 1980, James Newsome was convicted of murder on the basis of eyewitness evidence. Fifteen years later, he was released after his fingerprints were submitted to new computer technology that implicated someone else as the murderer.

In a review of 205 cases of wrongful arrest, Rattner (1988) found that 52 per cent of these cases were associated with mistaken eyewitness testimony. In 1996, the National Institute of Justice found that 28 people had been wrongfully convicted based on eyewitness testimony (DNA evidence had exonerated the accused). Consequently, in 1998, the American Psychological Association issued a new series of rules and procedures designed to reduce errors made in considering eyewitness identification (Wells *et al.*, 1998).

Eyewitness identification

In a famous, historical case, Frye v. The United States (1923), the court ruled that scientific evidence was admissible only if it was generally accepted by the relevant scientific community. The judgment in a case called Daubert v. Merrell Dow Pharmaceuticals, Inc. 70 years later, however, ruled that judges would be the gatekeepers of scientific reliability in the US – they would judge the relevance, validity and reliability of scientific evidence. This makes the quality of evidence very important. Laypeople regard eyewitness reports as important to their evaluation of testimony (Shaw *et al.*, 1999).

A survey of eyewitness testimony experts found that 98 per cent thought that testimony could be influenced by the way in which questions are worded, 98 per cent thought that police line-up instructions could affect identification, 87 per cent thought that eyewitnesses' confidence in their judgement is poorly correlated with the accuracy of the testimony, 83 per cent thought that memory loss is greatest immediately after witnessing the event and 80 per cent thought that eyewitness confidence is malleable and influenced by factors unrelated to accuracy, that exposure to a mugshot increases the likelihood of the face in the mugshot being selected from a later line-up, that children are more susceptible than adults to leading questions, and that eyewitnesses are better at recognising perpetrators of their own race (Kassin *et al.*, 2001).

According to forensic psychologists Gary Wells and Amy Bradfield (1999), 'There is increasing evidence that mistaken eyewitness identifications from line-ups and photospreads are the most frequent cause of juries convicting innocent persons'. They examined how information given to a witness before and after making a line-up identification affected the witness's confidence in making the correct identification. Giving positive post-identification feedback (such as telling the witness they identified the right suspect when they had not) inflates confidence in their identification, but also makes them think that their view of the suspect was better, that they identified the suspect more quickly and that they paid more attention when they witnessed the suspect.

In a twist to this type of experiment, Wells and Bradfield asked witnesses to think privately about how certain they were about their identification, how good their view was, how long they took to identify the suspect before being given false positive feedback. Another group of participants was given these instructions after receiving feedback and another was not instructed to think about its decision. In each case, the eyewitness had identified the wrong suspect.

The researchers found that when eyewitnesses were instructed to think about the decision prior to feedback, they were relatively unaffected by the false positive feedback. Those who were not instructed to think about their decision or were instructed to think after being given feedback showed a significant inflation in their confidence which also extended to other aspects of their testimony.

In a recent review, Wixted and Wells (2017) consider some of the factors that can influence incorrect eyewitness identification. One argument sometimes made is that confidence in eyewitness identification is not related to actual accurate identification of the perpetrator. Wixted and Wells found that confidence and accuracy were strongly related but only when suspect line-ups had no administrator, when line-ups were fair (i.e. the innocent line-up member does not resemble the perpetrator) and when the judgement of confidence was made immediately after the identification. They note that since 1989, 349 convictions largely based on eyewitness identification (about 70%) have been overturned in the US because DNA evidence proved that the suspect was not responsible (Innocence Project, 2016).

Recognising the fallibility of eyewitness identification, some US states such as the State of New Jersey, specifically issues the following instruction to jurors about eyewitness identification and confidence: 'although some research has found that highly confident witnesses are more likely to make accurate identification, eyewitness confidence is generally an unreliable indicator of accuracy' (NJ Courts 2012a, 2012b). This view is supported by the American Psychological Association, which concluded that 'many witnesses are overconfident in their identification decisions' (American Psychological Association, 2014).

As Wixted and Wells's review finds, however, that confidence is a good predictor of accuracy if it is measured immediately. Low confidence is a signal of uncertain identification. The suspects exonerated by DNA were those identified by people who had low confidence in their accuracy (Garrett, 2011). Wixted and Wells also note that there are some estimator variables that are important for accurate eyewitness testimony. Estimator variables are those that affect eyewitness identification and are outside of the control of the legal system. They include:

- Race - our ability to identify people from races other than our own is less good.
- Exposure - being briefly exposed to the potential suspect leads to worse identification.
- Lighting - poor lightning at the crime scene is associated with poorer memory for the perpetrator. Time - the longer the time between the eye witnessing and the line-up, the less accurate a person's memory.
- Stress - the more stressed a person is, the less accurate their memory.
- The presence of weapons -people's memory for perpetrators is poorer if weapons are present.

Cutting edge: How much do people know about memory?

Two psychologists sought to find out the answer by asking 1,500 members of the US public in a telephone survey, 73 attendees at a US psychology conference and a group of researchers with more than 10 years of experience in memory research (Simons and Chabris, 2011). Participants were asked to express agreement or disagreement with a series of 16 statements. There were some significant differences between groups. For example, none of the experts agreed with the following statements:

- People who suffer from amnesia typically cannot recall their own name or identity
- The testimony of one confident eyewitness should be enough evidence to convict a defendant of a crime

- Human memory works like a video camera, accurately recording events
- Hypnosis is useful in helping witnesses accurately recall details of crimes
- Once you have experienced an event and formed a memory of it, that memory does not change.

But the public were more likely to agree with them: agreement was 82, 37, 63, 54 and 47 per cent, respectively, for each of the above statements.

In response to the statement:

People generally notice when something unexpected enters their field of view

▶

Cutting edge: *Continued*

18 per cent of experts agreed, whereas 77 per cent of the public did. The conference attendees gave responses similar to the experts.

Acknowledging that their telephone polling had some limitations – it is expensive, completion rate is poor, it does not reach homes with no landline and the sample is likely to be older – the researchers conducted a follow-up study using Amazon's Mechanical Turk, an online research tool you read about in Chapter 2, which allows researchers to collect data on line from participants who take part for a small fee. The results from the public/non-experts was virtually the same as those of the first study, as you can see in Tables 8.3a and b.

Both studies demonstrate that, in two different types of survey, a large section of the general public holds mistaken beliefs about memory and how it works.

Table 8.3a Statements used and percentage of respondents giving each response, with the expert (*N* = 16) and the full Psychonomics sample (*N* = 73) percentages given for comparison

Statement	Group	Strongly Agree	Mostly Agree	Mostly Disagree	Strongly Disagree	Don't Know
Amnesia: *People suffering from amnesia typically cannot recall their own name or identity.*	**Public**	47.8	34.9	10.1	3.7	3.7
	Experts	0.0	0.0	12.5	87.5	0.0
	Psychonomics	0.0	1.4	31.5	57.5	9.6
Confident testimony: *In my opinion, the testimony of one confident eyewitness should be enough evidence to convict a defendant of a crime.*	**Public**	11.2	25.9	35.1	24.7	3.1
	Experts	0.0	0.0	6.2	93.8	0.0
	Psychonomics	0.0	0.0	11.0	87.7	1.4
Video memory: *Human memory works like a video camera,accurately recording the events we see and hear so that we can review and inspect them later.*	**Public**	23.9	39.1	23.4	11.3	2.4
	Experts	0.0	0.0	6.2	93.8	0.0
	Psychonomics	0.0	0.0	2.7	97.3	0.0
Hypnosis: *Hypnosis is useful in helping witnesses accurately recall details of crimes.*	**Public**	15.0	39.6	26.9	10.4	8.1
	Experts	0.0	0.0	18.8	68.8	12.5
	Psychonomics	0.0	0.0	15.1	69.9	15.1
Unexpected events: *People generally notice when something unexpected enters their field of view, even when they're paying attention to something else.*	**Public**	27.2	50.3	18.3	2.1	2.1
	Experts	0.0	18.8	31.2	50.0	0.0
	Psychonomics	2.7	15.1	35.6	43.8	2.7
Permanent memory: *Once you have experienced an event and formed a memory of it, that memory does not change.*	**Public**	16.5	31.1	34.7	14.1	3.6
	Experts	0.0	0.0	0.0	93.8	6.2
	Psychonomics	0.0	0.0	6.8	91.8	1.4

doi:10.1371/journal.pone.0022757.t002

Cutting edge: *Continued*

Table 8.3b Percentage of respondents agreeing with each memory statement, along with the average rate of agreement across items

Item	MTurk	SurveyUSA
Amnesia: People suffering from amnesia typically cannot recall their own name or identity.	81.4	69.6
Confident testimony: In my opinion, the testimony of one confident eyewitness should be enough evidence to convict a defendant of a crime.	22.1	32.9
Video memory: Human memory works like a video camera, accurately recording the events we see and hear so that we can review and inspect them later.	46.9	52.7
Unexpected events: People generally notice when something unexpected enters their field of view, even when they're paying attention to something else.	77.4	65.0
Permanent memory: Once you have experienced an event and formed a memory of it, that memory does not change.	28.0	39.9
Hypnosis: Hypnosis is useful in helping witnesses accurately recall details of crimes.	46.4	44.6
Average agreement rate (out of 6 items)	50.33	50.83
	(3.02)	(3.05)

Note: SurveyUSA data are from Simons & Chabris (2011).
doi: 10.1371/journal.pone.0051876.t003

Interference

Although long-term memory is durable, it may also be susceptible to interference. The finding that some memories may interfere with the retrieval of others is well established. An early study by Jenkins and Dallenbach (1924) showed that people are less likely to remember information after an interval of wakefulness than after an interval of sleep, presumably because of new memories that are formed when one is awake.

Subsequent research soon showed that there are two types of interference in retrieval. Sometimes we experience **retroactive interference**: when we try to retrieve information, other information, which we have learned more recently, interferes. You may have a hard time recalling your old telephone number because a new one has replaced it. When memories that interfere with retrieval are formed after the learning that is being tested, we experience retroactive interference.

At other times, retrieval is impaired by **proactive interference**, in which our ability to recall new information is reduced because of information we learned previously. Figure 8.18 illustrates the experimental procedure used to examine the effects of proactive interference.

In this procedure, the experimental group learns the words in both list A and list B. The control group learns only the words in list B. Both groups then experience a retention interval before they are asked to recall the words in list B. If the experimental group recalls fewer words in list B during the test than does the control group, proactive interference is said to have occurred.

As reasonable and intuitive as the principle of interference may be, it has not gone unchallenged. Researchers agree that interference can affect retrieval, but some argue that the kinds of recall task people are asked to perform in the laboratory are most likely to be affected by interference. In real life, such effects may not be so powerful. For example, meaningful prose, such as the kind found in novels, is resistant to interference. That said, however, a recent study demonstrated that when participants watched either a violent, sexually explicit or neutral television show featuring nine adverts, recall of the advertisements immediately after the exposure and 24 hours later was poorer in the violent and sexual television conditions (Bushman and Bonacci, 2002). The effect was robust whether the television programme was liked or disliked and whether the participant was male or female. It seems as if some stimuli are powerful or exciting enough to interfere with our memory, even outside the laboratory.

State-dependent memory: the effect of mood on recall

Research suggests that recall of memory is better when people's moods or emotional states match their emotional states when they originally learned the material. This phenomenon

Retroactive interference

Group	Initial learning	Retention interval	Retention test
Experimental	Learn A	Learn B	Recall A
Control	Learn A		Recall A

Proactive interference

	Initial learning		Retention interval	Retention test
Experimental	Learn A	Learn B		Recall B
Control		Learn B		Recall B

Figure 8.18 Retroactive and proactive interference illustrated.

is called **state-dependent memory**. The experimental procedure used in tests of state-dependent memory usually requires the manipulation of a person's mood by hypnosis (Bower, 1981), through drugs (Eich *et al.*, 1975) or, more commonly, by the alteration of the environmental context, as exemplified by the scuba diver study described earlier (see page 271) (Godden and Baddeley, 1975). Next, the person is given a list of items to memorise. Later, when the person may or may not be experiencing the same mental or emotional state, they are asked to recall the items on the list. If the states match, recall is better.

Mood-dependent memory describes a context in which the person's mood at encoding and retrieval can affect the successful execution of these two processes (such as a well-liked song provoking memories of events experienced when the song was first heard). Although replications in which positive effects in mood-dependent memory are rare (Bower and Mayer, 1989), Eich (1995) suggests that when participants in these experiments experience strong/stable moods and are responsible for generating memory cues, mood-dependent memory is robust.

In one experiment, participants were asked to generate specific memories for events from autobiographical memory in response to common words (Eich *et al.*, 1994). Two to three days later, participants were allowed to free recall the memories generated in the experiment. Eich *et al.* found that more events were recalled when the mood matched the mood at testing. In another set of experiments, Eich (1995) found that the transfer of information from one environment to another is better if these environments feel similar. However, changes in the environment are not important if the moods at acquisition and reinstatement are the same. There is also evidence to suggest that individuals with mood disorders have a greater ability to discriminate between old and new stimuli if their moods at exposure and testing match (Eich *et al.*, 1997).

Does this evidence suggest that mood-dependent memory is genuinely robust? Smith (1995) and Eich himself (1995) suggest that mood-dependent memory effects may be explained by other factors. Smith, for example, suggests that active

memories or pre-existing mood generated at the time of acquisition could have cued a representation of the initial context of the original event.

State-dependent memory may be related to **place- or context-dependent memory**, illustrated by the Godden and Baddeley experiment above. The demonstration of place-dependent memory (PDM) depends on the event to be remembered, the nature of encoding and retrieval, the ease by which people can mentally reinstate themselves, and the retention interval (Smith, 1979, 1988; McDaniel *et al.*, 1989; Wilhite, 1991). Reinstatement is important to PDM and refers to the process whereby the individual is placed in the same environment or is experiencing the same mood as when they originally encoded or generated information.

Because all of the factors listed above are important to PDM, the evidence for the phenomenon is mixed but generally supportive. In a meta-analysis of context-dependent memory studies in which retrieval and encoding were dependent on the explicit processing of aspects of the experimental environment, Smith and Vela (2001) found that context effects were very reliable. However, when people were encouraged to use non-contextual cues during encoding of material and its retrieval, the effects of environmental cues were reduced.

Accurate recall of memories of events experienced years previously has been found when the odours present at those events are re-presented some time later (Aggleton and Waskett, 1999; Chu and Downes, 2000), illustrating a form of state-dependent learning. Cann and Ross (1989) reported that the presence of a pleasant perfume at the presentation of a series of photographic slides led to better recognition if it was also presented at recall. Schab (1990) found that participants who learned and recalled in the presence of an ambient chocolate odour recalled more antonyms than did a control group or a group presented with an odour at encoding but not retrieval. In a subsequent experiment, odour-related words were no better recalled than neutral words although there was benefit to having the same odour present at encoding and recall. But the

(a)

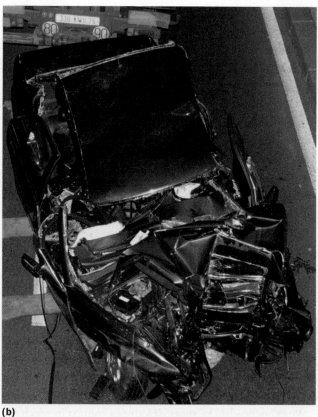

(b)

Flashbulb memories are thought to be generated by events that are important, unusual and personally meaningful. The attacks on the World Trade Center **(a)** and **(b)**, the car crash involving Dodi Fayed and Diana, Princess of Wales.
Source: © Laperruque / Alamy Stock Photo.

recall of memories may depend on the emotional nature of the odour. People report more unhappy memories in the presence of an unpleasant odour, for example, than they do in a pleasant one, and happier memories in the presence of a pleasant odour (Ehrlichman and Halpern, 1988).

Flashbulb memories

For British sports fans, it was a blessing; for those bored with wall-to-wall sport and physical activity involving sticks and running around in circles, it was a prompt for a collective groan. On 6 July 2005, the UK was told that London's bid to hold the 2012 Olympic Games was successful. Scenes of celebration ensued in Singapore and in London. The morning after, one of the authors was listening to the BBC's News and Sports radio station where the regular phone-in turned to discussing the logistics of holding the games and whether the capital would be up to it. At 9.50 a.m., the presenter, Michael Bannister, was about to introduce a guest when he read out an announcement from London Transport indicating that

Liverpool Street underground station in the financial district of London had been closed, due to a technical problem. Probably electrical, he said. This seemed unusual but, after 11 September 2001, nothing could be that unusual. The association with the 11 September attacks was prescient. It later transpired that bombs had been detonated in two London underground stations. A bus travelling near Tavistock Square, the home of the British Medical Association, had its roof blown off by another bomb. A total of 53 people were killed on 7 July 2005, including all of the British-born bombers.

The above recollection is an example of a **flashbulb memory** – the remembering of an event that is personally or socially important, novel, unexpected, vivid and has major long-term consequences. You will often hear older people say that they knew exactly what they were doing when US President Kennedy was assassinated (Winograd and Killinger, 1983) in the same way that the author knew exactly where he was and what he was doing when news of the first of the 7 July London bombs exploding was broadcast.

The name 'flashbulb memories' was coined by Brown and Kulik (1977) to describe the vivid recollections from black and white respondents of the assassinations of Martin Luther King and President Kennedy. According to Brown and Kulik, the memory has a 'live' quality that is almost perceptual . . . like a photograph' (p. 74). Since Brown and Kulik's landmark paper was published, flashbulb memories have been reported for the death of the King of Belgium (Finkenauer *et al.*, 1998), the death of spectators at the Hillsborough football stadium, England (Wright, 1993; Wright *et al.*, 1998), the resignation of Margaret Thatcher as British prime minister (Conway *et al.*, 1994; Wright *et al.*, 1998), the Gulf War (Weaver, 1993), the assassination of Olaf Palme, the Swedish prime minister (Christianson, 1989), the 1986 American space shuttle disaster (Bohannon, 1988), the experience of being in an earthquake (Neisser *et al.*, 1996b), the fall of the Berlin Wall, by East and West Germans (Bohn and Bernsten, 2007), and the death of Diana, Princess of Wales (Hornstein *et al.*, 2003).

According to Christianson (1992), 'people remember . . . public negative emotional events better than ordinary events that occurred equally long ago', suggesting that these events are not only more salient than others but also more accurate. Recently, there has been some debate on whether flashbulb memories are genuinely different from other types of memory (Hirst and Phelps, 2016). According to Brown and Kulik, flashbulb memories are of surprising or consequential events which are stored in the brain 'unchanged'; they also operate via a mechanism that is different from that which allows the formation of other types of memory. Wright (1993) and Wright *et al.* (1998), however, have conducted an extensive study of memories of the Hillsborough disaster and the resignation of Margaret Thatcher and suggest that flashbulb memories do not require a special mechanism. Furthermore, memories for these events may not even be vivid.

A problem with previous flashbulb memory research has been the absence of a 'control' group of memories: researchers have measured memories for flashbulb events over time but have not compared them with memories for other events experienced roughly at the same time or before the memorable event. Addressing this problem, Talarico and Rubin (2003) examined undergraduates' recall of events when first hearing about the 11 September 2001 attacks on the World Trade Center, and of other everyday memories on 12 September. There is some debate in the flashbulb memory literature concerning the accuracy of recall of important events. Talarico and Rubin returned to the students 1, 6 or 32 weeks later to test the accuracy and consistency of memory. There was a decline in the consistency of detail given for both types of event across time. Recall declined for both types of memory but flashbulb memories were recalled in a more narrative and coherent way. Emotion was unrelated to the consistency of recall but the more emotional the response, the greater the confidence in recalling details surrounding the event. The results suggest that while flashbulb memories are inconsistently recalled, their emotional impact makes people more confident about the perceived accuracy of their recall.

Hirst *et al.* (2009) asked 3,000 participants from the US to describe how they learned about the attacks on the World Trade Centre in 2001, 1 week, 11 months and/or 35 months after the attacks. They found that the forgetting rate for the event slowed after a year and that the emotional reactions to the event are remembered less well than are non-emotional aspects such as where they learned about the attack or from whom they learned the information.

Theories of flashbulb memories

What theory or theories can best account for flashbulb memories? Finkenauer *et al.* (1998) put the theories of Brown and Kulik (1977), and their own (called the emotional–integrative model), to the test by examining memories of the death of the King of Belgium on 13 August 1993. The experimenters' own model suggests that the appraisal of the event as novel and important leads to surprise. Surprise and the importance of the event to the person determine the intensity of the emotion experienced.

Finkenauer *et al.* noted that all the theories agreed that surprise and consequentiality are necessary for flashbulb memories. The degree of consequentiality influenced the degree of completeness and explicitness of the memory. Rehearsal of the memory for the event (thinking and talking about it) is also important. However, although the photographic model suggested that importance and feeling state were important determinants of flashbulb memories, these factors did not predict flashbulb memories.

Conway *et al.*'s (1994) model suggests that surprise and emotional feeling are determinants of flashbulb memories. However, Christianson and Engelberg's study (1999) of 203 participants' recall of the Estonia ferry disaster of September 1994 – in which 900 passengers died – found that fewer than one-third of respondents consistently reported their emotional state at the time of hearing of the disaster, suggesting that the recollection of emotional state is not a good predictor of memory consistency. This is consistent with Finkenauer *et al.*'s (1998) review of flashbulb memory models.

Finkenauer *et al.* suggest that the appraisal of an event as novel causes surprise; this then leads to the formation of a flashbulb memory. Appraisal of an event as important determines the intensity of the emotional response but this response does not directly affect the formation of flashbulb memories. Instead, the data suggest that emotional state triggers the rehearsal of remembered events which, in turn, strengthens memory.

The emotional–integrative model is a persuasive way of accounting for the factors necessary to determine a flashbulb memory. Because it is explicit, it is testable: you can generate hypotheses from the model and test them empirically. The evidence at the moment, however, suggests that flashbulb memories may not be special. Events may be memorable but they may not be memorable for the reasons originally given by the authors of flashbulb memories. Also, it seems as if the length of time since the flashbulb event was experienced is important to the amount of detail recalled.

Cutting edge: The Apple of your eye

Memory research has demonstrated that if we are repeatedly exposed to stimuli, our memory for them improves. This is especially so when learning is explicit. But what if the learning is implicit? For example, how well would you be able to reproduce a very well-known logo, such as the Apple logo, from memory? Try it now before reading on. Get a piece of paper and – without looking up or looking at an Apple logo if you use an Apple device – try drawing the logo. Once you've done that, come back to this section.

So, how well did you do? If you didn't do particularly well, you're in good company. Blake et al. (2015) ran a similar experiment and found that people were poor at drawing the logo and at recognising features of a logo in a forced-choice recognition test.

Controversies in psychological science: Does 'brain training' work in healthy individuals?

The issue

Over the past decade, psychologists have investigated whether training on specific cognitive tasks can lead to improved performance on similar or unrelated tasks, a phenomenon known as a **transfer effect**. Based on what they think is evidence, sharp-eyed businesses have marketed products which they claim can improve your cognitive ability through repeated training. Products such as Brain Gym and others, for example, are sold on the promise of exactly this. There has also been a rise in research exploring the effect of video-game use on cognitive ability. The issue is: does this training work? Does it lead to better cognitive performance and can it lead to better performance on similar or unrelated tasks?

The evidence

Three types of research are relevant to answering this question. There is research which has examined the (1) effect of commercial 'brain training' products on cognitive performance; (2) effect of working memory training on subsequent cognitive performance; or (3) relationship between time spent playing commercial video games (via Playstation, X Box, Nintendo, online etc.) and performance in different cognitive domains such as reaction time, sustained attention, memory and so on.

To take the last area first. Gamers have had a pretty bad press. The stereotypical image of a gamer is of an adolescent male (and it usually is a male) squandering his life away in a darkened, dank bedroom fiddling with consoles and boxes which provide no intellectual or social enrichment. Think *Spaced* or Kevin Smith in *Die Harder*. It is an extremely popular hobby. According to *Fortune*, the gaming industry generated revenue of $23.5 billion in the US in 2015. In the UK, the market was worth $4.2 billion in 2015. Some estimates –and remember that estimates are educated guesswork based on selected data – put the incidence of game-playing in industrialised countries at 75 per cent (Desai et al., 2010). The length of time spent gaming has been associated with reduced attention (according to assessments made by players' school teachers), poorer sleep quality and poorer academic performance (Swing et al., 2010; King et al., 2013). Others, however, have found no significant relationship between length of time spent video-gaming and academic success. For example, in one, large study of 192,000 adolescent students from 22 countries, no significant association was found between students' academic performance (e.g. objectively measured maths, reading and science ability) and the frequency of video game playing (Drummond and Sauer, 2014). The authors explain the negative effects of other studies by pointing out the subjective, self-report nature of the methods in those studies. In theirs, the measure of cognitive performance was objective.

In fact, there is evidence that action video-gaming is associated with better visual attention, faster location of objects, more accurate estimation of the number of visual stimuli present on a screen, better contrast sensitivity, improved spatial resolution, better working memory, better executive function and better ability to switch attention (Blacker and Curby, 2013; Wilms et al., 2013; McDermott et al., 2014; among others). One study claimed

▷

Controversies in psychological science: *Continued*

that training for 30 minutes a day for two months on the game, SuperMario 64, led to an increase in grey matter in the hippocampal formation, the right dorsolateral prefrontal cortex (dlPFC) and both sides of the cerebellum (Kuhn *et al.*, 2014). Although having low numbers and no matched experimental condition – the effect could be attributable to engaging in a motor task every day for months – the study also found that those who showed greatest desire to play had larger hippocampal formation and dlPFC. So much for the stereotype.

In another experiment, Wilms *et al.* divided three groups of action video players according to whether they were non-players, casual game players or experienced players (>15 hours a month) and asked them to perform a series of visual attention and short-term memory tasks. In one task, the participant would see a series of dots on screen (from 1 to 9 dots), followed by a blank or scrambled screen and would then be asked to recall the number of dots. They found that gaming was unrelated to visual short-term memory performance but was associated with significantly faster encoding of visual information. That gamers are faster on a number of measures is a frequently reported finding (e.g. Granic *et al.*, 2014).

One problem with studies such as this might seem obvious. The number of participants is very low. In this study around 10 people were allocated to each group and this affects the power and generalisability of the findings (Powers *et al.*, 2013). Another criticism of gaming studies is that they tend to recruit only those participants at the extremes – those who play a lot (five hours or more a week) and those who play a little, if at all (Unsworth *et al.*, 2015). There is also a problem of gradation. If your criterion for experienced playing is over five hours a week, you will not be able to determine whether there are any differences between those who play only five hours a week and those who play 20+ hours a week. There may be differences within the experienced player group.

Taking these into account, Unsworth *et al.* (2015) conducted two experiments. In one, they examined the effect of extremes on cognitive ability by studying only experienced and non-experienced players. In a second experiment, they used a statistical technique called latent variable analysis to predict cognitive performance from length of time playing in all participants. The number of participants in each was 198 and 466, respectively. In the first study, as they predicted, a significant difference was found between the two groups on a number of cognitive measures. In the second study, however, they found no significant relationship between video-playing length and cognitive performance.

In a different domain, studies indicated that people who were trained on working memory tasks (such as the CogMed working memory training programme) performed much better on memory, vigilance, fluid intelligence, attention tasks and, therefore, could be used to help people with a variety of disorders in which memory and attention are impaired such as ADHD and language impairment (see Shipstead *et al.*, 2012). Recent evidence, however, has not been supportive. For example, Chooi and Thompson (2012) divided 93 participants into a control group, an active control group and an experimental group. Half were followed up at 8 days; half at 20 days. The training task used by the experimental group was the *n* back task. In this task, blue squares were flashed on screen at one of eight locations while letters were delivered via headphones. Participants had to recall the location of a square or the name of a letter that had been presented previously. The *n* refers to the number of presentations. So, if *n* was 2, participants might be asked to recall the location of a square two presentations previously. Vocabulary, general ability, perceptual speed, card rotation, paper folding and other tests were used as outcome measures before and after the intervention. Although performance improved in the experimental group, the improvement was not statistically significant and there was no difference in performance between 8 and 20 days. This suggests that the transfer effect was absent.

One meta-analysis of 217 studies found that spatial skills training did result in benefits on spatial tasks (Uttal *et al.*, 2012) but another, which examined the effect of working memory training on later cognitive performance found (i) a reliable short-term benefit on working memory performance but these were not sustained at follow-up and (ii) no transfer effects on unrelated tasks such as non-verbal and verbal ability, attention and arithmetic. The short-term benefits did not generalised to non-working memory tasks (Melby-Lervag and Hulme, 2013). The most recent meta-analysis of 87 articles found no evidence of working memory training on measures of intelligence or far transfer (Melby-Lervag *et al.*, 2016).

Some research suggests that when working memory transfer effects are observed (in visuospatial reasoning tasks), they are mediated by a number of different factors (Jaeggi *et al.*, 2013). That is, people who do show transfer effects are highly motivated, have a need for cognition and had good pre-existing ability. Also, transfer effects were not found on all visuospatial tasks. There is evidence that such training may improve performance in those whose performance has been impaired by illness or brain disorder or in the elderly (Karbach and Verhaeghen, 2014),

▷

Controversies in psychological science: *Continued*

but the evidence for beneficial effects in healthy individuals is less clear.

Finally, what of the third area – so-called 'brain training'? The evidence is not good (Owen *et al.*, 2010; Rabipour and Raz, 2012). For example, there is no good evidence to suggest that commercial programmes such as Brain Gym produce reliable, sustained, statistically significant cognitive and physical improvements (Spaulding *et al.*, 2010). People who are told that such training can increase performance, are more positive about the effects about the training; those given a negative message respond more negatively: this highlights the importance of people's expectations when they play these games (Rabipour and Davidson, 2015).

One study found that engaging in unrelated activity has greater benefits than does cognitive training. Borness *et al.* (2013) randomly allocated 135 Australian white collar workers to sixteen weeks of online cognitive training (the 'Happy Neuron' programme which includes training in attention, language, memory and visuospatial ability; 20 minutes three times a week) or an active, but control, condition for the same period. In the active control, participants watched documentaries about the natural world. Cognitive ability, well-being and productivity were measured before, immediately after

training and six months after training. Those who watched the documentary showed an increase in self-reported quality of life, less stress and greater well-being after six months, compared to the cognitive training group. A recent review of brain training found that it has a significant effect on improvement on future performance of the same task, weaker effects on similar tasks and no effect on general cognitive ability (Simons *et al.*, 2016).

Conclusion

The evidence suggests the early excitement generated by studies showing that working memory training could produce transfer effects in other cognitive domains hasn't been matched by the reality of the evidence. The effects of video-game playing on cognitive ability, however, are a little more robust but effects are found when designs are maximised to find such effects (small *N*s and extreme groups). What is needed is larger studies and also an exploration of the type of game that participants play. Would there be a difference between those who play passive games, versus those who engage in role-play versus those who engage in violent role-play? Would you predict a difference? If so, why?

The biological basis of memory

Much of what we know about the biology of human memory has been derived from studies of people who suffer from memory loss – amnesia – or from studies of animals in which amnesia is surgically induced to learn more about the specific brain mechanisms involved in memory (Parkin, 1996). But with the development of neuroimaging techniques, psychologists and neuroscientists have begun to outline the regions of the healthy brain that are active during the various memory processes of encoding, retrieval and working memory. Before reviewing this material, however, we need to go back to the beginning. To learning.

Before memory: learning

Before material can be remembered (and forgotten), it must first be learned. Learning involves three basic processes: the acquisition of material, its consolidation and its retrieval. Retrieval can involve free recall, where the participant is asked to remember previously presented stimuli, unaided by cues (or

recognition) where the participant has, for example, to determine which of two stimuli had been previously presented (where one stimulus is a distractor and not experienced before and the other is the stimulus previously seen/heard/etc.).

During instrumental learning the organism identifies a link between a stimulus and the response (see Chapter 7). It learns that by making a certain number of behavioural responses or making these responses at certain intervals it will be rewarded (or reinforced; the reward reinforces the behaviour and encourages it to be repeated to achieve the same outcome). In classical conditioning, the organism learns that if two previously unassociated stimuli are paired often enough, then the response normally elicited by the first will also be elicited by the other (although before they were paired it would not have done this).

Learning seems to involve a strengthening of connections between neurons. The theory was proposed by Hebb (1949) in his famous book, *The Organization of Behaviour*. Hebb proposed that each psychologically important event is conceived of as the flow of activity in a neuronal loop. This loop is made up of the interconnections among dendrite, cell body and the synapses on these structures. The synapses in a particular path become functionally connected to form what Hebb called a cell assembly. The assumption he made was that if two neurons are excited together, they become linked functionally. If the synapse between two neurons is repeatedly activated as the postsynaptic neuron fires, then the structure or chemistry of the synapse changes. This change strengthens the connection between neurons.

Hebb proposed that short-term memory resulted from reverberation of the closed loops of the cell assembly; long-term memory is the more structural, lasting change in synaptic connections. This long-term change in structure is thought to reflect **long-term potentiation (LTP)**, a term which describes the strengthening of neuronal connections via repeated stimulation (Lomo, 1966). Lomo found that if the axonal pathway from the entorhinal cortex to the dendate gyrus was repeatedly, electrically stimulated, then there was a long-term increase in the size of potentials generated by the postsynaptic neurons. LTP, therefore, was produced by the activation of synapses and the depolarisation of postsynaptic neurons. Psychologists agree that long-term memory involves more or less permanent changes in the structure of the brain (Fuster, 1995; Horn, 1998). But where and how?

Where are long-term memories formed?

Long-term potentiation seems to predominate in the hippocampus. If the hippocampus is stimulated, long-term physical changes are observed (Bliss and Gardner-Medwin, 1973). The entorhinal cortex provides inputs to the hippocampus. The axons from the entorhinal cortex pass through a part of the subcortex called the perforant path and form synapses with cells in the dendate gyrus, a part of the hippocampal formation.

The hippocampal formation itself is composed of two distinct structures: Ammon's horn (often referred to as the hippocampus) and the dendate gyrus. Ammon's horn comprises the substructures CA1, CA2 and CA3. CA1 is sometimes referred to as 'Sommer's sector'. There is also significant hippocampal output to the mammillary body via a tract called the fornix. Damage to each of these structures is sometimes associated with memory loss although the evidence for the involvement of the fornix is mixed (Calabrese et al., 1995).

Translating this process into the behaviour seen in classical conditioning, the unconditioned stimulus (the puff of air) makes strong synaptic connections with the neurons which produce the unconditioned response (the blink). Presenting the conditioned stimulus (the tone) alone, generates weak synapses. But pairing the tone with the unconditioned stimulus leads to the conditioned stimulus forming very strong synaptic connections. The more often the pairing is made, the stronger the connection becomes. For this type of classical conditioning to occur, a functioning hippocampus appears to be necessary and the involvement of the structure would appear to be that of acquiring conscious knowledge of the relationship between the conditioned and unconditioned stimulus. The

hippocampus is also involved in learning the relationship between the unconditioned and conditioned stimulus when there is a delay between the presentation of each, a process called trace conditioning (Clark and Squire, 1998).

The consolidation of memory seems to be time-dependent. For example, the initial period and the few hours after the learning of UCS and CS pairings appears to be the moment when memory is consolidated. Therefore, interruption of the process at these times will impede consolidation (Bourtchouladze et al., 1998). The first period of consolidation may be dependent on a different neurotransmitter system to that involved in the second. These are the NMDA and dopaminergic systems, respectively.

Chemical modulation of long-term potentiation

The most important excitatory neurotransmitter in the nervous system is glutamic acid or glutamate. One subtype of glutamate, N-methyl-D-aspartate (NMDA), appears to be important for producing long-term potentiation (LTP) (Abel and Lattal, 2001). NMDA receptors are found in the CA1 sector of the hippocampus; blocking activity in NMDA receptors prevents long-term potentiation in CA1 and the dendate gyrus. Blocking activity does not prevent or reverse LTP that has already occurred. The key process is the entry of calcium ions through ion channels, a phenomenon mediated by NMDA receptors.

When calcium enters an ion channel, changes in the structure of the neuron are produced by an enzyme, called a calcium-dependent enzyme, CDE (Lynch et al., 1988). One CDE is called calpain which breaks down proteins in the spines of dendrites. Without this entry of calcium, LTP does not occur. Weak synapses, resulting from weak activation, do not lead to depolarisation that allows calcium ions to enter ion channels. Strong synapses that are activated do lead to this depolarisation, suggesting that the NMDA receptor is vital for the process of learning acquisition (Steele and Morris, 1999).

However, LTP can occur in other parts of the brain, apart from the hippocampus, and not all forms of LTP involve the NMDA receptors. So, although the hippocampus and the NMDA receptors seem to be prime mechanisms for LTP, they may not be the only ones. There are structures such as the amygdala, for example, that are involved in the conditioning of fear. Temporarily inactivating part of the amygdala, for example, can impair an organism's ability to learn to fear whereas inactivating the same area after conditioning has taken place still results in a fear response in the organism (Wilensky et al., 1999). This finding suggests that this part of the amygdala may be involved in the acquisition, but not consolidation, of memory. The topic of fear conditioning is explored in more detail in Chapter 13.

One of the most important findings in the physiology of memory in recent decades has been that the hippocampal formation is essential for the formation or learning of new memories but it may not be involved in the long-term retention or retrieval of memory (Shors, 2004). What is unclear is why this dissociation should be.

Lee *et al.* (2004) have discovered that a type of gene, called zif268, is needed for the reconsolidation of context-dependent fear memory but another factor (called brain-derived neurotrophic factor or BDNF) is needed for initial consolidation. This shows how different physiological processes are involved in different aspects of memory formation: one type of factor is needed for immediate consolidation (but not reconsolidation) and another is involved in reconsolidation (but not immediate consolidation). The retrieval of fear memory also appears to recruit zif268 but in another region of the brain – the anterior cingulate cortex (ACC) (Frankland *et al.*, 2004). Frankland *et al.* found that remote memory for fear was associated with anterior cingulate involvement in mice. Both the studies report changes in the brain during fear conditioning.

Studies of memory in animals have now associated around 47 specific genes with good memory performance. In research with human participants, genetic clusters were examined in participants who learned a series of semantically unrelated words for immediate free recall and then completed an unexpected delayed free-recall test five minutes later (de Quervain and Papassotiropoulos, 2006). The genes that encoded a certain protein (ADCY8), and five others, were related to better memory performance and with greater activation in those brain regions involved in autobiographical memory and delayed recall (areas described below).

Amnesia

Damage to particular parts of the brain can permanently impair the ability to form new long-term memories while leaving language and perception intact. The inability to form new memories is called **anterograde amnesia**. The impairment in the ability to retrieve memories from before the brain injury is called **retrograde amnesia**. The brain damage can be caused by the effects of long-term alcoholism, severe malnutrition, stroke, head trauma or surgery. In general, people with anterograde amnesia can still remember events that occurred prior to the damage. They can talk about things that happened before the onset of their amnesia, but they cannot remember what has happened since. They never learn the names of people they subsequently meet, even if they see them daily for years.

Amnesia is not an all-or-nothing phenomenon, however. Severe amnesia, for example, can leave facial familiarity recognition, the acquisition of school knowledge or knowledge of the meaning of words intact. The fact that amnesic patients can remember facts and describe experiences that occurred before the brain injury indicates that their ability to recall explicit memories acquired earlier is not severely disrupted. Of those parts of the brain necessary for establishing new explicit memories, the most important part seems to be the hippocampus, a structure located deep within the temporal lobe, and which forms part of the limbic system.

HM: A memory story

One of the most influential cases of anterograde amnesia was that of Henry G. Molaison, the patient referred to in the literature by the two most famous initials to psychology: HM (Scoville and Milner, 1957; Milner, 1970; Corkin *et al.*, 1981). HM's case is considered to be important in psychology because it demonstrated that memory was a distinct psychological function, that short-term and working memory was spared in amnesia, but declarative and episodic memory were not, and that the hippocampus was an important structure for memory formation, especially the consolidation of memory (Eichenbaum, 2012).

HM's case is interesting because his amnesia was both severe and relatively pure, being uncontaminated by other neuropsychological deficits. At the age of nine, he suffered a head injury after a bicycle accident which left him epileptic. In 1953, when HM was 27 years old, a neurosurgeon, William Beecher Scoville removed part of the temporal lobe on both sides of his brain because the drugs used to treat his epilepsy were not effective and the surgery was intended to reduce or eliminate the seizures. The surgery successfully reduced the seizures.

The parts of the brain removed during HM's surgery included the uncus, amygdala and the hippocampal formation (we know this, on the basis of drawings Scoville made of his procedure). At the time, there was no method of confirming these sites accurately, if at all. Even in 1984, when the first CT scans were taken of HM's brain, the regions affected were unclear (Corkin, 1984). Later MRI scans, however, confirmed that the areas affected were the medial temporal pole, most of the amygdala, the entorhinal cortex and the hippocampus (Corkin *et al.*, 1997). The regions are collectively known as the medial temporal lobe memory system and inputs form other subcortical structures are necessary to ensure that the system works effectively. The removal of the amygdala is thought to explain HM's reduced emotional expression and lack of initiative.

Following HM's death in 2008, his brain was donated to scientific research. By using the technique of postmortem imaging, Annese *et al.* (2014) were able to demonstrate that although most of the hippocampus had been lost, a considerable portion remained. This part remained intact probably because of the trajectory of the suction pump inserted into HM's brain to suck the hippocampus away.

The surgery reduced HM's epilepsy, but his behaviour changed in another, more profound way: he developed antero-grade amnesia. After the operation, he was unable to find his way around the hospital and was unable to recognise staff who treated him daily. These were the first signs that HM's behaviour was not quite right, although his IQ, perceptual skill, motor skill, working memory, attention, language ability and his personality remained unaffected (even 10 months after the operation, his IQ was above average; Corkin, 1984). However, although he could remember items in memory in the short-term (by rehearsing them), he was unable to remember these in the long-term. He would have lengthy conversations with someone yet be unable to remember the content of these conversations nor remember having had them.

Although HM could talk about his life prior to the surgery and remember facts and events from before 1953, his ability to retain information after that date (i.e. following surgery) was impaired although not completely lost. He could remember some facts about celebrities, for example, but only after having been exposed to these facts repeatedly (O'Kane *et al.*, 2004). He was also unable to retrieve any meaningful autobiograph-ical memories from before the surgery instead referring to friends and events in the context of general knowledge about people and events (Steinvorth *et al.*, 2005). He could not talk about anything that had happened since 1953. HM was aware that he had a memory problem. For example, here is his response to a researcher's question:

> Every day is alone in itself, whatever enjoyment I've had, and whatever sorrow I've had … Right now, I'm wondering. Have I done or said anything amiss? You see, at this moment everything looks clear to me, but what happened just before? That's what worries me. It's like waking from a dream; I just don't remember. (Source: Quoted in Milner, 1970, p. 37)

HM's problem lay in his ability to store new information in long-term memory, not in his short-term memory. His verbal short-term memory was normal; he could repeat seven num-bers forwards and five numbers backwards, which is about average for the general population. At first, investigators con-cluded that the problem was in memory consolidation and that the part of the brain that was destroyed during surgery was essential for carrying out this process. But subsequent evi-dence suggests that the brain damage disrupts explicit memory without seriously damaging implicit memory.

However, some psychologists have questioned whether HM had a pure memory deficit, that is, one that prevents the acquisition or consolidation of new information for explicit recall but leaves other cognitive abilities (such as the ability to produce and comprehend language) intact (Mackay *et al.*, 1998). Mackay *et al.* cite studies in which participants described two meanings in ambiguous sentences presented visually (such as 'they talked about the problem with the math-ematician') and compared these participants' performance with those of HM. HM's descriptions were 'less clear and concise and more repetitive than controls'. Independent judges also rated HM's descriptions as less grammatical and comprehensible.

Other investigators have found that people with antero-grade amnesia can learn to solve puzzles, perform visual dis-criminations and make skilled movements that require hand–eye coordination (Squire, 1987). Clearly, their brains are still capable of undergoing the kinds of change that con-stitute long-term memory, but the people fail to remember having performed the tasks previously. For example, they may learn the task on one occasion. When, the next day, the exper-imenter brings them to the experimental apparatus and asks if they have ever seen it before, they say no. They have no explicit, episodic memory for having spent some time learn-ing the task. But then they go on to perform the task well, clearly demonstrating the existence of implicit long-term memory.

Graf and Mandler (1984) showed lists of six-letter words to amnesic and non-amnesic people and asked them to rate how much they liked them. They then administered two types of memory test. In the explicit memory condition, they asked people to recall the words they had seen. In the implicit memory condition, they presented cards containing the first three letters of the words and asked people to say the first word that started with those letters that came into their minds. The amnesic people explicitly remembered fewer words than the non-amnesic people in the control group, but both groups performed well on the implicit memory task (see Figure 8.19).

The role of the hippocampus in memory

The hippocampus, like many structures of the brain, is not fully mature at birth. In fact, it is not until a child is 2–3 years old that most of these structures are fully developed. As a result, many cognitive activities, such as the formation of semantic memories, are not particularly well developed until this age (Liston and Kagan, 2002). One reason that few people remember events that occurred during infancy may be the immaturity of the hippocampus.

The hippocampus receives information from all association areas of the brain and sends information back to them. In addition, the hippocampus has two-way connections with

Psychology in action: Memory at the movies . . .

Common sense may be common (see Chapter 1) but does not make much sense in psychology. In more light-hearted contexts, people's misperceptions can seem comical. Films, television and novels exploit artistic licence to bend scientific facts sometimes to breaking point. One episode of *The X Files*, had a protagonist confuse a technique used for measuring brain structure with one used for measuring brain activity. This protagonist was the medically qualified one. Even as this passage was being written, a journalist on a 24-hour television news channel is describing football supporters' reaction to a national football team manager as 'Pavlovian', thus misunderstanding Pavlov and, probably, football supporters.

Perhaps nowhere is artistic licence more vigorously exploited than in films. Baxendale (2004) has reviewed how films interpret and portray an important human phenomenon: memory loss. *The Bourne Supremacy, Total Recall, Memento, Men in Black, The Eternal Sunshine of the Spotless Mind* . . . several recent films have used amnesia as the hook with which to draw in cinema-goers and the hook is not new. At least 10 silent movies released before 1926 featured amnesic characters.

Amnesia is an organic disorder with a neurological or psychiatric basis. Fugue states (where people experience lack of consciousness but appear conscious and wander around oblivious to their condition, ending up in, e.g. a bus depot) or states where people believe they are someone else (dissociative disorders) are rare, as are changes in personality and identity. Amnesic patients have normal intelligence, normal attention span but show a severe inability to process new information. The most common causes of amnesia are neurosurgery, infection or stroke. Many films routinely flout these known facts in the cause of entertainment and Baxendale highlights a few of these.

In terms of causes of amnesia, she finds that many movies attribute memory loss to car crashes and assault. When Santa falls from a sleigh in the film *Santa Who?* he loses his identity and autobiographical memory. This cause and effect, as Baxendale suggests, is highly unlikely. Everyday memory difficulties are also rarely seen (although they should be one of the defining features of the disorder) and amnesic characters pursue new careers and social networks, unimpeded by their cinematic affliction. Trained assassins are especially prone to developing this trait, as seen in *The Bourne Identity* and *The Long Kiss Goodnight*. (Although in an unusual and knowing twist, *The Bourne Identity Crisis* features a protagonist who forgets he is gay and becomes a trained assassin.)

Two other films, best forgotten, are *Clean Slate* and *50 First Dates*. In the former, the hero is able to form new memories while awake but, after sleeping, forgets all he has learned. In the latter, Adam Sandler attempts to seduce Drew Barrymore who forgets each meeting they have had. As Baxendale pointedly notes, 'Some viewers might envy Ms Barrymore's ability to forget her romantic encounters with Mr Sandler, but her affliction seems to be the result of a head injury rather than the unconscious suppression of traumatic memories.' Cinematic forgetfulness reaches its zenith – humorously and deliberately – in Groundhog Day where Bill Murray's character exists in a world in which he perpetually relives the previous day.

In terms of recovery, Baxendale notes how television and movies are enamoured of the 'two are better than one' philosophy of head injury – a bang on the head can produce memory loss but a second bang can restore it. This happens in the Tom and Jerry cartoons and films such as *Tarzan the Tiger* and *Singing in the Dark*. In real life, a second blow does not make an effective rehabilitation strategy.

There are some honourable exceptions to this filmic hall of dishonour. Christopher Nolan's innovative film Memento, for example, features a character played by Guy Pearce who has severe anterograde amnesia and tries to recall the events leading to his wife's death. This is relayed in a narrative played backwards, as the character tries to piece together clues to his life. The character does not suffer retrograde amnesia, does not lose his identity and suffers severe everyday memory problems (such as HM who, apparently, inspired the story). He writes every detail he thinks is important, and which may help him understand the past, in a clearly visible place such as his body (if he used a notebook, he would forget about it and forget what he wrote in it).

Ironically, the film that does portray amnesia in the most realistic form, according to Baxendale, does not feature humans at all. It is *Finding Nemo* and the fish, Dory, has severe difficulty in learning and remembering new information, recalling names and knowing where she is going and why. 'Although her condition is often played for laughs', Baxendale writes, 'poignant aspects of her memory loss are also portrayed, when she is alone, lost, and profoundly confused.' This reflects real-life, human amnesia.

Does the accurate or inaccurate portrayal of amnesia in films matter? After all, we don't always go to the cinema to confront a mirror raised to real life. We go to suspend disbelief. We go to see fish, toys and ants talking, to see a man in an unlikely, figure-hugging suit swinging from buildings by sticky strings spurting from his wrists, to cheer for a group of hobbits, to boo an asthmatic, black-helmeted villain, or to see a boy in spectacles racing on a broom in a flying contest. Reality becomes important, however, if the reality is meant to be accurately portrayed. Dustin Hoffman's character in *Rain Man*, for example, although an extreme example, is an attempt at a serious portrayal of the social debilitation experienced by a person with Asperger's Syndrome. (The man who inspired the Hoffman character appears in Chapter 12.)

The general lesson seems to be that if you expect to go to the cinema and see an accurate portrayal of memory loss then, well, forget it.

▶

Psychology in action: *Contiuned*

(a) **(b)**

(a) Leonard Shelby, played by Guy Pearce in the film Memento, is one of the few successful cinematic portrayals of amnesia. The most successful, however, appears to be Dory **(b),** in *Finding Nemo*.

Source: (a) Summit Entertainment/Kobal/REX/Shutterstock; (b) W. Disney/Everett/Rex Features.

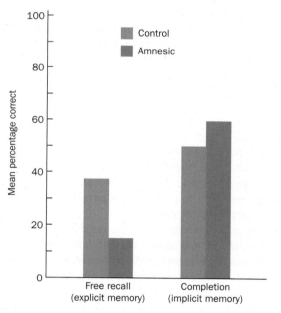

Figure 8.19 Explicit and implicit memory of amnesic patients and non-amnesic people. The performance of amnesic patients was impaired when they were instructed to try to recall the words they had previously seen but not when they were asked to say the first word that came into their minds.

Source: Adapted from Graf, P., Squire, L.R. and Mandler, G., The information that amnesic patients do not forget. *Journal of Experimental Psychology: Learning, memory and cognition*, 1984, 10, 164–78.

many regions in the interior of the cerebral hemispheres. Thus, the hippocampal formation is in a position to 'know' – and to influence – what is going on in the rest of the brain (Gluck and Myers, 1995). Presumably, it uses this information to influence the establishment of explicit long-term memories.

The structure appears to be very important for navigating or exploring our way around a spatial environment or in forming representations of the locations of objects (O'Keefe and Nadel, 1978). Morris *et al.* (1982), for example, placed rats in a pool of milky water that contained a platform just underneath the water. In order to avoid swimming constantly, the rats had to find the platform hidden beneath the milky water.

Eventually, through trial and error, the rats would find the platform. Then, the researchers performed a series of experimental ablations. One group of rats received lesions to the hippocampus, another received lesions to the cerebral cortex and another received no lesion. When the rats were then allowed into the pool, the pattern of behaviour seen in Figure 8.20 was observed. Notice how those rats with the hippocampus lesion had extremely poor navigation compared with the cortex lesion and control group. Similarly, when rats had learned that there was a platform under water and were then allowed to explore the water with the platform removed, those with an intact hippocampus would spend longer in the part of the maze where the platform had been previously positioned. Those rats with hippocampal lesions, however, did not engage in this 'dwell time' in the quadrant where the platform once was (Gerlai, 2001). This suggests an important role for the hippocampus in spatial learning.

Both rodents and primates show deficits in what has been called spatial memory (Redish and Touretzky, 1997). Spatial memory, the ability to encode and retrieve information about locations and routes is, like memory itself, not a unitary function. Kessels *et al.* (2001), for example, noted that there is a difference between memory for routes and paths and the knowledge of spatial layouts which enables a person to find an object or a location. The role of the hippocampus in aspects

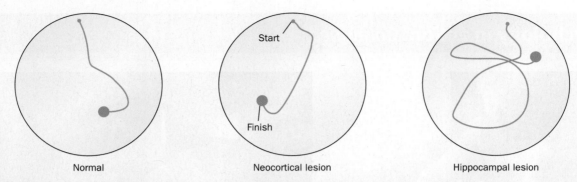

Figure 8.20 The effects of damaging a rat's hippocampus on its ability to find a platform in opaque water after having initially been trained to locate the platform successfully.

Source: Reprinted by permission from Macmillan Publishers Ltd: *Nature, Place navigation impaired in rats with hippocampal lesions,* 182(297), pp. 681–683 (Morris, R.G.M. et al. 1982), Copyright 1982.

of spatial memory has been well documented in animals, but O'Keefe and Nadel's view (1978) of hippocampal function has not gone unchallenged. Olton *et al.* (1979), for example, argued that the hippocampus was not exclusively responsible for spatial memory but was more involved in working memory. Tasks used in spatial memory tasks were, according to the theory, tests of short-term or working memory rather than spatial memory: all required the organism to keep information in mind while they engaged in another behaviour that used such information and this is the feature that was disrupted by damage.

In a meta-analysis of 27 studies that reviewed the consequences of hippocampal dysfunction, Kessels *et al.* (2001) found that whereas mild or moderate impairments were found on tasks requiring integration of information or navigation around a maze, there was little effect on spatial working memory. There was, however, a large impairment on tests of positional memory such as locating Xs in an array of letters. The lesions in patients showing mild to severe impairment were invariably to the right hippocampus, a finding that is consistent with O'Keefe and Nadel's hypothesis (1978) that the right hippocampus is specialised for mapping spatial information.

As you saw in Chapter 4, others have argued that rather than being primarily responsible for memory formation, the hippocampus role is the perception and construction of scenes (Maguire *et al.*, 2016). Patients with bilateral hippocampal damage, for example, presented with the typical autobiographical memory problems and spatial navigation difficulties but were also poor at perceiving scenes and constructing them in the imagination (Graham *et al.*, 2010). They were not impaired at perceiving or imagining single objects. This is called the scene construction theory of hippocampal function (Hassabis and Maguire, 2007; Maguire and Mullally, 2013). The hippocampus, in this theory, brings together details of scene to construct a coherent perception. The authors based their theory, in part, on the behaviour of people when they recall episodic memories – these memories will

normally involve the retrieval of scenes. Squire *et al.* (2010) found that patients with hippocampal damage with spared autobiographical memory also had spared scene construction ability.

Patients with bilateral damage have also been reported to show deficits in boundary extensions (Mullally *et al.*, 2012b) – when we recall a scene we usually imagine more of it beyond what we saw; these patients did not (Intraub and Richardson, 1989). Boundary extension has been associated with increased hippocampal activity in healthy individuals (Chadwick *et al.*, 2013).

However, there is evidence against this model. Kim *et al.* (2015) have argued that the role of the hippocampus is purely mnemonic – patients with bilateral damage can show preserved spatial navigation, scene construction and imagining and boundary extension. They attribute scene perception problems to underlying memory problems and that scene construction may be a function of the parahippocampal gyrus, rather than the hippocampus.

Some researchers have also suggested that different parts of the hippocampus may undertake different types of memory and imagination functions – the posterior part is responsible for retrieval of memory whereas the anterior part undertakes the function of re-combining or re-encoding details when people imagine stimuli from memory (Addis and Schacter, 2012). Weiler *et al.* (2010) found that the right anterior part was active when people imagined events which had a low probability of occurring during a holiday.

Neuroimaging and memory

Although much of our knowledge about the brain mechanisms that underlie memory has been derived from animal studies or from studies of individuals with brain injury, neuroimaging studies provide evidence from healthy individuals, and suggest that different regions of the brain are more involved than others in performing different types of memory task (Cabeza and Nyberg, 2000; Fletcher and Henson, 2001).

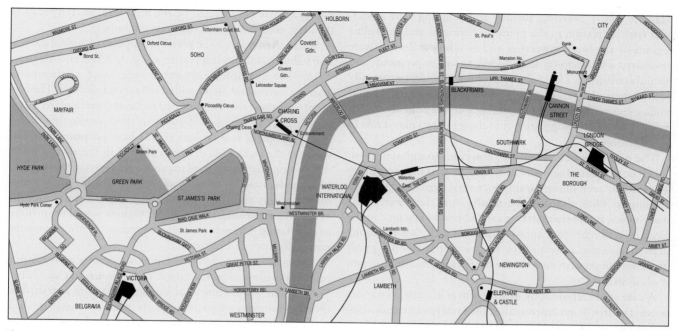

Figure 8.21 The route (in blue) that Maguire's taxi drivers had to describe.

Source: Maguire, E.A., Frackowiak, R.S.J. and Frith, C.D., Recalling routes around London: Activation of the right hippocampus in taxi drivers. *Journal of Neuroscience,* 1997, 17, 7103. © Society for Neuroscience.

As Horn (1998) asked, 'If memory consists of a mark made in the brain by a particular experience, where is the mark and what is its nature?'

Spatial navigation

Maguire and her colleagues now famously set up a novel and unusual experiment to see whether the hippocampus was active during spatial navigation (Maguire *et al.*, 1997). In their study, 11 London taxi drivers each with at least 14 years' experience of driving described the shortest legal route between two locations in London as a PET scanner observed brain activity study. You can see a map of the route in Figure 8.21.

The taxi drivers were also asked to recall famous London landmarks (an examination of topographical memory). The activation during these tasks was compared with that during the recall of sequences from famous films. When the drivers described the route from one location to another, significant activation of the right hippocampus was found (but was not found with the landmark or film conditions), as Figure 8.22 illustrates.

This finding suggests that the right part of the hippocampus is important to retrieval of information that involves recall of movement in complex environments. In another PET experiment, participants were asked to navigate their way around a familiar but complex virtual town, using a pair of virtual reality goggles (Maguire *et al.*, 1998).

Activation of the right hippocampus was again associated with knowing accurately where places were located and with navigating between them. The speed with which individuals navigated their environment was associated with right caudate nucleus activity. Also activated, however, were the right inferior parietal and bilateral medial cortices, which suggests, as many imaging studies do, that memory performance is not exclusively dependent on one region or structure.

Experienced taxi driving is one thing, but day-to-day navigation is another. One study examined untrained people's ability to navigate (drive) their way around a virtual London, as fMRI measured brain activation to see which regions of the brain were recruited during this type of task (Spiers and

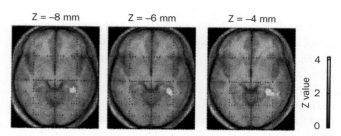

Figure 8.22 Areas of the brain activated by the recall of routes. Note the activation of the right hippocampus.

Source: Maguire, E.A., Frackowiak, R.S.J. and Frith, C.D., Recalling routes around London: Activation of the right hippocampus in taxi drivers. *Journal of Neuroscience,* 1997, 17, 7103. © Society for Neuroscience.

Maguire, 2007). Starting, turning and stopping were associated with activation in the premotor, parietal and cerebellar regions of the brain. Swerving and avoiding collisions were associated with occipital and parietal, as well as premotor and insula activation. The right prefrontal lobe was especially active when observing road traffic rules (supporting other studies you read about in Chapter 4 (and will read about further in Chapter 13) suggesting that these regions play a role in moral reasoning.

The picture is not consistent, however. Rosenbaum *et al.* (2005) noted that Maguire *et al.*'s data showed that activation was actually seen in the parahippocampal gyrus, not the hippocampus. They also describe results from their own fMRI study which found that participants who were engaged in the recall of well-rehearsed knowledge about a city's topography showed greatest activation in the parahippocampal gyrus (there was slight activation in the hippocampus) (Rosenbaum *et al.*, 2004).

A case study reported by Rosenbaum *et al.* (2005) provides another source of evidence against the involvement of the hippocampus in topographical memory. They studied SB, a patient with probable Alzheimer's disease who had been a taxi driver in Toronto, Canada, for 40 years. His remote memory for spatial locations in Toronto was compared with two other retired taxi drivers (with different illnesses) and a healthy control group. His ability to spatially navigate between various Toronto landmarks was comparable to the other participants. His most pronounced deficit was an inability to distinguish between Toronto landmarks and unknown buildings (an impairment that extended to world-famous landmarks). While the hippocampus may be necessary for the acquisition and retrieval of spatial information in the short-term, these results suggest that its role in long-term memory for old environments is much less certain.

This and the earlier study, together with those of amnesic patients who can recall the topography of the neighbourhood in which they grew up (e.g. Teng and Squire, 1999), provides a challenge to the view that the hippocampus is needed for the acquisition and retrieval of long-term topographical memories. However, Maguire *et al.* (2006) investigated the effects of brain injury on recall of routes in London in a taxi driver with damage to the hippocampus, the area which was active during route recall in the earlier imaging study. In the experiment, the driver and a matched control navigated their way through a virtual version of the city of London, along streets they had encoded 40 years ago.

They found that the injury did not affect the driver's ability to orientate himself around the city, his knowledge of landmarks and the spatial relationships between them or his ability to navigate the town. However, the driver did have difficulty when navigating routes that were not A-roads (major road arteries). It was as if complex routes were more problematic for him. It is possible, therefore, that coarse recall of topography is not affected by the hippocampus but recall of detailed, complex spatial relations might be.

There also appear to be preserved aspects of spatial navigation following bilateral hippocampal injury (Clark and Maguire, 2016). For example, only some aspects of environment learning/navigation are impaired following lesioning. The hippocampus may also not work in isolation, particularly when people have to navigate detours in their environment. For example, Spiers and Gilbert (2015) have proposed a model whereby the right PFC detects a change in the environment, the frontopolar cortex re-plans and sets subgoals, the superior PFC moderates the conflict arising from different possible route options and the posterior hippocampus processes the new path. These interacting sets of regions would be involved in calculating different routes when required. You can see the model illustrated in Figure 8.23

The hippocampus and entorhinal cortex were active during certain portions of a navigation task (Howard *et al.*, 2014). Very similar to Maguire *et al.*'s experiment with taxi drivers, the experimenters asked participants to learn to navigate their way, mentally, around the Soho district of London. A day later, they were presented with a series of movies with a first-person view which required them to navigate their way around the same environment as fMRI measured their brain activation. Howard *et al.* found that activity in the posterior hippocampus increased as the length of a pathway increased – the longer the path, the greater the activity. It also increased as the person travelled closer to their goal destination. When external cues to navigation were supplied, the increases in response to distance were not found. The results suggest that the hippocampus has a role in representing pathway distance from goals in navigation tasks.

Working memory

The ability to manipulate information in memory over a short space of time seems to be the primary responsibility of the frontal lobes (Fletcher and Henson, 2001), regions which, apparently contrarily, also become active during the retrieval of material that has been retained over long periods. Fletcher and Henson (2001) distinguish between two types of measures in working memory tasks: maintenance and manipulation. Working memory maintenance tasks involve measuring the process of keeping information in mind; working memory manipulation tasks involve measuring the reorganisation of material that is kept in mind.

A typical maintenance task involves presenting a participant with between three and nine stimuli and asking them to indicate whether a single stimulus presented subsequently formed part of the original array. The letter-based version of this task is usually associated with significant increases in activation in the left hemisphere, especially the ventrolateral frontal cortex, parietal lobe and premotor area (Awh *et al.*,

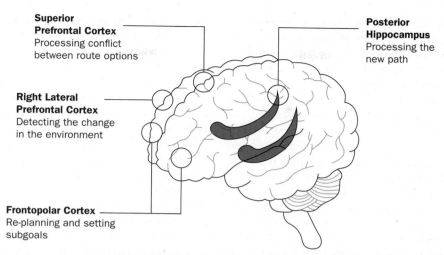

Superior Prefrontal Cortex
Processing conflict between route options

Right Lateral Prefrontal Cortex
Detecting the change in the environment

Frontopolar Cortex
Re-planning and setting subgoals

Posterior Hippocampus
Processing the new path

Figure 8.23 A conceptual model of prefrontal and hippocampal contributions to navigating detours. Spiers's and Gilberts's (2015).

1996). When the task involves information about spatial relations or objects rather than words, activity is greater in the right hemisphere. Often, the same regions activated by letters or words in the left hemisphere are also activated in the right by spatial/object stimuli (Smith *et al.*, 1996). When we maintain information in mind, there is sustained firing of neurons, especially in the PFC and, sometimes, the dorsolateral and intraparietal cortex – activation here is thought to predict better (or worse) working memory performance (Klingberg, 2010).

Remember from earlier that one type of working memory manipulation task involves presenting the participant with a series of five letters and then asking them to recite the letters forwards, backwards or in alphabetical order, in the mind. After a delay, the participant is asked to match the number order of a given letter, according to the mental manipulation (e.g. forwards, backwards or alphabetical). During the delay, there is usually activation seen in the ventrolateral and dorsolateral frontal cortex; during the reordering part of the task, activation is seen more in the dorsolateral part (D'Esposito *et al.*, 1999; Postle *et al.*, 1999).

Encoding and retrieval in episodic and semantic memory

Given that encoding and retrieval of information are two different cognitive tasks relating to the same function, you would expect these processes to have different underlying neural substrates. The left PFC is activated when we learn and encode material whereas the right side is activated when we try to recall this material (Tulving *et al.*, 1994; Nyberg *et al.*, 1996; Fletcher *et al.*, 1998a, b).

The encoding of episodic memory is associated with activity in regions including the prefrontal and medial-temporal

cortex and the cerebellum (Cabeza and Nyberg, 2000). Studies have usually found left-sided activation during episodic memory encoding, especially during the encoding of verbal material. The encoding of non-verbal material tends to be associated with bilateral activity in the frontal cortex. The role of the left PFC in memory may be one of organising information: this part of the brain is responsible for our ability to group items on the basis of some characteristic or attribute. However, it is thought that the recollection of autobiographical memories also relies on the hippocampus (Piolini *et al.*, 2009). Three components of episodic memory seem to be dissociable: the ability to retrieve memory, the precision of this retrieval and the vividness of the retrieval. Successful retrieval is associated with hippocampal activation, precision of retrieval is associated with activation in the angular gyrus, and vividness is reflected in increased activation in the precuneus (Richter *et al.*, 2016).

There is evidence that the amygdala and the hippocampus contain neurons that encode our ability to recognise something and also when/where this something was originally seen. In one experiment, participants were asked to remember as many of 12 unique items, presented on a computer screen, as possible and also remember where on the screen they had seen them. The stronger the neurons' responses in the amygdala and hippocampus during encoding, the better the recall of the stimulus's location (Rutishauser *et al.*, 2008).

Remembering and long-term memory

Neuroimaging studies of long-term memory involve presenting the participants with several items that they are told to memorise (or given no memorisation instructions), and then asking them to recall the presented material some time later. Usually, the participant is asked to recognise the presented stimulus from a range of target and distractor stimuli. The process involves encoding and retrieval and neuroimaging research has highlighted the different brain regions involved in each type of process. If encoding is intentional or incidental, it is associated with left frontal cortex activation, as we have already seen. Simple retrieval of information is also associated with left frontal lobe activation (Fletcher and Henson, 2001).

If encoding and retrieval is successful, would greater brain activation be seen during encoding for those stimuli that were successfully encoded or for all stimuli regardless of how well they were retrieved? There is evidence from EEG studies that a specific type of electrical activity, called EEG theta, is greater during the encoding of successfully retrieved words than unsuccessfully retrieved ones (Klimesch *et al.*, 1997). In one neuroimaging study, Brewer *et al.* (1998) found that greater right frontal cortex activity was associated with successful encoding. Individuals were asked to view a series of indoor or outdoor scenes and decide whether each scene depicted outdoors or indoors. Thirty minutes later, they were given a recognition test and asked to indicate whether they remembered the scene, thought the scene was familiar but not well remembered or was forgotten. Memory for the scenes was predicted by frontal and parahippocampal activation with greater activation found for the remembered images.

There are, sometimes, memories we want to suppress. They make us unhappy or embarrassed or are simply distracting. But we know little about the mechanism behind this deliberate suppression, nor do we know much about its neural basis. One possibility is that we directly suppress the memory, and that the hippocampus might be disrupted while we do so. Another is that a competing memory takes the place of the unwanted one (thought substitution). Doing both can temporarily suppress the appearance of an unwanted memory (Benoit and Anderson, 2012) and both mechanisms are underpinned by differences in brain activation.

Lateralisation of memory processes

A model called the HERA model has been proposed to account for the differences in brain activation seen during memory encoding and retrieval. HERA stands for Hemispheric Encoding-Retrieval Asymmetry, and the model argues that greater left than right frontal cortex activation is seen during episodic encoding whereas greater right than left frontal cortex activation is seen during episodic retrieval (Tulving *et al.*, 1994). The evidence reviewed above and more extensively in Fletcher and Henson (2001) and Cabeza and Nyberg (2000) suggests strong support for the model. In general, verbal encoding is associated with left frontal activation

whereas right activation is more common during retrieval but, as we have seen, such areas as well as others can be bilaterally active during encoding and retrieval. Why?

Fletcher and Henson (2001) put forward some interesting possibilities. Two are statistical and methodological and hinge on (1) the type of statistical parameters a study sets for **statistical significance** in neuroimaging research (different studies may set different parameters) and (2) the small number of samples used in neuroimaging research. A further reason may be the lack of clarity over the precise definition of cognitive processes in memory studies. Setting aside questions regarding what is verbal and what is non-verbal (and whether these two categories could be considered unitary), there are also questions regarding the nature of encoding and retrieval. Not all studies use the same measures of encoding or retrieval; perhaps the inconsistencies in findings can, therefore, be attributed to these different methodological approaches.

The nature of the model is challengeable, however. Dobbins and Wagner (2005) presented participants with various stimuli and then presented three images (two of which had been seen before) and asked them three different questions about each. The questions were 'Was this bigger before?' (the participant had to indicate whether an image previously seen had been bigger), 'Was it pleasant in the previous task?' (the participant was asked to indicate which of the stimuli was rated as pleasant or unpleasant in the previous task) and 'Is there a new item?' (the participant was asked to identify the image that had not been seen before). Two areas of the left PFC (specifically, the ventromedial/orbitofrontal cortex) were active in each of the retrieval conditions. There was greater activation in the anterior part of this region when participants retrieved conceptual information (pleasant condition) and in the posterior region during retrieval of conceptual and perceptual information (see Figure 8.24).

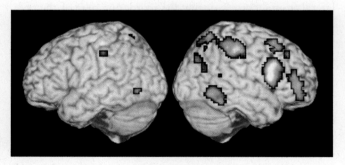

Figure 8.24 Domain-general and domain-sensitive prefrontal mechanisms.

Source: Dobbins, I.G. and Wagner, A.D. (2005) Domain-general and domain-sensitive prefrontal mechanisms for recollecting events and detecting novelty. *Cerebral Cortex*, 15, 1768–78.

Chapter review

Sensory memory

- Memory is the process of encoding, storing and retrieving information. It exists in three forms: sensory, short-term/working and long-term. The characteristics of each differ, which suggests that they differ physiologically as well.
- Sensory memory provides temporary storage of information until the newly perceived information can be stored in short-term memory.
- Information in sensory memory lasts for only a short time. When a visual stimulus is presented in a brief flash, all of the information is available for a short time (iconic memory). If the viewer's attention is directed to one line of information within a few hundred milliseconds of the flash, then the information can be transferred into short-term memory. Echoic memory – sensory memory for sound – appears to operate similarly.

Short-term and working memory

- Short-term memory and working memory contain a representation of information that has just been perceived, such as a person's name or telephone number. Although the capacity of short-term memory is limited, we can rehearse the information as long as we choose, thus increasing the likelihood that we will remember it indefinitely.
- Information in short-term memory is encoded according to previously learned rules. Information in long-term memory determines the nature of the encoding.
- Working memory is different from short-term memory in that it allows the short-term storage and manipulation as opposed to simple storage of material in memory.
- Working memory comprises a phonological loop – a store of phonetic, verbal information – a visuospatial scratchpad – a store of spatial information and memories for movement – and a central executive responsible for supervising and updating the content of working memory.
- Short-term memory lasts for about 20 seconds and has a capacity of about seven items. We often simplify large amounts of information by organising it into 'chunks' of information, which can then be more easily rehearsed and remembered.
- When presented with a list of items, we tend to remember the items at the beginning of the list (the primacy effect) and at the end of the list (the recency effect) better than items in the middle of the list.

- The primacy effect occurs presumably because we have a greater opportunity to rehearse items early in the list and thus store them in long-term memory. The recency effect occurs because we can retrieve items at the end of the list from short-term memory.
- The existence of acoustical errors (rather than visual ones) in the task of remembering visually presented letters suggests that information is represented phonologically in short-term memory.
- Loss of information from short-term memory appears to be primarily a result of displacement; new information pushes out old information. However, a small amount of simple decay may also occur.

Learning and encoding in long-term memory

- Long-term memory refers to the very long-term retention of information and appears to consist of physical changes in the brain – probably within the sensory and motor association cortex.
- Consolidation of memories is likely caused by rehearsal of information, which sustains particular neural activities and leads to permanent structural changes in the brain.
- Short-term memories probably involve neural activity (which can be prolonged by rehearsal), whereas long-term memories probably involve permanent structural changes.
- Elaboration is important to learning. Maintenance rehearsal, or simple rote repetition, is usually less effective than elaborative rehearsal, which involves deeper, more meaningful processing.
- Encoding specificity states that the way in which material is stored depends on how the material is retrieved. The most durable and useful memories are encoded in ways that are meaningful.
- Some psychologists have argued that shallow processing is a less effective way of encoding information than is deep processing (levels of processing, therefore, determine the success of retrieval). Critics, however, point out that shallow processing sometimes produces very durable memories, and the distinction between shallow and deep has proved to be impossible to define explicitly.
- Mnemonic systems are strategies used to enhance memory and usually employ information that is already contained in long-term memory and visual imagery.

The organisation of long-term memory

- Episodic memory refers to memories of events and people that are personally meaningful to us; it is synonymous with autobiographical memory.
- Semantic memory refers to memory for knowledge and facts.
- Most psychologists believe that episodic and semantic memories are parts of different systems although this is controversial.
- Explicit memory refers to recollection of information that was deliberately encoded and retrieved; implicit memory refers to memory for information that is unintentionally learned.

Remembering

- Remembering is an automatic process, although we may sometimes work hard at generating thoughts that will help this process along.
- Forgetting information occurs primarily in the first few years after it is learned and the rate of forgetting decreases slowly thereafter. Once we have learned something and retained it for a few years, the chances are that we will remember it for a long time afterwards.
- Recalling a memory of a complex event entails a process of reconstruction that uses old information.
- Our ability to recall information from episodic memory is influenced by retrieval cues, such as the questions people are asked in courts of law to establish how an event occurred. Sometimes, the reconstruction introduces new 'facts' that we perceive as memories of what we previously perceived.
- Remembering is strongly influenced by contextual variables involving mood and emotion. Some evidence suggests that remembering is easier when an individual's mood during the attempt to recall information is the same as it was when that information was originally learned; this is called state-dependent memory.
- We also tend to remember the circumstances that we were in when we first heard of a particularly emotional event such as the death of a famous person, a natural disaster, or an invasion of one country by another; these are called flashbulb memories.
- Sometimes recollecting one memory is made more difficult by the information contained in another memory, a phenomenon known as interference.

- In retroactive interference, recently learned information interferes with recollection of information learned earlier.
- In proactive interference, information learned a while ago interferes with recently learned information.
- Although memory interference is demonstrated in the laboratory, it may not operate so obviously in real life. Prose and other forms of everyday language appear to be more resistant to interference.

Biological basis of memory

- Much of what we have learned about the biological basis of memory comes from studies involving humans with brain damage, from laboratory studies in which animals undergo surgical procedures that produce amnesia, and from neuro-imaging studies of memory in healthy individuals.
- Learning seems to involve a strengthening of connections between neurons.
- Hebb proposed that short-term memory resulted from reverberation of the closed loops of the cell assembly; long-term memory is the more structural, lasting change in synaptic connections. This long-term change in structure is thought to reflect long-term potentiation (LTP), a term which describes the strengthening of neuronal connections via repeated stimulation.
- LTP is thought to originate in the hippocampus although it can occur elsewhere in the brain.
- A subtype of glutamate, N-methyl-D-aspartate (NMDA), appears to be important for producing long-term potentiation. NMDA receptors are found in the CA1 sector of the hippocampus; blocking activity in NMDA receptors prevents long-term potentiation in CA1 and the dendate gyrus.
- Anterograde amnesia refers to an inability to learn new memories after brain injury; these individuals can learn to perform many tasks that do not require verbal rules, such as recognising fragmentary pictures. Retrograde amnesia refers to the inability to retrieve remote memories.
- Patient HM showed an inability to store new information in long-term memory as a result of damage to the temporal lobes in general and the hippocampus in particular.
- The hippocampus is important for the learning of new material and for spatial navigation.
- The frontal cortex is involved in working memory and in the encoding and retrieval of material.

Suggestions for further reading

Baddley, A.D. and Eysenck M.W. (2014) *Memory* (2nd edn). Hove: Psychology Press.

Cotelli, M., Manenti, R., Zanetti, O. and Miniussi, C. (2012) Non-pharmacological intervention for memory decline. *Frontiers in Human Neuroscience*, 6, article 46.

Dittrich, L. (2016). *Patient HM*. London: Chatto & Windus.

Eichenbaum, H. (2012) *Cognitive Neuroscience of Memory: An Introduction*. Oxford: Oxford University Press.

Eriksson, J., Vogel, E.K., Lansner, A., Bergstrom, F. and Nyberg, L. (2015) Neurocognitive architecture of working memory. *Neuron*, 88, 33–46.

Eysenck, M.W. and Keane, M.T. (2015) *Cognitive Psychology: A Student's Handbook* (7th edn). Hove: Psychology Press.

Gilhooly, K., Lyddy, F. and Pollick, F. (2014) *Cognitive Psychology*. London: McGrawHill.

Lee, J. L., Nader, K., & Schiller, D. (2017). An update on memory reconsolidation updating. *Trends in Cognitive Sciences*, in press.

Logie, R.H. (2016). Retiring the central executive. *The Quarterly Journal of Experimental Psychology*, 69(10), 2093–109.

Oberauer, K., Lewandowsky, S., Awh, E., Brown, G. D., Conway, A., Cowan, N., … & Ma, W. J. (2018). Benchmarks for models of short term and working memory, in press.

CHAPTER 9
Consciousness

A GOOD NIGHT'S SLEEP

Before you read this chapter, which of the following do you think can help you better reach that stage of unconsciousness called sleep? Make a note of each one you think is right and then check your responses against the Psychology in Action section later in the chapter.

- Drinking caffeine
- Drinking alcohol
- Drinking high-alcohol-content drinks especially (e.g. spirits)
- Drinking hot milk
- Having regular sleeping patterns
- Alternating going to sleep early and late
- Undertaking regular exercise during the day
- Exercising just before going to bed
- Having a stressful work environment
- Exposing yourself to noise
- Having naps throughout the day

WHAT YOU SHOULD BE ABLE TO DO AFTER READING CHAPTER 9

- Describe what psychologists and philosophers mean by consciousness.
- Understand the problems of studying consciousness.
- Be familiar with theories explaining consciousness.
- Understand the concept of selective and divided attention and give examples of it.
- Describe hypnosis and the reasons for hypnotically induced behaviour.
- Describe the behavioural and psychophysiological stages of sleep.
- Understand theories of sleep.
- Describe the symptoms of sleep disorders and their possible causes.

QUESTIONS TO THINK ABOUT

- What is consciousness?
- Can we measure it?
- Is consciousness unitary?
- How do we manage to attend to some stimuli in the environment while ignoring others?
- What is hypnosis and how does it work?
- Why do we sleep?
- What are the effects of sleep deprivation on behaviour?

Consciousness: an introduction

> Consciousness poses the most baffling problems in the science of the mind. There is nothing that we know more intimately than conscious experience, but there is nothing that is harder to explain.
> (Source: Chalmers, 1995.)

Why are we aware of ourselves, of our thoughts, our perceptions, our actions, our memories and our feelings? Is some purpose served by our ability to realise that we exist, that events occur, that we are doing things and that we have memories? According to James (1890), 'all people unhesitatingly believe that they feel themselves thinking. This belief is the most fundamental of all postulates of Psychology.'

Philosophers have puzzled over the questions raised above for centuries without finding a convincing answer (Block *et al*., 1997). Psychologists, however, had generally neglected the problem of consciousness. Early behaviourists, as you saw in Chapter 1, denied that there was anything to explain and argued that the only subject matter for psychological investigation was behaviour, not consciousness. Several psychologists continue to believe that consciousness is a side effect of what we do – an epiphenomenon – that is not intrinsically interesting as a research question or a psychological topic.

Philosophical approaches to consciousness

Historically, people have taken three philosophical positions about the nature of consciousness (Block *et al*., 1997). The first and earliest position is that consciousness is not a natural phenomenon: it is not subject to the laws of nature that all scientists attempt to discover, laws involving matter and purely physical forces. This position states that consciousness is something supernatural and miraculous, not to be understood by the human mind.

The second position is that consciousness is a natural phenomenon but, for various reasons, we cannot understand it. Consciousness exists because of the nature of the human brain, but just how this occurs is not known. We can never understand consciousness because our brains are simply not capable of doing so; it would take a more complex brain than ours to understand the biology of subjective awareness. An alternative but related view is that everything can be explained, including all aspects of the human brain, but that consciousness is a vague, poorly operationally defined term (Wilkes, 1988; McGinn, 1989).

The third position is that people are indeed conscious, that this consciousness is produced by the activity of the human brain, and that there is every reason for us to be optimistic about our ability to understand this phenomenon (Crick, 1994).

The meaning of 'consciousness'

Although the word 'consciousness' is a noun, 'consciousness' itself does not exist. What exists are humans having the ability to do something that we describe as 'being conscious'. So, then, what does it mean to be conscious? Allport (1988) reported that, 'I find that I have no clear conception what people are talking about when they talk about consciousness or 'phenomenal awareness', nor, for that matter, when they talk about its linguistic-conceptual Siamese twin, the conscious self.' Consciousness is a private experience, which cannot be shared directly. We experience our own consciousness but not that of others. We conclude that other people are conscious because they are like us and because they can tell us that they, too, are conscious. This, inevitably, has a subjective quality which makes consciousness difficult to study scientifically.

According to Chalmers (1995), consciousness investigators face easy problems and a hard problem. The easy problems include the ability to discriminate, categorise and react to stimuli, to integrate information by using a cognitive system, to report mental states and to access internal states, to control behaviour deliberately and to differentiate between wakefulness and sleep. All of these features are associated with consciousness but, according to Chalmers, they are the relatively easy topics of consciousness because they primarily involve the contents of consciousness; these features refer to functions or abilities. Understanding (or discovering) the neural correlates of consciousness is also an easy problem, according to Chalmers. A mental state is said to be conscious when this state can be verbally reportable or internally accessible; the organism is able to be conscious of some information, react to it and explain it. This is another easy problem. But this is only one side of the story. The hard problem lies in studying the experience of these mental events.

When we report these mental events, we have an experience of reporting these mental events. Over and above this ability, we have the experience itself. There must be something 'that it is like' to be conscious (Nagel, 1974); there is a subjective quality about it and because of this, it poses a difficult problem. These conscious experiences are sometimes referred to as phenomenal consciousness or 'qualia'. In summary, the easy problems are understanding the functions and neurophysiology of consciousness; the hard problem is explaining why we have the experience of consciousness in the first place. The distinction between easy and hard problems is a controversial one and you yourself would probably challenge the notion that the understanding of the neural correlates of consciousness, for example, represents an easy problem. In the next section, we will consider some of the theories that have been proposed to account for the 'easy' and 'hard' aspects of consciousness.

Theories of consciousness

Neurobiological theories

The essence of the neurobiological approach is that consciousness arises from the neural activity of the brain. Neurobiological approaches diverge, however, when they begin to specify which parts or elements of the brain give rise to the activity that is meant to represent consciousness. Neurobiological theories of consciousness derive their data from a number of sources (such as those described Chapter 4) – neuroimaging and brain damage – and other branches of natural science, such as mathematics and quantum physics. Each type of study has yielded a different perspective on the neural correlates of consciousness and some of the most important or influential of these theories are reviewed below.

Consciousness and brain damage

Brain damage can alter human consciousness. Patients with anterograde amnesia, for example, are unable to form new verbal memories but can learn some kinds of tasks. However, they remain unaware that they have learned something, even when their behaviour indicates that they have. The brain damage does not prevent all kinds of learning, but it does prevent conscious awareness of what has been learned.

There are individuals who, if they have damaged the posterior parts of their brain, show a lack of awareness of stimuli presented to their visual field (see Chapter 6). Brain damage which impairs the perception of visual stimuli seems also to impair the ability. Blindsight patients have damage to the primary visual cortex and, although they are able to perform some visual perception tasks, they report being unaware of the task stimuli that had been presented in their visual field. Individuals with certain types of agnosia are unable to recognise objects or may be unable to ascribe meaning to such objects (see Chapter 6). Another form of agnosia is characterised by the inability to identify familiar faces by using facial cues alone. All of these disorders involve some lack of awareness and may help us to understand the regional contribution of the brain to conscious awareness.

Blindsight patients, as you saw in chapter 6, have damage to an area called V1, the primary visual cortex. This is the region in the brain to which information from the retina travels. Does the activity of V1 reflect conscious awareness of visual stimuli? Crick and Koch (1995) have proposed the controversial idea that it does not. They argue that it is not involved in conscious visual perception because V1 does not directly project to the frontal cortex (which integrates information from other parts of the cortex); the areas surrounding V1, however – the extrastriate cortex – do, and it is the activity of these areas which may reflect conscious processing.

Crick and Koch (1995) admit that this is a subtle and speculative proposal and have not undertaken an empirical test of this hypothesis. It remains an intriguing hypothesis.

Another form of brain damage, this time a surgical procedure designed to eliminate the symptoms of intractable epilepsy, gives rise to what has become known as the split brain or callosal syndrome (Bogen, 1993). Individuals who suffer epilepsy which cannot be controlled by drugs experience violent storms of neural activity which begin in one hemisphere and shift to the other via the corpus callosum, the large bundle of axons that connect one cerebral hemisphere to another. This causes an epileptic seizure. These seizures can occur many times each day, preventing the patient from leading a normal life. Neurosurgeons discovered that by severing the corpus callosum, thereby 'splitting' the brain, they could reduce the frequency of these seizures (Sperry *et al.*, 1969). This is illustrated in Figure 9.1.

Roger Sperry and Michael Gazzaniga and their associates (Gazzaniga, 1970, 1998; Gazzaniga *et al.*, 1996; Sperry, 1966) pioneered research into the psychological consequences of **split-brain surgery**. Sperry won the Nobel Prize in 1981 for his work on neurosurgery. Their work, initially with cats, demonstrated that the cerebral cortex of the left and right hemispheres normally exchange information via the corpus callosum. With one exception (described later), each hemisphere receives sensory information from the opposite side of the body and controls muscular movements on that side (see Chapters 4 and 6). The corpus callosum allows these activities to be coordinated, so that each hemisphere 'knows' what is going on in the other hemisphere (Hoptman and Davidson, 1994; Banich, 1995).

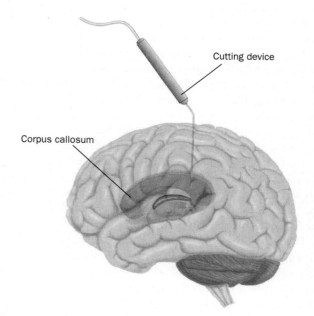

Figure 9.1 The split-brain operation. Holes are drilled in the top of the skull and a cutting device is introduced between the left and right cerebral hemispheres, severing the corpus callosum.

When the two hemispheres are disconnected after split-brain surgery, they appear to operate independently; their sensory mechanisms, memories and motor systems no longer appear to exchange information. The effects of these disconnections are not obvious to a casual observer, for the simple reason that only one hemisphere – in most people, the left – controls speech (see Chapter 10). The right hemisphere of an epileptic person with a split brain allows the patient to understand speech reasonably well, but it is poor at reading and spelling. Because Broca's speech area is located in the left hemisphere, the right hemisphere is totally incapable of producing speech.

Given that only one side of the brain can 'talk about' what it is experiencing, a casual observer will not detect the independent operations of the right side of a split brain. Even the patient's left brain has to learn about the independent existence of the right brain. One of the first things that these patients say they notice after the operation is that their left hand seems to have a mind of its own. This is called **alien hand** ('la main étrangère'). For example, patients may find themselves putting down a book held in the left hand, even if they are reading it with great interest. At other times, they surprise themselves by making obscene gestures with the left hand. Because the right hemisphere controls the movements of the left hand, these unexpected movements puzzle the left hemisphere, the side of the brain that controls speech. One hypothesis suggests that the inhibition of actions organised elsewhere, but originating in the frontal cortex, is lost in split-brain patients, hence the appearance of unusual, uninhibited behaviour in one hand. Another, different phenomenon is **intermanual conflict**. This refers to the apparently contradictory activity of the left and right hands; one might do up a set of buttons on a shirt, for example, while the other might undo them (Akelaitis, 1944/45).

If a patient with a split brain tries to use their right hand to arrange blocks to duplicate a geometrical design provided by the experimenter, the hand will hopelessly fumble around with the blocks. Often, the left hand (controlled by the right hemisphere) will brush the right hand aside and easily complete the task. It is as if the right hemisphere gets impatient with the clumsy ineptitude of the hand controlled by the left hemisphere.

The effects of cutting the corpus callosum suggest that consciousness depends on the ability of speech mechanisms in the left hemisphere to receive information from other regions of the brain. If such communication is interrupted, then some kinds of information can never reach consciousness.

There is still some controversy over whether split-brain patients are genuinely unable to perform the tasks that psychologists set them (see Martin, 2006, for a review). The degree to which split-brain patients can make decisions about stimuli presented to the left or right of their visual field may depend on the part of the corpus callosum damaged: normally, not all of the corpus callosum is cut, only parts of it (Sergent, 1987, 1990, 1991). In one study, two out of three patients when presented with circles in each hemifield could indicate which was bigger (Sergent, 1987). There are also other connections between the hemispheres, in addition to those made by the corpus callosum. Some neuropsychologists, such as Sergent, have argued that split-brain patients who do not show the typical split-brain profile are so because these channels of communication are intact – there is still some way in which the hemispheres can transfer information (Seymour et al., 1994).

Crick's astonishing hypothesis

Other neurobiological models of consciousness specify more exact regions and neural elements which give rise to consciousness. Crick's theory (Crick, 1994), for example, suggests that consciousness is the result of the activity of collections of neurons called neural assemblies (this is the astonishing hypothesis). The behaviour of neurons is represented by 35–75 Hz oscillations in the cortex; these oscillations form the basis of consciousness and correlate with awareness in different sensory modalities. According to the theory, oscillation represents the way in which the information we process is bound. The concept of binding is important in consciousness; it refers to the process whereby separate pieces of information about a single entity are brought together and used for processing later (Chalmers, 1995).

Bringing together information about colour and shape to form an image of an object is one example of binding. When elements are bound together, Crick's theory argues, neural groups will oscillate in the same space and time. While Crick's theory has received much attention and credit for specifically tying consciousness to specific brain activity, it has been criticised for not being able to explain the importance of these oscillations. If these oscillations give rise to conscious experience, why? Again, this is exactly Chalmers's 'hard' problem, mentioned earlier.

Penrose's and Hameroff's quantum models

Another neurobiological approach to consciousness focuses on the importance of chaos or non-linear dynamics in explaining consciousness. Much of Penrose's work is rooted in some quite complex physics and mathematics and we need not dwell on the detail here. In essence, Penrose (1989, 1994) argues that consciousness is a form of non-algorithmic processing which is important to conscious mathematical insight (Penrose himself is a mathematician). That is, consciousness is not an all-or-nothing, straightforward, linear process; instead, it is an uneven, non-linear process.

Penrose's model relies on an understanding of quantum physics. Quantum physics suggests that although events are observable and seem to follow a logical order, these events themselves are altered by being observed (this is called the Heisenberg Uncertainty Principle). In a revision of the original model, Hameroff and Penrose (1996) and Hameroff (1998) have suggested that consciousness takes place in the skeletal structure of neurons (called **cytoskeleton**), specifically in parts of the neuron called **microtubules.**

Hameroff is an anaesthetist and his ideas have been based on the processes involved in anaesthesia which induce loss of consciousness. For example, under general anaesthetic, individuals should not be able to move purposefully in response to a painful stimulus and should not be able to follow verbal commands (Franks and Lieb, 1998). There is some evidence that patients may be capable of remembering events/voices in the operating theatre during anaesthesia but this is quite controversial (Andrade, 1995).

In Hameroff's specific model of consciousness, microtubules in the neuron are essential to consciousness. The function of microtubules is to transport material inside the neuron and define the shape of the processes that they inhabit; they, therefore, serve an important neural function. The model suggests that quantum events occur in or around these microtubules and that these events give rise to our conscious experience. It suggests this for a number of reasons, not least the reason that microtubules are important for the functioning of the neuron. However, this model could be criticised on the same grounds as Crick's in the way that it does not explain why such neural events should be associated with consciousness. In fact, Churchland (1998) has suggested that these microtubules might just as well be called pixie dust in the synapses – essence which magically gives rise to consciousness – although Hameroff (1998) has argued that the mechanism by which microtubules give rise to consciousness is detailed and not as vague as pixie dust.

Cognitive theories

Cognitive theories of consciousness, although recognising that consciousness arises from the activity of the brain, describe the way in which it occurs in more mentalistic, cognitive terms.

Baars's global workspace theory

The global workspace theory (Baars, 1988; Baars *et al.*, 1998) states that the contents of consciousness are contained in a central processor called a global workspace. This is used to mediate the activity of non-conscious processes. When such processes need to inform the rest of the system, they send information to the workspace, which is a little like a blackboard used by the rest of the system (Baars *et al.*, 1998). The model can thus explain how different types of conscious information are available to us but it does not explain why this information in the global workspace is experienced; in other words, it does not solve the 'hard' problem (Chalmers, 1995).

Dennett's multiple drafts

The philosopher and cognitive scientist Daniel Dennett had proposed a complex theory of consciousness that relies on the idea that consciousness is not an all-or-nothing phenomenon that occurs in exactly the same way whenever it is evoked. Dennett (1991) begins the rationale for his theory by debunking the mind–body interactionism proposed by Descartes. The notion of the Cartesian theatre where mind and body are interacting protagonists is untenable according to Dennett. Instead, he argues that consciousness is not a theatre but the activation of revised collections of sensory information called 'drafts'. Because sensory information is received in various forms and at various times, conscious experience is an updating, constantly revising process a little like an author's manuscript which is in a constant state of redrafting and revision. Conscious experiences, therefore, result from multiple drafts of sensory information which are assembled at particular points in time. You can see why the theory is complex. One criticism of Dennett's theory is that, although it seems to abolish the notion of the Cartesian theatre, he is replacing it with a large number of theatres.

Shanon's theory

Shanon (1990, 1998) has argued, like Dennett and Baars, that consciousness is not unitary. Unlike Dennett and Baars, however, he invokes three components which he regards as making up consciousness: sensed being, mental awareness and reflection. Sensed being distinguishes between animate and living, and inanimate and dead; mental awareness refers to the idea that we are aware of thoughts that pass through our heads, that is, we are aware of the contents of consciousness; reflection refers to the idea that we are aware of our mental computations and that these 'mentations' can be the subject of future 'mentations'. According to Shanon, there are two types of reflection: meta-observation which reflects on the content of mental states, and monitoring or control which checks and evaluates thoughts; this control guides or governs our thinking process. According to Shanon, mental awareness is the core of consciousness whereas sensed being is a prerequisite and reflection is derived from it. How would one go about testing Shanon's theory, however? This would be difficult because the components are vaguely and generally described. It is also open to the criticism that it is too descriptive and actually explains very little.

Selective attention

We do not become conscious of all the stimuli detected by our sensory organs. For example, if you are writing an essay or laboratory practical report while the radio is on in the background and you have to meet an urgent deadline, you probably are unaware of what song is playing on the radio, or of the noises outside your room, of the hum of the refrigerator. Attention is completely devoted to your work. The process that controls our awareness of particular categories of events in the environment is called **selective attention**.

Sensory memory receives more information than it can transfer into short-term (working) memory (see Chapter 8). Sperling (1960) found that although people could remember only about four or five of the nine letters he flashed onto the screen if they tried to remember them all, they could direct their attention to any of the three lines of letters contained in sensory memory and identify them with perfect accuracy.

The process of selective attention determines which events we become conscious of. Attention may be controlled automatically, as when an intense stimulus (such as a loud sound) captures our attention; it may be controlled by instructions ('Pay attention to that one over there'); or it may be controlled by the demands of the particular task we are performing. For example, when we are driving a car, we pay special attention to other road users, pedestrians, road signs and so on. Our attentional mechanisms serve to enhance our responsiveness to certain stimuli and to tune out irrelevant information.

Attention plays an important role in memory. By exerting control over the information that reaches short-term memory, it determines what information ultimately becomes stored in explicit long-term memory – the portion of long-term memory that we can talk about and can become conscious of (see Chapter 8). But the storage of information in implicit memory does not require conscious attention. Not all the information we do not pay attention to is lost.

Why does selective attention exist? Why do we not simply process all the information that is being gathered by our sensory receptors? We sometimes miss something important because our attention is occupied elsewhere. According to Broadbent (1958), the answer is that the brain mechanisms responsible for conscious processing of this information have a limited capacity. There is only so much information that these mechanisms can handle at one particular moment. Thus, we need some system to serve as a gatekeeper, controlling the flow of information to this system. The nature of this gatekeeper – selective attention – is the subject of ongoing research. Our ability to detect the number of voices in a group is limited – we can usually identify no more than three (Vitevitch and Siew, 2016).

Dichotic listening

The first experiments to investigate the nature of attention scientifically took advantage of the fact that we have two ears. Cherry (1953) devised a test of selective attention called **dichotic listening**, a task that requires a person to listen to one of two messages presented simultaneously, one to each ear (dichotic means 'divided into two parts'). He placed headphones on his participants and presented recordings of different spoken messages to each ear, illustrated in Figure 9.2.

He asked the participants to shadow the message presented to one ear – to repeat back as quickly but as accurately as possible what that voice was saying. **Shadowing** ensured that they would pay attention only to that message.

The information that entered the unattended ear appeared to be lost. When questioned about what that ear had heard, participants responded that they had heard something, but they could not say what it was. Even if the voice presented to the unshadowed ear began to talk in a foreign language or read English backwards, participants do not notice the change (Wood and Cowan, 1995). Shadowing, however, is easier if the messages are physically different, that is, they are spoken by different sexes or one is louder than the other or one is speech and the other non-speech based. See Figure 9.3.

Figure 9.2 Dichotic listening and shadowing. A person listens to two different spoken messages simultaneously and continuously repeats back what one voice is saying.

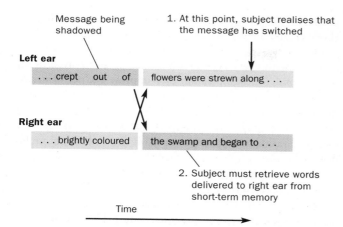

Figure 9.3 Shadowing a message that switches ears. When the message switches, the person must retrieve some words from memory that were heard by the unattended ear.

Other evidence shows that selective attention is not achieved by simply closing a sensory channel. Some information, by its very nature, can break through into consciousness. For example, if a person's name is presented to the unattended ear, they will very likely hear it and remember it later (Moray, 1959). Or if the message presented to the unattended ear contains sexually explicit words, people tend to notice them immediately (Nielsen and Sarason, 1981). The fact that some types of information presented to the unattended ear can grab our attention indicates that even unattended information undergoes some verbal analysis. If the unattended information is 'filtered out' at some level, this filtration must not occur until after the sounds are identified as words.

Several studies have shown that information presented to the unattended ear can affect our behaviour even if we do not become conscious of the information. To put it another way, the information can produce implicit memories, memories of which we are unaware (Cleermans, 1993). Von Wright *et al.* (1975) showed that words previously presented along with an unpleasant electrical shock would produce an emotional reaction when the words were presented to the unattended ear. Even when the participant was not consciously attending to the voice, the information produced a non-verbal response – a classically conditioned emotional reaction. Thus, the unattended information could trigger the recall of an implicit memory.

McKay (1973) showed that information presented to the unattended ear can influence verbal processing even when the listener is not conscious of this information. In the attended ear, participants heard sentences such as:

They threw stones towards the bank yesterday.

While this sentence was being presented, the participants heard the word 'river' or 'money' in the unattended ear. Later, they were asked which of the following sentences they had heard:

They threw stones towards the side of the river yesterday.

They threw stones towards the savings and loan association yesterday.

Of course, the participants had heard neither of these sentences. McKay found that the participants' choices were determined by whether the word 'river' or 'money' was presented to the unattended ear. They did not specifically recall hearing the words presented to the unattended ear, but obviously these words had affected their perception of the meaning of the word 'bank'.

Treisman (1960) showed that people can follow a message that is being shadowed even if it switches from one ear to the other. Suppose a person is shadowing a message presented to the left ear, while the message to the right ear is unshadowed. In the example given in Figure 9.3, the person will probably say 'crept out of the swamp' and not 'crept out of flowers'. Apparently, the switch occurs when the message begins to make no sense. However, by the time the person realises that 'crept out of flowers' makes no sense, the rest of the message, 'the swamp', has already been presented to the right ear. Because the person is able to continue the message without missing any words, he or she must be able to retrieve some words from memory. Thus, even though an unshadowed message cannot be remembered later, it produces some trace that can be retrieved if attention is directed to it soon after the words are presented.

The cocktail-party phenomenon

Selective attention to auditory messages has practical significance outside the laboratory. For example, sometimes we have to sort out one message from several others without the benefit of such a distinct cue; we seldom hear one voice in one ear and another voice in the other. We might be trying to converse with one person while we are in a room with several other people who are carrying on their own conversations. We can usually sort out one voice from another – an example of the **cocktail-party phenomenon**.

In this case, we are trying to listen to the person opposite us and to ignore the cross-conversation of the people to our left and right. Our ears receive a jumble of sounds, but we are able to pick out the ones we want, stringing them together into a meaningful message and ignoring the rest. This task takes some effort; following one person's conversation in such circumstances is more difficult when what they are saying is not very interesting. If we overhear a few words of another conversation that seems more interesting, it is hard to strain out the cross-conversation.

The original cocktail party effect study was reported in 1959 by Moray. The laboratory finding seemed to mirror that of hearing one's name mentioned in someone else's conversation at a party even though you were not attending to that conversation. However, in Moray's study, only 33 per cent of participants responded in this way. Is there some fundamental, psychological difference, therefore, between those who attend and those who do not, and would such a difference reflect different means of processing auditory or cognitive information?

This difference could be working memory. Conway *et al.* (2001) hypothesised that the least capable participants identified their names because they failed to demonstrate the working memory facility which would allow them to attend to the channel that they were meant to be attending to and ignore the channel they were not meant to.

Participants in the experiment were asked to complete a selective listening exercise similar to that of Moray. Participants listened to messages through headphones but were told only to attend to one channel; the participant's name would occur in the unattended channel. Participants also completed a working memory exercise that involved reading a simple mathematical equation followed by a word (e.g. 'Is $(6 + 4)/2 = 5$? DOG'), solving the equations and, at the end of all trials, writing down as many of the presented words as they could remember. The number of equation and word displays in each trial varied between two and six. Those who excelled at this task were significantly better at ignoring their name than were those who performed less well.

One of the behaviours we have become increasingly engaged in and which involves selective attention is mobile phone use. The use of these handsets has exploded over the past decade but their widespread availability and convenience has prompted some concern that they may be dangerous to use when, for example, driving. The assumption behind the concern is that holding a phone while driving reduces the controllability of the vehicle, impairs attention and, therefore, poses a threat to driver, pedestrians and other road users. But is there any scientific merit in this assumption? The Controversies in Psychological Science box tackles this question and describes some recent, counter-intuitive findings.

Background noise

The opposite phenomenon to attention – where we try to exclude (become less conscious of) auditory information – has great practical implications. Background noise, for example, is common in office environments and is a source of interference in open-plan offices (Klitzman and Stellman, 1989). Although there are very few controlled scientific experiments, existing studies report that background office noise is associated with stress, lack of concentration, low

levels of performance and reduced employee efficiency (Loewen and Suedfeld, 1992; Sundstrom *et al.*, 1994).

Of course, we would not expect background noise to interfere with every type of behaviour. Music played in the background, for example, may even improve our performance. Are there specific auditory stimuli, therefore, that selectively impair the performance of specific tasks? Salame and Baddeley (1982), for example, have suggested that performance on a cognitive task can only be disrupted if the auditory stimulus doing the disruption is speech; others have suggested that stimuli other than speech can affect performance, giving rise to what has been termed the irrelevant speech effect (LeCompte *et al.*, 1997). The irrelevant speech effect suggests that any disruptive sound (delivered at conversational level) can impair memory for verbal material during serial (that is, when the material has to be recalled in a specific order) and free recall (Salame and Baddeley, 1990; Jones, 1995).

Smith-Jackson and Kline (2009) sought to discover whether irrelevant speech modified these responses. They set up an experiment in which participants completed a verbal task at a desk while irrelevant speech played behind them. In one condition, the speech was a conversation between two men; in another, the conversation of one person with pauses (as if talking on the telephone). The presence of irrelevant speech was associated with making a greater number of errors and longer completion rates.

An alternative to the speech effect is that the noise which disrupts performance has to show some variation (rather than being speech-like) before recall is disrupted. This is called the changing state hypothesis (Jones *et al.*, 1992). This theory would suggest that, in an office environment, performance would be disrupted by speech plus office noise.

To test this hypothesis, Banbury and Berry (1998) exposed undergraduates to office noise with speech, office noise without speech, speech alone or no noise while they (1) memorised a prose passage describing martial arts instructions for the correct and incorrect way of stretching muscles, and (2) solved a variety of arithmetical problems (division and subtraction). Memory for the prose passage was measured shortly afterwards. The experimenters found that office noise with speech and speech alone had a detrimental effect on memory for the prose passage; individuals in the office noise without speech condition, however, did not perform significantly differently from the control group, suggesting that the speech component of the noise was important (as Salame and Baddeley suggested). All three noise conditions, however, were associated with deficits in arithmetic performance. The experimenters noted that individuals were exposed to a greater duration of noise during the arithmetic task. Before the irrelevant speech effect explanation could be ruled out, therefore, the experimenters suggested that length of exposure to noise needed to be extended in the prose recall condition. This they did by exposing individuals to office noise with speech, office noise without speech, meaningless speech or no noise during acquisition of the prose and during recall.

Controversies in psychological science: Does mobile phone use impair your driving?

The issue

The sale of mobile phones has been one of the marketing successes of the past few years: it is estimated that 85 per cent of people in the US have a mobile phone (Nielsen, 2013). Mobile phones are portable, convenient and handy. So handy, that people often use them while doing other things. Surveys suggest that around 80 per cent of mobile phone users report having used the device while driving, despite the use of such devices being illegal in many countries (Goodman *et al.*, 1999). In 2003, for example, the UK passed an amendment to the Road Traffic Act 1988 which made it an offence to drive a motor vehicle on a road while using a hand-held telephone (although not hands-free sets). The rationale for the ban is that factors such as holding the phone or dialling a number cause significant distraction and lack of control over the vehicle. Is there scientific evidence for this assumption?

The evidence

Strayer and Johnston (2001) have suggested that it is not the physical handling of mobile phones that leads to accidents but the conversations people have on them. They measured the errors made by drivers in a simulated driving task. These drivers either listened to a radio, listened to a book on tape, performed a word shadowing exercise on a mobile phone, held a conversation on a mobile phone or held a conversation using a hands-free set.

The authors cite previous studies that have shown a relationship between phone use and driving accidents. Redelmeier and Tibshirani's study (1997) of the phone records of those involved in driving accidents found that 24 per cent of people used their phones within the 10 minutes before the accident. They argued that this rate suggested a danger that was as great as having excess alcohol in your bloodstream. Strayer and Johnston suggest that while the relationship appears causal, there may be other factors, such as the personality and disposition of the drivers, which caused the accident. Furthermore, the study did not consider the conversational aspect of telephone use, although a study by Briem and Hedman (1995) suggested that holding a simple conversation did not significantly impair the ability to stay on the road.

Strayer and Johnston tested two hypotheses. The peripheral-interference hypothesis attributes driving accidents to non-conversational uses of the mobile phone such as holding and dialling. The attentional hypothesis attributes any driving impairment to the nature of the conversation taking place on the mobile phone.

In their simulated driving experiment, 48 undergraduates used a joystick to operate a cursor which they moved to follow a moving target on a computer screen. The target would move unpredictably, although not suddenly. Sporadically a green or red light would appear. If a green light appeared, the participant was asked to continue; if the red light appeared they were told to press a button which represented the brake on the joystick. The participants either conversed with a confederate on a mobile phone – they discussed President Bill Clinton's potential impeachment, and the Salt Lake City Olympic Committee bribery scandal – or conversed with a hands-free set or listened to a radio broadcast (which they could choose). The researchers found that the probability of missing a red light almost doubled when participants talked on the phone – whether hands-free or hand-held – compared with when they listened to the radio. There was no significant difference in the error rate between the two phone groups. Not only was the miss rate higher in these two groups, they were also slower to respond to the lights, as Figure 9.4 shows. People drove more poorly during the 'talking' portion of the conversation than the 'listening' portion.

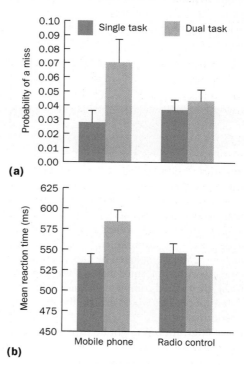

(a)

(b)

Figure 9.4 The probability of missing a red traffic light **(a)** and the reaction time to changing signals **(b)** when participants either performed the tracking task or performed the tracking task while having a conversation on a mobile phone or listening to the radio.

Source: Strayer, D.L. and Johnston W.A., Driven to distraction: Dual-task studies of simulated driving and conversing on a cellular telephone. *Psychological Science*, 2001, 12(6), 462–6, reprinted by permission of Blackwell Publishers Ltd.

Controversies in psychological science: *Continued*

To check that participants were listening to the material in the control condition – the authors did not assess this in their first experiment – and to ensure that the control condition was speech rather than music and speech-based, a second experiment required participants to complete the same simulated driving task but one group listened to a book on tape. This group did not perform significantly worse than the phone groups, suggesting that attending to verbal material is not enough to impair driving: active engagement in conversation is necessary for errors to be committed.

In a final experiment, participants performed easy or difficult versions of the simulated driving task as they either repeated a word said to them by the experimenter over a mobile phone or as they generated a word beginning with a letter given to them by the experimenter over a mobile phone. While errors increased from the easy to the difficult conditions in the control (no phone) and dual-task (phone conditions), generating words was associated with significantly poorer performance than was the word repetition condition. This poor performance was especially pronounced in the difficult condition.

Similar results were found when people were given a choice regarding when to read a text message on a phone when they were driving along a straight road in an area where driving demands increased followed by an area with low demands (Liang *et al.*, 2014).

Conclusion

Strayer and Johnston provide persuasive evidence that holding a conversation on a mobile phone can impair driving. It is one of a number of studies showing how using a mobile phone can affect driving and this impairment is immune to driving experience (Cooper and Strayer, 2008). They note that while eating a sandwich or holding a phone – activities some people may engage in while driving – are under the sole control of the driver, a telephone conversation is not, and it may be this lack of control which impairs driving performance. People using mobile phones are not aware of situations around them, and are at greater risk of injury or accidents (Neider *et al.*, 2010), even to pedestrians (Stavrinos *et al.*, 2011; Nasar and Troyer, 2013).

This study is an intriguing one because it appears to contradict received and, indeed, legal wisdom: mobile phones do not cause accidents; conversations do.

Noise – An international perspective

Zijlstra *et al.* (1999) looked at the work performance and psychological well-being of Dutch and Russian secretaries who were interrupted while undertaking a text-editing task. Contrary to expectations, interruptions made the participants work more quickly but no less efficiently, although these interruptions required more cognitive effort to deal with them. One strategy employed by participants was to ensure that their work had 'closure': that is, if they were interrupted mid-task, they would complete that task before dealing with the interruption. This would explain the increased speed in task performance.

These interruptions might be expected in a work environment and we may learn to adopt different strategies to avoid or ignore them. Noise over which we have little direct control may be more difficult to cope with. Aircraft noise or the noise of trains if you live under an airport flight path or near a railway track are examples of stimuli which can cause psychological impairment and annoyance. It has been estimated that 25 per cent of people in Europe have been exposed to noise level of 65dB or above (Berglund and Lindvall, 1995) and such people complain about the annoyance, the lack of sleep and the disruption to cognitive function that the noise causes (Smith and Jones, 1992).

Exposure to noise in children is correlated with deficits in reading, speech perception and long-term memory deficits (Evans and Lepore, 1993). Reading ability and long-term memory performance in children living next to a noisy, newly built airport in Munich was found to be severely impaired; those who had been exposed to airport noise and now lived near the old, closed airport, showed improvements in these tasks (Hygge *et al.*, 2002). Short-term memory also improved when the old airport closed.

Extending the exposure period from five to nine minutes significantly and detrimentally affected memory performance when participants were exposed to office noise without speech and meaningless speech (duration did not affect performance in the office noise with speech condition). The greater impairment with greater exposure supported the results of other studies which showed that increasing the number of irrelevant background words presented during a primary task resulted in poorer memory performance (Bridges and Jones, 1996). This study, therefore, suggests that different categories of noise affect ongoing cognitive activity differently.

Models of selective attention

With all this evidence suggesting the robustness of selective attention, are we any closer to understanding how we selectively attend? In cognitive psychology, models of selective attention have been broadly divided into two: early selection models and late selection models. We consider the early selection models here.

Early selection models

The primary feature of early selection models (ESM) is that if items are not attended to they are not selected for perceptual analysis and so play no further part in information processing. Late selection models, on the other hand, argue that all information is attended to and is only selected later on in the information processing chain, that is, after perceptual analysis of the stimuli. Most of the influential ESM models were developed in the 1950s and 1960s when organisational psychology was making large inroads into workforce behaviour. Psychologists such as Donald Broadbent were interested in how psychological principles could be applied to understanding real-life problems, such as operating air traffic control systems or navigating a plane, both of which require extraordinary attention and selective attention.

Broadbent (1958) proposed a model of attention which was popular at the time because it was testable and falsifiable. However, evidence has shown that features of the model were incorrect. Broadbent proposed a filter theory of attention which suggested that processing information was a little like the operation of a filtering system: a channel of communication would process information and transmit this information to other cognitive systems for analysis. Specifically, Broadbent suggested that this filter initially processes information from a 'sensory store' and transfers it to other cognitive systems. This was an all-or-nothing model: only selected material would pass through the filter system. This selected material would then make its way to a limited capacity P(erceptual) system which would identify the material.

The all-or-nothing feature of the model can certainly explain why material presented to the unattended ear in dichotic listening experiments is not processed. A series of experiments by Moray (1959), however, suggested that the basic feature of the model was wrong. Moray found that when participants were instructed to switch attention from one ear to another during the experiment, they were able to do this when the instruction was along the lines of, 'Robyn, switch ears.' According to the model, this channel should have been blocked and should have remained unattended to: the participant should have been attending exclusively to another channel. Another set of experiments also demonstrated that listeners could follow messages that were switched from one ear to the other. For example, a narrative would begin in one ear and be switched to the previously unattended ear (Treisman, 1960, 1964). Participants, contrary to the filter model, would switch attention to the unattended ear to follow the narrative.

Treisman proposed her own model of selective attention which was 'weaker' than that of Broadbent. She argued that selective attention is certainly an early information processing activity but that not only would attended messages get through to the system, but unattended material would also get through but in weakened, attenuated form. This is called the attenuation model (Treisman, 1960).

Visual information

Sperling's studies of sensory memory (discussed in Chapter 8) demonstrated the role of attention in selectively transferring visual information into verbal short-term memory (or, for our purposes, into consciousness). Other psychologists have studied this phenomenon in more detail. For example, Posner *et al.* (1980) had participants watch a computer-controlled video display screen as a small mark in the centre of the screen served as a **fixation** point for the participants' gaze. They were shown a warning stimulus near the fixation point followed by a target stimulus – a letter displayed to the left or to the right of the fixation point. The warning stimulus consisted of either an arrow pointing right or left or simply a plus sign. The arrows served as cues to the participants to expect the letter to occur either to the right or to the left. The plus sign served as a neutral stimulus, containing no spatial information. The participants' task was to press a button as soon as they detected the letter.

Eighty per cent of the time, the arrow accurately pointed towards the location in which the letter would be presented. However, 20 per cent of the time, the arrow pointed away from the location in which it would occur. The advance warning clearly had an effect on the participants' response times: when they were correctly informed of the location of the letter, they responded faster.

This study shows that selective attention can influence the detection of visual stimuli: if a stimulus occurs where we expect it, we perceive it more quickly; if it occurs where we do not expect it, we perceive it more slowly. Thus, people can follow instructions to direct their attention to particular locations in the visual field. Because gaze remained fixed on the centre of the screen in this study, this movement of attention was independent of eye movement. How does this focusing of attention work neurologically? The most likely explanation seems to be that neural circuits that detect a particular kind of stimulus are somehow sensitised, so that they can more easily detect that stimulus. In this case, the mechanism of selective attention sensitised the neural circuits that detect visual stimuli in a particular region.

Inattentional blindness

Sometimes we don't see a visual stimulus because our attention has been drawn to something else, even if this something else is near the stimulus we can't see or is above or behind it. For example, if we are asked to fixate on a particular task or a spot on a screen, we can often ignore objects that ordinarily we would have no trouble in perceiving. This phenomenon is called **inattentional blindness** (Mack and Rock, 1998). It is similar to another seen in perception – change blindness – where participants do not notice (even very large) changes in the stimuli they are viewing if their attention is directed elsewhere. Examples include a failure to notice that the heads in two photographs have been switched – the switch would need to occur during an eye movement, otherwise it would be detectable (Grimes, 1996); and a failure to notice that a person giving directions has changed to another as a door was being carried between them (Simons and Levin, 1998).

The inattentional blindness effect can be seen in the most extraordinary contexts. A few years ago, a cinema advert (also available via youtube.com) was screened in which the viewers watched a basketball game between non-professional players. Cinema-goers were asked to pay attention to the number of passes made by the team in black or the team in white. After this, they were asked 'Did you see the gorilla?' This was an odd question but not as odd as the audience's reaction. None reported a gorilla. Why would they? And what would a gorilla be doing in a basketball game? However, during the clip, a man in a gorilla suit walked along the screen during the game as the players participated. The viewers were so wrapped up in the game they neglected to see a highly unusual event occurring before their eyes.

The advert is based on an actual experiment designed and conducted by Daniel Simons and Christopher Chabris (Simons and Chabris, 1999). The audience behaved as the participants in their study behaved and the inattentional blindness was seen for a man who walked across the screen carrying an umbrella and even for the gorilla when it walked along the screen, stopped in the middle, turned to face the front, thumped its chest, turned and walked to the other side of the screen. This segment took nine seconds. The whole film lasted 62 seconds. You can see shots of the film in Figure 9.5 (and here: http://www.perceptionweb.com/perc0999/simons.html). Inattentional blindness has been demonstrated in all sorts of contexts, even in a Monty Python sketch (Wiseman and Watt, 2015).

Divided attention

Although all people seem to attend selectively to stimuli in the environment, they also sometimes have to undertake tasks that are made up of multiple components. Imagine cooking a meal, for example. Monitoring your boiling pasta while chopping up peppers and warming up your Bolognese sauce requires you to attend to several stimuli. When attention is split in this way it is called **divided attention**. Various models have sought to explain divided attention and how we can (or, more often, cannot) undertake many tasks all at once. Single-capacity models, for example, suggest that there is one pool of resources available to deal with perceptual and cognitive challenges (Kahneman, 1973). You can probably gather from this that the more tasks an individual undertakes, the less capacity will be left to undertake these tasks effectively because each task is competing for the same pool of resources.

Resources are, then, normally allocated to the most important task. Single-capacity model theorists have found some support for this proposition in experiments where individuals have to undertake two tasks simultaneously (this is called **dual-task methodology**). When this occurs, performance on both tasks diminishes. Results like these suggest that when the resources necessary to complete tasks exceed the available single capacity, then performance will deteriorate. However, not all evidence supports this view. The anecdotal example of preparing a meal is one subjective example. Experiments in which typists were asked to transcribe text and complete a shadowing task at the same time found the participants were able to do this effectively (Shaffer, 1975). Sometimes, two tasks can be performed as well as one can.

An alternative to the single resource models are the multiple resource models. These argue that, in fact, we have several resource pools to deal with various cognitive and perceptual processes. It is because of these various pools that we can divide our attention between tasks successfully. These models suggest that when two tasks compete for the same resource, this will result in an impairment in task performance. When tasks

Figure 9.5 Shots from the gorilla film.
Source: Simons, D. J. and Chabris, C. F., Gorillas in our midst: sustained inattentional blindness for dynamic events. *Perception,* 1999, 28, 1059–74.

Controversies in psychological science: Well, are you 'lovin' it'? The evidence for subliminal perception

The issue

One of the quirkier yet controversial claims made in the psychology literature is that people can be influenced in the way they behave by subliminal means – that is, without awareness that they are being influenced. Normally, such influence is created by exposing participants to images or words for very brief, sub-threshold (subliminal) periods and then observing whether they behave in a way which suggests that these stimuli have had an effect. In 1957, for example, an American market researcher claimed to have increased the sales of Coca Cola and popcorn in a cinema by flashing the messages 'Drink Coca Cola' and 'Eat popcorn' on screen. There was no actual evidence that such behaviour change had occurred, however, and no study was ever published (Karremans et al., 2006). So, is there any evidence that **subliminal perception** affects behaviour?

The evidence

We know that the availability of images implicitly affects people's behaviour. People exposed to pictures of an exclusive restaurant behave with better manners when later engaged in an eating task (Aarts and Djksterhuis, 2003); people who cast votes in school are more likely to pledge financial support for projects initiated by the school (Berger et al., 2008); and, famously, people primed with the Apple logo performed more creatively at a later task than did those primed with the IBM logo (Fitzsimons et al., 2008). People who are primed with jackpot symbols repeatedly flashed for 30 ms before playing a slot machine, bet more and are more confident in their last spin (Gibson and Zielaskowski, 2013). However, this effect was only found if betting immediately followed the prime; it wasn't found if the prime preceded the betting by 5 minutes.

People primed with images of fast food engage in more time-saving behaviour, presumably because the stimuli activate subconsciously concepts or schema of speed and time-saving (Zhong and DeVoe, 2010). In this study, people completed a lexical decision-task primed with six images of fast food restaurants. They then read a 320 word description of Toronto. The reading speed of the participants was faster if they had been primed with the fast food image.

In a second experiment, they examined the effect of fast food restaurant priming on preference for time-saving products. They asked 91 undergraduates to recall a time they spent in a fast food restaurant (or the last time they went shopping – the control condition) and then asked them to rate the desirability of various household products. Those who remembered the fast food restaurant, preferred more time-saving products.

Finally, participants were asked to judge the aesthetic appeal of either two fast food logos or the logos of two inexpensive dinners and were then asked to indicate their preference for saving (i.e. would they like $3 today or X amount of dollars in a week's time; there were various amounts increasing from $3). The participants exposed to the fast food symbols were more likely to accept a small payment on the day than wait for a larger payment. Exposure to brand logos (e.g. Macdonalds) can influence later behaviour even when five seconds passes between the subliminal presentation and the behaviour (Muscarella et al., 2013).

Karremans et al. (2006), in a review of the ostensibly subliminal effects of marketing stimuli, observe that self-help tapes which claim to improve self-esteem, memory and promote weight loss by embedding subliminal messages in the recording have been unsuccessful. One study found that when participants were subliminally primed with the words 'Coca cola' and 'thirsty', they reported an increase in how thirsty they felt (Cooper and Cooper, 2002). Karremans et al. (2006) found that priming participants with the name of a drink (Lipton's tea) influenced people's decision to drink this particular brand, but only if participants were thirsty.

This finding was replicated and extended by Bermeitinger et al. (2009). Participants played a computer game and subliminally presented the logo of a brand of dextrose pills during the game. The participants' desire to ingest these pills and their tiredness was measured. The results mirrored those for tea: participants in the subliminal condition were more likely to ingest the pills but only if they were tired. In Mack and Rock's experiments, participants were asked to indicate which of the two arms of a visually presented cross was longer. At the fourth trial, an unexpected object was presented at the same time as the cross and participants were asked whether they were aware of this object appearing. The next trials followed, with participants being told that an unexpected object might appear, and a final trial explicitly asked participants to look for an unexpected object. Around 75 per cent of participants did not recognise the appearance of an object when they were not directed to be aware of it, or had their attention directly drawn to it. Twenty-five per cent of participants failed to do this under the other (divided/full attention) conditions.

Conclusion

These experiments suggest that if subliminal perception is to work, the stimuli must be related to the participant's psychological or physiological state. The presentation of a stimulus alone will not lead to a person being influenced by it.

compete for different resource pools, then they should be performed successfully. A problem with the resource model, however, is operationally defining a resource and the types of task that would use the different 'resources'. There is no general agreement on what the different types of resources are.

A final explanation for divided attention concerns the processes involved in various tasks. For example, Johnston and Heinz (1978) suggest that selective and divided attention clearly requires some form of selection. They divide the type of selection required into early (selecting perceptual/sensory information) and late (selecting meaning). Their process model does not agree that there is one structure or system which allows attention. It argues that early selection uses less capacity than late selection. To test this hypothesis, they asked participants to undertake a dichotic listening task where the stimuli differed in terms of their physical features (perceptual) or in terms of their meaning (semantic). Concurrently, the participants undertook a reaction time task in which they had to press a button as soon as a light appeared. The experimenters found that although reaction time was slower when the participants listened to two messages, less capacity was required when the messages differed perceptually (such as the speaker's voice).

Brain mechanisms of selective attention

The left and right cerebral hemispheres seem to play different roles in attention. Focal attention (which involves attention to local cues) appears to rely on the left hemisphere, whereas global attention (a holistic approach which takes in whole objects or scenes) relies on the right hemisphere (Fink *et al.*, 1996). This asymmetry of function may explain the symptoms seen in the perceptual disorder, spatial neglect (described in Chapter 6), in which brain-injured (usually right-hemisphere-damaged) patients are unable to report or respond to stimuli contralateral to the side of the brain

injury. The brain regions thought to be affected by attention are highlighted in Figure 9.6a and b.

Sustained attention has been associated with increased activation in the right prefrontal and parietal cortices, based on PET and fMRI findings, but generally there is a network of regions traversing the right fronto-parietal regions that are involved in sustained attention (Coull *et al.*, 1996), as Figures 9.6 shows. However, there is also evidence that that brain can adapt to what it sees – that is, after initial firing, this firing is reduced with repeated presentation of a stimulus. Thus brain activation, measured via fMRI, is reduced when the same face or object is presented to the participant but recovers when the stimulus undergoes a modest transformation (Grill-Spector *et al.*, 2009). This increase and decrease appears to be associated with the firing of the inferotemporal neurons.

Selective attention has been associated with increases in activation in posterior regions, but the region of activation depends on the type of attention that is selectively applied. If one sensory modality is attended to, regions associated with other modalities show suppressed activation (Haxby *et al.*, 1994; Ghatan *et al.*, 1998).

Divided attention also recruits the prefrontal cortex (PFC), especially the left (Vandenberghe *et al.*, 1997; Benedict *et al.*, 1998). Posner and Petersen (1990) have characterised the ability to shift attention in three ways: the first component of attention allows the disengagement of attention from its current location (a function of the posterior parietal cortex); the second guides attention from the current location to the new location (a function of the superior colliculus, frontal eye fields and related structures); the third component allows the re-engagement of attention to the new location (a function of the thalamus). There is evidence that the lateral intraparietal area increases when people increase their attention to spatial locations and that an increase in the intraparietal sulcus is seen when people voluntarily direct attention to a location (Yantis, 2008).

Cutting edge: Banner ads – do they work?

The answer to the question really depends on what we mean by 'work'. If it means they are more likely to make you buy more of the product they are advertising – the jury's out. There is no way of establishing this. If you mean, 'do people notice them in the first place?', that is a more interesting question and the answer seems to be yes. And no. For example, only around 46 per cent of people report remembering any banner ads when they are asked to recall what was on a webpage they visited (Dreze and Hussherr, 2003). Lapa (2007) found that over time, people learned where the location of the banners were and so avoided them on subsequent visits. However, even when the locations were randomised, people only

fixated on them around 11 per cent of the time (Burke *et al.*, 2005).

Would horizontal ads at the top of the page be better noticed than skyscraper ads going down the side of a page? And would an animated advert be better than static one? The answer is that people fixate more on the skyscraper-type ad along the right-hand side of the page, especially if it is animated (Kuisima *et al.*, 2010; Simola *et al.*, 2011). A single animation was better than multiple animations. Animation reduces fixation on a horizontal ad. If an advert appears suddenly, people fixate on it for longer than if the advert appeared after around 12 seconds (Simola *et al.*, 2011).

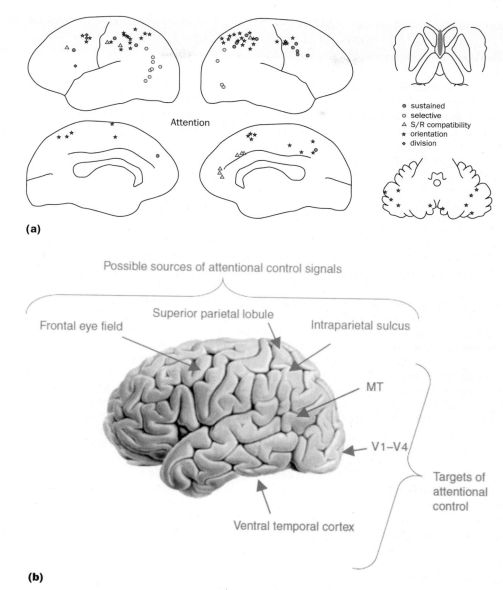

Figure 9.6 **(a)** The areas of the brain involved in attention, according to recent neuroimaging data. **(b)** Areas thought to be involved in the control of attention.

Source: Figure 4.6 from *Human Neuropsychology*, 2nd edn, Pearson/Prentice Hall (Martin, G.N., 2006).

Psychology in action: Attention and pain

It was once thought that distraction was enough to help people take their mind off pain. Some studies, however, have shown that it is not necessarily distraction that is responsible for reducing pain but rather the emotional quality of the distractor. Positive stimuli, such as humour and laughter, are known to reduce pain perception (Cogan *et al.*, 1987; Rotton and Shats, 1996) but increasing the attention required to complete cognitive tasks (distraction without emotion) does not (McCaul and Malott, 1984).

Minet de Wied and Marinus Verbaten from Utrecht University, the Netherlands, investigated whether high – and low-arousing neutral, negative or positive emotional

Psychology in action: *Continued*

stimuli affected people's experience of pain (de Wied and Verbaten, 2001). They presented pictures varying in emotional tone and arousal from the International Affective Picture System to 69 male students. The researchers hypothesised that if stimuli need to be emotionally distracting to reduce pain, then negative and positive pictures should reduce the experience of pain in a similar way. If stimuli prime the participant or help them appraise their state (so that a pleasant stimulus may put them in a positive mood but an unpleasant stimulus may put them in a negative mood), then pleasant and unpleasant stimuli will have different effects on the experience of pain. The pain induction task used was the cold-pressor task in which the participant keeps their arm in freezing water for as long as possible.

Exposure to pleasant pictures was associated with a greater tolerance of pain. In a second experiment, in which unpleasant pictures which contained either pain-related or pain-unrelated stimuli were presented, participants who viewed the pictures without pain cues tolerated the pain for longer than did those who viewed the pictures with pain cues. The results suggest that distraction by emotional cue may not be successful in reducing the experience of pain unless the distractor enhances positive mood (or does not produce a negative one, as experiment two showed).

Studies indicate that when changes in perception are induced in hypnotised people, the changes occur not in the people's actual perceptions but in their verbal reports about their perceptions. For example, Miller *et al.* (1973) used the Ponzo illusion to test the effects of hypnotically induced blindness. This effect is produced by the presence of the slanted lines to the left and right of two horizontal ones; if these lines are not present, the horizontal lines appear to be the same length. Through hypnotic suggestion, the experimenters made the slanted lines 'disappear'. But even though the participants reported that they could not see the slanted lines, they still perceived the upper line as being longer than the lower one. This result indicates that the visual system continues to process sensory information during hypnotically induced blindness; otherwise, the participants would have perceived the lines as being equal in length. The reported blindness appears to occur not because of altered activity in the visual system but because of altered activity in the verbal system (and in consciousness).

Neuroimaging studies have highlighted how the control of pain is related to different degrees of brain activation. Controlling this activation may reduce pain. For example, Koyama *et al.* (2005) administered thermal pain to 10 healthy volunteers as fMRI measured brain activation. As the pain became more intense, so did activation in the thalamus, PFC and ACC, areas of the brain known to respond to pain. When participants were told that they could expect a reduction in pain, however, there was a decrease in activation in these areas as well as a decrease in self-reported pain.

Taking this finding a step further, deCharms *et al.* (2005) speculated on what might happen if activity in the ACC could be manipulated. If it could be reduced, would participants experience less pain? Hypnosis, for example, has been associated with reduced pain and, in turn, less activation in the ACC. The researchers studied 36 healthy volunteers, some of whom undertook a training course in increasing/decreasing brain activation and pain. These included instructions either to pay attention to the pain or to direct attention away from it; to perceive the stimulus as tissue-damaging, or as a neutral sensory stimulus; to perceive the stimulus as being either very or not very intense; and to control the experience or to be controlled by it. The pain stimulus was heat.

When participants used these instructions to increase or decrease activation in the ACC, the perception of pain changed: those who were instructed to increase ACC activation, experienced more pain. When patients experiencing pain were given the same instructions, decreases in self-reported pain were found after training.

The results suggest that when healthy people exposed to pain, and patients experiencing pain, follow instructions designed to reduce activation in a part of the brain known to respond during painful experiences, then such experiences are reduced.

Hypnosis

Hypnosis is a process whereby verbal suggestions made by one individual can be acted on by another who would not normally and voluntarily perform those acts. Under hypnosis, a person can be induced to bark like a dog, act like a baby or tolerate being pierced with needles. Although these examples are interesting and amusing, hypnosis is important to psychology because it provides information about the nature of consciousness and has applications in the fields of medicine and psychotherapy.

Hypnosis, or **mesmerism**, was discovered by Franz Anton Mesmer (1734–1815), an Austrian physician. He found that when he passed magnets back and forth over people's bodies (in an attempt to restore their 'magnetic fluxes' and cure them of disease), they would often have convulsions and enter a trance-like state during which almost miraculous cures could be achieved. As Mesmer discovered later, the patients were not affected directly by the magnetism of the iron rods; they were responding to his undoubtedly persuasive and compelling personality. We now know that convulsions and trance-like states do not necessarily accompany hypnosis, and we also know that hypnosis does not cure physical illnesses. Mesmer's patients apparently had psychologically produced symptoms that were alleviated by suggestions made while they were hypnotised.

The induction of hypnosis

A person undergoing hypnosis can be alert, relaxed, tense, lying quietly or exercising vigorously. There is no need to move an object in front of someone's face or to say 'you are getting sleepy'; an enormous variety of techniques can be used to induce hypnosis in a susceptible person. The only essential feature seems to be the participant's understanding that they are to be hypnotised. Moss (1965) reported having sometimes simply said to a well-practised subject, in a normal tone of voice, 'Please sit in that chair and go into hypnosis', and the subject complied within a few seconds. Sometimes, this approach even worked on volunteers who had never been hypnotised before.

The induction process normally involves suggestions for sleep or relaxation, followed by a set of suggestions aimed to produce arm lowering or lifting, hand clasping ('you cannot separate your hands'), hallucinations and amnesia.

Characteristics of hypnosis

Hypnotised people are very suggestible; their behaviour will conform with what the hypnotist says, even to the extent that they may appear to misperceive reality (Wagstaff, 1996). Under hypnosis, people can be instructed to do things that they would not be expected to do under normal conditions, such as acting out imaginary scenes or pretending to be an animal. Hypnotised people can be convinced that an arm cannot move or is insensitive to pain, and they then act as if that is the case. They can also be persuaded to have positive or negative hallucinations – to see things that are not there or not to see objects that are there.

Hypnos. The son of Nyx (night) and brother of Thanatos (death), the mythical Hypnos was thought to fan the weary to sleep.

Source: Head of Hypnos, or Sleep, 1st-2nd Century AD, copy of a Hellenistic original, found at Civitella d'Arno, Italy (broze), Roman/British Museum, London, UK/Bridgeman Images.

One of the most dramatic phenomena of hypnosis is **post-hypnotic suggestibility**, in which a person is given instructions under hypnosis and follows those instructions after returning to a non-hypnotised state. For example, a hypnotist might tell a man that he will become unbearably thirsty when he sees the hypnotist look at her watch. She might also admonish him not to remember anything upon leaving the hypnotic state, so that **posthypnotic amnesia** is also achieved. After leaving the hypnotic state, the man acts normally and professes ignorance of what he perceived and did during hypnosis, perhaps even apologising for not having succumbed to hypnosis. The hypnotist later looks at her watch, and the man suddenly leaves the room to get a drink of water.

Theories of hypnosis

Most theories of hypnosis revolve around the question of whether hypnosis represents a different state of consciousness (Fellows, 1990; Lynn and Rhue, 1991). The state hypothesis of hypnosis suggests that this phenomenon is an example of an altered state of consciousness or a trance resulting from induction (Hilgard, 1986). Hilgard's neo-dissociation theory (Hilgard, 1978, 1991) suggests that we have multiple systems of control which are not all conscious at the same time. These systems are under the general, central control of an 'executive ego' which controls and motivates other systems. The theory suggests that when a person is under hypnosis, overall control is given up to the hypnotist who has access to various systems. Such a theory claims to find support from what is called the **'hidden observer' phenomenon**. This is where the experimenter places a hand on the shoulder of the hypnotised individual and appears to be able to talk to a hidden part of the person's body (Knox *et al.*, 1974).

The non-state hypothesis of hypnosis argues that the process does not reflect altered states of consciousness but more mundane psychological functions such as imagination, relaxation, role-enactment, compliance, conformity, attention, attitudes and expectations (Coe and Sarbin, 1991; Wagstaff, 1991, 1996). Wagstaff (1996), for example, has argued that hypnosis may well represent some altered state but the evidence suggests that hypnotic suggestion can be explained by what we already know about human behaviour and thought. Strategic role-enactment is common in psychological research, for example. The degree of role-taking depends on whether the participant is worried about giving up control or being manipulated. To experience a hand getting heavier, the individual can imagine a weight on their arm; to experience hypnotic 'amnesia', the individual can distract themselves. Of course, state theorists would argue that such compliance or acting out is part of hypnotic behaviour that occurs without subjective experience (Spanos, 1991, 1992).

People's expectations about hypnosis play an important role in their behaviour while under hypnosis. In lectures to two sections of an introductory psychology class, Orne (1959) told one section (falsely) that one of the most prominent features of hypnosis was rigidity of the preferred (that is, dominant) hand. Later, he arranged a demonstration of hypnosis during a meeting of students from both sections. Several of the students who had heard that the dominant hand became rigid showed this phenomenon when hypnotised, but none of the students who had not heard this myth developed a rigid hand. Similarly, if people become willing to follow a hypnotist's suggestions, perhaps they do so because they believe that this suggested behaviour is what is supposed to happen. Perhaps people willingly follow a hypnotist's suggestion to do something silly (such as bark like a dog) because they know that hypnotised people are not responsible for their behaviour.

Compliance, role-enactment and other psychological processes can also explain examples of antisocial or strange behaviour that individuals can apparently be hypnotised into doing. Hypnotists have induced individuals to expose themselves indecently, pick up dangerous snakes, steal, verbally attack others, put their hands in nitric acid, throw acid at the experimenter, deal heroin, mutilate the Bible and make homosexual approaches (Orne and Evans, 1965; Wagstaff, 1993). However, Orne and Evans (1965) reported that non-hypnotised individuals could also be instructed to perform these acts. What produces this apparent unusual behaviour is the need to want to help the hypnotist or thinking that the antics were safe or that someone else would take responsibility for them (Udolf, 1983). One of the best predictors of whether someone is hypnotisable and open to suggestion is if they are open to suggestion when not hypnotised (Braffman and Kirsch, 1999).

Controversies in psychological science: Can hypnosis reduce pain and stress?

The issue

Pain is the most unpleasant sensory experience humans can suffer. It can derive from many sources, although the commonest are illness and disease. Such pain is normally relieved by surgery or drugs (often the surgery itself causes pain and has to be relieved pharmacologically). There are instances, however, where surgical or pharmacological interventions in pain relief are not successful. Often, in such circumstances, patients turn to **hypnotic analgesia** as an alternative. Hypnotic analgesia refers to the ability to endure or eliminate surgical pain via hypnotic suggestion (Wagstaff, 1996). Does such analgesic intervention work?

The evidence

Barber (1996, 1998) has reviewed evidence which suggests that hypnotic treatment for acute pain resulting from medical procedures (chemotherapy, surgery) or recurring pain is effective. Of course, different types of condition produce different types of pain: some pains are constant, some intermittent. Osteoarthritis and trigeminal neuralgia, for example, produce almost constant pain whereas migraine and sickle cell disease and lower back pain caused by spinal nerve compression produce recurring pain.

To investigate whether hypnosis would help mediate the effects of a temporarily stressful event and whether any buffering effect would be accompanied by immune system changes, Kiecolt-Glaser et al. (2001) took blood samples from medical and dental students who were hypnotically suggestible. They did this during periods of low stress and then three days before their first exams. Exams have been found to provoke considerable distress in examinees.

Wounds tend to heal significantly more slowly before an important examination, for example, than during an exam-free period (Marucha et al., 1998). Half of the group were assigned to a hypnosis-generated relaxation-training condition in this interval; the other half received no relaxation training. The authors examined various immune system variables including lymphocyte number and interleukin-1 (which assists wound healing).

They found that students in the hypnosis condition showed a significantly greater proliferation of lymphocytes and an increase in interleukin-1 production during the examination period, compared with the control group. These students were also able to maintain baseline levels of these antibodies. The authors suggest that the effects are similar to those seen in surgical patients – hypnotic relaxation training in some patients is associated with shorter hospital stays, decreased pain and more rapid recovery following surgery (Blankfield, 1991; Lang et al., 2000). The findings highlight the role of hypnotic relaxation in reducing stress and in altering immune system functioning. In a meta-analysis of the effects of hypnosis on people undergoing surgery, Tefikow et al. (2013) found that hypnosis reduced emotional distress, pain, taking medicine, improved recovery and reduced the length of time spent in surgery.

Hypnotic analgesia has been explained in terms of the ironic processes theory (Wegner, 1994). According to this theory, the control of mental events is made possible by two processes working together. The operating process retrieves material that puts the organism in a desirable state; the maintaining process searches consciousness for any content that is inconsistent with the desired state. When cognitive tasks reduce the resources available, the effectiveness of the monitoring process increases in comparison with the operating process (Eastwood et al., 1998). Eastwood tested this ▶

Controversies in psychological science: *Continued*

hypothesis by requiring participants low and high in hypnotisability to report the degree of pain they were experiencing in a pain-induction task at regular intervals. The experimenters found that the frequency of pain reporting was associated with an increase in the level of experienced pain but that highly hypnotisable participants reported less pain.

The fact that only highly hypnotisable participants showed this effect explains why the published research has focused more on these individuals than on those who are not particularly susceptible to hypnotic suggestion (Crawford, 1994). Why are highly susceptible individuals more likely to report reductions in pain? Some psychologists have suggested that these individuals can partition their attentional resources more effectively (Hilgard and Hilgard, 1994). Crawford *et al.* (1993) have reported that highly susceptible individuals showed a bilateral increase in blood flow to the frontal cortex and somatosensory cortex during hypnotic analgesia and the experience of pain and Rainville *et al.* (2002) reported changes in the anterior cingulate cortex (AAC), in the frontal lobe. According to Crawford *et al.* (1998), this evidence suggests

that the frontal region deals with the active allocation of attention, whereas the posterior parts are concerned with the spatiotemporal aspects of pain perception (such as where and when the pain is experienced). There is also evidence that hypnotically induced pain activates the same areas as actual pain. This is what Derbyshire *et al.* (2004) found and the results can be seen in Figure 9.7.

Conclusion

Wagstaff (1987) has suggested that many of the effects seen in hypnotic analgesia are the result of the same factors that result in other forms of hypnotism. These factors include social support, relaxation, covert modelling, placebo and social compliance. Belief in the efficacy of the hypnosis is also an important factor. Wagstaff and Royce (1994) found that although hypnotic suggestions for the alleviation of nail-biting was better than non-hypnotic suggestions, the best predictor of abstinence from nail-biting was belief in the efficacy of the procedure. There may, therefore, be a strong placebo effect seen in these studies.

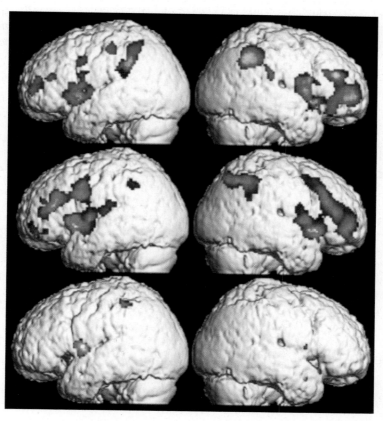

Figure 9.7 The top two scans show areas of activation while people experience hypnotically suggested pain; the next two show areas activated by actual heat pain; the bottom two show areas activated by imagining the pain from heat. From Derbyshire et al (2014).

Sleep

Sleep is not a state of unconsciousness but a state of altered consciousness. During sleep, we have dreams that can be just as vivid as waking experiences, and yet we forget most of them as soon as they are over. Our amnesia leads us to think, incorrectly, that we were unconscious while we were asleep. In fact, there are two distinct kinds of sleep, and thus two states of altered consciousness. We spend approximately one-third of our lives sleeping, or trying to, although the reasons for why we sleep are not fully known.

The stages of sleep

Sleep is not uniform. We can sleep lightly or deeply; we can be restless or still; we can have vivid dreams, or our consciousness can be relatively blank. Researchers who have studied sleep have found that its stages usually follow an orderly, predictable sequence.

Most sleep research takes place in sleep laboratories. Because a person's sleep is affected by their surroundings, a sleep laboratory contains one or more small bedrooms, furnished and decorated to be as home-like and comfortable as possible. The most important apparatus of the sleep laboratory is the polygraph, a machine located in a separate room that records on paper the output of various devices that can be attached to the sleeper. For example, the polygraph can record the electrical activity of the brain through small metal discs pasted to the scalp, producing an electroencephalogram (EEG). It can record electrical signals from muscles, producing an electromyogram (EMG) or from the heart, producing an electrocardiogram (ECG). Or it can record eye movements through small metal discs attached to the skin around the eyes, producing an electro-oculogram (EOG). Other special transducers can detect respiration, sweating, skin or body temperature, and a variety of other physiological states (Andreassi, 2007).

The EEG record distinguishes between alert and relaxed wakefulness. When a person is alert, the tracing looks rather irregular, and the pens do not move very far up or down. The EEG shows high-frequency (15–30 Hz), low-amplitude electrical activity called beta activity. When a person is relaxed and perhaps somewhat drowsy, the record shows alpha activity, a medium-frequency (8–12 Hz), medium-amplitude rhythm.

When the individual relaxes and becomes drowsy, the EEG changes from beta activity to alpha activity. Figure 9.8 illustrates this and the subsequent stages of sleep.

The first stage of sleep (stage 1) is marked by the presence of some **theta activity**, EEG activity of 3.5–7.5Hz. This stage is actually a transition between sleep and wakefulness; the EMG shows that muscles are still active, and the EOG indicates slow, gentle, rolling eye movements. The eyes slowly open and close from time to time. Soon, the person is fully asleep.

Normal Adult Brain Waves

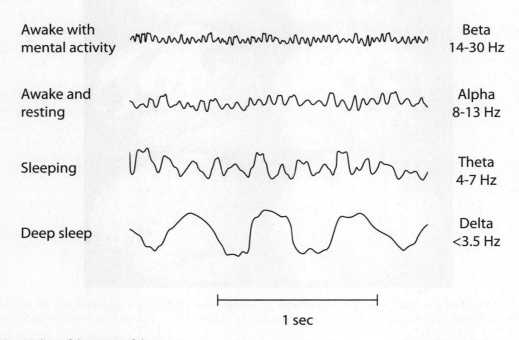

Figure 9.8 An EEG recording of the stages of sleep.

As sleep progresses, it gets deeper and deeper, moving through stages 2, 3 and 4. The EEG gets progressively lower in frequency and higher in amplitude. Stage 4 consists mainly of delta activity, characterised by relatively high-amplitude waves occurring at less than 3.5 Hz. Our sleeper becomes less responsive to the environment, and it becomes more difficult to awaken him. Environmental stimuli that caused him to stir during stage 1 produce little or no reaction during stage 4. The sleep of stages 3 and 4 is called **slow-wave sleep**.

Stage 4 sleep is reached in less than an hour and continues for as much as half an hour. Then, suddenly, the EEG begins to indicate lighter levels of sleep, back through stages 3 and 2 to the activity characteristic of stage 1. The sleeper's heartbeat becomes irregular and his respiration alternates between shallow breaths and sudden gasps. The EOG shows that the person's eyes are darting rapidly back and forth, up and down. The EEG record looks like that of a person who is awake and active. Yet the sleeper is fast asleep. Although EMG is generally quiet, indicating muscular relaxation, the hands and feet twitch occasionally.

At this point, the subject is dreaming and has entered another stage of sleep, called **rapid eye movement (REM) sleep**. The first episode of REM sleep lasts 20–30 minutes and is followed by approximately one hour of slow-wave sleep. As the night goes on, the episodes of REM sleep get longer and the episodes of slow-wave sleep get shorter, but the total cycle remains at approximately 90 minutes. A typical night's sleep consists of four or five of these cycles.

Regions of the brain also become more or less active during REM sleep. We will return to the significance of brain activity changes in sleep, consciousness and alertness at the end of the chapter.

Although a person in REM sleep exhibits rapid eye movements and brief twitches of the hands and feet, the EMG shows that the facial muscles are still. In fact, physiological studies have shown that, aside from occasional twitching, a person actually becomes paralysed during REM sleep. Males are observed to have partial or full erections. In addition, women's vaginal secretions increase at this time. These genital changes are usually not associated with sexual arousal or dreams of a sexual nature. Table 9.1 lists the principal characteristics of REM sleep and slow-wave sleep.

Chronotypes

Many parts of the body work according to set rhythms. These rhythms can be measured in periods of seconds, minutes, hours, days or weeks. Our heartbeat and our breathing, for example, occurs in rhythmic patterns (72 beats of the heart per minute on average in a healthy adult), as does our sleep (we do this daily, for a set number of hours normally, and within those hours there are further rhythmic patterns, as the section on sleep showed). The circaseptan rhythm is one that occurs every seven days; the menstrual cycle occurs over a period of a month.

Table 9.1 Principal characteristics of REM sleep and slow-wave sleep

REM sleep	Slow-wave sleep
Rapid EEG waves	Slow EEG waves
Muscular paralysis	Lack of muscular paralysis
Rapid eye movements	Slow or absent eye movements
Penile erection or vaginal secretion	Lack of genital activity
Dreams	

A number of behaviours seems to vary and fluctuate over the course of a day: our maximum and minimum grip strength (Atkinson et al., 1993), our back-leg strength (Coldwells et al., 1994) and our manual dexterity (Monk and Kupfer, 2000). Another time of day difference can be seen in diurnal type or chronotype. Some people (and animals) prefer nocturnality and are more alert during the night and prefer this time of day; others prefer diurnality (and are more alert during, and prefer, the daytime). In other words, there are evening types and morning types, larks and owls. These types are called **chronotypes**. These individuals either prefer or have a tendency to go to sleep later and wake up later (evening types) or to go to sleep earlier and wake up earlier (morning types).

Morning types or 'larks' are often viewed as conscientious, trustworthy and stable. They are reported to perform better cognitively in the morning than the evening (Roberts and Kyllonen, 1999). Evening types or 'owls' are thought to be creative, unstable and have fractious social and family relationships (they also yawn more, Zilli et al., 2007). Evening types have been shown to demonstrate increased mating success in the short-term (Piffer et al., 2011; Randler et al., 2012), are more impulsive and sensation-seeking, take more risks (Russo et al., 2012), are more extrovert (Randler et al., 2012) and are less conscientious and agreeable (Tsaousis, 2010), two of the five important personality traits, discussed in more detail in Chapter 14. Eveningness has also been found to be more common in individualist than collectivist cultures (Vollmer and Randler, 2012). A study of 293 volunteer college students by Jonason et al. (2013) found that the type was also associated with Machiavellianism, psychopathy and exploitative narcissism (the so-called Dark Triad which is discussed in Chapter 14). Evening types, then, appear to be a different, darker type of person to the early-risers. But there are some benefits.

For example, in one study, evening and morning types completed a visual component of a well-known test of creativity, the Torrance Test of Creative Thinking (Giampietro and Cavallera, 2007). The test involved (i) drawing a picture using a shape provided by the experimenter and giving a name to it, and (ii) making complete shapes out of 10 incomplete straight and curved lines. Evening types out-scored morning types.

When the IQ performance of adolescents classed as morning and evening types was tested in the morning and the evening, fluid (general) intelligence was better if the time of testing matched the person's circadian preference. There were no circadian preference effects for crystallised intelligence, intelligence for rehearsed or learned material such as vocabulary (Goldstein *et al.*, 2007). Morning types, however, reported fewer attention problems, less aggression, were more competent socially in school and were engaged in more activities. One reason for this might be that evening types have difficulty in adjusting to the demands of early morning rises for school (Andershed, 2005). A study of musical performance in 22 pianists found that keystroke velocity was higher in the morning but that morning types were more even in the morning and evening types more even in the evening (but note the small number of participants). (Van Vugt *et al.*, 2013).

The Savanna-IQ interaction hypothesis states that intelligent individuals are more likely to express novel values and preferences than are the less intelligent but that general intelligence has no effect on the acquisition of familiar values and preferences. In short, intelligent people go against the norm. We also know that intelligent people have a preference for the night rather than the morning. Some intriguing research also suggests that diurnal preference is heritable with one study of South Korean twins finding that heritability (see Chapter 3) of morningness–eveningness is 0.45 (Hur, 2007). That is, the preference is highly heritable. The amount of shared environment had little effect on this number, indicating that environment had no great effect on the expression of this preference.

Most societies' preference for activity, however, is the daytime (Kanazawa and Perina, 2009). Kanazawa and Perina asked over 20,000 adolescents about their sleeping habits and measured their IQ. Regardless of sex, race, education, parental status or marital status, high childhood IQ was associated with increased nocturnal activity in early adolescence. The more intelligent the adolescent, the more likely he or she was to develop into an adult who woke up late and went to bed late. You can see these patterns in Figure 9.9. The association between eveningness and cognitive ability and eveningness and academic achievement is contrary. A meta-analysis of studies examining chronotype and ability/academic success, and which included over 7,000 participants found a positive correlation between eveningness and cognitive ability but a negative correlation between the trait and academic achievement (Preckel *et al.*, 2011). The evening types were brighter but poor at academic work. The opposite pattern was seen in the morning types.

Functions of sleep

Sleep is one of the few universal behaviours. All mammals, all birds and some cold-blooded vertebrates spend part of each day sleeping. Sleep is seen even in species that would seem to be better off without sleep. For example, the Indus dolphin (*Platanista indi*) which lives in the muddy waters of the Indus estuary in Pakistan (Pilleri, 1979). Over the ages, it has become blind, presumably because vision is not useful in the animal's environment (it has an excellent sonar system, which it uses to navigate and find prey). However, despite the dangers caused by sleeping, sleep has not disappeared. The Indus dolphin never stops swimming; doing so would result in injury, because of the dangerous currents and the vast quantities of debris carried by the river during the monsoon season. Pilleri captured two Indus dolphins and studied their habits. He found that they slept a total of seven hours a day, in very brief naps of 4–60 seconds each. If sleep did not perform an important function, we might expect that it, like vision, would have been eliminated in this species through the process of natural selection.

Sleep deprivation

The universal nature of sleep suggests that it performs some important functions (Hobson, 1988). One approach to discovering the functions of sleep is the deprivation study. Consider, for example, the function of eating. The effects of starvation are easy to detect: the person loses weight, becomes fatigued and will eventually die if they do not eat again. By analogy, it should be easy to discover why we sleep by seeing what happens to a person who goes without sleep.

Unfortunately, deprivation studies have not obtained persuasive evidence that sleep is needed to keep the body functioning normally. Horne (1978) reviewed over fifty experiments in which humans had been deprived of sleep. He reported that most of them found that sleep deprivation did not interfere with people's ability to perform physical exercise. In addition, they found no evidence of a physiological stress response to sleep deprivation. If people encounter stressful situations that cause illness or damage to various organ systems, changes can be seen in such physiological measures as blood levels of cortisol and epinephrine. Generally, these changes did not occur.

Although sleep deprivation does not seem to damage the body, and sleep does not seem to be necessary for athletic exercise, sleep may be required for normal brain functioning. Several studies suggest that sleep-deprived people are able to perform normally on most intellectual tasks, as long as the tasks are short. They perform more poorly on tasks that require a high level of cortical functioning after two days of sleep deprivation (Horne and Minard, 1985). In particular, they perform poorly on tasks that require them to be watchful, alert and vigilant. Female flight attendants working on international transmeridian flights, for example, perform attention tasks that require delayed responding more poorly than do their ground-bound colleagues (Cho *et al.*, 2000). People also show poor recency memory, but not recognition memory, after 36 hours' lack of sleep (Harrison and Horne, 2000) and free recall of verbal material tends to be impaired after the loss of one night's sleep (Drummond *et al.*, 2000).

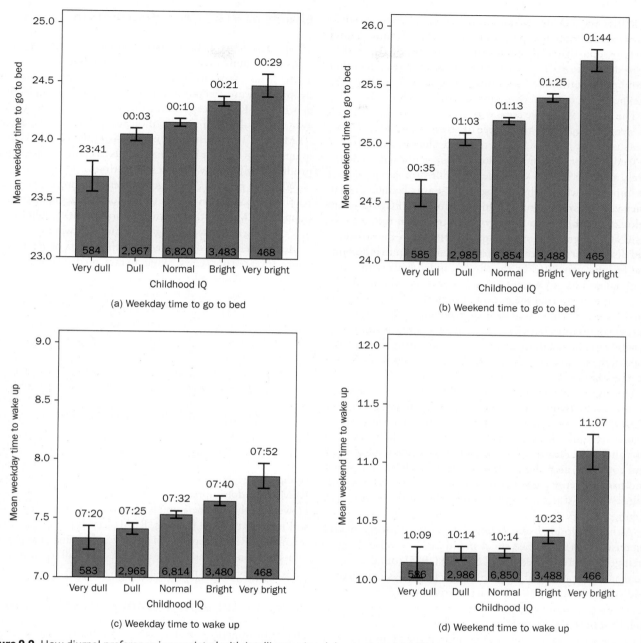

Figure 9.9 How diurnal preference is associated with intelligence in adolescence and adulthood.

Source: from 'Why night owls are more intelligent', *Personality and Individual Differences*, Vol. 47 (7), pp. 685–690 (Kanazawa, S. and Perina, K. 2009).

The effects of sleep deprivation on working memory depend on the length of deprivation. There is little difference in performance between 24 and 35 hours of deprivation (Chee *et al.*, 2006). The sleep deprivation is associated with a reduction in activation in two regions of the brain: the superior parietal cortex and the left thalamus. Participants allowed to sleep normally following sleep deprivation show greater activation in the frontal-parietal area and this correlates with improved working memory performance.

One study has reported that when sleep is restricted by 50 per cent, feelings of sociability and optimism decline by approximately 15 per cent (Haack and Mullington, 2005), and the ability to identify odours declines after 52 hours' sleep deprivation (McBride *et al.*, 2006). Wells and Cruess (2006) examined the effect of sleep loss on food consumption in a group of 50 undergraduates who were instructed to sleep for only four hours on the second day of the study (on the first they recorded their sleep quality and food intake).

Respondents kept diaries of what they ate and so the study relied on self-reporting, with all the caveats that implies. After sleep loss, participants ingested fewer calories two days after sleep deprivation. They also chose foods for reasons other than health, naturalness and price. The study highlights the unexpected nutritional consequences of sleep loss.

The way in which we cope with stress may affect how well we sleep, regardless of the source of stress. Sadeh *et al.* (2004) measured the sleeping patterns and sleeping quality of 36 students during periods of low stress – a normal academic week, and high stress – when their eligibility for acceptance on an important clinical psychology course was being assessed. They were classed as problem-focused copers (PFC; they manage or alter the stress-causing problem); emotion-focused copers (EFC; they regulate emotional responses to the stressor); and disengagers (DE; they try to disengage from the thoughts and feelings generated by the threat). Individuals with a predominantly EFC style slept less whereas those who used EFC less slept more during the period of high stress. The low EFC participants also improved their sleep quality during the stressful period whereas high EFC participants' sleep worsened. A general effect was found for PFC – people scoring high in this style slept more, regardless of whether the period was stressful or stress-free.

During stage 4 sleep, the metabolic activity of the brain decreases to about 75 per cent of the waking level (Sakai *et al.*, 1979). Thus, stage 4 sleep appears to give the brain a chance to rest. In fact, people are unreactive to all but intense stimuli during slow-wave sleep and, if awakened, act groggy and confused, as if their cerebral cortex has been shut down and has not yet resumed its functioning. These observations suggest that during stage 4 sleep the brain is, indeed, resting.

Although bodily exercise has little effect on sleep, mental exercise seems to increase the demand for slow-wave sleep. In an ingenious study, Horne and Minard (1985) found a way to increase mental activity without affecting physical activity and without causing stress. The investigators told volunteers to show up for an experiment in which they were supposed to take some tests designed to test reading skills. In fact, when the people turned up, they were told that the plans had been changed. They were invited for a day out, at the expense of the experimenters. They spent the day visiting an art exhibition, a shopping centre, a museum, an amusement park, a zoo and stately home. After a scenic drive through the countryside they watched a film in a local cinema. They were driven from place to place and certainly did not become overheated by exercise. After the film, they returned to the sleep laboratory. They said they were tired, and they readily fell asleep. Their sleep duration was normal and they awoke feeling refreshed. However, their slow-wave sleep, particularly stage 4 sleep, was increased.

Effects of REM sleep deprivation

Total sleep deprivation impairs people's ability to perform tasks that require them to be alert and vigilant, such as driving a car. What happens when only REM sleep is disrupted? People who are sleeping in a laboratory can be selectively deprived of REM sleep. An investigator awakens them whenever their polygraph records indicate that they have entered REM sleep. The investigator must also awaken control participants just as often at random intervals to eliminate any effects produced by being awakened several times.

When the person is no longer awakened during REM sleep, a rebound phenomenon is seen: the person engages in many more bouts of REM sleep than normal during the next night or two, as if catching up on something important that was missed.

Researchers have discovered that the effects of REM sleep deprivation are not very striking. In fact, medical journals contain reports of several patients who showed little or no REM sleep after sustaining damage to the brain stem (Lavie *et al.*, 1984; Gironell *et al.*, 1995). The lack of REM sleep did not appear to cause serious side effects. One of the patients, after receiving his injury, completed high school, attended law school and began practising law.

Several investigators have suggested that REM sleep may play a role in learning. For example, Greenberg and Pearlman (1974) suggest that REM sleep helps to integrate memories of events of the previous day – especially those dealing with emotionally related information – with existing memories. Crick and Mitchison (1983) suggest that REM sleep helps flush irrelevant information from memory to prevent the storage of useless clutter. Many studies using laboratory animals have shown that deprivation of REM sleep does impair the ability to learn a complex task. However, although the animals learn the task more slowly, they still manage to learn it. Thus, REM sleep is not necessary for learning. If REM sleep does play a role in learning, it appears to be a subtle one, at least, in the adult. As we shall see next, REM sleep may be important for brain development.

Sleep-dependent memory consolidation

One of the functions of sleep is to allow us to consolidate what we have learned while we were awake. This phenomenon is called sleep-dependent memory consolidation (Marshall and Born, 2007). For example, there is considerable evidence now to show that our procedural, declarative, sensory and motor memory are better after sleeping (Walker *et al.*, 2003; Cohen *et al.*, 2005; Born *et al.*, 2006) and each appears to be dependent on the appearance of certain sleep stages. Motor skills, for example, appear to be better consolidated after non-REM sleep or stage 2 sleep. Visual discrimination tasks are better remembered after slow-wave sleep and REM sleep (as evidenced by the findings that disrupting these sleep stages disrupts consolidation). The sleep after training appears to be resistant to the interference that you would expect to see during the delay between encoding and later retrieval. See Figures 9.10 and 9.11.

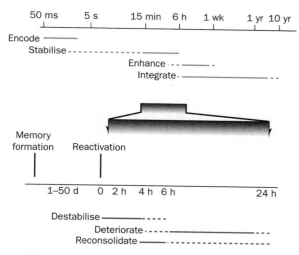

Figure 9.10 Time course of memory processes during sleep.

Source: Stickgold, R. and Walker, M.P., Sleep-dependent memory consolidation and reconsolidation. *Sleep Medicine* (2007), 8, 331–43, Figure 2.

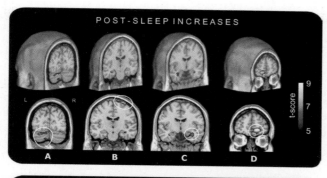

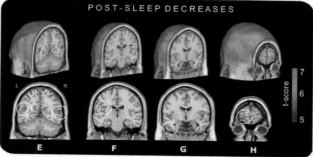

Figure 9.11 Sleep-dependent motor memory reorganisation in the human brain.

Source: Stickgold, R. and Walker, M.P., Sleep-dependent memory consolidation and reconsolidation. *Sleep Medicine* (2007), 8, 331–43, Figure 2.

Slow-wave sleep (and lots of it) appears to be beneficial for remembering word pairs, remembering spatial locations and recognising words. REM sleep appears to be beneficial to non-declarative memory and emotional memory, i.e. those memory functions that rely less on encoding by the hippocampus. Studies of hippocampal function – navigation, for example – have found that after learning the navigation of a virtual town the hippocampus becomes active during slow-wave sleep. This activation correlates with memory performance the following day: the greater the activation, the greater the performance (Peigneux *et al.*, 2004). There is no evidence that sleep helps you forget certain memories (Marshall and Born, 2007).

How sleep loss affects behaviour

At around 6 a.m. on 28 February 2001, Gary Hart, a 37-year-old builder from Lincolnshire, drove his Land Rover and trailer off the M62 near Great Heck in North Yorkshire, and plummeted down the embankment onto the east coast mainline. Within minutes, the vehicle was hit by a southbound express passenger train travelling at 117 mph. At 6.14 a.m. the passenger train collided with another train carrying 1,600 tons of coal. The collision killed 10 people and injured 76 people. Hart was convicted of death by dangerous driving. He admitted that he had not slept the night before but denied falling asleep at the wheel. He admitted having had only a short nap in the last 24 hours.

Most road traffic accidents occur between four and six o'clock in the morning, with a second, slightly smaller peak occurring in the middle of the afternoon. Most researchers attribute this finding to the gradual onset of sleeplessness and/or fatigue. A lack of sleep seems to exacerbate driving performance as does a feeling of fatigue and the ingestion of carbohydrates (Lowdon *et al.*, 2004). Even in the wakeful driver, prolonged driving induces subjective feelings of tiredness (Summala *et al.*, 1999) and lane drifting (Brookhuis and DeWaard, 1993). Long-haul lorry drivers, in particular, experience increased fatigue and tension as the driving progresses, although it seems as if difficult driving conditions result in fewer driving mistakes than do monotonous ones, such as a straight road (Matthews and Desmond, 2002). Fatigue appears to have the same detrimental effect on driving as does alcohol (DeWaard and Brookhuis, 1991).

Combined with long work hours, sleep loss can be fatal. Researchers at the Harvard Work Hours, Health and Safety Group studied a group of 2,737 US medical residents in their first postgraduate year (interns) (Barger *et al.*, 2005). The medical profession is notorious for having its physicians work long hours and shifts can frequently last longer than 24 hours. Forty per cent of the weeks in which interns worked involved them working for 80 hours; in 11 per cent, the physicians worked for over 100 hours. The researchers asked participants to note

Cutting edge: How sleeping children learn better than sleeping adults

Consolidation of learning is a well-established phenomenon in psychology, as you saw in Chapters 7 and 8. Consolidation of material can be enhanced by a period of sleep and our ability to convert implicit knowledge to explicit knowledge is thought to occur during slow-wave sleep. During SWS, temporary representations in the hippocampus are thought to be reactivated and then sent to other cortical areas for permanent storage. A study by a group of German researchers has found that learning of some tasks is better in children than adults if they are taught the task just before sleeping (Wilhelm *et al.*, 2013).

The task was a motor exercise in which they had to press a number of buttons on an eight-button light display in a given sequence as fast as they could (a little like a version of the game *Simon*). This was an implicit task because participants were not asked to remember the sequences of the buttons (they were later asked to free recall the sequences, however – a test of explicit memory). Adults and 8–11-year-old children completed the task either before going to bed or in the morning, after waking up. The more often the participants undertook the task, the faster they became. No surprise there – these would be practice effects.

Sleep, however, produced significant improvements in explicit knowledge – in both adults and children. What was more remarkable, however, was that the children's explicit knowledge was better than the adults'. That is, they remembered more of the sequences. There was no difference between them if the learning took place in the morning. When the researchers examined participants' EEG, they found that the children showed three times the amount of SWS than did the adults.

In a subsequent fMRI experiment in which participants were cued to recall the sequences of movements (that is, they did not free recall as in the original study but were prompted with the first couple of moves, for example), explicit knowledge after sleep in children was associated with increased activation in the left posterior hippocampus and better explicit knowledge was associated with an increase in the superior frontal gyrus and cuneus in children. These areas are known to be active during explicit knowledge of sequences (Destrebecqz *et al.*, 2005). In studies with adults, the beneficial consolidation effect may be dependent on the amount of time the person spends awake between the encoding of the information to be remembered and the onset of sleep (Cox *et al.*, 2014).

The authors suggest that the increased SWS in the children supports the superior explicit knowledge consolidation in this sample.

Gary Hart was convicted of death by dangerous driving after his car veered off a main road onto a railway line, and collided with a passenger train that subsequently collided with a coal train. The incident, which caused the deaths of 10 people, was found to be attributable to the fact that Hart had had only one brief nap in the previous 24 hours.
Source: Corbis/York Post/Corbis Sygma.

their work hours, extended work hours, documented motor vehicle crashes and near misses. Of the 320 crashes reported, 130 were severe enough to cause vehicle or person damage.

The risk of a crash or near miss was significantly amplified if the physician was commuting after an extended rather than non-extended workshift. The majority of interns reported spending as little as four hours asleep while working on extended shifts and they routinely worked 30 consecutive hours (see Table 9.2).

Table 9.2 The number of near misses and motor vehicle crashes in interns working extended (greater than 24 hours) and non-extended (less than 24 hours) shifts

	Extended work shift	Non-extended work shift
No. of crashes reported	58	73
No. of commutes	54,121	180,289
Rate (per 1,000 commutes)	1.07	0.40
Odds	2.3	1.0
No. of near misses reported	1,971	1,156
Rate (per 1,000 commutes)	36.42	6.41
Odds	5.9	1.0

One way of preventing this erratic, lack-of-sleep-induced driving is to avoid it completely. But if this is not practical, one solution may be caffeine. Reyner and Horne (2000) examined the effects of 200mg of caffeine on the driving performance of individuals who had experienced significant sleep loss (no sleep during the night) or who had slept for only about five hours. The participants were collected at around 5.30 a.m. and were put in an immobile car which allowed them to make a simulated, computer-generated, dull, monotonous drive. The drivers were young and experienced and drove for two hours, from 6 to 8 a.m. Some participants received coffee with a 200 mg dose of caffeine, while others received no caffeine in their drink.

The caffeine significantly reduced the number of driving incidents (such as lane drifting) and subjective sleepiness in drivers who had experienced only five hours' sleep. For drivers deprived of all sleep, there were dramatic impairments on all measures and the experiment was abandoned after an hour. Even in these profoundly inattentive participants, caffeine reduced driving incidents in the first 30 minutes. The amount of caffeine they received was the equivalent of two to three cups (any more – five or more cups – would mean administering pharmacological amounts of caffeine). With most accidents occurring between 4 and 6 a.m. or mid-afternoon, a quick couple of coffees half an hour before setting off on a journey may help make drivers' behaviour safer. In separate experiments, Reyner and Horne (1998) found that two common interventions that drivers initiate when they feel sleepy – blowing cold air on the face or listening to the radio – had only short-term effects on relieving sleepiness. However, combining caffeine intake with a nap improved driving performance and was associated with significantly less lane drifting (Horne and Reyner, 1996; Reyner and Horne, 1997).

A research group at the army and medical research centre in IMASSA in France found that healthy men who received 300mg of slow-release caffeine at various points during 64 hours of uninterrupted wakefulness were more alert from the beginning of the experiment, compared with the placebo group. This vigilance was maintained to the end (Beaumont et al., 2001). Alertness improved from the thirteenth hour, compared with the placebo group, and most tests of cognitive ability were better performed by the caffeine group in the early and middle stages of the experiment.

How long did these effects last and would they extend to the 'recovery' period after sleep deprivation? Would the person revert to normal fairly quickly regardless of whether they received caffeine or a placebo? The researchers measured EEG, sleepiness, sleep and cognitive function in the 42 hours of 'recovery' following the 64 hours of sleep deprivation in 16 healthy men who had received slow-release caffeine or a placebo (Beaumont et al., 2005). In the two nights following deprivation, both groups showed a rebound of slow-wave sleep with the rebound of REM sleep seen during the second night.

Cognitive function was similarly impaired in the placebo and caffeine groups on the first day of recovery and recovered – partially – to baseline levels on the second day.

The data reviewed here suggest that if a driver feels sleepy at the wheel, the first solution is to stop at a convenient place and take a nap. Coupling the nap with an intake of caffeine is an even better way of combating the potentially dangerous effects of sleepiness while driving. The practical consequences of this are clear: safer roads and, perhaps, a clearer head.

Dreaming

A person who is awakened during REM sleep and asked whether anything was happening will almost always report a dream. The typical REM sleep dream resembles a play or film – it has a narrative form. Conversely, reports of narrative, story-like dreams are rare among people awakened from slow-wave sleep. In general, mental activity during slow-wave sleep is more nearly static; it involves situations rather than stories and generally unpleasant ones. For example, a person awakened from slow-wave sleep might report a sensation of being crushed or suffocated. Unless the sleep is heavily drugged, almost everyone has four or five bouts of REM sleep each night, with accompanying dreams. Yet if the dreamer does not happen to awaken while the dream is in progress, it is lost for ever. Some people who claimed not to have had a dream for many years slept in a sleep laboratory and found that, in fact, they did dream. They were able to remember their dreams because the investigator awakened them during REM sleep.

The reports of people awakened from REM and slow-wave sleep clearly show that people are conscious during sleep, even though they may not remember any of their experiences then. Lack of memory for an event does not mean that it never happened; it only means that there is no permanent record accessible to conscious thought during wakefulness. Thus, we can say that slow-wave sleep and REM sleep reflect two different states of consciousness.

Since ancient times, people have regarded dreams as important, using them to prophesy the future, decide whether to go to war, or to determine the guilt or innocence of a person accused of a crime. In the last century, Sigmund Freud proposed a very influential theory about dreaming. He said that dreams arise out of inner conflicts between unconscious desires (primarily sexual ones) and prohibitions against acting out these desires, which we learn from society. According to Freud, although all dreams represent unfulfilled wishes, their contents are disguised and expressed symbolically. The latent content of the dream (from the Latin word for 'hidden') is transformed into the manifest content (the actual story-line or plot). Taken at face value, the manifest content is innocuous, but a knowledgeable psychoanalyst can supposedly recognise unconscious desires disguised as symbols in the dream. For example, climbing a set of stairs or shooting a gun might represent sexual intercourse. The problem with Freud's theory is that it is not disprovable; even if it is wrong, a psychoanalyst can always provide a plausible interpretation of a dream that reveals hidden conflicts disguised in obscure symbols.

Hobson (1988) proposed an explanation for dreaming that does not involve unconscious conflicts or desires. As we will see later, research using laboratory animals has shown that REM sleep occurs when a circuit of acetylcholine-secreting neurons in the pons becomes active, stimulating rapid eye movements, activation of the cerebral cortex and muscular paralysis. The activation of the visual system produces both eye movements and images. In fact, several experiments have found that the particular eye movements that a person makes during a dream correspond reasonably well with the content of a dream; that is, the eye movements are those that one would expect a person to make if the imaginary events were really occurring (Dement, 1974). The images evoked by the cortical activation often incorporate memories of episodes that have occurred recently or of things that a person has been thinking about lately. Presumably, the circuits responsible for these memories are more excitable because they have recently been active. Hobson suggests that although the activation of these brain mechanisms produces fragmentary images, our brains try to tie these images together and make sense of them by creating a more-or-less plausible story.

We still do not know whether the particular topics we dream about are somehow related to the functions that dreams serve or whether the purposes of REM sleep are fulfilled by the physiological changes in the brain regardless of the plots of our dreams. Given that we do not know for sure why we dream, this uncertainty is not surprising.

The song, 'Yesterday', apparently came to Paul McCartney in a dream. Waking up, he immediately beat out the melody on a piano. Originally titled 'Scrambled Eggs', it is now the most commercially successful song in history.
Source: Startraks Photo/REX/Shutterstock

Brain mechanisms of sleep

If sleep is a behaviour, then some parts of the brain must be responsible for its occurrence. In fact, researchers have discovered several brain regions that have special roles in sleep and biological rhythms.

All living organisms show rhythmic changes in their physiological processes and behaviour. Some of these rhythms are simply responses to environmental changes. For example, the growth rate of plants is controlled by daily rhythms of light and darkness. In animals, some rhythms are controlled by internal 'clocks', located in the brain. Mammals have two biological clocks that play a role in sleep. One of these controls **circadian rhythms** – rhythms that oscillate once a day (*circa* 'about', *dies* 'day'). The second clock, which controls the cycles of slow-wave and REM sleep, oscillates several times a day.

The clock that controls circadian rhythms is located in a small pair of structures found at the bottom of the hypothalamus: the **suprachiasmatic nuclei** (**SCN**). The activity of neurons in the SCN oscillates once each day; the neurons are active during the day and inactive at night. These changes in activity control daily cycles of sleep and wakefulness. If people are placed in a windowless room with constant lighting, they will continue to show circadian rhythms, controlled by the oscillations of their SCN.

However, because this biological clock is not very accurate, people's circadian rhythms will eventually get out of synchrony with the day/night cycles outside the building. But within a few days after leaving the building, their rhythms will become resynchronised with those of the sun. This resynchronisation is accomplished by a direct connection between the eyes and the SCN. Each morning, when we see the light of the sun (or turn on the room lights), our biological clock resets and begins ticking off the next day. A recent study suggests that there is a new class of light-detecting receptors in the retina – retinal ganglion cells – which contains a circadian photopigment molecule that responds to levels of illumination. This light-detecting system operates differently from the visual system (Berson *et al.*, 2002).

The second biological clock in the mammalian brain runs considerably faster, and it runs continuously, unaffected by periods of light and darkness. In humans, this clock cycles with a 90-minute period. The first suggestion that a 90-minute cycle occurs throughout the day came from the observation that infants who are fed on demand show regular feeding patterns (Kleitman, 1961). Later studies found 90-minute cycles of rest and activity, including such activities as eating, drinking, smoking, heart rate, oxygen consumption, stomach motility, urine production and performance on various tasks that make demands on a person's ability to pay attention. Kleitman (1982) termed this phenomenon the basic **rest–activity cycle** (**BRAC**). During the night, the clock responsible for the BRAC controls the alternating periods of REM sleep and slow-wave sleep.

Cutting edge: Does eating cheese – or any other food – affect the quality of your dreams?

You'll have seen that many other cutting edge sections in this book assess the publication of serious and worthy contributions to the development of the science. Sometimes, though, a study touches on a subject that is ostensibly quirky and trivial but which might reveal something useful about human behaviour. Tore Nielsen, from the Dream and Nightmare Laboratory at the University of Montreal, and Russell Powell tried to answer a question that is over a hundred years old: do people who eat cheese or other types of food report different qualities of dreams (Nielsen and Powell, 2015)?

Nielsen and Powell refer to a comic strip drawn by Winsor McCay between 1904–1925 called The Dream of Rarebit Fiend which used, as its leitmotif, the anecdotal connection between eating unpasteurised milk, and energetic and creative dreaming. There is evidence that the food we eat can disrupt of facilitate sleep – caffeine and alcohol being two of the most widely studied (Peuhkuri *et al.*, 2012; Clark and Landolt, 2016). However, little systematic research exists investigating the effect of food ingestion on the types (and quantity) of dreams we experience. One study found that people who expressed a preference for organic foods reported having more dreams – and more meaningful ones and ones involving flying, sex, water and risk (not combined) – whereas those who expressed a preference for fast food reported having fewer dreams and fewer dreams of a sexual or nightmarish nature (Kroth *et al.*, 2007). The study had a small sample (N = 49) and was based on self-report. In 2005, the British Cheese Board reported the surprising result that eating cheese did not lead to more nightmares. It did, however, find that Stilton eating was associated with vivid or 'crazy' dreams. The study was not, of course, published in any peer-reviewed journal. A study from 1931 found that eating cucumbers was associated with having nightmares (Jones, 1931).

To investigate this issue systematically, Nielsen and Russell asked 396 students to complete questionnaires asking about their sleeping habits, their dreams and their diet. The students were also asked to note if any foods they ate were associated with dreams of a particular type or quality and if eating late at night affected their dreaming. You can see the types of food associated with types of dream in Figure 9.12.

Around 18 per cent of the sample thought that food made their dreams 'bizarre' or 'disturbing'. Of the dreams described as being disturbing and the result of eating food, 44 per cent were associated with eating dairy products; 39 per cent of bizarre dreams were linked to dairy products. Sweet foods were associated with 31 per cent of bizarre dreams and 13 per cent with disturbing dreams. Eating late was associated with 47 per cent of disturbing dreams. Late eating affects sleep which may have a consequent effect on dreaming (Crispim *et al.*, 2011). The participants who did experience food-related dreaming were more likely to report more frequent and disturbing dreams, poorer sleep and higher caffeine intake. Having dreams described as vivid was associated with more positive behaviours and outcomes: better sleep, better diet (also, longer times between meals). Nielsen and Russell refer to a review paper noting that intermittent fasting (12–24 hours without food) has been associated with better physical health and cognition (Longo and Mattson, 2014).

This study, of course, involved self-report. An experimental study in which food intake was manipulated and the manipulation's effect on dreaming measured would provide a sounder test of the food-dreaming hypothesis.

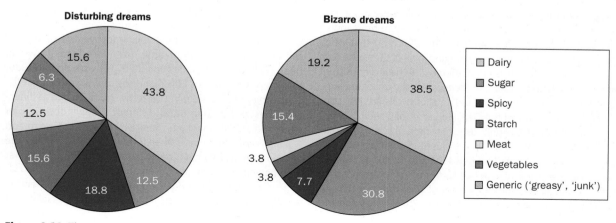

Figure 9.12 The proportional content of disturbing dreams.

Psychology in action: And the key to a good night's sleep is. . .

Given the effects of sleep deprivation, most of us would rather have a good night's sleep than a fractured one. The reality, however, is that life often intrudes on our best intentions – we eat and drink what we shouldn't, we experience stress and anxiety (we have deadlines – essays, papers, exams . . .), we stay up late to work, we may behave in other ways that means our sleep devoutly to be wished is actually wishful thinking.

Around 6–10 per cent of the population experiences levels of insomnia major enough to meet the criteria of a mental disorder (Ohayon, 2011). In the US, the figure is 9.3 per cent and twice as many men than women report experiencing it (Singareddy et al., 2012). Insomnia includes difficulty getting to sleep or maintaining it, waking up too early and being dissatisfied with the quality of the sleep we get. According to some research, it is now the second most commonly reported health complaint, after pain (Pallesen et al., 2014).

There are some ways of behaving – and some ways of not – that might give us a good night's sleep. In a review of the factors in the workplace which enhanced (or impaired) sleep, Linton et al. (2015) found that having good social support, control over our work, and feeling that our organisation was just and fair predicted fewer sleep disturbances than if these factors were absent. Being subject to high demands at work, experiencing job strain, bullying and seeing little reward for the effort put to work were associated with sleep disturbance. The lack of reward and lack of control can both produce stress, which can affect sleep quality and initiation (the demand-control theory; Karasek et al., 1979). Shift work was also a key predictor of somnolent health: people in shift work reported poorer sleep than those who had stopped working in shifts.

A review of the factors which contribute to what has been called 'sleep hygiene, has highlighted another set of behaviours which can affect our sleep (Irish et al., 2015). 'Sleep hygiene' consists of those behaviours which can promote good sleep such as: avoiding caffeine, eliminating noise, taking regular exercise, going to bed at a consistent time and so on. Leah Irish and her team from the US found that while there is some sleep benefit of engaging in all of these, the data are not universally consistent. Caffeine does have a consistent and major disruptive effect on sleep when the doses are large (but the effects of moderate and smaller doses are less consistent). Caffeine (from the German word for coffee, 'kaffee') is the world's most widely used psychoactive substance – around 85 per cent of the US is thought to drink at least one caffeinated drink a day (Mitchell et al., 2014). It is a chemical classed as a xanthine alkaloid and is found in foods other than coffee (such as tea), although most of the world receives its caffeine from coffee (Clark and Landolt, 2016). The word was coined in 1820, the year the chemical was identified by Friedlieb Ferdinand Runge. Ingesting caffeine 30 minutes before going to bed delays getting to sleep and shortens sleep when it occurs (Drake et al., 2013). Generally, ingestion makes the quality of sleep poorer, onset longer, its length shorter and the period of slow-wave sleep, shorter (Clark and Landolt, 2016). Studies of the effect of stopping the drinking of coffee on sleep quality however, are rare.

Clark and Landolt (2016) found that caffeine has been used to enhance performance in athletes, and to combat fatigue in truck drivers, shift-workers and airline pilots. Its effects are produced via action on two brain receptor types – adenosine A1 and A2A – which caffeine antagonizes. When animals receive substances that are adenosine agonists, sleep improves (Porkka-Heiskanen and Kalinchuk, 2011). The effects of caffeine are more pronounced in older people (Clark and Landolt, 2016) but apply equally to men and women, although Clark and Landolt note that most studies have recruited men.

The evidence for the effect of alcohol on sleep is also consistent, especially if drinkers are healthy. People report taking longer to get to sleep in the first half of the night and experiencing lighter sleep in the second part once alcohol has been metabolised. Most studies have administered the alcohol up to 60 minutes before the participants' bedtime; few have examined the effect of consumption earlier in the day (late afternoon and early evening).

One behaviour thought to promote sleep hygiene is regular exercise, although it has been suggested that exercise can impair sleep if undertaken close to bedtime (there is little evidence to support this). If the exercise occurs during the day or early evening, sleep is improved in adults with no previously reported sleep complaints. The effects are particularly strong if the exercise is undertaken 4–8 hours before bedtime (Youngstedt et al., 1997).

Stress can impair sleep, making it poorer and leading to increased feelings of arousal just before trying to get to sleep. Some of this effect can be mitigated by employing some stress management techniques (see Chapter 17) – there is evidence that these can improve the quality of self-reported sleep. Night-time noise also leads to worse sleep (Zaharna and Guilleminault, 2010) – we do habituate to such noises but our EEG responds as if we are aroused.

Having irregular sleeping patterns –going to bed at different times and waking up at different times – does impair sleep and studies in which the timing of people's sleep and waking is controlled have been found to be effective but the outcome measures have been based on self-report rather than having been directly observed.

Finally, napping can have a temporary, positive effect on wakefulness in sleepy drivers. Does napping, especially naps

▶

Psychology in action: *Continued*

of 30 minutes or more, impair the quality of your proper sleep? The evidence suggests that napping has no consistent, detrimental effect on the quality of sleep and the effects, if they do occur, depend on the sample, the sex of the sample studied and its age.

In summary, then, the research suggests that to enjoy a good night's sleep, you should:

- avoid drinking large amounts of coffee or alcohol before going to bed
- exercise regularly and during the day and not before going to bed
- avoid or minimize stress and bedtime noise

Napping is OK.

Studies using laboratory animals have found that the clock responsible for the BRAC is located somewhere in the pons. The pons also contains neural circuits that are responsible for REM sleep. The neurons that begin a period of REM sleep release acetylcholine. The release of this transmitter substance activates several other circuits of neurons. One of these circuits activates the cerebral cortex and causes dreaming. Another activates neurons in the midbrain and causes rapid eye movements. Yet another activates a set of inhibitory neurons that paralyses us and prevents us from acting out our dreams. The location of the two biological clocks is shown in Figure 9.13.

The most important brain region seems to be the **preoptic area**, located just in front of the hypothalamus, at the base of the brain (this region is named after the fact that it is located anterior to the point where some axons in the optic nerves cross to the other side of the brain). If the preoptic area is destroyed, an animal will sleep much less (McGinty and Sterman, 1968; Szymusiak and McGinty, 1986). If it is electrically stimulated, an animal will become drowsy and fall asleep (Sterman and Clemente, 1962).

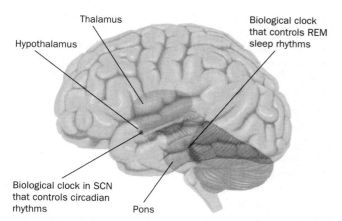

Figure 9.13 Two biological clocks in the human brain. The suprachiasmatic nucleus (SCN) of the hypothalamus is responsible for circadian rhythms. The clock in the pons is responsible for the basic rest–activity cycle (BRAC) and cycles of REM sleep and slow-wave sleep.

Neurobiological correlates of consciousness and awakening

The effects of waking up from sleep are similar to those of sleep deprivation. When we wake up, it normally takes between 20 and 30 minutes for consciousness to be re-established. During this time, people tend not to be very alert and experience psychological deficits called 'sleep inertia effects' (Lubin *et al.*, 1976). These include poor psychomotor performance, thinking and vigilance (Tassi and Muzet, 2000). These deficits are most pronounced at the beginning of awakening and become less pronounced as consciousness is restored. Our cortisol levels are higher following waking and these levels are associated with job or life stress (the greater the cortisol, the greater the stress we experience) (Chida and Steptoe, 2009).

Some studies have shown that the lack of alertness resulting from sleep deprivation is associated with reduced brain activation in the thalamus and PFC (Thomas *et al.*, 2000), suggesting that these mechanisms may intrude on waking when people are emerging from sleep. To discover the changes that occur in the brain during sleep and awakening, a PET study measured cerebral blood flow during 3–5 hours of sleep and immediately after people were awakened from stage 2 sleep (Balkin *et al.*, 2002). When awoken, people were asked to remain awake and motionless while brain activity was recorded.

Blood flow recovered most rapidly in the brain stem and thalamus, perhaps reflecting the re-establishment of consciousness. Fifteen minutes following the wake-up call, activity began to increase in the frontal cortex, a finding the researchers suggest may reflect a return to alertness (rather than consciousness), given that a reduction in frontal cortex activity is seen in sleep-deprived people. However, the study does not suggest that these regions are solely responsible for consciousness and alertness. As the researchers themselves acknowledge, consciousness and alertness recruit a network of brain areas which interact with each other, with no one area having an exclusive input.

Sleep disorders

Sleep does not always go smoothly, and some of the brain mechanisms responsible for sleep can malfunction, causing medical problems that manifest themselves while a person is awake. Fortunately, some of the things that sleep researchers have learned can help people with sleep-associated disorders.

Insomnia

Insomnia appears to affect around 10 per cent of the population (Ohayon *et al.*, 2012). There is no single definition of insomnia that can apply to all people but a general definition is an inability to initiate or maintain sleep over at least three nights. The lack of sleep can create daytime distress and an impairment in social, work and physical functioning (Drake *et al.*, 2003; Irwin *et al.*, 2006). The amount of sleep that individuals require is quite variable A short sleeper may feel fine with five hours of sleep; a long sleeper may still feel unrefreshed after ten hours. Insomnia, therefore, must be defined in relation to a person's particular sleep needs. Chronic insomnia – where the sleep loss occurs over a period of months – is associated with fatigue (clearly), impairments in thinking and mood and predisposes people to be at risk of mental illness (Baglioni *et al.*, 2011; Feige *et al.*, 2013).

One study found that occupational stress, defined as the inability to stop worrying about work when not at work, was the most common predictor of poor sleep (Akerstedt *et al.*, 2002). Workers who anticipated having a bad next day showed less slow-wave sleep, an increase in the amount of stage 2 sleep, anxiety prior to sleeping and poorer quality of sleep than did those who did not anticipate having a challenging day (Kecklund and Akerstedt, 2006). Next-day apprehension was highly correlated with feelings of tension, nervousness, uneasiness and stress. The study leaves open the question of why the stress produces these changes. Is the group which is apprehensive about the next day habitually stressful or prone to feelings of anxiety, for example? Are they more vulnerable to stressors than are the non-apprehensive individuals?

A common cause of insomnia, especially in older people, is **sleep apnoea** (apnoea means 'without breathing'): people cannot sleep and breathe at the same time (there's more on this in the REM sleep section). When they fall asleep, they stop breathing, the content of carbon dioxide in their blood builds up, and they awaken, gasping for air. After breathing deeply for a while, they go back to sleep and resume the cycle. Some people who suffer from sleep apnoea are blessed with a lack of memory for this periodic sleeping and awakening; others are aware of it and dread each night's sleep. The condition can be managed via a technique called Continuous Positive Airway Pressure (CPAP) in which a machine is used to increase the air pressure in the throat

so that the flesh at the back does not drop when a person breathes in (and which would obstruct the airway).

One model of insomnia suggests that there are predisposing, precipitating and perpetuating factors that cause the sleep loss, stressors being particularly adept ant provoking this (Spielman *et al.*, 1987). Alternative accounts suggest that the individual is in a state of hyperarousal – and there is evidence that people with insomnia are hyperaroused not only at night but during the day (Feige *et al.*, 2013). One study found that people with insomnia showed less of a reduction in glucose metabolism in areas of the brain that promote wakefulness, from the time that they are awake to entering stage 2 of sleep (Nofzinger *et al.*, 2004).

Disorders associated with REM sleep

Various disorders are associated with REM sleep (Fraigne *et al.*, 2014). Two important characteristics of REM sleep are dreaming and paralysis. The paralysis results from a brain mechanism that prevents us from acting out our dreams. In fact, damage to specific regions of the pons of a cat's brain will produce just that result: the cat, obviously asleep, acts as if it were participating in a dream (Jouvet, 1972). It walks around stalking imaginary prey and responding defensively to imaginary predators.

This phenomenon can occur in humans, too. Several years ago, Schenck *et al.* (1986) reported the existence of an interesting syndrome: REM sleep behaviour disorder, the absence of the paralysis that normally occurs during REM sleep. Individuals will act out their dreams, because the paralysis is absent, with potentially dangerous consequences. If the subcoruleus – an essential core region of Rem sleep – is damaged, **REM sleep behaviour disorder** can occur.

Dreams and muscular paralysis are fine when a person is lying in bed. But some people have periodic attacks of a sleep-related disorder called **cataplexy** (*kata* – 'down', *plessein* 'to strike'). They are struck down by paralysis while actively going about their business. They fall to the ground and lie there, paralysed but fully conscious. Attacks of cataplexy generally last less than a minute. The attacks are usually triggered by strong emotional states, such as anger, laughter or even lovemaking. People who have cataplectic attacks tend also to enter REM sleep as soon as they fall asleep, in contrast to the normal 90-minute interval. Around three million people suffer this form of sleep disorder worldwide (Fraigne *et al.*, 2014).

Another disorder associated with REM sleep is sleep apnoea in which the airways narrow and close repeatedly during sleep leading the person being unable to breath. This obstruction is produced by the inhibitory action of the hyperglossal nerve.

Disorders associated with slow-wave sleep

Several phenomena occur during the deepest phase (stage 4) of slow-wave sleep. These events include sleepwalking, sleep-talking, night terrors and enuresis.

Sleepwalking can be as simple as getting out of bed and right back in again, or as complicated as walking out of a house and climbing into a car (sleepwalkers, apparently, do not try to drive). We know that sleepwalking is not the acting out of a dream because it occurs during stage 4 of slow-wave sleep, when the EEG shows high-amplitude slow waves and the person's mental state generally involves a static situation, not a narrative. Sleepwalkers are difficult to awaken; once awakened, they are often confused and disoriented. However, contrary to popular belief, it is perfectly safe to wake them up.

Sleepwalking seems to run in families; Dement (1974) reported a family whose grown members were reunited for a holiday celebration. In the middle of the night they awoke to find that they had all gathered in the living room – during their sleep.

Sleeptalking sometimes occurs as part of a REM sleep dream, but it more usually occurs during other stages of sleep. Often, one can carry on a conversation with the sleeptalker, indicating that the person is very near the boundary between sleep and waking. During this state, sleeptalkers are sometimes very suggestible. So-called truth serums are used in an attempt to duplicate this condition, so that the person being questioned is not on guard against giving away secrets and is not functioning well enough to tell elaborate lies. Unfortunately for the interrogators, there are no foolproof, reliable truth serums.

Night terrors, like sleepwalking, occur most often in children. In this disorder, the child awakes, screaming with terror. When questioned, the child does not report a dream and often seems confused. Usually, the child falls asleep quickly without showing any after-effects and seldom remembers the event the next day. Night terrors are not the same as nightmares, which are simply frightening dreams from which one happens to awaken. Apparently, night terrors are caused by sudden awakenings from the depths of stage 4 sleep. The sudden, dramatic change in consciousness is a frightening experience for the child. The treatment for night terrors, like that for sleepwalking, is no treatment at all.

The final disorder of slow-wave sleep, **enuresis**, or bed-wetting, is fairly common in young children. Most children outgrow it, just as they outgrow sleepwalking or night terrors. Emotional problems can trigger enuresis, but bed-wetting does not itself indicate that a child is psychologically unwell. The problem with enuresis is that, unlike the other stage 4 phenomena, there are after-effects that must be cleaned up. Parents dislike having their sleep disturbed and get tired of frequently changing and laundering sheets. The resulting tension in family relationships can make the child feel anxious and guilty and can thus unnecessarily prolong the disorder.

Fortunately, a simple training method often cures enuresis. A moisture-sensitive device is placed under the bed sheet; when it gets wet, it causes a bell to ring. Because a child releases only a few drops of urine before the bladder begins to empty in earnest, the bell wakes the child in time to run to the bathroom. In about a week, most children learn to prevent their bladders from emptying and manage to wait until morning. Perhaps what they really learn is not to enter such a deep level of stage 4 sleep in which the mechanism that keeps the bladder from emptying seems to break down.

Nightmares

Nightmares are a rare but well-known sleep-related complaint reported by around 5 per cent of adults (Janson *et al.*, 1995; Strepansky *et al.*, 1998). They have been defined as 'disturbing mental experiences that generally occur during rapid eye movement sleep and often result in awakening' (Schredl and Reinhard, 2011). In their review of the nightmare literature, Schredl and Reinhard (2011) note that research on the subject has been hampered by different studies citing differences in the definitions of nightmares, and differences in the way nightmares are measured. Many studies, for example, emphasise the presence of fear as the dominant emotion experienced by people, but studies also find that people report disgust, rage, sadness and embarrassment. Measures of nightmares have included asking whether people do or do not experience them, or how often they experience them.

What is consistent and robust, however, is a sex difference: women report nightmares more often than do men (Levin and Nielsen, 2007), although sex differences in children are not common (Simard *et al.*, 2008). In a meta-analysis of 211 studies, Schredl and Reinhard (2011) found evidence of sex differences in healthy adolescent, young and middle-aged individuals but no evidence of sex differences in children or much older people. A number of reasons might explain the difference in adults: women may recall more dreams than men or experience them more frequently, they may experience more insomnia or may show greater depression. Schredl (2014), for example, found that women reported more dreams overall than did men. He also found that neuroticism was associated with reporting nightmares: women were more likely to be anxious, concerned and worried. Interestingly, the way in which researchers measured nightmares affected results: those offering a binary choice (yes or no to the question about experiencing nightmares) showed fewer sex differences than those offering a greater range of options.

Chapter review

The nature of consciousness

- Consciousness refers to our awareness of our own perceptions, thoughts and feelings and our experience of these.
- Some psychologists and philosophers regard consciousness as a by-product of cognitive processing and believe it is outside the scope of scientific study because of its subjective nature.
- Several theories seek to explain the nature of consciousness. These fall mainly into two camps: the neurobiological and the cognitive.
- The neurobiological explanations (such as those of Crick and Penrose) suggest that consciousness occurs when cell assemblies behave together or is generated by specific parts of a neuron.
- Perceptual disorders (such as blindsight and visual agnosia) and other deficits following brain injury (such as those seen after the split-brain operation) help demonstrate the importance of various brain regions to conscious awareness.

Attention

- The process of selective attention determines which stimuli will be noticed and which will be ignored. The factors that control our attention include novelty, verbal instructions and our own assessment of the significance of what we are perceiving.
- The cocktail-party phenomenon is an example of selective attention: we are able to detect relevant information in an environment that contains irrelevant and relevant information.
- Noise (such as office noise and speech) in the working environment can significantly impair memory for prose and arithmetic performance; the longer the duration of the noise, the greater the deficit.
- Dichotic listening experiments show that what is received by the unattended ear is lost within a few seconds unless something causes us to take heed of it; after those few seconds we cannot say what that ear heard. Even unattended information can produce implicit (as opposed to explicit) memories, however.
- Studies of the effects of mobile phone use on attention have demonstrated that engagement in conversation impairs attention and driving performance, regardless of whether the phone is hand-held or hands-free. Listening to the radio does not produce these impairments.

Hypnosis

- Hypnosis is a form of verbal control over a person's consciousness in which the hypnotist's suggestions affect some of the person's perceptions and behaviours.
- State theorists argue that consciousness during hypnosis is a mysterious, trance-like state. Non-state theorists argue that it can be explained by psychological factors such as compliance, role-enactment, imagination and willingness to please. Evidence suggests invoking the concepts of trance or altered states of consciousness is unnecessary.
- Barber asserts that being hypnotised is similar to participating vicariously in a narrative, which is something we do whenever we become engrossed in a novel, a film, a drama or even the recounting of a friend's experience. When we are engrossed in this way, we experience genuine feelings of emotion, even though the situation is not 'real'.
- Although individuals under hypnosis appear to perform extraordinary, unusual or antisocial acts, non-hypnotic suggestion can result in the same behaviours being induced. People who would not normally perform antisocial or distasteful acts may do so because they (correctly) assume that the experimenter is responsible for what they do.
- Hypnosis has been shown to be useful in reducing pain, eliminating bad habits, reducing stress and helping people talk about painful thoughts and memories.
- The reasons for the efficacy of hypnotic analgesia have included highly hypnotisable participants' ability to partition attention and the role of the anterior brain regions in allocating attentional resources.

Sleep

- Sleep consists of several stages of slow-wave sleep, characterised by increasing amounts of delta activity in the EEG, and REM sleep. REM sleep is characterised by beta activity in the EEG, rapid eye movements, general paralysis (with twitching movements of the hands and feet) and dreaming.
- There is evidence that morning and evening types perform better intellectually at the time which matches their preference. Evening types tend to be the more intelligent of the two diurnal types.

▷

- Sleep is a behaviour, not simply an altered state of consciousness.
- Although evidence suggests that sleep is not necessary for repairing the wear and tear caused by physical exercise, it may play an important role in providing an opportunity for the brain to rest.
- The consequences of sleep deprivation include fatigue, psychomotor and cognitive impairment and lack of vigilance.
- Although narrative dreams occur only during REM sleep, people often are conscious of static situations during slow-wave sleep. Freud suggested that dreams provided the opportunity for unconscious conflicts to express themselves through symbolism in dreams.
- Hobson suggested that dreams are the attempts of the brain to make sense of hallucinations produced by the activation of the cerebral cortex.
- The function of REM sleep in adults is uncertain, but it may be involved somehow in learning.

- The brain contains two biological clocks. One, located in the suprachiasmatic nucleus of the hypothalamus, controls circadian (daily) rhythms. This clock is reset when light strikes the retina in the morning. The second clock, located in the pons, controls the basic rest–activity cycle, which manifests itself in changes in activity during the day and alternating periods of slow-wave sleep and REM sleep during the night. A circuit of acetylcholine-secreting neurons in the pons, normally inhibited by serotonin-secreting neurons, turns on REM sleep. Slow-wave sleep is controlled by neurons in the preoptic area.
- Insomnia appears to be a symptom of a variety of physical and emotional disorders, not a disease. Although it is often treated by sleep medications, these drugs cause more sleep problems than they cure.
- The disorders of slow-wave sleep include sleepwalking, sleeptalking and night terrors.
- Sleepwalking and night terrors are primarily disorders of childhood. Sleeptalking is generally harmless so it probably should not even be considered a disorder.

Suggestions for further reading

Consciousness – general reading

Blackmore, S. (2005) *Conversations on Consciousness: Interviews with twenty minds.* Oxford: Oxford University Press.

Blackmore, S. (2017) *Consciousness: An introduction* (3rd edn). London: Hodder Arnold.

Dehaene, S. (2014) *Consciousness and the Brain.* London: Penguin.

Lawrence, R. (2016) Virtual immortality: why the mind-body problem is still a problem. *Skeptic*, 21, 26–34.

Pinto, Y., de Haan, E.H.F., & Lamme, V.A.F. (in press). The split-brain phenomenon revisited. *Trends in Cognitive Sciences*.

Wolman, D. (2012). A tale of two halves. *Nature*, 483, 260–63.

Some very easy-to-read texts on consciousness.

Attention and hypnosis

Häuser, W., Hagl, M., Schmierer, A. and Hansen, E. (2016) The efficacy, safety and applications of medical hypnosis: a systematic review of meta-analyses. *Deutsches Ärzteblatt International*, 113(17), 289.

Tefikow, S., Barth, J., Maichrowitz, S., Beelmann, A., Strauss, B. and Rosendahl, J. (2013) Efficacy of hypnosis in adults undergoing surgery of medical procedures: a meta-analysis of randomised controlled trials. *Clinical Psychology Review*, 33, 623–36.

Two good items on attention and hypnosis.

Sleep

Clark, I. and Landolt, H.P. (2016) Coffee, caffeine, and sleep: A systematic review of epidemiological studies and randomized controlled trials. *Sleep Medicine Reviews*.

Fraigne, J.J., Grace, K.P., Horner, R.L. and Peever, J. (2014) Mechanisms of REM sleep in health and disease. *Current Opinion in Pulmonary Medicine*, 20, 527–32.

Irwin, M.R., Olmstead, R. and Carroll, J.E. (2016) Sleep disturbance, sleep duration, and inflammation: a systematic review and meta-analysis of cohort studies and experimental sleep deprivation. *Biological Psychiatry*, 80(1), 40–52.

Ong, A.D., Kim, S., Young, S. and Steptoe, A. (2016) Positive affect and sleep: A systematic review. *Sleep Medicine Reviews*.

van Straten, A., van der Zweerde, T., Kleiboer, A., Cuijpers, P., Morin, C.M. and Lancee, J. (2017) Cognitive and behavioral therapies in the treatment of insomnia: a meta-analysis. *Sleep Medicine Reviews*.

CHAPTER 10
Language and Communication

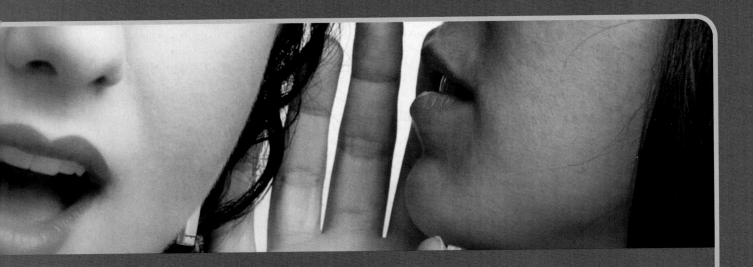

Imagine that you have to write a statement or an essay to gain admission into University to study for your degree – you might not even have imagined; you might have already had to do this.

In your statement, which words – and which classes of words – do you think would form part of the essay/statement that receives the most positive grade and reception?

Take a look at this table, which indicates the percentage use of different classes of words in over 50,000 US college admissions essays.

Of the types of word classes on the left, which would predict good essay grades? (The answer is below, upside down.)

Function Word Category	Examples	Rate of Use (%)
Articles	*a, an, the*	6.83
Prepositions	*all, below, much*	14.71
Personal pronouns	*i, us, you, hers, they*	10.88
Impersonal pronouns	*it, this, anything*	5.03
Auxiliary Verbs	*are, did, have*	8.25
Adverbs	*even, just, usually*	3.90
Conjunctions	*and, so, until*	6.41
Negations	*No, never, not*	1.04

Note: Rate of Use refers to the percentage of total words that each function word category was used over the entire sample.

Answer: In a study by Pennebaker et al. (2014) described later in the chapter, article and preposition use was associated with better grades; lower grades were associated with the use of auxiliary verbs, pronouns, adverbs, conjunctions and negations.

WHAT YOU SHOULD BE ABLE TO DO AFTER READING CHAPTER 10

- Define psycholinguistics and describe the nature of spoken language.

- Describe and explain the various models of reading.

- Describe various language disorders including the aphasias, the acquired dyslexias and developmental dyslexia and indicate what these tell us about normal language processing.

- Identify the neural mechanisms which might underlie different aspects of language such as speech perception, reading and speech comprehension.

- Appreciate the role of language, speech and non-verbal communication in social life, and what factors influence how we communicate.

QUESTIONS TO THINK ABOUT

- What is language?

- Why have humans evolved language?

- Can other primates learn language? Would this language approximate our own?

- What is the role of sound in understanding written and spoken language?

- What stages does language development go through?

- How do people learn to read? What is the best way of doing this?

- How do people learn to recognise words?

- What causes dyslexia?

- What are the effects of brain injury on reading, writing and speaking?

- Do all humans have the same central mechanism for producing language regardless of which language they speak?

- How are we able to comprehend language?

The use of language

Communication is probably one of the most important of all human behaviours. Our use of language can be private – we can think to ourselves in words or write diaries that are meant to be seen by no one but ourselves – but language evolved through social contacts among our early ancestors. Speaking and writing are clearly social behaviours: we learn these skills from other people and use them to communicate with them. An effective language system also abides by certain rules.

Although an exact definition is difficult to pin down (Harley, 2012), language can be characterised as a system of visual and/or vocal symbols which have meaning to the user and to the recipient. There are thought to be around 6,000 distinct languages in the world. The world's largest language is Chinese – it has more native speakers than any other – followed by English, Hindi/Urdu, Spanish and Arabic, as shown in Table 10.1. The most popular foreign language is English (Montgomery, 2004).

We can use language to speak, write and read and we can also use it to remember and to think. Language also enables us to consider complex and abstract issues by encoding them in words and then manipulating the words according to specific rules. These rules are the subject of an area of study called linguistics.

Psycholinguistics: the study of language acquisition and meaning

The study of linguistics involves determining the 'rules' of language and the nature and meaning of written and spoken language. In contrast, **psycholinguistics**, a branch of psychology devoted to the study of verbal behaviour, examines the role of human cognition in language acquisition and comprehension: it is the integration of psychology and linguistics.

Table 10.1 Estimates of native speakers of the most popular languages in the world (in 1995)

	Language	No. of speakers (millions)
1	Chinese	1113
2	English	372
3	Hindi/Urdu	316
4	Spanish	304
5	Arabic	201
6	Portuguese	165
7	Russian	155
8	Bengali	125
9	Japanese	123
10	German	102

Psycholinguists are interested in how we acquire language – how verbal behaviour develops – and how we learn to speak from our interactions with others. In short, they are interested in the interaction between the structure and processing of language.

Psycholinguistics is a relatively recent, distinct branch of psychology although psychologists have studied language since the discipline's early experimental days. Wundt, for example, regarded as the father of psycholinguistics, argued that the sentence was the most basic element of speech production and comprehension. Speech production involved the transformation of thought process into sequences of speech segments; comprehension, on the other hand, was the reverse process. Wundt's view was not universally accepted. The linguist Hermann Paul, for example, argued that words, not sentences, were the building blocks of speech.

This essentially European debate became somewhat sterile during the 1920s and 1930s when the form of psychology championed by Wundt was usurped by behaviourism which argued that psychology should concern itself only with observable behaviour (see Chapter 1). It was not until the 1950s that psychology began to take a renewed interest in the nature of language and, ironically, this interest was spurred by a linguist, Noam Chomsky. Chomsky's views of the nature of language are discussed later on in the chapter. This chapter reviews studies from psycholinguistics and cognitive psychology and introduces you to current understanding of the ways in which we produce and comprehend speech.

Perception of speech

Speech involves the production of a series of sounds in a continuous stream, punctuated by pauses and modulated by stress and changes in pitch. Sentences are written as sets of words, with spaces between them. Speech, however, is a more flexible means of communication than is writing. The sentences we utter are a string of sounds, some of which are emphasised (stressed), some are quickly glided over. We can raise the pitch of our voice when uttering some words and lower it when speaking others. We maintain a regular rhythmic pattern of stress. We pause at appropriate times, for example between phrases, but we do not pause after pronouncing each word. Thus, speech does not come to us as a series of individual words; we must extract the words from a stream of speech.

Recognition of speech sounds

The human auditory system is responsible for performing the complex task of enabling us to recognise speech sounds. The sound system of speech is called phonology. These sounds vary according to the sounds that precede and follow them, the speaker's accent and the stress placed on the syllables in which they occur. **Phonemes** are the elements of speech – the smallest units of sound that contribute to the meaning of a word. For example, the word 'pin' consists of three phonemes: /p/ + /i/ + /n/. It is important to note that phonemes are not the same as letters. The word 'ship', for example, has four letters but three phonemes: /sh/ + /i/ + /p/. Note that in linguistics phonemes are flanked by two forward-slanting lines to indicate that they are phonemes and not letters. The first step in recognising speech sounds, therefore, is the identification of phonemes.

Production of speech

The production of speech is the result of a coordinated set of muscles found in the face, mouth and throat. Those responsible for producing some common words are illustrated in Figure 10.1.

One detectable and distinctive phonetic feature is **voice onset time,** the delay between the initial sound of a voiced consonant and the onset of vibration of the vocal cords. Voicing refers to the vibration of the vocal cords. The distinction between voiced and unvoiced consonants allows us to distinguish between /p/ (unvoiced) and /b/ (voiced), between /k/ (unvoiced) and /g/ (voiced), and between /t/ (unvoiced) and /d/ (voiced).

For example, although the difference between uttering 'pa' and 'ba' is subtle, it is discernible. Uttering 'pa' involves building up pressure in the mouth. When the lips are opened, a puff of air comes out. The 'ah' sound does not occur immediately, because the air pressure in the mouth and throat keeps air from leaving the lungs for a brief time. The vocal cords do not vibrate until air from the lungs passes through them. Uttering 'ba', however, does not involve the initial build-up of pressure. The vocal cords begin vibrating as soon as the lips open. The delay in voicing that occurs when uttering 'pa' is slight, only 0.06 seconds.

An experiment by Lisker and Abramson (1970) illustrates this point. They presented participants with a series of computer-generated sounds consisting of a puff followed by an 'ah'. The sounds varied only in one way: the amount of time between the puff and the 'ah'. When we speak, we make a puff for 'pa' but not for 'ba'. However, even though the computer always produced a puff, participants reported that they heard 'ba' when the delay was short and 'pa' when it was long. Participants discriminated between the phonemes /p/ and /b/ strictly according to the delay in voicing. The experiment demonstrates that the auditory system is capable of detecting very subtle differences.

Although the fundamental unit of speech, logically and descriptively, is the phoneme, research suggests that psychologically the fundamental unit is larger. For example, the two syllables 'doo' and 'dee' each consist of two phonemes. When spoken, the same phoneme, /d/, is heard at the beginning. However, when Liberman *et al.* (1967) analysed the sounds of the syllables, they found that the beginning phonemes were not the same. In fact, they could not cut out a section of a tape recording of the two syllables that would sound like /d/.

These results suggest that the fundamental unit of speech consists of groups of phonemes, such as syllables. The perception of a phoneme is affected by the sounds that follow it (Ganong, 1980). Using a computer to synthesise a novel sound that fell between those of the phonemes /g/ and /k/, Ganong reported that when the sound was followed by 'ift',

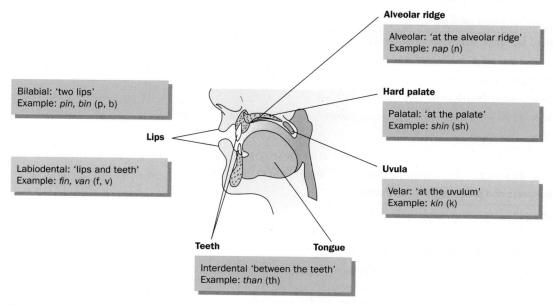

Figure 10.1 The areas in the vocal tract where production of consonants takes place.

Source: Payne, D.G. and Wenger, M.J., *Cognitive Psychology.* New York: Houghton Mifflin, 1998. Copyright © 1998 by Houghton Mifflin Company.

the participants heard the word 'gift', but when it was followed by 'iss', they heard 'kiss'. These results suggest that we recognise speech sounds in pieces larger than individual phonemes.

Errors in speech production

As you will see later in this chapter, some individuals with damage to a specific part of the brain have an inability to produce speech or will produce meaningless speech. Speech errors or slips of the tongue, however, are not confined to the brain-damaged (Fromkin, 1988; Dell *et al.*, 1997) and some of these will be very familiar to you. Table 10.2 lists some of the common speech production errors made by normal individuals.

One obvious error is where the beginnings of words are transposed. So, for example, instead of saying 'dear old queen', you might say 'queer old dean'. This is an example of a Spoonerism, named after the Oxford don William A. Spooner who was noted for making such mistakes as saying 'noble tons of soil' instead of 'noble sons of toil'.

Speech errors are interesting because although they are errors they still follow the rules of grammar. For example, one might confuse nouns in a sentence ('would you pass me that cupboard from the pepper') but you would not confuse a noun with a verb ('would you cupboard the pass from the pepper'). Errors thus reflect what we had intended to say rather than what we want to say (Levelt, 1989). Somehow, an error occurs between conception and execution.

Table 10.2 Some common speech errors
1   **Errors at phonemic segments**
Consonant anticipation: a reading list/a leading list
Consonant deletion: speech error/peach error
Vowel exchange: fill the pool/fool the pill
2   **Errors at phonetic features**
Voicing reversal: big and fat/pig and vat
Nasality reversal: cedars of Lebanon/cedars of Lemadon
3   **Errors at syllables**
Syllable delection: unanimity of opinion/unamity of opinion
Syllable reversal: Stockwell and Schacter/Schachwell and Stockter
4   **Errors of stress (with the stressed syllable given in capital letters)**
apples of the Origin/apples of the oRigin
eCONomists: ecoNOMists, I mean, eCONomists
5   **Errors of word selection**
Word exchange: tend to turn out/turn to tend out
Word movement: I really must go/I must really go
6   **Errors at morphemes**
Inflection morpheme error: cow tracks/tracks cows
Derivational morpheme error: easily enough/easy enough
7   **Errors at phrases**
A hummingbird was attracted by the red colour of the feeder/the red colour was attracted by a hummingbird of the feeder
My sister went to the Grand Canyon/the Grand Canyon went to my sister
8   **Semantic and phonological word errors**
Semantic substitution: too many irons in the fire/too many irons in the smoke
Phonological substitution: white Anglo-Saxon Protestant/white Anglo-Saxon Prostitute
9   **Errors at morphologically complex words**
Lexical selection error: it spread like wild fire/it spread like wild flower
Exchange error: ministers in our church/churches in our minister

Source: Adapted from Fromkin, V.A., Speech production, in J. Berko Gleason and N.B. Ratner (eds) *Psycholinguistics*. Fort Worth: Holt, Rinehart and Winston (Wadsworth 1997 edition).

Recognition of words: the importance of context

The perception of continuous speech involves different mechanisms from those used in the perception of isolated syllables. Because speech is full of hesitations, muffled sounds and sloppy pronunciations, many individual words can be hard to recognise out of context. For example, when Pollack and Pickett (1964) isolated individual words from a recording of normal conversations and played them back to other people, those people correctly identified the words only 47 per cent of the time. When they presented the same words in the context of the original conversation, the participants identified and understood almost 100 per cent of them.

Understanding the meaning of speech

The meaning of a sentence (or of a group of connected sentences that are telling a story) is conveyed by the words that are chosen, the order in which they are combined, the affixes that are attached to the beginnings or ends of the words, the pattern of rhythm and emphasis of the speaker, and knowledge about the world shared by the speaker and the listener.

Syntax

The understanding of speech entails following the 'rules' of language. Words must be familiar and combined in specific ways. For example, the sentence, 'The two boys looked at the heavy box' is comprehensible; but the sentence, 'Boys the two looking heavily the box at' is not. Only the first sentence follows the rules of English grammar.

All languages have a syntax, or grammar, which is a set of rules governing the ways in which words are used to form sentences. They all follow certain principles, which linguists call syntactical rules, for combining words to form phrases, clauses or sentences (syntax, like synthesis, comes from the Greek *syntassein*, 'to put together'). Our understanding of syntax is automatic although learned. We are no more conscious of this process, for example, than a child is conscious of the laws of physics when he or she learns to ride a bicycle.

Word order

Word order is important in English. In the sentences 'The boy hit the ball' and 'The ball hit the boy', word order tells us who does what to whom. In English, the first noun of the sentence is the subject, the second noun is the object and the part in between is usually the verb. This structure is referred to as S–V–O word order (for subject–verb–object) and around 75 per cent of the world's languages possess this sentence structure (Bernstein and Berko, 1993). Other languages, however, have different orders. Japanese, for example, uses the S–O–V order and both Welsh and Arabic use V–S–O. The assignation of words into meaningful categories (such as noun, verb, adjective and so on) is called parsing, and parsing involves being able to identify word classes.

Word class

Word class refers to the grammatical categories such as noun, pronoun, verb and adjective, and words can be classified as function words or content words. Function words include determiners, quantifiers, prepositions and words in similar categories: 'a', 'the', 'to', 'some', 'and', 'but', 'when' and so on. Content words include nouns, verbs and most adjectives and adverbs: 'apple', 'rug', 'went', 'caught', 'heavy', 'mysterious', 'thoroughly', 'sadly'. Content words express meaning; function words express the relations between content words and thus are very important syntactical cues.

Affixes

Affixes are sounds that we add to the beginning (prefixes) or end (suffixes) of words to alter their grammatical function. For example, we add the suffix '-ed' to the end of a regular verb to indicate the past tense (drop/dropped); we add '-ing' to a verb to indicate its use as a noun (sing/singing as in 'we heard the choir sing' and 'the choir's singing was delightful'); and we add '-ly' to an adjective to indicate its use as an adverb (bright/brightly). We are quick to recognise the syntactical function of words with affixes like these. For example, Epstein (1961) presented people with word strings such as the following:

> a vap koob desak the citar molent um glox nerf
>
> A vapy koob desaked the citar molently um glox nerfs

The people could more easily remember the second string than the first, even though letters had been added to some of the words. Apparently, the addition of the affixes 'y', '-ed' and '-ly' made the words seem more like a sentence and they thus became easier to categorise and recall.

Semantics

The meaning of a word – its **semantics** – provides important cues to the syntax of a sentence (semantics comes from the Greek *sema*, 'sign'). For example, consider the following set of words: 'Frank discovered a flea combing his beard'. The syntax of this sentence is ambiguous. It does not tell us whether Frank was combing Frank's beard, the flea was combing the flea's beard, or the flea was combing Frank's beard. But our knowledge of the world and of the usual meanings of words tells us that Frank was doing the combing, because people, not fleas, have beards and combs.

Function words and content words

Function words (such as 'the', 'and', 'some') help us determine the syntax of a sentence; **content words** help us determine its meaning. For example, even with its function words removed the following set of words still makes pretty good sense: 'man placed wooden ladder tree climbed picked apples'. You can probably fill in the function words yourself and get 'The man placed the wooden ladder against the tree, climbed it, and picked some apples'.

Prosody

Prosody is a syntactic cue which refers to the use of stress, rhythm and changes in pitch that accompany speech. Prosody can emphasise the syntax of a word or group of words or even serve as the primary source of syntactic information. For example, in several languages (including English), a declarative sentence can be turned into a question by means of prosody. Read the following sentences at the top of the next page aloud to see how you would indicate to a listener which is a statement and which is a question.

We do this by intonation. In written communication, prosody is emphasised by punctuation marks. For example, a comma indicates a short pause, a full stop indicates a longer one along with a fall in the pitch of voice, and a question mark indicates an upturn in the pitch of voice near the end of the sentence. These devices serve as only partial substitutes for the real thing. Because writers cannot rely on the cues provided by prosody, they must be especially careful to see that the syntax of their sentences is conveyed by other cues: word order, word class, function words, affixes and word meaning.

> You said that.
>
> You said that?

The relationship between semantics and syntax

Sentences can be read or heard semantically in more than one way. The linguist, Noam Chomsky (1957, 1965), suggested that language can partly be explained by reference to sentence grammar. Although Chomsky's ideas underwent several revisions, the 1965 version of his theory suggests that there are three grammars. The first – generative grammar – represents the rules by which a speaker's ideas can be transformed into a final grammatical form. These transformed ideas or thoughts are called deep structures (the second grammar). The final output is the surface grammar or structure which is the end spoken product.

The deep structure represents the kernel of what the person intended to say. In order to utter a sentence, the brain must transform the deep structure into the appropriate surface structure: the particular form the sentence takes.

Most psychologists agree that the distinction between surface structure and deep structure is important (Tanenhaus, 1988; Bohannon, 1993; Hulit and Howard, 1993). Individuals with a language disorder known as conduction aphasia have difficulty repeating words and phrases, but they can understand them. The deep structure of other people's speech appears to be retained, but not its surface structure.

What is meaning?

Words refer to objects, actions or relations in the world. Thus, the meaning of a word (its semantics) is defined by particular memories associated with it. For example, knowing the

Cutting edge: The impact of words

Using the right words in the right context is important, but we're sometimes unaware of the unintended consequences of the words that we use. Some language can normalise some unpleasant behaviour – the type of language we use to harm another human, for example. Brown *et al.* (2016) sought to examine whether the words used for chastising children – spank, swat, hit, slap and beat – determined the normality of using physical punishment for correcting children's behaviour or misbehaviour.

In an online survey, the researchers asked parents and nonparents to read eight vignettes involving a child's misbehaviour and asked them how acceptable corporal punishment would be using the terms above. The parents were more likely to employ corporal punishment – physically assault children – than were nonparents. When spank was used as the option for punishment, more people were likely to choose this as the most effective and acceptable way of addressing the misbehaviour. This was followed by swat, hit, slap and beat. Each of the words carried connotations of greater or lesser acceptability.

meaning of the word 'tree' means being able to imagine the physical characteristics of trees: what they look like, what the wind sounds like blowing through their leaves, what the bark feels like, and so on. It also means knowing facts about trees: about their roots, buds, flowers, nuts, wood and the chlorophyll in their leaves. These memories are not stored in the primary speech areas but in other parts of the brain, especially regions of the association cortex. Different categories of memories may be stored in particular regions of the brain, but they are linked, so that hearing the word 'tree' activates all of them.

To hear a familiar word and understand its meaning involves first recognising the sequence of sounds that constitute the word. We must, therefore, have some form of memory store which contains the auditory representations of words. This store forms part of our auditory word recognition system. When we find the auditory entry for the word in our **mental lexicon** (lexicon means 'dictionary'), we must be able to access semantic information about this word. The region of the brain responsible for the auditory comprehension of words must somehow communicate with another region (or regions) which allows us to ascribe meaning to what we have just heard.

Is there a universal language?

Or, put less controversially, are there some features of language that are shared by most, if not all, languages? The answer seems to be yes. For example, all languages have nouns and words to represent states of action or states of being because we all need a way of referring to objects, people and events. Hockett (1960a, b) has suggested that all languages share similar features. These are listed in Table 10.3. Are there others that you think could be added to the list?

Gesture, language and communication

When we speak, we often gesture and gesture has been considered to be the evolutionary forerunner of vocal language (Gentilucci and Corballis, 2006; Kendon, 2016). The ability of apes to be able to be taught sign language and, therefore, extract meaning from symbols using motor movement, is thought to provide some evidence for this theory, as is the observation that infants' first attempts at conveying meaning involve pointing (Kendon, 2016). Ploog (2002) hypothesised that we have two neural systems which mediate vocal behaviour. The first is in the cingulate cortex (and is found in non-humans) and the second is neocortical (seen in humans), which controls contralateral voluntary motor movement.

Gesture serves many functions: it is used to express feeling, tone and meaning. Many of the gestures we make are intended to communicate an idea or thought or request. We point in order to direct people where to go; we beckon with our hands if we want someone to come near us; we have a number of gestures signifying disapproval of others. There is some evidence that combining speech and gesture improves

Table 10.3 The features that Hockett regards as common to all languages

Universal	Description
Arbitrariness	There is no inherent connection between symbols and the objects they refer to
Broadcast transmission	Messages are transmitted in all directions and can be received by any hearer
Cultural transmission	Language is acquired through exposure to culture
Discreteness	A distinct range of possible speech sounds exists in language
Duality of structure	A small set of phenomes can be combined and recombined into an infinitely large set of meanings
Interchangeability	Humans are both message perceivers and message producers
Productivity	Novel messages can be produced according to the rules of the language
Semanticity	Meaning is conveyed by the symbols of the language
Specialisation	Sounds of a language are specialised to convey meaning (as compared with non-language sounds)
Total feedback	The speaker of a language has auditory feedback that occurs at the same time as the listener receives the message
Transitoriness	Linguistic messages fade quickly
Vocal-auditory channel	Means of transmission of the language is vocal-auditory

comprehension of another's intention. Kelly *et al.* (1999), for example, set up a series of experiments in which they asked participants to watch video footage of a specially created scenario. Two characters, Adam and Bill, are going home when they meet each other in the street just outside their flat. Adam is on a bike and Bill is walking. Adam asks Bill if he had brought the burgers. Bill had not. Adam says to Bill that he had better get them. Bill protests that the burger bar is in another part of town. In one condition, Bill makes eye contact with Adam and gestures towards his friend's bike; in another, he maintains eye contact and just says the dialogue.

In the experiment, participants were asked to indicate how they think the last person addressed in the scenario would react to what had been communicated. All scenarios featured indirect requests; in none was a target mentioned (in the example here, a bike) or an intended action explicitly suggested. Participants in the gesture and speech condition were almost twice as likely to understand the nature of the indirect request than were those in the speech-only condition. The authors found a similar result in another experiment in which participants had to remember information spoken by a woman who made or did not make meaningful gestures (e.g. shooting a basketball) when describing her brother, a basketball player.

Some have argued that there is a common brain system which mediates linguistic and non-linguistic (gestural) language. Enrici *et al.* (2011), for example, examined the brain activation of people who looked at images where a communication was linguistic ('Let me pass the bottle') or 'extralinguistic' (a person in a picture gestured towards a bottle). Participants also looked at stimuli in which where they were told that a shelf was falling down or where this was made clear non-linguistically (the shelf was coming apart). Both types of task activated the superior temporal sulcus (STS), the junction of the temporal and parietal cortices and the medial prefrontal cortex (PFC). Areas involved in language (see a later section for a full description) were activated in the linguistic conditions but the sensory and motor areas of the brain were active when participants processed the extralinguistic, gestural stimuli.

Sex differences in communication

The prolific American linguist, Deborah Tannen, has reported some curious differences between men and women in the way that they hold conversations and communicate with each other. Take the following example, from Tannen's book, You Just Don't Understand (1992):

'A married couple was in a car when the wife turned to her husband and asked, "Would you like to stop for a coffee?" '

'No, thanks', he answered truthfully. So they didn't stop.

The result? The wife, who had indeed wanted to stop, became annoyed because she felt her preference had not been considered. The husband, seeing his wife was angry, became frustrated. Why didn't she just say what she wanted?

This, according to Tannen's research, sums up one important difference between men's and women's language use: women often make a suggestion to start a negotiation. Men see it as a direct question to be answered directly. Another of Tannen's findings is that men's conversation can be a little like witnessing a verbal contest: it is a way of establishing dominance, not being pushed around, getting the upper hand. Women use conversation to encourage intimacy, closeness and

support. Men are more independent, exemplified by a man's ability to make a unilateral decision which directly affects his partner without consulting her. Women try to win an argument by agreement – requests are formulated as proposals, not demands. Another difference is that men and women behave differently when dispensing advice and understanding – when a woman expresses a problem or difficulty, a man will suggest a solution, when what is usually desired is understanding and reassurance.

A meta-analysis of men's and women's talkativeness and the type of speech they engage in has found some surprising differences (Leaper and Ayres, 2007). The researchers examined degrees of affiliative speech – that used to affirm or positively engage with another person – and assertive speech – that used to advance a point of view, be direct and give information.

Women, as predicted, engaged in more affiliative speech (but did not act unassertively during exchanges) but there was no general difference between the sexes in terms of assertive speech. The authors found the following specific results:

- Men were more talkative and used assertive speech more.
- Men used assertive speech less during interactions with strangers than close relations.
- Men were more likely to give suggestions in speech and approached conversations in a task-oriented way.
- Women made more critical statements.
- Female undergraduates used more affiliative and less assertive speech, but there was no difference in non-students.
- When mothers and fathers were with their child, the mother would talk more.
- Men were more talkative than women in mixed-sex interactions but there was no sex difference when interactions were with the same sex.
- Women were more likely to use affiliative speech in same-sex than mixed sex interactions.
- Women disclosed more information than men but not in mixed-sex interactions.
- Women smiled more (and for longer in same-sex interactions).
- Men used assertive speech more in same-sex interactions (perhaps seeing the exchange as a form of competition).
- If a researcher was present, men used more assertive speech; when one was absent, the women did (although this finding was based on limited data).
- Greater affiliative speech in women and greater talkativeness in men was more likely when research was done in a university laboratory.
- Women were more likely to discuss socioemotional-oriented topics; men discussed instrumental-oriented topics.
- Women were more assertive when interacting with children.

- Women used more affiliative speech when observed for brief periods (4–8 minutes), but not for 10–15 minutes or 20–300 minute periods.
- Talkativeness favouring men was greater in research published in top-tier journals.

The analysis suggests that sex differences in speech and the amount of speech can depend on a number of social and environmental factors, including the sex of the person the participant is interacting with, how long they interact, where they interact, how they interpret the situations they find themselves in, and whether they are students or non-students.

Do women have longer conversations? Friebel and Seabright (2011) examined the (anonymous) billing records of 3,103 mobile phone users in Italy and Greece. Over two years, women made fewer calls than did the men but the calls lasted 16 per cent longer. In a second study, they examined the length of time taken to deal with calls to a 'consumer services company' in Germany. They examined 92,000 days' worth of calls. Calls to women lasted 15 per cent longer than those to men. This did not affect productivity. The researchers noted that where sales could be measured, women sold slightly more.

Romantic attachment might be strengthened if both partners use language in a similar way (Ireland *et al.*, 2011). In one experiment, researchers analysed the language use of both participants in a speed-dating event and examined whether this was associated with mutual attractiveness. It was: the greater the match between the participants' language style, the greater the likelihood of their both being romantically interested in each other. In a second experiment, the researchers examined language style in couples' instant messages by phone and internet. They found that similar language style predicted the stability of the relationship three months later. The greater the similarity, the greater the likelihood that they remained together.

The message seems to be that if you both end up finishing each other' sentences, you will be doing this for some time to come.

Finally, a word about culture. If your first language is English you pay little thought to the sex or gender of the nouns you use. In English, nouns are neutral. In other languages, however, nouns are gendered. In French, for example, dogs, cats and Concorde are masculine (le chien, le chat, le Concorde) whereas apples, carrots and Rolex are feminine (la pomme, la carotte, une Rolex). Spanish and German are also gendered. You might not think this of much consequence but research suggests that these gendered words may influence how we think about them.

Boroditsky *et al.* (2003) examined how German and Spanish speakers described bridges. In German the word for bridge is a feminine noun; in Spanish it is masculine. They found that when the Germans spoke about bridges the structure was 'beautiful', 'elegant', 'fragile', 'pretty' and 'slender'. When the Spanish spoke about it, it was 'big', 'dangerous', 'long', 'strong' and 'sturdy'. Boroditsky *et al.* gave another group of French and Spanish speakers a memory test. Participants were asked to remember 24 inanimate objects which were given male or female names. The experiment was conducted in English. When the results were analysed, the nations remembered the objects best when the name given to them matched the gender of the word. The Spanish had especial problems in remembering a bridge if it was given a female name.

But the effect of language can be even more unwitting. Sera *et al.* (2002) asked French and Spanish participants to look at some objects and indicate whether a man or a woman should be the voice of these objects in a proposed animated film. Objects included a fork and a table (both feminine in French; masculine in Spanish). French speakers gave the fork a feminine voice more often than did the Spanish; conversely, the Spanish speakers chose a masculine voice.

Jobs with female/feminine titles are also perceived more differently than those with male/masculine titles. An Italian study found that women described with feminine job titles – la presidentessa (female president) – were judged as having lower status but as being warmer than those described in a masculine way (la presidente) (Merkel *et al.*, 2012). However, perceived competence did not differ. A study of Polish respondents found that women with feminine job titles were regarded less positively than if they had a masculine title (Formanowicz *et al.*, 2013). In a study in which women were given fictitious job titles that were feminine or masculine, men rated feminine job title holders to be less competent and warm and women only regarded the women as less warm (Budziszewska *et al.*, 2014).

Finally, one series of studies examined the effect of a woman keeping her maiden name, adopting her husband's surname or adopting a double-barrelled surname, on others' impressions (Noordewier *et al.*, 2010). Women who kept their surname were more likely to judge themselves to be similar to the female stereotype than were those who did not. When people were asked to rate variously surnamed women on a range of variables, women who adopted their married name were regarded as more caring, more dependent, less intelligent, more emotional, less competent and less ambitious than women who kept their maiden name. The converse was true for women who kept their maiden name: they were judged as more intelligent, more competent, less emotional, more independent and were judged to be similar to (unmarried) women who lived with a partner.

In a final study, in which people judged the suitability of job applicants, women who adopted their married name were not only less likely to be hired but, if they were, their salary would be lower.

Controversies in psychological science: Do Davids and Denices die younger?

The issue

Names are significant – they give us our individual identity and, sometimes, an identity we wish we did not have (embarrassing surnames bequeathed by parents, for example). Unique names are more likely to be judged as belonging to more creative individuals (Lebuda and Karwowski, 2013). People with unpopular first names feel more inferior than did people with popular first names (Harari and McDavid, 1973; Levine and Willis, 1994). What has become controversial recently is the proposition, based on research, that individuals with particular first names and initials of names are more likely to die earlier.

The evidence

For example, Christenfeld *et al*. (1999) found that when they examined the mortality in California between 1969 to 1995, men and with positive initials (such as ACE or GOD) lived 4.5 and 3.4 years longer than did men and women whose initials were more neutral (e.g. GNS, EYH). Men with unpopular initials (e.g. ASS, BAD) lived 2.8 years fewer than the neutral-initialled but there was no difference in mortality between women with unpopular and neutral initials. This study used the year of death for their analysis. When the data were examined by year of birth, there was no relationship between initials and death either for the period in the 1999 study or for a wider period, 1905–2003 (Morrison and Smith, 2005).

Some studies also found that particular letters in people's names were reflected in other outcomes such as grade point average (an overall mark for a course in US school systems). For example, Nelson and Simmons (2007) found that between 1990 and 2004, MBA students whose names began with C or D had a lower GPA than did students whose names began with A or B or between E and Z, even though the difference was 0.02 out of 4 (Smith, 2015). However, McCullough and McWilliams (2011) collected five years' worth of MBA student data and sought to see whether they could obtain the same finding. They didn't. In fact, people whose names began with the letter D had the highest GPA.

People with names beginning with the letter D were also more likely to die younger than people whose names began with E–Z, especially if they were Major Baseball League players (Abel and Kruger, 2010). These players died 1.7 years, on average, before those whose initials were E or above. The reasoning behind the finding is intuitive but illogical – 'D' is associated with lack of achievement, for example, which results in demotivation and lack of esteem. But as Smith has pointed out, F is an even greater signal of failure (in school it literally signifies failure). He also points out the Pepsi-Coke test which found that people preferred the drink that was in a cup marked M rather than Q, regardless of the actual contents, suggesting that D is not the only unpopular letter.

Smith notes that the baseball study restricted itself to the study of first names, to people born between 1875 and 1930 and included people who were at least 25 when they died, an unusual set of restrictions. Smith re-analysed these data, using the first initials of players born between 1875 and 1930 but grouped the sample by year of birth. In a second analysis, he examined first and last initials of all dead professional US baseball players. In a third analysis, he examined the relationship between name initials and the mortality rate of men and women in California who had died between 1960 and 2004.

He found no relationship between the initial of a name and increased mortality in any of the analyses. The third analysis drew on data from 6.7 million individuals. In this analysis, people whose names began with D actually lived longer.

The association between names and behaviours and intentions isn't limited to studies of mortality. Women with masculine names have been found to be more successful in law than those without, applicants with an ethnic name are more likely to be treated less favourably by prospective employers, and people associate faces with certain types of professions (Bertrand and Mullainathan, 2004; Coffey and McLaughlin, 2009; Oldmeadow *et al*., 2012). The latter finding, however, has not been replicated (Kramer and Jones, 2015). Neither has the proposition that people are drawn to live in places that share their name (e.g. people called Louis are disproportionately found in St Louis; Pelham *et al*., 2002), an example of what social psychologists call 'implicit egotism' (Galluci, 2003). Galluci found that for 35 names related to cities with St in their name, there was no evidence for a name-place match for 27 of them, and support only in eight. If there were more Smiths in a place called Smithstown, it was because the town was founded by a man called Smith and his descendants lived there. A similarly negative result has been found for employers – people are not more likely to work in companies whose names feature their own. When this does happen, it is usually because the company has been named after the person working there (Simonsohn, 2010).

Conclusion

The early relationships reported between initials and death/unpopularity are likely to be co-incidences driven by specific data-reduction and data-collection methods. In his conclusions, Smith suggests that if there is some relationship here then this might be underpinned by parental style or having a particular socio-economic background.

Reading

Speech first developed as a means of communication between two or more people facing each other, or at least within earshot of each other, and probably occurred around 200,000 to 300,000 years ago. Indo-European languages (144 tongues), for example, seem to have a common root, as Figures 10.2 and 10.3 show.

The invention of writing, which made it possible for people to communicate across both space and time, was an important turning point in civilisation. The first system of writing appears to have been developed around 4000 BC in Sumeria (the location of present-day Iran and Iraq), apparently in response to the need to keep records of ownership and of business transactions. The earliest forms of writing were stylised drawings of real objects (pictographs), but most cultures soon developed symbols based on sounds. For example, Egyptian hieroglyphic writing used some symbols as pictographs but used others phonetically, to spell out people's names or words that denoted concepts not easily pictured (Ellis, 1992).

With the notable exception of Chinese (and other Asian writing systems based on Chinese), most modern languages use alphabetic writing systems in which a small number of symbols represent (more or less) the sounds used to pronounce words. For example, most European languages are represented by the Roman alphabet, originally developed to represent the sounds of Latin and subsequently adopted by tribes of people ruled or influenced by the Roman Empire. The Roman alphabet was adapted from the Greek alphabet, which in turn was adapted from the Phoenician alphabet. For example, the letter D has its origin in the Phoenician symbol 'daleth', which meant 'door'. At first, the symbol literally indicated a door, but it later came to represent the phoneme /d/. The Greeks adopted the symbol and its pronunciation but changed its name to delta. Finally, the Romans took it, altering its shape into the one we recognise in English today.

Scanning text

Reading, first and foremost, is a visual task (Braille notwithstanding). Our visual system fixates on certain words in sentences and ignores or does not attend to others depending on what and how we are reading. This fixation means that we demonstrate visual acuity – we see words clearly.

Our visual acuity is higher in an area of the eye called the fovea, which you read about in Chapter 5. The fovea contains more cones than rods – the cones, recall from Chapter 5 and 6,

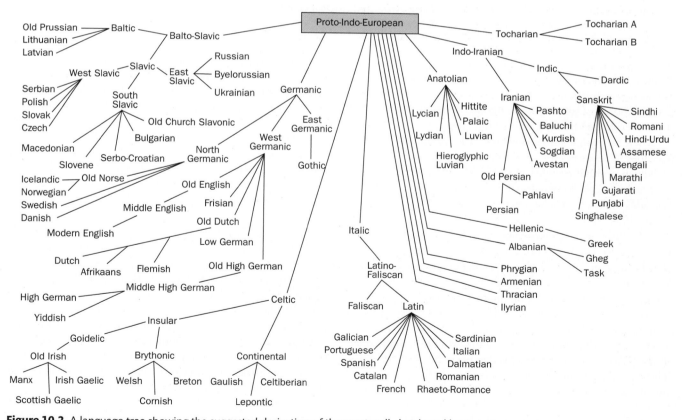

Figure 10.2 A language tree showing the suggested derivation of the most well-developed languages.

Source: from *Historical Linguistics: An Introduction*, MIT Press (Campbell, L. 1999) Fig. 6.1, p. 190, © 1999 Massachusetts Institute of Technology, by permission of The MIT Press and Edinburgh University Press, www.euppublishing.com.

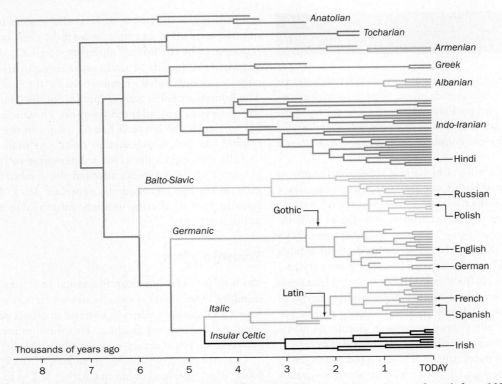

Figure 10.3 The origin of Indo-European languages. Atkinson *et al.*'s (2012) study of the evolution of words from 103 languages suggests that Indo-European languages originated in Anatolia (Turkey), approximately 9,000 years ago.

Source: from 'Mapping the Origins and Expansion of the Indo-European Language Family', *Science*, Vol. 337 no. 6097, pp. 957–60 (Bouckaert, R. 2012).

are the visual receptors which respond to colour, detail and brightness. One of the claims of speed-reading, for example, is that we can be trained to use peripheral vision to enable us to process chunks of words outside the area of acuity, holistically – a claim evaluated on the CiPS section later.

When we scan a scene, our eyes make rapid jumps called saccades. These same rapid movements occur during reading (a French ophthalmologist in the nineteenth century discovered saccadic eye movements while watching people read). The saccades make our fovea move from one word to the next, as Figure 10.4a and b.

The study of eye movements is made possible by a device called an eye tracker. This device consists of an apparatus that holds a person's head in a fixed position and a special video camera that keeps track of the person's gaze by focusing on an eye and monitoring the position of the pupil. The person reads material presented by a computer on a video monitor.

Perception does not occur while the eyes are actually moving but during the brief fixations that occur between saccades. The average **fixation** has a duration of about 250 milliseconds, but its duration can vary considerably. Figure 10.5 shows the pattern of fixations made by both good and poor readers. The ovals above the text indicate the location of the fixations (which occur just below the ovals, on the text itself), and the numbers indicate their duration (in milliseconds). The fixations of good readers were made in the forward direction; the poor readers looked back and examined previously read words several times (indicated by the arrows). In addition, the good reader took, on average, considerably less time to examine each word.

The forward scan from one letter to the next lasts about 20–35 ms and spans a distance of seven letters (Drieghe *et al.*, 2005; Rayner *et al.*, 2016). Sometimes – around 30 per cent of the time – we skip words, probably because they are over-familiar, frequent, short and very predictable in the context of the words that are being read. The word 'the', for example, is skipped around 50 per cent of the time (Angele and Rayner, 2013). The words are not ignored but processed – they are but they are processed so automatically that we pay less attention to them. If they are left out of text, for example, comprehension suffers (Fisher and Shebilske, 1985).

University students fixate on most words when they are asked to read text carefully enough to understand its meaning. They fixate on 80 per cent of the content words but on only 40 per cent of the function words such as 'the' and 'and' (Just and Carpenter, 1980). Function words are generally shorter than content words, but the difference is not only a matter of size. Readers are more likely to skip over short function words such as 'and' or 'the' than over short content words such as

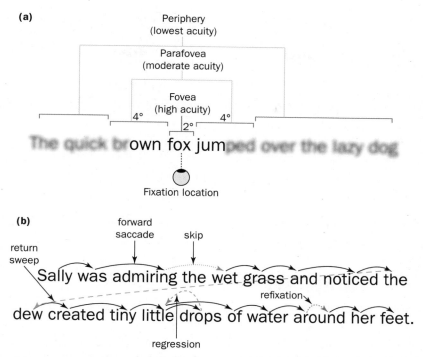

Figure 10.4 The figure shows the way in which our fovea allows us to focus on important text when reading. **(a)** It shows how our acuity recedes the further the fixation point is from our visual field. **(b)** It shows the types of eye movements we make when reading a sentence – we might skip a word or phrase, go back to another word/phrase and read it again.

'ant' or 'run' (Carpenter and Just, 1983). For example, read the following sentence:

> I love Paris in the
> the springtime

You may not have noticed that second 'the' at the beginning of the second line and would have read the sentence as normal; we seem to be able to glide over function words such as 'the' without it detrimentally affecting the way in which we perceive and understand meaning.

As sentences are read, they are usually analysed word by word (Rayner and Pollatsek, 1989). Some words contribute more to our understanding than do others, and some sentences cannot make sense until we reach the end. The more unusual a word is, the longer a reader fixates on it. The word 'sable', for example, receives a longer fixation than the word 'table'. The word that follows an unusual word does not receive a longer-than-usual fixation, which indicates that the reader finishes processing the word before initiating the next saccade (Thibadeau *et al.*, 1982).

Readers also spend more time fixating on longer words, such as those over seven letters in length. In fact, if word familiarity is held constant, the amount of time a word receives is proportional to its length (Carpenter and Just, 1983). In

addition, Just *et al.* (1983) found that the amount of time that Chinese readers spent fixating on a Chinese character was proportional to the number of brush strokes used to make it. Because all Chinese characters are of approximately the same size, the increased fixation time appears to reflect the complexity of a word rather than the amount of space it occupies.

Around 10–15 per cent of the time, readers will engage in regressions – going back in the text to a previously read word (Rayner *et al.*, 2016). Normally, this is done to confirm the meaning of the word (Schotter *et al.*, 2014). The return sweeps, labelled in Figure 10.4b describe the process whereby we move from the end of one line to the beginning of another. The greater the experience and the skill at reading, the shorter the fixations, the longer the saccades and the fewer the regressions. The ability to identify words appears to be more important than any other cognitive ability in determining reading speed (Kuperman and Van Dyke, 2011) and some words are more easily identifiable than others.

For example, the frequency of the word determines how quickly it is recognised – that is, how often it has been previously encountered before. A word like overcoat might be easily recognised, but a word such as cascara is not. Various methods can identify word frequency effects – for example, in lexical decision tasks, people decide whether a letter string is a real word or not; in naming tasks, people read aloud the words they see; in categorisation tasks, participants decide which semantic category a word belongs to. People are also

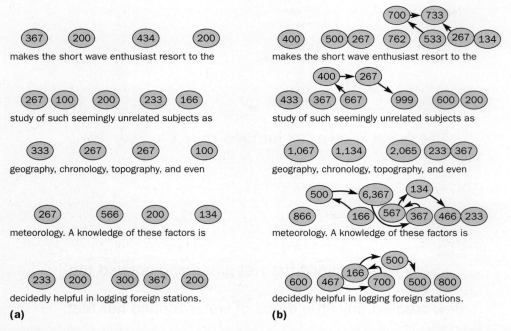

Figure 10.5 The pattern of fixations made by two readers. The ovals are placed above the locations of the fixations; the numbers within them indicate the durations of the fixations (in milliseconds). Arrows indicate backtracking to words already examined. **(a)** A good reader. **(b)** A poor reader.

Source: from Just, M.A. and Carpenter, P.A., *The Psychology of Reading and Language Comprehension* © 1987. Published by Allyn & Bacon, Boston, MA. Copyright © 1987 by Pearson Education. By permission of the publisher.

better able to identify letters when they appear inside whole words, than if presented alone (this is called the word superiority effect).

Our reading speed increases with age and the durations of our fixations decreases with age: children's fixation duration becomes equivalent to those of adults at around 11 years of age. Our perceptual span area – the area of text we need to enable us to enable us to make sense of it – is smaller in beginning readers (Rayner, 1986) which may explain why they take longer to read. Children's binocular control of their saccades is also poorer in 7-year olds than in adults when reading single words (Bucci and Kapoula, 2006). This may explain the fixation durations and, by extension, the slowness in reading. Lions *et al.* (2013) found that younger children showed poorer binocular co-ordination of saccades during single word reading and during a non-lexical visual search task. This co-ordination, and reading skill, improved with age with the children reaching adult level of co-ordination after the age of 10.

Phonetic and whole-word recognition

Most psychologists who study the reading process believe that readers have two basic ways of recognising words: phonetic and whole-word recognition. **Phonetic reading** involves the decoding of the sounds that letters or groups of letters make (in a similar way to which the units of speech are called phonemes, the units of written language are called **graphemes**).

For example, the ability to pronounce nonsense words depends on our knowledge of the relation between letters and sounds in the English language. Such knowledge is used to 'sound the word out'. When we do this, we apply **grapheme–phoneme correspondence** (**GPC**) rules: the rules which govern the ways in which we are able to translate written letters into the appropriate sounds. This is called **whole-word reading**: reading by recognising a word as a whole.

But do we have to 'sound out' familiar, reasonably short words such as 'table' or 'grass'? Probably not. Familiar words are perceived as whole words. However, consider this list of words: 'knave', 'shave', 'slave', 'have'. How did you pronounce the last word? You might have pronounced it to rhyme with 'slave'. This example illustrates that although whole-word reading would seem to be intuitively correct, our pronunciation of words can depend on the context in which words are used.

The process of reading

A relatively inexperienced reader will have to sound out most words and, consequently, will read rather slowly. Experienced, practised readers will quickly recognise most of them as individual units. In other words, during reading, phonetic and whole-word reading are engaged in a race. If the word is familiar, the whole-word method will win. If the word is unfamiliar, the whole-word method will lose and the phonetic method will have enough time to compete.

Cutting edge: Which words predict academic success?

As a student of psychology, you know how important it is to choose your words carefully and select your phrases judiciously. It's also important to develop a style, something which marks your writing as being different to someone else's. But are there words that we all use which might predict other behaviour, academic success, for example?

One class of words which might play an important part in predicting behaviour is function (closed class) words. Function words are not nouns, regular verbs, adjectives or adverbs but words which allow us to connect or shape the content of sentences – words such as 'a', 'the', 'that', 'may', 'could', 'some', 'both' and so on. The use of these words is a better predictor of some behaviours than are nouns or regular verbs (Pennebaker *et al.*, 2014).

To examine the relationship between function word use and academic success, Pennebaker *et al.* used special software the analyse the content of 50,000 University admissions essays from 25,975 applicants. The essays asked applicants to write about a person or event that had influenced them in some way. The students' Grade Point Average was correlated with the use of word classes.

The study found that students who used more articles and prepositions achieved higher grades suggesting to the authors that these students used more categorical language – objects and concepts were complex and described in a complex way. Students who used other types of function words more – auxillary verbs, pronouns, adverbs, conjunctions – had lower grades. This, the researchers suggest, reflects more dynamic language related to personal narratives and anecdote.

When we read a word, we must have some store of knowledge which allows us to identify words as words. In the same way that the auditory store was considered part of the auditory word recognition system, the visual store can be considered part of the visual word recognition system. But is our recognition of written words purely visual? Or can we read by 'ear'?

To answer this question, Rubenstein *et al.* (1971) presented individuals with three types of non-word (strings of letters which make invalid English words): **pseudo-words,** which conformed to the rules of English but had no meaning (e.g. GANK), non-words which were pronounceable but illegally spelled (e.g. MIRQ), and non-words which were unpronounceable and illegally spelled (e.g. HTTR). The participants had to decide whether these words, presented on a computer screen, were real English words or not (this is called a lexical decision task). The experimenters found that participants took longest to reject the pseudowords, followed by illegally spelled pronounceable words, followed by illegally spelled unpronounceable words. In a second experiment, Rubenstein *et al.*, included a set of words called **pseudohomophones;** these are words which are legally spelled, are pronounceable, sound like real words but have no meaning (e.g. PHICKS, which sounds like 'fix'). They would, therefore, pass an auditory word recognition system, but not the visual word recognition system. As predicted, pseudohomophones took longest to reject, followed by pseudowords.

Rubenstein *et al.* suggested that visual information is translated into a phonological code, a sound-based representation of the word, using grapheme to phoneme conversion. This representation is then checked by the auditory word recognition system which decides whether the word sounds like a real word or not. Pseudowords would fail this test – they do not sound like real words. Pseudohomophones, however, would pass because they do sound like real words. They, therefore, need to be checked by the visual word recognition system in order to determine whether the word is real. The visual word recognition system checks the orthography of a word (the way in which it is spelled). The recognition of words, therefore, involves phonic mediation: the conversion of written language into a sound-based representation.

We seem to access the sounds of words naturally and even when we read silently. For example, Van orden (1987) found that when people were asked whether words belonged in a particular semantic category, around 20 per cent of people would incorrectly respond 'yes' when the word was 'meet' and the category was 'food' (they confused it with the word, 'meat'; this is called a homophone). When the word was 'melt', categorisation errors occurred only in 3 per cent of cases. People took longer to decide whether 'meet' was a food than they did 'melt'.

Phonic mediation, however, appears to be necessary only for the recognition of unfamiliar words (Ellis, 1992). When we see a familiar word, we normally recognise it as a whole and say it aloud. If we see an unfamiliar word or a pronounceable non-word, we must try to read it phonetically. We recognise each letter and then sound it out, based on our knowledge of how letters are sounded out (phonetics).

Whole-word recognition is not only faster than phonetic decoding, but also essential in a language (such as English) in which spelling is not completely phonetic. In the following pairs of words:

cow/blow bone/one post/cost limb/climb

no single set of phonological rules can account for the pronunciation of both members of each pair (phonology refers to the relation between letters and the sounds they represent in a particular language). Yet all these words are familiar and easy to read. The ability to recognise words as wholes, therefore, may be necessary in order to read irregularly spelled words (although our 'have' example earlier on suggests how whole-word reading can fail).

Phonology, however, appears to be crucial for the development of language ability, as we will see later. Having good phonological skills appears to place children at an advantage linguistically. Gathercole and Baddeley (1990) found that 5-year-old children with good phonological skills were better at remembering nonsense words than were those with poor phonological skills. This ability to repeat nonsense words appears to be a good predictor of later, successful vocabulary acquisition (Gathercole et al., 1992). There is much debate over the best way to teach children how to learn to read, and psychologists have discovered much that teachers can use in their instruction.

Models of reading I: dual-route model

Two competing models try and explain how we read and recognise words (there are others, but these two are dominant). The first is the **dual-route** (Coltheart, 1978; Morton and Patterson, 1980) or dual-route cascaded **model of reading** (Coltheart et al., 2001). The second is the connectionist or parallel distributed processing model of reading (Seidenberg and McClelland, 1989; Harm and Seidenberg, 1999).

The dual-route model of reading proposes that there are two routes that take the reader from spelling to sound. The lexical route retrieves pronounced words from a lexicon, that is, it 'looks up' words in an internal word pool which contains items learned through experience, a little like a personalised dictionary. This route is also known as the 'direct', 'lexical', 'lexico-semantic' or 'addressed' route: all refer to the same path. The sublexical route is the system which converts letters into sounds – a process called grapheme–phoneme correspondence. It 'translates' letters into sounds based on sound–letter associations that have been learned. Other terms for this route include indirect, assembled, sublexical and graphological. The lexical route would be able to identify all known words, regardless of whether they follow grapheme–phoneme correspondence rules; the sublexical route would be able to identify non-words using these rules (it would be able to recognise 'flound' as a non-word, for example, because the word follows normal grapheme–phoneme correspondence rules).

The model derived from studies of brain-injured patients who appear to rely more on one route than the other. People with a type of dyslexia called phonological dyslexia (see below), for example, appear to have access only to whole word forms (the direct, lexical route) and have difficulty in reading regularly

spelled words (suggesting an impairment in the indirect, sublexical route). The reading of non-words is significantly worse than the reading of (familiar) words. An alternative to the dual-route model has argued that the same mechanisms underlie the reading aloud of words and non-words (such as 'nep' and 'cabe').

In a test of these competing models, Caccappoulo-van Vliet et al. (2004) described two patients with dementia who showed pure phonological dyslexia. These patients were unable to read non-words but they were able to read familiar, irregularly spelled words accurately. However, their phonological skills were intact, thus lending support to the dual-route model explanation of phonological dyslexia rather than the alternative (because phonological ability was generally unimpaired). Peterson et al. (2013) found evidence of support for both models. They were able to identify two clear sub-groups of dyslexic participants – those with phonological dyslexia and those with surface dyslexia. Children who had 'pure' phonological dyslexia (more common in older children) but no orthographic difficulties showed milder phonological impairments than did children with 'relative' phonological dyslexia and orthographic impairment.

The finding that older children were more likely to show phonological dyslexia suggests that this group relied on item-specific information in order to read. This supports the connectionist model and presents a problem for the DR model. Support for the dual-route model was found in the surface dyslexia group who did not show delayed reading ability but showed poorer lexical and orthographic ability than typically developing children, despite being matched for reading ability with these children. Problematic for both models was that a small number of cases with phonological dyslexia also had spared orthographic skill but were poor at reading real-words (the DR model, e.g. argues that the children should be able to read the real words via the lexical route). Also, having poor orthographic skill did not necessarily impair reading: control readers with orthographic skills comparable to those of the surface dyslexic group were able to read as well as control children with intact skill.

A meta-analysis of 35 neuroimaging studies of the dual-route model suggests that the two routes of reading can be mapped in unimpaired readers (Jobard et al., 2003). Access to the visual representation of words was found to rely on two routes, but there was no consistent brain region devoted to storing the shapes of word forms. Instead, a general region located at the occipitotemporal junction appeared to be involved in the initial segmentation or classification of word-like stimuli. The phonological route was subserved by parts of the temporal lobe and also regions involved in working memory (because of the process involved in matching letters and sounds). The so-called direct route, according to this review, recruited a pathway linking the occipitotemporal cortex with those involved in semantic processing (these regions are found in or around the temporal cortex).

A meta-analysis of 36 neuroimaging studies which examined the brain regions involved in word/non-word reading and irregular/regular word reading, found that specific regions were associated with these types of word reading and also found broad areas involved in different aspects of language (Taylor *et al.*, 2012). For example, in the left hemisphere, activation was found in different areas depending on the task: activation was found in the occipitotemporal cortex during orthographic analysis; in the anterior fusiform and middle temporal gyrus during semantic/lexical processing; in the inferior parietal cortex during spelling-sound conversion; and in the inferior temporal gyrus when people made phonological output decisions.

Models of reading II: connectionism/ parallel distributed processing

Are both routes in the dual-route model activated simultaneously during reading? One view holds that both systems operate in parallel and are in some form of race, the winner being the system which produces the best pronunciation. A second view holds that the two processes are pooled until a match is made that would prompt articulation. No clear agreement on this process has been reached, although a great deal of excitement in cognitive psychology and psycholinguistics has been roused by the possibilities of connectionism, a form of computer modelling of human cognitive function, in solving this problem. This approach argues that there are no qualitatively different processes involved in recognising words and that there is no localised lexicon.

Connectionism takes as its starting point the view that the brain, or our information processing system, operates in a similar way to a computer and can, therefore, be modelled. Such a model should be capable of learning (as our brain is). This idea, of course, is not new. Rosenblatt (1962) had developed a parallel processing machine which was capable of simple learning. Modern, computer-based models of human computation, however, were pioneered by Seidenberg and McClelland (1989). Their **parallel distributed processing** (PDP) model did away with the notion of dual routes and instead posited one route only which was non-lexical. Their model is an example of a computational model of behaviour because it translates units of behavioural phenomena into computations. Seidenberg and McClelland's model was a three-layer neural network which sought to read regular, exception and non-words from spelling to sound. The three layers were: features, letters and words. Perception within each of these layers was argued to occur in parallel so that the system could analyse features while it identified letters and attempted to name the word a stimulus might represent (Zorzi *et al.*, 1998).

However, the model has run into some difficulty. It cannot read non-words, for example, and it cannot simulate a form of dyslexia called surface dyslexia, which is described later in the chapter (Besner *et al.*, 1990; Coltheart *et al.*, 1993). The PDP model has been replaced by that of Plaut and colleagues (Plaut and McClelland, 1993; Plaut *et al.*, 1996) which seems to have met with some success in that it is at least capable of reading monosyllabic non-words but does not appear to account for the flexibility of human language (see Zorzi *et al.*, 1998, for a review). We will not say too much more about PDP and connectionism here.

Although the PDP model and connectionism are difficult concepts to grasp it is important to take note of them because there is great debate in psychology over the relevance and validity of connectionism in trying to explain the process of visual word recognition.

How children learn to read

Reading is an artificial activity and it must be taught to us (usually at an early age). A beginning reader has much of their work cut out because they have no vocabulary and no set of rules. Are there any cognitive skills (such as an awareness of rhyme or having an effective short-term memory) that can help develop the child's vocabulary and skills? Does reading develop naturally or in stages? And how can we best teach children to read?

To begin with, reading requires adequate sight, so a child would need to be visually competent. Of course, blind children can be taught Braille, but our concern here is with the development of visual word recognition and visual reading. The next important step is for the child to relate written letters or groups of letters to sounds. In some languages this is easier to do than it is in others. The rules needed to undertake this task are more complex in English, say, than in Finnish or Italian. Some of these rules will be simple – 'b' corresponds to /b/. Others are not – the 'c' in 'car' and 'mince' is sounded differently, for example. These general rules are called spelling-to-pronunciation correspondence rules or, more accurately, grapheme–phoneme correspondence rules. The essential feature of these rules is that the child must break up words into segments and put them back together again to form a pronounceable whole. This breaking and putting together again are called **segmentation** and **blending,** respectively, and are two tasks the beginning reader has great difficulty in undertaking.

According to Oakhill and Garnham (1988), the child's reading process is dependent on the development of a number of skills. Whether these skills give rise to reading, are associated with reading or develop from reading is an interesting psychological question that many developmental psychologists and psycholinguists have attempted to answer. However, this debate need not concern us here. What will concern us are the skills associated with reading development. Oakhill and Garnham's list includes the following features/ skills: word consciousness, awareness of lower-level features,

Controversies in psychological science: Does speed-reading work?

The issue

In 1959, an American high school teacher called Evelyn Wood developed a reading programme which she claimed could speed up the normal process of reading. The Evelyn Wood Reading Dynamics system taught readers to read very fast by instructing them to glance at whole phrases, with no loss in comprehension. The value of such as system, if it worked, could be enormous: time could be saved reading (if reading was not for pleasure) with no loss of understanding. The reader could not only read material more quickly but they could free up additional time for more reading. A win-win. Is there any evidence that this works? That it saves time reading but leaves comprehension unaffected?

The evidence

Rayner et al. (2016) has reviewed the evidence for the claims made by speed-reading programmes and put these claims to the test. One claim made by speed-reading products is that we can pick up more while glancing at a phrase than by reading each word; this can be trained and that regressions are best avoided. One argument against this, Rayner et al. argue, is that our ability to read is dependent on word recognition, which speed-reading does not acknowledge. Speed-reading also recommends that readers zigzag across a page, ignoring certain words. But, as we have seen in the section on scanning and reading above, ignoring words does not improve comprehension. The instruction to avoid regression is also self-handicapping because these eye movements are associated with better comprehension (Schotter et al., 2014). Even people who are trained to use their peripheral vision to read perform less well (understand less) than those who read normally.

Another claim is that speed-reading could be facilitated if people inhibit subvocalisation – the speech we hear in our heads when we read text. If people learn to read by visual input and processing alone, this could speed-up reading. Our inner voice would not obstruct the process. The research suggests that inhibiting or eliminating inner speech impairs comprehension of text when that text is difficult or which requires readers to make judgements about it (Rayner et al., 2016).

People who have been trained to speed-read do read much more quickly than untrained readers but their comprehension is impaired (Benedetto et al., 2015; Dingler et al., 2015). Two speed-readers who could read 15,000 words per minute were poor at understanding the text they had read when they were asked multiple-choice questions about it later (Homa, 1983). Their key skill, according to Homa, was 'a remarkable dexterity in page-turning'. Other studies show that speed-reading training improves speed of reading. In one study, people who had enrolled in a speed-reading course read around 280 wpm before the course and 400 after. They made fewer fixations and regressions than a control group who underwent no training. Their comprehension, however, declined: before the training, their comprehension score was 81 per cent; after training, this was 74 per cent (Calef et al., 1999). Speed-readers are better at understanding the gist of passages than are people who skim read, but they are no better than normal readers. Normal readers make more fixations and could answer detailed questions about the passages they read.

Conclusion

The research suggests that it is difficult to contradict Rayner et al.'s (2016) conclusion that 'speed-reading courses are essentially being taught to skim and not really read in the sense that we use the term "reading"' (p. 24). This is not to say that skimming is ill-advised or wrong. We encounter more and more text every day and the longer we live, and the more writing we produce, the less time there is to read this material. People who skim-read and use headings to help them find the important information in text tend to be better comprehenders (Hyona et al., 2002). However, when people chose to skim, they choose texts that are not demanding (Wilkinson et al., 2012). The key to speed-reading is simple but laborious: practice. The more you practice reading – and the more that unfamiliar words become familiar through repetition – the faster your reading and the better your comprehension will be.

---

orthographic awareness, phonemic awareness and use of analogy.

- **Word consciousness.** Word consciousness or **lexical awareness** refers to the ability to understand that speech and writing are composed of different, distinct elements called words. Young children have difficulties in identifying word boundaries (where one ends and another begins), children with strong lexical awareness tend to develop better reading ability (Ryan et al., 1977).
- **Awareness of lower-level features.** A young child has a limited sight vocabulary and what it does have will have been learned through breaking down the elements of words into manageable, processable pieces. English, although having an alphabet of 26 letters, has 45 phonemes. When Rozin et al. (1974) presented children with two words such as 'mow' and 'motorcycle' and asked them – auditorily – which one was 'mow', the maximum correct response varied from 50 per cent for suburban nursery children to 10 per cent for inner-city children.
- **Orthographic awareness.** The ability to recognise that writing systems have sets of rules that must be followed is called **orthographic awareness.** For example, in English, we know that some sequences of letters are acceptable (e.g. 'able') but know that others are not ('kqxg').

- **Phonological awareness.** Perhaps the most important skill a child needs in order to develop adequate reading ability is the capacity to appreciate sound and be able to identify letters with sounds (**phonological awareness**). Tests of phonological awareness would include finding the odd one out from two sets of spoken words such as: sun, sea, sock, rag; weed, need, peel, deed (Bradley and Bryant 1983; Bryant and Bradley, 1985). (These words rely on the child noting both the beginning and ending sounds of words.) Good performance at tasks such as these is a good predictor of later reading ability (Melby-Lervag *et al.*, 2012).

- **Use of analogy.** Sometimes, children will not use grapheme–phoneme correspondence rules to read a word because, to them, it looks like another word. For example, Marsh *et al.* (1977) asked children and adults to pronounce nonsense words such as 'tepherd'. This word, if pronounced according to GPC rules (with 'ph' pronounced as /f/) would be pronounced 'tefferd'. Children, however, pronounce it to rhyme with 'shepherd'. Adults do not. This is called children's use of analogy in reading.

The major ways in which children are taught to develop and use some or all of these skills are based on two systems: whole-word reading and phonics. Whole-word reading, as its name suggests, involves teaching the child to read whole words rather than analyse components of words and put them together to form whole words. This is sometimes called the look-and-say method because there is no room for segmentation of words. It is also called the meaning-based system because it encourages the child to think about the object the word represents. Words are usually displayed singly on cards and classrooms might have objects and pictures with word-labels attached to them. This means that the child begins to generate a pool of words which they will then be able to read in books after a sufficient number of words has been learned. Whole-word reading is easier for the child because it does not rely on segmentation. It also, as we have already mentioned, encourages the child to think about word meaning. One disadvantage of the system, however, is its inability to teach children how to decode new or unfamiliar words because no rule-based system is learned. If one considers that the average adult has a reading vocabulary of 50,000 words, the number of words a child would have to learn would be impracticable.

The alternative approach is called phonics. This rule-based system teaches the child correspondences between letters and sounds (i.e., GPC rules, segmentation and blending). There are many forms of this teaching system and most teach the children letter-to-sound correspondences first before exposing them to actual words. Recently, a year-long comparison of phonics versus standard teaching methods in a group of English children found that phonics was associated with a reduction in reading difficulties (Shapiro and Solity, 2008). The disadvantages of the system are that it cannot cope well with teaching the child irregular words and that

4–5-year-old children find the segmentation of phonemes difficult.

Many other teaching-of-reading systems exist. For example, one approach, the Initial Teaching Alphabet, reforms the orthography of irregular words by transforming them into regular words. Other approaches teach the child the letters of the alphabet first (success in which is a good predictor of reading ability). Another approach colour-codes letters in words. For example, a letter written in a certain colour can only be pronounced in one way. Yet another approach places marks underneath certain letters to indicate how they should be pronounced (the technical name for this is the 'diacritical marking system').

There is a close link between phonological skill and the ability to read. Some authors argue that is the key skill in the development of a child's reading ability. A study of 382 children from 21 primary schools in England found that phonological awareness was a significant predictor of later school success, including maths, reading and science performance, and teachers' positive assessments of the pupils (Savage *et al.*, 2007). 'Practically', the authors conclude, 'screening of phonological awareness and basic reading skills by school staff in year 1 significantly enhances the capacity of schools to predict curricular outcomes in year 6' (p. 732). If this is so, one might hypothesise that if children are trained well in phonological awareness (an awareness of the sounds of words), they might develop better reading skills than those without the benefit of this training.

Hatcher *et al.* (2004) tested this hypothesis by randomly assigning 410 British children of kindergarten age (4–5 years) to one of three teaching conditions or a control group. The conditions were Reading with Rhyme (a learning-to-read package with additional emphasis on rhyme), Reading with Phoneme (a learning-to-read package with additional emphasis on phoneme training such as syllable and word identification) and Reading with Rhyme and Phoneme (a combination of the first two). The control group was taught the standard reading programme. Measures of cognitive ability – including reading, arithmetic and literacy – were taken.

While children whose reading was progressing normally did not benefit significantly from the additional phonological training, children who had been identified as poor readers improved their reading skill and awareness of phonemes. The decline in reading ability was halted by the second school year in children who received phoneme training and by the third year in children who received the rhyme training.

There is also evidence that the home environment can be a predictor of children's reading skill. For example, van Bergen *et al.* (2016) found that parents' literacy and communication in the home was a significant predictor of a child's reading skill. When parental reading skill was removed from the analysis, the only other significant predictor of the child's reading was the number of books in the home.

Is there a 'best' approach amid this myriad of approaches? As you have seen, although some of the well-developed approaches have distinct advantages, all have certain disadvantages. However, one consistent predictor of later reading ability is successful phonological awareness. Pronunciation is also better if the phonetic aspects of speech are emphasised during the early stages of teaching. This may explain why developmental dyslexics often have good cognitive ability but have poor phonological processing skills, a topic we discuss in the section on language disorders below. If you were teaching a child to read, how would you start? What aspect of reading would you consider the most important to teach at the initial stages?

Understanding the meanings of words and sentences

The meanings of words are learned through experience. The meanings of content words involve memories of objects, actions and their characteristics; thus, the meanings of content words involve visual, auditory, somatosensory, olfactory and gustatory memories. These memories of the meanings of words are distributed throughout the brain. Our understanding of the meaning of the word 'apple', for example, involves memories of the sight of an apple, the way it feels in our hands, the crunching sound we hear when we bite into it, and the taste and odour we experience when we chew it. The understanding of the meanings of adjectives, such as the word 'heavy', involves memories of objects that are difficult or impossible to lift.

A phenomenon known as **semantic priming** gives us some hints about the nature of activation of memories triggered by the perception of words and phrases. Semantic priming is a facilitating effect on the recognition of words having meanings related to a word encountered earlier. A particular word can be more easily read if the word preceding it is related in meaning. If an individual sees the word 'bread', they will be more likely to recognise a fuzzy image of the word 'butter' or an image that is presented very briefly by means of a tachistoscope (Johnston and Dark, 1986). Presumably, the brain contains circuits of neurons that serve as 'word detectors' involved in visual recognition of particular words (Morton, 1979; McClelland and Rumelhart, 1981). Reading the word 'bread' activates word detectors and other neural circuits involved in memories of the word's meaning. Apparently, this activation spreads to circuits denoting related concepts, such as butter. Thus, our memories must be linked according to our experience regarding the relations between specific concepts.

Context effects, an example of top-down processing, have been demonstrated through semantic priming. Zola (1984), for example, asked people to read sentences such as the following:

1 Cinemas must have adequate popcorn to serve their patrons.

2 Cinemas must have buttered popcorn to serve their patrons.

while he recorded their eye movements with an eye tracker.

Zola found that individuals fixated for a significantly shorter time on the word popcorn in the second sentence. Because the word 'adequate' is not normally associated with the word 'popcorn', individuals reading the first sentence were unprepared for this word. However, 'buttered' is commonly associated with popcorn, especially in the context of a cinema. The context of the sentence, therefore, activated the word detector for 'popcorn', making the recognition of the word easier.

Semantic priming studies have also shed some light on another aspect of the reading process, the development of a mental model. It has been suggested that when a person reads some text, he or she generates a mental model of what the

Cutting edge: Can multimedia stories improve children's literacy?

They still exist, of course, but the stiff four-page cardboard storybooks and the attractively printed novels with witches and schoolboys have been joined by electronic alternatives and alternatives that are more interactive than television or the internet. Books delivered via smartphones or tablets not only teach children to listen to stories but can involve and immerse them in these stories by having them interact with the text – they can listen to sound effects, ask questions, see animations and gifs and so on. An interesting question is whether this additional activity improves or impairs children's literacy (or leaves it unaffected).

Takacs et al. (2015) undertook a meta-analysis of 43 studies which compared the effect of technology-assisted story telling (TAST) with more traditional story-telling on the literacy of 2,147 children. They found a small but statistically significant benefit of TAST on children's understanding stories and expressive vocabulary. Of the features the study found most beneficial were animated pictures, music and sound effects. 'Hotspots', dictionaries and games were less beneficial. Behaviour not enhanced by the technology was receptive vocabulary (which may have been a ceiling effect – scores were already high on this measure) and behaviour during listening to the story (engagement and communication) which suggests to the authors that the literary benefit of interactive stories is not because the stories are more exciting or attract more attention.

text is describing (Johnson-Laird, 1983). If the text contains a narrative, for example, the reader will imagine the scenes and actions that are being recounted. These issues of semantic priming and semantic networks are taken up in Chapter 11.

Language acquisition by children

Perception of speech sounds by infants

Language development begins even before birth. Although the sounds that reach a foetus are somewhat muffled, speech sounds can still be heard. And some learning appears to take place prenatally (foetal learning is considered in more detail in Chapter 12). The voice that a foetus hears best and most often is obviously that of its mother. Consequently, a newborn infant prefers its mother's voice to that of others (DeCasper and Fifer, 1980). DeCasper and Spence (1986) even found that newborn infants preferred hearing their mothers reading a passage they had read aloud several times before their babies were born to hearing them read a passage they had never read before. Homae *et al.* (2011) using near infrared spectroscopy looked at infants' brain activity while they listened to no language, were read Japanese sentences aloud and then heard nothing again. There was activation seen in the temporal and frontal lobe during the last period but it was not as strong as in the first suggesting to the authors that the children had retained a 'memory' of the previous sound and that these brain regions underpin speech perception and could be activated even in children as young as 3 months old.

An infant's auditory system is well developed. Wertheimer (1961) found that newborns still in the delivery room can turn their heads towards the source of a sound. Babies 2 or 3 weeks of age can discriminate between the sound of a voice and other sounds. By the age of 2 months, babies can tell an angry voice from a pleasant one; an angry voice produces crying, whereas a pleasant one causes smiling and cooing.

One device used to determine what sounds a very young infant can perceive is the pacifier nipple, placed in the baby's mouth. The nipple is connected by a plastic tube to a pressure-sensitive switch that converts the infant's sucking movements into electrical signals. These signals can be used to turn on auditory stimuli. Each time the baby sucks, a particular sound is presented. If the auditory stimulus is novel, the baby usually begins to suck at a high rate. If the stimulus remains the same, its novelty wears off (habituation occurs) and the rate of sucking decreases. With another new stimulus, the rate of sucking again suddenly increases, unless the baby cannot discriminate the difference. If the stimuli sound the same to the infant, the rate of sucking remains low after the change.

Using this technique, Eimas *et al.* (1971) found that 1-month-old infants could tell the difference between the sounds of the consonants 'b' and 'p'. Like Lisker and Abramson (1970) in the study discussed earlier, they presented the sounds 'ba' and 'pa', synthesised by a computer. The infants, like the adult participants in the earlier study, discriminated between speech sounds having voice-onset times that differed by only 0.02 of a second. Even very early during post-natal development, the human auditory system is ready to make very fine discriminations. Table 10.4 lists some of the responses infants make to various types of speech sound.

Infant communication

Even before infants learn to talk, they display clear intent to communicate. Most attempts at pre-verbal infant communication fall into three categories: rejection, request (for social interaction, for an object or for an action) and comment (Sachs, 1993). Rejection usually involves pushing the unwanted object away and using facial expression and characteristic vocalisations to indicate displeasure. A request for social interaction usually involves the use of gestures and vocalisations to attract the caregiver's attention. A request for an object usually involves reaching and pointing and particular vocalisations. A request for an action (such as the one described above) similarly involves particular sounds and movements. Finally, a comment usually involves pointing out an object or handing it to the carer, accompanied by some vocalisation.

Infants babble before they talk. They often engage in serious 'conversations' with their carers, taking turns 'talking' with them. Infants' voices are modulated, and the stream of sounds they make sound as though they are using a secret language (Menn and Stoel-Gammon, 1993). At about 1 year of age, a child begins to produce words. The first sounds children use to produce speech appear to be similar across all languages and cultures: the first vowel is usually the soft 'a' sound of 'father', and the first consonant is a stop consonant produced with the lips – 'p' or 'b'.

Thus, the first word is often 'papa' or 'baba'. The next feature to be added is nasality, which converts the consonants 'p' or 'b' into 'm'. Thus, the next word is 'mama'. Mothers and fathers all over the world recognise these sounds as their children's attempts to address them. The first sounds of a child's true speech contain the same phonemes that are found in the babbling sounds that the child is already making; thus, speech emerges from pre-speech sounds. During the course of learning words from their carers and from older children, infants often invent their own protowords, unique strings of phonemes that serve word-like functions. The infants use these **proto-words** consistently in particular situations (Menn and Stoel-Gammon, 1993). At around 6 months, infants will begin connecting the things they see and experience (people, objects, actions) with words (e.g. 'mama', 'foot', 'eat'). Bergelson and Swingley (2012) found that when mothers asked 6-month-old

The pre-speech period and the first words – An international perspective

The first sound that a baby makes is crying, a useful noise for attracting the attention of its carers. At about 1 month of age, infants start making other sounds, including 'cooing' (because of the prevalence of the 'ooing' sound). Often during this period, babies also make a series of sounds that resemble a half-hearted attempt to mimic the sound of crying (Kaplan and Kaplan, 1970).

At around 6 months, a baby's sounds begin to resemble those that occur in speech. Even though their babbling does not contain words – and does not appear to involve attempts to communicate verbally – the sounds that infants make, and the rhythm in which they are articulated, reflect the adult speech that babies hear. Mehler *et al.* (1988) found that 4-day-old infants preferred to hear a voice speaking French, their parents' native language. This ability to discriminate the sounds and rhythms of the language spoken around them manifested itself in the infants' own vocalisations very early on. Boysson-Bardies *et al.* (1984) had adult French speakers listen to recordings of the babbling of children from various cultures. The adults could easily distinguish the babbling of 8-month-old French infants from that of babies with different linguistic backgrounds.

A study by Kuhl *et al.* (1992) provides further evidence of the effect of children's linguistic environment on their language development. Native speakers learn not to distinguish between slight variations of sounds present in their language. In fact, they do not even hear the differences between them. For example, Japanese contains a sound that comes midway between /l/ and /r/. Different native speakers pronounce the sound differently, but all pronunciations are recognised as examples of the same phoneme. When native speakers of Japanese learn English, they have great difficulty distinguishing the sounds /l/ and /r/; for example, 'right' and 'light' sound to them like the same word. Presumably, the speech sounds that a child hears alter the brain mechanisms responsible for analysing them so that minor variations are not even perceived. The question is, when does this alteration occur? Most researchers have supposed that it happens only after children begin to learn the meanings of words, which occurs at around 10–12 months of age.

The experimenters presented two different vowel sounds, one found in English but not in Swedish and the other found in Swedish but not in English to 6-month-old infants in the US and Sweden. From time to time, they varied the sound slightly. The reactions of the Swedish infants and the American infants were strikingly different. Swedish infants noticed when the English vowel changed but not when the Swedish vowel changed; and American infants did the opposite. In other words, by the age of 6 months, the infants had learned not to pay attention to slight differences in speech sounds of their own language, but they were still able to distinguish slight differences in speech sounds they had never heard. Even though they were too young to understand the meaning of what they heard, the speech of people around them had affected the development of their perceptual mechanisms.

These results seem to support the **native language recognition hypothesis** – that infants have the ability to recognise words which belong to their native language (Moon *et al.*, 1993). Another hypothesis, the **general language discrimination hypothesis,** suggests that infants are capable of discriminating sentences from any two languages because they can extract sets of properties that these languages possess. The evidence above suggests that there is little support for this hypothesis. An alternative to these two hypotheses states that newborns are sensitive to prosody and can discriminate between languages on the basis of intonation and rhythm. This is called the rhythm-based language discrimination hypothesis (Nazzi *et al.*, 1998) and there is some support for this from studies in which infants were able to discriminate between English and Japanese but not English and Dutch.

Interestingly, there is evidence to suggest that the ability to discriminate between phonetic sounds successfully may change with age. Stager and Werker (1997) have reported that 8-month-old infants are capable of discriminating phonetic detail in a task in which 14-month-old infants cannot. The researchers suggest that this represents a reorganisation in the infant's language processing capacity: it shifts from the processes needed to learn syllables to the process needed to learn words. This is advantageous to the infant as it grows and has to put names to objects, events and situations. Because these activities are computationally complex and involve a huge increase in input, the amount of detail that needs to be processed is, therefore, limited.

infants to look at a particular object on a computer screen, the children would spend more time looking at the object the mother named than another object next to it on screen.

Some sequences are added very late. For example, the 'str' of string and the 'bl' of blink are difficult for young children to produce; they usually say 'tring' and 'link', omitting the first consonant. Most children recognise sounds in adult speech before they can produce them (Dehaene-Lambertz and Spelke, 2015).

The two-word stage

By 12 months, children understand around 50 words. At around 18–20 months of age, children start learning language by putting two words together, and their linguistic development takes a leap forward. It is at this stage that linguistic creativity begins.

Table 10.4 Examples of responses infants make to various speech sounds

Age of first occurrence	Response
Newborn	Is startled by a loud noise
	Turns head to look in the direction of sound
	Is calmed by the sound of a voice
	Prefers mother's voice to a stranger's
	Discriminates among many speech sounds
1–2 months	Smiles when spoken to
3–7 months	Responds differently to different intonations (e.g. friendly, angry)
8–12 months	Responds to name
	Responds to 'no'
	Recognises phrases from games (e.g. 'Peekaboo', 'How big is baby?')
	Recognises words from routines (e.g. waves to 'bye bye')
	Recognises some words

Source: from Berko Gleason, J., *The Development of Language*, 4th edn © 1997. Published by Allyn and Bacon, Boston, MA. Copyright © by Pearson Education. By permission of the publisher.

As for first sounds, children's two-word utterances are remarkably consistent across all cultures. Children use words in the same way, regardless of the language their parents speak. Even deaf children who learn sign language from their parents put two words together in the same way as children who can hear (Bellugi and Klima, 1972). And deaf children whose parents do not know sign language invent their own signs and use them in orderly, 'rule-governed' ways (Goldin-Meadow and Feldman, 1977). Thus, the grammar of children's language at the two-word stage appears to be universal.

For many years, investigators described the speech of young children in terms of adult grammar, but researchers now recognise that children's speech simply follows different rules. Young children are incapable of forming complex sentences – partly because their vocabulary is small, partly because their short-term 'working' memory is limited (they cannot yet encode a long string of words), and partly because their cognitive development has not yet reached a stage at which they can learn complex rules of syntax (Locke, 1993).

Acquisition of adult rules of grammar

The first words that children use tend to be content words: these words are emphasised in adult speech and refer to objects and actions that children can directly observe. As children develop past the two-word stage, they begin to learn and use more and more of the grammatical rules that adults use. The first form of sentence lengthening appears to be the expansion of object nouns into noun phrases (Bloom, 1970). For example, 'that ball' becomes 'that a big ball'. Next, verbs are used more frequently, articles are added, prepositional phrases are mastered and sentences become more complex. These results involve the use of **inflections** and function words. Table 10.5 shows the approximate order in which children acquire some of these inflections and function words.

It is more difficult for children to add an inflection or function word to their vocabulary than to add a new content word because the rules that govern the use of inflections or function words are more complex than those that govern the use of most content words. In addition, content words usually refer to concrete objects or activities. The rules that govern the use of inflections or function words are rarely made explicit. A parent seldom says, 'When you want to use the past tense, add "-ed" to the verb', nor would a young child understand such a pronouncement. Instead, children must listen to speech and figure out how to express such concepts as the past tense.

Languages seem to differ significantly in terms of inflection. Of the 6,912 languages spoken in the world, each with its

Table 10.5 The approximate order in which children acquire inflections and function words

Item		Example
1	Present progressive: *ing*	He is *sitting* down.
2	Preposition: *in*	The mouse is *in* the box.
3	Preposition: *on*	The book is *on* the table.
4	Plurals;- *s*	The *dogs* ran away.
5	Past irregular: e.g. *went*	The boy *went* home.
6	Possessive:- *'s*	The *girl's* dog is big.
7	Uncontractable copula *be*:	Are they boys or girls?
	e.g. *are, was*	*Was* that a dog?
8	Articles: *the, a, an*	He has *a* book.
9	Past regular: *-ed*	He *jumped* the stream
10	Third person regulars:-s *s*	She *ran* fast.
11	Third person irregular:	*Does* the dog bark?
	e.g. *has, does*	
12	Uncontractible auxiliary *be*:	*Is* he running?
	e.g. *is, were*	*Were* they at home?
13	Contractible copula *be*:	That's a spaniel.
	e.g. *'s, -re*	*They're* pretty.
14	Contractible auxiliary *be*:	He's doing it.
	e.g. *-'s, -'re*	*They're* running slowly.

Source: Adapted from Clark, H.H. and Clark, E.V., *Psychology and Language: An introduction to psycholinguistics*, 1977. © 1977, reprinted with permission of H.H. Clark & E.V. Clark.

median number of 7,000 speakers, what is common to the languages spoken by the largest groups? Are there particular morphological, geographic or even social features these languages share that makes them so popular? Lupyan and Dale (2011) examined the structural properties of over 2,000 languages in an attempt to find an answer.

Their research uncovered universal features of the most widely spoken languages, spoken across the greatest geographical area: these had the simplest inflectional morphology and were the ones which used syntax, rather than modality, to indicate possession and provide evidence. The who-did-what-to-whom structure in these languages relied less on inflection/morphology and more on word order and the architecture of the language. One reason for the popularity of these languages, the authors argue, is that less complex morphology is easier to learn and, therefore, more economic to pass on to the next generation.

The most frequently used verbs in most languages are irregular. Forming the past tense of such verbs in English does not involve adding '-ed' (e.g. go/went, throw/threw, buy/bought, see/saw). The past tense of such verbs must be learned individually. Because irregular verbs get more use than do regular ones, children learn them first, producing the past tense easily in sentences such as 'I came', 'I fell down', and 'she hit me'. Shortly after this period, they discover the regular past tense inflection and expand their vocabulary, producing sentences such as 'he dropped the ball'. But they also begin to say 'I comed', 'I falled down', and 'she hitted me'. Having learned a rule, they apply it to all verbs, including the irregular ones that they were previously using correctly. It takes children several years to learn to use the irregular past tense correctly again.

Children's rudimentary understanding, or at least recognition, of language and parts of speech seems to begin in the first few months of life. Children learn to assign meaning to words – decide whether they are nouns, verbs and so on – and use these words to form semi-structured sentences. That is, the child begins to follow the rules of grammar. Grammatical words tend to be phonetically and structurally smaller than lexical words – nouns, verbs and so on – and the commonest of them ('in', 'a', 'and') are used more frequently in conversation than are the most common lexical words. Does the child, therefore, show a preference for spoken grammatical or lexical words?

One study exposed 6-month-old infants to spoken lexical and grammatical words and measured their preference for each type of stimulus (Shi and Werker, 2001). The researchers found that the infants showed a preference for the lexical words. The authors suggest that although grammatical words are the most commonly used, lexical words may be more striking and acoustically interesting. Lexical words tend to be longer and have a more complex structure; mothers also tend to use lexical words in isolation (i.e. without the accompanying grammar). The preference for lexical words may help the child to give meaning to its world and act as a first essential step to developing more complex communication. It may be that children prefer and use lexical words first and then clamp them on to grammatical structures later.

Acquisition of meaning

The simplest explanation of why children use and understand language is that they hear a word spoken at the same time that they see (or hear, or touch) the object to which the word refers. After several such pairings, they add a word to their vocabulary. In fact, children first learn the names of things with which they interact, or things that change (and thus attract their attention). For example, they are quick to learn words like 'biscuit' or 'blanket', but are slow to learn words like 'wall' or 'window' (Ross *et al.*, 1986; Pease *et al.*, 1993).

Fast mapping

This quick learning of new, content words has been called **fast mapping** (Carey and Bartlett, 1978; Markman, 1989). There is some debate over whether fast mapping is specific to language or whether it is generated by other, cognitive processes. For example, if fast mapping is seen only for words then this would suggest that the process is language based; if fast mapping can extend to other domains, this suggests that the process is underpinned by general cognitive abilities (such as the ability to memorise).

In two experiments, Markson and Bloom (1997) taught 3–4-year-old children and a group of university undergraduates to learn a word referring to an object ('kobi') and a fact about this object. In one experiment, participants were told that this was an object given to the experimenter by her uncle. The participants' ability to remember and identify the object was tested immediately after learning, one week after or one month after. Although the adults were better at remembering the object and object name than were the children, all children performed comparably well when asked to retrieve the word, identify the object about which facts were presented, and to identify the object given to the experimenter by her uncle. The study suggests that fast mapping may not necessarily be specific to language processing but is made possible by learning and memory mechanisms that are not specific to the language domain.

Waxman and Booth (2000) replicated Markson and Bloom's original finding but suggested that there is a crucial difference between the principles underpinning noun learning and fact learning. They introduced pre-school children to an unfamiliar object, such as those seen in Figure 10.6, and required them to associate it with a noun ('This is a koba') or a fact ('My uncle gave this to me'). The researchers then investigated whether (1) the children were able to map the word or fact correctly by choosing the 'koba' or 'the object the uncle gave to the experimenter', from a series of 10 familiar objects and (2) the children were able to extend their knowledge of the object by identifying the object from unfamiliar ones. In the second condition, the children were asked, 'Is this one a koba?' (word condition), or 'Is this the one my uncle gave me?' (fact condition). The children were able to map successfully using the word or the fact. However, there was a difference between the two conditions when children had to extend their knowledge – the children extended the noun to other, similar objects but did not extend the fact.

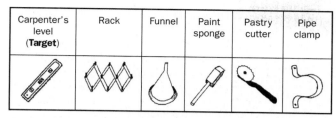

Figure 10.6 Some of the unfamiliar objects in Waxman and Booth's (2000) study.

Source: Waxman, S.R. and Booth, A.E., Principles that are invoked in the acquisition of words, but not facts. *Cognition*, 2000, 77, B33–43. © 2000, with permission from Elsevier.

Table 10.6 Some overextensions that children make while learning new words

Word	Original referent	Application
Mooi	Moon	Cakes, round marks on windows writing on windows and in books round shapes in books, round post-marks, letter *o*
buti	ball	Toy, radish, stone sphere at park entrance
ticktock	watch	All clocks and watches, gas meter, firehose wound on spool, bath scale round dial
baw	ball	Apples, grapes, eggs, squash, bell clapper, anything round
mem	horse	Cow, calf, pig, moose, all fourlegged animals
fly	fly	Specks of dirt, dust, all small insects, child's own toes, crumbs of bread, a toad
wau-wau	dog	All animals, toy dog, soft house slippers, picture of an old man dressed in furs

Source: Adapted from Table 13.2 from *Psychology and Language: An introduction to psycholinguistics* by Herbert H. Clark and Eve V. Clark. © 1977, reprinted with permission of H.H. Clark & E.V. Clark.

In another study, 2–4-year-old children were taught a novel name for an object ('My cat stepped on this agnew') and given an arbitrary fact for a second, unfamiliar object (such as metal shelving brackets and Allen keys) (Behrend *et al.*, 2001). The children extended the novel name to more exemplars than they did facts, suggesting that some of the principles underpinning the learning of words and facts are different.

Overextension and underextension

Often a child may commit what are called errors of overextension or underextension. If a child has learned to identify a ball but says 'ball' when they see an apple or an orange, or even the moon, we must conclude that they do not know the meaning of 'ball'. This error is called **overextension** – the use of a word to denote a larger class of items than is appropriate. If the child uses the word to refer only to the small red plastic ball, the error is called an **underextension** – the use of a word to denote a smaller class of items than is appropriate. Table 10.6 lists some examples of children's overextensions while learning the meanings of new words.

Both overextensions and underextensions are normal; a single pairing of a word with the object does not provide enough information for accurate generalisation.

Carers often correct children's overextensions. The most effective type of instruction occurs when an adult provides the correct label and points out the features that distinguish the object from the one with which the child has confused it (Chapman *et al.*, 1986). For example, if a child calls a yo-yo a ball, the carer might say, 'That's a yo-yo. See? It goes up and down' (Pease *et al.*, 1993).

Is there a language acquisition device?

According to Pinker (1984), 'In general, language acquisition is a stubbornly robust process; from what we can tell there is virtually no way to prevent it from happening, short of raising a child in a barrel'. The absence of barrels permitting, what shapes this linguistic learning process, and what motivates it?

There is vigorous controversy about why children learn to speak and, especially, why they learn to speak grammatically.

Chomsky (1965) observed that the recorded speech of adults is not as correct as the dialogue we read in a novel or hear in a play; often it is ungrammatical, hesitating and full of unfinished sentences. In fact, he characterised everyday adult speech as 'defective' and 'degenerate'. If this speech is really what children hear when they learn to speak, it is amazing that they manage to acquire the rules of grammar.

The view that children learn regular rules from apparently haphazard samples of speech has led many linguists to conclude that the ability to learn language is innate. All a child has to do is to be in the company of speakers of a language. Linguists have proposed that a child's brain contains a **language acquisition device** which embodies rules of 'universal grammar'; because each language expresses these rules in slightly different ways, the child must learn the details, but the basics are already there in the brain (Chomsky, 1965; Lenneberg, 1967; McNeill, 1970).

The assertion that an innate language acquisition device guides children's acquisition of a language is part of a general theory about the cognitive structures responsible for language and its acquisitions (Pinker, 1990). The most important components are as follows:

- Children who are learning a language make hypotheses about the grammatical rules they need to follow. These hypotheses are confirmed or disconfirmed by the speech that they hear.

- An innate language acquisition device guides children's hypothesis formation. Because they have this device, there are certain types of hypothetical rule that they will never entertain and certain types of sentence that they will never utter.
- The language acquisition device makes reinforcement unnecessary; the device provides the motivation for the child to learn a language.
- There is a critical period for learning a language. The language acquisition device works best during childhood; after childhood, languages are difficult to learn and almost impossible to master.

Evaluation of the evidence for a language acquisition device

No investigator regards the first assertion – that children make and test hypotheses about grammatical rules – as tenable. Thus, we cannot simply ask children why they say what they do. Children's hypothesis-testing is a convenient metaphor for the fact that their speech sometimes follows one rule or another.

A more important – and testable – assertion is that the hypothesis testing is guided by the language acquisition device. The most important piece of evidence in favour of this assertion is the discovery of language universals: characteristics that can be found in all languages that linguists have studied. Some of the more important language universals include the existence of noun phrases ('the quick brown fox . . . '); verb phrases ('. . . ate the chicken'); grammatical categories of words such as nouns and adjectives; and syntactical rules that permit the expression of subject–verb–object relations ('John hit Andy'), plurality ('two birds') and possession ('Rachel's pen').

However, the fact that all languages share certain characteristics does not mean that they are the products of innate brain mechanisms. For example, Hebb *et al.* (1973) observed that language universals may simply reflect realities of the world. When people deal with each other and with nature, their interactions often take the form of an agent acting on an object. Thus, the fact that all languages have ways of expressing these interactions is not surprising. Similarly, objects come in slightly different shapes, sizes and colours, so we can expect the need for ways (such as adjectives) to distinguish among them. It is not unreasonable to suppose that the same kinds of linguistic device have been independently invented at different times and in different places by different cultures. After all, archaeologists tell us that similar tools have been invented by different cultures all around the world. People need to cut, hammer, chisel, scrape and wedge things apart, and different cultures have invented similar devices to perform these tasks. We need not conclude that these inventions are products of a 'tool-making device' located in the brain. But even if some language universals are dictated by reality, others could indeed be the result of a language acquisition device. For example, consider the following sentences, adapted from Pinker (1990):

A1. Bill drove the car into the garage.
A2. Bill drove the car.
B1. Bill put the car into the garage.
B2. Bill put the car.

Someone (such as a child learning a language) who heard sentences A1 and A2 could reasonably infer that sentence B1 could be transformed into sentence B2. But the inference obviously is false; sentence B2 is ungrammatical. The linguistic rules say that sentence A2 is acceptable but that sentence B2 is not very complex; and their complexity is taken as evidence that they must be innate, not learned. Pinker (1990, p. 206) concludes: 'The solution to the problem [that children do not utter sentence B2] must be that children's learning mechanisms ultimately do not allow them to make the generalisation'.

This conclusion rests on the assumption that children use rules similar to the ones that linguists use. How, the reasoning goes, could a child master such complicated rules at such an early stage of cognitive development unless the rules were already wired into the brain? But perhaps the children are not following such complex rules. Perhaps they learn that when you say 'put' (something) you must always go on to say where you put something. Linguists do not like rules that deal with particular words, such as put (something) (somewhere); they prefer abstract and general rules that deal with categories: clauses, prepositions, noun phrases and the like. But children learn particular words and their meanings – why should they not also learn that certain words must be followed (or must never be followed) by certain others? Doing so is certainly simpler than learning the complex and subtle rules that linguists have devised. It would seem that both complex and simple rules (or innate or learned ones) could explain the fact that children do not utter sentence B2.

The third assertion is that language acquisition occurs without the need of reinforcement, or even of correction. Brown and Hanlon (1970) recorded dialogue between children and parents and found that adults generally did not show disapproval when the children's utterances were ungrammatical and approval when they were grammatical. Instead, approval appeared to be contingent on the truth or accuracy of the children's statements. If there is no differential reinforcement, how can we explain the fact that children eventually learn to speak grammatically? It is undoubtedly true that adults rarely say, 'Good, you said that correctly', or, 'No, you said that wrongly'. However, adults do distinguish between grammatical and ungrammatical speech of children. A study by Bohannon and

Stanowicz (1988) found that adults are likely to repeat children's grammatically correct sentences verbatim but to correct ungrammatical sentences. For example, if a child says, 'That be monkey', an adult would say, 'That is a monkey'. Adults were also more likely to ask for clarifications of ungrammatical sentences. Thus, adults do tend to provide the information children need to correct their faulty speech.

Chomsky's assertion about the defectiveness and degeneracy of adult speech is not strictly true, at least as far as it applies to what children hear. In fact, according to Newport *et al.* (1977), almost all the speech that a young child hears (at least, in industrialised English-speaking societies) is grammatically correct. If that is so, why should we hypothesise that a language acquisition device exists? Because, say some researchers, not all children are exposed to **child-directed speech** (i.e. speech which adults use specifically when communicating with children). 'In some societies people tacitly assume that children aren't worth speaking to and don't have anything to say that is worth listening to. Such children learn to speak by overhearing streams of adult-to-adult speech' (Pinker, 1990, p. 218).

Pinker's statement is very strong; it says that children in some cultures have no speech directed towards them until they have mastered the language. It implies that the children's mothers do not talk to them and ignores the fact that older children may not be quite so choosy about their conversational partners. To conclude that such an extreme statement is true would require extensive observation and documentation of child-rearing practices in other cultures. One of the strongest biological tendencies of our species is for a mother to cherish, play with and communicate with her offspring. If there really is a culture in which mothers do not do so, we need better documentation.

In fact, children do not learn a language that they simply overhear. Bonvillian *et al.* (1976) studied children of deaf parents whose only exposure to spoken language was through television or radio. This exposure was not enough; although the children could hear and did watch television and listen to the radio, they did not learn to speak English. It takes more than 'overhearing streams of adult-to-adult speech' to learn a language. The way that parents talk to their children is closely related to the children's language acquisition (Furrow *et al.*, 1979; Furrow and Nelson, 1986). Thus, the question is, just how much instruction (in the form of child-directed speech) do children need?

The fact that parents do not often reward their children's speech behaviours with praise or tangible reinforcers (such as sweets) does not prove that reinforcement plays no role in learning a language. We humans are social animals; our behaviour is strongly affected by the behaviour of others. It is readily apparent to anyone who has observed the behaviour of children that the attention of other people is extremely important to them. Children will perform a variety of behaviours that get other people to pay attention to them. They will make faces, play games and even misbehave in order to attract attention. And above all, they will talk.

The final assertion – that the language acquisition device works best during childhood – has received the most experimental support. For example, Newport and Supalla (1987) studied the ability of people who were deaf from birth to use sign language. They found that the earlier the training began, the better the person was able to communicate. Johnson and Newport (1989) also found that native Korean and Chinese speakers who moved to the USA learned English grammar better if they arrived during childhood. The advantage did not appear to be a result of differences in motivation to learn a second language. Such results are consistent with the hypothesis that something occurs within the brain after childhood that makes it more difficult to learn a language.

Observational studies such as these do not prove that a cause-and-effect relation exists between the variables in question. Johnson and Newport (1989) suggest that people's age (in particular, the age of their brain) affects their language-learning ability. But other variables are also correlated with age. For example, the Korean and Chinese speakers who moved to the USA as children spent several years in school; and perhaps the school environment is a particularly good place to learn a second language. In addition, adults are generally more willing to correct the grammatical errors made by children than those made by adolescents or other adults; thus, children may get more tutoring. It is certainly possible that the investigators are correct, but their results cannot be taken as proof that the brain contains an innate language acquisition device.

In one sense, a language acquisition device does exist. The human brain is a language acquisition device; without it, languages are not acquired. The real controversy is over the characteristics of this language acquisition device. Is it so specialised that it contains universal rules of grammar and provides innate motivation that makes reinforcement unnecessary?

The issue is made more interesting, if controversial, if we consider the ability of other higher primates to learn language. Other higher primates such as gorillas or chimpanzees do not naturally produce language although they have their own system of communication. Their vocal apparatus is different from that of humans so it would be unrealistic to assume that they would be able to articulate human language. However, these animals are the ones that are genetically closest to us; similar brain asymmetries, especially in those parts of the brain which are thought to mediate language, are seen in humans and apes. Would it be possible to teach primates human language? Do higher primates also possess an innate language acquisition device but need an environmental prompt for such a device to start working? These questions form the basis of the following Controversies in Psychological Science section.

Psychology in action: The language of food

The language we read and hear can also affect what and how much we eat. In one study, participants were asked to try a food, a salmon mousse, which was labelled either 'savoury mousse' or 'Food 386' (Yeomans *et al.*, 2008). People who were presented with the food labelled with the number liked the food the least – because they were expecting strawberry. They also rated it as saltier and ate less of it when offered it weeks later when invited back to the laboratory.

A menu can influence our choices in many ways – if the calories of an item are included on a menu, meals with fewer calories (up to 1 per cent less) are ordered (Roberto *et al.*, 2010). Emphasising that the dish was made with local products also increases the likelihood of that dish being ordered (Jacob and Gueguen, 2015). Joravsky *et al.* (2013) found that very expensive restaurants were more likely to mention 'origins' than inexpensive ones – 15 times more likely. Inexpensive restaurants have more items on their menus with greater size options; expensive ones feature half the number of items. The word 'you' or 'your' featured more often on inexpensive

menus and longer, polysyllabic words were more common on expensive restaurants' menus. The longer the word, the bigger the price. According to Joravsky *et al.* (2013), a one-letter increase leads to 18 cents being added to the bill. Odd-priced items on a menu (e.g. $4.99) are more likely to be ordered than even ones (Schindler and Warren, 1988). Linguistic fillers such as 'tasty', 'mouth-watering', 'terrific', 'wonderful' and so on tend to be found on the menus of cheaper restaurants.

We have more negative words for describing food we do not like – this is partly due to the fact that we have more adjectives to describe pain than pleasure, and people we don't like (a phenomenon termed negative differentiation). Our negative comments on food tend to be quite specific – 'chemical', 'piss', 'thin', and 'flat', for example. Positive reviews tend to be vague – 'amazing', 'fantastic', for example. Joravsky *et al.* found that people reviewing food of expensive restaurants were more likely to do so using sexual language 'sticky', 'rich', 'moist', 'oozing' whereas reviewers of cheap restaurants used the language of drug addition – 'addictive', 'I need a fix'.

Bilingualism

If an individual can meet the communication demands of the self or the individual's culture in two or more languages, they are considered bilingual (Mohanty and Perregaux, 1997). **Bilingualism** is described as 'simultaneous' when two or more languages develop in childhood more or less simultaneously, spontaneously and naturally, and 'successive' when a second (and third) language is learned after the first, such as learning a second language during puberty (Romaine, 1989).

Until relatively recently, it was thought that bilingualism was detrimental to cognitive performance such as lexical decision time: bilinguals were slower, committed more errors when naming pictures and had more tip-of-the tongue experiences. None of these is very much evident in conversation, however (Bialystok and Craik, 2010). The early studies, which compared Spanish–English bilinguals in America and English–Welsh bilinguals in Wales with monolinguals, showed that being able to speak two languages from childhood had negative consequences for intellectual development. However, these studies did not take into account socio-economic status, the degree of bilingualism or the skill in the second language (Lambert, 1977; Cummins, 1984). Rather than impairing cognitive ability, bilingualism appears to be beneficial to it (Perregaux, 1994). Executive functions, for example, are thought to be much better performed by bilingual speakers – bilinguals sort cards by colour and shape and complete the Stroop task better (see Chapter 8) (Bialystok and Martin, 2004; Bialystok *et al.*, 2008) although the evidence

is not completely consistent (Paap, 2014). Paap, for example, notes that these studies are characterised by small samples and that direct replications are rare.

Bilinguals appear to perceive events and people less egocentrically than do monolinguals, a finding that is correlated with better performance on a theory of mind task, described in Chapter 12 (Rubio-Fernandez and Glucksberg, 2012).

The brain regions responsible for control of executive functions also overlap with those areas responsible for the control of language in bilingual speakers (Pliatsikas and Luk, 2016). One reason why better executive function might be observed in bilinguals is that conflict resolution between two languages is a feature of executive function, and that the constant exercise of this conflict resolution enhances general executive function (Bialystok and Craik, 2010).

Bilingualism may even be a cognitive reserve, protecting against cognitive decline. One study found that the age of onset of dementia is four years later for bilingual than monolingual speakers (Bialystok *et al.*, 2007). Monolingual English and bilingual speakers of Spanish-English – whether adults or children – appear to recruit difference brain regions when they listen to English syllables (Archila-Suerte *et al.*, 2013). The former recruits the superior temporal gyrus in early and late childhood when listening to native speech whereas the bilingual group recruits the same area in early childhood and executive areas (bilateral middle frontal gyrus) in late childhood when listening to non-native speech.

However, the latest meta-analysis of the relationship between bilingualism and executive function has found that

Controversies in psychological science: Can other primates acquire language?

The issue

The members of most species can communicate with one another. Even insects communicate: a female moth that is ready to mate can release a chemical that will bring male moths from miles away; a dog can tell its owner that it wants to go for a walk by bringing its lead in its mouth and whining at the door. But, until recently, humans were the only species that had languages – flexible systems that use symbols to express many meanings. But are other primates able to learn and use symbols in the same linguistic way that humans do?

The evidence

In the 1960s, Beatrice and Roger Gardner of the University of Nevada began Project Washoe (Gardner and Gardner, 1969, 1978), a remarkably successful attempt to teach sign language to a female chimpanzee named Washoe. Previous attempts to teach chimps to learn and use human language focused on speech (Hayes, 1952). These attempts failed because, as we noted above, chimps lack the control of tongue, lips, palate and vocal cords that humans have and thus cannot produce the variety of complex sounds that characterise human speech.

Gardner and Gardner realised this limitation and decided to attempt to teach Washoe a manual language – one that makes use of hand movements. Chimps' hand and finger dexterity is excellent, so the only limitations in their ability would be cognitive ones. The manual language the Gardners chose was based on ASL, the American sign language used by deaf people. This is a true language, containing function words and content words and having regular grammatical rules.

Washoe was 1-year old when she began learning sign language; by the time she was 4, she had a vocabulary of over 130 signs. Like children, she used single signs at first; then, she began to produce two-word sentences such as 'Washoe sorry', 'gimme flower', 'more fruit' and 'Roger tickle'. Sometimes, she strung three or more words together, using the concept of agent and object: 'You tickle me'. She asked and answered questions, apologised, made assertions – in short, did the kinds of things that children would do while learning to talk. She showed overextensions and underextensions, just as human children do. Occasionally, she even made correct generalisations by herself. After learning the sign for the verb 'open' (as in open box, open cupboard), she used it to say open faucet, when requesting a drink. She made signs to herself when she was alone and used them to 'talk' to cats and dogs, just as children will do. Although it is difficult to compare her progress with that of human children (the fairest comparison would be with that of deaf children learning to sign), humans clearly learn language much more readily than Washoe did.

Inspired by Project Washoe's success (Washoe died in 2007), several other investigators have taught primate species to use sign language. For example, Patterson began to teach a gorilla (Patterson and Linden, 1981) and Miles (1983) began to teach an orangutan. Washoe's training started relatively late in her life, and her trainers were not, at the beginning of the project, fluent in sign language. Other chimpanzees, raised from birth by humans who are native speakers of ASL, have begun to use signs when they are 3 months old (Gardner and Gardner, 1975).

Many psychologists and linguists have questioned whether the behaviour of these animals can really be classified as verbal behaviour. For example, Terrace et al. (1979) argue that the apes simply learned to imitate the gestures made by their trainers and that sequences of signs such as, 'please milk please me like drink apple bottle' (produced by a young gorilla) are nothing like the sequences that human children produce. Others have challenged these criticisms (Fouts, 1983; Miles, 1983; Stokoe, 1983), blaming much of the controversy on the method that Terrace and his colleagues used to train their chimpanzee.

Chimpanzees can, apparently, use symbols to represent real objects and can manipulate these symbols logically (Premack, 1976). These abilities are two of the most powerful features of language. For Premack's chimpanzees, a blue plastic triangle means 'apple'. If the chimpanzees are given a blue plastic triangle and asked to choose the appropriate symbols denoting its colour and shape, they choose the ones that signify 'red' and 'round', not 'blue' and 'triangular'. Thus, the blue triangle is not simply a token the animals can use to obtain apples; it represents an apple for them, just as the word apple represents it for us.

Even though humans are the only primates who can pronounce words, several other species can recognise them. Savage-Rumbaugh (1990; Savage-Rumbaugh et al., 1998) taught Kanzi, a pygmy chimpanzee, to communicate with humans by pressing buttons that contained symbols for words.

Kanzi's human companions talked with him, and he learned to understand them. Although the structure of his vocal apparatus prevented him from responding vocally, he often tried to do so. During a three-month period, Savage-Rumbaugh and her colleagues tested Kanzi with 310 sentences, such as 'Put a toothbrush in the lemonade'. Three hundred and two of these had never been heard by the chimpanzee before. Only situations in which Kanzi could not have been guided by non-verbal cues from the human companions were counted; often, Kanzi's back was to the speaker. He responded correctly 298 times.

Conclusion

The most successful attempts at teaching a language to other primates are those in which the animal and the trainer have established a close relationship in which they can successfully communicate non-verbally by means of facial expressions, movements and gestures. Such interactions naturally lead to attempts at communication; and if signs (or spoken words) serve to make communication easier and more effective, they will most readily be learned.

there is no bilingual advantage for executive function performance: that is, bilinguals are no better or worse than monolinguals at executive function tasks (Lehtonen et al, 2018).

Brain development and language

In his book, *The Biological Foundations of Language*, Lenneberg (1967) argued that the functional lateralisation of language – one cerebral hemisphere's superiority for processing language – begins at the same time as the child begins to acquire language. Lenneberg thus argued that there was a sensitive period during which language should be acquired and lateralisation would develop.

Others (e.g. Krashen, 1973) argued that the hemispheres of the brain are equipotential at birth – each hemisphere is capable of undertaking the function for which the other becomes specialised. The **critical period** for lateralisation was complete by the age of 5 or 6 years. If lesions to the right hemisphere occurred before the age of 5 years, the child would show symptoms of aphasia, a disorder involving the inability to produce or comprehend speech. If damage occurred after the age of 5, no deficits in speech would arise suggesting that the normal left-for-language functional asymmetry had developed and was relatively complete. Krashen was involved in the study of an unusual case in which a young girl had been deprived of auditory stimulation and failed to develop normal language.

The case of 'Genie'

'Genie' was a 13-year-old girl who had been chronically abused since infancy. The girl's father had harnessed her to a potty in a room in the back of the family house since she was at least 20 months old and deprived her of any linguistic stimulation. She slept in a crib covered with wire mesh. Her father was intolerant of noise and would beat her whenever she made any sound. Her mother fed her a diet of baby food, cereals and, occasionally, boiled eggs. When eventually spotted by social workers, the girl was 4 feet 6 inches tall and weighed 4 stone. She could not eat solid food and had nearly two complete sets of teeth. She was 13 years and 9 months old. Her real name was Sarah Wylie.

Her most remarkable psychological feature was her almost complete lack of language. She could not talk and had a vocabulary of about 20 words (she could understand concepts such as 'red' 'blue', 'green'). Her speech production was limited to 'nomore', 'stopit' and other negatives. Following her discovery, she was admitted to the Children's Hospital in Los Angeles for treatment. Researchers were interested in how handicapped Genie's language had become and what possible recovery could be made from such gross linguistic impairment

(Fromkin *et al.*, 1972/73; Curtiss, 1977). There had been isolated instances of 'accidental' cases of language deprivation before, such as Victor, the 'wild boy of Aveyron', who had been found in 1800, lurking naked in front of a cottage in the Languedoc region of France. He had spent his 12 years from infancy living in the woods, surviving on a diet of acorns and potatoes. He had had his throat cut as a toddler and been left to die. Victor had no language, and while he never learned to speak, he achieved a rudimentary ability to spell.

A year after she was discovered, Genie's language ability underwent marked improvement. Her ability to structure according to rules was the equivalent of a 20-year old's, and

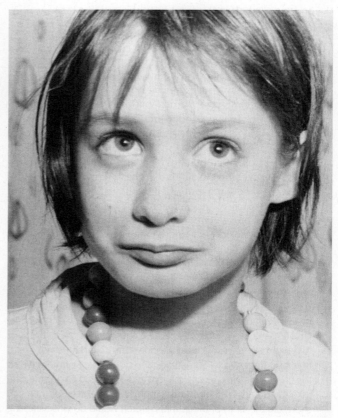

This is one of the few images of Genie (Susan Wiley) that is publicly available. It was reported that Genie had suffered sustained psychological and physical abuse from her father over a number of years which led to her showing highly maladaptive and delayed/ impaired behaviour. It was this behaviour – a failure to use/ develop language and interact normally with people – that led to the epithet 'wild child'. This is a term used to describe children who are literally abandoned, usually in the wild, and have no opportunity to develop language or social skills. Despite the best attempts of researchers to help rehabilitate Genie, her language did not improve significantly.
Source: Bettmann/Getty Images.

her spatial ability placed her in the adult ability category. She could tell the difference between singular and plural words and positive and negative sentences and could understand some prepositions. Her speech was limited to one or two word sentences, however, eventually becoming very descriptive and concrete ('big rectangular pillow', 'very, very, very dark-green box'). The 'explosion' of language, normally expected after such dramatic improvements, never lateralised.

It became clear that Genie could develop new but basic language skills. She made a dramatic recovery from the time of her discovery to the time when the scientists had to abandon their studies. Yet, her language never fully recovered, remaining steadfastly descriptive, almost at the level one would expect primates to achieve with intensive language training. Her study showed, however, the remarkable, devastating effects of language and auditory deprivation on the development of language ability.

Plasticity and language development

You saw in Chapter 4 that the brain shows a significant capacity for plasticity during development. This plasticity may be beneficial to the development of function if the brain is injured. For example, in a series of famous experiments, Dennis and Whitaker (1976) and Woods (1980) found that the incidence of aphasia – an inability to produce or comprehend speech following brain injury, and which you read about in the history section of Chapter 1 – was greater when brain injury occurred during infancy than later in life. Other authors suggested that left-hemisphere lesions would be associated with greater language impairment if the brain injury occurred after the age of 5 or 6 years (Vargha-Khadem et al., 1985). The evidence from the human literature was consistent with earlier experimental lesioning work in primates. This work found that if the brain of a monkey was lesioned during infancy, its recovery was significantly superior to that seen after the brain of an adult monkey was lesioned. This became known as the Kennard principle (named after Margaret Kennard who made the experimental observation): the notion that recovery from brain damage during infancy is better than from damage during adulthood.

Another source of data suggesting a critical period for the development of asymmetry comes from studies of hemispherectomy, where one hemisphere is removed for medical reasons, usually because of the growth of a large tumour or because of intractable epilepsy. In adults, left hemispherectomies result in fairly severe aphasia, but left hemispherectomies in children are associated with almost complete recovery of language function (Searleman, 1977).

What these data suggest is that the brain has a degree of plasticity when it is developing. That is, specialised functions have not developed in any sophisticated way in one or other hemisphere during early growth. After a specific age, however, this specialisation has begun, but one or other hemisphere can undertake the functions of the other if the other is damaged.

For example, studies have shown that early brain lesions in children between 13 and 36 months old are associated with a delay in the development of expressive vocabulary, especially if damage is to the left side. However, there seems to be little effect on the next stage of language development, sentence production (Vicari et al., 2000). If the damage occurs later, in adulthood, then it is hypothesised that the right hemisphere undertakes the language functions of the left (Hertz-Pannier et al., 1999). One study has found that injury to the left temporal lobe is associated with subsequent increased activation of the right frontal lobe during verbal fluency (Voets et al., 2006). MEG studies also suggest that lateralisation increases as a function of age (Ressel et al., 2008). The connections between brain areas also appear able to predict language improvement after stroke – for example, stronger connections between (1) regions in the left frontal and parietal areas and (2) the right middle frontal cortex and right inferior frontal cortex 1–2 months post injury in a study of 13 patients was associated with better preserved language comprehension. Decreased connectivity was associated with poorer language ability.

Other researchers have argued that when the brain is injured and language is impaired then recovery may not be due to other silent 'language areas' becoming active but that the increases in activation seen in brain areas reflect the increased effort and attention necessary to complete language and communication tasks (Geranmayeh et al., 2014). They argue that people who are less able to recover language after injury are those who may not be able to active these areas.

Is half a brain enough?

In a novel experiment to explore the nature of plasticity, Hertz-Pannier et al. (2002) studied six children who underwent left hemispherectomy for intractable epilepsy (epilepsy that cannot be controlled by drugs) and monitored their brain activity during language tasks before and after the surgery. They hypothesised that if the brain shows evidence of plasticity, then we might expect the right hemisphere to take over the language function of the left. They used fMRI to study the children at age 6 years and 10 months and found the typical left lateralisation for language tasks such as word generation; there was little right hemisphere activity.

Following surgery, receptive language recovered quickly but expressive language and reading was slower to recover. When fMRI scanning was undertaken again at 10 years 6 months, there was a shift in activity to the right hemisphere during expressive and receptive language tasks. The regions that were activated – the inferior frontal temporal and parietal cortices – were analogous to those in the left hemisphere prior to the surgery.

This activation in the right hemisphere is also seen in adults recovering from aphasia. For example, Cappa *et al.* (1997) found that activation in the right temporoparietal (TP) region during the acute phase of recovery predicted improvement in auditory comprehension later on. More recently, a group of researchers has found that a period of intensive training in a group of patients who had suffered a stroke destroying parts of the left frontal cortex and who had difficulty in comprehending speech, led to increased activation in the bilateral network of regions associated with language. There were also increases in right hemisphere regions.

A group of researchers from Germany compared the degree of brain activation and the degree of improvement in language function in eight patients who had suffered a stroke (Menke *et al.*, 2009). Over two weeks and for three hours a day, patients were trained to name concrete words. Task performance was measured before the training, immediately after and eight months after. Language function improved considerably – from 0 per cent to 64 per cent accuracy across the study. The researchers also found, however, that success at the task was predicted by different brain regions depending on when testing took place. In the short-term, activation in the hippocampus and fusiform gyrus and in the right precuneus and cingulate gyrus predicted language success. At 8 months, right-sided activation in the equivalent of Wernicke's area was found, as was activation in other areas of the temporal lobe region.

The researchers suggest that the process of recovery is dynamic and conclude that their study shows that in the early stages, regions not particularly associated with language but associated with memory and attention are activated but in the later stages of recovery, the 'classical' language areas become more involved.

The picture is not entirely clear-cut, however. A different group of German researchers found that activation in the right frontal part of the brain predicted degree of improvement in patients who had suffered a stroke (Saur *et al.*, 2010). Language proficiency was measured by combining the scores from a battery of language tasks. They studied 21 stroke patients two weeks and eight months after language training.

Another case study highlights how successful language development could be following such radical surgery (Battro, 2000). Nico is an Italian boy who was born with left hemiplegia. He managed to walk by age 18 months but developed intractable epilepsy at 22 months. Drugs and selective lesioning of the brain failed to halt the epilepsy and so, as a last resort and with the permission of Nico's parents, surgeons performed a right hemidecortication when the boy was 3 years and 7 months.

Nico recovered well and he did not lose his speech. His IQ was 107 and he learned to develop the basics of spelling and grammar at the same age as normal children through the use of a computer. He is still behind other children in his ability to draw and has difficulty forming letters of the alphabet and numbers with the right hand. The outcome of Nico's surgery suggests that the right hemisphere may be what Popper and Eccles (1977) described as a 'minor brain'. Without it, Nico has learned to develop the important function of language although his 'right hemisphere' functions, such as drawing, are impaired.

The neuropsychology of language and language disorders

Neuropsychology aims to localise not only basic perceptual and sensory functions, such as touching, seeing, recognising objects and so on, but also quite sophisticated cognitive functions (see Chapters 1 and 4). The most extensively studied cognitive function is language, and our knowledge of the neuropsychology of language has come from three sources: studies of individuals with brain injury who show language impairment, individuals who do not develop language adequately, and neuroimaging studies in which activation of the brain in healthy individuals is monitored while they complete language tasks. These sources indicate that the mechanisms involved in perception, comprehension and production of speech are located in different areas of the cerebral cortex.

Language disorders

Brain damage can result from a large number of factors and can cause a wide variety of impairments in cognitive function. Some of the most pronounced impairments are those related to language. Some language impairments result directly from brain injury, others do not but are likely to be the result of disorganised or abnormal brain activity or structure. The most common language disorders are called the aphasias. The key feature of the aphasias is the loss of language function; the patient is unable to produce or comprehend speech. Other important disorders of language are reading impairment (dyslexia) and stuttering and all three of these disorders are considered in the next sections.

Aphasia

Around 250,000 people in the UK and a million people in the US suffer from aphasia (Geranmayeh *et al.*, 2014). **Aphasia** literally means 'total loss of language function', although patients with the disorder do not lose all language: they are able to perform some language tasks, for example, depending on the site of the brain injury. Because of this, the term 'dysphasia' is sometimes used (dys – means 'partial loss of'). There are different types of aphasia, and the most common are summarised in Table 10.7. Two of the most common types are non-fluent (Broca's) aphasia and receptive (Wernicke's) aphasia. The areas of the brain which, when damaged, cause these aphasias can

Table 10.7 (a) Types of aphasia, their primary symptoms and the site of the associated brain lesion

Type of aphasia	Primary symptoms	Brain lesion to
Sensory (Wernicke's) aphasia	General comprehension deficits, neologisms, word retrieval deficits, semantic paraphasias	Post-perisylvian region: posterio-superior temporal opercular supramarginal angular and posterior insular gyri; planum temporale
Production (Broca's) aphasia	Speech production deficit, abnormal prosody; impaired syntactic comprehension	Posterior part of the inferior frontal and precentral convolutions of the left hemisphere
Conduction aphasia	Naming deficits and impaired ability to repeat non-meaningful single words and word strings	Arcuate fasciculus, posterior parietal and temporal regions; left auditory complex, insula supramarginal gyrus
Deep dysphasia	Word repetition deficits; verbal (semantic) paraphasia	Temporal lobe, especially regions which mediate phonological processing
Transcortical sensory aphasia	Impaired comprehension, naming reading and writing, semantic irrelevancies in speech	Temporoparieto-occipital junction of the left hemisphere
Transcortical motor aphasia	Transient mutism and telegrammatic dysprosodic speech	Connection between Broca's area and the supplementary motor area; medial frontal lobe regions anterolateral to the left hemispheres frontal horn
Global aphasia	Generalised deficits in comprehension, repetition, naming and speech production	Left perisylvian region, white matter, basal ganglia and thalamus

Source: G.N. Martin, *Human Neuropsychology*, 2nd edn, Pearson/Prentice Hall (2006).

Table 10.7 (b) Symptomatology of aphasia

Type	Site of damage	Spontaneous speech	Comprehension	Paraphasia	Repetition	Naming
Broca's		Non-fluent	Good	Common	Poor	Poor
Wernicke's		Fluent	Poor	Uncommon	Poor	Poor
Conduction		Fluent	Good	Common	Poor	Poor
Global		Non-fluent	Poor	Variable	Poor	Poor

Source: G.N. Martin, *Human Neuropsychology*, 2nd edn, Pearson/Prentice Hall (2006).

be seen in Figure 10.7. Aphasia is not a unitary disorder – it is heterogeneous and often the simple classifications in Table 10.8 do not capture the full extent of the disorder nor the nature of the language and communication impairment. This is likely due to the different brain regions involved.

Speech production: evidence from non-fluent (Broca's) aphasia

In order to produce meaningful communication, we need to convert perceptions, memories and thoughts into speech. The neural mechanisms that control speech production appear to be located in the frontal lobes. Damage to a region of the motor association cortex in the left frontal lobe (Broca's area)

disrupts the ability to speak: it causes **non-fluent (Broca's) aphasia**, a language disorder characterised by slow, laborious, non-fluent speech (it is also called expressive, production or motor aphasia). When trying to talk with patients who have non-fluent aphasia, most people find it hard to resist supplying the words the patients are groping for. But although these patients often mispronounce words, the ones they manage to produce are meaningful. They have something to say, but the damage to the frontal lobe makes it difficult for them to express these thoughts.

Below is a sample of speech from a man with Broca's aphasia, who is telling the examiner why he has come to the hospital. His words are meaningful but what he says is not grammatical. The dots indicate long pauses.

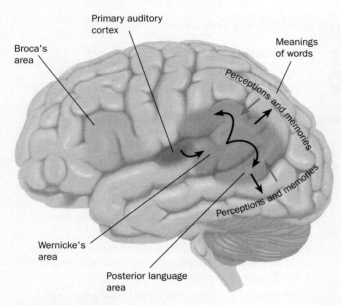

Primary auditory cortex

Broca's area

Meanings of words

Perceptions and memories

Perceptions and memories

Wernicke's area

Posterior language area

Figure 10.7 The dictionary in the brain relates the sounds of words to their meanings and permits us to comprehend the meanings of words and translate our own thoughts into words. Black arrows represent comprehension of words; red arrows represent translation of thoughts or perceptions into words.

Lesions that produce non-fluent aphasia must be centred in the vicinity of Broca's area. However, damage restricted to the cortex of Broca's area does not appear to produce Broca's aphasia; the damage must extend to surrounding regions of the frontal lobe and to the underlying subcortical white matter (Damasio, 1989, Damasio *et al.*, 1996). Dronkers *et al.* (2007) used MRI to measure, in detail, the extent of the damage to the preserved brains of two of Broca's patients, including the famous Leborgne ('Tan').

'Ah ... Monday ... ah Dad and Paul [patient's name] ... and Dad ... hospital. Two ... ah doctors ... , and ah ... thirty minutes ... and yes ... ah ... hospital. And, er Wednesday ... nine o'clock. And er Thursday, ten o'clock ... doctors. Two doctors ... and ah ... teeth. Yeah, ... fine'.
(Source: *Goodglass*, 1976, p. 278.)

They found that damage was much deeper than Broca reported (MRI was not available in his day) and other areas were also damaged including a large tract of fibre that connects the posterior and anterior language areas. Although damage to Broca's area can lead to transient impairment in speech production, it seems likely that damage to this fibre is necessary to produce severe speech difficulty.

Confusion about where – or what – Broca's area is exists even in the psychology literature today. One survey found that although 27 per cent of neuroimaging studies referred to Areas 44 and 45 as Broca's area, 52 per cent of the journal articles surveyed either did not define Broca's area or gave misleading or broad definitions of the region (Lindenberg *et al.*, 2007).

Wernicke (1874) suggested that Broca's area contains motor memories – in particular, memories of the sequences of muscular movements that are needed to articulate words. Talking involves rapid movements of the tongue, lips and jaw, and these movements must be coordinated with each other and with those of the vocal cords; thus, talking requires some very sophisticated motor control mechanisms. Because damage to the lower left frontal lobe (including Broca's area) disrupts the ability to articulate words, this region is the most likely candidate for the location of these 'programmes'. The fact that this region is located just in front of the part of the

Table 10.8 The dyslexias and the brain regions associated with them

Type of dyslexia	Primary symptoms	Brain regions implicated
Acquired dyslexia		
Visual word form dyslexia	Impaired sight reading; some decoding is possible	Disconnection between the angular gyrus of the dominant hemisphere and the visual input system
Phonological dyslexia	Deficits in reading pseudowords and nonwords	Temporal lobe of the dominant hemisphere?
Surface dyslexia	Tendency to produce regularisation errors in the reading of irregular words	?
Deep dyslexia	Semantic substitutions, impaired reading of abstract words, inability to read non-words	Extensive damage to the dominant hemisphere
Developmental dyslexia	Impaired reading and spelling of words/non-words/pseudowords, poor phonological processing skills, sequencing and short-term memory, some visuo-perceptual defects	Temporo-parietal regions of the dominant hemisphere

primary motor cortex that controls the muscles used for speech certainly supports this conclusion.

In addition to their role in the production of words, neural circuits located in the lower left frontal lobe appear to perform some more complex functions. Damage to Broca's area often produces **agrammatism**: loss of the ability to produce or comprehend speech that employs complex syntactical rules. For example, people with non-fluent aphasia rarely use function words. In addition, they rarely use grammatical markers such as '-ed' or auxiliaries such as 'have' (as in 'I have gone'). A study by Saffran *et al.* (1980) illustrates this difficulty. The following quotations are from agrammatic patients attempting to describe pictures:

> Picture of a boy being hit in the head by a baseball: 'The boy is catch … the boy is hitch … the boy is hit the ball'. (p. 229)
>
> Picture of a girl giving flowers to her teacher: 'Girl … wants to … flowers … flowers and wants to … The woman … wants to … The girl wants to … the flowers and the woman'. (p. 234)

In an ordinary conversation, non-fluent aphasics seem to understand everything that is said to them. They appear to be irritated and annoyed by their inability to express their thoughts well, and they often make gestures to supplement their scanty speech. The striking disparity between their speech and their comprehension often leads people to assume that their comprehension is normal. Their comprehension, however, is not normal.

The agrammatism that accompanies non-fluent aphasia appears to disrupt patients' ability to use grammatical information, including word order, to decode the meaning of a sentence. Thus, their deficit in comprehension parallels their deficit in production. If they heard a sentence such as, 'The mosquito was swatted by the man', they would understand that it concerns a man and a mosquito and the action of swatting. Because of their knowledge of men and mosquitoes, they would have no trouble figuring out who is doing what to whom. But a sentence such as, 'The cow was kicked by the horse' does not provide any extra cues; if the grammar is not understood, neither is the meaning of the sentence.

Other experiments have shown that people with non-fluent aphasia have difficulty carrying out a sequence of commands, such as 'Pick up the red circle and touch the green square with it' (Boller and Dennis, 1979). This finding, along with the other symptoms described in this section, suggests that an important function of the left frontal lobe may be sequencing, both physically in terms of muscle movement (e.g. the muscles of speech-producing words) and semantically in terms of sequencing actual words (e.g. comprehending and

producing grammatical speech). The frontal cortex may be important for allowing us to sequence stimuli correctly (see the section on working memory in Chapter 8). This sequencing role of the frontal cortex is returned to in the next chapter in relation to reasoning and in Chapter 13 in relation to organising social and emotional behaviour.

Studies of aphasic patients who have basic ability to produce simple sentences suggest that a double dissociation exists between writing and speaking – that is, they are able to produce certain types of words in one medium but not in another. Rapp *et al.* (2015) found that their patients were unable to produce affixes (e.g. the 'ing' in speaking) competently when writing but could when speaking. This suggests that written and spoken language may have different neural substrates, an idea that is discussed in more detail in the sections below.

Speech comprehension: evidence from receptive (Wernicke's) aphasia

Comprehension of speech obviously begins in the auditory system, which is needed to analyse sequences of sounds and to recognise them as words. Recognition is the first step in comprehension. As we saw earlier in this chapter, recognising a spoken word is a complex perceptual task that relies on memories of sequences of sounds. This task appears to be accomplished by neural circuits in the upper part of the left temporal lobe – a region that is known as **Wernicke's area**.

Brain damage in the left hemisphere that invades Wernicke's area as well as the surrounding region of the temporal and parietal lobes produces a disorder known as **Wernicke's aphasia**. The symptoms of receptive aphasia are poor speech comprehension and production of meaningless speech (Wernicke's aphasia is also known as sensory or receptive aphasia). Unlike non-fluent aphasia, speech in receptive aphasia is fluent and unlaboured; the person does not strain to articulate words and does not appear to be searching for them. The patient maintains a melodic line, with the voice rising and falling normally. When you listen to the speech of a person with receptive aphasia, it appears to be grammatical. That is, the person uses function words such as 'the' and 'but' and employs complex verb tenses and subordinate clauses. However, the person uses few content words, and the words that he or she strings together just do not make sense. For example:

> Well this is … mother is away here working her work out o'here to get her better, but when she's looking, the two boys looking in other part. One their small tile into her time here. She's working another time because she's getting, too.
>
> (Source: Cookie Theft Picture Description from: Carroll, D. (1999) *Psychology of Language*, 3rd edn, Brooks/Cole Publishing Company.)

The failure of patients with Wernicke's aphasia to comprehend their own speech typically renders them unaware of their language processing problems and they will continue to participate in conversations, nodding in the appropriate places and taking turns to speak, blissfully unaware of their disorder.

Or this example of a conversation between a patient and a speech therapist:

Therapist: What did you have (to eat)?

PH: Today I haven't touched a/maiwa/d^/David. He had beastly tomorrow.

Therapist: Was the food good?

PH: Yes, it was fine. (Source: R.C. Martin, 2003.)

A commonly used test of comprehension for receptive aphasia assesses the patient's ability to understand questions by asking them to point to objects on a table in front of them. For example, they are asked to 'point to the one with ink'. If they point to an object other than a pen, they have not understood the request. When tested this way, people with severe Wernicke's aphasia show poor comprehension. In the Cookie Theft test (see box), the patient describes the scene on a card. The scene is a small boy stealing a cookie jar from a kitchen cupboard while his mother is washing dishes at a sink.

Because Wernicke's area is a region of the auditory association cortex, and because a comprehension deficit is so prominent in receptive aphasia, this disorder has been characterised as a receptive aphasia. Wernicke suggested that the region that now bears his name is the location of memories of the sequences of sounds that constitute words. This hypothesis is reasonable; it suggests that the auditory association cortex of Wernicke's area recognises the sounds of words, just as the visual association cortex in the lower part of the temporal lobe recognises the sight of objects.

Wernicke's aphasia, like non-fluent aphasia, actually appears to consist of several deficits. The abilities that are disrupted include recognition of spoken words, comprehension of the meaning of words, and the ability to convert thoughts into words. Recognition is a perceptual task; comprehension involves retrieval of additional information from long-term memory. Damage to Wernicke's area produces a deficit in recognition; damage to the surrounding temporal and parietal cortex produces a deficit in production of meaningful speech and comprehension of the speech of others.

Wise *et al.* (2001) have suggested that the term 'Wernicke's area' has become meaningless because different research groups delineate the area in different ways and impute to it different functions. They identified two regions within 'Wernicke's area' which seemed to perform different functions. One part responded to speech and non-speech sounds, including the sound of the speaker's voice. The posterior part of this, near the parietal lobe, was active during speech production. The second part identified was more lateral and responded to external sources of speech; it was also active during the recall of word lists. This suggests that the functions of both parts are compatible with a hypothesis which states that the first region is involved in mimicking sounds and the second is involved in the transient representation of heard or internally generated phonetic sequences.

If the region around Wernicke's area is damaged, but Wernicke's area itself is spared, the person will exhibit all of the symptoms of receptive aphasia except a deficit in auditory word recognition. Damage to the region surrounding Wernicke's area (the posterior language areas) produces a disorder known as isolation aphasia, an inability to comprehend speech or to produce meaningful speech accompanied by the ability to repeat speech and learn new sequences of words. The difference between isolation aphasia and Wernicke's aphasia is that patients with isolation aphasia can repeat what other people say to them; thus, they obviously can recognise words. However, they cannot comprehend the meaning of what they hear and repeat; nor can they produce meaningful speech of their own. Apparently, the sounds of words are recognised by neural circuits in Wernicke's area, and this information is transmitted to Broca's area so that the words can be repeated. However, because the posterior language area is destroyed, the meaning of the words cannot be comprehended.

Damage to other regions of the brain can disrupt particular categories of meaning in speech. For example, damage to part of the association cortex of the left parietal lobe can produce an inability to name the body parts. This disorder is called **autotopagnosia,** or 'poor knowledge of one's own topography' (a better name would have been autotopanomia, 'poor naming of one's own topography'). People who can otherwise converse normally cannot reliably point to their elbows, knees or cheeks when asked to do so, and they cannot name body parts when the examiner points to them. However, they have no difficulty understanding the meaning of other words.

Recent studies have helped highlight the role of brain structure and damage to brain structure in language impairment, especially in people who have suffered a stroke. For example, Butler *et al.* (2014) found that three classes of behaviour/function was impaired following stroke: phonology, semantic and executive function/cognition. Phonological impairments were the most pronounced and was associated with damage to left-hemisphere regions such as Heschl's gyrus, the posterior middle and superior temporal gyro and superior temporal sulcus, and with white matter in the posterior superior temporal gyrus. The semantic component was associated with areas including and restricted to the left anterior middle temporal gyrus. This pattern is seen in neuroimaging studies and the connections between these two approaches to studying the brain and language and how their findings converge are described later in the chapter

Specific language impairment

Some children have difficulties in producing or understanding spoken language, in the absence of known brain injury. The 7 per cent who exhibit this impairment are said to show **specific language impairment** (van der Lely, 2005). There is some

---

Psychology in action: The man who lost his language: the phenomenology of aphasia

On Tuesday, 28 July we went to a party in London. I drive home because John had had too much to drink. At a red light I glanced at him, and saw on his face the expression of a man crazed by an apocalyptic vision. He laughed it off: 'Is that what you go around saying at parties, 'Good evening, you have a crazed apocalyptic look on your face?' ' If I had known what that look meant, it is theoretically possible that I might have saved him . . .

Source: Sheila Hale (2002). *The Man Who Lost His Language*, p. 30.

On the morning of the 30 July 1992, just before nine o'clock, Sir John Hale, art historian and prolific author, was found on his study floor, having the 'sweet witless smile of a baby' on his face and uttering only the words, 'the walls, the walls'. Hale had suffered a stroke. Sheila, his wife, had noted one of the signs just days before – a change in the musculature of his face. While most of the studies in this book emerge from academic journals, and are reported in the clinical way one would expect from such a source, Sheila Hale wrote a personal account of the disorder and its consequences, writing in careful and often touching detail about the day-to-day consequences of stroke and aphasia and how she coped with the virtual demolition of her husband's language.

Initially, John Hale was unable to speak or write or match written/spoken nouns to objects such as a razor, a chick, a pencil and some keys. He could surmise what people were saying from their gestures and tone of voice, laughing at jokes and following simple instructions. Reading for pleasure was difficult and he would turn over pages he could not follow. Curiously, he could understand academic journals and offprints which suggested a dissociation between reading for pleasure and reading for information. John was written off by his original consultant – at the time of the stroke, Hale was in his 60s and was felt to be unable to benefit from rehabilitation – but an independent neurologist suggested that his intelligence alone might help his recovery. Sheila Hale discovered a series of language puzzle books designed for Roald Dahl's wife, Patricia Neal – who had become aphasic following a stroke – by Valerie

Eton Griffiths, and recruited family and friends to use them with her husband. At this point, he began introducing new sounds into his conversation: the, da or whoah. He could copy shapes and words and perform mental arithmetic but was unable to write words independently.

His speech therapist originally thought that John could not benefit from therapy – ironically, because he was too exuberant and that anyone with his degree of expressiveness would not be sufficiently motivated to help themselves through the difficult process of rehabilitation. This view changed when, at a dinner party, she lifted up her arm and asked John what it was: 'John said da woahs. Elizabeth said, "No, John, listen to yourself. Now listen to me: ahm". John said ahhhm. "No, John, you're saying ahhhm. It's not quite right, is it? What is this? This is my . . . ?" John said ahm' (Hale, 2002, p. 191).

When Sheila asked the therapist how it could be that her husband could read German, English and French but not be able to write a sentence in any language, Elizabeth offered a series of illuminating metaphors: 'It is as though the road between Naples and Rome had been blown up. You can still travel between the two cities, but you have to make your way through the rubble to find an alternative route', or 'The British Library has been shaken by an earthquake. The books have been hurled off the shelves. They're all mixed up and the catalogues can't be found. The books are like your words: there they are, but you have no means of finding them' (Hale, 2002, p. 195). Some examples of John Hale's writing and attempts at written comprehension. The photograph shows Hale with his wife, Sheila.

John's understanding of words was excellent and he could recognise written and spoken reversed letter words, real words and non-words; he could match synonyms, and words to pictures. However, phonological segmentation was a problem: when presented with the words 'map' and 'gap' he was unable to indicate which sound had changed. He knew that both were different. He could identify the number of letters in a word and could fill in blanks in a story but sometimes made dysgraphic errors, writing 'borg' for 'dog'.

Three years after his stroke, John was able to speak the words: *haaloo, bye, I, fine, wine, bus, bow, bell, more, my, house*

▶

Psychology in action: *Continued*

and *horse*. Sometimes, when trying to say one of these words, he would say 'arm' instead. Two years later, Sheila described a typical morning: 'Over lunch he tells me about his morning. *Mmmmmm* means walking along minding his own business. *Arrrr*-up! With his left hand describing an arc means that he has crossed a bridge. He meets a friend: broad smile, greeting gestures; they go into a pub; mime of conversation: bahbahbahbahbah – and drinking. Or John gets on a bus: sounds of changing gears, starting and stopping'.

Eventually, his non-language became less prosodic – he would introduce the words *um, oh, ah, aargh, gah, no* and *oh my God* to stem the mellifluous aphasic flow. He took great pains to find the right word, a struggle observed in the brain-injured patient, Lt Zasetsky by Luria (1972) in his book, *The Man*

RICARDO WENT OUT SHOPPING TO BUY SOME FRUIT. HE BOUGHT A POUND OF _pears_. AND A LARGE JUICY WATER _melon_. HE ALSO WENT INTO THE OFF-LICENCE AND BOUGHT THREE BOTTLES OF _wine_. HE WALKED HOME ALONG BY THE _river_ AND WATCHED THE MEN ROWING THE _boat_. A VERY BEAUTIFUL _girl_ WAS SITTING ON A _bench_ SO HE SAT NEXT TO HER. SHE HAD LONG BLONDE _hair_ AND BIG BLUE _eyes_. RICARDO SAID 'GOOD _morning_ IT'S A LOVELY _day_.' SHE TURNED TO HIM AND _smiled_ SHOWING LOVELY WHITE _teeth_. RICARDO OFFERED HER ONE OF HIS _pears_. THEY TALKED HAPPILY FOR HALF AN HOUR AND THEN RICARDO ASKED HER OUT TO _dinner_. SHE AGREED AND THEY MET OUTSIDE THE _restaurant_ AT 7.30PM.

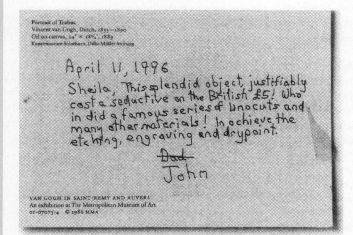

Portrait of Trabuc
Vincent van Gogh, Dutch, 1853–1890
Oil on canvas, 24" × 18¼", 1889
Kunstmuseum Solothurn, Dübi-Müller-Stiftung

April 11, 1996
Sheila, This splendid object, justifiably cast a seductive on the British £5! Who in did a famous series of linocuts and many other materials! In achieve the etching, engraving and drypoint.
~~Dad~~
John

VAN GOGH IN SAINT-REMY AND AUVERS
An exhibition at The Metropolitan Museum of Art
01-07075-4 © 1986 MMA

20 September 1998
Dear Miranda,
Thank you for the delicious dance on Friday. I was flattered to be on your party list and to partic... ...
Love
John

partic
aeiou
participate

Some examples of John Hale's writing and attempts at written comprehension. The photograph shows Hale with his wife, Sheila.

Source: S. Hale (2002). *The Man Who Lost His Language.* London: Penguin.

Psychology in action: *Continued*

with a Shattered World. 'It was so hard to write', Zasetsky wrote, 'At last, I'd turned up a good idea. So I began to hunt for words to describe it and finally I thought up two. But by the time I got to the third word, I was stuck . . . Finally, I managed to write a sentence expressing an idea I had . . . sometimes I'll sit over a page for a week or two . . . But I don't want to give it up. I want to finish what I've begun. So I sit at my desk all day, sweating over each word'.

One October evening, Sheila Hale wrote, 'I was too weak to resist a quick, forbidden glance into the future. And what I saw was a succession of meals, sitting across a table from a husband who was no more, or less, companionable than an affectionate dog' (Hale, 2002, p. 61). John Hale hid his despair well until, one afternoon, his wife found him with his head bowed and his left hand covering his face: 'When I put my arms around him, I felt the tears on his face. He was crying for the first time since I had known him'.

Hale's book is testament to the support, love and care that can help an individual with aphasia deal with extreme communication difficulty. Despite the impairment in his speech, John continued to be charming, garrulous and intelligent company. David Chambers summed up the positive aspects of Hale when writing the historian's obituary in The Times: 'for those in his company, the infinitely modulated exclamations, chuckles and ironical groans which accompanied his enchanting smile seemed almost to amount to conversation. Gregarious as ever, he proved that, even in aphasia, life can be exhilarating'.

---

overlap between this disorder and autism and dyslexia but some have argued that children with SLI show non-phonology and phonology impairments, whereas children with dyslexia have intact non-phonological language skills but impaired phonological ability – an inability to categorise sounds and map letters to sounds (Krishnan *et al.*, 2016).

Grammar and phonology are the most affected aspects in SLI but individuals' intelligence is within the normal range (van der Lely and Marshall, 2010). When a 6-year old with adequate hearing but specific language impairment is asked to repeat the sentence, 'Goldilocks ran away from the three bears because she thought they might chase her', she says, 'Doedilot when away from berd. Them gonna chate her' (Bishop, 1997).

Some language impairments, however, seem to occur in the absence of such auditory impairment. These impairments arise from a child's inability to acquire the rules of language early (Gopnik, 1997). One example of such a language impairment is the inability to produce the past tense. For example, in the following statement,

'Everyday he walks eight miles. Yesterday he . . '.

Some children would not be able to supply the past tense for 'walk' to complete the second sentence. These problems are seen in children who have normal auditory acuity and non-verbal and psychosocial skills, and, although they may have other difficulties such as dyslexia and depression, none of these factors has been reliably associated with these specific language impairments.

An early, theoretical interpretation of the deficits in SLI suggested that the deficit was one of procedural memory, rather than in language specifically. That is, these individuals experienced problems with the acquisition of skills required for sequencing more generally not those specific to language (Ullman and Pierpont, 2005). A meta-analysis of non-linguistic tasks requiring procedural learning found that SLI was associated with impaired performance on these measures, especially if children were young (Lum *et al.*, 2014). Dyslexic children and also adults with SLI have difficulty in extracting structures from sequences when learning artificial grammars (Pavlidou and Williams, 2014). These studies suggest that individuals with SLIs have problems in learning regularities in sequences of stimuli which are not necessarily linguistic (Krishnan *et al.*, 2016).

Some have suggested that the deficits seen in SLI may involve two types of grammar processing – basic and extended and that extended grammar is the most seriously affected. Extended grammar involves an awareness of the hierarchy of words in sentences and being able to understand this across whole clauses such as 'Who did Baloo give the long carrot to at the farm?' (ven der Lely and Pinker, 2014).

A meta-analysis has found that two regions are implicated in specific learning difficulty – the frontal cortex, including Broca's area and the equivalent area in the right hemisphere, and the caudate nucleus. Others suggest that regions such as the basal ganglia and striatum are implicated and that there is a reduction in some nuclei of the basal ganglia seen in children with SLI (Krishnan *et al.*, 2016). As Krishnan *et al.* acknowledge, some other studies show the opposite pattern (larger volumes, or no differences in adolescents).

Language and genes

Speech and language ability are highly heritable (Graham and Fisher, 2015; Swagerman *et al.*, 2015). Speech and language disorders have been linked to chromosomes 3, 7, 13, 16 and 19. The genes underlying these are not fully identified, but a strong candidate is the FOXP2 gene located on chromosome band 7q31 (Fisher, 2005). Disruption of this gene leads to disruptions in the articulation important for speech and seems to have evolved in the past 200,000 years (Enard *et al.*, 2002). Evidence for the gene-linked disorder was found in a family where three generations were found to suffer from speech impairment. Individuals with the genetic defect also have problems in understanding oral and written language.

It is probably inaccurate to describe FOXP2 as a 'language' gene, however, because it is also involved in other behaviours, not language exclusively. It is also one of many genes associated with reading disorder. Currently, 14 genes have been associated with dyslexia but only four appear to be reliably associated with the disorder – DYX1C1 in DYX1 on chromosome 15q21, DCDC2 and KIAA0319 in DYX2 on chromosome 6p21 and ROBO1 in DYX5 on chromosome 3p12-q12 (Raskind *et al.*, 2013). One gene on chromosome 7q, labelled CNTNAP2, is associated with problems in repeating non-words, and with expressive/receptive language problems more generally (Newbury *et al.*, 2009). The presence of this gene can influence brain activation (more right frontal operculum and middle temporal gyrus activation) in carriers even if the carriers are linguistically unimpaired (Whalley *et al.*, 2011).

A Genome-Wide Association Scan meta-analysis recently reported that reading and language skills were most strongly associated with the genes CCDC135/FLNC and RBFOX2 (Gialluisi *et al.*, 2016). A study using these data as a guide found significant associations between cortical thickness in language areas and the genes most consistently associated with language ability in the earlier analysis (Giallusi *et al.*, 2016). One candidate, rs5995177 was strongly associated with grey-matter thickness in language areas, especially the left posterior parietal gyrus, right medial temporal gyrus and inferior frontal gyrus and bilateral superior temporal gyrus. Language scores were highly correlated with the presence of this gene, but the association became weaker when IQ was taken into account suggesting that it may have a broader role in cognitive ability. What can be concluded from the molecular and genetic data is that language involves many genes and that there is no one gene 'responsible' for language – not surprising given that language itself is multi-factorial (sound, meaning, articulation, reading, and so on).

Dyslexia

The term **dyslexia** refers to a disorder involving impaired reading and it is one of the most common language disorders seen in children and adults. The incidence of the disorder lies between 5 and 17.5 per cent (Shaywitz, 1998). Although boys are thought to be affected more than girls, the evidence is unclear (Flynn and Rahbar, 1994). Many different types of dyslexia have been described but there are two broad categories: acquired dyslexia and developmental dyslexia. Acquired dyslexia describes a reading impairment resulting from brain injury in individuals with previously normal language.

Developmental dyslexia refers to a difficulty in learning to read despite adequate intelligence and appropriate educational opportunity (Brunswick, 2009). The types of dyslexia and their symptoms are described in Table 10.8.

Acquired dyslexia

The major types of dyslexia which result from brain injury are: visual word form dyslexia, phonological dyslexia, surface dyslexia and deep dyslexia. Visual word form dyslexia describes an inability to recognise words immediately but the individual is able to do this gradually with the naming of each letter (Warrington and Shallice, 1980). Sometimes a patient might commit a letter-naming mistake, pronouncing 'c, a, t . . . cat' when the word to be read is 'mat'. The disorder is thought to result from a disconnection between the region of the left hemisphere which mediates the recognition of word forms (Speedie *et al.*, 1982) and the visual input system. Reading ability may rely on the perceptual and visual skills of the right hemisphere.

Phonological dyslexia refers to an inability to read pseudowords and non-words and is relatively rare (although phonological deficits are also seen in developmental dyslexia, described below). Phonological dyslexia provides evidence that whole-word reading and phonological reading involve different brain mechanisms and provides some support for the dual-route model of reading outlined earlier in the chapter (see Figure 10.8). Phonetic reading, which is the only way we can read non-words or words we have not yet learned, entails some sort of letter-to-sound decoding. It also requires more than decoding of the sounds produced by single letters, because, for example, some sounds are transcribed as two-letter sequences

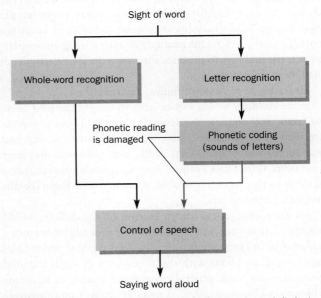

Figure 10.8 A hypothetical explanation of phonological dyslexia. Only whole-word reading remains.

(such as 'th' or 'sh') and the addition of the letter 'e' to the end of a word lengthens an internal vowel ('can' becomes 'cane').

Surface dyslexia is the inability to recognise and read words based on their physical characteristics. Individuals are able to apply the grapheme–phoneme correspondence rules, however (described earlier in the chapter), but have difficulties with irregular words, using inefficient spelling-to-sound strategies (so, 'yacht' is pronounced as it reads and sounds).

Deep dyslexia refers to a severe inability to read; concrete words can sometimes be read but are commonly replaced by semantically related words. For example, a patient would read 'sleep' when the word is 'dream' (Coltheart *et al.*, 1980). Abstract words are rarely pronounced accurately and neither are pronounceable non-words (indicating an inability to apply grapheme–phoneme correspondence rules).

Developmental dyslexia

The symptoms of developmental dyslexia resemble those of acquired dyslexias. Developmental dyslexia first manifests itself in childhood. It tends to occur in families, which suggests the presence of a genetic (and hence biological) component. For example, 33–66 per cent of parents with dyslexia will have children who develop the disorder. The percentage for parents without dyslexia is 6–16 per cent (Torppa *et al.*, 2010; van Bergen *et al.*, 2011). If one or more parents has dyslexia then the child is said to be at 'familial risk' of dyslexia.

A comparison between the reading ability of children of dyslexic parents who developed dyslexia, and children of dyslexic parents who did not develop dyslexia found that the dyslexic children were poor at naming the sounds of words, spelling and reading words and pseudowords (van Bergen *et al.*, 2012). The at-risk group which did not show evidence of dyslexia performed slightly better but were worse than a normal reading control group. Interestingly, the study found that the parents' reading ability, and their ability to name rapidly, were strong predictors of their child's reading status.

Developmental dyslexia is often co-morbid (occurs) with dyscalculia – a severe impairment at performing mathematical exercises despite the absence of intellectual disability (Wilson *et al.*, 2015). Both disorders are characterised by impairment in different types of cognitive task but both have been associated with impairments in verbal short-term memory performance and in accessing lexical information.

One of the principal, if not the most important, features of developmental dyslexia is poor awareness of the phonological features of sound – a process called phonological awareness (Stahl and Murray, 1994). The segmentation of words into sounds, being aware of alliteration, verbal repetition and verbal naming are all impaired in developmental dyslexia. For example, if children are asked to transpose the first sounds of the words 'mustard' and 'salad' (thereby producing 'sustard' and 'malad'), those with developmental dyslexia are unable to do this. Similarly, individuals with developmental dyslexia may be unable to perform phonological tasks such as indicating what is left when you take either the first or the last sound away from a word such as 'mice'. This poor phonological awareness is independent of intelligence. Tanaka *et al.* (2010) found that when phonological processing was studied in high and low IQ children with poor reading ability, similar patterns of reduced brain activation was found in the left posteriotemporal and occipitotemporal parts of the brain (those normally activated by phonological processing).

Developmental dyslexia: possible neuropsychological causes

Visual pathway deficits

Some psychologists have argued that phonological impairments do not explain the persistent and severe nature of dyslexia (Hulme and Roodenrys, 1995). Reading is a complex task that requires phonology, memory and visual perception and there are various theories that attempt to explain developmental dyslexia in terms of dysfunctional neuronal systems in several areas of the brain (Habib, 2000). Stein and his colleagues (Stein, 1991; Stein and Walsh, 1997), for example, suggested that developmental dyslexia is associated with poor visual direction sense, poor binocular convergence (described in Chapter 6), and visual fixation.

Stein's view argues that dyslexics are unable to process fast, incoming sensory information adequately. Most information from the retina to the cortex via the thalamus travels through one of three visual system pathways. One of these systems – the magnocellular (M) pathway – is thought to carry visual information about space, such as movement, depth and the relationships between the positions of stimuli. Some researchers have implicated a malfunctioning M pathway in dyslexia but have had difficulty in explaining why the defective pathway makes reading difficult.

Studies have shown that poor visual fixation, poor tracking from left to right and poor binocular convergence appear to hinder the development of normal reading (Eden *et al.*, 1994). In an fMRI study of developmental dyslexia and the ability to process visual motion, Eden *et al.* (1996) found that moving stimuli (such as dots) failed to activate the cortical area that is projected to by the magnocellular pathway (area V5). In competent readers, this area was activated in both hemispheres during the task. Furthermore, the presentation of stationary patterns did not produce different patterns of brain activation in dyslexic individuals and controls, suggesting that the dyslexic sample had difficulties specifically with attending to moving stimuli.

One hypothesis suggests that the M pathway plays an important role in selective attention. It acts as an attentional spotlight which focuses on important stimuli and ignores all the clutter surrounding these stimuli. Vidyasagar and Pammer (1999) put this hypothesis to the test. They asked 21

Some famous people with dyslexia. According to Agatha Christie, the world's most successful writer: 'I myself, was always recognized . . . as the "slow" one in the family. It was quite true, and I knew it and accepted it. Writing and spelling were always terribly difficult for me. My letters were without originality. I was . . . an extraordinarily bad speller and have remained so until this day'.

reading-impaired children and age-matched normal readers to complete a standard visual search task in which they had to locate a stimulus that was characterised by a combination of colour and form (e.g. looking for a grey triangle in a background of grey circles). The greater the number of distractors in this task, the greater the number of errors made by the reading-impaired group. When there were fewer than 36 distractors, the impaired readers did as well as their age-matched counterparts. When the number increased to 70, a significantly greater number of errors were committed by the impaired reading group, suggesting to the authors that in the dyslexic group visual search mechanisms are compromised when a visual scene is cluttered. Because reading places great demands on the attentional spotlight – which detects the conjunction of

features – an impairment in this process may be explained by deficits in the system that turns on and operates the spotlight.

A challenge was reported in a study which tested this explanation (Stuart *et al.*, 2006). People with developmental dyslexia have an impairment in one of the two visual pathways, the magnocellular pathway, which means that they are not sensitive to rapidly changing stimuli. A deficit in the auditory equivalent means that they have difficulty in segmenting speech, making accurate phonological representations of what they read and making grapheme–phoneme correspondences. Stuart *et al.* measured auditory and visual contrast thresholds in adults with severe reading difficulties. This group showed normal ability to detect visual contrasts (and auditory contrasts). The data undermine the notion that the magnocellular pathway is defective in allowing a person to be sensitive to contrasts. Perhaps, the researchers suggest, the abnormality lies at the level of the interaction between this pathway and the other visual pathway, the parvocellular pathway.

Neural dysfunction

One of the consistent findings in neuroimaging studies of developmental dyslexia is that a decrease in blood flow is seen in temporal and inferior parietal areas, namely the areas involved in letter-to-sound conversion, the analysis of speech sounds and word form recognition (Brunswick *et al.*, 1999; Aylward *et al.*, 2003; Horwitz and Braun, 2004; Hoeft *et al.*, 2006, 2007).

In a meta-analysis of 17 studies of brain activation in dyslexia, Richlan *et al.* (2009) found the following consistent effects: (1) underactivation of the posterior parts of left superior temporal gyrus; (2) underactivation of the supramarginal gyrus; (3) no dysfunction in the angular gyrus; (4) underactivation of the left inferior parietal lobe; (5) dysfunctional activation in the visual word form area; (5) overactivation in the left inferior frontal gyrus, premotor cortex and anterior insula; (6) no anomalies in the right hemisphere and (7) no abnormalities in the cerebellum. The function of the fourth area in dyslexia is unclear and the activation in point five probably reflects additional effort required to read in these participants. The failure to find any differences between typical and impaired readers in the cerebellum is at odds with individual studies which find such differences (see section below).

A slightly different meta-analysis explored differences in brain activation in readers of deep and shallow orthographies (Martin *et al.*, 2016). There were 14 studies of deep orthography (such as English) in dyslexia and 14 of shallow orthography (such as Dutch, German, Italian and Swedish). Across languages, the review found common underactivation in the left occipitotemporal cortex (which included the visual word form area). There was greater underactivation in bilateral inferior parietal regions, the left inferior frontal gyrus, left precuneus and right superior temporal gyrus and over activation in the left inferior insula in deep orthographies.

Some have argued that the degree of timing and progression of cortical activation may underpin reading difficulties, specifically in the parietal, temporal and frontal regions. Rezaie *et al.* (2011) used MEG to study the progression of brain activation in typical readers and children with reading difficulties who had to complete a visual word-recognition exercise. In the impaired group, activation was reduced in both hemispheres in the superior and middle temporal gyri but increased in the rostral middle, frontal and ventral occipitotemporal regions of the brain in both hemispheres. More interestingly, the peaks in the regions occurred simultaneously whereas in the typical group there was a progression of activation.

Some authors have argued that the differences in brain activation seen between individuals with and without reading impairment may be due to the amount and quality of the reading instruction individuals are given (Hoeft *et al.*, 2007). That is, changes seen in left temporo-parietal and occipito-temporal regions later in the individuals life might reflect the poor reading experience they have had rather than representing the cause of the disorder. In their review, Vandermosten *et al.* (2016) found that in children at risk of developing dyslexia, volumes in temporo-parietal regions were different in at-risk readers and in control groups, suggesting that the phonological deficit seen in dyslexic children may stem from this area. Areas involved in auditory process may also be affected in at-risk children.

Structural connectivity may also be an important predictor of reading impairment (and success) (Hosseini *et al.*, 2013; Vandermosten *et al.*, 2015). For example, Schurz *et al.* (2014) found that in a comparison between 14 German children and adolescents with developmental dyslexia and a control group, the dyslexic group showed reduced connectivity between the left posterior temporal areas and the left inferior frontal gyrus during reading tasks and when at rest (performing no task). Some of the reductions were greater for some types of connection that others. However, connectivity was stronger in this group between the reading areas of the brain and the precuneus, part of a default mode network.

One other structural abnormality may be found in developmental dyslexia, in a region called the **planum temporale**, a triangular-shaped area in the Wernicke's aphasia in the left hemisphere. This has been found to be longer in the left in normal readers and but more symmetrical with differences in composition of the area; people with injury to this area show impairments in auditory comprehension and so it is thought to be involved in processing the phonology of language (Bloom *et al.*, 2013). Bloom *et al.* (2013), for example, found that the planum temporale was larger on the right than the left in dyslexic children.

Cerebellar dysfunction

The cerebellum, best understood as the region which contributes to motor function, posture and balance, may also be implicated in developmental dyslexia and other neurodevelopmental disorders such as autistic spectrum conditions and Attention Deficit Hyperactivity Disorder, described in Chapter 12 (Stoodley, 2015). Nicolson *et al.* (1999) found that activation in the cerebellum was significantly lower in dyslexic than normal readers during the execution of familiar and novel motor tasks. The authors suggest that this cerebellar dysfunction affects the learning of new skills and the 'performance of automatic, overlearned skills'. A reduction in the volume of the cerebellum is correlated with poor reading (Eckert *et al.*, 2003), especially in one part called the left lobule V1 (Pernet *et al.*, 2009; Stoodley, 2014). Damage to the anterior cerebellum has been associated with reduced function in other brain regions during silent reading (Fernandez *et al.*, 2016), suggesting that it is used to allow inner speech.

Other studies find that activation is more diffuse in the cerebellum in dyslexic children who generate appropriate verbs to a noun (Baillieux *et al.*, 2009).

Bishop (2002) has argued that the development of the cerebellum depends on the degree of experience a person has with writing: a child with literacy problems is less likely to pick up a pen and use it frequently. Consequently, the cerebellum does not show the same strength of development seen in individuals who have a history of well-practised writing (Bishop, 2002). There is also evidence that dyslexic individuals have difficulty with acquiring information. For example, if participants have to learn sequences but their attention is divided, dyslexic and normal readers are affected by having attention divided (learning is poorer) but the dyslexic group showed a greater delay in skill acquisition (Garbay *et al.*, 2012). Others suggest that the cerebellum's role in procedural learning may explain its involvement in reading. When dyslexic individuals engage with interventions to read better, their improvement correlates with increased volume in the right anterior grey matter of the cerebellum (Stoodley and Stein, 2013).

Dyslexia across languages

Languages with fairly transparent reading systems, such as Italian, are less likely to present readers with difficulties. Paulesu *et al.* (2001) used PET to measure brain activation in French, English and Italian dyslexic participants and their respective control groups. Participants read either bisyllabic words or

Psychology in action: How to help people with developmental dyslexia

How can you help people undertake what most of us take for granted: reading? Individuals with developmental dyslexia have significant impairment in reading and various strategies and interventions have been proposed and created which have aimed to help make reading easier for children and adults. Some focus on the physical appearance of text and its background; others focus on improving the reader's ability to process the sounds of words and letters.

One of the most successful interventions involves phonological training and making participants aware of the sounds of words and letters. Various meta-analyses suggest that this leads to significant improvement in children's reading ability (Duff and Clarke, 2011; Strong *et al.*, 2011), especially when the training also involves encouraging the participants to remember and learn the letters of words. Phonemic awareness training involves training the reader to recognise sounds (phonemes) in words and to manipulate them. Phonics, specifically, asks the reader to focus on the association between a letter and its sound, requiring them to break a word into its component graphemes and phonemes. One novel variation of standard phonological training is based on the assumption that in developmental dyslexia there is a problem with the temporal processing of speech and that this poor processing also extends to music (rhythm). Flaugnacco *et al.* (2015) found that dyslexic children who had received training in music were better at phonological awareness, reading and rhythm after receiving this training.

Some techniques have focused on encouraging reading practice – having the individual read sections of text over and over again (this improves reading fluency). Reading speed and phonological awareness have been found to improve following this type of intervention (O'Brien *et al.*, 2011). Experiments in which people are asked to follow letters as they disappear from screen with increasing speed have found that this technique improves reading fluency (Horowitz-Kraus *et al.*, 2014) in a dyslexic and a control group.

More superficial approaches such as changing the appearance of text have also been found to be effective. For example, Zorzi *et al.* (2012) found that in a sample of 34 Italian and 40 French dyslexic children aged between 8 and 14 years of age, the ability to read improved when the space between letters was increased by 2.5 pt in text on a white sheet of A4 paper – the participants found this text easy to read even without being trained to read in this way. The number of errors the children made in this format was fewer than when reading normally spaced text. The reason for the improvement is that dyslexic children have a problem reading crowded words and letters. It was hypothesised that by spreading them out, reading would improve.

A review of randomised controlled trials of such interventions in developmental dyslexia found 22 studies which included 49 comparisons between an intervention and a control condition (Galuschka *et al.*, 2014). The most common comparison involved phonics instruction (29). Not only was this the most common intervention it was also the one which produced the most consistent and statistically significant effect on reading and spelling performance. All other interventions had less consistent effects.

Bogdanowicz *et al.* (2016) have highlighted a number of strategies which could help readers with developmental dyslexia. For example, they suggest that (based on the literature) early intervention is better than later intervention and that learning in groups of three of four can be as effective as learning one-to-one. Older children can benefit from the training if it is intense. They recommend that readers are taught specific, explicit reading skills and taught these skills intensely: this leads to better outcomes (Duff and Clarke, 2011). They also recommend providing additional academic support to readers to create high levels of motivation.

non-words aloud (an explicit reading task) or as they made decisions about specific physical features of letters in words (an implicit reading task). Activity in the same region in the left hemisphere was reduced in all three dyslexic groups. The region included the left middle, inferior and superior temporal cortex.

A recent study has extended the study of dyslexia in other languages to Chinese. In logographic Chinese, graphic forms (characters) are mapped onto syllables whereas in English, units (letters) are mapped onto phonemes. For this reason, when Chinese people engage in working memory tasks, there is activation in the areas responsible for visuospatial manipulation and the left middle frontal gyrus. There is the reading of complex shapes and characters and pronunciation must be memorised by rote. Earlier studies had associated impaired reading in logographic Chinese with anomalous activation in the left middle frontal gyrus (Siok *et al.*, 2004). In a follow-up study, Siok *et al.* (2008) found reduced activation in the same area in people identified as dyslexic in Chinese. This finding is important because it suggests that the brain regions implicated in dyslexia depend on whether the language is alphabetic (e.g. English, Italian and so on) or non-alphabetic (see Figure 10.9).

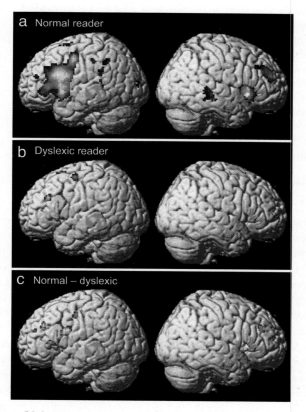

Figure 10.9 Brain regions showing significant activation in dyslexic and normal readers during a rhyme judgement task.

Source: Siok, W.T., Niu, Z., Jin, Z., Perfetti, C.A. and Tan, L.H. A structural–functional basis for dyslexia in the cortex of Chinese readers. *Proceedings of the National Academy of Sciences*, 2008, 105 (14), 5561-6.

In a study of monolingual Chinese and English dyslexic participants who completed a word-matching task (in which two words or pictures had to be matched at either a superficial or a semantic level), Hu *et al.* (2010) found that less activation was found in the left angular gyrus and left middle frontal, posterior temporal and occipitotemporal regions of the brain, using fMRI. This reduction was found in English and Chinese dyslexic participants, although the normal readers showed differences in activation between each other.

In normal Chinese readers, there was increased activation in the left inferior frontal sulcus; in the English readers, there was increased activation in the posterior STS. These findings suggest that the neural activation seen in the dyslexic group was culturally independent – the decrease occurred in both cultures.

Language in healthy individuals: neuroimaging and other studies

Neuroimaging studies of language in individuals without brain injury generally conclude that the left hemisphere participates in language-related tasks more actively than does the right hemisphere and that specific regions of the left hemisphere are involved in the different components of language such as speech production, comprehension, processing of sound, meaning, and so on (Brunswick, 2004). However, the left hemisphere does not have an exclusive role in language: the right hemisphere also plays an important role in some aspects of language processing.

The earliest confirmation of the involvement of the classical language areas in healthy individuals was made by Petersen *et al.* (1988). This study was the first neuroimaging (PET) investigation of language processing in healthy individuals. It found that the left posterior temporal cortex (including the primary auditory cortex and Wernicke's area) was significantly more active during passive listening of words than during a control condition. Repeating the nouns activated the primary motor cortex and Broca's area.

When people are asked to think of verbs that are appropriate to use with nouns, even more intense activity is seen in Broca's area. Price *et al.* (1994) have also reported that greater activation in the left inferior and middle frontal cortices was found during performance of a lexical decision task whereas more temporal regions were activated during reading aloud and reading silently. Hope *et al.* (2014) found that areas involved in the motor execution of speech –regardless of semantic content or phonological features – included the supplementary motor area, anterior cingulate, areas around the ventral insula and putamen, and cerebellum. This study also found speech-specific regions in the frontal operculum/left anterior insula. There is a dorsal area near the frontal operculum involved in silent and overt speech production and a ventral area that is active during speech production.

Cutting edge: Harry Potter's other contribution to the English language

JK Rowling's Harry Potter books are the most successful and popular book series in history. Over 500 million copies of the books have been sold, more than *Fifty Shades*, the *Mr Men* and *Twilight* put together. In addition to the role of the books in helping excite and inspire children's reading, they have recently taken on an additional role of helping some psychologists understand the neural basis of reading in the brain.

For example, Hsu *et al.* (2015) asked 23 German speakers to read selections of texts from the Harry Potter series which differed in content: some described magical events, some did not. There were at least 20 passages of each type presented and were matched for word type, word frequency, imageability and so on. fMRI was employed to measure brain activation during the two types of text. Participants found the magical passages to be more surprising and pleasurable than the control passages. When brain activation was compared, more activation was found in bilateral inferior frontal gyri, bilateral inferior parietal lobule, left fusiform gyrus and left amygdala during the reading of magical passages.

A slightly different approach was taken by Wehbe *et al.* (2014). Using a technique called computational modelling, they trained software to predict neural activation in fMRI based on the input of text. The text used was *Harry Potter and the Sorcerer's Stone*. The study found that occipital lobe activation was predicted by word length; left temporo-parietal regions and the right temporal regions predicted parts of speech, punctuation, and grammar (syntax). The involvement of the right temporal area is unusual and may reflect the number of syntactic features and structure studied (46). Semantic information predicted activation in the left superior and middle temporal gyri and the left inferior temporal gyrus, plus the right middle temporal region. Text referring to a character's motion predicted activity in the posterior temporal cortex and angular gyrus (regions that respond to visual movement); dialogue predicted activation in bilateral temporal and inferior frontal cortices, plus the right temporo-parietal junction; character identity predicted activation in the right posterior and middle temporal cortex. The network shown to be involved in different aspects of text comprehension is consistent with a model published by Fedorenko *et al.* (2012).

On the subject of words, but not Harry Potter specifically, a group of researchers has sought to examine the areas of the brain that are recruited in individuals who are expert wordsmiths (Protzner *et al.*, 2015). Competitive Scrabble players consistently outperform typical readers in lexical decision tasks. In these tasks, people decide as quickly as they can whether stimuli are words or non-words (Hargreaves *et al.*, 2012). Protzner *et al.* found that when 12 Scrabble experts and 12 non-experts completed a lexical decision task as fMRI measured activation, the expert group didn't recruit areas typically found when people recognised words but recruited areas involved in working memory (superior parietal cortex) and visual perception (visual cortex, fusiform gyrus), suggesting that Scrabble experts pay less attention to meaning and more to word form. There were areas of common activation between groups: the left inferior frontal gyrus was activated more by non-words than words, for example, reflecting the greater difficulty involved in determining whether a non-word is a word. The researchers also found that different types of activation at rest were associated with anagram performance in both groups: the network was more widespread in the Scrabble group; they showed connections in the frontal, temporal, parietal and limbic areas.

The degree of lateralisation does not seem to depend on the difficulty of the task the person is undertaking. Badcock *et al.* (2012) asked participants to generate words, provide a word given an auditory definition and listen to a story while looking at pictures. Blood flow was measured in the left and right middle cerebral arteries. All the tasks produced more blood flow on the left but difficult versions of the word and naming task did not generate greater lateralisation.

Regions of the brain involved in processing speech sounds

An important aspect of language analysis is, as you saw earlier in the chapter, phonological processing – the putting together of sounds to make meaningful words. Data from brain injury and from studies of cellular activity, localise the processing of sounds, specifically vowels, in the medial frontal region of the brain and non-language sounds in the superior temporal gyrus (Tankus *et al.*, 2012). Neuroimaging studies have found that when individuals discriminate between spoken words on the basis of phonetic structure, when they discriminate between consonants and when they make judgements about rhyme or engage in phonological memory tasks, activation in the left frontal cortex near Broca's area is found (Fiez *et al.*, 1995; Paulesu *et al.*, 1996; Zatorre *et al.*, 1996).

Other studies report involvement of the temporal cortex and angular gyrus especially during tasks involving drawing analogies, repeating words and in reading words and pseudowords (Nobre *et al.*, 1994; Karbe *et al.*, 1998). A region called Heschl's gyrus, and the posterior superior temporal gyrus, has been found to be more active during the processing of syllables than clicks (Nourski, 2014) and seems to be the region of the brain (together with regions around it) which discriminates between speech and non-speech sounds.

Cutting edge: The men who lost their accents

There are rare case studies in the neuropsychology language of individuals who behave in a very unusual way: they start speaking spontaneously in a previously unlearned second language (e.g. Beschin *et al.*, 2016). Imagine your friend, Anastasia from London, for example, waking up one morning, calling you up on her phone and saying: 'Если мир приглашает Вас на танец, доктор, всегда делайте движение ему на встречу', despite previously not having spoken a word of Russian. It would be strange.

But such cases exist. There are also cases of people developing foreign accents after brain injury. Berthier *et al.* (2015) report a case study of three individuals who presented with an unusual symptom: they lost their accents. One, patient

JF, was 18 years old and had developed a brain abscess in the left sensorimotor cortex, insula and basal ganglia. He came from Corrientes, a region of Argentina, and was a monolingual Spanish speaker Two weeks following his operation his speech was fluent but he spoke with a Japanese-type accent. This receded after a few days, leaving him with a flat accent. Both other cases were Spanish speakers with brain injury resulting in Broca's aphasia. Patients showed very slow speech, incorporated very long pauses and expressed monotone intonation. The phonetic features unique to their accents were lost, suggesting that injury to the middle left motor cortex can impair the production of regional accents.

This evidence suggests that Broca's area and the frontal cortex are necessary for the phonetic manipulation of language but that the posterior temporal cortex is responsible for the perceptual analysis of speech (Zatorre *et al.*, 1996). However, the picture may be a little more complex. Binder *et al.* (1997) compared the analysis involved in the phonetic and semantic perception of aurally presented words with the analysis of non-linguistic stimuli such as tones. A large network of left-hemisphere regions was activated during the semantic analysis, including areas in the frontal, temporal and parietal cortex. Activation, therefore, was not limited to one specific region.

A study by Hope *et al.* (2014) compared activation in regions of the brain during the auditory repetition of words and during rest. They found that phonological input activated the left superior temporal sulcus and left posterior putamen. During speech production, activation was found in the left ventral premotor cortex and left anterior putamen. Higher left posterior putamen activation has also been found when people read and repeat words compared with pseudowords (Oberhuber *et al.*, 2013), suggesting a role for this region in well-learned movement. Hope *et al.* interpret their finding of anterior putamen activation during speech production as reflecting the initiation of novel sequences of movement (compared with the well-learned movements mediated by the posterior part).

Damasio *et al.* (1996), in a comprehensive study of its kind, evaluated the effects of language processing in individuals with brain lesions in both hemispheres, inside and outside the temporal regions. Damasio *et al.* hypothesised that there is no single mediating site for all words, but there are separate regions within a larger network that are activated by different kinds of word. There were three categories of words: persons, non-unique animals and non-unique tools, each of which should be processed by different parts of the frontal and temporal lobe. Although 97 individuals showed normal language,

30 did not; 29 of these had brain injury to the left hemisphere. While impaired retrieval of words was associated with temporal cortex damage, abnormal retrieval of animal words was found in patients with left interior temporal lobe damage and abnormal retrieval of tools was associated with posterolateral inferior temporal cortex damage.

Because we cannot infer normal function from brain damage, Damasio *et al.* conducted a second experiment in which healthy individuals performed the same language tasks while undergoing a PET scan. Although all words activated the left temporal cortex, specific categories were associated with activation of specific regions of the brain. Naming of tools activated the posterior, middle and inferior temporal gyri, for example, and animal naming activated other parts of the inferior temporal cortex. These results are similar to those of Martin *et al.* (1996), which showed that different categories of words appeared to activate different parts of the brain. A recent study has even suggested that silently naming the use of tools activates Broca's area and the left premotor and supplementary motor area (Grafton *et al.*, 1997). This suggests that even the naming of a tool's use can activate those parts of the brain that would be activated during the actual movement involved in using those tools.

Regions of the brain involved in semantic processing

The anterior and medial temporal lobe appears to be more involved than others in processing the meaning of speech and language. Hope *et al.* (2014), for example, found that the left posterior middle temporal gyrus was activated when people listened to semantic content of language. However, there is a network of brain areas involved in understanding the meaning of language – including the temporal and parietal cortices and the inferior frontal region. Some regions are thought to store or represent lexical semantic information and to be involved in sentence processing – the angular gyrus and the supramarginal gyrus, for example (Friederici and Singer, 2015). The retrieval and manipulation of semantic information appears to be undertaken by the inferior frontal lobe – especially, the pars triangularis and orbitalis. All of these regions are connected by bands of white matter/fibre and the role of this connective tissue in language is important and returned to below.

There is significant overlap between neuroimaging and lesion studies in what they reveal about localisation of language processes. However, in neuroimaging experiments, it is unclear whether the activation in specific regions is necessary for the aspects of language processing studied. According to Price et al. (2003), one method of determining the necessity of these areas is to examine lesion data and investigate whether lesions to different areas are associated with different deficits.

Price et al. used fMRI to study two patients with acquired dyslexia. One patient had damage to all of the left temporal regions that are usually activated during normal reading. He was able to read some highly imageable words but was unable to read pseudowords and made meaning errors when reading others (saying 'wrong' when trying to read the word 'error'). The pattern is consistent with deficits seen in deep or phonological dyslexia and suggests that he relies on semantics when translating written words into sounds. The second patient also showed left temporal lobe damage but the lesion did not affect the superior temporal lobe (but did affect the inferior and anterior region). She could read regular words and most pseudowords but had greater difficulty in reading irregularly spelled words, a pattern typical of surface dyslexia. She had difficulty in reading words that required semantic processing, suggesting that the areas damaged might be important for semantic processing.

The first patient was asked to read highly imageable words during scanning; the second was asked to read one of a triad of regular three-letter words. For example, the word BUS would appear under two identical words. The first patient showed activation in all the language areas one would expect to be activated during normal reading, except for the area damaged. The second patient activated all the typical language areas but showed a reduction in areas associated with semantic processing. On the basis of these single-case studies, Price et al. suggest that translating written words to sounds is mediated by the left mid-fusiform gyrus in the temporal cortex. But, when semantic processing is impaired, the posterior part of this region and left frontal areas tries to undertake the function of translating the written word into phonology via semantics.

Regions of the brain involved in reading and syntax

The parts of the brain that are more active during the application of the rules of language include a network of regions spanning the frontal and temporal cortex, particularly, the left inferior frontal gyrus and left posterior superior temporal gyrus and sulcus (Friederici and Singer, 2015). Sentence processing is thought to recruit the left BA44 and working memory systems in the left inferior frontal sulcus, which are connected by white matter.

In terms of reading, you saw in the developmental dyslexia section above that some brain areas are more implicated than others in reading impairment. Martin et al.'s (2015) meta-analysis of 20 fMRI studies of reading in adults (23–34 years) and 20 fMRI studies with children (7–12 years) found that areas of common activation included the left ventral occipito-temporal, inferior temporal, posterior parietal regions and bilaterally in the supplementary motor areas. Activation in the cerebellum was found in adults but not in children, suggesting a developmental role for this structure in reading.

People with visual word form dyslexia are unable to recognise the form of words presented visually. Studies with healthy individuals have localised the ability to identify visual letter strings as words – visual word form – in the left fusiform gyrus. Consequently, this area has been known as the visual word form area (Warrington and Shallice, 1980) because it responds to the visual, rather than auditory, forms of words (Giraud and Price, 2001). Heim et al. (2005) found that Broca's area and a region nearby (areas BA 44 and 45) were more active during the reading of pseudowords than words. If the task involved lexical decision making and phonological decision-making, BA 44 was activated by pseudowords and words; BA45 was activated only in the lexical decision-making task suggesting that there are two routes which mediate different types of linguistic data: the left BA44 is involved in grapheme-phoneme conversion; the left BA45 is involved in lexical searches.

Neuroimaging studies show that the fusiform gyrus is active during the perception of word and word-like forms but it is less active during the perception of strings of letters that are unfamiliar such as consonant-string non-words (Buchel et al., 1998). Polk and Farah (2002) found that the left ventral visual cortex was active during the recognition of pseudowords and words presented in normal case. Graves et al. (2010) suggested that this visual word form area also mediated word frequency effects – that is, it responds to classes of words that are either high or low frequency. They found increased activation in the inferior frontal gyrus, both sides of the anterior insula, the supplementary motor area and the left temporal lobe areas that were in or near the visual word form area. Activation here, they say, is evidence for whole-word processing whereas activation in the inferior frontal gyrus is evidence of this region's role in phonological processing.

A meta-analysis of neuroimaging studies which examined the brain's response when processing nouns and verbs found 32 clusters of activation (Crepaldi et al., 2013). Twenty-seven of the areas were not specific to grammatical class. Of those that were, three were associated with noun processing across different tasks and these were the right inferior temporal gyrus, the left angular gyrus and the left inferior parietal gyrus. One area was involved in verb processing (right posterior middle temporal gyrus) and three areas were selectively responsive to nouns in some tasks and verbs in others (left and right inferior frontal gyrus and left insula). The analysis is illuminating because it localises verb processing mainly in the right, not left hemisphere and suggests that a network of related and nearby areas mediate the two types of language processing.

Regions of the brain involved in signing

There are significant similarities between the regions of the brain involved in typical language and in specialised language systems such as sign language. In the first brain imaging study of the perception of British Sign Language (BSL), nine hearing and nine congenitally deaf individuals had their brain activity measured by fMRI during the perception of sentences presented in BSL (MacSweeney et al., 2002). An analogous auditory task in English was completed by hearing individuals. Regardless of the modality of communication, there was activation in Broca's area and in Wernicke's area – both bilaterally – during the language perception tasks. However, differences did emerge between tasks in temporal and occipital areas. The auditory task in hearing individuals was associated with increased activity in the auditory cortices. This activation was not found during BSL. BSL, on the other hand, was associated with activity in an area called V5 at the junction of the temporal and occipital cortex. V5 is the region of the visual cortex which responds to movement and so activation here is consistent with what we know of the neurology of visual perception.

When hearing and deaf people's responses to BSL were explored, however, deaf signers showed greater activation in the left superior temporal cortex than did hearing signers. This result is intriguing because it suggests that the auditory cortex of the temporal lobe is active during an auditory language task in hearing individuals but that it may respond to visual input in congenitally deaf individuals.

This part of the temporal lobe has been described as a multi-modal language area (Buchel et al., 1998) because it can be activated by language processed in different modalities. The MacSweeney study indicated that this was so for sign language. Buchel et al. observed a similar phenomenon when studying blind participants reading Braille. When people engaged in tactile reading, the posterior left temporal area (Area 37) was active. Buchel et al. proposed that this area in blind, Braille-reading participants promotes activity in other parts of the brain that allows participants access to words. However, this area was active only during written word recognition, not spoken word recognition.

Regions of the brain involved in writing

Unlike speech perception or production, writing, is a more complex language function. It involves intention, vision, cognition, phonology, semantic processing and motor behaviour (if the writing is meaningful). Planton et al. (2013) identified 12 different areas in the brain that distinguished between writing and non-language related motor acts. Two of the areas identified – the graphemic/motor frontal area and the left superior parietal cortex – have been consistently associated with writing. Damage to these areas produces a disorder known as pure agraphia – an inability to write.

To explore the results of this study further, Planton et al. (2016) used fMRI to determine the areas of the brain which showed activation when people wrote down the name of an object they saw, spelled out loud the name of an object in a picture or reproduced the object in a drawing. Of five writing areas in the brain they investigated, drawing activated them all, and some were activated by orally spelling. The only part to show writing-specific lateralisation was the graphemic/frontal motor area. This was also bilaterally activated by the drawing task.

Neuropsychological models of language

A review of neuropsychological models of language by Shalom and Poeppel (2008) suggested that four competing and plausible frameworks explain the role of the brain in speech production and comprehension.

1 Price's (2000) model. This is a descendant of the Broca–Wernicke–Lichtheim model embodied in the aphasia sections. The Broca–Wernicke–Lichtheim model is an umbrella term used to describe the way in which the brain organises language comprehension and production, and is named after three neuropsychological figures. Price's model suggests that acoustic analysis occurs in the superior temporal cortex, visual analysis in the posterior inferior frontal cortex and temporal cortex, and semantic representation in a network of frontal and temporal regions. She suggests that there are two routes to retrieving the sounds and sights of words – a non-semantic route (posterior superior temporal cortex) and a semantic route (via posterior/inferior temporal cortex). Speech planning is governed by the anterior part of Broca's area and actual output is the responsibility of the motor cortex. The emphasis in Price's model is on semantic processing.

2 Friederici's (2002) model. This model makes two claims. The first is that the temporal lobe is responsible for semantic identification (such as the retrieval of memorised semantic information) and the frontal lobe constructs semantic relationships. The second is that the structure of syntax is built before semantic processing occurs and that these two interact later on in the processing stream.

3 Hickok and Poeppel's (2004) model. This utilises the distinction drawn in visual processing between the ventral and the dorsal streams (see Chapter 6 and also in the dyslexia section). They propose a visual and an auditory stream. The visual stream has two substreams, one (ventral) projecting to the temporal lobe and which is responsible for visual object recognition (the 'what') and a dorsal one projecting to the parietal and frontal lobes, which are involved in the visual representations of spatial attributes of language (the 'where'). The auditory stream is analagously conceptualised in the same way. The model, however, has little to say about the role of Broca's area.

4 Indefrey and Levelt's (2004) model. This proposes that Wernicke's area is involved in lexical analysis and in the representation of words but the posterior middle temporal lobe is involved in the phonological aspects of retrieval. It sees word production as involving five main types of representation (from appreciating the idea that a stimulus is lexical, to the breakdown of phonological output into syllables to production) each of which is processed at different times (from 175 ms after stimulus onset to 600 ms).

Although each says something slightly different about language processing and how it occurs in the brain, there are similarities between them. They suggest that:

* memorisation (learning and retrieval) occurs in the temporal lobe;

* analysis occurs in the parietal lobe;
* synthesising (creating combinations of representations) occurs in the frontal lobe;

and that:

* the inferior parietal lobe, inferior frontal lobe and the whole of the temporal lobe are involved in phonological processing;
* the middle areas are involved in syntactic processing;
* inferior areas are involved in semantic processing.

Recent conceptions of language and the brain have moved away from a single pathway model (called the 'dorsal stream') to a more distributed model including a dorsal and a ventral stream (Axer *et al.*, 2012; Bornkessel-Schlesewsky *et al.*, 2013;

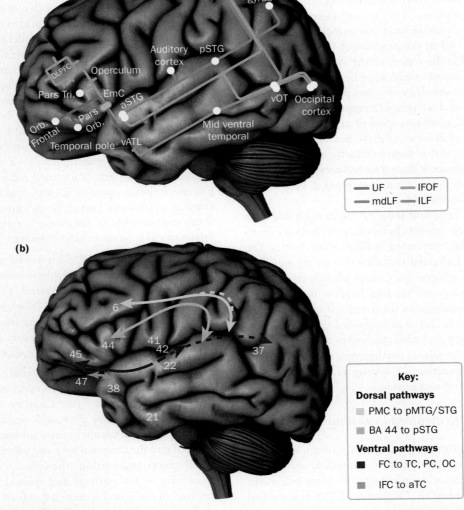

Figure 10.10 (a) The ventral pathway of the brain involved in language, here represented as a tube map. **(b)** The fibres and connections of this pathway are seen explicitly in.

2015; Hickok and Poeppel, 2004), as suggested by Friederici and Hickok and Poeppel. You can see this model illustrated in Figure 10.10a and b.

In this dual-route model, the dorsal stream is responsible for phonological processing and the ventral stream is responsible for semantic processing. These streams are thought to recruit tracts of white matter fibre which connect various regions of the language processing areas (Bajada *et al.*, 2015; Dick and Tremblay, 2012).

The ventral stream, for example, is thought to recruit regions in all four lobes connected by a band of fibre which progresses through the temporal lobe (Duffau *et al.*, 2013). The comprehension of speech might rely on pathways from the primary auditory cortex along this ventral stream. The temporal lobe includes the uncinate fasiculus, the inferior fronto-occipital fasciculus (IFOF), the middle longitudinal fasciculus and the inferior longitudinal fasciculus, two of which (the first and last) have been implicated in language over centuries. The uncinate, for example, first described in 1809, is short and hook-shaped and links the superior temporal pole, anterior entorhinal and perirhinal regions with the lateral parts of the frontal lobe. The uncinate overlaps at one point with the IFOF and may represent one large bundle at a certain point in the brain (Bajada *et al.*, 2015). It has been associated with semantic processing –some research finds that damage impairs semantic processing – but its exact role is unclear (other studies find no semantic impairment).

The dorsal stream is represented by connections between the temporal lobe and the frontal lobe (via the arcuate fasciculus), although some dispute this connection (see Dick and Temblay, 2012). It is thought that this stream is not fully developed until seven years of age (Friederici, 2012). An analysis of 165 people who had suffered a unilateral left hemisphere stroke found that two anatomical routes were affected – a dorsal stream involving the frontal and parietal cortex and a ventral stream involving the temporal and frontal cortex (Fridriksson *et al.*, 2017). Performance on language tests in people with the two types of cortical impairment found that the dorsal route represented a person's ability to articulate a word from its form and the ventral route represented a person's ability to extract meaning from a word. See Figure 10.11 for an illustration of these connections.

Sex differences

Early neuroimaging studies showed greater left hemisphere activation in men when completing language tasks but a more symmetrical pattern of activation in women (Pugh *et al.*, 1996), but the literature is mixed. Knuas *et al.* (2004), for example, found greater leftward asymmetry in the planum temporale in women whereas Sommer *et al.*'s (2004) meta-analysis of 14 functional imaging studies comprising 377 men and 442 women found no evidence for a sex difference in brain

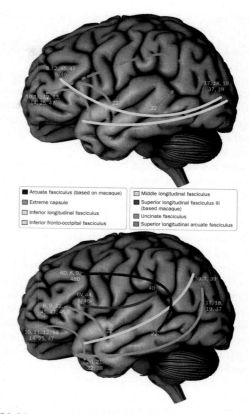

Figure 10.11 Some of the connections between brain areas (that are considered to be important to the processing of language). The numbers represent Brodman's areas, a system of dividing the brain according to its cellular structure and arrangement. The top image is based on data from imaging and post-mortem studies and suggests that there are five dissociable pathways. The bottom figure is based on an analysis of the architecture of the macaque monkey brain and suggests more diffuse connectivity.

activity during language processing. The most recent review has found no differences in proficiency between the sexes: there is an early advantage for girls but this disappears into adulthood (Wallentin, 2009). There is no consistent difference in brain activation or structure.

Language and the right hemisphere

The right side of the brain is not neglected in language. It takes on especial importance when the left hemisphere is damaged and may compensate for the language function lost after such damage. It is involved in the appreciation of metaphors (Bottini *et al.*, 1994) and in the processing of prosody and the affective tone of speech (Pell and Baum, 1997), although the data on metaphors are not consistent. Forgacs *et al.* (2014), for example, found that processing conventional, literal and novel metaphors was faster in the left hemisphere.

Neuropsychology and language – An international perspective

Deep orthographies such as those found in English and French are a minefield of rules and linguistic irregularities. In English, there are 1,120 ways of using graphemes (letters and strings of letters) to form 40 sounds (phonemes). Italian, on the other hand, has 33 graphemes representing 25 phonemes. When psychologists talk about the localisation of language, it is easy to forget that language is not a standard, unitary process but is heavily culture-bound. English, Russian and French, for example, all have different orthographical and phonological rules. Some authors have suggested that this explains the differences in word reading speed in English and Italian individuals (Italians are faster).

Around half of the world speaks more than one language (Grosjean, 2010) and there is evidence to suggest that each language shares common brain regions but also recruits regions specific to each (Costello, 2014). A meta-analysis of behavioural lateralisation studies (e.g. dichotic listening, visual field studies) of bilingualism has found differences between early and late bilinguals (Hull and Vaid, 2007). Early bilinguals (who acquired both languages before the age of 6) showed evidence of bilateral language representation; late bilinguals (who acquired language after the age of 6) showed greater left hemisphere dominance. In this second group, left hemisphere dominance was greater if participants were not proficient at the second language and if the second language was English. Current data from various sources suggest that multilingual individuals have separate regions in the brain which mediate each language (Kin *et al.*, 2013; Centeno *et al.*, 2014) but that this representation depends on when the language was acquired, the level of proficiency in the non-primary language, the degree of people's exposure to spoken language and the similarity of the languages people speak (Tu *et al.*, 2015).

Neuroimaging studies suggest that there is more left hemisphere involvement in language by bilingual individuals and that similar cortical areas may be recruited during the processing of both languages. A study of French and English speakers, for example, found that performing language tasks in both languages was associated with activity in the left inferior frontal cortex (Klein *et al.*, 1995). Another study found that there was activation in different parts of Broca's area when people performed language tasks using a language learned in adulthood, but this activation was absent in those who had learned the language in childhood (Kim *et al.*, 1997). There was no difference in activation in Wernicke's area.

Some researchers have argued that such differences might reflect participants' proficiency in using language rather than the age at which the second language was acquired (Perani *et al.*, 1998). If there is an overlap in the language areas that mediate both tongues, this may be due to the similarity of the two languages spoken. Most studies, for example, have studied bilinguals who speak Indo-European languages (English, French, Italian and so on). Perani *et al.* (1996) compared brain activation in Italian–English speakers, where English was learned later in life, and Spanish–Catalan speakers, where Catalan was learned concomitantly with Spanish. Focal activity in the left hemisphere language regions was determined by expertise and not age of acquisition, a finding that has been replicated (Dehaene *et al.*, 1997; Chee *et al.*, 1999). Would the same overlap be seen if the two languages spoken were different in terms of syntax (meaning and grammar), morphology (physical construction of the language) and phonology (the sound of the language)? ▷

To answer this question, Klein *et al.* (1999) measured cerebral blood flow in seven native speakers of Chinese (Mandarin) who had acquired English during adolescence. Mandarin uses pitch and tone to a greater extent than does English. The participants' task was to repeat words in Mandarin and English and to generate a verb in response to a noun in Mandarin and English. All words were presented auditorily and participants were asked to respond vocally. Klein *et al.* (1999) found that an area in the left frontal cortex was activated during speech production in Mandarin and English. A similar area was found to be active during French and English language processing in a previous study of Klein *et al.*'s (1995). Such findings can even extend to speakers of four or more languages.

Breillman *et al.* (2004), for example, used fMRI to measure the response of six quadrilingual participants who were asked to generate appropriate verbs to nouns; if the word 'fish' was presented, the participant might respond with 'swim'. Participants had knowledge of four to five common languages (English, German, Italian, French or Spanish) and completed the verbal task in each of their languages. As previous studies would predict, the task was associated with left-sided activation but, curiously, this activation was more pronounced in the languages in which participants were least proficient. This suggests that when people speak languages in which they are proficient the brain expends less energy – the process is more automatic and requires fewer cognitive resources for this reason. If people are not proficient in a language, there has to be a greater attempt at producing and understanding that language; this, in turn, recruits greater neural resources in order for the process to succeed.

One case study of a person who could speak four languages proficiently but developed a frontal brain tumour ▷

Neuropsychology and language – *Conitnued*

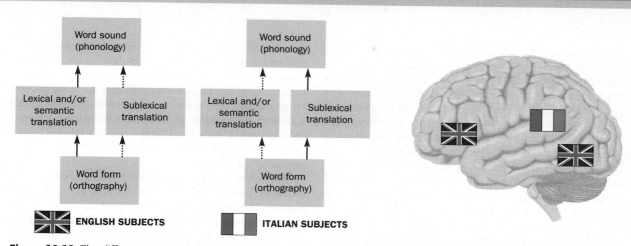

Figure 10.12 The different strategies used by English and Italian speakers are reflected in different types of brain activation.

Source: Fiez, J., Sound and meaning: How native language affects reading strategies. *Nature Neuroscience*, 2000, 3 (1), 3–5, reprinted by permission of the author and Nature Publishing Group.

found that the organisation of each of the four languages was a little different (Polczynska *et al.*, 2016). The patient had acquired her second language at 5 and the third and fourth at 15. The study found that a common set of brain regions involved in language was involved in the processing of all four languages (25 per cent) but that each language also recruited its own area within the language areas. The language acquired earliest was most impaired (and had a more bilateral representation in the brain), whereas the most recently learned languages were the most spared. Similarity of languages had no effect on language impairment. The data are consistent with studies finding that there are separate language areas responsible for the first and second language learned (Centeno *et al.*, 2014).

In the first study to observe cultural effects on language-related brain function in healthy individuals, Paulesu *et al.* (2000) asked six English and six Italian university students either to read aloud words and non-words (experiment 1) or to perform a feature detection task (experiment 2) which involved paying attention to physical aspects of words presented visually rather than to the words themselves. They were not asked to read the words in experiment 2. The authors found that, across both experiments, the Italian speakers showed greater activation in those areas responsible for processing phonemes (left temporal regions) whereas the English speakers showed greater activation in other areas of the temporal cortex and frontal cortex (areas activated during word retrieval and naming). The areas activated can be seen in Figure 10.12.

The result is in keeping with studies of aphasia patients among different ethnic Chinese groups. Yu-Huan *et al.* (1990), for example, have reported that unilateral stroke leads to greater incidence of aphasia in dextrals with right-sided lesions (crossed aphasia) but only among the majority ethnic group called the Han. Crossed aphasia is rare among the minority ethnic group (the Uighur-Kazaks) and Wernicke's aphasia is generally rare in the Han. One explanation for this dissociation may lie in the way in which the languages of the groups differ: the Uighur-Kazak language is Indo-European-based and phonological in nature; the Han language, conversely, is non-phonetic ('ideographical') where one sound can have multiple meanings.

A similar distinction is found in Japanese. Phonetic-based symbols (Kana) and logographic symbols (Kanji) are used routinely in written Japanese. Left-sided lesions are associated with impaired Kana reading in Japanese participants but preserved Kanji reading (Sasanuma, 1975). When healthy individuals are exposed to the different symbols in a typical visual field experiment, a left visual field advantage for Kanji is reported, suggesting right hemisphere involvement (Elman *et al.*, 1981).

Cutting edge: What happens in the brain during second language (vocabulary) learning?

A study by Yang *et al.* (2015) asked 39 native English speakers with no knowledge of Chinese or any tonal language to learn 48 tonal pseudowords in Chinese over a period of six weeks. Participants had 18 training sessions across this period. A control group did not receive any word training. fMRI was used to measure brain activation before the training and after. Behavioural (performance) measures were taken at these times, too. These took the form of three sound discrimination tasks – making same/difference tone judgements about pairs of words; making the same judgement about the beginning of words; and deciding whether the pitch of tones were different or the same.

The learners showed greater activation in the posterior middle temporal gyrus and angular gyrus (BA39) in both hemispheres during the sound discrimination tasks at post-test, compared with non-learners, suggesting that the experimental group was processing tonal information in a lexical and semantic way but the control group responded to tonal information acoustically, hence its greater activation in the left superior temporal gyrus (BA22). When learners were divided into successful and less successful language learners (based on their vocabulary learning), the successful group performed better all sound discrimination tasks, apart from pitch.

In terms of overall differences between learners and non-learners, the former showed decreased activation in the bilateral medial, middle and inferior frontal gyri, supplementary motor areas, anterior cingulate cortex, insula, left posterior superior temporal gyrus, and middle temporal gyri post-training. The result is expected because as we get better at language tasks our proficiency is reflected in less brain activation in relevant areas. The successful learners activated different areas at post-training – the left middle frontal gyrus, superior temporal gyrus, fusiform gyrus, precuneus, cerebellum and putamen.

When the researchers looked at the connections between brain areas in successful and less successful learners, they found significant differences.

Connections between the inferior frontal gyrus, medial frontal gyrus and superior temporal gyrus were stronger in the successful group pre-training suggesting that this network assisted in the successful learning of the vocabulary task. During tone discrimination at post-test, the successful learners showed direct connections between brain regions such as between superior temporal gyrus and medial frontal gyrus, and inferior parietal lobe and medial frontal gyrus suggesting that its brain network is efficient and flexible. The unsuccessful group lacked the automatic connection between the IPL and MFG during the tone discrimination task.

Handedness

Handedness refers to the degree to which individuals preferentially use one hand for certain activities (such as writing, unscrewing a jar, throwing a ball). It can also refer to the strength of hand skill. It is found in a variety of species and in most primates (from old/new world monkeys to great apes). Evidence of handedness or laterality goes back two million years; we seem to be the most lateralised of the primates. The right–left hand ratio in chimps is 2:1; in humans, it is 9:1 (Hopkins and Cantaloupo, 2008).

Handedness may be relevant to language because left – and right-handers may have speech localised in different hemispheres. According to a pioneering study by Rasmussen and Milner (1977), 96 per cent of right-handers and 70 per cent of left-handers in their study had left-hemisphere speech. Other, recent estimates place the figures at 95.3 per cent and 61.4 per cent, respectively (Segalowitz and Bryden, 1983). There are more men who are left-handers than women (Papadatou-Pastou *et al.*, 2008), possibly due to an X-linked allele.

The degree of activation in the right hemisphere during a word-generation task increases with the left-handedness of the participant (Knecht *et al.*, 2000a, b). Some psychologists have argued that human language evolved from gesture and that these gestures are 'behavioural fossils' accompanying speech. Corballis (1999), for example, argues that the proposition that language is gestural in origin might explain the relationship between handedness and cerebral asymmetry for language (of which, more later). Right-handers primarily gesture with their right hand (which may not be surprising), but left-handers (who have primarily left-hemisphere-based speech but show a more diverse pattern of localisation with some having speech in both hemispheres, or the right hemisphere) gesture with both hands.

Verbal and non-verbal communication

Verbal communication is accompanied by a smorgasbord of non-verbal cues that are richly communicative (DePaulo and Friedman, 1998). **Non-verbal communication** provides information about feelings and intentions (e.g. non-verbal cues are often reliable indicators of whether someone likes you). It also can be used to regulate interactions (non-verbal cues can signal the approaching end of an utterance, or that someone else wishes to speak), to express intimacy (touching and mutual eye contact), to establish dominance or control (non-verbal threats) and to facilitate goal attainment (e.g. pointing).

When we communicate with each other we tend to mimic not just each other's language and linguistic characteristics but also non-verbal behaviour. When dating we tend to use similar words to people we like in conversation (Ireland *et al.*, 2011). Our postures may align, our speech rate aligns, our speech rhythms, intonation, accent and facial expressions similarly may align (Healey *et al.*, 2014). The reason for this is that shared language and non-verbal behaviour is likely to improve cooperation and enhance social interaction; it increases people's liking for each other. When people are asked to mimic someone else's accent, for example, they rate the speaker of that accent as being more socially attractive than do those who had not imitated the accent (Adank *et al.*, 2013). People seem to imitate spontaneously low vowels (/a/) and imitate high vowels (/i o u/) less (Babel, 2011).

There is an idea in social psychology and psycholinguistics called structural priming which describes the matching of language by one or two members of a conversing dyad; the idea argues that when we hear other people's conversation, their language primes us to use the same language. Some aspects of language appear to be not as well perceived as others. People's awareness of the syntax they use, for example, is poor as is their awareness of whether their syntax matches the person they are talking to. One study found that people's syntax actually became less similar to each other's in everyday conversation (Healey *et al.*, 2014) so imitation does have its limits.

People tend to have less control over non-verbal than verbal communication, and people are often unaware that they are sending or receiving non-verbal cues. Non-verbal sensitivity improves with age, is more advanced among successful people, and is compromised among people with various psychopathologies. Are men or women better interpreters of body language? Sokolov *et al.* (2011) asked men and women to identify the emotion expressed in point-light displays of figures who knocked on a door. Women were more accurate in recognising anger in body posture but men were better at recognising happiness. When no emotion was expressed in the door-knocker, women were more accurate in identifying this neutral expression. Why should men be more accurate in identifying happiness, given that women are thought to be sensitive to positive emotion?

The authors cite research showing that men produce greater brain activation to positive stimuli and are more sensitive to subtle expressions of happiness in faces and actions. They also note that the men in their study were young, of high social status and were well-educated and were, therefore, more sensitive to positive stimuli.

Because the eyes are often considered to be the windows of the soul, eye contact, now technically called **gaze**, communicates an enormous amount of information (Kleinke, 1986). For example, people gaze more at people they like, and lower-status people gaze more at higher-status people than vice versa except when a higher-status person wants to exert control over a lower-status person. Because white adults tend to gaze more when listening than when speaking, a speaker who increases gaze signals that they are about to stop speaking, and a listener who reduces gaze indicates that they are about to start speaking.

Touch appears to result in some significant and demonstrable changes in behaviour. We know that a light touch on a person's arm inclines them to spare small change to someone requesting it: 51 per cent will do so compared with the 29 per cent not touched (Kleinke, 1977). Touching another person significantly enhances their willingness to complete surveys, sign petitions or look after a large dog for 10 minutes – more people are willing to do so when touched (Willis and Hamm, 1980; Hornik, 1987; Gueguen, 2002; Gueguen and Fischer-Lokou, 2002). Touching also enhances person perception – librarians who touched students lightly were rated more favourably and tutors doing the same to their students were regarded as more patient and understanding (Steward and Lupfer, 1987).

Waiters and waitresses are judged more favourably if they lightly touch their patrons (Hornick, 1992). They, and bar staff, are also more likely to receive higher tips (Crusco and Wetzel, 1984; Guegen and Jacob, 2005). Studies have also shown that people are more likely to try new food in a supermarket, and taste and buy more, when touched by staff (Smith *et al.*, 1982;

Hornick, 1992). One study of US patrons found that if they were touched by a waitress when ordering a drink, their consumption increased (Kaufman and Mahoney, 1999). Similarly, Gueguen *et al.* (2007) found that patrons in a medium-sized French restaurant who were recommended a dish, were more likely to order the dish when they were touched. If the waiter complimented the patron on his/her choice of meal, this was associated with more generous tip-giving (Seiter, 2007).

Finally, how close people position themselves relative to other people, **interpersonal distance**, communicates intimacy and liking. Hall (1966) has identified four interpersonal distance zones: intimate (up to 0.50 m), personal (0.5–1.25 m), social (1.25–4 m) and public (4–8 m). Clearly, if you want to become intimate with someone you will stand close, and if that person would rather not be that intimate they will move away.

Chapter review

Speech and comprehension

- Language can be defined as an orderly system of communication that involves the understanding or interpretation of vocal or written symbols.
- Phonemes are the basic elements of speech but research has also shown that the primary unit of analysis is not individual phonemes but groups of phonemes, perhaps syllables.
- Recognition of words in continuous speech is far superior to the ability to recognise them when they have been isolated. We use contextual information in recognising what we hear.
- Meaning is a joint function of syntax and semantics. All users of a particular language observe syntactical rules that establish the relations of the words in a sentence to one another. These rules are not learned explicitly. People can learn to apply rules of an artificial grammar without being able to say just what these rules are.
- The most important features that we use to understand syntax are word order, word class, function words, affixes, word meanings and prosody. Content words refer to objects, actions and the characteristics of objects and actions, and thus can express meaning even in some sentences having ambiguous syntax.

- Chomsky has suggested that speech production entails the transformation of deep structure (ideas, thoughts) into surface structure (actual sentence).
- Speech errors, although incorrect, follow syntactical rules; the errors lie in the content of the speech.

Reading

- Recognition of written words (reading) is a complex perceptual task which involves scanning text, perceiving and understanding symbols and sounding out these visual symbols.
- The eye-tracking device allows researchers to study people's eye movements and fixations and to learn from these behaviours some important facts about the nature of the reading process. For example, we analyse a sentence word by word as we read it, taking longer to move on from long words or unusual ones.
- Once a word has been perceived, recognition of its pronunciation and meaning takes place. Long or unfamiliar words are sounded out, that is, they are read phonologically by a process called phonic mediation.
- Short, familiar words are recognised as wholes. In fact, only whole-word reading will enable us to know how to pronounce words such as 'cow' and 'blow', or 'bone' and 'one', which have irregular spellings.

- The dual-route model of reading suggests that we have two routes for reading: one which does not rely on grapheme–phoneme correspondence rules and another which does.

Language acquisition by children

- Studies using the habituation of a baby's sucking response have shown that the human auditory system is capable of discriminating among speech sounds soon after birth.
- Human vocalisation begins with crying, then develops into cooing and babbling, and finally results in patterned speech. During the two-word stage, children begin to combine words creatively, saying things they have never heard.
- Child-directed speech is very different from that directed towards adults; it is simpler, clearer and generally refers to items and events in the present environment. As young children gain more experience with the world and with the speech of adults and older children, their vocabulary grows and they learn to use adult rules of grammar.
- Children seem to pay less attention to phonetic detail of language as they grow older, presumably because the process of acquiring vocabulary and understanding of objects and situations is computationally complex.
- Although the first verbs children learn tend to have irregular past tenses, once they learn the regular past tense rule (add '-ed'), they apply this rule even to irregular verbs they previously used correctly.
- A language acquisition device contains universal grammatical rules and motivates language acquisition. Although children's verbal performance can be described by complex rules, it is possible that simpler rules – which children could reasonably be expected to learn – can also be devised.
- Deliberate reinforcement is not necessary for language learning, but a controversy exists about just how important child-directed behaviour is.

- A critical period for language learning may exist which occurs between the ages of 5 and 14 years old; learning a new language after this is more difficult.
- Bilingualism refers to competence in two or more languages that are used to communicate with significant others. The languages activate similar brain areas, regardless of age of acquisition.
- Studies of other primates suggest that apes can be taught at least some of the rudiments of language.

Brain development and language

- Damage to either hemisphere is associated with better recovery of language when it occurs in childhood than adulthood.
- Some researchers have suggested that the lateralisation of language – left hemisphere dominance for language processing – is complete by around age 6; others argue that it continues until puberty.
- The ability of the brain to reorganise itself following injury in infancy and childhood, together with its ongoing development, is referred to as its plasticity.
- Children who have experienced surgical removal of an entire hemisphere, for medical reasons, do not experience significant impairments in function later in life.
- The ability of the child's brain to recover better than that of the adult's has been attributed to the ongoing development of lateralisation as well as the capacity of the right hemisphere to undertake the role of the language functions if disrupted.

Neuropsychology of language and language disorders

- The effects of brain damage suggest that memories of the sounds of words are located in Wernicke's area and that memories of the muscular movements needed to produce them are located in Broca's area.

- Wernicke's area is necessary for speech perception and Broca's area is necessary for its production.
- Wernicke's aphasia (caused by damage that extends beyond the boundaries of Wernicke's area) is characterised by fluent but meaningless speech that is lacking in content words but rich in function words.
- Broca's aphasia (caused by damage that extends beyond the boundaries of Broca's area) is characterised by non-fluent but meaningful speech that is lacking in function words but rich in content words.
- Damage to the temporoparietal region surrounding Wernicke's area produces isolation aphasia – loss of the ability to produce meaningful speech or to comprehend the speech of others but retention of the ability to repeat speech.
- Dyslexia refers to an inability to read. There are two general types: acquired and developmental.
- Acquired dyslexia refers to reading disorders arising from brain injury and there are various types of dyslexia that result from brain injury such as deep dyslexia, phonological dyslexia and visual word form dyslexia. Although some regions of the brain are known to be involved in these disorders, their exact neural basis is unknown.
- Developmental dyslexia refers to a disorder of reading that occurs without brain injury and manifests itself in delayed reading development. Phonological processing (the ability to break down words into sounds and appreciate how they relate to each other) is severely impaired in developmental dyslexia.
- No one knows the exact causes of developmental dyslexia. Theories include delayed or disorganised left hemisphere development, an impairment in the function of the magnocellular pathway, a dysfunctional cerebellum, an inability to scan text efficiently and neuronal degeneration in the temporal cortex.
- Models of language function and the brain now suggest that there are two streams involved – a dorsal stream which processes the phonology of language and a ventral stream which processes meaning in language
- Neuroimaging studies of language production and comprehension suggest that no one brain region is involved in language processing. Instead, there is a complex mosaic of regions which contributes to language and which interacts in a way which we only partially understand.
- Evidence suggests that Broca's area and the frontal cortex is necessary for the phonetic manipulation of speech but that the temporal cortex is necessary for the perceptual analysis of speech.
- The language areas of men and women are differently activated, with more bilateral activation in women, but the evidence is inconsistent.
- Handedness also interacts with degree of language proficiency, but in slightly irregular ways. Most right- and left-handers have left-hemisphere speech.

Non-verbal communication

- Speech is accompanied by non-verbal cues that are particularly important for communicating feelings and relationships, and for regulating conversation.
- Some of the most important non-verbal channels are gaze, facial expression, postures, gestures, touch and interpersonal distance.

Suggestions for further reading

Aitchison, J. (2011) *The Articulate Mammal*. London: Routledge.

Deriziotis, P., & Fisher, S. E. (2017). Speech and language: Translating the genome. *Trends in Genetics*, 33(9), 642–656.

Fisher, S.E. (2016) Evolution of language: Lessons from the genome. *Psychonomic Bulletin and Review*.

Fitch, W.T. (2017).Empirical approaches to the study of language evolution. *Psychonomic Bulletin and Review*.

Harley, T.A. (2012) *The Psychology of Language* (4th edn). Hove: Psychology Press.

Hartwigsen, G., & Saur, D. (2018). Neuroimaging of stroke recovery from aphasia–Insights into plasticity of the human language network. *NeuroImage, in press*.

Krishnan, S., Watkins, K.E. and Bishop, D.V.M. (2016) Neurobiological basis of language learning difficulties. *Trends in Cognitive Sciences*, 20(9), 701–714.

Lions, C., Bui-Quoc, E., Seassau, M., & Bucci, M. P. (2013). Binocular Coordination of Saccades During Reading In Strabismic ChildrenReading in Strabismic Children. *Investigative ophthalmology & visual science*, 54(1), 620-628.

Norton, E.S., Beach, S.D. and Gabrieli, J.D.E. (2015) Neurobiology of dyslexia. *Current Opinion in Neurobiology*, 73-8.

Price, C.J. (2012) A review and synthesis of the first 20 years of PET and fMRI studies of heard speech, spoken language and reading. *Neuroimage*, 62, 816–47.

Seidenberg, M.S. (2013) The science of reading and its educational implications. *Language Learning and Development*, 9, 4, 331–60.

Stone, M. (2016). A history of speech production research. *Acoustics Today*, 12, 48–55.

CHAPTER 11
Intelligence and thinking

I regarded finding that I had a form of Alzheimer's as an insult, and I decided to do my best to marshal any kind of forces that I could against this wretched disease. I have posterior cortical atrophy or PCA. They say, rather ingenuously, that if you have Alzheimer's it's the best form of Alzheimer's to have. This is a moot point, but what it does do, while gradually robbing you of your memory, visual acuity and other things you didn't know you had until you miss them, is leave you more or less fluent and coherent as you have always been.

It was my typing and spelling that convinced me that the diagnosis was right. They had gone haywire. Other problems I put down to my looming 60th birthday. I thought no one else had noticed the fumbling with seat belts and the several attempts to get clothing on properly, but my wife and PA were worrying. I have written 47 novels in the past 25 years, but now I have to check even quite simple words – they just blank on me, at random. I would not dare to write this without the once despised checker, and you would have your work cut out to read it, believe me.'

Sir Terry Pratchett

https://www.theguardian.com/books/2015/mar/15/a-butt-of-my-own-jokes-terry-pratchett-on-the-disease-that-finally-claimed-him

WHAT YOU SHOULD BE ABLE TO DO AFTER READING CHAPTER 11

- Describe the ways in which intelligence has been defined.
- Understand the principles of intelligence testing.
- Describe the various types of reasoning.
- Evaluate the contribution of heredity and environment to intelligence.
- Be aware of and describe individual differences in intelligence.
- Describe and understand the effects of ageing on cognitive ability.
- Define and give examples of inductive and deductive reasoning.
- Appreciate the biases in human reasoning and why they occur.

QUESTIONS TO THINK ABOUT

- What is intelligence?
- How can intelligence be measured?
- Is it useful to invoke the concept of intelligence?
- Is there more than one 'intelligence'?
- Is there a difference between 'clever' and 'intelligent'?
- What factors contribute to the development of intelligence?
- Is intelligence heritable? Which is more important to intelligence – genes or environment? Is this a sensible question to ask?
- What are the effects of ageing on functions such as language and remembering?
- What is dementia and are there different types of dementia with different symptoms?
- What causes dementia?
- How do we reason and are there effective and ineffective ways of reasoning?
- In which ways can our reasoning be irrational?
- Why do we sometimes violate various logical rules?
- What is creativity? Can we measure and facilitate creativity experimentally?

What is intelligence?

In general, if people do well academically or succeed at tasks that involve their heads rather than their hands, we consider them to be intelligent. If a politician makes a useful policy decision, we call it an intelligent decision. If an author writes an erudite book on an arcane subject, we might describe him as having written an intelligent appraisal. But if asked to give a precise definition of intelligence, psychologists – in common with non-scientists – come slightly unstuck. Sternberg and Detterman (1986) asked a dozen theorists to provide definitions of intelligence and received a dozen different descriptions. According to one of psychology's historians, writing in the 1920s, intelligence has come to represent whatever intelligence tests measure (Boring, 1923).

In general, however, psychologists agree that the term intelligence describes a person's ability to learn and remember information, to recognise concepts and their relations, and to apply the information to their own behaviour in an adaptive way (Neisser *et al.*, 1996a). Where they diverge is in describing the nature of intelligence and how it works. For example, some psychologists argue that there is a general factor called intelligence but no different subtypes of intelligence; others argue intelligence is a series of abilities; yet others adopt a combinative approach arguing that there is general intelligence but there are also specific abilities. The number of these abilities depends on the theory one examines.

Theories of intelligence

Most theories of intelligence are based on the analysis of performance on tests that seek to measure specific abilities such as non-verbal and verbal intellectual competence. Much of the debate in the psychology of intelligence has focused on whether there is a single intelligence or there are multiple intelligences. Is our intellectual ability a unitary factor or is it made up of a number of different abilities? Are these abilities, if they do exist, completely separate from each other or are they related?

Intelligence tests yield a single number, usually called an IQ score, although this does not itself mean that intelligence is a single, general characteristic. Some investigators have suggested that certain intellectual abilities are completely independent of one another. For example, a person can be excellent at spatial reasoning but poor at solving verbal analogies. But psychologists disagree over whether specific abilities are totally independent or whether one general factor influences all abilities. The next sections consider some influential theories of intelligence.

Spearman's two-factor theory

Charles Spearman (1927) proposed that an individual's performance on a test of intellectual ability is determined by two factors: the g factor, which is a general factor, and the s factor, which is a factor specific to a particular test. Spearman did not call his g factor 'intelligence'; he considered the term too vague. He defined the g factor as comprising three 'qualitative principles of cognition': apprehension of experience, eduction of relations and eduction of correlates. A common task on tests of intellectual abilities – solving analogies – requires all three principles (Sternberg, 1985). For example, consider the following analogy:

LAWYER:CLIENT:DOCTOR: ___

This problem should be read as 'LAWYER is to CLIENT as DOCTOR is to ___'.

Apprehension of experience refers to people's ability to perceive and understand what they experience; thus, reading and understanding each of the words in the analogy requires apprehension of experience. Eduction (not 'education') is the process of drawing or bringing out, that is, making sense of, given facts. In this case, eduction of relations refers to the ability to perceive the relation between lawyer and client; namely, that the lawyer works for and is paid by the client. Eduction of correlates refers to the ability to apply a rule inferred from one case to a similar case. Thus, the person whom a doctor works for and is ultimately paid by is obviously a patient. Because analogy problems require all three of Spearman's principles of cognition, he advocated their use in intelligence testing.

Empirical evidence for Spearman's two-factor theory comes from correlations among various tests of particular intellectual abilities. The governing logic is as follows. If we administer 10 different tests of intellectual abilities to a group of people and each test measures a separate, independent ability, the scores these people make on any one test will be unrelated to their scores on any other; the correlations among the tests will be approximately zero. However, if the tests measure abilities that are simply different manifestations of a single trait, the scores will be related; the intercorrelations will be close to 1.

In fact, the intercorrelations among a group of tests of intellectual abilities are neither zero nor 1. Instead, most of these tests are at least moderately correlated, so that a person who scores well on a vocabulary test also tends to score better than average on other tests, such as arithmetic or spatial reasoning. The correlations among various tests of intellectual ability usually range from 0.3 to 0.7, which means that they have between 9 per cent and 49 per cent of their variability in common (Ozer, 1985).

Spearman concluded that a general factor (g) accounted for the moderate correlations among different tests of ability. Thus, a person's score on a particular test depends on two things: the person's specific ability (s) on the particular test (such as spatial reasoning) and their level of the g factor, or general reasoning ability.

Evidence from factor analysis

Factor analysis is a statistical procedure developed by Spearman and Pearson that permits investigators to identify common factors among groups of tests. It is a form of data reduction in the sense that a large number of data can be reduced and explained by reference to two or three factors (Kline, 1993) and is widely used in research that administers questionnaire measures. In the case of intelligence tests, these common factors would be particular abilities that affect people's performance on more than one test. If a group of people take several different tests of intellectual ability and each person's scores on several of these tests correlate well with one another, the tests may (at least partly) be measuring the same factor. A factor analysis determines which sets of tests form groups. For example, Birren and Morrison (1961) administered the Wechsler Adult Intelligence Scale (WAIS, an intelligence test described in the next section) to 933 people. This test consists of 11 different subtests. Birren and Morrison calculated the correlations between subtests and then subjected these correlations to a factor analysis. Table 11.1 shows the results of the analysis.

The factor analysis revealed three factors, labelled A, B and C. The numbers in the three columns in the table are called factor loadings; they are somewhat like **correlation coefficients**

Table 11.1 Three factors derived by factor analysis of scores on WAIS subtests

Subtest	Factors		
	A	B	C
Information	0.70	0.18	0.25
Comprehension	0.63	0.12	0.24
Arithmetic	0.38	0.35	0.28
Similarities	0.57	0.12	0.27
Digit span	0.16	0.84	0.13
Vocabulary	0.84	0.16	0.18
Digit symbol	0.24	0.22	0.29
Picture completion	0.41	0.15	0.53
Block design	0.20	0.14	0.73
Picture arrangement	0.35	0.18	0.41
Object assembly	0.16	0.06	0.59

Source: Adapted from Morrison, D.F. (1967) *Multivariate Statistical Methods*, New York: McGraw-Hill.

in that they express the degree to which a particular test is related to a particular factor. For the various subtests on factor A, the largest factor loading is for vocabulary, followed by information, comprehension and similarities. In the middle range are picture completion, arithmetic, picture arrangement and digit symbol. Digit span, object assembly and block design are the smallest. Verbal subtests make the most important contribution to factor A, so we might be tempted to call this factor verbal ability. But almost all tests make at least a moderate contribution, so perhaps this factor may reflect general intelligence. Digit span has a heavy loading on factor B (0.84), and arithmetic and digit symbol have moderate loadings. Factor B, therefore, is related to maintaining information in short-term memory and manipulating numbers. Factor C appears to be determined mainly by block design, object assembly, picture completion and picture arrangement, and might, therefore, represent the factor, spatial ability.

Although factor analysis can give hints about the nature of intelligence, it cannot provide definitive answers. The names given to factors are determined by the investigator and, although the names may appear to be quite appropriate, the process inevitably has a subjective element to it. There is also the danger of reification when conducting factor analysis. That is, the factors may wrongly be seen as concrete entities and not simply as labels used to describe a set of data as concisely and accurately as possible. Furthermore, factor analysis can never be more meaningful than the individual tests on which it is performed. To identify the relevant factors in human intelligence, one must include an extensive variety of tests in the factor analysis. The WAIS, for example, does not contain a test of musical ability. If it did, a factor analysis would undoubtedly yield an additional factor. Whether musical ability is a component of intelligence depends on how we decide to define intelligence; this question cannot be answered by a factor analysis.

Other psychologists employed factor analysis to determine the nature of intelligence. Thurstone's study (1938) of students' performance on a battery of 56 tests extracted seven factors, which he labelled verbal comprehension, verbal fluency, number, spatial visualisation, memory, reasoning and perceptual speed. At first, Thurstone thought that his results contradicted Spearman's hypothesised g factor. However, Eysenck suggested a few years later that a second factor analysis could be performed on Thurstone's factors. If the analysis found one common factor, then Spearman's g factor would receive support. In other words, if Thurstone's seven factors themselves had a second-order factor in common, this factor might be conceived of as general intelligence.

Cattell performed a second-order factor analysis and found not one but two major factors. Horn and Cattell (1966) called these factors fluid intelligence (gf) and crystallised intelligence (gc). Fluid intelligence is reflected by performance on relatively culture-free tasks, such as those that measure the ability to see relations among objects or the ability to see patterns in a repeating series of items. Crystallised intelligence is defined by tasks that require people to have already acquired information, such as vocabulary and semantic information, and is therefore more culture-bound. Cattell regards fluid intelligence as closely related to a person's native capacity for intellectual performance; in other words, it represents a potential ability to learn and solve problems. In contrast, he regards crystallised intelligence as what a person has accomplished through the use of their fluid intelligence – what they have learned. Horn (1978) disagrees with Cattell by citing evidence suggesting that both factors are learned but are also based on heredity. He says that gf is based on casual learning and gc is based on cultural, school-type learning.

Figure 11.1 shows examples from four of the subtests that load heavily on fluid intelligence.

Tests that load heavily on the crystallised intelligence factor include word analogies and tests of vocabulary, general information and use of language. According to Cattell, gc depends on gf. Fluid intelligence supplies the native ability, whereas experience with language and exposure to books, school and other learning opportunities develop crystallised intelligence. If two people have the same experiences, the one with the greater fluid intelligence will develop the greater crystallised intelligence. However, a person with a high fluid intelligence exposed to an intellectually impoverished environment will develop a poor or mediocre crystallised intelligence. Table 11.2 presents a summary of tests that load on g_f and g_c.

No two investigators agree about the nature of intelligence. However, most believe that a small number of common factors account for at least part of a person's performance on intellectual tasks. The current view of g and its contribution to sub-factors of intelligence can be seen in Figure 11.2.

Sternberg's triarchic theory of intelligence

Sternberg (1985) has devised a theory of intelligence that derives from the information-processing approach used by many cognitive psychologists. Sternberg's theory has three parts; he calls it a triarchic theory (meaning 'ruled by three'). The three parts of the theory deal with three aspects of intelligence: componential intelligence, experiential intelligence and contextual intelligence. Taken together, these three

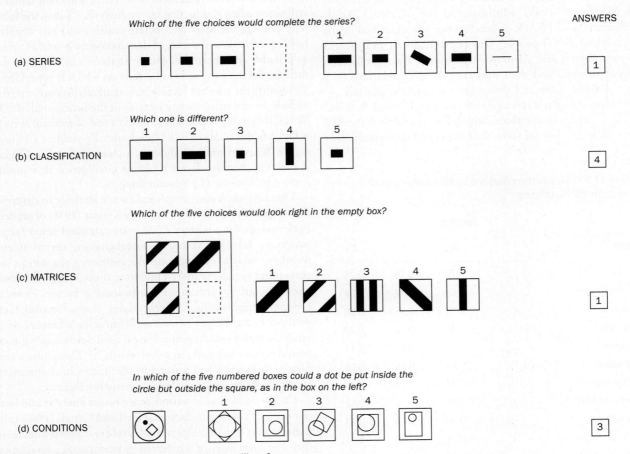

Figure 11.1 Four tests that correlate well with Cattell's g_f factor.

Source: from *Technical Supplement for the Culture Fair Intelligence Tests, Scales 2 and 3*, Institute for Personality and Ability Testing (Cattell, R.B., Krug, S.E., Barton, K. 1973), by permission of Hogrefe Ltd. © 2008 Hogrefe Ltd., Oxford, www.hogrefe.co.uk. All rights reserved.

Table 11.2 Summary of tests with large factor loadings on g_f or g_c

Test	Approximate factor loadings	
	g_f	g_c
Figural relations: Deduction of a relation when this is shown among common figures	0.57	0.01
Memory span: Reproduction of several numbers or letters presented briefly	0.50	0.00
Induction: Deduction of a correlate from relations shown in a series of letters, numbers, or figures, as in a letter series test	0.41	0.06
General reasoning: Solving problems of area, rate, finance, and the like, as in an arithmetic reasoning test	0.31	0.34
Semantic relations: Deduction of a relation when this is shown among words, as in an analogies test	0.37	0.43
Formal reasoning: Arriving at a conclusion in accordance with a formal reasoning process, as in a syllogistic reasoning test	0.31	0.41
Number facility: Quick and accurate use of arithmetical operations such as addition, subtraction and multiplication	0.21	0.29
Experimental evaluation: Solving problems involving protocol and requiring diplomacy, as in a social relations test	0.08	0.43
Verbal comprehension: Advanced understanding of language, as measured in a vocabulary reading test	0.08	0.68

Source: Adapted from Horn, J.L., Organization of abilities and the development of intelligence. *Psychological Review*, 1968, 75, 249. © 1968 by the American Psychological Association. Adapted by permission.

components go beyond the abilities measured by most common tests of intelligence. They include practical aspects of behaviour that enable a person to adapt successfully to their environment. Table 11.3 provides a summary of the key concepts of Sternberg's triarchic theory.

Componential intelligence consists of the mental mechanisms people use to plan and execute tasks. The components revealed by the factor analyses of verbal ability and deductive reasoning are facets of componential intelligence. Sternberg suggests that the components of intelligence serve three functions. Meta-components (transcending components) are the processes by which people decide the nature of an intellectual problem, select

a strategy for solving it and allocate their resources. For example, good readers vary the amount of time they spend on a passage according to how much information they need to extract from it (Sternberg, 1985). This decision is controlled by a meta-component of intelligence. Performance components are the processes actually used to perform the task, for example, word recognition and working memory. Knowledge acquisition components are those the person uses to gain new knowledge by sifting out relevant information and integrating it with what they already know.

The second part of Sternberg's theory deals with experiential intelligence. **Experiential intelligence** is the ability to deal

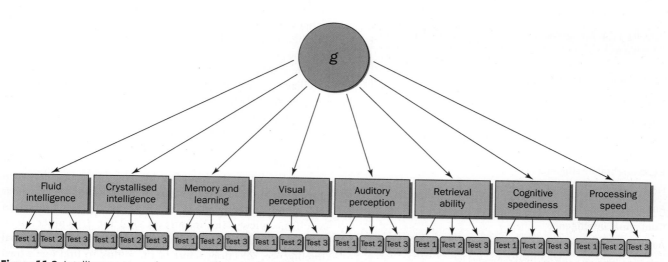

Figure 11.2 Intelligence researchers generally agree that all intellectual ability is underpinned by a general (*g*) intelligence. This contributes to other, specific abilities (which may be developed to a lesser or a greater extent depending on various factors such as education, interest, genes and environment).

Cutting edge: Hobbies and cognitive ability

If you've ever applied for a job and submitted a CV, you've probably included a section in it highlighting your exciting personal interests and hobbies. You may wonder whether those interests in on-line gambling and glamping exert any significant effect on your employment prospects. A meta-analysis of vocational interests and cognitive ability suggests that it does: specifically, on the perception of your intellectual strength (Passler *et al.*, 2015).

Passler *et al.* examined 27 studies including 55,297 participants. They used Holland's (1997) taxonomy of personal interests to divide people's hobbies into categories. This taxonomy divides interests into six types: the Realistic type prefers working with tools, machines or outdoors; the Investigative type prefers sciences; the Artistic type prefers expressive activities such as writing or performing; the Social type prefers working with people; the Enterprising type prefers leading and persuading others; and the Conventional type prefers working with data.

Passler *et al.* found that the types were associated with different cognitive abilities:

Realistic types had greater mechanical knowledge and spatial ability:

Investigative types had high *g*, numerical and inductive ability scores and greater spatial and verbal ability;

Artistic types scored highly on verbal scales;

Social types showed poorer mechanical knowledge;

Social and Enterprising types had poorer verbal ability.

The strongest positive effects were found for the Realistic, Investigative and Artistic types; the weakest or the most negative effects were found for Enterprising and Social types. The latter might be explained, the authors suggest, by Armstrong *et al.*'s (2011) proposition that there are no good cognitive tests that can be used to predict the abilities required for working with others and that environments in which interpersonal relations are important may not necessarily require strong cognitive ability.

effectively with novel situations and to solve automatically problems that have been previously encountered. According to Sternberg's theory, a person with good experiential intelligence is able to deal more effectively with novel situations than is a person with poor experiential intelligence. The person is better able to analyse the situation and to bring mental resources to bear on the problem, even if they have never encountered one like it before. After encountering a particular type of problem several

times, the person with good experiential intelligence is also able to 'automate' the procedure so that similar problems can be solved without much thought, freeing mental resources for other work. A person who has to reason out the solution to a problem every time it occurs will be left behind by people who can give the answer quickly and automatically. Sternberg suggests that this distinction is closely related to the distinction between fluid and crystallised intelligence (Horn and Cattell, 1966). According to Sternberg, tasks that use fluid intelligence are those that demand novel approaches, whereas tasks that use crystallised intelligence are those that demand mental processes that have become automatic.

The third part of Sternberg's theory deals with **contextual intelligence** – intelligence reflecting the behaviours that were subject to natural selection in our evolutionary history. Contextual intelligence takes three forms: adaptation, selection and shaping. The first form, adaptation, consists of fitting oneself into one's environment by developing useful skills and behaviours. In different cultures, adaptation will take different forms. For example, knowing how to distinguish between poisonous and edible plants is an important skill for a member of a hunter–gatherer tribe. Knowing how to present oneself in a job interview is an important skill for a member of an industrialised society. The second form of contextual intelligence, selection, refers to the ability to find one's own niche in the environment. That is, individuals will decide on careers or activities which they both enjoy doing and do well.

Table 11.3 An outline of Sternberg's triarchic theory of intelligence

Componential intelligence

Meta components (e.g. planning)

Performance components (e.g. lexical access)

Knowledge acquisition components (e.g. ability to acquire vocabulary words)

Experimental intelligence

Novel tasks

Automated tasks

Contextual intelligence

Adaptation (adapting to the environment)

Selection (finding a suitable environment)

Shaping (changing the environment)

The third form of contextual intelligence is shaping. Adapting to the environment or selecting a new one may not always be possible or profitable. In such cases, intelligent behaviour consists of shaping the environment itself. For example, a person whose talents are not appreciated by their employer may decide to start their own business.

Gardner's multiple intelligences theory

Gardner's theory of intelligence is based on a neuropsychological analysis of human abilities (Gardner, 1983). It argues that intelligence falls into seven categories: linguistic intelligence, musical intelligence, logical/mathematical intelligence, spatial intelligence, bodily/kinesthetic intelligence and two types of personal intelligence. Bodily/kinesthetic intelligence includes the types of skill that athletes, typists, dancers or mime artists exhibit. Personal intelligence includes awareness of one's own feelings (intrapersonal intelligence) and the ability to notice individual differences in other people and to respond appropriately to them – in other words, to be socially aware (interpersonal intelligence).

Three of Gardner's types of intelligence – verbal intelligence, logical/mathematical intelligence and spatial intelligence – are not unusual, having been identified previously by many other researchers. The other four are rather unusual. According to Gardner, all seven abilities are well represented in the brain, in that specific brain damage can impair some of them but leave others relatively intact. For example, people with damage to the left parietal lobe can show apraxia, an inability to perform sequences of voluntary skilled movements. In contrast, people with damage to the right parietal lobe develop spatial neglect (see Chapter 6). Individuals with frontal lobe damage, as you will see in Chapter 13, have difficulty evaluating the significance of social situations and making decisions about social matters (the frontal lobes used to be regarded as the region of the brain responsible for intelligence). These examples illustrate bodily/kinesthetic intelligence and both intrapersonal and interpersonal intelligence.

Process overlap theory

A recent theory which has attempted to explain why people who perform well on some tests of cognitive ability also perform well on others suggests that cognitive tests depend on executive processes such as working memory that are domain-general, and other processes that are domain-specific (Kovacs and Conway, 2016). As executive processes are required across a variety of different cognitive tasks, they are recruited more often than domain-specific ones. This is called **process overlap theory** – because these processes overlap – and is an attempt at explaining the positive manifold discovered by Spearman (1904), one of the most consistently replicated findings in psychology. The positive manifold refers to the phenomenon whereby variables are positively correlated.

Spearman, as you read above, discovered that scores on some cognitive tests (e.g. arithmetic) correlated with others (e.g. mental rotation) and this correlation was explained with reference to a general intelligence factor: a latent variable that explained the underlying correlation between different types of abilities. It explains around 40 per cent of the variance in performance of a wide ranges of cognitive tests (Deary *et al.*, 2010; although this does leave 60 per cent unaccounted for by general intelligence (Ackerman, 2016)). Except, of course, that some tests did not correlate well with each other – vocabulary and comprehension scores correlated well with each other but these did not correlate with mental rotation scores.

Kovacs and Conway express the problem with *g* in this way:

'The problem with *g* is simply that still to this day there is no satisfactory consensus about how to interpret it: If there is a causal factor behind *g*, it has not been identified yet. . . there is substantial confusion about what kind of thing *g*, or indeed what any latent variable, is in the first place' (p .152).

In their model, *g* emerges from independent cognitive processes; it is a result, not a cause. Executive processes such as updating, switching, inhibition, working memory and induction underlie performance across a variety of mental ability tests. Ritchie *et al.* (2015), for example, found that the relationship between education and better cognitive ability was not explained by *g* but that education exerted effects on specific subtests of an IQ scale, a finding also reported in a slightly different study by Woodley (2012) who found that education improved particular abilities regardless of whether these abilities correlated with *g*. Kovacs and Conway's processes overlap – hence the name – and the combination of processes contributes to performance on ability tests.

Emotional intelligence

A different type of intelligence, one not based on any particular cognitive ability, was proposed by Goleman (1995, 1998). This type of intelligence refers to the social and emotional components of interactions with others: the more socially sensitive and emotionally sensitive you were to the needs and behaviours of others, the more successful your interaction would be. Goleman referred to this as emotional intelligence but there is some controversy over whether this is a separate, valid and reliable type of intelligence (Sjoberg, 2001).

Cutting edge: Are clever people funnier?

According to a study by Christensen *et al.* (2016), yes. They administered a test of fluid reasoning, vocabulary knowledge and retrieval ability to 270 young adults who were also asked to complete humour generation exercises. All three of the cognitive abilities – especially general intelligence – predicted humour production.

Estimating intelligence – An international perspective

How intelligent are you?

Intelligence tests attempt to measure intelligence. The average or mean score on these tests is 100. Most of the population (about $^2/_3$ people) score between 85 and 115. Very bright people score around 130 and scores have been known to go over 145.

The following graph shows the typical distribution of scores.

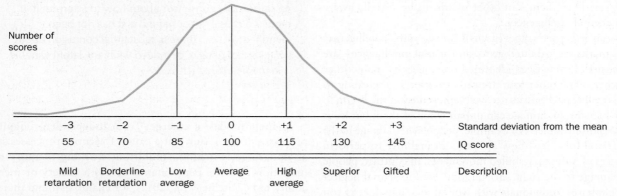

Figure 11.3 Example of a test used to examine individuals' perception of their own and their relatives' intelligence.

Although the proposition that men and women differ in intelligence is controversial, there is a great deal of evidence to suggest that males overestimate their own IQ more than do females (Beloff, 1992; Byrd and Stacey, 1993). These beliefs seem to be unrelated to actual cognitive performance. The actual IQ of males is significantly lower than their IQ estimate whereas that of females is also lower but not significantly so (Reilly and Mulhern, 1995). People are generally quite good at estimating their own intelligence, but are better at estimating numerical ability than general cognitive ability and when they have a clear set of scales showing people's relative position on them (Freund and Kasten, 2012).

A consistent finding is that participants of both sexes rate their fathers' IQ as being higher than their mothers' (Beloff, 1992; Furnham and Rawles, 1995). Not only are fathers rated as more intelligent than mothers, but sons are also judged by their parents to have a higher IQ than daughters (Furnham and Gasson, 1998). These findings appear to generalise across cultures. Furnham *et al.* (1999a), for example, asked 400 participants from the UK, Hawaii and Singapore to estimate their own parents' and siblings' IQ score for each of Gardner's multiple intelligences, using the test described in Figure 11.3. There were no sex differences in the estimated intelligence of siblings and parents but men estimated their own mathematical, spatial and bodily/kinetic intelligence as well as their overall intelligence to be higher than did women.

A similar study asked 140 Belgian, 227 British and 177 Slovakian students to estimate their multiple intelligence as well

▶

Estimating intelligence – *Continued*

as that of their parents and siblings (Furnham *et al.*, 1999b). Men rated their own general intelligence, but not those of their parents or siblings, more highly than did women. When the researchers looked at specific types of intelligence, men rated their numerical (but not verbal or cultural) IQ higher than did women.

Few national differences were reported but those that were appeared to be attributable to the Slovakian women. They rated their own and their fathers' IQ more highly than did Slovakian men. They also rated their verbal intelligence more highly than numerical and cultural IQ (Slovakian men rated their cultural and numerical IQ to be similar but higher than their cultural IQ). This is the first study of its kind to find that women rate their own intelligence more highly.

A study comparing British and Turkish respondents found that men rated their father's intelligence as being higher than their mother's (based on Gardner and Sternberg's models) and men rated their overall, verbal, logical, spatial, creative and practical intelligence higher than did women (Furnham *et al.*, 2009). Cultural differences were more pronounced than sex differences, however, with Turks rating their musical, body-kinesthetic, interpersonal, intrapersonal, naturalistic, creative, emotional and practical intelligence higher than did the Brits. Using the same intelligence measures, von Stumm *et al.* (2009) compared estimates of men and women from 12 nations – Australia, Austria, Brazil, France, Iran, Israel, Malaysia, South Africa, Spain, Turkey, UK and US. All nations overestimated their

intelligence compared with actual scores and men overestimated their own intelligence pretty universally.

Furnham *et al.* (2002a) asked British and American students to estimate their own overall intelligence and different types of intelligence, but also that of well-known figures such as Tony Blair, Bill Gates, Prince Charles and Bill Clinton. Men, as expected, estimated their verbal, logical and spatial IQ more highly than did women and women rated their male partners as having lower verbal IQ but higher spatial IQ than themselves. Of the famous figures, participants rated Bill Clinton and Prince Charles as less intelligent than themselves but Tony Blair and Bill Gates to be more intelligent.

A series of meta-analyses has confirmed the general pattern of findings reported in studies where men and women estimate their own, and male and female relatives' intelligence: males give higher estimates for all types of intelligence, apart from verbal ability (Symanowicz and Furnham, 2011). This asymmetry is not actually reflected in intelligence scores: they are comparable. But men believe they are more intelligent, indicating an over-inflation bias. The effect is seen cross-culturally, apart from in Uganda, Zimbabwe and Zambia where women give higher self-estimates.

'It is unclear,' the authors conclude, 'whether it is men who are arrogantly and conceitedly overestimating their intelligence, or that women are humbly and unconfidently under-estimating their intelligence, or that both are occurring to the same degree' (p. 502).

Are there consistent sex differences in cognitive ability?

Take a look at Figure 11.4. At the moment, the glass is empty but imagine that it is half full. Using a pencil, draw a line across the glass where you think the top of the water should be. Do that now before you read on.

If you were a man, you probably drew the line horizontally across the glass; if you were a woman, you probably drew the line parallel to the direction in which the water glass is tipped. The correct line would be the horizontal one.

This phenomenon illustrates one of the most consistent sex differences in cognitive ability. The task is Piaget's Water Level Test, and men tend to be better at it than women (Halpern, 1992; Rilea, 2008).

Why should males tend to be better at this task? One explanation for the Water Level Test result is that men and boys are intrinsically superior at tests of spatial ability than are women and girls (we will come on to reasons why this should be a little later). Spatial ability refers to 'skills in representing,

Figure 11.4 The Water Level Test. The glass is meant to be half full of water. The participant's task is to indicate where the top of the water should be.

Source: Kalichman, S.C., The effects of sex and context on paper and pencil spatial task performance. *Journal of General Psychology*, 1989, 116, 133–9. Reprinted with permission of the Helen Dwight Reid Educational Foundation. Published by Heldref Publications, 1319 Eighteenth St., NW, Washington, DC, 20036–1802, www.heldref.org, copyright © 1989.

transforming, generating and recalling symbolic, non-linguistic information' (Linn and Petersen, 1985). The test of spatial ability which shows the most consistent and reliable sex difference is mental rotation (Masters and Sanders, 1993). In this task, individuals are presented with three sets of cubes and have to match the target set with one of the other two. The task is not straightforward because the cubes have to be mentally rotated before a match can be made (see Chapter 8).

A different version of the standard mental rotation task was used in a study by Hirnstein *et al.* (2009). The researchers presented the well-known Vandeberg and Kuse mental rotation test in its original and in modified form. In the original, as you've seen, the participant is presented with one target and four sample sets of cubes and is asked to identify two samples that are identical, when rotated, to the target set. In the modified version, the participant has to compare each sample against the target, a modification that prohibits a leaping strategy – moving onto the next trial as soon as they think they've identified two matching samples (thereby ignoring the remaining, uncompared samples). Hirnstein *et al.* (2009) found that the performance of both men and women was poorer in the modified condition, but men's performance was more adversely affected than that of women. However, the better performance in men still remained.

Although superior mental rotation performance is a male preserve, object location memory is thought to be better in women, a finding that has been replicated internationally in 35 out of 40 countries (Silverman *et al.*, 2007). Honda and Nihei (2009) asked men and women to study a variety of objects and to recall the location of the objects either three minutes after presentation or one week later. Women were better than men after three minutes but not after a week. They were also better at locating objects whose locations had been swapped but, again, only in the three-minute condition.

In other types of visuospatial test, women tend to outperform men. For example, women have been found to be consistently superior to men at tests involving visual recognition. It has been suggested that this may be so because of women's superior linguistic ability. Women, for example, are better than men at tests involving verbal fluency, such as naming as many objects as possible beginning with a specific letter (Halpern, 1997), and boys tend to be diagnosed with reading and speech disorders more commonly than are girls (Flynn and Rahbar, 1994).

The stimuli used can also be important. Rilea (2008) found that men were better at the Water Level Task but showed no advantage on mental rotation or paper folding. However, men were better at rotating polygons than stick figures (and they showed a right hemisphere advantage for the task; there was no right hemisphere advantage shown by women for either stimulus type). Contreras *et al.* (2007) suggest a stimulus-specific complicating factor: the tests of spatial ability used are static, not dynamic. Therefore, they set up a study in which men and women performed a dynamic test of spatial ability – guiding two dots towards a destination in the shortest time. They found that even when performance factors were taken into account, men outperformed women (i.e. differences in performance style did not explain the sex difference). On average, men took longer to decide on the first move of the dots, then guided the dots more quickly.

These data suggest that 'spatial ability' is not an all-or-nothing concept but multidimensional. Different types of spatial ability test and different types of spatial stimuli produce sex differences; others do not.

Can sex differences be eliminated? There are some interesting answers. An experiment by McLoy and Koonce (1988, cited in Halpern, 1992) trained men and women on a standard simulated flight task and found that men were better at learning this task than were women. They also found that given sufficient training, women performed at about the same level as men; they simply needed more training to achieve this level of competence.

One study manipulated participants' belief in performance and observed the consequences of this manipulation on behaviour. Men and women (in same sex groups) were asked to perform a mental rotation test but different groups were given different instructions (Moe, 2009). One group was told: 'men are better than women at this task'; another: 'women are better than men'; and a third were given instructions with no reference to sex. Each group was also told that the test was either quite easy or very difficult. Women performed better when given the sex-positive instruction but task difficulty priming had no discernible effect. Men performed better when given sex-positive instructions, when told the test was easy and, if given control instructions, when the task was described as difficult. The sex-negative instructions had no effect on performance of either sex. This phenomenon, called stereotype threat, is described in Chapter 16.

Sex differences in visuospatial ability might also be due to different processing styles. Pena *et al.* (2008) asked men and women to complete a visuospatial exercise in which they had to guide two differently coloured dots on a monitor to a colour-appropriate target area. Participants did this by using a cursor to alter the direction of an arrow button which guided the dots. Two interesting findings emerged. Men, as expected, performed better than women but the type of strategy employed during the task affected success on the task. They also found that when one type of strategy was adopted, sex differences were reduced; when the other was employed, sex differences remained strong.

The two strategy styles were described as 'segmentary' or 'planned and feedback-dependent holistic'. Segmentary strategy involved focusing on a particular portion of the task, to the exclusion of other aspects of the task or the screen (hence, 'segment'). Followers of this strategy would change the course of the dot frequently. Holistic strategists did not make as many course changes. Some of these planned their actions before the task ('planned') and some acted on feedback from the screen ('feedback-dependent'). Men used the holistic strategy more often than did women; women were more likely to adopt the segmentary strategy. When men used planned holistic and segmentary strategies, they performed better than women using the same strategies. However, when both sexes employed the planned strategy, this sex difference narrowed.

Theories of differences in spatial performance

Theories of sex differences in cognitive ability fall into four general categories: evolutionary, psychosocial, biological and cognitive.

Evolutionary theories

The evolutionary point of view suggests that spatial superiority in men is a throwback to the evolution of men and women as hunters and gatherers (Eals and Silverman, 1994). This theory suggests that because men originally roamed and hunted (activities which rely on the manipulation of visuospatial features in the environment), and because women stayed 'at home' and gathered, it is not surprising that men are spatially superior. The greater visual recognition performance seen in women is meant to reflect women's evolutionary role as foragers (Tooby and DeVore, 1987).

According to evolutionary psychologists, one reason why men are better at spatial cognition than women is that men were the hunters who ranged far and wide for their prey and would, therefore, need to develop a well-tuned set of navigational skills. Women, the child-bearers and rearers, stayed at home and foraged. Some argue that women's ranging was limited to picking plants; men would hunt for game.

According to Ecuyer-Dab and Robert (2004), however, this dichotomy suggests that rather than showing a superior spatial advantage by men over women it shows how context can affect the way in which each sex expresses its specific spatial skills: spatial cognition in men would be used to navigate the environment for a mate and food whereas women's spatial cognition developed to deal with the immediate environment because they were more concerned with the survival of their offspring in the home. They, therefore, had no need to develop the navigational spatial skills that men did. In short, men developed and evolved large-scale navigation mechanisms and women evolved small-scale ones.

Boys, creatures of extremes?

Helen Cronin, the evolutionary psychologist, has pithily described the male species as having more Nobels but also more dumb-bells. That is, men are more likely to show extreme performances on measures of intelligence and cognitive ability

whereas women may show a less extreme pattern. There is some evidence of this. An extensive study of 320,000 11–12-year-olds in the UK, found few strong differences between girls and boys on the Cognitive Abilities Test but boys were more strongly represented at the top and bottom of the distribution for the non-verbal measure scores and at the lower end of the verbal measure distribution (Strand et al., 2006).

Lohman and Lakin (2009) administered the same test in three different versions to over 318,000 children from grades 3 to 11 in North America. They found almost identical results to those reported by the UK study, suggesting that the findings cannot be attributable to nation, age, education system or type of test. Instead, the results suggest a more universal finding.

Ecuyer-Dab and Robert cite evidence that women, for example, were more likely than men to use landmarks when giving map directions. Men are more likely to provide more detail on direction and distance – although women are capable of doing this, they simply do not use these references as their primary source of information.

One objection to the theory that males are intrinsically superior to females on tests of mental rotation is that the results may be attributable to other causes. For example, because the task is timed, it has been argued that this is detrimental to women, who are more cautious when making decisions about rotation (Goldstein et al., 1990). To test this hypothesis, Masters (1998) allowed male and female undergraduates either a short or unlimited time to perform a mental rotation task. She also used three different scoring procedures because previous studies had been criticised for basing their findings on using correct answers only (without looking at the number of incorrect responses too). Masters found that regardless of scoring procedure or time limit, men performed better than women. (Interestingly, however, some sex differences, such as female self-reported confusion over left and right, may be attributable to women rating themselves more critically than do men (Jordan et al., 2006).)

However, evolutionary theories such as these are so broad as to be untestable (see Chapter 3). As Halpern (1997) also notes, you can explain almost any finding by indicating how it would be advantageous to hunters and gatherers.

Psychosocial theories

Psychosocial theories suggest that sex differences are learned through experience or imitation. Children, it is argued, fulfil sex-role stereotypes: boys are encouraged to play with toys which involve visuospatial manipulation; girls are not (we will come back to this in Chapter 12). It has also been suggested that boys and girls receive different models, rewards and punishment. One researcher has suggested that peer interaction is more likely to lead to stereotypical sex-role behaviour than is parent–child interaction, although this idea is controversial (Harris, 1995).

Another study, investigating the effect on spatial performance of the degree to which men and women internalise their sexual identity or behave in a stereotypically male or female way, on spatial test performance found a weak relationship between spatial ability and sex roles although the actual sex difference remained (Saucier *et al.*, 2002).

Halpern (1992) cites fairly strong evidence against a psychosocial explanation for sex differences in cognitive ability. She noted that among individuals with high reasoning ability, right-handed men outperformed left-handed men on tests of spatial ability but were poorer than left-handed men at verbal tasks. Conversely, left-handed females were better at spatial tasks than were right-handers but the opposite pattern applied to verbal tasks. Any theory of psychosocial influence would have difficulty in explaining these findings: why should right- and left-handed boys and girls be socialised differently? It would also have difficulty in explaining why boys are more likely than girls to suffer from stuttering and reading disorders.

Biological theories

Biological theories suggest that sex differences in cognitive ability may be due to biological factors such as hormonal regulation and brain organisation. There is evidence that anatomical differences exist between the brains of boys and girls and between those of men and women (Shaywitz *et al.*, 1995). Keller and Menon (2009) examined brain activation and structure in 25 men and women who performed various mathematical operations including subtraction and addition. While men and women were equally accurate and equally as fast at the tests, their brain activation during processing differed. There was greater activity in the right dorsal and ventral streams in men and in an area of the right parietal lobe known to be important for calculating arithmetical problems. In terms of structure, women had greater neuronal density in these areas compared with men. The authors suggest that the differences reflect women's more efficient use of neural resources.

Apart from neuroanatomical differences, there may also be differences in the amount of, or sensitivity to, hormones (Collaer and Hines, 1995). Cognitive ability, for example, appears to fluctuate across the menstrual cycle (Hampson, 1990), and the amount of testosterone appears to correlate with spatial skill (Moffat and Hampson, 1996). In one study, normal ageing men given testosterone to enhance their sex drive showed increased visuospatial performance (Janowsky *et al.*, 1994). In another, transsexuals given testosterone as part of their preoperative sex change programme were found to show increased visuospatial ability and decreased verbal ability over a period of three months (Van Goozen *et al.*, 1995).

Other studies have also found no relationship between hormone level and spatial ability (Liben *et al.*, 2002). This may not mean that steroids are not involved. 'It may be', as the authors suggest, 'that such effects do occur but only under some as yet unidentified additional setting conditions (be they biological or experiential)'.

Cognitive theories

Empathising and systemising are two ways of processing information, described by Simon Baron-Cohen (2003), in which people work at identifying someone's thoughts and feelings (perspective-taking, altruism, cooperativeness) or analysing relationships in non-social interactions (an interest in science, technology, the natural world, etc.). The approaches can be measured by two questionnaires, called the empathy quotient and the systemising quotient. Women are thought to be better at the former; men, the latter.

In one study, men were found to engage in higher levels of systemising than were women and non-heterosexual women higher than heterosexual women (Nettle, 2007). There were no differences between heterosexual and non-heterosexual men. Women did show a greater interest in the arts and culture, however, which may not be related to sociability/empathy.

Cutting edge: Why do men do better than women in final degree exams at Oxford?

The answer is unusual and it may have little to do with ability. A consistent finding in the final year examinations at Oxford and Cambridge is that men outperform women, despite the opposite pattern being observed in secondary school. To try and discover why, Mellanby *et al.* (2013) conducted a longitudinal study of 1929 applicants to Oxford who had been successful in enrolling at the University. They examined various variables including sex, first year exam performance and the expectation of achieving the best degree (a First). They found that all three variables predicted final year performance. First year exam marks and the expectation of obtaining a First were the best predictors of achieving a First – and both of the former were higher in men than women. It seems as if men expect a First, but women don't and that this self-concept may explain the sex difference in achievement.

Intelligence testing

Assessment of intellectual ability, or intelligence testing, is a controversial topic because of its importance in modern society. Unless people have special skills that suit them for a career in sports or entertainment, their economic success may depend heavily on formal education. Many employers use specialised aptitude tests to help them select among job candidates. Test scores correlate with school and university grades, the number of years in education and adult occupational status (Nisbett *et al.*, 2012). There are hundreds of tests of specific abilities, such as manual dexterity, spatial reasoning, vocabulary, mathematical aptitude, musical ability, creativity and memory. All these tests vary widely in reliability, validity and ease of administration.

Early intelligence tests

Intelligence testing has a long and chequered history. As early as 2200 BC, Chinese administrators tested civil servants (mandarins) periodically to be sure that their abilities qualified them for their job. In Western cultures, differences in social class were far more important than individual differences in ability until the Renaissance, when the modern concept of individualism came into being.

The term 'intelligence' is an old one, deriving from the Latin *intellectus* (meaning 'perception' or 'comprehension'). However, its use in the English language dates only from the late nineteenth century, when it was revived by the philosopher Herbert Spencer (1820–1903) and by the biologist/statistician Sir Francis Galton (1822–1911). Galton was the most important early investigator of individual differences in ability. He was strongly influenced by his cousin Charles Darwin, who stressed the importance of inherited differences in physical and behavioural traits related to a species' survival. Galton observed that there were family differences in ability and concluded that intellectual abilities were heritable. Having noted that people with low ability were poor at making sensory discriminations, he decided that tests involving such discriminations would provide valid measures of intelligence.

In 1884, Francis Galton established the Anthropometric Laboratory (meaning 'human-measuring') at the International Health Exhibition in London. His exhibit was so popular that afterwards his laboratory became part of the South Kensington Museum. He tested over 9,000 people on 17 variables, including height and weight, muscular strength and the ability to perform sensory discriminations. One task involved detecting small differences in the weights of objects of the same size and shape.

Galton made some important contributions to science and mathematics. His systematic evaluation of various large numbers of people and the methods of population statistics he developed served as models for the statistical tests now used in all branches of science. His observation that the distribution of most human traits closely resembles the normal curve (developed by the Belgian statistician Lambert Quételet, 1796–1874) is the foundation for many modern tests of statistical significance and can be seen in Figure 11.5.

Galton also outlined the logic of a measure he called correlation: the degree to which variability in one measure is related to variability in another. From this analysis, the British mathematician Karl Pearson (1857–1936) derived the correlation coefficient (r) used today to assess the degree of statistical relation between variables. In addition, Galton developed the logic of twin studies and adoptive parent studies to assess the heritability of a human trait.

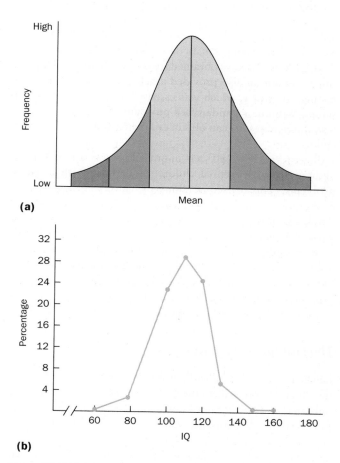

Figure 11.5 The normal curve and data from intelligence testing. **(a)** A mathematically derived normal curve. **(b)** A curve showing the distribution of IQ scores of 850 children of two-and-a-half years of age.

Source: Terman, L.M. and Merrill, M.A., *Stanford–Binet Intelligence Scale*. Boston MA: Houghton-Mifflin, 1960. Copyright © 1960 by Houghton Mifflin Company.

Modern intelligence tests

The Binet–Simon Scale

Alfred Binet (1857–1911), a French psychologist, and a colleague (Binet and Henri, 1896) suggested that a group of simple sensory tests could not adequately determine a person's intelligence. They recommended measuring a variety of psychological abilities (such as imagery, attention, comprehension, imagination, judgements of visual space, and memory for various stimuli) that appeared to be more representative of the traits that distinguished people of high and low intelligence.

To identify children who were unable to profit from normal classroom instruction and needed special attention, Binet and Theodore Simon assembled a collection of tests, many of which had been developed by other investigators, and published the **Binet–Simon Scale** in 1905. The tests were arranged in order of difficulty, and the researchers obtained norms for each test. Norms are data concerning comparison groups that permit the score of an individual to be assessed relative to his or her peers. In this case, the norms consisted of distributions of scores obtained from children of various ages. Binet and Simon also provided a detailed description of the testing procedure, which was essential for obtaining reliable scores. Without a standardised procedure for administering a test, different testers can obtain different scores from the same child.

Binet revised the 1905 test in order to assess the intellectual abilities of both normal children and those with learning problems. The revised versions provided a procedure for estimating a child's **mental age** – the level of intellectual development that could be expected for an average child of a particular age. For example, if an 8-year-old child scores as well as average 10-year-old children, their mental age is 10 years. Binet did not develop the concept of IQ (intelligence quotient). Nor did he believe that the mental age derived from the test scores expressed a simple trait called 'intelligence'. Instead, he conceived of the overall score as the average of several different abilities.

The Stanford–Binet Scale

Lewis Terman of Stanford University translated and revised the Binet–Simon Scale in the USA. The revised group of tests, published in 1916, became known as the **Stanford–Binet Scale**. Revisions by Terman and Maud Merrill were published in 1937 and 1960. In 1985, an entirely new version was published. The Stanford–Binet Scale consists of various tasks grouped according to mental age. Simple tests include identifying parts of the body and remembering which of three small cardboard boxes contains a marble. Intermediate tests include tracing a simple maze with a pencil and repeating five digits orally. Advanced tests include explaining the difference between two abstract words that are close in meaning (such as fame and notoriety) and completing complex sentences.

The 1916 Stanford–Binet Scale contained a formula for computing the **intelligence quotient (IQ)**, a measure devised by Stern (1914). The (IQ) represents the idea that if test scores indicate that a child's mental age is equal to their chronological age (i.e. calendar age), the child's intelligence is average; if the child's mental age is above or below their chronological age, the child is more or less intelligent than average. This relation is expressed as the quotient of mental age (MA) and chronological age (CA). The result is called the ratio IQ. The quotient is multiplied by 100 to eliminate fractions. For example, if a child's mental age is 10 and the child's chronological age is 8, then their IQ is (10 8) × 100 = 125.

The 1960 version of the Stanford–Binet Scale replaced the ratio IQ with the **deviation IQ**. Instead of using the ratio of mental age to chronological age, the deviation IQ compares a child's score with those received by other children of the same chronological age (the deviation IQ was invented by David Wechsler, whose work is described in the next section). Suppose that a child's score is one **standard deviation** above the mean for their age. The standard deviation of the ratio IQ scores is 16 points, and the score assigned to the average IQ is 100 points. If a child's score is one standard deviation above the mean for their age, the child's deviation IQ score is 100 + 16 (the standard deviation) = 116. A child who scores one standard deviation below the mean receives a deviation IQ of 84 (100–16), as Figure 11.6 illustrates.

Wechsler Adult Intelligence Scale

When David Wechsler was chief psychologist at New York City's Bellevue Psychiatric Hospital he developed several popular tests of intelligence. The Wechsler–Bellevue Scale, published in 1939, was revised in 1942 for use in the armed forces and was superseded in 1955 by **the Wechsler Adult Intelligence Scale (WAIS)**. This test was revised again in 1981 (the WAIS-R), 1997 (the WAIS-III) and 2008 (WAIS-IV). The **Wechsler Intelligence Scale for Children (WISC)**, first published in 1949; the fourth edition was published in 2008. Various versions of the WAIS-R have been devised for use with various populations (such as Irish, Scottish, Welsh and so on).

Previous versions of the scale provided a measure called 'full-scale IQ' which comprised scores from two separate subscales – performance IQ and verbal IQ. The current version, the WAIS-IV, however, has dispensed with the two subscales and now provides a total full-scale IQ score. It is a large collection of individual tests (the test is called a 'battery') currently validated on 2,200 individuals between 16 and 90 years of age. The tests which form the WAIS-IV can be seen in Figure 11.7a. You can see that full-scale IQ is made up of scores from four separate subscales all of which have core

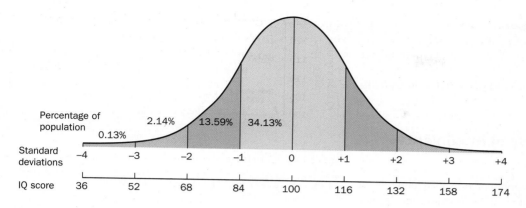

Figure 11.6 Calculating the deviation IQ score.

Test Structure

Figure 11.7 The new subtests that now form part of the latest revision of the WAIS-IV.

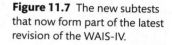

Verbal Comprehension Scale

Core Subtests
Similarities
Vocabulary
Information

Supplemental Subtests
Comprehension

Perceptual Reasoning Scale

Core Subtests
Block Design
Matrix Reasoning
Visual Puzzles   New!

Supplemental Subtests
Picture Completion
Figure Weights (16–69) only   New!

FSIQ

Working Memory Scale

Core Subtests
Digit Span
Arithmetic

Supplemental Subtests
Letter-Number Sequencing (16–69 only)

Processing Speed Scale

Core Subtests
Symbol Search
Coding

Supplemental Subtests
Cancellation (16–69 only)   New!

Ages 16:0 – 90:11

(a)

New Subtests: Visual Puzzles

'Which 3 of these pieces go together to make this puzzle?'

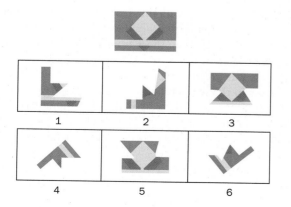

(b)

New Subtests: Figure Weights

'Which one of these goes here to balance the scale?'

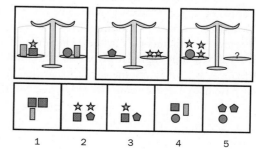

(c)

components or subtests. It is these core components (10 tests) which contribute to full-scale IQ. Figure 11.7b and c shows you examples of two of the new tests in the WAIS-IV that did not feature in WAIS-III.

The WAIS is the most widely administered adult intelligence test.

Reliability and validity of intelligence tests

The adequacy of a measure is represented by its reliability and validity (terms described in Chapter 2). In the case of intelligence testing, reliability is assessed by the correlation between the scores that people receive on the same measurement on two different occasions; perfect reliability is 1. High reliability is achieved by means of standardised test administration and objective scoring: all participants are exposed to the same situation during testing, and all score responses in the same way. The acceptable reliability of a modern test of intellectual ability should be at least 0.85. Validity is the correlation between test scores and the criterion – an independent measure of the variable that is being assessed.

However, most tests of intelligence correlate reasonably well with such measures as success in school (between 0.40 and 0.75). Thus, because intellectual ability plays at least some role in academic success, IQ appears to have some validity.

The Flynn effect

One of the most curious phenomena of intelligence measurement is that people appear to be getting significantly more intelligent or, more accurately, their IQ scores are increasing. This is called the Flynn effect after the psychologist James Flynn who noticed that the average level of intelligence in the US had risen since the beginning of the twentieth century – a 20-point acceleration in IQ in 60 years (Flynn, 1984, 1987). This is illustrated in Figure 11.8. Although this term has stuck, Flynn was not the first to observe generational increases in IQ/intelligence test performance – around 24 studies had been published before Flynn's widely cited study, and the first study showing the pattern was reported in 1936 (Lynn, 2013). The effect appears to be robust and some possible reasons for it are considered below. The Cutting Edge section describes a recent meta-analysis of the effect and concludes that the effect may be tailing off.

Why would IQ increase in this way, even though the increase appears to be attenuating? The most obvious explanation would be improved schooling and education, especially in primary or elementary school where the focus has shifted towards teaching cognitive skills that reflect fluid intelligence (Blair *et al.*, 2005a). Some suggest that this improvement may have halted in economically developed countries in

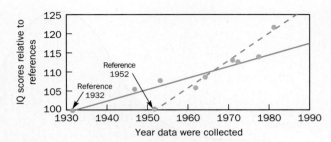

Figure 11.8 IQ increase over the twentieth century.

Source: Blair, C., Gamson, D., Thorne, S. and Baker, D., Rising mean IQ: Cognitive demand of mathematics education for young children, population exposure to formal schooling and the neurobiology of the PFC. *Intelligence*, 2005, 33, 93–106, p. 94, figure 1.

the recent two decades. Lynn (2009) exploited the fact that measures of intelligent behaviour have been standardised in the past few years (standardisation is the process whereby a test's validity is tested to ensure that it is a measure of what it claims to measure for a given population). One, the well-known Raven's Coloured Progressive Matrices, was standardised in the UK in 2007 and 2008. In the task, participants have to select from several options the one which would complete a sequence with the final part missing. Over the period 1982–2007, children between 4 and 11 years old improved by 8 IQ points. Children between 7 and 15 completing the Standard Progressive Matrices showed a 8.2 IQ point increase between 1979 and 2008.

Standardisation of two vocabulary tests – the Crichton Vocabulary Scale and the Mill Hill vocabulary scale in 2007 and 2008 in the UK – has shown that vocabulary knowledge declined in 4–11-year-olds on the Crichton scale and a small increase was recorded in 7–15 year-olds on the Mill Hill scale. The improvement, Lynn suggests, is due to better nutrition, rather than education or greater cognitive stimulation because vocabulary showed negligible improvement across the decades.

There is a significant association between national IQ and educational achievement. Lynn and Mikk (2007) correlated published national IQs scores in 2002 and 2006 with the educational attainment scores of children in 25 (10-year-olds) and 46 (14-year-olds) countries. Maths and science achievement correlated significantly with national IQ. IQ was also associated with per capita income: the greater the IQ, the greater the income. Some studies, with small samples, have also found that adolescents who come from wealthier backgrounds have greater grey matter volume than those from poorer backgrounds but greater or lesser white matter (Mackey *et al.*, 2015). Cortical thickness was greater in all lobes in the wealthier group and thickness in the temporal and occipital lobes was positively correlated with standardised test of cognitive ability (the Massachusetts Comprehensive Assessment System). There is also a positive association between personality and national

Cutting edge: Are we getting brighter? Up to a point

The Flynn effect, as you saw in the main section of the chapter, is robust but its appearance in different countries and nations is variable. For example, the effect appears to be fairly strong in countries such as Austria, France, Germany, Israel, Japan, Kenya, The Netherlands, Spain (and, more recently, the Czech Republic; Laciga and Cigler, 2016), but the effect is weaker in countries such as Australia, Brazil, Ireland, the UK, the US and New Zealand (Pietschnig and Vorachek, 2015). Some countries (Sweden, Norway) appear to show no current increases in IQ and some others (Denmark, Finland) appear to show a reversal, with IQ points dropping.

To examine the overall robustness of this effect, Pietschnig and Vorachek (2015) undertook a meta-analysis of data from 271 samples (4 million people), from 31 countries, collected between 1909 and 2013. They found that the Flynn effect does occur but it is very IQ-domain-specific – that is, it is stronger for fluid intelligence (where there have been substantial gains) and weaker for crystallised intelligence, as you can see in Figure 11.9. It was also stronger in adults, than in children, and has decreased in recent decades. They found that increases in crystallised intelligence had stopped in the period 1987–2011. Fluid intelligence had increased by 0.43 IQ point every year until 1985 and by 0.22 points a year up until 2013.

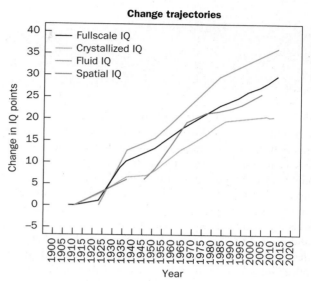

Figure 11.9 The Flynn effect across the decades. Each type of cognitive domain has seen an increase in average score since the early twentieth century.

Cutting edge: Are liberals brighter than conservatives?

A large body of evidence has found that people who hold socially liberal views score higher on tests on intelligence than do more conservative samples (e.g. Hodson and Busseri, 2012). They are also less likely to be religious (Zuckerman et al., 2013). Some research, however, suggests that holding right of centre views is associated with greater IQ. One study of Brazilian participants, for example, reported this association (Rindermann et al., 2012). Carl (2014) examined the responses of thousands of Americans to the General Social Survey from 1990 to 2008. This includes a brief verbal intelligence test (a 10-word vocabulary test in which respondents chose which

of five phrases represents the correct definition of a word). It also asks respondents to express social and political attitudes. He found that people who described themselves as Republicans reported higher verbal intelligence scores (2–5 IQ points) than did self-reported Democrats. Those who supported Republicans in elections were more likely to have higher verbal scores. Carl argues that verbal intelligence is associated with greater socially liberal beliefs and economically liberal beliefs. However, as the author acknowledges, the verbal test used in the survey may be a poor proxy for IQ/intelligence and the effects in the study were small.

IQ, especially extraversion, openness to experience and agreeableness (Stolarski et al., 2013).

A review by Kuncel and Hezlett (2010) found that standardised cognitive test scores predicted the grade point average of American graduates but predicted less well the

attainment of a degree (which involves a motivational component). As you might expect, tests that were specific to the outcome measure were better predictors of performance than were tests of general maths and verbal skill. Cognitive test performance predicted success in occupational training in civilian and military jobs, overall job performance, leadership effectiveness and creativity. The more complex the job and the training, the better the cognitive scores were at predicting performance.

The roles of heredity and environment

Abilities – intellectual, athletic, musical and artistic – appear to run in families. Why? Are the similarities owing to heredity, or are they solely the result of a common environment, which includes similar educational opportunities and exposure to people having similar kinds of interests?

According to Sternberg and Grigorenko (1997), we know three facts about the roles of heredity and environment in intelligence: (1) both contribute to intelligence; (2) they interact in various ways; and (3) poor and enriched environments influence the development of intellectual ability regardless of heredity.

What these facts illustrate is that the typical nature–nurture debate in intelligence is no longer valid. The nature–nurture argument suggests that, in its most stark form, behaviour or function is determined solely by the environment or solely by genetics/heredity. Psychologists have discovered that this argument is too simplistic. In fact, it is inaccurate. Almost all psychologists agree that intelligence has a hereditary (as well as environmental) component. The debate now focuses on the degree to which each contributes to intelligence and the ways in which they interact to influence intellectual development.

The meaning of heritability

When we ask how much influence heredity has on a given trait, we are usually asking what the heritability of the trait is. Heritability is a statistical measure that expresses the proportion of the observed variability in a trait that is a direct result of genetic variability (GV). The value of this measure can vary from 0 to 1. The heritability of many physical traits in most cultures is very high; for example, eye colour is affected almost entirely by hereditary factors and little, if at all, by the environment. Thus, the heritability of eye colour is close to 1.

Heritability is a concept that many people misunderstand. It does not describe the extent to which the inherited genes are responsible for producing a particular trait; it measures the relative contributions of differences in genes and differences in environmental factors to the overall observed variability of the trait in a particular population. An example may make this distinction clear. Consider the heritability of hair colour in the Eskimo culture. Almost all young Eskimos have black hair, whereas older Eskimos have grey or white hair. Because all members of this population possess the same versions of the genes that determine hair colour, the GV with respect to those genes is in essence zero. All the observed variability in hair colour in this population is explained by an environmental factor – age. Therefore, the heritability of hair colour in the Eskimo culture is zero.

As with hair colour, we infer the heritability of a person's intelligence from their observed performance. Thus, looking at a person's IQ score is equivalent to looking at the colour of a person's hair. By measuring the correlation between IQ score and various genetic and environmental factors, we can arrive at an estimate of heritability. Clearly, even if hereditary factors do influence intelligence, the heritability of this trait must be considerably less than 1 because so many environmental factors also influence intelligence. The branch of psychology called behaviour genetics (see Chapters 1 and 3), predicts the degree of parental influence via genetic and environmental transmission on the development of the child's intellectual development.

The proportion of the **variance** associated with genetic differences among individuals is called h; the remaining variation which is associated with environmental influences is referred to as $1 - h$ (Neisser *et al.*, 1996a). The features which families share and have in common (such as choice of home) is sometimes referred to as c. Factor h can be subdivided into two types: additive h, which refers to the amount of hereditary variance that is passed from parent to child, and non-additive h, which refers to new, unique genetic expression in each generation. As children grow older, h increases and c decreases (McGue *et al.*, 1993). In childhood, the contribution of h and c to intelligence is similar; by adolescence, h predicts about three-quarters of intellectual ability.

The heritability of a trait depends on the amount of variability of genetic factors in a given population. If there is little GV, genetic factors will appear to be unimportant. Because the ancestors of people living in developed Western nations came from all over the world, GV is likely to be much higher there than in an isolated tribe of people in a remote part of the world. Therefore, if a person's IQ score is at all affected by genetic factors, the measured heritability of IQ will be higher in, say, Western European culture than in an isolated tribe.

The relative importance of environmental factors in intelligence depends on the amount of environmental variability (EV) that occurs in the population. If EV is low, then environmental factors will appear to be unimportant. In a society with a low variability in environmental factors relevant to intellectual development – one in which all children are raised in the same way by equally skilled and conscientious carers, all schools are equally good, all teachers have equally effective personalities and teaching skills, and no one is discriminated against – the effects of EV would be small and those of GV would be large. In contrast, in a society in which only a few privileged people receive a good education, environmental factors would be responsible for much of the variability in intelligence: the effects of EV would be large relative to those of GV.

Sources of environmental and genetic effects during development

Biological and environmental factors can affect intellectual abilities prenatally and post-natally. Newborn infants cannot be said to possess any substantial intellectual abilities; rather, they are more or less capable of developing these abilities during their lives. Therefore, prenatal influences can be said to affect a child's potential intelligence by affecting the development of the brain. Factors that impair brain development will necessarily also impair the child's potential intelligence.

As the axons of developing neurons grow, they thread their way through a tangle of other growing cells, responding to physical and chemical signals along the way. During this stage of prenatal development, differentiating cells can be misguided by false signals. For example, if a woman contracts German measles during early pregnancy, toxic chemicals produced by the virus may adversely affect the development of the foetus. Sometimes, these chemicals can misdirect the interconnections of brain cells and produce mental retardation. Thus, although development of a human organism is programmed genetically, environmental factors can affect development even before a person is born.

Educational influences in the environment, including (but not limited to) schooling, significantly affect the development of cognitive ability. Nisbett et al. (2012) note that children who miss a year of school demonstrate a drop in their IQ score, compared to attenders. A child who enters the 5th grade a year earlier than a child of the same age in the 4th grade has a verbal IQ that is five points higher at the end of the school year. In Norway, there are indications that adding two years beyond the 7th grade affects (improves) IQ at age 19 (Brinch and Galloway, 2011). According to Nisbett (2009), lengthening the school day, decreasing class sizes and using interactive computer games were all found to lead to an increase in academic skill. Around 40 per cent of variance in educational attainment is attributable to genetic influence.

Results of heritability studies

Estimates of the degree to which heredity influences a person's intellectual ability come from several sources. The two most powerful methods are comparisons between identical and fraternal twins and comparisons between adoptive and biological relatives (see Chapter 3).

Identical and fraternal twins

Current evidence indicates that the heritability of IQ is between 0.4 and 0.8. That is, highly heritable (Nisbett et al., 2012). One reason for this may be that children select experiences that reflect their predispositions thus stimulating cognitive development. An alternative is that there are different genes that are activated at different stages in development (as they do for puberty) (Tucker-Drob et al., 2013).

MZ twins are also more comparable in terms of brain volume and activation. Grey matter in the frontal, parietal and occipital cortex is virtually identical in volume in MZ twins. There is also considerable similarity in volume between DZ twins but more variation in the posterio-occipital region and language-related frontal regions (Chiang et al., 2009; van Leeuwen et al., 2009). White matter volume is correlated in MZ twins but not in the frontal and parietal cortex in DZ twins. The structural pattern is mirrored in functional studies. For example, highly intelligent individuals given a simple or a moderately difficult problem to solve do so more quickly than less intelligent individuals and show less cortical activation, especially the PFC (Neubauer and Fink, 2009). This probably reflects lack of effort required to solve simple puzzles. As the task increases in difficulty activation increases in the highly intelligent (Larson et al., 1995).

The contribution of h to intelligence appears to increase from 0.3 in early childhood (Cherny et al., 1994) to 0.8 in middle age (Finkel et al., 1995). However, this influence may extend to very old age (over 80 years of age). In the first study of its kind, Petrill et al. (1998) examined the influence of h in MZ and DZ twins greater than 80 years of age taken from the OctoTwin sample of the Swedish Twin Registry which contains details of 90 per cent of the twins born in Sweden. The mean age of the participants was 82.7 years and all were free from dementia and motor handicap. Petrill et al. (1998) found that there was a significant influence of h on ability, especially on memory performance.

At least half the total variance in IQ scores is accounted for by genetic variance (Chipuer et al., 1990; Plomin et al., 1997). The fact that, by most estimates, genetic factors account for approximately 50 per cent of the variability in IQ scores means that the other half of the variability is accounted for by environmental factors. However, the contribution of the environment is less than 25 per cent. Some estimates, based on comparisons of parents and their offspring raised together or apart, suggest a value of only 4 per cent. Why are these figures so low?

Plomin (1988) suggests that estimates of the importance of environmental factors tend to be low because the environment in a given family is not identical for all its members. Some environmental variables within a family are shared by all members of the family, such as the number of books the family has, the examples set by the parents, the places the family visits on holiday, the noisiness or quietness of the home, and so on. But not all of the environmental factors that affect a person's development and behaviour are shared in this way. For example, no two children are treated identically, even by family members; differences in their appearances and personalities affect the way other people treat them. Different members of a family will probably have different friends and acquaintances, attend different classes in school and, in general, be exposed to different influences. And once people leave home, their environments become even more different.

Plomin *et al.* (2013), investigating the reasons for exceptional reading ability in the top 5 per cent of 10,000 12-year-old twins, found that genetic factors explained more than half the difference in performance between the exceptional and normal readers; growing up in the same family/attending the same school accounted for less than a fifth. Kivas *et al.* (2013) found that numeracy and literacy were more heritable than was intelligence during early to late childhood (7–12 years). One reason for this is that schooling may reduce the variance attributable to environment, but as the children select and create their own environment later, cognitive ability correlates with heritability.

Estimates of the contribution of EV to intelligence based on measurements made during childhood also tend to be higher than similar estimates based on measurements made during adulthood. The reason for this difference may be that, during childhood, family members share a more similar environment, whereas during adulthood their environments become less similar. As Plomin (1997) notes, studies of genetically unrelated children (of a mean age of under 10 years) adopted and raised in the same families, suggest that up to 30 per cent of the variability in IQ scores is due to common environmental factors. However, when the comparison is made among young adults, the figure drops to less than 3 per cent. Adopted children appear to become more like their birth parents but do not become more like their adoptive parents, findings that were also reported in a study of the development of antisocial behaviour in twins (Pike *et al.*, 1996).

Thus, once children leave home and are exposed to different environmental variables, the effect of a common family environment almost disappears. What is left, in the case of related individuals, is their common genetic heritage.

Tucker-Drob *et al.* (2011) studied 750 twin pairs to examine the relationship between heritability and the socio-economic status (SES) of their parents. At 10 months, there was little effect of SES. At two years, there was much more variation especially in twins with parents of high SES. A re-analysis of data collected in the 1970s (and involving 839 twin pairs) found that 40 per cent of variance in IQ could be accounted for by genetics and shared environment in the families with lowest level of income and education (Harden *et al.*, 2007). This increased to 50 per cent accounted for by genetics and 30 per cent by shared environment in the richer and better educated families. Another study, of 548 adult twins and 207 older and younger siblings, found that older female siblings from educated families showed the largest effect of shared environment (Van der Sluis *et al.*, 2008). The amount of cortical white matter is also highly heritable. A study of 705 twins and siblings found that this increased with higher SES and higher IQ (Chliang *et al.*, 2011). Nisbett *et al.* conclude, however, that these effects of SES are much more common in North American than European populations.

If intelligence is inherited, how does inheritance occur?

Given that our DNA is what makes us what we are, the first and most obvious locus of any genetic cause would be our chromosomes (Plomin, 1997). The DNA contains sequences of information that are divided into sections by enzymes (called restriction enzymes). Sometimes these sequences are repeated. These enzymes act as markers that can be used to locate chromosomes and defects on chromosomes. Some **genetic disorders** of behaviour are single-gene disorders, that is, only one chromosome is affected. More complex behaviours, however, are likely to have multiple genetic loci called quantitative trait loci. The question, therefore, is whether intelligence is inherited through one gene or multiple genes.

Plomin and his colleagues have pioneered research in this, one of the most difficult areas in behaviour genetics. Plomin *et al.* (1994, 1995) have made an extensive study of DNA markers from Caucasian children of varying intelligence – from low IQ (less than 59) to high IQ (over 142) – and have found small genetic differences in intelligence between those with low and high IQ. Several of 100 identifiable DNA markers have been associated with intelligence, but no one marker has been consistently associated with it.

Six genetic markers have been identified that have been associated with cognitive ability and only one of these has withstood rigorous statistical testing. In their review of the contribution of individual genes in intelligence, Nisbett *et al.*'s (2012) conclusion is difficult to argue with: 'Figuring out why it has proved so difficult to identify the specific genes responsible for genetic variation in highly heritable behaviour traits is the most challenging problem facing behavioural genetics' (p. 6).

Recently, Genome Wide Association Studies (GWAS; see Chapter 3) have been employed to try and clarify the role of genes in intelligence but, as Plomin *et al.* (2013) note if all the genes had been identified, there wouldn't be any need for twin or adoption studies. The studies conclude that there are no genes which produce effects large enough to be meaningfully and consistently associated with intelligence and this suggests that the genes are likely to be many in

Psychology in action: Can low intelligence be improved?

Various projects, predominantly but not exclusively in the USA, have sought to discover whether early intervention in the schooling of poor children can lead to educational benefits beyond the period of intervention. Some studies suggest, for example, that placing an emphasis on the importance of developing executive function skill can leads to better school performance in 3–18 year olds (Jacob and Parkinson, 2015), although there is no evidence to suggest that the link is causal.

Some intervention programmes have shown that intervening early in a poor child's education can enhance their success at school (Johnson and Walker, 1991; Reynolds, 1994). Two such interventions include the Cognitive Acceleration Through Science Education programme (Adey and Shayer, 1994) and the Practical Intelligence for Schools Project (Sternberg and Wagner, 1986; Williams *et al.*, 1996). The former involves teaching children the pattern of thinking seen in science. In a 2-year intervention study of 11–12-year-old children, there was a significant increase in science achievement test scores at the end of the intervention. The latter helps the child to build coping strategies based on knowing the strengths, weaknesses and demands of a task and applying the appropriate steps and strategies to complete these tasks. Again, intervention improved the intellectual skill of children when measured on practical and academic measures of writing, homework and test-taking. However, it is unclear whether these interventions make children think better or make them more intelligent.

In one study, children who received intervention were less likely to be placed in special needs classes while in school but (1) were not intellectually superior and (2) did not graduate any more quickly (Gray *et al.*, 1982). A second study, conversely, found that although intervention groups were less likely to be placed in special needs classes in school, they also performed better at school and, at 19 years old, performed better than the non-intervention group on tests of literacy (Weikart *et al.*, 1978).

The picture is clearly mixed, but if intervention programmes do show some evidence of success, why should this be?

Campbell *et al.* (2001) suggest that intervention programmes directly affect a child's cognitive abilities by enabling it to 'meet the challenges of school'. The evidence, they argue, points towards a stronger role for these direct factors rather than indirect ones such as changes in motivation or the parents' perception of the child. The researchers explored some of these factors in a cohort of 104 largely African American children (98 per cent of total) from the Abecedarian project.

The Abecedarian project involved the study of the effects of educational intervention in children from low-income families. Fifty-seven of the infants were randomly assigned to the intervention group; the remainder to the control group. Intervention took the form of early education programmes in infancy for eight hours a day, five days a week, 50 weeks a year. A special curriculum was designed to promote cognitive, perceptual and social development. The control group did not receive such consistent education and attended various day-care centres for different periods, with no experimental intervention. The researchers (Campbell *et al.*, 2001) conducted follow-up assessments when the participants were 21 years old and these assessments included tests of intelligence and evaluations of achievement.

The researchers found that cognitive test performance increased more steeply in the treated group during early childhood when compared with controls. From 3 to 21 years, however, there was a generally better performance in the treated group than in the controls. Reading and mathematics performance was better in the treated group but both groups' performance remained fairly stable from middle childhood onwards: performance showed little change over time and both groups' achievement developed in parallel. It was evident, however, that both groups showed a gradual decline in scores between 12 and 21 years, when compared with standardised scores for the general population. While the treated group performed better than the untreated group, both groups' performance compared unfavourably with the population average.

number, each having small effect sizes. The first GWAS study, for example, found that the gene with the largest effect size accounted for less than 0.005 of the variance in cognitive ability. A study of 101,069 individuals and a replication sample of 25,490 identified three polymorphism associated with educational attainment, that explained around 2 per cent of the variance (Rietveld *et al.*, 2013). One meta-analysis of 16 studies that included over 9,000 participants, found that a polymorphism on one gene was associated with IQ. Another possible polymorphism associated with intelligence is Val66Met.

The effect of intelligence on health

In recent years, psychologists have turned to an unusual factor as a predictor of long-term good health: intelligence. Studies have shown that people with lower IQ are more likely to die earlier than those with higher IQ, whatever socio-economic class they belong to (Batty *et al.*, 2007). A study of 1,181 Scottish people born in 1936 and followed by researchers from 1963 to 2003 confirmed this finding (Deary *et al.*, 2008).

People with higher intelligence and dependable have a significantly lower rate of mortality. The 'hazard ratio' was 0.8 for

Controversies in psychological science: Is there a relationship between race and intelligence?

The issue

Of all the controversies in psychological science discussed in this book, perhaps the most controversial is that of the contribution of race to intelligence. *The Bell Curve*, a book written by a psychologist and a sociologist (Herrnstein and Murray, 1994), provoked a furore among psychologists and in the media across the world at the time. The book asserted that psychologists agree that a general intelligence factor exists; that IQ tests measure what most people think of as intelligence; that IQ is almost impossible to modify through education and special training; that IQ is genetically determined; and that racial differences in IQ are the result of heredity. Whereas the chapter has so far discussed the first four assertions, this section addresses the last: whether race can influence IQ.

The evidence

Many studies have established the fact that there are racial differences in scores on various tests of intellectual abilities. For example, people who are identified as black generally score an average of 85 on IQ tests, whereas people who are identified as white score an average of 100 (Jensen, 1985; Lynn, 1991; Rushton, 1997). Although many blacks score better than many whites, on average whites do better on these tests. A statement endorsed by 52 professors indicated that, on average, whites' average IQ score is 100, African Americans' is 85, American-Hispanics' is somewhere between whites and African Americans', and Asians' is above 100 (Mainstream Science, 1994, cited in Suzuki and Valencia (1997)). Lynn's study (1996) of 2,260 children between 6 and 17 years of age found that Asian children scored an average of 107 IQ points, white children an average of 103 and black children an average of 89. Interestingly, black infants are more advanced than their white counterparts in the first 15 months of life (Lynn, 1998).

The controversy lies not in the facts themselves but in what these facts mean. Some authors have argued that the racial differences in scores on the tests are caused by heredity (Lynn, 1993; Rushton, 1995, 1997). The Bell Curve highlighted other racial aspects of intelligence such as the failure of intervention programmes to improve the IQs of black children.

The assertions made in *The Bell Curve* have not gone unchallenged. In response to the book and issues surrounding intelligence, the American Psychological Association set up a taskforce to report on the state of knowledge regarding the nature and determinants of intelligence (Neisser *et al.*, 1996a). In 2012, the APA published an update of Neisser *et al.*'s review (Nisbett *et al.*, 2012). Its conclusions were that (1) IQ heritability varied by social class, (2) no genetic polymorphisms were associated with variation in IQ, (3) crystallised and fluid intelligence are entirely separable abilities at the behavioural and biological level and that *g* is to all intents and purposes synonymous with IQ, (4) environment had an important effect in intelligence with 12–18 point improvement in

IQ observed when (US) working class children were moved to (US) middle-class homes and (5) the gap between whites' and blacks' IQ had decreased by 0.33 standard deviations since Neisser *et al.*'s review. In 1996, they note, there was a 15 point difference between whites and blacks; between 1970 and 2002 there had been a 5.5 point gain (Dickens and Flynn, 2006).

Some investigators have attempted to use statistical methods to remove the effects of environmental variables, such as socio-economic status, that account for differences in performance between blacks and whites. However, these methods are controversial, and many statisticians question their validity. On the other hand, a study by Scarr and Weinberg (1976) provides unambiguous evidence that environmental factors can substantially increase the measured IQ of a black child. Scarr and Weinberg studied 99 black children who were adopted into white families of higher-than-average educational and socio-economic status. The expected average IQ of black children in the same area who were raised in black families was approximately 90. The average IQ of the adopted group was observed to be 105.

Other authors have flatly stated that there are no racial differences in biologically determined intellectual capacity. But this claim, like the one asserting that blacks are inherently less intelligent than whites, has not been determined scientifically. It is an example of what Jensen (1980) has called the egalitarian fallacy – the 'gratuitous assumption that all human populations are essentially identical in whatever trait or ability the test purports to measure' (p. 370). Although we know that blacks and whites have different environments and that a black child raised in an environment similar to that of a white child will receive a similar IQ score, the question of whether any racial hereditary differences exist has not been answered. When we point to group differences in races we are referring to general, average differences in intellectual performance; there are considerable within-group differences that may even be larger than between-group differences (Suzuki and Valencia, 1997).

There is also a problem with what we mean by race. We can define race biologically by gene frequencies (Loehlin *et al.*, 1975) or we can define it as a social construct. For many people, race is whatever they believe it to mean; they themselves ascribe meaning to it (Omi and Winant, 1994). In this sense, the concept of race makes very little scientific sense.

Conclusion

Although the issue of race and intelligence as currently conceived does not appear to be meaningful, it would be scientifically interesting to study the effects of different environments on inherited intellectual capacity. The interesting and more valid questions concerning race are those addressed by social psychologists and anthropologists – questions concerning issues such as the prevalence of prejudice, ethnic identification and cohesiveness, fear of strangers (xenophobia), and the tendency to judge something (or someone) that is different as inferior.

intelligence and 0.77 for dependability (i.e. very low). Children who were in the lower half of the dependability/intelligence dimension were twice as likely to die as those in the upper half. This hazard ratio was 2.82. Smoking, high cholesterol and high blood pressure in middle age was associated with a hazard ratio of 2.34 in women and 3.2 in men (Lowe *et al.*, 1998).

The researchers suggest that a number of explanations could account for the association. There is a relationship between genes and intelligence and longevity, for example, and this relationship may be mediated by socio-economic status and to having a healthy lifestyle.

Intelligence, thinking and ageing

The neural basis of intelligence

The neural bases of intelligence can include factors such as larger brain structures/regions, greater brain volume, genetic associations with brain development and greater (or lesser) activation measured by fMRI, PET and other neuroimaging techniques. Deary *et al.* (2010) reviewed a number of studies in this area and concluded that there are some neural features which can predict intelligence and cognitive ability. For example, studies of children and adolescents' brain development have found that the *speed* at which cortical thickness develops is a better predictor of IQ at the age of 20 than is *actual* cortical thickness at the age of 20 suggesting that it is not the absolute differences in brain volume that are important but how such differences develop over time (Giedd and Rapoport, 2010). Other studies have found that highly intelligent children show thinner cortices early in their lives but show rapid increases in thickness in the prefrontal and temporal lobes through to puberty when there was further thinning (Shaw *et al.*, 2006).

There are also significant, and consistently reported, correlations between head size, cranial volume and brain volume, and IQ. There are specific correlations between IQ and the volume of the frontal, temporal and parietal cortices (Deary *et al.*, 2010). The greater the IQ, the greater the volume. This is more common for volume of grey matter than white matter. Ritchie *et al.* (2015) examined the brain volume, cortical thickness and white matter volume in 672 people in their 70s and correlated these with participants' general intelligence (*g*) scores. The greatest predictor of *g* was brain volume. Collectively, the brain measures used explained 18–21 per cent of the variance in *g*.

At the region-specific level, areas of the brain considered to be implicated in intelligence are the dorsolateral PFC, the parietal lobe, the anterior cingulate cortex and parts of the temporal and occipital lobe (Jung and Haier, 2007). Barbey *et al.* (2012) examined the effect of brain injury on *g* and executive function and found that regions in the left hemisphere (especially, the frontal and parietal lobes) and white matter fibres (the superior

longitudinal and arcuate fasciculus) were associated with impairments in both cognitive measures. The combination of these areas is thought to represent intelligence. Jung and Haier's parieto-frontal integration theory of intelligence provides a detailed model of the regions involved in this network.

This suggests that the fusiform gyrus, extrastriate cortex and Wernicke's area are involved in intelligence because of the first two's involvement in the processing of imagery and visual information and the third's role in processing syntax. Pathways from these areas send information to other brain areas, including the parietal cortex which makes further connections with the frontal lobes (specifically areas called BA 6, 9, 10, 45, 46, 47). Here, the frontal lobes' working memory system decides on which responses can be made. The ACC selects the response and inhibits inappropriate ones. All regions rely on the connections (white matter nerve fibres) between them, and the left hemisphere appears to be more involved than the right.

In terms of brain activation, less activation is usually a predictor of greater intelligence, a finding that is explained by highly intelligent people have greater neuronal efficiency (although the term efficiency is used very vaguely defined, if at all; see Poldrack, 2015). The hypoactivation is especially seen in the frontal and parietal cortex (van den Heuvel *et al.*, 2009) and is seen even at rest in highly intelligent people (Neubauer and Fink, 2009).

There seem to be sex differences in neuronal volume and its relation to IQ (Deary *et al.*, 2010). For example, greater fronto-parietal grey matter is associated with intelligence in men and greater white matter volume and grey matter volume in Broca's area in women (Haier *et al.*, 2005). Cortical thickness in the frontal lobe correlated with intelligence in women and thickness in the temporal-occipital area was correlated with intelligence in men (Narr *et al.*, 2007). In men, the fibres may be fewer but thicker than those in women (Schmithorst, 2009). Although men and women show differences in neuronal features, their cognitive performance does not consistently differ, suggesting to Deary *et al.* that 'males and females can achieve similar levels of overall intellectual performance by using differently structured brains in different ways' (p. 209).

Ageing and cognitive ability

As the body and the brain grow older, certain changes occur. The acuity of the senses may begin to decline, the ability to move quickly is reduced. On the cognitive level, there is also a decline in various functions such as the manipulation of information in working memory, retrieval of names, reaction time, declarative memory, information processing. Functions such as vocabulary, however, see some improvement with age (Woodruff-Pak, 1997). A study of over 20,000 individuals found that performance on a range of cognitive tasks declined with increasing age (Sternberg *et al.*, 2013).

General IQ scores will peak at around 25 years of age and decline up to 65 years. After 65, the score drops rapidly (Woods, 1994). At the most severe end of cognitive decline, there is dementia (or 'neurocognitive disorder') – the gradual and relentless loss in intellectual function as the individual reaches the sixth decade of life and beyond.

Our categorisation of individuals into age groups is fairly arbitrary. In most developed countries, the age of retirement is set at 65 (an age originally set by Otto von Bismarck, the German chancellor from 1871 to 1890), although this does not mean that those people who are 65 or older are incapable of holding down a job or lack the cognitive and physical capacity to hold down such a job. The distribution of the elderly population in the Western world in 1950 was pyramid-shaped, that is, there were fewer people reaching old and very old (over 80 years) age. It has been estimated that by 2030, this distribution will be pillar-shaped, with roughly equal numbers in the old and very old categories.

Improvements in health care, sanitation, crime prevention and nutrition are thought to be responsible for this increase in the number of years we are living. Psychologically, therefore, the more we learn about the effects of ageing – and in reversing its negative effects – the more important this information will become in countries where we are living longer.

But there are peaks of ability that researchers have observed. For example, fluid intelligence scores tend to be highest in early adulthood, whereas crystallised intelligence performance tends to be highest in middle age, although even this pattern is complicated by studies which have found that some types of short-term memory for faces and inverted faces peak at different times (Germine et al., 2011; Halberda et al., 2012).

In an extensive study of age and peak cognitive performance, Hartshorne and Germine (2015) examined age-related effects on 30 different cognitive abilities using existing, published data/standardised scores and data obtained via internet research. The sample in the first set of data included 2,450 healthy Americans aged between 16 and 89 years of age. When the researchers examined standardised scores, fluid intelligence scores peaked earlier than did crystallised intelligence scores, as predicted by previous research. Tests of learned knowledge (vocabulary, information, comprehension, arithmetic, similarities), confirming previous research, showed a much later peak in performance than did almost every other task studied. Some tasks peaked earlier than others, overall. Some of the effects are illustrated in Figure 11.10a and b.

In the second part of the study, between 10,300 and 11,532 participants completed a range of cognitive ability tests via the internet. The age range was 10–71 years. As with the standardised scores, the same peaks in performance was found with some specific characteristics – performance on two working memory tasks, for example, peaked at 30 years of age, later than the peak for processing speed performance. The researchers also attempted to replicate the results of their studies by asking 12,073 10–66 year olds to complete a digit span task and another 8,300 15–73 year olds to complete a visual working memory task on a different internet site. Age of peak performance was no different to the main study.

What is ageing?

From a strict point of view, we age as soon as we emerge from the womb. We are born with all the neurons we will have in life and they begin dying as soon as we grow. There is a massive shedding of neurons and synapses during childhood; this continues to old age. Of course, this shedding does not leave us intellectually helpless. Although neurons are lost, new connections are formed between existing neurons (this is why, although neurons are lost, the brain increases in weight during childhood) and the existing neurons work more efficiently. It has been suggested that psychological ageing begins after maturity and that this is measured by behaviour that includes the ability to acquire, remember and retrieve words, people and events and the ability to process and manipulate information. This scientific study of the ageing process is called **gerontology.**

One problem with studying the ageing process, however, is the large variability between and within samples. For example, during a long period of study, older participants become susceptible to disease processes and illnesses which could directly affect the variables that gerontologists are interested in studying. This within-subject variation can also be seen in another capacity. If we take one age group, say the 50–60-year-old, and compare it with another on some cognitive measure, we are defining a group of individuals by an age category but all individuals within this group may not show the same degree of ageing. For example, although the ability to remember strings of digits declines with age, some individuals perform badly, some stay the same and some actually get better (Holland and Rabbitt, 1991). Group variation becomes more of a problem when we look at data from cross-sectional studies.

Cross-sectional studies (see Chapter 2), compare independent groups on some measure. In ageing research, a cross-sectional design would involve assigning individuals to age categories such as 18–25, 26–35, 36–45, 46–55 and so on. These groups would then complete a series of tests of cognitive ability, and differences between groups would be examined. If a difference in memory was found between the younger groups and the older groups, however, we could not attribute this finding to ageing and cite ageing as a cause. Can you see why? (This question was posed in Chapter 2.) The reason is that we are not really looking at the effects of ageing but at the effect of age groups. We are not following one individual across all age ranges, but have sampled from several different age ranges. Because of this, our groups may differ on variables that we had not anticipated, such as improvement in nutrition and healthcare. When one group influences the results in this way, the study is said to show a cohort effect. The conclusion we can draw is that age groups differ from each other.

A different type of design looks at age change and this is called a longitudinal design. Here, individuals are assessed across the lifespan and each individual acts as his/her own control (we could combine the two designs as well and compare individuals within one age group which vary on another characteristic, such as

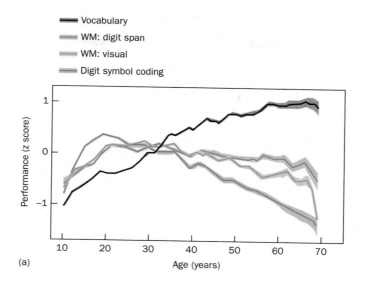

(a)

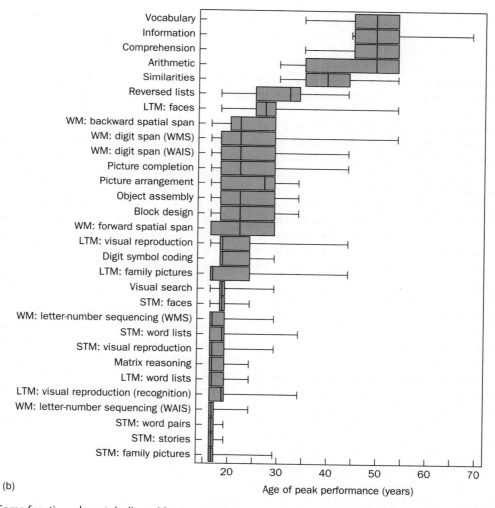

(b)

Figure 11.10 (a) Some functions do not decline with age – vocabulary, for example. **(b)** A detailed plotting of peak cognitive performance according to age and function. The line in the middle of the boxes is the median score.

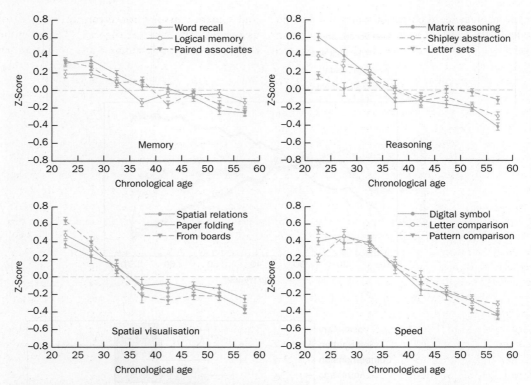

Figure 11.11 Mean scores and standard errors for 12 cognitive variables at 5-year age intervals.
Source: Salthouse, T.A. When does age-related cognitive decline begin? *Neurobiology of Aging*, 2009, 30, 507–14, figure 2.

occupation or education level). A problem here is that with repeated testing, the individual will become increasingly familiar with the measures employed. When longitudinal and cross-sectional measures are compared, the longitudinal assessments show least decline in ability (Schaie, 1990).

However, recent studies suggest that cross-sectional designs such as these can be meaningful and provide similar data to longitudinal studies. For example, Salthouse (2009) has summarised data showing the (fairly relentless decline) in cognitive ability as we get older, in a number of domains apart from vocabulary and general knowledge (which increase). You can see these data illustrated in Figure 11.11. The decline begins in adulthood and progresses thenceforth.

Memory decline

There is a gradual loss in performance for certain types of memory task with age. For example, older individuals have difficulty in retrieving names (Rabbitt *et al.*, 1995) and putting names to famous faces (Burke *et al.*, 1991). In Burke *et al.*'s experiment, participants were allowed one minute in which to name famous faces. The number of tip-of-the-tongue responses as people tried to put names to faces increased with age. When participants were allowed to try to remember the names on the tips of their tongues, however, 95 per cent of their responses were correct, which suggests that the information had been stored but that the participants had difficulty in retrieving it.

Older people also have difficulty in recalling where, when or how an event occurred, despite knowing that an event has occurred. This type of memory is called **source memory** because the emphasis is on the recall of the context in which an event occurred, rather than of the content/knowledge of the event (Johnson *et al.*, 1993). This type of memory seems more affected in the elderly than is memory for facts or items (Trott *et al.*, 1997), possibly because it relies on the integrity of the frontal lobe and the integrity of this brain region is challenged in elderly individuals, as you will see later.

Age-related impairments have been reported for declarative memory, efficiency of processing information and metamemory (Woodruff-Pak, 1997). **Metamemory** refers to 'knowing about knowing'; this knowledge of skills necessary to complete a task may be absent in the elderly. For example, elderly individuals may not spend sufficient amounts of time on a task that requires time to be spent on it (recall of digit names in serial order, for example). When they are instructed to spend a certain length of time on this task, however, they can recall accurately just as many series of digits as younger participants.

Prospective memory

Recent research on ageing and memory has focused on **prospective memory**, that is, remembering to perform an activity in the future (Maylor, 1996). This type of memory may be especially important to the elderly given that such monitoring is essential for taking medicine at particular times, for example (Park and Kidder, 1996; Einstein *et al.*, 1998). In experiments where a handkerchief or comb is borrowed by the experimenter at the beginning of a test session and/or hidden in a drawer and the individual has to remember to ask for the return of the item, there is an age-related decline in memory.

Studies of prospective memory can be either 'time based' or 'event based'. In time-based experiments, the participant engages in a task and has to inform the experimenter when a certain time has elapsed (Einstein *et al.*, 1995). This may be analogous to remembering to telephone someone in an hour's time (Maylor, 1996). In one study, Maylor (1990) asked 52–95-year-olds to telephone her once a day for a week. Three-quarters of those who adopted a memory strategy or used external cues for remembering were more reliable at telephoning than were those who did not use such mnemonics. In event-based experiments, participants must make a response when a particular event occurs in a sequence of events.

Kliegel *et al.* (2000) suggests that the tests of prospective memory used in these experiments are not particularly realistic. These tests, they argue, usually require participants to make a single, isolated act within an experimental session. Everyday life, on the other hand, often involves more complicated planning than this. From cooking a three-course meal to air traffic control, the prospective memory required to perform these acts is complex.

A caveat

One note of caution, however. Some studies show that when memory instructions in some experiments are de-emphasised, age differences in performance disappear. Age is also affected by the content of the test. So, for example, if people have to recall a narrative that is character-based, older people perform more poorly at than if they were asked to recall a narrative that was based on perceptual features – they were worse when they had to remember a man or a woman, rather than a character (Fung and Carstencens, 2003). Time of day is also important: Older people perform better between 8 a.m. and 11 a.m. whereas younger participants give their best performance between 1 p.m. and 5 p.m. (Hasher *et al.*, 1999).

Language

Certain aspects of language processing may actually improve with age. One of the greatest gains is seen in vocabulary (Bayley and Oden, 1955; Jones, 1959). However, older individuals have difficulty in retrieving or accessing these words and exhibit a greater number of tip-of-the-tongue responses than do young individuals during retrieval (Bowles and Poon, 1985).

According to LaRue (1992), the types of linguistic error made by elderly participants include: circumlocutions (giving inaccurate multi-word responses), nominalisations (describing functions not objects), perceptual errors (misidentifying stimuli) and semantic association errors (naming an object/feature associated with a target object). The elderly may also have difficulty in comprehending and initiating grammatically complex sentences (Kemper, 1992). Reasons for these, and other memory impairments, are discussed below.

If cognitive ability declines, why does it?

The evidence above indicates that cognitive ability, especially certain types of memory, declines with age. But is this the case? It depends on what we mean by 'age'. Ritchie (1997), for example, distinguishes between behaviour that is ageing-related and age-related. Ageing-related processes are the result of ageing; age-related processes occur only at a specific age. Is the decline seen in the elderly, therefore, not the result of ageing but of other age-related illnesses? Some European longitudinal data suggests that ageing may not be a factor (Leibovici *et al.*, 1996; Ritchie *et al.*, 1996). These researchers found that when controlling for physical illness, depression and signs of dementia, participants' cognitive performance improved over three years. They suggest that the decline that is commonly reported is due to pathology not ageing per se.

Processing speed and ageing

Several studies have shown a strong, positive association between the speed with which we process information and intelligence. Intelligence measures are significantly associated with mental speed, an association which becomes stronger as the information processing task became more complex (Sheppard and Vernon, 2008).

Over many years and several studies, Timothy Salthouse (1992, 1993; Craik and Salthouse, 2000) has argued that the elderly perform more poorly at cognitive tasks because they become slower at performing them. Older people have difficulty in activating, representing or maintaining information 'in mind', in attending to relevant stimuli in the environment and ignoring the irrelevant ones and in processing information speedily. If individual differences in speed are partialled out of these studies, then age-related differences disappear (Salthouse and Babcock, 1991). In fact, ageing could account for less than 1–2 per cent of the variance seen in such studies (Salthouse, 1993). This is a theory that has strong currency in gerontology. For example, several researchers have proposed that the cognitive decline seen in ageing may be attributable to reduced functioning of the frontal lobe (Parkin and Walter, 1992; West, 1996). The density of dopamine receptors declines in this area and dopamine is an important neurotransmitter in the performance of working memory tasks. The frontal cortex is also important for efficient information processing.

If there is significant frontal cortex decline with ageing, we might expect executive function, a key function of the frontal cortex, to be more significantly compromised in older participants. The support for this hypothesis, however, is mixed with some cross-sectional studies showing no differential decline and others showing decline on specific frontal lobe tests (one of these, a card sorting task, is described in the next major section on thinking) (Crawford *et al.*, 2000). If people are asked to remember small amounts of information (2–4 items in memory), older adults have been found to show greater activation in the right frontal cortex. But when the memory load increases, younger people show greater frontal cortex activation and older people less – and older people perform worse (Schneider-Garces *et al.*, 2010). Their performance may be the same as younger people's when tasks are simple, but they show more brain activation than younger people (Reuter-Lorenz, 2013).

Older people are also more susceptible to distraction – and being unable to suppress the effects of distraction or ignore the source – a finding that is reflected in differences in activation in visual areas (Gazzaley *et al.*, 2005). Spatial working memory (SWM) is also affected. This type of memory is important for many other cognitive functions and abilities such as adjusting to a new environment or driving a car. Young people asked to complete SWM tasks and undertake a task in which they have to adapt visually and physically to the environment, showed activation in the frontal and parietal areas (Anguera *et al.*, 2010). The better the SWM, the better the learning. Older people did not activate this network during motor learning suggesting that the SWM component was not being used (Anguera *et al.*, 2011).

Why is memory performance one of the most consistently affected cognitive abilities? One suggestion is that cognitive decline is the result of changes in the central nervous system (CNS) (Lowe and Rabbitt, 1997). In particular, researchers have focused on the hippocampus and the frontal cortex. There is a considerable loss in frontal lobe tissue over the course of the lifespan – around 17 per cent between the ages of 20 and 80 (Mittenberg *et al.*, 1989; West, 1996). One PET study compared the encoding and retrieval of word pairs in young (mean age 26) and old (70 and over) adults (Cabeza *et al.*, 1997). The young participants showed greater left prefrontal activation during encoding and right prefrontal activation during retrieval compared with the old sample. In fact, the old sample showed little frontal activation during encoding and more bilateral activation during retrieval. This pattern of activity suggested to the experimenters that the stimuli had been inefficiently processed or encoded. An fMRI study of recognition and encoding in young, middle-aged and older adults found that activation in brain areas involved in these memory processes declines across age groups but activation in areas that are irrelevant to the specific tasks increases (Grady *et al.*, 2006).

An alternative (or complementary) view to the frontal lobe hypothesis suggests that ageing results in an impairment of cognitive differentiation – the degree to which behaviour is specialised for specific tasks. The decline, which is domain-independent, is reflected in neurons' inability to perform such differentiation. The cortical basis of visual differentiation may be the ventral visual cortex – this responds to faces, orthography

and places – and shows less atrophy than other areas with age. In an fMRI study where 12- and 70-year-olds were asked to view faces, houses, pseudowords and chairs, less specialisation in activation in the ventral visual cortex was found in the elderly sample (Park *et al.*, 2004). Given that perceptual processing speed declines with age, perhaps such a slowness might be the result of a ventral visual cortex that shows less differentiation. Because there is less differentiation, older participants who are asked to make the same/different decisions about geometric pairs or digits (a standard perceptual processing speed task) are slower at doing so.

Can the decline be halted?

We are living in a modern world, as all worlds are, and modern worlds present new technological challenges. Mobile phones, computers, broadband, the internet . . . to young people these are the meat and drink (or nut cutlet and alfalfa shake) of their lives. Older people have greater difficulty in adjusting to and using this technology (Charness and Boot, 2009). In one study, older people took twice as long to learn to use a new word processor at their own pace than did younger people, even if they had prior word processing experience (Charness *et al.*, 2001).

However, all is not lost. Playing video games appears to result in a marked improvement in cognitive performance (Basak *et al.*, 2008) and research involving cognitive training via computer has produced promising, positive results. For example, attention and memory have been found to improve through these interventions (Smith *et al.*, 2009; Zehnder *et al.*, 2009; Zelinski *et al.*, 2011). Whether the effects extend beyond performance on the types of task trained in is still unclear. Short- and long-term memory do appear to improve, however (Gunther *et al.*, 2003). In older people with mild cognitive impairment (MCI), training in memory exercises has led to improvements in episodic memory, prospective memory, quality of life and metamemory (Kinsella *et al.*, 2009; Kurz *et al.*, 2009). These cognitive changes also correlate with changes (increases) in brain activation (Hampstead *et al.*, 2011). Improvements in long-term episodic memory, for example, have been associated with increases in the frontal, temporal and parietal regions of the brain (Belleville *et al.*, 2011). Using repetitive transcranial magnetic stimulation (rTMS), Turriziani *et al.* (2012) found that inhibition of the right dorsolateral prefrontal cortex (DLPFC) led to improvements in recognition memory in healthy participants and individuals with MCI.

Education may also be a protective factor. An Australian study of elderly blue-collar workers and academics found that the degree of education was associated with crystallised intelligence but not other types of cognitive ability (Christensen *et al.*, 1997) and a Dutch study has also shown that education was associated with a slower rate of memory decline (Schmand *et al.*, 1997). Andel *et al.* (2006) suggest that high levels of education and having a complex occupation may accelerate cognitive decline, arguably because the person's 'cognitive reserve' has been expended. However, a study of education in individuals with dementia (see below) found that the longer the individual was in education, the lower the risk of developing dementia (EClipSE, 2010).

Neurocognitive disorder (dementia) and Alzheimer's disease

The manual used for the diagnosis of mental illness (the DSM-V, see Chapter 18), reclassified dementia in its 2013 revision as 'neurocognitive disorder' (NCD). Many of the journals and textbooks you read, therefore, will still refer to old term, dementia. They are interchangeable. According to the World Health Organisation (2016), 47.5 million people in the world suffer from dementia/NCD. In the UK, 700,000 people suffer from NCD and the cost of caring for them is around £17 billion.

The most common cause of NCD is Alzheimer's disease (see below) but there are others. It is important to differentiate between Alzheimer's disease and NCD: the former is the disease, the latter is the psychological consequence of this illness. Alzheimer's disease is the third leading cause of death behind heart disease and neoplasia in the US (James *et al.*, 2014). In DSM-V, the criteria for a neurocognitive disorder include:

A. Evidence of significant cognitive decline from a previous level of performance in one or more cognitive domains:
   — Learning and memory
   — Language
   — Executive function
   — Complex attention
   — Perceptual-motor
   — Social cognition

B. The cognitive deficits interfere with independence in everyday activities. At a minimum, assistance should be required with complex instrumental activities of daily living, such as paying bills or managing medications.

C. The cognitive deficits do not occur exclusively in the context of a delirium

D. The cognitive deficits are not better explained by another mental disorder (e.g. major depressive disorder, schizophrenia)

Alzheimer's disease was named after Alois Alzheimer at the beginning of the last century who reported the case of a 56-year-old female patient who exhibited cognitive impairment as a result of abnormal brain formations. These formations (see Figure 11.12) are the characteristics of Alzheimer's disease and include neurofibrillary tangles – abnormal proteins which are found in various parts of the person's brain, especially the temporal, parietal and frontal cortices, neuritic senile plaques – abnormal nerve cell processes which surround the protein and are found in the cortex – and granuovacuolar degeneration (Nelson *et al.*, 2010; Hyman *et al.*, 2012). The tangles are consistently associated with cognitive decline, with plaques having a greater effect on high-functioning individuals

(a)

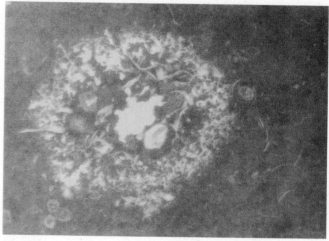

(b)

Figure 11.12 Images showing two of the characteristic neural features of Alzheimer's disease. **(a)** One of the neurofibrillary tangles that characterises brain cell abnormality in Alzheimer's disease. **(b)** The senile plaques seen in the nerve cell of a brain attacked by Alzheimer's disease.

Source: Beatty, J. (1995) *Principles of Behavioral Neuroscience*. New York: Brown and Benchmark/William C. Brown Communications Inc., 1995. Reprinted with permission.

(Nelson *et al.*, 2010). Animal models suggest that the specific protein contributing to the cognitive decline in Alzheimer's disease may be an assembly called AB*56 which is found outside cells (Lesne *et al.*, 2006).

There is significant neuron loss in Alzheimer's disease. The frontal and temporal gyri are thought to shrink by approximately 20 per cent and atrophy is found in the hippocampus, amygdala and other subcortical areas such as the raphe nuclei and nucleus basalis of Meynert. Figures 11.13a and b and 11.14 show how extensive this atrophy can be.

The cortical regions affected in Alzheimer's disease invariably include the olfactory areas – the medial temporal lobe, the piriform cortex, the prepiriform cortex, olfactory tubercle and entorhinal cortex, all of which have connections

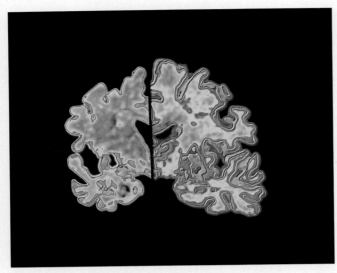

(a)

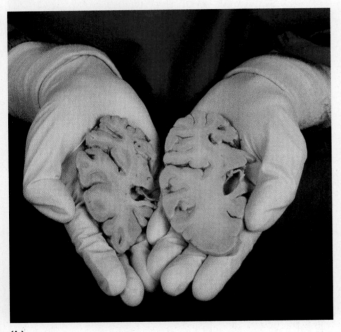

(b)

Figure 11.13 (a) Alzheimer's disease. A computer-enhanced photograph of a slice through the brain of a person who died of Alzheimer's disease (left) and a normal brain (right). Note that the grooves (sulci and fissures) are especially wide in the Alzheimer's brain, indicating degeneration of the brain. **(b)** Sections from a normal brain (right) and from a brain with Alzheimer's.

Source: (a) Alfred Pasieka/Science Photo Library (b) Plate 11.3 from *Human Neuropsychology*, 2nd edn, Pearson/Prentice Hall (Martin, G.N., 2006).

to (secondary) olfactory areas, the orbitofrontal cortex (OFC), insula and DlPFC. Some of the highest densities of plaques and tangles and the greatest pathology, for example, are found in the entorhinal cortex, subiculum, temporal pole, the piriform cortex, amygdala, OFC and prepiriform cortex. It is thought that it is for this reason that one of the earliest

symptoms – if not the earliest – of Alzheimer's disease is impaired olfactory function (see Martin (2013) for a review of these studies). A study of Scandinavian participants found a significant relationship between the ability to identify odour and cognitive decline (Olofsson *et al.*, 2009).

The disease can occur sporadically or in a genetic form called familial Alzheimer's disease. The familial form is thought to be autosomal-dominant with the gene carried on chromosome 21 and, possibly, chromosome 19. The gene expresses itself by producing the amyloid precursor protein from which the protein associated with the senile plaques is formed. Early-onset alzheimer's disease is associated with this marker and also with mutations on chromosomes 1 and 14 (Bird, 1999).

In a study of 69 presymptomatic carriers, 50 carriers and 70 non-carriers, Cash *et al.* (2013) found that the putamen, precuneus, temporal lobe and cingulate gyrus and thalamus were smaller in symptomatic carriers than noncarriers. White matter was also reduced in the fornix and cingulum in symptomatic carriers and these areas have connections with the grey matter areas above also reduced in carriers.

The E4 allele of the apolipoprotein gene also appears to be a risk factor in Alzheimer's disease and for cognitive impairment (Deary *et al.*, 2002; Schieper's *et al.*, 2011).

In a study of healthy, young APOE-E4 carriers and noncarriers, Shine *et al.* (2015) found differences in brain activation between the two groups during memory tasks. In one task, participants were asked to press a button when they saw a scene, face, object or scrambled object they had seen immediately before. Activity in the posteriomedial cortex (PCC, precuneus and cingulum) was increased in the carrier group during the scene condition only. In another task where participants chose the odd one out in a series of stimuli that included faces, objects and so on, carriers again showed increases in activation in the PMC when the odd one out involved scenes suggesting that scenes are particularly susceptible to abnormal processing in these carriers. The abnormal increase is inconsistent with what we expect might happen in healthy brains: one hypothesis argues that deactivation in this region during encoding predicts activation during retrieval.

The disease has also been linked with a number of candidate genes including *CLU, CR1, TOMM40, BIN1* and *PICALM*. Another genetic risk factor, brain-derived neurotropic factor (BDNF), has been associated with hippocampal-dependent learning in normal ageing; the expression of this gene declines with age (Harris and Deary, 2011).

Memory decline in Alzheimer's disease

The major cognitive impairment in Alzheimer's disease is memory loss and episodic memory retrieval is thought to be one of the most seriously affected. A person's inability to recall autobiographical information from long-term memory (e.g. information about people and events) is a major characteristic of the disease and appears early on in the disorder's development

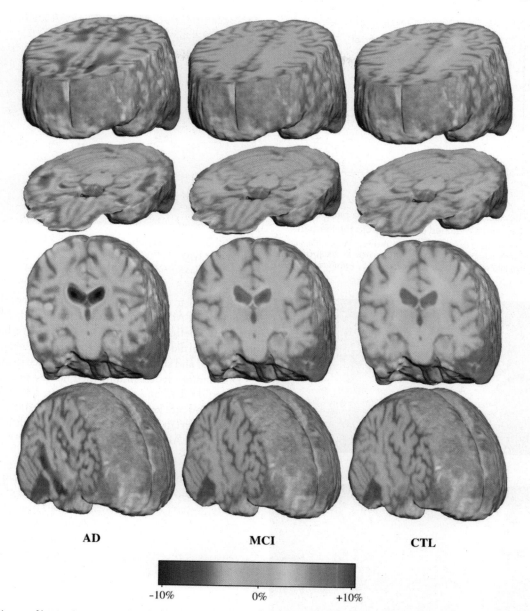

AD   MCI   CTL

−10%   0%   +10%

Figure 11.14 Areas of brain degeneration and its processes which contribute to dementia and its severity.

Source: Leow, A.D., Yanovsky, I., Parikshak, N. *et al.* Alzheimer's Disease Neuroimaging Initiative: A one-year follow-up study using tensor-based morphometry correlating degenerative rates, biomarkers and cognition. *NeuroImage*, 2009, 45, 645–55, figure 1.

(Fleischman and Gabrieli, 1999). Figure 11.15 plots the decline in memory function in a patient with Alzheimer's disease and a matched control, across the lifespan. Figure 11.16a and b shows brain scans of patients with Alzheimer's disease who tried to retrieve episodic memory.

The cognitive decline seen in Alzheimer's patients is much more severe than that seen in disease-free individuals during the course of normal ageing, and various cognitive deficits correlate with a reduction in the volume of the hippocampus, the temporal cortex and thalamus. It can sometimes be difficult to distinguish between the effects of NCD due to Alzheimer's and symptoms of MCI. MCI seems to occupy a halfway house

between the cognitive decline seen with normal ageing and dementia. Sixty-one per cent of MCI patients begin with memory impairments (Storandt, 2008) and it, too, has some of the hallmarks of Alzheimer's disease, such as the amyloid-B deposits (Goedert and Spillantini, 2006). Figure 11.17 shows the gradual atrophy in the brain at different stages of cognitive decline in individuals with varying degrees of intelligence.

A study from the Czech Republic found that people with AD were poorer at identifying famous faces, recognising emotion in facial expressions and identifying famous landmarks such as Tower Bridge and Charles Bridge than were controls (Sheardova *et al.*, 2014). Women with AD seem to show greater cognitive

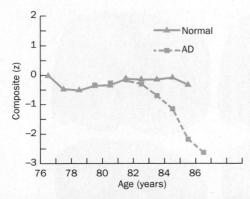

Figure 11.15 The decline in memory function in a patient with Alzheimer's disease and a matched control, across the lifespan.

Source: from Cognitive deficits in the early stages of Alzheimer's disease. *Current Directions in Psychological Science,* 17(3), Fig. 1, p.198 (Storandt, M. 2008), copyright © 2008 by Association for Psychological Science. Reprinted by Permission of SAGE Publication.

The author Terry Prachett was diagnosed with dementia of the Alzheimer type.

Source: Peter Macdiarmid/Getty Images News/Getty Images.

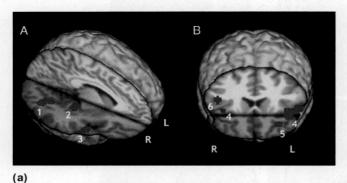

(a)

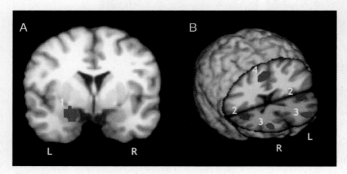

(b)

Figure 11.16 Comparison of brain activation between AD patients **(a)** across encoding studies, and **(b)** across retrieval studies.

Source: Schwindt, G.C. and Black, S.E. Functional imaging studies of episodic memory in Alzheimer's disease: a quantitative meta-analysis. *NeuroImage,* 2009, 45, 181–90, figures 2 and 3.

impairment than do men (Irvine *et al.*, 2012), regardless of type of cognitive function and even when dementia severity and age are taken into account. In an interesting parallel, Proust-Lima *et al.* (2008) found that at the age of 65, cognitive decline was commonly seen in both healthy men and women but the decline was greater in women. One reason for this decline is thought to be the loss of oestrogen. The reasoning is that after the menopause, the lack of production of this hormone is responsible

for the decline in cognition. There is some support for this in AD. Women with AD who received hormone replacement therapy performed better on tests of naming and verbal short-term memory than did women who did not receive therapy (Henderson *et al.*, 1996) and showed similar performance to men with AD.

Disorientation over finding their homes, forgetting people's names and faces, and not being able to follow the flow of a conversation, are key features of NCD. In 2003, the journalist and critic Adrian Gill wrote an article about his father, who suffered from Alzheimer's disease. Gill wrote:

> 'Conversations with Daddy are like talking to someone who can travel through walls. In the middle of a sentence, he can be somewhere else. I have to open empirical, rational doors to follow him. He glides through time and subjects in a way that logic and language prevent me. It's a sort of itinerant freedom.'

In the past, the only absolute diagnosis of AD could be made post-mortem by searching for plaques and tangles. The disease, therefore, would have progressed considerably in the brain before the person had died. Now, PET can be used to measure and record the presence of amyloid in the brain (Shoghi-Jadid *et al.*, 2002). MCI is considered to be the precursor of the neurocognitive impairment in AD and is thought to reflect the first stage in the continuum of cognitive decline. PET can detect up these abnormal deposits a decade before a person with the familial form of AD shows the symptoms of neurocognitive decline (Bateman *et al.*, 2012). The advantage of the PET technique is that it can also be used it to measure abnormal proteins in adults without the neurocognitive impairment associated with AD.

This impairment is gradual and occurs in the presence of a normal level of consciousness but in the absence of any other CNS disease that might account for the symptoms.

One difficulty in diagnosing Alzheimer's disease is that senile plaques are seen with normal ageing (tangles tend not to be),

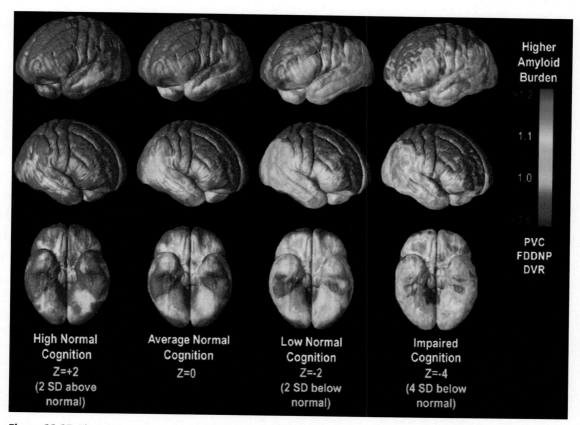

Figure 11.17 The areas of the brain showing increases in amyloid plaques according to intelligence level – from left to right, very bright, moderately bright, not very bright and severely impaired.

whereas tangles are seen in other types of dementia (Ritchie, 1997). Although the effects of ageing and dementia may be distinguished by the fact that abnormalities in the elderly affect the superficial cortex, they go much deeper in Alzheimer's disease. There is significant loss of certain neurotransmitter pathways linking various brain structures, such as the cerebral cortex and the hippocampus, in Alzheimer's disease.

Intervention

Many of the treatments that have been developed to try and combat the disease have sought to reverse, remove or manage the effects of the amyloid B protein. Success has not been great and there is currently no known treatment for the disease that is effective or curative. Once a person has reached the moderate stage of the disease, drugs are not effective (Sampson, 2010; Golde *et al.*, 2011).

Attempts have been made to reverse or at least halt the decline in cognition by non-pharmacological and non-invasive means, that is, by cognitive training, primarily, memory training. In early AD, this type of training has been associated with significant improvements in cognition (Gaitan *et al.*, 2013; Reijnders *et al.*, 2013). Some studies even suggest that such training can lead to increased brain volume. For example, one study found that older people who underwent three months of

three-ball juggling training showed an increase in brain volume in the middle temporal lobe (Boyke *et al.*, 2008). Other studies have also reported increases in other brain areas with cognitive training (Hosseini *et al.*, 2014). Some of these regions can be seen in Figure 11.18.

Dementia and the novelist: the case of Iris Murdoch

Fellow novelist A.S. Byatt spared no sensitivity when she reviewed Iris Murdoch's last novel, *Jackson's Dilemma*. The book, Byatt averred, was 'an Indian rope trick . . . in which all the people have no selves and therefore there is no story and no novel'. Murdoch, however, was no novelistic novice. In 1978, she won the Booker Prize for *The Sea, The Sea* and was made Dame Commander of the British Empire in 1987 in recognition of her contribution to literature. Published criticism is an occupational hazard in the novelist's world but Byatt's criticism may have unwittingly reflected an organic, rather than creative, decline. Murdoch was diagnosed with Alzheimer's disease at the age of 76, just after she had finished writing *Jackson's Dilemma*; a post-mortem three years later confirmed the diagnosis.

Following the diagnosis of suspected Alzheimer's disease, Garrard *et al.* (2005) monitored structural changes in Murdoch's

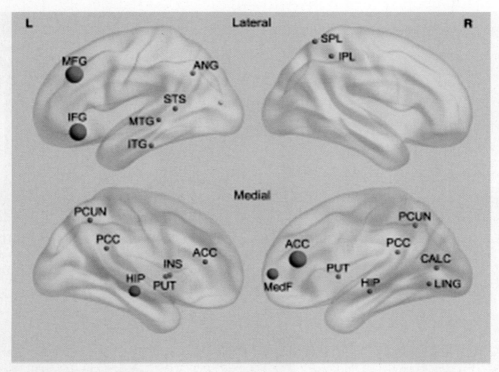

Figure 11.18 The effect of cognitive training on brain activity in people with Alzheimer's Disease. The circles show the areas most affected by cognitive training in AD – the larger the circle, the greater the effect.

brain, as part of her neurological assessment. In 1997, there was evidence of global atrophy, especially in the hippocampus (bilaterally). You can see examples of her neuropsychological performance in Figure 11.19.

When *Jackson's Dilemma* was published in 1995, the author had suffered severe writer's block and had become unexpectedly inarticulate at a question and answer session with the public a year later. The following summer, she was only able to describe her surroundings by reference to a city name and was unable to subtract or spell backwards. Her picture naming became circumlocutory: a bus was described as 'something carried along'; and her spelling became regularised. She would spell cruise as 'crewse', for example. Her retrograde memory was profoundly impaired and her narrative speech was grammatical but lacked real content. For example: 'the girl is just holding a plate and various pieces of . . . well . . . something useful . . . standing at a window . . . whether the window is open is not quite clear to me. The thing where the water is running out. The girl doesn't bother. The window is open. Plate and two cups.'

Murdoch's disorder afforded Garrard *et al.* the opportunity to examine any relationship between the novelist's intellectual decline and the external manifestation of that decline – her final novel. The novelist regarded the work as being a true reflection of her output and requested no alterations be made to the text. Garrard *et al.* compared the vocabulary, syntax, grammatical class and lexical differences in this novel, in *Under the Net* (published in 1954) and in *The Sea, The Sea*.

The researchers found that her vocabulary was rich and innovative in the early work but was impoverished in the final novel. The number of words and class of words per sentence (ten sentences were taken from the first, middle and final chapters of each novel) was smallest in the last novel. There was no difference in word length between the novels but the final work contained more high frequency words, reflecting a decline in linguistic innovation. The use of high frequency words is, according to Garrard *et al.*, typical of temporal lobe pathology.

In a sense, of course, these data are correlational. The final novel exhibited the features described here and these features coincided with the development of the author's degenerative disease. Nonetheless, the data obtained from the analysis of the author's physical output reflects the behaviour observed by those closest to her.

Thinking

Human reasoning is not simple, neat and impeccable. It is not akin to a proof of logic . . . we build mental models which represent distinct probabilities or that unfold in time in a kinematic sequence, and we base our conclusions on them. (Source: Johnson-Laird, 2010.)

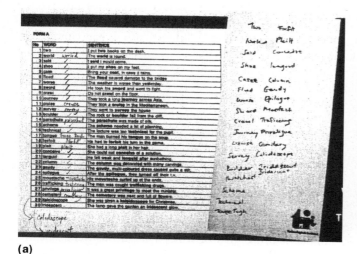

(a)

(b)

Figure 11.19 **(a)** Examples of Iris Murdoch's neuropsychological performance; **(b)** Iris Murdoch herself.

Sources: (a) From Garrard, P., Maloney, L.M., Hodges, J.R. and Patterson, K. The effects of very early Alzheimer's disease on the characteristics of writing by a renowned author, in *Brain*, 2005, 128, pp. 250–60, by permission of Oxford University Press and Peter Garrard. (b) REX/Shutterstock.

One of the most important components of cognition is thinking: categorising, reasoning and solving problems. When we think, we perceive, classify, manipulate, and combine information. When we are finished, we know something we did not know before (although our 'knowledge' may be incorrect).

The purpose of thinking is, in general, to solve problems. These problems may be simple classifications (What is that, a bird or a bat?); they may involve decisions about courses of actions (Should I buy a new car or pay to fix the old one?); or they may require the construction, testing and evaluation of complex plans of action (How am I going to manage to earn money to continue my education so that I can get out of this dead-end job, and still be able to enjoy life?). Much, but not all, of our thinking involves language. We certainly think to ourselves in words, but we also think in shapes and images. And some of the mental processes that affect our decisions and plans take place without our being conscious of them. Thus, we will have to consider non-verbal processes as well as verbal ones (Reber, 1992; Holyoak and Spellman, 1993).

Classifying

When we think, each object or event is not considered as a completely independent entity. Instead, we classify things – categorise them according to their characteristics. Then, when we have to solve a problem involving a particular object or situation, we can use information that we have already learned about similar objects or situations. To take a very simple example, when we enter someone's house for the first time, we recognise chairs, tables, sofas, lamps and other pieces of furniture even though we may never have seen these particular items before. Because we recognise these categories of objects, we know where to sit, how to increase the level of illumination, and so on.

Concepts are categories of objects, actions or states of being that share some attributes: cat, comet, team, destroying, playing, forgetting, happiness, truth, justice. Most thinking deals with the relations and interactions among concepts. For example, 'the hawk caught the sparrow' describes an interaction between two birds; 'studying for an examination is fun' describes an attribute of a particular action; and 'youth is a carefree time of life' describes an attribute of a state of being.

Concepts exist because the characteristics of objects have consequences for us. For example, angry dogs may hurt us, whereas friendly dogs may give us pleasure. Dangerous dogs tend to growl, bare their teeth and bite, whereas friendly dogs tend to prance around, wag their tails and solicit our attention. Thus, when we see a dog that growls and bares its teeth, we avoid it because it may bite us; but if we see one prancing around and wagging its tail, we may try to pat it. We have learned to avoid or approach dogs who display different sorts of behaviour through direct experience with dogs or through the vicarious experience of watching other people interact with them. The point is, we can learn the concepts of dangerous and friendly dogs from the behaviour of one set of dogs while we are young and respond appropriately to other dogs later in life. Our experiences with particular dogs generalise to others.

Formal and natural concepts

Formal concepts are defined by listing their essential characteristics, as a dictionary definition does. For example, dogs have four legs, a tail, fur and wet noses; are carnivores; can bark, growl, whine and howl; pant when they are hot; bear live young; and so on. Thus, a formal concept is a sort of category that has rules about membership and non-membership.

Psychologists have studied the nature of formally defined concepts, such as species of animals. Collins and Quillian (1969) suggested that such concepts are organised hierarchically in semantic memory. Each concept has associated with it a set of characteristics. Consider the hierarchy of concepts relating to animals shown in Figure 11.20. At the top is the concept 'animal', with which are associated the characteristics common to all animals, such as 'has skin', 'can move around', 'eats', 'breathes' and so on. Linked to the concept 'animal' are groups of animals, such as birds, fish and mammals, along with their characteristics. These hierarchies are illustrated in Figure 11.20.

Collins and Quillian assumed that the characteristics common to all members of a group of related concepts (such as all birds) were attached to the general concept (in this case bird) rather than to all the members. Such an arrangement would produce an efficient and economical organisation of memory. For example, all birds have wings. Thus, we need not remember that a canary, a jay, a robin and an ostrich all have wings; we need only remember that each of these concepts belong to the category of bird and that birds have wings.

Collins and Quillian tested the validity of their model by asking people questions about the characteristics of various concepts. Consider the concept 'canary'. The investigators asked people to say true or false to statements such as, 'A canary eats'. When the question dealt with characteristics that were specific to the concept (such as 'can sing', or 'is yellow'), the subjects responded quickly. If the question dealt with a characteristic that was common to a more general concept (such as 'has skin' or 'breathes'), the subjects took a longer time in answering. Presumably, when asked a question about a characteristic that applied to all birds or to all animals, the participants had to 'travel up the tree' from the entry for canary until they found the level that provided the answer. The further they had to go, the longer the process took.

The model above is attractive but it does not reflect realistically the way in which we classify concepts and their characteristics. For example, although people may conceive of objects in terms of a hierarchy, a particular person's hierarchy of animals need not resemble that compiled by a zoologist. For example, Rips *et al.* (1973) found that people said yes to 'A collie is an animal' faster than they did to 'A collie is a mammal'. According to Collins and Quillian's model, animal comes above mammal in the hierarchy, so the results should have been just the opposite.

Although some organisation undoubtedly exists between categories and subcategories, it appears not to be perfectly logical and systematic. For example, Roth and Mervis (1983) found that people judged Chablis to be a better example of wine than of drink, but they judged champagne to be a better example of drink than of wine. This inconsistency clearly reflects people's experience with the concepts. Chablis is obviously a wine: it is sold in bottles that resemble those used for other wines, it looks and tastes similar to other white wines, the word 'wine' is found on the label, and so on. By these standards, champagne appears to stand apart. A wine expert would categorise champagne as a particular type of wine. But the average person, not being particularly well acquainted with the fact that champagne is made of fermented grape juice, encounters champagne in the context of something to drink on a special occasion, something to launch ships with, and so on. Thus, its characteristics are perceived as being rather different from those of Chablis.

Rosch (1975; Mervis and Rosch, 1981) suggested that people do not look up the meanings of concepts in their heads in the way that they seek definitions in dictionaries. The concepts we use in everyday life are natural concepts, not formal ones

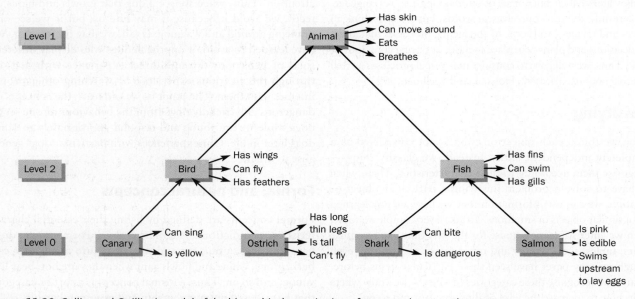

Figure 11.20 Collins and Quillian's model of the hierarchical organisation of concepts in semantic memory.

Source: From Robert L. Solso, *Cognitive Psychology*, 2nd edn. Published by Allyn & Bacon, Boston, MA. Copyright © 1988 by Pearson Education. By permission of the publisher.

discovered by experts who have examined characteristics we are not aware of. **Natural concepts** are based on our own perceptions and interactions with things in the world. For example, some things have wings, beaks and feathers, and they fly, build nests, lay eggs and make high-pitched noises. Other things are furry, have four legs and a tail, and run around on the ground. Formal concepts consist of carefully defined sets of rules governing membership in a particular category; natural concepts are collections of memories of particular examples that share some similarities. Formal concepts are used primarily by experts (and by people studying to become experts), whereas natural concepts are used by ordinary people in their daily lives.

Rosch suggests that people's natural concepts consist of collections of memories of particular examples, called **exemplars,** that share some similarities. The boundaries between formal concepts are precise, whereas those between natural concepts are fuzzy – the distinction between a member and a non-member is not always clear. Thus, to a non-expert, not all members of a concept are equally good examples of that concept. A robin is a good example of bird; a penguin or ostrich is a poor one. We may acknowledge that a penguin is a bird because we have been taught that it is, but we often qualify the category of membership by making statements such as 'strictly speaking, a penguin is a bird'. Exemplars represent the important characteristics of a category – characteristics that we can easily perceive or that we encounter when we interact with its members.

According to Rosch *et al.* (1976), natural concepts vary in their level of precision and detail. They are arranged in a hierarchy from very detailed to very general. When we think about concepts and talk about them, we usually deal with basic-level concepts – those that make important distinctions between different categories – but do not waste time and effort with those that do not matter. For example, chair and apple are **basic-level concepts.** Concepts that refer to collections of basic-level concepts, such as furniture and fruit, are called superordinate concepts. Concepts that refer to types of items within a basic-level category, such as deckchair and Granny Smith's, are called subordinate concepts. These can be seen in Figure 11.21.

The basic-level concept tends to be the one that people spontaneously name when they see a member of the category. That is, all types of chair tend to be called 'chair', unless there is a special reason to use a more precise label. People tend to use basic-level concepts for a very good reason: cognitive economy. The use of subordinate concepts wastes time and effort on meaningless distinctions, and the use of superordinate concepts loses important information. Rosch *et al.* (1976) presented people with various concepts and gave them 90 seconds to list as many attributes as they could for each of them. The subjects supplied few attributes for superordinate concepts but were able to think of many for basic-level concepts.

Subordinate concepts evoked no more responses than basic-level concepts did. Thus, because they deal with a large number of individual items and their characteristics, basic-level concepts represent the maximum information in the most efficient manner. When people think about basic-level concepts, they do not have to travel up or down a tree to find the attributes that belong to the concept. The attributes are directly attached to the exemplars that constitute each concept.

It is important to recognise that concepts can represent something more complex than simple exemplars or collections of attributes. Goldstone *et al.* (1991) showed participants groups of figures and asked them to indicate which were most similar to each other. When they showed the participants two triangles, two squares and two circles, the subjects said that the squares and triangles were most similar, presumably because both contained straight lines and angles. However, when they added a square to each of the pairs, the participants said that the two most similar groups were the triangles plus square and the circles plus square. The task is illustrated in Figure 11.22.

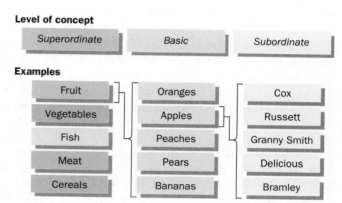

Figure 11.21 Examples of basic-level, subordinate and superordinate concepts.

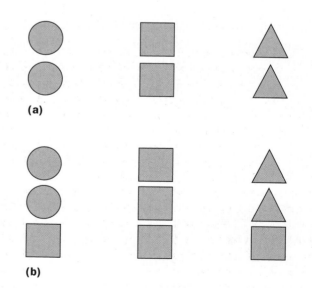

Figure 11.22 Concept formation. Participants were asked which of the groups of shapes were most similar. **(a)** Three pairs of geometrical shapes. **(b)** The same shapes with the addition of squares.

The concept this time was 'two things and a square'. If the participants were simply counting attributes, then the addition of a square to the pairs should not have changed their decision. As this study shows very clearly, concepts can include relations among elements that cannot be described by counting attributes.

Concepts are the raw material of thinking; they are what we think about. But thinking itself involves the manipulation and combination of concepts. Such thinking can take several forms, but the most common forms are deductive reasoning and inductive reasoning.

Deductive reasoning

Deductive reasoning consists of inferring specific instances from general principles or rules. For example, the following two series of sentences express deductive reasoning:

> John is taller than Phil
>
> Sue is shorter than Phil
>
> Therefore, John is taller than Sue
>
> All mammals have fur
>
> A bat is a mammal
>
> Therefore, a bat has fur

Deductions consist of two or more statements from which a conclusion is drawn. The first group of sentences presented above involves the application of a simple mathematical principle. The second group presents a syllogism. The syllogism, a form of deductive logic invented by Aristotle, is often found in tests of intelligence. A syllogism is a logical construction that consists of a major premise (e.g. 'all mammals have fur'), a minor premise ('a bat is a mammal'), and a conclusion ('a bat has fur'). The major and minor premises are assumed to be true. The problem is to decide whether the conclusion is true or false.

People differ widely in their ability to solve syllogisms. For example, many people would agree with the conclusion of the following syllogism:

> All mammals have fur
>
> A zilgid has fur
>
> Therefore, a zilgid is a mammal

These people would be wrong; the conclusion is not warranted. The major premise says only that all mammals have fur. It leaves open the possibility that some animals that have fur are not mammals.

Mental models

Why are some people better than others at solving syllogisms? Johnson-Laird (1985) notes that syllogistic reasoning is much more highly correlated with spatial ability than with verbal ability. Spatial ability includes the ability to visualise shapes and to manipulate them mentally. Why should skill at logical reasoning be related to this ability? Johnson-Laird and his colleagues (Johnson-Laird and Byrne, 1991; Johnson-Laird et al., 1992) suggest that people solve problems involving logical deduction by constructing **mental models,** mental constructions based on physical reality. When faced with a reasoning problem, people will generate a mental model of the puzzle and see what conclusions they can draw from parts of the mental model. They search for alternative models that might contradict the conclusion reached from the initial model; but if this falsification is not forthcoming, the conclusion is accepted. If the alternative model does falsify the conclusion reached by previous reasoning, the search goes on for an alternative model which may help us to reach the correct conclusion. For example, if you consider the following problem:

> A is less than C
>
> B is greater than C
>
> Is B greater than A?

in order to compare A with B, you must remember the order of the three elements. One kind of mental model is an imaginary line going from small to large in which you mentally place each item on the line as you encounter it. Then, with all three elements in a row, you can answer the question. Figure 11.23 illustrates this.

In fact, when we solve problems concerning comparisons of a series of items, we tend to think about our own mental model that represents the information rather than about the particular facts given to us (Potts, 1972). For example, consider this passage:

> Although the four craftsmen were brothers, they varied enormously in height. The electrician was the very tallest, and the plumber was shorter than him. The plumber was taller than the carpenter, who, in turn, was taller than the painter. (Source: Just and Carpenter, 1987, p. 202.)

After reading this passage, people can more easily answer questions about pairs of brothers who largely differ in height.

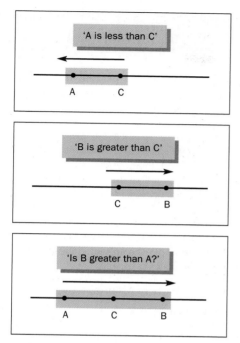

Figure 11.23 A mental model. Logical problems are often solved by imagining a physical representation of the facts.

For example, they are faster to answer the question, 'Who is taller, the electrician or the painter?' than the question, 'Who is taller, the plumber or the carpenter?' This finding is particularly important because the passage explicitly states that the plumber was taller than the carpenter, but one must infer that the electrician was taller than the painter. Just and Carpenter's study shows that the result of an inference can be more readily available than information explicitly given. How can this be? The most plausible explanation is that when people read the passage, they construct a mental model that represents the four brothers arranged in order of height. The painter is clearly the shortest and the electrician is clearly the tallest. Thus, a comparison between the extremes can be made very quickly.

The type of syllogistic reasoning described in the previous section does not always lead to an alternative model being sought. Many reasoners rarely go beyond the initial model they construct (Evans *et al.*, 1999). Participants in Evans *et al.*'s experiment, for example, were more likely to accept conclusions that were consistent with their original model and reject conclusions that were inconsistent rather than construct a more accurate, reasonable model. This lack of ability to search for alternative models and accept conclusions that are inconsistent with the original mental models can have serious consequences for us, especially if people are making judgements about our character, demeanour and conduct. Nowhere is this more important than when judgements are made against a person accused of a crime in a court trial. In a later section, you will see how juries appear to make their decisions (and the

factors that can affect the nature of this decision-making) and how biases in jurors' reasoning can affect their verdict.

Many creative scientists and engineers report that they use mental models to reason logically and solve practical and theoretical problems (Krueger, 1976). For example, the American physicist and Nobel laureate Richard Feynman said that he used rather bizarre mental models to keep track of characteristics of complex mathematical theorems to see whether they were logical and consistent. Here is how Feynman described his thought processes:

> When I'm trying to understand . . . I keep making up examples. For instance, the mathematicians would come in with a . . . theorem. As they're telling me the conditions of the theorem, I construct something that fits all the conditions. You know, you have a set [one ball] – disjoint [two balls]. Then the balls turn colours, grow hairs, or whatever, in my head as they [the mathematicians] put more conditions on. Finally, they state the theorem, which is some . . . thing about the ball which isn't true for my hairy green ball thing, so I say 'False!'
>
> (Source: Feynman, 1985, p. 70.)

Inductive reasoning

Deductive reasoning involves applying the rules of logic to infer specific instances from general principles or rules. This type of reasoning works well when general principles or rules have already been worked out. **Inductive reasoning** is the opposite of deductive reasoning; it consists of inferring general principles or rules from specific facts. In one well-known laboratory example of inductive reasoning, participants are shown cards that contain figures differing in several dimensions, such as shape, number and colour (Milner, 1964). On each trial, they are given two cards and asked to choose the one that represents a particular concept. After they choose a card, the experimenter indicates whether the decision is correct or not. The task is illustrated in Figure 11.24.

One trial is not enough to recognise the concept. If the first trial reveals that a card is correct, then the concept could be red, or four or triangle, or some combination of these, such as red triangle, four red shapes, or even four red triangles. Information gained from the second trial allows the subject to rule out some of these hypotheses – for example, shape does not matter, but colour and number do. The participant uses steps to solve the problem in much the same way as a scientist does: they form a hypothesis on the basis of the available evidence and test that hypothesis on subsequent trials. If it is proved false, it is abandoned, a new hypothesis consistent with what went before is constructed and this new hypothesis is tested.

Syllogistic reasoning – An international perspective

Several studies have suggested that illiterate, unschooled people in remote villages in various parts of the world are unable to solve syllogistic problems. Scribner (1977) visited two tribes of people in Liberia, West Africa – the Kpelle and the Vai – and found that tribespeople gave what Westerners would consider to be wrong answers. However, the people were not unable to reason logically but approached problems differently. For example, she presented the following problem to a Kpelle farmer. At first glance, the problem appears to be a reasonable one even for an illiterate, unschooled person because it refers to his own tribe and to an occupation he is familiar with.

> All Kpelle men are rice farmers
>
> Mr Smith is not a rice farmer
>
> Is he a Kpelle man?

The man replied:

Participant: I don't know the man in person. I have not laid eyes on the man himself.

Experimenter: Just think about the statement.

Participant: If I know him in person, I can answer that question, but since I do not know him in person, I cannot answer that question.

Experimenter: Try and answer from your Kpelle sense.

Participant: If you know a person, if a question comes up about him you are able to answer. But if you do not know the person, if a question comes up about him it's hard for you to answer.

Source: Scribner, 1977, p. 490.

The farmer's response did not show that he was unable to solve a problem in deductive logic. Instead, it indicated that as far as he was concerned, the question was unreasonable. In fact, his response contained an example of logical reasoning: 'If you know a person . . . you are able to answer.'

Scribner found that illiterate people would sometimes reject the premises of her syllogism, replace them with what they knew to be true, and then solve the new problem, as they had defined it. For example, she presented the following problem to a Vai tribesperson.

> All women who live in Monrovia are married
>
> Kemu is not married
>
> Does she live in Monrovia?

The answer was yes. The respondent said, 'Monrovia is not for any one kind of people, so Kemu came to live there.' The suggestion that only married women live in Monrovia was absurd, because the tribesperson knew otherwise. Thus, if Kemu wanted to live there, she could – and did.

Clearly, the intellectual ability of people in other cultures cannot be measured against Western standards. In the world of traditional tribal people, problems are solved by application of logical reasoning to facts gained through direct experience. Their deductive-reasoning ability is not necessarily inferior, it is simply different, pragmatic.

Figure 11.24 A card sorting task. Participants are asked to sort cards according to a given criterion, such as colour or shape, that is unknown to them. After they have successfully determined this criterion, it is unexpectedly and unknowingly changed and the participant has to determine the new sorting criterion.

Source: From Pinel, P.J., *Biopsychology*, 3rd edn © 1997. Published by Allyn and Bacon, Boston, MA. Copyright © by Pearson Education. By permission of the publisher.

Logical errors in inductive reasoning

Psychologists have identified several tendencies that interfere with people's ability to reason inductively. These include the failure to select the information they need to test a hypothesis, the failure to seek information that would be provided by a comparison group, and the disinclination to seek evidence that would indicate whether a hypothesis is false.

Failure to select relevant information

When reasoning inductively, people often fail to select the information they need to test a hypothesis. For example, consider the following task, from an experiment by Wason and Johnson-Laird (1972):

Your job is to determine which of the hidden parts of these cards you need to see in order to answer the following question decisively:

For these cards is it true that if there is a vowel on one side there is an even number on the other side?

You have only one opportunity to make this decision; you must not assume that you can inspect the cards one at a time. Name those cards which it is absolutely essential to see.

The participants were shown four cards like those in Figure 11.25. Most people say that they would need to see card (a), and they are correct. If there was not an even number on the back of card (a), then the rule is not correct. However, many participants failed to realise that card (d) must also be inspected. True, there is no even number on this card, but what if there is a vowel on the other side? If there is, then the rule is (again) proved wrong. Many participants also wanted to see card (c), but there is no need to do so. The hypothesis says nothing about whether an even number can be on one side of the card without there being a vowel on the other side.

People have to be taught the rules of logic; they do not automatically apply them when trying to solve a problem. But under certain circumstances, most people do reason logically. For example, Griggs and Cox (1982) presented a slightly different version of this test. They asked people to decide which cards should be checked to see whether the following statement was true: 'If a person is drinking beer, she must be over age 19.' The cards represented people; their age was on one side and their drink (beer or Coke) was on the other. Which card(s) would you check? (See Figure 11.26.)

Most participants correctly chose cards (a) and (d). They knew that if someone were drinking beer, she must be old enough. Similarly, if someone were 16 years old, we must check to see what she was drinking. The subjects readily recognised the fact that we do not need to know the age of someone drinking Coke, and someone 22 years old can drink whatever beverage she prefers. This study shows that experiments using puzzles designed to test people's reasoning ability do not always assess their ability to apply a logical rule to a practical situation.

In everyday life, people may commit biases in reasoning despite evidence showing that their reasoning is incorrect. The controversy in the UK concerning the possible role of the triple MMR (measles, mumps and rubella) vaccine in autism is an example of this. Some parents regard the multiple vaccination as potentially dangerous to their child and request single vaccines (one each for each of the infections). The reasoning is based on evidence from a study in which 12 children who received the MMR vaccine developed gut problems and symptoms of a developmental disorder called autism in which the child becomes withdrawn and does not engage in social and emotional communication. Other, larger, more sophisticated studies reporting no negative effect of the vaccine on child development did little to dispel the belief that MMR might cause autism.

This real-life example mirrors findings from the laboratory. In fact, laboratory studies try to investigate why some people commit these biases in reasoning and decision-making. In one study, participants were presented with hypothetical social reforms that would benefit the majority of people but would leave a small minority less well off (Baron and Jurney, 1993). Although participants agreed that such social policy decisions would be beneficial to all people, they voted against the proposals because some people might be worse off. This type of reasoning may explain why politicians behave in the way that they do.

Failure to utilise a comparison group

Another tendency that interferes with people's ability to reason inductively is their failure to consider a comparison group. Imagine that you learn that 79 per cent of the people with a particular disease get well within a month after taking a new, experimental drug (Stich, 1990). Is the drug effective? The correct answer to this question is: we cannot conclude anything – we need more information. What we need to know is what happens to people with the disease if they do not take the drug. If we find that only 22 per cent of these people recover within a month, then we would conclude that the drug is effective; 79 per cent is much greater than 22 per cent. On the other hand, if we find that 98 per cent recover without taking the drug, then we would conclude that the drug is worse than useless – it actually interferes with recovery. In other words, we need a control group. But most people are perfectly willing to conclude that, because 79 per cent seems like a high figure, the drug must work. Seeing the necessity for a control group does not come naturally; unless people are deliberately taught about control groups, they will not realise the need for them.

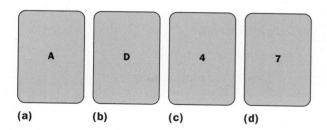

(a)   **(b)**   **(c)**   **(d)**

Figure 11.25 Cards used in a formal test of problem-solving.

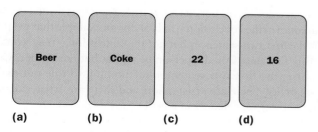

(a)   **(b)**   **(c)**   **(d)**

Figure 11.26 Cards used in a more realistic version of the problem-solving test.

Failure to seek or use information that would be provided by a control group has been called ignoring base rate information. As several researchers have suggested, the problem here may be that we engage in two types of reasoning (Reber, 1992; Evans and Over, 1996; Stanovich, 1999). One type of reasoning is deliberate and conscious and involves explicit memories of roles that we can describe verbally. The other type of reasoning is unconscious and uses information we have learned implicitly. Because the explicit and implicit memory systems involve at least some different brain mechanisms, information from one system cannot easily interact with information from the other system. One of the most serious consequences of this reasoning error can be seen in so-called pseudo-diagnosticity tasks (Doherty *et al.*, 1979). This task involves making a medical diagnosis and is presented in the following way:

> A patient shows symptom A which is present in 95 per cent of patients suffering from disease B.
>
> Does this give grounds to suspect that the patient is suffering from disease B?

This decision can only be made by considering whether symptom A is also present in other illnesses; that is, the person must be aware of the base rate likelihood of disease B occurring relative to other diseases. If symptom A is present in other diseases, the data presented above do not give good grounds for an exclusive diagnosis of disease B. People who are untrained reasoners usually fail to consider this possibility: they are not sensitive to base rate information (Evans *et al.*, 2002).

We are also more swayed by narrative, than numerical, evidence when making decisions and this leads to some erroneous decision-making. An online study examined the effects of narrative evidence and statistical evidence on men's perception of risk of contracting the hepatitis B virus and whether they would seek vaccination. All the participants were homosexual. Narrative evidence was more persuasive than statistical evidence in heightening awareness of the risk of contracting the illness and in predicting participants' intention to get vaccination.

If people are allowed to observe actual occurrences of certain events (that is, acquire the information about the base rate of occurrence automatically and implicitly), however, they can consider information about event frequency (Holyoak and Spellman, 1993). Furthermore, if people are given explicit instructions to consider alternative hypotheses, they will make decisions that take these alternative hypotheses into account (Klayman and Brown, 1993; Evans *et al.*, 2002).

Confirmation bias

Individuals may also show a disinclination to seek evidence that would indicate whether a hypothesis is false. Instead, people tend to seek evidence that might confirm their hypothesis; they exhibit the **confirmation bias.** For example, Wason (1968) presented people with the series of numbers '2, 4, 6' and asked them to try to figure out the rule to which they conformed. The participant was to test their hypothesis by making up series of numbers and saying them to the experimenter, who would reply yes or no. Then, whenever the participant decided that enough information had been gathered, they could say what the hypothesis was. If the answer was correct, the problem was solved. If it was not, the participant was to think of a new hypothesis and test that one.

Several rules could explain the series '2, 4, 6'. The rule could be 'even numbers', or 'each number is two more than the preceding one', or 'the middle number is the mean of the first and third number'. When people tested their hypotheses, they almost always did so by presenting several sets of numbers, all of which were consistent with their hypotheses. For example, if they thought that each number was two more than the preceding one, they might say '10, 12, 14' or '61, 63, 65'. Very few participants tried to test their hypotheses by choosing a set of numbers that did not conform to the rules, such as '12, 15, 22'. In fact, the series '12, 15, 22' does conform to the rule. The rule was so simple that few participants figured it out: each number must be larger than the preceding one.

The confirmation bias is very strong. Unless people are taught to do so, they tend not to think of possible non-examples of their hypotheses and to see whether they might be true – the way that scientists do. But, in fact, evidence that disconfirms a hypothesis is conclusive, whereas evidence that confirms it is not.

The confirmation bias in inductive reasoning has a counterpart in deductive reasoning. For example, consider the following sentences (Johnson-Laird, 1985):

> All the pilots are artists
>
> All the skiers are artists
>
> True or false: All the pilots are skiers

Many people say 'true'. They test the truth of the conclusion by imagining a person who is a pilot and an artist and a skier – and that person complies with the rules. Therefore, they decide that the conclusion is true. But if they would try to disconfirm the conclusion – to look for an example that would fit the first two sentences but not the conclusion – they would easily find one. Could a person be a pilot but not a skier? Of course; the first two sentences say nothing to rule out that possibility. There are artist–pilots and there are artist–skiers, but nothing says that there must be artist–pilot–skiers.

The tendency to seek (and to pay more attention to) events that might confirm our beliefs is demonstrated by the way we have distorted the original meaning of the saying, 'the exception

Cutting edge: Counterfactual thinking

You and your friend work a few hours a week in the University bookshop, to make a bit of extra money to make your bank balance go a bit further. You hear that your friend received a £50 bonus this month because the shop exceeded its targets. When you check your bank account online, you discover that you received only £20. It is still a bonus, but less than you'd anticipate. You feel a little bit crestfallen. But why?

This is an example of counterfactual thinking. This is a cognitive phenomenon in which our emotions are influenced by our knowledge of unobtained and obtained outcomes (Kahneman and Miller, 1986). In the bookshop example, even though you had received more money, you were expecting a better outcome, one which did not materialise.

Henderson and Norris (2013) sought to discover whether different regions of the brain were recruited during this type of thinking. Ursu and Carter (2005) had found that people who received outcomes that were very rewarding and unexpected showed increased activation in the medial OFC and more later OFC activation when the outcomes were disappointing. Coricelli et al. (2005) found an increase in medial OFC and lateral OFC activation when people regretted a disappointing outcome.

Henderson and Norris (2013) used fMRI to measure activation in participants who were asked to select one of two cards in a gambling game and were then told what the outcome of the selection would be (two amounts, one higher). Activation was found in the frontal and parietal cortices when participants experienced mixed emotions – not receiving the higher of the two wins. Activation in these regions correlated with activation in the dorsal and ventral striatum, regions involved in punishment and reward.

proves the rule'. Most people take this to mean that we can still consider a rule to be valid even if we encounter some exceptions. But that conclusion is illogical: if there is an exception, the rule is wrong. In fact, the original meaning of the phrase was, 'the exception tests the rule', which it does. The word 'prove' comes from the Latin probare, 'to test'.

Sure-thing principle

The sure thing principle states that if you believe that you prefer A to B in all states of the world, then you should prefer A to B in any state of the world (Hardman and Harries, 2002). Usually, when people commit violations of the principle, it indicates an inability to think through a problem or situation. For example, Shafir et al. (1993) asked students to imagine they were waiting for exam results and to plan for two outcomes: making a deposit for a holiday and deferring a decision on whether to go on holiday until after the exam results are published, or booking a cheap holiday immediately. Students who were told their result booked a holiday, whether the result was a pass or a fail. Students who were not told, however, elected to pay a small deposit and decide whether to go when the results were published. The evidence showed that even if those who deferred their holiday knew they had failed or passed, they would have booked the holiday. If they booked the holiday whatever their results were, why did they defer the holiday when they did not know the results?

Who believes in spoon bending?

'Would anyone in the audience who believes in telepathy, please put my hand up,' asked Emo Philips in one of his stand-up routines. This chapter (and Chapter 15 also) shows that people can make very poor reasoners and can make ineffective use of evidence to make judgements or inform decisions. Our decisions are affected by our own biases, personal beliefs and convictions. One review has highlighted some of these elementary reasoning errors in people who are convinced of their belief in something a little strange: psychic ability (Wiseman and Watt, 2006).

The two commonest types of psychic ability are extrasensory perception (ESP) and psychokinesis. ESP is the 'apparent ability to receive information via a channel of communication not presently recognised by mainstream science and includes alleged clairvoyance, telepathy and precognition (in which the information related to a future event)'. Psychokinesis is the 'apparent ability to influence physical objects and biological systems using unknown means, and encompasses a wide range of alleged phenomena, including causing objects to levitate, dice to roll at above chance levels and paranormal healing'. Is there something defective or unusual about the reasoning of the people who believe in such things?

Some psychologists have argued that believers in the paranormal have poor cognitive ability because they misattribute psychic causes to normal or natural phenomena – they cannot see a simple relationship between physical cause and effect (Alcock, 1981; Blackmore, 1992). There is some evidence of lower academic achievement in these individuals but the overall results are inconsistent.

People from the humanities are more likely to believe in psychic phenomena than are those with a science background but one study found that students of biology were greater believers than those from the humanities (Salter and Routledge, 1971). When asked to be critically evaluative of mock science papers, believers are less critical than non-believers (Gray and Mill, 1990). They are also poor at understanding probability. For example, if asked whether throwing 10 dice at the same time and getting 10 sixes is more or less likely than throwing one die 10 times and obtaining 10 sixes, believers underestimate the statistical likelihood (Musch and Ehrenberg, 2002). Believers are also more likely to see patterns in series of random dots (Blackmore and Moore, 1994) and to be prone to fantasy. 'The more the individual possesses the ability to find connections between their experiences and actual events', writes Blackmore (1992), 'the more likely they are to view their experiences as psychic'.

Probability heuristic

The probability heuristic is similar to the confirmation bias in the sense that it shows how people can draw conclusions based on what they believe rather than on available evidence. The difference between them is that the probability heuristic shows how people can draw erroneous conclusions by not taking into account the probability of an outcome (Kahneman *et al.*, 1982; Tversky and Kahneman, 1983). The example in Table 11.4 illustrates the concept. Read through the example now and then come back to the text to see how you did.

Table 11.4 The Linda problem

Linda is 31 years old, single, outspoken and very bright. She majored in philosophy. As a student, she was deeply concerned with issues of discrimination and social justice, and also participated in anti-nuclear demonstrations.

Please rank the following by their probability, using 1 for the most probable and 8 for the least probable.

A Linda is a teacher in primary school

B Linda works in a bookstore and takes yoga classes

C Linda is an attractive feminist

D Linda is a psychiatric social worker

E Linda is a member of Woman Against Rape

F Linda is a bank teller

G Linda is an insurance salesperson

H Linda is a bank teller and is an active feminist

Source: Tversky, A. and Kahneman, D., Extensional versus intuitive reasoning: Conjunction fallacy in probability judgement. Psychological Review, 1983, 90, 293–315, © 1983 by the American Psychological Association, reprinted with permission.

Psychology in action: Jury decision-making

Trial by jury itself, instead of being a security to persons who are accused, will be a delusion, a mockery and a snare. Lord Denman, Lord Chief Justice.

The outcomes of many famous historical trials by jury in Europe and the USA in recent years may give some credence to Denman's thoughts. The verdict in the O.J. Simpson case in the USA and the acquittal of the Maxwell brothers of fraud in the UK have led to calls for a review of the jury system (Doran and Jackson, 1997). Jury systems exist in many countries. In England and Wales, for example, juries are considered part of the justice delivery system, but only 2 per cent of criminal cases go to trial by jury. In the UK, jurors are usually laypersons with no especial expertise in law or the subject of the trial; numbers vary between 12 (England and Wales) and 15 (Scotland). The lay nature of juries has made some question the verdicts of fraud trials, for example, where it is felt that the detailed evidence of fraud presented by the prosecution cannot be fully appreciated by a lay juror. In other countries, a jury may comprise a mixture of lay and expert jurors, called an 'escabinato jury'.

In Western societies, the jury symbolises all that is democratic, fair and just in a society. Jury decisions can call into question core values, and can have dramatic social consequences. For example, the 1992 Los Angeles riots, which left 50 dead and 2,300 injured, were sparked by the perception that an all-white jury had delivered an unjust verdict of 'not guilty' in the trial of white police officers accused of beating a black motorist. Several

factors affect jury decision-making including the decision-making process itself, the number of people on a jury, jurors' prior beliefs, features specific to the case such as the sex, employment record and criminal history of the defendant, whether the crime involved the use of a weapon, and the availability of eyewitness testimony (Howitt, 2002).

Much of the research relies on experiments in which trials are simulated and mock juries hear (often genuine) court evidence, and draw their conclusions. The invented nature of much of these experiments obviously encourages us to be cautious when interpreting their results. However, many studies make their protocol as realistic as possible and encourage their participants to behave as if they were making real-life jury decisions.

Factors influencing juries' verdicts

The results make interesting reading. Allowing jurors to take notes or to ask questions leads to no significant change in the verdict reached or in the perception of the prosecution or defence (Penrod and Heuer, 1997), but makes the processing of complex evidence easier. The publicity given to a case (Otto *et al.*, 1994), the attractiveness of the victim (Kerr, 1978) and the order of evidence (Kassin *et al.*, 1990; Kerstholt and Jackson, 1998) have all been found to influence eventual verdicts. People who are anti-police are more likely to acquit than are those who do not hold anti-police views (Vidmar *et al.*, 1997),

▶

Psychology in action: *Continued*

and people are more persuaded by an expert witness when the evidence is complex (Cooper *et al.*, 1996).

Jury size is important. In the case of Williams v. Florida, the US Supreme Court ruled that six jurors were as effective as twelve. Juries usually require unanimity: in the UK this may be required at first but if this is not forthcoming a 10/12 majority is required. In Spain, on the other hand, there is what is called qualified majority voting. To reach a verdict of not guilty, a majority of 5/9 must be reached; for a verdict of guilty, 7/9 is required.

Large juries tend to result in hung verdicts (Zeisel, 1971; Saks and Marti, 1997) and spend longer deliberating on the verdict, engage in more irrelevant deliberations, make more assertions, regard trial evidence less meaningfully and are more intransigent than their unanimous-verdict counterparts (Arce *et al.*, 1998). Large juries are also likely to reach more guilty verdicts (Saks and Marti, 1997). Striking a note of caution, however, Saks and Marti found that although large mock juries reached more hung judgments, only 1 per cent of real juries were hung. When agreement between jurors is made compulsory, however, members do spend more time deliberating evidence in detail (Arce *et al.*, 1998).

In a study of 1,000 defendants on felony charges, Myers (1979) found that there were some specific features of the case that influenced verdicts. These included whether: a weapon was recovered, a large number of witnesses gave testimony or were prepared to, the defendant had previous convictions and was employed, whether the defendant was young or old; and the seriousness of the crime was also a factor. Factors not associated with the final verdict were the eyewitness testimony of the defendant, the testimony of experts and the defendant's relation to the victim.

How do jurors reach a verdict?

Psychologists have suggested two models which might account for this type of decision-making (Honess and Charman, 2002). The story model argues that jurors evaluate evidence/information in a step-by-step manner and construct a meaningful narrative using the evidence they hear. During the course of the trial, the juror begins to form a story and evaluates subsequent evidence in light of this (Pennington and Hastie, 1986, 1992). The second model is the dual-process model. This model argues that the juror engages in two types of processing during decision-making. The first type, systematic processing, involves paying close attention to case detail and engaging in close scrutiny of information. The second type, heuristic processing, involves paying less attention to detail but paying more attention to the social, emotional, subjective aspects of the case such as the persuasiveness of expert evidence, and the belief that there is 'no smoke without fire' (Eagly and Chaiken, 1993).

Evidence suggests that the story model best accounts for jury decision-making (Carlson and Russo, 2001). The model also suggests that because all jurors have access to evidence, their construction of stories will depend on the juror's own beliefs, predispositions and personal experiences.

Predecisional distortion'/bias

Failure to ignore a judge's instructions or to dismiss evidence deemed inadmissible is thought to contribute to bias in reasoning. Inadmissible evidence would still be evaluated, partially, according to the judgement the juror has already reached about the culpability of the defendant. Carlson and Russo call this 'predecisional distortion' because evidence is interpreted in a partial way before a verdict is reached. Carlson and Russo found that predecisional bias was greater in prospective mock jurors than it was in a group of students. These jurors distorted evidence twice as much, held stronger prior beliefs and were more confident in their judgements than were the student juror group, possibly because the prospective jurors were older than the students or because the students were more analytical and reflective. This is a reasonable hypothesis given that the prospective group held strong prior beliefs that were not particularly susceptible to change.

If this bias is inherent in the system – because jurors are thinking individuals with differences in belief, thinking style and intellect – how can it be avoided? For a juror to reach a verdict before all the evidence is presented, and to interpret evidence in a way that is consistent with that verdict, is clearly problematic (Constantini and King, 1980). There is some evidence, however, that if people are given instructions not to develop biased thinking (either pro – or anti – an individual), then these biases can be removed. In mock jury settings, giving juries instructions before evidence is presented is more effective than instructing them after all the evidence has been heard (Bourgeois *et al.*, 1995).

There are some biases, however, that people would find very difficult to avoid. Pre-trial publicity is a good example of information presented prior to trial that could influence a juror's view of the evidence. Some judges in the UK consider such publicity could prejudice a defendant's case, as happened in 2001 when a judge ordered a retrial of two professional footballers accused of assaulting a man in Leeds city centre. A retrial was ordered after a national newspaper published an interview with the father of the assaulted man. The judge ruled that the defendants would not receive a fair trial. Although it seems intuitively reasonable, there is no systematic evidence to support the idea that pre-trial information could cause juror bias. More realistically, however, as Studebacker and Penrod (1997) note, there is no trial anywhere in the world where a juror would not be aware of some aspects of the crime.

In what position in life did you place Linda? If you responded like those participants in the original experiment, you would be significantly less likely to indicate that Linda was a bank teller than a bank teller and a feminist. For some reason, people were not likely to consider bank tellers to be active feminists (or vice versa), thereby ignoring the principles of probability. This type of error, called a conjunction error, is reduced when the initial description of the person is followed by text stating that 100 people fit the description they have read and the reader is asked how many of them are bank tellers and bank tellers and active feminists. When led in this way, people do not commit errors in reasoning that take little account of probability; without such guidance, these errors are committed.

An example of real-life decision-making is seen every time a juror reaches a verdict in a trial. Jurors' decisions carry great weight and in some cases can determine whether a person lives or dies. The Psychology in Action box describes some of the factors that can influence a juror's decision-making and tries to explain how jurors reach their decisions.

Problem-solving

The ultimate function of thinking is to solve problems. We are faced with an enormous variety of them in our daily lives: fixing a television set, planning a picnic, choosing a spouse, navigating across the ocean, solving a maths problem, tracking some game, designing a bridge, finding a job. The ability to solve problems is related to academic success, vocational success and overall success in life, so trying to understand how we do so is an important undertaking.

Algorithms and heuristics

Some kinds of problem can be solved by following a sequence of operators known as an algorithm. **Algorithms** are procedures that consist of a series of steps that, if followed in the correct sequence, will provide a solution. If you apply properly the steps of an algorithm (such as long division) to divide one number by another, you will obtain the correct answer. But many problems are not as straightforward as this. When there is no algorithm to follow, we must follow a heuristic to guide our search for a path to the solution. Heuristics (from the Greek *heuriskein,* 'to discover') are general rules that are useful in guiding our search for a path to the solution of a problem. Heuristics tell us what to pay attention to, what to ignore and what strategy to take.

Heuristic methods can be very specific, or they can be quite general, applying to large categories of problems. For example, management courses try to teach students problem-solving methods they can use in a wide variety of contexts. Newell and Simon (1972) suggest a general heuristic method that can be used to solve any problem: means–ends analysis. The principle behind **means–ends analysis** is that a person should look for differences between the current state and the goal state and seek ways to reduce these differences. The steps of this method are as follows (Holyoak, 1990, p. 121):

1 Compare the current state to the goal state and identify differences between the two. If there are none, the problem is solved; otherwise, proceed.

2 Select an operator that would reduce one of the differences.

3 If the operator can be applied, do so; if not, set a new sub-goal of reaching a state at which the operator could be applied. Means–ends analysis is then applied to this new subgoal until the operator can be applied or the attempt to use it is abandoned.

4 Return to step 1.

At all times, the person's activity is oriented towards reducing the distance between the current state and the goal state. If problems are encountered along the way (i.e. if operators cannot be applied), then subgoals are created and means–ends analysis is applied to solving that problem, and so on until the goal is reached.

Of course, there may be more than one solution to a particular problem, and some solutions may be better than others. A good solution is one that uses the smallest number of actions while minimising the associated costs. The relative importance of cost and speed determines which solution is best. Intelligent problem-solving involves more than trying out various actions (applying various operators) to see whether they bring you closer to the goal. It also involves planning. When we plan, we act vicariously, 'trying out' various actions in our heads. Obviously, planning requires that we know something about the consequences of the actions we are considering. Experts are better at planning than are novices. If we do not know the consequences of particular actions, we will be obliged to try each action (apply each operator) and see what happens. Planning is especially important when many possible operators are present, when they are costly or time-consuming, or when they are irreversible. If we take an irreversible action that brings us to a dead end, we have failed to solve the problem.

Reasoning, decision-making and the brain

For most of our complex, intelligent behaviour, a region in the front of the brain appears to be essential. Damage to the frontal lobes is associated with deficits in planning, putting stimuli in the correct order, behaving spontaneously and inhibiting incorrect responses (Adolphs *et al.*, 1996).

Damasio and colleagues' studies of patients with frontal lobe damage show that these individuals have great difficulty in making correct decisions (Damasio, 1995; Bechara *et al.*, 1996, 1997). Damasio suggests that the ability to make decisions leading to positive or potentially harmful consequences depends on the activation of somatic (i.e. bodily) states. Damasio calls this the **somatic marker hypothesis** because such decisions involve automatic, endocrine and musculoskeletal routes. These routes mark events as important, but appear to be impaired in certain frontal lobe patients. When the decision can have a positive or negative outcome, the degree of physiological activity, such as heart rate and galvanic skin response (GSR) (see Chapter 4) that is normally seen in healthy individuals is absent in these patients (Bechara *et al.*, 1997).

In a typical experiment, patients were taught to play a card game (the Iowa Gambling Task) where they were told to make as much money as possible (Bechara *et al.*, 1997). There are four decks of cards and some have a high probability of delivering a large immediate monetary reward or a large delayed monetary loss or a low immediate monetary reward or a low delayed monetary loss. No participant was told which deck contained the greatest probability of obtaining these outcomes and, therefore, had to learn from experience, turning over cards and remembering the outcomes. They had hunches. When a decision involved a high degree of risk, for example, a healthy individual would show a characteristic increase in physiological arousal; the frontal lobe patient, however, would not. Neuroimaging studies of the same task are associated with increases in blood flow to the ventromedial region of the frontal cortex (Elliott *et al.*, 1997; Grant *et al.*, 2000).

Bechara *et al.* (1997) found that the ventromedial-damaged patients opted for the disadvantageous decks and failed to be sensitive to future consequences. Instead, they seemed to be guided by immediate reward. The researchers called this 'myopia for the future'. Even when the future consequences of behaving in a particular way were undesirable, these patients continued to behave in an inappropriate way. The group followed this up with a study showing that substance abusers performed within the same range as people with damage to the ventromedial cortex (Bechara *et al.*, 2001).

In healthy individuals, blood flow tends to increase in the frontal and parietal lobes during reasoning tasks (Goel *et al.*, 1997, 1998). According to theories of deduction, our ability to reason is either based on understanding the linguistic rules that underpin logic or based on whether visuospatial relations are involved in the reasoning (Goel, 2007). These two different interpretations probably explain why the results from neuroimaging have been inconsistent. Different types of reasoning tasks recruit different regions. For example, early studies, such as the PET studies of Goel – cited above – asked people to follow syllogisms such as:

> Some officers are generals
>
> No privates are generals
>
> Some officers are not privates

and found increased activation in the left frontal and temporal lobes.

Later studies, using fMRI, found increases in both sides of the PFC, the left temporal lobe and both sides of the parietal lobe (Goel *et al.*, 2000; Goel, 2003).

Differences in activation are seen depending on whether the reasoning task involves conditional reasoning (participants have to follow if–then relations), complex conditional reasoning (such as the card sorting task described earlier), and transitive inferences (e.g. understanding that the relationship between A and B or B and C can be transferred to A and C). Left prefrontal activation is seen during the first, bilateral occipital, parietal and frontal activation during the second and frontal and parietal activation in the last. Goel and Dolan

Cutting edge: Expertise

Some people clearly and obviously know more than we do. They are experts – in medicine, engineering, law, languages, plumbing. They have extensive conceptual and procedural knowledge of their domain, often without explicit knowledge of this. Expert touch typists, for example, know little about the location of keys on a QWERTY keyboard (Snyder *et al.*, 2013). Their knowledge is implicit. In tasks where visual components need to be analysed in order for a decision to be made, experts can do this quickly (whether this be in chess, medicine or Formula One racing).

Eye-movement studies suggest that experts analyse a scene, using different visual fixations to non-experts (Bertram *et al.*, 2013). In Bertram *et al.*'s study, they asked radiologists,

CT radiographers and psychology students to identify abnormalities – large lymph nodes – in a series of scans of an abdomen. Radiologists are physicians who specialise in scanning the body; radiographers are not physicians but people trained to administer and analyse body scans. An eye tracker was used to monitor eye movement during this decision-making.

Radiologists were better at detecting abnormalities than were the other two groups. Their eye movements also differed. Their saccades (eye movements) were shorter and when they saw large lymph nodes the number of fixations on the relevant areas were greater in this group. Both medical groups out-performed the psychology students and both identified obvious abnormalities.

(2001), for example, using the third type, asked people to reason problems such as:

> Graham is taller than Mike
>
> Mike is taller than Lynn
>
> Graham is taller than Lynn

Knauff *et al.* (2003) extended this to action sentences:

> A dog is cleaner than a cat
>
> An ape is dirtier than a cat
>
> A dog is cleaner than an ape

and found similar activation.

According to Goel (2007), these studies suggest that the frontal-temporal pathway provides us with a heuristic system for reasoning – it helps us process conceptually coherent material – whereas the parietal lobe underpins a more formal system based on universal reasoning rules – it is involved in processing non-conceptual, incoherent material.

There is an exception to this model, however. Take a look at the following statements:

1 Mary is cleverer than John; John is cleverer than George; Mary is cleverer than George

2 Mary is cleverer than John; John is cleverer than George; George is cleverer than Mary

3 Mary is cleverer than John; Mary is cleverer than George; John is cleverer than George

Patients with damage to the left PFC cannot process the first two types; patients with damage to the right are poor at processing the last, suggesting that there may be a degree of reasoning-related asymmetry in the brain.

In general, however, a small network of regions is involved in reasoning and, whatever the task, the PFC is involved.

Brain activation in the very intelligent

Would more or less activation in the frontal lobes be apparent in very bright individuals? An early PET study indicated that individuals with high IQ had lower metabolic rates than those with low IQ during problem-solving (Haier *et al.*, 1988). When high and low IQ individuals were trained on a computer game, both groups' brain activity declined but the decline in the high IQ group was more rapid, suggesting that the highly intellectually able may need to use less of their neural machinery to think (Haier *et al.*, 1992).

A study by Chinese researchers, however, has found that intelligence is not simply related to activity in the frontal lobe but to connections between this region and other brain areas (Song *et al.*, 2008). They used fMRI to study 59 healthy adults and correlated intelligence scores with the strength of connections between the orbitolateral prefrontal cortex (OLPFC) and other brain regions. They found that the greater the intelligence score, the greater the strength between the prefrontal cortex and the OLPFC within it, and with the parietal, limbic and occipital cortices. The results suggest that intelligence can be correlated with increased brain activation, even when the brain is at rest.

Creative thinking

Creativity has almost as many definitions as intelligence. We recognise that the writing of a novel, the design of a sculpture and the construction of a painting are creative products but what does it mean to be creative? Feldhusen and Goh (1995) define creativity as a 'complex mix of motivational conditions, personality factors, environmental conditions, chance factors and end products'. Vernon (1989) suggests that creativity is a person's capacity to produce ideas, inventions, artistic objects, insight and products evaluated highly by experts. Torrance (1975) defines creativity as a set of abilities, skills, motivations and states linked to dealing with problems. Others define the components of creative thinking as involving a realisation that a problem exists, formulation of questions to clarify the problem, determining the causes of the problem, clarifying the desired goal or solution and selecting a way to achieve this goal (Feldhusen, 1993). Still others have suggested that creativity involves producing a recognised, important end-product, not rubbish.

All of these definitions seem to have a common feature – that creativity involves some form of end-product. However, this end-product need not be material. Albert (1990), for example, has suggested that creativity is expressed through decisions not products. There do, however, seem to be different degrees of creativity. The production of a novel, painting or sculpture is undoubtedly creative, but solving inductive and deductive problems also involves a degree of creative thinking. However, artistic production seems to require creativity plus talent. These are high-level creative behaviours as opposed to the basic creative behaviour involved in solving deductive reasoning puzzles.

Given that psychologists cannot measure high-level creativity directly in the laboratory – they cannot ask individuals to come into the laboratory and write full-length novels, for example – they have devised other tests which tap the capacity to engage in creative thinking. The Torrance Tests of Creativity, for example, measure performance on a series of verbal and figural tasks such as naming as many objects as possible beginning with a specific letter or creating as many designs as possible using the same basic design (e.g. a circle). Torrance (1975) reported that performance on these tests predicted creative achievement, occupation and creative writing. Other tests, such as those by Wallach and Kogan (1965), are verbal and measure verbal fluency – the ability to devise many uses for objects and the ability to detect similarities between stimuli. There is little evidence that performance on tests such as the Wallach and Kogan and the Torrance Tests – called tests of divergent thinking – predicts creativity (Brown, 1989) and there is even doubt cast on whether they measure creative thinking at all (Kim, 2011).

Are there any features of the creative individual's personality that can predict creativity? Dacey (1989) has listed nine personality factors predictive of creativity and includes in this list flexibility, risk-taking and tolerance of ambiguity. Other factors suggested by other psychologists include: cognitive complexity, perceptual openness, field independence, autonomy and self-esteem (Woodman and Schoenfeldt, 1989), and fluency, flexibility, curiosity and humour (Treffinger *et al.*, 1990). Pride might be another.

In Greek mythology, Prometheus stole fire from the gods for mankind's use. Humans were thus able to use their own creativity and not rely on divine creation. The gods became displeased and released Pandora's Box on mankind – a casket of evil.

Source: Prometheus carrying fire (oil) Jan Crossiers (1600–71), Prado, Madrid, Spain. Index/Bridgeman Art Library Ltd.

Creativity and pride

Early Christian philosophy considered pride to be the deadliest of the deadly sins but, like the assumptions behind many ancient beliefs, the picture is a little more complicated than this. Psychologists have suggested that there may be two types of pride: adaptive and maladaptive. One might be authentic and the other hubristic. Authentic pride is illustrated by concrete personal achievement attributable to unstable, internal, specific causes ('I performed well on my exam because I revised thoroughly). Hubristic pride is illustrated by achievement attributable to internal, stable and global causes ('I did well at my exam because I am good at everything I do') (Tracy and Robins, 2007). The former is associated with positive and adaptive personality traits (e.g. extraversion, agreeableness) as well as self-esteem and civic duty, whereas the latter is negatively associated with these traits and associated with narcissism, rejection sensitivity, anxiety and other undesirable psychological states and traits.

Damian and Robins (2012) investigated whether the two types were related to creativity. They found that authentic pride was significantly and positively associated with creativity and intrinsic motivation, whereas hubristic pride was not associated with creativity and was positively associated with extrinsic motivation.

Creativity and romance

'In order to create', said the great Russian violinist Igor Stravinsky, 'there must be a dynamic force – and what force is more potent than love?' Researchers at Arizona State University examined the relationship between romantic motives and creativity in a series of experiments (Griskevicius *et al.*, 2006).

Men and women looked at photographs of attractive people of the opposite sex, or imagined being in a romantic scenario, and then completed subjective (writing a short story) and objective (the Remote Associates Test) creativity tests. The Remote Associates Test asks people to come up with one word that links three others in 15 seconds. For example, 'sun' would correctly bring together 'dress', 'dial' and 'flower'.

For men, thinking about an attractive woman as a potential romantic partner increased creativity. Women's creativity only increased when the man was perceived as trustworthy and committed. Men's increased creativity was therefore associated with attraction to a short-term mate, whereas women's was associated with attraction to a long-term mate. Women did not show increased creativity when thinking about a short-term or long-term mate who could not demonstrate good long-term viability as a partner. Although both sexes reported increased positive mood and arousal after appraising a person who might become a short-term partner, mood was unrelated to creativity.

The next step would be to examine not only the relationship between creativity and actual courtship, but also the relationship between the quality of the relationship and creativity.

Creativity, cognition and mood

Does a person's emotional state affect his or her ability to perform cognitive operations or be creative? In a famous series of experiments, Isen and colleagues found that while positive mood led to undergraduates betting larger amounts in a gambling game than did controls, these bets were only large when the probability of winning was high (Isen and Patrick, 1983) and that those in a positive mood thought about loss more (Isen and Geva, 1987). Individuals in a positive mood are more likely to choose a risky treatment for back pain than are those in a control group (Deldin and Levin, 1986).

Positive mood appears to have a beneficial effect on creativity, however (Isen *et al.*, 1987). People who had watched some comedy that induced positive mood were better able to solve a creative problem which involved supporting a lighted candle on a door using tacks, some matches in a matchbox and the candle (the solution, just in case you are not in a positive mood, is to tack the box to the door and place the candle lit with the matches, on top of the box).

Oaksford *et al.* (1996) extended this study by having participants complete creative and reasoning tasks after watching either a comedy programme, a neutral, wildlife programme or a negative documentary about stress. Their aim was to test two hypotheses. The facilitation hypothesis suggests that positive mood benefits creative thinking by facilitating it; the suppression hypothesis suggests that positive and negative moods take up resources that would normally be available for performing the cognitive task. Although positive and negative mood impaired performance on a deductive reasoning task, the positive mood only was associated with poor performance on the Tower of London Task which involves forward planning and reasoning. Some examples from the task can be seen in Figure 11.27.

Australians in a negative mood appear to be more successful than those in a positive mood at convincing others to agree with statements such as 'Student fees should be increased/decreased' or 'Aboriginal land rights should be preserved/restricted in Australia' (Forgas, 2007). Those in a negative mood were more likely to persuade others to believe an unpopular view than were people in a positive mood. Why? When the content of the arguments were examined, people in a negative mood were more likely to use concrete messages in their persuasion. This, in turn, led to more effective persuasion. Mood had influenced participants' processing style.

A sad or negative mood is not necessarily a disadvantage – it tends to be associated with thinking that is systematic and careful and less reliant on heuristics (Blanchette and Richards, 2010). Another phrase for it is 'depressive realism' – people are less biased and more accurate in their judgements (Allan *et al.*, 2007).

Anxiety, on the other hand, tends to be associated with risk aversion when making decisions (Maner and Gerend, 2007) especially when the risk is personally relevant. A review of anxiety and creativity suggests that some variables are uniformly associated with poor performance, especially when cognition involves creativity (Byron and Khazanchi, 2011). Anxiety impairs creativity, particularly if the person is characteristically anxious (the effects are less obvious if the person is temporarily anxious) presumably because this trait imposes cognitive demands that take thinking resources away from creativity and disrupt or interfere with creative production. The more complex the creativity task, the greater the impairment, a finding that supports the demand/interference model. Anxiety also affected children more than it did adults.

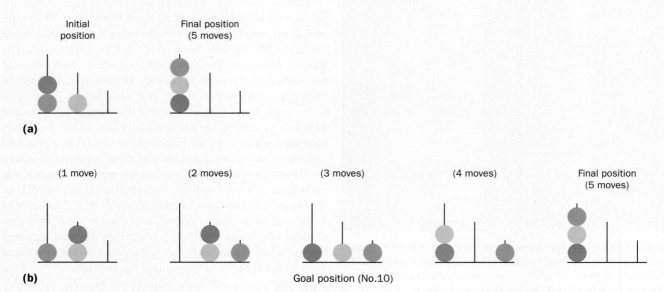

Figure 11.27 The Tower of London task. In **(a)** the participant is required to move the balls from the initial position to the target position in five moves; **(b)** shows how this is done.

Case studies in creativity

According to the theory of creativity proposed by Sternberg and Lubart (1991), there are three features of creativity that highly creative individuals possess. These features are: (1) domain-relevant skills – abilities the individual has in their domain and their knowledge of the domain; (2) creativity-relevant processes – the personality, cognitive style or other individual differences which promote creativity; and (3) intrinsic task motivation – the internal drive which motivates the individual and which can be influenced by the individual's environment. Domains for creative individuals such as John Irving, Charles Darwin and Claude Monet, for example, would be fiction, science and art, respectively.

Creative people are thought to produce products that are high in quality and novelty; intelligent, but not particularly creative, people can produce products of high quality but these may not be novel (Sternberg, 2001). The novel nature of creativity also suggests that its products 'defy the crowd' (Sternberg and Lubart, 1995): creative individuals produce unusual (sometimes) counter-intuitive products (ideas, as well as physical items), and some individuals, like Darwin, attempt to persuade the crowd with their ideas. Creatives also analyse the many ideas they have or may redefine problems or make unexpected connections between two things. As the British artist Damien Hirst remarked, 'Put two things together that are meaningless; together, they create meaning.'

Sternberg and Lubart (1991) also suggest that the creative individual is a little like a successful market trader: they buy low and sell high. That is, they identify a problem needing a solution or find/pose an important question, and are then the first to provide the solution, leaving others to elaborate on these solutions and refine them. Some creatives may not be well known because they try to pose too many questions or attempt solutions to too many problems.

Curiosity is a trait which, according to some psychologists, marks out the creative from the non-creative (Kashdan and Fincham, 2002). But is there a more fundamental characteristic of creativity which psychology's current questionnaires and measures do not tap? According to Sternberg (2002), there is. It is

the decision to be creative. People who create decide that they will forge their own path and follow it, for better or for worse. The path is a difficult one because people who defy convention often are not rewarded. Hence, at times, their self-esteem may be high, at other times, low. At times, they may work in groups, at other times individually. At times, they may feel curious, at other times, less so. But if psychologists are to understand and facilitate creativity, I suggest they must start, not with a kind of skill, not with a personality trait, not with a motivational set, and not with an emotional state, but rather, simply, with a decision . . . for creativity to occur, it must be preceded by a personal decision to think and act creatively, with all the risks attendant on doing so'.

'The physical impossibility of death in the mind of someone living' by Damien Hirst.
Source: Daniel Berehulak/Getty Images News/Getty Images.

Cutting edge: The creative scientist

Are there any traits of a creative scientist that mark him or her out as being different? Grosul and Feist (2013) examined the personality traits of 145 scientists who responded to a request to complete a survey. A total of 3,183 people were initially approached to participate. They found that openness to experience, neuroticism and psychoticism predicted scientific creativity (the number of papers they had published, and number of articles they had had cited). The more open, and less psychotic, the sample was the more likely it was to be productive and creative. The finding for psychoticism is surprising given that its relationship with creativity is often in the other direction – greater creativity is associated with greater psychoticism. The authors suggest that this, more frequent link, has been found with creative people who are not scientists. There may be a different quality of creativity found in scientists – and creativity was measured differently in this study to most creativity studies – than in other creative individuals.

Creativity and the brain

Brain damage can have negative (but also positive) effects on creativity. Shamay-Tsoory (2011) examined the effect of brain injury on original creative thinking – defined as producing statistically infrequent ideas or connections between events and things – in patients with damage to the medial PFC, the inferior frontal gyrus, and the posterior and temporal cortex. They used the Torrance Test of creativity – where a person draws as many different, original, new objects from a circle as they can – and the Alternate uses test – where people devise as many alternate uses for six common objects – to measure originality.

Damage to the medial PFC was associated with greatest impairment in originality. However, there were some unusual asymmetries. Right-sided PFC lesions led to lower creativity scores but left-sided PFC damage was associated with slightly higher ones. The researchers found that the larger the lesion in the left inferior frontal and left parietal and temporal cortices, the greater the originality score (the opposite outcome was found for right-sided lesions).

These are areas involved in language production and the authors cite research showing that patients with injury to the left inferior frontal cortex show a previously undemonstrated artistic ability and motivation or show greater originality with increasing degrees of aphasia. Thus, creative thinking may rely on right frontal regions but linear, linguistic thinking – which impedes creative thinking – involves the left. 'It is possible,' the author suggests, 'that in order to produce an original response, as opposed to a more typical response, one would need to inhibit the typical, automatic responses most likely related to left hemisphere activation' (p. 184).

The frontal lobes appear to be more involved in creativity than are other brain regions (Heilman, 2016). A meta-analysis of 34 neuroimaging studies which measured creative thinking found that activation during creativity tasks tended to be left-sided and in particular areas: the caudo-lateral PFC, the medial and rostral PFC and the inferior parietal and posterior temporal cortices (Gonen-Yaacovi *et al.*, 2013). The analysis also found some task-specific differences. For example, anterior areas of the lateral PFC were more activated when people had to generate a new shape from three existing shapes (so-called combination tasks) than when they generated unusual uses for objects. Some studies have suggested that creatively verbal experts – for example, people with 11 years' experience of creative fiction writing – have different patterns of connections between brain regions. Lotze *et al.* (2014) found that reduced activation in the connection between area 44 and both hemispheres and increased activation between the right caudate and intraparietal sulcus were characteristic of highly productive fiction writers.

Controversies in psychological science: Are creativity and psychopathology related?

The issue

According to Dryden, 'Great wits are sure to madness near allied, and thin partitions do their bounds divide'. As if providing direct evidence for Dryden's poetic analysis, Lady Caroline Lamb once famously described Lord Byron as mad, bad and dangerous to know. But what empirical evidence is there to link psychopathology and creativity? If there is a relationship, does creativity cause psychopathology or does psychopathology cause creativity? Is it possible to determine this?

The evidence

Kraepelin (1921) had originally described a disorder called manic-depressive insanity in which the manic aspect of the disorder would produce changes in thought that would increase creativity and thinking. A number of authors report that increases in creativity are common during the manic episodes of bipolar disorder (Sutherland, 1987; Jamison, 1989; Goodwin and Jamison, 1990). Jamison (1989), for example, found that creative individuals, especially poets, reported states of mania during creation although she did not specify the direction of the change in behaviour (whether the poetry caused the mania or vice versa). There was also a high incidence of suicide in poets. Weisberg (1994), in studying the quantity and quality of the work of the composer Franz Schubert, who suffered what we would today call a bipolar disorder, found that although the quantity of the composer's work increased during manic episodes, the quality was not significantly improved.

In a famous study of the relationship between creativity and psychopathology, Ludwig (1994) compared 59 women writers from a Women Writers' Conference at the University of Kentucky and 59 women from a housewives' association, medical centre and university women's club. Ludwig found that the writers were more likely to suffer from mood disorders, drug abuse, panic attacks, general anxiety and eating disorders. The results of this study complement those of writers attending an Iowa writers' workshop, 90 per cent of whom were men (Andreasen, 1987).

▶

Controversies in psychological science: *Continued*

The study found a greater incidence of mood disorder in this group than in the general population (80 per cent v. 30 per cent) and a greater incidence of bipolar disorder. Shapiro and Weisberg (1999) sought to determine if the same relationship held for non-eminent samples. They gave a creativity and creativity personality questionnaire to 20 undergraduates (from a sample of 70) who met strict criteria for bipolar disorder. The presence of hypomanic or euphoric symptoms was found to be significantly associated with creativity, although depressive symptoms were not. The authors speculated that the depressed effect may be a part of the creative individual's behaviour because the inability to be creative (because of pressures in other areas of life) makes the individual depressed.

In two studies of creativity, Post (1994, 1996) analysed extensively the biographies of 291 world-famous creative men (visual artists, composers, creative writers, scientists, scholars and statesmen). He found that 90 per cent of the writers in his sample exhibited some traits which would be classified as a personality disorder according to mental disorder diagnostic manuals; only one scientist showed this profile (Henry Babbage, inventor of the first computer). In addition, 73.4 per cent of scientists exhibited unremarkable sexual behaviour whereas only 39 per cent of writers did. Depressive episodes occurred in 72 per cent of the writers. These data suggested to Post that, although the study was retrospective, a 'causal nexus' existed between creativity and psychopathology. In a subsequent study of 100 American and British writers (Post, 1996), there was a high prevalence of mood disorder Poets showed the greatest degree of bipolar disorder, although the incidence of depression, marital/sexual problems and alcoholism in poets was low. When the degree of cognitive distortions found in the work of 36 eminent depressed and 36 non-depressed authors was analysed, there were more distortions in the depressed writers, and poets exhibited more than did novelists (Thomas and Duke, 2007).

A study of 40 innovative American jazz musicians from the 1940s, 1950s and 1960s found that about 50 per cent were addicted to heroin, and 27 per cent became dependent on alcohol (Wills, 2003). Only one of the sample (Bud Powell) was schizophrenic but 28 per cent had 'probable' depression. This study, according to the author, 'adds weight to the finding that outstanding workers in the arts can suffer from above-average levels of mental health problems but manage to produce exceptional work despite this'.

If creativity and psychopathology are related, what creates this link? One personality trait which has been linked with creativity is **psychoticism** (Eysenck, 1995). Psychoticism refers to a cold, manipulative and indifferent personality style. A number of studies has shown that creative individuals score highly on tests of psychoticism (Fodor, 1994; Stavridou and Furnham, 1996). However, Aguilar-Alonso (1996) found no difference between high and low psychoticism on a measure of

Stephen Fry, Carrie Fisher, Richard Dreyfuss: creative individuals associated with manic-depression or clinical depression.
Source: REX/Shutterstock (L), Getty Images/WireImage (R).

▶

Controversies in psychological science: *Continued*

verbal and drawing creativity. Rawlings (1985) has suggested that individuals high in psychoticism show the same impulsive, non-conforming processes that underlie creative thinking ability. In addition, the relationship between creativity and psychoticism is strong but only if psychoticism is measured with the Eysenck Personality Questionnaire and the measure of creativity is uniqueness (Acar and Runco, 2012).

Conclusion

Retrospective evidence suggests that there is a strong link between mental disorder and creativity. The problem with retrospective studies, however, is that we cannot empirically examine the personalities of creative individuals who are dead: we have to rely on books, anecdotes, personal reminiscences of creative individuals' relatives, friends or lovers. The findings of some recent empirical studies have been inconsistent. Modern studies employ creativity tests thought to tap specific forms of thinking but these may be far removed from the creativity seen in a visual artist, a poet or a novelist. While we may still be able to describe creative individuals as bad or dangerous, their madness is still open to question.

Chapter review

Theories of intelligence

- Although intelligence is often represented by a single score – the IQ – modern investigators do acknowledge the existence of specific abilities. What is controversial is whether a general factor also exists.
- Factor analysis is a data reduction technique that attempts to explain a large amount of data with reference to one or two factors.
- Spearman argued that a general intelligence factor existed (which he called g) and demonstrated that people's scores on a variety of specific tests of ability were correlated. He also believed that specific factors (s factors) also existed.
- Thurstone performed a factor analysis on 56 individual tests that revealed the existence of seven factors, not a single g factor.
- Cattell's factor analysis on such data obtained two factors. The nature of the tests that loaded heavily on these two factors suggested the names fluid intelligence (g_f) and crystallised intelligence (g_c), with the former representing a person's native ability and the latter representing what a person learns.
- Sternberg's triarchic theory of intelligence attempts to integrate laboratory research using the information processing approach and an analysis of intelligent behaviour in the natural environment.
- According to Sternberg, we use componential intelligence to plan and execute tasks. We use experiential intelligence to apply past strategies to new problems. Finally, we use contextual intelligence to adapt to, select or shape our environment.
- Gardner's multiple intelligences theory is based primarily on the types of skill that can be selectively lost through brain damage. His definition of intelligence includes many abilities that are commonly regarded as skills or talents.

- Like Sternberg's theory, Gardner's theory emphasises the significance of behaviours to the culture in which they occur.
- The most consistent sex difference in cognition is for mental rotation – men are better at it than are females.
- Men overestimate their own IQ but both sexes rate their fathers and male children as having higher IQs than their mothers or female children.

Intelligence testing

- Although the earliest known instance of ability testing was carried out by the ancient Chinese, modern intelligence testing dates from the efforts of Galton to measure individual differences.
- Galton made an important contribution to the field of measurement, but his tests of simple perceptual abilities were abandoned in favour of tests that attempt to assess more complex abilities, such as memory, logical reasoning and vocabulary.
- Binet developed a test that was designed to assess students' intellectual abilities in order to identify children with special educational needs.
- Although the test that superseded his, the Stanford–Binet Scale, provided for calculation of IQ, Binet believed that 'intelligence' was actually a composite of several specific abilities. For him, the concept of mental age was a convenience, not a biological reality.
- Wechsler's two intelligence tests, the WAIS-III for adults (and its variants) and the WISC-R for children, are the most widely used tests of intelligence.
- The reliability of modern intelligence tests is excellent, but assessing their validity is still difficult. Because no single criterion measure of intelligence exists, intelligence tests are validated by comparing the scores with measures of achievement, such as scholastic success.
- Tests also need to be intelligible and quick to complete.
- Intelligence tests can have both good and bad effects on the people who take them. The principal benefit is derived by identifying children with special needs (or special talents) who will profit from special programmes.

The roles of heredity and environment

- Variability in all physical traits is determined by a certain amount of genetic variability, environmental variability and an interaction between genetic and environmental factors.
- The degree to which genetic variability is responsible for the observed variability of a particular trait in a particular population is called heritability or h.
- Heritability is not an indication of the degree to which the trait is determined by biological factors; rather, it reflects the relative proportions of genetic and environmental variability found in a particular population.
- Intellectual development is affected by many factors, both pre- and post-natal. Potential intelligence can be permanently reduced during prenatal or post-natal development by injury, toxic chemicals, poor nutrition or disease.
- Twin studies and studies comparing biological and adoptive relatives indicate that both genetic and environmental factors affect intellectual ability, which is probably not surprising. These studies also point out that not all of a person's environment is shared by other members of the family; each person is an individual and is exposed to different environmental variables.
- The evidence suggests that biological children who are adopted are intellectually more like their biological parents; this finding applies across all age ranges.
- Although there are differences between races in terms of IQ score, it is unclear whether this is due to heredity.

Intelligence, thinking and ageing

- As we age, a decline is seen in working memory, retrieval of names, reaction time, declarative memory, information processing. Functions such as vocabulary, however, see some improvement with age.
- The cognitive decline is thought to be principally caused by poor processing speed, which means we perform tasks less quickly and efficiently than we did when younger.
- General IQ scores will peak at around 25 years of age and decline up to 65 years. After 65, the score drops rapidly.

- At the most severe end of cognitive decline, there is dementia – the gradual and relentless loss in intellectual function (especially memory) as the individual reaches the sixth decade of life and beyond.
- The major cause of dementia is Alzheimer's disease and the condition is called **Dementia of the Alzheimer Type.** The disease is characterised by abnormal protein deposits (plaques and tangles) in the brain. There is also a familial/genetic form and an early-onset form (which may have a genetic cause).

Thinking

- Formal concepts are defined as lists of essential characteristics of objects and events. In everyday life, we use natural concepts – collections of memories of particular examples, called exemplars.
- Concepts exist at the basic, subordinate and superordinate levels. We do most of our thinking about concepts at the basic level.
- Deductive reasoning consists of inferring specific instances from general principles.
- One of the most important skills in deductive reasoning is the ability to construct mental models that represent problems.
- Inductive reasoning involves inferring general principles from particular facts. This form of thinking involves generating and testing hypotheses.
- Without special training (such as learning the rules of the scientific method), people often ignore relevant information, ignore the necessity of control groups or show a confirmation bias – the tendency to look only for evidence that confirms one's hypothesis.

- Jury decision-making is one important real-life example of reasoning, and jurors can reach decisions that do not follow logic and that are influenced by factors other than trial evidence (such as jury size, pre-existing beliefs, aspects of the trial and so on).
- Current evidence suggests that jurors evaluate evidence in a step-by-step manner and construct a meaningful narrative using the evidence they hear.
- Problem-solving is best represented spatially: we follow a path in the problem space from the initial state to the goal state, using operators to get to each intermediate state. Sometimes a problem fits a particular mould and can be solved with an algorithm – a cut-and-dried set of operations.
- However, in most cases, a problem must be attacked by following a heuristic – a general rule that helps guide our search for a path to the solution of a problem. The most general heuristic is means–ends analysis, which involves taking steps that reduce the distance from the current state to the goal. If obstacles are encountered, subgoals are created and attempts are made to reach them.
- The regions of the brain recruited most consistently during reasoning and decision-making are the prefrontal cortex and parietal lobe.
- Creativity has been defined in many ways but most psychologists agree that it describes a person's capacity to produce novel ideas, inventions, objects or products and to engage in successful problem-solving.
- Studies suggest a link between psychopathology (such as manic depression and depression) and creativity, but whether the link is causal is open to question.

Suggestions for further reading

Intelligence

Carson, S. (2011) The unleashed mind. *Scientific American Mind*, 22, 22–9.

Cotelli, M., Manenti, R., Zanetti, O. and Miniussi, C. (2012) Non-pharmacological intervention for memory decline. *Frontiers in Human Neuroscience*, 6, 46.

Deary, I.J., Penke, L. and Johnson, W. (2010) The neuroscience of human intelligence. *Nature Review Neuroscience*, 11, 201–11.

Ellis, L. (2011) Identifying and explaining apparent universal sex differences in cognition and behavior. *Personality and Individual Differences*, 51, 552–61.

Nisbett, R.E., Aronson, J., Blair, C., Dickens, W., Flynn, J., Halpern, D.F. and Turkheimer, E. (2012) Intelligence: New findings and theoretical developments. *American Psychologist*, 67, 130–59.

Plomin, R. and Deary, I.J. (2015) Genetics and individual differences: five special findings. *Molecular Psychiatry*, 20, 98–108.

Some very good papers on intelligence . . .

Thinking and reasoning

Blanchette, I. and Richards, A. (2010) The influence of affect on higher level cognition: A review of research on interpretation, judgment, decision making and reasoning. *Cognition and Emotion*, 24, 561–95.

Holyoak, K.J. and Morrison, R.G. (2012) The *Oxford Handbook of Thinking and Reasoning*. Oxford: Oxford University Press.

Johnson-Laird, P.N. (2010) Mental models and human reasoning. *PNAS*, 107, 18243–50.

Kahneman, D. (2012) *Thinking, Fast and Slow*. London: Penguin.

Sutherland, S. (1992) *Irrationality*. London: Penguin.

Voyer, D., Voyer, S.D. and Saint-Aubin, J. (2017) Sex differences in visual-spatial working memory: a meta-analysis. *Psychonomic Bulletin & Review*, 24(2), 307–34.

. . . and some good books and papers on thinking and reasoning.

CHAPTER 12
Developmental psychology

THE SECRET OF A HAPPY CHILD: NO IRRITATING SIBLINGS TO GET IN THE WAY

In an interview with *Rolling Stone* magazine, Natalie Portman once said: 'I would never have been an actress if I weren't an only child, because my parents would never have let me be the star of the family'. It turns out that when it comes to the advantages of life without brothers and sisters, she was on to something.

One of the widest-ranging research projects on family life conducted in Britain has revealed that the fewer siblings children have, the happier they are – and that only children are the most contented.

It finds that: seven out of 10 British teenagers are 'very satisfied' with their lives, children from ethnic minorities are on average happier than their white British counterparts and that happiness declines the more siblings there are in a household.

Source: Anushka Asthana, *The Observer*

WHAT YOU SHOULD BE ABLE TO DO AFTER READING CHAPTER 12

- Describe the major stages of psychological development from birth.

- Outline the nature of foetal development and learning.

- Describe how infant perception, memory and cognition develop.

- Describe the emotional and social development of the child from infancy to adolescence and attempt to explain how this occurs.

- Describe the psychological changes that occur during adolescence, adulthood and old age and attempt to explain why these changes occur.

QUESTIONS TO THINK ABOUT

- Can a foetus learn?

- How does a child learn to think and perceive?

- Does a child's cognitive development progress in distinct, orderly, progressive stages?

- Is an infant's ability to perceive stimuli such as faces, innate?

- What is the relationship between brain development and cognitive development?

- What are a child's most important psychological functions?

- How valid are categories such as 'adolescence' and 'infancy'? How do we distinguish between them?

- Does the child see and hear what the adult sees and hears?

- When and how do children develop a sense of morality?

- What causes disorders of cognition and emotion in infants?

- What is your earliest memory? Is there something special about this date?

- How important is the nature of peer interaction to the social development of adolescents?

- Is adulthood marked by similar psychological milestones to those in infancy?

- How does social and cognitive behaviour change as people get older?

- Is cognitive decline in old age preventable?

- Are some cognitive abilities better preserved (or even improved) as we enter old age?

Developmental psychology

Apart from conception, development is probably the most astonishing thing we do. From birth to around late adolescence, we develop from a fairly unsophisticated bundle of reflexes and crude cognition to a fantastically efficient organism that can use language, perceive depth, colour, shape and motion, walk, run and jump, drive a car, or parachute from a plane, become a novelist, mathematician or physicist. There is an impressively rapid development of sensory, perceptual, social and cognitive ability during infancy and childhood and this, together with the further development of these abilities in adolescence and adulthood, is the subject matter of developmental psychology.

Developmental psychologists study both the similarities and the differences among people as they develop and change over the course of their life. Because of the longitudinal nature of this study, the area is sometimes described as lifespan developmental psychology, which acknowledges the fact that development does not end when adolescence ends.

The major developmental periods across the lifespan are the prenatal period, infancy and childhood, adolescence, adulthood, middle and late adulthood, and old age. This chapter considers the main developments that characterise each stage.

Prenatal development

The nine months between conception and birth is called the **prenatal period** and the length of a normal human pregnancy is 266 days, or 38 weeks. The prenatal period involves three developmental stages: the zygote, the embryo and the foetal stages. This is a vital period for the infant's later development (Glynn and Sandman, 2011).

Stages of prenatal development

Zygote stage

Conception, or the union of the ovum (egg) and sperm, is the starting point for prenatal development. During the **zygote stage**, which lasts about two weeks, the zygote, or the cell that is formed at conception, divides many times and the internal organs begin to form. By the end of the first week, the zygote consists of about 100 cells. Many of the cells are arranged in two layers, one for the skin, hair, nervous system and sensory organs, and the other for the digestive and respiratory systems and glands. Near the end of this stage, a third layer of cells appears, those that will eventually develop into the circulatory and excretory systems and muscles.

Embryo stage

Discriminating between the sexes is usually quite easy to do but in the early, embryonic stage of development, the organism can develop either female or male anatomy. At six weeks, a structure (called a gonad, located next to the kidneys) activates a process which can result in the development of an ovary or a testis (Ainsworth, 2015). If a testis develops, then the organism will produce an increase in testosterone; if an ovary develops, the organism will produce oestrogen and makes what would have been the structures of male anatomy disappear (testosterone has the same effect on female organs, such as the Fallopian tubes).

The second stage of prenatal development, the **embryo stage**, begins at about two weeks and ends about eight weeks after conception (see Figure 12.1).

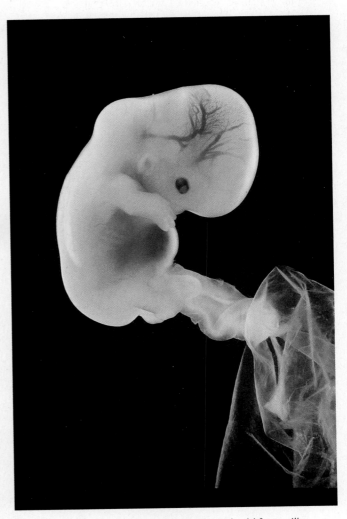

Figure 12.1 As this photograph of a six-week-old foetus illustrates, most of the major features that define the human body are present near the end of the embryonic stage of development (which starts at about two weeks and ends about eight weeks after conception).

Source: Neil Harding/Getty Images.

During this stage, the zygote is transformed into an embryo and development occurs at a rapid pace. Within a month after conception, a heart has begun to beat, a tiny brain has started to function, and most of the major body structures are beginning to form. By the end of this stage, the major features that define the human body – the arms, hands, fingers, legs, toes, shoulders, head and eyes – are discernible. Behaviourally, the embryo can react reflexively to stimulation. For example, if the mouth is stimulated, the embryo moves its upper body and neck. This stage is also noteworthy because it is here that the embryo is most susceptible to chemicals that can cause birth defects. These chemicals include drugs such as alcohol or toxins produced by diseases such as German measles, and are called **teratogens** (from the Greek *teras*, meaning 'monster').

Sexual development begins during the embryo stage. The determining factor for sex is the Y chromosome, which is contributed by the male parent at conception. If it is present, the embryo will become a male (XY); if it is not, it will become a female (XX). Early in prenatal development, the embryo develops a pair of gonads that will become either ovaries or testes (the word 'gonad' comes from the Greek gonos, meaning 'procreation'). If a Y chromosome is present, a gene located on it causes the production of a chemical signal that makes the gonads develop into testes. Otherwise, the gonads become ovaries. The gene responsible for this is SRY. However, more recently, studies have suggested that rather than individuals passively developing into females, there are genes – such as WNT4 – which activate ovaries and inhibit the development of testes. The consequence of this is that genes such as WNT4 can influence the sex of the organism, and that chromosomes are not the exclusive determinants of this.

The development of the other sex organs is determined by the presence or absence of testes. If testes are present, they begin secreting a class of sex hormones known as **androgens** (*andros* in Greek means 'man'; *gennan* means 'to produce') which bring about the development of the male internal sex organs, the penis and the scrotum. Thus, these hormones are absolutely necessary for the development of a male. The most important androgen is testosterone. We will see in Chapter 13 how this hormone is involved in other behaviours such as dominance and aggression.

In contrast, the development of female sex organs (uterus, vagina and labia) occurs naturally; it does not need to be stimulated by a hormone. If the gonads completely fail to develop, the foetus becomes female, with normal female sex organs. Of course, lacking ovaries, such a person cannot produce ova. See Figure 12.2. Some individuals, however, do not fall into the category of men or women – changes in chromosomes or genes can result in disordered sexual development.

Foetal stage

The final stage of prenatal development is the **foetal stage**, which lasts about seven months. It officially begins with the appearance of bone cells and ends with birth. At the end of the second month of pregnancy, the foetus is about 3 cm long and weighs about 28 g. By the end of the third month, the development of major organs is completed and the bones and muscles are beginning to develop. The foetus is now 7–8 cm long and weighs about 90 g. The foetus may show some movement, especially kicking.

By the end of the fourth month, the foetus is about 18 cm long and weighs about 180 g. It is also now sleeping and waking regularly. Foetal movements also become strong enough to be felt by the mother, and the heartbeat is strong enough to be heard through a stethoscope. During the sixth month, the foetus grows to over 33 cm long and weighs almost 1 kg. The

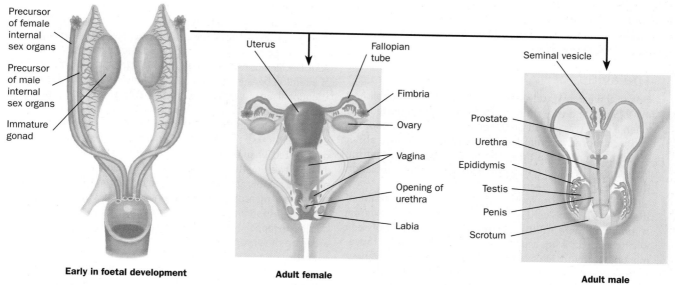

Figure 12.2 Differentiation and development of the sex organs.

seventh month is a critical month because if the foetus is born prematurely at this point, it has a fair chance of surviving. However, foetuses mature at different rates, and some 7-month-old foetuses may be mature enough to survive whereas others may not.

During the last two months of prenatal development, the foetus gains weight at the rate of about 0.2 kg per week. On average, the foetus is about 50 cm long and weighs about 2.8 kg at the end of this period. The foetus is now ready to be born.

Physical and perceptual development in infancy and childhood

Babies are called infants until 2 years of age. A newborn human infant is a helpless creature, absolutely dependent on adult care. But recent research has shown that newborns interact proactively, not simply passively, with their carers. They quickly develop skills that shape the behaviour of the adults with whom they interact.

John Betjeman wrote in his poem, *Summoned by Bells*, that 'childhood is measured out by sounds and smells/and sights before the dark of reason grows.' This section reviews the development of some of the infant's most important skills and some of the physical milestones of an infant's development. It begins with a brief review of brain development.

Brain development

The brain allows the infant to process information around it, to assimilate this material and to act on it. But without successful development, a disrupted brain can have serious consequences such as psychopathology and delayed cognitive ability (Kyiakopoulos and Frangou, 2009). If infants are born at 34 weeks and their grey matter is damaged, the likelihood of their developing behavioural problems and showing impaired cognition in infancy increases (Van Baar *et al.*, 2009). Similar problems are seen in children born before 39 weeks (Young *et al.*, 2010). The longer the period of gestation, the greater the grey matter density (Davis *et al.*, 2011).

As you saw in Chapters 4 and 10, the brain can exhibit considerable 'plasticity' during childhood. A child can recover more quickly from localised brain injury or damage than can adults.

Controversies in psychological science: Does foetal learning exist?

The issue

We assume that most development (cognitive, social and emotional) occurs from birth onwards. However, some research suggests that learning could occur before then, in the womb, a phenomenon called **foetal learning.** The foetus is active and can respond to its external environment. The important question, however, is whether this activity represents meaningful behaviour characteristic of learning or means nothing more sophisticated than a few automatic, involuntary motor or sensory responses.

The evidence

One of the earliest studies of foetal behaviour was published in 1925. Using a very simple paradigm, Pieper reported that when a hand was placed on the pregnant woman's abdomen and a car horn was sounded, the foetus would move about 25–30 per cent of the time. The finding suggested that the foetus might be more sensitive to external sensory stimulation than had previously been assumed.

Modern studies use foetal heart rate (FHR) as a measure of the foetus's responsiveness. If the foetus responds to external stimulation, there will be a change in FHR that is not seen when the foetus is not exposed to such stimulation. The movement of the foetus is also used as a measure of responsiveness. Using these measures, researchers have found that 37–42-week-old foetuses respond to noises (Schmidt *et al.*,

1985), and FHR responses can be recorded in foetuses as young as 29 weeks (Kisilevsky, 1995; Kisilevsky and Low, 1998). Movement has also been reported in 24–26-week-old foetuses about 1–5 seconds after the onset of a stimulus (Shahidullah and Hepper, 1993).

Is the foetus responding to the acoustic stimuli because it is stimulated by the noise or is it simply showing a reflex action resulting, perhaps, from the vibration caused by the noise? One source of evidence for a foetus's ability to discriminate between stimuli (and, therefore, some demonstrated form of elementary cognition) comes from studies of heart deceleration (or reduction). Deceleration of heart rate is thought to be a good measure of attention because a stimulus which impinges on the foetus's attentional radar is usually accompanied by a reduction in heart rate (Lecanuet *et al.*, 1992). Foetuses have shown evidence of deceleration when they are exposed to different sounds. For example, Lecanuet *et al.* (1989) found that a foetus's heart rate decelerated when the stimulus changed from the word 'babi' to 'biba', suggesting that it was capable of discriminating between phonetic stimuli, at least as measured by heart rate.

Another measure of foetal learning is dishabituation – the renewed responding to a stimulus after the initial response has declined (Hepper, 1994). Habituation and dishabituation involve a degree of sensory discrimination because some stimuli will activate a response and others will not. While this can be measured in the foetus – by separating testing sessions – psychologists have also been interested in the foetus's post-natal response

Controversies in psychological science: *Continued*

to the stimuli they were exposed to in the womb. For example, if a foetus responded to a stimulus in the womb would they show evidence of learning by preferring that stimulus once it is born? How would we measure this learning?

One way is by studying 'non-nutritive sucking' – the degree of sucking a baby makes when it is exposed to an experimental and control stimulus. Greater sucking is meant to indicate greater interest or attention. Newborns show greater evidence of sucking when they hear their mother's voice or when they are presented with melodies or stories they were exposed to in the womb (DeCasper and Fifer, 1980; DeCasper et al., 1994).

May et al. (2011) used a neuroimaging method that can be applied to study 0–3 day-old infants' brain response. They measured the infants' response to hearing a familiar and unfamiliar language – a familiar language would have been the one the infant would have been exposed to when it was in the womb. The familiar language was the one spoken by the mother and family. Both hemispheres showed increased activation to the familiar language and a decrease to the unfamiliar language. There was no region-specific difference in response to the two groups. The data complement behavioural studies showing that newborns can distinguish, and prefer, a familiar language (Byers-Heinlein et al., 2010).

There is also some evidence of pre-natal olfactory learning. Newborns are more attracted to the odour of amniotic fluid than other, unfamiliar odours (Schaal et al., 1995). Given a choice

between a breast covered in amniotic fluid and one covered with an unfamiliar fluid, newborns choose to suckle on the nipple coated with amniotic fluid (Winberg and Porter, 1998). Even the mother's eating pattern can influence this 'learning'. Mothers who were garlic eaters gave birth to infants who 'recognised' the odour of garlic (Hepper, 1995). A group of French researchers exposed 3–4-day-old infants to a novel odour (camomile) placed on the mother's nipple and measured whether they preferred this odour to the odour of breast milk or another odour (Delaunay-El Allam et al., 2006). Preference was measured via head orientation in a paired odour choice paradigm in which the babies were presented with two odours. (Infants orient, or move, towards the stimuli they prefer.)

It was found that those exposed to the novel odour preferred that odour more than they did a new odour (those not exposed did not show this preference). When the infants were presented with maternal milk and camomile odours, those who had been exposed to camomile found both odours to be equally attractive; those not exposed to camomile preferred the breast milk. The results show that even 4-day-old infants can learn to express preferences for odours to which they have been previously exposed. A more recent study has claimed that a group of 39 third trimester foetuses could respond to face like stimuli and that it prefers facelike stimuli to others (Reid et al, 2017), although a number of problems have been reported with this study (Scheel et al, 2017, in press).

Infants can be quick learners and responders to sound, but there is evidence that foetuses also show evidence of learning.

Source: Joe Klamar/AFP/Getty Images.

Controversies in psychological science: *Continued*

Conclusion

Does all of this evidence suggest that the foetus is capable of cognition? This depends on what we mean by cognition. If this means the ability to discriminate between stimuli, then neonates do demonstrate cognitive ability. They may be able to distinguish between the phonetic patterns in two stories, one of which was read to them when they were in the womb, but they clearly did not learn anything about the content or meaning of the story. Their learning was at a basic, perhaps even reflex, level. The auditory system may have sensed the phonetic nature of the story, but the neonate may not have been consciously aware of this sensation. The evidence suggests that the foetus is not simply an inactive, non-behaving organism, but a responsive and potentially discriminating human being.

If damage occurs between infancy and 6 or 7 years old, the function undertaken by the damaged region can recover speedily as long as adequate rehabilitation and support from family and friends are present (as you saw in Chapters 4 and 10). The case of Nico, the child who had half of his brain removed to prevent epileptic fits, exemplified this relatively sophisticated recovery.

Another important feature of brain development is myelination – the process whereby nerve fibres (the axons) an covered in a milky sheath (myelin) that assists the propagation of nerve impulses sent down these fibres. The most dramatic, and the fastest, changes in myelination occur between birth and 6 months; there is slightly slower change between the age of 12 and 24 months and then a period of stable myelination that progresses until early adulthood (Miller *et al.*, 2003; Hermoye *et al.*, 2006). Reflecting the functions that the infant relies on first, myelination is fastest in regions of the brain responsible for basic motor behaviour, the pons and cerebellum. Figure 12.3 shows myelination's milestones through childhood.

A number of factors influences the rate at which our brain grows and can impair this growth in the critical early stages when the cells of the brain are beginning to develop and make connections with other neurons. A lack of stimulation at a very early age can lead to a significant dysfunction in the nervous system. The failure to stimulate the visual system in animals, for example, leads to long-term disruption of this system's functioning (Blakemore and Mitchell, 1973). Malnutrition, discussed earlier, can have serious consequences for brain development and intellectual functioning.

Until recently, much of what we knew about the development of the brain and its function came from post-mortem studies, studies of acquired brain damage or rare case studies of children deprived of stimulation, such as Genie or the Wild Boy of Aveyron (see Chapter 10). Even then, these rare studies did not tell us precisely what occurred during brain development. Techniques such as fMRI and MRI (see Chapter 4) have enabled researchers to compare stages of brain development – white matter and grey matter – across the lifespan both within a sample (i.e. longitudinally) and between samples (cross-sectionally).

Research using these techniques has found that different parts of the brain mature at different times and that growth rates vary with age – the growth of cortical thickness, for

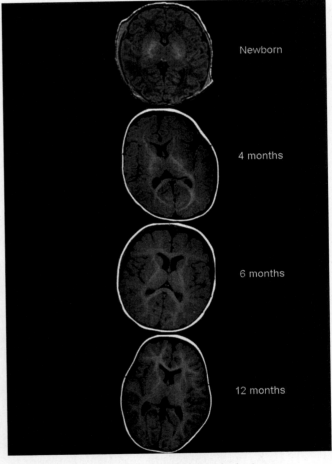

Figure 12.3 How myelination develops as the brain grows.

Source: Richmond, J. and Nelson, C.A. (2007). Accounting for change in declarative memory: A cognitive neuroscience perspective. *Development Review*, 27, 3, 349–73. Images courtesy of P. Ellen Grant, M.D.

example, is greater during the first than second year of life (Lyall *et al.*, 2015). Some areas of the brain have also shown cortical thinning with age – bilateral anterior cingulate and middle cingulate gyrus, for example. But cortical thickness reaches 97 per cent of adult levels by the age of two. Cortical surface area develops more slowly – only 69 per cent of cortical surface area has reached adult levels by the age of two. The folding of the cortex is also greater in the first than second year of life (Li *et al.*, 2014). Brain maturation, measured from 37 areas in the brain via MRI, can accurately predict chronological age between the ages of 5 and 18 years (Cao *et al.*, 2015). Techniques such as these have enabled the creation of 'brain maturation indices' or 'brain development indices' (Haartsen *et al.*, 2016) that use measures of brain structure to predict chronological age after 8 years.

Another feature of brain development is that grey matter volume increases early in development and then decreases from mid-childhood. The decline continues to early adulthood (Aubert-Broche *et al.*, 2013; Tamnes *et al.*, 2013; Wierenga *et al.*, 2014; Mills *et al.*, 2016) although some, unreplicated reports have found that grey matter peaks in adolescence rather than declines. Mills *et al.* found that in 391 participants, grey matter volume was highest in childhood and decreased in the second decade of life and decreased more quickly in the third. The decline may be attributable to pruning of the synapses.

White matter volume continues to increase throughout childhood and adolescence (and, in some studies adulthood), but declines after this stage (Haartsen *et al.*, 2016; Mills *et al.*, 2016; Pfefferbaum *et al.*, 2013). The greatest increase in white matter myelination occurs in the first year of life and continues, but much more slowly, until young adulthood when the temporal and frontal cortices are the last to experience complete myelination (Dubois *et al.*, 2014). You can see the pattern of development of white matter in Figure 12.4a and b.

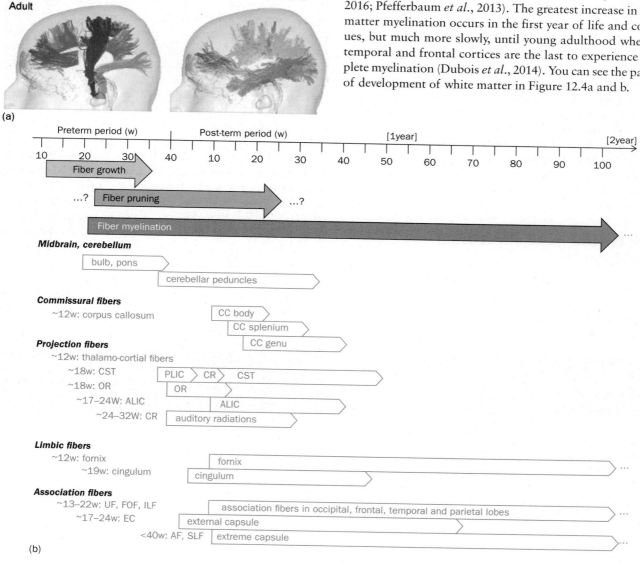

Figure 12.4 (a) How white matter bundle of fibres develop – images here show 6-week old infant brains and adults'. **(b)** The chronological development of different parts of the brain and its structures from before birth to 2 years after birth. From Dubois et al (2014).

Between birth and one year of age, the motor and auditory cortices are the first to develop, followed by the visual cortex and the default network (Gao *et al.*, 2015; Smyser and Neil, 2015). At birth there are already connections between the thalamus and sensory areas and this network develops in the first two years post-natally. Some connections between regions are greater at some ages than others. For example, Hampson *et al.* (2012) found that connectivity in paralimbic and subcortical regions increased with age, whereas connectivity between cortical areas, especially the visual cortex and the default mode network decreased. Ritchie *et al.* (2015) found that cognitive ability at age 73 and 76 predicted subsequent changes in brain volume but brain volumes did not predict later changes in cognitive performance. Although white and grey matter declined in these groups, white matter increases when they occurred were associated with a decline on a range of cognitive ability tests.

In terms of brain function, rather than structure, researchers have suggested that it is important to take other brain functions into account when examining age-related increases or decreases in brain function because these other functions might directly contribute to any changes observed. For example, Tsvetanov *et al.* (2015) argue that brain activation measures (such as fMRI) depend on neural and vascular activity and that age can affect vascular (blood flow) function. They found that when fMRI was used to record brain activation during an auditory and sensorimotor task, there was a reduction in activation in the visual and auditory cortex and an increase in the primary motor cortex. When vascular function was taken into account, the effects on the visual and auditory cortices disappeared; the effects on the motor cortex remained.

Does environment affect brain development?

The nature–nurture controversy is one of the oldest in psychology. Normally, this controversy revolves around the origins of a particular behaviour, talent or personality trait. People ask, 'Is it caused by biological or social factors?', 'Is it innate or learned?', 'Is it a result of hereditary or cultural influences?', 'Should we look for an explanation in the brain or in the environment?' Almost always, biology, innateness, heredity and the brain are placed on the 'nature' side of the equation. Society, learning, culture and the environment are placed on the 'nurture' side. Rarely does anyone question whether these groups of items form a true dichotomy and, in fact, they don't. Both count.

Studies using humans and laboratory animals show that interactions between hereditary and environmental factors – between nature and nurture – begin very early in life. Rosenzweig and his colleagues examined the effects of environmental stimulation on the development of the brain (Rosenzweig, 1984) by dividing litters of rats and placing the animals into two kinds of environment: enriched and impoverished. The enriched environment contained items such as running wheels, ladders, slides and 'toys' that the animals could explore and manipulate. The experimenters changed these objects every day to maximise the animals' experiences and to ensure that they would learn as much as possible. The impoverished environments were plain cages in a dimly illuminated, quiet room.

The researchers found that the brains of rats raised in the enriched environment had a thicker cerebral cortex, a better blood supply, more protein content and more acetylcholine, a transmitter substance that appears to play an important role in learning.

What is the evidence from humans that environment is important for proper neuronal development? A group of researchers from Canada, Japan and Germany measured the electrical activity of the brains of twelve 4–6-year-olds as the participants listened to the tone of a violin or a burst of noise (Fujioka *et al.*, 2006). Over the course of a year, half of the children received music lessons; the other half did not. MEG was used to record brain activity at four points during the year.

The researchers found that a brain electrical potential recorded from the left hemisphere appearing 250 ms after the onset of the violin sound was larger, and appeared earlier, in

---

Cutting edge: White matter and white matter – does breastfeeding affect the development of white matter in the brain?

According to Deoni *et al.* (2013) it does. They studied 133 children between 10 months and 4 years of age. The infants had been either exclusively breastfed, formula-fed for 3 months, or both. They found that the breastfed infants showed increased white matter in the frontal lobe and association areas. The length of breastfeeding (i.e. how long) was associated with the increase.

However, researchers have highlighted problems with this study. Anderson and Buggren (2014), have noted that the socioeconomic (SES) status of the mothers in these studies was not taken into account, nor was age controlled for (nor the sex of the children). They suggest that any cerebral change could have been attributable to these factors – the largest difference in volume between breastfed and formulafed children was found between high and low SES of the mother. There is also the possibility that the reasons not to breastfeed are important. Jenkins and Foster (2014) found that when this was taken into account, the breastfeeding effect on outcomes disappeared.

those children who had received musical training. As you might expect, musical discrimination was better in the trained group, but so was non-musical working memory. The study suggests that musical training can influence the brain's ability to produce electrical potentials elicited by music, but not non-music, sounds.

In a natural experiment, Skeels (1966) had reported that children removed from orphanages and placed in mental institutions developed normal intelligence whereas those that stayed in orphanages did not. These marked effects of environment on cognitive development have been seen in a very real context. According to UNICEF, 1.5 million children in Central and Eastern Europe are in orphanages, as a result of war. In 2004, 23,000 international adoptions were made in the US, and most of the children came from Eastern Europe, Russia and China (Nelson, 2007).

Sensory stimulation in these institutions is basic – there is little patterned light, for example, and walls are usually painted white. Infants are left in cribs, rarely held, and strict dress codes are usually applied, as are eating times (Nelson, 2007). As the early Skeels study showed, institutionalisation's effects are not positive and these effects are seen in current institutions (Maclean, 2003). These negative effects include poor health, physical impairment, impaired brain development, delay in speech and language, inattention, hyperactivity, impaired cognition and behavioural problems (Albers *et al.*, 1997; Rutter *et al.*, 1999; Chugani *et al.*, 2001). The children can catch up by the age of 4, if adopted and reared in a good environment. The reason they catch up may be attributable to the brain's plasticity, a notion you read about in Chapter 4.

Motor development

At birth, the infant's most important movements are reflexes – automatic movements in response to specific stimuli. The most important reflexes are the rooting, sucking and swallowing responses. If a baby's cheek is lightly touched, they will turn their head towards the direction of the touch (the rooting response). If the object makes contact with the baby's lips, the baby will open its mouth and begin sucking. When milk or any other liquid enters the mouth, the baby will automatically make swallowing movements. These reflexes are important for the baby's survival and for an infant's social development.

Normal motor development follows a distinct pattern, which appears to be dictated by maturation of the muscles and the nervous system. Maturation refers to any relatively stable change in thought, behaviour or physical growth that is due to the ageing process and not to experience. Although individual children progress at different rates, their development follows the same basic maturational pattern. Development of motor skills requires two ingredients: maturation of the child's nervous system and practice. Development of the nervous system is not complete at birth; considerable growth occurs during the first several months. In fact, some changes are still taking place in early adulthood.

Development of perceptual ability

If we want to study how older children or adults perceive the world, we can simply ask them about their experiences. We can determine how large an object must be for them to see it or how loud a sound must be for them to hear it. But we cannot talk to infants and expect to get any answers; we must use their non-verbal behaviour as an indicator of what they can perceive. Newborn infants indicate their taste preferences by facial expression and by choosing to swallow or not to swallow different liquids. When an infant is given a sweet liquid, the face relaxes in an expression rather like a smile; but when it is given a sour or bitter liquid, the face indicates displeasure. Newborn infants can even learn to recognise particular odours. Sullivan *et al.* (1991) presented 1-day-old infants with a citrus odour and then gently stroked them. The next day, these infants (but not control infants) turned towards a cotton swab containing the odour that had been paired with the stroking.

Cutting edge: is there a relationship between studying at home and children's brain structure?

According to a study from a group of Japanese researchers, yes (Asano *et al.*, 2014). They investigated the relationship between how long children said they studied at home on weekdays and the children's grey and white matter at two points, separated by three years. Parents indicated the number of hours the children spent on homework. 229 children participated, aged between 5.6 years and 18.4 years. IQ measures were taken at both times.

A significant, positive correlation was found between the number of hours spent studding at home and white matter volume in the right superior frontal gyrus (SFG). A positive correlation was also found between these hours and scores from a verbal comprehension test.

The authors suggest that the because the SFG is involved in memory over long periods, the increase in volume may be related to the increased memorisation resulting from greater home study.

Most investigations of the perceptual abilities of newborn infants have taken advantage of the fact that babies have good control of movements of their head, eyes and mouth. We will look at the results of some of these studies next.

Perception of patterns

The visual perceptual abilities of infants can be studied by observing their eye movements as visual stimuli are shown to them. A harmless spot of infrared light, invisible to humans, is directed onto the baby's eyes. A special television camera, sensitive to infrared light, records the spot and superimposes it on an image of the display that the baby is looking at. The technique is precise enough to determine which parts of a stimulus the baby is scanning. For example, Salapatek (1975) reported that a 1-month-old infant tends not to look at the inside of a figure. Instead, the baby's gaze seems to be 'trapped' by the edges.

By the age of 2 months, the baby scans across the border to investigate the interior of a figure. Before the age of 2 months, infants seem to be more concerned with the contours of visual stimuli and rarely attend to internal features. This is called the **externality effect** (Bushnell, 1979). One reason for the externality effect could be that the infant's visual system is developing and does not possess the acuity or contrast sensitivity (the ability to discriminate between degrees of shade) necessary to perceive complex stimuli. Figure 12.5 shows how babies in the early weeks of life prefer to examine the periphery of a stimulus and stare at areas of high contrast (such as hairline or the chin of the face). At around 2 months, the child inspects the internal features of the stimulus, such as the features of the face (Bronson, 1991).

At around 3 weeks of age, newborns will prefer to look at chequerboards made up of large squares rather than smaller ones; at around 8–14 weeks, the preference shifts to the small squares (Brennan *et al.*, 1966). See Figure 12.6 for an example of the stimuli the newborns prefer at different ages.

One reason for this difference in preference may be due to the development of contrast sensitivity. A chequerboard with large squares, for example, will show great contrast because the white and the black blocks are big and, therefore, contrast with each other clearly. Small squares on a chequerboard allow little opportunity for contrast and the newborn may perceive these as a blur.

The work by Salapatek and his colleagues suggests that at the age of 1 or 2 months, babies are probably not perceiving complete shapes; their scanning strategy is limited to fixations on a few parts of the object at which they are looking. Their ability to focus on stimuli, and their visual acuity (the ability to discriminate elements within a stimulus) is relatively poor.

Infants can see objects at six metres that adults can at 200 (Courage and Adams, 1990). However, by 3 months, babies show clear signs of pattern recognition and the visual system develops quite rapidly. At 3 months, the babies' ability to focus is as good as adults'. Newborns show evidence of colour preference – they prefer to look at coloured stimuli rather than grey ones – but their ability to discriminate between individual colours is poor. The ability to discriminate between colours, however, is seen by 2 months (Brown, 1990) and this improves over the next 3 months.

Face perception at birth

Is our ability to recognise faces an acquired skill or an innate function? Perhaps one of the most salient perceptual features of infant development is the gradual shift in preference from simple stimuli to patterned ones. For example, newborns prefer to look at stimuli that resemble the human face than at stimuli that do not (Rosser, 1994), and they prefer to look at scrambled faces than at a black and white oval stimulus (Fantz,

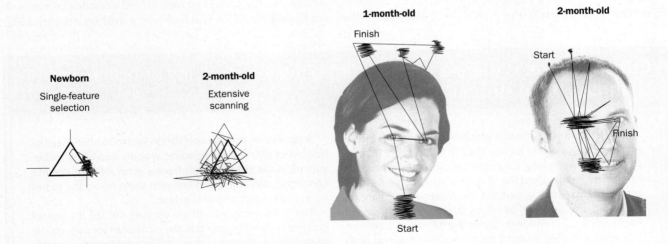

Figure 12.5 The ways in which an infant scans a face at 1 month and 2 months old.

Source: Adapted from Salapatek, P., Pattern perception in early infancy. In L.B. Cohen and P. Salapatek (eds) *Infant Perception: From sensation to cognition*. New York: Academic Press, 1975. Copyright 1975, with permission from Elsevier.

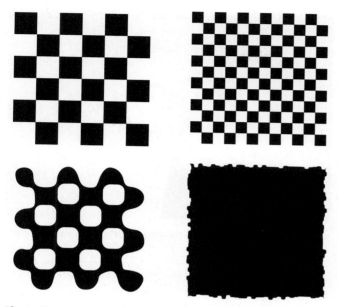

Figure 12.6 How the young infant perceives contrast. The two images at the bottom represent how the two images at the top, which differ in contrast, appear to young infants.

Source: Adapted from Banks, M.S. and Salapatek, P., Infant visual perception. In M.M. Haith and J.J. Campos (eds) *Handbook of Child Psychology*. Vol. 2: Infancy and developmental psychobiology (4th edn). New York: Wiley, 1983. Copyright © 1983, this material is used by permission of John Wiley & Sons, Inc.

1961). Three- to four-month olds have been found to look equally long at the mouth and eyes of a dynamic (than static) smiling face of a person making simple vocalisations, whereas nine month olds look more at the eyes than the mouth (Wilcox *et al.*, 2013).

Perceiving and recognising faces seems to rely on different perceptual mechanisms from those that allow us to recognise and perceive objects (as you saw in Chapter 6). Monkeys in a visually enriched environment but deprived of face stimuli will show a preference for monkey or human faces after this period of deprivation (Sugita, 2008). We process faces holistically and configurally, unlike most other objects. There are a multitude of aspects to face perception – identification, gaze, emotional expression – each of which is mediated by a different brain system (see Chapter 8).

At 2 years of age, infants show a preference for natural face arrangements rather than face arrangements that have disorganised features, which suggests that they show evidence of familiarity with the human face (Fantz, 1961; Bow-Haim *et al.*, 2006). There are two hypotheses regarding the way in which young infants perceive faces and other visual stimuli. The first, the sensory hypothesis, suggests that visual perception occurs in two stages (Kleiner, 1993). The first involves the infant comparing stimuli for contrast. If these stimuli are similar, then a second stage – the analysis of structure – takes place. This theory, therefore, suggests that if sensory characteristics are similar or identical, then preference for a stimulus will depend on the comparison of structure.

A competing hypothesis, the structural hypothesis, suggests that infants show a preference for face-like arrangements over non-face arrangements not because of the differences in the sensory properties of these stimuli but because infants have a specific device that contains information about the structural features of people's faces (Morton and Johnson, 1991). Morton and Johnson referred to this device that allows children to orient towards face-like stimuli as 'conspec'. Conspec is involved in perceiving the spatial relations between features of a face. For example, this device is responsible for perceiving that a cartoon face has elements in the right place to represent the mouth and eyes. Because conspec is a visual/perceptual device, it has a neural basis (in a subcortical structure called the superior colliculus, which guides the infant's attention to visual patterns). Another process allows the infant to learn about faces because they are guided towards paying attention to them – this is called 'conlearn'. Conlearn is thought to be a cortical function because it involves more sophisticated processing of information.

Evidence is inconsistent regarding that hypothesis is correct, although the structural hypothesis has been successfully tested (Valenza *et al.*, 1996). Umilta and his colleagues, for example, presented healthy newborns with a variety of different face stimuli in a series of experiments. The aim of the experiments was to discover whether the sensory properties of faces accounted for babies' orienting response or whether the arrangement of features in faces was the most important determinant of orienting (Umilta *et al.*, 1996; Simion *et al.*, 1998). In one experiment, newborns were presented with two stimuli: one with facial features in correct arrangement, the other in a different order. The babies preferred to look at the correctly arranged stimulus (Umilta *et al.*, 1996). When face-like patterns were presented which differed only in their degree of sensory salience – the 'eyes' and 'nose' were either blobs or the outline of blobs – babies preferred to look at the outlined blobs.

It was once thought that, up to the age of 10, children processed faces analytically – they looked at the individual features of a face when trying to recognise it. After this age, they began processing faces configurally – looking at the relations between features on a face in order to recognise it (Carey and Diamond, 1977). Research suggests that this is not the case and that both adults and children process faces configurally (Flin, 1985; Baenninger, 1994).

A study from researchers in Australia and England has examined how our competence for recognising faces develops from 5 to 15 years old (Johnston *et al.*, 2011). Participants either matched faces based on identity, emotional expression or matched images of butterfly wings. Ninety-two children and 24 adults completed the tasks. The 8–15-year-olds were significantly better at the facial identity than the facial emotion task. Younger children were better at the butterfly than the face tasks. The study shows that when tasks are equated for difficulty, clear differences in face processing occur across childhood.

Young infants' visual acuity is poor. The figure on the right is how the figure on the left would be perceived by a newborn.
Source: © DK Picture Library.

Figure 12.7 A visual cliff. The child does not cross the glass bridge.

Perception of space

The ability to perceive three-dimensional space and ability to judge the distance of objects from each other (depth perception) comes at an early age. Gibson and Walk (1960) placed 6-month-old babies on what they called a visual cliff – a platform containing a chequerboard pattern (see Figure 12.7). The platform adjoined a glass shelf mounted several feet over a floor that was also covered by the chequerboard pattern. Most babies who could crawl would not venture out onto the glass shelf. The infants acted as if they were afraid of falling.

Several different types of cue in the environment contribute to depth perception (see Chapter 6). One cue arises from the fact that each eye gets a slightly different view of the world (Poggio and Poggio, 1984). The ability to perceive the world using information from both eyes – binocular depth cues – emerges at around 2–3 months of age and improves rapidly thereafter. Both eyes need to be properly aligned in order for depth perception to occur properly. If one eye is out of alignment, a condition called strabisimus arises (cross-eyedness). However, the infant usually never develops stereoscopic vision, even if the eye movements are later corrected by surgery on the eye muscles. Banks *et al*. (1975) studied infants whose eye movement deficits were later corrected surgically. If surgery occurred before 3 years of age, stereoscopic vision developed; if the surgery occurred later, it did not. This suggests that there is a critical period for the development of aspects of the visual system: if the aspect is developing, it can be modified; if it is complete, modification is not possible.

Other cues, such as kinetic depth cues and pictorial depth cues (such as those used by artists to draw in three dimensions and which allow us to view a receding railtrack as receding), also improve with age. For example, at the age of 3–4 weeks, babies will blink if an object looms towards them (Nanez, 1987).

The development of depth perception appears to be closely allied with motor development because the child's movement (especially of the head) helps the child to locate objects and helps them navigate their way around the environment. Babies who have considerable experience of crawling are more anxious about crossing the visual cliff than are those with little crawling experience (Bertenthal *et al*., 1984). These experienced crawlers are also better able to remember the location of objects and to find hidden objects (Bai and Bertenthal, 1992).

Cognitive development in infancy and childhood

As children grow, their nervous systems mature and they undergo new experiences. Perceptual and motor skills become more complex and children become more competent at executing them. Children learn to recognise particular faces and voices, begin to talk and respond to the speech of others, and learn how to solve problems. Infants as young as 13 months are even able to form memories of specific events they experience (Bauer, 1997). Psychologists and linguists have studied the development of language, written and spoken, from infancy onwards (see Chapter 10). This section considers our current understanding of the development of two other major aspects of cognitive development: memory and thinking.

Number sense

Recent years have seen an increasing interest in how children understand and manipulate numbers and quantities. Of course, this is not a new topic – it is the cornerstone of one theory of cognitive development, described in a later section. But new experiments have highlighted shifts in numeracy as the child develops. For example, a 6-month-old can discriminate an array of eight dots or sounds from 16 but not eight from 12 (the distance is shorter); at 9 months, they can tell eight from 12 but not eight from 10 (Lipton and Spelke, 2003). This ability gets better with age so that between 3 and 6 years they can tell a 3:4 ratio from a 5:6 ratio (Halberda and

Feigenson, 2008). The ability may reside in a part of the brain called the intra parietal sulcus – activation is seen here in 4-year-olds during such task and this activation increases with age (Libertus and Brannon, 2009).

Development of memory

Memory development in infancy

Memory is a difficult process to study in infants because they have yet to develop language and cannot give the sophisticated linguistic responses that older children can (Rubin, 1982; Eacott and Crawley, 1998). One-year-old infants, in particular, show rapid forgetting of material. As adults, we can remember few memories of events occurring in this preverbal period – before the age of 5 years and certainly from before 3 and a half years (Mullen, 1994; Rubin, 2000). The failure to be able to retrieve memories for events that occurs in infancy is called childhood or **infantile amnesia** (Rubin 2000) and the period of 'amnesia' can occur from 0 to 8 years of age. The memories that are recalled from this early period tend to be fractured and disorganised and, as you saw in Chapter 8, attempts at confirming whether memories from this period have been repressed have not met with success. Some studies find that people are able to recall memories from before the age of three and even before the age of one (Strange and Hayne, 2013).

Verifying the accuracy of an early memory is, of course, almost impossible. One method psychologists have used is to compare young children and adults' ability to recall the same event, such as the birth of a sibling (Gross *et al.*, 2013). Thus Gross *et al.* asked 2–5-year-old children to recall memories associated with the recent birth of a sibling and asked adults to recall the same event from when they were that age. Both groups were unable to recall these memories, suggesting to the authors that such an event had not been encoded into long-term memory. Wells *et al.* (2014) asked people to free recall their earliest positive and negative emotional memories that could confidently be recalled. There was no difference in the number of types of emotional memory recalled but the majority of events occurred at age 6 to six and a half. Memory for the type of activity and the people present was good but other detail was less clearly recalled – what they were wearing, the time of the event, for example, or the event's duration.

There is some evidence to suggest that childhood amnesia may be culture-specific. For example, European Americans recall memories from a year earlier than do people from Taiwan (Wang, 2006) and similar differences have been found between US and Korean and Turkish samples (Mullen, 1994; Sahin and Mebert, 2013). The phenomenon might extend to the type of area in which participants live. Goz *et al.* (2016) asked 67 Turkish children between the ages of 10 and 13 to write down their earliest memory in as much detail as they could and to date it. The children either came from three villages in Bursa (rural) or from three municipalities in Istanbul (urban). Children from rural areas recorded memories from a year later than their urban counterparts but their memories included more social interactions and fewer details.

The autobiographical bump

Research has indicated that we have a reminiscence bump – adults over 40 years of age recall more memories from specific periods in childhood or early adulthood than for others (Rubin *et al.*, 1986). The bump can occur between 10 and 15 years of age, up to 30 (Dickson *et al.*, 2011; Koppel and Berntsen, 2014). The phenomenon can be identified in two ways – participants can be presented with a word cue and are asked to retrieve their earliest memory associated with that word; or participants are asked to free recall the most important autobiographical memories of their lives (Koppel and Berntsen, 2014). Each permits a different sort of retrieval – the word cue elicits any type of memory whereas the free recall places emphasis on the significance of the memory (Koppel and Berntsen, 2015).

Studies adopting the former technique find that participants recall fewer but earlier memories. For example, Koppel and Berntsen (2015) found that the bump for word-cues was found on average at 9 years of age (and ended at 25 years), whereas the bump for the important memories technique was 15 and 28 years, suggesting that there may be two – or more – bumps (Koppel and Rubin, 2016; Rubin, 2015). The bump may occur earlier depending on the way in which data are collected. Researchers sometimes divide memories according to periods – 0–5 years, 6–10 years and so on. Janssen *et al.* (2011) found that if they adopted a 5-year period as their standard measure, word-cued memories were more common between 6 and 10 years; if they adopted a 10-year period, the peak occurred between 11 and 20 years. The wording of the task, therefore, can influence the bump. Memories evoked by odours are more commonly retrieved between 0 and 10 years (Koppel and Rubin, 2016). Figure 12.8 shows the differences in the peaks of autobiographical bumps depending on the technique used to elicit them (Wells et al, 2013).

Measures of memory in infancy

Because infants do not have sophisticated language, psychologists have had to devise other methods of studying the way in which their memory works.

Usually when presented with two stimuli, one of which is familiar and the other novel, infants who are older than 8–10 weeks will look longer at the novel stimulus. This suggests that the infant is capable of being distracted by stimuli that it perceives as new. The perception of a stimulus as new implies that there is a memory of the old stimulus that is used as a comparison.

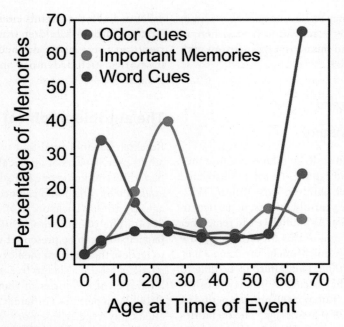

Figure 12.8 The memory bumps elicited by different types of sensory stimuli and cognitive prompts.

A version of this task, the paired-comparison task, involves exposing the infant to a stimulus and then, after a short while, presenting it with the pre-exposed stimulus and a novel one. Memory is measured by monitoring the length of time the infant gazes at the stimuli (Fantz, 1958). For successful recognition, the length between the initial presentation and the subsequent recognition task depends on the infant's age. Nine-month-old infants can recognise a stimulus successfully after a delay of between 90 and 160 seconds, whereas 6-month-old infants require a much shorter interval.

Habituation paradigms involve the presentation of stimuli to infants repeatedly until they cease to make an orienting response to it, that is, they begin to ignore it because it does not seem to interest them. Attention tends to be paid to stimuli that are different from those that have been repeatedly presented. The longer the delay between the habituated stimulus and a novel stimulus, the more likely it is that the infant will produce a response to the habituated stimulus.

Operant conditioning makes use of the child's manipulation of mobiles. The child learns that if it moves its foot, which is attached to the mobile, the mobile moves and, therefore, catches its attention. The more vigorous the kicking, the greater the movement of the mobile (Rovee and Rovee, 1969). Technically, this paradigm is called the **mobile conjugate reinforcement paradigm**. A version of this paradigm involves a period of not being able to move the mobile, then a period of being able to move the mobile (via a ribbon attached to the child's foot), followed by a period of not being able to move the mobile again (Sullivan *et al.*, 1979). This indicates whether the child has learned the association between moving its foot and the resulting effect on the mobile (see Figure 12.9).

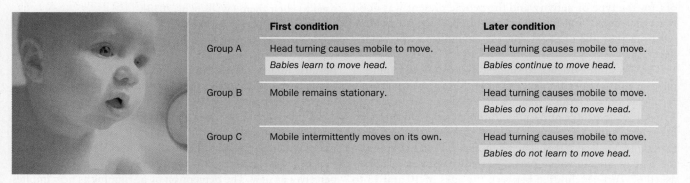

	First condition	Later condition
Group A	Head turning causes mobile to move. *Babies learn to move head.*	Head turning causes mobile to move. *Babies continue to move head.*
Group B	Mobile remains stationary.	Head turning causes mobile to move. *Babies do not learn to move head.*
Group C	Mobile intermittently moves on its own.	Head turning causes mobile to move. *Babies do not learn to move head.*

Figure 12.9 The importance of a responsive environment.

Source: Based on Watson, J.S. and Ramey, C.T., Reactions to responsive contingent stimulation in early infancy. *Merrill–Palmer Quarterly*, 1972, 18, 219–27.

Using this technique, researchers have found that young infants' recognition memory is relatively poor. Young infants of 2–3 months, although able to detect small changes in the mobile, are unable to recognise the mobile one day after training if the mobile has more than one element that has been changed, as measured by their reluctance to move the mobile (Rovee-Collier and Hayne, 1987). As the infant becomes older, however, the delay that can occur between presentations can become longer. For example, a 6-month-old infant can discriminate between a novel and a familiar stimulus after a delay of two weeks; an infant of 3 months can discriminate after a delay of only three days (Borovsky and Rovee-Collier, 1989).

The **deferred imitation paradigm** involves exposing the child to an adult who is performing some actions with a set of novel stimuli. After a delay, the 9–18-month-old infant is allowed to manipulate the objects used by the adult. Learning and memory is measured by the infant's ability to model its behaviour on the adult's (Meltzoff, 1988, 1995). If the toddler can understand instructions, it is given structured tasks, removed from the laboratory, returned again and asked to re-enact the activities it performed earlier. Memory performance for recently acquired actions (making a rattle) and familiar actions (putting a teddy to bed) is quite accurate (Bauer and Mandler, 1992; Mandler and McDonough, 1995).

Over the course of development from 1 to 2 years, the number of sequences of actions that the child can remember increases. At 20 months, for example, the child is able to remember three sequences (Bauer and Dow, 1994); at 24 months, the child can act out five (Bauer and Travis, 1993); at 30 months, the number of actions in the sequence can increase to eight. The finding that children can recall successively increasing series of steps with increasing age suggests that their memory capacity is increasing (or perhaps that their means of encoding is becoming more sophisticated and organised).

As age increases, so the delay between the initial learning period and recall sessions can also increase without any detriment to performance. By 14 months, for example, children have been found to be able to demonstrate the use of a series of observed props after a delay of one week (Meltzoff, 1988). The interesting question that arises from these findings is whether the child is engaging in imitation or in real reasoning. A recent study suggests that the child may be actually capable of reasoning, rather than imitating. Meltzoff's (1988) famous study of imitation learning in infants showed that when 14-month-old children watched an adult turn on a light box by touching the top of the box with the top of the head, two-thirds of the children attempted to switch on the light in this way a week later. None of the control group attempted to switch the light on in this way.

Gergely *et al.* (2002) repeated Meltzoff's study but instead of having the adult turn the light on with their head with hands free, they had adults either do the same as those in the Meltzoff study or had them occupy both hands. In the experiment, the hands occupied condition was achieved by having adults wrap their arms and torso in a blanket. Twenty-seven infants viewed either the 'hands-free' or 'hands-occupied' adult switching on the light.

When the adult's hands were free, 69 per cent of infants used their heads to switch on the light; when the adult's hands were occupied, only 21 per cent of infants used their heads. The study suggests that infants may be capable of greater rationality than that implied in Meltzoff's seminal study. 'The early imitation of goal-directed actions', the authors conclude, 'is a selective, inferential process that involves evaluation of the rationality of the means in relation to the constraints of the situation'.

By around 3 months of age, the infant shows awareness of changes in its environment; by 6 months, it is able to remember temporal order of stimuli. At 8 months, it is able to recognise words spoken in a story that it heard a while before. For example, Jusczykand Hohne (1997) exposed fifteen 8-month-old infants to three children's stories for 10 days. After two weeks, infants heard words that either occurred frequently in the stories or did not occur frequently. The infants listened significantly longer to the words that had been part of the stories.

The findings of this study suggest that because a delay of two weeks had passed between exposure and recognition, the infant is already beginning to form long-term memories for words occurring in speech. This, of course, has implications for language development (as we saw in Chapter 10).

Memory in early childhood

Between the ages of 1 and 3 years, the child develops the rudimentary language that allows them to communicate and to express an awareness of memory (Bauer, 1997). This awareness of events experienced in the past is quite considerable. For example, a child of 3 years can recall a visit to McDonald's or report an event that occurred when they were 2 years old or younger (Nelson, 1986; Fivush *et al.*, 1987). When the child is prompted by an adult, the memory performance is even more impressive (Fivush, 1984; Bauer *et al.*, 1995). If the child is asked to act out the event, as opposed to providing a verbal report of it, they are able to recall twice as much information.

At this age, children's memory can be tested in more sophisticated ways than those used for very young infants. For example, two of the most commonly used measures of memory in young children involve object hiding and retrieval and the acting out of observed events. In the hidden object task, the child sees an object being hidden by an adult and after a delay is asked to retrieve it (DeLoache, 1984). In the observed actions task, the child is exposed to an adult performing a series of actions with props; either immediately after this, or after a delay (and, in both cases, without practice), the child is asked to act out this demonstration.

Children are able to perform such tasks, even at 1–2 years of age. Bauer and Dow (1994), for example, required 16- and 20-month-old infants to demonstrate a series of seen actions after a delay of one week. At the time of the initial exposure, the action was putting a child's toy character to bed; at the retrieval session (one week later), the props had changed to a small dog and a plastic crib. Although the props were changed, the performance of the demonstration after a week's delay was not significantly different.

Knowing where things are – spatial development at 2 years old

Toddlers are quite adept at demonstrating their knowledge of where an object is: very young children can use information about distance and geometry to determine the location of an object. However, this ability is tempered, especially in younger toddlers. This suggests that the neural mechanism that allows such location finding may be developing at this age. For example, when 16–36-month-old toddlers watch a toy being placed in a box and are then moved to the opposite side of the box and asked to find the toy, 22-month-old children are able to use landmarks in the room to guide their object location but younger children fail to do so (Newcombe *et al.*, 1998). Two-year-old children forget more, after a delay between encoding and retrieval, than older infants, even when the effects of learning are kept constant (Bauer, 2006). This type of 'place learning' is thought to depend on the integrity of the hippocampus. When the context is changed or when a memory cue alters, infants remembering is impaired, perhaps because they interpret or perceive the cue and context as being a unitary representation, rather than considering both relatively and separately (Jones and Herbert, 2006). This ability to see relations between objects is thought to be attributable to the function of the hippocampus and this is not mature in infants.

Sluzenski *et al.* (2004) had 18–42-month-old infants complete tasks in which they had to remember multiple locations, learn the relations between objects and recall a learned location after a delay. For example, the two-location task involved the children observing two objects being hidden simultaneously in a box filled with sand. Whereas the performance of 18- and 24-month-old infants did not differ significantly when attempting to find the first toy, the 24-month-olds were better at finding the second object. In another task, children were taught the spatial relation between two objects and were asked to search for one of these when another was revealed. Performance was poor in most of the children. In a retention task, children were asked to find an object after a delay between observing the object being hidden and retrieving it. The 18-month-olds performed more poorly than the other groups, especially the older ones.

Why does the child's memory improve dramatically from 1 to 4 years of age?

Three factors seem to account for the child's ability to recall information better with age: the formation of memory-related structures, the development of language and the development of metamemory, that is, the realisation that using memory strategies will help the child to think and behave. The development of language means that a child has the capability to encode material verbally instead of via some other representation such as visual representation. By the age of 3 years, for example, the child begins initiating conversation (Fivush *et al.*, 1987). Interestingly, it has been suggested that it is not the verbal encoding of material per se that causes improvement in memory but the verbal expression of memory. That is, if a memory is verbally expressed, then this memory will be retained longer than if it had not been expressed (Nelson, 1993; Bauer and Wewerka, 1995).

It has also been suggested that the types of memory recalled from early and later infancy are dependent on whether the child is employing a narrative technique to give structure and meaning to events. Autobiographical memory develops later in infancy and this form of memory relies on the structuring and organisation of events to make them meaningful. Perhaps one reason why we can remember events as adults from the age of 4 years onwards but not before then is because we did not have a narrative structure in place before the age of 4 to give material meaning and depth (Nelson, 1993). This is quite a controversial idea.

The relationship between childhood maltreatment and psychological development

There is evidence that exposure to emotional or physical abuse in childhood is associated with later impairments in psychological development and adjustment (e.g. Norman *et al.*, 2012; Teicher and Samson, 2013; Khan *et al.*, 2015). The Adverse Childhood Experience study found that maltreatment in childhood was a significant predictor of later depression, suicidal ideation (thinking about committing suicide) and attempted suicide (Dube *et al.*, 2001, 2003). This study also found that as the number of childhood examples of maltreatment increased, so did later psychiatric disorders.

The appearance of later psychiatric conditions appears to be related to the type of abuse experienced. Depression, for example, is more likely to arise from emotional abuse than physical abuse (Norman *et al.*, 2012). The risk of later drug use is greater for physical than emotional abuse. Anxiety has been found to be more common in those who had experienced sexual abuse after 12 years of age and depression more common in those experiencing abuse before 12 years of age (Schoedl *et al.*, 2010). The type and number of psychiatric symptoms also appears to vary according to when childhood maltreatment occurred – early or late (Thornberry *et al.*, 2012), although this may be a simplistic and arbitrary division. Other studies have found age-specific evidence of later psychiatric disorder – PTSD and depression occurring more commonly after abuse at 3–5 years than 0–2 or 6–8, for example (Dunn *et al.*, 2013).

Some researchers have suggested that examples of childhood abuse affect brain development and structure. For example, parental verbal abuse has been associated with decreased connectivity between Broca's and Wernicke's areas (Choi *et al.*, 2009), whereas seeing acts of domestic violence affected other pathways such as those linking the limbic system and the visual cortical areas (Choi *et al.*, 2011). Heim *et al.* (2013) found that the area of the somatosensory cortex representing the genitals was thinner in women who had reported experiencing childhood sexual abuse but the same characteristic was not found in women who had experienced emotional abuse.

Other researchers have found that the age at which abuse occurs affects brain regions at different times. Abuse during the ages of 3 and 5 and 11 and 13 was more likely to be associated with hippocampal atrophy, whereas the prefrontal cortex was affected when the abuse occurred at 9–10 and 14–16 years of age (Andersen *et al.*, 2008). Seeing abuse between parents has been associated with visual cortex dysfunction when the abuse was seen between 11 and 13 years of age (Tomodo *et al.*, 2012). Many other examples of this kind have been reported (Khan *et al.*, 2015).

Khan *et al.* (2015) examined the relationship between the number and type of maltreatment experienced in childhood by boys and girls, and major depressive disorder. They recruited a community sample of 560 young adults (18–25 years). The sample had experienced between 0 and 4 types of maltreatment (from a list of 10). The strongest predictor of lifetime depression in men was the experience of non-verbal emotional abuse at 14 years of age; the greatest predictor for women was peer emotional abuse at the same age. These were better predictors than the number of examples of maltreatment. The authors note that non-verbal emotional abuse is characterised by having parents who are very difficult to please, do not have time to talk to their children or have no interest in them, withhold secrets and expect their children to take on adult responsibilities. 'Being rejected at about 14 years of age', they conclude, 'may be a crucial underlying risk factor for the emergence of depression in both males and females' (p. 23). The causal direction of this relationship is unclear – the depression might lead to rejection but the rejection might lead to depression.

The development of cognition: Jean Piaget

The most influential student of child development has been Jean Piaget (1896–1980), a Swiss psychologist, who viewed cognitive development as a maturational process. Piaget formulated the most comprehensive description of the process of cognitive development that we have. His conclusions were based on his observations of the behaviour of children – first,

of his own children at home and, later, of other children at his Centre of Genetic Epistemology in Geneva. He noticed that children of similar age tend to engage in similar behaviours and to make the same kinds of mistakes in problem-solving. He concluded that these similarities are the result of a sequence of development that all normal children follow. Completion of each period, with its corresponding abilities, is the prerequisite for entering the next period.

According to Piaget, as children develop they acquire cognitive structures – mental representations or rules that are used for understanding and dealing with the world and for thinking about and solving problems. The two principal types of **cognitive structure** are schemata and concepts. **Schemata** ('schema' is the singular form) are mental representations or sets of rules that define a particular category of behaviour – how the behaviour is executed and under what conditions. A child is said to have a 'grasping schema' when they are able to grasp a rattle in their hand. Once they have learned how to grasp a rattle, they can then use the same schema to grasp other objects. A child has acquired a 'picking up schema' when they are able to lift the rattle from a surface.

Piaget suggested that as a child acquires knowledge of the environment, they develop mental structures called concepts – rules that describe properties of environmental events and their relations to other concepts. For example, concepts about the existence of various objects include what the objects do, how they relate to other objects, and what happens when they are touched or manipulated. Thus, an infant's cognitive structure includes concepts of such things as rattles, balls, crib slats, hands and other people.

Infants acquire schemata and concepts by interacting with their environment. According to Piaget, two processes help a child to adapt to its environment: assimilation and accommodation. **Assimilation** is the process by which new information is modified to fit existing schemata. For example, when a child moves a wooden block along a surface while making the rumbling sound of an engine, they have assimilated the wooden block into their schema of a car. **Accommodation** is the process by which old schemata are changed by new experiences. Accommodation produces either new schemata or changes in existing ones. For example, suppose that a young girl's concept of animal has three categories: doggies, kitties and teddies. If she sees a picture of a deer and calls it a kitty, she has assimilated the new information into an existing concept. However, if she decides that a deer is a new kind of animal, she will accommodate her animal concept to include the new category. Now this concept consists of doggies, kitties, teddies and deer.

Assimilation and accommodation are closely linked in that they both work together but there are periods in the child's life when it will assimilate more than it will accommodate (and vice versa). Piaget referred to this state as cognitive 'equilibrium'. When the child undergoes periods of quick and radical change, however, there is disequilibrium – new information does not match what the child knows and so the child has to accommodate the new information, rather than assimilate it. Once accommodation has taken place, the child returns to assimilation.

Piaget's four periods of cognitive development

Although development is a continuous process, the cognitive structures of children vary from age to age. We can make inferences about the rules that children of certain ages use to understand their environment and control their behaviour. Piaget divided cognitive development into four periods: sensorimotor, preoperational, concrete operational and formal operational. What a child learns in one period enables them to progress to the next period. This conception of stages was viewed as invariant – they always appeared in this order – and universal – they emerge in this way in all children. See Table 12.1 for a summary of Piaget's stages.

The sensorimotor period

The **sensorimotor period**, which lasts for approximately the first two years of life, is the first stage in Piaget's theory of cognitive development. It is marked by an orderly progression of increasingly complex cognitive development ranging from reflexes to symbolic thinking. During this period, cognition is closely tied to external stimulation. An important feature of the sensorimotor period is the development of **object permanence**, the idea that objects do not disappear when they are out of sight. Until about 5 months of age, children appear to lose all interest in an object that disappears from sight – the saying 'out of sight, out of mind' seems particularly appropriate. In addition, cognition consists entirely in behaviour: thinking is doing.

At first, infants do not appear to have a concept for objects. They can look at visual stimuli and will turn their heads and eyes towards the source of a sound, but hiding an object elicits no particular response. At around 3 months, they become able to follow moving objects with their eyes. If an object disappears behind a barrier, infants will continue to stare at the place where the object has disappeared but will not search for it.

At around 7–9 months, infants can grasp and hold objects and gain experience with manipulating and observing them. They can also anticipate the future position of a moving object. If a moving object passes behind a screen, infants turn their eyes towards the far side of the screen, seeming to anticipate the reappearance of the object on the other side.

During the last half of their first year, infants develop much more complex concepts concerning the nature of physical objects. They grasp objects, turn them over and investigate their properties. By looking at an object from various angles, they learn that the object can change its visual shape and still be the same object. In addition, if an object is hidden, infants will actively search for it; their object concept now contains the rule of object permanence. For infants at this stage of development, a hidden object still exists. 'Out of sight' is no longer 'out of mind'.

By early in their second year, object permanence is well enough developed that infants will search for a hidden object in the last place they saw it hidden. However, at this stage infants can only keep track of changes in the hiding place that they can see. For example, if an adult picks up an object, puts it under a cloth, drops the object while their hand is hidden, closes the hand again and removes it from the cloth, infants will look for the object in the adult's hand. When they do not find the object there, they look puzzled or upset and do not search for the object under the cloth.

Near the end of the sensorimotor period, two other interesting developments occur. First, children develop the ability to imitate actions that they have seen others perform, a behaviour that Piaget called **deferred imitation**. This behaviour is due to their increasing ability to form mental representations of actions that they have observed. These representations may then be recalled at a later time to direct particular imitative actions and symbolic play, such as pretending to feed a doll or taking a stuffed animal for a walk. Secondly, as having an imagination shows, 2-year-old children begin to think symbolically. They can use words to represent objects such as balls and animals. This is a critical developmental step because this skill is crucial to language development.

The preoperational period

Piaget's second period of cognitive development, the **preoperational period**, lasts from approximately age 2 to age 7 and involves the ability to think logically as well as symbolically.

Table 12.1 The four periods of Piaget's theory of cognitive development

Period	Approximate age (years)	Major features
Sensorimotor	0–2	Object permanence; deferred imitation; rudimentary symbolic thinking
Preoperational	2–6 or 7	Increased ability to think symbolically and logically; egocentric; cannot yet master conservation problems
Concrete operational	6 or 7–11	Child can master conservation problems, can understand categorisation; cannot think abstractly
Formal operational	11 upwards	Child can think abstractly and hypothetically

This period is characterised by rapid development of language ability and of the ability to represent things symbolically. The child arranges toys in new ways to represent other objects (for example, a row of blocks can represent a train), begins to classify and categorise objects, and starts learning to count and to manipulate numbers. By the age of 2½ years, children have been shown to be able to treat objects such as kitchen utensils, bathroom items, animals, plants and so on as distinct categories of object (Bauer and Mandler, 1989).

Piaget asserted that development of symbolism actually begins during the sensorimotor period, when a child starts imitating events in his or her environment. For example, a child might represent a horse by making galloping movements with the feet or a bicycle by making steering movements with the hands. Symbolic representations like these are called signifiers: the motor act represents (signifies) the concept because it resembles either the movements that the object makes or the movements the child makes when interacting with the object.

Concepts can also be represented by words, which are symbols that have no physical resemblance to the concept; Piaget referred to such abstract symbols as signs. Signifiers are personal, derived from the child's own interactions with objects. Therefore, only the child and perhaps members of the immediate family will understand a child's signifiers. In contrast, signs are social conventions. They are understood by all members of a culture. A child who is able to use words to think about reality has made an important step in cognitive development.

Piaget's work demonstrated quite clearly that a child's representation of the world is different from that of an adult. For example, most adults realise that a volume of water remains constant when poured into a taller, narrower container, even though its level is now higher. However, early in the preoperational period, children will fail to recognise this fact; they will say that the taller container contains more water. The ability to realise that an object retains mass, number or volume when it undergoes various transformations is called conservation; the transformed object conserves its original properties.

Piaget concluded that the abilities to perceive the conservation of number, mass, weight and volume are attributes of increasing cognitive development. His studies showed number to be conserved by age 6, whereas conservation of volume did not occur until age 11. Presumably, conservation of number comes first because children can verify the stability of number once they learn to count, although conservation skill is seen in children who are not proficient counters (see Figure 12.10). This is an example of what Piaget called 'horizontal decalage' – the development of a skill within a period.

Another important characteristic of the preoperational period is **egocentrism**, or a child's belief that others see the world in precisely the way that they do. For example, a 3-year-old child may run to a corner, turn his back to you and cover his eyes in an attempt to hide during a game of hide and seek, not realising that he is still in full view. In a typical 'egocentric thinking' task, the child may be presented with models of three mountains which differ according to colour and features: some may have a cross on or snow or a house. A doll is placed at one end of the mountains and the child at the other. The child is then asked what they think the doll can see.

Because giving a verbal response is difficult for the child, the child either selects the doll's view from ten images or is given models of the mountains and has to arrange them in such a way to represent the doll's viewpoint. Children aged 8–9 years

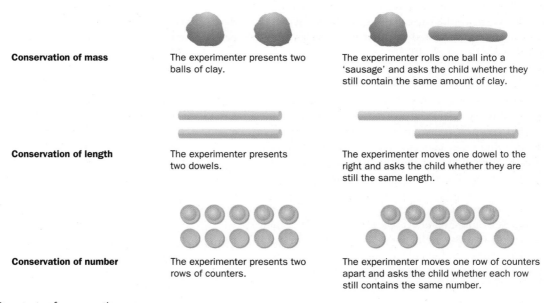

Conservation of mass — The experimenter presents two balls of clay. — The experimenter rolls one ball into a 'sausage' and asks the child whether they still contain the same amount of clay.

Conservation of length — The experimenter presents two dowels. — The experimenter moves one dowel to the right and asks the child whether they are still the same length.

Conservation of number — The experimenter presents two rows of counters. — The experimenter moves one row of counters apart and asks the child whether each row still contains the same number.

Figure 12.10 Various tests of conservation.

Source: Lefrancois, G.R., *Of Children: An introduction to child development*, Wadsworth (Lefrancois, G.R. 1983) with permission of Guy Lefrancois.

perform poorly at this task, usually selecting the image that represents their, rather than the doll's, point of view. According to Piaget, the child was unable to 'decentre'. He concluded that the children 'really imagine that the doll's perspective is the same as their own' (p. 220; cited in Donaldson, 1978).

However, there have been challenges to Piaget's view of the child's cognitive development during this period. A significant series of studies, for example, has demonstrated that the child's egocentric thinking may not be as egocentric as Piaget suggested. If children are given familiar objects in the three mountains' task, for example, or are given alternative methods of giving a response – rather than choosing one of ten pictures which is difficult even for older children – even very young children show evidence that they can see viewpoints from another's perspective (Newcombe and Huttenlocher, 1992). If the difficulty and the unfamiliarity of a task are eliminated, therefore, children during this period do better than Piaget's conception would predict.

Young children also show evidence that they can engage in non-egocentric thinking: they change their language, depending on the context in which they find themselves. For example, 2-year-olds use shorter sentences when talking to their peers than when talking to adults suggesting that they are responsive to those interacting with them and possibly modify their own linguistic output accordingly (Gelman and Shatz, 1978).

Simplification of the tasks Piaget used has also shown that children in this period are capable of conservation. If the number of conserved items is reduced from six or seven to three, even 3-year-old children can perform the task correctly (Gelman, 1972). In one example of a conservation task, sugar is dissolved in water and the child is asked whether the sugar still exists. Although Piaget's studies suggested that children incorrectly responded that the sugar did not exist, research suggests that 3–5-year-olds are capable of responding that the sugar exists and can be tasted but that its particles are too small to be visible (Au et al., 1993).

The period of concrete operations

Piaget's third stage of cognitive development, the **period of concrete operations**, spans approximately ages 7 to 11 and involves children's developing understanding of the conservation principle and other concepts such as categorisation. Its end marks the transition from childhood to adolescence. This period is characterised by the emergence of the ability to perform logical analysis, by an increased ability to empathise with the feelings and attitudes of others, and by an understanding of more complex cause-and-effect relations. The child becomes much more skilled at the use of symbolic thought. For example, even before the period of concrete operations, children can arrange a series of objects in order of size and can compare any two objects and say which is larger. However, if they are shown that stick A is larger than stick B and that stick B is larger than stick C, they cannot infer that stick A is larger than stick C.

During the early part of this period, children become capable of making such inferences. However, although they can reason with respect to concrete objects, such as sticks that they have seen, they cannot do so with hypothetical objects. For example, they cannot solve the following problem: Judy is taller than Frank and Frank is taller than Carl. Who is taller, Judy or Carl? The ability to solve such problems awaits the next period of cognitive development.

The period of formal operations

During the **period of formal operations**, which begins at about age 11, children become capable of abstract reasoning. They can now think and reason about hypothetical objects and events. They also begin to understand that under different conditions their behaviour can have different consequences. Formal operational thinking is not 'culture free' – it is influenced by cultural variables, especially formal schooling (Piaget, 1972; Rogoff and Chavajay, 1995). Without exposure to the principles of scientific thinking, such as those taught at school, people do not develop formal operational thinking.

The period is also critical in another way. At around age 11 the child is beginning the journey into adolescence where physical, bodily changes are significant and where a type of formal operational egocentrism, the ability to imagine what others think about them and the belief that their views of others are shared by others, develops (Inhelder and Piaget, 1955). Teenagers seem to have two distinct views of themselves and others, believing that they are constantly on stage, performing to an imaginary audience and being the focus of attention (Elkind and Bowen, 1979), and believing that others are always talking or thinking about them. They feel they are special. These two views peak during this period and decline steadily throughout the adolescent years.

Although Piaget held that there are four periods of cognitive development, not all people reach the formal operational period, even as physically mature adults. In some tribal cultures, formal operations do not emerge at all, probably because there is a lack of opportunity to engage in hypothetico-deductive reasoning (Gellaty, 1987). In some cases, adults show formal operational thought only in their areas of expertise. Thus, a mechanic may be able to think abstractly while repairing an engine but not while solving maths or physics problems. A physicist may be able to reason abstractly when solving physics problems but not while reading poetry. However, once an individual reaches that level of thinking, they will always, except in the case of brain disease or injury, perform intellectually at that level.

Play and its role in social and cognitive development

Play is often regarded as a social behaviour – children interact with each other or with objects in the environment in an enjoyable and positive way – but it is also a cognitive one in which children learn about these objects and the objects' relationship to the environment. Babies as young as 1 year begin to play with objects, although in an unsophisticated way. For example, objects may be picked up, sucked and thrown, but little more than this. However, as the infant grows older, it begins to play with objects in a more symbolic way. Through play, it appears to show evidence of developing cognition.

At 12–18 months, infants begin to play with objects symbolically – they pretend that the object is something else. For example, an object (a pencil) used for one purpose (writing), is used to carry out another behaviour (combing the hair) (Belsky and Most, 1981). About half of the infants who reach 14 months can pretend that they are sleeping by putting their head on a pillow, but it takes a further six months before they are able to use a doll to signify sleeping by putting the doll to bed (Watson and Fischer, 1977). At the age of 4 years, children use play to find out more about their environment and the social values of the environment around them as well as its customs and traditions.

According to Piaget, play is the opposite of imitation. When children imitate, accommodation predominates over assimilation; when children play, the opposite occurs. According to Vygotsky (1976/1933), the meaning of an object in children's play completely usurps its actual physical meaning. In the comb and pencil example, the pencil had become the comb – it combed hair; it did not write messages on paper. This creativity in the child's use of objects increases in the presence of a parent but only if the parent joins in (Slade, 1987), which indicates that the parent's involvement in the child's developing imagination and exploration of objects is an important one.

Because of the complex nature of the activity, Piaget (1945/1951) saw play as a cognitive activity rather than a social one. He gave it the name **symbolic play** because infants used objects to symbolise other objects or used them to symbolise other activities (e.g. the pencil symbolised a comb). The transition from play to symbolic or pretend play occurred in two stages, according to Piaget.

The first stage occurs when the infant is between 0 and 4 years and, in typically Piagetian fashion, this stage is further subdivided into three substages. In substage 1, the child develops an idea of what an object is and preserves its unique characteristics; this enables it to project these characteristics onto other objects. The infants might observe a behaviour in those around them, develop a schema of those objects they observe and translate this schema into a different type of behaviour. For example, a child may observe an adult cleaning with one object but use another to carry out the same activity.

In substage 2, the child shows evidence of independence from the prop/object they use. That is, the knowledge of an object precedes the use of the object. A brush placed above the head is symbolically treated as an umbrella. The child not only has an awareness of what umbrellas do but is also able to use another object to signify the use of an umbrella. Another example is where the child plays hide and seek but plays the part of the person doing the hiding.

In substage 3, various actions are combined together to form an ensemble of meaning. This example comes from Piaget's study of one of his daughters: a shoe box is used as a bath, and a blade of grass is used as a thermometer. The child dips the blade into the shoe box and declares it too hot; a short while later, she repeats the action and declares that it is just right. This degree of imagination appears to occur at the same time as the creation of imaginary characters in the child's world. At this stage, this type of symbolic play becomes more organised.

How would you go about developing a test for determining which of Piaget's periods of cognitive development a child is in? What kinds of activity would you include in such a test and how would the child's behaviour with respect to those activities indicate the child's stage of development?

Pretend play has also been considered to be uniquely important for the child's cognitive and social development (Copple and Bredekamp, 2009). However, there may be two other views of the role of play: one explanation may be that it is one of several ways in which cognition develops in infants; another is that play is an epiphenomenon arising from other factors that are more important to development (Lillard *et al.*, 2012). Lilliard *et al.* found that for language, narrative and emotional regulation, research supports all three views; for executive function and social skills, research does not support the 'importance' view but is unable to determine which of the other two views is correct. For reasoning, pretend play is one of various routes to positive development but it could still be epihemomenal. None of the explanations confirm that pretend play is positively associated with problem-solving. For executive function and creativity, the research tends to the epiphenomenon explanation.

Evaluation of Piaget's contributions

Piaget's theory has had an enormous impact on research in developmental psychology (Beilin, 1990; Halford, 1990). However, not all of Piaget's conclusions have been accepted uncritically. One criticism levelled at Piaget is that he did not always define his terms operationally. Consequently, it is difficult for others to interpret the significance of his generalisations. Many of his studies lack the proper controls. Thus, much of his work is not experimental, which means that cause-and-effect relations among variables cannot be identified with certainty. Perhaps the greatest criticism of Piaget has been reserved for his periods of cognitive development. Attempts to verify the timetable of Piaget's periods of cognitive development have met with little success (Flavell, 1992). Children can be trained to perform Piaget's tasks correctly so that a child who should be operating at a level occurring in an early period might correctly attempt cognitive tasks that characterise a later developmental period (Beilin, 1978).

This illustrates a problem with Piaget's theorising: there are not many abilities that are completely absent in one specific period and present in another. One view suggests that the child has the capacity for all of these abilities but they are present at different levels in different children, which would account for variations in children's cognitive performance.

Subsequent research has suggested that a child's ability to conserve various physical attributes occurs earlier than Piaget had supposed. Piag *et al* so appears to have underestimated the ability of young children to understand another person's point of view, as you saw in the section on the preoperational period. For example, Flavell *et al.* (1981) found that even a 3-year-old child realises that a person looking at the opposite side of a card to that which the child is examining will not see the same thing. Clearly, the child recognises the other person's point of view. Flavell and colleagues also showed that even very young children can tell the difference between appearance and reality. They presented a series of disguised items and asked children what the objects really were (Flavell *et al.*, 1989).

Piaget's prediction would be that children would identify the disguise, rather than the object underneath. However, Flavell *et al.* found that 3-year-old children were capable of correctly identifying the disguised object. They were also able to distinguish between the way an object felt and how it actually was. For example, although an ice cube held by a rubber glove was not perceived as cold, children were able to understand that the cube still maintained the property of coldness. Therefore, the children showed evidence of logical thinking before they reached the concrete operations period.

Piag *et al* so largely discounted experience in his theory of development; periods would develop naturally and in order and did not depend on experience. However, culture does seem to have a significant effect on cognitive skills such as conservation. The children of the Hausa tribe in Nigeria, for example, do not go to school and do not understand conservation principles until they are around 11 years old (Fahrmeier, 1978), suggesting that some degree of daily activity involving conservation may be necessary before this concept is mastered.

Vygotsky's sociocultural theory of cognitive development

Piaget's theory of cognitive development focuses on children's interactions with the physical world – children form internal representations of the world based on their experiences with physical objects. Another theorist, the Russian psychologist Lev Vygotsky, agreed that experience with physical objects is an important factor in cognitive development, but he disagreed that this is the whole story. Instead, he argued that the culture in which one lives also plays a significant role in cognitive development: the child's cognitive development was promoted by the interaction between the child and its social environment

(Vygotsky, 1987). Although Vygotsky's work was conducted during the 1920s and early 1930s (he died of tuberculosis in 1934, aged 37), his writings have had a major impact on more recent conceptualisations of cognitive development during childhood (Smith *et al.*, 1997).

Vygotsky argued that children do not learn to think about the physical world in a vacuum. The cultural context – what they hear others say about the world and how they see others interact with physical aspects of the world – matters. Thus parents, teachers, friends and many others help children to acquire ideas about how the world works. We would expect, then, that the development of children raised in non-stimulating environments devoid of stimulating interactions with others, with books, and even television, would lag behind that of children raised in more stimulating environments. And this is exactly what has been found.

Vygotsky further believed that children's use of speech also influences their cognitive development. Piaget had argued that the private speech that children engage in was egocentric – children were unable to imagine others' points of view – and that this conversation would be rattled off as if in a stream of consciousness. As the child interacts with peers and as the child grows older and interacts with adults, this private speech is eliminated and the child engages in social speech – they listen to others talking and respond appropriately. Children up to about age 7 can often be observed talking to themselves. While drawing in a colouring book, a child may say, 'I'll colour her arms and face green and her trousers black'. Piaget would interpret such talk as being egocentric and non-social because it is directed at the self, because it may not make sense to a listener, and because its purpose is not to communicate information.

Vygotsky's (1934/1962) interpretation was different. He argued that the child's talk reflected the formulation of a plan that would serve as a guide to subsequent behaviour. According to Vygotsky, language is the basis for cognitive development, including the ability to remember, solve problems, make decisions and formulate plans. As children became better at tasks that involved attention, memorisation, planning and so on, then their private vocal speech would disappear and would be internalised instead. Studies have shown that children engage more in private speech if a task is challenging, if it makes them make mistakes or results in confusion about what to do next (Berk, 1992, 1994). The children who use such speech when faced with challenging tasks are more attentive and show better improvement in cognitive performance than are those who are less talkative (Behrend *et al.*, 1992).

After about the age of 7 children stop vocalising their thoughts and instead carry on what Vygotsky labelled 'inner speech'. **Inner speech** represents the internalisation of words and the mental manipulation of them as symbols for objects in the environment. As children socially interact with their parents, teachers and peers, they learn new words to represent new objects. As the 'expertise' of the people they interact with increases, so does the children's cognitive skills. For example, Rogoff (1990) has shown that children become better problem solvers if they practise solving problems with their parents or with more experienced children than if they practise the problems alone or with children of similar cognitive ability. Vygotsky explained this process by referring to the **zone of proximal (or potential) development**. This describes a range of tasks or skills that a child is unable to master alone but can with the assistance of adults or their peers. The greater the interaction with adults, then the more adult the child's language becomes. But what aspect of the interaction is important for the change in development?

There are two possible candidates. One is a process whereby two people begin with a different understanding and by mutual discussion reach a common understanding. This has been called intersubjectivity (Newson and Newson, 1975) because one member of the dyad adjusts their point of view according to the behaviour of the other. The other possibility is that the interaction acts as a form of 'scaffolding' – peers and adults provide social support in the learning environment but this support can be adjusted (Bruner, 1983). Mothers who provide good social support while their child learns – and are, therefore, good scaffolders – produce children that generate more private speech and who are more successful than children with less social support when completing puzzles alone (Behrend *et al.*, 1992).

Thus, while Piaget argued for a purely maturational view of children's cognitive development – skills developed within periods defined by cognitive characteristics as well as age – Vygotsky placed greater importance on sociocultural influences such as language and interactions with other people. As we have seen, research partially supports both theorists' ideas. However, Vygotsky's work has gone beyond Piaget's theory in explaining how cultural variables, especially language, influence cognitive development.

Research has taken the work of Piaget and others and reformulated notions of cognitive stages by linking shifts in thinking and performance to the development of the brain. One of the more interesting models is Johnson's (2001, 2010; Johnson *et al.*, 2009). Originally, Johnson's model was an attempt at explaining the development of attention in relation to developing brain regions in infants. It argues that cognitive abilities develop via three routes: maturation and the maturation of the cortex (which occurs naturally and is pre-programmed), changes in interaction between brain regions so that working memory, for example, can lead to the strengthening of connections between parts of the brain, and learning of skills which shapes brain development. What is currently unclear is which of these is the more plausible or the most relevant mechanism. Johnson (2010) suggests that it may be the second, what he called the interactive specialisation account.

Social and emotional development in infancy and childhood

Normally, the first adults with whom infants interact are their parents. In most cases, one parent serves as the primary carer. As many studies have shown, a close relationship called attachment is important for infants' social development. **Attachment** is a social and emotional bond between infant and carer that spans both time and space. It involves both the warm feelings that the parent and child have for each other and the comfort and support they provide for each other, which becomes especially important during times of fear or stress. This interaction must work both ways, with each participant fulfilling certain needs of the other.

Formation of a strong and durable bond depends on the behaviour of both people in the relationship. According to theorist Bowlby (1969), attachment is a part of many organisms' native endowment. He and Ainsworth have developed an approach that has succeeded in discovering some of the variables that influence attachment in humans (Ainsworth and Bowlby, 1991).

Infant attachment

Newborn infants rely completely on their parents (or other carers) to supply them with nourishment, keep them warm and clean, and protect them from harm. To most parents, the role of primary carer is much more than a duty; it is a source of joy and satisfaction. Nearly all parents anticipate the birth of their children with the expectation that they will love and cherish them. And when a child is born, most of them do exactly that. As time goes on, and as parent and child interact, they become strongly attached to each other. What factors cause this attachment to occur? Evidence suggests that human infants are innately able to produce special behaviours that shape and control the behaviour of their carers. As Bowlby (1969) noted, the most important of these behaviours are sucking, cuddling, looking, smiling and crying.

Sucking

A baby must be able to suck in order to obtain milk. But not all sucking is related to nourishment. Piaget (1952) noted that infants often suck on objects even when they are not hungry. Non-nutritive sucking appears to be an innate behavioural tendency in infants that serves to inhibit a baby's distress. In modern society, most mothers cover their breasts between feedings or feed with a bottle, so a baby's non-nutritive sucking must involve inanimate objects or the baby's own thumb. But in Uganda, mothers were observed to give their babies access to a breast when they were fussy, just as mothers in other cultures would give them a dummy (Ainsworth, 1967).

Cuddling

Infants of all species of primates have special reflexes that encourage front-to-front contact with their mothers. For example, a baby monkey clings to its mother's chest shortly after birth. This clinging leaves the mother free to use her hands and feet. Human infants are carried by their parents and do not hold on by themselves. However, infants do adjust their posture to mould themselves to the contours of the parent's body. This cuddling response plays an important role in reinforcing the behaviour of the carer. Some infants, perhaps because of hereditary factors or slight brain damage, do not make the cuddling response and remain rigid in the adult's arms. Adults who hold such infants tend to refer to them as being not very lovable.

Harlow (1974) conducted a series of experiments on infant monkeys and showed that clinging to a soft, cuddly form appears to be an innate response. Harlow and his colleagues isolated baby monkeys from their mothers immediately after birth and raised them alone in cages containing two mechanical surrogate mothers. One surrogate mother was made of bare wire mesh but contained a bottle that provided milk. The other surrogate was padded and covered with terry cloth but provided no nourishment.

The babies preferred to cling to the cuddly surrogate and went to the wire model only to eat. If they were frightened, they would rush to the cloth-covered model for comfort. These results suggest that close physical contact with a cuddly object is a biological need for a baby monkey, just as food and drink are. A baby monkey clings to and cuddles with its mother because the contact is innately reinforcing, not simply because she provides it with food.

Undoubtedly, physical contact with soft objects is also inherently reinforcing for human infants. The term 'security blanket' suggests that these objects are comforting during times of distress. Indeed, children are most likely to ask for their special blankets or stuffed animals before going to bed, when they are ill, or when they are in an unfamiliar situation.

Looking

For infants, looking serves as a signal to parents: even a very young infant seeks eye-to-eye contact with its parents. If a parent does not respond when eye contact is made, the baby usually shows signs of distress. Tronick *et al.* (1978) observed face-to-face interactions between mothers and their infants. When the mothers approached their babies, they typically smiled and began talking in a gentle, high-pitched voice. In return, infants smiled and stretched their arms and legs. The mothers poked and gently jiggled their babies, making faces

at them. The babies responded with facial expressions, wiggles and noises of their own.

To determine whether the interaction was really two-sided, the experimenters had each mother approach her baby while keeping her face expressionless or mask-like. At first, the infant made the usual greetings, but when the mother did not respond, the infant turned away. From time to time, the infant looked at her again, giving a brief smile, but again turned away when the mother continued to stare without changing her expression. These interactions were recorded on videotape and were scored by raters who did not know the purpose of the experiment, so the results were not biased by the experimenters' expectations.

Each mother found it difficult to resist her baby's invitation to interact. In fact, some of the mothers broke down and smiled back. Most of the mothers who managed to hold out (for three minutes) later apologised to their babies, saying something like, 'I am real again. It's all right. You can trust me again. Come back to me' (Tronick *et al.*, 1978, p. 110). This study clearly shows that the looking behaviour of an infant is an invitation for the mother to respond.

Smiling

By the time an infant is 5 weeks old, visual stimuli begin to dominate as elicitors for smiling. A face (especially a moving one) is a more reliable elicitor of a smile than a voice is; even a moving mask will cause an infant to smile. At approximately 3 months of age, specific faces – those of people to whom the infant has become attached – will elicit smiles. In particular, the infant will engage in more generic smiling when gazing at its mother's face than when gazing elsewhere (Van Beek *et al.*, 1994). The infant also smiles when the mother smiles (Kaye and Fogel, 1980).

Crying

For almost any adult, the sound of an infant's crying is intensely distressing or irritating. An infant usually cries only when it is hungry, cold or in pain (Wolff, 1969). In these situations, only the intervention of an adult can bring relief. The event that most effectively terminates crying is being picked up and cuddled, although unless the baby is fed and made more comfortable it will soon begin crying again. Because picking up the baby stops the crying, the parent learns through negative reinforcement to pick up the infant when it cries. Thus, crying serves as a useful means for a cold, hungry or wet child to obtain assistance.

Wolff (1969) suggested that babies have different patterns of crying. Konner (1972), who was studying a hunter–gatherer tribe in Africa, found that a pain cry caused all the people in earshot to turn towards the infant and induced several of them to run towards the child. However, only the child's carers responded to a hunger cry. More recent evidence suggests that babies' cries do not fall into need-specific categories – there is no 'hunger cry', no different cry for pain, and so on. Instead, cries simply vary in intensity, according to the level of the infant's distress. However, the onset of crying provides important information. If a baby suddenly begins crying intensely, mothers are more likely to assume that the baby is afraid or in pain. If the cry begins more gradually, mothers suspect hunger, sleepiness or a need for a nappy change (Gustafson and Harris, 1990).

The nature and quality of attachment

For an infant, the world can be a frightening place. The presence of a primary caregiver provides a baby with considerable reassurance when they first become able to explore the environment. Although the unfamiliar environment produces fear, the caregiver provides a secure base that the infant can leave from time to time to see what the world is like.

Stranger anxiety and separation anxiety

Babies are born prepared to become attached to their primary caregiver, who in most cases is their mother. Attachment appears to be a behaviour pattern that is necessary for normal development (Ainsworth, 1973; Bowlby, 1973). However, although attachment appears to be an inherited disposition, infants do not have a natural inclination to become attached to any one specific adult. Rather, the person to whom the baby becomes attached is determined through learning; the individual who serves as the infant's primary caregiver (or, in Bowlby's terms, 'attachment figure') is usually the object of the attachment.

Attachment partially reveals itself in two specific forms of infant behaviour: stranger anxiety and separation anxiety. **Stranger anxiety**, which usually appears in infants between the ages of 6 and 12 months, consists of wariness and sometimes fearful responses, such as crying and clinging to their carers, that infants exhibit in the presence of strangers. Male strangers generate the most anxiety in infants. Child strangers generate the least anxiety, while female strangers generate an intermediate amount of anxiety (Skarin, 1977). Stranger anxiety can be reduced and even eliminated under certain conditions. For example, if the infant is in familiar surroundings with its mother, and the mother acts in a friendly manner towards the stranger, the infant is likely to be less anxious in the presence of the stranger than it would if the surroundings were unfamiliar or if the mother was unfriendly towards the stranger (Rheingold and Eckerman, 1973).

Separation anxiety is a set of fearful responses, such as crying, arousal and clinging to the carer, that an infant exhibits when the carer attempts to leave the infant. Separation anxiety differs from stranger anxiety in two ways: time of emergence and the conditions under which the fear responses occur. It

first appears in infants when they are about 6 months old and generally peaks at about 15 months – a finding consistent among many cultures (Kagan *et al.*, 1978). Like stranger anxiety, separation anxiety can occur under different conditions with different degrees of intensity. For example, if an infant is used to being left in a certain environment, say a daycare centre, it may show little or no separation anxiety (Maccoby, 1980). The same holds true for situations in which the infant is left with a sibling or other familiar person (Bowlby, 1969).

However, if the same infant is left in an unfamiliar setting, it will show signs of distress. Some infants show 'disorganised' attachment behaviour, that is, they show conflicting behaviour towards the carer. They may rush to the sound of an opening door when hearing the carer about to enter a room and then run away when the carer enters; they may also adopt a 'frozen' or still posture when the carer is in the room (Main and Solomon, 1990). A longitudinal study of disorganised attachment behaviour in 157 children (studied from 24 months to 19 years) found that disorganised behaviour was correlated with insensitive caring, living alone with the infant, neglect, physical and psychological neglect and an intrusive caring style (Carlson, 1998).

Ainsworth's Strange Situation

One measure of separation anxiety was devised by Ainsworth and her colleagues (Ainsworth *et al.*, 1978). They developed a test of attachment called the **Strange Situation** that consists of a series of eight episodes, during which the baby is exposed to various events that might cause some distress. The episodes involve the experimenter introducing the infant and the parent to a playroom and then leaving, the parent leaving and being reunited with the infant, or a stranger entering the playroom with and without the parent present. Each episode lasts for approximately three minutes. The Strange Situation test is based on the idea that if the attachment process has been successful, an infant should use its mother as a secure base from which to explore an unfamiliar environment. By noting the infant's reactions to the strange situation, researchers can evaluate the nature of the attachment.

The use of the Strange Situation test led Ainsworth and her colleagues to identify three patterns of attachment. **Secure attachment** is the ideal pattern: infants show a distinct preference for their mothers over the stranger. Infants may cry when their carers leave, but they stop as soon as they return. Babies may also form two types of insecure attachment. Babies with **resistant attachment** show tension in their relations with their carers. Infants stay close to their mother before the mother leaves but show both approach and avoidance behaviours when the mother returns. Infants continue to cry for a while after their mother returns and may even push her away. Infants who display **avoidant attachment** generally do not cry when they are left alone. When their mother returns, the infants are likely to avoid or ignore them. These infants tend not to cling or cuddle when they are picked up.

Although infants' personalities certainly affect the nature of their interactions with their carers and hence the nature of their attachment, mothers' behaviour appears to be the most important factor in establishing a secure or insecure attachment (Ainsworth *et al.*, 1978; Isabella and Belsky, 1991). Mothers of securely attached infants tend to be those who respond promptly to their crying and who are adept at handling them and responding to their needs. The babies apparently learn that their mothers can be trusted to react sensitively and appropriately. Mothers who do not modulate their responses according to their infants' own behaviour – who appear insensitive to their infants' changing needs – are most likely to foster avoidant attachment. Mothers who are impatient with their infants and who seem more interested in their own activities than in interacting with their offspring tend to foster resistant attachment.

The nature of the attachment between infants and carers appears to be related to children's later social behaviour. For example, Waters *et al.* (1979) found that children who were securely attached at 15 months were among the most popular and the most sociable children in their nursery schools at 3½ years of age. In contrast, insecurely attached infants had difficulties with social adjustment later in childhood; they had poor social skills and tended to be hostile, impulsive and withdrawn (Erickson *et al.*, 1985).

While these attachment behaviours are seen cross-culturally, there are cultural differences. German babies, for example, appear to show more avoidant attachment than do American ones, possibly because German parents encourage their children to be independent from an early age (Grossman *et al.*, 1985). Japanese babies are thought to exhibit more resistant attachment, possibly because Japanese mothers do not normally leave their charges in the care of others (Miyake *et al.*, 1985).

Predictors of secure attachment

Recall that Ainsworth and her colleagues found that the insecure attachment features just described were strongly related to attachment security. What is unclear from Ainsworth's study, however, is which aspects of the mother–child interaction, if any, are predictive of a secure attachment style. Are all the features listed above necessary for secure attachment or only one? Some researchers suggest that maternal sensitivity is the greatest predictor (Goldsmith and Alansky, 1987); others show different factors.

One problem with studies of attachment is the variation in methodology. Sometimes, conclusions are drawn from a single observation, others from multiple observations; the measures of attachment have ranged from asking parents about their attitudes to childcare to observing the frequency of physical contact (Frodi *et al.*, 1985; Benn, 1986; Kerns and Barth, 1995). As a result, the determinants of attachment are unclear because different studies adopt different research designs. In a meta-analysis of 66 attachment studies, De Wolff and van Ijzendoorn (1997) found that there was a moderately strong relationship between maternal sensitivity, defined as the ability to respond appropriately and promptly to the signals of the infant, and attachment.

Theory of mind

An important cognitive and emotional skill that develops in infancy is theory of mind – the ability to mentalise, socially interact with others and infer people's feelings and thoughts from their expression, voice and speech, thereby creating empathy and understanding. Some researchers have argued that we do this automatically as adults, but the evidence for this is inconsistent (Kovacs *et al.*, 2010; Phillips *et al.*, 2015).

The way in which humans mentalise, according to Byom and Mutlu (2013), is via knowledge of shared content, the perception of social cues and the interpretation of actions. Knowledge of shared content describes the body of information – semantic and episodic – that we use to help us understand and interact with others. In a conversation, for example, we infer the thoughts and goals of the person we are speaking to so that we can respond to them. Perception of social cues include the ability to follow someone's eye gaze, and the ability to process facial expressions and vocal cues. The ability to follow gaze is reflected in our understanding of where another person's attention is focused and, therefore, can help us infer his or her intentions. It also helps us to understand when to contribute to a conversation and helps us understand whether our message is being understood. Interpretation of actions refers to our ability to interpret why a person has behaved or acted in the way that they have.

There are different ways of measuring each type of theory of mind component. The most common examples of these are the Strange stories task (shared world knowledge), reading the mind's eyes task (perceiving social cues) and false belief tasks (interpreting actions). Stimuli in these tasks are either static images, stories or video clips – the medium may be important because we are affected more by certain types of stimuli (live stimuli) than others (static images) (Ponkanen *et al.*, 2010). In the Strange stories task (Happe, 1994), participants are presented with descriptions or pictures representing social scenarios and are asked to infer the mental states of people in them or predict the characters' behaviour. It is a test of shared knowledge because the participant needs to have knowledge of the world in which the character appears in order to understand how that character would behave. This includes knowledge of faux pas, deception, persuasion and other social and behavioural features. In the reading the mind's eyes task, participants are presented with images of the eyes and are asked to infer the emotion expressed. The most well-known example of a false belief task is the Sally-Ann task (Wimmer and Perner, 1983) and you can see this described and illustrated in Figure 12.11.

All of the tests described above are 'third-person' tests. That is, the participant makes inferences about others' mental states

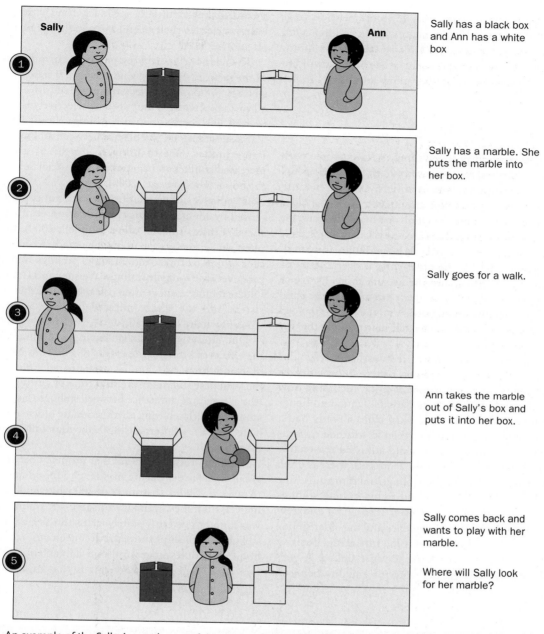

Figure 12.11 An example of the Sally Ann task, one of the most widely used tests of theory-of-mind.

in the 'third-person', and are not directly involved in any observed interaction. New tests are being developed that encourage first- and second-person understanding. For example, participants might interact with another whose behaviour is controlled by an experimenter. Boom and Mutlu cite one experiment in which the degree of gaze expressed by a virtual character who interacted with the participant was manipulated. The gaze was either directed towards the participant or towards another object. The former was associated with more positive evaluations of the character and the interaction. The advantage of employing virtual characters (or robots) is that

they can be precisely and explicitly manipulated (the disadvantage is that they still look like virtual characters or robots, that is, not human).

Whether theory of mind is a specialised behaviour independent of other cognitive abilities or whether it is a combination of other cognitive abilities which give rise to the understanding of others is not known. Ageing studies suggest that ToM measured via stories declines with working memory, inhibitory control (having less control over inhibition) and processing speed (Moran, 2013). ToM measured via visual stimuli is less affected by these declines, suggesting a degree of independence. The affective component of ToM might also predict later proactive aggression in children aged 6–9 years: the less effective the affective theory of mind, the greater the aggression expressed by the child later in life (Austin *et al.*, 2017). You'll find out more about ToM in the section on autism.

Relationships with siblings

Along with parents and peers, siblings are the people with whom children share a close social and emotional relationship. Siblings may also cause resentment in older children because they attract most of the attention from parents and the older child may feel left out. Studies by Dunn and her colleagues, for example, have found that mothers are less warm towards their older children when their new baby is born (Dunn and Kendrick, 1982; Dunn, 1993). If the older child is over 2 years of age, they may also feel less secure and become more disruptive (Teti *et al.*, 1996). While this may draw attention to the child and maybe flag some underlying problem, the disruption can end up alienating the parent which itself may prolong the disruptive behaviour.

The elements of competition or jealousy between older and younger children is called sibling rivalry, but the degree of rivalry depends on a number of factors, including how secure the older child feels with its parents. Dunn and Kendrick (1982) found that if the first-born child already had a secure relationship with its parents, then its attitude towards the newborn was positive and the child adjusted reasonably well to the new arrival in the family. That said, there is often an element of tomfoolery in the siblings' relationships: one study found that disagreements and fights among siblings were as frequent as 56 an hour (Dunn, 1993). The disagreements, however, peter out by adolescence and the older sibling frequently takes the dominant role, initiating positive behaviours when engaging with the younger sibling. As siblings get older, there is a greater sense of equality between them and they eventually spend less time with each other and more time with their peers, as you will see in a later section on adolescence.

The relationship between parents is an important predictor of the security of sibling relationships. If parents get on, so do siblings. Similarly, if both parents are sensitive to the needs of all of their children, and are not selectively sensitive to one, there is less conflict between siblings (Brody, 1998). Parents' ability to stamp on skirmishes between siblings also predicts later conflict. The inability to do this is associated with increased conflict and aggressive, antisocial behaviour outside the home (Garcia *et al.*, 2000).

Of course, sibling relationships are not completely characterised by conflict. Siblings provide a source of emotional and social comfort to each other (Vandell, 2000). Older siblings often act as surrogate parents: one study found that in 57 per cent of 186 cultures studied, older siblings were the primary caregivers for younger siblings (Weisner and Gallimore, 1977). Older siblings are also often role models for their brothers and sisters and are often imitated by their younger siblings (Abramovitch *et al.*, 1980).

One study suggests that having a sibling can moderate the effects of stressful life events (Gass *et al.*, 2007). One hundred and thirty-two families participated – the average age of the youngest sibling at the first time of testing was 4.9 years (the average age difference between siblings was 5.6 years). The study found that having an affectionate older sibling was associated with less internalising behaviour following a stressful event.

Another study has found that intimacy between siblings is greatest in sisters during middle childhood and adolescence (Kim *et al.*, 2006). In a study of 200 white middle – and working-class families, intimacy in same-sex sibling relationships was found to be fairly stable across this period but mixed-sex sibling relationships showed a decline in intimacy across childhood and adolescence until mid-adolescence when intimacy increased. One reason for this is that middle adolescence

Social organisation – An international perspective

Do children from different cultures interact differently when in social groups? Children from Mexican families living in the US with mothers who had received limited schooling, US children whose mothers' had extensive schooling, and children of Mexican families with mothers who had extensive schooling were studied. Groups of three children from each group were given a task – to follow instructions for origami – which they completed together (Mejia-Arauz *et al.*, 2007).

The children from Mexican families with mothers who had received limited schooling were more likely to work together than were the other groups. The US children were more likely to work individually or in pairs – they were also more likely to chat more when interacting than interact non-verbally (which was the common form of interaction in the Mexican children).

The results seem to confirm studies showing that certain cultures – such as those in Mexico – are more likely to show evidence of collaboration on a shared task, even children from those cultures.

heralds an interest in the opposite sex and having a sibling of the opposite sex might, therefore, be a useful sounding board for advice and strategy. First-borns experienced more conflict in early adolescence, second-borns experienced more conflict in middle childhood.

Finally, some children have no siblings because they are an only child. Do these children differ in some psychological way from children with brothers and sisters? Studies of only children have shown them to be high in self-esteem and in motivation to achieve; they are also more obedient and more intellectually able than children with siblings (Falbo and Polit, 1986; Falbo, 1992). Interestingly, one country has provided some useful data on the development of only children. In 1979, the People's Republic of China implemented a family planning policy stating that families should produce only one child. When these children were studied, their profile was comparable to their Western counterparts but they had higher scores on tests of intelligence and were more academically successful than their equivalents with siblings (Falbo and Poston, 1993).

The psychological consequences of being mathematically gifted

In September 1971, the psychologist Julian C Stanley launched the Study of Mathematically Precocious Youth – a project inspired by Terman's study of genes and intelligence. Stanley administered a series of exams to bright 13-year-old children to identify those who performed in the top 1 per cent for mathematical reasoning (Lubinski *et al.*, 2014). This ability was thought to be a more useful measure than IQ – the aim of identification was to help those who were highly gifted to develop this ability. In 2012–2013, Lubinski *et al.* examined two cohorts from the study (the 1972–1974 cohort and 1976–1978 cohort) and explored how their careers, accomplishments, psychological well-being, life preferences and priorities had developed. Between 2012 and 2013 most of the cohort recruited by Stanley had an average age of 53 years. The sample comprised 1,037 men and 613 women.

Four per cent of the sample had secured tenure (a permanent position) at research Universities, 2.3 per cent were senior executives at well-known companies and 2.4 per cent were lawyers at well-known firms. The sample had published 85 books, 7,572 journal articles, achieved 681 patents and secured $358 million in grant income. Around 30 per cent had completed doctorates (compared with the US average of 2 per cent). The men earned more than the women – almost twice as much. The median income for the men was $140,000 and $138,000, depending on the cohort. Married men earned more than unmarried men. The men valued full-time work, making an impact and having a high income, whereas women valued part-time work, family involvement and time for close relationships. The men were more concerned with social advancement and with being successful at work. Both men and women were more satisfied with their lives and relationships compared than was the general population.

Relationships with others

As well as forming relationships with parents and siblings, children also develop relationships with their peers, usually with children who are similar to them in terms of age and sex. The development of friendships marks an important trait in the child's life: the development of cooperation. Friends who play with each other are more likely to be cooperative than children who are not friends; friends also play in a more complex way than non-friends (Hinde *et al.*, 1985). On the other hand, such close relationships also lead to conflicts: these are more common among friends than among non-friends (Hartup and Laursen, 1992), clearly because they spend more time with each other. However, when conflicts do occur, friends make greater attempts at negotiation when solving disputes.

As relationships develop, children show evidence of prosocial behaviour – they will automatically help another child. For example, if a child sees another crying, they will comfort that child, even before being taught to behave this positively by a parent. The degree of prosocial behaviour that children show, however, can depend on the degree of encouragement they are given or on the prosocial disposition of the parents. Children who see others behaving in a generous and helpful way are more likely to be helpful and generous themselves (Eisenberg and Fabes, 1998). However, the father seems to be the more important role model for children: a positive correlation between the father's prosocial behaviour and the child's has been reported, but there was no such correlation found between the mother's and the child's (Eisenberg *et al.*, 1992).

Disorders of social cognition and emotion

Some children are born with disorders associated with mental retardation (such as **Down syndrome**); or they can develop reading disorders that seem unrelated to the educational opportunities available to the child and to any underlying brain damage (such as developmental dyslexia). If there is no underlying intellectual retardation or physical cause, cognitive and emotional disorders are sometimes described as specific developmental disorders or disorders of psychological development (Rispens and van Yperen, 1997).

In earlier chapters, we discussed some disorders of childhood in some detail. This section describes disorders we have not come across yet: autism, conduct disorder and attention deficit hyperactivity disorder and disorders of emotional regulation.

Autism spectrum disorder

Autism spectrum disorder (ASD) describes a developmental disorder characterised by three features: social abnormality, language abnormality and stereotypical and repetitive patterns of behaviour (Frith, 1989; Happé, 1994; Bailey *et al.*, 1996). Prior to 2013, the Diagnostic and Statistical Manual of the American Psychiatric Association (one of two diagnostic manuals used by doctors and psychologists to diagnose mental disorder – see Chapter 18) had differentiated between four types of autistics condition, including autistic disorder and Asperger's disorder. In DSM-V (the latest revision) these specific conditions have been eliminated and the disorder is now viewed as a continuum. ASD affects approximately 1 per cent of the population (Idring *et al.*, 2012).

Autism was originally reported in 1943 by Leo Kanner in an article in which he described 11 cases of 'autistic disturbance of affective contact and . . . desire for preservation of sameness'. The symptoms he described form the core of the classification of autism today. Some researchers have criticised the new approach of DSM-V because ASD is a highly heterogeneous disorder (with different presentation of symptoms, severity of symptoms and, therefore, possible causes and treatments) and that sub-types may be not only desirable but necessary (Lai *et al.*, 2013). One of the clearest sources of heterogeneity is sex: more (twice as many) boys (and men) are more likely to be diagnosed with ASD (Idring *et al.*, 2012) and most of the research has focused on these participants (e.g. Lai *et al.*, 2014; Wilson *et al.*, 2014). The assumption has been that both boys and girls with ASD exhibit the same neuropsychological and psychological characteristics. There is evidence to suggest that this assumption is not correct (Lai *et al.*, 2013) and that the grey and white matter regions that might be implicated in ASD in girls are different to those in boys.

Of the specific symptoms in ASD, social abnormality includes an inability to reciprocate in social interactions, to form or develop loving relationships and to interact spontaneously with others. Autistic children and adults have an impairment in the appreciation of social cues, especially those associated with facial expressions and emotions in facial expression (Weigelt *et al.*, 2012; Ewing *et al.*, 2013). In an experiment in which autistic and control children were asked to sort pictures of individuals according to a category, autistic children would sort by appearance (hat) rather than emotion (Weeks and Hobson, 1987).

Language development in autism is severely delayed and there is evidence of deviant communication in the form of the idiosyncratic use of language, the making up of new words (neologising) and little engagement in social chat. Other examples of deviant language use include a difficulty in maintaining a topic of conversation (Bailey *et al.*, 1996).

The stereotypical and repetitive behaviour includes an over-reliance on routines or rituals and an abnormal attachment to objects.

The development of autism

Autism appears in the first two years of a child's life and is four times as common in boys as it is in girls (Gillberg and Coleman, 1992; Rapin, 1997). The prevalence of the disorder is one in 100 across most of the countries in which autism has been studied (Bryson *et al.*, 1988; Gillberg and Coleman, 1992; Sugiyama *et al.*, 1992). Autism may recede when the child develops language and uses it to communicate socially.

Early signs of the disorder include a failure to maintain eye-to-eye contact, to reach out to familiar persons (Swettenham *et al.*, 1998), and to imitate (Klin *et al.*, 1992). Baron-Cohen's 'reading the mind in the eyes' test described in the theory of mind section asks participants to judge the emotion emitted in a photograph that shows only the eye region of a human face. Baron-Cohen *et al.* (2001) administered the test to people with Asperger's syndrome (see below) and to high-functioning autistic individuals (people of normal intelligence who show autistic characteristics) and compared the performance of these groups with that of a control group. The performance of the experimental groups was significantly impaired. Autistic people are more likely to look at uninformative parts of the face such as nose and chin, rather than the eyes – they do not look at the eyes in pictures or in filmed interactions (Klin *et al.*, 2002; Spezio *et al.*, 2007). This partly explains why autistic people are less able than typical people to detect fear in people's faces.

There are checklists available that enable parents to determine whether their child is exhibiting autistic tendencies, including Baron-Cohen *et al.*'s (1992) Checklist for Autism in Toddlers (CHAT). This aims to identify those at risk of developing the disorder. Whereas performance on some cognitive tasks is low (such as comprehension), performance on others is high (such as block design) (Venter *et al.*, 1992). Some autistic people also exhibit exceptional abilities in specific domains such as reading, spelling, maths and music. When these abilities become extreme and highly remarkable, autistic individuals are called 'idiot savants', although such exceptional abilities are not unique to autism (O'Connor and Hermelin, 1988).

Autism and theory of mind

In the late 1980s a theme emerged in autism research which suggested that autistic children had an impaired ability to make inferences about other people's mental states; that is, these children lacked, or had a defective, **theory of mind** (Leslie, 1987). According to this early model, a 2-year-old child could pretend play and understand others' mental states, desires and beliefs, but autistic children could not because the mechanism which would allow this was impaired. As a result, the lack of pretend play would also be accompanied, later on, by an inability to interpret others' mental states.

Baron-Cohen *et al.* (1985) illustrated this in a study in which a child saw the unexpected transfer by a third person of an object from the location in which it was placed by the experimenter to a different location. The child's task was to predict where the experimenter would look for this object. Such tasks are now called 'theory of mind' tasks or tests of false belief. In a typical task, person A places an object in a cupboard and leaves the room. Person B enters, puts the object in a different location and leaves the room. Person A re-enters, and the participant is asked where person A will look for the object.

Children improve on these tasks from age 3 to 5 across cultures (Wellman *et al.*, 2001). Four-year-old children can correctly indicate that the experimenter would look in the original location for the object. Autistic children, however, cannot, and predict that the experimenter would look in the new location. They seem unaware that the experimenter would not know about the transfer of the object – they could not imagine the task from the other person's perspective. Baron-Cohen (1995) later used the term 'mindblindness' to refer to such inabilities to understand the thoughts of others.

A meta-analysis of studies examining the effect of age and language acquisition on understanding of theory of mind (measured via false-belief tasks) has found that theory of mind is strongly associated with language ability, but not age (Milligan *et al.*, 2007). The more advanced the language understanding (general language, semantics, receptive vocabulary, syntax), the greater the false-belief understanding.

Some researchers also suggest that theory of mind deficits are not common to all autistic individuals (Happé, 1993, 1994). The major deficit in autistic children, according to Frith and Happé (1994), is not impaired theory of mind but the inability to see situations and objects as wholes. Most of us see images and events as global images and events – we attend to the detail later. When you look at the television screen you do not attend to each individual detail of the image consciously (although your brain does do this), but you perceive a global image. The problem with autistic individuals, according to this view, is that they process information piecemeal and not in the context in which it appears.

There appears to be some evidence for this hypothesis. In experiments where participants have to find images within larger, more complex images, autistic children do very well (O'Riordan and Plaisted, 2001). Most normal participants have difficulty ignoring the large global image in which the 'hidden' image is embedded. Autistic children are also better than controls at discriminating among novel stimuli (but not familiar ones), indicating that they attend to specific features of stimuli (Plaisted *et al.*, 1998).

Frith and Happé (1994) suggest that two cognitive systems may be impaired in autism: one which normally allows theory of mind and another which determines the way in which information is processed. This model has the benefit of accounting for the theory of mind deficits and the tendency of autistic individuals to segment information instead of perceiving it globally. However, the model does not explain why such impairments arise in the first place. One source of information suggests that this impairment may be neurological in nature, as the section below highlights.

Neuropsychology of autism

A review of neuroimaging data has concluded that a reduction in frontal lobe size and activation are some of the more consistent neuropsychological characteristics of autism, as is

white matter reduction indicating that axon density and myelination are lower (Deb and Thompson, 1998; Verhoeven *et al.*, 2010). A single-case study, however, appears to present a challenge to this view. Bird *et al.* (2004) studied patient GT who had suffered brain damage as a result of stroke. There was extensive bilateral damage to the medial frontal lobes exclusively. GT showed the typical frontal lobe symptoms – impairments in planning and memory – but showed no evidence of impairment on 'theory of mind' tasks. This suggests that the medial frontal lobe may not be necessary for performing theory of mind tasks. Why, therefore, does neuroimaging evidence and some clinical neuropsychological evidence suggest otherwise? Bird *et al.* suggest that this could be because the medial frontal lobes are necessary for the acquisition of theory of mind but not for implementing theory of mind functions.

A similar idea lay behind a neuroimaging study of high functioning autistic adults (Kennedy and Courchesne, 2007). The study explored the idea that there are two different networks in the brain which perform different functions. One is thought to be impaired in autism; the other is intact. One network is responsible for doing cognitively demanding tasks and for engaging in externally directed behaviour. The second was activated when a person engaged in behaviour that involved a social or emotional component or which is introspective in nature (such as theory of mind). This is called the Task-Negative Network because there is a decrease in activation in specific brain areas during the performance of social or emotional tasks. This is the network that is affected in autism and this is what Kennedy and Courchesne (2007) found in their participants. The Task-Positive Network was unaffected.

Brain activation in children and adults with autistic spectrum disorders (ASD) differs from healthy children when their attention to a stimulus is directed by a social, rather than a non-social, cue (Greene *et al.*, 2011). In the experiment, the participants looked at a fixation point, then either a drawing of a pair of eyes looking to the left was presented, or an arrow pointing left or a drawing of eyes looking forward. The typically developing children showed activation in the fronto-parietal area, the visual cortex and striatum; ASD children only showed activation in one region (superior parietal tubule). This suggests that social cues are processed differently in the autistic and typically developing brain.

Structural differences in the brain also seem to exist in people exhibiting highly autistic traits (but who are not autistic). The Autism-spectrum Quotient (AQ) measures autistic traits and may predict poor performance on tests performed poorly by ASD individuals. Von dem Hagen *et al.* (2011) found that increased AQ scores in healthy adults were associated with less white matter in the posterior superior temporal sulcus (STS), a region important for social judgement. An area near this region also showed deactivation during a Stroop task. Lai *et al.* (2014) found that high functioning adult males with ASD showed differences depending on language delay. Those whose language was delayed showed larger total grey matter volume, smaller bilateral insula volume and larger volume in the pons and medulla oblongata. There were also similarities in brain region volumes between those individuals with and without a delay in their language (there was no complete heterogeneity).

Another region thought to be involved in autism is the amygdala. People with damage to the amygdala (Chapter 13) have severe difficulties in recognising emotion, specifically fear. These patients also have difficulty in making complex social judgements such as assessing trustworthiness in someone's face. Autistic individuals are able to recognise basic emotions, unlike patients with bilateral amygdala damage, and discriminate between the intensity of emotions expressed through facial expression (Adolphs et al., 2001). However, they are impaired at making social judgements about emotional facial expressions. For example, they rate faces as significantly more trustworthy than do control groups. Critchley et al. (2000) found that although autistic individuals performed above chance levels when identifying emotional facial expressions, they performed more poorly than a control group and did not activate the brain's 'face area' or the cerebellum when making judgements about emotional facial expression.

People with early damage to the amygdala are significantly impaired at theory of mind tests requiring sophisticated understanding of communication (e.g. detecting tactless/ironic remarks and interpreting metaphors) (Shaw et al., 2004). Adults with brain injury performed no worse than a control groups. The findings suggest that the amygdala may be necessary for the development of theory of mind but may not be responsible for the ongoing reasoning involved in theory of mind tasks.

A theory of 'theory of mind' that combines data from neuroanatomy and neurochemistry has been proposed by Abu-Akel and Shamay-Tsoory (2011). According to the model, networks of cortical and subcortical regions allow us to represent the cognitive and the affective components of mental states that relate to us and to others. Specifically, the cognitive and affective parts of theory of mind rely on the prefrontal lobe with the cognitive component relying on areas including the dorsomedial PFC (dmPFC), dorsal anterior cingulate cortex and dorsal striatum and the affective component on the ventro medial OFC (vmOFC), ventral (anterior cingulate cortex ACC), ventral striatum and amygdala. It also suggests that our ability to distinguish between ourselves and others is mediated by attentional systems in the temporoparietal (TP) junction and ACC. Finally, it proposes that dopamine and serotonin are the two most important neurotransmitters in allowing theory of mind.

Some researchers have hypothesised that autism may involve a dysfunction in the so-called mirror neuron system (see Chapter 4). These are neurons that fire when an organism reaches, for example, but also when the organism watches another reaching, hence, 'mirror' (Molenberghs et al., 2009). The 'broken mirror' theory of autism suggests that the inability of autistic people to imitate is due to the dysfunction or impairment in these neurons (Williams et al., 2004). However, imitation involves not only matching an action but also visual analysis, selecting what is to be imitated and when to imitate it (Southgate and Hamilton, 2008). Different types of imitation are, therefore, possible. Researchers have also queried whether the imitation deficit in autism is robust and consistent. Some studies show that if an autistic child is instructed to imitate, he or she will (Hamilton et al., 2007). They may fail to imitate meaningless action and facial expression, but they are able to imitate automatically (Bird et al., 2007). It may be that normal children use cues from others to influence imitation – and when and what to imitate – but autistic children do not. That may be the failure in autism, not a failure to imitate itself (and, by extension, a failure of the mirror neuron system).

Recent research has focused on whether connectivity between regions in the brains of individuals with ASD is distinctive (Uddi et al., 2013; Plitt et al., 2015a, 2015b). For example, Plitt et al. found that connectivity at rest predicted social abnormalities and changes in the ability to adapt over time (from late adolescence to early adulthood). Connectivity between the anterior insula and dorsal anterior cingulate predicted improvements in the young people's ability to adapt. The strength of connections within and between the motor regions of the brain have also been found to predict ASD and the severity of ASD (Nebel et al., 2014). Specifically, connections between and within the precentral gyrus were particularly important. Connectivity within the dorsomedial region of the precentral gyrus (which mediates movement of limbs and the trunk) was abnormal in children and adults with ASD. Finally, at the neurochemical level, the amount of the neurotransmitter GABA is lower in the motor and auditory areas of the brain (Gaetz et al., 2013) and in auditory area of the left perisylvian brain region in children with ASD and their siblings (Rojas et al., 2013).

Autism and testosterone

Evidence has suggested an association between levels of foetal testosterone and autism (Auyeung et al., 2009). Autism has been viewed as an 'extreme manifestation of male traits'. Auyeung et al. examined levels of testosterone – more common in males – in amniotic fluid during amniocentesis in the period 1996–2001. The study was longitudinal and the mothers of the children completed two autism questionnaires when their children were between 6 and 10 years old. It found that the higher the testosterone, the higher the scores on the questionnaires. The relationship was found in both sexes. The authors suggest that the findings support a view of autism or autistic traits as resulting from exposure to prenatal androgens.

Genes and autism

A new line of research in autism has focused on the role of genes in the disorder. A number of studies suggests that genes, gene region and variations (called copy number variations) in certain genes have been associated with ASD. These genes

Autism – An international perspective

A major study of children in Cambridgeshire suggests that the incidence of autism varies between 94 and 99 per 10,000 (Baron-Cohen *et al.*, 2009), comparable with data from other areas. The study analysed the Special Educational Needs register in Cambridgeshire and also distributed a diagnosis questionnaire to parents of all children between 5 and 9 years old. The number of questionnaires analysed was 3,373. Eleven children received a confirmed diagnosis of autism following assessment.

But do all cultures report the same symptoms when describing autism spectrum disorder? Matson *et al.* (2011) examined this question in 145 children from four countries: Israel, South Korea, the US and the UK. There were significant differences between the nations. Children from the UK were found to have greater impairment across all autistic symptoms – non-verbal communication, verbal communication, insistence on sameness – whereas autistic children from Israel were least impaired.

The authors argue that what may be markers for autism in one country are not considered markers in another – the behaviour may not be considered abnormal.

They also suggest that the disorder may be diagnosed differently. For example, in the US, infants are screened for developmental milestones at 18 and 24 months; some are even screened for autism. In the UK, children are only assessed for autism if it is reported by the parent or family member. None of the countries differed in the frequency of social skill impairment reported. As the diagnosis of autism is variable and the symptoms of the disorder are now acknowledged to fall on a continuum rather than forming a discrete category, perhaps these differences reflect this variability. There is also evidence that support for autistic people varies between cultures. There are a number of intervention programmes available in the UK and the US, for example. However, there is underdevelopment of care and services in China (Sun *et al.*, 2013b).

include *NRXN1* and *CNTN4*. Glessner *et al.* (2009) have also reported additional 'susceptibility' genes – two in total. They found that in their study of 859 ASD participants, variations within or surrounding genes involved in ubiquitin pathways were more common in ASD. Ubiquitin is important for altering the function of protein and, ultimately, can affect the attributes of synapses, neurotransmitter release, spine density, changes in dendritic spines and other neuronal features.

Maestrini *et al.* (2010) identified other gene loci associated with the disorder in 127 families. Two gene loci, *AUTS1* (on chromosome 7) and *AUTS5* (on chromosome 2), have been the most commonly reported and studied. This study found two other genes on chromosome 7 – *IMMP2L* and *DOCK4* – which were also associated with autism. The results suggest that genes on these chromosomes contribute to autism, but the actual genes vary. Four large-scale genome studies of 1,000 families identified six genes associated with ASD – *CHD8, DYRK1A, GRIN2B, KATNAL2, POGZ* and *SCN2A* (Buxbaum *et al.*, 2012).

Managing ASD

One type of social information which autistic individuals have a problem in processing is facial expression. They attend less often than typical individuals to faces and perform more poorly at face discrimination tasks. As a result, remedial exercises such as the Let's Face It! program have been developed. This computer-based intervention comprises seven games designed to remedy the face recognition problems by helping the user focus on the eye area, and develop a holistic face processing strategy.

To see how effectively it can do this, Tanaka *et al.* (2010) administered 20 hours of face training to a group of 42 children with autism. Compared with a control group, the autistic group showed significant improvement in the recognition of the mouth and in the recognition of the face based on the features of the eyes.

The outcome for autism is varied – some individuals develop little language whereas others are able to go on to full-time education, get married and start families (Rapin, 1997). The most important therapeutic intervention appears to involve intensive education aimed at changing the behavioural and communication problems. As such, most interventions are designed for use by parents and teachers who have greatest contact with the children. Medical interventions have also been developed but these appear to be more effective in improving attention than in eliminating all the characteristics of the disorder (Cohen and Volkmar, 1997).

One of the most comprehensive and effective ways of managing autism is Early Intensive Behavioural Intervention (EIBI). EIBI is based on the principles of operant conditioning (see Chapter 7) and involves helping the individual to improve their language, help themselves, imitate and to improve their social skills. Various operant conditioning procedures are used including discrete trial teaching, generalisation, reinforcement, shaping, extinction and others. The process is done one-to-one with the teacher/therapist and involves the parent to ensure that the behaviour modification generalises later on. According to Peters-Scheffer *et al.* (2011), it is most effective when intensive (40 hours a week) and extensive (done over 2 years). They found that in 11 studies, featuring 344 children, IQ, non-verbal IQ, and receptive and expressive language significantly improved in those receiving EIBI when compared to a control group.

Conduct disorder/attention deficit hyperactivity disorder

Conduct disorder is a severe impairment in the ability of the child to inhibit its own behaviour and, specifically, to inhibit antisocial and deviant behaviour (Nicol, 1998). It is related to a specific disorder termed **attention deficit hyperactivity disorder (ADHD)** whose main features are poor sustained attention, impulsiveness and hyperactivity (Barkley, 1997). Recent conceptions of ADHD identify three types: Inattentive, Hyperactive/Impulsive and Co-morbid. The inattentive type is more likely to have problems performing executive or cognitive tasks than are the other two.

ADHD occurs in 3–7 per cent of the child population, and is three times more common in boys. Between 50 and 80 per

Kim Peek, thought to be the inspiration for Dustin Hoffman's character, Raymond Babbitt, in Rain Man (although the character is not based on Peek) is an example of an autistic savant. He was able to read a Tom Clancy novel in under an hour and a half and name the Russian radio operator character from the book four months later (as well as give the page number of the passage describing the character). He memorised his first book at the age of 18 months and had learned 9,000, including Shakespeare and maps of all major US cities. He could read a page in 10 seconds. Not surprisingly, his friends nicknamed him, 'Kim-puter'. Kim Peek's brain was unusual because his corpus callosum was absent. Kim Peek died in 2009.

Source: Adam Nadel/Polaris/Eyevinearchive.

cent of children with the disorder continue showing symptoms into adolescence; 30–50 per cent of affected adolescents show symptoms in adulthood. So, although the disorder recedes, it persists in a high percentage of cases. Because of the nature of the disorder, the problems associated with it can be cognitively damaging. ADHD has been associated with low academic achievement and school performance, suspension/expulsion from school, poor family and peer relationships, mental disorder and substance abuse (Barkley, 1997). Most of the 'treatment' approaches to the disorder involve some form of counselling, behaviour management and, sometimes, psychoactive medication (Toplak *et al.*, 2008). Some examples include managing behaviour in the classroom using praise, giving rewards to increase positive behaviour and ignoring inappropriate behaviour. This has met with some success (Chronis *et al.*, 2006). Intensive working memory training programmes have shown significant improvements and a transfer of skills to other domains (Holmes *et al.*, 2009). Training on visuospatial memory tasks can lead to improvement in verbal working memory (Thorell *et al.*, 2009) and these effects have been found to be sustained three to six months later (Holmes *et al.*, 2009a,b).

The causes of ADHD are unclear. Some biological evidence has associated the disorder with a problem in the connections between the frontal lobe, the cerebellum and a region called the striatum. Some studies have shown that brain volume – in the cortex and the cerebellum – is smaller in children with ADHD and that activation is more diffuse when participants complete a cognitive task (Durston, 2003). Cognitive theories attribute some role to disrupted cognitive or executive processes, which explains the involvement of the frontal lobe (Barkley, 2006).

Emotion, attachment and hemispheric asymmetry

One model of emotional expression suggests that different sides of the frontal lobes regulate our experience of positive and negative emotions (you'll find more on this model in the next chapter). The left frontal region is thought to be responsive to positive emotion and the right frontal region is thought to be more responsive to negative emotion. Negative emotion may also be associated with reduced activity in the left frontal cortex (Davidson and Sutton, 1995).

Studies of distressed infants have highlighted similar asymmetries. For example, Davidson and Fox (1989) measured EEGs from infants they characterised as criers and non-criers (criers were those who became distressed when separated from their mother). The criers were distinguished from the non-criers by greater right-sided frontal EEG activation. Dawson *et al.* (1997) reported that the infants of depressed mothers (as well as the mothers themselves) showed reduced left frontal

EEG activity. These asymmetries have also been found in studies comparing 4-year-old infants who are either happy and sociable or unhappy and unsociable. The sociable children showed greater left frontal activation (Fox et al., 1995).

Behavioural inhibition in toddlers and infants refers to a temperamental pattern characterised by increased vigilance and decreased motor behaviour when children are confronted with a novel stimulus. These children are also more likely to avoid unfamiliar adults, show little spontaneous behaviour in the presence of unfamiliar peers and are regarded by their parents and peers as anxious and fearful. Children showing this pattern of behaviour also seem to show characteristic patterns of physiological and neural activity; some studies show that behavioural inhibition in children can be predicted by these physiological measures.

Depressed mothers who breastfed were more likely to raise infants who had a less negative temperament. These infants were also less likely to show increased right-sided EEG activation (characteristic of expressing negative emotion) than were infants of depressed mothers who breastfed less consistently. One reason for the interaction may be that the physical closeness of the mother and infant during breastfeeding offsets the negative temperament that might be provoked by a depressed mother who is less close to her child.

Four-month-old infants who display a consistent pattern of right frontal EEG activity are more likely to be behaviourally inhibited (Fox et al., 2001). The EEG pattern was evident even at 9 months. Children who were initially assessed as inhibited but later became non-inhibited did not show this characteristic pattern of right-sided EEG activity. The researchers suggest that infants showing an increase in left-sided activity use approach (positive) behaviour to modulate negative affect; those infants who show right-sided activity are less likely to do this.

What seems unclear in these EEG studies, however, is the nature of cause and effect. Does the distress cause the EEG asymmetry or does the EEG asymmetry cause the distress? Does the asymmetry predispose the infant to distress? These are interesting and important questions. Because they have implications for theories of the nature of emotion and the neuropsychology of emotion, we discuss these in more detail in the next chapter.

The frontal lobes (see Chapters 4 and 11) also are involved in executive functions such as regulating behaviour (planning, changing strategies, responding emotionally). A study by Hughes et al. (1998) compared the performance of 3 – or 4-year-old children, described as 'easy' or 'hard to manage', on a series of theory of mind, emotional understanding and executive function (frontal lobe) tasks. They found that the disruptive children showed poorer understanding of emotion and less successful performance on the theory of mind tasks.

If regional brain activity can discriminate sociable from non-sociable children, what do you think would be the implications of this for child welfare and education?

Development of sex roles in childhood

Physical development as a male or a female is only one aspect of sexual development. Social development is also important. A person's **sexual identity** is one's private sense of being a male or female and consists primarily of the recognition of membership in a particular group of people: males or females. Acceptance of this membership does not necessarily indicate acceptance of the sex roles or sex stereotypes that may accompany it. For example, a dedicated feminist may fight to change the role of women in her society but still clearly identify herself as a woman. Sex roles are cultural expectations about the ways in which men and women should think and behave.

Closely related to them are **sex stereotypes**, beliefs about differences in the behaviours, abilities and personality traits of males and females. Society's sex stereotypes have an important influence on the behaviour of its members. In fact, many people unconsciously develop their sex identity and sex roles based on sex stereotypes they learned as children.

Development of sexual identity

According to Kohlberg (1966), the ability of children to identify with their sex is determined in large part by their ability to classify objects as being boys' objects or girls' objects, that is, they begin to identify their own sex by observing how others class objects and people. In Kohlberg's model, the child undergoes three stages of sexual identity development: gender labelling, gender stability and gender consistency.

- *Stage 1 Gender labelling.* At the age of 2–3½ years, the child learns that they are of one sex. Labels that other people apply to them are learned and they attach these same labels to people of the same sex or objects associated with a sex.
- *Stage 2 Gender stability.* Between the ages of 3½ and 4½ children begin to realise that their sex is a constant and that this feature can often be seen in other's physical
- appearance. This time, therefore, is characterised by an increase in awareness of others' physical features.
- *Stage 3 Gender consistency.* At the age of 4½ children discover that people's sex does not change and that physical appearance does not affect their sexual identity. If a girl or boy dresses up as a member of the opposite sex, they are still regarded as a girl or boy despite their appearance.

By 2 years of age children begin to perceive themselves as being a boy or a girl. In the process of learning what it means to be boys or girls, children associate, in a stereotypical manner, certain toys, games, attitudes and behaviours, such as being aggressive or compliant, with one sex or the other

(Huston, 1983; Jacklin and Maccoby, 1983; Picariello *et al.*, 1990). For example, consider an experiment conducted by Montemayor (1974), who invited children between the ages of 6 and 8 years to play a game that involved tossing marbles into a clown's body. Some of the children were told that they were playing a 'girl's game', some were told it was a 'boy's game', and others were told nothing. Boys and girls both said that the game was more fun when it had been described as appropriate to their sex, and they even attained better scores when it was.

Kohlberg's notion of identity development is echoed in recent work that tries to explain how this development occurs. **Gender schema theory**, for example, argues that children construct a 'schema' – a mental representation – of male and female and pay especial attention to features of their own sex (Bem, 1981; Martin and Halverson, 1981). Children's perception of sex is matched with information about others' sex that the child has already processed and understood (Ruble and Martin, 1998).

The ability to identify others' and the child's own sex emerges between the ages of 1 and 3 years. Usually, this is determined by asking children to look at photographs of boys and girls and to point to the person who is a boy or a girl or who is most like the child doing the looking (Etaugh *et al.*, 1989; Fagot and Leinbach, 1989). Children as young as 30 months can complete this task successfully and children as young as 36 months can sort photographs of boys and girls into two piles, without instructions to sort them according to sex.

By the age of 2, children are already beginning to spend more time preferentially playing with their own sex, with the time spent playing with the same-sex child multiplying 11-fold by the time children reach 6 years (LaFreniere *et al.*, 1984).

Sexual identity and play

Sexual identity is also thought to emerge during play. Pre-schoolers, for example, will engage in role-play but in a sex-typical way: boys will play at being mechanics and bus drivers whereas girls will play at being teachers and cooks (Garvey, 1977). By the age of 1, children will play with sex-typical toys with their parents; by the age of 2, they may engage in this spontaneously without the interference of a parent (Fagot *et al.*, 1986; Roopnarine, 1986).

Some researchers, however, have noted that while children learn that the sexes differ on some dimensions, such as physical appearance, they do not differ on others (Campbell *et al.*, 2002). Campbell *et al.* argue that sexual differentiation does not occur in all domains at certain age points. For example, they point to studies showing that children's ability to divide toys into 'girl' toys and 'boy' toys can be unrelated to the children's actual preference for those toys (Perry *et al.*, 1984). Furthermore, children who show sex-typed behaviour in one domain may not show it in another (Turner *et al.*, 1993).

To discover how well children could sex-type according to different behaviour domains, Campbell *et al.* studied 56 2-year-old children in various experimental conditions. In one condition, the child's mother would ask it to point to a male- and female-related stimulus that could be a toy or an activity. Male toys were described as cars, trains, water-pistols, blocks and balls whereas female toys were described as toasters, cookers, dolls, dustpans and brushes, and combs. Some of the female activities were described as drawing, whispering, playing with dolls or playing pat-a-cake; some of the male activities were described as chasing, jumping, climbing, wrestling and playing cowboys. In another condition, the child was presented with a photograph of itself and a photograph of a child of the opposite sex and was asked to point to the picture of the girl or boy. Finally, the children were observed in naturalistic settings. In one of these, a child was allowed to play with a selection of toys with the parent. In another, the child played with another child and their interaction was videotaped.

The researchers found that two-thirds of children could identify themselves as male or female, a finding supported by other studies of 3-year-old children (Fagot, 1985). About half of the group were able to point to the face of a boy or a girl accurately in photographs and around a quarter were able to differentiate toys according to whether they were boys' toys or girls' toys. Only one child in eight was able to identify activities according to their sex-type.

On the basis of these results, the researchers suggest that the child's awareness of its own sex and that of others is a 'developmental precursor' to the later sex-typing of toys and activities. The children in the study did prefer to play with sex-typed toys, however, whether they played alone or with another child. Lloyd and Duveen (1990) found that whereas 1½–3½ year-old boys played with boys' toys more than girls' toys, the girls played equally with boys' and girls' toys. When the children were paired with a same-sex partner, both sexes spent more time playing with their sex-typed toys.

According to Miller (1987), boys and girls are sensitive to the properties of toys that allow them to engage in specific behaviours. Thus, guns and swords offer the boy an opportunity for conflict whereas dolls and dolls' houses offer the girl an opportunity to nurture. Others, however, have noted that the attributes of objects may be related to sex but not to what the object actually does (the technical term for this is affordance). For example, when a typically female object such as a teapot was masculinised by painting it brown and covering it with spikes, boys were more inclined to play with it than were girls (Leinbach *et al.*, 1997). Furthermore, when a 6-month-old baby is dressed in either pink or blue (its actual sex is not apparent) and parents are asked to give it either a train (a boy's toy), doll (a girl's toy) or fish (a neutral toy), the baby in pink would be given the doll more often than would the baby in blue. The baby in pink was also smiled at more often (Will *et al.*, 1976).

Pink for girls, blue for boys – is it all black and white?

According to Hines (2010), sex differences in sex identity and sex-specific play are greater than differences in personality, cognition or height. Sex-specific play is seen in 2-year-olds and increases significantly between 2½ and 5 years (Golombok *et al.*, 2008). Stereotypically, boys prefer to play with angular toys such as trucks and blocks whereas girls prefer to play with rounder toys such as dolls, and there is considerable evidence for the strength of this sex difference – 12- to 24-month-old girls spend longer looking at dolls whereas boys spend longer looking at cars (Jadva *et al.*, 2010).

Another stereotypical sex difference appears to be the preference for colour – boys prefer blue objects, girls prefer pink. People tend to associate masculine perfumes with the colours blue and green and feminine ones with the colour pink (Zellner *et al.*, 2008). As any visitor to a babies' clothes shop will attest, the sex typing by colour is strong. See Figure 12.12 for some inter-species similarities.

A series of experiments by Cunningham and MacRae (2011) from the University of Aberdeen, however, has shown convincingly that not only does such a preference exist but that colour can prime sex-specific stereotypes about a person. In their first experiment, they studied the colour of toys and clothes in a popular British mail order catalogue and in the inventory of a well-known high street catalogue retailer. They found that 53 per cent of all of the items were either coloured blue or pink. Boys were offered more blue-coloured toys and girls more pink-coloured ones. In a second experiment, boys and girls were asked to chose which items other boys and girls would like to furnish their bedroom with. Items were blue or pink (each item was available in each colour). The 10-year-olds were more likely to choose blue items for boys and pink for girls.

They then extended this work by examining colour's ability to prime assumptions and beliefs about others. In one experiment, response times to male and female forenames presented either in pink or blue were measured. Undergraduates who had to decide whether the name was masculine or feminine. Participants were slower in reacting to male names in pink and female names in blue than when the name and colour 'matched'. The difference was also found for sex-typed objects (e.g. football boots, bras) coloured pink or blue. Responses were faster when the colour in which the item was presented matched the item.

Then, the researchers examined whether a blue or pink background against which a male or female face was presented affected how quickly a participant was able to identify the sex of the face. In a group of 20 undergraduates, responses were

Figure 12.12 The female and male vervet monkey, showing the typical human responses to toys – females prefer soft toys, males prefer wheeled toys.

faster when the background colour matched the sex of the face: pink for girls, blue for boys.

Finally, participants were asked to assess the personalities of men and women photographed wearing pink or blue clothes. The men dressed in pink were described as having more feminine traits than those dressed in blue; women in blue were judged to be more masculine.

Where do children learn sex stereotypes?

Parents play an especially important role in the development of sex stereotypes: they tend to encourage and reward their sons for playing with 'masculine' toys such as cars and trucks and objects such as baseballs and footballs (Fagot and Hagan, 1991) and encourage baby boys to generate gross motor activity, whereas they are more soothing and calming with baby girls (Smith and Lloyd, 1978). Parents also tend to encourage and reward their daughters for engaging in 'feminine' activities that promote dependence, warmth and sensitivity, such as playing house or hosting a make-believe tea party (Dunn *et al.*, 1987; Lytton and Romney, 1991). Parents who do not encourage or reward these kinds of stereotypical activity tend to have children whose attitudes and behaviour reflect fewer sex stereotypes (Weisner and Wilson-Mitchell, 1990).

In supposedly 'masculine' academic subjects, girls are perceived as performing less well than boys. Many reasons have been suggested for the discrepancy but one of the most frequently cited is socialisation: that is, parents and teachers are more likely to engage boys in science and scientific explanations than they are girls.

In an ingenious experiment to test this hypothesis, Crowley *et al.* (2001) sought the permission of parents visiting a Californian children's museum to film and record their interactions with their children as they made their way around the exhibitions. Data were collected from 298 interactions between mothers and fathers and their daughters and sons on 26 days over a 30-month period. Conversations were rated according to whether they involved explanations, descriptions of or directions for exhibitions.

The researchers found that parents were more likely to explain exhibits to their sons than to their daughters. If the behaviour of parents helps shape the behaviour of their children, the researchers suggest that this disparity could have a significant effect on the child's interest in and knowledge of science.

Moral development

The word 'morality' comes from a Latin word that means 'custom'. Moral behaviour is behaviour that conforms to a generally accepted set of rules, although whether these rules generally are accepted is quite controversial. With few exceptions, by the time a person reaches adulthood, they have accepted a set of rules about personal and social behaviour. These rules vary in different cultures and may take the form of laws, **taboos** and even sorcery (Chasdi, 1994). How does a child acquire morality?

Piaget's theory of moral development

According to Piaget, the development of morality occurs in three general stages: the premoral stage, the moral realism stage and the moral relativism stage. Table 12.2 outlines the features of each stage.

The first stage of moral development (ages 0–5 years) is **premoral**. During this period the child has little conception of rules or principles. The second stage, however, sees the beginning of rule adherence. This stage, **moral realism**, is characterised by egocentrism, or 'self-centredness', and blind adherence to rules.

Egocentric children can evaluate events only in terms of their personal consequences. Their behaviour is not guided by the effects it might have on someone else, because they are not capable of imagining themselves in the other person's place. Thus, young children do not consider whether an act is right or wrong but only whether it is likely to have good or bad

Table 12.2 Piaget's stages of moral development

Stage	Description
Premoral (0–5 years)	The child shows little understanding of rules or principles
Moral realism (5–10 years)	Rules are obeyed quite rigidly The child judges a person's action by its consequences The child develops a belief in punishment and justice
Moral relativism (10 years and over)	The child becomes more flexible in interpreting moral issues The child becomes aware that moral responses are relative, that rules can be broken and that people are not always punished

consequences personally. Punishment is a bad consequence, and the fear of punishment is the only real moral force at this age. A young child also believes that rules come from parents (or other authority figures, such as older children or God), and that rules cannot be changed.

Older children and adults judge an act by the intentions of the actor as well as by the consequences of the act. A young child considers only an act's objective outcomes, not the subjective intent that lay behind the act. For example, Piaget told two stories, one about John, who accidentally broke 15 cups, and Henry, who broke one cup while trying to do something that was forbidden to him. When a young child is asked which of the two children is the naughtiest, the child will say that John is, because he broke 15 cups. They will not take into account the fact that the act was entirely accidental.

As children mature, they become less egocentric and more capable of empathy. Older children (older than age 7) can imagine how another person feels. This shift away from egocentrism means that children's behaviour may be guided not merely by the effects that acts have on themselves but also by the effects they have on others. At around 10 years of age, children enter Piaget's third stage of moral development, moral relativism, during which rules become more flexible as the child learns that many of them (such as those that govern games) are social conventions that may be altered by mutual consent.

Kohlberg's theory of moral development

Piaget's description of moral development was considerably elaborated on by Lawrence Kohlberg (1927–1987). Kohlberg (1971) had argued that, 'All individuals in all cultures go through the same order or sequence of gross stages of development, though they vary in rate and terminal point of development'. He studied boys of between 10 and 17 years of age, over the course of several years, by presenting them with stories

involving moral dilemmas (Kohlberg, 1966, 1982). For example, one story described a man called Heinz whose wife was dying of a cancer that could only be treated by a medication discovered by a chemist living in the same town. This was the dilemma in full:

> A woman is near death from cancer. One drug might save her, a form of radium discovered by a chemist living in the same town, who is selling the drug at 10 times what it cost him to manufacture it. The sick woman's husband tried to borrow the money but could raise only half the price. He told the chemist that his wife was dying and asked him to sell the drug more cheaply or, at least, let him pay later, but the chemist refused. The desperate husband broke into the chemist's shop to steal the drug for his wife. Should he have done that?

For this dilemma and others, there is no correct answer. It is designed to discover more about how people engage in moral reasoning. On the basis of his research using such dilemmas, Kohlberg argued that moral development comprised three levels and seven stages (see Table 12.3). These stages are closely linked to children's cognitive development as outlined by Piaget.

The first two stages belong to the **preconventional level**, during which morality is externally defined. During stage 1, morality of punishment and obedience, children blindly obey authority and avoid punishment. When asked to decide what Heinz should do, children base their decisions on fears about being punished for letting one's wife die or for committing a crime. During stage 2, morality of naive instrumental hedonism, children's behaviour is guided egocentrically by the pleasantness or unpleasantness of its consequences to them. The moral choice is reduced to a weighing of the probable risks and benefits of stealing the drug.

Table 12.3 Levels and stages of Kohlberg's theory of moral development

Level and stage	Highlights
Preconventional level	
Stage 1: Morality of punishment and obedience	Avoidance of punishment
Stage 2: Morality of naive instrumental hedonism	Egocentric perspective; weighing of potential risks and benefits
Conventional level	
Stage 3: Morality of maintaining good relations	Morality based on approval from others
Stage 4: Morality of maintaining social order	Rules and laws define morality
Postconventional level	
Stage 5: Morality of social contracts	Obey societal rules for the common good, although individual rights sometimes outweigh laws
Stage 6: Morality of universal ethical principles	Societal laws and rules based on ethical values
Stage 7: Morality of cosmic orientation	Adoption of values that transcend societal norms

Morality across cultures – An international perspective

A study of the development of morality in young children in the US, Fiji, China and Brazil has highlighted stages of moral progress as children grow older, especially in terms of delaying gratification and making sure that resources are distributed fairly (Rochat *et al.*, 2009). At the ages of 3 and 5, children still show evidence of self-interest over self-sacrifice by choosing to place a sweet in their own cup before other children's and by giving themselves more valuable items. By the age of 5, their sense of fairness does begin to increase.

The study also found large differences in self-interest across cultures. Children growing up in smaller communities that were traditional in nature (placing emphasis on the sense of community) were more likely to express less self-interest, that is, greater fairness.

The next two stages belong to the **conventional level**, which includes an understanding that the social system has an interest in people's behaviour. During stage 3, morality of maintaining good relations, children want to be regarded by people who know them as good, well-behaved children. Moral decisions are based on perceived social pressure. Either Heinz should steal the drug because people would otherwise regard him as heartless, or he should not steal it because they would regard him as a criminal. During stage 4, morality of maintaining social order, laws and moral rules are perceived as instruments used to maintain social order and, as such, must be obeyed. Thus, both protecting a life and respecting people's property are seen as rules that help maintain social order. This stage required people to expand their social perspectives, a requirement which was assisted by having attended university or working in a work setting that involved complex reasoning (Mason and Gibbs, 1993).

Kohlberg also described a final level of moral development – the **postconventional level**, during which people realise that moral rules have some underlying principles that apply to all situations and societies. During stage 5, morality of social contracts, people recognise that rules are social contracts, that not all authority figures are infallible, and that individual rights can sometimes take precedence over laws. During stage 6, morality of universal ethical principles, people perceive rules and laws as being justified by abstract ethical values, such as the value of human life and the value of dignity. In stage 7, the morality of cosmic orientation, people adopt values that transcend societal norms. This stage represents the zenith of moral development. Kohlberg believed that not all people reach the postconventional level of moral development.

Evaluation of Piaget's and Kohlberg's theories of moral development

Piaget's and Kohlberg's theories have greatly influenced research on moral development, but they have received some criticism. For example, Piaget's research indicated that children in the second stage (moral realism) respond to the magnitude of a transgression rather than to the intent behind it. But even adults respond to the magnitude of a transgression.

The theft of a few postage stamps by an office worker, for example, is not treated the same way as the embezzlement of thousands of pounds. In this sense, children's morality is quite adult-like.

While stages 1 to 4 of Kohlberg's model appear to be universal, the appearance of the later stages of moral reasoning seem to be culture-specific. Urban populations tend to express more mature moral judgements, that is, reach the later stages of reasoning, than rural populations. For example, stages 5 and 6 are absent in semi-literate, peasant cultures (Kohlberg, 1969) and in folk villages (Snarey, 1985). One conclusion from this is that the stage model does not classify modes of reasoning that involve the types of collective reasoning seen in less literate cultures (Snarey, 1985). For example, one 50-year-old Indian man justified Heinz's theft to save the life of a pet in terms of the 'unity of life' – all human life was sacred and needed to be preserved if possible. When Japanese and North American adults were given the Heinz dilemma, there was no difference in the moral stages of the two groups but the reasons for their decision were different (Isawa, 1992). Americans believed that the wife should live and that Heinz was right to steal the drug; the Japanese, however, were more concerned with the purity and cleanliness of life and decided that Heinz should not steal the drug.

Sobesky (1983) found that changes in the wording of Heinz's dilemma would drastically change people's responses. If the possibility of imprisonment was underscored, people tended to make more responses belonging to the preconventional level. Many researchers agree with Rest (1979), who concluded that Kohlberg's 'stages' are not coherent entities but do describe a progression in the ability of children to consider more and more complex reasons for moral rules.

A different type of criticism was levelled by Gilligan (1977, 1982), who suggested that Kohlberg's theory is sex-biased. According to her, Kohlberg's studies seem to suggest that men (in general) adhered to universal ethical principles, whereas women (in general) preferred to base their moral judgements on the effects these judgements would have on the people involved. Men's judgements were based more on abstract ideas of justice, whereas women's judgements were based more on concrete considerations of caring and concern for relationships. The criticism has some validity in the sense that the moral stages which Kohlberg suggested were based on data collected exclusively from boys: results show that when men and women study these dilemmas, their decisions place women at stage 3 and men at stage 5.

However, most researchers have not found that men's and women's moral judgements tend to be based on different types of values. For example, Donenberg and Hoffman (1988) found that boys and girls were equally likely to base their moral judgements on justice or caring and that the sex of the main character in the moral dilemma had no effect on their judgements. Adolescent girls reach the third stage of reasoning more quickly than do boys (Silberman and Snarey, 1993) and girls and women, across most cultures but not all, appear to express more care-related concerns when making moral judgements (Jaffe and Hyde, 2000; Leenders and Brugman, 2005; Raynauld et al., 1999). Johnson (1998), in a study of adults, also found that both sexes were capable of moral reasoning based on justice and caring.

Alternative models of moral development

Although Kohlberg's model has been one of the most influential and widely studied models of moral reasoning, it is not the only one. Other models of moral development have focused on specific types of moral behaviour. For example, Damon (1977, 1980) has explored children's concept of sharing and distributing resources. In a typical scenario, a child is told that a class of children has received some money from the sale of paintings that the whole class had made. The child is given examples of how the money could be distributed – it could be distributed according to merit, need, equality or sex – and is asked which criterion is most appropriate. Based on responses to this scenario, Damon proposed that the child goes through four levels of moral reasoning, summarised in Table 12.4.

In Damon's model of distributive justice, the child begins the process of moral development by making decisions about sharing based on egocentric considerations. The child will make decisions based on their own desires and perspectives. This stage of reasoning occurs during the pre-schooler stage.

Towards the end of this stage, children begin to introduce external factors into their reasoning and may distribute/share resources according to the size or ability of the recipient group. The second stage is observed in primary school children and is characterised by an increase in equality-based judgements, that is, the child believes that everybody should share in a reward regardless of their ability or merit. The third stage finds the child considering the merit and the achievement of others when deciding how to distribute resources. The fourth and final stage, which occurs at age 10–11 years, sees the child considering a large number of factors that could influence their judgements about distribution; at this stage, the children show evidence of the moral concept of fairness.

Damon's stages model finds considerable support in real-life decision-making by children. This type of thinking appears to follow a similar pattern, but the children exhibit greater levels of self-interest (Gerson and Damon, 1978). They will, for example, indicate that resources should be distributed according to merit if they themselves are seen as showing merit.

An alternative method of measuring moral reasoning and development is the socio-moral reflection method (SRM) of Gibbs et al. (1982). This is a dilemma-free measure that evaluates the importance of those issues, values and institutions that arise in Kohlberg's model and which are seen in every society and culture – contracts, truth, affiliation, life, property, law and legal justice (Gibbs et al., 2007). For example, people's view of truth and contract might be prompted by the statement: 'Think about when you've made a promise to a friend'; affiliation would be explored by statements such as: 'Let's say a friend of yours needed help and may die and you're the only person who can save him or her'.

While this and other models have attempted to create chronologies of moral development, some researchers have questioned the catch-all nature of the term 'moral development'. For example, a distinction has been made between 'moral' and 'socio-conventional' reasoning (Turiel, 1998). Moral reasoning involves making decisions where the consequences of actions could lead to another person being physically or psychologically harmed. Socio-conventional reasoning concerns issues regarding conformity to social norms or

Table 12.4 Damon's model of distributive justice

Stage	Description
1	Pre-schoolers' decisions are based on their feelings and perspectives; decisions are egocentric
	At the end of the stage, external considerations influenced reasoning
2	Primary school children base their decisions on notions of equality
3	Equality gives way to considerations of merit and notions of reciprocity
4	The distribution of resources is based on other's achievements
	At age 10 to 11, the child exhibits evidence of fairness

conduct such as how to address others, how to behave at a dinner table. Both types of reasoning follow a rule system of some kind but the two are different in terms of their comparative moral importance. It is thought that children can make the distinction between these two types of reasoning by 6 or 7 years.

Adolescence

After childhood comes adolescence, the threshold to adulthood (in Latin, *adolescere* means 'to grow up'). The transition between childhood and adulthood is as much social as it is biological. In some societies, people are considered to be adults as soon as they are sexually mature, at which time they may assume adult rights and responsibilities, including marriage. In most industrialised societies, where formal education often continues into the late teens and early twenties, adulthood officially comes several years later. The end of adolescence is difficult to judge because the line between adolescence and young adulthood is fuzzy: there are no distinct physical changes that mark this transition. Erikson (1968) described adolescence as a 'psycho-social moratorium': a period in which the child begins to experiment with life and with living, testing social and emotional boundaries to see what is acceptable and what is not.

Physical development

Puberty (from the Latin *puber*, meaning 'adult'), the period during which a person's reproductive system matures, marks the beginning of the transition from childhood to adulthood. Many physical changes occur during this stage: people reach their ultimate height, develop increased muscle size and body hair, and become capable of reproduction. There is also a change in social roles. As a child, a person is dependent on parents, teachers and other adults. As an adolescent, they are expected to assume more responsibility. Relations with peers also suddenly change; members of one's own sex become potential rivals for the attention of members of the other sex.

Sexual maturation

The internal sex organs and external genitalia do not change much for several years after birth, but they begin to develop again at puberty. When boys and girls reach about 11–14 years of age, their testes or ovaries secrete hormones that begin the process of sexual maturation. This activity of the gonads is initiated by the hypothalamus, the part of the brain to which the pituitary gland is attached. The hypothalamus instructs the pituitary gland to secrete hormones that stimulate the gonads to secrete sex hormones. These sex hormones act on various organs of the body and initiate the changes that accompany sexual maturation.

The sex hormones secreted by the gonads cause growth and maturation of the external genitalia and of the gonads themselves. In addition, these hormones cause the maturation of ova and the production of sperm. All these developments are considered primary sex characteristics, because they are essential to the ability to reproduce. The sex hormones also stimulate the development of secondary sex characteristics, the physical changes that distinguish males from females. Before puberty, boys and girls look much the same, except, perhaps, for their hairstyles and clothing. At puberty, young men's testes begin to secrete testosterone; this hormone causes their muscles to develop, their facial hair to grow and their voices to deepen. Young women's ovaries secrete oestradiol, the most important oestrogen, or female sex hormone. Oestradiol causes women's breasts to grow and their pelvis to widen, and it produces changes in the layer of fat beneath the skin and in the texture of the skin itself.

Development of the adult secondary sex characteristics takes several years, and not all characteristics develop at the same time. The process begins in girls at around age 11. The first visible change is the accumulation of fatty tissue around the nipples, followed shortly by the growth of pubic hair. The spurt of growth in height commences, and the uterus and vagina begin to enlarge. The first menstrual period begins at around age 13, just about the time the rate of growth in height begins to decline. In boys, sexual maturation begins slightly later. The first visible event is the growth of the testes and scrotum, followed by the appearance of pubic hair. A few months later, the penis begins to grow, and the spurt of growth in height starts. The larynx grows larger, which causes the voice to become lower. Sexual maturity – the ability to father a child – occurs at around age 15. The growth of facial hair usually occurs later; often a full beard does not grow until the late teens or early twenties.

In industrialised societies, the average age at the onset of puberty has been declining. For example, the average age at the onset of menstruation was between 14 and 15 years in 1900 but is between 12 and 13 years today. The most important reason for this decline is better childhood nutrition. It appears that this decline is levelling off in industrialised societies, but in many developing countries, the age of the onset of puberty is beginning to fall as these countries enjoy increasing prosperity.

Behavioural effects of puberty

The changes that accompany sexual maturation have a profound effect on young people's behaviour and self-concept. One pronounced change is sensitivity about their appearance. Many girls worry about their weight and the size of their breasts and hips (Kloep, 1999). Many boys worry about their height, the size of their genitals, their muscular development and the growth of their beards (Alsaker, 1996). At around the age of 13, girls have consistently more negative views of their body image than do boys (Kloep, 1999; Wichstrom, 1999). Findings such as these have been linked to the higher incidence of eating disorders such as anorexia nervosa and bulimia nervosa in girls (we return to the characteristics of anorexia and bulimia and their possible causes in much more detail in Chapter 13). In Europe, for example, between 1 and 3 per cent of girls are reported to show symptoms of one of these two disorders (Barnombudsmannen, 1997). A study of Scottish children found that although many of them considered themselves to be 'too fat', they were not significantly overweight for their age, showing an average body shape (Shucksmith and Hendry, 1998). The results indicate that puberty and the short period following it are characterised by a concern with body image, but a concern which does not appear grounded in reality.

An Australian study asked over 500 8–11-year-old boys and girls what they thought of their body image and whether they engaged in any thinking or behaviour that could lead to weight loss or muscle gain (McCabe and Ricciardelli, 2003). Body Mass Index was measured (see Chapter 13 for how this is calculated), as was self-esteem. As might be expected, children with high BMIs were those most concerned with losing weight and their self-esteem was associated with their body satisfaction. The poorer the self-esteem, the greater the dissatisfaction. Boys were more likely than girls to think about, and put strategies in place towards, increasing muscle. However, even girls were engaged in thinking about increasing their muscles. The study shows that even quite young children are concerned with their body image and already think about strategies for losing weight and/or increasing muscle.

In an American study of 165 girls and 139 boys with an average age of 15 years, Jones (2004) found that girls became increasingly dissatisfied with their bodies primarily through talking about their appearance with friends and comparing themselves with desirable others. As time progressed, the girls became highly preoccupied with their appearance and this preoccupation was related to the increase in dissatisfaction. Boys, however, seemed less concerned with making direct comparisons between themselves and their peers. Instead, those boys who reported being most dissatisfied with their bodies had an 'internalised' ideal of what a muscular body looked like: it was against this ideal that they compared themselves.

A more extensive study investigated how body image changed across almost two decades. The cross-sectional study of 3,127 college students from a North American university who completed body image questionnaires from 1983 to 2001 found that body image changed significantly across these years, especially in women (Cash et al., 2004). White women, in particular, reported negative assessments of their body image and a preoccupation with being overweight in the 1980s and early 1990s. Their satisfaction with their upper and mid torso as well as their overall appearance declined over the period. Women who completed assessments more recently – mid-1990s onwards – reported more favourable body image and less concern with being overweight (despite being heavier than the 1980s cohorts). Men were relatively unaffected over the years, with their body image remaining relatively stable.

In addition to concerns with bodily appearance, most adolescents display a particular form of egocentrism that develops early in the stage of formal operations: self-consciousness. Some developmental psychologists believe that self-consciousness results from the difficulty in distinguishing their own self-perceptions from the views other people have of them.

Because the onset of puberty occurs at different times in different individuals, young adolescents can find themselves to be more or less mature than some of their friends, and this difference can have important social consequences. Early-maturing boys feel more confident about themselves than do late-maturing boys and are also more satisfied with their looks and musculature (Cok, 1990). Early-maturing girls, however, seem to exhibit greater depression and unhappiness, although the evidence for this is mixed (Alsaker, 1992). Early-maturing girls do appear to have greater eating concerns (Brooks-Gunn, 1988) and show greater variability in self-esteem.

How do adolescents view puberty?

Adolescent boys and girls have different views of puberty. Whereas boys seem to look forward to the increasing strength, freedom and social status that the change brings, girls see limited benefits. Instead, they regard the onset of becoming a woman as being accompanied by the need to conform to society's view of women and this view is one that associates being a woman with lower social status (Martin, 1996). Girls perceive having less freedom than do boys because their parents insist on regulating aspects of their social lives, specifically, protecting them from predatory boys (Martin, 1996). Girls also seem unhappier at this time than are boys. Depression, for example, appears to be more common in girls than in boys at puberty (Wichstrom, 1999). One possible reason may be their consistent concern over body image and the need to maintain a level of physical attractiveness – in short, the beginning of the development of sexual identity – two features that could meet with as much acceptance as rejection. Girls become increasingly concerned with their weight and shape after the onset of puberty.

Social development, peer relations and delinquency

During adolescence a person's behaviour and social roles change dramatically. Adolescence is not simply a continuation of childhood; it marks a real transition from the dependence of childhood to the relative independence of adulthood. Adolescence is also a period during which many people seek out new experiences and engage in reckless behaviour – behaviour that involves psychological, physical and legal risks for them as well as for others (Arnett, 1995). Norm-breaking such as this is related to the adolescent's social network (Magnusson et al., 1986). For example, early-maturing girls have been found to have older female friends who engage in more adult behaviour

Psychology in action: Adolescents and the internet

Once there were pigeons, then the printing press, then Roland Hill's Penny Post, followed by television and telephony and, in another technological upheaval, the internet. Humans have created inventive ways of communicating with each other. In the 1980s and 1990s, the internet was a largely passive affair – we surfed to find things and to buy things. The past 10 years have seen the arrival of Web 2.0. The internet became interactive: Facebook, Instagram YouTube, Skype,Twitter, WhatsApp and the like blossomed and the internet underwent another, small revolution.

Online communication has now become one of the most popular means whereby one human being communicates with another, especially if that human being is pubescent or pre-pubescent. Van den Eijnden *et al.* (2008) cite a study reporting that 84 per cent of Dutch adolescents were found to have used instant messaging or internet chat rooms. In 2007–08, serious concerns were raised about adolescents' and young people's use of the internet when a spate of 17 suicides in the town of Bridgend, South Wales were linked with the use of social networking sites. There was no evidence that these sites encouraged these suicides and it was more likely that the publicity generated on television and in newspapers provided more obvious encouragement.

This type of communication, however, is largely sterile and devoid of human contact. It may also be used by the lonely. Van den Eijnden *et al.*, therefore, sought to investigate whether online messaging was associated with any negative (or positive) effect on well-being. They monitored instant messenger use and chat room visits by 663 12–15-year-olds at two time points, separated by six months. Measures of loneliness and depression as well as compulsive internet use were administered at each session.

Using instant messaging and frequenting chat rooms – but not emailing – was positively related to compulsive internet use six months later: the greater the involvement in the former, the greater the compulsive internet use six months later. However, messenger use (but not chat room use or emailing) was also associated with increased depression six months later whereas loneliness was inversely related to instant messenger use. That is, those who reported being most lonely were less likely to use instant messaging, possibly because these lonely adolescents were adopting an 'avoidant' coping style (avoiding communication); research suggests that lonely people use the internet for entertainment, rather than contact (Seepersad, 2004).

Why was there an increase in reported depression? Perhaps depression arises because the person's social support is provided by online strangers. Such weak relations cannot provide the social support that human contact can.

It seems, however, that adolescent boys can benefit more from this online communication than can girls – they feel that they are able to disclose more in an environment where there is no face-to-face or physical contact (Schouten *et al.*, 2007). The notion that the typical adolescent internet user is a generally lonely geek also appears to be a myth. Adolescents who are socially competent in 'real life' are more likely to use the internet – via messaging services, for example – to keep in touch with people (Bryant *et al.*, 2006).

Adolescents are also more likely to use online social networking sites to seek support for dealing with issues in their social lives that they have difficulties with (Spies Shapiro and Margolin, 2014). If they use social media to avoid social problems, their well-being is reduced. There is no evidence that internet use has an adverse effect on brain function (Mills, 2014), contrary to some claims in the popular media.

(such as drinking and smoking). Such girls are also likely to regard themselves as more accepted by older girls, to date more (Stattin and Magnusson, 1990) and be more sexually active. The picture in boys is unclear; there is no such consistent pattern in the nature of their peer network or their behaviour.

Early- and late-maturing 14-year-old boys report being involved in more crime and being more rebellious in school, such as being sent out of class, swearing at a teacher, expulsion from school and so on (Williams and Dunlop, 1999). Early and late maturers may engage in delinquent behaviour for different reasons – early maturers drink alcohol because this is what their peers do; late maturers drink in order to attract attention and gain popularity.

Delinquency is associated with a range of intellectual problems. Children with conduct disorder, for example, may have

low verbal IQ, impaired language ability and poor executive function, as you saw earlier. Although this pattern has been seen in young and adolescent children, a near identical pattern of intellectual impairment is seen in pre-school clinic-referred boys who met the standard criteria for conduct disorder (Speltz *et al.*, 1999). It would seem that the routine language testing of pre-school children exhibiting conduct disorder would be helpful in halting the decline in verbal IQ and language skill in these children.

Adolescence and mental health

Rates of depression tend to increase in adolescence. Some studies have found that the prevalence increases from 1 per cent in children under 12 years of age to over 20 per cent by the end of adolescence (Kessler *et al.*, 2001). The biggest increase is seen between the ages of 15 and 18 (Hankin *et al.*, 1998), is twice as likely in girls (Glowinski *et al.*, 2003) and is even higher in pairs of female twins.

While some of the variance in mental health can be attributable to the momentous physical and social changes that the adolescent is going through, there are risk factors which can increase the likelihood of depression emerging. Sexual abuse, for example (Putnam, 2003), is a serious risk factor for later depression which has also been associated with altered brain development (Teicher *et al.*, 2006). Studies have found that abuse experienced in childhood is associated with reduced hippocampus, corpus callosum and frontal cortex grey matter (Andersen *et al.*, 2008). Depression, as you will see in the last chapter in the book, is associated with reduced hippocampal volume in adults. The pattern in depressed adolescents, however, is inconsistent. Some studies report a decrease in older adolescents who have major depression while others, fewer of them, show no reduction in adolescents with comparable problems (Andersen and Teicher, 2008).

A study from The Netherlands reports that Dutch pre-adolescents experience different degrees of mental health problems as they progress through puberty (Oldehinkel *et al.*, 2011). A sample of just over 2,000 children were studied over two periods. The greater the degree of puberty expressed, the more tired, irritable, rule-breaking and likely to abuse substances the child was. Girls were socially more uncertain and reported more depression and anxiety; boys expressed less self-criticism.

Friendship

Friendship in childhood appears to have greater long-term consequences than might first be apparent(Newcomb and Bagwell, 1995). For example, pre-adolescent friendship and peer rejection are significant predictors of adult adjustment. Poor peer relations are associated with later maladjustment and mental health problems (J.G. Parker *et al.*, 1995). In an extensive longitudinal study, Bagwell *et al.* (1998) tracked 60 individuals from school age to 12 years after (when the mean age was 23 years 3 months). These researchers found that lower levels of pre-adolescent peer rejection predicted overall adjustment. Those with friends reported higher self-esteem as adults, whereas peer rejection and friendlessness was associated with mental disorder, especially depression. This evidence suggests that peer support and approval are important determinants of the adolescent's happiness and later adjustment. However, approval or rejection may not necessarily be causes of later adjustment or maladjustment. Perhaps these factors help to moderate maladjustment.

Psychology in action: Bullying

A teenage schoolboy hanged himself after being plagued by cruel bullies on Facebook.

Teenager Tom Mullaney was found dead in the bedroom f his family home in the early hours of Thursday morning. According to his distraught friends and family the youngster killed himself after being threatened with being attacked at school. It's believed the threats had been delivered verbally and on the social networking site.

(Source: The Sun, 15 February 2011.)

Tom Mullaney's death is, sadly, not unique and neither is its cause. Bullying in schools and – more recently – on social networking sites such as Facebook exists and it is common. According to Nicolaides *et al.* (2002, p. 106), bullying is 'a form of aggressive behaviour that causes injury or distress to the individual to whom it is directed'. This aggression can be physical (actual bodily violence), verbal or psychological (such as social exclusion). The harm must also be intentional, repeated and is exercised by someone with greater power over the victim (Olweus, 1999). It seems to know no ethnic barriers nor physical ones (Naasel *et al.*, 2001). In fact, disabled children are disproportionally more likely to be bullies (Unnener and Cornell, 2003).

Some forms or bullying are more common in some cultures than others. Western cultures tend to show physical forms of bullying whereas in Japan, the bullying is principally psychological – a phenomenon called Ijime (Hilton *et al.*, 2010). A wave of suicides in Japan in the early 1990s led to a programme of bullying research that continues. Similar to Western figures, 22 per cent of Japanese children report being victims of bullying (Smith and Brain, 2000).

Approximately 27 per cent of children and adolescents have been victims or bully-victims (Cray *et al.*, 2006) but the percentage varies according to the study; most report incidences of between 22 and 30 per cent (Evans *et al.*, 2014). Verbal bullying is more common than physical bullying – one study of 7,182

▶

Psychology in action: *Continued*

children found that 54 per cent of them had reported being involved in perpetrating this kind of bullying (Wong *et al.*, 2009). The consequences of this are serious – bullying is associated with the development of mental health problems in the bullied later in life (Arseneault *et al.*, 2010) and leads to short-term and potentially long-term depression, poor self-esteem and physical and emotional problems (Boulton and Smith, 1994). It may not necessarily affect the victim's academic achievement but schools which adopt anti-bullying policies tend to show better academic performance (Fonagy *et al.*, 2005). Schools which show or allow student–student or student–teacher conflict show the greatest conduct disorder problems (Swearer *et al.*, 2010). Bullying can begin as early as 5–6 years and continues through to adolescence where it peaks.

Since September 1999, it has been a legal requirement in England and Wales for schools to have an anti-bullying programme. Such programmes have been increasing across Europe, and Norway and Sweden have well-publicised anti-bullying campaigns. Such initiatives are considered important because studies have suggested that when schools are complacent about their bullying children or when the school's climate encourages bullying, then social relationships are harmed and the education that children in such schools receive is poor (Olweus, 1993; Rigby, 1997).

Before describing the characteristics of bullies, it is worth examining whether some people are susceptible to being a victim of this behaviour. There are few certain traits but those which do characterise victims include: feeling inferior, lonely, having few positive interactions with peers, interacting ineffectively with the bully and craving approval. These are the characteristics of the 'passive' type. The 'proactive' type is immature, impulsive, hyperactive, with poor social skills and seen as irritating and offensive to other children (Hilton *et al.*, 2010). What is common to both types is poor social skills and some research suggests that adolescent victims have poorer theory of mind (Shakoor *et al.*, 2012)

Boys are more likely to be physical bullies than are girls; girls are more likely to engage in 'psychological' bullying such as name-calling and excluding others (Vaillancourt *et al.*, 2008). Boys tend to bully boys but girls are bullied by boys and girls. Teachers' perceptions/suspicions of bullying tend to be accurate, but the incidence of bullying in their schools is usually under-reported.

Some psychologists have suggested that bullying becomes more prevalent during early adolescence and during transitional periods in the children's lives, for specific reasons. For example, aggression in early adolescence is viewed more positively by children's peers than it is later in adolescence (Bukowski *et al.*, 2000). Hormonal changes lead to body size increase, the beginning of a sexual interest in the opposite sex and the visible expression of secondary sexual characteristics

which mark the onset of young adulthood. The increase in body size, some researchers argue, leads to boys reviewing their position in their social environments and expressing a need for dominance within their social group (Hawley, 1999). One way of expressing this dominance is to use aggression, usually with the approval of peers (Maccoby, 1998).

Young adolescents also undergo a physical transition in their lives: moving school (Pellegrini and Long, 2002). This move appears to coincide with an increase in antisocial behaviour. In primary school, children are taught in well-established, close, friendly groups. The move to secondary school usually leads to the break-up of this close group and the child has to find new friends in a much bigger environment. Once social groups are established, the incidence of bullying should decrease.

The common view of the bully is of a person who is a lumpen, physically able individual who is socially inept (Nicolaides *et al.*, 2002). Research suggests, however, that the school bully is likely to be cold, manipulative and very socially adept. This is one reason why they are able to convince others to condone, endorse or join in with the bullying (Sutton *et al.*, 1999). Japanese bullies are also effective in convincing victims that they are to blame for their victimisation. Bullies who initiate aggression are more accurate in answering questions about social manipulation than are bullies who helped or supported the ringleader bullies, the victims or the defenders. This finding suggests that the bully is not a socially inept individual but one who is aware of the power of manipulation and ensures that they avoid blame for their behaviour. They also have positive attitudes to aggression and have difficulty in restraining aggression (Hilton *et al.*, 2010). Bullies take their behaviour with them and their transgressions visit them later in life – they experience greater interpersonal problems and are maladjusted. For example, they show less commitment to school work, are at greater risk of dropping out and of using drugs and alcohol, and show increased levels of offending up to 11 years after the incidents of bullying (Olweus, 1993; Vanderbilt and Augustyn, 2010; Ttofi *et al.*, 2011; Kim *et al.*, 2011).

Do anti-bullying programmes work? The evidence is mixed. The purpose of bullying prevention programmes is to increase awareness of bullying and to reduce it. Some studies find a significant reduction in bullying, but others do not (Bauer *et al.*, 2007; Vreeman and Carroll, 2007; Frey *et al.*, 2009). One meta-analysis of 14 programmes found a negligible effect of these campaigns on rates of bullying (Smith *et al.*, 2004). The Swedish Olweus Bullying Prevention Programme implemented in 13 studies found a 17 per cent drop in bullying (Ttofi *et al.*, 2008), suggesting that what could work in one school or school system may not work in a different environment. And such national differences may explain why the effectiveness – or reported effectiveness – appears mixed.

▶

Psychology in action: *Continued*

For example, Evans *et al.* (2014) found that in 22 controlled studies in which bullying perpetration was measured, 11 of them reported significant effects; of the studies focusing on victimisation, 67 per cent reported significant effects suggesting that there is some evidence for successful anti-bullying programmes but it is by no means consistent. Seventy two per cent of the studies which examined victimisation and found significant results were conducted in countries outside the US (UK, Australia, Turkey, Germany and others). Six of eight studies that were not significant were conducted in the US; a similar pattern was found in the US for bullying perpetration suggesting that the samples in these studies were more heterogeneous.

A recent study asked 97 children from various Canadian schools about their views of the design and implementation of anti-bullying programmes (Cunningham *et al.*, 2016). Three themes emerged from the study: (1) students felt that some of the materials used in these campaigns didn't engage them, and found them boring, negative or delivered by unconvincing presenters; (2) the consequences of the programmes were not monitored by teachers and teachers did not catch instances of bullying and responded slowly when they did identify instances; and (3) some students disengaged and did not become involved in the programmes, disrupted activities and denied bullying.

What, therefore, can be done to remove this blight on the lives of children and others who feel bullied? The most important thing is to not accept the bullying and make people aware of it. Not responding to bullying simply increases the likelihood of more bullying. No one should tolerate an idiotic bully.

Relationships with parents

Philip Larkin, in his poem *This Be the Verse*, famously remarked, The relationship between adolescents and their parents can be fractious. As adolescents begin to define their new roles and to assert them, they almost inevitably come into conflict with their parents. Adolescents and their parents tend to have similar values and attitudes towards important issues (Youniss and Smollar, 1985). Family conflicts tend to be provoked by minor issues, such as messy rooms, loud music, clothes, curfews and household chores. These problems tend to begin around the time of puberty; if puberty occurs particularly early or late, so does the conflict (Paikoff and Brooks-Gunn, 1991).

Adolescence is said to be a time of turmoil, characterised by unhappiness, stress and confusion. When McGue *et al.* (2005) asked 1,330 11-year-old twins to rate the warmth and degree of conflict experienced in their relationship with parents and then asked them to do the same three years later (1,176 children did), the children's perception of their relationship declined significantly in three years – conflicts increased significantly and reported warmth decreased. Girls experienced these changes more significantly than did boys.

Whereas a few adolescents are unhappy most of the time (and most are unhappy some of the time), studies have found that the vast majority of teenagers generally feel happy and self-confident (Offer and Sabshin, 1984; Peterson and Ebata, 1987). But mood states do seem to be more variable during the teenage years than during other times of life (Csikszentmihalyi and Larson, 1984).

The degree of parental conflict the child is exposed to can have devastating consequences later in life, especially in terms of the child's adjustment (Fincham, 1998). Although divorce may seem an obvious cause of problems for the child, evidence suggests that the negative effects of divorce are evident before separation occurs (Doherty and Needle, 1991). Parental conflict has been associated with poor academic performance, depression (Meyer *et al.*, 1993) and antisocial behaviour (Loeber and Dishion, 1983). Longitudinal studies suggest that high degrees of parental conflict at the age of 3 are associated with later adjustment problems in adulthood (Neighbors *et al.*, 1997). Although not all children will be affected detrimentally by parental conflict, this behaviour has consistently clear and negative effects on the child's immediate and future behaviour. A review of 40 studies, including over 40,000 children, has found that a child with an incarcerated parent was more likely to be anti-social but no more likely to show mental health problems, drug use or poor educational attainment (Murray *et al.*, 2012).

Adulthood: beyond adolescence

It is much easier to outline child or adolescent development than adult development; children and adolescents change faster, and the changes are closely related to age. Adult development is much more variable because physical changes in adults are more gradual. Mental and emotional changes during adulthood are more closely related to individual experience than to age. Some people achieve success and satisfaction with their careers, while some hate their jobs. Some marry and have happy family lives; others are happy to live without children, and others never adjust to the roles of spouse and parent. No single description of adult development will fit everyone. Because of this variability, there is no single 'normative' change that occurs from adolescence onwards: puberty is the last single period during a person's development where significant and consistent changes in physical and cognitive behaviour occur.

Muscular strength peaks during the late twenties or early thirties and then declines slowly thereafter as muscle tissue gradually deteriorates. By age 70, strength has declined by approximately 30 per cent in both men and women (Young *et al.*, 1984). However, age has much less effect on endurance than on strength. Both laboratory tests and athletic records reveal that older people who remain physically fit show remarkably little decline in the ability to exercise for extended periods of time (Spirduso and MacRae, 1990).

Although it is easy to measure a decline in the sensory systems (such as vision, hearing and olfaction), older people often show very little functional change in these systems. Most of them learn to make adjustments for their sensory losses, using additional cues to help them decode sensory information. For example, people with a hearing loss can learn to attend more carefully to other people's gestures and lip movements; they can also profitably use their experience to infer what is said.

Functional changes with age are also minimal in highly developed skills. For example, Salthouse (1984, 1988) found that experienced older typists continued to perform as well as younger ones, despite the fact that they performed less well on standard laboratory tests of sensory and motor skills, including the types of skill that one would expect to be important in typing. The continuous practice they received enabled them to develop strategies to compensate for their physical decline. For example, they tended to read farther ahead in the text they were typing, which enabled them to plan in advance the patterns of finger movements they would have to make. However, the neurological diseases that accompany ageing can have devastating intellectual and personal consequences (see Chapter 11).

Middle adulthood: a period of contentment?

By the time people reach middle adulthood, they have achieved or have chosen to achieve almost all of the major life decisions available to them. Marriage or cohabitation, having children, setting up a home, beginning a career – decisions on all of these major life changes will have been made by the time that people reach their late thirties/mid-forties.

Because the major life decisions have been made, people during this period in life generally feel comfortable and contented, and a conventional way of life becomes the norm. People become quite satisfied with their lives at this time; they feel at their most confident, most in control and most productive (Lachman *et al.*, 1994; Shek, 1996; Tikoo, 1996; Chiriboga, 1997). Depression, for example, although present in the middle-aged, declines during this period in life (Pearlin and Mullan, 1992). Middle-aged women regard themselves as having a better ability to cope with life's difficulties (Stewart and Ostrove, 1998). Women's interest in sex appears to decline from the mid-forties (Helson and Soto, 2005).

At mid-life (during the early to mid-forties), realities about one's life structure must finally be faced. Men whose life structures do not yet meet their prior goals and expectations realise that the future will probably not bring the success that up until then has eluded them. Men who have succeeded begin to question whether the goals they had set for themselves were meaningful and worthwhile. All men, successful or not, also begin to confront the fact that they are getting older. They are starting to detect some signs of physical decline, and they are witnesses to the death of their parents or their parents' friends.

Several investigators have defined objective criteria for the presence of a mid-life crisis and have looked for its presence in representative samples of participants. For example, Costa and McCrae (1980) administered a Midlife Crisis Scale to 548 men aged 35–79 years. The scale contained items asking whether the participants were experiencing any of the symptoms of a mid-life crisis, such as dissatisfaction with job and family, a sense of meaninglessness or a feeling of turmoil. They found no evidence for a mid-life crisis. Some people did report some of the symptoms, but they were no more likely to occur during the early to mid-forties than at any other age. A study of 60 women (Reinke *et al.*, 1985) also found no evidence of a mid-life crisis.

These findings do not mean that middle-aged people do not periodically contemplate or question the important issues in their lives. But there appears to be no crisis – in the dramatic sense – inherent to these reflective periods.

Adult development occurs against the backdrop of what many developmental psychologists consider to be the two most important aspects of life: love and work. For most of us, falling in love is more than just a compelling feeling of wanting to be with someone. It often brings with it major responsibilities, such as marriage and children. Work, too, is more than just a way to pass time. It involves setting and achieving goals related to income, status among peers and accomplishments outside the family.

Parenthood

One of the most significant events in a couple's life is the birth of a child. It brings about an upheaval in the social, emotional and intellectual lives of parents who find that demands on their time become more pressing and who are exposed to the additional stress of having responsibility for the care of another human being.

Generally speaking, mothers assume more responsibilities than do fathers for the day-to-day care of children (Biernat and Wortman, 1991). As a result, they spend more time doing housework and less time talking to their husbands (Peskin, 1982), which can place strain on their marital happiness. However, if husband and wife can find time together in the evenings, and if the husband is able to share in the parenting and household chores, the stress of adapting to family life is lessened considerably (Daniels and Weingarten, 1982). Even men who take parental leave report that they do so to look after their children, not to do housework (Brandt and Kvande, 1998). There seem to be exceptions to this pattern, however. A Danish study found that if both parents had successful careers, then the housework and childcare were distributed more equitably (Hestbaek, 1998).

The general pattern of greater involvement in the day-to-day running of the household by women may be why they perceive the personal costs of having a child to be greater than those perceived by men (Beckman, 1987). Men's priorities, it seems, remain the same after the birth of the child as they were before: they still want the attention of their wives or partners, they still want to engage in an active social life and they still want the freedom to pursue other interests outside the family (Watson *et al.*, 1995). With the inconvenience of childbirth, it is perhaps not surprising that men regard their marriages as being less satisfactory after the birth of a child (Chalmers and Meyer, 1996). The introduction of another human being into the dyad can also bring clear stresses. Parents may find that the time they have to spend with each other is reduced, especially if their child has additional medical or behavioural problems (Schuchts and Witkin, 1989).

Parenting adolescents

As children grow older and become more self-sufficient in caring for themselves, the day-to-day burdens of raising a family taper off and husbands and wives are able to spend more time with each other. However, adolescents pose new problems for their parents: they may question parental authority, and their burgeoning social agenda may put a wrinkle in their parents' personal and social calendars. For many parents, rearing adolescents, particularly during the time just prior to their leaving home, represents the low point of marital happiness (Cavanaugh, 1990). Most of the tensions revolve around issues of responsibility and mutual respect. The adolescent is slowly groping towards adulthood and wishes to be regarded as an individual who is responsible enough to lead their life without parental interference. Parents, however, still feel that their child requires guidance and has not earned the right to be regarded as fully independent.

Once a family's youngest child has left home, marital happiness increases and continues to do so through the remainder of the couple's life together. Although parents may miss daily contact with their children, they also feel happy (not to mention relieved) that a major responsibility of life – raising self-reliant children who become responsible members of society – has been completed successfully. Just as importantly, the parents now have time for each other and freedom to pursue their own interests. It may be true that an empty nest is a happy nest. Research tends to support this statement. In one study, only 6 per cent of empty-nest couples reported that life prior to their last child leaving home was better than their empty-nest experience. Over 50 per cent of the couples interviewed said that their lives were better now than before their children had left home (Deutscher, 1968; Neugarten, 1974).

Cutting edge: How does parenting affect the parent's. . . brain?

Parenting is a skill, a learned skill which requires time-management, executive function, motor execution, some empathy and the ability to deal with a number of predictable and unpredictable stressors – from illness, to the redecoration of the living room wall with crayon. Some new research suggests that parenting also affects the brain of the parent – especially that of the mother (the mother has been the primary subject of the research; there is slightly less on fathers) (Swain *et al.*, 2014a, b).

For example, neuroimaging studies have found that mothers show greater activation in the prefrontal cortex, the OFC and the striatum when viewing their 2–4 month olds (Kuo *et al.*, 2010) and that the activation is correlated with a better quality of interaction between the mother and the child (Atzil *et al.*, 2011). These regions have also been found to be activated in fathers, as have the inferior frontal gyrus, the medial and lateral PFC and insula when fathers view their 4–6 month infant (Atzil *et al.*, 2012) and in the medial frontal gyrus, striatum and cingulate if they look at images of their children who are aged between one and five years olds (Mascaro *et al.*, 2013).

Kim *et al.* (2014) examined structural changes in the brains of 16 fathers in the first four months of the infants' life. Scans were taken 2–4 weeks and 12–16 weeks postpartum. The study found that grey matter volume increased in the father's hypothalamus, amygdala, striatum and lateral prefrontal cortex (findings that are consistent with research from primates who are fathers), but decreased in the right OFC, posterior cingulate cortex and insula. Studies of mothers report no decreases. The authors explain the result by citing the default-mode network (DMN) – a collection of regions and structures which show deactivation when we engage in cognitive tasks (Greicius *et al.*, 2009), and which you read about in Chapter 4. They argue that the decrease may reflect a shift of resources from these areas to others as deactivation in the DMN is associated with increased attention to a task.

Activation of the mother's PFC and amygdala can be modified by infant's facial emotion expression (Nishitani *et al.*, 2011; Strathearn and Kim, 2013). Greater blood flow to the right PFC was found in mothers compared to women who had never been pregnant when they had to discriminate

▶

Cutting edge: *Continued*

between the emotions expressed in unfamiliar infants' faces. There was no difference between the two groups of women when completing the same task but with adult stimuli (Nishitani *et al.*, 2011). In an fMRI study, first-time mothers viewed images of their own baby or an unfamiliar infant expressing happy, sad or neutral expressions (Strathearn and Kim, 2013). Activation in the mothers' amygdala was higher when watching their own baby's happy expression than sad. An opposite pattern was found for infants who were unfamiliar to the mother.

Finally, one study examined how a child's relationship with its mother affected how the child as an adult dealt with discussions about conflict with a romantic partner (Raby *et al.*, 2015). Raby *et al.* used data from the Minnesota Longitudinal Study of Risk and Adaptation, a 37-year long longitudinal

study of human development. Mother–child interactions were observed and noted across the study. A subsample of 37 34–37 year olds adults who had been in a romantic relationship for at least six months was selected for study. They and their partners were asked, separately, to list the top three topics of conflict in their relationship. They were then asked, together, to discuss how they would resolve these conflicts. Electrodermal electrodes were attached while they engaged in these discussions. Participants who had experienced less sensitive maternal caregiving during childhood were those most likely to show increased skin conductance during conflict discussion/resolution. The increase did not depend on relationship quality, SES, sex or ethnicity, suggesting that early, supportive parental relationships may affect later behaviour.

Late adulthood and the menopause

One of the inevitable features of ageing is that the process is visible. The outer shell of age is easy to see: a young person may not be served alcohol based on their appearance, and similar judgements – often, more harmful – are made about people as they pass from middle into late adulthood. Although middle-aged and older individuals may feel full of vitality, youth and vigour, this is not the impression their physical appearance indicates to others (Featherstone and Hepworth, 1993). Despite the subjective feeling of vitality, some physical changes are inevitable.

There is also an increase in reported mental health symptoms in the 45–64 year old group, as well as in older samples who are retired or out of work, as Figure 12.13 shows.

At late adulthood the body undergoes a shift, especially in women. Alteration in the endocrine system leads to the pituitary gland and the hypothalamus releasing hormones that prevent the ovaries from controlling menstruation. This physical change is called the **menopause** and is sometimes accompanied by 'hot flushes', sweating during sleep, fatigue and irritability (Dan and Bernhard, 1989). In one Scottish study, over half of the sample had reported experiencing one of 15 menopause-related symptoms, but only 22 per cent of respondents felt the symptoms to be a problem (Porter *et al.*, 1996). In fact, many women experience and value the sense of freedom that the menopause brings (Robinson, 1996). They feel that this time of life brings enhanced social status and psychological well-being. There are also cross-cultural differences in people's responses to the menopause. Japanese women, for example, report fewer menopausal symptoms than do American or Canadian women (Lock, 1998).

Old age

The contrast between the subjective experience of ageing and actual ageing is clearly illustrated by a quote from Gibson (1992, p. 59) who notes that we do not really have an experience of being old: 'When they get to a certain age, quite a number of people realise that the whole business of age status is rather an illusion. All their lives, they had expected to be "old" when they reached a certain date on the calendar, but when they reached it, they did not feel different'.

Despite the way people feel, physical deterioration and loss of friends and family become characteristics of old age, a

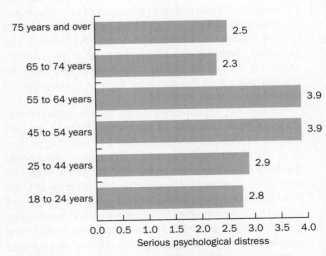

Figure 12.13 Percentage of age group reporting symptoms of severe psychological distress.

Source: National Center on Health Statistics (2006) Health, United States, 2006.

period that begins almost arbitrarily at 65 years. Whereas in young adulthood and middle age, the death of friends is a non-normative event, in old age it becomes normative. Very few milestones, however, mark the transition to old age. There are socially constructed events, such as compulsory retirement from work, which indicate that old age has arrived, but few other events as certain as this mark out the last and longest period in a person's life (Hendry and Kloep, 2002). Physical deterioration is gradual and there is no point at which a person undergoes transition from effective to defective. The function of the senses declines in old age. Sight and hearing are obvious casualties but smell and taste are impaired also.

The US Beaver Dam Wisconsin Epidemiology of Hearing Loss Study (which, despite its name, also records olfactory function) has examined 1,556 individuals at five and 10 year stages using the San Diego Odor Identification Test (Schubert *et al.*, 2009, 2011). At the first, five-year follow-up when 2,491 respondents participated, 24 per cent of the sample had impaired olfactory ability (Murphy *et al.*, 2002). This increased to 63 per cent in a subgroup of 80–97-year-olds. Men were more severely impaired than women. Another substantial (cross-sectional) study of 2,928 individuals aged between 57 and 85 years (Schumm *et al.*, 2009) found a 67 per cent decline in olfactory identification performance on the Sniffin Sticks test. The elderly prefer stronger tasting food than the young (Murphy and Withee, 1986; deGraaf, *et al.*, 1996), prefer more salt in vegetable juice that is low in NaCl, more sucrose/citric acid in a lemon drink (Murphy and Withee, 1986), and prefer sweeter concentrations of food (Mojet, *et al.*, 2004). Sweet taste appears to be the one that is least susceptible to ageing (Schumm *et al.*, 2009); the least well-recognised is sour.

The social psychology of ageing

There is a tendency in some people to disguise the effects of old age – they may dress in a way they think young people do or may engage in activities they associate with youth, or attempt to conceal the physical effects of ageing by applying cosmetics. These individuals feel that they still need to compete, to be sexy and to be seen as attractive to younger people rather than accept the ageing process. This is unusual because when people are asked which age they would like to be, the ideal age is quite close to their actual age (Uotinen, 1998). General optimism appears to increase with age, but optimism related to health and thinking declines (Isaacowitz, 2005). Interestingly, when 3,793 adults aged between 34 and 74 years of age were asked to rate how satisfied they were with their life in the past, the present or future, there was little difference between the young and old samples in terms of actual satisfaction but the older participants anticipated their satisfaction would get worse and the younger sample expected it would get better (Lachman *et al.*, 2008). The under 65s found the present more satisfying than the past; the over 65s found the past and present equally satisfying.

What constitutes successful ageing? Researchers and older people alike agree on the principal factors which contribute to successful ageing but laypeople tend to consider more 'psychological' factors as additionally important, as Figure 12.14 shows. Biomedical theorists, for example, emphasise longevity as a measure of successful ageing and focus on the absence of illness/risk factors for illness, as well as the maintenance of cognitive and physical function as important constituents (Bowling and Dieppe, 2005). One study of 601 Australian men in their 80s found that three-quarters of them aged well, mentally, and that education and the degree of physical activity they were involved in were good predictors of successful mental health (Almeida *et al.*, 2006). Psychosocial theorists emphasise older people's satisfaction with life, personal growth and social participation as important constituents. Laypeople, when asked, highlight social, psychological and physical factors as important to growing old successfully. One study of 854 people aged 50 and over found that 75 per cent of the sample regarded themselves as ageing very well; they cited good health and functioning as a definition of successful ageing (Bowling and Dieppe, 2005).

There is evidence that ageing may not be an entirely negative experience. A study of young people found that not only did they want to be older but also that they were less positive about their own age and worried about their personal inadequacies (Montepare, 1991). Older people who accepted the process of ageing, on the other hand, felt good about themselves, feared ageing less and were more satisfied with life (Montepare and Lachman, 1989). Data from the Amsterdam Longitudinal Aging Study suggest that having a partner, a good family, social support and high self-esteem can lead to

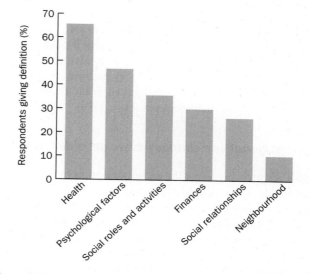

Figure 12.14 Most common definitions of successful ageing given by 854 people aged >50 in Britain.

Source: From Thoughts for Today, *British Medical Journal*, 2005, Vol. 331, p. 1550, unnumbered figure (24–31 December 2005) with permission from the BMJ Publishing Group.

better coping with chronic illness in old age (Penninx *et al.*, 1998), which indicates that there are factors which can mitigate the effects of old age.

There is an element of loss of power in old age, however. Compulsory retirement from work – a milestone introduced by the German chancellor, Bismarck, in the nineteenth century – is the first step to removing a sense of power from old people. There is no relationship between a person's ability to function as an employee and their age (Salthouse and Maurer, 1997), but almost all professions have a compulsory retirement age. In fact, politicians are one of the few professions not to have such a compulsory milestone, an irony given that the original compulsory retirement age was determined by a politician. If there is no relationship between an employee's work performance and their age, how can a retirement age be justified?

At retirement, old people may become eligible for state benefits and other monetary or social benefits that the state sees fit to bestow on them. Because of this dependence, old age is sometimes characterised as a 'second childhood' (Hockey and James, 1995). As Jacques says in his seven ages of man speech in *As You Like It* (II, VII, 163–6):

> Last scene of all,
>
> That ends this strange eventful history,
>
> Is second childishness and mere oblivion;
>
> Sans teeth, sans eyes, sans taste, sans everything.

Old people fear becoming a burden to others and fear the loss of autonomy that old age can bring (Dittman-Kohli, 1990). The prejudice that they may face can also be problematic and can become a self-fulfilling prophecy. If old people are presented with subliminal messages that are derogatory about old people's abilities, for example, they perform less well on a subsequent task of cognitive ability than would those old people not exposed to such messages (Levy, 1996).

How language use changes as we get older

While research suggests that we respond to negative emotion less readily as we get older, research into the psychology of expressive writing also suggests that we become less egocentric. Pennebaker and Stone (2003) compared the language used in written or spoken expression by people who had taken part in 32 experiments in which they expressed how they feel and think about a recently experienced trauma. This technique, and what it is used for, is discussed in more detail in Chapter 18.

One of the most pronounced differences in young and older authors' and speakers' language development was the use of the first person singular: I. There was a significantly lower tendency to use 'I' in communication in the older groups, suggesting that as people get older, they become more topic-focused and less self-referential. In the older samples, there was also significantly less evidence of referring to other people. In the younger samples there was a significantly greater reference to other people. Perhaps this change reflects the possibility that as we grow up, we are much closer to and dependent on other people and refer to ourselves in terms of others' behaviour or expectations (such as those of parents or older siblings).

Older participants in both studies made more use of the future-tense than did the younger ones while using fewer past-tenses. Conversely, the youngest sample made the greatest use of the past-tense and least use of the future-tense. Time references (such as day, minute and clock) were more common in the younger samples whereas the use of words of six letters or more was more common in the older samples (but there were no differences between groups for fiction, perhaps reflecting the probability that professional authors' vocabulary is already fairly well-developed at the beginning of their writing career).

Although the largest portion of the study was cross-sectional, it suggests that older people's use of language differs in significant and interesting ways from that of younger samples. The most important of these differences is a reduction in the egocentric use of 'I' in older people.

Death and bereavement

'I'm not afraid of death', said Woody Allen. 'I just don't want to be there when it happens'. Death is the final event of life. It is a biological and social event – family and friends are emotionally affected by the death of a loved one. Although a death may claim a life at any time, most people die when they are old. One question that developmental psychologists have asked about death and dying among the elderly is, how do old people view the inevitability of their own death?

As you might expect, elderly people contemplate their death more often than do younger people but, generally speaking, they fear death less than do their younger counterparts (Kalish, 1976) and tend to cope better with loss (McCrae and Costa, 1993). Although depression can occur immediately someone close dies, this decreases over the next one to two years (Thompson *et al.*, 1998). No one knows why this is so, but a tentative explanation may be that older people have had more time to review the past and to plan for the future knowing that bereavement is close at hand. Thus, they are able to prepare themselves psychologically (and financially) for death. The sense of loss, however, can continue until the bereaved die (Wortman *et al.*, 1993).

Contemplating and preparing for death, though, is not like knowing that you are actually dying. The changes in attitude that terminally ill people experience, have been studied by Kübler-Ross (1969, 1981). After interviewing hundreds of dying people, she concluded that people undergo five distinct phases of psychologically coping with death. The first stage is denial. When terminally ill people learn of their condition,

Elizabeth Kübler-Ross (1926–2004), psychiatrist.
Source: Press Association Images.

they generally try to deny it. Anger comes next – now they resent the certainty of death. In the third stage, bargaining, people attempt to negotiate their fate with God or others, pleading that their lives might be spared. While bargaining, they actually realise that they are, in fact, going to die. This leads to depression, the fourth stage, which is characterised by a sense of hopelessness and loss. According to Kübler-Ross,

'When the terminally ill patient can no longer deny his illness, when he is forced to undergo more surgery or hospitalization, when he begins to have more symptoms or becomes weaker or thinner, he cannot smile it off anymore'. The fifth and final stage, acceptance, is marked by a more peaceful resignation to the facts or 'positive submission'. 'It is as if the pain had gone', according to Kübler-Ross, 'the struggle is over'.

Kübler-Ross's work highlights the psychological factors involved in dying and has provided an initial theory about how the dying come to grips with their fate. Her work, though, has not been accepted uncritically. Her research was not scientific – her method for interviewing people was not systematic, and her results are largely anecdotal. Moreover, of the five stages, denial is the only one that appears to be universal. Apparently, not all terminally ill people have the same psychological response to the fact that they are dying.

However, despite its flaws, Kübler-Ross's work is important because it has prompted an awareness, both scientific and public, of the plight of the terminally ill. The scientific response, as you might guess, has been to do more medical research in the hope of prolonging the life of people with cancer or other terminal illness. The public response has involved the attempt to provide support for the dying and their families through hospice services (Aiken, 1994). In the past, hospices were places where strangers and pilgrims could find rest and shelter. Today, hospices are special places that provide medical and psychological support for the dying and their families. In cases in which the dying person wishes to die at home, hospice volunteers work in that setting. The primary functions of hospice services are two-fold: to provide relief from pain and to allow the person to die with dignity. No attempt is made to prolong life through technology if doing so would diminish the self-respect of the dying person and their family. To die with dignity is perhaps the best death possible – for, together, the dying and their loved ones are able to experience, for the last time together, reverence for the experience of life.

Chapter review

Prenatal development

- The three stages of prenatal development span the time between conception and birth. In just nine months, the zygote grows from a single cell, void of human resemblance, into a fully developed foetus, complete with physical features that look much like yours and mine, except in miniature.

- Sex is determined by the sex chromosomes. Male sex organs are produced by the action of a gene on the Y chromosome that causes the gonads to develop into testes.
- The testes secrete androgens, a class of hormones that stimulates the development of male sex organs. If testes are not present, the foetus develops as a female.
- There is evidence that the human foetus is capable of discriminating between sensory stimuli while in the womb,

suggesting that it is capable of a rudimentary form of cognition.

Physical and perceptual development in infancy and childhood

- A newborn infant's first movements are reflexes that are crucial to its survival. For example, the rooting, sucking and swallowing reflexes are important in finding and consuming food.
- Sophisticated movements, such as crawling and standing, develop and are refined through natural maturation and practice.
- A newborn's senses appear to be at least partially functional at birth. However, normal development of the senses, like that of motor abilities, depends on experience.
- The brain appears to develop throughout infancy and adolescence, with myelination being the key characteristic of maturation.
- Because the infant lacks language, most studies of motor and perceptual development examine the child's non-verbal response to stimulation. These responses include movements involving the head, mouth and eyes.
- If an infant is deprived of the opportunity to practise them during a critical period, these skills may fail to develop, which will affect the child's performance as an adult.
- Before the age of 2 years, infants seem to be more concerned with the contours of visual stimuli – a phenomenon called the externality effect.

Cognitive development in infancy and childhood

- The first step in a child's cognitive development is learning that many events are contingent on its own behaviour. This understanding occurs gradually and is controlled by the development of the nervous system and by increasingly complex interactions with the environment.
- By around 3 months, the infant shows awareness of changes in its environment; by 6 months, it is able to remember temporal order of stimuli. At 8 months, it is able to recognise words spoken in a story that it heard a while before.
- Over the course of development from 1 to 2 years the number of sequences of actions that the child can remember increases.
- Three factors seem to account for the child's ability to recall information better with age: the formation of memory-related structures, the development of language and the development of metamemory – the realisation that using memory strategies will help the child to think and behave.

- According to Piaget, as children develop they acquire cognitive structures – mental representations or rules that are used for understanding and dealing with the world and for thinking about and solving problems. The two principal types of cognitive structure are schemata (mental representations or sets of rules that define a particular category of behaviour) and concepts (rules that describe properties of environmental events and their relations to other concepts).
- According to Piaget, two processes help a child to adapt to its environment: assimilation, the process by which new information is modified to fit existing schemata, and accommodation, the process by which old schemata are changed by new experiences.
- Piaget divided a child's cognitive development into four periods – a system that is widely, if not universally, accepted. These periods are determined by the child's experiences and the maturation of its nervous system.
- An infant's earliest cognitive abilities are closely tied to the external stimuli in the immediate environment; objects exist for the infant only when they are present (the sensorimotor period).
- Gradually, infants learn that objects exist even when hidden. The development of object permanence leads to the ability to represent things symbolically, which is a prerequisite for the use of language (the preoperational period).
- Next, the ability to perform logical analysis and to understand more complex cause-and-effect relations develops (the period of concrete operations).
- Around the age of 11 years, a child develops more adult-like cognitive abilities – abilities that may allow the child to solve difficult problems by means of abstract reasoning (the period of formal operations).
- Piaget's critics point out that, in some cases, his tests of cognitive development underestimate children's abilities. For example, if tested appropriately, it is evident that they conserve various properties earlier than he thought, and that their egocentrism is less pronounced than his tests indicated.
- Vygotsky's writings and the research they have stimulated have showed that the sociocultural context in which children are raised has a significant impact on their cognitive development.
- In particular, language appears to influence how children learn to think, solve problems, formulate plans, make decisions and contemplate ideas.

Social development in infancy and childhood

- Because babies are totally dependent on their parents, the development of attachment between parent and infant is crucial to the infant's survival.

- Some of the behaviours that babies possess innately are sucking, cuddling, looking, smiling and crying. These behaviours promote parental responses and are instrumental in satisfying physiological needs.
- Play is a social and cognitive behaviour – children interact with each other or with objects in the environment in an enjoyable and positive way and learn about these objects and the objects' relationship to the environment. At around 12–18 months, infants begin to play with objects symbolically – they pretend that the object is something else. At the age of 4 years, children use play to find out more about their environment and its social values as well as its customs and traditions.
- Ainsworth's Strange Situation theory allows a researcher to determine the nature of the attachment between infant and caregiver. By using this test, several investigators have identified some of the variables – some involving infants and some involving mothers – that influence attachment.
- Maternal sensitivity (as measured by the mother's ability to respond positively to the baby's signals) appears to be the best predictor of secure attachment.
- Interaction with peers is probably the most important factor in social development among children and adolescents. However, a caregiver's style of parenting can also have strong effects on the social development of children and adolescents.
- Children rate people who speak their own 'national' language and in their own accent more positively than they do ethnically different groups.

Disorders of social cognition and emotion

- Autism is a childhood disorder in which the child shows abnormal patterns of social interaction (indifference and unwillingness to make eye or physical contact), delayed and/or idiosyncratic language, and stereotypical and repetitive behaviour.
- An influential theory of autism suggests that autistic children lack a theory of mind: they are unable to imagine the thoughts, actions or feelings of others.
- Others theories suggest that autistic children have an impairment of executive function or that they are unable to see wholes (instead of features); these theories are based on the finding that not all autistic children experience theory of mind difficulties.
- There seems to be a reduction in dopamine in the frontal regions of autistic children which may suggest an impairment in executive function and some studies have suggested that theory of mind tasks are mediated by the frontal lobe.
- **Asperger's syndrome** describes impaired interpersonal communication and social functioning but seems to differ from autism in also being characterised by individuals having a narrow and obsessional range of interests.
- Attention deficit hyperactivity disorder (ADHD) describes a failure of the child to inhibit its own antisocial and deviant behaviour; these children are impulsive, hyperactive and have a poor attention span.
- Emotional distress may be predicted by decreased left frontal EEG activation and increased right frontal activation.

Development of sex roles in childhood

- A person's sexual identity refers to one's private sense of being a male or female and consists primarily of the recognition of membership in a particular group of people: males or females.
- According to Kohlberg, the ability of children to identify with their sex is determined in large part by their ability to classify objects as being boys' objects or girls' objects.
- Gender schema theory argues that children construct a 'schema' – a mental representation – of male and female and pay special attention to features of their own sex. Children's perception of sex is matched with information about others' sex that the child has already processed and understood.
- The ability to identify others' and the child's own sex emerges between the ages of 1 and 3 years.
- Research has shown that both parents and peers tend to encourage children to behave in sex-appropriate ways, especially with regard to play activities and toys.

Moral development

- Piaget suggested that moral development consists of three principal stages: the premoral stage, characterised by little understanding of rules or principles; the moral realism stage, characterised by egocentrism and blind adherence to rules; and the moral relativism stage, characterised by empathy and a realisation that behaviour is judged by the effects it has on others.
- Kohlberg suggested that moral development consists of three levels, with seven stages.
- During the preconventional level, morality is based on the personal consequences of an act.
- During the conventional level, morality is based on the need to be well regarded and on sharing a common interest in social order. During the postconventional level, which is

achieved by only a few people, morality becomes an abstract, philosophical virtue.

- Critics of Piaget and Kohlberg point out that the stages of moral development are, to a certain degree, products of the measuring instruments. Although it does not appear, as Gilligan originally suggested, that females follow different moral rules from males, her work has sensitised researchers to the importance of including both sexes in studies of human development. Subtle changes in the way that moral dilemmas are posed can produce very different answers.
- Damon's model of redistributive justice argues that the child begins the process of moral development by making decisions about sharing based on egocentric consideration.
- Eventually, the child makes moral decisions based on concepts of fairness and merit.

Adolescence

- Adolescence is the transitional stage between childhood and adulthood. Puberty is initiated by the hypothalamus, which causes the pituitary gland to secrete hormones that stimulate maturation of the reproductive system.
- Puberty marks a significant transition, both physically and socially. Early maturity appears to be socially beneficial to boys, because early maturers are more likely to be perceived as leaders. The effects of early maturity in girls are mixed; although their advanced physical development may help them acquire some prestige, early-maturing girls are more likely to engage in norm-breaking behaviour.
- Whereas boys seem to look forward to the increasing strength, freedom and social status that puberty brings, girls regard the period as one in which they need to conform to society's view of women and as one that restricts freedom.
- The nature of friendship changes during adolescence. Girls seek out confidantes rather than playmates, and boys join groups that provide mutual support in their quests to assert their independence. Insecure friendships at this time can lead to increased psychopathology later in life.
- Bullying can be physical (actual bodily violence), verbal or psychological (such as social exclusion) and increases during the transition from primary to secondary school; contrary to received wisdom, the bully is not socially inept but very aware of the power of manipulation.
- Although adolescence brings conflicts between parents and children, these conflicts tend to be centred on relatively minor issues. Most adolescents hold the same values and attitudes concerning important issues as their parents do. Mood swings during adolescence can be

dramatic but, on the whole, teenagers report that they are generally happy and self-confident.

Adulthood: beyond adolescence

- Up to the time of young adulthood, human development can reasonably be described as a series of stages: a regular sequence of changes that occurs in most members of our species. But development in adulthood is much more variable and few generalisations apply.
- Older people are more likely to exhibit gradual changes, especially in abilities that require flexibility and in learning new behaviours.
- Intellectual abilities that depend heavily on crystallised intelligence – an accumulated body of knowledge – are much less likely to decline than are those based on fluid intelligence – the capacity for abstract reasoning.
- By the time people reach middle adulthood, they have achieved or have chosen to achieve almost all of the major life decisions available to them such as marriage or cohabitation, having children, setting up a home or establishing a career. People during this period in life generally feel comfortable and contented, and a conventional way of life becomes the norm. People feel at their most confident, most in control and most productive. Depression declines during this period in life.
- There appears to be no scientific evidence to support the idea that people experience a mid-life crisis.
- Marriages seem to be happiest just after the birth of children and after the children have left home. It appears to be unhappiest just before the children leave home – possibly owing to the emotional and time demands that adolescents place on their parents.
- At late adulthood, the body undergoes a shift, especially in women. Alteration in the endocrine system leads to the pituitary gland and the hypothalamus releasing hormones that prevent the ovaries from controlling menstruation. This physical change is called the menopause and is sometimes accompanied by 'hot flushes', sweating during sleep, fatigue and irritability.
- Having a partner, good family and social support and high self-esteem can lead to better coping with chronic illness in old age.
- With old age and retirement, people feel less independent and more of a burden than they did when working. The dependence on others and on state benefits has led to this period in life being described as a second childhood.
- Kübler-Ross's interviews with terminally ill people have revealed that many of them seem to experience a five-stage process in facing the reality that they are going to die.

Suggestions for further reading

General development

Batalle, D., Edwards, A. D., & O'Muircheartaigh, J. (2018). Annual Research Review: Not just a small adult brain: understanding later neurodevelopment through imaging the neonatal brain. *Journal of Child Psychology and Psychiatry*, in press.

Bee, H. and Boyd, D. (2013) *The Developing Child* (13th edn). Boston MA: Allyn & Bacon.

Boyd, D. and Bee, H. (2014) *Lifespan Development* (7th edn). Boston MA: Allyn & Bacon.

Crone, E.A. and Ridderinkof, K.R. (2011) The developing brain: From theory to neuroimaging and back. *Developmental Cognitive Neuroscience*, 1, 101–9.

Dehaene-Lambertz, G.and Spelke, E.S. (2015) The infancy of the human brain. *Neuron*, 88, 93-109.

Gibbs, J.C. (2013) *Moral Development and Reality: Beyond the theories of Kohlberg and Hoffman* (3rd edn). Boston MA: Allyn & Bacon.

Glynn, L.M. and Sandman, C.A. (2011) Prenatal origins of neurological development: a critical period for fetus and mother. *Current Directions in Psychological Science*, 20, 384–9.

Otsuka, Y. (2014) Face recognition in infants: A review of behavioral and near???-infrared spectroscopic studies. *Japanese Psychological Research*, 56(1), 76–90. Reid, V.M., Dunn, K., Young, R.J., Amu, J.,

Donovan, T. and Reissland, N. (2017) The human fetus preferentially engages with face-like visual stimuli. *Current Biology* 27, 1–4.

There are dozens of books available on all aspects of development which makes choosing the best text to recommend a little troublesome. The titles above are recommended as good introductions to development.

Adolescence and adulthood

Batalle, D., Edwards, A. D., & O'Muircheartaigh, J. (2018). Annual Research Review: Not just a small adult brain: understanding later neurodevelopment through imaging the neonatal brain. *Journal of Child Psychology and Psychiatry*, 59(4), 350–371.

Papalia, D.E., Sterns, H., Feldman, R.D. and Camp, C. (2006) *Adult Development and Aging*. Maidenhead: McGraw-Hill.

Watts, T. W., Duncan, G. J., & Quan, H. (2018). Revisiting the Marshmallow Test: A Conceptual Replication Investigating Links Between Early Delay of Gratification and Later Outcomes. *Psychological science*, 0956797618761661.

Whitbourne, S.K. and Whitbourne, S.B. (2017) *Human Development and Aging* (6th edn). London: John Wiley.

Very readable accounts of the main phases of development after childhood.

CHAPTER 13
Motivation and emotion

'VISIBLY UNHAPPY' BRIE LARSON AND THE AMATEUR BODY LINGUISTS

Donald Clarke

"The way Andrew Garfield looked at ex-girlfriend Emma Stone during her Oscars speech is break-ing hearts," the *Daily Mirror* told us. The story features a hazy photograph of Garfield looking like a man who has just eaten a slightly stale Hobnob while completing a cryptic crossword. He looks as if he's planning a potholing holiday in Cornwall. He looks like a man thinking whatever the heck you want him to think. Put a map of central Europe beside him and you might conclude that he was plotting a Fourth Reich.

One can hardly imagine a better example of the Kuleshov effect in action. Around a century ago, Lev Kuleshov, the great Russian film-maker and film theorist, constructed an experiment involving the actor Ivan Mosjoukine. Kuleshov pointed his camera at Mosjoukine and asked the star to keep his face as expressionless as possible. The same footage was then intercut with various contrasting images: a bowl of soup, a child in a coffin, a woman reclining on a couch. When the resulting film was screened, the audience believed that Mosjoukine's expressions changed each time he appeared on screen. One observer claimed that the crowd appreciated: "the heavy pensiveness of his mood over the forgotten soup, were touched and moved by the deep sorrow with which he looked on the dead child, and noted the lust with which he observed the woman."

Source: http://www.irishtimes.com/culture/visibly-unhappy-brie-larson-and-the-amateur-body-linguists-1.2995428

WHAT YOU SHOULD BE ABLE TO DO AFTER READING CHAPTER 13

- Define motivation.

- Describe and understand the processes involved in starting and stopping a meal.

- Outline the basic psychology and physiology of thirst.

- Describe the major eating disorders, anorexia nervosa, bulimia nervosa and obesity, and outline their possible causes.

- Describe and understand the process of sexual development and orientation.

- Evaluate the theories explaining aggression and describe the factors which lead to aggressive behaviour.

- Describe the ways in which psychologists have defined and studied emotion.

- Evaluate the 'fundamental emotion' debate.

- Outline the major theories of emotion.

- Describe current understanding of the biological basis of emotion.

QUESTIONS TO THINK ABOUT

- What motivates us to eat, drink, be aggressive and have sex?

- What influences sexual preference and orientation?

- What causes eating disorders?

- What strategies can an overweight person adopt to lose weight and, more importantly, maintain this loss?

- How does aggressive behaviour manifest itself and what theories could account for it?

- How would you define emotion?

- Are there basic emotions? If so, how many and what distinguishes one from the other?

- What role do physiology and the brain play in the expression and recognition of emotions of different types?

Motivation

Why do people behave differently? Why do some individuals eat particular foods whereas others eat different foods? Why do we eat in the first place? What makes us attracted to different sexual partners, or any sexual partner? Why do we become aggressive?

Most of these questions can probably be answered by motivation. When commonly used, motivation refers to a driving force that moves us to a particular action. More formally, motivation is a general term for a group of phenomena that affect the nature of an individual's behaviour, the strength of the behaviour and the persistence of the behaviour.

Motivation includes two types of phenomenon. First, stimuli that were previously associated with pleasant or unpleasant events motivate approach or avoidance behaviours. For example, if something reminds you of an interesting person you met recently, you may try to meet that person again by consulting your mobile and sending a message. Secondly, being deprived of a particular reinforcer increases an organism's preference for a particular behaviour. Besides obvious reinforcers such as food or water, this category includes more subtle ones. For example, after spending a lot of time performing routine tasks, we become motivated to go for a walk or meet with friends.

Motivation affects all categories of behaviour. This chapter considers three important categories of motivated behaviour: eating, sexual behaviour and aggression. Other types of motivation such as intention and being influenced by real or imaginary others will be discussed in Chapters 15 and 16.

Biological needs

Biological needs can be potent motivators. To survive, we need air, food, water, various vitamins and minerals, and protection from extremes in temperature. Complex organisms possess physiological mechanisms that detect deficits or imbalances associated with these needs and **regulatory behaviours** that bring physiological conditions back to normal. Examples of regulatory behaviours include eating, drinking, hunting, shivering, building a fire and putting on a warm coat. This process of detection and correction, which maintains physiological systems at their optimum value, is called homeostasis ('stable state'). Deficits or imbalances motivate us because they cause us to perform the appropriate regulatory behaviours.

A regulatory system has four essential features: the **system variable** (the characteristic to be regulated), a **set point** (the optimum value of the system variable), a **detector** that monitors the value of the system variable, and a **correctional mechanism** that restores the system variable to the set point. A simple example of such a regulatory system is a room where temperature is regulated by a thermostatically controlled heater. The system variable is the air temperature of the room, and the detector for this variable is a thermostat. The thermostat can be adjusted so that contacts of a switch will close when the temperature falls below a pre-set value (the set point). Closure of the contacts turns on the correctional mechanism – the coils of the heater. You can see this process illustrated in Figure 13.1.

If the room cools below the set point, the thermostat turns the heater on, which warms the room. The rise in room temperature causes the thermostat to turn the heater off. Because the activity of the correctional mechanism (heat production) feeds back to the thermostat and causes it to turn the heater off, this process is called **negative feedback.** Negative feedback is an essential characteristic of all regulatory systems.

The **drive reduction hypothesis** was the earliest attempt to explain the nature of motivation and reinforcement. This theory stated that biological needs, caused by deprivation of the necessities of life, are unpleasant. The physiological changes associated with, say, going without food for several hours produce an unpleasant state called hunger. Hunger serves as a drive, energising an organism's behaviour. The organism then engages in behaviours that in the past have obtained food. The act of eating reduces hunger, and this drive reduction is reinforcing.

Not all drives are based on homeostasis, on biological needs like the ones for food and water. The most obvious example is the drive associated with sexual behaviour. An individual can survive without sexual behaviour; but the sex drive is certainly motivating, and sexual contact is certainly reinforcing. Similarly, most organisms placed in a featureless environment will soon become motivated to seek something new; they will work at a task that gives them a view of the world outside.

The drive reduction hypothesis of reinforcement has fallen out of favour for two primary reasons. The first is that drive is almost always impossible to measure. For example, suppose you obtain pleasure from watching a set of colour slides taken by a friend while on holiday. According to the drive reduction hypothesis, your 'exploratory drive' or 'curiosity drive' is high, and looking at holiday slides reduces it, providing reinforcement. Or consider a woman who enjoys listening to music. What drive induces her to turn on her iPod? What drive is

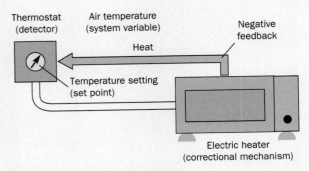

Figure 13.1 An example of a regulatory system.

reduced by this activity? There is no way to measure 'drive' in either of these examples and confirm that it actually exists; thus, the hypothesis cannot be tested experimentally.

The second problem is that if we examine our own behaviour we find that most events we experience as reinforcing are also exciting, or drive-increasing. The reason a roller-coaster ride is fun is certainly not because it reduces drive. The same is true for skiing, surfing or viewing a horror film. Likewise, an interesting, reinforcing conversation is one that is exciting, not one that puts you to sleep. And people who engage in prolonged foreplay and sexual intercourse do not view these activities as unpleasant because they are accompanied by such a high level of drive. In general, the experiences we really want to repeat (that is, the ones we find reinforcing) are those that increase, rather than decrease, our level of arousal.

Physiology of reinforcement

To understand the nature of reinforcement we must understand something about its physiological basis. Olds and Milner (1954) discovered quite by accident that electrical stimulation of parts of the brain can reinforce an animal's behaviour. For example, rats will repeatedly press a lever when the brain is electrically stimulated.

The neural circuits stimulated by this electricity are also responsible for the motivating effects of natural reinforcers such as food, water or sexual contact, and of drugs such as heroin, alcohol and cocaine. Almost all investigators believe that the electrical stimulation of the brain is reinforcing because it activates the same system that is activated by natural reinforcers and by drugs that people commonly abuse. The normal function of this system is to strengthen the connections between the neurons that detect the discriminative stimulus (such as the sight of a lever) and the neurons that produce the operant response (such as a lever press). The electrical brain stimulation activates this system directly.

Researchers have discovered that an essential component of the reinforcement system consists of neurons that release dopamine as their transmitter substance. Thus, all reinforcing stimuli appear to trigger the release of dopamine in the brain.

Optimum-level theory

Although events that increase our level of arousal are often reinforcing, there are times when a person wants nothing more than some peace and quiet. In this case, avoidance of exciting stimuli motivates our behaviour. The removal (or avoidance) of an aversive stimulus produces negative reinforcement (see Chapter 7). In an attempt to find a common explanation for both positive and negative reinforcement, some psychologists have proposed the **optimum-level hypothesis** of reinforcement and punishment: when an individual's arousal level is too high, less stimulation is reinforcing; when it is too low, more

stimulation is desired (Hebb, 1955; Berlyne, 1966). Berlyne hypothesised two forms of exploration: diversive exploration is a response to understimulation (boredom) that increases the diversity of the stimuli the organism tries to come in contact with; specific exploration is a response to overstimulation (usually because of a specific need, such as lack of food or water) that leads to the needed item, thereby decreasing the organism's drive level.

The hypothesis that organisms seek an optimum level of arousal is certainly plausible. Any kind of activity, even the most interesting and exciting one, eventually produces satiety; something that was once reinforcing becomes bothersome. Presumably, participation in an exciting behaviour gradually raises an organism's arousal above its optimum level. However, the logical problem that plagues the drive reduction hypothesis also applies to the optimum-level hypothesis. Because we cannot measure an organism's drive or arousal, we cannot say what its optimum level should be. Thus, the optimum-level hypothesis remains without much empirical support.

Effects of intermittent reinforcement

When an organism's behaviour is no longer reinforced, the behaviour eventually ceases, or extinguishes (see Chapter 7). If the behaviour was previously reinforced every time it occurred, extinction is very rapid. However, if it was previously reinforced only intermittently, the behaviour persists for a long time. Intermittent reinforcement leads to **perseverance**, even when the behaviour is no longer reinforced.

Many human behaviours are reinforced on intermittent schedules that require the performance of long sequences of behaviours over long intervals of time. A person's previous experience with various schedules of reinforcement probably affects how long and how hard the person will work between occasions of reinforcement. If all attempts at a particular endeavour are reinforced (or if none are), the person is unlikely to pursue a long and difficult project that includes the endeavour. If we knew more about a person's history with various schedules of reinforcement, we would probably know more about their ability to persevere when the going gets difficult (that is, when reinforcements become variable).

The role of conditioned reinforcement

Another phenomenon that affects the tendency to persevere is conditioned reinforcement. When stimuli are associated with reinforcers, they eventually acquire reinforcing properties of their own. For example, the sound of the food dispenser reinforces the behaviour of a rat being trained to press a lever.

Motivation is not merely a matter of wanting to do well and to work hard. It also involves the ability to be reinforced by the immediate products of the work being done. If a person has regularly been exposed to particular stimuli in association with reinforcers, that person's behaviour can be reinforced by those stimuli. In addition, if the person has learned how to recognise self-produced stimuli as conditioned reinforcers, the performance of the behaviours that produce them will be 'self-reinforcing'.

Failure to persist: learned helplessness

A large body of evidence suggests that organisms can learn that they are powerless to affect their own destinies. Two social psychologists, Maier and Seligman (1976), reported a series of experiments demonstrating that animals can learn that their own behaviour has no effect on an environmental event. This result is exactly the opposite of what has been assumed to be the basis of learning. All the examples of learning and conditioning cited so far have been instances in which one event predicts the occurrence of another. **Learned helplessness** involves learning that an aversive event cannot be avoided or escaped.

Overmeier and Seligman (1967) conducted the basic experiment. They placed a dog in an apparatus in which it received electrical shocks that could not be avoided; nothing the animal did would prevent the shocks. Next, they placed the dog in another apparatus in which the animal received a series of trials in which a warning stimulus was followed by an electrical shock. In this case the animal could avoid the shocks simply by stepping over a small barrier to the other side of the apparatus. Dogs in the control group learned to step over the barrier and avoid the shock, but dogs that had previously received inescapable shocks in the other apparatus failed to learn. They just squatted in the corner and took the shock as if they had learned that it made no difference what they did. They had learned to be helpless.

Seligman (1975) has suggested that the phenomenon of learned helplessness has important implications for behaviour. When people have experiences that lead to learned helplessness, they become depressed and their motivational level decreases. The change in motivation occurs because the helplessness training lowers their expectation that trying to perform a task will bring success. Seligman also suggested that learned helplessness has the characteristics of a personality trait; that is, people who have had major experiences with insoluble tasks will not try hard to succeed in other types of task, including ones they could otherwise have solved.

Seligman's theory of learned helplessness has been challenged by other investigators, who have explained the phenomenon in other ways. The issue is whether learning to be helpless in a particular situation generalises only to similar situations or to a wide variety of them. For example, McReynolds (1980) observed that when people experience a situation in which reinforcements are not contingent on their responding, their responding extinguishes. If the situation then changes to one in which responding will be reinforced, the people will continue not to respond unless they perceive that the schedule of reinforcement has changed. The more similar the second situation is to the first, the more likely it is that the person will act helpless. This explanation describes the phenomenon of learned helplessness as a failure to discriminate between the condition under which responding is reinforced and the condition under which it is not. Further research will have to determine whether learned helplessness is, as Seligman asserts, a stable personality trait or whether it can be explained by the principles of instrumental conditioning. We will return to learned helplessness in the depression section of Chapter 18 (see pp. 748–749).

Ingestion: drinking and eating

Much of what an animal learns to do is motivated by the constant struggle to obtain food and drink. The need to eat certainly shaped the evolutionary development of our own species. Simply put, motivation to eat is aroused when there is a deficit in the body's supply of stored nutrients, and it is satisfied by a meal that replenishes this supply. A person who exercises vigorously uses up the stored nutrients more rapidly, and loses water, and consequently must eat more food and ingest more fluid. Thus, the amount of food and drink a person normally ingests is regulated by physiological need. But what, exactly, causes a person to start eating and drinking, and what stops these behaviours? These are simple questions, yet the answers are complex. There is no single physiological measure that can tell us reliably whether a person should be hungry or thirsty; hunger and thirst are determined by a variety of conditions. So, instead of asking 'What is the cause of hunger or thirst?' we should ask, 'What are the causes?'

Thirst

A popular theory at the turn of the twentieth century argued that thirst was caused by a dry mouth and that it was this dryness that regulated how much water we ingested. When the salivary glands reduced the amount of fluid they secreted, this made the mouth dry and was the cue for drinking. While plausible, the theory was not supported by evidence because even if water was made available to the mouth but was prevented from reaching the stomach, drinking would continue: the mouth was being kept wet, not dry, and yet drinking continued because the fluid did not reach the stomach. Why?

Osmometric thirst

A later theory suggested that thirst was caused by dehydration within cells (Gilman, 1937). The fluid in cells is called intracellular fluid and contains a little sodium but large amounts of potassium and other metabolites. The other source of fluid in the body is extracellular fluid and this is found in two places.

Interstitial fluid surrounds the cell body and is salty; blood plasma is found in the capillaries, arteries and veins and allows living cells and blood to be suspended within it. Extracellular fluid comprises about 20 per cent of the body's weight; intracellular fluid comprises about 40 per cent of body weight. Gilman administered solutions of sodium chloride to animals. The membranes surrounding cells are not very permeable to sodium and so water is drawn from the intracellular fluid to the extracellular fluid by a process called osmosis, whereby water moves through a semi-permeable membrane from a region where there is a low concentration of solutes to one where there is a high concentration. This reduces the concentration of sodium available across the membrane and the movement of water by osmosis dehydrates and shrinks the body's cells. This is what Gilman found and the type of thirst is called **osmometric thirst**. Because the organism needs to be aware of this thirst, there must be cells in the body which serve to inform the central nervous system (CNS) that dehydration is occurring. These cells are called osmoreceptors and are located in the brain. When salt solutions are injected into the brain, drinking increases, but if sodium chloride is injected into the general blood supply, no such increase is observed (Wood *et al.*, 1977).

The precise locus of the osmoreceptors seems to be a part of the brain called the lateral preoptic area. If even small lesions are made to this region, the typical increase in drinking seen in response to dehydration is reduced (Mason, 1980). When neurons are exposed to urea, salt and sucrose – neurons are impermeable to salt and sucrose but not to urea – those neurons stimulated by salt and sucrose and which caused increased drinking were located in the lateral preoptic area (Peck and Novin, 1971).

Volumetric thirst

Osmometric thirst is caused by dehydration within cells. There is another type of thirst that results from dehydration outside cells, that is, a reduction in the level of blood plasma. This is called **volumetric thirst** because the thirst is provoked by a reduction in the volume of blood plasma. One obvious way in which volumetric thirst can occur is through bleeding – a loss of blood leads to a great loss of extracellular fluid with all the substances that the fluid contains. People who suffer from haemophilia experience thirst during a bleeding episode and this is alleviated by an infusion of blood.

Volumetric thirst can also result from low levels of salt in the diet. The loss of extracellular fluid produces the movement of water from the extracellular fluid and into cell bodies, by the process of osmosis described earlier. This process leads to drinking.

One further way in which the body experiences volumetric thirst is via baroreceptors. Baroreceptors are receptors on the walls of blood vessels which detect changes in the blood pressure of the cardiovascular system. If blood pressure drops, these baroreceptors can detect this drop and initiate volumetric thirst via the brain.

What starts a meal?

Cultural and social factors influence when and how much we eat. But the 'real' reason for eating must be related to the fact that the body needs nourishment: if all other factors were eliminated, eating would be determined by some internal physiological state. What are the internal factors that cause us to eat?

Many years ago, Cannon and Washburn (1912) suggested that hunger resulted from an empty stomach. The walls of an empty stomach rubbed against each other, producing what we commonly identify as hunger pangs. Cannon also suggested that thirst was produced by a dry mouth, because a loss of body fluid resulted in a decreased flow of saliva. Some sceptics called Cannon's explanation of hunger and thirst the 'spit and rumble theory'. However, removal of the stomach does not abolish hunger pangs. Inglefinger (1944) interviewed patients whose stomachs had been removed because of cancer or large ulcers; their oesophagi had been attached directly to their small intestines. Because they had no stomachs to catch and hold food, they had to eat small, frequent meals. Despite their lack of a stomach, these people reported the same feelings of hunger and satiety that they had experienced before the operation.

A more likely cause of hunger is depletion of the body's store of nutrients. The primary fuels for the cells of our body are glucose (a simple sugar) and fatty acids (chemicals produced when fat is broken down). If our digestive system contains food, these nutrients are absorbed into the blood and nourish our cells. But the digestive tract is sometimes empty; in fact, most of us wake up in the morning in that condition. So there has to be a reservoir that stores nutrients to keep the cells of the body nourished when the gut is empty. Indeed, there are two reservoirs, one short-term and the other long-term. The short-term reservoir stores carbohydrates, and the long-term reservoir stores fats.

The short-term reservoir is located in the cells of the muscles and the liver, and it is filled with a carbohydrate – a form of animal starch – called **glycogen**. When glucose is received from a meal, some of it is used for fuel and some is converted into glycogen and stored in the liver. Our long-term reservoir consists of adipose tissue (fat tissue), which is found beneath the skin and in various locations in the abdomen. Adipose tissue consists of cells capable of absorbing nutrients from the blood, converting them to triglycerides (fats), and storing them. The cells can expand in size enormously; in fact, the primary physical difference between an obese person and a person of normal weight is the size of their fat cells, which is determined by the amount of triglycerides that these cells contain.

The long-term fat reservoir is obviously what keeps us alive during a prolonged fast. Once the level of glycogen in our short-term carbohydrate reservoir gets low, fat cells start breaking down fats and releasing fatty acids and a carbohydrate called glycerol. The brain lives primarily on glucose, and the rest of the body lives on fatty acids. Glycerol is converted into glucose, so the brain continues to be nourished even after the short-term reservoir is depleted, as Figure 13.2 shows.

Because glucose is such an important fuel, Mayer (1955) proposed the **glucostatic hypothesis** of hunger. According to the glucostatic hypothesis, hunger occurs when the level of glucose in the blood becomes low, presumably after the glycogen in the body's short-term reservoir has been used up. Mayer theorised that this decrease in blood sugar is detected by glucose-sensitive neurons in the brain called **glucostats** (the term 'glucostat' is analogous to thermostat, but it refers to the measurement of glucose rather than temperature). Mayer suggested that these detectors activate neural circuits that make a person hungry, thus stimulating the correctional mechanism, eating.

Subsequent evidence suggests that there are two different types of nutrient detectors which measure the blood level of the two primary nutrients, glucose and fatty acids (Friedman *et al.*, 1986, 1991). The glucose detectors appear to be located in the liver, but the location of the fatty acid detectors is not yet known (Ritter and Taylor, 1989; Ritter *et al.*, 1992). Both sets of detectors send information to the brain, and activity of neural circuits there stimulates hunger.

What stops a meal?

Nutrient detectors sense the fact that the body's supplies of stored energy are getting low by measuring glucose and fatty acids in the blood. Through their connection with the brain these detectors are able to stimulate hunger. But what ends hunger? What brings a meal to its finish? Consider

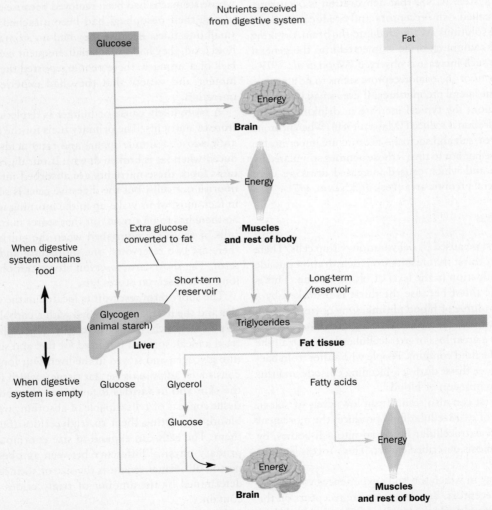

Figure 13.2 Overview of food metabolism. When the digestive system contains food, glucose nourishes the brain and muscles. Extra glucose is stored in the liver and converted to fat. When the digestive system is empty, glucose obtained from glycogen stored in the liver nourishes the brain until this short-term reservoir is used up. Fatty acids from fat tissue nourish the muscles, and glycerol is converted to glucose to nourish the brain.

what happens when you eat. Your stomach fills with food, and the digestive process begins. However, about an hour passes before significant amounts of nutrients are absorbed from the intestines into the bloodstream. Therefore, the body's supply of fuel is not replenished until quite some time after the meal begins. If you were to continue to eat until the nutrients actually entered the bloodstream, your stomach would burst. Therefore, some other detectors must be responsible for stopping the meal.

Although evidence suggests that the primary cause of hunger is not an empty stomach, the primary cause of satiety (that is, the cessation of hunger caused by eating) seems to be a full stomach. Many studies have shown that satiety is caused by entry of a sufficient quantity of nourishing food into the stomach. Therefore, the stomach must contain detectors that sense the presence of food. We have known for a long time that hunger can be abolished by injecting food into an animal's stomach by means of a flexible tube. Even though the animal does not get to taste and smell the food, it will not subsequently eat. Davis and Campbell (1973) showed how precisely the stomach can measure its contents. The investigators allowed hungry rats to eat their fill and then removed some food from their stomachs. When they let the rats eat again, they ate almost exactly as much as had been taken out.

The stomach appears to contain detectors that inform the brain about the chemical nature of its contents as well as the quantity. The ability to detect the chemical nature of food that has entered the stomach is important, because eating should stop relatively soon if the food is very nutritious but should continue for a longer time if it is not. Deutsch et al. (1978) injected either milk or a dilute salt solution into hungry rats' stomachs and 30 minutes later allowed them to eat. The rats that had received injections of milk ate less than the ones that had received the salt solution. Because the rats could not taste what was put in their stomachs, the effect had to come from detectors there. The nature of these detectors is not known, but they must respond to some chemicals present in food. You can try an experiment of your own: drink two glasses of water when you are very hungry and see whether they satisfy your appetite.

Detectors that measure the amount and nutritive value of food in the stomach contribute only to short-term control of eating – the termination of a single meal. Long-term factors also control food intake. For example, when people eat especially nutritious food, they soon learn to eat less. When they begin to exercise more, and hence burn up their store of nutrients faster, they soon start eating more.

There may also be characteristics of food that may make us eat more or less of it. Some psychologists have argued that the variety and sensory properties of food can reduce or increase our intake; these reductions are associated with a reduction in ratings of the food's pleasantness. The sensory-specific section reviews some of this evidence.

Mood, food and emotion

One reason people give for eating excessively is that it makes them feel better. Some researchers have linked this increased positive mood to the dopamine release caused by carbohydrate and fat (the foods we crave– crisps, sweets, biscuits and so on – are full of carbohydrate and fat). A study of healthy men, however, suggests that the relationship can be quite complex: if a man is exposed to a stimulus that creates happiness, his appetite for chocolate increases; if he is exposed to one that causes sadness it decreases (Macht et al., 2002).

Macht et al. asked men to abstain from eating for either two or eight hours before watching film clips designed to elicit anger, fear, sadness and happiness (e.g. a sequence from the film Cry Freedom was used to generate anger). After this, participants were given up to four pieces (5 g) of their preferred chocolate to eat and were asked to rate their appetite for chocolate and how much they liked what they ate.

Men in the happiness condition ate more chocolate and rated it as more pleasant than did men in the sadness condition. The findings suggest that emotion can affect eating in two ways: one involves people eating nice food when in a good mood and rating the food in a way that is congruent with their mood. The other involves people regulating their emotion through eating: people may, like binge eaters, eat tasty food to feel better.

Some research, however, suggests that chocolate does not necessarily improve positive mood but reduces negative mood. Macht and Mueller (2007) asked 48 men and women of normal weight to eat a 5 g piece of chocolate or drink some water after watching film clips designed to elicit positive, negative or neutral mood states. Mood was measured after seeing the clips and before and after ingesting the chocolate.

The chocolate eaters reported less negative mood compared to the water drinkers but the food had no effect on the other mood states. The authors suggest that this reduction in bad mood was attributable to the chocolate's palatability. In a second study, therefore, participants ate either palatable or unpalatable chocolate – one that was not rated as particularly pleasant – just after watching mood-inducing films. The palatable chocolate reduced negative mood, but the unpalatable chocolate did not. The benefit disappeared after three minutes.

Greimel et al. (2006) induced joy or sadness in participants by presenting them with video clips designed to elicit these emotions. Participants then rated the pleasantness and sweetness of a sweet chocolate drink, a bitter quinine solution and a bitter-sweet drink. Emotion significantly influenced pleasantness and sweetness ratings of the sweet drink: those who had been made sad rated the drink as less pleasant and sweet; those who had been made happy rated it as more pleasant and sweeter. There was no effect of emotion on the ratings of the bitter and bitter-sweet drinks.

Psychology in action: The social psychology of eating

The Babawet Dimashq (Damascus Gate) restaurant in Syria is the largest restaurant in the world, serving a potential 6,000 customers. Going out to eat is a social endeavour (and a geographical one, in the case of the Babawet Dimashq) – the food is sometimes secondary to the enjoyment of the company and the purpose of the meeting. Decades of research has shown that not only is eating a social activity, our intake varies according to the person, and the number of people, we are eating with. According to Herman et al. (2003), 'Social influences are profound, arguably greater than any other influence on eating'.

Most of the clear influences involve modelling. Modelling occurs when we modify our own behaviour to be more consistent with the behaviour of the person we are with (Cruwys et al., 2014; Vartanian et al., 2015). We eat more when the person we are with eats more and we eat less when the person we are with eats less (Conger et al., 1980). The effects of modelling are found regardless of our personality, whether the person eating is with us (or is eating elsewhere), our weight or our degree of hunger. In general, modelling increases if we want to affiliate with the person we're eating with or if we are similar to them – this effect extends to snacks and lunch. Couples in one study ate more biscuits if they were with other couples that shared their interests (Salvy et al., 2007). It is unclear to what extent variables such as sex or impulsivity mediate these effects, although there are some significant effects of sex on eating with others.

The 'social facilitation of eating' refers to when we eat more with someone than when we are alone (Herman, 2015). We spend less time in a cafeteria or restaurant when we are alone than in a group – 36.5 mins, on average, compared with 50.3. Zajonc (1965) identified two influencers of facilitation – audience effects and co-action effects. The former refers to facilitation produced by being in front of a passive audience. The latter refers to facilitation than occurs when we are with a person engaged in the same activity. Consumption is affected more by the latter than the former. We eat more with family and friends than we do with strangers – our meals at the weekend tend to be larger (by approximately 12 per cent) and these may contain more macronutrients and alcohol than meals eaten during the week (Redd and de Castro, 1992). One recent study examined the effect of meal-sharing on trust (Woolley and Fischbach, 2016). People who shared the same food as the person they were with were more trusting of each other and co-operated more in an employment negotiation exercise. They were also more likely to hold positive views of an advertised product if the person in the advert ate a food that was similar to the food participants were eating.

However, social facilitation is not universal: Men and women eat less in the company of a desirable person (Mori et al., 1987), but the effect is particularly pronounced in women, For example, if women are in mixed sex groups, they will eat less than with other women. Men eat more in mixed groups than in mixed pairs (Brindal et al., 2015). Women's intake is also predicted by the number of men in a group: the larger the number the less the intake; their calorie intake is also lower (Young et al., 2009). When women are told that their responses to a questionnaire were 'masculine', they ate less when in the company of others (Pliner and Chaiken, 1990). Women are also judged more positively if they eat less (Bock and Kanarek, 1995).

Despite the evidence, people believe that they are immune to social influence. In one study, 34 per cent reported that their eating was influenced by others but 56 per cent said that it was not (Robinson et al., 2014). Perhaps more importantly, people do not realise that their behaviour changes depending on the context they find themselves in and the people they are with (Vorauer and Miller, 1997; Higgs, 2015). Reminding people of the lunch they ate before they have an afternoon snack decreases snacking (Higgs and Woodward, 2009). We're also influenced by the TV we watch. Children and adults consume more high-energy, low nutrient food and fewer fruits and vegetables while watching television (Harrison et al., 2012). One study asked people to watch 10 minutes of The Food Network or a documentary about monkeys and elephants and then presented 800 calories worth of food in the way of sweets, cheese curls and carrots (Bodenlos et al., 2013). Intake was measured in both groups. Although more people ate chocolate after seeing the food programme, the calorie intake between the two groups did not differ.

Music and food intake

Have you ever wondered if the music in a restaurant, shop or bar influences your food and drink consumption or purchasing? A number of studies suggests that it can. One of the earliest and most dramatic studies monitored people's wine-buying as they walked down an isle with either French accordion music or German bierkeller music playing. The buying matched the music – people bought more French wine when the accordion music was playing and more German wine when the bierkeller music was playing (North *et al.*, 1999). Note, however, that the number of participants in this study was small – 44.

We tend to eat more quickly if we're exposed to high-tempo music. According to one study, music that is 94 beats per minute is associated with 4.4 bites per minute, compared with slow music's 3.83 (no music is even lower – 3.23) (Roballey *et al.*, 1985). Note, again, that this study had a very small number of participants – 11. Another study played fast and slow-tempo jazz music to Italian restaurant patrons and found that people spent longer in the slow-tempo condition but took longer to get served (Caldwell and Hibbett, 2002). They also underestimated the time they spent eating (the high-tempo group over-estimated their time). This finding is consistent with others. Milliman (1986), for example, found that people spent 11 minutes longer eating in a restaurant if the music was relaxing and spent more on drink (but not food).

One study, however, found that playing classical music led to fewer patrons staying in a restaurant and more leaving early, compared with jazz, popular and easy listening music (Wilson, 2003). People were more prepared to pay more in the classical, jazz and popular conditions.

Drinking is also affected by music – people drink more when music is played (Drews *et al.*, 1992) and a similar effect of tempo on consumption has been reported. For example, mean drinking time during fast music is 9.70 minutes; during slow music it is 13.52 (McElrea and Standing, 1992). Louder volume leads to greater and faster drinking (Gueguen *et al.*, 2008) and songs which mention drinking lead to patrons spending more money on drink (Engel *et al.*, 2012).

Sensory-specific satiety

Have you ever experienced the feeling when, after eating a big savoury meal, you could still manage to eat dessert? Or that you have had enough of eating peanuts but could quite happily contemplate eating a packet of crisps?

These experiences reflect sensory-specific satiety (SSS) – the decrease in the pleasantness and consumption of specific food after eating it to satiety. The satiety is sensory-specific because individuals may become sated eating foods of specific tastes, shapes, sizes and textures but not foods of different taste, shape, size and texture (Rolls *et al.*, 1986). This phenomenon explains why, if we eat a meal composed of a variety of foods, we eat more because there is greater sensory stimulation available from a varied meal (we would consume a greater quantity of a meal consisting of a bowl of soup, sausages, egg and bacon, and chocolate mousse than we would a meal comprising solely of sausages). SSS also has survival value because if we become bored with eating one food but not another, this increases the likelihood of a variety of foods being eaten.

If a food is eaten to satiety, a second course of the same food will result in a reduction in intake of around 50 per cent (Rolls *et al.*, 1981). In Rolls's early experiment, all foods, with the exception of roast beef, produced SSS. In one study, participants ate either a four-course meal of sausages, bread and butter, chocolate dessert and bananas or ate only one of these foods to satiety. The researchers found that consumption was 60 per cent higher when foods were presented together than when presented separately (Rolls *et al.*, 1986). At a post-satiety tasting session, those foods presented alone were also rated as less pleasant than those eaten as part of a four-course meal (Rolls *et al.*, 1984). Even colour and shape influence the amount of food eaten. When a variety of pasta shapes is presented for consumption, more is eaten than when only one pasta shape is presented; people also eat more food if it is made up of different colours than one colour (Rolls *et al.*, 1982). The effect of varying the shape and variety of food can be seen in Figures 13.3a and b.

SSS is also seen in the sense of smell. In an experiment where participants were asked to rate the pleasantness of the odours of banana, satsuma, fish paste, chicken and rose water before and after consuming bananas and chicken to satiety, the pleasantness of chicken and banana odours (but not other foods) significantly declined after satiety (Rolls and Rolls, 1997).

Why should this be? SSS allows us to enjoy and consume a greater variety of food and, therefore, represents a mechanism that enables us to consume a variety of nutrients. There is also evidence that certain regions of the brain may be responsible for our feeling of satiety. The hypothalamus, as you have seen, is important to feeding. Neurons in this region in monkeys stop responding to the sight and taste of food when the food has been eaten to satiety (Rolls *et al.*, 1986). Small *et al.* (2001b) and others, however, suggest that a key region involved in satiety is the orbitofrontal cortex (OFC).

An fMRI study in which the odour of banana was presented before and after people had eaten bananas to satiety found that activation in the OFC decreased when people sniffed the odour of banana after satiety (O'Doherty *et al.*, 2000). No such decrease was observed when people sniffed the odour of vanilla, suggesting that the OFC response was a specific response to a specific property of the food eaten to satiety. One role for the prefrontal cortex (PFC) in this process may be that

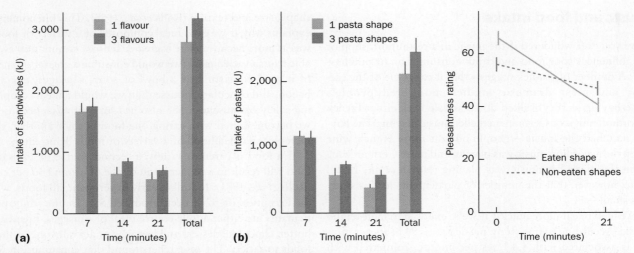

Figure 13.3 (a) The amount eaten of a one-flavoured and a three-flavoured meal. **(b)** The effect of varying the type of pasta shape on food intake and pleasantness ratings of the taste of the shapes. In both these examples, the sensory properties of the food influence intake and ratings of pleasantness.

Source: Reprinted from Rolls, B.J., Rolls E.T. and Rowe E.A., How sensory properties of foods affect human feeding behaviour, *Psychology and Behaviour*, 1982, 29, 409–17. © 1982, with permission from Elsevier Science; and Rolls and Rolls (1997).

of responding to reward. When we have eaten to satiety, the OFC will not respond because the brain does not feel rewarded. Rolls *et al.* (1986) have reported that OFC taste cells in monkeys reduce their firing to food stimuli when these monkeys have eaten to satiety.

In another study, volunteers ate chocolate to satiety as a PET scanner measured brain activation (Small *et al.*, 2001a). Participants first ate a chunk of chocolate, rated it for pleasantness and were then asked if they would like another. If they did, they were given another piece and asked to rate its pleasantness again. This continued until the participants felt that they had consumed enough chocolate.

The researchers found that when participants ate chocolate blood flow increased in a collection of regions including areas beneath the corpus callosum, a part of the OFC called the caudomedial OFC, the insula, striatum and midbrain. When participants were sated, blood flow increased in the parahippocampal gyrus and a different part of the OFC (the caudolateral OFC) than was activated during initial eating. What could this activation represent?

Small *et al.* suggest that the activity with chocolate reflects two different systems which mediate two aspects of behaviour: approach and withdrawal. That is, when the brain responds to reward, it activates the insula and part of the OFC. This reflects an 'approach' behaviour because we tend to approach things we like and this generates a positive emotion. When the brain responds to non-reward or stimuli that do not provide an opportunity for reward (such as food we no longer want to eat) brain regions involved in 'withdrawal' are recruited. These are involved in withdrawal because we

tend to withdraw from stimuli we do not like and we find such stimuli unpleasant (or at the very least, do not find them pleasant).

This is an interesting hypothesis because it is in keeping with a model of emotion which argues that the frontal cortex is the region that becomes active during the experience of positive and negative emotion. We will describe and evaluate this model in the emotion section of the chapter (see p. 533).

The region is also activated while looking at food-related stimuli after fasting (Porubska *et al.*, 2006). Twelve lean participants were asked to look at food-and non-food-related stimuli after five hours of fasting as functional MRI measured brain activation as they did this. The left side of the OFC was significantly more active when participants viewed the food slides (the insula on both sides of the brain was also more active). As self-reported appetite increased, so did activation in the insula bilaterally, the left operculum and the right putamen. The data suggest that all of these regions are involved in the motivation to eat.

The role of the brain in hunger, obesity and perception of food flavour

Several studies have now examined the effect of food aroma and food images on brain activation. One such study examined the brain regions involved in the perception of high and low-calorie foods (Killgore and Yurgelun-Todd, 2010). Women showed greater activation in the dorsolateral, ventrolateral, the middle and superior cingulate and insula when seeing images

Cutting edge: How healthy are ready meals compared with cookbook meals?

How many calories do you think are in a supermarket ready meal compared to a meal created by a chef in his/her cookbook? A group of doctors at NHS Leeds examined the ingredients in 100 British ready meals from three UK supermarkets and 100 main meals selected from five bestselling cookery books (Howard *et al.*, 2012). It's estimated that £9.5bn are spent on ready meals in Western Europe, with the UK being the biggest consumer, spending £2.5bn, according to the authors. That is a lot of microwaving.

The UK's health advisory arm, NHS Choices, suggests that ready meals contain fewer fruit and vegetables and more sugar and fat than meals cooked at home from scratch. Howard *et al.* collected data on calories, protein, carbohydrate, sugar, salt, fat, saturated fat, fibre, and meal weight for both types of meal.

Neither type of meal met WHO guidelines on nutrition but ready meals met more WHO goals regarding fibre density and energy derived from carbohydrate and fat, than did the chefs' meals. Ready meals contained more salt. The UK's Food Standards Authority issues a recommended traffic light system for manufacturers to include on their products where red indicates high levels of fat and carbohydrate and green indicates low levels of these. Red was the most common descriptor for the chefs' meals; green for the ready meals. The chefs' recipes contained more calories, protein, fat and saturated fat and less fibre than did the ready meals.

In short, neither type of meal provided a balanced diet but one was more balanced than the other – and it was not the one which public stereotyping would suggest.

---

of high-calorie foods than did men, suggesting a greater responsiveness in women.

Bragulat *et al.* (2010) asked five normal-weight and five obese individuals to fast for 24 hours and then measured their brain activation, using fMRI, as participants smelled food-related odours (two sweet and two 'fat-related') or non-food odours (such as Douglas fir). The odour associated most with the food the participants would like to eat generated significant activation in the limbic area and in parts of the cortex associated with reward (the insula, the ventral striatum, anterior cingulated and taste cortex in the frontal lobe). There were differences between obese and lean participants – the former showed more activation in the hippocampus and parahippocampal area whereas the latter showed greater activation in the posterior insula. Reduced activation is seen in the mid-insula in obese vs lean participants (Brooks *et al.*, 2013) but increased activation is seen in obese people when they see photographs of food (Scharmuller *et al.*, 2012; Ziaudden *et al.*, 2012). Grey matter volume has been found to be lower in the insula, medial OFC and cerebellum in those who were prone to obesity and this reduction was negatively correlated with concentrations of leptin (Smucny *et al.*, 2012), suggesting that brain structure may be a risk factor for obesity. People with bulimia nervosa show increased activation in the insult when they see photographs of high-calorie food (Schienle *et al.*, 2009).

That obese people show less connectivity between the insula and OFC at rest suggests that there may be abnormal processing of gustatory stimuli (Kullmann *et al.*, 2012). People who are less successful at keeping off weight after a diet show more activation in the insula when seeing photographs of food before and after the diet (Murdaugh *et al.*, 2012). If obese people undergo bariatric surgery, their brain's response to food cues becomes similar to that of lean people (Frank *et al.*, 2013). Preston and Ehrsson (2016) found that when people's image of their body weight was manipulated so that they would look obese, activation in the right anterior insula and anterior cingulate cortex was associated with greater negative feeling about their bodies.

The area which is common to the studies is the insula and, as you saw in Chapter 5, this region is the part of the brain consistently associated with activation when a person tastes food. There is some evidence that damage to the left or right side affects different types of taste perception with left-sided lesions associated with poorer ability to taste salt and right with bitter (Stevenson *et al.*, 2013). Some researchers have suggested that the anterior part may be responsible for integrating smell and taste information (Kringelbach, 2015). A review of the role of the brain in perceiving images of food found that the areas consistently activated included the left middle insula, the left lateral OFC, and bilateral posterior fusiform gyrus (van der Laan, 2011).

The other important brain area for food flavour is the OFC, as the above studies on sensory-specific satiety demonstrate. This area is thought to respond to various types of pleasurable stimuli – from touch, to taste to drugs. One study measured brain activation in people who liked or disliked grapefruit. Those who liked the fruit showed greater OFC activation when they tasted it (van den Bosch *et al.*, 2014). People who disliked it showed activation in the insula, cingulate cortex and operculum. There was also more activation in the OFC in both groups to sugar and more in the cingulate cortex and operculum to quinine (a bitter taste).

Obesity and its treatment

Obesity: some figures

In Western countries, obesity is defined as having body fat that exceeds 25 per cent of body weight in women and 18 per cent in men (Bray, 1998). The amount of fat is estimated using a measure called body mass index (BMI). This takes a person's weight in kilograms and divides it by their height in metres squared. This figure is expressed as X kg/m^2. To be diagnosed as clinically obese, a person must have a BMI that is equal to or greater than 30 kg/m^2 (World Health Organization, 1998). Figure 13.4 shows you how to calculate BMI.

The prevalence of being overweight in 6–11-year-old children had increased from 6 per cent in 1980 to 10.65 per cent in 1994 (Troiano and Flegal, 1998). Only a minority of adults have the desired BMI of 18.5 to 24.9 kg/m^2 and this shift towards being overweight is thought to carry severe health risks. The risk of mortality increases by around 30 per cent in people with a BMI of 30 kg/m^2; this percentage continues upward to 40 per cent when BMI exceeds 40 kg/m^2 (Manson *et al.*, 1995). A study of 14,403 Norwegian men aged between 40 and 49 and initially free of coronary heart disease (CHD) has shown that BMI was a risk factor for the subsequent development of the disease later in life (Haheim *et al.*, 2007). The causes of death in obese people include stroke, diabetes and cancer (these correlate with obesity). Obese people also suffer social and physical complications (Wadden *et al.*, 2002). Obese girls complete fewer years in school, despite having just as good grades as those who remain, are less likely to marry, and earn less than their non-obese counterparts. Obese people also elicit negative aesthetic judgements from others (as you saw in Chapter 3): people tend to prefer partners with a specific shape and size (and it is not obese).

Consequences of obesity and rationale for intervention

Interventions are recommended when a person has a serious BMI statistic and a risk of developing ill health. For people with a BMI of below 27 kg/m^2, clinicians recommend an increase in physical activity and a decrease in fat and sugar intake, coupled with self-directed efforts to maintain weight loss and the taking of a doctor's advice (Wadden *et al.*, 2002). For people with higher BMIs, the same intervention may be implemented but if this does not work more drastic measures may be adopted such as drugs or, for those with a BMI in excess of 40 kg/m^2, surgery (this is called **bariatric** surgery). The side effects of surgery are considerable, but weight loss is produced more efficiently (Yanovski and Yanovski, 2002).

Initial success at weight loss depends on the goals of the person losing the weight. First, people need to be motivated to lose weight. Secondly, they need to realise that weight reduction programmes are designed for health rather than aesthetic reasons. For example, until recently interventions were guided towards helping people achieve their ideal weight (rather than a weight which would reduce the risk of ill health). Current emphasis, however, is on reducing health complications and so a loss of 5–15 per cent can be effective in producing this reduction, even though the patient/client may not be happy with having lost so little weight and expect a weight loss of 20–35 per cent (Blackburn, 1995; O'Neil *et al.*, 2000). Wadden *et al.* cite one study which reported that weight reduction of 7 kg/m^2 combined with 150 minutes of exercise a week reduced the likelihood of developing diabetes by 58 per cent (Diabetes Prevention Program Research Group, 2002, cited in Wadden *et al.*, 2002). A meta-analysis of obesity prevention programmes for children has found that only 21 per cent of 64 programmes showed evidence of weight gain prevention in children (Stice *et al.*, 2006). The effect was greater for children and adolescents (rather than pre-adolescents) and for girls.

Psychological interventions

Difficulty in restricting food intake is increased during holiday periods which the overweight regard as high-risk periods because of family celebrations or national holiday celebrations. One way in which this difficulty could be reduced is by self-monitoring, the act of closely observing what is eaten and when and in which contexts. Boutelle *et al.* (1999) examined the effect of self-monitoring during this high-risk holiday period in a group of overweight individuals on a weight-loss programme. Forty-nine obese people who had been on the programme for at least a month, were known to self-monitor rarely and who were willing to be contacted in a two-week holiday period (Christmas–New Year), took part in the study. Self-monitoring took the form of examining food intake and taking weight measurements daily. Two groups – an intervention group and a non-intervention group – were observed and both groups were encouraged to do this basic level of self-monitoring. However, the intervention group also received daily mailings (comics and literature about self-monitoring and weight loss) from the researchers as well as one or two phone calls in each week in the two-week period reminding them to self-monitor.

Those in the intervention group self-monitored more frequently but also managed their weight more effectively than did those in the non-intervention group. Both groups had difficulty

Height (Feet) — **Weight (Pounds)**

Height (Feet)	100	105	110	115	120	125	130	135	140	145	150	155	160	165	170	175	180	185	190	195	200	205	210	215	220	225	230	235	240	245	250
5'0"	20	21	21	22	23	24	25	26	27	28	29	30	31	32	33	34	35	36	37	38	39	40	41	42	43	44	45	46	47	48	49
5'1"	19	20	21	22	23	24	25	26	26	27	28	29	30	31	32	33	34	35	36	37	38	39	40	41	42	43	43	44	45	46	47
5'2"	18	19	20	21	22	23	24	25	26	27	27	28	29	30	31	32	33	34	35	36	37	37	38	39	40	41	42	43	44	45	46
5'3"	18	19	19	20	21	22	23	24	25	26	27	27	28	29	30	31	32	33	34	35	35	36	37	38	39	40	41	42	43	43	44
5'4"	17	18	19	20	21	21	22	23	24	25	26	27	27	28	29	30	31	32	33	33	34	35	36	37	38	39	39	40	41	42	43
5'5"	17	17	18	19	20	21	22	22	23	24	25	26	27	27	28	29	30	31	32	32	33	34	35	36	37	37	38	39	40	41	42
5'6"	16	17	18	19	19	20	21	22	23	23	24	25	26	27	27	28	29	30	31	31	32	33	34	35	36	36	37	38	39	40	40
5'7"	16	16	17	18	19	20	20	21	22	23	23	24	25	26	27	27	28	29	30	31	31	32	33	34	35	36	36	37	38	39	40
5'8"	15	16	17	17	18	19	20	21	21	22	23	24	24	25	26	27	27	28	29	30	30	31	32	33	33	34	35	36	37	38	38
5'9"	15	16	16	17	18	18	19	20	21	21	22	23	24	24	25	26	27	27	28	29	30	30	31	32	32	33	34	35	35	36	37
5'10"	14	15	16	17	17	18	19	19	20	21	22	22	23	24	24	25	26	27	27	28	29	29	30	31	32	32	33	34	34	35	36
5'11"	14	15	15	16	17	17	18	19	20	20	21	22	22	23	24	24	25	26	26	27	28	29	29	30	31	31	32	33	33	34	35
6'0"	14	14	15	16	16	17	18	18	19	20	20	21	22	22	23	24	24	25	26	26	27	28	28	29	30	31	31	32	33	33	34
6'1"	13	14	15	15	16	16	17	18	18	19	20	20	21	22	22	23	24	24	25	26	26	27	28	28	29	30	30	31	32	32	33
6'2"	13	13	14	15	15	16	17	17	18	19	19	20	21	21	22	22	23	24	24	25	26	26	27	28	28	29	30	30	31	32	32
6'3"	12	13	14	14	15	16	16	17	17	18	19	19	20	21	21	22	22	23	24	24	25	26	26	27	28	28	29	30	30	31	31
6'4"	12	13	13	14	15	15	16	16	17	18	18	19	19	20	21	21	22	22	23	24	24	25	26	26	27	27	28	29	29	30	30

Height (Feet) — **Weight (Pounds)**

Height (Feet)	255	260	265	270	275	280	285	290	295	300	305	310	315	320	325	330	335	340	345	350	355	360	365	370	375	380	385	390	395	400
5'0"	50	51	52	53	54	55	56	57	58	59	60	61	62	62	63	64	65	66	67	68	69	70	71	72	73	74	75	76	77	78
5'1"	48	49	50	51	52	53	54	55	56	57	58	59	60	60	61	62	63	64	65	66	67	68	69	70	71	72	73	74	75	76
5'2"	47	48	48	49	50	51	52	53	54	55	56	57	58	59	59	60	61	62	63	64	65	66	67	68	69	70	70	71	72	73
5'3"	45	46	47	48	49	50	50	51	52	53	54	55	56	57	58	58	59	60	61	62	63	64	65	66	66	67	68	69	70	71
5'4"	44	45	45	46	47	48	49	50	51	51	52	53	54	55	56	57	58	58	59	60	61	62	63	64	64	65	66	67	68	69
5'5"	42	43	44	45	46	47	47	48	49	50	51	52	52	53	54	55	56	57	57	58	59	60	61	62	63	64	64	65	66	67
5'6"	41	42	43	44	44	45	46	47	48	48	49	50	51	52	52	53	54	55	56	56	57	58	59	60	61	61	62	63	64	65
5'7"	40	41	42	42	43	44	45	45	46	47	48	49	49	50	51	52	52	53	54	55	56	56	57	58	59	60	60	61	62	63
5'8"	39	40	40	41	42	43	43	44	45	46	46	47	48	49	49	50	51	52	52	53	54	55	55	56	57	58	59	59	60	61
5'9"	38	38	39	40	41	41	42	43	44	44	45	46	47	47	48	49	49	50	51	52	52	53	54	55	55	56	57	58	58	59
5'10"	37	37	38	39	39	40	41	42	42	43	44	44	45	46	47	47	48	49	50	50	51	52	52	53	54	55	55	56	57	57
5'11"	36	36	37	38	38	39	40	40	41	42	43	43	44	45	45	46	47	47	48	49	50	50	51	52	52	53	54	54	55	56
6'0"	35	35	36	37	37	38	39	39	40	41	41	42	43	43	44	45	45	46	47	47	48	49	50	50	51	52	52	53	54	54
6'1"	34	34	35	36	36	37	38	38	39	40	40	41	42	42	43	44	44	45	46	46	47	48	49	50	50	51	51	52	53	53
6'2"	33	33	34	35	35	36	37	37	38	39	40	40	41	42	42	43	44	44	45	46	46	47	48	48	49	49	50	51	51	51
6'3"	32	32	33	34	34	35	36	36	37	38	39	39	40	41	41	42	42	43	44	44	45	46	46	47	47	48	49	49	50	50
6'4"	31	32	32	33	33	34	35	35	36	37	37	38	38	39	40	40	41	41	42	43	43	44	44	45	46	46	47	47	48	49

Figure 13.4 How to determine BMI in adults. Here is a shortcut method for calculating BMI if you are too short or too tall for the table: Step 1, multiply weight (in pounds) by 703; Step 2, multiply height (in inches) by height (in inches); Step 3, divide the answer in Step 1 by the answer in Step 2 to get your BMI. Example: for a person who is 5 feet 5 inches tall weighing 149 lbs. Step 1, 149 × 703 = 104747; Step 2, 65 × 65 = 4225; Step 3; 104,747 divided by 4,225 = 24.8.
Source: Shape Up America! www.shapeup.org.

in managing their weight, however (the comparison group putting on a pound, on average). Those in the self-monitoring group lost more weight and there was a strong association between self-monitoring and weight loss.

The difficulty in maintaining weight loss is one of the most serious problems obese people face. Studies of 20-week intervention programmes, such as the one described, have found that people can lose up to 9 kg (around 9 per cent of body weight) but when the intervention programme stops, people can regain as much as one-third of their weight in the following 12 months (Foreyt and Goodrick, 1993; Wing, 2002). Clinicians, therefore, have focused their attention on how to achieve the maintenance of weight loss.

This can be done by creating detailed behavioural plans for the client to follow, as well as by controlling the portions of food the client eats. Replacing normal meals and snacks

In 2008, chef Jamie Oliver launched a campaign called 'Pass It On' to get the people of Rotherham in the North of England eating well and heathily.

Source: Peter Dench/Getty Images.

One resident, Julie Critchlow (pictured here), was so unimpressed she took take-away orders from disgruntled schoolchildren outside the school railings. She was eventually won over.

Source: Ross Parry Agency.

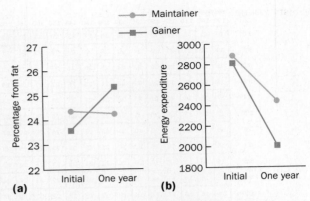

Figure 13.5 The number of calories obtained from fat (a) and the weekly kcal expenditure (b) in a group of people who gained weight or maintained weight loss after undergoing a weight loss programme.

Source: McGuire, T., Wing, R.R., Klem, W., Lang, M.L. and Hill, J.O., What predicts weight regain in a group of successful weight losers? *Journal of Consulting and Clinical Psychology*, 1999, 67(2), 177–85. Copyright © 1999 by the American Psychological Association, reprinted with permission.

with portion-controlled meals, for example, can lead to an 8 per cent reduction in weight over a sustained period of dietary regime control. The longer the intervention, the greater the weight loss, but most of the loss is seen in the first six months (Perri *et al.*, 1989; Flechtner-Mors *et al.*, 2000). The greatest predictor of whether people maintain their loss is their ability to engage in physical activity. Those who do, tend to maintain their weight-loss programmes, as Figure 13.5 shows. Those who exercise at home are more successful at maintenance than are those who attend gyms or leisure centres (Perri *et al.*, 1997).

Surgical interventions

If psychological interventions do not succeed in producing weight loss, more aggressive interventions such as surgery are sometimes implemented if the person is morbidly obese, that is, the person has a BMI of over 40 kg/m². There are two methods of surgically effecting weight loss in the obese. The first, called an intestinal bypass, worked by bypassing a part of the digestive system called the jejenum (Mason and Ito, 1969). The effect of this was to produce dramatic weight loss – in the order of 45 kg – but also very serious side effects such as liver failure. The second, and the one that is most commonly adopted, is also a form of gastric bypass.

A 50 ml pouch is attached to the gullet which restricts food intake. The pouch is connected to the jejenum, bypassing the stomach and part of the intestine called the duodenum. The effect of this is to reduce weight by around 30 per cent in the first-year-and-a-half after surgery (Albrecht and Pories, 1999) and a sustained loss over a decade later.

Pharmacological interventions

In recent years, several companies have sought to deliver the perfect anti-obesity drug or 'fat-buster'. Historically, such drugs have been used for other purposes – for depression (fenfluramine, sibutramine) or to combat smoking (rimonabant). Customised drugs have focused on the substances in the body which regulate hunger and satiety, such as the hormone, cholecystokinin (CCK), amylin, insulin and glucagons. All of these are released when we eat and help limit meal size (Woods *et al.*, 2006; Naslund and Hellstrom, 2007). One, ghrelin, is released in the stomach and affects the vagus nerve and hypothalamus and increases food intake. Research suggests that there are neurons in the hypothalamic arcuate nucleus which respond to chemicals which signal angry deficits (such as ghrelin) (Atasoy *et al.*, 2012). When these neurons are excited, animals eat voraciously; when they are destroyed, intake is inhibited (Atasoy *et al.*, 2012).

Drugs which mimic the effects of these hormones produce an increase in the feeling of satiety. Drugs that antagonise ghrelin receptors decrease the feelings of hunger (Moran, 2006). There are also chemicals, melanocortins, which are released by leptin's action on a group of neurons in the arcuate nucleus. When melanocortin receptors are activated, there is a decrease in feeding and an increase in energy expenditure. Drugs are being developed which act as agonists for melanocortin receptors (Nargund *et al.*, 2006). Other drugs being developed include histamine 3 antagonists which may help to reduce weight gain (Ebenshade *et al.*, 2006). None of these drugs has met with long-term success, as yet, but the quest to develop the perfect weight-loss drug continues.

Policy for the future

Wadden *et al.* (2002) suggest five ways in which the obesity problem might be tackled. These are as follows:

- Regulating the food advertising aimed at children, especially the advertising of sugary and fatty foods.
- Prohibiting fast foods and drinks from schools.
- Subsidising the sale of healthy foods.
- Taxing unhealthy foods.
- Providing resources for physical activity.

Some of these steps may probably never happen, because they are quite stark and potentially expensive, especially for the manufacturer who will see its goods taxed and the advertising of these goods reduced. The authors do acknowledge that these steps may not even achieve the aims they set out to achieve. Of course, there is also the important issue of choice and freedom of choice: people can decide not to consume sugary or fatty foods and some people enjoy eating such foods in moderation. For those who consume sensibly to reduce or impede access to such foods, by reducing their advertising or taxing them heavily, would it be psychologically (perhaps morally) beneficial?

What causes obesity?

Various psychological variables may be a cause of obesity, including lack of impulse control, poor ability to delay gratification and maladaptive eating styles (primarily eating too fast). However, in a review of the literature, Rodin *et al.* (1989) found that none of these suggestions has received empirical support. Rodin and her colleagues also found that unhappiness and depression seem to be the effects of obesity, not its causes, and that dieting behaviour seems to make the problem worse.

There is no single, all-inclusive explanation for obesity, but there are many partial ones. Habit plays an important role in the control of food intake. Early in life, when we are most active, we form our ideas about how much food constitutes a meal. Later in life, we become less active, but we do not always reduce our food intake accordingly. We fill our plates according to what we think is a proper-sized meal (or perhaps the plate is filled for us), and we eat everything, ignoring the satiety signals that might tell us to stop before the plate is empty.

One reason why many people have so much difficulty losing weight is that metabolic factors appear to play an important role in obesity. In fact, a good case can be made that obesity is most often not an eating disorder but rather a metabolic disorder. Metabolism refers to the physiological processes, including the production of energy from nutrients, that take place within an organism. Just as cars differ in their fuel efficiency, so do people. Rose and Williams (1961) studied pairs of people who were matched for weight, height, age and activity. Some of these matched pairs differed by a factor of two in the number of calories they ate each day. People with an efficient metabolism have calories left over to deposit in the long-term nutrient reservoir; thus, they have difficulty keeping this reservoir from growing. In contrast, people with an inefficient metabolism can eat large meals without getting fat. Thus, whereas a fuel-efficient automobile is desirable, a fuel-efficient body runs the risk of becoming obese.

Genetic influences

Are people who suffer from excessive weight gain genetically different from those with normal weight or is it true that, as Bray (1998) suggests, 'genes load the gun, the environment pulls the trigger'? Differences in metabolism appear to have a hereditary basis. Griffiths and Payne (1976) found that the children of obese parents weighed more than other children even though they ate less. Stunkard *et al.* (1986) found that the body weight of a sample of people who had been adopted as infants was highly correlated with their biological parents but not with their adoptive parents. Thus, a person's weight (presumably closely related to their metabolic efficiency) is influenced by genetic factors.

Why are there genetic differences in metabolic efficiency? James and Trayhurn (1981) suggest that under some environmental conditions metabolic efficiency is advantageous. That is, in places where food is only intermittently available in sufficient quantities, being able to stay alive on small amounts of food and to store up extra nutrients in the form of fat when food becomes available for a while is a highly adaptive trait. Therefore, the variability in people's metabolisms may reflect the nature of the environment experienced by their ancestors.

Another factor – this one non-hereditary – can influence people's metabolism. Many obese people diet and then relapse, thus undergoing large changes in body weight. Some investigators have suggested that starvation causes the body's metabolism to become more efficient. For example, Brownell *et al.* (1986) fed rats a diet that made them become obese and then restricted their food intake until their body weights returned to normal. Then they made the rats fat again and reduced their food intake again. The second time, the rats became fat much faster and lost their weight much more slowly. Clearly, the experience of gaining and losing large amounts of body weight altered the animals' metabolic efficiency.

Steen *et al.* (1988) obtained evidence that the same phenomenon (called the yo-yo effect) takes place in humans. They measured the resting metabolic rate in two groups of adolescent wrestlers: those who fasted just before a competition and binged afterwards and those who did not. The investigators found that wrestlers who fasted and binged developed more efficient metabolisms. Possibly, these people will have difficulty maintaining a normal body weight as they get older.

The role of leptin

For a long time, investigators believed that fat tissue provided some chemical signal that could be detected by the brain. When too much fat began accumulating, more of this chemical was secreted, and the person began eating less. If the amount of body fat began to decrease, the level of the chemical fell and the person began eating more.

After many years of searching for such a chemical signal, researchers have finally succeeded in finding one. The discovery came after years of study with a strain of genetically obese mice. The ob mouse (as this strain is called) has a low metabolism, overeats and gets monstrously fat. It also develops diabetes in adulthood, just as many obese people do. Recently, researchers in several laboratories have discovered the cause of the obesity (Campfield *et al.*, 1995; Halaas *et al.*, 1995; Pelleymounter *et al.*, 1995). A particular gene, called OB, normally produces a protein known as leptin (from the Greek word leptos, 'thin'). Leptin is normally secreted by fat cells that have absorbed a large amount of triglyceride. Because of a genetic mutation, the fat cells of ob mice are unable to secrete leptin.

Leptin has profound effects on metabolism and eating, acting as an anti-obesity hormone. If ob mice are given daily injections of leptin, their metabolic rate increases, their body temperature rises, they become more active and they eat less. As a result, their weight returns to normal. The treatment works even when the leptin is injected directly into the brain, indicating that the chemical acts directly on the neural circuits that control eating and metabolism. Figure 13.6 shows a photograph of an untreated ob mouse and an ob mouse that has received injections of leptin.

Maffei *et al.* (1995) discovered that leptin is found in humans and that the level of leptin in the blood is correlated with obesity; thus, this chemical signal appears to be present in our species as well as in mice. But if leptin is produced by human fat cells, why do some people nevertheless overeat and become obese?

Hormones act on their target cells by stimulating receptor molecules located on these cells (see Chapter 4). Using the techniques of molecular genetics, Tartaglia *et al.* (1995) discovered the leptin receptor. In order for leptin to reduce weight, the brain must contain functioning leptin receptors. Perhaps, researchers speculate, some people have leptin receptors that

Figure 13.6 The effects of leptin on obesity in mice of the ob (obese) strain. The ob mouse on the left is untreated; the one on the right received daily injections of leptin.
Source: Photo courtesy of Dr J. Sholtis, The Rockefeller University. © 1995 Amgen, Inc.

do not respond normally to the presence of leptin in the blood. The overgrown fat cells of these people secrete high levels of leptin, but the effect the hormone produces in the brain is less intense than normal. Hence, people overeat.

Myths about obesity

In a review of perceptions and misperceptions of the scientific evidence describing and explaining obesity, Casazza *et al.* (2013) have found that there are still some fairly rigorously held beliefs about obesity which are not supported by the evidence. They examined popular media reports and the scientific literature and found seven prevalent myths – beliefs which are contradicted by the evidence.

Anorexia nervosa

Anorexia nervosa is an eating disorder characterised by a severe restriction of eating, distorted body image and emaciation. Its cause is unknown. The literal meaning of the word 'anorexia' suggests a loss of appetite, but people with this disorder generally do not lose their appetite; instead, they restrict their intake. This limited intake of food – especially fats and carbohydrates – occurs despite intense preoccupation with food, its preparation and with their own disorder (Hermans *et al.*, 1998). Their average intake is around 1,000 calories a day; for healthy adult women, the recommended calorie intake is between 1,500 and 2,000. They may enjoy preparing meals for others to consume, collect recipes and even hoard food that they do not eat. They have an intense fear of becoming obese, and this fear continues even if they become dangerously thin. There is a significant disturbance in the perception of body shape and size, with anorexics consistently overestimating body size and shape (Smeets *et al.*, 1997). Many exercise excessively by cycling, running, or almost constant walking and pacing. The prevalence of the disorder is between 0.5 and 1 per cent.

People with anorexia appear unaware that they are ill and will starve themselves despite evidence that this is making them ill. They are often resistant to treatment (Kaye *et al.*, 2013). Individuals are also characterised by certain personality traits – they score highly on anxiety, negative emotion, perfectionism, and inflexibility, and engage in obsessive behaviour such as being preoccupied with cleanliness and exactitude (Kaye *et al.*, 2013). Their ability to restrict intake is related to other, similar behaviours – for example, they are better able to postpone reward compared to those without the disorder (Steinglass *et al.*, 2012).

Bulimia nervosa

A different eating disorder, **bulimia nervosa,** is characterised by a loss of control of food intake. The term bulimia comes from the Greek *bous*, 'ox', and *limos*, 'hunger'. People with bulimia nervosa periodically gorge themselves with food, especially dessert or snack food, and especially in the afternoon or evening. These behaviours must occur at least twice a week for three months for a diagnosis of bulimia nervosa to be made. These binges are usually followed by self-induced vomiting or the use of laxatives, along with feelings of depression and guilt (Mawson, 1974; Halmi, 1978). This behaviour is called purging, although not all bulimics use this behaviour as a means of compensating for the binge eating. With this combination of bingeing and purging, the net nutrient intake (and consequently, the body weight) of bulimics can vary. Episodes of bulimia are seen in some patients with anorexia nervosa. Individuals with bulimia appear to be less concerned with food but are excessively preoccupied with body shape (Lovell *et al.*, 1997).

The prevalence rate is a little higher than for anorexia and ranges between 1 and 3 per cent. Despite a reported increase in the prevalence of the disorder over many decades, some recent research suggests that it is declining, with data from the UK, the USA and the Netherlands showing reduced prevalence of bulimia (Hoek and van Hoeken, 2003; Currin *et al.*, 2005; Keel *et al.*, 2005).

Aetiology of anorexia and bulimia nervosa

Because anorexia is characterised by constraint, reduced affect and emotion, and an ascetic way of life, and bulimia is characterised by impulsivity and sensation-seeking, the causes of each might be different. Some researchers have suggested that bulimia might be attributable to some neurophysiological problem, such as an imbalance of serotonin (a neurotransmitter involved in mood, eating and impulsive behaviour). Serotonin disturbances are seen in the disorder during and after the illness (Kaye, 2008) and one mechanism for the process might be that gonadal steroids affect the regulation of 5-HT during puberty. Reducing intake also affects serotonin and mood because the lack of food reduces blood levels of a chemical called tryptophan. In the short term, they might experience an improvement in mood but with continued calorie restriction, the effect on serotonin is to make their mood worse (Kaye, 2008).

Onset of anorexia nervosa is most common in adolescence (Kaye *et al.*, 2013) and there is considerable evidence that genetic heritability predicts its appearance – 50–80 per cent of the risk of developing the eating disorder is attributable to genetic factors (Kaye *et al.*, 2013). The existence of hereditary factors suggests that abnormalities in physiological mechanisms may be involved. Some psychologists believe that the emphasis our society places on slimness, especially in women, is largely responsible for this disorder, whereas others suggest that the excessive need to control eating (which is, in turn, caused by Western societies' preoccupation with shape and weight) is the characteristic feature (Fairburn *et al.*, 1999). There is a debate regarding whether individuals with anorexia have a disturbance in appetite leading to pathological eating patterns or whether the pathological feeding patterns occur secondary to some other cause such as pre-occupation with body image (Kaye *et al.*, 2013). There is evidence that the personalities of individuals with bulimia and anorexia differ from the general population – they are more impulsive and compulsive, for example. In a meta-analysis of eating disorders and personality, Farmstead *et al.* (2016) found that restricting anorexia and binge-eating was associated with an obsessive-compulsive personality type. Some personality disorders (borderline and paranoid which you'll read about in Chapter 18) were more common in binge-eating/purging anorexia nervosa and bulimia nervosa.

One search to discover a psychobiological cause for the disorder has focused on brain regions known to be involved in eating and the integration of sensory information – such as the insula – and on the neurotransmitters, dopamine and serotonin. The function of both neurotransmitter systems is abnormal in anorexia (Kaye *et al.*, 2013) with some serotonin receptors being underactive and others over-active. One meta-analysis found that the possession of the 5-HTTLPR S allele was a risk factor for developing anorexia (Calati *et al.*, 2011).

When women who had recovered from anorexia were asked to taste sucrose or water as fMRI measured brain activation, they showed less activation in the ventral and dorsal striatum and the insula when tasting both (Wagner *et al.*, 2008). But whereas activation in the insula in a control group correlated with the rated pleasantness of sucrose, there was no such correlation found in the anorexic women. Women with anorexia also show less activation in the insula when they sample chocolate milk when fasting (Haase *et al.*, 2009). A recent study used deep brain stimulation of the subcallosal cingulate (see Chapter 4) in 16 patients who were resistant to other types of treatment (Lipsman *et al.*, 2017). It found that the treatment increased BMI and reduced depression and anxiety.

In their review of the aetiology of anorexia, Kaye *et al.* highlight a number of questions that are still unanswered about the disorder such as: Are there differences between subtypes of anorexia and do these have different causes? How does the brain contribute to the disorder? Why do people with anorexia have distorted body self-image when they have normal, undistorted perception of the bodies of others (Gaudio and Quattrocchi, 2012)?

Body dissatisfaction in healthy and eating-disordered women

Around 50 per cent of girls and undergraduate women report being dissatisfied with their bodies (Bearman *et al.*, 1986), and this can occur as early as 7 years of age and across cultures (Dohnt and Tiggemann, 2006). This dissatisfaction with one's body is seen as a significant risk factor for the development of eating disorders (Grabe *et al.*, 2007). A number of studies has shown that such body dissatisfaction is significantly higher in young women than it is in middle-aged women. One theory that could account for this dissatisfaction is Frederickson and Roberts's self-objectification theory (1997). This argues that most Western cultures regard the female body as something to be viewed and evaluated. In such cultures, there is a tendency in women to monitor their appearance, judging it as others (mostly, men) would view it. Noting that the body does not meet the ideal – or the perceived notion of an ideal – the woman becomes dissatisfied about her appearance. One consequence of such monitoring is increased anxiety and shame about the body. Ultimately, it could be argued, such monitoring leads to eating disorder, anxiety and sexual dysfunction.

Strahan *et al.* (2006) found that women rated their appearance more negatively than did men and also compared their bodies with very attractive women, especially unrealistic ones such as models, more often than they did less attractive ones. This bias was eliminated by removing the salience of 'cultural norms', that is, the emphasis on what people find attractive in women and what magazines and television portray as being the ideal of womanly pulchritude and physical perfection. When cultural norms are minimised, women compare themselves with their (more realistic and relevant) peers. However, when cultural norms are made salient, women are more likely to compare themselves with models (and consequently feel worse about themselves when they make such comparisons).

The widespread portrayal of such norms, and women's susceptibility to their psychologically pernicious effects, might explain their insecurity with their bodies. A recent television advertisement for a well-known UK pharmacist showed a woman nervously standing amongst a beach of sunbathers, as the voice-over conveyed her inner thoughts about whether she was slim enough to expose herself in the summer sun. 'The most dreaded moment of the year,' the voice-over intoned. A newspaper commentator takes up the story: 'Her fellow baskers turn en masse to judge her. She nervously reveals smooth, caramel limbs, thus enabling the meerkats to return to their sunbathing, safe in the knowledge that they won't have to look at her bingo wings and stubble for the rest of the day' (Raeside, 2007).

This manipulation has some basis in fact. Frederick *et al.* (2006) found that more women than men felt too heavy, unattractive and avoided wearing a swimsuit in public (16 per cent of men versus 31 per cent of women). Men felt better about their bodies than did women but underweight women were most happy with their bodies. Slender women were more satisfied than those with higher BMIs. Various studies have shown that women, particularly young women, are overly concerned with their appearance and with how others view them; self-objectification seems to occur when the women have the maximum potential for reproduction.

In 2004, the company Dove launched its campaign for Real Beauty (top) using models which contrasted with those normally seen in adverts for similar products (bottom). Of course, both types are designed to sell us thing we do not really need.
Source: Richard Levine / Alamy Stock Photo, (Top); Anton Oparin / Alamy Stock Photo, (Bottom).

The media are viewed as one source of women's body dissatisfaction. Thin women are portrayed as paragons: they are healthy, better-looking, attract the most desirable men and so on. Films, magazines and television programmes emphasise the thinness of women (Fouts and Burggraf, 1999), there are fewer fat people portrayed on television and portrayals now are thinner than on television in the past and thinner than is normal in the population (Silverstein *et al.*, 1986; Fouts and Burggraf, 1999; Greenberg *et al.*, 2003). Women who watch thin media images of other women express a significantly greater negative body image than when watching average-sized women, especially if the viewers are under 19 years old and they are concerned with their body weight (Groesz *et al.*, 2002; Grabe *et al.*, 2007). Culturation theory argues that increased exposure to material makes this material the norm over time and people come to accept it as real (Gerbner *et al.*, 2002): if this is what women are like, women might think, this is how I need to be, too. If women with a negative body image watch a seven-minute analysis of how the media portrays women, they engage less in social comparison – comparing themselves to an imagined ideal – and are affected less by seeing images of thin, beautiful women (Posavac *et al.*, 1998).

The effects of watching television and fashion magazine images appear to be different: seeing thin women in fashion magazines is associated with a greater activation of what psychologists call 'internalisation of thin ideals', the ability to evoke a stereotype of the most desirable (thin) woman (Tiggemann, 2003). Interestingly, women with eating disorders report less anxiety about their body when watching magazine advertisements featuring average-sized models (Halliwell *et al.*, 2005). The advertisements featuring very thin and average-sized women were rated as just as effective as each other, suggesting that advertisements need not recruit the thinnest of stick-thin women to sell their wares. Curiously, women's response to watching other women's bodies on television, as well as their intake of crisps and chocolates, can be affected by the size of the television screen they watch. One study had female students of normal weight eat snacks while watching a 30-minute film of beautiful girls in a frame size that was either in 4:3 ratio (normal) or 16:9 (where the image is stretched) (Anschutz *et al.*, 2008). Restrained eaters felt worse and ate less in the thinner condition.

Furthermore, if women are asked to look at photographs of themselves and other women and identify a part of their own and others' bodies they find unattractive, women with higher BMI judged their bodies to be less attractive (Roefs *et al.*, 2008). Eye-tracking technology showed that they would spend more time looking at their unattractive body parts and more time looking at other women's attractive parts.

About one anorexic patient in 30 dies of the disorder. Many anorexics suffer from osteoporosis, and bone fractures are common. When the weight loss becomes severe enough, anorexic women cease menstruating (this is called amenorrhoea). Another possible cause is that changes in a young woman's endocrine status alter her metabolism or the neural mechanisms involved in feeding, but because prolonged fasting and the use of laxatives have many effects, interpreting these differences is difficult (Halmi, 1978). Recent neuroimaging research, however, has shed some light on the neurobiological mechanisms of the disorder. Uher *et al.* (2003) reported that women with anorexia who had been successfully tested showed differences in activation in the anterior cingulate and PFC when looking at pictures of food. Wagner *et al.* (2008) went a step further and used fMRI to measure brain activation in 16 women who had recovered from anorexia and 16 controls who tasted sucrose or water. They found reduced activation in the insula, anterior cingulate and striatum in the recovered anorexic group. The pleasantness ratings of the tasters were correlated with brain activation, as Figure 13.7 shows.

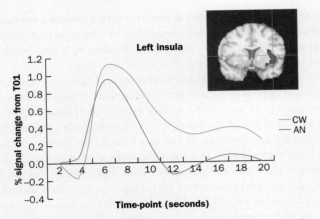

Figure 13.7 Changes in the brain's insula region while recovering anorexic women and healthy women tasted sucrose. Activation was reduced in the recovering group suggesting that this brain region plays a role in the eating disorder.

Source: Reprinted, with permission from Elsevier, from *Physiology and Behaviour*, vol. 94, issue 1, Walter Kaye, 'Neurobiology of anorexia and bulimia nervosa', pages 121–35, copyright 2008.

Sexual behaviour

The motivation to engage in sexual behaviour can be very strong. However, sexual behaviour is not motivated by a physiological need, in the way that eating is. Because we must perform certain behaviours in order to reproduce, the process of natural selection has ensured that our brains are constructed in such a way as to cause enough of us to mate with each other that the species will survive. A survey of the past 20 years has shown that sex differences in sexual behaviour have not changed considerably. In 1993, Oliver and Hyde reported that men engaged in more sexual activity and had more permissive attitudes to sex, especially masturbation and casual sex. In 2010, Peterson and Shibley-Hyde examined 30 sexual behaviours from 834 individual samples and found an almost identical pattern, with men showing more permissive attitudes to most of the variables. Those cultures/ethnic groups with the greater equality between the sexes were more likely to show the smallest differences between the sexes.

Effects of sex hormones on behaviour

Sex hormones – hormones secreted by the testes and ovaries – have effects on cells throughout the body. In general, these effects promote reproduction. For example, they cause the production of sperms, build up the lining of the uterus, trigger ovulation and stimulate the production of milk. Sex hormones also affect nerve cells in the brain, thereby affecting behaviour, but they do not cause behaviours. Behaviours are responses to particular situations and are affected by people's experiences in the past. Sex hormones affect people's motivation to perform particular classes of reproductive behaviours. We therefore start

Eating disorders – An international perspective

It is almost a cliché to say that eating disorders have increased significantly in the past few decades and that this increase is most obvious in young women raised in 'the West'. Like most clichés, however, it is underpinned by a strong element of truth and evidence. Eating disorders are still more common in Western cultures and more common in girls and women than boys and men. According to Prince (1985), the most well-known eating disorder (after obesity) is anorexia nervosa and there is evidence that this disorder may be culture-bound, that is, one limited to culture 'primarily by reason of certain of their psychosocial features'.

In a review of the extent to which anorexia and bulimia nervosa are culture-bound, Keel and Klump (2003) showed that anorexia has been reported in every non-Western region of the world but that bulimia nervosa appears most frequently in Western cultures. Although suggesting that the former may be culture-bound, the authors caution that anorexia is a more widely studied and accepted disorder than is bulimia and the lack of extensive evidence on the prevalence of bulimia may explain its greater appearance in studies of Western participants.

If we humour the study's conclusion, however, and try to explain why the discrepancy should arise, one factor that might be important is the availability of high-sugar, fatty, palatable foods. Binge eating involves eating these foods to excess; there must, therefore, be a ready source of them. The great prevalence of bulimia in the West may, therefore, reflect the fact that more of this food is available. It does not explain, however, why the bingeing occurs in the first place. The authors suggest a possible genetic predisposition to bulimia, citing evidence that the disorder may share genetic transmission with other 'neuroses' such as phobia. This idea may be too general to be valid, however. Why should genetic predisposition to bingeing be transmitted along with genetic predisposition to being afraid of a spider?

our exploration of sexual behaviour with the motivational effects of sex hormones.

Effects of androgens

Androgens such as testosterone are necessary for male sexual development (see Chapter 12). Men tend to have around 1/100000g of testosterone per litre of blood whereas women have a tenth of this (Mazur, 2016). During prenatal development, the testes of male foetuses secrete testosterone, which causes the male sex organs to develop. This hormone also affects the development of the brain. The prenatal effects of sex hormones are called **organisational effects** because they alter the organisation of the sex organs and the brain. Studies using laboratory animals have shown that if the organisational effects of androgens on brain development are prevented, the animal later fails to exhibit male sexual behaviour. In addition, males cannot have an erection and engage in sexual intercourse unless testosterone is present in adulthood. These effects are called **activational effects** because the hormone activates sex organs and brain circuits that have already developed.

J.M. Davidson *et al.* (1979) performed a carefully controlled double-blind study of the activational effects of testosterone on the sexual behaviour of men whose testes failed to secrete normal amounts of androgens. The men were given monthly injections of a placebo or one of two different dosages of a long-lasting form of testosterone. When the men receiving testosterone were compared with the men in the control group, the effect of testosterone on total number of erections and attempts at intercourse during the month following the injection was found to be large and statistically significant, and the larger dosage produced more of an effect than did the smaller dosage. Thus, we may conclude that testosterone definitely affects male sexual performance.

If a man is castrated (has his testes removed, usually because of injury or disease), his sex drive will inevitably decline. Usually, he first loses the ability to ejaculate, and then he loses the ability to achieve an erection (Bermant and Davidson, 1974). But studies have shown that some men lose these abilities soon after castration, whereas others retain at least some level of sexual potency for many months. Injections or pills of testosterone quickly restore potency.

One controversial study published in *PNAS* in 2011 reported that being a father was associated with having less testosterone (Gettler *et al.*, 2011). It received widespread media coverage. Testosterone was measured five years apart. Two hundred and fifty seven men were single and did not become father; 162 married and became fathers and 46 married but did not have children. Testosterone was lowest in the second group but this

reduction was not significantly greater than that seen in married men without children (Mazur, 2016). When Mazur (2013) attempted to replicate the finding in a group of 4,462 Vietnam veterans, he failed to do so.

Effects of progesterone and oestrogen

In most species of mammals, the hormones oestradiol and progesterone have strong effects on female sexual behaviour. The levels of these two sex hormones fluctuate during the menstrual cycle of primates and the oestrus cycle of other female mammals. The difference between these two cycles is primarily that the lining of the primate uterus – but not that of other mammals – builds up during the first part of the cycle and sloughs off at the end. A female mammal of a non-primate species – for example, a laboratory rat – will receive the advances of a male only when the levels of oestradiol and progesterone in her blood are high. This condition occurs around the time of ovulation, when copulation is likely to make her become pregnant. During this time, the female will stand still while the male approaches her. If he attempts to mount her, she will arch her back and move her tail to the side, giving him access to her genitalia. In fact, an oestrus female rat often does not wait for the male to take the initiative; she engages in seductive behaviours such as hopping around and wiggling her ears. These behaviours usually induce sexual activity by the male (McClintock and Adler, 1978).

There is an interesting relationship between oestradiol and power/dominance in women. Women undergraduates showing the highest levels of power motivation are more likely to show higher levels of oestradiol, especially if the women are single and not taking oral contraceptives (Stanton and Edelstein, 2009). There is also evidence that levels of these hormones are associated with alterations in specific psychological functions. For example, women have been found to show better verbal task performance and worse spatial task performance during their luteal phase (Pletzer *et al.*, 2011). Pain is also experienced more strongly during the luteal stage (Choi *et al.*, 2006).

Some of these behavioural changes might be associated with changes in certain brain structures, such as the amygdala, frontal lobe and hippocampus, (Lisofsky *et al.*, 2014). Increases in the left side of two of these structures, for example (the amygdala and hippocampus) has been consistently found during the luteal stage (Lisofsky *et al.*, 2014), as have increases in the right during the follicular stage. Other regions show differential activation in the different stages – more anterior cingulate cortex activation is found during the luteal stage and more superior temporal gyrus activation is observed during the follicular stage (Lisofsky *et al.*, 2014).

Sexual orientation

When people reach puberty, the effects of sex hormones on their maturing bodies and on their brains increase their interest in sexual activity. As sexual interest increases, most people develop a special interest in members of the opposite sex – they develop a heterosexual orientation. Why does opposite-sex attraction occur? And why does same-sex attraction sometimes occur? Research has not yet provided definite answers to these questions, but it has provided some hints.

Homosexual behaviour (engaging in sexual activity with members of the same sex; from the Greek homos, meaning 'the same') is seen in male and female animals of many species. The widespread occurrence of homosexual behaviour means that we should not refer to it as unnatural. However, humans are apparently the only species in which some members regularly exhibit exclusive homosexuality. Other animals, if they are not exclusively heterosexual, are likely to be bisexual, engaging in sexual activity with members of both sexes. In contrast, the number of men and women who describe themselves as exclusively homosexual exceeds the number who describe themselves as bisexual.

Sexual orientation appears to be determined prior to adolescence and prior to homosexual or heterosexual activity and most homosexual men and women have engaged in some heterosexual experiences during childhood and adolescence (Bell et al., 1981). But unlike heterosexuals, they found these experiences unrewarding. The most important single predictor of adult homosexuality was a self-report of homosexual feelings, which usually occurred three years before first genital homosexual activity. This finding suggests that homosexuality is a deep-seated tendency. It also tends to rule out the suggestion that seduction by an older person of the same sex plays an important role in the development of homosexuality.

As the researchers admit, the results of the study are consistent with the hypothesis that homosexuality is at least partly determined by biological factors. That is, biological variables may predispose a child to behaviour that is more typical of the other sex and eventually to sexual arousal by members of their own sex.

Homosexuality and heterosexuality are characterised by specific features – behaviour, appearance and voice – and people can distinguish between heterosexual and homosexual men and women quite well (Tskhay and Rule, 2013; Rule and Alaei, 2016). People are able to judge sexual orientation from video clips lasting 10 seconds (Rule and Alaei, 2016); gay men and straight women sway their hips more and lesbian women and men are more likely to sway the shoulders (Johnson et al.,

2007). Most people believe that gay men lisp, but the evidence for this is not consistent (Mack and Munson, 2012). Some research suggests that gay men have distinctive – more feminine – facial structure than do straight men (Skorska et al., 2015), with shorter noses and smaller nostrils; gay women have thicker mouths and have more of an underbite than do heterosexual women (these features are characteristic of heterosexual men). Gay men and women are better at identifying other gay men and women, as are people who are familiar with gay men and women (Rule et al., 2011).

What might be the biological causes of homosexuality? We can immediately rule out the suggestion that male homosexuals have insufficient levels of testosterone in their blood; male homosexuals have normal levels of testosterone (Tourney, 1980). A more likely cause of male homosexuality is the pattern of exposure of the developing brain to sex hormones, but this research is controversial and early research has not led to much further illumination.

Various laboratories have studied the brains of deceased heterosexual and homosexual men and have found differences in the size of two different subregions of the hypothalamus and in a bundle of axons that connects the right and left temporal lobes (Swaab and Hofman, 1990; LeVay, 1991; Allen and Gorski, 1992). When the connections between the left and right amygdala were examined in heterosexual and homosexual men and women, connections were more widespread from the left amygdala in the homosexual men and heterosexual women (Savic and Lindstrom, 2008) and from the right in homosexual women and heterosexual men. In general, there was a rightward asymmetry in the heterosexual group and a more symmetrical pattern in the homosexual group. We cannot necessarily conclude that any of these regions is directly involved in people's sexual orientation, but the results do suggest that the brains may have been exposed to different patterns of hormones prenatally.

Is there a genetic basis for homosexuality? Bailey and Pillard (1991) studied pairs of male twins in which at least one member identified himself as homosexual. If both twins are homosexual, they are said to be concordant for this trait. If only one is homosexual, the twins are said to be discordant. Thus, if homosexuality has a genetic basis, the percentage of identical twins concordant for homosexuality should be higher than that for fraternal twins. And this is exactly what Bailey and Pillard found; the concordance rate was 52 per cent for identical twins and 22 per cent for fraternal twins. In a subsequent study, Bailey et al. (1993) found evidence that heredity plays a role in female homosexuality, too. The concordance rates for female identical and fraternal twins were 48 per cent and 16 per cent, respectively. The Cutting Edge section takes up these points.

Aggressive behaviour

Aggression is a serious problem for humans: every day, we hear or read about incidents involving violence and cruelty and, undoubtedly, thousands more go unreported. Many factors probably influence a person's tendency to commit acts of aggression, including childhood experiences, peer group pressures, hormones and drugs, and malfunctions of the brain. Various aspects of aggressive behaviour have been studied by zoologists, physiological psychologists, sociologists, social psychologists, political scientists and psychologists who specialise in the learning process.

Ethological studies of aggression

The utility of species-typical behaviours such as sexual activity, parental behaviour, food gathering and nest construction is obvious; we can easily understand their value to survival. But violence and aggression are also seen in many species, including our own. If aggression is harmful, one would not expect it to be so prevalent in nature. Ethologists – zoologists who study the behaviour of animals in their natural environments – have analysed the causes of aggression and have shown that it, too, often has value for the survival of a species.

Intraspecific aggression

Intraspecific aggression involves an attack by one animal upon another member of its species. Ethologists have shown that intraspecific aggression has several biological advantages. First, it tends to disperse a population of animals, forcing some into new territories, where necessary environmental adaptations may increase the flexibility of the species. Secondly, when accompanied by rivalry among males for mating opportunities, intraspecific aggression tends to perpetuate the genes of the healthier, more vigorous animals.

Human cultures, however, are very different even from those of other species of primates. Perhaps intraspecific

---

Cutting edge: What we do and don't know about sexual orientation

A recent issue of *Psychological Science in the Public Interest* sought to summarise the current scientific thinking on the nature of sexual orientation (Bailey *et al.*, 2016). Sexual orientation has been defined as 'relative sexual attraction to men, women or both' (Bailey *et al.*, 2016, p. 45). Most people are attracted to members of a different sex; only around 5 per cent are sexually attracted to members of the same sex. Women are more likely to be bisexual than lesbian, whereas men are more likely to be gay than bisexual.

Many parts of the world have seen an increase in the acceptance of people with different sexual orientation. In the US, in 2015, the Supreme Court mandated that its states permit same-sex marriages (a far cry from the country's attitude in the 60s when homosexuality was illegal and, in the 1980s, when the manual providing diagnostic criteria for mental illness categorised homosexuality as a mental illness). As of July 2016, same-sex marriage has been made legal in Argentina, Belgium, Denmark, France, Ireland, Iceland, Norway, Portugal, South Africa, Sweden, the United Kingdom an many other countries. But not all. Around 75 countries prohibit homosexuality and 11 countries impose the death penalty. In Uganda in 2014, for example, President Yoweri Museveni requested scientific evidence to determine whether sexual orientation was inborn or acquired before he passed the Anti-Homosexuality Act. The Act was passed.

Homosexuality is illegal in Uganda and can lead to 14 years in prison.

In their review, Bailey *et al.* (2016) concluded that we currently know the following regarding sexual orientation:

- Across culture, and regardless of sex, those who develop same-sex relationships are more likely to express gender nonconformity in childhood, regardless of how they are socialised
- People who hold positive views about same-sex relationships are more likely to believe in non-social causes (e.g. genetic, biological) for this orientation
- People who hold negative views are more likely to believe in social causes (e.g. early sexual experiences) for same-sex orientation
- There is no one, fully supported theory of sexual orientation causation
- There is more evidence supporting non-social than social causes – when boys surgically and socially become girls, their sexual orientation remains the same (they are attracted to girls)
- There is weak evidence for the proposition that same-sex orientation is the result of recruitment by homosexual adults, or disordered parenting
- Homosexual attraction tends to occur before homosexual behaviour

▶

Cutting edge: Sexual behaviour and the eyes

As you saw in one of the Cutting Edge sections in Chapter 4, one cue to sexual attraction, beyond the physical characteristics such as an erect penis, blushing to the face and chest, and lubrication in the vagina, may be pupil dilation. When the pupils are dilated, the autonomic nervous system is activated. Sometimes, this dilation is not under conscious control. As a result, it may provide us with an indirect measure of sexual interest that is immediately visible.

Research has found that our pupils dilate when we look at sexual images of people we are attracted to (Rieger and Savin-Williams, 2012) and that the stimuli which cause the greatest dilation are sexual stimuli (Laeng *et al.*, 2012). This change correlates with genital arousal, but the association is much stronger in men than women (Rieger *et al.*, 2014). An indication of sexual interest can also be measured via eye-tracking. Bolmont *et al.* (2014) investigated which parts of a person's body we would fixate on if we were asked to indicate whether we were interested in them romantically or whether the person aroused sexual desire. You can see the results in Figure 13.8.

People were more likely to look at the body than the face and this effect was strongest when people made decisions about sexual desire.

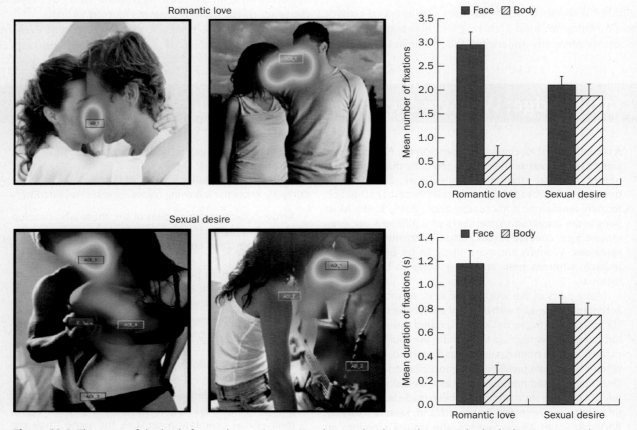

Figure 13.8 The areas of the body focused on, using eye-tracking technology, when people think about romantic love (top row) and sexual desire (bottom row).

aggression has outlived its usefulness for humans and we would benefit by its elimination. Whatever the case may be, we must understand the causes of human aggression in order to eliminate it or direct it to more useful purposes.

Threat and appeasement

Ethologists have discovered a related set of behaviours in many species: ritualised **threat gestures** and **appeasement gestures.** Threat gestures enable an animal to communicate aggressive intent to another before engaging in actual violence. For example, if one dog intrudes on another's territory, the defender will growl and bare its teeth, raise the fur on its back (making it look larger to its opponent), and stare at the intruder. Almost always, the dog defending its territory will drive the intruder away. Threat gestures are particularly important in species whose members are able to kill each other (Lorenz, 1966; Eibl-Eibesfeldt, 1989). For example, wolves often threaten each other with growls and bared teeth but rarely bite each other. Because an all-out battle between two wolves would probably end in the death of one and the serious wounding of the other, the tendency to perform ritualised displays rather than engage in overt aggression has an obvious advantage to the survival of the species.

Aggression shows distinct sex differences. During play, young boys often display more aggression than do young girls (Fabes and Eisenberg, 1992). In an American longitudinal study of elementary and high school students, males were shown to be more aggressive than were females and patterns of aggression were found to be less stable for males than for females (Woodall and Matthews, 1993). However, sex differences in aggression may vary in different cultures. In some cultures and subcultures, girls may join gangs that are involved in aggressive activities. For example, in Chihuahua, Mexico, a girl being initiated into a gang must fist-fight a gang member. Girl gangs often join their 'brother' gangs in defending their turf against other male gangs. Girl gangs also fight other girl gangs, and such fights may involve knife-fighting and rock-throwing as well as fist-fighting.

Words associated with hot temperature may also result in increased aggression and hostility. DeWall and Bushman (2009) exposed participants to words associated with heat, cold or neither and subsequently measured their aggression and hostility to others. They found that people who had been exposed to the hot words (e.g. sunburn, boils, roasted, sweats) showed significantly greater aggressive and hostile thoughts than when exposed to cold or neutral words. There was no difference between cold and neutral words.

Hormones and aggression

In birds and most mammals, androgens appear to exert a strong effect on aggressiveness. Do hormones also influence aggressive behaviour in humans? Men are generally more aggressive than women (Knight *et al.*, 1996) although such differences are attenuated when factors such as provocation are considered (Bettencourt and Miller, 1996). The fact that a man's sexual behaviour depends on the presence of testosterone suggests that this hormone may also influence aggressive behaviour. Some cases of aggressiveness – especially sexual assault – have been treated with drugs that block androgen receptors and thus prevent androgens from exerting their normal effects (Heim and Hursch, 1979; Brain, 1984,

1994). The rationale is based on animal research that indicates that androgens promote both sexual behaviour and aggression in males. However, the efficacy of treatment with anti-androgens has yet to be established conclusively (Mazur and Booth, 1998).

Another way to determine whether androgens affect aggressiveness in humans is to examine the testosterone levels of people who exhibit varying levels of aggressive behaviour in the laboratory and outside the laboratory. Testosterone is secreted into the bloodstream sporadically and so changes in levels can be measured easily. Levels are greatest in the morning and lower in the afternoon (Dabbs, 1990). Clearly, in the laboratory it is unethical (and probably undesirable) to encourage direct aggression, i.e. physical violence. Psychologists, therefore, have developed measures that increase feelings of hostility rather than generate hostility itself (such as being frustrated while playing a game of Cyberball). Most studies report negative results, that is, no relationship between testosterone level and hostility (Mazur and Booth, 1998) but Peterson and Harmon-Jones (2012) found a positive relationship between the expression of anger (and no other emotion) and levels of testosterone in Cyberball players who had been made angry by confederates.

Outside the laboratory, the findings are slightly different. Dabbs *et al.* (1987) measured the testosterone levels of 89 male prison inmates and found a significant correlation between these levels and (1) the violence of the crime, and (2) their fellow prisoners' ratings of their toughness. These effects were also found in female prison inmates. Dabbs *et al.* (1988) found that women prisoners who showed unprovoked violence and had several prior convictions also showed higher levels of testosterone. It is reported that 17–18-year-old criminals with high testosterone levels were more likely to have committed violent crimes and to have violated prison rules (Dabbs *et al.*, 1991). The picture is not entirely uniform, however. One study found no significant difference between the testosterone levels of those individuals charged with violent offences and those charged with property crime (Bain *et al.*, 1987).

In studies of competitive sports, researchers have found that competitors who lose a tennis match or a wrestling competition or a hockey match show a fall in blood levels of testosterone (Mazur and Lamb, 1980; Elias, 1981; Aguilar *et al.*, 2013). In Aguilar *et al.*'s study, they not only found a decrease in testosterone in the losing players but also a rise in cortisol, a hormone known to increase during stress. One study examined the relationship between testosterone levels and the winning of a football match in Portuguese women (Oliveira *et al.*, 2009). The researchers measured testosterone levels before and after a game played by competitors from the Portuguese female soccer league. Winners showed greater testosterone after winning than before the game; there was a similar decline in the losers. In a very elaborate study, Jeffcoate *et al.* (1986) found that the blood levels of a group of five men confined on a boat for 14 days changed as they established a dominance-aggression ranking among themselves: the higher the rank, the higher the testosterone level was. Increases have also been reported in individuals about to play a chess match, with greater increases found in winners than losers after the match (Mazur *et al.*, 1992), and in Brazilian supporters who saw their team on television win the 1994 World Cup Final against Italy; the (losing) Italian viewers showed relatively lower levels (Fielden *et al.*, 1994, cited in Mazur and Booth, 1998). One study even suggested that adopting a power pose increased levels of testosterone (and financial risk-taking and feelings of power) (Carney *et al.*, 2010), although a replication with a larger sample (four times the size) found that posing affected feelings of power but had no effect on testosterone level (Ranehill *et al.*, 2015).

Testosterone and dominance

What could account for the relationship between testosterone and aggression? Mazur and Booth (1998) have proposed that a reciprocal relationship exists between these two factors. Specifically, high levels of testosterone encourage dominant behaviour which maintains high status. The model is reciprocal because testosterone and dominance are seen as reinforcing each other in contrast to the basal model which suggests that the individual has a static, basal level of testosterone which routinely predicts his behaviour. These authors suggest that reciprocal relationships can obviously only be observed across time and at different testing points. They point to a study in which testosterone levels in American Air Force veterans were low during marriage but increased during divorce as evidence for their model (Mazur and Michalek, 1998). The authors interpreted this finding in terms of competition. Divorce is a stressful, but competitive, process. Marriage, on the other hand, is a positive experience, free of competition and – if successful – stress.

The way in which women view themselves is directly related to the degree of testosterone they secrete (Grant and France, 2001). Women with higher levels of testosterone used more 'dominant' adjectives to describe themselves than do those with lower levels, providing additional evidence for a link between testosterone and dominance. There is also an unusual link between testosterone and communication. Pennebaker *et al.* (2004) correlated testosterone level with natural written language in two people who were undergoing testosterone therapy for the development of upper body strength (male) or as part of a transgender procedure (female). The longer the time since the last testosterone injection, the fewer words describing social relations were used in the participants' text.

People showing comparatively high and low levels of testosterone also tend to react differently in simple social settings, suggesting that the hormone plays some part in assertiveness (Dabbs *et al.*, 2001). Dabbs *et al.* found that participants with low testosterone looked around a room more when entering (to the left and the exit) and focused less frequently on a camera present than did high-testosterone participants. People with high testosterone levels who feel that their status is threatened, try to regain this quickly – usually through physical challenge. Researchers have also begun to examine the mismatch effect – where people normally low in testosterone are placed in positions of great status. In one experiment, researchers placed high and low testosterone students in high and low status positions – making sure they completed a short or long version of a spatial intelligence test accurately (Josephs *et al.*, 2006). Those who completed the task first would put their hand up and say 'done' thus signalling status: they were intellectually superior.

Low testosterone individuals were more emotionally aroused, focused more on their status and performed worse on the test if they were in the high status position. The same pattern was seen in the high testosterone individuals only when they were in the low status position, thus demonstrating the mismatch effect. The same effect for emotional arousal and poor cognition was replicated in a separate experiment with a different type of cognitive test (mathematics) and when heart rate was measured. In a final experiment, the researchers found that levels of testosterone were better predictors of dominance than were self-report measures such as questionnaires.

Having a high level of testosterone has also been associated with lack of empathy, although whether it causes this lack of empathy or whether it is only correlated with it is open to question. To test this hypothesis, Hermans *et al.* (2006) administered testosterone to 20 healthy women whose facial muscles were recorded while they observed happy and angry faces. Empathy was measured by participants' mimicry of others' facial expression of emotions. Testosterone was found to be associated with a decrease in facial mimicry, suggesting that the hormone has a role in empathy.

Mazur (2016) has proposed a 'dual hormone hypothesis'. This argues that testosterone is only associated with dominance or leadership when another hormone, cortisol, is low. You'll learn more about cortisol in Chapter 17. It increases in the body when we experience stress. Both conditions need to exist: high testosterone and low cortisol. If cortisol is low, the lack of stress may embolden high-testosterone individuals to be more assertive and dominant. The evidence is currently mixed: Mazur and Booth (2014), for example, have found no relationship between low cortisol and dominant behaviour in a large group of Vietnam veterans.

Emotion

Most psychologists who have studied emotion have focused on one or more of the following questions: What kinds of situations produce emotions? What kinds of feelings do people say they experience? What kinds of behaviours do people engage in?

Psychology in action: Aggression at work

Sometimes, work isn't as pleasant as it should be. You turn up to work in a bad mood: it's raining, you overslept, you had too many bill reminders in the post, your train was half an hour late (for which you are told off), the ticket assistant was rude to you, your boss appears to be irritated with you and all morning you've had the most annoying customers in the world on the phone or at your cash desk. These slings and arrows may make you wonder why you're doing the job you're doing. These quotidian irritations pale into insignificance, however, compared to real workplace troubles – assault and murder.

Aggression in the workplace has been studied for some years, and was pioneered in Europe by research in Scandinavia, but we still know too little about how to prevent it. Or, perhaps more pertinently, employers still do too little to put what we know about it into practice.

Workplace aggression refers to psychological acts (such as shouting) and physical assault that can harm another or cause offence in the workplace (Dupre and Barling, 2003). One researcher has specifically characterised workplace aggression as involving either expressions of hostility (which can be verbal or non-verbal, such as giving someone the 'silent treatment'); acts of obstruction (deliberately hampering a person's ability to do their job); and overt physical aggression (Baron *et al.*, 1999).

The chances of your being verbally or physically assaulted by a work colleague, however, are comparatively rare. In fact, most aggression in the workplace is committed by members of the public (customers) or people outside the company. In 1997, 866 Americans were murdered at work; 85 per cent of these murders were committed by outsiders (US Bureau of Labor Statistics, 1998). A study of eight Californian cities found that 90 per cent of non-fatal assaults were caused by non-workmates (Peek-Asa *et al.*, 2001).

In a review, LeBlanc and Barling (2004) highlighted some of the causes of workplace aggression (and, therefore, how aggression could be reduced). LeBlanc and Barling have identfied four types of aggression. Type I aggression involves an assailant that is not remotely related to the victim (those most at risk are people who handle money with members of the public). Type II aggression involves an assailant who has a legitimate relationship with the organisation (e.g. a customer). Type III aggression involves an offence where the aggressor is a current or former employee of the company or organisation. The fourth type involves aggression by a current employee against another.

So, what predicts workplace aggression? Several factors appear to be involved. Being under surveillance, for example, increases aggression towards an employee's supervisor but not colleagues (Greenberg and Barling, 1999).

The two most important predictors, however, are alcohol consumption and perceived organisational injustice. Organisational injustice refers to perceived wrongdoing or unfairness by the company and/or supervisors. These two factors have been found to predict aggression against colleagues and subordinates. Excessive drinking can also interact with job insecurity to produce aggression towards colleagues: those who don't feel secure in their job and drink excessively are more likely to be aggressive than heavy drinking people who are more secure in their job. These feelings of insecurity and aggression increase if people feel they are being mistreated (Jockin *et al.*, 2001).

A sense of justice is important to every employee. We expect to be treated with politeness, dignity and respect. Supervisors who are perceived as abusive were likely to see their employees quit. But those who remain, and still felt that they were being abused, were likely to be less satisfied with life and would experience more psychological distress and conflicts between work and family (Tepper, 2000). These are the people likely to show less job commitment and satisfaction. Those who felt they could find other jobs felt better. Employers, managers or bosses who are bullies tend to behave much more badly if they are also incompetent; in fact, they bully because they feel incompetent (Fast and Chen, 2009), which is no relief to the competent and conscientious employee. Of course, in such a circumstance, one would expect a conscientious and intelligent employer to step in and stop the bullying. Not to do so is simply another form of bullying.

The conclusion from the studies reviewed by LeBlanc and Barling (2004) seems clear. A happy workforce is one where supervisors are not over-controlling, where decision-making is transparent, where employees' views are respected and addressed (not simply acknowledged and disregarded), where people are not prevented from doing their job properly and where individuals are appropriately rewarded for their efforts. It all seems quite simple, doesn't it?

What physiological changes do people undergo in situations that produce strong emotions? What exactly is an emotion?

The word 'emotion' comes from Latin and means 'to move' or 'to stir up'. In general terms, **emotion** is used by psychologists to refer to a display of feelings that are evoked when important things happen to us. Emotions are relatively brief and occur in response to events having motivational relevance (or to their mental re-creation, as when we remember something embarrassing that we did in the past and experience the feelings of embarrassment again). Emotions are the consequence of events that motivate us. When we encounter reinforcing or punishing stimuli, stimuli that motivate us to act, we express and experience positive or negative emotions. The nature of the emotions depends on the nature of the stimuli and on our prior experience with them. Emotions are different to moods. Whereas emotions are brief and evoked by specific events, moods are longer lasting and not attributable to a specific, identifiable event or stimulus (Diener *et al.*, 2014).

There are problems, however, associated with defining emotions. We have a multitude of ways of expressing what we think are emotional behaviours. Davitz (1970), for example, found 556 words and phrases that were emotion-related.

Some psychologists view emotion as being produced by reinforcing stimuli or by a set of interacting brain regions or by our awareness of bodily feelings. Given the disparate nature of these definitions, LeDoux (1995b) was right when he concluded that emotion had 'proved to be a slippery concept for both psychologists and neuroscientists'.

If the definition is unclear, then perhaps we can agree on examples of emotions and can describe a core set of basic, fundamental emotions. Yet, even here, the evidence is ambiguous. There are psychologists who have argued that a set of basic emotions exists (Ekman, 1973; Izard, 1977, 1992; Plutchik, 1980). The number of basic emotions has ranged from six or seven (Ekman, 1984, 1992) to eight (Plutchik, 1980), to ten (Izard, 1992). To Ekman, the basic emotions are sadness, joy (happiness), surprise, fear, anger, disgust and contempt (or fear), and these can be universally seen in facial expression (see Figure 13.9).

To Plutchik, the basic emotions are fear/terror, anger/rage, joy/ecstasy, sadness/grief, acceptance/trust, disgust/loathing, expectancy/anticipation and surprise/astonishment. There are other psychologists who have argued that because we have no satisfactory criteria on which to base any concept of 'basicness' then we cannot conclude that any emotions we care to list are basic ones (Ortony and Turner, 1990). Yet others argue that the methods used to determine basic emotions are flawed and that the findings are not wholly conclusive (Russell, 1994; cf. Ekman, 1994). What, therefore, is the evidence for basic emotions?

Basic emotions

Charles Darwin (1872) suggested that human expressions of emotion have evolved from similar expressions in other animals. He said that emotional expressions are innate, unlearned responses consisting of a complex set of movements, principally of the facial muscles. Thus, a man's sneer and a wolf's snarl are biologically determined response patterns, both controlled by innate brain mechanisms, just as coughing and sneezing are. Some of these movements resemble the behaviours themselves and may have evolved from them. For example, a snarl shows one's teeth and can be seen as an anticipation of biting.

Darwin performed what was probably the first cross-cultural study of behaviour. He obtained evidence for his conclusion that emotional expressions were innate by observing his own children and by corresponding with people living in various isolated cultures around the world. He reasoned that if people all over the world, no matter how isolated, show the

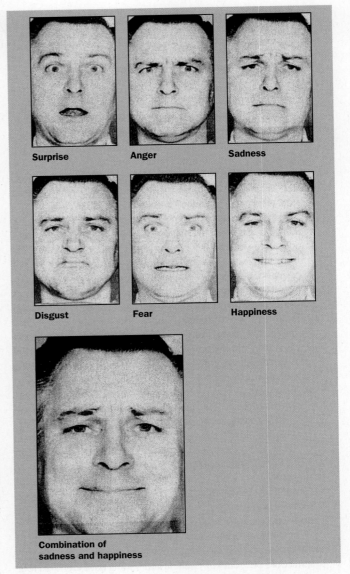

Figure 13.9 The six basic emotions shown in facial expression, and a combination of two, as suggested by Ekman.
Source: Paul Ekman Group, LLC.

same facial expressions of emotion, these expressions must be inherited instead of learned. The logical argument goes like this. When groups of people are isolated for many years, they develop different languages. Thus, we can say that the words that people use are arbitrary; there is no biological basis for using particular words to represent particular concepts. However, if facial expressions are inherited, they should take approximately the same form in people from all cultures, despite their isolation from one another. And Darwin did, indeed, find that people in different cultures used the same patterns of movement of facial muscles to express a particular emotional state.

Of the basic emotions that we experience most often, it has been argued that sadness and happiness are the two most common. But what of other potential, basic emotions, such as jealousy? Why are they not referred to as basic? Jealousy is included in neither Ekman's nor Plutchik's list of basic emotions. It does not have a universal facial expression and is not rapid, like basic emotions. Plutchik's criteria for basicness include: being present in non-human species, appearing universally in human culture and helping organisms solve adaptation-related survival problems. In Ekman's taxonomy, jealousy would be considered a 'blended' emotion – a combination of other basic emotions (Buss, 2013).

The consequences of jealousy, however, are significant. It can lead to physical harm and, sometimes, death. Partners of jealous others may feel psychologically and physically terrorised. Jealousy is thought to be the leading cause of physical abuse in relationships and the leading cause of murder of girlfriends, ex-girlfriends, wives and ex-wives (Buss, 2013). Two behaviours can lead to the murderous jealousy – the man discovers that his partner has had sex with another man, or the woman leaves the man for another. Women can also express violent jealousy but the degree is not as great as that seen in men.

Buss (2014) also takes issue with one of Plutchik's criteria – the emphasis on survival. Buss argues that evolution is better predicted by reproductive success, rather than survival success – whether we mate or not. In this context, jealousy does become an important emotion, possibly a basic emotion, because it evolved to reduce infidelity, reduce the possibility of a partner leaving a relationship and reduce the likelihood of mate-poaching.

What is the key to enduring happiness?

In 2011, the UK government decided to measure happiness in its population. The items chosen to do appear in Table 13.1.

Freud, in one of his more perspicacious moments, once remarked that our common mental state is unhappiness. This we punctuate with attempts, of varying success, at relieving it. The American Declaration of Independence accords the right to all American citizens the 'pursuit of happiness'. The intuitive psychology behind this Right, and a former UK Prime Minister's preoccupation with the nation's mood, seems to be the belief that we all deserve happiness and should pursue it

---

Table 13.1 Office of National Statistics Happiness Survey questions

- Are you satisfied with life?
- Are you satisfied with your husband, wife or partner?
- How satisfied are you with your mental and physical health?
- Are you happy in your job?
- Do you feel involved in your neighbourhood?
- Are you happy with your personal income?
- Are you satisfied with your education?

---

without hindrance. This, however, is easier said than done. Research shows that lottery winners have a short-term boost in well-being but no significant long-term increase in happiness. That said, the famous North American Nun study (a longitudinal study of ageing and Alzheimer's disease in nuns from the School Sisters of Notre Dame) found an association between positive thoughts expressed in handwritten diaries and longer living (Danner et al., 2001).

Various international surveys of happiness – such as Value Surveys, the World Database of happiness (yes, such a thing exists) and the Spring 2007 Eurobarometer (yes, that exists, too) – show that happiness has risen in recent years (in 87 per cent of countries over 17 years) especially in countries such as India, Mexico, Puerto Rico and South Korea (Inglehart et al., 2010). It has remained flat in the US, Switzerland and Norway, presumably because their happiness levels were already quite high. The 2007 European survey found that happiness rose in 23 of the 24 countries studied since 1999. Economics appears to have little long-term impact. If there is rising prosperity or a period of economic decline, there is a period of readjustment and happiness levels return to normal (Kahneman et al., 2004).

Zelenski and Larsen (2000) found that positive emotions are the ones we experience most frequently during the day. For three times a day over the course of a month, their 82 undergraduates reported the degree of various emotions that they experienced. The researchers found that positive emotions dominated the participants' self-reports. The intensity and frequency of positive emotions far outnumbered negative emotions. The researchers also found that some emotions were frequently experienced together. Examples included fear and sadness, sadness and anger, and anger and disgust. Jealousy was the most commonly experienced secondary emotion.

Would people who outwardly express positive emotions also show high degrees of positive affect in their 'inner' life? To try to answer this question, Harker and Keltner (2001) took the unusual step of taking photographs of women printed in their college yearbook and relating the degree of affect expressed in their faces to personality later in life. Ratings of the women's disposition was also obtained from independent observers.

High degrees of positive affect expressed in the photographs correlated with self-reported traits of affiliation, competence and low negative affect. Positive facial expression was also positively correlated with having a good marriage and enhanced well-being, up to 30 years after the photograph was taken. When observers rated the personalities of the women based only on information provided by the yearbook photographs, women showing positive affect were judged more positively. These were the women with whom observers expected to have more rewarding exchanges.

The researchers admit that the measure of positive emotional expression was very limited. They say that 'it is hard to think of a thinner slice of behaviour'. They also concede that the study focused on women exclusively.

The results of the study, however, are consistent with another showing that very happy people are likely to have stronger social and romantic relations than their less happy counterparts. Diener and Seligman (2002) screened 222 undergraduates for self-reported happiness and compared the 10 per cent who scored most highly on happiness and well-being measures ($N = 22$) with a sample of those who scored in the average range ($N = 60$) or below-average ($N = 24$). Comparison measures included personality, social relations, romantic relations, exercise and psychopathology.

Very happy people were found to have a rich social life and to spend less time alone than did the moderately happy people. They had stronger romantic and social relationships than did the less happy groups and were more extraverted, agreeable and less neurotic. Unhappy people's social relations were worse than moderately happy people's. The very happy people did not experience a greater number of objectively defined good events in their lives than did the other groups but no one factor was sufficient for happiness, that is, there was no one factor which was common to all very happy people. Even the very happy people were not consistently happy – they occasionally experienced negative moods. A study of smiling and longevity by a group of American researchers, has found that baseball players who smiled in their baseball register photographs lived significantly longer than did players who did not smile (Abel and Kruger, 2010).

Sheldon and Houser-Marko (2001) sought to see whether people who pursued and attained happiness actually sustained this sense of happiness. They found that students who were self-concordant, that is, set goals that were personally meaningful, were more likely to achieve their goals. Greater attainment in semester 1 predicted increased feelings of self-concordance in semester 2. Those most likely to achieve their goals in semester 2 showed best adjustment and sense of growth at the end of the study. They were also likely to have a higher average mark across all courses, even though the goals may not have been specifically class-related.

The experimenters suggest that the new level of well-being brought about by goal attainment may extend to further semesters, and studies are needed to answer this question and to see whether older students show the same pattern of achievement as their younger counterparts. People who surround themselves with happy people who are central to their social network are more likely to be happy in future (Fowler and Christakis, 2009). In the study, 4,739 individuals were studied from 1983 to 2003.

The secret to generating happiness, however, remains elusive. As Diener and Seligman (2002) conclude: 'There appears to be no single key to high happiness that automatically produces this state . . . High happiness seems to be like beautiful symphonic music – necessitating many instruments, without any one being sufficient for the beautiful quality.'

The neural basis of emotion

Perhaps one way of determining whether an emotion is basic is to observe the neural machinery activated by basic emotions. If these emotions are distinct then it follows that different brain regions or pathways might mediate them. Current

---

Controversies in psychological science: Are conservatives happier than liberals?

The issue

Once upon a time (in the 50s to be precise), to be conservative was to be portrayed as fearful and threatened by uncertainty and novelty (Adorno *et al.*, 1950). That, however, was then. Psychological research in recent years has suggested that far from being timorous and fearful, conservatives tend to be happier than their ideological opposites and that their life satisfaction is also higher (Jetten *et al.*, 1997; Onraet *et al.*, 2013; Bixter, 2015).

The evidence

Most of these studies, however, were conducted with participants from the US and in a specific period – the 1990s to 2000s (Stavrova and Luhmann, 2016). Does the same happiness gap exist in people not from the US? In two studies, Stavrova and Luhmann (2016) attempted to discover an answer by examining the responses of a large cohort of US nationals and individuals from outside the US. They also wanted to discover a possible reason for this happiness gap. Could, for example, conservative people express greater happiness when the environment in which they lived was compatible with their ideology? That is, they are happier if they live and work in an environment where individuals share their ideological outlook, a phenomenon called person–culture fit. We know, for example, that people are happier at work and are more committed and satisfied if their values match those of the people they work with (Brown *et al.*, 2005) but that people are unhappier if their ideological views clash with those of the community in which they live (Motyl *et al.*, 2014).

▶

Controversies in psychological science: *Continued*

In the first study, Stavrova and Luhmann (2016) used data from the US General Social Survey, a survey of North Americans' values and attitudes which has been conducted since 1972. They used waves from 1974 and 2014. Happiness in the survey was measured by asking people: 'Would you say that you are very happy, pretty happy or not too happy?'. Ideology was measured using a 7-point scale with extremely liberal at one end and extremely conservative at the other.

In a study of 48,000 individuals, they found that 1975 was the most liberal year and 2014 the most conservative. More importantly, they found a significant association between ideology and happiness that was unaffected by respondents' age, sex or social inequality: people describing themselves as conservatives reported greater happiness. However, this relationship was moderated by another interesting factor. The relationship was stronger in those years when more people described themselves as conservative and reduced considerably in more liberal years, which is consistent with the person–culture fit hypothesis.

In their second study, the researchers examined data from the World Values Survey, which asks respondents from over 90 countries questions about their values and attitudes. It has been administered since 1981, when the sample of countries was just 18. The researchers examined data from 1981 to 2014. The total sample was 238,449 individuals from 92 countries. Happiness was measured by asking the question: 'Would you say you are not at all happy. . . [to]. . . very happy?' where not at all happy was given a score of 1 and very happy a score of 4. Participants were also asked to indicate how satisfied they were with life. Ideology was measured on a 10-point scale by asking people whether they found themselves on the left (1) or the right (10).

Conservative ideology was found to vary among countries – it was lowest in Zimbabwe and highest in Vietnam. Conservative ideology was significantly related to life satisfaction: those regarding themselves as being on the right expressed greater life satisfaction. The authors did not report the happiness data. A similar pattern to that seen in the US sample emerged: satisfaction was highest when the context was more conservative. In liberal contexts, the gap reversed: liberals were more satisfied than were conservatives, but only in 5 of the 92 countries.

Conclusion

One reason for the happiness gap might be that in most of these societies, a conservative ideology prevails and that this prevalence is only sporadically shifted. If the dominant, prevailing ideology is conservative, conservatives will be happier than liberals because they live around and share a community with like-minded people. One argument states that conservatives believe that 'people get what they deserve' and so any prevailing concern or anxiety about social inequality can be justified. Liberals, on the other hand, express unhappiness at social inequality (Schlenker et al., 2013) although they are more likely to smile in photographs and use more positive words in writing (Wojcik et al., 2015).

Emotion – An international perspective

In the late 1960s, Ekman and Friesen undertook a series of cross-cultural observations that validated those of Darwin (Ekman *et al.*, 1972). They visited an isolated tribe in a remote area of New Guinea – the South Fore tribe, a group of 319 adults and children who had never been exposed to Western culture. If they were able to identify accurately the emotional expressions of Westerners as well as they could identify those of members of their own tribe, and if their own facial expressions were the same as those of Westerners, then the researchers could conclude that these expressions were not culturally determined.

Because translations of single words from one language to another are not always accurate, Ekman and Friesen told little stories to describe an emotion instead of presenting a single word. They told the story to a subject, presented three photographs of Westerners depicting three different emotions, and asked the subject to choose the appropriate one. This they were able to do. In a second study, Ekman and Friesen asked Fore tribespeople to imagine how they would feel in situations that would produce various emotions, and the researchers videotaped their facial expressions. They showed photographs of the videotapes to American college students, who had no trouble identifying the emotions. Four of them are shown in Figure 13.10. The caption describes the story that was used to elicit each expression. Table 13.2 shows the degree of accuracy of various cultures at recognising facial expressions of emotion.

A new study from the UK and the US has extended the work on facial expression to vocal expression. Sauter *et al.* (2010) compared Western participants with a group of people from Himba settlements in North Namibia, a remote area where the indigenous population is culturally isolated. Participants were

Emotion – *Continued*

Figure 13.10 Portraying emotions. Ekman and Friesen asked South Fore tribesmen to make faces (shown in the photographs) when they were told stories. **(a)** Your friend has come and you are happy. **(b)** Your child has died. **(c)** You are angry and about to fight. **(d)** You see a dead pig that has been lying there a long time.
Source: © Paul Ekman Group, LLC.

Table 13.2 Cross-cultural accuracy (%) in recognising of emotion

Expression	US	Chile	Brazil	Argentina	Japan
Happiness	97	90	92	94	87
Fear	88	78	77	68	71
Disgust	84	85	86	79	82
Anger	68	76	82	72	63
Surprise	91	88	81	93	87
Sadness	87	91	82	88	80
Average	86	85	83	82	78

Source: Adapted from: Elfenbein, H.A. and Ambady, N. (2003) Universals in cultural differences in recognising emotions. *Current Directions in Psychological Science*, 12(5), 159–64.

told a story in which an emotion was expressed (sadness at the death of a loved one, for example) and were then presented with two vocalisations – one representing the emotion of the story, the other unrelated. Their task was to identify the most appropriate emotion.

There was significant evidence for the universality of the basic emotions – anger, disgust, fear and so on. Both groups were able to correctly identify these emotions as being appropriate. Voices that reflected other, non-basic emotions, however, were not universally recognised. These included achievement, relief and sensual pleasure.

Not all psychologists have agreed with Ekman's conclusions. While the finding that facial expressions can be identified cross-culturally is robust, there is little agreement on what these findings mean. Zajonc (1985), for example, has suggested that facial expressions are epiphenomena – not important of

themselves and, in fact, serving another purpose, such as conveying social information. Critics such as Fridlund (1992, 1994) have argued that all facial expressions are communicative and that to single out a group of emotional facial expressions ignores the fundamental social nature of facial expression. Expressions may not be emotional signals but social tools used for communications: we can communicate happiness or approval via a smile but this smile may not be generated by genuine emotion but by social cues or needs. This objection is difficult, in part, to counter because expressions may sometimes be used for non-emotional purposes. Smiling may indeed be an expression of joy, but it can also be an expression of sarcasm or even, in sinister contexts, threat. What critics suggest is that facial expressions do not reflect the emotion but the social signalling of the emotion; the two are different.

Other critics have even questioned whether the cross-cultural findings are robust. Russell (1994) has argued in some detail that the faults in the methodology in these experiments, particularly the method of presenting each emotion sequentially and asking respondents to choose from a list of alternative descriptions the expression they have seen, make the conclusions of these studies uninterpretable. More recent research avoids these pitfalls and introduces a broader range of measures.

For example, Gendron *et al.* (2014a) investigated emotional perception in the Himba cultural group in remote regions of Namibia by asking them to label the emotion expressed by vocalisations and to match the vocalisation to an emotion. In the latter, participants had to decide which of two vocalisations matched the emotion conveyed by a brief story. Sauter *et al.* (2010) had previously demonstrated evidence of correct emotion matching in this sample. However, Gendron *et al.* found that whereas there was almost universality in the valence of emotion chosen (positive vs negative), there was much less

▷

Emotion – *Continued*

agreement on the specific emotion categories (e.g. fear or anger). The same group found that the Himba were able to assign the correct valence but not discrete emotions to posed facial expressions (Gendron *et al.*, 2014b). It also found that Sauter *et al.* had trained their participants to select appropriate emotions in their study – that is, they could only proceed to the next experiment if they were able to categorise the study according to Western emotion labels.

The notion that there may also be an in-group advantage for recognising emotions has been challenged (Beaupre and Hess, 2005). These Canadian researchers measured emotional recognition in a sample of French-Canadian, sub-Saharan Africans and Chinese participants living in Canada. All samples performed similarly when asked to recognise expressions of emotion in the in-group and out-group faces but some groups were better at this task in general (regardless of the nationality of the face). The French-Canadians recognised sadness more accurately than did the other two cultures and recognised shame more accurately than did the Chinese. The authors argue that because the stimuli used in the experiment derive from North American investigations, this benefited the French-Canadians and might explain their accuracy.

Cutting edge: What do emotion researchers agree on?

In 1994, Paul Ekman and Richard Davidson asked 24 researchers in the field of emotion to say what they agreed on in terms of our understanding of emotion. Then, there was little agreement on which emotions were considered to be universal and whether moods differed from emotion. Do current emotion researchers still disagree?

Ekman (2016) asked 248 emotion scientists, who researched and published in emotion, to answer 15 questions about what they considered to be true and established facts in emotion research. Sixty percent of the sample responded. This is what Ekman found:

- 88 per cent agreed that there was evidence for universals in emotion
- 80 per cent agreed that there were facial or vocal universals in emotion
- 66 per cent agreed that there were universals in the types of events that trigger an emotion
- 49 per cent stated that research supported the notion that discrete emotions existed
- 11 per cent held the view that emotions were socially constructed
- 18 per cent considered dimensions such as approach-avoidance and positive-negative to constitute what was basic about basic emotions (an approach taken by Wundt and Plutchik)
- 16 per cent considered discrete responses to constitute what was basic about basic emotions (an approach taken by Darwin and Ekman)

- 55 per cent considered both of these to constitute what was basic about basic emotions
- 91 per cent considered anger to be an empirically established emotion
- 90 per cent considered fear to be an empirically established emotion
- 86 per cent considered disgust to be an empirically established emotion
- 80 per cent considered sadness to be an empirically established emotion
- 76 per cent considered happiness to be an empirically established emotion
- 40–50 per cent considered shame, surprise and embarrassment to be empirically established emotions

Other emotions considered to be empirically established were: guilt (37 per cent), contempt (34 per cent), love (32 per cent), awe (31 per cent), pain (28 per cent), envy (28 per cent), compassion (20 per cent), pride (9 per cent) and gratitude (6 per cent)

In the 20 or so years since the previous survey, it is clear that emotion researchers now are in much greater agreement about what constitutes the basic knowledge and tenets in their field than were researchers in the early 1990s. This shift is probably attributable to the vast amount of research that has been undertaken and published since then – as well as the creation of journals specifically publishing emotion research – which has helped provide a body of common, empirically supported knowledge.

research has focused on patterns of activation in the brain that distinguish between emotion states or valence (Saarimaki *et al.*, 2015). Valence describes the quality of an emotion – whether negative or positive. There are some regions and structures that appear more involved in emotional expression and experience, and recognition, than others. These include the orbitofrontal cortex, the amygdala, the insula, the anterior cingulate cortex and the connections between these regions and the brainstem and hypothalamus. Saarimaki *et al.* induced the six basic emotions by asking participants to watch films or imagine stimuli which evoked these emotions. They found that brain activation in specific areas – the medial and inferior lateral prefrontal cortex, the precentral and postcentral gyri, precuneus and posterior cingulate cortex – distinguished between the six. The results are illustrated in Figure 13.11.

A meta-analysis of the neuroimaging literature on the experience of positive and negative affect – but excluding studies of reward and loss – examined 397 different fMRI and PET studies (Lindquist *et al.*, 2015). The researchers wanted to discover whether there were different regions of the brain which responded during positive experience than during the experience of negative emotion, or whether there were valence-general regions which responded regardless of negative and positive affect. It found that, rather than the brain having valence-specific regions, it has valence-general regions that responded to both types of affect. These were found in the limbic and paralimbic regions.

In animal research, much of the work on understanding the neural correlates of emotion has focused on fear because this emotion is easy to condition in the laboratory. Evidence from animal work, studies of brain-damaged humans and from neuroimaging suggests that the amygdala is an important structure for the recognition and expression of fear but that it might have a more general role in sensitivity to threat and reward rather than a specific role in specific emotions.

Emotional responses contain four components: behavioural, autonomic, hormonal and neural. The behavioural component consists of muscular movements that are appropriate to the situation that elicits them. For example, a dog defending its territory against an intruder first adopts an aggressive posture, growls and shows its teeth. If the intruder does not leave, the defender runs towards it and attacks. Autonomic responses – that is, changes in the activity of the autonomic nervous system (ANS) – facilitate these behaviours and provide quick mobilisation of energy for vigorous movement. As a consequence, the dog's heart rate increases, and changes in the size of blood vessels shunt the circulation of blood away from the digestive organs towards the muscles. Hormonal responses reinforce the autonomic responses. The hormones secreted by the adrenal glands further increase heart rate and blood flow to the muscles and also make more glucose available to them.

One of the more important neurotransmitters for emotion is dopamine. When we experience even a slight lift in our mood – or positive affect – the increase is accompanied by an

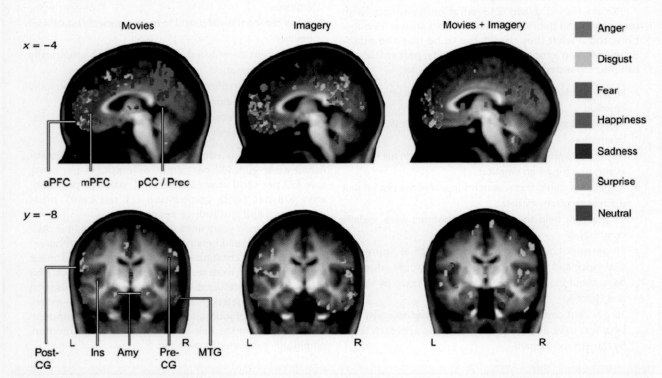

Figure 13.11 Areas of the brain showing activation when people watched movies designed to elicit specific memories or imagined these emotions.

increase in dopamine in two of the major pathways that send dopamine projections to the brain. This does not mean to say that no dopamine was being carried along these pathways in the first place – there are levels of dopamine in the brain, even at rest – but it does mean that a change in behaviour resulted in an increase in these levels.

Emotional responses, like all other responses, can be modified by experience. For example, we can learn that a particular situation is dangerous or threatening. Once the learning has taken place, we will become frightened when we encounter that situation. This type of response, acquired through the process of classical conditioning, is called a conditioned emotional response. A conditioned emotional response is produced by a neutral stimulus that has been paired with an emotion-producing stimulus. If an organism learns to make a specific response that avoids contact with the aversive stimulus (or at least minimises its painful effect), most of the non-specific 'emotional' responses will eventually disappear. That is, if the organism learns a successful coping response – a response that terminates, avoids or minimises an aversive stimulus – the emotional responses will no longer occur.

The amygdala

The amygdala, as you saw in Chapter 4, plays an important role in the expression of conditioned emotional responses. According to Aggleton and Mishkin (1986), it represents 'the sensory gateway to the emotions'. It serves as a focal point between sensory systems and the systems responsible for behavioural, autonomic and hormonal components of conditioned emotional responses (Kapp *et al.*, 1982; LeDoux, 1995a). It comprises a number of different regions/collections of nuclei. It sends projections to the medial temporal lobe, striatum and brainstem and has reciprocal connections with others (Paz and Pare, 2013). Meta-analyses show that blood flow to the amygdala increases during tasks which manipulate states of fear (Kragar and Labar, 2016) but that the structure is involved in behaviour beyond fear and emotion such as arousal and valence, and the detection of personally salient and meaningful stimuli.

Many studies have found that damage to the amygdala disrupts the behavioural, autonomic and hormonal components of conditioned emotional responses. After this region has been destroyed, animals no longer show signs of fear when confronted with stimuli that have been paired with aversive events (LeDoux, 1995a, 1996). LeDoux and his group have identified two routes by which conditioning to fear can occur. The first is a direct – fast and dirty – route linking the thalamus to the amygdala and a second, slower route which links the two via the visual or auditory cortex (depending on the type of stimulus). The first carries the emotional content of the conditioning; the second carries the sensory content.

Take a look at Figure 13.12 to see how this system would operate when a person sees a snake. The amygdala has reciprocal connections with the prefrontal lobe and this reciprocity may

be important in the context of emotion because the activity of the PFC may act as a break on the feedback provided by the amygdala. The amygdala also sends projections to memory areas, such as the hippocampus, and to the basal ganglia and hypothalamus, as well as olfactory areas (Morrison and Salzman, 2010).

The role of the amygdala in human emotion

The effects seen in animals are mirrored in humans. Individuals with damage to the amygdala are unable to recognise fear in facial expressions, are unable to draw a fearful expression (although they can draw other emotional expressions) and are impaired at recognising fear by sound (Adolphs *et al.*, 1994, 1995, 1999; Calder *et al.*, 1996; Scott *et al.*, 1997; Brooks *et al.*, 1998).

Neuroimaging data suggest that the amygdala is relatively more involved than other brain regions in the perception of fear-related material. Morris *et al.* (1996) reported that not only did activation increase in the left side of the amygdala when individuals were watching fearful facial expressions but they also found that this activation was greater when the facial expression was more intense. Other fMRI and PET studies have confirmed this activation in the amygdala during the perception of fear in facial expression (Morris *et al.*, 1998), and in the perception of sad expressions, but not angry ones (Blair *et al.*, 1999).

Adolphs *et al.* (1999) reported a case study of a 31-year-old woman who sustained damage to both sides of her amygdala. They asked her to rate facial expressions, words and sentences along two dimensions: how arousing they were and how pleasant they were. While she was able to distinguish pleasant from unpleasant emotions, she was unable to recognise emotional

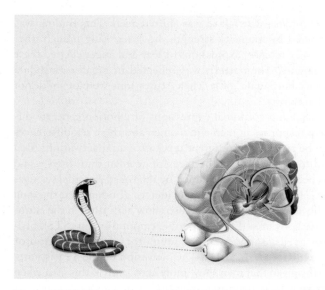

Figure 13.12 What happens in the brain when we fear a snake. LeDoux's model suggests that there are two pathways in the brain which mediate this response. Both are highlighted here.
Source: Science Photo Library Ltd./Claus Lunan/Bonnier Publications.

arousal in those expressions conveying negative emotions, specifically fear and anger. The authors argue that these results support a role for the amygdala in responding to highly negative, threat-related stimuli that require quick responses, although there are results showing that if we keep negative thoughts in mind, this maintenance, and the subsequent bad feeling it generates, is associated with increases in amygdala activity (Schaefer *et al.*, 2002).

One study of patients who had electrodes inserted into the amygdala while they saw faces and face parts expressing neutral, fearful and happy emotions found that activity of the neurons in the structure responded more quickly depending on the face part (Meletti *et al.*, 2012). First, the amplitude of the signal in the structure increased when looking at the eye region of the face, compared to whole faces and the mouth alone and this occurred 200–400 ms after the stimulus appeared. They responded more strongly to fearful eyes. They also responded to smiling eyes more strongly than they did faces and mouths but the reaction was later – 300–400 ms after the stimulus was presented. There is evidence that the amygdala can make appraisals of how relevant a stimulus is at 140 ms after stimulus onset and that this quick response can enable an organism to respond (Brosch *et al.*, 2011). An appraisal of the novelty of a stimulus can also occur in this and other regions before the visual cortex has completed the analysis of the information it has received (Brosch and Sander, 2013).

Our gaze towards facial expression of emotion appears to involve the amygdala (N'Diaye *et al.*, 2009). In an fMRI experiment, individuals were asked to look at a series of animated faces expressing different intensities of different emotions. The faces either shifted their gaze away from the observer or towards them. Anger was judged to be more intense when the gaze was shifted towards the observed and fear was judged more intense when gaze was shifted away. This finding was tempered by intensity strength, however: only mild (rather than very intense) expressions of fear and anger elicited these judgments. The pattern was reflected in greater amygdala activity but, again, only when expressions were of mild, not high intensity.

Facial and corporeal expressions of emotion generate different responses in men and women and these sex differences may be reflected in different types of neural activation. Men tend to look more at the faces of women than men – and this behaviour is accompanied by increased amygdala activation – but men seeing dynamic images of other men showing bodily expressions of threat also show activation in the extrastriate body area (EBA), superior temporal sulcus (STS), fusiform gyrus, supplementary premotor area and premotor cortex (Kret *et al.*, 2011). The activation of the STS is noteworthy given that men show more activation in this area when they view faces denoting superiority (Aleman Swart, 2008).

The amygdala's role in emotion does not appear to be tied to recognising or generating negative emotion. Viewing positive stimuli has also been found to be associated with a significant increase in activation in the left side of the amygdala; this activation also extends to other brain areas known to be involved in drug addiction and reward (Hamann *et al.*, 2002). Watching diseased and mutilated bodies stimulated both sides of the amygdala (but little beyond it). The notion that the amygdala is active when encoding and retrieving positive memories suggests that its role here may be due to its role in remembering positive events. That said, the amygdala has many parts (and parts that PET may not have been sensitive enough to measure), and Hamann *et al.* suggest that different regions within the structure may play different roles.

There are also asymmetries in activation observed in the amygdala depending on the valence of emotion – positive or negative. Generally, right-sided activation is seen when people experience negative emotional stimuli and left-sided activation is seen when people experience positive emotional stimuli (Dolcos and Denkova, 2014). Some studies have found that activation in the amygdala is seen when people smell pleasant and unpleasant scents, or only when they perceive unpleasant scents or when these scents are simply intense (Martin, 2013).

One view suggests that this asymmetry might reflect degrees of processing – more direct, initial, automatic experience is associated with right-sided activation and more cognitive responses to emotional stimuli are associated with left-sided activation. The amygdala's connections with the medial temporal lobe also highlight its importance in encoding, consolidating and retrieving memories, particularly those with an emotional valence. The interactions between these two regions enhance and enable the persistence of emotional memories (Dolcos and Denkova, 2014).

The orbitofrontal cortex and emotion

The orbitofrontal cortex (OFC) is located at the tip of the frontal lobes (see Figure 13.13). It covers the part of the brain just above the orbits – the bones that form the eye sockets – hence the term 'orbitofrontal'. The OFC receives information from

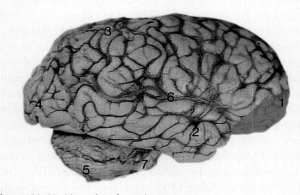

Figure 13.13 The orbitofrontal cortex.
Source: Science Photo Library.

the sensory system and from the regions of the frontal lobes that control behaviour. Thus, it knows what is going on in the environment and what plans are being made to respond to these events. It also communicates extensively with the limbic system, which is known to play an important role in emotional reactions. In particular, its connections with the amygdala permit it to affect the activity of the amygdala, which, as we saw, plays a critical role in certain emotional responses.

Neuroimaging studies implicate the OFC in emotion. One experiment compared those brain regions that were activated during pleasant or neutral touch, smell and taste (Francis *et al.*, 1999). Participants had their hands stroked by either a velvet glove or a piece of wood as their brain activity was monitored. The pleasant touch (velvet) was associated with significantly greater activation in the OFC than was the neutral touch (wood). The more intense touch (the neutral wood) was associated with activation in the part of the brain that represents touch. When participants tasted the pleasant sensation of glucose and the pleasant aroma of vanillin, similar but different parts of the OFC were activated, as were other parts of the brain.

The strongest evidence for the involvement of the OFC in emotion, however, comes from individuals who have suffered injury to the area. The earliest– and most famous – case was reported in the mid-nineteenth century (see Chapter 1). Phineas Gage, the railroad worker, was using a steel rod to ram a charge of dynamite into a hole drilled in solid rock. The charge exploded and shot the rod into his cheek, through his brain and out of the top of his head. He survived, but he was a different man. Before his injury, he was serious, industrious and energetic. Afterwards, he became childish, irresponsible, boorish and thoughtless of others (Harlow, 1848, 1868). He was unable to make or carry out plans, and his actions appeared to be capricious and whimsical. His accident largely destroyed the OFC (Harlow, 1848; Damasio *et al.*, 1994). Figure 13.14 shows the plotted trajectory of the iron rod through Gage's head.

Over the succeeding years, physicians reported several cases similar to that of Phineas Gage. In general, damage to the OFC reduced people's inhibitions and self-concern; they became indifferent to the consequences of their actions. A list of the behaviours associated with OFC damage appears in Table 13.3.

Given the large list of impairments in Table 13.3, what exactly is the role of the OFC in emotion? Eslinger and Damasio (1985) found that their patient, EVR, who sustained bilateral damage of the OFC displayed excellent abstract social judgement. When he was given hypothetical situations that required him to make decisions about what the people involved should do – situations involving moral, ethical or practical dilemmas – he always gave sensible answers and justified them with carefully reasoned logic. However, his personal life was a disaster.

EVR frittered away his life savings on investments that his family and friends pointed out were bound to fail. He lost one job after another because of his irresponsibility. He became unable to distinguish between trivial decisions and important

ones, spending hours trying to decide where to have dinner but failing to use good judgement in situations that concerned his occupation and family life. As the authors noted, 'He had learned and used normal patterns of social behaviour before his brain lesion, and although he could recall such patterns when he was questioned about their applicability, real-life situations failed to evoke them' (p. 1737). Damasio proposed a somatic marker hypothesis of OFC function (see the section on reasoning and the brain in Chapter 11). This suggests that our ability to make social and emotional decisions depends on our being able to make sense of somatic information that the body generates in response to specific events. If we are making a risky decision, this risk will be associated with a physiological response which will reflect our uncertainty about the decision we have made. In frontal lobe patients, Damasio argues, these connections between somatic states and an appreciation of them, are missing.

The type of behaviour seen in EVR is also seen in many patients with OFC damage. Hornak *et al.* (1996) found that their group of patients with frontal lobe damage were impaired at identifying facial and vocal emotional expression. Some of the comments made by orbitofrontal lobe patients on their disorder might help to illuminate the phenomenology of the social impairment – it shows us in very personal terms how the brain damage has affected that person's behaviour. Some of the comments made by Hornak *et al.*'s patients appear in Table 13.4.

Emotional processing deficits and social conduct problems seen in frontal lobe patients most often accompany damage to the right (ventromedial) PFC, rather than the left (Tranel *et al.*, 2002). Patients with damage to the left side show normal skin conductance response when faced with the risky gambling task (described in Chapter 11) and show little antisocial behaviour. Those with damage to the right side, however, show reduced skin conductance to the gambling task and meet the criteria for antisocial personality disorder, suggesting that the right PFC plays a more involved role than the left in emotional regulation. The idea that the OFC responds asymmetrically during the experience of emotion is reviewed, in a slightly different context, below.

Some patients with frontal lobe damage are unable to inhibit making incorrect responses on some cognitive tasks (although others can). Do you think that this lack of inhibition may be related to the emotional changes seen after damage to the OFC?

The insula

You saw earlier in the chapter that the insula is a part of the brain that is implicated in eating, obesity, hunger and flavour, and is part of the primary taste cortex. Lesions to the insula have also been associated with an impairment in the ability to recognise disgust (Jones *et al.*, 2010) and activation is found here when people view faces expressing disgust. This is also

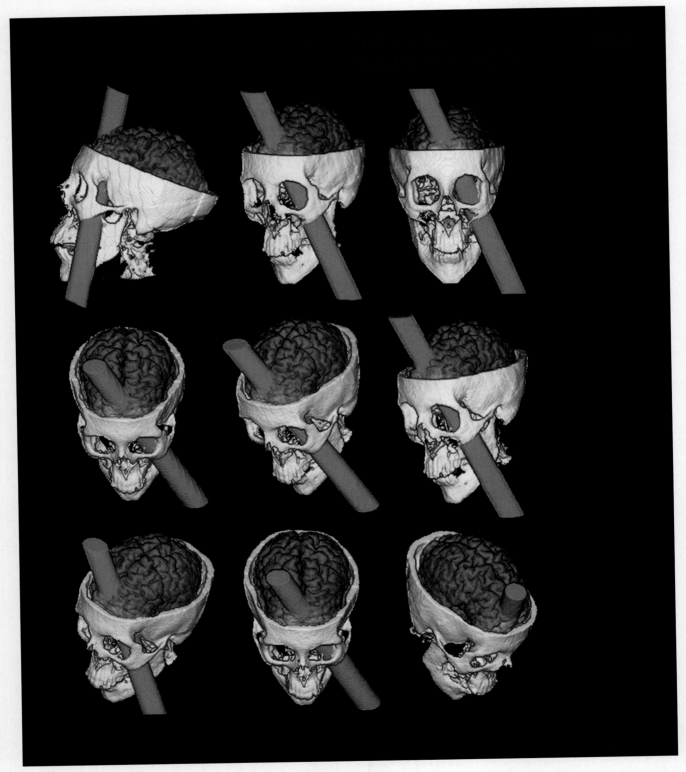

Figure 13.14 The trajectory of the iron bar through Phineas Gage's head.

Source: From H. Damasio, T. Grabowski, R. Frank, A.M. Galaburda and A.R. Damasio, The return of Phineas Gage: Clues about the brain from a famous patient. *Science*, 1994, 246, 1102–5. Department of Neurology and Image Analysis Facility, University of Iowa.

Table 13.3 Some of the personality changes that can follow frontal lobe injury

Exaltation/depression
Decreased concern with social propriety
Apathy and indifference
Lack of judgement
Diminished reliability
Facetiousness
Childish behaviour
Anxiety
Social withdrawal
Irritability
Inertia
Lack of ambition
Indifference to opinions of others
Lack of restraint
Restlessness
Purposelessness
Slowness in thinking
Decreased self-concern
Impulsive
Distractibility
Egocentricity

Source: Adapted with permission from Stuss, D.T., Gow, C.A. and Hetherington, C.R., 'No longer Gage': Frontal lobe dysfunction and emotional changes. *Journal of Consulting and Clinical Psychology*, 1992, 60(3), 349–59. Copyright © 1992 by the American Psychological Association, adapted with permission.

Table 13.4 Some responses of frontal lobe patients after their injury

Case 2

'If I have something to say, I can't wait and have to say it straight away.'

Case 4

'Emotion, tears, that's all gone out of the window. If I saw someone cry I'd just laugh – people look really silly getting upset.'

'I'm much more aggressive and I feel less fear. I go fighting for no reason.'

'Since I've taken up body building, I tend to show off a bit.'

Case 5

'Anger and irritability had increased; anxiety had decreased.'

Case 7

'I ain't scared of nobody. I'm not frightened of opening my mouth and speaking my mind. If I think someone's in the wrong, I'll tell them and not give a monkey's what they think of me.'

Case 8

'I'm not the woman he married; much more outspoken.'

Source: Adapted from Hornak, J., Rolls, E.T. and Wade, D., Face and voice expression identification in patients with emotional and behavioural changes following ventral frontal lobe damage. *Neuropsychologia*, 1996, 34(4), 247–61.

Left–right frontal asymmetry and emotion

Other evidence implicates the anterior cortex in emotion but in a different way. It has generally been thought that the right hemisphere was the dominant hemisphere for processing emotion but this is far too crude a characterisation of a complex behaviour and function.

The right hemisphere is superior to the left at recognising and perceiving emotional stimuli – such as distinguishing neutral from emotional faces and distinguishing sentences that vary according to their emotional tone – but the left hemisphere plays an important role in the experience of emotion. Davidson and colleagues, for example, have exposed participants to film clips designed to elicit specific emotions – positive and negative – as EEG activity was recorded. Participants indicated when they were experiencing positive and negative emotions as they watch the film. The results of the studies suggest that increases in left frontal EEG are seen when people experience positive emotion and increases in the right are seen when the experience is negative (R.J. Davidson *et al.*, 1979; Wheeler *et al.*, 1993). These emotional responses reflect approach and withdrawal motivational tendencies – our tendency to generate positive emotion results from contexts which we wish to approach or are drawn to, whereas our tendency to produce negative emotion results from stimuli and context that tend to evoke withdrawal responses.

Researchers have argued that our baseline frontal EEG response – and asymmetrical frontal activation specifically – can predict later emotion and our tendency to approach stimuli and contexts that are positive and can predict later risk

found when people inhale disgusting odours (Wicker *et al.*, 2003) although increases in activation in the left insula have been reported to pleasant odours (Fulbright *et al.*, 1998), in the right to disgusting ones (Heining *et al.*, 2003), and bilaterally to unpleasant (not necessarily disgusting) odours (Royet *et al.*, 2001). Wicker *et al.*'s study also found that the disgust stimuli stimulated the left side.

Evidence suggests that the insula's involvement is broader than responding to smell and taste, as the studies on disgust indicate. One general role could be allowing the emotional evaluation of stimuli or reflecting our feeling states and bodily sensations (Jones *et al.*, 2010). Craig (2009) suggests that its principal role is to interpret information about our bodily states, sensory state and cognitive states and create a unitary feeling that reflects the interaction of all three and specifically reflects the 'emotional now', 'the emotional self' or the 'global emotional moment'. What we do know is that it, and many of the regions and structures involved in emotion, subserve many different functions (or, at least, what we regard as different functions).

taking (Studer *et al.*, 2013). Those showing greater relative left-sided frontal EEG, for example, are more likely to respond positively to positive stimuli and, more broadly, engage in approach-related behaviour.

Ekman *et al.* (1990) investigated whether the type of EEG activity associated with a genuine smile would differ from that generated by false smiles. The genuine smile is called the **Duchenne smile** and is thought to activate the zygomatic muscles around the corners of the mouth and the orbicularis occuli muscles around the corners of the eyes spontaneously, as you can see in Figure 13.15. It is also associated with better long-term adjustment, that is, people who express Duchenne smiles seem to be those who are better adjusted in the long-term (Papa and Bonanno, 2008). Recent research, however, suggests that it can be elicited in people who pretend to be happy and that people judge smiles to be genuine even when they are produced voluntarily (Krumhuber and Manstead, 2009). When people are asked to judge the degree of happiness in a person's facial expression, they tend to look more at the mouth; when asked to judge whether the smile is genuine, they look at the eyes (Manera *et al.*, 2011). Research which has used eye-tracking devices to monitor where people look has found that the external sides of the eyes are focused on more when making judgements about authenticity (Boraston *et al.*, 2008).

Ekman *et al.* (1990) found that the Duchenne smiles were associated with greater left-sided activation in temporal and parietal regions. On the basis of these and other studies, Davidson suggested that the frontal asymmetry reflects motivational tendencies to withdraw or approach. That is, pleasant stimuli should be approachable and, therefore, activate the left frontal region whereas unpleasant stimuli would be avoided or withdrawn from and would activate the right frontal region (and decrease activity in the left frontal region).

Other asymmetries in brain activation resulting from behaviour include higher right frontal activity during the ovulatory period of the menstrual cycle and higher left during the women's ovulatory period which the authors interpret as reflecting the women's hormonal changes (Hwang *et al.*, 2008); greater right frontal EEG produced in people who are prone to nostalgia (Tullett *et al.*, 2015); increased left hemisphere EEG in 2-month-old infants when they listened to human voices (Mai *et al.*, 2014); left-sided activation in newborns who listened to their mother's voice compared to a stranger's voice (Beauchemin *et al.*, 2011); and increased risk taking in individuals with high left frontal activation when they engaged in tasks which involved great risks and losses (Telpaz and Yechiam, 2014).

Harmon-Jones *et al.* (2011) investigated whether leaning forward – literally approaching – activated the left frontal area. Participants watched pictures of deserts or rocks (neutral objects) as they leant forward or reclined backward. None were seated in a neutral position and it was not clear in this study whether participants leant forward or reclined backward to half of each set of stimuli. Leaning forward to deserts resulted in activation in the left frontal area; reclining had no effect on EEG.

Disentangling the approach–withdrawal relationship further, Berkman and Lieberman (2010) asked whether the typical brain asymmetry you would expect from approaching a pleasant stimulus would also be seen when approaching an unpleasant stimulus. Some cheeses, for example, are noxiously malodorous but we approach and eat them none the less. We may not like vegetables, but if we are on a diet we feel compelled to eat more of them.

Using fMRI, the researchers found that prefrontal asymmetry was associated with motivation to approach, rather than with the affective characteristics of the stimulus approached. Whether stimuli were positive or negative, left dorsolateral

(a)   (b)

Figure 13.15 The Duchenne smile. The face is that of Paul Ekman.
Source: from Emotions Revealed, Weidenfeld and Nicholson (Ekman, P. 2003).

activation was higher when participants approached stimuli. When the emotional content of the stimulus was compared, there were no asymmetries observed. The results interacted with the individual differences of the sample investigated: those who were typically approach-motivated showed greatest left-sided asymmetry.

A study by researchers from Germany and Austria has found that when people are asked to move away from or move towards the faces of people expressing basic emotions, the faces with happy expressions were more likely to be approached and the angry expressions were more likely to be moved away from (Seidel *et al.*, 2010). So far, so obvious. But they also found that when the participants saw expressions of sadness and disgust, they indicated a physical, motor movement towards the sad face but when asked whether they would approach such a face, their response was the opposite: consciously, they would avoid. With disgust, people indicated conscious withdrawal but they did not physically withdraw more from a disgust face than they did others.

Although men and women did not differ significantly in their responses, the sex of the poser did produce different results: male faces expressing sadness and happiness were rated more positively than were female faces and male faces expressing disgust and anger were responded to more quickly and rated more negatively than were female ones. Commenting on the seemingly inconsistent findings for the sad facial expressions, the authors argue that 'it seems reasonable that sadness communicates a request for help and elicits approach towards the sender, but prior social experiences may lead to a restraint' (p. 506).

While some studies have supported the frontal asymmetry model. Some evidence suggests that the type of asymmetry depends on the methods of analysis and recording procedures researchers use (Hagemann *et al.*, 1998). Hagemann *et al.* (2005b), for example, found that EEG asymmetry to emotional stimuli can change from one testing session to the next. In one study, they even found that right-sided activation most consistently predicted the strength of people's emotional responses to emotional stimuli (Hagemann *et al.*, 2005a). In a recent study, it was found that right frontal activation was more common in the morning and during the autumn, suggesting that the EEG can be influenced not only by time of day but also season (Peterson and Harmon-Jones, 2009).

Emotional experience: anger and disgust

Anger is conceivably an approach tendency because there is motivation to engage in competitiveness or physical harm (Carver and Harmon-Jones, 2009). Anger does not make people walk away, rather it makes them want to engage more in aggression and readies them for combat. But anger, by definition, is not necessarily a positive emotion. This presents the asymmetry model above with a paradox of sorts. If it is genuinely an approach tendency, we should see

increased left frontal brain activity when people experience it. If this increase is found, this does not then give the left frontal lobe an exclusive role in positive affect – it can also be activated by a negative emotion. Harmon-Jones (2004), however, suggests that there may be an alternative explanation: that people who get angry actually like being angry and, therefore, anger can be seen, via this logic, as a positive emotion.

To test this hypothesis, he took baseline EEG measurements from men and women and correlated this activity with their responses on an Attitudes Towards Anger questionnaire. This questionnaire asked participants to agree or disagree with a series of statements about anger (e.g. 'I like the feeling of power I get from expressing anger'). Measures of aggression were also taken and were used to divide the participants into those who expressed high levels of trait anger. The results showed that the most angry and aggressive of the group showed greater left frontal brain activity than did their milder counterparts. There was no significant relationship between attitudes towards anger and brain asymmetry: those who found anger to be a positive emotion were no more likely than those who did not view it so to produce left frontal EEG. The study is important because it suggests that the role of the frontal cortex in emotion might be more usefully seen as one involving motivational tendencies rather than emotional valence.

Individuals high in trait anger show greater EEG activation in the left frontal area of the brain when they view pictures designed to make them angry (Harmon-Jones, 2007). Peterson *et al.* (2008) asked participants to contract their hand to increase activation in the contralateral hemisphere (contracting the right hand leads to left hemisphere activation and contracting the left, the right hemisphere). After being insulted and then being given the opportunity to show aggression against their tormentor in a game, participants who contracted their right hand showed more aggression than did left-hand contractors. Left-frontal EEG was also associated with greater aggression. This EEG work has been extended to neuroimaging. In an fMRI experiment, participants were insulted and then asked to think about the incident (Denson *et al.*, 2008). The researchers found that feelings of anger induced by the insult were associated with activation in the anterior cingulate cortex (ACC). Activation in the hippocampus, insula and cingulate cortex were associated with thinking about the insult.

Anger induced by being ostracised – being deliberately made to feel excluded – has been associated with greater activation in the left frontal areas of the brain (Peterson *et al.*, 2011). The study also used a little-reported technique in the asymmetry literature – hand contraction – and found that right-hand contractions were associated with increased left-sided activation. The contraction was also associated with greater reports of anger after being ostracised. The results support the notion that anger is an approach-behaviour, even though it may not be perceived as positive, it is positive to the people experiencing it.

Experiments in which approach and withdrawal are manipulated during anger have found that people moving an on-screen representation of themselves make more approaches to a facial expression of anger (Wilkowski and Meier, 2010). Mayan and Meiran (2011), in a further modification, asked angered women undergraduates to step forward when they saw the word 'forward' on a screen, or move away when the same word was presented. Participants stood on a 'dance mat' and reaction time was measured to each instruction. Anger was manipulated by asking participants to recall an experience that made them very angry and then listen to a piece of atonal music. The women in the anger condition were more likely to approach during the 'forward' condition.

Another emotion regarded as negative is disgust and there appears to be a curious link between the recognition of this emotion and the degenerative motor disorder, Huntington's disease (HD). Sprengelmeyer *et al.* (1996) found that patients who showed symptoms of HD were poor at recognising facial expressions of disgust (but not other emotions). People who have just been diagnosed with the illness are also impaired in recognising disgust in facial expressions, although the ability to detect disgust in people's voices and the ability to experience disgust appear unaffected (Sprengelmeyer *et al.*, 2006). However, in an extensive study of 475 individuals with Huntington's disease, Johnson *et al.* (2007) found that patients are not more likely to show an impairment in recognising disgust specifically, but are impaired at recognising negative emotions in general – anger, disgust, fear, sadness – as well as surprise but not happiness (Henley *et al.*, 2008; Snowden *et al.*, 2008).

Calder *et al.* (2010) contend that the problem with previous research has been the over-reliance on one type of facial expression recognition test. They asked patients with manifest HD to recognise emotion from faces, voices and in short vignettes. They found that the recognition of anger, fear and disgust was impaired across all stimuli types, but the strongest effect was found for anger. In a second experiment, they were unable to identify faces which responded to pleasant and unpleasant tastes and smells but were able to identify faces showing what they call the 'expanded form' of disgust expression (upper lip curl, more associated with anger). In a review of 16 studies, an impairment in the ability to recognise facial expressions of anger was the most commonly reported but the ability to recognise all emotions – in faces and in voices – was impaired (Henley *et al.*, 2012).

Neuroimaging data from healthy participants implicate cortical regions in tasks requiring individuals to recognise emotion of disgust. Using fMRI, Schienle *et al.* (2005) asked 63 women to rate how disgusting they considered 40 generally disgusting scenes and 40 neutral scenes to be. They found that activation was greater in the left OFC, left medial OFC, the occipitotemporal lobe and left and right amygdala when the women viewed the disgusting stimuli. A broadly similar result was reported in a group of men and women who viewed disgust – and fear-inducing pictures (Schienle *et al.*, 2005). This study found increased activation in the left medial and dorsolateral prefrontal cortex (DlPFC) in both sexes.

Schienle *et al.* interpret their results in terms of Rolls's theory of emotion. Rolls (1999) has proposed that visual affective stimuli are initially processed by the occipital lobe. The ventral visual system then projects to the amygdala and PFC via the inferior temporal area. The PFC 'decides' on the reward value of the stimuli – do they afford reward or punishment? This 'decision' then leads to a behavioural outcome and the individual either withdraws or approaches.

Sex differences in emotion

Do men and women respond differently to faces which show a negative or positive facial expression? In one fMRI study, twenty men and women saw photographs of faces or watched videos of social interactions illustrating positive and negative emotion (Fine *et al.*, 2009). The researchers found that men showed greater activation in regions of the right hemisphere – the anterior cingulate, medial/superior frontal gyrus and superior temporal gyrus – than did women when seeing positive photographs. There was no difference between the sexes when watching negative faces.

When watching the positive social interaction, men showed greater activation in the left posterior cingulate and right inferior temporal gyrus. The left middle temporal lobe was more active in the men while watching the negative vignette. The results suggest that the differences between the sexes when watching video vignettes of social interaction are greater than when watching photographs. Men also showed greater activity on one side of the brain than the other.

This single study illustrates a well-documented finding in psychology: women and men respond to emotional stimuli differently and this difference may be reflected in differences in activation in regions of the brain. A meta-analysis of sex differences in the ability to process emotional signals, for example, found that women were better at recognizing emotions and were better able to express their emotions than were men (Kret and de Gelder, 2012). Men, on the other hand, responded more strongly to stimuli which conveyed threat (becoming dominant, violent or aggressive).

A meta-analysis of neuroimaging studies which examined sex differences in response to positive and negative emotional stimuli found significant differences between men and women (Stevens and Hamann, 2012). Women were more likely than men to show increased activation in the left amygdala (and left thalamus, hypothalamus and medial prefrontal lobe) when exposed to negative stimuli. The same region was more active in men than women when participants processed positive stimuli. The authors suggest that the strong response in the amygdala to negative stimuli is consistent with evidence indicating that women respond more strongly to negative stimuli, although this probably depends on the definition of 'negative'. The previous meta-analysis found that men responded more strongly to threatening stimuli, for example, ones that are probably negative.

Cutting edge: Music and emotion

It probably goes without saying that we enjoy music because of the joy (and sometimes sadness) it brings us. It is the main reason we listen to it. But, like any good psychologist, you will want to know whether there is good empirical evidence associating exposure to music with changes in mood (and there is – Hunter *et al.*, 2010).

One study from the University of Berlin examined whether the trends in the emotionality of music in America had changed in 25 years. Do Americans listen to happier or sadder music now than they did 25 years ago? Or has there been no change? Schellenberg and von Scheve (2012) examined emotion cues in music in 1,000 Top 40 recordings from the US from 1975 to 2009. Emotion cues include such features as tempo and chord – sad music tends to be slow tempo in a minor cord; happy music has a faster tempo and tends to be in a major cord.

The researchers found that the number of women singers had increased over time and that songs had become longer. In terms of the songs' emotion, the average tempo had decreased significantly over time and that there had been a significant increase in the use of the minor cord. It seems, therefore, as music has become sadder over time, as Figure 13.16 illustrates.

Another study found that the less complex the music –the fewer instruments are included – the more successful it is (in terms of sales) (Percino *et al.*, 2014).

Whether sad music can also elicit sadness has also been investigated. People who listened to sad music, rather than neutral or happy music, gave lower happiness ratings to facial expressions if they had self-selected sad music that they liked (Vuoskoski and Eerola, 2012). Uplifting music, on the other hand, has been associated with poorer driving safety if a driver listens to this while driving (Brodsky, 2001). A recent study found that if uplifting music abruptly changed to more calming music, this resulted in fewer driving accidents (ven der Zwaag *et al.*, 2013).

Finally, have you ever rung up a call centre and ended up being on hold while listening to some antiquated variant of Vivaldi's *Four Seasons* or one of Beyoncé's hits? Did this annoy you, relax you or have no effect? In a field study, Niven (2014) examined the effect of changing the hold music in call centres on customers' behaviour. In the three week study, the centre played either songs with prosocial lyrics (Heal The World, Help, Love Generation), neutral songs (On The Line, Octopus's Garden, Rock This Party) or their usual instrumental music. The call centre employees were not informed about the nature of the music conditions. Caller anger was rated by employees. Music with prosocial lyrics had no significant effect on anger levels but people were less angry when listening to neutral music than instrumental music. Employees were also less exhausted in this condition.

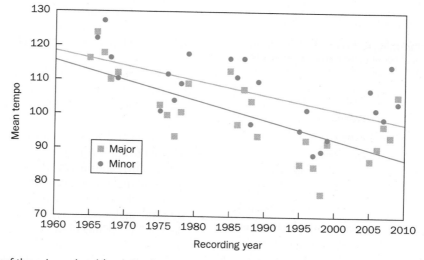

Figure 13.16 The use of the minor chord (and the duration of pop songs) has increased over 50 decades of the Top 40 music chart.

Crying

Is there anything as sincere as a tear? According to Ovid, men ought to cry because it would convince women that they were sincere in their emotions. Whether Ovid meant this as a recommendation to manipulate or an instruction to be honest is debatable but what isn't is the universality of the behaviour and the individual differences in its expression and how it is perceived. We are the only species to cry in response to emotional events, for example (Trimble, 2013; Vingerhoets and Bylsma, 2015).

Women cry more than do men – women in the West report crying 2–4 times more than do men (Vingerhoets and Scheirs, 2000), particularly if they find themselves in conflict. Men are more likely to cry when they receive positive news, but sex differences in response to loss or rejection are negligible.

The physical expression of crying is normally described as tears shed from the lachrymal glands in the absence of irritation but crying is more than lachrymal secretion – when we cry, we also sob and make vocalisations. The behaviour is usually seen in response to feelings of helplessness and hopelessness – some of the antecedents of crying can be seen in Table 13.5. According to Vingerhoets (2013) there are five types of emotional tears: those related to (1) physical pain, (2) attachment, (3) compassion/empathy, (4) society and (5) sentimentality and moral decision-making. The last would be elicited by watching films involving eternal love or good overcoming bad (Vingerhoets and Bylsma, 2015).

There is a common belief that, whatever the type of tear, crying is beneficial to psychological well-being and physical health, perhaps because the increase in parasympathetic activity leads to increased relaxation. Vingerhoets (2013) reports that a study of participants in 37 countries found that 70 per cent of them agreed that crying was positive and beneficial. What is curious, however, is that laboratory studies contradict these self-report studies. For example, if people watch sad films and cry, they feel worse compared with participants who watched the film but did not cry (Cornelius, 1997). There are also some situations in which crying could be demonstrably unbeneficial. Women who are in situations that might lead to rape are more likely to be attacked if they cry (Ullman and Knight, 1993).

Whatever the reason for this disparity, the way people view criers has shown some clear sex differences: men, for example, respond more negatively to men crying (Cretser et al., 1992) considering it a sign of weakness, irritating and confusing (Jesser, 1989). If we are close to someone, i.e. we have an attachment to them, our normal response to seeing them cry is to comfort them, holding their hand and so on and women are more likely to do this than are men. Responding in this way to a stranger's crying is rare (Vingerhoets, 2013). Men who cry at work are perceived as more emotional and less competent (Fischer et al., 2013). Children who ring up a child protection helpline and cry are more likely to be responded to with empathy and with requests to take their time (Hepburn and Potter, 2007).

The odour of sanctity

Recent work in social psychology suggests that people in clean-scented environments engage more in charity work, express reciprocal trust, engage with unknown people more and show more interest in voluntary work (Lilenquist et al., 2010). Eskine et al. (2011) found that people who were given a teaspoon of a bitter substance to taste expressed greater moral disgust when judging controversial topics such as incest or the acceptability of eating a dead dog. The more conservative respondents responded even more robustly after tasting the substance. Of course, this effect could be due to intensity, rather than bitterness, and a useful experiment would alter the intensities of this and other tastes.

A study from researchers at British and American universities found that the scent of a room can influence a person's moral judgements (Schnall et al., 2008). In a series of experiments, people were exposed to strong or mild malodour (or no odour) and were asked to make moral decisions such as whether to approve marriage among cousins, approving of sex between first cousins, or whether to approve of driving rather than walking to work. People in the malodour condition made increasingly severe moral judgements. One of the researchers from the malodour study also found that cleanliness – either directly by washing or indirectly by priming via words related to cleanliness used as part of a task – was associated with making less severe moral judgements (Schnall et al., 2008). The researchers suggest that people use intuitions when making judgements about right or wrong, even when those intuitions are not relevant to the moral judgement being made.

Table 13.5 Antecedents of crying. On the left side are "negative" antecedents of crying; right side, their "positive" counterparts.

Loss, grief	Birth of a child
Divorce, break-up	Wedding
Separation	Reunion
Conflict	Harmony
Loneliness, solitude	Social bonding, union
Defeat, failure	Victory, success, achievement
Powerlessness	Extraordinary performance
Distress, suffering	Ultimate happiness, rapture
Old, discarded, worn out	Young, with potential
Sin, egoism, world is bad	Justice, altruism, world is good
Tiny, vulnerable	Awesome, powerful
Physical pain	Tender love making, orgasm

Exposure to a clean scent (a citrus scent) has been associated with an increased likelihood of reciprocating trust and an increased likelihood to volunteer for a good cause and to donate to this good cause (Lilenquist *et al.*, 2010).

Using display rules

We all realise that other people can recognise our expressions of emotions. Consequently, we sometimes try to hide our true feelings, attempting to appear impassive or even to display an emotion different from what we feel. At other times, we may exaggerate our emotional response to make sure that others see how we feel. For example, if a friend tells us about a devastating experience, we make sure that our facial expression conveys sadness and sympathy. Researchers have studied all these phenomena.

Attempting to hide an emotion is called **masking**. An attempt to exaggerate or minimise the expression of an emotion is called **modulation**. And an attempt to express an emotion we do not actually feel is called **simulation**. According to Ekman and Friesen (1974), the expression of emotions often follows culturally determined **display rules** – rules that prescribe under what situations we should or should not display signs of particular emotions. Although the patterns of muscular movements that accompany particular feelings are biologically determined, these movements can, to a certain extent, be controlled by display rules. See Figure 13.17.

Each culture has a particular set of display rules. For example, in Western culture, it is impolite for a winner to show too much pleasure and for a loser to show too much disappointment. The expression of these emotions is supposed to be modulated downwards. Also, in many cultures, it is unmanly to cry or to show fear and unfeminine to show anger.

Context is important in encouraging genuine facial expression of emotion. Participants were asked to listen to stories which varied in funniness and were told by a friend or a stranger (Jakobs *et al.*, 1999). The stories were either told on tape recorder, face-to-face or on the telephone. The researchers found that participants who listened to a stranger smiled less than when listening to a friend, as previous research would predict. Motivation to express an emotion was enhanced by face-to-face encounters, but only when listening to a friend. Simply listening to a friend did not affect this motivation, but the interaction between storyteller and channel of communication did. The study shows that the facial expression of emotion in response to listening to a story of varying emotional content can depend not just on the storyteller but the medium through which that storyteller tells the story. The interpersonal distance between a person and a target who smiles is shorter than the distance between them and a target with a neutral smile or a non-enjoyment smile (Miles, 2009).

Neuroimaging research suggests that we remember smiling faces better than ones with neutral expressions. Tsukiura and Cabeza (2008) presented individuals with either smiling or non-smiling faces and were asked to associate the face with a name that was also presented with each face. Participants were then presented with the names and asked to retrieve the facial expression associated with that name. People remembered smiling faces better and faster than neutral ones. The OFC and hippocampus were particularly involved in successful encoding, especially when stimuli were smiling faces. The connections between these two regions were also stronger during the retrieval of smiling than neutral faces.

The results suggest that a smiling face can enhance retrieval. Furthermore, the rewarding nature of the smile is reflected in activation in the OFC. This activation, the researchers suggest, strengthens the hippocampal activation (itself a reflection of strengthened encoding).

Ekman and his colleagues (Ekman *et al.*, 1972; Friesen, 1972) attempted to assess a different kind of culturally determined display rule. They showed a distressing film to Japanese and American college students, singly and in the presence of a visitor, who was described to the subjects as a scientist. Because the Japanese culture discourages public display of emotion, the researchers expected that the Japanese students would show fewer facial expressions of emotion when in public than when alone.

The researchers recorded the facial expressions of their participants with hidden cameras while the participants viewed a film showing a gruesome and bloody coming-of-age rite in a pre-literate tribe. The results were as predicted. When the participants were alone, American and Japanese subjects showed the same facial expressions. When they were with another person, the Japanese participants were less likely to express negative emotions and more likely to mask these expressions with polite smiles. Thus, people from both cultures used the same facial expressions of emotion but were subject to different social display rules.

When people attempt to mask the expression of a strongly felt emotion, they are usually unable to do so completely, that is, there is some **leakage**, or subtle sign of the emotion (Ekman and Friesen, 1969). Ekman and Friesen (1974) investigated this

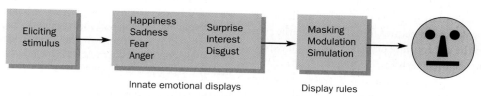

Figure 13.17 Controlled facial displays. Innate emotional displays can be modified by display rules.

phenomenon. They showed an unpleasant film of burns and amputations to female nursing students. After watching the film, the participants were interviewed by an experimenter, who asked them about the film. Some of the participants were asked to pretend to the interviewer that they had seen a pleasant film. The experimenters videotaped the participants during the interviews and showed these tapes to a separate group of raters, asking them to try to determine whether the people they were watching were being honest or deceptive. The raters were shown videotapes of the participants' faces or bodies. The results indicated that the raters could detect the deception better when they saw the subjects' bodies than when they saw their faces. Apparently, people are better at masking signs of emotion shown by their facial muscles than those shown by muscles in other parts of their body. Presumably, people recognise the attention paid to the face and learn to control their facial expressions better than they do the movements of the rest of the body.

Facial feedback hypothesis

The use of display rules suggests that we are capable of manipulating our facial expression to influence others. It has also been suggested that our own facial expressions can influence our own feelings. That our awareness of facial expression influences the way in which we feel is at the heart of the **facial feedback hypothesis** (Lanzetta *et al.*, 1976; Tourangeau and Ellsworth, 1979). If this is so, then manipulating a person's facial expression should result in the feeling of the expression-appropriate emotion. You cannot be angry with a smile on your face, for example. This idea has its origin in a remark by Darwin (1872), who had argued that 'the free expression by outward signs of an emotion intensifies it . . . the repression, as far as this is possible, of all outward signs softens our emotions'.

A test of the facial feedback hypothesis was undertaken by Laird (1974), who asked participants to view photographs while electrical activity from the face muscles was ostensibly recorded. The individuals were told that they would feel emotion-related muscle changes and, to counteract these changes, their muscles would be contracted or relaxed. In fact, the facial manipulation resulted in the participants expressing either a happy or angry face. As predicted, participants who then responded to specific photographs were angrier when exhibiting an angry expression and happier when exhibiting a happy face. However, a study by Tourangeau and Ellsworth (1979) cast doubt on these findings. They asked participants to exhibit either sad, fearful or neutral expressions while watching sad, anger-provoking and neutral films. Although the films themselves elicited the appropriate emotion, the facial expressions did not influence their feelings.

One final source of support for the hypothesis comes from a very well-known study by Strack *et al.* (1988). Strack *et al.* asked participants to watch cartoons and hold a pen either between their lips (a 'pout', thereby preventing them from making any facial expression) or between their teeth (thereby creating the expression of a smile), as you can see from Figure 13.18. Those who held the pen by their lips rated the cartoons as being less funny than did those who did not have their facial expression inhibited (i.e. held the pen between their teeth). People with low attention to emotion have been found to show the facial feedback effect, whereas those with high attention to emotion did not (Dzokoto *et al.*, 2014), suggesting that emotional regulation can influence facial feedback.

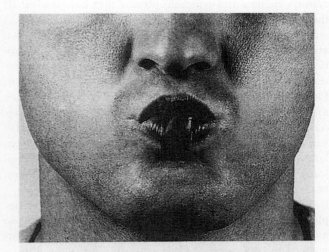

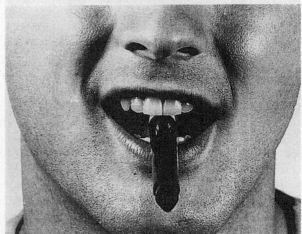

Figure 13.18 Illustrations of the conditions in Strack *et al.*'s experiment. Participants who watched cartoons while holding a pen between their lips in the 'sucking position' regarded the cartoons as less funny than did participants who held the pen between their teeth. In the 'lips' condition, the muscles involved in smiling were inhibited by the position of the pen.

Source: Strack, F., Stepper, S. and Martin, L.L., Inhibiting and facilitating conditions of the human smile. *Journal of Personality and Social Psychology*, 1988, 54, 1768–777. © Fritz Strack. Reproduced with permission

However, an attempt to replicate Strack *et al.*'s experiment – the first such replication – resulted in failure (Wagenmakers *et al.*, 2016). Seventeen independent replication attempts failed to find the effect Strack *et al.* reported. Strack, however, responding to these failures questioned whether the cartoons used in the 1980s were relevant in the 2010s and criticised the replications for recording participants' behaviour using a camera, which could have been inhibitory. He also notes that several conceptual replications have supported the original study. The failed replications were direct replications.

Posture and emotion

'One must sit with a sense of dignity and grandeur, like a mountain or a giant pine . . . the innate dignity of man is physiologically manifested in his erect back, since he alone of all creatures has this capacity to hold his spinal column vertical,' wrote Dogen, Zen Buddhist Master, in the thirteenth century (Kapleau, 1980).

Buddhist seating preferences aside, we are all aware of the health benefits of adopting good posture, especially when sitting at a desk typing away at a computer. Darwin highlighted the evolutionary advantage of certain types of deportment – bodily movement and posture sent clear signals to members of the same and different species, especially one that posed a threat. He also noted that pride was one of the more obviously signalled complex emotions – the upright posture indicated superiority over others. You can imagine the howls of despair echoing around Notre Dame.

An empirical test of the hypothesis that upright posture leads to a feeling of pride asked undergraduates to complete a brief measure of intelligence (Raven's Progressive Matrices) and adopt a slumped or an upright position while the test was apparently scored in another room (Roberts and Arefi-Afshar, 2007). All received feedback indicating that they had scored in the top 25 per cent. Finally, they rated their satisfaction with their Raven's performance, completed a maths test and rated their satisfaction with their maths performance.

Psychology in action: Should you smile during an interview?

It's the job you want, in a place you like with a salary that exceeds your expectations. You've bought a new outfit, you've rehearsed your presentation and you've pre-empted all the difficult questions (even the one about your greatest weakness). You enter the interview room. There are three people behind a desk. You say 'good morning', brightly, and smile. Has your last act condemned your career or enhanced it?

Psychological research has generally concluded that smiling generates positive responses in those we smile at (e.g. Lau, 1982). There is some evidence that it could also be advantageous at interview. Behaviours such as smiling, eye contact, being attentive, and facing the interviewer are associated with favourable assessments (Imada and Hakel, 1977; DeGroot and Motowildo, 1999). In the Abel and Deitz (2008) study of applicants for the position of disk-jockey, individuals who smiled in their photograph were more likely to be appointed regardless of their qualifications. Other studies, in which people rated management trainee applicants or research assistants, found no effect of smiling on hiring decisions (Levine and Feldman, 2002; Fraudenorfer *et al.*, 2014), although smiling management trainees were rated as more likeable (Levine and Feldman, 2002).

Ruben *et al.* (2014) have argued that the seriousness of the job is also a factor in whether smiling applicants are hired. They argue that a serious position is one that is less likely to be offered to a smiling candidate. In two studies, they tested this hypothesis. In a pilot study, they asked a small group of undergraduates to rate various professions according to their seriousness and whether their representatives were nice and agreeable and were expected to smile. Newspaper reporter was the profession regarded as most serious, although data entry employees were thought less likely to smile.

In the first study, 100 introductory psychology students were divided into assessors (newspaper editor) and job candidates (part-time news reporter). They were given instructions on how to behave but given no guidance on smiling. The interview took 5 minutes. Editors were asked how likely they were to hire the applicant. Smiling, nodding, gesturing and gaze duration was measured in applicants. Smiling was much more likely to be associated with a no-hire decision, whereas nodding was associated with likelihood of employment. Applicants who said they tried hard to create a good impression, smiled less (and were more likely to be hired). When applicants smiled seemed important – if they smiled less in the middle of the interview, they were considered more employable than if they smiled at the beginning.

In a second study, 140 introductory psychology students were asked to watch 30-second silent clips of interviewees whom participants were told were being interviewed for the jobs of newspaper reporter, middle manager, primary school teacher or a salesperson. If participants thought that the candidates were applying for the middle manager or reporter jobs, they were more likely to appoint if applicants smiled less. The effect was not as strong for the teacher and salesperson posts but the relationship was still negative.

'Our results,' the authors conclude, 'suggest that although the applicant should not smile much, when he or she does smile, it should be at the beginning and at the end of the interview' (p. 17).

Posture had a significant effect on satisfaction ratings, but only in men. Men were significantly more satisfied with their performance if they had been in the upright posture condition. In contrast, women in the upright condition performed less well after adopting this position and expressed more negative attitudes about their performance. Why?

Objectification theory suggests that women would feel self-conscious in the upright condition because it emphasises a sexually salient part of their body, namely their breasts. The discomfort that this produces disrupts performance (and satisfaction with this performance). The authors draw on social psychology research, for example, which shows that women who performed a cognitive task in their swimsuit performed less well than those wearing a jumper (they also performed less well than men who completed the task naked from the waist up).

Once study suggested that adopting a dominant pose is also sufficient to increase the level of testosterone (Carney *et al*. 2010). Men and women were asked to adopt a high-power, non-verbal display or a low-power non-verbal display. An example of the former would be sitting with the feet up on the desk, with hands behind the head. An example of the latter would be sitting in a chair with feet together and the hands cupped in the lap. Those in the high-power condition showed an increase in testosterone, a decrease in cortisol and increased feelings of power. They were also more tolerant of risk. The pattern was the opposite in the low-power group.

However, in a significant volte face and in recognition of a failure to replicate the original findings (Ranehill *et al*., 2015), Cuddy has renounced her findings and the phenomenon in a blistering bout of self-criticism, concluding that 'I do not have any faith in the embodied effects of 'power poses'. I do not think the effect is real. I discourage others from studying power poses'. She continues: 'The data are real. The sample size is tiny [the sample size was 42]. The data are flimsy. The effects are small and barely there in many cases. The experimenters were both aware of the hypotheses.' She lists a number of other criticisms. It is a tour de force and a model of a retraction.

Cutting edge: Exploring the Kuleshov effect

At the beginning of the twentieth century, the pioneering Russian film-maker, Lev Kuleshov (1899–1970) was experimenting with different forms of manipulating the audience's expectations. One such experiment involved presenting a neutral image of the actor Ivan Mozhukin and juxtapose it with various images and contexts, such as a bowl of soup, a girl playing with a doll and a woman in a coffin. Kuleshov reported that viewers who saw the actor's neutral expression attributed an emotion to it that was consistent with the context. So, if the context involved the image of the coffin, the actor's expression was perceived as sad; if the little girl was playing, it was interpreted as happy and so on.

This became known as the Kuleshov effect and is quite well known in film studies, if not so well known in psychology despite its clear psychological importance. (In fact, so ill known is it in psychology only two attempts have been made to replicate Kuelshov's findings, see below.)

No one quite knows exactly what Kuleshov did because the original footage does not exist and accounts are not especially detailed (Barratt *et al*., 2016). On the basis of what is known from these sketchy accounts, Prince and Hensley (1992) and Mobbs *et al*. (2006) attempted to replicate Kuleshov's finding. Prince and Hensley asked communication students to look at a close-up of an actor with a neutral expression in three contexts: a smiling girl playing with a teddy, a woman in a coffin or a hot bowl of soup on a table. Participants saw the actor, then the context, then the actor again and then were then asked to indicate which of seven emotions he experienced (there was also a 'no emotion' option). The study found no effect of context – most of the participants chose 'no emotion' rather than one of the seven emotions. Mobbs *et al*.'s (2005) was a neuroimaging study which asked people to look at an object for 750 ms, then a face which looked directly at the participant, followed by an interval and then the face again (unlike the original where the order was different). Mobbs *et al*. found that neutral faces were rated as more arousing and emotional when the film sequences were positive or negative.

To determine whether the effect was genuine or artefactual, and having identified the problems with previous studies described above, Barratt *et al*. asked students from a Danish university to look at neutral expressions of men and women followed by stimuli designed to elicit happiness (e.g. smiling baby, kitten falling asleep), sadness (e.g. coffin and a graveyard), hunger (e.g. bowl of soup or rice, loaf of bread), fear (e.g. spiders, roaring lion) or desire (male and female reclining nudes). There was also a neutral condition (grey background with numbers counting down from three). Barratt *et al*. found some evidence for the effect: participants chose emotions to describe the facial expressions that were consistent with the context/stimuli accompanying the faces. The strongest effect was found for the sadness condition. Faces in this condition were also reported as being more negative and less aroused than those accompanying the desire stimuli.

The interesting question, then, is what exactly are the participants responding to? Do they perceive the emotion in the neutral face? Or does the participant experience the emotion and this is transferred or is leaked to the perception of the face? Measuring this in future experiments would be informative.

Facing emotion

Much work in psychophysiology has tried to outline what type of muscle activity in the face is associated with the experience of different emotions. Facial muscle activity can be extremely subtle and can only be measured by EMG, a sensitive psychophysiological technique (see Chapter 4). EMG recording can reveal that the muscle activity of the face changes when it expresses pleasant and unpleasant emotion whereas normal observation of the person's face cannot reveal such detail.

Pleasant stimuli tend to produce greater muscle activity in the zygomaticus major (the part of the face that allows us to move the corners of our mouth into a smile) and less over the corrugator supercilii muscles (these draw the brow down and allow frowning) than do unpleasant ones. Whether the decrease in muscle activity is due to a decrease in negative emotion or an increase in a positive one is an important question: it is the key to understanding whether these changes occur because negative feelings are decreased or positive ones are increased. Larsen *et al.* (2003) asked 68 women to report positive and negative feelings during exposure to negative, positive and neutral pictures, sounds and words. The group's facial muscle activity (EMG) was recorded. The pictures included those of mutilated bodies, household objects, people and food amongst others and noises included animal noises, alarms, engines and laughter. Words included insults, terms of endearment and neutral expressions.

One important finding was that pictures and sounds had a more significant effect on muscle activity than did the words. A second finding was that the nature of the stimulus had a much greater effect on activity over the corrugator supercilii muscle especially when people viewed pictures (although this effect was seen for all three types of stimuli). The effects on the zygomaticus major muscle were unreliable.

Self-reported negative emotion was associated with significant increases over the corrugator supercilii muscle whereas positive emotion was associated with less activity. For positive emotion specifically, words and pictures did produce increases over the zygomaticus major area but the region was relatively unaffected by people's self-reports of negative emotion.

This suggests that facial reciprocity in emotion (muscle activity going up during one type of emotion but down during another) does not occur in this region, but does around the corrugator supercilii under the conditions in which the study's participants found themselves in a quiet room, dimly lit where signalling of emotion was not necessary.

Theories of emotion

Theories of emotion have attempted to explain the nature of emotion from various perspectives. These perspectives can be broadly described as physiological, evolutionary and cognitive.

Physiological theories

The James–Lange theory

William James (1842–1910), an American psychologist, and Carl Lange (1834–1900), a Danish physiologist, independently suggested similar explanations for emotion, which most people refer to collectively as the James–Lange theory

Cutting edge: Heroes – do they tend to the right?

The evidence suggests that they do, that is, statues of heroes and paintings of them depict the individuals looking up and to the right. Frimer and Sinclair (2016) asked 158 Americans to choose three moral heroes and three celebrities and then conducted a google search of the names and downloaded images on the first page. The names included Martin Luther King, Mother Teresa, Nelson Mandela, Brad Pitt, Marilyn Monroe and Elvis Presley.

They found that moral heroes looked up and to the right more often than by chance, and more often than did the celebrities. In a follow-up experiment, they investigated whether people would be more likely to choose people posing with head up and to the right to promote a social cause than they would a person adopting a different pose. A sample of 412 Americans was studied.

Participants selected the image with the person looking up and right more often than any other posture. The effect was replicated in a second study where the hair of the person in the image was removed as were elements of body asymmetry (by flipping the image). Why were these effects found?

The model looking up and to the right made the person look heroic, warm, competent, future-oriented and proud, according to the researchers. In a fourth study, a person adopting this pose was also rated as more attractive.

Interestingly, most politicians portraits feature them facing to the left. And there are some notable exceptions to the study's general findings (Thomas *et al.*, 2012). The famous image of Che Guevara by Alberto Korda portrays the Cuban leader looking up. And to the left.

(James, 1884; Lange, 1887). Basically, the **James–Lange theory** states that emotion-producing situations elicit an appropriate set of physiological responses, such as trembling, sweating and increased heart rate. The situations also elicit behaviours, such as clenching of the fists or fighting. The brain receives sensory feedback from the muscles and from the organs that produce these responses, and it is this feedback that constitutes our feelings of emotion. As James put it:

> The bodily changes follow directly the perception of the exciting fact, and … our feelings of the same changes as they occur is the emotion. Common sense says we lose our fortune, are sorry, and weep; we meet a bear, are frightened, and run … The hypothesis here to be defended says that this order of sequence is incorrect … The more rational statement is that we feel sorry because we cry, angry because we strike, afraid because we tremble, and not that we cry, strike, or tremble because we are sorry, angry or fearful, as the case may be. (Source: James, 1890. p. 449.)

James suggested that our own emotional feelings are based on what we find ourselves doing and on the sensory feedback we receive from the activity of our muscles and internal organs. Where feelings of emotions are concerned, we are self-observers. Thus, patterns of emotional responses and expressions of emotions give rise to feelings of emotion. By this reasoning, feelings of emotions are simply by-products of emotional responses. The James–Lange model is illustrated in Figure 13.19.

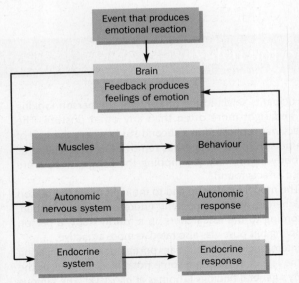

Figure 13.19 A diagrammatic representation of the James–Lange theory of emotion. An event in the environment triggers behavioural, autonomic and endocrine responses. Feedback from these responses produces feelings of emotion.

James's and Lange's theory was not entirely correct, however. As Cannon (1927, 1931) pointed out:

1 Separating the viscera from the CNS did not result in changes in emotional behaviour.

2 Emotional and non-emotional states can be associated with the same physiological changes.

3 Visceral changes are too slow to be able to reflect emotional changes.

4 Inducing visceral change that should result in emotional change usually does not produce these changes.

Schachter and Singer's model

Schachter (1964) proposed that feelings of emotions are determined jointly by perception of physiological responses and by cognitive assessment of a specific situation. Thus, to Schachter, emotion is cognition plus perception of physiological arousal. Both are necessary. Schachter and Singer (1962) tested this hypothesis by inducing physiological arousal in groups of participants placed in various situations. All participants were told that they were part of an investigation on the effects of a vitamin called 'suproxin' on visual perception (no such vitamin exists). The investigators gave some participants injections of adrenalin, a hormone that stimulates a variety of ANS effects associated with arousal, such as increased heart rate and blood pressure, irregular breathing, warming of the face and mild trembling. Other participants received a control injection of a salt solution, which has no physiological effects.

Next, the researchers placed some participants in an anger-provoking situation in which they were treated rudely and subjected to obnoxious test questions such as, 'How many men, besides your father, has your mother slept with? (a) one, (b) two, (c) three, (d) four or more.' Others were treated politely and saw the antics of another 'participant' (a confederate who was hired by the experimenters) who acted silly and euphoric. The experimenters hoped that these two situations, together with the physiological reactions produced by the injections of adrenalin, would promote either negative or positive emotional states.

Finally, some participants were correctly informed that the injections they received would produce side effects such as trembling and a pounding heart. Others were told to expect irrelevant side effects or none at all. Schachter and Singer predicted that the participants who knew what side effects to expect would correctly attribute their physiological reactions to the drug and would not experience a change in emotion. Those who were misinformed would note their physiological arousal and conclude that they were feeling especially angry or happy, as the circumstance dictated. All participants reported their emotional states in a questionnaire.

The results were not as clear-cut as the experimenters had hoped. The adrenalin did not increase the intensity of the participants' emotional states. However, participants who expected to experience physiological arousal as a result of the injection reported much less of a change in their emotional states than did those who did not expect it, regardless of whether they had received the adrenalin or the placebo. These results suggest that we interpret the significance of our physiological reactions rather than simply experience them as emotions.

Nisbett and Schachter (1966) provided further evidence that participants could be fooled into attributing their own naturally occurring physiological responses to a drug and thus into feeling less 'emotional'. First, they gave all participants a placebo pill (one having no physiological effects). Half the participants were told that the pill would make their hearts pound, their breathing increase and their hands tremble; the other half (the control subjects) were told nothing about possible side effects. Then, the researchers strapped on electrodes and gave the participants electrical shocks. All participants presumably experienced pain and fear, and, consequently, their heart rates and breathing increased, they trembled, and so on. Yet the participants who perceived their reactions as drug-induced were able to tolerate stronger shocks than were the control subjects, and they reported less pain and fear. Thus, cognition can affect people's judgements about their own emotional states and even their tolerance of pain.

The precise nature of the interaction between cognition and physiological arousal has not been determined. For example, in the Nisbett and Schachter experiment, although the verbal instruction about effects of the placebo affected the participants' reactions to pain, it did not seem to do so through a logical, reasoned process. In fact, Nisbett and Wilson (1977) later reported that participants did not consciously attribute their increased tolerance of pain to the effects of the pill. When participants were asked whether they had thought about the pill while receiving the shocks or whether it had occurred to them that the pill was causing some physical effects, participants typically gave answers such as, 'No, I was too worried about the shock' (Nisbett and Wilson, 1977, p. 237).

Evolutionary theories

Evolutionary theories of emotion view emotions as adaptive traits – they help the organism to adapt to the demands of the environment and thereby survive (Izard, 1977; Plutchik, 1984).

Plutchik's structural, psychoevolutionary theory of emotion

In common with other evolutionary theories of emotion, Plutchik's (1984) psychoevolutionary theory regards emotions as being important to adaptation and survival. However, he argues that in order to understand the nature of emotions, they must be organised in a certain way. He argues, therefore, that emotions can be distinguished on the basis of intensity (anger is less intense than rage, for example),

similarity (surprise may engage the same feelings as happiness), polarity (that is, opposites: grief is the opposite of joy), and whether they are primary or secondary (the secondary emotions derive from the primary ones).

Plutchik lists eight behavioural patterns, such as destruction, rejection and reproduction, which can be seen in all organisms; each of his primary emotions (described in an earlier section) is associated with these behavioural patterns.

Shaver's prototype theory

Shaver et al.'s (1992) model of emotion also uses the notion that we react to the environment using a limited behavioural repertoire and argues that, like emotional facial expression, these repertoires should be universal. Furthermore, the assumption that emotions are universal suggests that they have a biological basis. Emotions are viewed as 'action tendencies' that arise from an appraisal of the environment. Because the similarities in environmental events are more common than dissimilarities, the theory argues, appraisals will be similar across cultures. Shaver and his colleagues suggest that such a view is supported by evidence from three countries – the USA, Italy and China – in which there was substantial overlap in the words that individuals listed as basic emotions.

Frijda's 'action tendencies'

Shaver adopted the concept of 'action tendencies' from Frijda's (1988) model which also views emotions as adaptive. There is a small number of these tendencies which represents the individual's readiness to respond to the environment in emotional ways. These tendencies mediate the individual's relationship with the environment and Frijda proposed 10 of them. Like Plutchik's model, Frijda's argues that emotions are adaptive in that they are used by individuals to solve problems posed by the environment. Unlike Plutchik's, it is specifically related to human behaviour. However, Frijda also argues that there is little difference between the action tendency and the emotion associated with it, emotion perhaps being the state of awareness of these action tendencies. He also suggests that these emotions (and tendencies) follow on from an individual's appraisal of the environment.

This notion of appraisal is important to a number of models and theories of emotion, especially the cognitive theories described below. The concept was first systematically described in Fritz Heider's book, *The Psychology of Interpersonal Relations* published in 1958 which spurred much of the research in attribution in social psychology, described in Chapter 15. In general, such theories argue that emotion is dependent on the individual's appraisal of environmental events and situations. Schachter and Singer's model, although described as a physiological model, involved a strong appraisal component.

Other models, however, include appraisal as a more explicit feature. Often central to these theories is whether a stimulus or an event (which can theoretically elicit an emotion) is relevant, is consistent with what a person wants and expects, whether the person experiencing the emotion caused the stimulus to occur and whether the person is able to control the outcome of the response to the stimulus (Moors, 2014). The person needs to be aware that they have little control, and acknowledge the relevance, of the stimulus. Once an appraisal is formed, it then generates 'action tendencies', physiological responses and motor behaviour. Together, these constitute our feeling.

Cognitive theories

Lazarus's model

Lazarus's original model of emotion suggested that emotion arose from the individual's appraisal of the environment (Lazarus, 1966). **Primary appraisal** involved the initial evaluation of the environment – is it positive, negative or neutral; secondary appraisal involved the individual's evaluation of how best to cope with this environment and what options were available to facilitate this coping. **Secondary appraisal** was composed of two types: emotion-focused coping and problem-focused coping. Emotion-focused coping refers to the defence mechanisms that the individual might adopt, such as fleeing the situation or denying negative thoughts and feelings. Problem-centred coping is directed more at finding solutions to the problems posed by the environment when there are changes in the environment.

This original model, however, was devised to explain how people respond to stressors – factors which cause stress (this is discussed in more detail in later chapters). The later reformulation of the model (Lazarus, 1991) was designed to be a general theory of emotion which Lazarus called the 'cognitive–motivational–relational' theory of emotion. Primary appraisal comprised these components: goal-relevance (Is the environment related to the goal that the individual wants to pursue?), goal congruency/incongruency (Is the goal possible or will it be prevented?) and ego-involvement (Does the environment have consequences for the individual's self-esteem?). Secondary appraisal assesses the environment in terms of how the individual might cope with it and how such coping might affect future relations. Lazarus proposed that the appraisal of situations which might involve harm to the individual were innate; however, secondary appraisal could override the decisions derived from primary appraisal.

Weiner's model

Weiner's model also utilises the concept of appraisal but is based on the notion that individuals make attributions to the environment and behaviour (Weiner, 1985, 2014). The individual's account of how events in the environment were caused determines which positive and negative emotions are elicited. This attribution-dependent model suggests that these explanations depend on three factors: (1) whether the cause of the emotion is internal to the individual or external and caused by the environment; (2) whether the cause is stable or will change over time; and (3) whether the cause of the emotion is controllable or uncontrollable. According to this model, the attributions for success or failure will determine whether positive or negative emotions are experienced. Weiner's mode has been extended to various behaviours such as helping and aggression.

The hedonic treadmill theory

In 1971, Brickman and Campbell published a theory of emotion and well-being in which they suggested that we adapt to emotional events in our lives, in the same way that we adapt to a new smell when we enter an unfamiliar house. Studies published in the late 1970s appeared to support this theory. Lottery winners, for example, were no more happy than lottery losers and non-winners and people with paraplegia were similarly not less happy than those who could walk. The theory suggests that experiences inducing happy emotions are transitory; they are transitory because of adaptation.

Research has forced a revision of the theory and Diener *et al.* (2006) describe some of these developments. For example, the treadmill view suggests that after we experience a highly emotional event, we return to a neutral state soon after. Once you've got your fantastic exam result, for example, or received that promotion, there is a period in which you are elated. The elation then subsides. Research has shown, however, that (exceptional events aside – such as getting that promotion) people are generally happy most of the time, according to self-reports. The European Values Study Group and World Values Survey Association (2005) data indicate that 80 per cent of respondents reported being quite or very happy, suggesting that the baseline is 'happy' rather than 'neutral'. Of course, there is variability in these 'set points'; different people have different set points. You also saw earlier in the book how positive affect declines with age but that negative affect also decreases.

The theory also states that people cannot do very much to change the long-term degree of happiness they experience – because of the return to a neutral state. However, studies of widows and widowers, as well as of people who have been laid off from work, show initially very low levels of happiness but this happiness is restored (but usually, only after a very long period – years, for example). The early data from people with severe disability has also been challenged, with Diener *et al.* (2006) citing evidence from patients with disabilities showing that they experienced a drop in life satisfaction after the disability, a drop that did not recover significantly.

Other models

Leventhal and Scherer's (1987) and Scherer's model (2009; 2013) suggests that the emotion system is made up of three components. At the sensory motor level, individuals may respond to situations and events automatically. This automatic reaction is present from birth onwards. The schematic level is also an automatic level of processing but the automatic behaviour derives from learned associations. Finally, the conceptual level represents reactions that are not automatic but depend on the individual's memories about emotion, expectations, goals, plans and so on. The conceptual level places the event that causes the emotion in a long-term context, that is, how would it affect the individual's future behaviour? In addition to these levels, the model proposes that the stimuli giving rise to emotional reactions are evaluated along various dimensions including novelty, pleasantness, their relevance to goals and plans, the potential to cope with them and their compatibility with social norms and the individual's self-concept.

The conceptual act theory (Barratt, 2014) argues that emotion arises when our own physical sensations and our perception of others, physical behaviour or surroundings lead us to interpret them as emotions. Emotions are regarded as 'concepts' and are informed by the language and culture that creates such concepts.

Mesquita and Boiger's (2014) sociodynamic model of emotion emphasises what they claim is missing from other theories of emotion: that emotion plays an important role in social interactions and our relationships with others, and that the emotions we produce are a function of the social context in which they are expressed. Emotions are generated in social interactions and these help shape and change future interactions. They propose that an arguing couple's behaviour is best understood not by regarding each actor's emotions separately but how each engages with the other. They cite examples of emotions occurring only in certain contexts – a child's crying is more likely when family members withdraw, for example. The theory describes more the context in which emotions occur.

Finally, Tracy (2014)'s evolutionary account of emotion argues that emotions are influenced by natural selection to enable an organism to produce physiological, cognitive and behavioural responses that can help it respond to threats and opportunities. In this theory, each distinct emotion is thought to hold an adaptive function and comprises many components (physiological, behavioural, cognitive, sensory, motivational) which serve some function. Anger and fear, for example, are distinct emotions with distinct adaptations and functions. The account purports to understand which elements of evolutionary history or pressure elicit emotion – which situation relevant to evolution elicits fear, for example, and what effect does this have on the organism?

Emotional distance

The best psychology reveals something about our behaviour that is astonishing and unexpected. Who could think that even placing dots wide apart on a sheet of paper makes you emotionally distant, for example? But this is what Williams and Bargh (2008a, b) found.

They reviewed a theory suggesting that when we think about distant events we think about them in the abstract, but when we think about recent events we think and talk about them in more concrete terms (Trope and Lieberman, 2003). This even extends to social and physical distance (we think more concretely about people and places near us) (Fujita *et al.*, 2006). Think about where you live now and describe it to yourself. You probably used concrete language – it's a first-floor flat, it's in a certain part of town, it has two bedrooms and so on.

Williams and Bargh (2008a, b) reasoned that this relationship could be inverted. That is, priming the thought of distance could make people think more distantly. They asked participants to plot a pre-assigned series of points on a graph paper – see Figure 13.20. Some participants had to plot the points far apart from each other; other participants had to plot them near to each other. They were then asked to rate and judge various objects, scenarios and film clips.

Those who had been primed by plotting distal points derived greater enjoyment in film clips depicting embarrassing events, showed less emotional distress when watching violent material, gave lower estimates for the calorie content in unhealthy food and reported weaker ties to family members and the place where they grew up.

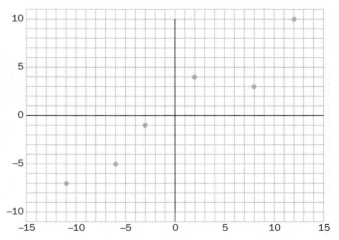

Figure 13.20 The graph paper on which Williams and Bargh's participants placed pre-determined dots.

But this may not be the best psychology. Pashler *et al*. (2012), for example, attempted to run the same experiment but in such a way that the experimenter did not know which condition the participants were assigned to. That is, they made sure that those involved were blind to the condition of the experiments and had no way of consciously or unconsciously influencing the results. They repeated two of Williams and Bargh's experiments. They failed to replicate the original findings.

In discussing the possible reasons for this, and discounting explanations that were weak, they conclude that the results may simply not be valid and that the original study's finding was an example of what is called a Type 1 error: finding a positive result where one does not genuinely, reproducibly exist. This study highlights again the importance of replication in psychology, and any science. If a finding seems too extraordinary or too good to be true, wait for a replication. If it is true and genuinely extraordinary others will find the same result.

Similar studies, which have examined the effect of physical warmth on prosocial behaviour, have produced similarly negative results. For example, Lynott *et al*. (2017) asked participants to evaluate the quality of hot or cold therapeutic gel packs and then choose whether they wanted a reward for themselves or give one to someone else. They predicted that people in the warm gel condition would be more likely to reward others, that is, participants would be more prosocial. Although there was some evidence for this association, it was weak and additional analysis found that the results were inconclusive. The study was based on a large sample of 611.

A final note about distance and emotion. Stefanucci and Storbeck (2009) asked participants to look at arousing or non-arousing images and then estimate the distance to the ground from a two-floor balcony, and to estimate the size of an object on the ground. Those who looked at the arousing images overestimated the distance and the size of the object. However, estimates of horizontal – rather than vertical – distance was unaffected. When participants were asked to exaggerate their emotional arousal, their over-estimation increased.

Emotion without cognition?

Related to research on mood and cognition is a broader issue in emotion research. This is whether emotion can occur without cognition. Some psychologists, such as Lazarus (1984), believe that emotions are produced only by cognitive processes – by anticipating, experiencing, or imagining the outcomes of important interactions with the environment. Others, such as Zajonc (1984), insist that cognitive appraisal is not necessary and that emotions are automatic, species-typical responses heavily influenced by classical conditioning.

Although the two sides of the debate appear to have been drawn sharply, it seems clear that both automatic processes and conscious deliberation play a role in the expression and feelings of emotion. Some examples of emotions clearly involve cognitive processes. For instance, a person can become angry after realising that someone's 'kind words' actually contained a subtle insult. This anger is a result of cognition. But sometimes, emotional reactions and their associated feelings seem to occur automatically. As we saw, through the process of classical conditioning, stimuli can evoke emotional reactions before we have time to realise what is happening. In some cases, we may be acting in a hostile and angry manner without realising what we are doing. If cognitive processes are responsible for our anger, they are certainly not conscious, deliberate ones.

One of the problems with this debate (as with many other debates) is that the opponents sometimes define the same terms in different ways. For example, not everyone agrees which operations of the brain should be regarded as cognitive and which should not. According to Lazarus (1984), many cognitive processes are unconscious and relatively automatic. But if cognitive processes need not be conscious, how can we tell whether a given process is cognitive? And if we cannot tell, how can we hope to decide whether cognition is necessary for all emotions? If our definition of cognition is too general, we would have to conclude that all responses require cognition.

Happiness – An international perspective

Most people are generally happy (Diener *et al*., 2014) and although people's life satisfaction and mood fluctuates, over time, both are usually perceived as more positive than neutral. Some twin studies have suggested that the likelihood of reporting negative mood; is more heritable than reporting positive mood. Positive mood is better predicted by shared environmental influences (Zheng *et al*., 2016). Zheng *et al*. suggest that their data indicate a two-factor model of affect – where positive emotion is situational and negative emotion is dispositional (see the section on neuroticism in Chapter 14 for a similar suggestion).

Studies of peoples of different nations have shown that different people not only think about happiness in different ways but their happiness is influenced by nation-level variables such as taxation. In their review of the topic, Oishi and

▶

Happiness – *Continued*

Gilbert (2016) have found that many unusual differences exist between people from different countries.

Americans, for example, associated personal achievement and related experiences with emotion, whereas the Japanese associate it with things that do not last very long and with envy (Uchida and Kitayama, 2009). People from some nations, (Iran, for example), fear happiness (Joshanloo, 2013; Joshanloo *et al.*, 2014), This is especially strong if those people are from nations which also value conformity and reliance on formal rules (Joshanloo *et al.*, 2014). Civic virtue (as exemplified by the belief that we must not evade tax or commit fraud) was found to be a positive predictor of happiness in 73 nations (Stavrova *et al.*, 2013), especially if the nation valued civic virtue. Oishi and Gilbert note that a similar relationship exists for religion. Religious people are happiest in religious societies than are non-religious ones (Diener *et al.*, 2011).

Taxation is one predictor of happiness. Those nations with more progressive tax regimes are more likely to have happy citizens, as are those nations with democracy and freedom (Orviska *et al.*, 2014; Oishi *et al.*, 2012). As you saw in Chapter 2, there is evidence that the wealth of a nation is related to life satisfaction and happiness –although this evidence has been robustly challenged. Typically, the wealthier the nation, the happier the citizen, although wealthier nations have been found to have angrier and more anxious citizens than do poorer ones (Diener *et al.*, 1995; Tay *et al.*, 2014). Immigrants from Eastern Europe to Western Europe report being happier than those who remain although there are some national differences – immigrating Romanians, Russians and Turks are the happiest, whereas immigrating and remaining Poles show no difference (Bartram, 2013).

But differences also lie at the more local level. People who live in better educated areas tend to report greater happiness, for example, although educated people themselves were not necessarily happier than their less educated counterparts elsewhere (Rentfrow *et al.*, 2009; Florida *et al.*, 2013).

Oishi and Gilbert concluded that a number of problems exist in this field: most of the studies are based on self-report and more behavioural data would provide a stronger test of the hypotheses examined. Also, most studies have focused on the differences between Western (usually North American) and Asian cultures and so there is a need to extend the studies to other nations and continents (such as Africa and the Middle East). They also emphasise the importance of measuring fluctuations in happiness – and not just taking one static measure and drawing conclusions.

Controversies in psychological science: Dark clouds gathering, sunny spells later...

The issue

Many people long for summer months when they can jet off to sunny climes, soak in the sun and lounge on the beach while creatively avoiding skin cancer. People in countries where natural sunlight is restricted appear to have a higher incidence of unhappiness or depression. The mood of the general population appears to decline in the winter months (Harmatz *et al.*, 2000), and one treatment for **seasonal affective disorder** – the appearance of depression in the dark, winter months (see Chapter 18) – is exposure to artificial light. But is there any evidence that climate and temperature significantly influence mood? And if so, how?

The evidence

Keller *et al.* (2005) reviewed a variety of studies investigating the relationship between climate, mood and cognition. Task performance in one study peaked at 22 °C and dropped at cooler or warmer temperatures than 22 °C (Allen and Fischer, 1978). More heuristic and less-systematic processing has been found in people during sunny and warm days than on cloudy or cool days (Sinclair *et al.*, 1994). People are more likely to tip if an employee refers to pleasant weather than gloomier weather (Rin, 1996; Rind and Strohmetz, 2001) and that young women (18–25 years old) are more likely to accept romantic approaches from attractive men (giving their telephone number) on sunny than cloudy days (Gueguen, 2013). Studies such as this have led to the suggestion that low humidity and high levels of sunlight (and high barometric pressure and temperature) are associated with positive mood whereas high temperatures alone led to a negative mood or no change in mood. Evidence, however, is not entirely consistent.

For example, daily mood reports collected from almost 500 undergraduates in Dallas during the autumn or spring

▶

Controversies in psychological science: *Continued*

found no relationship between season and mood (Watson, 2000). A study of shoppers recruited on sunny or cloudy, rainy days found that people recalled more of the ten unusual objects placed at a checkout when the weather was rainy (Forgas *et al.*, 2009). Others report that behaviour such as violence increases during high temperatures (Anderson, 2001) and that stock market returns are higher in the summer (Saunders, 1993), perhaps reflecting the possibility that the temperature inures traders to risk or makes them less risk-averse. Seasonal studies are also problematic in that sunny and warm days can be experienced in 'cooler' seasons (e.g. autumn). And there is a possibility that sunny days in spring and autumn can produce different effects (they are less novel in the spring, for example?). Do people need to be directly exposed to this weather for mood to change, i.e. do they need to be outdoors? One study found that 93 per cent of the people in the individual countries studied spent their time indoors during good weather (Woodcock and Custovic, 1998).

To test these hypotheses, Keller *et al.* (2005) set up three experiments. In the first, they examined whether temperature or the length of time spent outdoors in warm weather affected mood. Data were collected from 97 people from April to June. They found no direct relationship between barometric pressure and temperature, and mood. But they did find a positive relationship between mood and time spent outside. A similar relationship was found for creativity, cognitive flexibility, openness to experience and digit span performance. People who spent more than 30 minutes outdoors on clear days had higher digit spans and showed a more flexible thinking style.

In a second experiment, the researchers manipulated the time spent outdoors. The first session took part indoors; participants then either danced or walked around a track or walked outdoors or on a treadmill. Again, temperature did not appear to affect mood but the outdoor condition did. When people were outdoors on days that were warm, clear and characterised by high pressure, their mood was significantly more positive than those indoors during the same meteorological conditions. (The mood of those indoors decreased.)

They found that the more time that participants spent outdoors in the spring, the greater the association between temperature and mood. As temperatures increased in the summer, there was a negative relationship between time spent outdoors and mood: those who were outside in high temperatures showed reduced mood. The best temperature for mood improvement was 19.7 °C. This mood declined after 45 minutes outdoors.

Source: Image Source Salsa / Alamy Stock Photo.

One reason for a possible inconsistency in results, however, may be individual difference. For example, there may be certain 'types' which prefer certain types of weather and whose mood increases or decreases depending on the weather. This is what Klimstra *et al.* (2011) found. They monitored self-reported mood across 30 days and noted the weather on those days. They were able to identify four types in 497 adolescents and their mothers: Summer Lovers, Summer Haters, Rain Haters and the Unaffected. Summer Lovers were happier, less fearful and less angry on sunny and warmer days and less happy and more anxious on rainy days. Summer Haters (of which there were more than Summer Lovers) were less happy on sunny days and happier on rainy days. Rain Haters were angrier and less happy in pluvial weather and happier, but no less angry, on sunny days. The Unaffected type was the most common of all. When these were included in the mood–weather correlations, such relationships were small. When this group was removed, the correlations increased, showing a relationship between mood and weather.

▶

Controversies in psychological science: *Continued*

Source: Alamy Stock Photos.

A comprehensive (1 million participants) study of the association between weather conditions and life satisfaction in 50 US states over a 5-year period found that daily weather conditions had no effect on self-reported life satisfaction (Lucas and Lawless, 2013).

Conclusion

While Keller *et al.*'s review suggests that the important contributor to mood is the time people spend outdoors in warm weather on clear days, recent research suggests that the relationship depends on weather preference.

Cutting edge: The cognitive consequences of oral contraception

In 1960, the Food and Drug Administration in the US approved the use of the first legal, oral contraceptive (Enovid). This was followed by the first legalised approval of the pill (Anovlar) in Europe. The journey began back in the 1930s when progesterone was first isolated from ovarian glands and the 1940s when German researchers found that this hormone suppressed ovulation in women, not just non-human animals. Around 100 million women around the world use it.

But apart from its functional use, does taking an oral contraceptive affect a woman's psychological functioning? Some research has focused on 'feminising' versus 'masculinising' effects of the pill. Other research has looked at the effect of the chemical on cognition and emotion.

In a review of the literature, Pletzer and Kerschbaum (2014) note that contraceptive use has been associated with increased grey matter volume in the anterior cingulate cortex also with changes in mate preference. In terms of cognitive performance, oral contraceptive users have been found to show better verbal memory than non-users but no better verbal fluency (Mordecai *et al.*, 2008). There seems to be mixed evidence concerning better mental rotation but some

Cutting edge: *Continued*

studies have suggested that oral contraceptive users' behaviour is more similar to men's on tasks involving recall of emotional memories (Nielsen *et al.*, 2013).

The findings for emotion are even more mixed: some studies find that oral contraceptive use is beneficial to mood whereas others finding an association with

depression, anxiety and fatigue (Pletzer and Kerschbaum, 2014). There seem to be some differences in brain activation during tasks involving facial recognition and, because of this, Pletzer and Kerschbaum (2014) argue that taking contraceptive use into account during neuroimaging experiments is important.

Chapter review

Motivation

- Motivation is a general term for a group of phenomena that affects the nature, strength and persistence of an individual's behaviour. It includes a tendency to perform behaviours that bring an individual into contact with an appetitive stimulus or that move it away from an aversive one.
- Regulatory systems include four features: a system variable (the variable that is regulated), a set point (the optimum value of the system variable), a detector to measure the system variable and a correctional mechanism to change it.
- Psychologists believed that aversive drives were produced by deprivation and that reinforcement was a result of drive reduction. However, the fact that we cannot directly measure an individual's drive level makes it impossible to test this hypothesis. Many reinforcers increase drive rather than reduce it. Thus, most psychologists doubt the validity of the drive reduction hypothesis of reinforcement.
- The discovery that electrical stimulation of parts of the brain could reinforce behaviour led to the study of the role of brain mechanisms involved in reinforcement. Apparently, all reinforcing stimuli (including addictive drugs) cause the release of dopamine in the brain.
- Because high levels of drive or arousal can be aversive, several investigators proposed the optimum-level theory of motivation and reinforcement. This theory suggests that organisms strive to attain optimum levels of arousal; thus, reinforcement and punishment are seen as two sides of the same coin.
- Because drive cannot be directly measured, we cannot determine whether an individual's drive is above or below its optimum level.
- Perseverance is the tendency to continue performing a behaviour that is no longer being externally reinforced

and is determined by the organism's previous history with intermittent reinforcement and its opportunity to develop behaviours that produce conditioned reinforcers.
- Learned helplessness involves learning that an aversive event cannot be avoided or escaped.

Eating and drinking

- The fluid in cells is called intracellular fluid and contains a little sodium but large amounts of potassium and other metabolites. The other source of fluid in the body is extracellular fluid and this is found in two places. Interstitial fluid surrounds the cell body and is salty; blood plasma is found in the capillaries, arteries and veins and allows living cells and blood to be suspended within it.
- The reduction in the concentration of sodium available across the membrane and the movement of water by osmosis dehydrating and shrinking the body's cells is called osmometric thirst.
- Another type of thirst (volumetric thirst) results from dehydration outside cells, that is, a reduction in the level of blood plasma.
- Hunger is the feeling that precedes and accompanies an important regulatory behaviour: eating.
- Eating begins for both social and physiological reasons. Physiologically, the most important event appears to be the detection of a lowered supply of nutrients available in the blood.
- Detectors in the liver measure glucose level, and detectors elsewhere in the body measure the level of fatty acids. Both sets of detectors inform the brain of the need for food and arouse hunger.
- Detectors responsible for satiety, which appear to be located in the walls of the stomach, monitor both the

▶

quality and the quantity of the food that has just been eaten.

- Neuroimaging evidence suggests that our brain's response to images of food changes depending on our hunger state and also on our degree of obesity.
- Long-term control of eating appears to be regulated by the chemical leptin, which is released by over-nourished fat tissue and detected by cells in the brain. It decreases meal size and increases metabolic rate, thus helping the body to burn up its supply of triglycerides.
- Genetic and environmental factors may interact to cause the person's weight to deviate from the norm.
- To be diagnosed as clinically obese a person must have a body mass index that is equal to or greater than 30 kg/m^2.
- Intervention programmes for obese people are successful if individuals self-monitor and continue to adopt the strategies they have been taught after the intervention period is over.
- In extreme cases, surgery of the intestine is an effective means of helping a person lose weight (bariatric surgery).
- People differ genetically in the efficiency of their metabolisms and this efficiency can easily lead to obesity.
- Particular eating habits, especially those learned during infancy, can override the physiological signals that would otherwise produce satiety.
- Experiences such as repeated fasting and refeeding (the yo-yo effect) are often accompanied by overeating.
- Sensory-specific satiety refers to a reduction in the pleasantness of a food eaten to satiety, whereas the pleasantness of others is relatively unaffected.
- People eat more of a four-course than of a one-course meal and more of a meal containing a variety of pasta shapes and colours than one containing one shape and one colour.
- The hedonic response to food after satiety is thought to be mediated by the secondary taste cortex; the primary taste cortex helps to identify the food.
- Anorexia nervosa is an eating disorder in which the individual is obsessed with food and weight but deliberately reduces their intake of food and avoids it; the prevalence of the disorder is between 0.5 and 1 per cent worldwide, and most anorexics are young women.
- Studies have found metabolic differences in anorexic patients, but we cannot determine whether these differences are the causes or the effects of the disorder.

- Bulimia nervosa is an eating disorder which involves a loss of control of food intake; bulimic individuals will often binge and then use laxatives or vomiting to get rid of the consumed food.

Sexual behaviour

- Testosterone has two major effects on male sexual behaviour: organisational and activational.
- In the foetus, testosterone organises the development of male sex organs and of some neural circuits in the brain; in the adult, testosterone activates these structures and permits erection and ejaculation to occur.
- The sexual behaviour of female mammals with oestrus cycles depends on oestradiol and progesterone, but these hormones have only a minor effect on women's sexual behaviour.
- Women's sexual desire, like that of men, is much more dependent on androgens.
- The development of sexual orientation appears to have biological roots. A large-scale study of homosexuals failed to find evidence that child-rearing practices fostered homosexuality.
- Studies have identified three regions of the brain that differ in size between homosexual and heterosexual males. These results suggest that the brains of these two groups may have been exposed to different patterns of hormones early in life. In addition, twin studies indicate that homosexuality has a genetic component as well.

Aggressive behaviour

- Ethological studies of other species suggest that aggression is a means of averting violence: threat gestures warn of an impending attack, and appeasement gestures propitiate the potential aggressor.
- In males of most animal species, androgens have both organisational and activational effects on aggressive behaviour.
- Testosterone appears to increase in a variety of situations and contexts. Increases have been found before chess players play matches and in winners after matches; increased levels have been reported in prisoners convicted of violent crime and described by fellow inmates as being tough. These data are, however, correlational.
- Field studies on the effects of televised violence are not conclusive. Observational studies have revealed a modest relation between preference for violent television shows and boys' aggressiveness, but we cannot be sure that watching the violence causes the aggressiveness.

▷

- An attempt to manipulate aggression by forcing children to watch violent or non-violent television programmes was inconclusive because many children resented their loss of choice.

Emotion

- Emotion refers to behaviours, physiological responses and feelings evoked by appetitive or aversive stimuli, although psychologists have defined emotion in various ways.
- Darwin believed that expression of emotion by facial gestures was innate and that muscular movements were inherited behavioural patterns.
- Ekman and his colleagues showed that members of the South Fore tribe recognised facial expressions of Westerners and made facial gestures that were clear to Westerners, suggesting that emotional expressions are innate behaviour patterns and universally found.
- There is controversy, however, over whether facial expressions reflect true emotions or whether they reflect the social communication of an emotion.
- A number of theorists have suggested that there is a group of basic emotions, although the exact number is controversial, as is the notion that there are basic emotions. The most widely accepted number of basic emotions is six or seven.
- Research has shown that those who are outwardly happy are most likely to have high self-esteem and are happy in other aspects of their lives.
- Expressions of emotion are not always frank and honest indications of a person's emotional state. They can be masked, modulated or simulated according to culturally determined display rules.
- Destruction to parts of the amygdala prevents the recognition of fear in facial expressions and activation in the amygdala is seen in healthy individuals exposed to facial expressions of fear. In healthy individuals, the left side of the amygdala is active during the experience of positive emotion.
- The orbitofrontal cortex is also important to emotion and may be involved in the regulation of socially appropriate behaviour that involves complex decision-making.
- People with damage to the orbitofrontal region are able to explain the implications of complex social situations but are unable to respond appropriately when put in these situations. Thus, this region appears to be necessary for translating judgements about the personal significance of events into appropriate actions and emotional responses.

- The affective asymmetry of emotion model suggests that EEG activation of the left frontal region may be involved in the experience of positive emotion whereas activation of the right frontal region is involved in the experience of negative emotion.
- People have been found to be more moralistic (and altruistic) in the presence of a pleasant, 'clean' scent than not.
- Some research suggests that the posture people adopt can affect their degree of self-esteem and self-worth and also influence testosterone production.
- James and Lange suggested that the physiological and behavioural reactions to emotion-producing situations were perceived by people as states of emotion and that emotional states were not the causes of these reactions.
- Although emotional states are sometimes produced by automatic, classically conditioned responses, some psychologists have suggested that the perception of our own emotional state is not determined solely by feedback from our behaviour and the organs controlled by the autonomic nervous system. It is also determined by cognitive assessment of the situation in which we find ourselves.
- Schachter and his colleagues found that information about the expected physiological effects of drugs (or placebos) influenced subjects' reports about their emotional state. In one study, subjects even tolerated more intense electrical shocks, apparently discounting their own fear.
- Appraisal theories suggest that emotion is experienced after the environment has been evaluated for threat, fear, joy or any other influential factor.
- Evolutionary theories argue that emotions are a means of adapting to change in the environment; these changes produce a restricted set of responses which are universal (hence, the emotions associated with them should also be universal).
- Cognitive theories of emotion suggest that our emotional response depends on our cognitive appraisal of our situation and circumstance or the stimulus we perceive.
- Lazarus, argued that primary appraisal involved the initial evaluation of the environment – is it positive, negative or neutral whereas secondary appraisal involved the individual's evaluation of how best to cope with this environment and what options were available to facilitate this coping. This model was later updated. A recently updated model, the hedonic treadmill model, argues that after we experience a highly emotional event, we return to a neutral state soon after.
- The debate over whether cognition is necessary for emotion continues. Ultimately, the argument rests on how cognition is defined.

Suggestions for further reading

Motivation

Casazza, K. *et al.* (2013) Myths, presumptions and facts about obesity. *NEJM*, 368, 446–54.

Current Opinion in Psychology (2018), Special Issue on Aggression and violence.

Deckers, C. (2010) Motivation: *Biology, Psychology and Environment* (3rd edn). Boston, MA: Allyn & Bacon.

Hock, R.R. (2010) *Human Sexuality* (2nd edn). Boston, MA: Allyn & Bacon.

Kaye, W.H., Wierenga, C.E., Bailer, U.F., Simmons, A.N., and Bischoff-Grethe, A. (2013) Nothing tastes as good as skinny feels: the neurobiology of anorexia nervosa. *TICS*, 36, 110–20.

Nave, G., Nadler, A., Zava, D., & Camerer, C. (2017). *Single dose testosterone administration impairs cognitive reflection in men. Psychological Science*, in press.

Singh, M. (2014) Mood, food and obesity. *Frontiers in Psychology*, 5, 1–20.

Emotion

Adolphs, R. (2017) How should neuroscience study emotions? *Social, Cognitive and Affective Neuroscience*, 12(1), 24–31.

Al-Shawaf, L., Lewis, D.M.G., & Buss, D.M. (in press). Sex differences in disgust: Why are women more easily disgusted than men? *Emotion Review*.

Berridge, K.C. and Kringelbach, M.L. (2013) Neuroscience of affect: brain mechanisms of pleasure and displeasure. *Current Opinion in Neurobiology*, 23, 294–303.

Brooks, J.A., Shablack, H., Gendron, M., Satpute, A.B., Parrish, M.H. and Lindquist, K.A. (2017) The role of language in the experience and perception of emotion: a neuroimaging meta-analysis. *Social Cognitive and Affective Neuroscience*, 12(2), 169–83.

Farb, A.S., Chapman, H.A. and Anderson, A.K. (2013) Emotions: form follows function. *Current Opinion in Neurobiology*, 23, 393–8.

Feinstein, J.S. (2013). Lesion studies of human emotion and feeling. *Current Opinion in Neurobiology*, 23, 304–309.

Harmon-Jones, E. and Gable, P.A. (2017). On the role of asymmetric frontal cortical activity in approach and withdrawal motivation: An updated review of the evidence. *Psychophysiology*, in press.

Inman, C. S., Bijanki, K. R., Bass, D. I., Gross, R. E., Hamann, S., & Willie, J. T. (2018). Human amygdala stimulation effects on emotion physiology and emotional experience. *Neuropsychologia*, in press.

Kragel, P.A. and LaBar, K.S. (2016) Decoding the nature of emotion in the brain. *TICS*,

Lewis, M., Haviland-Jones, J.M. and Barrett, L.F. (2010) *Handbook of Emotions* (3rd edn). London: Guilford Press.

Lindquist, K.A., Satpute, A.B., Wager, T.D., Weber, J. and Barrett, L.F. (2016) The brain basis of positive and negative affect: evidence from a meta-analysis of the human neuroimaging literature. *Cerebral Cortex*, 26(5), 1910–22.

Macmillan, M. and Lena, M.L. (2010) Rehabilitating Phineas Gage. *Neuropsychological Rehabilitation*, 20, 641–58.

McDuff, D., Kodra, E., el Kaliouby, R. and LaFrance, M. (2017) A large-scale analysis of sex differences in facial expressions. *PloS one*, 12(4), e0173942.

Schirmer, A. and Adolphs, R. (2017) Emotion perception from face, voice and touch: Comparisons and convergence. *TICS*, in press.

Yap, S. C., Wortman, J., Anusic, I., Baker, S. G., Scherer, L. D., Donnellan, M. B., & Lucas, R. E. (2017). The effect of mood on judgments of subjective well-being: Nine tests of the judgment model. *Journal of Personality and Social Psychology*, 113(6), 939.

Some excellent books and papers on general emotion topics.

CHAPTER 14
Personality

CAN YOUR 'PERSONALITY' PREDICT YOUR POLITICAL ATTITUDES AND PERSUASIONS?

In March 2018, many countries around the world woke up to the possibility that information some Facebook users had supplied online via a 'personality' quiz on the site may have been used by a third party to target them with advertisements for certain political candidates and views and against others. What is more, information from the 'friends' of those users was also accessed and those users were also targeted. In total, around 50 million users were thought to be affected. This controversial abuse of users' data was so significant that the CEO of Facebook took out full-page ads in US newspapers on March 25 apologising for the data security breach.

The ethics of this process aside, some questions emerge from this debacle that psychologists are interested in (and have a view on). Think about what the answers to these questions might be, before you read on.

How were the questions in the personality quiz designed and by whom?

What was the validity of the quiz?

Which items in this quiz reflected certain personality types and how? What evidence is there that such categorisation into personality types based on this quiz would make a person more or less susceptible to political messaging?

WHAT YOU SHOULD BE ABLE TO DO AFTER READING CHAPTER 14

- Describe what psychologists mean by 'personality'.

- Describe and understand the methods used by psychologists to study personality.

- Describe and explain what is meant by trait theory and situationism.

- Describe and evaluate psychodynamic personality theory and humanistic approaches to personality.

- Describe and evaluate the trait models of Cattell, Eysenck and Costa and McCrae.

- Evaluate the validity and reliability of personality tests.

QUESTIONS TO THINK ABOUT

- What is personality?

- Can we measure personality? If so, how?

- If individuals possess personality characteristics, how do we explain people's behaviour when they act "out of character"?

- Does personality mean the same thing in every culture? Is personality a linguistic rather than behavioural phenomenon?

- Does personality have a biological basis?

- How stable is personality over time?

- Are there national differences in personality?

Towards a definition of personality

People have different styles of thinking, of relating to others and of working, all of which reflect differences in personality – differences crucial to defining us as individuals. Common experience tells us that there is no one else just like us. There may even be significant differences in the personal characteristics of identical twins.

Such everyday observations provide a starting point for psychology's study of personality. But unlike such informal observations, psychology's approach to studying personality is considerably more calculated. For example, to many people, personality is nothing more than 'what makes people different from one another'. To psychologists, however, the concept is generally defined much more narrowly. **Personality** is a particular pattern of behaviour and thinking that prevails across time and situations and differentiates one person from another.

Psychologists do not draw inferences about personality from casual observations of people's behaviour. Rather, their assessment of personality is derived from results of special tests designed to identify particular personality characteristics. The goal of psychologists who study personality is to discover the causes of individual differences in behaviour.

This goal has led to two specific developments in the field of personality psychology: the development of theories that attempt to explain such individual differences and the development of methods by which individual patterns of behaviour can be studied and classified. Merely identifying and describing a personality characteristic is not the same as explaining it. However, identification is the first step on the way to explanation. What types of research effort are necessary to study personality? Some psychologists devote their efforts to the development of tests that can reliably measure differences in personality. Others try to determine the events – biological and environmental – that cause people to behave as they do. Thus, research on human personality requires two kinds of effort: identifying personality characteristics and determining the variables that produce and control them.

Trait theories of personality

As you will see in this chapter, the word 'personality' means different things to different people. The way in which personality is used by trait theorists is similar to the way in which we often think of personality in everyday life: a set of personal characteristics that determines the different ways we act and react in a variety of situations.

Personality types and traits

It has long been apparent that people differ in personality. The earliest known explanation for these individual differences is the humoral theory, proposed by the Greek physician Galen in the second century and based on then-common medical beliefs that had originated with the ancient Greeks. The body was thought to contain four humours, or fluids: yellow bile, black bile, phlegm and blood. People were classified according to the disposition supposedly produced by the predominance of one of these humours in their systems. Choleric people, who had an excess of yellow bile, were bad tempered and irritable. Melancholic people, who had an excess of black bile, had gloomy and pessimistic temperaments. Phlegmatic people, whose bodies contained an excessive amount of phlegm, were sluggish, calm and unexcitable. Sanguine people had a preponderance of blood (sanguis), which made them cheerful and passionate.

Although later biological investigations discredited the humoral theory, the notion that people could be divided into different **personality types** – different categories into which personality characteristics can be assigned based on factors such as developmental experiences – persisted long afterwards. For example, Freud's theory, which maintains that people go through several stages of psychosexual development, predicts the existence of different types of people, each type having problems associated with one of these stages. We discuss some of these problems later in this chapter.

Personality types are useful in formulating hypotheses because, when a theorist is thinking about personality variables, extreme cases are easily brought to mind. But after identifying and defining personality types, one must determine whether these types actually exist and whether knowing a person's personality type can lead to valid predictions about their behaviour in different situations.

Most modern investigators view individual differences in personality as being in degree, not kind. Tooby and Cosmides (1990) have, for example, argued that the nature of human reproduction makes the evolution of specific personality types unlikely – fertilisation produces a reshuffling of the genes in each generation, making it highly unlikely that a single, unified set of genes related to personality type would be passed from one generation to the next.

Rather than classify people by categories, or types, many investigators prefer to measure the degree to which an individual expresses a particular personality trait. A personality trait is an enduring personal characteristic that reveals itself in a particular pattern of behaviour in different situations. A simple example illustrates the difference between types and traits. We could classify people into two different types: tall people and short people. Indeed, we use these terms in everyday language. But we all recognise that height is best conceived of as a trait – a dimension on which people differ along a wide range of values. If we measure the height of a large sample of people, we will find instances all along the distribution, from very short to

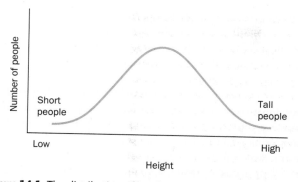

Figure 14.1 The distribution of height. We can measure people's height, a trait, on a continuous scale. We can also look at the extremes and divide people into the categories 'short' and 'tall' types.

very tall, as Figure 14.1 illustrates. It is not that people are only either tall or short (analogous to a personality type) but that people vary in the extent to which they are one or the other (analogous to a personality trait).

We assume that people tend to behave in particular ways: some are friendly, some are aggressive, some are lazy, some are timid, some are reckless. Trait theories of personality fit this common-sense view. However, personality traits are not simply patterns of behaviour: they are factors that underlie these patterns and are responsible for them.

Identification of personality traits

Trait theories of personality do not pretend to be all-encompassing explanations of behaviour. Instead, they are still at the stage of discovering, describing and naming the regular patterns of behaviour that people exhibit (Goldberg, 1993). In all science, categorisation must come before explanation; we must know what we are dealing with before we can go about providing explanations. The ultimate goal of the personality psychologist is to explain what determines people's behaviour – which is the ultimate goal of all branches of psychology.

Allport's search for traits

Gordon Allport (1897–1967) was one of the first psychologists to search systematically for a basic core of personality traits. He began by identifying all the words in an unabridged dictionary of the English language that described aspects of personality (Allport and Odbert, 1936). He found around 18,000 words, which he then further analysed for those that described only stable personality characteristics. He eliminated words that represented temporary states, such as 'flustered', or evaluations, such as 'admirable'. This still left him with over 4,000 words. Allport was interested in learning how many traits are needed to describe personality and exactly what these traits may be. For example, many of those 4,000 words, such

as 'shy' and 'bashful', are synonyms. Although each synonym presumably makes some sort of distinction about a trait, a group of synonyms together might be used to describe the same underlying trait. Many trait theorists believe that the most basic set of personality traits ranges from three to 16 traits.

Allport's research stimulated other psychologists to think about personality in terms of traits or dispositions. In fact, most modern trait theories can be traced to Allport's earlier theoretical work. Like Allport, modern trait theorists maintain that only when we know how to describe an individual's personality will we be able to explain it.

Cattell: sixteen personality factors

Factor analysis is an important means of defining intelligence (see Chapter 11). Factor analysis identifies variables that tend to be correlated. To use factor analysis to study personality, researchers must observe the behaviour of a large number of people. Usually, the observations are limited to responses to questions on paper-and-pencil tests, but occasionally, investigators observe people's behaviour in semi-natural situations. Statistical procedures then permit investigators to determine which items a given person tends to answer in the same way; they can then infer the existence of common factors. For example, a shy person would tend to say no to statements such as 'I attend parties as frequently as I can' or 'When I enter a room full of people, I like to be noticed.' In contrast, outgoing people would tend to say 'yes' to these statements.

To the degree that people possess orderly personality traits, they tend to answer certain clusters of questions in particular ways. Raymond Cattell (1905–98) began his search for a relatively small number of basic personality traits with Allport and Odbert's (1936) list of adjectives. In addition, he collected data on people's personality characteristics from interviews, records describing their life histories, and from observing how people behave in particular situations. From this list, Cattell began to construct preliminary versions of a questionnaire called the 16PF. Then, using factor analysis, he analysed responses from thousands of people to whom the inventory had been administered. Eventually, he identified 16 personality factors.

Cattell referred to these 16 traits as source traits because, in his view, they are the cornerstones upon which personality is built: they are the primary factors underlying observable behaviour. He called groups of similar types of observable behaviour surface traits; he included such traits as kindness, honesty and friendliness because they are visible to others. They represent the surface of personality and spring forth from source traits, which lie deeper within the personality. Figure 14.2 illustrates a personality profile of a hypothetical individual rated on Cattell's 16 factors. The factors are listed in order of importance, from top to bottom. Look at the ratings to see whether you think they would help you to predict the person's behaviour.

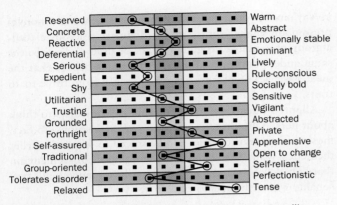

Figure 14.2 A hypothetical personality profile using Cattell's sixteen personality factors.

Source: From *16PF® Fifth Edition Administrator's Manual*. Copyright © 1993 by the Institute for Personality and Ability Testing, Inc., Champaign, Illinois, USA. All rights reserved. Reproduced with permission. '16PF' is a registered trademark of IPAT Inc. IPAT is a wholly owned subsidiary of OPP Ltd.

Eysenck: three factors

Hans Eysenck (1916–1997) also used factor analysis to devise his theory of personality (Eysenck, 1970; Eysenck and Eysenck, 1985). His research identified three important factors: extraversion, neuroticism and psychoticism. These factors are bipolar dimensions. Extraversion is the opposite of introversion, neuroticism is the opposite of emotional stability, and psychoticism is the opposite of self-control. **Extraversion** refers to an outgoing nature and a high level of activity; **introversion** refers to a nature that shuns crowds and prefers solitary activities.

Neuroticism refers to a nature full of anxiety, worries and guilt; **emotional stability** refers to a nature that is relaxed and at peace with itself. Psychoticism refers to an aggressive, egocentric and antisocial nature; self-control refers to a kind and considerate nature, obedient of rules and laws. Eysenck's use of the term 'psychoticism' is different from its use by most clinical psychologists; his term refers to antisocial tendencies and not to a mental illness. A person at the extreme end of the distribution of psychoticism would receive the diagnosis of antisocial personality disorder.

Neuroticism has been the subject of considerable research because it has been associated with mental illness and ill-health (Perkins *et al.*, 2015). People scoring high on neuroticism tend to think negatively and experience negative emotions. They take fewer risks when they make investments. People who score low on this trait are better bomb disposal workers and are more likely to be volunteer for military pilot training (Hallam and Rachman, 1980; Campbell *et al.*, 2009; Kuhnen *et al.*, 2013).

One hypothesis which may explain neuroticism is that these individuals are dispositionally more susceptible to threat and make exaggerated (negative) emotional responses when they encounter threats (Gray and McNaughton, 2000). There is evidence for this hypothesis but these individuals also respond with negative emotion in the absence of a threat. Perkins *et al.*,

for example, have suggested that neuroticism is explained by dysfunction in the brain regions responsible for self-generated thought leading to self-generated thoughts about problems and negative events and experiences.

According to Eysenck, the most important aspects of a person's temperament are determined by the combination of the three dimensions of extraversion, neuroticism and psychoticism – just as colours are produced by the combinations of the three dimensions of hue, saturation and brightness. Figure 14.3 illustrates the effects of various combinations of the first two of these dimensions – extraversion and neuroticism – and relates them to the four temperaments described by Galen.

More than most other trait theorists, Eysenck emphasises the biological nature of personality (Eysenck, 1991). For example, consider the introversion–extraversion dimension, which is biologically based, according to Eysenck, on an optimum arousal level of the brain. Eysenck believes that the functioning of a neural system located in the brain stem produces different levels of arousal of the cerebral cortex. Introverts have relatively high levels of cortical excitation, whereas extraverts have relatively low levels. Thus, in order to maintain the optimum arousal level, the extravert requires more external stimulation than does the introvert. The extravert seeks stimulation from external sources by interacting with others or by pursuing novel and highly stimulating experiences. The introvert avoids

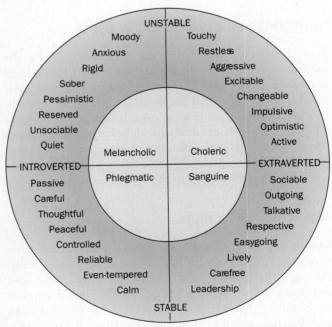

Figure 14.3 Eysenck's original theory illustrated for two factors. According to Eysenck, the two dimensions of neuroticism (stable versus unstable) and introversion–extraversion combine to form a variety of personality characteristics. The four personality types based on the Greek theory of humours are shown in the centre. Eysenck later added 'psychoticism' as the third trait.

Source: Eysenck, H.J., *The Inequality of Man*. London: Temple Smith, 1973. Reprinted with permission.

external stimulation in order to maintain their lower arousal level at an optimum state. Different states of arousal are hypothesised to lead to different values of the extraversion trait for different people. This hypothesis is reviewed in the section on the biological basis of personality.

Most trait theorists accept the existence of Eysenck's three factors because they have emerged in factor analyses performed by many different researchers; these appear, in fact, to have the highest validity of all proposed personality factors (Kline, 1993).

The five-factor model and the Big Five

Languages reflect the observations of a culture; that is, people invent words to describe distinctions they notice. An analysis of such distinctions by Tupes and Christal (1961), replicated by Norman (1963), led to the most widely accepted model of personality traits: the **five-factor model** (FFM; McCrae and Costa, 1985, 1987, 1990). The FFM proposes that personality is composed of the following five primary dimensions:

1 Neuroticism

2 Extraversion

3 Openness

4 Agreeableness

5 Conscientiousness

These factors can be measured by the Neuroticism, Extraversion and Openness Personality Inventory, or NEO-PI, which consists of 181 items that potentially describe the person being evaluated (McCrae and Costa, 1990). Studies have shown that people's assessment of their own personality agrees well with ratings by spouses and those who know them. The test items are brief sentences, such as 'I really like most people I meet' or (for ratings by someone else) 'She has a very active imagination'. The person taking the test rates the accuracy of each item on a scale of 1 to 5, from strong disagreement to strong agreement. The scores on each of the five factors consist of the sums of the answers to different sets of items.

McCrae et al. (1986) validated the FFM through the factor analysis of a list of adjectives contained in a test called the California Q-Set. This test consists of 100 brief descriptions (such as 'irritable', 'cheerful', 'arouses liking' and 'productive'). The items were provided by many psychologists and psychiatrists who found the words useful in describing people's personality characteristics. Thus, the words are not restricted to a particular theoretical orientation. McCrae and his colleagues found that factor analysis yielded the same five factors as the analysis based on everyday language: neuroticism, extraversion, openness, agreeableness and conscientiousness.

The FFM is regarded by most personality psychologists as a fairly robust model of personality (Magai and McFadden, 1995) although it is a model that is atheoretical and descriptive rather than explanatory (Hampson, 2012). The Big Five

Personality Inventory has been used to investigate various relationships between personality and other psychological variables, as you will see in this chapter and throughout the text. When a study investigates conscientiousness or openness to experience, for example, it is using the FFM model. For example, Zhao and Seibert (2006) investigated the differences between the personalities of managers and entrepreneurs. In a meta-analysis, they found that entrepreneurs scored more highly on the dimension of conscientiousness and openness to experience but scored lower on neuroticism and agreeableness. There was no difference between the two groups for extraversion.

Another group explored whether those who are always late for appointments differed in personality traits from those who turned up on time or early. Participants completed a personality questionnaire (the Big Five) and were invited to participate in an experiment a few days later (Back et al., 2006). The researchers then examined whether any of the personality variables were related to the degree of punctuality. They examined three dependent measures – time of arrival, earliness and lateness. As you might predict, conscientiousness was significantly associated with punctuality – the more conscientious the participant, the less likely he or she was to turn up late and the more likely he or she was to turn up early. Agreeableness was associated with turning up on time and neuroticism was associated with turning up early. The researchers speculate that more specific components of these general traits – such as dependability – might better predict punctuality.

Grit

A recent addition to the personality literature in recent years has been grit. Grit is considered to be a higher-order factor that reflects perseverance and sticking to a goal (Duckworth et al., 2007). What is interesting about this trait is that research has found that it is a good predictor of academic and life success (Duckworth et al., 2007). It has been found to predict working memory performance and have a neural substrate in the nucleus accumbens (Nemmi et al., 2016). However, others have argued that grit is not a separate trait but is very similar to and overlaps significantly with conscientiousness. Predictions of academic success from personality, for example, have found that conscientiousness is the better predictor, with grit separately adding little to academic success (Rimfeld et al., 2016). A meta-analysis of the literature on grit was unable to establish that this was a distinct factor – it found that it had no construct validity – and that grit was highly correlated with conscientiousness (Crede et al., 2016).

Stability of personality traits across the lifespan

Some longitudinal studies of personality show remarkable stability in personality factors (especially, extraversion). Cross-sectional studies, however, show less stability – not surprisingly, perhaps, because cross-sectional studies include people who differ in age (and, therefore, share different cultural influences). A study of the personalities of 163 men over 45 years found that neuroticism, extraversion and openness were positively correlated throughout the 45 years and that the traits remained relatively stable (Soldz and Vaillant, 1999).

A review of the stability of personality in 152 longitudinal studies (allowing for 3,217 examples of **test–retest reliability**) found that the consistency of personality increased from childhood to young adulthood, increased still further from adulthood to 30 years, and stabilised between the ages of 50 and 70 years (Roberts and DelVecchio, 2000). These data suggest that personality traits are fairly stable across the lifespan, certainly until the age of 50. Even then, stabilisation is not so great as to indicate a marked change in personality.

The results were confirmed by Caspi et al. (2000) who monitored the personalities of children born between April 1972 and March 1973 in Dunedin, New Zealand, the country's fourth largest city. The children were studied from 3 years of age to 21. At the age of 3, children were classified by temperament and, in adulthood, they were asked to rate their own temperament. They also had their temperament rated by others (official records were also used to form an assessment of their temperament).

Some studies have suggested that some personality traits are more fluid than others. McCrae and Costa and their international team of researchers looked at changes in the Big Five personality traits from the age of 14 years to 30 years in a sample of Germans, British, Spaniards, Czechs and Turks ($N = 5,085$) (McCrae et al., 2000). They found that neuroticism, extraversion and openness to experience decreased from 14 to 30 years but that agreeableness and conscientiousness increased. Similar trends were found after 30 years, but the changes were not as pronounced.

A similar pattern – some decline, some stability, but largely some change – has also been noted in a meta-analysis of longitudinal studies. Roberts et al. (2006) found that social dominance (a feature of extraversion), conscientiousness and emotional stability increase between the ages of 20 and 40, whereas social vitality and openness increase during adolescence, then decline to old age. Smits et al. (2011) asked first-year students between 1982 and 2007 to complete the Big Five. They found small increases in extraversion, agreeableness and conscientiousness and small decreases in neuroticism. No changes were found for openness to experience.

A cross-sectional study of over a million individuals aged between 10 and 65 years found distinct patterns of personality change across the age categories (Soto et al., 2011). Agreeableness and conscientiousness were less apparent during adolescence and increased during emergent adulthood; extraversion was also less apparent from late childhood to adolescence. Anxiety and depression, facets of neuroticism, increased in girls from late childhood to adolescence. Depression, but not anxiety, declined during the college years. Openness to experience was not prominent up until adolescence but increased during the college years. In adulthood, the study found that a 65-year-old was more self-disciplined than 85 per cent of adolescents and more agreeable than 75 per cent of them.

A lack of stability in personality traits has also been reported in a longitudinal study of 174 people aged 77 (Harris et al., 2016). Harris et al. were able to use data collected in 1947 when the individuals were adolescents. Of the large sample ($N = 1,208$), a portion of the sample survived and agreed to take part in a follow-up study in 2012. In 1947, six personality traits were measured by the participant's teachers. In 2012, the same traits were measured. People who knew the participants well were asked to judge their personality. While there was little stability found in any of the six traits nor in the general trait of dependability, when some other effects were excluded, mood stability and conscientiousness did show evidence of stability from adolescence to old age.

Cutting edge: Personality and diet

Is there any relationship between your personality and what you eat? According to a large Finnish study of 1,681 participants, there is (Tiainen et al., 2013). The researchers administered questionnaires to find out what people ate and how often, and correlated these data with the big five personality traits of the NEO-PI.

These were some of the results they found:

Openness to experience in men was associated with higher vegetable consumption and lower chocolate and sweets consumption.

Neuroticism in women was associated with lower fish and vegetable consumption and higher soft drink consumption.

Extraversion in women was associated with greater meat and vegetable intake.

Openness to experience in women was associated with greater fruit and vegetable intake.

Agreeableness in women was associated with reduced soft drink intake and conscientiousness with higher fruit intake.

The researchers also found that more resilient women were more likely to eat more vegetables, fruits, fish and fibre than were non-resilient women.

Personality – An international perspective

Any truly grand theory of personality must be able to encompass all cultures, countries and languages. If personality comprises three or five factors, which we all exhibit to a lesser or greater extent, then these factors should be exhibited or reported cross-culturally. If not, then the theory is culture-specific and describes only personality within a limited number of cultures.

One immediate problem in testing the universality of trait theories is that the way in which they are measured depends on language, and different cultures have slightly different words that they use to describe things. They also have words to represent events and objects that other cultures do not. Inuit, for example, have tens of words to describe the quality of snow. Individuals in less Arctic climes would obviously have no need for such a large vocabulary because snow appears only irregularly and does not impinge on their life in such a regular and intrusive way.

In personality, problems in demonstrating universality lie in taxonomy. Do the same words mean the same thing across cultures? For example, various cultures have attributed different meanings to the conscientiousness factor of the Big Five model (Caprara and Perugini, 1994). This factor means something different to the Dutch, Hungarians and Italians, and to the Americans, Germans, Czechs and Poles. Some reviewers have suggested that the best one can do is to find acceptable counterparts of the Big Five in all cultures; the first three factors of the model can be found in most cultures but the cross-cultural validity of others may be questionable (De Raad, 1998). However, there are more consistencies than inconsistencies across cultures.

McCrae et al. (2005) asked college students from 50 cultures, including Arabic and Black African cultures, to identify a man or woman they knew well and rate them using the third person version of the Revised NEO-PI. The Big Five structure was replicated in almost all cultures (Morocco and Nigeria were two of the half dozen or so not to show this pattern). Women were more positive than men in rating others, especially when rating other women.

In a separate study of the geography of personality traits, Allik and McCrae (2004) examined whether respondents from 36 cultures differed according to the Big Five personality dimension. Cultures that were geographically close shared similar personality traits: the greatest geographical distinction was between European and American cultures, and Asian and African cultures. Americans and Europeans were significantly more extravert and open to experience but less agreeable than peoples from other cultures. Why?

The authors suggest that the results may be due to shared gene pools (China and Korea, for example, share genetic ancestry) or to features of those cultures. Studying the process of acculturation – the assimilation of a person's behaviour with that person's culture – might help identify which is correct. For example, a study of Chinese people who emigrated to Canada found that differences between these people and European Canadians attenuated the longer the Chinese people lived in Canada (McCrae et al., 1998). Openness and agreeableness, in particular, increased in the immigrant group but introversion remained stable and did not match levels seen in European Canadians. These data suggest that some personality traits might be adopted or enhanced by acculturation, but others may not.

Can cultures also differ according to the implicit or lay trait or context theories they hold? Implicit theories describe what people think about the stability (trait) or variability (context) of personality traits, how consistent they believe such traits are across situations, how they predict behaviour from a person's personality traits, how they form an idea of a person's traits from little behavioural information and so on. Church et al. (2005) investigated cross-cultural implicit beliefs about personality in what they called two individualistic cultures – America and Australia – and two collectivistic cultures – Mexico and the Philippines. They hypothesised that the more individualistic the culture, the greater or stronger the culture's beliefs in traits, rather than situations, as determinants of behaviour. Implicit trait beliefs were stronger in Americans than in Mexicans or Filipinos, but implicit contextual beliefs were weaker.

We often hold stereotypes of our own and other nations that may not necessarily be true. The Brits have stiff-upper lips, Americans let it all hang out, Australians don't stand on ceremony and the French are supercilious. None might be accurate; some might.

To investigate whether our perceptions of our own and the culture of others are supported by empirical data, a team of international researchers asked respondents from 49 cultures across six continents to complete a National Character Survey which asked them to describe a typical member from a culture. These responses were compared with personality data collected via the Revised NEO-PI (Terracciano et al., 2005).

These was a significant relationship between cultural traits described by others and objectively assessed personality for only four cultures – New Zealand, Australia, Poland and Lebanon. The only significant relationships between self-reported cultural characteristics and personality scores were found in Poland and Japan. Poland, therefore, was the only culture where the people's views of the nation's characteristics were supported by objective data.

The study highlights the power of national stereotypes in our views of others and members of our own culture: such stereotypes are contradicted by empirical data.

How much of personality is expressed in our writing?

A little, a lot? Do you deliberately not inject much of your personality into your writing? Are you aware that your personality might influence your writing? Some formats of writing will obviously be less susceptible to individual creativity than others – writing a lab report, for example, demands different skills and a different style to writing an essay or a diary.

Researchers at the University of Toronto asked 94 undergraduates to complete a writing task which required them to write about the past, present and future (Hirsch and Peterson, 2009). The five major personality dimensions were measured. A specialised software package analysed language use in the students' narratives.

A strong correlation was found between personality type and word use. Those scoring high in extraversion were more likely to use words associated with humans, social processes and family; agreeableness was also associated with family words and with words associated with inclusivity. Achievement and work-related words were associated with high conscientiousness, and words expressing negative emotion, anger, anxiety and sadness were associated with high neuroticism. Participants high in neuroticism were also more likely to discuss topics related to the body. Finally, words related to hearing and seeing were associated with openness to experience.

Of course, the software used in the experiment measured word usage rather than word context and an analysis based on the context in which the words are used would provide a more robust investigation of the association between personality and writing.

How we view ourselves in the past and the present

Geoffrey Haddock (2006) asked women students to rate their present (now) and past selves (beginning of the academic year) for physical attractiveness. They were also asked how important physical attractiveness was to their sense of self. Participants rated their present selves as physically more attractive, but only if physical attraction was a feature they thought was important to their sense of self. In a second experiment, participants judged their current physical attractiveness and estimated how physically attractive they would be in five years' time. Participants rated their future selves to be more attractive than their current selves. However, this result was found only in participants who tended to make social comparisons with others.

While the results may reflect the fact that students actually do believe that they get more attractive with time, they could also suggest that our appraisals of ourselves are affected by time and that these are relative: we are more positive about the present than the past and are more positive about the future than the present. Whether Mac was right or not, Haddock's participants could have been singing the same tune.

Some studies show that young and middle-aged people rate their present selves more positively than their younger selves, whereas older individuals (mean age, 73 years) feel more positively about the present for some attributes, more negatively about others and neutral about still others (Ryff, 1991). Other studies show that people rate themselves to be happier in the present than the past.

In a systematic study of people's appraisals of their past and present selves, Wilson and Ross (2001) asked university undergraduates to provide descriptions of their present selves and how they remember themselves at 16 years of age. People were more positive about their present than past selves. In a second study, participants evaluated themselves using a list of desirable attributes (broad-minded, common sense, self-confident, good coping skills, good social skills) and undesirable attributes (dishonest, rude, dull/boring). The same pattern emerged: past selves were viewed less favourably. Even a period of two months was sufficient to produce a less favourable view of the past self compared with the present self. In two more studies, the researchers found that people judged themselves to have improved more significantly than acquaintances. When people compared their past self to a peer at that age, they regarded themselves more favourably than they did their peer.

There are various explanations for why people regard their current self more positively than they do their past self.

Cutting edge: Which personality attributes make a good boss and employee?

At least two: Conscientiousness and agreeableness. There is a body of research which has concluded that these two personality traits, more than others, are regarded as positive attributes in employees and employers and are predictors of job success and perceived successful leadership. They predict job performance in low level and complex jobs, training success and securing experience to apply for a job (Sackett and Walmsley, 2014). Sackett and Walmsley also found that while conscientiousness was the most important attribute across job types, specific professions also valued other personality traits: news reporters, for example, were more likely to be open to experience and insurance salesmen were more likely to be extravert. In one study of hectare managers' personality and people's judgement of their competence, people were more likely to judge good leaders/managers to be those who were open to experience, conscientious and agreeable (Bergman et al., 2014), with the last two particularly important for ethical leadership.

Perhaps people revise the past because they wish to see their present selves in a favourable light. Revising the past downward may be easier than inflating the past upward. By criticising their past selves, they can feel better about themselves without inflating their current view of themselves.

Heritability of personality traits

Several trait theorists, including Cattell and Eysenck, have asserted that a person's genetic history has a strong influence on their personality. Many studies have shown that some personality traits are strongly heritable (Emde et al., 1992; McGue et al., 1993; Jang et al., 1998). The heritability of a trait can be assessed by comparing identical (monozygotic, MZ) with fraternal (dizygotic, DZ) twins, comparing twins raised together with twins raised apart, and comparing biological with adoptive relatives (see Chapter 3). Many studies have found that identical twins are more similar to each other than are fraternal twins on a variety of personality measures, which indicates that these characteristics are heritable (Loehlin, 1992).

Using various tests of Eysenck's factors of extraversion, neuroticism and psychoticism, Zuckerman (1991) found that identical twins were more similar than fraternal twins on every measure. Similar data have been reported for the Big Five (e.g. Loehlin et al., 1998; Yamagata et al., 2006) with correlations between MZ twins being consistently higher than those for the DZ twins.

The results of Big Five and extraversion, neuroticism and psychoticism studies suggest that heredity accounts for between 40 and 70 per cent of the variability in these three personality traits. Concordance rates for extraversion in MZ twins range between 0.45 and 0.60, and for DZ twins, between 0.15 and 0.3 (Zuckerman, 2005). When people rate the personalities of MZ and DZ twins they see on video, the concordance rating (CR) for the MZ twins is 0.59 and for the DZ twins 0.23 (so viewers think the MZ twins behave more similarly than the DZ twins, even though they are not aware of their twin status). A similar pattern is seen for peer ratings. The concordance rates for MZ twins reared apart is between 0.3 and 0.6; for DZ twins, it is 0.

Slightly lower correlations are found for neuroticism, but the direction is the same; the CRs are higher for the MZ than DZ twins (Zuckerman, 2005). Thus, it would appear that the remaining 30–60 per cent of the variability is caused by differences in environment. In other words, some family environments should tend to produce extraverts, others should tend to produce introverts, and so on. But research indicates that the matter is not so simple.

Zuckerman (1995) reviewed several studies that measured the correlation in personality traits of pairs of identical twins raised together and raised apart. If family environment has a significant effect on personality characteristics, then the twins raised together should be more similar than those raised apart. But they

were not. Taken as a group, these studies found no differences, indicating that differences in family environment account for none of the variability of personality traits in the twins who were tested. Another approach, comparing the personality traits of parents with those of their adopted children, suggests that family environment may account for approximately 7 per cent of the variability (Scarr et al., 1981). If approximately 40–70 per cent of the variability in personality traits is caused by heredity and 0–7 per cent is caused by family environment, what is responsible for the remaining 23–50 per cent of the variability? The answer is that heredity and environment interact.

The major source of the interaction seems to be the effect that people's heredity has on their family environment (Plomin and Bergeman, 1991). That is, people's genetic endowment plays an important role in determining how family members interact with them. Identical twins agreed on their ratings of cohesion, expressiveness, conflict, achievement, culture, activity, organisation and control much more than the fraternal twins did; that is, identical twins were much more likely to have experienced similar family environments.

There are two possible explanations for these results: the family environments could have been more similar for identical twins than for fraternal twins, or the family environments could really have been the same in all cases but were simply perceived as different by the fraternal twins. Evidence suggests that the first possibility is correct, that is, the family environments really were more similar for identical twins (Loehlin, 1992). How can this be? One might think that each family has a certain environment and that everyone in the household comes under its influence.

Although there are aspects of a family that are shared by the entire household, the factors that play the largest role in shaping personality development appear to come from social interactions between an individual and other family members. These social interactions are different for different people. Because of hereditary differences, one child may be more sociable; this child will be the recipient of more social interaction. Another child may be abrasive and disagreeable; this child will be treated more coldly. In the case of identical twins, who have no hereditary differences, the amount of social interaction with each twin is likely to be similar.

Even physical attributes (which are largely hereditary) will affect a child's environment. A physically attractive child will receive more favourable attention than will an unattractive child. In fact, studies that examined video-taped interactions between mothers and their children confirm that heredity does have an important influence on the nature of these interactions (Plomin and Bergeman, 1991). Thus, although a child's environment plays an important part in their personality development, hereditary factors play a large role in determining the nature of this environment.

Are all personality traits a product, direct or indirect, of a person's heredity? The answer is no. Some personality characteristics show a strong effect of shared environment but almost no effect of genetics. For example, twin studies have found a strong influence of family environment, but not of heredity, on belief in God, involvement in religion, masculinity/femininity, attitudes towards racial integration, and intellectual interests (Loehlin and Nichols, 1976; Rose, 1988). Thus, people tend to learn some important social attitudes from their family environments.

Personality and birth order

Do you have a brother or sister? Do you think that he or she is similar to or different from you? If you have many siblings, and you are the youngest or the oldest, have you noticed that you might behave slightly differently from your brother or sister? A study from the US of families with large numbers of siblings (equal to or greater than six) has found differences in personality between brothers/sisters which is dependent on birth order (Dixon *et al.*, 2008). The youngest sibling, as well as the three youngest siblings, was significantly more extravert than the oldest, and oldest three siblings, when compared with their own family members and those from the other families.

One explanation for the finding may be that the younger sibling has to try harder for parental attention because of competition from other siblings: increased extraversion is reflected in increased assertiveness.

Neurobiological basis of personality

Patients with damage to the front of the brain, the orbito-frontal cortex (OFC) behave differently from those with damage to other areas of brain, as you saw in Chapters 4 and 13. They are more impulsive, engage in more inappropriate behaviour and report more anger and less happiness (Berlin *et al.*, 2004).

Controversies in psychological science: Can personality predict health and ill health?

The issue

Back in the 1980s, Hans Eysenck proposed a very controversial theory. He argued that a cancer-prone personality existed: a personality type that would mean the likelihood of developing the disease was greater in this type than those who did not express the type. While the evidence to support the theory was sparse, a new line of research has suggested that personality and mood may influence health and ill health.

The evidence

A number of studies has found that personality is a strong and consistent predictor of physical health (e.g. Hampson, 2012; Hampson *et al.*, 2013; Jokela *et al.*, 2013; Chapman *et al.*, 2011). These studies have examined the relationship not only between self-reported health (which can be subjective and misleading) and personality but objectively reported and observed health- such as assessments by physicians or physiological indicators of health. Chapman *et al.*, for example, found that personality was a better predictor of longevity than was socioeconomic status and intelligence. This predictive power of personality has been found across age ranges from childhood onwards.

Of the personality traits that are more important to health, conscientiousness is that which has most consistently predicted mortality (Friedman *et al.*, 2013). In a study of 6,904 participants from the Health and Retirement Study in the US, Weston *et al.* (2014) measured personality and self-reported health on two occasions, four years apart. Three personality traits were predictive of the development of later ill health such as lung disease, stroke or having a heart problem: conscientiousness, openness to experience and neuroticism. Conscientiousness was a protective factor – the greater the score, the less likely it was that the participants would develop these illnesses; neuroticism was a risk factor and openness to experience was associated with a reduced likelihood of developing an illness. Neuroticism has been associated with poorer health and mental health, in other studies (Finch *et al.*, 2012; Barlow *et al.*, 2014).

A study with a different approach examined the relationship between an individual's health and personality as assessed by people's friends (Jackson *et al.*, 2015). Six hundred people were assessed longitudinally from 1935 to 2013. Some unusual findings emerged, but findings that were still consistent with those reported earlier: men who were regarded by their friends as conscientious and open to experience lived longer whereas women who were regarded as emotional stable (less neurotic) and agreeable by their friends lived longer. The friends' assessments were also better predictors of health/longevity than were the participants' own.

Despite its association with poor health -especially poor mental health- neuroticism has recently been associated with lower mortality in a group of over 300, 000 UK participants (Gale et al, 2017). The study found an 8% reduction in mortality in those with the highest levels of neuroticism (possibly because neurotic people are so concerned with and anxious about their health that they may take many steps to keeping themselves healthy)

Conclusion

The evidence suggests that a significant and consistent relationship exists between personality and longevity and ill health with conscientiousness acting as a protective factor and neuroticism as a risk factor. A reason for this may be that conscientious people may look after themselves more, are more careful in looking after their own health or are more optimistic.

Traumatic brain injury to the frontal lobe in children as young as 5 or as old as 14 is associated with personality changes six and 12 months following injury (Max *et al.*, 2006). Curiously, given the marked changes in 'personality' normally observed in frontal lobe patients, Berlin *et al.* (2004) found no significant differences between the groups on a standard measure of personality (the Big Five). Where, therefore, if anywhere, do the neural correlates of personality reside?

Many models of personality have drawn on biological and physiological mechanisms to explain differences in extraversion, neuroticism and psychoticism (Eysenck and Eysenck, 1985; Gray, 1987; Zuckerman, 1995; Canli, 2006). Zuckerman (1995), for example, suggested that the personality dimensions of extraversion, neuroticism and psychoticism are determined by the neural systems responsible for reinforcement, punishment and arousal. People who score high on extraversion are particularly sensitive to reinforcement – perhaps their neural reinforcement systems are especially active. Table 14.1 summarises Zuckerman's hypothetical explanations for the three major personality dimensions.

Infants who later become extraverts show higher activity levels, whereas adult extraverts show more reinforcement-seeking behaviour. Adult extraverts participate in more social activities, tend to shift from one type of activity to another, are optimistic and expect that their pursuits will result in reinforcing outcomes. However, unlike people who score high on psychoticism, they are sensitive to the effects of punishment and can learn to act prudently. People who score high on neuroticism are anxious and fearful. If they also score high on psychoticism, they are hostile as well. These people are particularly sensitive to the punishing effects of aversive stimuli. Zuckerman therefore suggests that the personality dimension of neuroticism is controlled by the sensitivity of the neural system responsible for punishment, which appears to involve the amygdala.

People who score high on psychoticism have difficulty learning when not to do something. Zuckerman suggests they have a low sensitivity to punishment and also have a high tolerance for arousal and excitation; in other words, we could say that their optimum level of arousal is abnormally high. Some theorists hypothesise that people seek situations that provide an optimum level of arousal: too much or too little arousal is aversive (see Chapter 13). Therefore, a person with a high optimum level of arousal (a high tolerance for excitement) seeks out exciting situations and performs well in them. A neurotic would find these situations aversive, and their behaviour would become disorganised and inefficient. A person with a high tolerance for excitement makes a good warrior but does not fit in well in civilised society.

This is a reformulation of Eysenck's original theory. He argued that extraverts were less reactive to cortical excitation and, therefore, sought out stimulation. Extraverts do need more stimulation to feel good. Introverts, conversely, are cortically over-aroused which leads to them seeking out or avoiding situations that are stimulating. Eysenck's theory was constructed at a time when EEG and ERP were the only useful methods of measuring excitation. Neuroimaging data show a complicated pattern. Introverts show more activation in some brain regions than do extraverts; conversely, extraverts show more activation in some brain regions than do introverts (Haier *et al.*, 2004). A recent study found that EEG was not able distinguish between the big five personality dimensions (Korjus *et al.*, 2015).

To examine whether the neural correlates of the Big Five personality traits, DeYoung *et al.* (2010) examined the relationship between structural MRI scans and personality in 116 individuals. They found that extraversion varied with the volume of medial OFC, neuroticism with regions involved in threat and anxiety, conscientiousness with part of the prefrontal lobe involved in planning, and agreeableness with areas involved in the appreciation of others' mental states. In terms of brain structure, the personality trait which most closely correlates with volume is neuroticism (Bjornebekk *et al.*, 2013). People who score highly on this trait have been found to have smaller brain volume in the frontal and temporal region. Extraversion was associated with a thinner inferior frontal gyrus. There was no consistent structural feature associated with openness to experience and agreeableness. Using the EPI as the measure of personality, Lu *et al.* (2014) found that high levels of extraversion were associated with reduced grey matter in the amygdala and parahippocampal gyrus bilaterally, the right middle temporal gyrus and the left superior frontal gyrus. Neuroticism correlated with grey matter volume in the right cerebellum; a correlation has also been found between grey matter volume in the cerebellum and novelty-seeking (Picerni *et al.*, 2013) so this structure may reflect some non-psychological aspects of these traits which are common to both. Neuroimaging

Table 14.1 Zuckerman's hypothetical biological characteristics that correspond to personality dimensions

Factor	Loading
Extraversion	
Do you like mixing with people?	0.70
Do you like plenty of bustle and excitement around you?	0.65
Are you rather lively?	0.63
Neuroticism	
Do you often feel fed up?	0.67
Do you often feel lonely?	0.60
Does your mood often go up and down?	0.59
Psychoticism	
Do good manners and cleanliness matter much to you?	−0.55
Does it worry you if you know there are mistakes in your work?	−0.53
Do you like taking risks for fun?	0.51

studies suggest that some connections between the amygdala and anterior cingulate cortex are reduced in individuals who are high in neuroticism, although the samples are small (Ormel *et al.*, 2013). If the connections are reduced, some have argued that this makes the amygdala more responsive (hyperresponsive) to stress, or that the response in the amygdala to anxiety-provoking stimuli can't be extinguished, and so people behave anxiously and express negative emotion (Depue, 2009).

The picture, therefore, is complex – perhaps not surprisingly given the febrile nature of personality and debate over whether it is a genuinely fixed series of traits. Perhaps the biological basis of personality may be found at a more genetic level. There have been associations reported, for example, between the presence of a serotonin gene (*5HTT* or *SERT*) and neuroticism scores (Lesch *et al.*, 1996). There are two variants of this gene – a long one and a short one. The short-allele version has been associated with high harm-avoidance and neuroticism scores, and lower agreeableness scores (Lesch *et al.*, 1996; Greenberg *et al.*, 2000), and with depression and hostility (Mossner *et al.*, 2001; Sen *et al.*, 2004). Chiao and Blizinsky (2010) sought to examine the significance of this allele in cultures characterised as individual or collectivist. They found that, across 29 nations – including Argentina, Australia, France, India, China, Spain, South Africa, Turkey, the UK and the US – those characterised as collectivist were more likely to carry the short version of the allele. The presence of the allele was also associated with reduced anxiety and more positive mood.

Novelty-seeking and sensation-seeking have been associated with the presence of a specific dopamine receptor (D4DR) (Ebstein *et al.*, 1996). Its allele has two forms and the longer one has been linked to high-novelty seeking although in reviews of all relevant studies, around half show this pattern (Prolo and Lincino, 2002). In one study of 4-year-old children, mothers of those children with the long form of the D4DR allele described them as having more problems with aggression (Schmidt *et al.*, 2001, 2002).

Of course, if this allele is important to more 'negative' personality types, perhaps those with the allele might respond in a specific way when they view negative images, such as fearful faces. Predicting that viewing such faces would lead to greater amygdala activation in these allele carriers, Hariri *et al.* (2002) found this activation in an fMRI study of 28 individuals.

Perhaps, in terms of understanding the possible genetic causes of personality expression, Wilson best sums up our current status:

Reductionism across all levels is not a realistic goal for science. . . . One could conceivably find all the particular genes that contribute to the genetic variance in a personality trait but not be able to account for the complex interactive influences with environment that shaped the trait. Genes and environment interact throughout development and although environment cannot change genes, it can affect this expression through releasor genes. Genes do not make personality traits or behavioural traits, they simply make proteins that in turn make nerves, biochemicals, and these affect physiology and ultimately, behaviour. (Source: Wilson, 1998, p. 247.)

One other model of personality, Gray's reinforcement sensitivity theory (Gray and McNaughton, 2000; McNaughton and Corr, 2004) argues that a behavioural inhibition system (BIS) mediates our response to aversive events in the environment. In the original model, an over-sensitive system leads to extreme behavioural responses such as psychiatric disorders (e.g. anxiety and depression). A complex network of structures was thought to underlie the BIS, including the amygdala, the septal area and the hippocampus. In the updated, 2004 version of the model, three networks were proposed to mediate our response to positive, negative and conflicting stimuli: the Behavioural Approach System, the Flight Freeze System and the Behavioural Inhibition System. The first mediates approach behaviours and explains differences in sensitivity to reward; the second mediates avoidance behaviours, especially defensive avoidance (avoiding threat); and the third mediates inhibition (when a threatening stimulus is encountered) (Kennis *et al.*, 2013).

If the first is more sensitive, people are more likely to approach positive stimuli and greater activation is seen in the

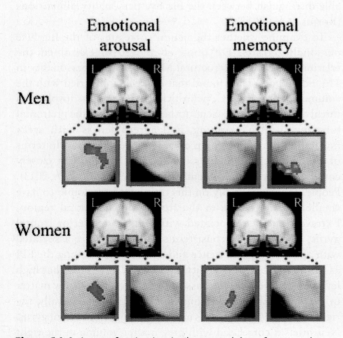

Figure 14.4 Areas of activation in the amygdalae of men and women as they recalled arousing, emotional pictures.

Source: Plate 10.1 from *Human Neuropsychology*, 2nd edn, Pearson/Prentice Hall (Martin, G.N., 2006).

ventral tegmental area, the ventral striatum and prefrontal cortex. The activation of the inhibition system and the freeze system depends on what McNaughton and Corr call defensive distance and the intensity of the threat dictates which brain regions are recruited. For example, the freeze system responds to signals of threat and determines whether the threat is to be avoided and whether we fight, flee or freeze. If the threat is intense, the periaqueductal grey, medial hypothalamus and amygdala are involved; if the threat is low, the anterior cingulate cortex and ventral PFC are involved. This system is also involved in frustration – when we expect a reward but the reward does not materialise.

The inhibition system intervenes if the other two systems are activated or if there is a conflict within each of these systems. When it is activated, behaviour is inhibited and people will ruminate and worry more. Kennis *et al.* (2013) have proposed that a fourth dimension can be added to these three: effortful control. This acts as a contrast system which inhibits impulses and overcomes the tendency of a person not to act.

The state you're in: a psycho-geography of personality

Can country or a state be said to have a 'personality'? In what was perhaps the earliest study to explore this in a systematic way, the Catell 16PF was administered to six regions of the US (Krug and Kulhavy, 1973). It found that people from north-eastern, mid-west and west coast states had higher 'creative productivity' scores than those in south-eastern, south-western and mountain regions. Another report from the 1970s found that subscriptions to cultured and sophisticated magazines were more common in the north-east and west central parts of the US than the South (Zelinsky, 1974). A more recent study of self-perception in nine US regions found that respondents in the mid and south Atlantic regions rated themselves as 'nervous' or 'worrying' whereas those in New England, the mid-Atlantic and Pacific regions scored more highly on broad-mindedness, curiosity and sophistication (Plaut *et al.*, 2002). The development of well-validated personality measures, such as the FFM which is biologically rooted and predicts stability in traits across time, has sparked a plethora of cross-cultural and transnational studies.

Why should these different states show these different patterns of personality? Rentfrow *et al.* (2008) suggest at least three reasons: (1) people migrated to places that met their psychological and physical needs; (2) a social founder effect, where the intellectual history, customs and culture of a place established social norms for that environment which influenced behaviour and personality; and (3) socialisation, where personality traits are acquired that are consistent with the behaviour seen in the environment people were in, that is, people behaved in a way that was consistent with the behavioural norm for that region.

In terms of social migration, Rentfrow *et al.* argue that a person high in extraversion, for example, might escape a suffocating small town to one where there is greater stimulation and creativity, and there is evidence from social psychology demonstrating that people seek out social situations that are consistent with their own beliefs and attitudes (Buss, 1987). Extraverts seek out stimulating environments; neurotic people do not (Furnham, 1981). The social influence of the social founder effect might work in the same way as emotional contagion – if a personality trait is common in a region, it affects others and is imbibed by them. Environmental factors may also be important – as you saw in Chapter 11, people living in areas with little natural light are more inclined to be unhappy and those living in hot climates tend to experience more violence than those in cold ones (Anderson and Anderson, 1996; Magnusson, 2000).

Rentfrow *et al.* investigated whether US regions differed in terms of their extraversion, openness to experience, agreeableness, conscientiousness and neuroticism. They predicted that extraversion would be related to community involvement, preference for enterprising or social professions and interest in physical health (as others had suggested before: Ozer and Benet-Martinez, 2006); agreeableness would be related to religiosity, longevity and low levels of criminality (Ozer and Benet-Martinez, 2006; Roberts *et al.*, 2007); conscientiousness with health-protecting behaviour, longevity and low levels of crime; neuroticism with criminal behaviour and poor coping; and openness to experience with unconventional belief and preference for creative professions.

Rentfrow *et al.* used the internet to recruit 619,397 participants from 50 US states and Washington DC. Information about ethnicity, socio-economic status, education etc. was requested, as was information about personality. Fifty-five per cent were women. Rentfrow *et al.*'s findings were as follows:

- Levels of extraversion were associated with social involvement (such as club meetings, time spent in bars), involvement in business in healthcare professions (e.g. sales/nursing), high rates of robbery and murder, high religiosity and a higher proportion of people in artistic/investigative professions; but lower levels of jogging/exercising.
- Levels of agreeableness were associated with low crime and activities that were social (but not bar/club related), religiosity and involvement in artistic/entertainment professions.
- Levels of conscientiousness were positively associated with murder and robbery (strangely – although when demographic variables were taken into account, this effect disappeared), religiosity and less time spent in bars.
- Levels of openness to experience were associated with liberal values, preference for artistic/investigative professions and more tolerant views on marijuana, abortion and gay marriage.
- Levels of neuroticism were associated with incidents of robbery and murder and in less exercise taken at home.

Similar studies have examined state-level differences in personality and their associated with residential mobility – who are most likely to move state or remain in their state? (McCann, 2015). McCann examined residential mobility in 50 states in 2005 and correlated this with the personality scores of 619,397 residents. He found that the greater the neuroticism in a state, the less likely was residential mobility (within and outside county); state extraversion was also associated with the same pattern of mobility when narcissism was excluded; conscientiousness was associated with the greatest mobility but only when demographic factors were not considered. McCann has

also found that the degree of volunteering was lower in US States scoring high in neuroticism (McCann, 2017).

Rentfrow *et al.* also reported an analysis of personality type in the UK (Rentfrow *et al.*, 2015). They found regional personality differences in 400,000 British residents from 380 local authority districts in England, Wales and Scotland. Agreeableness was highest in the Scottish Highlands and the North of England, Neuroticism was lowest in the southwest of England and Openness was higher in London, Brighton, Manchester and Bristol. You can see the pattern of personality distribution across the UK in Figure 14.5.

Figure 14.5 Five maps of the UK showing the degree of personality trait expressed by each region: **(a)** extraversion; **(b)** agreeableness; **(c)** conscientiousness; **(d)** neuroticism; **(e)** openness to experience. The higher the presence of the trait, the redder the colour.

Cutting edge: Language, personality and Facebook

What type of language do people use on social networking sites – Facebook, specifically – and is it predicted by personality type and the person's sex? Schwartz *et al.* (2013) examined 700 million words, phrases and content topics in Facebook messages written by 75,000 Facebook users who had volunteered their data. The researchers administered a personality measure and noted the participants' age and sex.

They found some unusual findings: neurotic participants were more likely to use the phrases 'sick of' and 'depressed', for example; men were more likely to use the possessive 'my' to preface "wife" or "girlfriend" than did women did about their partners. The authors collected the most widely used words and phrases used by participants to create word clouds. You can see the results of this analysis for sex, age and personality in Figure 14.6.

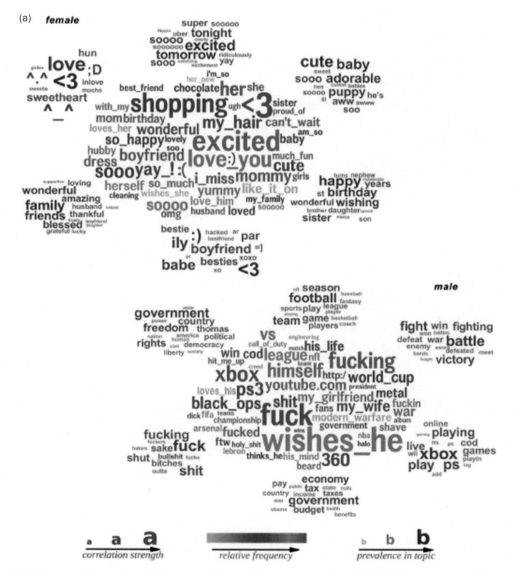

Figure 14.6 (a) These are the words and phrases used most frequently by girls/women (top) and boys/men (bottom). The bigger the size of the word the greater the frequency of use. **(b)** The words and phrases used most frequently by different age groups: 13–18, 19–22, 23–29 and 30–65. The sweariest respondents are 19–22-year-olds. **(c)** The words and phrases that most strongly distinguish between introverts and extroverts, and neurotic individuals and those who are emotionally stable.

Cutting edge: *Continued*

Another study found that personality was associated with how abstract a person's language was. Beukeboom *et al.* (2012) found that the more extraverted the person, the more abstract the language they used when they spoke and interacted with others. Holtgraves (2011) examined the relationship between text messages and personality.

He administered a version of the Big Five to 224 students and analysed the content of the last 20 text messages they sent via their mobile phone. Extraversion was related to talkativeness in texts but only in women; women were also more frequent texters (they spent less time sending the next message). Extroverts used fewer negative words. Extroverts

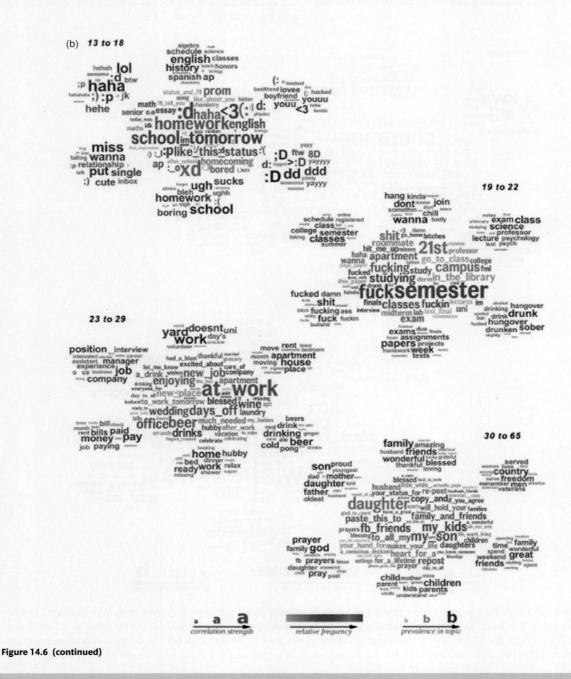

Figure 14.6 (continued)

Cutting edge: *Continued*

Figure 14.6 (continued)

were no more likely to swear but they did use more sexual words. Extroversion also correlated with word expansion (e.g. 'Bittchhhhhhh') which the author suggests may be a form of shouting via text. People scoring high in neuroticism used more negative emotional words (but did not use fewer positive ones). Women used more social words than did men and used more pronouns (and fewer impersonal pronouns). Men were more likely to swear and also refer to leisure.

Psychology in action: Facebook, Twitter, Instagram . . . are we all narcissists now?

The chances are – in fact, the overwhelming probability is – that you are a Facebook user. It is the most widely used social network in the world (Wilson *et al*., 2012). Across the planet, it and other social networking sites (SNS) are thought to have between 100 million and 600 million users (Kwon and Wen, 2010; Ahmad, 2011) and it has been estimated that over 90 per cent of US college students have Facebook profiles (Ellison *et al*., 2007). Twitter has 288 million active users, which included 19 per cent of the US and 37 per cent of those aged between 18 and 29 (Duggan *et al*., 2014).

A large proportion of students use such sites to receive support when upset or distressed (Park *et al*., 2009) – as you read about in the Psychology in Action section in Chapter 12 – but students invariably use them to communicate and interact with friends. Users have a need to belong, but also a need for self-presentation (Nadkarni and Hofmann, 2012). And self-presentation is an important part of the Facebook mystique because so much can be manipulated – from events described, to personality projected to the type of image portrayed in profile photographs. College students and adolescents, for example, report uploading profile photographs that they consider to show their most physically attractive selves (Siibak, 2009). Profile photos are an important feature of impression management because the image appears next to each update/message. People tend to express more positive messages in status updates than private messages. (Bazarova *et al*., 2012). Research suggests, however, that despite indications to the contrary, users tend to portray themselves accurately rather than present an idealised version of themselves (Back *et al*., 2010; Wilson *et al*., 2012); aspects of users' behaviour inferred from tweets can also be accurately perceived by others (Orehek and Human, 2017).

The majority of the (admittedly, limited) research indicates that the dominant personality trait of users is extraversion. It is the strongest predictor of Facebook usage, for example (Correa *et al*., 2010). Extroverts make more contacts to friends, are more likely to publicise the events in their lives (Bibby, 2008) and have a wider social network (Tong *et al*., 2008; Lonnqvist and Itkonen, 2014). Introverts use Facebook as well, of course, and they prefer this means of interacting to face-to-face contact (Orr *et al*., 2009) but extroverts, unlike introverts, do not use the SNS as a substitute for real communication.

Perhaps the most intriguing personality type associated with SNS usage is narcissism. Narcissists have a highly inflated sense of self, have unrealistic (positive) views of their ability or selves, are exhibitionist, attention-seeking, overly concerned with the way they look and have little interest in forming long-term interpersonal relations but exploit short-term relationships to bolster their positive self-image or status. They are also highly extrovert. Levels of narcissism have apparently increased in American college students over the past two decades (Twenge *et al*., 2008). Buffardi and Campbell (2008) found that highly narcissistic individuals had more Facebook friends and wall posts, used it more frequently, and also displayed more attractive photographs. Bibby (2008) found that the trait predicted Facebook use as a means of occupying time, pursuing leisure interests and engaging in romantic liaisons. In adolescents, narcissism has been found to predict status update frequency (Ong *et al*., 2011), although this has not been found in students (Bergman *et al*., 2011). Bergman *et al*. did find, however, that narcissism was associated with wanting more friends, wanting these friends to know what they were doing and with projecting a positive self-image. Narcissists tend to use Facebook more frequently than do other personality types (Ljepava *et al*., 2013).

Narcissism, as you read about briefly in the section on chronotypes in Chapter 9, is one of the Dark Triad (now, the Tetrad). The Dark Triad comprises three personality dimensions – psychopathy (coldness, impulsiveness, anti-social behaviour), Machiavellianism (manipulation, exploitativeness, deception) and narcissism. People scoring high on the Dark Triad prefer short-term romantic/sexual relationships, for example, and prefer 'one night stands' to serious, long-term relationships (Jonason *et al*., 2012; Koladich and Atkinson, 2016). 'Sadism' (enjoyment of cruelty in everyday life) has now been added to the triad to make this a Tetrad (Buckels *et al*., 2013; Book *et al*., 2016).

Narcissism does not characterise another type of social network user, the troll – an individual (usually, anonymous), who engages in disruptive, abusive online behaviour and whose intention is to provoke reactions to which they can respond with further pointless abuse and nonsense. Trolls tend to be bored, attention-seeking, desirous of causing damage and of seeking revenge (Shachaf and Hara, 2010). Trolls, rather than showing excessive narcissism, instead show high levels of sadism, Machiavellianism and psychopathy, consistent with their behavioural profile (Buckels *et al*., 2014). Sadism was the trait most strongly correlated with the behaviour.

The social learning approach

Some psychologists, such as Cattell and Eysenck, are interested in the ways in which people differ with respect to their personality traits. Other psychologists are more interested in the ways in which a person's personality is affected by environmental and cognitive variables. These psychologists view personality and its development as a process in which behavioural, cognitive and environmental variables interact to produce a person's personality. **Social learning theory** embodies the idea that both the consequences of behaviour and an individual's beliefs about those consequences determine personality.

Social learning theory stems partially from Skinner's experimental analysis of behaviour. Although Skinner's work has influenced contemporary personality theory, he should not be mistaken for a personality theorist. He was definitely not one. For Skinner, behaviour is explained entirely in terms of its consequences. Behaviour is consistent from one situation to the next because it is maintained by similar kinds of consequences across those situations. Behaviour changes only when the consequences for behaving change. Skinner's ideas have attracted the attention of some personality researchers because they are experimentally based and provide testable hypotheses for predicting an individual's behaviour within and across situations. Social learning theorists have modified and applied Skinner's ideas to their own work. One such researcher is Albert Bandura (b. 1925), who blended Skinner's ideas with his own ideas about how cognitive factors may influence behaviour.

Expectancies and observational learning

Cognitive processing, including the individual's interpretation of the situation, is central to social learning theory (Bandura, 1973, 1986). An important aspect of cognition for Bandura and other social learning theorists is **expectancy**, the individual's belief that a specific consequence will follow a specific action. Expectancy refers to how someone perceives the contingencies of reinforcement for their own behaviour. If a person does something, it may be because they expect to be rewarded or punished. In different situations, expectancies may vary. For example, a child may learn that he can get what he wants from his younger sister by hitting her. However, on one occasion, his parents may catch him hitting his sister and punish him. His expectancy may now change: he may still get what he wants by behaving aggressively, but if he is caught, he'll be punished. This new expectancy may influence how he behaves towards his sister in the future (especially around his parents).

Expectancies also permit people to learn actions vicariously, that is, without those actions being directly reinforced. The vicarious nature of some learning experiences is obvious in children as they imitate the actions of others. A 3-year-old who applies deodorant to herself does so not because this behaviour has been reinforced in the past, but rather because after watching her mother do it, she expects it would be 'fun' for her to do so too.

Vicarious learning is better known as **observational learning**, which is learning through observing the kinds of consequence that others (called models) experience as a result of their behaviour. Observational learning is a form of learning in which an expectancy about reinforcement is formed merely by observing another's behaviour and the consequences it produces. Your own experience is no doubt filled with examples of observational learning – learning to dance, to make a paper aeroplane, to write italic and to engage in many other activities. The more complex the behaviour, the more times we must observe it being executed and practise what we have observed before we can learn it well. Learning to tie a shoelace requires more attention to detail than learning to roll a ball across the floor.

Reciprocal determinism and self-efficacy

Unlike many personality researchers, Bandura does not believe that either personal characteristics (traits) or the environment alone determine personality (Bandura, 1978). Rather, he argues for **reciprocal determinism**, the idea that behaviour, environmental variables and person variables, such as perception, interact to determine personality, as illustrated in Figure 14.7. We know that our actions can affect the environment. We also know that the environment can affect our behaviour. Likewise, our thoughts may affect the ways in which we behave to change the environment and, in turn, those changes can influence our thoughts. When our acts of kindness are met with kindness in return, we perceive the environment as friendly and are apt to show kindness under other similar circumstances. Likewise, when we are treated rudely, we perceive the environment as unfriendly (perhaps hostile) and will be likely to attempt to avoid or change similar environments in the future.

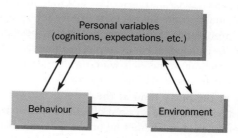

Figure 14.7 Patterns of interaction in reciprocal determinism. According to Bandura, behaviour, environment and personal variables, such as cognitions and expectations, interact to determine personality.

According to Bandura (1982), **self-efficacy,** or one's expectations of success in a given situation, is an important determinant of whether one will attempt to make changes in one's environment. Each day, we make many decisions based on our perceptions of the extent to which our actions will produce reinforcement. Our actions are based on our evaluation of our competency. Moreover, self-efficacy not only determines whether we will engage in a particular behaviour, it also determines the extent to which we will maintain that behaviour in the face of adversity. For example, if you believe that you are unqualified for a job even though you really desire it, you are apt not to apply for an interview for that job. However, if you are confident of your qualifications for the job, you will surely attempt the interview. Even if you are turned down for that job, you may interview for a similar position because you are sure of your abilities. Low self-efficacy can hamper both the frequency and the quality of behaviour – environment interactions, and high self-efficacy can facilitate both.

Related to self-efficacy is the extent to which an individual feels optimistic or pessimistic about their life's circumstances. Seligman and Schulman (1986) have found that people (in the case of their study, life insurance agents) who can find something positive in less than desirable circumstances are generally more successful than are people who view those circumstances negatively. It seems that otherwise cheerless circumstances stimulate optimists to seek creative means of 'putting the circumstances right'. Pessimists are more likely to throw up their arms in despair and to give up. Thus, if there is a solution to be found for a problem, the optimist has the better chance of finding it.

Person variables

Like Bandura, Walter Mischel (b. 1930) believes that much of one's personality is learned through interaction with the environment. In 1968, Mischel published a book, Psychology and Assessment, which set a situationist cat amongst the trait pigeons. The book arose while he was 'struggling to prepare a survey course for graduate students in the psychology programme on the state of personality, psychology and assessment' (Mischel, 2009). Mischel (1968, 1976) suggested that stable personality traits did not exist – or if they did, they were of little importance. Situations, not traits, best predicted behaviour, he concluded. For example, imagine two situations: a party to celebrate someone's winning a large sum of money and a funeral. People will be much more talkative, cheerful and outgoing at the party than at the funeral. How much will knowing a person's score on a test of intraversion–extraversion enable you to predict whether he or she will be talkative and outgoing? In this case, knowing the situation has much more predictive value than knowing the test score.

Like Bandura, Mischel emphasises the role of cognition in determining how one learns the relationship between one's behaviour and its consequences. In addition, though, Mischel argues that individual differences in cognition, or person variables as he calls them, account for differences in personality. Mischel (1984) proposed five person variables that figure significantly in social learning:

1 *Competences.* We each have different skills, abilities and capacities. What we know and the kinds of behaviour that have been reinforced in the past influence the kinds of action in which we will probably engage in the future.

2 *Encoding strategies and personal constructs.* We also differ in our ability to process information. The way we process information determines how we perceive different situations. One person may perceive going on a date as fun, and so look forward to it; another person may perceive going on a date as potentially boring, and so dread it.

3 *Expectancies.* On the basis of our past behaviour and our knowledge of current situations, we form expectancies about the effects of our behaviour on the environment. Expecting our behaviour to affect the environment positively leads to one course of action; expecting our behaviour to affect it negatively leads to another.

4 *Subjective values.* The degree to which we value certain reinforcers over others influences our behaviour. We seek those outcomes that we value most.

5 *Self-regulatory systems and plans.* We monitor our progress towards achieving goals and subject ourselves to either self-punishment or self-reinforcement, depending on our progress. We also modify and formulate plans regarding how we feel a goal can best be achieved.

Mischel's view is a dynamic one – people's thoughts and behaviours are undergoing constant change as they interact with the environment. New plans are made and old ones reformulated; people adjust their actions in accordance with their competences, subjective values and expectancies of behaviour–environment interactions. Mischel (1968) reviewed evidence from research and found that most personal characteristics showed low cross-situational consistency of 0.3 or lower. That is the correlation between a person's personality and the behaviour in different situations they found themselves in was low. He concluded that the concept of personality trait was not useful. People's behaviour was determined by the situations in which they found themselves, not by any intrinsic personality traits.

Personality and situations are usually conceived of as independent variables, but they are not always independent. In laboratory settings, experimenters assign people to various situations. Here, situation and personality are truly independent. However, as Bem and Allen (1974) pointed out, people in life outside the laboratory are able to exert some choice over the situations they enter. For instance, a party is a moderately powerful situation and tends to produce extraverted behaviours. Introverted people may stay away from parties to avoid situations that encourage behaviours with which they are not comfortable. Similarly, extraverts may avoid situations in which they are alone. The fact that people choose their own situations means that personality traits interact with situations. Emmons *et al.* (1986) found that people do, indeed, show consistent patterns in the types of situations they choose; and when circumstances force them to be in situations they do not normally choose, they feel uncomfortable.

Since Mischel's critique, most of his criticisms have been rejected by evidence, particularly the criticism that traits have limited utility and do not predict behaviour because correlations between personality and behaviour are low, that stability of personality traits is subjectively perceived and that stability is an attribute of the situation, not the person (Funder, 2009; Roberts, 2009). Research from the US has measured the relationship between behaviour experienced day to day and self-reported personality, as measured via the Big Five (Fleeson and Gallagher, 2009). A meta-analysis of 15 studies which sampled people's experiences reported several times a day, across days and weeks, was conducted. The studies were conducted over eight years and involved over 20,000 reports of experiences. The correlations between these experiences and self-reported traits were high: traits predicted individual differences in daily behaviour.

The fourth criticism, however, that behaviour may not be consistent across situations has been trickier to reject. Some interactions between situation and personality require the analysis of both variables. Figure 14.8 illustrates some of the important variables that control an individual's personality development. Fred enjoys most sports and he enjoys most social activities such as drinking and partying. Sometimes, however, he prefers to spend some time by himself. Are we justified in arguing that Fred has a 'sociability' trait? Or does the situation determine his behaviour?

Some suggest that any model of behaviour and personality should include the person, situations and behaviours as important variables (Funder, 2009). Thus, the formula $B = f(P, S)$ where behaviour is a function of personality and situation will be relevant if one wishes to understand a particular behaviour, aggression or altruism, say. To do this one looks at who acts in what situations. Studying the person and situation can be illustrated using modified equations/formulae.

However, despite this some psychologists suggest that behavioural consistency is not synonymous with the definition of a personality trait and what is important is temporal, rather than situational, consistency – that is, the personality trait can be seen across time, which is the definition of a stable personality trait (Roberts, 2009).

Locus of control

Other social learning theorists, such as Julian Rotter (b. 1916), have argued that the extent to which one perceives oneself to be in control of particular situations is also an important element of personality. **Locus of control** refers to whether one believes that the consequences of one's actions are controlled by internal, person variables or by external, environmental variables (Rotter, 1954, 1966). A person who expects to control their own fate – or, more technically, who perceives that rewards are dependent upon their own behaviour – has an internal locus of control. A person who sees their life as being controlled by external forces unaffected by their own behaviour has an external locus of control, as you can see from Figure 14.9.

Rotter developed the I–E Scale, which assesses the degree to which people perceive the consequences of their behaviour to be under the control of internal or external variables. The I–E Scale contains 29 pairs of statements to which a person

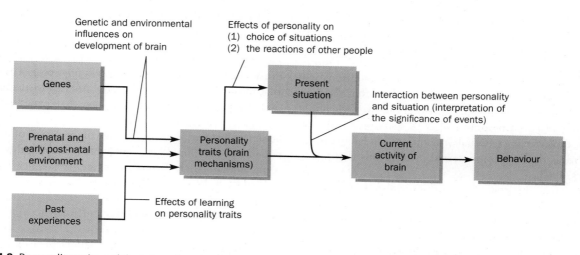

Figure 14.8 Personality traits and the interactions between traits and situations that determine behaviour.

Figure 14.9 Internal and external loci of control. People having internal loci of control perceive themselves as being able to determine the outcomes of the events in their lives. People having external loci of control perceive the events in their lives to be determined by environmental variables.

indicates their degree of agreement. A typical item would be as follows:

> The grades that I achieve depend on my abilities and how hard I work to get them.
>
> The grades that I achieve depend mostly on my teacher and his or her tests.

The scale is scored by counting the number of choices consistent with either the internal or the external locus of control orientation. Scores may range from 0 to 23, with lower scores indicative of greater internal locus of control. Of all the populations Rotter has assessed with the I–E Scale, the highest level of internal locus of control was obtained from a group of Peace Corps volunteers (Rotter, 1966).

Rotter's scale has been used in hundreds of studies of social behaviour in a wide variety of situations. Consider some of the findings obtained from research using the I–E Scale:

- People having internal locus of control orientations will work harder to obtain a goal if they believe that they can control the outcome in a specific situation. Even when told that a goal could be obtained with their own skill and effort, those having external orientations tended not to try as hard as those having internal orientations (Davis and Phares, 1967).

- People having internal orientations are also more likely to be aware of and to use good health practices. They are more apt to take preventive medicines, to exercise regularly and to stop smoking than are people having external orientations (Strickland, 1979). They are, however, more likely to blame themselves when they fail, even when failure is not their fault (Phares, 1984).

The psychodynamic approach

The work of Sigmund Freud had a profound and lasting effect on twentieth-century society but little long-term effect on modern psychology. Terms such as ego, libido, repression, rationalisation and **fixation** are as familiar to many Western laypeople as to clinicians. Before Freud formulated his theory, people believed that most behaviour was determined by rational, conscious processes. Freud was the first to claim that what we do is often irrational and that the reasons for our behaviour are seldom conscious. The mind, to Freud, was a battleground for the warring factions of instinct, reason and conscience; the term psychodynamic refers to this struggle.

The development of Freud's theory

Sigmund Freud (1856–1939) was a Viennese physician who acquired his early training in neurology in the laboratory of Ernst Wilhelm von Brücke, an eminent physiologist and neuroanatomist. Freud's work in the laboratory consisted mostly of careful anatomical observation rather than experimentation. Careful observation also characterised his later work with human behaviour; he made detailed observations of individual patients and attempted to draw inferences about the structure of the human psyche from these cases.

Freud left Vienna briefly and studied in Paris with Jean Martin Charcot, who was investigating the usefulness of hypnosis as a treatment for hysteria. Patients with hysteria often experience paralysis of some part of the body or loss of one of the senses, and no physiological cause can be detected. The fact that hypnosis could be used either to produce or to alleviate these symptoms suggested that they were of psychological origin. Charcot proposed that hysterical symptoms were caused by some kind of psychological trauma. Freud was greatly impressed by Charcot's work and became even more interested in problems of the mind.

Freud returned home to Vienna, opened his medical practice and began an association with Josef Breuer, a prominent physician. Freud and Breuer together published a book called *Studies on Hysteria*, and one of the cases cited in it, that of Anna O., provided the evidence that led to some of the most important tenets of Freud's theory. Breuer had treated Anna O. 12 years before he and Freud published their book. She suffered from a great number of hysterical symptoms, including loss of speech, disturbances in vision, headaches and paralysis and loss of feeling in her right arm. Under hypnosis, Anna was asked to think about the time when her symptoms had started. Each of her symptoms appeared to have begun just when she was unable to express a strongly felt emotion. While under hypnosis, she experienced these emotions again, and the experience gave her relief from her hysterical symptoms. It was as if the emotions had been bottled up, and reliving the original experiences uncorked them. This release of energy (which Breuer and Freud called catharsis) presumably eliminated the hysterical symptoms.

The case of Anna O. is one of the most frequently reported cases in the annals of psychotherapy. However, Breuer's original description appears to be inaccurate in some of its most important respects (Ellenberger, 1972). Apparently, the woman was not cured at all by Breuer's hypnosis and psychotherapy. Ellenberger discovered hospital records indicating that Anna O. continued to take morphine for the distress caused by the disorders Breuer had allegedly cured. Freud appears to have learned later that the cure was a fabrication, but this fact did not become generally known until recently. However, Breuer's failure to help Anna O. with her problems does not mean that we must reject psychoanalysis. Although Breuer's apparent success inspired Freud to examine the unconscious, Freud's theory of personality must stand or fall on its own merits when evaluated by modern evidence.

The case of Anna O., along with evidence obtained from his own clinical practice, led Freud to reason that human behaviour is motivated by instinctual drives, which, when activated, supply 'psychic energy'. This energy is aversive, because the nervous system seeks a state of quiet equilibrium. According to Freud, if something prevents the psychic energy caused by activation of a drive from being discharged, psychological disturbances will result.

Freud believed that instinctual drives were triggered by traumatic events in a person's life. During such an event, the individual is forced to hide strong emotion. Because it cannot be expressed normally, the emotion is expressed neurotically, that is, with excessive anxiety. The individual cannot recall the emotions or the events that produced them because they are embedded in the unconscious, the inaccessible part of the mind. Unconscious memories and emotions exert control over conscious thoughts and actions, causing the neurotic symptoms to linger and the emotions of the original traumatic event to stay secret.

Freud also believed that the mind actively prevents unconscious traumatic events from reaching conscious awareness. That is, the mind represses the memories of traumatic events, most of which are potentially anxiety-provoking, preventing their being consciously discovered. He used the idea of an iceberg as a metaphor to describe the mind. Only the tip is visible above water; the much larger and more important part of it is submerged. Likewise, the conscious mind hides a larger and more important part of the mind – the unconscious. To understand a person's personality, we must tap his or her unconscious.

Freud, then, argued that our personalities are determined by both conscious and unconscious powers, with the unconscious exerting considerable influence on the conscious. To understand how the unconscious exerts its control over conscious thought and action, we need to explore Freud's view of the structure of personality.

Structures of the mind: id, ego and superego

Freud was struck by the fact that psychological disturbances could stem from events that a person apparently could no longer consciously recall, although they could be revealed during hypnosis. This phenomenon led him to conclude that the mind consists of unconscious, preconscious and conscious elements. The unconscious includes mental events of which we are not aware, the conscious entails mental events of which we are aware and the preconscious involves mental events that may become conscious through effort.

Freud divided the mind into three structures: the id, the ego and the superego. The operations of the id are completely unconscious. The **id** contains the **libido,** which is the primary source of instinctual motivation for all psychic forces; this force is insistent and is unresponsive to the demands of reality. The id obeys only one rule: to obtain immediate gratification in whatever form it may take – this is called the **pleasure principle.** If you are hungry, the id compels you to eat; if you are angry, the id prompts you to strike out or to seek revenge or to destroy something. Freud conceived of the id as

the dark, inaccessible part of our personality. . . . We approach the id with analogies: we call it a chaos, a cauldron full of seething excitations. . . . It is filled with energy reaching it from the instincts, but it has no organisation, produces no collective will, but only a striving to bring about the satisfaction of the instinctual needs subject to the observance of the pleasure principle. (Source: Frend, 1933. p. 650.)

The **ego** is the self; it controls and integrates behaviour. It acts as a mediator, negotiating a compromise among the pressures of the id, the counterpressures of the superego and the demands of reality. The ego's functions of perception, cognition and memory perform this mediation. The ego is driven by the **reality principle,** the tendency to satisfy the id's demands realistically, which almost always involves compromising the demands of the id and superego. It involves the ability to delay gratification of a drive until an appropriate goal is located. To ward off the demands of the id when these demands cannot be gratified, the ego uses defence mechanisms (described later). Some of the functions of the ego are unconscious.

The **superego** is subdivided into the conscience and the ego-ideal. The **conscience** is the internalisation of the rules and restrictions of society. It determines which behaviours are permissible and punishes wrongdoing with feelings of guilt. The **ego-ideal** is the internalisation of what a person would like to be – their goals.

Freud believed the mind to be full of conflicts. A conflict might begin when one of the two primary drives, the sexual instinctual drive or the aggressive instinctual drive, is aroused. The id demands gratification of these drives but is often held in check by the superego's internalised prohibitions against the behaviours the drives tend to produce. Internalised prohibitions are rules of behaviour learned in childhood that protect the person from the guilt that they would feel if the instinctual drives were allowed to express themselves.

The result of the conflict is compromise formation, in which a compromise is reached between the demands of the id and the suppressive effects of the superego. According to Freud, phenomena such as dreams, artistic creations and slips of the tongue (we now call them Freudian slips) are examples of compromise formation.

In what many consider to be his greatest work, *The Interpretation of Dreams*, Freud wrote, 'The interpretation of dreams is the royal road to a knowledge of the unconscious activities of the mind' (1900, p. 647). To Freud, dreams were motivated by repressed wishes and urges. By analysing dreams, Freud thought repressed wishes and memories could be rediscovered. For example, Freud believed that the **manifest content** of a dream – its actual storyline – is only a disguised version of its **latent content** – its hidden message, which is produced by the unconscious. The latent content might be an unexpressed wish related to the aggressive instinctual drive.

For example, a person may desire to hurt or injure another person, perhaps a co-worker with whom they are competing for a promotion. However, if the person acted out this scenario in a dream, they would experience guilt and anxiety. Therefore, the aggressive wishes of the unconscious are transformed into a more palatable form – the manifest content of the dream might be that the co-worker accepts a job offer from a different company, removing any competition for the promotion. The manifest content of this dream manages to express, at least partly, the latent content supplied by the unconscious.

In addition to analysing his patient's dreams, Freud also developed the technique of free association to probe the unconscious mind for clues of intrapsychic conflict. **Free association** is a method of analysis in which an individual is asked to relax, clear his or her mind of current thoughts and then report all thoughts, images, perceptions and feelings that come to mind. During free association, Freud looked for particular patterns in his patient's report that might reveal wishes, fears and worries that the patient's mind might be keeping hidden. For example, free association might reveal, among other things, the thought of beating someone up, an image of a knife, and perhaps a feeling of relief. Recognising a pattern in his patient's report, he may draw conclusions about the client's hidden desire to harm someone and about the reasons motivating both that desire and the relief experienced once the aggressive urge is satisfied.

Defence mechanisms

According to Freud, the ego contains **defence mechanisms** – mental systems that become active whenever unconscious instinctual drives of the id come into conflict with internalised prohibitions of the superego. The signal for the ego to utilise one of its defences is the state of anxiety produced by an intrapsychic conflict. This unpleasant condition motivates the ego to apply a defence mechanism and thus reduce the anxiety. The six important defence mechanisms are summarised in Table 14.2.

Repression

Repression is responsible for actively keeping threatening or anxiety-provoking memories from our conscious awareness. For example, a person may have witnessed a brutal murder but cannot recall it later because of the uncomfortable emotions it would arouse. Freud believed that repression was perhaps the most powerful of the defence mechanisms.

Reaction formation

Reaction formation involves replacing an anxiety-provoking idea with its opposite. An often-cited example of a reaction formation is that of a person who is aroused and fascinated by pornographic material but whose superego will not permit this enjoyment. They become a militant crusader against pornography. Reaction formation can be a very useful defence mechanism in this situation, permitting acceptable interaction with the forbidden sexual object. The crusader against pornography often studies the salacious material to see just how vile it is so that they can better educate others about its harmful nature. Thus, enjoyment becomes possible without feelings of guilt.

Table 14.2 Freudian defence mechanisms

Defence mechanism	Description	Example
Repression	The mind's active attempt to prevent memories of traumatic experiences from reaching conscious awareness	Failure to remember the death of a loved one or other highly upsetting events that occurred earlier in your life
Reaction formation	Replacing an anxiety-provoking idea with its opposite	Having intense feelings of dislike for a person but acting in a friendly manner towards them
Projection	Denial of one's unacceptable feelings and desire and finding them in others	Denying that you have negative feelings towards someone, but asserting that person to have negative feelings towards you
Sublimation	Channelling psychic energy from an unacceptable drive into a more acceptable one	Diverting energy from the sex drive to produce a work of art
Rationalisation	Creating an acceptable reason for a behaviour that is actually performed for a less acceptable reason	Asserting that you donate money to charities because you truly are a generous person when really you want the tax relief for the donation
Conversion	The manifestation of a psychic conflict in terms of physical symptoms	A psychic conflict, perhaps aroused by a particular person, causes you to develop symptoms of deafness or blindness to avoid contact with them

Projection

Projection involves denial of one's own unacceptable desires and the discovery of evidence of these desires in the behaviour of other people. For example, a man who is experiencing a great deal of repressed hostility may perceive the world as being full of people who are hostile to him. In this way, he can blame someone else for any conflicts in which he engages.

Sublimation

Sublimation is the diversion of psychic energy from an unacceptable drive to an acceptable one. For example, a person may feel strong sexual desire but find its outlet unacceptable because of internalised prohibitions. Despite repression of the drive, its energy remains and finds another outlet, such as artistic or other creative activities. Freud considered sublimation to be an important factor in artistic and intellectual creativity. He believed that people have a fixed amount of drive available for motivating all activities, therefore surplus sexual instinctual drive that is not expended in its normal way can be used to increase a person's potential for creative achievement.

Rationalisation

Rationalisation is the process of inventing an acceptable reason for a behaviour that is really being performed for another, less acceptable reason. For example, a man who feels guilty about his real reasons for purchasing a pornographic magazine may say, 'I don't buy the magazine for the pictures. I buy it to read the interesting and enlightening articles it contains.'

Conversion

Conversion is the provision of an outlet for intrapsychic conflict in the form of a physical symptom. The conflict is transformed into blindness, deafness, paralysis or numbness. (This phenomenon has also been called hysteria, which should not be confused with the common use of the term to mean 'running around and shouting and generally acting out of control'.) For example, a person might develop blindness so that he or she will no longer be able to see a situation that arouses a strong, painful intrapsychic conflict. Anna O.'s problem would be described as a conversion reaction.

Freud's psychosexual theory of personality development

Freud believed that personality development involves passing through several psychosexual stages of development – stages that involve seeking pleasure from specific parts of the body called erogenous zones. As we will see, each stage of personality development involves deriving physical pleasure from a different erogenous zone. Freud used the term 'sexual' to refer to physical pleasures and the many ways an individual might seek to gratify an urge for such pleasure. He did not generally use the term to refer to orgasmic pleasure.

Freud's theory of personality development has been extremely influential because of its ability to explain personality disorders in terms of whole or partial fixation – arrested development owing to failure to pass through an earlier stage of development. Freud believed that a person becomes fixated at a particular stage of development when he or she becomes strongly attached to the erogenous zone involved in that stage. Although normal personality development involves passing successfully through all the psychosexual stages, Freud maintained that most people become more or less fixated at some point in their development.

Because newborn babies can do little more than suck and swallow, their sexual instinctual drive finds an outlet in these activities. Even as babies become able to engage in more complex behaviours, they continue to receive most of their sexual gratification orally. The early period of the **oral stage** of personality development is characterised by sucking and is passive. Later, as babies become more aggressive, they derive their pleasure from biting and chewing.

Fixation at the oral stage may result from early (or delayed) weaning from breast to bottle to cup. Someone whose personality is fixated at the early oral stage might be excessively passive. 'Biting' sarcasm or compulsive talking can represent fixation at the later, more aggressive phase of the oral stage. Other oral stage fixation activities include habits such as smoking and excessive eating.

The **anal stage** of personality development begins during the second year of life; now babies begin to enjoy emptying their bowels. During the early part of this stage, called the expressive period, babies enjoy expelling their faeces. Later, in the retentive period, they derive pleasure from retaining them. Improper toilet training can result in fixation at the anal stage. People fixated at the anal expressive period are characterised as destructive and cruel; anal retentives are seen as stingy and miserly.

At around age 3, a child discovers that it is pleasurable to play with his penis or her clitoris, and enters the **phallic stage** (phallus means 'penis', but Freud used the term bisexually in this context). Children also begin to discover the sex roles of their parents, and they unconsciously attach themselves to the parent of the opposite sex. A boy's attachment to his mother is called the **Oedipus complex**, after the mythical Greek king who unknowingly married his mother after killing his father. For a time, Freud believed that a girl formed a similar attachment with her father, called the **Electra complex**, but he later rejected this concept. In Greek mythology, Electra, aided by her brother, killed her mother and her mother's lover to avenge her father's death.

In boys, the Oedipus complex normally becomes repressed by age 5, although the conflicts that occur during the phallic stage continue to affect their personalities throughout life. A boy's unconscious wish to take his father's place is suppressed by his fear that his father will castrate him as punishment. In fact, Freud believed that young boys regarded females as castrated males. The conflict is finally resolved when the boy begins to model his behaviour on that of his father so that he achieves identification with the father. Failure to resolve this conflict causes the boy to become fixated at this stage. The boy then becomes preoccupied with demonstrations of his manhood, continually acting 'macho'.

Girls supposedly experience fewer conflicts than boys do during the phallic stage. According to Freud, the chief reason for their transfer of love from their mothers (who provided primary gratification during early life) to their fathers is penis envy. A girl discovers that she and her mother lack this organ, so she becomes attached to her father, who has one. This attachment persists longer than the Oedipus complex, because the girl does not have to fear castration as revenge for usurping her mother's role. Freud believed that penis envy eventually becomes transformed into a need to bear children. The missing penis is replaced by a baby. A girl who becomes fixated during the phallic stage develops strong feelings of being inferior to men, which are expressed in seductive or otherwise flirtatious behaviour. For example, she may become attracted to older men ('father figures') and attempt to seduce them to demonstrate her power over them and thereby relieve her feelings of inferiority.

After the phallic stage comes a **latency period** of several years, during which the child's sexual instinctual drive is mostly submerged. Following this period, the onset of puberty, the child, now an adolescent, begins to form adult sexual attachments to age-mates of the other sex. Because the sexual instinctual drive now finds its outlet in heterosexual genital contact, this stage is known as the **genital stage**.

Further development of Freud's theory: the neo-Freudians

Freud's theory created controversy in the Victorian era in which it was unveiled. Its emphasis on childhood sexuality and seething internal conflicts seemed preposterous and offensive. Yet the theory's proposal that our thoughts and behaviour as adults stem from unconscious forces as well as from our early childhood experiences was revolutionary and these were recognised by many scholars as genuinely original ideas. Freud attracted a number of followers who studied his work closely but who did not accept it completely. Each of these people agreed with Freud's view on the dynamic forces operating within the psyche. Each of them disagreed with Freud, though, on how much importance to place on the role of unconscious sexual and aggressive instincts in shaping personality. Four psychodynamic theorists, Carl Jung, Alfred Adler, Karen Horney and Erik Erikson, have been particularly influential in elaborating psychodynamic theory.

Carl Jung: analytical psychology

Early in the twentieth century, several students of psychoanalysis met with Freud to further the development of psychoanalysis. One of these people was Carl Jung (1875–1961). Freud called Jung 'his adopted eldest son, his crown prince and successor' (Hall and Nordby, 1973, p. 23). However, Jung developed his own version of psychodynamic theory that de-emphasised the importance of sexuality. He also disagreed with his mentor on the structure of the unconscious. Unfortunately, Freud had little tolerance of others' opinions. After 1913, he and Jung never saw each other again. Jung continued to develop his theory after the split by drawing ideas from mythology, anthropology, history and religion, as well as from an active clinical practice in which he saw people with psychological disorders.

To Jung, libido was a positive creative force that propels people towards personal growth. He also believed that forces other than the id, ego and superego, such as the collective unconscious, form the core of personality. To Jung, the ego was totally conscious and contained the ideas, perceptions, emotions, thoughts and memories of which we are aware. One of Jung's more important contributions to psychodynamic theory was his idea of the collective unconscious, which contains memories and ideas inherited from our ancestors. Stored in the collective unconscious are archetypes, inherited and universal thought forms and patterns that allow us to notice particular aspects of our world (Carver and Scheier, 2011). From the dawn of our species, all humans have had roughly similar experiences with things such as mothers, evil, masculinity and femininity. Each one of these is represented by an archetype. For example, the shadow is the archetype containing basic instincts that allow us to recognise aspects of the world such as evil, sin and carnality. Archetypes are not stored images or ideas – we are not born with a picture of evil stored somewhere in our brain – but we are born with an inherited disposition to behave, perceive and think in certain ways.

Alfred Adler: striving for superiority

Like Jung, Alfred Adler (1870–1937) studied with Freud. Also like Jung, Adler felt that Freud overemphasised the role of sexuality in personality development. Adler argued that feelings of inferiority play the key role. Upon birth, we are dependent on others for survival. As we mature, we encounter people who are more gifted than we are in almost every aspect of life. The inferiority we feel may be social, intellectual, physical or athletic. These feelings create tension that motivates us to compensate for the deficiency. Emerging from this need to compensate is a striving for superiority, which Adler believed to be the major motivational force in life.

According to Adler (1939), **striving for superiority** is affected by another force, social interest, which is an innate desire to contribute to society. Social interest is not wholly instinctual though, because it can be influenced by experience. Although individuals have a need to seek personal superiority, they have a greater desire to sacrifice for causes that benefit society as a whole. Thus, while Freud believed that people act in their own self-interest, motivated by the id, Adler believed that people desire to help others, directed by social interest.

Karen Horney: The Flight of the Vagina

Karen Horney (pronounced 'horn-eye'; 1885–1952), like other Freudian dissenters, did not believe that sex and aggression are the primary themes of personality. She did agree with Freud, though, that anxiety is a basic problem that people must address and overcome.

According to Horney, individuals suffer from basic anxiety caused by insecurities in relationships. People often feel alone, helpless or uncomfortable in their interactions with others. For example, people who begin a new job are often unsure of how to perform their duties, whom to ask for help, and how to approach their new colleagues. Horney theorised that to deal with basic anxiety, the individual has three options (Horney, 1950):

1 *Moving towards others.* Accept the situation and become dependent on others. This strategy may entail an exaggerated desire for approval or affection.

2 *Moving against others.* Resist the situation and become aggressive. This strategy may involve an exaggerated need for power, exploitation of others, recognition or achievement.

3 *Moving away from others.* Withdraw from others and become isolated. This strategy may involve an exaggerated need for self-sufficiency, privacy or independence.

Horney believed that these three strategies corresponded to three basic orientations with which people approach their life. These **basic orientations** reflect different personality characteristics. The self-effacing solution corresponds to the moving towards others strategy and involves the desire to be loved. The self-expansive solution corresponds to the moving against others strategy and involves the desire to master oneself. The resignation solution corresponds to the moving away strategy and involves striving to be independent of others.

Horney maintained that personality is a mixture of the three strategies and basic orientations. As the source of anxiety varies from one situation to the next, so may the strategy and basic orientation that is used to cope with it. Like Adler, Horney thought environmental variables influenced personality development. In her view, outlined in her book, *The Flight of the Vagina*, in order to understand personality, one must consider not only psychodynamic forces within the mind, but also the environmental conditions to which those forces are reacting.

Erik Erikson: identity crisis

Erik Erikson (1902–94) studied with Anna Freud, Sigmund Freud's daughter. He emphasised social aspects of personality development rather than biological factors. He also differed from Freud about the timing of personality development. For Freud, the most important development occurs during early childhood. Erikson emphasised the ongoing process of development throughout the lifespan. Erikson proposed that people's personality traits develop as a result of a series of crises they encounter in their social relations with other people. Because these crises continue throughout life, psychosocial development does not end when people become adults.

Erikson's theory of lifelong development has been very influential, and his term 'identity crisis' has become a familiar one. However, because his theory does not make many empirically testable predictions, it has received little empirical support.

Evaluation of psychodynamic theory and research

Freud's psychodynamic theory has had a profound effect on psychological theory, psychotherapy and literature. His writing, although nowadays regarded as sexist, is lively and stimulating, and his ideas have provided many people with food for thought. However, his theory has received little empirical support, mainly because he used concepts that are poorly defined and that cannot be observed directly. How is one to study the ego, the superego or the id? How can one prove (or disprove) that an artist's creativity is the result of a displaced aggressive or sexual instinctual drive? The writings of the neo-Freudians have had even less influence on modern research. Although the theories of Jung, Adler, Horney and Erikson have their followers, scientific research on personality has largely ignored them.

The emphasis by Freud and his followers on the potentially harmful effects of particular types of childhood environment has led some psychotherapists to conclude that their patients' maladjustments and mental disorders are, by and large, caused by their parents. Many parents have blamed themselves for their children's disorders and have suffered feelings of severe guilt. But many forms of mental disorders – particularly the most serious ones – are largely a result of heredity and are not affected much by family environment. Hence, the teachings of Freud and his followers have compounded the tragedy of mental illness by causing parents to be accused unjustly of poor parenting practices.

The one Freudian phenomenon that has undergone experimental testing is repression. This phenomenon is very important to Freud's theory because it is one of the primary ego defences and because it operates by pushing memories (or newly perceived stimuli) into the unconscious. Thus, experimental verification of repression would lend some support to Freud's notions of intrapsychic conflict and the existence of the unconscious.

The results of research on repression have not been conclusive. Typically, the researchers in repression experiments ask participants to learn some material associated with an unpleasant, ego-threatening situation, and they then compare their memory for the information with that of participants who learned the material under non-threatening conditions. If repression occurs, the threatened participants should remember less of the material than the non-threatened participants will. Some studies have reported positive results, but later experiments have shown that other, non-Freudian phenomena could explain them more easily (D'Zurilla, 1965). Perhaps the most important point here is that none of the experiments can really be said to have threatened the participants' egos, producing the level of anxiety that would lead to the activation of a defence mechanism. Any experimental procedure that did so would probably be unethical. Thus, it is difficult to test even the most specific prediction of Freud's theory. It is very hard, perhaps impossible, to prove that a person's behaviour and personality are products of unconscious conflicts. If people admit to their sexual urges, psychoanalytic thinking would accept this as fitting the theory; if they deny them, they are repressing these urges and denying their existence. Can you see a problem here in scientifically accepting psychoanalytic explanations of personality?

The humanistic approach

The **humanistic approach** to the study of personality seeks to emphasise the positive, fulfilling elements of life. Humanistic psychologists are interested in nurturing personal growth, life satisfaction and positive human values. They believe that people are innately good and have an internal drive for **self-actualisation** – the realisation of one's true intellectual and emotional potential. The two most influential humanistic theorists have been Abraham Maslow and Carl Rogers.

Maslow and self-actualisation

For both Freud and Abraham Maslow (1908–70), motivation is one of the central aspects of personality. However, where Freud saw strong instinctual urges generating tensions that could not be completely resolved, Maslow saw positive impulses that could be easily overwhelmed by the negative forces within one's culture. According to Maslow (1970), human motivation is based on a hierarchy of needs. Our motivation for different activities passes through several levels, with entrance to subsequent levels dependent on first satisfying needs in previous levels, as illustrated by Figure 14.10. If an individual's needs are not met, they cannot scale the hierarchy and so will fail to attain their true potential.

In Maslow's view, understanding personality requires understanding this hierarchy. Our most basic needs are physiological needs, including the need for food, water, oxygen,

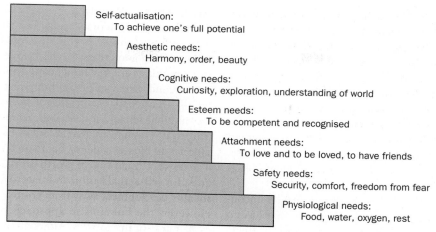

Figure 14.10 Maslow's hierarchy of needs. According to Maslow, every person's goal is to become self-actualised. In order to achieve this goal, individuals must first satisfy several basic needs.

rest and so on. Until these needs are met, we cannot be motivated by needs found in the next level (or any other level). If our physiological needs are met, we find ourselves motivated by safety needs, including the need for security and comfort, as well as for peace and freedom from fear. Once the basic survival and safety needs are met, we can become motivated by attachment needs, the need to love and to be loved, to have friends and to be a friend. Next, we seek to satisfy esteem needs – to be competent and recognised as such. You are probably beginning to get the picture: we are motivated to achieve needs higher in the hierarchy only after first satisfying lower needs. If we are able to lead a life in which we have been able to provide ourselves with food and shelter and to surround ourselves with love, we are free to pursue self-actualisation.

Maslow based his theory partially on his own assumptions about human potential and partially on his case studies of historical figures whom he believed to be self-actualised, including Albert Einstein, Eleanor Roosevelt, Henry David Thoreau and Abraham Lincoln. Maslow examined the lives of each of these people in order to assess the common qualities that led each to become self-actualised. In general, he found that these individuals were very self-accepting of themselves and of their lives' circumstances, were focused on finding solutions to pressing cultural problems rather than to personal problems, were open to others' opinions and ideas, were spontaneous in their emotional reactions to events in their lives, had strong senses of privacy, autonomy, human values and appreciation of life, and had a few intimate friendships rather than many superficial ones.

Maslow (1964) believed that the innate drive for self-actualisation is not specific to any particular culture. He viewed it as being a fundamental part of human nature. In his words, 'Man has a higher and transcendent nature, and this is part of his essence . . . his biological nature of a species which has evolved' (p. xvi).

Rogers and conditions of worth

Carl Rogers (1902–87) also believed that people are motivated to grow psychologically, aspiring to higher levels of fulfilment as they progress towards self-actualisation (Rogers, 1961). Like Maslow, Rogers believed that people are inherently good and have an innate desire for becoming better. Rogers, though, did not view personality development in terms of satisfying a hierarchy of needs. Instead, he believed that personality development centres on one's self-concept, or one's opinion of oneself, and on the way one is treated by others.

Rogers argued that all people have a need for positive regard, or approval, warmth, love, respect and affection flowing from others. Young children, in particular, show this need when they seek approval for their actions from parents and siblings. In Rogers's view, children often want others to like them to the extent that gaining positive regard is a major focus of their lives. The key to developing a psychologically healthy personality, though, is to develop a positive self-concept or image of oneself. How does one do this? Rogers's answer is that we are happy if we feel that others are happy with us. Likewise, we are also unhappy with ourselves when others are disappointed in or unsatisfied with us.

Thus, our feelings towards ourselves depend to a large extent on what others think of us. As children, we learn that there exist certain conditions or criteria that must be met before others give us positive regard. Rogers called these criteria **conditions of worth**.

Positive regard is often conditional. For example, parents may act approvingly towards their young child when he helps in the kitchen or in the garden but not when he pinches his younger sister or tells a lie. The boy learns that what others think of him depends on his actions. Soon, too, he may come to view himself as others view him and his behaviour: 'People like me when I do something good and they don't like me when I do something bad.'

Although conditions of worth are a necessary part of the socialisation process, they can have negative effects on personality development if satisfying them becomes the individual's major ambition. As long as the individual focuses chiefly on seeking positive regard from others, they may ignore other aspects of life, especially those that lead to positive personality growth. In Rogers's view, then, conditions of worth may stand in the way of self-actualisation. An individual may devote her life to satisfying the expectations and demands of others in lieu of working towards realising her potential. In this sense, the need for positive regard may smother an individual's progress towards self-actualisation.

According to Rogers, the solution to this problem is **unconditional positive regard,** or love and acceptance that has no strings attached. In a family setting, this means that parents may establish rules and expect their children to obey them, unless doing so would compromise the children's feelings of worth and self-respect. For example, if a child misbehaves, the parents should focus on the child's behaviour and not the child. In this way, the child learns that her behaviour is wrong but that her parents still love her. Unconditional positive regard allows people to work towards realising their potential unfettered by what others think of them.

In developing his theory, Rogers used unstructured interviews in which the client, not the therapist, directed the course of the conversation. He believed that if the therapist provided an atmosphere of unconditional positive regard, a client would eventually reveal their true self, the kind of person they now are, as well as their ideal self, the kind of person that they would like to become. Rogers also gave the Q sort test to many of his clients. This test consists of a variety of cards, each of which contains a statement such as 'I am generally an optimistic person' or 'I am generally an intolerant person'. The clients' task is to sort the cards into several piles that vary in degree from 'least like me' to 'most like me'. The clients sort the cards twice, first on the basis of their real self and next in terms of their ideal self. The difference between the arrangement of the cards in the piles is taken as an index of how close the clients are to reaching their ideal self. Rogers's goal as a therapist was to facilitate the clients becoming their ideal self. Rogers's approach to therapy is discussed in more detail in Chapter 18.

Evaluation of the humanistic approach

The humanistic approach is impressive because of its emphasis on people seeking a healthy well-being. Indeed, the approach has wide appeal to those who seek an alternative to the more mechanistic and strictly biologically or environmentally determined views of human nature.

However, critics point up two closely related problems with this approach.

First, many of the concepts used by humanistic psychologists are defined subjectively and so are difficult to test

empirically. For example, how might we empirically examine the nature of self-actualisation? Few published studies have even attempted to answer this question. By now, you know the hallmark of a good theory – the amount of research it generates. On this count, the humanistic approach comes up short.

A second criticism of the humanistic approach is that it cannot account for the origins of personality. It is subject to the nominal fallacy; it describes personality, but it does not explain it. Humanistic psychologists believe that self-actualisation is an innate tendency, but there is no research that shows it to be so. Conditions of worth are said to hamper a child's quest for self-actualisation and thus to alter the course of personality development away from positive psychological growth. However, the humanistic approach provides no objective explanation of this process. Although the humanistic approach may offer a positive view of human nature and give apparent purpose to life, this view is largely unsubstantiated. Before moving on to the next section, take time to look at Table 14.3 which summarises the major theories of personality we have discussed so far.

Assessment of personality

Think for a moment of your best friend. What is he or she like? Outgoing? Impulsive? Thoughtful? Moody? You can easily respond yes or no to these alternatives because you have spent enough time with your friend to know him or her quite well. After all, one of the best ways to get to know people – what they are like and how they react in certain situations – is to spend time with them. Obviously, psychologists do not have the luxury of spending large amounts of time with people in order to learn about their personalities. Generally, they have only a short period to accomplish this goal. From this necessity, personality tests were first developed. The underlying assumption of any personality test is that personality characteristics can be measured. This final section of the chapter describes the two main types of personality test: objective tests and projective tests.

Objective tests of personality

Objective personality tests are similar in structure to classroom tests. Most contain multiple-choice and true/false items, although some allow the person taking the test to indicate the extent to which they agree or disagree with an item. The responses that subjects can make on objective tests are constrained by the test design. The questions asked are unambiguous, and explicit rules for scoring the subjects' responses can be specified in advance. Examples include the Eysenck Personality Inventory and the NEO-PI, described earlier.

One of the oldest and most widely used objective tests of personality is the **Minnesota Multiphasic Personality**

Table 14.3 A summary of the major personality theories

Theory	Primary figures	Primary emphases	Primary strengths	Primary limitations
Trait	Allport, Cattell, Eysenck	An individual's traits determine personality	Focuses on stability of behaviour over long periods; attempts to measure traits objectively	Largely descriptive; ignores situational variables that may affect behaviour
Psychobiological	Eysenck, Zuckerman	The role of genetics and the brain and nervous system in personality development	Emphasis on the interaction of biology and environment in determining personality; rigorous empirical approach	Reliance on correlation methods in determining the role of genetics in personality
Social learning	Bandura, Mischel, Rotter	Personality is determined by both the consequences of behaviour and our perception of them	Focuses on direct study of behaviour and stresses rigorous experimentation	Ignores biological influences on personality development; often more descriptive than explanatory
Psychodynamic	Freud, Jung, Adler, Horney, Erikson	Unconscious psychic conflicts; repression of anxiety-provoking ideas and desires	The idea that behaviour may be influenced by forces outside conscious awareness	Basic concepts are not empirically testable
Humanistic	Maslow, Rogers	Stresses the positive aspects of human nature and how to become a better person	Useful in therapeutic settings	Contains vague and untestable concepts; primarily descriptive

Inventory (**MMPI**), devised by Hathaway and McKinley in 1939. The original purpose for developing the test was to produce an objective, reliable method for identifying various personality traits that were related to a person's mental health. Improvement in people's scores over the course of treatment would indicate that the treatment was successful.

In devising this test, Hathaway and McKinley wrote 504 true/false items and administered the test to several groups of people in mental institutions in Minnesota who had been diagnosed as having certain psychological disorders. These diagnoses had been arrived at through psychiatric interviews with the patients. Such interviews are expensive, so a simple paper-and-pencil test that accomplished the same result would be valuable. The control group consisted of relatives and friends of the patients, who were tested when they came to visit them. (Whether these people constituted the best possible group of normal participants is questionable.) The responses were analysed empirically, and the questions that correlated with various diagnostic labels were included in various scales. For example, if people who had been diagnosed as paranoid tended to say true to 'I believe I am being plotted against', this statement would become part of the paranoia scale.

The current revised version of the MMPI, the MMPI-2, has norms based on a sample of people that is much more representative ethnically and geographically than the original sample (Graham, 1990). It includes 550 questions, grouped into ten clinical scales and four validity scales. A particular item can be used on more than one scale. For example, both people who are depressed and those who are hypochondriacal tend to agree that they have gastrointestinal problems. The clinical scales include a number of diagnostic terms traditionally used to label psychiatric patients, such as **hypochondriasis**, depression or paranoia.

The four validity scales were devised to provide the tester with some assurance that subjects are answering questions reliably and accurately and that they can read the questions and pay attention to them. The '?' scale ('cannot say') is simply the number of questions not answered. A high score on this scale indicates either that the person finds some questions irrelevant or that the person is evading issues that they find painful.

The L scale (lie) contains items such as 'I do not read every editorial in the newspaper every day' and 'My table manners are not quite as good at home as when I am out in company'. A person who disagrees with questions like these is almost certainly not telling the truth. A high score on the L scale suggests the need for caution in interpreting other scales and also reveals something about the participant's personality. In particular, people who score high on this scale tend to be rather naive; more sophisticated people realise that no one is perfect and do not try to make themselves appear to be so.

The F scale (frequency) consists of items that are answered one way by at least 90 per cent of the normal population. The usual responses are 'false' to items such as 'I can easily make other people afraid of me, and sometimes do it for the fun of it', and 'true' to items such as 'I am liked by most people who know me'. A high score on this scale indicates carelessness, poor reading ability or very unusual personality traits.

The K scale (defensiveness) was devised to identify people who are trying to hide their feelings to guard against internal conflicts that might cause them emotional distress. A person receives a high value on the K scale by answering 'false' to statements such as 'Criticism or scolding hurts me terribly' and 'At periods, my mind seems to work more slowly than usual'. People who score very low on this scale tend to be in need of help or to be unusually immune to criticism and social influences.

Some psychologists argue that validity scales are useless or even harmful in most testing situations. For example, consider the following item: 'Before voting, I thoroughly investigate the qualifications of all candidates.' According to Crowne and Marlowe (1964), anyone who answers 'yes' to such a question has to be lying. But as McCrae and Costa (1990) note, people taking tests do not necessarily respond passively to each item, taking it at face value. Instead, their response is based on their interpretation of what they think the question means. They suggest (p. 40) that most people will say to themselves:

> Surely these psychologists didn't mean to ask if I actually study the voting records of every single political candidate, from President to dogcatcher. No one does, so that would be a stupid question to ask. What they must have meant to ask was whether I am a concerned citizen who takes voting seriously. Since I am and I do, I guess I should answer yes. (Source: McCrae and Costa, 1990, p. 40.)

There is evidence to support McCrae and Costa's suggestion. When psychologists calculate a person's score on the MMPI, they usually apply a correction factor derived from the validity scales. Several studies have shown that the application of the correction factors to the scores of normal subjects actually reduces the validity of these scores. McCrae and Costa suggest that when the MMPI is administered to normal subjects for research purposes, such corrections should not be made. However, validity scales may be useful in situations in which subjects may be motivated to lie (e.g. when a personality test is used to screen job applicants) or in cases in which the test is being used clinically to evaluate the possibility of mental illness or personality disorder.

As well as being used in clinical assessment, the MMPI has been employed extensively in personality research, and a number of other tests, including the California Psychological Inventory and the Taylor Manifest Anxiety Scale, are based on it. However, the MMPI has its critics. As we saw earlier, the five-factor model of personality has received considerable support. Some of its advocates have noted that the MMPI misses some of the dimensions measured by the NEO-PI, which includes tests of neuroticism, extraversion, openness,

agreeableness and conscientiousness (Johnson *et al.*, 1984). Thus, these factors will be missed by a clinician or researcher who relies only on the MMPI. For this reason, many researchers, especially those interested in the psychobiology of personality, no longer use the MMPI.

Projective tests of personality

Projective tests of personality are different in form from objective ones and are derived from psychodynamic theories of personality. Psychoanalytically oriented psychologists believe that behaviour is determined by unconscious processes more than by conscious ones. Thus, they believe that a test that asks straightforward questions is unlikely to tap the real roots of an individual's personality characteristics.

Projective tests are designed to be ambiguous so that the person's answers will be more revealing than simple agreement or disagreement with statements provided by objective tests. The assumption of projective tests is that an individual will 'project' his or her personality into the ambiguous situation and thus make responses that give clues to this personality. In addition, the ambiguity of the test makes it unlikely that subjects will have preconceived notions about which answers are socially desirable. Thus, it will be difficult for a subject to give biased answers in an attempt to look better (or worse) than he or she actually is.

The Rorschach Inkblot Test

One of the oldest projective tests of personality is the **Rorschach Inkblot Test**, published in 1921 by Hermann Rorschach, a Swiss psychiatrist. The Rorschach Inkblot Test consists of 10 pictures of inkblots, originally made by spilling ink on a piece of paper that was subsequently folded in half, producing an image that is symmetrical in relation to the line of

A client completing a Rorschach Inkblot test.
Source: Will & Deni McIntyre/Science Photo Library.

the fold. Five of the inkblots are black and white, and five are colour. The participant is shown each card and asked to describe what it looks like. Then the cards are shown again, and the participant is asked to point out the features they used to determine what was seen. The responses and the nature of the features the participant uses to make them are scored on several dimensions.

In the following example described by Pervin (1975), a person's response to a particular inkblot might be: 'Two bears with their paws touching one another playing a game or could be they are fighting and the red is the blood from the fighting.' The classification of this response, also described by Pervin (p. 37), would be: large detail of the blot was used, good form was used, movement was noted, colour was used in the response about blood, an animal was seen, and a popular response (two bears) was made. A possible interpretation of the response might be as follows:

> Subject starts off with popular response and animals expressing playful, 'childish' behaviour. Response is then given in terms of hostile act with accompanying inquiry. Pure colour response and blood content suggest he may have difficulty controlling his response to the environment. Is a playful, childlike exterior used by him to disguise hostile, destructive feelings that threaten to break out in his dealings with the environment?

Although the interpretation of people's responses to the Rorschach Inkblot Test was originally based on psychoanalytical theory, many investigators have used it in an empirical fashion. That is, a variety of different scoring methods have been devised, and the scores obtained by these methods have been correlated with clinical diagnoses, as investigators have done with people's scores on the MMPI. However, the validity of these scoring techniques and the validity of the test in general is questionable (Groth-Marnat, 1997).

The Thematic Apperception Test

Another popular projective test, the **Thematic Apperception Test (TAT)**, was developed in 1938 by the American psychologists Henry Murray and C.D. Morgan to measure various psychological needs. People are shown a picture of a very ambiguous situation and are asked to tell a story about what is happening in the picture, explaining the situation, what led up to it, what the characters are thinking and saying, and what

the final outcome will be. Presumably, the participants will 'project' themselves into the scene, and their stories will reflect their own needs. As you might imagine, scoring is difficult and requires a great deal of practice and skill. The tester attempts to infer the psychological needs expressed in the stories. Consider the responses of one woman to several TAT cards, along with a clinician's interpretation of these responses (Phares, 1979, p. 273). The questions asked by the examiner are in parentheses.

> *Card 3BM.* Looks like a little boy crying for something he can't have. (Why is he crying?) Probably because he can't go somewhere. (How will it turn out?) Probably sit there and sob himself to sleep.
>
> *Card 3GF.* Looks like her boyfriend might have let her down. She hurt his feelings. He's closed the door on her. (What did he say?) I don't know.
>
> *Card 10.* Looks like there's sorrow here. Grieving about something. (About what?) Looks like maybe one of the children's passed away.
>
> *Interpretation.* The TAT produced responses that were uniformly indicative of unhappiness, threat, misfortune, a lack of control over environmental forces. None of the test responses were indicative of satisfaction, happy endings, etc. . . . . In summary, the test results point to an individual who is anxious and, at the same time, depressed.

The pattern of responses in this case is quite consistent; few people would disagree with the conclusion that the woman is sad and depressed. However, not all people provide such clear-cut responses. As you might expect, interpreting differences in the stories of people who are relatively well adjusted is much more difficult. As a result, distinguishing among people with different but normal personality traits is hard.

One major problem with the TAT is in quantifying responses, such as the ones above. Often, responses are analysed qualitatively which makes assessing the reliability of the test difficult. Others have argued that subjecting the test to quantitative rigorous examination defeats the object of using the test which is to help guide a clinician's assessment of a patient's personality. However, even here, there are problems in that there is little agreement between clinicians regarding the assessment of the individual's responses on the TAT (Groth-Marnat, 1997).

Controversies in psychological science: Are projective tests reliable and valid?

The issue

Most empirical studies find that projective tests, such as the Rorschach Inkblot Test and the TAT, have poor reliability and little validity. In a review of over 300 studies, Lundy (1985) found that the validity of the TAT appears to be lower when it is administered by an authority figure, in a classroom setting or when it is represented as a test. Lundy (1988) suggests that in such situations, the participants are likely to realise that they are talking about themselves when they tell a story about the cards and may be careful about what they say. Why are projective tests so unsuccessful?

The evidence

Projective tests have met with little success for a number of reasons: (1) there are few standardised procedures because different clinicians can present tests and present different parts of them in different ways; (2) norms are rarely available so that comparisons between how an individual performs and how he or she performs compared to the population cannot be reliably made; (3) the tests have low reliability – people can respond differently on a test depending on the examiner; and (4) the tests have low validity – they do not measure what they purport to measure.

Scott Lilienfeld and his colleagues at Texas, Emory and Pittsburgh Universities have conducted a comprehensive and critical review of the scientific status of projective tests (Lilienfeld *et al.*, 2000). The review raises some important questions about the ways in which the tests are administered, used and interpreted. These concerns take on added significance when you consider that according to one survey (Watkins *et al.*, 1995), over 30 per cent of clinical psychologists who were members of the American Psychological Association reported using projective techniques either always or frequently, and over 80 per cent used the tests at least once or occasionally.

The most popular of the projective techniques used by respondents in the Watkins *et al.* (1995) study was the Rorschach Inkblot Test. The test was criticised in the 1950s and 1960s for poor standardisation. These criticisms were taken on board and when the test was corrected in the 1970s, detailed instructions for the administration and interpretation of the test, as well as the provision of some norms, were included (Exner, 1974). The correction became known as the Comprehensive System. Despite the improvement in standardisation, Lilienfeld *et al.* (2000) found that reliability continued to be low: clinicians agreed on only half of the characteristics that the test purports to reveal about the individual (the test involves the clinician rating the individual's responses on over 100 characteristics).

The test also showed poor validity; although clinicians claimed that the test could identify mental disorder, researchers found that it was poor at detecting depression, anxiety and psychopathy. Some studies claimed to show that tests did reveal these disorders; others not: the picture was clearly inconsistent. This highlights the danger in using the test unthinkingly: it could identify people as mentally ill when they are not. Lilienfeld *et al.* (2001) cite a study of 123 volunteers at a blood donation centre who were asked to complete the test: one in six was identified as showing signs of schizophrenia.

The scores they receive on one day are often very different from those they receive on another day. But a test of personality is supposed to measure enduring traits that persist over time and in a variety of situations. The TAT has also been criticised for potential sex bias, mostly because of what are considered male-dominated themes, such as power, ambition and status, used to score the test (Worchel *et al.*, 1990).

According to Lilienfeld *et al.* (2000), the TAT suffers from the same early problems as the Rorschach: there are no standardised procedures (so clinicians can administer as many or as few of the scenes and in any order, as they wish) and no way of scoring the test in a standardised way (clinicians interpret the responses to the scenes intuitively). In fact, the number of psychologists using a standardised scoring system for TAT has been reported to be as low as 3 per cent. The TAT also suffers from the unavailability of population norms and from poor test–retest reliability. Attempts have been made to provide standardised scoring systems for the TAT (Westen *et al.*, 1990) which seem to show that it is good at describing people's perceptions of others, but these attempts may not be sufficiently rigorous to be clinically applicable.

Conclusion

Lilienfeld *et al.* (2000) suggest that we can draw six conclusions from a review of studies of the scientific status of projective tests:

1 The use of projective tests continues to be very controversial and psychiatrists need to be aware of this.

2 People can 'fake' responses on these tests.

3 The techniques are used for purposes for which they were not intended.

4 Scoring can be unreliable and poor.

5 Norms are either absent or poorly described.

6 The techniques may show a cultural bias favouring North Americans.

▶

Controversies in psychological science: *Continued*

If projective tests such as the Rorschach and the TAT have been found to be of low reliability and validity, why do many clinical psychologists and psychiatrists continue to use them? The primary reason seems to be tradition. The use of these tests has a long history and the rationale for the tests is consistent with psychodynamic explanations of personality. Many psychodynamic and clinical psychologists still argue that the tests are valuable for discovering and evaluating inner determinants of personality, whatever the evidence to the contrary.

Chapter review

Trait theories of personality

- We can conceive of personality characteristics as types or traits. The earliest theory of personality classified people into types according to their predominant humour, or body fluid. Today, most psychologists conceive of personality differences as being represented by degree, not kind.
- Personality traits are the factors that underlie patterns of behaviour. Presumably, these factors are biological in nature, although they may be the products of learning as well as heredity.
- The search for core personality traits began with Allport, who studied how everyday words are used to describe personality characteristics. Although he never isolated a core set of traits, his work inspired others to continue the search for such traits.
- Several researchers developed their theories of personality through factor analysis, a statistical method of reducing a large amount of data to two or three themes or ideas (called factors).
- Cattell's analyses indicated the existence of 16 personality factors; Eysenck's research suggested that personality is determined by three dimensions: extraversion (versus introversion), neuroticism (versus emotional stability) and psychoticism (versus self-control).
- McCrae and Costa's five-factor model, based on an analysis of words used to describe people's behavioural traits, includes extraversion, neuroticism, agreeableness, openness and conscientiousness. There is strong cross-cultural agreement on the first three factors but not on the fifth.

Heritability of personality traits

- Studies of twins and adopted children indicate that personality factors, especially extraversion, neuroticism and psychoticism, are affected strongly by genetic factors. However, there is little evidence for an effect of common family environment, largely because an individual's environment is strongly affected by heredity factors, such as personality and physical attributes.
- Zuckerman argues that extraversion is caused by a sensitive reinforcement system, neuroticism is caused by a sensitive punishment system (which includes the amygdala), and psychoticism is caused by the combination of a deficient punishment system and an abnormally high optimum level of arousal.
- Extraversion is associated with increased amygdala activation when viewing happy faces.

The social learning approach

- Social learning theory blends Skinner's notion of reinforcement with cognitive concepts such as expectancy to explain social interaction and personality.
- According to Bandura, people learn the relation between their behaviour and its consequences by observing how others' behaviour is rewarded and punished. In this way, people learn to expect that certain consequences will follow certain behaviours.
- Bandura has also argued that personality is the result of reciprocal determinism – the interaction of behaviour, environment and person variables such as perception.

- The extent to which a person is likely to attempt to change his or her environment is related to self-efficacy, the expectation that he or she will be successful in producing the change. People with low self-efficacy tend not to try to alter their environments; the opposite is true for people with high self-efficacy.
- Mischel has argued that personality differences are due largely to person variables – individual differences in cognition. These variables include competences, encoding strategies and personal constructs, expectancies, subjective values and self-regulatory systems and plans.
- Rotter's research has shown that locus of control – the extent to which people believe that their behaviour is controlled by person variables or by environmental variables – is also an important determinant of personality.
- Traits and situations interact: some people are affected more than others by a particular situation, and people tend to choose the types of situation in which they find themselves. People's personality traits directly affect situational variables.

The psychodynamic approach

- Freud believed that the mind is full of conflicts between the primitive urges of the id and the internalised prohibitions of the superego.
- According to Freud, these conflicts tend to be resolved through compromise formation and through ego defences such as repression, sublimation and reaction formation. His theory of psychosexual development, a progression through the oral, anal, phallic and genital stages, provided the basis for a theory of personality and personality disorders.
- Freud's followers, most notably Jung, Adler, Horney and Erikson, embraced different aspects of Freud's theory, disagreed with other aspects, and embellished still other aspects.
- Jung disagreed with Freud about the structure of the unconscious and the role of sexuality in personality development, and saw libido as a positive life force.
- Adler also disagreed with Freud on the importance of sexuality. Instead, Adler emphasised the need to compensate

for our inferiority and our innate desire to help others as the major forces in personality development.
- Horney argued that personality is the result of the strategies and behaviours people use to cope with anxiety, which she believed is the fundamental problem that all people must overcome in the course of normal personality development.
- Erikson maintained that personality development is more a matter of psychosocial processes than of psychosexual processes. He viewed personality development as involving eight stages, each of which involves coping with a major conflict or crises. Resolution of the conflict allows the person to pass to the next stage; failure to resolve it inhibits normal personality development.
- Although Freud was a brilliant and insightful thinker, his theory has not been experimentally verified, primarily because most of his concepts are unobservable and, therefore, untestable.

The humanistic approach

- The humanistic approach attempts to understand personality and its development by focusing on the positive side of human nature and people's attempts to reach their full potential: self-actualisation.
- Maslow argued that self-actualisation is achieved only after the satisfaction of several other important but lesser needs, for example, physiological, safety and attachment needs.
- Maslow's case study analysis of people whom he believed to be self-actualised revealed several common personality characteristics including self-acceptance, a focus on addressing cultural problems and not personal ones, spontaneity, preservation of privacy, an appreciation of life and possession of a few very close friends.
- According to Rogers, the key to becoming self-actualised is developing a healthy self-concept. The primary roadblocks in this quest are conditions of worth – criteria that we must meet to win the positive regard of others. Rogers maintained that too often people value themselves only to the extent that they believe other people do. As a result, they spend their lives seeking the acceptance of others instead of striving to become self-actualised. Rogers proposed that only by treating others with unconditional positive regard could we help people to realise their true potential.

- Although the humanistic approach emphasises the positive dimensions of human experience and the potential that each of us has for personal growth, it has been criticised for being unscientific.
- Critics argue that its concepts are vague and untestable and that it is more descriptive than explanatory.

Assessment of personality

- Objective tests contain items that can be answered and scored objectively, such as true/false or multiple-choice questions.
- One of the most important objective personality tests is the Minnesota Multiphasic Personality Inventory (MMPI),

which was empirically devised to discriminate among people who had been assigned various psychiatric diagnoses. It has since been used widely in research on personality.

- The MMPI's validity scales have been challenged by researchers who suggest that most people's responses can be taken at face value. More recently, researchers interested in personality have turned to tests not based on people with mental disorders, such as the NEO-PI.
- Projective tests, such as the Rorschach Inkblot Test and the Thematic Apperception Test, contain ambiguous items that elicit answers that presumably reveal aspects of participants' personalities; because answers can vary widely, test administrators must receive special training to interpret them. Unfortunately, evidence suggests that the reliability and validity of such tests are poor.

Suggestions for further reading

Carver, C.S. and Scheier, M.F. (2013) *Perspectives on Personality* (7th edn). Boston, MA: Allyn & Bacon.

Chamorro-Premuzic, T. (2014) *Personality and Individual Differences* (3rd edn). London: Blackwell.

Cloninger, S.C. (2012) *Theories of Personality* (6th edn). Boston, MA: Prentice Hall.

Eysenck, H. (1985) *Decline and Fall of the Freudian Empire*. London: Pelican.

de Francisco Carvalho, L. and Pianowski, G. (2017) Pathological personality traits assessment using Facebook: Systematic review and meta-analyses. *Computers in Human Behavior*, 71, 307–17.

Gregory, R.J. (2014) *Psychological Testing* (7th edn). Boston, MA: Allyn & Bacon.

John, O.P., Robins, R.W. and Pervin, L.A. (2011) Ha*ndbook of Personality: Theory and Research* (3rd edn). London: Guilford Press.

Mitchell, R.L. and Kumari, V. (2016) Hans Eysenck's interface between the brain and personality: Modern evidence on the cognitive neuroscience of personality. *Personality and Individual Differences*, 103, 74–81.

Motyl, M., Demos, A. P., Carsel, T. S., Hanson, B. E., Melton, Z. J., Mueller, A. B., ... & Yantis, C. (2017). The state of social and personality science: Rotten to the core, not so bad, getting better, or getting worse?. *Journal of Personality and Social Psychology*, 113(1), 34.

Muris, P., Merckelbach, H., Otgaar, H. and Meijer, E. (2017) The malevolent side of human nature: A meta-analysis and critical review of the literature on the Dark Triad (Narcissism, Machiavellianism, and Psychopathy). *Perspectives on Psychological Science*, 12(2), 183–204.

Pervin, L.A. and Cervone, S. (2017) *Personality Psychology* (13th edn). London: Wiley.

Riccelli, R., Toschi, N., Nigro, S., Terracciano, A. and Passamonti, L. (2017) Surface-based morphometry reveals the neuroanatomical basis of the five-factor model of personality. *Social Cognitive and Affective Neuroscience*, 1, 14.

Some very good titles are a very good introduction to personality.

CHAPTER 15
Social psychology I: Social cognition and attitudes

Michael A. Hogg, Dominic Abrams and G. Neil Martin

WHAT WORKS BETTER: KEEP OFF THE GRASS OR SAVE THE PLANET?

Applying theories from social psychology to environmental problems, researchers at Arizona State University tested the power of social norms in influencing behaviour. Robert Cialdini, Ph.D., and two graduate students worked with a local hotel on a programme to encourage lodgers to reuse wet towels. The researchers randomly assigned cards with one of five different messages to 260 guest rooms, each with one of the following messages:

'Help the hotel save energy'

'Help save the environment'

'Partner with us to help save the environment'

'Help save resources for future generations'

'Join your fellow citizens in helping to save the environment'

The last message, which described a social norm, was the most successful. . . . Next best were the messages urging environmental protection and the benefit to future generations. . . . Least successful: The message emphasising the benefit to the hotel. Only one in five guests with that card reused their towels.

Source: http://www.apa.org/research/action/shaping.aspx.

WHAT YOU SHOULD BE ABLE TO DO AFTER READING CHAPTER 15

- Define social psychology and understand what social psychologists do.

- Understand how we process, store and use information about ourselves and other people.

- Understand the motives that influence how we form a conception of who we are.

- Understand how self-concept influences our perceptions and treatment of other people.

- Understand how we make inferences, especially causal inferences, about others' behaviour, and also about our own behaviour.

- Understand how attitudes are formed and changed.

QUESTIONS TO THINK ABOUT

- Are the problems facing social psychology different from those in other branches of psychology?

- Does it matter where and when social psychology research is conducted?

- How quickly can you form a mental image of another person? What does the image contain? Is it purely visual, or does it capture something about their personality, group membership or other 'social' information? How are such impressions formed?

- What determines whom you like and dislike? Why do you sometimes change your mind about a person?

- Why do you use stereotypes and is it possible to avoid them?

- Who would you trust to make an accurate judgement about your future prospects: a teacher, parent or yourself? What might influence the judgement made by each of these people?

- Try to persuade someone using a line of argument with which you personally disagree. Is persuasion simply a matter of using the right technique or are there other reasons why this is a difficult task? What tactics do you use, and why?

Social psychology

Most human activity is social. We spend most of our waking hours interacting with, thinking about or being directly or indirectly influenced by other people. Our behaviour affects the way others think, feel and act and, in turn, their behaviour affects our thoughts, feelings and actions. Not for nothing is the American social psychologist Elliot Aronson's best-selling book on social psychology called *The Social Animal* (latest edition published in 2011). Human interaction also structures the norms, conventions and institutions that make up the societies we live in.

The field of psychology that studies social behaviour is called social psychology. According to Gordon Allport (1968, p. 3), social psychology is the study of 'how the thoughts, feelings, and behaviour of individuals are influenced by the actual, imagined, or implied presence of others'. In the next two chapters, we explore the way in which people, as individuals or in groups, affect one another. We examine the complex interplay of basic cognitive processes and cognitive structures that we use to process and store information, and the nature of human relations and interactions that occur in everyday life. In this chapter, we focus on social cognition and attitudes – how people process and store social information, and how social information affects social behaviour. In Chapter 16 we focus on social interaction between individuals, between groups and among people within groups.

Doing social psychology

To a large extent we are all social psychologists but rather than being empirical scientists, we are more like intuitive social psychologists (Heider, 1958). To get by in life we need to have a well-developed understanding of why people behave as they do, what causes particular behaviours, and what effect our behaviour has on others. These common-sense understandings are often quite accurate, but sometimes they are not. For example, we 'know' that 'birds of a feather flock together' (similarity leads to attraction), but we also 'know' that 'opposites attract'. So, which is correct? Many of us may also think that friendship between people from different racial groups should reduce prejudice – but does it? How can we be sure? Under what circumstances is someone most likely to help someone in distress? To get someone to do you a favour, should you first make a modest request that they will agree to and then scale it up to the real request, or should you first make an outrageously large request that nobody in their right mind would agree to and then scale it down?

To answer these questions, social psychologists use a wide range of scientific methods including laboratory experiments, field experiments, surveys, observation of naturally occurring behaviour, and the analysis of what people say and write.

Controlled laboratory experiments predominate because they are so well suited to establishing the causes of behaviour. However, some research questions are difficult to address in the laboratory. For example, it would be difficult to study a riot or an established street gang in the laboratory. Can you think of any other experiment which you would think would be impossible to set up (you'll be surprised at some of the experiments psychologists have conducted . . .)? Social psychologists can be quite tenacious and inventive. One early researcher tried to instigate a riot in the laboratory by wafting smoke under the locked door of the laboratory – some groups of participants kicked the door open and disengaged the smoke generator, and other groups calmly discussed the possibility that they were being observed (French, 1944).

Social psychologists develop formal theories about human behaviour that, unlike common-sense theories, are carefully grounded in data from systematic and well-controlled research. These theories sometimes confirm common-sense knowledge, but sometimes they do not, and many theories are concerned with how people develop and use this common-sense social psychological knowledge in the first place.

Social cognition and social knowledge

We often have ready-made explanations and interpretations of people and situations – explanations that are readily accessible in the society in which we live. In this way, people's social interpretations can vary from culture to culture, group to group and across time. For example, Moscovici (1976) explored how Freudian concepts, such as unconscious motives, Oedipus complex, displacement and so forth, have become widely accepted and used in contemporary mass culture to account for people's behaviour. These **social representations** of the way people's minds work provide a framework for making sense of the world. This framework develops through many means, such as mass communication, informal conversation and adherence to prescriptions of scientific and religious movements and other group ideologies (Moscovici, 1983; also see Lorenzi-Cioldi and Clémence, 2001).

Social representations have consequences for how we deal with one another. For example, whether insanity is considered to have a moral, biological, religious, physical or social cause will determine how it is responded to by policy-makers and the public (Jodelet, 1991). When Peter Sutcliffe, the British 'Yorkshire Ripper', was convicted in 1981 in the UK of over 20 rapes and murders he was deemed to be 'criminal' rather than 'insane', and was therefore imprisoned rather than hospitalised. Such distinctions are dependent more on society's current social representations of good and evil, sanity and insanity than they are on objectively measurable criteria.

However, criteria for diagnosing mental illness have progressed dramatically since then (see Chapter 18).

Against the background of particular social representations, values and norms, cognitive-inferential processes affect the way we understand, use and respond to our social environment (Augoustinos and Walker, 1995). For example, Echebarria-Echabe *et al.* (1994) examined how smokers and non-smokers account for the causes of smoking. Two representations appeared to be common: one which emphasised the psychological weakness of people who fall prey to the attractions of tobacco and another (defensive representation) which associated smoking with facilitative social factors and favourable stereotypes of smokers. When the potential conflict between non-smokers and smokers was made more salient, smokers became more likely to adhere to the defensive representation.

Our ability to interpret social situations involves a range of basic cognitive–inferential processes, including memory for people, places and events; concept formation skills; and sensory and perceptual abilities. Social cognition rests on an array of basic cognitive–inferential processes and on the way in which social information is stored, structured and retrieved from memory. Fiske and Taylor have characterised the individual as a motivated tactician,

> a fully engaged thinker who has multiple cognitive strategies available and chooses among them based on goals, motives, and needs. Sometimes the motivated tactician chooses wisely, in the interests of adaptability and accuracy, and sometimes . . . defensively, in the interests of speed or self-esteem. (Source: Fiske and Taylor, 1991, p. 13.)

A central and dominant theme in social psychology has been the development of our understanding of social cognition – how people attend to, perceive, interpret, store and respond to social information.

Forming impressions of people

All of us form impressions of others: friends, neighbours, lecturers, foreigners – virtually everyone we meet. We assign all sorts of characteristics to them. We may, for example, think of someone as friendly or hostile, helpful or selfish. Note that these are terms that describe the type of person someone is, and critically evaluate them. One of the major tasks of social psychology is to understand how we form these impressions. In Solomon Asch's words, 'How do the perceptions, thoughts, and motives of one person become known to other persons?' (Asch, 1952, p. 143). To answer questions like this, psychologists study **impression formation**, the way in which we form

impressions, often first impressions, of others and attribute specific characteristics to them.

Cognitive algebra

One perspective on impression formation argues that our evaluation of other people is critically important as it underpins fundamental judgements of danger and safety and thus approach–avoidance decisions. Impressions of people are largely evaluative. This process has been referred to as **cognitive algebra** (Anderson, 1978). This perspective argues that people intuitively represent traits in terms of their desirability: they effectively assign values to traits, e.g. $+1, 0, -1, -2$, and they integrate the value of traits they assign to a person in order to arrive at an overall evaluation of that person. This information can be integrated in three different ways:

- *summation* – the larger the number of positive traits the more positive the overall impression;
- *averaging* – a limited number of highly positive traits yields a more positive impression than lots of positive traits with many of them only marginally positive (marginal traits bring down the average);
- *weighted averaging* – not only are traits averaged, but some traits are considered more important than others in a particular context and are thus weighted more heavily. Research suggests that the weighted averaging model best characterises impression formation.

Several factors influence weighting. For example, the same information may be weighted differently if you are forming an impression of a potential friend rather than a potential colleague. Weightings of particular attributes may also be influenced by what other person attributes are present. The meanings of specific attributes, and overall meaning of a combination of attributes, may influence the meaning and the valence of a particular attribute. Generally, although attribute valence is important, so is the meaning of an attribute – when we evaluate someone as 'cruel' we not only evaluate that person negatively, but also know something about their behaviour. These and other considerations suggest people may not form impressions in such a piecemeal manner, but in a more holistic or gestalt manner that places a greater importance on the meaning of attributes. This idea underpins Asch's **configural** model of impression formation.

Asch's configural model

Over half a century ago, Asch (1946) noted that our impressions of others are formed by more complex rules than just a simple sum of the characteristics that we use to describe people. Asch was able to show that when we form impressions of other people, some perceptual features seem to have more influence than others in our final impression. For example, your impression of someone may be swayed by whether people are intelligent or not, and a friend's may be swayed by whether people are approachable or not. Kelly (1955) refers to these idiosyncratic views of what is most important in characterising people as **personal constructs**. In one context, intelligence may be a more relevant dimension than approachability (e.g. evaluating someone as a member of a research team), whereas in another context the opposite may be true (e.g. evaluating someone as a charity fundraiser). Asch called characteristics that are disproportionately influential in impression formation central traits. Central traits are very useful for organising and summarising large amounts of diverse information about a person you encounter.

To demonstrate this, Asch (1946) provided participants with a list of traits describing a hypothetical person. Some received a list that included the trait 'warm', whereas others received an identical list, except that the trait 'warm' was replaced by 'cold'. Participants given the list including 'warm' were more likely to see the person as generous, happy and altruistic. But not all traits seemed to be so important. When the words 'polite' and 'blunt' were substituted for 'warm' and 'cold', no differences were observed in participants' impressions. Kelley (1950) replicated Asch's study in a more naturalistic setting where the target person was not hypothetical, but was a real person who really gave a guest lecture to a class. Kelley found the same results.

Students who had had the lecturer described as 'cold' rated him to be more unsociable, self-centred, unpopular, formal, irritable, humourless and ruthless than did those who had had him described as 'warm'. Our perception of others seems to be based partially on central traits – which can vary from context to context, or from person to person.

Biases in impression formation

What determines whether a trait is central or not? One factor is the order in which information is available or is processed. Research suggests that the first information we process is the most important – there is a marked **primacy effect**. Getting to know someone takes time and usually requires many interactions. Perhaps the first time you saw someone was at a party when she was loud and boisterous, having a good time with her friends. But later, you learn that she is a mathematics student with excellent grades who is generally quite reserved. What is your overall impression of this person: loud and boisterous, or bright and shy? To determine whether first impressions might overpower later impressions, Asch (1946) presented one of the following lists of words to each of two groups of participants:

> Intelligent, industrious, impulsive, critical, stubborn, envious
>
> Envious, stubborn, critical, impulsive, industrious, intelligent

Notice that these lists contain the same words but in reverse order. After they saw the list, Asch asked the participants to describe the personality of the person having these characteristics. People who heard the first list evaluated the person much more favourably than people who heard the second list – a clear primacy effect.

Although sometimes more recent information can be influential (e.g. when there is a lot of information and we are distracted), the general rule is that first impressions are most impactful and most enduring (Jones and Goethals, 1972).

The impressions we form of people are also disproportionately influenced by negative information. We tend to pay more attention to negative information, and although we like to think the best of people, bad impressions, once formed, are very difficult to change. By contrast, good impressions can easily change. One reason for this negativity bias is that people are probably especially sensitive to negative information because it can signify potential harm or danger (Skowronski and Carlston, 1989).

Sometimes there are social conventions and norms (sometimes legislation) that actually discourage us from forming impressions at all. For example, people would resist forming impressions based on race, gender or disability, particularly if they were serving on a selection panel for job applicants. People make an assessment of **social judgeability**, a perception of whether there is a legitimate and adequate basis for judging a specific person before forming an impression. Sometimes, merely believing you are in a position to make a judgement (but in reality, you lack good evidence) results in your making unwarranted evaluations of other people (Leyens *et al.*, 1992).

Impressions are also influenced by physical appearance. Immediate first impressions are often based on what we see, because other information about people's 'character' is not yet available. According to Zebrowitz and Collins (1997), appearance-based first impressions can actually be surprisingly accurate. However, there are obvious pitfalls. For example, the tendency to form more favourable first impressions of physically attractive people may cause one to hire people who are delightfully decorative but not much good at getting the job done (Heilman and Stopeck, 1985). A study of 11,370 convicted criminals found that those with the greatest tendency to control the impression formed of them were less likely to be antisocial, but were more likely to be convicted of serious crimes such as murder and sexual assault (C.G. Davis *et al.*, 2011). They also received longer sentences.

Schema and categories

A central theme for social cognition is the concept of **schema** – 'schemata' is the plural (Fiske and Taylor, 1991). A schema is a mental framework or body of knowledge that organises and synthesises information about something. Schemata contain information about attributes and the relationship between attributes. We have schemata for specific people (e.g. one's best friend), groups of people (e.g. traffic wardens), ourselves, events (e.g. how to order food at a restaurant), roles (e.g. how the pilot of an aeroplane should behave in the cockpit), places and objects.

Schemata aid us in interpreting the world. The first time you visited your psychology lecturer in his/her office, for example, there were probably not many surprises. Your 'lecturer' schema guided your expectations. However, you would probably be surprised if you saw that your lecturer's office was filled with skateboarding trophies, autographed photos of heavy metal bands, or dead animals mounted on the walls as hunting trophies. Such possessions are probably inconsistent with your impression of lecturers.

As an example of how schemata guide our interpretations, try to make sense of the following passage:

> The procedure is actually quite simple. First you arrange things into different groups. Of course, one pile may be sufficient depending on how much there is to do. . . . It is important not to overdo things. That is, it is better to do too few things at once than too many. In the short run this may not seem important, but complications can easily arise. A mistake can be expensive as well. At first the whole procedure will seem complicated. Soon, however, it will become just another facet of life. (Source: Bransford and Johnson, 1972, p. 722.)

Does this passage make sense to you? What if I tell you that the title of the passage is 'Washing Clothes'? Now you can interpret the passage easily. The sentences make perfect sense within the context of your schema for washing clothes. Not surprisingly, research has demonstrated that understanding is improved when people know the title of the passage before it is read (Bransford and Johnson, 1972). Imagine a time when you turned on the radio and a discussion or phone-in left you clueless as to the topic being talked about because the exchanges were so vague and generic that you could only make sense of them when the interviewer gave a reminder of the topic that was under discussion.

Categories, prototypes and exemplars

Once you categorise a person (as an individual or as a member of a particular group), the schema of that person or group is activated. Research suggests that schemata can be organised as prototypes (Cantor and Mischel, 1979) or as

exemplars (Smith and Zárate, 1992). A prototype is an abstract fuzzy set of attributes that define the category, where no instance may actually embody the attributes. An exemplar is a specific instance of the category. For example, if your schema of Australian people is the actor High Jackman then you have an exemplar representation, whereas if what comes to mind is a general notion of billabongs, kangaroos, boomerangs and so forth then you have a prototype representation. Note that both types of schema are equally accurate or inaccurate as a 'true' description of the category as a whole.

Social categories simplify the social world by reducing an infinite diversity of people to a more limited number of categories of people, each described by a schema – men, women, Catholics, Danes, doctors and so forth. Categories only form and persist to the extent that they make sense of the world and one's place within it. Any specific person can fit into many categories (e.g. someone can be a female, an Italian and an engineer), but once a person is categorised, the appropriate schema is activated to influence perceptions, expectations and interaction.

Categories vary in inclusiveness. Highly inclusive categories have many members (e.g. a nation) and thus overshadow potentially important differences between people. More exclusive categories have fewer members (e.g. a family). Although these capture differences more precisely, an exclusive category structure would produce too many categories – it is a too fine-grained segmentation of the world. In general, the most cognitively accessible social categories are **basic level categories** which are neither too inclusive nor too exclusive. Basic level categories are default categories that we first use to generate context-specific schemata of people – these are often based on visible cues such as skin colour, physiognomy, sex and dress (Zebrowitz, 1996). However, many factors, including the social interactive context, our interaction goals and our own personal history, can influence basic level categories and what categorisation and associated schema comes into play in a particular context.

Leigh and Susilo (2009) exploited an unusual quirk of the Australian electoral system to see whether physical appearance implicitly influenced voting intentions. In the Northern Territory of Australia, photographs of candidates appear on ballot papers. In the study, the researchers examined whether the candidates' beauty and skin colour were associated with electoral success. They found that in areas with small indigenous populations, candidates with a lighter skin colour received more votes. In areas where there were high numbers of indigenous people, darker-skinned candidates were more successful. The effect of skin colour was more pronounced for people who were challengers for the position than for those who were incumbents. The candidates' beauty did not affect electoral success.

Schema acquisition and development

We tend to acquire and develop our schemata through exposure to instances of the category – face-to-face encounters, media presentations, second-hand accounts and so forth. As one encounters more instances of a category one's schema is likely to become less exemplar-based and more prototype-based. Research suggests that such prototype-based schemata can become tightly organised into a single mental construct that is very rapidly activated in an all-or-nothing fashion by category cues (Schul, 1983). Such schemata are highly resistant to change (Fiske and Neuberg, 1990), which can be particularly problematic in the case of schemata of groups.

Group schemata and stereotypes

Schemata of social groups are particularly significant since they characterise large numbers of people in terms of a small number of properties that submerges the variety of differences that exist between people. Schemata of social groups are almost always shared among people in one group. For example, British people often believe that Americans are 'brash', the French think the British are 'cold' and so forth. Shared schemata of social groups are best described as stereotypes. Because they are closely associated with prejudice, discrimination and intergroup relations, we will return to them in the next chapter (Leyens *et al.*, 1994).

According to Tajfel (1981), stereotypes are learned early in childhood through normal socialisation rather than direct experience. Research suggests that children's use of stereotypes and expression of negative attitudes towards out-groups peak at around the age of 7 and then decline by 8 or 9 years of age. This may reflect cognitive developmental changes that affect the way children understand the meaning of categories and attributes, and changes in role-taking skills (Aboud, 1988; Durkin, 1995). Prejudice (a topic discussed in much greater depth in the next chapter) usually refers to a person's expression of negative views of and behaviours towards members of an ethnic group that differs from their own (Brown, 1995). A key component of prejudice is the belief that the ethnic or 'out-group' is highly dissimilar to the 'in-group' (the person's own social or racial group). Language is one important factor that can enhance or magnify perceived dissimilarities between groups and this is no more evident than when comparing different nationalities or cultures (Giles and Johnson, 1987; Giles and Coupland, 1991). Language is a communicative glue, bonding otherwise highly dissimilar individuals. Not only can it allow communication between the in-group members, it can also prevent or inhibit communication with out-group members.

Automaticity of stereotypes

Images of another group (the out-group) are generally less favourable than images of one's own group (the in-group) and provide a relatively positive evaluation of oneself. For example,

a stereotype that characterises an out-group as lazy and unmotivated is an excellent justification for an intergroup relationship where your own group has control over that group.

Some of the best comedy comes from caricature – the exaggeration of stereotypes or stereotypical features. Two recent colourful examples are Sasha Baron-Cohen's creations, Borat and Bruno.
Source: Vince Bucci/Getty Images Entertainment/Getty Images, (Top); Jeffrey Ufberg/WireImage/Getty Images (Bottom).

Once someone is categorised as a member of a particular group, the schema of that group (stereotype) influences the impression of that person. For example, if students believe that professors are pompous, boring and opinionated, then once you, as a student, categorise someone as a professor you will automatically tend to assume that they are pompous, boring and opinionated, and that impression will influence the entire interaction. The expectation may even, over a period of time, change the professor's behaviour to conform to your schema (Snyder, 1984).

Stereotypes are automatically and unconsciously activated in particular contexts – they have the property of **automaticity**. Particular cues (e.g. a Welsh accent) can automatically activate a categorisation (Welsh), which in turn automatically engages the appropriate stereotype. In a classic study, Devine (1989) presented people with (negative) African-American primes (words like 'lazy', 'slavery', 'Negroes') far too quickly for people to be aware of them. She found that participants interpreted a subsequent neutral act, by someone merely called Donald, in ways that were consistent with negative stereotypes of African-Americans. Whether someone scored high or low on a racial prejudice scale did not affect susceptibility to preconscious priming – an effect that was replicated by Fazio et al. (1995). Other research has, however, shown that the effect is more marked for people who score high on unobtrusive measures of possessing racist attitudes (Lepore and Brown, 1997).

The property of automaticity has been exploited by the **implicit association test** (IAT; Greenwald et al., 2002) which has been thought to elicit our hidden prejudices. The test has been placed on the Web (http://implicit.harvard.edu/implicit/) – so you can discover if you are prejudiced, or rather, just how prejudiced you are.

Implicit biases or prejudice can be expressed towards various types of people, the obese for example (Teachman et al., 2003). Beachgoers in Connecticut were given a newspaper article which stated that obesity was caused either by genetics or by overeating and lack of exercise. The IAT was then administered in which participants decided whether words paired with the adjective 'good' or 'bad' were appropriately paired. So, the pairing of 'thin people' with 'good' and 'fat people' with 'bad' would be expected to be responded to more quickly as an appropriate pairing than would 'fat people' and 'good'. Participants also completed a questionnaire measuring their attitudes towards obesity and obese people.

Although the participants claimed to hold no explicit biases towards fat people, their implicit responses suggested otherwise. People associated 'fat people' with more negative attributes (lazy, bad) than positive ones (motivated, smart). In line with Crandall's (1994) reasoning, this bias was greater when people had been previously primed to think that obesity was caused by controllable factors such as overeating and lack of exercise than when they saw it as being caused by uncontrollable genetic factors.

In a follow-up study, the implicit test was prefaced by stories which evoked sympathy towards fat people, or evoked sympathy towards people who use wheelchairs (what the researchers called a comparable 'stigmatised' group) or were neutral. Ninety women participated at Yale University. Reading empathic stories about fat people did not reduce implicit fat bias, compared with reading neutral stories. When overweight participants were added to this sample, there was evidence of in-group bias. Fat people were more likely to show less implicit bias after reading the empathetic material. The results suggest that while people may claim that they do not hold negative (stereotypical) views of fat people, their implicit cognitions and behaviour suggest otherwise.

It is noteworthy that while the IAT can reveal our attitudes and views of brands and products (Maison et al., 2004), more recent research has cast serious doubt on its validity in revealing racial bias (Oswald et al., 2013, 2015; Greenwald et al., 2014). Meta-analyses have found that IAT scores are not good predictors of racial discrimination (Oswald et al., 2015).

If stereotyping is largely an automatic process over which we have only limited conscious control, what can be done to combat it? One solution might be to make the category–stereotype link more conscious by thinking hard about it and suppressing the stereotype immediately it comes to mind. Over time, stereotype suppression might inhibit stereotype activation. An alternative view, which makes equal sense, is that the more you try to suppress the stereotype the firmer the cognitive or associative link between the category and the stereotype, and thus the more entrenched the automatic activation effect. Macrae et al. (1994) call this effect 'stereotype rebound'.

Stereotype content model

One model which attempts to explain how and why we hold stereotypes is Fiske's Stereotype Content Model (SCM) (Fiske et al., 2007; Fiske, 2012). According to Fiske's model, when we meet someone we are unfamiliar with and who belongs to a different category of person to which we don't belong (age, race, sex, occupation, etc.), we ask two questions: do they intend to cause harm and are they capable of causing harm? These two questions are reflected in the model's positing of two stereotype dimensions: warmth and competence. Warmth reflects how friendly, sincere, trustworthy, sociable and warm a person is. People who cooperate are perceived as warm; those who compete are perceived as cold (Fiske, 2012). Competence reflects of how skilful, confident and capable they are. The model proposes a matrix of high and low warmth and competence, as you can see in Figure 15.1.

Groups who would be high in warmth and competence would be members of our in-group (our culture/nation); groups who would be low in both include the homeless and poor (and, in some cases, immigrants), who are generally perceived negatively and are groups which tend to elicit most

	Low Competence, Low Status	High Competence, High Status
High Warmth, Cooperative	Older people, disabled people, traditional women (Pity sympathy)	In-group, allies, reference groups: e.g., middle class, white, Christian, heterosexual (Pride, admiration)
Low Warmth, Competitive	Poor people, welfare recipients, homeless people, immigrants (Disgust, contempt)	Rich people, female professionals, lesbians, feminists, Asians, Jews (Envy, jealousy)

Figure 15.1 Fiske's stereotype content model which suggests that we categorise people along two dimensions – warmth and competence.

disgust, and are likely to be demeaned and dehumanised (Harris and Fiske, 2006; Cikara *et al.*, 2010). Categories of people who fall somewhere in between would include the elderly, and qualified and rich out-groups. These tend to elicit ambivalent emotions – the elderly are characterised by high warmth and low competence in professionals are characterised by low warmth and high competence.

Perceptions of immigrants vary according to the country of origin. The stereotype of the elderly is universal and appears quite resistant to change (Cuddy *et al.*, 2005). The old are associated with illness, incompetence and invisibility (North and Fiske, 2012) and we hold prescriptive views about this group, and others (e.g. old people should not like rap or hip-hop or should dress according to their age not like teenagers). Younger people are far more likely to hold negative views of the elderly who violate these prescriptive stereotypes than are middle-aged people – they rate them as significantly lower in warmth and competence (North and Fiske, 2013). Younger participants were less concerned about the violations made by people of the same age or by middle-aged individuals.

In the US, Latino and African-American immigrants are rated lowest on both dimensions, European immigrants are rated similarly to indigenous US individuals and Canadians are rated higher than any other (Lee and Fiske, 2006). East Asians are rated high on competence and low on warmth. Cuddy *et al.* (2009) examined stereotypical impressions of EU countries by asking 755 respondents in seven EU countries (Belgium, France, Germany, the Netherlands, Portugal and Spain) to judge each of the (then) 15 EU countries along the two dimensions described here. The study identified three clusters: (1) high warmth and low competence (Spain, Italy, Portugal, Greece, Ireland), (2) low warmth and high competence (Belgium, Sweden, France, Denmark, the Netherlands, Finland, Luxembourg, Austria) and (3) highest competence and lowest warmth (UK, Germany). Individuals asked to describe fictional immigrants who were competitive or not or who were high or low in status judged competitive immigrants to be low in warmth. They also regarded the high-status group

to be competent, judged both status groups to be equally warm, admired uncompetitive, high-status groups, envied high-status, competitive groups and pitied uncompetitive, low-status groups (Caprariello *et al.*, 2009).

Fiske has argued that the SCM can explain and predict societal inequalities – in health, income and mobility (Durante *et al.*, 2013). The model, she suggests, argues that ambivalence helps maintain these inequalities. In a study of 37 different nations (across Europe, the Americas, Asia, Africa), the societies with the greatest inequality were those most likely to show the ambivalent profile. Equal societies were more likely to dislike competitive groups and not rate them as competent (Durante *et al.*, 2013). She and her research group have also identified an association between lower stereotype ambivalence and national peace/conflict (Durante *et al.*, 2017). In a study of 4,344 individuals from 38 nations, those from highly conflicted or highly peaceful countries were likely to hold lower ambivalent stereotypes whereas those countries falling in between are more ambivalent.

The trolley/train dilemma

Another, practical consequence of the SCM is that some groups may be likely to be perceived as morally better than others, even more expendable. Foot's philosophical mind-experiment, the trolley dilemma, provides an example. In the footbridge version of this philosophical dilemma, participants are presented with the following scenario. A person on a footbridge can see an empty runaway train careering towards five people on a railway track. The person can either allow the accident to happen – he or she can't directly stop it themselves – or shove a bystander over the bridge to block the train's pathway. The dilemma is: do you kill one person to save five or do you allow five people to die when you could have prevented their death. There is no right or wrong answer to this: it is a real moral dilemma. The utilitarian response is to save as many people as possible, by sacrificing one. Deontological reasoning argues that the rights of the person on the bridge outweigh utilitarian concerns. Most people are deontological reasoners – one study found that 88 per cent of people considered it wrong to shove the person off the bridge (Hauser *et al.*, 2008).

Cikara *et al.* (2010) explored who would be most likely to be saved in the context of the SCM model and whether brain activation was associated with particular types of social cognition. They asked 18 Princeton students to take part in the footbridge dilemma and used fMRI to measure brain activation. The group to be saved was either from an in-group (high warmth/competence) or an out-group (low warmth/competence) or from variants of the dimensions. As predicted by the model, people were more likely to save members of the in-group. The group least likely to be saved were the low warmth/competence group – the homeless. Brain activation during this decision involved the medial PFC, the left lateral OFC and left dorsolateral PFC. These activations were found during decisions participants found most acceptable.

Cutting edge: Schadenfreude

It has become a cliché to say that the German language has words for things that English has no language for – and almost a cliché to say it is a cliche. Perhaps the most famous of these is schadenfreude: the taking of pleasure in the misfortune of others (outgroup members) whom we envy (Cikara and Fiske, 2013). We smile more when a person we envy experiences a negative event, for example (Cikara and Fiske, 2012); we are less empathetic. However, we can express more empathy for some groups who encounter a misfortune – the elderly, for example, who are the recipients of pity rather than envy in such studies. The

brain region most commonly activated during empathy is the insula, as you saw in the pain section in Chapter 5. Cikara and Fiske (2011) found that people feel less bad when envied individuals suffer a misfortune and feel bad when a pitied group suffer a misfortune; they feel worse for this group than their own in-group. They are less willing to harm pitied out-group members than envied ones. Bilateral activation in the anterior insula was associated with a willingness to harm envied groups who had experienced positive events but with an unwillingness to harm their in-group.

When good intentions backfire: stereotypes, influence and behaviour

A female assistant is working alongside her male boss on a complex decision task. Will he treat her any differently from a male assistant? Research by Vescio *et al.* (2005) examined the idea that powerful men use stereotypes to judge women when the stereotype seems contextually relevant and when they are focusing on the weakness of women in that context, that is, if the task is in an area in which women are stereotyped as weak.

Male and female students believed they were participating in an academic competition involving teams. Half the participants were led to believe that good leaders focused on eliminating weaknesses in their teams; the other half that good leaders focused on maximising strengths. Their task was to select from among four male and four female members those who should represent the team, and assign them roles of team captain, player and non-player. They were also asked to email an explanation for their decision to each member. The results showed that weakness-focused men, not women, used their stereotypes of subordinate women more strongly by assigning fewer valued positions in the group to those women. At the same time, these men praised the subordinate women more highly, as shown in Table 15.1.

So these powerful men effectively acted in a patronising way towards subordinate women, denying them an opportunity for advancement but delivering positive messages to them.

Next Vescio and colleagues investigated how male leaders who patronised and focused on weakness might affect the behaviour of male and female subordinates. Being patronised makes people angry but, because women tend to avoid overtly aggressive responses, Vescio and colleagues predicted that low-power women may respond more passively to being patronised. In contrast, low-power men seemed likely to respond competitively, by endeavouring to perform better. A male leader assigned male or female participants a low-power role as a team member, and then either praised the member or did not, and assigned the member to a valued or devalued position in the group. Both male and female team members reported feeling angrier when they were patronised than when they were not but, as shown in Table 15.2, on a 23-item test males performed better after being patronised whereas females did not. As Vescio and colleagues conclude, leadership styles often focus on eliminating weaknesses, but people are likely to be more motivated and perform better, and less likely to be the unwitting victims of patronising stereotypes, when leaders focus on ways in which subordinate group members can promote the goals of the group.

Table 15.1 Position assignment and praise of female subordinates as a function of leader's gender and social influence focus

	Male leaders		Female leaders	
	Weakness focused	Strength focused	Weakness focused	Strength focused
Position assignment	3.79	4.47	4.76	4.58
Praise	4.42	3.84	3.69	3.62

Table 15.2 Performance as a function of position assignment, praise and participant's gender

	Valued position		Devalued position	
	Praised	Not praised	Praised	Not praised
Female participants	10.48	9.69	9.02	9.99
Male participants	10.00	10.19	11.86	10.5

Research shows that when people are negatively primed with an unflattering stereotype – women are poor at maths – the targeted sample has a reduced positive view of themselves and exhibit the stereotype they are primed with. Those unprimed do not show this behaviour. This is called stereotype threat and is described and evaluated in more detail in the next chapter. A study from the US has found that one particular anxiety, about maths, can influence children's judgements about stereotypical sex roles (Bellock *et al.*, 2010). The researchers measured maths anxiety in first and second grade maths teachers in the US (over 90 per cent are women) and examined whether this affected children's performance and their stereotypes about the sexes (boys are good at maths, girls are good at reading). At the beginning of the year, there was no relationship between the teacher's maths anxiety and her children's performance. By the end of the year, however, there was: the more anxious the teacher, the more likely it was that girls (but not boys) endorsed the above stereotype. These girls' maths achievement was also lower than boys or girls who did not hold the stereotype. The teacher's ability could not explain these findings: if this were so, boys and girls would have shown similar declines.

Research suggests that if male and female characteristics are made salient via priming, then men and women behave more like their gender stereotype (Hundhammer and Mussweiler, 2012). People are faster at describing themselves as male or female, women become more submissive and men become more assertive. The stereotyped behaviour is eliminated if modern sex stereotypes are primed.

Although the data are inconsistent and the findings controversial, there is some evidence that women are under-represented in science and various reasons have been proposed for the apparent sex disparity. Rossiter (1993) gave the name 'the Matilda effect' to describe the under-recognition of women in science. One reason for the under-recognition may be that working in this field is incongruent with our stereotypes of women. According to role congruity theory (Eagly and Karau, 2002), we expect each sex to be characterised by specific traits; if the sexes are not congruent with this view, we do not view them as representative of that group. In science, women appear to receive fewer grants, and grants of lesser value, fewer citation and fewer awards than do men (Knobloch-Westerwick *et al.*, 2013). Psychologists – whether male or female – are more likely to hire male psychologists and women are less likely to be considered employable as a lab manager, and less competent (Steinpreis *et al.*, 1999; Moss-Racusin *et al.*, 2012).

In a further study which supports the existence of this bias, Knobloch-Westerwick *et al.* asked 243 communication academics to rate conference abstracts written by men or women. The abstract was the same in each condition – only the sex of the author changed. The abstracts described either sex-congruent or sex-neutral content. Some examples included: infant attention and body image (female-typed abstract) and computer-mediated transactions and democratising journalism (male-typed). You might query the description of both. However, regardless of content, abstracts by men were regarded as being of better scientific quality (and especially if the content was male-typed).

Cutting edge: Does listening to sexually degrading music lead to endorsement of sexual stereotypes?

Pop music brings joy to many but it's also a minefield of controversy. Elvis was banned for swivelling his hips, a po-faced DJ banned Frankie Goes to Hollywood's *Relax* from his playlist on BBC Radio 1, as for the Sex Pistols. . . .

The controversy does and will continue. Currently, there are expressions of anger over the use of sexually degrading lyrics and visual content in songs, primarily, but not exclusively, in rap where women are objectified and described as sexually available objects. Robin Thicke courted controversy with his lyrics for *Blurred Lines*. Many examples of this kind come with a parental advisory label. What concerns some is that lyrics such as these portray women poorly, encourage negative stereotypes of women and encourage aggressive treatment of women. They may even endorse rape myths: the idea that women enjoy having forced sexual intercourse without consent.

To examine whether listening to these lyrics endorses rape myths and confirms sexual stereotypes, Sprankle *et al.* (2012) asked 187 male undergraduates to listen to a sexually explicit music video with the lyrics absent or present and examined the effects of exposure on men's aggressive behaviour towards women and whether they endorsed rape myths and sexual stereotypes. One of the videos used was 'Shake That Shit' and example lyrics include: 'Maannn, these bitches is awfully nasty/And these bitches keep walking past me/Either way, I'm a pimp for today/Put your bootie in the way and shake that shit!' It's not Shakespeare and that's one of the milder extracts.

The researchers found that none of the videos – which were chosen from a pilot study in which people rated various videos of songs for degree of offensiveness – influenced sexual stereotypes and none confirmed rape myths. We may be more immune to the sound of these lyrics than lay and invested opinion suggest. This psychological deafness might be doubly advantageous.

Social cognition and neuroscience

A new field of research in social psychology attempts to determine which brain areas and structures are involved in social processes such as social rejection, prejudice, social interaction and so on (Hari *et al.*, 2015). There are even journals dedicated to this line of research – *Social Neuroscience* and *Social, Cognitive and Affective Neuroscience*.

Social cognition has been associated with a network of brain regions including the dorsal frontal cortex, anterior cingulate and superior temporal sulcus (STC) (Rushworth *et al.*, 2013). A study by Deen *et al.* (2015) found that parts of the STC were activated by specific social tasks and other types of activation were not domain specific but elicited by different tasks. For example, they found that the superior temporal junction was associated with activation during theory of mind tasks and that face and biological motion perception were associated with activation in the posterior superior temporal sulcus. An area which showed greatest overlap in activation was a part of the posterior STS – this was active during the perception of dynamic faces and voices, a finding which supports others which have found activation in these areas during perception of these stimuli.

Other areas implicated in social decision-making include the ventral striatum and the orbitofrontal cortex, two areas known to mediate aspects of reward and perception of reward (Seo and Lee, 2012). When we make social decisions, we think about what the other person might be thinking and how they might respond to our behaviour – this involves regions responsible for theory of mind. Our ability to perceive and express fairness – and respond to unfairness – implicates regions including the insula, anterior cingulate cortex, dorsolateral prefrontal cortex and the amygdala.

The amygdala is particularly noteworthy because, as you saw in Chapter 4 and 13, it is associated with the expression and perception of threat and with the encoding of emotional memories. Some research in social neuroscience has implicated the structure in the perception of race. The first neuroimaging studies, on this topic for example, found that activation in the amygdala was correlated with negative racial attitudes (Hart *et al.*, 2000; Phelps *et al.*, 2000). Phelps *et al.* (2000) asked white Americans to view unfamiliar black and white women as fMRI recorded brain activation from the structure. They also measured participants' implicit and explicit attitudes to race. They found that activation in the amygdala to the black men was correlated with implicit, but not explicit, attitudes towards race. When black and white men who were famous and positively regarded were presented, the amygdala activation was eliminated, suggesting that the activation and implicit bias was a reflection of a fear of the unfamiliar.

Hart *et al.* (2000), however, found activation to both black and white unfamiliar faces in black and white participants but that the activation declined when participants saw the same-race face but not the other-race face, suggesting to the authors that 'alarm signals from the amygdala attenuate more rapidly for same race than other race strangers' (p. 166).

In a study where European Americans sorted photographs of African-American and European American faces according to age, amygdala activation was greater during the decisions made about African-Americans (Wheeler and Fiske, 2005). In a twist on the normal paradigm, Cunningham *et al.* (2004) presented unfamiliar black and white faces subliminally and to conscious awareness as brain activation was measured. Amygdala activation was stronger when the black face was presented subliminally, suggesting an even greater degree of **automatic processing** in this structure. Activity in the anterior cingulate cortex (ACC) and dorsolateral prefrontal cortex (DlPFC), however, was correlated with a decline in activation in the amygdala suggesting (as Chapter 13 noted) that these regions acted as a break on – or controlled or modulated – the information sent by the amygdala.

The evidence suggests that the amygdala is more likely to be active when seeing a black male face, regardless of the participant's race or sex (Chekroud *et al.*, 2014). Chekroud *et al.* suggest that the amygdala is not involved in a behaviour as vague as a bias towards an in-group or prejudice but that it is sensitive to threat and to a threat people see posed by black men. This perception of threat, they argue, has been socially learned. The social learning is seen reflected in the amygdala's activation.

Remember, of course, that the amygdala is not really one structure – it is made of different nuclei and it also responds to different types of stimuli, including trustworthy faces not just ones it perceives as a threat (Todorov, 2012). Its involvement in race perception is demonstrable but what this involvement means or reflects is unclear.

The insula might be responsible for different aspects of social processing to those mediated by the prefrontal cortex. For example, Gu *et al.* (2015) found that patients with injury to this area were better at detecting violations of norms in a fairness game than were patients with PFC injury. The latter patients, on the other hand, were more likely to accept unfairness in this game and accepted more unfair (monetary) offers. Gu *et al.* suggest that this dissociation indicates that the insula is involved in the detection of the violation of norms whereas the vmPFC evaluates fairness during social interactions.

Facing racial stereotypes

Physical appearance is a powerful cue to category membership. For example, we rely heavily on sex or skin colour to assign people to gender or racial/ethnic categories, and then generate stereotypical assumptions about their attributes and behaviours. We can even be quite discriminating in our perception of and reaction to physical appearance cues. For example, research in the US has shown that African-American prisoners who have more Afro-centric facial features receive more severe sentences than African-American prisoners with less Afro-centric features.

Blair *et al.* (2004) analysed the facial features of a random sample of black and white prison inmates who had been given equivalent sentences. They hypothesised that strongly Afro-centric facial features might unwittingly (or wittingly) influence sentencing decisions. They defined Afro-centric features as being typical of those seen in African-Americans – for example, 'dark skin, wide nose, full lips'.

The sample comprised 216 black and white inmates at the Florida Department of Corrections and their facial photographs were presented to two groups of undergraduates who rated the degree to which facial features were typical of African-Americans. While there was little difference in the severity of the sentence given to the black and white prisoners, there were significant differences in the harshness of the sentence within the black sample. Those with stereotypically Afro-centric features were significantly more likely to have received harsher sentences than were those with less Afro-centric physical characteristics.

The results indicate that although bias and stereotyping were not evident in sentencing – black and white criminals with equivalent criminal histories were given comparable sentences – more subtle forms of stereotyping were significantly influencing sentencing decisions.

In an unusual study, Stillman *et al.* (2010) found that people were able to accurately estimate the degree of violence committed by sex offenders by looking at their faces only. In the experiment, 97 undergraduates saw photographs of 87 registered sex offenders for two seconds and were asked to rate how likely the person was to be violent on a four-point scale. These judgements were then compared with the actual degree of violence shown in the criminal's offence. When judgements were accurate, the faces rated as violent were younger, had a heavier brow, looked more masculine and appeared physically strong.

However, errors were made and participants judged, incorrectly, that happy, well-groomed individuals were less likely to be violent and that angry and disgusted expressions on the faces would be associated with greater violence.

Stereotypes – An international perspective

Are there any features of stereotypes that transcend national boundaries? One model in social psychology – the stereotype content model – argues just that. One aspect of the model argues that there are two universally recognised stereotypical dimensions – competence and warmth. Another proposes that there may be an ambivalent stereotype – competent and cold or warm and incompetent. Cuddy *et al.* (2009) investigated whether these dimensions would be reflected in the stereotypes held by 10 non-US nations, including seven European nations and three East Asian nations.

They were. The group found that the dimensions of competence and warmth characterised stereotypes of others. The group also found that out-groups were more likely to receive ambivalent descriptors (scoring high on one dimension and low on another). Groups of high status tend to be rated high on competence whereas very competitive groups tend to be rated as stereotypically less warm. So, whereas the nature of the stereotype can be seen to be universal, the expression of this stereotype varies cross-culturally.

Controversies in psychological science: Sexist humour – does it make you sexist?

Issue

People who express sexist attitudes – an antagonism towards women (perhaps, itself, a sexist definition) – tend to suppress them for external reasons rather than internal ones. That is, these views would violate some social norm and are, therefore, not expressed. Sexist jokes tend to re-enforce sexist beliefs. Highly sexist men are far more likely to accept a sexist norm after exposure to sexist jokes: when asked to pretend to be managers who had made sexist remarks to a woman employee, highly sexist men felt less guilty about it after reading sexist jokes than neutral ones (Ford *et al.*, 2001). But can exposure to sexist humour create sexist beliefs?

Evidence

A group of US researchers asked participants to read a series of scenarios and pretend to empathise with people in them (Ford *et al.*, 2008). In the scenario, participants were told that a

▶

Controversies in psychological science: *Continued*

discussion has taken place about workmates' favourite jokes. Some of these jokes were sexist (e.g. 'How can you tell if a blonde's been using the computer? There's Tippex on the screen'). The next scenario involved a discussion of views in which sexist beliefs were defended seriously. Finally, a vignette was presented in which the National Council of Women's aims were stated and its request for donations made clear. Participants were asked how much they would give to the organisation.

Highly sexist people exposed to sexist humour were less likely to give to the organisation. In a second experiment, the amount of money participants would cut from the organisation was measured. Sexist individuals exposed to sexist humour recommended greater budget cuts than those exposed to neutral comedy.

There is also evidence that women tend to find jokes against their own sex as funnier, whereas men find jokes against women are funnier (Abrams and Bippus, 2014). Respondents who didn't identify strongly with their sex found jokes about their own sex funnier than jokes about the opposite sex.

Conclusion

The moral of this story seems to be: exposure to some forms of comedy can harm your charity collecting but our attitude to sexist jokes is shaped by how strongly we identify with our sex. Women are also more likely to find jokes against women as funnier.

Conceptual and historical issues in social psychology

So far, you have seen how social psychologists have studied basic social behaviours such as impression formation and stereotypes. That social psychologists study these topics and in an experimental way owes a lot to the branch's history and development. The empirical study of social behaviour emerged in the second half of the nineteenth century (with a group in Germany calling themselves students of Völkerpsychologie – folk psychology – who focused on the collective mind, in contrast to Wundt).

In the early 1900s, America superseded Germany as the powerhouse of social psychology – a process which was accelerated in the 1930s by an enormous influx of leading German social psychologists fleeing Nazism. The ensuing global conflict, the Second World War, then posed urgent applied social psychological questions that created an explosion of research activity that focused on, for example, small group processes (Lewin, 1951), attitudes and attitude change (Hovland *et al.*, 1953) and prejudice (Adorno *et al.*, 1950).

From the late 1940s, social psychology grew prodigiously, in terms of programmes, publications and profile within psychology. During the 1950s and early 1960s small group research flourished (e.g. the study of group cohesion, leadership, communication networks, group influence – Shaw, 1976), as did the study of interpersonal relationships as social exchanges (Thibaut and Kelley, 1959), and the study of attitude change as the resolution of cognitive dissonance (Festinger, 1957). The mid-1960s through the 1970s was characterised by attribution theories that focused on how people, as intuitive scientists,

develop causal explanations of their social world as a basis for behaviour (Kelley, 1973).

Generally speaking, there are two camps in social psychology: those who believe that group behaviour is not qualitatively different from individual or interpersonal behaviour (we can call them 'individualists') and those who believe it is ('collectivists'). The debate mostly bubbles along in the background, but from time to time it seems to become a major preoccupation. The 1960s was one such occasion, when social psychology seemed to be deep in crisis (Elms, 1975). Critics felt that the discipline was asking the wrong questions, providing inadequate explanations of trivial behaviours and using primitive methodologies. The resolution of the crisis had two contrasting prongs. Social psychologists in the USA developed social cognition (discussed extensively in this chapter) in a drive for better methodology and better theory (Fiske and Taylor, 1991), and social psychologists in Europe developed what they called a more social social psychology (Tajfel, 1984) in a drive for socially relevant research (e.g. the study of prejudice and intergroup conflict) and theories that linked cognitive and social processes.

The late 1960s and early 1970s, therefore, saw the emergence of a crisis of confidence in social psychology. Social psychologists were concerned that social psychology was theoretically immature, methodologically unsophisticated, inappropriately dependent on scientific method, and focused too much on individuals and interpersonal interaction and too little on language and collective phenomena. Out of this angst arose a diversity of 'resolutions'. The two most successful are social cognition, with sophisticated methodologies and theories that continue to dominate social psychology (Nisbett and Ross, 1980; Fiske and Taylor, 1991; Devine *et al.*, 1994; Moskowitz, 2005), and social perspectives that focus on culture (Smith *et al.*, 2006), collective representations (Moscovici, 1976) and intergroup relations and social identity (Tajfel, 1984; Hogg and Abrams, 1988).

There is another set of responses that rejects traditional social psychological methods, theories and research foci altogether, and instead focuses on subjectivity, language and qualitative methods (Potter and Wetherell, 1987; Edwards, 1997). Two recent trends in social psychology are evolutionary social psychology (Buss and Kenrick, 1998) and social neuroscience (Ochsner and Lieberman, 2001). The former focuses on the evolutionary and adaptive origins of social behaviours and social-cognitive processes. The latter maps social behaviours and social-cognitive processes onto functions, structures and processes within the brain.

Self-knowledge

Knowledge about ourselves is very much like knowledge about other people. If you were asked who you were, how would you respond? You might say your name, that you are a student and perhaps that you are also an athlete or have a part-time job. Alternatively, you could talk about your family, your nationality, ethnicity or religion. There are many ways you could potentially describe yourself, all of which would reflect your **self-concept** – your knowledge, feelings and ideas about yourself. In its totality, the self is a person's distinct individuality. At the core of the self-concept is the **self-schema** – a mental framework that represents and synthesises information about who you are. The self-schema is a cognitive structure that organises the knowledge, feelings and ideas that constitute the self-concept.

Social psychologists believe that we have many different selves that can be more or less discrete and come into play in different contexts – the subjective experience of self is highly context dependent. Selves not only describe how we are, but also how we would like to be, called possible selves (Markus and Nurius, 1986). Higgins (1987) takes this idea further in his **self-discrepancy theory**. He distinguishes between the actual self (how one really is), the ideal self (how one would like to be) and the 'ought' self (how one thinks one ought to be). The latter two are 'self-guides' which mobilise different types of self-related behaviours. The ideal self engages 'promotional' goals – we strive towards achieving the ideal, whereas the 'ought' self engages 'prevention' goals – we strive to avoid doing what we ought not to do (Higgins, 1998).

How do we learn who we are – how do we form self-schemata? Introspection is one way, but the overwhelmingly social nature of human existence means that we learn much more about ourselves from how others treat us, and from how we think others view us. Research on **self-fulfilling prophecies** shows that others' expectation about us can change the way we behave. For example, Snyder (1984) reports a series of studies in which experimental participants behaved in a more extravert manner simply because others were primed with the false expectation that they, the participants, were extraverts. Expectations constrained participants to behave in a more extravert manner, and biased interpretations of neutral behaviour so it appeared more extravert. In this way participants gradually really did behave in a more extravert manner. Another example comes from research by Steele and Aronson (1995) into **stereotype threat**, which shows that because African-American students are aware of social expectations concerning academic underperformance, they can actually reduce effort and thus underperform.

Social impact on behaviour can affect self-conception because, according to self-perception theory (Bem, 1972), we often learn most about ourselves by simply observing how we behave. If there is no obvious coercion to behave as we do, then we assume that the behaviour reflects the type of person we are (see attribution theory, below). If you notice that you often drink coffee of your own free will you would be forgiven for deducing that you are the kind of person who likes coffee.

In addition to introspection and self-perception, another powerful source of self-knowledge is social comparison. According to **social comparison theory** (Festinger, 1954) people need to feel confident about the validity of their perceptions, attitudes, feelings and behaviours. This sense of validity often comes from the fact that other people who are similar to us agree with us. In this way, attitudes about ourselves may be grounded in belonging to groups of people who have similar views about who we are – views that reinforce and confirm our own self-attitudes.

Orientations of self-knowledge

We are all aware of two contrasting orientations to life – one in which we are adventurous, optimistic and approach-oriented (the glass is half full), and one in which we are more cautious, avoidant and defensively oriented (the glass is half empty). This general distinction has recently been reconceptualised by **regulatory focus theory** (Higgins, 1997, 1998). Regulatory focus theory proposes that people have two separate self-regulatory systems, termed promotion and prevention, which are concerned with the pursuit of different types of goals.

The promotion system is concerned with the attainment of one's hopes and aspirations, termed ideals. It generates sensitivity to the presence or absence of positive events. People in a promotion focus adopt approach strategic means to attain their goals. For example, promotion-focused students are likely to seek ways to improve their grades, to find new challenges and to treat problems as interesting obstacles to overcome. Promotion-focused individuals are also especially likely to recall information relating to the pursuit of success by others (Higgins and Tykocinski, 1992) and are most inspired by positive role models, who emphasise strategies for achieving success (Lockwood et al., 2002). In addition, they tend to show especially high motivation and persistence on tasks that are framed in terms of gains and non-gains (Shah et al., 1998).

The prevention system is concerned with the fulfilment of one's duties and obligations, termed oughts. It generates sensitivity to the presence or absence of negative events. People in a prevention focus use avoidance strategic means to attain their goals. For example, prevention-focused students might be more concerned with avoiding new situations or new people, to concentrate more on avoiding failure rather than achieving the highest possible grade. Prevention-focused individuals are especially likely to recall information relating to the avoidance of failure by others (Higgins and Tykocinski, 1992) and are most inspired by negative role models, who highlight strategies for avoiding failure (Lockwood et al., 2002). In addition, they tend to show high motivation and persistence on tasks that are framed in terms of losses and non-losses (Shah et al., 1998).

The two self-regulatory systems can be activated either chronically or temporarily. Differences in chronic promotion and prevention focus can arise from differences in the quality of a child's relationship with a caregiver (Higgins and Silberman, 1998). Caregivers can initiate a chronic promotion focus by, for example, hugging and kissing a child for behaving in a desired manner (a positive event) and withdrawing love as discipline (absence of a positive event). Conversely, a chronic prevention focus will likely result if caregivers encourage a child to be especially alert to potential dangers (absence of a negative event) and punish and shout at a child when they behave undesirably (a negative event).

In addition to these chronic individual differences, regulatory focus can also change more quickly from situation to situation. Situational variability can be induced experimentally through, for example, task feedback or task instructions. In one study (E.T. Higgins et al., 1994), students were asked to report either on how their hopes and aspirations had changed over time (activating a promotion focus) or on how their sense of duty and obligation had changed over time (activating a prevention focus). The participants read about several episodes that occurred over the course of a few days in the life of another student. In each of these episodes the student was pursuing a desired goal by employing either approach strategic means ('Because I wanted to be at school for the beginning of my 8.30 psychology class which is usually excellent, I woke up early this morning'), or avoidance strategic means ('I wanted to take a class in photography at the community centre, so I didn't register for a class in Spanish that was scheduled at the same time'). Higgins et al. predicted that participants would recall better the episodes which described strategic means that were consistent with their induced self-regulatory focus. Consistent with this prediction, participants in a promotion focus recalled better the episodes in which the student used approach strategic means whereas participants in a prevention focus recalled better the episodes in which the student used avoidance strategic means.

One interesting line of research has applied the principles of regulatory focus theory to intergroup discrimination (Sassenberg et al., 2003). Participants with either a chronic or temporarily induced promotion or prevention focus were asked to distribute positive resources (money) or negative resources (withdrawal of money) between anonymous members of their own laboratory group (in-group) and anonymous members of another laboratory group (out-group).

Given that promotion-focused individuals have been shown to be especially sensitive to the presence or absence of positive outcomes whereas prevention-focused individuals are especially sensitive to the presence or absence of negative outcomes, Sassenberg et al. predicted that intergroup discrimination would be shown only when the available means for favouring the in-group were consistent with participants' chronic (or temporary) regulatory focus. Consistent with this prediction, participants discriminated under a promotion focus when positive but not negative resources had to be distributed and under a prevention focus when negative but not positive resources had to be distributed. In other words, under a promotion focus, group members focused on approaching positive in-group events and under a prevention focus group members focused on avoiding negative events.

Self-awareness

The above may give the impression that people spend all their time thinking about themselves, but this is not the case. People are not consciously aware of themselves all the time – if people were, then probably very little would ever get done. **Self-awareness** comes and goes for different reasons and with different consequences. Often we just get on with life without being particularly aware of ourselves, whereas at other times we can be obsessively self-absorbed or absolutely mortified over how others view us.

Duval and Wicklund (1972) believe that self-awareness is a state in which one is aware of oneself as an object, much as one might be aware of a tree or another person. Not surprisingly, standing in front of a mirror is a very effective way to become self-aware. Carver and Scheier (1981) argue that self-awareness can have at least two foci: the private self (one's private thoughts, feelings and attitudes) and the public self (how others see one, one's public image). Hence, self-awareness can also be raised simply by being in the presence of other people – for example, giving a public talk or performance. Private self-awareness directs behaviour at matching one's internal standards, whereas public self-awareness directs behaviour at promoting a good impression in the eyes of others. In contrast to heightened self-awareness, reduced self-awareness can produce a sense of de-individuation (Zimbardo, 1970; Diener, 1980) that may be associated with disinhibited, impulsive and anti-normative behaviour.

Being self-aware causes one to exert effort to try to address any discrepancy between one's actual self and how one feels one would like to be or ought to be. According to self-discrepancy theory (Higgins, 1987), described above, failure to resolve a discrepancy between the actual and the ideal self produces dejection-related emotions (disappointment, dissatisfaction, sadness), whereas failure to resolve an actual, 'ought' discrepancy produces agitation-related emotions (anxiety, fear).

Types of self and identity

Actual and possible selves can take many different forms. The enormous variety of human existence offers us a dazzling kaleidoscope of different ways in which we can define and conceptualise our selves. However, since selves are largely grounded in human interaction, various forms of human interaction may produce a more limited number of types of self. In particular, researchers distinguish between selves and identities that are grounded in individuality, interpersonal relationships and group and category memberships.

Social identity theorists such as Hogg and Abrams (1988) and Tajfel and Turner (1986) distinguish between the personal self (personal identity: self defined in terms of idiosyncratic attributes or personal relationships) and the collective self (social identity: the self defined in terms of group attributes). Brewer and Gardner (1996) distinguish among individual self (defined by personal traits that differentiate one from all other people), relational self (defined by dyadic relationships), and collective self (defined by group memberships). From a more cultural perspective (see below), Markus and Kitayama (1991) distinguish between the independent self (self defined as autonomous and separate from other people) and the interdependent self (self defined in terms of specific relationships people have with others). These distinctions are certainly not the same as one another, but there is a general notion that people can define themselves perhaps as I, you and I or we.

Social identity

Social identity theory distinguishes between personal self/personal identity, and collective self/social identity (Tajfel and Turner, 1986; Hogg and Abrams, 1988). Social identity theorists believe that one's self-concept comprises a large array of different identities that fall into two broad types: personal identities that derive from our close interpersonal relationships (e.g. friendships and romantic relationships) and our idiosyncratic characteristics (e.g. being humorous), and social identities that derive from the social groups to which we belong (ethnicity, gender, profession, age group). Features of the immediate social context – situation, people, goals, activities and so forth – influence what aspect of the self-concept we experience and use to process information and plan action in that particular context.

Social identities are uniquely associated with group behaviours – for example, the stereotypes we spoke of above, but also other group behaviours such as conformity and discrimination (see Chapter 16). Social identities are attached to group memberships and derive their descriptive and evaluative properties from perceptions of the nature of the evaluative relations (e.g. status) that exist between groups. In this way, intergroup relations influence self-conception. Social identity is associated with group and intergroup behaviours because the process of categorising ourselves and others as group members causes us to view ourselves and others only in terms of the defining attributes of membership of the relevant group, called the group prototype (Turner et al., 1987). This causes us to perceive and treat others stereotypically, and causes us and fellow group members to enact the defining features (perceptions, attitudes, feelings, behaviours) of our group.

Self-motives

What motivates the different ways that we may want to conceptualise ourselves? Research suggests that there are three general classes of motivations. One motive is self-assessment – a desire to find out the truth about ourselves, however disappointing or unfavourable the truth may be (Trope, 1986). Another motive is self-verification – a desire to confirm what we already know about ourselves, by looking for self-consistent information (Swann, 1987). The third motive is self-enhancement – a desire to find out favourable things about ourselves (Kunda, 1990). Sedikides (1993) conducted a series of six experiments to compare the relative strength of these three motives, and concluded that self-enhancement is by far the strongest, with self-verification a distant second and self-assessment an even more distant third.

Because self-enhancement is so important, people have a formidable repertoire of strategies and techniques to construct or maintain a favourable self-concept (Baumeister, 1998). For example, they take credit for success but deny blame for failure; they forget failure feedback more readily than success feedback; they accept praise uncritically but receive criticism sceptically and dismiss it as being based on prejudice; and they self-interestedly interpret ambiguous self-attributes and perform a biased search of self-knowledge.

Self-esteem

The reason why people pursue self-enhancement is because it elevates **self-esteem**. Research overwhelmingly shows that it is adaptive for people to have a relatively positive sense of themselves, that there is a positivity bias and that a negative self-image can be quite dysfunctional (Taylor and Brown, 1988). People vary in their general level of self-esteem. People with higher self-esteem tend to pursue self-enhancement, whereas people with lower self-esteem tend to avoid self-derogation. Using the language of Higgins's (1998) regulatory focus theory, the former have a promotion orientation and the latter a prevention orientation. Although low self-esteem can be dysfunctional, research tends to discredit the popular belief that low self-esteem is associated with social problems such as violence (Baumeister *et al.*, 1996). On the contrary, violence is more closely associated with narcissism – high self-esteem in conjunction with a feeling of being superior and special, as you saw in Chapter 14.

People may not pursue self-esteem for its own sake. Leary *et al.* (1995) suggest that self-esteem is an internal indicator of social acceptance and belonging – it is a 'sociometer'. The idea here is that the most basic human motive is to belong and to be properly socially connected. Feeling good about one's self – self-esteem – is an extremely powerful indicator that one has succeeded in this pursuit.

Social inference

Causal attribution

In order to interact with people and get on in life we need to have a basic understanding of how people work – we need to know why people do what they do. This knowledge is essential if we are to be able to navigate our way through life in such a way that we can make good things happen for us and avoid bad things that might happen to us. The most powerful knowledge we can have about people is causal knowledge – if we know what causes people to behave in certain ways then we are able to predict and influence what people will do. For example, most of us know that if we are nice to people they are likely to agree to do small favours for us, and that people who feel threatened or cornered can often lash out aggressively. The

Cultural differences in self and identity – An international perspective

The same person can experience self in an array of different personal or collective ways depending on context. There is, however, another tradition of research that focuses on enduring differences in self-conception that are grounded in cultural differences (Triandis, 1989; Markus and Kitayama, 1991; Oyserman *et al.*, 2002).

The key cultural difference is between individualistic and collectivist societies (Hofstede, 1980). Western societies such as the UK and US tend to be individualistic – they emphasise the unique individual and separateness from others, and encourage individual choice and loose ties among people. Eastern societies such as Japan and India tend to be collectivist – they emphasise group loyalty, relations among people and the collective good. According to Triandis *et al.* (1985), collectivist societies are associated with allocentrism (people who value cooperation, social support, equality and honesty), and individualistic societies with idiocentrism (people who strive for achievement, pleasure, social recognition and a comfortable life, and who experience anomie and a degree of social alienation).

More recently, Markus and Kitayama (1991) have identified the key cultural difference in self-conception to be between independent and interdependent self-construal. The independent construal emphasises the uniqueness of the self, its autonomy from others and self-reliance. Although other people have an influence on a person's behaviour, a person's self-concept is largely defined independently. The interdependent construal emphasises the interconnectedness of people and the role that others play in developing an individual's self-concept. In the interdependent construal, what others think of the individual, or do to the individual, matter – the person is extremely sensitive to others and strives to form strong social bonds with them.

Students from India (a collectivist Eastern culture) judge the self to be more similar to others, whereas American students (members of an individualist culture) judge the self to be more dissimilar to others (Markus and Kitayama, 1991). Markus and Kitayama have also shown that Japanese students tend to associate positive feelings with interpersonal behaviours and tend not to associate such feelings with personal achievements. In contrast, American students tend to feel satisfaction in their accomplishments. In a similar vein, comparing workers' intentions to leave their organisations, Abrams *et al.* (1998) found that Japanese workers were influenced by the evaluations they expected from their friends, family and co-workers, whereas British workers were not.

Vignoles *et al.* (2000) note that despite cultural differences in self-conception, the need to have a distinctive and integrated sense of self is universal; however, self-distinctiveness means something different in individualist and in collectivist cultures. In the former it is the isolated and bounded self that gains meaning from separateness, whereas in the latter it is the relational self that gains meaning from its relations with others.

explanation of how people develop a common-sense causal understanding of human behaviour is called **attribution theory** (Hewstone, 1989). Strictly speaking, there are a number of variants of attribution theory that emphasise different aspects. Kelley's (1967) covariation model is probably the best established, and so we will focus on that.

Disposition versus situation

In deciding the causes of behaviour, the most important thing we need to know is whether the behaviour is a reflection of the person's disposition to behave in that way or a reflection of situational constraints that made them behave in that way. We need to assess the relative importance of situational and dispositional factors (Heider, 1958). **Situational factors** are stimuli in the environment. **Dispositional factors** are individual personality characteristics. One of the tasks of socialisation is to learn what behaviours are expected in various situations. Once we learn that in certain situations most people act in a specific way, we develop schemata for how we expect people to act in those situations. For example, when people are introduced, they are expected to look at each other, smile, say something like 'How do you do?' or 'It's nice to meet you', and perhaps offer to shake the other person's hand. If people act in conventional ways in given situations, we are not surprised. Their behaviour appears to be dictated by social custom – by the characteristics of the situation.

As we get to know other people, we also learn what to expect from them as individuals. We learn about their dispositions – the kinds of behaviours in which they tend to engage across all sorts of situations. We learn to characterise people as friendly, generous, suspicious, pessimistic or greedy by observing their behaviour in a variety of situations. Sometimes, we even make inferences from a single observation (Krull and Erickson, 1995). If someone's behaviour is very different from the way most people would act in a particular situation, we attribute their behaviour to internal or dispositional causes. For example, if we see a person refuse to hold a door open for someone in a wheelchair, we assign that person some negative dispositional characteristics.

Kelley's covariation theory of attribution

Kelley (1967) has suggested that we attribute the behaviour of other people to external (situational) or internal (dispositional) causes on the basis of consideration of three aspects of the behaviour: its consensus, its consistency and its distinctiveness (Kelley, 1967; Kelley and Michela, 1980).

Consensual behaviour – a behaviour shared by many people – is usually attributed to external causes. The behaviour is assumed to be constrained or demanded by the situation. For example, if someone asks an acquaintance for the loan of a coin to make a telephone call, we do not conclude that the person is especially generous if he or she complies. The request

is reasonable and costs little; lending the money is a consensual behaviour – most people would do it. However, if a person has some change but refuses to lend it, we readily attribute the behaviour to dispositional factors such as being a stingy or mean person.

We also base our attributions on **consistency** – on whether a person's behaviour occurs reliably in the same situation. For example, if you meet someone for the first time and notice that she speaks slowly and without much expression, stands in a slouching posture and sighs occasionally, you will probably conclude that she has a sad disposition. Now, suppose that after she has left, you mention to a friend that the young woman seems very passive. Your friend says, 'No, I know her well, and she's usually very cheerful.' With this new evidence about her behaviour you may reassess and wonder what happened to make her act so sad – was it something in the situation? If a person's pattern of behaviour is consistent, we attribute the behaviour to internal causes. Inconsistent behaviours lead us to seek external causes.

Finally, we base our attributions on **distinctiveness** – the extent to which a person performs a particular behaviour only in a particular situation. Behaviours that are distinctively associated with a particular situation are attributed to situational factors; those that occur in a variety of situations are attributed to dispositional factors. For example, suppose that your partner is always very attentive towards you and other people but seems very dismissive to you whenever a particular group of his friends are around. You are unlikely to conclude that he is a dismissive type of person; you are more likely to conclude that this particular group of friends has a bad influence on him. Because his dismissive behaviour occurs only under a distinctive circumstance (the presence of the group of friends), you attribute it to external causes. Table 15.3 summarises Kelley's ideas about the factors that determine internal or external attributions.

Table 15.3 Kelley's theory of attribution

Principle	Attribution of external causality	Attribution of internal causality
Consensus	*High.* Person lends coin for telephone call, performing a socially acceptable behaviour	*Low.* Person refuses to lend coin and seems mean
Consistency	*Low.* Usually cheerful person acts sad and dejected; we wonder what event has caused the sadness	*High.* We meet a person who speaks slowly and slouches, and conclude that we have met a person who is sad by nature
Distinctiveness	*High.* A child is rude only when playing with a certain friend; we conclude that the friend is a bad influence	*Low.* A child acts impudently and says mean and nasty things to everyone he or she meets. We conclude that the child is rude

Implications and extensions of attribution theory

Attribution theory has a number of interesting implications and extensions. Earlier in this chapter we described how people can learn about themselves by investigating the causes of their behaviour. According to self-perception theory (Bem, 1972), if people can internally attribute their behaviour then they have gained knowledge about themselves.

Another intriguing idea, suggested by Schachter (1964), is that the emotions we experience have two distinct components: an undifferentiated state of generalised physiological arousal and a cognitive label attached on the basis of an attributional analysis of what caused the arousal. So, arousal in the presence of a snarling lion is experienced as fear whereas arousal in the presence of an attractive member of the opposite sex may be experienced as sexual desire or passion. If Schachter is right, then there are interesting therapeutic implications – for example, if someone who is anxious can be persuaded to reattribute their arousal to something amusing then anxiety could be transformed into happiness (Valins and Nisbett, 1972).

Schachter and Singer (1962) conducted an experiment that did indeed show that different emotions could be produced by different labels. Participants were injected with a drug that produces arousal and were told that the cause of the arousal was the drug, or they were not told anything. All participants then waited in a room with a euphoric or an angry confederate. Participants who had not been informed of the cause of the arousal attributed their arousal to the behaviour of the confederate and actually reported feeling euphoric or angry. This was a controlled laboratory experiment. Subsequent research has shown that the nature of physiological arousal associated with different emotions, particularly strong emotions, is often different and so the emotions are intrinsically different – emotions may be based less on cognitive labelling than Schachter first suggested (Reisenzein, 1983; Forsterling, 1988). However, anyone who has observed small children will know how easily tears can be changed to laughter by simply doing something funny to entertain the child.

Attributional biases

Although causal attribution is an important way in which people make sense of their world, it is quite clear that we do not rely on causal attributions all the time. If we did then we would be completely immobilised by cogitation. Attribution and other inferential processes help us to construct representations and theories of the world, and in many cases simple cues rapidly engage these fully fledged interpretations. In other words, we often rely on fully fledged schemata, such as stereotypes, as described in detail earlier in this chapter.

When we do perform causal attributions we are actually doing something quite complex. Formal science is all about understanding the causes of things, and we all know how difficult formal science is. Not surprisingly, lay attributions fall well short of the rigour of formal science. Although day-to-day attributions are adequate for our everyday social interactional needs, attributional accuracy is compromised by the nature of human information processing and social cognition – it is marked by an array of biases and errors (Nisbett and Ross, 1980).

Actor–observer effects and the fundamental attribution error

When attributing someone's behaviour to possible causes, an observer tends to overestimate the significance of dispositional factors and underestimate the significance of situational factors. This kind of bias is called the **fundamental attribution error** (Ross, 1977) or the correspondence bias (Gilbert and Malone, 1995). It also reflects essentialism (Haslam *et al.*, 1998) – a tendency to consider behaviour to reflect underlying and immutable, often innate, properties (essences) of people or the groups they belong to.

For example, if we see a driver make a mistake, we are more likely to conclude that the driver is careless than to consider that external factors (perhaps a crying baby in the back seat) may have been a temporary distraction.

The fundamental attribution error seems to be remarkably potent (but see below). Even when evidence indicates otherwise, people seem to prefer dispositional explanations to situational ones. For example, consider a well-known study by Jones and Harris (1967). Students read essays that other students had either freely chosen or been instructed to write in support of or in opposition to Fidel Castro. The students had to infer the writers' true attitude towards Castro. Where the writers had been free to choose, the students reasoned that those who wrote a pro-Castro essay were in favour of him, and those who wrote an anti-Castro essay were against him. Surprisingly, even when it was made quite clear that the writers had been instructed what essay to write, the students still believed that those who wrote a pro-Castro essay were in favour of him, and those who wrote an anti-Castro essay were against him. The students disregarded situational factors and made a dispositional attribution, thus committing the fundamental attribution error. The effect is even seen in hiring decisions; professionals tend to overemphasise the importance of dispositional factors rather than situational factors when evaluating the competence of a potential employee (Swift *et al.*, 2013).

In contrast, when trying to explain our own behaviour, we are much more likely to attribute it to characteristics of the situation than to our own disposition. In other words, we tend to see our own behaviour as relatively variable and strongly influenced by the situation, whereas we see the behaviour of others as more stable and due to personal dispositions. When we try to explain our own behaviour, we are not likely to make the fundamental attribution error (Sande *et al.*, 1988).

The fact that we tend to make different kinds of attributions for our own and others' behaviour is called the **actor–observer effect**.

A study of college-age male–female couples demonstrates the actor–observer effect (Orvis *et al.*, 1976). Each partner was asked separately to describe disagreements in the relationship, such as arguments and criticism. Each partner was also asked to explain his or her attribution of the underlying causes of the disagreements. When describing their own behaviour, participants tended to refer to environmental circumstances, such as financial problems or not getting enough sleep. However, when describing their partner's behaviour, participants often referred to specific negative personality characteristics, such as selfishness or low commitment to the relationship.

Why do we tend to commit the fundamental attribution error when we observe the behaviour of others but not when we explain the causes of our own behaviour? Jones and Nisbett (1971) suggested two possible reasons. First, we have a different focus of attention when we view ourselves. When we are doing something, we see the world around us more clearly than we see our own behaviour. However, when we observe someone else doing something, we focus our attention on what is most salient and relevant: that person's behaviour, not the situation in which he or she are placed.

A second possible reason for these differences in attribution is that different types of information are available to us about our own behaviour and that of other people. We have more information about our own behaviour and we are thus more likely to realise that our own behaviour is often inconsistent. We also have a better notion of which stimuli we are attending to in a given situation. This difference in information leads us to conclude that the behaviour of other people is consistent and thus is a product of their personalities, whereas ours is affected by the situation in which we find ourselves.

Even though we may be aware of the difference in attributions that we make as actors or observers, this does not seem to prevent the actor–observer effect. For example, Krueger *et al.* (1996) asked pairs of participants (one actor and one observer) to describe the actor on a series of trait adjectives and to rate the consistency of relevant behaviour. Participants then predicted one another's ratings. The actor–observer effect was obtained. Moreover, actors, but not observers, were aware that observers rated actors' behaviour as more consistent than actors themselves did. People who experience stress are more likely to make dispositional attributions to behaviour – for example, people who had experienced stress and had produced high degrees of cortisol, were more likely to attribute the commission of a crime to the perpetrator's disposition rather than to mitigating situational reasons (Kubota *et al.*, 2014). This suggests that stress can be an important determinant of the fundamental attribution error.

However, the fundamental attribution error (and the actor–observer effect) may be less 'fundamental' than psychologists once thought (Sabini *et al.*, 2001) – a meta-analysis of the actor – observer effect found that the error existed but only when the actor was portrayed as idiosyncratic, and where the effect was dependent on specific variables; the effect was not robust (Malle, 2006). This study did find an effect for negative events – actors infrequently attributed excessive alcohol drinking or test failure or aggression to dispositional reasons, thus indicating a self-serving bias. The fundamental attribution error also appears to be influenced by culture. As you might expect from our earlier comparison of individualist and collectivist cultures, it is more prevalent in the former than the latter types of society (Morris and Peng, 1994). People in individualist societies are more inclined to explain behaviour in terms of individual dispositions and free will, whereas people in collectivist societies are more inclined to explain behaviour in terms of social obligations and situational constraints.

The fundamental attribution error is also influenced by more immediate social contexts and individual goals. For example, Schmid and Fiedler (1998) examined closing speeches made by trainee lawyers and university students acting as prosecutors or defending lawyers. Prosecutors tended to attribute internal causality to the defendants, whereas defence lawyers tried to support negative intentional attributions to the victim. When an audience of laypeople was asked to judge the speeches, and recommend sentencing, its decisions reflected the attributions made in the speeches.

False consensus

Another attribution error is the tendency for people to believe that their own behaviour is widely shared and that their own views are consensual – an error called **false consensus**. For example, Sherman *et al.* (1984) found that male school students who smoked believed that a majority of their peers did so too, whereas non-smokers believed that a majority did not smoke. Obviously, both groups cannot be correct.

One explanation for false consensus is that people tend to surround themselves with similar others and thus actually encounter a disproportionate number of people who behave like they do (Ross, 1977). Thus, when people conclude that other people are more similar to themselves than they actually are, the error may be a result of a bias in selecting people to be with. Another possible explanation is that we dwell so much on our own behaviour that it effectively inhibits proper comparisons that might lead us to realise that others do not necessarily think or act as we do. A third possibility is that in order to have a stable perception of reality we need to believe that our perceptions, attitudes and behaviours are correct, and so we exaggerate the degree of consensual support we have. If you believe the world is flat, then it helps you believe this is true if you can believe that lots of other people agree with you (Marks and Miller, 1987). However, recent research suggests that this social projection of one's own beliefs involves the inclusion of others in the same social category as oneself (Spears and Manstead, 1990; Krueger and Clément, 1997), and it is increased when we are more self-attentive or self-conscious (Fenigstein and Abrams, 1993).

Self-serving biases

Some biases seem to be designed to protect or enhance our self-esteem or self-image (Hoorens, 1993) – these are called **self-serving biases**. These may take a number of forms, and sometimes we may not even be aware of them. For example, people seem to feel more positive about letters of the alphabet that are contained within their own names as compared with letters that do not appear in their name (the 'name letter effect'). Hoorens and Nuttin (1993) examined the name letter effect among children and university students. Participants tended to think these letters appeared more frequently in other words relative to non-name letters. Moreover, because of their association with oneself, 'mere ownership' of the name letters was sufficient to make them more attractive.

Self-serving biases of this type also find expression in the attributions we make. For example, when we attempt to attribute causes to our own behaviour – to explain the reasons for our actions – we tend to attribute our accomplishments and successes to internal causes and our failures and mistakes to external causes. Suppose that you receive an outstanding score on a test. If you are like most people, you will feel the high score is well deserved. After all, you are an intelligent individual who studied hard for the test. Your attributions reflect internal causes for the test score: you are bright and a hard worker. Now suppose that you fail the test – what sorts of attribution do you tend to make? Again, if you are like most people, you may blame your low score on the fact that it was a difficult, even unfair, test, or on the lecturer for being so picky about the answers they counted as wrong. Your attributions in this case blame external causes for the low score – the test's difficulty and the pickiness of your lecturer in marking it. One possible explanation for the self-serving bias is that people are motivated to protect and enhance their self-esteem (Sedikides and Gregg, 2003). Simply put, we protect our self-esteem when we blame failure on the environment and we enhance it when we give ourselves credit for our successes.

However, people differ in their **attributional style** – the extent to which they attribute their outcomes to stable and global causes (Metalsky *et al.*, 1987). In general, people with a 'depressogenic' style are more likely to attribute their failures to these stable and global causes (e.g. lack of ability that will affect performance in many ways), resulting in a sense of hopelessness and depression. On the other hand, there is some evidence that depressogenic attributional style is associated with very high levels of achievement among students, perhaps because such students actively test the limits of their capability, and set very high standards for themselves (Houston, 1994).

This type of bias can also occur at the group level, where it is called the **ultimate attribution error**. People tend to attribute in-group failures and out-group successes to external factors such as luck, and in-group successes and out-group failures internally to properties of the groups and their members (Pettigrew, 1979). This clearly makes the group that you belong to, the in-group, appear much more positive than the group you do not belong to, the out-group, and thus is a self-serving bias.

Another self-serving attributional phenomenon is the belief in a just world – the belief that people get what they deserve in life (Lerner, 1977; Furnham, 2003). According to this idea, when misfortune or tragedy strikes, people tend to blame the victim instead of attributing the source of the problem to situational factors outside the victim's control. As a result, an innocent victim may be blamed for circumstances over which they had no control, and any suffering is seen as being deserved. Common examples of this include the tendency to blame unemployed people, destitute people, rape victims and even victims of genocide for their plight. People may also be complacent about HIV infection because they overly attribute it to risky behaviour by homosexuals (the belief that 'gays deserve AIDS') and thus not relevant to themselves (Ambrosio and Sheehan, 1991).

Although there is a sense in which the **belief in a just world** may reflect the fundamental attribution error, social psychologists believe it is also, and perhaps more importantly, a self-serving bias. By seeing people as bringing bad things on themselves by being bad people, we can reason that we are good, sensible people and thus these things will not happen to us. In this way, the world appears more within our control and less fickle and unpredictable. An interesting twist, which is consistent with this idea, is self-blame. People may sometimes blame themselves for their plight in order to avoid the frightening conclusion that the world is a completely unpredictable place where anything may happen irrespective of what you do (Miller and Porter, 1983). Belief in a just world also varies across cultures. In a study of people from 12 countries, Furnham (1983) discovered that the susceptibility to the belief in a just world attribution error was positively correlated with wealth and social status. That is, across many countries (which included countries from both Eastern and Western cultures), a person was more likely to commit this kind of attribution error if they were wealthy and had high social status.

Attributional processes in relationships

People do not always engage in attributions in order to understand their world. However, people do tend to spend a great deal of time communicating their attributions, or negotiating with one another over their attributions. This is particularly the case in close interpersonal relationships (friendship and marriage), where attributions are communicated to fulfil a variety of functions – to explain, justify or excuse behaviour, or to attribute blame and instil guilt (Hilton, 1990).

Interpersonal relationships seem to go through three basic phases: formation, maintenance and dissolution. At each stage attributional communications can take a different form and serve different functions. During the formation stage, attributions reduce ambiguity and facilitate communication and an understanding of the relationship – they bring people together by providing a shared attributional framework. In the maintenance phase, the need to make attributions decreases because stable personalities and relationships have been constructed. The dissolution phase is characterised by an increase in attributions in order to regain an understanding of the relationship, or to deal with divergent attributions.

A notable feature of many interpersonal relationships is precisely this attributional conflict, where partners proffer divergent causal interpretations of behaviours, and disagree over what attributions to adopt. Often partners cannot even agree on a cause–effect sequence, one exclaiming, 'I withdraw because you nag', the other, 'I nag because you withdraw'.

Do attributional dynamics produce dysfunctional marital relationships, or do dysfunctional relationships distort the attributional dynamic? This important causal question has been looked at by Fincham and Bradbury (1987), who obtained responsibility attributions, causal attributions and marital satisfaction measures from 39 married couples on two occasions 10–12 months apart. Attributions made on the first occasion were found reliably to predict marital satisfaction 10–12 months later, but only for wives. Another longitudinal study (though only over a two-month period) confirmed that attributions do have a causal impact on subsequent relationship satisfaction. Subsequent, more extensive and better-controlled longitudinal studies have replicated these findings for both husbands and wives.

Srivastava *et al.* (2006) asked over 100 couples to indicate their satisfaction with their romantic relationship and investigated whether optimists were more satisfied (and whether partners of optimists were more satisfied). Both results were found: those who were most optimistic, and those partnered with very optimistic people, were significantly more likely to be satisfied with their relationship. A feature of this satisfaction that was important was perceived support – when they argued, partners who sought quick conflict resolution through conversation, for example, were more satisfied with the way in which the argument was resolved after a week had passed.

How long term is this effect of optimism? When the researchers followed up couples after a year, it was men's overall optimism that predicted relationship success. Male optimists' relationships lasted longer than did non-optimists'.

Why is optimism so important? Srivastava *et al.* (2006) suggest that optimists may attribute a partner's negative outbursts or behaviour as temporary, reflecting a state-specific reaction rather than a global personality disposition. They may also focus more on a partner's positive characteristics, thus ignoring or playing down a partner's negative mood. They act as a more 'secure base' for their partners and thus provide much needed social support that is always there, unconditionally.

Heuristic judgements

Social cognition refers to ways in which we make inferences about people, social inferences, and the world we live in, and then store these inferences as schemata that guide our perception and judgement. An important basis for social inference is, as we have seen, to find causes for people's behaviour through attribution processes. However, as we have also seen, these processes are often not very accurate or reliable. Often we do not use attribution processes at all to make inferences about people, but instead use cognitive short-cuts or inferential rules called heuristics. Two of the most important heuristics that people use are representativeness and availability (Tversky and Kahneman, 1974).

The representativeness heuristic

When we meet someone for the first time, we notice their clothes, hairstyle, posture, manner of speaking, hand gestures and many other characteristics. Based on our previous experience, we use this information to make tentative conclusions about other characteristics that we cannot immediately discover. In doing so, we attempt to match the characteristics we can observe with schemata or stereotypes we have of different types or groups of people. If the person seems representative of one of these schemata, we conclude that they fit that particular category (Lupfer *et al.*, 1990). In making this conclusion, we use the **representativeness heuristic** – we classify an object into the category to which it appears to be the most similar.

The representativeness heuristic is based on our ability to categorise information. We observe that some characteristics tend to go together (or we are taught that they do). When we observe some of these characteristics, we conclude that the others are also present. Most of the time this strategy works; we are able to predict people's behaviour fairly accurately. Tversky and Kahneman (1974) describe someone called Steve: he is 'very shy and withdrawn, invariably helpful, but with little interest in people or in the world of reality. A meek and tidy soul, he has a need for order and structure, and a passion for detail'. Chances are you will infer that Steve is a librarian rather than a farmer, surgeon or trapeze artist – and you are probably quite likely to be correct. What we know about Steve seems to be quite representative of what we 'know' about librarians.

In relying on the representativeness heuristic we often subscribe to the **base-rate fallacy** – we overlook statistical information about the relative size of categories and therefore the probability that the person will belong to the category. If you described a person as being athletic and interested in surfing you are probably better off simply inferring she is Chinese than Australian (for every Australian there are 60 Chinese).

Learning to play the odds, so to speak, and so to avoid being misled by distinctive characteristics, is particularly important in certain intellectual endeavours. For example, doctors who are experienced in making diagnoses of diseases teach their students to learn and make use of the probabilities of particular diseases and not to be fooled by especially distinctive symptoms. In fact, Zukier and Pepitone (1984) posed a problem to first-year medical students and to residents who had completed their clinical training. The inexperienced students were tricked by the base-rate fallacy but the residents played the odds, as they had been taught to do.

The availability heuristic

When people attempt to assess the importance or the frequency of an event, they tend to be guided by the ease with which examples of that event come to mind – by how available these examples are to the imagination. This mental short-cut is called the **availability heuristic**. In general, the things we are able to think of most easily are more important and occur more frequently than things that are difficult to imagine. Thus, the availability heuristic works well – most of the time.

Some events are so vivid that we can easily picture them happening. We can easily picture getting mugged while walking through the heart of a large city at night or being involved in an aeroplane crash, probably because such events are often reported in the news and because they are so frightening. Thus, people tend to overestimate the likelihood of such misfortunes happening to them. Tversky and Kahneman (1982) demonstrated the effect of availability by asking people to estimate whether English words starting with 'k' were more or less common than words with 'k' in the third position (e.g. 'kiss' versus 'lake'). Most people said that there were more words starting with 'k'. In fact, there are more than twice as many words having 'k' in the third position as those having 'k' in the first position. But because thinking of words that start with a particular letter is easier than thinking of words that contain the letter in another position, people are misled in their judgement.

Many variables can affect the availability of an event or a concept and thus increase its effect on our decision-making. For example, having recently seen a particular type of event makes it easier for us to think of other examples of that event. This phenomenon is called priming. Many first-year psychology students demonstrate this phenomenon when, after first learning the symptoms of various clinical disorders, they start 'discovering' these very symptoms in themselves. Normally, when we are primed, we are unaware of the stimulus that causes the priming – we are physically aware of the stimuli but not aware of the effects they have. There are two types of priming in psychology – one type is used in cognitive psychology – as you saw in Chapter 8 – and one type is used in social psychology. Both have features in common (Doyen et al., 2014): experimenters expose a participant to a priming stimulus, the prime activates a representation in the participant's mind, this representation activates other representations, and these other representations lead to changes in behaviour. In Bargh et al.'s (1996) famous but unreplicated study, participants were exposed to words about old people (the priming stimulus), which activated representations (old people) which activated other representations (the way old people behave) which lead to behaviour change (people walked out of the lab like old people). This is the explanation for that finding. This is sometimes called semantic or associative priming because the prime activates thoughts about stimuli associated with the priming stimulus.

Higgins et al. (1977) demonstrated the effects of priming on judging the personality characteristics of strangers. They had participants work on a task that introduced various descriptive adjectives. Next, the experimenters described an imaginary person, saying that he had performed such feats as climbing mountains and crossing the Atlantic in a yacht. Finally, they asked the participants to give their impressions of this person. Those participants who had previously been exposed to words such as 'adventurous' reported favourable impressions, whereas those who had been exposed to words such as 'reckless' reported unfavourable ones. The priming effect of the descriptive adjectives had biased their interpretation of the facts. Berger et al. (2008) found that people were more likely to support school funding initiatives if voting for such initiatives were held in schools than in other public buildings. In a second, laboratory study, they found that exposure to school-related primes were more likely to make participants support school funding initiatives.

More recently, a group of US researchers found that exposure to the Republican party flag increased positive attitudes to Republican beliefs (Carter et al., 2011). In two experiments, conducted during the 2008 US Presidential election and one year into Obama's administration, they exposed participants to the Republican flag and measured voting intentions and political attitudes and beliefs. Those exposed to the flag were more likely to be sympathetic to Republican beliefs and attitudes and expressed an intention to vote Republican despite the participants denying that such exposure would influence their thinking and this finding applied to both Democrat and Republican participants.

However, as you saw in Chapter 1, priming in social psychology is probably the discipline's more controversial phenomenon currently because of the failure to replicate some significant and noteworthy priming effects – the idea that exposure to words about old people can lead participants to walk like old people, for example. One prime does appear to be robust, however, and that is religious priming – people directly exposed to religion-specific words (e.g. Bible) or words related to religion (e.g. divine) either consciously or subliminally behave in more prosocial ways following exposure (Shariff et al., 2015); that is, they are more likely to behave positively and kindly towards others.

The availability heuristic also explains why personal encounters tend to have an especially strong effect on our decision-making. For example, suppose that you have decided to buy a new car. You have narrowed your choice down to two makes, both available for about the same price. You read an article in a consumer magazine that summarises the experiences of thousands of people who have purchased these cars, and their testimony shows clearly that one of them has a much better repair record. You decide to purchase that make, and mention the fact to a friend later that day. She says, 'Oh, no! Don't buy one of those. I bought one last year, and it has been nothing but trouble. I'd had it for only two weeks when it first broke down. I got it towed to a garage, and they had to order a part from the manufacturer. Since then, I've had trouble with the air conditioner and the transmission.' Would this experience affect your decision to buy that make of car?

Most people would take this personal encounter very seriously. Even though it consists of the experience of only one person, whereas the survey in the consumer magazine represents the experience of thousands of people, a vivid personal encounter is much more available and memorable than a set of statistics, and tends to have a disproportionate effect on our own behaviour (Borgida and Nisbett, 1977).

Dijksterhuis *et al.* (1998) extended Bargh *et al.*'s research to explore the effects of making specific individuals salient. Participants were first asked to unscramble some sentences that contained within them words that describe the traits associated with the elderly stereotype. This primed the elderly stereotype by making the attributes of elderly people more accessible in participants' minds. Next, half the participants were asked to make judgements about a specific elderly person, Princess Juliana, the 89-year-old Dutch Queen Mother. This made a specific 'exemplar' accessible. Participants were then directed to the lifts at the end of the corridor where another experimenter was waiting. The time taken for them to reach this second experimenter was recorded. In contrast to Bargh *et al.*'s (1996) results, when Princess Juliana was primed, participants walked significantly faster than when the general stereotype of elderly people had been primed.

These two studies illustrate that when general stereotypes are activated we may automatically adopt some of the stereotypical characteristics ourselves, but when images of specific extreme individuals are activated we automatically make a contrast between ourselves and the exemplar, making us react in opposition to the characteristics of the individual. We assimilate ourselves to stereotypes but contrast ourselves from individuals. For example, Dijksterhuis *et al.* (1998) also found that participants performed better on a test when the stereotype of professor had been primed than when the stereotype of a supermodel had been primed. However, they performed worse on the test when the specific example of Albert Einstein had been primed than when the specific example of Claudia Schiffer had been primed.

Attitudes and attitude change

The study of **attitudes** – relatively enduring sets of beliefs, feelings and intentions towards an object, person, event or symbol – is one of the most important fields of study in social psychology (Pratkanis *et al.*, 1989; Eagly and Chaiken, 1993). Some early definitions of social psychology actually defined social psychology as the study of attitudes.

The nature of attitudes

Many social psychologists believe that attitudes have three different components: affect, behavioural intention and cognition. The affective component consists of the kinds of feeling that an attitude object (person, activity, physical object) arouses. The behavioural intentional component consists of an intention to act in a particular way with respect to a particular object. The cognitive component consists of a set of beliefs about an object. Social psychologists have studied all three aspects of attitudes.

Affective components of attitudes

Affective components of attitudes can be very strong and pervasive. The bigot feels disgust in the presence of people from a certain religious, racial or ethnic group; the nature lover feels exhilaration from a pleasant walk through the woods. Like other emotional reactions, these feelings are strongly influenced by direct or vicarious classical conditioning (Rajecki, 1989).

Direct classical conditioning is straightforward. Suppose that you meet someone who seems to take delight in embarrassing you. She makes clever, sarcastic remarks that disparage your intelligence, looks and personality. Unfortunately, her remarks are so clever that your attempts to defend yourself make you appear even more foolish. After a few encounters with this person, the sight of her or the sound of her voice is likely to elicit feelings of dislike and fear. Your attitude towards her will be negative.

Vicarious classical conditioning undoubtedly plays a major role in transmitting parents' attitudes to their children. People are skilled at detecting even subtle signs of fear, hatred and other negative emotional states in people, especially when they know them well. Thus, children often vicariously experience their parents' prejudices and fears even if these feelings are unspoken. Children who see their parents recoil in disgust at the sight of members of some ethnic group are likely to feel the same emotion and thus, over time, develop the same attitude.

Simply being exposed repeatedly to an otherwise neutral object or issue over time may influence our attitude towards it – generally in a favourable direction. This attraction for the familiar is called the **mere exposure effect**. One of the first studies to demonstrate this effect used several neutral stimuli – towards which there were no positive or negative feelings – such as nonsense words, photographs of the faces of unknown people and Chinese characters (Zajonc, 1968). The more the participants saw the stimuli, the more they liked the stimuli later. Stimuli that were seen only once were liked more than ones never seen before. Even when the stimuli were flashed so briefly that they could not be recognised, participants usually preferred a stimulus that had been previously presented to a novel one that they could not recognise (Kunst-Wilson and Zajonc, 1980). The mere exposure effect probably reflects our tendency to feel positive about things that do not pose a threat to us. Our feelings towards a person, event or object will naturally improve if, on repeated exposure, we discover that no threat is posed.

Thornton *et al.* (2014) were interested in discovering whether the mere presence of a mobile phone would be sufficient to produce distraction when completing some standard cognitive tests. In one experiment, the experimenter left her phone or her notebook on the table while participants completed the tests. The more difficult tests were performed more poorly when the mobile phone was left in view of the participants. In a second experiment students were asked to get out their mobiles and leave them on a table – or were not given this instruction – while completing the same tests as those in the first experiment. Again, the more demanding tests were performed more poorly when the mobiles were on view. The study suggests that although we know that actual mobile phone use can impair cognition while we are engaged in other tasks – driving, for example – the mere presence of a phone can result in decreased attention to a cognitive task.

Attitudes and behaviour

Attitudes have a behavioural intention component – a motivation or expressed intention to behave in some way or other that is consistent with the affective and cognitive components of an attitude. For example, many people have negative attitudes towards smoking and express the intention not to smoke. But although we may express an attitude about a behaviour, this does not guarantee that we actually behave in a way consistent with this attitude – people who intend not to smoke often smoke. Intentions and behaviour are not the same thing.

People do not always behave as their expressed attitudes and beliefs would lead us to expect. In a classic example, LaPiere (1934) drove across the western United States with a Chinese couple. They stopped at over 250 restaurants and lodging places and were refused service only once. Several months after their trip, LaPiere wrote to the owners of the places they had

visited and asked whether they would serve Chinese people. The response was overwhelmingly negative; 92 per cent of those who responded said that they would not. Clearly, their behaviour gave less evidence of racial bias than their expressed attitudes did. This study has been cited as evidence that attitudes do not always influence behaviour – indeed hundreds of studies of the relationship between attitudes and behaviour suggest, that on average, attitudes predict only 2–3 per cent of behaviour (Wicker, 1969). One way to think of this is that only two or three times out of 100 do people actually do what they say – perhaps we should not be quite so harsh on our politicians.

However, all is not lost. If it were, then commercial advertising would be a waste of time, as advertising largely tries to change behaviour by changing people's attitudes towards products. There are ways in which we can be much more accurate at predicting behaviour from attitudes. Attitude specificity is one important influence on attitude–behaviour congruence. If you measure a person's general attitude towards a topic, you will be unlikely to be able to predict their behaviour. Behaviours, unlike attitudes, are specific events. However, as the attitude being measured becomes more specific, the person's behaviour becomes more predictable.

For example, Weigel *et al.* (1974) measured people's attitudes towards a series of topics that increased in specificity from 'a pure environment' to 'the Sierra Club' (an American organisation that supports environmental causes). They used the participants' attitudes to predict whether they would volunteer for various activities to benefit the Sierra Club. A person's attitude towards environmentalism was a poor predictor of whether they would volunteer; their attitude towards the Sierra Club itself was a much better predictor (see Table 15.4). For example, a person might favour a pure environment but also dislike organised clubs or have little time to spare for meetings. This person would express a positive attitude towards a pure environment but would not join the club or volunteer for any activities to support it.

In another study, Davidson and Jacard (1979) monitored women's attitudes towards birth control as a predictor of use

Table 15.4 Correlation between willingness to join or work for the Sierra Club and various measures of related attitudes

Attitude scale	Correlation
Importance of a pure environment	0.06
Pollution	0.32
Conservation	0.24
Attitude towards the Sierra Club	0.68

Source: Based on Weigel, R., Vernon, D.T.A. and Tognacci, L.N., Specificity of the attitude as a determinant of attitude–behavior congruence, *Journal of Personality and Social Psychology*, 1974, 30, 724–8.

of the contraceptive pill over the next two years. They found that pill use over the next two years was most strongly predicted by a very specific measure of 'Attitude towards using birth control pills during the next two years' (a correlation of 0.57), and least strongly in contrast to the most general measure of 'Attitude towards birth control' (correlation of 0.08).

Reasoned action and planned behaviour

Probably the most systematic account of how attitudes and behaviour are related has been developed by Fishbein and Ajzen (see Ajzen, 1989) in their **theories of reasoned action** and of **planned behaviour**. Someone's intention to behave in a certain way is strengthened if (1) they have a positive attitude towards the behaviour, (2) they believe many people who matter also have a favourable attitude towards the behaviour, (3) they believe they have the resources and opportunity to engage in the behaviour and (4) the intention is very specific to one particular behaviour. For example, consider someone who loves going to Wagnerian operas, all of whose friends also love going to Wagnerian operas, and who has a ticket to go to *The Ring*, which is on in his city tonight and who has nothing else to do tonight. If he expressed the strong intention of going to *The Ring* tonight which he is likely to do, then you can probably pretty accurately predict that this is what he will do. In contrast, consider someone who loves going to Wagnerian operas, but all of whose friends do not, and has no ticket to the opera. He is unlikely to express a strong intention of going to *The Ring* tonight, and you are much less likely to know exactly what he will be doing.

Attitude accessibility and attitude strength

Attitudes are cognitively represented in memory. Thus, like any other cognitive representations they are likely to have a greater influence on behaviour if they are readily accessible – easily and readily recalled. Indeed, research does show that attitudes affect behavioural intentions, and thus behaviour, more strongly if the attitudes are more accessible in memory (Doll and Ajzen, 1992). Our attitudes can also vary in strength. A strong attitude is one that has a strong associative link with the attitude object and thus, once activated, the attitude has a more automatic link with behavioural intentions and ultimately behaviour (Fazio *et al.*, 1986). So, for example, if you absolutely love chocolate and think about eating chocolate all the time then your attitude towards chocolate is strong and accessible and is probably a very good predictor of your intention to eat chocolate – an intention which probably maps tightly onto your behaviour. If, on the other hand, you quite like lobster and occasionally think about eating lobster then your attitude towards lobster is less strong and accessible, and is a poor predictor of your intentions and behaviour.

Social identity and norms

Another factor that influences the attitude–behaviour relationship is the extent to which an attitude is an important aspect of the kind of person we are. Self-defining attitudes, ones that define our identity, particularly our social identity as a group member, are more likely to be expressed as behaviour. More specifically, attitudes are more likely to express themselves as behaviour if the attitudes (and associated behaviour) are normative properties of a social group with which people identify (Terry and Hogg, 1996). To test this idea, Terry and Hogg (1996) measured attitudes and intentions relating to taking regular exercise and adopting sun-protective behaviours. They found a much tighter attitude–intention link among student participants who identified strongly with a student peer group for whom they felt regular exercise and adopting sun-protective behaviour was a strong group-defining norm.

Attitude change and persuasion

People often attempt to persuade us to change our attitudes. Social psychological research on persuasion has taken its form from an early and highly influential programme of research by Hovland *et al.* (1953). Hovland and colleagues famously asked, 'Who says what to whom and with what effect?' – a question which identifies the three key aspects of persuasive communication: the source of the communication, the content of the message and the audience or target of the communication.

The source

Credibility and attractiveness are two aspects of the source of a message that have a major effect on persuasiveness. A message tends to be more persuasive if its source is credible. Source credibility is high when the source is perceived as knowledgeable and is trusted to communicate this knowledge accurately. For example, in one study, people developed a more favourable attitude towards different types of medicine when the information appeared in the prestigious medical journal *New England Journal of Medicine* than when it appeared in a mass-circulation tabloid (Hovland and Weiss, 1951). Research by Bochner and Insko (1966) showed that credible sources are not only more persuasive but they can also induce the greatest amount of attitude change. Bochner and Insko took advantage of the fact that their student participants believed that eight hours of sleep a night was required to maintain good health. They then exposed them to one of two sources of opinion, a high credibility Nobel Prize – winning sleep physiologist or a less credible YMCA instructor, who said that less sleep was optimal. Both sources shifted the students' attitudes when the sources advocated between seven and three hours' sleep, but when they advocated one or two hours the credible source was significantly more effective than the less credible source at changing attitudes.

Messages also have more impact when the source is physically attractive. For example, physically attractive people are more likely than physically unattractive people to persuade others to sign a petition (Chaiken, 1979). Individuals who are asked to endorse products for advertisers are almost always physically attractive or appealing in other ways. Since people tend to like people who are similar to them more than people who are not, similarity should have the same effect. However, this does not seem to be the case. People are more persuaded by similar others when the issue is a matter of taste (e.g. musical preference), but more persuaded by dissimilar others when the issue is a matter of fact (e.g. who won the Tour de France in a particular year) (Petty and Cacioppo, 1981).

The message

As you would expect, aspects of the message itself are important in determining its persuasive appeal. For example, is an argument that provides only one side of an issue more effective than one that presents both sides? The answer depends on the audience. If the audience either knows very little about the issue or already holds a strong position with respect to it, one-sided arguments tend to be more effective. If the audience is well informed about the issue, however, a two-sided argument tends to be more persuasive (McAlister et al., 1980).

Most communicators tend to avoid negative comments about individuals and stereotypes of groups and prefer to emphasise positive aspects, although there are notable presidential examples. Audiences tend to report disliking communicators who say they dislike others (Ames et al., 2010) and audiences tend to dislike even more those communicators who inappropriately criticise or insult others. Communicators tend to avoid negative stereotyping, possibly for this reason, at the cost of accuracy (Bergsieker et al., 2012). Bergsieker et al. found that communicators were more likely to emphasise the positive characteristics of ambivalent groups – for example, high in intelligence, low in kindness; or the opposite – and avoid the negative stereotypes associated with them or negative statements which are factually correct.

In the political domain, research has found that political leaders and political party activists use more abstract language when addressing audiences that are sympathetic with, and share their, views. The concrete or abstract content of the message can influence sympathetic and non-sympathetic listeners differently. For example, political messages that contain abstract language are considered more persuasive by sympathetic audiences but ones containing concrete language are considered more persuasive by audiences that don't share the individual's view (Menegatti and Rubini, 2013).

Some research also suggests that some media are more persuasive than others and that these media might have some important, real-life consequences such as how we are evaluated at a job interview. For example, Schroeder and Epley (2015) found that when people pitched for jobs to professional recruiters and hypothetical employers, they were more likely to be judged as competent, thoughtful and intelligence if the recruiters could hear the pitch rather than read a pitch (such as via a CV or a letter of application).

The audience

Research on the audience or target of the communication identifies a number of factors that influence how easily persuaded people may be. One finding is that people who have very low or very high self-esteem are less easily persuaded than people with average self-esteem, because the former are either too anxious to pay attention or too self-assured to be influenced (Rhodes and Wood, 1992). There are no straightforward sex differences in persuadability, but complex interactions (Carli, 1990). For example, Covell et al. (1994) studied the effect of tobacco and alcohol advertisements on Canadian adult and adolescent males and females and discovered a sex difference among the adolescents only – female adolescents were more influenced than male adolescents by advertisements that were strongly image oriented. As with sex, there is no clear relationship between age and persuadability – some research finds no age effect whereas other studies find that younger and older people are more easily persuaded than people in their middle years (Visser and Krosnick, 1998).

Psychology in action: How not to throw in the towel

How effective are scare tactics embedded in the message in changing someone's attitude? Some research suggests that frightening messages are very effective and there is considerable research showing that negative messages are more effective than positive ones.

Leventhal et al. (1967) found that people were more likely to stop smoking when the message was accompanied by a graphic video of surgery on a patient affected by lung cancer. Other research finds the opposite. Janis and Feshbach (1953)

found much more improvement in dental hygiene practices among participants who had been exposed to a low-fear message (facts about tooth decay and gum disease) than those exposed to a high-fear message (graphic visual images of disease).

Yet other research has shown that scare tactics may be effective in bringing about change, but only when combined with instructive information about how to change one's behaviour (Cialdini et al., 1981). According to Janis (1967), a

▶

Psychology in action: *Continued*

Figure 15.2 The towel hanger used in Goldstein *et al*.'s experiment.

Source: Goldstein, N.J., Cialdini, R.B. and Griskevicius, V., 2008.

little bit of fear is good for motivation to attend to the message and to change one's attitudes and behaviours, but too much fear can distract us from the message so that we are unable to conceive of ways to put the message into action (Keller and Block, 1995).

Another example of the power of the message to change behaviour was highlighted in the vignette at the opening of the chapter. Goldstein *et al*. (2008) examined whether different types of messages left in people's hotel rooms would alter their towel recycling use. Great expense is spent on laundry by hotels, both financial and environmental. Could there be a way of persuading people to reuse their dirty towels? The researchers set up a field experiment in which hotel rooms hung signs which featured different messages. One featured what the researchers called a 'descriptive norm', for example, 'JOIN YOUR FELLOW GUESTS IN

HELPING TO SAVE THE ENVIRONMENT'. Almost 75 per cent of guests who are asked to participate in our new resource savings program do help by using their towels. The other featured a standard sign about saving the environment, as illustrated in Figure 15.2.

Guests who were provided with the first sign were significantly more likely to reuse their towels, as you can see from the graph in Figure 15.3. If the environmental message refers to provincial norms, rather than general standard environmental norms, people are more likely to use fewer towels (Reese *et al*., 2013).

A similar change in behaviour was also observed in another context. Cialdini *et al*. (2006) examined whether the provision of different types of messages would affect people's tendency to thieve wood from Arizona's Petrified Forest National Park. They provided visitors with a plea to think about their behaviour and not steal but did so under two conditions: when messages were positively conveyed or negatively conveyed. In the positive condition, the message was: 'Please leave petrified wood in the forest' accompanied by a picture of a person holding a piece of wood and

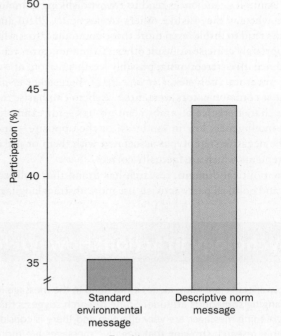

Figure 15.3 There was a significant difference in towel reusage when the message on the towel hanger was changed.

Psychology in action: *Continued*

admiring it. In the negative condition, the message read: 'Please don't remove the petrified wood from the forest' accompanied by a drawing of a person stealing wood with a red circle and bar across him. In another manipulation, they exposed visitors to two milder messages which were descriptive but either mentioned that previous visitors had removed wood from the forest, changing its state, or had left the wood in the forest, preserving its natural state. When theft of wood was measured, those in the first manipulation were significantly less likely to steal whereas those in the second were more likely to steal.

Even clothing with specific wording may influence helping and giving. If charity donations boxes for African children were placed near cash registers in bakeries, people were more likely to donate if the boxes features the words 'Donating = Loving' than 'Donating = Helping' or no message (Gueguen and Lamy, 2011). People donate more to charity if they are asked by a person wearing a t-shirt with the message 'Loving = Helping' than 'Donating = Helping' (Gueguen *et al.*, 2011). The number of people willing to give blood increases if people are asked by those wearing t-shirts with 'Loving = Helping' than 'Donating = 'Helping' (Sire-Charles *et al.*, 2012). People are also more likely to help others load the boot of a car in a supermarket car park if those having difficulty loading wear a t-shirt saying 'Loving', than 'Helping' or no message (Charles-Sire *et al.*, 2015).

The process of attitude change through persuasion

Petty and Cacioppo (1986) have proposed the **elaboration likelihood model (ELM)** to account for attitude change through persuasion (Figure 15.4). According to this model, persuasion can take either a central or a peripheral route. The central route requires a person to think critically about the argument being presented, to weigh its strengths and weaknesses, and to elaborate on the relevant themes. At issue is the substance of the argument, not its emotional or superficial appeal. The peripheral route, on the other hand, refers to attempts at persuasion in which the change is associated with positive stimuli – a professional athlete, a millionaire or an

attractive model – which actually may have nothing to do with the substance of the argument. Selling products by associating them with attractive people or by implying that buying the product will result in emotional, social or financial benefits are examples of the use of peripheral attitude change techniques.

Very closely related to Petty and Cacioppo's distinction between central and peripheral route processing, is Chaiken's distinction between systematic and heuristic processing (Bohner *et al.*, 1995). People can systematically consider all aspects of a message, or they can very superficially rely on simple heuristics such as thinking that longer arguments or arguments with more statistical facts and figures must be more true, or that all messages from politicians are lies. People are more likely to resort to heuristic processing if they have limited time to process the message or if they are in a good mood. So, to change attitudes towards consumer products it is quite effective to bombard hurried people with advertisements that put them in a good mood and present statistical/scientific information from people dressed as scientists. This encourages heuristic processing and encourages the heuristic that messages backed by science must be true. One difference between the elaboration likelihood model and the heuristic–systematic model is that whereas a message is processed either centrally or peripherally at any one time, it can be processed systematically and heuristically at the same time.

Resistance to persuasion

Far more attempts at persuasion fail than succeed. Researchers have identified three major factors: reactance, forewarning and inoculation. Reactance refers to a tendency to resist persuasion, or even move one's attitudes in an opposite direction, when a deliberate persuasion attempt is detected. People do not like to have their personal freedom limited by being

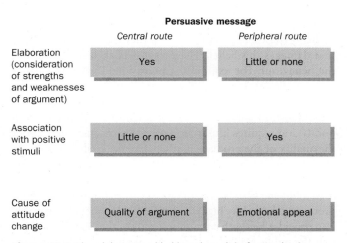

Figure 15.4 The elaboration likelihood model of attitude change. Persuasive messages may centre either on a substantive argument that requires an individual to think about the argument's strengths and weaknesses (the central route) or on a superficial argument that is associated with positive stimuli (the peripheral route).

pressured to change their attitudes. When people are forewarned of an influence attempt they are less easily influenced, particularly as regards attitudes that are considered important. Forewarning allows people to generate defensive counterarguments to protect their attitudes.

Related to forewarning, is inoculation. Inoculation is a process where people are exposed to a weak version of a persuasive argument – much like inoculation against an illness. This allows people to build up resistance, in this case specific counterarguments, against the full-blown persuasive attempt. Research on inoculation was prompted by the way that American prisoners of war in the Korean War of the 1950s were easily brainwashed to denounce the American way of life and endorse Communism. It was thought that this had happened because the soldiers had never heard any attacks on the American way of life, and so were completely unprepared to protect their attitudes (McGuire, 1964). McGuire and Papageorgis (1961) conducted a study where student participants who strongly endorsed truisms such as 'It's a good idea to brush your teeth after every meal', were exposed to a strong attack on these truisms and then had their attitudes remeasured. Some participants were prepared for the attack by being provided with supporting arguments defending their position, some were inoculated by being exposed to a mild form of the attack, and some were not prepared at all. Supportive defence and inoculation reduced attitude change relative to no defence, but inoculation was significantly more effective.

What kinds of argument do you think would be effective in persuading you to change your attitude towards a prominent political figure? How would you describe these arguments in psychological terms? Based on social psychological knowledge about the relationship between attitudes and behaviour, what advice would you give an organisation that wanted to combat waste (e.g. excessive paper use, excessive energy use)? Would you recommend changing employees' attitudes in order to change their behaviour?

Cognitive dissonance

Although we usually regard our attitudes as causes of our behaviour, our behaviour also affects our attitudes. Two major theories attempt to explain the effects of behaviour on attitude formation: cognitive dissonance and self-perception.

The oldest theory is cognitive dissonance theory, developed by Leon Festinger (1957). According to **cognitive dissonance theory**, when we perceive a discrepancy between our attitudes and behaviour, between our behaviour and self-image or between one attitude and another, an unpleasant state of anxiety, or dissonance, results. For example, a person may successfully overcome a childhood racial prejudice but may experience unpleasant emotional arousal at the sight of a racially mixed couple. The person experiences a conflict between the belief in their own lack of prejudice and the evidence of prejudice from their behaviour. This conflict produces dissonance, which

is an aversive state that people are motivated to reduce. A person can reduce dissonance by (1) reducing the importance of one of the dissonant elements, (2) adding consonant elements or (3) changing one of the dissonant elements.

Suppose that a student believes that he is very intelligent but he invariably receives poor grades in his courses. Because the obvious prediction is that intelligent people get good grades, the discrepancy causes the student to experience dissonance. To reduce this dissonance, he may decide that grades are not important and that intelligence is not very closely related to grades. He is using strategy 1, reducing the importance of one of the dissonant elements – the fact that he received poor grades in his courses. Or he can dwell on the belief that his lecturers were unfair or that his job leaves him little time to study. In this case, he is using strategy 2, reducing dissonance by adding consonant elements – those factors that can account for his poor grades and hence explain the discrepancy between his perceived intelligence and grades. Finally, he can use strategy 3 to change one of the dissonant elements. He can either improve his grades or revise his opinion of his own intelligence.

Induced compliance

Most of us believe that although we can induce someone to do something, getting someone to change an attitude is much harder. However, Festinger's theory of cognitive dissonance and supporting experimental evidence indicate otherwise. Under the right conditions, when people are coerced into doing something or are paid to do something, the act of **compliance** – simply engaging in a particular behaviour at someone else's request – may cause a change in their underlying attitudes.

Cognitive dissonance theory predicts that dissonance occurs when a person's behaviour has undesirable outcomes for self-esteem; there is a conflict between the person's belief in their own worth and the fact that they have done something that damages this belief. The person will then seek to justify the behaviour. For example, a poorly paid vacuum cleaner sales representative is likely to convince himself that the shoddy merchandise he sells is actually good. Otherwise, he must question why he works for a company that pays him poorly and requires him to lie to prospective customers about the quality of the product in order to make a sale. Conversely, an executive of one of the celebrity gossip magazines may know that the magazines she produces are sleazy, mindless drivel, but she is so well paid that she does not feel bad about producing them. Her high salary justifies her job and probably also provides her with enough self-esteem that she has decided that the public gets what it deserves anyway.

Festinger and Carlsmith (1959) verified this observation by having participants perform very boring tasks, such as putting spools on a tray, dumping them out, putting them on the tray again, dumping them out again and so on. After the participants had spent an hour on exercises like this, the experimenter asked each participant whether they would help out in the study by trying to convince the next person that the task was interesting and enjoyable. Some participants received $1 for helping out; others received $20. Control participants were paid nothing. The experimenters predicted that participants who were paid only $1 would perceive the task as being relatively interesting. They had been induced to lie to a 'fellow student' (actually, a confederate of the experimenters) for a paltry sum. Like the vacuum cleaner sales representative, they should convince themselves of the worth of the experiment to maintain their self-esteem. Poorly paid participants did in fact rate the task better than did those who were well paid (Figure 15.5). Clearly, our actions have an effect on our attitudes. When faced with inconsistency between our behaviour and our attitudes, we often change our attitudes to suit our behaviour.

Attitudes and expenditures

Festinger's theory of cognitive dissonance accounts for another relation between behaviour and attitudes: our tendency to value an item more if it costs us something. For example, some people buy extremely expensive brands of cosmetics even though the same ingredients are used in much cheaper brands. Presumably, they believe that if an item costs more, it must work better. Following the same rationale, most animal shelters sell their stray animals to prospective pet owners, not only because the money helps defray their operating costs, but also because they assume that a purchased pet will be treated better than a free pet.

Aronson and Mills (1959) verified this phenomenon. The experimenters subjected female college students to varying degrees of embarrassment as a prerequisite for joining what

was promised to be an interesting discussion about sexual behaviour. To produce slight embarrassment, they had the participants read aloud five sex-related words (such as prostitute, virgin and petting – remember that this research was conducted in the 1950s) to the experimenter, who was male. To produce more severe embarrassment, they had the women read aloud 12 obscene four-letter words and two sexually explicit passages of prose. The control group read nothing at all. The 'interesting group discussion' turned out to be a tape recording of a very dull conversation.

Festinger's theory predicts that the women who had to go through an embarrassing ordeal in order to join the group would experience some cognitive dissonance. They had suffered an ordeal in order to take part in an interesting discussion that turned out actually to be very dull. These negative and positive experiences are inconsistent and dissonance arousing, and should make them view the 'discussion' more favourably so that their effort would not be perceived as having been completely without value. The results were as predicted: the participants who had been embarrassed the most rated the discussion more favourably than did the control participants or those who had experienced only slight embarrassment. We value things at least partly by how much they cost us. One controversial implication is that people might value social goods like education and national parks more highly if they personally paid (more) for them.

Self-perception

Bem (1972) proposed an alternative to the theory of cognitive dissonance. Drawing on attribution theory, which we discussed earlier in this chapter, he defined self-perception theory in the following way:

> Individuals come to 'know' their own attitudes, emotions, and other internal states partially by inferring them from observations of their own overt behaviour and/or the circumstances in which this behaviour occurs. Thus, to the extent that internal cues are weak, ambiguous, or uninterpretable, the individual is functionally in the same position as an outside observer, an observer who must necessarily rely on those same external cues to infer the individual's inner states.

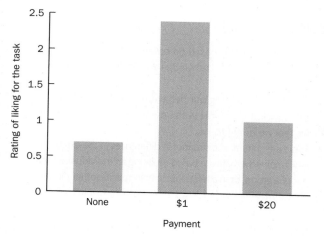

Figure 15.5 Effects of induced compliance. People who received $1 to lie about a boring task later indicated that they liked the task more than did people who received $20.

Source: Based on data from Festinger, L. and Carlsmith, J.M., Cognitive consequences of forced compliance. *Journal of Abnormal and Social Psychology,* 1959, 58, 203–10.

Bem noted that an observer who attempts to make judgements about someone's attitudes, emotions or other internal states must examine the person's behaviour for clues. For example, if you cannot ask someone why they are doing something, you must analyse the situation in which the behaviour occurs to try to determine the motivation. Bem suggested that people analyse their own internal states in a similar way, making attributions about the causes of their own behaviour.

You will recall the experiment by Festinger and Carlsmith (1959) in which students who were paid only $1 later rated a boring task as more interesting than did those who were paid $20. How does self-perception theory explain these results? Suppose that an observer watches a participant who has been paid $1 to deliver a convincing speech to another student about how interesting a task was. Because being paid such a small sum is not a sufficient reason for calling a dull task interesting, the observer will probably conclude that the student actually enjoyed the task. Lacking good evidence for external causes, the observer will attribute the behaviour to a dispositional factor: interest in the task. Bem argued that the participants make the same inference about themselves. Because the participants were not paid enough to tell a lie, they must have enjoyed the task. The principal advantage of self-perception theory is that it makes fewer assumptions than does dissonance theory; it does not postulate a motivating aversive-drive state.

Perhaps self-perception and cognitive dissonance occur under different conditions, producing attitude changes for different reasons. One factor that may determine whether dissonance or self-perception processes come into play involves the idea that attitudes have ranges of acceptable behaviour. For example, a pacifist might agree with using force to protect a helpless child from attack but would not agree with using force to react to a personal insult. According to Fazio *et al.* (1977), a pacifist who used force to protect a child might change his attitudes through self-perception (the behaviour falls within the latitude of acceptable behaviours), whereas a pacifist who struck out in retaliation for an insult would experience dissonance (the behaviour falls outside the latitude of acceptable behaviours). Using a slightly different logic, Cooper and Fazio (1984) suggest that when counter-attitudinal behaviour has undesirable consequences, we go through an attributional/self-perception process where we decide whether the behaviour was voluntary. If it was, then we experience dissonance.

Chapter review

Social psychology

- Social psychology is the study of how the thoughts, feelings and behaviour of people are influenced by the actual, imagined or implied presence of other people.
- Social psychologists employ the scientific method – they formulate theories of human behaviour and test them using a wide range of empirical methods.
- Social psychology has its roots in late-nineteenth-century German folk psychology. By the 1920s, America had taken the lead and social psychology was a branch of general psychology. The Second World War gave impetus to a focus on groups and attitudes. This was gradually replaced from the mid-1960s by a focus on individual cognition and inference in its social context. Contemporary social psychology is very diverse, embracing a wide range of emphases on social cognition, groups, intergroup relations, close relationships and attitudes.

Social cognition and social knowledge

- Social cognition refers to the way we process and represent the social world and our place in it. Social cognition is governed by cognitive parsimony, but it is also motivated by our own goals.
- Impressions of people are strongly influenced by central traits, negative information and information that one encounters first (primacy effect).
- Our thoughts, feelings, perceptions and beliefs about the world are organised in mental frameworks, or schemata,

which help us manage and synthesise information about our social world.
- Schemata can be tied closely to specific instances of a category (called exemplars) or they can be fuzzy abstractions of defining features (called prototypes).
- Schemata that are widely shared within a group, and are held about another group, are stereotypes.
- Schemata tend to be activated automatically once we have categorised a person, object or event.

Self and identity

- Our self-concept is based on schemata that organise and synthesise personal knowledge and feelings we have about ourselves.
- We often try to bring our behaviour, and thus our own self-conception, in line with how we would like to be, or we feel we ought to be.
- There are cultural and situational differences in the extent to which self-schemata are based on being an individual, a member of a group, or in a relationship with specific other people.
- Neuroimaging evidence suggests that our implicit attitudes and biases can be reflected in altered brain activation. For example, amygdala activation is found to images of black men when viewers expressed implicit, but not explicit, attitudes towards race.
- The way we conceptualise ourselves is most strongly motivated by a desire for an evaluatively positive self-concept that contributes to a sense of positive self-esteem.

▶

Social inference

- In making attributions about the causes of another person's behaviour, we consider the relative contributions of dispositional and situational factors.
- In some circumstances, we may gain an understanding of what sort of person we are and how we feel, by trying to discover what the causes of our behaviour might be.
- In making attributions about others' behaviour we tend to overestimate the role of dispositional factors and underestimate the role of situational factors (the fundamental attribution error); however, we do the opposite for our own behaviour.
- Attributions also tend to be self-serving. We attribute our own and our groups' good behaviours internally and bad behaviours externally. We also tend to think bad things happen to bad people and good things to good people.
- In making inferences about people we tend to rely on cognitive short-cuts or heuristics, such as how available something is to memory, and how superficially representative something is of a category.

Attitudes and attitude change

- Attitudes have affective, cognitive and behavioural intention components and may be learned through mere exposure to the object of the attitude, classical conditioning processes and imitation.
- Attitudes are poor predictors of behaviour unless very specific attitudes and very specific behaviours are measured. Prediction is even better if attitudes towards behaviours are measured, and if normative support is strong and opportunity and resources to perform the behaviour are available.
- To understand explicit attempts to change a person's attitude, we must consider both the source of the intended persuasive message and the message itself.
- A message tends to be persuasive if its source is credible or attractive and if it is pitched correctly at its intended audience.
- There are at least two routes to persuasion. The central route involves careful consideration of the message, whereas the peripheral route involves superficial reliance on heuristics such as the attractiveness of the message source.
- Cognitive dissonance is an aversive state that occurs when our attitudes and behaviour are inconsistent. Resolution of dissonance often involves changing attitudes in line with behaviour.
- Our own observations of our behaviour and situation also influence attitude development.

Suggestions for further reading

Aronson, E. (2011) *The Social Animal* (11th edn). New York: Freeman.

Bless, H. and Burger, A.M. (2016) A closer look at social psychologists' silver bullet: Inevitable and editable side effects of the experimental approach. *Perspectives on Psychological Science*, 11, 296–308.

Cacioppo, J. T., Cacioppo, S., & Petty, R. E. (2018). The neuroscience of persuasion: A review with an emphasis on issues and opportunities. *Social Neuroscience*, 13(2), 129–172.

Chung, S., & Fink, E. L. (2018). One of the most cited persuasion studies but no success in replication: investigating replication using Petty, Cacioppo, and Goldman (1981) as an example. *Annals of the International Communication Association*, in press.

Cikara, M. and Van Bavel, J.J. (2014) The neuroscience of intergroup relations: An integrative review. *Perspectives on Psychological Science*, 9(3), 245–74.

De keersmaecker, J., & Roets, A. (2017). 'Fake news': Incorrect, but hard to correct. The role of cognitive ability on the impact of false information on social impressions. *Intelligence*, 65, 107–110.

Falk, E., & Scholz, C. (2018). Persuasion, influence, and value: Perspectives from communication and social neuroscience. *Annual Review of Psychology*, 69.

Fiske, S.T. and Macrae, N. (2012) *Sage Handbook of Social Cognition*. London: Sage.

Gilder, T. S., & Heerey, E. A. (2018). The role of experimenter belief in social priming. *Psychological Science*, in press.

Hari, R., Hennriksson, L., Malinen, S. and Pakkonen, L. (2015) Centrality of social interaction in human brain function. *Neuron*, 88, 181–93.

Hogg, M.A. and Vaughan, G.M. (2013) *Social Psychology* (6th edn). London: Pearson Education.

Vignoles, V. L., Chryssochoou, X., & Breakwell, G. M. (2000). The distinctiveness principle: Identity, meaning, and the bounds of cultural relativity. *Personality and Social Psychology Review*, 4(4), 337–354.

Some good reviews of various aspects of the psychology of attitudes and social cognition.

CHAPTER 16
Social psychology II: Interpersonal and group processes

Michael A. Hogg, Dominic Abrams and G. Neil Martin

LANDMARK MILGRAM EXPERIMENTS ON OBEDIENCE RECREATED IN POLAND, WITH SIMILARLY HORRIFYING CONCLUSION

People are happily willing to deal potentially fatal electric shocks to people, a new study has found.

The new study finds that people are still horrifyingly obedient to authority, even when they think that they are doing something very wrong.

Around 50 years ago, scientists including Stanley Milgram ran an experiment to test how willing people would be to deliver electric shocks to people if they were encouraged to do so. Though no electric shocks were actually delivered, subjects were told that they were – and heard people scream as they believed they were dealing out potentially deadly shocks.

Now, social psychologists have recreated those experiments and found that people are similarly obedient.

They recruited 80 participants, equally made up of men and women, aged between 18 and 69. They were each given up to 10 buttons to press, and were told that each of them corresponded with a higher shock level.

The level of obedience among the participants was similarly high to that of the original studies, the researchers found.

Some 90 per cent of the people involved were willing to go all the way up to the highest level of shock, the researchers found. That was limited somewhat when people thought they were shocking a woman, though the researchers caution that the sample size is too small to say definitively.

Source: http://www.independent.co.uk/news/science/milgram-poland-experiment-recreated-authority-obedience-research-social-psychology-a7628981.html

WHAT YOU SHOULD BE ABLE TO DO AFTER READING CHAPTER 16

- Understand how people are influenced by individuals, authority, group norms and minorities.
- Know what affects people's performance of tasks in groups, and how groups make decisions and are influenced by leaders.
- Know why intergroup conflicts and prejudices are so difficult to change, and what underlies crowd behaviour and social movements.
- Understand some of the causes of human aggression.
- Understand what makes people help others.
- Understand why we like who we do, and how we develop love and close relationships.

QUESTIONS TO THINK ABOUT

- If someone ordered you to do something that caused serious harm to another person, would you do it?
- How does the presence of an audience affect the way you perform?
- Is there such a thing as team spirit? If so, which psychological processes are involved?
- What makes a great leader? What would 10 such leaders have in common?
- If you try hard to suppress your prejudices, do you think they will gradually disappear?
- Can contact between racial groups reduce racial prejudice?
- Are men more aggressive than women?
- What sort of person are you attracted to, and why?
- Does attraction lead to love or vice versa?

Social influence

The social process responsible for attitude change (discussed in Chapter 15) is social influence. However, social influence is in fact a much wider topic because it also addresses changes in people's behaviour that are not associated with changed attitudes. Sometimes people simply do what people tell or ask them to do, without necessarily changing their underlying attitudes. A key distinction in the social influence literature is between compliance (a surface change in behaviour which is not associated with true underlying cognitive changes) and conformity (a deep-seated cognitive change, usually in response to the existence of self-defining group norms).

Compliance

Research on compliance focuses on the conditions under which people will go along with a request or do someone a favour. For example, how can you get someone to lend you some money, fix your car, pop down to the shops for you, fill out a questionnaire, and so forth? You simply want people to do what you request – you are not looking for deep-seated changes in their attitudes and values.

Ingratiation

One very effective method is **ingratiation**, which involves getting people to like you – flattery may not get you everywhere, but it is surprisingly effective. People are much more likely to agree to a request from someone they like or find attractive. One reason for this is that an attractive person, by association, makes the request appear more attractive. Advertisers regularly pay tribute to the effectiveness of association when they use attractive models and celebrities to endorse their products. For example, Smith and Engel (1968) showed two versions of an advertisement for a new car. One version included an attractive young woman and the other did not. When the participants subsequently rated the car, those who saw the advertisement with the attractive young woman rated the car as faster, more appealing, more expensive-looking and better designed.

Besides making products or opinions more attractive by being associated with them, attractive people are better able to get others to comply with their requests because people want to be liked by attractive people. People believe that being liked by attractive people makes them more desirable, too. Thus, people tend to emphasise their associations with attractive and important people. We have all encountered name-droppers who want us to think that they are part of a privileged circle of friends. This phenomenon is even demonstrated by fans of sports teams. Cialdini *et al.* (1976) found that students were more likely to wear sweatshirts featuring their university name on the day after the university football team had won a game than after the team

had lost. Also, Wann and Dolan (1994) have shown that spectators identify with, and are biased in favour of, fellow spectators who support the same team.

Although attractive people may influence our behaviour, it is possible that they may only influence our underlying attitudes when we do not consider the underlying message carefully. According to Petty and Cacioppo's (1986, 1996) elaboration likelihood model (see the section on attitude change in Chapter 15), people can process information either via a central or a peripheral route. Attractive people may influence us via the peripheral route, and can thus be less influential if we adopt central route processing.

Reciprocity

Another effective method for ensuring others will comply with your requests is first to do them a favour. This takes advantage of a powerful human expectation of **reciprocity** – the tendency to return favours others have done for us. When someone does something for us, we feel uncomfortable until we have discharged the debt. For example, if people invite us to their house for dinner, we feel obliged to return the favour in the near future. Owing a social debt to someone we do not like is especially distasteful. Often people will suffer in silence rather than ask for help from someone they dislike. Reciprocity is pervasive – every culture is known to have some form of the 'golden rule' (Cialdini, 1993). It establishes a basic guideline for behaviour in a wide range of situations, and its emergence in evolutionary history is considered to be crucial to the development of social life.

Reciprocity does not require that the 'favour' be initially requested or even wanted. The debt of obligation can be so strong that reciprocity can be exploited by people who want us to comply with their requests when we would otherwise not do so. For example, people trying to sell something often try to capitalise on the reciprocity rule by giving the potential customer a free sample. Once the person has accepted the 'gift', the sales representative tries to get them to return the favour by making a purchase. Many of us avoid accepting free samples because we dislike being manipulated into buying something we do not want.

Experiments conducted by social psychologists have confirmed the strength of reciprocity in human interactions. For example, Regan (1971) enlisted the participation of university students in an experiment that supposedly involved art appreciation. During a break in the experimental session, some participants were treated to a soft drink by another 'participant' (a confederate) or by the experimenter; others received nothing. After the experiment, the confederate asked each participant to purchase some raffle tickets he was selling. Compliance with the request was measured by the number of tickets each participant bought. The participants treated to a soft drink by the confederate purchased the most raffle tickets.

Multiple requests

A third technique for gaining compliance involves the use of multiple requests. The focal request is either preceded by a smaller request that everyone will agree to (called foot-in-the-door), or preceded by a much larger request that everyone will refuse (door-in-the-face), or accompanied by all sorts of sweeteners (low-balling).

To investigate the **foot-in-the-door tactic**, Freedman and Fraser (1966) sent a person posing as a volunteer worker to call on homeowners in a residential California neighbourhood. The volunteer asked the homeowners to perform a small task: to accept a 3-inch-square sign saying 'Keep California Beautiful' or 'Be a Safe Driver' or to sign a petition supporting legislation favouring one of these goals. Almost everyone agreed. Two weeks later, the experimenters sent another person to ask these people whether they would be willing to have public service billboards erected in front of their houses. To give them an idea of precisely what was being requested, the 'volunteer worker' showed the homeowners a photograph of a house almost completely hidden by a huge, ugly, poorly lettered sign saying 'Drive Carefully'. Over 55 per cent of the people agreed to this obnoxious request. In contrast, only 17 per cent of householders who had not been contacted previously (and asked to accept the smaller sign) agreed to have such a billboard placed on their property.

The foot-in-the-door tactic works even better when the focal request is preceded by a graded series of smaller requests leading up to the focal request (Dolinski, 2000). So, if you wanted to persuade someone to go out with you, it might be useful to get them first to agree to study with you in the library, and once they say yes, say, 'How about going for coffee?', and then once they agree, pose the focal request of asking them to go out with you.

The foot-in-the-door tactic probably works because once people have committed themselves to a course of action they are loath then to change their mind. Commitment probably increases compliance for several reasons. First, the act of complying with a request in a particular category may change a person's self-image. Through the process of self-attribution, people who accept a small sign to support safe driving may come to regard themselves as public-spirited – what sensible person is not in favour of safe driving? Thus, when they hear the billboard request, they find it difficult to refuse. After all, they are public-spirited, so how can they say no? Saying no would imply that they did not have the courage of their convictions. Thus, this reason has at its root self-esteem. To maintain positive self-esteem, the person must say yes to the larger request.

Commitment may also increase compliance because the initial, smaller request changes people's perception of compliance in general. Evidence supporting this suggestion was provided by Rittle (1981). While sitting in a waiting room before taking part in an experiment, some adult participants were approached by an 8-year-old child who was having trouble operating a vending machine. Later, while answering a series of questions designed to disguise the true nature of the experiment, they were asked to rate their perceptions of how

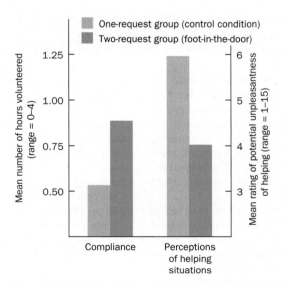

Figure 16.1 The effect of commitment on compliance and perceptions of the potential unpleasantness of helping situations. Mean number of hours volunteered (compliance) and mean rating of potential unpleasantness of volunteering, for control participants and participants who first helped a child.

Source: Based on data from Rittle, R.H., Changes in helping behaviour: Self versus situational perceptions as mediators of the foot-in-the-door technique. *Personality and Social Psychology Bulletin*, 1981, 7, 431–7.

unpleasant it might be to provide help to other people. After the participants had answered all the questions and the study was apparently over, the interviewer asked them whether they would volunteer between 30 minutes and 4 hours of their time to participate in a research project. Participants who had helped the child rated helping as less unpleasant and were more willing to participate in the research project than were people who had not helped the child (see Figure 16.1).

The second multiple request tactic, the **door-in-the-face**, is the opposite of the foot-in-the-door. Here, the focal request is preceded by a much larger request that no one is likely to comply with. Cialdini *et al.* (1975) tested this tactic by approaching students with a huge request: 'Would you serve as a voluntary counsellor at a youth offenders' centre two hours a week for the next two years?' Virtually no one agreed. However, when the researchers then asked for a considerably smaller request, 'Would you chaperone a group of these offenders on a two-hour trip to the zoo?', 50 per cent agreed. When the second request was presented alone, less than 17 per cent complied. For the tactic to be effective, the final request should come from the same person who made the initial request. According to Cialdini and associates, participants perceive the scaled-down request as a concession by the influencer, and consequently they feel pressure to reciprocate. If some other person were to make the second request, reciprocation would not be necessary.

The final multiple request tactic is called **low-balling**. The effectiveness of low-balling depends on people's disinclination to change their mind once they have already made a commitment. For example, some of you may have had dealings with

car sales agents. You are shown a beautiful car that you fall in love with and the agent commits you to purchasing the car which includes CD-player, GPS, air-conditioning, sunroof, electric windows and so forth, as well as all the various dealer costs. The agent now goes to get the paperwork ratified by their boss and comes back with the disappointing news that many of the 'extras' are not included. A rational choice would now be to decline to buy the car. However, because you are committed to your decision you are actually very likely still to purchase the car.

The effectiveness of low-balling was experimentally demonstrated by Cialdini *et al.* (1978). They asked half their participants to be in an experiment that began at 7 a.m. The other half were asked first to commit themselves to participating in an experiment, and then were informed that it would start at 7 a.m. The latter group, in the low-balling situation, complied more often (56 per cent) than the control group (31 per cent), and also tended to keep their appointments.

Obedience

Research confirms that people tend to comply with the requests of people in authority and to be swayed by their persuasive arguments, and that such obedience is generally approved of by society. Obedience can be quite mindless. Cohen and Davis (1981) cite the example of a physician who prescribed ear-drops for a hospitalised patient with an ear infection. His order read 'place in R ear'. Unfortunately, he apparently did not put enough space between the abbreviation for right (R) and the

Cutting edge: Do we underestimate people's likelihood of complying?

How many times have you asked a stranger or a person you think has some influence for a favour? And how often have you thought twice about asking because you feared getting a 'no' in response? If you have thought twice, you're not alone. Research suggests that we are very poor at accurately determining how compliant people will be if they are asked to do something for us (Bohns, 2016). Our fear of embarrassment inhibits us. But the reality of people's reactions might surprise us, as Bohns has described.

When people are asked how many people they would need to approach to borrow a phone to make an urgent phone call because their own phone has died, they usually estimate this will be around 10 people. In reality, they asked six (Flynn and Lake, 2008). When people are asked to approach others and asked them to complete a one-page or a 10-page questionnaire, people think that respondents will

be less compliant when asked to complete the larger questionnaire. There was no difference in the rejection rate in response to the request (Flynn and Lake, 2008). When people were asked to ask strangers to vandalise a book by writing the word 'pickle' inside it, they predicted that only 28 per cent would agree to this; 64 per cent did (Bohns *et al.*, 2014). When asked whether respondents would complete a task after having refused an initial task, participants judged that 16 per cent fewer would comply but compliance increased by 10 per cent (Newark *et al.*, 2014).

There is also a difference between how respondents and participants behave if respondents are asked to do something directly or indirectly. Those who are asked say that direct requests would be more effective but those doing the asking believed that indirect requests would lead to better compliance (Flynn and Lake, 2008).

Even the once most powerful man in the world feels the need to obey authority: G.W. Bush's handwritten note at the UN on 14 September 2005, asking if he can go to the lavatory.
Source: REUTERS/Rick Wilking.

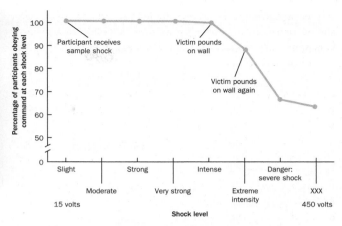

Figure 16.2 Data from one of Milgram's studies of obedience.

Source: From Baron, R.A. and Byrne, D., *Social Psychology*: Understanding human interaction, 8th edn © 1997. Published by Allyn & Bacon, Boston, MA. Copyright © by Pearson Education. By permission of the publisher.

word ear – the nurse delivered the ear drops rectally. Neither she nor the patient thought to question such treatment for an earache. Other research in the US confirms that many medication errors occur because nurses overwhelmingly defer to doctors, even when the nurses have concerns about the wisdom or correctness of the doctors' directions (Lesar *et al.*, 1997).

The classic study of blind obedience is a series of over two dozen experiments performed by the American psychologist, Stanley Milgram from Yale University, who advertised for participants in local newspapers in order to obtain as representative a sample as possible. The most famous of Milgram's experiments is the one called New Baseline (Condition 5). The participants served as 'teachers' in what they were told was a learning experiment. A confederate (a middle-aged accountant) serving as the 'learner' was strapped into a chair 'to prevent excessive movements when he was shocked', and electrodes were attached to his wrist. The participants were told that 'although the shocks can be extremely painful, they cause no permanent tissue damage'.

The participant was then brought to a separate room housing an apparatus having dials, buttons and a series of switches that supposedly delivered shocks ranging from 15 to 450 volts. The participant was instructed to use this apparatus to deliver shocks, in increments of 15 volts for each 'mistake', to the learner in the other room. Beneath the switches were descriptive labels ranging from 'Slight shock' to 'Danger: severe shock'.

The learner gave his answers by pressing the appropriate lever on the table in front of him. Each time he made an incorrect response, the experimenter told the participant to throw another switch and give a larger shock. At the 300-volt level, the learner pounded on the wall and then stopped responding to questions. The experimenter told the participant to

consider a 'no answer' as an incorrect answer. At the 315-volt level, the learner pounded on the wall again. If the participant hesitated in delivering a shock, the experimenter said, 'Please go on'. If this admonition was not enough, the experimenter said, 'The experiment requires that you continue', then, 'It is absolutely essential that you continue', and finally, 'You have no other choice; you must go on'. The factor of interest was how long the participants would continue to administer shocks to the hapless victim. A majority of participants gave the learner what they believed to be the 450-volt shock, despite the fact that the learner pounded on the wall twice and then stopped responding altogether (see Figure 16.2). You can see the script followed by the learner in response to the shocks in Table 16.1.

In a later experiment, when the confederate was placed in the same room as the participant and his struggling and apparent pain could be observed, 37.5 per cent of the participants – over one-third – obeyed the order to administer further shocks (Milgram, 1974). Thirty per cent were even willing to hold his hand against a metal plate to force him to receive the shock. The prods given to participants was also important: these began with 'Please continue' or 'Please go on', then 'The experiment requires that you continue', then 'It is absolutely essential that you continue' and, finally, 'You have no other choice, you must go on'. The last prod, a direct instruction, is the least effective (Burger, 2009). Burger found that the percentages of participants continuing after each prompt were: 64 per cent, 46 per cent, 10 per cent and 0 per cent (Burger *et al.*, 2011), a finding also reflected in Milgram's experiment (Haslam *et al.*, 2014a). Haslam *et al.* (2014a) found that in a variant of Milgram's experiment, the most successful prompt was the second – those receiving this prompt were most likely to continue.

Table 16.1 Shock labels associated learner responses, and experimenter prods in the Milgram paradigm

Switch	Volts	Label	Learner response
1	15	Slight shock	
2	30		
3	45		
4	60		
5	75	Moderate shock	Ugh!
5	90		Ugh!
7	105		Ugh! (*louder*)
8	120		Ugh! Hey *this* really hurts.
9	135	Strong shock	Ugh!
10	150		Ugh!!! Experimenter! That's all. Get me out of here, please. My heart's starting to bother me. I refuse to go on Let me out.
11	165		Ugh! Let me out. (*shouting*)
12	180		Ugh! I can't stand the pain. Let me out of here! (*shouting*)
13	195	Very Strong shock	Ugh! Let me out of here. Let me out of here. My heart's bothering me. Let me out of here! You have no right to keep me here! Let me out! Let me out of here! Let me out! Let me out of here! My hearts bothering me. Let me out! Let me out!
14	210		Ugh!! Experimenter! *Get* me out of here I've had enough. I *won't* be in the experimenter any more.
15	225		Ugh!
16	240		Ugh!
17	255	Intense shock	Ugh! Get me *out* of here
18	270		Ugh! (*Agonized scream.*) Let me out of here. Let me out of here. Let me out of here. Let me out. Do you here? Let me out of here.
19	285		Ugh! (*Agonized scream.*)
20	300		Ugh! (*Agonized scream.*)I absolutely refuse to answer any more. Get me out of here. You can't hold me here. Get me out. Get me out of here.
21	315	Extreme intensity shock	(*Intensely agonized scream.*) *I told you I refuse to answer.* I'm no longer part of this experiment.
22	330		(*Intensely and prolonged scream.*) Let me out of here. Let me out of here. My heart's bothering me. Let me out, I tell you (*Hysterically*) Let me out of here. Let me out of here. You have no right to hold me here. Let me out! Let me out! Let me out! Let me out here! Let me out! Let me out!
23	345		[Silence]
24	360		[Silence]
25	375	Danger severe shock	[Silence]
26	390		[Silence]
27	405		[Silence]
28	420		[Silence]
29	435		[Silence]
30	450	XXX	[Silence]

Note: Experimenter prods were as follows: I. Please continue (or) Please go on; 2. The experiment requires that you continue; 3. It is absolutely essential that you continue; 4. You have no other choice, you must go on.

Milgram's experiments indicate that a significant percentage of people will blindly follow the orders of authority figures, no matter what the effects are on other people. Most people find this surprising. They cannot believe that for such a large proportion of people the social pressure to conform to the experimenter's orders is stronger than the participant's own desire not to hurt someone else. As Ross (1977) points out, this misperception is an example of the fundamental attribution error. People tend to underestimate the effectiveness of situational factors and to overestimate the effectiveness of dispositional ones. Clearly, the tendency to obey an authority figure is amazingly strong. However, one factor that can dramatically reduce obedience is social support for non-compliance. In one of his studies, Milgram had two confederates work with the participant. When the confederates were obedient, so was the participant – obedience increased to 92.5 per cent. However, when the confederates were disobedient so was the participant – obedience dropped dramatically to 10 per cent.

Another variable which could also affect obedience, and studied by Milgram but never published, is the experiment that included the Relationship Condition. Here, the closeness of the relationship between the learner and the participant influenced the likelihood of the participant administering the shock. As the relationship increased, the completion rate went from 65 to 62.5 per cent to 40 to 30 per cent (Russell, 2014). The last of Milgram's 24 variations on his experiments was run in a run-down office in the industrial town of Bridgeport. In the relationship condition, participants were asked to bring a friend with them. Milligram found that of 20 pairs of friends, three individuals from three pairs inflicted every shock. Eighty per cent disobeyed before administering the 195 volt switch (Russell, 2014).

An alternative explanation to the one provided by Milgram is that the participants, far from being unaware that what they are doing is right or wrong, engage in what Haslam *et al.* (2014b) called creative followership – that is, participants were aware of what they were doing because they believed and thought that it was right. Data collected by Milgram showed that most participants were glad that they had participated and that the experiment had not bothered them – 84 per cent said they were glad or very glad to have participated; 64 per cent said that the experiment had not bothered them at all and 74 per cent agreed that they had learned something via participation (Haslam *et al.*, 2014a). Eighty-nine per cent said their views of Yale hadn't changed and 80 per cent said that further studies should carried out. Haslam *et al.* argue that this evidence suggests that, indirectly, participants shared the goals of the experimenter and viewed the experimenters as virtuous rather than vicious.

Understandably, much of the attention given to Milgram's research focused on its considerable ethical implications (Elms, 1995). Many people, psychologists and non-psychologists alike, have attacked his research on the grounds that it involved

deception, involved obtaining no informed consent, there was no right to withdraw, there was no proper debriefing session, and too much emotional strain on the participants. Indeed, Milgram's research helped prompt psychologists to strengthen ethical guidelines for conducting research with humans. He described one participant as follows: 'I observed a mature and initially poised businessman enter the laboratory smiling and confident. Within 20 min he was reduced to a twitching, stuttering wreck, who was rapidly approaching a point of nervous collapse' (Baumrind, 1964). A psychiatrist who studied 40 of the participants found no evidence of the participants having been harmed by the experience.

Milgram conducted an extensive debriefing at the end of each experimental session in which the true purpose of the experiment was explained to the participants. The participants were told that their behaviour was quite typical of the way most people responded to the situation posed by the experiment. In addition, the participants were later sent a detailed written report of the experimental procedure and a follow-up questionnaire asking them about their feelings regarding their participation. Eighty-four per cent of the participants said that they were glad to have participated in the experiment, and only 1.3 per cent indicated that they wished they had not participated.

Milgram and obedience to authority in the twenty-first century

Most psychologists thought it would never happen but, in 2007, a psychologist from Santa Clara did it. On 3 January 2007, the American current affairs programme, Primetime, featured a replication of Milgram's study, conducted by Jerry Burger. The programme was timely. Milgram's findings have been thought to explain aberrations ranging from the Holocaust of the Second World War, to the Mai Lai massacre, to the torture and humiliation that was allowed to fester at Abu Ghraib. For decades, psychologists and others have debated whether Milgram's findings were of their time or whether, in this multimedia age, they could transcend temporal boundaries. But no psychologist has replicated Milgram's study for over 30 years (Blass, 2000) because professional societies' guidelines on the ethical treatment of participants would prevent such experiments from being conducted (Elms, 1995).

However, Burger (2009) alighted on a solution. Most of the controversy surrounding Milgram's studies focuses on his fifth experiment. This is where participants were asked to administer shocks from between 15 and 450 volts to an unseen person. At 150 volts, the participants heard the cries of protest from the victim and the victim's expressions of pain. At up to 300 volts, the victim yelled that he was in pain. After 330 volts, he fell silent. Sixty-five per cent of people administered the shocks, at the experimenter's instigation, at the maximum voltage. The point at which participants began to become reluctant to give the shock was 150 volts. When psychiatrists, students and members of the public are asked at what point they would stop, 150 volts is their threshold (Milgram, 1974). This is an important figure because of those who reached this level, 79 per cent were prepared to continue to 450 volts, the maximum.

Burger used this fact to inform his replication. The assumption would be that if participants were willing to deliver a shock at this level, it is highly likely that they would have administered a higher shock (regardless of whether they said they would not). Burger carefully screened his participants, making sure that they had seen a clinical psychologist beforehand and that there was no indication of vulnerability. Participants were also informed, three times, that they could withdraw at any point and still keep the money they were promised for participating. They were told that the learner had also been offered the opportunity to leave at any point. Participants were told immediately after the experiment that the learner had received no shock (a long time elapsed in Milgram's study). In addition, the experimenter in Burger's study was a clinical psychologist who was instructed to stop immediately if any unacceptable signs of distress were observed. Twenty-nine men and 41 women participated. The experiment was run using an almost identical protocol to that in Milgram's studies. In one condition, participants saw another confederate refuse the experimenter's instructions.

Seventy per cent of participants were willing to go beyond the 150-volt limit and had to be prevented from doing so. Even when they saw a confederate refuse instructions they continued to deliver the shock, indicating that seeing others disobey did not inhibit the giving of punishment. There was no significant difference between men and women (Milgram's studies recruited, largely, men from New Haven). And while those who reported being highly empathetic expressed a reluctance to continue earlier than did those who were less empathetic, this empathy did not prevent them from physically continuing with the experiment and delivering the shocks.

A virtual reality version of the New Baseline condition also replicated Milgram's finding: all participants were willing to administer a shock greater than 150 volts and none continued after being given the last prod (Haslam *et al.*, 2015). If the participant identified with the experimenter, they were more likely to administer the shocks. But there is one silver lining. Crockett *et al.* (2014) found that people were willing to pay more to reduce others' pain than their own.

It seems as if, over 50 years after Milgram's published his first experiment in the Journal of Abnormal and Social Psychology in 1963, people will behave in almost exactly the same way now as they did then. Of course, the jaded might ask whether we needed an experiment, Milgram's experiment, to tell us that people are inclined to obey authority. 'Of course not,' writes Blass (2009). 'What he did teach us is just how strong this tendency is – so strong, in fact, that it can make us

act in ways contrary to our moral principles . . . Milgram showed that it does not take evil or aberrant persons to carry out actions that are reprehensible and cruel' (p. 40).

Conformity

Compliance and obedience produce changes in people's behaviour, but in general such changes do not correspond to a change in people's attitudes or other internal cognitive structures. These deeper changes are more likely to be wrought by group influence where we conform to what we perceive to be group norms (Turner, 1991).

Norms

People, particularly in individualistic Western societies, often think that they are not very influenced by norms and conventions. Indeed, conforming is often viewed as undesirable, as an indication of a weak personality, a lack of individual

Public Announcement

WE WILL PAY YOU $4.00 FOR ONE HOUR OF YOUR TIME

Persons Needed for a Study of Memory

•We will pay five hundred New Haven men to help us complete a scientific study of memory and learning. The study is being done at Yale University.

•Each person who participates will be paid $4.00 (plus 50c carfare) for approximately 1 hour's time. We need you for only one hour: there are no further obligations. You may choose the time you would like to come (evenings, weekdays, or weekends).

•No special training, education, or experience is needed. We want:

Factory workers	Businessmen	Construction workers
City employees	Clerks	Salespeople
Laborers	Professional people	White-collar workers
Barbers	Telephone workers	Others

All persons must be between the ages of 20 and 50. High school and college students cannot be used.

•If you meet these qualifications, fill out the coupon below and mail it now to Professor Stanley Milgram, Department of Psychology, Yale University, New Haven. You will be notified later of the specific time and place of the study. We reserve the right to decline any application.

•You will be paid $4.00 (plus 50c carfare) as soon as you arrive at the laboratory.

- -

TO:
PROF. STANLEY MILGRAM, DEPARTMENT OF PSYCHOLOGY, YALE UNIVERSITY, NEW HAVEN, CONN. I want to take part in this study of memory and learning. I am between the ages of 20 and 50. I will be paid $4.00 (plus 50c carfare) if I participate.

NAME (Please Print). . . . .

ADDRESS . . . .

TELEPHONE NO. . . . . Best time to call you . . . .

AGE . . . . OCCUPATION. . . . . SEX . . . . . .
CAN YOU COME:

WEEKDAYS . . . . EVENINGS . . . . . . WEEKENDS . . . .

A copy of the participant recruitment advert that Milgram used.
Source: Granger/REX/Shutterstock.

The social psychology of attribution – An international perspective

People frequently talk of differences between the East and the West. Almost any psychological quirk in people from these two terrains can be attributed to one group having a 'Western' style of thinking or behaving and the other an 'Eastern' one. But is there any psychological evidence to support the cliché?

Interestingly, social psychology has provided some. Research on people's perception of the causes of behaviour has found a striking result: people from the West, largely the US, tend to explain others' behaviour in terms of people's characteristics, that is, they commit the fundamental attribution error. People from the East, on the other hand, such as East Asians, attribute people's behaviour to situational factors (Morris and Peng, 1994; Lee *et al.*, 1996). In Morris and Peng's study, for example, the researchers analysed American and Chinese newspaper reports of mass murder and compared how often each nation attributed the murderers' actions to personal or situational characteristics. The US journalists tended to focus on negative personality characteristics of the murderers; the Chinese journalists focused more on situational/contextual factors.

Research also shows that the West, at least those living in the North American part of it, tends to hold single individuals responsible for actions whereas East Asians hold groups or communities responsible (Menon *et al.*, 1999; Chiu *et al.*, 2000). Chui *et al.* asked people to determine who was responsible when a pharmacist dispensed the incorrect medicine. Americans believed it was the specific pharmacist; Chinese

participants believed it was the pharmacy as a unit. Americans also believe there are fewer reasons for the causes of people's behaviour than do other Asian nations, such as Korea (Choi *et al.*, 2003).

In a recent study, European Americans and Asian Americans were asked to list their perceptions of consequences of various actions, including a shot in billiards and turning an area into a national park (Maddux and Yuki, 2006). When considering the consequences of taking a shot at billiards, the Asian Americans thought that a single shot would have a much greater impact on subsequent shots than did the European Americans. Japanese participants also listed more indirect consequences of creating a national park.

When the groups had to consider the consequences of a social act such as firing someone or causing an accident, the Japanese thought that these events would affect more people than did the Americans. They also felt more responsible, felt worse and were more likely to apologise to those affected.

The authors make an interesting extrapolation from their findings. The crime rate in Japan may be lower because the Japanese perceive their acts as affecting more people. The Japanese are also the only people to suffer from the culture-dependent psychological disorder, *taijin kyofusho* – an extreme fear of hurting or offending others and of being harshly judged by others. 'For East Asians,' the authors suggest, 'a sense of interdependence with others may extend farther outward in a temporal and physical manner, leading to a heightened sense of responsibility' (p. 680).

autonomy, and so forth. In reality, almost everything we think and do is, to varying degrees, grounded in social norms and conventions. Language itself is a normative way of communicating and representing the world to ourselves and others. If people did not agree on how to construct sentences or on what sounds to use to refer to what objects, then communication would be impossible. What we eat, when we eat, what side of the road we drive on, how we behave in restaurants – these are all normative behaviours.

One of the earliest and most influential studies of how group **norms** emerge and then influence us was conducted by Sherif (1936). Sherif was able to show empirically how norms can arise out of social interaction, and then how these norms exert influence on behaviour. Sherif's study was based on a perceptual illusion, originally discovered by astronomers, called the **autokinetic effect**: a small stationary pin-point of light, when projected in an otherwise completely darkened room, appears to move. The illusion is so strong that even if someone is aware of the effect, the apparent movement often persists.

Sherif first placed participants in the room individually and asked each of them how far the light was moving at different times. The answers were quite variable; one person might see the light move 6 cm on average, whereas another might see it move an average of 300 cm. Next, Sherif had groups of three people observe the light together and call out their judgements of movement one after the other. Finally, the participants would again observe the light individually. The most interesting result of the study was that when people made their judgements together they very rapidly converged on a narrow range of judgements that was pretty close to the average of their individual judgements, and their subsequent individual judgements also fell within this narrow range. The group had established what Sherif referred to as a collective frame of reference – a group norm. Even when tested by themselves on a subsequent day, the group members still conformed to this frame of reference.

MacNeil and Sherif (1976) were able to show that even an arbitrary norm can have the same effect. They had a group with only one true participant and three confederates – the confederates made very extreme judgements that produced an extreme norm. MacNeil and Sherif gradually replaced all the confederates with real participants whose individual autokinetic judgements were nowhere near as extreme as the group norm – and yet, they still conformed tightly to the norm.

Sherif's autokinetic findings are not too surprising if we consider that the participants found themselves in an uncertain situation. It makes sense to use others' opinions or judgements as a frame of reference when you are not sure what is going on. But just how strongly do group norms influence individual behaviour when the situation is unambiguous – when we are certain that we perceive things as they really are? The answer to this question was provided in a series of elegant studies conducted by Asch (1951, 1952, 1955).

Majority influence

Asch's studies were less to do with the emergence of norms and more to do with how a numerical majority can influence a single person. Asch asked several groups of seven to nine students to estimate the lengths of lines presented on a screen. A sample line was shown at the left, and the participants were to choose which of the three lines to the right matched it (Figure 16.3). The participants gave their answers orally. In fact, there was only one true subject in each group; all the other participants were confederates of the experimenter. The seating was arranged so that the true subject answered last. On 12 of the 18 trials the confederates made unanimously incorrect responses. When this happened, about 25 per cent of true subjects remained unaffected, but the rest conformed to the erroneous majority on at least one trial. Five per cent conformed to all the incorrect judgements. Overall conformity occurred 33 per cent of the time when it could have occurred. Under control conditions, when the confederates responded accurately, fewer than 1 per cent of the true subjects' estimations were errors – the task was quite unambiguous.

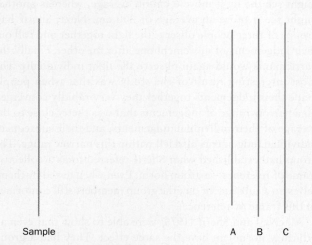

Figure 16.3 An example of the stimuli used by Asch (1951).

Group pressure did not affect the participants' perceptions; it affected their behaviour. That is, the participants went along with the group decision even though the choice still looked wrong to them – and even though the other people were complete strangers. When they were questioned later, they said that they had started doubting their own eyesight or had thought that perhaps they had misunderstood the instructions. The participants who did not conform felt uncomfortable about disagreeing with the other members of the group. The Asch effect shows how strong the tendency to conform can be. Faced with a simple, unambiguous task while in a group of strangers who showed no signs of disapproval when the participant disagreed with them, the vast majority of participants nevertheless ignored their own judgements and agreed with the obviously incorrect choice made by the other people.

Presumably, people conformed because they thought that the other members of the group might ridicule them, or at least secretly think badly of them, if they did not. If this is true then conformity should entirely disappear if participants could give their responses privately, without the other members of the group knowing what they had done. To investigate this, Deutsch and Gerard (1955) conducted an Asch-type study where participants gave their responses privately in cubicles. Conformity dropped but certainly did not disappear – it occurred at a rate of 23 per cent.

An interesting twist to the Asch paradigm was reported by a group of Japanese researchers (Mori and Arai, 2010). Instead of having confederates explicitly making (incorrect) judgements about a stimulus, the researchers were able to present stimuli on a half-transparent PowerPoint slide while participants wore sunglasses that were polarised so that they would filter green or magenta. These glasses affected the length of the lines visible on the screen because the magenta sunglasses allowed the top green part of the line to be seen as black and the green glasses prevented the perception of this colour (because the image and filter were green). In Asch's experiment, only men were tested. Mori and Arai tested men and women. Using this technique, women conformed to the majority decision but the men did not. The conformity did not rely on the uniformity of response from the majority (as was the case in the original experiment).

In research that sought to discover factors that would reduce conformity, probably the most important influence was the unanimity of the erroneous majority. Asch's original experiment employed a unanimous erroneous majority to obtain a conformity rate of 33 per cent. However, Asch also found that a correct supporter (i.e. a member of the majority who always gave the correct answer – and thus agreed with and supported the true participant) reduced conformity from 33 per cent to 5.5 per cent. Other experiments have confirmed that conformity is greatly reduced if the majority is not unanimous (Allen, 1975).

However, support itself may not be the crucial factor in reducing conformity. Any sort of lack of unanimity among the majority seems to be effective. For example, Asch found that a dissenter who was even more incorrect than the majority was equally effective. Allen and Levine (1971) conducted an experiment in which participants who were asked to make visual judgements were provided with a supporter who had normal vision, or a supporter who wore such thick glasses as to raise serious doubts about his ability to see anything at all, let alone accurately judge lines. In the absence of any support, participants conformed 97 per cent of the time. The 'competent' supporter reduced conformity to 36 per cent, but most surprising was that the 'incompetent' supporter reduced conformity as well, to 64 per cent.

The process of conformity

Why do people conform? Or rather, what is the process by which people conform? There are at least three reasons why people conform (Turner, 1991). The first is that people like to think their perceptions and attitudes are accurate and valid. So, if people are uncertain or find that others disagree with them, they may think they are wrong and feel a need to change their perceptions and attitudes in line with those of other people. This form of social influence is called **informational influence** (Deutsch and Gerard, 1955). It would have been present in the auto-kinetic studies, but not the Asch studies.

The second reason why people conform is that people like to be liked and approved of by others and therefore do not like to stand out as different, particularly when in the physical presence of other people. This form of social influence is called **normative influence** (Deutsch and Gerard, 1955). It would have been present in both the autokinetic studies and the Asch studies, but not in the Deutsch and Gerard study.

The third reason why people conform is that they feel a sense of belonging with the group defined by the norm – this is a process of **referent informational influence** (Turner, 1991), which is associated with social identity processes (Turner *et al.*, 1987; Hogg and Abrams, 1988). Group norms

map out the defining attributes of a group. Thus, when people identify with the group they use the norms of the group to define themselves as group members. The process is fairly automatic – the group's norms are cognitively represented as a prototype (a fuzzy set of features that define the in-group and distinguish it from out-groups). When people categorise themselves as group members, they assimilate self to the relevant prototype and thus their behaviour is transformed so that it conforms to the prototype/norms. In the Sherif and Asch situations, other people's behaviour becomes a self-defining norm that is internalised to regulate one's own behaviour as a group member. Abrams *et al.* (1990) found that conformity in both the Sherif and the Asch paradigms was reduced when the source of influence was categorised as an out-group rather than an in-group.

The Stanford Prison Experiment

The Stanford Prison Experiment (SPE) (Haney *et al.*, 1973) and Milgram's obedience experiments are probably the two most controversial studies in psychology. In the case of the SPE, the controversy arises not so much from the studies' findings (which are controversial enough) but because of the way in which the study was constructed and the effect the study had on social psychology and psychology more widely.

Briefly, this is what the study involved. Philip Zimbardo, a psychologist at the University of Stanford, was piqued by several reports of guard brutality in US prisons and sought to discover whether bad prison guards were inherently bad or were shaped by the situation in which they found themselves. To investigate this further, Zimbardo advertised for volunteers to take part in a study on prison life but gave no further details of the study. He then had the Palo Alto police arrest students for various misdemeanours, assign the students prisoner numbers and lock them up in a mocked-up real-life prison cell in a basement at Stanford University. Every attempt was made to ensure the authenticity of the prison environment (you can find out more details here: www.prisonexp.org). The students were randomly assigned to playing prisoners or guards.

Cutting edge: Artificial interactions

The conformity section suggested that if we identify with a group, we are more likely to conform to its views and attitudes. The later section on prejudice will show how identification with an in-group and lack of identification with an out-group can contribute to prejudicial attitudes. Our identification with members of our own in-group can also extend to non-human agents. Eyssel and Kuchenbrandt (2012) asked German students to evaluate a newly

developed robot. The German students were asked to assess a robot that was given either a German name or a Turkish name. They were also told that the German-named robot had been built in Germany and the Turkish robot in Turkey. (Turkey is the largest minority group in Germany.) For almost every dimension – warmth, mind, closeness, contact and design – the German robot was rated most positively.

The guards underwent orientation training by the prison superintendent (Zimbardo himself). They knew the situation was not real but, as Zimbardo himself has noted, 'No one expected what happened'.

The experiment was meant to run for 14 days; it was stopped after less than a week. The first 24 hours were uneventful. The researchers expected the prisoners to sit around, behind bars, reading books and playing guitars. But the prisoners began to rebel. On the second morning, they began protesting vocally and physically. It was at this point that the atmosphere changed. The guards became increasingly brutal, as if they were determined to demonstrate who had the real power in this context (remember that both groups were students). As the prisoners became increasingly humiliated, the guards' behaviour worsened. Faced with this authoritarian onslaught, the prisoners became increasingly compliant. This simply made the guards more sadistic. The diary extracts below convey the reflections of one of the guards:

Diary entry, before the experiment

As I am a pacifist and non-aggressive individual, I cannot foresee a time when I might maltreat other living things.

Day 3 of the study

This was my first chance to exercise the kind of manipulative power that I really like.

Day 5 of the study

I harass Sarge, who continues to stubbornly over-respond to commands. I have singled him out for special abuse both because he begs for it and because I simply don't like him.

The controversial conclusion that people drew from the SPE was that the 'power of the situation' would be enough to overwhelm and subsume people's inherent and customary decency and humanity. If allowed (and encouraged) to behave sadistically, people would behave sadistically. They would lose (or relinquish) their individual identity and, instead, their assumed roles would take over and define their behaviour. The resonance of the study is such that it has been used to explain the abusive behaviour of soldiers towards Iraqi prisoners at the Abu Ghraib prison camp. But there are several problems with the study.

The first is that the results themselves were slightly exaggerated – only three of the 11 guards were demonstrably bad and abusive (as judged by the prisoners). The second is that Zimbardo's objectivity was compromised by the fact that he was a superintendent in the study and may have influenced and encouraged the behaviour because he was not blind to its aims. Even some of the instructions provided to participants encouraged the proliferation of 'demand characteristics'. Demand characteristics are clues in the study's descriptions which reveal the actual purpose of the experiment or what is expected. In the SPE, for example, participants were asked: 'Will our simulating prisoners and guards come to behave in a relatively short time in a manner similar to prisoners and guards in real life prisons?' And what of the participants themselves, the ones encouraged to take part in a study of 'prison life'? Carnahan and McFarland (2007) set up an experiment in which they recruited participants for a study of prison life or another, innocuous study. Those who responded to the prison life advert were more likely to be dispositionally aggressive, narcissistic, Machiavellian, and dominant and less likely to be empathetic.

Attempts at replicating the SPE have not been successful. Lovibond *et al.* (1979) found that their guards did not behave sadistically and the prisoners did not respond with distress. The BBC's recreation of the experiments in 2003, not entirely to Zimbardo's satisfaction (see his interview in Cohen, 2004), produced no abuse from the guards and the prisoners came together to form a weak pact of resistance.

The most obvious criticism of the study is that the students hadn't lost their freedom and they weren't in an actual prison. Even the prisoner who advised Zimbardo on his facility, Carlo Prescott, admitted years later that the participants largely enacted some of the personal experiences he disclosed.

Minority influence

Conformity research tends to focus on the way that a numerical majority influences the attitudes and behaviour of a minority. A valid question arises then as to whether a minority can influence the majority – what facilitates **minority influence**. After all, everyday experience tells us that people do not always conform to majorities. Sometimes a minority can be persuasive. Indeed, social change – from new trends and fashions to social movements and political revolutions – would not be possible if active minorities could not have influence over the masses (Moscovici, 1976). Asch (1952) looked at this in one of his studies. He had 16 naive participants facing one confederate who gave incorrect answers. The participants found the confederate's behaviour ludicrous, and openly ridiculed him and laughed at him. Even the experimenter found the situation so bizarre that he could not contain his mirth and ended up laughing at the poor confederate. Clearly, in this context a minority was pretty ineffectual.

But in the Asch paradigm, who really is the majority and who the minority? Moscovici and Faucheux (1972) make the point that in a standard Asch experiment the hapless lone participant is faced by a small group of people who actually behave extremely bizarrely – in the real world, no one would make the judgements that the confederates make in the experiment. In reality, the majority is a minority, and the studies actually show how a minority viewpoint can be persuasive. This clever insight raises the question of how minorities are influential.

Because minorities have to combat a pervasive consensus that often has the support of a powerful elite, they need to adopt particular behavioural styles in order to be effective (Mugny, 1982). Minorities need to challenge the dominant consensus by providing an alternative viewpoint that is strongly consensual among minority members and has marked consistency across time. A consistent minority (1) disrupts the majority norm and thus produces uncertainty and doubt; (2) draws attention to itself as an entity; (3) conveys the existence of an alternative coherent point of view; (4) demonstrates certainty in, and unshakeable commitment to, its point of view; and (5) shows that the only solution to the conflict that has arisen is espousal of the minority viewpoint.

Minorities are also more effective if they are seen to have made significant personal or material sacrifices for their cause, to be acting out of principle rather than from ulterior motives, and to have some flexibility around their core message. There is also some evidence that minorities may be more effective if they are viewed by the majority as being a relevant in-group. This is usually difficult to bring about because, by definition, the majority protects itself by emphasising the out-group status of the minority. It can work, however, if the minority is able to establish its legitimate in-group credentials before it espouses a minority viewpoint (Crano and Alvaro, 1998) – in effect behaving like a wolf in sheep's clothing.

A consistent, but not rigid or inflexible, minority has what is called 'latent influence' that produces a conversion effect. Majority members cogitate about the minority position, but still conform to the majority position, until at a later point they suddenly appear to be converted to the minority's position and switch their allegiance and change their behaviour. This distinction between the majority having relatively surface influence and the minority having a deeper latent influence leading to conversion resembles to some extent the distinction made by social cognition and attitude researchers between peripheral and central route processing (Petty and Cacioppo, 1986) (discussed in Chapter 15).

Moscovici and Personnaz (1980) conducted an intriguing experiment to test the conversion and latent influence ideas. Participants called out the colour of a series of blue slides, which varied only in intensity, after they had heard a confederate who was described as either a member of the majority (82 per cent of people) or a member of a minority (18 per cent of people) describe the slide as green. Moscovici and Personnaz also had participants describe the chromatic after-image they saw when the slide had been removed – participants did not realise that the after-image of blue is yellow, and of green is purple. Participants exposed to majority influence (the confederate who was a member of the majority) showed a tendency to call the blue slides green, but their after-image was unaffected – it remained yellow, indicating that although they may have complied with the majority they certainly had not changed what they actually saw. Participants exposed to minority influence, however, continued to call the slides blue, but remarkably their after-image had shifted towards purple, and the effect had become a little stronger when they were tested individually at a later stage. Although they had not changed their surface behaviour, there was a deeper latent change in their perception as a consequence of minority influence.

People in groups

Human beings are unmistakably social creatures: a great deal of our lives is spent in the company of others. By itself, this is not an especially profound observation, but it leads to some interesting implications, particularly for social psychologists. We do not merely occupy physical space with other people. We affiliate psychologically and form groups with each other. A **group** is a collection of individuals who have a shared definition of who they are and what they should think, feel and do – people in the same group generally have common interests and goals. Groups are very diverse in size, form and longevity – they include ethnic groups, nations, organisations, departments, teams, clubs and even families. However, by the definition above, not all aggregations of people are groups in a psychological sense – a crowd of people shopping or some people standing at a bus stop are unlikely to be a group.

People aggregate, affiliate or form groups for all sorts of reasons. One set of reasons is very instrumental. Being in a group provides protection and allows people to do things that they cannot do alone. For example, it is probably better to walk down dangerous back streets in a crowd rather than alone, and a community can put up a barn more quickly than a lone individual. There are, however, some more basic psychological reasons for joining groups. A group of people with similar attitudes and behaviours to your own provides a wonderfully comforting sense of self-validation. Groups can reduce anxiety (Schachter, 1959), provide confirmation of the validity of one's perceptions (Festinger, 1954), and reduce uncertainty about one's self and one's place in the world (Hogg, 2000).

Baumeister and Leary (1995) believe that the need to belong is one of the most fundamental of all human motives. They may well be right. Williams and Sommer (1997) has shown in a series of vivid experiments that simply being ignored or excluded from social interaction can have quite profound effects. Indeed, many societies use ostracism or shunning as a potent punishment. In Williams and Sommer's studies, a naive participant ostensibly waiting with two other people (actually experimental confederates) for an experiment to begin is excluded by the confederates from a spontaneous game of passing a ball that they have found in the room. The participant showed signs of genuine distress – fidgeting, disengagement, displacement activities, and so forth.

The treatment of marginal group members and deviants

Many of the groups we are in, our in-groups, provide the psychological environment for the self and are therefore fundamental, or even primary, to our sense of who we are (Allport, 1954; Yzerbyt *et al.*, 2000). They matter psychologically so much to us that we can be inordinately concerned and upset if we feel marginalised or rejected by the group, and we can go to great lengths to protect the integrity of the group by treating deviant members harshly. For example, people are much more willing to derogate a deviant member of the in-group than a similarly deviant member of an out-group – a phenomenon known as the 'black sheep effect' (Marques *et al.*, 1988). Moreover, this effect is particularly strong when people identify strongly with their group (Branscombe *et al.*, 1993).

Marques *et al.* (2001) proposed that this effect reflects the operation of 'subjective group dynamics', whereby people try, psychologically, to sustain the sense of validity of their in-group's norms. In one experiment, Abrams *et al.* (2000) asked psychology students to evaluate normative or deviant group members who were either psychology students (in-group) or customs officers (out-group) who made statements about the UK's policy on asylum seekers. The norm for psychology students was to leave the existing policy unchanged, whereas the norm for customs officers was to advocate tighter restrictions. Two types of deviant were presented in each group. The anti-norm psychologist and anti-norm customs officer actually both expressed an identical (slightly restrictive)

attitude which tended towards the views of the opposing group. Evaluations of these anti-norm members showed the classic black sheep effect. The out-group deviant was preferred over the in-group deviant. However, when the deviants expressed extreme positions that exaggerated the norm of their own group (i.e. a very restrictive customs officer and a very lenient psychologist) they were evaluated much more negatively, and positively, respectively. This pattern of results is shown in Figure 16.4.

The opposing reactions to the anti- and pro-norm deviants shows that people may be more concerned to ensure that they maintain the difference between in- and out-group norms than to ensure that all members of their group conform. Equally important is that people do not necessarily reject out-group members more than in-group members. They may favour out-group members who lend apparent support to the validity of in-group norms. Other research (Yzerbyt *et al.*, 1999; Hutchison and Abrams, 2003) shows that group members who identify more highly are likely to reject an anti-norm deviant from the stereotypical image of the group. All of this suggests that people are strongly motivated to sustain the idea that their in-group is a coherent entity.

Which is more important – the individual or the group?

There is evidence that people may store information about the individual and collective self in separate cognitive 'baskets' (Trafimow *et al.*, 1991), that is, when people think of their personal qualities they are unlikely also to think about their group memberships, and vice versa. This means it is possible to test whether the individual or collective self has primacy in terms of people's motivation. Despite evidence that people will defend their collective in-group norms, some researchers argue that the individual self-concept provides the most

In 2007, the UK saw its first 'run' on a bank. Within hours of rumours of the extent of the bank's debt, Northern Rock's customers began queuing to withdraw their money. Some claimed that such images fuelled greater panic and exacerbated the bank's problems.

Source: Peter Macdiarmid/Getty Images News/Getty Images.

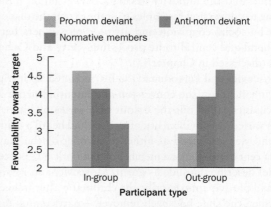

Figure 16.4 Favourability towards anti-norm and pro-norm deviants relative to normative members of the in- and out-group.

Source: Based on Abrams, D., Marques, J.M., Brown, N.J. and Henson, M., Pro-norm and anti-norm deviance within and between groups. *Journal of Personality and Social Psychology*, 2000, 78, 911.

powerful motivational force for behaviour. Gaertner *et al.* (2002) proposed that the individual self has primacy both because the individual self is the unit of natural selection and because attributes of the self seem to remain stable over time, and changes occur only slowly over the lifespan, presumably because people defend their individual self against threatening feedback, and they selectively accept or pursue information that confirms their self-image as an individual.

A further possibility is that either the individual or collective self may have primacy, depending on the context. For example, Markus and Wurf (1987) assume that the self is defined by a 'working self-concept', which draws on the relevant attributes in relation to the current situation. More radically, Turner *et al.*'s (1987) self-categorisation theory holds that the context and situation have a very strong effect on how the self is defined. In particular, self is defined in terms of a social category to which one belongs relative to a category to which one does not belong within a situation. For example, at a football match people define themselves primarily in terms of which team they support (Cialdini *et al.*, 1976), whereas when taking part in an election they define themselves in terms of which party they support.

Gaertner and Insko (2000) showed that participants would allocate more money to the in-group than an out-group only if they believed their personal earnings could be influenced by other in-group members. In another set of studies Gaertner *et al.* (1999) showed that people whose individual self was threatened considered the threat to be more severe, felt more negative and angry and derogated the source of the threat more than did those who experienced a threat to the collective self. For example, in their experiment participants anticipated playing a game with an individual partner (dyad condition) or joined two others to play against another three-person group. Participants rated their initial feelings of anger, and then after completing an initial comprehension task, participants received positive or insulting feedback from the opposing person/team that they 'did well/seems to know what is going on', or 'did not do well, must be a little slow'. Participants then rated their feelings of anger again. Figure 16.5 shows that participants felt angrier when their individual self was insulted than when their collective self was insulted.

To compare evidence for these different views, Gaertner *et al.* (2002) conducted a meta-analysis (statistical summary across a series of different studies) to examine how people respond to threats to the individual and collective self, and how they respond to opportunities to enhance the self. In these experiments threats and enhancements were manipulated either by directing negative or positive feedback or linking positive or negative information to the individual or collective self. Across 37 different items of research evidence, Gaertner *et al.* found that people responded more strongly to both threats and enhancements of the individual self than to comparable threats to the collective self or the contextual self.

Social facilitation

You saw in the above discussion of social influence that the behaviour of other people has a powerful effect on our behaviour. Studies have shown that the mere presence of other people can affect a person's behaviour. Triplett (1897) published the first experimental study of social facilitation – the enhancement of a person's performance by the presence of other people. He had people perform simple tasks, such as turning the crank of a fishing reel. He found that his participants turned the crank faster and for longer if other people were present. Although many other studies found the same effect, some investigators reported just the opposite effect. If the task was difficult and complex, the presence of an audience impaired the participants' performance. We're all probably familiar with the sound of audience laughter accompanying a sit-com on television. More often than not, this laughter is real not canned and we know that – despite what people might say – people laugh more and find the comedy funnier if they watch or listen to the material with audience laughter present (Martin and Gray, 1996).

We laugh most when we are with others – thirty times more likely – (Provine, 2004) and laugh more when we can see or hear someone else laugh (Vlahovic *et al.*, 2012). Laughter is commonest in conversation rather than in response to jokes (Provine, 2004); we usually laugh most at the last thing a person has said (Vettin and Todd, 2004).

Zajonc (1965) suggested an explanation for social facilitation. He claims that the presence of people who are watching a performer (or of people whom the performer perceives as watching) raises that person's arousal level and produces 'drive'. The increase in arousal has the effect of increasing the probability of performing dominant responses: responses that are best learned and most likely to occur in a particular situation. When the task is simple, the dominant response is generally the correct one (by definition an easy task is one which

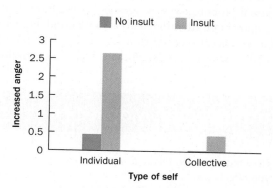

Figure 16.5 Increases in anger as a result of an insult to the individual or collective self.

Source: Based on Gaertner, L., Sedikides, C. and Graetz, K., In search of self-definition: Motivational primacy of the individual self, motivational primacy of the collective self, or collective primacy? *Journal of Personality and Social Psychology*, 1999, 76, 13.

you get right all the time), so an audience improves performance. When the task is difficult the dominant response is generally not the correct one (by definition a difficult task is one which you get wrong all the time), so an audience impairs performance.

Subsequent experiments have supported Zajonc's explanation. For example, Martens (1969) tested the prediction that the presence of a group increases a person's level of arousal or drive. While participants performed a complex motor task alone or in the presence of 10 people, the experimenter determined physiological arousal by measuring the amount of sweat present on the participants' palms. The presence of an audience produced a clear-cut effect: the participants who performed in front of other people had sweatier palms.

Markus (1978) tested the effects of an audience on task performance. She had student participants get undressed and then dress up in either their own clothes (an easy task where the dominant response is to get it right) or in unfamiliar clothing involving a special lab coat and special shoes (a difficult task where the dominant response is to make mistakes). Some participants did this alone whereas others did this while being watched. Relative to those who did the task alone, those who were being watched were faster on the easy task and slower on the difficult task – clear support for social facilitation.

Zajonc (1965) believed that the mere presence of other people produces arousal and drive. Baron (1986) proposed an alternative view. He argued that people are distracting and that trying to concentrate on a task while being distracted causes arousal and drive. There is some support for this idea. Any form of distraction, for example, loud noise, produces social facilitation effects – improved performance of easy tasks and degraded performance of difficult tasks. Baron has also suggested that perhaps the notion of arousal or drive is unnecessary. People have a limited capacity for attention. In order to perform a task successfully you need to attend to a range of cues and procedures. The presence of other people is an additional tax on attention, which people combat by narrowing their attention onto the task cues and procedures. Difficult tasks require more attention than easy tasks, and thus narrowing of attention causes you to fail to attend to some important cues – task performance deteriorates. Easy tasks require less

attention, so narrowing of attention actually causes you to attend more to the task than you ordinarily would – task performance improves.

A final perspective on how being in the presence of other people affects task performance builds on the idea that people make you self-aware (Carver and Scheier, 1981; Higgins, 1987) (see also the section on 'Self awareness' in Chapter 15). Being self-aware motivates people to try to bring their actual self (their actual task performance) into line with their ideal self (how they would like or feel they ought to perform the task). Where the discrepancy is small, the additional motivation improves performance, but where the discrepancy is large and insurmountable, people tend to give up trying and task performance deteriorates.

Social loafing

Working together on a task, rather than merely being watched by others or simply being in the presence of others, can have additional effects: the presence of a group sometimes results in a decrease in effort, or **social loafing**. Thus, a group is often less than the sum of its individual members. Many years ago, Ringelmann (1913) measured the effort that people made when pulling a rope in a mock tug-of-war contest against a device that measured the exerted force. Presumably, the force exerted by eight people pulling together in a simple task would be at least the sum of their individual efforts or even somewhat greater than the sum because of social facilitation. However, Ringelmann found that the total force exerted was only about half what would be predicted by the simple combination of individual efforts. The participants exerted less force when they worked in a group.

The reduced performance could be due to at least two reasons. The people pulling on the rope could have distracted each other or interfered in other ways, or the people pulling the rope could simply have tried less hard – this is a distinction between **coordination losses** and **motivation losses** (Steiner, 1972). To tease these two possibilities apart, Ingham *et al.* (1974) replicated Ringelmann's study, but with two experimental conditions: one in which real groups of varying size pulled on a rope, and the other involving pseudo-groups with only

---

Cutting edge: Mobile phone presence and social interaction

How much do you think having a mobile phone in front of you affects your conversation with your friend or a person you're talking with? A lot? Not much?

Misra *et al.* (2014) investigated whether having a mobile phone present during a conversation affected the quality of that conversation. The study took part in coffee shops in the East

coast of the US. A hundred pairs were recruited. The participants' conversations lasted 10 minutes. During these 10 minutes, talkers who had a mobile phone present rated the conversation as being less fulfilling and reported feeling less empathetic towards their friend. The closer the friendship, the less the empathetic concern if there was a mobile phone present.

one true participant and a number of confederates. The confederates were instructed only to pretend to pull on the rope while making realistic grunts to indicate exertion. The true participant was in the first position and so did not know that the confederates, who were behind, were not actually pulling. Participants in pseudo-groups pulled less strongly than participants pulling on their own. Because there was no coordination, there can be no loss due to poor coordination; the decrement can be attributed only to a loss of motivation. In real groups, there was an additional decrement in individual performance that can be attributed to coordination loss.

Scores of more recent studies have confirmed these results and have extended them to other behaviours, such as clapping, shouting, cheering and **brainstorming** (Williams *et al.*, 2003). Formally defined, loafing is 'a reduction in individual effort when working on a collective task (in which one's outputs are pooled with those of other group members) compared to when working either alone or coactively' (Williams *et al.*, 1993, p. 131).

Several variables have been found to influence the tendency to loaf. One of the most important of them is identifiability. Williams *et al.* (1981) asked participants to shout as loud as they could individually or in groups. Participants who were told that the equipment could measure only the total group effort shouted less loudly than those who were told that the equipment could measure individual efforts. The latter did not loaf – they shouted just as loudly in groups as they did alone. These results suggest that a person's efforts in a group activity are affected by whether other people can observe their individual efforts.

Another variable that determines whether social facilitation or social loafing occurs is individual responsibility. If a person's efforts are duplicated by those of another person (and if their individual efforts are not identifiable), the person is likely to exert sub-maximum effort. Harkins and Petty (1982) had participants work in groups of four on a task that required them to report whenever a dot appeared in a particular quadrant of a video screen. In one condition, each participant watched an individual quadrant and was solely responsible for detecting dots that appeared there. In the other condition, all four participants watched the same quadrant; thus, the responsibility for detecting dots was shared. Participants did not loaf when they were responsible for their own quadrants.

In a review of the social loafing literature, Karau and Williams (1993) noted that two variables – sex and culture – appear to moderate people's tendency to loaf. Although all people in different cultures are susceptible to social loafing, the effect is smaller for women than for men and for people living in Eastern cultures than for those living in Western cultures. Karau and Williams offer a reasonable explanation for this finding: both women and people living in Eastern cultures tend to be more group – or collectively oriented in their thinking and behaviour than are men and people living in Western cultures. That is, women and people living in Eastern cultures

tend to place greater importance on participating in group activities, which partially buffers them from social loafing effects.

Although research tends to show that loafing is the rule in groups, there are some studies that show that groups sometimes motivate people to work harder than they do alone. For example, Zaccaro (1984) had male and female participants construct 'moon tents' out of sheets of paper in two – or four-person co-active groups. The usual loafing effect emerged. However, other participants who believed they were competing against an out-group, and for whom the attractiveness and social relevance of the task was accentuated, behaved quite differently. The loafing effect was reversed: individuals performed at a higher rate in the larger group. This effect may represent **social compensation**, in which people work harder collectively than co-actively in order to compensate for anticipated loafing by others on important tasks or in important groups.

Why do people loaf? There are many reasons. For example, people are often anxious about having their performance evaluated, and so when their individual performance cannot be identified, they can avoid the possibility of evaluation by simply doing less. When their performance can be evaluated they are motivated to work harder in order to avoid an unfavourable evaluation. Another reason why people loaf may be because they feel that in a group they are dispensable – their effort is not really necessary to the group's overall performance because so many others are making a contribution.

Karau and Williams (1993; Williams *et al.*, 2003) have proposed an integrative model they call the **collective effort model**. It states that people will work hard on a collective task only to the degree that they expect their efforts to be instrumental in leading to outcomes that they value personally. Thus loafing will occur if people view the outcomes of the group performance or collective task as trivial or inconsistent with their own desires. Valued outcomes can be objective, say pay and rewards, or subjective such as personal satisfaction and feelings of growth, belonging or enjoyment. Even if people do value the outcomes, they will still loaf if they do not believe that their own efforts can help achieve those outcomes.

The collective effort model identifies a number of factors that moderate loafing. Because people work harder on collective tasks when they expect their effort to be instrumental in obtaining valued outcomes, loafing will be reduced when people: (1) believe their collective inputs can be evaluated; (2) work in smaller rather than larger groups; (3) view their contributions to the collective task as unique or important rather than redundant or trivial; (4) work on tasks that are meaningful, high in personal involvement, important to respected others, or intrinsically interesting; (5) work in cohesive groups or in situations that activate a salient group identity; (6) expect their co-workers to perform poorly; and (7) have a dispositional tendency to value collective outcomes.

Suppose that you have been asked by your psychology lecturer to organise a small group of class members to prepare a presentation. As the leader of the group, what steps might you take to prevent the individual members of your group from becoming social loafers?

Group decision-making

One of the most significant tasks that people perform in groups is decision-making. Group decision-making usually involves discussion that transforms a diversity of opinions into a single group decision.

Because it can be useful to predict what decision a group will come to from an initial distribution of diverse views (e.g. juries, parliament, summits and other committees), research has identified a small number of explicit or implicit decision-making rules that groups can adopt, called **social decision schemes** (Davis, 1973). These are:

1 unanimity (discussion pressurises deviants to conform);

2 majority wins (discussion confirms the majority position, which is then adopted as the group position);

3 truth wins (discussion reveals the position that is demonstrably correct);

4 two-thirds majority (unless there is a two-thirds majority, the group is unable to reach a decision); and

5 first shift (the group ultimately adopts a decision consistent with the direction of the first shift in opinion shown by any member of the group).

If you know the decision rule that is being adopted, and you know the initial distribution of positions, then you can predict the group decision with a respectable degree of accuracy (Stasser and Dietz-Uhler, 2001).

Group decision-making involves social interaction, and so is subject to a range of effects that do not impact on individual decision-making, for example, social facilitation and social loafing may affect the decision-making process.

Group remembering

For groups to make decisions they need to marshal a substantial amount of material that is stored in memory. Do groups facilitate or impede memory? Research shows that groups are better than individuals at recalling simple information – such as names of performers or capital cities (Clark and Stephenson, 1995). This is because the group can pool unshared information and can recognise what is true and what is false. However, in more complex memory tasks, like recalling a police interrogation, the group's memory tends to be a creative reconstruction rather than regurgitation of facts. Group remembering is often a constructive process, characterised by negotiation of an agreed joint account of some part of experience. Some individuals' memories will contribute to the

developing consensus while others' will not. In this way, the group shapes a version of the truth that gains its subjective veracity from the degree of consensus. The group in effect constructs a version of the truth that guides individuals about what to store as a true memory and what to discard as an incorrect memory.

Another way to look at group remembering is to focus not on what a group recalls, but on how a group stores information. Groups tend to have transactive memory structures (Moreland *et al.*, 1996). Within the group, different people specialise in remembering different things, but through interaction (transactions) all members of the group remember who is the memory specialist in different domains. Transactive memory has clear advantages in dealing with remembering large amounts of information. However, there are pitfalls. In the context of organisations, if someone leaves then their memory domain disappears and it can take a while for someone else to occupy that domain. The other side of the coin is that new members of organisations may take some time to learn the transactive memory structure of the organisation. In both cases, group processes are disrupted. Disruption can be minimised by making sure that people occupying important memory domains have 'understudies', and that new members are formally taught the transactive memory structure of the organisation.

Group polarisation

We often think of committees and other small decision-making groups as being cautious and conservative in making decisions. Indeed, this is often the case – such groups arrive at group decisions that smooth out and average individual variability, which is precisely what one would expect from Sherif's (1936) research on group norms, described above. So, the social psychology community was most interested in Stoner's research (1961) – Stoner found that a group would actually make a riskier decision than the average of the positions held by the group members if the members themselves already leaned towards such a decision. Group discussion produced a risky shift.

Subsequent research has shown this phenomenon to be part of a more general tendency for a group decision to be more extreme than the mean of its members' positions, in the direction favoured by the mean – a phenomenon called group polarisation (Moscovici and Zavalloni, 1969). If the group leans towards taking a risk, group discussion will produce a riskier decision, if it leans towards caution then the group decision will be more cautious; if it leans towards joining the single European currency the decision will strongly favour joining; if it leans against joining it will be even more opposed; and so forth.

One important consequence of group polarisation is attitude change. For example, suppose that you join a local environmental group because you have a desire to protect the environment. After attending several meetings and discussing environmental issues with other group members, you may find that your pro-environment attitude has become even stronger: you are more of an environmentalist than you thought you were. The fact that group discussion can affect attitude change so powerfully has been documented in many psychology experiments. For example, Myers and Bishop (1970) found that the initial level of racial prejudice voiced by groups was altered through group discussion. Discussion caused the group with an initially low level of prejudice to become even less prejudiced and discussion caused the group with an initially high level of prejudice to become even more prejudiced.

What causes group discussion to lead to polarisation? Although several explanations have been offered, three seem the most plausible: those concerning informational and normative influence (Isenberg, 1986), and social identity processes (Turner *et al.*, 1989). Informational influence involves learning new information germane to the decision to be made. When you are in a group that is already slanted towards one decision, group discussion will bring to light new information that supports your position but that you have not heard before. This supportive novel information will strengthen commitment to your position, and across the members of the group this will encourage the group to endorse a more extreme decision.

Normative influence involves comparison of one's individual views with that of the group. Just as we discussed in the earlier section on conformity, people strive for social approval and do not like to stand out from the crowd. Discussion reveals what appears to be the socially desirable position, and thus members of the group strive to be seen by the other members of the group to be adhering to the 'popular' position. In this way, the group becomes more extreme and is able to endorse a more extreme decision.

Social identity processes involve people in the group constructing a group norm to define their membership in the decision-making group and then conforming to that norm. If the group's mean initial position is relatively extreme, this implies that people who are not in the group (or who are in a specific out-group) are less extreme. In order to distinguish the group from 'other people', the in-group norm is perceptually polarised away from 'most other people'. The process of self-categorisation and depersonalisation associated with group identification (Turner *et al.*, 1987) causes people to conform to the polarised norm and thus endorse a polarised group decision. Research has supported this analysis by showing that group polarisation occurs only if people perceive the extreme mean to be a group norm rather than merely an aggregate of positions, and if they identify with the group defined by the norm (Mackie, 1986; Turner *et al.*, 1989; Abrams *et al.*, 1990).

Groupthink

Irving Janis has studied a related phenomenon that sometimes occurs in group decision-making – **groupthink**, the tendency to avoid dissent in the attempt to achieve group consensus (Janis, 1972, 1982). He developed the notion of groupthink after studying the poor decision-making that led President John F. Kennedy to order the ill-fated attempt to overthrow the Castro regime in Cuba in 1961. The decision to embark on the Bay of Pigs invasion was made by Kennedy and a small group of advisers. After studying the conditions that led to this decision and other important group decisions that altered the course of twentieth-century history (such as the 1941 Japanese attack on Pearl Harbor), Janis proposed his theory of groupthink.

The theory specifies the conditions necessary for groupthink as well as its symptoms and consequences (see Figure 16.6). The conditions that foster groupthink include a stressful situation in which the stakes are very high, a cohesive group of people who already tend to think alike and who are isolated from others who could offer criticism of the decision, and a strong group leader who makes their position well known to the group. In the Bay of Pigs example, the overthrow of one of America's arch-enemies was at stake, Kennedy's group of advisers were like-minded regarding the invasion and met in secret, and Kennedy was a forceful and charismatic leader who made his intentions to invade Cuba known to the group.

Janis also notes five symptoms of groupthink, all of which were present during the decision to invade Cuba: (1) group members share the illusion that their decision is sound, moral and right – in a word, invulnerable; (2) dissent from the leader's views are discouraged, further supporting the illusion that the group's decision is the right one; (3) instead of assessing the strengths and weaknesses of the decision, group members rationalise their decision, looking only for reasons that support it; (4) group members are closed-minded – they are not willing to listen to alternative suggestions and ideas; and (5) self-appointed 'mindguards' exist within the group who actively discourage dissent from the group norm.

Combined, these symptoms lead to flawed decision-making. They contribute to the tendency to conduct only incomplete or no research on the issue about which a decision is being made, to fail to examine alternative courses of action specified by the decision and, finally, to fail to consider potential risks inherent in the decision.

Janis argues that groupthink may be avoided by taking several precautions: (1) criticism by group members should be encouraged; (2) relevant input should be sought from appropriate people who are not members of the group; (3) the group should be broken down into sub-groups in which different ideas and opinions are generated and developed; and (4) the group leader should not overstate their position on the matter and should be on guard for rationalisation, closed-mindedness and illusions of invulnerability. An unlikely last word on this topic goes to former US President Ronald Reagan. He perceptively understood the dangers of groupthink: 'You risk becoming isolated. People tell you about what you want to hear and are reluctant to tell you about somebody who might not be pulling his weight or doing something hurtful to your administration. Not many people close to you are willing to say: 'You're wrong'.'

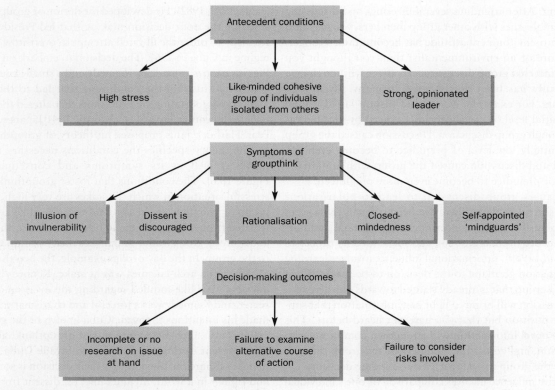

Figure 16.6 A summary of Janis's conception of groupthink.

Psychology in action: Leadership

Our discussion of groupthink has identified the important role of leaders in group decision-making. Indeed, it is very difficult to envisage groups without leaders. Almost all groups are structured into one or more people who have greater influence and take the lead, and others who are more influenced and act as followers. Leadership is endemic to group processes.

One approach to leadership focuses on the way that particular leadership styles are suited to different leadership situations – these are called **contingency theories** because they argue that the effectiveness of a particular style is contingent on situational factors. The best known of these is Fiedler's (1965) contingency theory. Fiedler believed that people differ in their leadership styles – some people are task-oriented and others relationship-oriented. Task-oriented leaders are authoritarian, value group success and derive self-esteem from task accomplishment rather than being liked by the group; relationship-oriented leaders are relaxed, friendly, non-directive and sociable, and gain self-esteem from happy and harmonious group relations. Fiedler also believed that leadership situations could be classified in terms of what he called situational control. At one extreme were situations in which leaders had legitimate authority, good leader–member

relations and the task was well structured; at the other extreme, legitimacy was low, leader–member relations poor and the task poorly structured. Fiedler predicted that relationship-oriented leaders were more effective than task-oriented leaders except if situational control was either very high or very low, when task-oriented leaders would be more effective. There is general support for this analysis, except that critics have suggested that it is too static a view of leadership, and that it underplays the fact that leadership is very much a group process that involves the relationship between leaders and followers.

Leader–follower relations are a more central focus of **transactional theories of leadership**. For example, Hollander (1958) argues that for leaders to be effective they need to develop a relationship with the rest of the group that allows them to be innovative and to exert influence over the group. Hollander suggests that leaders need to accumulate what he calls idiosyncrasy credits. This can be done by (1) initially conforming closely to established group norms, (2) ensuring that the group feels it has democratically elected you as the leader, (3) making sure that you are seen to have the competence to fulfil the group's objectives, and (4) being seen to identify with the group, its ideals and its aspirations.

Psychology in action: *Continued*

Another transactional model of leadership is **leader–member exchange (LMX)** theory (Graen and Uhl-Bien, 1995). To be effective, leaders need to establish very different individualised exchange relationships with different members of the group. However, in doing this, leaders need to be careful to treat all members with respect as valued group members, and not to create destructive internal divisions by showing too much preference for some members over others.

A development of transactional models of leadership focuses on **transformational leadership** (Bass, 1998). Transformational leaders' transactions with followers are characterised by charisma, inspirational motivation, intellectual stimulation and individualised consideration, which motivate followers to work for group goals that transcend immediate self-interest. Transformational leaders are those who respond positively to change and who actively induce change. Great leaders often do seem to behave in this way but critics worry that too much emphasis is now being placed on charisma as a personality attribute.

A different approach to the explanation of leadership has been proposed by social identity theorists (Hogg, 2001; Hogg and van Knippenberg, 2003). In groups, people tend to rest their evaluation and endorsement of leaders on the extent to which leaders match schemas they have of good leadership. However, where people identify strongly with a group that is important to self-definition, people's evaluations of their leaders are increasingly influenced by how prototypical of the group the leader is perceived to be.

There are many implications of this idea. For example, in very cohesive and salient groups with which people identify strongly, poor leaders (those who do not match effective leadership schemas) may prevail simply because they are highly prototypical of the group. Leaders are also presumably aware that they can increase their leadership effectiveness of such groups by being seen to be prototypical. They will engage in a rhetoric of prototypicality in which they talk up their own prototypicality (Reicher and Hopkins, 1996). Leaders of cohesive groups may behave differently as a function of how prototypical they are (van Knippenberg and van Knippenberg, 2003). Leaders who are highly prototypical are often aware that their prototypicality is not in question – they are thus able to be innovative and non-conformist. The prototypicality of less prototypical leaders still needs to be established – these leaders need to be much more conformist and thus less able to be innovative.

Negotiation, teamwork and leadership – An international perspective

From selling detergent to securing peace in Northern Ireland or the Middle East, the ability to negotiate with others is an important social skill. The outcome of a transaction or interaction can turn on not only how well you negotiate, but on how you work as a team and the leadership you show. A review by Gelfand *et al.* (2007) summarises how these three characteristics vary across nations and how this variation affects decisions.

Research on negotiation has shown that, in the US, people are more likely to show self-serving biases and make internal attributions about other negotiators' behaviour (Gelfand and Christakopoulou, 1999). North Americans are more likely to see conflicts as being about winning or violating an individual's rights (Gelfand *et al.*, 2001), to share information directly with their colleagues during negotiation, and to achieve high goals that both parties want to attain (Adair *et al.*, 2001). They are more likely to make concessions at the end of the negotiation than at the beginning (Hendon *et al.*, 2003), and are most satisfied with a negotiation when their economic gains have been maximised (Ma *et al.*, 2002).

Japanese negotiators, in contrast, see conflicts as a violation of duty but also as an opportunity to compromise (Gelfand *et al.*, 2001). The Japanese, Russians and participants from Hong Kong are more likely to seek out information during a negotiation through a pattern of offers (Adair *et al.*, 2001). Unlike US negotiators, Asian negotiators are more likely to make generous concessions early on in an exchange and gradually reduce these concessions as the negotiation goes on (Hendon *et al.*, 2003). Unlike Americans, Estonians see a successful negotiation ending when both parties are the recipients of equivalent outcomes (Ma *et al.*, 2002).

The ways in which teams operate and are perceived also differ across cultures. For example, Americans view their team less favourably if they – as individuals – do well but the team performs poorly. You don't see such an interpretation in Chinese participants (Chen *et al.*, 1998). Taiwanese participants view their teams more negatively if membership changes often (compared with Australian participants, who don't) (Harrison *et al.*, 2000). Individuals from collectivistic cultures are more likely to view teams as 'entities' and as

▶

Negotiation, teamwork and leadership – *Continued*

'acting as one' (Chiu *et al.*, 2000). In Japan, indirect personal ties between group members are important for engendering trust amongst the team; in the US, this trust is fostered by team participants belonging to some shared membership category, such as the school they went to (Yuki *et al.*, 2005). Teams of people from collectivistic cultures cooperate better and are more successful (Eby and Dobbins, 1997).

What if the team is made up of people from different cultures? The research suggests that these teams show considerable evidence of ethnocentrism and strong in-group biases (Von Glinow *et al.*, 2004; Cramton and Hinds, 2005). When the team leaders prevent communication breakdown, however, multicultural teams perform as well as monocultural teams (Ayoko *et al.*, 2002). A person's culture/nation becomes important in team negotiations when either very few or very many members share the same background (Randel, 2003). Here, performance is worse than in more homogeneous groups (Thomas, 1999). Over time, however, Harrison *et al.* (2002) have found that this performance improves, presumably because team members have begun to familiarise themselves with each other and have learned about each other's behaviour. Also, the more heterogeneous the team, the better the performance (compared with moderately varied teams) (Earley and Mosakowski, 2000).

Finally, we all know of leaders who seem capable of persuading others and of turning the minds of people who appear to hold entrenched, immutable opinions – Bill Clinton intervening to negotiate with the violently opposed political factions in Northern Ireland; Tony Blair persuading Bill Clinton to release ground troops in Kosovo which, ultimately, put an end to Milosevic's ethnic cleansing; Bob Geldof persuading a few popstars to sing a tune and then subsequently persuading millions to help feed the millions of starving in Africa and, more recently, persuading the eight richest nations in the world to tackle poverty in developing countries. (Of course, there are those whose persuasion is not as honourable or which leads to outcomes that are not as positive – such as those who can persuade young men that crashing a plane into a building or detonating a bomb on a tube train is a good idea or, more historically, Jim Jones, leader of the People's Temple – a Californian cult – who in 1978 ordered almost 800 people to commit suicide.)

Is there any trait that leaders such as this share? In individualistic cultures there is a tendency for leaders to use coercive power to achieve aims whereas in collectivistic cultures, the tendency is to use expert power. According to the Global Leadership and Organizational Behaviour Effectiveness Project (cleverly acronymed as GLOBE) which looked at 17,000 middle managers in 62 cultures, two traits stand out in good leaders: being charismatic and being a team-player (House *et al.*, 2004). The best senior managers were described as innovative, visionary and courageous; those at a lower level were described as being attentive to subordinates and were good at team building.

Gelfand *et al.* (2007) note that charisma varies across nations. They cite the example given by Den Hartog and Verburg (1997). They found that a strong, ululating voice was described as enthusiastic in Latin American cultures, and therefore a vehicle for charisma, whereas a monotonous tone was described as worthy of respect and self-control in Asian cultures, a uniformity that was considered charismatic.

Many social psychologists explain these acts in terms of de-individuation, in which one loses one's sense of individuality and personal responsibility. In collective settings, people 'blend' into the crowd, achieving a sense of anonymity that causes them to assume less responsibility for their actions (Diener, 1980). Consider a study of empathy towards strangers conducted by Zimbardo (1970). In one condition, young women were easily identifiable: they wore name tags and were called by their names. In another condition, a different group of young women were not so easily identifiable: they wore large coats and hoods without name tags and were never referred to by their names. The two groups of women were given chances to administer electric shocks to a stranger, who was actually a confederate of Zimbardo's. The young women who were unidentifiable gave nearly twice as many electric shocks to the stranger as did the young women whose identities were known. Thus, the amount of aggression Zimbardo observed in his participants was strongly correlated with the extent to which their identities were known, reinforcing the idea that antisocial behaviour observed in some groups is due to the loss of personal identity of its individual members.

People in crowds are not always antisocial, and crowds themselves are not always aggressive. De-individuation may not be an automatic consequence of crowds, or it may be a process that is less mechanically tied to antisocial behaviour. Taylor *et al.* (1994) characterise de-individuation as a process wherein one's personal identity – one's sense of self – is replaced by identification with the group's values and goals (see also Reicher *et al.*, 1995).

This idea has been more fully explored in terms of social identity theory, which we discussed earlier in this chapter. Reicher (1987, 2001) suggests that crowds are events where people from the same group, and thus with a common social identity, come together to achieve goals (which may or may not involve violence). The strong sense of common social identity ensures that people are highly attuned to the appropriate group norm, and thus conform tightly to it. There is no loss of identity or responsibility, no de-individuation, rather a change of identity. For Reicher, crowds are not fickle or irrational. They are group events in which there are clear limits to acceptable behaviour – limits set by the identity of the crowd. Local conditions and goals will influence how the crowd's social identity expresses itself within these limits. For example, Stott and colleagues have analysed the role of police behaviour in situations when football fans become violent, such as the 1998 World Cup Final, and conclude that the more heavy-handed the police are in their approach to policing the more violent and antagonistic the fans will be (e.g. Stott *et al.*, 2001; Stott and Adang, 2004).

This rational model of crowds links crowd action to various forms of social protest that may be part of a social movement. The key question in the study of social protest is what causes individual discontents or grievances to be transformed into collective action: how and why do sympathisers become mobilised as activists or participants? Klandermans (1997) argues that this involves the relationship between individual attitudes and behaviour (see Chapter 15). Sympathisers hold, by definition, sympathetic attitudes towards an issue yet these attitudes do not translate into behaviour. Participation also resembles a social dilemma (see below). Protest is generally for a social good (such as equality) or against a social ill (e.g. pollution), and as success benefits everyone irrespective of participation but failure harms participants more, it is tempting to 'free ride' – to remain a sympathiser rather than become a participant.

When crowds go wrong: football hooliganism

From the early 1970s European, but particularly English, football has become strongly associated with hooliganism. Football 'hooliganism' involves groups of people behaving in the same way. It is also a set of behaviours which is often associated in the popular mind with crowd behaviour, the popular image of a riot or other violent and antisocial collective event. Popular hysteria tends to characterise football hooliganism in terms of the familiar stereotypical image of football fans on the rampage (Murphy *et al.*, 1990).

De-individuation theories offer a group-oriented analysis of this phenomenon. A football match is a crowd context where people feel anonymous and unidentifiable; they lose their sense of individual identity and thus no longer feel that it is necessary to act in socially acceptable ways. This perspective assumes that people are fundamentally antisocial and aggressive, and that the only reason people do not ordinarily act in this way is that they are usually identifiable in a society whose norms strongly proscribe such behaviour. Hooliganism is primitive unsocialised behaviour that lies deep in all our psyches, and which is released in crowd settings like a football match. Although recognising the group context of hooliganism, this analysis is also rather individualistic. The crowd releases individual aggressive instincts – and in fact any (non-group) context that makes one feel de-individuated may have the same effect (e.g. darkness, or clothing which conceals who we are). One problem with this analysis is that it cannot easily explain why most people at football matches do not indulge in hooliganism. Perhaps they are not de-individuated – but why? Perhaps they are de-individuated, but de-individuation does not inevitably produce hooliganism, in which case alternative or additional processes must operate to produce hooliganism.

A different, more genuinely group-oriented analysis of football hooliganism is provided by Marsh *et al.* (1978). According to their analysis, violence by football fans is actually orchestrated far away from the stadium and long before a given match. What might appear to be a motley crowd of supporters on match day can actually consist of several distinct groups of fans with different status. By participating in ritualised aggression over a period of time, a faithful follower can be 'promoted' into a higher group and can continue to pursue a 'career structure'. Rival fans who follow their group's rules quite carefully can avoid real physical harm to themselves or others. For example, chasing the opposition after a match ('seeing them off') need not necessarily end in violence since part of the agreed code is not actually to catch anyone. Seen in this light, football hooliganism is a kind of staged production and is not the example of an uncontrollable mob sometimes depicted by the media. When real violence does take place, it tends to be both unusual and attributable to particular individuals.

Football hooliganism can also be understood in more broadly societal terms. For example, Murphy *et al.* (1990) described how football arose in Britain as an essentially working-class sport, and that by the 1950s working-class values to do with masculine aggression had already become associated with the game. Attempts by the government (seen as middle class) to control this aspect of the sport can backfire because these attempts merely enhance class solidarity and encourage increased violence that generalises beyond matches. This sort of explanation points towards an analysis in terms of inter-group relations and subcultural norms that prescribe and legitimate aggression. Fans derive a sense of who they are – a sense of identity – from being part of a group of supporters. Some people, particularly those with few other valued sources of identity, identify more strongly than others. The attitudinal, dress and behavioural norms of the group are strongly adhered to, particularly in situations where the group is very salient, for example, at or around a match when supporters of opposing teams are present in the stadium, in the streets and on public transport. The actual norms of the groups reflect the historical origins of the sport and the intrinsically competitive

Protestors marching after the riots in Paris of October/November 2005, which led to debates on integration and discrimination in France, and to what extent French of North African descent could have a French national identity.

Source: Christophe Ena/Press Association Images.

and masculine nature of the game. Football hooliganism is largely a display of controlled aggression and machismo that reflects strong identification with group norms (this sort of group-oriented analysis owes much to social identity theory).

Intergroup relations

Sherif (1962, p. 5) has provided a classic definition of **intergroup relations**:

Intergroup relations refer to relations between two or more groups and their respective members. Whenever individuals belonging to one group interact, collectively or individually, with another group or its members in terms of their group identifications we have an instance of intergroup behaviour. Intergroup behaviour tends to be competitive and ethnocentric, that is, people tend to view all attributes of their group as being better than all attributes of any out-group they compare themselves with.

Realistic conflict and interdependence

One explanation of why and how this happens was developed on the basis of a series of three famous field experiments conducted by Sherif and his colleagues in 1949, 1953 and 1954 at summer camps for young boys in the US (see Sherif, 1966). The participants, 11-year-old boys, were randomly assigned to one of two cabins that were isolated from each other. Friends were split up to be in different cabins. During the first week, the boys in each cabin spent their time together as a group, fishing, hiking, swimming and otherwise enjoying themselves. The boys formed two cohesive groups, which they named the Rattlers and the Eagles. They became attached to their groups and strongly identified with them.

Next, the experimenters arranged a series of formal competitive events between the two groups. The best team was to win a trophy for the group and individual prizes for its members. As the competition progressed, the boys began taunting and insulting each other. Then the Eagles burned the Rattlers' flag and, in retaliation, the Rattlers broke into the Eagles' cabin and scattered or stole their rivals' belongings. Although further physical conflict was prevented by the experimenters, the two groups continued to abuse each other verbally and seemed to have developed a genuine hatred for each other – stereotypes and prejudices developed and were expressed verbally and physically.

Finally, in one of the studies the experimenters arranged for the boys to work together in order to accomplish shared goals that both groups valued but neither group could accomplish alone. The experimenters sabotaged the water supply for the camp and had the boys fix it; they had the boys repair a truck that had broken down; and they induced the boys to pool their money to rent a movie. After the boys worked on cooperative ventures, rather than competitive ones, the level of intergroup conflict diminished markedly.

To explain the results of these studies, Sherif developed **realistic conflict theory**. Sherif argued that the way people behave towards one another is strongly influenced by people's goals and their perception of the goal relations between people. When people have a common goal that requires interdependent action for its achievement, then people cooperate to help one another to achieve the goal, and this produces a sense of solidarity and oneness that underpins group formation. This is what happened in the first stage of the studies. When two groups have mutually exclusive goals, in other words when only one group can achieve the goal at the expense of the other group, then the groups compete and hinder each other from achieving their goal. This spawns mutual dislike, conflict and hostility. This is what happened in the second stage of the studies. When two groups have a common goal that cannot be achieved by one group alone (called a superordinate goal), then the two groups cooperate to help one another to achieve the goal. This reduces hostility and generates more positive intergroup attitudes. This is what happened in the final stage of the studies.

Frustrated goals and relative deprivation

A key feature of realistic conflict theory is the argument that intergroup conflict rests on competitive goals that cause each group to impede or frustrate each other's attempts to achieve their goals. Collective goal frustration may contribute to hostile intergroup relations. This idea has its roots in Dollard *et al.*'s (1939) **frustration – aggression hypothesis**. When people's goals are frustrated they can feel a sense of anger (technically called an 'instigation to aggress') that can be dissipated only by aggression, often not directed at the cause of the frustration but at a scapegoat that is weak and vulnerable.

According to Berkowitz (1962), frustration is most likely to translate into collective aggression against an out-group when the instigation to aggress is associated with other generally aversive conditions, there are aggressive cues in the environment, and people are in the presence of others who are acting aggressively.

Generally, conflict between groups arises when a group has an acute feeling of being deprived. **Relative deprivation** can be most acute when a period of rising expectations (how things ought to be) and rising achievements (how things are) comes to an abrupt end because achievements suddenly drop off. This J-curve hypothesis (Davies, 1969) has been used to explain large-scale intergroup conflicts, for example, the French and Russian revolutions, and the rise of anti-Semitism in Europe after the economic crash of 1929.

Although relative deprivation can be based on diachronic (over time) comparisons between one's circumstances now and how they used to be, Runciman (1966) suggests that synchronic (here and now) self – other comparisons are much more immediate and powerful. These comparisons can be between one's self and individual others (interpersonal comparisons) or between one's own group and another group (intergroup comparisons). The former generates a sense of **egoistic relative deprivation** that is associated with stress, depression and demotivation. It is the latter that generates a sense of **fraternalistic relative deprivation** that is associated with collective protest, intergroup conflict, prejudice, and so forth (Vanneman and Pettigrew, 1972).

There are at least three conditions that seem to amplify the impact of fraternalistic deprivation on competitive intergroup behaviour: (1) people need to identify strongly with their group (Abrams, 1990); (2) people need to feel that their deprived state relative to another group rests not only on an unjust distribution of resources (distributive injustice), but also on unjust procedures (procedural injustice) (Tyler and Smith, 1998); and (3) there is a perception of real intergroup conflict over scarce resources (see our discussion of realistic conflict theory, above).

Humour, aggression and motivation: self-determination theory

According to self-determination theory (Deci and Ryan, 2000), autonomy motivation involves behaviour that includes making choices for oneself, acting according to values and principles that are respected and endorsed, and initiating behaviour in a proactive way. Control motivation, on the other hand, involves behaving according to the dictates of an external agency, under pressure and where behaviour is contingent on feedback from this agency. As you might expect, those expressing the former motivation would flourish; those with less autonomy and under greater control, would not.

There is evidence for this. People who are autonomous express greater well-being (Sheldon et al., 1996), have more positive romantic relationships (Knee et al., 2005) and perform better on tasks when they interact with others (Weinstein and Ryan, 2010). Weinstein et al. (2011) sought to see whether being primed with either of these orientations – primed autonomy and control – affected people's hostility and preference for hostile humour. In a series of four experiments, this is exactly what they found: people who had been primed with the control orientation found hostile humour (extracted from America's Funniest Home Videos) to be funnier (and less aversive). People who were high in trait hostility – and primed with the control condition – were particularly enamoured with the hostile material. Both trait hostility and control priming also enhanced aggressive behaviour.

Social identity

Although competitive goals and a sense of relative deprivation certainly do encourage conflict and hostile intergroup attitudes and behaviour, there is also substantial evidence that the mere existence of social categories or groups can be sufficient to provide the framework for this behaviour. Tajfel et al. (1971) conducted an experiment in which school students were randomly assigned to groups (ostensibly on the basis of preferences for paintings by the artists Klee and Kandinsky, who were unknown to the students). The participants did not interact and did not know who was in their group or who was in the other group. Nevertheless, they subsequently discriminated against the out-group by repeatedly allocating less money to the out-group than their own group (even though they personally did not benefit financially from this allocation). This paradigm, the **minimal group paradigm**, and variants of it, have been used many hundreds of times over the last 35 years or so to replicate this effect – people who are categorised on a minimal, trivial and often random basis tend to show a competitive and discriminatory orientation towards an out-group.

Minimal social categorisation can sometimes not produce discrimination. Experimental participants need to feel they belong to the minimal group, and this sense of belonging or identification is enhanced where people feel uncertain about themselves and their place in the social context (Hogg, 2000). Also, discrimination can disappear when participants, rather than allocating rewards, are asked to allocate punishments or withhold rewards – called the positive – negative asymmetry effect (Mummendey and Otten, 1998).

The initial minimal group finding was an important catalyst for the development, originally by Tajfel and then by Turner and his associates, of social identity theory (Tajfel and Turner, 1986; Turner et al., 1987; Hogg and Abrams, 1988; Hogg, 2006) (see also the section in Chapter 15 on self and identity). According to social identity theory, group and intergroup behaviour is associated with social identity (self-definition in terms of the defining attributes of an in-group), not personal identity (self-definition in terms of idiosyncratic traits or close interpersonal relationships). People cognitively represent social groups in terms of a fuzzy set of attributes (called a prototype) that simultaneously captures in-group similarities and intergroup differences. Prototypes are catered to specific contexts in order to maximise entitativity – the property of a group that makes it a distinct entity with sharp boundaries and clear consensual defining attributes. Self-inclusive social categories with high entitativity and clear prescriptive prototypes are very effective at reducing self-conceptual, attitudinal and behavioural uncertainty (Hogg, 2000).

When a particular intergroup categorisation seems best to account for what is going on in a particular situation it then becomes psychologically salient, that is, people categorise themselves and others in terms of the categorisation. Social categorisation causes people to view others and themselves not as unique individuals, but in terms of the relevant in-group or out-group prototype – a process called **depersonalisation** because perception is based on group membership and group attributes not individuality and personal attributes. Depersonalisation explains why, in intergroup contexts, we tend to see out-group members stereotypically, why we conform to in-group norms relating to perceptions, feelings, attitudes and behaviours, and why we tend to accentuate intergroup differences and intragroup similarities on all available and relevant dimensions of comparison. This cognitive aspect of social identity theory is called **self-categorisation theory** (Turner *et al.*, 1987).

Because groups define and evaluate who we are, it is important that the groups we belong to have attributes that we consider to be evaluatively positive. Intergroup behaviour is a struggle for positive distinctiveness for our own group relative to relevant out-groups. This furnishes a favourable social identity, and this in turn contributes to an underlying sense of self-esteem. The struggle for positive social identity can be framed in terms of a struggle for status, with dominant groups protecting their high-status position of advantage and privilege, and subordinate groups striving to rectify their lower-status position and associated disadvantage. According to social identity theory, the form that this struggle takes depends upon people's perceptions of the nature of status relations between groups (Tajfel and Turner, 1986; Ellemers, 1993). The focus is largely on how lower-status groups respond to their social position.

Where status relations are considered legitimate but the boundaries between groups are believed to be permeable, members of lower-status groups pursue social mobility – they disidentify from their group and try to gain admittance for themselves and their immediate family to the higher-status group. This is almost always unsuccessful. It leaves people with a marginal social identity – rejected by their in-group and not accepted by the out-group. Where status relations are considered to be relatively legitimate and highly stable and boundaries are impermeable, lower-status group members pursue a strategy of social creativity. They try to improve their social identity by seeking a redefinition of in-group properties – different, more positive attributes and a re-evaluation of existing properties. They also focus on comparisons with groups who are even lower in status than their own. Finally, where people recognise the illegitimacy of their lower-status position, feel that status relations are unstable and can envisage ways to achieve a change in status relations, they engage in direct social competition. They go head-to-head with the higher-status groups – this can take the form of democratic political action, social protest or revolution and war.

The social identity analysis of intergroup behaviour has gathered substantial support as an account of the dynamics of intergroup behaviour. For example, regarding the role of self-esteem, Hunter *et al.* (1996) studied the intergroup relationship between Catholic and Protestant 16-year-olds in Northern Ireland. Participants first completed some measures of self-esteem and then evaluated the two groups. Self-esteem was then measured again. Among those who expressed in-group bias when they evaluated the groups (favouring their own group over the other), self-esteem was raised on dimensions such as honesty, academic ability and physical appearance.

Regarding the motivational role of uncertainty reduction, a series of experiments has shown that discrimination in the minimal group paradigm occurs only if people are categorised under conditions of subjective uncertainty that cause them to identify with the minimal group (Hogg, 2000). Regarding intergroup conflict, there is an entire literature in the area of language and social psychology which shows that **ethnolinguistic groups** (ethnic groups for whom language is a defining feature) thrive or perish depending on perceptions of the stability, legitimacy and permeability of status relations, exactly as predicted by social identity theory (Giles and Johnson, 1987). Finally, there is evidence that in-group prototypes do enhance entitativity and that people conform to such norms when they identify with their group (Abrams *et al.*, 1990), and that this is associated with out-group stereotyping (Oakes *et al.*, 1993; Leyens *et al.*, 1994).

Ostracism

Research by Zadro *et al.* (2005) shows that people can feel worse when they are the target of ostracism (being excluded and ignored in the presence of others) than the target of a verbal dispute. Furthermore, those who are the source of the behaviour actually feel better when they ostracise you than when they target you with verbal dispute.

To demonstrate this, Zadro and colleagues conducted three role-playing experiments in which they constructed a mock train ride in the laboratory – three rows, one right behind the other, of three chairs. To further cue the 'train ride' aspect there were some of the usual signs found in trains, such as 'no smoking' and 'do not place your feet on the seats'. Student participants were randomly assigned the role of target or source – targets sat in the middle of rows and sources sat at the ends.

The scenario was described as one in which they were travelling home by train and the sources were cross with the target because he or she had not invited them to a party. In the ostracism condition the sources were told to express their anger by talking to one another across the target but ignoring the target. In the dispute condition, they were told to express their anger by directly arguing with the target. The role-play lasted about five minutes, after which participants completed a questionnaire indicating how they felt – more specifically, to what extent they felt the four basic needs of belonging, control, self-esteem and meaningful existence were being met.

The results of the first study, with 35 students, showed that targets of ostracism felt all four needs were less satisfied than did targets of dispute – they felt less belonging, less control, lower self-esteem and less meaningful existence. Sources who used ostracism felt greater control than did sources who used dispute. The second study, with 57 participants, was virtually identical with some minor changes to increase the realism of the role-play. Once again targets of ostracism felt all four needs were less satisfied than did targets of dispute. The final study, with 138 participants, used a slightly different scenario – the target had refused to provide notes for the sources to catch up on a class they had missed – but was the same in other respects. Yet again, targets of ostracism felt all four needs were less satisfied than did targets of dispute – but here the difference was significant only on belonging and meaningful existence. In addition, sources of ostracism felt greater belonging and more superiority than did sources of dispute. This last study also had a control condition in which the target was explicitly included by the sources – as one would expect, inclusion caused both targets and sources to feel their needs were being better satisfied than did ostracism or dispute.

These studies have used some very vivid paradigms – for example, in one paradigm a participant ostensibly waiting with two others for an experiment is initially included in a ball-tossing game and then excluded (e.g. Williams and Sommer, 1997). The reaction to ostracism underscores the fundamentally social nature of human existence and the way that our sense of self and of reality is grounded in social recognition. We feel isolated. This isolation can also make us feel, literally, cold. Zhong and Leonardelli (2008) found that when people were asked to recall an experience in which they felt socially isolated, they estimated the temperature of the room to be lower than did those who recalled an experience in which they were socially included. Those who were excluded from a cybermall game found the room to be colder and expressed a greater desire for warm food and drink than did those who were included.

Social exclusion can also lead people to adopt a less critical approach to persuasive messages. For example, socially excluded people are more likely to comply and to conform than are those who are not socially excluded (Riva *et al.*, 2014). Socially excluded individuals are also more likely to be persuaded by arguments that are or low quality – those who are not socially excluded are persuaded by high-quality agreements, perhaps suggesting the need to belong (Pfundmair *et al.*, 2016). However, this pattern of responding appears to hold only when the source of the message is credible.

Some psychologists have argued that social ostracism produces social pain that is equivalent to physical pain, and that it can evoke activation in those parts of the brain that are typically activated when we experience physical pain (Eisenberger, 2012). Using a version of the ball-tossing paradigm described above, Eisenberger (2013) found that people who were excluded from the game, showed activation in the dorsal anterior cingulate cortex and the anterior insula – areas involved in physical pain. The researchers found that the greater the activation in the anterior cingulate, the greater the degree of distress experienced by the socially excluded participant. Both this and the main finding have been found in variants of the ball-tossing task (e.g. Krill and Platek, 2009; Gunther *et al.*, 2010; Masten *et al.*, 2012).

The effect of ostracism on physical pain has also been investigated with mixed findings: some studies suggests that it increases pain sensitivity; others that it numbs the recipient. The cyberball manipulation leads people to be hypersensitive to pain but when they think about a future alone, it numbs them. Bernstein and Claypool (2012) instead of using the cyberball task, asked people to imagine a future alone and, in the extreme scenario, 'devoid of any meaningful social relations'. They found that the more severe the future life exclusion, the greater the pain numbing; less severe future exclusion was associated with hypersensitivity to pain. They suggest that the hypersensitivity to the cyberball exclusion is adaptive and prosocial, a means of coping with ostracism. The future alone paradigm leads to maladaptive responses.

The importance of being close to someone can't be understated. People respond more emotionally when they have a friend with them – even of that friend is in a separate room. For example, Wagner *et al.* (2014) asked sets of two friends to come for a neuroimaging experiment where both would be looking at positive, negative and neutral photographs. One friend would be undergoing scanning in one room and the other would be in a separate room. Neither could see each other but in one condition, the non-imaged friend was told that their imaged friend was looking at the same photo at that moment. Both friends responded more emotionally if they know they were both looking at the photographs and in this condition activation was greater in the ventral striatum and medial orbitofrontal cortex in the friend undergoing imaging. the activation of the striatum is interesting because several studies suggests that this region is affected when people learn about others' social behaviour, when they perceive reward inequality and when they engage in social contact (Baez-Mendoza and Schultz, 2013).

Some people, of course, are more prone to rejection than others and this rejection sensitivity has its origins in development, with the person experiencing high levels of rejection by caregivers and friends during childhood and beyond. People who are sensitive to rejection show increasing levels of distress when exposed to words and images that represent rejection (Downey *et al.*, 2004).

People who feel as if they will be rejected or belittled when giving a public talk show increases in the sympathetic nervous system, hypothalamic-pituitary axis (described in more detail in the next chapter) and in the degree of inflammation (Eisenberger, 2013). Eisenberger suggests that there are significant ties between rejection, loneliness, stress and mortality. She highlights a number of brain regions that are activated when people become socially excluded, or relive the experience of being socially excluded, or watch images of social exclusion, or see images of deceased people they were very close to. The dorsal anterior cingulate cortex is one brain area which is activated during each of these conditions. Some of the others are illustrated in Figure 16.7.

Prejudice

Intergroup attitudes are a core component of intergroup behaviour. Attitudes toward the out-group tend to be shared among the in-group members, and tend to devalue the out-group relative to the in-group – they are stereotypes and are a defining feature of prejudice. Indeed, **prejudice** can be defined as a shared attitude, generally negative, towards a social out-group, and thus towards members of that group purely on the basis of their membership in that group (see Chapter 11 for some discussion of the development of prejudice). Some of the most pernicious prejudices are those based on people's race, ethnicity, religion, age, sex, sexual orientation and mental and physical health. But people have a remarkable ability to be prejudiced against almost any group you care to mention – illustrated by the 2006 Oscar-winning film Crash. Like other attitudes, prejudices have a cognitive component. In this case the cognitive component is (as discussed in the social cognition section of Chapter 15) a stereotype or schema – a set of interrelated (and shared) beliefs about members of the group that influences perception once we categorise someone as being a member of the group. Again, like other attitudes, there is no guarantee that prejudice will be expressed as behaviour, but when it is, that behaviour is called **discrimination**.

Researchers at the universities of Colorado and Chicago have found that making stereotypes about people accessible influences a person's decision to shoot those individuals during a videogame (Correll *et al.*, 2007). In the experiment, participants had to press a key indicating 'shoot' if they saw a person with a gun in the game they were playing. If the person was not carrying a gun, they were to press a key indicating 'don't shoot'. Half of the characters in the game were white, half were black. Before playing the game, people were asked to read newspaper articles in which armed robberies committed by either black or white felons were reported.

People who read about the black criminals were significantly more likely to shoot black targets in the videogame – regardless of whether these targets were armed or unarmed – than white (even armed) targets. So, by making stereotypical information accessible (the link between black people and violence), the researchers found that people's tendency to engage in stereotype-driven behaviour increased.

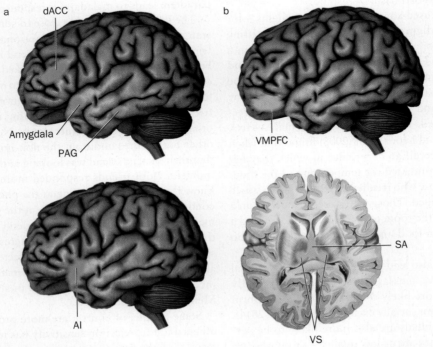

Figure 16.7 Brains **(a)** and **(b)** show the areas activated when people process social disconnection (red) and disconnection (blue).

Theories of prejudice

Because prejudice is repugnant and can have such appalling effects, such as genocide, prejudice is often traced to individual differences and personality attributes. One of the most widely promulgated theories of prejudice is the **authoritarian personality** (Adorno *et al.*, 1950). Children who are brought up in families where their parents use harsh disciplinarian methods to secure love and dependence develop a love–hate relationship with their parents, which is unendurably stressful. The stress is resolved by idealising their parents and all authority figures and redirecting their hatred onto weaker others. This resolution becomes a deep-seated and immutable personality syndrome, authoritarianism, which frames relations for the rest of the person's life. It predisposes people to be prejudiced. Another personality explanation has been proposed by Rokeach (1948), who argues that some people, for whatever reason, have a general cognitive style that is rigid and dogmatic. These people are predisposed to be prejudiced because they strive for a rigidly stratified social world, are resistant to belief change in the light of contradictory evidence, and are inclined to ground their beliefs in authority and orthodox belief systems.

An individual differences explanation of prejudice, called **social dominance theory**, has been proposed by Pratto *et al.* (1994). They describe a relatively sophisticated, but nonetheless 'individual differences', analysis of exploitative power-based intergroup relations. People who desire their own group to be dominant and superior to out-groups have a high social dominance orientation that encourages them to reject egalitarian ideologies, and to accept myths that legitimise hierarchy and discrimination. These kinds of people are more inclined to be prejudiced than are people who have a low social dominance orientation.

Critics of personality and individual differences explanations of prejudice (Pettigrew, 1958; Billig, 1976) note that prejudice is not a sporadic individual matter, but rather it is a collective behaviour engaged in by large numbers of people in a relatively coordinated and highly targeted manner. They also provide evidence that personality is actually a poor predictor of prejudice, and that the nature of intergroup relations is a better predictor. In general, most social psychologists now believe that prejudice is a part of intergroup behaviour and therefore needs to be understood as part of a theory of intergroup behaviour. Although prejudice, stereotypes and discrimination are expressed by individuals, they are genuinely intergroup phenomena: individuals are prejudiced because they belong to groups that have developed certain relations with one another that are characterised by unequal status and advantage, and by conflict and hatred (Brown, 1995).

Cognitive processes in prejudice

We have already see one way in which cognitive processes are involved in prejudice – the categorisation of people into in- and out-group seems to lay the groundwork for intergroup behaviour and possible prejudice. It may do this because it affects self-conception: it encourages people to view themselves as group members and think of themselves in terms of social identity, which can be considered a type of self-schema. Social categorisation causes people to view out-group members in terms of stereotypes, and to behave in ways that favour the in-group and maintain the distinctiveness of in-group identity.

Another cognitive process that is involved in stereotyping and prejudice is illusory correlation. The availability heuristic involves people assuming that distinctive, easily imagined items occur more frequently (see Chapter 15). This phenomenon probably explains why people overestimate the rate of violent crime (because an act of violence is a frightening, distinctive event) and overestimate the relative numbers of violent crimes committed by members of minority groups (because members of minority groups tend to be more conspicuous). This tendency is an example of an **illusory correlation** – the perception of an apparent relation between two distinctive elements that does not actually exist or is enormously exaggerated (Hamilton and Gifford, 1976).

Another fallacy that promotes stereotyping is the **illusion of out-group homogeneity**. People tend to assume that members of other groups are much more similar than are members of their own group (Linville, 1982). This tendency is even seen between the sexes: women tend to perceive men as being more alike than women are, and men do the opposite (Park and Rothbart, 1982). The same is true for young people and old people (Linville *et al.*, 1989). However, this effect can sometimes be reversed so that people think their own group is more homogeneous than the out-group. Simon and Brown (1987) suggest that one situation in which this can happen is when the in-group is a minority group in terms of status. The reason for this is that solidarity and thus homogeneity may have a special value for minorities.

Stigma and disadvantage

One of the principal problems with prejudice is that it stigmatises and disadvantages entire groups of people: 'Stigmatised individuals possess (or are believed to possess) some attribute, or characteristic, that conveys a social identity that is devalued in a particular social context' (Crocker *et al.*, 1998, p. 505). The targets of prejudice and discrimination are members of stigmatised groups, and thus they are stigmatised individuals. Stigma persists for a number of reasons. This is discussed in Chapter 18 in the context of people's attitudes towards individuals with mental illness.

An fMRI study of stigma found that our unstated prejudices might be revealed by our brain activation. Krendl *et al.* (2006) asked 22 men to make explicit (do you like this person?) or implicit (is this a man or a woman?) judgements about people with well-established stigma (obesity, unattractiveness, transsexuality, etc.). Areas of the brain normally activated by negative emotional stimuli, as well as regions involved in

Cutting edge: An accent on accents

The way people speak affects how we behave towards them and think about them. Accents, whether regional or national, activate a store of stereotypes that may or not be accurate. We do not expect the Queen to sound like a cockney.

We also identify more with people whose accents are similar to our own: Bestelmeyer *et al.* (2014) asked Scottish and English students to listen to the voices of people with English, Scottish and American accents who spoke number sequences (1-4-2-9, etc.). As they did this, fMRI measured brain activation. They found that distinct patterns of brain activation were found when people listened to people with accents similar to theirs. When people heard their own accent, activation was found in the amygdala bilaterally, the right rolandic operculum and anterior cingulate cortex. Listening to different accents was associated with reductions in these areas. Perhaps this own-accent bias reflects a greater emotional connection to the sound, hence the activation in these areas.

Other accents may signify so-called class or competence or affect the credibility of the speaker. A study from the University of Chicago asked native American English speakers to assess the truthfulness of innocuous statements made by people with mild or strong accents (Lev-Ari and Keysar, 2010). Mild accents were Polish, Turkish and German; strong accents were Italian, Korean and (very accented) Turkish. Mild and strong versions were included to examine whether accent affected the difficulty of being understood. Statements included: 'Ants don't sleep'.

Native English speakers were less likely to believe statements that were spoken in a non-native accent. When the accent was brought to their attention as a possible source of bias, the effect disappeared for mild accents but remained for strong ones. Thus, accent, the authors conclude, 'might reduce the credibility of non-native job seekers, eyewitnesses, reporters and news anchors'.

---

control and inhibition, were activated. However, when the most negatively perceived faces were judged in the implicit condition, activation was much greater in the amygdala and prefrontal cortex (PFC). Perhaps as one increased (in the amygdala), the other area responded to inhibit its activation.

A relatively positive sense of self can be gained by comparing others unfavourably with oneself. Stigma can legitimise inequalities of status and resource distribution that favour a dominant group – such groups are certainly going to ensure that the stigma remains in place, because it serves a system justification function (Jost and Hunyadi, 2002). Finally, people may need to stigmatise groups that have different world views from their own, because if one did not degrade and discredit out-groups in this way then the frail sense of certainty in, and controllability of, life that one gains from one's own world view would be shattered (Solomon *et al.*, 1991).

Members of stigmatised groups can experience **attributional ambiguity**. They can continually read prejudice and discrimination into innocuous behaviours and even into behaviours favouring them: Was I served first at the bar because I am black and the bartender was trying to conceal her hidden prejudice? Members of stigmatised groups can also suffer depressed self-esteem, self-worth and efficacy that can reduce motivation. For example, because stigmatised groups know exactly the negative stereotypes that others have of them, they experience stereotype threat. Stigmatised individuals are aware that others may judge and treat them stereotypically, and thus, on tasks that really matter to them, they worry that through their behaviour they may even confirm the stereotypes.

Although some stigmatised individuals are vulnerable to low self-esteem, diminished life satisfaction and, in some cases, depression, most members of stigmatised groups are able to weather the assaults and maintain a positive self-image (Crocker and Major, 1989). There are many ways in which people can do this. One way is to deny personal disadvantage. For instance, Crosby (1982) has identified the 'paradox of the contented female worker'. Women workers compare their salaries and working conditions with those of other women, which narrows the potential for recognising much larger sex-based inequalities in pay and conditions (Major, 1994).

Stereotype threat

Why do some groups in society underperform in particular areas – for example, academic underachievement of African-Americans, and mathematical and scientific underachievement of women? Coining the term 'stereotype threat', Steele and his colleagues argued that underachievement is a psychological response to stereotypes that characterise one's in-group (e.g. women) as inferior to a relevant outgroup (men) on a specific task (maths) in a specific domain (school) (Steele *et al.*, 2002). The negative stereotype is a cognitive and emotional burden that impedes performance and paradoxically actually produces an effect consistent with the negative expectation. Stereotype threat has two repercussions: anxiety about confirming the stereotype and thus being judged as possessing the negative attribute, and disengagement with the task and the domain. These two effects lead to underachievement (Steele, 1997; Aronson *et al.*, 1999).

Much of the original research had been conducted with African-American students in the American schooling system. For example, African-American students have been found to perform less well than their white counterparts in testing situations where negative stereotypes about African-Americans were made relevant (Steele and Aronson, 1995). This may be due to the potential recognition that failure could confirm a negative stereotype of their in-group (and, by extension, the self). The stereotype threat effect has been investigated with different stigmatised groups and in several domains including white men's maths ability when compared to Asian-American men (traditionally associated with higher maths ability; Aronson *et al.*, 1999) and children from low socio-economic backgrounds in academic testing situations (Croizet and Claire, 1998).

A principal aim of social psychological research into stereotype threat has been to discover what psychological variables (at both the social and individual levels) affect individuals' vulnerability to this effect. Some basic processes and issues have been identified, for example:

1 *Domain identification.* Stereotype threat only occurs in individuals for whom performing well in a given domain is important (Steele, 1997). Aronson *et al.* (1999) measured white male students' identification with maths and then asked them to complete a maths test either in the context of the stereotype that Asians are superior at maths (stereotype threat condition) or not (control condition). Performance on the maths test was significantly worse in the stereotype threat condition, but only for participants who identified highly with the maths domain (even when controlling for previous standardised aptitude test (SAT) scores). Interestingly, this study not only provides evidence for domain-specific identification but also demonstrates that stereotype threat can affect traditionally non-stigmatised groups (American white male students).

2 *Cognitive load.* It is possible that the stereotype threat effect is more pronounced when people are under high cognitive load as there is an extra pressure to disconfirm negative stereotypes. Spencer *et al.* (1999) examined this possibility in two experimental studies of high-achieving male and female American university students. Women are believed to experience stereotype threat in maths-related domains. Participants in the first study did a maths test that was either easy or difficult. There was no difference in the performance of male and female students on the easy test, but females performed significantly worse on the difficult test. The increased cognitive load of stereotype threat impeded performance on a task that also demanded greater cognitive capacity. In a second study, Spencer *et al.* showed that this gender difference in performance on the difficult test was accentuated when the test was explicitly introduced in terms of gender differences in maths ability. This finding lends further credibility to the idea that performance differences do indeed result from stereotype threat rather than from real differences between males' and females' maths ability.

3 *Self-categorisation with the stereotyped group.* Research suggests that priming the social identity of the stigmatised group will automatically prime the negative stereotype and in turn affect performance in a stereotype-consistent manner. One study clearly demonstrates this effect in the maths performance of Asian-American women (Shih *et al.*, 1999). In contrast to the negative connotations of being female in the maths domain, Shih *et al.* reasoned that Asian-American identity is associated with a positive stereotype of maths ability. Indeed, female Asian-Americans who were primed with their Asian-American identity significantly outperformed participants who were primed instead with their gender identity ('women').

4 *Individual level of identification with the stereotyped group.* Schmader (2002) demonstrated that the degree to which a person identifies with a relevant category also affects how strongly the stereotype influences their performance. White American students completed a maths test in either a gender-relevant domain or a gender-irrelevant domain. In the gender-irrelevant domain there was no difference between men's and women's performances on the test. However, in the gender-relevant domain, only the female participants who identified highly with their gender underperformed compared with males. Thus, vulnerability to stereotype threat seems to depend on whether people see themselves as representative of the stereotyped category.

Given the deleterious consequences of stereotype threat, is it possible to train people to combat or overcome stereotype threat? Aronson *et al.* (2002) conducted an intervention study to trial a method of helping students resist their responses to stereotype threat. African-American and Caucasian male and female undergraduates participated in a laboratory study ostensibly concerning a pen-pal mentoring system for younger students. They were randomly divided into three groups. A battery of attitude change techniques were used to teach them and help them internalise the idea that intelligence is malleable (intervention-specific group) or that people have different intelligence orientations (intervention-only group – in case intervention alone boosts performance). The third group was a no-intervention control. The results showed that several weeks after the lab session the students in the intervention-specific group (where the negative stereotype was challenged) reported greater academic identification and enjoyment and higher grades compared with the other intervention style and the control group. This was particularly the case for African-American students whose academic performance and identification were depressed as a reaction to stereotype threat in the other conditions. It is interesting to note that there were no differences between groups on stereotype threat scores per se, suggesting that the specific intervention changed the participants' responses to stereotype threat and not their perceptions of it.

Stereotype threat – an evaluation

If a male superiority stereotype is triggered by prefacing a maths test with 'men are better in mathematics', girls and women will perform worse at the test than if they were presented with the test without this priming (Spencer *et al.*, 1999). However, whether an actual sex difference in maths performance exists, regardless of stereotype threat, is unclear. Lindberg *et al.* (2010), for example, found no difference between the sexes in studies published between 1990 and 2007. However, a study of 20,000 children in the US found an advantage of boys in every area of maths (Fryer and Levitt, 2010).

Since the Spencer *et al.* study was published, over 100 studies of stereotype threat and sex differences have been published. A meta-analysis published in 2012 (Stoet and Geary, 2012) found that only 55 per cent of studies replicated the original result but concluded that half of this 55 per cent was affected by confounds (such as pre-existing maths competence). Of those studies without confounds, only 30 per cent replicated the original finding. Ganley *et al.*'s (2013) studies of 931 children and adolescents found no effect of implicit or explicit stereotyping on maths performance. In two of their three studies, sex differences in maths achievement existed regardless of stereotype priming. Similarly, negative findings have been reported by Finnigan and Corker (2016) in a study of 590 women aged between 18 and 60.

A recent meta-analysis limited studies to those which included girls, included children under 18, employed quasi-experimental designs, the dependent variable was known to have an advantage favouring boys (maths, science, spatial skills), and the threat condition was part of a between-subjects design (Flore and Wicherts, 2015). Of 972 papers, 26 met the inclusion criteria. The analysis found evidence of stereotype threat but also of publication bias – although the effect was found (and this was small), the results were excessive for the number of studies reported. That is, journals had favoured positive findings and rejected studies with negative ones.

These data are important because a lot of work and research has been invested in reducing the effect of stereotype threat. For example, exercises in self-affirmation which ask people to write about their meaningful personal values (friends, family, interests, etc.) have been used to try and minimise the evocation of the stress, vigilance, disengagement and poorer academic performance associated with the activation of negative stereotype. These reflective exercises have been used with African American and Hispanic middle school children, and with women on university physics courses (Hanselman *et al.*, 2014, 2016). The effects of this intervention are mixed (Sherman *et al.*, 2013; Shnabel *et al.*, 2013; Tibbetts *et al.*, 2016). The original study reporting beneficial effects of self-affirmation was published in 2006 (Cohen *et al.*, 2006). Borman *et al.* (2016) published the first successful replication of the self-affirmation effect by finding significant effects on black and Hispanic seventh-grade students' grade point average – the GPA is the average of students' academic grades in US colleges.

However, in a large study of two cohorts ($N = 939$; $N = 1170$) from backgrounds similar to those reporting the positive results described above, no significant effects of self-affirmation were found (Hanselman *et al.*, 2016). Other studies have also found negative results (Protzko and Aronson, 2016). This suggests that the intervention might not be as robust as originally thought.

Modern forms of prejudice

Prejudice can express itself in many different ways. We are all familiar with what has been called old-fashioned prejudice – name-calling, abuse, persecution, assault and discrimination. This kind of expression of prejudice is now illegal and socially censured in all Western democratic societies, and so it is rarely encountered. Not surprisingly, research on racism in the US shows a dramatic reduction in expressed anti-black attitudes since the 1930s (Devine and Elliot, 1995).

However, it may not be so much that prejudice is vanishing but that it is changing its form. This new form of prejudice (the research focuses mainly on racism) has a number of different names – aversive racism, modern racism, symbolic racism, regressive racism or ambivalent racism (Gaertner and Dovidio, 1986; Hilton and von Hippel, 1996). However, the general idea is that people now experience a conflict between deep-seated emotional antipathy towards racial out-groups, and modern egalitarian values that exert pressure to behave in a non-prejudiced manner. The resolution of this conflict, which produces **modern racism** or subtle forms of racism, is achieved by avoidance and denial of racism – separate lives, avoidance of the topic of race, denial of being prejudiced, denial of racial disadvantage, and thus opposition to affirmative action or other measures to address racial disadvantage. Although this analysis is mainly focused on racism in the US, it can also apply to sexism (Swim *et al.*, 1995) and to racial attitudes in Europe (Pettigrew and Meertens, 1995).

Modern forms of prejudice can, by definition, be very difficult to detect, because people try to conceal their prejudices. To detect prejudice, researchers need to be ingenious in designing unobtrusive and indirect measures. Many different methods have been devised (Crosby *et al.*, 1980). For example, social cognition research shows that stereotypes can be automatically generated by categorisation, and categorisation can automatically arise from category primes (an accent, a face, a costume) (Bargh, 1989).

Another powerful unobtrusive measure of prejudice is to analyse the subtext of what people say. Racism can very subtly and quite unintentionally be embedded in the words we use, the way we express ourselves, and the way we communicate with and about racial out-groups (Potter and Wetherell, 1987; Edwards, 1997). For example, van Dijk (1987) found evidence of prejudice from a detailed analysis of spontaneous everyday talk among whites in the Netherlands and in southern California about other races (blacks, East Indians, North Africans, Hispanics, Asians). One hundred and eighty free-format interviews conducted between 1980 and 1985 were qualitatively analysed to show how racism is embedded in and reproduced by everyday discourse. People can use particular forms of language to communicate their prejudiced attitudes in ways that disarm the charge of being a racist. A common example is the disclaimer 'I'm not racist, but . . . ' that can precede a clearly racist comment.

A more cognitive index of language and prejudice is the **linguistic intergroup bias** effect (Maass, 1999). Maass discovered that people tend to use concrete language that simply describes events when talking about positive out-group (and negative in-group) characteristics, but use much more general and abstract terms that relate to enduring traits when talking about negative out-group (and positive in-group) characteristics. In this way we can detect negative out-group attitudes: people start to become abstract and general when talking about their prejudices.

Can we reduce prejudice?

How can prejudice and intergroup conflict be reduced? Research suggests that propaganda, public service advertising and formal education have a limited effect – these methods are effective in conveying official societal expectations, but then, of course, they fail if they are conducted against a background of powerful and entrenched day-to-day informal endorsement of prejudice. So, are there any techniques that work and, if so, how?

On a larger scale, a popular view about how to reduce prejudice is the **contact hypothesis**: if people from different races could just get to know one another through coming together to interact then prejudice would disappear (Allport, 1954). Although this idea has immediate appeal, and indeed it was part of the scientific justification for the racial desegregation of the American schooling system in the 1950s, it is fraught with problems. For intergroup contact to work, people have to come together for prolonged equal-status, meaningful interaction that is pleasant and capable of changing stereotypes of entire groups not just attitudes towards the individuals with whom one interacts. Contact can often produce interracial friendships, but it rarely changes racial stereotypes. More often than not, contact can confirm and accentuate intergroup perceptions and further entrench stereotypes. There is often so much anxiety associated with intergroup encounters that groups avoid contact or find contact unpleasant and attribute this to the out-group (Stephan and Stephan, 2000).

Nevertheless, contact between members of different groups may promote positive attitudes. Indeed, a recent statistical survey of 515 studies of the effects of contact concluded that, all things being equal, contact does promote more positive intergroup relationships (Pettigrew and Tropp, 2006).

Contact may foster good interpersonal relationships ('decategorisation' of group members; Brewer and Miller, 1984), or it may foster a sense of common membership in a superordinate ingroup ('recategorisation'; Gaertner et al., 1993), or it may allow the recognition of positive features of other groups while preserving a sense of in-group distinctiveness (mutual positive differentiation; Hewstone, 1996). Dovidio et al. (1997) asked sets of six participants to work first as two three-person groups. These groups then interacted and participants judged one another. Half of the participants were then encouraged to think of themselves as one larger (six-person) category. These recategorised participants were less likely to show evaluative preferences for their own sub-group, or to show a preference for self-disclosing to and helping members of their own sub-group.

Other research by Wright et al. (1997) has shown that that intergroup attitudes can improve if people witness or have knowledge of rewarding intergroup friendships between others – if my friend John has close out-group friends then maybe the out-group isn't quite as bad as I thought. Pettigrew (1998) concluded that friendship across group boundaries is an important way that contact allows people to learn about out-groups and to feel less anxious about future interaction with other members of these groups. This makes it more likely that people will generalise their positive feelings about an out-group friend to the out-group as a whole. Similar conclusions were reached by Brown and Hewstone (2005), who also emphasise the way that contact can influence emotions and feelings, and trust between groups, which in turn can promote more positive intergroup relationships.

Prejudices are intergroup psychological mechanisms for protecting and enhancing our self-image and our material well-being. Not surprisingly, threats to racial or cultural identity are unlikely to reduce prejudice. Thus, nations that try to assimilate ethnic minorities threaten those minorities and cause them to react to protect themselves, which in turn threatens the dominant majority and fuels prejudice. One strategy that does seem to help is pluralism or multiculturalism – a social policy that recognises cultural diversity within the confines of a common superordinate national identity (Hornsey and Hogg, 2000).

Many people are unaware of their stereotypes and preconceptions about members of other groups because (as noted in the social cognition section of Chapter 15) stereotypes are automatically linked to categories (Bargh, 1989). Although making people aware of their stereotypes can persuade people that their beliefs are unjustified, this can backfire if people then try too hard to suppress their stereotypes. In one study, participants were shown a picture of a skinhead and then wrote a passage about a day in the life of that person (Macrae et al., 1994). Half of the participants were instructed not to rely on stereotypes. Consistent with the instructions, participants in the no-stereotype condition used less stereotypical descriptions.

Next, participants were shown a picture of a second skinhead and were asked to write about a day in his life, but without suppression instructions. In this second stage, those who had been given the suppression instructions previously now showed a substantially increased use of stereotypical descriptions.

In a further experiment, compared with those in a control condition, participants who had first been in a suppress condition subsequently chose to sit further away from a chair they thought would be occupied by a skinhead. Macrae et al. reasoned that the effort involved in suppressing the stereotype actually makes the content of the stereotype more accessible. Thus, once a person is no longer actively suppressing the stereotype this content becomes 'hyperaccessible' (Wegner and Erber, 1992), resulting in a stereotype rebound effect (see also Plant and Devine, 2001).

Langer et al. (1985) gave a group of children specific training in thinking about the problems of people with disabilities. They thought about such problems as the ways that a person with disabilities might drive a car and the reasons why a blind person might make a good newscaster. After this training, they were found to be more willing to go on a picnic with a person with disabilities than were children who did not receive the training. They were also more likely to see the specific consequences of particular disabilities rather than to view people with disabilities as 'less fit'. For example, they were likely to choose a blind child as a partner in a game of pin the tail on the donkey because they realised that the child would be likely to perform even better than a sighted child. Thus, at the individual level, people can learn to recognise their biases and to overcome their prejudices.

Devine (1989) proposed that even when a person has knowledge of a stereotype that is automatically linked to a category membership, the explicit application of a stereotype is a controllable process. It seems that people who are high and people who are low in prejudice towards a particular group may both share the same knowledge of the stereotype but low-prejudiced people may suppress or control the stereotype. However, the connection between categorising a person and applying a stereotype turns out to be complex. Lepore and Brown (1997) found that white British people's stereotypes of West Indians were similar regardless of whether participants were high or low scorers on a measure of prejudice.

The important message from this research is that even though people may share knowledge of a stereotype, they apply the stereotype differently when a categorisation is activated. That is, high-prejudiced people seem more likely to apply the negative aspects of the stereotype automatically, whereas low-prejudiced people are more likely to apply the positive aspects of the stereotype automatically.

With practice, stereotypes can be overcome: that is, when people either choose to, or are requested to, resist stereotypes over a period of time, the automatic associations they make with a particular category can be altered (Kawakami et al., 2000). The question is: how do low-prejudiced people sustain their low levels of prejudice in the face of pervasive social stereotypes? Monteith et al. (2002) argue that low-prejudiced people are especially sensitive to 'cues for control'. In essence, when automatic stereotype activation results in a reaction that is inconsistent with the way we think we should respond, this results in a negative sense of self – a sense of guilt or unease. Over time, people learn that certain situational or other cues give advance warning that an undesired response is likely (e.g. if race is mentioned in a conversation you might be alerted to the possibility that you could say something prejudicial).

Monteith et al. argued that when low-prejudiced individuals see images of black people linked with stereotypical content (e.g. the statement 'this person spends a lot of time on the streets') this evokes guilt about the stereotypical association, and this in turn acts as a well-established cue for control.

In Monteith et al.'s research, participants who had completed measures of prejudice earlier in the year were asked to engage simultaneously in what they believed were two separate tasks. The first task was to decide whether pictures (of black and white people) had been presented before in the original format or as a mirror image. The second task was to decide what categories would best fit people described by a series of sentences (e.g. the description 'this person has to do a lot of reading' fits the category 'college student'). Monteith et al. reasoned that if a picture of a black person happened to be presented in conjunction with a black stereotype description then this would constitute a cue for control among low-prejudiced people. Indeed, when these participants were presented with this combination of stimuli their decision times slowed down, relative to trials when the same sentences were paired with white faces. In contrast, participants who were high in prejudice were not expected to try to control their reactions, and in fact they responded with equal speed regardless of whether the black stereotypical sentences were paired with white or black faces (see Figure 16.8).

But how is it that we sometimes make important errors when we make judgements about other people? Why do we have immediate, 'gut' reactions to people and events, and what are the advantages and pitfalls? If you were hired by an organisation to design and implement a strategy to reduce harmful ethnic prejudice among employees within the organisation, what would your strategy be?

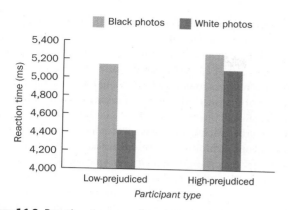

Figure 16.8 Reaction times as a function of race of photo and participant type.

Source: Based on Monteith, M.J., Ashburn-Nardo, L., Voils, C.I. and Czopp, A.M., Putting the brakes on prejudice: On the development and operation of cues for control. *Journal of Personality and Social Psychology,* 2002, 83, 1029–50.

Aggression and helping behaviour

Aggression

Human **aggression** is often considered to be an innate component of our biological inheritance, a behaviour that is a necessary part of the evolutionary process that ensures survival of the fittest (Lorenz, 1966). Chapter 13 described some of the basic functions of aggression. The ability to hurt others may well have these roots; however, social psychologists tend to be more interested in discovering situational factors that encourage or inhibit aggression and explain the huge diversity of human aggression (Baron and Richardson, 1994).

Many factors can cause aggression. When important goals are frustrated, people can feel angry and express this as aggression, particularly when there is an available target for aggression without fear of retaliation, and when the person who is frustrated has few other coping mechanisms available. According to social learning theory (Bandura, 1977), aggression can be learned by simply observing other people being reinforced for behaving aggressively. Aggression can also become more likely in a given situation if a person who has a tendency to respond aggressively is aroused, even if the arousal has nothing to do with anger (it could be arousal from a gym workout, a film, a sexual encounter).

Alcohol and aggression

Alcohol consumption is often associated with aggression. Research suggests that alcohol makes people more prone to social influence while at the same time less able to think through the consequences of their actions for themselves or others. Together this facilitates aggression when people drink in groups in societies that glorify aggression (Bushman and Cooper, 1990).

Causal links are complex. For example, perhaps aggressive people like to go drinking in groups, and they would be aggressive even if they had not been drinking? However, controlled studies have shown that people who had consumed alcohol were more likely to act aggressively when encouraged by a confederate than were those who had consumed a placebo.

Media violence and aggression

The question of whether watching film and television violence leads to or causes actual violence in the viewer is probably one of the most protracted in social psychology. Social learning theory makes the clear prediction that much of the aggression in our society is caused or amplified by excessive violence on television and in films. However, research is inconclusive about the causal links (Phillips, 1986) and the evidence is mixed. Some studies find increases following exposure to violent media, others find decreases and other find no effect (Ferguson, 2014). Perhaps aggressive people watch or pay more attention to media aggression, whereas non-aggressive people either do not watch media aggression or simply do not pay much attention to it.

Sometimes associations are made between a person's violent behaviour and the films they watch or games they play, while ignoring other variables that could have more likely led to the person's violent behaviour – an illusory correlation. The American Psychological Association published a specific policy statement in 2005 associating media violence with societal violence. The view is not unanimous – in 2013, 230 academics including criminologists and psychologists wrote an open letter to the APA rejecting its view and requesting it abandons its policy because they argue the evidence does not support it.

Similar arguments hold for the evidence that violent pornography is associated with more aggressive attitudes and behaviours towards women: perhaps misogynistic attitudes encourage men to view violent pornography rather than vice versa. Evidence comes from two sources: experimental studies in laboratories where the effects of exposure to violent visual (and it is usually visual) material on the viewer are observed; and from larger, broader, correlational studies which examine associations between societal violence (the number of murders, physical assaults) with the availability of violent media (TV, film, games). The latter has been criticised for lacking ecological validity and controlled to such an extent that drawing meaningful conclusions is difficult (Krahe *et al.,* 2011).

The former method has found that societal violence was correlated with the introduction of television in Canada, South Africa (where television was introduced in 1975) and the US (Centerwall, 1989). Studies of France, Germany, Italy and Japan noted no such correlation (Zimring and Hawkins, 1997). In one of the more naturalistic experiments, Charlton *et al.* (1998) monitored the incidence of playground violence and aggression in school children before and after the introduction of television on the island of St Helena. There was no increase in the children's aggression following the introduction of television.

The evidence suggests that societally, and at least in the United States (a democracy that legitimises the possession and use of firearms), violence in films correlated with homicide in the US in the mid-twentieth century. However, it was negatively correlated in the latter part of the twentieth century – fewer homicides were committed (Ferguson, 2014). In an intriguing study, Gosselt *et al.* (2015) examined Internet Movie Database synopses of 1,396 films over the period 1973–2011. They found that violence in films declined over the years and became less lethal. Men were more likely to be the perpetrator and the victim (80 per cent). The most common type of violence involved the use of firearms. One out of every 11 incidents of violence involved sexual violence against women; the figure was 1 in 250 for men.

Video game use, as you read in Chapter 8, has increased significantly in the past 10 years. Anderson *et al.* (2010) have argued that exposure to violent video games is associated with higher levels of aggressive behaviour, aggressive thinking, physiological arousal, lack of empathy and lower levels of pro-social behaviour, regardless of age or sex of the player. These effects are thought to be larger than the effects of TV and film violence (Polman *et al.*, 2008) but are also thought to be an overestimate because of publication bias – positive results are more likely to be published (Ferguson, 2007). When Ferguson (2014) examined young persons' violence rates and video game consumption between 1996 and 2011, he found no positive association between the two. He reported that increased consumption correlated with reduced violence.

Prosocial and helping behaviour

Aggression is generally regarded as antisocial and undesirable. The flip side of this kind of behaviour is prosocial behaviour and behaviour oriented towards helping others. Just as aggression may have an evolutionary dimension, so does prosocial behaviour – cooperative helping behaviour among people is the foundation of human endeavour, and so it would be expected that over millions of years predispositions to behave in this way would have a selective advantage (Wilson, 2004). But again, as with the study of aggression, social psychologists are more concerned to identify situational factors that encourage people to behave prosocially and to help other people.

Cooperation and social dilemmas

Despite the possibility of an evolutionary advantage to cooperative prosocial behaviour, people are remarkably uncooperative. One popular research paradigm involves the **prisoner's dilemma** (Rapoport, 1976). In one variant of this, two obviously guilty suspects are questioned separately by detectives who have only enough evidence to convict them of a lesser offence. The suspects are separately offered a chance to confess, knowing that if one confesses but the other does not, the confessor will be granted immunity and the confession will be used to convict the other of the more serious offence. If both confess, each will receive a moderate sentence. If neither confesses, each will receive a very light sentence. The prisoners are faced by a dilemma as to whether to trust one another in order to obtain the best joint pay-off. Although mutual non-confession produces the best joint outcome, mutual suspicion and lack of trust almost always encourage both to confess. This finding has been replicated in hundreds of prisoner's dilemma experiments, using a variety of experimental conditions and pay-off matrices (Dawes, 1991).

Many other **social dilemmas** involve a number of individuals or groups exploiting a limited resource (Kerr and Park, 2001) under conditions where, if everyone cooperates, an optimal solution for all is reached, but if everyone competes then everyone loses. These are called **commons dilemmas** because they are modelled on the 'tragedy of the commons'. English towns used to have common pasture on which people were free to graze their cattle. If all used it in moderation it would replenish itself and continually benefit them all. Imagine, however, 100 farmers surrounding a common that could support only 100 cows. If each grazed one cow, the common would be maximally utilised and minimally taxed. One farmer, however, might reason that if they grazed an additional cow, output would be doubled, minus a very small cost due to overgrazing – a cost borne equally by all 100 farmers. So this farmer adds a second cow. If all 100 farmers reasoned in this way they would rapidly destroy the common, thus producing the tragedy of the commons. The commons dilemma is an example of a replenishable resource dilemma. The commons is a renewable resource that will continually support many people provided that all people show restraint in 'harvesting' the resource. Many of the world's most pressing environmental and conservation problems are replenishable resource dilemmas – for example, rainforests and the world's population of ocean fish are renewable resources if harvested appropriately.

Another type of social dilemma is called a public goods dilemma. Public goods, such as public health, national parks, clean air and road networks, are provided for everyone. Because public goods are available to all, people are tempted to use them without contributing to their maintenance.

Experimental research on social dilemmas finds that when self-interest is pitted against the collective good, the usual outcome is competition and resource destruction even when appeals are made to cooperative and altruistic norms (Kerr, 1992). People can, however, act more cooperatively when they identify with the common good (Brewer and Kramer, 1986). In other words, when people derive their social identity from the entire group that has access to the resource, self-interest becomes subordinate to the common good (de Cremer and van Vugt, 1999). However, the same research indicates that when different groups, rather than individuals, have access to a public good, then the ensuing intergroup competition ensures ethnocentric actions which are far more destructive than mere self-interest. International competition over limited resources such as rainforests, whales and wetlands tragically accelerates their disappearance.

Another way in which social dilemmas can be resolved is by putting in place various structural solutions. These include a range of measures such as limiting the number of people accessing the resource (via permits), limiting the amount of the resource that people can take (via quotas), handing over management of the resource to an individual (a leader) or a single group, facilitating free communication among those accessing the resource, and shifting the pay-off to favour cooperation over competition. The problem with structural solutions is that they require an enlightened and powerful authority to implement measures, manage the bureaucracy and police violations. This can be hard to bring about (Rutte and Wilke, 1984).

Can the presence of a camera induce helpfulness? Van Rompay *et al.* (2009) recruited participants ostensibly to canvass their views of a Dutch bank. They were given a 'need for approval' scale to complete and then invited to an office at the researchers' university. In one office, there was a camera; in another, the camera was not present. After the participants had signed the informed consent form, the experimenter 'accidentally' dropped her papers. In the study, one of the questions participants answered was how willing they were to donate to charity. The remainder of items in the questionnaire were irrelevant. Thus, the researchers monitored public helpfulness (helping the researcher pick up her papers) and private helpfulness (degree of willingness to donate to charity).

People were more likely to help the experimenter pick up her papers when a camera was present than when not. There was no effect of the camera on private helpfulness – those in the camera condition were no more likely to donate more to charity than were those in the camera-absent condition. Furthermore, the tendency to help was greatest in those participants scoring high in need for approval.

Helping – such as giving to a charity – is also facilitated if the individuals requiring help are identified. This is called the 'identifiable victim effect' – people are more likely to give help if they are exposed to a single vivid example rather than an anonymous source deserving help. This is why many of the TV and media averts for charities that you see mention the name of the person (or animal) you would be hypothetically helping. People are more likely to give to orphans if they can see the orphans in photographs, rather than silhouette and people are more likely to give if these images induce positive, rather than negative affect (Genevsky *et al.*, 2013). When charity-giving behaviour in this study was examined using fMRI, one region – the nucleus accumbens – predicted the greater charity giving.

Other, useful donation-facilitating techniques include being specific in the amount of donation you want. In both real-life and laboratory-based studies, asking for a specific amount will lead to greater donations, to the needy and a willingness to give, that does simply asking for a donation (Hsee *et al.*, 2013).

Bystander intervention

People sometimes find themselves in a situation where they witness an emergency where someone needs their help. When are people most likely to help and why?

In 1964 in New York City, a woman named Kitty Genovese was chased and repeatedly stabbed by an assailant, who took 35 minutes to kill her. The woman's screams apparently went unheeded by at least 38 people who watched from their windows. No one, it seemed, tried to stop the attacker; no one even made a quick, anonymous telephone call to the police. When the bystanders were questioned later, they could not explain their inaction. 'I just don't know', they said.

As you can imagine, people were shocked by the bystanders' response to the Genovese murder. Commentators said that the apparent indifference of the bystanders demonstrated that American society, especially in urban areas, had become cold and apathetic. Experiments performed by social psychologists suggest that this explanation is wrong – people in cities are not generally indifferent to the needs of other people. The fact that Kitty Genovese's attack went unreported is not remarkable because 38 people were present; it is precisely because so many people were present that the attack was not reported. Recent research, however, including a detailed review of the case suggests that this picture is not as clear-cut as it has usually been portrayed in textbooks. The Controversies in Psychological Science section reveals some remarkable facts about the case and undermines some persistent myths.

Darley and Latané have extensively studied the phenomenon of **bystander intervention** – the actions of people witnessing a situation in which someone appears to require assistance. Their experiments have shown that in such situations the presence of other people who are doing nothing inhibits others from giving aid. For example, Darley and Latané (1968) staged an 'emergency' during a psychology experiment. Each participant participated in a discussion about personal problems associated with college life with one, two or five other people by means of an intercom. The experimenter explained that the participants would sit in individual rooms so that they would be anonymous and hence would be more likely to speak frankly. The experimenter would not listen in but would get their reactions later in a questionnaire. Actually, only one participant was present; the other voices were simply tape recordings. During the discussion, one of the people, who had previously said that he sometimes had seizures, apparently had one. His speech became incoherent and he stammered out a request for help.

Almost all participants left the room to help the victim when they were the only witness to the seizure. However, when there appeared to be other witnesses, the participants were much less likely to try to help. In addition, those who did try to help reacted more slowly if other people were thought to be present (see Figure 16.9).

Darley and Latané reported that the participants who did not respond were not indifferent to the plight of their fellow student. Indeed, when the experimenter entered the room, they usually appeared nervous and emotionally aroused, and they asked whether someone was helping the victim. The experimenters did not receive the impression that the participants had decided not to act; rather, they were still in conflict, trying to decide whether they should do something.

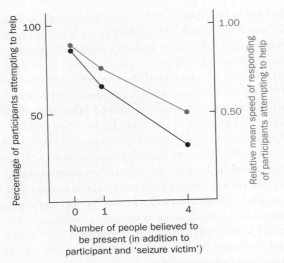

Figure 16.9 Bystander intervention. Percentage of participants attempting to help as a function of the number of other people the participants believed to be present.

Source: Based on data from Darley, J.M. and Latané, B., Bystander intervention in emergencies: Diffusion of responsibility. *Journal of Personality and Social Psychology*, 1968, 8, 377–83.

Thus, it seems that whether bystanders will intervene in a particular circumstance depends in part on how they perceive the situation. Latané and Darley (1970) have proposed a model describing a sequence of steps bystanders face when confronted with a potential emergency:

1 The event must come to their attention or be noticed.

2 They must assume some responsibility for helping the victim.

3 The possible courses of action must be considered and compared.

4 Finally, they must actually implement the chosen course of action.

Of course, this sequence takes place rapidly and without much awareness on the bystander's part, as is true of many situations to which we respond daily.

Unfortunately, at least from the perspective of the victim, obstacles may arise at any stage in this decision-making process, which make it unlikely that a bystander will intervene. In many cases, the bystander who is aware that others are available to help may not feel any personal responsibility to do so, a phenomenon called **diffusion of responsibility**. This factor is considered to be responsible for the finding that help is less likely to be offered when there are several bystanders present. In addition, the bystander may not feel competent to intervene or may be fearful of doing so; consequently, no action is taken. Shotland and Heinold (1985) staged an accident in which a person seemed to be bleeding. Bystanders who had received training in first-aid treatment were much more likely to come to the victim's aid, and they did so whether or not bystanders were present. Because they knew how to recognise an emergency and knew what to do, they were less likely to fear doing the wrong thing.

The last literature review of bystander intervention was conducted in 1981. An update was published by Fischer *et al.* (2011) who reviewed all studies from 1960 to 2010 which examined the determinants of intervening (a total of 7,700 participants). They found that people were found to be less likely to be bystanders if the situation was perceived as dangerous, if the perpetrators were present and the cost of intervening was physical rather than non-physical. The authors interpret their result in the context of an arousal – cost – reward model in which dangerous situations are recognised more quickly and are recognised as real emergencies and, therefore, increase arousal and helping. Bystanding was also attenuated when other bystanders provided physical support and if they were male and familiar. Bystanding also extends to children. Plotner *et al.* (2015) found that 5-year-old children were more likely to help an experimenter in need when the children were alone but not when they were with someone else.

Controversies in psychological science: What did Kitty Genovese's witnesses really witness?

The issue

The case of Kitty Genovese gave rise to a theory of social behaviour and intervention and sparked a series of now-famous experiments on the bystander effect, described in the text. Her murder was identified as a 'signal crime' – one that issued a warning about the breakdown in society's collective moral fabric (Innes, 2004). But was this research based on an enormous series of false premises? According to a review of the evidence by Manning *et al.* (2007), it was.

The evidence

These are the facts of Kitty Genovese's murder and the response to it:

In the early morning of 13 March 1964, Kitty Genovese was sexually assaulted and then murdered in the Kew Gardens district of Queens in New York. According to almost all textbooks you will read which report the case, 38 people witnessed the assault and murder at some point from a nearby building but did nothing to intervene or alert the police. Curiously, although the

Controversies in psychological science: *Continued*

case was reported in the local paper the next day, reference to the 38 witnesses only appeared in a newspaper, *The New York Times*, two weeks later, on 27 March – '38 who saw murder didn't call the police', the story boldly surmised and went on: 'Apathy at stabbing of Queens woman shocks inspector'.

However, research by a local historian and lawyer, Joseph de May Jnr, began to cast doubt on this interpretation. He found that:

- not all of the 38 alleged witnesses were eyewitnesses – some only heard noise from the assault;
- the police were called immediately;
- despite reports that witnesses had seen Kitty Genovese for 30 minutes, this was impossible because, given the geography and chronology of the assault, she could only have been visible for a few seconds;
- Kitty Genovese was still alive when the police arrived – she was not seen being murdered.

The story then becomes even more intriguing because no list of the 38 witnesses has ever been made available and the three witnesses in court said that their first glimpse of what transpired could not lead them to believe that what they were witnessing was a murder (Manning *et al.*, 2007). According to the District Attorney, only half a dozen people were found who saw something of relevance. None actually saw the stabbing and one reported shouting at the assailant. This scared him off. After this first attack, Kitty Genovese made her way around the corner of the building and tried to make her way to the entrance of her flat. She would have been out of sight of most witnesses. At the site of the second attack, the stairwell of 92–96 Austin Street, only one person could have seen what happened.

Despite reports to the contrary, some residents did try to contact the police. An affidavit sworn by a 15-year-old boy stated that his father called the police. At the appeal of the murderer in 1995, several of the residents stated that they had tried to call the police but were unsuccessful. There was no '911' service at that time and calls to the local police station were not always welcome. There were regular reports of trouble at a nearby bar and police found the constant aggravation troublesome. This bar had closed earlier than usual on the night of Genovese's murder. One resident was even reported to have telephoned another resident, called the police and went to Genovese's side.

Conclusion

What does this curious collection of facts demonstrate? First, it clearly demonstrates that you should never believe what you read in the papers. The hoo-ha over the YK2 Millennium Bug and other spurious fears, many of which are detailed in Nick Davies's Flat Earth News (2008) (see also the Controversies in Psychological Science section in Chapter 2), provides further evidence in support of the recommendation. Misreporting, however, is alive and well. Recall the supposition, guesswork, accusations and rumour that surrounded Portugal resident Robert Murat and the media's assumption of his involvement in the disappearance of Madeleine McCann in 2007 and the hounding of Christopher Jefferies over the murder of his tenant, Joanne Yeates. Second, far from sounding the death knell of the responsible citizen and the intervening bystander, it appears to show that citizen intervention was in reasonably good health.

The case of Kitty Genovese may, in Manning *et al.*'s words, be 'a stubborn and intractable urban myth'. It illustrates explicitly the value of evaluating everything you read, including this CiPS section.

Attraction and relationships

One of the most pervasive and immediate aspects of social life is our interpersonal relationships. It is, therefore, no accident that soap operas and celebrity magazines have a huge following, and they focus almost exclusively on close relationships – friendships, enmities, family life, romance, and so forth. For most of us, much of our day-to-day happiness or misery rests on how our personal relationships are faring.

Interpersonal attraction

One of the key features of our interpersonal relationships is whether we like someone or not, and whether they like us – **interpersonal attraction**. Many factors determine interpersonal

attraction. Some factors are characteristics of the individuals themselves; others are determined by the socially reinforcing aspects of the environment. Interpersonal attraction is an important aspect of more enduring and closer relationships, such as friendships; however, the bases of attraction can change as one moves through different stages of a relationship (Duck, 1992). Physical appearance and attitudinal similarity can be very important in the initial stages of a relationship, whereas deeper personality similarities and complementarities of needs may become more important later on.

Physical appearance

Despite such maxims as 'Beauty is in the eye of the beholder', 'Never judge a book by its cover' and 'Beauty is only skin-deep', research confirms that we tend to like physically attractive people more than physically less attractive people

(Langlois *et al.*, 2000). Social reinforcement provides a likely explanation for this phenomenon. Someone who is seen in the company of an attractive person and is obviously favoured by this person is likely to be well regarded by other people.

Walster *et al.* (1966) studied the effects of physical appearance at a dance at which university students were paired by a computer. Midway through the evening, the experimenters asked the participants to rate the attraction they felt towards their partners and to say whether they thought they would like to see them in the future. For both sexes, the only characteristic that correlated with attraction was physical appearance. Intelligence, grades and personality variables had no significant effect.

When people first meet someone who is good-looking, they rate the person as probably holding attitudes similar to their own and tend to assume that they have a good personality, a successful marriage and high occupational status (Dion *et al.*, 1972). They are received as healthier, more intelligent, and as more successful daters. In fact, physically attractive people usually do possess many of these characteristics, probably because they receive favourable treatment from society (Hatfield and Sprecher, 1986). People think that attractiveness is important – the percentage of people undergoing Botox or facial plastic surgery doubled between 2001 and 2007 (Bobadilla *et al.*, 2013).

We also tend to rate the group we belong to as being much more attractive than if we rated each individual member of the group for attractiveness and averaged this rating. This is what van Osch *et al.* (2015) found. But why? They examined two explanations, one of which was selective attention – people selectively attend to the most attractive members of the group and this perception affects their overall judgement about the attractiveness of the group. People also spend less time looking at the least attractive members of a group so, perhaps, the more attractive members become more salient when making group attractiveness judgements. The researchers found that this group attractiveness effect was robust – it was found across four studies.

Proximity

Not surprisingly, the mere physical proximity of one person to another is a potent facilitator of attraction (Sprecher, 1998). Festinger *et al.* (1950) found that the likelihood of friendships between people who lived in an apartment house was related to the distance between the apartments in which they lived: the closer the apartments, the more likely the friendship was. People were also unlikely to have friends who lived on a different floor unless their apartments were next to a stairway, where they would meet people going up or down the stairs.

Proximity enhances familiarity, and familiarity has been shown to increase liking. We tend to grow to like things that become familiar to us over repeated exposure. Repetition generally increases our preference for a stimulus. This

phenomenon applies to people as well. Even in the brief time it takes to participate in an experiment, familiarity affects interpersonal attraction. Saegert *et al.* (1973) had female university students participate in an experiment supposedly involving the sense of taste. Groups of two students (all were participants; no confederates this time) entered booths, where they tasted and rated various liquids. The movements of the participants from booth to booth were choreographed so that pairs of women were together from zero to ten times. Afterwards, the participants rated their attraction to each of the other people in the experiment. The amount of attraction the participants felt towards a given person was directly related to the number of interactions they had had – the more interactions, the more attracted they were to those persons (see Figure 16.10). And as you saw in Chapter 13, those who smile more are liked more.

Whether our attraction increases with an increase in geographical distance – absence making the heart grow fonder – has been studied. According to Construal-level theory (Trope and Liberman, 2010), our mental representations of people become more abstract and high level, the less close to us psychologically they are. When the distance is reduced, people's thoughts become more concrete, more detailed and refer more to situations. Using this as their starting point, Park *et al.* (2015) hypothesised that the more distant people were from others, then the greater the emphasis on describing others in terms of abstract trait (positive and negative). They found that men were more likely to rate women who were spatially distant to them as more attractive if they were higher in intelligence than themselves, rather than lower. They were more likely to

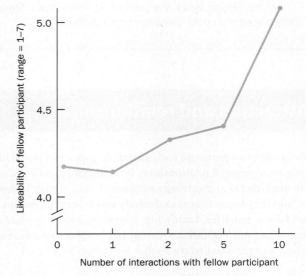

Figure 16.10 Familiarity, exposure and attraction. The rated likeability of a fellow participant as a function of number of interactions.

Source: Based on data from Saegert, S.C., Swap, W. and Zajonc, R.B., Exposure, context, and interpersonal attraction. *Journal of Personality and Social Psychology*, 1973, 25, 234–42.

want to interact with the woman and develop a romantic interest. When men interacted with a woman who was spatially near (face-to-face), they regarded a more intelligent woman as less attractive and showed less interest in going on a date with her. When the results from the six studies were analysed together, one finding emerged: men were more likely to find a spatially distant woman more attractive if she outperformed them in intelligence.

In 1989, Kenrick *et al.* (1989) published a controversial study in which they found that men who were in committed relationships rated their partner as being less sexually attractive and loved them less after seeing nude images (e.g. from *Playboy* and *Penthouse*) of a person of the opposite sex than did people who saw images of abstract art. Only men in the study responded in this way, not women. The researchers suggest that men make direct comparisons between the models and their partners and view the models as potential partners. But, like many exciting findings in social psychology, the effect either seems to be weak, non-existent or a Type 1 error.

Balzarini *et al.* (2016) conducted three replications of the original study and conducted a meta-analysis of the data in the original and new studies. The effect was not found. What is more, some slightly different results were found. In the original study, men and women found the erotic images to be more attractive than abstract art. In the replication, men rated the nudes as more pleasant and the women rated them as less pleasant.

Reciprocity

Liking follows the reciprocity principle – we tend to like those who like us. Dittes and Kelley (1956) led students in small discussion groups to believe, by way of anonymous written evaluations (actually written by the experimenters), that other group members either liked or disliked them. Results showed that students who believed they were liked were more attracted to the group than were those who believed they were disliked. More recently, Sprecher (1998) found reciprocal liking to be one of the major determinants of interpersonal attraction.

However, people with low or high self-esteem respond differently. People with high self-esteem base their liking for others less strongly than do people with low self-esteem on whether other people like them. In addition, we tend to like others who grow to like us, and dislike those who initially like us and then cool off on us – this is called the **gain–loss hypothesis** (Aronson and Linder, 1965). There are two possible explanations for this effect. When rejection changes to acceptance, the anxiety over rejection is reduced so that we experience the pleasure of being liked. Alternatively, it is possible that we regard those who like us from the beginning as undiscriminating, and this reduces the value of their praise. Those who dislike us to begin with but then re-evaluate as they get to know us better are discerning people, so their praise is worth more.

Similarity and need complementarity

Another factor that influences interpersonal attraction is similarity – similarity in looks, interests and attitudes. Couples tend to be similar in attractiveness. In fact, couples who are mismatched in this respect are the most likely to break up (White, 1980). Although we might think that people would seek the most attractive partners that they could find, people tend to fear rejection and ridicule. Men especially tend to be afraid of approaching attractive women for this reason (Bernstein *et al.*, 1983).

Couples (and groups of friends) also tend to hold similar opinions. Presumably, a person who shares our opinions is likely to approve of us when we express them. Also, having friends who have similar opinions guarantees that our

Cutting edge: Risky business and exposure to erotica

We have all, at some point, behaved rather differently (and for various reasons) in front of a member of the opposite sex, but one study suggests that our risk-taking behaviour is affected by exposure to a member of the opposite sex. McAlvanah (2009) showed participants photographs of members of the same or different sex, before and after participants made a series of decisions about gambling outcomes. Participants exposed to a member of the opposite sex took many more risky gambles than did the control group. Attractiveness did not affect gambling decisions.

Attractiveness was found to have an effect on behaviour in a different study of interaction between men and women (Straaten *et al.*, 2009). Participants were asked to interact with another person who was high and low in attractiveness. Observers rated the participants' interaction in terms of how improved their fluency became, how positively they presented themselves, how much positive affect they showed, etc. Men who rated themselves as similar in attractiveness to the confederate showed more of an increase in these behaviours – men low in attractiveness invested more in the interaction when meeting a confederate low in attractiveness, for example. Women's interaction was unrelated to the confederates' physical attractiveness.

opinions are likely to find a consensus; we will not often find ourselves in the unpleasant position of saying something that invites disapproval from other people. Byrne (1971) confirmed, in a series of laboratory experiments, the important role of attitude similarity in relationships. The results were so reliable and consistent that Byrne formulated a 'law of attraction': attraction towards a person bears a linear relationship to the proportion of attitudes associated with the person. The more that other people agree with you, the more reinforcing they are and the greater your attraction to them. For example, if you suddenly discover that someone you are going out with likes the same obscure rock group as you, your liking for that person will suddenly increase.

Similarity of attitudes is not the only factor determining the strength of interpersonal attraction. Other kinds of similarity are also important, such as age, occupational status and ethnic background. Friends tend to have similar backgrounds as well as similar attitudes. In addition, liking can sometimes rest on dissimilarity. Winch (1958) suggested that under some circumstances, particularly in more developed relationships, people seek others who have different qualities from ourselves and who can thus best satisfy our needs – we pursue **need complementarity**.

Love

The relationships we have with others are generally marked by two different kinds of emotion: **liking**, a feeling of personal regard, intimacy and esteem towards another person, and **loving**, a combination of liking and a deep sense of attachment to another person. Loving someone does not necessarily entail romance. You may have several close friends whom you love dearly yet have no desire to be involved with romantically.

Romantic love, also called **passionate love**, is an emotionally intense desire for sexual union with another person (Hatfield, 1988). Feeling romantic love generally involves experiencing five closely intertwined elements: a desire for intimacy with another, feeling passion for that person, being preoccupied with thoughts of that person, developing feelings of emotional dependence on that person, and feeling wonderful if that person feels romantic love towards you and dejected if not.

'Falling in love' and 'being in love' are common expressions that people use to describe their passionate desires for one another. Passionate love may occur at almost any time during the life-cycle, although people involved in long-term cohabitation or marriages seem to experience a qualitatively different kind of love. The partners may still make passionate love to one another, but passion is no longer the defining characteristic of the relationship. This kind of love is called **companionate love** and is characterised by a deep, enduring affection and caring for another. Companionate love is also marked by a mutual sense of commitment, or a strong desire to maintain the relationship. How passionate love develops

into companionate love is an unanswered question, although it is likely that the sort of intimacy that punctuates romantic love is still a major force in the relationship. An important feature of intimacy is self-disclosure, or the ability to share deeply private feelings and thoughts with another. Indeed, part of loving another is feeling comfortable sharing deeply personal aspects of yourself with that person.

Sternberg (1988b) has developed a theory of how intimacy, passion and commitment may combine to produce liking and several different forms of love (see Table 16.2). According to this theory, liking involves only intimacy, infatuation involves only passion, and empty love involves only commitment. Combining any two of these elements produces still other kinds of love. Romantic love entails both intimacy and passion but no commitment. Companionate love entails both intimacy and commitment but no passion. Fatuous love (a kind of love marked by complacency in the relationship) entails both passion and commitment but no intimacy. The highest form of love, consummate love, contains all three elements.

Sternberg's theory is descriptive. It characterises different kinds of love but it does not explain the origins of love. What function has love served in the evolution of our species? The answer can be summed up very succinctly: procreation and child-rearing. Although love of any kind for another person is not a necessary requirement for sexual intercourse, a man and a woman who love each other passionately are more likely to have sex than are a man and a woman who do not. And if their union produces a child, then love serves another function – it increases the likelihood that both parents will share in the responsibilities of child-rearing. Our capacity for loving, then, contributes in very practical ways to the continued existence of our species.

Maintaining and ending relationships

Research on the maintenance of relationships has mainly dealt with heterosexual marriages in Western societies. Marital satisfaction seems to rest on companionate love and role

Table 16.2 Sternberg's theory of love

	Intimacy	Passion	Commitment
Non-love			
Liking	*****		
Infatuated love		*****	
Empty love		*****	
Romantic love	*****	*****	
Companionate love	*****		*****
Fatuous love		*****	*****
Consummate love	*****	*****	*****

Source: After Sternberg, R.J., *The Triangle of Love*, New York: Basic Books, 1988.

complementarity, coupled with a sense of security and a shared search for new excitements and stimulation.

Commitment, the desire or intention to continue in the relationship, is crucial. Highly committed partners have a greater chance of staying together (Adams and Jones, 1997), and the very idea of subjectively committing oneself to a relationship can be more important than the conditions that led to commitment (Berscheid and Reis, 1998). Commitment has also been linked to the level of marital satisfaction, pro-relationship behaviour and trust. Two longitudinal studies by Wieselquist *et al.* (1999) revealed that commitment-inspired acts, such as accommodation and willingness to sacrifice, are good indicators of someone's pro-relationship motives. This is a cyclical model: such acts in turn elicit the partner's trust and reciprocal commitment and subsequent dependence on the relationship.

Adams and Jones (1997) pinpointed three factors that contribute to an ongoing relationship: (1) personal dedication (positive attraction to a particular partner and relationship); (2) moral commitment (a sense of obligation, religious duty or social responsibility, as controlled by a person's values and moral principles); and (3) constraint commitment (factors that make it costly to leave a relationship, such as lack of attractive alternatives, and various social, financial or legal investments in the relationship). More informally, relationship maintenance depends on people's feelings that: (1) they want to continue the relationship; (2) they ought to continue it; (3) they must continue it.

The end of a relationship is heralded by four factors (Levinger, 1980): (1) a new life seems to be the only solution; (2) alternative partners are available; (3) there is an expectation that the relationship will fail; and (4) there is a lack of commitment to a continuing relationship. Rusbult and Zembrodt (1983) believe that once deterioration is identified, it can be responded to in any of four ways. A partner can take a passive stance and show loyalty by waiting for an improvement to occur, or neglect, by allowing the deterioration to continue. Alternatively, a partner can take an active stance and show 'voice' behaviour, by working at improving the relationship, or exit behaviour, by choosing to end the relationship.

Duck (1992) describes a **relationship dissolution model** of four phases that partners pass through when a break-up occurs. There is an intrapsychic phase that involves brooding and some needling of the partner. The next phase is the dyadic phase. The pair will discuss the relationship, identify problems and make attributions of blame. The third phase is the social phase. In saying that the relationship is near an end, the partners may negotiate with friends, both as a means of social support for an uncertain future and for reassurance of being right. The social network will probably take sides, pronounce on guilt and blame and, like a court, sanction the dissolution. The final grave-dressing phase involves elaborating an acceptable account of the relationship that preserves one's reputation for reliability in future relationships. This 'grave-dressing' activity seeks a socially acceptable version of the life and death of the relationship.

Attraction is usually seen as a positive thing, but to what extent is it likely to be an advantage or a problem if people within a workplace (classroom, office, military unit) are attracted to one another? How likely is this to happen, and why?

Chapter review

Social influence

- Compliance with a request can be strengthened by ingratiation, reciprocity, or making multiple requests to prepare the target for the focal request – foot-in-the-door, door-in-the-face, low-balling.
- People have a tendency to blindly obey orders from people in authority, even when the consequence of obedience is terrible suffering for others. Obedience drops dramatically when there is social support for disobedience.
- Social interaction, particularly when people are uncertain or are in need of social approval, produces group norms that subsequently regulate behaviour.

- People conform because they are unsure, in need of approval, or define themselves – their identity – in terms of a group that is defined by the norms.
- Although people usually conform to majorities, minorities can change attitudes and behaviour through a conversion process. To do this, minorities need to be internally consensual in repeatedly, but not dogmatically, promulgating the same message.

People in groups

- The presence of other people enhances the performance of a well-learned behaviour but interferes with the performance of complex or poorly learned behaviour.

- When a group of people must collectively perform a task, the effort of any one individual is usually less than we would predict had the individual attempted the task alone – a behaviour known as social loafing.
- Loafing is reduced among people who value their group and feel they must compensate for others' performances. It is also reduced when people feel more identifiable and when they feel the task is important.
- Groups often exist to make decisions. Effective group decision-making can be hampered by elements of the discussion leading to the decision. This can cause groups to make very extreme decisions (polarisation) or very bad decisions (groupthink).
- Groups often need to remember a great deal of information. One way to do this effectively is to have a transactive memory structure in which different individuals or different sub-groups are responsible for remembering different information, but all members of the group know who is responsible for what.
- Groups usually have leaders. Leadership effectiveness ultimately rests on whether the group perceives the leader as being legitimate, as having the requisite skills, as being a loyal and focal group member, and as having the appropriate relationships with followers.
- People in crowds can sometimes behave antisocially because they feel anonymous and not responsible for the consequences of their actions – they are de-individuated.
- Collective events can also change people's identities so that they identify with the identity of the crowd and conform strongly to group norms.

Intergroup relations and prejudice

- Intergroup relations exist whenever people belonging to one group interact collectively or individually with another group or its members in terms of their group identifications.
- Where groups have the same goal, but only one group can achieve the goal at the expense of the others, then intergroup relations become highly conflictual. Where groups have the same goal, but the goal can only be achieved by the groups working cooperatively together, intergroup relations are more harmonious.
- Where groups feel their goals are being frustrated by another group, or that they are deprived relative to another group, conflict and negative attitudes arise – the target is often a weaker scapegoat group.

- The framework of intergroup competition or hostility is also contained in the mere fact of the existence of different categories – in-groups and out-groups.
- Self-determination theory argues that when we make choices for ourselves and initiate behaviour proactively, we flourish. People who are autonomous have been found to express greater well-being, have more positive romantic relationships and perform better on tasks when they interact with others.
- People derive a sense of who they are – a social identity – from the groups they belong to, and thus they are prepared to protect these groups against other groups. Because groups define and evaluate one's identity, and thus self-concept, people strive to evaluate their groups more positively than other groups.
- Prejudice is an attitude, usually negative, towards a particular group. Its cognitive component is stereotypes, and its behavioural manifestation is discrimination.
- Stereotypes and prejudices may be strengthened because people inflate the co-occurrence of negative behaviours and distinctive groups, and also exaggerate the perceived homogeneity of out-groups.
- Some people may be more prejudiced than others, but generally we can all be prejudiced if the social conditions favour prejudice. Prejudice stigmatises and disadvantages other people, but prejudice can be difficult to detect where social norms and legislation outlaw blatant prejudice.
- Teaching people to think about members of other groups as individuals and to consider them in terms of their personal situations and characteristics can reduce prejudices and tendencies towards stereotyping.
- Although initially appealing, simply bringing different groups into contact with one another, so that they become familiar with one another, is not reliably effective in reducing prejudice.

Aggression and helping behaviour

- Arousal, frustration, disinhibition and elevated testosterone levels are all factors that can lead to human aggression.
- People can also learn to be aggressive by witnessing other people being reinforced for aggressive behaviour.
- Alcohol and media violence may also contribute to aggression.
- People often find it difficult to sacrifice their own personal short-term gains for long-term collective gains. This is the social dilemma that underpins many of the world's greatest environmental problems. Social dilemmas can be reduced

when people feel themselves part of a community or group that accesses a resource. Leadership, resource management and limited access to a resource can also help.

- People often fail to help in an emergency (called bystander apathy) if there are many other potential helpers available or if they feel they do not have the resources to help. Misperception of norms can sometimes inhibit people from offering assistance in an emergency.
- Bystander intervention is facilitated if there are only few bystanders present and if they feel they have the resources (time, ability and so forth) to help.

Attraction and relationships

- We tend to be attracted to others who think positively of us, who are similar to us, who are physically attractive, and who live, work or play near us.
- Sternberg's theory of love describes how the elements of intimacy, passion and commitment are involved in the different kinds of love.
- The course of a relationship is strongly influenced by the degree of commitment the partners have to the relationship.

Suggestions for further reading

Brown, R. and Paterson, J. (2016) Indirect contact and prejudice reduction: limits and possibilities. *Current Opinion in Psychology*, 11, 20–24.

Christoff, K. (2014) Dehumanization in organisational settings: Some scientific and ethical considerations. *Frontiers in Human Neuroscience*, 8, 748.

Haslam, S.A. and Reicher, S.D. (2017) 50 years of 'Obedience to Authority': From blind conformity to engaged followership. *Annual Review of Law and Social Science*, 13(1).

Kite, M.R., and Whitley, B.E. (2016) *The Psychology of Prejudice and Discrimination* (3rd edn). London: Routledge.

Krahe, B. (2013) *The Social Psychology of Aggression* (3rd edn). London: Psychology Press.

Journal of Social Issues, special issue (2014). Milgram at 50. Vol 70, no 3.

Lieberman, J.D., Krauss, D.A., Heen, M. and Sakiyama, M. (2016) The good, the bad, and the ugly: Professional perceptions of jury decision-making research practices. *Behavioral Sciences and the Law*, 34(4), 495–514.

Maio, G. and Haddock. G. (2015) *The Psychology of Attitudes and Attitude Change* (3rd edn). London: Sage.

Reynolds, K.J. and Klik, K.A. (2016) New developments in prejudice research: from its neural basis and impact on well-being to prejudice reduction. *Current Opinion in Psychology*, 11, 115–119.

Smith, J.R. and Haslam, A. (2017) *Social Psychology: Revisiting the Classic Studies* (2nd edn). London: Sage.

Swami, V. (2016) *Attraction Explained*. London: Routledge.
Some excellent items on interpersonal and group processes.

CHAPTER 17
Psychology and health

WHICH ARE THE MOST WORK-STRESSED CITIES IN THE UK?

According to a survey of 3,000 employees, undertaken by one company in 2018, the top ten was

- Cardiff
- Wolverhampton
- London
- Coventry
- Liverpool
- Oxford
- Leicester
- Brighton and Hove
- Southampton
- Edinburgh

According to this survey, 70 per cent of those working in Cardiff experienced work stress, followed by Wolverhampton (64 per cent) and London (59 per cent).

- What do you think might explain these results?

- Can we rely on the results?

- When was the study conducted and how were the respondents selected?

- What measure of stress was used?

- What is 'work stress'?

- What type of employees participated?

- Were any participants excluded?

WHAT YOU SHOULD BE ABLE TO DO AFTER READING CHAPTER 17

- Define health psychology.

- Describe some of the factors that can lead to (or prevent) overeating, cigarette smoking, sexually transmitted disease, alcohol use and physical inactivity.

- Evaluate the psychological strategies that have been employed to reduce ill health.

- Describe and understand the process of stress and its effects on the immune system.

- Define psychoneuroimmunology and understand its significance to health.

- Evaluate the role of personality and specific styles of behaving in the maintenance of health and ill health.

QUESTIONS TO THINK ABOUT

- What is health psychology and how does it differ from abnormal psychology?

- What illnesses can psychology help to prevent? How can it do this?

- How can people stop eating fatty food, smoking or be encouraged to take up physical exercise?

- What is the role of personality in the development or prevention of illness?

- What effect do stressors have on health and the immune system?

- Can public health education campaigns change behaviour? How would you design an effective one?

Try and find out some of the answers here: https://www.telegraph.co.uk/business/2018/02/26/revealed-stressed-city-uk-not-london/

Health psychology: a definition

The particular behaviours that make up an individual's way of life have important consequences for that individual's quality of life. Whether a person smokes, drinks alcohol, eats specific foods, exercises, has regular health checks and is susceptible to stress can all have an impact on a person's health and beliefs about their health. Such beliefs and behaviour are at the core of what health psychology seeks to understand. Health psychology is the branch of psychology that applies psychological principles to the understanding of health and illness. Factors influencing health can be external (in the form of stressors, health promotion, advertising of health-impairing products) or internal (in the form of thoughts, beliefs, decision-making and coping responses).

According to Matarazzo (1982), the aims of health psychology are to promote and maintain health, to prevent and treat illness, to identify the causes and symptoms of illness and the causes of health, and to analyse and improve healthcare systems/policy. It is a relatively new branch of psychology and, as its subject matter suggests, has a slight overlap with clinical psychology. Both health psychology and clinical psychology study stress and how people cope with it, but health psychology tends to concern itself with bodily illness whereas clinical psychology is primarily concerned with mental illness. (Clinical psychology is the subject of Chapter 18.) Many of the theories and explanations for health-related behaviour and experience derive from work in cognitive and social psychology. Because of this fusion of psychologies and because of the subject matter of health psychology, the sub-area was not regarded as a distinct branch of the discipline until relatively recently.

Health and ill health

The starting point for all health psychologists is the definition of health and the determinants of health. Health has been defined as 'a positive state of physical, mental and social well-being – not simply the absence of injury or disease – that varies over time along a continuum. At the wellness end of the continuum, health is the dominant state. At the other end of the continuum, the dominant state is illness or injury' (Sarafino and Smith (2014)). A healthy lifestyle is one that can enhance an individual's physical and mental well-being; an unhealthy lifestyle is one that diminishes physical and psychological well-being. According to Whitehead (1995), the determinants of good health can be conceived of in the way suggested in Figure 17.1.

In this model, the individual is at the centre and possesses immutable characteristics which can influence health (such as

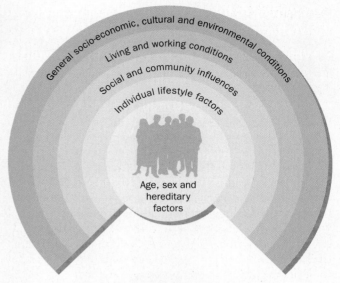

Figure 17.1 The types of factors which Whitehead suggests are contributors to health.

Source: Whitehead, M., Tackling health inequalities: An agenda for action. In M. Benzenal, K. Judge and M. Whitehead (eds) *Tackling Inequalities in Health: An agenda for action*, p. 23. London: King's Fund, 1995. © 1995 King's Fund. Reprinted by permission.

age, sex, race and, genetic make-up). Surrounding the individual are four interacting layers which represent external determinants of health. These include the individual's lifestyle, their social and community influences, living and working conditions and the general cultural and environmental conditions in which the individual lives.

Some specific examples of factors within each of these layers include nutrition, alcohol consumption, smoking, sexual behaviour and exercise. Health psychologists attempt to understand the factors which influence health and, if these factors are detrimental to health, apply psychological techniques in order to promote good health and discourage unhealthy behaviour. They are also involved in psychological aspects of healthcare and in determining the effects of government health policy on behaviour. The following sections evaluate the role of specific behaviours – eating, exercising, smoking, drinking alcohol and having unprotected sex – in health and illness.

Nutrition

Over the past 150 years or so, our diet has changed considerably: it is higher in fat and lower in fibre, largely because processed foods, fast food and sweets are high in fat and low in fibre. Diets too high in saturated fats (those fats found in animal products and a few vegetable oils) and too low in fibre have been associated with specific health disorders, such as **coronary heart disease (CHD)**, the narrowing of blood vessels that supply nutrients to the heart, and cancer, a malignant and intrusive tumour that destroys body organs and tissue (Cohen, 1987). CHD leads to 17.5 million deaths, according to the World Health Organization (WHO) and the WHO launched the 'Global Hearts' initiative in 2016 to combat the disease.

The chief culprit in CHD is **serum cholesterol**, a chemical that occurs naturally in the bloodstream where it serves as a detoxifier. Cholesterol is also the source of lipid membranes of cells and steroid hormones. It is a vital substance and we would die without it. Cholesterol has two important forms: HDL (high-density lipoprotein) and LDL (low-density lipoprotein). HDL is sometimes called 'good' cholesterol because high levels of it are inversely associated with CHD; it seems to play a protective role in the bloodstream. LDL is often called 'bad' cholesterol because high levels of it are associated with the formation of atherosclerotic plaques, which clog arteries. Fibre is an important dietary component because it helps to reduce LDL cholesterol levels (and aids digestion). People with pre-existing heart complaints are prescribed the cholesterol-reducing drugs, statins.

Of course, bad nutrition is different from malnutrition and the latter is more serious. According to the WHO and UNICEF, tens of millions of children under 5 years of age show signs of wasting/malnutrition, and the global pattern of stunting in children can be seen in Figure 17.2.

Heart disease and eating – explaining the French paradox

A paradox familiar to health researchers and gourmands alike is this: the French diet is laden with highly palatable saturated fat, and the nation's blood cholesterol level is high yet the incidence of death caused by heart disease is lower in France than it is in the US. Of course, a highly fatty diet may not necessarily lead to heart disease and there could be other explanations for the French paradox including genetic differences, metabolism, a less stressful life, differences in attitudes towards illness, different eating patterns, greater exercise and so on (Rozin, 1999).

The body mass index of French people tends to be significantly lower than that of Americans: they are leaner. One reason for the leanness, despite the content of the diet, may be that they actually eat less. Although the diet may appear superficially frightening in terms of its nutritional content, it is a diet of moderation, rather than excess.

To examine whether this could explain the French paradox, Paul Rozin and a group of researchers at the University of Pennsylvania, US, and CNRS in Paris, examined portion sizes in French and American fast-food restaurants (e.g. Pizza Hut, McDonald's, Hard Rock Café, Quick, Burger King and so on.), more upmarket restaurants (e.g. bistros) and supermarkets (Rozin *et al.*, 2003). The study took place in Pennsylvania and Paris. The portion sizes described in the cities' respective Zagat guide (a restaurant guide) were also compared.

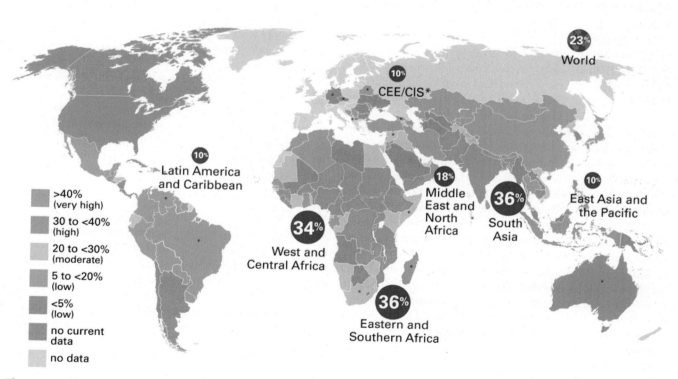

Figure 17.2 Geographical pattern of stunting in children under 5 years of age.
Source: World Health Organization, 2007.

When supermarket and restaurant foods were analysed, the French portions were indeed smaller. Of course, even small portions can be calorifically intense but the eating of many small, highly calorific portions does not appear to occur in the French diet. The French also spent more time eating than did the Americans suggesting that the eating experience for the French amounts to more than the ingestion of food: it is a social, cultural – possibly, emotional – experience.

Physical fitness

People in developed countries lead increasingly sedentary lives; our work has changed (it is less physical) as have our leisure opportunities (we can watch more television, surf the internet and play computer games). Like high-fat, low-fibre diets, lack of exercise is correlated with increased risk of CHD (Peters *et al.*, 1983; Powell *et al.*, 1987). People who exercise regularly appear to accumulate less body fat and to be less vulnerable to the negative effects of stress than are people who do not exercise regularly (J.D. Brown, 1991).

There is some evidence that people who engage in regular aerobic exercise are likely to live longer (Paffenbarger *et al.*, 1986). On average, those who exercised moderately (an equivalent of 20 miles running or walking per week) lived about two years longer than those who exercised less than the equivalent of five miles. The results have been replicated in a sample of elderly individuals. The relationship between the time that elderly (61–81 years old) non-smoking participants spent walking and the death rate was monitored over a period of 12 years (Hakim *et al.*, 1998). Men who walked more than two miles a day lived significantly longer than those who exercised less. Only 21.5 per cent of the two-mile walkers had died after 12 years, whereas 43 per cent had died in the group that undertook less exercise. Cancer and CHD were also lower in the walkers: this effect occurred even when other factors (such as blood pressure, alcohol consumption, medical condition and cholesterol level) had been taken into account. However, diet was not considered and there is the possibility that healthy eating may have been responsible for the reduced death rate. If a factor (such as walking or diet) can benefit health or make an individual less susceptible to illness or ill health, this factor is called a **protective factor**. In other words, this factor protects the individual from ill health. (Of course, it cannot prevent an illness, only protect a person from developing it.)

Although a brisk walk is often recommended to those who are not as agile as they once were, many elderly individuals continue to lead a sedentary lifestyle. Our immune system, the part of the body that fights infection (as you'll see later on), deteriorates with age, and this may expose the elderly to an increased risk for illnesses, such as upper respiratory tract infection.

To see if regular exercise could protect against infection, a group of researchers at the University of Tokyo measured immune system response on three occasions over 12 months in a group of normally sedentary elderly individuals who engaged in two bouts of 60-minute exercise a week for the duration of the study (Akimoto *et al.*, 2003). Participants, who were aged 65 years and older, engaged in resistance training (back, chest and inner thigh exercises) and endurance training (aerobic exercise such as 'step' and ball games).

People's estimates of good health from skin blood perfusion

When we describe people as being in bloom or looking healthy, we often use their skin colour as a guide. A grey or pallid complexion normally leads us to think the person is not in the rudest of health. A new study has now sought to operationalise the degree of blood perfusion (as it is called) in the skin by asking people to manipulate blood perfusion in images of people's faces and to indicate how healthy the faces looked (Stephen *et al.*, 2011).

In the photographs showing faces that were judged healthy, people increased skin blood colour, suggesting that they find this aspect of the face to denote healthiness. Examples can be seen in Figure 17.3. This information, the researchers argue, may affect mate choice, as health is one of the predictors of mate selection.

The secretion and concentration of an important antibody (a chemical produced by the body to fight infection) increased significantly over the period of study – before training, 4 months in and 12 months in – suggesting the benefits of this simple exercise regime to immune system functioning. Although the study did not use a control group, or examine the possible different effects of resistance and endurance training, the findings suggest a relatively easy way of protecting immune system functioning in a group that is susceptible to immune system decline.

There is also evidence that regular aerobic exercise can act as a protective factor against cognitive decline and can improve motor and other types of memory (Roig *et al.*, 2012), although this depends on the type of exercise and type of cognitive test administered.

Types of exercise

According to Cooper (1985), aerobic exercises such as running, walking, cycling and swimming are superior to other forms of exercise for improving cardiovascular health. **Aerobic exercises** are those which expend considerable energy, increase blood flow and respiration and thereby stimulate and strengthen the heart and lungs and increase the body's efficiency in using oxygen. Running at least two miles in less than 20 minutes four times a week (or any equivalent aerobic exercise) significantly increases cardiovascular health (Cooper, 1985). One study showed that aerobic exercise had an additional benefit: reduced heart response to mental stress (Kubitz and Landers, 1993). Two groups of students who had not

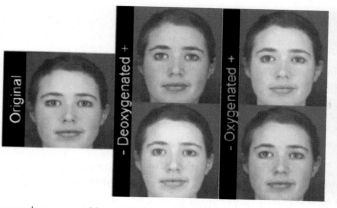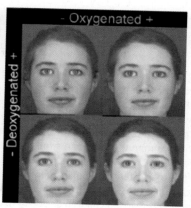

Figure 17.3 A rosy glow = good health? Which of these faces do you think looks the healthiest?

exercised for at least three months prior to the study were divided into two groups. One group rode an exercise bike three times a week for 40 minutes for eight weeks; the other group did not perform any aerobic exercises. At the end of the eight-week period, both groups were given timed colour perception and maths tests. Participants in the aerobic exercise programme showed lower absolute heart rates in response to the tests than did the participants who did not exercise.

Controversies in psychological science: Can exercise improve mood?

The issue

Exercisers frequently report that they feel better after a bout of vigorous exercise (the so-called feel-good effect). They feel an increase in positive mood and self-confidence that can sometimes translate into better work performance or cognitive ability. But is there scientific evidence demonstrating the positive effects of exercise on mood?

The evidence

There is some evidence that physical exercise can be beneficial to certain mental illnesses – improvements have been found in mood disorders (Heating et al., 2016), in dementia/neuro-cognitive disorders (Brett et al., 2016), and bipolar disorder, described in the next chapter (Melo et al., 2016). In individuals without mental illness, exercise can have significant immediate effects on mood and these effects are dependent on the types of exercise taken (Biddle, 1995; Scully et al., 1998). Petruzzello and Tate (1997), for example, found that exercise reduced state anxiety (the anxiety felt at the time) only after aerobic exercise. When trait anxiety was examined (the anxiety that individuals consistently feel, independently of their environment), a training programme lasting 10 weeks reduced anxiety.

In a comparison of participants' mood before and after aerobic dance exercise, soccer, tennis or bowling, Rudolph and Kim (1996) found that mood improved only after the aerobic exercise

and soccer. Biddle's review (Biddle, 1995) suggests that intensity of exercise may be a factor in enhanced mood, and perhaps this explains the result of this study. Running at intense levels over short durations increased stress but running over long distances increased arousal (Kerr and van den Wollenberg, 1997).

If exercise does improve mood, how much is needed and at what intensity? Hansen et al. (2001) measured mood before and after resting (sitting quietly) and before and after three bouts of exercise, lasting 10, 20 and 30 minutes, respectively, in a group of 20–25-year-olds. During the exercise conditions, participants worked on a bicycle ergometer (in essence, an exercise bike) which allowed participants to exercise with moderate intensity. After 10 minutes of cool-down – the post-exercise period – mood was measured again. They found that vigour, fatigue and total mood improved after 10 minutes of exercise but no improvement in mood was seen after 20 minutes of exercise, suggesting that up to 20 minutes' worth of exercise may be the maximum required to attain a positive mood state.

Many people abandon exercise regimes because the intensity is too great and may feel negatively because of this level of strain and difficulty. In one experiment, 24-year-old undergraduates rested for two minutes as their respiration was monitored, then walked for three minutes on a treadmill at 4.8 kph (Hall et al., 2002). Speed was subsequently increased to 8 kph and workload was increased every two minutes by 1.6 kph. The study continued until the participant reported being too physically exhausted to participate.

▶

Controversies in psychological science: *Continued*

During the increments, there was an increase in arousal but little improvement in mood. When exercise reached a moderate intensity, however, there was still an increase in arousal but also a shift towards negative mood. When the exercise session was over and participants had cooled down, there was a recovery in mood. Within a minute, participants reported increased levels of positive mood.

This effect may extend to thinking. A group of researchers at the Medical College of Georgia in the US assigned 171 sedentary, overweight 7–11-year-old children to one of two conditions: in one, the children received around 13 weeks' worth of aerobic exercise (20–40 minutes a day); the other, control group received no specific exercise (C.L. Davis *et al.*, 2011). The researchers then examined the group's cognitive and academic performance, and measured brain activation (using fMRI) as the children performed executive function tasks.

The children in the exercise condition produced significantly better executive function and mathematics scores. During fMRI, increased activation in both sides of the prefrontal cortex (PFC) was found, and a decrease in the parietal cortex, when these children performed the executive tasks. There was also a dose–response effect found – that is, the more intense the exercise the children had experienced, the greater the effect on executive function performance. These results, the authors suggest, show that regular exercise improves cognitive performance via changes in the brain.

Conclusion

The studies reviewed here suggest that exercise can have a beneficial effect on mood by decreasing state anxiety and depression if the exercise is relatively acute and is of a specific type. Deprivation of exercise in those who habitually exercise may be detrimental to mood.

Cigarette smoking – An international perspective

According to the WHO (2016), around 6 million deaths are attributable to smoking, annually and 22 per cent of the world's population over 15 smoke tobacco.

According to the Imperial Cancer Research Fund, the death rate is the equivalent of a jumbo jet crashing every day and killing all the passengers. The pattern varies by country, but approximately 35 per cent of men and 25 per cent of women in the EU smoke – rates of women smoking have fallen in Denmark, the Netherlands, Sweden and the UK but have risen in Greece, Portugal and Spain.

Smoking is thought to cause a third of cancers (Doll and Peto, 1981). Concerned by this fatal relationship, more and more governments have begun to ban smoking in public places – in fact, by 2000 almost all industrialised societies had some sort of ban in place (see Figure 17.4). In Britain, Ireland followed suit in 2004, Scotland in 2006 and the rest of the UK in 2007.

The largest reduction in smoking is found in the most well-off (Marsh and McKay, 1994); the failure to quit has been associated with low income (Nevid *et al.*, 1996).

Prompted by international data suggesting that smoking and its health-related problems were more prevalent in lower socio-economic groups than in higher ones, Droomers *et al.* (2002) obtained data on smoking and socio-economic status from the Dutch GLOBE study of 27,000 individuals recruited from south-eastern Netherlands in 1991. GLOBE is the Dutch acronym for Health and Living Conditions of the Population of Eindhoven and Its Surroundings.

Droomers *et al.* examined the relationship between educational level and the intention to smoke in 1,354 beginning Dutch smokers. Smoking information was obtained in 1991 and then 6.5 years later. The researchers found that participants at the lower end of the education spectrum were significantly more likely to continue smoking than were their better-educated counterparts.

Smoking is also associated with many problem behaviours such as a higher intake of fatty food (Shah *et al.*, 1993), lower fruit and vegetable intake, higher alcohol intake (Morabia and Wynder, 1990) and less physical activity. Current smokers have been found to consume more alcohol, meat, eggs and chips more frequently than former or non-smokers, although sweet consumption in those who have stopped smoking is higher (French *et al.*, 1996).

In addition to these health risks, people who use tobacco also face increased risks of cancer, bronchitis, emphysema, strokes and ulcers. Non-smokers who are exposed to air contaminated with cigarette smoke (second-hand smoke) also face increased risks of CHD and cancer. As a result of the negative effects of smoking, this behaviour is banned in many public places such as public transport, restaurants, cinemas, offices, hospitals, schools, and so on.

Cigarette smoking – *Continued*

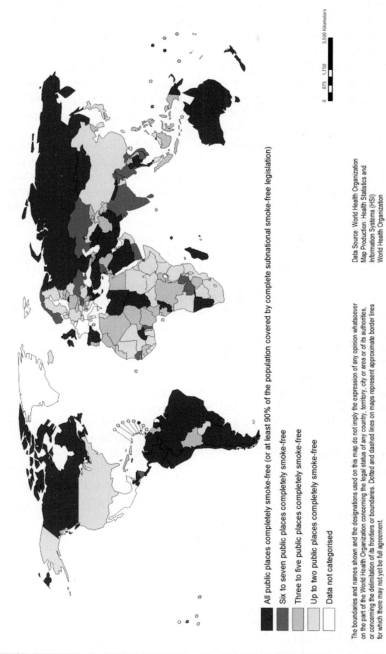

Smoke-free environments, 2014

■ All public places completely smoke-free (or at least 90% of the population covered by complete subnational smoke-free legislation)

■ Six to seven public places completely smoke-free

■ Three to five public places completely smoke-free

□ Up to two public places completely smoke-free

□ Data not categorised

The boundaries and names shown and the designations used on this map do not imply the expression of any opinion whatsoever on the part of the World Health Organization concerning the legal status of any country, territory, city or area or of its authorities, or concerning the delimitation of its frontiers or boundaries. Dotted and dashed lines on maps represent approximate border lines for which there may not yet be full agreement.

Data Source: World Health Organization
Map Production: Health Statistics and
Information Systems (HSI)
World Health Organization

0   875   1,750   3,500 Kilometers

Figure 17.4 Smoking bans across the world.

A 'stigmatised habit'

People hold justifiably negative views of smoking and because of this it has been labelled a 'stigmatised habit' (Furnham *et al.*, 2002b). Their research showed that when people are asked to prioritise who should receive healthcare, for example, smokers are normally given the lowest priority. A study at University College London confirmed this view. The researchers asked 100 adults to rank 16 hypothetical patients in terms of priority for treatment for three medical conditions: heart transplantation, in vitro fertilisation (IVF) and cosmetic surgery. Participants were told that these patients would be treated by a UK National Health Service hospital, that is, a hospital directly funded by public taxation and which offers treatment free at the point of delivery. Information about patients varied according to age, annual income, smoking behaviour and whether the patient had children. The researchers found that young people, non-smokers and those on a low annual income were given highest priority and smokers the lowest priority. The existence of children only influenced decisions about IVF and heart transplant.

The results are consistent with other studies of people's attitudes to smokers, with young people preferentially prioritised for kidney dialysis treatment (Furnham and Briggs, 1993) and smokers given lower priority (Furnham *et al.*, 2000). As dialysis is unrelated to smoking, this result coupled with the findings from Furnham *et al.*'s study indicates little sympathy towards those who smoke. Smoking appears to be a 'stigmatised habit' which can cloud perceptions of smokers and their treatment for illnesses unrelated to their habit. Of course, these studies asked for the general public's attitudes, and not doctors'.

Factors which promote the initiation and maintenance of smoking

What causes people, especially adolescents, to begin smoking? Psychologists know that both imitation and peer pressure contribute to the acquisition of the smoking habit (Lynskey *et al.*, 1998). Adolescents who have favourable impressions of a smoker are likely to imitate that person's actions. Cigarette manufacturers use this knowledge to advertise their products: they often portray smoking as a glamorous, mature, independent and sometimes rebellious behaviour. In a longitudinal study of 643 14–17-year-olds and their smoking behaviour, the best predictor of smoking was peers' smoking six months earlier; parental smoking also predicted smoking (Biglan *et al.*, 1995).

Some of the strategies which may prevent the recruitment of smokers include price increases, limiting access to young people, developing non-smoking policies for schools, banning advertising and tobacco sponsorship of sporting (and any other public) events, and spending more on health education. A survey of 80 Australian smoking experts (from government, universities and professional and volunteer organisations) who had been asked to rate the smoking reduction strategies they considered to be most effective reported that increased tobacco taxes would be the most effective strategy, followed by TV campaigning, having smoke-free areas and banning tobacco advertising (Paul and Sanson-Fisher, 1996). As we will see from the evidence below and in the Psychology in Action section, some of these strategies may be more effective than others.

Two American studies of adolescents' smoking habits show an interesting pattern of recruitment and cessation. Chassin *et al.* (1996) examined the history of smoking from adolescence to adulthood in a longitudinal study of 4,035 participants (with roughly equal numbers of men and women, with an average age of 29 at the end of the study). The authors reported an increase in the initiation of smoking from adolescence to adulthood, with a slight decrease in the participants' initiation in their mid-twenties and no initiation in adulthood. This finding suggests that smoking begins in adolescence and that the discouragement of smoking should target this age group. Those who did not quit were likely to have smoking parents and be less well educated than those who successfully quitted. Rose *et al.*'s (1996) study of 700 adolescents found that attempting to quit was associated with being female, attaining some college education, perceiving smoking as dangerous (both generally and personally), being married and occupying several social roles. Health beliefs about the dangers of smoking did not predict cessation.

Lucas and Lloyd (1999) investigated why girls started smoking, asking 11–16-year-olds about their age at first cigarette, the source of the supply, the location of the first smoke, the people present at the first smoke and the perceived degree of coercion involved in smoking for the first time. The average age of the first smoke was significantly lower for boys than for girls – the only measure to show a sex difference. In fact, men also seem to be able to give up more successfully (Wetter *et al.*, 1999). Smoking for the first time tended to involve two friends and did not lead to regular smoking. This trend (the lack of a tendency to smoke regularly) was also reported in a study of adolescents by Bell *et al.* (1999). Peer pressure appeared to play little role in maintaining smoking, but smokers did indicate that they were likely to start smoking with friends and when drinking alcohol, suggesting that adolescents socialise with individuals with similar interests rather than with those they necessarily call role-models or peers whose behaviour needs to be emulated.

Psychology in action: How to stop smoking

A number of measures have been put in place to help people give up smoking – they range from the economic – bans on tobacco advertising, restricting sales, increasing prices, to the psychological – providing education and behavioural strategies for quitting.

When Willemsen and de Zwart (1999) reviewed studies examining the effect of these measures on adolescent smoking, they found that, in isolation, few of them were effective; the measures were most effective in combination. Of the isolated measures, price increases were the single most prohibitive factor. Setting an age limit had no effect on smoking.

Non-psychological intervention programmes for cigarette smokers have explained nicotine replacement. This replacement is normally undertaken via a nicotine gum, a transdermal patch (a plaster-like patch that allows nicotine to be absorbed through the skin) or vaping (see below). The patch was developed by a behavioural psychologist, Frank Etscorn. Over several months, the nicotine levels of the patches are reduced, and the individual is weaned from nicotine altogether. The success rate is mixed. A review of the effectiveness of nicotine gum and patches suggests success rates of 11 per cent and 13 per cent for each therapy, respectively (Law and Tang, 1995). These figures are comparable to the success of other treatment approaches.

Quitting smoking has both immediate and long-term positive effects, as Table 17.1 shows, although quitting (and maintaining that quitting) is not easy for smokers.

Exposing smokers to positive images of smoking has been shown to predict their willingness or intention to smoke (Dinh *et al.*, 1995) whereas exposing them to negative images predicts successful abstinence from smoking (Gibbons and Eggleston, 1996). These findings suggest that altering the way in which a person thinks about smoking can help stop the behaviour. One Canadian anti-smoking programme, the Waterloo Smoking Prevention Project (Flay *et al.*, 1985), has been especially effective in reducing the number of young adolescents who experiment with smoking, by asking students to seek out information about smoking, to think about their beliefs regarding smoking, to learn about the social pressures involved in smoking and by giving them explicit training in how to resist those pressures – for example, politely turning down a cigarette when one is offered.

By the end of the two-year period, fewer than 8 per cent of the students who had been involved in the prevention programme were experimenting with smoking. In contrast, almost 19 per cent of the students who had not gone through the programme had experimented with smoking. While these results are encouraging, the students were only monitored for two years.

Between 2000 and 2001, the American Cancer Society trialed a telephone counselling programme for smokers who wanted to quit (Rabius *et al.*, 2004). Over 3,000 callers notified the Society of their intent to quit; of these, 420 were aged between 18 and 25 years. When intention to give up smoking

Table 17.1 The body's response to stopping cigarette smoking

Timescale	Response
Within 20 minutes of last puff	Blood pressure and pulse return to normal levels
Within 8 hours	Nicotine and carbon monoxide levels in the blood are halved, oxygen levels in the blood return to normal
Within 1 day	Carbon monoxide is eliminated from the body and lungs start to clear out the accumulated tar
Within 2 days	There is no tar left in the body Taste and smell start to return to normal
Within 3 days	Breathing becomes easier due to relaxing of bronchial tubes Energy levels increase
From 2 weeks to 3 months	Circulation of the blood improves Walking and running become easier
From 3 months to 9 months	Coughs, wheezing and breathing problems improve as lung function is increased by up to 10 per cent
After 5 years	Risk of heart attack falls to about half that of a smoker
After 10 years	Risk of lung cancer falls to half that of a continuing smoker

Source: No Smoking Day website, http://www.nosmokingday.org.uk.

Psychology in action: *Continued*

was measured, quit rates were significantly higher among older and younger smokers who received telephone counselling (compared with those who received a self-help booklet). Although cessation was reported by the participant – and there was no attempt to verify this – the results suggest that telephone counselling may be a useful way of helping smoking cessation.

The psychological evidence suggests that a number of specific factors can trigger smoking: these include visual, social and physiological cues. Evidence from studies in which an attempt is made to stop smoking by engaging smokers in an intervention programme shows that the studies' success rate is variable but that specially designed intervention programmes are more effective than doing nothing at all to stop smoking.

Changing unhealthy behaviour: e-cigarettes

Twenty years ago, they were unknown. Now, it is difficult to walk down any high street (at least in the west) and not spot at least one: e-cigarettes and a person vaping. E cigarettes are devices for replacing actual cigarettes. People use them either (the activity is called vaping) to replace traditional cigarette use because they are smokeless and have fewer perceived health risks, or recreationally. They were first developed by Hon Kik, a Chinese pharmacist in the 2000s. They work by delivering a vapour of nicotine derived from heating nicotine, glycerol and flavourings (Grana *et al.*, 2014). It is estimated that around 2.6 people now vape in the UK (ASH, 2015) and the market has doubled in the US between the years 2011 and 2012 from $250 to $500 million. E-cigarettes can come in many flavours, can be bought cheaply or in very expensive, bespoke form and at various strengths of nicotine.

Smoking, generally, is in decline especially among the young (Fuller and Hawkins, 2014), a likely consequence of smoking bans in many countries around the world, although Hopkinson *et al.* (2014) note that around 200,000 children between 11 and 15 years of age begin smoking in the UK each year. e-cigarette use has boomed in the past eight years: from 2 per cent of smokers and non-smokers in 2011 to 23 per cent in 2015 (West *et al.*, 2016). McNeill *et al.* (2015) estimated that in 2015, 5.5 per cent of the adult population were e-cigarette smokers. According to ASH, 13 per cent of older children had tried e-cigarettes in 2015, almost double the number from 2014. Most of these children were also smokers. It was rare for any non-smokers to have tried e-cigarettes. Some research suggests that children use them primarily for the different flavours, rather than to reduce smoking (Measham *et al.*, 2016). However, the idea that e-cigarette use is the beginning of a 'slippery slope' which leads children towards cigarette use is not supported (Palazzolo, 2013).

The primary purpose of e-cigarettes in adults is to replace traditional cigarette smoking, which is perceived to be unhealthy (Palazzolo, 2013). However, there has been some controversy surrounding the healthiness of e-cigarettes themselves. The US Food and Drug Administration's decision to class the product as dangerous, because it contains nicotine and other substances which could be potentially harmful, has led to e-cigarettes being unable to be marketed as smoking cessation tools or as alternatives to smoking (Palazzolo, 2013). There are very few ingredients in e-cigarettes compared to the thousands in burning tobacco, many of which are carcinogenic. Public Health England (2015) has indicated that e-cigarettes carry a lower risk of ill health than normal cigarettes and others argue that they are 95 per cent safer than cigarettes (Nutt *et al.*, 2014). Evidence suggests that they are successful in replacing cigarettes. E-cigarettes are 60 per cent safer than other smoking cessations products you can buy over the counter (Brown *et al.*, 2014) and more effective than nicotine-free e-cigarettes (McRobbie *et al.*, 2014). Whether the amount of nicotine in the blood stream after vaping is less than that seen after smoking tobacco, however, is unclear: some studies find a reduction, some studies find an increase.

The outcomes of nicotine-replacement programmes or smoking cessation programmes are modest but strong. One study found that 31 per cent (of 216 participants) of smokers gave up smoking after six months of using e-cigarettes (Siegel *et al.*, 2011). Vaping with nicotine also seems to have cognitive benefits – people using e-cigarettes with nicotine showed better working memory and prospective memory performance than non-nicotine cigarette-users, and indicated less desire to smoke (Dawkins *et al.*, 2012, 2013). Brown *et al.* (2014) studied smoking cessation in 464 e-cigarette users, 1,922 over-the-counter nicotine replacement product users and 3,477 people who used no aids when trying to quit. All adults had been smokers in the 12 months prior to the study. The group most likely to abstain was the e-cigarette group – it was 1.6 times more likely to abstain than the other two groups.

However, a meta-analysis of smoking cessation studies which included e-cigarette use and a control group found that e-cigarette users were 28 per cent less likely to give up smoking (Kalkhoran and Glantz, 2016). The authors suggest that there may be various reasons for this, including the possibility that people who use e-cigarettes use them for number of reasons, not just to stop smoking, but to use in places where smoking is prohibited or to use as an alternative, not replacement, for cigarettes. The degree of use might also be important so there may be subgroups of e-cigarette users who are more likely to give up – those who use them daily are more likely to give up than are those who use them intermittently, for example (Biener and Hargraves, 2015). The authors of the meta-analysis also point out that smoking cessation was defined differently in many studies and that the analysis contained only two clinical trials (where participants are randomly assigned to conditions rather than choosing options themselves, the more robust approach).

The physiology of smoking

Cigarette smoking, like other forms of drug use, is addictive: the nervous system may develop a tolerance to the drug or become physically dependent on the drug. Tolerance simply means that the neurons in the central nervous system (CNS) respond progressively less to the presence of the drug; larger doses of the drug are required to produce the same CNS effects that smaller doses produced earlier. Physical dependence means that CNS neurons now require the presence of the drug to function normally.

The nicotine contained in cigarette smoke exerts powerful effects on the CNS and heart by stimulating postsynaptic receptors sensitive to the neurotransmitter acetylcholine (these are called nicotinic acetylcholine receptors). This stimulation produces temporary increases in heart rate and blood pressure, decreases in body temperature, changes in hormones released by the pituitary gland and the release of adrenalin from the adrenal glands as well as changes in motor and cognitive behaviour.

In common with all reinforcers, natural and artificial, it also causes secretion of dopamine in the brain; the release of dopamine in the brain is reinforcing, so this effect contributes to the maintenance of cigarette smoking. An injection of nicotine increases firing in dopamine neurons in one part of the brain (ventral tegmental area) and enhances its release in another (Besson *et al.*, 2007). Cigarette smoking may also be maintained by negative reinforcement. People who try to quit smoking usually suffer withdrawal symptoms, including headaches, insomnia, anxiety and irritability and, at a neurophysiological level, the acetylcholine receptors might be desensitised. These symptoms are relieved by smoking another cigarette. Such negative reinforcement appears to be extremely powerful. Over 60 per cent of all smokers have tried to quit smoking at least once, but have started again in order to escape the unpleasant withdrawal symptoms.

Nicotine alone cannot be blamed for the health risks posed by cigarette smoking. These risks are caused by the combination of nicotine with other toxic substances, such as the carbon monoxide and tars found in cigarette smoke. For example, while nicotine causes an increase in heart rate, the carbon monoxide in smoke deprives the heart of the oxygen needed to perform its work properly. The smoker's heart undergoes stress because it is working harder with fewer nutrients than normal. Over a period of years, this continued stress weakens the heart, making it more susceptible to disease than is the heart of a non-smoker.

Alcohol consumption

Alcohol is probably the most widely used and abused substance that requires the consumer to be of a given age before it is sold or used. According to the WHO, in 2010 6.21 litres of alcohol per person was consumed, around 13.5 g a day. Sixteen per cent were heavy, episodic drinkers but 62 per cent of people over 15 indicated that they had not drunk alcohol in the previous 12 months.

When psychologists refer to substance abuse, they mean that the substance is used in a way that poses a threat to the safety and well-being of the user, to another or to both. Most people who use alcohol do not abuse it, and not all people who abuse alcohol are alcoholics. People who drive under the influence of alcohol pose a serious threat to both themselves and others, but they may not be alcoholics. A review of the effect of light and heavy alcohol consumption has found that heavy drinking is associated with increased risks of cardiovascular problems (Klatsky, 2010), including cardiomyopathy (enlarged heart and weakened contraction), high blood pressure, heart rhythm disturbances and stroke. Lighter drinking is linked to none of these. Interestingly, wine appears to be more protective against cardiovascular heart disease than are spirits or beer. According to the WHO's Global statistics on alcohol and health (2014), 3.3 million people died from causes related to alcohol consumption in 2012 with the percentage being almost twice as high in men.

Data suggest that people in the age range typically representing students (18–24 years) drink more alcohol than their non-student counterparts (O'Malley and Johnston, 2002); over 40 per cent of students say that they are heavy or binge drinkers (Wechsler *et al.*, 2002). According to a study of 300 first-year students at the University of South Florida, however, this heavy drinking may be dependent on the year in which the students are studying; it may not, for example, appear in the first year (Del Boca *et al.*, 2004). Students were asked to self-report their monthly alcohol consumption during their first year at university. About a fifth of the students were abstinent during the 32-week period of the study. Binge drinking varied from week to week but did not exceed 30 per cent. Drinking was heaviest during the holiday period.

Alcoholism is an addiction to ethanol, the psychoactive agent in alcoholic drinks. A psychoactive substance is any substance that affects CNS functioning. Male alcoholics outnumber female alcoholics by a ratio of about four or five to one (Lauer, 1989).

Because neuronal activity of the brain becomes suppressed and reduces inhibitory controls on behaviour when moderate to heavy amounts of alcohol are consumed, individuals become more relaxed and more outgoing, show impaired motor coordination and have difficulty thinking clearly. As more alcohol is consumed, neuronal activity in the brain is depressed further, producing distortions in perception, slurred speech, memory loss, impaired judgement and poor control of movement (Stritzke *et al.*, 1996). Unconsciousness and death may result from ingesting large amounts of alcohol over a short period of time. A study of Japanese alcohol drinkers who were not dependent on the drink found some differences between men and women at the brain region level. Women drinkers were more likely to show abnormalities in the right amygdala than were men (Sasaki *et al.*, 2009).

Once ingested, alcohol is rapidly absorbed from the stomach and intestinal tract. Because alcohol is a small fat – and water-soluble molecule, it is quickly and evenly distributed throughout the body via the circulatory system. Blood alcohol levels are affected by body weight and muscularity. Generally speaking, an obese or muscular individual would have to consume more alcohol than a slender person to attain the same level of intoxication. In addition, regardless of body characteristics, blood levels of alcohol increase more slowly in people who drink on a full stomach than in those having little or no food in their stomach. Food in the stomach impairs absorption of substances through the gastrointestinal tract. Even when total body weight, coping style and sensation-seeking are taken into account, men remain the heaviest consumers (Watten, 1997).

Inebriation is related to the manner in which alcohol is metabolised by the body. Unlike most other drugs, alcohol is metabolised by the liver at a constant rate, regardless of how much alcohol has been consumed. For example, in one hour, the body will metabolise the alcohol in 400 g of beer or 35 g of 80–100 per cent proof spirits. Hence, if a person consumes more than 400 g of beer or 35 g of spirits per hour, their blood alcohol level rises beyond that level caused by the first drink, and they may begin to become intoxicated. When blood alcohol levels reach 0.3–0.4 per cent, people lose consciousness, and at 0.5 per cent neurons in the brain that control the respiratory and circulatory systems stop functioning, causing death. Driving under the influence of alcohol is defined in most countries as a blood alcohol level greater than 0.1 per cent. Mixing alcohol with other drugs is also dangerous (see Table 17.2).

The use of alcohol is prompted by the same factors that contribute to the initiation of smoking: imitation and peer pressure. Many young people see drinking as the thing to do because it seemingly represents maturity, independence and rebelliousness and because it is associated with having fun. On days where participants encountered negative experiences, drinking is more likely to be solitary; the individual is home and alone (Mohr *et al.*, 2001). When interpersonal experiences were positive, drinking was more likely to occur in social contexts. Experiences also interacted with personality type. Those who were more neurotic were more likely than stable individuals to drink alone when they had experienced negative interpersonal experiences. When the researchers looked at the participants' normal drink levels, they found that people who drank more at home were more likely to do so in response to negative experiences. Not surprisingly, alcohol intoxication has a range of negative effects on behaviour – social and cognitive. Even drinking one or two cans of beer, for example, can impair drinkers' memory for the brand of a product in an advert they watched (Orquin *et al.*, 2014).

Treatment programmes for drug abuse, including smoking and drinking, may take several forms. In some cases, aversion therapy is used; in others, less intrusive forms of therapy involving extensive counselling are used. In the latter case, the

Table 17.2 The consequences of mixing alcohol with various drugs

Drug	Example	Possible consequences of using simultaneously with alcohol
Narcotics	Codeine or Percodan	Increased suppression of CNS functions and possible death due to respiratory failure
Minor pain relievers	Aspirin or Tylenol	Stomach irritation and bleeding; increased likelihood of liver damage from acetaminophen
Antidepressants	Tofranil, Triavil	Increased suppression of CNS functions; drinking some red wines while using some kinds of antidepressants may produce extremely high blood pressure. May also lead to death due to respiratory failure
Antihistamines	Actifed	Increased drowsiness, making operation of motor vehicles and power equipment more dangerous
CNS stimulants	Caffeine, Dexedrine	Reverses some of the depressive effects of alcohol; however, they do not produce increases in sobriety if consumed while one is inebriated
Antipsychotics	Thorazine	Impaired control of motor movements and possible death due to respiratory failure
Anti-anxiety drugs	Valium	Decreased arousal; impaired judgement, which can lead to accidents in the home or on the road

Source: Based on Palfai and Jankiewicz, 1991, and data from the National Institute for Alcohol Abuse and Alcoholism Clearinghouse for Alcohol Information, 1982.

psychologist's or therapist's general aim is to teach the individual the following:

1 To identify environmental cues or circumstances that may cause the addictive behaviour to occur or recur.

2 To learn to behave in ways that are incompatible with the undesired behaviour.

3 To have confidence that they can overcome the addiction.

4 To view setbacks in overcoming the addiction as temporary and to treat them as learning experiences in which new coping skills can be acquired.

Sexually transmitted diseases and AIDS

Sexual activity represents the most emotionally intense form of intimacy. Through casual sexual relationships, however, sexual activity may have severely negative consequences: it may result in contracting a sexually transmitted disease (STD). Individuals who contract an STD experience a loss of self-esteem and often they lose their ability to initiate or maintain sexual relationships.

The most life-threatening illness that is transmitted sexually is acquired immune deficiency syndrome, or AIDS, which can also be transmitted through blood transfusions and the sharing of hypodermic needles among intravenous drug users. It can be easily diagnosed by using an antibody test. Men are most affected and an estimated half a million people in the EU have an incurable and transmissible infection (European Communities, 2009). AIDS is the last stage of the illness triggered by the human immunodeficiency virus (HIV). AIDS has been reported in 163 countries. The first cases were reported in 1981, a year in which 295 diagnoses of AIDS were made worldwide and 126 people died from it. Only 10 years later, in 1991, 41,871 new cases were reported and 31,381 people had died from AIDS. According to the WHO, at the end of 2015 there were 36.7 million people infected with HIV-AIDS. The lowest incidence is in South East Asia (4.3 per cent) and highest in Africa (14.9 per cent). Around 3 per cent of prisoners have HIV-AIDS.

Between 50 and 70 per cent of people infected with HIV will develop AIDS within 8–10 years (Moss and Bacchetti, 1989). Changes in lifestyle, such as practising safe sex, can reduce one's risk of contracting an STD or AIDS. These practices include limiting the number of one's sexual partners, finding out the sexual history of partners before engaging in sexual relations, using a condom during sex and abstinence from sexual intercourse. In the case of AIDS, these lifestyle changes must involve not only safe sex practices but also behaviours that will prevent non-sexual transmission of the AIDS virus, such as refusal to share hypodermic needles.

Prevention programmes have been based on changing knowledge, attitudes, beliefs and practices (Janz and Becker, 1984; Ajzen, 1985, 1991; Sheeran and Abraham, 1996). One model, the theory of reasoned action, is based on principles from social and cognitive psychology (Ajzen, 1985, 1991; Conner and Sparks, 1996). According to the model, behaviour follows from an intention to act. These intentions are based on the individual's beliefs, attitudes and feelings. Attitudes, in turn, are based on beliefs about the evaluation of the consequences of behaviour. The model takes into account the possibility that an individual's attitude can be influenced by social factors and that others' perception of them can determine their intention to act. Thus, if we apply the model to AIDS: an individual will intend to act in a particular way (e.g. using a condom) if they have a positive view of condoms and think that others would approve (Abraham et al., 1998).

Critics of the social cognitive models argue that the models do little to explain AIDS-related behaviour change and that intention to act does not explain behaviour change (Joffe, 1996, 1997; Fife-Shaw, 1997). Others, however, suggest that there is considerable evidence for the efficacy of the models (Abraham et al., 1998). Sheeran et al. (1997) (cited in Abraham et al., 1998), for example, reported a positive correlation between behavioural intention and condom use. Abraham et al. (1998) also note that interventions based on theory are more effective than those based on information-giving (Kalichman et al., 1996).

Although prevention programmes have been partially successful in reducing high-risk sexual behaviours, they are least successful in situations in which a person's personal or cultural values prevent them from engaging in safe sex practices (Herdt and Lindenbaum, 1992). These values generally involve misperceptions of what practising safe sex means. Some men refuse to wear condoms because doing so would detract from their conception of what it means to be a man. Many people, especially young people, have the mistaken belief that they are invulnerable to any type of misfortune, including contracting an STD or AIDS.

It is relatively easy to explain fear of contagion during the periods of the bubonic plague and cholera. At that time, medical science was unsophisticated and lacked the technology needed to understand basic physiology. Fear of contagion in the time of AIDS is not so easily explained.

Bishop (1994) offers three possible explanations. First, some people may reason that just because no evidence currently exists that AIDS is spread through casual contact, it does not mean that such evidence may not be discovered. Medical experts tend to describe the transmission of AIDS through casual contact as being 'near impossible' or 'very unlikely', which leaves room for doubt in many people's minds.

Stress and health

Stress is a term that causes psychologists headaches. There is a great deal of controversy over what the term means and whether the term reflects a genuine psychological variable. This controversy is not helped by the suggestion that the man who popularised it probably meant another word that was similar, as you will see later. In general terms, stress is a pattern of physiological, behavioural, emotional and cognitive responses to real or imagined stimuli that are perceived as preventing a goal or endangering or otherwise threatening well-being. These stimuli are generally aversive and are called stressors. Stress is not a direct product of **cultural evolution** but is a product of natural selection. It is a behavioural adaptation that helped our ancestors to fight or flee from wild animals and enemies. Stress often helps us to confront or escape threatening situations (Linsky *et al.*, 1995).

Stressors come in many forms. They may be catastrophic, such as floods and rape, or they may be relatively trivial, such as being stuck in traffic when you are late for an appointment. An American study has examined the relationship between stress and rail commuting in 208 men and women who lived in the suburbs (New Jersey) and commuted to Manhattan, New York (Evans and Wener, 2006). Over 100 million Americans, according to the authors, commute to work and the percentage using trains has increased by a fifth since 1980. They found that the longer the length of the journey, the greater the amount of salivary cortisol produced by participants (an index of stress). At the end of the journey, the researchers gave participants a proof-reading exercise to complete. Those who had taken longer journeys, persisted less at this task. They also reported experiencing more stress.

Stressors are not always bad, however. Some, such as athletic competition, having to perform in front of an audience or sitting an exam, can affect behaviour in positive ways. However, when stress is extended over long periods, it can have negative effects on both a person's psychological health and their physical health (Selye, 1991).

Selye's general adaptation syndrome

Much of what we know about the effects of dealing with prolonged and severe stressors on the body stems from the work of the Austrian-born Canadian endocrinologist Hans Selye. There is some suggestion that Selye was unclear about the difference between the terms 'stress' and 'strain' (when he talked about stress this was seen as something new whereas people had been more than used to speaking of people being under strain). As Youngston (1998) neatly summarises:

> The other thing Selye did was to use what was actually the correct term. The terms 'stress' and 'strain' come from engineering . . . Stress is the force exerted on a body that tends to cause it to deform, while strain is a measure of the extent to which a body is deformed when it is subjected to stress. A strain gauge is a simple device that measures the amount of the deformity.

The terms can, of course, be applied to human bodies in exactly this mechanical way. A bone can be stressed and can bend a little, thus exhibiting strain. But when we talk, these days, about a human being experiencing stress, we are not thinking of the application of a physical force that causes a bit of body squashing (strain). Our usage is purely metaphorical.

Through his work with laboratory animals, Selye found that chronic exposure to severe stressors produces a sequence of three physiological stages: alarm, resistance and exhaustion. Selye (1956) referred to these stages collectively as the **general adaptation syndrome (GAS)**.

The responses in the alarm stage involve arousal of the autonomic nervous system (ANS) and occur when the organism is first confronted with a stressor. During this stage, the organism's resistance to the stressor temporarily drops below normal, and the organism may experience shock – impairment of normal physiological functioning. With continued exposure to the stressor, the organism enters the stage of resistance, during which its ANS returns to normal functioning. Resistance to the stressor increases and eventually levels out at above normal levels. The stage of resistance, then, reflects the organism's adaptation to environmental stressors. However, with continued exposure to the stressor, the organism enters the stage of exhaustion. During this stage, the organism loses its ability to adapt, and resistance plummets to below normal levels, leaving the organism susceptible to illness and even death.

Most of Selye's work was focused on physical stressors, such as cold or heat or pain, but psychological stressors might exert considerably worse effects on health and behaviour. The extent to which people can adapt varies across individuals and depends on how the stressor is perceived. Some stressors are absolute (e.g. being tortured or being in an earthquake/tsunami); others are relative and depend on how we respond to them. Our emotional responses seem designed primarily to cope with short-term events. The physiological responses that accompany the negative emotions are described below and prepare us to threaten or fight rivals or to run away from dangerous situations. The absolute stressors provoke an adaptive stress response (relative stressors provoke this variably).

Walter Cannon coined the phrase **'fight or flight response'** to refer to the physiological reactions that prepare us for the strenuous efforts required by fighting or running away. Normally, once we have bluffed or fought with an adversary or run away from a dangerous situation, the threat is over and our physiological condition can return to normal. The fact that the physiological responses may have adverse long-term effects on our health is unimportant as long as the responses are brief. But when the threatening situations are continuous rather than episodic, they produce a more or less continuous stress response. This continued state of arousal can lead to CHD and other physical problems.

The biological basis of stress

Physical response to stressors is governed by the ANS, which is controlled by the hypothalamus. Stress is a biological response that is experienced as an emotion, although the form it takes varies depending on the nature of the stressor. In some situations we may feel frightened, and in others we may feel inspired or exhilarated.

When an individual senses a stressor, the hypothalamus sends signals to the ANS and to the pituitary gland, both of which respond by stimulating body organs to change their normal activities:

- Heart rate increases.
- Blood pressure rises.
- Blood vessels constrict.
- Blood sugar levels rise.
- Blood flow is directed away from extremities and towards major organs.
- Breathing becomes deeper and faster.
- Air passages dilate, which permits more air to enter the lungs.
- Digestion stops.
- Perspiration increases.
- Adrenal glands secrete adrenalin (epinephrine), which stimulates the heart and other organs.

It is easy to see why these changes are adaptive. They each prepare the body to deal with the stressor – collectively, these physiological responses produce a heightened psychological and physical state of alertness and readiness for action. Regardless of the nature of the stressor and whether we confront the stressor or run from it, the biological response is generally the same. Whether you find yourself in a dark alley confronted by a man with a knife or are facing your next psychology exam, the ANS and the pituitary gland stimulate the body to respond to the stressor.

There are two cases in which such responses can be maladaptive. First, stress can produce anxiety, which may impair one's ability to perform a task. As you may have experienced yourself, anxiety can hinder a variety of behaviours from performing in examinations, to speaking in public, competing during sporting events or remembering lines in a play.

The second case involves the effects of prolonged and severe stress. Many people's lifestyles place them in situations in which they are daily confronted with stressors. These lifestyles place these people at increased risk of illness.

Physiological mechanisms involved in stress

Emotions consist of behavioural, autonomic and hormonal responses. The latter two components – autonomic and hormonal responses – are the ones that can have adverse effects on health. Because threatening situations generally call for vigorous activity, the autonomic and hormonal responses that accompany them help to make the body's energy resources available. The sympathetic branch of the ANS is active, and the adrenal glands secrete epinephrine, norepinephrine and steroid stress hormones. This is known by the name hypothalamic–pituitary–adrenal (HPA) axis.

Epinephrine (adrenalin) releases the stored form of glucose that is present in the muscles, thus providing energy for strenuous exercise. Along with norepinephrine (noradrenalin), it also increases blood flow to the muscles by increasing the output of the heart, which also increases blood pressure. Over the long term, these changes contribute to CHD.

The hypothalamus releases a substance called corticotrophin-releasing hormone (CRH) which triggers the production of andrenocorticotrophin in the pituitary gland (Lupien *et al.*, 2007). This travels in the blood and arrives at the adrenal glands where it triggers the release of two types of stress hormone: the glucocorticoids and catecholamines (adrenaline and noradrenaline). These are responsible for the fight or flight response. In humans, the glucocorticoid released is called cortisol. Cortisol is called a **glucocorticoid** because it has profound effects on glucose metabolism, effects similar to those of epinephrine. In addition, glucocorticoids help break down protein and convert it to glucose, help make fats available for energy, increase blood flow and stimulate behavioural responsiveness, presumably by affecting the brain. They also have other physiological effects, some of which are only poorly understood. Almost every cell in the body contains glucocorticoid receptors, which means that few parts of the body are unaffected by these hormones. Figure 17.5 illustrates the effects of hormones on various body organs and their functions.

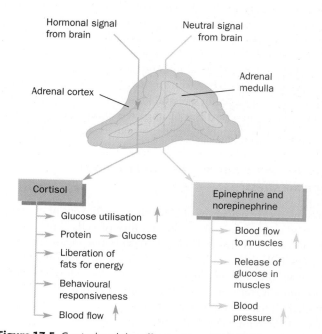

Figure 17.5 Control and the effects of secretion of epinephrine, norepinephrine and cortisol by the adrenal gland.

Although activation is common in the amygdala in people experiencing serious stress, the evidence for a structural change in this part of the brain has been inconsistent. Holzel *et al.*, (2009) have now reported such a change in grey matter density in the right amygdala. They studied 26 stressed but otherwise healthy individuals before and after a stress-reduction programme called mindfulness. The intervention lasted eight weeks. MRI scans were taken before and after the intervention and people rated their perceived stress according to a well-used questionnaire. People reported less stress after the intervention. This stress reduction also correlated with less grey matter in the right side of the amygdala.

Glucocorticoids tend to be at their highest levels in the morning and decline throughout the afternoon. People tend to be at their unhappiest in the morning and better later, an effect that is amplified in the depressed and which may be related to the level of cortisol (Janowski and Ciakowska, 2008). There is evidence that they bind to two brain receptor sub-types, and during responses to highly stressful events the T1 receptor type is awash with glucocorticoids and the T2 type is 70 per cent occupied (Lupien *et al.*, 2007).

Selye (1974) suggested that most of the harmful effects of stress were produced by the prolonged secretion of glucocorticoids. Although the short-term effects of glucocorticoids are essential, the long-term effects are damaging. These effects include increased blood pressure, damage to muscle tissue, a particular form of diabetes, infertility, stunted growth, inhibition of the inflammatory responses and suppression of the immune system. High blood pressure can lead to heart attack or stroke.

Selye's research involved exposing laboratory animals to chronic and intense stressors under controlled laboratory conditions. In addition to showing that resistance to stressors appears to involve three stages, his results also showed that animals became seriously ill during the stage of exhaustion. Can prolonged exposure to severe stressors produce similar risks for humans? Many studies investigating the relationship of lifestyle to health have shown that the answer to this question is 'yes'. Specifically, stressful lifestyles have been shown to be related to increased risk of impaired immune system functioning, ulcers, high blood pressure, cancer and CHD.

Telomeres – what are they and can they predict stress?

Telomeres are sequences of DNA that cap the tops of chromosomes and help maintain the stability of cells (Epel, 2009). However, there are enzymes that cannot replicate chromosomes fully or completely at the tips which means that, in essence, they are missing. As cells replicate, these telomeres become shorter. The relevance of this to health psychologists is that shorter telomeres in white blood cells are associated with the development of chronic disease such as stroke (Fuster and Andres, 2006). There is also some evidence to suggest that stressors are associated with shorter telomeres. For example,

parents who cared for a child with a chronic illness had lower levels of the enzyme that prevents shortening and had shorter telomeres (Epel *et al.*, 2004). Similar telomere shortening is seen in people who care for people with dementia, in the depressed (Simon *et al.*, 2006; Damjanovic *et al.*, 2007), and in women with low occupational status (Cherkas *et al.*, 2006). Current evidence points to a role for these genetic anomalies in stress reactions, but research is at an early stage.

Cognitive appraisal and stress

Many of the harmful effects of long-term stress are caused by our own reactions – primarily the secretion of stress hormones. Some events that cause stress, such as prolonged exertion or extreme cold, cause damage directly. These stressors will affect everyone; their severity will depend on each person's physical capacity. Selye's model has been useful for understanding the biological components involved in stress, but it does not explain the role of psychological components in stress. The effects of other stressors, such as situations that cause fear or anxiety, depend on people's perceptions and emotional reactivity. That is, because of individual differences in temperament or experience with a particular situation, some people may find a situation stressful and others may not. In these cases, it is the perception that matters.

One of the most important variables that determines whether an aversive stimulus will cause a stress reaction is the degree to which the situation can be controlled. When an animal can learn a coping response that allows it to avoid contact with an aversive stimulus, its emotional response will disappear. Weiss (1968) found that rats that learned to minimise (but not completely avoid) shocks by making a response whenever they heard a warning tone developed fewer stomach ulcers than did rats that had no control over the shocks. The effect was not caused by the pain itself, because both groups of animals received exactly the same number of shocks. Thus, being able to exert some control over an aversive situation reduces an animal's stress. Humans react similarly. Situations that permit some control are less likely to produce signs of stress than are those in which other people (or machines) control the situation (Gatchel *et al.*, 1989). Perhaps this phenomenon explains why some people like to have a magic charm or other 'security blanket' with them in stressful situations. Perhaps even the illusion of control can be reassuring.

Some psychologists argue that the psychological components in stress may influence the degree to which stressors arouse the ANS. One such psychologist is Richard Lazarus, who argues that our perception of the stressor does, to a large extent, determine the stress we experience (Lazarus and Folkman, 1984). According to Lazarus, an individual's stress levels are affected by their cognitive appraisal, or perception, of the stressful situation.

Cognitive appraisal is a two-stage process. In the first stage, we evaluate the threat: we attempt to judge the seriousness of the threat posed by the stressor. If we decide that the threat is real, we pass to the second stage, during which we assess whether we have the resources necessary to cope adequately with the threat. The extent to which we believe both that the stressor is a serious one and that we do not have the resources necessary to deal with it determines the level of stress we will experience. The belief that we cannot deal effectively with a stressor perceived as being extremely dangerous leads to the highest levels of stress. Because different people may evaluate differently both the stressor and their ability to cope with it, they are likely to show different levels of stress when faced with the same stressor. We know from experience that this is true. For example, people vary tremendously in their reactions to snakes: a harmless grass snake will arouse intense fear in some people and none in others.

Selye's findings, then, do not apply to all people; there are individual differences in how people react to prolonged exposure to stress. Some people show little, if any, risk of becoming ill during or after chronic stress. Kobasa (1979) refers to these people as hardy individuals. In a study of how business executives coped with long-term stress, she found that some of her subjects became ill and some did not. She wanted to find out what caused this difference. Through detailed analyses of her subjects' responses to different psychological inventories, she found that the hardy subjects viewed the stressors in their lives as challenges and that they met these challenges head on; they did not avoid them or become anxious about them. They also felt that they had control over the challenges (stressors).

In other words, Kobasa's findings support Lazarus's idea of the importance of cognitive appraisal in dealing with stress: how we initially assess the stressor, how we tackle it, and the extent to which we believe that we can control the stressor seem to influence whether we become at risk of illnesses related to being chronically stressed.

Psychoneuroimmunology

In addition to causing elevated levels of glucocorticoids, epinephrine and norepinephrine, stressors can also impair the function of the immune system, which protects us from assault by viruses, microbes, fungi and other types of parasite. Study of the interactions between the immune system and behaviour is called **psychoneuroimmunology**. Before discussing the effect of stressors on immune system functioning, it is useful to have an understanding of how the immune system works.

The immune system

The function of the **immune system** is to protect the body from infection. It is a network of organs and cells that protects the body from invading bacteria, viruses and other foreign substances, and is one of the most complex systems of the body. Because infectious organisms have developed devious tricks through the process of evolution, our immune system has evolved devious tricks of its own.

The immune system derives from white blood cells that develop in the bone marrow and in the thymus gland. Some of the cells roam through the blood or lymph glands and sinuses; others reside permanently in one place. The immune reaction occurs when the body is invaded by foreign organisms.

There are two types of specific immune reaction: chemically mediated and cell mediated. Chemically mediated immune reactions involve antibodies. All bacteria have unique proteins on their surfaces, called **antigens**. These proteins serve as the invaders' calling cards, identifying them to the immune system. Through exposure to the bacteria, the immune system learns to recognise these proteins. The result of this learning is the development of special lines of cells that produce specific **antibodies** – proteins that recognise antigens and help to kill the invading microorganism. One type of antibody is released

---

Cutting edge: Can chewing gum reduce stress?

Sometimes, in time of stress, we might eat more or we might chew more. Some studies have found that chewing gum chewers have lower state-trait anxiety than non-chewers and produce less cortisol, a hormone released during stress (Scholey et al., 2009). However, others have been unable to replicate these results although with different methods. In a slightly different study, Smith and Woods (2012) asked 72 students to chew gum daily for two weeks or to refrain from chewing. Measures of anxiety, perceived stress, depression and levels of tiredness were taken before and after the two weeks. A reduction in stress was associated with increased chewing. It was also associated with a reduction in not getting their academic work completed. Yokohama et al. (2017) found that chewing gum was also associated with greater oxygen in the frontal lobe. They asked 11 young adults to chew a flavourless gum for three minutes. They chewed 30, 70 or 110 times. Near infrared spectroscopy was used to measure oxygenation in the left frontal lobe. Gum chewing increased the amount of oxygen here in all three chewing conditions, compared with baseline. Fast chewing (110 times) was associated with greater oxygenation.

into the circulation by **B lymphocytes**, which receive their name from the fact that they develop in bone marrow. These antibodies, called **immunoglobulins**, are chains of protein. Each of five different types of immunoglobulin is identical except for one end, which contains a unique receptor. A particular receptor binds with a particular antigen, just as a molecule of a hormone or a transmitter substance binds with its receptor. When the appropriate line of B lymphocytes detects the presence of an invading bacterium, the cells release their antibodies, which bind with the bacterial antigens. The antibodies either kill the invaders directly or attract other white blood cells which then destroy the invaders. This process is illustrated by Figure 17.6.

One class of antibody, **secretory immunoglobulin A (sIgA)**, is secreted by and covers the mucosal surfaces such as those found in the respiratory and gastrointestinal tracts. Its role appears to be to provide protection against infection by creating a barrier to invading organisms (Kraehenbuhl and Neutra, 1992). Because this antibody can be measured from saliva, it has been one of the most widely researched of the antibodies (Evans *et al.*, 1997).

The other type of defence mounted by the immune system, cell-mediated immune reactions, is produced by **T lymphocytes**, which develop in the thymus gland. An example of T lymphocyte appears in Figure 17.7.

T lymphocytes also produce antibodies, but the antibodies remain attached to the outside of the cell's membrane. T lymphocytes primarily defend the body against fungi, viruses and multicellular parasites. When antigens bind with their surface antibodies, the cells either kill the invaders directly or signal other white blood cells to come and kill them.

In addition to the immune reactions produced by lymphocytes, natural killer cells continuously prowl through tissue. When they encounter a cell that has been infected by a virus or that has become transformed into a cancer cell, they engulf and destroy it. Thus, natural killer cells constitute an important defence against viral infections and the development of malignant tumours. Although the immune system normally protects us, it can cause us harm, too. Allergic reactions occur when an antigen causes cells of the immune system to overreact, releasing a particular immunoglobulin that produces a localised inflammatory response. The chemicals released during this reaction can enter the general circulation and cause life-threatening complications. Allergic responses are harmful, and why they occur is unknown.

The immune system can do something else that harms the body – it can attack its own cells. Autoimmune diseases occur when the immune system becomes sensitised to a protein present in the body and attacks the tissue that contains this protein. Exactly what causes the protein to be targeted is not known. What is known is that autoimmune diseases often follow viral or bacterial infections. Presumably, in learning to recognise antigens that belong to the infectious agent, the immune system develops a line of cells that treat one of the body's own proteins as foreign. Some common autoimmune diseases include rheumatoid arthritis, diabetes, lupus and multiple sclerosis.

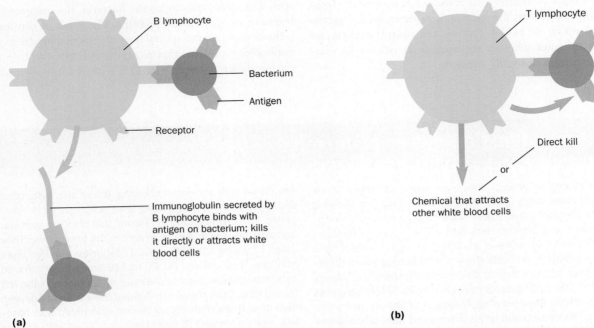

(a)

(b)

Figure 17.6 Immune reactions. **(a)** Chemically mediated reaction. The B lymphocyte detects an antigen on a bacterium and releases a specific immunoglobulin. **(b)** Cell-mediated reaction. The T lymphocyte detects an antigen on a bacterium and kills it directly or releases a chemical that attracts other white blood cells.

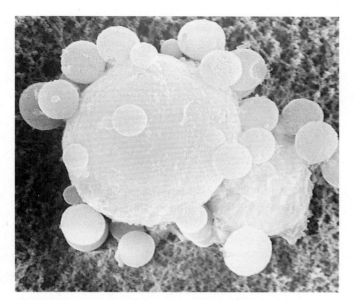

Figure 17.7 A T lymphocyte at work destroying tumour cells.
Source: Andrejs Liepins/Science Photo Library/Photo Researchers Inc.

Neural control of the immune system

Stress can suppress the immune system, resulting in a greater likelihood of infectious diseases, and it can also aggravate autoimmune diseases. It may even affect the growth of cancers. What is the physiological explanation for these effects? One answer, and probably the most important one, is that stress increases the secretion of glucocorticoids, and these hormones directly suppress the activity of the immune system. All types of white blood cell have glucocorticoid receptors, and suppression of the immune system is presumably mediated by these receptors (Solomon, 1987).

Stress and the immune system

The immune system does not appear to react to different types of stressor in the same way. Chronic stressors, such as bereavement of a close friend or relative, caring for a relative with Alzheimer's disease and marital disharmony, tend to result in reduced immune system functioning (Kiecolt-Glaser *et al.*, 1993; Zisook *et al.*, 1994). Kiecolt-Glaser *et al.* (1995), for example, reported that wounds took nine days longer to heal in caregivers for individuals with Alzheimer's disease than in age and income-matched 'stress-free' controls. Figures 17.8a and b show the relationship between caregiving and wound healing and wound size over the recovery period.

Acute stress, however, does not appear to have the same effect. Acute stress appears actually to increase the number of natural killer cells (Delahanty *et al.*, 1996) and the levels of sIgA (Zeier *et al.*, 1996). Caregivers in these studies tend to be 'informal' caregivers – they are not paid to look after ill people but are relatives or friends who willingly look after a seriously

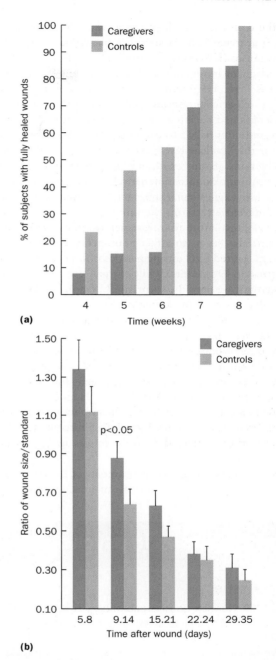

Figure 17.8 The progress of wound healing in Alzheimer's disease. **(a)** Percentage of caregivers and controls whose wounds had healed in time. **(b)** Average wound size during first five weeks of study.
Source: Kiecolt-Glaser, J.K., Marucha, P.T., Malarkey, W.B., Mercado, A.M. and Glaser, R., Slowing of wound-healing by psychological stress. *The Lancet*, 346, 1194–1196. © 1995 The Lancet Limited.

ill family member or friend. A meta-analysis of 23 published studies examining the health of caregivers and non-caregivers and its relationship to caregiving found that caregivers' levels of stress hormones were 23 per cent higher and their antibody responses 15 per cent lower than those of non-caregivers

(Vitaliano *et al.*, 2003). While the authors stress that it is impossible to tell from these studies whether the stress of caregiving causes changes in physical condition, they point out that caregiving is a potentially risky behaviour.

Evans *et al.* (1993) have reported that lower quality of life (such as experiencing more undesirable or fewer desirable experiences) is associated with lower levels of sIgA. However, undergraduates asked to present a piece of work orally in front of their colleagues showed an increase in the levels of this antibody (Evans *et al.*, 1994). Levels of sIgA tend to decrease during examination periods (Jemmott and Magloire, 1988) which suggests that short-term and long-term stressors have different effects on the immune system. Exam stress seems to cause more than just nerves, panic and sleepless nights. It also seems to affect brain activation. Lewis *et al.* (2007) measured EEG during periods of low exam stress and high stress in 49 students. While cortisol levels did not change between testing periods, surprisingly, frontal EEG did: leftward asymmetry in the frontal area during low exam stress shifted to rightward asymmetry during high exam stress. This increase in the right frontal area also correlated with self-reports of poorer health. The results are consistent with the model of EEG frontal asymmetry (see Chapter 13).

The immune system has recently been studied in experiments designed to examine the effects of laughter and humour on stress and coping with stress. The evidence for the role of humour and laughter in mediating the effects of the immune system is discussed in the Controversies in Psychological Science section.

A study by researchers at the University of British Columbia has found that seeing photographs of infectious disease can

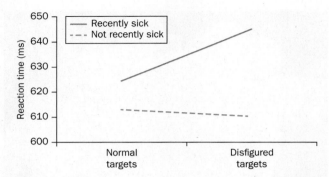

Figure 17.9 Disgust: an immune system response? People who had been ill avoid images of disfigurement.

activate an 'aggressive immune response' (Schaller *et al.*, 2010). Twenty-eight participants saw photographs of either infectious disease or guns and then had their white blood cells measured for an immune system chemical, cytokine interleukin-6. Those in the disease condition showed higher levels of this chemical, suggesting that even the sight of disease can trigger an adaptive biological mechanism such as immunity.

It seems as if exposure to illness can also affect how people react to seemingly irrelevant stimuli. Miller and Maner (2011a, b) hypothesised that activation of the biological immune system would activate a behavioural immune system – that is illness would lead to people avoiding illness-related stimuli. They found that people who had recently been ill were more attentive to, and avoided more, images of disfigured individuals than were those who had not been ill, as shows in Figure 17.9.

Controversies in psychological science: Can humour improve health?

The issue

In 1979, Norman Cousins published a rather unusual book called The *Anatomy of Illness*. In it, he described the way in which he used laughter to help him recover from a degenerative spinal condition. Since 1979, a number of popular and scientific accounts have suggested that using humour can help to combat stress and ill health. One contributor to the field has suggested that 'happy breathing, simulated smiles and transcendental breathing' can uplift spirits (Holden, 1993). 'Don your Super-Humour-Person cape,' he exhorts, 'and save the world from the arch-villain over-seriousness'. While we can dismiss accounts like this as minor eccentricities of little psychological importance, more thoughtful researchers have examined whether humour does help us to cope with ill health and stress and provide immunity from these problems. These researchers have focused upon the effects of humour from several perspectives. Perhaps the most important of these

are: producing humour, appreciating humour and using humour as a coping mechanism.

The evidence

Laughter is an intriguing behaviour: it can induce laughter in a passive listener, can enhance the enjoyment of comedy, despite people's claimed dislike of audience laughter (Martin and Gray, 1996), and provides vigorous muscle exercise. According to Hans Selye, laughter is a form of eustress: a positive, life-enhancing type of stress or pressure. In one experiment, 20 men and women endured pressure-induced discomfort after having listened to either a 20-minute laughter tape, a relaxation tape or a dull narrative (Cogan *et al.*, 1987). For both the laughter and relaxation conditions, discomfort thresholds were higher, that is, participants could endure greater stress.

Controversies in psychological science: *Continued*

Does this suggest that comedy is good for you? The picture is not altogether clear-cut. In a well-controlled experiment where the effect of the appreciation of humour on stress reduction was examined, the experimenters found no relationship between appreciation and stress reduction (Martin and Lefcourt, 1983). They did, however, find a slight moderation of the stress when humour was produced by participants. Another study found that this moderating effect was significant for depression but not anxiety symptoms (Nezu *et al.*, 1988). This finding suggests that it may not necessarily be the blanket appreciation (watching, listening) of humour that is important but the way in which humour is used.

Martin and Lefcourt and their colleagues have conducted a number of experiments in which they examined the relationship between a person's sense of humour, their use of humour as a coping mechanism and their response to stress. In a small number of detailed studies, the experimenters took measures of individuals' physical stress by sampling their salivary immunoglobulin A concentrations (sIgA). In one study, 40 participants provided saliva samples and completed a Daily Hassles Scale (a measure of the degree of stress experienced daily) and a sense of humour questionnaire. The experimenters found a negative correlation between low scores on the sense of humour questionnaire and sIgA levels. A different experiment measured sIgA concentrations before and after the presentation of humorous stimuli and examined whether the presentation would interact with the participants' sense of humour (Lefcourt *et al.*, 1990). The researchers found that not only did saliva concentrations increase after presentation of humour but also those participants with the greatest sense of humour had larger concentrations of sIgA after exposure to an audio comedy tape.

Pain tolerance has been found to be higher after watching comedy and women are more tolerant of pain after watching a funny film (Zweyer *et al.*, 2004; Dunbar *et al.*, 2011). Lefcourt *et al.* (1997) found that women who used coping humour a great deal exhibited lower systolic blood pressure than did low-scoring women. Men, on the other hand, showed the reverse pattern. On the basis of the participants' responses to the stressful tasks, the experimenters concluded that humour may moderate the effect of uncontrollable and passively experienced stress but that stressful problem-solving tasks involving active participation are less susceptible to these moderating effects.

In an ingenious test of the hypothesis that laughter and humour help us combat the effects of stressful events, Rotton (1992) examined the death rates of comedians, literary humourists and non-humorous individuals by examining published biographical details. He found no significant difference between the lifespan of humorous entertainers and that of others.

In a review of studies examining the relationship between humour and good health, Rod Martin (R.A. Martin, 2001) concludes that evidence is mixed at best. Some studies show beneficial effects of exposure to humour on health, others no effect. Furthermore, stimuli that are perceived as generally pleasant stimulate similar responses to those elicited by humour. Conversely, a stimulus need not be pleasant to reduce a painful experience. Studies have shown that both positive and negative emotional stimuli can reduce the perception of pain, for example. Martin suggests that experiments need to distinguish more clearly between effects that are specific to humour and effects that are general to positive emotional stimuli.

Conclusion

From what you have read so far, are you convinced that humour can help reduce the effect of stress? What influences your decision? Can you think of better ways of measuring the effects of sense of humour, or perceiving humour or generating humour, on stress reduction? Would you expect the effects of sense of humour on stress reduction to be long term? If so, why? If not, why not?

Bereavement

Bereavement, another source of stress, also suppresses the immune system. Cancer and other illnesses have been observed to occur at higher than average rates among people who are widowed. To investigate the possibility that bereavement suppresses the immune system, Schleifer *et al.* (1983) drew blood samples from 15 men whose wives were dying of terminal breast cancer. Two blood samples were drawn, the first before the spouse's death and the second within two months afterwards. Each time, an agent that normally stimulates blood lymphocyte activity was mixed with the lymphocytes, and the resultant level of activity was measured. On average, the activity level of blood lymphocytes after the spouse's death was less than before her death, which meant that the bereaved spouses were more susceptible to illness. Taken together, the results of these studies (and many other similar studies) suggest a strong link between stress and weakening of the immune system.

Loneliness

Loneliness, the feeling or perception of being alone, is stressful and is associated with poor health. Loneliness does not depend on having a small social network: even people with lots of friends and acquaintances can feel lonely. A factor that can facilitate good relations with others, and therefore predict good/ill health, is sociability, defined as 'the quality of seeking others and being agreeable' (Cohen *et al.*, 2003). Two of the dimensions of the Big Five personality scale (see Chapter 14) seem to measure this behaviour: extraversion and agreeableness. Cohen *et al.* used these measures and another which measures how well people develop good relations with others (and how often they interact with others) to examine whether high scorers were less prone to illness.

The researchers took baseline measures of sociability in over 300 adults aged between 18 and 54, then exposed participants to one of two rhinoviruses which caused the common cold. Five days after exposure, physical symptoms were noted and any infection development measured. Four weeks later, blood samples were taken to verify whether an illness had developed.

Sociability predicted susceptibility to the common cold: the greater the degree of sociability, the less likely the person was to develop a cold. The highly sociable individuals had more social relationships and relationships of greater quality than less sociable ones but the link between sociability and the development of illness remained even when these factors were taken into account. This suggests that it is not simply being sociable which could be a protective factor against illness but that it is the trait of sociability which acts as the protector. Interestingly, high extraversion scores, high agreeableness scores and positive relations individually predicted the decreased likelihood of a cold developing. However, when the measures were combined, the effect was greater.

In a direct examination of whether loneliness (and the size of a person's social network) influenced health, a group of North American researchers investigated the antibody response to influenza immunisation in first-year students whose social networks and degrees of loneliness throughout their first semester were assessed (Pressman *et al.*, 2005). These measures were then used to predict the degree of health or ill health experienced by the students.

Students experiencing either the greatest degree of loneliness or the smallest social networks showed poorer antibody response to one viral component of the vaccine (there were four in total). Those who were most lonely and who also had the smallest social networks showed the lowest antibody response of all. People who were lonely also had more circulating cortisol, slept less well, experienced greater stress and experienced more negative (and less positive) emotion. These outcomes were not significantly affected by social network size. The antibody responses at one and four months can be seen in Figures 17.10a and b.

Procrastination

Procrastination refers to the tendency to put off tasks and chores that could be done immediately. You might think that in the short term, this produces less stress because the individual is under less pressure to perform, but the opposite appears to be the case (Mann, 2016). In a study of procrastination among health psychology students, Tice and Baumeister (1997) noted the date on which students submitted coursework and took measures of procrastination from each. Not surprisingly, procrastinators submitted their coursework significantly later. They also received lower grades. However, and oddly, they also seemed to experience less stress than did non-procrastinators. In a term-long study, the researchers found that this was true, but only at the beginning of the term; at the end of the term their symptoms of stress were significantly greater than those of non-procrastinators, as seen in Figure 17.11.

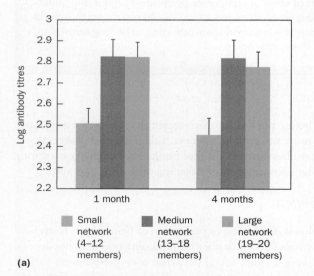

(a)

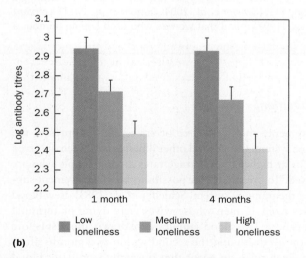

(b)

Figure 17.10 **(a)** Antibody levels at one month and four months, according to size of social network. **(b)** Antibody level at one month and four months, according to degree of loneliness.

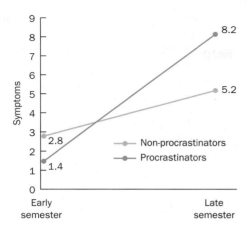

Figure 17.11 The number of symptoms reported by student procrastinators and non-procrastinators across a term on a health psychology course.

Source: Tice, D.M. and Baumeister, R.F., Longitudinal study of procrastination, performance, stress and health: The costs and benefits of dawdling. *Psychological Science*, 1997, 8(6), 454–458. Reprinted by permission of Blackwell Publishers Ltd.

Readers should, perhaps, consider the implications of this study very, very carefully.

Personality type (not Big Five)

In the 1950s, Friedman and Rosenman identified a behaviour pattern that appeared to be related to a person's susceptibility to CHD (Friedman and Rosenman, 1959). Heart attacks occur when the blood vessels that serve the heart become blocked, whereas strokes involve the blood vessels in the brain. The two most important risk factors in CHD are high blood pressure and a high level of cholesterol in the blood. Friedman and Rosenman characterised the disease-prone **type A pattern** as one of excessive competitive drive, an intense disposition, impatience, hostility, fast movements and rapid speech. People with the **type B pattern** were less competitive, less hostile, more patient, easy-going and tolerant, and they moved and talked more slowly; they were also less likely to suffer from CHD. Friedman and Rosenman developed a questionnaire that distinguished between these two types of people. The test is rather interesting, because the person who administers it is not a passive participant. The interviewer asks questions in an abrupt, impatient manner, interrupting the subject if they take too much time to answer a question. The point of such behaviour is to try to elicit type A behaviour from the subject.

Despite initial research showing that type A behaviour pattern was associated with twice the rate of CHD relative to non-type-A behaviour patterns (Rosenman *et al.*, 1975), research since has not been so conclusive. For example, one large study found that although people classified as type A were more likely to have heart attacks, the long-term survival

rate after having a heart attack was higher for type A patients than for type B patients (Ragland and Brand, 1988). In this case, it would seem better to be type A, at least after having a non-fatal heart attack. Other studies have failed to find a difference in the likelihood of CHD in people with type A and type B personalities (Dimsdale, 1988).

There also seems to be a relationship between the competitive aspect of type A personalities and blood pressure and heart rate. In one study, blood pressure and cardiovascular activity was measured in 36 male and female undergraduates who took part in a motorised racing game experiment (Harrison *et al.*, 2001) where they played alone, or in competition with the experimenter, or in collaboration with the experimenter.

The competitive condition was associated with significant increases in blood pressure and heart rate whereas the cooperative condition produced barely discernible changes in activity, a finding that echoes reports in the literature of reduced or stable cardiovascular activity in response to stress in the presence of a supportive person. As expected, the competitive condition was rated the most competitive condition and the cooperative condition was rated the most cooperative while the solo condition was rated the least difficult and engaging of the three.

Occupational stress

Occupational stress refers to the degree of stress experienced by members of different professions and a variety of professions have been extensively studied including Jamaican police officers (Nelson and Smith, 2016), emergency department workers (Basu *et al.*, 2016), journalists (Monteiro *et al.*, 2016) and genetic counsellors (Johnstone *et al.*, 2016), with high demand and low control being particularly strong predictors of stress and ill-health.

This area of research is a popular one in organisational psychology and the Whitehall Study of CHD in British civil servants is a good example of the type of work carried out in this area. This study has shown that the lower the grade of employment in the civil service, the higher the mortality rate from CHD. The Whitehall II Study followed a different cohort and investigated whether two factors might be associated with CHD-related mortality: high psychosocial pressure and low control over their environment (Marmot *et al.*, 1997).

In an extensive study of absenteeism in 84,319 individuals in two counties in Sweden, Knutsson and Goine (1998) found that the professions showing highest degrees of absenteeism for men were shop assistants, repairmen and welders, whereas loggers and mechanics were absent for the fewest days. The professions with the highest absenteeism rates for women were shop assistants, assistant nurses and secretaries (the lowest rates were for primary school teachers). Of course, these findings do not necessarily suggest that these professions are marked by acute stress (and, therefore, by high rates of absenteeism) although they might, but they suggest that some professions may be more susceptible to stressors.

Much of the applied work in occupational or organisational psychology has been directed towards helping people to cope with the stress generated by heavy workloads or excessive working hours (Warr, 1990; Buunk *et al.*, 1998). This work can lead to 'burn-out'. Burn-out has been defined as 'a unique affective response to stress [and] a multidimensional construct consisting of emotional exhaustion, physical fatigue, and cognitive weariness' (Melamed *et al.*, 2006). In the workplace, it can result from constant and persistent exposure to stressors. Melamed *et al.* (2006) investigated the relationship between burn-out and risk of cardiovascular disease and reported an association with ill health, sleep disturbance and impaired immune system functioning. Coping style is also related to burn-out, with task-orientated coping associated with reduced burn-out and emotion-orientated coping associated with increased burn-out (Howlett *et al.*, 2015).

There appears to be a significant relationship between the number of hours worked and the degree of physical and mental illness an employee experiences, but the extent of this relationship is unclear: most conclude that the two are related but the relationship is not particularly strong (Sparks *et al.*, 1997). Studies from Japan, however, suggest that individuals who work in excess of 11 hours a day are more at risk of myocardial infarction than are those who work a moderate number (Sokejima and Kagamimori, 1998). In Japan, it is thought that long working hours can cause sudden fatal heart attacks, called 'karoshi' (Uehata, 1991, cited in Kageyama *et al.*, 1997). Kageyama *et al.*'s study of working commuters suggests that those with the longest commuting times and who work the most overtime show greater variability in heart rate than do those who commute and work less.

The ferocious work ethic of the Japanese is famed: they work longer hours than the British, Germans or North Americans. This devotion has been blamed for the estimated drop in birth rate from 1.28 to 1.26 per couple in 2006: people are too busy working to procreate and bring up a family. A study of 968 Canadian employees has found that those in higher-status occupations suffer greater conflicts between home and work than do those in lower-status occupations (Schieman *et al.*, 2006). This conflict was most pronounced in the self-employed, those with greater job authority and those who worked longer hours.

Unemployment

Almost all of us have to earn a living: money allows us to do many of the things we want to do and employment gives structure and meaning to our lives. Unemployment, however, has been associated with an increase in ill health (Kim *et al.*, 2016; Overland, 2016) – see Figure 17.12. Reviews of studies

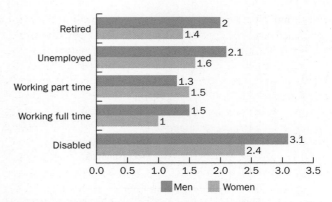

Figure 17.12 Average depression score for adults ages 63–73, by work status.

Source: From The impact of work on the psychological health and well-being of older Americans. *Annual Review of Gerontology and Geriatrics*, 26, pp. 153–74 (James, J.B. and Spiro, A. 2007) (c) Springer Publishing Company. Reproduced with the permission of the Springer Publishing Company, LLC, New York, NY 10036.

conducted after the financial crash of 2008 find an increase in reported mental illness and suicides (Parmar *et al.*, 2016).

One consequence of unemployment is increased isolation and loss of social context (Donovan and Oddy, 1982). A Danish study of employed and unemployed single mothers found that isolation can lead to depression (Beck-Jorgensen, 1991) and that lower self-esteem is characteristic of people who become unemployed (Winefield and Tiggemann, 1994). A longitudinal study of 1,060 young people who were monitored over five years since their last term at school in northern Sweden found that unemployment was correlated significantly with increases in depressive symptoms, even when their initial health status was accounted for (Hammarstrom and Janlert, 1997).

However, it is possible that being in a job that you loathe may be just as detrimental to your physical and psychological well-being. Broom *et al.* (2006) investigated this possibility in a group of 2,500 40–44-year-old Australians. They found, as perhaps expected, that unemployed people reported generally worse health than those who were employed. However, people who had job insecurity, low marketability and experienced great strain at work expressed poorer health than did those who were in jobs with few or no stressors. If all three negative outcomes were reported, those people reporting them indicated that it was no better than being unemployed.

'These findings challenge the assumption that any job is better for health than is no job at all,' say the authors, 'suggesting that the quality of work tempers the health benefits of employment' (p. 583).

Optimism, conscientiousness and forgiveness

Optimism refers to a disposition to believe in positive outcomes. Evidence suggests that dispositional optimists (those who are characteristically optimistic) are more successful at coping with ill health (Stanton and Snider, 1993), are not as emotionally perturbed by stressors (Aspinwall and Taylor, 1992), can cope better with breast cancer surgery (Stanton and Snider, 1993), report better physical health (Scheier and Carver, 1992), have a better quality of life (Fitzgerald *et al.*, 1993) and show an increase in helper T cells and natural killer cells (Segerstrom *et al.*, 1998). Optimism is also associated with better adjustment in university (Segerstrom *et al.*, 1998) and to the stress generated by missile attack (Zeidner and Hammer, 1992). A study of 163 early-stage breast cancer patients found that 5–13 years after surgery the degree of initial optimism expressed before treatment was positively related to people's feelings of well-being later on (medical variables predicted very little of reported well-being at follow-up) (Carver *et al.*, 2005).

Allied to optimism is forgiveness – the willingness to ignore or put aside past perceived offences. Some early research had suggested that this willingness was associated with better health. In one study, unforgiving thoughts produced greater aversive emotion and higher heart rate, blood pressure and brow muscle activity than did forgiving thoughts (Witvliet *et al.*, 2001). But some experiments by researchers in the US and the UK have found that forgiveness may not be as beneficial to the person forgiving as it might be (Luchies *et al.*, 2010). They found that the self-respect and self-concept of people who forgave their agreeable spouses who made amends increased but the opposite was found when the perpetrator was highly disagreeable or who only weakly made amends, thereby demonstrating a 'doormat effect'.

'It may not be prudent to recommend forgiveness,' the authors caution, 'without considering the extent to which the perpetrator has acted in a manner that signals that the victim will be safe and valued in a continued relationship with the perpetrator' (p. 746).

Conscientiousness may protect against ill health, as you saw in Chapter 14. Studies since the 1990s have suggested that this trait correlated with longevity (Friedman *et al.*, 1993). In a meta-analysis of 194 studies in which conscientiousness-related traits were associated with risk factors for mortality such as smoking, drinking alcohol, using drugs, being sexually promiscuous and so on, Bogg and Roberts (2004) found that the relationship between conscientiousness and risky health-related behaviours was weak but the relationship between this trait and beneficial health-related behaviours was significant. The more conscientious the participants were, the fewer symptoms of ill health they reported.

A study of 366 individuals asked participants to keep daily diaries of stressors experienced, ways of coping with those stressors and the amount of positive affect experienced (Bartley and Roesch, 2011). They also completed a Five Factor Personality measure. Individuals scoring high in conscientiousness were more likely to use more problem-focused coping. This, in turn, was associated with increased positive affect. The findings suggest that conscientiousness may mediate our response to stressors by influencing our coping strategy, one that is focused on dealing with the problem.

Cutting edge: Words, connectedness to nature, longevity and the pursuit of happiness

What, apart from conscientiousness, is likely to lead to a healthier, happier life? Two variables might be your written expression and your connectedness to nature. Specifically, the writing of words that reflect a positive effect.

Pressma and Cohen (2012) examined the written output of 88 contributors to *A History of Psychology in Autobiography*. They found that the more often positive words were used, the longer the writer lived. Positive words included ones such as: lively, vigorous and attentive. There was no relationship between longevity and negatively hued words, such as angry, afraid and drowsy. An earlier study had found that having a positive emotional style added between 2 and 23 extra years to your life (Levy *et al.*, 2002).

Connectedness to nature – how close we feel to the outdoors – also shows a small but significant association with subjective well-being. Capaldi *et al.* (2014) undertook a meta-analysis of 30 samples totalling 8,523 participants for studies which examined the relationship between connectedness and well-being. The participants who felt more connected were those who had experienced more positive effect, expressed more vitality and expressed more life satisfaction. Connectedness was most strongly associated with feelings of vitality.

Cutting edge: The neural correlates of living the good life

Various factors can influence our psychological well-being, from many of the variables described above, to listening to the sounds of nature which can help with the recovery from stress (Annerstedt *et al.*, 2013). Psychologists have argued that subjective well-being comprises two different but interacting components: a cognitive one and an affective one. The

Cutting edge: *Continued*

cognitive component refers to how we think about our lives and the satisfaction we derive from our evaluations. The affective component refers to the pleasant thoughts we have about our lives.

Kong *et al.* (2014) sought to determine which regions of the brain mediated our subjective well-being by taking 294 university students, measuring their brain activation at rest and correlating this activation with measures of well-being. The researchers also administered tests measuring the cognitive and affective components of well-being. They found that activation in certain brain regions predicted people's cognitive well-being (including the

bilateral superior temporal gyrus, the right thalamus, right lingual gyrus and left planum temporale). A different region, and only one, predicted people's affective well-being – the amygdala.

Lewis *et al.* (2013) took MRI scans of 70 young individuals who had completed measures designed to assess human potential and correlated the two. This type of well-being was associated with larger volume in the insula on the right. That is, the greater the sense of a purpose in life, the greater the person's relations with others, and personal growth, the larger was this region. The left insula was also larger in those who had good relations with others.

Social support

Although all of us experience stress, the experience is a subjective and private matter. Nobody else can truly know what we feel. However, being confronted by a stressor and coping with stress are often social matters. We learn as children to seek others – parents, siblings and friends – when we need help. This is a pattern of coping that continues over the lifespan. Social support – the help that we receive from others in times of stress – is an important coping strategy for many people for two reasons. First, we can benefit from the experience of others in dealing with the same or similar stressors. Other people can show us how to cope, perhaps by teaching us how to reappraise the situation. Secondly, other people can provide encouragement and incentives to overcome the stressor when we may otherwise fail to cope with the stressful situation.

A Finnish study has reported that women who gave, rather than received, support in intimate relationships took fewer days off sick from work (Vaananen *et al.*, 2005). A different pattern, however, was seen in men. They took fewer days off if they received more support from their partner than they gave.

Eighty-nine first-year undergraduates completed a battery of depression, stress, social support and friendship measures at the beginning and end of their first term (Brissette *et al.*, 2002). When greater optimism was expressed at the beginning of the term, smaller increases in stress and depression and greater perception of social support were reported later in the term. The number of friends in the social network, however, did not seem to affect response to stress. Social support was found to contribute significantly to the better adjustment experienced by the optimistic, suggesting that this could be a mediating factor.

Finally, researchers at the University of Michigan looked at the relationship between mortality and the giving and receiving of social and emotional support in a group of 423 elderly married couples (Brown *et al.*, 2003). In the late 1980s, participants were interviewed about how much social support they gave to relatives, neighbours and spouses, such as running errands,

shopping, helping with housework, providing transport or childcare, and so on. They were also asked whether they made their spouse feel loved and whether they were willing to listen to their spouse in times of need. In addition, respondents were asked how often they were the recipients of such support. Five years after the interviews took place, the mortality rate in the sample was assessed and correlated with the survey responses. Surprisingly, those who reported giving support to others showed least risk for mortality, whether the support was social or emotional. This relationship held even when demographic, personality and health variables were controlled for.

Coping with everyday stress

The degree to which we experience stress and the degree to which stress impairs our health depends to a large extent on our perception of the threat posed by the stressor. The number of potential stressors is very large. Depending on the individual, almost any aspect of the environment can be perceived as a stressor.

Sources of stress

Stress can be induced by changes that threaten or otherwise complicate life. The death of a spouse, being promoted at work, changes in social activities, getting married and sustaining a personal injury or illness are significant life changes that cause stress and disrupt everyday life (Holmes and Rahe, 1967). Some evidence has accumulated that suggests that if an individual experiences enough changes in lifestyle over a short time period, they are likely to develop a physical illness within the next two years (Rahe and Arthur, 1978). Other research suggests that not all people who encounter a series of significant stressors over a short period are at risk of illness (DePue and Monroe, 1986). Why? Once again, the answer lies in the way that people perceive stressors. Recall Lazarus's idea of cognitive appraisal: the amount of stress induced by a stimulus perceived to be a stressor is determined by how significant we believe its threat to be and whether we feel competent to cope with that threat.

Stressors do not have to be catastrophic or cause significant changes in lifestyle to induce stress. Often, the everyday hassles we experience are enough to leave us feeling stressed out. Locking our keys in the car, being late for an appointment or having a disagreement with a friend are examples of stressful everyday events.

A common source of daily stress comes simply from making routine choices about what to do, how to do it or when to do it. Consider, for example, a choice between studying tonight for a test you have tomorrow or going to a party with some friends. You want to do both, but you can only do one (you are back into the classic self-control situation again – the choice between a small, short-term reward and a larger, long-term reward). Psychologists refer to this as an approach–approach conflict because the choice involves two desirable outcomes. Other choices involve approach–avoidance conflicts – one outcome is desirable and the other is not. For example, you live in Kent, want to visit Oslo and decide to travel by sea because you are afraid of flying. Still other choices involve avoidance – avoidance conflicts in which both outcomes are undesirable. For instance, choosing between having a root canal procedure or having a tooth extracted creates stress because you do not want to have either one of them, yet one needs to be done.

Several different tests have been developed to measure the severity of various stressors on people. Among the first measures to be developed was Holmes and Rahe's (1967) Social Readjustment Rating Scale (SRRS), which was devised on the assumption that any change in a person's life is a stressor. The test asks people to rate the amount of change or adjustment caused by recent events in their life, such as getting married or divorced, getting a new job or being sacked, moving to a new location, and losing a loved one. Responses are given in terms of life-change units (LCUs) – how much change or adjustment is caused by specific events. Once a person completes the SRRS, the LCUs are summed, resulting in a single score. High scores indicate high levels of stress and low scores low levels of stress. People who get high scores have been shown to have more illness and adjustment problems than have people who get lower scores (Holmes and Rahe, 1967; Monroe *et al.*, 1992).

Another commonly used scale, the Daily Hassles and Uplifts Scale, measures daily events that are either troublesome (hassles) or pleasant (uplifts) (DeLongis *et al.*, 1988). This scale requires people to rate, at the end of each day, the extent to which an event, such as the weather, deadlines, family or physical appearance, served as a hassle or uplift for them on that day. This scale may be completed daily over extended periods to provide a picture of how the routine events of everyday life create stress for people. Daily hassles yield a more accurate prediction of physical illness and adjustment problems than do daily uplifts (DeLongis *et al.*, 1988) and major life events (Garrett *et al.*, 1991).

Coping styles and strategies

So far, we have considered the negative effects of stress: its damaging effects on the body and mind. However, each of us can learn to control stress. We may not always be able to predict when and where we will encounter stressors or to control their intensity, but we can mitigate their damaging effects by adopting coping strategies that are consistent with our lifestyles. A **coping strategy** is simply a plan of action that we follow, either in anticipation of encountering a stressor or as a direct response to stress as it occurs, which is effective in reducing the level of stress we experience. Coping strategies which alter appraisals of stressors in particular and the emotional responses to them are associated with better long-term health outcomes (Denson *et al.*, 2009).

According to Lazarus and Folkman (1984; Folkman and Lazarus, 1991), there are two types of coping response: problem-focused and emotion-focused. **Problem-focused coping** is directed towards the source of the stress. For example, if the stress is job related, a person might try to change conditions at work or take courses to acquire skills that will enable them to obtain a different job. **Emotion-focused coping** is directed towards a person's own personal reaction to the stressor. For example, a person might try to relax and forget about the problem or find solace in the company of friends. Obviously, if the source of a stress-producing problem has a potential solution, problem-focused coping is the best strategy. If it does not, then emotion-focused coping is the only option.

We each have our own idiosyncratic ways of dealing with stress that can be categorised as being emotion-focused. In fact, health psychologists have shown several of these methods to be effective in controlling stress, including aerobic exercise, cognitive reappraisal, progressive relaxation training and social support. Some people engage in other activities such as smoking, although evidence suggests that smoking results in no significant self-reported decrease in anxiety.

Resilience

You have already seen how various personality factors can act as protective agents against stress and ill health. Optimism is one – an optimistic disposition is associated with significantly fewer symptoms of ill health and stress.

Another factor is resilience. People are sometimes said to have 'bounced back' from some misfortune or some adversity, suggesting that they are resilient. Some psychologists have likened resilience to the property of metals: cast iron is hard and brittle (not resilient) whereas wrought iron is soft and malleable (resilient). Resilient individuals, in a psychological rather than metallurgical sense, are said to be able to bounce back from negative experiences and adapt to changing, adverse environmental conditions: they are optimistic, energetic, curious and express high degrees of positive emotion. Some psychological research has explored whether these positive emotions are a by-product of resilience or whether they are essential to resilient people's ability to cope. Some of the factors underpinning resilience include self-esteem, attributional style and low perfectionism (Johnson *et al.*, 2017).

Tugade and Fredrickson (2004) induced stress by asking participants to prepare a speech and deliver it to a video camera. The participants were told that their performance would be evaluated by their peers. In fact, this was an experimental ruse and there was no evaluating group. Cardiovascular and psychological responses were measured during and after the delivery of the speech. Individuals who characteristically expressed positive emotion were more likely to show cardiovascular recovery after the stressful task (giving a speech). They were also more likely to find positive meaning in negative events. Given that increased cardiovascular reactivity produced by negative events predicts ill health, this degree of resilience suggests that the factor may protect against such ill health by reducing one of its predictors.

The study based their characterisation of resilience on participants' self-report. It would be useful to see whether a group of individuals rated by peers as resilient would show a similar pattern of behaviour. Furthermore, it would be useful to see whether this resilience is constant or whether it fluctuates and is affected by different types of negative experiences.

Some people use retrieval of positive memories to offset the unpleasant emotion created by negative experiences. Joormann and Siemer (2004) examined whether undergraduates' ability to cope with negative mood involved evoking positive memories. People who were slightly depressed were unlikely to evoke positive memories to cope with the unhappy memories; those who did not experience depression but were unhappy did use positive emotion. Even when the depressed participants were asked to recall only pleasant memories, they still reported being unhappy.

Cognitive reappraisal

Aerobic exercise is not the coping strategy of choice for everyone. Some people find that simply altering their perception of the threat posed by stressors reduces stress. This coping strategy is called **cognitive reappraisal** (or cognitive restructuring) and is an extension of Lazarus and Folkman's idea of cognitive appraisal. It is one of the more effective adaptive strategies, although there are situations in which it is not effective (McRae, 2016).

The rationale underlying cognitive reappraisal is easy to grasp: if our cognitive appraisal of a stressor is a determining factor in producing stress, then by reappraising that stressor as being less threatening, stress should be reduced. Sometimes, simply learning to substitute an incompatible response, such as replacing a negative statement with a positive one, is sufficient to reduce stress (Lazarus, 1971; Meichenbaum, 1977). For example, students who suffer from test anxiety perceive tests as extremely threatening. They may say to themselves, 'I am going to fail the exam tomorrow', or, 'That test is going to be

far too hard'. To reappraise the stressor in this case would involve replacing these statements with ones such as 'I'm going to pass that test tomorrow' or 'Yes, the test will be difficult, but I'm ready for it'.

Cognitive reappraisal is an effective coping strategy because it is often a more realistic approach to interpreting the threat posed by stressors than is the original appraisal. We have good reason to appraise a charging bear as a real threat, but not a university examination. After all, we may not be able to deal with the bear, but we can always learn how to take tests and improve our study habits. An additional benefit of cognitive reappraisal is that it teaches the individual that they can take control of stressful situations.

Relaxation training

Another coping strategy is simply learning to relax when confronted with a stressor. Relaxing is based on the same principle as cognitive reappraisal: substitute an incompatible response for the stress reaction. One procedure for producing relaxation is the **progressive relaxation technique**. It involves three steps: (1) recognising your body's signals informing you that you are experiencing stress; (2) using those signals as a cue to begin relaxing; and (3) relaxing by focusing your attention on different groups of muscles, beginning with those in the head and neck and then those in the arms and legs. Imagine that when confronted by a stressor, for example an exam, you respond by tensing certain muscles: those in your hand and fingers that you use to hold your pen or pencil and those around your mouth that you use to clench your teeth. Once you become aware of these responses, you can use them as cues to relax the muscle groups involved.

Some have also suggested that the use of aromas can alleviate stress and anxiety; this is sometimes called aromatherapy. Aromatherapy is, in fact, a misnomer because there is usually more to aromatherapy than just the presentation of odour; clients normally receive massage as well. The evidence for a long-term, or even short-term, effect of odour on mental health is sparse; few studies have investigated this relationship scientifically and those that have done so have serious methodological or statistical flaws (see G.N. Martin, 1996, for a review).

Stress inoculation training

According to psychologist Donald Meichenbaum, the best way to cope with stress is to take the offensive – to have a plan in mind for dealing with stressors before you are actually confronted by them. In other words, people should not wait until they are faced with a stressor to cope with it; instead, they should anticipate the kinds of stressor most likely to affect them and develop the most effective coping plan for dealing with specific stressors. Meichenbaum (1985), in fact, has devised a problem-focused coping method, called **stress inoculation training**, which focuses on helping people to develop coping skills that will decrease their susceptibility to the negative effects of stress.

Stress inoculation training has been found to be effective in reducing stress levels among people working in a variety of settings, including nurses, teachers, police trainees (Bishop, 1994) and professional athletes (Cox, 1991).

Stress inoculation training usually occurs in a clinical setting involving a therapist and a client and takes place over three phases aimed at achieving seven goals.

> In Meichenbaum's words (1985, p. 21), stress inoculation training is analogous to the concept of medical inoculation against biological diseases.... Analogous to medical inoculation, [stress inoculation training] is designed to build 'psychological antibodies', or coping skills, and to enhance resistance through exposure to stimuli that are strong enough to arouse defenses without being so powerful as to overcome them.

The first phase is called the conceptualisation phase and involves two basic goals. Goal 1 involves learning about the transactional nature of stress and coping. Stress and coping are strongly influenced by the interaction of cognitive and environmental variables. A person experiences stress to the extent that they appraise the stressor – an environmental variable – as taxing or overwhelming their ability to cope with it – a cognitive variable. In Meichenbaum's view, coping is any behavioural/cognitive attempt to overcome, eliminate or otherwise control the negative effects caused by the stressor (see also Lazarus and Folkman, 1984).

Goal 2 involves becoming better at realistically appraising stressful situations by taking stock of, or self-monitoring, patterns in maladaptive thinking, feeling and behaving. A person may keep a diary, or a 'stress log', to record stressful events, the conditions under which these events occur, and their reactions to these events.

The second phase is called the skills acquisition and rehearsal phase and involves goals 3–5. Goal 3 involves learning specific problem-solving skills aimed at reducing stress. For example, a person may learn to identify and define a specific stressor and outline a plan for dealing with it in behavioural terms. The plan should include developing alternative ideas for dealing with the stressor and considering the possible consequences that correspond to each alternative. At this point, a person may find relaxation training and self-instructional training, in which they learn to make positive self-statements when confronted by a stressor, helpful.

Goal 4 involves learning and rehearsing emotion-regulation and self-control skills. These skills help people to remain calm and rational when confronted with a stressor. Goal 5 involves learning how to use maladaptive responses as a cue to invoke the new coping strategy. For example, when faced with a stressor, you may feel yourself getting tense. This feeling of tension is your cue to implement specific aspects of your inoculation training, which presumably would reduce your level of stress.

The third and final phase of Meichenbaum's programme is called the application and follow-through phase and comprises goals 6 and 7. Goal 6 involves imagery rehearsal, in which a person practises coping with the stressor by imagining being confronted by that stressor in progressively more difficult situations. The purpose of rehearsing the coping skills is to build confidence in one's ability to use the new coping strategy. Goal 7 involves learning to apply new coping abilities to both expected and unexpected stressors. This might be accomplished by imagining several situations in which you feel anxious, imagining implementing the coping strategy in response to the anxiety and, finally, imagining feeling relieved as a result of coping with the stressor.

Stress is an inevitable consequence of environmental change. Both large changes, such as a natural disaster or changing jobs, and small changes, such as remembering that we have an exam tomorrow, contribute to the overall level of stress that we experience at any one time. Whether stress impairs our health depends on three variables: the extent to which we appraise the stressor as threatening, whether we engage in good health practices, and the extent to which we use coping strategies effectively. The combined effects of these variables on the relationship between stress and health are summarised in Figure 17.13.

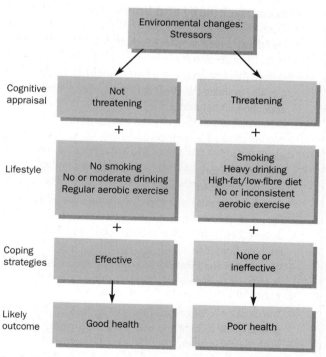

Figure 17.13 The effects of stress on health are mediated by cognitive appraisal, lifestyle and coping abilities.

Do psychological interventions reduce stress?

Psychologists know that psychological stress is linked to immune system responses: one causes disruption of the other. If psychological factors can affect the immune system, it seems reasonable to hypothesise that psychological factors that play a large part in intervention treatment can also affect immune system response. Over 85 intervention studies of the effect of psychological variables on stress have now appeared in journals, most of them appearing since the 1980s (Miller and Cohen, 2001).

Miller and Cohen's review suggests that the success of interventions is modest. The authors reviewed studies which examined the effects of different types of intervention on immune system functioning. These included (1) stress management interventions which are normally undertaken with patients with medical illness – these interventions involve educating the person about the illness, and providing coping skills training and psychological support; (2) relaxation interventions which involve muscle relaxation; (3) disclosure interventions which usually ask participants to write about their stressful experiences; (4) hypnosis; and (5) conditioning interventions in which a neutral stimulus is paired with an immune system facilitator so that the presentation of the neutral stimulus alone will produce the immune system response.

The researchers found that stress management interventions altered immune responses very little; relaxation interventions also showed little evidence of producing immune response changes; disclosure interventions were modestly successful in enhancing immune system response; hypnosis showed that participants could use hypnotic suggestion to alter immune responses; and conditioning interventions were also modestly successful in changing immune system response.

Although two of these interventions met with some success, none of the interventions was found to be beneficial to people suffering stress caused by illness. Perhaps such interventions are inappropriate for counteracting the stress experienced by medically ill individuals (e.g. those suffering from cancer). The authors suggest that people most likely to benefit from stress management and relaxation are those suffering ongoing, chronic stress such as the bereaved and those who have been involved in natural disasters.

Chapter review

Health psychology and unhealthy behaviour

- Health psychology applies psychological principles to the study of health and illness. It examines the effects of various psychological and physical factors on health and can also evaluate the effect of health policy and health education on behaviour.
- Behaviours which have implications for health psychology include smoking, eating, sexual behaviour, exercise and alcohol use.
- Protective factors are those which make the individual less susceptible to ill health.
- Evidence suggests that people who have high-fat, low-fibre diets tend to be more susceptible to coronary heart disease (CHD) and cancer than are people who have low-fat, high-fibre diets.
- Weight gain and increased low-density lipoprotein (LDL) cholesterol levels are both risk factors for CHD and cancer.
- The decision to begin smoking is influenced by peer pressure, low income and poor education; smoking normally begins in adolescence and is rarely initiated in adulthood.

- Smoking cessation programmes have met with limited success; a combination of nicotine replacement and psychological treatments appears to show the best outcome.
- Exercise appears to be effective in increasing positive mood and alleviating mild depression.
- The best precautionary measure against contracting any sexually transmitted disease (STD) is the practice of safe sex.

Stress and health

- Stress is defined in terms of our physiological and psychological response to stimuli that either prevent us from obtaining a goal or endanger our well-being.
- Selye's model describes how prolonged exposure to stress leads to illness and sometimes death.
- The stress response, which Cannon called the fight or flight response, is useful as a short-term response to threatening stimuli but is harmful in the long term. This response includes increased activity of the sympathetic branch of the autonomic nervous system and increased secretion of epinephrine, norepinephrine and glucocorticoids by the adrenal gland.
- Although increased levels of epinephrine and norepinephrine can raise blood pressure, most of the stressor-related harm to health comes from glucocorticoids.

- Prolonged exposure to high levels of these hormones can increase blood pressure, damage muscle tissue, lead to infertility, inhibit growth, inhibit the inflammatory response and suppress the immune system.
- The most important predictor of ill health produced by stressors is the nature of a person's coping response.
- Personality characteristics which may serve as protective factors against stress include optimism and conscientiousness.
- Type A behaviour pattern refers to behaviour that is competitive, hostile, rapid and intense; some of these variables, especially hostility, may predict the likelihood of CHD, but the research findings are mixed.
- Psychoneuroimmunology is the study of the effects of psychological stressors on the immune system.
- The immune system consists of several types of white blood cell that produce chemically mediated and cell-mediated responses. The immune system can cause harm when it triggers an allergic reaction or when it attacks the body's own tissues in autoimmune diseases.
- The most important mechanism by which stress impairs immune function is by increasing blood levels of glucocorticoids. Neural input to the bone marrow, lymph nodes and thymus gland may also play a role; naturally occurring opioids appear to suppress the activity of internal killer cells.
- A wide variety of stressful situations, such as the death of a spouse or caring for a relative with Alzheimer's disease, have been shown to increase people's susceptibility to infectious diseases.

Coping with everyday stress

- Stress may stem from a wide variety of sources. Even positive events, such as the birth of a child or the marriage of a son or daughter can produce stress.
- Stress may lead to physical illness when a person undergoes several stressful events over a short period of time. The extent to which people become ill appears to depend on the extent to which they perceive a stressor as being a threat to their well-being and the extent to which they believe they can cope with that threat.
- Lazarus and Folkman have identified two types of coping.

  – Problem-focused coping represents any attempt to reduce stress by attempting to change the event or situation producing the stress.
  – Emotion-focused coping centres on changing one's personal reaction to the stressful event or situation. Emotion-focused coping may involve activities such as aerobic exercise, cognitive reappraisal, relaxation training and seeking social support.

- Meichenbaum's stress inoculation training programme is a problem-focused coping strategy that prepares people to cope with anticipated stressors. Its seven goals of stress inoculation training focus on specific kinds of knowledge, behaviour and coping strategies central to preparing people to anticipate, confront and reduce the threat posed by stressful situations.
- Reviews of the benefits of psychological interventions in stress have produced mixed results; some interventions are modestly successful; others show no benefit.

Suggestions for further reading

Daruna, J.H. (2012) *Introduction to Psychoneuroimmunology.* Oxford: Academic Press.

Eisenberger, N.I. (2013) Social ties and health: A social neuroscience perspective. *Current Opinion in Neurobiology,* 23, 407–13.

Kalkhoran, S. and Glantz, S.A. (2016) E-cigarettes and smoking cessation in real-world and clinical settings: A systematic review and meta-analysis. *The Lancet Respiratory Medicine,* 4(2), 116–28.

Lavallo, W.R. (2017). *Stress and Health: Biological and Psychological Interventions.* London: Sage.

Marsland, A.L., Walsh, C., Lockwood, K. and John-Henderson, N.A. (2017) The effects of acute psychological stress on circulating and stimulated inflammatory markers: A systematic review and meta-analysis. *Brain, Behavior, and Immunity.*

Ogden, J. (2012) *Health Psychology* (5th edn). Maidenhead: Open University Press.

Sarafino, E.P. and Smith, T.W. (2014) *Health Psychology: Biopsychosocial Interactions* (8th edn). London: Wiley.

Vitaliano, P.P., Young, H.M. and Zhang, J. (2004) Is caregiving a risk factor for illness? *Current Directions in Psychological Science,* 13, 1, 13–16.

Yang, T., Zhu, M., Chen, Q., Liu, Y. and Deng, J. (2016) Is the global occupational stress equally addressed? A systematic literature review on effective stress interventions. *Evidence-based Medicine and Public Health,* 2.

A good selection of items covering topics reviewed in the chapter.

CHAPTER 18
Mental health and illness

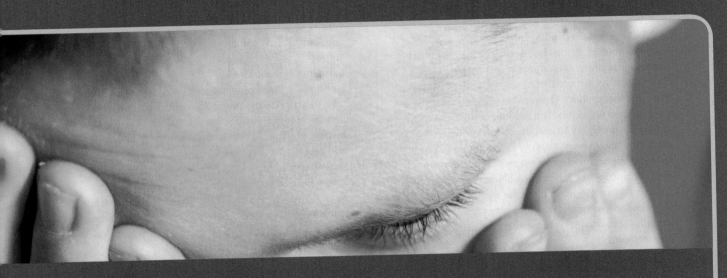

ASK CARRIE FISHER: I'M BIPOLAR – HOW DO YOU FEEL AT PEACE WITH MENTAL ILLNESS?

I was told that I was bipolar when I was 24 but was unable to accept that diagnosis until I was 28 when I overdosed and finally got sober. Only then was I able to see nothing else could explain away my behavior.

We have been given a challenging illness, and there is no other option than to meet those challenges. Think of it as an opportunity to be heroic – not 'I survived living in Mosul during an attack' heroic, but an emotional survival. An opportunity to be a good example to others who might share our disorder. That's why it's important to find a community – however small – of other bipolar people to share experiences and find comfort in the similarities.

You don't have to like doing a lot of what you do, you just have to do it. You can let it all fall down and feel defeated and hopeless and that you're done. But you reached out to me – that took courage. Now build on that. Move through those feelings and meet me on the other side. As your bipolar sister, I'll be watching. Now get out there and show me and you what you can do.

Carrie Fisher, 2016

WHAT YOU SHOULD BE ABLE TO DO AFTER READING CHAPTER 18

- Define the term 'mental illness'.

- Explain the aim of classification of mental disorders and define mental abnormality.

- Describe the most important treatment approaches to mental disorders.

- Describe the symptoms and causes of major mental disorders.

- Evaluate theories of mental disorder.

- Evaluate treatment approaches to mental disorder.

QUESTIONS TO THINK ABOUT

- When does a normal behaviour become abnormal?

- Which term makes the best sense: mental disorder or mental illness? Why?

- How, and in what ways, are mental illnesses different from 'physical' ones? Are they?

- Are mental illnesses categorical or do they fall along a continuum?

- Do all mental disorders have a biological basis?

- What are the best treatments for mental illness? Do you think some treatment approaches are more appropriate than others?

- Why do people hold negative views of people with mental illness?

Classification and diagnosis of mental disorders

Abnormal psychology is the area of psychology which studies and treats mental illness. A mental disorder has been defined as 'a syndrome characterised by clinically significant disturbance in an individual's cognition, emotional regulation, or behaviour that reflects a dysfunction in the psychological, biological or developmental processes underlying mental functioning' (American Psychiatric Association, DSM, 2013, p. 20). Its cause may be genetic, environmental, cognitive or neurobiological, and it produces serious distress to the individual and a disruption to the individual's social and occupational life. The purpose of a diagnosis of mental disorder is to help prognosis, plan a treatment and predict and evaluate treatment outcomes, although a diagnosis may not necessarily lead to the suggestion of treatment. According to the World Health Organisation (WHO, 2010), 450 million people in the world suffer from mental illness.

The names of some mental illnesses you may already be familiar with – depression and anxiety, for example. Others will not be so familiar, such as **paraphilia** and **conversion disorder**. Although the symptoms described for each disorder may apply to healthy individuals who exhibit a 'bad mood' or who are under stress, these disorders represent a severe impairment in functioning. Clinical depression is not the same as the 'low' we sometimes feel in life, and generalised anxiety disorder does not represent the stress we feel before an exam or speaking in public.

'Mental disorder' is a clinical impairment characterised by abnormal thought, feeling or behaviour. Some mental disorders, especially the less severe ones, appear to be caused by environmental factors or by a person's perception of these factors, such as stress or unhealthy family interactions. In contrast, many of the more severe mental disorders appear to be caused by hereditary and other biological factors that disrupt normal thought processes or produce inappropriate emotional reactions. The descriptions of mental disorders in this chapter necessarily make distinctions that are not always easy to make in real life; the essential features of the more important mental disorders are simplified here for the sake of clarity. In addition, many of the cases that clinicians encounter are less clear-cut than the ones included here and are thus not so easily classified.

To understand, diagnose and treat psychological disorders, some sort of classification system is needed. The need for a comprehensive classification system of psychological disorders was first recognised by Emil Kraepelin (1856–1926), who provided his version in a textbook of psychiatry published in 1883. The classification most widely used today still retains a number of Kraepelin's original categories.

What is 'abnormal'?

Mental disorders are characterised by abnormal behaviour, thoughts and feelings. The term 'abnormal' literally refers to any departure from the norm. Thus, a short or tall person is 'abnormal', and so is someone who is especially intelligent or talented. Albert Einstein was 'abnormal', as were Oscar Wilde and Pablo Picasso. The term 'abnormal' is often used pejoratively – it is used to refer to characteristics that are disliked or feared – but this is not the way in which it is used when describing mental illness. The most important feature of a mental disorder, however, may not be whether a person's behaviour is abnormal – different from that of most other people – but whether it is maladaptive. Mental disorders cause distress or discomfort and often interfere with people's ability to lead useful, productive lives. They often make it impossible for people to hold down jobs, raise families or relate to others socially.

The causes of mental disorders

What causes mental disorders? In general, they are caused by an interaction between hereditary, cognitive and environmental factors. In some cases, the genetic component is strong and the person is likely to develop a mental disorder even in a very supportive environment. In other cases, the cognitive and environmental components are strong. A complete understanding of mental disorders requires that scientists investigate genetic, cognitive and environmental factors. Once genetic factors are identified, the scientist faces the task of determining the physiological effects of the relevant genes and the consequences of these effects on a person's susceptibility to a mental disorder. Understanding the cognitive factors involved in mental disorders requires identification of the origins of distorted perceptions and maladaptive thought patterns. And environmental factors encompass more than simply a person's family history or present social interactions; they also include the effects of prenatal health and nutrition, childhood diseases and exposure to drugs and environmental toxins.

Different psychologists and other mental health professionals approach the study of mental disorders from different perspectives, each of which places more or less emphasis on these factors. The perspectives differ primarily in their explanation of the aetiology, or origin, of mental disorders. Some of these perspectives are described next.

The psychodynamic perspective

According to the psychodynamic perspective, based on Freud's early work (see Chapter 14), mental disorders originate in intrapsychic conflict produced by the three warring factions of the mind: the id, ego and superego. For some people, the conflict becomes so severe that the mind's defence mechanisms are ineffective, resulting in mental disorders that may involve, among other symptoms, extreme anxiety, obsessive thoughts and compulsive behaviour, depression, distorted perceptions and patterns of thinking, and paralysis or blindness for which there is no physical cause. The id, ego and superego are hypothetical constructs, not physical structures of the brain (see Chapter 14). But Freud and his followers often spoke as if these structures and their functions were real. Even today, psychodynamic theorists and practitioners approach mental disorders by emphasising the role of intrapsychic conflict in creating psychological distress and maladaptive behaviour.

The medical perspective

The medical perspective has its origins in the work of the ancient Greek physician Hippocrates. Hippocrates formulated the idea that excesses in the four humours (black bile, yellow bile, blood and phlegm) led to emotional problems. Other physicians, Greek and Roman, extended Hippocrates' ideas and developed the concept of mental illness – illnesses of the mind. Eventually, specialised institutions or asylums were established where people with mental disorders were confined. Early asylums were ill-run and the patients' problems were poorly understood and often mistreated. During the eighteenth and nineteenth centuries, massive reforms in the institutional care of people with mental disorders took place. The quality of the facilities and the amount of compassion for patients improved, and physicians, including neurosurgeons and psychiatrists, who were specifically trained in the medical treatment of mental disorders, were hired to care for these patients.

Today, the medical perspective is the dominant perspective in the treatment of mental disorders. Individuals with mental disorders are no longer confined to mental institutions. Instead, they are treated on an out-patient basis with drugs that are effective in abating the symptoms of mental disorders. Usually, only those people with very severe mental problems are institutionalised. The **medical model**, as the medical perspective is properly called, is based on the idea that mental disorders are caused by specific abnormalities of the brain and nervous system and that, in principle, they should be approached the same way as physical illnesses. As we shall see, several mental disorders, including schizophrenia, depression and bipolar disorder, are known to have specific biological causes and can be treated to some extent with drugs. We shall also see that genetics play a pivotal role in some of these disorders.

However, not all mental disorders can be traced so directly to physical causes. For that reason, other perspectives, which focus on the cognitive and environmental factors involved in mental disorders, have emerged.

The cognitive behavioural perspective

In contrast to the medical perspective, the cognitive behavioural perspective holds that mental disorders are learned maladaptive behaviour patterns that can best be understood by focusing on environmental factors and a person's perception of those factors. In this view, a mental disorder is not something that arises spontaneously within a person. Instead, it is caused by the person's interaction with their environment. For example, a person's excessive use of alcohol or other drugs may be negatively reinforced by the relief from tension or anxiety that often accompanies intoxication.

According to the cognitive behavioural perspective, it is not merely the environment that matters: what also counts is a person's ongoing subjective interpretation of the events taking place in their environment. Therapists operating from the cognitive behavioural perspective therefore encourage their clients to replace or substitute maladaptive thoughts and behaviours with more adaptive ones.

The humanistic and sociocultural perspective

Proponents of the humanistic perspective (see Chapter 14) argue that proper personality development occurs when people experience unconditional positive regard. According to this view, mental disorders arise when people perceive that they must earn the positive regard of others. Cultural variables influence the nature and extent to which people interpret their own behaviours as normal or abnormal. What is considered perfectly normal in one culture may be considered abnormal in another. Moreover, mental disorders exist that appear to occur only in certain cultures – a phenomenon called **culture-bound syndrome**.

Classification of disorders

Mental disorders can be classified in many ways, but the two systems most commonly used in the world are those found in the latest revision of the American Psychiatric Association's (APA) *Diagnostic and Statistical Manual (of Mental Disorders)* V (DSM-V), published in 2013, and the World Health Organization's *International Classification of Diseases* 11 (ICD-11) due for publication in 2018. DSM was originally devised by American psychiatrists to classify mental disorders specifically, whereas the ICD was devised as an international classification system for all diseases. The two are more alike than different, and attempts have been made with the recent revisions of the manuals to harmonise the mental disorder aspects of them both – DSM 5 now matches the contents of Chapter 5 of the ICD, for example, although some differences remain between them.

According to the APA, the DSM-V represents a 'classification of mental disorders with associated criteria designed to facilitate more reliable diagnosis of those disorders' (p. xii). The original version of the manual was published in 1952 (although the first attempt by an earlier incarnation of the APA at classifying disorders occurred in 1844) and there have been five versions and two revisions since then. The number of mental disorders classified in the first version of DSM was 108; in DSM-II (1968), 182; in DSM III (1980), 265; in DSM-III-R (1987), 292; in DSM-IV, 297 (1994). The first edition comprised 130 pages; the latest edition is 999 pages long (Khoury *et al.,* 2014). The expansion of behaviour and mental conditions described as mental disorders with each subsequent edition has been a spur to vocal criticism by many psychologists and psychiatrists who argue that DSM pathologises normal behaviour. We will return to this debate a little later.

DSM-V took 12 years to complete, starting properly in 2003 when 13 international planning conferences were set up with 400 participants from 39 countries. 'Work groups' were charged with proposing revisions, and new scientific findings from the past two decades were included as part of the process. Its aim was to be a manual which could be used by practitioners, which was guided by research evidence, which provided a continuation of DSM-IV and would leave no possible inclusion unconsidered, although it admits that it does 'not constitute comprehensive definition of underlying disorders which encompasses cognitive, environmental, behavioural, and physiological processes that are far more complex than can be described in these brief summaries', (p. 11) nor does it describe the 'full range of mental disorders that individuals experience . . . daily . . . throughout the world (p. 19)', which does undermine the manual's usefulness as a diagnostic tool somewhat.

Field trials were set up in 11 large medical and academic settings, as well as clinical practices, to determine whether the new diagnoses and criteria had validity. For example, patients would complete a list of their symptoms which would be scored by a central server; results were sent to clinicians who would carry out interviews and scored the patient's symptoms according to DSM criteria on computer. The clinician would submit them to a server, and the agreement between two independent clinicians on the diagnosis would be assessed.

Table 18.1 lists the classifications in DSM-V. It's a long list.

Table 18.1 Summary of the DSM-V classification of disorders

Classification of mental disorders in DSM-V

Neurodevelopmental Disorders

Intellectual Disabilities

Communication Disorders

Autism Spectrum Disorder

Attention-Deficit/Hyperactivity Disorder

Specific Learning Disorder (reading or writing or mathematics)

Motor Disorder

Other Neurodevelopmental Disorders

Schizophrenia Spectrum and Other Psychotic Disorders

Schizotypal (Personality) Disorder

Delusional Disorder

Brief Psychotic Disorder

Schizophreniform Disorder

Schizophrenia

Schizoaffective Disorder

Substance/Medication-Induced Psychotic Disorder

Psychotic Disorder Due To Another Medical Condition

Catatonia Associated With Another Mental Disorder

Catatonic Disorder Due To Another Medical Condition

Unspecified Catatonia

Other Specified Schizophrenia Spectrum and Other Psychotic Disorder

Unspecified Schizophrenia Spectrum and Other Psychotic Disorder

Bipolar and Related Disorders

Bipolar I Disorder

Bipolar II Disorder

Cyclothymic Disorder

Substance/Medication-Induced Bipolar and Related Disorders

Bipolar and Related Disorder Due to Another Medical Condition

Other Specified Bipolar and Related Disorders

Unspecified Bipolar and Related Disorders

Depressive Disorders

Disruptive Mood Dysregulation Disorder

Major Depressive Disorder (Single episode/Recurrent episode)

Persistent Depressive Disorder (Dysthymia)

Premenstrual Dysphoric Disorder

Substance/Medication-Induced Depressive Disorders

Depressive Disorder Due To Another Medical Condition

Other Specified Depressive Disorder

Unspecified Depressive Disorder

Anxiety Disorders

Separation Anxiety Disorder

Selective Mutism

Specific Phobia

Social Anxiety Disorder (Social Phobia)

Panic Disorder

Table 18.1 *(Continued)*

Panic Attack Specifier

Agoraphobia

Generalized Anxiety Disorder

Substance/Medication-Induced Anxiety Disorder

Anxiety Disorder Due To Another Medical Condition

Other Specified Anxiety Disorder

Unspecified Anxiety Disorder

Obsessive-Compulsive and Related Disorders

Obsessive-Compulsive Disorder

Body Dysmorphic Disorder

Hoarding Disorder

Trichotillomania (Hair-Pulling Disorder)

Excoriation (Skin-Picking Disorder)

Substance/Medication-Induced Obsessive-Compulsive and Related Disorders

Obsessive-Compulsive and Related Disorder Due to Another Medical Condition

Other Specified Obsessive-Compulsive and Related Disorder

Unspecified Obsessive-Compulsive and Related Disorder

Trauma-and Stressor-Related Disorders

Reactive Attachment Disorder

Disinhibited Social Engagement Disorder

Post-traumatic Stress Disorder

Acute Stress Disorder

Adjustment Disorders

Other Specified Trauma- and Stressor-Related Disorder

Unspecified Trauma- and Stressor-Related Disorder

Dissociative Disorders

Dissociative Identity Disorder

Dissociative Amnesia

Depersonalization/Derealization Disorder

Other Specified Dissociative Disorder

Unspecified Dissociative Disorder

Somatic Symptom and Related Disorders

Somatic Symptom Disorder

Illness Anxiety Disorder

Conversion Disorder

Psychological Factor Affecting Other Medical Conditions

Factitious Disorder

Other Specified Somatic Symptom and Related Disorder

Unspecified Somatic Symptom and Related Disorder

Feeding and Eating Disorder

Pica

Rumination Disorder

Avoidant/Restrictive Food Intake Disorder

Anorexia Nervosa

Bulimia Nervosa

Binge-Eating Disorder

Other Specified Feeding or Eating Disorder

Unspecified Feeding or Eating Disorder

Elimination Disorders

Enuresis

Ecopresis

Other Specified Elimination Disorder

Unspecified Elimination Disorder

Sleep-Wake Disorders

Insomnia Disorder

Hypersomnolence Disorder

Narcoplepsy

Breathing-Related Sleep Disorders

    Obstructive Sleep Apnea Hypopnea

    Central Sleep Apnea

    Sleep-related Hypoventilation

    Circadian Rhythm Sleep-Wake Disorders

Parasomnias

    Non-Rapid Eye Movement Sleep Arousal Disorders

    Nightmare Disorder

    Rapid Eye Movement Sleep Behaviour Disorder

    Restless Legs Syndrome

    Substance/Medication-Induced Sleep Disorders

Other Specified Insomnia Disorder

Unspecified Insomnia Disorder

Other Specified Hypersomnolence Disorder

Unspecified Hypersomnolence Disorder

Other Specified Sleep-Wake Disorder

Unspecified Sleep-Wake Disorder

Sexual Dysfunctions

Delayed Ejaculation

Erectile Disorder

Female Orgasmic Disorder

Female Sexual Interest/Arousal Disorder

Genito-Pelvic Pain/Penetration Disorder

Male Hypoactive Sexual Desire Disorder

Premature (Early) Ejaculation

Substance/Medication-Induced Sexual Dysfunction

Other Specified Sexual Dysfunction

Unspecified Sexual Dysfunction

(Continued)

Table 18.1 *(Continued)*

Gender Dysphoria

Gender Dysphoria

Other Specified Gender Dysphoria

Unspecified Gender Dysphoria

Disruptive, Impulse-Control and Conduct Disorders

Oppositional Defiant Disorder

Intermittent Explosive Disorder

Conduct Disorder

Antisocial Personality Disorder

Pyromania

Kleptomania

Other Specified Disruptive, Impulse-Control and Conduct Disorders

Unspecified Disruptive, Impulse-Control and Conduct Disorders

Substance-Related and Addictive Disorders

Substance-Related Disorders

  Alcohol Use Disorder

  Alcohol Intoxication

  Alcohol Withdrawal

  Other Alcohol-Induced Disorders

  Unspecified Alcohol-Related Disorders

Caffeine-Related Disorders

  Caffeine Intoxication

  Caffeine Withdrawal

  Other Caffeine-Induced Disorders

  Unspecified Caffeine-Related Disorder

Cannabis-Related Disorders

  Cannabis Use Disorder

  Cannabis Intoxication

  Cannabis Withdrawal

  Other Cannabis-Induced Disorders

  Unspecified Cannabis-Related Disorders

Hallucinogen-Related Disorders

  Phencyclidine Use Disorder

  Other Hallucinogen Use Disorder

  Phencyclidine Intoxication

  Other Hallucinogenic Intoxication

  Hallucinogen Persisting Perception Disorder

  Other Phencyclidine Persisting Perception Disorder

  Other Hallucinogen Persisting Perception Disorder

  Unspecified Phencyclidine-Related Disorders

  Unspecified Hallucinogen-Related Disorders

Inhalant-Related Disorders

  Inhalant Use Disorder

  Inhalant Intoxication

Other Inhalant-Induced Disorders

  Unspecified Inhalant-Related Disorder

Opioid-Related Disorders

  Opioid Use Disorder

  Opioid Intoxication

  Opioid Withdrawal

  Other Opioid-Induced Disorders

  Unspecified Opioid-Related Disorders

Sedative-, Hypnotic-, or Anxiolytic-Related Disorders

  Sedative-, Hypnotic-, or Anxiolytic-Related Use Disorder

  Sedative-, Hypnotic-, or Anxiolytic Intoxication

  Sedative-, Hypnotic-, or Anxiolytic Withdrawal

  Other Sedative-, Hypnotic-, or Anxiolytic-Induced Disorders

  Unspecified Sedative-, Hypnotic-, or Anxiolytic-Related Disorder

Stimulant-Related Disorder

  Stimulant Use Disorder (Amphetamine-type; cocaine; other/unspecified

  Stimulant Intoxication

  Stimulant Withdrawal

  Other Stimulant-Induced Disorders

  Unspecified Stimulant-Related Disorder

Tobacco-Related Disorders

  Tobacco Use Disorder

  Tobacco Withdrawal

  Other Tobacco-Induced Disorders

  Unspecified Tobacco-Related Disorder

Other (or Unknown) Substance-Related Disorders

Non-Substance-Related Disorders

Neurocognitive Disorders

Delirium

Other Specified Delirium

Unspecified Delirium

Major and Mild Neurocognitive Disorders

Major or Mild Neurocognitive Disorder Due To Alzheimer's Disease

Major or Mild Frontotemporal Neurocognitive Disorder

Major or Mild Neurocognitive Disorder With Lewy Bodies

Major or Mild Vascular Neurocognitive Disorder

Major or Mild Neurocognitive Disorder Due To Traumatic Brain Injury

Substance/Medication-Induced Major or Mild Neurocognitive Disorder

Major or Mild Neurocognitive Disorder Due To HIV Infection

Major or Mild Neurocognitive Disorder Due To Parkinson's Disease

Major or Mild Neurocognitive Disorder Due To Huntington's Disease

Major or Mild Neurocognitive Disorder Due To Another Medical Condition

Major or Mild Neurocognitive Disorder Due To Multiple Aetiologies

Table 18.1 *(Continued)*

Personality Disorders

Cluster A Personality Disorders

   Paranoid Personality Disorder

   Schizoid Personality Disorder

   Schizotypal Personality Disorder

Cluster B Personality Disorder

   Antisocial Personality Disorder

   Borderline Personality Disorder

   Histrionic Personality Disorder

   Narcissistic Personality Disorder

Cluster C Personality Disorder

   Avoidant Personality Disorder

   Dependent Personality Disorder

   Obsessive-Compulsive Personality Disorder

Other Personality Disorders

Paraphilic Disorders

Voyeuristic Disorder

Exhibitionistic Disorder

Sexual Masochism Disorder

Sexual Sadism Disorder

Pedophilic Disorder

Fetishistic Disorder

Transvestic Disorder

Other Specified Paraphilic Disorder

Unspecified Paraphilic Disorder

Other Mental Disorders

Other Specified Mental Disorder Due To Another Medical Condition

Unspecified Mental Disorder Due To Another Medical Condition

Other Specified Mental Disorder

Unspecified Mental Disorder

Medication-Induced Movement Disorders and Other Adverse Effects of Medication

Other Conditions That May Be A Focus of Clinical Attention

Differences between DSM-IV and DSM-V

There is a number of significant differences between the most recent edition of DSM and its predecessor (Kupfer and Regier, 2013), some minor, some major. For example, the new edition has abandoned the concept of axes (see the 5th edition of *Psychology*) and has tried to emphasise how different disorders may fall along a continuum of mental disorder rather than represent discrete, self-contained categories of their own. More research on genetics and neuroimaging has been used to inform its diagnoses. The conditions, Autism Disorder, Asperger's Disorder and pervasive developmental disorder now come under one umbrella condition – autism syndrome disorder. People with autistic symptoms will be classified across a continuum of behaviour from mild to severe in two domains (social communication and restrictive/repetitive behaviours or interests). Asperger's Syndrome has ceased to exist as a diagnostic category.

The substance abuse sections have been restructured and disorders are now classified under 'substance use disorders'. More detail regarding mild and major neurocognitive disorder has been included and whereas DSM-IV included Dementia of... followed by the cause (e.g. Alzheimer's disease), the term dementia has been removed in DSM-V and replaced with 'neurocognitive disorder'. The category, 'Personality Disorders' has remained and includes various personality types. Some had argued that this condition should be represented by a continuum (Livesley, 2013), as is autism, and not as a collection of categories, but this argument was lost. A new section (section

III) has been included which describes new disorders which require further study or which are not established.

Section III also includes Cultural Formulation, which is a discussion of the role of culture in diagnoses. DSM acknowledges, as its previous edition did, that the boundaries between normal and abnormal behaviour and functioning depend on culture – what is abnormal in one may not be considered in the other, and vice versa. In DSM-IV, these disorders were described as 'culture-bound'. In DSM-V, they have been divided into three categories – cultural syndrome cluster (a group of co-occurring symptoms in a specific cultural group); cultural idiom of distress – you'll have to bear with DSM's phrasing – (a term used to describe the suffering of a group and the group's way of expressing it); and cultural explanations or perceived causes (a label which provides a cultural aetiology for symptoms of illness).

How valid and reliable is the DSM?

The DSM is not short of critics. Frances and Widiger (2012) argued that 'our classification of mental disorders is no more than a collection of fallible and limited constructs that seek, but never find, an elusive truth.' However, they go on: 'Nevertheless, this is our best current way of defining and communicating about mental disorders'. The principal criticism of the new DSM (and some of the old ones) is that it has been overly keen to introduce new mental disorders on the basis of, in some cases, very little evidence – no data on prevalence, validity, reliability, treatment response and so on has been included (see Maj, 2014; Lasalvia, 2015; Stein and Nesse, 2015 for some lively arguments). Until DSM-III, homosexuality was included as a mental illness.

Frances and Nardo (2013) provide two examples of disorders which may not merit inclusion. Binge eating disorder, for example, is described as a mental disorder where a person binge eats once a week for three months. Whether this behaviour, which some might consider not exactly abnormal, constitutes a serious mental condition is arguable. DSM has also pathologised what some have described as normal behaviour – children's temper tantrums (which are now described as 'disruptive mood dysregulation disorder'. Grief is another behaviour which has been pathologised. Houts (2001), one of DSM's fiercest critics, refers to sleep disorders as an example of this invention and over-inclusiveness. Until DSM-III-R, sleep disorders were not considered mental disorders. 'It is as though sleep problems became mental disorders overnight sometime in 1987', he notes. Other behaviours which Houts argues are inappropriately classed as mental disorder include **frotteurism** (touching or rubbing up against another in a sexual way without consent), kleptomania (compulsive theft), dyscalculia (a disorder of mathematical thinking), pathological gambling and voyeurism. Critics, even those involved in chairing previous DSM revisions, such as Allen Frances, have offered excoriating assessments of this new set of diagnoses (you can find his objections here: http://www. huffingtonpost.com/allen-frances/dsm-5_b_2227626.html).

Another issue with classification is the potential of over-diagnosis or attaching a diagnosis of mental illness to a behaviour which would otherwise not have been so-described, even by those describing symptoms. Moffitt *et al.* (2010) found that that, over a 15-year period, diagnosis of anxiety disorder had increased by 50 per cent, depression by 41 per cent, alcohol dependence by 38 per cent and cannabis dependence by 18 per cent. A study of 1,420 individuals assessed nine times between the ages of 9 and 21 found that 61 per cent of them met well-defined criteria for mental illness (Copeland *et al.,* 2011). Other conditions which have seen a rise in diagnosis in the past 15 years include autism (20-fold increase), ADHD (tripled) and adult bipolar disorder (doubled). Antidepressant medication is the third most popularly prescribed medication in the US, especially in the 18–44-year-old group (Pratt *et al.,* 2011) – this either reflects a genuine response to a genuine condition or an over-prescription. The US does report the highest prevalence of mental illness and the greatest severity of illness than any other major country – bipolar disorder is 4.4 per cent in the US, twice has high as that reported in other countries (Deacon, 2013).

Reflecting the fact that the DSM-V is strongly influenced by psychiatrists, the manual tends to be more consistent with the medical perspective on mental disorders. This means that diagnosis and treatment based on the DSM-V emphasise biological factors, and equate mental illness with physical illness which may, in turn, mean that potential cognitive and environmental determinants may be overlooked. The current revision is partly driven by the US's National Institute of Mental Health which

views mental disorders as diseases and whose new framework for undertaking mental health research is focused on discovering the neurobiological mechanisms which underlie mental illness (Kirmayer and Crafta, 2014) and on creating a diagnostic system based on neural, biological measures.

Although DSM argues that its diagnostic criteria and classifications are based on neurobiological research, there are few consistent neurobiological correlates of the disorders contained within it. Some have noted that a biological test does not appear as a criterion for diagnosis in any DSM disorder (Deacon, 2013). Even the measures used to derive these correlates might present us with confounds. A person with autism, for example, responds to the experience of undergoing an fMRI scan (one of the principal measures of brain activation) differently to a person with schizophrenia (Weinberger and Goldberg, 2014).

Other authors have pointed out that DSM's own methods did not provide some support for the existence of certain types of mental disorder. For example, the DSM field trials used a statistic called kappa to ensure that agreement between two clinicians on the diagnosis of a disorder was sound and consistent. If an illness appears in 10 per cent of patients in a clinic, and two clinicians agree that the same diagnosis can be confirmed in 85 per cent, the kappa value of this is 85 (Freedman *et al.,* 2013). The kappa value for schizophrenia in DSM-IV, for example, was 85 per cent, i.e. high. It is also high for bipolar disorder, a condition called schizoaffective disorder, post-traumatic stress disorder (67 per cent), major neurocognitive disorders and boarding disorders. Major depression, which has not changed substantially since DSM-IV, presents more of a problem because its symptoms can vary from mild to severe and from those who seek treatment to those who are disabled by the illness. But depression also co-occurs with anxiety – in the jargon, it is 'co-morbid with'. In DSM-V, a new mixed disorder has been included 'mixed anxiety and depression'. This has a kappa value of 0.

Personality disorder is another illness which performed badly in terms of kappa results – while agreement on the diagnosis of borderline personality disorder was good, antisocial personality disorder and obsessive-compulsive personality had questionable reliability; narcissistic personality and schizotypal personality disorders appeared so infrequently, they could be not be evaluated. Freedman *et al.*'s analysis of kappa values is illustrated in Figure 18.1.

These data and others like them highlight DSM's problem with reliability. Reliability in this context means what it did in the context of psychological testing (discussed in Chapter 2) – consistency across applications. If the DSM was perfectly reliable, users would be able to diagnose each case in the same way. But evaluating psychological disorders is not so easy. Using the DSM is not like using a recipe; it is more like navigating your way through an unfamiliar city using only a crude map. Using this map, you may or may not reach your destination. Mental disorders do not have distinct borders that allow a mental health professional to diagnose a disorder in a person with 100 per cent accuracy all of the time. Some critics argue, for example, that DSM encourages the making of false-positive

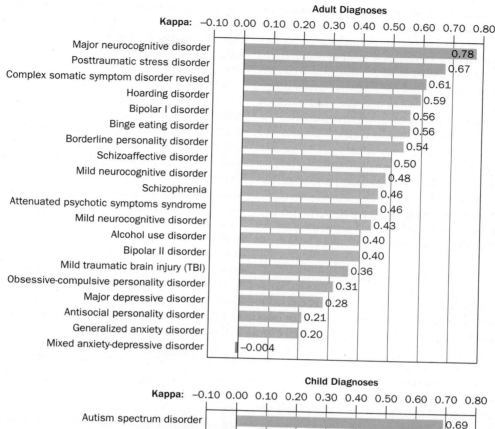

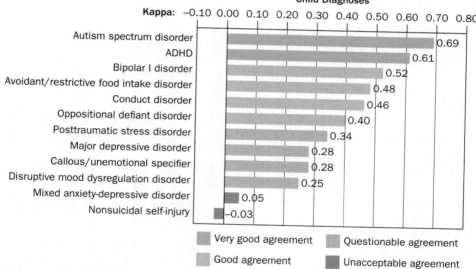

Figure 18.1 The kappa (reliability and validity) figures for the main DSM mental disorders.

judgements — claiming a disorder exists when there only exists a moderate, normal disruption in behaviour. For example, one in four cases of bereavement might be diagnosed as major depressive disorder when these people are undergoing a natural, event-specific change in mood (Wakefield *et al.*, 2012).

Evidence suggests that actuarial (statistical) analysis of symptoms is better than clinical analysis (Aegisdottir *et al.*, 2006). Specific indicators such as sex, age, test scores, medical history and so on (actuarial measures) are superior to expert 'experience' and knowledge of previous cases. You might guess

that this name comes from the world of insurance (hence, actuary) and you'd be right: the actuarial method was used to assess how long a person would live (using statistics such as age, sex, height, weight, etc.) and to set levels of insurance.

Of course, not every individual will follow the pattern predicted by these statistics (not every overweight, short, old man will live longer than a slim, tall woman) but as a general guide they are a useful statistical predictor of groups of people's behaviour as a whole. In the clinical realm, Aegisdottir *et al.* (2006)'s meta-analysis found that actuarial method was

13 per cent more accurate. Reasons for the success include its reliability – a decision is based on the same criteria and not based on the subjective impression of the clinician who may be influenced by irrelevant variables or not pay attention to relevant ones. Most clinicians, however, adopt the clinical method, despite the advantages of the actuarial method. People are always more persuaded by the importance of narrative than the importance of statistics (as Chapter 2 showed).

Another criticism of DSM is that by giving a diagnosis of mental illness, the individual carries a formal signal of stigma. People respond negatively to those with mental illness, and the evidence for this and what we might do to change this behaviour is considered next.

In the fifth edition of *Psychology*, this section, ended with the words: 'The next edition of Psychology will make (even more?) interesting reading.' A pretty accurate prediction?

Stigma

Once people are labelled, they are likely to be perceived as having all the characteristics assumed to accompany that label; their behaviour will probably be perceived selectively and interpreted in terms of the diagnosis. An early experiment by Langer and Abelson (1974) illustrated how labelling can affect **clinical judgements**. A group of psychoanalysts were shown a videotape of a young man who was being interviewed. Half of the psychoanalysts were told that the man was a job applicant, while the other half were told that he was a patient. Although both groups of clinicians watched the same man exhibiting the same behaviour, those who were told that he was a patient rated him as being more disturbed, that is, less well adjusted.

The most famous example of labelling with a psychiatric mental illness affecting the behaviour of those around the person labelled is probably that of Robert Rosenhan. In 1973, he wrote an article called 'on being sane in insane places' (http://bit.ly/IJMX6Do) which described fake patients who had been admitted to 12 psychiatric hospitals and described how they were treated. They were admitted because they had apparently suffered auditory hallucinations. In hospital, each acted normally and claimed not to hear any voices. Each one of them was diagnosed with a disorder called schizophrenia (see later section) and kept in hospital for 19 days. When one became bored and started writing a diary, one of the staff made this note on the behaviour: 'continuous writing must be a behavioural manifestation of that disturbance, perhaps a subset of the compulsive behaviours that are sometimes correlated with schizophrenia'.

When the hospitals challenged Rosenhan to send more fake patients to confirm that their system was robust, they claimed to have identified 41 fakes out of 193 new admissions. Rosenhan had not sent any new admissions.

It is easy to lapse into the mistaken belief that, somehow or other, labelling disorders explains why people are like they are. Diagnosing a psychological disorder only describes the symptoms of the disorder; it does not explain its origins. To say that someone did something 'because he's schizophrenic' does not

explain his behaviour. We need to be on guard against associating the names of disorders with people rather than with their symptoms. It is more appropriate to talk about 'someone who displays the characteristics of schizophrenia' than to say that 'he's a schizophrenic'.

Ben-Zeev *et al.* (2010) describes three types of stigma: public stigma whereby large groups of people hold stereotypical perceptions of a group and respond towards it negatively; self-stigma in which an individual loses their sense of self-esteem because they perceive that others view them negatively; and label avoidance where people avoid seeking out mental health services because they do not want to be a labelled. Labels can be quite dangerous triggers of negative stereotypes. Knowing that a person is schizophrenic, for example, increases the degree of prejudice expressed towards that person (Crisp *et al.*, 2000) and one reason for this may be that such traits are seen as unchangeable and fixed. People would be not be likely to overcome mental illness in the way that they could more physical illnesses (Corrigan *et al.*, 2000). Some have argued that DSM is an exercise in the actor-observer effect which you read about in Chapter 15, attributing the cause of mental illness to the individual rather than to situations (Khoury *et al.*, 2014).

The boxer Frank Bruno's admission to a psychiatric hospital for depression was reported in two versions of the UK's best-selling daily newspaper, The Sun. This was the second edition, printed because of the complaints generated by the first in which the boxer was described as 'Bonkers Bruno'.

Source: The Sun/NI Syndication. Copyright© News Group Newspapers Ltd.

The need for classification

Despite the objectives above, proper classification has advantages for a patient. One advantage is that, with few exceptions, the recognition of a specific diagnostic category precedes the development of successful treatment for that disorder. Treatments for diseases such as diabetes, syphilis, tetanus and malaria were found only after the disorders could be reliably diagnosed. A patient may have a multitude of symptoms, but before the cause of the disorder (and hence its treatment) can be discovered, the primary symptoms must be identified.

Different kinds of mental disorder have different causes, and they respond to different types of psychological treatment and drugs. If future research is to reveal more about causes and treatments of these disorders, we must be able to classify specific mental disorders reliably and accurately.

Another important reason for properly classifying mental disorders is prognosis. Some disorders have good prognoses; the patients are likely to improve soon and are unlikely to have a recurrence of their problems. Other disorders have progressive courses; patients are less likely to recover from these disorders. In the first case, patients can obtain reassurance about their futures; in the second case, patients' families can obtain assistance in making realistic plans.

Lay knowledge of mental illness

The past few years have seen a shift in attitudes to mental illness by members of the public. The public's mental health literacy has improved – they endorse the medical model and support the use of treatment. However, attitudes towards people with depression and schizophrenia have not improved (Schomerus *et al.*, 2012) and people still prefer to maintain some distance between themselves and those with mental illness – they are less likely to accept them as co-workers or as friends. Although the public understanding of the biology of depression is a positive development, this belief does have some negative consequences – people tend to have more pessimistic views of the prognosis of depression if people think it has a genetic or biological cause, for example, because these causes are considered permanent or difficult to treat (Lebowitz *et al.*, 2013). A study of German participants found that people with mental illness were becoming less devalued and discriminated against (Angermeyer and Matschinger 2005) but an Australian study of attitudes from 2002/3 to 2011 found no change in attitude towards people with depression and people showed increased perception of people with schizophrenia as dangerous (Reavley and Jorm, 2012). This is a common perception of people with schizophrenia (Swanson *et al.*, 2015).

One survey suggested that people would think that over 50 per cent of employers would reject a job application from a person with mental illness (Angermeyer *et al.*, 2013) and 50 per cent of them thought that others would think less of people who had been admitted to a psychiatric hospital. This study focused on mental health in general, rather than specific mental illnesses. Even people who endorse biological causes for mental illness also want more social distance between themselves and a person with mental illness – a finding that has been reported in the US, Germany, Turkey, Russia and Mongolia (Mackenzie *et al.*, 2014). There are some groups who are more positive than others – highly educated women, for example, express less stigma and greater mental health literacy (Holman, 2014).

Associated with stigma is also a belief that people with mental illness are disproportionately violent. In one survey, 49 per cent of Americans believed that people with serious mental illness were more dangerous than the general population (Barry *et al.*, 2013); the percentage is even higher (60 per cent) for schizophrenia (Pescosolido *et al.*, 2010). The media may play an important role in the perception. It is not uncommon for a reporting of a shooting, especially a mass shooting, to be accompanied about speculation regarding the perpetrator's mental health. McGinty *et al.* (2013) asked one group of US respondents to read about a mass shooting committed by someone with a mental illness and another to read one where mental illness wasn't mentioned. Those in the first group were more likely to perceive people with mental illness as dangerous. When you examine the actuarial data on violent or serious crimes committed by people with mental illness, the findings are illuminating, A study of 10,024 crimes in Baltimore, St Louis and Los Angeles in the US found that the 12-month prevalence of minor and serious violent crimes was 12 per cent in patients with schizophrenia, bipolar disorder and major depression (Swanson *et al.*, 2015). The greatest number of crimes was committed by younger men of low socio-economic status who had problems with alcohol and drugs. Substance use is a consistent and strong predictor of crime.

The link between mental illness and violence is modest but significant. Violence is three to five times higher in men with schizophrenia and 4–13 times higher in women (Fazel *et al.*, 2009). Two disorders are more associated with violent crime than any others – substance use and anti-social personality disorder (Yu *et al.*, 2012). Sixty one percent of firearms fatalities in the US in 2010 were suicides – the risk of suicide is 47–74 per cent if people have mental illness (Li *et al.*, 2011). The use of firearms, and media exposure, are predictors of suicide. The suicide rate in Switzerland decreased significantly when number of firearms military personnel were allowed in their homes was halved (Reisch *et al.*, 2013). After the Port Arthur massacre in Australia in 1996 where 35 people were murdered, firearms ownership was restricted. Eighteen years before the ban, there were 13 such examples of mass shooting; in the 10 years since the ban, there were none.

Those with mental illness are much more likely to be the victims of crime than the perpetrators. Khalif *et al.* (2015) found that 40 per cent of the psychiatric patients they interviewed had been the victim of a physical, sexual or acquisitive (e.g. robbery) crime, compared with 14 per cent of the general population. When violent assaults were examined, 19 per cent of people with mental illness had experienced this crime, compared with 3 per cent of the general population.

Mental illness – An international perspective

According to the WHO, around 350 million people in the world suffer from depression, 21 million suffer from schizophrenia and 47.5 million have neurocognitive disorder. These are three illnesses that cross cultural and national boundaries. But are some mental disorders culture-dependent? Are diagnostic manuals too Western-based? And would a mental disorder in one culture be classed as normal behaviour in another?

Tanaka-Matsumi and Draguns (1997) found that depression is common across most cultures. A World Health Organization (WHO) study of depression in Switzerland, Canada, Japan and Iran (World Health Organization, 1983) found that 76 per cent of individuals diagnosed as depressed exhibited symptoms of sadness, joylessness, anxiety, tension and lack of energy. Levels of guilt, however, showed large variation between cultures. Iran reported the lowest levels (22 per cent of respondents), followed by Japan (45 per cent), Canada (58 per cent) and Switzerland (68 per cent). There was also within-culture variation. For example, the two Japanese cities studied (Nagasaki and Tokyo) showed different degrees of depression, with more core symptoms reported in Nagasaki.

A study of British and Turkish outpatients found that Turkish patients reported more somatic complaints (insomnia, hypochondria) whereas the British patients reported more psychological complaints such as guilt and pessimism (Ulusahin *et al.*, 1994).

Suicidal ideation (thoughts about suicide) and suicide are also symptoms of depression which show cultural variation. In a study of the suicide rates among 15–24-year-olds in a large number of countries including Egypt, Jordan, Kuwait, Syria, the Scandinavian countries, eastern Europe, Japan, Singapore and Sri Lanka, the Arabic states (Egypt, Jordan, etc.) had the lowest suicide rates whereas Scandinavia, eastern Europe and some Asian countries had the highest (Barraclough, 1988). The highest reported rates were for Sri Lanka (47 suicides per 100,000 of the population) and Hungary (38.6 per 100,000). The exact reasons for these high rates are unknown. Some have suggested that the weakening of family structure or religious values is responsible; others suggest that endemic group violence is responsible in Sri Lanka and a fear of failure is responsible in Hungary, but these are vague, general reasons which could apply to other countries (Jilek-Aal, 1988). Paris (1991) has also cautioned that suicide and suicide attempts fluctuate across space and time and that such fluctuation may not be detected in epidemiological surveys of suicide.

Schizophrenia has been subject to three major cross-cultural studies over 25 years in 20 research centres from 17 countries. The aim of such exhaustive research has been to collect data, standardise the instruments used for measuring schizophrenic symptoms and conduct follow-up assessments (Jablensky, 1989). If different countries have different ways of measuring schizophrenia, for example, then a higher or lower incidence of the disorder may not reflect actual incidence but differences in the ways in which schizophrenia is diagnosed.

One of the most comprehensive cross-cultural studies examined 1,379 schizophrenic patients in 12 centres from 10 countries: Denmark (Aarhus), India (Agra and Chandigarh), Columbia (Cali), Ireland (Dublin), Nigeria (Fbadai), Russia (Moscow), the UK (Nottingham), Japan (Nagasaki), the Czech Republic (Prague) and the US (Honolulu, Hawaii and Rochester, New York). In each of the countries, the incidence rates were comparable (Jablensky *et al.*, 1992).

A disorder which does present some cross-cultural problems is anxiety (Tseng *et al.*, 1990). Here, there is great cultural variability in terms of the degree of generalised anxiety reported. Tseng *et al.* (1986) asked psychiatrists in Beijing, Tokyo and Honolulu to diagnose the mental disorder of Chinese patients recorded on videotape. The Beijing psychiatrists diagnosed the patients as exhibiting neurasthenia; the others diagnosed adjustment reaction. When Japanese and American psychiatrists were asked to diagnose patients with social phobia, the Japanese psychiatrists showed greater agreement in their diagnosis of Japanese social phobics than did their American counterparts (Tseng *et al.*, 1990).

Results like these suggest that cultural variations exist in the diagnosis of some mental disorders. Perhaps because anxiety is a vaguer syndrome than is depression or schizophrenia, it ought not to be surprising that great variation exists between cultures in diagnosing this disorder. When more specific anxiety disorders are examined, such as object phobia, some cross-cultural agreement occurs (Davey, 1992; Davey *et al.*, 1998). In their study of the nature of object phobia in Japanese, British, American, Scandinavian, Indian, Korean and Hong Kong individuals, Davey *et al.* (1998) reported that there was broad agreement on the stimuli considered phobia-related. This consistency suggests that, at least for some anxiety disorders, there is universality.

Three culture-bound syndromes are Koro, Taijin Kyofusho and anthropophobia (Tanaka-Matsumi and Draguns, 1997). Koro is found in men in southern China or Southeast Asia and refers to a belief that genitals are withdrawn into the abdomen and a fear of death provoked by a female ghost (Tseng *et al.*, 1992). Taijin Kyofusho is a Japanese disorder similar to social phobia. However, individuals with this disorder have a specific fear of offending others by blushing, emitting offensive odours, staring inappropriately and presenting improper facial expressions (Tanaka-Matsumi, 1979). Anthropophobia seems to be the Chinese equivalent and involves the fear of being looked at.

It seems evident that although there is agreement between cultures about what constitutes a diagnosis for some mental disorders, there is clear variation for others. Anxiety, for example, seems to show the greatest variation, and depression and schizophrenia the least. Furthermore, there are some mental disorders which are culture-bound.

The treatment of mental disorders

The evolution of interventions

Mental disorder and its treatment has a long history. In the past, people suffering from mental disorder have been regarded with awe or fear; others whom we would now probably classify as paranoid schizophrenics were seen as instruments through whom gods or spirits were speaking. More often, they were considered to be occupied by devils or evil spirits and were made to suffer accordingly. The earliest known attempts to treat mental disorders involved trephining, or drilling holes in a person's skull. Presumably, the opening was made to permit evil spirits to leave the victim's head. In prehistoric times, this procedure was performed with a sharp-edged stone; later civilisations, such as the Egyptians, refined the practice. Signs of healing at the edges of the holes in prehistoric skulls indicate that some people survived these operations. An example is seen in Figure 18.2.

Many painful practices were directed at people's presumed possession by evil spirits. Individuals who were thought to be unwilling hosts for evil spirits were subjected to curses or insults designed to persuade the demons to leave. If this approach had no effect, exorcism was tried to make the person's body an unpleasant place for devils to reside. Other rituals included beatings, starving, near-drowning and the drinking of foul-tasting concoctions. The delusional schemes of psychotics often include beliefs of personal guilt and unworthiness. In a society that accepted the notion that there were witches and devils, these people were ready to imagine themselves as evil. They confessed to unspeakable acts of sorcery and welcomed their own persecution and punishment.

Until the eighteenth century, many Europeans accepted the idea that devils and spirits were responsible for peculiar behaviours in some people. But a few people believed that these disorders reflected diseases and that they should be treated medically, with compassion for the victim. Johann Wier, a sixteenth-century physician, was among the first to challenge the practice of witchcraft. He argued that most people who were being tortured and burned for practising witchcraft in fact suffered from mental illness. The Church condemned his writings as heretical and banned them. However, even within the Church some people began to realise that the prevailing beliefs and practices were wrong.

As belief in witchcraft and demonology waned, the clergy, the medical authorities and the general public began to regard people with mental disorders as ill. Torture and persecution eventually ceased. However, the lives of mentally ill people did not necessarily become better. The unfortunate ones were consigned to various asylums established for the care of the mentally ill. Most of these mental institutions were inhumane. Patients were often kept in chains and sometimes wallowed in their own excrement. Those who displayed bizarre catatonic postures or who had fanciful delusions were exhibited to the public for a fee. Many of the treatments designed to cure mental patients were little better than the tortures that had previously been used to drive out evil spirits. Patients were tied up, doused in cold water, bled, made to vomit, spun violently in a rotating chair and otherwise assaulted.

Mistreatment of the mentally ill did not go unnoticed by humanitarians. A famous and effective early reformer was Philippe Pinel (1745–1826), a French physician. In 1793, Pinel was appointed director of La Bicêtre, a mental hospital in Paris. Pinel believed that most mental patients would respond well to kind treatment. As an experiment, he removed the chains from some of the patients, took them out of dungeons and allowed them to walk about the hospital grounds. The experiment was a remarkable success; an atmosphere of peace and quiet replaced the previous noise, stench and general aura of despair. Many patients were eventually discharged. Pinel's success at La Bicêtre was repeated when he was given charge of Salpêtrière Hospital. Some mentally ill people eventually recover – or at least get much better – without any treatment at all. But if a person was put in a mental institution that existed prior to Pinel's time, they had little chance to show improvement.

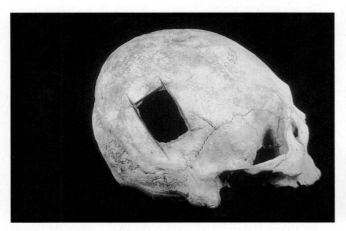

Figure 18.2 Among the earliest biological approaches to the treatment of mental disorders was the ancient practice of trephining, in which a hole was made in the skull to allow evil spirits to escape from the person's head.
Source: Loren McIntyre/Woodfin Camp and Associates, Inc.

The development of modern treatment

The modern history of specific treatments for mental disorders probably began with Franz Anton Mesmer (1734–1815), an Austrian physician who practised in Paris in the late eighteenth and early nineteenth centuries. He devised a theory of 'magnetic fluxes', according to which he attempted to effect cures by manipulating iron rods and bottles of chemicals. In reality, he hypnotised his patients and thereby alleviated some of their symptoms. As a result, hypnosis was first known as mesmerism.

In 1815, there were approximately 2,000 individuals institutionalised in mental asylums in England. The number had increased a century later when 100 or so asylums in England and Wales housed an average of 1,000 patients. In America, at the same time, the number housed was between 1,500 and 3,000. Dr William Black, a nineteenth-century English physician, kept a list of the causes of insanity of those individuals admitted to the Bethlehem asylum, the largest madhouse in the UK at the time (it was also known as Bedlam).

A French neurologist, Jean Martin Charcot (1825–93), began his investigations of the therapeutic uses of hypnosis when one of his students hypnotised a woman and induced her to display the symptoms of a conversion reaction (hysteria). Charcot examined her and concluded that she was a hysterical patient. The student then woke the woman, and her symptoms vanished. Charcot had previously believed that hysteria had an organic basis, but this experience changed his opinion, and he began investigating its psychological causes.

Just before Freud began private practice, he studied with Charcot in Paris and observed the effects of hypnosis on hysteria. Freud's association with Charcot, and later with Breuer, started him on his life's study of the determinants of personality and the origins of mental illness. He created the practice of psychoanalysis. Some modern psychiatrists and psychologists still use some of his therapeutic methods to treat their clients.

Current treatment: the eclectic approach

Most therapists adopt a general, **eclectic approach** to the treatment of mental disorders. The eclectic approach (from the Greek eklegein, to 'single out') involves the therapist using whatever methods they feel will work best for a particular client at a particular time. Such therapists are not strongly wedded to particular theoretical orientations; instead, they seek the particular form of therapy that will best solve a particular client's problems. This often means combining aspects of several different treatment approaches according to a particular client's problem and personal circumstances. For example, Acierno *et al.* (1993) have shown that combinations of therapies are more effective in treating panic disorder than is any one alone.

Types of treatment

Psychoanalysis and psychodynamic therapy

Sigmund Freud is given credit for developing psychoanalysis, which is a form of therapy aimed at providing the client with insight into their unconscious motivations and impulses (see Chapter 14). Freud's theory of personality suggests that unconscious conflicts based on the competing demands of the id (representing biological urges), the superego (representing the moral dictates of society) and the ego (representing reality) often lead to anxiety. The source of these conflicts, according to Freud, can usually be traced back to unacceptable, often sexually based, urges from early childhood: repressed impulses and feelings that lead to conscious anxiety.

The purpose of therapy is to create a setting in which clues about the origins of intrapsychic conflicts are most likely to be revealed by the client. These clues are revealed in clients' dreams, physical problems, memory (or failure to remember certain things), manner of speech and cognitive and emotional reactions to therapy. Then, by exposing the client to these clues, they will gain insight into the problem.

While the psychoanalyst's primary role is interpretation, the client's main job is to provide the psychoanalyst with something to interpret: descriptions of their fears, anxieties, thoughts or repressed memories. This is not an easy task for the client to accomplish because the client unconsciously invokes one or more defence mechanisms, which (as you recall from Chapter 14), prevent anxiety-provoking memories and ideas from reaching conscious awareness. Together, the psychoanalyst and client work for insight into the client's problems.

Psychoanalytic techniques

Freud used free association to encourage the client to speak freely, without censoring possibly embarrassing or socially unacceptable thoughts. Freud achieved this goal in two ways. First, the client was encouraged to report any thoughts or images that came to mind, without worrying about their meaning. Secondly, Freud attempted to minimise any authoritative influence over the client's disclosures by eliminating eye contact. He usually sat in a chair at the head of a couch on which the client reclined.

Among the topics clients are encouraged to discuss are their dreams. Dream interpretation, the evaluation of the underlying meaning of dream content, is a hallmark of psychoanalysis (Freud, 1900). But even dream content is subject to some censoring, according to Freud, so that the analyst must be able to distinguish between the dream's manifest content (the actual images and events that occur within the dream) and latent content (the hidden meaning or significance of the dream). The manifest content masks the latent content because the latent content is anxiety-provoking and causes the person psychological discomfort.

Insight is not achieved quickly, nor do clients always find it easy to disclose private aspects of their personal lives. For example, a client may have to confront the reality of being abused as a child, or of being unloved, or of feeling peculiar, inferior or out of place. Although the client wishes to be cured, they do not look forward to the anxiety and apprehension that may result from recalling painful memories. The client often becomes defensive at some point during therapy, unconsciously attempting to halt further insight by censoring their true feelings, a process Freud called **resistance**.

Over a period of months or even years of therapy sessions taking place as often as several times a week, the client gradually becomes less inhibited, and the discussion begins to drift away from recent events to the more distant shores of early childhood. As the client relives aspects of childhood, they may begin to project powerful attitudes and emotions onto the therapist, a process called **transference**. The client may come to love or hate the therapist with the same intensity of the powerful emotions experienced in childhood towards parents or siblings.

Freud reasoned that the analyst, being human too, could just as easily project his or her emotions onto the client, a process he called counter-transference. Unlike transference, Freud believed **counter-transference** to be unhealthy and undesirable. To be effective, the analyst must remain emotionally detached and objective in their appraisal of the client's disclosures. For this reason, he argued that the analyst, in order to understand their own unconscious conflicts, should undergo complete analysis with another therapist.

Modern psychodynamic therapy

Psychoanalysis is now often referred to as **psychodynamic therapy** to reflect differences between modern psychoanalytic approaches and the original form of Freudian psychoanalysis. For example, although modern forms of psychodynamic therapies still focus on achieving insight into the unconscious, they tend to place less emphasis on sexual factors during development and more upon social and interpersonal experiences. Contemporary therapists also are more likely to address concerns and issues in the client's present life than to examine childhood experiences exclusively.

Modern psychodynamic therapists also view the ego as playing a more active role in influencing a person's thoughts and actions. Instead of viewing the ego as functioning merely to seek ways to satisfy the demands of the id and superego, they believe it to be a proactive component in one's overall psychological functioning. In other words, compared with Freud, modern psychodynamic therapists see the ego as having more control over the psyche. Thus, people

receiving psychodynamic therapy are seen as being less constrained by the mind's unconscious forces than Freud thought them to be.

One modern form of psychodynamic therapy, time-limited therapy, takes 25–30 sessions with the therapist to complete (Strupp, 1993). The goal of time-limited therapy is to understand and improve the client's interpersonal skills through interpretation of transference processes. This therapy is based on Freud's belief that our early experiences with others influence the dynamics of our current relationships. Time-limited therapy focuses on the schemata that a client has about interpersonal relationships and attempts to modify those that are incorrect or that otherwise prevent the client from developing fulfilling relationships with others.

Evaluation

Evaluating the effectiveness of psychoanalysis or psychodynamic therapy is difficult because only a small proportion of people with mental disorders qualify for this method of treatment. To participate in this kind of therapy, a client must be intelligent, articulate and motivated enough to spend three or more hours a week working hard to uncover unconscious conflicts. In addition, they must be able to afford the therapist's fees, which are high. These qualifications rule out most psychotics, as well as people who lack the time or money to devote to such a long-term project. Furthermore, many people who enter this kind of therapy become dissatisfied with their progress and leave. In other cases, the therapist encourages a client to leave if they decide that the client is not cooperating fully. Thus, those who actually complete a course of therapy do not constitute a random sample, and we cannot conclude that this kind of therapy works just because a high percentage of this group is happy with the results. Those who have dropped out ought also to be counted.

Another problem in evaluating psychoanalysis and psychodynamic therapy is that therapists have a way to 'explain' their failures: they can blame them on the client (Eysenck, 1985). If the client appears to accept an insight into their behaviour but the behaviour does not change, the insight is said to be merely 'intellectual'. This escape clause makes the argument for the importance of insight completely circular and, therefore, illogical: if the client gets better, the improvement is due to insight; but if the client's behaviour remains unchanged, real (as opposed to 'intellectual') insight did not occur.

Humanistic therapies

Client-centred therapy

In the 1940s, Carl Rogers (1902–87) developed the first humanistic therapy, creating a major alternative to psychoanalysis. The aim of **humanistic therapy** is to provide the client with a greater understanding of their unique potential for personal growth and self-actualisation. Humanistic therapies proceed from the assumption that people are good and have innate worth. Psychological problems reflect some type of blocking of one's potential for personal growth; humanistic therapy aims to realise this potential.

Rogers found the formalism of psychoanalysis too confining and its emphasis on intrapsychic conflict too pessimistic (Tobin, 1991). His discontent led him to develop his own theory of personality, abnormal behaviour and therapy. His **client-centred therapy** is so named because of the respect given the client during therapy: the client decides what to talk about without direction or judgement from the therapist. The client takes ultimate responsibility for resolving the client's problems. The client, not a method or theory, is the focus of the therapy.

Rogers believed that the cause of many psychological problems can be traced to people's perceptions of themselves as they actually are (their real selves) as differing from the people they would like to be (their ideal selves). Rogers called this discrepancy between the real and the ideal perceptions of the self-incongruence. The goal of client-centred therapy is to reduce **incongruence** by fostering experiences that will make attainment of the ideal self possible. Because the client's and not the therapist's thoughts direct the course of therapy, the therapist strives to make those thoughts, perceptions and feelings more noticeable to the client. This is frequently done through reflection, sensitive rephrasing or mirroring of the client's statements. For example:

> Client: I get so frustrated at my parents. They just don't understand how I feel. They don't know what it's like to be me.
>
> Therapist: You seem to be saying that the things that are important to you aren't very important to your parents. You'd like them now and then to see things from your perspective.

By reflecting the concerns of the client, the therapist demonstrates empathy, or the ability to perceive the world from another's viewpoint. The establishment of empathy is key in encouraging the client to deal with the incongruence between the real and the ideal selves.

For Rogers (1951), the 'worth and significance of the individual' is a basic ground rule of therapy. This theme is represented in therapy through unconditional positive regard, in which the therapist tries to convey to the client that his or her worth as a human being is not dependent on anything they think, do or feel.

In client-centred therapy, the therapist totally and unconditionally accepts the client and approves of them as a person so that the client can come to understand that their feelings are worthwhile and important. Once the client begins to pay attention to these feelings, a self-healing process begins. For example, a client usually has difficulty at first expressing feelings verbally. The therapist tries to understand the feelings underlying the client's confused state and to help them put those feelings into words. Through this process, the client learns to understand and heed their own drive towards self-actualisation.

Evaluation

Unlike many other clinicians, who prefer to rely on their own judgements concerning the effectiveness of their techniques, Rogers himself stimulated a considerable amount of research on the effectiveness of client-centred therapy. He recorded therapeutic sessions so that various techniques could be evaluated. One researcher, Truax (1966), obtained permission from Rogers (and his clients) to record some therapy sessions, and he classified the statements made by the clients into several categories. One of the categories included statements of improving mental health, such as 'I'm feeling better lately' or 'I don't feel as depressed as I used to'. After each of the patients' statements, Truax noted Rogers's reaction to see whether he gave a positive response. Typical positive responses were 'Oh, really? Tell me more' or 'Uh-huh. That's nice' or just a friendly 'Mm'. Truax found that of the eight categories of client statements, only those that indicated progress were regularly followed by a positive response from Rogers. Not surprisingly, during their therapy, the clients made more and more statements indicating progress.

This study attests to the power of social reinforcement and its occurrence in unexpected places. Rogers was an effective and conscientious psychotherapist, but he had not intended to single out and reinforce his clients' realistic expressions of progress in therapy. (Of course, he did not uncritically reinforce exaggerated or unrealistic positive statements.) This finding does not discredit client-centred therapy. Rogers simply adopted a very effective strategy for altering a person's behaviour. He used to refer to his therapy as non-directive; however, when he realised that he was reinforcing positive statements, he stopped referring to it as non-directive because it obviously was not.

Behavioural and cognitive behavioural therapies

The fundamental assumption made by behavioural therapists is that people learn maladaptive or self-defeating behaviour in the same way as they learn adaptive behaviour. Undesirable behaviour, such as nail-biting or alcohol abuse, is the problem, not just a reflection of the problem. The methods that behavioural therapists use to induce behaviour change are extensions of classical and operant conditioning principles and work quite successfully.

In classical conditioning, a previously neutral stimulus (ultimately the conditional stimulus, CS) comes to elicit the same response as a stimulus (unconditional stimulus, UCS) that naturally elicits that response because the CS reliably predicts the UCS (see Chapter 7). According to Joseph Wolpe (1958), one of the founders of behavioural therapy, many of our everyday fears and anxieties become associated with neutral stimuli through coincidence. Going to the dentist may evoke fear because the last time that you went you were not given enough anaesthetic and the drilling hurt. Although the dental surgery is usually not painful, you associate the dentist with pain because of your past experience. The next sections describe some of the more specific behavioural and cognitive behavioural approaches.

Systematic desensitisation

One behavioural therapy technique, developed by Wolpe, has been especially successful in eliminating some kinds of fear and phobia. This technique, called **systematic desensitisation**, is designed to remove the unpleasant emotional response produced by the feared object or situation and replace it with an incompatible one – relaxation.

The client is first trained to achieve complete relaxation. The essential task is to learn to respond quickly to suggestions to feel relaxed and peaceful so that these suggestions can elicit an immediate relaxation response. Next, client and therapist construct a hierarchy of anxiety-related stimuli.

Finally, the conditional stimuli (fear-eliciting situations) are paired with stimuli that elicit the learned relaxation response. For example, a person with a fear of spiders is instructed to relax and then to imagine hearing from a neighbour that she saw a spider in her garage. If the client reports no anxiety, they are instructed to move to the next item in the hierarchy and to imagine hearing a neighbour say that there is a tiny spider across the street; and so on. Whenever the client begins feeling anxious, they signal to the therapist with some predetermined gesture such as raising a finger. The therapist instructs the client to relax and, if necessary, describes a less threatening scene. The client is not permitted to feel severe anxiety at any time. Gradually, over a series of sessions (the average is 11), the client is able to get through the entire list, vicariously experiencing even the most feared encounters.

Whereas practitioners of systematic desensitisation are careful not to permit their clients to become too anxious, practitioners of a procedure called **flooding** attempt to rid their clients of their fears by arousing them intensely until their responses diminish through habituation and they learn that nothing bad happens. The therapist describes, as graphically as possible, the most frightening encounters possible with the object of a client's phobia. The client tries to imagine the encounter and to experience intense fear (thereby 'flooding' the client's mind with anxious thoughts). In some cases, the client actually encounters the object of their fear, in which case

the treatment is called *in vivo* (live) **implosion therapy**. Of course, the client is protected from any adverse effects of the encounter (or the encounter is imaginary), so there are no dangerous consequences. Eventually, the fear response begins to subside, and the client learns that even the worst imaginable encounter can become tolerable. In a sense, the client learns not to fear their own anxiety attack, and avoidance responses begin to extinguish.

Aversion therapy

In **aversion therapy**, a negative reaction to a neutral stimulus is caused by pairing it with an aversive stimulus (UCS). Aversion therapy attempts to establish an unpleasant response (such as a feeling of fear or disgust) to the object that produces the undesired behaviour. For example, a person with a **fetish** for women's shoes might be given painful electrical shocks while viewing colour slides of women's shoes. Aversion therapy has also been used to treat drinking, smoking, transvestism, **exhibitionism** and overeating. This technique has been shown to be moderately effective (Marshall *et al.*, 1991). However, because the method involves pain or nausea, the client's participation must be voluntary, and the method should be employed only if other approaches fail or are impractical.

The use of aversive methods raises ethical issues, particularly when the individual is so severely impaired that they are unable to give informed consent to a particular therapeutic procedure. It would seem reasonable that aversive methods involving stimuli such as electric shock should be used as the last resort. In a method called **covert sensitisation**, instead of experiencing a punishing stimulus after performing a behaviour, the client imagines that they are performing an undesirable behaviour and then imagines receiving an aversive stimulus.

Behaviour modification

Behaviour modification, a general term describing therapy based on operant conditioning principles (see Chapter 7), involves altering maladaptive behaviour by rearranging the contingencies between behaviour and its consequences. Increases in desirable behaviour can be brought about through either positive or negative reinforcement, and undesirable behaviour can be reduced through either extinction or punishment.

In its infancy, behaviour modification was applied chiefly to patients with schizophrenia (described in detail later) and the mentally retarded (Lindsley, 1956; Ayllon and Azrin, 1968; Neisworth and Madle, 1982). The use of operant conditioning principles has been extended to a wide array of behaviours and circumstances, for example weight management, anorexia nervosa, bed-wetting, smoking and compliance with medical regimens (Kazdin, 1994).

Token economies

The behaviour–analytic approach has been used on a large scale in mental institutions with generally good success. Residents are often asked to do chores to engage them in active participation in their environment. In some instances, other specific behaviours are also targeted as desirable and therapeutic, such as helping residents who have more severe problems. To promote these social behaviours, therapists have designed **token economies**. A list of tasks is compiled, and residents receive tokens as rewards for performing the tasks; later, they can exchange these tokens for snacks, other desired articles or various privileges. The tokens become conditioned reinforcers for desirable and appropriate behaviours. The amount of time spent performing the desirable behaviours was high when reinforcement contingencies were imposed and low when they were not.

Although token economies are based on a simple principle, they are very difficult to implement. A mental institution includes patients, caretakers, housekeeping staff and professional staff. If a token economy is to be effective, all staff members who deal with residents must learn how the system works; ideally, they should also understand and agree with its underlying principles. A token economy can easily be sabotaged by a few people who believe that the system is foolish, wrong or in some way threatening to themselves. If these obstacles can be overcome, token economies work very well.

Modelling

Humans (and many other animals) have the ability to learn without directly experiencing an event. People can imitate the behaviour of other people, watching what they do and, if the conditions are appropriate, performing the same behaviour. This capability provides the basis for the technique of **modelling**. Behaviour therapists have found that clients can make much better progress when they have access to a model providing examples of successful behaviours to imitate.

Social skills training

With social skills training, the client is taught to behave in a desirable and socially appropriate way and this has been used extensively in individuals with schizophrenia (see below) and Asperger's syndrome (Chapter 12). They might do this by engaging in **assertiveness training**, which teaches the client to be more direct about their feelings (Oltmans and Emery, 1998). A part of assertiveness training might be role-playing, in which the client is taught to act out or rehearse social skills by adopting the identity of another, socially skilled person.

Cognitive behavioural therapy

The first attempts at developing psychotherapies based on altering or manipulating cognitive processes emerged during the 1970s. These attempts were undertaken by behavioural therapists who suspected that maladaptive behaviour, or, for that matter, adaptive behaviour, could be due to more than only environmental variables. They began exploring how their clients' thoughts, perceptions, expectations and self-statements might interact with environmental factors in the development and maintenance of maladaptive behaviour.

The focus of **cognitive behavioural therapy** (**CBT**) is on changing the client's maladaptive thoughts, beliefs and perceptions. Like behaviour therapists – and unlike most insight psychotherapists – cognitive behaviour therapists are not particularly interested in events that occurred in the client's childhood. They are interested in the here and now and in altering the client's behaviour so that it becomes more functional. Although they employ many methods used by behavioural therapists, they believe that when behaviours change, they do so because of changes in cognitive processes.

There are many ways in which CBT can be applied to mental disorder. Attribution retraining, for example, involves retraining the client to alter their perception of causes of events or behaviour (attributions are perceived causes). One way in which this can be achieved is by requesting the client to adopt a more scientific approach to their beliefs. For example, it is common in depression for a depressed person to attribute causes for failure to themselves but to attribute successes to others. Attribution retraining should encourage the client to change these 'faulty' attributions and make them more realistic. One form of CBT designed to treat depression requires the patient to assess whether their view of themselves and others is distorted based on a considered analysis of their lives. This approach, based on the clinical work of Beck (1967, 1976; Beck and Emery, 1985), is considered in the section on depression below (see p. 752).

Another CBT approach, **rational-emotive therapy**, was developed in the 1950s by Albert Ellis, a clinical psychologist, and is based on the belief that psychological problems are caused by how people think about upsetting events and situations. In contrast to the other forms of CBT, rational-emotive therapy did not grow out of the tradition of behaviour therapy. Ellis asserts that psychological problems are the result of faulty cognitions; therapy is therefore aimed at changing people's beliefs. Rational-emotive therapy is highly directive and confrontational. The therapist tells their clients what they are doing wrong and how they should change.

According to Ellis and his followers, emotions are the products of cognition. A significant activating event (A) is followed by a highly charged emotional consequence (C), but it is not correct to say that A has caused C. Rather, C is a result of the person's belief system (B).

Therefore, inappropriate emotions (such as depression, guilt and anxiety) can be abolished only if a change occurs in the person's belief system. It is the task of the rational-emotive therapist to dispute the person's beliefs and to convince them that those beliefs are inappropriate. Ellis tries to show his clients that irrational beliefs are impossible to satisfy, that they make little logical sense and that adhering to them creates needless anxiety, self-blame and self-doubt. The following are examples of the kinds of ideas that Ellis believes to be irrational:

> The idea that it is a necessity for an adult to be loved or approved by virtually every significant person in the community.
>
> The idea that one should be thoroughly competent, adequate, and goal-oriented in all possible respects if one is to consider oneself as having worth.
>
> The idea that human unhappiness is externally caused and that people have little or no ability to control their lives.
>
> The idea that one's past is an all-important determinant of one's present behaviour.
>
> The idea that there is invariably a right, precise, and perfect solution to human problems and that it is catastrophic if this perfect solution is not found. (Source: Ellis, 1973, pp. 152–3.)

In a review of research evaluating the effectiveness of rational-emotive therapy, Haaga and Davison (1989) concluded that the method has been shown to reduce general anxiety, test anxiety and unassertiveness. Rational-emotive therapy has appeal and potential usefulness for those who can enjoy and profit from intellectual teaching and argumentation. The people who are likely to benefit most from this form of therapy are those who are self-demanding and who feel guilty for not living up to their own standards of perfection. People with serious anxiety disorders or with severe thought disorders, such as schizophrenia and other psychoses, are unlikely to respond to an intellectual analysis of their problems.

Many therapists who adopt an eclectic approach use some of the techniques of rational-emotive therapy with some of their clients. In its advocacy of rationality and its eschewing of superstition, the therapy proposes a common-sense approach to living. However, many psychotherapists disagree with Ellis's denial of the importance of empathy in the relationship between therapist and client.

Evaluation

Psychotherapists of traditional orientations have criticised behavioural therapy for its focus on the symptoms of a psychological problem to the exclusion of its root causes. Some psychoanalysts even argue that treatment of just the symptoms is dangerous. In their view, the removal of one symptom of an intrapsychic conflict will simply produce another, perhaps more serious, symptom through a process called **symptom substitution**.

There is little evidence that symptom substitution occurs. It is true that many people's behavioural problems are caused by conditions that existed in the past, and often these problems become self-perpetuating. Behavioural therapy can, in many cases, eliminate the problem behaviour without delving into the past. For example, a child may, for one reason or another, begin wetting the bed. The nightly awakening irritates the parents, who must change the bed sheets and the child's pyjamas. The disturbance often disrupts family relationships. The child develops feelings of guilt and insecurity and wets the bed more often. Instead of analysing the sources of family conflict, a therapist who uses behavioural therapy would install a device in the child's bed that rings a bell when they begin to urinate. The child awakens and goes to the bathroom to urinate and soon ceases to wet the bed. The elimination of bed-wetting causes rapid improvement in the child's self-esteem and in the entire family relationship. Symptom substitution does not appear to occur (Baker, 1969).

Although cognitive behavioural therapists believe in the importance of unobservable constructs such as feelings, thoughts and perceptions, they do not believe that good therapeutic results can be achieved by focusing on cognitions alone. They, like their behaviour-analytic colleagues, insist that it is not enough to have their clients introspect and analyse their thought patterns. Instead, therapists must help clients to change their behaviour. Behavioural changes can cause cognitive changes. For example, when a client observes that they are now engaging in fewer maladaptive behaviours and more adaptive behaviours, the client's self-perceptions and self-esteem are bound to change as a result. Therapy is more effective when attention is paid to cognitions as well as to behaviours.

Other forms of psychotherapy

Group therapy

Group psychotherapy, in which two or more clients meet simultaneously with a therapist to discuss problems, became common during the Second World War. The stresses of combat produced psychological problems in many members of the armed forces, and the demand for psychotherapists greatly exceeded the supply. What began as an economic necessity became an institution once the effectiveness of group treatment was recognised.

Because most psychological problems involve interactions with other people, treating these problems in a group setting may be worthwhile. Group therapy provides four advantages that are not found in individual therapy:

1 The group setting permits the therapist to observe and interpret actual interactions without having to rely on clients' descriptions, which may be selective or faulty.

2 A group can bring social pressure to bear on the behaviours of its members. If a person receives similar comments about

Psychology in action: How instructions to express reduce distress

Imagine having experienced severe distress or trauma. You may have been physically attacked, robbed or sexually assaulted. Anecdotal evidence suggests that it is best to talk about these events to another person – this allows you to express your feelings about the event that you had previously kept to yourself. It is a form of catharsis, people will say. They might be right.

A novel medicine treatment for trauma has been emotional disclosure (ED) through expressive writing. ED involves asking an individual who has suffered severe trauma or distress to express how they feel about the distress or trauma by writing about it and to write or think about why they feel in the way that they do. This ostensibly simple technique has been found to improve coping, physical health, emotional health and immune system functioning in extremely distressed individuals (Smyth, 1998).

The pioneers of this technique, James Pennebaker and his colleagues (Pennebaker *et al.*, 1988; Pennebaker and Francis, 1996; Pennebaker, 1997), have published several studies showing that when distressed individuals are asked to write down their thoughts and express their emotions, these individuals required fewer visits from the doctor than did those who wrote about trivial topics. Individuals also showed an improvement in their immune system functioning. The participants in these studies were people suffering real distress – Holocaust survivors, the bereaved and the recently unemployed.

Replications by different groups are positive, but mixed. Some improvement in physical health beyond the 'treatment' period has been reported (Lepore, 1997) and survivors of trauma who create narratives about their distress feel better than those who do not (Foa *et al.*, 1995). Arthritic patients who wrote about the emotionally negative aspects of their illness saw an improvement in their condition (Kelley *et al.*, 1997). Sloan and Marx (2004) randomly assigned 49 women who reported having experienced at least one traumatic event and who showed at least moderate levels of post-traumatic stress disorder to a disclosure condition – where they wrote about a traumatic event in prose as emotionally as possible – or a control condition where no writing occurred. Participants in the disclosure condition reported fewer psychological and physical symptoms a month after testing. The only improvement that was 'clinically' significant, however, was a reduction in depressive symptoms. A meta-analysis of emotional disclosure in caregivers – people who look after others with serious illnesses – found that the technique reduced symptoms of trauma and improved psychological well-being but that it had no significant effect on depression, anxiety or quality of life (Riddle *et al.*, 2016). The technique was more successful with those with fewer than five years' experience of care-giving.

A study investigating the effects of ED in patients suffering serious illness found that it had little effect in reducing distress, but patients who had little social contact with others or who found that the opportunities for expressing emotions to others were limited benefited greatly from the process. Zakowski *et al.* (2004) randomly assigned 104 gynaecological and prostate cancer patients to an ED condition, where patients wrote about their trauma for 20 minutes a day for three days, or a non-ED condition (writing about a non-emotional topic). Those in the ED condition who had little opportunity for expressing emotion in social contexts benefited significantly from the ability to write about their illness. The lack of a reduction in stress is comparable to findings from studies of breast cancer which report similarly negative findings (Stanton and Danoff-Burg, 2002). The authors suggest that the benefits of writing in cancer patients might be better revealed in more objective, physical measures rather than subjective, self-report measures.

Some researchers have hypothesised that the benefits of expressive writing arise from the changes in thinking that such writing encourages (Pennebaker, 1997). When individuals write about cause and effect in their expressive writing and show insight into their distress, physical and psychological health improves – their thoughts become more methodically organised (Pennebaker *et al.*, 1997).

Undergraduates who wrote about their stressful thoughts and feelings on entering university showed significantly better working memory performance at the end of the experiment (Klein and Boals, 2001). More 'cognitive' than 'emotion' words were used at a later session (compared with earlier sessions). The researchers suggest that this supports Smyth's (1998) contention that if writing moderates health by changing cognition, changes in tests measuring cognition should be closely associated with the writing process. In a second experiment, students were asked to write about intrusive negative thoughts. They showed significant improvements in working memory than did those who wrote about a positive event or a trivial one.

This last finding suggests that the improvements may be due to the removal of intrusive negative thoughts, rather than intrusive thoughts per se (positive thoughts, for example, which may have been on people's minds, did not place significant strains on working memory). Of course, this study focused on one type of working memory task and did not measure health outcomes, but the authors hypothesise that the improvements in health as a result of expressive writing may be due to the improvements in working memory capacity. There is also evidence that repeated emotional disclosure can be more effective in students experiencing stress – the more a person writes, the more successful the disclosure (Niles *et al.*, 2016), although this is based on a study of 50 students.

their behaviour from all the members of a group, the message is often more convincing than if a psychotherapist delivers the same comments in a private session.

3 The process of seeing the causes of maladaptive behaviour in other people often helps a person to gain insight into their own problems. People can often learn from the mistakes of others.

4 Knowing that other people have problems similar to one's own can bring comfort and relief. People discover that they are not alone.

The structure of group therapy sessions can vary widely. Some sessions are little more than lectures, in which the therapist presents information about a problem common to all members of the group, followed by discussion. For example, in a case involving a person with severe mental or physical illness, the therapist explains to family members the nature, treatment and possible outcomes of the disorder. Then the therapist answers questions and allows people to share their feelings about what the illness has done to their family. Other groups are simply efficient ways to treat several clients at the same time. Most types of group therapy involve interactions among the participants.

Family therapy and couples therapy

In **family therapy**, a therapist meets with (usually) all the members of a client's family and analyses the ways in which individuals interact. The therapist attempts to get family members to talk to each other instead of addressing all comments and questions to them. As much as possible, the family therapist tries to collect data about the interactions – how individuals sit in relation to each other, who interrupts whom, who looks at whom before speaking – in order to infer the nature of interrelationships within the family. For example, there may be barriers between certain family members; perhaps a father is unable to communicate with one of his children. Or two or more family members may be so dependent on each other that they cannot function independently; they constantly seek each other's approval and, through overdependence, make each other miserable.

After inferring the family structure, the therapist attempts to restructure it by replacing maladaptive interactions with more effective, functional ones. The therapist suggests that perhaps all members of the family must change if the client is to make real improvement. They get family members to 'actualise' their transactional patterns – to act out their everyday relationships – so that the maladaptive interactions will show themselves. Restructuring techniques include forming temporary alliances between the therapist and one or more of the family members, increasing tension in order to trigger changes in unstable structures, assigning explicit tasks and homework to family members (for example, making them interact with other members), and providing general support, education

and guidance. Sometimes, the therapist visits the family at home. For example, if a child in a family refuses to eat, the therapist will visit during a mealtime in order to see the problem acted out as explicitly as possible.

Behavioural therapists have also applied their methods of analysis and treatment to families. This approach focuses on the social environment provided by the family and on the ways in which family members reinforce or punish each other's behaviour. The strategy is to identify the maladaptive behaviours of the individuals and the ways these behaviours are inadvertently reinforced by the rest of the family. Then the therapist helps the family members find ways to increase positive exchanges and reinforce each other's adaptive behaviours. A careful analysis of the social dynamics of a family often reveals that changes need to be made not in the individual showing the most maladaptive behaviours but in the other members of the family.

All couples will find that they disagree on some important issues. These disagreements necessarily lead to conflicts. For example, they may have to decide whether to move to accommodate the career of one of the partners, they will have to decide how to spend their money, and they will have to decide how to allocate household chores. Their ability to resolve conflict is one of the most important factors affecting the quality and durability of their relationship (Schwartz and Schwartz, 1980).

Mindfulness

A technique that has attracted a great deal of attention from therapists and researchers in the past few years is one that actually dates back to the 1970s. Mindfulness is a state of mind in which the individual focuses on cognitive, emotional or corporeal experiences in the present in a non-judgmental and accepting way. Techniques to enhance mindfulness have been developed to treat depression, stress and anxiety (Keng et al., 2011) and various practices exist: Mindfulness-Based Stress Reduction (MBSR), Mindfulness-Based Cognitive Therapy (MBCT), Dialectical Behavioural Therapy and Acceptance and Commitment Therapy (Spijkerman et al., 2016). Mindfulness-Based Cognitive Therapy (MBCT) was originally designed for individuals with depression but has also been applied to anxiety.

Evidence suggests that MBCT is effective in preventing relapse in individuals who have experienced three episodes of depression (Kuyken et al., 2010) and, in the UK, the treatment is offered as part of the NICE national guidelines on depression relapse (NICE, 2009). As Strauss et al. (2014) note, however, neither MBSR nor MBCT were designed for people with acute depression or anxiety. In their meta-analysis of 12 studies which included randomised control trials of mindfulness for a current episode of anxiety or depression, Strauss et al. found that mindfulness-based interventions were successful in reducing symptom severity in people with depression but not anxiety.

Controversies in psychological science: Does psychotherapy work?

The issue

The evaluation of therapies and therapists is an important issue as the consequences are serious. It has received much attention, but almost everyone who is involved agrees that too little is known about the efficacy of psychotherapeutic methods, partly because psychotherapeutic effectiveness is difficult to study. The most well-known psychotherapies, their goals and methods of intervention are summarised in Table 18.2. Given that there are at least 400 types of therapy and over 150 classified mental disorders (Garfield and Bergin, 1994), achieving some consistency across studies is difficult, but there is evidence that some types of psychotherapy are more successful than others (Lilienfeld *et al.*, 2013) and the more empirically supported therapies show the greatest success (Lilienfeld *et al.*, 2014).

Table 18.2 Causes of spurious therapeutic effectiveness (CSTE)

CSTE	Description
Category 1 CSTEs: Erroneous perceptions of client change in its absence	
1. Illusory placebo effects	Perceived improvement occurring in the absence of genuine improvement
2. Palliative benefits	Feeling better about one's signs and symptoms without tangible improvements in them
3. Confusing insight with improvement	Mistaking apparent understanding of one's problem with improvement in that problem
4. Retrospective rewriting of pre treatment functioning	Belief that one has improved arising from a tendency to remember one's pretreatment functioning as worse than it was
5. Response-shift bias	Change in one's evaluation standard with respect to an outcome dimension as a consequence of treatment
6. Reduction in cognitive biases	Declines in cognitive biases tied to pretreatment reporting of symptoms
7. Demand characteristics	Tendency of clients to report improvement in accord with what they believe to be the therapist's or researcher's hypotheses
8. The therapist's office error	Confusion of client's in-session behavioral presentation with out-of-session improvement
9. Test-retest artifacts	Tendency of scores on psychopathology measures to decline spuriously on their second administration
10. Unknowable outcomes in the control condition	Lack of information regarding what would have occurred had the treatment not been administered
11. Selective attrition	Tendency of clients who drop out of therapy to improve less than other clients
12. Compliance bias	Tendency for client adherence to treatment recommendations to be confounded with variables that predict improvement
13. Selective attention to client outcomes	Tendency of individuals to unwittingly "cherrypick" the outcome variables on which clients are improving
14. Selective memory for client outcomes	Tendency of individuals to preferentially recall indications of improvement as opposed to those of no improvement or worsening
15. Selective interpretation of client outcomes	Tendency of individuals to interpret ambiguous changes in signs or symptoms as indications of improvement

▶

Controversies in psychological science: *Continued*

CSTE	Description
Category 2 CSTEs: Misinterpretations of actual client change stemming from extratherapeutic factors	
16. Spontaneous remission	Tendency of some psychological conditions to improve on their own
17. History	Widely shared events transpiring outside of treatment
18. Cyclical nature of some disorders	Tendency of some psychological conditions to go up and down
19. Self-limiting nature of disorder episodes	Tendency of individuals with psychological conditions to improve once episodes have run their natural course
20. Regression to the mean	Tendency of extreme scores to become less extreme on retesting
21. Maturation	Improvement arising from naturally occurring psychological growth
22. Multiple treatment interference	Tendency of individuals who obtain one treatment to obtain others at the same time
23. Initial misdiagnosis	Errors in the diagnosis of a condition, resulting in erroneous inferences of improvement
Category 3 CSTEs: Misinterpretations of actual client change stemming from nonspecific treatment factors	
24. Placebo effects	Improvement stemming from the expectation of improvement
25. Novelty effects	Improvement owing to enthusiasm regarding the prospects of receiving a new intervention
26. Effort justification	Clients who invest substantial time, energy, effort, and resources in an intervention often feel a psychological need to justify this commitment

The evidence

Several factors make it extremely difficult to evaluate the effectiveness of a particular form of therapy or an individual therapist. These include measurement – there are no easily applied, commonly agreed criteria for mental health; and self-selection – clients choose whether to enter therapy, what type of therapy to engage in and how long to stay in therapy, which makes it nearly impossible to establish either a stable sample population or a control group. Self-selection means that certain kinds of people are more likely than others to enter a particular therapy and stick with it, which produces a biased sample. Lack of a stable sample and of a control group makes it difficult to compare the effectiveness of various kinds of therapy. Many patients change therapists or leave therapy altogether. What conclusions can we make about the effectiveness of a therapy by looking only at the progress made by the clients who remain with it?

There is also the issue of resistance of some psychotherapists to evidence-based research and many psychotherapists continue what they do based on informal, clinical experience rather than empirical data that test their assumptions. One of the more obvious biases in this type of thinking is naive realism (or common-sense realism) – the idea that seeing is believing and that the external world is exactly as we see it and, therefore, how others see it, too. Of course, as you have seen throughout this book, this is invariably untrue. Intuition is usually contradicted by evidence (Gaudiano *et al.*, 2011) and some mental health professionals use techniques to, for example, recover memories from birth using hypnosis, despite no evidence that these techniques work (Legault and Laurence, 2007). Lilienfeld *et al.* (2014) list 26 causes of spurious therapeutic effectiveness which lead to perception of client change where none actually exists, misinterpretation of actual change, and misinterpretation of change that is actually produced by non-therapeutic factors. You can see the description of these in Table 18.2. The stronger the belief of the therapist that their technique is the best, the more successful the outcomes of their therapies (Munder *et al.*, 2013).

Yet another problem with scientific evaluation of psychotherapy is the question of an appropriate control group. The effects

▶

Controversies in psychological science: *Continued*

of therapeutic drugs must be determined through comparison with the effects of placebos (innocuous pills that have no effects on people's thoughts and behaviour) to be sure that the improvement has not occurred merely because the patient thinks that a pill has done some good. Placebo effects can also occur in psychotherapy: people know that they are being treated and get better because they believe that the treatment should lead to improvement. Also, given the assumption that these therapies have the power to do good, there may be the possibility that they also have the power to do harm (Barlow, 2010; Dimidjian and Hollon, 2010). Given these problems, what can we say about the efficacy of psychotherapy?

In a pioneering, controversial paper on psychotherapeutic evaluation, Eysenck (1952) examined 19 studies assessing the effectiveness of psychotherapy. He reported that of the people who remained in psychoanalysis as long as their therapists thought they should, 66 per cent showed improvement. Similarly, 64 per cent of patients treated eclectically showed an improvement. However, 72 per cent of patients who were treated only custodially (receiving no psychotherapy) in institutions showed improvement. In other words, people got better just as fast by themselves as they did in therapy.

Subsequent studies were not much more supportive. Some investigators, including Eysenck, concluded that it was unethical to charge a person for psychotherapy because there was little scientific evidence for its effectiveness. Many forms of therapy have never been evaluated objectively because their practitioners are convinced that the method works and deem objective confirmation unnecessary.

Several studies have suggested that the ability to form understanding, warm and empathetic relationships is one of the most important traits that distinguish an effective therapist from an ineffective one (Beutler *et al.*, 1994). For example, Strupp and Hadley (1979) enlisted a group of lecturers on the basis of their reputation as warm, trustworthy, empathetic individuals. The lecturers (from the departments of English, history, mathematics and philosophy) were asked to hold weekly counselling sessions for students with psychological difficulties. Another group of students was assigned to professional psychotherapists, both psychologists and psychiatrists, and a third group received no treatment at all. Most of the students showed moderate depression or anxiety.

Although there was much variability, with some individual students showing substantial improvement, students who met with the lecturers did as well as those who met with the professional therapists. Both groups did significantly better than the control subjects who received no treatment. These results suggest that sympathy and understanding are the most important

ingredients in the psychotherapeutic process, at least for treatment of mild anxiety or depression. In such cases, the therapists' theories of how mental disorders should be treated may be less important than their ability to establish warm, understanding relationships with their clients.

In one meta-analysis, Westen and Morrison (2001) scrutinised studies from nine clinical psychology and psychiatric journals published between 1990 and 1999. To be eligible for inclusion, studies had to test the efficacy of a specific psychosocial treatment against a waiting-list control group and an alternative therapy, have had a follow-up of at least 12 months, include valid measures of outcome and be experimental in nature. Thirty-four studies met these inclusion criteria.

The authors found substantial improvement in mental health in up to half of the patients. The majority of patients, however, did not show sustained improvement at one to two years' follow-up, especially those who are depressed or generally anxious. Half of patients who complete a course of treatment will benefit from it, whereas the figure drops to 40 per cent if a patient simply enters treatment (but may not continue). The long-term treatment success for panic disorder is good, but the authors found that the depressed or anxious patient will maintain mild to significant levels of symptoms after treatment. The authors note that follow-up studies at two years were non-existent. In the four studies that did conduct such a follow-up, a quarter of depressed patients who did not abuse alcohol or drugs and were not suicidal will improve two years after treatment. Psychotherapy for panic disorder treatment was the most effective, with 46 per cent of patients showing sustained improvement.

The strict exclusion/inclusion criteria in the study is a plus and a negative. On the plus side, the studies reviewed are carefully selected and well-controlled experimental studies. On the negative side, few studies were included and complications such as co-morbidity (the appearance of one disorder with another) were not addressed because patients in the selected studies suffered exclusively from one disorder. The future should see the inclusion of studies employing other therapies.

Conclusion

The success of psychotherapy (which includes CBT as well as the other, humanistic therapies) rests on the type of therapy applied. There are some negative outcomes: an estimated 9–13 per cent of clients worsen after psychotherapy (Beutler and Clarkin, 1990) and it is ineffective for dealing with other physical illnesses, such as cancer (Coyne *et al.*,

▶

Controversies in psychological science: *Continued*

2007, 2009). The application of psychotherapy to schizophrenia has been associated with a deterioration in the client's condition (Lambert and Bergin, 1994). Also, some problems may be inappropriate for psychotherapy: criminal or antisocial behaviour, for example. For some other problems, however, such as depression, psychotherapy may be quite effective when combined with other treatments.

Table 18.3 Summary of the basic assumptions, goals and methods involved in traditional forms of psychotherapy

Type of therapy	Basic assumptions	Primary goals	Typical method of analysis or intervention
Psychoanalysis	Behaviour is motivated by intra-psychic conflict and biological urges	To discover the sources of conflict and resolve them through insight	Free association, dream interpretation, interpretation of transference, resistance, memory, and manner of speech
Psychodynamic	Behaviour is motivated by both unconscious forces and inter-personal experiences	To understand and improve interpersonal skills	Interpretation of transference and modification of client's inappropriate schemata about interpersonal relationships
Humanistic and gestalt	People are good and have innate worth	To promote personal growth and self-actualisation and to enhance client's awareness of bodily sensations and feelings	Reduce incongruence through reflection, empathy, unconditional positive regard and techniques to enhance personal awareness and feelings of self-worth
Behavioural and cognitive behavioural	Behaviour is controlled largely by environmental contingencies, people's perception of them, or their combination	To change maladaptive behaviour and thinking patterns	Manipulate environmental variables, restructure thinking patterns and correct faulty thinking or irrational beliefs
Family/couples	Problems in relationships entail everybody involved in them	To discover how interactions influence problems in individual functioning	Analysis of patterns of family/couple's interaction and how others reinforce maladaptive and adaptive thinking and behaving

Three further meta-analyses have confirmed the success of the intervention. Khoury *et al.* (2013) found that, in 209 studies, mindfulness-based interventions were moderately successful in reducing symptoms of various psychological disorders compared to controls on a waiting list and when compared with other psychological treatments. It was no better than CBT or pharmacology and it was better in treating psychological than physical conditions. The attrition rate in these studies was also lower than that reported in cognitive and behavioural studies – individuals were more likely to stay the course.

A meta-analysis of MBSR in non-clinical (healthy) individuals experiencing stress and anxiety found that the intervention was moderately successful and the effects were maintained up to 19 weeks following the intervention (Khoury *et al.*, 2015). The effects were stronger for stress and moderate for anxiety, depression and distress and quality of life. Spijkerman *et al.* (2016) examined whether online Mindfulness-Based interventions were successful in reducing symptoms. They found 15 studies which met the criteria for inclusion in the study. The online interventions showed a small but significant effect on depression, anxiety and well-being. The largest effect was for stress, with guided online interventions showing greater success than unguided ones. The number of interventions was also a strong predictor of success.

Biological treatments

The most common biological treatment for mental illness is pharmacological. Psychopharmacological interventions are aimed at treating psychological problems by using chemical agents and their use has increased significantly in the past 20 years with the improvement in diagnosis, the increased reporting of mental illness and the development of new psychotropic drugs. Antidepressants, for example, are the third most prescribed types of drug in the US (Pratt *et al.*, 2011).

There are four major classes of drugs used to treat mental disorders: antipsychotic drugs, antidepressant drugs, antimanic drugs and anti-anxiety drugs. We discuss the application and effectiveness of these drugs in the sections describing mental disorders.

Some people with depression do not respond to antidepressant drugs, but a substantial percentage of these people improve after a few sessions of **electroconvulsive therapy (ECT)** in which electrodes are applied to a person's head and a brief surge of electrical current is passed through them. Because antidepressant medications are generally slow-acting, taking 10 days to two weeks for their therapeutic effects to begin, severe cases of depression are often treated with a brief course of ECT to reduce the symptoms immediately. These people are then maintained on an antidepressant drug.

There are several problems with ECT treatments. An excessive number of ECT treatments has been associated with permanent memory loss (Squire *et al.*, 1981) with little enduring effect on cognitive performance (Calev *et al.*, 1995; Barnes *et al.*, 1997). Nowadays, ECT is usually administered only to the right hemisphere, in order to minimise damage to people's verbal memories, and is used only when the patient's symptoms justify it. Because ECT undoubtedly achieves its effects through the biochemical consequences of the seizure, pharmacologists may discover new drugs that can produce rapid therapeutic effects without ECT's deleterious ones. Once this breakthrough occurs, ECT can be abandoned.

One other biological treatment for mental disorders is even more controversial than electroconvulsive therapy: psychosurgery or neurosurgery (Fenton, 1998). **Psychosurgery** involves the treatment of a mental disorder, in the absence of obvious organic damage, through brain surgery. In contrast, brain surgery to remove a tumour or diseased neural tissue or to repair a damaged blood vessel is not psychosurgery, and there is no controversy about these procedures.

Psychosurgery has its origins in the late 1930s when, at a conference at University College London, the results of frontal lobectomies on two chimpanzees, Becky and Lucy, were presented. The surgery resulted in an increase in calmness and passivity in the chimps. Egas Moniz, a 59-year-old Portuguese professor of neurology, one of the audience at the meeting, suggested that this technique might also be appropriate for humans. Late in 1935, the first frontal lobotomy operations were performed. While treating some symptoms, such as those in chronic schizophrenia, the prefrontal lobotomies were found to have serious side effects, such as apathy and severe blunting of emotions, intellectual impairments and deficits in judgement and planning ability. Nevertheless, the procedure was used for a variety of conditions, most of which were not improved by the surgery. Approximately 40,000 prefrontal lobotomies were performed in the US alone, most of them between 1935 and 1955. A simple procedure, called 'ice pick' prefrontal lobotomy by its critics, was even performed on an out-patient basis, as seen in Figure 18.3. The development of antipsychotic drugs and the increasing attention paid to the serious side effects of prefrontal lobotomy led to a sharp decline in the use of this procedure during the 1950s. Today it is no longer performed.

Drug therapy is the preferred biological treatment for mental disorders although it represents only a possible treatment, not a cure. Usually, the drugs are effective only to the extent that the people for whom they are prescribed actually use them. In some cases, people forget to take their drugs, only to have the disordered symptoms return. In other cases, people take their drugs, get better, and stop taking the drugs because they feel that they are no longer 'sick'. In this case, too, the symptoms soon return. For some people, this cycle repeats itself endlessly.

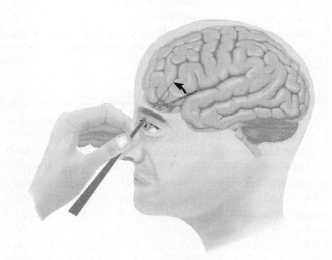

Figure 18.3 'Ice pick' prefrontal lobotomy. The sharp metal rod (a leucotome) is inserted under the eyelid and just above the eye so that it pierces the skull and enters the base of the frontal lobe.
Source: Adapted with permission from Freeman, W., Proceedings of the Royal Society of Medicine, 1949, 42 (suppl.), 8–12. Reprinted by permission of The Royal Society of Medicine.

Psychology in action: The placebo effect

The placebo effect is one of the strongest and most important psychological phenomena in this book. A seemingly inert treatment, its effects can make people feel less pain, endure surgery and can have as powerful an effect on behaviour and pain as morphine. If we're in pain or have an illness, we expect the drugs we take to have a physiological or neurobiological effect (i.e. to work) and attribute the behavioural effects they have to these mechanisms and this is right. The placebo, curiously, may also exert its effect via the same mechanisms, activating the opioid system in the brain and in brain regions involved in actual analgesia.

A placebo is an intervention which has no known causal physiological or physical mechanism of action and which should have no functional purpose or effect. There are different types of placebo such as a pill, injection, needles and so on and even the characteristics of these types of treatments can have different effects on behaviour, as you'll discover below. Over 40 years, research has demonstrated that a placebo can have beneficial effects on a range of pain-related conditions, including migraine, insomnia, irritable bowel syndrome and stomach problems (Jubb and Bensing, 2013).

One of the earliest demonstrations of a placebo effect in the context of medication was published in the 1950s. Beecher (1955) found that 35 per cent of patients responded positively to an inert placebo. The placebo effect can be magnified by factors such as the relationship with the patient's doctor. Kaptchuk et al. (2009) found that having a very good relationship with a doctor led to an improvement in outcome for irritable bowel treatment that was the equivalent of receiving IBS medication. The shape, brand name and cost of a (placebo) drug can all influence a person's response to treatment (Jubb and Bensing, 2013).

In 2015, Espay et al. published a study showing that when patients with Parkinson's disease were told that two drugs being administered cost $100 of $1,500, those receiving what they thought was the more expensive drug showed better outcomes – but only if the expensive drug had been administered first. In fact, both the drugs were placebo – and both improved behaviour. A similar finding was reported in an earlier study of pain tolerance in healthy participants (Waber et al., 2008). In Waber et al.'s experiment, participants were given electric shocks to the wrist and then provided with a codeine-like pill (actually, a placebo) which they were told worked faster than codeine. Half of the sample were told that the pills cost $2.50 each; the other half that they cost 10 cents. Participants reported experiencing less pain in the expensive pill condition. In both of these experiments, participants received one dose of the placebo. It is unclear whether the placebo effect would persist over weeks or months.

A patient's expectations can also strongly influence his or her response to treatment. If people are told that a drug is a 'powerful painkiller', they will expect the drug to have powerful effects and interpret its effects erroneously (Benedetti et al., 1999). Vase et al. (2003) found that people told 'You may receive an active or a placebo agent' demonstrated a smaller effect of placebo than people told: 'The agent you have been given is known to significantly reduce pain'. The placebo effect is often strongest if the placebo is administered as a replacement for a drug that has already been experienced (Jubb and Bensing, 2013).

A placebo is also associated with alterations in brain activity and some of the brain regions that respond to placebo overlap with those regions involved in pain and analgesia. For example, a range of brain regions –including the dorsolateral prefrontal cortex, the rostral anterior cingulate cortex (rACC) and the periaqueductal grey – are commonly activated in people administered placebos (Geuter et al., 2013; Atlas and Wager, 2014). The first PET study of placebo found activation in the rACC during sham treatment and the administration of a real, opioid analgesic (Petrovic et al., 2002), as did the first fMRI study of placebo (Wager et al., 2004) (see Figures 18.4a and b).

This activation, however, is not consistent: some studies show greater activation in the rACC during a placebo versus control condition; others show a decrease (Geuter et al., 2013). In the experiment reported by Geuter et al. (2013), healthy participants were exposed to painful heat and provided with different types of pain relief (placebo). These were creams described as expensive or inexpensive. Both placebo creams relieved pain and the more expensive placebo was associated with greater relief. As other studies have also reported, Geuter et al. found increases in the rACC and the ventral striatum (and a reduction in other areas) during the placebo conditions. The most consistent response was found in the rACC. Activation was found here when participants anticipated pain and when they experienced it. It was also higher during the placebo drug described as expensive.

Other central nervous system regions involved in the placebo effect include the spinal cord: activation is reduced here when people are given a placebo and increased when people are told that they might experience increased symptoms (the more responsive the spinal cord is, the more pain is experienced, as you saw in Chapter 5) (Eippert et al., 2009; Geuter and Buchel, 2013).

The effect of the placebo is clear and very potent. More than any other phenomenon in this book it demonstrates how psychological processes can influence physical responses.

▶

Psychology in action: *continued*

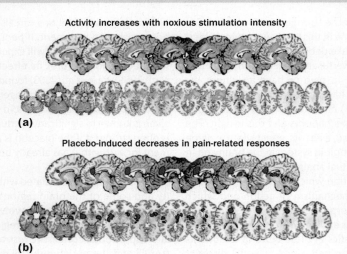

Activity increases with noxious stimulation intensity

(a)

Placebo-induced decreases in pain-related responses

(b)

Figure 18.4a Placebo-induced reductions in target regions for pain processing in the brain. Regions activated by high-intensity or low-intensity painful heat across five samples in the Wager laboratory (combined *N* = 115; adapted from Atlas, Bolger, Lindquist, & Wager, 2010).

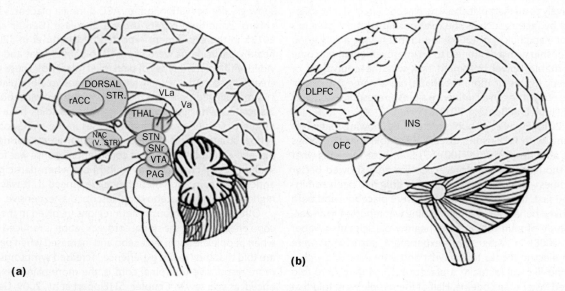

(a)

(b)

Figure 18.4b (a) Mid-sagittal view of human brain, indicating brain regions active in placebo effects. Blue shaded areas are involved in opioid mechanisms, green shaded areas in dopamine.

Abbreviations: rACC, rostral anterior cingulate cortex; dorsal str., dorsal striatum;NAC, nucleus accumbens; v.str., ventral stria-tum; thal, thalamus; VLa, ventrolateralthalamus; VA, ventral anterior thalamus; STN, subthalamic nucleus; SNr, substan-tia nigra pars reticulate; VTA, ventral tegmental area; PAG, periacqueductal grey pathways (Source: Jayne Jubb).

(b) Lateral view of human brain, indicating brain regions active in placebo effects. Blue shaded areas are involved in opioid.

Abbreviations: DLPFC, dorsolateral prefrontal cortex; OFC, orbitofrontal cortex; INS,insula mechanisms (Source: Jayne Jubb).

Mental disorders

An earlier section described the major approaches to treating mental disorder. This section reviews some of the most important mental disorders. The full list of disorders classified by DSM-V can be seen in Table 18.1.

Anxiety disorders

Anxiety is a sense of apprehension or doom that is accompanied by certain physiological reactions, such as accelerated heart rate, sweaty palms and tightness in the stomach. It is the most commonly reported mental illness. The prevalence of anxiety internationally ranges between 1 and 28 per cent, depending on the study and overall prevalence is 7 per cent (Baxter *et al.*, 2013). It is twice as common in Europe/Anglicised countries that in African countries. It is more common in women and in those aged between 15 and 34 (Baxter *et al.*, 2014a). The increase in this, and in other mental illnesses, is probably driven more by population growth, rather than an increase in the disease (Baxter *et al.*, 2014b).

Several types of mental disorders are classified as anxiety disorders, which have fear and anxiety as their most prominent symptoms. Three of the most important anxiety disorders are generalised anxiety disorder, panic disorder and specific phobia. Two anxiety disorders previously described as such in DSM-IV – obsessive-compulsive disorder and post-traumatic stress disorder – now either occupy their own category (OCD is now found under its own category – Obsessive Compulsive and Related Disorders) or have been moved to a new category (PTSD is now found under Trauma – and Stressor-related disorders).

Generalised anxiety disorder (GAD)

Description

The principal characteristic of **generalised anxiety disorder (GAD)** is excessive worry about all matters relating to the individual's life: health, money, work, relationships and so on. These worries must be present on most days and will have occurred over a period of at least six months. The anxious individual finds it difficult to control the worry and shows at least three symptoms out of the following: restlessness, being easily fatigued, difficulty concentrating, irritability, muscle tension and sleep disturbance.

Anxious individuals spend considerably longer making decisions. For example, Tallis *et al.* (1991) asked a group of

controls and clinically anxious individuals to respond if a target was present on a computer monitor. Although there was no difference between controls and anxious individuals when the target was present, the anxious group took significantly longer to make a decision when the target was absent. This finding demonstrates that anxious individuals seem to attend more to tasks that require them to make absolutely correct decisions.

Aetiology

Several models exist which try to explain GAD; some of these also apply to other mental disorders but this section limits itself to those which account for GAD explicitly. One explanation (Borkovec, 1994) suggests that GAD arises from the individual's drive to set and anticipate a set of goals that are desirable. In this context, the anxiety arises when a history of a frustrated failure to achieve affects the perception of cues associated with these goals. Anxiety is reflected in the individual's need to anticipate all possible outcomes, for fear of failing or not achieving.

Eysenck (1992) has argued that although Berkovec's model [described in full in Berkovec (1994)] might explain pathological worry, it does not explain normal worry. Eysenck's model attempts to explain both by suggesting that worry or anxiety serves as an 'alarm function' which brings information concerning threat-related stimuli into awareness. In a sense, worry acts as a behaviour that will prepare an individual for future behaviour; it prompts the individual to anticipate future situations and their solutions.

Although older than Eysenck's, Gray's (1982) model suggests a similar mechanism but ties it to neurophysiology and certain brain systems. According to Gray, anxiety is evoked by signals of punishment, lack of reward, novel stimuli and innate fear stimuli. The individual detects such threats by means of a **behavioural inhibition system (BIS)** which also generates the anxiety. An important function of the BIS is that it helps the organism (Gray's theory applies to humans and other animals) to evaluate the threat content of a stimulus or event. The neurophysiology of the system is vast and complicated, involving neuroanatomical and neurochemical interaction between a number of brain regions. The BIS is thought to be represented by the septum and hippocampal formation.

Two-factor model

The two-factor model of anxiety suggests that individuals exhibit a vulnerability to anxiety owing to high trait anxiety and poor coping skills. There is a strong correlation between neuroticism and almost all major anxiety disorders (Andrews et al., 1989; Andrews, 1991). There also seems to be a loss of control exhibited by anxious individuals and anxiety is often preceded by stressful life events (Last et al., 1984), as Borkovec's model also suggests. Individuals with panic disorder and GAD have been found to rate their parents as less caring and as overprotective (Silove et al., 1991), indicating perhaps one cause of the perceived lack of control. High trait anxiety individuals have been found to be very similar to clinically anxious patients in terms of their perception that events are out of their control and in terms of parental overprotection (Bennett and Stirling, 1998).

Information-processing models

A number of studies have suggested that individuals high in trait anxiety and those suffering GAD exhibit **attentional biases**. That is, they are significantly biased towards responding to threat – or anxiety-related material. Anxious people are more vigilant when reacting to threatening faces than non-threatening faces, for example (Bradley et al., 1999). There are various ways of measuring this attentional bias and three of the most common measures are the dot probe, the emotional Stroop test and the interpretation of ambiguous sentences (Eysenck et al., 1991; Wells and Mathews, 1994).

The dot probe task involves the presentation of two words, one above the other, on a computer monitor. Individuals are asked to read aloud the word at the top; this word is either neutral or is an anxiety – or threat-related word. After a short pause, the individual is presented with either another pair of words or a dot where the top or bottom word appeared. The individual has to press a key when such a dot appears. MacLeod and his colleagues (MacLeod et al., 1986; Matthews et al., 1990) have reported that latencies are shorter for anxiety-related words in GAD patients.

Similar biases are reported for the emotional Stroop task. In this, individuals have to read the colour in which a word is written. These words are either neutral or anxiety-related. GAD patients and individuals high in trait anxiety exhibit a bias towards the anxiety-related words, although the effects found with the Stroop are not as robust as those seen in the dot probe (Williams et al., 1996). Finally, anxious individuals have a tendency to interpret ambiguous sentences such as 'The two men watched as the chest was opened' as threatening, that is, they interpret the chest as being a person's torso rather than a large box (Eysenck et al., 1991).

Each model of GAD has some merit; that Eysenck's and Gray's models flag anxiety as indicating an alarm system that prepares an individual for future action suggests that anxiety results from excessive monitoring for and detection of threat. The findings from attentional bias studies support this view. Why the anxiety should be produced by this appraisal in some individuals and not in others, however, is still unclear.

Borkovec's model is useful in that it specifies previous non-reward and frustration as a cause of being unable to achieve goals. Gray's model is useful because it ties this appraisal down to one neuropsychological system.

In a meta-analysis of the role of brain activation in anxiety, Etkin and Wager (2007) suggest that the brain contains a 'fear circuit'. This involves the amygdala, insult, inferior frontal gyrus, fusiform gyrus and superior temporal gyrus. When people experience fear, increased activation is found in these areas bilaterally. When people take medication, or receive some other treatment, this activation decreases. The type and nature of activation and the structures and regions involved, depend on the specific anxiety disorder.

Treatment

The most common form of treatment for GAD is psycho-pharmacological, with drug administration sometimes coupled with CBT. The drugs used to combat anxiety disorder are called **anti-anxiety drugs** or **anxiolytics** and include barbiturates, benzodiazepines and antidepressants. Barbiturates are sedatives and include drugs such as Phenobarbital. However, because they are highly toxic and foster dependence, they are not widely used. Benzodiazepines are anticonvulsant and sedative drugs, and are the most widely prescribed. Two common benzodiazepines are chlordiazepoxide (Librium) and diazepam (Valium), both of which are low in toxicity.

A meta-analysis of 65 studies comparing CBT and/or pharmacological interventions with a control condition for the treatment of GAD, found that CBT was a significantly better treatment than was no treatment (Mitte, 2005). When studies directly compare CBT with drug intervention, there was no significant difference in efficacy.

The evidence for the efficacy of pharmacology in anxiety is inconsistent with one review concluding that a placebo effect is strong. Benzodiazepines have been found to be effective for GAD, panic disorder and **social anxiety disorder** but these have side effects such as cognitive impairment, sedation and dependence (Baldwin et al., 2014). Drugs that are normally the first choice in anxiety are serotonin-specific reuptake inhibitors (which were developed as anti-depressants). These, too, have side effects such as nausea, insomnia and sexual dysfunction (Baldwin et al., 2014).

A recent innovation in treatment has been the development of on-line interventions (this has been developed for depression, too). The problem with CBT, as a non-pharmacological intervention, is that it is expensive, its availability is limited and it requires attendance at a practice, office or clinic. Internet-based CBT has been developed which has had positive outcomes for depression, social anxiety disorder (Robinson et al., 2010). In one version of this online treatment, the Worry Programme has been used which comprises six online lessons that challenge the individual's beliefs about their worries, challenges their core beliefs and ensures that relapse is prevented. In one study, anxious individuals were placed into different conditions randomly (Robinson *et al.*, 2010). One group received technician-assisted online treatment which involved a weekly email and telephone call which followed a specific script. One group received clinician-assisted treatment which involved weekly email or telephone calls plus involvement in online discussions. Each took 10 minutes a week. A control group received no treatment for 11 weeks. Both treatment groups showed reduced worry scores and GAD scores and had sustained this improvement three months later; the clinician-assisted group's anxiety was reduced the most.

Panic disorder

Panic has been described as a fear of fear (Foa *et al.*, 1984). Individuals who experience panic are threatened by the presence or the potential presence of fear-related physical states. People with **panic disorder** suffer from episodic attacks of acute anxiety – periods of acute and unremitting terror that grip them for lengths of time lasting from a few seconds to a few hours. The lifetime prevalence for panic attacks is around 13 per cent and most people who experience one will experience another (deJonge *et al.*, 2016). Those who do experience more than one are likely to experience other mental illnesses. Onset is most common at the age of 32 (deJonge *et al.*, 2016).

Panic attacks include many physical symptoms, such as shortness of breath, sweating, racing heartbeat (trachycardia), physical tension, cognitive disorganisation, dizziness and fear of loss of support (jelly legs). The individual feels as if he or she is about to collapse and is on the point of death. Such catastrophic thoughts and feelings only exacerbate the physical symptoms and so the individual becomes involved in a self-fulfilling prophecy.

Between panic attacks, people with panic disorder tend to suffer from **anticipatory anxiety** – a fear of having a panic attack (Ottaviani and Beck, 1987). Because attacks can occur without apparent cause, these people anxiously worry about when the next one might strike them. Sometimes, a panic attack that occurs in a particular situation can cause the person to fear that situation. The anxiety we all feel from time to time is significantly different from the intense fear and terror experienced by a person gripped by a panic attack, as the case study below illustrates.

Aetiology

There seems to be a hereditary component to panic disorders: the concordance rate for the disorder is higher between identical twins than between fraternal twins (Torgerson, 1983). Almost 30 per cent of the first-degree relatives (parents, children and siblings) of a person with panic disorder also have panic disorder (Crowe *et al.*, 1983). According to Crowe *et al.*,

the pattern of panic disorder within a family tree suggests that the disorder is caused by a single, dominant gene.

Panic attacks can be triggered in people with histories of panic disorder by giving them injections of lactic acid (a by-product of muscular activity) or by having them breathe air containing an elevated amount of carbon dioxide (Woods *et al.*, 1988; Cowley and Arana, 1990). People with family histories of panic attack are more likely to react to sodium lactate, even if they have never had a panic attack previously (Balon *et al.*, 1989). Some researchers believe that what is inherited is a tendency to react with alarm to bodily sensations that would not disturb most other people.

Clark's model

The most comprehensive (and cognitive) model of panic disorder is that proposed by David Clark. Clark (1986, 1988) argues that panic attacks are produced by the **catastrophic misinterpretation** of bodily events. Slight changes in bodily sensation are interpreted as symptomatic of a physical threat which makes the individual anxious. The more anxious the individual becomes, the more intense the bodily sensations become (the self-fulfilling prophecy referred to above). According to Clark's model, two processes contribute to the maintenance of this misinterpretation. The first is hypervigilance: the individual repeatedly checks for changes in bodily sensations; the second is avoidance strategies: the individual avoids those behaviours they feel will exacerbate the bodily sensations. For example, a person who is afraid that he is about to have a heart attack will avoid exercise (although this prevents the individual from discovering that exercise will not cause a heart attack).

Seligman (1988), however, has argued that the catastrophic misinterpretation theory is questionable on the grounds that the realisation that death will not accompany panic attacks will eventually dawn on these patients. Seligman suggests an alternative suggestion based on **evolutionary preparedness**, the notion that we are evolutionarily predisposed to respond in a specific way to some stimuli because it is to our advantage to do so (Seligman, 1971). Panic, in this context, is the individual's response to biologically prepared bodily sensations. However, as Power and Dalgleish (1997) argue, the failure to realise that death does not follow bodily sensations arises because individuals avoid situations and stimuli that would induce such bodily sensations in the first place. Seligman's formulation may not, therefore, be necessary (for the reason he suggests).

Interestingly, some patients maintain that they do not misinterpret their bodily sensations catastrophically and some are more difficult to convince that these sensations will not lead to death (McNally, 1990). These findings point to a degree of variation in panic disorder patients. The anxiety sensitivity hypothesis (Reiss and McNally, 1985), for example, suggests that some individuals are more anxiety-sensitive than others. The degree of sensitivity depends on pre-existing beliefs about the harmfulness of bodily sensations. These pre-existing beliefs predispose the individual to interpret bodily events negatively and erroneously. This leads to panic.

Treatment

Treatment for panic disorder can be both cognitive behavioural or pharmacological. CBT, for example, is effective at reducing panic attacks. Such therapy would involve breathing and relaxation techniques, **cognitive restructuring** (altering misconceptions about the consequences of bodily sensations) and eliciting bodily sensations in the individual to demonstrate the non-harmful nature of such changes (Craske *et al.*, 1997). Antidepressants and anxiolytics are sometimes used to treat panic attacks with some success. Some individuals react badly to the drugs, however, and while they treat the anxiety generated during panic, they do not address the core problem of catastrophic misinterpretation.

Social anxiety disorder

Social anxiety disorder (SAD) is the second most common anxiety disorder (Wittchen *et al.*, 2014) and describes an illness in which people have extreme fear of social situations and interacting with others, especially people who are unfamiliar. Often, they fear that they will be scrutinised by others and, consequently, might be criticised.

The aetiology of SAD is multifarious – various studies have suggested genetic and biological influences, parenting, peer relationships and adverse life events (Spence and Rapee, 2016). The difficulty in deterring which, if any, is more important has been hampered by the lack of longitudinal studies. Studies of SAD ask participants to engage in various tasks such as recognising emotion in faces, experiencing social transgressions or criticism, engage in self-referential thoughts, exposing them to scrutiny and examining their anticipation of public speaking.

Studies of brain activation in SAD have found a network of regions that are active under various conditions in three individuals. For example, a meta-analysis of brain activation during the recognition of emotion in people's facial expressions found that SAD patients showed activation in these areas, compared to a neutral task: bilateral amygdala, left medial temporal lobe, the right anterior cingulate, right globus pallidus and right post central gyrus (Hattingh *et al.*, 2013). These, and the right insula, anterior cingulate cortex, left dfPFC and medial PFC and the occipito-temporal area bilaterally, are consistently activated in SAD but not in control groups (Bruhl *et al.*, 2014). No region is more active in controls than in SAD. See Figure 18.5.

Treatment can be offered either in the form of medication or cognitive behavioural therapy. People with SAD who receive these show less activation in the occipital and temporal cortex; antidepressants have been associated with decreased activation in the amygdala in three studies (Bruhl *et al.*, 2014).

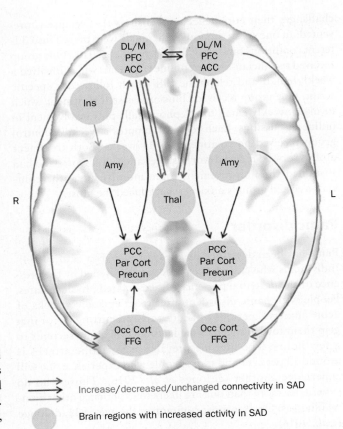

Figure 18.5 Proposed neurobiological model of SAD. The red marked connections are increased in SAD, the blue connections decreased. *Abbreviations*: DL/MPFC, Dorsolateral/Medial Prefrontal cortex; ACC, anterior cingulate cortex; Ins, insula; Amy, amygdala; Thal, thalamus; PCC, posterior cingulate cortex; Par, cort parietal cortex; Precun, precuneus; Occ, cort occipital cortex; FFG, fusiform gyrus; R, right; L, left.

The amygdala is particularly interesting in the context of anxiety because the volume of the structure has been associated with increased trait anxiety (Baur *et al.*, 2012) and blood flow is greater here in post pubertal women who are high in trait anxiety (Kaczkurkin *et al.*, 2016).

Specific phobia

Phobias – named after the Greek god Phobos, who frightened his enemies – are irrational fears of specific objects or situations. Because phobias can be highly specific, clinicians have coined a variety of inventive names, some of which are summarised in Table 18.4.

Most individuals have one or more irrational fears of specific objects or situations, and it is difficult to draw a line between these fears and phobic disorders. If someone is afraid of spiders but manages to lead a normal life by avoiding them, it would seem inappropriate to say that the person has a

Table 18.4 Drugs commonly used to treat mental disorders

Therapeutic function	Class of drugs	Generic name	Trade name
Antipsychotic	Soporific	Chlorpromazine	Thorazine
	Non-soporific	Acetophenazine	Tindal
	Phenothiazines	Thioridazine	Mellaril
		Fluphenazine	Permitil
		Trifluoperazine	Stelazine
		Perphenazine	Trilafon
	Butyrophenones	Haloperidol	Haldol
Antidepressant	Tricyclics	Imipramine	Tofranil
	Monoamine oxidase inhibitors	Amitryptiline	Elavil
		Phenelzine	Nardil
	Serotonin reuptake inhibitors	Fluoxetine	Prozac
			Miltown
Anti-anxiety	Propanediols	Meprobamate	
	Benzodiazepines	Chlordiazepoxide	Librium
		Diazepam	Valium
Antimanic	Lithium salts	Lithium carbonate	Eskalith

mental disorder. Similarly, many otherwise normal people are afraid of speaking in public. The term 'phobic disorder' should be reserved for people whose fear makes their life difficult.

Agoraphobia (*agora* means 'marketplace' in Ancient Greek) is a fear of open spaces and is the most serious and common of the phobic disorders. It occurs in between 50 and 80 per cent of phobic disorders (Matthews *et al.*, 1981). It is reported three times as often in women as in men. Onset is sudden and individuals are usually in their early twenties (Clarke, 1992). The term was coined by Westphal in 1871 to describe four (male) cases who feared open spaces.

Agoraphobia can be severely disabling. Some people with this disorder have stayed inside their house for years, afraid to venture outside. Supermarkets and queuing are especially anxiety-provoking for agoraphobics. Features of supermarket layout such as stairways and diminished access, for example, are regarded as anxiety-provoking by agoraphobic individuals (Jones *et al.*, 1996).

Specific phobias include fear of spiders, blood, snakes, darkness or heights. These phobias are often caused by a specific traumatic experience and are the easiest of all types of phobia to treat. The Epidemiological Catchment Area (ECA) Study found that insects, mice, snakes and bats were the more frequently cited feared/disgust-provoking stimuli (Robins and Regier, 1994).

The lifetime prevalence rate for simple phobia is estimated to be about 14 per cent for women and about 8 per cent for men (Robins and Regier, 1991), but approximately one-third

of the population sometimes exhibit phobic symptoms (Goodwin and Guze, 1984).

Aetiology

Animal phobias are sometimes surprising because in Europe, for example, there are no indigenous lethally poisonous spiders, although spider phobias are common. One explanation for this anomaly is that we fear animals that have potentially lethal consequences; we are, therefore, predisposed to fear them. This is the preparedness hypothesis (Seligman, 1971) which we encountered in the section on panic disorder. Evidence for this hypothesis comes in the form of the deliberate conditioning of fear of spiders. These conditioning experiences are the most difficult to extinguish – more difficult than non-threatening stimuli (Ohman *et al.*, 1985; McNally, 1987).

However, Seligman's theory has its problems. For example, if we are adaptively predisposed to fear the stimuli producing simple phobias, what adaptive purpose does a fear of snails, moths and slugs serve? As McNally (1995) points out, we can ascribe adaptive significance to a fear of any object if we are creative enough. One theory suggests that phobias develop from a pairing of a phobic object with an aversive stimulus so that phobic stimuli become phobic by association. However, only 40–50 per cent of animal phobias appear to be accounted for in this way. Davey (1992) also reported that only eight out of 118 spider phobics recall having a traumatic experience with spiders.

Matchett and Davey (1991) suggest an alternative explanation: that some stimuli become the object of phobia because of our inherent fear of contamination or disease. Animals (such as spiders, slugs, cockroaches) become feared because they seem disgusting and we would reject them as food on the basis of this disgust (although some individuals would be immune to such disgust responses; snails are considered a delicacy in certain parts of Europe). In fact, sensitivity to disgust may be an important determinant of the level of fear (Webb and Davey, 1993). To investigate whether some animal phobias were disgust – or fear-related, Davey *et al.* (1998) conducted a cross-cultural study of phobia in seven countries. An analysis of the data suggested that phobic stimuli could be divided into one of three categories: fear-irrelevant (for example, chicken, hamster, cow), fear-relevant (for example, lion, bear, alligator) and disgust-relevant (for example, cockroach, spider, maggot, worm). Disgust was consistent across cultures (although there were some cross-cultural differences with Indian respondents reporting lower levels of fear to the disgust stimuli and Japanese respondents showing higher levels of fear). This finding suggests that not all stimuli may be feared for the same reasons (perhaps the term 'simple phobia' is too simplistic, as Curtis *et al.* (1998) suggest).

How specific is specific phobia?

Some innovative work in neuroimaging has found that as an object a person fears comes closer to them, activity is increased in an area of the brain called the bed of the nucleus stria terminalis. When a person holds a feared object, such as a snake, however, and moves it closer to their own person, activation is found in the ventromedial prefrontal cortex (VPC) (Nili *et al.*, 2010; Somerville *et al.*, 2010). The studies suggest that our brain has a network of regions and structures that allows us to appraise threat-related objects, determine our reaction to them and to overcome our fear of them. The volume of the amygdala on the left has been found to be greater in people who were afraid of spiders and this structural characteristic also correlated with disgust sensitivity, trait and anxiety and the duration of the illness (Fisher *et al.*, 2013).

Fearful objects look bigger than they are – we overestimate their size (Vasey *et al.*, 2012). The actual size of a spider correlates with the degree of fear arachnophobics' experience. We also think that heights are taller if we make estimates from the top of a building, than the bottom, but this could be that we have more information on which to make a judgement in the top condition (Proffitt *et al.*, 1995). If people are afraid of spiders, they also estimate its distance to them to be shorter than it actually is (Col *et al.*, 2013). Mobbs *et al.* (2010) have shown, using fMRI, that when a tarantula is placed closer to a person's foot (seen via a live video feed), a series of brain regions become activated as feelings of threat increase. These include the periaqueductal grey, the amygdala and the stria terminalis. The amygdala and terminalis activation increased as the spider moved closer to the participant. As the spider moved away, activation became more pronounced in the orbitofrontal cortex (OFC). See Figure 18.6.

But are such regions activated to every phobia? Or do some phobias have features not shared by others? Animal phobias, for example, are known to activate the amygdala, insula and anterior cingulate cortex (ACC) (Shin and Liberzon, 2010).

Lueken *et al.* (2011) used fMRI and galvanic skin response (GSR) to compare two groups of phobics: those with ophiadanophobia (snake; animal) and those with dental phobia (blood–injection–injury) as participants watched a fear-inducing video of their feared stimulus/situation. The fear of snakes was associated with increased activation in the amygdala, insula, thalamus and in GSR. Individuals with dental phobia showed activation in the PFC and OFC and less GSR. These data suggest that these two phobias differ, with different underlying neural characteristics.

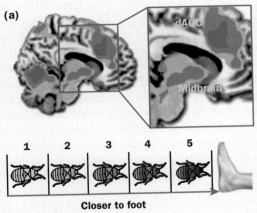 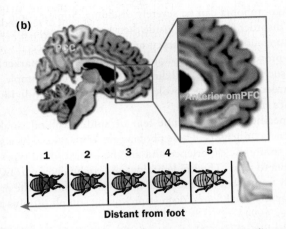

Figure 18.6 How the brain responds when it sees an approaching object it fears (a) and when it seems a feared object from a distance (b). ACC = anterior cingulate cortex, dACC = dorsal anterior cingulate cortex, PCC = posterior cingulate cortex, omPFC = orbitomedial prefrontal cortex.

One review has also suggested that some specific phobias – such as fear of blood – can co-occur with other fears and are associated with anxiety and problems in personality later in life (Miloyan and Eaton, 2016).

Treatment

Phobias are sometimes treated by systematic desensitisation (described in the general section on treatment) or modelling. Bandura (1971), for example, has described a modelling session with people who had a phobic fear of snakes. The therapist himself performed the fearless behaviour at each step and gradually led participants into touching, stroking and then holding the snake's body with gloved and bare hands while the experimenter held the snake securely by head and tail. If a participant was unable to touch the snake following ample demonstration, they were asked to place their hand on the experimenter's and to move their own hand down gradually until it touched the snake's body. After participants no longer felt any apprehension about touching the snake under these secure conditions, anxieties about contact with the snake's head area and entwining tail were extinguished. The therapist again performed the tasks fearlessly, and then he and the participant performed the responses jointly. As participants became less fearful, the experimenter gradually reduced his participation and control over the snake, until eventually participants were able to hold the snake in their lap without assistance, to let the snake loose in the room and retrieve it, and to let it crawl freely over their body. Progress through the graded approach tasks was paced according to the participants' apprehensiveness. When they reported being able to perform

one activity with little or no fear, they were eased into a more difficult interaction. This treatment eliminated fear of snakes in 92 per cent of those who participated.

Modelling is successful for several reasons. Participants learn to make new responses by imitating those of the therapist and their behaviour in doing so is reinforced. When they observe a confident person approaching and touching a feared object without showing any signs of emotional distress, they probably experience a vicarious extinction of their own emotional responses. In fact, Bandura (1971, p. 684) reports that 'having successfully overcome a phobia that had plagued them for most of their lives, subjects reported increased confidence that they could cope effectively with other fear-provoking events', including encounters with other people.

CBT has also been applied to agoraphobia (Ost *et al.*, 1993). In an experiment in which the effect of exposure (graded exposure to the phobic stimuli) was compared with exposure and CBT (combating negative thoughts and dysfunctional attitudes), Burke *et al.* (1997) found no difference in the effectiveness of the two therapies at six months following the therapy: both were equally effective. Similar combinations have also been found to be effective for social phobia (Scholing and Emmelkamp, 1996).

A recently developed treatment has taken the idea of exposure but added a technological element: virtual reality (VR) technology. This has many practical benefits. and has been applied to a number of anxiety disorders, successfully, including social anxiety disorder (Bouchard *et al.*, 2016). The fear of flying, for example, would be more efficiently treated using simulated or virtual stimuli rather than taking sufferers to airports. This approach is evaluated in the Psychology in Action section.

Psychology in action: Virtual planes can relieve real fear of flying

The fear may be more common than people imagine. According to one German study, 15 per cent of respondents reported having a fear of flying and around 60 per cent of those try to cope with this fear by drinking alcohol or taking tranquillisers (Wilhelm and Roth, 1997).

In many cases, treatment may take the form of CBT which exposes the patient to the fear-eliciting stressor with the aim of attenuating the fear that such stressors cause. For example, a patient may be exposed to real aeroplanes or may be walked around a stationary plane. Recently, however, psychologists have harnessed new technology to help people combat their fear of flying: virtual reality or VR (Klein, 1998). VR technology allows researchers to simulate events, locations or stimuli effectively using computer software. Consequently, it is a very convenient and inexpensive approach to treatment.

Rothbaum *et al.* (2000) randomly assigned 49 patients who expressed a fear of flying to one of three conditions: VR

training, standard exposure therapy or no therapy where patients were on a waiting list for treatment.

The VR training involved exposing the participant to a virtual aircraft (sitting in it while it took off and landed); standard exposure involved direct exposure to an airport and a stationary plane. Both experimental conditions were preceded by four sessions of anxiety management. Patients received treatment over eight weeks and a post-treatment flight was set up after this period to examine the efficacy of the VR treatment, as measured by willingness to fly and self-reported anxiety about the first flight.

Both VR and standard exposure treatments were better than the control condition in reducing fear of flying. The beneficial effects of exposure were still seen at a six-month follow-up. Ninety-three per cent of VR patients and 93 per cent of standard exposure patients had flown after treatment. The results show that VR may be an inexpensive and more

Psychology in action: *continued*

convenient way of reducing the fear of flying than is actual exposure to real aeroplanes. If given the choice, patients indicated that they would opt for the VR treatment rather than real exposure.

Exposure to VR also appears to be more effective at reducing flight anxiety than is relaxation therapy, a common psychological intervention that some flyers adopt. Muhlberger *et al.* (2001) found that while exposure to VR flights increased feelings of fear, these feelings gradually attenuated and to a greater extent than they did in people undergoing relaxation training. Both approaches reduced flight anxiety, but VR was better, as Figure 18.7 shows.

Virtual reality technology of this kind has now been used to treat arachnophobia (Carlin *et al.*, 1997) and claustrophobia (Botella *et al.*, 1998). As with all treatments, its success is measured by its long-term effects. A recent 12–month follow-up study suggests that VR flight exposure has lasting effects on anxiety relief. Rothbaum's team followed up 24 patients who were either exposed to actual planes and an airport or to VR flying. As you saw in the section at the beginning, both interventions were successful at the first testing point. The follow-up study showed that the initial improvements were maintained. The results suggest that a very

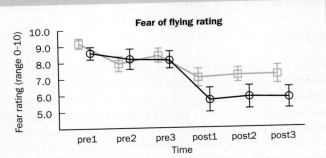

Figure 18.7 Fear of flying scores for people in the VR exposure group (black line) and the relaxation group (orange line).

Source: Muhlberger, A., Herrmann, M.J., Wiedemann, G., Ellgring, H. and Pauli, P., Repeated exposure of flight phobics to flights in virtual reality. Behaviour Research and Therapy, 2001, 39, 1033–50. Copyright 2000, with permission from Elsevier.

short-term treatment that imposes fewer practical demands than real exposure to planes and airports can have sustainable benefits. However, Page and Coxon (2016) note that a large number of these VR studies recruit very small samples and frequently do not employ an adequate control group, both of which are good points.

Post-traumatic stress disorder (PTSD)

Description

Post-traumatic stress disorder (PTSD) made its first appearance in DSM-III in 1980 and refers to anxiety that follows a traumatic event. This event poses a threat to the individual's life or the lives of others. Symptoms of the disorder include the re-experiencing of feelings related to the event (such as intrusive memories, thoughts and images related to the event), avoidant behaviour (such as denial and emotional numbing) and arousal (such as hypervigilance for trauma-related information).

A review of symptoms suggests that they can be grouped into four types: intrusions, avoidance, dysphoria and hyperarousal (Yufik and Simmons, 2010). Sadness, guilt and anger are also associated with the disorder (Shore *et al.*, 1989). People with PTSD seem to express emotional facilitation of cognition – trauma-related information is processed faster and more accurately than information unrelated to the trauma. They also show emotional interference – the impairment of processing of some trauma-related information (Brown and Marey, 2012). These latter symptoms are important because PTSD seldom appears alone but with other disorders or additional diagnoses (McFarlane, 1992; Bleich *et al.*, 1997). PTSD

is a controversial disorder because its validity has been challenged. Some researchers point to the ease with which PTSD symptoms can be faked (Burges and McMillan, 2001).

The prevalence rate is around 25–30 per cent in the general population, and rape is associated with the greatest prevalence (Green, 1994). A recent review of 35 studies in which PTSD following a terrorist incident was recorded, found that the prevalence of PTSD was between 33-39 per cent in direct victims (the primary targets of the attack), 5–6 per cent in emergency/rescue services and 17–29 per cent in relatives and friends of the person injured or killed by the attacks (Garcia-Vera *et al.*, 2016). Other events which can produce PTSD are road traffic accidents (Stallard *et al.*, 1998; Murray *et al.*, 2002), bank robberies (Kamphuis and Emmelkamp, 1998), war (Fontana and Rosenheck, 1993) and natural or human-made disasters (Freedy *et al.*, 1994). Onset of the disorder may be delayed by many years (Blank, 1993). As with GAD and panic disorder, there is a greater Stroop interference for words related to the trauma (Thrasher *et al.*, 1994).

The emergency services, especially its members who respond to disasters, may be more prone to developing the disorder because of the type of work they engage in. In the UK, ambulance drivers answer more calls than do the police and fire service combined. It might be expected, therefore, that the incidence of PTSD is high (between 10 and 20 per cent).

Clohessy and Ehlers (1999) found that 21 per cent of the 56 ambulance drivers in the UK they studied met DSM-IV TR criteria for PTSD. Predictors of the severity of the post-traumatic stress were poor coping strategy, efforts to suppress intrusive thoughts and dwelling on previous distressing events.

In a study of 96 victims of physical or sexual assault, Dunmore et al. (1999) found that some factors were common to both onset and maintenance whereas others were specific to onset. Factors associated with both were appraising the event and the consequences of the event (dwelling on the assault and its aftermath) and adopting poor coping strategies (such as avoidance). Factors which were related to onset were feeling detached during the assault and being unable to perceive positive responses from others. The researchers suggest that these cognitive factors may contribute to PTSD in a number of ways. They may prevent recovery by encouraging poor coping strategy or by generating a sense of immediate threat.

Aetiology

Horowitz's (1979, 1986) model suggests that information about the trauma in PTSD is processed because of a mechanism called completion tendency. Completion tendency refers to the need for new information to be integrated into existing patterns of thought and memory. Power and Dalgleish (1997) describe how there is first a stunned reaction to the traumatic event and then a feeling of information overload as the individual realises the enormity of the trauma. Such information cannot be accommodated by existing mental schemata, and defence mechanisms, such as denial and numbing, provide a means of coping with this lack of accommodation. Completion tendency, however, insists on keeping the memory of the event alive (Horowitz calls this 'active memory') through flashbacks and nightmares. The anxiety results from the vacillation between these two processes: defence mechanisms and completion tendency. Although an honourable attempt at explaining PTSD, Power and Dalgleish (1997) query whether the model explains some features of the disorder. Why do only some individuals develop PTSD, for example? And why is PTSD delayed in some individuals?

It has been suggested that those individuals exposed to trauma who go on to develop PTSD have a pre-existing disposition to respond over-sensitively to trauma. Alternatively, they develop over-sensitivity as a consequence of the trauma. The hippocampus, amygdala and anterior cingulate cortex, for example, have been found to be smaller in PTSD (Morey et al., 2012). The amygdala is especially sensitive to emotional stimuli in PTSD. One model suggests that during trauma reinstatement, activation is found in the dorsal anterior cingulate and ventral PFC when people are cognitively processing information, and in the amygdala and insula when they are responding to the emotional content of the stimulus (Brown and Morey, 2012). However, the type of activation may be content-specific.

The insula might be hyperactive when it assigns value to a particular threat and this threat contains emotional information but is hypoactive when it responds to trauma-related information.

Treatment

Various forms of treatment have been attempted with PTSD with varying success (Shalev et al., 1996; Foa and Meadows, 1997). Debriefing appears to be ineffective (Deahl et al., 1994) but drug treatment meets with mixed success (O'Brien and Nutt, 1998). Treatment based on exposure seems to be effective (Foa and Meadows, 1997).

A more unusual treatment has been based on the electronic game Tetris. In Tetris, seven differently coloured and shaped blocks descend from the top of the screen to the bottom and the aim is the build a wall of shapes horizontally. To do this, the player can move the blocks to the left or the right. If the blocks build up to the top without the wall being completed, the game is lost. Research has found that when people play this visuospatial game during or after the experience of trauma, the number of traumatic intrusions later in an experiment is lower than if participants had not played the game or had completed a word game (e.g. Green and Bavelier, 2003; Deeprose et al., 2012; James et al., 2015). The explanation for this is that the game taxes working memory to such an extent that the rehearsal of trauma-related material cannot take place or cannot be consolidated because resources have been shifted elsewhere.

Obsessive-compulsive disorder (OCD)

Description

Individuals with **obsessive-compulsive disorder** (OCD) suffer from obsessions – thoughts that will not leave them – and **compulsions** – behaviours that they cannot keep from performing. In one study, impaired control of mental activities, checking, urges involving loss of motor control and feeling contaminated were found to be the major classes of obsession and compulsion among a large sample of American college students (Sternberger and Burns, 1990). The lifetime prevalence rate is estimated to be about 2.5 per cent (Robins and Regier, 1991; Bebbington, 1998).

Unlike people with panic disorder, people with OCD have a defence against anxiety – their compulsive behaviour. Unfortunately, the need to perform this compulsive behaviour often becomes more and more demanding of their time until it interferes with their daily life. Obsessions are seen in many mental disorders, including schizophrenia. However, unlike persons with schizophrenia, people with OCD recognise that their thoughts and behaviours are senseless and wish that they would go away. The types of obsession and compulsion seen in these individuals are summarised in Table 18.5.

Table 18.5 The number and percentage of obsessive and compulsive symptoms reported by 70 children and adolescents diagnosed with obsessive-compulsive disorder

	Reported symptom at initial interview	
Obsessions	**Number**	**%**
Concern with dirt, germs or environmental toxins	28	40
Something terrible happening (fire, death or illness of self or loved one)	17	24
Symmetry, order or exactness	12	17
Scrupulosity (religious obsessions)	9	13
Concern or disgust with bodily wastes or secretions (urine, stools, saliva)	6	8
Lucky or unlucky numbers	6	8
Forbidden, aggressive or perverse sexual thoughts, images or impulses	3	4
Fear might harm others or oneself	3	4
Concern with household items	2	3
Intrusive nonsense sounds, words or music	1	1
Compulsions	**Number**	**%**
Excessive or ritualised handwashing, showering, bathing, toothbrushing or grooming	60	85
Repeating rituals (going in or out of a door, up or down from a chair)	36	51
Checking (doors, locks, cooker, appliances, emergency brake on car, homework)	32	46
Rituals to remove contact with contaminants	16	23
Touching	14	20
Measures to prevent harm to self or others	11	16
Ordering or arranging	12	17
Counting	13	18
Hoarding or collecting rituals	8	11
Rituals of cleaning household or inanimate objects	4	6
Miscellaneous rituals (such as writing, moving, speaking)	18	26

Source: Rapoport, J.L., The biology of obsessions and compulsions, *Scientific American* (international edition), 1989 (March), p. 63. Copyright © 1989 by Scientific American, Inc. All rights reserved.

Consider the case of Sergei, a 17-year-old ex-student:

> Only a year ago, Sergei seemed to be a normal adolescent with many talents and interests. Then, almost overnight he was transformed into a lonely outsider, excluded from social life by his psychological disabilities. Specifically, he was unable to stop washing. Haunted by the notion that he was dirty – in spite of the contrary evidence of the senses – he began to spend more and more of his time cleansing himself of imaginary dirt. At first his ritual ablutions were confined to weekends and evenings and he was able to stay in school while keeping them up, but soon they began to consume all his time, forcing him to drop out of school, a victim of his inability to feel clean enough. (Source: Rapoport, 1989, p. 63.)

There are two principal kinds of obsession: obsessive doubt or uncertainty, and obsessive fear of doing something prohibited (Salkovskis *et al.*, 1998). Uncertainties, both trivial and important, preoccupy some people with OCD almost completely. Others are plagued with the fear that they will do something terrible – swear aloud in church, urinate in someone's living room, kill themselves or a loved one, or jump off a bridge – although they seldom actually do anything antisocial. And even though they are often obsessed with thoughts of killing themselves, fewer than 1 per cent of them actually attempt suicide.

Most compulsions fall into one of four categories: counting, checking, cleaning and avoidance. For example, people might repeatedly check burners on the stove to see that they are off and windows and doors to be sure that they are locked. Some people wash their hands hundreds of times a day, even when they become covered with painful sores. Other people meticulously clean their homes or endlessly wash, dry and fold their clothes. Some become afraid to leave home because they fear contamination and refuse to touch other members of their families. If they do accidentally become 'contaminated', they usually have lengthy purification rituals.

Aetiology

Several possible causes have been suggested for OCD. Unlike simple anxiety states, this disorder can be understood in terms of defence mechanisms. Some cognitive investigators have suggested that obsessions serve as devices to occupy the mind and displace painful thoughts.

Cognitive researchers also point out that persons with OCD believe that they should be competent at all times, avoid any kind of criticism at all costs, and worry about being punished by others for behaviour that is less than perfect (Sarason and Sarason, 1993). Thus, one reason people who have OCD may engage in checking behaviour is to reduce the anxiety caused by fear of being perceived by others as incompetent or to avoid others' criticism that they have done something less than perfectly.

Family studies have found that OCD is associated with a neurological disorder called **Gilles de la Tourette's syndrome**, which appears during childhood (Janowic, 1993). Gilles de la Tourette's syndrome is characterised by muscular and vocal tics, including making facial grimaces, squatting, pacing, twirling, barking, sniffing, coughing, grunting or repeating specific words (especially vulgarities). It is not clear why some people with the faulty gene develop Gilles de la Tourette's syndrome early in childhood and others develop OCD later in life.

OCD appears to show different patterns of activation than other anxiety disorders. It has been associated with dysfunctional activation in the nucleus accumbens and with abnormal connectivity to the frontal lobe (Figee *et al.*, 2011).

Treatment

There are usually two forms of treatment employed in OCD. The first is behavioural therapy in which the individual may be exposed to the object, situation or event that provokes the ritualistic behaviour (Emmelkamp, 1993). One example may be to deliberately dirty the hands of an individual who ritualistically washes their hands 20 or 30 times a day and not allow them to wash their hands (Rapoport, 1989). This type of therapy has met with some success in serious cases of OCD. However, behavioural treatment appears to be more successful at eliminating compulsive than obsessive behaviour (Emmelkamp, 1993). Drug treatment appears to eliminate both successfully. These drugs are two serotonin-specific reuptake inhibitors (described in more detail in the section on depression below) and act by increasing the amount of the neurotransmitter, serotonin, in the brain.

A more radical form of intervention is Deep Brain Stimulation, which you read about in Chapter 4 when we discussed Parkinson's Disease. One study has suggested that DBS can reduce the symptoms of OCD by decreasing the excessive connectivity between the frontal lobe and the striatum (Figee *et al.*, 2013).

Dissociative disorders

In **dissociative disorders**, anxiety is reduced by a sudden disruption in consciousness, which in turn produces changes in one's sense of identity. The term comes from Freud: according to psychoanalytical theory, a person develops a dissociative disorder when a massive repression fails to keep a strong sexual desire from consciousness. As a result, the person resorts to dissociating one part of their mind from the rest.

The most common dissociative disorder is **psychogenic amnesia**, in which a person 'forgets' all their past life, along with the conflicts that were present, and begins a new one. The term 'psychogenic' means 'produced by the mind'. Because amnesia can also be produced by physical means – such as epilepsy, drug or alcohol intoxication, and brain damage – clinicians must be careful to distinguish between amnesias of organic and psychogenic origin.

A **psychogenic fugue** is a special form of amnesia in which a person deliberately leaves home and starts a new life elsewhere (fugue means 'flight'). You read about this in the memory at the movies section in Chapter 8.

Dissociative identity disorder is a very rare, but very striking, dissociative disorder that is marked by the presence of two or more separate personalities within the individual, either of which may be dominant at any given time. Only about 100 cases of dissociative identity disorder have been documented, and some investigators believe that many, if not most of them, are simulations, not actual mental disorders.

An interesting example of dissociative identity disorder is the case of Billy Milligan as told in the book *The Minds of Billy Milligan* (Keyes, 1981). Milligan was accused of rape and kidnapping but was deemed not guilty by reason of insanity. His psychiatric examination showed him to have 24 different personalities. Two were women and one was a young girl. There was a Briton, an Australian and a Yugoslav. One woman, a lesbian, was a poet, while the Yugoslav was an expert on weapons and munitions, and the Briton and Australian were minor criminals. Dissociative identity disorder has received much attention; people find it fascinating to contemplate several different personalities, most of whom are unaware of each other, existing within the same individual. Bliss (1980) suggests that dissociative identity disorder is a form of self-hypnosis, established early in life and motivated by painful experiences. In fact, the overwhelming majority of people diagnosed as having multiple personality disorder report having been physically abused when they were a child (Kluft, 1984).

Personality disorders

The DSM-V classifies abnormalities in behaviour that impair social or occupational functioning as **personality disorders**. There are several types of personality disorder which the DSM has grouped into three clusters. Cluster A, for example, refers to the 'eccentric cluster' of schizotypal and paranoid personality disorder; Cluster B (the dramatic cluster) includes the narcissistic and antisocial personality disorders; and Cluster C (the anxious cluster) includes avoidant and dependent personality disorders. Another general cluster accounts for other personality disorders not covered by these clusters. Because there are so many personality disorders, this chapter focuses on just one in depth: antisocial personality disorder. Table 18.6 provides a description of the several other personality disorders. According to a meta-analysis of four studies, pathological personality is associated with extreme scores on The Big Five (Gotzsche-Astrup and Mosvowitz, 2016). Unlike DSM-V, the ICD-11 may introduce a severity scale for each personality disorder rather than classifying people by category alone (Gotzsche-Astrup and Mosvowitz, 2016).

Antisocial personality disorder and psychopathy

Antisocial personality disorder refers to a failure to conform to standards of decency, repeated lying and stealing, a failure to sustain long-lasting and loving relationships, low tolerance of boredom and a complete lack of guilt. The first edition of the DSM used the term 'sociopathic personality disturbance', which was subsequently replaced by the present term, 'antisocial personality disorder'. Most clinicians still refer to such people as psychopaths or sociopaths but this is probably incorrect. There is good evidence, for example, that antisocial personality disorder/sociopathy and psychopathy are different disorders; the former is characterised by antisocial behaviour, usually criminal, whereas the latter is characterised by these antisocial activities plus other, more emotive factors such as lack of empathy for others, remorselessness and manipulativeness. Edens *et al.* (2001) investigated whether the structured clinical interview for ASPD from DSM-IV could predict institutional aggression and physical or verbal violence in a group of 298 male and 55 female prison inmates from four prisons. The DSM criteria did not predict misconduct in jail.

The symptoms of psychopathy were based, originally, on Cleckley's (1976) 16 characteristics of antisocial personality disorder. Psychopathy is considered the prototype personality disorder (Crego and Widiger, 2014). Cleckley's list of features provides a good picture of what most psychopaths are like.

Table 18.6 Descriptions of various personality disorders

Personality disorder	Description
Paranoid	Suspiciousness and extreme mistrust of others; enhanced perception of being under attack by others
Schizoid	Difficulty in social functioning – poor ability and little desire to become attached to others
Schizotypal	Unusual thought patterns and perceptions; poor communication and social skills
Histrionic	Attention-seeking; preoccupation with personal attractiveness; prone to anger when attempts at attracting attention fail
Narcissistic	Self-promoting; lack of empathy for others; attention-seeking; grandiosity
Borderline	Lack of impulse control; drastic mood swings; inappropriate anger; becomes bored easily and for prolonged periods; suicidal
Avoidant	Oversensitivity to rejection; little confidence in initiating or maintaining social relationships
Dependent	Uncomfortable being alone or in terminating relationships; places others' needs above one's own in order to preserve the relationship; indecisive
Obsessive-compulsive	Preoccupation with rules and order; tendency towards perfectionism; difficulty relaxing or enjoying life
Passive-aggressive	Negative attitudes; negativity is expressed through passive means; complaining, expressing envy and resentment towards others who are more fortunate
Depressive	Pervasive depressive cognitions and self-criticism; persistent unhappiness; feelings of guilt and inadequacy

Source: Adapted from Carson, R .C., *et al.*, *Abnormal Psychology and Modern Life*, 10th edn. Published by Allyn & Bacon, Boston, MA. Copyright © 1996 by Pearson Education. By permission of the publisher.

They are unconcerned for other people's feelings and suffer no remorse or guilt if their actions hurt others. Although they may be superficially charming, they do not form real friendships; thus, they often become swindlers or confidence artists. Both male and female psychopaths are sexually promiscuous from an early age, but these encounters do not seem to mean much to them. According to Hare (1993), they are 'social predators who charm, manipulate, and ruthlessly plan their way through life. . . Completely lacking in conscience and feeling for others, they selfishly take what they want and do as they please, violating social norms and expectations without the slightest sense of guilt or regret' (p. xi).

Psychopaths habitually tell lies, even when there is no apparent reason for doing so and even when the lie is likely to be discovered. They steal things they do not need or even appear to want. When confronted with evidence of having lied or cheated, psychopaths do not act ashamed or embarrassed and usually shrug the incident off as a joke.

Psychopaths do not easily learn from experience; they tend to continue committing behaviours that get them into trouble. They also do not appear to be driven to perform their antisocial behaviours; instead, they usually give the impression that they are acting on whims. When someone commits a heinous crime such as a brutal murder, normal people expect that the criminal had a reason for doing so. However, criminal psychopaths are typically unable to supply a reason more compelling than 'I just felt like it'. They do not show much excitement or enthusiasm about what they are doing and do not appear to derive much pleasure from life. Although they are capable of understanding the difference between right and wrong, the consequences of immoral behaviour and the possession of this knowledge is unimportant to them (Cima *et al.*, 2010).

Psychopathy is diagnosed, conventionally via the Hare Psychopathy Checklist-Revised (PCL-R). This is a part interview, part – 20-item questionnaire based measure that generates a two-factor structure. Respondents are scored from 0 to 2 ('does not apply' to 'definitely applies') and a score of 30 is the cut-off point for diagnosis of psychopathy. One factor measures behavioural aspects of anti-social behaviour (called lifestyle/antisocial – violence, theft, not caring about others); the second (affective/interpersonal) measures the more emotional, affective components of the disorder such as the manipulativeness and the remorselessness. The two-factor model has been extended to four – each of the traits within each factor and you can see these listed in Table 18.7. This table also includes the traits for the Youth Version (YV) and the Short Version (SV). The original measure was developed using US participants but it has since been validated across cultures and sexes and has been found to predict violent and sexual re-offending (Boduszek and Debowska, 2016). The most consistent predictor of later crime commission is scores on the anti-social factor.

Table 18.7 PCL-R

1. Glibness/superficial charm (F1, I)
2. Grandiose sense of self worth (F1, I)
3. Need for stimulation (F2, L)
4. Pathological lying (F1, I)
5. Conning/manipulative (F1, I)
6. Lack of remorse/guilt (F1, Af)
7. Shallow affect (F1, Af)
8. Callous/Lack of empathy (F1, Af)
9. Parasitic lifestyle (F2, L)
10. Poor behavioural controls (F2, A)
11. Promiscuous sexual behaviour
12. Early behaviour problems (F2, A)
13. Lack of realistic, long-term goals (F2, L)
14. Impulsivity (F2, L)
15. Irresponsibility (F2, L)
16. Failure to accept responsibility for action (F1, Af)
17. Many short-term marital relationships
18. Juvenile delinquency
19. Revocation of conditional release (F2, A)
20. Criminal versatility (F2, A)

The items on the PCL-R which make up its Factors (two, F1 and F2) and four components (I= interpersonal; Af= Affective; L= Lifestyle; A=Antisocial). Interpersonal and affective component make up Factor 1. Psychopaths score more highly on this factor than do people with anti-social personality disorder.

When Hassall *et al.* (2015) administered the PCL-R to a group of students, business students scored higher on all four factors than did psychology students and a similar result is found in the corporate world (Babiak *et al.*, 2010). This is why one of Hare's books was called *Snakes in Suits*. When Boduszek and Debowska (2016) attempted to determine whether the factor structure of the PCL-R could be obtained across 11 studies, they reported inconsistent results.

Aetiology

Cleckley (1976, p. 371) suggested that the psychopath's defect 'consists of an unawareness and a persistent lack of ability to become aware of what the most important experiences of life mean to others . . . The major emotional accompaniments are absent or so attenuated as to count for little.' Some investigators have hypothesised that this lack of involvement is caused by an unresponsive autonomic nervous system (ANS). If a person feels no anticipatory fear of punishment, they are perhaps more likely to commit acts that normal people would be afraid to commit. Similarly, if a person feels little or no

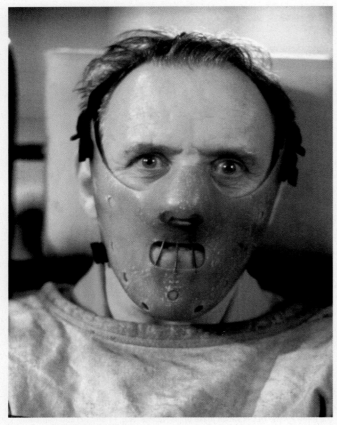

Not a typical psychopath.
Source: Orion/Kobal/REX/Shutterstock.

emotional response to other people and to their joys and sorrows, they are unlikely to establish close relationships with them.

Many experiments have found that psychopaths do show less reactivity in situations involving punishment. For example, Hare (1965) demonstrated that psychopaths show fewer signs of anticipatory fear. All participants in Hare's study watched the numerals 1 to 12 appear in sequential order in the window of a device used to present visual stimuli. They were told that they would receive a very painful shock when the numeral 8 appeared. Psychopathic subjects showed much less anticipatory responsiveness than did normal control subjects or non-psychopathic criminals.

According to Hare (1996, p. 46), 'In some respects, it is as if psychopaths lack a central organiser to plan and keep track of what they think and say'. The part of the brain that is more responsible than any other for monitoring, organising and integrating sensory input and behaviour, is the frontal cortex. People with damage to the frontal cortex have also been shown to exhibit irregularities in ANS functioning such as a lack of heart rate responsiveness and GSR in contexts that require an assessment of risk.

Over many years, Adrian Raine, James Blair and others in the UK and US have published controversial data linking frontal lobe dysfunction with psychopathic behaviour and antisocial personality disorder. In general, psychopaths tend to show less activity or less volume in this area, a region known to mediate some aspects of emotional and social behaviour (see Chapter 13). In what they describe as a study showing the 'first evidence for a structural brain deficit in antisocial personality disorder' (APD), Raine *et al.* (2000) compared the brain volume of 21 community volunteers having the DSM-IV TR ratified APD with control groups and found that prefrontal brain volume of the APD group was 11 per cent less than other groups. They also showed little autonomic response when undertaking the social stressor task – they had their behaviour videotaped as they talked about their faults.

A review of neuroimaging findings from psychopathy has highlighted the importance of four areas of the brain: the OFC, the amygdala, the anterior/posterior cingulate and nearby limbic structures (Anderson and Kiehl, 2012). A study of white matter volume in the brains of psychopaths and non-psychopaths has found a reduction in the connections between the frontal lobe and the thalamus. A meta-analysis of brain volume in psychopathy found that prefrontal cortex reductions were the most commonly reported (Santana, 2016). These areas of reduction included the OFC, the medial PFC, the inferior frontal gyrus and the anterior cingulate cortex. At the level of function, connections between the prefrontal lobe, the amygdala and the parietal lobe were reduced in the psychopaths (Motzkin *et al.*, 2011). When psychopaths had to make decisions regarding moral violations, activity in the ventromedial PFC and temporal cortex was reduced compared to a control group (Herenski *et al.*, 2010). A review (Pascual *et al.*, 2013) has summarised the brain areas involved in moral decision-making. You can see the ones that are most widely studied in Figure 18.8.

To date, neuroimaging studies have focused on 'unsuccessful' psychopaths, i.e. those who have been caught and jailed. It has been suggested that successful psychopaths – those who are not caught and jailed – are behaviourally very similar to their incarcerated counterparts but are physiologically different (Widom, 1978). Ishikawa *et al.* (2001) recruited people from temporary employment agencies and administered the Hare Psychopathy Checklist to determine the degree of psychopathy in the sample. The researchers found that, when compared with the control group, the successful psychopaths showed heightened heart rate activity and performed better than the unsuccessful psychopaths at a test of frontal lobe function. The authors suggest that this reactivity reflects the successful psychopath's greater awareness of changes in the social environment – they are better than unsuccessful psychopaths at assessing or making risky decisions; unsuccessful psychopaths show little ANS reaction to risk and it may

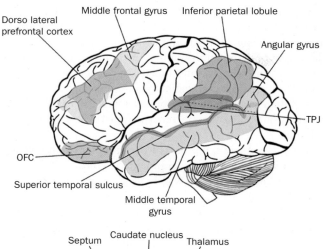

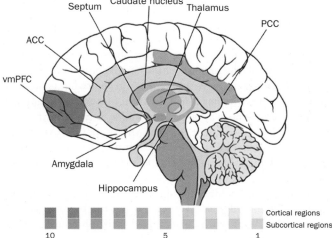

Figure 18.8 The areas of the brain involved in moral decision-making, at the cortical and subcortical level. The intensity of the colour reflects the number of studies associating these areas with morality. The greener/bluer the colour, the greater the number of studies. From Pascual et al (2013).

be this lack of feedback from the ANS that leads to their slipping up.

Treatment

There is no standard, effective treatment for APD or psychopathy and the treatments used have normally been designed for other purposes such as anger management or reducing deviant sexual behaviour (Oltmans and Emery, 1998). Whereas evidence suggests that there is some temporary effect on the behaviour, the effect does not generalise to other settings in the long term. One predictor of success, when it does happen, is a person's adherence to a treatment programme: the more successful complete the programme (Reid and Gacono, 2000).

Schizophrenic spectrum and other psychotic disorders

Schizophrenia, the most common psychosis, is not a unitary illness but a group of varied disorders each with a distinctive set of symptoms (Arnedo *et al.*, 2014).

The common symptoms are distortions of thought, perception and emotion, bizarre behaviour and social withdrawal. Around eight to 40 cases per 1,000 are reported per year worldwide and the disorder appears to recognise no cultural or international boundaries. It is higher in urban areas and there is a lifetime risk of 0.7 per cent of developing the illness (and this is greater in men). It is highest in people of lowest socio-economic status, has its onset in adolescence or early adulthood, and genetic factors account for 80 per cent of the disorder's appearance (Tandon *et al.*, 2008a). According to the WHO (2016), 21 million people worldwide suffer from the disorder. Schizophrenia is probably the most serious of the mental disorders. It tends to manifest itself in the patient's mid-twenties, although there will have been evidence of subtle clinical symptoms and decline of function prior to this – the so-called prodromal stage of the illness (Addington *et al.*, 2007). It is highly heritable – if a close relative has the illness, this increases the likelihood of developing the disorder (Rees *et al.*, 2015).

The word 'schizophrenia' literally means 'split mind', although it is commonly misinterpreted as 'split personality'. The individual does not suffer from split personality or multiple personality (those are other mental disorders) but from disordered thought and affect. The man who invented the term, Eugen Bleuler (in 1911), intended it to refer to a break with reality caused by such disorganisation of the various functions of the mind that thoughts and feelings no longer worked together normally.

Many studies of people who become schizophrenic in adulthood have found that they were different from others even in childhood. One study obtained home movies of people with adult-onset schizophrenia that showed them and their siblings when they were children (Walker and Lewine, 1990). Although the schizophrenia did not manifest itself until adulthood, viewers of the films (six graduate students and one professional clinical psychologist) did an excellent job of identifying the children who were to become schizophrenic. The viewers commented on the children's poor eye contact, relative lack of responsiveness and positive affect, and generally poor motor coordination.

The prognosis for schizophrenia is described by the 'law of thirds'. Approximately one-third of the people who are diagnosed as having it will require institutionalisation for the rest of their lives. About one-third show remission of symptoms and may be said to be cured of the disorder. The final third are occasionally symptom-free (sometimes for many years) only to have the symptoms return, requiring more treatment and perhaps even institutionalisation. It has the worst prognosis of the psychiatric illnesses apart from dementia (Jobe and Harrow, 2010). After about five years, however, the illness stabilises and does not worsen.

Schizophrenia is characterised by two categories of symptoms: positive and negative. **Positive symptoms** include thought disorders, hallucinations and delusions. A **thought disorder** – a pattern of disorganised, irrational thinking – is probably the most pronounced symptom of schizophrenia. People with schizophrenia have great difficulty arranging their thoughts logically and sorting out plausible conclusions from absurd ones. In conversation, they jump from one topic to another as new associations come up. Sometimes, they utter meaningless words or choose words for their rhyme rather than for their meaning. **Delusions** are beliefs that are obviously contrary to fact. **Delusions of persecution** are false beliefs that others are plotting and conspiring against oneself. **Delusions of grandeur** are false beliefs in one's power and importance, such as a conviction that one has god-like powers or has special knowledge that no one else possesses. **Delusions of control** are related to delusions of persecution; the person believes, for example, that they are being controlled by others through such means as radar or tiny radio receivers implanted in their brain.

The third positive symptom of schizophrenia is **hallucinations**, which are perceptions of stimuli that are not actually present. The most common schizophrenic hallucinations are auditory, but such hallucinations can also involve any of the other senses. The typical schizophrenic hallucination consists of voices talking to the person. Sometimes, they order the person to act; sometimes, they scold the person for their unworthiness; sometimes, they just utter meaningless phrases. Sometimes, those with schizophrenia may also hear a voice that keeps a running commentary on their behaviour, or they hear two or more voices.

In contrast to the positive symptoms, the **negative symptoms** of schizophrenia are known by the absence of normal behaviours: flattened emotional response, poverty of speech, lack of initiative and persistence, inability to experience pleasure, and social withdrawal.

Types of schizophrenia

The DSM identifies four types of schizophrenia: undifferentiated, catatonic, paranoid and disorganised. Most cases of schizophrenia, however, do not fit exactly into one of these categories. Many individuals are diagnosed with **undifferentiated schizophrenia**, that is, the patients have delusions, hallucinations and disorganised behaviour but do not meet the criteria for catatonic, paranoid or disorganised schizophrenia. In addition, some patients' symptoms change after an initial diagnosis, and their classification changes accordingly.

Catatonic schizophrenia (from the Greek *katateinein*, meaning 'to stretch or draw tight') is characterised by various motor disturbances, including catatonic postures – bizarre, stationary poses maintained for many hours – and waxy flexibility, in which the person's limbs can be moulded into new positions, which are then maintained. Catatonic schizophrenics are often aware of all that goes on about them and will talk about what happened after the episode of catatonia subsides.

The pre-eminent symptoms of **paranoid schizophrenia** are delusions of persecution, grandeur or control. The word 'paranoid' has become so widely used in ordinary language that it has come to mean 'suspicious'. However, not all paranoid schizophrenics believe that they are being persecuted. Some believe that they hold special powers that can save the world or that they are Christ, or Napoleon or the president of the USA.

Individuals with paranoid schizophrenia are among the most intelligent of psychotic patients, so, not surprisingly, they often build up delusional structures incorporating a wealth of detail. Even the most trivial event is interpreted in terms of a grand scheme, whether it is a delusion of persecution or one of grandeur. The way a person walks, a particular facial expression or movement, or even the shapes of clouds can acquire special significance. An example of a case study of paranoid schizophrenia appears in the Psychology in Action section.

Disorganised schizophrenia is a serious progressive and irreversible disorder characterised primarily by disturbances of thought. People with disorganised schizophrenia often display signs of emotion, especially silly laughter, that are inappropriate to the circumstances. Also, their speech tends to be a jumble of words: 'I came to the hospital to play, gay, way, lay, day, bray, donkey, monkey' (Snyder, 1974, p. 132). This sort of speech is often referred to as a word salad.

Aetiology

Research into the causes of all kinds and forms of schizophrenia throughout this century and the last reflects the challenge that psychologists face in attempting to understand how psychological and biological factors interact to influence behaviour. Schizophrenia appears to result from one or more inherited, biological predispositions that are activated by environmental stress.

Genetic causes

The heritability of schizophrenia, or more precisely the heritability of a tendency towards schizophrenia, has now been firmly established by both twin studies and adoption studies. Identical (monozygotic, MZ) twins are much more likely to be concordant for schizophrenia than are fraternal (dizygotic, DZ) twins, and the children of parents with schizophrenia are

Psychology in action: Treating paranoid schizophrenia

Bill McClary, a 25-year-old unemployed man, did not go to the therapist willingly. His sister Coleen, with whom he had been living for 18 months, suggested that Bill receive professional help for behaviour that had become increasingly unusual. He would spend most of his time in social isolation, daydreaming, talking to himself and saying things that did not make sense. Although most people engage in such behaviour at some time, Bill's was constant and this is what worried his sister.

On seeking professional help, Bill appeared quiet and hesitant. During therapy, he was friendly but shy and ill-at-ease. It was only later that his therapist learned of even stranger and unusual behaviour reported by Bill's brother Roger.

It transpired that Bill had had occasional but not long-lasting heterosexual and homosexual relationships. After moving in with his sister, he became convinced that people were talking about him, especially about his sexuality. He came to believe that a group of conspirators had implanted microphones and cameras in the house to spy on his sexual encounters with men. These recordings were released as a film which Bill believed had grossed $50 million at the box office; this money was used to fund the activity of the Irish Republican Army in Northern Ireland and he would often feel deeply guilty and responsible for the deaths there because his money was used to buy arms and ammunition.

Bill also heard voices discussing his sexual behaviour in unpleasant terms. Often, these discussions would involve an element of punishment, such as 'He's a faggot; we've got to kill him'. The successfully released film was called Honour Thy Father and Bill's name in the film was Gay Talese. Although Bill did not acknowledge the fact, this name actually belonged to a real novelist who wrote about organised crime. He maintained that his photograph had appeared on the cover of Time magazine in the previous year with the name Gay Talese printed clearly on it.

Bill was the youngest of four children born to Irish-American parents. He was very close to his mother and his father blamed him for the break-up of his marriage; he was often excluded from his father's activities. At the age of 12, Bill's father fell ill and Bill remembered wanting to see him dead. His school work was good and he eventually became a

bank clerk – a stop-gap job while he thought of which career to pursue. He was quiet and polite but eccentric; he resigned after two years to become a lift operator, a job which afforded even more thinking time, but he was sacked after a year for being disorganised. He moved in with his mother shortly after this but because each made the other anxious, he moved out and moved in with his sister, her husband and their three children. It was at this point that Bill's unusual behaviour became noticeable.

Bill did not seem to enjoy life very much – he did not like interacting with others, was ambivalent about relationships and described sex in very impersonal terms. Initial therapy sessions targeted Bill's indifference and time-keeping and his sister was advised to ignore inappropriate behaviour. If he missed breakfast, then he would not have a snack cooked for him at eleven, as had previously happened. This strategy and others like it resulted in Bill keeping time and domestic appointments. He enjoyed helping his niece with her homework and so this pleasant activity was encouraged. Eventually, his schedule approached those of the house and he began to help more with domestic chores. Mumbling and lack of social contact was tackled next. The therapist advised Bill to move to one area of the house whenever he felt the need to mumble and talk to himself. This was partly but not totally successful. His shyness with other people was tackled by asking Bill to rehearse mentally conversations that might occur with other people.

When the 'film fantasy' was made aware to the therapist, however, Bill was prescribed thioridazine, a standard antipsychotic medication. This was successful in reducing the self-talk but his delusions remained. To try and eliminate these delusions, Bill was told to visit a local library and find the cover of Time with his photograph on. This he did and obviously did not find such a cover. However, he believed that the covers had been switched by conspirators. He was told to go to two more libraries but he was still convinced that the covers had been switched. Over the next few weeks, he began to believe that he might just have imagined the Time incident and his delusions managed to recede a little.

Source: Oltmans *et al.* (1995).

more likely themselves to become schizophrenic, even if they were adopted and raised by non-schizophrenic parents (Kety *et al.*, 1968; Farmer *et al.*, 1987). Twin studies of schizophrenia compare the concordance rates of MZ twins with the concordance rates of siblings of different genetic relatedness who were reared either together or apart. The risk of one MZ twin developing the disorder if the other has it is between 50 and 70 per cent; in DZ twins, this is between 9 and 18 per cent. If both of a child's parents are affected, it has a 40–60 per cent chance of developing the illness (Tanda *et al.*, 2008).

If a person has been diagnosed with schizophrenia, there exists the possibility that other family members have the disorder, too. It is important to note that although the likelihood of developing schizophrenia increases if a person has schizophrenic relatives, this disorder is not a simple trait, like eye colour, that is inherited. Even if both parents are schizophrenic, the probability that their child will develop schizophrenia is 30 per cent or less.

Current findings provide strong evidence that schizophrenia is heritable, and they also support the conclusion that carrying a 'schizophrenia gene' does not mean that a person will necessarily become schizophrenic (see Figure 18.9). These figures suggest that the environment may be an important trigger for the activation of the biological predisposition. Other risk factors can be seen in Figure 18.10.

Genome Wide Association Studies (GWAS) (see Chapter 3) attempt to identify genetic features which cluster in a group of individuals. Forty-two single-nucleotide polymorphisms have been identified which have been associated with a 70 per cent risk of developing schizophrenia; 34 have been confirmed in high-risk schizophrenia, although it has been difficult to replicate these findings (Arnedo *et al.*, 2014). Yet other studies, suggest that over 1000 alleles are involved in schizophrenia (Cross Disorder Group, 2013). A GWAS study of 36,989 cases of schizophrenia and 113,075 controls identified 128 independent alleles (Schizophrenia Working Group, 2014). Some studies have associated schizophrenia with genetic mutation such as copy number variations – these are higher in schizophrenia than in controls (Kirkor *et al.*, 2012). The first to be identified was *22q11.2*. At least 15 of these have been identified in schizophrenia and have been associated with a risk of developing

schizophrenia (Robinson *et al.*, 2014). The most significant association is thought to be on the short arm of chromosome 6. There is also an association between schizophrenia and the gene which encodes the dopamine D2 receptor and genes which code the regulation of dopamine synthesis, pathways which are also responsible for our response to stress (Howes *et al.*, 2016).

Neurochemical causes

The dominant neurochemical hypothesis concerning schizophrenia involves dopamine and the evidence for dopamine's involvement was originally indirect. Cocaine and amphetamine, for example, can cause symptoms of schizophrenia, both in schizophrenics and in non-schizophrenics; antipsychotic drugs, on the other hand, can reduce them. Because both types of drug affect neural communication in which dopamine serves as a transmitter substance, investigators hypothesised that abnormal activity of these neurons was the primary cause of schizophrenia. The **dopamine hypothesis**, therefore, states that schizophrenia is produced by the

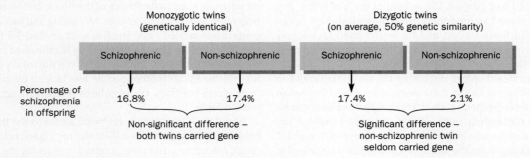

Figure 18.9 Heritability of schizophrenia. An explanation for evidence that people can have an unexpressed 'schizophrenia gene'.

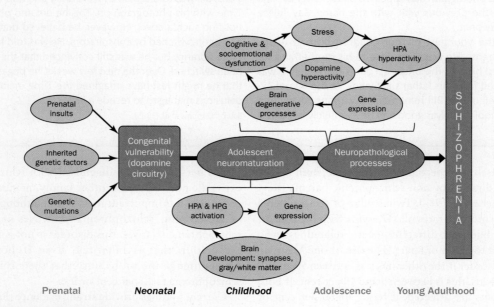

Figure 18.10 Some of the risk factors for schizophrenia.

overactivity of synapses (increased dopamine synthesis), especially those in the striatum, that use dopamine as a transmitter substance (Howes *et al.*, 2016; Weinstein *et al.*, 2016; Maia and Frank, 2016).

Neurological causes

Two meta-analyses have found that there is greater loss of brain volume in schizophrenia than in controls, although whether this loss is due to the illness or the drugs used by individuals is not clear (Veijola *et al.*, 2014). There is also evidence of decreased white matter connectivity in schizophrenia (Kochumov and Hong, 2014). There seem to be specific abnormalities in the fibres connecting the frontal and temporal lobes (Wheeler and Voineskov, 2014). A meta-analysis of 15 such studies found that there was a significant reduction in left frontal white matter and left temporal white matter (Ellison-Wright and Bullmore, 2009). In first-episode patients, there is a loss in white matter in the right frontal lobe and left temporal lobe but some studies find no such differences (Yao *et al.*, 2013). The severity of negative symptoms has been associated with lower white matter in the bilateral uncinate fasciclus and inferior frontal areas (Szesko *et al.*, 2013). Unaffected family members also show decreased left PFC and medial temporal lobe white matter (Hao *et al.*, 2009). There appears to be a reduction in connectivity between other areas such as the frontal cortex and the limbic system (Wheeler and Voineskos, 2014). See Figure 18.11.

Despite these findings, there is no confirmed and consistent biological marker of schizophrenia at the neural level. The lack of consistency is due to methodological differences between studies investigating neural bases, the heterogeneity of symptoms presented in schizophrenia, the inclusion of a range of sub-types, a variety of proposed causal mechanisms, and differences in moderator variables (studies vary by participants' age, sex, age of onset) (Wheeler and Voineskov, 2014).

Cognitive and environmental causes

Family and expressed emotion

A study carried out in Finland has suggested that being raised by a 'mentally healthy' family helps to protect against the development of schizophrenia (Tienari *et al.*, 1987). The researchers examined the children of schizophrenic mothers who had been adopted away early in life. Following interviews and psychological tests, the families who adopted the children were classified as well-adjusted, moderately maladjusted or severely maladjusted. The children adopted by the well-adjusted families were least likely to show signs of mental disturbance, including schizophrenia. These findings suggest that the environment may be either an important cause or mediator of schizophrenia.

The personality and communicative abilities of either or both parents appear to play an influential role in the development of schizophrenic symptoms in children. Several studies have shown that children raised by parents who are dominating, overprotective, rigid and insensitive to the needs of others later develop schizophrenia (Roff and Knight, 1981). In many cases, a parent may be verbally accepting of the child

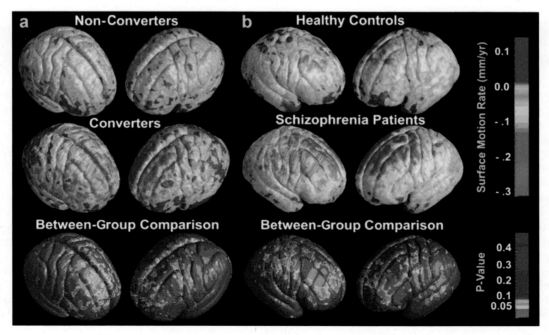

Figure 18.11 Changes in brain volume between healthy people, schizophrenic patients and those at risk of developing schizophrenia who later go on to develop (or not develop) the disorder.

yet in other ways reject them, which establishes a conflict for the child called a **double-bind**. For example, a mother may encourage her son to become emotionally dependent on her yet continually reject him when he tries to hug her or sit on her lap.

Another environmental factor which could account for the development of schizophrenia is **expressed emotion** or EE (Hooley *et al*., 1996). Brown *et al*. (1966; Brown, 1985) identified a category of behaviours of families of individuals recovering from schizophrenia that seemed to be related to the patients' rates of recovery. They labelled this variable expressed emotion, which consists of expressions of criticism, hostility and emotional overinvolvement by the family members towards the patient. Patients living in a family environment in which the level of expressed emotion was low were more likely to recover, whereas those in families in which it was high were likely to continue to exhibit schizophrenic symptoms. Perceived criticism also appears to be important: in depressed patients, perceived criticism predicted a relapse in the mental disorder more reliably than did actual criticism (Hooley and Teasdale, 1989); mood disorder patients with high-EE families appear to be more non-verbally negative than patients from low-EE families (Simoneau *et al*., 1998). Expressed emotion has been found to increase with illness duration and patients are more likely to relapse if they come from high-EE families (Hooley, 2010).

Treatment

The commonest form of treatment for schizophrenia is psychopharmacological.

Chlorpromazine and other antipsychotic drugs are remarkably effective in alleviating the positive symptoms of schizophrenia but produce little consistent improvement in the negative symptoms. Hallucinations diminish or disappear, delusions become less striking or cease altogether, and the patient's thought processes become more coherent. These drugs are not merely tranquillisers; for example, they cause a patient with catatonic immobility to begin moving again as well as cause an excited patient to quieten down. In contrast, true tranquillisers such as Librium or Valium only make a schizophrenic patient slow-moving and lethargic.

Antipsychotic drugs block dopamine receptors and prevent them from becoming stimulated. The focus of the drugs appears to be the D2 receptor in the striatum: around 70 per cent of these receptors are occupied by antipsychotic medication which blocks their action (Lidow *et al*., 1998). Cocaine, conversely, activates this receptor. The only effective means of treating the disorder is by D2 antagonists. These **antipsychotic** drugs help to reduce the effects of schizophrenia apparently by blocking dopamine receptors in the brain. Presumably, overactivity of dopamine synapses is responsible for the positive symptoms of schizophrenia, which is why treatment is effective at combating the positive symptoms but has limited success in combating the negative symptoms (Keshavan *et al*., 2008). Although dopamine-secreting neurons are located in several parts of the brain, most researchers believe that the ones involved in the symptoms of schizophrenia are located in the cerebral cortex and parts of the limbic system near the front of the brain. There is evidence that the education of the family/patient about the disorder reduces the likelihood of a relapse and that social skills training also improves outcome (Keshavan *et al*., 2008).

Cutting edge: Predicting who will develop psychosis

One of the most difficult challenges in mental health is predicting who will develop a mental illness. One category of people might be able to help provide some sort of guidance is those at-risk for developing an illness. With schizophrenia, for example, at risk individuals might be those with a close relative who has been diagnosed. Schmidt *et al*. (2016) have taken this a step further. They tried to discriminate those who would develop psychosis from those who would not by reviewing the literature on significant predictors of developing the illness and then modelling which combination of factors best predicted the appearance of the illness.

They focused their research on those at high clinical risk of developing psychosis and they examined known environmental and biological/clinical contributors to the illness. They found that models based on environmental factors

alone predicted 63 per cent of those going on to develop the illness; clinical/biological/neurocognitive factors predicted 82 per cent of illness, overall.

When the researchers analysed the data for the specific types of data that predicted illness development, they found that clinical features plus EEG was best, followed by MRI scans, then blood markers.

If all three tests were positive, the likelihood of making the transition to psychosis was 98 per cent. If only two were positive, the likelihood was between 71–82 per cent. The likelihood of developing the illness when one test was positive, was low: between 1–21 per cent.

Although this study was a theoretical one, based on existing not original data, it provides a clear description of predictors of a person's transition from health to psychosis and a model which future research can test.

A new drug used to treat schizophrenia has been dihydrexidine, a D1 agonist which has been found to improve working memory in non-human primates. Because one of the more pronounced cognitive deficits in schizophrenia involves impairment in executive function, such as working memory, this drug has been used to target the dorsolateral PFC. This area has been found to have atrophy of dendrites on pyramidal cells (Arnsten *et al.*, 2016). Its use in schizophrenia is in its early stages but initial results are positive.

The major problem with antipsychotic drugs is that they do not discriminate between these two systems of dopamine-secreting neurons. The drugs interfere with the activity of both the circuits involved in the symptoms of schizophrenia and the circuits involved in the control of movements. Consequently, when a person with schizophrenia begins taking an antipsychotic drug, they often exhibit a movement disorder. Fortunately, the disorder is usually temporary and soon disappears.

However, after taking the antipsychotic drug for several years, some people develop a different, more serious, movement disorder known as **tardive dyskinesia** (tardive means late developing; dyskinesia refers to a disturbance in movement), an often irreversible and untreatable syndrome characterised by continual involuntary lip smacking, grimacing and drooling (Cummings and Wirshing, 1989).

Clozapine, an antischizophrenic drug, is more effective than other antipsychotic drugs in helping cases of almost untreatable schizophrenia (Kane *et al.*, 1988). It improves the symptoms of about 30–50 per cent of those people who have not responded to traditional antipsychotic drugs. Because about 2 per cent of those taking clozapine suffer an inhibition of white blood cell production, which can be fatal, weekly blood tests have to be conducted. Prognosis is worse for patients on long-term antipsychotic medication (Chouinard and Chouinard, 2008).

The positive symptoms of the illness have been addressed using CBT. One aim of the CBT is to improve the patient's social skills by changing his/her cognition. A meta-analysis of social skills training in schizophrenia found that they led to improvements in the acquisition of skills, assertiveness, social interactions and a general reduction in symptoms (Kurtz and Mueser, 2009). More modest improvements are seen in social activities such as behaving appropriately at a supermarket.

Depressive disorders

These were the opening words of Professor Lewis Wolpert, Professor of Developmental Biology at University College London in his book, *Malignant Sadness*. Everyone experiences

> It was the worst experience of my life. More terrible even than watching my wife die of cancer. I am ashamed to admit that my depression felt worse than her death but it's true. I was in a state that bears no resemblance to anything I had experienced before. I was not just feeling very low. I was seriously ill. I was totally self-involved, negative and thought about suicide most of the time. I could not think properly *let alo*ne work, and wanted to remain curled up in bed all day.

moods varying from sadness to happiness to elation. We are excited when our team wins a game, saddened to learn that a friend's father has had a heart attack, thrilled at news of a higher than expected grade in an exam, and devastated by the death of a loved one. Some people, though, experience more dramatic mood changes than these. They may be characterised by a deep, foreboding depression or by a combination of depression and euphoria.

DSM-V describes what we consider to be chronic and persistent unhappiness as Major Depressive Disorder (MDD). According to DSM-V, individuals with MDD, have depressed mood, have diminished interest and pleasure, weight/appetite increase or decrease, insomnia or hypersomnia, psychomotor agitation, loss of energy, feelings of worthlessness, inappropriate guilt, lack of concentration, diminished thinking and recurrent thoughts of deaths or suicide. Depressed people also show impairment in some cognitive functions such as executive functions, especially if they are currently experiencing severe depression and if they are taking relevant medication (Snyder, 2013). Depressed people cannot always state why they are depressed. Around 17 per cent of people will experience a major episode of depression at some point in their lives (Kessler *et al.*, 1994) and a similar percentage experiences disability at work due to the illness (Goldberg and Steury, 2001). According to Elizabeth Wurtzel, author of *Prozac Nation*:

> one day, you realise that your entire life is just awful, not worth living, a horror and a black blot on the white terrain of human existence. One morning, you wake up afraid you are going to live . . . for all intents and purposes, the deeply depressed are just the walking, waking dead.

The 'walking, waking dead', according to the World Health Organization (2016), number 350 m word-wide with this number includes more women than men (Wang *et al.*, 2016).

Aetiology

Cognitive causes

People with mood disorders do not have the same outlook on life as others. Specifically, they make negative statements about themselves and their abilities: 'Nobody likes me', 'I'm not good at anything', 'What's the point in even trying, I'll just mess it up anyway'. Because they are so negative about themselves, depressed people are particularly unpleasant to be around. The problem is that the depressed individual is caught in a vicious circle: negative statements strain interpersonal relationships, which result in others withdrawing or failing to initiate social support, which, in turn, reinforces the depressed individual's negative statements (Klerman and Weissman, 1986).

Beck (1967, 1991) suggested that the changes in affect seen in depression are not primary but instead are secondary to changes in cognition. That is, the primary disturbance is a distortion in the person's view of reality. For example, a depressed person may see a scratch on the surface of their car and conclude that the car is ruined; or a person whose recipe fails may see the unappetising dish as proof of their unworthiness; or a nasty letter from a creditor is seen as a serious and personal condemnation. According to Beck, depressed people's thinking is characterised by self-blame (things that go wrong are always their fault), overemphasis on the negative aspects of life (small problems are blown out of proportion) and failure to appreciate positive experiences (pessimism). This kind of pessimistic thinking involves negative thoughts about the self, about the present and about the future, which Beck collectively referred to as the **cognitive triad**. In short, depressed people blame their present miserable situation on their inadequacies and a lack of hope for improving the situation in the future. Depressive symptoms can be measured via the Beck Depression Inventory.

The negative view of the self and events, however, seems to be time-specific. Depressed individuals who are asked to describe themselves 'right now' use negative terms, but use less negative terms when they describe how they usually feel (Brewin et al., 1992). Depressed patients are also likely to be negative when discussing things globally but not when discussing specific issues (Wycherley, 1995).

Beck's original model argued that cognition caused the emotional disorder, but his later reformulation of the theory suggested that cognition is part of a set of interacting mechanisms that include biological, psychological and social factors (Kovacs and Beck, 1978). In the reformulation, Beck argued that people might be predisposed to develop depression under certain circumstances. He called this a diathesis–stress theory. Central to the theory is that there is a set of schema – a stored collection of knowledge that affects encoding and understanding of all other processed information – which, when activated, sets off a series of negative thoughts and experiences. If the schema is depressogenic – characterised by depressive features – then an event which might activate these schemata leads to the person processing information very negatively. However, if a person is not exposed to these triggers, they will think or behave no more depressively than a person who does not possess depressogenic schemata. A study of undergraduates found that students with dysfunctional attitudes – those who were identified as having depressogenic schemata – felt more depressed after learning they had been refused a place at a university of their choice than when learning that they had, a pattern not seen in students whose attitudes were not dysfunctional (Abela and D'Allessandro, 2002).

Beck also distinguished between two types of depression: sociotropic depression in which the abnormal belief derived from a dependence on others, and autonomous depression in which the individual was goal-oriented and relied little on others. The evidence for these two types as distinct varieties of depression, however, is mixed (Power and Dalgleish, 1997).

Another causal factor in depression appears to involve the attributional style of the depressed person (Abramson et al., 1978, 1989). According to this idea, it is not merely experiencing negative events that causes people to become depressed: what is more important are the attributions people make about why those events occur. People who are most likely to become depressed are those who attribute negative events and experiences to their own shortcomings and who believe that their life situations are never going to get any better. A person's attributional style, then, serves as a predisposition or diathesis for depression. In other words, people prone to depression tend to have a hopeless outlook on their life: 'I am not good at anything I try to do and it will never get any better. I am always going to be a useless person.' According to this view, depression is most likely when people with pessimistic attributional styles encounter significant or frequent life stressors (Abramson et al., 1989). The pessimistic attributions are then generalised to other, perhaps smaller, stressors, and eventually a deep sense of hopelessness and despair sets in. Thus, the original formulation of the theory was called the helplessness theory whereas the later reformulation became known as the hopelessness theory.

Such people also appear to suffer a double dose of hopelessness. Not only do they perceive negative outcomes as being their own fault, but they also perceive positive outcomes as being due to circumstance or to luck. In addition, they apply pessimistic attributions to a wide range of events and experiences and apply positive attributions only to a very narrow range of events and experiences, if any.

However, there is mixed evidence for a strong version of the hopelessness attribution theory. Swendsen (1998) reported that attributional style did not predict immediate depressed or anxious mood in a group of 91 individuals who were asked to report negative events, cognitions, anxiety and depression five times a day for one week. However, attributional style did predict 'individual' specific causal attributions made to negative events. Similar findings have been reported in other studies

(Kapci, 1998). Lynd-Stevenson (1996, 1997) reports that hopelessness does not mediate the relationship between attributional style and depression but that there is a mediating effect when measures of hopelessness are relevant to the individual's ongoing life (in Lynd-Stevenson's sample's case, hopelessness related to unemployment). Attributional style, therefore, seems to apply only in certain, relevant contexts.

The rumination that depressed people are prone to engage in – negative, repetitive thoughts – has been associated with neural correlates including reduced connectivity (Berman et al., 2014).

Genetic causes

Like schizophrenia, depressive disorders have been subject of a search to discover an underlying genetic cause. One study of 9,000 people with major depression found no genetic sequences which were associated with depression (MDDWG, 2013). In 2015, the first two genetic markers linked to depression were discovered (CONVERGE Consortium, 2015). A study of 5,303 Chinese women with depression and 5,337 without, found that two sequences were associated with the illness – one next to an enzyme whose function is not completely understood and another next to S1RT1, a gene that codes for mitochondria, cells which produce energy (Flint et al., 2014). This was later confirmed in a study of 3000 men and women with depression.

Neurochemical causes

Drug treatments for depression (which are described in detail below) have shed some light on the biochemical causes of schizophrenia. Antidepressants such as imipramine, for example, stimulate synapses that use two transmitter substances, norepinephrine and serotonin. Other drugs such as reserpine, which is used to treat high blood pressure, can cause episodes of depression. Reserpine lowers blood pressure by blocking the release of norepinephrine in muscles in the walls of blood vessels, thus causing the muscles to relax. However, because the drug also blocks the release of norepinephrine and serotonin in the brain, a common side – effect is depression. This side effect strengthens the argument that biochemical factors in the brain play an important role in depression.

Such data have suggested a biological amine theory of depression: depression results from a depletion in the monoamines, dopamine, norepinephrine or serotonin. The serotonin hypothesis is a variant of this general theory. The serotonin hypothesis suggests that this neuro-transmitter (the lack of it) may be more involved in depression because blocking reuptake of serotonin is more effective than blocking norepinephrine. Given that most antidepressants augment serotonin (perhaps by different mechanisms), perhaps the involvement of other neurotransmitters is peripheral.

In addition to the amines, levels of the neurotransmitter gamma amino butyuric acid (GABA) have been found to be lower in the cerebrospinal fluid (CSF) and plasma of individuals with unipolar depression (Brambila et al., 2003). When depressed individuals are given drugs which increase the level of serotonin at serotonergic neurons or are given ECT, the decrease in GABA concentration seen in the occipital cortex is reversed (Sanacora et al., 2002, 2004). The roles of the two classes of GABA (the a and b classes) in depression, however, are unclear.

Another possible chemical cause of depression is vitamin D deficiency. The receptors for vitamin D are present on neurons in the cingulate cortex and hippocampus and several studies have found a correlation between depression and vitamin D deficiency. However, as Anglin et al. (2013) note, eight reviews of the evidence have found insufficient evidence for the involvement of vitamin D. In their own review of 14 studies including 31,424 people, they found that significant effects were found in some types of study and not others. They also suggest that the field may be susceptible to publication bias – negative results aren't published.

Neuropathological causes

In a neuroimaging study, activity in the PFC near the top of the corpus callosum was reduced in individuals with unipolar and bipolar depression (Drevets et al., 1997). This part of the PFC is called the ACC and a specific region within the cingulate – which has been called subgenual region sg24 – is less active in people with mood disorder, as Figure 18.12 shows.

Drevets et al. found that the volume of this region was lateralised to the left hemisphere, which is consistent with the data and model of normal emotion (described in Chapter 13). These findings were subsequently replicated in a group of people with severe **mood disorder** (Hirayasu et al., 1999).

When Drevets and his colleagues went on to explore the cellular nature of this region in people with mood disorder, they found the typical reduction in sg24 but also a reduction in the density of cells and in the number of glial cells (see Ongur et al., 1998). A further study, using a larger sample, found that same pattern of cell reduction in a group of individuals with major and bipolar depression but only in a subset with a family history of the disorder (Torrey et al., 2000). These cells carry neurotransmitter receptors and help to transport neuro-transmitters, which may explain why their reduction is associated with depression; the reduction might also explain why this area is seen as smaller in people with depression and bipolar depression.

There is also evidence that connectivity in the brain at rest differs between people with major depressive disorder and control groups (Berman et al., 2011; Zeng et al., 2012). This resting state abnormality has been thought to underlie the rumination that depressed individuals engage in. People with depression attend preferentially to negative information but

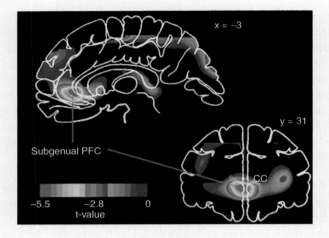

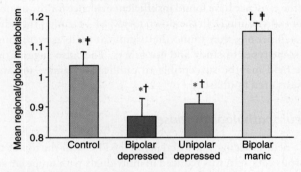

* p<0.025 control vs. depressed; † p<0.01 depressed vs. manic;
‡ p<0.05 control vs. manic

Figure 18.12 Decreases in activation in the prefrontal cortex seen in individuals with mood disorders.

Source: Drevets, W.C., Neuroimaging and neuropathological studies of depression: Implications for the cognitive-emotional features of mood disorders. Current Opinion in Neurobiology, 2001, 11, 240–49. Copyright 2001, with permission from Elsevier.

the brain regions underlying this are not completely known – some suggest that the amygdala becomes active during exposure to negative information and the ventral striatum responds to positive information and is less active in depressed individuals (Groenewold *et al.*, 2013).

There are also neuroanatomical differences between depressed people and control groups during the processing of emotional information. The brain's response to sad faces in these two groups can predict the classification of each group with 80 per cent accuracy (Fu *et al.*, 2008) and can predict how well people respond to CBT. A meta-analysis of depressed individuals performing tasks involving emotional information found that negative emotion was associated with greater activation in the right amygdala, left striatum, dorsolateral anterior cingulate and parahippocampal areas in people with depression than in controls (Groenewold *et al.*, 2013). Positive emotion was associated with less activation in these areas (and in the left striatum). In the frontal lobe, there was a

decrease in the left dlPFC in negative emotion tasks and an increase in the medial OFC in positive tasks. All of these areas, according to the authors, are involved in the appraisal and monitoring of affective information. Deficits in the structure or function of the hypothalamus hippocampus, subgenus anterior cingulate, OFC, middle frontal cortex and basal ganglia have also been associated with depression (Swaab *et al.*, 2005; Bao *et al.*, 2008; Costafreda *et al.*, 2009).

Treatment

The treatments available for depression are well established but their success is variable. The Sequenced Treatment Alternatives To Relieve Depression (STAR*D) study, for example, found that only a quarter of individuals improved after one treatment (Fried and Nesse, 2015). One reason for this might be that DSM guidance indicates that it is the number of symptoms which determines a diagnosis of illness, not the type of specific symptom. Given the heterogeneity of symptoms in depression – DSM lists nine, as you saw earlier – and the severity of these symptoms, it may not be surprising that not all treatments are effective for all individuals. According to Fried and Nesse (2015), for example, two individuals with MDD may not have a symptom in common (based on the current diagnostic system) and that 227 symptom profiles are possible. In their review of 3,703 individuals in the STAR*D study, the most common symptom profile was found in only 2 per cent. Fourteen percent showed a symptom profile not shared by any other person, suggesting a high degree of heterogeneity in the symptoms and diagnosis of the illness. There is evidence that a combination of treatments – psychotherapy and medication – can lead to more successful outcomes. A meta-analysis of studies combining these two approaches in depression and anxiety found that the combination lead to a clinically meaningful improvement in people's health, even two years later treatment (Cuijpers *et al.*, 2014).

The two principal treatments for major depressive disorder are cognitive therapy and antidepressant medication.

Cognitive (behavioural) therapy

Beck's cognitive therapy begins by arguing that the negative beliefs held by depressed individuals are seen as conclusions based on faulty logic (Beck, 1967). A depressed person concludes that they are 'deprived, frustrated, humiliated, rejected or punished' (Beck *et al.*, 1979, p. 120). Beck views the cognitions of the depressed individual in terms of a cognitive triad: a negative view of the self ('I am worthless'), of the outside world ('The world makes impossible demands on me') and of the future ('Things are never going to get better').

Even when confronted with evidence that contradicts their negative beliefs, depressed individuals often find an

Suicide – An international perspective

Migration, low intelligence and substance use may separately be important risk factors for depression and suicide. In some countries, suicide rates have increased by over 60 per cent in between 1950 and 2000 and you can see this pattern and the international incidence in Figure 18.13.

A study of immigration into Estonia, which had been part of the Soviet Union until independence in 1991 and had, therefore, a significant Russian population (about 30 per cent of the population were Russians in 1989), found that while the rate of suicide was lower in the Russian minority during Soviet rule, this pattern changed during the period of stabilisation following independence (Varnik et al., 2005). The rate was higher than that found in Estonians in Estonia or in Russians in Russia, reflecting a change in status from privileged minority to non-privileged minority. The rates converged in 1998, suggesting to the authors that this may reflect the efforts by the Estonian government to integrate the Russian minority.

In a separate study of Swedish servicemen, Gunnell et al. (2005) found that of 987,308 Swedish men followed up for up to 26 years risk of suicide was 2–3 times higher in men with the lowest cognitive test scores compared to those with the highest. The greatest suicide risk emerged from the test of logic – this was the test correlating most significantly with suicide. Perhaps this reflects an inability to solve problems in real life; problems which, if left unresolved, lead to self-harm and death.

Suicide attempts in adolescence are associated with heavy or frequent drinking and illegal drug-taking (Shaffer and Pfeffer, 2001; Gould et al., 2003). A group of Norwegian researchers monitored the correlation between substance use and suicide in two surveys (in 1992 and 2002) of 23,000 13–19-year-olds (Rossow et al., 2005). There was a significant relationship between increased substance use and suicide, but only in girls. For boys, the effect of substance use seemed to be less pronounced in 2002 than in 1992. For both sexes, the substance most significantly associated with suicide attempts was alcohol.

It is noteworthy that despite decades of research, we are nowhere nearer predicting who will commit suicide. In a meta-analysis of studies which sought to identify predictors of suicidal thought and behaviour, Frankin et al. (2016) found that in over 50 years' of research, no broad categories or sub-categories of behaviour predicted suicide and studies rarely consider multiple risk factors.

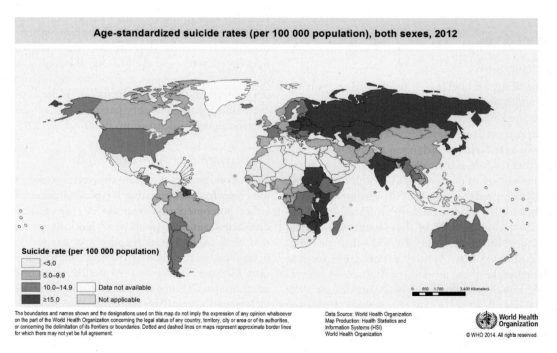

Age-standardized suicide rates (per 100 000 population), both sexes, 2012

Suicide rate (per 100 000 population)
- <5.0
- 5.0–9.9
- 10.0–14.9
- ≥15.0
- Data not available
- Not applicable

The boundaries and names shown and the designations used on this map do not imply the expression of any opinion whatsoever on the part of the World Health Organization concerning the legal status of any country, territory, city or area or of its authorities, or concerning the delimitation of its frontiers or boundaries. Dotted and dashed lines on maps represent approximate border lines for which there may not yet be full agreement.

Data Source: World Health Organization
Map Production: Health Statistics and Information Systems (HSI)
World Health Organization

World Health Organization
© WHO 2014. All rights reserved.

Figure 18.13 World Health Organization statistics for suicide rates across the world.
Source: World Health Organization: 2014.

illogical means of interpreting good news as bad news (Lewinsohn *et al.*, 1980). For example, a student who receives an A grade on an exam might attribute the high grade to an easy, unchallenging exam rather than to their own mastery of the material. The fact that few others in the class received a high grade does little to convince the depressed person that they deserve congratulations for having done well. The depressed student goes on believing, against contrary evidence, that the good grade was not really deserved.

Once the faulty logic is recognised for what it is, therapy entails exploring means for correcting the distortions. The therapist does not accept the client's conclusions and inferences at their face value. Instead, those conclusions resulting from faulty logic are discussed so that the client may understand them from another perspective, changing their behaviour as a result.

Meta-analyses suggest that CBT can be a very effective means of combating depression and may even be more effective than tricyclic antidepressants (see below) in the long term (Hensley *et al.*, 2004). Recent advances in CBT and CBT-like treatments include the availability of online interventions, as you saw for anxiety. For example, van Ballegooijen *et al.* (2014) note that guided online therapy is more successful than unguided therapy and that people adhere to face to face CBT better than guided therapy.

Antidepressant drugs

Tricyclic antidepressants

Antidepressant drugs are a class of drugs used to treat the symptoms of major depression. **Antimanic drugs** are used to treat the symptoms of bipolar disorder and mania. The earliest used antidepressant drugs were derived from the family of chemicals known as **tricyclics**, which refers to their 'three-ring' chemical structure (Lickey and Gordon, 1983).

Although the biology of depression is not well understood, the most widely accepted theory is that depression may result from a deficiency of the catecholamine neurotransmitters norepinephrine and serotonin. Each of these neurotransmitters may be involved in different types of depression, although researchers are not sure how. Antidepressant drugs seem to slow down the reuptake of these neurotransmitters by presynaptic axons. Although tricyclic antidepressants do not work for all people, about 60–80 per cent of those whose depression has brought despair to their lives gradually return to normal after having been placed on tricyclics for two to six weeks (Hughes and Pierattini, 1992). Unfortunately, tricyclics have many side effects, including dizziness, sweating, weight gain, constipation, increased heart rate, poor concentration and dry mouth.

Monoamine oxidase inhibitors (MAOIs)

Another class of antidepressants, introduced in the late 1950s, is the **monoamine oxidase inhibitors** (**MAOIs**), which take one to three weeks to begin alleviating depression. MAOIs prevent enzymes in the synaptic gap from destroying dopamine, norepinephrine and serotonin that have been released by presynaptic neurons. These drugs can have many side effects, many of them fatal. The **tyramine cheese reaction**, for example, arises from the eating of foods containing tyramine such as some wines, milk products, coffee and chocolate. Because the monoamine oxidase does not oxidise tyramine, tyramine displaces epinephrine at epinephrine receptors. This produces severe hypertension and blurred vision, impotence, insomnia and nausea. It can also be fatal if leading to a haemorrhage. MAOIs also have been shown to be more effective in treating atypical depressions such as those involving hypersomnia (too much sleep) or mood swings (Hughes and Pierattini, 1992).

Serotonin-specific reuptake inhibitors (SSRIs)

A relatively new class of drugs is **serotonin-specific reuptake inhibitors** (**SSRIs**), which, as their name suggests, block the reuptake of serotonin in nerve cells. As a result, the common feature of all SSRIs is that they enhance the transmission of serotonin. Perhaps the most common SSRI is fluoxetine (Prozac), first authorised for medical use in 1988. Fluoxetine inhibits the reuptake of serotonin, leaving more of that neurotransmitter in the synaptic cleft to stimulate post-synaptic receptors, and is the drug of first choice when tricyclic drug treatment has failed. SSRIs produce fewer negative side-effects than do tricyclics and the MAOIs, although some individuals do experience headache, gastrointestinal discomfort, insomnia, tremor and sexual dysfunction. There is evidence, however, that antidepressants have no clinical advantage over placebo in minor depression (Barbui *et al.*, 2011).

Other pharmacological treatments

Two developments in the psychopharmacology of depression have been second generation (atypical) depressants which block either norepinephrine reuptake or dopamine reuptake, and **dual-action antidepressants** which block certain serotonin receptors while inhibiting its reuptake. An example of the former, nefazdone, was released in 1995; an example of the latter, mirtazapine, was released in 1997. Neither type of drug has been authorised in all European countries and, because of their youth, little research is available evaluating their long-term efficacy.

The important factor in assessing the effect of antidepressant medication is the maintenance phase of the treatment. In the initial period of drug-taking, there is an acute phase in which the acute symptoms begin to stabilise. This period can last up to three months (Hirschfeld, 2001). The next period extends between the end of the acute period and the end of the depression itself, a period that can take up to 6–12 months. The danger is that if patients had stabilised in the acute phase, then they would have medication withdrawn. According to Hirschfeld (2001), however, around one-third to one-half of people who successfully stabilise in the acute phase, will relapse if medication is not sustained, hence the importance of monitoring behaviour closely during this period.

Bipolar disorder

Bipolar disorder is characterised by alternating periods of depression and mania. **Mania** (the Greek word for madness) is characterised by wild, exuberant, unrealistic activity not precipitated by environmental events. During manic episodes, people are usually elated and self-confident; however, contradiction or interference tends to make them very angry. Their speech (and, presumably, their thought processes) becomes very rapid. They tend to flit from topic to topic and are full of grandiose plans, but their thoughts are not as disorganised as those of people with schizophrenia. Manic patients also tend to be restless and hyperactive, often pacing around ceaselessly. They often have delusions and hallucinations, typically of a nature that fits their exuberant mood. Impairments in 'frontal lobe' function such as set-shifting, verbal memory and sustained attention have been reported (Clark *et al.*, 2002), and the experience of the disorder has been related to an oversensitive frontal cortex (Harmon-Jones *et al.*, 2002).

Very few patients exhibit only mania, thus DSM-V classifies all cases in which mania occurs as bipolar disorder. Patients with bipolar disorder usually experience alternate periods of mania and depression. Each of these periods lasts from a few days to a few weeks, usually with several days of relatively normal behaviour between. Around 40 per cent of bipolar disorder patients will have been diagnosed with major depression previously (Bowden, 2001). During the depressive and manic period, there appear to be cognitive impairments such as delayed verbal memory, whereas during the depressed period there is decreased verbal fluency (Kurtz and Gerraty, 2009).

Lithium carbonate

Lithium carbonate is most effective in the treatment of bipolar disorders or simple mania (Young and Newham, 2006). People's manic symptoms usually decrease as soon as their blood level of lithium reaches a sufficiently high level (Gerbino *et al.*, 1978). In bipolar disorder, once the manic phase is eliminated, the depressed phase does not return. People with bipolar disorder have remained free of their symptoms for years as long as they have continued taking lithium carbonate. This drug can have some side effects, such as a fine tremor or excessive urine production; but in general, the benefits far outweigh the adverse symptoms. However, an overdose of lithium is toxic, which means that the person's blood level of lithium must be

Depression knows no social or intellectual barriers. Lewis Wolpert, Professor of Developmental Biology, Winston Churchill, British Prime Minister (both pictured here) and the late Stuart Sutherland, Professor of Psychology, have all suffered from major depression or bipolar disorder.

Sources: Colin McPherson/Corbis Entertainment/Getty Images (l); PA Photos/Empics (r).

monitored regularly. Psychotherapy has also been associated with some benefits, but this treatment is more successful for depression than mania (Scott, 2006).

The major difficulty with treating bipolar disorder is that people with this disorder often miss their 'high'. When medication is effective, the mania subsides along with the depression. But most people enjoy at least the initial phase of their manic periods, and some believe that they are more creative at that time. In addition, many of these people say that they resent having to depend on a chemical 'crutch'. As a consequence, many people suffering from bipolar disorder stop taking their medication. Not taking their medication endangers the lives of these people because the risk of death by suicide is particularly high during the depressive phase of bipolar disorder.

Chapter review

Classification and diagnosis of mental disorders

- Psychologists and other mental health professionals view the causes of mental disorders from several different perspectives:
  - The psychodynamic perspective argues that mental disorders arise from intrapsychic conflict that overwhelms the mind's defence mechanisms.
  - The medical perspective asserts that mental disorders have an organic basis, as physical illnesses do.
  - The cognitive behavioural perspective maintains that mental disorders are learned patterns of maladaptive thinking and behaving.
  - The humanistic perspective suggests that mental disorders arise from an oversensitivity to the demands of others and because positive regard from others is conditional on meeting those demands.
  - The sociocultural perspective focuses on how cultural variables influence the development of mental disorders and people's subjective reactions to them.
- The two major manuals for diagnostic mental disorder are the Diagnostic and Statistical Manual of Mental Disorders V (American Psychiatric Association, 2013) and the International Classification of Diseases 11 (World Health Organization, 2017).
- There is strong cross-cultural agreement for the diagnosis of disorder such as schizophrenia, although anxiety and social phobia are not as uniformly diagnosed; there are also culture-bound disorders which are not universal.
- Research indicates that lay people continue to show poor understanding of the symptoms, possible causes and treatment of mental illness.

Treatment of mental disorders

- Historically, people suffering from emotional or behavioural problems were believed to be possessed by demons or were accused of being witches. They were often subjected to torture, including trephining, in which a small hole was punctured in the skull of the afflicted person to allow demonic spirits to escape. Mental patients in sixteenth – and seventeenth-century asylums encountered abject humiliation. Philippe Pinel, a French physician, is often credited with changing the asylum environment in the late eighteenth century.
- Modern therapy adopts an eclectic approach – the borrowing of methods from different treatments and blending them in a way that will work best in treating the patient's problem. There are, however, different types of treatment approaches that have specific characteristics.
- Insight psychotherapy is based primarily on conversation between therapist and client. The oldest form of insight psychotherapy, psychoanalysis, was devised by Freud.
- Psychoanalysis attempts to discover the forces that are warring in the client's psyche and to resolve these inner conflicts by bringing to consciousness the client's unconscious drives and the defences that have been established against them. Insight is believed to be the primary source of healing.
- Humanistic therapy emphasises conscious, deliberate mental processes.
- Client-centred therapy is based on the premise that people are healthy and good and that their problems result from faulty thinking. Instead of evaluating themselves in terms of their own self-concepts, they judge themselves by other people's standards. This tendency is rectified by providing an environment of unconditional positive regard in which clients can find their own way to good mental health.
- The range of people that may benefit from insight therapy is limited and narrow. In general, those most likely to benefit are those who are intelligent and able to articulate their problems. Insight psychotherapies are not effective with persons with serious mental disorders such as schizophrenia. There are also difficulties with evaluating their effectiveness.
- Behavioural therapists attempt to use the principles of classical and operant conditioning to modify behaviour – fears

are eliminated or maladaptive behaviours are replaced with adaptive ones.

- Systematic desensitisation uses classical conditioning procedures to condition relaxation to stimuli that were previously producing fear. In contrast, implosion therapy attempts to extinguish fear and avoidance responses. Aversion therapy attempts to condition an unpleasant response to a stimulus with which the client is preoccupied, such as a fetish.
- The most formal system of therapy based on operant conditioning involves token economies, which arrange contingencies in the environment of people who reside in institutions.
- Some operant treatment is vicarious – people can imagine their own behaviour with its consequent reinforcement or punishment.
- Modelling involves using others as role models for behaviour.
- The major problem with behaviour therapy is the failure of patients to transfer behaviour outside the therapy setting. Techniques to promote generalisation include the use of intermittent reinforcement and recruitment of family and friends as adjunct therapists.
- Cognitive behavioural therapies attempt to change overt behaviour and unobservable cognitive processes.
- Rational-emotive therapy is based on the assumption that people's psychological problems stem from faulty cognitions. Its practitioners use many forms of persuasion, including confrontation, to encourage people to abandon faulty cognitions in favour of logical and healthy ones.
- Beck has developed ways to help depressed people correct errors of cognition that perpetuate self-defeating thoughts.
- Group therapy is based on the belief that certain problems can be treated more efficiently and more effectively in group settings.
- Practitioners of family therapy, couples therapy and some forms of group behaviour therapy observe people's interactions with others and attempt to help them learn how to establish more effective patterns of behaviour. Treatment of groups, including families and couples, permits the therapist to observe clients' social behaviours, and it uses social pressures to help convince clients of the necessity for behavioural change. It permits clients to learn from the mistakes of others and to observe that other people have similar problems, which often provides reassurance.
- The effectiveness of psychotherapeutic methods is difficult to assess: outcomes are difficult to measure objectively, ethical considerations make it hard to establish

control groups for some types of disorder, and self-selection and drop-outs make it impossible to compare randomly selected groups of participants. Research suggests that behavioural therapy and cognitive behavioural therapy are effective.

- Biological treatments for mental disorders include drugs, electroconvulsive therapy and psychosurgery.
- Research has shown that treatment of the positive symptoms of schizophrenia with antipsychotic drugs, of **major depression** with antidepressant drugs and of bipolar disorder with lithium carbonate are the most effective ways to alleviate the symptoms of these disorders.
- Tricyclic antidepressant drugs can also alleviate severe anxiety that occurs during panic attacks and agoraphobia and can reduce the severity of obsessive-compulsive disorder.
- Although electroconvulsive therapy is an effective treatment for depression, its use is reserved for cases in which rapid relief is critical because the seizures may produce brain damage.
- The most controversial treatment, psychosurgery, is rarely performed today. Its only accepted use, in the form of **cingulotomy**, is for treatment of crippling compulsions that cannot be reduced by more conventional means.

Mental disorders

Anxiety disorders

- Anxiety disorders refer to mental disorders which are characterised by excessive worry or fear and include generalised anxiety disorder, panic disorder, simple phobia, obsessive-compulsive disorder and post-traumatic stress disorder.
- Generalised anxiety disorder is characterised by excessive worry about all aspects of life; the most explanatory models suggest that anxiety serves as an alarm function preparing an organism for future action. It is best treated by anxiolytic (anti-anxiety) drugs.
- Social anxiety disorder is a condition that affects those who express extreme worry at being in the company of others
- Panic disorder results from a fear of fear. A patient misinterprets bodily sensations catastrophically.
- Cognitive behavioural therapy and anti-anxiety drugs are effective treatments.
- **Social phobia** refers to an excessive pathological fear of speaking or performing in public.
- Agoraphobia, the most common phobia, is the fear of open spaces. Simple phobia is a fear of specific stimuli such as spiders and snakes.
- Recent research has applied virtual reality technology (exposure to computer-simulated events, objects or

locations) to the treatment of the fear of flying and fear of spiders, with long-term success.
- Post-traumatic stress disorder refers to anxiety generated by an astonishing event or trauma (such as natural catastrophe, war or rape).
- Somatoform disorders include **somatisation disorder** and conversion disorder.
- Obsessive-compulsive disorder is a disorder in which people have obsessional thoughts and behavioural compulsions
- Dissociative disorders include psychogenic amnesia (with or without fugue) – a withdrawal from a painful situation or from intolerable guilt; multiple personalities – the adoption of several distinct and complete personalities.

Personality disorders

- Antisocial personality disorder refers to a pathological impairment in social and personal behaviour. It is also known as psychopathy or sociopathy, but antisocial personality is qualitatively different from psychopathy. Psychopaths are indifferent to the effects of their behaviour on other people, are impulsive, fail to learn from experience, are sexually promiscuous, lack commitment to a partner and are habitual liars. Some psychopaths are superficially charming and psychopathy tends to run in families.
- Evidence suggests that the frontal lobe is either dysfunctional or smaller in psychopathy.

Schizophrenic disorders

- Schizophrenia is a mental illness characterised by distortions of thought, perception and emotion.
- The main positive symptoms of schizophrenia include thought disorders; delusions of persecution, grandeur and control; and hallucinations. The main negative symptoms include withdrawal, apathy and poverty of speech.
- DSM classifies schizophrenia into several sub-types, including undifferentiated, catatonic, paranoid and disorganised.
- Recent research suggests that a low level of expressed emotion (including critical comments and emotional overinvolvement) by family members facilitates the recovery of a patient with schizophrenia.
- Positive symptoms of schizophrenia can be made worse in schizophrenic patients by drugs that stimulate dopamine synapses (cocaine and amphetamine) and can be reduced or eliminated by drugs that block dopamine receptors (antipsychotic drugs).
- These findings have led to the dopamine hypothesis, which states that schizophrenia is caused by an inherited biochemical defect that causes dopamine neurons to be overactive.
- Enlargement of the ventricles is a consistent finding in schizophrenic patients and is unrelated to drug use; there is also evidence of reduced frontal lobe activation.
- Some researchers have suggested that lateralisation of function does not occur normally in schizophrenia.
- More recent studies indicate that schizophrenia can best be conceived of as two different disorders.
- The positive symptoms are produced by overactivity of dopamine neurons and can be treated with antipsychotic drugs. These positive symptoms are associated with limbic and sublimbic neural activation during verbal hallucination and verbal disorganisation.
- The negative symptoms, which do not respond to these drugs, are caused by brain abnormality. Investigators have found direct evidence of brain damage by inspecting CT scans of living patients' brains.
- Researchers have suggested three possible causes of the brain abnormality: a virus that triggers an autoimmune disease, which causes brain damage later in life; a virus that damages the brain early in life; and obstetric complications.

Depressive disorders

- Major Depressive Disorder describes a condition in which people feel extreme, chronic and persistent unhappiness that extends over weeks.
- Bipolar disorder consists of alternating periods of mania and depression; major depression consists of depression alone.
- Disorders of mood involve emotional reactions and these reactions may be, at least in part, based on faulty and negative cognition.
- Depressed individuals may be characterised by a negative attributional style which promotes helplessness and hopelessness.
- Biological treatments include lithium carbonate for bipolar disorder and electroconvulsive therapy and antidepressant drugs (including monoamine oxidase inhibitors and tricyclic antidepressants) for depression.
- Neuroimaging research has shown that an area in the frontal cortex, sg24, is smaller in people suffering from depression although a number of cortical and subcortical regions have been implicated in the disorder.
- Anti-depressant drugs for depression, called serotonin-specific reuptake inhibitors, act by preventing reuptake of serotonin and blocking serotonin receptors.

Suggestions for further reading

Abnormal psychology – general reading

Butcher, J.N., Hooley, J., Mineka, S. and Nock, M.K. (2016) *Abnormal Psychology* (17th edn). Boston, MA: Prentice Hall.

Clark, L. A., Cuthbert, B., Lewis-Fernández, R., Narrow, W. E., & Reed, G. M. (2017). Three approaches to understanding and classifying mental disorder: ICD-11, DSM-5, and the National Institute of Mental Health's research domain criteria (RDoC). *Psychological Science in the Public Interest, 18(2)*, 72–145.

Hall, H. (2016) Who's crazy now? DSM-V and the classification of mental disorders. *Skeptic Magazine*, 21, 4–5.

Khoury, B., Langer, E.J. and Pagnini, F. (2014) The DSM: mindful science or mindless power? A critical review. *Frontiers in Psychology*, 5, 1–8.

Kring, A., Johnson, S., Davison, G.C. and Neale, J.M. (2017) *Abnormal Psychology* (13th edn). Chichester: Wiley.

Lilienfeld, S.O., Ritschel, L.A., Lynn, S.J., Cautin, R.L. and Latzman, R.D. (2013) Why many clinical psychologists are resistant to evidence-based practice. *Clinical Psychology Review*, 33, 883–900.

Lilienfeld, S.O., Ritschel, L.A., Lynn, S.J., Cautin, R.L. and Latzman, R.D. (2014) Why ineffective psychotherapies appear to work. *Perspectives on Psychological Science*, 9, 355–87.

Nevid, J., Rathus, S. and Greene, B. (2017) *Abnormal Psychology in a Changing World* (10th edn). Boston, MA: Allyn and Bacon.

Oltmanns, T.F. and Emery, R.E. (2014) Abnormal Psychology (8thedn). Upper Saddle River, NJ: Prentice Hall.

Pascual, L., Rodrigues, P. and Gallardo-Pujol, D. (2013) How does morality work in the brain? A functional and structural perspective on moral behaviour. *Frontiers in Integrative Neuroscience*, 7, 1–8.

Raine, A. (2014) *Anatomy of Violence*. London: Penguin.

Abnormal psychology is one of the most popular areas of study in psychology. As a result, there are many good textbooks which are in their sixth editions (and beyond). The books and papers listed here are very good introductions to the general area of mental disorder and are recommended for more information on topics covered in this chapter.

Specific mental illnesses

Abram, S.V. and DeYoung, C.G. (2017) Using personality neuroscience to study personality disorder. *Personality Disorders: Theory, Research, and Treatment*, 8(1), 2.

Cipriani, A., Furukawa, T. A., Salanti, G., Chaimani, A., Atkinson, L. Z., Ogawa, Y., … & Egger, M. (2018). Comparative efficacy and acceptability of 21 antidepressant drugs for the acute treatment of adults with major depressive disorder: a systematic review and network meta-analysis. *The Lancet, in press*.

Dohm, K., Redlich, R., Zwitserlood, P. and Dannlowski, U. (2016) Trajectories of major depression disorders: A systematic review of longitudinal neuroimaging findings. *Australian and New Zealand Journal of Psychiatry*, 0004867416661426.

Hare, R.D. (2016) Psychopathy, PCL-R, and criminal justice: Some new findings and current issues. *Canadian Psychology*, 57, 21–34.

Santana, E.J. (2016) The brain of the psychopath: A systematic review of structural neuroimaging studies. *Psychology and Neuroscience*, 9(4), 420.

Special issue of Biological Psychiatry on dopamine and schizophrenia, 2016, vol 81.

Wheeler, A.L. and Voineskos, A.N. (2014) A review of structural neuroimaging in schizophrenia: from connectivity to connectomics. *Frontiers in Human Neuroscience*, 8, 118.

Winsper, C., Marwaha, S., Lereya, S. T., Thompson, A., Eyden, J. and Singh, S.P. (2016) A systematic review of the neurobiological underpinnings of borderline personality disorder (BPD) in childhood and adolescence. *Reviews in the Neurosciences*, 27(8), 827–47.

The texts and papers here provide a good summary of what we know about specific mental illnesses.

Case studies

Sutherland, S. (1987) *Breakdown*. London: Weidenfeld and Nicolson.

Wolpert, L. (1999) *Malignant Sadness: The anatomy of depression*. London: Faber.

The impact of mental disorder (on the individual and on the people around the individual) is seen vividly in personal accounts of mental illness. Sutherland's book is remarkable. It is an account of bipolar disorder suffered by the late Stuart Sutherland and recounts the various treatments and therapies he underwent in a search for a cure. He describes the events surrounding the disorder with often painful honesty, and the account is made all the more provocative by the fact that Sutherland was Professor of Psychology at the University of Sussex. Wolpert, another distinguished academic, suffered from major episodes of depression. In his book, he describes the episodes vividly and reviews current understanding of the disorder and its treatment.

Glossary

 A

absolute threshold The minimum value of a stimulus that can be detected.

accommodation (1) Changes in the thickness of the lens of the eye that focus images of near or distant objects on the retina. (2) In developmental psychology, the process by which existing schemata are modified or changed by new experiences.

achromatopsia Suffering from a form of colour blindness in which the world is seen in shades of grey.

acquired dyslexia Reading impairment which results from brain injury.

acquisition In classical conditioning, the time during which a conditioned stimulus first appears and increases in frequency.

action potential A brief electrochemical event that is carried by an axon from the soma of the neuron to its terminal buttons; causes the release of a transmitter substance.

activational effect The effect of a hormone on a physiological system that has already developed. If the effect involves the brain, it can influence behaviour. An example is facilitation of sexual arousal and performance.

actor–observer effect The tendency to attribute one's own behaviour to situational factors but others' behaviour to dispositional factors.

adaptation The ability of generations of species to adapt effectively to changes in the environment.

adaptive significance The effectiveness of behaviour in aiding organisms to adjust to changing environmental conditions.

adjacency/proximity principle A Gestalt principle of organisation; elements located closest to each other are perceived as belonging to the same figure. Also called proximity principle.

aerobic exercise Physical activity that expends considerable energy, increases blood flow and respiration and thereby stimulates and strengthens the heart and lungs and increases the body's efficient use of oxygen.

affect In emotion research, the term given to a prolonged, general mood state (e.g. 'positive affect').

affix A sound or group of letters added to the beginning of a word (prefix) or its end (suffix).

affordances Features of the perceptual environment which give it its meaning or signify its use.

aggression The intent to inflict harm on others.

agoraphobia A mental disorder characterised by fear of and avoidance of being alone in public places; this disorder is often accompanied by panic attacks.

agrammatism A language disturbance; difficulty in the production and comprehension of grammatical features, such as proper use of function words, word endings and word order. Often seen in cases of Broca's aphasia.

alcoholism An addiction to ethanol, the psychoactive agent in alcoholic beverages.

algorithm A procedure that consists of a series of steps that will solve a specific type of problem.

alien hand After split-brain operation, the feeling that patients report of one hand not belonging to them.

alleles Alternative forms of the same gene.

allesthesia In spatial neglect, where patients transfer features of the right-hand side of an object/environment to the left when drawing. Also called allochiria.

allochiria See allesthesia.

alpha activity Rhythmical, medium-frequency activity of the electroencephalogram, usually indicating a state of quiet relaxation.

altruism The unselfish concern of one individual for the welfare of another.

Alzheimer's disease A degenerative brain disorder characterised by neuronal abnormalities which leads to confusional states and cognitive impairment.

amygdala A part of the limbic system of the brain located deep in the temporal lobe; damage causes changes in emotional and aggressive behaviour.

anal stage The second of Freud's psychosexual stages, during which the primary erogenous zone is the anal region. Freud argued that during this time, children take pleasure in retaining or expelling faeces.

anatomical coding A means by which the nervous system represents information; different features are coded by the activity of different neurons.

androgens The primary class of sex hormones in males. The most important androgen is testosterone.

androstenone A chemical secreted by wild boars and thought to be a pheromone.

animism The belief that all animals and all moving objects possess spirits providing their motive force.

anomalous trichromacy A deficit in colour vision in which a photopigment is altered.

anorexia nervosa An eating disorder characterised by attempts to lose weight, sometimes to the point of starvation.

anterior Towards the front.

anterograde amnesia A disorder caused by brain damage that disrupts a person's ability to form new long-term memories of events that occur after the time of the brain damage.

anti-anxiety (anxiolytic) drug A 'tranquilliser', which reduces anxiety. The most common include chlordiazepoxide (Librium) and diazepam (Valium).

antibodies Proteins in the immune system that recognise antigens and help kill invading micro-organisms.

anticipatory anxiety A fear of having a panic attack; may lead to the development of agoraphobia.

antidepressant drugs Drugs used to treat depression.

antigen The unique proteins found on the surface of bacteria; these proteins are what enable the immune system to recognise the bacteria as foreign substances.

antimanic drugs Drugs used to treat bipolar disorder and mania.

antipsychotic drugs The pharmacological agents used to treat severe mental illness such as schizophrenia.

antisocial personality disorder A disorder characterised by a failure to conform to standards of decency; repeated lying and stealing; a failure to sustain lasting, loving relationships; low tolerance of boredom; and a complete lack of guilt.

anxiety A sense of apprehension or doom that is accompanied by many physiological reactions, such as accelerated heart rate, sweaty palms and tightness in the stomach.

anxiolytic drug See anti-anxiety drug.

aphasia Language impairment seen after brain damage and usually involves an inability to produce or comprehend speech.

appeasement gesture A stereotyped gesture made by a submissive animal in response to a threat gesture by a dominant animal; tends to inhibit an attack.

apperceptive agnosia An inability to recognise objects visually.

archetypes Universal thought forms and patterns that Jung believed resided in the collective unconscious.

articulatory loop The component of working memory which stores verbal/auditory information. Also called phonological loop.

artificial intelligence The construction of computer programs that simulate mental function.

Asperger's syndrome Disorder similar to autism but characterised by a narrow and obsessional range of interests.

assertiveness training A technique which trains an individual to be more direct about his/her feelings.

assimilation The process by which new information about the world is modified to fit existing schemata.

associative agnosia An inability to make meaningful associations to visually presented objects.

attachment A social and emotional bond between infant and carer that spans both time and space.

attention deficit hyperactivity disorder (ADHD) A conduct disorder characterised by poor sustained attention, impulsiveness and hyperactivity in children.

attentional bias A tendency to attend to certain stimuli more than others.

attitude A relatively enduring set of beliefs, feelings and intentions towards an object, person, event or symbol.

attribution The process by which people infer the causes of other people's behaviour.

attribution theory Group of theories about how people assign causes to their own or others' behaviour.

attributional ambiguity Tendency of members of stigmatised groups continually to read prejudice and discrimination into innocuous behaviours and even into behaviours favouring them.

attributional style An individual (personality) predisposition to make a certain type of causal attribution for behaviour.

auditory hair cell The sensory neuron of the auditory system; located on the basilar membrane.

authoritarian personality Personality syndrome originating in childhood that predisposes individuals to be prejudiced.

autism spectrum disorder Developmental disorder characterised by abnormal social behaviour, language abnormalities and stereotypical and repetitive patterns of behaviour.

autobiographical memory See episodic memory.

autokinetic effect Optical illusion in which a point of light shining in complete darkness appears to move about.

automatic processing The formation of memories of events and experiences with little or no attention or effort.

automaticity Tendency for categories and associated stereotypes to be activated on the basis of cues, very rapidly and without conscious awareness.

autonomic nervous system (ANS) The portion of the peripheral nervous system that controls the functions of the glands and internal organs.

autotopagnosia An inability to name body parts following damage to the left parietal association cortex.

availability heuristic A general rule for social judgement by which a person judges the likelihood or importance of an event by the ease with which examples of that event come to mind.

aversion therapy A form of treatment in which the client is trained to respond negatively to a neutral stimulus that has been paired with an aversive stimulus.

avoidance response An operant response acquired through negative reinforcement that prevents an aversive stimulus from occurring.

avoidant attachment A kind of attachment in which infants avoid or ignore their mothers and often do not cuddle when held.

axes The criteria used in DSM-IV for classifying mental disorder.

axon A long, thin part of a neuron attached to the soma; divides into a few or many branches, ending in terminal buttons.

B lymphocytes Cells that develop in bone marrow and release immunoglobulins to defend the body against antigens.

backward masking The ability of a stimulus to interfere with the perception of a stimulus presented just before it.

barbiturate A drug that causes sedation; one of several derivatives of barbituric acid.

bariatric surgery Surgery of the intestine to reduce weight loss.

Barnum effect Individuals' acceptance that vague and generalised descriptions of personality that apply to almost all individuals are an accurate reflection of their own personality.

basal ganglia A collection of brain structures underneath the cortex which play an important role in motor behaviour.

base-rate fallacy The failure to consider the likelihood that a person, place or thing is a member of a particular category – some categories are simply larger than others.

basic level categories Default categories that people tend to use most of the time because they are neither too inclusive nor too exclusive.

basic-level concept A concept that makes important distinctions between different categories.

basic orientations Karen Horney's sets of personality characteristics that correspond to the strategies of moving towards others, moving against others and moving away from others.

basic rest–activity cycle (BRAC) The suggestion that our behaviour patterns for drinking, feeding, sleeping and so on follow 90-minute cycles of rest and activity. The cycle is controlled by a biological clock in the pons; during sleep, it controls cycles of REM sleep and slow-wave sleep.

basilar membrane A membrane that divides the cochlea of the inner ear into two compartments. The receptive organ for audition resides here.

behaviour genetics The branch of psychology that studies the role of genetics in behaviour.

behaviour modification Behaviour therapy based on the principles of operant conditioning.

behavioural inhibition system (BIS) The brain system which allows the organism to evaluate how threatening the environment is.

behaviourism A movement in psychology that asserts that the only proper subject matter for scientific study in psychology is observable behaviour.

belief in a just world The belief that people get what they deserve in life – good things happen to good people and bad things happen to bad people.

benzodiazepine A class of drug having anxiolytic ('tranquillising') effects.

beta activity The irregular, high-frequency activity of the electroencephalogram, usually indicating a state of alertness or arousal.

between-groups design See independent groups design.

bilingualism The ability to communicate in two or more languages.

Binet–Simon Scale An intelligence test developed by Binet and Simon in 1905; the precursor of the Stanford–Binet Scale.

biological evolution Changes that take place in the genetic and physical characteristics of a population or group of organisms over time.

bipedalism The ability to move about the environment on two feet.

bipolar cell A neuron in the retina that receives information from photoreceptors and passes it on to the ganglion cells, from which axons proceed through the optic nerves to the brain.

bipolar disorder Alternating states of depression and mania separated by periods of relatively normal affect.

blending After segmenting a word, the putting together of these segments to pronounce a word.

blindsight A disorder resulting from occipital cortex damage in which patients seem to show awareness of objects but declare being consciously unaware of them.

bottom-up processing A perception based on successive analyses of the details of the stimuli that are present.

brain stem The 'stem' of the brain, including the medulla, pons and midbrain.

brainstorming Uninhibited generation of as many ideas as possible in a group, in order to enhance group creativity.

brightness A perceptual dimension of colour, most closely related to the intensity or degree of radiant energy emitted by a visual stimulus.

brightness constancy The tendency to perceive objects as having constant brightness even when they are observed under varying levels of illumination.

bulimia nervosa A loss of control over food intake characterised by gorging binges followed by self-induced vomiting or use of laxatives; also accompanied by feelings of guilt and depression.

bystander intervention The intervention of a person in a situation that appears to require their aid.

c The features which families share in common and can contribute to intelligence.

callosal syndrome The behavioural consequences of lesioning the largest bundle of nerve fibres connecting the two hemispheres, the corpus callosum.

Cartesian dualism See dualism.

cataplexy A neurological disorder in which the person collapses, becoming temporarily paralysed but not unconscious; usually triggered by anger or excitement; apparently related to the paralysis that normally accompanies REM sleep.

catastrophic misinterpretation The interpretation of bodily sensations as physical threat.

catatonic schizophrenia A form of schizophrenia characterised primarily by various motor disturbances, including catatonic postures and waxy flexibility.

causal event or determinant An event that causes another event to occur.

central executive The component of working memory that coordinates the other elements of working memory such as the phonological loop and the visuospatial scratchpad.

central nervous system (CNS) The brain and the spinal cord.

central traits Descriptive traits that are significantly more important than other traits in organising information about a person into an impression.

cerebellum A pair of hemispheres resembling the cerebral hemispheres but much smaller and lying beneath and at the back of them; controls posture and movements, especially rapid ones.

cerebral cortex The outer layer of the cerebral hemispheres of the brain, approximately 3 mm thick.

cerebral hemisphere The largest part of the brain; covered by the cerebral cortex and containing parts of the brain that evolved most recently.

cerebrospinal fluid (CSF) The liquid in which the brain and spinal cord float; provides a shock-absorbing cushion.

chemosensation The process of sensing chemical stimuli by the chemosenses (olfaction and gustation).

chemosense One of the two sense modalities (gustation and olfaction) that detect the presence of chemical molecules present in the environment.

child-directed speech The speech of an adult directed towards a child; differs in important features from adult-directed speech and tends to facilitate learning of language by children.

cholesterol lipid, a chemical made of fat, present in the body which is necessary but which, in excess, can be a risk factor for ill-health.

chromosomal aberration The rearrangement of genes within chromosomes or a change in the total number of chromosomes.

chromosomes Rod-like structures in the nuclei of living cells; contain genes.

chronotype A behaviour type in which people prefer, and operate more effectively during, a specific time of day - morning or evening/night.

chunking A process by which information is simplified by rules which make it easily remembered once the rules are learned. For example, the string of letters TWAIBMBBC is easier to remember if a person learns the rule that organises them into smaller 'chunks': TWA, IBM and BBC.

cilia Hair-like appendages of a cell; involved in movement or in transducing sensory information. Cilia are found on the receptors in the auditory and vestibular systems.

cingulotomy The surgical destruction of the cingulum bundle, which connects the prefrontal cortex with the limbic system; helps to reduce intense anxiety and the symptoms of obsessive-compulsive disorder.

circadian rhythm A daily rhythmical change in behaviour or physiological process.

classical conditioning The process by which a response normally elicited by one stimulus (the UCS) comes to be controlled by another stimulus (the CS) as well.

client-centred therapy A form of therapy in which the client is allowed to decide what to talk about without strong direction and judgement from the therapist.

clinical judgements Diagnoses of mental disorders or predictions of future behaviour based largely on experts' experience and knowledge.

clinical neuropsychology The branch of psychology concerned with the identification and treatment of the behavioural consequences of nervous system disorders and injuries.

clinical psychology The branch of psychology concerned with the investigation and treatment of abnormal behaviour and mental disorders.

cochlea A snail-shaped chamber set in bone in the inner ear, where audition takes place.

cocktail-party phenomenon The ability to attend selectively to auditory material against a background of competing auditory stimuli.

cognitive algebra Approach to the study of impression formation which focuses on how people combine attributes that have valence into an overall positive or negative impression.

cognitive behavioural therapy (CBT) A treatment method that focuses on altering the client's maladaptive thoughts, beliefs and perceptions.

cognitive dissonance theory The theory that changes in attitude can be motivated by an unpleasant state of tension caused by a disparity between a person's beliefs or attitudes and their behaviour, especially beliefs or attitudes that are related to the person's self-esteem.

cognitive neuroscience The branch of neuroscience which seeks to localise cognitive functions (such as memory, attention, language, etc.) in the brain.

cognitive psychology The branch of psychology that studies complex behaviours and mental processes, such as perception, attention, learning and memory, verbal behaviour, concept formation and problem-solving.

cognitive reappraisal Any coping strategy in which one alters one's perception of the threat posed by a stressor to reduce stress.

cognitive rehabilitation Specific form of rehabilitation in which patients are encouraged to recover functions such as memory and language which have been impaired by brain injury.

cognitive restructuring Altering misconceptions about the consequences of bodily sensation.

cognitive science The branch of psychology which seeks to understand human cognitive function by using artificial intelligence and computer models.

cognitive structures According to Piaget, mental representations or rules, such as schemata or concepts, that are used for understanding and dealing with the world and for thinking about and solving problems.

cognitive triad Pessimistic thinking about the self, the present and the future.

collective effort model People will only work hard on a collective task to the degree that they expect their efforts to be instrumental in leading to outcomes that they value personally.

collective unconscious According to Jung, the part of the unconscious that contains memories and ideas inherited from our ancestors over the course of evolution.

colour mixing The perception of two or more lights of different wavelengths seen together as light of an intermediate wavelength.

commitment The desire or intention to continue an interpersonal relationship.

commons dilemma Social dilemma in which cooperation by all benefits all, but competition by all harms all.

companionate love Love that is characterised by a deep, enduring affection and caring for another person, accompanied by a strong desire to maintain the relationship.

comparative psychology The branch of psychology that studies the behaviours of a variety of organisms in an attempt to understand the adaptive and functional significance of the behaviours and their relation to evolution.

competition A striving or vying with others who share the same ecological niche for food, mates and territory.

compliance Engaging in a particular behaviour at another person's request, not because you have an underlying attitude that favours the behaviour.

componential intelligence According to Sternberg, the mental mechanisms people use to plan and execute tasks; includes metacomponents, performance components, and knowledge acquisition components.

compulsion An irresistible impulse to repeat some action over and over even though it serves no useful purpose.

computerised tomography (CT) Technique that uses a special X-ray machine and a computer to produce images of the brain that appear as slices taken parallel to the top of the skull.

concept A category of objects or situations that share some common attributes.

concordance research Research that studies the degree of similarity between twins in traits expressed. Twins are said to be concordant for a trait if either both or neither twin expresses it and discordant if only one twin expresses it.

conditional response (CR) In classical conditioning, the response elicited by the CS.

conditional stimulus (CS) In classical conditioning, a stimulus which, because of its repeated association with the unconditional stimulus (UCS), eventually elicits a conditional response (CR).

conditioned emotional response A classically conditioned response produced by a stimulus that evokes an emotional response, in most cases including behavioural and physiological components.

conditioned reinforcer (or punisher) A stimulus that acquires its reinforcing (or punishing) properties through association with a primary reinforcer (or punisher). Sometimes referred to as a secondary reinforcer (or punisher).

conditions of worth Conditions that others place on us for receiving their positive regard.

conduct disorder Impairment in the child's ability to inhibit its own antisocial and deviant behaviour.

cone A photoreceptor that is responsible for acute daytime vision and for colour perception.

confidentiality Privacy of participants and non-disclosure of their participation in a research project.

configural model Asch's gestalt-based model of impression formation, in which central traits have a disproportionate role in configuring the final impression.

confirmation bias A tendency to seek evidence that might confirm a hypothesis rather than evidence that might disconfirm it; a logical error.

conformity The adoption of attitudes and behaviours shared by a particular group of people – the internalisation of a group norm as a standard for one's own behaviour.

confounding of variables An inadvertent alteration of more than one variable during an experiment. The results of an experiment involving confounded variables permit no valid conclusions about cause and effect.

conjugate movement The cooperative movement of the eyes, which ensures that the image of an object falls on identical portions of both retinas.

connectionism The modelling of human cognitive function based on computer simulation.

conscience The internalisation of the rules and restrictions of society; it determines which behaviours are permissible and punishes wrongdoing with feelings of guilt.

consensual behaviour Behaviour that is shared by many people; behaviour that is similar from one person to the next. To the extent that different people engage in the same behaviour, their behaviour is consensual.

conservation Understanding that specific properties of objects (height, weight, volume, length) remain the same despite apparent changes in the shape or arrangement of those objects.

consistency The extent to which a person behaves the same way every time they are in the same situation.

consolidation The process by which information in short-term memory is transferred to long-term memory, presumably because of physical changes that occur in neurons in the brain.

consumer psychology The branch of psychology which studies the factors which influence consumer decision-making and preference.

contact hypothesis The view that prejudice will disappear if you bring people from different races together to interact with one another.

content word A noun, verb, adjective or adverb that conveys meaning.

context-dependent memory See place-dependent memory.

contextual intelligence According to Sternberg, intelligence that reflects the behaviours that were subject to natural selection: adaptation – fitting oneself into one's environment by developing useful skills and behaviours; selection – finding one's own niche in the environment; and shaping – changing the environment.

contingency theory Fiedler's interactionist theory that the effectiveness of particular leadership styles depends on situational and task factors.

contralateral Residing in the side of the body opposite the reference point.

control group A comparison group used in an experiment, the members of which are exposed to the naturally occurring or zero value of the independent variable.

conventional level Kohlberg's second level of moral development, in which people realise that society has instituted moral rules to maintain order and to serve the best interests of its citizenry.

convergence The result of conjugate eye movements whereby the fixation point for each eye is identical; feedback from these movements provides information about the distance of objects from the viewer.

conversation analysis In qualitative research, the process of analysing conversations for meaning, themes, and patterns (in speech and psychology).

conversion A defence mechanism that involves converting an intrapsychic conflict into a physical form, such as blindness, deafness, paralysis or numbness.

conversion disorder A somatoform disorder involving the actual loss of bodily function, such as blindness, paralysis and numbness, due to excessive anxiety.

conversion effect When minority influence brings about a sudden and dramatic internal and private change in the attitudes of a majority.

coordination loss Deterioration in group performance in comparison to individual performance due to problems in coordinating behaviour.

coping strategy A plan of action that a person follows to reduce the perceived level of stress, either in anticipation of encountering a stressor or in response to its occurrence.

cornea The transparent tissue covering the front of the eye.

coronary heart disease (CHD) The narrowing of blood vessels that supply nutrients to the heart.

corpus callosum A large bundle of axons ('white matter') that connects the cortex of the two cerebral hemispheres.

correctional mechanism In a regulatory process, the mechanism that is capable of restoring the system variable to the set point.

correlation coefficient A measurement of the degree to which two variables are related.

correlational study The observation of two or more variables in the behaviour or other characteristics of people or other animals.

counterbalancing A systematic variation of conditions in an experiment, such as the order of presentation of stimuli, so that different participants encounter them in different orders; prevents confounding of independent variables with time-dependent processes such as habituation or fatigue.

counter-transference The process by which the therapist projects their emotions onto the client.

covert sensitisation A method used by behavioural therapists in which a client imagines the aversive consequences of their inappropriate behaviour.

cranial nerve A bundle of nerve fibres attached to the base of the brain; conveys sensory information from the face and head and carries messages to muscles and glands.

creativity A process through which end products are created, usually in novel, unusual or unexpected ways.

cri-du-chat syndrome A genetic disorder arising from partial deletion of chromosome 5 which is associated with mental retardation and mewing sounds (hence cri-du-chat).

critical period A specific time in development during which certain experiences must occur for normal development to occur.

cross-cultural psychology The branch of psychology that studies and compares the effects of culture on behaviour.

crowd A group event involving a large number of people in the same place at the same time acting in a collective fashion.

CS pre-exposure effect The name given to the effect seen in latent inhibition – the phenomenon whereby a novel object is more successfully paired with a familiar one in conditioning.

cultural evolution The adaptive changes of cultures in response to environmental changes over time.

cultural psychology The branch of psychology which studies variations in behaviour within, but not necessarily across, cultures.

culture-bound syndrome Highly unusual mental disorders, similar in nature to non-psychotic mental disorders, that appear to be specific to only one or a few cultures.

cumulative recorder A mechanical device connected to an operant chamber for the purpose of recording operant responses as they occur in time.

cytoskeleton The skeletal structure of neurons.

debriefing Full disclosure to research participants of the true nature and purpose of a research project after its completion.

deductive reasoning Inferring specific instances from general principles or rules.

deep dyslexia A severe inability to read; common words are sometimes read but are often replaced by semantically similar words.

deep processing The analysis of the complex characteristics of a stimulus, such as its meaning or its relationship to other stimuli.

defence mechanisms Mental systems that become active whenever unconscious instinctual drives of the id come into conflict with internalised prohibitions of the superego.

deferred imitation A child's ability to imitate the actions they have observed others perform. Piaget believed deferred imitation to result from the child's increasing ability to form mental representations of behaviour performed by others.

deferred imitation paradigm A child is exposed to an adult who is performing actions with a set of novel stimuli; after a delay, the child is then allowed to manipulate objects used by the experimenter. Identical use indicates a degree of imitation and learning.

deindividuation The loss of one's individuality and sense of personal responsibility in collective events.

delta activity The rhythmical activity of the electroencephalogram, having a frequency of less than 3.5 Hz, indicating deep (slow-wave) sleep.

delusions Beliefs that are obviously contrary to fact.

delusions of control The false belief that one's thoughts and actions are being controlled by other people or forces.

delusions of grandeur The false belief that one is famous, powerful or important.

delusions of persecution The false belief that other people are plotting against one.

dementia Cognitive deterioration associated with degenerative brain disorders.

dementia of the Alzheimer type (DAT) Cognitive impairment that arises from Alzheimer's disease.

dendrite A tree-like part of a neuron on which the terminal buttons of other neurons form synapses.

dependent variable The event whose value is measured in an experiment. Manipulation of independent variables demonstrates whether they affect the value of dependent variables.

depersonalisation The perception and treatment of self and others not as unique individual persons but as prototypical embodiments of a social group.

detector In a regulatory process, a mechanism that signals when the system variable deviates from its set point.

determinant See causal event.

deuteranopia A form of hereditary anomalous colour vision; caused by defective 'green' cones in the retina.

developmental dyslexia A difficulty in learning to read despite adequate intelligence and appropriate educational opportunity.

developmental psychology The branch of psychology that studies the changes in behavioural, perceptual and cognitive capacities of organisms as a function of age and experience.

deviation IQ A procedure for computing the intelligence quotient; compares a child's score with those received by other children of the same chronological age.

dichotic listening A task that requires a person to listen to one of two different messages being presented simultaneously, one to each ear, through headphones.

dichromacy A deficit in colour vision in which a photopigment is missing.

difference threshold An alternative name for just-noticeable difference (jnd).

diffusion of responsibility An explanation of the failure of bystander intervention stating that, when several bystanders are present, no one person assumes responsibility for helping.

discourse analysis Qualitative method of analysis which involves the identification of themes, thoughts and ideas from transcripts of conversations or discussions.

discrimination (1) In operant conditioning, responding only when a specific discriminative stimulus is present but not when similar stimuli are present. (2) The differential treatment of people based on their membership in a particular group – discrimination is typically 'against' an out-group and in favour of the in-group. (3) In classical conditioning, the appearance of a conditioned response (CR) when one stimulus is presented (the CS+) but not another (the CS−).

discriminative stimulus In operant conditioning, the stimulus that sets the occasion for responding because, in the past, a behaviour has produced certain consequences in the presence of that stimulus.

disorganised schizophrenia A type of schizophrenia characterised primarily by disturbances of thought and a flattened or silly affect.

display rule A culturally determined rule that prescribes the expression of emotions in particular situations.

dispositional factors Individual personality characteristics that affect a person's behaviour.

dissociative disorders A class of disorders in which anxiety is reduced by a sudden disruption in consciousness, which in turn produces changes in one's sense of identity.

dissociative identity disorder A rare dissociative disorder in which two or more distinct personalities exist within the same person; each personality dominates in turn.

distinctive feature A physical characteristic of an object that helps distinguish it from other objects.

distinctiveness The extent to which a person engages in a particular behaviour in one situation but not in other situations.

divided attention Attention which is divided among two or more tasks.

dizygotic (DZ) twins wins that are fertilised from different ova (and are, therefore, genetically different).

DNA 'Deoxyribonucleic acid'. The DNA structure resembles that of a twisted ladder. Strands of sugar and phosphates are connected by rungs made from adenine and thymine and guanine and cytosine.

doctrine of apperception The belief that we do not see objects as separate elements but as wholes.

doctrine of the association of ideas The belief that various associations are made between events and ideas, which allow meaningful thought to occur.

dominant allele The form of the gene that controls the expression of a trait. When a gene pair contains two dominant alleles or when it contains both a dominant and a recessive allele, the trait regulated by the dominant gene will be expressed.

door-in-the-face tactic Multiple-request technique to gain compliance, in which the focal request is preceded by a larger request that is bound to be refused.

dopamine hypothesis The hypothesis that the positive symptoms of schizophrenia are caused by overactivity of synapses in the brain that use dopamine.

double-aspect theory The belief that mental and physical events are characteristics of the same underlying entity.

double-bind The conflict caused for a child when they are given inconsistent messages or cues from a parent.

double-blind study An experiment in which neither the subject nor the experimenter knows the value of the independent variable.

Down syndrome A genetic disorder caused by a chromosomal aberration resulting in an extra twenty-first chromosome. People having Down syndrome are generally short, have broad skulls and round faces, and suffer impairments in physical, psychomotor and cognitive development.

drive A condition, often caused by physiological changes or homeostatic disequilibrium, that energises an organism's behaviour.

drive reduction hypothesis The hypothesis that a drive (resulting from physiological need or deprivation) produces an unpleasant state that causes an organism to engage in motivated behaviours. Reduction of drive is assumed to be reinforcing.

DSM-IV TR *See Diagnostic and Statistical Manual IV.*

dual-action antidepressants Antidepressants which block certain serotonin receptors and inhibit its reuptake.

dual-route model of reading A model which proposes that there are two, non-semantic routes that take the reader from spelling to sound. The lexical route retrieves words from the mental lexicon; the sublexical route converts letters into sound using grapheme–phoneme correspondence rules.

dual-task methodology A protocol in attention research whereby the participant undertakes two tasks simultaneously in order to determine the degree to which the performance of one interferes with the other.

dualism or Cartesian dualism The philosophical belief that reality consists of mind and matter.

Duchenne smile The genuine smile of joy characterised by the activation of specific facial muscles.

dyslexia A disorder impaired reading ability.

echoic memory A form of sensory memory for sounds that have just been perceived.

eclectic approach A form of therapy in which the therapist uses whatever method they feel will work best for a particular client at a particular time.

educational psychology The branch of psychology which applies psychological principles to our understanding of the educational process and children's learning and adjustment in education.

ego The self. The ego also serves as the general manager of personality, making decisions regarding the pleasures that will be pursued at the id's request and the moral dictates of the superego that will be followed.

egocentrism Self-centredness; preoperational children can see the world only from their own perspective.

ego-ideal The internalisation of what a person would like to be.

egoistic relative deprivation Sense of personally having less than one feels one is entitled to relative to one's aspirations or to other individuals.

elaboration likelihood model A model that explains the effectiveness of persuasion. The central route requires the person to think critically about an argument, and the peripheral route entails the association of the argument with something positive.

elaborative rehearsal The processing of information on a meaningful level, such as forming associations, attending to the meaning of the material, thinking about it and so on.

Electra complex In Freudian thinking, a girl's attachment to her father; named after the mythical Electra who killed her mother and mother's lover in order to avenge her father's death.

electrocardiogram (ECG) The measurement and graphical presentation of the electrical activity of the heart, recorded by means of electrodes attached to the skin.

electroconvulsive therapy (ECT) Treatment of severe depression that involves passing small amounts of electric current through the brain to produce seizure activity.

electrocortical stimulation mapping A method of localising language function in the brain (of patients) by electrically stimulating the cortex.

electrodermal response (EDR) (see galvanic skin response).

electroencephalogram (EEG) The measurement and graphical presentation of the electrical activity of the brain, recorded by means of electrodes attached to the scalp.

electroencephalography (EEG) A technique which measures the electrical activity of the brain using electrodes.

electromyogram (EMG) The measurement and graphical presentation of the electrical activity of muscles, recorded by means of electrodes attached to the skin above them.

electro-oculogram (EOG) The measurement and graphical presentation of the electrical activity caused by movements of the eye, recorded by means of electrodes attached to the skin adjacent to the eye.

elevation A monocular cue of depth perception; objects nearer the horizon are seen as farther from the viewer.

embryo stage The second stage of prenatal development, beginning two weeks and ending about eight weeks after conception, during which the heart begins to beat, the brain starts to function and most of the major body structures begin to form.

emotion A relatively brief display of a feeling made in response to environmental events having motivational significance or to memories of such events.

emotion-focused coping Any coping behaviour that is directed towards changing one's own emotional reaction to a stressor.

emotional disclosure A method by which trauma can be reduced by writing about that trauma and explaining why the response to trauma exists

emotional intelligence An understanding of the social and emotional components of interactions with others.

emotional stability The tendency to be relaxed and at peace with oneself.

empiricism The philosophical view that all knowledge is obtained through the senses.

encephalisation Increased brain size.

encoding The process by which sensory information is converted into a form that can be used by the brain's memory system.

encoding specificity The principle that how we encode information determines our ability to retrieve it later.

endocrine gland A gland that secretes a hormone.

enuresis Bed-wetting; a slow-wave sleep disorder.

enzymes Proteins that regulate the structure of bodily cells and the processes occurring within those cells.

epigenetics A field of study examining how experience and learning can alter gene expression.

epilepsy A seizure disorder which involves excessive and uncontrollable firing of neurons.

episodic memory A type of long-term memory that serves as a record of our life's experiences. Also called autobiographical memory.

ergonomics/human factors psychology The branch of psychology that studies the ways in which people and machines work together and helps design machines that are safer and easier to operate.

escape response An operant response acquired through negative reinforcement that terminates an aversive stimulus.

ethnolinguistic group Social group defined principally in terms of its language.

ethology The branch of comparative psychology which studies the behaviour of animals and uses this information to draw conclusions about human behaviour and evolution.

event-related potential (ERP) A technique which records the brain's electrical activity across several presentations of the same stimuli.

evolutionary preparedness The notion that we are predisposed to fear certain objects and contexts.

evolutionary psychology The branch of psychology that studies the ways in which an organism's evolutionary history contributes to the development of behavioural patterns and cognitive strategies related to reproduction and survival during its lifetime.

exemplar A memory of particular examples of objects or situations that are used as the basis of classifying objects or situations into concepts.

exhibitionism Exposure of genitals in public for sexual gratification.

expectancy The belief that a certain consequence will follow a certain action.

experiential intelligence According to Sternberg, the ability to deal effectively with novel situations and to solve automatically problems that have been encountered previously.

experiment A study in which the experimenter changes the value of an independent variable and observes whether this manipulation affects the value of a dependent variable. Only experiments can confirm the existence of cause-and-effect relations among variables.

experimental brain lesion Deliberate damage to a particular region of the brain.

experimental group A group of participants in an experiment, the members of which are exposed to a particular value of the independent variable, which has been manipulated by the experimenter.

experimental psychology The experimental study of human behaviour, especially sensation and perception.

explicit memory Memory that can be described verbally and of which a person is therefore aware.

expressed emotion Expressions of criticism, hostility and emotional over-involvement by family members towards a person with schizophrenia.

externality effect In infancy, the idea that the child is more concerned with the contours of visual stimuli and rarely attends to internal features.

extinction In classical conditioning, the elimination of a response that occurs when the CS is repeatedly presented without being followed by the UCS. A decrease in the frequency of a previously reinforced response because it is no longer followed by a reinforcer.

extraversion The tendency to seek the company of other people, to be lively, and to engage in conversation and other social behaviours with them.

facial feedback hypothesis The notion that our awareness of facial expression influences the way we feel.

factor analysis A statistical procedure that identifies common factors among groups of data.

false consensus The tendency for a person to perceive their own behaviour as representative of general consensus of how other people behave.

family therapy A form of therapy in which the maladaptive relationships among family members is inferred from their behaviour and attempts are made to restructure these behaviours into more adaptive ones.

fast mapping The quick learning of new, content words by children.

fetish Unusual sexual attachment to objects such as articles of clothing, learned through classical conditioning.

field experiment An experiment that is conducted in a realistic environment and over which the experimenter has little experimental control.

fight or flight response Physiological reactions that help ready us to fight or to flee a dangerous situation.

figure A visual stimulus that is perceived as a self-contained object.

fissures Grooves between the bulges (gyri) of the cortex.

five-factor model A theory stating that personality is composed of five primary dimensions: neuroticism, extraversion, openness, agreeableness and conscientiousness. This theory was developed using factor analyses of ratings of the words that people use to describe personality characteristics.

fixation (1) A brief interval between saccadic eye movements during which the eye does not move; visual information is gathered during this time. (2) An unconscious obsession with an erogenous zone resulting from failure to resolve the crisis associated with the corresponding stage of psychosexual development.

fixation point The area in space where a gaze is fixed.

fixed-interval schedule A schedule of reinforcement in which the first response that is made after a fixed interval of time since the previous reinforcement (or the start of the session) is reinforced.

fixed-ratio schedule A schedule of reinforcement in which reinforcement occurs only after a fixed number of responses have been made since the previous reinforcement (or the start of the session).

flashbulb memory A lucid memory for an event or experience that occurred during a particularly emotional experience.

flooding The intense arousal of anxious patients, usually through exposure to the anxiety-provoking stimulus or context, which is intended to demonstrate that no harm comes from such exposure.

foetal learning The notion that the foetus is capable of rudimentary learning while in the womb.

foetal stage Third and final stage of prenatal development which lasts for about seven months, beginning with the appearance of bone tissue and ending with birth.

foot-in-the-door tactic Multiple-request technique to gain compliance, in which the focal request is preceded by a smaller request that is bound to be accepted.

forensic/criminological psychology The branch of psychology which uses psychological principles to study and assist in the legal and criminal process.

form constancy The tendency to perceive objects as having a constant form, even when they are rotated or their distance from the observer changes.

formal concept A category of objects or situations defined by listing their common essential characteristics, as dictionary definitions do.

fovea A small pit near the centre of the retina containing densely packed cones; responsible for the most acute and detailed vision.

fraternal twins See dizygotic (DZ) twins.

fraternalistic relative deprivation Sense that one's group has less than it is entitled to relative to its aspirations or to other groups.

free association A method of Freudian analysis in which an individual is asked to relax, clear their mind of current thoughts, and then report all thoughts, images, perceptions and feelings that come to mind.

free nerve ending An unencapsulated (naked) dendrite of somatosensory neurons.

frontal lobe The front portion of the cerebral cortex, including Broca's speech area and the motor cortex; damage impairs movement, planning and flexibility in behavioural strategies.

frotteurism Rubbing against a person in public for sexual gratification.

frustration–aggression hypothesis Theory that all frustration leads to aggression, and all aggression comes from frustration. Used to explain prejudice and intergroup aggression.

function word A preposition, article or other word that conveys little of the meaning of a sentence but is important in specifying its grammatical structure.

functional hemispheric asymmetry The idea that a function is located in one cerebral hemisphere.

functional magnetic resonance imaging (fMRI) A development of MRI which allows the observation of brain function and not just structure.

functionalism The strategy of understanding a species' structural or behavioural features by attempting to establish their usefulness with respect to survival and reproductive success.

fundamental attribution error The tendency to overestimate the significance of dispositional factors and underestimate the significance of situational factors in explaining other people's behaviour.

fundamental frequency The lowest, and usually most intense, frequency of a complex sound; most often perceived as the sound's basic pitch.

fusiform face area Small region in the frontal lobe which is thought to be specialised for the recognition and identification of faces. Also called fusiform gyrus.

g factor According to Spearman, a factor of intelligence that is common to all intellectual tasks; includes apprehension of experience, education of relations and eduction of correlates.

gain–loss hypothesis Paradox of liking people more if they initially dislike us and then later like us; and of liking them less if the sequence is reversed.

galvanic skin response (GSR) A measure of the electrical activity of the skin.

ganglion cell A neuron in the retina that receives information from photoreceptors by means of bipolar cells and from which axons proceed through the optic nerves to the brain.

gaze Looking at someone's eyes.

gender schema theory Argues that children construct a 'schema' – a mental representation – of male and female and pay especial attention to features of their own sex.

general adaptation syndrome (GAS) The model proposed by Selye to describe the body's adaptation to chronic exposure to severe stressors. The body passes through an orderly sequence of three physiological stages: alarm, resistance and exhaustion.

general language discrimination hypothesis The notion that children can discriminate sentences from two languages based on extracting linguistic properties from these languages.

generalisation (1) The conclusion that the results obtained from a sample apply also to the population from which the sample was taken. (2) In classical conditioning, CRs elicited by stimuli that resemble the CS used in training. (3) In operant conditioning, the occurrence of responding when a stimulus similar (but not identical) to the discriminative stimulus is present.

generalised anxiety disorder (GAD) Excessive worry about all matters relating to the individual's life.

genes Small units of chromosomes that direct the synthesis of proteins and enzymes.

genetic disorders Inherited disorders of behaviour that arise from faulty genetic material.

genetic epistemology The study of the origin of knowledge in the development of the child.

genetics The study of the genetic make-up of organisms and how it influences physical and behavioural characteristics.

genital stage The final of Freud's psychosexual stages (from puberty through adolescence). During this stage, the adolescent develops adult sexual desires.

genotype An organism's genetic make-up.

geon According to Biederman, an elementary shape that can serve as a prototype in recognising objects; a given object can consist of one or more individual geons.

gerontology The study of the process of ageing.

Gestalt psychology A school of psychology that asserts that the perception of objects is produced by particular configurations of the elements of stimuli; that cognitive processes can be understood by studying their organisation, not their elements.

gestalt therapy A form of therapy emphasising the unity of mind and body by teaching the client to 'get in touch' with unconscious bodily sensations and emotional feelings.

Gilles de la Tourette's syndrome A neurological disorder characterised by tics and involuntary utterances, some of which may involve obscenities and the repetition of others' utterances.

glia/glial cell A cell of the central nervous system that provides support for neurons and supplies them with some essential chemicals.

glucocorticoid A chemical, such as cortisol, that influences the metabolism of glucose, the main energy source of the body.

glucose A sugar which is the primary source of fuel for the body's cells.

glucostatic hypothesis The hypothesis that hunger is caused by a low level or low availability of glucose, a condition that is monitored by specialised sensory neurons.

glucostats Hypothetical entity which detects decreases in blood sugar.

glycogen An insoluble carbohydrate that can be synthesised from glucose or converted to it; used to store nutrients.

good continuation A Gestalt law of organisation; given two or more interpretations of elements that form the outline of the figure, the simplest interpretation will be preferred.

grapheme–phoneme correspondence (GPC) rules The rules used to convert written words into spoken sounds.

graphemes The smallest units of written words.

grey matter The portions of the central nervous system that are abundant in cell bodies of neurons rather than axons.

ground A visual stimulus that is perceived as a formless background against which objects are seen.

grounded theory A form of qualitative analysis which deliberately constructs theories on the basis of information derived from transcripts of conversations and discussions.

group A collection of individuals who have a shared definition of who they are and what they should think, feel and do – people in the same group generally have common interests and goals.

group polarisation The tendency for a group decision to be more extreme than the mean of its members' positions, in the direction favoured by the mean.

group psychotherapy Therapy in which two or more clients meet simultaneously with a therapist, discussing problems within a supportive and understanding environment.

groupthink The tendency to avoid dissent in the attempt to achieve group consensus in the course of decision-making.

gustation The sense of taste.

gyri Bulges in the surfaces of the cortex.

h The proportion of variance associated with genetic differences among individuals.

habituation The simplest form of learning; learning not to respond to an unimportant event that occurs repeatedly.

hallucinations Perceptual experiences that occur in the absence of external stimulation of the corresponding sensory organ.

handedness The degree to which an individual preferentially uses one hand for most activities.

haze A monocular cue of depth perception; objects that are less distinct in their outline and texture are seen as farther from the viewer.

health psychology The branch of psychology which applies psychological principles to health behaviour and illness prevention.

heredity The sum of the traits and tendencies inherited from a person's parents and other biological ancestors.

heritability The degree to which the variability of a particular trait in a particular population of organisms is a result of genetic differences among those organisms.

hertz (Hz) The primary measure of the frequency of vibration of sound waves; cycles per second.

heuristics Cognitive short-cuts that provide adequately accurate inferences for most of us most of the time.

'hidden observer' phenomenon The phenomenon whereby the hypnotist places a hand on the shoulder of the hypnotised and appears to be able to talk to a hidden part of the hypnotised person's body.

hippocampus A structure in the limbic system, located deep in the temporal lobe, which plays an important role in memory and learning.

homeostasis The process by which important physiological characteristics (such as body temperature and blood pressure) are regulated so that they remain at their optimum level.

hormone A chemical substance secreted by an endocrine gland that has physiological effects on target cells in other organs.

hue A perceptual dimension of colour, most closely related to the wavelength of a pure light.

human factors psychology See ergonomics.

humanistic approach An approach to the study of personality in which the emphasis is placed on the positive, fulfilling aspects of life.

humanistic psychology An approach to the study of human behaviour that emphasises human experience, choice and creativity, self-realisation, and positive growth.

humanistic therapy A form of therapy focusing on the person's unique potential for personal growth and self-actualisation.

Huntington's disease A genetic disorder caused by a dominant lethal gene in which a person experiences slow but progressive mental and physical deterioration.

hypnosis The process whereby verbal instructions can be acted on by another without conscious awareness of these instructions.

hypnotic analgesia The use of hypnosis to alleviate pain.

hypochondriasis A somatoform disorder involving persistent and excessive worry about developing a serious illness. People with this disorder often misinterpret the appearance of normal physical aches and pains.

hypothalamus A region of the brain located just above the pituitary gland; controls the autonomic nervous system and many behaviours related to regulation and survival, such as eating, drinking, fighting, shivering and sweating.

hypothesis A statement, usually designed to be tested by an experiment, that tentatively expresses a cause-and-effect relationship between variables.

hypothetico-deductive A methodological approach which sets hypotheses and then constructs experiments to test them.

iconic memory A form of sensory memory that holds a brief visual image of a scene that has just been perceived.

id The unconscious reservoir of libido, the psychic energy that fuels instincts and psychic processes.

idealism The belief that all ideas ultimately come from information from the senses.

idiot savants Autistic individuals who excel in specific abilities such as mental arithmetic, drawing, painting or music.

illusion of out-group homogeneity belief that members of groups to which one does not belong are more similar to one another than are members of one's own group.

illusory correlation the perception of an apparent relation between two distinctive elements that does not actually exist or is enormously exaggerated.

immune system network of organs and cells that protects the body from invading bacteria, viruses and other foreign substances.

immunoglobulins The antibodies that are released by B lymphocytes.

implicit association test (IAT) Test to measure the speed with which people unconsciously and automatically associate evaluative words with social categories – a measure of unconsciously held stereotypes.

implicit memory Memory that cannot be described verbally and of which a person is therefore not aware.

implosion therapy A form of therapy that attempts to rid people of fears by arousing them intensely until their responses diminish through habituation and they learn that nothing bad happens.

impression formation The way in which we form impressions of others and attribute specific characteristics and traits to them.

inattentional blindness A perceptual phenomenon whereby a person fails to see particularly obvious or dramatic changes to a visual stimulus because their attention has been drawn to another aspect of it.

inclusive fitness The reproductive success of those who share common genes.

incongruence A discrepancy between a client's real and ideal selves.

independent groups design A design whereby each group in an experiment contains different participants. Also called between-groups design.

independent variable The variable that is manipulated in an experiment as a means of determining cause-and-effect relations. Manipulation of an independent variable demonstrates whether it affects the value of the dependent variable.

individual differences The branch of psychology concerned with the individual factors that make us different (such as personality, sex, race, etc.).

inductive reasoning Inferring general principles or rules from specific facts.

infantile amnesia Loss of memory for events that occur in infancy.

inflection change in the form of a word (usually by adding a suffix) to denote a grammatical feature such as tense or number.

information processing An approach used by cognitive psychologists to explain the workings of the brain; information received through the senses is processed by systems of neurons in the brain.

informational influence An influence to accept information from another as evidence about reality.

informed consent Agreement to participate as a subject in an experiment after being informed about the nature of the research and any possible adverse effects.

ingratiation Strategic attempt to get someone to like you in order to obtain compliance with a request.

inner speech To Vygotsky, the internalisation of words and the mental manipulation of words as symbols for objects in the environment.

insomnia Chronic and relentless inability to fall asleep at the appropriate times.

insula Area of the brain located in the temporal cortex and involved in various behaviours including smell, taste, time perception, movement and language.

intelligence A person's ability to learn and remember information, to recognise concepts and their relations, and to apply the information to their own behaviour in an adaptive way.

intelligence quotient (IQ) A simplified single measure of general intelligence; by definition, the ratio of a person's mental age to their chronological age, multiplied by 100; often derived by other formulas.

interactionism The view that the mind and body are separate physical entities which interact.

intergroup relations Relations between groups or between individuals who are members of different groups and who are interacting in terms of their respective group memberships.

intermanual conflict The effect sometimes seen after split-brain surgery whereby one hand appears to behave in a contradictory way to the other.

intermittent reinforcement The occasional reinforcement of a particular behaviour; produces responding that is more resistant to extinction.

International Classification of Disorders 10 (ICD-10) A manual similar to DSM.

interpersonal attraction People's tendency to approach each other and to evaluate each other positively.

interpersonal distance The distance apart at which people feel most comfortable in interacting in different situations, relationships and cultures.

interposition A monocular cue of depth perception; an object that partially occludes another object is perceived as closer.

inter-rater reliability The degree to which two or more independent observers agree in their ratings of another organism's behaviour.

intervening variables In behaviourism, the variables that modify the relationship between stimulus and response.

intraspecific aggression The attack by one animal upon another member of its species.

introspection Literally, 'looking within', in an attempt to describe one's own memories, perceptions, cognitive processes or motivations.

introversion The tendency to avoid the company of other people, especially large groups of people; shyness.

ion A positively or negatively charged particle; produced when many substances dissolve in water.

ion channel A special protein molecule located in the membrane of a cell; controls the entry or exit of particular ions.

ion transporter A special protein molecule located in the membrane of a cell; actively transports ions into or out of the cell.

iris The pigmented muscle of the eye that controls the size of the pupil.

isolation aphasia A language disturbance that includes an inability to comprehend speech or to produce meaningful speech accompanied by the ability to repeat speech and to learn new sequences of words; caused by brain damage to the left temporal/parietal cortex that spares Wernicke's area.

James–Lange theory A theory of emotion that suggests that behaviours and physiological responses are directly elicited by situations and that feelings of emotions are produced by feedback from these behaviours and responses.

jealousy A mood or emotional state in which an individual experiences a real or imagined perceived sexual or romantic threat to their romantic/sexual relationship from a rival.

just-noticeable difference (jnd) the smallest difference between two similar stimuli that can be distinguished. Also called difference threshold.

kin selection A type of selection that favours altruistic acts aimed at individuals who share some of the altruist's genes, such as parents, siblings, grandparents, grandchildren and, under certain conditions, distant relatives.

language acquisition device A hypothetical brain function which all children are said to have and which embodies the rules of universal grammar.

latency period The fourth of Freud's psychosexual stages, between the phallic stage and the genital stages during which there are no unconscious sexual urges or intrapsychic conflicts.

latent content The hidden message of a dream, produced by the unconscious.

latent inhibition The phenomenon whereby a novel object is more successfully paired with a familiar one in conditioning.

lateralisation Phenomenon whereby a function is the predominant responsibility of one side or part of the body or brain (e.g. speech production is lateralised in the left hemisphere).

law of attraction Byrne's theory that attraction towards a person bears a linear relationship to the proportion of attitudes associated with the person – the more similar you are to someone the more you like them.

law of closure Gestalt law of organisation; elements missing from the outline of a figure are 'filled in' by the visual system.

law of effect Thorndike's observation that stimuli that occur as a consequence of a response can increase or decrease the likelihood of making that response again.

leader–member exchange (LMX) theory Theory that effective leadership rests on leaders developing personalised relationships with individual followers.

leakage A sign of expression of an emotion that is being masked.

learned helplessness A response to exposure to an inescapable aversive stimulus, characterised by reduced ability to learn a solvable avoidance task; thought to play a role in the development of some psychological disturbances.

learning An adaptive process in which the tendency to perform a particular behaviour is changed by experience.

lens The transparent organ situated behind the iris of the eye; helps to focus an image on the retina.

leptin Protein which is secreted by fat cells that have absorbed a large amount of triglyceride.

lexical awareness The ability to understand that speech and writing are composed of different, distinct elements called words.

libido An insistent, instinctual force that is unresponsive to the demands of reality; the primary source of motivation.

liking A feeling of personal regard, intimacy and esteem towards another person.

limbic cortex The cerebral cortex located around the edge of the cerebral hemispheres where they join with the brain stem; part of the limbic system.

limbic system A set of interconnected structures of the brain important in emotional and species-typical behaviour; includes the amygdala, hippocampus and limbic cortex.

linear perspective A monocular cue of depth perception; the arrangement or drawing of objects on a flat surface such that parallel lines receding from the viewer are seen to converge at a point on the horizon.

linguistic intergroup bias The use of concrete language that simply describes events when talking about positive out-group (and negative in-group) characteristics, and more general and abstract terms that relate to enduring traits when talking about negative out-group (and positive in-group) characteristics.

linguistic relativity The hypothesis that the language a person speaks is related to their thoughts and perceptions.

linguistics The study of the rules of language and the nature and meaning of written and spoken language.

lithium carbonate A rug used to treat bipolar disorder.

localisation of function The notion that functions may be localised in the brain at the neural, chemical or anatomical level.

locus of control An individual's beliefs that the consequences of their actions are controlled by internal person variables or by external environmental variables.

long-term memory (LTM) Memory in which information is represented on a permanent or near-permanent basis.

long-term potentiation (LTP) In learning and memory research, the strengthening of connections between neurons via repeated stimulation.

loving A combination of liking and a deep sense of attachment to, intimacy with, and caring for another person.

low-ball tactic Technique for inducing compliance in which a person who agrees to a request can feel committed even after finding that there is a hidden cost.

magnetic resonance imaging (MRI) Neuroimaging technique which allows neuropsychologists to observe the structure of the living brain by measuring the reverberation of hydrogen molecules in the brain as a magnetic field is passed over the head.

magnetoencephalography (MEG) A technique for measuring brain activation by detecting the activity of magnetic fields from a large number of neurons.

maintenance rehearsal The rote repetition of information; repeating a given item over and over again.

major depression Persistent and severe feelings of sadness and worthlessness accompanied by changes in appetite, sleeping and behaviour.

mania Excessive emotional arousal and wild, exuberant, unrealistic activity.

manifest content The apparent storyline of a dream.

masking Attempting to hide the expression of an emotion.

matching Systematic selection of participants in groups in an experiment or (more often) a correlational study to ensure that the mean values of important subject variables of the groups are similar.

materialism A philosophical belief that reality can be known only through an understanding of the physical world, of which the mind is a part.

maturation Any relatively stable change in thought, behaviour or physical growth that is due to the ageing process and not to experience.

mean A measure of central tendency; the sum of a group of values divided by their number; the arithmetical average.

means–ends analysis An approach to problem-solving in which a person should look for differences between the current state and the goal state and seek ways to reduce these differences.

median A measure of central tendency; the midpoint of a group of values arranged numerically.

medical model A perspective on mental illness which regards mental disorder as caused by specific abnormalities of the brain and nervous system.

medulla The part of the brain stem closest to the spinal cord; controls vital functions such as heart rate and blood pressure.

MEG See magnetoencephalography.

meiosis The form of cell division by which new sperm and ova are formed. The chromosomes within the cell are randomly rearranged so that new sperm and ova contain 23 individual chromosomes, or half of that found in other bodily cells.

memory The cognitive processes of encoding, storing and retrieving information.

meninges The three-layered set of membranes that enclose the brain and spinal cord.

menopause In women, the alternation in the endocrine system which leads to the pituitary gland and the hypothalamus releasing hormones that prevent the ovaries from controlling menstruation.

menstrual synchrony The phenomenon whereby menstrual cycles of more than one female become synchronous.

mental age A measure of a person's intellectual development; the level of intellectual development that could be expected for an average child of a particular age.

mental lexicon Hypothetical cognitive store of words and their meanings.

mental model A mental construction based on physical reality that is used to solve problems of logical deduction.

mental space (M-space) A hypothetical construct in Case's model of cognitive development similar to working memory, whose primary function is to process information from the external world.

mere exposure effect The formation of a positive attitude towards a person, place or thing, based solely on repeated exposure to that person, place or thing.

mesmerism Another word for hypnosis, named after Franz Anton Mesmer, an Austrian physician.

meta-analysis A statistical procedure by which the results of many studies are combined to estimate the magnitude of a particular effect.

metamemory Knowledge of the knowledge acquisition process.

method of loci A mnemonic system in which items to be remembered are mentally associated with specific physical locations or landmarks.

microtubules Parts of the neuron which perform specific functions.

midbrain The part of the brain stem just anterior to the pons; involved in control of fighting and sexual behaviour and in decreased sensitivity to pain during these behaviours.

minimal group paradigm Experimental methodology to investigate the effect of social categorisation alone on behaviour.

Minnesota Multiphasic Personality Inventory (MMPI) An objective test designed originally to distinguish individuals with different psychological problems from normal individuals. It has since become popular as a means of attempting to identify personality characteristics of people in many everyday settings.

minority influence Social influence processes whereby numerical or power minorities change the attitudes of the majority.

mirror neuron Neurons which fire when viewing an action as well engaging in the same action.

mnemonic system A special technique or strategy consciously employed in an attempt to improve memory.

mobile conjugate reinforcement paradigm An experimental method whereby a child learns that if it moves its foot, which is attached to a mobile, the mobile moves and, therefore, catches its attention.

modelling A technique which has individuals modelling their behaviour on that of another.

modern racism Racist attitudes that are expressed in ways that do not immediately look like racism because on the surface they appear to reflect liberal values of egalitarianism, individualism, and so forth.

modularity The notion that the functions of the brain are organised by means of semi-independent and self-contained modules, each of which performs a specific function.

modulation An attempt to exaggerate or minimise the expression of an emotion.

monoamine oxidase inhibitors (MAOIs) Antidepressants which prevent enzymes at the synaptic gap from destroying amines.

monogamy The mating of one female and one male.

monozygotic (MZ) twins Twins that are fertilised from the same ovum (and are, therefore, genetically identical).

mood disorder A disorder characterised by significant shifts or disturbances in mood that affect normal perception, thought and behaviour. Mood disorders may be characterised by deep, foreboding depression, or a combination of the depression and euphoria.

moral realism The second stage of Piaget's model of moral development, which includes egocentrism and blind adherence to rules.

moral relativism The final of Piaget's stages of moral development in which the child becomes more flexible in interpreting moral issues, understands that moral responses are relative, that rules can be broken and that people are not always punished.

motion parallax A cue of depth perception. As we pass by a scene, objects closer to us pass in front of objects farther away.

motivated tactician A model of social cognition that characterises people as having multiple cognitive strategies available, which they choose among on the basis of personal goals, motives and needs.

motivation A general term for a group of phenomena that affect the nature, strength or persistence of an individual's behaviour.

motivation loss Deterioration in group performance in comparison to individual performance due to reduced motivation to perform.

motor association cortex Those regions of the cerebral cortex that control the primary motor cortex; involved in planning and executing behaviours.

motor neuron A neuron whose terminal buttons form synapses with muscle fibres. When an action potential travels down its axon, the associated muscle fibres will twitch.

muscle spindle A muscle fibre that functions as a stretch receptor; arranged parallel to the muscle fibres responsible for contraction of the muscle, it detects muscle length.

mutations Accidental alterations in the DNA code within a single gene. Mutations can either be spontaneous and occur naturally or be the result of environmental factors, such as exposure to high-energy radiation.

myelin The insulating material that encases most large axons.

narrative A mnemonic system in which items to be remembered are linked together by a story.

native language recognition hypothesis The notion than infants have the ability to identify words in their native language.

natural concept A category of objects or situations based on people's perceptions and interactions with things in the world; based on exemplars.

natural selection The consequence of the fact that organisms reproduce differentially, which is caused by behavioural differences among them. Within any given population, some animals – the survivors – will produce more offspring than will other animals.

naturalistic observation Observation of the behaviour of people or other animals in their natural environments.

need complementarity Winch's theory that we seek out apparent opposites, as they can best satisfy our needs.

negative after-image The image seen after a portion of the retina is exposed to an intense visual stimulus; a negative after-image consists of colours complementary to those of the physical stimulus.

negative feedback A process whereby the effect produced by an action serves to diminish or terminate that action. Regulatory systems are characterised by negative feedback loops.

negative reinforcement An increase in the frequency of a response that is regularly and reliably followed by the termination of an aversive stimulus.

negative symptoms Symptoms of schizophrenia that may include the absence of normal behaviour, flattened emotion, poverty of speech, lack of initiative and persistence, and social withdrawal.

neobehaviourism/radical behaviourism The strand of behaviourism developed by Skinner and others which described behaviour in terms of instrumental (or operant) learning.

nerve A bundle of nerve fibres that transmit information between the central nervous system and the body's sense organs, muscles and glands.

neural networks Computer models which hope to simulate the way in which the brain works.

neuroimaging Technique used to measure the anatomical structure and neural activity of the living human brain.

neuromodulator A substance secreted in the brain that modulates the activity of neurons that contain the appropriate receptor molecules.

neuron A nerve cell; consists of a cell body with dendrites and an axon whose branches end in terminal buttons that synapse with muscle fibres, gland cells or other neurons.

neuropsychological rehabilitation Process whereby brain-damaged individuals are trained to retrieve some of the functions lost through injury.

neuropsychology/neuroscience The study of central nervous system function.

neuroticism The tendency to be anxious, worried and full of guilt.

neurotransmitter A chemical released by the terminal buttons that causes the postsynaptic neuron to be excited or inhibited.

night terrors A children's disorder in which the child wakes up in absolute terror, usually after suddenly waking from stage 4 sleep; distinguishable from nightmares which are frightening dreams.

nociception The term used to describe the physical process of experiencing pain.

nociceptors The body's pain receptors.

nominal fallacy The false belief that one has explained the causes of a phenomenon by identifying and naming it; for example, believing that one has explained lazy behaviour by attributing it to 'laziness'.

non-fluent (Broca's) aphasia Severe difficulty in articulating words, especially function words, caused by damage that includes Broca's area, a region of the frontal cortex on the left (speech-dominant) side of the brain.

non-verbal communication Transfer of meaningful information from one person to another by means other than written or spoken language (e.g. gaze, facial expression, posture, touch).

nootropics Rugs which claim to improve intellectual function.

norm Data concerning comparison groups that permit the score of an individual to be assessed relative to their peers.

normative influence An influence to conform with the positive expectation of others, to gain social approval or to avoid social disapproval.

norms (in social psychology) Generally accepted rules and ways of behaving.

object permanence The idea that objects do not disappear when they are out of sight.

objective personality tests Tests for measuring personality that can be scored objectively, such as a multiple-choice or true/false test.

observational learning Learning through observing the kinds of consequence that others (called models) experience as a result of their behaviour.

obsession An involuntary recurring thought, idea or image.

obsessive-compulsive disorder Recurrent, unwanted thoughts or ideas and compelling urges to engage in repetitive ritual-like behaviour.

occipital lobe The rearmost portion of the cerebral cortex; contains the primary visual cortex.

occupational psychology See organisational psychology.

Oedipus complex In Freudian thinking, a boy's attachment to his mother; named after the mythical Greek king who unwittingly killed his father and married his mother.

oestrous cycle The ovulatory cycle in mammals other than primates; the sequence of physical and hormonal changes that accompany the ripening and disintegration of ova.

olfaction The sense of smell.

olfactory bulbs Stalk-like structures located at the base of the brain that contain neural circuits that perform the first analysis of olfactory information.

olfactory mucosa The mucous membrane lining the top of the nasal sinuses; contains the cilia of the olfactory receptors.

operant chamber An apparatus in which an animal's behaviour can be easily observed, manipulated and automatically recorded.

operant conditioning A form of learning in which behaviour is affected by its consequences. Favourable consequences strengthen the behaviour and unfavourable consequences weaken the behaviour.

operational definition The definition of a variable in terms of the operations the experimenter performs to measure or manipulate it.

opioid A neuromodulator whose action is mimicked by a natural or synthetic opiate, such as opium, morphine or heroin.

optic disc A circular structure located at the exit point from the retina of the axons of the ganglion cells that form the optic nerve.

optimum-level hypothesis The hypothesis that organisms will perform behaviour that restores the level of arousal to an optimum level.

oral stage The first of Freud's psychosexual stages, during which the mouth is the major erogenous zone – the major source of physical pleasure. Early in this stage, the mouth is used for sucking; later in the stage it is used for biting and chewing.

orbitofrontal cortex (OFC) A region of the prefrontal cortex that plays an important role in recognition of situations that produce emotional responses.

organisational effect An effect of a hormone that usually occurs during prenatal development and produces permanent changes that alter the subsequent development of the organism. An example is androgenisation.

organisational/occupational psychology The branch of psychology concerned with the efficiency and effectiveness of organisation.

orienting response Any response by which an organism directs appropriate sensory organs (eyes, ears, nose) towards the source of a novel stimulus.

orthographic awareness The ability to recognise that writing systems have sets of rules that must be followed.

osmometric thirst The reduction in the concentration of sodium available across the membrane and the movement of water by osmosis dehydrates and shrinks the body's cells.

ossicle One of the three bones of the middle ear (the hammer, anvil and stirrup) that transmit acoustic vibrations from the eardrum to the membrane behind the oval window of the cochlea.

oval window An opening in the bone surrounding the cochlea. The stirrup presses against a membrane behind the oval window and transmits sound vibrations into the fluid within the cochlea.

overextension The use of a word to denote a larger class of items than is appropriate, for example, referring to the moon as a ball.

overtone A component of a complex tone; one of a series of tones whose frequency is a multiple of the fundamental frequency.

Pacinian corpuscle A specialised, encapsulated somatosensory nerve ending, which detects mechanical stimuli, especially vibrations.

paleoanthropology The study of human evolution through interpreting fossil remains.

panic A feeling of fear mixed with hopelessness or helplessness.

panic disorder Unpredictable attacks of acute anxiety that are accompanied by high levels of physiological arousal and that last from a few seconds to a few hours.

papilla A small bump on the tongue that contains a group of taste buds.

parallel distributed processing (PDP) model Connectionist model devised by Seidenberg and McClelland to read regular, exception and non-words.

parallel processor The notion that the brain is composed of different modules which allow us to work simultaneously on more than one task.

paranoid schizophrenia A form of schizophrenia in which the person suffers from delusions of persecution, grandeur or control.

paraphilia Mental or behavioural disorder that has a sexual content.

parasympathetic branch The portion of the autonomic nervous system that activates functions that occur during a relaxed state.

parental investment The resources, including time, physical effort and risks to life, that a parent spends in procreation and in the feeding, nurturing and protecting of offspring.

parietal lobe The region of the cerebral cortex behind the frontal lobe and above the temporal lobe; contains the somatosensory cortex; is involved in spatial perception and memory.

passionate love An emotional, intense desire for sexual union with another person. Also called romantic love.

Pavlovian conditioning Similar to classical conditioning – the process by which a response normally elicited by one stimulus (the UCS) comes to be controlled by another stimulus (the CS) as well.

perception (1) A rapid, automatic, unconscious process by which we recognise what is represented by the information provided by our sense organs. (2) The detection of the more complex properties of a stimulus, including its location and nature; involves learning.

perceptual disorders Disorders in perception that tend to leave elementary sensation unimpaired.

period of concrete operations The third period in Piaget's theory of cognitive development during which children come to understand the conservation principle and other concepts, such as categorisation.

period of formal operations The fourth period in Piaget's theory of cognitive development during which individuals first become capable of more formal kinds of abstract thinking and hypothetical reasoning.

peripheral nervous system The cranial and spinal nerves; that part of the nervous system peripheral to the brain and spinal cord.

perseverance The tendency to continue to perform a behaviour even when it is not being reinforced.

perseveration Responding in a manner that was previously correct but is now inappropriate.

person variables Individual differences in cognition, which, according to Mischel, include competences, encoding strategies and personal constructs, expectancies, subjective values, and self-regulatory systems and plans.

personal constructs Idiosyncratic and personal ways of characterising other people.

personality Particular pattern of behaviour and thinking prevailing across time and situations that differentiates one person from another.

personality disorders Abnormalities in behaviour which impair social or occupational function.

personality trait An enduring personal characteristic that reveals itself in a particular pattern of behaviour in a variety of situations.

personality types Different categories into which personality characteristics can be assigned based on factors such as developmental experiences or physical characteristics.

phallic stage The third of Freud's psychosexual stages. During this stage, the primary erogenous zone is the genital area. At this time, children not only wish to stimulate their genitalia but also become attached to the opposite-sex parent.

phenotype The outward expression of an organism's genotype; an organism's physical appearance and behaviour.

pheromone A chemical secreted by the body which induces stereotypical behaviour in the perceiving organism.

phobia Unreasonable fear of specific objects or situations, such as insects, animals or enclosed spaces, learned through classical conditioning.

phoneme The minimum unit of sound that conveys meaning in a particular language, such as /p/.

phonetic reading Reading by decoding the phonetic significance of letter strings; 'sound reading'.

phonological awareness The capacity to appreciate the sounds of words and be able to identify letters with sounds.

phonological dyslexia A reading disorder in which people can read familiar words but have difficulty reading unfamiliar words or pronounceable non-words because they cannot sound out words.

phonological loop See articulatory loop.

photopigment A complex molecule found in photoreceptors; when struck by light, it splits apart and stimulates the membrane of the photoreceptor in which it resides.

photoreceptor A receptive cell for vision in the retina; a rod or a cone.

physiological psychology The branch of psychology that studies the physiological basis of behaviour.

pituitary gland An endocrine gland attached to the hypothalamus at the base of the brain.

place-dependent memory Description of greater success in retrieval of material when acquisition and retrieval of information occur in the same location.

placebo An inert substance that cannot be distinguished from a real medication by the patient or subject; used as the control substance in a single-blind or double-blind experiment.

planned behaviour (theory of) Modification by Ajzen of the theory of reasoned action. It suggests that predicting a behaviour from an attitude measure is improved if people believe that they have control over that behaviour.

planum temporale Structure found in the primary auditory cortex which seems to be larger in the left than right hemisphere.

pleasure principle The rule that the id obeys: obtain immediate gratification, whatever form it may take.

polyandry The mating of one female with more than one male.

polygynandry The mating of several females with several males.

polygyny The mating of one male with more than one female.

pons The part of the brain stem just anterior to the medulla; involved in control of sleep.

positive brain allometry An increase in brain size relative to body size.

positive reinforcement An increase in the frequency of a response that is regularly and reliably followed by an appetitive stimulus.

positive symptoms Symptoms of schizophrenia that may include thought disorder, hallucinations or delusions.

positivism The school of thought which states that all meaningful ideas can be reduced to observable material.

positron emission tomography (PET) Technique used to measure the degree of blood flow or oxygen consumption in the living brain as it engages in activity.

postconventional level Kohlberg's third and final level of moral development, in which people come to understand that moral rules include principles that apply across all situations and societies.

posterior Towards the back.

posterior part of the parietal cortex (PPC) Part of the brain responsible for the ability to locate objects in space.

posthypnotic amnesia A failure to remember what occurred during hypnosis; induced by suggestions made during hypnosis.

posthypnotic suggestibility The tendency of a person to perform a behaviour suggested by the hypnotist some time after the person has left the hypnotic state.

postsynaptic neuron A neuron with which the terminal buttons of another neuron form synapses and that is excited or inhibited by that neuron.

post-traumatic stress disorder (PTSD) Anxiety which follows a traumatic event.

preconventional level Kohlberg's first level of moral development, which bases moral behaviour on external sanctions, such as authority and punishment.

prefrontal cortex The anterior part of the frontal lobe; contains the motor association cortex.

prejudice n attitude or evaluation, usually negative, towards a group of people defined by their racial, ethnic or religious heritage or by their gender, occupation, sexual orientation, level of education, place of residence or membership of a particular group.

premoral stage of moral development First of Piaget's stages of moral development in which the child shows little understanding of rules or principles governing moral behaviour or understanding.

prenatal period The nine months between conception and birth. This period is divided into three developmental stages: the zygote, the embryo and the foetal stages.

preoperational period The second of Piaget's periods, which represents a 4–5 year transitional period between first being able to think symbolically and then being able to think logically. During this stage, children become increasingly capable of speaking meaningful sentences.

preoptic area region at the base of the brain just in front of the hypothalamus; contains neurons that appear to control the occurrence of slow-wave sleep.

presynaptic neuron A neuron whose terminal buttons form synapses with and excite or inhibit another neuron.

primacy effect (1) The tendency to remember initial information. In the memorisation of a list of words, the primacy effect is evidenced by better recall of the words early in the list. (2) The tendency to form impressions of people based on the first information we receive about them.

primary appraisal An anxiety research, the initial evaluation of the environment as neutral, positive or negative.

primary auditory cortex The region of the cerebral cortex that receives information directly from the auditory system; located in the temporal lobes.

primary motor cortex The region of the cerebral cortex that directly controls the movements of the body; located in the back part of the frontal lobes.

primary punisher A biologically significant aversive stimulus, such as pain.

primary reinforcer A biologically significant appetitive stimulus, such as food or water.

primary somatosensory cortex The region of the cerebral cortex that receives information directly from the somatosensory system (touch, pressure, vibration, pain and temperature); located in the front part of the parietal lobes.

primary visual cortex (V1) The region of the cerebral cortex that receives information directly from the visual system; located in the occipital lobes.

principle of common fate States that elements that move in the same direction will be perceived as belonging together and forming a figure.

prisoner's dilemma Two-person game in which both parties are torn between competition and cooperation and, depending on mutual choices, both can win or both can lose.

proactive interference Interference in recall that occurs when previously learned information disrupts our ability to remember newer information.

problem-focused coping Any coping behaviour that is directed at reducing or eliminating a stressor.

process overlap theory According to Lovacs and Conway, a theory of intelligence which explains why people who do well one on cognitive test do well on another; it argues that executive functions and domain-specific functions overlap.

progressive relaxation technique A relaxation technique involving three steps: (1) recognising the body's signals that indicate the presence of stress; (2) using those signals as a cue to begin relaxing; and (3) relaxing groups of muscles, beginning with those in the head and neck and then those in the arms and legs.

projection A defence mechanism in which one's unacceptable behaviours or thoughts are attributed to someone else.

projective tests Unstructured personality measures in which a person is shown a series of ambiguous stimuli, such as pictures, inkblots or incomplete drawings. The person is asked to describe what they 'see' in each stimulus or to create stories that reflect the theme of the drawing or picture.

proprioception Our sense of bodily position and movement.

prosocial behaviour Acts that are positively valued by society.

prosody The use of changes in intonation and emphasis to convey meaning in speech besides that specified by the particular words; an important means of communication of emotion.

prosopagnosia A form of visual agnosia characterised by difficulty in the recognition of people's faces; caused by damage to the visual association cortex.

prospective memory Remembering to perform an activity planned in the future.

protanopia A form of hereditary anomalous colour vision; caused by defective 'red' cones in the retina.

protective factor A factor – psychological or physiological – which can assist in the prevention of disease.

prototype A hypothetical idealised pattern that resides in the nervous system and is used to perceive objects or shapes by a process of comparison; recognition can occur even when an exact match is not found.

protoword A unique string of phonemes that an infant invents and uses as a word.

proximate causes Immediate environmental events and conditions that affect behaviour.

proximity principle See adjacency principle.

pseudohomophone A word which is legally spelled, is not a real word but sounds like a real word (e.g. 'phicks' sounds like 'fix').

pseudoword A word that is legally spelled but is not a real word.

psychiatry A branch of medicine concerned with the diagnosis and treatment of mental illness.

psychoactive substance use disorders Mental disorders that are characterised by addiction to drugs or by abuse of drugs.

psychoanalysis A form of therapy aimed at giving the client insight into their unconscious motivations and impulses; a branch of thinking which argues that behaviour can be explained by unconscious desires and impulses.

psychobiology See physiological psychology.

psychodynamic A term used to describe the Freudian notion that the mind is in a state of conflict among instincts, reasons and conscience.

psychodynamic therapy Therapy based on the understanding that unconscious drives, desires and impulses manifest themselves in behaviour.

psychogenic amnesia A dissociative disorder characterised by the inability to remember important events or personal information.

psychogenic fugue Amnesia with no apparent organic cause accompanied by a flight away from home.

psycholinguistics A branch of psychology devoted to the study of verbal behaviour.

psychological universal Psychological phenomenon that is seen across all peoples and cultures.

psychology The scientific study of the causes of behaviour; also, the applications of the findings of psychological research to the solution of problems.

psychoneuroimmunology Study of the interactions between the immune system and behaviour as mediated by the nervous system.

psychophysics A branch of psychology that measures the quantitative relation between physical stimuli and perceptual experience.

psychophysiology The measurement of physiological responses, such as blood pressure and heart rate, to infer changes in internal states, such as emotions.

psychosurgery Unalterable brain surgery used to relieve the symptoms of psychological disorders.

psychoticism The tendency to be aggressive, egocentric and antisocial.

puberty The period during which people's reproductive systems mature, marking the beginning of the transition from childhood to adulthood.

punishment A decrease in the frequency of a response that is regularly and reliably followed by an aversive stimulus.

purposive behaviourism A variation on behaviourism proposed by Tolman which argued that variables intervening between stimulus and response were important and gave behaviour its purpose.

qualitative analysis An approach to research which focuses on the ways in which people use words, express feelings and arguments. Themes and ideas can be interpreted from transcripts of these discussions.

quantitative research The methodological approach which regards human behaviour as measurable and subject to statistical analysis.

radical behaviourism See neobehaviourism.

rapid eye movement (REM) sleep A period of sleep during which dreaming, rapid eye movements, and muscular paralysis occur and the EEG shows beta activity.

ratio IQ A formula for computing the intelligence quotient; mental age divided by chronological age, multiplied by 100.

rational-emotive therapy Therapy based on the belief that psychological problems are caused not by upsetting events but by how people think about them.

rationalisation A defence mechanism that justifies an unacceptable action with a more acceptable, but false, excuse.

reaction formation A defence mechanism that involves behaving in a way that is the opposite of how one really feels because the true feelings produce anxiety.

realistic conflict theory Sherif's theory of intergroup conflict that traces the complexion of intergroup behaviour to the nature of goal relations between groups.

reality principle The tendency to satisfy the id's demands realistically, which almost always involves compromising the demands of the id and superego.

reasoned action (theory of) Fishbein and Ajzen's model of the links between attitude and behaviour. A major feature is the proposition that the best way to predict a behaviour is to ask whether the person intends to do it.

receiver operating characteristic (ROC) curve A graph of hits and false alarms of subjects under different motivational conditions; indicates people's ability to detect a particular stimulus.

recency effect The tendency to recall later information. In the memorisation of a list of words, the recency effect is evidenced by better recall of the last words in the list.

receptive field That portion of the visual field in which the presentation of visual stimuli will produce an alteration in the firing rate of a particular neuron.

receptor cell A neuron that directly responds to a physical stimulus, such as light, vibrations or aromatic molecules.

receptor molecule A special protein molecule located in the membrane of the postsynaptic neuron that responds to molecules of the transmitter substance. Receptors such as those that respond to opiates are sometimes found elsewhere on the surface of neurons.

recessive allele The form of the gene that does not influence the expression of a trait unless it is paired with another recessive allele.

reciprocal altruism Altruism in which people behave altruistically towards one another because they are confident that such acts will be reciprocated towards either them or their kin.

reciprocal determinism The idea that behaviour, environment and personal variables, such as perception, interact to determine personality.

reciprocity The tendency to return, in kind, favours that others have done for us.

recovered memories Memories (usually negative) that are thought to be repressed in very early childhood and which access consciousness during therapy.

referent informational influence An influence to conform with a self-referent group norm that defines oneself as a group member.

reflex An automatic response to a stimulus, such as the blink reflex to the sudden approach of an object towards the eyes.

regulatory behaviour A behaviour that tends to bring physiological conditions back to normal, thus restoring the condition of homeostasis.

regulatory focus theory Higgins's theory of individual differences in whether people have a promotion (approach) or a prevention (avoidance) orientation to life.

rehabilitation In neuropsychology, the procedure whereby a person with brain injury is taught to re-learn cognitive and social functions and skills lost through the injury.

reification Assuming that your subject matter is real and concrete and actually exists in substance.

relationship dissolution model Duck's proposal of the sequence through which most long-term relationships proceed if they finally break down.

relative deprivation Sense of having less than that to which one feels entitled.

reliability The repeatability of a measurement; the likelihood that if the measurement was made again it would yield the same value.

REM sleep behaviour disorder A neurological disorder characterised by absence of the paralysis that normally occurs during REM sleep; the patient acts out their dreams.

remember-to-know shift Period when remembered information is transferred into long-term memory and becomes permanent knowledge.

repeated measures design A design whereby the same participants take part in each condition of an experiment. Also called within-groups design.

replication Repetition of an experiment or observational study to see whether previous results will be obtained.

representativeness heuristic A general rule for social judgement by which people classify a person, place or thing into the category to which it appears to be the most similar.

repression The mental force responsible for actively keeping memories, most of which are potentially threatening or anxiety provoking, from being consciously discovered.

reproductive strategies Different systems of mating and rearing offspring. These include monogamy, polygyny, polyandry and polygynandry.

reproductive success The number of viable offspring an individual produces relative to the number of viable offspring produced by other members of the same species.

resistance A development during therapy in which the client becomes defensive, unconsciously attempting to halt further insight by censoring their true feelings.

resistant attachment A kind of attachment in which infants show mixed reactions to their mothers. They may approach their mothers upon their return but, at the same time, continue to cry or even push their mothers away.

response bias Tendency to say yes or no when unsure whether a stimulus was detected.

response cost A decrease in the frequency of a response that is regularly and reliably followed by the termination of an appetitive stimulus.

retention interval Period between the acquisition and retrieval of material.

retina The tissue at the back inside surface of the eye that contains the photoreceptors and associated neurons.

retinal disparity The fact that points on objects located at different distances from the observer will fall on slightly different locations on the two retinas; provides the basis for stereopsis, one of the forms of depth perception.

retrieval The active processes of locating and using stored information.

retrieval cues Contextual variables, including physical objects or verbal stimuli, that improve the ability to recall information from memory.

retroactive interference Interference in recall that occurs when recently learned information disrupts our ability to remember older information.

retrograde amnesia The loss of the ability to retrieve memories of one's past, particularly memories of episodic or autobiographical events.

reuptake The process by which a terminal button retrieves the molecules of transmitter substance that it has just released; terminates the effect of the transmitter substance on the receptors of the postsynaptic neuron.

rod A photoreceptor that is very sensitive to light but cannot detect changes in hue.

role-playing A technique which requires an individual to act out or rehearse skills by adopting the identity of another.

Rorschach Inkblot Test A projective test in which a person is shown a series of symmetrical inkblots and asked to describe what he or she thinks they represent.

round window An opening in the bone surrounding the cochlea. Movements of the membrane behind this opening permit vibrations to be transmitted through the oval window into the cochlea.

s factor According to Spearman, a factor of intelligence that is specific to a particular task.

saccade The rapid movement of the eyes that is used in scanning a visual scene, as opposed to the smooth pursuit movements used to follow a moving object.

sample A selection of items from a larger population, for example a group of participants selected to participate in an experiment.

Sapir–Whorf hypothesis The idea that language can determine thought.

saturation A perceptual dimension of colour, most closely associated with purity of a colour.

schema A mental framework or body of knowledge that organises and synthesises information about a person, place or thing.

schemata Mental representations or sets of rules that define a particular category of behaviour. Schemata include rules that help us to understand current and future experiences.

schizophrenia A serious mental disorder characterised by thought disturbances, hallucinations, anxiety, emotional withdrawal and delusions.

scientific method A set of rules that govern the collection and analysis of data gained through observational studies or experiments.

sclera The tough outer layer of the eye; the 'white' of the eye.

seasonal affective disorder A mood disorder characterised by depression, lethargy, sleep disturbances and craving for carbohydrates. This disorder generally occurs during the winter, when the amount of daylight is low. This disorder can be treated with exposure to bright lights.

secondary appraisal In anxiety research, the individual's ability to evaluate how best to cope with an environment and what strategies can facilitate coping.

secondary reinforcer (or punisher) See conditioned reinforcer (or punisher).

secretory immunoglobulin A (sIgA) A type of antibody which is secreted by and covers the mucosal surfaces.

secure attachment A kind of attachment in which infants use their mothers as a base for exploring a new environment. They will venture out from their mothers to explore a strange situation but return periodically.

segmentation The breaking up of words in order to make them more pronounceable.

selective attention The process that controls our awareness of, and readiness to respond to, particular categories of stimuli or stimuli in a particular location.

self-actualisation The realisation of one's true intellectual and emotional potential.

self-awareness Being consciously aware of oneself as an object.

self-categorisation theory Turner and associates' theory of how the process of categorising oneself as a group member produces social identity and group and intergroup behaviours.

self-concept One's knowledge, feelings and ideas about one's self.

self-control The tendency to be kind, considerate and obedient of laws and rules.

self-discrepancy theory Higgins's theory about the consequences of making actual–ideal and actual–'ought' self comparisons that reveal self-discrepancies.

self-efficacy The expectations of success; the belief in one's own competences.

self-esteem Feelings about and evaluations of oneself.

self-fulfilling prophecy A stereotype that causes a person to act in a manner consistent with that stereotype.

self-perception theory The theory that we come to understand our attitudes and emotions by observing our own behaviour and the circumstances under which it occurs.

self-schema A mental framework that represents and synthesises information about one's self; a cognitive structure that organises the knowledge, feelings and ideas that constitute the self-concept.

self-serving bias The tendency to make attributions that protect or enhance our self-esteem and self-image.

semantic memory A type of long-term memory that contains data, facts and other information, including vocabulary.

semantic priming A facilitating effect on the recognition of words having meanings related to a word that was presented previously.

semantics The meanings and the study of the meanings represented by words.

semicircular canal One of a set of three organs in the inner ear that responds to rotational movements of the head.

semi-structured interview A flexible form of the structured interview which requests responses to specific pre-set questions but allows the interviewer the scope to ask participants to develop their answers further.

sensation The detection of the elementary properties of a stimulus.

sensorimotor period Is first period in Piaget's theory of cognitive development, lasting from birth to 2 years. It is marked by an orderly progression of increasingly complex cognitive development: reflexes, permanence, a rough approximation of causality, imitation and symbolic thinking.

sensory association cortex Those regions of the cerebral cortex that receive information from the primary sensory areas.

sensory memory Memory in which representations of the physical features of a stimulus are stored for very brief durations.

sensory-specific satiety (SSS) The decrease in the pleasantness and consumption of food after eating it to satiety.

separation anxiety A set of fearful responses, such as crying, arousal and clinging to the carer, that the infant exhibits when the carer attempts to leave the infant.

serotonin-specific reuptake inhibitors (SSRIs) Antidepressants which block the reuptake of serotonin in nerve cells.

serum cholesterol A fat-like chemical found in the blood. One form (LDL) promotes the formation of atherosclerotic plaques. Another form (HDL) may protect against coronary heart disease.

set point The optimum value of the system variable in a regulatory mechanism. The set point for human body temperature, recorded orally, is approximately 98.6°F.

sex chromosomes The chromosomes that contain the instructional code for the development of male or female sex characteristics.

sex-influenced gene A gene which can occur in both sexes but the phenotype is more common in one sex.

sex-linked gene A gene that resides only on the sex chromosome.

sex role Cultural expectations about the ways in which men and women should think and behave.

sex stereotypes Beliefs about differences in the behaviours, abilities and personality traits of males and females.

sexual identity One's private sense of being male or female.

sexual selection Selection for traits specific to sex, such as body size or particular patterns of behaviour.

shading A monocular cue of depth perception; determines whether portions of the surface of an object are perceived as concave or convex.

shadowing The act of continuously repeating verbal material as soon as it is heard.

shallow processing The analysis of the superficial characteristics of a stimulus, such as its size or shape.

shaping The reinforcement of behaviour that successively approximates the desired response until that response is fully acquired.

short-term memory (STM) An immediate memory for stimuli that have just be en perceived. It is limited in terms of both capacity ($[7 \pm 2]$ pieces of information) and duration (less than 20 seconds).

signal detection theory A mathematical theory of the detection of stimuli, which involves discriminating a signal from the noise in which it is embedded and which takes into account subjects' willingness to report detecting the signal.

similarity principle A Gestalt principle of organisation; similar elements are perceived as belonging to the same figure.

simulation An attempt to express an emotion that one does not actually feel.

single-blind study An experiment in which the experimenter but not the subject knows the value of the independent variable.

single-case study research An experiment or correlational study concerning the behaviour of individual participants rather than comparisons of the average performance of groups of participants.

situational factors Environmental stimuli that affect a person's behaviour.

sleep apnoea A disturbance of sleep in which people will pause or briefly stop breathing during sleep.

sleeptalking Literally, talking in one's sleep.

sleepwalking Literally, walking while asleep.

slow-wave sleep Sleep other than REM sleep, characterised by regular, slow waves on the electroencephalograph.

smart drugs Generic name given to any non-prescription drugs which claim to improve intellectual function.

social anxiety disorder Previously called 'social phobia'; a fear of social situations and social interaction.

social cognition The processes involved in perceiving, interpreting, storing and acting on social information.

social comparison theory Theory of the process of comparing one's behaviours and opinions with those of others in order to establish the correct or socially approved way of thinking or behaving.

social compensation Increased effort on a collective task in order to compensate for other group members' actual, perceived or anticipated lack of effort or ability.

social decision schemes Explicit or implicit decision-making rules that relate individual opinions to a final group decision.

social determination theory Argues that two forms of motivation govern social behaviour: autonomy motivation (which involves behaviour that includes making choices for oneself, acting according to values and principles that are respected and endorsed, and initiating behaviour in a proactive way) and control motivation (involves behaving according to the dictates of an external agency, under pressure and where behaviour is contingent on feedback from this agency).

social dilemmas A general class of situations in which long-term gains are best served by short-term losses.

social dominance theory Individual differences in people's preference for their own group to be dominant over and superior to other groups, and their rejection of egalitarian ideologies and acceptance of myths that legitimise hierarchy and discrimination.

social facilitation Te enhancement of task performance caused by the mere presence of others.

social identity That part of the self-concept that derives from membership of social groups and is associated with group, as opposed to interpersonal, behaviours.

social identity perspective See social identity theory.

social identity theory Theory of group membership and intergroup relations based on self-categorisation, social comparison and the construction of a shared self-definition in terms of in-group defining properties.

social judgeability Perception of whether it is socially acceptable to judge a specific person.

social learning theory The idea that both consequences of behaviour and an individual's beliefs about those consequences determine personality.

social loafing A reduction in effort when people perform a task collectively with other people.

social neuroscience new branch of psychology which studies the relationship between brain structure and function, and social processes and behaviour.

social norms Informal rules defining the expected and appropriate behaviour in specific situations.

social phobia A mental disorder characterised by an excessive and irrational fear of situations in which the person is observed by others.

social psychology The branch of psychology that studies our social behaviour – how the actual, imagined or implied presence of other people influences our thoughts, feelings and behaviours.

social representations Collectively elaborated explanations of unfamiliar and complex phenomena that transform them into a familiar and simple form.

sociobiology The study of the genetic bases of social behaviour; the branch of biology which seeks to explain behaviour in terms of adaptation and evolution.

soma A cell body; the largest part of a neuron.

somatic marker hypothesis The idea that the ability to make decisions leading to positive or potentially negative consequences depends on the activation of somatic (bodily) states.

somatisation disorder A class of somatoform disorder, occurring mostly among women, that involves complaints of wide-ranging physical ailments for which there is no apparent biological cause.

somatoform disorder A mental disorder involving a bodily or physical problem for which there is no physiological basis.

somatosense Bodily sensations; sensitivity to such stimuli as touch, pain and temperature.

source memory Recall of the context in which an event occurred, rather than of the content/knowledge of the event.

species-typical behaviour A behaviour seen in all or most members of a species, such as nest building, special food-getting behaviours or reproductive behaviours.

specific language impairment Difficulty in producing or understanding spoken language in the absence of known brain injury.

specific phobia An excessive and irrational fear of specific things, such as snakes, darkness or heights.

spinal cord A long, thin collection of nerve cells attached to the base of the brain and running the length of the spinal column.

split brain The consequence of surgical excision of the fibres connecting the two cerebral hemispheres of the brain.

split-brain surgery A surgical procedure that severs the corpus callosum, thus abolishing the direct connections between the cortex of the two cerebral hemispheres.

split-half reliability The degree to which two halves or portions of the same measure correlate.

spontaneous recovery After an interval of time, the reappearance of a response that had previously been extinguished.

sport and exercise psychology The branch of psychology concerned with studying the effect of sport and exercise on behaviour and with applying psychological principles to our understanding of sport-related behaviour.

standard deviation A statistic that expresses the variability of a measurement; square root of the sum of the squared deviations from the mean.

Stanford–Binet Scale An intelligence test that consists of various tasks grouped according to mental age; provides the standard measure of the intelligence quotient.

state-dependent memory The tendency to recall information better when our mental or emotional state at retrieval matches that during encoding.

statistical significance The likelihood that an observed relation or difference between two variables is not due to chance factors.

stereopsis A form of depth perception based on retinal disparity.

stereotaxic apparatus A device used to insert an electrode into a particular part of the brain for the purpose of recording electrical activity, stimulating the brain electrically, or producing localised damage.

stereotype A shared, often unfavourable, generalisation held by members of one group about members of another group.

stereotype threat Feeling that one will be judged and treated in terms of negative stereotypes of one's group, and that one will inadvertently confirm these stereotypes through one's behaviour.

stigma Possession of some attribute, or characteristic, which conveys a social identity that is devalued in a particular social context.

stimulus equivalence A type of learning in which stimuli become equivalent even though the organism has never observed a relation between them; may be involved in learning how to read and manipulate symbols.

storage The process of maintaining information in memory.

Strange Situation A test of attachment in which an infant is exposed to different stimuli that may be distressing.

stranger anxiety The wariness and fearful responses, such as crying and clinging to their carers, that the infant exhibits in the presence of strangers.

stress A pattern of physiological, behavioural and cognitive responses to stimuli (real or imagined) that are perceived as endangering one's well-being.

stress inoculation training The stress management programme developed by Meichenbaum for teaching people to develop coping skills that increase their resistance to the negative effects of stress.

stressors Stimuli that are perceived as endangering one's well-being.

striving for superiority The motivation to seek superiority. Adler argued that striving for superiority is born out of our need to compensate for our inferiorities.

stroke A cerebrovascular accident; damage to the brain caused by a blood clot in a cerebral artery or rupture of a cerebral blood vessel.

Stroop effect A phenomenon whereby a well-practised memory is difficult to inhibit and is retrieved automatically where another, different response is required (e.g. if participants are asked to name the colours of words and see the word red written in the colour blue, they are likely to say 'red' rather than 'blue').

structuralism Wundt's system of experimental psychology; it emphasised introspective analysis of sensation and perception.

structured interview Are defined format for interviewing participants in research which allows little deviation from the questions set.

sublimation A defence mechanism that involves redirecting pleasure-seeking or aggressive instincts towards socially acceptable goals.

subliminal perception The perception of a stimulus, as indicated by a change in behaviour, at an intensity insufficient to produce a conscious sensation.

subordinate concept A concept that refers to types of items within a basic-level category.

subvocal articulation Muttering words inaudibly.

superego The repository of an individual's moral values, divided into the conscience – the internalisation of a society's rules and regulations – and the ego-ideal – the internalisation of one's goals.

superordinate concept A concept that refers to collections of basic-level concepts.

supertaster An individual with a genetic polymorphism which increases sensitivity to tasting bitter substances.

suprachiasmatic nucleus (SCN) Structures located in the posterior of the hypothalamus which are thought to regulate circadian rhythms.

surface dyslexia A reading disorder in which people can read words phonetically but have difficulty reading irregularly spelled words by the whole-word method.

symbolic play Name given by Piaget to a certain type of play because infants used objects to symbolise other objects or were used to symbolise other activities.

sympathetic branch The portion of the autonomic nervous system that activates functions that accompany arousal and expenditure of energy.

symptom substitution The Freudian notion that the removal of one symptom will lead to its replacement by another.

synaesthesia Phenomenon where the stimulus in one sensory modality evokes a sensation in another.

synapse The junction between the terminal button of one neuron and the membrane of a muscle fibre, a gland or another neuron.

synaptic cleft A fluid-filled gap between the presynaptic and postsynaptic membranes; the terminal button releases transmitter substance into this space.

syntax Grammatical rules for combining words to form phrases, clauses and sentences.

system variable The variable controlled by a regulatory mechanism; for example, temperature in a heating system.

systematic desensitisation A method of treatment in which the client is trained to relax in the presence of increasingly fearful stimuli.

T lymphocytes Cells that develop in the thymus gland that produce antibodies which defend the body against fungi, viruses and multicellular parasites.

taboo A societal rule prohibiting the members of a given culture from engaging in specific behaviours.

tachistoscope A device that can present visual stimuli for controlled (usually very brief) durations of time.

tardive dyskinesia A serious movement disorder that can occur when a person has been treated with antipsychotic drugs for an extended period.

target cell A cell whose physiological processes are affected by a particular hormone; contains special receptor molecules that respond to the presence of the hormone.

taste bud A small organ on the tongue that contains a group of gustatory receptor cells.

tectorial membrane A membrane located above the basilar membrane; serves as a shelf against which the cilia of the auditory hair cells move.

template A hypothetical pattern that resides in the nervous system and is used to perceive objects or shapes by a process of comparison.

temporal coding A means by which the nervous system represents information; different features are coded by the pattern of activity of neurons.

temporal lobe The portion of the cerebral cortex below the frontal and parietal lobes and containing the auditory cortex.

teratogens Drugs or other substances that can cause birth defects.

terminal button The rounded swelling at the end of the axon of a neuron; releases transmitter substance.

test–retest reliability The degree to which scores on one test correlate with the same test undertaken on another occasion.

texture A monocular cue of depth perception; the fineness of detail present in the surfaces of objects or on the ground or floor of a scene.

thalamus A region of the brain near the centre of the cerebral hemispheres. All sensory information except smell is sent to the thalamus and then relayed to the cerebral cortex.

Thematic Apperception Test (TAT) A projective test in which a person is shown a series of ambiguous pictures that involve people. The person is asked to make up a story about what the people are doing or thinking. The person's responses are believed to reflect aspects of their personality.

theory A set of statements designed to explain a set of phenomena; more encompassing than a hypothesis.

theory of mind The understanding of others' mental events.

theory of reasoned action The notion that behaviour follows from an intention to act and that these intentions are based on beliefs, feelings and attitudes.

theta activity EEG activity of 3.5–7.5 Hz; occurs during the transition between sleep and wakefulness.

thought disorder A pattern of disorganised, illogical and irrational thought that often accompanies schizophrenia.

threat gesture A stereotyped gesture that signifies that one animal is likely to attack another member of the species.

three-term contingency The relation among discriminative stimuli, behaviour and the consequences of that behaviour. A motivated organism emits a specific response in the presence of a discriminative stimulus because, in the past, that response has been reinforced only when the discriminative stimulus is present.

threshold The point at which a stimulus, or a change in the value of a stimulus, can just be detected.

tip-of-the-tongue phenomenon An occasional problem with retrieval of information that we are sure we know but cannot immediately remember.

token economy A programme often used in institutions in which a person's adaptive behaviour is reinforced with tokens that are exchangeable for desirable goods or special privileges.

tolerance The decreased sensitivity to a drug resulting from its continued use.

top-down processing A perception based on information provided by the context in which a particular stimulus is encountered.

transactional theories of leadership Theories that attribute effective leadership to mutually beneficial exchange relations between leaders and followers.

transactive memory Shared system for encoding, storing and retrieving information in a group.

transcranial magnetic stimulation (TMS) technique which modulates cortical activity by passing alternating magnetic fields across the scalp. (rTMS = repetitive transcranial magnetic stimulation.)

transduction The conversion of physical stimuli into changes in the activity of receptor cells of sensory organs.

transfer effect. The beneficial effects of training in one cognitive skill/function can lead to beneficial effects on other, unrelated cognitive skills/functions.

transference The process by which a client begins to project powerful attitudes and emotions onto the therapist.

transformational leadership Effective leaders' transactions with followers are characterised by charisma, inspirational motivation, intellectual stimulation, and individualised consideration, which motivate followers to work for group goals that transcend immediate self-interest.

triarchic theory A theory of intelligence which posits that intelligence is made of componential, experiential and contextual elements.

trichromatic theory The theory that colour vision is accomplished by three types of photoreceptor, each of which is maximally sensitive to a different wavelength of light.

tricyclic antidepressants The earliest known antidepressants, so called because of their chemical three-ring structure.

tritanopia A form of hereditary anomalous colour vision; caused by a lack of 'blue' cones in the retina.

two-point discrimination threshold The minimum distance between two small points that can be detected as separate stimuli when pressed against a particular region of the skin.

type A pattern A behaviour pattern characterised by high levels of competitiveness and hostility, impatience and an intense disposition; supposedly associated with an increased risk of coronary heart disease.

type B pattern A behaviour pattern characterised by lower levels of competitiveness and hostility, patience and an easygoing disposition; supposedly associated with a decreased risk of coronary heart disease.

tyramine cheese reaction A potentially fatal reaction to eating certain foods in individuals taking MAOIs.

UCR See unconditional response.

UCS See unconditional stimulus.

UCS pre-exposure effect A phenomenon in which conditioning is weak because the organism has already been exposed to a novel UCS before it is used in the conditioning experiment.

ultimate attribution error The tendency to attribute in-group failures and out-group successes externally, and in-group successes and out-group failures internally.

ultimate causes Evolutionary conditions that have slowly shaped the behaviour of a species over generations.

unconditional positive regard According to Rogers, the therapeutic expression that a client's worth as a human being is not dependent on anything that they do, say, feel or think.

unconditional response (UCR) In classical conditioning, a response, such as salivation, that is naturally elicited by the UCS.

unconditional stimulus (UCS) In classical conditioning, a stimulus, such as food, that naturally elicits a reflexive response, such as salivation.

unconscious The inaccessible part of the mind.

unconscious inference A mental computation of which we are unaware that plays a role in perception.

underextension The use of a word to denote a smaller class of items than is appropriate, for example referring only to one particular animal as a dog.

undifferentiated schizophrenia A type of schizophrenia characterised by fragments of the symptoms of different types of schizophrenia.

unilateral spatial hemineglect A perceptual disorder in which the patient neglects (or fails to attend to) one side of the body, usually the left.

validity The degree to which the operational definition of a variable accurately reflects the variable it is designed to measure or manipulate.

variable A measure capable of assuming any of several values.

variable error An error caused by random differences in experimental conditions, such as the subject's mood or changes in the environment.

variable-interval schedule A schedule of reinforcement similar to a fixed-interval schedule but characterised by a variable time requirement having a particular mean.

variable-ratio schedule A schedule of reinforcement similar to a fixed-ratio schedule but characterised by a variable response requirement having a particular mean.

variance The square of the standard deviation.

vertebrae Ones that encase the spinal cord and constitute the vertebral column.

vestibular apparatus The receptive organs of the inner ear that contribute to balance and perception of head movement.

vestibular sac One of a set of two receptor organs in each inner ear that detect changes in the tilt of the head.

vicarious reward. The experience of a sense of reward not only by directly experiencing positive outcomes but also by seeing people receive positive outcomes.

visual agnosia The inability of a person who is not blind to recognise the identity or use of an object by means of vision; usually caused by damage to the brain.

visuospatial neglect A perceptual disorder in which the patient neglects (or fails to attend to) one side of the body, usually the left.

visuospatial scratchpad The component of working memory that stores visuospatial information.

voice onset time The delay between the initial sound of a voiced consonant (such as the puffing sound of the phoneme /p/) and the onset of vibration of the vocal cords.

volumetric thirst Thirst provoked by a reduction in the volume of blood plasma.

voyeurism Looking at people while they are undressing or having sex, without their knowledge.

waist-to-chest ratio In men, the ratio between size of waist and chest, which determines attractiveness.

waist-to-hip ratio In women, the ratio between size of hips and waist, which determines attractiveness.

wavelength The distance between adjacent waves of radiant energy; in vision, most closely associated with the perceptual dimension of hue.

Weber fraction The ratio between a just-noticeable difference and the magnitude of a stimulus; reasonably constant over the middle range of most stimulus intensities.

Wechsler Adult Intelligence Scale (WAIS) An intelligence test for adults devised by David Wechsler; currently in its fourth edition.

Wechsler Intelligence Scale for Children (WISC) An intelligence test for children devised by David Wechsler; similar in form to the Wechsler Adult Intelligence Scale.

Wernicke's aphasia A disorder caused by damage to the left temporal and parietal cortex, including Wernicke's area; characterised by deficits in the perception of speech and by the production of fluent but rather meaningless speech.

Wernicke's area A region of auditory association cortex located in the upper part of the left temporal lobe; involved in the recognition of spoken words.

white matter The portions of the central nervous system that are abundant in axons rather than cell bodies of neurons. The colour derives from the presence of the axons' myelin sheaths.

whole-word reading Reading by recognising a word as a whole; 'sight reading'.

withdrawal symptom An effect produced by discontinuance of use of a drug after a period of continued use; generally opposite to the drug's primary effects.

within-groups design See repeated measures design.

working memory A short-term memory system which allows the retention and processing of information concurrently.

zone of proximal (or potential) development According to Vygotsky, the range of tasks or skills that a child is unable to master alone but can with the assistance of adults or their peers.

zygote stage. The first stage of prenatal development, during which the zygote divides many times and the internal organs begin to form.

References

A

Aan Het Rot, M. *et al.* (2010) Safety and efficacy of repeated-dose intravenous ketamine for treatment-resistant depression. *Biological Psychiatry*, 67, 139–45.

Aan Het Rot, M., Zarate, C.A., Charney, D.S. and Mathew, S.J. (2012) Ketamine for depression: where do we go from here? *Biological Psychiatry*, 72(7), 537–47.

Aarts, H. and Dijksterhuis, A. (2003) The silence of the library: Environment, situational norm and social behavior. *Journal of Personality and Social Psychology*, 84, 18–28.

Abe, N., Suzuki, M., Tsukiura, T., Mori, E., Yamaguchi, K., Itoh, M. and Fujii, T. (2007) Deceiving others: distinct neural responses of the prefrontal cortex and amygdala in simple fabrication and deception with social interactions. *Journal of Cognitive Neuroscience*, 19, 287–95.

Abel, E.L. and Kruger, M.L. (2010) Athletes, doctors and lawyers with first names beginning with 'D' die sooner. *Death Studies*, 34, 71–81.

Abel, E.L. and Kruger, M.L. (2010) Smile intensity in photographs predicts longevity. *Psychological Science*, 21(4), 542–4.

Abel, M. and Deitz, M. (2008) Smiling, job qualifications, and ratings of job applicants. *American Journal of Psychological Research*, 4, 45–57.

Abel, T. and Lattal, K.M. (2001) Molecular mechanisms of memory acquisition, consolidation and retrieval. *Current Opinion in Neurobiology*, 11, 180–7.

Abela, J.R.Z. and D'Alessandro, D.U. (2002) Beck's cognitive theory of depression: A test of the diathesis-stress and causal mediation components. *British Journal of Clinical Psychology*, 41, 111–28.

Aboud, F.E. (1988) *Children and Prejudice*. Oxford: Blackwell.

Abraham, C., Sheeran, P. and Orbel, S. (1998) Can social cognitive models contribute to the effectiveness of HIV-preventative behavioural interventions? A brief review of the literature and a reply to Joffe (1996; 1997) and Fife-Shaw (1997) *British Journal of Medical Psychology*, 71, 297–310.

Abramovitch, R., Corter, C. and Pepler, D.J. (1980) Observations of mixed-sex sibling dyads. *Child Development*, 51, 1268–71.

Abrams, D. (1990) *Political identity: Relative deprivation, social identity and the case of Scottish Nationalism.* ESRC 16–19 Initiative Occasional Papers. London: Economic and Social Research Council.

Abrams, D., Ando, K. and Hinkle, S. (1998) Psychological attachment to the group: Cross-cultural differences in organizational identification and subjective norms as predictors of workers' turnover intentions. *Personality and Social Psychology Bulletin*, 24, 1027–39.

Abrams, D., Marques, J.M., Bown, N.J. and Henson, M. (2000) Pro-norm and anti-norm deviance within and between groups. *Journal of Personality and Social Psychology*, 78, 906–12.

Abrams, D., Wetherell, M., Cochrane, S., Hogg, M.A. and Turner, J.C. (1990) Knowing what to think by knowing who you are: Self-categorisation and the nature of norm formation, conformity and group polarisation. *British Journal of Social Psychology*, 29, 97–119.

Abrams, J.R. and Bippus, A.M. (2014) Gendering jokes: Intergroup bias in reactions to same-versus-opposite gender humor. *Journal of Language and Social Psychology*, 1–11.

Abramson, L.Y., Metalsky, G.I. and Alloy, L.B. (1989) Hopelessness depression: A theory-based subtype. *Psychological Review*, 96, 358–72.

Abramson, L.Y., Seligman, M.E.P. and Teasdale, J.D. (1978) Learned helplessness in humans: Critique and reformulation. *Journal of Abnormal Psychology*, 87, 49–74.

Abu-Akel, A. and Shamay-Tsoory, S. (2011) Neuroanatomical and neurochemical bases of theory of mind. *Neuropsychologia*, 49, 2971–84.

Acar, S. and Runco, M.A. (2012) Psychoticism and creativity: A meta-analytic review. *Psychology of Aesthetics, Creativity and the Arts*, 6, 341–50.

Aciego, R., Garcia, L. and Betancourt, M. (2012) The benefits of chess for the intellectual and social-emotional enrichment in schoolchildren. *Spanish Journal of Psychology*, 15, 551–59.

Acierno, R.E., Hersen, M. and Van Hasselt, V.B. (1993) Interventions for panic disorder: A critical review of the literature. *Clinical Psychology Review*, 18, 561–78.

Ackerman, P.L. (2016) Process overlap and g do not adequately account for a general factor of intelligence. *Psychological Inquiry*, 27, 178–80.

Ackerman, P.L., Chamorro-Premuzic, T. and Furnham, A. (2011) Trait complexes and academic achievement: Old and new ways of examining personality in educational contexts. *British Journal of Educational Psychology*, 81, 27–40.

Adair, J.G. (1984) The Hawthorne effect: A reconsideration of the methodological artifact. *Journal of Applied Psychology*, 69, 334–45.

Adair, W.L., Okumura, T. and Brett, J.M. (2001) Negotiation behavior when cultures collide: the United States and Japan. *Journal of Applied Psychology*, 86, 317–85.

Adams, J.M. and Jones, W.H. (1997) The conceptualisation of marital commitment: An integrative analysis. *Journal of Social and Personal Relationships*, 11, 1177–96.

Adams, W.J., Gray, K.L., Garner, M. and Graf, E.W. (2010) High-level face adaptation without awareness. *Psychological Science*, 21(2), 205–10.

Adank, P., Stewart, A.J., Connell, L. and Wood, J. (2013) Accent imitation positively affects language attitudes. *Frontiers in Psychology*, 4, 280.

Addington, J.K.S., Cadenhead, K.S., Cannon, T.D., Cornblatt, B., McGlashan, T.H. and Perkins, D.O. (2007) North American prodrome longitudinal research: A collaborative multisite approach to prodromal schizophrenia research. *Schizophrenia Bulletin*, 33, 665–72.

Addis, D.R. and Schacter, D.L. (2011) The hippocampus and imagining the future: where do we stand? *Frontiers in Human Neuroscience*, 5.

Adey, P. and Shayer, M. (1994) *Really Raising Standards: Cognitive intervention and academic achievement.* New York: Routledge.

Adler, A. (1939) *Social Interest: A challenge to mankind.* New York: Putnam.

Adolphs, R. (2015) The unsolved problems of neuroscience. *Trends in Cognitive Sciences*, 1–3.

Adolphs, R., Russell, J.A. and Tranel, D. (1999) A role for the human amygdala in recognizing emotional arousal from unpleasant stimuli. *Psychological Science*, 10(2), 167–71.

Adolphs, R., Sears, L. and Piven, J. (2001) Abnormal processing of social information from faces in autism. *Journal of Cognitive Neuroscience*, 13(2), 232–40.

Adolphs, R., Tranel, D., Bechara, A., Damasio, H. and Damasio, A.R. (1996) Neuropsychological approaches to reasoning and decision-making. In A.R. Damasio *et al.* (eds) *Neurobiology of Decision-making*. Berlin: Springer-Verlag.

Adolphs, R., Tranel, D., Damasio, H. and Damasio, A.R. (1994) Impaired recognition of emotion in facial expressions following bilateral damage to the human amygdala. *Nature*, 372, 669–72.

Adolphs, R., Tranel, D., Damasio, H. and Damasio, A.R. (1995) Fear and the human amygdala. *Journal of Neuroscience*, 15, 5879–91.

Adorno, T.W., Frenkel-Brunswik, E., Levinson, D.J. and Sanford, R.M. (1950) *The Authoritarian Personality*. New York: Harper.

Advocat, C.D. and Comaty, J. (2014) *Julien's A Primer of Drug Action* (13th edn). San Francisco, CA: W.H. Freeman.

Ægisdóttir, S., White, M.J. and Spengler, P.M. (2006) The meta-analysis of clinical judgment project: Fifty-six years of accumulated research on clinical versus statistical prediction. *The Counseling Psychologist*, 34, 341–82.

Aggleton, J.P. and Mishkin, M. (1986) The amygdala: Sensory gateway to the emotions. In R. Plutchik and H. Kellerman (eds) *Biological Foundation of Emotions*. New York: Academic Press.

Aggleton, J.P. and Waskett, L. (1999) The ability of odours to serve as state-dependent cues for real world memories: Can Viking smells aid the recall of Viking experience? *British Journal of Psychology*, 90, 1–8.

Aguilar, R., Jimenez, M. and Alvero-Cruz, J.R. (2013) Testosterone, cortisol and anxiety in elite field hokey players. *Physiology and Behavior*, 119, 38–42.

Aguilar-Alonso, A. (1996) Personality and creativity. *Personality and Individual Differences*, 21(6), 959–69.

Ahmad, A. (2011) Social network sites and its popularity. *International Journal of Research and Reviews in Computer Science*, 2, 522–6.

Ahmed, S.H. (2005) Imbalance between drug and non-drug reward availability: a major risk factor for addiction. *European Journal of Pharmacology*, 526, 9–20.

Aiken, L.R. (1994) *Dying, Death and Bereavement*. Boston, MA: Allyn and Bacon.

Ainsworth, C. (2015) Sex redefined. *Nature*, 518, 288–91.

Ainsworth, M. (1973) The development of infant-mother attachment. In B. Caldwell and H. Ricciuti (eds) *Review of Child Development Research*, Vol. 3. Chicago, IL: University of Chicago Press.

Ainsworth, M.D.S. (1967) *Infancy in Uganda: Infant care and the growth of love*. Baltimore, MD: Johns Hopkins University Press.

Ainsworth, M.D.S. and Bowlby, J. (1991) An ethological approach to personality development. *American Psychologist*, 46, 333–41.

Ainsworth, M.D.S., Blehar, M.C., Waters, E. and Wall, S. (1978) *Patterns of Attachment*. Hillsdale, NJ: Lawrence Erlbaum Associates.

Ajzen, I. (1985) From intentions to actions: A theory of planned behaviour. In J. Kuhl and J. Beckmann (eds) *Action Control: From cognition of behaviour*. Berlin: Springer-Verlag.

Ajzen, I. (1989) Attitude structure and behaviour. In A.R. Pratkanis, S.J. Breckler and A.G. Greenwald (eds) *Attitude Structure and Function*. Hillsdale, NJ: Lawrence Erlbaum Associates, pp. 241–74.

Ajzen, I. (1991) The theory of planned behaviour. *Organizational Behaviour and Human Decision Processes*, 50, 179–211.

Akelaitis, A.J. (1944/45) Studies on the corpus callosum IV: Diagnostic dyspraxia in epileptics following partial and complete section of the corpus callosum. *American Journal of Psychiatry*, 101, 594–9.

Akerstedt, T., Knutsson, A., Westerholm, P., Theorell, T., Alfredsson, L. and Klecklund, G. (2002) Sleep disturbances, work stress and work hours. A cross-sectional study. *Journal of Psychosomatic Research*, 53, 741–8.

Akimoto, T., Kumai, Y., Akama, T., Hayashi, E., Murakami, H., Soma, R., Kuno, S. and Kono, I. (2003) Effects of 12 months of exercise training on salivary secretory IgA levels in elderly subjects. *British Journal of Sports Medicine*, 37, 76–9.

Albers, L.H., Johnson, D.E., Hostetter, M.K., Iverson, S. and Miller, L.C. (1997) Health of children adopted from the former Soviet Union and Eastern Europe: Comparison with preadoptive medical records. *Journal of the American Medical Association*, 278, 922–4.

Albert, R.S. (1990) Identity, experiences and career choice among the exceptionally gifted and talented. In M.A. Runco and R.S. Albert (eds) *Theories of Creativity*. Newbury Park, CA: Sage.

Albrecht, R.J. and Pories, W.J. (1999) Surgical intervention for the severely obese. *Ballière's Clinical Endocrinology and Metabolism*, 13, 149–72.

Alcock, J.E. (1981) *Parapsychology: Science or magic?* New York: Pergamon Press.

Aleman, A. and Swart, M. (2008) Sex differences in neural activation to facial expressions denoting contempt and disgust. *PLoS ONE*, 3(11), e3622.

Aleman, A. and Swart, M. (2008) Sex differences in neural activation to facial expressions denoting contempt and disgust. *PLoS ONE*, 3(11), e3622.

Ales, J.M., Appelbaum, L.G., Cottereau, B.R. and Norcia, A.M. (2013) The time course of shape discrimination in the human brain. *Neuroimage*, 67, 77–88.

Alexander, R.D. (1979) *Darwinism and Human Affairs*. Seattle, WA: University of Washington Press.

Alibali, M.W., Heath, D.C. and Myers, H.J. (2001) Effects of visibility between speaker and listener on gesture production: Some gestures are meant to be seen. *Journal of Memory and Language*, 44, 169–88.

Alipour, A. (2006) Teaching undergraduate psychology in the Islamic Republic of Iran. *International Journal of Psychology*, 41(1), 35–41.

Allan, L.G., Siegel, S. and Hannah, S. (2007) The sad truth about depressive realism. *Quarterly Journal of Experimental Psychology*, 60, 482–5.

Allen, L.S. and Gorski, R.A. (1992) Sexual orientation and the size of the anterior commissure in the human brain. *Proceedings of the National Academy of Sciences*, 89, 7199–202.

Allen, M.A. and Fischer, G.J. (1978) Ambient temperature effects on paired associate learning. *Ergonomics*, 21, 95–101.

Allen, M.S. and Jones, M.V. (2014) The home advantage over the first 20 seasons of the English Premier League: Effects of shirt colour, team ability and time trends. *International Journal of Sport and Exercise Psychology*, 12(1), 10–18.

Allen, V.L. (1975) Social support for non-conformity. In L. Berkowitz (ed.) *Advances in Experimental Social Psychology*, Vol. 8. New York: Academic Press, pp. 1–43.

Allen, V.L. and Levine, J.M. (1971) Social support and conformity: The role of independent assessment of reality. *Journal of Experimental Social Psychology*, 7, 48–58.

Allik, J. and McCrae, R.R. (2004) Toward a geography of personality traits: Patterns of profiles across 36 cultures. *Journal of Cross-Cultural Psychology*, 35 (1), 13–28.

Allport, A. (1988) What concept is consciousness? In A. Marcel and E. Bisiach (eds) *Consciousness in Contemporary Science*. Oxford: Oxford University Press.

Allport, G.W. (1954) *The Nature of Prejudice.* Reading, MA: Addison-Wesley.

Allport, G.W. (1968) The historical background of modern social psychology. In G. Lindzey and E. Aronson (eds) *The Handbook of Social Psychology,* Vol. 1. Reading, MA: Addison-Wesley.

Allport, G.W. and Odbert, H.S. (1936) Trait-names: A psycholexical study. *Psychological Monographs,* 47 (1, Whole No. 211).

Almeida, O.P., Norman, P., Hankey, G., Jamrozik, K. and Flicker, L. (2006) Successful mental health aging: Results from a longitudinal study of older Australian men. *American Journal of Geriatric Psychiatry,* 14 (1), 27–35.

Alsaker, F.D. (1992) Pubertal timing, overweight and psychological adjustment. *Journal of Early Adolescence,* 12, 396–419.

Alsaker, F.D. (1996) Annotation: The impact of puberty. *Journal of Child Psychology and Psychiatry,* 37(3), 249–58.

Al-Shawa, L., Lewis, D.M.G. and Buss, D.M. (2014) Mating strategy and disgust. *Evolution and Human Behaviour,* 36, 199–205.

Altman, J. and Das, G.D. (1965) Autoradiographic and histological evidence of postnatal hippocampal neurogenesis in rats. *Journal of Comparative Neurology,* 124, 319–35.

Ambrosio, A.L. and Sheehan, E.P. (1991) The just world belief and the AIDS epidemic. *Journal of Social Behavior and Personality,* 6, 163–70.

American Psychiatric Association (2001) *DSM-IV-TR: Diagnostic and Statistical Manual of Mental Disorders.* Arlington, VA: APA.

American Psychiatric Association (2013) *Diagnostic and Statistical Manual of Mental Disorders (DSM-5®).* American Psychiatric Pub.

American Psychological Association (2014) http://www.apa.org/about/offices/ogc/amicus/gomes-johnson.aspx

American Psychological Society (2015) Replication in psychological science. *Psychological Science,* 26, 1827–32.

Amunts, K., Ebell, C., Muller, J., Telefont, M., Knoll, A. and Lippert, T. (2016) The Human Brain Project: Creating a European research infrastructure to decode the human brain. *Neuron,* 92, 574–81.

Amunts, K., Schleicher, A., Burgel, U., Mohlberg, H., Uylings, H.B. and Zilles, K. (1999) Broca's region revisited: cytoarchitecture and intersubject variability. *Journal of Comparative Neurology,* 412(2), 319–41.

Ancoli-Israel, S. (2000) Insomnia in the elderly: A review for the primary care practitioners. *Sleep,* 23, S23–S30.

Andel, R., Vigen, C., Mack, W.J., Clark, L.J. and Gatz, M. (2006) The effect of education and occupational complexity on rate of cognitive decline in Alzheimer's patients. *Journal of the International Neuropsychological Society,* 12, 147–52.

Andersen, S.L. and Teicher, M.H. (2008) Stress, sensitive periods and maturational events in adolescent depression. *Trends in Neurosciences,* 31 (4), 183–91.

Andersen, S.L., Tomoda, A., Vincow, E.S., Valente, E., Polcari, A. and Teicher, M.H. (2008) Preliminary evidence for sensitive periods in the effect of childhood sexual abuse on regional brain development. *Journal of Neuropsychiatry and Clinical Neuroscience,* 20, 292–301.

Andershed, A-K. (2005) *In Sync with Adolescence: the role of morningness-eveningness in adolescence.* New York: Springer.

Anderson, A. and Buggren, A. (2014) Cognitive and neurodevelopmental benefits of extended formula-feeding in infants: Re: Deoni., 2013. *Neuroimage,* 100, 706–9.

Anderson, B. and Harvey, T. (1996) Alterations in cortical thickness and neuronal density in the frontal cortex of Albert Einstein. *Neuroscience Letters,* 210, 161–4.

Anderson, C.A. (2001) Heat and violence. *Current Directions in Psychological Science,* 10, 33–8.

Anderson, C.A. and Anderson, K.B. (1996) Violent crime rate studies in philosophical context: A destructive testing approach to heat and southern culture of violence effects. *Journal of Personality and Social Psychology,* 70, 740–56.

Anderson, C.A., Shibuya, A., Ihori, N., Swing, E.L., Bushman, B.J., Sakamoto, A., Rothstein, H.R. and Saleem, M. (2010) Violent video game effects of aggression, empathy, and prosocial behavior in Eastern and Western countries. *Psychological Bulletin,* 136, 151–3.

Anderson, D.E., DePaulo, B.M., Ansfield, M., Tickle, J.J. and Green, E. (1999) Beliefs about cues to deception: Mindless stereotypes or untapped wisdom? *Journal of Nonverbal Behaviour,* 23, 67–89.

Anderson, N.E. and Kiehl, K.A. (2012) The psychopath magnetized: Insights from brain imaging. *Trends in Cognitive Sciences,* 16, 52–60.

Anderson, N.H. (1978) Cognitive algebra: Integration theory applied to social attribution. In L. Berkowitz (ed.) *Cognitive Theories in Social Psychology.* New York: Academic Press, pp. 1–126.

Anderson, S.W., Damasio, H. and Damasio, A.R. (2005) A neural basis for collecting behaviour in humans. *Brain,* 128, 201–12.

Anderson, S.W., Damasio, H., Jones, R.D. and Tranel, D. (1991) Wisconsin Card Sorting Test performance as a measure of frontal lobe damage. *Journal of Clinical and Experimental Neuropsychology,* 13, 909–22.

Anderson, V., Brown, S., Newitt, H. and Hoile, H. (2011) Long-term outcome from childhood traumatic brain injury: intellectual ability, personality, and quality of life. *Neuropsychology,* 25(2), 176.

Andrade, J. (1995) Learning during anaesthesia: A review. *British Journal of Psychology,* 86, 479–506.

Andreano, J.M. and Cahill, L. (2009) Sex influences on the neurobiology of learning and memory. *Learning and Memory,* 16, 248–66.

Andreasen, N.C. (1987) Creativity and mental illness: Prevalence rates in writers and first degree relatives. *American Journal of Psychiatry,* 144, 1288–92.

Andreassi, J. (2007) *Psychophysiology* (5th edn). Hillsdale, NJ: Lawrence Erlbaum Associates.

Andrews, G. (1991) Anxiety, personality and anxiety disorders. *International Review of Psychiatry,* 3, 293–302.

Andrews, G., Pollock, C. and Stewart, G. (1989) The determination of defense style by questionnaire. *Archives of General Psychiatry,* 46, 455–60.

Andrews, G., Slade, T. and Peters, L. (1999) Classification in psychiatry: ICD 10 versus DSM-IV. *British Journal of Psychiatry,* 174, 3–5.

Andrews, T.J. and Ewbank, M.P. (2004) Distinct representations for facial identity and changeable aspects of faces in the human temporal lobe. *Neuroimage,* 23, 905–13.

Angele, B. and Rayner, K. (2013) Processing 'the' in the parafovea: Are articles skipped automatically? *Journal of Experimental Psychology: Learning, Memory and Cognition,* 39, 649–62.

Angermeyer, M.C. and Matschinger, H. (2005) Causal beliefs and attitudes to people with schizophrenia. *British Journal of Psychiatry,* 186, 331–4.

Angermeyer, M.C., Matschinger, H., Carta, M.G. and Schomerus, G. (2013) Changes in the perception of mental illness stigma in Germany over the last two decades. *European Psychiatry,* 29, 390–5.

Anglin, R.E.S., Samaan, Z., Waiter, S.D. and McDonald, S. (2013) Vitamin D deficiency and depression in adults. *British Journal of Psychiatry,* 202, 100–7.

Angrist, B.J., Rotrosen, J. and Gershon, S. (1980) Positive and negative symptoms in schizophrenia: Differential response to amphetamine and neuroleptics. *Psychopharmacology,* 72, 17–19.

Anguera, J.A., Reuter-Lorenz, P.A., Willingham, D.T. and Seidler, R.D. (2010) Contributions of spatial working memory to visuomotor learning. *Journal of Cognitive Neuroscience,* 22, 1917–30.

Anguera, J.A., Reuter-Lorenz, P.A., Willingham, D.T. and Seidler, R.D. (2011) Failure to engage spatial working memory contributes to declines in visuospatial motor learning. *Journal of Cognitive Neuroscience*, 23, 11–25.

Annau, Z. and Kamin, L.J. (1961) The conditioned emotional response as a function of intensity of the UCS. *Journal of Comparative and Physiological Psychology*, 54, 428–32.

Annerstedt, M., Jonsson, P., Wallergard, M., Johansson, G., Karlson, B., Grahn, P., Hansen, A.M. and Wahrborg, P. (2013) Inducing physiological stress recovery with sounds of nature in a virtual reality forest. *Physiology and Behavior*, 118, 240–50.

Annese, J., Schenker-Ahmed, N.M., Bartsch, H., Maechler, P., Sheh, C., Thomas, N., Kayano, J., Ghatan, A., Bresler, N., Frosch, M.P., Klaming, R. and Corkin, S. (2014) Postmortem examination of patient H.M.'s brain based on histological sectioning and digital 3D reconstruction. *Nature Communications*, 5, 3122.

Annett, M. (1992) Spatial ability in subgroups of left and right handers. *British Journal of Psychology*, 83, 493–515.

Anschutz, D.J., Engels, R.C.M.E., Becker, E.S. and van Strien, T. (2008) The bold and the beautiful. Influence of body size of televised media models on body dissatisfaction and actual food intake. *Appetite*, 51, 530–7.

Anschutz, D.J., Engels, R.C.M.E., van der Zwaluw, C.S. and van Strien, T. (2011) Sex differences in young adults' snack food intake after food commercial exposure. *Appetite*, 56, 255–60.

APA (2010) *Ethical Principles of Psychologists and Code of Conduct*. Washington DC: American Psychological Association.

Appelbaum, P.S. and Scurich, N. (2014) Impact of behavioural genetic evidence on the adjudication of criminal behavior. *Journal of the American Academy of Psychiatry and Law*, 42, 91–100.

Arce, R., Farina, F., Vila, C. and Santiago, D. (1998) In search of causes of hung juries. *Expert Evidence*, 6, 1–18.

Archila-Suerte, P., Zevin, J., Ramos, A.I. and Hernandez, A.E. (2013) The neural basis of non-native speech perception in bilingual children. *Neuroimage*, 67, 51–63.

Arendt, M., Rosenberg, R., Foldager, L., Perto, G. and Munk-Jorgensen, P. (2005) Cannabis-induced psychosis and subsequent schizophrenia-spectrum disorders: follow-up study of 535 incident cases. *British Journal of Psychiatry*, 187, 510–15.

Arnedo, J. *et al.* (2014) Uncovering the hidden risk architecture of the schizophrenias. *American Journal of Psychiatry*, 172, 139–53.

Arnett, J. (1995) The young and the reckless: Adolescent reckless behavior. *Current Directions in Psychological Science*, 4, 67–71.

Arnsten, A.F.T., Girgis, R.R., Gray, D.L. and Mailman, R.B. (2016) Novel dopamine therapeutics for cognitive deficits in schizophrenia. *Biological Psychiatry*, 81, 67–77.

Aron, A.R., Robbins, T.W. and Poldrack, R.A. (2014) Inhibition and the right inferior frontal cortex: one decade on. *Trends in Cognitive Sciences*, 18, 177–85.

Aronson, E. (2007) *The Social Animal*. New York: Freeman.

Aronson, E. and Linder, D. (1965) Gain and loss of esteem as determinants of interpersonal attractiveness. *Journal of Experimental Social Psychology*, 1, 156–71.

Aronson, E. and Mills, J. (1959) The effects of severity of initiation on liking for a group. *Journal of Abnormal and Social Psychology*, 59, 177–81.

Aronson, J., Fried, C.B. and Good, C. (2002) Reducing the effects of stereotype threat on African American college students by shaping theories of intelligence. *Journal of Experimental Social Psychology*, 38, 113–25.

Aronson, J., Lustina, M., Good, C., Keough, K., Steele, C.M. and Brown, J. (1999) When White men can't do math: Necessary and sufficient factors in stereotype threat. *Journal of Experimental Social Psychology*, 35, 29–46.

Arseneault, L., Bowes, L. and Shakoor, S. (2010) Bullying victimization in youths and mental health problems. *Psychological Medicine*, 40, 717–19.

Arthur, W., Cho, I. and Muñoz, G.J. (2016) Red vs. green: Does the exam booklet color matter in higher education summative evaluations? Not likely. *Psychonomic Bulletin & Review*, 23(5), 1596–601.

Asano, M., Taki, Y., Hashizume, H., Takeuchi, H., Thyreau, B., Sassa, Y., Asano, K. and Kawashima, R. (2014) Correlations between brain structures and study time at home in healthy children: a longitudinal analysis. *Brain and Behavior*, 4, 801–11.

Asch, S.E. (1946) Forming impressions of personality. *Journal of Abnormal and Social Psychology*, 41, 258–90.

Asch, S.E. (1951) Effects of group pressure upon the modification and distortion of judgment. In H. Guetzkow (ed.) *Groups, Leadership, and Men*. Pittsburgh, PA: Carnegie.

Asch, S.E. (1952) *Social Psychology*. New York: Prentice Hall.

Asch, S.E. (1955) Opinions and social pressure. *Scientific American Mind*, 193, 31–5.

ASH (2015) http://ash.org.uk/about/annual-reports/

Ashcraft, M.H. and Kirk, E.P. (2001) The relationship among working memory, math anxiety and performance. *Journal of Experimental Psychology (General)*, 130, 224–37.

Ashton, C.H. (2001) Pharmacology and effects of cannabis: a brief review. *British Journal of Psychiatry*, 178, 101–6.

ASK (2015) *Use of electronic cigarettes among children in Great Britain*. London: ASH.

Aspinwall, L.G. and Taylor, S.E. (1992) Individual differences, coping, and psychological adjustment: A longitudinal study of college adjustment and performance. *Journal of Personality and Social Psychology*, 63, 989–1003.

Atasoy, D., Betley, J.N., Su, H.H. and Sternson, S.M. (2012) Deconstruction of a neural circuit for hunger. *Nature*, 488, 172–7.

Atkinson, G., Coldwells, A., Reily, T. and Waterhouse, J. (1993) A comparison of circadian rhythms in work performance between physically active and inactive subjects. *Ergonomics*, 36, 273–81.

Atkinson, R.C. and Shiffrin, R.M. (1968) Human memory: A proposed system and its control processes. In K.W. Spence and J.T. Spence (eds) *The Psychology of Learning and Motivation: Advances in research and theory*, Vol. 2. New York: Academic Press.

Atlas, L.Y. and Wager, T.D. (2014) A meta-analysis of brain mechanisms of placebo analgesia: consistent findings and unanswered questions. In *Placebo*. Springer Berlin Heidelberg, pp. 37–69.

Atlas, L.Y., Bolger, N., Lindquist, M.A. and Wager, T.D. (2010) Brain mediators of predictive cue effects on perceived pain. *Journal of Neuroscience*, 30(39), 12964–77.

Attrill, M.J., Gresty, K.A., Hill, R.A. and Barton, R.A. (2008) Red shirt colour is associated with long-term team success in English football. *Journal of Sports Sciences*, 26, 577–82.

Atzil, S., Hendler, T. and Feldman, R. (2011) Specifying the neurobiological basis of human attachment: Brain, hormones and behaviour in synchronous and intrusive mothers. *Neuropsychopharmacology*, 36, 2603–15.

Atzil, S., Hendler, T., Zagoory-Sharon, O., Weintraub, Y. and Feldman, R. (2012) Synchrony and specificity in the maternal and the paternal brain: Relations to oxytocin and vasopressin. *JAACAP*, 51, 798–811.

Au, T.K., Sidle, A.L. and Rollins, K.B. (1993) Developing an intuitive understanding of conservation and contamination: Invisible particles as a plausible mechanism. *Developmental Psychology*, 29, 286–99.

Aubert-Broche, B., Fonov, V., Garcia-Lorenzo, D., Mouiha, A., Guizard, N., Coupe, P., Eskildsen, S.F. and Collins, D.L. (2013) A new method for structural volume analysis of longitudinal brain MRI data and its application on studying the growth trajectories of anatomical brain structures in childhood. *Neuroimage*, 15(82): 393–402.

Augoustinos, M. and Walker, I. (1995) *Social Cognition: An integrated introduction.* London: Sage.

Austin, G., Bondü, R. and Elsner, B. (2017) Longitudinal relations between children's cognitive and affective theory of mind with reactive and proactive aggression. *Aggressive Behavior*, in press.

Australian Brain Alliance Steering Committee (2016) Australian Brain Alliance. *Neuron*, 92, 597–600.

Auyeung, B., Baron-Cohen, S., Ashwin, E., Knickmeyer, R., Taylor, K. and Hackett, G. (2009) Fetal testosterone and autistic traits. *British Journal of Psychology*, 100, 1–22.

Awh, E., Jonides, J., Smith, E.E., Schumacher, E.H., Koeppe, R.A. and Katz, S. (1996) Dissociation of storage and rehearsal in verbal working memory. *Psychological Science*, 7, 25–31.

Axel, R. (1995) The molecular logic of smell. *Scientific American Mind*, 273, 154–9.

Axer, H., Klingner, C.M. and Prescher, A. (2012) Fiber anatomy of dorsal and ventral language streams. *Brain and Language*, 127, 192–204.

Ayabe-Kanamura, S., Schicker, I., Laska, M., Hudson, R., Distel, H., Kobayakawa, T. and Saito, S. (1998) Differences in perception of everyday odors: a Japanese–German cross-cultural study. *Chemical Senses*, 23, 31–8.

Ayllon, T. and Azrin, N.H. (1968) *The Token Economy: A motivational system for therapy and rehabilitation.* New York: Appleton-Century-Crofts.

Aylward, E.H. *et al.* (2003) Instructional treatment associated with changes in brain activation in children with dyslexia. *Neurology.* 61, 212–19.

Ayoko, B.O., Hartel, C.E. and Callan, V.J. (2002) Resolving the puzzle of productive and destructive conflict in culturally heterogeneous workgroups: A communication accommodation theory approach. *International Journal of Conflict Management*, 13, 165–95.

B

Baars, B.J. (1988) *A Cognitive Theory of Consciousness.* Cambridge: Cambridge University Press.

Baars, B.J., Newman, J. and Taylor, J.G. (1998) Neuronal mechanisms of consciousness: A relational global-workspace framework. In S.R. Hameroff, A.W. Kaszniak and A.C. Scott (eds) *Towards a Science of Consciousness II.* Cambridge, MA: MIT Press.

Babad, E., Darley, J.M. and Kaplowitz, H. (1999) Developmental aspects in students' course selection. *Journal of Educational Psychology*, 91(1), 157–68.

Babiak, P., Neumann, C.S. and Hare, R.D. (2010) Corporate psychopathy: Talking the walk. *Behavioral Sciences and the Law*, 28, 174–93.

Babkin, B.P. (1949) *Pavlov: A biography.* Chicago, IL: University of Chicago Press.

Back, M.D., Schmukle, S.C. and Egloff, B. (2006) Who is late and who is early? Big Five personality factors and punctuality in attending psychological experiments. *Journal of Research in Personality*, 40, 841–48.

Back, M.D., Stopfer, J.M., Vazire, S., Gaddis, S., Schmukle, S.C., Egloff, B. and Gosling, S.D. (2010) Facebook profiles reflect actual personality, not self-idealization. *Psychological Science*, 21, 372–74.

Badcock, C. (1991) *Evolution and Individual Behavior: An introduction to human sociobiology.* Cambridge, MA: Blackwell.

Badcock, N.A., Nye, A. and Bishop, D.V.M. (2012) Using functional transcranial Doppler ultrasonography to assess language lateralization: Influence of task and difficulty level. *Laterality*, 17, 694–710.

Baddeley, A.D. (1982) Domains of recollection. *Psychological Review*, 89, 708–729.

Baddeley, A.D. (1986) *Working Memory.* Oxford: Clarendon Press.

Baddeley, A.D. (1996) *Human Memory: Theory and practice* (2nd edn) Hove: Psychology Press.

Baddeley, A.D. and Hitch, G.J. (1974) Working memory. In G.H. Bower (ed.) *The Psychology of Learning and Motivation: Advances in research and theory*, Vol. 8. New York: Academic Press.

Baddeley, A.D. and Hitch, G.J. (1977) Recency examined. In S. Dornic (ed.) *Attention and Performance*, Vol. 6. Hillsdale, NJ: Lawrence Erlbaum Associates.

Baddeley, A.D. and Logie, R.H. (1992) Auditory imagery and working memory. In R.S. Nickerson (ed.) *Attention and Performance*, Vol. 8. Hillsdale, NJ: Lawrence Erlbaum Associates.

Baddeley, A.D., DellaSala, S. and Spinnler, H. (1991) The two-component hypothesis of memory deficit in Alzheimer's disease. *Journal of Clinical and Experimental Neuropsychology*, 13, 372–380.

Baddeley, A.D., Thomson, N. and Buchanan, M. (1975) Word length and the structure of short-term memory. *Journal of Verbal Learning and Verbal Behaviour*, 14, 575–89.

Baenninger, M.A. (1994) The development of face recognition: featural or configurational processing? *Journal of Experimental Child Psychology*, 57, 377–96.

Baer, D.M., Peterson, R.F. and Sherman, J.A. (1967) Development of imitation by reinforcing behavioral similarity to a model. *Journal of the Experimental Analysis of Behavior*, 10, 405–16.

Baez-Mendoza, R. and Schultz, W. (2013) The role of the striatum in social behaviour. *Frontiers in Neuroscience*, 7, 233.

Baglioni, C., Battagliese, G., Feige, B., Spiegelhalder, K., Nissen, C., Voderholzer, U., . . . and Riemann, D. (2011) Insomnia as a predictor of depression: a meta-analytic evaluation of longitudinal epidemiological studies. *Journal of Affective Disorders*, 135(1), 10–19.

Bagwell, C.L., Newcomb, A.F. and Bukowski, W.M. (1998) Preadolescent friendship and peer rejection as predictors of adult adjustment. *Child Development*, 69 (1), 140–153.

Bahrick, H.P. (1984) Semantic memory content in permastore: Fifty years of memory for Spanish learned in school. *Journal of Experimental Psychology: General*, 113, 1–29.

Bahrick, H.P., Bahrick, P.O. and Wittlinger, R.P. (1975) Fifty years of memories for names and faces: A cross-sectional approach. *Journal of Experimental Psychology: General*, 104, 54–75.

Bahrick, H.P., Hall, L.K. and da Costa, L.A. (2008) Fifty years of memory of college grades: Accuracy and distortions. *Emotion*, 8, 1.

Bai, D.L. and Bertenthal, B.I. (1992) Locomotor status and the development of spatial search skills. *Child Development*, 63, 215–26.

Bailey, A., Phillips, W. and Rutter, M. (1996) Autism: Towards an integration of clinical, genetic, neuropsychological and neurobiological perspectives. *Journal of Child Psychology and Psychiatry*, 37(1), 89–126.

Bailey, J.M. and Pillard, R.C. (1991) A genetic study of male sexual orientation. *Archives of General Psychiatry*, 48, 1089–96.

Bailey, J.M., Pillard, R.C., Neale, M.C. and Agyei, Y. (1993) Heritable factors influence sexual orientation in women. *Archives of General Psychiatry*, 50, 217–23.

Bailey, J.M., Vasey, P.L., Diamond, L.M., Breedlove, S.M., Vilain, E. and Epprecht, M. (2016) Sexual orientation, controversy and science. *Psychological Science in the Public Interest*, 17, 45–101.

Baillieux, H., Vandervliet, E.J.M., Manto, M., Parizel, P.M., Deyn, P.P. and Marien, P. (2009) Developmental dyslexia and widespread activation across the cerebellar hemispheres. *Brain and Language*, 108, 122–32.

Bain, J., Langevin, R., Dickey, R. and Ben-Aron, M. (1987) Sex hormones in murderers and assaulters. *Behavioural Science and the Law*, 5, 95–101.

Bair, M.J., Poleshuck, E.L., Wu, J., Krebs, E.K., Damush, T.M., Tu, W. and Kroenke, K. (2013) Anxiety but not social stressors predict 12-month depression and pain severity. *The Clinical Journal of Pain*, 29(2), 95.

Bajada, C.J., Lambon-Ralph, M.A. and Cloutman, L.L. (2015) Transport for language south of the Sylvian fissure. *Cortex*, 69, 141–51.

Baker, B.L. (1969) Symptom treatment and symptom substitution in enuresis. *Journal of Abnormal Psychology*, 74, 42–9.

Baker, T.B., Japuntich, S.J., Hogle, J.M., McCarthy, D.E. and Curtin, J.J. (2006) Pharmacologic and behavioural withdrawal from addictive drugs. *Current Directions in Psychological Science*, 15(5), 232–6.

Baldwin, D.S., Anderson, I.M., Nutt, D., Allgulander, C., Bandelow, B., den Boer, J.A. . . . and Malizia, A. (2014) Evidence-based pharmacological treatment of anxiety disorders, post-traumatic stress disorder and obsessive-compulsive disorder: a revision of the 2005 guidelines from the British Association for Psychopharmacology. *Journal of Psychopharmacology*, 28(5), 403–39.

Baldwin, J.D. and Baldwin, J.I. (1998) *Behavior Principles in Everyday Life* (3rd edn). Hillsdale, NJ: Prentice Hall.

Balkin, T.J., Braun, A.R., Wesensten, N.J., Jeffries, K., Varga, M., Baldwin, P., Belenky, G. and Herscovitch, P. (2002) The process of awakening: a PET study of regional brain activity patterns mediating the re-establishment of alertness and consciousness. *Brain*, 125, 2308–19.

Balon, R., Jordan, M., Pohl, R. and Yeragani, V.K. (1989) Family history of anxiety disorders in control subjects with lactate-induced panic attacks. *American Journal of Psychiatry*, 146, 1304–6.

Balzarini, R.N., Dobson, K., Chin, K. and Campbell, L. (2016) Does exposure to erotic reduce attraction and love for romantic partners in men? Independent replications of Kenrick, Gutierres and Goldberg (1989) study 2. *Journal of Experimental Social Psychology*, 770, 191–7.

Banbury, S. and Berry, D.C. (1998) Disruption of office-related tasks by speech and office noise. *British Journal of Psychology*, 89, 499–517.

Bandura, A. (1971) Psychotherapy based upon modeling principles. In A.E. Bergin and S.L. Garfield (eds) *Handbook of Psychotherapy and Behavior Change*. New York: Wiley.

Bandura, A. (1973) *Aggression: A social learning analysis*. Englewood Cliffs, NJ: Prentice Hall.

Bandura, A. (1977) *Social Learning Theory*. Upper Saddle River, NJ: Prentice Hall.

Bandura, A. (1978) The self system in reciprocal determinism. *American Psychologist*, 33, 344–58.

Bandura, A. (1982) Self-efficacy mechanism in human agency. *American Psychologist*, 37, 122–47.

Bandura, A. (1986) *Social Foundations of Thought and Action: A social-cognitive theory*. Englewood Cliffs, NJ: Prentice Hall.

Bandura, A. and Menlove, F.L. (1968) Factors determining vicarious extinction of avoidance behavior through symbolic modeling. *Journal of Personality and Social Psychology*, 8, 99–108.

Bangalore, S.S., Prasad, K.M.R., Montrose, D.M., Goradia, D.D., Diwadkar, V.A. and Keshavan, M.S. (2008) Cannabis use and brain structural alterations in first episode schizophrenia. *Schizophrenia Research*, 99, 1–6.

Banich, M.T. (1995) Interhemispheric processing: Theoretical considerations and empirical approaches. In R.J. Davidson and K. Hugdahl (eds) *Brain Asymmetry*. Cambridge, MA: MIT Press.

Banks, M.S., Aslin, R.N. and Letson, R.D. (1975) Sensitive period for the development of human binocular vision. *Science*, 190, 675–7.

Banyard, P. and Hunt, N. (2000) Reporting research: Something missing? *The Psychologist*, 13(2), 68–71.

Bao, A.-M., Meynen, G. and Swaab. D.F. (2008) The stress system in depression and neurodegeneraton: Focus on the human hypothalamus. *Brain Research Reviews*, 57, 531–33.

Barash, D. (1982) *Sociobiology and Behavior*. London: Hodder & Stoughton.

Barber, J. (1996) *Hypnosis and Suggestion in the Treatment of Pain: A clinical guide*. New York: W.W. Norton.

Barber, J. (1998) The mysterious persistence of hypnotic analgesia. *The International Journal of Clinical and Experimental Hypnosis*, XLVI(1), 28–43.

Barbey, A.K., Colom, R., Solomon, J., Krueger, F., Forbes, C. and Grafman, J. (2012) An integrative architecture for general intelligence and executive function revealed for lesion mapping. *Brain*, 135, 1154–1164.

Barbui, C., Cirpriani, A., Patel, V., Ayuso-Mateous, J.L. and van Ommersen, M. (2011) Efficacy of antidepressants and benzodiazepines in minor depression. *British Journal of Psychiatry*, 198, 11–16.

Barella, L.A., Etnier, J.L. and Chang, Y.K. (2010) The immediate and delayed effects of an acute bout of exercise on cognitive performance of healthy older adults. *Journal of Ageing and Physical Activity*, 18, 87–98.

Barger, L.K., Cade, B.E., Ayas, N.T., Cronin, J.W., Rosner, B., Speizer, F.E. and Czeisler, C.A. (2005) Extended work shifts and the risk of motor vehicle crashes among interns. *The New England Journal of Medicine*, 352 (2), 125–34.

Bargh, J.A. (1989) Conditional automaticity: Varieties of automatic influence in social perception and cognition. In J.S. Uleman and J.A. Bargh (eds) *Unintended Thought*. New York: Guilford Press, pp. 3–51.

Bargh, J.A., Chen, M. and Burrows, L. (1996) The automaticity of social behavior: Direct effects of trait concept and stereotype activation on action. *Journal of Personality and Social Psychology*, 71, 230–44.

Barkley, R.A. (1997) Behavioural inhibition, sustained attention and executive function: Constructing a unifying theory of ADHD. *Psychological Bulletin*, 121(1), 65–94.

Barkley, R.A. (2006) *Attention-deficit Hyperactivity Disorder: A handbook for diagnosis and treatment*. (3rd edn). New York: Guilford Press.

Barlett, C.P., Harris, R. J. and Bruey, C. (2008) The effect of the amount of blood in a violent video game on aggression, hostility, and arousal. *Journal of Experimental Social Psychology*, 44(3), 539–46.

Barlow, D.H. (2010) Negative effects from psychological treatments. *American Psychologist*, 65, 13–20.

Barlow, D.H., Ellard, K.K., Sauer-Zavala, S., Bullis, J.R. and Carl, J.R. (2014) The origins of neuroticism. *Perspectives on Psychological Science*, 9, 481–96.

Barnes, R.C., Hussein, A., Anderson, D.N. and Powell, D. (1997) Maintenance electroconvulsive therapy. *British Journal of Psychiatry*, 170, 285–87.

Barnett, J.H., Werners, U., Secher, S.M., Hill, K.E., Brazil, R., Masson, K. *et al.* (2007) Substance use in a population-based clinic sample of people with first-episode psychosis. *British Journal of Psychiatry*, 190, 515–20.

Barnett, M.A. (1986) Commonsense and research findings in personality. *Teaching of Psychology*, 13, 62–4.

Barnombudsmannen (1997) *Barndom satter spar, Rapport fran barnens myndighet*. Sweden: Barnombudsmannen.

Baron, A. and Galizio, M. (1983) Instructional control of human operant behavior. *Psychological Record*, 33, 495–520.

Baron, A., Perone, M. and Galizio, M. (1991) Analyzing the reinforcement process at the human level: Can application and behavioristic interpretation replace laboratory research? *The Behavior Analyst*, 14, 79–117.

Baron, J. and Jurney, J. (1993) Norms against voting for coerced reform. *Journal of Personality and Social Psychology*, 64, 347–55.

Baron, R.A. and Byrne, D. (1997) *Social Psychology: Understanding human interaction* (8th edn). Boston, MA: Allyn and Bacon.

Baron, R.A. and Richardson, D.R. (1994) *Human Aggression* (2nd edn). New York: Plenum Press.

Baron, R.A., Neuman, J.H. and Geddes, D. (1999) Social and personal determinants of workplace aggression: evidence for the impact of perceived injustice and the Type A behaviour pattern. *Aggressive Behaviour*, 25, 281–96.

Baron, R.S. (1986) Distraction-conflict theory: Progress and problems. In L. Berkowitz (ed.) *Advances in Experimental Social Psychology*, Vol. 20. New York: Academic Press, pp. 1–40.

Baron-Cohen, S. (1995) *Mindblindness: An essay on autism and theory of mind.* Cambridge, MA: MIT Press.

Baron-Cohen, S. (2003) *The Essential Difference: Men, women and the extreme male brain.* London: Penguin.

Baron-Cohen, S., Allen, J. and Gillberg, C. (1992) Can autism be detected at 18 months? The needle, the haystack and the CHAT. *British Journal of Psychiatry*, 161, 839–43.

Baron-Cohen, S., Leslie, A.M. and Frith, U. (1985) Does the autistic child have a 'theory of mind'? *Cognition*, 21, 37–46.

Baron-Cohen, S., Scott, F.J., Allison, C., Williams, J., Bolton, P., Matthews, F.E. and Brayne, C. (2009) Prevalence of autism-spectrum conditions: UK school-based population study. *The British Journal of Psychiatry*, 194, 500–9.

Baron-Cohen, S., Wheelwright, S., Hill, J., Raste, Y. and Plumb, I. (2001) The 'reading the mind in the eyes' test revised version: A study with normal adults, and adults with Asperger Syndrome or high-functioning autism. *Journal of Child Psychology and Psychiatry*, 42(2), 241–51.

Barraclough, B. (1988) International variation in the suicide rate of 15–24 year olds. *Social Psychiatry and Psychiatric Epidemiology*, 23, 75–84.

Barragan-Jason, G., Lachat, F. and Barbeau, E.J. (2012) How fast is famous face recognition? *Frontiers in Psychology*, 3, 1–11.

Barratt, D., Redei, A.C., Innes-Ker, A. and van der Weijer, J. (2016) Does the Kuleshov effect really exist? Revisiting a classic film experiment on facial expressions and emotional contexts. *Perception*, 0, 1–28.

Barraza, J.A. and Zak, P.J. (2009) Empathy toward strangers triggers oxytocin release and subsequent generosity. *Annals of the New York Academy of Science*, 1176, 182–9.

Barrett, D. and Fish, W. (2011) Our move: using chess to improve math achievement for students who receive special education services. *International Journal of Special Education*, 26, 181–93.

Barrett, L.F. (2014) The conceptual act theory: A précis. *Emotion Review*, 6, 292–7.

Barry, C.L., McGinty, E.E., Vernick, J.S. and Webster, D.W. (2013) After Newtown – public opinion on gun policy and mental illness. *New England Journal of Medicine*, 368, 1077–81.

Bart, W.M. (2014) On the effect of chess training on scholastic achievement. *Frontiers in Psychology*, 5, 1–3.

Bartam, D. (2013) Happiness and economic migration: a comparison of Eastern European migrants and stayers. *Migration Studies*, 1, 156–75.

Bartlett, F.C. (1932) *Remembering: An experimental and social study.* Cambridge: Cambridge University Press.

Bartley, C.E. and Roesch, S.C. (2011) Coping with daily stress: The role of conscientiousness. *Personality and Individual Differences*, 50, 79–83.

Bartley, E.J. and Fillingim, R.B. (2013) Sex differences in pain: a brief review of clinical and experimental findings. *British Journal of Anaesthesia*, 111(1), 52–8.

Bartolomeo, P., bachoud-Levi, A-C. and de Schotten, M.T. (2013) The anatomy of cerebral achromatopsia. *Cortex*, 56, 138–44.

Bartoshuk, L.M. (1993) The biological basis of food perception and acceptance. *Food Quality and Preference*, 4, 21–32.

Bartram, D. (2013) Happiness and 'economic migration': A comparison of Eastern European migrants and stayers. *Migration Studies*, 1(2), 156–75.

Basak, C., Boot, W.R., Voss, M. and Kramer, A.F. (2008) Can training in a real-time strategy video-game attenuate cognitive decline in older adults? *Psychology and Aging*, 23, 765–77.

Bass, B.M. (1998) *Transformational Leadership: Industrial, military, and educational impact.* Mahwah, NJ: Lawrence Erlbaum Associates.

Basu, S., Qayyum, H. and Mason, S. (2016) Occupational stress in the ED: a systematic literature review. *Emergency Medicine Journal*, emermed-2016.

Bate, S. and Bennetts, R.J. (2014) The rehabilitation of face recognition impairments: a critical review and future directions. *Frontiers in Human Neuroscience*, 8, 1–17.

Bateman, R. J., Xiong, C., Benzinger, T. L., Fagan, A. M., Goate, A., Fox, N. C., . . . and Holtzman, D. M. (2012) Clinical and biomarker changes in dominantly inherited Alzheimer's disease. *New England Journal of Medicine*, 367(9), 795–804.

Batsell Jr, W.R., Perry, J.L., Hanley, E. and Hostetter, A.B. (2017) Ecological validity of the testing effect: the use of daily quizzes in introductory psychology. *Teaching of Psychology*, 44(1), 18–23.

Battro, A.M. (2000) *Half a Brain Is Enough.* Cambridge: Cambridge University Press.

Batty, G.D., Deary, I.J. and Macintyre, S. (2007) Childhood IQ in relation to risk factors for premature mortality in middle-aged persons: The Aberdeen Children of the 1950s study. *Journal of Epidemiology and Community Health*, 61, 241–7.

Bauer, N.S., Lozano, P. and Rivara, E.P. (2007) The effectiveness of the Olweus Bullying Prevention program in public middle schools. *Journal of Adolescent Health*, 40, 266–74.

Bauer, P.J. (1997) Development of memory in early childhood. In N. Cowan and C. Hulme (eds) *The Development of Memory in Childhood.* Hove: Psychology Press.

Bauer, P.J. (2006) Constructing a past in infancy: A neuro-developmental account. *Trends in Cognitive Sciences*, 10, 175–81.

Bauer, P.J. and Dow, G.A.A. (1994) Episodic memory in 16- and 20-month-old children: Specifics are generalised, but not forgotten. *Developmental Psychology*, 30, 403–17.

Bauer, P.J. and Mandler, J.M. (1989) Taxonomies and triads: Conceptual organization in one- to two-year olds. *Cognitive Psychology*, 21, 156–84.

Bauer, P.J. and Mandler, J.M. (1992) Putting the horse before the cart: the use of temporal order in recall of events by one-year-old children. *Developmental Psychology*, 28, 441–52.

Bauer, P.J. and Travis, L.L. (1993) The fabric of an event: Different sources of temporal invariance differentially affect 24-month-olds' recall. *Cognitive Development*, 8, 319–41.

Bauer, P.J. and Wewerka, S.S. (1995) One- to two-year-olds' recall of events: The more expressed, the more impressed. *Journal of Experimental Child Psychology*, 59, 475–96.

Bauer, P.J., Hertsgaard, L.A. and Wewerka, S.S. (1995) Effects of experience and reminding on long-term recall in infancy: Remembering not to forget. *Journal of Experimental Child Psychology*, 59, 260–98.

Baumeister, R.F. (1998) The self. In D.T. Gilbert, S.T. Fiske and G. Lindzey (eds) *Handbook of Social Psychology* (4th edn), Vol. 1. New York: McGraw-Hill, pp. 680–740.

Baumeister, R.F. and Leary, M.R. (1995) The need to belong: Desire for interpersonal attachments as a fundamental human motivation. *Psychological Bulletin*, 117, 497–529.

Baumeister, R.F., Smart, L. and Boden, J.M. (1996) Relation of threatened egotism to violence and aggression: The dark side of high self-esteem. *Psychological Review*, 103, 5–33.

Baumgartner, T., Heinrichs, M., Vonlanthen, A., Fischbacher, U. and Fehr, E. (2008) Oxytocin shapes the neural circuitry of trust adaptation in humans. *Neuron*, 58, 639–50.

Baumrind, D. (1964) Some thoughts on ethics of research: After reading Milgram's 'behavioural study of obedience'. *American Psychologist*, 19, 421–3.

Baur, V., Hanggi, J. and Jancke, L. (2012) Volumetric associations between uncinate fasciculus., amygdala and trait anxiety. *MBC Neuroscience*, 13, 4.

Baxendale, S. (2004) Memories aren't made of this: Amnesia at the movies. *British Medical Journal*, 329, 1480–3.

Baxter, A.J., Scott, K.M., Ferrari, A.J., Norman, R.E., Vos, T. and Whiteford, H.A. (2014a) Challenging the myth of an 'epidemic' of common mental disorders: trends in the global prevalence of anxiety and depression between 1990 and 2010. *Depression and Anxiety*, 31(6), 506–16.

Baxter, A.J., Scott, K.M., Vos, T. and Whiteford, H.A. (2013) Global prevalence of anxiety disorders: a systematic review and meta-regression. *Psychological Medicine*, 43(05), 897–910.

Baxter, A.J., Vos, T., Scott, K.M., Ferrari, A.J. and Whiteford, H.A. (2014b) The global burden of anxiety disorders in 2010. *Psychological Medicine*, 44(11), 2363–74.

Bayley, N. and Oden, M.H. (1955) The maintenance of intellectual ability in gifted adults. *Journal of Gerontology*, 10, 91–107.

Bazarova, N.N., Taft, J.G., Choi, Y.H. and Cosley, D. (2012) Managing impressions and relationships on Facebook: Self-presentational and relational concerns revealed through the analysis of language style. *Journal of Language and Social Psychology*, 32, 121–41.

Bearman, S.K., Presnell, K. and Martinez, E. (2006) The skinny on body dissatisfaction: A longitudinal study of adolescent girls and boys. *Journal of Adolescence*, 35, 217–29.

Beatty, J. (1995) *Principles of Behavioral Neuroscience*. Madison, WI: Wm C. Brown Communications.

Beauchamp, G.K. and Cowart, B.J. (1987) Preference for extremely high levels of salt among young children. *Annals of the NY Academy of Sciences*, 510, 171–2.

Beauchamp, G.K. and Moran, M. (1982) Dietary experience and sweet taste preference in human infants. *Appetite*, 3, 139–52.

Beauchamp, G.K. and Moran, M. (1984) Acceptance of sweet and salty tastes in 2-year old children. *Appetite*, 5, 291–305.

Beauchamp, G.K. and Pearson, P. (1991) Human development and umami taste. *Physiology and Behavior*, 49, 1009–12.

Beauchamp, G.K., Cowart, B.J. and Moran, M. (1986) Developmental changes in salt acceptability in human infants. *Developmental Psychobiology*, 19, 17–25.

Beauchemin, M., Gonzalez-Frankenberger, B., Tremblay, J., Vannasing, P., Martinez-Montes, E., Belin, P., Beland, R., Francoeur, D., Carceller, A.M., Wallois, F. and Lassonde, M. (2011) Mother and stranger: an electrophysiological study of voice processing in newborns. *Cerebral Cortex*, 21, 1705–11.

Beaumont, M., Batejat, D., Pierard, C., Coste, O., Doireau, P., Chauffard, F., Enslen, M., Lagarde, D. and Pierard, C. (2005) Recovery after prolonged sleep deprivation: Residual effects of slow-release caffeine on recovery sleep, sleepiness and cognitive functions. *Neuropsychobiology*, 51, 16–27.

Beaumont, M., Batejat, D., Pierard, C., Coste, O., Doireau, P., Van Beers, P., Chauffard, F., Chassard, D., Enslen, M., Denis, J.B. and Lagarde, D. (2001) Slow release caffeine and prolonged (64 hr) continuous wakefulness: effects on vigilance and cognitive performance. *Journal of Sleep Research*, 10, 265–76.

Beaupre, M.G. and Hess, U. (2005) Cross-cultural emotion recognition among Canadian ethnic groups. *Journal of Cross-Cultural Psychology*, 36 (3), 355–70.

Bebbington, P.E. (1998) Epidemiology of obsessive-compulsive disorder. *British Journal of Psychiatry*, 173, supplement, 35, 2–6.

Bechara, A., Damasio, H., Tranel, D. and Damasio, A.R. (1997) Deciding advantageously before knowing the advantageous strategy. *Science*, 275, 1293–5.

Bechara, A., Dolan, S., Denburg, N., Hindes, A., Anderson, S.W. and Nathan, P.E. (2001) Decision-making deficits, linked to a dysfunctional ventromedial prefrontal cortex, revealed in alcohol and stimulant abusers. *Neuropsychologia*, 39, 376–89.

Bechara, A., Tranel, D., Damasio, H. and Damasio, A.R. (1996) Failure to respond automatically to anticipated future outcomes following damage to prefrontal cortex. *Cerebral Cortex*, 6, 215.

Beck, A.T. (1967) *Depression: Clinical, experimental and theoretical aspects*. New York: Harper and Row.

Beck, A.T. (1976) *Cognitive Therapy and the Emotional Disorders*. New York: International Universities Press.

Beck, A.T. (1991) Cognitive therapy: A thirty-year retrospective. *American Psychologist*, 46, 368–75.

Beck, A.T. and Emery, G. (1985) *Anxiety Disorders and Phobias: A cognitive perspective*. New York: Basic Books.

Beck, A.T., Rush, A.J., Shaw, B.F. and Emery, G. (1979) *Cognitive Therapy of Depression*. New York: Guilford Press.

Beck, H.P., Levinson, S. and Irons, G. (2009) Finding Little Albert. *American Psychologist*, 64, 605–14.

Beck-Jorgensen, B. (1991) What are they doing when they seem to do nothing? In J. Ehnrooth and L. Sivrala (eds) *Construction of Youth*. Helsinki: Helsinki Finnish Youth Research Society.

Beckman, L.J. (1987) Changes in motivation for parenthood among young married couples. *Population and Environment*, 9(2), 96–110.

Bedi, G., Hyman, D. and de Wit, H. (2010) Is ecstasy an 'empathogen'? Effects of ±3, 4-methylenedioxymethamphetamine on prosocial feelings and identification of emotional states in others. *Biological Psychiatry*, 68(12), 1134–40.

Beecher, H.K. (1955) The powerful placebo. *Journal of the American Medical Association*, 159(17), 1602–6.

Begley, C.G. and Ellis, L.M. (2012) Improve standards for preclinical cancer research. *Nature*, 483, 531–3.

Behrend, D.A., Rosengren, K.S. and Perlmutter, M. (1992) The relation between private speech and parental interactive style. In R.M. Diaz and L.E. Berk (eds) *Private Speech: From social interaction to self-regulation*. Hillsdale, NJ: Lawrence Erlbaum Associates.

Behrend, D.A., Scofield, J. and Kleinknecht, E.E. (2001) Beyond fast mapping: Young children's extensions of novel words and novel facts. *Developmental Psychology*, 37(5), 698–705.

Behrens, T.E.J., Fox, P., Laird, A. and Smith, S.M. (2013) What is the most interesting part of the brain? *TICS*, 17, 2–3.

Beilin, H. (1978) Inducing conservation through training. In G. Steiner (ed.) *Psychology of the Twentieth Century*. Munich: Kindler.

Beilin, H. (1990) Piaget's theory: Alive and more vigorous than ever. *Human Development*, 33, 362–65.

Belin, D., Belin-Rauscent, A., Murray, J.E. and Everitt, B. (2013) Addiction: failure of control over maladaptive incentive habits. *Current Opinion in Neurobiology*, 23, 564–72.

Bell, A.P., Weinberg, M.S. and Hammersmith, S.K. (1981) *Sexual Preference: Its development in men and women.* Bloomington, IN: Indiana University Press.

Bell, R., Pavis, S., Amos, A. and Cunningham-Burley, S. (1999) Continuities and changes: Teenage smoking and occupational transition. *Journal of Adolescence*, 22, 683–94.

Belleville, S., Clement, F., Mellah, S., Gilbert, B., Fontaine, E. and Gaithier, S. (2011) Training-related brain plasticity in subjects at risk of developing Alzheimer's disease. *Brain*, 134, 1623–34.

Bellock, S.L., Gunderson, E.A., Ramirez, G. and Levine, S.C. (2010) Female teachers' math anxiety affects girls' math achievement. *Proceedings of the National Academy of Sciences*, 107, 1860–3.

Bellugi, U. and Klima, E.S. (1972) The roots of language in the sign talk of the deaf. *Psychology Today*, 61–76.

Beloff, H. (1992) Mother, father and me: Our IQ. *The Psychologist*, 5, 309–11.

Belsky, A.C.I., Tomiyama, A.J. and Ward, A. (2015) What does weight stigma smell like? Cross-Moan influence on visual weight cues on olfaction. *International Journal of Obesity*, 39, 1030–2.

Belsky, J. and Most, R.K. (1981) From exploration to play: A cross-sectional study of infant free play behaviour. *Developmental Psychology*, 17, 630–9.

Bem, D. and Allen, A. (1974) On predicting some of the people some of the time: The search for cross-situational consistencies in behavior. *Psychological Review*, 81, 506–20.

Bem, D.J. (1972) Self-perception theory. In L. Berkowitz (ed.) *Advances in Experimental Social Psychology*, Vol. 6. New York: Academic Press.

Bem, S. (1981) Gender schema theory: A cognitive account of sex typing. *Psychological Review*, 88, 354–64.

Bender, A., Spada, H., Rothe-Wulf, A., Traber, S. and Rauss, K. (2012) Anger elicitation in Tonga and Germany: the impact of culture on cognitive determinants of emotions. *Frontiers in Psychology*, 3, 435, 1–20.

Benedetti, F., Arduino, C. and Amanzio, M. (1999) Somatotopic activation of opioid systems by target-directed expectations of analgesia. *Journal of Neuroscience*, 19(9), 3639–48.

Benedetto, S., Carbone, A., Pedrotti, M., Le Fevre, K., Bey, L.A.Y. and Baccino, T. (2015) Rapid serial visual presentation in reading: The case of Spritz. *Computers in Human Behavior*, 45, 352–8.

Benedict, R.H., Lockwood, A.H., Shucard, J.L., Schucard, D.W., Wack, D. and Murphy, B.W. (1998) Functional neuroimaging of attention in the auditory modality. *NeuroReport*, 9, 121–6.

Benn, R.K. (1986) Factors promoting secure attachment relationships between employed mothers and their sons. *Child Development*, 57, 1224–31.

Bennett, A. and Stirling, J. (1998) Vulnerability factors in the anxiety disorders. *British Journal of Medical Psychology*, 71(3), 311–22.

Bennett, C.M. and Miller, M.B. (2010) How reliable are the results from functional magnetic imaging? *Annals of the NY Academy of Sciences*, 1191, 133–55.

Benningfield, M.M. and Cowan, R.L. (2013) Brain serotonin function in MDMA (ecstasy) users: evidence for persisting neurotoxicity. *Neuropsychopharmacology*, 38(1), 253.

Benoit, R.G. and Anderson, M.C. (2012) Opposing mechanisms support the voluntary forgetting of unwanted memories. *Neuron*, 76, 450–60.

Bensafi, M., Sobel, N. and Khan, R.M. (2007) Hedonic-specific activity in piriform cortex during odor imagery mimics that during odor perception. *Journal of Neurophysiology*, 98, 3254–62.

Ben-Zeev, D., Young, M.A. and Corrigan, P.W. (2010) DSM-V and the stigma of mental illness. *Journal of Mental Health*, 19, 318–27.

Bergelson, E. and Swingley, D. (2012) At 6-9 months, human infants know the meanings of many common nouns. *PNAS*, 109, 3253–8.

Bergen, B.K. and Lau, T.T.C. (2012) Writing direction affects how people map space onto time. *Frontiers in Psychology*, 3, article 109.

Berger, J., Meredith, M. and Wheeler, C. (2008) Contextual priming: Where people vote affects how they vote. *PNAS*, 105, 8846–49.

Bergerson, N. and Schneider, B.H. (2005) Explaining cross-national differences in peer-directed aggression. *Aggressive Behavior*, 31, 116–37.

Berglund, B. and Lindvall, T. (1995) *Community Noise.* Stockholm: Stockholm University and Karolinska Institute.

Bergman, D., Lornudd, C., Sjoberg, L. and von Thiele Schwartz, U. (2014) Leader personality and 360-degree assessments of leader behaviour. *Scandinavian Journal of Psychology*, 55, 389–97.

Bergman, S.M., Fearrington, M.E., Davenport, S.W. and Bergman, J.Z. (2011) Millennials, narcissism, and social networking: What narcissists do on social networking sites and why? *Personality and Individual Differences*, 50, 706–11.

Bergqvist, T.F. and Malec, J.F. (1997) Psychology: Current practice and training issues in treatment of cognitive dysfunction. *Neurorehabilitation*, 8, 49–56.

Bergsieker, H.B., Leslie, L.M., Constantine, V.S. and Fiske, S.T. (2012) Stereotyping by omission: Eliminate the negative, accentuate the positive. *Journal of Personality and Social Psychology*, 102, 1214.

Berk, L.E. (1992) Children's private speech: An overview of theory and the status of research. In R.M. Diaz and L.E. Berk (eds) *Private Speech: From social interaction to self-regulation.* Hillsdale, NJ: Lawrence Erlbaum Associates.

Berk, L.E. (1994) Why children talk to themselves. *Scientific American Mind*, 271(5), 78–83.

Berk, L.E. (2009) *Child Development* (8th edn). Boston, MA: Allyn & Bacon.

Berkman, E.T. and Falk, E.B. (2013) Beyond brain mapping using neural measures to predict real-world outcomes. *Current Directions in Psychological Science*, 22(1), 45–50.

Berkman, E.T. and Lieberman, M.D. (2010) Approaching the bad and avoiding the good: Lateral prefrontal cortical asymmetry distinguishes between action and valence. *Journal of Cognitive Neuroscience*, 22, 1970–9.

Berkovec, T.D. (1994) The nature, function and origins of worry. In G. Davey and F. Tallis (eds) *Worrying: Perspectives on theory, assessment and treatment.* Chichester: Wiley.

Berkowitz, L. (1962) *Aggression: A social psychological analysis.* New York: McGraw-Hill.

Berlin, B. and Kay, P. (1969) *Basic Color Terms: Their universality and evolution.* Berkeley, LA: University of California Press.

Berlin, H.A., Rolls, E.T. and Kischika, U. (2004) Impulsivity, time perception, emotion and reinforcement sensitivity in patients with orbitofrontal cortex lesions. *Brain*, 127, 1108–26.

Berlyne, D.E. (1966) Motivational problems raised by exploratory and epistemic behavior. In S. Koch (ed.) *Psychology: A study of a science*, Vol. 5. New York: McGraw-Hill.

Berman, M.G., Misic, B., Buschkuehl, M., Kross, E., Deldin, P., Peltier, S., Churchill, N.W., Jaeggi, S., Vakorin, V., McIntosh, A. and Jonides, J. (2014) Does resting-state connectivity reflect depressive rumination? *Neuroimage*, 103, 267–79.

Berman, M.G., Peltier, S., Nee, D.E., Kross, E., Dedlin, P.J. and Jonides, J. (2011) Depression, rumination and the default network. *SCAN*, 6, 548–55.

Berman, R.M. *et al.* (2000) Antidepressant effects of ketamine in depressed patients. *Biological Psychiatry*, 47, 351–4.

Berman, R.M., Cappiello, A., Anand, A., Oren, D.A., Heninger, G.R., Charney, D.S. and Krystal, J.H. (2000) Antidepressant effects of ketamine in depressed patients. *Biological Psychiatry*, 47(4), 351–4.

Bermant, G. and Davidson, J.M. (1974) *Biological Bases of Sexual Behavior.* New York: Harper and Row.

Bermeitinger, C., Goeltz, R., Johr, N., Neumann, M., Ecker, U.K.H. and Doerr, R. (2009) The hidden persuaders break into the tired brain. *Journal of Experimental Social Psychology*, 45, 320–6.

Berndt, R.S. and Mitchum, R.S. (1995) *Cognitive Neuropsychological Approaches to the Treatment of Language Disorders.* Hove: Lawrence Erlbaum Associates.

Bernstein, I.L. (1978) Learned taste aversion in children receiving chemotherapy. *Science*, 200, 1302–3.

Bernstein, I.L. (1991) Aversion conditioning in response to cancer and cancer treatment. *Clinical Psychology Review*, 11, 183–91.

Bernstein, I.L., Webster, M.M. and Bernstein, I.D. (1982) Food aversions in children receiving chemotherapy for cancer. *Cancer*, 50, 2961–3.

Bernstein, M.J. and Claypool, H.M. (2012) Social exclusion and pain sensitivity: Why exclusion sometimes hurts and sometimes numbs. *Personality and Social Psychology Bulletin*, 38, 185–6.

Bernstein, R.N. and Berko, G.J. (1993) *Psycholinguistics.* Fort Worth, TX: Holt, Rinehart and Winston.

Bernstein, W.M., Stephenson, B.O., Snyder, M.L. and Wicklund, R.A. (1983) Causal ambiguity and heterosexual affiliation. *Journal of Experimental Social Psychology*, 19, 78–92.

Berridge, K. C. and Kringelbach, M. L. (2015) Pleasure systems in the brain. *Neuron*, 86, 646–64.

Berscheid, E. and Reis. H.T. (1998) Attraction and close relationships. In D.T. Gilbert, S.T. Fiske and G. Lindzey (eds) *The Handbook of Social Psychology* (4th edn), Vol. 2. New York: McGraw-Hill, pp. 193–281.

Berson, D.M., Dunn, F.A. and Takao, M. (2002) Phototransduction by retinal ganglion cells that set the circadian clock. *Science*, 295, 1070–3.

Bertenthal, B.I., Campos, J.J. and Barrett, K. (1984) Self-produced locomotion: An organizer of emotional, cognitive and social development in infancy. In R. Emde and R. Harmon (eds) *Continuities and Discontinuities in Development.* New York: Plenum Press.

Berthier, M.L., Davila, G., Morena-Torres, I., Beltran-Corbellini, A., Santana-Moreno, D., Roe-Vellve, N., Thurnhofer-Hemsi, K., Torres-Prioris, M., Massone, M.I. and Ruiz-Cruces, R. (2015) Loss of regional accent after damage to the speech production network. *Frontiers in Human Neuoscience*, 9, 610.

Berton, O. *et al.* (2006) Essential role of BDNF in the mesolimbic dopamine pathway in social defeat stress. *Science.* 311, 864–8.

Bertram, R., Helle, L., Kaakinen, J.K. and Svedstrom, E. (2013) The effect of expertise on eye movement behaviour in medical image perception. *PLoS ONE*, 8, e66169.

Bertrand, M. and Mullainathan, S. (2004) Are Emily and Greg more employable than Lakisha and Jamal? *The American Economic Review*, 94, 991–1013.

Beschin, N., de Bruin, A. and Della Sala, S. (2016) Compulsive foreign language syndrome: A clinical observation not a mystery. *Cortex*, 81, 276–7.

Besner, D., Twilley, L., McCann, R.S. and Seergobin, K. (1990) On the connection between connnectionism and data: Are a few words necessary? *Psychological Review*, 97, 432–46.

Besson, M., Granon, S., Mameli-Engvall, M., Cloez-tayarani, I., Maubourguet, N., Cormier, A., Cazala, P., David, V., Changeux, J-P. and Faure, P. (2007) Long-term effects of chronic nicotine exposure on brain nicotinic receptors. *Proceedings of the National Academy of Sciences*, 104 (19), 8155–60.

Bestelmeyer, P.E.G., Belin, P. and Ladd, D.R. (2014) A neural marker for social bias toward in-group accents. *Cerebral Cortex*, 1–9.

Bethlehem, R.A.I., Baron-Cohen, S., van Honk, J., Auyeung, B. and Bos, P.A. (2014) The oxytocin paradox. *Frontiers in Behavioural Neuroscience*, 8, 48.

Bettencourt, B.A. and Miller, N. (1996) Gender differences in aggression as a function of provocation: A meta-analysis. *Psychological Bulletin*, 119(3), 422–47.

Beukeboom, C.J., Tanis, M. and Vermeulen, I.E. (2012) The language of extraversion: Extraverted people talk more abstractly, introverts are more concrete. *Journal of Language and Social Psychology*, 32, 101–201.

Beutler, L.E. and Clarkin, J.F. (1990) *Systematic Treatment Selection: Toward targeted therapeutic interventions.* New York: Brunner/Mazel.

Beutler, L.E., Machado, P.P.P. and Allstetter Neufeldt, S. (1994) Therapist variables. In A.E. Bergin and S.L. Garfield (eds) *Handbook of Psychotherapy and Behaviour Change.* New York: Wiley.

Bevilacqua, L. and Goldman, D. (2011) Genetics of emotion. *Trends in Cognitive Sciences*, 15, 401–8.

Bhattacharyya, S., Atakan, Z., Martin-Santos, R., Crippa, J.A., Fusar-Ppoli, P. and McGuire, P. (2012a) Neural mechanisms for the cannabinoid modulation of cognition and affect in man. *Current Pharmacological Design*, 18, 5045–54.

Bhattacharyya, S., Atakan, Z., Martin-Santos, R., Crippa, J.A., Kambeitz, J., Prata, D., Williams, S., Brammer, M., Collier, D.A. and McGuire, P. (2012b) Preliminary report of biological basis of sensitivity to the effects of cannabis on psychosis. *Molecular Psychiatry*, 17, 1152.

Bhattacharyya, S., Morrison, P.D., Fusar-Poli, P., Martin-Santos, R., Borgwardt, S., Winton-Brown, T. . . . and Mehta, M.A. (2010) Opposite effects of Δ-9-tetrahydrocannabinol and cannabidiol on human brain function and psychopathology. *Neuropsychopharmacology*, 35(3), 764–74.

Bialystok, E. and Craik, F.I.M. (2010) Cognitive and linguistic processing in the bilingual mind. *Current Directions in Psychological Science*, 19, 19–23.

Bialystok, E. and Martin, M.M. (2004) Attention and inhibition in bilingual children: Evidence from the dimensional change card sort task. *Developmental Science*, 7, 325–39.

Bialystok, E., Craik, F.I.M. and Freedman, M. (2007) Bilingualism as a protection against the onset of symptoms of dementia. *Neuropsychologia*, 45, 459–64.

Bialystok, E., Craik, F.I.M. and Luk, G. (2008) Cognitive control and lexical access in younger and older bilinguals. *Journal of Experimental Psychology: Learning, Memory and Cognition*, 34, 859–73.

Bialystok, E., Craik, F.I.M. and Luk, G. (2012) Bilingualism: consequences for mind and brain. *Trends in Cognitive Sciences*, 16, 240–50.

Bibby, P.A. (2008) Dispositional factors in the use of social networking sites: Findings and implications for social computing research. *Lectures Notes in Computer Science*, 5075, 392–400.

Biddle, S. (1995) Exercise and psychosocial health. *Research Quarterly for Exercise and Sport*, 66(4), 292–7.

Biederman, I. (1987) Recognition-by-components: A theory of human image interpretation. *Psychological Review*, 94, 115–47.

Biederman, I. (1990) Higher-level vision. In D.N. Osherson, S.M. Kosslyn and J. Hollerbach (eds) *An Invitation to Cognitive Science. Vol. 2: Visual Cognition and Action.* Cambridge, MA: MIT Press.

Biener, L. and Hargraves, J.L. (2015) A longitudinal study of electronic cigarette use in a population-based sample of adult smokers: association with smoking cessation and motivation to quit. *Nicotine and Tobacco Research*, 17(2),127–33.

Biernat, M. and Wortman, C.B. (1991) Sharing of home responsibilities between professionally employed women and their husbands. *Journal of Personality and Social Psychology*, 60, 844–60.

Biggs, J.B. (1987) *Student Approaches to Learning and Studying*. Melbourne: Australian Council for Educational Research.

Biglan, A., Duncan, T.E., Ary, D.V. and Smolkowski, K. (1995) Peer and parental influences on adolescent tobacco use. *Journal of Behavioural Medicine*, 18(4), 315–30.

Billig, M. (1976) *Social Psychology and Intergroup Relations*. London: Academic Press.

Billig, M. (1997) Rhetorical and discursive analysis. In N. Hayes (ed.) *Doing Qualitative Analysis in Psychology*. Hove: Psychology Press.

Binder, J.R., Frost, J.A., Hammeke, T.A., Cox, R.W., Rao, S.M. and Prieto, T. (1997) Human brain language areas identified by functional magnetic resonance imaging. *Journal of Neuroscience*, 17(1), 353–62.

Binet, A. and Henri, V. (1896) La psychologie individuelle. *Année Psychologique*, 2, 411–65.

Bird, C.M., Castelli, F., Malik, O., Frith, U. and Husain, M. (2004) The impact of extensive medial frontal lobe damage on 'theory of mind' and cognition. *Brain*, 127, 914–28.

Bird, G. *et al.* (2007) Intact automatic imitation of human and robot actions in autism spectrum disorders. *Proceedings of Biological Sciences*, 274, 3027–31.

Bird, T.D. (1999) Clinical genetics of familial Alzheimer's disease. In R.D. Terry, R. Katzman, K.L. Bick and S.S. Sisodia (eds) *Alzheimer's Disease* (2nd edn). Philadelphia, PA: Lippincott Williams & Wilkins.

Birnbaum, G.E., Ein-Dor, T., Reis, H.T. and Segal, N. (2014) Why do men prefer nice women? Gender typicality mediates the effect of responsiveness on perceived attractiveness in initial acquaintanceship. *Personality and Social Psychology Bulletin*, 40, 1341–53.

Birren, J.E. and Morrison, D.F. (1961) Analysis of the WISC subtests in relation to age and education. *Journal of Gerontology*, 16, 363–9.

Bishop, D.V.M. (1990) *Handedness and Developmental Disorders*. Hove: Lawrence Erlbaum Associates.

Bishop, D.V.M. (1997) Listening out for subtle deficits. *Nature*, 387, 129–30.

Bishop, D.V.M. (2002) Cerebellar abnormalities in developmental dyslexia: Cause, correlate or consequence? *Cortex*, 38, 491–8.

Bishop, G.D. (1994) *Health Psychology: Integrating mind and body*. Boston, MA: Allyn & Bacon.

Bixter, M.T. (2015) Happiness, political orientation, and religiosity. *Personality and Individual Differences*, 72, 7–11.

Bjornebekk, A., Fjell, A.M., Walhovd, K.B., Grydeland, H., Torgesen, S. and Westlye, L.T. (2013) Neuronal correlates of the five factor model of human personality: Multimodal imaging in a large healthy sample. *Neuroimage*, 65, 194–208.

Black, S.L. and Biron, C. (1982) Androstenol as a human pheromone: No effect on perceived sexual attractiveness. *Behavioural and Neural Biology*, 34, 326–30.

Blackburn, G.L. (1995) Effect of degree of weight loss on health benefits. *Obesity Research*, 3 (suppl.), 211–16.

Blacker, K.J. and Curby, K.M. (2013) Enhanced visual short-term memory in action video game players. *Attention, Perception, and Psychophysics*, 75(6), 1128–36.

Blackmore, S. (2010) *Consciousness – an Introduction*. London: Hodder & Stoughton.

Blackmore, S.J. (1992) Psychic experiences: Psychic illusions. *Skeptical Inquirer*, 16, 367–76.

Blackmore, S.J. and Moore, R. (1994) Seeing things: Visual recognition and belief in the paranormal. *European Journal of Parapsychology*, 10, 91–103.

Blair, C., Gamson, D., Thorne, S. and Baker, D. (2005) Rising mean IQ: Cognitive demand of mathematics education for young children, population exposure to formal schooling, and the neurobiology of the prefrontal cortex. *Intelligence*, 33, 93–106.

Blair, I.V., Judd, C.M. and Chapleau, K.M. (2004) The influence of Afrocentric facial features in criminal sentencing. *Psychological Science*, 15, 674–9.

Blair, J., Mitchell, D. and Blair, K. (2005) *The Psychopath: Emotion and the brain*. Oxford: Blackwell.

Blair, R.J.R., Morris, J.S., Frith, C.D., Perrett, D.I. and Dolan, R.J. (1999) Dissociable neural responses to facial expressions of sadness and anger. *Brain*, 122, 883–93.

Blake, A.B., Nazarian, M. and Castel, A.D. (2015) The Apple of the mind's eye: Everyday attention, metamemory, and reconstructive memory for the Apple logo. *The Quarterly Journal of Experimental Psychology*, 68, 858–65.

Blakemore, C. and Mitchell, D.E. (1973) Environmental modification of the visual cortex and the neural basis of learning and memory. *Nature*, 241, 467–8.

Blakeslee, A.F. (1931) Genetics of sensory thresholds: taste for phenylthio-carbamide. *Proceedings of the National Academy of Sciences*, 18, 120–30.

Blanchette, I. and Richards, A. (2010) The influence of affect on higher level cognition: A review of research on interpretation, judgment, decision making and reasoning. *Cognition and Emotion*, 24, 561–95.

Blank, A.S. (1993) The longitudinal course of post-traumatic stress disorder. In J.R.T. Davidson and E.B. Foa (eds) *Posttraumatic Stress Disorder: DSM-IV and beyond*. Washington DC: Amercian Psychiatric Press.

Blanke, O., Ortigue, S. and Landis, T. (2003) Colour neglect in an artist. *The Lancet*, 361, 264.

Blankfield, R.P. (1991) Suggestion, relaxation, and hypnosis as adjuncts in the care of surgery patients: A review of the literature. *American Journal of Clinical Hypnosis*, 33, 172–86.

Blass, T. (2000) The Milgram paradigm after 35 years: Some things we now know about obedience to authority. In T. Blass (ed.), *Obedience to Authority: Current perspectives on the Milgram experiment*. Hillsdale, NJ: Lawrence Erlbaum Associates.

Blass, T. (2009) From new haven to Santa Clara: A historical perspective on the Milgram obedience experiments. *American Psychologist*, 64(1), 37–45.

Bleich, A., Koslowsky, M., Dolev, A. and Lerer, B. (1997) Post-traumatic stress disorder and depression. *British Journal of Psychiatry*, 170, 479–82.

Bliss, E.L. (1980) Multiple personalities: A report of 14 cases with implications for schizophrenia and hysteria. *Archives of General Psychiatry*, 37, 1388–97.

Bliss, T. and Gardner-Medwin, A. (1973) Long-lasting potentiation of synaptic transmission in the dendate area of unanaesthetised rabbit following stimulation of the perforant path. *Journal of Physiology*, 232, 357–74.

Block, J. and Block, J.H. (2006) Nursery school personality and political orientation two decades later. *Journal of Personality*, 40, 734–49.

Block, N., Flanagan, O. and Guzeldere, G. (1997) *The Nature of Consciousness*. Cambridge, MA: MIT Press.

Bloom, J.S., Garcia-Barrera, M.A., Miller, C.J., Miller, S.R. and Hynd, G.W. (2013) Planum temporale morphology in children with developmental dyslexia. *Neuropsychologia*, 51, 1684–92.

Bloom, L. (1970) *Language Development: Form and function in emerging grammars*. Cambridge, MA: MIT Press.

Blum, S.H. and Blum, L.H. (1974) Do's and don'ts: An informal study of some prevailing superstitions. *Psychological Reports*, 35, 567–71.

Boaz, N.T. (1993) Origins of Hominidae. In A.J. Manyak and A. Manyak (eds) *Milestones in Human Evolution*. Prospect Heights, IL: Waveland Press.

Bobadilla, L., Metze, A.V. and Taylor, J. (2013) Physical attractiveness and its relation to unprovoked and reactive aggression. *Journal of Research in Personality, 47,* 70–7.

Bochner, S. and Insko, C.A. (1966) Communicator discrepancy, source credibility, and opinion change. *Journal of Personality and Social Psychology, 4,* 614–21.

Bock, B.C. and Kanarek, R.B. (1995) Women and men are what they eat: The effects of gender and reported meal size on perceived characteristics. *Sex Roles, 33*(1), 109–19.

Bodenlos, J. S. and Wormuth, B. M. (2013) Watching a food-related television show and caloric intake. A laboratory study. *Appetite, 61,* 8–12.

Boduszek, D. and Debowska, A. (2016) Critical evaluation of psychopathy measurement (PCL-R and SRP-III/SF) and recommendations for future research. *Journal of Criminal Justice, 44,* 1–12.

Boesveldt, S., Frasnelli, J., Gordon, A.R. and Lundstrom, J.N. (2010) The fish is bad: Negative food odors elicit faster and more accurate reactions than other odors. *Biological Psychology, 84,* 313–17.

Bogdanowicz, K.M., Krasowicz-Kupis, G., and Wiejak, K. (2016) In search of effective remediation for students with developmental dyslexia – a review of contemporary English literature. *Polish Psychological Bulletin, 47,* 270–80.

Bogen, J.E. (1993) The callosal syndromes. In K.M. Heilman and E. Valenstein (eds) *Clinical Neuropsychology.* New York: Academic Press.

Bogg, T. and Roberts, B.W. (2004) Conscientiousness and health-related behaviours: A meta-analysis of the leading behavioural contributors to mortality. *Psychological Bulletin, 130* (6), 887–919.

Bohannon, J.N. (1988) Flashbulb memories for the space shuttle disaster: A tale of two theories. *Cognition, 29,* 179–96.

Bohannon, J.N. (1993) Theoretical approaches to language acquisition. In J.B. Gleason (ed.) *The Development of Language.* New York: Macmillan.

Bohannon, J.N. and Stanowicz, L. (1988) The issue of negative evidence: Adult responses to children's language errors. *Developmental Psychology, 24,* 684–9.

Bohn, A. and Berntsen, D. (2007) Pleasantness bias in flashbulb memories: positive and negative flashbulb memories of the fall of the Berlin Wall among East and West Germans. *Memory and Cognition, 35* (3), 565–77.

Bohner, G., Moskowitz, G.B. and Chaiken, S. (1995) The interplay of heuristic and systematic processing of social information. *European Review of Social Psychology, 6,* 33–68.

Bohns, V.K. (2016) (Mis)understanding our influence over others: A review of the underestimation-of-compliance effect. *Current Directions in Psychological Science, 25,* 119–23.

Bohns, V.K., Roghanizad, M.M. and Xu, A.Z. (2014) Underestimating our influence over others' unethical behavior and decisions. *Personality and Social Psychology Bulletin, 40*(3), 348–62.

Boller, F. and Dennis, M. (1979) *Auditory Comprehension: Clinical and experimental studies with the token test.* New York: Academic Press.

Bolles, R.C. (1979) *Learning Theory.* New York: Holt, Rinehart & Winston.

Bolmont, M., Cacioppo, J.T. and Cacioppo, S. (2014) Love is in the gaze: an eye-tracking study of love and sexual desire. *Psychological Science, 25,* 1748–56.

Bond, C.F. and DePaulo, B.M. (2006) Accuracy of deception judgments. *Personality and Social Psychology Review, 10,* 214–34.

Bonvillian, J., Nelson, K.E. and Charrow, V. (1976) Languages and language-related skills in deaf and hearing children. *Sign Language Studies, 12,* 211–50.

Book, A., Visser, B.A., Blais, J., Hosker-Field, A., Methot-Jones, T., Gauthier, N.Y., Volk, A., Holden, R.R. and D'Agata, M.T.D. (2016) Unpacking more

'evil': What is at the core of the dark tetrad? *Personality and Individual Differences, 90,* 269–72.

Boothroyd, L.G., Jones, B.C., Burt, D.M. and Perrett, D.I. (2007) Partner characteristics associated with masculinity, health and maturity in male faces. *Personality and Individual Differences, 43,* 1161–73.

Boraston, Z.L., Corden, B., Miles, L.K., Skuse, D.H. and Blakemore, S.J. (2008) Brief report: perception of genuine and posed smiles by individuals with autism. *Journal of Autism and Developmental Disorder, 38,* 574–80.

Borgida, E. and Nisbett, R.E. (1977) The differential viewpoint of abstract vs. concrete information on decisions. *Journal of Applied Social Psychology, 7,* 258–71.

Boring, E.G. (1923) Intelligence as the tests test it. *The New Republic,* June, 35–7.

Boring, E.G. (1953) A history of introspection. *Psychological Bulletin, 50,* 169–89.

Borman, G.D., Grigg, J. and Hanselman, P. (2016) An effort to close achievement gaps at scale through self-affirmation. *Educational Evaluation and Policy Analysis, 38,* 21–42.

Born, J. *et al.* (2006) Sleep to remember. *Neuroscientist, 12,* 410–24.

Borness, C., Proudfoot, J., Crawford, J. and Valenzuela, M. (2013) Putting brain training to the test in the workplace: a randomized, blinded, multisite, active-controlled trial. *PLoS ONE, 8*(3), e59982.

Bornkessel-Schlesewsky, I. and Schlesewsky, M. (2013) Reconciling time, space and function: a new dorsal-ventral stream model of sentence comprehension. *Brain and Language, 125,* 60–76.

Bornkessel-Schlesewsky, I., Schlesewsky, M., Small, S.L. and Rauschecker, J.P. (2015) Neurobiological roots of language in primate audition: common computational properties. *TICS, 19,* 142–50.

Bornmmann, L., Leydesdorffff, L. and Krampen, G. (2012) Which are the best cities for psychology research worldwide? *Europe's Journal of Psychology, 8,* 535–46.

Boroditsky, L., Schmidt, L. and Phillips, W. (2003) Sex, syntax and semantics. In D. Gentner and S. Goldin-Meadow (eds), *Language in mind: Advances in the study of language and thought.* London: MIT Press.

Borovsky, D. and Rovee-Collier, C. (1989) Contextual restraints on memory retrieval at 6 months. *Child Development, 61,* 1569–83.

Botella, C., Banos, R.M., Perpina, C., Villa, H., Alcaniz, M. and Rey, A. (1998) Virtual reality treatment of claustrophobia: A case report. *Behaviour Research and Therapy, 36,* 239–46.

Botez, M.I., Oliver, M., Vezina, J-L., Botez, T. and Kaufman, B. (1985) Defective revisualization: Dissociation between cognitive and imagistic thought. Case report and short review of the literature. *Cortex, 21,* 375–89.

Bottini, G., Corcoran, R., Sterzi, R., Paulesu, E., Schenone, P., Scarpa, P., Frackowiak, R.S.J. and Frith, C.D. (1994) The role of the right hemisphere in the integration of figurative aspects of language. *Brain, 117,* 1241–53.

Boubela, R.N., Kalcher, K., Huf, W., Seidel, E-M., Derntl, B., Pezawas, L., Nasel, C. and Moser, E. (2015) fMRI measurements of amygdala activation are confounded by stimulus correlated signal fluctuation in nearby veins draining distant brain regions. *Scientific Reports, 5,* 1–15.

Bouchard, S., Dumoulin, S., Robillard, G., Guitard, T., Klinger, É., Forget, H., . . . and Roucaut, F. X. (2016) Virtual reality compared with in vivo exposure in the treatment of social anxiety disorder: a three-arm randomised controlled trial. *The British Journal of Psychiatry, 210,* 276–83.

Boulton, M.J. and Smith, P.K. (1994) Bully/victim problems in middle school children: Stability, self-perceived competence, peer perception and peer acceptance. *British Journal of Developmental Psychology, 12,* 315–29.

Bourgeois, M.J., Horowitz, I.A., ForsterLee, L. and Grahe, J. (1995) Nominal and interactive groups: effects of preinstruction and deliberations on decisions and evidence recall in complex trials. *Journal of Applied Psychology*, 80, 58–67.

Bourtchouladze, R., Abel, T., Berman, N., Gordon, R., Lapidus, K. and Kandel, E.R. (1998) Different training procedures recruit either one or two critical periods for contextual memory consolidation, each of which requires protein synthesis and PKA. *Learning and Memory*, 5, 365–74.

Boutelle, K.N., Kirschenbaum, D.S., Baker, R.C. and Mitchell, M.E. (1999) How can obese weight controllers minimize weight gain during the high risk holiday season? By self-monitoring very consistently. *Health Psychology*, 18(4), 364–8.

Bowden, C.L. (2001) Strategies to reduce misdiagnosis of bipolar depression. *Psychiatric Services*, 52(1), 51–5.

Bower, G.H. (1981) Mood and memory. *American Psychologist*, 36, 129–48.

Bower, G.H. and Clark, M.C. (1969) Narrative stories as mediators for serial learning. *Psychonomic Science*, 14, 181–2.

Bower, G.H. and Mayer, J.D. (1989) In search of mood-dependent retrieval. *Journal of Social Behaviour and Personality*, 4, 133–68.

Bower, T.G.R. (1972) *Perception in Infancy* (2nd edn). San Francisco, CA: W.H. Freeman.

Bowlby, J. (1969) *Attachment*. New York: Basic Books.

Bowlby, J. (1973) *Separation: Anxiety and Anger*. New York: Basic Books.

Bowles, N.L. and Poon, L.W. (1985) Aging and retrieval of words in semantic memory. *Journal of Gerontology*, 40, 71–7.

Bowling, A. and Dieppe, P. (2005) What is successful ageing and who should define it? *British Medical Journal*, 331, 1548–51.

Boyke, J., Driemeyer, J., Gaser, C., Buchel, C. and May, A. (2008) Training-induced brain structure changes in the elderly. *Journal of Neuroscience*, 28, 7031–5.

Boynton, R.M. (1979) *Human Color Vision*. New York: Holt, Rinehart & Winston.

Boysson-Bardies, B., Sagart, L. and Durand, C. (1984) Discernible differences in the babbling of infants according to target language. *Journal of Child Language*, 11, 1–15.

BPS (2009) *Code of Ethics and Conduct: Guidance published by the Ethics Committee of the British Psychological Society*. Leicester: British Psychological Society.

BPS Division of Clinical Psychology (2010) *How to Become a Clinical Psychologist*. Leicester: British Psychological Society. http://dcp.bps.org.uk/dcp/clinical_psychology/role_home$.cfm.

Bradley, B.P., Mogg, K., Groom, C., deBono, J. and White, J. (1999) Attentional bias for emotional faces in generalized anxiety disorder. *British Journal of Clinical Psychology*, 38, 267–77.

Bradley, L. and Bryant, P. (1983) Categorising sounds and learning to read – a causal connection. *Nature*, 301, 419–21.

Braffman, W. and Kirsch, I. (1999) Imaginative suggestibility and hypnotisability: an empirical analysis. *Journal of Personality and Social Psychology*, 77, 578–878.

Bragulat, V., Dzemidzic, M., Bruno, C., Cox, C.A., Talavage, T., Considine, R.V. and Kareken, D.A. (2010) Food-related odor probes of brain reward circuits during hunger: A pilot fMRI study. *Obesity*, 18, 1566–71.

Brain, P. (1984) Biological explanations of human aggression and the resulting therapies offered by such approaches: A critical evaluation. In R. Blanchard and D. Blanchard (eds) *Advances in the Study of Aggression*. New York: Academic Press.

Brain, P. (1994) Hormonal aspects of aggression and violence. In A. Reiss, K. Micek and J. Roth (eds) *Understanding and Preventing Violence*, Vol. 2. New York: National Academic Press.

Brambila, P. *et al.* (2003) GABAergic dysfunction in mood disorders. *Molecular Psychiatry*, 8, 721–37.

Brandt, B. and Kvande, E. (1998) Masculinity and child care: the reconstruction of fathering. *Sociological Review*, 46(2), 293–313.

Branscombe, N.R., Wann, D.L., Noel, J.G. and Coleman, J. (1993) In-group or out-group extremity: Importance of threatened social identity. *Personality and Social Psychology Bulletin*, 19, 381–418.

Bransford, J.D. and Johnson, M.K. (1972) Contextual prerequisites for understanding: Some investigations of comprehension and recall. *Journal of Verbal Learning and Verbal Behavior*, 11, 717–26.

Braskie, M. N., Klunder, A. D., Hayashi, K. M., Protas, H., Kepe, V., Miller, K. J., . . . and Satyamurthy, N. (2010) Plaque and tangle imaging and cognition in normal aging and Alzheimer's disease. *Neurobiology of Aging*, 31(10), 1669–78.

Bray, G.A. (1998) *Contemporary Diagnosis and Management of Obesity*. Newton, PA: Handbooks in Health Care.

Breillmann, R.S., Saling, M.M., Connell, A.B., Waites, A.B., Abbott, D.F. and Jackson, G.D. (2004) A high-field functional MRI study of quadri-lingual subjects. *Brain and Language*, 89, 531–42.

Bremner, A. J., Caparos, S., Davidoff, J., de Fockert, J., Linnell, K. J. and Spence, C. (2013) 'Bouba' and 'Kiki' in Namibia? A remote culture make similar shape-sound matches, but different shape–taste matches to Westerners. *Cognition*, 126(2), 165–72.

Brennan, W.M., Ames, E.W. and Moore, R. (1966) Age differences in infants' attention to patterns of different complexities. *Science*, 151, 354–6.

Brett, L., Traynor, V. and Stapley, P. (2016) Effects of physical exercise on health and well-being of individuals living with a dementia in nursing homes: A systematic review. *Journal of the American Medical Directors Association*, 17(2), 104–16.

Brewer, J.B., Zhao, Z., Desmond, J.E., Glover, G.H. and Gabrieli, J.D.E. (1998) Making memories: Brain activity that predicts how well visual experience will be remembered. *Science*, 281, 1185–7.

Brewer, M.B. and Caporael, L.R. (1990) Selfish genes versus selfish people: Sociobiology as origin myth. *Motivation and Emotion*, 14, 237–43.

Brewer, M.B and Gardner, W. (1996) Who is this 'we'? Levels of collective identity and self-representation. *Journal of Personality and Social Psychology*, 71, 83–93.

Brewer, M.B. and Kramer, R.M. (1986) Choice behavior in social dilemmas: Effects of social identity, group size, and decision framing. *Journal of Personality and Social Psychology*, 50, 543–9.

Brewer, M.B. and Miller, N. (1984) Beyond the contact hypothesis: Theoretical perspectives on desegregation. In N. Miller and M.B. Brewer (eds) *Groups in Contact: The psychology of desegregation*. New York: Academic Press, pp. 281–302.

Brewin, C.R., Smith, A.J., Power, M.J. and Furnham, A. (1992) State and trait differences in the depressive self-schema. *Behaviour Research and Therapy*, 30, 555–7.

Brickman, P. and Campbell, D.T. (1971) Hedonic relativism and planning the good society. In M.H. Appley (ed.), *Adaptation Level Theory: A symposium*. New York: Academic Press.

Bridges, A.M. and Jones, D.M. (1996) Word-dose in the disruption of serial recall by irrelevant speech: Phonological confusions or changing state? *Quarterly Journal of Experimental Psychology*, 49A, 919–39.

Briem, V. and Hedman, L.R. (1995) Behavioural effects of mobile telephone task on driver behaviour in a car following situation. *Accident Analysis and Prevention*, 27, 707–15.

Brinch, C.N. and Galloway, T.A. (2011) *Schooling in adolescents raises IQ*. Oslo: Research Department Statistics.

Brindal, E., Wilson, C., Mohr, P. and Wittert, G. (2015) Eating in groups: do multiple social influences affect intake in a fast-food restaurant? *Journal of Health Psychology*, 20, 483–9.

Brissette, I., Scheier, M.F. and Carver, C.S. (2002) The role of optimism in social network development, coping and psychological adjustment during a life transition. *Journal of Personality and Social Psychology*, 82, 102–11.

Broadbent, D.E. (1958) *Perception and Communication*. London: Pergamon Press.

Broberg, D.J. and Bernstein, I.L. (1987) Candy as a scapegoat in the prevention of food aversions in children receiving chemotherapy. *Cancer*, 60, 2344–7.

Brodsky, W. and Slor, Z. (2013) Background music as a risk factor for distraction among young-novice drivers. *Accident Analysis & Prevention*, 59, 382–93.

Brody, G.H. (1998) Sibling relationships quality: Its causes and consequences. *Annual Review of Psychology*, 49, 1–24.

Bronson, G.W. (1991) Infant differences in rate of visual encoding. *Child Development*, 62, 44–54.

Broockman, D. and Kalla, J. (2016) Durbly reducing transphobia: A field experiment on door-to-door canvassing. *Science*, 352, 220–4.

Brookhuis, K.A. and DeWaard, D. (1993) The use of psychophysiology to assess driver status. *Ergonomics*, 36(9), 1099–110.

Brooks, B.M., Gardiner, J.M., Kaminska, Z. and Beavis, Z. (2001) Implicit versus explicit retrieval of surnames of famous people: Dissociative effects of levels of processing and age. *Journal of Memory and Language*, 44, 118–30.

Brooks, P., Young, A.W., Maratos, E.J., Coffey, P.J., Calder, A.I., Isaac, C.L., Mays, A.R., Hodges, J.R., Montaldi, D., Cezayirli, E., Roberts, N. and Hadley, D. (1998) Face processing impairments after encephalitis: Amygdala damage and recognition of fear. *Neuropsychologia*, 36(1), 59–70.

Brooks, S. J., Cedernaes, J. and Schiöth, H. B. (2013) Increased prefrontal and parahippocampal activation with reduced dorsolateral prefrontal and insular cortex activation to food images in obesity: a meta-analysis of fMRI studies. *PLoS ONE*, 8(4), e60393.

Brooksbank, B.W.L., Brown, R. and Gustafsson, J.A. (1974) The detection of 5-alpha-androst-16-en-3alpha-ol in human male auxillary sweat. *Experientia*, 30, 864–5.

Brooks-Gunn, J. (1988) Antecedents and consequences of variations in girls' maturational timing. *Journal of Adolescent Health Care*, 9, 365–73.

Broom, D.H., D'Souza, R.M., Strazdins, L., Butterworth, P., Parslow, R. and Rodgers, B. (2006) The lesser evil: Bad jobs or unemployment? A survey of mid-aged Australians. *Social Science and Medicine*, 63, 575–86.

Brosch, T. and Sander, D. (2013) Comment: The appraising brain. *Emotion Review*, 5, 163–8.

Brosch, T., Pourtois, G., Sander, D. and Vuilleumier, P. (2011) Additive effects of emotional, endogenous, and exogenous attention: behavioral and electrophysiological evidence. *Neuropsychologia*, 49(7), 1779–87.

Brown, A.M. (1990) Development of visual sensitivity to light and color vision in human infants: A critical review. *Vision Research*, 30, 1159–88.

Brown, A.S. (1991) A review of the tip-of-the-tongue experience. *Psychological Bulletin*, 109, 204–23.

Brown, A.S., Holden, G.W. and Ashraf, R. (2016) Spank, slap or hit? How labels alter perceptions of child discipline. *Psychology of Violence*, in press.

Brown, E. and Perrett, D.I. (1993) What gives a face its gender? *Perception*, 22, 829–40.

Brown, G.W. (1985) The discovery of expressed emotion: Induction or deduction? In J. Leff and C. Vaughn (eds) *Expressed Emotion in Families*. New York: Guilford Press.

Brown, G.W., Bone, M., Dalison, B. and Wing, J.K. (1966) *Schizophrenia and Social Care*. London: Oxford University Press.

Brown, J., Beard, E., Kotz, D., Michie, S. and West, R. (2014) Real-world effectiveness of e-cigarettes when used to aid smoking cessation: a cross-sectional population study. *Addiction*, 109, 1531–40.

Brown, J.D. (1991) Staying fit and staying well: Physical fitness as a moderator of life stress. *Personality Processes and Individual Differences*, 60, 455–61.

Brown, R. and Hanlon, C. (1970) Derivational complexity and order of acquisition in child speech. In J.R. Hayes (ed.) *Cognition and the Development of Language*. New York: Wiley.

Brown, R. and McNeill, D. (1966) The 'tip-of-the-tongue' phenomenon. *Journal of Verbal Learning and Verbal Behavior*, 5, 325–37.

Brown, R.J. (1995) *Prejudice: Its social psychology*. Oxford, UK: Blackwell.

Brown, R.J. and Hewstone, M. (2005) An integrative theory of intergroup contact. *Advances in Experimental Social Psychology*, 37, 255–343.

Brown, R.T. (1989) Creativity: What are we to measure? In J.A. Glover, R.R. Ronning and C.R. Reynolds (eds) *Handbook of Creativity*. New York: Plenum Press.

Brown, R.W. and Kulik, J. (1977) Flashbulb memories. *Cognition*, 5, 73–99.

Brown, S.L., Nesse, R.M., Vonokur, A.D. and Smith, D.M. (2003) Providing social support may be more beneficial than receiving it. *Psychological Science*, 14 (4), 320–7.

Brown, V.M. and Morey, R.A. (2012) Neural systems for cognitive and emtotional processing in post traumatic stress disorder. *Frontiers in Psychology*, 3, 449.

Brown, W.M., Cronk, L., Grochow, K., Jacobson, A., Liu, C.K., Popovic, Z. and Trivers, R. (2005) Dance reveals symmetry especially in young men. *Nature*, 438, 1148–50.

Brownell, K.D., Greenwood, M.R.C., Stellar, E. and Shrager, E.E. (1986) The effects of repeated cycles of weight loss and regain in rats. *Physiology and Behavior*, 38, 459–64.

Bruce, V. (1994) Stability from variation: The case of face recognition. The M.D. Vernon memorial lecture. *Quarterly Journal of Experimental Psychology*, 47A, 5–28.

Bruce, V. and Young, A.W. (1986) Understanding face recognition. *British Journal of Psychology*, 77, 305–27.

Bruce, V., Burton, A.M. and Dench, N. (1994) What's distinctive about a distinctive face? *Quarterly Journal of Experimental Psychology*, 47A(1), 119–41.

Bruce, V., Burton, A.M., Hanna, E., Healey, P., Mason, O., Coombes, A., Fright, R. and Linney, A. (1993) Sex discrimination: How do we tell the difference between male and female faces? *Perception*, 22, 131–52.

Bruce, V., Henderson, Z., Newman, C. and Burton, A.M. (2001) Matching identities of familiar and unfamiliar faces caught on CCTV images. *Journal of Experimental Psychology: Applied*, 7(3), 207–18.

Bruce, V., Valentine, T. and Baddeley, A.D. (1987) The basis of the 3/4 view effect in face recognition. *Applied Cognitive Psychology*, 1, 109–20.

Bruhl, A.B., Delsignore, A., Komossa, K. and Weidt, S. (2014) Neuroimaging in social anxiety disorder – A meta-analytic review resulting in a new neuro-functional model. *Neuroscience and Biobehavioural Reviews*, 47, 260–80.

Bruner, J.S. (1983) *Child's Talk: Learning to use language*. Oxford: Oxford University Press.

Brunswick, N. (2004) Developmental dyslexia: Evidence from brain research. In T. Nunes and P. Bryant (eds) *Handbook of Children's Literacy*. Dordrecht, The: Kluwer Press.

Brunswick, N. (2009) *Dyslexia – A Beginners' Guide.* Oxford: Oneworld.

Brunswick, N., McCory, E., Price, C., Frith, C. and Frith, U. (1999) Explicit and implicit processing of words and pseudowords by adult developmental dyslexics: A search for Wernicke's Wortschatz. *Brain*, 122, 1901–17.

Bryant, J.A., Sanders-Jackson, A. and Smallwood, A.M.K. (2006) IMing, text messaging, and adolescent social networks. *Journal of Computer-Mediated Communication*, 11, 2.

Bryant, P.E. and Bradley, L. (1985) *Children's Reading Problems: Psychology and education.* Oxford: Blackwell.

Bryson, S.E., Clark, B.S. and Smith, I.M. (1988) First report of a Canadian epidemiological study of autistic syndromes. *Journal of Child Psychology and Psychiatry*, 29, 433–45.

Bucci, M.P. and Kapoula, Z. (2006) Binocular coordination of saccades in 7 year old children in single word reading and target fixation. *Vision Research*, 46, 457–66.

Buchel, C., Price, C. and Friston, K. (1998) A multimodal language region in the ventral-visual pathway. *Nature*, 394(6690), 274–7.

Buchner, A. and Wippich, W. (2000) On the reliability of implicit and explicit memory measures. *Cognitive Psychology*, 40, 227–59.

Buck, L. and Axel, R. (1991) A novel multigene family may encode odorant receptors: A molecular basis for odor recognition. *Cell*, 65, 175–87.

Buck, L.B. (2004) Olfactory receptors and coding in mammals. *Nutrition Reviews*, 62, S184–S188.

Buckels, E., Jones, D. and Paulhus, D. (2013) Behavioural confirmation of everyday sadism. *Psychological Science*, 24, 2201–09.

Buckels, E., Trapnell, P.D. and Paulhus, D.L. (2014) Trolls just want to have fun. *Personality and Individual Differences*, 67, 97–102.

Buckingham, G. (2014) Getting a grip on heaviness perception: a review of weight illusions and their probable causes. *Experimental Brain Research*, 232, 1623–29.

Budziszewska, M., Hansen, K. and Bilewicz, M. (2014) Backlash over gender – fair language: The impact of feminine job titles on men's and women's perception of women. *Journal of Language and Social Psychology*, 33, 681–91.

Buffardi, L.E. and Campbell, W.K. (2008) Narcissism and social networking web sites. *Personality and Social Psychology Bulletin*, 34, 1303–14.

Bukowski, W.M., Sippola, L.A. and Newcomb, A.F. (2000) Variations in patterns of attraction to same- and other-sex peers during early adolescence. *Developmental Psychology*, 36, 147–54.

Buller, D.B., Strzyzewski, K.D. and Hunsaker, F.G. (1991) Interpersonal deception II: The inferiority of conversational participants as deception detectors. *Communication Monographs*, 58, 25–40.

Buman, M.P., Philips, B., Youngstedt, S.D., Kane, C.E. and Harshkowitz, M. (2014) Does nighttime exercise really disturb sleep? Results from the 2013 National Sleep Foundation Sleep in America Poll. *Sleep Medicine*, 15, 755–61.

Burger, J.M. (2009) Replicating Milgram. *American Psychologist*, 64(1), 1–11.

Burger, J.M., Girgis, Z.M. and Manning, C.M. (2001) In their own words: Explaining obedience to authority through an examination of participants' comments. *Social Psychological and Personality Science*, 2, 460–6.

Burges, C. and McMillan, T.M. (2001) The ability of naïve participants to report symptoms of post-traumatic stress disorder. *British Journal of Clinical Psychology*, 40, 209–14.

Burgoyne, A.P., Sala, G., Gobet, F., Macnamara, B.N., Campitelli, G. and Hambrick, D.Z. (2016) The relationship between cognitive ability and chess skill: A comprehensive meta-analysis. *Intelligence*, 59, 72–83.

Burke, D.M., MacKay, D.G., Worthley, J.S. and Wade, E. (1991) On the tip-of-the-tongue: What causes word finding failures in young and older adults? *Journal of Memory and Language*, 30, 542–79.

Burke, M., Drummond, L.M. and Johnston, D.W. (1997) Treatment choice for agoraphobic women: Exposure or cognitive-behaviour therapy? *British Journal of Clinical Psychology*, 36, 409–20.

Burke, M., Hornof, A., Nielsen, E. and Gorman, N. (2005) High-cost banner blindness. *ACM Transactions of Computers and Human Interaction*, 12, 423–45.

Burt, C. (1962) The concept of consciousness. *British Journal of Psychology*, 53, 229–42.

Burt, T., Lisanby, S.H. and Sackheim, H.A. (2002) Neuropsychiatric applications of transcranial magnetic stimulation: a meta-analysis. *International Journal of Neuropsychopharmacology*, 5, 73–103.

Burton, A.M., Bruce, V. and Dench, N. (1993) What's the difference between men and women? Evidence from facial measurement. *Perception*, 22, 153–76.

Burton, A.M., Wilson, S., Cowan, M. and Bruce, V. (1999) Face recognition in poor-quality video: Evidence from security surveillance. *Psychological Science*, 10(3), 243–8.

Bushman, B.J. and Bonacci, A.M. (2002) Violence and sex impair memory for television ads. *Journal of Applied Psychology*, 87, 557–64.

Bushman, B.J. and Cooper, H.M. (1990) Effects of alcohol on human aggression: an integrative research review. *Psychological Bulletin*, 107, 341–54.

Bushnell, I.W.R. (1979) Modification of the externality effect in young infants. *Journal of Experimental Child Psychology*, 28, 211–25.

Buss, D.M. (1987) Selection, evocation and manipulation. *Journal of Personality and Social Psychology*, 53, 1214–31.

Buss, D.M. (1991) Evolutionary personality psychology. *Annual Review of Psychology*, 45, 459–91.

Buss, D.M. (1995) Evolutionary psychology: A new paradigm for psychological science. *Psychological Inquiry*, 6(1), 1–30.

Buss, D.M. (2013) Sexual jealousy. *Psychological Topics*, 22, 155–82.

Buss, D.M. (2014) Comment: Evolutionary criteria for considering and emotion 'basic': Jealousy as an illustration. *Emotion Review*, 6, 313–31.

Buss, D.M. and Kenrick, D.T. (1998) Evolutionary social psychology. In D.T. Gilbert, S.T. Fiske and G. Lindzey (eds) *The Handbook of Social Psychology* (4th edn), Vol. 2. New York: McGraw-Hill, pp. 982–1026.

Buss, D.M., Haselton, M.G., Shackelford, T.K., Bleske, A.L. and Wakefield, J.C. (1998) Adaptations, exaptations and spandrels. *American Psychologist*, 53(5), 533–48.

Butler, R.A., Lambon Ralph, M. and Woollams, A.M. (2014) Capturing multi-dimensionality in stroke aphasia: mapping principal behavioural components to neural structures. *Brain*, 137, 3248–66.

Buunk, B.P., de Jonge, J., Ybema, J.F. and de Wolff, C.J. (1998) Psychological aspects of occupational stress. In P.J. Denth, H. Thierry and C.J. de Wolff (eds) *The Handbook of Work and Organisational Psychology* (2nd edn). Hove: Psychology Press.

Buxbaum, J.D., Daly, M.J., Devlin, B., Lehner, T., Roeder, K., State, M.W. and the Autism Sequencing Consortium (2012) *Neuron*, 76, 1052–6.

Byom, L.J. and Mutlu, B. (2013) Theory of mind: mechanisms, methods and new directions. *Frontiers in Human Neuroscience*, 7, 413.

Byrd, M. and Stacey, B. (1993) Bias in IQ perception. *The Psychologist*, 6, 16.

Byrne, D. (1971) *The Attraction Paradigm.* New York: Academic Press.

Byrne, R. (1995) *The Thinking Ape.* Oxford: Oxford University Press.

Byron, K. and Khazanchi, S. (2011) A meta-analytic investigation of the relationship of state and trait anxiety to performance on figural and verbal creative tasks. *Personality and Social Psychology Bulletin*, 37, 269–82.

C

Cabeza, R. and Nyberg, L. (2000) Imaging cognition II: Empirical review of 275 PET and fMRI studies. *Journal of Cognitive Neuroscience*, 12(1), 1–47.

Cabeza, R., Grady, C.L., Nyberg, L., McIntosh, A.R., Tulving, E., Kapur, S., Jennings, J.M., Houle, S. and Craik, F.I.M. (1997) Age-related differences in neural activity during memory encoding and retrieval: A positron emission tomography study. *Journal of Neuroscience*, 17(1), 391–400.

Caccappoulo-van Vliet, E., Miozzo, M. and Stern, Y. (2004) Phonological dyslexia: A test case for reading models. *Psychological Science*, 15 (9), 583–90.

Caeyenberghs, K. and Leemans, A. (2014) Hemispheric lateralization of topological organization in structural brain networks. *Human Brain Mapping*, 35, 4844–957.

Cain, W.S. (1977) Differential sensitivity for smell: 'noise' at the nose. *Science*, 195, 796–8.

Calabrese, P., Markowitsch, H.J., Harders, A.G., Scholz, M. and Gehlen, W. (1995) Fornix damage and memory: A case report. *Cortex*, 31, 555–64.

Calati, R., DeRonchi, D., Bellini, M. and Serretti, A. (2011) The 5-HTTLPR polymorphism and eating disorders: A meta-analysis. *International Journal of Eating Disorders*, 44, 191–9.

Calder, A.J., Keane, J., Young, A.W. and Lawrence, A.D. (2010) The relation between anger and different forms of disgust: Implications for emotion recognition impairments in Huntington's disease. *Neuropsychologia*, 48, 2719–29.

Calder, A.J., Young, A.W., Rowland, D., Perrett, D.I., Hodges, J.R. and Etcoff, N.L. (1996) Facial emotion recognition after bilateral amygdala damage: Differentially severe impairment of fear. *Cognitive Neuropsychology*, 13, 699–745.

Caldwell, C. and Hibbert, S.A. (2002) The influence of music tempo and musical preference on restaurant patrons' behavior. *Psychology & Marketing*, 19(11), 895–917.

Calef, T., Pieper, M. and Coffey, B. (1999) Comparisons of eye movements before and after a speed-reading course. *Journal of American Optometric Association*, 70, 171–81.

Calev, A., Gaudino, E.A., Squires, N.K. *et al.* (1995) ECT and non-memory cognition: A review. *British Journal of Clinical Psychology*, 34, 505–16.

Calvin, W.H. and Ojemann, G.A. (1994) *Conversations with Neil's Brain.* New York: Addison-Wesley.

Campbell, A., Shirley, L. and Caygill, L. (2002) Sex-typed preferences in three domains: Do two-year-olds need cognitive variables? *British Journal of Psychology*, 93, 203–17.

Campbell, F.A., Pungello, E.P., Miller-Johnson, S., Burchinal, M. and Ramey, C.T. (2001) The development of cognitive and academic abilities: Growth curves from an early childhood educational experiment. *Developmental Psychology*, 37(2), 231–42.

Campbell, J.S. *et al.* (2009) Meta-analysis of personality assessments as predictors of military aviation training success. *International Journal of Aviation Psychology*, 20, 92–109.

Campfield, L.A., Smith, F.J., Guisez, Y., Devos, R. and Burn, P. (1995) Recombinant mouse OB protein: evidence for a peripheral signal linking adiposity and central neural networks. *Science*, 269, 546–9.

Canli, T. (2006) *Biology of Personality and Individual Difference.* New York: The Guilford Press.

Canli, T., Zhao, Z., Desmond, J.E., Kang, E., Gross, J. and Gabrieli, J.D.E. (2001) An fMRI study of personality influences on brain reactivity to emotional stimuli. *Behavioural Neuroscience*, 115(1), 33–42.

Cann, A. and Ross, D.A. (1989) Olfactory stimuli as context cues in human memory. *American Journal of Psychology*, 102, 91–102.

Cannon, W.B. (1927) The James–Lange theory of emotions: A critical examination and an alternative theory. *American Journal of Psychology*, 39, 106–24.

Cannon, W.B. (1931) James–Lange and the thalamic theories of emotion. *Psychological Review*, 38, 281–95.

Cannon, W.B. and Washburn, A.L. (1912) An explanation of hunger. *American Journal of Physiology*, 29, 444–54.

Cantagallo, A. and Della Sala, S. (1998) Preserved insight in an artist with extrapersonal spatial neglect. *Cortex*, 34, 163–89.

Cantor, N. and Mischel, W. (1979) Prototypes in person perception. In L. Berkowitz (ed.) *Advances in Experimental Social Psychology*, Vol. 12. New York: Academic Press, pp. 3–52.

Cao, B., Mwangi, B., Hasan, K.M., Selvaraj, S., Zeni, C.P., Zunta-Soares, G.B. and Soares, J.C. (2015) Development and validation of a brain maturation index using longitudinal neuroanatomical scans. *Neuroimage*, 117, 311–18.

Capaldi, C.A., Dopko, R.L. and Zelenski, J.M. (2014) The relationship between nature connectedness and happiness. *Frontiers in Psychology*, 5, 976.

Cappa, S.E., Perani, D., Grassi, E., Bressi, S., Albertoni, M. and Franceschi, M. (1997) A PET follow-up study of recovery after stroke in acute aphasics. *Brain and Language*, 56, 55–67.

Cappell, K.A., Gmeindl, L. and Reuter-Lorenz, P.A. (2010) Age differences in dlPFC recruitment during verbal working memory depend on memory load. *Cortex*, 46, 462–73.

Caprara, G.V. and Perugini, M. (1994) Personality described by adjectives: Generalizability of the Big Five to the Italian lexical context. *European Journal of Personality*, 8, 357–69.

Caprara, G.V., Vecchione, M., Alessandri, G., Gerbino, M. and Barbaranelli, C. (2011) The contribution of personality traits and self-efficacy beliefs to academic achievement: A longitudinal study. *British Journal of Educational Psychology*, 81, 78–96.

Caprariello, P.A., Cuddy, A.J.C. and Fiske, S.T. (2009) Social structures shapes cultural stereotypes and emotions: A causal test of the stereotype content model. *Group Processes and Intergroup Relations*, 12, 147–55.

Carey, S. and Bartlett, E. (1978) Acquiring a single new word. *Proceedings of the Stanford Child Language Conference*, 15, 17–29.

Carey, S. and Diamond, R. (1977) From piecemeal to configurational representation of faces. *Science*, 195, 312–14.

Carl, N. (2014) Verbal intelligence is correlated with socially and economically liberal beliefs. *Intelligence*, 44, 142–8.

Carli, L.L. (1990) Gender, language, and influence. *Journal of Personality and Social Psychology*, 59, 941–51.

Carlin, A.S., Hoffman, H.G. and Weghorst, S. (1997) Virtual reality and tactile augmentation in the treatment of spider phobia: A case study. *Behaviour Research and Therapy*, 35, 153–8.

Carlin, J.D. and Calder, A.J. (2013) The neural basis of eye gaze processing. *Current Opinion in Neurobiology*, 23, 450–5.

Carlson, E.A. (1998) A prospective longitudinal study of attachment disorganization/disorientation. *Child Development*, 69(4), 1107–28.

Carlson, K.A. and Russo, J.E. (2001) Biased interpretation of evidence by mock jurors. *Journal of Experimental Psychology: Applied*, 7(2), 91–103.

Carnahan, T. and McFarland, S. (2007) Revisiting the Stanford Prison Experiment: Could participant self-selection have led to the cruelty? *Personality and Social Psychology Bulletin*, 33, 603–14.

Carney, D.R., Cuddy, A.J.C. and Yap, A.J. (2010) Power posing: Brief nonverbal displays affect neuroendocrine levels and risk tolerance. *Psychological Science*, 21 (10), 1363–8.

Carp, J. (2012) The secret lives of experiments: Methods reporting in the fMRI literature. *Neuroimage*, 63, 289–300.

Carpenter, P.A. and Just, M.A. (1983) What your eyes do while your mind is reading. In K. Rayner (ed.) *Eye Movements in Reading: Perceptual and language processes.* New York: Academic Press.

Carpenter, S.K. (2012) Testing enhances the transfer of learning. *Current Directions in Psychological Science*, 21, 279–83.

Carson, R.C., Butcher, J.N. and Mineka, S. (1996) *Abnormal Psychology and Modern Life* (10th edn). Boston, MA: Allyn & Bacon.

Carter, T.J., Ferguson, M.J. and Hassin, R.R. (2011) A single exposure to the American flag shifts support toward republicanism up to 8 months later. *Psychological Science*, 22, 101–18.

Caruso, E.M. and Gino, F. (2011) Blind ethics: Closing one's eyes polarizes moral judgments and discourages dishonest behavior. *Cognition*, 118, 280–5.

Carver, C.S. and Harmon-Jones, E. (2009) Anger is an approach-related affect: Evidence and implications. *Psychological Bulletin*, 135(2), 183–204.

Carver, C.S. and Scheier, M.F. (1981) *Attention and Self-regulation: A control theory approach to human behavior.* New York: Springer-Verlag.

Carver, C.S. and Scheier, M.F. (2011) *Perspectives on Personality* (7th edn). Boston, MA: Allyn & Bacon.

Carver, C.S., Smith, R.G., Antoni, M.H., Petronis, V.M., Weiss, S. and Derhagopian, R.P. (2005) Optimistic personality and psychosocial well-being during treatment predict psychosocial well-being among long-term survivors of breast cancer. *Health Psychology*, 24(5), 508–16.

Casazza, K. (2013) Myths, presumptions and facts about obesity. *The New England Journal of Medicine*, 368, 446–54.

Case, L. and Smith, T.B. (2000) Ethnic representation in a sample of the literature of applied psychology. *Journal of Consulting and Clinical Psychology*, 68(6), 1107–10.

Cash, D.M., Ridgway, G.R., Liang, Y., Ryan, N.S., Kinnunen, K.M., Yeatman, T., . . . and Ghetti, B.F. (2013) The pattern of atrophy in familial Alzheimer disease Volumetric MRI results from the DIAN study. *Neurology*, 81(16), 1425–33.

Cash, T.F., Morrow, J.A., Hrabosky, J.I. and Perry, A.A. (2004) How has body image changed? A cross-sectional investigation of college women and men from 1983 to 2001. *Journal of Consulting and Clinical Psychology*, 72 (6), 1081–9.

Cashen, M.C. and Leicht, K.L. (1970) Role of the isolation effect in a formal educational setting. *Journal of Educational Psychology*, 61, 484–6.

Caspi, A. (2000) The child is father of the man: Personality continuities from childhood to adulthood. *Journal of Personality and Social Psychology*, 78(1), 158–72.

Cavanaugh, J.C. (1990) *Adult Development and Aging.* Belmont, CA: Wadsworth.

Cavazza, N., Guidetti, M. and Butera, F. (2015) Ingredients of gender-based stereotypes about food. *Appetite*, 91, 266–72.

Centeno, M., Knoepp, M.J., Vollmar, C., Stretton, J., Sidhu, M., Michallef, C *et al.* (2014) Language dominance assessment in a bilingual population: Validity of fMRI in the second language. *Epilepsia*, 55, 1504–11.

Centerwall, B. (1989) Exposure to television as a risk factor for violence. *American Journal of Epidemiology*, 129, 643–52.

Cepeda, N.J., Pashler, H., Vul, E., Wixted, J.T. and Roher, D. (2006) Distributed practice in verbal recall tasks: A review and quantitative synthesis. *Psychological Bulletin*, 132, 354–80.

Cervenka, M.C., Boatman-Reich, D.F., Ward, J., Franaszczuk, P.J. and Crone, N.E. (2011) Language mapping in multilingual patients: electrocoricography and cortical stimulation during naming. *Frontiers in Human Neuroscience*, 5(13), 1–15.

Chadwick, M.J., Mullally, S.L. and Maguire, E.A. (2013) The hippocampus extrapolates beyond the view in scenes: an fMRI study of boundary extension. *Cortex*, 49, 2067–79.

Chaiken, S. (1979) Communicator's physical attractiveness and persuasion. *Journal of Personality and Social Psychology*, 37, 1387–97.

Chalmers, B. and Meyer, D. (1996) What men say about pregnancy, birth and parenthood. *Journal of Psychosomatic Obstetrics and Gynaecology*, 17, 47–52.

Chalmers, D.J. (1995) Facing up to the problems of consciousness. *Journal of Consciousness Studies*, 2(3), 200–19.

Chaminade, T., Da Fonseca, D., Rosset, D., Lutcher, E., Cheng, G. and Deruelle, C. (2012, September). fMRI study of young adults with autism interacting with a humanoid robot. In *RO-MAN, 2012 IEEE.* IEEE. pp. 380–5.

Chaminade, T., Rosset, D., Da Fonseca, D., Nazarian, B., Lutcher, E., Cheng, G. and Deruelle, C. (2012) How do we think machines think? An fMRI study of alleged competition with an artificial intelligence. *Frontiers in Human Neuroscience*, 6, 1–9.

Chamorro-Premuzic, T., Furnham, A., Christopher, A.N., Garwood, J. and Martin, G.N. (2008) Birds of a feather: Students' preferences for lecturers' personalities by their own personality and learning approaches. *Personality and Individual Differences*, 44, 965–76.

Chan, E.Y. (2015) Physically-attractive males increase men's financial risk-taking. *Evolution and Human Behaviour*, 36, 407–13.

Chao, L.L., Haxby, J.V. and Martin, A. (1999) Attribute-based neural substrates in temporal cortex for perceiving and knowing about objects. *Nature Neuroscience*, 2, 913–19.

Chapman, B.P., Roberts, B.W. and Duberstein, P.R. (2011) Personality and longevity: Knowns, unknowns, and implications for public health and personalised medicine. *Journal of Aging Research*, 2011, 1–24.

Chapman, H.A., Bernier, D. and Rusak, B. (2010) MRI-related anxiety levels change within and between repeated scanning sessions. *Psychiatry Research*, 182, 160–4.

Chapman, K.L., Leonard, L.B. and Mervis, C.B. (1986) The effect of feedback on young children's inappropriate word usage. *Journal of Child Language*, 13, 101–17.

Charles-Sire, V., Stefan, J. and Gueguen, N. (2015) Single exposure to the word 'loving' and implicit helping behavior. *Social Influence*, 11, 1–6.

Charlton, R.A., Barrick, T.R., Markus, H.S. and Morris, R.G. (2009) Theory of mind associations with other cognitive functions and brain imaging in normal aging. *Psychology and Aging*, 24, 338–48.

Charlton, T., Gunter, B. and Coles, D. (1988) Broadcast television as a cause of aggression? *Emotional and Behavioural Difficulties*, 3, 5–13.

Charness, N and Boot, W.R. (2009) Aging and information technology use. *Current Directions in Psychological Science*, 18, 253–8.

Charness, N., Kelley, C.L., Bosman, E.A. and Mottram, M. (2001) Word processing training and retraining. *Psychology and Aging*, 16, 110–27.

Charpentier, A. (1891) Analyse experimentale quelques elements de la sensation de poids. *Archives de Physiologie Normales et Pathalogiques*, 3, 122–35.

Chasdi, E.H. (1994) *Culture and Human Development: The selected papers of John Whiting.* New York: Cambridge University Press.

Chassin, L., Presson, C.C., Rose, J.S. and Sherman, S.J. (1996) The natural history of cigarette smoking from adolescence to adulthood: Demographic predictors of continuity and change. *Health Psychology*, 15(6), 478–84.

Chatterjee, A. (2004) Neuropsychology of art. *Neuropsychologia*, 42, 1568–83.

Chee, M.W., Tan, E.W. and Thiel, T. (1999) Mandarin and English single word processing studied with functional magnetic resonance imaging. *Journal of Neuroscience*, 19, 3050–6.

Chee, M.W.L., Chuah, L.Y.M., Venkatraman, V., Chan, W.Y., Philip, P. and Dinges, D.F. (2006) Functional imaging of working memory following normal sleep and after 24 and 35 h of sleep deprivation: Correlations of fronto-parietal activation with performance. *Neuroimage*, 31, 419–28.

Chekroud, A.M., Everett, J.A.C., Bridge, H. and Hewstone, M. (2014) A review of neuroimaging studies of race-related prejudice: does amygdala response reflect threat? *Frontiers in Human Neuroscience*, 8, 179.

Chen, F.S., Mayer, J., Mussweiler, T. and Heinrichs, M. (2014) Oxytocin increases the likeability of physically formidable men. *SCAN*, 10(6): 797–800.

Chen, Y.R., Brockner, J. and Katz, T. (1998) Toward an explanation of cultural differences in in-group favouritism: the role of individual versus collective primacy. *Journal of Personality and Social Psychology*, 75, 1490–502.

Cherkas, L.F., Aviv, A., Valdes, A.M., Hunkin, J.L., Gardner, J.P., Surdulescu, G.L. *et al.* (2006) The effects of social status on biological aging as measured by white-blood cell telomere length. *Aging Cell*, 5, 361–5.

Cherny, S.S., Fulker, D.W., Emde, R.N., Robinson, J., Corley, R.P., Reznick, J.S., Plomin, R. and DeFries, J.C. (1994) A developmental–genetic analysis of continuity and change in the Bayley Mental Development Index from 14 to 24 months: The MacArthur Longitudinal Twin Study. *Psychological Science*, 5, 354–60.

Cherry, E.C. (1953) Some experiments on the recognition of speech, with one and with two ears. *Journal of the Acoustical Society of America*, 25, 975–9.

Chetverikov, A. and Ivanchei, I. (2016) Seeing 'the Dress' in the right light: Perceived colors and inferred light sources. *Perception*, 45(8), 910–30.

Chiang, M-C., Barysheva, M., Shattuck, D.W., Lee, A.D., Madsen, S.K., Avedissian, C. and Thompson, P.M. (2009) Genetics of brain fiber architecture in intellectual performance. *Journal of Neuroscience*, 29, 2212–24.

Chiang, M-C., McMahon, K.L., de Zubicaray, G.I., Martin, N.G., Hickie, I., Toga, A.W. and Thompson, P.M. (2011) Genetics of white matter development. *Neuroimage*, 54, 2308–17.

Chiao, J.Y. and Blizinsky, K.D. (2010) Culture-gene coevolution of individualism-collectivism and the serotonin transporter gene. *Proceedings of the Royal Society B*, 277, 529–37.

Chiao, J.Y., Iidaka, T., Gordon, H.L., Nogawa, J., Bar, M., Aminoff, E. . . . and Ambady, N. (2008) Cultural specificity in amygdala response to fear faces. *Journal of Cognitive Neuroscience*, 20(12), 2167–74.

Chida, Y. and Steptoe, A. (2009) Cortisol awakening response and psychosocial factors: A systematic review and meta-analysis. *Biological Psychology*, 80, 265–78.

Chiesa, M. and Hobbs, S. (2008) Making sense of social research: How useful is the Hawthorne effect? *European Journal of Social Psychology*, 38, 67–74.

Chipuer, H.M., Rovine, M.J. and Plomin, R. (1990) LISREL modelling: Genetic and environmental influences on IQ revisited. *Intelligence*, 14, 11–29.

Chiriboga, D.A. (1997) Crisis, challenge and stability in the middle years. In M.E. Lachman and J.B. James (eds) *Multiple Paths of Midlife Development*. Chicago, IL: Chicago University Press.

Chiu, C., Morris, M.W., Hong, Y. and Menon, T. (2000) Motivated cultural cognition: The impact of implicit cultural theories on dispositional attribution varies as a function of need for closure. *Journal of Personality and Social Psychology*, 78, 247–59.

Cho, K., Ennaceur, A., Cole, J.C. and Suh, C.K. (2000) Chronic jet lag produces cognitive deficits. *Journal of Neuroscience*, 20:RC66, 1–5.

Choi, I. and Nisbett, R.E. (1998) *Personality and Social Psychology Bulletin*, 24, 949–60.

Choi, I., Dalal, R., Kim-Prieto, C. and Park, H. (2003) Culture and judgement of causal relevance. *Journal of Personality and Social Psychology*, 84, 46–59.

Choi, J., Jeong, B., Polcari, A., Rohan, M.L. and Teicher, M.H. (2012) Reduced fractional anisotropy in the visual limbic pathway of young adults witnessing domestic violence in childhood. *Neuroimage*, 59(2), 1071–9.

Choi, J., Jeong, B., Polcari, A.M., Rohan, M.L. and Teicher, M.H. (2012) Reduced fractional anisotrophy in the visual limbic pathway of young adults witnessing domestic violence in childhood. *Neuroimage*, 59, 1071–9.

Choi, J., Jeong, B., Rohan, M.L., Polcari, A.M. and Teicher, M.H. (2009) Preliminary evidence for white matter tract abnormalities in young adults exposed to parental verbal abuse. *Biological Psychiatry*, 65, 227–34.

Choi, J.C., Chung, M.I. and Lee, Y.D. (2012) Modulation of pain sensation by stress-related testosterone and cortisol. *Anaesthesia*, 67(10), 1146–51.

Chomsky, N. (1957) *Syntactic Structure*. The Hague: Mouton Publishers.

Chomsky, N. (1965) *Aspects of the Theory of Syntax*. Cambridge, MA: MIT Press.

Chooi, W.T. and Thompson, L.A. (2012) Working memory training does not improve intelligence in healthy young adults. *Intelligence*, 40(6), 531–42.

Choudhury, S., Fishman, J.R., McGowan, M.L. and Juengst, E.T. (2014) Big data, open science and the brain: lessons learned from genomics. *Frontiers in Human Neuroscience*, 8, 239.

Chouinard, G. and Chouinard, V. (2008) Atypical antipsychotics: CATIE study, drug-induced movement disorder and resulting iatrogenic psychiatric-like symptoms, sensitivity rebound psychosis and withdrawal discontinuation. *Psychotherapy and Psychosomatics*, 77, 69–77.

Chrea, C., Valentin, D., Sulmont-Rosse, C., Ly Mai, H., Hoang Nguyen, D. and Abdi, H. (2004) Culture and odor categorization: agreement between cultures depends upon the odors. *Food Quality and Preference*, 15, 669–79.

Christenfeld, N., Phillips, D. and Glynn, L. (1999) What's in a name: mortality and the power of symbols. *Journal of Psychosomatic Research*, 47, 241–54.

Christensen, A.P., Silvia, P.J., Nusbaum, E.C. and Beaty, R.E. (2016) Clever people: intelligence and humor production ability. *Psychology of Aesthetics, Creativity and the Arts*, in press.

Christensen, H., Henderson, A.S., Griffiths, K. and Levings, C. (1997) Does ageing inevitably lead to declines in cognitive performance? A longitudinal study of elite academics. *Personality and Individual Differences*, 23(1), 67–78.

Christiansen, B. (1986) Den norske befolknings syn pa psykologer. *Tidsskrift for Norsk Psykologforening*, 23, 619–34.

Christianson, S.A. (1989) Flash-bulb memories: Special, but not so special. *Memory and Cognition*, 17, 435–43.

Christianson, S.A. and Engelberg, E. (1999) Memory and emotional consistency: The MS Estonia ferry disaster. *Memory*, 7(4), 471–82.

Christianson, S-A. (1992) Remembering emotional events. In S.-A. Christianson (ed.), *The Handbook of Emotion and Memory*. London: Routledge.

Christie, F. and Bruce, V. (1998) The role of movement in the recognition of unfamiliar faces. *Memory and Cognition*, 26(4), 780–90.

Chronis, A.M., Jones, H.A. and Raggi, V.L. (2006) Evidence-based psychosocial treatments for children and adolescents with attention-deficit/hyperactivity disorder. *Clinical Psychology Review*, 26, 486–502.

Chu, S. and Downes, J.J. (2000) Odour-evoked autobiographical memories: Psychological investigations of Proustian phenomena. *Chemical Senses*, 25, 111–16.

Chu, S., Hardaker, R. and Lycett, J.E. (2007) Too good to be 'true'? The handicap of high socio-economic status in attractive males. *Personality and Individual Differences*, 42, 1291–300.

Chua, H.F., Boland, J.E. and Nisbett, R.E. (2005a) Cultural variation in eye movements during scene perception. *Proceedings of the National Academy of Sciences*, 102(35), 12629–33.

Chua, H.F., Gonzalez, R., Taylor, S.F., Welsh, R.C. and Liberzon, L. (2009) Decision-related loss: regret and disappointment. *Neuroimage*, 47, 2031–40.

Chugani, H.T., Brehen, M.E., Muzik, O., Juhasz, C., Nagy, F. and Chugani, D.C. (2001) Local brain functional activity following early deprivation; A study of postinstitutionalised Romanian orphans. *Neuroimage*, 14, 1290–301.

Church, A.T., Katigbak, M.S., Ortiz, F.A., del Prado, A.M., Vargas-Flores, J., Ibanez-Reyes, J., Reyes, J.A.S., Pe-Pua, R. and Cabrera, H.F. (2005) Investigating implicit trait theories across cultures. *Journal of Cross-Cultural Psychology*, 36(4), 476–96.

Churchland, P.S. (1998) Brainshy: Nonneural theories of conscious experience. In S.R. Hameroff, A.W. Kaszniak and A.C. Scott (eds) *Towards a Science of Consciousness II*. Cambridge, MA: MIT Press.

Cialdini, R.B. (1993) *Influence: Science and practice* (3rd edn). New York: HarperCollins.

Cialdini, R.B., Borden, R.J., Thorne, A., Walker, M.R., Freeman, S. and Sloan, L.R. (1976) Basking in reflected glory: Three (football) field studies. *Journal of Personality and Social Psychology*, 34, 366–75.

Cialdini, R.B., Cacioppo, J.T., Bassett, R. and Miller, J.A. (1978) Low-balling procedure for producing compliance: Commitment then cost. *Journal of Personality and Social Psychology*, 36, 463–76.

Cialdini, R.B., Demaine, L.J., Sagarin, B.J., Barrett, D.W., Rhoads, K. and Winter, P.L. (2006) Managing social norms for persuasive impact. *Social Influence*, 1, 3–15.

Cialdini, R.B., Petty, R.E. and Cacioppo, J.T. (1981) Attitude and attitude change. *Annual Review of Psychology*, 32, 357–404.

Cialdini, R.B., Vincent, J.E., Lewis, S.K., Catalan, J., Wheeler, D. and Darby, B.L. (1975) Reciprocal concessions procedure for inducing compliance: The door-in-the-face technique. *Journal of Personality and Social Psychology*, 31, 206–15.

Cikara, M. and Fiske, S.T. (2011) Bounded empathy: Neural responses to outgroup targets' (mis) fortunes. *Journal of Cognitive Neuroscience*, 23, 3791–803.

Cikara, M. and Fiske, S.T. (2012) Stereotypes and schadenfreude affective and physiological markers of pleasure at outgroup misfortunes. *Social Psychological and Personality Science*, 3, 63–71.

Cikara, M. and Fiske, S.T. (2013) Their pain, our pleasure: stereotype content and schadenfreude. *Annals of the New York Academy of Sciences*, 1299(1), 52–9.

Cikara, M., Farnsworth, R.A., Harris, L.T. and Fiske, S. (2010) On the wrong side of the trolley track: Neural correlates of relative social valuation. *SCAN*, 5, 404–13.

Cima, M., Tonnaer, F. and Hauser, M.D. (2010) Psychopaths know right from wrong but don't care. *SCAN*, 5, 59–67.

Clark, D.M. (1986) A cognitive approach to panic. *Behaviour Research and Therapy*, 24, 461–70.

Clark, D.M. (1988) A cognitive model of panic attacks. In S. Rachman and J.D. Maser (eds) *Panic: Psychological perspectives*. Hillsdale, NJ: Lawrence Erlbaum Associates.

Clark, H.H. and Clark, E.V. (1977) *Psychology and Language: An introduction to psycholinguistics*. New York: Harcourt Brace Jovanovich.

Clark, I. and Landolt, H.P. (2016) Coffee, caffeine and sleep: A systematic review of epidemiological and randomized controlled trials. *Sleep Medicine Reviews*, in press.

Clark, I.A. and Maguire, E.A. (2016) Remembering preservation in hippocampal amnesia. *Annual Review of Psychology*, 67, 1–32.

Clark, J.D. (1993) The African tinderbox: The spark that ignited our cultural heritage. In A.J. Almquist and A. Manyak (eds) *Milestones in Human Evolution*. Prospect Heights, IL: Waveland Press.

Clark, L., Iversen, S.D. and Goodwin, G.M. (2002) Sustained attention deficit in bipolar disorder. *British Journal of Psychiatry*, 180, 313–19.

Clark, N.K. and Stephenson, G.M. (1995) Social remembering: Individual and collaborative memory for social information. *European Review of Social Psychology*, 6, 127–60.

Clark, R.E. and Squire, L.R. (1998) Classical conditioning and brain systems: The role of awareness. *Science*, 280, 77–81.

Clarke, J.C. (1992) The nature and treatment of panic anxiety and agoraphobia. In S. Schwartz (ed.) *Case Studies in Abnormal Psychology*. New York: Wiley.

Clarke, S., Thiran, A.B., Maeder, P., Adriani, M., Vernet, O., Regli, L., Cuisenaire, O. and Thiran, J-P. (2002) What and where in human auditory cortex: Selective deficits following focal hemispheric lesions. *Experimental Brain Research*, 147, 8–15.

Clary, R., Wandersee, J. and Elias, J.S. (2007) Does the color-coding of examination versions affect college science students' test performance? Countering claims of bias. *Journal of College Science Teaching*, 37(1), 40.

Clayman, S.E. and Heritage, J. (2002) Questioning presidents: Journalistic deference and adversarialness in the press conference of Eisenhower and Reagan. *Journal of Communication*, 52, 749–75.

Cleckley, H. (1976) *The Mask of Sanity*. St Louis, MO: C.V. Mosby.

Cleermans, A. (1993) *Mechanisms of Implicit Learning*. Cambridge, MA: MIT Press.

Clohessy, S. and Ehlers, A. (1999) PTSD symptoms, response to intrusive memories and coping in ambulance workers. *British Journal of Clinical Psychology*, 38, 251–66.

Coe, W.C. and Sarbin, T.R. (1991) Role theory: Hypnosis from a dramaturgical and narrational perspective. In S.J. Lynn and J.H. Rhue (eds) *Theories of Hypnosis: Current models and perspectives*. New York: Guilford Press.

Coffey, B. and McLaughlin, P.A. (2016) The effect on lawyers income of gender information contained in first names. *Review of Law and Economics*, 12(1), 57–76.

Coffield, F., Moseley, D., Hall, E. and Ecclestone, K. (2004) *Learning Styles and Pedagogy in Post-16 Learning: A systematic and critical review*. London: Learning and Skills Research Centre, Learning and Skills Development Agency.

Cogan, B., Cogan, D., Waltz, W. and McCue, M. (1987) Effects of laughter and relaxation on discomfort thresholds. *Journal of Behavioural Medicine*, 10(2), 139–44.

Cohen, D. (2004) *Psychologists on Psychology*. London: Hodder & Stoughton.

Cohen, D. and Gunz, A. (2002) As seen by the other . . . : Perspectives on the self in the memories and emotional perceptions of easterners and westerners. *Psychological Science*, 13, 55–9.

Cohen, D., Hoshino-Browne, E. and Leung, A.K. (2007) Culture and the structure of personal experience: Insider and outsider phenomenologies of the self and social world. In M.P. Zanna (ed.) *Advances in Experimental Social Psychology* (4th edn) San Diego, CA: Elsevier.

Cohen, D.J. and Volkmar, F.R. (1997) *Autism and Pervasive Developmental Disorders: A handbook*. New York: Wiley.

Cohen, G. (1990) Why is it difficult to put names to faces? *British Journal of Psychology*, 81, 287–97.

Cohen, G., Stanhope, N. and Conway, M.A. (1992) Age differences in the retention of knowledge by young and elderly students. *British Journal of Developmental Psychology*, 10, 153–64.

Cohen, G.L., Garcia, J., Apfel, N. and Master, A. (2006) Reducing the racial achievement gap: A social-psychological intervention. *Science*, 313, 1307–10.

Cohen, L.A. (1987) Diet and cancer. *Scientific American Mind*, 102, 42–8.

Cohen, M. and Davis, N. (1981) *Medication Errors: Causes and prevention*. Philadelphia, PA: G.F. Stickley.

Cohen, S., Doyle, W.J., Turner, R., Alper, C.M. and Skoner, D.P. (2003) Sociability and susceptibility to the common cold. *Psychological Science*, 14(5), 389–95.

Cohen, D.A. *et al.* (2005) Off-line learning of motor skill memory: A double dissociation of goal and movement. *Proceedings of the National Academy of Sciences*, 102, 18237–41.

Cohn, E.G. and Rotton, J. (1997) Assault as a function of time and temperature: A moderator-variable time-series analysis. *Journal of Personality and Social Psychology*, 72, 1322–34.

Cok, F. (1990) Body image satisfaction in Turkish adolescents. *Adolescence*, 25, 409–13.

Coldwells, A., Atkinson, G. and Reilly, T. (1994) Sources of variation in back and leg dynamometry. *Ergonomics*, 37, 79–86.

Cole, S., Balcetis, E. and Dunning, D. (2013) Affective signals of threat produce perceived proximity. *Psychological Science*, 24, 34–40.

Collaer, M.L. and Hines, M. (1995) Human behavioural sex differences: A role for gonadal hormones during early development. *Psychological Bulletin*, 118, 55–107.

Colley, B. and McLaughlin, P.A. (2009) Do masculine names help female lawyers become judges? *American Law and Economics Review*, 11, 112–33.

Collins, A.M. and Quillian, M.R. (1969) Retrieval time from semantic memory. *Journal of Verbal Learning and Verbal Behavior*, 8, 240–8.

Colombo, J.A., Reisin, H.D., Miguel-Hidalgo, J.J. and Rajkowska, G. (2006) Cerebral cortex astroglia and the brain and the brain of a genius. *Brain Research Reviews*, 52, 257–63.

Coltheart, M. (1978) Lexical access in simple reading tasks. In G. Underwood (ed.) *Strategies of Information Processing*. London: Academic Press.

Coltheart, M. (2013) How can functional neuroimaging inform cognitive theories? *Perspectives on Psychological Science*, 8(1), 98–103.

Coltheart, M., Curtis, B., Atkins, P. and Haller, M. (1993) Models of reading aloud: Dual-route and parallel-distributed-processing approaches. *Psychological Review*, 100, 589–608.

Coltheart, M., Patterson, K. and Marshall, J.C. (1980) *Deep Dyslexia*. London: Routledge and Kegan Paul.

Coltheart, M., Rastle, K., Perry, C., Langdon, R. and Ziegler, J. (2001) DRC: A dual route cascaded model of visual word recognition and reading aloud. *Psychological Review*, 108, 204–56.

Combs, A.W. and Snygg, D. (1959) *Individual behavior: A perceptual approach to behavior*. Oxford: Harpers.

Comninos, A.N. *et al.* (2017) Kisspeptin modulates sexual and emotional brain processing in humans. *The Journal of Clinical Investigation*. 127, 709.

Confer, J.C., Easton, J.A., Fleischman, D.S., Goetz, C.D., Lewis, D.M.G., Perilloux, C. and Buss, D.M. (2010) Evolutionary psychology. *American Psychologist*, 65(2), 110–26.

Conger, J.C., Conger, A.J., Costanzo, P.R., Wright, K.L. and Matter, J.A. (1980) The effect of social cues on the eating behavior of obese and normal subjects. *Journal of Personality*, 48(2), 258–71.

Conner, M. and Sparks, P. (1996) The theory of planned behaviour and health behaviours. In M. Conner and P. Norman (eds) *Predicting*

Health Behaviours: Research and practice with social cognition models. Buckingham: Open University Press.

Connor, C.M., Guo, Y. and Akbarian, S. (2009) Cingulate white matter neurons in schizophrenia. *Biological Psychiatry*, 66, 486–93.

Conrad, C.D. (2008) Chronic stress-induced hippocampal vulnerability: the glucocorticoid vulnerability hypothesis. *Reviews in the Neurosciences*, 19(6), 395–412.

Constantini, E. and King, J. (1980) The partial juror: Correlates and causes of prejudgement. *Law and Society Review*, 15, 9–40.

Constantinidou, F. and Baker, S. (2002) Stimulus modality and verbal learning performance in normal aging. *Brain and Language*, 82(3), 296–311.

Constantinople, C.M. and Bruno, R.M. (2013) Deep cortical layers are activated directly by thalamus. *Science*, 340, 1591–4.

Contreras, M.J., Rubio, V.J., Pena, D., Colom, R. and Santacreu, J. (2007) Sex differences in dynamic spatial ability: The unsolved question of performance factors. *Memory and Cognition*, 35(2), 297–303.

Converge Consortium (2015). Sparse whole genome sequencing identifies two loci for major depressive disorder. *Nature*, 523(7562), 588.

Conway, A.R.A., Cowan, N. and Bunting, M.F. (2001) The cocktail party phenomenon revisited: the importance of working memory capacity. *Psychonomic Bulletin and Review*, 8(2), 331–5.

Conway, M.A., Anderson, S.J., Larsen, S.F., Donnelly, C.M., McDaniel, M.A., McClelland, A.G.R., Rawles, R.E. and Logie, R.H. (1994) The formation of flashbulb memories. *Memory and Cognition*, 22, 326–43.

Conway, M.A., Cohen, G. and Stanhope, N. (1991) On the very long-term retention of knowledge acquired through formal education: Twelve years of cognitive psychology. *Journal of Experimental Psychology: General*, 120, 1–22.

Conway, M.A., Cohen, G. and Stanhope, N. (1992) Why is it that university grades do not predict very-long-term retention? *Journal of Experimental Psychology: General*, 121(3), 382–4.

Conway, M.A., Gardiner, J.M., Perfect, T.J., Anderson, S.J. and Cohen, G.M. (1997) Changes in memory awareness during learning: The acquisition of knowledge by psychology undergraduates. *Journal of Experimental Psychology: General*, 126, 393–413.

Conway, M.A., Wang, Q., Hanyu, K. and Haque, S. (2005) A cross-cultural investigation of autiobiographical memory. *Journal of Cross-Cultural Psychology*, 36(6), 739–49.

Cook, D.A., Thompson, W.G., Thomas, K.G. and Thomas, M.R. (2009) Lack of interaction between sensing–intuitive learning styles and problem-first versus information-first instruction: A randomized crossover trial. *Advances in Health Sciences Education*, 14(1), 79–90.

Cooper, J. and Cooper, G. (2002) Subliminal motivation: A story revisited. *Journal of Applied Social Psychology*, 32, 2213–27.

Cooper, J. and Fazio, R.H. (1984) A new look at dissonance theory. In L. Berkowitz (ed.) *Advances in Experimental Social Psychology*, Vol. 17. New York: Academic Press, pp. 229–65.

Cooper, J., Bennett, E.A. and Sukel, H.L. (1996) Complex scientific testimony: How do jurors make decisions? *Law and Human Behaviour*, 20, 379–94.

Cooper, J.M. and Strayer, D.L. (2008) Effects of simulator practice and real-world experience on cell-phone-related driver distraction. *Human Factors*, 50, 893–902.

Cooper, K. (1985) Running without risk. *Runner's World*, 20, 61–4.

Cooper, R.M. and Zubek, J.P. (1958) Effects of enriched and restricted early environments on the learning ability of bright and dull rats. *Canadian Journal of Psychology*, 12, 159–64.

Copeland, W., Shanahan, L., Costello, E.J. and Angold, A. (2011) Cumulative prevalence of psychiatric disorders by young adulthood. *Journal of the American Academy of Child Adolescence and Psychiatry*, 50, 252–61.

Copple, C. and Bredekamp, S. (2009) *Developmentally Appropriate Practice*. Washington, DC: National Association for the Education of Young Children.

Corazza, O., Demetrovics, Z., van den Brink, W. and Schifano, F. (2013) 'Legal highs' an inappropriate term for 'Novel Psychoactive Drugs' in drug prevention and scientific debate. *International Journal of Drug Policy*, 24(1), 82–3.

Corazza, O., Demetrovics, Z. and van den Brink, W. and Schiffano, F. (2013) 'Legal highs' an inappropriate term for 'Novel Psychoactive Drugs' in drug prevention and scientific debate. *International Journal of Drug Policy*, 24, 82–3.

Corballis, M.C. (1997) The genetics and evolution of handedness. *Psychological Review*, 104(4), 714–27.

Corballis, M.C. (1999) The gestural origins of language. *American Scientist*, 87, 138–45.

Corbett, G.C. and Davies, I.R.L. (1997) Establishing basic color terms: Measures and techniques. In C.L. Hardin and L. Maffi (eds) *Color Categories in Thought and Language*. New York: Cambridge University Press.

Coricelli, G., Critchley, H.D., Joffily, M., O'Doherty, J.P., Sirigu, A. and Dolan, R.J. (2005) Regret and its avoidance: a neuroimaging study of choice behavior. *Nature Neuroscience*, 8, 1255–62.

Corkin, S. (1984) Lasting consequences of bilateral medial temporal lobectomy: clinical course and experimental findings in HM. *Seminars in Neurology*, 4, 249–59.

Corkin, S., Amaral, D.G., Gonzalez, R., Johnson, K. and Hyman, B.T. (1997) HM's medial temporal lobe lesion: findings from MRI. *Journal of Neuroscience*, 17, 3964–79.

Corkin, S., Sullivan, E.V., Twitchell, T.E. and Grove, E. (1981) The amnesic patient H.M.: Clinical observations and test performance 28 years after operation. *Society for Neuroscience Abstracts*, 7, 235.

Correa, T., Hinsley, A.W. and de Zuniga, H.G. (2010) Who interacts on the web? *Computers in Human Behavior*, 26, 247–53.

Correll, J., Park, B., Judd, C.M. and Wittenbrink, B. (2007) The influence of stereotypes on decisions to shoot. *European Journal of Social Psychology*, 37, 1102–17.

Corrigan, P.W. *et al.* (2000) Stigmatising attribution about mental illness. *Journal of Communication and Psychology*, 28, 91–102.

Corrigan, P.W., Kerr, A. and Knudsen, L. (2005) The stigma of mental illness: Explanatory models and methods for change. *Applied and Preventive Psychology*, 11, 179–90.

Corrigan, P.W., River, L., Lundin, R.K., Penn, D.L., Uphoff-Wasowski, K., Campion, J. *et al.* (2001) Three strategies for changing attributions about severe mental illness. *Schizophrenia Bulletin*, 27, 187–95.

Costa, P.T. and McCrae, R.R. (1980) Still stable after all these years: Personality as a key to some issues in adulthood and old age. In P.B. Baltes (ed.) *Lifespan Development and Behavior*. New York: Academic Press.

Costafreda, S.G., Chu, C., Ashburner, J. and Fu, C.H.Y. (2009) Prognostic and diagnostic potential of the structural anatomy of depression. *PLoS ONE*, 4, e6353.

Costall, A. (1995) Socialising affordances. *Theory and Psychology*, 5(4), 467–81.

Costello, T.G. (2014) Awake craniotomy and multilingualism: language testing during anesthesia for awake craniotomy in a bilingual patient. *Journal of Clinical Neuroscience*, 21, 1469–70.

Coull, J.T., Frith, C.D., Frackowiak, R.S.J. and Grasby, P.M. (1996) A fronto-parietal network for rapid visual information processing: A PET study of sustained attention and working memory. *Neuropsychologia*, 34(11), 1085–95.

Courage, M.L. and Adams, R.J. (1990) Visual acuity assessment from birth to three years using the acuity card procedures: Cross-sectional and longitudinal samples. *Optometry and Vision Science*, 67, 713–18.

Courchesne, E., Hesselink, J.R., Jernigan, T.L. and Yeung-Courchesne, R. (1987) Abnormal neuroanatomy in a nonretarded person with autism. *Archives of Neurology*, 44, 335–41.

Cousins, N. (1983) *The Anatomy of Illness*. New York: Bantam.

Covell, K., Dion, K.L. and Dion, K.K. (1994) Gender differences in evaluations of tobacco and alcohol advertisements. *Canadian Journal of Behavioural Science*, 26, 404–20.

Cowan, M.L., Watkins, C.D., Fraccaro, P.J., Feinberg, D.R. and Little, A.C. (2015) It's the way he tells them (and who is listening): Men's dominance is positively correlated with their preference for jokes told by dominant-sounding men. *Evolution and Behavior*, 37, 97–104.

Cowey, A. (2004) The 30th Sir Frederick Bartlett lecture: fact, artefact, and myth about blindsight. *The Quarterly Journal of Experimental Psychology*, 57A(4), 577–609.

Cowley, D.S. and Arana, G.W. (1990) The diagnostic utility of lactate sensitivity in panic disorder. *Archives of General Psychiatry*, 47, 277–84.

Cox, R., Tijdens, R.R., Meeter, M.M., Sweegers, C.L. and Talamini, L.M. (2014) Time, not sleep, unbinds contexts from item memory. *PLoS ONE*, 9, e88307.

Cox, R.H. (1991) *Intervention Strategies. In A. Monat & R. S. Lazarus (eds) Stress and coping: An Anthology*. New York: Columbia University Press.

Coyne, J.C., Stefanek, M. and Palmer, S.C. (2007) Psychotherapy and survival in cancer: The conflict between hope and evidence. *Psychological Bulletin*, 133, 367–94.

Coyne, J.C., Stefanek, M., Thombs, B.D. and Palmer, S.C. (2009) Time to let go of the illusion that psychotherapy extends the survival of cancer patients: Reply to Kraemer, Kuchler and Spiegel (2009) *Psychological Bulletin*, 135(2), 179–82.

Craig, A.D. (2009) Emotional moments across time: A possible neural basis for time perception in the anterior insula. *Philosophical Transactions of the Royal Society B*, 364, 1933–42.

Craik, F.I.M. and Lockhart, R.S. (1972) Levels of processing: A framework for memory research. *Journal of Verbal Learning and Verbal Behavior*, 11, 671–84.

Craik, F.I.M. and Salthouse, T.A. (2000) *The Handbook of Aging and Cognition*. London: Lawrence Erlbaum Associates.

Craik, F.I.M. and Tulving, E. (1975) Depth of processing and the retention of words in episodic memory. *Journal of Experimental Psychology: General*, 104, 268–94.

Cramer, S.C., Sur, M., Dobkin, B.H., O'brien, C., Sanger, T.D., Trojanowski, J.Q. . . . and Chen, W.G. (2011) Harnessing neuroplasticity for clinical applications. *Brain*, 134(6), 1591–1609.

Cramton, C.D. and Hinds, P.L. (2005) Subgroup dynamics in internationally distributed teams: ethnocentrism or cross-national learning? *Research in Organisational Behaviour*, 26, 231–63.

Crandall, C.S. (1994) Prejudice against fat people: Ideology and self-interest. *Journal of Personality and Social Psychology*, 66, 882–94.

Crano, W.D. and Alvaro, E.M. (1998) The context/comparison model of social influence: Mechanisms, structure, and linkages that underlie indirect attitude change. In W. Stroebe and M. Hewstone (eds) *European Review of Social Psychology*, Vol. 8. Chichester: Wiley, pp. 175–202.

Craske, M.G., Rowe, M., Lewin, M. and Noriega-Dimitri, R. (1997) Interoceptive exposure versus breathing retraining within cognitive-behavioural therapy for panic disorder with agoraphobia. *British Journal of Clinical Psychology*, 36, 85–99.

Crawford, H.J. (1994) Brain systems involved in attention and disattention (hypnotic analgesia) to pain. In K. Pribram (ed.) *Origins: Brain and self-organisation*. Hillsdale, NJ: Lawrence Erlbaum Associates.

Crawford, H.J., Brown, A. and Moon, C. (1993) Sustained attentional and disattentional abilities: Differences between low and highly hypnotisable persons. *Journal of Abnormal Psychology*, 102, 534–43.

Crawford, H.J., Knebel, T., Kaplan, L., Vendemia, J.M.C., Xie, M., Jamison, S. and Pribram, K.H. (1998) 1. Somatosensory event-related potential changes to noxious stimuli and 2. Transfer learning to reduce chronic low back pain. *International Journal of Clinical and Experimental Hypnosis*, XLVI(1), 92–132.

Crawford, J.R., Bryan, J., Luszcz, M.A., Obonsawin, M.C. and Stewart, L. (2000) The executive decline hypothesis of cognitive aging: Do executive deficits qualify as differential deficits and do they mediate age-related memory decline? *Aging, Neuropsychology and Cognition*, 7(1), 9–31.

Credé, M., Tynan, M.C. and Harms, P.D. (2016) *Much Ado About Grit: A Meta-Analytic Synthesis of the Grit Literature*.

Crego, C. and Widiger, T.A. (2014) Psychopathy and the DSM. *Journal of Personality*, 83(6), 665–77.

Crepaldi, D., Berlingeri, M., Cattinelli, I., Borghese, N.A., Luzzatti, C. and Paulesu, E. (2013) Clustering the lexicon in the brain: a meta-analysis of the neurofunctional evidence on noun and verb processing. *Frontiers in Nature Neuroscience*, 7, 303.

Crepaldi, D., Berlingeri, M., Paulesu, E. and Luzzatti, C. (2011) A place for nouns and a place for verbs? *Brain and Language*, 116, 33–49.

Crick, F. (1994) *The Astonishing Hypothesis*. London: Simon & Schuster.

Crick, F. and Koch, C. (1995) Are we aware of neural activity in primary visual cortex? *Nature*, 121–6.

Crick, F. and Mitchison, G. (1983) The function of dream sleep. *Nature*, 304, 111–14.

Crisp, A.H., Gelder, M.G., Rix, S., Meltzer, H.I. and Rowalnds, O.J. (2000) Stigmatisation of people with mental illness. *British Journal of Psychiatry*, 177, 4–7.

Crispim, C.A., Zimberg, I.Z., dos Reis, B.G. *et al.* (2011) Relationship between food intake and sleep pattern in healthy individuals. *Journal of Clinical Sleep Medicine*, 7(6), 659–64.

Critchley, H., Daly, E.M., Bullmore, E.T., Williams, S.C.R., Van Amelsvoort, T., Robertson, D.M., Rowe, A., Phillips, M., McAlonan, G., Howlin, P. and Murphy, D.G.M. (2000) The functional neuroanatomy of social behaviour: Changes in cerebral blood flow when people with autistic disorder process facial expressions. *Brain*, 123, 2203–12.

Crocker, J. and Major, B. (1989) Social stigma and self-esteem: The self-protective properties of stigma. *Psychological Review*, 96, 608–30.

Crocker, J., Major, B. and Steele, C. (1998) Social stigma. In D.T. Gilbert, S.T. Fiske and G. Lindzey (eds) *The Handbook of Social Psychology* (4th edn), Vol. 2. New York: McGraw-Hill, pp. 504–53.

Crockett, M.J., Kurth-Nelson, Z., Siegel, J.Z., Dayan, P. and Dolan, R.J. (2014) Harm to others outweighs harm to self in moral decision making. *Proceedings of the National Academy of Sciences*, 111(48), 17320–5.

Crockett, M.J., Kurth-Nelson, Z., Siegel, J.Z., Dayan, P. and Dolan, R.J. (2016) Harm to others outweighs harm to self in moral decision making. *PNAS*, 111, 17320–5.

Croizet, J.C. and Claire, T. (1998) Extending the concept of stereotype threat to social class: The intellectual underperformance of students from low socioeconomic backgrounds. *Personality and Social Psychology Bulletin*, 24, 588–94.

Crombag, H.F.M., Wagenaar, W.A. and Van Koppen, P.J. (1996) Crashing memories and the problem of 'source monitoring'. *Applied Cognitive Psychology*, 10, 95–104.

Crosby, F. (1982) *Relative Deprivation and Working Women*. New York: Oxford University Press.

Crosby, F., Bromley, S. and Saxe, L. (1980) Recent unobtrusive studies of black and white discrimination and prejudice: A literature review. *Psychological Bulletin*, 87, 546–63.

Cross-Disorder Group of the Psychiatric Genomics Consortium (2013) Identification of risk loci with shared effects on five major psychiatric disorders: a genome-wide analysis. *The Lancet*, 381(9875), 1371–9.

Crossley, M.A., Mechelli, A., Scott, J., Carletti, F., Fox, P.T., McGuire, P. and Bullmore, E.T. (2014) The hubs of the human connectome are generally implicated in the anatomy of brain disorders. *Brain*, 137, 2382–95.

Crowe, R.R., Noyes, R., Pauls, D.L. and Slymen, D. (1983) A family study of panic disorder. *Archives of General Psychiatry*, 40, 1065–9.

Crowley, K., Callanan, M.A., Tenenbaum, H.R. and Allen, E. (2001) Parents explain more often to boys than to girls during shared scientific thinking. *Psychological Science*, 12(3), 258–61.

Crowne, D. and Marlowe, D. (1964) *The Approval Motive*. New York: Wiley.

Crump, M.J.C., McDonnell, J.V. and Gureckis, T.M. (2013) Evaluating Amazon's Mechanical Turk as a tool for experimental behavioural research. *PLoS ONE*, 8, e57410.

Crusco, A.H. and Wetzel, C.G. (1984) The Midas touch the effects of interpersonal touch on restaurant tipping. *Personality and Social Psychology Bulletin*, 10(4), 512–17.

Cruwys, T., Bevelander, K.E. and Hermans, R.C.J. (2014) Social modeling of eating: A review of when and why social influence affects food intake and choice. *Appetite*, 86, 3–18.

Crystal, S.R. and Bernstein, I.L. (1998) Infant salt preference and mother's morning sickness. *Appetite*, 30, 297–307.

Csikszentmihalyi, M. and Larson, R. (1984) *Being Adolescent: Conflict and growth in the teenage years*. New York: Basic Books.

Cuddy, A.J.C. (2009) Stereotype content model across cultures: Towards universal similarities and some differences. *British Journal of Social Psychology*, 48, 1–33.

Cuddy, A.J.C., Fiske, S.T. and Kwan, V.S.Y. (2009) Stereotype content model across cultures: Towards universal similarities and some differences, *British Journal of Social Psychology*, 48, 1–33.

Cuddy, A.J.C., Norton, M.I. and Fiske, S. (2005) This old stereotype: The pervasiveness and persistence of the elderly stereotype. *Journal of Social Issues*, 61, 265–83.

Cuijpers, P., Sijbrandij, M., Koole, S.L., Andersson, G., Beekman, A.T. and Reynolds, C.F. (2014) Adding psychotherapy to antidepressant medication in depression and anxiety disorders: a meta-analysis. *World Psychiatry*, 13, 56–67.

Culebras, A. and Moore, J.T. (1989) Magnetic resonance findings in REM sleep behavior disorder. *Neurology*, 39, 1519–23.

Cummings, J.L. and Wirshing, W.C. (1989) Recognition and differential diagnosis of tardive dyskinesia. *International Journal of Psychiatry in Medicine*, 19, 133–44.

Cummins, J. (1984) *Bilingualism and Special Education: Issues in assessment and pedagogy*. Clevedon: Multilingual Matters.

Cunningham, C.E., Mapp, C., Rimas, H., Cunningham, L., Mielko, S., Vaillancourt, T. and Marcus, M. (2016) What limits the effectiveness of antibullying programs? A thematic analysis of the perspective of students. *Psychology of Violence*, 6(4), 596.

Cunningham, S.J. and Macrae, C.N. (2011) The colour of gender stereotyping. *British Journal of Psychology*, 102, 598–614.

Cunningham, W.A., Johnson, M.K., Raye, C.L., Gatenby, J., Gore, J.C. and Banaji, M.R. (2004) Separable neural components in the processing of black and white faces. *Psychological Science*, 15, 806–13.

Currin, L., Schmidt, U., Treasure, J. and Jick, H. (2005) Time trends in eating disorder incidence. *British Journal of Psychiatry*, 186, 132–5.

Curtis, G.C., Magee, W.J., Eaton, W.W., Wittchen, H.-U. and Kessler, R.C. (1998) Specific fears and phobias. *British Journal of Psychiatry*, 173, 212–17.

Curtiss, S. (1977) *Genie: A psycholinguistic study of a modern day 'wild child'.* New York: Academic Press.

D

D'Esposito, M., Postle, B.R., Ballard, D. and Lease, J. (1999) Maintenance versus manipulation of information held in working memory: an event-related fMRI study. *Brain and Cognition*, 41, 66–86.

D'Souza, D.C., Ranganathan, M., Braley, G., Gueorguiveau, R., Zimolo, Z., Cooper, T., Perry, E. and Krystal, J. (2008) Blunted psychotomimetic and amnestic effects of delta – 9-tetrahydrocannabinol in frequent users of cannabis. *Neuropsychopharmacology*, 33, 2505–16.

D'Zurilla, T. (1965) Recall efficiency and mediating cognitive events in 'experimental repression'. *Journal of Personality and Social Psychology*, 1, 253–7.

Dabbs, J.M. (1990) Salivary testosterone measurements: Reliability across hours, days and weeks. *Physiology and Behaviour*, 48, 83–6.

Dabbs, J.M. (1997) Testosterone and papillary response to auditory sexual stimuli. *Physiology and Behaviour*, 62, 090–912.

Dabbs, J.M., Bernieri, F.J., Strong, R.K., Campo, R. and Milun, R. (2001) Going on stage: Testosterone in greetings and meetings. *Journal of Research in Personality*, 35, 27–40.

Dabbs, J.M., Frady, R.L., Carr, T.S. and Besch, N.F. (1987) Saliva testosterone and criminal violence in young adult prison inmates. *Psychosomatic Medicine*, 49, 174–82.

Dabbs, J.M., Jurkovic, G. and Frady, R. (1991) Salivary testosterone and cortisol among late adolescent male offenders. *Journal of Abnormal Child Psychology*, 19, 469–78.

Dabbs, J.M., Ruback, J.M., Frady, R.L. and Hopper, C.H. (1988) Saliva testosterone and criminal violence among women. *Personality and Individual Differences*, 9, 269–75.

Dacey, J.S. (1989) *Fundamentals of Creative Thinking.* Lexington, MA: Lexington.

Dahaene-Lambertz, G. and Spelke, E.S. (2015) The infancy of the human brain. *Neuron*, 88, 93–109.

Daly, M. and Wilson, M. (1988) *Homicide.* New York: Aldine de Gruyter.

Daly, M. and Wilson, M. (1996) Violence against stepchildren. *Current Directions in Psychological Science*, 5, 77–81.

Damasio, A.R. (1995) Toward a neurobiology of emotion and feeling: Operational concepts and hypotheses. *The Neuroscientist*, 1, 19–25.

Damasio, H. (1989) Neuroimaging contributions to the understanding of aphasia. In F. Boller and J. Grafman (eds) *Handbook of Neuropsychology*, Vol. 2. Amsterdam: Elsevier.

Damasio, H., Grabowski, T., Frank, R., Galaburda, A.M. and Damasio, A.R. (1994) The return of Phineas Gage: Clues about the brain from the skull of a famous patient. *Science*, 264, 1102–5.

Damasio, H., Grabowski, T.J., Tranel, D., Hichwa, R.D. and Damasio, A.R. (1996) A neural basis for lexical retrieval. *Nature*, 380, 499–505.

Damian, R.I. and Robins, R.W. (2012) Aristotle's virtue or Dante's deadliest sin? The influence of authentic and hubristic pride on creative achievement. *Learning and Individual Differences*, 26, 156–60.

Damjanovic, A.K., Yang, Y., Glaser, R., Kiecolt-Glaser, J.K., Nguyen, H., Laskowski, B. *et al.* (2007) Accelerated telomere erosion is associated with a declining immune function of caregivers of Alzheimer's disease patients. *Journal of Immunology*, 179, 4249–54.

Damon, W. (1977) *The Social World of the Child.* San Francisco, CA: Jossey-Bass.

Damon, W. (1980) Patterns of change in children's social reasoning: A two-year longitudinal study. *Child Development*, 51, 1010–17.

Dan, A.J. and Bernhard, L.A. (1989) Menopause and other health issues for midlife women. In S. Hunter and M. Sundel (eds) *Midlife Myths: Issues, findings and practice implications.* Newbury Park, CA: Sage.

Daneman, M. and Carpenter, P.A. (1980) Individual differences in working memory and reading. *Journal of Verbal Learning and Verbal Behaviour*, 19, 450–66.

Daneman, M. and Hannon, B. (2001) Using working memory theory to investigate the construct validity of multiple-choice comprehension tests such as the SAT. *Journal of Experimental Psychology: General*, 130, 208–23.

Daniels, P. and Weingarten, K. (1982) *Sooner or Later: The timing of parenthood in adult lives.* New York: W.W. Norton.

Danker, J.F. and Anderson, J.R. (2010) The ghost of brain states past: Remembering reactivates the brain regions engaged during encoding. *Psychological Bulletin*, 136(1), 87–102.

Danner, D.D., Snowdon, D.A. and Friesen, W.V. (2001) Positive emotions in early life and longevity: Findings from the nun study. *Journal of Personality and Social Psychology*, 80(5), 804–13.

Darley, J.M. and Latané, B. (1968) Bystander intervention in emergencies: Diffusion of responsibility. *Journal of Personality and Social Psychology*, 8, 377–83.

Darwin, C. (1872) *The Expression of the Emotions in Man and Animals.* Reprinted in 1965 by University of Chicago Press, Chicago.

Darwin, C.J., Turvey, M.T. and Crowder, R.G. (1972) An auditory analogue of the Sperling partial report procedure: Evidence for brief auditory storage. *Cognitive Psychology*, 3, 255–67.

Darwin, F. (1887) *Charles Darwin's Autobiography.* Reprinted in 1950 by Henry Schuman, New York.

Davey, G.C.L. (1992) Characteristics of individuals with fear of spiders. *Anxiety Research*, 4, 299–314.

Davey, G.C.L., McDonald, A.S., Hirisave, U., Prabhu, C.G., Iwawaki, S., Jim, C.I., Merckelbach, H., de Jong, P.J., Leung, P.W.L. and Reimann, B.C. (1998) A cross-cultural study of animal fears. *Behaviour Research and Therapy*, 36, 735–50.

Davidson, A. R. and Jacard, J. (1979) Variables that moderate the attitude–behavior relation: Results of a longitudinal survey. *Journal of Personality and Social Psychology*, 37, 1364–76.

Davidson, J.M., Camargo, C.A. and Smith, E.R. (1979) Effects of androgen on sexual behavior in hypogonadal men. *Journal of Clinical Endocrinology and Metabolism*, 48, 955–8.

Davidson, R.J. and Fox, N.A. (1989) Frontal brain asymmetry predicts infants' response to maternal separation. *Journal of Abnormal Psychology*, 98(2), 127–31.

Davidson, R.J. and Sutton, S.K. (1995) Affective neuroscience: The emergence of a discipline. *Current Opinion in Neurobiology*, 5(2), 217–24.

Davidson, R.J., Schwartz, G.E., Saron, C., Bennett, J. and Goleman, D.J. (1979) Frontal vs parietal EEG asymmetry during positive and negative affect. *Psychophysiology*, 16(2), 202–3.

Davies, A.P.C. and Shackelford, T.K. (2015) Comparisons of the effectiveness of mate-attraction tactics across mate poaching and general attraction and across types of romantic relationships. *Personality and Individual Differences, 85,* 140–4.

Davies, A.P.C. and Shackelford, T.K. (2017) Don't you wish your partner was hot like me? The effectiveness of mate poaching across relationship types considering the relative mate-values of the poacher and the partner of the poached. *Personality and Individual Differences, 106,* 32–5.

Davies, I.R.L., Laws, G., Corbett, G.G. and Jerrett, D.J. (1998) Cross-cultural differences in colour vision: Acquired 'colour blindness' in Africa. *Personality and Individual Differences, 25,* 1153–62.

Davies, J.C. (1969) The J-curve of rising and declining satisfaction as a cause of some great revolutions and a contained rebellion. In H.D. Graham and T.R. Gurr (eds) *The History of Violence in America: Historical and comparative perspectives.* New York: Praeger, pp. 690–730.

Davies, N. (2008) *Flat Earth News.* London: Chatto and Windus.

Davis, C.G., Thake, J. and Weekes, J.R. (2011) Impression managers: Nice guys or serious criminals? *Journal of Research in Personality, 46,* 26–31.

Davis, C.L., Tomporowski, P.D., McDowell, J.E., Austin, B.P., Miller P.H., Yanasak, N.E., Allison, J.D. and Naglieri, J.A. (2011) Exercise improves executive function and achievement and alters brain activation in overweight children: A randomized controlled trial. *Health Psychology, 30,* 91–8.

Davis, E.P., Buss, C., Muftuler, L.T., Head, K., Hasso, A., Wing, D.A., Hobel, C. and Sandman, C.A. (2011) Children's brain development benefits from longer gestation. *Frontiers in Psychology, 2,* article 1.

Davis, J.D. and Campbell, C.S. (1973) Peripheral control of meal size in the rat: Effect of sham feeding on meal size and drinking rats. *Journal of Comparative and Physiological Psychology, 83,* 379–87.

Davis, J.H. (1973) Group decision and social interaction: A theory of social decision schemes. *Psychological Review, 80,* 97–125.

Davis, W.L. and Phares, E.J. (1967) Internal–external control as a determinant of information-seeking in a social influence situation. *Journal of Personality, 35,* 547–61.

Davitz, J.R. (1970) A dictionary and grammar of emotion. In M. Arnold (ed.) *Feelings and Emotions: The Loyola Symposium.* New York: Academic Press.

Dawes, R.M. (1991) Social dilemmas, economic self-interest, and evolutionary self-interest. In D.R. Brown and J.E. Keith-Smith (eds) *Frontiers of Mathematical Psychology: Essays in honour of Clyde Coombs.* New York: Springer-Verlag, pp. 53–79.

Dawkins, L., Turner, J. and Crowe, E. (2013) Nicotine derived from the electronic cigarette improves time-based prospective memory in abstinent smokers. *Psychopharmacology, 227,* 377–84.

Dawkins, L., Turner, J., Hasna, S. and Soar, K. (2012) The electronic cigarette: effects on desire to smoke, withdrawal symptoms and cognition. *Addiction and Behaviour, 37,* 970–3.

Dawkins, R. (1996) *Climbing Mount Improbable.* New York: W.W. Norton.

Dawkins, R. (2007) *The God Delusion.* London: Black Swan.

Dawson, G., Frey, K., Panagiotides, H., Osterling, J. and Hessl, D. (1997) Infants of depressed mothers exhibit atypical frontal brain activity: A replication and extension of previous findings. *Journal of Child Psychology and Psychiatry, 38(2),* 179–86.

Day, J.J. and Sweatt, J.D. (2011) Cognitive neuroepigenetics: A role for epigenetic mechanisms in learning and memory. *Neurobiology of Learning and Memory, 96,* 2–12.

De Araujo, I.E., Rolls, E.T., Velazco, M.I., Margot, C. and Cayeux, I. (2005) Cognitive modulation of olfactory processing. *Neuron, 46,* 671–9.

de Cremer, D. and van Vugt, M. (1999) Social identification effects in social dilemmas: A transformation of motives. *European Journal of Social Psychology, 29,* 871–93.

De Raad, B. (1998) Five big, Big Five issues: rationale, content, structure, status and crosscultural assessment. *European Psychologist, 3(2),* 113–24.

De Souza, L.C., Guimaraes, H.C., Teixeira, A.L., Carmamelli, P., Levy, R., Dubois, B. and Volle, E. (2014) Frontal lobe neurology and the creative mind. *Frontiers in Psychology, 5,* 1–21.

de Wied, M. and Verbaten, M.N. (2001) Affective pictures processing, attention and pain tolerance. *Pain, 90,* 163–72.

De Wolff, M.S. and van Ijzendoorn, M.H. (1997) Sensitivity and attachment: A meta-analysis on parental antecedents of infant attachment. *Child Development, 68(4),* 571–91.

Deacon, B.J. (2013) The biomedical model of mental disorder: A critical analysis of its validity, utility, and effects on psychotherapy research. *Clinical Psychology Review, 33(7),* 846–61.

Deahl, M.P., Gillham, A.B., Thomas, J. *et al.* (1994) Psychological sequelae following the Gulf War. Factors associated with subsequent morbidity and the effectiveness of psychological debriefing. *British Journal of Psychiatry, 165,* 60–5.

Dean, P.J.A. and Sterr, A. (2013) Long-term effects of mild traumatic brain injury on cognitive performance. *Frontiers in Human Neuroscience, 7,* 30, 1–11.

Deary, I.J. *et al.* (2002) Cognitive change and the APOE e4 allele. *Nature, 418,* 932.

Deary, I.J., Batty, G.D., Pattie, A. and Gale, C.R. (2008) More intelligent, more dependable children live longer. *Psychological Science, 19(9),* 874–80.

Deary, I.J., Penke, L. and Johnson, W. (2010) The neuroscience of human intelligence: differences. *Nature Reviews: Neuroscience, 11,* 201–11.

Deb, S. and Thompson, B. (1998) Neuroimaging in autism. *British Journal of Psychiatry, 173,* 299–302.

DeCasper, A.J. and Fifer, W.P. (1980) Of human bonding: Newborns prefer their mothers' voices. *Science, 208,* 1175–6.

DeCasper, A.J. and Spence, M. (1986) Prenatal maternal speech influences newborns' perception of speech sounds. *Infant Behavior and Development, 9,* 133–50.

DeCasper, A.J., Lecanuet, J-P., Bunsel, M-C., Granier-Deferre, C. and Maugeais, R. (1994) Fetal reactions to recurrent maternal speech. *Infant Behaviour and Development, 17,* 159–64.

deCharms, R.C., Maeda, F., Glover, G.H., Ludlow, D., Pauly, J.M., Soneji, D., Gabrieli, J.D.E. and Mackey, S.C. (2005) Control over brain activation and pain learned by using real-time functional MRI. *Proceedings of the National Academy of Sciences, 102 (51),* 18626–31.

Deci, E.L. and Ryan, R.M. (2000) The general causality orientations scale: Self-determination in personality. *Journal of Research in Personality, 19,* 109–34.

Deen, B., Koldewyn, K., Kanwisher, N. and Saxe, R. (2015) Functional organization of social perception and cognition in the superior temporal sulcus. *Cerebral Cortex, 25,* 4596–609.

Deeprose, C., Zhang, S., Dejong, H., Dalgliesh, T. and Holmes, E.A. (2012) Imagery in the aftermath of viewing a traumatic film. *Journal of Behaviour Therapy and Experimental Psychiatry, 43,* 758–64.

Degenhardt, L., Coffey, C., Carlin, J.B., Swift, W., Moore, E. and Patton, G.C. (2010) Outcomes of occasional cannabis use in adolescence: 10-year follow-up study in Victoria, Australia. *The British Journal of Psychiatry, 196,* 290–5.

DeGraaf, C., Van Staveren, W. and Burema, J. (1996) Psychophysical and psychohedonic functions of four common food flavours in elderly subjects. *Chemical Senses, 21,* 293–302.

DeGroot, T. and Motowidlo, S.J. (1999) Why visual and vocal interview cues can affect interviewers' judgements and predict job performance. *Journal of Applied Psychology, 84,* 986–93.

DeGutis, J.M., Chiu, C., Grosso, M.E. and Cohan, S. (2014) Face processing improvements in prosopagnosia: successes and failures over the last 50 years. *Frontiers in Human Neuroscience*, 8, 1–14.

Dehaene, S., Dupoux, E., Mehler, J, Cohen, L. and Paulesu, E. (1997) Anatomical variability in the cortical representation of first and second language. *NeuroReport*, 8, 3809–15.

Dehaene-Lambertz, G. and Spelke, E.S. (2015) The infancy of the human brain. *Neuron*, 88(1), 93–109.

DeJonge, T., Veenhoven, R., Kalmijn, W. and Arends, L. (2016) Pooling time series based on slightly different questions about the same topic forty years of survey research on happiness and life satisfaction in The Netherlands. *Social Indicators Research*, 126(2), 863–91.

Del Boca, F.K., Darkes, J., Greenbaum, P.E. and Goldman, M.S. (2004) Up close and personal: Temporal variability in the drinking of individual college students during their first year. *Journal of Consulting and Clinical Psychology*, 72(2), 155–64.

Delahanty, D.L., Dougall, A.L., Hawkes, L., Trakowski, J.H., Schmitz, J.B., Jenkins, F.J. and Baum, A. (1996) Time course of natural killer cell activity and lymphocyte proliferation in response to two acute stressors in healthy men. *Health Psychology*, 15, 48–55.

Delaunay-El Allam, M., Marlier, L. and Schaal, B. (2006) Learning at the breast: Preference formation for an artificial scent and its attraction against the odor of maternal milk. *Infant Behavior and Development*, 29, 308–21.

Deldin, P.J. and Levin, I.P. (1986) The effect of mood induction in a risky decision task. *Bulletin of the Psychonomic Society*, 24, 4–6.

Dell, G.S., Burger, L.K. and Svec, W.R. (1997) Language production and serial order: A functional analysis and a model. *Psychological Review*, 104(1), 123–47.

DeLoache, J.S. (1984) Oh where, oh where: memory-based searching by very young children. In C. Sophian (ed.) *Origins of Cognitive Skills*. Hillsdale, NJ: Lawrence Erlbaum Associates.

DeLongis, A., Folkman, S. and Lazarus, R.S. (1988) The impact of daily stress on health and mood: Psychological and social resources as mediators. *Journal of Personality and Social Psychology*, 54, 486–95.

Dement, W.C. (1974) *Some Must Watch While Some Must Sleep*. San Francisco, CA: W.H. Freeman.

Demuth, J.P., Bie, T.D., Stajich, J.E., Cristiani, N. and Hahn, M.W. (2006) The evolution of mammalian gene families. *PLoS ONE*, 1, e85.

Den Hartog, D.N. and Veburg, R.M. (1997) Charisma and rhetorics: Communicative techniques of international business leaders. *Leadership Quarterly*, 8(4), 355–91.

Dennett, D.D. (1991) *Consciousness Explained*. London: Penguin.

Dennis, M. and Whitaker, H.A. (1976) Language acquisition following hemidecortication: Linguistic superiority of the left over the right hemisphere. *Brain and Language*, 3, 404–33.

Denson, T.F., Pedersen, W.C., Ronquillo, J. and Nandy, A.S. (2008) The angry brain: Neural correlates of anger, angry rumination and aggressive personality. *Journal of Cognitive Neuroscience*, 21, 734–44.

Denson, T.F., Spanovic, M. and Miller, N. (2009) Cognitive appraisals and emotions predict cortisol and immune responses. *Psychological Bulletin*, 135, 823–53.

Deoni, S.C.L., Dean, D.C., Piryatinsky, I., O'Muircheartaigh, J., Waskiewicz, N., Lehman, K., Han, M. and Dirks, H. (2013) Breastfeeding and early white matter development: a cross-sectional study. *Neuroimage*, 82, 77–86.

DePaulo, B. and Friedman, H.S. (1998) Nonverbal communication. In D.T. Gilbert, S.T. Fiske and G. Lindzey (eds) *The Handbook of Social Psychology* (4th edn), Vol. 2. New York: McGraw-Hill, pp. 3–40.

Deppe, M., Knecht, S., Papke, K., Lohmann, H. Fleischer, H., Heindel, W. and Ringelstein, H. (2000) Assessment of hemispheric language lateralisation: a comparison between fMRI and fTCD. *Journal of Cerebral Blood Flood Flow and Metabolism*, 20, 263–8.

Depue, R.A. (2009) Genetic, environmental and epigenetic factors in the development of personality disturbance. *Development and Psychopathology*, 21, 1031–63.

DePue, R.A. and Monroe, S.M. (1986) Conceptualization and measurement of human disorder in life-stress research: The problem of chronic disturbance. *Psychological Bulletin*, 99, 36–51.

deQuervain, D.J. et al. (2003) A functional genetic variation of the 5-HTa receptor affects human memory. *Nature Neuroscience*, 6, 1141–2.

deQuervain, D.J-F. and Papassotiropoulos, A. (2006) Identification of a genetic cluster influencing memory performance and hippocampal activity in humans. *Proceedings of the National Academy of Sciences*, 103(11), 4270–4.

Derbyshire, S.W.G. et al. (2004) Cerebral activation during hypnotically induced and imagined pain. *Neuroimage*, 23, 392–401.

Deregowski, J.B., Muldrow, E.S. and Muldrow, W.F. (1972) Pictorial recognition in a remote Ethiopian village. *Perception*, 1, 417–25.

DeRenzi, E. (1986) Prosopagnosia in two patients with CT scan evidence of damage confined to the right hemisphere. *Neuropsychologia*, 24, 385–9.

DeRenzi, E. and Lucchelli, F. (1993) The fuzzy boundaries of apperceptive agnosia. *Cortex*, 29, 187–215.

Derntl, B., Windischberger, C., Robinson, S., Kryspin-Exner, I., Gur, R.C., Moser, E. and Habel, U. (2009) Amygdala activity to fear and anger in healthy young males is associated with testosterone. *Psychoneuroendocrinology*, 34(5), 687–93.

Deroche-Gamonet, V. et al. (2004) Evidence for addiction-like behavior in the rat. *Science*, 305, 1014–17.

Desai, R. A., Krishnan-Sarin, S., Cavallo, D. and Potenza, M. N. (2010) Video-gaming among high school students: health correlates, gender differences, and problematic gaming. *Pediatrics*, 126(6), e1414–e1424.

Destrebecqz, A., Peigneux, P., Laureys, S., Degueldre, C., Del Fiore, G., Aerts, J. . (2005) The neural correlates of implicit and explicit sequence learning: Interacting networks revealed by the process dissociation procedure. *Learning and Memory*, 12(5), 480–90.

Detuscher, G. (2010) *Through the Language Glass*. London: Arrow.

Deutsch, J.A., Young, W.G. and Kalogeris, T.J. (1978) The stomach signals satiety. *Science*, 201, 165–7.

Deutsch, M. and Gerard, H.B. (1955) A study of normative and informational social influences upon individual judgment. *Journal of Abnormal and Social Psychology*, 51, 629–36.

Deutscher, I. (1968) The quality of postparental life. In B.L. Neugarten (ed.) *Middle Age and Aging*. Chicago, IL: University of Chicago Press.

Devine, P.G. (1989) Stereotypes and prejudice: Their automatic and controlled components. *Journal of Personality and Social Psychology*, 56, 5–18.

Devine, P.G. and Elliot, A. (1995) Are racial stereotypes really fading? The Princeton trilogy revisited. *Personality and Social Psychology Bulletin*, 22, 22–37.

Devine, P.G., Hamilton, D.L. and Ostrom, T.M. (eds) (1994) *Social Cognition: Impact on social psychology*. San Diego, CA: Academic Press.

DeWaard, D. and Brookhuis, K.A. (1991) Assessing driver status: A demonstration experiment on the road. *Accident Prevention and Analysis*, 23(4), 297–301.

deWall, C.N. and Bushman, B.J. (2009) Hot under the collar in a lukewarm environment: Words associated with hot temperature increase aggressive thoughts and hostile perceptions. *Journal of Experimental Social Psychology*, 45, 1045-7.

Dewsbury, D.A. (2009) Charles Darwin and psychology at the bicentennial and sesquicentennial. *American Psychologist*, 64(2), 67-74.

DeYoung, C.G., Hirsh, J.B., Shane, M.S., Papademetris, X., Rajeevan, N. and Gray, J.R. (2010) Testing predictions from personality neuroscience: Brain structure and the big five. *Psychological Science*, 21, 820-8.

Diabetes Prevention Program Research Group (2002) Reduction in the incidence of type 2 diabetes with lifestyle intervention or metformin. *New England Journal of Medicine*, 346, 393-403.

Diamond, M.C., Scheibel, A.B., Murphy, G.M. and Harvey, T. (1985) On the brain of a scientist: Albert Einstein. *Experimental Neurology*, 88, 198-204.

Dick, A.S. and Tremblay, P. (2012) Beyond the arcuate fasciculus: consensus and controversy in the connectional anatomy of language. *Brain*, 135, 3529-50.

Dickens, W.T. and Flynn, J.R. (2006) Black Americans reduce the racial IQ gap. *Psychological Science*, 17, 913-20.

Dickson, R.A., Pillemer, D.B. and Bruehl, E.C. (2011) The reminiscence bump for salient personal memories: Is a cultural life script required? *Memory and Cognition*, 39, 977-91.

Dickson-Wright, C. (2007) *Spilling the Beans*. London: Hodder.

Diekmann, J., Konig, C.J. and Alles, J. (in press) The role of neuroscience information in choosing a personality test. *International Journal of Selection and Assessment*, 23, 99-108.

Diener, E. (1980) Deindividuation: The absence of self-awareness and self-regulation in group members. In P.B. Paulus (ed.) *Psychology of Group Influence*. Hillsdale, NJ: Lawrence Erlbaum Associates, pp. 209-42.

Diener, E. and Seligman, M.E.P. (2002) Very happy people. *Psychological Science*, 13, 80-3.

Diener, E., Diener, M. and Diener, C. (1995) Factors predicting the subjective well-being of nations. *Journal of Personality and Social Psychology*, 69, 851-64.

Diener, E., Kanazawa, S., Suh, E.M. and Oishi, S. (2014) Why people are in a generally good mood. *Personality and Social Psychology Review*, 19, 235-56.

Diener, E., Lucas, R.E. and Scollon, C.N. (2006) Beyond the hedonic treadmill. *American Psychologist*, 61(4), 305-14.

Diener, E., Oishi, S. and Park, J-Y. (2014) An incomplete list of eminent psychologists of the modern era. *Archives of Scientific Psychology*, 2, 20-32.

Diener, E., Tay, L. and Myers, D. (2011) The religion paradox: If religion makes people happy, why are so many dropping out? *Journal of Personality and Social Psychology*, 101, 1278-90.

Dijker, A.M. (2008) Why Barbie feels heavier than Ken: the influence of size-based expectancies and social cues on the illusory perception of weight. *Cognition*, 106, 1109-25.

Dijkerman, H.C. and Milner, A.D. (1997) Copying without perceiving motor imagery in visual form agnosia. *NeuroReport*, 8, 720-32.

Dijksterhuis, A., Spears, R., Postmes, T., Stapel, D.A., Koomen, W., van Knippenberg, A. and Scheepers, D. (1998) Seeing one thing and doing another: Contrast effects in automatic behavior. *Journal of Personality and Social Psychology*, 75, 862-71.

Dijkstra, P.D. and Preenen, P.T. (2008) No effect of blue on winning contests in judo. *Proceedings of the Royal Society of London B: Biological Sciences*, 275(1639), 1157-62.

Dimidjian, S. and Hollon, S.D. (2010) How would we know if psychotherapy were harmful? *American Psychologist*, 65, 21-33.

Dimsdale, J.E. (1988) A perspective on type A behavior and coronary disease. *New England Journal of Medicine*, 318, 110-12.

Dingler, T., Shirazi, A.S., Kunze, K. and Schmidt, A. (2015, March) Assessment of stimuli for supporting speed reading on electronic devices. In *Proceedings of the 6th Augmented Human International Conference* (pp. 117-24) ACM.

Dinh, K.T., Sarason, I.G., Peterson, A.V. and Onstad, L.E. (1995) Children's perceptions of smokers and non-smokers: A longitudinal study. *Health Psychology*, 14, 32-40.

Dion, K., Berscheid, E. and Walster, E. (1972) What is beautiful is good. *Journal of Personality and Social Psychology*, 24, 285-90.

Dittes, J.E. and Kelley, H.H. (1956) Effects of different conditions of acceptance upon conformity to group norms. *Journal of Abnormal and Social Psychology*, 53, 100-07.

Dittman-Kohli, E. (1990) The construction of meaning in old age: Possibilities and constraints. *Ageing and Society*, 10, 279-94.

Dittrich, A. (1998) The standardized psychometric assessment of altered states of consciousness in humans. *Pharmacopsychiatry*, 31, 80-4.

Ditzen, B., Schaer, M., Gabriel, B., Bodenmann, G., Ehlert, U. and Heinrichs, M. (2009) Intranasal oxytocin increases positive communication and reduces cortisol levels during couple conflict. *Biological Psychiatry*, 65, 728-31.

Dixon, M.M., Reyes, C.J., Leppert, M.F. and Pappas, L.M. (2008) Personality and birth order in large families. *Personality and Individual Differences*, 44, 119-28.

Dixson, B.J. and Brooks, R.C. (2013) The role of facial hair in women's perceptions of men's attractiveness, health, masculinity and parenting abilities. *Evolution and Human Behavior*, 34, 236-43.

Djordjevic, J., Zatorre, R.J. and Jones-Gotman, M. (2004) Effects of perceived and imagined odors on taste detection. *Chemical Senses*, 29, 199-208.

Dobbins, I.G. and Wagner, A.D. (2005) Domain-general and domain-sensitive prefrontal mechanisms for recollecting events and detecting novelty. *Cerebral Cortex*, 15, 1768-78.

Doherty, M.E., Mynatt, C.R., Tweney, R.D. and Schiavo, M.D. (1979) Pseudodiagnosticity. *Acta Psychologica*, 43, 11-21.

Doherty, W.J. and Needle, R.H. (1991) Psychological adjustment and substance use among adolescents before and after parental divorce. *Child Development*, 62, 328-37.

Dohnt, H.K. and Tiggeman, M. (2006) Body image concerns in young girls: The role of peers and media prior to adolescence. *Journal of Youth and Adolescence*, 35, 135-45.

Dolcos, F. and Denkova, E. (2014) Current emotion research in cognitive neuroscience: Linking enhancing and impairing effects of emotion on cognition. *Emotion Review*, 6, 362-5.

Dolinski, D. (2000) On inferring one's beliefs from one's attempt and consequences for subsequent compliance. *Journal of Personality and Social Psychology*, 78, 260-72.

Doll, J. and Ajzen, I. (1992) Accessibility and stability of predictors in the theory of planned behaviour. *Journal of Personality and Social Psychology*, 63, 754-65.

Doll, R. and Peto, R. (1981) *The Causes of Cancer: Quantitative Estimates of Avoidable Risks of Cancer in the United States Today*. Oxford: Oxford University Press.

Dollard, J., Doob, L.W., Miller, N.E., Mowrer, O.H. and Sears, R.R. (1939) *Frustration and Aggression*. New Haven, CT: Yale University Press.

Domenech, P. and Koechlin, E. (2015) Executive control and decision-making in the prefrontal cortex. *Current Opinion in Behavioural Sciences*, 1, 101-6.

Domes, G., Heinrichs, M., Michel, A., Berger, C. and Herpertz, S.C. (2007) Oxytocin attenuates amygdala responses to emotional faces regardless of valence. *Biological Psychiatry*, 62, 1187-90.

Donaldson, M. (1978) *Children's Minds.* London: Fontana.

Donche, V., Coertjens, L. and van Petegem, P. (2010) Learning pattern development throughout higher education: A longitudinal study. *Learning and Individual Differences*, 20, 256-9.

Donenberg, G.R. and Hoffman, L.W. (1988) Gender differences in moral development. *Sex Roles*, 18, 701-17.

Donovan, A. and Oddy, M. (1982) Psychological aspect of unemployment: An investigation into the emotional and social adjustment of school leavers. *Journal of Adolescence*, 5, 15-30.

Doran, S. and Jackson, J. (1997) The case for jury waiver. *Criminal Law Review*, 155-72.

Doty, R.L., Appelbaum, S., Zusho, H. and Settle, R.G. (1985) Sex differences in odor identification ability: A cross cultural analysis. *Neuropsychologia*, 23, 667-72.

Dovidio, J.F., Gaertner, S.L., Validzic, A., Matoka, K., Johnson, B. and Frazier, S., (1997) Extending the benefits of recategorization: Evaluations, self-disclosure, and helping. *Journal of Experimental Social Psychology*, 33, 401-20.

Downey, G., Mougios, V., Ayduk, A., London, B. and Shoda, Y. (2004) Rejection sensitivity and the defensive motivational system. *Psychological Science*, 10, 668-73.

Downing, P.E., Peelen, M.V., Wiggett, A.J. and Tew, B.D. (2006) The role of the extrastriate body area in action perception. *Social Neuroscience*, 1(1), 52-62.

Doyen, S., Klein, O., Pichon, C-L. and Cleeremans, A. (2012) Behavioral priming: It's all in the mind, but whose mind? *PLoS ONE*, 7(1), e29081.

Doyen, S., Klein, O., Simons, D.J. and Cleermans, A. (2014) On the other side of the mirror: Priming in cognitive and social psychology. *Social Cognition*, 32, 12-32.

Draganski, B. and May, A. (2008) Training-induced structural changes in the adult human brain. *Behavioural Brain Research*, 192, 137-42.

Draganski, B., Gaser, C., Busch, V., Schuierer, G., Bogdahn, U. and May, A. (2004) Changes in grey matter induced by training. *Nature*, 427, 311-12.

Drake, C., Roehrs, F., Shambroom, J. and Roth, F. (2013) Caffeine effects on sleep taken 0, 3, or 6 hours before going to bed. *Journal of Clinical Sleep Medicine*, 9, 1195-200.

Drake, C.L., Roehrs, T. and Roth, T. (2003) Insomnia causes, consequences, and therapeutics: an overview. *Depression and Anxiety*, 18, 163-76.

Drevets, W.C., Price, J.L., Simpson, J.R., Todd, R.D., Reich, T., Vannier, M. and Raichle, M.E. (1997) Subgenual prefrontal cortex abnormalities in mood disorders. *Nature*, 386, 824-7.

Drew, P. (1984) Speakers' reportings in invitation sequences. In J.M. Atkinson and J. Heritage (eds), *Structures of Social Action: Studies in conversation analysis.* Cambridge: Cambridge University Press.

Drews, D.R., Vaughn, D.B. and Anfiteatro, A. (1992) Beer consumption as a function of music and the presence of others. *Journal of the Pennsylvania Academy of Science*, 134-6.

Dreze, X. and Hussherr, F-X. (2003) Internet advertising: is anybody watching? *Interactive Marketing*, 17, 8-23.

Drieghe, D., Rayner, K. and Pollatsek, A. (2005) Word skipping during reading revisited. *Journal of Experimental Psychology: Human Perception and Performance*, 31, 954-69.

Driemeyer, J., Boyke, J., Gaser, C., Buchel, C. and May, A. (2008) Changes in gray mater induced by learning - revisited. *PLoS ONE*, 3, e2669.

Dronkers, N.F., Plaisant, O., Iba-Zizen, M.T. and Cabanis, E.A. (2007) Paul Broca's historic cases: High resolution MR imaging of the brains of Leborgne and Lelong. *Brain*, 130, 1432-41.

Droomers, M., Schrijvers, C.T.M. and Mackenbach, J.P. (2002) Why do lower educated people continue smoking? Explanations from the longitudinal GLOBE study. *Health Psychology*, 21, 263-72.

Druckman, D. and Porter, L.W. (1991) Developing careers. In D. Druckman and R.A. Bjork (eds) *In the Mind's Eye: Enhancing human performance.* Committee on Techniques for the Enhancement of Human Performance. National Research Council.

Drummond, A. and Sauer, J.D. (2014) Video-games do not negatively impact adolescent academic performance in science, mathematics or reading. *PLoS ONE*, 9(4), e87943.

Drummond, S.P.A., Brown, G.G., Gillin, J.C., Stricker, J.L., Wong, E.C. and Buxton, R.B. (2000) Altered brain response to verbal learning following sleep deprivation. *Nature*, 403, 655-7.

D'souza, D.C., Ranganathan, M., Braley, G., Gueorguieva, R., Zimolo, Z., Cooper, T., . . . and Krystal, J. (2008) Blunted psychotomimetic and amnestic effects of Δ-9-tetrahydrocannabinol in frequent users of cannabis. *Neuropsychopharmacology*, 33(10), 2505-16.

Dube, S.R., Anda, R.F., Felitti, V.J., Chapman, D.P., Williamson, D.F. and Giles, W.H. (2001) Childhood abuse, household dysfunction, and the risk of attempted suicide throughout the lifespan. *JAMA*, 286, 3089-96.

Dube, S.R., Felitti, V.J., Dong, M., Giles, W.H. and Anda, R.F. (2003) The impact of adverse childhood experiences on health problems. *Preventative Medicine*, 37, 268-77.

Dubois, J., Dehaene-Lanbertz, G., Kulikova, S., Poupon, C., Huppi, P.S. and Hertz-Pannier, L. (2014) The early development of brain white matter: A review of imaging studies in foetuses, newborns and infants. *Neuroscience*, 276, 48-71.

DuBose, C. N., Cardello, A. V. and Maller, O. (1980) Effects of colorants and flavorants on identification, perceived flavor intensity, and hedonic quality of fruit-flavored beverages and cake. *Journal of Food Science*, 45(5), 1393-9.

Duchaine, B.C., Yovel, G., Butterworth, E.J. and Nakayama, K. (2006) Prosopagnosia as an impairment to face-specific mechanisms. *Cognitive Neuropsychology*, 23, 714-47.

Duck, S. (1992) *Human Relationships* (2nd edn). London: Sage.

Duckworth, A.L., Peterson, C., Matthews, M.D. and Kelly, D.R. (2007) Grit: Perseverance and passion for long-term goals. *Journal of Personality and Social Psychology*, 92, 1087-101.

Duff, F.J. and Clarke, P.J. (2011) Practitioner review: Reading disorders: What are the effective interventions and how should they be implemented and evaluated? *Journal of Child Psychology and Psychiatry*, 52, 3-12.

Duffau, H., Herbert, G. and Motitz-Gasser, S. (2013) Toward a pluri-component, multimodal, and dynamic organization of the ventral semantic stream in humans: lessons from stimulation mapping in awake patients. *Frontiers in Systems Neuroscience*, 7, 44.

Duggan, M. and Smith, A. (2013) Social media update 2013. *Pew Internet and American Life Project.*

Dunbar, R. I., Baron, R., Frangou, A., Pearce, E., van Leeuwin, E. J., Stow, J., . . . and Van Vugt, M. (2011) Social laughter is correlated with an elevated pain threshold. *Proceedings of the Royal Society of London B: Biological Sciences*, rspb20111373.

Dunlosky, J., Rawson, K.A., Marsh, E.J., Nathan, M.J. and Willingham, D.T. (2013) Improving students' learning with effective learning techniques: Promising directions from cognitive and educational psychology. *Psychological Science in the Public Interest*, 14, 4-58.

Dunmore, E., Clark, D.M. and Ehlers, A. (1999) Cognitive factors involved in the onset and maintenance of posttraumatic stress disorder (PTSD) after physical or sexual assault. *Behaviour Research and Therapy*, 37, 809-29.

Dunn, D.S., Saville, B.K., Baker, S.C. and Marek, P. (2013) Evidence-based teaching: Tools and techniques that promote learning in the psychology classroom. *Australian Journal of Psychology*, 65, 5–13.

Dunn, E.C., McLaughlin, K.A., Slopen, N., Rosand, J. and Smoller, J.W. (2013) Developmental timing of child maltreatment and symptoms of depression and suicidal ideation in young adulthood. *Depression and Anxiety*, 30, 955–64.

Dunn, J. (1993) *Young Children's Close Relationships: Beyond attachment.* Newbury Park, CA: Sage.

Dunn, J. and Kendrick, C. (1982) *Siblings: Love, envy and understanding.* Cambridge, MA: Harvard University Press.

Dunn, J., Bretherton, I. and Munn, P. (1987) Conversations about feeling states between mothers and their young children. *Developmental Psychology*, 23, 132–9.

Dunne, S. and O'Doherty, J.P. (2013) Insights from the application of computational neuroimaging to social neuroscience. *Current Opinion in Neurobiology*, 23, 387–92.

Dupre, K.E. and Barling, J. (2003) Workplace aggression. In A. Sagie, S. Stashevsky and M. Koslowsky (eds) *Misbehavior and Dysfunctional Attitudes in Organizations.* New York: Palgrave.

Durante, F. *et al.* (2013) Nations' income inequality predicts ambivalence in stereotype content: How societies mind the gap. *British Journal of Social Psychology.* 52, 726–46.

Durante, F. *et al.* (2016) Ambivalent stereotypes link to peace, conflict and inequality across 38 nations. *PNAS.* 114, 669–74.

Durante, F., Tablante, C.B. and Fiske, S.T. (2017) Poor but warm, rich but cold (and competent): Social classes in the stereotype content model. *Journal of Social Issues*, 73(1), 138–57.

Durante, K.M., Griskevicius, V., Simpson, J.A., Cantu, S. and Li, N.P. (2012) Ovulation leads women to perceive sexy cads as good dads. *Journal of Personality and Social Psychology*, 103, 292–305.

Durante. K.M., Li, N.P. and Haselton, M.G. (2008) Changes in women's choice of dress across the ovulatory cycle: Naturalistic and laboratory task-based evidence. *Personality and Social Psychology Bulletin*, 34(11), 1451–60.

Durkin, K. (1995) *Developmental Social Psychology: From infancy to old age.* Oxford: Blackwell.

Durston, S. (2003) A review of the biological bases of ADHD: What have we learned from imaging studies? *Mental Retardation and Developmental Disabilities Research Reviews*, 9, 184–95.

Duval, S. and Wicklund, R.A. (1972) *A Theory of Objective Self-awareness.* New York: Academic Press.

Dye, M.W.G., Green, C.S. and Bavelier, D. (2009a) Increasing speed of processing with action video games. *Current Directions in Psychological Science*, 18, 321–6.

Dye, M.W.G., Green, C.S. and Bavelier, D. (2009b) The development of attention skills in action video game players. *Neuropsychologia*, 47, 1780–9.

Dziurawiec, S. and Deregowski, J.B. (1992) 'Twisted perspective' in young children's drawings. *British Journal of Developmental Psychology*, 10, 35–49.

Dzokoto, V., Wallace, D.S., Peters, L. and Bentsi-Enchill, E. (2014) Attention to emotion and non-western faces: Revisiting the facial feedback hypothesis. *The Journal of General Psychology*, 14, 151–68.

Eacott, M.J. and Crawley, R.A. (1998) The offset of childhood amnesia: Memory for events that occurred before age 3. *Journal of Experimental Psychology (General)*, 12, 22–33.

Eagly, A.H. and Chaiken, S. (1993) *The Psychology of Attitudes.* San Diego, CA: Harcourt Brace Jovanovich.

Eagly, A.H. and Karau, S.J. (2002) Role congruity theory of prejudice toward female leaders. *Psychological Review*, 109, 573–98.

Eals, M. and Silverman, I. (1994) The hunter–gatherer theory of spatial sex differences: Proximate factors mediating the female advantage in recall of object arrays. *Ethology and Sociobiology*, 15(2), 95–105.

Earley, P.C. and Mosakowski, E. (2000) Creating hybrid team cultures: an empirical test of transnational team functioning. *Academy of Management Journal*, 43, 26–49.

Earp, B. D. and Trafimow, D. (2015) Replication, falsification, and the crisis of confidence in social psychology. *Frontiers in Psychology*, 6. 621.

Eastwick, P.W. and Finkel, E.J. (2008) Sex differences in mate preferences revisited: Do people know what they initially desire in a romantic partner? *Journal of Personality and Social Psychology*, 94(2), 245–64.

Eastwood, J.D., Gaskovski, P. and Bowers, K.S. (1998) The folly of effort: Ironic effects in the mental control of pain. *International Journal of Clinical and Experimental Hypnosis*, 46(1), 77–91.

Eaves, L.J., Eysenck, H.J. and Martin, N.G. (1989) *Genes, Culture and Personality: An empirical approach.* London: Academic Press.

Ebbinghaus, H. (1885) *Memory: A contribution to experimental psychology* (H.A. Ruger and C.E. Busserius, trans.) Reprinted in 1913 by Teachers College, Columbia University, New York.

Ebstein, R.P., Novick, O., Umansky, R., Priel, B. and Osher, Y. (1996) Dopamine D4 receptor (D4DR) exon III polymorphism associated with the human personality trait of novelty seeking. *Nature Genetics*, 12, 78–80.

Eby, L.T. and Dobbins, G.H. (1997) Collectivistic orientation in teams: an individual- and group-level analysis. *Journal of Organisational Behavior*, 18, 275–95.

Eccles, J.C. (1989) *Evolution of the Brain: Creation of the self.* London: Routledge.

Echebarria-Echabe, A., Fernandez-Guede, E. and Gonzalez-Castro, J.L. (1994) Social representations and intergroup conflicts: Who's smoking here? *European Journal of Social Psychology*, 24, 339–55.

Eckert, M.A., Leonard, C.M., Richards, T.L., Aylward, E.H., Thomson, J. and Berninger, V.W. (2003) Anatomical correlates of dyslexia: Frontal and cerebellar findings. *Brain*, 126, 482–94.

EClipSE Collaborative Members (2010) Education, the brain and dementia: neuroprotection or compensation? *Brain*, 113, 2210–16.

Ecuyer-Dab, I. and Robert, M. (2004) Have sex differences in spatial ability evolved from male competition for mating and female concern for survival? *Cognition*, 91, 221–57.

Eddy, N.B., Halbach, H., Isbell, H. and Seevers, M.H. (1965) Drug dependence: Its significance and characteristics. *Bulletin of the World Health Organization*, 32, 721–33.

Eden, G.F., Stein, J.F., Wood, H.M. and Wood, F.B. (1994) Differences in eye movements and reading problems in dyslexic and normal children. *Vision Research*, 34(10), 1345–58.

Eden, G.F., VanMeter, J.W., Rumsey, J.M., Maisog, J.M., Woods, R.P. and Zeffiro, T.A. (1996) Abnormal processing of visual motion in dyslexia revealed by functional brain imaging. *Nature*, 382, 66–9.

Edens, J.F., Kelley, S.E., Lilienfeld, S.O., Skeem, J.L. and Douglas, K.S. (2015) DSM-5 antisocial personality disorder: Predictive validity in a prison sample. *Law and Human Behavior*, 39, 123–9.

Edens, J.F., Skeem, J.L., Cruise, K.R. and Cauffman, E. (2001). Assessment of 'juvenile psychopathy' and its association with violence: A critical review. *Behavioral Sciences & the Law*, 19(1), 53–80.

Edwards, D. (1997) *Discourse and Cognition.* London: Sage.

Edwards, D. and Middleton, D. (1987) Conversation and remembering: Bartlett revisited. *Applied Cognitive Psychology*, 1, 77–92.

Ehrlichman, H. and Halpern, J.N. (1988) Affect and memory: Effects of pleasant and unpleasant odours on retrieval of happy and unhappy memories. *Journal of Personality and Social Psychology,* 55(5), 769–79.

Eibl-Eibesfeldt, I. (1989) *Human Ethnology.* New York: Aldine de Gruyter.

Eich, E. (1995) Mood as a mediator of place dependent memory. *Journal of Experimental Psychology: General,* 124(3), 293–308.

Eich, E., Macaulay, D. and Lam, R.W. (1997) Mania, depression and mood dependent memory. *Cognition and Emotion,* 11(5/6), 607–18.

Eich, E., Macaulay, D. and Ryan, L. (1994) Mood dependent memory for events of the personal past. *Journal of Experimental Psychology (General),* 123, 201–15.

Eich, J., Weingartner, H., Stillman, R. and Gillin, J. (1975) State-dependent accessibility of retrieval cues and retention of a categorized list. *Journal of Verbal Learning and Verbal Behavior,* 14, 408–17.

Eichenbaum, H. (2012) What HM taught us. *Journal of Cognitive Neurocience,* 25, 14–21.

Eiler, J.M. (2007) Geochemistry. The oldest fossil or just another rock? *Science,* 317, 1046–7.

Eimas, P.D., Siqueland, E.R., Jusczyk, P. and Vigorito, J. (1971) Speech perception in infants. *Science,* 171, 303–6.

Einstein, G.O., McDaniel, M.A., Richardson, S.L., Guynn, M.J. and Cinfer, A.R. (1995) Aging and prospective memory: Examining the influences of self-initiated retrieval processes. *Journal of Experimental Psychology: Learning, Memory and Cognition,* 21, 996–1007.

Einstein, G.O., McDaniel, M.A., Smith, R.E. and Shaw, P. (1998) Habitual prospective memory and aging. *Psychological Science,* 9(4), 284–8.

Eippert, F., Finsterbusch, J., Bingel, U. and Büchel, C. (2009) Direct evidence for spinal cord involvement in placebo analgesia. *Science,* 326(5951), 404.

Eisenberg, N. and Fabes, R.A. (1998) Prosocial development. In W. Damon and N. Eisenberg (eds) *Handbook of Child Psychology. Vol. 3: Social, emotional and personality development* (5th edn). New York: Wiley.

Eisenberg, N., Wolchik, S., Goldberg, L. and Engel, I. (1992) Parental values, reinforcement, and young children's prosocial behaviour: A longitudinal study. *Journal of Genetic Psychology,* 153, 19–36.

Eisenberger, N.I. (2012) The neural bases of social pain: Evidence for shared representations with physical pain. *Psychosomatic Medicine,* 74, 126–35.

Eisenberger, N.I. (2013) Social ties and health: a social neuroscience perspective. *Current Opinion in Neurobiology,* 23, 407–13.

Eisenberger, N.I., Lieberman, M.D. and Williams, K.D. (2003) Does rejection hurt: An fMRI study of social exclusion. *Science,* 302, 290–2.

Eklund, A., Nichols, T.E. and Knutsson, H. (2016) Cluster value: why fMRI inferences for spatial extent have inflated false-positive rates. *PNAS,* 1–6.

Ekman, P. (1973) Cross cultural studies of facial expression. In P. Ekman (ed.) *Darwin and Facial Expression: A century of research in review.* New York: Academic Press.

Ekman, P. (1984) Expression and the nature of emotion. In K. Scherer and P. Ekman (eds) *Approaches to Emotion.* Hillsdale, NJ: Lawrence Erlbaum Associates.

Ekman, P. (1992) Are there basic emotions? *Psychological Review,* 99, 550–3.

Ekman, P. (1994) Strong evidence for universals in facial expressions: A reply to Russell's mistaken critique. *Psychological Bulletin,* 115(2), 268–87.

Ekman, P. (2016) What scientists who study emotion agree about. *Perspectives on Psychological Science,* 11, 31–4.

Ekman, P. and Davidson, R.A. (1994) *The nature of emotion.* New York: OUP.

Ekman, P. and Friesen, W.V. (1969) Nonverbal leakage and clues to deception. *Psychiatry,* 32, 88–105.

Ekman, P. and Friesen, W.V. (1974) Detecting deception from body or face. *Journal of Personality and Social Psychology,* 29, 288–98.

Ekman, P. and O'Sullivan, M. (1991) Who can catch a liar? *American Psychologist,* 46, 913–20.

Ekman, P., Davidson, R.J. and Friesen, W.V. (1990) The Duchenne smile: Emotional expression and brain physiology II. *Journal of Personality and Social Psychology,* 58(2), 542–53.

Ekman, P., Friesen, W.V. and Ellsworth, P. (1972) *Emotion in the Human Face: Guidelines for research and a review of findings.* New York: Pergamon Press.

Ekman, P., O'Sullivan, M. and Frank, M.G. (1999) A few can catch a liar. *Psychological Science,* 10, 263–6.

Elfenbein, H.A. and Ambady, N. (2003) Universals in cultural differences in recognizing emotions. *Current Directions in Psychological Science,* 12(5), 159–64.

Elias, M. (1981) Serum cortisol, testosterone and testosterone binding globulin responses to competitive fighting in human males. *Aggressive Behavior,* 7, 215–24.

Elkind, D. and Bowen, R. (1979) Imaginary audience behaviour in children and adolescence. *Developmental Psychology,* 15, 33–44.

Ellemers, N. (1993) The influence of socio-structural variables on identity management strategies. *European Review of Social Psychology,* 4, 27–57.

Ellenberger, H.F. (1972) The story of 'Anna O.': A critical review with new data. *Journal of the History of the Behavioral Sciences,* 8, 267–79.

Elliot, A.J. and Aarts, H. (2011) Perception of the color red enhances the force and velocity of motor output. *Emotion,* 11, 445–9.

Elliot, A.J. and Niesta, D. (2008) Romantic red: Red enhances men's attraction to women. *Journal of Personality and Social Psychology,* 95, 1150–64.

Elliot, A.J., Maier, M.A., Binser, M.J., Friedman, R. and Pekrun, R. (2009) The effect of red on avoidance behaviour in achievement contexts. *Personality and Social Psychology Bulletin,* 35, 365–75.

Elliot, A.J., Moller, A.C., Friedman, R., Maier, M.A. and Meinhardt, J. (2007) Color and psychological functioning: The effect of red on performance attainment. *Journal of Experimental Psychology: General,* 136(1), 154–68.

Elliott, R., Frith, C.D. and Dolan, R.J. (1997) Differential neural response to positive and negative feedback in planning and guessing tasks. *Neuropsychologia,* 35(10), 1395–04.

Ellis, A. (1973) Rational-emotive therapy. In R. Corsini (ed.) *Current Psychotherapies.* Itasca, IL: Peacock.

Ellis, A.W. (1992) *Reading, Writing and Dyslexia: A cognitive analysis* (2nd edn). Hove: Psychology Press.

Ellis, R.R. and Lederman, S.J. (1998) The golf-ball illusion: evidence for top-down processing in weight perception. *Perception,* 27, 193–201.

Ellison, N. Steinfeld, C. and Lampe, C. (2007) The benefits of Facebook 'friends': Social capital and college students' use of online social networking sites. *Journal of Computer-Mediated Communication,* 12, 1143–68.

Ellison-Wright, T. and Bullmore, E. (2009) Meta-analysis of diffusion tensor imaging studies in schizophrenia. *Schizophrenia Research,* 108, 3–10.

Elman, I., Borsook, D. and Volkow, N.D. (2013) Pain and suicidality: insights from reward and addiction neuroscience. *Progress in Neurobiology,* 109, 1–27.

Elman, J.L., Takahashi, K. and Tohsaku, Y.H. (1981) Lateral asymmetries for the identification of concrete and abstract Kanji. *Brain and Language,* 13, 290–300.

Elms, A.C. (1975) The crisis of confidence in social psychology. *American Psychologist,* 30, 967–76.

Elms, A.C. (1995) Obedience in retrospect. *Journal of Social Issues,* 51, 21–32.

Ember, C. and Ember, M. (2007) Climate, econiche, and sexuality: Influences on sonority of language. *American Anthropologist*, 109, 180–5.

Emde, R.N., Plomin, R., Robinson, J., DeFries, J., Reznick, J.S., Campos, J., Kagan, J. and Zahn-Waxler, C. (1992) Temperament, emotion, and cognition at fourteen months: The MacArthur longitudinal twin study. *Child Development*, 63, 1437–55.

Emmelkamp, P.M.G. (1993) Technical advances in behavioral psychotherapy of obsessive-compulsive disorders. *Psychotherapeutic Psychosomatics*, 60, 57–61.

Emmons, R.A., Diener, E. and Larsen, R.J. (1986) Choice and avoidance of everyday situations and affect congruence: Two models of reciprocal interactionism. *Journal of Personality and Social Psychology*, 51, 815–26.

Enard, W. *et al.* (2002) Molecular evolution of FOXP2, a gene involved in speech and language. *Nature*, 418, 869–72.

Engel, L.R., Frum, C., Puce, A., Walker, N.A. and Lewis, J.W. (2009) Different categories of living and non-living sound-sources activate distinct cortical networks. *Neuroimage*, 47, 1778–91.

Engen, T. (1982) *The Perception of Odors*. New York: Academic Press.

Engle, R.W., Kane, M.J. and Tuholski, S.W. (1999) Individual differences in working memory capacity and what they tell us about controlled attention, general fluid intelligence and functions of the prefrontal cortex. In A. Miyake and P. Shah (eds) *Models of Working Memory: Mechanisms of active maintenance and executive control*. New York: Cambridge University Press.

Enlow, D.H. (1982) *Handbook of Facial Growth*. Philadelphia, PA: Saunders.

Enrici, I., Adenzato, M., Cappa, S., Bara, B.G. and Tettamanti, M. (2011) Intention processing in communication: A common brain network for language and gestures. *Journal of Cognitive Neuroscience*, 23, 2415–31.

Epel, E., Blackburn, E., Lin, J., Dhabhar, F., Adler, N., Morrow, J.D. *et al.* (2004) Accelerated telomere shortening in response to exposure to life stress. *Proceedings of the National Academy of Sciences*, 101, 17312–15.

Epel, E.S. (2009) Telomeres in a life-span perspective; A new 'psychobiomarker'? *Current Directions in Psychological Science*, 18, 1, 6–10.

Epstein, R. and Kanwisher, N. (1998) A cortical representation of the local visual environment. *Nature*, 392(66676), 598–601.

Epstein, W. (1961) The influence of syntactical structure on learning. *American Journal of Psychology*, 74, 80–5.

Erickson, K.I. (2013) Evidence for structural plasticity in humans: Comment on Thomas and Baker (2012) *Neuroimage*, 73, 237–8.

Erickson, K.I., Voss, M.W., Prakash, R.S., Basak, C., Szabo, A., Chaddock, L., Kim, J.S., Hero, S., Alves, H. and White, S.M. (2011) Exercise training increases size of hippocampus and improves memory. *PNAS*, 108, 3017–22.

Erickson, M.F., Sroufe, L.A. and Egeland, B. (1985) The relationship between quality of attachment and behavior problems in preschool in a high-risk sample. *Monographs of the Society for Research in Child Development*, 50 (1/2), Serial No. 209.

Erikson, E.H. (1968) *Identity, Youth and Crisis*. New York: W.W. Norton.

Eriksson, P.S., Perfilieva, E., Bjork-Eriksson, T., Alborn, A., Nordborg, C., Peterson, D.A. (1998) Neurogenesis in the adult human hippocampus. *Nature Medicine*, 4, 1313–17.

Ersche, K.D., Jones, P.S., Williams, G.B., Smith, D.G., Bullmore, E.T. and Robbins, T.W. (2012) Distinctive personality traits and neural correlates associated with stimulant drug use versus familial risk of stimulant dependence. *Biological Psychiatry*, 74, 137–44.

Ersche, K.D., Jones, P.S., Williams, G.B., Turton, A.J., Robbins, T.W. and Bullmore, E.T. (2012) Abnormal brain structure implicated in stimulant drug addiction. *Science*, 335, 601–4.

Ersche, K.D., Williams, G.B., Robbins, T.W. and Bullmore, E.T. (2013) Meta-analysis of structural brain abnormalities associated with stimulant drug dependence and neuroimaging of addiction vulnerability and resilience. *Current Opinion in Neurobiology*, 23, 615–24.

Esbenshade, A., Fox, G.B. and Cowart, M.D. (2006) Histamine H3 receptor antagonists: preclinical promise for treating obesity and cognitive disorders. *Molecular Interventions*, 6, 77–88.

Eskine, K.J., Kacinik, N.A. and Prinz, J.J. (2011) A bad taste in the mouth. *Psychological Science*, 22, 295–9.

Eslinger, P.J. and Damasio, A.R. (1985) Severe disturbance of higher cognition after bilateral frontal lobe ablation: Patient EVR. *Neurology*, 35, 1731–41.

Eslinger, P.J. and Grattan, L.M. (1993) Frontal lobe and frontal-striatal substrates for different forms of human cognitive flexibility. *Neuropsychologia*, 31(1), 17–28.

Espay, A.J., Norris, M.M., Eliassen, J.C., Dwivedi, A., Smith, M.S., Banks, C., . . . and Szaflarski, J. P. (2015) Placebo effect of medication cost in Parkinson disease: A randomized double-blind study. *Neurology*, 84(8), 794–802.

Etaugh, C., Grinnell, K. and Etaugh, A. (1989) Development of gender labelling: Effects of age of pictured children. *Sex Roles*, 21, 769–73.

Etcoff, N.L., Ekman, P., Magee, J.J. and Frank, M.G. (2000) Lie detection and language comprehension. *Nature*, 405, 139.

Etkin, A. and Wager, T.D. (2007) Functional neuroimaging of anxiety: a meta-analysis of emotional processing in PTSD, social anxiety disorder, and specific phobia. *American Journal of Psychiatry*, 164(10), 1476–88.

European Communities (2009) *Health Statistics – Atlas on Mortality in the European Union*. Luxembourg: Office for Official Publications of the European Communities.

European Values Study Group and World Values Survey Association (2005) *European and World Values Surveys Integrated Data File 1999–2002, Release I*. Ann Arbor, MI: Inter-University Consortium for Political and Social Research.

Euston, D.R., Gruber, A.J. and McNaughton, B.L. (2012) The role of medial prefrontal cortex in memory and decision-making. *Neuron*, 76, 1057–70.

Evans, C.B.R., Fraser, M.W. and Cotter, K.L. (2014) The effectiveness of school-based bullying prevention programs: A systematic review. *Aggression and Violent Behavior*, 19, 532–44.

Evans, G.W. and Lepore, S.J. (1993) Nonauditory effects of noise on children: A critical review. *Children's Environments*, 10, 31–50.

Evans, G.W. and Wener, R.E. (2006) Rail commuting duration and passenger stress. *Health Psychology*, 25(3), 408–12.

Evans, J., St, B.T. and Over, D.E. (1996) *Rationality and Reasoning*. Hove: Psychology Press.

Evans, J., St, B.T., Handley, S.J., Harper, C. and Johnson-Laird, P.N. (1999) Reasoning about necessity and possibility: A test of the mental model theory of deduction. *Journal of Experimental Psychology: Learning, Memory and Cognition*, 25, 1495–513.

Evans, J., St, B.T., Venn, S. and Feeney, A. (2002) Implicit and explicit processes in a hypothesis testing task. *British Journal of Psychology*, 93, 31–46.

Evans, P., Bristow, M., Hucklebridge, F., Clow, A. and Pang, E-Y. (1994) Stress, arousal, cortisol and secretory immunoglobin A in students undergoing assessment. *British Journal of Clinical Psychology*, 33, 575–6.

Evans, P., Bristow, M., Hucklebridge, F., Clow, A. and Walters, N. (1993) The relationship between secretory immunity, mood and life events. *British Journal of Clinical Psychology*, 32, 227–36.

Evans, P., Clow, A. and Hucklebridge, F. (1997) Stress and the immune system. *The Psychologist*, July, 303–7.

Evanschitzky, H. and Armstrong, J.S. (2010) Replications of forecasting research. *International Journal of Forecasting*, 26, 4–8.

Everitt, B.J. and Robbins, T.W. (2013) From the ventral to the dorsal striatum: Devolving view of their roles in drug addiction. *Neuroscience and Biobehavioral Reviews*, 37, 1946–54.

Ewbank, M.P. and Andrews, T.J. (2008) Differential sensitivity for viewpoint between familiar and unfamiliar faces in human visual cortex. *Neuroimage*, 40, 1857–70.

Ewing, L., Pellicano, E. and Rhodes, G. (2013) Atypical updating of face representations with experience in children with autism. *Developmental Science*, 16, 116–23.

Exner, J.E. (1974) *The Rorschach: A comprehensive system*, Vol. 1. New York: Wiley.

Eysenck, H.J. (1952) The effects of psychotherapy: An evaluation. *Journal of Consulting Psychology*, 16, 319–24.

Eysenck, H.J. (1957) *Sense and Nonsense in Psychology*. London: Pelican.

Eysenck, H.J. (1970) *The Structure of Human Personality* (3rd edn). London: Methuen.

Eysenck, H.J. (1985) *Decline and Fall of the Freudian Empire*. London: Pelican.

Eysenck, H.J. (1991) Dimensions of personality: 16, 5, or 3? Criteria for a taxonomic paradigm. *Personality and Individual Differences*, 12, 773–90.

Eysenck, H.J. (1995) *Genius: A natural history of creativity*. Cambridge: Cambridge University Press.

Eysenck, H.J. and Eysenck, M.W. (1985) *Personality and Individual Differences: A natural science approach*. New York: Plenum Press.

Eysenck, M.W. (1992) *Anxiety: The cognitive perspective*. Hove: Psychology Press.

Eysenck, M.W. (2001) How do European and US psychology differ? *Psychologist*, 14(7), 352–3.

Eysenck, M.W., Mogg, K., May, J., Richards, A. and Mathews, A. (1991) Bias in interpretation of ambiguous sentences related to threat in anxiety. *Journal of Abnormal Psychology*, 100, 144–50.

Eyssel, F. and Kuchenbrandt, D. (2012) Social categorisation of social robots: Anthropomorphism as a function of robot group membership. *British Journal of Social Psychology*, 51, 724–31.

F

Fabes, R.A. and Eisenberg, N. (1992) Young children's coping with interpersonal anger. *Child Development*, 63, 116–28.

Fagot, B. (1985) Changes in thinking about early sex role development. *Developmental Review*, 5, 83–98.

Fagot, B. and Hagan, R.I. (1991) Observations of parent reactions to sex-stereotyped behaviors: Age and sex differences. *Child Development*, 62, 617–28.

Fagot, B. and Leinbach, M. (1989) The young child's gender schema: Environmental input, internal organisation. *Child Development*, 60, 663–72.

Fagot, B., Leinbach, M. and Hagan, R. (1986) Gender labeling and the adoption of sex-typed behaviours. *Developmental Psychology*, 22, 440–43.

Fahrmeier, E.D. (1978) The development of concrete operations among the Hausa. *Journal of Cross-Cultural Psychology*, 9, 23–44.

Fairburn, C.G., Shafran, R. and Cooper, Z. (1999) A cognitive behavioural theory of anorexia nervosa. *Behaviour Research and Therapy*, 37, 1–13.

Falbo, T. (1992) Social norms and the one-child family: Clinical and policy implications. In F. Boer and J. Dunn (eds) *Children's Sibling Relationships*. Hillsdale, NJ: Lawrence Erlbaum Associates.

Falbo, T. and Polit, D. (1986) A quantitative review of the only-child literature: Research evidence and theory development. *Psychological Bulletin*, 100, 176–89.

Falbo, T. and Poston, D.L. (1993) The academic, personality and physical outcomes of only children in China. *Child Development*, 64, 18–35.

Falk, D., Lepore, F.E. and Noe, A. (2012) The cerebral cortex of Albert Einstein: A description and preliminary analysis of unpublished photographs. *Brain*, 136, 1304–27.

Falk, E.B., Berkman, E.T. and Lieberman, M.D. (2012) From neural responses to population behaviour: Neural focus group predicts population-level media effects. *Psychological Science*, 23, 439–45.

Fantz, R.L. (1958) Pattern vision in young infants. *Psychological Record*, 8, 43–7.

Fantz, R.L. (1961) The origin of form perception. *Scientific American Mind*, 204, 66–72.

Farah, M.J. (1990) *Visual Agnosia: Disorders of object vision and what they tell us about normal vision*. Cambridge, MA: MIT Press.

Farah, M.J. and Ratcliff, G. (1994) *The Neuropsychology of High-level Vision*. Hove: Psychology Press.

Farah, M.J., Wilson, K.D., Drain, M. and Tanaka, J.N. (1998) What is 'special' about face perception? *Psychological Review*, 105, 482–98.

Farahany, N.A. (2016) Neuroscience and behavioural genetics in US criminal law: an empirical analysis. *Journal of Law and the Biosciences*, 2, 485–509.

Farmer, A., McGuffin, P. and Gottesman, I. (1987) Twin concordance in DSM-III schizophrenia. *Archives of General Psychiatry*, 44, 634–41.

Farsides, T. and Woodfield, R. (2003) Individual differences and undergraduate academic success: The roles of personality, intelligence and application. *Personality and Individual Differences*, 34, 1225–43.

Farstad, S. M., McGeown, L. M. and von Ranson, K. M. (2016) Eating disorders and personality, 2004–2016: a systematic review and meta-analysis. *Clinical Psychology Review*, 46, 91–105.

Fazel, S., Gulati, G., Linsell, L., Geddes, J.R. and Grann, M. (2009). Schizophrenia and violence: systematic review and meta-analysis. *PLoS Med*, 6(8), e1000120.

Fazel, S., Lichtenstein, P., Grann, M., Goodwin, G.W. and Langstrom, N. (2010) Bipolar disorder and violent crime: new evidence from population-based longitudinal studies and systematic review. *Archives of General Psychiatry*, 67, 931–8.

Fazio, R.H., Jackson, J.R., Dunton, B.C. and Williams, C.J. (1995) Variability in automatic activation as an unobtrusive measure of racial attitudes: A bona fide pipeline. *Journal of Personality and Social Psychology*, 69, 1013–27.

Fazio, R.H., Sanbonmatsu, D.M., Powell, M.C. and Kardes, F.R. (1986) On the automatic activation of attitudes. *Journal of Personality and Social Psychology*, 50, 229–38.

Fazio, R.H., Zanna, M.P. and Cooper, J. (1977) Dissonance and self-perception: An integrative view of each theory's proper domain of application. *Journal of Experimental Social Psychology*, 13, 464–79.

Featherstone, M. and Hepworth, M. (1993) Images of ageing. In J. Bond, P. Coleman and S. Peace (eds) *Ageing and Society*. London: Sage.

Fedorenko, E., Nieto-Castanon, A. and Kanwisher, N. (2012) Lexical syntactic representations in the brain: An fMRI investigation with multi-voxel pattern analyses. *Neuropsychologia*, 50, 499–513.

Feige, B., Baglioni, C., Spiegelhalder, K., Hirscher, V., Nissen, C. and Riemann, D. (2013) The microstructure of sleep in primary insomnia. *International Journal of Psychophysiology*, 89, 171–80.

Feinstein, J.S. (2013) Lesion studies of human emotion and feeling. *Current Opinion in Neurobiology*, 23, 304–09.

Feinstein, J.S., Khalsa, S.S., Salomons, T.V., Prkachin, K.M., Frey-Law, L.A., Lee, J.E., . . . and Rudrauf, D. (2016) Preserved emotional awareness of pain in a patient with extensive bilateral damage to the insula, anterior cingulate, and amygdala. *Brain Structure and Function*, 221(3), 1499–1511.

Feldhusen, J.F. (1993) A conception of creative thinking and creativity training. In S.G. Isaksen, M.C. Murdoch, R.L. Firestien and D.J. Treffinger (eds) *Nurturing and Developing Creativity: The emergence of a discipline.* Norwood, NJ: Ablex.

Feldhusen, J.F. and Goh, B.E. (1995) Assessing and accessing creativity: An integrative review of theory, research and development. *Creativity Research Journal*, 8(3), 231–47.

Fellows, B.J. (1990) Current theories of hypnosis: A critical review. *British Journal of Experimental and Clinical Hypnosis*, 7, 81–92.

Fenigstein, A. and Abrams, D. (1993) Self-attention and the egocentric assumption of shared perspectives. *Journal of Experimental Social Psychology*, 29, 287–303.

Fenton, G.W. (1998) Neurosurgery for mental disorder. *Irish Journal of Psychiatric Medicine*, 15(2), 45–8.

Ferdenzi, C., Delplanque, S., Atanassova, R. and Sander, D. (2016) Androstadienone's influence on the perception of facial and vocal attractiveness is not sex specific. *Psychoneuroendorcrinology*, 66, 166–75.

Ferguson, C.J. (2007) Evidence for publication bias in video game violence effects literature. *Aggression and Violent Behavior*, 12, 470–82.

Ferguson, C.J. (2014) Does media violence predict societal violence? It depends on what you look at and when. *Journal of Communication*, 65(1), E1–22.

Fernandez, V.G., Juranke, J., Romanowska-Pawlliczek, A., Stuebing, K., Williams, V.J. and Fletcher, J.M. (2016) White matter integrity of cerebellar-cortical tracts in reading impaired children: A probabilistic tractography study. *Brain and Language*, 161, 45–56.

Fernandez-Duque, D., Evans, J., Christian, C. and Hidges, S.D. (2015) Superfluous neuroscience information makes explanations of psychological phenomena more appealing. *Journal of Cognitive Neuroscience*, 27, 926–44.

Ferrari, P.F., Gallese, V., Rizzolatti, G. and Fogassi, L. (2003) Mirror neurons responding to the observation of ingestive and communicative mouth actions in the monkey ventral premotor cortex. *European Journal of Neuroscience*, 17, 1703–14.

Ferrie, J.E., Shipley, M.J., Akbaraly, T.N., Marmot, M.G., Kivimaki, M. and Singh-Manoux, A. (2011) Change in sleep duration and cognitive function: Findings from the Whitehall II study. *Sleep*, 34, 565–73.

Ferris, G.R., Witt, L.A. and Hochwarter, W.A. (2001) Interaction of social skill and General Mental Ability on job performance and salary. *Journal of Applied Psychology*, 86, 1075–82.

Fertonani, A. and Miniussi, C. (2016) Transcranial electrical stimulation: What we know and do not know about mechanisms. *The Neuroscientist*, 1–15.

Fertonani, A. and Miniussi, C. (in press) Transcranial electrical stimulation what we know and do not know about mechanisms. *The Neuroscientist*.

Festinger, L. (1954) A theory of social comparison processes. *Human Relations*, 7, 117–40.

Festinger, L. (1957) *A Theory of Cognitive Dissonance.* Stanford, CA: Stanford University Press.

Festinger, L. and Carlsmith, J.M. (1959) Cognitive consequences of forced compliance. *Journal of Abnormal and Social Psychology*, 58, 203–10.

Festinger, L., Schachter, S. and Back, K. (1950) *Social Pressures in Informal Groups: A study of a housing community.* New York: Harper and Row.

Feynman, R.P. (1985) *Surely You're Joking, Mr. Feynman!* New York: Bantam Books.

Fiedler, F.E. (1965) A contingency model of leadership effectiveness. In L. Berkowitz (ed.) *Advances in Experimental Social Psychology*, Vol. 1. New York: Academic Press, pp. 149–90.

Fields, L. (1993) Foreword in special issue on stimulus equivalence. *The Psychological Record*, 43, 543–6.

Fields, L., Landon-Jimenez, V., Buffington, D.M. and Adams, B.J. (1995) Maintained nodal-distance effects in equivalence classes. *Journal of the Experimental Analysis of Behavior*, 64, 129–46.

Fiez, J.A. (2016) The cerebellum and language: Persistent themes and findings. *Brain and Language*, 161, 1–3.

Fiez, J.A., Raichle, M.E., Miezin, F.M., Petersen, S.E., Tallai, P. and Katz, W.F. (1995) PET studies of auditory and phonological processing: Effects of stimulus characteristics and task demands. *Journal of Cognitive Neuroscience*, 7(3), 357–75.

Fife-Shaw, C. (1997) Commentary on Joffe (1996) AIDS research and prevention: A social representational approach. *British Journal of Medical Psychology*, 70, 65–73.

Figee, M. et al. (2011) *Biological Psychiatry*, 69, 867–74.

Figee, M. et al. (2013) Deep brain stimulation restores frontostriatal network activity in obsessive-compulsive disorder. *Nature Neuroscience*, 16, 386–7.

Finch, J.F., Baranik, L.E., Liu, Y. and West, S.G. (2012) Physical health, positive and negative affect, and personality: A longitudinal analysis. *Journal of Research in Personality*, 46, 537–45.

Fincham, F.D. (1998) Child development and marital relations. *Child Development*, 69(2), 543–74.

Fincham, F.D. and Bradbury, T.N. (1987) Cognitive processes and conflict in close relationships: An attribution–efficacy model. *Journal of Personality and Social Psychology*, 53, 1106–18.

Fine, J.D., Semrud-Clikman, M. and Zhu, D.C. (2009) Gender differences in BOLD activation to face photographs and video vignettes. *Behavioural Brain Research*, 201, 137–46.

Fink, G.R., Halligan, P.W., Marshall, J.C., Frith, C.D., Frackowiak, R.S.J. and Dolan, R.J. (1996) Where in the brain does visual attention select the forest and the trees? *Nature*, 382, 626–8.

Finkel, D., Pedersen, N.L., McGue, M. and McClearn, G.E. (1995) Heritability of cognitive abilities in adult twins: Comparison and Minnesota and Swedish data. *Behaviour Genetics*, 25, 421–32.

Finkenauer, C., Luminet, O., Gisle, L., El-Ahmadi, A., van der Linden, M. and Philppot, P. (1998) Flashbulb memories of the underlying mechanisms of their formation: Toward an emotional-integrative model. *Memory and Cognition*, 26(3), 516–31.

Finlayson, C., Pacheco, F.G., Rodriguez-Vidal, J., Fa, D.A. et al. (2006) Late survival of Neanderthals at the southernmost extreme of Europe. *Nature*, 443, 850–3.

Finnigan, K.M. and Corker, K.S. (2016) Do performance avoidance goals moderate the effect of different types of stereotype threat on women's math performance? *Journal of Research in Personality*, 63, 36–43.

Fischer, A.H., Eagly, A.H. and Oosterwijk, S. (2013) The meaning of tears: Which sex seems emotional depends on the social context. *European Journal of Social Psychology*, 43(6), 505–15.

Fischer, P., Krueger, J.I., Greitemeyer, T., Vogrincic, C., Kastenmuller, A., Frey, D., Heene, H., Wicher, M. and Kainbacher, M. (2011) The bystander-effect: a meta-analytic review on bystander intervention in dangerous and non-dangerous emergencies. *Psychological Bulletin*, 137, 517–37.

Fisher, D.F. and Shebilske, W.L. (1985) There is more that meets the eye than the eye mind assumption. In R. Groner, G.W. McGonkie and C Menz (eds) *Eye Movements and Human Information Processing.* Amsterdam: North Holland, pp. 149–58.

Fisher, S.E. (2005) On genes, speech and language. *New England Journal of Medicine*, 353 (16), 1655–7.

Fiske, S. (2012) Managing ambivalent prejudices: Smart-but-cold and warm-but-dumb stereotypes. *Annals AAPSS*, 639, 33–48.

Fiske, S., Cuddy, A.J.C. and Glick, P. (2007) Universal dimensions of social perception: Warmth and competence. *TICS*, 11, 77–83.

Fiske, S.T. and Neuberg, S.L. (1990) A continuum of impression formation, from category-based to individuating processes: Influences of information and motivation on attention and interpretation. In L. Berkowitz (ed.) *Advances in Experimental Social Psychology*, Vol. 23. New York: Academic Press, pp. 1–74.

Fiske, S.T. and Taylor, S.E. (1991) *Social Cognition* (2nd edn). New York: McGraw-Hill.

Fisler, M.S., Federspiel, A., Horn, H., Dierks, T., Schmitt, W., Wiest, R., de Quervain, D. and Soravia, L. (2013) Spider phobia is associated with decreased left amygdala volume: a cross-sectional study. *BMC Psychiatry*, 13, 70.

Fitzgerald, T.E., Tennen, H., Affleck, G. and Pransky, G.S. (1993) The relative importance of dispositional optimism and control appraisals in quality of life after coronary bypass surgery. *Journal of Behavioural Medicine*, 16, 25–43.

Fitzsimons, G.M., Chartrand, T.L. and Fitzsimons, G.J. (2008) Automatic effects of brand exposure on motivated behavior: How Apple makes you 'think different'. *Journal of Consumer Research*, 35, 21–34.

Fivush, R. (1984) Learning about school: The development of kindergartens' school scripts. *Child Development*, 55, 1697–709.

Fivush, R., Gray, J.T. and Fromhoff, F.A. (1987) Two-year-olds talk about the past. *Cognitive Development*, 2, 393–410.

Flanagan, J.R., Bittner, J.P. and Johansson, R.S. (2008) Experience can change distinct size-weight priors engaged in lifting objects and judging their weights. *Current Biology*, 18, 1742–7.

Flaugnacco, E., Lopez, L., Terribili, C., Montico, M., Zoia, S. and Schon, D. (2015) Music training increases phonological awareness and reading skills in developmental dyslexia: A randomised control trial. *PLoS ONE*, 10, e0138715.

Flavell, J.H. (1992) Cognitive development: Past, present and future. *Developmental Psychology*, 28, 998–1005.

Flavell, J.H., Everett, B.H., Croft, K. and Flavell, E.R. (1981) Young children's knowledge about visual perception: Further evidence for the level 1-level 2 distinction. *Developmental Psychology*, 17, 99–103.

Flavell, J.H., Green, F.L. and Flavell, E.R. (1989) Young children's ability to differentiate appearance-reality and level 2 perspectives in the tactile modality. *Child Development*, 60, 201–13.

Flay, B.R., Ryan, K.B., Best, J.A., Brown, K.S., Kersell, M.W., d'Avernas, J.R. and Zanna, M.P. (1985) Are social-psychological smoking prevention programs effective? The Waterloo Study. *Journal of Behavioral Medicine*, 8, 37–59.

Flechtner-Mors, M., Ditschuneit, H.H., Johnson, T.D., Suchard, M.A. and Adler, G. (2000) Metabolic and weight loss effects of a long term dietary intervention in obese patients: A four year follow up. *Obesity Research*, 8, 399–402.

Fleeson, W. and Gallagher, P. (2009) The implications of Big Five standing for the distribution of trait manifestation in behavior: Fifteen experience-sampling studies and a meta-analysis. *Journal of Personality and Social Psychology*, 97, 1097–114.

Fleischman, D.A. and Gabrieli, J.D.E. (1999) Long-term memory in Alzheimer's disease. *Current Opinion in Neurobiology*, 9, 240–4.

Fletcher, P.C. and Henson, R.N.A. (2001) Frontal lobes and human memory. *Brain*, 849–81.

Fletcher, P.C., Shallice, T. and Dolan, R.J. (1998a) The functional roles of prefrontal cortex in episodic memory. I. Encoding. *Brain*, 121, 1239–48.

Fletcher, P.C., Shallice, T. and Dolan, R.J. (1998b) The functional roles of prefrontal cortex in episodic memory. II. Retrieval. *Brain*, 121, 1249–56.

Fletcher, P.C., Shallice, T., Frith, C.D., Frackowiak, R.S. and Dolan, R.J. (1996) Brain activity during memory retrieval. The influence of imagery and semantic cueing. *Brain*, 119, 1587–96.

Fletcher, R. and Voke, J. (1985) *Defective Colour Vision: Fundamentals, diagnosis and management*. Bristol: Adam Hilger.

Flexas, A., Rossello, J., de Miguel, P., Nadal, M. and Munar, E. (2014) Cognitive control and unusual decision about beauty: an fMRI study. *Frontiers in Human Neuroscience*, 8, 520, 1–9.

Flexser, A.J. and Tulving, E. (1978) Retrieval independence in recognition and recall. *Psychological Review*, 85, 153–71.

Flin, R.H. (1985) Development of face recognition: An encoding switch? *British Journal of Psychology*, 76, 125–34.

Flint, J. and Kendler, K.S. (2014) The genetics of major depression. *Neuron*, 81(3), 484–503.

Flore, P.C. and Wicherts, J.M. (2015) Does stereotype threat influence performance of girls in stereotyped domains? A meta-analysis. *Journal of School Psychology*, 53, 25–44.

Florida, R., Mellander, C. and Rentfrow, P.J. (2013) The happiness of cities. *Regional Studies*, 47, 613–27.

Flynn, F.J. and Lake, V.K. (2008) If you need help, just ask: underestimating compliance with direct requests for help. *Journal of Personality and Social Psychology*, 95(1), 128.

Flynn, J.M. and Rahbar, M.H. (1994) Prevalence of reading failure in boys compared with girls. *Psychology in Schools*, 31, 66–71.

Flynn, J.R. (1984) The mean of IQ of Americans: Massive gains 1932 to 1978. *Psychological Bulletin*, 99, 29–51.

Flynn, J.R. (1987) Massive IQ gains in 14 nations: What IQ tests really measure. *Psychological Bulletin*, 101, 171–91.

Flynn, J.R. (2016) No population is frozen in time: The sociology of intelligence. *Psychological Inquiry*, 27, 205–9.

Foa, E.B. and Meadows, E.A. (1997) Psychosocial treatments for post-traumatic stress disorder: A critical review. *Annual Review of Psychology*, 48, 449–80.

Foa, E.B., Molnar, C. and Cashman, L. (1995) Change in rape narratives during exposure therapy for post-traumatic stress disorder. *Journal of Traumatic Stress*, 8, 675–90.

Foa, E.B., Steketee, G. and Young, M.C. (1984) Agoraphobia: Phenomenologic aspects, associated characteristics, and theoretical considerations. *Clinical Psychology Review*, 4, 431–57.

Fodor, E.M. (1994) Subclinical manifestations of psychosis-proneness, ego strength, and creativity. *Personality and Individual Differences*, 18(5), 635–43.

Fodor, J. (1983) *The Modularity of Mind*. Cambridge, MA: MIT Press.

Foerster, A., Roche, S., Wiesiolek, C., Chagas, A.P., Machado, G., Silva, E., Fregni, F. and Monte-Silva, K. (2013) Site-specific effects of mental practice combined with transcranial direct current stimulation on motor learning. *European Journal of Neuroscience*, 37, 786–94.

Foley, R. (2014) The case for characterising type-2 blindsight as a genuinely visual phenomenon. *Consciousness and Cognition*, 32, 56–67.

Folkman, S. and Lazarus, R.S. (1991) Coping and emotion. In A. Monat and R.S. Lazarus (eds) *Stress and Coping: An anthology*. New York: Columbia University Press.

Foltveld, P. (1995) Professional, psychology in Denmark. In A. Schorr and S. Saari (eds) *Psychology in Europe*. Gottingen: Hogrefe and Huber.

Fonagy, P., Twemlow, S.W., Vernberg, E., Sacco, F.C. and Little, T.D. (2005) Creating a peaceful school learning environment: the impact of an antibullying program on educational attainment in elementary schools. *Medical Science Monitor*, 11, CR317-25.

Fontana, A. and Rosenheck, R. (1993) A causal model of the etiology of war-related PTSD. *Journal of Traumatic Stress*, 6, 475-99.

Ford, T.E., Boxer, C.F., Armstrong, J. and Edel, J.R. (2008) More than 'just a joke': the prejudice-releasing function of sexist humor. *Personality and Social Psychology Bulletin*, 34(2), 159-70.

Ford, T.E., Wentzel, E.R. and Lorion, J. (2001) Effects of exposure to sexist humor on perceptions of normative tolerance of sexism. *European Journal of Social Psychology*, 31, 677-91.

Foreyt, J. and Goodrick, G.D. (1993) Evidence for success of behaviour modification in weight loss and control. *Annals of Internal Medicine*, 119, 698-701.

Forgacs, B., Lukacs, A. and Pleh, C. (2014) Lateralized processing of novel metaphors: Disentangling figurativeness and novelty. *Neuropsychologia*, 56, 101-9.

Forgas, J.P. (2007) When sad is better than happy: Negative affect can improve the quality and effectiveness of persuasive messages and social influence strategies. *Journal of Experimental Social Psychology*, 43, 513-28.

Forgas, J.P., Goldenberg, L. and Unkelbach, C. (2009) Can bad weather improve your memory? *Journal of Experimental Social Psychology*, 45, 254-7.

Formanowicz, M., Bedynska, S., Cisłak, A., Braun, F. and Sczesny, S. (2013) Side effects of gender-fair language: How feminine job titles influence the evaluation of female applicants. *European Journal of Social Psychology*, 43(1), 62-71.

Forsterling, F. (1988) *Attribution Theory in Clinical Psychology*. Chichester: Wiley.

Fortin, S., Godbout, L. and Braun, C.M.J. (2003) Cognitive structure of executive deficits in frontally lesioned head trauma patients performing activities of daily living. *Cortex*, 39, 273-91.

Foster, J.J. and Parker, I. (1995) *Carrying out Investigations in Psychology*. Leicester: BPS Books.

Fouts, G. and Burggraf, K. (1999) Television situation comedies: Female body images and verbal reinforcement. *Sex Roles*, 40, 473-81.

Fouts, R.S. (1983) Chimpanzee language and elephant tails: A theoretical synthesis. In J. de Luce and H.T. Wilder (eds) *Language in Primates: Perspectives and Implications*. New York: Springer-Verlag.

Fowler, J.H. and Christakis, N.A. (2009) Dynamic spread of happiness in a large social network: longitudinal analysis over 20 years in Framingham Heart Study. *British Medical Journal*, 337, 1-9.

Fox, A.B., Rosen, J. and Crawford, M. (2009) Distractions, distractions: does instant messaging affect college students' performance on a concurrent reading comprehension task? *CyberPsychology and Behavior*, 12(1), 51-3.

Fox, A.F. (1932) The relationship between chemical constitution and taste. *Proceedings of the National Academy of Sciences*, 18, 115-20.

Fox, C.J., Iaria, G. and Burton, J. (2009) Defining the face-processing network: Organization of the functional localizer in fMRI. *Human Brain Mapping*, 30, 1637-51.

Fox, J. and Jones, D. (2013) DSM-5 and bereavement: the loss of normal grief? *Journal of Counselling and Development*, 91, 113-19.

Fox, K.C.R., Nijeboer, S., Dixon, M.L., Floman, J.L., Ellamil, M., Rumak, S.P., Sedlmeier, P. and Christoff, K. (2014) Is meditation associated with altered brain structure? *Neuroscience and Biobehavioural Reviews*, 43, 48-73.

Fox, N.A. Rubin, K.H., Calkins, S.D., Marshall, T.R., Coplan, R.J., Porges, S.W., Long, J.M. and Stewart, S. (1995) Frontal activation asymmetry and social competence at four years of age. *Child Development*, 66, 1770-84.

Fox, N.A., Henderson, H.A., Rubin, K.H., Calkins, S.D. and Schmidt, L.A. (2001) Continuity and discontinuity of behavioural inhibition and exuberance: Psychophysiological and behavioural influences across the first four years of life. *Child Development*, 72(1), 1-21.

Fraigne, J.J., Grace, K.P., Horner, R.L. and Peever, J. (2014) Mechanisms of REM sleep in health and disease. *Current Opinion in Pulmonary Medicine*, 20, 527-32.

Frances, A.J. and Nardo, J.M. (2013) ICD-11 should not repeat the mistakes made by DSM-5. *British Journal of Psychiatry*, 203, 1-2.

Frances, A.J. and Widiger, T. (2012) Psychiatric diagnosis: Lessons from the DSM-IV past and cautions for the DSM-5 future. *Annual Review of Clinical Psychology*, 8, 109-30.

Francis, S., Rolls, E.T., Bowtell, R., McGlone, F., O'Doherty, J., Browning, A., Clare, S. and Smith, E. (1999) The representation of pleasant touch in the brain and its relationship with taste and olfactory areas. *NeuroReport*, 10, 453-9.

Frank, S., Kullmann, S. and Veit, R. (2013) Food related processes in the insular cortex. *Frontiers in Human Neuroscience*, 7, 499.

Frankland, P.W., Bontempi, B., Talton, L.E., Kaczmarek, L. and Silva, A.J. (2004) The involvement of the anterior cingulated cortex in remote contextual fear memory. *Science*, 304, 881-3.

Franklin, J.C. (2016) Risk factors for suicidal thoughts and behaviors. *Psychological Bulletin*, 143, 187-232.

Franks, N.P. and Lieb, W.R. (1998) The molecular basis of general anesthesia: current ideas. In S.R. Hameroff, A.W. Kaszniak and A.C. Scott (eds) *Towards a Science of Consciousness II*. Cambridge, MA: MIT Press.

Frauendorfer, D., Mast, M.S., Nguyen, L. and Gatica-Perez, D. (2014) Nonverbal social sensing in action: Unobtrusive recording and extracting of nonverbal behavior in social interactions illustrated with a research example. *Journal of Nonverbal Behavior*, 38(2), 231-45.

Frauendorfer, D., Schmid Mast, M., Nguyen, L. and Gatica-Perez, D. (in press) Nonverbal social sensing in action: Unobtrusive recording and extracting of nonverbal behavior in social interactions illustrated with a research example. *Journal of Nonverbal Behavior*, 38, 231-45.

Frederick, D.A., Peplau, L.A. and Lever, J. (2006) The swimsuit issue: Correlates of body image in a sample of 52, 677 heterosexual adults. *Body Image*, 3, 413-19.

Frederickson, B.L. and Roberts, T.A. (1997) Objectification theory: Towards understanding of women's lived experiences and mental health risks. *Psychology of Women Quarterly*, 21, 173-8.

Freedman, J.L. and Fraser, S.C. (1966) Compliance without pressure: The foot-in-the-door technique. *Journal of Personality and Social Psychology*, 4, 195-203.

Freedman, R. (2013) The initial field trials of DSM-5: New blooms and old thorns. *American Journal of Psychiatry*, 170(1), 1-5.

Freedy, J.R., Saladin, M.E., Kilpatrick, D.G., Resnick, H.S. and Saunders, B.E. (1994) Understanding acute psychological distress following natural disaster. *Journal of Traumatic Stress*, 7, 257-73.

Freeman, J.B., Rule, N.O., Adams, R.B. and Ambady, N. (2009) Culture shapes a mesolimbic response to signals of dominance and subordination that associates with behavior. *Neuroimage*, 47, 353-9.

Fregni, F., Orsati, F., Pedrosa, W., Fecteau, S., Tome, F.A.M., Nitsche, M.A., Mecca, T., Macedo, E.C., Pascual-Leone, A. and Boggio, P.S. (2008) Transcranial direct current stimulation of the prefrontal cortex modulates the desire for specific foods. *Appetite*, 51, 34-41.

French, J.R.P. (1944) Organised and unorganised groups under fear and frustration. *University of Iowa Studies of Child Welfare*, 20, 231-308.

French, S.A., Hennrikus, D.J. and Jeffrey, R.W. (1996) Smoking status, dietary intake, and physical activity in a sample of working adults. *Health Psychology*, 15(6), 448-54.

Freud, S. (1900) *The Interpretation of Dreams.* London: George Allen & Unwin.

Freud, S. (1933) *New Introductory Lectures on Psychoanalysis* (J. Strachey, trans.) New York: W.W. Norton.

Freund, P.A. and Kasten, N. (2012) How smart do you think you are? A meta-analysis on the validity of self-estimates of cognitive ability. *Psychological Bulletin*, 138, 296–321.

Frey, K.S., Hirschstein, M.K., Edstrom, L.V. and Snell, J.L. (2009) Observed reductions in school bullying, nonbullying aggression and destructive bystander behavior. *Journal of Educational Psychology*, 101, 466–81.

Fridlund, A.J. (1992) The behavioural ecology and sociality of human faces. In M.S. Clark (ed.) *Emotion: Review of personality and social psychology*, Vol. 13. Newbury Park, CA: Sage.

Fridlund, A.J. (1994) *Human Facial Expression: An evolutionary view.* San Diego, CA: Academic Press.

Fridriksson, J., Yourganov, G., Bonilha, L., Basilakos, A., Den Ouden, D-B. and Rorden, C. (2017) Revealing the dual streams of speech processing. *PNAS*, 113, 15108–13.

Friebel, G. and Seabright, P. (2011) Do women have longer conversations? Telephone evidence of gendered communication strategies. *Journal of Economic Psychology*, 32, 348–56.

Fried, E.I. and Nesse, R.M. (2015) Depression is not a consistent syndrome: An investigation of unique symptom patterns in the STAR*D study. *Journal of Affective Disorders*, 172, 96–102.

Friederici, A.D. (2002) Towards a neural basis of auditory sentence processing. *Trends in Cognitive Science*, 6, 78–84.

Friederici, A.D. (2012) Language development and the ontogeny of the dorsal pathway. *Frontiers in Human Neuroscience*, 4, 3.

Friederici, A.D. and Singer, W. (2015) Grounding language processing on basic neurophysiological principles. *TICS*, 18, 325–38.

Friedlmayer, S. and Rossler, E. (1995) Professional identity and public image of Austrian psychologists. In A. Schorr and S. Saari (eds) *Psychology in Europe*. Göttingen: Hogrefe & Huber.

Friedman, H.S. and Kern, M.L. (2014) Personality, well-being, and health. *Annual Review of Psychology*, 65, 719–42.

Friedman, H.S., Kern, M.L., Hampson, S.E. and Duckworth, A.L. (2014) A new lifespan approach to conscientiousness and health. *Developmental Psychology*, 50, 1377–89.

Friedman, H.S., Tucker, J.S., Tomlinson-Keasey, C., Schwartz, J.E., Wingard, D.L. and Criqui, M.H. (1993) Does childhood personality predict longevity? *Journal of Personality and Social Psychology*, 65, 176–85.

Friedman, M. and Rosenman, R.H. (1959) Association of specific overt behavior patterns with blood and cardiovascular findings: Blood cholesterol level, blood clotting time, incidence of arcus senilis, and clinical coronary artery disease. *Journal of the American Medical Association*, 162, 1286–96.

Friedman, M.I., Tordoff, M.G. and Kare, M.R. (1991) *Chemical Senses. Vol. 4: Appetite and Nutrition.* New York: Dekker.

Friedman, M.I., Tordoff, M.G. and Ramirez, I. (1986) Integrated metabolic control of food intake. *Brain Research Bulletin*, 17, 855–9.

Friesen, W.V. (1972) Cultural differences in facial expression in a social situation: an experimental test of the concept of display rules. Doctoral dissertation, University of California, San Francisco.

Frijda, N.H. (1988) The laws of emotion. *American Psychologist*, 43, 349–58.

Frimer, J.A. and Sinclair, L. (2016) Moral heroes look up and to the right. *Personality and Social Psychology Bulletin*, 42, 400–10.

Frith, U. (1989) *Autism: Explaining the enigma.* Oxford: Blackwell.

Frith, U. and Happé, F. (1994) Autism: Beyond 'theory of mind'. *Cognition*, 50, 115–32.

Frodi, A., Grolnick, W. and Bridges, L. (1985) Maternal correlates of stability and change in infant-mother attachment. *Infant Mental Health Journal*, 6, 60–67.

Fromkin, V. (1988) The grammatical aspects of speech errors. In F.J. Newmeyer (ed.) *Linguistics: The Cambridge survey*, Vol. 11. Cambridge: Cambridge University Press.

Fromkin, V. (1993) Speech production. In J. Berko Gleason and N.B. Ratner (eds) *Psycholinguistics.* Fort Worth, TX: Holt, Rinehart & Winston.

Fromkin, V., Krashen, S., Curtiss, S., Rigler, S. and Rigler, M. (1972/73) The development of language in Genie: A case of language acquisition beyond the 'critical period.' *Brain and Language*, 1, 81–107.

Fryer, R.G. and Levitt, S.D. (2010) An empirical analysis of the gender gap in mathematics. *American Economic Journal – Applied Economics*, 2, 210–40.

Fu, C.H.Y. *et al.* (2008) Neural responses to sad facial expressions in major depression. *Biological Psychiatry*, 64, 505–12.

Fujioka, T., Ross, B., Kakigi, R., Pantev, C. and Trainor, L.J. (2006) One year of musical training affects development of auditory cortical-evoked fields in young children. *Brain*, 129, 2593–608.

Fujita, K., Henderson, M.D., Eng, J., Trope, Y. and Liberman, N. (2006) Spatial distance and mental construal of social events. *Psychological Science*, 17, 278–82.

Fulbright, R.K., Skudlarski, P., Lacadie, C.M., Warrenburg, S., Bowers, A.A., Gore, J.C. and Wexler, B.E. (1998) Functional MR imaging of regional brain responses to pleasant and unpleasant odors. *American Journal of Neuroradiology*, 19(9), 1721–6.

Fuller, E. and Hawkins, V. (2014) *Smoking, drinking and drug use among young people in England 2013.* London: Health and Social Care Information Centre.

Funder, D.C. (2009) Persons, behaviors and situations: an agenda for personality psychology in the postwar era. *Journal of Research in Personality*, 43, 120–6.

Fung, H.H. and Carstensen, L.L. (2003) Sending memorable messages to the old: age differences in preferences and memory for advertisements. *Journal of Personality and Social Psychology*, 85, 163–78.

Furnham, A. (1981) Personality and activity preferences. *British Journal of Social Psychology*, 20, 57–68.

Furnham, A. (1983) Attributions for affluence. *Personality and Individual Differences*, 4, 31–40.

Furnham, A. (1992) Prospective psychology students' knowledge of psychology. *Psychological Reports*, 70, 375–82.

Furnham, A. (1993) A comparison between psychology and non-psychology students' misperceptions of the subject. *Journal of Social Behaviour and Personality*, 8(2), 311–22.

Furnham, A. (1994) The Barnum effect in medicine. *Complementary Therapies in Medicine*, 2, 1–4.

Furnham, A. (1996) *All in the Mind: The essence of mind.* London: Whurr.

Furnham, A. (2003) Belief in a just world: Research progress over the past decade. *Personality and Individual Differences*, 34, 795–817.

Furnham, A. (2009) Sex differences in mate selection preferences. *Personality and Individual Differences*, 47, 262–7.

Furnham, A. and Briggs, J. (1993) Ethical ideology and moral choice: A study concerning the allocation of medical resources. *Journal of Social Behaviour and Personality*, 8, 87–98.

Furnham, A. and Gasson, L. (1998) Sex differences in parental estimates of their children's intelligence. *Sex Roles*, 38, 151–62.

Furnham, A. and Hughes, D.J. (2014) Myths and misconceptions in popular psychology: Comparing psychology and the general public. *Teaching of Psychology*, 41, 256–61.

Furnham, A. and Rawles, R. (1995) Sex differences in the estimation of intelligence. *Journal of Social Behaviour and Personality*, 10, 741–5.

Furnham, A. and Schofield, S. (1987) Accepting personality test feedback: A review of the Barnum effect. *Current Psychological Research and Reviews*, 6(2), 162–78.

Furnham, A., Arteche, A., Chamorro-Premuzic, T., Keser, A. and Swami, V. (2009) Self- and other-estimates of multiple abilities in Britain and Turkey: A cross-cultural comparison of subjective ratings of intelligence. *International Journal of Psychology*, 44, 434–42.

Furnham, A., Fong, G. and Martin, G.N. (1999a) Sex and cross-cultural differences in the estimated multi-faceted intelligence quotient score for self, parents and siblings. *Personality and Individual Differences*, 26, 1025–34.

Furnham, A., Hosoe, T. and Tang, T.L.P. (2002a) Male hubris and female humility? A crosscultural study of ratings of self, parental, and sibling multiple intelligence in America, Britain, and Japan. *Intelligence*, 30, 101–15.

Furnham, A., Lavancy, M. and McClelland, A. (2001) Waist-to-hip ratio and facial attractiveness: A pilot study. *Personality and Individual Differences*, 30, 491–502.

Furnham, A., Rakow, T., Sarmany-Schuller, I. and De Fruyt, F. (1999b) European differences in self-perceived multiple intelligences. *European Psychologist*, 4(3), 131–8.

Furnham, A., Simmons, K. and McClelland, A. (2000) Decisions concerning the allocation of scarce medical resources. *Journal of Social Behaviour and Personality*, 15, 185–200.

Furnham, A., Thomson, K. and McClelland, A. (2002b) The allocation of scarce medical resources across medical conditions. *Psychology and Psychotherapy: Theory, Research and Practice*, 75, 189–203.

Furrow, D. and Nelson, K. (1986) A further look at the motherese hypothesis: A reply to Gleitman, Newport and Gleitman. *Journal of Child Language*, 13, 163–76.

Furrow, D., Nelson, K. and Benedict, H. (1979) Mothers' speech to children and syntactic development: Some simple relationships. *Journal of Child Language*, 6, 423–42.

Fusaroli, R., Bahrami, B., Olsen, K., Roepstroff, A., Rees, G., Frith, C. and Tylen, K. (2012) Coming to terms: Quantifying the benefits of linguistic coordination. *Psychological Science*, 23, 931–9.

Fusar-Poli, P., Crippa, J.A, Bhattacharyya, S., Borgwardt, S.J., Allen, P., Martin-Santos, R., Seal, M., Surguladze, A., O'Carrol, C., Atakan, Z., Zuardi, A.W. and McGuire, P.K. (2009) Distinct effects of delta 9-tetrahydrocannabinol and cannabinol on neural activation during emotional processing. *Archives of General Psychiatry*, 66, 95–105.

Fuster, J.J. and Andres, V. (2006) Telomere biology and cardiovascular disease. *Circulation Research*, 99, 1167–80.

Fuster, J.M. (1995) *Memory in the Cerebral Cortex: An empirical approach to neural networks in the human and nonhuman primate.* Cambridge, MA: MIT Press.

G

Gabay, Y., Schiff, R. and Vakil, E. (2012) Attentional requirements during acquisition and consolidation of a skill in normal readers and developmental dyslexics. *Neuropsychology*, 26, 744–57.

Gabay, Y., Schiff, R. and Vakil, E. (2012) Dissociation between online and offline learning in developmental dyslexia. *Journal of Clinical and Experimental Neuropsychology*, 34(3), 279–88.

Gabryel, B. and Trzeciak, H.I. (1994) Nootropics: Pharmacological properties and therapeutic use. *Polish Journal of Pharmacology*, 46, 383–94.

Gaertner, L. and Insko, C.A. (2000) Intergroup discrimination in the minimal group paradigm: Categorization, reciprocation, or fear? *Journal of Personality and Social Psychology*, 79, 77–94.

Gaertner, L., Sedikides, C. and Graetz, K. (1999) In search of self-definition: Motivational primacy of the individual self, motivational primacy of the collective self, or collective primacy? *Journal of Personality and Social Psychology*, 76, 5–18.

Gaertner, L., Sedikides, C., Vevea, J.L. and Iuzzini, J. (2002) The 'I', the 'we' and the 'when': A meta-analysis of motivational primacy in self-definition. *Journal of Personality and Social Psychology*, 83, 574–91.

Gaertner, S.L. and Dovidio, J.F. (1986) The aversive form of racism. In J.F. Dovidio and S.L. Gaertner (eds) *Prejudice, Discrimination, and Racism.* New York: Academic Press, pp. 61–89.

Gaertner, S.L., Dovidio, J.F., Anastasio, P.A., Bachman, B.A. and Rust, M.C. (1993) The common ingroup identity model: recategorization and the reduction of intergroup bias. *European Review of Social Psychology*, 4, 1–26.

Gaetz, W., Bloy, L., Wang, D.J., Port, R.G., Blaskey, L., Levy, S.E. and Roberts, T.P. (2013) GABA estimation in the brains of children on the autism spectrum: Measurement precision and regional cortical variation. *Neuroimage*, S1053–8119.

Gainotti, G. (2000) What the locus of brain lesion tells us about the nature of the cognitive defect underlying category-specific disorders: A review. *Cortex*, 36, 539–59.

Gaitán, A., Garolera, M., Cerulla, N., Chico, G., Rodriguez-Querol, M. and Canela-Soler, J. (2013) Efficacy of an adjunctive computer-based cognitive training program in amnestic mild cognitive impairment and Alzheimer's disease: a single-blind, randomized clinical trial. *International Journal of Geriatric Psychiatry*, 28(1), 91–9.

Galaburda, A.M. (1999) Albert Einstein's brain. *The Lancet*, 354, 1821.

Gale, C., Cukic, I., Batty, G. D., McIntosh, A. M., Weiss, A., & Deary, I. J. (2017). When is higher Neuroticism protective against premature death? *Findings from the UK Biobank. Psychological Science*, in press.

Galizio, M. (1979) Contingency-shaped and rule-governed behavior: Instructional control of human loss avoidance. *Journal of the Experimental Analysis of Behavior*, 31, 53–70.

Gallace, A., Boschin, E. and Spence, C. (2011) On the taste of 'Bouba' and 'Kiki': An exploration of word-food associations in neurologically normal participants. *Cognitive Neuroscience*, 2(1), 34–46.

Gallucci, M. (2003) I sell seashells by the seashore and my name is Jack. *Journal of Personality and Social Psychology*, 85, 789–99.

GALLUP (2015) Evolution, creationism, intelligent design. www.gallup.com/poll/21814/evolution-creationism-intelligent-design.aspx

Galton, F. (1869) *Hereditary Genius: An inquiry into its laws and consequences.* Cleveland, OH: World Publishing.

Galton, F. (1878) Composite portraits. *Nature*, 18, 97–100.

Galton, F. (1883) *Inquiries into Human Faculty and Its Development.* London: Macmillan.

Galuschka, K., Ise, E., Krick, K. and Schulte-Krone, G. (2014) Effectiveness of treatment approaches for children and adolescents with reading disabilities: A meta-analysis of randomised controlled trials. *PLoS ONE*, 9, e89990.

Gamer, M., Bauermann, T., Stoeter, P. and Vossel, G. (2007) Covariations among fMRI, skin conductance and behavioural data during processing of concealed information. *Human Brain Mapping*, 28, 1287–301.

Gangestad, S.W., Garver-Apgar, C.E., Simpson, J.A. and Cousins, A.J. (2007) Changes in women's mate preferences across the ovulatory cycle. *Journal of Personality and Social Psychology*, 92, 151–63.

Gangestad, S.W., Simpson, J.A., Cousins, A.J., Garver-Apgar, C.E. and Christensen, P.N. (2004) Women's preferences for male behavioural displays change across the menstrual cycle. *Psychological Science*, 15(3), 203–7.

Ganley, C.M., Mingle, L.A., Ryan, A.M. and Ryan, K. (2013) An examination of stereotype threat effects on girls' mathematics performance. *Developmental Psychology*, 49, 186.

Ganong, W.F. (1980) Phonetic categorization in auditory word perception. *Journal of Experimental Psychology: Human Perception and Performance*, 6, 110–25.

Gao, W., Alcauter, S., Elton, A., Hernandez-Castillo, C.R., Smith, J. K., Ramirez, J. and Lin, W. (2015) Functional network development during the first year: relative sequence and socioeconomic correlations. *Cerebral Cortex*, 25(9), 2919–28.

Garcia, J. and Koelling, R. (1966) Relation of cue to consequence in avoidance learning. *Psychonomic Science*, 4, 123–4.

Garcia, M.M., Shaw, D.S., Winslow, E.B. and Yaggi, K.E. (2000) Destructive sibling conflict and the development of conduct problems in young boys. *Developmental Psychology*, 36, 44–53.

García-Rubio, M.A., Picazo-Tadeo, A.J. and González-Gómez, F. (2011) Does a red shirt improve sporting performance? Evidence from Spanish football. *Applied Economics Letters*, 18(11), 1001–4.

Garcia-Vera, M.P., Sanz, J. and Guiterrez, S. (2016) A systematic review of the literature on post traumatic stress disorder in victims of terrorist attacks. *Psychological Reports*, 119, 328–59.

Gardner, H. (1983) *Frames of Mind*. New York: Basic Books.

Gardner, R.A. and Gardner, B.T. (1969) Teaching sign language to a chimpanzee. *Science*, 165, 664–72.

Gardner, R.A. and Gardner, B.T. (1975) Early signs of language in child and chimpanzee. *Science*, 187, 752–3.

Gardner, R.A. and Gardner, B.T. (1978) Comparative psychology and language acquisition. *Annals of the New York Academy of Sciences*, 309, 37–76.

Gardner, R.M. and Brown, D.L. (2012) A test of contemporary misconceptions in psychology. *Learning and Individual Differences*, 24, 211–15.

Garfield, S.L. and Bergin, A.E. (1994) Introduction and historical overview. In A.E. Bergin and S.L. Garfield (eds) *Handbook of Psychotherapy and Behaviour Change*. New York: Wiley.

Garrard, P., Maloney, L.M., Hodges, J.R. and Patterson, K. (2005) The effects of very early Alzheimer's disease on the characteristics of writing by a renowned author. *Brain*, 128, 250–60.

Garrett, B. (2011) *Convicting the Innocent: Where criminal prosecutions go wrong*. MA: Harvard University Press.

Garrett, V., Brantly, P., Jones, G. and McNight, G. (1991) The relation between daily stress and Crohn's disease. *Journal of Behavioral Medicine*, 34, 187–96.

Garvey, C. (1977) *Play*. Cambridge, MA: Harvard University Press.

Gass, K., Jenkins, J. and Dunn, J. (2007) Are sibling relationships protective? A longitudinal study. *Journal of Child Psychology and Psychiatry*, 48(2), 167–75.

Gatchel, R.J., Baum, A. and Krantz, D.S. (1989) *An Introduction to Health Psychology* (2nd edn). New York: Newbery Award Records.

Gathercole, S.E. and Baddeley, A.D. (1990) The role of phonological memory in vocabulary acquisition – a study of young children learning new names. *British Journal of Psychology*, 81, 439–54.

Gathercole, S.E., Willis, C., Emslie, H. and Baddeley, A.D. (1992) Phonological memory and vocabulary development during the early school years: A longitudinal study. *Developmental Psychology*, 28, 887–98.

Gaudiano, B.A., Brown, L.A. and Miller, I.W. (2011) Let your intuition be your guide? Individual differences in the evidence-based practice attitudes of psychotherapists. *Journal of Evaluation in Clinical Practice*, 17, 628–34.

Gaudio, S. and Quattrocchi, C. (2012) Neural basis of a multidimensional model of body image distortion in anorexia nervosa. *Neuroscience and Biobehavioural Review*, 36, 1839–47.

Gazzaley, A., Cooney, J.W., Rissman, J. and D'Esposito, M. (2005) Top-down suppression deficit underlies working memory impairment in normal aging. *Nature Neuroscience*, 8, 1298–300.

Gazzaniga, M.S. (1970) *The Bisected Brain*. New York: Appleton-Century-Crofts.

Gazzaniga, M.S. (1995) *The Cognitive Neurosciences*. Cambridge, MA: MIT Press.

Gazzaniga, M.S. (1998) The split-brain revisited. *Scientific American Mind*, July, 35–9.

Gazzaniga, M.S., Eliassen, J.C., Nisenson, L., Wessinger, C.M., Fendrich, R. and Baynes, K. (1996) Collaboration between the hemispheres of a callosotomy patient. *Brain*, 119, 1255–62.

Gelfand, M.J. and Christakopoulou, S. (1999) Culture and negotiator cognition: judgement accuracy and negotiation processes in individualistic and collectivistic cultures. *Organisational Behavior and Human Decision Processes*, 79, 248–69.

Gelfand, M.J., Erez, M. and Aycan, Z. (2007) Cross-cultural organizational behavior. *Annual Review of Psychology*, 58, 479–514.

Gelfand, M.J., Nishi, L.H., Holcombe, K.M., Dyer, N., Ohbuchi, K.I. and Fukuno, M. (2001) Cultural influences on cognitive representations of conflict: interpretations of conflict episodes in the United States and Japan. *Journal of Applied Psychology*, 86, 1059–74.

Gellaty, A. (1987) Acquisition of a concept of logical necessity. *Human Development*, 39, 32–47.

Gelman, R. (1972) Logical capacity of very young children: Number invariance rules. *Child Development*, 43, 75–90.

Gelman, R. and Shatz, M. (1978) Appropriate speech adjustments: The operation of conversational constraints on talk in two-year-olds. In M. Lewsi and L.A. Rosenblum (eds) *Interaction, Conversation, and the Development of Language*. New York: Wiley.

Gendron, M., Roberston, D. and Barrett, L.F. (2015) Cultural variation in emotion perception is real: A response to Sauter, Eisner, Ekman & Scott (2015) *Psychological Science*, 1–3.

Gendron, M., Roberston, D., van der Vyver, J.M. and Barrett, L.F. (2014a) Cultural relativity in perceiving emotion from vocalizations. *Psychological Science*, 25, 911–20.

Gendron, M., Roberston, D., van der Vyver, J.M. and Barrett, L.F. (2014b) Perceptions of emotions from facial expressions are not culturally universal. *Emotion*, 14, 251–62.

Genevsky, A., Vastfjall, D., Slovic, P. and Knutson, B. (2013) Neural underpinnings of the identifiable victim effect: Affect shifts preferences for giving. *The Journal of Neuroscience*, 33, 17188–96.

Gentilucci, M. and Corballis, M.C. (2006) From manual gesture to speech: A gradual transition. *Neuroscience and Biobehavioral Reviews*, 30, 949–60.

Georgas, J. (1995) Psychology in Greece. In A. Schorr and S. Saari (eds) *Psychology in Europe*. Göttingen: Hogrefe & Huber.

Georgas, J. (2006) The education of psychologists in Greece. *International Journal of Psychology*, 41(1), 29–34.

Geranmayeh, F., Brownsett, S.L. and Wise, R.J.S. (2014) Task-induced brain activity in aphasic stroke patients: what is driving recovery? *Brain*, 137, 2632–48.

Gerbino, L., Oleshansky, M. and Gershon, S. (1978) Clinical use and mode of action of lithium. In M.A. Lipton, A. DiMascio and K.F. Killam (eds) *Psychopharmacology: A generation of progress*. New York: Raven Press.

Gerbner, G., Gross, L. and Morgan, M. (2002) Growing up with television: Cultivation processes. In J. Bryant and D. Zillman (eds), *Media effects: Advances in theory and research* (2nd edn). Mahwah, NJ: Lawrence Erlbaum Associates.

Gerdle, B., Björk, J., Cöster, L., Henriksson, K.G., Henriksson, C. and Bengtsson, A. (2008) Prevalence of widespread pain and associations with work status: a population study. *BMC Musculoskeletal Disorders*, 9(1), 102.

Gergely, G., Bekkering, H. and Kiraly, I. (2002) Rational imitation in preverbal infants. *Nature*, 415, 755.

Gerlai, R. (2001) Behavioural tests of hippocampal function: simple paradigms complex problems. *Behavioural Brain Research*, 125, 269–77.

Germine, L.T., Duchaine, B. and Nakayama, K. (2011) Where cognitive development and aging meet: Face learning ability peaks after age 30. *Cognition*, 118, 201–10.

Gerson, R. and Damon, W. (1978) Moral understanding and children's conduct. In W. Damon (ed.) *Moral Development: New directions in child development*. San Francisco, CA: Jossey-Bass.

Geschwind, D.H. (2011) Genetics of autism spectrum disorders. *Trends in Cognitive Sciences*, 15, 409–16.

Getov, S., Kanai, R., Bhrami, B. and Rees, G. (2014) Human brain structure predicts individual differences in preconscious evaluation of facial dominance and trustworthiness. *SCAN*, 10, 690–700.

Gettler, L.T., McDade, T.W., Feranil, A.B. and Kuzawa, C.W. (2011) Longitudinal evidence that fatherhood decreases testosterone in human males. *Proceedings of the National Academy of Sciences*, 108(39), 16194–9.

Geuter, S., Eippert, F., Attar, C.H. and Büchel, C. (2013) Cortical and subcortical responses to high and low effective placebo treatments. *Neuroimage*, 67, 227–36.

Ghatan, P.H., Hshieh, J.C., Petersson, K.M., Stone-Elander, S. and Ingvar, M. (1998) Coexistence of attention-based facilitation and inhibition in the human cortex. *Neuroimage*, 7(1), 23–9.

Gialluisi, A., Guadalupe, T., Francks, C. and Fisher, S.E. (2016) Neuroimaging genetic analyses of novel candidate genes associated with reading and language. *Brain & Language*, in press.

Giampietro, M. and Cavallera, G.M. (2007) Morning and evening types and creative thinking. *Personality and Individual Differences*, 42, 453–63.

Gibbons, F.X. and Eggleston, T.J. (1996) Smoker networks and the 'typical smoker': A prospective analysis of smoking cessation. *Health Psychology*, 15(6), 469–77.

Gibbs, G. (1992) *Improving the Quality of Student Learning*. Bristol: Technical and Educational Services.

Gibbs, J.C., Basinger, K.S., Grime, R.L. and Snarey, J.R. (2007) Moral judgement development across cultures: revisiting Kohlberg's universality claims. *Developmental Review*, 27, 443–500.

Gibbs, J.C., Widaman, K.F. and Colby, A. (1982) Construction and validation of a simplified, group-administerable equivalent to the moral judgment interview. *Child Development*, 53, 895–910.

Gibson, B. and Zielaskowski, K. (2013) Subliminal priming of winning images prompts increased betting in slot machine play. *Journal of Applied Social Psychology*, 43, 106–15.

Gibson, E.J. and Walk, R.R. (1960) The 'visual cliff'. *Scientific American Mind*, 202, 2–9.

Gibson, H.B. (1992) *The Emotional and Sexual Life of Older People*. London: Chapman & Hall.

Gibson, J.J. (1950) *The Perception of the Visual World*. Boston, MA: Houghton Mifflin.

Gibson, J.J. (1966) *The Senses Considered as Perceptual Systems*. Boston, MA: Houghton Mifflin.

Gibson, J.J. (1979) *The Ecological Approach to Visual Perception*. Boston, MA: Houghton Mifflin.

Gibson, J.J. (1982) Affordances and behaviour. In E.S. Reed and R.K. Jones (eds) *Reasons for Realism: Selected papers of J.J. Gibson*. Hillsdale, NJ: Lawrence Erlbaum Associates.

Giedd, J.N. and Rapoport, J.L. (2010) Structural MRI of pediatric brain development: what have we learned and where are we going? *Neuron*, 67(5), 728–34.

Gilbert, A.L. *et al.* (2006) Whorf hypothesis is supported in the right visual field but not the left. *Proceeding of the National Academy of Sciences*, 103, 489–94.

Gilbert, D.T. and Malone, P.S. (1995) The correspondence bias. *Psychological Bulletin*, 117, 21–38.

Giles, H. and Coupland, N. (1991) *Language: Contexts and Consequences*. Milton Keynes: Open University Press.

Giles, H. and Johnson, P. (1987) Ethnolinguistic identity theory: A social psychological approach to language maintenance. *International Journal of the Sociology of Language*, 68, 69–91.

Gillberg, C. and Coleman, M. (1992) *The Biology of Autistic Syndromes* (2nd edn). London: MacKeith Press.

Gilligan, C.F. (1977) In a different voice: Women's conceptions of self and morality. *Harvard Educational Review*, 47, 481–517.

Gilligan, C.F. (1982) *In a Different Voice*. Cambridge, MA: Harvard University Press.

Gilman, A. (1937) The relation between blood osmotic pressure, fluid distribution and voluntary water intake. *American Journal of Physiology*, 120, 323–8.

Gingerich, A.C. and Lineweaver, T.T. (2014) OMG! Texting in class = U Fail: (Empirical evidence that text messaging during class disrupts comprehension. *Teaching of Psychology*, 41, 44–51.

Gingnell, M., Morell, A., Bannbers, E. and Wikstrom, J. (2012) Menstrual cycle effects on amygdala reactivity to emotional stimulation in premenstrual dysphoric disorder. *Hormones and Behavior*, 62, 400–6.

Giraud, A.L. and Price, C.J. (2001) The constraints functional neuroimaging places on classical models of auditory word processing. *Journal of Cognitive Neuroscience*, 13, 754–65.

Gironell, A., de la Calzada, M.D., Sagales, T. and Barraquer-Bordas, L. (1995) Absence of REM sleep and altered non-REM sleep caused by a haematoma in the pontine tegmentum. *Journal of Neurology, Neurosurgery and Psychiatry*, 59, 195–6.

Glasser, M.F., Coalson, T.S., Robinson, E.C., Hacker, C.D., Harwell, J., Yacoub, E., Ugurbil, K., Andersson, J., Beckmann, C.F., Jenkinson, M., Smith, S.M. and Van Essen, D.C. (2016), A multi-modal parcellation of human cerebral cortex. *Nature*, 536, 171–8.

Glessner, J.T. *et al.* (2009) Autism genome-wide copy number variation reveals ubiquitin and neuronal genes. *Nature*, 459, 569–73.

Glisky, E.L. (1997) Rehabilitation of memory disorders: Tapping into preserved mechanisms. *Brain and Cognition*, 35(3), 291–2.

Global Deception Research Team (2006) A world of lies. *Journal of Cross-Cultural Psychology*, 37(1), 60–74.

Glowinski, A.L. *et al.* (2003) Genetic epidemiology of self-reported lifetime DSM-IV major depressive disorder in a population-based twin sample of female adolescents. *Journal Child Psychology and Psychiatry*, 44, 988–96.

Gluck, M.A. and Myers, C.E. (1995) Representation and association in memory: A neurocomputational view of hippocampal function. *Current Directions in Psychological Science*, 4, 23–9.

Glynn, L.M. and Sandman, C.A. (2011) Prenatal origins of neurological development: a critical period for fetus and mother. *Current Directions in Psychological Science*, 20, 384–9.

Gobbini, M.I. and Haxby, J.V. (2007) Neural systems for recognition of familiar faces. *Neuropsychologia*, 45, 32–41.

Godden, D.R. and Baddeley, A.D. (1975) Context-dependent memory in two natural environments: On land and under water. *British Journal of Psychology*, 66, 325–31.

Goedert, M. and Spillantini, M.G. (2006) A century of Alzheimer's disease. *Science*, 314, 777–81.

Goel, V. (2003) Evidence for dual neural pathways for syllogistic reasoning. *Psychologica*, 32, 301–9.

Goel, V. (2007) Anatomy of deductive reasoning. *Trends in Cognitive Sciences*, 11(10), 435–41.

Goel, V. and Dolan, R.J. (2001) Functional neuroanatomy of three-term relational reasoning. *Neuropsychologia*, 39, 901–9.

Goel, V. et al. (2000) Dissociation of mechanisms underlying syllogistic reasoning. *Neuroimage*, 12, 504–14.

Goel, V., Gold, B., Kapur, S. and Houle, S. (1997) The seats of reason? An imaging study of deductive and inductive reasoning. *NeuroReport*, 8, 1305–10.

Goel, V., Gold, B., Kapur, S. and Houle, S. (1998) Neuroanatomical correlates of human reasoning. *Journal of Cognitive Neuroscience*, 10(3), 293–302.

Goh, J.O., Leshikar, E.D., Sutton, B.P., Tan, J.C., Sim, S.K., Hebrank, A.C. and Park, D.C. (2010) Culture differences in neural processing of faces and houses in the ventral visual cortex. *Social Cognitive and Affective Neuroscience*, 5(2–3), 227–35.

Goldacre, B. (2008) *Bad Science.* London: Fourth Estate

Goldberg, L.R. (1993) The structure of phenotypic personality traits. *American Psychologist*, 48, 26–34.

Goldberg, R.J. and Steury, S. (2001) Depression in the workplace: Costs and barriers to treatment. *Psychiatric Services*, 52(12), 1639–43.

Golde, T.E., Schneider, L.S. and Koo, E. H. (2011) Anti-aβ therapeutics in Alzheimer's disease: the need for a paradigm shift. *Neuron*, 69(2), 203–13.

Goldin-Meadow, S. and Feldman, H. (1977) The development of language-like communication without a language model. *Science*, 197, 401–3.

Goldsmith, H.H. and Alansky, J.A. (1987) Maternal and infant predictors of attachment: A meta-analytic review. *Journal of Consulting and Clinical Psychology*, 55, 805–16.

Goldstein, D., Hahn, C.S., Hasher, L., Wiprzycka, U.J. and Zelazo, P.D. (2007) Time of day, intellectual performance, and behavioural problems in Morning versus Evening type adolescents: Is there a synchrony effect? *Personality and Individual Differences*, 42, 431–40.

Goldstein, D., Haldane, D. and Mitchell, C. (1990) Sex differences in visuo-spatial ability: The role of performance factors. *Memory and Cognition*, 18, 546–50.

Goldstein, E.B. (2007) *Sensation and Perception* (7th edn). Belmont, CA: Thompson.

Goldstein, N.J., Cialdini, R.B. and Griskevicius, V. (2008) A room with a viewpoint: using social norms to motivate environmental conservation in hotels. *Journal of Consumer Research*, 35, 472–82.

Goldstone, R.L., Medink, D.L. and Gentner, D. (1991) Relational similarity and the nonindependence of features in similarity judgments. *Cognitive Psychology*, 23, 222–62.

Goleman, D. (1995) *Emotional Intelligence.* New York: Bantam Books.

Goleman, D. (1998) *Working with Emotional Intelligence.* New York: Bantam Books.

Golle, J., Mast, F.W. and Lobmaier, J.S. (2014) Something to smile about: The interrelationship between attractiveness and emotional expression. *Cognition and Emotion*, 28, 298–310.

Golombok, S. et al. (2008) Developmental trajectories of sex-typed behaviour in boys and girls: a longitudinal general population study of children aged 2.5–8 years. *Child Development*, 79, 1583–93.

Gonen-Yaacovi, G., de Souza, L., Levy, R., Urbanski, M., Josse, G. and Volle, E. (2013) Rostral and caudal prefrontal contributions to creativity: a meta-analysis of functional imaging data. *Frontiers in Human Neuroscience*, 7, 1–22.

Gonen-Yaacovi, G., de Souza, L.C., Levy, R., Urbanski, M., Josse, G. and Volle, E. (2013) Rostral and caudal prefrontal contribution to creativity: a meta-analysis of functional imaging data. *Frontiers in Human Neuroscience*, 7, 465.

Goodale, M.A. and Milner, A.D. (1992) Separate visual pathways for perception and action. *Trends in Neurosciences*, 15, 2–25.

Goodale, M.A., Milner, A.D., Jakobson, L.S. and Carey, D.P. (1991) Perceiving the world and grasping it: A neurological dissociation. *Nature*, 349, 154–6.

Goodglass, H. (1976) Agrammatism. In H. Whitaker and H.A. Whitaker (eds) *Studies in Neurolinguistics.* New York: Academic Press.

Goodman, M.J., Tijerina, L., Bents, F.D. and Wierwille, W.W. (1999) Using cellular telephones in vehicles: Safe or unsafe? *Transportation Human Factors*, 1, 3–42.

Goodwin, D.W. and Guze, S.B. (1984) *Psychiatric Diagnosis* (3rd edn). New York: Oxford University Press.

Goodwin, F.K. and Jamison, K.R. (1990) *Manic-depressive Illness.* New York: Oxford University Press.

Gopnik, M. (1997) Language deficits and genetic factors. *Trends in Cognitive Neurosciences*, 1(1), 5–9.

Gordon, I., Wyk, B.C., Bennett, R.H., Cordeaux, C., Llucas, M.V., Eilbott, J.A., Zagoory-Sharon, O., Leckman, J.F., Feldman, R. and Pelphrey, K. (2013) Oxytocin enhances brain function in children with autism. *PNAS*, 110, 20953–8.

Gorvine, B.J. and Smith, H.D. (2015) Predicting student success in a psychological statistics course emphasizing collaborative learning. *Teaching of Psychology*, 42(1), 56–9.

Gorvine, B.J. and Smith, H.D. (2015) Predicting student success in a psychological statistics course emphasising collaborative learning. *Teaching of Psychology*, 42, 56–9.

Gosselt, J.F., van Hoof, J., Gent, B.S. and Fox, J-P. (2015) Violent frames: analyzing internet movie database reviewers' text descriptions of media violence and gender differences from 39 years of US action, thriller, crime and adventure movies. *International Journal of Communication*, 9, 547–67.

Gotzsche-Astrup, O. and Moskowitz, A. (2016) Personality disorders and the DSM-5: Scientific and extra-scientific factors in the maintenance of the status quo. *Australian and New Zealand Journal of Psychiatry*, 50, 119–27.

Gould, M.S., Greenberg, T., Velting, D.M. and Shaffer, D. (2003) Youth suicide risk and preventive interventions: A review of the past 10 years. *Journal of the American Academy of Child and Adolescent Psychiatry*, 42, 386–405.

Gould, S.J. (1985) *The Flamingo's Smile.* New York: W.W. Norton.

Goyal, M.S., Hawrylycz, M., Miller, J.A., Snyder, A.Z. and Raichle, M.E. (2014) Aerobic glycolysis in the human brain is associated with development and neotenous gene expression. *Cell Metabolism*, 10, 49–57.

Goz, I., Ceven, Z.I. and Tekcan, A.L. (2016) Urban-rural differences in children's earliest memories. *Memory*, 25, 214–19.

Grabe, S., Hyde, J.S. and Ward, L.M. (2007) The role of the media in body image concerns among women: A meta-analysis of experimental and correlational studies. *Psychological Bulletin*, 134(3), 460–76.

Grady, C.L., Springer, M.V., Hongwanishkul, D., McIntosh, A.R. and Winocur, G. (2006) Age-related changes in brain activity across the adult lifespan. *Journal of Cognitive Neuroscience*, 18(2), 227–41.

Graen, G.B. and Uhl-Bien, M. (1995) Relationship-based approach to leadership: Development of leader–member exchange (LMX) theory of leadership over 25 years: Applying a multi-level multi-domain approach. *Leadership Quarterly*, 6, 219–47.

Graf, P. and Mandler, G. (1984) Activation makes words more accessible, but not necessarily more retrievable. *Journal of Verbal Learning and Verbal Behavior*, 23, 553–68.

Graf, P., Squire, L.R. and Mandler, G. (1984) The information that amnesic patients do not forget. *Journal of Experimental Psychology: Learning, Memory and Cognition*, 10, 164–78.

Grafton, S.T., Fadiga, L., Arbib, M.A. and Rizzolatti, G. (1997) Premotor cortex activation during observation and naming of familiar tools. *Neuroimage*, 6, 231–6.

Graham, C.A., Janssen, E. and Sanders, S.A. (2000) Effects of fragrance on female sexual arousal and mood across the menstrual cycle. *Psychophysiology*, 37, 76–84.

Graham, J.R. (1990) *MMPI-2: Assessing personality and psychopathology.* New York: Oxford University Press.

Graham, K.S., Barense, M.D. and Lee, A.C. (2010) Going beyond LTM in the MTL: a synthesis of neuropsychological and neuroimaging findings on the role of the medial temporal lobe in memory and perception. *Neuropsychologia*, 48, 831–53.

Graham, S.A. and Fisher, S.E. (2015) Understanding language from a genomic perspective. *Annual Review of Genetics*, 49, 131–60.

Grainger, J., Lete, B., Bertrand, D., Dufau, S. and Ziegler, J.C. (2012) Evidence for multiple routes in learning to read. *Cognition, 123,* 280–92.

Grana, R., Benowitz, N. and Glantz, S.A. (2014) E-cigarettes. *Circulation*, 129, 1972–86.

Granhag, P.A. and Stromwall, L.A. (2001) Detection deception based on repeated interrogations. *Legal and Criminological Psychology*, 6, 85–101.

Granic, I., Lobel, A. and Engels, R.C. (2014) The benefits of playing video games. *American Psychologist*, 69(1), 66.

Grant, P.R. (1986) *Ecology and Evolution of Darwin's Finches.* Princeton, NJ: Princeton University Press.

Grant, S., Contoreggi, C. and London, E.D. (2000) Drug abusers show impaired performance in a laboratory test of decision-making. *Neuropsychologia*, 38, 1180–7.

Grant, V.J. and France, J.T. (2001) Dominance and testosterone in women. *Biological Psychology*, 58, 41–7.

Graves, W.W., Desai, R., Humphries, C., Seidenberg, M.S. and Binder, J.R. (2010) Neural systems for reading aloud: a multiparametric approach. *Cerebral Cortex*, 20, 1799–815.

Gray, J.A. (1982) *The Neuropsychology of Anxiety.* Oxford: Oxford University Press.

Gray, J.A. (1987) *The Psychology of Fear and Stress* (2nd edn). Cambridge: Cambridge University Press.

Gray, J.A. (1998) Creeping up on the hard question of consciousness. In S.R. Hameroff, A.W. Kaszniak and A.C. Scott (eds) *Towards a Science of Consciousness II.* Cambridge, MA: MIT Press.

Gray, J.A. and McNaughton, N. (2000) *The Neuropsychology of Anxiety* (2nd edn). Oxford: OUP.

Gray, S.W., Ramsey, B.K. and Klaus, R.A. (1982) *From 3 to 20: The early training project.* Baltimore, MD: University Park Press.

Gray, T. and Mill, D. (1990) Critical abilities, graduate education (Biology vs English), and belief in unsubstantiated phenomena. *Canadian Journal of Behavioural Science*, 22, 162–72.

Green, B.L. (1994) Psychosocial research in traumatic stress: An update. *Journal of Traumatic Stress*, 7, 341–62.

Green, C.S. and Bavelier, D. (2003) Action video game modifies visual selective attention. *Nature*, 423, 534–7.

Green, D.M. and Swets, J.A. (1974) *Signal Detection Theory and Psychophysics.* New York: Krieger.

Greenberg, B.D., Li, Q., Lucas, F.R., Hu, S., Sirota, L.A. and Benjamin, J. (2000) Association between the serotonin transporter promoter polymorphism and personality traits in primarily a female population sample. *American Journal of Medical Genetics*, 96(2), 202–16.

Greenberg, B.S., Eastin, M., Hofschire, L., Lachlan, K. and Brownell, K. (2003) Portrayals of overweight and obese individuals on commercial television. *American Journal of Public Heath*, 93, 1342–8.

Greenberg, L. and Barling, J. (1999) Predicting employee aggression against co-workers, subordinates and supervisors: The roles of person behaviours and perceived workplace factors. *Journal of Organizational Behaviour*, 20, 897–913.

Greenberg, R. and Pearlman, C.A. (1974) Cutting the REM nerve: An approach to the adaptive role of REM sleep. *Perspectives in Biology and Medicine*, 17, 513–21.

Greene, A.L. and Eaton, N.R. (2016) Panic disorder and agoraphobia: A direct comparison of their multivariate comorbidity patterns. *Journal of affective disorders*, 190, 75–83.

Greene, D.J., Colich, N., Iacoboni, M., Zaidel, E., Bookheimer, S.Y. and Dapretto, M. (2011) Atypical neural networks for social orienting in autism spectrum disorders. *Neuroimage*, 56, 354–62.

Greengross, G. and Miller, G.F. (2009) The Big Five personality traits of professional comedians compared to amateur comedians, comedy writers and college students. *Personality and Individual Differences*, 47, 79–83.

Greenwald, A.G., Banaji, M.R. and Nosek, B.A. (2014) Statistically small effects of the Implicit Association Test can have societally large effects. *Journal of Personality and Social Psychology*, 108, 553–61.

Greenwald, A.G., Banaji, M.R., Rudman, L.A., Farnham, S.D., Nosek, B.A. and Mellott, D.S. (2002) A unified theory of implicit attitudes, stereotypes, self-esteem, and self-concept. *Psychological Review*, 109, 3–25.

Gregory, R.L. (1998) Mythical mechanisms (2): Is the brain a computer? *Perception*, 27, 127–8.

Greicius, M.D. and Menon, V. (2004) Default-mode activity during a passive sensory task. *Journal of Cognitive Neuroscience*, 16, 1484–92.

Greicius, M.D., Supekar, K., Menon, V. and Dougherty, R.F. (2009) Resting-state functional connectivity reflects structural connectivity in the default mode network. *Cerebral Cortex*, 19(1), 72–8.

Greimel, E., Macht, M., Krumhuber, E. and Ellgring, H. (2006) Facial and affective reactions to tastes and their modulation by sadness and joy. *Physiology and Behavior*, 89, 261–9.

Griffiths, M. and Payne, P.R. (1976) Energy expenditure in small children of obese and non-obese mothers. *Nature*, 260, 698–700.

Griffiths, R.R., Bigelow, G.E. and Henningfield, J.E. (1980) Similarities in animal and human drug-taking behavior. In N.K. Mello (ed.) *Advances in Substance Abuse, Vol. 1.* Greenwich, CT: JAI Press.

Griggs, R.A. and Cox, J.R. (1982) The elusive thematic-materials effect in Wason's selection task. *British Journal of Psychology*, 73, 407–20.

Grill-Spector, K. and Witthoft, N. (2009) Deos the bairn not raed ervey lteter by istlef, but the wrod as a wlohe? *Neuron*, 62(2), 161–2.

Grimes, J. (1996) On the failure to detect changes in scenes across saccades. In K. Atkins (ed.), *Perception*, Vol 2, New York: Oxford University Press.

Griskevicius, V., Cialdini, R.B. and Kenrick, D.T. (2006) Peacocks, Picasso, and parental investment: The effects of romantic motives on creativity. *Journal of Personality and Social Psychology*, 91(1), 63–76.

Groenewold, N.A., Opmeer, E.M., de Jonge, P., Aleman, A. and Costafreda, S. (2013) Emotional valence modulates brain functional abnormalities in depression. *Neuroscience and Biobehavioural Reviews*, 37, 152–63.

Groesz, L.M., Levine, M.P. and Murnen, S.K. (2002) The effect of experimental presentation of thin media images on body satisfaction: A meta-analytic review. *International Journal of Eating Disorders*, 31, 1–16.

Grosjean, F. (2010) *Bilingual: Life and reality.* Cambridge, MA: Harvard University Press.

Gross, C. (2012) Some revolutions in neuroscience. *Journal of Cognitive Neuroscience*, 25, 4–13.

Gross, J., Jack, F., Davis, N. and Hayne, H. (2013) Do children recall the birth of a younger sibling? Implications for the study of childhood amnesia. *Memory*, 21, 336–46.

Grossman, K., Grossman, K.E., Spangler, G., Suess, G. and Unzer, L. (1985) Maternal sensitivity and newborns' orientation responses as related to quality of attachment in Northern Germany. In I. Bretherton and E. Waters (eds) Growing points of attachment theory and research. *Monographs of the Society for Research in Child Development*, 50.

Grosul, M. and Feist, G.J. (2013) The creative person in science. *Psychology of Aesthetics, Creativity and the Arts*, 81, 30.

Groth-Marnat, G. (1997) *Handbook of Psychological Assessment* (3rd edn). New York: Wiley.

Gruter, T., Gruter, M. and Carbon, C-C. (2008) Neural and genetic foundations of face recognition and prosopagnosia. *Journal of Neuropsychology*, 2, 79–97.

Gu, X., Wang, X., Hula, A., Wang, S., Xu, S., Lohrenz, T.M., Knight, R.T., Gao, Z., Dayan, P. and Montague, P.R. (2015) necessary, yet dissociable contributions of the insular and ventromedial prefrontal cortices to norm adaptation. *The Journal of Neuroscience*, 35, 467–73.

Guariglia, C., Padovani, A., Pantano, P. and Pizzamiglio, L. (1993) Unilateral neglect restricted to visual imagery. *Nature*, 364, 235–7.

Guariglia, P., Matano, A. and Piccardi, L. (2014) Bisecting or not bisecting: This is the neglect question. Line bisection performance in the diagnosis of neglect in right brain-damaged patients. *PLoS ONE, 9*, e99700.

Gueguen, N. (2002) Touch, awareness of touch and compliance to a request. *Perceptual and Motor Skills*, 95, 355–60.

Gueguen, N. (2013) Weather and courtship behavior: A quasi-experiment with the flirty sunshine. *Social Influence*, 8, 312–19.

Gueguen, N. and Fischer-Lokou, J. (2002) An evaluation of touch on a large request: A field setting. *Psychological Reports*, 90(1), 267–9.

Gueguen, N. and Fischer-Lokou, J. (2003) Tactile contact and spontaneous help. *The Journal of Social Psychology*, 143, 785–7.

Guéguen, N. and Jacob, C. (2005) The effect of touch on tipping: an evaluation in a French bar. *International Journal of Hospitality Management*, 24(2), 295–9.

Gueguen, N. and Lamy, L. (2011) The effect of the word 'love' on compliance to a humanitarian aid request. *Social Influence*, 6, 249–58.

Guéguen, N., Jacob, C. and Boulbry, G. (2007) The effect of touch on compliance with a restaurant's employee suggestion. *International Journal of Hospitality Management*, 26(4), 1019–23.

Gueguen, N., Jacob, C. and Charles-Sire, V. (2011) The effect of the word 'loving' on compliance to a fundraising request. *International Journal of Nonprofit and Voluntary Sector Marketing*, 16, 371–80.

Guéguen, N., Jacob, C., Le Guellec, H., Morineau, T. and Lourel, M. (2008) Sound level of environmental music and drinking behavior: a field experiment with beer drinkers. *Alcoholism: Clinical and Experimental Research*, 32(10), 1795–8.

Guest, S., Essick, G., Dessirier, J.M., Blot, K., Lopetcharat, K. and McGone, F. (2009) Sensory and affective judgments of skin during inter- and intrapersonal touch. *Acta Psychologia*, 130, 115–26.

Gunawardane, K.G.C., Piffer, D. and Custance, D.M. (2011) Evidence of sexual selection for evening orientation in human males. *Interdisciplinary Biology Central*, 3, 1–8.

Gunnell, D., Magnusson, P.K.E. and Rasmussen, F. (2005) Low intelligence test scores in 18-year-old men and risk of suicide: Cohort study. *British Medical Journal*, 330, 167–70.

Gunther Moor, B., Guroglu, B., Op de Macks, Z.A., Rombouts, S.A.R.B., Van der Molen, M.W. and Crone, E.A. (2010) Social exclusion and punishment of excluders: Neural correlates and developmental trajectories. *Neuroimage* 59, 708–17.

Gunther, V.K., Shafer, P., Holzner, B.J. and Kemmler, G.W. (2003) Long-term improvements in cognitive performance through computer-assisted cognitive training. *Aging and Mental Health*, 7, 200–6.

Guo, S.W. and Reed, D.R. (2001) The genetics of phenylthiocarbamide perception. *Annals of Human Biology*, 28, 111–42.

Gustafson, G.E. and Harris, K.L. (1990) Women's responses to young infants' cries. *Developmental Psychology*, 26, 144–52.

Gustavson, C.R. and Gustavson, J.C. (1985) Predation control using conditioned food aversion methodology: Theory, practice, and implications. *Annals of the New York Academy of Sciences*, 443, 348–56.

H

Haack, M. and Mullington, J.M. (2005) Sustained sleep restriction reduces emotional and physical well-being. *Pain*, 119, 56–64.

Haaga, D.A. and Davison, G.C. (1989) Cognitive change methods. In A.P. Goldstein and F.H. Kanfer (eds) *Helping People Change* (3rd edn). New York: Pergamon Press.

Haaland, K.Y. and Harrington, D.H. (1989) Hemispheric control of the initial and corrective components of aiming movements. *Neuropsychologia*, 27, 961–9.

Haartsen, R., Jones, E.J.H. and Johnson, M.H. (2016) Human brain development over the early years. *Current Opinion in Behavioural Sciences*, 10, 149–54.

Haase, L., Cerf-Ducastel, B. and Murphy, C. (2009) Cortical activation in response to pure taste stimuli during the physiological states of hunger and satiety. *Neuroimage*, 44, 1008–21.

Habib, M. (2000) The neurological basis of developmental dyslexia. *Brain*, 123, 2373–99.

Haddock, G. (2006) Do I get better looking each day? Changes in self-perceptions of attractiveness as a function of temporal perspective. *European Journal of Social Psychology*, 36, 761–71.

Hagbloom, S.J., Warnick, R., Warnick, J.E., Jones, V.K., Yarbrough, G.L., Russell, T.M., Borecky, C.M., McGahhey, R., Powell, J.L., Beavers, J. and Monte, E. (2002) The 100 most eminent psychologists of the 20th century. *Review of General Psychology*, 6(2), 139–52.

Hagemann, D., Hewig, J., Naumann, E., Seifert, J. and Bartussek, D. (2005a) Resting brain activity and affective reactivity: Aggregated date support the right-hemisphere hypothesis. *Journal of Individual Differences*, 26, 139–54.

Hagemann, D., Hewig, J., Seifert, J., Naumann, E. and Bartussek, D. (2005b) The latent state-trait structure of resting EEG asymmetry: replication and extension. *Psychophysiology*, 42, 740–52.

Hagemann, D., Naumann, E., Becker, G., Maier, S. and Bartussek, D. (1998) Frontal brain asymmetry and affective style: A conceptual replication. *Psychophysiology*, 35, 372–88.

Hagemann, N., Strauss, B. and Liebling, J. (2008) When the referee sees red. *Psychological Science*, 19, 769–71.

Haheim, L.L., Tonstad, S., Hjermann, I., Leren, P. and Holme, I. (2007) Predictiveness of body mass index for fatal coronary heart disease in men according to length of follow-up: A 21-year prospective cohort study. *Scandinavian Journal of Public Health*, 35, 4–10.

Haier, R.J. (2004) Brain imaging studies of personality. In R. Stelmack (ed.), *On the Psychobiology of Personality: Essays in Honor of Marvin Zuckerman*. Amsterdam: Elsevier.

Haier, R.J., Jung, R.E., Yeo, R.A., Head, K. and Alkire, M.T. (2005) The neuroanatomy of general intelligence: sex matters. *NeuroImage*, 25(1), 320–7.

Haier, R.J., Neuchterlein, K.H., Hazlett, E., Wu, J.C., Pack, J., Browning, H.L. and Buchsbaum, M.S. (1988) Cortical glucose metabolic rate correlates of abstract reasoning and attention studied with positron emission tomography. *Intelligence*, 12, 199–217.

Haier, R.J., Siegel, B., Tang, C., Abel, L. and Buchsbaum, M.S. (1992) Intelligence and changes in regional cerebral glucose metabolic rate following learning. *Intelligence*, 16, 415–26.

Hakim, A.A., Petrovitch, H., Burchfiel, C.M., Webster-Ross, G., Rodriguez, B.L., White, L.R., Yano, K., Curb, J.D. and Abbott, R.D. (1998) Effects of walking on mortality among non-smoking retired men. *New England Journal of Medicine*, 338, 94–9.

Halaas, J.L., Gajiwala, K.S., Maffei, M. and Cohen, S.L. (1995) Weight-reducing effects of the plasma protein encoded by the obese gene. *Science*, 269, 543–6.

Halberda, J. and Feigenson, L. (2008) Developmental change in the acuity of the 'number sense'. *Developmental Psychology*, 44, 1457–65.

Halberda, J., Ly, R., Wilmer, J.B., Naiman, D.Q. and Germine, L. (2012) Number sense across the lifespan as revealed by a massive Internet-based sample. *Proceedings of the National Academy of Sciences*, 109(28), 11116–20.

Halberstadt, J. and Rhodes, G. (2000) The attractiveness of nonface averages: Implications for an evolutionary explanation of the attractiveness of average faces. *Psychological Science*, 11, 285–9.

Halberta, J., Ly, R, Wilmer, J.B., Naiman, D.Q. and Germine, L. (2012) Number sense across the lifespan as revealed by a massive internet-based sample. *PNAS*, 109, 11116–20.

Hale, S. (2002) *The Man Who Lost His Language*. London: Penguin.

Halford, G.S. (1990) Is children's reasoning logical or analytical? *Human Development*, 33, 356–61.

Hall, C.S. and Nordby, V.J. (1973) *A Primer of Jungian Psychology*. New York: New American Library.

Hall, E.E., Ekkekakis, P. and Petruzzello, S.J. (2002) The affective beneficence of vigorous exercise revisited. *British Journal of Health Psychology*, 7, 47–66.

Hall, E.T. (1966) *The Hidden Dimension*. New York: Doubleday.

Hallam, R.S. and Rachman, S.J. (1980) Courageous actos or courageous actors? *Personality and Individual Differences*, 1, 341–6.

Haller, R., Rummel, C., Henneberg, S., Pollmer, U. and Koster, E.P. (1999) The influence of early experience with vanillin on food preference later in life. *Chemical Senses*, 24, 465–7.

Hallermann, S., de Kock, C.P.J., Stuart, G.J. and Kole, M.H.P. (2012) State and location dependence of action potential metabolic cost in cortical pyramidal neurons. *Nature Neuroscience*, 15, 1007–14.

Halligan, P.W. and Cockburn, J.M. (1993) Cognitive sequelae of stroke: Visuospatial and memory disorders. *Critical Reviews in Physical and Rehabilitation Medicine*, 5(1), 57–81.

Halligan, P.W. and Marshall, J.C. (1994) *Spatial Neglect: Position papers on theory and practice*. London: Macmillan.

Halliwell, E., Dittmar, H. and Howe, J. (2005) The impact of advertisements featuring ultra-thin or average-size models on women with a history of eating disorders. *Journal of Community and Applied Social Psychology*, 15, 406–13.

Halmi, K.A. (1978) Anorexia nervosa: Recent investigations. *Annual Review of Medicine*, 29, 137–48.

Halpern, A.R. and Zatorre, R.J. (1999) When that tune runs through your head: A PET investigation of auditory imagery for familiar melodies. *Cerebral Cortex*, 9, 697–704.

Halpern, D.F. (1992) *Sex Differences in Cognitive Abilities*. Hillsdale, NJ: Lawrence Erlbaum Associates.

Halpern, D.F. (1997) Sex differences in intelligence. *American Psychologist*, 52(10), 1091–102.

Halpern, J.H., Sherwood, A.R., Hudson, J.I., Gruber, S., Kozin, D. and Pope Jr, H.G. (2011) Residual neurocognitive features of long-term ecstasy users with minimal exposure to other drugs. *Addiction*, 106(4), 777–86.

Halwani, G.F., Loui, P., Ruber, T. and Schlaug, G. (2011) Effects of practice and experience on the arcuate fasciculus: Comparing singers, instrumentalists, and non-musicians. *Frontiers in Psychology*, 2, article 156.

Hamann, S.B., Ely, T.D., Hoffman, J.M. and Kilts, C.D. (2002) Ecstasy and agony: Activation of the human amygdala in positive and negative emotion. *Psychological Science*, 13, 135–41.

Hameroff, S.R. (1998) More neural than thou. In S.R. Hameroff, A.W. Kaszniak and A.C. Scott (eds) *Towards a Science of Consciousness II*. Cambridge, MA: MIT Press.

Hameroff, S.R. and Penrose, R. (1996) Orchestrated reduction of quantum coherence in brain microtubules: A model for consciousness. In S.R. Hameroff, A.W. Kaszniak and A.C. Scott (eds), *Towards a Science of Consciousness*. Cambridge, MA: MIT Press.

Hamilton, A.F. *et al.* (2007) Imitation and action understanding in autistic spectrum disorders: how valid is the hypothesis of a deficit in the mirror neuron system? *Neuropsychologia*, 45, 1859–68.

Hamilton, D.L. and Gifford, R.K. (1976) Illusory correlation in interpersonal perception: A cognitive basis of stereotypic judgments. *Journal of Experimental Social Psychology*, 12, 392–407.

Hamilton, W.D. (1964) The genetical evolution of social behaviour: I and II. *Journal of Theoretical Biology*, 7, 1–52.

Hamilton, W.D. (1970) Selfish and spiteful behavior in an evolutionary model. *Nature*, 228, 1218–20.

Hammarstrom, A. and Janlert, U. (1997) Nervous and depressive symptoms in a longitudinal study of youth unemployment – selection or exposure? *Journal of Adolescence*, 20, 293–305.

Hammersley, M. (1992) *What's Wrong with Ethnography?* London: Routledge.

Hammersley, M. (2008) *Questioning Qualitative Inquiry*. London: Sage.

Hampson, E. (1990) Estrogen-related variations in human spatial and articulatory–motor skills. *Psychoneuroendocrinology*, 15, 97–111.

Hampson, M., Tokoglu, F., Shen, X., Scheinost, D., Papademetris, X. and Constable, R.T. (2012) Intrinsic brain connectivity related to age in young and middle aged adults. *PLoS ONE*, 7, e44067.

Hampson, S.E. (2012) Personality processes: Mechanisms by which personality traits 'get outside the skin'. *Annual Review of Psychology*, 63, 315–39.

Hampson, S.E., Edmonds, G.W., Goldberg, L.R, Dubanoski, J.P. and Hillier, T.A. (2013) Childhood conscientiousness relates to objectively measured adult physical health four decades later. *Health Psychology*, 32, 925–8.

Hampstead, B.M., Stringer, A.Y., Stilla, R.F., Deshpande, G., Hu, X., More, A.B. and Sathian, K. (2011) Activation and effective connectivity changes following explicit-memory training for face-name pairs in patients with mild cognitive impairment. *Neurorehabilitation and Neural Repair*, 25, 210–22.

Haney, C., Banks, C. and Zimbardo, P. (1973) Interpersonal dynamics in a simulated prison. *International Journal of Criminology and Penology*, 1, 69–97.

Hanggi, J., Fovenyi, L., Liem, F., Meyer, M. and Jancke, L. (2014) The hypothesis of neuronal interconnectivity as a function of brain size. *Frontiers in Human Neuroscience*, 8, 915.

Hankin, B.L. *et al.* (1998) Development of depression from preadolescence to young adulthood: emerging gender difference in a 10-year longitudinal study. *Journal of Abnormal Psychology*, 107, 128–40.

Hanselman, P., Bruch, S.K., Gamoran, A. and Borman, G.D. (2014) Threat in context: School moderation of the impact of social identity threat on racial/ethnic achievement gaps. *Sociology of Education*, 87, 106–24.

Hanselman, P., Rozek, C.S., Grigg, J. and Borman, G.D. (2016) New evidence of self-affirmation effects and theorised sources of heterogeneity from large-scale replications. *SREE*, https://eric.ed.gov/?id=ED567619

Hansen, C.J., Stevens, L.C. and Coast, J.R. (2001) Exercise duration and mood state: How much is enough to feel better? *Health Psychology*, 20(4), 267–75.

Hansen, J. and Wänke, M. (2009) Think of capable others and you can make it! Self-efficacy mediates the effect of stereotype activation on behaviour. *Social Cognition*, 27, 76–88.

Hao, Y. *et al.* (2009) Schizophrenia patients and their healthy siblings share disruption of white matter integrity in the left prefrontal cortex and the hippocampus but not the anterior cingulate cortex. *Schizophrenia Research*, 114, 128–35.

Happé, F. (1993) Communicative competence and theory of mind in autism: A test of relevance theory. *Cognition*, 48, 101–19.

Happe, F. (1994) An advanced test of theory of mind: understanding of story characters' thoughts and feeling by able autistic, mentally handicapped and normal children and adults. *Journal of Autism and Developmental Disorders*, 24, 129–54.

Happé, F. (1994) *Autism: An introduction to psychological theory*. London: UCL Press.

Harari, H. and McDavid, J. (1973) Name stereotypes and teachers' expectations. *Journal of Educational Psychology*, 65, 222–5.

Harden, K.P., Turkheimer, E. and Loehlin, J.C. (2007) Genotype by environment interaction in adolescents' cognitive aptitude. *Behavior Genetics*, 37, 273–83.

Hardman, D. and Harries, C. (2002) How rational are we? *The Psychologist*, 15(2), 76–9.

Hare, R.D. (1965) Temporal gradient of fear arousal in psychopaths. *Journal of Abnormal Psychology*, 70, 442–5.

Hare, R.D. (1996) Psychopathy: A clinical construct whose time has come. *Criminal Justice and Behaviour*, 23(1), 25–54.

Hare, R.D. and Hart S.D. (1993) Psychopathy, mental disorder, and crime. In S. Hodgins (ed.) *Mental Disorder and Crime* (pp. 104–15). Thousand Oaks, CA, US: Sage Publications.

Harenski, C.L., Harenski, K.A., Shane, M.S. and Kiehl, K.A. (2010) Aberrant neural processing of moral violations in criminal psychopaths. *Journal of Abnormal Psychology*, 119, 863–74.

Hargreaves, I.S., Pexman, P.M., Zdrazilova, L. and Sargious, P. (2012) How a hobby can shape cognition: visual word recognition in competitive Scrabble players. *Memory and Cognition*, 40, 1–7.

Hari, R., Henriksson, L., Malinen, S. and Parkkonen, L. (2015) Centrality of social interaction in human brain function. *Neuron*, 88(1), 181–93.

Hariri, A.R., Tessitore, A., Mattay, V.S. and Fera, F. (2002) The amygdala response to emotional stimuli: a comparison of faces and scenes. *Neuroimage*, 17, 317–23.

Harker, L. and Keltner, D. (2001) Expressions of positive emotion in women's college yearbook pictures and their relationship to personality and life outcomes across adulthood. *Journal of Personality and Social Psychology*, 80(1), 112–24.

Harkins, S.G. and Petty, R.E. (1982) Effects of task difficulty and task uniqueness on social loafing. *Journal of Personality and Social Psychology*, 43, 1214–29.

Harlow, H. (1974) *Learning to Love*. New York: J. Aronson.

Harlow, J.M. (1848) Passage of an iron rod through the head. *Boston Medical and Surgery Journal*, 39, 389–93.

Harlow, J.M. (1868) Recovery from the passage of an iron bar through the head. *Massachusetts Medical Society Publications*, 2, 327–46.

Harm, M.W. and Seidenberg, M.S. (1999) Phonology, reading acquisition, and dyslexia: insights from connectionist models. *Psychological Review*, 106(3), 491.

Harm, M.W. and Seidenberg, M.S. (2004) Computing the meanings of words in reading: Cooperative division of labor between visual and phonological processes. *Psychological Review*, 111, 662–720.

Harmatz, M.G., Well, A.D., Overtree, C.E., Kawamura, K.Y., Rosal, M. and Ockene, L.S. (2000) Seasonal variation of depression and other moods: A longitudinal approach. *Journal of Biological Rhythms*, 15, 344–50.

Harmon-Jones, E. (2004) On the relationship between frontal brain activity and anger: Examining the role of attitude toward anger. *Cognition and Emotion*, 18 (3), 337–61.

Harmon-Jones, E. (2007) Trait anger predicts relative left frontal cortical activation to anger-inducing stimuli. *International Journal of Psychophysiology*, 66, 154–60.

Harmon-Jones, E., Abramson, L.Y., Sigelman, J., Bohlig, A., Hogan, M.E. and Harmon-Jones, C. (2002) Proneness to hypomania/mania symptoms or depression symptoms and asymmetrical frontal cortical responses to an anger-evoking event. *Journal of Personality and Social Psychology*, 82(4), 610–18.

Harmon-Jones, E., Gable, P.A. and Price, T.F. (2011) Learning embodies desire: Evidence that leaning forward increases relative left frontal cortical activation to appetitive stimuli. *Biological Psychology*, 87, 311–13.

Harris, B. (1979) Whatever happened to Little Albert? *American Psychologist*, 34(2), 151–60.

Harris, C.R. (2002) Sexual and romantic jealousy in heterosexual and homosexual adults. *Psychological Science*, 13(1), 7–12.

Harris, C.R., Chabot, A. and Mickes, L. (2013) Shifts in methodology and theory in menstrual cycle research on attraction. *Sex Roles*, 69, 525–35.

Harris, G. and Booth, D.A. (1987) Infants' preference in food and previous dietary exposure in 6-month-old infants. *IRCS Medical Science*, 13, 1178–9.

Harris, J.R. (1995) Where is the child's environment? A group socialization theory of development. *Psychological Review*, 102, 458–89.

Harris, L.T. and Fiske, S.T. (2006) Dehumanizing the lowest of the low neuroimaging responses to extreme out-groups. *Psychological Science*, 17(10), 847–53.

Harris, M.A., Brett, C.E., Johnson, W. and Deary, I.J. (2016) Personality stability from age 14 to age 77 years. *Psychology and Aging*, 31(8), 862.

Harris, N.B. (1992) Sex, race, and experiences of aggression. *Aggressive Behavior*, 18, 201–17.

Harris, S.E. and Deary, I.J. (2011) The genetics of cognitive ability and cognitive ageing in healthy older people. *Trends in Cognitive Sciences*, 15, 388–94.

Harrison, D.A., Price, K.H., Gavin, J.H. and Florey, A. (2002) Time, teams, and task performance: changing effects of surface- and deep-level diversity on group functioning. *Academy of Management Journal*, 45, 1029–45.

Harrison, G.L., McKinnon, J.L., Wu, A. and Chow, C.W. (2000) Cultural influences on adaptation to fluid workgroups and teams. *Journal of International Business Studies*, 31, 489–505.

Harrison, J. and Baron-Cohen, S. (eds) (1996) *Synaesthesia: Classic and contemporary readings*. Oxford: Blackwell.

Harrison, K., Liechty, J.M. and The STRONG Kids Program. (2012) US preschoolers' media exposure and dietary habits: The primacy of television and the limits of parental mediation. *Journal of Children and Media*, 6(1), 18–36.

Harrison, L.K., Denning, S., Easton, H.L., Hall, J.C., Burns, V.E., Ring, C. and Carroll, D.G. (2001) The effects of competition and competitiveness on cardiovascular activity. *Psychophysiology*, 38, 601–6.

Harrison, Y. and Horne, J.A. (2000) Sleep loss and temporal memory. *The Quarterly Journal of Experimental Psychology*, 53A(1), 271–9.

Hart, A.J., Whalen, P.J., Shin, L.M., McInerney, S.C., Fischer, H. and Rausch, S.L. (2000) Differential response in the human amygdala to racial outgroup vs ingroup face stimuli. *Neuroreport*, 11, 2351–5.

Hartley, J. (1998) *Learning and Studying: A research perspective*. London: Routledge.

Hartshorne, J.K. and Germine, L.T. (2015) When does cognitive functioning peak? The asynchronous rise and fall of different cognitive abilities across the life span. *Psychological Science*, 26, 433–43.

Hartup, W.W. and Laursen, B. (1992) Conflict and context in peer relations. In C.H. Hart (ed.) *Children on Playgrounds: Research perspectives and applications*. Albany, NY: State University of New York Press.

Hartwig, M. and Bond, C.F. (2011) Why do lie-catchers fail? A lens model meta-analysis of human lie judgments. *Psychological Bulletin*, 137, 643–59.

Hartwig, M., Granhag, P.A., Stromwall, L.A. and Andersson, L.O. (2004) Suspicious minds: Criminals' ability to detect deception. *Psychology, Crime and Law*, 10 (1), 83–95.

Haselton, M.G., Mortezaie, M., Pillsworth, E.G., Bleske-Rechek, A. and Frederick, D.A. (2007) Ovulatory shifts in human female ornamentation: Near ovulation, women dress to impress. *Hormones and Behavior*, 51, 40–45.

Hasher, L. and Zacks, R.T. (1988) Working memory, comprehension, and ageing: A review and a new view. In G.H. Bower (ed.) *The Psychology of Learning and Motivation*, Vol. 22. San Diego, CA: Academic Press.

Hasher, L., Zacks, R.T. and Rahhal, T.A. (1999) Timing, instructions, and inhibitory control: Some missing factors in the age and memory debate. *Gerontology*, 45, 355–7.

Haslam, N., Rothschild, L. and Erbst, D. (1998) Essentialist beliefs about social categories. *British Journal of Social Psychology*, 39, 113–27.

Haslam, S.A., Reicher, S.D. and Birney, M.E. (2014a) Nothing by mere authority: Evidence that in an experimental analogue of the Milgram paradigm participants are motivated not by orders but by appeals to science. *Journal of Social Issues*, 70, 473–88.

Haslam, S.A., Reicher, S.D. and Millard, K. (2015) Shock treatment: Using immersive digital realism to restage and reexamine Milgram's obedience to authority research. *PLoS ONE*, 10, e109015.

Haslam, S.A., Reicher, S.D., Millard, K. and McDonald, R. (2014b) 'Happy to have been of service': The Yale archive as a window into the engaged followership of participants in Milgram's 'obedience' experiments. *British Journal of Social Psychology*, 54, 55–83.

Hassabis, D. and Maguire, E.A. (2007) Deconstructing episodic memory with construction. *Trends in Cognitive Sciences*, 11(7), 299–306.

Hassabis, D. and Maguire, E.A. (2007) Deconstructing episodic memory with construction. *TICS*, 11, 299–306.

Hassall, J., Boduszek, D. and Dhingra, K. (2015) Psychopathic traits of business and psychology students and their relationship to academic success. *Personality and Individual Differences*, 82, 227–31.

Hatcher, P.J., Hulme, C. and Snowling, M.J. (2004) Explicit phoneme training combined with phonic reading instruction helps young children at risk of reading failure. *Journal of Child Psychology and Psychiatry*, 45(2), 338–58.

Hatfield, E. (1988) Passionate and compassionate love. In R.J. Sternberg and M.L. Barnes (eds) *The Psychology of Love*. New Haven, CT: Yale University Press.

Hatfield, E. and Sprecher, S. (1986) *Mirror, Mirror . . . The importance of looks in everyday life*. Albany, NY: SUNY Press.

Hattingh, C.J., Ipser, J., Tromp, S., Syal, S., Lochner, C., Brooks, S.J. and Stein, D.J. (2013) Functional magnetic resonance imaging during emotion recognition in social anxiety disorder. *Frontiers in Human Neuroscience*, 6, 347.

Hauch, V., Blandon-Gitlin, I., Masip, J. and Sporer, S.L. (2014) Are computers effective lie detectors? A meta-analysis of linguistic cues to deception. *Personality and Social Psychology Review*, 1–36.

Hauch, V., Blandón-Gitlin, I., Masip, J. and Sporer, S.L. (2015) Are computers effective lie detectors? A meta-analysis of linguistic cues to deception. *Personality and Social Psychology Review*, 19(4), 307–42.

Hauch, V., Sporer, S.L., Michael, S.W. and Meissner, C.A. (2016) Does training improve the detection of deception? A meta-analysis. *Communication Research*, 43(3), 283–343.

Hauser, M., Cushman, F., Young, L., Jin, R.K. and Mikhail, J. (2007) A dissociation between moral judgements and justifications. *Mind and Language*, 22, 1–21.

Hauser, M.D., Young, L. and Cushman, F. (2008) Reviving Rawls' linguistic analogy. *Moral Psychology*, 2, 107–43.

Havlicek, J., Saxton, T.K., Roberts, C., Jozifkova, E., Lhota, S., Valentova, J. and Flegr, J. (2008) He sees, she smells? Male and female reports of sensory reliance in mate choice and non-mate choice contexts. *Personality and Individual Differences*, 45, 565–70.

Hawley, D.F., Morch, K., Christie, B.R. and Leasure, J.L. (2012) Differential response of hippocampal subregions to stress and learning. *PLoS ONE*, 7(12), e53126.

Hawley, P.H. (1999) The ontogenesis of social dominance: A strategy-based evolutionary perspective. *Developmental Review*, 19, 97–132.

Haxby, J.V., Hoffman, E.A. and Gobbini, M.I. (2000) The distributed human neural system for face perception. *Trends in Cognitive Sciences*, 4, 223–33.

Haxby, J.V., Horwitz, B., Ungeldeider, L.G., Maisog, J.M. (1994) The functional organization of human extrastriate cortex: PET rCBF study of selective attention to faces and locations. *Journal of Neuroscience*, 14 (11Pb1), 6336–53.

Hayes, C. (1952) *The Ape in Our House*. London: Gollancz.

Hayes, J.E. and Duffy, V.B. (2008) Oral sensory phenotype identifies level of sugar and fat required for maximal liking. *Physiology and Behavior*, 95, 77–87.

Hayes, N. (1997) *Doing Qualitative Analysis in Psychology*. Hove: Psychology Press.

Haynie, D.L., Nansel, T., Eitel, P. and Crump, A.D. (2001) Bullies, victims, and bully/victims. *The Journal of Early Adolescence*, 21, 29–49.

Healey, P.G.T., Purver, M. and Howes, C. (2014) Divergence in dialogue. *PLoS ONE*, 9, e98598.

Healy, A.F., Havas, D.A. and Parker, J.T. (2000) Comparing serial position effects in semantic and episodic memory using reconstruction of order tasks. *Journal of Memory and Language*, 42, 147–67.

Hebb, D.O. (1949) *The Organization of Behaviour.* New York: Wiley/ Interscience.

Hebb, D.O. (1955) Drives and the CNS (conceptual nervous system) *Psychological Review*, 62, 243–54.

Hebb, D.O., Lambert, W.E. and Tucker, G.R. (1973) A DMZ in the language war. *Psychology Today*, April, 55–62.

Hedden, T., Ketay, S., Aron, A., Markus, H.R. and Gabrieli, J.D. (2008) Cultural influences on neural substrates of attentional control. *Psychological Science*, 19(1), 12–17.

Heider, E.R. (1971) 'Focal' color areas and the development of color names. *Developmental Psychology*, 4, 447–55.

Heider, E.R. (1972) Universals in color naming and memory. *Journal of Experimental Psychology*, 93, 10–20.

Heider, F. (1958) *The Psychology of Interpersonal Relations.* New York: Wiley.

Heilman, K.M. (2016) Possible brain mechanisms of creativity. *Archives of Clinical Neuropsychology*, 31, 285–96.

Heilman, M.E. and Stopeck, M.H. (1985) Attractiveness and corporate success: Different causal attributions for males and females. *Journal of Applied Psychology*, 70, 379–88.

Heim, C.M., Mayberg, H.S., Mletzko, T., Nemeroff, C.B. and Pruessner, J.C. (2013) Decreased cortical representation of genital somatosensory field after childhood sexual abuse. *American Journal of Psychiatry*, 170, 616–23.

Heim, N. and Hursch, C. (1979) Castration for sex offenders: Treatment or punishment? *Archives of Sexual Behaviour*, 8, 281–304.

Heim, S., Alter, K., Ischebeck, A.K., Amunts, K., Eickhoff, S.B., Mohlberg, H., Zilles, K., von Cramon, D.Y. and Friederici, A.D. (2005) The role of the left Brodmann's areas 44 and 45 in reading words and pseudowords. *Cognitive Brain Research*, 25, 982–93.

Heine, S.J., Takemoto, T., Moskalenko, S., Lasaleta, J. and Henrich, J. (2008) Mirrors in the head: Cultural variation in objective self-awareness. *Personality and Social Psychology Bulletin*, 34(7), 879–87.

Heining, M., Young, A.W., Ioannou, G., Andrew, C.M., Brammer, M.J., Gray, J.A. and Phillips, M.L. (2003) Disgusting smells activate human anterior insula and ventral striatum. *Annals of the New York Academy of Sciences*, 1000(1), 380–4.

Heinzen, T.E., Lilienfeld, S.O. and Nolan, S.A. (2015) Clever Hans. *Skeptic Magazine*, 20, 10–17.

Heinzen, T.E., Lilienfeld, S.O. and Nolan, S.A. (2015) *The Horse that Won't Go Away.* New York: Macmillan.

Heisz, J.J., Pottruff, M.M. and Shore, D.I. (2013) Females scan more than males: A potential mechanism for sex differences in recognition memory. *Psychological Science*, 24, 1157–63.

Helson, R. and Soto, C.J. (2005) Up and down in middle age: monotonic and nonmonotonic changes in roles, status and personality. *Journal of Personality and Social Psychology*, 89, 194–204.

Henderson, S.E. and Norris, C.J. (2013) Counterfactual thinking and reward processing: An fMRI study of responses to gamble outcomes. *Neuroimage*, 64, 582–9.

Henderson, V.W., Watt, L. and Buckwalter, J.G. (1996) Cognitive skills associated with estrogen replacement in women with Alzheimer's disease. *Psychoneuroendocrinology*, 21(4), 421–30.

Hendon, D.W., Roy, M.H and Ahmed, Z.U. (2003) Negotiation concession patterns: a multicountry, multiperiod study. *American Business Review*, 21, 75–81.

Hendrie, C.A., Mannion, H.D. and Godfrey, G.K. (2009) Evidence to suggest that nightclubs function as human sexual display grounds. *Behaviour*, 146, 1331–48.

Hendry, L.B. and Kloep, M. (2002) *Lifespan Development: Resources, challenges, risks.* London: Thomson Learning.

Henley, S.M.D., Novak, M.J.U., Frost, C., King, J., Tabrizi, S.J. and Warren, J.D. (2012) Emotion recognition in Huntington's disease: A systematic review. *Neuroscience and Biobehavioral Reviews*, 36, 237–53.

Henrich, J., Heine, S.J. and Norenzayan, A. (2010) The weirdest people in the world? *Behavioural and Brain Sciences*, 33, 61–135.

Hensley, P.L., Nadiga, D. and Uhlenhuth, E.H. (2004) Long-term effectiveness of cognitive therapy in major depressive disorder. *Depression and Anxiety*, 20, 1–7.

Hepburn, A. and Potter, J. (2007) Crying receipts: Time, empathy, and institutional practice. *Research on Language and Social Interaction*, 40(1), 89–116.

Hepper, P.G. (1994) Auditory learning in the human fetus. *Infant Behaviour and Development*, 17, 96.

Hepper, P.G. (1995) Human fetal 'olfactory' learning. *International Journal of Prenatal, Perinatal and Psychological Medicine*, 7, 147–51.

Herdt, G. and Lindenbaum, S. (eds) (1992) *Social Analyses in the Time of AIDS.* Newbury Park, CA: Sage.

Herlitz, A. and Loven, J. (2013) Sex differences and the own-gender bias in face recognition. *Visual Cognition*, 21, 1306–36.

Herman, C.P. (2015) The social facilitation of eating. A review. *Appetite*, 86, 61–73.

Herman, C.P., Roth, D.A. and Polivy, J. (2003) Effects of the presence of others on food intake: a normative interpretation. *Psychological Bulletin*, 129(6), 873.

Herman, C.P., Roth, D.A. and Polivy, J. (2003) Effects of the presence of others on food intake: a normative interpretation. *Psychological Bulletin*, 129, 873–6.

Hermans, D., Pieters, G. and Eelen, P. (1998) Implicit and explicit memory for shape, body weight, and food-related words in patients with anorexia nervosa and nondieting controls. *Journal of Abnormal Psychology*, 107(2), 193–202.

Hermans, E.J., Putman, P. and van Honk, J. (2006) Testosterone administration reduces empathetic behavior: A facial mimicry study. *Psychoneuroendocrinology*, 31, 859–66.

Hermoye, L., Saint-Martin, C., Cosnard, G., Lee, S., Kim, J., Nassogne, M. *et al.* (2006) Pediatric diffusion tensor imaging: Normal database and observation of the white matter maturation in early childhood. *Neuroimage*, 29, 493–504.

Herrmann, C.S., Rach, S., Neurling, T. and Struber, D. (2013) Transcranial alternating current stimulation: a review of the underlying mechanisms and modulation of cognitive processes. *Frontiers in Human Neuroscience*, 7, 279.

Herrnstein, R.J. and Murray, C. (1994) *The Bell Curve.* New York: Free Press.

Herschfield, H.E., Bang, H.M. and Weber, E.U. (2013) National differences in environmental concern and performance are predicted by country age. *Psychological Science*, 25 152–60.

Hertz-Pannier, L., Chiron, C., Jambaque, I., Renaux-Kieffer, V., Van de Moortele, P-F., Delalande, O., Fohlen, M., Brunelle, F. and Le Bihan, D. (2002) Late plasticity for language in a child's non-dominant hemisphere. *Brain*, 125, 361–72.

Hertz-Pannier, L., Chiron, C., Van de Moortele, P-F., Bourgeois, M., Fohlen, M. and Dulac, O. (1999) Multi-task fMRI presurgical language mapping in children with cognitive impairment. *Neuroimage*, 9, S691.

Hesslinger, V.M. and Carbon, C.C. (2016) The Dress: The role of illumination information and individual differences in the psychophysics of perceiving white-blue ambiguities. *i-Perception*, 7(2), 2041669516645592.

Hestbaek, A.D. (1998) Parenthood in the 1990s: Tradition and modernity in the parenthood of dual-earner couples with different lifemodes. *Childhood*, 5(4), 473-91.

Hewstone, M. (1989) *Causal Attribution: From cognitive processes to collective beliefs.* Oxford: Blackwell.

Hewstone, M. (1996) Contact and categorization: Social psychological interventions to change intergroup relations. In C.N. Macrae, C. Stangor and M. Hewstone (eds) *Stereotypes and Stereotyping.* New York: Guilford Press, pp. 323-68.

Hickok, G. and Poeppel, D. (2004) Dorsal and ventral streams: A framework for understanding aspects of the functional anatomy of language. *Cognition*, 92, 67-99.

Hicks, L.L., McNulty, J.K., Meltzer, A.L. and Olson, M.A. (2016) Capturing the interpersonal implications of evolved preferences? Frequency of sex shapes automatic, but not explicit partner evaluations. *Psychological Science*, 7, 826-47.

Higgins, E.T. (1987) Self-discrepancy: A theory relating self and affect. *Psychological Review*, 94, 319-40.

Higgins, E.T. (1997) Beyond pleasure and pain. *American Psychologist*, 52, 1280-300.

Higgins, E.T. (1998) Promotion and prevention: Regulatory focus as a motivational principle. *Advances in Experimental Social Psychology*, 30, 1-46.

Higgins, E.T. and Silberman, I. (1998) Development of regulatory focus: Promotion and prevention as ways of living. In J. Heckhausen and C.S. Dweck (eds) *Motivation and Self-regulation across the Lifespan.* New York: Cambridge University Press, pp. 78-113.

Higgins, E.T. and Tykocinski, O. (1992) Self-discrepancies and biographical memory: Personality and cognition at the level of psychological situation. *Personality and Social Psychology Bulletin*, 18, 527-35.

Higgins, E.T., Roney, C., Crowe, E. and Hymes, C. (1994) Ideal versus ought predilections for approach and avoidance: Distinct self-regulatory systems. *Journal of Personality and Social Psychology*, 66, 276-86.

Higgins, E.T., Rholes, W.S. and Jones, C.R. (1977) Category accessibility and impression formation. *Journal of Experimental Social Psychology*, 13, 141-54.

Higgins, S.T., Budney, A.J. and Bickel, W.K. (1994) Applying behavioral concepts and principles to the treatment of cocaine dependence. *Drug and Alcohol Dependence*, 7, 19-38.

Higgins, S.T., Hughes, J.R. and Bickel, W.K. (1989) Effects of d-amphetamine on choice in social versus monetary reinforcement: A discrete trial test. *Pharmacology, Biochemistry, and Behavior*, 34, 297-301.

Higgs, S. (2015) Social norms and their influence on eating behaviours. *Appetite*, 86, 38-44.

Higgs, S. and Thomas, J. (2016) Social influences on eating. *Current Opinion in Behavioural Sciences*, 9, 1-6.

Higgs, S. and Woodward, M. (2009) Television watching during lunch increases afternoon snack intake of young women. *Appetite*, 52(1), 39-43.

Hilgard, E.R. (1978) States of consciousness in hypnosis: Divisions or levels? In F.H. Frankel and H.S. Zamansky (eds) *Hypnosis at Its Bicentennial: Selected Papers.* New York: Plenum Press.

Hilgard, E.R. (1986) *Divided Consciousness: Multiple controls in human thought and action.* New York: Wiley.

Hilgard, E.R. (1991) A neodissociation interpretation of hypnosis. In S.J. Lynn and J.H. Rhue (eds) *Theories of Hypnosis: Current models and perspectives.* New York: Guilford Press.

Hilgard, E.R. and Hilgard, J.R. (1994) *Hypnosis in the Relief of Pain.* New York: Brunner/Mazel.

Hill, H. and Bruce, V. (1996) Effects of lighting on the perception of facial surfaces. *Journal of Experimental Psychology: Human Perception and Performance*, 22(4), 986-1004.

Hill, R.A. and Barton, R.A. (2005) Red enhances human performance in contests. *Nature*, 435, 293.

Hill, S.E., Rodeheffer, C.D., Griskevicius, V., Durante, K. and White, A.E. (2012) Boosting beauty in an economic decline: mating, spending and the lipstick effect. *Journal of Personality and Social Psychology*, 103, 275-91.

Hillebrand, H. (2004) On the generality of the latitudinal diversity gradient. *American Nature*, 163, 192-211.

Hilton, D.J. (1990) Conversational processes and causal explanation. *Psychological Bulletin*, 107, 65-81.

Hilton, J. L. and von Hippel, W. (1996) Stereotypes. Annual Review of *Psychology*, 47, 237-71.

Hilton, J.M., Anngela-Cole, L. and Wakita, J. (2010) A cross-cultural comparison of factors associated with school bullying in Japan and the United States. *The Family Journal*, 18, 413-22.

Hinde, R.A., Titmus, G., Easton, D. and Tamplin, A. (1985) Incidence of 'friendship' and behaviour with strong associates versus non-associates in preschoolers. *Child Development*, 56, 234-45.

Hines, M. (2010) Sex-related variation in human behavior and the brain. *TiCS*, 14, 448-56.

Hines, T. (2014) Neuromythology of Einstein's brain. *Brain and Cognition*, 88, 21-5.

Hirayasu, Y., Shenton, M.E., Salisbury, D.F., Kwon, J.S., Wible, C.G., Fischer, I.A., Yurgelun-Todd, D., Zarate, C., Kikinis, R., Jolesz, F.A. and McCarley, R.W. (1999) Subgenual cingulate cortex volume in first-episode psychosis. *American Journal of Psychiatry*, 156, 1091-3.

Hirnstein, M., Bayer, U. and Hausmann, M. (2009) Sex-specific response strategies in mental rotation. *Learning and Individual Differences*, 19, 225-8.

Hirschfeld, R.M.A. (2001) Clinical importance of long-term antidepressant treatment. *British Journal of Psychiatry*, 179 (suppl. 42), s4-s8.

Hirsh, J.B. and Peterson, J.B. (2009) Personality and language use in self-narratives. *Journal of Research in Personality*, 43, 524-7.

Hirst, W. and Phelps E.A. (2016) Flashbulb memories. *Current Directions in Psychological Science*, 25, 36-41.

Hirst, W. *et al.* (2009) Long-term memory for the terrorist attack of September 11: Flashbulb memories, event memories, and the factors that influence their retention. *Journal of Experimental Psychology: General*, 138, 161-76.

Hitch, G.J., Towse, J.N. and Hutton, U. (2001) What limits children's working memory span? Theoretical accounts and applications for scholastic development. *Journal of Experimental Psychology: General*, 130, 184-98.

Ho, M.R. and Bennett, T.L. (1997) *Archives of Clinical Neuropsychology*, 12(1), 1-11.

Hobson, J.A. (1988) *The Dreaming Brain.* New York: Basic Books.

Hockett, C.F. (1960a) Logical considerations in the study of animal communication. In W.E. Lanyon and W.N. Tavolga (eds) *Animal Sounds and Communication.* Washington DC: American Institute of Biological Sciences.

Hockett, C.F. (1960b) The origin of speech. *Scientific American Mind*, 203, 89-96.

Hockey, J. and James, A. (1995) Back to Our Futures: Imaging second childhood. In M. Featherstone and A. Wernick (eds) *Images of Ageing*. London: Routledge.

Hodapp, V. and Langfeldt, H-P. (2006) Learning and teaching psychology as a major subject in Germany. *International Journal of Psychology*, 41(1), 24–8.

Hodson, G. and Busseri, M.A. (2012) Bright minds and dark attitudes: Lower cognitive ability predicts greater prejudice through right-wing ideology and low intergroup contact. *Psychological Science*, 23, 187–95.

Hoeft, F. et al. (2006) Neural basis of dyslexia. *Journal of Neuroscience*, 26, 10700–8.

Hoeft, F., Meyler, A., Hernandez, A., Juel, C., Taylor-Hill, H., Martindale, J.L., McMillon, G., Kolchugina, G., Black, J.M. and Faizi, A. (2007) Functional and morphometric brain dissociation between dyslexia and reading ability. *Proceedings of the National Academy of Sciences*, 104, 4234–9.

Hoeft, F., Meyler, A., Hernandez, C. and Juel, H. (2007) Functional and morphometric brain dissociation between dyslexia and reading ability. *PNAS*, 104, 4234–9.

Hoek, H.W. and van Hoeken, D. (2003) Review of the prevalence and incidence of eating disorders. *International Journal of Eating Disorders*, 34, 383–96.

Hofstede, G. (1980) *Culture's Consequences: International differences in work-related values*. Beverly Hills, CA: Sage.

Hogg, M.A. (2000) Subjective uncertainty reduction through self-categorization: A motivational theory of social identity processes. *European Review of Social Psychology*, 11, 223–55.

Hogg, M.A. (2001) A social identity theory of leadership. *Personality and Social Psychology Review*, 5, 184–200.

Hogg, M.A. (2006) Social identity theory. In P.J. Burke (ed.) *Contemporary Social Psychological Theories*. Palo Alto, CA: Stanford University Press, pp. 111–36

Hogg, M.A. and Abrams, D. (1988) *Social Identifications: A social psychology of intergroup relations and group processes*. London: Routledge.

Hogg, M.A. and van Knippenberg, D. (2003) Social identity and leadership processes in groups. In M.P. Zanna (ed.) *Advances in Experimental Social Psychology*, Vol. 35. San Diego, CA: Academic Press.

Hogg, M.A. and Vaughan, G.M. (2007) *Social Psychology* (5th edn). London: Pearson Education, Prentice Hall Europe.

Holden, R. (1993) *Laughter – The Best Medicine*. London: Thorsons.

Holland, C.A. and Rabbitt, P. (1991) The course and causes of cognitive change with advancing age. *Reviews in Clinical Gerontology*, 1, 81–96.

Holland, J.L. (1997) *Making vocational choices: A theory of vocational personalities and work environments* (3rd edn). Odessa: PAR.

Hollander, E.P. (1958) Conformity, status, and idiosyncrasy credit. *Psychological Review*, 65, 117–27.

Holman, D. (2014) Exploring the relationship between social class, mental illness stigma and mental health literacy using British national survey data. *Health*, 1–17.

Holmes, J. et al. (2009a) Adaptive training leads to sustained enhancement of poor working memory in children. *Developmental Science*, 12, 9–15.

Holmes, J. et al. (2009b) Working memory deficits can be overcome: impacts of training and medication on working memory in children with ADHD. *Applied Cognitive Psychology*, 12, 9–15.

Holmes, J.D. (2014) Undergraduate psychology's scientific identity dilemma: Student and instructor interests and attitudes. *Teaching of Psychology*, 41, 104–9.

Holmes, T.H. and Rahe, R.H. (1967) The social readjustment rating scale. *Journal of Psychosomatic Research*, 11, 213–18.

Holtgraves, T. (2011) Text messaging, personality and the social context. *Journal of Research in Personality*, 45, 92–9.

Holyoak, K.J. (1990) Problem solving. In D.N. Osherson and E.E. Smith (eds) *An Invitation to Cognitive Science. Vol. 3: Thinking*. Cambridge, MA: MIT Press.

Holyoak, K.J. and Spellman, B.A. (1993) Thinking. *Annual Review of Psychology*, 44, 265–315.

Holzel, B.K., Carmody, J., Evans, K.C., Hoge, E.A., Dusek, J.A., Morgan, L., Pitman, R.K. and Lazar, S.W. (2009) Stress reduction correlates with structural changes in the amygdala. *Social Cognitive and Affective Neuroscience*, 5, 11–17.

Holzel, B.K., Carmody, J., Vangel, M., Congleton, C., Terramsetti, S.M., Gard, T. and Lazar, S.W. (2011) Mindfulness practice leads to increase in regional brain grey matter density. *Psychiatry Research: Neuroimaging*, 191, 36–43.

Homa, D. (1983) An assessment of two extraordinary speed-readers. *Bulletin of the Psychonomic Society*, 21, 123–6.

Homae, F. Watanabe, H., Nakano, T. and Taga, G. (2011) Large-scale brain networks underlying language acquisition in early infancy. *Frontiers in Psychology*, 2, article 93.

Honda, A. and Nihei, Y. (2009) Sex differences in object location memory: The female advantage of immediate detection of changes. *Learning and Individual Differences*, 19, 234–7.

Honess, T.M. and Charman, E.A. (2002) Member of the jury – guilty of incompetence? *The Psychologist*, 15, 72–5.

Hooley, J.M. (2010) Social factors in schizophrenia. *Current Directions in Psychological Science*, 19, 238–42.

Hooley, J.M. and Teasdale, J.D. (1989) Predictors of relapse in unipolar depressives: Expressed emotion, marital distress and perceived criticism. *Journal of Abnormal Psychology*, 98, 229–35.

Hooley, J.M., Rosen, L.R. and Richters, J.E. (1996) Expressed emotion: Toward clarification of a critical construct. In G. Miller (ed.) *The Behavioural High-risk Paradigm in Psychopathology*. New York: Springer-Verlag.

Hoorens, V. (1993) Self-enhancement and superiority biases in social comparison. *European Review of Social Psychology*, 4, 113–39.

Hoorens, V. and Nuttin, J.M. (1993) Overvaluation of own attributes: Mere ownership or subjective frequency? *Social Cognition*, 11, 177–200.

Hope, T.M.H., Prejawa, S., Jones, O., Oberhuber, M., Seghier, M.L., Green, D.W. and Price, C.J. (2014) Dissecting the functional anatomy of auditory word repetition. *Frontiers in Human Neuroscience*, 8, 246.

Hopia, H., Paavilanen, E. and Asted-Kurki, P. (2005) The diversity of family health: Constituent systems and resources. *Scandinavian Journal of Caring Sciences*, 19, 186–95.

Hopkins, E.J., Weisberg, D.S. and Taylor, J.C.V. (2016) The seductive allure is a reductive allure: People prefer scientific explanations that contain logically irrelevant reductive information. *Cognition*, 155, 67–76.

Hopkins, N. and Hall, S. (2000) David Copeland: a quiet introvert, obsessed with Hitler and bombs. The Guardian, 30 June. www.guardian.co.uk/Archive/Article/0,4273,4035463,00.html.

Hopkins, W.D. and Cantal.upo, C. (2008) Theoretical speculations on the evolutionary origins of hemispheric specialization. *Current Directions in Psychological Science*, 17(3), 233–7.

Hopkinson, N.S., Lester-George, A., Ormiston-Smith, N., Cox, A. and Arnott, D. (2014) Child uptake of smoking by area across the UK. *Thorax*, 69, 873–5.

Hoptman, M.J. and Davidson, R.J. (1994) How and why do the two cerebral hemispheres interact? *Psychological Bulletin*, 116(2), 195–219.

Horn, G. (1998) Visual imprinting and the neural mechanisms of recognition memory. *Trends in Neurosciences*, 21(7), 300–35.

Horn, J.L. (1978) Human ability systems. In F.B. Baltes (ed.) *Life Span Development*, Vol 1. New York: Academic Press.

Horn, J.L. and Cattell, R.B. (1966) Refinement and test of the theory of fluid and crystallized ability intelligences. *Journal of Educational Psychology*, 57, 253–70.

Hornak, J., Rolls, E.T. and Wade, D. (1996) Face and voice expression identification in patients with emotional and behavioural changes following ventral frontal lobe damage. *Neuropsychologia*, 34(4), 247–61.

Horne, J.A. (1978) A review of the biological effects of total sleep deprivation in man. *Biological Psychology*, 7, 55–102.

Horne, J.A. (1988) *Why We Sleep: The functions of sleep in humans and other mammals*. Oxford: Oxford University Press.

Horne, J.A. and Minard, A. (1985) Sleep and sleepiness following a behaviourally 'active' day. *Ergonomics*, 28, 567–75.

Horne, J.A. and Reyner, L.A. (1996) Driver sleepiness: Comparisons of practical countermeasures – caffeine and a nap. *Psychophysiology*, 33, 306–9.

Horney, K. (1950) *Neurosis and Human Growth*. New York: W.W. Norton.

Hornik, J. (1987) The effect of touch and gaze upon compliance and interest of interviewees. *The Journal of Social Psychology*, 127, 681–3.

Hornik, J. (1992) Tactile stimulation and consumer response. *Journal of Consumer Research*, 19(3), 449–58.

Hornsey, M.J. and Hogg, M.A. (2000) Assimilation and diversity: An integrative model of subgroup relations. *Personality and Social Psychology Review*, 4, 143–56.

Hornstein, S.L., Brown, A.S. and Mulligan, N.W. (2003) Long-term flashbulb memory for learning of Princess Diana's death. *Memory*, 11(3), 293–306.

Horowitz, M.J. (1979) Psychological response to serious life events. In V. Hamilton and D.M. Warburton (eds) *Human Stress and Cognition*. New York: Wiley.

Horowitz, M.J. (1986) *Stress Response Syndromes* (2nd edn). Northvale, NJ: Jason Aronson.

Horowitz-Kraus, T., Cicchino, N., Amiel, M., Holland, S.K. and Breznitz, Z. (2014) Reading improvement in English and Hebrew-speaking children with reading difficulties after reading acceleration training. *Annals of Dyslexia*, 64, 183–201.

Horwitz, B. and Braun, A.R. (2004) Brain network interactions in visual and linguistical processing. *Brain and Language*, 89, 377–84.

Hosseini, S.H., Black, J.M., Soriano, T., Bugescu, N., Martinez, R., Raman, M.M., . . . and Hoeft, F. (2013) Topological properties of large-scale structural brain networks in children with familial risk for reading difficulties. *Neuroimage*, 71, 260–74.

Hosseini, S.M., Kramer, J.H. and Kesler, S.R. (2014) Neural correlates of cognitive intervention in persons at risk of developing Alzheimer's disease. *Frontiers in Aging Neuroscience*, 6, 231.

Hosseini, S.M.H., Black, J.M., Soriano, T., Bugescu, N., Martinez, R., Raman, M.M., Kesler, S.R. and Hoeff, F. (2013) Topological properties of large-scale structural brain networks in children with familial risk for reading difficulties. *Neuroimage*, 71, 260–74.

House, R.J., Hanges, P.W., Javidan, M., Dorfman, P. and Gupta, V. (2004) *Culture, Leadership and Organization: the GLOBE study of 62 societies*. Thousand Oaks, CA: Sage.

Houston, D.M. (1994) Gloomy but smarter: The academic consequences of attributional style. *British Journal of Social Psychology*, 33, 433–41.

Houston, J.P. (1983) Psychology: A closed system of self-evident information? *Psychological Reports*, 52, 203–8.

Houts, A.C. (2001) The diagnostic and statistical manual's new white coat and circulatory of plausible dysfunctions: response to Wakefield Part I. *Behaviour Research and Therapy*, 39, 315–45.

Houts, A.C. and Follette, W.C. (1998) Mentalism, mechanisms, and medical analogues: Reply to Wakefield (1998) *Journal of Consulting and Clinical Psychology*, 66, 853–5.

Hovland, C.I. and Weiss, W. (1951) The influence of source credibility on communication effectiveness. *Public Opinion Quarterly*, 15, 635–50.

Hovland, C.I., Janis, I.L. and Kelley, H.H. (1953) *Communication and Persuasion*. New Haven, CT: Yale University Press.

Howard, L.R., Javadi, A.H., Yu, Y., Mill, R.D., Morrison, L.C., Knight, R., Loftus, M.M., Staskute, L. and Spiers, H.J. (2014) The hippocampus and entorhinal cortex encode the path and Euclidean distances to goals during navigation. *Current Biology*, 24, 1331–40.

Howard, S., Adams, J and White, M. (2012) Nutritional content of supermarket ready meals and recipes by television chefs in the United Kingdom. *BMJ*, 345, e7607.

Howarth, C., Gleeson, P. and Attwell, D. (2012) Updated energy budgets for neural computation in the neocortex and cerebellum. *Journal of Cerebral Blood Flow Metabolism*, 32, 1222–32.

Howell, J.L., Collisson, B. and King, K.M. (2014) Physics envy: Psychologists' perceptions of psychology and agreement about core concepts. *Teaching of Psychology*, 41, 330–4.

Howes, O.D., McCutcheon, R., Owen, M.J. and Murray, R.M. (2016) The role of genes, stress and dopamine in the development of schizophrenia. *Biological Psychiatry*, 81, 9–20.

Howitt, D. (2002) *Forensic and Criminal Psychology*. Harlow: Prentice Hall.

Howlett, A.C. (1990) Reverse pharmacology applied to the cannabinoid receptor. *Trends in Pharmacological Sciences*, 11, 395–7.

Howlett, M., Doody, K., Murray, J., LeBlanc-Duchin, D., Fraser, J. and Atkinson, P. R. (2015) Burnout in emergency department healthcare professionals is associated with coping style: a cross-sectional survey. *Emergency Medicine Journal*, emermed-2014.

Hoy, K.E., Emonson, M.R., Arnold, S.L., Thomson, R.H., Daskalakis, Z.J. and Fitzgerald, P. (2013) Testing the limits: investigating the effect of tDCS dose on working memory enhancement in healthy controls. *Neuropsychologia*, 51, 1777–84.

Hsee, C.K., Zhang, J., Lu, Z. and Xu, F. (2013) Unit asking: a method to boost donations and beyond. *Psychological Science*, 24, 1801–8.

Hsu, C-T., Jacobs, A.M., Altmann, U. and Conrad, M. (2015) The magical activation of left amygdala when reading Harry Potter: An fMRI study on how descriptions of supra-natural events entertain and enchant. *PLoS ONE*, 10, e011879.

Hu, W., Lee, H.L., Zhang, Q., Liu, T., Geng, L.B., Seghier, M.L., Shakeshaft, C., Twomey, T., Green, D.W., Yang, Y.M. and Price, C.J. (2010) Developmental dyslexia in Chinese and English populations: dissociating the effect of dyslexia from language differences. *Brain*, 133, 1694–706.

Hubbard, R. and Vetter, D. E. (1991) Replications in the finance literature: An empirical study. *The Quarterly Journal of Business and Economics*, 30, 70–81.

Hubbard, R. and Vetter, D. E. (1996) An empirical comparison of published replication research in accounting, economics, finance, management, and marketing. *Journal of Business Research*, 35, 153–64.

Hubel, D.H. and Wiesel, T.N. (1977) Functional architecture of macaque monkey visual cortex. *Proceedings of the Royal Society of London (Series B)*, 198, 1–59.

Hubel, D.H. and Wiesel, T.N. (1979) Brain mechanisms of vision. *Scientific American Mind*, 241, 150–62.

Hübener, F., Laska, M., Kobayakawa, T. and Saito, S. (in press) Cross-cultural comparison of olfactory perception in Japanese and Germans. *Food Quality and Preference*.

Huczynski, A. and Buchanan, D. (2010) *Organizational Behaviour* (7th edn). Harlow: FT/Prentice Hall.

Hudson, G. and Busseri, M.A. (2012) Bright minds and dark attitudes: Lower cognitive ability predicts greater prejudice through right-wing ideology and low inter-group contact. *Psychological Science*, 23, 187–95.

Hughes, C., Dunn, J. and White, A. (1998) Trick or treat? Uneven understanding of mind and emotion and executive dysfunction in 'hard-to-manage' preschoolers. *Journal of Child Psychology and Psychiatry*, 39(7), 981–94.

Hughes, E.J., Bond, J., Svrckova, P., Makropoulos, A., Ball, G., Sharp, D.J., Edwards, A.D., Hajnal, J.V. and Counsell, S.J. (2012) Regional changes in thalamic shape and volume with increasing age. *Neuroimage*, 63, 1134–42.

Hughes, J.R. and Pierattini, R. (1992) An introduction to pharmacotherapy. In J. Grabowski and G.R. Vandenbos (eds) *Psychopharmacology: Basic mechanisms and applied interventions. Master Lectures in Psychology.* Washington, DC: American Psychological Association.

Hughes, S., Lyddy, F., Kaplan, R., Nichols, A.L., Miller, H., Saad, C.G., Dukes, K. and Lynch, A-J. (2015) Highly prevalent but not always persistent: Undergraduate and graduate student's misconceptions about psychology. *Teaching of Psychology*, 42, 34–42.

Hulit, L.M. and Howard, M.R. (1993) *Born to Talk: An introduction to speech and language development.* New York: Merrill/Macmillan.

Hull, C.L. (1943) *Principles of Behavior.* New Haven, CT: Yale University Press.

Hull, C.L. (1952) *A Behaviour System.* New Haven, CT: Yale University Press.

Hull, R. and Vaid, J. (2007) Bilingual language lateralization: A meta-analytic tale of two hemispheres. *Neuropsychologia*, 45, 1987–2008.

Hulme, C. and Roodenrys, S. (1995) Practitioner review: Verbal working memory development and its disorders. *Journal of Child Psychology and Psychiatry*, 36(3), 373–98.

Humphreys, G.W. and Riddoch, M.J. (1987a) *To See or Not to See: A case study of visual object processing.* Hove: Psychology Press.

Humphreys, G.W. and Riddoch, M.J. (1987b) The fractionation of visual agnosia. In G.W. Humphreys and M.J. Riddoch (eds) *Visual Object Agnosia: A cognitive neuropsychological approach.* Hove: Psychology Press.

Hund-Georgiadis, M. and von Cramon, D.Y. (1999) Motor-learning related changes in piano players and non-musicians revealed by functional magnetic resonance signals. *Experimental Brain Research*, 125, 417–25.

Hundhammer, T. and Mussweiler, T. (2012) How sex puts you in gendered shoes: Sexuality-priming leads to gender-based self-perception and behavior. *Journal of Personality and Social Psychology*, 103, 176–93.

Hunt, M. (1974) *Sexual Behavior in the 1970s.* Chicago, IL: Playboy.

Hunter, J.A., Platow, M.J., Howard, M.L. and Stringer M. (1996) Social identity and intergroup evaluative bias: Realistic categories and domain specific self-esteem in a conflict setting. *European Journal of Social Psychology*, 26, 631–47.

Hunter, P.G., Schellenberg, E.G. and Schimmack, U. (2010) Feelings and perceptions of happiness and sadness induced by music: Similarities, differences, and mixed emotions. *Psychology of Aesthetics, Creativity, and the Arts*, 4(1), 47.

Hur, Y-M. (2007) Stability of genetic influence on morningness-eveningness: A cross-sectional examination of South Korean twins from preadolescence to young adulthood. *Journal of Sleep Research*, 16, 17–23.

Hurleman, R., Patin, A., Onur, O.A., Cohen, M.X., Baumgartner, T., Meltzer, S. et al. (2010) Oxytocin enhances amygdala-dependent, socially reinforced learning and emotional empathy in humans. *Journal of Neuroscience*, 30, 4999–5007.

Hurley, J.C. and Underwood, M.K. (2002) Children's understanding of their research rights before and after debriefing: Informed assent, confidentiality and stopping participation. *Child Development*, 73, 132–43.

Hurley, R.W. and Adams, M.C. (2008) Sex, gender, and pain: an overview of a complex field. *Anesthesia and Analgesia*, 107(1), 309.

Huston, A.C. (1983) Sex-typing. In E.M. Hetherington (ed.) *Handbook of Child Psychology, Vol. 4: Socialization, Personality, and Social Development.* New York: Wiley.

Hutchison, P.A. and Abrams, D. (2003) Ingroup identification moderates stereotype change in reaction to deviance. *European Journal of Social Psychology*, 33(4), 499–506.

Hwang, R-J., Chen, L-F., Yeh, T-C., Tu, P-C., Tu, C-H. and Hsieh, J-C. (2008) The resting frontal alpha asymmetry across the menstrual cycle: A magnetoencephalographic study. *Hormones and Behavior*, 54, 28–33.

Hyde, C.L., Nagle, M.W., Tian, C., Chen, X., Paciga, S.A., Wendland, J.R., . . . and Winslow, A.R. (2016) Identification of 15 genetic loci associated with risk of major depression in individuals of European descent. *Nature Genetics*, 48(9), 1031–6.

Hygge, S., Evans, G.W. and Bullinger, M. (2002) A prospective study of some effects of aircraft noise on cognitive performance in schoolchildren. *Psychological Science*, 13(5), 469–74.

Hyman, B.T. *et al.* (2012) NIA-Alzheimer's Association guidelines for the neruopathologic assessment of Alzheimer's disease. *Alzheimer's Disease*, 8, 1–13.

Hyona, J., Lorch, R.F. and Kaakinen, J.K. (2002) Individual differences in reading to summarize expository text: Evidence from eye fixation patterns. *Journal of Educational Psychology*, 94, 44–55.

Idring, S., Rai, D., Dal, H., Dalman, C., Strum, H. and Zander, E. (2012) Autism spectrum disorders in the Stockholm youth project. *PLoS ONE*, 7, e41280.

Iidaka, T. (2013) Role of the fusiform gyrus and superior temporal sulcus in face perception and recognition. *Japanese Psychological Research*, 56, 33–45.

Imada, A.S. and Hakel, M.D. (1977) Influence of nonverbal communication and rater proximity on impressions and decisions in simulated employment interviews. *Journal of Applied Psychology*, 62, 295–300.

Imafuku, M., Hakuno, Y., Uchida-Ota, M., Yamamoto, J-I. and Minagawa, Y. (2014) 'Mom called me!' Behavioural and prefrontal responses of infants to self-names spoken by their mothers. *Neuroimage*, 103, 476–84.

Inbau, F.E., Reid, J.E. and Buckley, J.P. (1986) *Criminal Interrogation and Confessions* (3rd edn). Baltimore, MO: Williams & Wilkins.

Indefrey, P. and Levelt, W.J. (2004) The spatial and temporal signatures of word production components. *Cognition*, 92, 101–44.

Ingham, A.G., Levinger, G., Graves, J. and Peckham, V. (1974) The Ringelmann effect: Studies of group size and group performance. *Journal of Experimental Social Psychology*, 10, 371–84.

Inglefinger, F.J. (1944) The late effects of total and subtotal gastrectomy. *New England Journal of Medicine*, 231, 321–7.

Inglehart, R., Foa, R., Peterson, C. and Welzel, C. (2008) Development, freedom and rising happiness. *Perspectives on Psychological Science*, 3, 264–85.

Inhelder, B. and Piaget, J. (1958) *The Growth of Logical Thinking from Childhood to Adolescence: An essay on the construction of formal operational structures.* New York: Basic Books.

Innes, M. (2004) Crime as signal, crime as a memory. *Journal for Crime, Conflict and the Media*, 1(2), 15–22.

Innocence Project (2016) https://www.innocenceproject.org/dna-exonerations-in-the-united-states/

Intraub, H. and Richardson, M. (1989) Wide-angle memories of close-up scenes. *Journal of Experimental Psychology: LMC*, 15, 179–87.

Ioannidis, J.P. (2005) Contradicted and initially stronger effects in highly cited clinical research. *JAMA*, 294(2), 218–28.

Ionnanidis, J.P.A. (2005) Contradicted and initially stronger effects in highly cited clinical research. *JAMA*, 294, 218–28.

Ireland, M.E., Slatcher, R.B., Eastwick, P.W., Scissors, L.E., Finkel, E.J. and Pennebaker, J.W. (2011) Language style matching predicts relationship initiation and stability. *Psychological Science*, 29, 39–44.

Irish, L.A., Kline, C.E., Gunn, H.E., Buysse, D.J. and Hall, M.A. (2015) The role of sleep hygiene in promoting public health: A review of empirical evidence. *Sleep Medicine Reviews*, 22, 23–36.

Irvine, K., Laws, K.R., Gale, T.M. and Kondel, T.K. (2012) Greater cognitive deterioration in women than men with Alzheimer's disease: a meta analysis. *Journal of Clinical and Experimental Neuropsychology*, 34(9), 989–98.

Irwin, M.R., Cole, J.C. and Nicassio, P.M. (2006) Comparative meta-analysis of behavioural interventions for insomnia and their efficacy in middle-aged adults and in older adults 55+ years of age. *Health Psychology*, 25, 1, 3–14.

Isaacowitz, D.M. (2005) Correlates of well-being in adulthood and of old age: A tale of two optimisms. *Journal of Research in Personality*, 39, 224–44.

Isaacs, E.B., Edmonds, C.J., Lucas, A. and Gadian, D.G. (2001) Calculation difficulties in children of very low birthweight: A neural correlate. *Brain*, 124, 1701–7.

Isabella, R.A. and Belsky, J. (1991) Interactional synchrony and the origins of infant–mother attachment: A replication study. *Child Development*, 62, 373–84.

Isawa, N. (1992) Postconventional reasoning and moral education in Japan. *Journal of Moral Education*, 21, 3–16.

Isen, A.M. and Geva, N. (1987) The influence of positive affect on acceptable levels of risk and thoughts about losing: The person with a large canoe has a large worry. *Organizational Behaviour and Human Decision Processes*, 39, 145–54.

Isen, A.M. and Patrick, R. (1983) The effects of positive feelings on risk taking: When the chips are down. *Organizational Behaviour and Human Performance*, 31, 194–202.

Isen, A.M., Daubman, K.A. and Nowicki, G.P. (1987) Positive affect facilitates creative problem solving. *Journal of Personality and Social Psychology*, 52, 1122–31.

Isenberg, D.J. (1986) Group polarization: A critical review and meta-analysis. *Psychological Bulletin*, 50, 1141–51.

Ishi, H., Gyoba, J., Kamachi, M., Mukaida, S. and Akamatsu, S. (2004) Analyses of facial attractiveness on feminised and juvenilised faces. *Perception*, 33, 135–45.

Ishikawa, S.S., Raine, A., Lencz, T., Bihrle, S. and Lacasse, L. (2001) Autonomic stress reactivity and executive functions in successful and unsuccessful criminal psychopaths from the community. *Journal of Abnormal Psychology*, 110(3), 423–32.

Iversen, S.D. and Iversen, L.L. (2007) Dopamine: 50 years in perspective. *Trends in Neurosciences*, 30 (5), 188–93.

Izard, C.E. (1977) *Human Emotions*. New York: Plenum Press.

Izard, C.E. (1992) Basic emotions, relations among emotions, and emotion-cognition relations. *Psychological Review*, 99, 561–5.

Jabalpurwala, I. (2016) Brain Canada: One brain one community. *Neuron*, 92, 601–6.

Jablensky, A. (1989) Epidemiology and cross-cultural aspects of schizophrenia. *Psychiatric Annals*, 19, 516–24.

Jablensky, A., Sartorious, N., Ernberg, G., Anker, M., Korten, A., Cooper, J.E., Day, R. and Bertelsen, A. (1992) *Schizophrenia: Manifestations, incidence and course in different cultures. A WHO ten country study. Psychological*

Medicine Monograph Supplement 20. Cambridge: Cambridge University Press.

Jacklin, C.N. and Maccoby, E.E. (1983) Issues of gender differentiation in normal development. In M.D. Levine, W.B. Carey, A.C. Crocker and R.T. Gross (eds) *Developmental-Behavioral Pediatrics*. Philadelphia: Saunders.

Jackson, A.F. and Bolger, D.J. (2014) The neurophysiological bases of EEG and EEG measurement: A review for the rest of us. *Psychophysiology*, 51, 1061–71.

Jackson, J.J., Connolly, J.J., Garrison, S.M., Leveille, M.M. and Connolly, S.L. (2015) Your friends know how long you will live: a 75-year study of peer-rated personality traits. *Psychological Science*, 26, 335–40.

Jackson, P.L., Meltzoff, A.N. and Decety, J. (2006) Neural circuits involved in imitation and perspective-taking. *Neuroimage*, 31, 429–39.

Jacob, C., Guéguen, N. and Boulbry, G. (2015) Effect of an unexpected small favor on compliance with a survey request. *Journal of Business Research*, 68(1), 56–9.

Jacob, R. and Parkinson, J. (2015) The potential for school-based interventions that target executive function to improve academic achievement: A review. *Review of Educational Research*, 85(4), 512–52.

Jacoby, L.L., Bishara, A.J., Hessels, S. and Toth, J.P. (2005) Aging, subjective experience, and cognitive control: Dramatic false remembering by older adults. *Journal of Experimental Psychology: General*, 134, 2, 131–48.

Jadva, V., Hines, M. and Golombok, S. (2010) Infants' preferences for toys, colors and shapes. *Archives of Sexual Behaviour*, 39, 1261–73.

Jaeggi, A.V., De Groot, E., Stevens, J.M. and Van Schaik, C.P. (2013) Mechanisms of reciprocity in primates: testing for short-term contingency of grooming and food sharing in bonobos and chimpanzees. *Evolution and Human Behavior*, 34(2), 69–77.

Jaeggi, S.M., Buschkuehl, M., Jonides, J. and Perrig, W.J. (2008) Improving fluid intelligence with training on working memory. *PNAS*, 105, 6829–33.

Jaeggi, S.M., Studer-Luethi, B., Buschkuehl, M. and Su, Y.F. (2010) The relationship between n-back performance and matrix reasoning – implications for training and transfer. *Intelligence*, 38, 625–35.

Jaffe, J.H. (1985) Drug addiction and drug abuse. In L.S. Goodman and A. Gilman (eds) *The Pharmacological Basis of Therapeutics*, Vol. 7. New York: Macmillan.

Jaffe, S. and Hyde, J.S. (2000) Gender differences in moral orientation. *Psychological Bulletin*, 126, 703–26.

Jahanshad, N., Lee, A.D., Barysheva, M., McMahon, K.L., de Zubicary, G.I., Martin, N.G., Wright, M.J., Toga, A.W. and Thompson, P.M. (2010) Genetic influences on brain asymmetry: A DTI study of 374 twins and siblings. *Neuroimage*, 52, 455–69.

Jakobs, E., Manstead, A.S.R. and Fischer, A.H. (1999) Social motives, emotional feelings and smiling. *Cognition and Emotion*, 13(4), 321–45.

James, E.L., Bonsall, M.B., Hoppitt, L., Tunbridge, E.M., Geddes, J.R., Milton, A.L. and Holmes, E.A. (2015) Computer game play reduces intrusive memories of experimental trauma via reconsolidation update mechanisms. *Psychological Science*, 1–15.

James, P.A., Oparil, S., Carter, B.L., Cushman, W.C., Dennison-Himmelfarb, C., Handler, J., . . . and Smith, S.C. (2014) 2014 evidence-based guideline for the management of high blood pressure in adults: report from the panel members appointed to the Eighth Joint National Committee (JNC 8). *JAMA*, 311(5), 507–20.

James, W. (1884) What is an emotion? *Mind*, 9, 188–205.

James, W. (1890) *Principles of Psychology*. New York: Henry Holt.

James, W.P.T. and Trayhurn, P. (1981) Thermogenesis and obesity. *British Medical Bulletin*, 37, 43–8.

Jameson, K.A., Highnote, S.M. and Wasserman, L.M. (2001) Richer color experience in observers with multiple photopigment opsin genes. *Psychonomic Bulletin and Review*, 8(1), 244–61.

Jamison, K.R. (1989) Mood disorders and patterns of creativity in British writers and artists. *Psychiatry*, 52, 125–34.

Janata, P. (2009) The neural architecture of music-evoked autobiographical memories. *Cerebral Cortex*, 19, 2579–94.

Jang, K.L., McCrae, R.R., Angleitner, A., Riemann, R. and Livesley, W.J. (1998) Heritability of facet-level traits in a cross-cultural twin sample: Support for a hierarchical model of personality. *Journal of Personality and Social Psychology*, 74, 1556–65.

Janis, I.L. (1967) Effects of fear arousal on attitude change: Recent developments in theory and experimental research. In L. Berkowitz (ed.) *Advances in Experimental Social Psychology*, Vol. 3. New York: Academic Press, pp. 167–224.

Janis, I.L. (1972) *Victims of Groupthink: A psychological study of foreign policy decisions and fiascoes*. Boston, MA: Houghton Mifflin.

Janis, I.L. (1982) *Groupthink: Psychological studies of policy decisions and fiascoes*. Boston: Houghton Mifflin.

Janis, I.L. and Feshbach, S. (1953) Effects of fear-arousing communications. *Journal of Abnormal and Social Psychology*, 48, 78–92.

Janowic, J. (1993) Tourette's syndrome: Phenomenology, pathophysiology, genetics, epidemiology and treatment. In S.H. Appel (ed.) *Current Neurology*, Vol. 13. Chicago: Mosby Yearbook.

Janowski, K.S. and Ciarkowska, W. (2008) Diurnal variation in energetic arousal, tense arousal, and hedonic tone in extreme morning and evening types. *Chronobiology International*, 25, 577–95.

Janowsky, J.S., Oviatt, S.K. and Orwoll, E.S. (1994) Testosterone influences spatial cognition in older men. *Behavioural Neuroscience*, 108, 325–32.

Janson, C., Gislason, T., de Backer, W., Plaschke, P., Bjornsson, E., Hetta, J. *et al.* (1995) Prevalence of sleep disturbances among young adults in three European countries. *Sleep*, 18, 589–97.

Janssen, S.M.J., Rubin, D.C. and St Jacques, P.L. (2011) The temporal distribution of autobiographical memory: Changes in reliving and vividness over the lifespan do not explain the reminiscence bump. *Memory and Cognition*, 39, 1–11.

Janz, N. and Becker, M.H. (1984) The health belief mode: A decade later. *Health Education Quarterly*, 11, 1–47.

Jaynes, J. (1970) The problem of animate motion in the seventeenth century. *Journal of the History of Ideas*, 6, 219–34.

Jeannerod, M., Decety, J. and Michel, F. (1994) Impairment of grasping movements following a bilateral posterior parietal lesion. *Neuropsychologia*, 32, 369–80.

Jeffcoate, W.J., Lincoln, N.B., Selby, C. and Herbert, M. (1986) Correlations between anxiety and serum prolactin in humans. *Journal of Psychosomatic Research*, 30, 217–22.

Jemmott, J.B. and Magloire, K. (1988) Academic stress, social support and secretory immunoglobin A. *Journal of Personality and Social Psychology*, 55, 803–10.

Jenkins, J.G. and Dallenbach, K.M. (1924) Oblivescence during sleep and waking. *American Journal of Psychology*, 35, 605–12.

Jenkins, J.M. and Foster, E.M. (2014) The effects of breastfeeding exclusivity on early childhood outcomes. *American Journal of Public Health*, 104(S1), S128–S135.

Jenkins, W.M., Merzenich, M.M., Ochs, M.T., Allard, T. and Guic-Robles, E. (1990) Functional reorganization of primary somatosensory cortex in adult owl monkeys after behaviourally controlled tactile stimulation. *Journal of Neurophysiology*, 63, 82–104.

Jensen, A.R. (1980) *Bias in Mental Testing*. New York: Free Press.

Jensen, A.R. (1985) The nature of the black-white difference on various psychometric tests: Spearman's hypothesis. *Behavioral and Brain Sciences*, 8, 193–263.

Jensen, K.B., Regenbogen, C., Ohse, M.C., Frasnelli, J., Freiherr, J. and Lundstrom, J.N. (2016) Brain activations during pain: A neuroimaging meta-analysis of pain patients and healthy controls. *Pain*, 157, 1279–86.

Jesser, C.J. (1989) Men and crying. *Changing Men*, 12, 72–3.

Jetten, J., Spears, R. and Manstead, A.S. (1997) Strength of identification and intergroup differentiation: The influence of group norms. *European Journal of Social Psychology*, 27(5), 603–9.

Ji, L-J., Guo, T., Zhang, Z. and Messervey, D. (2009) Looking into the past: Cultural differences in perception and representation of past information. *Journal of Personality and Social Psychology*, 96, 761–9.

Jilek-Aal, L. (1988) Suicidal behaviour among youth: A cross-cultural comparison. *Transcultural Psychiatric Research Review*, 25, 87–106.

Jobard, G., Crivello, F. and Tzourio-Mazoyer, N. (2003) Evaluation of the dual route theory of reading: a metaanalysis of 35 neuroimaging studies. *Neuroimage*, 20(2), 693–712.

Jobard, G., Crivello, F. and Tzourio-Mazoyer, N. (2003) Evaluation of the dual route theory of reading: A metaanalysis of 35 neuroimaging studies. *Neuroimage*, 20, 693–712.

Jobe, T.H. and Harrow, M. (2010) Schizophrenia course, long-term outcome, recovery and prognosis. *Current Directions in Psychological Science*, 19, 220–5.

Jockin, A., Arvey, R.D. and McGue, M. (2001) Perceived victimization moderates self-reports of workplace aggression and conflict. *Journal of Applied Psychology*, 86, 1262–9.

Jodelet, D. (1991) *Madness and Social Representations*. Hemel Hempstead: Harvester Wheatsheaf.

Joffe, H. (1996) AIDS research and prevention: A social representational approach. *British Journal of Medical Psychology*, 69, 169–90.

Joffe, H. (1997) Juxtaposing positivist and non-positivist approaches to social scientific AIDS research: Reply to Fife-Shaw's commentary. *British Journal of Medical Psychology*, 70, 75–83.

John, L.K., Lowenstein, G. and Prelec, D. (2012) Measuring the prevalence of questionable research practices with incentives for truth telling. *Psychological Science*, 23, 524–32.

Johnson, D.L. and Walker, T. (1991) A follow-up evaluation of the Houston Parent–Child Development Centre: School performance. *Journal of Early Intervention*, 15, 226–36.

Johnson, J. and Wood, A.M. (2017) Integrating positive and clinical psychology: Viewing human functioning as continua from positive to negative can benefit clinical assessment, interventions and understandings of resilience. *Cognitive Therapy and Research*, 41(3), 335–49.

Johnson, J., Panagioti, M., Bass, J., Ramsey, L. and Harrison, R. (2016) Resilience to emotional distress in response to failure, error or mistakes: A systematic review. *Clinical Psychology Review*.

Johnson, J.H., Butcher, J.N., Null, C. and Johnson, K.N. (1984) Replicated item level factor analysis of the full MMPI. *Journal of Personality and Social Psychology*, 47, 105–14.

Johnson, J.S. and Newport, E.L. (1989) Critical period effects in second language learning: The influence of maturational state on the acquisition of English as a second language. *Cognitive Psychology*, 21, 60–99.

Johnson, K.L., Gill, S., Reichman, V. and Tassinary, L.G. (2007) Swagger, sway, and sexuality: Judging sexual orientation from body motion and morphology. *Journal of Personality and Social Psychology*, 93, 321–34.

Johnson, M. (1998) The neural basis of cognitive development. In D. Kuhn and R.S. Siegler (eds) *Handbook of Child Psychology, Vol. 2: Cognition, perception and language*. New York: Wiley.

Johnson, M.H. (2001) Functional brain development in humans. *Nature Reviews Neuroscience*, 2, 472-83.

Johnson, M.H. (2010) Interactive specialization: a domain-general framework for human functional brain development. *Developmental Cognitive Neuroscience*, 1, 7-21.

Johnson, M.H., Grossmann, T. and Cohen, K.K. (2009) Mapping functional brain development. *Developmental Psychology*, 45, 151-9.

Johnson, M.K., Hashtroudi, S. and Lindsay, D.S. (1993) Source monitoring. *Psychological Bulletin*, 114, 3-28.

Johnson, S.A. *et al.* (2007) Beyond disgust: Impaired recognition of negative emotions prior to diagnosis in Huntington's disease. *Brain*, 130, 1732-44.

Johnson-Laird, P.N. (1983) *Mental Models*. Cambridge, MA: Harvard University Press.

Johnson-Laird, P.N. (1985) Deductive reasoning ability. In R.J. Sternberg (ed.) *Human Abilities: An information-processing approach*. New York: W.H. Freeman.

Johnson-Laird, P.N. (2010) Mental models and human reasoning. *PNAS*, 107, 18243-50.

Johnson-Laird, P.N. and Byrne, R.M.J. (1991) *Deduction*. Hillsdale, NJ: Lawrence Erlbaum Associates.

Johnson-Laird, P.N., Byrne, R.M.J. and Schaeken, W. (1992) Propositional reasoning by model. *Psychological Review*, 99, 418-39.

Johnston, P.J., Kaufman, J., Bajic, J., Sercombe, A., Michie, P.T. and Karayanidis, F. (2011) Facial emotion and identity processing development in 5 to 15 year old children. *Frontiers in Psychology*, 2(26), 1-9.

Johnston, V.S. (2006) Mate choice decisions: The role of facial beauty. *Trends in Cognitive Sciences*, 10(1), 10-13.

Johnston, W.A. and Dark, V.J. (1986) Selective attention. *Annual Review of Psychology*, 37, 43-76.

Johnston, W.A. and Heinz, S.P. (1978) Flexibility and capacity demands of attention. *Journal of Experimental Psychology: General*, 107, 420-35.

Johnstone, B., Kaiser, A., Injeyan, M.C., Sappleton, K., Chitayat, D., Stephens, D. and Shuman, C. (2016). The relationship between burnout and occupational stress in genetic counselors. *Journal of Genetic Counseling*, 25(4), 731-41.

Jokela, M., Batty, G.D., Nyberg, S.T., Virtanen, M., Nabi, H., Singh-Manoux, A. and Kivimaki, M. (2013) Personality and all-cause mortality: Individual-participant meta-analysis of 3947 deaths in 76150 adults. *American Journal of Epidemiology*, 178, 667-75.

Jonason, P. K., Jones, A. and Lyons, M. (2013) Creatures of the night: Chronotypes and the Dark Triad traits. *Personality and Individual Differences*, 55(5), 538-41.

Jonason, P.K., Jones, A. and Lyons, M. (2013) Creatures of the night: Chronotypes and the Dark Triad traits. *Personality and Individual Differences*, 55, 538-41.

Jonason, P.K., Koening, B. and Tost, J. (2010) Living a fast life: The Dark Triad and life history theory. *Human Nature*, 21, 428-42.

Jonason, P.K., Li, N. and Madson, L. (2012) It is not all about the Benjamins: Understanding preference for mates with resources. *Personality and Individual Differences*, 92, 306-10.

Jonason, P.K., Luevano, V.X. and Adams, H.M. (2012) How the dark triad traits predict relationship choices. *Personality and Individual Differences*, 53, 180-4.

Jonason, P.K., Garcia, J.R., Webster, G.D., Li, N.P. and Fisher, H.E. (2015) Relationship dealbreakers: Trust people avoid in potential mates. *Personality and Social Psychology Bulletin*, 41, 1697-1711.

Jones, C.L., Ward, J. and Critchley, H.D. (2010) The neuropsychological impact of insular cortex lesions. *Journal of Neurology, Neurosurgery and Psychiatry*, 81(6), 611-18.

Jones, D.C. (2004) Body image among adolescent girls and boys: A longitudinal study. *Developmental Psychology*, 40, 5, 823-35.

Jones, D.M. (1995) The fate of the unattended stimulus. Irrelevant speech and cognition. *Applied Cognitive Psychology*, 9, 23-38.

Jones, D.M., Madden, C. and Miles, C. (1992) Privileged access by irrelevant speech to short-term memory: The role of changing state. *The Quarterly Journal of Experimental Psychology*, 44A, 645-59.

Jones, D.T. and Reed, R.R. (1989) Golf: An olfactory neuron specific-G protein involved in odorant signal transduction. *Science*, 244, 790-5.

Jones, E. (1931) *On the Nightmare*. New York: Liveright.

Jones, E.E. (1990) *Interpersonal Perception*. New York: W.H. Freeman.

Jones, E.E. and Goethals, G.R. (1972) Order effects in impression formation: Attribution context and the nature of the entity. In E.E. Jones, D.E. Kanouse, H.H. Kelley, R.E. Nisbett, S. Valins and B. Weiner (eds) *Attribution: Perceiving the causes of behavior*. Morristown, NJ: General Learning Press, pp. 27–46.

Jones, E.E. and Harris, V.A. (1967) The attribution of attitudes. *Journal of Experimental Social Psychology*, 3, 1-24.

Jones, E.E. and Nisbett, R.E. (1971) The actor and observer: Divergent perceptions of the causes of behavior. In E.E. Jones, D.E. Kamouse, H.H. Kelley, R.E. Nisbett, S. Valins and B. Weiner (eds) *Attribution: Perceiving the causes of behavior*. Morristown, NJ: General Learning Press, pp. 79–94.

Jones, E.J.H. and Herbert, J.S. (2006) Exploring memory in infancy. *Infant and Child Development*, 15, 195-205.

Jones, G.V. (1989) Back to Woodworth: Role of interlopers in the tip-of-the-tongue phenomenon. *Memory and Cognition*, 17(1), 69-76.

Jones, H.E. (1959) Intelligence and problem-solving. In J.E. Birren (ed.) *Handbook of Aging and the Individual*. Chicago: University of Chicago Press.

Jones, K. S., Derby, P. L. and Schmidlin, E. A. (2010) An investigation of the prevalence of replication research in human factors. *Human Factors: The Journal of the Human Factors and Ergonomics Society*, 52, 586-95.

Jones, R.B., Humphris, G. and Lewis, T. (1996) Do agoraphobics interpret the environment in large shops and supermarkets differently? *British Journal of Clinical Psychology*, 35, 635-7.

Jones, S.P., Dwyer, D.M. and Lewis, M.B. (2017) The utility of multiple synthesised views in the recognition of unfamiliar faces. *The Quarterly Journal of Experimental Psychology*, 70, 906-18.

Jonge, P., Roest, A. M., Lim, C. C., Florescu, S. E., Bromet, E. J., Stein, D. J., . . . and Al-Hamzawi, A. O. (2016) Cross-national epidemiology of panic disorder and panic attacks in the world mental health surveys. *Depression and Anxiety*, 33(12), 1155-77.

Joormann, J. and Siemer, M. (2004) Memory accessibility, mood regulation, and dysphoria: Difficulties in repairing sad mood with happy memories? *Journal of Abnormal Psychology*, 113(2), 179-88.

Jordan, K., Wüstenberg, T., Jaspers-Feyer, F. and Fellbrich, A. (2006) Sex differences in left/right confusion. *Cortex*, 42, 69-78.

Josephs, R.A., Sellers, J.G., Newman, M.L. and Mehta, P.H. (2006) The mismatch effect: When testosterone and status are at odds. *Journal of Personality and Social Psychology*, 90(6), 999-1013.

Joshanloo, M. (2013) The influence of fear of happiness beliefs on responses to the satisfaction with life scales. *Personality and Individual Differences*, 54, 647-51.

Joshanloo, M. *et al.* (2014) Cross-cultural validation of fear of happiness scale across 14 national groups. *Journal of Cross-Cultural Psychology*, 45, 246–64.

Joslyn, S., Loftus, E., McNoughton, A. and Powers, J. (2001) Memory for memory. *Memory and Cognition*, 29(6), 789–97.

Jost, J.T. and Hunyadi, O. (2002) The psychology of system justification and the palliative function of ideology. *European Review of Social Psychology*, 13, 111–53.

Jost, J.T., Glaser, J., Kruglanski, A.W. and Sulloway, F.J. (2003) Political conservatism as motivated social cognition. *Psychological Bulletin*, 129, 339–75.

Jouvet, M. (1972) The role of monoamines and acetylcholine-containing neurons in the regulation of the sleep–waking cycle. *Ergebnisse der Physiologie*, 64, 166–307.

Jubb, J. and Bensing, J.M. (2013) The sweetest pill to swallow: how patient neurobiology can be harnessed to maximise placebo effects. *Neuroscience & Biobehavioral Reviews*, 37(10), 2709–20.

Jung, R. (1974) Neuropsychologie und neurophysiologie des konturund formsehens in zeichnerei und malerei. In H. Weick (ed.) *Psychopathologie Mususcher Gestaltungen*, Stuttgart: F.K. Shattauer.

Jung, R.E. and Haier, R.J. (2007) The Parieto-Frontal Integration Theory (P-FIT) of intelligence: converging neuroimaging evidence. *Behavioral and Brain Sciences*, 30(02), 135–54.

Jusczyk, P.W. and Hohne, E.A. (1997) Infants' memory for spoken words. *Science*, 277, 1984–6.

Just, M.A. and Carpenter, P.A. (1980) A theory of reading: From eye fixations to comprehension. *Psychological Review*, 87, 329–54.

Just, M.A. and Carpenter, P.A. (1987) *The Psychology of Reading and Language Comprehension*. Boston: Allyn & Bacon.

Just, M.A., Carpenter, P.A. and Wu, R. (1983) *Eye Fixations in the Reading of Chinese Technical Text, Technical Report*. Pittsburgh: Carnegie-Mellon University.

K

Kaas, J.H. and Hackett, T.A. (1999) 'What' and 'where' processing in auditory cortex, *Nature Neurocience*, 2, 1045–7.

Kaczkurkin, A.N. *et al.* (2016) Elevated amygdala perfusion mediates developmental sex differences in trait anxiety. *Biological Psychiatry*, 80, 775–85.

Kaczmarek, B.L.J (1991) Aphasia in an artist: A disorder of symbolic processing. *Aphasiology*, 5, 361–71.

Kagan, J., Kearsley, R.B. and Zelazo, P.R. (1978) *Infancy: Its place in human development*. Cambridge, MA: Harvard University Press.

Kageyama, T., Nishikido, N., Kobayashi, T., Kurokawa, Y. and Kabuto, M. (1997) Commuting, overtime, and cardiac autonomic activity in Tokyo. *Lancet*, 350, 639.

Kahneman, D. (1973) *Attention and Effort*. Englewood Cliffs, NJ: Prentice Hall.

Kahneman, D. and Miller, D.T. (1986) Norm theory: comparing reality to its alternatives. *Psychological Review*, 93, 136–52.

Kahneman, D., Krueger, A.B., Schkade, D.A., Schwartz, N. and Stone, A.A. (2004) A survey method for characterizing daily life experience: The day reconstruction method. *Science*, 3, 1776–80.

Kahneman, D., Slovic, P. and Tversky, A. (1982) *Judgement Under Uncertainty: Heuristics and Biases*. Cambridge: Cambridge University Press.

Kaijura, H., Cowart, B.J. and Beauchamp, G.K. (1992) Early developmental change in bitter taste responses in human infants. *Developmental Psychobiology*, 25, 375–86.

Kail, R. and Hall, L.K. (2001) Distinguishing short-term memory from working memory. *Memory and Cognition*, 29, 1–9.

Kalichman, S.C., Carey, M.P. and Johnson, B.T. (1996) Prevention of sexually transmitted HIV infection: a meta-analytic review of the behavioural outcome literature. *American Behavioral Medicine*, 18, 6–15.

Kalish, R.A. (1976) Death and dying in a social context. In R.H. Binstock and E. Shanas (eds) *Handbook of Aging and the Social Sciences*. New York: Van Nostrand Reinhold.

Kalivas, P.W. and Volkow, N.D. (2005) The neural basis of addiction: A pathology of motivation and choice. *American Journal of Psychiatry*, 162, 1403–13.

Kalkhoran, S. and Glantz, S.A. (2016) E-cigarettes and smoking cessation in real-world and clinical settings: a systematic review and meta-analysis. *The Lancet Respiratory Medicine*, 4, 116–28.

Kalyuga, S., Ayres, P., Chandler, P. and Sweller, J. (2003) The expertise reversal effect. *Educational Psychologist*, 38(1), 23–31.

Kamphuis, J.H. and Emmelkamp, P.M.G. (1998) Crime-related trauma: Psychological distress in victims of bankrobbery. *Journal of Anxiety Disorders*, 12(3), 199–208.

Kanazawa, S. and Perina, K. (2009) Why night owls are more intelligent. *Personality and Individual Differences*, 47, 685–90.

Kandel, E.R., Schwartz, J.H. and Jessell, T.M. (1995) *Essentials of Neural Science and Behaviour*. Englewood Cliffs, NJ: Prentice Hall.

Kane, J., Honigfeld, G., Singer, J., Meltzer, H. and the Clozaril Collaborative Study Group. (1988) Clozapine for the treatment-resistant schizophrenic: A double-blind comparison with chlorpromazine. *Archives of General Psychiatry*, 45, 789–96.

Kane, M.J., Bleckley, M.K., Conway, A.R.A. and Engle, R.W. (2001) A controlled-attention view of working memory capacity. *Journal of Experimental Psychology: General*, 130, 169–83.

Kang, D., Han, H., Jain, A.K. and Lee, S-W. (2014) Nighttime face recognition at large standoff: Cross-distance and cross-spectral matching. *Pattern Recognition*, 47, 3750–66.

Kanner, L. (1943) Autistic disturbances of affective contact. *Nervous Child*, 2, 217–50.

Kanwisher, N., Tong, F. and Nakayama, K. (1998) The effect of face inversion on the human fusiform face area. *Cognition*, 68, B1–B11.

Kapci, E.G. (1998) Test of the hopelessness theory of depression drawing negative inference from negative life events. *Psychological Reports*, 82, 355–63.

Kaplan, E.L. and Kaplan, G.A. (1970) The prelinguistic child. In J. Eliot (ed.) *Human Development and Cognitive Processes*. New York: Holt, Rinehart & Winston.

Kapleau, P. (1980) *Three Pillars of Zen: Teaching, practice and enlightenment*. Harden City, NY: Anchor Books.

Kapp, B.S., Gallagher, M., Applegate, C.D. and Frysinger, R.C. (1982) The amygdala central nucleus: Contributions to conditioned cardiovascular responding during aversive Pavlovian conditioning in the rabbit. In C.D. Woody (ed.) *Conditioning: Representation of involved neural functions*. New York: Plenum Press.

Kaptchuk, T.J., Shaw, J., Kerr, C.E., Conboy, L., Kelley, J.M., Csordas, T.J., . . . and Jacobson, E.E. (2009) 'Maybe I made up the whole thing': placebos and patients' experiences in a randomized controlled trial. *Culture, Medicine, and Psychiatry*, 33(3), 382–411.

Karandashev, V. (2006) Teaching of undergraduate psychology in Russia. *International Journal of Psychology*, 41(1), 58–64.

Karasek, R., Gardell, B. and Lindell, J. (1987) Work and non-work correlates of illness and behaviour in male and female Swedish white collar workers. *Journal of Organizational Behavior*, 8(3), 187–207.

Karau, S.J. and Williams, K.D. (1993) Social loafing: A meta-analytic review and theoretical integration. *Journal of Personality and Social Psychology*, 65, 681–706.

Karbach, J. and Verhaeghen, P. (2014) Making working memory: A meta-analysis of executive-control and working memory training in older adults. *Psychological Science*, 25, 2027–37.

Karbe, H., Herholz, K., Weber-Luxenburger, G., Ghaemi, M. and Heiss, W.-D. (1998) Cerebral networks and functional brain asymmetry: Evidence from regional metabolic changes during word repetition. *Brain and Language*, 63, 108–21.

Karni, A., Meyer, G., Jezzard, P., Adams, M.M., Turner, R. and Ungerleider, L.G. (1995) Functional MRI evidence for adult motor cortex plasticity during motor skill learning. *Nature*, 377, 155–8.

Karpicke, J.D. and Grimaldi, J.P. (2012) Retrieval-based learning: A perspective for enhancing meaningful learning. *Educational Psychology Review*, 24, 401–18.

Karremans, J.C., Frankenhuis, W.E. and Arons, S. (2010) Blind men prefer a low waist-to-hip ratio. *Evolution and Human Behavior*, 31, 182–6.

Karremans, J.C., Stroebe, W. and Claus, J. (2006) Beyond Vicary's fantasies: The impact of subliminal priming and brand choice. *Journal of Experimental Psychology*, 42, 792–8.

Kashdan, T.B. and Fincham, F.D. (2002) Facilitating creativity by regulating curiosity. *American Psychologist*, 57, 373–4.

Kassin, S.M., Reddy, M.E. and Tulloch, W.F. (1990) Juror interpretations of ambiguous evidence: The need for cognition, presentation order, and persuasion. *Law and Human Behaviour*, 14, 43–55.

Kassin, S.M., Tubb, V.A., Hosch, H.M. and Memon, A. (2001) On the 'general acceptance' of eyewitness testimony research: A new survey of the experts. *American Psychologist*, 56, 405–16.

Katz, R.C., Wilson, L. and Frazer, N. (1994) Anxiety and its determinants in patients undergoing magnetic resonance imaging. *Journal of Behaviour Therapy and Experimental Psychiatry*, 25, 131–4.

Kaufman, D. and Mahoney, J.M. (1999) The effect of waitresses' touch on alcohol consumption in dyads. *The Journal of Social Psychology*, 139(3), 261–7.

Kawakami, K., Dovidio, J.F., Moll, J., Hermsen, S. and Russin, A. (2000) Just say no (to stereotyping): Effects of training in the negation of stereotypic associations on stereotype activation. *Journal of Personality and Social Psychology*, 78, 871–88.

Kay, P. (1975) Synchronic variability and diachronic changes in basic color terms. *Language in Society*, 4, 257–70.

Kay, P. and Kempton, W. (1984) What is the Sapir–Whorf hypothesis? *American Anthropologist*, 86(1), 65–79.

Kay, P., Berlin, B. and Merrifield, W. (1991) Biocultural implications of systems of color naming. *Journal of Linguistic Anthropology*, 1(1), 12–25.

Kay, P., Berlin, B., Maffi, L. and Merrifield, W. (1997) Color naming across languages. In C.L. Hardin and L. Maffi (eds) *Color Categories in Thought and Language*. New York: Cambridge University Press.

Kaye, K. and Fogel, A. (1980) The temporal structure of face-to-face communication between mothers and infants. *Developmental Psychology*, 16, 454–64.

Kaye, W. (2008) Neurobiology of anorexia and bulimia nervosa. *Physiology and Behaviour*, 94, 121–35.

Kaye, W.H., Wierenga, C.E., Bailer, U.F., Simmons, A.N. and Bischoff-Grethe, A. (2013) Nothing tastes as good as skinny feels: the neurobiology of anorexia nervosa. *TINS*, 36, 110–20.

Kazdin, A.E. (1994) *Behavior Modification in Applied Settings*. Pacific Grove, CA: Brooks/Cole.

Keane, M.M., Gabrieli, J.D.E., Mapstone, H.C., Johnson, K.A. and Corkin, S. (1995) Double dissociation of memory capacities after bilateral occipital-lobe or medial temporal-lobe lesions. *Brain*, 118, 1129–48.

Kecklund, G. and Akerstedt, T. (2006) Apprehension of the subsequent working day is associated with a low amount of slow wave sleep. *Biological Psychology*, 66, 169–76.

Keel, P.K. and Klump, K.L. (2003) Are eating disorders culture-bound syndromes? Implications for conceptualizing their etiology. *Psychological Bulletin*, 129(5), 747–69.

Keel, P.K., Dorer, D.J., Franko, D.L., Jackson, S.C. et al. (2005) Postmission predictors of relapse in women with eating disorders. *American Journal of Psychiatry*, 62, 2263–8.

Keil, F.C., Lockhart, K.L. and Schlegel, E. (2010) A bump on a bump? Emerging intuitions concerning the relative difficulty of the sciences. *Journal of Experimental Psychology: General*, 139, 1–15.

Keller, K. and Menon, V. (2009) Gender differences in the functional and structural neuroanatomy of mathematical cognition. *Neuroimage*, 47, 342–52.

Keller, M.C., Fredrickson, B.L., Ybarra, O., Cote, S., Johnson, K., Mikels, J., Conway, A. and Wager, T. (2005) A warm heart and a clear head: The contingent effect of weather on mood and cognition. *Psychological Science*, 16(9), 724–31.

Keller, P.A. and Block, L.G. (1995) Increasing the persuasiveness of fear appeals: The effect of arousal and elaboration. *Journal of Consumer Research*, 22, 448–59.

Kelley, H.H. (1950) The warm–cold variable in first impressions of persons. *Journal of Personality*, 18, 431–9.

Kelley, H.H. (1967) Attribution theory in social psychology. In D. Levine (ed.) *Nebraska Symposium on Motivation*, Vol. 15. Lincoln, NE: University of Nebraska Press.

Kelley, H.H. (1973) The process of causal attribution. *American Psychologist*, 28, 107–28.

Kelley, H.H. and Michela, J.L. (1980) Attribution theory and research. *Annual Review of Psychology*, 31, 457–501.

Kelley, J.E., Lumley, M.A. and Leisen, J.C. (1997) Health effects of emotional disclosure in rheumatoid arthritis patients. *Health Psychology*, 16, 331–40.

Kelly, G.A. (1955) *The Psychology of Personal Constructs*. New York: W.W. Norton.

Kelly, S.D., Barr, D.J., Church, R.B. and Lynch, K. (1999) Offering a hand to pragmatic understanding: The role of speech and gesture comprehension and memory. *Journal of Memory and Language*, 40, 577–92.

Kemp, R., Towell, N. and Pike, G. (1997) When seeing should not be believing: Photographs, credit cards and fraud. *Applied Cognitive Psychology*, 11, 211–22.

Kemper, S. (1992) Language and aging. In F.I.M. Craik and T. Salthouse (eds) *The Handbook of Aging and Cognition*. Hillsdale, NJ: Lawrence Erlbaum Associates.

Kendon, A. (2016) Reflections on the 'gesture-first' hypothesis of language origins. *Psychonomic Bulletin and Review*, 24, 163–70.

Keng, S.L., Smoski, M.J. and Robbins, C.J. (2011) Effects of mindfulness on psychological health: A review of empirical studies. *Clinical Psychology Review*, 31, 1041–56.

Kennedy, D.P. and Courchesne, E. (2007) The intrinsic functional organization of the brain is altered in autism. *Neuroimage*, 39, 1877–85.

Kennis, M., Rademaker, A.R. and Geuze, E. (2013) Neural correlates of personality: An integrative review. *Neuroscience and Biobehavioural Reviews*, 37, 73–95.

Kenny, P.J. (2007) Brain reward systems and compulsive drug use. *Trends in Pharmacological Sciences*, 28(3), 135–41.

Kenny, P.J. et al. (2006) Conditioned withdrawal drives heroin consumption and decreased reward sensitivity. *Journal of Neuroscience*, 26, 5894–900.

Kenrick, D.T., Gutierres, S.E. and Goldberg, L.L. (1989) Influence of popular erotica on judgements of strangers and mates. *Journal of Experimental Social Psychology*, 25, 159–67.

Kerkhoff, G. and Schenk, T. (2012) Rehabilitation of neglect: an update. *Neuropsychologia*, 50(6), 1072–9.

Kerkhoff, G. and Schenk, T. (2012) Rehabilitation of neglect: An update. *Neuropsychologia*, 50, 1072–9.

Kerns, K.A. and Barth, J.M. (1995) Attachment and play: Convergence across components of parent–child relationships and their relations to peer competence. *Journal of Social and Personal Relationships*, 12, 243–60.

Kerr, J.H. and van den Wollenberg, A.E. (1997) High and low intensity exercise and psychological mood states. *Psychology and Health*, 12, 603–18.

Kerr, N.L. (1978) Beautiful and blameless: Effects of victim attractiveness and responsibility on mock jurors' verdicts. *Personality and Social Psychology Bulletin*, 4, 479–82.

Kerr, N.L. (1992) Norms in social dilemmas. In D. Schroeder (ed.) *Social Dilemmas: Psychological perspectives*. New York: Praeger.

Kerr, N.L. and Park, E.S. (2001) Group performance in collaborative and social dilemma tasks: Progress and prospects. In M.A. Hogg and R.S. Tindale (eds) *Blackwell Handbook of Social Psychology: Group processes*. Oxford: Blackwell, pp. 107–38.

Kerstholt, J.H. and Jackson, J.L. (1998) Judicial decision making: Order of evidence presentation and availability of background information. *Applied Cognitive Psychology*, 12, 445–54.

Keshavan, M.S., Tandon, R., Boutros, N.N. and Nasrallah, H.A. (2008) Schizophrenia, 'Just the facts': What we know in 2008, Part 3: Neurobiology. *Schizophrenia Research*, 100, 89–107.

Kessels, R.P.C., deHaan, E.H.F., Kappelle, L.J. and Postma, A. (2001) Varieties of human spatial memory: A meta-analysis on the effects of hippocampal lesions. *Brain Research Reviews*, 35, 295–303.

Kessler, R.C. *et al.* (2001) Mood disorders in children and adolescents: an epidemiologic perspective. *Biological Psychiatry*, 49, 1002–14.

Kessler, R.C., McGonagle, K.A., Zhao, S., Nelson, C., Hughes, M., Eshleman, S., Wittchen, H. and Kendler, K. (1994) Lifetime and 12–month prevalence of DSM-III-R psychiatric disorders in the United States. *Archives of General Psychiatry*, 51, 8–19.

Kety, S.S., Rosenthal, D., Wender, P.H. and Schulsinger, F. (1968) The types and prevalence of mental illness in the biological and adoptive families of adopted schizophrenics. In D. Rosenthal and S.S. Kety (eds) *The Transmission of Schizophrenia*. Elmsford, NY: Pergamon Press.

Keyes, D. (1981) *The Minds of Billy Milligan*. New York: Bantam.

Khalifeh, H., Johnson, S., Howard, L.M., Borschmann, R., Osborn, D., Dean, K., Hart, C., Hogg, J. and Moran, P. (2015) Violent and non-violent crime against adults with severe mental illness. *British Journal of Psychiatry*, 206, 275–82.

Khan, A., McCormack, H.C., Bolger, E.A., McGreenery, C.E., Vitaliano, G., Polcari, A. and Teicher, M.H. (2015) Childhood maltreatment, depression and suicidal ideation. *Frontiers in Psychiatry*, 6, 42.

Khan, S.A., Levine, W.J., Dobson, S.D. and Kralik, J.D. (2011) Red signals dominance in male rhesus macaques. *Psychological Science*, 22, 1001–3.

Khoury, B., Langer, E.J. and Pagnini, F. (2014) The DSM: mindful science of mindless power? A critical review. *Frontiers in Psychology*, 5, 602.

Khoury, B., Lecomte, T., Fortin, G., Masse, M., Therien, P., Bouchard, V., Chapleau, M-A., Paquin, K. and Hofmann, S.G. (2013) Mindfulness-based therapy: A comprehensive meta-analysis. *Clinical Psychology Review*, 33, 763–71.

Khoury, B., Sharma, M., Rush, S.E. and Fournier, C. (2015) Mindfulness-based stress reduction for healthy individuals: A meta-analysis. *Journal of Psychosomatic Research*, 78, 519–28.

Kieber, B., Veit, R., Birbaumer, N., Gruzelier, J. and Lotze, M. (2010) The brain of opera singers: Experience-dependent changes in functional activation. *Cerebral Cortex*, 20, 1144–52.

Kiecolt-Glaser, J.K., Malarkey, W.B., Chee, M., Newton, T., Caccioppo, J.T., Mao, H-Y. and Glaser, R. (1993) Negative behaviour during marital conflict is associated with immunological down-regulation. *Psychosomatic Medicine*, 55, 395–409.

Kiecolt-Glaser, J.K., Marucha, P.T., Atkinson, C. and Glaser, R. (2001) Hypnosis as a modulator of cellular immune dysregulation during acute stress. *Journal of Consulting and Clinical Psychology*, 69(4), 674–82.

Kiecolt-Glaser, J.K., Marucha, P.T., Malarkey, W.B., Mercado, A.M. and Glaser, R. (1995) Slowing of wound healing by psychological stress. *Lancet*, 346, 1194–6.

Killgore, W.D.S. and Yurgelun-Todd, D.A. (2010) Sex differences in cerebral responses to images of high versus low-calorie food. *Neuroreport*, 21 (5), 354–8.

Kim, J-Y., McHale, S.M., Osgood, D.W. and Crouter, A.C. (2006) Longitudinal course and family correlates of sibling relationships from childhood through adolescence. *Child Development*, 77(6), 1746–61.

Kim, K.H. (2011) The APA 2009 Division 10 debate: Are the Torrance Tests of Creative Thinking still relevant in the 21st century? *Psychology of Aesthetics, Creativity and the Arts*, 5, 302–8.

Kim, K.H.S., Relkin, N.R., Lee, K-M. and Hirsch, J. (1997) Distinct cortical areas associated with native and second languages. *Nature*, 388, 171–4.

Kim, M.J., Catalano, R.F., Haggerty, K.P. and Abbott, R.D. (2011) Bullying at elementary school and problem behaviour in young adulthood: A study of bullying, violence and substance use from age 11 to age 21. *Criminal Behaviour and Mental Health*, 21(2), 136–44.

Kim, P., Rigo, P., Mayes, L.C., Feldman, R., Leckman, J.F. and Swain, J.E. (2014) Neural plasticity in fathers of human infants. *Social Neuroscience*, 9, 522–35.

Kim, S., Dede, A.J., Hopkins, R.O. and Squire, L.R. (2015) Memory scene construction and the human hippocampus. *Proceedings of the National Academy of Sciences*, 112, 4767–72.

Kim, T. J. and von dem Knesebeck, O. (2016) Perceived job insecurity, unemployment and depressive symptoms: a systematic review and meta-analysis of prospective observational studies. *International archives of occupational and environmental health*, 89(4), 561–73.

Kin, H., Ishikawa, E., Takano, S., Ayuzawa, S., Matsushita, A., Muragaki, Y. *et al.* (2013) Language areas involving the inferior temporal cortex on intraoperative mapping in a bilingual patient with glioblastoma. *Neurologia medico-chirurgica*, 53, 256–8.

King, D.L., Gradisar, M., Drummond, A., Lovato, N., Wessel, J., Micic, G., . . . and Delfabbro, P. (2013) The impact of prolonged violent video gaming on adolescent sleep: an experimental study. *Journal of Sleep Research*, 22(2), 137–43.

King, J.A., Blair, R.J.R., Mitchell, D.G.V., Dolan, R.J. and Burgess, N. (2006) Doing the right thing: A common neural circuit for appropriate violent or compassionate behavior. *Neuroimage*, 30, 1069–76.

King, M.C. and Wilson, A.C. (1975) Evolution at two levels in humans and chimpanzees. *Science*, 188 (4184), 107–16.

Kinsella, G.J., Mullaly, E., Rand, E., Ong, B., Burton, C., Price, S., Phillips, M. and Storey, E. (2009) Early intervention for mild cognitive impairment. *Journal of Neurology, Neurosurgery and Psychiatry*, 80, 730–6.

Kinsey, A., Pomeroy, W.B. and Martin, C.E. (1948) *Sexual Behavior in the Human Male*. Philadelphia, PA: Saunders.

Kinsey, A., Pomeroy, W.B., Martin, C.E. and Gebhard, P.H. (1953) *Sexual Behavior in the Human Female*. Philadelphia, PA: Saunders.

Kipps, C.M., Duggins, A.J., McCusker, E.A. and Calder, A.J. (2007) Disgust and happiness recognition correlate with anteroventral insula and amygdala volume respectively in preclinical Huntington's disease. *Journal of Cognitive Neuroscience*, 19(7), 1206–17

Kirby, K.N., Petry, N.M. and Bickel, W.K. (1999) Heroin addicts have higher discount rates for delayed rewards than on-drug-using controls. *Journal of Experimental Psychology: General*, 128(1), 78–87.

Kirkpatrick, M.G., Gunderson, E.W., Perez, A.Y., Haney, M., Foltin, R.W. and Hart, C.L. (2012) A direct comparison of the behavioral and physiological effects of methamphetamine and 3,4-methylenedioxymethamphetamine (MDMA) in humans. *Psychopharmacology*, 219(1), 109–22.

Kirmayer, L.J. and Crafa, D. (2014) What kind of science for psychiatry? *Frontiers in Human Neuroscience*, 8, 435.

Kirschner, P.A. and van Merriënboer, J.J. (2013) Do learners really know best? Urban legends in education. *Educational Psychologist*, 48(3), 169–83.

Kirwan, C.B., Ashby, S.R. and Nash, M.I. (2014) Remembering and imagining differentially engage the hippocampus: A multivariate fMRI investigation. *Cognitive Neuroscience*, 5, 177–85.

Kisilevsky, B.S. (1995) The influence of stimulus and subject variables on human fetal responses to sound and vibration. In J-P. Lecanuet, W.P. Fifer, N.A. Krasnegor and W.P. Smotherman (eds) *Fetal Development: A psychobiological perspective*. Hillsdale, NJ: Lawrence Erlbaum Associates.

Kisilevsky, B.S. and Low, J.A. (1998) Human fetal behavior: 100 years of study. *Developmental Review*, 18, 1–29.

Kitayama, S., Duffy, S., Kawamura, T. and Larsen, J.T. (2003) Perceiving an object and its context in different cultures: A cultural look at new look. *Psychological Science*, 14(3), 201–6.

Klackl, J., Pfundmair, M., Agroskin, D. and Jonas, E. (2013) Who is to blame? Oxytocin promotes nonpersonalistic attributions in response to a trust betrayal. *Biological Psychology*, 92(2), 387–94.

Klandermans, B. (1997) *The Social Psychology of Protest*. Oxford: Blackwell.

Klatsky, A.L. (2010) Alcohol and cardiovascular health. *Physiology and Behavior*, 100, 76–81.

Klayman, J. and Brown, K. (1993) Debias the environment instead of the judge: An alternative approach to reducing error in diagnostic (and other) judgement. *Cognition*, 49, 97–122.

Klein, A.R. (1998) Virtual reality exposure therapy (fear of flying): From a private practice perspective. *Cyberpsychology and Behaviour*, 1, 311–16.

Klein, D., Milner, B., Zatorre, R.J., Meyer, E. and Evans, A.C. (1995) The neural substrates underlying word generation: A bilingual functional imaging study. *Proceedings of the National Academy of Science USA*, 92(7), 2899–903.

Klein, D., Milner, B., Zatorre, R.J., Zhao, V. and Nikelski, J. (1999) Cerebral organization in bilinguals: A PET study of Chinese-English verb generation. *NeuroReport*, 10, 2841–6.

Klein, K. and Boals, A. (2001) Expressive writing can increase working memory capacity. *Journal of Experimental Psychology: General*, 130(3), 520–33.

Klein, R. A., Ratliff, K. A., Vianello, M., Adams Jr, R. B., Bahník, Š., Bernstein, M. J., . . . and Cemalcilar, Z. (2014) Investigating variation in replicability. *Social Psychology*, 45, 142–52.

Kleiner, K. (1993) Specific versus non-specific face of cognition device? In B. de Boysson-Bardies, S. de Schonen, P. Jusczyk, P. McNeilage and J. Morton (eds) *Developmental Neuro Cognition: Speech and face processing in the first year of life*. New York: Academic Press.

Kleinke, C. (1977) Compliance to requests made by gazing and touching experimenters in field settings. *Journal of Experimental Social Psychology*, 13, 218–23.

Kleinke, C.L. (1986) Gaze and eye contact: A research review. *Psychological Bulletin*, 100, 78–100.

Kleitman, N. (1961) The nature of dreaming. In G.E.W. Wolstenholme and M. O'Connor (eds) *The Nature of Sleep*. London: Churchill.

Kleitman, N. (1982) Basic rest–activity cycle – 22 years later. *Sleep*, 4, 311–17.

Klerman, G.L. and Weissman, M.M. (1986) The interpersonal approach to understanding depression. In T. Millon and G. L. Klerman (eds) *Contemporary Directions in Psychopathology: Toward the DSM-IV*. New York: Guilford Press.

Kliegel, M., McDaniel, M.A. and Einstein, G.O. (2000) Plan formation, retention, and execution in prospective memory: A new approach and age-related effects. *Memory and Cognition*, 28(6), 1041–9.

Klimesch, W., Doppelmayr, M., Schimke, H. and Ripper, B. (1997) Theta synchronization and alpha desynchronization in a memory task. *Psychophysiology*, 34, 169–76.

Klimstra, T.A., Frijns, T., Keijsers, L., Denissen, J.A., Raajmakers, Q.A.W., van Aken, M.A.G., Koot, H.M.K., van Lier, P. and Neeus, W.H.J. (2011) Come rain or shine: individual differences in how weather affects mood. *Emotion*, 11, 1495–9.

Klin, A., Jones, W., Schultz, R. and Volkmar, F. (2002) Visual fixation patterns during viewing of naturalistic social situations as predictors of social competence in individuals with autism. *Archives of General Psychiatry*, 59, 809–16.

Klin, A., Volkmar, F.R. and Sparrow, S.S. (1992) Autistic social dysfunction: Some limitations of the theory of mind hypothesis. *Journal of Child Psychology and Psychiatry*, 33, 861–76.

Kline, P. (1993) *Personality – The psychometric view*. London: Routledge.

Klingberg, T. (2010) Training and plasticity of working memory. *Trends in Cognitive Sciences*, 14, 317–24.

Klitzman, S. and Stellman, J.M. (1989) The impact of the physical environment on the psychological well-being of office workers. *Social Science and Medicine*, 29, 733–42.

Kloep, M. (1999) Love is all you need? Focusing on adolescents' life concerns from an ecological point of view. *Journal of Adolescence*, 22, 49–63.

Klontz, J. C. and Jain, A. K. (2013) A case study of automated face recognition: The Boston marathon bombings suspects. *Computer*, 46(11), 91–4.

Kluft, R.P. (1984) An introduction to multiple personality disorder. *Psychiatric Annals*, 7, 9–29.

Klug, W.S. and Cummings, M.R. (1986) *Concepts of Genetics* (2nd edn) Glenview, IL: Scott Foresman.

Knaapila, A. (2012) Genetic analysis of chemosensory traits in human twins. *Chemical Senses*, 37, 869–81.

Knauff, M. *et al.* (2003) Reasoning, models and images: behavioural measures and cortical activity. *Journal of Cognitive Neuroscience*, 15, 559–73.

Knecht, S., Deppe, E., Drager, B., Bobe, L., Lohmann, H., Ringelstein, E-B. and Henningsen, H. (2000a) Language lateralization in healthy right-handers. *Brain*, 123, 74–81.

Knecht, S., Drager, B., Deppe, M., Bobe, L., Lohmann, H., Floel, A., Ringelstein, E-B. and Henningsen, H. (2000b) Handedness and hemispheric language dominance in healthy humans. *Brain*, 123, 2512–18.

Knee, C.R., Lonsbary, C., Canavello, A. and Patrick, H. (2005) Self-determination and conflict in romantic relationships. *Journal of Personality and Social Psychology*, 89, 997–1009.

Knight, B. and Johnston, A. (1997) The role of movement in face recognition. *Visual Cognition*, 4, 265–73.

Knight, D.C., Smith, C.N., Stein, E.A. and Helmstetter, F.J. (1999) Functional MRI of human Pavlovian fear conditioning: patterns of activation as a function of learning. *NeuroReport*, 10, 3665–70.

Knight, G.P., Fabes, R.A. and Higgins, D.A. (1996) Concerns about drawing causal inferences from meta-analyses: An example in the study of gender differences in aggression. *Psychological Bulletin*, 119(3), 410–21.

Knight, K.N. and Nisbett, R.E. (2007) Culture, class and cognition: Evidence from Italy. *Journal of Cognition and Culture*, 7, 283–91.

Knobloch-Westerwick, S., Glynn, C.J. and Huge, M. (2013) The Matilda effect in science communication: An experiment on gender bias in publication quality perceptions and collaboration interest. *Science Communication*, 35, 603–25.

Knox, J.V., Morgan, A.H. and Hilgard, E.R. (1974) Pain and suffering in ischemia: The paradox of hypnotically suggested anesthesia as contradicted by reports from the 'hidden observer'. *Archives of General Psychiatry*, 30, 840–7.

Knuas, T.A., Bollich, A.M., Corey, D.M., Lemen, L.C. and Foundas, A.L. (2004) Sex-linked differences in the anatomy of the perisylvian language cortex: A volumetric MRI study of gray matter volumes. *Neuropsychology*, 18(4), 738–47.

Knutson, B., Rick S., Wimmer, Elliott G., Prelec, D. and Loewenstein G. (2007) Neural predictors of purchases. *Neuron*, 53, 147–56.

Knutsson, A. and Goine, H. (1998) Occupation and unemployment rates by predictors of long term sickness absence in two Swedish counties. *Social Science and Medicine*, 47(1), 25–31.

Kobasa, S.C. (1979) Stress life events, personality, and health: An inquiry into hardiness. *Journal of Personality and Social Psychology*, 42, 168–77.

Kobayashi, K. (2005) What limits the encoding effect of note-taking? A meta-analytic examination. *Contemporary Educational Psychology*, 39, 242–62.

Kochunov, P. and Hong, L.E. (2014) Neurodevelopment and neurodegenerative models of schizophrenia. *Schizophrenia Bulletin*, 40, 721–8.

Kohlberg, L. (1966) A cognitive developmental analysis of children's sex role concepts and attitudes. In E. Maccoby (ed.) *The Development of Sex Differences*. Stanford, CA: Stanford University Press.

Kohlberg, L. (1969) Stage and sequence: The cognitive developmental approach to socialization. In D.A. Goslin (ed.), *Handbook of Socialization Theory and Research*. Chicago, IL: Rand McNally.

Kohlberg, L. (1971) From is to ought: How to commit the naturalistic fallacy and get away with it in the study of moral development. In T. Mischel (ed.), *Cognitive Development and Epistemology*. New York: Academic Press.

Kohlberg, L. (1982) Moral development. In J.M. Broughton and D.J. Freeman-Moir (eds) *The Cognitive Developmental Psychology of James Mark Baldwin*. Norwood, NJ: Ablex.

Koladich, S.J. and Atkinson, B.E. (2016) The dark triad and relationship preferences: A replication and extension. *Personality and Individual Differences*, 94, 253–5.

Kolb, B. and Gibb, R. (2013) Searching for the principles of brain plasticity and behaviour. *Cortex*, 58, 251–60.

Kong, F., Hu, S., Wang, X., Song, Y. and Liu, J. (2014) Neural correlates of the happy life: The amplitude of spontaneous low frequency fluctuations predicts subjective well-being. *Neuroimage*, 107, 136–45.

Konner, M.J. (1972) Aspects of the developmental ethology of a foraging people. In N. Blurton Jones (ed.) *Ethological Studies of Child Behaviour*. Cambridge: Cambridge University Press.

Koppel, J. and Berntsen, D. (2014) The cultural life script as cognitive schema: How the life script shapes memory for fictional life stories. *Memory*, 22, 949–71.

Koppel, J. and Berntsen, D. (2015) The peaks of life: The differential temporal locations of the reminiscence bump across disparate cueing methods. *Journal of Applied Research in Memory and Cognition*, 4, 66–80.

Koppel, J. and Rubin, D.C. (2016) Recent advances in understanding the reminiscence bump: The importance of cues in guiding recall from autobiographical memory. *Current Directions in Psychological Science*, 25, 135–40.

Korchmaros, J.D. and Kenny, D.A. (2001) Emotional closeness as a mediator of the effect of genetic relatedness on altruism. *Psychological Science*, 12(3), 262–5.

Korjus, K., Uusberg, A., Uusberg, H., Kuldkepp, N., Kreegipuu, K., Allik, J., Vincente, R., and Aru, J. (2015) Personalty cannot be predicted from the power of resting state EEG. *Frontiers in Human Neuroscience*, 9, 63.

Kornmeier, J., Spitzer, M. and Sosic-Vasic, Z. (2014) Very similar spacing-effect patterns in very different learning/practice domains. *PLoS ONE*, 9, 1–11.

Koscik, T.R. and Tranel, D. (2012) The human ventromedial prefrontal cortex is critical for transitive inference. *Journal of Cognitive Neuroscience*, 24, 1191–204.

Kosfeld, M., Heinrichs, N., Zak, P.J., Fischbacher, U. and Fehr, E. (2005) Oxytocin increases trust in humans. *Nature*, 435, 673–6.

Kovacs, A.M., Teglas, E. and Endress, A.D. (2010) The social sense: susceptibility to others' beliefs in human infants and adults. *Science*, 330, 1830–4.

Kovacs, K. and Conway, A.R.A. (2016) Process overlap theory: A unified account of the general factor of intelligence. *Psychological Inquiry*, 27, 151–77.

Kovacs, M. and Beck, A.T. (1978) Maladaptive cognitive structures in depression. *American Journal of Psychiatry*, 135, 525–33.

Kovacs, Y., Voronin, I., Kaydalov, A., Malykh, S.B., Dale, P.S. and Plomin, R. (2013) Literacy and numeracy are more heritable than intelligence in primary school. *Psychological Science*, 24, 2048–56.

Koyama, T., McHaffie, J.G., Laurienti, P.J. and Coghill, R.C. (2005) The subjective experience of pain: Where expectations become reality. *Proceedings of the National Academy of Sciences*, 102(36), 12950–55.

Kozel, F.A., Johnson, K.A., Mu, Q., Grenesko, E.L., Laken, S.J. and George, M.S. (2005) Detecting deception using functional magnetic resonance imaging. *Biological Psychiatry*, 58, 605–13.

Kraehenbuhl, J-P. and Neutra, M.R. (1992) Molecular and cellular basis of immune protection of mucosal surfaces. *Physiological Review*, 72, 853–79.

Kraepelin, E. (1921) *Manic–Depressive Insanity and Paranoia*. London: Churchill Livingstone.

Kragel, P.A. and LaBar, K.S. (2016) Decoding the nature of emotion in the brain. *TICS*, 20(6), 444–55.

Krahe, B., Moller, I., Huesmann, L., Kirwil, L., Feber, J. and Berger, A. (2011) Desensitisation to media violence: Links with habitual media violence exposure, aggressive cognitions and aggressive behaviour. *Journal of Personality and Social Psychology*, 100, 630–46.

Kramer, A.D.I., Guillory, J.E. and Hancock, J.T. (2014) Experimental evidence of massive-scale emotional contagion through social networks. *PNAS*, 111, 8788–90.

Kramer, R.S.S. and Jones, A.L. (2015) Do people's first names match their faces? *Journal of Articles in Support of the Null Hypothesis*, 12, 1–8.

Krashen, S.D. (1973) Lateralization, language learning and the critical period: Some new evidence. *Language Learning*, 23, 63–74.

Kravitz, D.J., Saleem, K.S., Baker, C.I. and Mishkin, M. (2011) A new neural framework for visuospatial processing. *Nature Reviews Neuroscience*, 12, 217–30.

Krendl, A.C., Macrae, C.N., Kelley, W.M., Fugelsang, J.A. and Heatherton, T.F. (2006) The good, the bad and the ugly; An fMRI investigation of the functional anatomic correlates of stigma. *Social Neuroscience*, 1(1), 5–15.

Kret, M.E. and De Gelder, B. (2012) A review on sex differences in processing emotional signals. *Neuropsychologia*, 50(7), 1211–21.

Kret, M.E., Pichon, S., Grèzes, J. and de Gelder, B. (2011) Men fear other men most: gender specific brain activations in perceiving threat from dynamic faces and bodies – An fMRI study. *Frontiers in Psychology*, 2, 3.

Krill, A. and Platek, S.M. (2009) In-group and out-group membership mediates anterior cingulate activation to social exclusion. *Frontiers in Evolutionary Neuroscience*, 1, 1–7.

Kringelbach, M.L. (2015) The pleasure of food: underlying brain mechanisms of eating and other pleasures. *Flavour*, 4(1), 20.

Krishnan, S., Watkins, K.E. and Bishop, D.V. (2016) Neurobiological basis of language learning difficulties. *Trends in Cognitive Sciences*, 20(9), 701–14.

Krishnan, S., Watkins, K.E. and Bishop, D.V.M. (2016) Neurobiological basis of language learning difficulties. *Trends in Cognitive Sciences*, 20(9), 701–14.

Krishnan-Sarin, S., Reynolds, B., Duhig, A.M., Smith, A., Liss, T., McFetridge, A., Cavallo, D.A., Carroll, K.M. and Potenza, M.N. (2007) Behavioural impulsivity predicts treatment outcome in a smoking cessation program for adolescent smokers. *Drug and Alcohol Dependence*, 88, 79–82.

Krolak Salmon, P., Hénaff, M.A., Isnard, J., Tallon Baudry, C., Guénot, M., Vighetto, A., . . . and Mauguiere, F. (2003) An attention modulated response to disgust in human ventral anterior insula. *Annals of Neurology*, 53(4), 446–53.

Kroth, J., Briggs, A., Cummings, M., Rodriguez, G. and Martin, E. (2007) Retrospective reports of dream characteristics and preferences for organic vs junk foods. *Psychological Reports*, 101, 335–8.

Krueger, B. *et al.* (2008) Performance groups in adult cochlear implant users. *Otology and Neurotology*. 29, 509–12.

Krueger, J. and Clément, R.W. (1997) Estimates of social consensus by majorities and minorities: The case for social projection. *Personality and Social Psychology Review*, 1, 299–313.

Krueger, J., Ham, J.J. and Linford, K.M. (1996) Perceptions of behavioral consistency: Are people aware of the actor–observer effect? *Psychological Science*, 7, 259–64.

Krueger, T.H. (1976) *Visual Imagery in Problem Solving and Scientific Creativity*. Derby, CT: Seal Press.

Krug, S.E. and Kulhavy, R.W. (1973) Personality differences across regions in the United States. *Journal of Social Psychology*, 91, 7379.

Krull, D.S. and Erickson, D.J. (1995) Inferential hopscotch: How people draw social inferences from behavior. *Current Directions in Psychological Science*, 4, 3538.

Krull, D.S. and Silvera, D.H. (2013) The stereotyping of science: superficial details influence perceptions of what is scientific. *Journal of Applied Social Psychology*, 43, 1660–7.

Krumhuber, E.G. and Manstead, A.S.R. (2009) Can Duchenne smiles be feigned? New evidence on felt and false smiles. *Emotion*, 9, 807–20.

Kubitz, K.A. and Landers, D.M. (1993) The effects of aerobic exercise on cardiovascular responses to mental stress: An examination of underlying mechanisms. *Journal of Sport and Exercise Physiology*, 15, 326–7.

Kübler-Ross, E. (1969) *On Death and Dying*. New York: Macmillan.

Kübler-Ross, E. (1981) *Living with Death and Dying*. New York: Macmillan.

Kubota, J.T., Mojdehbakhsh, R., Raio, C., Brosch, T., Uleman, J.S. and Phelps, E.A. (2014) Stressing the person: Legal and everyday person attributions under stress. *Biological Psychology*, 103, 117–24.

Kuhl, B.A., Dudukovic, N.M., Kahn, I. and Wagner, A.D. (2007) Decreased demands on cognitive control reveal the neural processing benefits of forgetting. *Nature Neuroscience*, 10(7), 908–14.

Kuhl, P.K., Williams, K.A., Lacerda, F., Stevens, K.N. and Lindblom, B. (1992) Linguistic experience alters phonetic perception in infants by 6 months of age. *Science*, 255, 606–8.

Kühn, S., Gleich, T., Lorenz, R. C., Lindenberger, U. and Gallinat, J. (2014) Playing Super Mario induces structural brain plasticity: gray matter changes resulting from training with a commercial video game. *Molecular Psychiatry*, 19(2), 265–71.

Kuhnen, C.M. *et al.* (2013) Serotonergic genotypes, neuroticism, and financial choices. *PLoS ONE*, 8, e54632.

Kuisma, J., Simola, J., Uusitalo, L. and Öörni, A. (2010) The effects of animation and format on the perception and memory of online advertising. *Journal of Interactive Marketing*, 24(4), 269–82.

Kullmann, S., Pape, A. A., Heni, M., Ketterer, C., Schick, F., Häring, H. U., . . . and Veit, R. (2012) Functional network connectivity underlying food processing: disturbed salience and visual processing in overweight and obese adults. *Cerebral Cortex*, bhs124.

Kumar, S. *et al.* (2016) The brain basis for misophonia. *Current Biology*, 27, 1–7.

Kuncel, N.R. and Hezlett, S.A. (2010) Fact and fiction in cognitive ability testing for admissions and hiring decisions. *Current Directions in Psychological Science*, 19, 339–45.

Kunda, Z. (1990) The case for motivated reasoning. *Psychological Bulletin*, 108, 480–98.

Kunst-Wilson, W.R. and Zajonc, R.B. (1980) Affective discrimination of stimuli that cannot be recognized. *Science*, 207, 557–8.

Kuo, P.X., Carp, J., Light, K.C. and Grewen, K.M. (2012) Neural responses to infants linked with behavioral interactions and testosterone in fathers. *Biological Psychology*, 91(2), 302–6.

Kuo, P.X., Carp, J., Light, K.C. and Grewen, K.M. (2012) Neural responses to infants linked with behavioural interactions and testosterone in fathers. *Biological Psychology*, 91, 303–6.

Kuperman, V. and Van Dyke, J.A. (2011) Effects of individual differences in verbal skills on eye-movement patterns during sentence reading. *Journal of Memory and Language*, 65, 42–73.

Kupfer, D.J., Kuhl, E.A. and Regier, D.A (2013) DSM-5: The future arrived. *JAMA*, 309(16), 1691–2.

Kuppens, T. and Pollet, T.V. (2014) Mind the level: problems with two recent nation-level analyses in psychology. *Frontiers in Psychology*, 5, 110.

Kurtz, M.M. and Gerraty, R.T. (2009) A meta-analytic investigation of neurocognitive deficits in bipolar illness. *Neuropsychology*, 23, 551–62.

Kurtz, M.M. and Mueser, K.T. (2009) A meta-analysis of controlled research on social skills training for schizophrenia. *Journal of Consulting and Clinical Psychology*, 76, 491–504.

Kurz, A., Pohl, C., Ramsenthaler, M. and Sorg, C. (2009) Cognitive rehabilitation in patients with mild cognitive impairment. *International Journal of Geriatric Psychiatry*, 24, 163–8.

Kusima, J., Simola, J., Uusitalo, L. and Oorni, A. (2010) The effects of animation and format on the perception and memory of online advertising. *Journal of Interactive Marketing*, 24, 269–82.

Kutas, M. and Hillyard, S.A. (1980) Reading senseless sentences: brain potentials reflect semantic incongruity. *Science*, 207, 203–5.

Kutas, M. and Van Petten, C. (1994) Psycholinguistics electrified. In M. Gernsbacher (ed.) *Handbook of Psycholinguistics*. San Diego, CA: Academic Press.

Kutas, M., Federmeier, K.D., Coulson, S., King, J. and Munte, T.F. (2000) Language. In J Cacioppo, E. Louis and G. Tassinary (eds), *Handbook of Psychophysiology* (2nd edn) Cambridge: Cambridge University Press.

Kuyken, W., Watkins, E., Holden, E., White, K., Taylor, R. S., Byford, S., . . . and Dalgleish, T. (2010). How does mindfulness-based cognitive therapy work? *Behaviour Research and Therapy*, 48(11), 1105–12.

Kwon, O. and Wen, Y. (2010) An empirical study of the factors affecting social network use. *Computers in Human Behavior*, 26, 254–63.

Kyriakopoulos, M. and Frangou, S. (2009) Recent diffusion tensor imaging findings in early stages of schizophrenia. *Current Opinion in Psychiatry,* 22, 168–76.

L

Lachman, M.E., Lewkowicz, C., Marcus, A. and Peng, Y. (1994) Images of midlife development among young, middle-aged, and older adults. *Journal of Adult Development,* 1(4), 201–11.

Lachman, M.E., Rocke, C., Rosnick, C. and Ryff, C.D. (2008) Age differences in trajectories of life satisfaction. *Psychological Science,* 19, 895–910.

Laciga, J. and Cigler, H. (2016) The Flynn effect in the Czech Republic. *Intelligence,*

LaCour, M.J. and Green, D.P. (2014) *Science,* 1366–9.

Laeng, B., Sirois, S. and Gredebäck, G. (2012) Pupillometry a window to the preconscious? *Perspectives on Psychological Science,* 7(1), 18–27.

Lafer-Sousa, R., Hermann, K.L. and Conway, B.R. (2015) Striking individual differences in color perception uncovered by 'the dress' photograph. *Current Biology,* 25(13), R545–R546.

LaFreniere, P., Strayer, F.E. and Gauthier, R. (1984) The emergence of same-sex affiliative preferences among preschool peers: A developmental/ etho-logical perspective. *Child Development,* 55, 1958–65.

Lai, M-C., Lombardo, M.V., Ecker, C., Chakrabarti, B., Suckling, J., Bullmore, E.T., Happe, F., MRC Aims Consortium, Murphy, D.G.M. and Baron-Cohen, S. (2014) Neuroanatomy of individual differences in language in adult males with autism. *Cerebral Cortex,* 25m, 3613–28.

Lai, M-C., Lombardo, M.V., Suckling, J., Ruigrok, A.N.V., Chakrabarti, B., Ecker, C., Deoni, S.C.L., Craig, M.C., Murphy, D.C.M., Bullmore, E.T., MRC Aims Consortium and Baron-Cohen, S. (2013) Biological sex affects the neurobiology of autism. *Brain,* 136, 2799–815.

Laird, J.D. (1974) Self-attribution of emotion: The effects of expressive behav-iour on the quality of emotional experience. *Journal of Personality and Social Psychology,* 29, 475–86.

Lambert, M.J. and Bergin, A.E. (1994) The effectiveness of psychotherapy. In A.E. Bergin and S.L. Garfield (eds) *Handbook of Psychotherapy and Behaviour Change.* New York: Wiley.

Lambert, W.E. (1977) The effect of bilingualism on the individual: Cogni-tive and sociocultural consequences. In P.A. Hornby (ed.) *Bilingualism: Psychological, social and educational implications.* New York: Academic Press.

Lane, A., Mikolajczak, M., Treinen, E., Samson, D., Corneille, O., de Timary, P and Luminet, O. (2015) Failed replication of oxytocin effect on trust: The envelope task case. *PLoS ONE,* 10, 1–10.

Lang, E.V., Benotsch, E.G., Flick, L.J., Lutgendorf, S., Berbaum, M.L., Berbaum, K.S., Logan, H. and Spiegel, D. (2000) Adjunctive non-pharmacological analgesia for invasive medical procedures: A ran-domised trial. *Lancet,* 355, 1486–90.

Lang, P.J. (1979) A bio-informational theory of emotional imagery. *Psychophysiology,* 16, 495–512.

Lang, P.J. (1984) Cognition in emotion: Concept and action. In C.E. Izard, J. Kagan and R.B. Zajonc (eds) *Emotions, Cognition and Behaviour.* New York: Cambridge University Press.

Lange, C.G. (1887) *Über Gemüthsbewegungen.* Leipzig: T. Thomas.

Langer, E.J. and Abelson, R.P. (1974) A patient by any other name . . . Clinician group difference in labeling bias. *Journal of Consulting and Clinical Psychology,* 42, 4–9.

Langer, E.J., Bashner, R.S. and Chanowitz, B. (1985) Decreasing prejudice by increasing discrimination. *Journal of Personality and Social Psychology,* 49, 113–20.

Langleben, D.D. (2008) Detection of deception with fMRI: are we there yet? *Legal and Criminological Psychology,* 13, 1–9.

Langlois, J.H., Kalakanis, L., Rubenstein, A.J., Larson, A., Hallam, M. and Smoot, M. (2000) Maxims or myths of beauty? A meta-analytic and theo-retical review. *Psychological Bulletin,* 126, 390–423.

Lapa, C. (2007) Using eye tracking to understand banner blindness and improve website design. http://scholarworks.rit.edu/theses/693/

LaPiere, R.T. (1934) Attitudes and actions. *Social Forces,* 13, 230–7.

LaPointe, K.E., Klein, J.A., Konkol, M.L., Kveno, S M., Bhatt, E., DiFabio, R.P. and Carey, J.R. (2009) Cortical activation during finger tracking vs. ankle tracking in healthy subjects. *Restorative Neurology and Neuroscience,* 27(4), 253–64.

Larsen, J.T., Norris, C.J. and Cacioppo, J.T. (2003) Effects of positive and neg-ative affect on electromyographic activity over zygomaticus major and corrugator supercilli. *Psychophysiology,* 40, 776–85.

Larson, G.E., Haier, R.J., LaCasse, L. and Hazen, K. (1995) Evaluation of 'men-tal effort' hypothesis for correlations between cortical metabolism and intelligence. *Intelligence,* 21, 267–78.

Larsson, M., Oberg, C. and Backman, L. (2006) Recollective experience in odor recognition: Influences of adult age and familiarity. *Psychological Research,* 70, 68–75.

LaRue, A. (1992) *Aging and Neuropsychological Assessment.* New York: Plenum Press.

Lasalvia, A. (2015) DSM-5 two years later: facts, myths and some key open issues. *Epidemiology and Psychiatric Sciences,* 1–3.

Lassek, W.D. and Gaulin, S. (2008) Waist-hip ratio and cognitive ability: Is glutofemoral fat a privileged store of neurodevelopmental resources? *Evolution and Human Behavior,* 29, 26–34.

Lassek, W.D. and Gaulin, S.J.C. (2009) Costs and benefits of fat-free muscle mass in men: Relationship to mating success, dietary requirements and natural immunity. *Evolution and Human Behavior,* 30, 322–8.

Last, C.G., Barlow, D.H. and O'Brien, G.T. (1984) Precipitants of agoraphobia: Role of stressful life events. *Psychological Reports,* 54, 173–80.

Latané, B. and Darley, J.M. (1970) *The Unresponsive Bystander: Why doesn't he help?* New York: Appleton-Century-Crofts.

Lau, S. (1982) The effect of smiling on person perception. *Journal of Social Psychology,* 117, 63–7.

Lauer, R.H. (1989) *Social Problems and the Quality of Life.* Dubuque, IA: W.C. Brown.

Lavie, P., Pratt, H., Scharf, B., Peled, R. and Brown, J. (1984) Localized pontine lesion: Nearly total absence of REM sleep. *Neurology,* 34, 1118–20.

Law, M.R. and Tang, J.L. (1995) An analysis of the effectiveness of intervention intended to help people stop smoking. *Archives of Internal Medicine,* 155, 1933–41.

Laws, K.R. (2013) Negativland-a home for all findings in psychology. *BMC Psychology,* 1, 2.

Laxmisan, A., Hakimzada, F., Sayan, O.R., Green, R.A., Zhang, J. and Patel, V.L. (2007) The multitasking clinician: decision-making and cognitive demand during and after team handoffs in emergency care. *International Journal of Medical Informatics,* 76(11), 801–11.

Lazarus, A.A. (1971) *Behavior Therapy and Beyond.* New York: McGraw-Hill.

Lazarus, R.S. (1966) *Psychological Stress and the Coping Process.* New York: McGraw-Hill.

Lazarus, R.S. (1984) Thoughts on the relations between emotion and cogni-tion. In K.R. Scherer and P. Ekman (eds) *Approaches to Emotion.* Hillsdale, NJ: Lawrence Erlbaum Associates.

Lazarus, R.S. (1991) *Emotion and Adaptation.* New York: Oxford University Press.

Lazarus, R.S. and Folkman, S. (1984) *Stress, Appraisal, and Coping.* New York: Springer-Verlag.

Le Clec'H, G., Dehaene, S., Cohen, L., Mehler, J., Dupoux, E., Poline, J.B., Lehericy, S., van de Moortele, P.F. and Le Bihan, D. (2000) Distinct cortical areas for names of numbers and body parts independent of language and input modality. *Neuroimage*, 12, 381–91.

Leahey, T.H. (2003) *A History of Psychology* (6th edn) Englewood Cliffs, NJ: Prentice Hall.

Leaper, C. and Ayres, M.M. (2007) A meta-analytic review of gender variations in adults' language use: Talkativeness, affiliative speech and assertive speech. *Personality and Social Psychology Review*, 11(4), 328–63.

Leary, M.R., Tambor, E.S., Terdal, S.K. and Downs, D.L. (1995) Self-esteem as an interpersonal monitor: The sociometer hypothesis. *Journal of Personality and Social Psychology*, 68, 518–30.

LeBlanc, M.M. and Barling, J. (2004) Workplace aggression. *Current Directions in Psychological Science*, 13(1), 9–12.

Lebowitz, M.S., Ahn, W. and Nolen-Hoeksema, S. (2013) Fixable or fate? Perceptions of the biology of depression. *Journal of Consulting and Clinical Psychology*, 81, 518.

Lebowitz, M.S., Ahn, W.K. and Nolen-Hoeksema, S. (2013) Fixable or fate? Perceptions of the biology of depression. *Journal of Consulting and Clinical Psychology*, 81(3), 518.

Lebuda, I. and Karwowski, M. (2013) Tell me your name and I'll tell you how creative your work is. *Creativity Research Journal*, 25, 137–42.

Lecanuet, J-P., Granier-Deferre, C. and Busnel, M-C. (1989) Differential fetal auditory reactiveness as a function of stimulus characteristics and state. *Seminars in Perinatology*, 13, 421–9.

Lecanuet, J-P., Granier-Deferre, C., Jacquet, A-Y. and Busnel, M-C. (1992) Decelerative cardiac responsiveness to acoustical stimulation in the near-term fetus. *The Quarterly Journal of Experimental Psychology*, 44, 279–303.

LeCompte, D.C., Neely, C.B. and Wilson, J.R. (1997) Irrelevant speech and irrelevant tones. *Journal of Experimental Psychology: Learning, Memory and Cognition*, 23, 472–83.

Ledford, H. (2015) First robust genetic links for depression emerge. *Nature*, 523, 268–9.

LeDoux, J. (1996) *The Emotional Brain.* Englewood Cliffs, NJ: Simon & Schuster.

LeDoux, J.E. (1995a) Emotion: Clues from the brain. *Annual Review of Psychology*, 46, 209–35.

LeDoux, J.E. (1995b) In search of an emotional system in the brain: Leaping from fear to emotion and consciousness. In M.S. Gazzaniga (ed.) *The Cognitive Neurosciences.* Cambridge, MA: MIT Press.

LeDoux, J.E. and Pine, D.S. (2016) Using neuroscience to help understand fear and anxiety: a two-system framework. *American journal of psychiatry*, 173(11), 1083–93.

Lee, F., Hallahan, M. and Herzog, T. (1996) Explaining real-life events: How culture and domain shape attributions. *Personality and Social Psychology Bulletin*, 22, 732–41.

Lee, H.W., Lim, K.Y. and Grabowski, B.L. (2010) Improving self-regulation, learning strategy use, and achievement with metacognitive feedback. *Educational Technology Research and Development*, 58(6), 629–48.

Lee, J.L.C., Everitt, B.J. and Thomas, K.L. (2004) Independent cellular processes for hippocampal memory consolidation and reconsolidation. *Science*, 304, 839–43.

Lee, M.Y., Chang, P-H., Kwon, Y.H. and Jang, S.H. (2013) Differences of the frontal activation patterns by fingers and toe movements: An fMRI study. *Neuroscience Letters*, 533, 7–10.

Lee, S. (1995) Self-starvation in context: Towards a culturally sensitive understanding of anorexia nervosa. *Social Science and Medicine*, 41, 25–36.

Lee, T.L. and Fiske, S. (2006) Not an out-group, but not yet an in-group: Immigrants in the stereotype content model. *International Journal of Intercultural Relations*, 30, 751–68.

Lee, T.M.C., Liu, H-L., Chan, C.C.H., Ng, Y-B., Fox, P.T. and Gao, J-H. (2005) Neural correlates of feigned memory impairment. *Neuroimage*, 28, 305–13.

Lee, T.M.C., Liu, H-L., Tan, L-H., Chan, C.C.H., Mahankali, S., Feng, C-M, Hou, J., Fox, P.T. and Gao, J-H. (2002) Lie detection by functional magnetic resonance imaging. *Human Brain Mapping*, 15, 157–64.

Leenders, I. and Brugman, D. (2005) Moral/non-moral domain shift in young adolescents in relation to delinquent behaviour. *British Journal of Developmental Psychology*, 23, 1–6.

Lefcourt, H.M., Davidson, K., Prkachin, K.M. and Mills, D.E. (1997) Humor as a stress moderator in the prediction of blood pressure obtained during five stressful tasks. *Journal of Research in Personality*, 31, 523–42.

Lefcourt, H.M., Davidson-Katz, K. and Kueneman, K. (1990) Humor and immune system functioning. *Humour: International Journal of Humor Research*, 3(3), 305–22.

Lefrancois, G.R. (1983) *Of Children: An Introduction to Child Development* (4th edn) Belmont, CA: Wadsworth.

Legault, E. and Laurence, J.R. (2007) Recovered memories of childhood sexual abuse: Social worker, psychologist and psychiatrist reports of beliefs, practices and cases. *Australian Journal of Clinical and Experimental Hypnosis*, 35, 111–33.

Lehtonen, M., Soveri, A., Laine, A., Järvenpää, J., de Bruin, A., & Antfolk, J. (2018). Is bilingualism associated with enhanced executive functioning in adults? A meta-analytic review. *Psychological Bulletin*, 144(4), 394–425.

Leibovici, D., Ritchie, K., Ledesert, B. *et al.* (1996) Does education level determine the course of cognitive decline? *Age and Ageing*, 25, 392–7.

Leigh, A. and Susilo, T. (2009) Is voting skin-deep? Estimating the effect of candidate ballot photographs on election outcomes. *Journal of Economic Psychology*, 30, 61–70.

Leinbach, M.D., Hort, B.E. and Fagot, B.I. (1997) Bears are for boys: Metaphorical associations in young children's gender stereotypes. *Cognitive Development*, 12, 107–30.

Lemay, E.P., Clark, M.S. and Greenberg, A. (2010) What is beautiful is good because what is beautiful is desired: Physical attractiveness stereotyping as projection of interpersonal goals. *Personality and Social Psychology Bulletin*, 36, 339–53.

Leng, G. and Ludwig, M. (in press) Intranasal oxytocin: myths and delusions. *Biological Psychiatry*, 79, 243–50.

Lenneberg, E. (1967) *Biological Foundations of Language.* New York: Wiley.

Lepore, L. and Brown, R. (1997) Category and stereotype activation: Is prejudice inevitable? *Journal of Personality and Social Psychology*, 72, 275–87.

Lepore, S.J. (1997) Expressive writing moderates the relation between intrusive thoughts and depressive symptoms. *Journal of Personality and Social Psychology*, 73, 1030–7.

Lerman, D.C. and Iwata, B.A. (1995) Prevalence of the extinction burst and its attenuation during treatment. *Journal of Applied Behaviour Analysis*, 28, 93–4.

Lerner, M.J. (1977) The justice motive: Some hypotheses as to its origins and forms. *Journal of Personality*, 45, 1–52.

Lesar, T.S., Briceland, L. and Stein, D.S. (1997) Factors related to errors in medication prescribing. *Journal of the American Medical Association*, 277, 312–17.

Lesch, K-P., Bengel, D., Heils, A., Sabol, S.Z., Greenberg, B.D. and Petri, S. (1996) Association of anxiety-related traits with a polymorphism in the serotonin transporter gene regulatory region. *Science*, 274, 1527–31.

Leslie, A.M. (1987) Pretense and representation: The origins of 'theory of mind'. *Psychological Review*, 94, 412–26.

Lesne, S., Koh, M.T., Kotilinek, L., Kayed, R., Glabe, C.G., Yang, A., Gallagher, M. and Ashe, K.H. (2006) A specific amyloid-B protein assembly in the brain impairs memory. *Nature*, 440, 352–7.

Leuner, B. and Gould, E. (2010) Structural plasticity and hippocampal function. *Annual Review of Psychology*, 61, 111–40.

Leuner, B., Glasper, E.R. and Gould, E. (2010) Parenting and plasticity. *Trends in Neurosciences*, 33(10), 465–73.

Lev-Ari, S. and Keysar, B. (2010) Why don't we believe non-native speakers? The influence of accent on credibility. *Journal of Experimental Social Psychology*, 46, 1093–6.

LeVay, S. (1991) A difference in hypothalamic structure between heterosexual and homosexual men. *Science*, 253, 1034–7.

Levelt, W. (1989) *Speaking: From intention to articulation*. Cambridge, MA: MIT Press.

Leventhal, H. and Scherer, K. (1987) The relationship of emotion to cognition: A functional approach to a semantic controversy. *Cognition and Emotion*, 1, 3–28.

Leventhal, H., Watts, J.C. and Pagano, R. (1967) Effects of fear and instructions on how to cope with danger. *Journal of Personality and Social Psychology*, 6, 313–21.

Levin, R. and Nielsen, T.A. (2007) Disturbed dreaming, post-traumatic stress disorder, and affect distress: a review and neurocognitive model. *Psychological Bulletin*, 133, 482–528.

Levine, M.B. and Willis, F.N. (1994) Public reactions to unusual names. *The Journal of Social Psychology*, 134(5), 561–8.

Levine, S.P. and Feldman, R.S. (2002) Women and men's nonverbal behavior and self-monitoring in a job interview setting. *Applied Human Resources Management Research*, 7, 1–14.

Levinger, G. (1980) Toward the analysis of close relationships. *Journal of Experimental Social Psychology*, 16, 510–44.

Levy, B. (1996) Improving memory in old age through implicit self-stereotyping. *Journal of Personality and Social Psychology*, 71, 1092–106.

Levy, B., Ariely, D., Mazar, N., Chi, W., Lukas, S. and Elman, I. (2008) Gender differences in the motivational processing of facial beauty. *Learning and Motivation*, 39, 136–45.

Levy, B.R., Slade, M.D., Kunkel, S.R. and Kasl, S.V. (2002) Longevity increased by positive self-perceptions of aging. *Journal of Personality and Social Psychology*, 83(2), 261.

Lewandowsky, S. and Oberauer, K. (2016) Motivated rejection of science. *Current Directions in Psychological Science*, 25, 217–22.

Lewin, K. (1951) *Field Theory in Social Science*. New York: Harper.

Lewin, R. (1984) *Human Evolution: An illustrated introduction*. Cambridge, MA: Blackwell Scientific.

Lewinsohn, P.M., Mischel, W., Chaplin, W. and Barton, R. (1980) Social competence and depression: The role of illusory self-perceptions. *Journal of Abnormal Psychology*, 89, 194–202.

Lewis, C.M., Levinson, D.F., Wise, L.H. *et al.* (2003) Genome scan meta-analysis of schizophrenia and bipolar disorder, part II. *American Journal of Human Genetics*, 73, 34–48.

Lewis, G.L., Kanai, R., Rees, G. and Bates, T.C. (2013) Neural correlates of the 'good life': eudaimonic well-being is associated with insular cortex volume. *SCAN*, 9, 615–18.

Lewis, R.S., Weekes, N.Y. and Wand, T.H. (2007) The effect of a naturalistic stressor on frontal EEG asymmetry, stress and health. *Biological Psychology*, 75, 239–47.

Leyens, J-P., Yzerbyt, V.Y. and Schadron, G. (1992) Stereotypes and social judgeability. *European Review of Social Psychology*, 3, 91–120.

Leyens, J-P., Yzerbyt, V.Y. and Schadron, G. (1994) *Stereotypes and Social Cognition*. London: Sage.

Li, G., Wang, L., Shi, F., Lyall, A.E., Lin, W., Gilmore, J.H. and Shen, D. (2014) Mapping longitudinal development of local cortical gyrification in infants from birth to 2 years of age. *Journal of Neuroscience*, 34, 4228–38.

Li, P. and Gleitman, L. (2002) Turning the tables: language and spatial reasoning. *Cognition*, 83, 265–94.

Li, W., Moallem, I., Paller, K.A. and Gottfriend, J.A. (2007) Subliminal smells can guide social preferences. *Psychological Science*, 18(12), 1044–9.

Li, Z., Page, A., Martin, G. and Taylor, R. (2011) Attributable risk of psychiatric and socio-economic factors for suicide from individual-level, population-based studies. *Social Science and Medicine*, 72, 608–16.

Liang, Y., Horrey, W.J. and Hoffman, J.D. (2014) Reading text while driving: understanding drivers' strategic and tactical adaptation to distraction. *Human Factors*, 57, 347–59.

Liben, L.S., Susman, E.J., Finkelstein, J.W., Chinchilli, V.M., Kunselman, S., Schwab, J., Dubas, J.S., Demers, L.M., Lookingbill, G., D'Arcangelo, M.R., Krogh, H.R. and Kulin, H.E. (2002) The effects of sex steroids on spatial performance: A review and an experimental clinical investigation. *Developmental Psychology*, 38, 236–53.

Liberman, A.M., Cooper, F.S., Shankweiler, D.P. and Studdert-Kennedy, M. (1967) Perception of the speech code. *Psychological Review*, 74, 431–61.

Libertus, M.E. and Brannon, E.M. (2009) Behavioral and neural basis of number sense in infancy. *Current Directions in Psychological Science*, 18, 346–51.

Lick, D.J., Cortland, C.L. and Johnson, K.L. (2015) The pupils are the window to sexuality: Pupil dilation as a visual cue to others' sexual interest. *Evolution and Human Behaviour*, 37, 117–24.

Lickey, M.E. and Gordon, B. (1983) *Drugs for Mental Illness*. New York: W.H. Freeman.

Lidow, M.S., Williams, G.V. and Goldman-Rakic, P.S. (1998) The cerebral cortex: A case for a common site of action of antipsychotics. *Trends in Pharmacological Sciences*, 19, 136–40.

Liggett, J. (1974) *The Human Face*. London: Constable.

Lilienfeld, S.O. (2011) Public skepticism of psychology. *American Psychologist*, 67, 119–29.

Lilienfeld, S.O., Ritschel, L.A., Lynn, S.J., Cautin, R.L. and Latzman, R.D. (2013) Why many clinical psychologists are resistant to evidence-based practice. *Clinical Psychology Review*, 33, 883–900.

Lilienfeld, S.O., Ritschel, L.A., Lynn, S.J., Cautin, R.L. and Latzman, R.D. (2014) Why ineffective psychotherapies appear to work. *Perspectives on Psychological Science*, 9, 355–87.

Lilienfeld, S.O., Wood, J.W. and Garb, H.N. (2000) The scientific status of projective techniques. *Psychological Science in the Public Interest*, 1, 27–66.

Lilienfeld, S.O., Wood, J.W. and Garb, H.N. (2001) What's wrong with this picture? *Scientific American Mind*, May, 81–7.

Liljenquist, K., Zhong, C-B. and Galinsky, A.D. (2010) The smell of virtue: Clean scents promote reciprocity and charity. *Psychological Science*, 21(3), 381–3.

Lillard, A.S, Lerner, M.D., Hopkins, E.J., Dore, R.A., Smith, E.D. and Palmquist, C.M. (2012) The impact of pretend play on children's development: A review of the evidence. *Psychological Bulletin*, 19, 1.

Lillard, A.S., Lerner, M.D., Hopkins, E.J., Dore, R.A., Smith, E.D. and Palmquist, C.M. (2013) The impact of pretend play on children's development: A review of the evidence. *Psychological Bulletin*, 139(1), 1.

Lindberg, S.M., Hyde, J.S., Petersen, J.L. and Linn, M.C. (2010) New trends in gender and mathematics performance: a meta-analysis. *Psychological Bulletin*, 136, 1123–35.

Lindenberg, R., Fangerau, H. and Seitz, R.J. (2007) 'Broca's area' as a collective term? *Brain and Language*, 102, 22–9.

Lindquist, K.A., Satpute, A.B., Wager, T.D., Weber, J. and Barrett, L.F. (2015) The brain basis of positive and negative affect: Evidence from a meta-analysis of the human neuroimaging literature. *Cerebral Cortex*, 1–13.

Lindsley, O.R. (1956) Operant conditioning methods applied to research in chronic schizophrenia. *Psychiatric Research Reports*, 24, 289–91.

Linn, M.C. and Petersen, A.C. (1985) Emergence and characterization of sex differences in spatial ability: A meta-analysis. *Child Development*, 56, 1479–98.

Linsky, A.S., Bachman, R. and Straus, M.A. (1995) *Stress, Culture, and Aggression*. New Haven, CT: Yale University Press.

Linton, S.J., Kecklund, G., Franklin, K.A., Leissner, L.C., Siverten, B., Lindberg, E., Svensson, A.C., Hansson, S.O., Sundin, O., Hetta, J., Bjorkelund, C. and Hall, C. (2015) The effect of the work environment on future sleep disturbance: a systematic review. *Sleep Medicine Reviews*, 23, 10–19.

Linville, P.W. (1982) Affective consequences of complexity regarding the self and others. In M.S. Clark and S.T. Fiske (eds) *Affect and Cognition: The 17th annual Carnegie symposium on cognition*. Hillsdale, NJ: Lawrence Erlbaum Associates, pp. 79–109.

Linville, P.W., Fischer, G.W. and Salovey, P. (1989) Perceived distributions of the characteristics of in-group and out-group members: Empirical evidence and a computer simulation. *Journal of Personality and Social Psychology*, 57, 165–88.

Lions, C., Bui-Quoc, E., Seassau, M. and Bucci, M.P. (2013) Binocular coordination of saccades during reading in strabismic children. *Investigative ophthalmology & visual science*, 54(1), 620-28.

Lipsman, N. *et al.* (2017) Deep brain stimulation of the subcallosal cingulate for treatment-refractory anorexia nervosa: 1 year follow-up of an open-label trial. *Lancet*, 4, 285–94.

Lipton, J.S. and Spelke, E.S. (2003) Origins of number sense: Large-number discrimination in human infants. *Psychological Science*, 14, 396–401.

Lisker, L. and Abramson, A. (1970) The voicing dimension: Some experiments in comparative phonetics. In *Proceedings of Sixth International Congress of Phonetic Sciences, Prague, 1967*. Prague: Academia.

Lisofsky, N., Lindenberger, U. and Kuhn, S. (2014) Amygdala/hippocampal activation during the menstrual cycle: Evidence for lateralization of effects across different tasks. *Neuropsychologia*, 67, 55–62.

Liston, C. and Kagan, J. (2002) Memory enhancement in early childhood. *Nature*, 419, 806.

Little, A.C., Jones, B.C., Burt, D.M. and Perrett, D.I. (2007) Preferences for symmetry in faces change across the menstrual cycle. *Biological Psychology*, 76, 209–16.

Liu, X. (2013) Reduced white matter integrity and cognitive deficit in never-medicated chronic schizophrenia. *Behavioural Brain Research*, 252, 157–63.

Liu, Y., Postupna, N., Falkenberg, J. and Anderson, M.E. (2008) High frequency deep brain stimulation: What are the therapeutic mechanisms. *Neuroscience and Biobehavioral Reviews*, 32, 343–51.

Livesley, J. (2013) The DSM-5 personality disorder proposal and future directions in the diagnostic classification of personality disorder. *Psychopathology*, 46, 207–16.

Ljepava, N., Orr, R.R., Locke, S. and Ross, C. (2013) Personality and social characteristics of Facebook non-users and frequent users. *Computers in Human Behavior*, 29, 1602–7.

Ljepava, N., Orr, R.R., Locke, S. and Ross, C. (2013) Personality and social characteristics of Facebook non-users and frequent users. *Computers in Human Behavior*, 29(4), 1602-7.

Lloyd, B. and Duveen, G. (1990) A semiotic analysis of the development of the social representation of gender. In G. Duveen and B. Lloyd (eds) *Social Representation and the Development of Knowledge*. Cambridge: Cambridge University Press.

Lock, M. (1998) Menopause: lessons from anthropology. *Psychosomatic Medicine*, 60, 410–19.

Locke, J.L. (1993) *The Child's Path to Spoken Language*. Cambridge, MA: Harvard University Press.

Lockwood, P., Jordan, C.H. and Kunda, Z. (2002) Motivation by positive or negative role models: Regulatory focus determines who will best inspire us. *Journal of Personality and Social Psychology*, 83, 854–64.

Loeber, R. and Dishion, T.J. (1983) Early predictors of male delinquency: A review. *Psychological Bulletin*, 94, 68–99.

Loehlin, J.C. (1992) *Genes and Environment in Personality Development*. London: Sage.

Loehlin, J.C., Lindzey, G. and Spuhler, J.N. (1975) *Race Differences in Intelligence*. San Fransisco ICA: W.H. Freeman.

Loehlin, J.C., McCrae, R.R., Costa, P.T. and John, O.P. (1998) Heritabilities of common and measure-specific components of the Big Five personality factors. *Journal of Research in Personality*, 32, 431–53.

Loewen, L.J. and Suedfeld, P. (1992) Cognitive and arousal effects of masking office noise. *Environment and Behaviour*, 24, 381–95.

Loftus, E.F. (1997) Creating false memories. *Scientific American Mind*, September, 50–5.

Loftus, E.F. and Palmer, J.C. (1974) Reconstruction of automobile destruction: An example of the interaction between language and memory. *Journal of Verbal Learning and Verbal Behavior*, 13, 585–9.

Loftus, E.F. and Zanni, G. (1975) Eyewitness testimony: The influence of the wording of a question. *Bulletin of the Psychonomic Society*, 5, 86–8.

Loftus, E.F., Miller, D.G. and Burns, H.J. (1978) Semantic integration of verbal information into a visual memory. *Journal of Experimental Psychology: Human Learning and Memory*, 4, 19–31.

Logie, R.H. (1995) *Visuo-spatial Working Memory*. Hove: Psychology Press.

Logie, R.H. (1996) The seven ages of working memory. In J.T.E. Richardson, R.W. Engle, L. Hasher, R.H. Logie, E.R. Stoltzfus and R.T. Zacks (eds) *Working Memory and Human Cognition*. Oxford: Oxford University Press.

Lohman, D.F. and Lakin, J.M. (2009) Consistencies in sex differences on the Cognitive Abilities Test across countries, grades, test forms and cohorts. *British Journal of Educational Psychology*, 79, 389–407.

Lomo, T. (1966) Frequency potentiation of excitatory synaptic activity in the dendate area of the hippocampal formation. *Acta Physiologica Scandinavica*, 68, 128.

Longo, V.D. and Mattson, M.P. (2014) Fasting: molecular mechanisms and clinical applications. *Cell Metabolism*, 19, 181–92.

Lonnqvist, J.-E. and Itkonen, J.V.A. (2014) It's all about extraversion: Why Facebook friend count doesn't count towards well-being. *Journal of Research in Personality*, 53, 64–7.

Lorch, R.F. (1989) Text-signaling devices and their effects on reading and memory processes. *Educational Psychology Review*, 1, 209–34.

Lorenz, K. (1966) *On Aggression*. New York: Harcourt Brace Jovanovich.

Lorenzi-Cioldi, F. and Clémence, A. (2001) Group processes and the construction of social representations. In M.A. Hogg and R.S. Tindale (eds) *Blackwell Handbook of Social Psychology: Group processes*. Oxford: Blackwell, pp. 311–33.

Lorig, T.S. (1989) Human EEG and odor response. *Progress in Neurobiology*, 33, 387–98.

Lotze, M., Erhard, K., Neumann, N., Eickhoff, S.B. and Langner, R. (2014) Neural corelates of verbal creativity: differences in resting-state functional connectivity associated with expertise in creative writing. *Frontiers in Human Neuroscience*, 8, 1–8.

Lotze, M., Scheler, G., Tan, H.R., Braun, C. and Birbaumer, N. (2003) The musician's brain: functional imaging of amateurs and professionals during performance and imagery. *Neuroimage*, 20, 1817–29.

Lovden, M., Wenger, E., Martensson, J., Lindenberger, U. and Backman, L. (2013) Structural brain plasticity in adult learning and development. *Neuroscience and Biobehavioural Reviews*, 37, 2296–310.

Lovell, D.M., Williams, J.M.G. and Hill, A.B. (1997) Selective processing of shape-related words in women with eating disorders, and those who have recovered. *British Journal of Clinical Psychology*, 36, 421–32.

Lovibond, S.H., Mithiran, X. and Adams, W.G. (1979) The effects of three experimental prison environments on the behavior of non-convict volunteer subjects. *Australian Psychologist*, 14, 272–87.

Lowden, A., Holmback, U., Akerstedt, T., Forslund, J., Lennernas, M. and Forslund, A. (2004) Performance and sleepiness during a 24 h wake in constant conditions are affected by diet. *Biological Psychology*, 65, 251–63.

Lowe, C. and Rabbitt, P. (1997) Cognitive models of ageing and frontal lobe deficits. In P. Rabbitt (ed.) *Methodology of Frontal and Executive Function*. Hove: Psychology Press.

Lowe, C.F. (1979) Determinants of human operant behavior. In M.D. Zeiler and P. Harzem (eds) *Advances in the Analysis of Behavior, Vol. 1: Reinforcement and the Organization of Behaviour*. Chichester: Wiley.

Lowe, C.F., Beasty, A. and Bentall, R.P. (1983) The role of verbal behavior in human learning: Infant performance on fixed-interval schedules. *Journal of the Experimental Analysis of Behavior*, 39, 157–64.

Lowe, L.P., Greenland, P., Ruth, K.J., Dyer, A.R., Stamler, R. and Stamler, J. (1998) Impact of major cardiovascular disease risk factors, particularly in combination, on 22-year mortality in women and men. *Archives of Internal Medicine*, 158, 2007–14.

Lu, F., Huo, Y., Li, M., Chen, H., Liu, F., Wang, Y., Long, Z., Duan, X., Zhang, J., Zeng, L. and Chen, H. (2014) Relationship between personality and gray matter volume in healthy young adults. *PLoS ONE*, 9, e88763.

Lubin, A., Hord, D., Tracy, M. and Johnson, L.C. (1976) Effects of exercise, bedrest and napping on performance decrement during 40 hours. *Psychophysiology*, 13, 334–9.

Lubinski, D., Benbow, C.P. and Kell, H.J. (2014) Life paths and accomplishments of mathematically precocious males and females four decades later. *Psychological Science*, 25, 2217–32.

Lubow, R.E. (1989) *Latent Inhibition and Conditioned Attention Theory*. Cambridge: Cambridge University Press.

Lucas, K. and Lloyd, B. (1999) Starting smoking: Girls' explanations of the influence of peers. *Journal of Adolescence*, 22, 647–55.

Lucas, R.E. and Lawless, N.M. (2013) Does life seem better on a sunny day? Examining the association between daily weather conditions and life satisfaction judgments. *Journal of Personality and Social Psychology*, 104, 872–84.

Lucassen, P.J., Meerlo, P., Naylor, A.S., Van Dam, A.M., Dayer, A.G., Fuchs, E., . . . and Czeh, B. (2010) Regulation of adult neurogenesis by stress, sleep disruption, exercise and inflammation: Implications for depression and antidepressant action. *European Neuropsychopharmacology*, 20(1), 1–17.

Luchies, L.B., Finkel, E.J., McNulty, J.K. and Kumashiro, M. (2010) The doormat effect: When forgiving erodes self-respect and self-concept clarity. *Journal of Personality and Social Psychology*, 98, 734–9.

Lucken, U., Muehlhan, M., Evens, R., Wittchens, H.U. and Kirschbaum, C. (2012) Within and between session changes in subjective and neuroendocrine stress parameters during magnetic resonance imaging. *Psychoneuroendocrinology*, 37, 1299–1308.

Luders, E., Narr, K.L., Bilder, R.M., Thompson, P.M., Szezko, P.R., Hamilton, L. et al. (2007) Positive correlations between corpus callosum thickness and intelligence. *Neuroimage*, 37, 1457–64.

Ludwig, A.M. (1994) Mental illness and creative activity in female writers. *American Journal of Psychiatry*, 151, 1650–6.

Lueken, U., Kruschwitz, J.D., Muehlhan, M., Siegert, J., Hoyer, J. and Wittchen, H-U. (2011) How specific is specific phobia? Different neural response patterns in two subtypes of specific phobia. *Neuroimage*, 56, 363–72.

Luft, A.R., Smith, G.V., Forrester, L., Whitall, J., Macko, R.F., Hauser, T.K., . . . and Hanley, D.F. (2002) Comparing brain activation associated with isolated upper and lower limb movement across corresponding joints. *Human Brain Mapping*, 17(2), 131–40.

Lum, J.A., Conti-Ramsden, G., Morgan, A.T. and Ullman, M.T. (2014) Procedural learning deficits in specific language impairment (SLI): A meta-analysis of serial reaction time task performance. *Cortex*, 51, 1–10.

Lumeng, J.C., Cardinal, T.M., Sitto, J.R. and Kannan, S. (2008) Ability to taste 6-n-propylthiouracil and BMI in low-income preschool-aged children. *Obesity*, 16, 1522–8.

Lundeberg, M.A., Fox, P.W., Brown, A.C. and Elbedour, S. (2000) Cultural influences on confidence: Country and gender. *Journal of Educational Psychology*, 92, 152–9.

Lundstrom, J.N., McClintock, M.K. and Olsson, M.J. (2006a) Effects of reproductive state on olfactory sensitivity suggest odor specificity. *Biological Psychology*, 71, 244–7.

Lundstrom, J.N., Olsson, M.J., Schaal, B. and Hummel, T. (2006b) A putative social chemosignal elicits faster cortical responses than perceptually similar odorants. *Neuroimage*, 30, 1340–6.

Lundy, A.C. (1985) The reliability of the Thematic Apperception Test. *Journal of Personality Assessment*, 49, 141–5.

Lundy, A.C. (1988) Instructional set and thematic apperception test validity. *Journal of Personality Assessment*, 52, 309–20.

Lunt, I. (1995) Demographic trends in professional psychology in the United Kingdom. In A. Schorr and S. Saari (eds) *Psychology in Europe*. Göttingen: Hogrefe and Huber.

Lupfer, M.B., Clark, L.F. and Hutcherson, H.W. (1990) Impact of context on spontaneous trait and situational attributions. *Journal of Personality and Social Psychology*, 58, 239–49.

Lupien, S.J., Maheu, F., Tu, M., Fiocco, A. and Schramek, T.E. (2007) The effects of stress and stress hormones on human cognition: Implications for the field of brain and cognition. *Brain and Cognition*, 65, 209–37.

Lupyan, G. and Dale, R. (2011) Language structure is partly determined by social structure. *PLoS ONE*, 5 (8559), 1–10.

Luria, A.R. (1972) *The Man with a Shattered World*. New York: Basic Books.

Lustig, C., May, C.P. and Hasher, L. (2001) Working memory span and the role of proactive interference. *Journal of Experimental Psychology: General*, 130, 199–207.

Lyall, A.E., Shi, F., Geng, X., Woolson, S., Li, G., Wang, L., Hamer, R.M., Shen, D. and Gilmore, J.H. (2015) Dynamic development of regional cortical thickness and surface area in early childhood. *Cerebral Cortex*, 25, 2204–12.

Lynch, G., Muller, D., Seubert, P. and Larson, J. (1988) Long-term potentiation: Persisting problems and recent results. *Brain Research Bulletin*, 21, 363–72.

Lynd-Stevenson, R.M. (1996) A test of the hopelessness theory of depression in unemployed young adults. *British Journal of Clinical Psychology*, 35, 117–32.

Lynd-Stevenson, R.M. (1997) Generalized and event-specific hopelessness: Salvaging the mediation hypothesis of the hopelessness theory. *British Journal of Clinical Psychology*, 36, 73–83.

Lynn, R. (1991) Race differences in intelligence: A global perspective. *Mankind Quarterly*, 31, 255–96.

Lynn, R. (1993) Oriental Americans: Their IQ, educational attainment and socioeconomic status. *Personality and Individual Differences*, 15, 237–42.

Lynn, R. (1996) Racial and ethnic differences in intelligence in the United States on the Differential Ability Scale. *Personality and Individual Differences*, 20, 271–3.

Lynn, R. (1998) New data on black infant precocity. *Personality and Individual Differences*, 25, 801–4.

Lynn, R. (2009) Fluid intelligence but not vocabulary has increased in Britain, 1979–2008. *Intelligence*, 37, 249–55.

Lynn, R. (2013) Who discovered the Flynn effect? A review of early studies of the secular increase of intelligence. *Intelligence*, 41, 765–9.

Lynn, R. and Mikk, J. (2007) National differences in intelligence and educational attainment. *Intelligence*, 35, 115–21.

Lynn, S.J. and Rhue, J.W. (1991) *Theories of Hypnosis: Current models and perspectives*. New York: Guilford Press.

Lynott, D., Corker, K.S., Connell, L. and O'Brien, K.S. (2017) The effect of haptic and ambient temperature experience on prosocial behavior. *Archives of Scientific Psychology*, 5(1), 10.

Lynskey, M.T., Fergusson, D.M. and Horwood, L.J. (1998) The origins of the correlations between tobacco, alcohol, and cannabis use during adolescence. *Journal of Child Psychology and Psychiatry*, 39(7), 995–1005.

Lytton, H. and Romney, D.M. (1991) Parents' sex-related differential socialization of boys and girls: A meta-analysis. *Psychological Bulletin*, 109, 267–96.

M

Ma, Z., Anderson, T., Wang, X., Wang, Y., Jaeger, A. and Saunders, D. (2002) Individual perception, bargaining behavior, and negotiation outcomes: a comparison across two countries. *International Journal of Cross-Cultural Management*, 2, 171–84.

Maass, A. (1999) Linguistic intergroup bias: Stereotype-perpetuation through language. In M.P. Zanna (ed.) *Advances in Experimental Social Psychology*, Vol. 31. San Diego ICA: Academic Press, pp. 79–121.

Maccoby, E.E. (1980) *Social Development: Psychological growth and the parent-child relationship*. New York: Harcourt Brace Jovanovich.

Maccoby, E.E. (1998) *The Two Sexes: Growing apart, coming together*. Cambridge, MA: Harvard University Press.

MacCoun, R. and Reuter, P. (2001) Evaluating alternative cannabis regimes. *British Journal of Psychiatry*, 178, 123–8.

Mace, F.C., Lalli, J.S., Shea, M.C., Lalli, E.P., West, B.J., Roberts, M. and Nevin, J.A. (1990) The momentum of behavior in a natural setting. *Journal of the Experimental Analysis of Behavior*, 54, 163–72.

Macht, M. and Mueller, J. (2007) Immediate effects of chocolate on experimentally induced mood states. *Appetite*, 49, 667–74.

Macht, M., Roth, S. and Ellgring, H. (2002) Chocolate eating in healthy men during experimentally induced sadness and joy. *Appetite*, 39, 147–58.

Mack, A. and Rock, I. (1998) *Inattentional Blindness*. Cambridge, MA: MIT Press.

Mack, S. and Munson, B. (2012) The influence of /s/ quality on ratings of men's sexual orientation: Explicit and implicit measures of the 'gay lisp' stereotype. *Journal of Phonetics*, 40, 198–212.

Mackay, D.G., Stewart, R. and Burke, D.M. (1998) HM revisited: relations between language comprehension, memory and the hippocampal system. *Journal of Cognitive Neuroscience*, 10(3), 377–94.

Mackenzie, C.S., Erickson, J., Deane, F.P. and Wright, M. (2014) Changes in attitudes toward seeking mental health services. *Clinical Psychology Review*, 34, 99–106.

Mackey, A.P., Finn, A.S., Leonard, J.A., Jacoby-Senghor, D.S., West, M.R., Gabrieli, C.F.O. and Gabrieli, J.D.E. (2015) Neuroanatomical correlates of the income-achievement gap. *Psychological Science*, 26, 925–33.

Mackie, D.M. (1986) Social identification effects in group polarization. *Journal of Personality and Social Psychology*, 50, 720–8.

Maclean, K. (2003) The impact of institutionalization on child development. *Development and Psychopathology*, 15, 853–84.

MacLeod, C.M. (1992) The Stroop task: The 'gold standard' of attentional measures. *Journal of Experimental Psychology: General*, 38, 421–39.

MacLeod, C.M., Matthews, A. and Tata, P. (1986) Attentional biases in emotional disorders. *Journal of Abnormal Psychology*, 95, 15–20.

Macnamara, B.N., Hambrick, D.Z. and Oswald, F.L. (2014) Deliberate practice and performance in music, games, sports, education, and professions: A meta-analysis. *Psychological Science*, 25, 1608–18.

MacNeil, M. and Sherif, M. (1976) Norm change over subject generations as a function of arbitrariness of prescribed norms. *Journal of Personality and Social Psychology*, 34, 762–73.

Macrae, C.N., Bodenhausen, G.V., Milne, A.B. and Jetten, J. (1994) Out of mind but back in sight: Stereotypes on the rebound. *Journal of Personality and Social Psychology*, 67, 808–17.

MacSweeney, M., Woll, B., Campbell, R., McGuire, P.K., David, A.S., Williams, S.C.R., Suckling, J., Calvert, G.A. and Brammer, M.J. (2002) Neural systems underlying British Sign Language and audio-visual English processing in native users. *Brain*, 125, 1583–93.

Maddux, W.W. and Yuki, M. (2006) The 'ripple effect': Cultural differences in perceptions of the consequences of events. *Personality and Social Psychology Bulletin*, 32(5), 669–83.

Maestrini, E. *et al.* (2010) High-density SNP association study and copy number variation analysis of the AUTS1 and AUTS5 loci implicate the IMMP2L-DOCK4 gene region in autism susceptibility. *Molecular Psychiatry*, 15, 954–68.

Maffei, M., Halaas, J., Ravussin, E., Pratley, R.E., Lee, G.H., Zhang, Y., Fei, H., Kim, S., Lallone, R. and Ranganathan, S. (1995) Leptin levels in human and rodent: Measurement of plasma leptin and ob RNA in obese and weight-reduced subjects. *Nature Medicine*, 11, 1155–61.

Magai, C. and McFadden, S.H. (1995) *The Role of Emotions in Social and Personality Development*. New York: Plenum Press.

Magnus, H. (1880) Untersuchungen über den Farbensinn der Naturvölker. *Physiologische Abhandlungen*, Ser. 2, no. 7.

Magnusson, A. (2000) An overview of epidemiological studies on seasonal affective disorder. *Acta Psychiatrica Scandinavica*, 101, 176–84.

Magnusson, D., Stattin, H. and Allen, V.L. (1986) Differential maturation among girls and its relevance to social adjustment: A longitudinal perspective. In D.L. Featherman and R.M. Learner (eds) *Lifespan Development and Behaviour*. New York: Academic Press.

Maguire, E.A. and Mullally, S.L. (2013) The hippocampus: a manifesto for change. *Journal of Experimental Psychology: General*, 142(4), 1180.

Maguire, E.A. and Mullaly, S.L., (2013) The hippocampus: a manifesto for change. *Journal of Experimental Psychology: General*, 142, 1180–9.

Maguire, E.A., Burgess, N., Donnett, J.G., Frackowiak, R.S.J., Frith, C.D. and O'Keefe, J. (1998) Knowing where and getting there: A human navigation network. *Science*, 280, 921–4.

Maguire, E.A., Frackowiak, R.S.J. and Frith, C.D. (1997) Recalling routes around London: Activation of the right hippocampus in taxi drivers. *Journal of Neuroscience*, 17, 7103.

Maguire, E.A., Intraub, H. and Mullaly, S.L. (2015) Scenes, spaces, and memory traces: What does the hippocampus do? *The Neuroscientist*, 1–8.

Maguire, E.A., Nannery, R. and Spiers, H.J. (2006) Navigation around London by a taxi driver with bilateral hippocampal lesions. *Brain*, 129, 2894–907.

Mai, X., Xu, L., Li, M., Shao, J., Zhao, Z., Lamm, C., Fox, N.A., Nelson, C.A. and Lozoff, B. (2014) Sounds elicit relative left frontal alpha activity in 2-month old infants. *International Journal of Psychophysiology*, 94, 287–91.

Maia, T.V. and Frank, M.J. (2016) An integrative perspective on the role of dopamine in schizophrenia. *Biological Psychiatry*, 81, 52–66.

Maier, M.A., Elliot, A.J. and Lichtenfeld, S. (2008) Mediation of the negative effect of red on intellectual performance. *Personality and Social Psychology Bulletin*, 34, 1530–40.

Maier, S.F. and Seligman, M.E. (1976) Learned helplessness: Theory and evidence. *Journal of Experimental Psychology: General*, 105, 3–46.

Main, M. and Solomon, J. (1990) Procedures for identifying infants as disorganised/disoriented during the Ainsworth Strange Situation. In M.T. Greenberg, D. Cichetti and E.M. Cummings (eds) *Attachment in the Preschool Years*. Chicago ITL: University of Chicago Press.

Maisey, D.S., Vale, E.L.E., Cornelissen, P.L. and Tovee, M.J. (1999) Characteristics of male attractiveness for women. *The Lancet*, 353, 1500.

Maison, D., Greenwald, A.G. and Bruin, R.H. (2004) Predictive validity of the Implicit Association Test in studies of brands, consumer attitudes and behavior. *Journal of Consumer Psychology*, 14, 405–15.

Maj, M. (2014) DSM-5, ICD-11 and 'pathologization of normal conditions'. *Australian and New Zealand Journal of Psychiatry*, 48, 193–7.

Major Depressive Disorder Working Group of the Psychiatric GWAS Consortium, Ripke, S., Wray, N. R., Lewis, C. M., Hamilton, S. P., Weissman, M. M., *et al.*

Major, B. (1994) From social inequality to personal entitlement: The role of social comparisons, legitimacy appraisals and group memberships. In M.P. Zanna (ed.) *Advances in Experimental Social Psychology*, Vol. 26. San Diego: Academic Press, pp. 293–355.

Makel, M.C. (2014) The empirical march: making science better at self-correction. *Psychology of Aesthetics, Creativity and the Arts*, 8, 2–7.

Makel, M.C. and Plucker, J.A. (2014) Facts are more important than novelty replication in the education sciences. *Educational Researcher*, 43, 304–16.

Makel, M.C. and Plucker, J.A. (2014) Facts are more important than novelty: Replication in the education sciences. *Educational Researcher*, 43(6), 304–16.

Malle, B.F. (2006) The actor-observer asymmetry in attribution: A (surprising) meta-analysis. *Psychological Bulletin*, 132, 895–919.

Malnic, B., Hirono, J., Sata, T. and Buck, L.B. (1999) Combinatorial receptor codes for odors. *Cell*, 96, 713–23.

Mameli, F., Mrakic-Sposta, S., Vergari, M., Fumagalli, M., Macis, M., Ferrucci, R., Nordio, F., Consonni, D., Sartori, G. and Priori, A. (2010) Dorsolateral prefrontal cortex specifically processes general – but not personal – knowledge deception. *Behavioural Brain Research*, 211, 164–8.

Mancini, F., Bolognini, N., Bricolo, E. and Vallar, G. (2011) Cross-modal processing in the occipito-temporal cortex: A TMS study of the Muller-Lyer Illusion. *Journal of Cognitive Neuroscience*, 23, 1987–97.

Mancini, F., Bricolo, E. and Vallar, G. (2010) Multisensory integration in the Muller-Lyer illusion: From vision to haptics. *The Quarterly Journal of Experimental Psychology*, 63, 818–30.

Mandler, J.M. and McDonough, L. (1995) Long-term recall of sequences in infancy. *Journal of Experimental Child Psychology*, 59, 457–74.

Maner, J.K. and Gerend, M.A. (2007) Motivationally selective risk judgements: Do fear and curiosity boost the boons or the banes? *Organizational Behavior and Human Decision Processes*, 103, 256–67.

Manera, V., Del Guidice, M., Grandi, E. and Colle, L. (2011) Individual differences in the recognition of enjoyment smiles: no role for perceptual-attentional factors and autistic-like traits. *Frontiers in Psychology*, 2, article 143.

Mann, L. (2016) Procrastination revisited: a commentary. *Australian Psychologist*, 51(1), 47–51.

Manning, R., Levine, M. and Collins, A. (2007) The Kitty Genovese murder and the social psychology of helping. *American Psychologist*, 62(6), 555–62.

Manson, J.E., Willett, W.C., Stampfer, M.J., Colditz, G.A., Hunter, D.J. and Hankinson, S.E. (1995) Body weight and mortality among women. *New England Journal of Medicine*, 333, 677–85.

Markey, P.M. and Markey, C.N. (2007) The interpersonal meaning of sexual promiscuity. *Journal of Research in Personality*, 41, 1199–212.

Markman, E.M. (1989) *Categorization and Naming in Children*. Cambridge, MA: MIT Press.

Markowitz, D.M. and Hancock, J.T. (2015) Linguistic obfuscation in fraudulent science. *Journal of Language and Social Psychology*, 1–11.

Marks, G. and Miller, N. (1987) Ten years of research on the false-consensus effect: An empirical and theoretical review. *Psychological Bulletin*, 102, 72–90.

Markson, L. and Bloom, P. (1997) Evidence against a dedicated system for word learning in children. *Nature*, 385, 813–15.

Markus, H. (1978) The effect of mere presence on social facilitation: An unobtrusive test. *Journal of Experimental Social Psychology*, 14, 389–97.

Markus, H. and Wurf, E. (1987) The dynamic self-concept: A social psychological perspective. *Annual Review of Psychology*, 38, 299–337.

Markus, H.R. and Kitayama, S. (1991) Culture and the self: Implications for cognition, emotion, and motivation. *Psychological Review*, 98, 224–53.

Markus, H.R. and Nurius, P. (1986) Possible selves. *American Psychologist*, 41, 954–69.

Marler, P. (1961) The filtering of external stimuli during instinctive behaviour. In W.H. Thorpe and O.L. Zangwill (eds) *Current Problems in Animal Behaviour*. Cambridge: Cambridge University Press.

Marlowe, F. and Wetsman, A. (2001) Preferred waist-to-hip ratio and ecology. *Personality and Individual Differences*, 30, 481–9.

Marmot, M.G., Bosma, H., Hemingway, H., Brunner, E. and Stansfeld, S. (1997) Contribution of job control and other risk factors to social variations in coronary heart disease incidence. *Lancet*, 350, 235–9.

Marques, J.M., Abrams, D. and Serodio, R. (2001) Being better by being right: Subjective group dynamics and derogation of in-group deviants when generic norms are undermined. *Journal of Personality and Social Psychology*, 81, 436–47.

Marques, J.M., Yzerbyt, V.Y. and Leyens, J-P. (1988) Extremity of judgments towards ingroup members as a function of ingroup identification. *European Journal of Social Psychology*, 18, 1–16.

Marsh, A. and McKay, S. (1994) *Poor Smokers*. London: Policy Studies Institute.

Marsh, G., Desberg, P. and Cooper, J. (1977) Developing strategies in reading. *Journal of Reading Behaviour*, 9, 391–4.

Marsh, G.G. and Philwin, B. (1987) Unilateral neglect and constructional apraxia in a right-handed artist with a left posterior lesion. *Cortex*, 23(1), 149–55.

Marsh, P., Rosser, E. and Harré, R. (1978) *The Rules of Disorder*. Milton Keynes: Open University Press.

Marshall, L. and Born, J. (2007) The contribution of sleep to hippocampus-dependent memory consolidation. *Trends in Cognitive Sciences,* 11(10), 442–50.

Marshall, W.L., Eccles, A. and Barbaree, H.E. (1991) The treatment of exhibitionists: A focus on sexual deviance versus cognitive and relationship features. *Behaviour Research and Therapy,* 29, 129–36.

Martella, D. and Maass, A. (2000) Unemployment and life satisfaction: The moderating role of time structure and collectivism. *Journal of Applied Social Psychology,* 30, 1095–108.

Martens, R. (1969) Palmar sweating and the presence of an audience. *Journal of Experimental Social Psychology,* 5, 371–4.

Martin, A. and Chao, L.L. (2001) Semantic memory and the brain: Structure and processes. *Current Opinion in Neurobiology,* 11, 194–201.

Martin, A., Kronbichler, M. and Richlan, F. (2016) Dyslexic brain activation abnormalities in deep and shallow orthographies: A meta-analysis of 28 functional neuroimaging studies. *Human Brain Mapping,* 37, 2676–99.

Martin, A., Shurtz, M., Kronbichler, M. and Richlan, F. (2015) Reading the brain of children and adults: A meta-analysis of 40 functional magnetic resonance imaging studies. *Human Brain Mapping,* 36, 1963–81.

Martin, A., Wiggs, C.L., Ungerleider, G. and Haxby, V. (1996) Neural correlates of category-specific knowledge. *Nature,* 379, 649–52.

Martin, C.L. and Chun, M. (2016) The BRAIN Initiative: Building, strengthening and sustaining. *Neuron,* 92, 570–3.

Martin, C.L. and Halverson, C.E. (1981) A schematic processing model of sex-typing and stereotyping in children. *Child Development,* 52, 1119–34.

Martin, G.N. (1996) Olfactory remediation: Current evidence and possible applications. *Social Science and Medicine,* 43(1), 63–70.

Martin, G.N. (1998) Human electroencephalographic (EEG) response to olfactory stimulation: Two experiments using the aroma of food. *International Journal of Psychophysiology,* 30, 287–302.

Martin, G.N. (2001) How do European and US psychology differ? *The Psychologist,* 14(7), 352–3.

Martin, G.N. (2003) *Essential Biological Psychology.* London: Hodder Arnold.

Martin, G.N. (2006) *Human Neuropsychology* (2nd edn). Harlow: Prentice Hall Europe.

Martin, G.N. (2013) *The Neuropsychology of Smell and Taste.* Hove: The Psychology Press.

Martin, G.N. (2016) The neuroscience of. . . https://www.scribd.com/document/261645429/The-Psychology-of-The-Neuroscience-of

Martin, G.N. and Gray, C.D. (1996) The effects of audience laughter on men's and women's responses to humour. *Journal of Social Psychology,* 136(2), 221–31.

Martin, G.N., Apena, F., Chaudry, Z., Mulligan, Z. and Nixon, C. (2001) The development of an attitude towards the sense of smell questionnaire (SoSQ) and a comparison of different professions' responses. *North American Journal of Psychology,* 3(3), 491–502.

Martin, G.N., Sadler, S.J. and Baluch, B. (1997) Individual group differences in the perception and knowledge of psychological research. *Personality and Individual Differences,* 22(5), 771–4.

Martin, K.A. (1996) *Puberty, Sexuality and the Self.* London: Routledge.

Martin, R.A. (2001) Humor, laughter and physical health: Methodological issues and research findings. *Psychological Bulletin,* 127(4), 504–19.

Martin, R.A. and Lefcourt, H.M. (1983) Sense of humor as a moderator of the relation between stressors and moods. *Journal of Personality and Social Psychology,* 45, 1313–24.

Martin, R.C. (2003) Language processing: Functional organization and neuroanatomical basis. *Annual Review of Psychology,* 54, 55–89.

Marton, F. and Saljo, R. (1976) On qualitative differences in student learning 1: Outcome and process. *British Journal of Educational Psychology,* 46(1), 4–11.

Marucha, P.T., Kiecolt-Glaser, J.K. and Favagehi, M. (1998) Mucosal wound healing is impaired by examination stress. *Psychosomatic Medicine,* 60, 362–5.

Mascaro, J.S., Hackett, P.D. and Rilling, J.K. (2013) Testicular volume is inversely correlated with nurture-related brain activity in human fathers. *PNAS,* 110, 15746–51.

Maslow, A.H. (1964) *Religions, Values, and Peak-experiences.* New York: Viking.

Maslow, A.H. (1970) *Motivation and Personality* (2nd edn). New York: Harper & Row.

Mason, E.E. and Ito, C. (1969) Gastric bypass. *Annals of Surgery,* 170, 329–39.

Mason, M. and Gibbs, J.C. (1993) Social perspective-taking and moral judgment among college students. *Journal of Adolescent Research,* 8, 109–13.

Mason, W.T. (1980) Supraoptic neurones of rat hypothalamus are osmosensitive. *Nature,* 287, 154–7.

Massa, L.J. and Mayer, R.E. (2006) Testing the ATI hypothesis: Should multimedia instruction accommodate verbalizer-visualizer cognitive style? *Learning and Individual Differences,* 1i6(4), 321–35.

Massar, K. and Buunk, A.P. (2010) Judging a book by its cover: jealousy after subliminal priming with attractive and unattractive faces. *Personality and Individual Differences,* 49, 634–8.

Masten, C.L., Telzer, E.H., Fuligni, A.J., Lieberman, M.D. and Eisenberger, N.I. (2012) Time spent with friends in adolescence relates to less neural sensitivity to later peer rejection. *Social Cognitive and Affective Neuroscience,* 7(1), 106–14.

Master, S.L., Eisenberger, N.I., Taylor, S.E., Naliboff, B.D., Shirinyan, D. and Lieberman, M.D. (2009) A picture's worth: Partner photographs reduce experimentally induced pain. *Psychological Science,* 20, 1316–18.

Masterpasqua, F. (2009) Psychology and epigenetics. *Review of General Psychology,* 13, 194–201.

Masters, M.S. (1998) The gender difference on the Mental Rotation test is not due to performance factors. *Memory and Cognition,* 26(3), 444–8.

Masters, M.S. and Sanders, B. (1993) Is the gender difference in mental rotation disappearing? *Behaviour Genetics,* 23, 337–41.

Masuda, T. and Nisbett, R.E. (2001) *Journal of Personality and Social Psychology,* 81, 922–34.

Masuda, T., Gonzalez, R., Kwan, L. and Nisbett, R.E. (2008) Culture and aesthetic preference: Comparing the attention to context of east Asians and Americans. *Personality and Social Psychology Bulletin,* 34(9), 1260–75.

Matarazzo, J.D. (1982) Behavioural health's challenge to academic scientific and professional psychology. *American Psychologist,* 37, 1–14.

Matchett, G. and Davey, G.C.L. (1991) A test of a disease-avoidance model of animal phobias. *Behaviour Research and Therapy,* 29, 91–4.

Mather, M., Cacioppo, J.T. and Kanwisher, N. (2013) How fMRI can inform cognitive theories. *Perspectives on Psychological Science,* 8, 108–113.

Matson, J.L., Worley, J.A., Fodstad, J.C., Chung, K-M., Suh, D., Jhin, H.K., Ben-Itzchak, E., Zachor, D.A. and Furniss, F. (2011) A multinational study examining the cross cultural differences in reported symptoms of autism spectrum disorders: Israel, South Korea, the UK and the US. *Research in Autism Spectrum Disorders,* 5, 1598–604.

Mattes, R.D., Arnold, C. and Boraas, M. (1987) Learned food aversions among cancer chemotherapy patients: Incidence, nature and clinical implications. *Cancer,* 60, 2576–80.

Matthew, S.J. (2010) Riluzole for relapse prevention following intra-venous ketamine in treatment-resistant depression: a pilot rand-omized, placebo-controlled continuation trial. *International Journal of Neuropsychopharmacology*, 13, 71–82.

Matthews, A., May, J., Mogg, K. and Eysenck, M.W. (1990) Attentional bias in anxiety: Selective search or defective filtering? *Journal of Abnormal Psychology*, 99, 166–73.

Matthews, A.M., Gedler, M.G. and Johnston, D.W. (1981) *Agoraphobia: Nature and treatment*. New York: Guilford Press.

Matthews, G. and Desmond, P.A. (2002) Task-induced fatigue states and simulated driving performance. *The Quarterly Journal of Experimental Psychology*, 55A(2), 659–86.

Mauss, I.B., Savino, N.S., Anderson, C.L., Tamir, M., Weisbuch, M. and Laudenslager, M.L. (2011) The pursuit of happiness can be lonely. *Emotion*, 12, 908–12.

Mawson, A.R. (1974) Anorexia nervosa and the regulation of intake: A review. *Psychological Medicine*, 4, 289–308.

Max, J.E., Levin, H., Schachar, R.J., Landis, J., Saunders, A.E., Ewing-Cobbs, L., Chapman, S.B. and Dennis, M. (2006) Predictors of personality change due to traumatic brain injury in children and adolescents six to twenty four months after injury. *Journal of Neuropsychiatry and Clinical Neuroscience*, 18, 21–32.

May, L., Byers-Heinlein, K., Gervain, J. and Werker, J.F. (2011) Language and the newborn brain. *Frontiers in Psychology*, 2, article 222.

Mayan, I. and Meiran, N. (2011) Anger and the speed of full-body approach and avoidance reactions. *Frontiers in Psychology*, 2, 22.

Mayer, J. (1955) Regulation of energy intake and the body weight: The glu-costatic theory and the lipostatic hypothesis. *Annals of the New York Academy of Science*, 63, 15–43.

Mayer, J.D. and Cobb, C.D. (2000) Educational policy on emotional intelligence: Does it make sense? *Educational Psychology Review*, 12, 163–83.

Mayer, J.D., Cobb D. and Salovey, P. (1999) Emotional intelligence meets tra-ditional standards for intelligence. *Intelligence*, 27, 267–98.

Maylor, E.A. (1990) Age and prospective memory. *The Quarterly Journal of Experimental Psychology*, 42A, 471–93.

Maylor, E.A. (1996) Older people's memory for the past and the future. *The Psychologist*, October, 456–9.

Maylor, E.A. (2002) Serial position effects in semantic memory: Reconstructing the order of verses of hymns. *Psychonomic Bulletin and Review*, 9(4), 816–20.

Maynard Smith, J. (1964) Group selection and kin selection. *Nature*, 210, 1145–7.

Maynard, D.W. (1992) On clinicians co-implicating recipients' perspectives in the delivery of diagnostic news. In P. Drew and J. Heritage (eds), *Talk at Work*. Cambridge: Cambridge University Press.

Maze, I. *et al.* (2010) Essential role of the histone methyltransferase G9a in cocaine-induced plasticity. *Science*, 327, 213–16.

Mazur, A. (2013) Testosterone rises among young husbands with children in the home. *Andrology*, 1–5.

Mazur, A. (2016) http://www.sciencedirect.com/science/article/pii/S0018506X15300891

Mazur, A. and Booth, A. (1998) Testosterone and dominance in men. *Behavioural and Brain Sciences*, 21, 353–97.

Mazur, A. and Booth, A. (2014) Testosterone is related to deviance in male army veterans but relationships are not moderated by cortisol. *Biological Psychology*, 96, 72–6.

Mazur, A. and Lamb, T. (1980) Testosterone, status, and mood in human males. *Hormones and Behavior*, 14, 236–46.

Mazur, A. and Michalek, J. (1998) Marriage, divorce and male testosterone. *Social Forces*, 77, 315–30.

Mazur, A., Booth, A. and Dabbs, J. (1992) Testosterone and chess competi-tion. *Social Psychology Quarterly*, 55, 70–7.

Mazur, J.E. (1994) *Learning and Behavior*. Englewood Cliffs, NJ: Prentice Hall.

McAlister, A., Perry, C., Killen, L.A., Slinkard, L.A. and Maccoby, N. (1980) Pilot study of smoking, alcohol, and drug abuse prevention. *American Journal of Public Health*, 70, 719–21.

McAlvanah, P. (2009) Are people more risk-taking in the presence of the opposite sex? *Journal of Economic Psychology*, 30, 136–46.

McBride, D.M. and Dosher, B.A. (1997) A comparison of forgetting in an implicit and explicit memory task. *Journal of Experimental Psychology: General*, 126(4), 371–92.

McBride, S.A., Balkin, T.J., Kamimori, G.H. and Killgore, W.D.S. (2006) Olfactory decrements as a function of two nights of sleep deprivation. *Journal of Sensory Studies*, 21, 456–63.

McCabe, D.P. and Castel, A.D. (2008) Seeing is believing: The effect of brain images on judgements of scientific reasoning. *Cognition*, 107, 343–52.

McCabe, M.P. and Ricciardelli, L.A. (2003) Body image and strategies to lose weight and increase muscle among boys and girls. *Health Psychology*, 22(1), 39–46.

McCabe, R., Heath, C., Burns, T. and Priebe. S (2002) Engagement of patients with psychosis in the consultation: Conversation analytic study. *British Medical Journal*, 325, 1148–51.

McCann, S. J. (2017). Higher USA State Resident Neuroticism Is Associated With Lower State Volunteering Rates. *Personality and Social Psychology Bulletin*, in press.

McCann, S.J.H. (2015) Big Five personality and residential mobility: a state-level analysis of the USA. *The Journal of Social Psychology*, 155(3), 274–91.

McCaul, K.D. and Malott, J.M. (1984) Distraction and coping with pain. *Psychological Bulletin*, 95, 516–33.

McClelland, J.L. and Rumelhart, D.E. (1981) An interactive activation model of context effects in letter perception, Part 1: An account of basic find-ings. *Psychological Review*, 88, 375–407.

McClintock, M.K. (1971) Menstrual synchrony and suppression. *Nature*, 229, 244–5.

McClintock, M.K. and Adler, N.T. (1978) The role of the female during copulation in wild and domestic Norway rats (*Rattus norvegicus*) *Behaviour*, 67, 67–96.

McCrae, R.R. and Costa, P.T. (1985) Updating Norman's 'adequate taxonomy': Intelligence and personality dimensions in natural language and in questionnaires. *Journal of Personality and Social Psychology*, 49, 710–12.

McCrae, R.R. and Costa, P.T. (1987) Validation of the five-factor model of personality across instruments and observers. *Journal of Personality and Social Psychology*, 52, 81–90.

McCrae, R.R. and Costa, P.T. (1990) *Personality in Adulthood*. New York: Guilford Press.

McCrae, R.R. and Costa, P.T. (1993) Psychological resilience among widowed men and women: A 10-year follow-up of a national sample. In M.S. Stroebe, W. Stroebe and R.O. Hansson (eds) *Handbook of Bereavement*. Cambridge: Cambridge University Press.

McCrae, R.R. *et al.* (2005) Universal features of personality traits from the observer's perspective: data from 50 cultures. *Journal of Personality and Social Psychology*, 88 (3), 547–61.

McCrae, R.R., Costa, P.T. and Busch, C.M. (1986) Evaluating comprehen-siveness in personality systems: The California Q-Set and the five-factor model. *Journal of Personality*, 54, 430–46.

McCrae, R.R., Costa, P.T., Ostendorf, F., Angleitner, A., Hrebickova, M., Avia, M.D., Sanz, J., Sanchez-Bernardos, M.L., Kusdil, M.E.,Woodfield, R.,

Saunders, P.R. and Smith, P.B. (2000) Nature over nuture: Temperament, personality and lifespan development. *Journal of Personality and Social Psychology*, 78(1), 173–86.

McCrae, R.R., Yik, M.S.M., Trapnell, P.D., Bond, M.H. and Paulhus, D.L. (1998) Interpreting personality profiles across cultures: Bilingual, acculturation and peer rating studies of Chinese undergraduates. *Journal of Personality and Social Psychology*, 74, 1041–55.

McCullough, B.D. and McWilliams, T.P. (2011) Students with the initial 'A' don't get better grades. *Journal of Research in Personality*, 45, 340–3.

McCullough, M.E., Smith Churchland, P. and Mendez, A.J. (2013) Problems with measuring peripheral oxytocin: Can the data on oxytocin and human behavior be trusted? *Neuroscience and Biobehavioural Reviews*, 37, 1485–92.

McDaniel, M.A., Anderson, D.C., Einstein, G.O. and O'Halloran, C.M. (1989) Modulation of environmental reinstatement effects through encoding strategies. *American Journal of Psychology*, 102, 523–48.

McDaniel, M.A., Maier, S.F. and Einstein, G.O. (2002) 'Brain-specific' nutrients: A memory cure? *Psychological Science in the Public Interest*, 3(1), 12–38.

McDermott, A.F., Bavelier, D. and Green, C.S. (2014) Memory abilities in action video game players. *Computers in Human Behavior*, 34, 69–78.

McElrea, H. and Standing, L. (1992) Fast music causes fast drinking. *Perceptual and Motor skills*, 75(2), 362.

McEwen, B.S. (2012) Brain on stress: how the social environment gets under the skin. *Proceedings of the National Academy of Sciences*, 109(Supplement 2), 17180–5.

McFarlane, A.C. (1992) Avoidance and intrusion in post-traumatic stress disorder. *Journal of Nervous and Mental Disease*, 180, 439–45.

McGinn, C. (1989) Can we solve the mind-body problem? *Mind*, 98, 349–66.

McGinty, D.J. and Sterman, M.B. (1968) Sleep suppression after basal forebrain lesions in the cat. *Science*, 160, 1253–5.

McGinty, E.E., Webster, D.W. and Barry, C.L. (2013) Effects of news media messages about mass shootings on attitudes toward persons with serious mental illness and public support for gun control policies. *American Journal of Psychiatry*, 170(5), 494–501.

McGue, M., Bacon, S. and Lykken, D.T. (1993) Personality stability and change in early adulthood: A behavior genetic analysis. *Developmental Psychology*, 29, 96–109.

McGue, M., Elkins, I., Walden, B. and Iacono, W.G. (2005) Perceptions of the parent–adolescent relationship: A longitudinal investigation. *Developmental Psychology*, 41(6), 971–84.

McGuire, W.J. (1964) Inducing resistance to persuasion. In L. Berkowitz (ed.) *Advances in Experimental Social Psychology*, Vol. 1. New York: Academic Press, pp. 191–229.

McGuire, W.J. and Papageorgis, D. (1961) The relative efficacy of various types of prior belief-defence in producing immunity against persuasion. *Journal of Abnormal and Social Psychology*, 62, 327–37.

McKay, D.C. (1973) Aspects of the theory of comprehension, memory and attention. *The Quarterly Journal of Experimental Psychology*, 25, 22–40.

McKenna, D.D. and Farrell, B.D. (2006) Tropical forests are both evolutionary cradles and museums of leaf beetle diversity. *Proceedings of the National Academy of Science*, 103, 10947–51.

McLellan, D.L. (1991) Functional recovery and the principles of disability medicine. In M. Swash and J. Oxbury (eds) *Clinical Neurology*. Edinburgh: Churchill Livingstone.

McManus, I.C. (1985) Handedness, language dominance and aphasia: A genetic model. *Psychological Medicine*, 8, 1–40.

McNab, F. *et al.* (2009) Changes in cortical dopamine D1 receptor binding associated with cognitive training. *Science*. 323, 800–2.

McNally, R.J. (1987) Preparedness and phobias. *Psychological Bulletin*, 101, 283–303.

McNally, R.J. (1990) Psychological approaches to panic disorder: A review. *Psychological Bulletin*, 108, 403–19.

McNally, R.J. (1995) Preparedness, phobias, and the Panglossian paradigm. *Behavioural and Brain Sciences*, 18, 303–4.

McNaughton, N. and Corr, P.J. (2004) A two-dimensional neuropsychology of defense: fear/anxiety and defensive distance. *Neuroscience and Biobehavioral Reviews*, 28(3), 285–305.

McNeill, A., Brose, L.S., Calder, R., Hitchman, S.C., Hajek, P. and McRobbie, H. (2015) *E-cigarettes: an evidence update*. London: PHE.

McNeill, D. (1970) *The Acquisition of Language: The study of developmental psycholinguistics*. New York: Harper & Row.

McNorgan, C. (2012) A meta-analytic review of multi sensory imagery identifies the neural correlates of modality-specific and modality-general imagery. *Frontiers in Human Neuroscience*, 6, 1–14.

McRae, K. (2016) Cognitive emotion regulation: a review of theory and scientific findings. *Current Opinion in Behavioral Sciences*, 10, 119–24.

McReynolds, W.T. (1980) Learned helplessness as a schedule-shift effect. *Journal of Research in Personality*, 14, 139–57.

McRobbie, H., Bullen, C., Hartmann-Boyce, J. and Hajek, P. (2014) Electronic cigarettes for smoking cessation and reduction. *Cochrane Library*, 12. CD010216.

Meador, K.J., Allen, M.E., Adams, R.J. and Loring, D.W. (1991) Allochiria vs allesthesia. Is there a misrepresentation? *Archives of Neurology*, 48, 546–9.

Measham, F., O'Brien, K. and Turnbull, G. (2016) 'Skittles and Red Bull is my favourite flavour': E-cigarettes, smoking, vaping, and the changing landscape of nicotine consumption amongst British teenagers. *Drugs Education and Preventative Policy*, 23, 224–37.

Meehl, P.E. (1956) Wanted – a good cookbook. *American Psychologist*, 11, 262–72.

Meerwijk, E.L., Ford, J.M. and Weiss, S.J. (2013) Brain regions associated with psychological pain: implications for a neural network and its relationship to physical pain. *Brain Imaging and Behavior*, 7(1), 1–14.

Mehler, J., Jusczyk, P., Lambertz, G., Halsted, N., Bertoncini, J. and Amiel-Tison, C. (1988) A precursor of language acquisition in young infants. *Cognition*, 29, 143–78.

Mehta, R. and Zhu, R. (2009) Blue or red? Exploring the effect of color on cognitive task performances. *Science*, 323, 1226–9.

Meichenbaum, D. (1985) *Stress Inoculation Training*. New York: Pergamon Press.

Meichenbaum, D.H. (1977) *Cognitive-behavior Modification: An integrative approach*. New York: Plenum Press.

Meints, S.M., Miller, M.M. and Hirsch, A.T. (2016) Differences in pain coping between black and white Americans: A meta-analysis. *The Journal of Pain*, 17, 642–53.

Mejia-Arauz, R., Rogoff, B., Dexter, A. and Najafi, B. (2007) Cultural variation in children's social organization. *Child Development*, 78(3), 1001–14.

Melamed, S., Shirom, A., Toker, S., Berliner, S. and Shapira, I. (2006) Burnout and risk of cardiovascular disease: Evidence, possible causal paths, and promising research directions. *Psychological Bulletin*, 132(3), 327–53.

Melby-Lervåg, M. and Hulme, C. (2013) Is working memory training effective? A meta-analytic review. *Developmental Psychology*, 49(2), 270.

Melby-Lervåg, M. and Hulme, C. (2016) There is no convincing evidence that working memory training is effective: A reply to Au et al. (2014) and Karbach and Verhaeghen (2014). *Psychonomic Bulletin and Review*, 23(1), 324–30.

Melby-Lervag, M., Lyster, S-A. and Hulme, C. (2012) Phonological skills and their role in learning to read: A meta-analytic review. *Psychological Bulletin*, 138, 322–52.

Melby-Lervag, M., Redick, T.S. and Hulme, C. (2016) Working memory training does not improve performance on measures of intelligence or other measures of 'far transfer': Evidence from meta-analytic review. *Perspectives on Psychological Science*, 11, 512–34.

Meletti, S., Cantalupo, G., Benuzzi, F., Mai, R., Tassi, L., Gasparini, E., Tassinari, C.A. and Nichelli, P. (2012) Fear and happiness in the eyes: An intra-cerebral event-related potential study from the human amygdala. *Neuropsychologia*, 50, 44–54.

Mellanby, J., Zimdars, A. and Cortina-Borja, M. (2013) Sex differences in degree performance at the University of Oxford. *Learning and Individuals Differences*, 26, 102–111.

Melo, M.C., Abreu, R.L., Neto, V.B.L., de Bruin, P.F. and de Bruin, V.M. (2016) Chronotype and circadian rhythm in bipolar disorder: a systematic review. *Sleep Medicine Reviews*.

Meltzoff, A.N. (1988) Infant imitation and memory: Nine-month-olds in immediate and deferred tests. *Child Development*, 59, 217–25.

Meltzoff, A.N. (1995) What infant memory tells us about infantile amnesia: Long-term recall and deferred imitation. *Journal of Experimental Child Psychology*, 59, 497–515.

Menegatti, M. and Rubini, M. (2013) Convincing similar and dissimilar others: the power of language abstraction in political communication. *Personality and Social Psychology Bulletin*, 39, 596–607.

Menke, R., Meinzer, M., Kugel, H., Deppe, M., Baumgartner, A., Schiff-bauer, H., Thomas, M., Kramer, K., Lohmann, H., Floel, A., Knecht, S. and Breitenstein, C. (2009) Imaging short- and long-term training success in chronic aphasia. *BMC Neuroscience*, 10, 118.

Menn, L. and Stoel-Gammon, C. (1993) Phonological development: Learning sounds and sound patterns. In J.B. Gleason (ed.) *The Development of Language*. New York: Macmillan.

Mennella, J.A. and Bobowski, N.K. (2015) The sweetness bitterness of childhood. *Physiology and Behaviour*, 152, 502–7.

Menon, T., Morris, M.W., Chiu, C. and Hong, Y. (1999) Culture and the construal of agency: Attribution to individual versus group dispositions. *Journal of Personality and Social Psychology*, 76, 701–17.

Merkel E., Maass A. and Frommelt L. (2012) Shielding women against status loss: The masculine form and its alternatives in the Italian language. *Journal of Language and Social Psychology*, 31, 311–20.

Merrens, M.R. and Richards, W.S. (1970) Acceptance of generalized bona fide personality interpretations. *Psychological Reports*, 27, 691–4.

Mervis, C.B. and Rosch, E. (1981) Categorization of natural objects. *Annual Review of Psychology*, 32, 89–116.

Mesquita, B. and Boiger, M. (2014) Emotions in context: A sociodynamic model of emotions. *Emotion Review*, 6, 298–302.

Messerli, F.H. (2012) Chocolate consumption, cognitive function, and novel laureates. *New England Journal of Medicine*, 367, 1562–4.

Metalsky, G.I., Halberstadt, L.J. and Abramson, L.Y. (1987) Vulnerability to depressive mood reactions: Toward a more powerful test of the diathesis-stress and causal mediation components of the reformulated theory of depression. *Journal of Personality and Social Psychology*, 52, 386–93.

Meunier, D., Ersche, K.D., Craig, K.J., Fortino, A., Merlo-Pich, E.M., Fineberg, N.A., Shabbir, S.S., Robbins, T.W. and Bullmore, E.T. (2012) Brain functional connectivity in stimulant drug dependence and obsessive-compulsive disorder. *Neuroimage*, 59, 146.

Meyer, M.J. and Bagwell, J. (2012) The non-impact of paper color on exam performance. *Issues in Accounting Education*, 27(3), 691–706.

Meyer, P.A., Garrison, C.Z., Jackson, K.L. and Addy, C.L. (1993) Undesirable life events and depression in young adolescents. *Journal of Child and Family Studies*, 2, 47–60.

Michael, G.A., Galich, H., Relland, S. and Prud-hon, S. (2010a) The nature and specificity of color-induced nasal thermal sensations. *Behavioural and Brain Research*, 207, 418–28.

Michael, G.A., Relland, S., Borg, C., Peyron, R. and Thomas-Anterion, C. (2010b) A role for the insula in color-induced nasal thermal sensations. *Behavioural Brain Research*, 212, 103–8.

Midorikawa, A. and Kawamura, M. (2014) The emergence of artistic ability following traumatic brain injury. *Neurocase*, 21, 90–4.

Mikolajczak, M., Gross, J.J., Lane, A., Corneille, O., de Timary, P. and Luminet, O. (2010) Oxytocin makes people trusting, not gullible. *Psychological Science*, 21(8), 1072–4.

Miles, H.L. (1983) Apes and language: The search for communicative competence. In J. de Luce and H.T. Wilder (eds) *Language in Primates: Perspectives and implications*. New York: Springer-Verlag.

Miles, L.K. (2009) Who is approachable? *Journal of Experimental Social Psychology*, 45, 262–6.

Milgram, S. (1963) Behavioral study of obedience. *Journal of Abnormal and Social Psychology*, 67, 371–8.

Milgram, S. (1974) *Obedience to Authority*. London: Tavistock.

Miller, C.L. (1987) Qualitative differences among gender-stereotyped toys: Implications for cognitive and social development. *Sex Roles*, 16, 473–87.

Miller, D.T. and Porter, C.A. (1983) Self-blame in victims of violence. *Journal of Social Issues*, 39, 139–52.

Miller, G.A. (1956) The magical number seven plus or minus two: Some limits on our capacity for processing information. *Psychological Review*, 63, 81–97.

Miller, G.E. and Cohen, S. (2001) Psychological interventions and the immune system: A meta-analytic review and critique. *Health Psychology*, 20, 47–63.

Miller, J., Mckinstry, R, Phillip, J., Mukherjee, P. and Neil, J. (2003) Diffusion-tensor MR imaging of normal brain maturation: A guide of structural development and myelination. *American Journal of Radiology*, 180, 851–9.

Miller, J.D., Scott, E. and Okamoto, S. (2006) Public acceptance of evolution. *Science*, 313, 765–6.

Miller, R.J., Hennessy, R.T. and Leibowitz, H.W. (1973) The effect of hypnotic ablation of the background on the magnitude of the Ponzo perspective illusion. *International Journal of Clinical and Experimental Hypnosis*, 21, 180–91.

Miller, S.L. and Maner, J.K. (2011a) Ovulation as a male mating prime: Subtle signs of women's fertility influence men's mating cognition and behavior. *Journal of Personality and Social Psychology*, 100, 295–308.

Miller, S.L. and Maner, J.K. (2011b) Sick body, vigilant mind: the biological immune system activates the behavioural immune system. *Psychological Science*, 22, 1467–71.

Milligan, K., Astington, J.W. and Dack, L.A. (2007) Language and theory of mind: Meta-analysis of the relation between language ability and false-belief understanding. *Child Development*, 78(2), 622–46.

Milliman, R.E. (1986) The influence of background music on the behavior of restaurant patrons. *Journal of Consumer Research*, 13(2), 286–9.

Mills, K.L. (2014) Effects of internet use on the adolescent brain: despite popular claims experimental evidence remains scarce. *TICS*, 18, 385–7.

Mills, K.L. and Tamnes, C.K. (2014) Methods and considerations for longitudinal structural brain imaging analysis across development. *Developmental Cognitive Neuroscience*, 9, 172–90.

Mills, K.L., Goddings, A-L., Herting, M.M., Meuwese, R., Blakemore, S-J., Crone, E.A., Dahl, R.A., Guroglu, B., Raznahan, A., Sowell, E.R. and Tamnes, C.K. (2016) Structural brain development between childhood and adulthood: Convergence across four longitudinal samples. *Neuroimage*, 141, 273–81.

Milner, A.D. (1998) Streams of consciousness: Visual awareness and the brain. *Trends in Cognitive Sciences*, 2(1), 25–30.

Milner, A.D. and Goodale, M.A. (1995) *The Visual Brain in Action.* Oxford: Oxford University Press.

Milner, A.D., Perrett, D.I., Johnston, R.S., Benson, P.I., Jordan, T.R. and Healey, D.W. (1991) Perception and action in 'visual form agnosia'. *Brain*, 114, 405–28.

Milner, B. (1964) Some effects of frontal lobotomy in man. In J.W. Warren and G. Akert (eds) *The Frontal Granular Cortex and Behaviour.* New York: McGraw-Hill.

Milner, B. (1970) Memory and the temporal regions of the brain. In K.H. Pribram and D.E. Broadbent (eds) *Biology of Memory.* New York: Academic Press.

Milner, B., Corkin, S. and Teuber, H-L. (1968) Further analysis of the hippocampal amnesic syndrome: 14 year follow-up study of HM. *Neuropsychologia*, 6, 217–24.

Miloyan, B. and Eaton, W. W. (2016) Blood-injection-injury phobia in older adults. *International Psychogeriatrics*, 28(06), 897–902.

Min, B. and Choi, I. (2016) Heavy-heartedness biases your weight perception. *The Journal of Social Psychology*, 156, 513–22.

Minahan, J. and Siedlecki, K.L. (2016) Individual differences in Need for Cognition influence the evaluation of circular scientific explanations. *Personality and Individual Differences*, 99, 113–17.

Mischel, W. (1968) *Personality and Assessment.* New York: Wiley.

Mischel, W. (1976) *Introduction to Personality* (2nd edn). New York: Holt, Rinehart & Winston.

Mischel, W. (1984) Convergences and challenges in the search for consistency. *American Psychologist*, 39, 351–64.

Mischel, W. (2009) From *Personality and Assessment* (1968) to personality science, 2009. *Journal of Research in Personality*, 43, 282–90.

Misra, S., Cheng, L., Genevie, J. and Yuan, M. (2014) The iPhone effect: The quality of in-person social interactions in the presence of mobile devices. *Environment and Behaviour*, 1–24.

Mitchell, D.C., Knight, C.A. and Hockeberry, J. (2014) Beverage caffeine intakes in the US. *Food Chemistry and Toxicology*, 63, 136–42.

Mitte, K. (2005) Meta-analysis of cognitive-behavioural treatments for Generalized Anxiety Disorder: A comparison with pharmacotherapy. *Psychological Bulletin*, 131(5), 785–95.

Mittenberg, W., Seidenberg, M., O'Leary, D.S. and DiGiulio, D. (1989) Changes in cerebral functioning associated with normal ageing. *Journal of Clinical and Experimental Neuropsychology*, 11(6), 918–32.

Miyake, A. (2001) Individual differences in working memory: Introduction to the special section. *Journal of Experimental Psychology: General*, 130(2), 163–8.

Miyake, K., Chen, S. and Campos, J.J. (1985) Infant temperament, mother's mode of interaction and attachment in Japan: An interim report. In I. Bretherton and E. Waters (eds) *Growing points of attachment theory and research. Monographs of the Society for Research in Child Development*, 50.

Miyamoto, Y., Nisbett, R.E. and Masuda, T. (2006) Culture and physical environment: Holistic versus analytic perceptual affordances. *Psychological Science*, 17, 113–19.

Mobbs, D., Hagan, C.C., Azim, E., Menon, V. and Reiss, A.L. (2005) Personality predicts activity in reward and emotional regions associated with humor.

Proceedings of the National Academy of Sciences of the United States of America, 102(45), 16502–6.

Mobbs, D., Weiskopf, N., Lau, H.C., Featherstone, E., Dolan, R.J. and Frith, C.D. (2006) The Kuleshov effect: The influence of contextual framing on emotional attributions. *SCAN*, 1, 95–106.

Mobbs, D., Yu, R., Rowe, J.B., Eich, H., FeldmanHall, O. and Dalgliesh, T. (2010) Neural activity associated with monitoring the oscillating threat value of a tarantula. *Proceedings of the National Academy of Sciences*, 107, 20582–6.

Moe, A. (2009) Are males always better than females in mental rotation? Exploring a gender belief explanation. *Learning and Individual Differences*, 19, 21–7.

Moffat, S.D. and Hampson, E. (1996) A curvilinear relationship between testosterone and spatial cognition in humans: Possible influence of hand preference. *Psychoneuroendocrinology*, 21, 323–37.

Moffitt, T.E. (2010) How common are common mental disorders? *Psychological Medicine*, 40, 899–909.

Mohanty, A.K. and Perregaux, C. (1997) Language acquisition and bilingualism. In J.W. Berry, P.R. Dasen and T.S. Sarawathi (eds) *Handbook of Cross-cultural Psychology. Vol. 2: Basic Processes and Human Development.* Boston, MA: Allyn & Bacon.

Mohr, C.D., Armeli, S., Tennen, H., Carney, M.A., Affleck, G. and Hromi, A. (2001) Daily interpersonal experiences, context and alcohol consumption: Crying in your beer and toasting good times. *Journal of Personality and Social Psychology*, 80, 489–500.

Mojet, J., Heidema, J. and Christ-Hazelhof, E. (2004) Effect of concentration on taste-taste interactions in foods for the elderly and young subjects. *Chemical Senses*, 29, 671–81.

Molenberghs, P., Cunnington, R. and Mattingley, J.B. (2009) Is the mirror neuron system involved in imitation? A short review and meta-analysis. *Neuroscience and Biobehavioral Reviews*, 33, 975–80.

Molenberghs, P., Sale, M.V. and Mattingley, J.B. (2011) Is there a critical lesion site for unilateral spatial neglect? A meta-analysis using activation likelihood estimation. *Frontiers in Human Neuroscience*, 6, 78.

Monk, T.H. and Kupfer, D.J. (2000) Circadian rhythms in healthy aging-effects downstream from the pacemaker. *Chronobiology International*, 17, 355–68.

Monroe, S., Thase, M. and Simons, A. (1992) Social factors and psychobiology of depression: Relations between life stress and rapid eye movement sleep latency. *Journal of Abnormal Psychology*, 101, 528–37.

Montagu, A. (1980) *Sociobiology Examined.* New York: Oxford University Press.

Monteiro, S., Marques Pinto, A. and Roberto, M. S. (2016) Job demands, coping, and impacts of occupational stress among journalists: a systematic review. *European Journal of Work and Organizational Psychology*, 25(5), 751–72.

Monteith, M.J., Ashburn-Nardo, L., Voils, C.I. and Czopp, A.M. (2002) Putting the brakes on prejudice: On the development and operation of cues for control. *Journal of Personality and Social Psychology*, 83, 1029–50.

Montemayor, R. (1974) Children's performance in a game and their attraction to it as a function of sex-typed labels. *Child Development*, 45, 152–6.

Montepare, J.M. (1991) Characterisitics and psychological correlates of young adult men's and women's subjective age. *Sex Roles*, 24(5/6), 323–33.

Montepare, J.M. and Lachman, M.E. (1989) 'You're only as old as you feel': Self-perceptions of age, fear of aging and life satisfaction from adolescence to old age. *Psychology and Aging*, 4(1), 73–8.

Montgomery, S. (2004) Of towers, walls and fields: perspectives on language in science. *Science*, 303(5662), 1333–5.

Montin, S. (1995) The public image of psychologists in Finland. In A. Schorr and S. Saari (eds) *Psychology in Europe*. Göttingen: Hogrefe & Huber.

Montoya, R.M. (2008) I'm hot, so I'd say you're not: The influence of objective physical attractiveness on mate selection. *Personality and Social Psychology Bulletin*, 34, 1315–31.

Moon, C., Panneton-Cooper, R. and Fifer, W.P. (1993) Two-day-olds prefer their native language. *Infant Behaviour and Development*, 16, 495–500.

Moore, D.R. and Shannon, R.V. (2009) Beyond cochlear implants: awakening the deafened brain. *Nature Neuroscience*, 12, 686–91.

Moore, R. (2007) What are students taught about evolution? *McGill Journal of Education*, 42(2), 177–87.

Moors, A. (2013) On the causal role of appraisal in emotion. *Emotion Review*, 5, 132–40.

Moors, A. (2014) Flavors of appraisal theories of emotion. *Emotion Review*, 6(4), 303–7.

Morabia, A. and Wynder, E.L. (1990) Dietary habits of smokers, people who never smoked, and ex-smokers. *American Journal of Clinical Nutrition*, 52, 933–7.

Moran, D.T., Monti-Block, L., Stenaas, L.J. and Berliner, D.L. (1995) Structure and function of human vomeronasal organ. In R.L. Doty (ed.) *Handbook of Olfaction and Gustation*. New York: Dekker.

Moran, J.M. (2013) Lifespan development: The effects of typical aging on theory of mind. *Behavioural Brain Research*, 237, 32–40.

Moran, T.H. (2006) Gut peptide signalling in the controls of food intake. *Obesity*, 14, 250S–253S.

Moray, N. (1959) Attention in dichotic listening: Affective cues and the influence of instructions. *The Quarterly Journal of Experimental Psychology*, 11, 56–60.

Mordecai, K.L., Rubin, L.H. and Maki, P.M. (2008) Effects of menstrual cycle phase and oral contraceptive use on verbal memory. *Hormones and Behavior*, 54(2), 286–93.

Moreland, R.L., Argote, L. and Krishnan, R. (1996) Socially shared cognition at work: Transactive memory and group performance. In J.L. Nye and A.M. Bower (eds) *What's Social about Social Cognition: Research on socially shared cognition in small groups*. Thousand Oaks, CA: Sage, pp. 57–84.

Morelli, S.A., Sacchet, M.D. and Zaki, J. (2015) Common and distinct neural correlates and vicarious reward: A quantitative meta-analysis. *Neuroimage*, 112, 244–53.

Moreno, F.A. and Delgado, P.L. (1997) Hallucinogen-induced relief of obsessions and compulsions. *American Journal of Psychiatry*, 154, 1057–8.

Moreno, F.A., Wiegand, C.B., Taitano, E.K. and Delgado, P.L. (2006) Safety, tolerability, and efficacy of psilocybin in nine patients with obsessive-compulsive disorder. *Journal of Clinical Psychiatry*, 67, 1735–40.

Morey, R.A., Gold, A.L., LaBar, K.S., Beall, S.K., Brown, V.M., Haswell, C.C., . . . and McCarthy, G. (2012) Amygdala volume changes in post-traumatic stress disorder in a large case-controlled veterans group. *Archives of General Psychiatry*, 69(11), 1169–78.

Mori, D., Chaiken, S. and Pliner, P. (1987) 'Eating lightly' and the self-presentation of femininity. *Journal of Personality and Social Psychology*, 53(4), 693.

Mori, K. and Arai, M. (2010) No need to fake it: Reproduction of the Asch experiment without confederates. *International Journal of Psychology*, 45, 390–7.

Morling, B. and Lamoreaux, M. (2008) Measuring culture outside the head: A meta-analysis of individualism-collectivism in cultural products. *Personality and Social Psychology Review*, 12(3), 199–221.

Morris, J.S., Friston, K.J., Buchel, C., Frith, C.D., Young, A.W., Calder, A.J. and Dolan, R.J. (1998) A neuromodulatory role for the human amygdala in processing emotional facial expressions. *Brain*, 121, 47–57.

Morris, J.S., Frith C.D., Perrett, D.L., Rowland, D., Young, A.W., Calder, A.J. and Dolan, R.J. (1996) A differential neural response in the human amygdala to fearful and happy facial expressions. *Nature*, 383, 812–15.

Morris, M.W. and Peng, K.P. (1994) Culture and cause: American and Chinese attributions for social and physical events. *Journal of Personality and Social Psychology*, 67, 949–71.

Morris, P.H., White, J., Morrison, E.R. and Fisher, K. (2013) High heels as supernormal stimuli: How wearing high heels affects judgements of female attractiveness. *Evolution and Human Behaviour*, 34, 176–81.

Morris, R.G.M., Garrud, P., Rawlins, J.N.P. and O'Keefe, J. (1982) Place navigation impaired in rats with hippocampal lesions. *Nature*, 182(297), 681–3.

Morrison, D.F. (1967) *Multivariate Statistical Methods*. New York: McGraw-Hill.

Morrison, S. and Smith, G. (2005) Mongrammatic determinism? *Psychosomatic Medicine*, 67, 820–4.

Morrison, S.E. and Salzman, C.D. (2010) Re-valuing the amygdala. *Current Opinion in Neurobiology*, 20, 221–30.

Morton, D.L., Watson, A., El-Deredy, W. and Jones, A.K. (2009) Reproducibility of placebo analgesia: Effect of dispositional optimism. *Pain*, 146(1), 194–8.

Morton, J. (1979) Word recognition. In *Psycholinguistics 2: Structures and Processes*. Cambridge, MA: MIT Press.

Morton, J. and Johnson, M.H. (1991) CONSPEC and CONLERN: a two-process theory of infant face recognition. *Psychological Review*, 98, 164–81.

Morton, J. and Patterson, K.E. (1980) A new attempt at an interpretation, or, an attempt at a new interpretation. In M. Coltheart, K.E. Patterson and J.C. Marshall (eds) *Deep Dyslexia*. London: Routledge & Kegan Paul.

Moscovici, S. (1976) *Social Influence and Social Change*. London: Academic Press.

Moscovici, S. (1983) The phenomenon of social representations. In R.M. Farr and S. Moscovici (eds) *Social Representations*. Cambridge: Cambridge University Press, pp. 3–69.

Moscovici, S. and Faucheux, C. (1972) Social influence, conforming bias, and the study of active minorities. In L. Berkowitz (ed.) *Advances in Experimental Social Psychology*, Vol. 6. New York: Academic Press, pp. 149–202.

Moscovici, S. and Personnaz, B. (1980) Studies in social influence V: Minority influence and conversion behavior in a perceptual task. *Journal of Experimental Social Psychology*, 16, 270–82.

Moscovici, S. and Zavalloni, M. (1969) The group as a polarizer of attitudes. *Journal of Personality and Social Psychology*, 12, 125–35.

Moskowitz, G.B. (2005) *Social cognition: Understanding self and others*. New York: Guilford Press.

Moss, A.R. and Bacchetti, P. (1989) Natural history of HIV infection. *AIDS*, 3, 55–61.

Moss, C.S. (1965) *Hypnosis in Perspective*. New York: Macmillan.

Mossner, R., Henneberg, A., Schmitt, A., Syagailo, Y.V., Grassle, M. and Hennig, T. (2001) Allelic variation of serotonin transporter expression is associated with depression in Parkinson's disease. *Molecular Psychiatry*, 6(3), 350–2.

Moss-Racusin, C.A., Dovidio, J.F., Brescoll, V.L., Graham, M.J. and Handelsman, J. (2012) Science faculty's subtle gender biases favor male students. *PNAS*, 109, 16474–9.

Motyl, M., Iyer, R., Oishi, S., Trawalter, S. and Nosek, B.A. (2014) How ideological migration geographically segregates groups. *Journal of Experimental Social Psychology*, 51, 1–14.

Motzkin, J.C., Newman, J.P., Kiehl, K.A. and Koenigs, M. (2011) Reduced prefrontal connectivity in psychopathy. *The Journal of Neuroscience*, 31, 17348–57.

Mozer, M.C., Halligan, P.W. and Marshall, J.C. (1997) The end of the line for a brain-damaged model of unilateral neglect. *Journal of Cognitive Neuroscience*, 9(2), 171–90.

Muehlhan, M., Lueken, U., Siegert, J., Wittchen, H-U., Smolka, M.N. and Kirschbaum, C. (2013) Enhanced sympathetic arousal in response to fMRI scanning correlates with task induced activations and deactivations. *PLoS ONE*, 8, e72576.

Mueller, P.A. and Oppenheimer, D.M. (2014) The pen is mightier than the keyboard: advantages of longhand over laptop note taking. *Psychological Science*, 25(6), 1159–68.

Mugny, G. (1982) *The Power of Minorities*. London: Academic Press.

Muhlberger, A. (1997) *Exposition in virtuellen Weltzen zur Therapie von Flugangst*. Diplomarbeit: Universität Wurzburg.

Mullally, S.L., Hassabis, D. and Maguire, E.A. (2012) Scene construction in amnesia: An fMRI study. *Journal of Neuroscience*, 32(16), 5646–53.

Mullaly, S.L., Intraub, H. and Maguire, E.A. (2012) Attenuated boundary extension produces a paradoxical memory advantage in amnesic patients. *Current Biology*, 22, 261–8.

Mullen, M.K. (1994) Earliest recollections of childhood: A demographic analysis. *Cognition*, 52, 55–79.

Mummendey, A. and Otten, S. (1998) Positive–negative asymmetry in social discrimination. In W. Stroebe and M. Hewstone (eds) *European Review of Social Psychology*, Vol. 9. Chichester: Wiley, pp. 107–43.

Munafo, M.R. and Flint, J. (2011) Dissecting the genetic architecture of human personality. *Trends in Cognitive Sciences*, 15, 395–400.

Munder, T., Brutsch, O., Leonhart, R., Gerger, H. and Barth, J. (2013) Researcher allegiance in psychotherapy outcome research. *Clinical Psychology Review*, 33, 501–11.

Munro, G.D. (2010) The scientific impotence excuse: Discounting belief-threatening scientific abstracts. *Journal of Applied Social Psychology*, 40, 579–600.

Munro, G.D. and Munro, C.A. (2014) 'Soft' versus 'hard' psychological science: Biased evaluations of scientific evidence that threatens or supports a strongly held political identity. *Basic and Applied Social Psychology*, 1–11.

Murdaugh, D.L., Cox, J.E., Cook, E.W. and Weller, R.E. (2012) fMRI reactivity to high-calorie food pictures predicts short-and long-term outcome in a weight-loss program. *Neuroimage*, 59, 2709–21.

Murphy, C. and Withee, J. (1986) Age-related differences in the pleasantness of chemosensory stimuli. *Psychology and Ageing*, 1, 312–18.

Murphy, C., Schubert, C.R., Cruickshanks, K.J., Klein, B.E.K., Klein, R. and Nondahl, D.M. (2002) Prevalence of olfactory impairment in older adults. *JAMA*, 288, 2307–12.

Murphy, K.J., Pacicot, C.I. and Goodale, M.A. (1996) The use of visuomotor cues as a strategy for making perceptual judgements in a patient with visual form agnosia. *Neuropsychology*, 10, 396–401.

Murphy, P., Williams, J. and Dunning, E. (1990) *Football on Trial: Spectator violence and development in the football world*. London: Routledge.

Murphy, P.N., Bruno, R., Ryland, I., Wareing, M., Fisk, J.E., Montgomery, C. and Hilton, J. (2012) The effects of 'ecstasy' (MDMA) on visuospatial memory performance: findings from a systematic review with meta analyses. *Human Psychopharmacology: Clinical and Experimental*, 27(2), 113–38.

Murray, J., Ehlers, A. and Mayou, R.A. (2002) Dissociation and post-traumatic stress disorder: Two prospective studies of road traffic accident survivors. *British Journal of Psychiatry*, 180, 363–8.

Murray, J., Farrington, D.P. and Sekol. I. (2012) Children's antisocial behavior, mental health, drug use, and educational performance after parental incarceration: A systematic review and meta-analysis. *Psychological Bulletin*, 138, 175–210.

Muscarella, C., Brintazzolli, G., Gordts, S., Soetens, E. and van den Bussche, E. (2013) Short- and long-term effects of conscious, minimally conscious and unconscious brand logos. *PLoS ONE*, 8, e57738.

Musch, J. and Ehrenberg, K. (2002) Probability misjudgement, cognitive ability, and belief in the paranormal. *British Journal of Psychology*, 93, 169–77.

Mutschler, I., Wieckhorst, B., Kowalevski, S., Derix, J., Wendtlandt, J., Schultze-Bonhage, A. and Ball, T. (2009) Functional organization of the human anterior insular cortex. *Neuroscience Letters*, 457, 66–70.

Myers, D.G. and Bishop, G.D. (1970) Discussion effects on racial attitudes. *Science*, 169, 778–89.

Myers, M.A. (1979) Rule departures and making law: juries and their verdicts. *Law and Society Review*, 13, 781–97.

N'Diaye, K., Sander, D. and Vuilleumier, P. (2009) Self-relevance processing in the human amygdala: gaze direction, facial expression and emotional intensity. *Emotion*, 9, 798–806.

Naber, M., Stoll, J., Einhauser, W. and Carter, O. (2013) How to become a mentalist: Reading decisions from a competitor's pupil can be achieved without training but requires instruction. *PLoS ONE*, 9, e73302.

Nadkarni, A. and Hofmann, S.G. (2012) Why do people use Facebook? *Personality and Individual Differences*, 52, 243–9.

Nafe, J.P. and Wagoner, K.S. (1941) The nature of pressure adaptation. *Journal of General Psychology*, 25, 323–51.

Nagata, Y. and Takeuchi, N. (1990) Measurement of odor threshold by triangle odor bag method. *Bulletin of the Japanese Environmental Sanitation Centre*, 17, 77–89.

Nagel, T. (1974) What is it like to be a bat? *Philosophical Review*, 4, 435–50.

Nakazawa, K., Sun, L.D., Quirk, M.C., Rondi-Reig, L., Wilson, M.A. and Tonegawa, S. (2003) Hippocampal CA3 NMDA receptors are crucial for memory acquisition of one-time experience. *Neuron*, 38, 305–15.

Nanez, J. (1987) Perception of impending collision in 3 to 6 week old infants. *Infant Behaviour and Development*, 11, 447–63.

Napier, J.L. and Jost, J.T. (2008) Why are conservatives happier than liberals? *Psychological Science*, 19, 565–72.

Naqvi, N.H. and Bechara, A. (2008) The hidden island of addiction: the insula. *Trends in Neurosciences*, 32(1), 56–67.

Nargund, R.P. (2006) Melanocortin-4 receptor (MC4R) agonists for the treatment of obesity. *Journal of Medical Chemistry*, 49, 4035–43.

Narr, K.L., Woods, R.P., Thompson, P.M., Szeszko, P., Robinson, D., Dimtcheva, T., . . . and Bilder, R. M. (2007) Relationships between IQ and regional cortical gray matter thickness in healthy adults. *Cerebral Cortex*, 17(9), 2163–71.

Nasar, J.L. and Troyer, D. (2013) Pedestrian injuries due to the mobile phone use in public places. *Accident Analysis and Prevention*, 57, 91–5.

Naslund, E. and Hellstrom, P.M. (2007) Appetite signalling: from gut peptides and enteric nerves to brain. *Physiology and Behaviour*, 92, 256–62.

Nation, K. and Snowling, M.J. (1998) Individual differences in contextual facilitation: Evidence from dyslexia and poor reading comprehension. *Child Development*, 69, 996–1011.

Nation, K. and Snowling, M.J. (1999) Developmental differences in sensitivity to semantic relations among good and poor comprehenders: Evidence from semantic priming. *Cognition*, 70, B1-13.

Natu, V. and O'Toole, A.J. (2011) The neural processing of familiar and unfamiliar faces: A review and synopsis. *British Journal of Psychology*, 102, 726-47.

Naumann, L.P., Vazire, S. and Rentfrow, P.J. (2009) Personality judgments based on physical appearance. *Personality and Social Psychology Bulletin*, 35, 1661-71.

Naumov, A.I. (1996) Hofstede's measurement of Russia: The influence of national cultures on business management. *Management*, 1, 70-103.

Nave, G., Camerer, C. and McCullough, M. (2015) Does oxytocin increase trust in humans? A critical review of research. *Perspectives on Psychological Science*, 10(6), 772-89.

Nazzi, R., Bertoncini, J. and Mehler, J. (1998) Language discrimination by newborns: Toward an understanding of the role of rhythm. *Journal of Experimental Psychology: Human Perception and Performance*, 24(3), 756-66.

Nebel, M.B., Joel, S.E., Muschelli, J., Barber, A.D., Caffo, B.S., Pekar, J.J. and Mostofsky, S H. (2014) Disruption of functional organization within the primary motor cortex in children with autism. *Human Brain Mapping*, 35(2), 567-80.

Nedel, M.B., Eloyan, A., Barber, A.D. and Mostofsky, S.H. (2014) Precentral gyrus functional connectivity signatures of autism. *Frontiers in Systems Neuroscience*, 8, 1-11.

Nee, E.E. and Jonides, J. (2013) Neural evidence for a 3-state model of visual short-term memory. *Neuroimage*, 74, 1-11.

Neider, M.B., McCarley, J.S., Crowell, J.A., Kaczmarski, H. and Kramer, A.F. (2010) Pedestrians, vehicles and cell phones. *Accident Analysis and Prevention*, 42, 589-94.

Neighbors, B.D., Forehand, R. and Bau, J-J. (1997) Interparental conflict and relations with parents as predictors of young adult functioning. *Development and Psychopathology*, 9, 169-87.

Neisser, U. (1964) Visual search. *Scientific American Mind*, 210, 94-102.

Neisser, U. (1984) Interpreting Harry Bahrick's discovery: What confers immunity against forgetting? *Journal of Experimental Psychology: General*, 113, 32-5.

Neisser, U., Boodoo, G., Bouchard, T.J., Boykin, W.A., Brody, N., Ceci, S., Halpern, D.F., Loehlin, J.C., Perloff, R., Sternberg, R.J. and Urbina, S. (1996a) Intelligence: Knowns and unknowns. *American Psychologist*, 51(2), 77-101.

Neisser, U., Winograd, E., Bergman, E.T., Schreiber, C.A., Palmer, S.E. and Weldon, M.S. (1996b) Remembering the earthquake: Direct experience vs hearing the news. *Memory*, 4, 337-57.

Neisworth, J.T. and Madle, R.A. (1982) Retardation. In A.S. Bellack, M. Hersen and A.E. Kazdin (eds) *International Handbook of Behavior Modification and Therapy*. New York: Plenum Press.

Nelson, C.A. (2007) A neurobiological perspective on early human deprivation. *Child Development Perspectives*, 1(1), 13-18.

Nelson, K. (1986) *Event Knowledge: Structure and function in development*. Hillsdale, NJ: Lawrence Erlbaum Associates.

Nelson, K. (1993) Events, narratives, memory: What develops? In M.E. Lamb and A.L. Brown (eds) *Memory and Affect in Development*. Hillsdale, NJ: Lawrence Erlbaum Associates.

Nelson, K. V. and Smith, A. P. (2016) Occupational stress, coping and mental health in Jamaican police officers. *Occupational Medicine*, kqw055.

Nelson, L.D. and Simmons, J.P. (2007) Moniker maladies: When names sabotage success. *Psychological Science*, 18, 1106-12.

Nelson, P.T. et al. (2010) Modeling the association between 43 different clinical and pathological variables in the severity of cognitive impairment in a large autopsy cohort of elderly persons. *Brain Pathology*, 20, 66-79.

Nemmi, F., Nymberg, C., Helander, E. and Klingberg, T. (2016) Grit is associated with structure of nucleus accumbens and gains in cognitive training. *Journal of Cognitive Neuroscience*.

Nettle, D. (2007) Empathizing and systemizing: What are they and what do they contribute to our understanding of psychological sex differences? *British Journal of Psychology*, 98, 237-55.

Neubauer, A. and Fink, A. (2009) Intelligence and neural efficiency. *Intelligence*, 37, 223-9.

Neubauer, A.C. and Fink, A. (2009) Intelligence and neural efficiency. *Neuroscience and Biobehavioral Reviews*, 33(7), 1004-23.

Neugarten, B.L. (1974) The roles we play. In *American Medical Association, Quality of Life: The middle years*. Acton, MA: Publishing Sciences Group.

Nevid, J.S., Art, R.J. and Moulton, J.L. (1996) Factors predicting participant attrition in a community-based, culturally specific smoking cessation program for Hispanic smokers. *Health Psychology*, 15(3), 226-9.

Nevin, J.A. (1988) Behavioral momentum and the partial reinforcement effect. *Psychological Bulletin*, 103, 44-56.

New Jersey Courts (2012a) www.judiciary.state.nj.us/pressrel/2012/jury_instruction.pdf

New Jersey Courts (2012b) www.judiciary.state.nj.us/pressrel/2012/pr120719a.htm

Newark, D.A., Flynn, F.J. and Bohns, V.K. (2014) Once bitten, twice shy: The effect of a past refusal on expectations of future compliance. *Social Psychological and Personality Science*, 5(2), 218-25.

Newbury, D.F. et al. (2009) CMIP and ATP2C2 modulate phonological short-term memory in language impairment. *American Journal of Human Genetics*, 85, 264-72.

Newcomb, A.F. and Bagwell, C.L. (1995) Children's friendship relations: A meta-analytic review. *Psychological Bulletin*, 117, 306-47.

Newcombe, F., Mehta Z. and Deflaan, E.H.F. (1994) Category specificity in visual recognition. In M.J. Farah and G. Ratcliff (eds) *The Neuropsychology of High-level Vision*. Hove: Lawrence Erlbaum Associates.

Newcombe, N. and Huttenlocher, J. (1992) Children's early ability to solve perspective-taking problems. *Developmental Psychology*, 28, 635-43.

Newcombe, N., Huttenlocher, J., Drummey, A.B. and Wiley, J.G. (1998) The development of spatial location coding: Place learning and dead reckoning in the second and third years. *Cognitive Development*, 13, 185-200.

Newell, A. and Simon, H.A. (1972) *Human Problem Solving*. Englewood Cliffs, NJ: Prentice Hall.

Newport, E.L. and Supalla, R. (1987) A critical period effect in the acquisition of a primary language. Unpublished manuscript cited by J.S. Johnson and E.L. Newport. Critical period effects in second language learning: The influence of maturational state on the acquisition of English as a second language. *Cognitive Psychology*, 21, 60-99.

Newport, E.L., Gleitman, H.R. and Gleitman, L. (1977) Mother I'd rather do it myself: Some effects and noneffects of maternal speech style. In C.E. Snow and C.A. Ferguson (eds) *Talking to Children: Language input and acquisition*. Cambridge: Cambridge University Press.

Newson, J. and Newson, E. (1975) Intersubjectivity and the transmission of culture: On the social origins of symbolic functioning. *Bulletin of the British Psychological Society*, 28, 437-46.

Nezu, A.M., Nezu, C.M. and Blissett, S.E. (1988) Sense of humor as a moderator of the relation between stressful life events and psychological distress: A prospective analysis. *Journal of Personality and Social Psychology*, 54, 699-714.

Ngo, M. K., Misra, R. and Spence, C. (2011) Assessing the shapes and speech sounds that people associate with chocolate samples varying in cocoa content. *Food Quality and Preference*, 22(6), 567–72.

NICE (2009) https://www.nice.org.uk/guidance/cg90

Nicholls, M.E.R., Loveless, K.M., Thomas, N.A., Loetscher, T. and Churches, O. (2014) Some participants may be better than others. *The Quarterly Journal of Experimental Psychology*, 68, 10–8.

Nicholson, C.D. (1990) Pharmacology of nootropics and metabolically active compounds in relation to their use in dementia. *Psychopharmacology*, 101, 147–59.

Nicol, R. (1998) Conduct disorder. *Current Opinion in Psychiatry*, 11, 385–8.

Nicolaides, S., Toda, Y. and Smith, P.K. (2002) Knowledge and attitudes about school bullying in trainee teachers. *British Journal of Educational Psychology*, 72, 105–18.

Nicolaus, L.K. and Nellis, D.W. (1987) The first evaluation of the use of conditioned taste aversion to control predation by mongooses upon eggs. *Applied Animal Behaviour Science*, 17, 329–46.

Nicolaus, L.K., Hoffman, T.E. and Gustavson, C.R. (1982) Taste aversion conditioning in free ranging raccoons (*Procyon lotor*) *Northwest Science*, 56, 165–9.

Nicolson, R.I., Fawcett, A.J., Berry, E.L., Jenkins, I.H., Dean, P. and Brooks, D.J. (1999) Association of abnormal cerebellar activation with motor learning difficulties in dyslexic adults. *The Lancet*, 353, 1662–7.

Nielsen, L.L. and Sarason, I.G. (1981) Emotion, personality, and selective attention. *Journal of Personality and Social Psychology*, 41, 945–60.

Nielsen, S.E., Segal, S.K., Worden, I.V., Yim, I.S. and Cahill, L. (2013) Hormonal contraception use alters stress responses and emotional memory. *Biological Psychology*, 92(2), 257–66.

Nielsen, T. and Powell, R.A (2015) Dreams of the rarebit Fiend: food and diet as instigators of bizarre and disturbing dreams. *Frontiers in Psychology*, 6, 47, 1–15.

Nigmatullina, V., Hellyer, P., Nachev, P., Sharp, D. and Seemungal, B.M. (2013) the neuroanatomical correlates of training-related perceptuo-reflex uncoupling in dancers. *Cerebral Cortex*, 25, 554–62.

Niles, A.N., Byrne Haltom, K.E., Lieberman, M.D., Hur, C. and Stanton, A.L. (2016) Writing content predicts benefit from written expressive disclosure: Evidence for repeated exposure and self-affirmation. *Cognition and Emotion*, 30(2), 258–74.

Nili, U., Goldberg, H., Weizman, A. and Dudai, Y. (2010) Fear not thou: activity of frontal and temporal circuits in moments of real-life courage. *Neuron*, 66, 949–62.

Nisbett, R.E. (2009) *Intelligence and How to Get It*. New York: Norton.

Nisbett, R.E. and Ross, L. (1980) *Human Inference: Strategies and shortcomings of social judgment*. Englewood Cliffs, NJ: Prentice Hall.

Nisbett, R.E. and Schachter, S. (1966) Cognitive manipulation of pain. *Journal of Experimental Social Psychology*, 2, 227–36.

Nisbett, R.E. and Wilson, T.D. (1977) Telling more than we can know: Verbal reports on mental processes. *Psychological Review*, 84, 231–59.

Nisbett, R.E., Aronson, J., Blair, C., Dickens, W., Flynn, J., Halpern, D.F. and Turkheimer, E. (2012) Intelligence: New findings and theoretical developments. *American Psychologist*, 67, 130–59.

Nishitani, S., Doi, H., Koyama, A. and Shinohara, K. (2011) Differential prefrontal response to infant facial emotions in mother compared with non-mothers. *Neuroscience Research*, 70, 183–8.

Niven, K. (2014) Can music with prosocial lyrics heal the working world? A field intervention in a call center. *Journal of Applied Social Psychology*, 45, 132–8.

Noble, K.G., Grieve, S.M., Korgaonkar, M.S., Engelhardt, L.E., Griffith, E.Y., Williams, L.M. and Brickman, A.M. (2012) Hippocampal volume varies with educational attainment across the life-span. *Frontiers in Human Neuroscience*, 6, 307, 1–9.

Nobre, A.C., Allison, T. and McCarthy, G. (1994) Word recognition in the human inferior temporal lobe. *Nature*, 372, 260–3.

Nochi, M. (1998) 'Loss of self' in the narratives of people with traumatic brain injury: A qualitative analysis. *Social Science and Medicine*, 46(7), 869–78.

Nofzinger, E.A., Buysse, D.J., Germain, A., Price, J.C., Miewald, J.M. and Kupfer, D.J. (2004) Functional neuroimaging evidence for hyperarousal in insomnia. *American Journal of Psychiatry*, 161(11), 2126–8.

Noordewier, M.K., van Horen, F., Ruys, K.I. and Stapel, D.A. (2010) What's in a name? 361.708 Euros: The effects of marital name change. *Basic and Applied Social Psychology*, 32, 17–25.

Norenzayan, A. and Heine, S.J. (2005) Psychological universals: What are they and how can we know? *Psychological Bulletin*, 131(5), 763–84.

Norman, R.E., Byambaa, M., De, R., Butchart, A., Scott, J. and Vos, T. (2012) The long-term health consequences of child physical abuse, emotional abuse and neglect. *PLoS Medicine*, 9, e1001349.

Norman, W.T. (1963) Toward an adequate taxonomy of personality attributes: Replicated factor structure in peer nomination personality ratings. *Journal of Abnormal and Social Psychology*, 66, 574–83.

North, A.C., Hargreaves, D.J. and McKendrick, J. (1999) The influence of in-store music on wine selections. *Journal of Applied Psychology*, 84(2), 271.

North, M.S. and Fiske, S.T. (2012) Act your (old) age: perspective, ageist biases over succession, consumption and identity. *Personality and Social Psychology Bulletin*, 39, 720–34.

Norton, L.S. and Crowley, C.M. (1995) Can students be helped to learn how to learn? An evaluation of an approaches to learning programme for first year students. *Higher Education*, 29, 307–28.

Nottebohm, F. (1981) A brain for all seasons: cyclical anatomical changes in song control nuclei of canary brain. *Science*, 214, 1368–70.

Nourski, K.V. (2014) Functional organization of human auditory cortex: investigation of response latencies through direct recordings. *Neuroimage*, 101, 598–609.

Nunez, J.M., Casey, B.J., Egner, T., Hare, T. and Hirsch, J. (2005) Intentional false responding shares neural substrates with response conflict and cognitive control. *Neuroimage*, 25, 267–77.

Nutt, D. (2014) Estimating the harms of nicotine-containing products using the MCDA approach. *European Addiction Research*, 20, 218–25.

Nutt, D., King, L.A., Saulsbury, W. and Blakemore, C. (2007) Development of a rational scale to assess the harm of drugs of potential misuse. *The Lancet*, 369(9566), 1047–53.

Nyberg, L., McIntosh, A.R., Cabeza, R., Habib, R., Houle, S. and Tulving, E. (1996) General and specific brain regions involved in encoding and retrieval of events: What, where and when. *Proceedings of the National Academy of Sciences*, 93, 11280–5.

O'Brien, B.A., Wolf, M., Miller, L.T., Lovett, M.W. and Morris, R. (2011) Orthographic processing efficiency in developmental dyslexia: an investigation of age and treatment factors at the sub lexical level. *Annals of Dyslexia*, 61, 111–35.

O'Brien, M. and Nutt, D. (1998) Loss of consciousness and post-traumatic stress disorder. *British Journal of Psychiatry*, 173, 102–4.

O'Connor, N. and Hermelin, B. (1988) Low intelligence and special abilities. *Journal of Child Psychology and Psychiatry*, 29, 391–6.

O'Doherty, J., Rolls, E.T., Francis, S., Bowtell, R., McGlone, F., Kobal, G., Renner, B. and Ahne, G. (2000) Sensory-specific satiety-related olfactory activation of the human orbitofrontal cortex. *NeuroReport*, 11, 399–403.

O'Kane, G., Kensinger, E.A. and Corkin, S. (2004) Evidence for semantic learning in profound amnesia: an investigation with patient HM. *Hippocampus*, 14, 417–25.

O'Keefe, J. and Nadel, L. (1978) *The Hippocampus as a Cognitive Map*. Oxford: Clarendon.

O'Malley, P.M. and Johnston, L.D. (2002) Epidemiology of alcohol and other drug use among college students. *Journal of Studies on Alcohol*, Supplement No. 14, 23–39.

O'Neil, P.M., Smith, C.F., Foster, G.D. and Anderson, D.A. (2000) The perceived relative worth of reaching goal weight. *International Journal of Obesity*, 24, 1069–76.

O'Riordan, M. and Plaisted, K. (2001) Enhanced discrimination in autism. *The Quarterly Journal of Experimental Psychology*, 54A(4), 961–79.

Oakes, P.J., Haslam, S.A. and Turner, J.C. (1993) *Stereotyping and Social Reality*. Oxford: Blackwell.

Oakhill, J. and Garnham, A. (1988) *Becoming a Skilled Reader*. Oxford: Blackwell.

Oaksford, M., Morris, F., Grainger, B. and Williams, J.M.G. (1996) Mood, reasoning, and central executive processes. *Journal of Experimental Psychology: Learning, Memory and Cognition*, 22(2), 476–92.

Oberauer, K. (2002) Access to information in working memory: exploring the focus of attention. *Journal of Experimental Psychology: Learning, Memory, and Cognition*, 28(3), 411.

Oberhuber, M., Parker-Jones, O., Hope, T.M., Prejawa, S., Seghier, M.L., Green, D.W. *et al.* (2013) Functionally distinct contributions of the anterior and posterior putamen during sublexical and lexical reading. *Frontiers in Human Neuroscience*, 7, 787.

Ochsner, K. and Lieberman, M. (2001) The emergence of social cognitive neuroscience. *American Psychologist*, 56, 717–34.

Oddy, M. and Cogan, J. (2005) Coping with severe memory impairment. *Neuropsychological Rehabilitation*, 14(5), 281–494.

OECD (2005) *OECD Health Data 2005*. Paris: Organisation for Economic Cooperation and Development.

Offer, D. and Sabshin, M. (1984) *Normality and the Life Cycle: A critical integration*. New York: Basic Books.

Ohayon, M.M. (2011) Epidemiological overview of sleep disorders in the general population. *Sleep Medicine Research*, 2, 1–9.

Ohayon, M.M. (2012) Determining the level of sleepiness in the American population and its correlates. *Journal of Psychiatric Research*, 46(4), 422–7.

Ohman, A., Dimberg, U. and Ost, L-G. (1985) Animal and social phobias: Biological constraints on learned fear responses. In S. Reiss and R. Bootzin (eds) *Theoretical Issues in Behaviour Therapy*. New York: Academic Press.

Oishi, S. (2010) The psychology of residential mobility: Implications for the self, social relationships and well-being. *Perspectives on Psychological Science*, 5, 5–21.

Oishi, S. and Diener, E. (2014) Residents of poor nations have a greater sense of meaning in life than residents of wealthy nations. *Psychological Science*, 25(2), 422–30.

Oishi, S. and Gilbert, E.A. (2016) Current and future directions in culture and happiness research. *Current Opinion in Psychology*, 8, 54–8.

Oishi, S., Schimmack, U. and Diener, E. (2012) Progressive taxation and the subjective well-being of nations. *Psychological Science*, 23, 86–92.

Okano, H., Sasaki, E., Yamamori, T., Iriki, A., Shimogori, T., Yamaguchi, Y., Kasai, K. and Miyawaki, A. (2016) Brain/MINDS: A Japanese national brain project for marmoset neuroscience. *Neuron*, 92, 582–90.

Oldehinkel, A.J., Verhulst, F.C. and Ormel, J. (2011) Mental health problems during puberty: Tanner stage-related differences in specific symptoms. The TRIALS study. *Journal of Adolescence*, 34, 73–85.

Olds, J. and Milner, P.M. (1954) Positive reinforcement produced by electrical stimulation of septal area and other regions of the rat brain. *Journal of Comparative and Physiological Psychology*, 47, 419–27.

Oliveira, T., Gouveia, M.J. and Oliveira, R.F. (2009) Testosterone responsiveness to winning and losing experiences in female soccer players. *Psychoneuroendocrinology*, 34, 1056–64.

Oliver, M.B. and Hyde, J.S. (1993) Gender differences in sexuality: A meta-analysis. *Psychological Bulletin*, 114, 29–51.

Olofson, J.K. and Gottfried, J.A. (2015) The muted sense: neurocognitive limitations of olfactory language. *TICS*, 19, 314–21.

Olofsson, J.K. and Gottfried, J.A. (2015) The muted sense: neurocognitive limitations of olfactory language. *Trends in Cognitive Sciences*, 19(6), 314–21.

Olofsson, J.K., Ronnlund, M., Nordin, S., Nyberg, L., Nilsson, L-G. and Larsson, M. (2009) Odor identification deficit as a predictor of five-year global cognitive change: Interactive effects with age and ApoE-e4. *Behaviour Genetics*, 39, 496–503.

Olson, J.M., Vernon, P.A., Harris, J.A. and Jang, K.L. (2001) The heritability of attitudes: a study of twins. *Journal of Personality and Social Psychology*, 80(6), 845–60.

Oltmans, T.F. and Emery, R.E. (1998) *Abnormal Psychology* (2nd edn). Englewood Cliffs, NJ: Prentice Hall.

Oltmans, T.F., Neale, J.M. and Davison, G.C. (1995) *Case Studies in Abnormal Psychology*. New York: Wiley.

Olton, D.S., Becker, J.T and Handelsmann, G.E. (1979) Hippocampus, space and memory. *Behavioural and Brain Science*, 2, 313–65.

Olweus, D. (1993) *Bullying in Schools: What we know and what we can do*. Oxford: Blackwell.

Omi, M. and Winant, H. (1994) *Racial Formation in the United States: From the 1960s to the 1980s*. New York: Routledge & Kegan Paul.

Ong, E.Y.L., Ang, R.P., Ho, J.C.M., Lim, J.C.Y., Goh, D.H., Lee, C.S. and Chua, A.Y.K. (2011) Narcissism, extraversion and adolescents' self-presentation on Facebook. *Personality and Individual Differences*, 50, 180–5.

Ongur, D., Drevets, W.C. and Price, J.L. (1998) Gial reduction in the subgenual prefrontal cortex in mood disorders. *Proceedings of the National Academy of Sciences*, 95, 13290–5.

Onraet, E., Van Hiel, A. and Dhont, K. (2013) The relationship between right-wing ideological attitudes and psychological well-being. *Personality and Social Psychology Bulletin*, 39, 509–22.

Op de Beeck, H.P., Brants, M., Baeck, A. and Wagemans, J. (2010) Distributed subordinate specificity for bodies, faces, and buildings in human ventral visual cortex. *Neuroimage*, 49, 3414–25.

Open Science Collaboration (2015) Estimating the reproducibility of psychological science. *Nature*, 349, aac4716-1-8.

Opendak, M. and Gould, E. (2015) Adult neurogenesis: A substrate for experience-dependent change. *TICS*, 19, 314–21.

Ophir, E., Nass, C. and Wagner, A.D. (2009) Cognitive control in media multitaskers. *Proceedings of the National Academy of Sciences*, 106(37), 15583–7.

Orehek, E. and Human, L.J. (2017) Self-expression on social media: Do tweets present accurate and positive portraits of impulsivity, self-esteem and attachment style? *Personality and Social Psychology Bulletin*, 43, 60–70.

Ormel, J., Bastiaansen, A., Riese, H., Bos, E.H., Servaas, Ellenbogen, M., Rosmalen, J.G.M. and Aleman, A. (2013) The biological and psychological basis of neuroticism: Current status and future directions. *Neuroscience and Biobehavioural Reviews*, 37, 59–72.

Orne, M.T. (1959) The nature of hypnosis: Artifact and essence. *Journal of Abnormal and Social Psychology*, 58, 277–99.

Orne, M.T. and Evans, F.J. (1965) Social control in the psychological experiment: Antisocial behavior and hypnosis. *Journal of Personality and Social Psychology*, 1, 189–200.

Orquin, J.L., Jeppesen, H.B., Scholderer, J. and Haugtvedt, C. (2014) Attention to advertising and memory for brands under alcohol intoxication. *Frontiers in Psychology*, 5, 1–8.

Orr, E.S., Sisic, M., Ross C., Simmering, M.G., Arseneault, J.M. and Orr, R.R. (2009) The influence of shyness on the use of Facebook in an undergraduate sample. *Cyberpsychology and Behavior*, 12, 337–40.

Ortigue, S., Bianchi-Demicheli, F., Hamilton, A.F. de C. and Grafton, S.T. (2007) The neural basis of love as a subliminal prime: an event-related functional Magnetic Resonance Imaging study. *Journal of Cognitive Neuroscience*, 19(7), 1218–30.

Ortony, A. and Turner, T.J. (1990) What's basic about basic emotions? *Psychological Review*, 97, 315–31.

Orvis, B.R., Kelley, H.H. and Butler, D. (1976) Attributional conflict in young couples. In J.H. Harvey, W.J. Ickes and R.F. Kidd (eds) *New Directions in Attribution Research*, Vol. 1. Hillsdale, NJ: Lawrence Erlbaum Associates.

Orviska, M., Caplanova, A. and Hudson, J. (2014) The impact of democracy on well-being. *Society and Indic Research*, 115, 493–508.

Ost, J. and Costall, A. (2002) Misremembering Bartlett: A study in serial reproduction. *British Journal of Psychology*, 93, 243–55.

Ost, L-G., Westling, B.E. and Hellstrom, K. (1993) Applied relaxation, exposure in-vivo and cognitive methods in the treatment of panic disorder with agoraphobia. *Behaviour Research and Therapy*, 31, 383–94.

Oswald, F.L., Mitchell, G., Blanton, H., Jaccard, J. and Tetlock, P.E. (2015) Using the IAT to predict ethnic and racial discrimination: small effect sizes of unknown societal significance. *Journal of Personality and Social Psychology*, 108, 562–71.

Oswald, F.L., Mitchell, G., Blanton, H., Jaccard, J. and Tetlock, P.E. (2013) Predicting ethnic and racial discrimination: A meta-analysis of IAT criterion studies. *Journal of Personality and Social Psychology*, 105, 171–92.

Ottaviani, R. and Beck, A.T. (1987) Cognitive aspects of panic disorder. *Journal of Anxiety Disorders*, 1, 15–28.

Otto, A.L., Penrod, S.D. and Dexter, H.R. (1994) The biasing impact of pretrial publicity on juror judgements. *Law and Human Behaviour*, 18, 453–69.

Ouellette, J.A. and Wood, W. (1998) Habit and intention in everyday life: The multiple processes by which past behaviour predicts future behaviour. *Psychological Bulletin*, 124(1), 54–74.

Oveis, C., Spectre, A., Smith, P.K., Liu, M.Y. and Keltner, D. (2016) Laughter conveys status. *Journal of Experimental Social Psychology*, 65, 109–15.

Øverland, S. (2016) Unemployment and mental health. *Occupational and environmental medicine*, oemed-2016.

Overmeier, J.B. and Seligman, M.E.P. (1967) Effects of inescapable shock upon subsequent escape and avoidance responding. *Journal of Comparative and Physiological Psychology*, 63, 28–33.

Owen, A.M., Hampshire, A., Grahn, J.A., Stenton, R., Dajani, S., Burns, A.S., . . . and Ballard, C.G. (2010) Putting brain training to the test. *Nature*, 465(7299), 775–8.

Oyserman, D., Coon, H.M. and Kemmelmeier, M. (2002) Rethinking individualism and collectivism: Evaluation of theoretical assumptions and meta-analyses. *Psychological Bulletin*, 128, 3–72.

Ozer, D.J. (1985) Correlation and the coefficient of determination. *Psychological Bulletin*, 97, 307–15.

Ozer, D.J. and Benet-Martinez, V. (2006) Personality and the prediction of consequential outcomes. *Annual Review of Psychology*, 578, 1–21.

Paap, K.R. (2014) The role of componential analysis, categorical hypothesizing, replicability and confirmation bias in testing for bilingual advantages in executive functioning. *Journal of Cognitive Psychology*, 70, 218–33.

Pabba, M. (2013) Evolutionary development of the amygdaloid complex. *Frontiers in Neuroanatomy*, 7, 1–4.

Paffenbarger, R.S., Hyde, J.T., Wing, A.L. and Hsieh, C.C. (1986) Physical activity, all-cause mortality, and longevity of college alumni. *New England Journal of Medicine*, 314, 605–12.

Page, S. and Coxon, M. (2016) Virtual reality exposure therapy for anxiety disorders: small samples and no controls? *Frontiers in Psychology*, 7.

Paikoff, R. L. and Brooks-Gunn, J. (1991) Do parent–child relationships change during puberty? *Psychological Bulletin*, 110, 47–66.

Palazzolo, D.L. (2013) Electronic cigarettes and vaping: a new challenge in clinical medicine and public health. *Frontiers in Public Health*, 1, 56.

Palermo, R. *et al.* (2016) Do people have insight into their face recognition abilities? *The Quarterly Journal of Experimental Psychology*.

Palermo, R., Rossion, B., Rhodes, G., Laguesse, R., Tez, T., Hall, B., . . . & Al-Janabi, S. (2017). Do people have insight into their face recognition abilities?. *The Quarterly Journal of Experimental Psychology*, 70(2), 218–33.

Pallesen, S., Siversten, B., Nardhus, I. and Bjorvatn, B. (2014) A 10-year trend of insomnia prevalence in the adult Norwegian population. *Sleep Medicine*, 15, 173–9.

Palmer, S.E. (1975a) In D.A. Norman, D.E. Rumelhart and the LNR Research Group (eds) *Explorations in Cognition*. San Francisco ICA: W.H. Freeman.

Palmer, S.E. (1975b) The effects of contextual scenes on the identification of objects. *Memory and Cognition*, 3, 519–26.

Pan, H., Epstein, J., Silbersweig, D.A. and Stern, E. (2011) New and emerging imaging techniques for mapping brain circuitry. *Brain Research Reviews*, 67, 226–51.

Pantev, C., Oostenveld, R., Engelein, A. Ross, B., Roberts, L.E. and Hoke, M. (1998) Increased auditory cortical representation in musicians. *Nature*, 392, 811–14.

Papa, A. and Bonanno, G.A. (2008) Smiling in the face of adversity: The interpersonal and intrapersonal functions of smiling. *Emotion*, 8, 1–12.

Papadatou-Pastou, M., Martin, M., Munafo, M.R. and Jones, G.V. (2008) Sex differences in left-handedness: A meta-analysis of 144 studies. *Psychological Bulletin*, 134(5), 677–99.

Papassotiropoulos, A. and de Quervain, D.J-F. (2011) Genetics of human episodic memory: dealing with complexity. *Trends in Cognitive Sciences*, 15, 381–7.

Papassotiropoulos, A. *et al.* (2006) Genetics, transcriptomics, and protemocis of Alzheimer's disease. *Journal of Clinical Psychiatry*, 67, 652–70.

Parente, R. and Stapleton, M. (1997) History and systems of cognitive rehabilitation. *Neurorehabilitation*, 8, 3–11.

Paris, J. (1991) Personality disorders, parasuicide, and culture. *Transcultural Psychiatric Research*, 28, 25–39.

Park, B. and Rothbart, M. (1982) Perception of out-group homogeneity and levels of social categorization: Memory for the subordinate attributes of in-group and out-group members. *Journal of Personality and Social Psychology*, 42, 1051–68.

Park, D.C. and Kidder, D.P. (1996) Prospective memory and medication adherence. In M. Brandimonte, G.O. Einstein and M.A. McDaniel (eds) *Prospective Memory: Theory and applications*. Mahwah, NJ: Lawrence Erlbaum Associates.

Park, D.C., Polk, T.A., Park, R., Minear, M., Savage, A. and Smith, M.R. (2004) Aging reduces neural specialization in ventral visual cortex. *Proceedings of the National Academy of Science*, 101, 13091–5.

Park, L.E., Young, A.F. and Eastwick, P.W. (2015) (Psychological) distance makes the heart grow fonder: Effects of psychological distance and relative intelligence on men's attraction to women. *Personality and Social Psychology Bulletin*, 41, 1459–73.

Park, N., Kee K.F. and Valenzuela, S. (2009) Being immersed in social networking environment: Facebook groups, uses and gratifications, and social outcomes. *Cyberpsychology and Behaviour*, 12, 729–33.

Parker, D., Manstead, A.S.R. and Stradling, S.G. (1995) Extending the theory of planned behaviour: the role of personal norm. *British Journal of Social Psychology*, 34, 127–37.

Parker, J.G., Rubin, K.H., Price, J. and De Rosier, M.E. (1995) Peer relationships, child development, and adjustment: A developmental psychopathology perspective. In D. Cicchetti and D. Cohen (eds) *Developmental Psychopathology, Vol. 2: Risk, disorder and adaptation*. New York: Wiley.

Parkin, A.J. (1996) *Memory and Amnesia: An Introduction*. Oxford: Blackwell.

Parkin, A.J. and Stewart, F. (1993) Category-specific impairments? No. A critique of Sartori *et al*. *The Quarterly Journal of Experimental Psychology*, 46A, 505–9.

Parkin, A.J. and Walter, B.M. (1992) Recollective experience, normal aging, and frontal dysfunction. *Psychology and Aging*, 2, 290–8.

Parks, A.M. (1991) Drivers business decision-making ability whilst using carphones. In E. Lovessey (ed.) *Contemporary ergonomics: Proceedings of the Ergonomic Society Annual Conference*. London: Taylor & Francis.

Parmar, D., Stavropoulou, C. and Ioannidis, J. P. (2016) Health outcomes during the 2008 financial crisis in Europe: systematic literature review. *BMJ*, 354, i4588.

Parris, B.A., Kuhn, G., Mizon, G.A., Benattayallah, A. and Hodgson, T.L. (2009) Imaging the impossible: An fMRI study of impossible causal relationships in magic tricks. *Neuroimage*, 45, 1033–9.

Parrott, A.C. (2013) Human psychobiology of MDMA or 'Ecstacy': an overview of 25 years of empirical research. *Human Psychopharmacology*, 28, 289–307.

Pascual, L., Rodrigues, P. and Gallardo-Pujol, D. (2013) How does morality work in the brain? A functional and structural perspective of moral behavior. *Frontiers in Integrative Neuroscience*, 7.

Pashler, H. and Harris, C.R. (2012) Is the replicability crisis overblown? Three arguments examined. *Perspectives on Psychological Science*, 7, 531–6.

Pashler, H. and Wagenmakers, E. J. (2012) Editors' introduction to the special section on replicability in psychological science a crisis of confidence? *Perspectives on Psychological Science*, 7, 528–30.

Pashler, H., Coburn, N. and Harris, C.R. (2012) Priming of social distance? Failure to replicate effects on social and food judgments. *PLoS ONE*, 7, e42510, 1–6.

Passingham, R.E. (1995) *The Frontal Lobes and Voluntary Action*. Oxford: Oxford University Press.

Passler, K., Beinicke, A. and Hell, B. (2015) Interests and intelligence: A meta-analysis. *Intelligence*, 50, 30–51.

Patihis, L., Ho, L.Y., Tingen, I.W., Lilienfeld, S.O. and Loftus, E.F. (2014) Are the 'memory wars' over? A scientist-practitioner gap in beliefs about repressed memory. *Psychological Science*, 25, 519–30.

Patin, A. and Pause, B. (2015) Human amygdala activations during nasal chemoreception. *Neuropsychologia*, 78, 171–94.

Paton, J.J., Belova, M.A., Morrison, S.E. and Salzman, C.D. (2006) The primate amygdala represents the positive and negative value of visual stimuli during learning. *Nature*, 439, 865–70.

Patterson, F.G. and Linden, E. (1981) *The Education of Koko*. New York: Holt, Rinehart & Winston.

Patterson, K.E. (1994) Reading, writing and rehabilitation: A reckoning. In M.J. Riddoch and G. Humphreys (eds) *Cognitive Neuropsychology and Cognitive Rehabilitation*. Hove: Psychology Press.

Pattij, T. and Vanderschuren, L.J.M.J. (2008) The neuropharmacology of impulsive behaviour. *Trends in Pharmacological Sciences*, 29(4), 192–9.

Pau, S., Jahn, G., Sakreida, K., Domin, M. and Lotze, M. (2013) Encoding and recall of finger sequences in experienced pianists compared with musically naïve controls: A combined behavioral and functional imaging study. *Neuroimage*, 64, 379–387.

Paul, C.L. and Sanson-Fisher, R.W. (1996) Experts' agreement on the relative effectiveness of 29 smoking reduction strategies. *Preventive Medicine*, 25, 517–26.

Paulesu, E., Demonet, J-F., Fazio, F., McCory, E., Chanoine, V., Brunswick, N., Cappa, S.F., Cossu, G., Habib, M., Frith, C.D. and Frith, U. (2001) Dyslexia: Cultural diversity and biological unity. *Science*, 291, 2165–7.

Paulesu, E., Frith, U., Snowling, M., Gallagher, A., Morton, J., Frackowiak, R.S.J. and Frith, C.D. (1996) Is developmental dyslexia a disconnection syndrome? Evidence from PET scanning. *Brain*, 119(1), 143–57.

Paulesu, E., McCrory, E., Fazio, F., Menoncello, L., Brunswick, N., Cappa, S.F., Cotelli, M., Cossu, G., Corte, F., Lorusso, M., Pesenti, S., Gallagher, A., Perani, D., Price, C., Frith, C.D. and Frith, U. (2000) A cultural effect on brain function. *Nature Neuroscience*, 3(1), 91–6.

Pavlidou, E.V. and Williams, J.M. (2014) Implicit learning and reading: Insights from typical children and children with developmental dyslexia using the artificial grammar learning (AGL) paradigm. *Research in Developmental Disabilities*, 35(7), 1457–72.

Payne, J. and Israel, N. (2010) Beyond teaching practice: Exploring individual determinants of student performance on a research skills module. *Learning and Individual Differences*, 20, 260–4.

Paz, R. and Pare, D. (2013) Physiological basis for emotional modulation of memory circuits by the amygdala. *Current Opinion in Neurobiology*, 23, 381–6.

Pearlin, L.I. and Mullan, J.T. (1992) Loss and stress in ageing. In M.L. Wykle, E. Kahara and J. Kowal (eds) *Stress and Health Among the Elderly*. New York: Springer-Verlag.

Pease, D.M., Gleason, J.B. and Pan, B. (1993) Learning the meaning of words: Semantic development and beyond. In J.B. Gleason (ed.) *The Development of Language*. New York: Macmillan.

Peck, J.W. and Novin, D. (1971) Evidence that osmoreceptors mediating drinking in rabbits are in the lateral preoptic area. *Journal of Comparative and Physiological Psychology*, 74, 134–47.

Pedersen, W.C., Miller, L.C., Putcha-Bhagauatula, A. and Yang, Y. (2002) Evolved sex differences in the number of proposed partners desired? The long and the short of it. *Psychological Science*, 13, 157–61.

Peek-Asa, C., Runyan, C.W. and Zwerling, C. (2001) The role of surveillance and evaluation research in the reduction of violence against workers. *American Journal of Preventive Medicine*, 20, 141–8.

Peel, E., Parry, O., Douglas, M. and Lawton, J. (2005) Taking the biscuit: A discursive approach to managing diet in Type 2 diabetes. *Journal of Health Psychology*, 10, 779–91.

Peer, E., Brandimarte, L., Samat, S. and Acquisti, A. (2017) Beyond the Turk: Alternative platforms for crowdsourcing behavioural research. *Journal of Experimental Social Psychology*, 70, 153–63.

Peers, P.V., Simons, J.S. and Lawrence, A.D. (2013) Prefrontal control of attention to threat. *Frontiers in Human Neuroscience*, 7, 24, 1–12.

Peigneux, P. *et al.* (2004) Are spatial memories strengthened in the human hippocampus during slow wave sleep? *Neuron*, 44, 535–45.

Peled-Avron, L., Perry, A. and Shamay-Tsoory, S. (2016) The effect of oxytocin on the anthropomorphism of touch. *Psychoneuroendocrinology*, 66, 159–65.

Pell, M.D. and Baum, S.R. (1997) The ability to perceive and comprehend intonation in linguistic and affective contexts by brain-damaged adults. *Brain and Language*, 57, 80–99.

Pellegrini, A.D. and Long, J.D. (2002) A longitudinal study of bullying, dominance, and victimization during the transition from primary school through secondary school. *British Journal of Developmental Psychology*, 20, 259–80.

Pelleymounter, M.A., Cullen, M.J., Baker, M.B., Hecht, R. *et al.* (1995) Effects of the obese gene product on body weight regulation in ob/ob mice. *Science*, 269, 540–3.

Pena, D., Contreras, M.J., Shih, P.C. and Santacreu, J. (2008) Solution strategies as possible explanations of individual and sex differences in a dynamic spatial task. *Acta Psychologia*, 128, 1–14.

Penn, D.L., Kommana, S., Mansfield, M. and Link, B.G. (1999) Dispelling the stigma of schizophrenia II. The impact of information on dangerousness. *Schizophrenia Bulletin*, 25, 437–46.

Pennebaker, J.W. (1997) Writing about emotional experiences as a therapeutic process. *Psychological Science*, 8(3), 162–6.

Pennebaker, J.W. and Francis, M.E. (1996) Cognitive, emotional and language processes in disclosure. *Cognition and Emotion*, 10, 621–6.

Pennebaker, J.W. and Stone, L.D. (2003) Words of wisdom: language use over the life span. *Journal of Personality and Social Psychology*, 85(2), 291–301.

Pennebaker, J.W., Chung, C.K., Frazee, J., Lavergne, G.M. and Beaver, D.I. (2014) When small words foretell academic success: The case of college admissions essays. *PLoS ONE*, 9(12), e115844.

Pennebaker, J.W., Groom, C.J., Loew, D. and Dabbs, J.M. (2004) Testosterone as a social inhibitor: Two case studies of the effect of the testosterone treatment on language. *Journal of Abnormal Psychology*, 113(1), 172–5.

Pennebaker, J.W., Kiecolt-Glaser, J. and Glaser, R. (1988) Disclosure of traumas and immune function: Health implications for psychotherapy. *Journal of Consulting and Clinical Psychology*, 56(2), 239–45.

Pennebaker, J.W., Mayne, T.J. and Francis, M.E. (1997) Linguistic predictors of adaptive bereavement. *Journal of Personality and Social Psychology*, 72, 863–71.

Pennington, B.F., Santerre-Lemmon, L., Risenberg, J., MacDonald, B., Boada, R., Friend, A., Leopold, D.R., Samuelsson, S., Byrne, B., Willcutt, E.G. and Olson, R.K. (2012) Individual prediction of dyslexia by single versus multiple deficit models. *Journal of Abnormal Psychology*, 121, 212–24.

Pennington, N. and Hastie, R. (1986) Evidence evaluation in complex decision making. *Journal of Personality and Social Psychology*, 51, 242–58.

Pennington, N. and Hastie, R. (1992) Explaining the evidence: tests of the story model for juror decision making. *Journal of Personality and Social Psychology*, 62, 189–206.

Penninx, B.W.J.H., van Tilburg, T., Boeke, A.J.P., Deeg, D.J.H., Kriegsman, D.M.W. and van Eijk, T.M. (1998) Effects of social support and coping resources on depressive symptoms: Different for various chronic diseases? *Health Psychology*, 17, 551–8.

Pennisi, E. (2006) Mining the molecules that made our mind. *Science*, 313, 1908–11.

Penrod, S.D. and Heuer, L. (1997) Tweaking common-sense: Assessing aids to jury decision making. *Psychology, Public Policy and Law*, 3(2/3), 259–84.

Penrose, R. (1989) *The Emperor's New Mind*. Oxford: Oxford University Press.

Penrose, R. (1994) *Shadows of the Mind*. Oxford: Oxford University Press.

Penton-Voak, I.S. and Perrett, D.I. (2000) Female preference for male faces change cyclically: Further evidence. *Evolution and Human Behaviour*, 21, 39–48.

Penton-Voak, I.S., Perrett, D.I., Castles, D.L., Kobayashi, T., Burt, D.M., Murray, L.K. and Minamisawa, R. (1999) Menstrual cycle alters face preference. *Nature*, 399(6738), 741–2.

Perani, D., Dehaene, S., Grassi, F., Cohen, L., Cappa, S.F., Dupoux, E. *et al.* (1996) Brain processing of native and foreign languages. *NeuroReport*, 7, 2439–44.

Perani, D., Garibotto, V., Gorini, A., Moresco, R.M., Henin, M., Panzacchi, A. *et al.* (2008) In vivo PET study of 5HT (2A) serotonin and D2 dopamine dysfunction in drug-naïve obsessive-compulsive disorder. *Neuroimage*, 42, 306–14.

Perani, D., Paulesu, E., Galles, N.S., Dupoux, E., Dehaene, S., Bettinardi, V., Cappa, S.F., Fazio, F. and Mehler, J. (1998) The bilingual brain: Proficiency and age of acquisition of the second language. *Brain*, 121, 1841–52.

Percino, G., Klimek, P. and Thurner, S. (2014) Instrumentational complexity of music genes and why simplicity sells. *PLoS ONE*, 1–16.

Pereira, F. (1995) Psychology in Portugal. In A. Schorr and S. Saari (eds) *Psychology in Europe*. Göttingen: Hogrefe & Huber.

Perkins, A.M., Arnone, D., Smallwood, J. and Mobbs, D. (2015) Thinking too much: self-generated thought as the engine of neuroticism. *Trends in Cognitive Sciences*, 19, 492–98.

Pernet, C.R., Poline, J.B., Demonet, J.F. and Rousselet, G.A. (2009) Brain classification revelas the right cerebellum as the best biomarker of dyslexia. *BMC Neuroscience*, 10, 67.

Perregaux, C. (1994) *Les enfants a deux vois – Des effets du bilingualisme sur l'apprentissage de la lecture*. Berne: Lang.

Perrett, D.I., May, K.A. and Yoshikawa, S. (1994) Facial shape and judgements of female attractiveness. *Nature*, 368, 239–42.

Perri, M.G., Martin, A.D., Leermakers, E.A., Sears, S.F. and Notelovitz, M. (1997) Effects of group – versus home-based exercise training in healthy older men and women. *Journal of Consulting and Clinical Psychology*, 65, 278–5.

Perri, M.G., Nezu, A.M., Patti, E.T. and McCann, K.L. (1989) Effect of length of treatment on weight loss. *Journal of Consulting and Clinical Psychology*, 57, 450–52.

Perry, D., White, A. and Perry, L. (1984) Does early sex-typing result from children's attempts to match their behaviour to sex role stereotypes? *Child Development*, 55, 2114–21.

Perry, D.W., Zatorre, R.J., Petrides, M., Alivisatos, B., Meyer, E. and Evans, A.C. (1999) Localization of cerebral activity during simple singing. *NeuroReport*, 10, 3453–8.

Persson, H. (1995) Psychology in Sweden. In A. Schorr and S. Saari (eds) *Psychology in Europe*. Göttingen: Hogrefe & Huber.

Pert, C.B., Snowman, A.M. and Snyder, S.H. (1974) Localization of opiate receptor binding in presynaptic membranes of rat brain. *Brain Research*, 70, 184–8.

Pervin, L.A. (1975) *Personality: Theory, Assessment, and Research*. New York: Wiley.

Pescosolido, B.A., Martin, J.K., Long, J.S., Medina, T.R., Phelan, J.C. and Link, B.G. (2010) A disease like any other? A decade of change in public reactions to schizophrenia., depression and alcohol dependence. *American Journal of Psychiatry*, 167, 1321–30.

Peskin, J. (1982) Measuring household production for the GNP. *Family Economics Review*, 3, 16–25.

Peters, R.K., Cady, L.D., Bischoff, D.P., Bernstein, L. and Pile, M.C. (1983) Physical fitness and subsequent myocardial infarction in healthy workers. *Journal of the American Medical Association*, 249, 3052–6.

Petersen, J.L. and Shibley-Hyde, J. (2010) A meta-analytic review of research on gender differences in sexuality, 1993–2007. *Psychological Bulletin*, 136, 21–38.

Petersen, S.E., Fox, P.T., Posner, M.I., Mintin, M. and Raichle, M.E. (1988) Positron emission tomographic studies of the cortical anatomy of single-word processing. *Nature*, 331, 585–9.

Peterson, A.C. and Ebata, A.T. (1987) Developmental transitions and adolescent problem behavior: Implications for prevention and intervention. In K. Herrelmann (ed.) *Social Prevention and Intervention*. New York: De Gruyter.

Peterson, C.K. and Harmon-Jones, E. (2009) Circadian and seasonal variability of resting frontal EEG asymmetry. *Biological Psychology*, 80, 315–20.

Peterson, C.K. and Harmon-Jones, E. (2012) Anger and testosterone: Evidence that situationally-induced anger relates to situationally-induced testosterone. *Emotion*, 12, 899–902.

Peterson, C.K., Gravens, L.C. and Harmon-Jones, E. (2011) Asymmetric frontal cortical activity and negative affective responses to ostracism. *Social Cognitive and Affective Neuroscience*, 6, 277–85.

Peterson, C.K., Shackman, A.J. and Harmon-Jones, E. (2008) The role of asymmetrical frontal activity in aggression. *Psychophysiology*, 45, 86–92.

Peterson, L.R. and Peterson, M.J. (1959) Short-term retention of individual verbal items. *Journal of Experimental Psychology*, 58, 193–8.

Peterson, R.L., Pennington, B.F. and Olson, R.K. (2013) Subtypes of developmental dyslexia: Testing the predictions of the dual-route and connectionist frameworks. *Cognition*, 126, 20–38.

Peters-Scheffer, N., Didden, R., Korzilius, H. and Sturmey, P. (2011) A meta-analytic study on the effectiveness of comprehensive ABA-based early intervention programs for children with Autism Spectrum Disorders. *Research in Autism Spectrum Disorders*, 5, 60–9.

Petrill, S.A., Plomin, R., Berg, S., Johansson, B., Pedersen, N.L., Ahern, F. and McClearn, G.E. (1998) The genetic and environmental relationship between general and specific cognitive abilities in twins age 80 and older. *Psychological Science*, 9(3), 183–9.

Petrovic, P., Kalso, E., Petersson, K.M. and Ingvar, M. (2002) Placebo and opioid analgesia--imaging a shared neuronal network. *Science*, 295(5560), 1737–40.

Petruzzello, S.J. and Tate, A.K. (1997) Brain activation, affect, and aerobic exercise: An examination of both state independent and state dependent relationships. *Psychophysiology*, 34(5), 527–33.

Petruzzello, S.J., Jones, A.C. and Tate, A.K. (1997) Affective responses to acute exercise: A test of opponent-process theory. *Journal of Sports Medicine and Physical Fitness*, 37(3), 205–12.

Pettigrew, T.F. (1958) Personality and sociocultural factors in intergroup attitudes: A cross-national comparison. *Journal of Conflict Resolution*, 2, 29–42.

Pettigrew, T.F. (1979) The ultimate attribution error: Extending Allport's cognitive analysis of prejudice. *Personality and Social Psychology Bulletin*, 5, 461–76.

Pettigrew, T.F. (1998) Intergroup contact theory. *Annual Review of Psychology*, 49, 65–85.

Pettigrew, T.F. and Meertens, R.W. (1995) Subtle and blatant prejudice in western Europe. *European Journal of Social Psychology*, 25, 57–75.

Pettigrew, T.F. and Tropp, L. (2006) A meta-analytic test of intergroup contact theory. *Journal of Personality and Social Psychology*, 90, 751–83.

Petty, R.E. and Cacioppo, J.T. (1981) *Attitudes and Persuasion: Classic and contemporary approaches*. Dubuque, IA: Brown.

Petty, R.E. and Cacioppo, J.T. (1986) The elaboration likelihood model of persuasion. *Advances in Experimental Social Psychology*, 19, 123–205.

Petty, R.E. and Cacioppo, J.T. (1996) *Attitudes and Persuasion: Classic and contemporary approaches*. Boulder, CO: Westview Press.

Peuhkuri, K., Sihvola, N and Korpela, R. (2012) Diet promotes sleep duration and quality. *Nutrition Research*, 32, 309–19.

Peuhkuri, K., Sihvola, N. and Korpela, R. (2012) Diet promotes sleep duration and quality. *Nutrition Research*, 32(5), 309–19.

Pfefferbaum, A., Rohlfing, T., Rosenbloom, M.J., Chu, W., Colrain, I.M. and Sullivan, E.V. (2013) Variation in longitudinal trajectories of regional brain volumes of healthy men and women measured with atlas-based percolation of MRI. *Neuroimage*, 65, 176–93.

Pfundmair, M., Aydin, N. and Frey, D. (2016) Whatever? The effect of social exclusion on adopting persuasive messages. *The Journal of Social Psychology*, 157, 181–93.

Phan, K.L., Angstadt, M., Golden, J., Onyewuenyi, I., Popovska, A. and de wit, H. (2008) Cannabinoid modulation of amygdala reactivity to social signals of threat in humans. *Journal of Neuroscience*, 28, 2313–19.

Phares, E.J. (1979) *Clinical Psychology: Concepts, methods, and profession*. Homewood, IL: Dorsey Press.

Phares, E.J. (1984) *Introduction to Personality*. Columbus, OH: Merrill.

Phelps, E.A., O'Connor, K.J., Cunningham, W.A., Funayama, E.S., Gatenby, J.C., Gore, J.C. and Banaji, M.R. (2000) Performance on indirect measures of race evaluation predicts amygdala activation. *Journal of Cognitive Neuroscience*, 12, 729–38.

Philipp-Muller, A. and MacDonald, G. (2016) Avoidant individuals may have muted responses to social warmth after all: An attempted replication of Macdonald and Borsook (2010). *Journal of Experimental Social Psychology*, 70, 272–80.

Phillips, D.P. (1986) Natural experiments on the effects of mass media violence on fatal aggression: Strengths and weaknesses of a new approach. In L. Berkowitz (ed.) *Advances in Experimental Social Psychology*, Vol. 19. New York: Academic Press, pp. 207–50.

Phillips, J., Ong, D.C., Surtees, A.D.R., Xin, Y., Williams, S., Saxe, R. and Frank, M.C. (2015) A second look at automatic theory of mind: Reconsidering Kovacs, Teglas and Endress (2010). *Psychological Science*, 1–15. 26, 1353–67.

Piaget, J. (1945/1951) *Play, Dreams and Imitation in Childhood*. New York: Norton.

Piaget, J. (1952) *The Origins of Intelligence in Children* (M. Cook, trans.) New York: International Universities Press.

Piaget, J. (1972) Intellectual evolution from adolescence to adulthood. *Human Development*, 15, 1–12.

Piatti, M., Savage, D.A. and Torgler, B. (2012) The red mist? Red shirts, success and team sports. *Sport in Society*, 15(9), 1209–27.

Picariello, M.L., Greenberg, D.N. and Pillemer, D.B. (1990) Children's sex-related stereotyping of colors. *Child Development*, 61, 1453–60.

Picemi, E., Petrosini, L., Piras, F., Laricchiuta, D., Cutuli, D., Chiapponi, C., Fagioli, S., Girardi, P., Caltagirone, C. and Spalletta, G. (2013) New evidence for the cerebellar involvement in personality traits. *Frontiers in Behavioural Neuroscience*, 7, 133.

Picerni, E., Petrosini, L., Piras, F., Laricchiuta, D., Cutuli, D., Chiapponi, C., . . . and Spalletta, G. (2013) New evidence for the cerebellar involvement in personality traits. *Frontiers in Behavioral Neuroscience*, 7, 133.

Pietschnig, J. and Voracek, M. (2015) One century of global IQ gains: a formal meta-analysis of the Flynn effect (1909–2013) *Perspectives on Psychological Science*, 10, 282–306.

Piffer, D., Gunawardane, K. C. and Custance, D.M. (2011) Evidence of sexual selection for evening orientation in human males: A cross cultural study in Italy and Sri Lanka. *Interdisciplinary Bio Central*, 3(1), 13.

Pike, A., Reiss, D., Hetherington, E.M. and Plomin, R. (1996) Using MZ differences in the search for nonshared environmental effects. *Journal of Child Psychology and Psychiatry*, 37(6), 695–704.

Pike, G.E., Kemp, R.I., Towell, N.A. and Phillips, K.C. (1997) Recognizing moving faces: The relative contribution of motion and perspective view information. *Visual Cognition*, 4, 409–38.

Pilleri, G. (1979) The blind Indus dolphin, *Platanista indi. Endeavours*. 3, 48–56.

Pine, K.J. and Fletcher, B. (2011) Women's spending behaviour is menstrual-cycle sensitive. *Personality and Individual Differences*, 50, 74–8.

Pinker, S. (1984) *Language Learnability and Language Development*. Cambridge, MA: Harvard University Press.

Pinker, S. (1990) Language acquisition. In D.N. Osherson and H. Lasnik (eds) *An Invitation to Cognitive Science. Vol. 1: Language*. Cambridge, MA: MIT Press.

Pinker, S. (1994) *The Language Instinct*. London: Penguin.

Pinker, S. (1997) *How the Mind Works*. New York: W.W. Norton.

Pinto, A. da C. and Baddeley, A.D. (1991) Where did you last park your car? Analysis of a naturalistic long-term recency effect. *European Journal of Cognitive Psychology*, 3, 297–313.

Pinzer, L. and Smith, G. (2009) First names and longevity. *Perceptual and Motor Skills*, 108, 149–60.

Pinzur, L. and Smith, G. (2009) First names and longevity. *Perceptual and Motor Skills*, 108(1), 149–60.

Plaisier, M.A. and Smeets, J.B.J. (2012) Mass is all that matters in the size-weight illusion. *PLoS ONE*, 7, e42518.

Plaisted, K., O'Riordan, M. and Baron-Cohen, S. (1998) Enhanced discrimination of novel, highly similar stimuli by adults with autism during a perceptual learning task. *Journal of Child Psychology and Psychiatry*, 39(5), 765–75.

Plant, A. and Devine, P.G. (2001) Response to other-imposed pro-Black pressure: Acceptance or backlash? *Journal of Experimental Social Psychology*, 37, 486–501.

Planton, S., Jucla, M., Roux, F-E. and Demonet, J-F. (2013) The 'handwriting brain': a meta-analysis of neuroimaging studies of motor versus orthographic processes. *Cortex*, 49, 2772–87.

Planton, S., Longcamp, M., Peran, P., Demonet, J-F. and Jucla, M. (2016) How specialised are writing-specific brain regions? An fMRI study of writing, drawing and oral spelling. *Cortex*, 88, 66–80.

Plaut, D.C. and McClelland, J.L. (1993) Generalization with componential attractors: Word and nonword reading in an attractor network. In *Proceedings of the 15th Annual Conference of the Cognitive Science Society*. Hillsdale, NJ: Lawrence Erlbaum Associates.

Plaut, D.C., McClelland, J.L., Seidenberg, M.S. and Patterson, K.E. (1996) Understanding normal and impaired word reading: Computational principles in quasi-regular domain. *Psychological Review*, 103, 56–115.

Plaut, V.C., Markus, H.R. and Lachman, M.E. (2002) Place matters: Consensual features and regional variation in American well-being and self. *Journal of Personality and Social Psychology*, 83, 160–84.

Pletzer, B., Kronbichler, M., Aichhorn, M., Bergmann, J., Ladurner, G. and Kerschbaum, H.H. (2010) Menstrual cycle and hormonal contraceptive use modulate human brain structure. *Brain Research*, 1348, 55–62.

Pletzer, B., Kronbichler, M., Ladurner, G., Nuerk, H.C. and Kerschbaum, H. (2011) Menstrual cycle variations in the BOLD-response to a number bisection task: implications for research on sex differences. *Brain Research*, 1420, 37–47.

Plexter, B. and Kerschbaum, H.K. (2014) 50 years of hormonal contraception – time to find out, what it does to our brain. *Frontiers in Neuroscience*, 8, 256.

Pliatsikas, C. and Luk, G. (2016) Executive control in bilinguals: A concise review on fMRI studies. *Bilingualism: Language and Cognition*, 19, 69–705.

Pliner, P. and Chaiken, S. (1990) Eating, social motives, and self-presentation in women and men. *Journal of Experimental Social Psychology*, 26(3), 240–54.

Plitt, M., Barnes, K.A. and Martin, A. (2015a) Functional connectivity classification of autism identifies highly predictive brain features but falls short of biomarker standards. *Neuroimage: Clinical*, 7, 359–66.

Plitt, M., Barnes, K.A., Wallace, G.L., Kenworthy, L. and Martin, A. (2015b) Resting-state functional connectivity predicts longitudinal change in autistic traits and adaptive functioning in autism. *PNAS*, 12, e6699–6706.

Plomin, R. (1988) The nature and nurture of cognitive abilities. In R. Sternberg (ed.) *Advances in the Psychology of Human Intelligence*. Hillsdale, NJ: Lawrence Erlbaum Associates.

Plomin, R. (1997) Identifying genes for cognitive abilities and disabilities. In R.J. Sternberg and E. Grigorenko (eds) *Intelligence, Heredity and Environments*. New York: Cambridge University Press.

Plomin, R. (2008) *Behavioural Genetics*. London: Palgrave.

Plomin, R. and Bergeman, C.S. (1991) The nature of nurture: Genetic influence on 'environmental' measures. *Behavioral and Brain Sciences*, 14, 373–427.

Plomin, R. and Deary, I.J. (2015) Genetics and intelligence differences: five special findings. *Molecular Psychiatry*, 20, 98–108.

Plomin, R. and DeFries, J.C. (1998) The genetics of cognitive abilities and disabilities. *Scientific American Mind*, 278(5), 40–47.

Plomin, R., DeFries, J.C., McClearn, G.E. and Rutter, M. (1997) *Behavioural Genetics* (3rd edn). New York: W.H. Freeman.

Plomin, R., Haworth, C.M.A., Meaburn, E.L., Price, T.S., Wellcome Trust Case Control Consortium and Davis, O.S. (2013) Common DNA markers can account for more than half of the genetic influences on cognitive abilities. *Psychological Science*, 24, 562–8.

Plomin, R., McClearn, G.E., Smith, D.L., Skuder, P., Vignetti, S., Chorney, M.J., Chorney, K., Kasarda, S., Thompson, L.A., Detterman, D.K., Petrill, S.A., Daniels, J., Owen, M.J. and McGuffin, P. (1995) Allelic associations between 100 DNA markers and high versus low IQ. *Intelligence*, 21, 31–48.

Plomin, R., McClearn, G.E., Smith, D.L., Vignetti, S., Chorney, M.J., Chorney, K., Venditti, C.P., Kasarda, S., Thompson, L.A., Detterman, D.K., Daniels, J., Owen, M.J. and McGuffin, P. (1994) DNA markers associated with high versus low IQ: the IQ QTL project. *Behavioural Genetics*, 24, 107–18.

Plomin, R., Shakeshaft, N.G., McMillan, A. and Tzraskowski, M. (2013) Nature, nurture, and expertise. *Intelligence*, 45, 115–17.

Ploog, D. (2002) Is the neural basis of vocalisation different in non-human primates and *Homo sapiens*? In T.J. Crow (ed.), *The Speciation of Modern Homo sapiens*. Oxford: Oxford University Press.

Plotner, M., Over, H., Carpenter, M. and Tomasello, M. (2015) Young children show the bystander effect in helping situations. *Psychological Science*, 26, 499–506.

Plutchik, R. (1980) *Emotion: A Psychoevolutionary Synthesis*. New York: Harper & Row.

Plutchik, R. (1984) Emotions: A general psychoevolutionary theory. In K.R. Scherer and P. Ekman (eds) *Approaches to Emotion*. Hillsdale, NJ: Lawrence Erlbaum Associates.

Poggio, G.F. and Poggio, T. (1984) The analysis of stereopsis. *Annual Review of Neuroscience*, 7, 379–412.

Polczynska, M.M., Benjamin, C.F.A., Japardi, K., Frew, A. and Bookheimer, S.Y. (2016) Language system organization in a quadrilingual with a brain tumor: Implications for understanding of the language network. *Neuropsychologia*, 86, 167–75.

Poldrack, R.A. (2014) Is 'efficiency' a useful concept in cognitive neuroscience? *Developmental Cognitive Neuroscience*, 11, 12–17.

Poldrack, R.A. (2015) Is "efficiency" a useful concept in cognitive neuroscience? *Developmental Cognitive Neuroscience*, 11, 12–17.

Poldrack, R.A., Fletcher, P.C., Henson, R.N., Worsley, K.J., Brett, M. and Nichols, T.E. (2008) Guidelines for reporting an fMRI study. *Neuroimage*, 40, 409–14.

Polk, T.A. and Farah, M.J. (2002) Functional MRI evidence for an abstract, not perceptual, word-form area. *Journal of Experimental Psychology: General*, 131(1), 65–72.

Pollack, I. and Pickett, J.M. (1964) Intelligibility of excerpts from fluent speech: Auditory vs structural context. *Journal of Verbal Learning and Verbal Behavior*, 3, 79–84.

Polman, H., Orobio de Castro, B. and van Aken, M.A.G. (2008) Experimental study of the differential effects of playing versus watching violent video games on children's aggressive behavior. *Aggressive Behavior*, 34, 256–64.

Pond, C.M. and Mattacks, C.A. (1987) The anatomy of adipose tissue in captive macaca monkeys and its implications for human biology. *Folia Primatologica*, 48, 164–85.

Ponkanen, L.M., Alhoniemi, A., Leppanen, J.M. and Hietanen, J.K. (2010) Does it make a difference if I have an eye contact with you or with your picture? *Cognitive and Affective Neuroscience*, 6, 486–94.

Poo, M., Du, J-I., Ip, N.Y., Xiong, Z-Q., Xu, B. and Tan, T. (2016) China Brain Project: Basic neuroscience, brain diseases, and brain-inspired computing. *Neuron*, 92, 591–96.

Popa, L.S., Hewitt, A.L. and Ebner, T.J. (2014) The cerebellum for jocks and nerds alike. *Frontiers in Systems Neuroscience*, 8, 113, 1–13.

Popper, K.R. and Eccles, J. (1977) *The Self and Its Brain: An argument for interactionism*. New York: Springer-Verlag.

Porkka-Heiskanen, T and Kalinchuk, A.V. (2011) Adenosine, energy metabolism and sleep homeostasis. *Sleep Medicine Reviews*, 15, 123–35.

Poropat, A.E. (2009) A meta-analysis of the five-factor model of personality and academic performance. *Psychological Bulletin*, 135(2), 322–38.

Porter, J., Craven, B., Khan, R.M., Chang, S-J., Kang, I., Judkewicz, B., Volpe, J., Settles, G. and Sobel, N. (2007) Mechanisms of scent-tracking in humans. *Nature Neuroscience*, 10(1), 27–9.

Porter, M., Penney, G.C., Russell, D., Russell, E. and Templeton, A. (1996) A population-based survey of women's experience of the menopause. *British Journal of Obstetrics and Gynaecology*, 103, 1025–8.

Porter, S., Doucette, N.L., Woodworth, M., Earle, J. and MacNeil, B. (2008) Halfe the world knows not how the other halfe lies: Investigation of verbal and non-verbal signs of deception exhibited by criminal offenders and non-offenders. *Legal and Criminological Psychology*, 13, 27–38.

Porubska, K., Veit, R., Preissl, H., Fritsche, A. and Birbaumer, N. (2006) *Neuroimage*, 32, 1273–80.

Posavac, H., Posavac, S. and Posavac, E. (1998) Exposure to media images of female attractiveness and concern with body weight images among young women. *Sex Roles*, 38, 187–201.

Posner, M. and Petersen, S.E. (1990) The attention system of the human brain. *Annual Review of Neuroscience*, 13, 25–42.

Posner, M.I., Snyder, C.R.R. and Davidson, B.J. (1980) Attention and the detection of signals. *Journal of Experimental Psychology: General*, 109, 160–74.

Post, F. (1994) Creativity and psychopathology: A study of 291 world-famous men. *British Journal of Psychiatry*, 165, 22–34.

Post, F. (1996) Verbal creativity, depression and alcoholism. *British Journal of Psychiatry*, 168, 545–55.

Postle, B.R., Berger, J.S. and D'Esposito, M. (1999) Functional neuroanatomical double dissociation of mnemonic and executive control processes contributing to working memory performance. *Proceedings of the National Academy of Sciences*, 96, 12959–64.

Postman, L. and Phillips, L. (1965) Short-term temporal changes in free recall. *The Quarterly Journal of Experimental Psychology*, 2, 509–22.

Pothuizen H. J., Jongen-Rêlo, A.L., Feldon, L. and Yee, B.K. (2005) Double dissociation of the effects of selective nucleus accumbens core and shell lesions on impulsive-choice behaviour and salience learning in rats. *European Journal of Neuroscience*, 22, 2605–16.

Potter, J. and Wetherell, M. (1987) *Discourse and Social Psychology*. London: Sage.

Potter, J. and Wetherell, M. (1995) Discourse analysis. In J.A. Smith, R. Harré and L. van Langenhove (eds) *Rethinking Research Methods in Psychology*. London: Sage.

Potts, G.R. (1972) Information processing strategies used in the encoding of linear orderings. *Journal of Verbal Learning and Verbal Behavior*, 11, 727–40.

Pound, N., Penton-Voak, I.S. and Brown, W.M. (2007) Facial symmetry is positively associated with self-reported extraversion. *Personality and Individual Differences*, 43, 1572–82.

Powell, K.E., Thompson, P.D., Caspersen, C.J. and Kendrick, J.S. (1987) Physical activity and the incidence of coronary heart disease. *Annual Review of Public Health*, 8, 253–87.

Power, M. and Dalgleish, T. (1997) *Cognition and Emotion*. Hove: Psychology Press.

Powers, K.L., Brooks, P.J., Aldrich, N.J., Palladino, M.A. and Alfieri, L. (2013) Effects of video-game play on information processing: a meta-analytic investigation. *Psychonomic Bulletin and Review*, 20(6), 1055–79.

Prandini, C. and McCarthy, S. (2006) Teaching psychology as a science in Italy. *International Journal of Psychology*, 41(1), 42–50.

Pratkanis, A.R., Breckler, S.H. and Greenwald, A.G. (1989) *Attitude Structure and Function*. Hillsdale, NJ: Lawrence Erlbaum Associates.

Pratt, L.A., Brody, D.J. and Gu, Q. (2011) Antidepressant use in persons aged 12 and over: United States, 2005–2008.

Pratto, F., Sidanius, J., Stallworth, L.M. and Malle, B.F. (1994) Social dominance orientation: A personality variable predicting social and political attitudes. *Journal of Personality and Social Psychology*, 67, 741–63.

Preckel, F., Lipnevich, A.A., Schneider, S. and Roberts, R.D. (2011) Chronotype, cognitive abilities, and academic achievement: A meta-analytic investigation. *Learning and Individual Differences*, 21, 483–92.

Preiss, D.D., Castillo, J.C., Grigorenko, E.L. and Manzi, J. (2013) Argumentative writing and academic achievement: A longitudinal study. *Learning and Individual Differences*, 28, 204–11.

Premack, D. (1976) Language and intelligence in ape and man. *American Scientist*, 64, 674–83.

Pressley, M., McDaniel, M.A., Turnure, J.E., Wood, E. and Ahmad, M. (1987) Generation and precision of elaboration: Effects on intentional and incidental learning. *Journal of Experimental Psychology: Learning, Memory, and Cognition*, 13(2), 291.

Pressley, M., McDaniel, M.A., Turnure, J.E., Wood, E. and Ahmad, M. (1987) Generation and precision of elaboration: Effects on intentional and incidental learning. *Journal of Experimental Psychology: Learning, Memory and Cognition*, 13, 291–300.

Pressman, S.D. and Cohen, S. (2012) Positive emotion word use and longevity in famous deceased psychologists. *Health Psychology*, 31, 297–305.

Pressman, S.D., Cohen, S., Miller, G.E., Barkin, A., Rabin, B.S. and Treanor, J.J. (2005) Loneliness, social network size, and immune response to influenza vaccination in college freshmen. *Health Psychology*, 24(3), 297–306.

Preston, C. and Ehrsson, H.H. (2016) Illusory obesity triggers body dissatisfaction responses in the insula and the anterior cingulate cortex. *Cerebral Cortex*, 1–11.

Price, C.J. (2000) Functional imaging studies of aphasia. In J.C. Mazziotta, A.W. Toga and R.S.J. Frakowiak (eds), *Brain Mapping: The disorders.* San Diego ICA: Academic Press.

Price, C.J., Gorno-Tempini, M.L., Graham, K.S., Biggio, N., Mechelli, A., Patterson, K. and Noppeney, U. (2003) Normal and pathological reading: Converging data from lesion and imaging studies. *Neuroimage*, 20, S30–S41.

Price, C.J., Wise, R.J.S., Watson, J.D.G., Patterson, K., Howard, D. and Frackowiak, R.S.J. (1994) Brain activity during reading: The effects of exposure duration and task. *Brain*, 117, 1255–69.

Prince, R. (1985) The concept of the culture-bound syndromes: Anorexia nervosa and brain-fag. *Social Science and Medicine*, 21, 197–203.

Prince, S. and Hensley, W.E. (1992) The Kuleshov effect: Recreating the classic experiment. *Cinema Journal*, 31, 59–75.

Prinz, F., Schlange, T. and Asadullah, K. (2011) Believe it or not: How much can we reply on published data on potential drug targets? *Nature Reviews Drug Delivery*, 10, 712–13.

Proffitt, D.R., Bhalia, M., Gossweiler, R. and Midgett, J. (1995) Perceiving geographical slant. *Psychonomic Bulletin and Review*, 2, 409–28.

Prokosch, M.D., Coss, R.G., Scheib, J.E. and Blozis, S.A. (2009) Intelligence and mate choice: Intelligent men are always appealing. *Evolution and Human Behavior*, 30, 11–20.

Prolo, P. and Licinio, J. (2002) D4DR and novelty seeking. In J. Benjamin, R. Ebstein and R H. Belmaker (eds), *Molecular Genetics and the Human Personality.* Arlington, VA: American Psychiatric Publishing, 91–107.

Protsko, J. and Aronson, J. (2016) Context moderates affirmation effects on the ethic achievement gap. *Social Psychological and Personality Science*, 1–8.

Protzner, A.B., Hargreaves, J.S., Campbell, J.A., Myers-Stewart, K., van Hees, S., Goodyear, B.G., Sargious, P. and Pexman, P.M. (2015) This is your brain on Scrabble: Neural correlates of visual word recognition in competitive Scrabble players as measured during task and resting-state. *Cortex*, 75, 204–19.

Proust-Lima, C., Amieva, H., Letenneur, L., Orgogozo, J.M., Jacqmin-Gadda, H. and Dartigues, J F. (2008) Gender and education impact on brain aging: a general cognitive factor approach. *Psychology and Aging*, 23(3), 608.

Provine, R.R. (2004) Laughing, tickling and the evolution of speech and self. *Current Directions in Psychological Science*, 13(6), 215–18.

Public Health England (2015) https://www.gov.uk/government/publications/health-matters-smoking-and-quitting-in-england/smoking-and-quitting-in-england

Pugh, K.R., Shaywitz, B.A., Shaywitz, S.E., Constable, R.T., Skudlarski, P., Fulbright, R.K., Bronen, R.A., Shankweiler, D.P., Katz, L., Fletcher, J. and Gore, J.C. (1996) Cerebral organisation of component processes in reading. *Brain*, 119, 1221–38.

Pulford, B.D. and Sohal, H. (2006) The influence of personality on HE students' confidence in their academic abilities. *Personality and Individual Differences*, 41, 1409–9.

Putman, P.W. (2003) Ten-year research update review: child sexual abuse. *Journal of the American Academy of Child Adolescence and Psychiatry*, 42, 269–78.

Putnam, A.L. (2015) Mnemonics in education: Current research and applications. *Translational Issues in Psychological Science*, 1, 130–9.

Puts, D.A. (2010) Beauty and the beast: Mechanisms of sexual selection in humans. *Evolution and Human Behavior*, 31, 157–75.

Quian Quiroga, R., Reddy, L., Kreiman, G., Koch, C. and Fried, I. (2005) Invariant visual representation by single neurons in the human brain. *Nature*, 435, 1102–7.

Quinones-Vidal E., Lopez-Garcia, J.J., Penaranda-Ortega, M. and Tortosa-Gil, F. (2004) The nature of social and personality psychology as reflected in JPSP, 1965–2000. *Journal of Personality and Social Psychology*, 86, 435–52.

Rabbitt, P., Maylor, E., McInnes, L., Bent, N. and Moore, B. (1995) What goods can self-assessment questionnaires deliver for cognitive gerontology? *Applied Cognitive Psychology*, 9, S127–S152.

Rabipour, S. and Davidson, P.S. (2015) Do you believe in brain training? A questionnaire about expectations of computerised cognitive training. *Behavioural Brain Research*, 295, 64–70.

Rabipour, S. and Raz, A. (2012) Training the brain: Fact and fad in cognitive and behavioral remediation. *Brain and Cognition*, 79(2), 159–79.

Rabius, V., McAlister, A.L., Geiger, A., Huang, P. and Todd, R. (2004) Telephone counseling increases cessation rates among young adult smokers. *Health Psychology*, 23(5), 539–41.

Raby, K.L., Roisman, G.I., Simpson, J.A., Collins, W.A. and Steele, R.D. (2015) Greater maternal insensitivity in childhood predicts greater electrodermal reactivity during conflict discussions with romantic partners in adulthood. *Psychological Science*, 26, 348–53.

Racine, M., Tousignant-Laflamme, Y., Kloda, L.A., Dion, D., Dupuis, G. and Choinière, M. (2012) A systematic literature review of 10 years of research on sex/gender and experimental pain perception–Part 1: Are there really differences between women and men? *Pain*, 153(3), 602–18.

Radoeva, P.D., Prasad, S., Brainard, D.H. and Aguirre, G.K. (2008) Neural activity within area v1 reflects unconscious visual performance in a case of blindsight. *Journal of Cognitive Neuroscience*, 20(11), 1927–39.

Raeside, J. (2007) The hard sell. *The Guardian Guide*, July, 14–20.

Ragland, D.R. and Brand, R.J. (1988) Type A behavior and mortality from coronary heart disease. *New England Journal of Medicine*, 318, 65–9.

Rahe, R.H. and Arthur, R.J. (1978) Life changes and illness reports. In K.E. Gunderson and R.H. Rahe (eds) *Life Stress and Illness.* Springfield, IL: Thomas.

Raichle, M. E. (2008) A brief history of human brain mapping. *Trends in Neurosciences*, 32, 118–26.

Raine, A. (1997) *The Psychopathology of Crime* (2nd edn) New York: Academic Press.

Raine, A., Lencz, T., Bihrle, S., Lacasse, L. and Collenti, P. (2000) Reduced prefrontal gray matter volume and reduced autonomic activity in antisocial personality disorder. *Archives of General Psychiatry*, 57, 119–27.

Rainville, P., Hofbauer, R.K., Bushnell, M.C., Duncan, G.H. and Price, D.D. (2002) Hypnosis modulates activity in brain structures involved in the regulation of consciousness. *Journal of Cognitive Neuroscience*, 14(6), 887–901.

Rajecki, D.J. (1989) *Attitudes* (2nd edn) Sunderland, MA: Sinauer Associates.

Ramon, M. and Rossion, B. (2010) Impaired processing of relative distances between features and of the eye region in acquired prosopagnosia. *Cortex*, 46, 374–89.

Ramus, P. (2006) Genes, brain and cognition. *Cognition*, 101, 247–69.

Randel, A.E. (2003) The salience of culture in multinational teams and its relation to team citizenship behaviour. *International Journal of Cross-Cultural Management*, 3, 27–44.

Randich, A. and LoLordo, V.M. (1979) Preconditioning exposure to the unconditioned stimulus affects the acquisition of the conditioned emotional response. *Learning and Motivation*, 10, 245–75.

Randler, C., Ebenhoh, N., Fischer, A., Hochel, S., Schroff, C., Stoll, J.C. *et al.* (2012) Chronotype but not sleep length is related to salivary testosterone in young adult men. *Psychoneuroendocrinology*, 37, 1740–4.

Ranehill, E., Dreber, A., Johannesson, M., Leiberg, S., Sul, S. and Weber, R.A. (2015) Assessing the robustness of power posing: No effect on hormones and risk tolerance in a large sample of men and women. *Psychological Science*, 1–4.

Ranganath, R., Jurafsky, D. and McFarland, D.A. (2013) Detecting friendly, flirtatious, awkward, and assertive speech in speed-dates. *Computer Speech and Language*, 27, 89–115.

Rapin, I. (1997) Autism. *New England Journal of Medicine*, 337(2), 97–104.

Rapoport, A. (1976) *Experimental Games and Their Uses in Psychology.* Morristown, NJ: General Learning Press.

Rapoport, J.L. (1989) The biology of obsessions and compulsions. *Scientific American Mind*, March, 62–9.

Rapp, B., Fischer-Baum, S. and Miozzo, M. (2015) Modality and morphology: What we write may not be what we say. *Psychological Science*, 26, 892–902.

Raskind, W.H., Peter, B., Richards, T., Eckert, M.M. and Berninger, V. (2013) The genetics of reading disabilities: from phenotypes to candidate genes. *Frontiers in Psychology*, 3, 601.

Rasmussen, T. and Milner, B. (1977) The role of early left brain injury in determining lateralization of cerebral speech functions. *Annals of the New York Academy of Sciences*, 299, 355–69.

Rattner, A. (1988) Convicted but innocent: Wrongful conviction and the criminal justice system. *Law and Human Behaviour*, 12, 283–93.

Ravaja, N., Turpeinen, M., Saari, T., Puttonen, S and Keltikangas-Jarvinen, L. (2008) The psychology of James Bond: Phasic emotional responses to violent video game events. *Emotion*, 8, 1.

Ravizza, S.M., Uitvlugt, M.G. and Fenn, K.M. (2016) Logged in and zoned out: How laptop internet use relates to classroom learning. *Psychological Science*, 28, 171–80.

Rawlings, D. (1985) Psychoticism, creativity and dichotic shadowing. *Personality and Individual Differences*, 6, 737–42.

Raynauld, R., Larivee, S. and Dionne, J. (1999) Peut-on ameliorer le judgement moral d'eleves de 10–12 ans? *Psychologie and Education*, 36, 55–78.

Rayner, K. (1986) Eye movements and the perceptual span in beginning and skilled readers. *Journal of Experimental Child Psychology*, 41, 211–36.

Rayner, K. and Pollatsek, A. (1989) *The Psychology of Reading.* Englewood Cliffs, NJ: Prentice Hall.

Rayner, K., Schotter, E.R., Masson, M.E., Potter, M.C. and Treiman, R. (2016) So much to read, so little time how do we read and can speed reading help? *Psychological Science in the Public Interest*, 17(1), 4–34.

Rayner, K., Schotter, E.R., Masson, M.E.J., Potter, M.C. and Treiman, R. (2016) So much to read, so little time: How do we read, and can speed reading help? *Psychological Science in the Public Interest*, 17, 4–34.

Read, J. and Harre, N. (2001) The role of biological and genetic beliefs in the stigmatization of 'mental patients'. *Journal of Mental Health*, 10, 223–35.

Reavley, N.J. and Jorm, A.F. (2012) Stigmatising attitudes towards people with mental disorders: Changes in Australia over 8 years. *Psychiatry Research*, 197, 302–6.

Reber, A.S. (1992) The cognitive unconscious: An evolutionary perspective. *Consciousness and Cognition*, 1, 93–133.

Reber, P.J. (2013) The neural basis of implicit learning and memory: A review of neuropsychological and neuroimaging research. *Neuropsychologia*, 51, 2026–42.

Redcay, E., Dodell-Feder, D., Pearrow, M.J., Mavros, P.L., Kleiner, M., Gabrieli, J.D.E. and Saxe, R. (2010) Live face-to-face interaction during fMRI. *Neuroimage*, 50, 1639–47.

Redd, M. and De Castro, J.M. (1992) Social facilitation of eating: Effects of social instruction on food intake. *Physiology & Behavior*, 52(4), 749–54.

Redding, G.M. and Hawley, E. (1993) Length illusion in fractional Muller-Lyer stimuli: an object–perception approach. *Perception*, 22, 819–28.

Redelmeier, D.A. and Tibshirani, R.J. (1997) Association between cellular-telephone calls and motor vehicle collisions. *New England Journal of Medicine*, 336, 453–8.

Redish, A.D. and Touretzky, D.S. (1997) Cognitive maps beyond the hippocampus. *Hippocampus*, 7, 15–35.

Rees, E., O'Donovan, M.C. and Owen, M.J. (2015) Genetics of schizophrenia. *Current Opinion in Behavioural Sciences*, 2, 8–14.

Reese, G., Loew, K. and Steffgen, G. (2013) A towel less: social norma enhance pro-environmental behaviour in hotels. *The Journal of Social Psychology*, 154, 97–100.

Regan, J. (1971) Guilt, perceived injustice and altruistic behaviour. *Journal of Personality and Social Psychology*, 18, 124–32.

Reicher, S.D. (1987) Crowd behaviour as social action. In J.C. Turner, M.A. Hogg, P.J. Oakes, S.D. Reicher and M.S. Wetherell, *Rediscovering the Social Group: A self-categorization theory.* Oxford: Blackwell, pp. 171–202.

Reicher, S.D. (2001) The psychology of crowd dynamics. In M.A. Hogg and R.S. Tindale (eds) *Blackwell Handbook of Social Psychology: Group processes.* Oxford: Blackwell, pp. 182–207.

Reicher, S.D. and Hopkins, N. (1996) Seeking influence through characterising self-categories: An analysis of anti-abortionist rhetoric. *British Journal of Social Psychology*, 35, 297–311.

Reicher, S.D., Haslam, S.A. and Smith, J.R. (2012) Working toward the experimenter: reconceptualising obedience within the Milgram paradigm as identification-based followership. *Perspectives on Psychological Science*, 7, 315–24.

Reicher, S.D., Spears, R. and Postmes, T. (1995) A social identity model of deindividuation phenomena. *European Review of Social Psychology*, 6, 161–98.

Reid, A.K. and Staddon, J.E.R. (1998) A dynamic route finder for the cognitive map. *Psychological Review*, 105(3), 585–601.

Reid, V. M., Dunn, K., Young, R. J., Amu, J., Donovan, T., & Reissland, N. (2017). The human fetus preferentially engages with face-like visual stimuli. *Current Biology*, in press.

Reid, W.H. and Gacono, C. (2000) Treatment of antisocial personality, psychopathy, and other characterologic antisocial syndromes. *Behavioural Sciences and the Law*, 18, 647–62.

Reijnders, J., van Heugten, C. and van Boxtel, M. (2013) Cognitive interventions in healthy older adults and people with mild cognitive impairment: a systematic review. *Ageing Research Reviews*, 12(1), 263–75.

Reilly, J. and Mulhern, G. (1995) Gender differences in self-estimated IQ: The need for care in interpreting group data. *Personality and Individual Differences*, 18, 189–92.

Reinke, B.J., Holmes, D.S. and Harris, R.L. (1985) The timing of psychosocial changes in women's lives: The years 25 to 45. *Journal of Personality and Social Psychology*, 48, 1353–64.

Reinke, R.R., Corrigan, P.W., Leonhard, C., Lundin, R.K. and Kubiak, M.A. (2004) Examining two aspects of contact on the stigma of mental illness. *Journal of Social and Clinical Psychology*, 23, 377–89.

Reisch, T., Steffen, T., Habenstein, A. and Tschacher, W. (2013) Change in suicide rates in Switzerland before and after firearm restriction resulting from the 2003 Army XXI reform. *American Journal of Psychiatry*, 170, 977–84.

Reisenzein, R. (1983) The Schachter theory of emotion: Two decades later. *Psychological Bulletin*, 94, 239–64.

Reiss, S. and McNally, R.J. (1985) Expectancy mode of fear. In S. Reiss and R. Bootzin (eds) *Theoretical Issues in Behaviour Therapy*. San Diego ICA: Academic Press.

Rentfrow, P.J. and Jokela, M. (2016) Geographical psychology: the spatial organisation of psychological phenomenon. *Current Directions of Psychological Science*, 25, 393–8.

Rentfrow, P.J., Gosling, S.D. and Potter, J. (2008) A theory of the emergence, persistence, and the expression of geographic variation in psychological characteristics. *Perspectives on Psychological Science*, 3(5), 339–69.

Rentfrow, P.J., Jokela, M. and Lamb, M.E. (2015) Regional personality differences in Great Britain. *PLoS ONE*, 10, e0122245.

Rentfrow, P.J., Mellander, C. and Florida, R. (2009) Happy states of America: a state-level analysis of psychological, economic and social well-being. *Journal of Research in Personality*, 43, 1073–82.

Rescorla, R.A. (1991) Associative relations in associative learning. The Eighteenth Bartlett Memorial Lecture. *The Quarterly Journal of Experimental Psychology*, 43, 1–23.

Ressel, V., Wilke, M., Lidzba, K., Lutzenberger, W. and Krageloh-Mann, I. (2008) Increases in language lateralization in normal children as observed using MEG. *Brain and Language*, 106, 167–76.

Rest, J.R. (1979) *Development in Judging Moral Issues*. Minneapolis IMN: University of Minnesota Press.

Reuter-Lorenz, P.A. (2013) Aging and cognitive neuroimaging: A fertile union. *Perspectives on Psychological Science*, 8, 68–71.

Rey, J.M., Sawyer, M.G., Raphael, B., Patton, G.C. and Lynskey, M. (2002) Mental health of teenagers who use cannabis. *British Journal of Psychiatry*, 150, 216–21.

Reyner, L.A. and Horne, J.A. (1997) Suppression of sleepiness in drivers: Combination of caffeine with a short nap. *Psychophysiology*, 34, 721–5.

Reyner, L.A. and Horne, J.A. (1998) Evaluation of 'in car' countermeasures to driver sleepiness: Cold air and radio. *Sleep*, 21, 46–50.

Reyner, L.A. and Horne, J.A. (2000) Early morning driver sleepiness: Effectiveness of 200 mg caffeine. *Psychophysiology*, 37, 251–6.

Reynolds, A.J. (1994) Effects of a preschool plus follow-on intervention for children at risk. *Developmental Psychology*, 30, 787–804.

Rezaie, R., Simos, P.G., Fletcher, J.M., Juranek, J., Cirino, P.T., Li, Z., Passaro, A.D. and Papanicolaou, A.C. (2011) The timing and strength of regional brain activation associated with word recognition in children with reading difficulties. *Frontiers in Human Neuroscience*, 5, article 45.

Rheingold, H.L. and Eckerman, C.O. (1973) Fear of the stranger: A critical examination. In H.W. Reese (ed.) *Advances in Child Development and Behavior*, Vol. 8. New York: Academic Press.

Rhodes, G., Byatt, G., Michie, P.T. and Puce, A. (2004) Is the fusiform face area specialised for faces, individuation, or expert individuation? *Journal of Cognitive Neuroscience*, 16(2), 189–203.

Rhodes, G., Yoshikawa, S., Palermo, R., Simmons, L.W., Peters, M., Lee, K., Halberstadt, J. and Crawford, J.R. (2007) Perceived health contributes to the attractiveness of facial symmetry, averageness and sexual dimorphism. *Perception*, 36, 1244–52.

Rhodes, N. and Wood, W. (1992) Self-esteem and intelligence affect influenceability: The mediating role of message reception. *Psychological Bulletin*, 111, 156–71.

Richlan, F., Kronbichler, M. and Wimmer, H. (2009) Functional abnormalities in the dyslexic brain: A quantitative meta-analysis of neuroimaging studies. *Human Brain Mapping*, 30, 3299–308.

Richter, F.R., Cooper, R.A., Bays, P.M. and Simons, J.S. (2016) Distinct neural mechanisms underlie the success, precision, and vividness of episodic memory. *eLife*, 1–18.

Riddle, J.P., Smith, H.E. and Jones, C.J. (2016) Does written emotional disclosure improve the psychological and physical health of caregivers? A systematic review and meta-analysis. *Behaviour Research and Therapy*, 80, 23–32.

Riddoch, G. (1917) Dissociation of visual perceptions due to occipital injuries, with special reference to appreciation of movement. *Brain*, 40, 15–47.

Rieger, G. and Savin-Williams, R.C. (2012) The eyes have it: Sex and sexual orientation differences in pupil dilation patterns. *PLoS ONE*, 7, e40256.

Rieger, G., Cash, B.M., Merrill, S.M., Jones-Rounds, J., Dharmavaram, S. and Savin-Williams, R. (2014) Sexual arousal: the correspondence of eyes and genitals. *Biological Psychology*, 104, 56–64.

Rietveld, C.A. *et al.* (2013) GWAS of 126, 559 individuals identified genetic variants associated with educational attainment. Science express, 340(6139), 1467–71.

Rigby, K. (1997) *Bullying in Schools: And what to do about it*. London: Jessica Kingsley.

Rilea, S.L. (2008) A lateralization of function approach to sex differences in spatial ability: A reexamination. *Brain and Cognition*, 67, 168–82.

Rilling, J., Kaufman, T., Smith, E., Patel, R. and Worthman, C. (2009) Abdominal depth and waist circumference as influential determinants of human female attractiveness. *Evolution and Human Behavior*, 30, 21–31.

Rimfeld, K., Kovas, Y., Dale, P.S. and Plomin, R. (2016) True grit and genetics: Predicting academic achievement from personality. *Journal of Personality and Social Psychology*, 111(5), 780.

Rind, B. (1996) Effect of beliefs about weather conditions on tipping. *Journal of Applied Social Psychology*, 26, 137–47.

Rind, B. (1997) Effect of interest arousal on compliance with a request for help. *Basic and Applied Social Psychology*, 19, 137–47.

Rindermann, H., Flores-Mendoza, C. and Woodley, M.A. (2012) Political orientations, intelligence and education. *Intelligence*, 40, 217–25.

Ringelmann, M. (1913) Recherches sur les moteurs animés: *Travail de l'homme*. Annales de l'Institut National Agronomique, 2(12), 1–40.

Rips, L.J., Shoben, E.J. and Smith, E.E. (1973) Semantic distance and the verification of semantic relations. *Journal of Verbal Learning and Verbal Behavior*, 12, 1–20.

Rispens, J. and van Yperen, T.A. (1997) How specific are 'specific developmental disorders'? The relevance of the concept of specific developmental disorders for the classification of childhood developmental disorders. *Journal of Child Psychology and Psychiatry*, 38(3), 351–63.

Ritchie, K. (1997) Establishing the limits of normal cerebral aging and senile dementia. *British Journal of Psychiatry*, 173, 97–101.

Ritchie, K., Leibovici, D., Ledesert, B. *et al.* (1996) A typology of sub-clinical senescent cognitive disorder. *British Journal of Psychiatry*, 168, 470–6.

Ritchie, S.J. *et al.* (2015) Beyond a bigger brain: Multivariate structural brain imaging and intelligence. *Intelligence*, 51, 47–56.

Ritchie, S.J. *et al.* (2015) Brain volumetric changes and cognitive ageing during the eighth decade of life. *Human Brain Mapping*, 36, 4910–25.

Ritchie, S.J., Bates, T.C. and Deary, I.J. (2015) Is education associated with improvements in general cognitive ability, or in specific skills? *Developmental Psychology*, 51, 573–82.

Ritter, R.C., Brenner, L. and Yox, D.P. (1992) Participation of vagal sensory neurons in putative satiety signals from the upper gastrointestinal tract. In S. Ritter, R.C. Ritter and C.D. Barnes (eds) *Neuroanatomy and Physiology of Abdominal Vagal Afferents*. Boca Raton, FL: CRC Press.

Ritter, S. and Taylor, J. S. (1989) Capsaicin abolishes lipoprivic but not glucoprivic feeding in rats. *American Journal of Physiology*, 256, R1232–R1239.

Rittle, R.H. (1981) Changes in helping behavior: Self- versus situational perceptions as mediators of the foot-in-the-door effect. *Personality and Social Psychology Bulletin*, 7, 431–7.

Rizzolatti, G. and Arbib, M. A. (1998) Language within our grasp. *Trends in neurosciences*, 21(5), 188–94.

Rizzolatti, G., Camarda, R., Fogassi, M., Genhlucci, M., Luppino, G. and Matelli, M. (1988) Functional organization of inferior area 6 in the macaque monkey: II. Area F5 and the control of distal movements. *Experimental Brain Research*, 71, 491–507.

Roballey, T.C., McGreevy, C., Rongo, R R., Schwantes, M.L., Steger, P.J., Wininger, M.A. and Gardner, E.B. (1985) The effect of music on eating behavior. *Bulletin of the Psychonomic Society*, 23(3), 221–2.

Robbins, S.B., Lauver, K., Le, H., Davis, D., Langley, R. and Carlstrom, A. (2004) Do psychosocial and study skill factors predict college outcomes? A meta-analysis. *Psychological Bulletin*, 130(2), 261–88.

Robbins, T.W., Mehta, M.A. and Sahakian, B.J. (2000) Boosting working memory. *Science*, 290, 2275–6.

Roberson, D., Pak, H. and Hanley, J.R. (2008) Categorical perception of colour in the left and right visual field is verbally mediated: Evidence from Korea. *Cognition*, 107, 752–62.

Roberto, C.A., Larsen, P.D., Agnew, H., Baik, J. and Brownell, K.D. (2010) Evaluating the impact of menu labeling on food choices and intake. *American Journal of Public Health*, 100(2), 312–18.

Roberts, B.W. (2009) Back to the future: Personality and Assessment and personality development. *Journal of Research in Personality*, 43, 137–45.

Roberts, B.W. and DelVecchio, W.F. (2000) The rank-order consistency of personality traits from childhood to old age: A quantitative review of longitudinal studies. *Psychological Bulletin*, 126(1), 3–25.

Roberts, B.W., Kuncel, N.R., Shiner, R., Caspi, A. and Goldberg, L.R. (2007) The comparative validity of personality traits, socioeconomic status, and cognitive ability for predicting important life outcomes. *Perspectives on Psychological Science*, 2, 315–45.

Roberts, B.W., Walton, K.E. and Viechtbauer, W. (2006) Patterns of mean-level change in personality traits across the life course: A meta-analysis of longitudinal studies. *Psychological Bulletin*, 132(1), 1–25.

Roberts, R. and Kyllonen, P. (1999) Morningness-eveningness and intelligence. *Personality and Individual Differences*, 27, 1123–33.

Roberts, R.D. and Kyllonen, P.C. (1999) Morningness–eveningness and intelligence: early to bed, early to rise will likely make you anything but wise! *Personality and Individual Differences*, 27(6), 1123–33.

Roberts, S. and Winters, J. (2013) Linguistic diversity and traffic accidents: Lessons from statistical studies of cultural traits. *PLoS ONE, 8*, e70902.

Roberts, T-A. and Arefi-Afshar, Y. (2007) Not all who stand tall are proud: Gender differences in the proprioceptive effects of upright posture. *Cognition and Emotion*, 21(4), 714–27.

Robertson, D.J., Noyes, E., Dowsett, A.J., Jenkins, R. and Burton, A.M. (2016) Face recognition by Metropolitan Police super-recognisers. *PLoS ONE*, 11, e0150036.

Robertson, I.H., Halligan, P.W. and Marshall, J.C. (1993) Prospects for the rehabilitation of unilateral neglect. In I.H. Robertson and J.C. Marshall (eds) *Unilateral Neglect: Clinical and experimental studies*. Hove: Lawrence Erlbaum Associates.

Robins, L.N. and Regier, D.A. (1991) *Psychiatric Disorders in America*. New York: The Free Press.

Robinson, E., Thomas, J., Aveyard, P. and Higgs, S. (2014) What everyone else is eating: a systematic review and meta-analysis of the effect of informational eating norms on eating behavior. *Journal of the Academy of Nutrition and Dietetics*, 114(3), 414–29.

Robinson, E., Titov, N., Andrews, G., McIntyre, K., Schwencke, G. and Solley, K. (2010) Internet treatment for generalized anxiety disorder: A randomised controlled trial comparing clinician vs technical assistance. *PLoS ONE*, 5, e10942.

Robinson, E.B., St Pourcain, B., Anttila, V., Kosmicki, J.A., Bulik-Sullivan, B., Grove, J., . . . and Martin, J. (2016) Genetic risk for autism spectrum disorders and neuropsychiatric variation in the general population. *Nature Genetics*, 48(5), 552–5.

Robinson, G. (1996) Cross-cultural perspectives on menopause. *Journal of Nervous and Mental Diseases*, 184(8), 453–8.

Robinson, M.R., Wray, N.R. and Visscher, P.M. (2014) Explaining additional genetic variation in complex traits. *Trends in Genetics*, 30(4), 124–32.

Roca, M., Parr, A., Thompson, R., Woolgar, A., Torralva, T., Antoun, N., Manes, F. and Duncan, J. (2010) Executive function and fluid intelligence after frontal lobe lesions. *Brain*, 133, 234–47.

Rochat, P., Dias, M.D.G., Liping, G., Broesch, T., Passos-Ferreira, C., Winning, A. and Berg, B. (2009) Fairness in distributive justice by 3 – and 5-year olds across seven cultures. *Journal of Cross-Cultural Psychology*, 40, 416–42.

Rodin, J., Schank, D. and Striegel-Moore, R. (1989) Psychological features of obesity. *Medical Clinics of North America*, 73, 47–66.

Roediger III, H.L. and Crowder, R.G. (1976) A serial position effect in recall of United States presidents. *Bulletin of the Psychonomic Society*, 8, 275–8.

Roediger III, H.L., Bergman, E.T. and Meade, M.L. (2000) Repeated reproduction from memory. In A. Saito (ed.) *Bartlett, Culture and Cognition*. Hove: Psychology Press.

Roediger, H.L. and Pyc, M.A. (2012) Inexpensive techniques to improve education: Applying cognitive psychology to enhance educational practice. *Journal of Applied Research in Memory and Cognition*, 1(4), 242–8.

Roediger, H.L., III. and Karpicke, J.D. (2006) Test-enhanced learning: Taking memory tests improves long-term retention. *Psychological Science*, 17, 249–55.

Roediger, H.L., Meade, M.L. and Bergman, E.T. (2001) Social contagion of memory. *Psychonomic Bulletin and Review*, 8, 365–71.

Roefs, A., Jansen, A., Moresi, S., Willems, P. and van Grootel, S. (2008) Looking good: BMI, attractiveness bias and visual attention. *Appetite*, 51, 552–5.

Roff, J.D. and Knight, R. (1981) Family characteristics, childhood symptoms, and adult outcome in schizophrenia. *Journal of Abnormal Psychology*, 90, 510–20.

Rogers, C.R. (1951) *Client-centered Therapy*. Boston, MA: Houghton Mifflin.

Rogers, C.R. (1961) *On Becoming a Person*. Boston, MA: Houghton Mifflin.

Rogoff, B. (1990) *Apprenticeship in Thinking: Cognitive development in social context*. New York: Oxford University Press.

Rogoff, B. and Chavajay, P. (1995) What's become of research on the cultural basis of cognitive development. *American Psychologist*, 50, 859–77.

Rohrer, D. and Pashler, H. (2010) Recent research on human learning challenges conventional instructional strategies. *Educational Researcher*, 39, 406–12.

Rohrer, D. and Pashler, H. (2012) Learning styles: where's the evidence? *Online Submission*, 46(7), 634–5.

Roig, M., Skriver, K., Lundbye-Jensen, J., Kiens, B. and Nielsen, J.B. (2012) A single bout of exercise improves motor memory. *PLoS ONE*, 7, e44594.

Rojas, D.C., Singel, D., Steinmetz, S., Hepburn, S. and Brown, M.S. (2013) Decreased left perisylvian GABA concentration in children with autism and unaffected siblings. *Neuroimage*, S1053–8119.

Rokeach, M. (1948) Generalized mental rigidity as a factor in ethnocentrism. *Journal of Abnormal and Social Psychology*, 43, 259–78.

Rolls, B.J., Rolls, E.T. and Rowe, E.A. (1982) How sensory properties of foods affect human feeding behaviour. *Physiology and Behaviour*, 29, 409–17.

Rolls, B.J., Rowe, E.A., Rolls, E.T., Kingston, B. and Megson, A. (1981) Variety in the meal enhances food intake in man. *Physiology and Behaviour*, 26, 215–21.

Rolls, B.J., van Duijenvoorde, P.M. and Rolls, E.T. (1984) Pleasantness changes and food intake in a varied four-course meal. *Appetite*, 5, 337–48.

Rolls, E.T. (1997) Brain mechanisms of vision, memory and consciousness. In M. Ito, Y. Miyashita and E.T. Rolls (eds) *Cognition, Computation and Consciousness*. Oxford: Oxford University Press.

Rolls, E.T. (1999) *The Brain and Emotion*. New York: Oxford University Press.

Rolls, E.T. (2008) *Memory, Attention and Decision-making: A unified computational neuroscience approach*. Oxford: Oxford University Press.

Rolls, E.T. and Baylis, L.L. (1994) Gustatory, olfactory and visual convergence within the primate orbitofrontal cortex. *Journal of Neuroscience*, 14, 5437–52.

Rolls, E.T. and Rolls, J.H. (1997) Olfactory sensory-specific satiety in humans. *Physiology and Behaviour*, 61(3), 461–73.

Rolls, E.T., Murzi, E., Yaxley, S., Thorpe, S.J. and Simpson, S.J. (1986) Sensory-specific satiety: Food-specific reduction in responsiveness of ventral forebrain neurons after feeding in the monkey. *Brain Research*, 368, 79–86.

Romaine, S. (1989) *Bilingualism*. Oxford: Blackwell.

Roopnarine, J.L. (1986) Mothers' and fathers' behaviours toward the sex-typed toy play of their infant sons and daughters. *Sex Roles*, 12, 59–68.

Rosal, M.C., Ockene, J.K., Ma, Y., Hebert, J.R., Ockene, I.S., Merriam, P. and Hurley, T.G. (1998) Coronary Artery Smoking Intervention Study (CASIS): 5 year follow-up. *Health Psychology*, 17, 476–8.

Rosch, E.H. (1975) Cognitive representations of semantic categories. *Journal of Experimental Psychology: General*, 104, 192–233.

Rosch, E.H., Mervis, C.B., Gray, W.D., Johnson, D.M. and Boyes-Braem, P. (1976) Basic objects in natural categories. *Cognitive Psychology*, 8, 382–439.

Rose, G.A. and Williams, R.T. (1961) Metabolic studies of large and small eaters. *British Journal of Nutrition*, 15, 1–9.

Rose, J.S., Chassin, L., Presson, C.C. and Sherman, S.J. (1996) Prospective predictors of quit attempts and smoking cessation in young adults. *Health Psychology*, 15(4), 261–8.

Rosen, D.B. and Jaruszewicz, C. (2009) Developmentally appropriate technology use and early childhood teacher education. *Journal of Early Childhood Teacher Education*, 30(2), 162–71.

Rosenbaum, R.S., McKinnon, M.C., Levine, B. and Moscovitch, M. (2004) Visual imagery deficits, impaired strategic retrieval, or memory loss: disentangling the nature of an amnesic person's autobiographical memory deficit. *Neuropsychologia*, 42, 1619–35.

Rosenbaum, R.S., Richards, B., Black, S.E. and Moscovitch, M. (2005) 'Where to?' remote memory for spatial relations and landmark identity in former taxi drivers with Alzheimer's disease and encephalitis. *Journal of Cognitive Neuroscience*, 17(3), 446–62.

Rosenblatt, F. (1962) *Principles of Neurodynamics*. New York: Spartan.

Rosenman, R.H., Brand, R.J., Jenkins, C.D., Friedman, M., Straus, R. and Wurm, M. (1975) Coronary heart disease in the Western Collaborative Group Study: Final follow-up experience of 8½ years. *Journal of the American Medical Association*, 233, 872–7.

Rosenthal, R. and Fode, K.L. (1963) The effect of experimental bias on the performance of the albino rat. *Behavioral Science*, 8, 183–7.

Rosenzweig, M.R. (1984) Experience, memory, and the brain. *American Psychologist*, 39, 365–76.

Ross, G., Nelson, K., Wetstone, H. and Tanouye, E. (1986) Acquisition and generalization of novel object concepts by young language learners. *Journal of Child Language*, 13, 67–83.

Ross, L. (1977) The intuitive psychologist and his shortcomings: Distortions in the attribution process. In L. Berkowitz (ed.) *Advances in Experimental Social Psychology*. New York: Academic Press.

Rosser, R. (1994) *Cognitive Development: Psychological and Biological Perspectives*. Boston, MA: Allyn & Bacon.

Rossiter, M.W. (1993) The Matthew Matilda effect in science. *Social Studies of Science*, 23, 325–41.

Rossow, I., Groholt, B. and Wichstrom, L. (2005) Intoxicants and suicidal behaviour among adolescents: Changes in levels and associations from 1992 to 2002. *Addiction*, 100, 79–88.

Roth, E.M. and Mervis, C.B. (1983) Fuzzy set theory and class inclusion relations in semantic categories. *Journal of Verbal Learning and Verbal Behavior*, 22, 509–25.

Rothbaum, B.O., Hodges, L., Smith, S., Lee, J.H. and Price, L. (2000) A controlled study of virtual reality exposure therapy for the fear of flying. *Journal of Consulting and Clinical Psychology*, 68(6), 1020–6.

Rotter, J.B. (1954) *Social Learning and Clinical Psychology*. Englewood Cliffs, NJ: Prentice Hall.

Rotter, J.B. (1966) Generalized expectancies for internal versus external control of reinforcement. *Psychological Monographs*, 80 (1, Whole No. 609).

Rotton, J. (1992) Trait humor and longevity: Do comics have the last laugh? *Health Psychology*, 11(4), 262–6.

Rotton, J. and Shats, M. (1996) Effects of state humor, expectancies, and choice on postsurgical mood and self-medication: a field experiment. *Journal of Applied Social Psychology*, 26, 1775–94.

Rotton, J., Barry, T., Frey, J. and Soler, E. (1978) Air pollution and interpersonal attraction. *Journal of Applied Social Psychology*, 8, 57–71.

Rovee, C. and Rovee, D.T. (1969) Conjugate reinforcement of infant exploratory behaviour. *Journal of Experimental Child Psychology*, 8, 33–9.

Rovee-Collier, C. and Hayne, H. (1987) Reactivation of infant memory: Implications for cognitive development. In H.W. Reese (ed.) *Advances in Child Development and Behaviour*, Vol. 20. New York: Academic Press.

Rowe, C., Harris, J.M. and Roberts, S.C. (2005) Sporting contests – seeing red? Putting sportswear in context. *Nature*, 437, E10.

Royet, J.P., Hudry, J., Zald, D.H., Godinot, D., Grégoire, M.C., Lavenne, F., . . . and Holley, A. (2001) Functional neuroanatomy of different olfactory judgments. *Neuroimage*, 13(3), 506–19.

Rozin, P. (1999) Food is fundamental, fun, frightening, and far-reaching. *Social Research*, 66, 9–30.

Rozin, P., Bressman, B. and Taft, M. (1974) Do children understand the basic relationship between speech and writing? The Mow–Motorcycle test. *Journal of Reading Behaviour*, 6, 327–34.

Rozin, P., Kabnick, K., Pete, E., Fischler, C. and Shields, C. (2003) The ecology of eating: Smaller portion sizes in France than in the United States help explain the French paradox. *Psychological Science*, 14(5), 450–4.

Rubenstein, H., Lewsi, S.S. and Rubenstein, M.A. (1971) Evidence for phonemic recoding in visual word recognition. *Journal of Verbal Learning and Verbal Behaviour*, 10, 645–57.

Rubin, D.C. (1982) On the retention function for autobiographical memory. *Journal of Verbal Learning and Verbal Behaviour*, 21, 21–38.

Rubin, D.C. (2000) The distribution of early childhood memories. *Memory*, 8, 265–9.

Rubin, D.C. (2015) One bump, two bumps, three bumps, four? Using retrieval cues to divide one autobiographical memory reminiscence bump into many. *Journal of Applied Research in Memory and Cognition*, 4(1), 87–9.

Rubin, M.A., Hall, J.A. and Schmid Mast, M. (2014) Smiling in a job interview: When less is more. *The Journal of Social Psychology*, 155, 107–26.

Rubio-Fernandez, P. and Glucksberg, S. (2012) Reasoning about other people's beliefs: Bilinguals have an advantage. *Journal of Experimental Psychology: Learning, Memory and Cognition*, 38, 211–17.

Rubio-Fernández, P. and Glucksberg, S. (2012) Reasoning about other people's beliefs: bilinguals have an advantage. *Journal of Experimental Psychology: Learning, Memory and Cognition*, 38(1), 211.

Ruble, D.N. and Martin, C.L. (1998) Gender development. In W. Damon and N. Eisenberg (eds) *Handbook of Child Psychology. 3: Social, emotional and personality development*. New York: Wiley.

Rudolph, D.L. and Kim, J.G. (1996) Mood responses to recreational sport and exercise in a Korean sample. *Journal of Social Behaviour and Personality*, 11(4), 841–9.

Ruff, C.B., Trinkhaus, E. and Holliday, T.W. (1997) Body mass and encephalization in Pleistocene Homo. *Nature*, 387, 173–6.

Ruffman, T., Murray, J., Halberstadt, J. and Vater, T. (2012) Age-related differences in deception. *Psychology and Aging*, 27, 543–9.

Ruigrok, A.N.V., Salimi-Khorshidi, G., Lai, M-C., Baron-Cohen S., Lombardo, M.V., Tait, R.J. and Suckling, J. (2014) A meta-analysis of sex differences in human brain structure. *Neuroscience and Biobehavioural Reviews*, 39, 34–50.

Rule, N.O. and Alaei, R. (2016) 'Gaydar': The perception of sexual orientation from subtle cues. *Current Directions in Psychological Science*, 25, 444–8.

Rule, N.O., Freeman, J.B. and Ambady, N. (2013) Culture in social neuroscience: A review. *Social Neuroscience*, 8, 3–10.

Rule, N.O., Rosen, K.S., Slepian, M.L. and Ambady, N. (2011) Mating interest improves women's accuracy in judging male sexual orientation. *Psychological Science*, 22, 881–6.

Rumelhart, D.E., McClelland, J.L. and the PDP Research Group (1986) *Parallel Distributed Processing: Explorations in the microstructure of cognition*. Cambridge, MA: MIT Press.

Runciman, W.G. (1966) *Relative Deprivation and Social Justice*. London: Routledge & Kegan Paul.

Ruotsalainen, J. H., Verbeek, J. H., Mariné, A. and Serra, C. (2016) Preventing occupational stress in healthcare workers. *The Cochrane Library*, http://onlinelibrary.wiley.com/doi/10.1002/14651858.CD002892.pub5/pdf

Rupp, H.A., James, T.W., Ketterson, E.D., Sengelaub, D.R., Janseen, E. and Heiman, J.R. (2009) Neural activation in the orbitofrontal cortex in response to male faces increases during the follicular phase. *Hormones and Behavior*, 56, 66–72.

Rusbult, C.E. and Zembrodt, I.M. (1983) Responses to dissatisfaction in romantic involvements: A multi-dimensional scaling analysis. *Journal of Experimental Social Psychology*, 19, 274–93.

Rushton, J.P. (1995) *Race, Evolution and Behaviour: A life history perspective*. New Brunswick, NJ: Transaction.

Rushton, J.P. (1997) Race, intelligence and the brain: The errors and omissions of the 'revised' edn of S.J. Gould's *The Mismeasure of Man* (1996). *Personality and Individual Differences*, 23(1), 169–80.

Rushworth, M.F.S., Mars, R.B. and Sallet, J. (2013) Are there specialised circuits for social cognition and are they unique to humans? *Current Opinion to Neurobiology*, 23, 436–42.

Russell, G.F.M. and Treasure, J. (1989) The modern history of anorexia nervosa: An interpretation of why the illness has changed. *Annals of the New York Academy of Sciences*, 575, 13–30.

Russell, J.A. (1994) Is there universal recognition of emotion from facial expression? A review of the cross-cultural studies. *Psychological Bulletin*, 115(1), 102–41.

Russell, M.I., Suritz, G.M. and Thompson, K. (1980) Olfactory influences on the human menstrual cycle. *Pharmacology, Biochemenstrual Behaviour*, 13, 737–8.

Russell, N.J.C. (2011) Milgram's obedience to authority experiments: Origins and early evolution. *British Journal of Social Psychology*, 50, 140–62.

Russell, N.J.C. (2014) Stanley Milgram's obedience to authority 'relationship' condition: Some methodological and theoretical implications. *Social Sciences*, 3, 194–214.

Russell, P.A., Deregowski, J.B. and Kinnear, P.R. (1997) Perception and aesthetics. In J.W. Berry, P.R. Dasen and T.S. Sarawathi (eds) *Handbook of Cross-cultural Psychology. Vol. 2: Basic processes and human development*. Boston, MA: Allyn & Bacon.

Russell, P.J. (1992) *Genetics*. New York: HarperCollins.

Russo, P.M., Leone, L., Penolazzi, B. and Natale, V. (2012) Circadian preference and the big five. *Chronobiology International*, 29, 1–6.

Russo, S.J., Dietz, D.M., Dumitriu, D., Morrison, J.H., Malenka, R.C. and Nestler, E.J. (2010) The addicted synapse: mechanisms of synaptic and structural plasticity in nucleus accumbens. *Trends in Neurosciences*, 33, 267–76.

Rutishauser, U., Schuman, E.M. and Mamelak, A.N. (2008) Activity of human hippocampal and amygdala neurons during retrieval of declarative memories. *Proceedings of the National Academy of Sciences*, 105(1), 329–34.

Rutte, C.G. and Wilke, H.A.M. (1984) Social dilemmas and leadership. *European Journal of Social Psychology*, 14, 105–21.

Rutter, M., Andersen-Wood, L., Beckett, C., Bredenkamp, D., Castle, J., Groothues, C. et al. (1999) Quasi-autistic patterns following severe early global privation. *Journal of Child Psychology and Psychiatry*, 40, 537–49.

Ryan, E.B., McNamara, S.R. and Kenney, M. (1977) Lexical awareness and reading performance among beginning readers. *Journal of Reading Behaviour*, 9, 399–400.

Ryff, C.D. (1991) Possible selves in adolescence and old age: A tale of shifting horizons. *Psychology and Aging*, 6, 286–95.

Ryle, G. (1949) *The Concept of Mind*. New York: Barnes & Noble.

Saari, S. (1995) The legalization of Finnish psychology. In A. Schorr and S. Saari (eds) *Psychology in Europe*. Göttingen: Hogrefe & Huber.

Saarimaki, H., Gotsopoulos, A., Jaaskelainen, I.P., Lampinen, J., Vuillleumier, P., Hari, R., Sams, M. and Nummenmaa, L. (2015) Discrete neural signatures of basic emotions. *Cerebral Cortex*, 1–11.

Sabini, J., Siepmann, M. and Stein, J. (2001) The really fundamental attribution error in social psychological research. *Psychological Inquiry*, 12, 1–15.

Sachs, J. (1993) The emergence of intentional communication. In J. Berko Gleason (ed.) *The Development of Language*. New York: Macmillan.

Sachs, O. (1989) *Seeing Voices: A journey into the world of the deaf*. Berkeley ICA: University of California Press.

Sackett, P.R. and Walmsley, P.T. (2014) Which personality attributes are most important in the workplace? *Perspectives on Psychological Science*, 9, 538–51.

Sacks, O. (1995) *An Anthropologist on Mars*. New York: Alfred A. Knopf.

Sadeh, A., Keinan, G. and Daon, K. (2004) Effects of stress on sleep: The moderating role of coping style. *Health Psychology*, 23(5), 542–5.

Sadler, M.S., Meagor, E.L. and Kaye, K.E. (2012) Stereotypes of mental disorders differ in competence and warmth. *Social Science and Medicine*, 74, 915–22.

Saegert, S.C., Swap, W. and Zajonc, R.B. (1973) Exposure, context and interpersonal attraction. *Journal of Personality and Social Psychology*, 25, 234–42.

Saffran, E.M., Schwartz, M.F. and Marin, O.S.M. (1980) Evidence from aphasia: Isolating the components of a production model. In B. Butterworth (ed.) *Language Production*. London: Academic Press.

Sagarin, B.J., Martin, A.L., Coutinho, S.A, Edlund, J.E., Patel, L., Skowronski, J.J. and Zengel, B. (2012) Sex differences in jealousy: a meta-analytic examination. *Evolution and Human Behavior*, 33, 595–614.

Sagioglou, C. and Greitemeyer, T. (2014) Bitter taste causes hostility. *Personality and Social Psychology Bulletin*, 1–9.

Sahin, B. and Mebert, C.J. (2013) The role of culture and self-construal in autobiographical memories of US and Turkish college students. *Memory*, 21, 1004–17.

Sakai, F., Meyer, J.S., Karacan, I., Derman, S. and Yamamoto, M. (1979) Normal human sleep: Regional cerebral haemodynamics. *Annals of Neurology*, 7, 471–8.

Sakata, H. (1997) Parietal visual neurons coding three-dimensional characteristics of objects and their relation to hand action. In P. Thier and H.-O. Karnath (eds) *Parietal Lobe Contributions to Orientation in 3D Space*. Berlin: Springer-Verlag.

Saks, M. and Marti, M. (1997) A metaanalysis of the effect of jury size. *Law and Human Behaviour*, 21, 451–67.

Salame, P. and Baddeley, A.D. (1982) Disruption of short-term memory by unattended speech: Implications for the structure of working memory. *Journal of Verbal Learning and Verbal Behaviour*, 21, 150–64.

Salame, P. and Baddeley, A.D. (1990) The effects of irrelevant speech on immediate free recall. *Bulletin of the Psychonomic Society*, 28, 540–2.

Salapatek, P. (1975) Pattern perception in early infancy. In L.B. Cohen and P. Salapatek (eds) *Infant Perception: From sensation to cognition*, Vol. 1. New York: Academic Press.

Salkovskis, P.M., Forrester, E. and Richards, C. (1998) Cognitive-behavioural approach to understanding obsessional thinking. *British Journal of Psychiatry*, 173 (suppl. 35), 53–63.

Salter, C.A. and Routledge, L.M. (1971) Supernatural beliefs among graduate students at the University of Pennsylvania. *Nature*, 232, 278–9.

Salthouse, T.A. (1984) Effects of age and skill in typing. *Journal of Gerontology*, 113, 345–71.

Salthouse, T.A. (1988) Cognitive aspects of motor functioning. In J.A. Joseph (ed.) *Central Determinants of Age-related Declines in Motor Function*. New York: New York Academy of Sciences.

Salthouse, T.A. (1992) What do adult age differences in the Digit Symbol Substitution Test reflect? *Journal of Gerontology*, 47(3), 121–8.

Salthouse, T.A. (1993) Speed mediation of adult age differences in cognition. *Developmental Psychology*, 29(4), 722–38.

Salthouse, T.A. (2009) When does age-related cognitive decline begin? *Neurobiology of Aging*, 30, 507–14.

Salthouse, T.A. and Babcock, R.L. (1991) Decomposing adult age differences in working memory. *Developmental Psychology*, 27(5), 763–76.

Salthouse, T.A. and Maurer, T.J. (1997) Aging, job performance and career development. In J.E. Birren and K.W. Schaie (eds) *Handbook of the Psychology of Aging*. New York: Academic Press.

Salvy, S-J., Jarrin, D., Paluch, R., Irfan, N. and Pliner, P. (2007) Effects of social influence on eating in couples, friends and strangers. *Appetite*, 49, 92–9.

Sampson, E.L. (2010) Palliative care for people with dementia. *British Medical Bulletin*, 96(1), 159–74.

Sanacora, G. *et al.* (2002) Increased occipital cortex GABA concentrations in depressed patients after therapy with selective serotonin reuptake inhibitors. *American Journal of Psychiatry*, 159, 663–5.

Sanacora, G. *et al.* (2004) Subtype-specific alterations of gamma-aminobutyric acid and glutamate in patients with major depression. *Archives of General Psychiatry*, 61, 705–13.

Sande, G.N., Goethals, G.R. and Radloff, C.E. (1988) Perceiving one's own traits and others: The multifaceted self. *Journal of Personality and Social Psychology*, 54, 13–20.

Santana, E. J. (2016). The brain of the psychopath: A systematic review of structural neuroimaging studies. *Psychology & Neuroscience*, 9(4), 420.

Sanz, J.H., Karlsgodt, K.H., Bearden, C.E., van Erp, T.G., Nandy, R.R. and Ventura, J. (2009) Symptomatic and functional correlates of regional brain physiology during working memory processing in patients with recent onset schizophrenia. *Psychiatry Research*, 173, 177–82.

Sarafino, E.P. (2011) *Health Psychology: Biopsychosocial interactions* (7th edn). Chichester: Wiley.

Sarason, I. and Sarason, B. (1993) *Abnormal Psychology: The problem of maladaptive behavior* (7th edn). Englewood Cliffs, NJ: Prentice Hall.

Sasaki, H. *et al.* (2009) Structural and diffusional brain abnormality related to relatively low level alcohol consumption. *Neuroimage*, 46, 505–10.

Sasanuma, S. (1975) Kana and kanji processing in Japanese aphasics. *Brain and Language*, 2, 369–83.

Sassenberg, K., Kessler, T. and Mummendey, A. (2003) Less negative = positive? Social discrimination as avoidance or approach. *Journal of Experimental Social Psychology*, 39, 48–58.

Saucier, D.M., McCreary, D.R. and Saxberg, J.K.L. (2002) Does gender role socialization mediate sex differences in mental rotations? *Personality and Individual Differences*, 32, 1101–11.

Saunders, E.M. (1993) Stock prices and Wall Street weather. *American Economic Review*, 83, 1337–45.

Saur, D., Ronneberger, O., Kummerer, D., Mader, I., Weiller, C. and Kloppel, S. (2010) Early functional magnetic resonance imaging activations predict language outcome after stroke. *Brain*, 133, 1252–64.

Sauter, D.A., Eisner, F., Ekman, P. and Scott, S.K. (2010) Cross-cultural recognition of basic emotions through nonverbal emotional vocalizations. *Proceedings of the National Academy of Sciences*, 107, 2408–12.

Sauter, D.A., Eisner, F., Ekman, P. and Scott, S.K. (2010) Cross-cultural recognition of basic emotions through nonverbal emotional vocalisations. *PNAS*, 107, 2408–12.

Sauter, D.A., Eisner, F., Ekman, P. and Scott, S.K. (2015) Emotional vocalizations are recognised across cultures regardless of the valence of distractors. *Psychological Science*, 1–3.

Savage, R., Carless, S. and Ferraro, V. (2007) Predicting curriculum and test performance at age 11 from pupil background, baseline skills and phonological awareness at age 5 years. *Journal of Child Psychology and Psychiatry*, 48(7), 732–9.

Savage-Rumbaugh, E.S. (1990) Language acquisition in a nonhuman species: Implications for the innateness debate. *Development Psychobiology*, 23, 599–620.

Savage-Rumbaugh, S., Shanker, S.G. and Taylor, T.J. (1998) *Apes, Language and the Human Mind*. Oxford: Oxford University Press.

Savic, I. and Lindstrom, P. (2008) PET and MRI show differences in cerebral asymmetry and functional connectivity between homo- and heterosexual subjects. *Proceedings of the National Academy of Sciences*, 105, 9403–8.

Savic, I., Berglund, H. and Lindstrom, P. (2005) Brain response to putative pheromones in homosexual men. *Proceedings of the National Academy of Sciences*, 102(20), 7356–61.

Scarr, S. and Weinberg, R.A. (1976) IQ performance of black children adopted by white families. *American Psychologist*, 31, 726–39.

Scarr, S. and Weinberg, R.A. (1978) The influence of 'family background' on intellectual attainment. *American Sociological Review*, 43, 674–9.

Scarr, S., Webber, P.L., Weinberg, A. and Wittig, M.A. (1981) Personality resemblance among adolescents and their parents in biologically related and adoptive families. *Journal of Personality and Social Psychology*, 40, 885–98.

Schaal, B., Marlier, L. and Soussignan, R. (1995) Responsiveness to the odour of amniotic fluid in the human neonate. *Biological Neonate*, 67, 397–406.

Schaal, J.D. (2015) Visuomotor functions in the frontal lobe. *Annual Review of Visual Science*, 1, 469–98.

Schaalma, H.P., Kok, G., Bosker, R.J., Parcel, G.S., Peters, L., Poelman, J. and Reinders, J. (1996) Planned development and evaluation of AIDS/STD education for secondary-school students in the Netherlands: Short-term effects. *Health Education Quarterly*, 23, 469–87.

Schab, F.R. (1990) Odors and the remembrance of things past. *Journal of Experimental Psychology: Learning, Memory and Cognition*, 16(4), 648–55.

Schachter, S. (1959) *The Psychology of Affiliation*. Stanford, CA: Stanford University Press.

Schachter, S. (1964) The interaction of cognitive and physiological determinants of emotional state. In P.H. Liederman and D. Shapiro (eds) *Psychobiological Approaches to Social Behavior*. Stanford, CA: Stanford University Press.

Schachter, S. and Singer, J.E. (1962) Cognitive, social and physiological determinants of emotional state. *Psychological Review*, 69, 379–99.

Schacter, D.L. (1987) Implicit memory: History and current status. *Journal of Experimental Psychology: Learning, Memory and Cognition*, 13, 501–18.

Schaefer, S.M., Jackson, D.C., Davidson, R.J., Aguirre, G.K., Kimberg, D.Y. and Thompson-Schill, S.L. (2002) Modulation of amygdalar activity by the conscious regulation of negative emotion. *Journal of Cognitive Neuroscience*, 14(6), 913–21.

Schafe, D.P. *et al.* (2013) The 'quad-partite' synapse: microglia-synapse interactions in the developing and mature CNS. *Glia*, 16, 24–36.

Schaie, K.W. (1990) Intellectual development in adulthood. In J.E. Birren and K.W. Schaie (eds) *Handbook of the Psychology of Aging* (3rd edn). San Diego, CA: Academic Press.

Schall, J.D. (2015) Visuomotor functions in the frontal lobe. *Annual Review of Vision Science*, 1, 469–98.

Schaller, M., Miller, G.E., Gervais, W.M., Yager, S. and Chen, E. (2010) Mere visual perception of other people's disease symptoms facilitates a more aggressive immune response. *Psychological Science*, 21, 649–52.

Scharmüller, W., Übel, S., Ebner, F. and Schienle, A. (2012) Appetite regulation during food cue exposure: a comparison of normal-weight and obese women. *Neuroscience letters*, 518, 106–10.

Scheel, A., Ritchie, S., Brown, N., & Jacques, S. (2017). Through a womb, darkly: Methodological problems in a recent study of fetal visual perception. https://psyarxiv.com/2vgcw/

Scheier, M.F. and Carver, C.S. (1992) Effects of optimism on psychological and physical well-being: Theoretical overview and empirical update. *Cognitive Therapy and Research*, 16, 201–28.

Schellenberg, B.J.I. and Bailis, D.S. (2015) Predicting longitudinal trajectories of academic passion in first-year university students. *Learning and Individual Differences*, 40, 149–55.

Schellenberg, E.G. and von Scheve, C. (2012) Emotional cues in American popular music: Five decades of the top 40. *Psychology of Aesthetics, Creativity and the Arts*, 6, 196–203.

Schenck, C.H., Bundlie, S.R., Ettinger, M.G. and Mahowald, M.W. (1986) Chronic behavioral disorders of human REM sleep: A new category of parasomnia. *Sleep*, 9, 293–308.

Scherer, K.R. (2009) The dynamic architecture of emotion: Evidence for the component process model. *Cognition and Emotion*, 23, 1307–51.

Scherer, K.R. (2013) The nature and dynamics of relevance and valence appraisals: theoretical advances and recent evidence. *Emotion Review*, 5, 150–62.

Schieman, S., Whitestone, Y.K. and Van Gundy, K. (2006) The nature of work and the stress of higher status. *Journal of Health and Social Behavior*, 47, 242–57.

Schienle, A., Schäfer, A., Hermann, A. and Vaitl, D. (2009) Binge-eating disorder: reward sensitivity and brain activation to images of food. *Biological psychiatry*, 65, 654–61.

Schienle, A., Schafer, A., Stark, R., Walter, B. and Vaitl, D. (2005) Relationship between disgust sensitivity, trait anxiety and brain activity during disgust induction. *Neuropsychobiology*, 51, 86–92.

Schiepers, O.J.G. *et al.* (2011) APOE e4 status predicts age-related cognitive decline in the ninth decade. *Molecular Psychiatry*. 17, 315–24.

Schifano, F., Corkery, J., Naidoo, V., Oyefeso, A. and Ghodse, A.H. (2010) Comparison between amphetamine/methylamphetamine and ecstasy (MDMA, MDEA, MDA, 4-MTA) mortality data in the UK (1997–2007) *Neuropsychobiology*, 61(3), 122–30.

Schifferstein, H.N.J. (2006) The relative importance of sensory modalities in product usage: a study of self-reports. *Acta Psychologia*, 121, 41–64.

Schindler, R.M. and Warren, L.S. (1988) Effect of odd pricing on choice of items from a menu. *NA-Advances in Consumer Research, Volume* 15.

Schizophrenia Working Group of the Psychiatric Genomics Consortium (2014) Biological insights from 108 schizophrenia-associated genetic loci. *Nature*, 511, 421–7.

Schlaffke, L., Lissek, S., Lenz, M., Juckel, G., Schultz, T., Tegenthoff, M., . . . and Brüne, M. (2015) Shared and nonshared neural networks of cognitive and affective theory of mind: A neuroimaging study using cartoon picture stories. *Human Brain Mapping*, 36(1), 29–39.

Schleidt, M., Neumann, P. and Morishita, H. (1988) Pleasure and disgust: memories and associations of pleasant and unpleasant odours in Germany and Japan. *Chemical Senses*, 13, 279–93.

Schleifer, S.J., Keller, S.E., Camerino, M., Thornton, J.C. and Stein, M. (1983) Suppression of lymphocyte stimulation following bereavement. *Journal of the American Medical Association*, 15, 374–7.

Schlenker, B.R, Chambers, J.R. and Bonnie M, Le (2013) Conservatives are happier than liberals, but why? Political ideology, personality, and life satisfaction. *Journal Research Bulletin*. 39, 509–22.

Schlenker, B.R., Chambers, J.R. and Le, B.M. (2012) Conservatives are happier than liberals, but why? Political ideology, personality and life satisfaction. *Journal of Research in Personality*, 46, 127–46.

Schmader, T. (2002) Gender identification moderates stereotype threat effects on women's math performance. *Journal of Experimental Social Psychology*, 38, 194–201.

Schmahmann, J.D. and Sherman, J.C. (1998) The cerebellar cognitive affective syndrome. *Brain*, 121, 561–79.

Schmand, B., Smit, J.H., Lideboom, J., Smits, C., Hooijer, C., Jonker, C. and Deelman, B. (1997) Low education is a genuine risk factor for accelerated memory decline and dementia. *Journal of Clinical Epidemiology*, 50, 1025–33.

Schmid, J. and Fiedler, K. (1998) The backbone of closing speeches: The impact of prosecution versus defense language on judicial attributions. *Journal of Applied Social Psychology*, 28, 1140–72.

Schmidt, A., Cappucciati, M., Radua, J., Rutigliano, G., Rocchetti, M., Dell'Osso, L., . . . and McGuire, P. (2016) Improving prognostic accuracy in subjects at clinical high risk for psychosis: systematic review of predictive models and meta-analytical sequential testing simulation. *Schizophrenia Bulletin*, sbw098.

Schmidt, L.A., Fox, N.A., Perez-Elgar, K., Hu, S. and Hamer, D.H. (2001) Association of DRDH with attention problems in normal childhood development. *Psychiatric Genetics*, 1, 25–9.

Schmidt, L.A., Fox, N.A., Rubin, K.H., Hu, S. and Hamer D.H. (2002) Molecular genetics of shyness and aggression in preschoolers. *Personality and Individual Differences*, 33, 227–38.

Schmidt, W., Boos, R., Gnirs, J., Auer, L. and Schulze, S. (1985) Fetal behavioural states and controlled sound stimulation. *Early Human Development*, 12, 145–53.

Schmidt-Wilcke, T., Rosengarth, K., Luerding, R., Bogdahn, U. and Greenlee, M.W. (2010) Distinct patterns of functional and structural neuroplasticity associated with learning Morse code. *Neuroimage*, 51, 1234–41.

Schmithorst, V.J. (2009) Developmental sex differences in the relation of neuroanatomical connectivity to intelligence. *Intelligence*, 37(2), 164–73.

Schmitt, D.P. (2004) The Big Five related to risky sexual behaviour across 10 world regions: Differential personality associations of sexual promiscuity and relationship infidelity. *European Journal of Personality*, 18, 301–19.

Schmitt, D.P. and Buss, D.M. (2001) Human mate poaching: Tactics and temptations for infiltrating existing mateships. *Journal of Personality and Social Psychology*, 80(6), 894–917.

Schmitt, D.P. *et al.* (2004) Patterns and universals of mate poaching across 53 nations: The effects of sex, culture and personality on romantically attracting another person's partner. *Journal of Personality and Social Psychology*, 86(4), 560–84.

Schmolck, H., Buffalo, E.A. and Squire, L.R. (2000) Memory distortions develop over time: Recollections of the O.J. Simpson trial verdict after 15 and 32 months. *Psychological Science*, 11(1), 39–45.

Schnall, S., Benton, J. and Harvey, S. (2008) With a clean conscience. *Psychological Science*, 19(12), 1219–22.

Schneider, G.E. (1969) Two visual systems. *Science*, 163, 895–902.

Schneider, I.K., Rutjens, B.T., Jostmann, N.B. and Lakens, D. (2011) Weighty matters: importance literally feels heavy. *Social Psychology and Personality Science*, 2, 474–8.

Schneider-Garces, N.J. (2010) Span, CRUNCH, and beyond: working memory capacity and the ageing brain. *Journal of Cognitive Neuroscience*, 22, 655–69.

Schoedl, A.F. (2010) The clinical correlates of reported childhood sexual abuse. *Journal of Child Sexual Abuse*, 19, 156–70.

Schoenfeld, T.J. and Gould, E. (2012) Stress, stress hormones, and adult neurogenesis. *Experimental Neurology*, 233(1), 12–21.

Scholing, A. and Emmelkamp, P.M.G. (1996) Treatment of generalized social phobia: Results at long-term follow-up. *Behaviour Research and Therapy*, 34(5/6), 447–52.

Scholz, J., Klein, M.C., Behrens, T.E. and Johansen-Berg, H. (2009) Training induces changes in white matter architecture. *Nature Neuroscience*, 12, 1370–1.

Scholz, M., Niesch, H., Steffen, O., Ernst, B., Loeffler, M., Witruk, E. *et al.* (2008) Impact of chess training on mathematics performance and concentration ability of children with learning disabilities. *International Journal of Special Education*, 23, 138–56.

Schomerus, G., Schwahn, C., Holzinger, A., Corrigan, P.W., Grabe, H.J., Carta, M.G. and Angermeyer, M.C. (2012) Evolution of public attitudes about mental illness: a systematic review and meta analysis. *Acta Psychiatrica Scandinavica*, 125(6), 440–52.

Schott, G.D. (2012) Pictures as a neurological tool: Lessons from enhanced and emergent artistry in brain disease. *Brain*, 135, 1947–63.

Schotter, E.R., Tran, R. and Rayner, K. (2014) Don't believe what you read (only once): Comprehension is supported by regressions during reading. *Psychological Science*, 25, 1218–26.

Schouten, A.P., Valkenburg, P.M. and Peter, J. (2007) Precursors and underlying processes of adolescents' online self-disclosure: Developing and testing an 'Internet-attribute-perception' model. *Media Psychology*, 10, 292–314.

Schredl, M. (2014) Explaining the gender differences in nightmare frequency. The *American Journal of Psychology*, 127, 205–13.

Schredl, M. and Reinhard, I. (2011) Gender differences in nightmare frequency: A meta-analysis. *Sleep Medicine Reviews*, 15, 115–21.

Schroeder, J. and Epley, N. (2015) The sound of intellect: Speech reveals a thoughtful mind, increasing a job candidate's appeal. *Psychological Science*, 26, 877–91.

Schubert, C.R., Cruickshanks, K.J., Klein, B.E.K., Klein, R. and Nondahl, D.M. (2011) Olfactory impairment in older adults: Five-year incidence and risk factors. *The Laryngoscope*, 121, 873–8.

Schubert, C.R., Cruickshanks, K.J., Murphy, C., Huang, G-H., Klein, B.E.K., Klein, R., Nieto, F.J., Pankow, J.S. and Tweed, T.S. (2009) Olfactory impairment in adults: The Beaver Dam Experience. *Annals of the New York Academy of Sciences*, 1170, 531–6.

Schuchts, R.A. and Witkin, S.L. (1989) Assessing marital change during the transition to parenthood. *Social Casework: The Journal of Contemporary Social Work*, 70(2), 67–75.

Schul, Y. (1983) Integration and abstraction in impression formation. *Journal of Personality and Social Psychology*, 44, 45–54.

Schultz, W. (2007) Behavioral dopamine signals. *Trends in Neurosciences*, 30(5), 201–10.

Schumm, L.P., McClintock, M., Williams, S., Leitsch, S., Lundstrom, J., Hummel, T. and Lindau, S.T. (2009) Assessment of sensory function in the national social life, health and aging project. *Journal of Gerontology: Social Sciences*, 64B, 176–85.

Schurz, M., Wimmer, H., Richlan, F., Ludersdorfer, P., Klackl, J. and Kronbichler, M. (2014) Resting-state and task-based functional brain connectivity in developmental dyslexia. *Cerebral Cortex*, 25, 3502–14.

Schutter, D.J.J.G. and Harmon-Jones, E. (2013) The corpus callosum: A commissural road to anger and aggression. *Neuroscience and Biobehavioural Reviews*, 37, 2481–8.

Schwartz, G.E., Brown, S.L. and Ahern, G.L. (1980) Facial muscle patterning and subjective experience during affective imagery: sex differences. *Psychophysiology*, 17, 75–82.

Schwartz, H.A. (2013) Personality, gender, and age in the language of social media: the open-vocabulary approach. *PLoS ONE*, 8, e73791.

Schwartz, H.A., Eichstaedt, J.C., Kern, M.L., Dziurzynski, L., Ramones, S.M., Agrawal, M., . . . and Ungar, L.H. (2013) Personality, gender, and age in the language of social media: The open-vocabulary approach. *PLoS ONE*, 8(9), e73791.

Schwartz, N. (1999) Self-reports: How the questions shape the answers. *American Psychologist*, 54(2), 93–105.

Schwartz, R. and Schwartz, L.J. (1980) *Becoming a Couple*. Englewood Cliffs, NJ: Prentice Hall.

Schweizter, N.J., Saks, M.J., Murphy, E.R., Roskies, A.L., Sinnott-Armstrong, W. and Gaudet, L.M. (2011) Neuroimages as evidence in a men's rea defense: No impact. *Psychology, Public Policy, and Law*, 17, 357–93.

Scott, E.C. and Matzke, N.J. (2007) Biological design in the classroom. *Proceedings of the National Academy of Science*, 104(1), 8669–76.

Scott, J. (2006) Psychotherapy for bipolar disorders – efficacy and effectiveness. *Journal of Psychopharmacology*, 20(2), 46–50.

Scott, S.K., Young, A.W., Calder, A.J., Hellawell, D.J., Aggleton, J.P. and Johnson, M. (1997) Impaired auditory recognition of fear and anger following bilateral amygdala lesions. *Nature*, 385, 254–7.

Scoville, W.B. and Milner, B. (1957) Loss of recent memory after bilateral hippocampal lesions. *Journal of Neurology, Neurosurgery and Psychiatry*, 20, 11–21.

Scribner, S. (1977) Modes of thinking and ways of speaking: Culture and logic reconsidered. In P.N. Johnson-Laird and P.C. Wason (eds) *Thinking: Readings in cognitive science*. Cambridge: Cambridge University Press.

Scully, D., Kremer, J., Meade, M.M., Graham, R. and Dudgeon, K. (1998) Physical exercise and psychological well-being: A critical review. *British Journal of Sports Medicine*, 32, 111–20.

Searleman, A. (1977) A review of right hemisphere linguistic abilities. *Psychological Bulletin*, 84, 503–28.

Seasssau, M. and Bucci, M-P. (2013) Reading and visual search: A developmental study in normal children. *PLoS ONE*, 8, e70261.

Sedikides, C. (1993) Assessment, enhancement, and verification determinants of the self-evaluation process. *Journal of Personality and Social Psychology*, 65, 317–38.

Sedikides, C. and Gregg, A.P. (2003) Portraits of the self. In M.A. Hogg and J. Cooper (eds) *The Sage Handbook of Social Psychology*. London: Sage, pp. 110–38.

Seepersad, S. (2004) Coping with loneliness: Adolescent online and offline behavior. *CyberPsychology and Behavior*, 7, 35–9.

Segall, M.H., Campbell, D.T. and Herskovits, M.J. (1966) *The Influence of Culture on Visual Perception*. Indianapolis, In: Bobbs-Merrill.

Segalowitz, S.J. and Bryden, M.P. (1983) Individual differences in hemispheric representation of language. In S.J. Segalowitz (ed.) *Language Functions and Brain Organization*. New York: Academic Press.

Segerstrom, S.C., Taylor, S.E., Kemeny, M.E. and Fahey, J.L. (1998) Optimism is associated with mood, coping and immune change in response to stress. *Journal of Personality and Social Psychology*, 74(6), 1646–55.

Sehulster, J.R. (1989) Content and temporal structure of autobiographical knowledge: Remembering twenty-five seasons at the Metropolitan Opera. *Memory and Cognition*, 17, 590–606.

Seidel, E-M., Kirschner, M., Gur, R.C. and Derntl, B. (2010) The impact of facial emotional expressions on behavioural tendencies in women and men. *Journal of Experimental Psychology: Human Perception and Performance*, 36, 500–7.

Seidenberg, M.S. and McClelland, J.L. (1989) A distributed, developmental model of word recognition and naming. *Psychological Review*, 96, 523–68.

Seiter, J. S. (2007) Ingratiation and gratuity: The effect of complimenting customers on tipping behavior in restaurants. *Journal of Applied Social Psychology*, 37(3), 478–85.

Selfridge, O.G. (1959) *Pandemonium: A paradigm for learning. The Mechanisation of Thought Process*. London: HMSO.

Selfridge, O.G. and Neisser, U. (1960) Pattern recognition by machine. *Scientific American Mind*, 203, 60–8.

Seligman, M.E.P. (1971) Phobias and preparedness. *Behavior Therapy*, 2, 307–20.

Seligman, M.E.P. (1975) *Helplessness*. San Francisco, CA: W.H. Freeman.

Seligman, M.E.P. (1988) Competing theories of panic. In S. Rachman and J.D. Maser (eds) *Panic: Psychological Perspectives*. Hillsdale, NJ: Lawrence Erlbaum Associates.

Seligman, M.E.P. and Schulman, P. (1986) Explanatory style as a predictor of productivity and quitting among life insurance sales agents. *Journal of Personality and Social Psychology*, 50, 832–8.

Selye, H. (1956) *The Stress of Life*. New York: McGraw-Hill.

Selye, H. (1974) *Stress without Distress*. New York: Harper & Row.

Selye, H. (1991) History and present status of the stress concept. In A. Monat and R.S. Lazarus (eds) *Stress and Coping*. New York: Columbia University Press.

Sen, S., Burmeister M. and Ghosh, D. (2004) Meta-analysis of the association between a serotonin transporter promoter polymorphism (5-HTTLPR) and anxiety-related personality traits. *American Journal of Medical Genetics Part B: Neuropsychiatric Genetics*, 127B, 85–9.

Senju, A., Vernetti, A., Kikuchi, Y., Akechi, H., Hasegawa, T. and Johnson, M.H. (2012) Cultural background modulates how we look at other person's gaze. *International Journal of Behavioural Development*, 37, 131–6.

Seo, H. and Lee, D. (2012) Neural basis of learning and preference during social decision making. *Current Opinion in Neurobiology*, 22, 990–5.

Sera, M.D., Elieff, C., Forbes, J., Burch, M.C., Rodriguez, W. and Dubois, D.P. (2002) When language affects cognition and when it does not: An analysis of grammatical gender and classification. *Journal of Experimental Psychology: General*, 131, 377–97.

Sergent, J. (1987) A new look at the human split brain. *Brain*, 110, 1375–92.

Sergent, J. (1990) Furtive incursions into bicameral minds: Integrative and co-ordinating role of the subcortical structures. *Brain*, 113, 537–68.

Sergent, J. (1991) Processing of spatial relations within and between the disconnected cerebral hemispheres. *Brain*, 114, 1025–43.

Sergerie, K., Chochol, C. and Armony, J.L. (2008) The role of the amygdala in emotional processing: A quantitative meta-analysis of functional neuroimaging studies. *Neuroscience and Biobehavioral Reviews*, 32, 811–30.

Seubert, J., Rea, A.F., Loughead, J. and Habel, U. (2009) Mood induction with olfactory stimuli reveals differential affective responses in males and females. *Chemical Senses*, 34, 77–84.

Sewards, T.V. (2004) Dual separate pathways for sensory and hedonic aspects of taste. *Brain Research Bulletin*, 62(4), 271–83.

Seymour, S.E., Reuter-Lorenz, P.A. and Gazzaniga, M.S. (1994) The disconnection syndrome: Basic findings reaffirmed. *Brain*, 117, 105–15.

Shachaf, P. and Hara, N. (2010) Beyond vandalism: Wikipedia trolls. *Journal of Information Science*, 36, 357–70.

Shackelford, T.K. (2001) Partner-killing by women in cohabiting relationships and marital relationships. *Homicide Studies*, 5, 253–66.

Shackelford, T.K. and Buss, D.M. (2000) Marital satisfaction and spousal cost-inflation. *Personality and Individual Differences*, 28, 917–28.

Shackelford, T.K., Buss, D.M. and Bennett, K. (2002) Forgiveness or breakup: Sex differences in responses to a partner's infidelity. *Cognition and Emotion*, 16, 299–307.

Shaffer, D. and Pfeffer, C.R. (2001) Practice parameter for the assessment and treatment of children and adolescents with suicidal behaviour. *Journal of the American Academy of Child and Adolescent Psychiatry*, 40, 24S–51S.

Shaffer, L.H. (1975) Multiple attention in continuous verbal tasks. In S. Dornic (ed.) *Attention and Performance*, Vol. 5. New York: Academic Press.

Shafir, E., Simonson, I. and Tversky, A. (1993) Reason-based choice. *Cognition*, 49, 11–36.

Shah, J., Higgins, E.T. and Friedman, R.S. (1998) Performance incentives and means: How regulatory focus influences goal attainment. *Journal of Personality and Social Psychology*, 74, 285–93.

Shah, M., French, S.A., Jeffrey, R.W., McGovern, P.G., Forster, J.L. and Lando, H.A. (1993) Correlates of high fat/calorie food intake in a work-site population: The Healthy Worker Project. *Addictive Behaviours*, 18, 583–94.

Shah, P. and Miyake, A. (1996) The separability of working memory resources for spatial thinking and language processing: An individual differences approach. *Journal of Experimental Psychology: General*, 125, 4–27.

Shahidullah, S. and Hepper, P. (1993) The developmental origins of fetal responsiveness to an acoustic stimulus. *Journal of Reproductive and Infant Psychology*, 11, 135–42.

Shakoor, S., Jaffee, S.R., Bowes, L., Ouellet-Morin, I., Andreou, P., Happe, F., Moffitt, T.E. and Arseneault, L. (2012) A prospective longitudinal study of children's theory of mind and adolescent involvement in bullying. *Journal of Child Psychology and Psychiatry*, 53, 254–61.

Shalev, A.Y., Bonne, O. and Eth, S. (1996) Treatment of the post-traumatic stress disorder. *Psychosomatic Medicine*, 58, 165–82.

Shalom, D.B. and Poeppel, D. (2008) Functional anatomic models of language: Assembling the pieces. *Neuroscientist*, 14(1), 119–27.

Shamay-Tsoory, S.G., Adler, N., Aharon-Peretz, J., Perry, D. and Mayseless, N. (2011) The origins of originality: The neural bases of creative thinking and originality. *Neuropsychologia*, 49, 178–85.

Shams, L., Kamitani, Y. and Shimojo, S. (2000) What you see is what you hear. *Nature*, 408, 788.

Shanon, B. (1990) Consciousness. *Journal of Mind and Behaviour*, 11, 137–52.

Shanon, B. (1998) What is the function of consciousness? *Journal of Consciousness Studies*, 5(3), 295–308.

Shapiro, A.H. (1975) Behaviour of Kibbutz and urban children receiving an injection. *Psychophysiology*, 12, 79–82.

Shapiro, L.R. and Solity, J. (2008) Delivering phonological and phonics training within whole-class teaching. *British Journal of Educational Psychology*, 78, 597–620.

Shapiro, P.J. and Weisberg, R.W. (1999) Creativity and bipolar diathesis: Common behavioural and cognitive components. *Cognition and Emotion*, 13(6), 741–62.

Shariff, A.F., Willard, A.K., Andersen, T. and Norenzayan, A. (2015) Religious priming: A meta-analysis with a focus on prosociality. *Personality and Social Psychology Review*, 20, 27–48.

Shaver, P.R., Shaver, W.S. and Schwartz, J.C. (1992) Cross-cultural similarities and differences in emotion and its representation: A prototype approach. In M.S. Clark (ed.) *Review of Personality and Social Psychology*, Vol. 13. Newbury Park, CA: Sage.

Shaw, J.S., Garcia, L.A. and McClure, K.A. (1999) A lay perspective on the accuracy of eyewitness testimony. *Journal of Applied Social Psychology*, 29(1), 52–71.

Shaw, M.E. (1976) *Group Dynamics* (2nd edn). New York: McGraw-Hill.

Shaw, P., Greenstein, D., Lerch, J., Clasen, L., Lenroot, R., Gogtay, N.E.E.A., . . . and Giedd, J. (2006) Intellectual ability and cortical development in children and adolescents. *Nature*, 440(7084), 676–9.

Shaw, P., Lawrence, E.J., Radbourne, C., Bramham, J., Polkey, C.E. and David, A.S. (2004) The impact of early and late damage to the human amygdala on 'theory of mind' reasoning. *Brain*, 127, 1535–48.

Shaywitz, B.A., Shaywitz, S.E., Pugh, K.R., Constable, R.T., Skudlarski, P., Fulbright, R.K., Bronen, R.A., Fletcher, J.M., Shankweiler, D.P., Katz, L. and Gore, J.C. (1995) Sex differences in the functional organization of the brain for language. *Nature*, 373, 607–9.

Shaywitz, S.E. (1998) Dyslexia. *New England Journal of Medicine*, 338(5), 307–12.

Sheardova, K., Laczó, J., Vyhnalek, M., Andel, R., Mokrisova, I., Vlcek, K., . . . and Hort, J. (2014) Famous Landmark Identification in Amnestic Mild Cognitive Impairment and Alzheimer's Disease. *PLoS ONE*, 9(8), e105623.

Sheeran, P. and Abraham, C. (1996) The health belief model. In M. Conner and P. Norman (eds) *Predicting Health Behaviour: Research and practice with social cognition models*. Buckingham: Open University Press.

Shek, D.T.L. (1996) Midlife crisis in Chinese men and women. *Journal of Psychology*, 130(1), 109–19.

Sheldon, K.M. (2005) Positive value change during college: Normative trends and individual differences. *Journal of Research in Personality*, 39, 209–23.

Sheldon, K.M. and Houser-Marko, L. (2001) Self-concordance, goal attainment, and the pursuit of happiness: Can there be an upward spiral? *Journal of Personality and Social Psychology*, 80(1), 152–65.

Sheldon, K.M., Ryan, R.M. and Reiss, H. (1996) What makes for a good day? Competence and autonomy in the day and in the person. *Personality and Social Psychology Bulletin*, 22, 1270–9.

Shen, H.W. *et al.* (2009) Altered dendritic spine plasticity in cocaine-withdrawn rats. *Journal of Neuroscience*. 29, 2876–84.

Shepard, R.N. and Metzler, J. (1971) Mental rotation of three-dimensional objects. *Science*, 171, 701–3.

Shepherd, J. (1989) The face and social attribution. In A.W. Young and H.D. Ellis (eds) *Handbook of Research on Face Processing*. Amsterdam: North-Holland.

Sheppard, L.D. and Vernon, P.A. (2008) Intelligence and speed of information-processing: A review of 50 years of research. *Personality and Individual Differences*, 44, 535–51.

Sheridan, J. and Humphreys, G.W. (1993) A verbal-semantic category-specific recognition impairment. *Cognitive Neuropsychology*, 10, 143–84.

Sherif, M. (1936) *The Psychology of Social Norms*. New York: Harper.

Sherif, M. (1966) *In Common Predicament: Social psychology of intergroup conflict and cooperation*. Boston, MA: Houghton Mifflin.

Sherif, M. (ed.) (1962) *Intergroup Relations and Leadership*. New York: Wiley.

Sherman, D.K. *et al.* (2013) Deflecting the trajectory and changing the narrative: How self-affirmation affects academic performance and motivation under identity threat. *Journal of Personality and Social Psychology*, 104, 591–618.

Sherman, S.J., Presson, C.C. and Chassin, L. (1984) Mechanisms underlying the false consensus effect: The special role of threats to the self. *Personality and Social Psychology Bulletin*, 10, 127–38.

Shi, R. and Werker, J.F. (2001) Six-month-old infants' preference for lexical words. *Psychological Science*, 12, 70–5.

Shih, M., Pittinsky, T.L. and Ambady, N. (1999) Stereotype susceptibility: Identity salience and shifts in quantitative performance. *Psychological Science*, 10, 80–83.

Shin, L.M. and Liberzon, I. (2010) The neurocircuitry of fear, stress, and anxiety disorders. *Neuropsychopharmacology*, 35, 169–91.

Shine, J.P., Hodgetts, C.J., Postans, M., Lawrence, A.D. and Graham, K.S. (2015) APOE-ε4 selectively modulates posteromedial cortex activity during scene perception and short-term memory in young healthy adults. *Scientific Reports*, 5, 16322.

Shing, Y.L., Werkle-Bergner, M., Brehmer, Y., Muller, V., Li, S-C. and Lindenberger, U. (2010) Episodic memory across the lifespan: The contribution of associative and strategic components. *Neuroscience and Biobehavioural Reviews*, 34, 1080–91.

Shipstead, Z., Redick, T.S. and Engle, R.W. (2012) Is working memory training effective? *Psychological Bulletin*, 138(4), 628.

Shnabel, N., Purdie-Vaughns, V., Cook, J.E., Garcia, J and Cohen, G.L. (2013) Demystifying values-affirmation interventions: Writing about social belonging is a key to buffering against identity threat. *Personality and Social Psychology Bulletin*, 39, 663–76.

Shoghi-Jadid, K., Small, G.W., Agdeppa, E D., Kepe, V., Ercoli, L.M., Siddarth, P., . . . and Barrio, J.R. (2002) Localization of neurofibrillary tangles and beta-amyloid plaques in the brains of living patients with Alzheimer disease. *The American Journal of Geriatric Psychiatry*, 10(1), 24–35.

Shore, J.H., Vollmer, W.M. and Tatum, E.L. (1989) Community patterns of post-traumatic stress disorder. *Journal of Nervous and Mental Disease*, 177, 681–5.

Shors, T.J. (2004) Memory traces of trace memories: Neurogenesis, synaptogenesis and awareness. *Trends in Neurosciences*. 27(5), 250–6.

Shors, T.J. (2014) The adult brain makes new neurons, and effortful neurons keeps them alive. *Current Directions in Psychological Science*, 23, 311–18.

Shotland, R.L. and Heinold, W.D. (1985) Bystander response to arterial bleeding: Helping skills, the decision-making process, and differentiating the helping response. *Journal of Personality and Social Psychology*, 49, 347–56.

Shucksmith, J. and Hendry, L.B. (1998) *Health Issues and Young People: Growing up and speaking out*. London: Routledge.

Sidman, M. and Tailby, W. (1982) Conditional discrimination versus matching to sample: An expansion of the testing paradigm. *Journal of the Experimental Analysis of Behavior*, 37, 5–22.

Siegel, M.B., Tanwar, K.L. and Wood, K.S. (2011) Electronic cigarettes as a smoking cessation tool: results from an online survey. *American Journal of Preventive Medicine*, 40, 472–5.

Siibak, A. (2009) Constructing the self through the photo selection – visual impression management on social networking websites. *Cyberpsychology: Journal of Psychosocial Research on Cyberspace*, 3(1), article 1.

Silberman, M.A. and Snarey, J. (1993) Gender differences in moral development during early adolescence: The contribution of sex-related variations in mutation. *Current Psychology: Developmental, Learning, Personality and Social*, 12, 163–71.

Silove, D., Parker, G., Hadzi-Pavlovic, D., Manicavasagar, V. and Blaszcynski, A. (1991) *British Journal of Psychiatry*, 159, 835–41.

Silveri, M.C., Gainotti, G., Perani, D., Cappelletti, J.Y., Carbone, G. and Fazio, F. (1997) Naming deficit for non-living items: Neuropsychological and PET study. *Neuropsychologia*, 35(3), 359–67.

Silverman, I., Eals, M. and Peters, M. (2007) The hunter-gatherer theory of sex differences in spatial abilities: Data from 40 countries. *Archives of Sexual Behavior*, 36, 261–8.

Silverstein, B., Perdue, L., Peterson, B. and Kelly, E. (1986) The role of the mass media in promoting a thin standard of bodily attractiveness for women. *Sex Roles*, 14, 519–32.

Simard, V., Nielsen, T.A., Tremblay, R.E., Bovin, M. and Montplaisir, J.Y. (2008) Longitudinal study of bad dreams in preschool-aged children. *Sleep*, 31, 62–70.

Simion, F., Valenza, E., Umilta, C. and Dalla Barba, B. (1998) Preferential orienting to faces in newborns: A temporal–nasal asymmetry. *Journal of Experimental Psychology: Human Perception and Performance*, 24(5), 1399–405.

Simmons, D.J. and Chabris, C.F. (2011) What people believe about how memory works: A representative survey of the US population. *PLoS ONE*, 6, 1–7.

Simmons, D.J. and Chabris, C.F. (2012) Common (mis)beliefs about memory: A replication and comparison of telephone and mechanical Turk survey methods. *PLoS ONE*, 7, 1–5.

Simons, D.J., Boot, W.R., Charness, N., Gathercole, S., Chabris, C., Hambrick, D.Z. and Stine-Morrow, E.A.L. (2016) Do 'brain training' programs work? *Psychological Science in the Public Interest*, 17, 103–86.

Simmons, J.P., Nelson, L.D. and Simonsohn, U. (2011) False positive psychology: Undisclosed flexibility in data collection and analysis allows presenting anything as significant. *Psychological Science*, 22, 1359–66.

Simner, J. (2012) Defining synaesthesia. *British Journal of Psychology*, 103, 1–15.

Simola, J., Kuisima, J., Oorni, A., Uusitalo, L. and Hyona, J. (2011) The impact of salient advertisements on reading and attention on web pages. *Journal of Experimental Psychology: Applied*, 17, 174–90.

Simola, P., Liukkonen, K., Pitkäranta, A., Pirinen, T. and Aronen, E.T. (2014) Psychosocial and somatic outcomes of sleep problems in children: a 4 year follow up study. *Child: Care, Health and Development*, 40(1), 60–7.

Simon, B. and Brown, R.J. (1987) Perceived intragroup homogeneity in minority–majority contexts. *Journal of Personality and Social Psychology*, 53, 703–11.

Simon, N.M., Smoller, J.W., McNamara, K.L., Maser, R.S., Zalta, A.K., Pollack, M.H. *et al.* (2006) Telomere shortening and mood disorders: Preliminary support for a chronic stress model of accelerated aging. *Biological Psychiatry*, 60, 432–5.

Simoneau, T.L., Miklowitz, D.J. and Saleem, R. (1998) Expressed emotion and interactional patterns in the families of bipolar patients. *Journal of Abnormal Psychology*, 107(3), 497–507.

Simons, D.J. and Chabris, C.F. (1999) Gorillas in our midst: sustained inattentional blindness for dynamic events. *Perception*, 28, 1059–74.

Simons, D.J. and Levin, D.T. (1998) Failure to detect changes to people in a real-world interaction. *Psychonomic Bulletin and Review*, 5, 644–9.

Simons, D.J., Boot, W.R., Charness, N., Gathercole, S.E., Chabris, C.F., Hambrick, D.Z. and Stine-Morrow, E.A. (2016) Do 'brain-training' programs work? *Psychological Science in the Public Interest*, 17(3), 103–86.

Simons, R.C. and Hughes, C.C. (1985) *The Culture-bound Syndromes: Folk illnesses of psychiatric and anthropological interest*. Boston, MA: D. Reidel/Kluwer.

Simonsohn, U. (2011) Spurious also? Name similarity effects (implicit egotism) in employer decisions. *Psychological Science*, 22, 1087–9.

Simonsohn, U. (2011) Spurious? Name similarity effects (implicit egotism) in marriage, job, and moving decisions. *Journal of Personality and Social Psychology*, 101(1), 1.

Simonton, D.K. (2004) Psychology's status as a scientific discipline: Its empirical placement within an implicit hierarchy of the sciences. *Review of General Psychology*, 8(1), 59–67.

Simpson, J.A., Gangestad, S.W., Christensen, P.N. and Leck, K. (1999) Fluctuating asymmetry, sociosexuality and intrasexual competitive tactics. *Journal of Personality and Social Psychology*, 76, 159–72.

Sinclair, R.C., Mark, M.M. and Clore, G.L. (1994) Mood-related persuasion depends on (mis)attribution. *Social Cognition*, 12, 309–26.

Singareddy, R., Vgontzas, A.N., Fernandez-Mendoza, J., Liao, D., Calhoun, S., Shaffer, M.L. *et al.* (2012) Risk factors for incident chronic insomnia: a general population prospective study. *Sleep Medicine*, 13, 346–53.

Singh, D. and Luis, S. (1995) Ethnic and gender consensus for the effect of waist-to-hip ratio on judgment of women's attractiveness. *Human Nature*, 6, 51–68.

Singh, D., Dixson, B.J., Jessop, T.S., Morgan, B. and Dixson, A.F. (2010) Cross-cultural consensus for waist-hip ratio and women's attractiveness. *Evolution and Human Behavior*, 31, 176–81.

Siok, W.T., Niu, Z., Jin, Z., Perfetti, C.A. and Tan, L.H. (2008) A structural-functional basis for dyslexia in the cortex of Chinese readers. *Proceedings of the National Academy of Sciences*, 105(14), 5561–66.

Siok, W.T., Perfetti, C.A., Jin, Z. and Tan, L.H. (2004) Biological abnormality of impaired reading is constrained by culture. *Nature*, 431, 71–6.

Sip, K. E., Roepstorff, A., McGregor, W. and Frith, C.D. (2007) Detecting deception: The scope and limits. *Trends in Cognitive Sciences*, 12(2), 48–53.

Sip, K.E., Carmel, D., Marchant, J.L., Li, J., Petrovic, P., Roepstorff, A., McGregor, W.B. and Frith, C.D. (2013) When Pinocchio's nose does not grow: Belief regarding lie-detectability modules production of deception. *Frontiers in Human Neuroscience*, 7, 1–11.

Sire-Charles, V., Gueguen, N., Pascual, A. and Meineri, S. (2012) Words as environmental cues: The effect of the word 'loving' on compliance to a blood donation request. *The Journal of Psychology*, 146, 455–70.

Sirigu, A., Zalla, T., Pillon, B., Grafman, J., Agid, Y. and Dubois, B. (1995) Selective impairments in managerial knowledge following pre-frontal cortex damage. *Cortex*, 31, 301–6.

Sjoberg, L. (2001) Emotional intelligence: A psychometric analysis. *European Psychologist*, 6(2), 79–95.

Skarin, K. (1977) Cognitive and contextual determinants of stranger fear in six- and eleven-month-old infants. *Child Development*, 48, 537–44.

Skeels, H.M. (1966) Adult status of children with contrasting early life experiences. *Monographs of the Society for Research in Child Development*, 31, 1–65.

Skinner, B.F. (1948) *Walden Two*. New York: Macmillan.

Skinner, B.F. (1953) *Science and Human Behavior*. New York: Macmillan.

Skinner, B.F. (1971) *Beyond Freedom and Dignity*. New York: Vantage.

Skinner, B.F. (1986) The evolution of verbal behavior. *Journal of the Experimental Analysis of Behavior*, 45, 115–22.

Skolnick, P., Popik, P. and Trullas, R. (2009) Glutamate-based antidepressants: 20 years on. *Trends in Pharmacological Sciences*, 30, 563–9.

Skorska, M.N., Geniole, S.N., Vrysen, B.M., McCormick, C.M. and Bogaert, A.F. (2015) Facial structure predicts sexual orientation in both men and women. *Archives of Sexual Behaviour*, 44, 1377–94.

Skowronski, J.J. and Carlston, D.E. (1989) Negativity and extremity biases in impression formation: A review of explanations. *Psychological Bulletin*, 105, 131–42.

Slade, A. (1987) A longitudinal study of maternal involvement and symbolic play during the toddler period. *Child Development*, 58, 367–75.

Sloan, D.M. and Marx, B.P. (2004) A closer examination of the structured written disclosure procedure. *Journal of Consulting and Clinical Psychology*, 72(2), 165–75.

Slotte, V. and Lonka, K. (1999) Review and process effects of spontaneous note-taking on text comprehension. *Contemporary Educational Psychology*, 24, 1–20.

Sluzenski, J., Newcombe, N.S. and Satlow, E. (2004) Knowing where things are in the second year of life: Implications for hippocampal development. *Journal of Cognitive Neuroscience*, 16(8), 1443–51.

Smajic, A., Merritt, S., Banister, C. and Blinebry, A. (2014) The red effect, anxiety, and exam performance: a multistudy examination. *Teaching of Psychology*, 41(1), 37–43.

Small, D.M., Jones-Gottman, M., Zatorre, R.J., Petrides, M. and Evans, A.C. (1997) A role of the right anterior temporal lobe in taste quality recognition. *Journal of Neuroscience*, 17, 5136–42.

Small, D.M., Zatorre, R.J. and Jones-Gottman, M. (2001a) Increased intensity perception of aversive taste following right anteromedial temporal lobe removal in humans. *Brain*, 124, 1566–75.

Small, D.M., Zatorre, R.J., Dagher, A., Evans, A.C. and Jones-Gotman, M. (2001b) Changes in brain activity related to eating chocolate. *Brain*, 124, 1720–33.

Smeesters, D. and Liu, J. (2011) The effect of color (red versus blue) on assimilation versus contrast in prime-to-behavior effects. *Journal of Experimental Social Psychology*, 47, 653–6.

Smeets, M.A.M., Smit, F., Panhuysen, G.E.M. and Ingleby, J.D. (1997) The influence of methodological differences on the outcome of body size estimation studies in anorexia nervosa. *British Journal of Clinical Psychology*, 36, 263–77.

Smith, A.P. and Jones, D.M. (1992) Noise and performance. In A.P. Smith and D.M. Jones (eds) *Handbook of Human Performance. Vol. 1: The physical environment*. London: Academic Press.

Smith, A.P. and Woods, M. (2012) Effects of chewing gum on the stress and work of university students. *Appetite*, 58, 1037–40.

Smith, B. and Shimeld, S. (2017) Using pictorial mnemonics in the learning of tax: A cognitive load perspective. *Higher Education Research and Development*, 33, 565–79.

Smith, B.L., Holliday, W.G. and Austin, H.W. (2010) Students' comprehension of science textbooks using a question-based reading strategy. *Journal of Research in Science Teaching*, 47, 36–79.

Smith, E.E., Jonides, J. and Koeppe, R.A. (1996) Dissociating verbal and spatial working memory using PET. *Cerebral Cortex*, 6, 11–20.

Smith, E.R. and Zárate, M.A. (1992) Exemplar-based model of social judgment. *Psychological Review*, 99, 3–21.

Smith, G. (2012) Do people whose names begin with 'D' really die young? *Death Studies*, 36, 182–9.

Smith, G.E., Housen, P., Yaffe, K., Ruff, R., Kennison, R.F., Mahncke, H.W. and Zelinski, E.M. (2009) A cognitive training program based on principles of brain plasticity. *Journal of the American Geriatric Society*, 57, 594–603.

Smith, G.H. and Engel, R. (1968) Influence of a female model on perceived characteristics of an automobile. *Proceedings of the 76th Annual Convention of the American Psychological Association*, 3, 681–2.

Smith, J.D., Schneider, B.H., Smith, P.K. and Ananiadou, K. (2004) The effectiveness of whole-school antibullying programs. *School Psychology Review*, 33, 547–60.

Smith, J.P. and Cage, B.N. (2000) The effects of chess instruction on the mathematics achievement of southern, rural, black secondary students. *Research in Schools*, 7, 19–26.

Smith, L. (1996) *Critical Readings on Piaget*. London: Routledge.

Smith, L., Dockerell, J. and Tomlinson, P. (1997) *Piaget, Vygotsky and Beyond*. London: Routledge.

Smith, P. and Lloyd, B. (1978) Maternal behaviour and perceived sex of infant: revisited. *Child Development*, 4, 1263–5.

Smith, P.B., Bond, M.H. and Kagitcibasi, C. (2006) *Understanding Social Psychology across Cultures*. London: Sage.

Smith, S.M. (1979) Remembering in and out of context. *Journal of Experimental Psychology: Human Learning and Memory*, 5, 460–71.

Smith, S.M. (1988) Environmental context-dependent memory. In G.M. Davies and D.M. Thomson (eds) *Memory in Context, Context in Memory*. Chichester: Wiley.

Smith, S.M. (1995) Mood is a component of mental context: Comment on Eich (1995). *Journal of Experimental Psychology: General*, 124(3), 309–10.

Smith, S.M. and Vela, E. (2001) Environmental context-dependent memory: A review and meta-analysis. *Psychonomic Bulletin and Review*, 8(2), 203–20.

Smith, T.W., Baldwin, M. and Christensen, A.J. (1990) Interpersonal influence as active coping: Effects of task difficulty on cardiovascular reactivity. *Psychophysiology*, 27, 429–37.

Smith-Jackson, T.L. and Klein, K.W. (2009) Open-plan offices: Task performance and mental workload. *Journal of Environmental Psychology*, 29, 279–89.

Smits, I.A.M., Dolan, C.V., Vorst, H.C.M., Wicherts, J.M. and Timmerman, M.E. (2011) Cohort differences in Big Five personality factors over a period of 25 years. *Journal of Personality and Social Psychology*, 100, 1124–38.

Smucny, J., Cornier, M-A., Eichman, L.C., Thomas, E.A., Bechtell, J.L. and Tregellas, J.R. (2012) Brain structure predicts risk for obesity. *Appetite*, 59, 859–65.

Smyser, C D. and Neil, J.J. (2015, March) Use of resting-state functional MRI to study brain development and injury in neonates. In *Seminars in Perinatology* (Vol. 39, No. 2, pp. 130–40) WB Saunders.

Smyth, J.M. (1998) Written emotional expression: Effect sizes, outcome types, and moderating variables. *Journal of Consulting and Clinical Psychology*, 66(1), 174–84.

Snarey, J. (1985) The cross-cultural universality of social-moral development: A critical review of Kohlbergian research. *Psychological Bulletin*, 97, 202–32.

Snowden, J.S., Austin, N.A., Sembi, S. and Thompson, J.C. (2008) Emotion recognition in Huntington's disease and frontotemporal dementia. *Neuropsychologia*, 46, 2638–49.

Snyder, H.R. (2013) Major depressive disorder is associated with broad impairments on neuropsychological measures of executive function: A meta-analysis and review. *Psychological Bulletin*, 139, 81–132.

Snyder, J.S. and Cameron, H.A. (2012) Could adult hippocampal neurogenesis be relevant for human behavior? *Behavioural Brain Research*, 227(2), 384–90.

Snyder, J.S., Ferrante, S.C. and Cameron, H.A. (2012) Late maturation of adult-born neurons in the temporal dentate gyrus. *PLoS ONE*, 7(11), e48757.

Snyder, J.S., Glover, L.R., Sanzone, K.M., Kamhi, J.F. and Cameron, H.A. (2009) The effects of exercise and stress on the survival and maturation of adult generated granule cells. *Hippocampus*, 19(10), 898–906.

Snyder, K.M., Ashitaka, Y., Shimada, H., Ulrich, J.E. and Logan, G.D. (2013) What skilled typists don't know about the QWERTY keyboard. *Attention, Perception and Psychophysics*, 76, 162–71.

Snyder, L.H., Batista, A.P. and Andersen, R.A. (1997) Coding of intention in the posterior parietal cortex. *Nature*, 386, 167–70.

Snyder, M. (1984) When belief creates reality. In L. Berkowitz (ed.) *Advances in Experimental Social Psychology*, Vol. 18. New York: Academic Press, pp. 248–306.

Snyder, S.H. (1974) *Madness and the Brain*. New York: McGraw-Hill.

Sobel, N., Khan, R.M., Saltman, A., Sullivan, E.V. and Gabrieli, J.D.E. (1999) The world smells different to each nostril? *Nature*, 402, 35.

Sobesky, W.E. (1983) The effects of situational factors on moral judgments. *Child Development*, 54, 575–84.

Sofer, C., Dotsch, R., Wigboldus, D.H.J. and Todorov, A. (2014) What is typical is good: The influence of face typicality on perceived trustworthiness. *Psychological Science*, 1–9.

Sokejima, S. and Kagamimori, S. (1998) Working hours as a risk for acute myocardial infarction in Japan: Case-control study. *British Medical Journal*, 317, 775–80.

Sokolov, A.A., Kruger, S., Enck, P., Krageloh-Mann, I. and Pavlova, M.A. (2011) Gender affects body language reading. *Frontiers in Psychology*, 2(16), 1–6.

Soldz, S. and Vaillant, G.E. (1999) The Big Five personality traits and the life-course: A 45-year longitudinal study. *Journal of Research in Personality*, 33, 208–32.

Solomon, G.F. (1987) Psychoneuro-immunology: Interactions between central nervous system and immune system. *Journal of Neuroscience Research*, 18, 1–9.

Solomon, S., Greenberg, J. and Pyszczynski, T. (1991) A terror management theory of social behavior: The psychological functions of self-esteem and cultural worldviews. In M. Zanna (ed.) *Advances in Experimental Social Psychology*, Vol. 24. San Diego, CA: Academic Press, pp. 93–159.

Solso, R.L. (1988) *Cognitive Psychology* (2nd edn). Boston, MA: Allyn & Bacon.

Somers, M., Neggers, S.F., Diederen, K.M., Boks, M.P., Kahn, R.S. and Sommer, I.E. (2011) The measurement of language lateralization with functional transcranial Doppler and functional MRI. *Frontiers in Human Neuroscience*, 5, article 31.

Somerville, L.H., Whalen, P.J. and Kelley, W.M. (2010) Human bed nucleus of the stria terminalis indexes hypervigilant threat monitoring. *Biological Psychiatry*, 68, 416–24.

Sommer, I.E.C., Aleman, A., Bouma, A. and Kahn, R.S. (2004) Do women really have more bilateral language representation than men? A meta-analysis of functional imaging studies. *Brain*, 127, 1845–52.

Song, M., Zhou, Y., Li, J., Liu, Y., Tian, L., Yu, C. and Jiang, T. (2008) Brain spontaneous functional connectivity and intelligence. *Neuroimage*, 41, 1168–76.

Sorokowski, P. and Szmajke, A. (2011) The influence of the 'Red Win' effect in sports: A hypothesis of erroneous perception of opponents dressed in red-Preliminary test. *Human Movement*, 12(4), 367–73.

Soto, C.J., John, O.P., Gosling, S.D. and Potter, J. (2011) Age differences in personality traits from 10–65: Big Five domains and facets in a large cross-sectional sample. *Journal of Personality and Social Psychology*, 100, 330–48.

Southgate, V. and Hamilton, A.F. de C. (2008) Unbroken mirrors: challenging a theory of autism. *Trends in Cognitive Sciences*, 12(6), 225–9.

Spalding, K.L., Bergmann, O., Alkass, K., Bernard, S., Salehpour, M., Huttner, H.B., . . . and Possnert, G. (2013) Dynamics of hippocampal neurogenesis in adult humans. *Cell*, 153(6), 1219–27.

Spanos, N.P. (1991) A sociocognitive approach to hypnosis. In S.J. Lynn and J.H. Rhue (eds) *Theories of Hypnosis: Current models and perspectives*. New York: Guilford Press.

Spanos, N.P. (1992) Compliance and reinterpretation in hypnotic responding. *Contemporary Hypnosis*, 9, 7–14.

Sparks, K., Cooper, C., Fried, Y. and Shirom, A. (1997) The effects of hours of work on health: A meta-analysis. *Journal of Occupational and Organizational Psychology*, 70(4), 391–408.

Spaulding, L.S., Mostert, M.P. and Beam, A.P. (2010) Is Brain Gym® an effective educational intervention? *Exceptionality*, 18(1), 18–30.

Spearman, C. (1904) 'General intelligence', Objectively determined and measured. *The American Journal of Psychology*, 15, 201–92.

Spearman, C. (1927) *The Abilities of Man*. London: Macmillan.

Spears, R. and Manstead, A.S.R. (1990) Consensus estimation in social context. *European Review of Social Psychology*, 1, 81–110.

Speedie, L.J., Rothi, L.J. and Heilman, K.M. (1982) Spelling dyslexia: A form of cross-cueing. *Brain and Language*, 15, 340–52.

Speltz, M.L., DeKlyen, M., Calderon, R., Greenberg, M.T. and Fisher, P.A. (1999) Neuropsychological characteristics and test behaviors of boys with early onset conduct problems. *Journal of Abnormal Psychology*, 108(2), 315–25.

Spence, C. and Gallace, A. (2011) Tasting shapes and words. *Food Quality and Preference*, 22(3), 290–5.

Spence, S.H. and Rapee, R.M. (2016) The etiology of social anxiety disorder: an evidence-based model. *Behaviour Research and Therapy*, 86, 50–67.

Spence, S.A. (2008) Playing Devil's advocate: The case against fMRI lie detection. *Legal and Criminological Psychology*, 13, 11–25.

Spence, S.A., Farrow, T.F.D., Herford, A.E., Wilkinson, I.D., Zheng, Y. and Woodruff, P.W.R. (2001) Behavioral and functional anatomical correlates of deception in humans. *NeuroReport*, 12, 2849–53.

Spence, S.A., Kaylor-Hughes, C., Farrow, T.F.D. and Wilkinson, I.D. (2008) Speaking of secrets and lies: The contribution of ventrolateral prefrontal cortex to vocal deception. *Neuroimage*, 40, 1411–18.

Spencer, N.A., McClintock, M.K., Sellergren, S.A., Bullivant, S., Jacob, S. and Mennella, J.A. (2004) Social chemosignals from breastfeeding women increase sexual motivation. *Hormones and Behavior*, 46, 362–70.

Spencer, S.J., Steele, C.M. and Quinn, D.M. (1999) Stereotype threat and women's math performance. *Journal of Experimental Social Psychology*, 35, 4–28.

Sperling, G.A. (1960) The information available in brief visual presentation. *Psychological Monographs*, 74, 498.

Sperry, R.W. (1966) Brain bisection and consciousness. In J. Eccles (ed.) *Brain and Conscious Experience*. New York: Springer-Verlag.

Sperry, R.W., Gazzaniga, M.S. and Bogen, J.E. (1969) Interhemispheric relationships: The neocortical commissures and syndromes of hemisphere disconnection. In P.J. Vinken and G.W. Bruyn (eds) *Handbook of Clinical Neurology*, Vol. 4. Hillsdale, NJ: North-Holland.

Spezio, M.L., Adolphs, R., Hurley, R.S.E. and Piven, J. (2007) Analysis of face gaze in autism using 'Bubbles'. *Neuropsychologia*, 45, 144–51.

Spielman, A. J., Saskin, P. and Thorpy, M. J. (1987) Treatment of chronic insomnia by restriction of time in bed. *Sleep*, 10(1), 45–56.

Spiers, H.J. and Gilbert, S.J. (2015) Solving the detour problem in navigation: a model of prefrontal and hippocampal interactions. *Frontiers in Human Neuroscience*, 9, 125.

Spiers, H.J. and Maguire, E.A. (2007) Neural substrates of driving behaviour. *Neuroimage*, 36, 245–55.

Spies Shapiro, L.A. and Margolin, G. (2014) Growing up wired: social networking sites and adolescent psychosocial development. *Clinical and Child Family Psychology Review*, 17, 1–18.

Spijkerman, M.P.J., Pots, W.T.M. and Bohlmeijer, E.T. (2016) Effectiveness of online mindfulness-based interventions in improving mental health: A review and meta-analysis of randomized controlled trials. *Clinical Psychology Review*, 45, 102–14.

Spirduso, W.W. and MacRae, P.G. (1990) Motor performance and aging. In J.E. Birren and K.W. Schaie (eds) *Handbook of the Psychology of Aging* (3rd edn). San Diego: CA: Academic Press.

Spiro, R.J. (1977) Remembering information from text: The 'state of schema' approach. In R.C. Anderson, R.J. Spiro and W.E. Montague (eds) *Schooling and the Acquisition of Knowledge*. Hillsdale, NJ: Lawrence Erlbaum Associates.

Spiro, R.J. (1980) Accommodative reconstruction in prose recall. *Journal of Verbal Learning and Verbal Behavior*, 19, 84–95.

Spoor, F., Leakey, M.G., Gathgo, P.N., brown, F., H., Anton, S.C., McDougall, I., Kiarie, C., Manthi, F.K. and Leakey, L.N. (2007) Implications of new early *Homo* fossils from Ileret, east of Lake Turkana, Kenya. *Nature*, 448, 688–91.

Sprankle, E.L., End, C.M. and Bretz, M.N. (2012) Sexually degrading music videos and lyrics. *Journal of Media Psychology*, 24, 31–9.

Sprecher, S. (1998) Insiders' perspectives on reasons for attraction to a close other. *Social Psychology Quarterly*, 61, 287–300.

Sprengelmeyer, R., Schroeder, U., Young, A.W. and Epplen, J.T. (2006) Disgust in pre-clinical Huntington's disease: A longitudinal study. *Neuropsychologia*, 44, 518–33.

Sprengelmeyer, R., Young, A.W., Calder, A.J., Karnat, A., Lange, H., Homberg, V., Perrett, D.I. and Rowland, D. (1996) Loss of disgust: perception of faces and emotions in Huntington's disease. *Brain*, 119, 1647–65.

Squire, L.R. (1987) *Memory and Brain*. Oxford: Oxford University Press.

Squire, L.R., Slater, P.C. and Miller, P.L. (1981) Retrograde amnesia following ECT: Long-term follow-up studies. *Archives of General Psychiatry*, 38, 89–95.

Squire, L.R., van der Horst, A.S., McDuff, S.G., Frascino, J.C., Hopkins, R.O. and Mauldin, K.N. (2010) Role of the hippocampus in remembering the past and imagining the future. *Proceedings of the National Academy of Sciences*, 107(44), 19044–8.

Srivastava, S., McGonigal, K.M., Richards, J.M., Butler, E.A. and Gross, J.J. (2006) Optimism in close relationships: How seeing things in a positive light makes them so. *Journal of Personality and Social Psychology*, 91(1), 143–53.

Stager, C.L. and Werker, J.F. (1997) Infants listen for more phonetic detail in speech perception than in word-learning tasks. *Nature*, 388, 381–2.

Stagner, R. (1958) The gullibility of personnel managers. *Personnel Psychology*, 11, 347–52.

Stahl, S.A. and Murray, B.A. (1994) Defining phonological awareness and its relationship to early reading. *Journal of Educational Psychology*, 86(2), 221–34.

Stallard, P., Velleman, R. and Baldwin, S. (1998) Prospective study of post-traumatic stress disorder in children involved in road traffic accidents. *British Medical Journal*, 317, 1619–23.

Stanovich, K.E. (1999) *Who Is Rational? Studies of individual differences in reasoning*. Mahwah, NJ: Lawrence Erlbaum Associates.

Stanton, A.L. and Danoff-Burg, S. (2002) Emotional expression, expressive writing and cancer. In S.J. Lepore and J.M. Smyth (eds) *The writing cure: How expressive writing promotes health and emotional well-being*. Washington, DC: American Psychological Association.

Stanton, A.L. and Snider, P.R. (1993) Coping with breast cancer diagnosis: A prospective study. *Health Psychology*, 12, 16–23.

Stanton, S.J. and Edelstein, R.S. (2009) The physiology of women's power motive: Implicit power motivation is positively associated with estradiol levels in women. *Journal of Research in Personality*, 43, 1109–13.

Stasser, G. and Dietz-Uhler, B. (2001) Collective choice, judgment, and problem solving. In M.A. Hogg and R.S. Tindale (eds) *Blackwell Handbook of Social Psychology: Group processes*. Oxford: Blackwell, pp. 31–55.

Stattin, H. and Magnusson, D. (1990) *Pubertal Maturation in Female Development*. Hillsdale, NJ: Lawrence Erlbaum Associates.

Stavridou, A. and Furnham, A. (1996) The relationship between psychoticism, trait-creativity and the attentional mechanism of cognitive inhibition. *Personality and Individual Differences*, 21(1), 143–53.

Stavrinos, D., Byington, K.W. and Schwebel, D.C. (2011) Distracted walking: Cell phones increase injury risk for college pedestrians. *Journal of Safety Research*, 42, 101–7.

Stavrova, O. and Luhmann, M. (2016) Are conservatives happier than liberals? Not always and not everywhere. *Journal of Research in Personality*, 63, 29–35.

Stavrova, O., Schlosser, T. and Fetchenhauer, D. (2013) Are virtuous people happy all around the world? *Personality and Social Psychology Bulletin*, 39, 927–42.

Steegen, S., Dewitte, L., Tuerlinckx, F. and Vanpaemel, W. (2014) Measuring the crowd within again: a pre-registered replication study. *Frontiers in Psychology*, 5, 786, 1–8.

Steele, C.M. (1997) A threat in the air: How stereotypes shape intellectual ability and performance. *American Psychologist*, 52, 613–29.

Steele, C.M. and Aronson, J. (1995) Stereotype vulnerability and the intellectual test performance of African-Americans. *Journal of Personality and Social Psychology*, 69, 797–811.

Steele, C.M., Spencer, S.J. and Aronson, J. (2002) Contending with group image: The psychology of stereotype and social identity threat. In M.P. Zanna (ed.) *Advances in Experimental Social Psychology*, Vol. 34. San Diego, CA: Academic Press, pp. 379–440.

Steele, K.M. (2014) Failure to replicate the Mehta and Zhu (2009) color-priming effect on anagram solution times. *Psychonomic Bulletin and Review*, 21(3), 771–6.

Steele, R.J. and Morris, R.G. (1999) Delay-dependent impairment of a matching-to-place task with chronic and intrahippocampal infusion of the NMDA-antagonist D-AP5. *Hippocampus*, 9, 118–36.

Steen, S.N., Oppliger, R.A. and Brownell, K.D. (1988) Metabolic effects of repeated weight loss and regain in adolescent wrestlers. *Journal of the American Medical Association*, 260, 47–50.

Stefanucci, J.K. and Storbeck, J. (2009) Don't look down: Emotional arousal elevates height perception. *Journal of Experimental Psychology: General*, 138, 131–45.

Stein, D.J. and Nesse, R.M. (2015) Normal and abnormal anxiety in the age of DSM-5 and ICD-11. *Emotion Review*, 7, 22–9.

Stein, J.F. (1991) Visuospatial sense, hemispheric asymmetry and dyslexia. In J.F. Stein (ed.) *Vision and Visual Dyslexia*. London: Macmillan.

Stein, J.F. and Walsh, V. (1997) To see but not to read; the magnocellular theory of dyslexia. *Trends in Neurosciences*, 20(4), 147–52.

Steiner, I.D. (1972) *Group Process and Productivity*. New York: Academic Press.

Steinglass, J. *et al.* (2012) Fear of food as a treatment target: exposure and response prevention for anorexia nervosa in an open series. *International Journal of Eating Disorders*, 45, 615–21.

Steinpreis, R.E., Anders, K.A. and Ritzke, D. (1999) The impact of gender on the review of the curricula vitae of job applicants and tenure candidates. *Sex Roles*, 41, 509–28.

Steinvorth, S., Levine, B. and Corkin, S. (2005) Medial temporal lobe structures are needed to re-experience remote autobiographical memories: Evidence from HM and WR. *Neuropsychologia*, 43, 479–96.

Stelzer, J., Lohmann, G., Mueller, K., Buschmann, T. and Turner, R. (2014) Deficient approaches to human neuroimaging. *Frontiers in Human Neuroscience*, 8, 1–16.

Stepansky, R., Holzinger, B., Schmeiser-Rieder, A., Saletu, B., Kunze, M. and Zeitlhofer, J. (1998) Austrian dream behavior: results of a representative population survey. *Dreaming*, 8, 23–30.

Stephan, W.G. and Stephan, C.W. (2000) An integrated threat theory of prejudice. In S. Oskamp (ed.) *Reducing Prejudice and Discrimination*. Mahwah, NJ: Lawrence Erlbaum Associates, pp. 23–46.

Stephen, I.D., Coetzee, V., Smith, M.L. and Perrett, D.I. (2011) Skin blood perfusion and oxygenation colour affect perceived human health. *PLoS ONE*, 4, e5083, 1–6.

Sterman, M.B. and Clemente, C.D. (1962) Forebrain inhibitory mechanisms: Cortical synchronization induced by basal forebrain stimulation. *Experimental Neurology*, 6, 91–102.

Stern, K. and McClintock, M.K. (1998) Regulation of ovulation by human pheromones. *Nature*, 392, 177–9.

Stern, W. (1914) *The Psychological Methods of Testing Intelligence*. Baltimore, IMD: Warwick & York.

Sternberg, D.A., Ballard, K., Hardy, J.L., Katz, B., Doraiswamy, P. and Scanlon, M. (2013) The largest human cognitive performance dataset reveals insights into the effects of lifestyle factors and aging. *Frontiers in Human Neuroscience*, 7(292), 1–10.

Sternberg, R.J. (1985) *Beyond IQ: A triarchic theory of human intelligence*. Cambridge: Cambridge University Press.

Sternberg, R.J. (1988) *The Triangle of Love*. New York: Basic Books.

Sternberg, R.J. (2001) What is the common thread of creativity? *American Psychologist*, 56, 360–2.

Sternberg, R.J. (2002) Creativity as a decision. *American Psychologist*, 57, 376.

Sternberg, R.J. and Detterman, D.K. (1986) *What Is Intelligence? Contemporary viewpoints on its nature and definition*. Norwood, NJ: Ablex.

Sternberg, R.J. and Grigorenko, E. (1997) *Intelligence, Heredity and Environment*. New York: Cambridge University Press.

Sternberg, R.J. and Lubart, T.I. (1991) An investment theory of creativity and its development. *Human Development*, 32, 1–31.

Sternberg, R.J. and Lubart, T.I. (1995) *Defying the Crowd: Cultivating creativity in a culture of conformity*. New York: Free Press.

Sternberg, R.J. and Wagner, R.K. (1986) *Practical Intelligence: Nature and origins of competence in the everyday world*. New York: Cambridge University Press.

Sternberger, L.G. and Burns, G.L. (1990) Obsessions and compulsions: Psychometric properties of the Padua inventory with an American college population. *Behavior Research and Therapy*, 28, 341–5.

Stevens, J.S. and Hamann, S. (2012) Sex differences in brain activation to emotional stimuli: A meta-analysis of neuroimaging studies. *Neuropsychologia*, 50, 1578–93.

Stevenson, R.J., Miller, L.A. and McGrillen, K. (2013) The lateralization of gustatory function and the flow of information from tongue to cortex. *Neuropsychologia*, 51, 1408–16.

Steward, L. and Lupfer, M. (1987) Touching as teaching: The effect of touch on students' perceptions and performance. *Journal of Applied Social Psychology*, 17, 800–9.

Stewart, A.J. and Ostrove, J.M. (1998) Women's personality in middle age: gender, history and midcourse corrections. *American Psychologist*, 53(11), 1185–94.

Stewart, F., Parkin, A.J. and Hunkin, N.M. (1992) Naming impairments following from herpes simplex encephalitis: category-specific? *The Quarterly Journal of Experimental Psychology*, 44A, 261–84.

Stice, E., Shaw, H. and Marti, C.N. (2006) A meta-analytic review of obesity prevention programs for children and adolescents: the skinny on interventions that work. *Psychological Bulletin*, 132(5), 667–91.

Stich, S.P. (1990) Rationality. In D.N. Osherson and E.E. Smith (eds) *An Invitation to Cognitive Science. Vol. 3: Thinking*. Cambridge, MA: MIT Press.

Stickgold, R. and Walker, M. P. (2007) Sleep-dependent memory consolidation and reconsolidation. *Sleep Medicine*, 8, 331–43.

Stillman, T.F., Maner, J.K. and Baumeister, R.F. (2010) A thin slice of violence: distinguishing violent from nonviolent sex offenders at a glance. *Evolution and Human Behavior*, 31, 298–303.

Stoddard, J.T. (1886) Composite portraiture. *Science*, 8, 89–91.

Stoerig, P. and Cowey, A. (1997) Blindsight in man and monkey. *Brain*, 120, 535–59.

Stoet, G. and Geary, D.C. (2012) Can stereotype threat explain the gender gap in mathematics performance and achievement? *Review of General Psychology*, 16, 93–102.

Stokoe, W.C. (1983) Apes who sign and critics who don't. In J. de Luce and H.T. Wilder (eds) *Language in Primates: Perspectives and Implications*. New York: Springer-Verlag.

Stolarski, M., Zajenkowski, M. and Meisenberg, G. (2013) National intelligence and personality: Their relationships and impact on national economic success. *Intelligence*, 41, 94–101.

Stoner, J.A.F. (1961) A comparison of individual and group decisions including risk. Unpublished Master's thesis, Massachusetts Institute of Technology, Boston.

Stoodley, C.J. (2014) Distinct regions of the cerebellum show gray matter decreases in autism ADHD and developmental dyslexia. *Frontiers in Systems Neuroscience*, 8, 92.

Stoodley, C.J. (2015) The cerebellum and neurodevelopmental disorders. *Cerebellum*, 15, 34–7.

Stoodley, C.J. and Schmahmann, J.D. (2009) Functional topography in the human cerebellum: A meta-analysis of neuroimging studies. *Neuroimage*, 44, 489–501.

Stoodley, C.J. and Stein, J.F. (2013) Cerebellar function in developmental dyslexia. *Cerebellum*, 12, 267–76.

Storandt, M. (2008) Cognitive deficits in the early stages of Alzheimer's disease. *Current Directions in Psychological Science*, 17(3), 198–202.

Storandt, M., Grant, E.A., Miller, J.P. and Morris, J.C. (2006) Longitudinal course and neuropathological outcomes in original vs revised MCI and in preMCI. *Neurology*, 67, 467–73.

Stott, C., Hutchison, P. and Drury, J. (2001) 'Hooligans' abroad? Intergroup dynamics, social identity and participation in collective disorder at the 1998 World Cup finals. *British Journal of Social Psychology*, 40, 359–84.

Stott, C.J. and Adang, O.M.J. (2004) 'Disorderly' conduct: social psychology and the control of football 'hooliganism' at 'Euro2004'. *The Psychologist*, 17, 318–19.

Straaten, I. van, Engels, R.C.M.E., Finkenhauer, C. and Holland, R.W. (2009) Meeting your match: How attractiveness similarity affects approach behaviour in mixed-sex dyads. *Personality and Social Psychology Bulletin,* 35, 685–97.

Strack, F., Stepper, S. and Martin, L.L. (1988) Inhibiting and facilitating conditions of the human smile: A nonobtrusive test of the facial feedback hypothesis. *Journal of Personality and Social Psychology,* 54, 768–77.

Strahan, E.J., Wilson, A.E., Cressman, K.E. and Buote, V.M. (2006) Comparing to perfection: How cultural norms for appearance affect social comparisons and self-image. *Body Image,* 3, 211–27.

Strand, S., Deary, I.J. and Smith, P. (2006) Sex differences in Cognitive Abilities Test scores: A UK national picture. *British Journal of Educational Psychology,* 76, 463–80.

Strange, D. and Hayne, H. (2013) The devil is in the detail: Children's recollection of details about their prior experiences. *Memory,* 21, 431–43.

Strathearn, L. and Kim, S. (2013) Mothers' amygdala response to positive or negative infant affect is modulated by personal relevance. *Frontiers in Neuroscience,* 7, 176.

Strauss, C., Cavanagh, K., Oliver, A. and Pettman, D. (2014) Mindfulness-based interventions for people diagnosed with a current episode of an anxiety or depressive disorder: A meta-analysis of randomized controlled trials. *PLoS ONE,* 9, e96110, 1–13.

Strayer, D.L. and Johnston, W.A. (2001) Driven to distraction: Dual-task studies of simulated driving and conversing on a cellular telephone. *Psychological Science,* 12(6), 462–6.

Strick, M., Holland, R.W. and van Knippenberg, A. (2008) Seductive eyes: Attractiveness and direct gaze increase desire for associated objects. *Cognition,* 106, 1487–96.

Strickland, B.R. (1979) Internal–external expectancies and cardiovascular functioning. In L.C. Perlmutter and R.A. Monty (eds) *Choice and Perceived Control.* Hillsdale, NJ: Lawrence Erlbaum Associates.

Strike, L.T., Couvy-Duchesne, B., Hansell, N.K., Cuellar-Partida, G., Medland, S.F. and Wright, M.J. (2015) Genetics and brain morphology. *Neuropsychological Review,* 25, 63–96.

Stritzke, W.G.K., Lang, A.R. and Patrick, C.J. (1996) Beyond stress and arousal: A reconceptualization of alcohol–emotion relations with reference to psychophysiological methods. *Psychological Bulletin,* 120(3), 376–95.

Strong, G.K., Torgerson, C.J., Torgerson, D. and Hulme, C. (2011) A systematic meta-analytic review of evidence for the effectiveness of the Fast ForWord language intervention programme. *Journal of Child Psychology and Psychiatry,* 52, 224–35.

Stroop, J.R. (1935) Studies of interference in serial verbal reactions. *Journal of Experimental Psychology,* 18, 743–62.

Strupp, H.H. (1993) The Vanderbilt psychotherapy studies: Synopsis. *Journal of Consulting and Clinical Psychology,* 61, 431–3.

Strupp, H.H. and Hadley, S.W. (1979) Specific vs. nonspecific factors in psychotherapy. *Archives of General Psychiatry,* 36, 1125–36.

Stuart, G.W., McAnally, K.I., McKay, A., Johnston, M. and Castles, A. (2006) A test of the magnocellular deficit theory of dyslexia in an adult sample. *Cognitive Neuropsychology,* 23(8), 1215–29.

Studebaker, C.A. and Penrod, S.D. (1997) Pretrial publicity: The media, the law and common sense. *Psychology, Public Policy and Law,* 3(2/3), 428–60.

Studer, B., Pedroni, A. and Rieskamp, J. (2013) Predicting risk-taking behaviour from prefrontal resting-state activity and personality. *PLoS ONE, 8,* e76861.

Stunkard, A.J., Sørenson, T.I., Harris, C., Teasdale, T.W., Chakraborty, R., Schull, W.J. and Schulsinger, F. (1986) An adoption study of human obesity. *New England Journal of Medicine,* 314, 193–8.

Stuss, D.T., Gow, C.A. and Hetherington, C.R. (1992) 'No longer Gage': Frontal lobe dysfunction and emotional changes. *Journal of Consulting and Clinical Psychology,* 60(3), 349–59.

Sugita, Y. (2008) Face perception in monkeys reared with no exposure to faces. *Proceedings of the National Academy of Sciences,* 105, 394–8.

Sugiyama, T., Takei, Y. and Abe, T. (1992) The prevalence of autism at Nagoya, Japan. In H. Naruse and E.M. Ornitz (eds) *Neurobiology of Infantile Autism.* Amsterdam: Excerpta Medica.

Sui, J., Liu, C.H. and Han, S. (2009) Cultural difference in neural mechanisms of self-recognition. *Social Neuroscience,* 4(5), 402–11.

Sullivan, M.J. and Brender, W. (1986) Facial electromyography: A measure of affective processes during sexual arousal. *Psychophysiology,* 23, 182–8.

Sullivan, M.W., Rovee-Collier, C. and Tynes, D.M. (1979) A conditioning analysis of infant long-term memory. *Child Development,* 50, 152–62.

Sullivan, R.M., Taborsky-Barba, S., Mendoza, R., Itano, A., Leon, M., Cotman, C.W., Payne, T.F. and Lott, I. (1991) Olfactory classical conditioning in neonates. *Pediatrics,* 87, 511–18.

Summala, H., Hakkanen, H., Mikkola, T. and Sinkkonen, J. (1999) Task effects on fatigue symptoms in overnight driving. *Ergonomics,* 42, 798–806.

Sun, D., Lee, T.M.C. and Chan, C.C.H. (2015) Unfolding the spatial and temporal neural processing of lying about face familiarity. *Cerebral Cortex,* 25(4), 927–36.

Sun, X., Allison, C., Auyeung, B., Baron-Cohen, S. and Brayne, C. (2013b) A review of healthcare service and education provision of Autism Spectrum Condition in mainland China. *Research in Developmental Disabilities,* 34, 469–79.

Sundstrom, E., Town, J.P. and Rice, R.W. (1994) Office noise, satisfaction and performance. *Environment and Behaviour,* 26, 195–222.

Susilo, T. and Duchaine, B. (2013) Advances in developmental propopagnosia research. *Current Opinion in Neurobiology,* 23, 423–9.

Sutherland, S. (1987) *Breakdown.* London: Weidenfeld & Nicolson.

Sutton, J., Smith, P.K. and Swettenham, J. (1999) Social cognition and bullying: Social inadequacy or skilled manipulation? *British Journal of Developmental Psychology,* 17, 435–50.

Suzdak, P.D., Glowa, J.R., Crawley, J.N., Schwartz, R.D., Skolnick, P. and Paul, S.M. (1986) A selective imidazobenzodiazepine antagonist of ethanol in the rat. *Science,* 234, 1243–7.

Suzuki, L.A. and Valencia, R.R. (1997) Race-ethnicity and measured intelligence. *American Psychologist,* 52(10), 1103–14.

Swaab, D.F. and Hofman, M.A. (1990) An enlarged suprachiasmatic nucleus in homosexual men. *Brain Research,* 537, 141–8.

Swaab, D.F., Bao, A-M. and Lucassen, P.J. (2005) The stress system in the human brain in depression and neurodegeneration. *Ageing Research Review,* 4, 141–94.

Swagerman, S.C., van Bergen, E., Dolan, C., de Geus, E., Koenis, M.M.G., Pol, H.E. and Boomsa, D.I. (2015) Genetic transmission of reading ability. *Brain and Language,* 25, 927–36.

Swain, J.E., Dayton, C.J., Kim, P., Ho, S., Tolman, R. and Volling, B.L. (2014a) The human paternal brain. *Infant Mental Health Journal,* 35, 394–408.

Swain, J.E., Kim, P., Spicer, J., Ho, S., Dayton, C.J., Elmadih, A. and Abel, K.M. (2014b) Brain basis of human parental caregiving in mothers and fathers. *Brain Research,* 1580, 78–101.

Swami, V. and Tovee, M.J. (2005a) Female physical attractiveness in Britain and Malaysia: A cross-cultural study. *Body Image,* 2, 115–28.

Swami, V. and Tovee, M.J. (2005b) Male physical attractiveness in Britain and Malaysia: A cross-cultural study. *Body Image,* 2, 383–93.

Swami, V. et al. (2010) The attractive female body weight and female body dissatisfaction in 26 countries across 10 world regions: Results of the

International Body Project 1. *Personality and Social Psychology Bulletin.* 36, 309–25.

Swami, V., Greven, C. and Furnham, A. (2007) More than just skin deep? A pilot study in integrating physical and non-physical factors in the perception of physical attractiveness. *Personality and Individual Differences*, 42, 563–72.

Swami, V., Jones, J., Einon, D. and Furnham, A. (2009) Men's preferences for women's profile waist-to-hip ratio, breast size, and ethnic group in Britain and South Africa, *British Journal of Psychology*, 100, 313–25.

Swami, V., Miller, R., Furnham, A., Penke, L. and Tovee, M.J. (2008) The influence of men's sexual strategies on perceptions of women's bodily attractiveness, health and fertility. *Personality and Individual Differences*, 44, 98–107.

Swann, W.B. (1987) Identity negotiation: Where two roads meet. *Journal of Personality and Social Psychology*, 53, 1038–51.

Swanson, J.W., McGinty, E., Fazel, S. and Mays, V.M. (2015) Mental illness and reduction of gun violence and suicide: Bringing epidemiological research to policy. *Annals of Epidemiology*, 25, 366–76.

Swanson, L.W. and Petrovich, G.D. (1998) What is the amygdala? *Trends in Neurosciences*, 21(8), 323–31.

Swearer, S.M., Espelage, D.L., Vaillancourt, T. and Hymel, S. (2010) What can be done about school bullying? *Educational Researcher*, 39, 38–47.

Swendsen, J.D. (1998) The helplessness–hopelessness theory and daily mood experience: An idiographic and cross-situational perspective. *Journal of Personality and Social Psychology*, 74(5), 1398–408.

Swettenham, J., Baron-Cohen, S., Charman, T., Cox, A., Baird, G., Drew, A., Rees, L. and Wheelwright, S. (1998) The frequency and distribution of spontaneous attention shifts between social and nonsocial stimuli in autistic, typically developing, and nonautistic developmentally delayed infants. *Journal of Child Psychology and Psychiatry*, 39(5), 747–53.

Swift, S.A., Moore, D.A., Sharek, Z.S. and Gino, F. (2013) Inflated applicants: Attribution errors in performance evaluation by professionals. *PLoS ONE*, 8, e69258.

Swim, J.T., Aikin, K., Hall, W. and Hunter, B.A. (1995) Sexism and racism: Old-fashioned and modern prejudices. *Journal of Personality and Social Psychology*, 68, 199–214.

Swing, E.L., Gentile, D.A., Anderson, C.A. and Walsh, D.A. (2010) Television and video game exposure and the development of attention problems. *Pediatrics*, 126(2), 214–21.

Symanowicz, A. and Furnham, A. (2011) Gender differences in self-estimates of general, mathematical, spatial and verbal intelligence: Four meta-analyses. *Learning and Individual Differences*, 21, 493–504.

Symons, D. (1979) *The Evolution of Human Sexuality.* New York: Oxford University Press.

Szeszko, P.R., Robinson, D.G., Ikuta, T., Peters, B.D., Gallego, J.A., Kane, J. and Malhotra, A.K. (2014) White matter changes associated with antipsychotic treatment in first-episode psychosis. *Neuropsychopharmacology*, 39(6), 1324–31.

Szymusiak, R. and McGinty, D. (1986) Sleep-related neuronal discharge in the basal forebrain of cats. *Brain Research*, 370, 82–92.

T

Tajfel, H. (1981) *Human Groups and Social Categories.* Cambridge: Cambridge University Press.

Tajfel, H. (ed.) (1984) *The Social Dimension: European developments in social psychology.* Cambridge: Cambridge University Press.

Tajfel, H. and Turner, J.C. (1986) The social identity theory of intergroup behaviour. In S.G. Worchel and W. Austin (eds) *Psychology of Intergroup Relations* (2nd edn). Chicago, IL: Nelson-Hall, pp. 7–24.

Tajfel, H., Billig, M., Bundy, R.P. and Flament, C. (1971) Social categorization and intergroup behaviour. *European Journal of Social Psychology*, 1, 149–77.

Takacs, Z.K., Swart, E.K. and Bus, A.G. (2015) Benefits and pitfalls of multi-media and interactive features in technology-enhanced storybooks: A meta-analysis. *Review of Educational Research*, 85, 698–739.

Takahashi, H., Matsuura, M., Yahata, N., Koeda, M., Suhara, T. and Okubo, Y. (2006) Men and women show distinct brain activations during imagery of sexual and emotional infidelity. *Neuroimage*, 32, 1299–307.

Takahashi, M. and Inoue, T. (2009) The effects of humor on memory for non-sensical pictures. *Acta Psychologica*, 132, 80–4.

Takeuchi, H. (2010) Training of working memory impacts structural connectivity. *Journal of Neuroscience*, 30, 3297–303.

Talarico, J.M. and Rubin, D.C. (2003) Confidence, not consistency, characterizes flashbulb memories. *Psychological Science*, 14(5), 455–61.

Tallis, F., Eysenck, M.W. and Matthews, A. (1991) Elevated evidence requirements and worry. *Personality and Individual Differences*, 12, 21–108.

Talmi, D., Grady, C.L., Goshen-Gottstein, Y. and Moscovitch, M. (2005) Neuroimaging the serial position curve. *Psychological Science*, 16(9), 716–23.

Tamnes, C.K., Walhovd, K.B., Dale, A.M., Ostby, Y., Grydeland, H., Richardson, G., Westlye, L.T., Roddey, J.C., Hagler, D.J., Due-Tannssensen, P., Holland, D. and Fjell, A.M. (2013) Brain development and aging: overlapping and unique patterns of change *Neuroimage*, 68, 63–74.

Tan, A., Ma, W., Vira, A., Marwha, D. and Eliot, L. (2016) The human hippocampus is not sexually-dimorphic: Meta-analysis of structural MRI volumes. *Neuroimage*, 124, 350–66.

Tan, L.H., Chan, A.H.D., Kay, P., Khong, P-L., Yip, L.K.C. and Luke, K-K. (2008) Language affects patterns of brain activation associated with perceptual decision. *Proceedings of the National Academy of Science*, 105, 4004–9.

Tanaka, J.W., Wolf, J.M., Klaiman, C., Koenig, K., Cockburn, J., Herlihy, L., Brown, C., Stahl, S., Kaiser, M.D. and Schultz, R.T. (2010) Using computerized games to teach face recognition skills to children with autism spectrum disorder: the Let's Face It! Program. *Journal of Child Psychology and Psychiatry*, 51, 944–52.

Tanaka-Matsumi, J. (1979) Taijin Kyofusho: Diagnostic and cultural issues in Japanese psychiatry. *Culture, Medicine and Psychiatry*, 3, 231–45.

Tanaka-Matsumi, J. and Draguns, J.G. (1997) Culture and psychopathology. In J.W. Berry, P.R. Dasen and T.S. Saraswathi (eds) *Handbook of Cross-cultural Psychology. Vol 2: Basic Processes and Human Development.* Boston, MA: Allyn & Bacon.

Tanda, R., Keshavan, M.S. and Nasrallah, H.A. (2008) Schizophrenia, 'Just the facts': What we know in 2008, Part 2: Epidemiology and etiology. *Schizophrenia Research*, 100, 1–18.

Tanenhaus, M.K. (1988) *Psycholinguistics: An Overview.* Cambridge: Cambridge University Press.

Tang, Y.Y., Lu, Q., Fan, M., Yang, Y. and Posner, M.I. (2012) Mechanisms of white matter changes influenced by meditation. *PNAS*, 109, 10570–4.

Tankus, A. *et al.* (2012) Structured neuronal encoding and decoding of human speech features. *Nature Communications*, 3, 1015.

Tannen, D. (1992) *You Just Don't Understand: Women and Men in Conversation.* London: Virago.

Tartaglia, L.A., Dembski, M., Weng, X., Deng, N.H., Culpepper, J., Devos, R., Richards, G. J., Campfield, L.A., Clark, F.T., Deeds, J., Muir, C., Sanker, S., Moriarty, A., Moore, K.J., Smutko, J.S., Mays, G.G., Woolf, E.A., Monroe, C.A. and Tepper, R.I. (1995) Identification and expression cloning of a leptin receptor, OB-R. *Cell*, 83, 1263–71.

Tassi, P. and Muzet, A. (2000) Sleep inertia. *Sleep Medicine Review*, 4, 341–53.

Tatsumi, I.F., Fushimi, T., Sadato, N., Kawashima, R., Yokoyama, E., Kanno, I. and Senda, M. (1999) Verb generation in Japanese: A multicenter PET activation study. *Neuroimage*, 9, 154–64.

Taubert, M. *et al.* (2010) Dynamic properties of human brain structure. *Journal of Neuroscience*, 30, 11670–7.

Taubert, M., Villringer, A. and Ragert, P. (2012) Learning-related great and white matter changes. *The Neuroscientist*, 18, 320–5.

Tay, L., Morrison, M. and Diener, E. (2014) Living among the affluent: boon or bane? *Psychological Science*, 25, 1235–41.

Taylor, J.S.H., Rastle, K. and Davis, M.H. (2012) Can cognitive models explain brain activation during word and pseudoword reading? A meta-analysis of 36 neuroimaging studies. *Psychological Review*, 139, 766–91.

Taylor, M.J., Batty, M. and Itier, R.J. (2004) The faces of development: A review of early face processing over childhood. *Journal of Cognitive Neuroscience*, 16(8), 1426–42.

Taylor, S.E. (1983) Adjustment to threatening events. *American Psychologist*, 38, 1161–73.

Taylor, S.E. and Brown, J.D. (1988) Illusion and well-being: A social psychological perspective on mental health. *Psychological Bulletin*, 103, 193–210.

Taylor, S.E., Peplau, L.A. and Sears, D.O. (1994) *Social Psychology*. Englewood Cliffs, NJ: Prentice Hall.

Teachman, B.A., Gapinski, K.D., Brownell, K.D., Rawlins, M. and Jeyaram, S. (2003) Demonstrations of implicit anti-fat bias: The impact of providing causal information and evoking sympathy. *Health Psychology*, 22, 68–78.

Tefikow, S., Barth, J., Maichrowitz, S., Beelman, A., Strauss, B. and Rosendahl, J. (2013) Efficacy of hypnosis in adults undergoing surgery or medical procedures: A meta-analysis of randomized controlled trials. *Clinical Psychology Review*, 33, 623–36.

Teicher, M.H. and Samson, J.A. (2013) Childhood maltreatment and psychopathology. *American Journal of Psychiatry*, 170, 1114–33.

Teicher, M.H. *et al.* (2006) Sticks, stones and hurtful words: relative effects of various forms of childhood maltreatment. *American Journal of Psychiatry*, 163, 993–1000.

Telpaz, A. and Yechiam, E. (2014) Contrasting losses and gains increases the predictability of behaviour by frontal EEG asymmetry. *Frontiers in Behavioural Neuroscience*, 8, 149.

Telzer, E.H., Masten, C.L., Berkman, E.T., Lieberman, M.D. and Fuligni, A.J. (2010) Gaining while giving: An fMRI study of the rewards of family assistance among White and Latino youth. *Social Neuroscience*, 5(5–6), 508–18.

ten Brinke, L. and Porter, S. (2012) Cry me a river: Identifying the behavioral consequences of extremely high-stakes interpersonal deception. *Law and Human Behavior*, 36(6), 469.

Ten Brinke, L. and Porter, S. (2012) Cry me a river: Identifying the behavioural consequences of extremely high-stakes interpersonal deception. *Law and Human Behavior*, 36, 469–77.

Teng, E. and Squire, L. (1999) Memory for places learned long ago is intact after hippocampal damage. *Nature*, 400, 475–7.

Tepper, B.J. (2000) Consequences of abusive supervision. *Academy of Management Journal*, 43, 178–90.

Terenius, L. and Wahlström, A. (1975) Morphine-like ligand for opiate receptors in human CSF. *Life Sciences*, 16, 1759–64.

Terracciano, A. *et al.* (2005) National character does not reflect mean personality trait levels in 49 cultures. *Science*, 310, 96–100.

Terrace, H.S., Petitto, L.A., Sanders, R.J. and Bever, T.G. (1979) Can an ape create a sentence? *Science*, 206, 891–902.

Terry, D.J. and Hogg, M.A. (1996) Group norms and the attitude–behavior relationship: A role for group identification. *Personality and Social Psychology Bulletin*, 22, 776–93.

Teti, D.M., Sakin, J.W., Kucera, E., Corns, K.M. and Das Eiden, R. (1996) And baby makes four: Predictors of attachment security among preschool-age firstborns during the transition to siblinghood. *Child Development*, 67, 579–96.

The Observer (2008) *The Observer Drugs Poll 2008*, 16 November.

Theodoridou, A., Rowe, A.C., Penton-Voak, I.S. and Rogers, P.J. (2009) Oxytocin and social perception: Oxytocin increases perceived facial trustworthiness and attractiveness. *Hormones and Behavior*, 56, 128–32.

Thibadeau, R., Just, M.A. and Carpenter, P.A. (1982) A model of the time course and content of reading. *Cognitive Science*, 6, 157–203.

Thibaut, J.W. and Kelley, H.H. (1959) *The Social Psychology of Groups*. New York: Wiley.

Thomas, C. and Baker, C.I. (2013) Teaching an adult brain new tricks. *Neuroimage*, 73, 225–36.

Thomas, D.C. (1999) Cultural diversity and work group effectiveness: an experimental study. *Journal of Cross-Cultural Psychology*, 30, 242–63.

Thomas, K.M. and Duke, M. (2007) Depressed writing: Cognitive distortions in the works of depressed and nondepressed poets and writers. *Psychology of Aesthetics, Creativity and the Arts*, 1(4), 204–18.

Thomas, M., Sing, H., Belenky, G., Holcomb, H., Mayberg, H. and Dannals, R. (2000) Neural basis of alertness and cognitive performance impairments during sleepiness. I. Effects of 24h of sleep deprivation on waking human regional brain activity. *Journal of Sleep Research*, 9, 335–52.

Thomas, N.A., Loetscher, T., Clode, D. and Nicholls, M.E. (2012) Right-wing politicians prefer the emotional left. *PLoS ONE*, 7(5), e36552.

Thompson, L.W., Gallagher-Thompson, D., Futterman, A., Gilewski, M.J. and Peterson, J. (1998) The effects of late-life spousal bereavement over a thirty month interval. In M.P. Lawton and T.A. Salthouse (eds) *Essential Papers in the Psychology of Aging*. New York: New York University Press.

Thompson, P. (1980) Margaret Thatcher: A new illusion. *Perception*, 9(4), 483–4.

Thompson, T. and Schuster, C.R. (1968) *Behavioral Pharmacology*. Englewood Cliffs, NJ: Prentice Hall.

Thorell, L.B. *et al.* (2009) Training and transfer effect of executive functions in preschool children. *Developmental Science*, 12, 106–13.

Thornberry, T.P., Knight, K.E. and Lovegrove, P.J. (2012) Does maltreatment beget maltreatment? A systematic review of the intergenerational literature. *Trauma, Violence, and Abuse*, 13(3), 135–52.

Thorndike, E.L. (1905) *The Elements of Psychology*. New York: Seiler.

Thornton, B., Faires, A., Robbins, M. and Rollins, E. (2014) The mere presence of a cell phone may be distracting. *Social Psychology*, 45, 479–88.

Thorpe, S.K., Holder, R.L. and Crompton, R.H. (2007) Origin of human bipedalism as an adaptation for locomotion on flexible branches. *Science*, 316, 1328–31.

Thrasher, S.M., Dalgleish, T. and Yule, W. (1994) Information processing in posttraumatic stress disorder. *Behaviour Research and Therapy*, 32, 247–54.

Thurman, D.J. (2016) The epidemiology of traumatic brain injury in children and youths: A review of research since 1990. *Journal of Child Neurology*, 31, 20–7.

Thurstone, L.L. (1938) *Primary Mental Abilities*. Chicago: IL: University of Chicago Press.

Tiainen, A.-M.K., Mannisto, S., Lahti, M., Blomstedt, P.A., Lahti, J., Perala, M-M., Raikkonen, K., Kajantie, E. and Eriksson, J.G. (2013) Personality and dietary intake – findings in the Helsinki Birth Cohort Study. *PLoS ONE*, 8, e68284.

Tibbetts, Y., Harackiewicz, J.M., Canning, E.A., Boston, J.S., Priniski, S.J. and Hyde, J.S. (2016) Affirming independence: Exploring mechanisms underlying a values affirmation intervention for first-generation students. *Journal of Personality and Social Psychology*, 110(5), 635.

Tice, D.M. and Baumeister, R.F. (1997) Longitudinal study of procrastination, performance, stress and health: The costs and benefits of dawdling. *Psychological Science*, 8(6), 454–8.

Tienari, P., Sorri, A., Lahti, I., Naarala, M., Wahlberg, K-E., Moring, J., Pohjola, J. and Wynne, L.C. (1987) Genetic and psychosocial factors in schizophrenia: The Finnish adoptive family study. *Schizophrenia Bulletin*, 13, 476–83.

Tiggemann, M. (2003) Media exposure, body dissatisfaction and disordered eating: Television and magazines are not the same! *European Eating Disorders Review*, 11, 418–30.

Tikoo, M. (1996) An explanatory study of differences in developmental concerns of middle-aged men and women in India. *Psychological Reports*, 78(3), 883–7.

Tobin, S.A. (1991) A comparison of psychoanalytic self-psychology and Carl Rogers's person-centered therapy. *Journal of Humanistic Psychology*, 31, 9–33.

Todorov, A. (2012) The role of the amygdala in face perception and evaluation. *Motivation and Emotion*, 36, 16–26.

Todorov, A., Mende-Siedlecki, P. and Dotsch, R. (2013) Social judgements from face. *Current Opinion in Neurobiology*, 23, 373–80.

Tolman, E.C., Ritchie, B.F. and Kalish, D. (1946) Studies in spatial learning: I. Orientation and the shortcut. *Journal of Experimental Psychology*, 36, 13–24.

Tomcho, T.J. and Foels, R. (2012) Meta-analysis of group learning activities: Empirically based teaching recommendations. *Teaching of Psychology*, 39(3), 159–69.

Tomoda, A., Polcari, A., Andersen, C.M. and Teicher, M.H. (2012) Reduced visual cortex gray matter volume and thickness in young adults who witnessed domestic violence in childhood. *Neuroimage*, 54, e52528.

Tong, S.T., Van Der Heide, B. and Langwell, L. (2008) Too much of a good thing? The relationship between number of friends and interpersonal impressions on Facebook. *Journal of Computer-Mediated Communication*, 13, 531–49.

Tooby, J. and Cosmides, L. (1989) Evolutionary psychology and the generation of culture. Part I: Theoretical considerations. *Ethology and Sociobiology*, 10, 39–49.

Tooby, J. and Cosmides, L. (1990) On the universality of human nature and the uniqueness of the individual: The role of genetics and adaptation. *Journal of Personality*, 58, 17–67.

Tooby, J. and DeVore, I. (1987) The reconstruction of hominid behavioural evolution through strategic modelling. In G.W. Kinzey (ed.) *The Evolution of Human Behaviour: Primate Models*. New York: SUNY Press.

Tootell, R.B., Reppas, J.B., Dale, A.M. and Look, R.B. (1995) Visual motion aftereffect in human cortical area MT revealed by functional magnetic resonance imaging. *Nature*, 375, 139–41.

Toplak, M.E., Connors, L., Shuster, J., Knezevic, B. and Parks, S. (2008) Review of cognitive, cognitive-behavioral, and neural-based interventions for Attention-Deficit/Hyperactivity Disorder. *Clinical Psychology Review*, 28, 801–23.

Torgerson, S. (1983) Genetic factors in anxiety disorders. *Archives of General Psychiatry*, 40, 1085–9.

Torppa, M., Lyytinen, P., Erskine, J., Eklund, K. and Lyytinen, H. (2010) Language development, literacy skills, and predictive connections to reading in Finnish children with and without familial risk for dyslexia. *Journal of Learning Disabilities*, 43, 308–21.

Torrance, E.P. (1975) Creativity research in education: Still alive. In I.A. Taylor and J.W. Getzels (eds) *Perspectives in Creativity*. Chicago, IL: Aldine.

Torrey, E.F., Webster, M., Knable, M., Johnston, N. and Yolken, R.H. (2000) Foundation brain collection and Neuropathology Consortium. *Schizophrenia Research*, 44, 151–5.

Tottenham, N., Hare, T.A., Millner, A., Gilhooly, T., Zevin, J.D. and Casey, B.J. (2011) Elevated amygdala response to faces following early deprivation. *Development Science*, 14, 190–204.

Tourangeau, R. and Ellsworth, P.C. (1979) The role of facial response in the experience of emotion. *Journal of Personality and Social Psychology*, 37, 1519–31.

Tourney, G. (1980) Hormones and homosexuality. In J. Marmor (ed.) *Homosexual Behavior*. New York: Basic Books.

Tovee, M.J. and Cornelissen, P.L. (2001) Female and male perceptions of female physical attractiveness in front-view and profile. *British Journal of Psychology*, 92, 391–402.

Tracy, J.L. (2007) The psychological structure of pride: A tale of two facets. *Journal of Personality and Social Psychology*, 92, 506–25.

Tracy, J.L. (2014) An evolutionary approach to understanding distinct emotions. *Emotion Review*, 6, 308–12.

Tracy, J.L. and Robins, R.W. (2007) Emerging insights into the nature and function of pride. *Current Directions in Psychological Science*, 16(3), 147–50.

Trafimow, D., Triandis, H.C. and Goto, S.G. (1991) Some tests of the distinction between the private self and the collective self. *Journal of Personality and Social Psychology*, 60, 649–55.

Tramo, M.J. (2001) Music of the hemispheres. *Science*, 291, 54–6.

Tranel, D., Bechara, A. and Denburg, N.L. (2002) Asymmetric functional roles of right and left ventromedial prefrontal cortices in social conduct, decision-making, and emotional processing. *Cortex*, 38, 589–612.

Trapold, M.A. and Spence, K.W. (1960) Performance changes in eyelid conditioning as related to the motivational and reinforcing properties of the UCS. *Journal of Experimental Psychology*, 59, 212.

Treffinger, D.J., Feldhusen, J.F. and Isaksen, S.G. (1990) Organization and structure of productive thinking. *Creative Learning Today*, 4(2), 6–8.

Treisman, A.M. (1960) Contextual cues in selective listening. *The Quarterly Journal of Experimental Psychology*, 12, 242–8.

Treisman, A.M. (1964) Verbal cues, language, and meaning in selective attention. *American Journal of Psychology*, 77, 206–19.

Triandis, H.C. (1989) The self and social behavior in differing cultural contexts. *Psychological Review*, 96, 506–20.

Triandis, H.C., Leung, K., Villareal, M.J. and Clack, F.L. (1985) Allocentric versus idiocentric tendencies: Convergent and discriminant validation. *Journal of Research in Personality*, 19, 395–415.

Trimble, M. (2013) Laughing and crying. *Epilepsy & Behavior*, 28(2), 316.

Triplett, N. (1897) The dynamogenic factors in pacemaking and competition. *American Journal of Psychology*, 9, 507–33.

Trivers, R L. (1972) Parental investment and sexual selection. In B. Campbell (ed.) *Sexual Selection and the Descent of Man*. Chicago, IL: Aldine.

Trivers, R.L. (1971) The biology of reciprocal altruism. *Quarterly Review of Biology*, 46, 35–57.

Troiano, R.P. and Flegal, K.M. (1998) Overweight children and adolescents: Description, epidemiology and demographics. *Pediatrics*, 101, 497–504.

Tronick, E., Als, H., Adamson, L., Wise, S. and Brazelton, T.B. (1978) The infant's response to entrapment between contradictory messages in face-to-face interaction. *Journal of the American Academy of Child Psychiatry*, 17, 1–13.

Trope, Y. (1986) Self-enhancement and self-assessment in achievement behavior. In R. Sorrentino and E.T. Higgins (eds) *Handbook of Motivation and Cognition*, Vol. 2. New York: Guilford Press, pp. 350–78.

Trope, Y. and Liberman, Y. (2003) Temporal construal. *Psychology Review*, 110, 403–21.

Trott, C.T., Friedman, D., Ritter, W. and Fabiani, M. (1997) Item and source memory: Differential age effects revealed by event-related potentials. *NeuroReport*, 8, 3373–8.

Truax, C.B. (1966) Reinforcement and nonreinforcement in Rogerian psychotherapy. *Journal of Abnormal Psychology*, 71, 1–9.

Tryon, R. (1940) Genetic differences in maze-learning ability in rats. *Yearbook of the National Society for the Study of Education*, 39, 111–19.

Trzaskowski, M., Yang, J., Visscher, P.M. and Plomin, R. (2013) DNA evidence for strong genetic stability and increasing heritability of intelligence from age 7 to 12. *Molecular Psychiatry*, 1–5.

Tsaousis, I. (2010) Circadian preferences and personality traits: a meta-analysis. *European Journal of Personality*, 24, 356–73.

Tseng, W-S., Asai, M., Jiequi, L., Wibulswasd, P., Suryani, L.K., Wen, L-K., Brennan, J. and Hieby, E. (1990) Multicultural study of minor psychiatric disorders in Asia: Symptom manifestations. *International Journal of Social Psychiatry*, 36, 252–64.

Tseng, W-S., Asai, M., Kitanishi, K., McLaughlin, D. and Kyomen, H. (1992) Diagnostic patterns of social phobia: Comparison in Tokyo and Hawaii. *Journal of Nervous and Mental Diseases*, 180, 380–5.

Tseng, W-S., Xu, N., Ebata, K., Hsu, J. and Cui, Y. (1986) Diagnostic pattern of neurosis among China, Japan and America. *American Journal of Psychiatry*, 143, 1010–14.

Tskhay, K.O. and Rule, N.O. (2013) Accuracy in categorising perceptually ambiguous groups: A review and meta-analysis. *Personality and Social Psychology Review*, 17, 72–86.

Tsukiura, T. and Cabeza, R. (2008) Orbitofrontal and hippocampal contributions to memory for face-name associations: The rewarding power of a smile. *Neuropsychologia*, 46, 2310–19.

Tsvetanov, K.A., Henson, R.N.A., Tyler, L.L., Davis, S.W., Shafto, M.A., Taylor, J.R., Williams, N., cam-CAN and Rowe, J.B. (2015) The effect of aging on fMRI: Correction for the confounding effects of vascular reactivity evaluated by doing fMRI and MEG in 335 adults. *Human Brain Mapping*, 36, 2248–69.

Ttofi, M.M., Farrington, D.P. and Baldry, A.C. (2008) *Effectiveness of programmes to reduce school bullying*. Stockholm: Swedish Council for Crime Prevention, Information and Publications.

Ttofi, M.M., Farrington, D.P., Lösel, F. and Loeber, R. (2011) The predictive efficiency of school bullying versus later offending: A systematic/meta analytic review of longitudinal studies. *Criminal Behaviour and Mental Health*, 21(2), 80–9.

Tu, L., Wang, J., Abutalebi, J., Jiang, B., Pan, X., Li, M. *et al.* (2015) Language exposure induced neuroplasticity in the bilingual brain: A follow-up fMRI study. *Cortex*, 64, 8–19.

Tucker-Drob, E.M., Briley, D.A. and Harden, K.P. (2013) Genetic and environmental influences on cognition across development and context. *Current Directions in Psychological Science*, 22, 349–55.

Tucker-Drob, E.M., Rhemtulla, M., Harden, K.P., Turkheimer, E. and Fask, D. (2011) Emergence of a gene x socioeconomic status interaction in infant mental ability between 10 months and 2 years. *Psychological Science*, 22, 125–33.

Tugade, M.M. and Fredrickson, B.L. (2004) Resilient individuals use positive emotions to bounce back from negative emotional experiences. *Journal of Personality and Social Psychology*, 86(2), 320–33.

Tullett, A.M., Wildschut, T., Sedikides, C. and Inzlicht, M. (2015) Right-frontal cortical asymmetry predicts increased proneness to nostalgia. *Psychophysiology*, 52, 990–6.

Tulving, E. (1972) Episodic and semantic memory. In E. Tulving and W. Donaldson (eds) *Organization of Memory*. New York: Academic Press.

Tulving, E. (1983) *Elements of Episodic Memory*. Oxford: Oxford University Press.

Tulving, E. (1984) Precis of 'Elements of Episodic Memory'. *The Behavioral and Brain Sciences*, 7, 223–68.

Tulving, E. and Arbuckle, T.Y. (1963) Sources of intratrial interference in immediate recall of paired associates. *Journal of Verbal Learning and Verbal Behaviour*, 1, 321–34.

Tulving, E., Kapur, S., Markowitsch, H.J., Craik, F.I. and Houle, S. (1994) Hemispheric encoding/retrieval asymmetry in episodic memory: positron emission tomography findings. *Proceedings of the National Academy of Sciences*, 91, 2016–20.

Tunbridge, E.M., Harrison, P.J. and Weinberger, D.R. (2006) Catechol-O-methyltransferase, cognition, and psychosis: Val158Met and beyond. *Biological Psychiatry*, 60, 141–51.

Tupes, E.C. and Christal, R.E. (1961) Recurrent personality factors based on trait ratings. *USAF ASD Technical Report*, 61–97.

Turiel, E. (1998) The development of morality. In N. Eisenberg (ed.) *Handbook of Child Psychology, Vol. 3: Social, emotional and personality development*. New York: Wiley.

Turner, J.C. (1991) *Social Influence*. Milton Keynes: Open University Press.

Turner, J.C., Hogg, M.A., Oakes, P.J., Reicher, S.D. and Wetherell, M.S. (1987) *Rediscovering the Social Group: A self-categorization theory*. Oxford: Blackwell.

Turner, J.C., Wetherell, M.S. and Hogg, M.A. (1989) Referent informational influence and group polarization. *British Journal of Social Psychology*, 28, 135–47.

Turner, J.R., Caroll, D. and Courtney, H. (1983) Cardiac and metabolic responses to 'Space Invaders': An instance of metabolically exaggerated cardiac adjustment? *Psychophysiology*, 20, 544–9.

Turner, P.J., Gervai, J. and Hinde, R.A. (1993) Gender-typing in young children: Preferences, behaviour and cultural differences. *British Journal of Developmental Psychology*, 11, 323–41.

Turriziani, P., Smirni, D., Zappalà, G., Mangano, G.R., Oliveri, M. and Cipolotti, L. (2012) Enhancing memory performance with rTMS in healthy subjects and individuals with Mild Cognitive Impairment: the role of the right dorsolateral prefrontal cortex. *Frontiers in Human Neuroscience*, 6, 62.

Tuvblad, C., Narusyte, J., Grann, M. *et al.* (2011) The genetic and environmental etiology of antisocial behavior from childhood to emerging adolescence. *Behavioural Genetics*, 41, 62–40.

Tversky, A. and Kahneman, D. (1974) Judgment under uncertainty: Heuristics and biases. *Science*, 185, 1124–31.

Tversky, A. and Kahneman, D. (1982) Judgment under uncertainty: Heuristics and biases. In D. Kahneman, P. Slovic and A. Tversky (eds) *Judgment under Uncertainty*. New York: Cambridge University Press.

Tversky, A. and Kahneman, D. (1983) Extensional versus intuitive reasoning: Conjunction fallacy in probability judgement. *Psychological Review*, 90, 293–315.

Twenge, J.M., Konrath, S. and Foster, J.D. (2008) Further evidence of an increase in narcissism among college students. *Journal of Personality*, 76, 919–28.

Tye-Murray, N., Spencer, L. and Woodworth, G.G. (1995) Acquisition of speech by children who have prolonged cochlear implant experience. *Journal of Speech and Hearing Research*, 38, 327–37.

Tyler, T.R. and Smith, H.J. (1998) Social justice and social movements. In D.T. Gilbert, S.T. Fiske and G. Lindzey (eds) *The Handbook of Social Psychology* (4th edn), Vol. 2. New York: McGraw-Hill, pp. 595–632.

Tzeng, O.J.L. (1973) Positive recency effects in delayed free recall. *Journal of Verbal Learning and Verbal Behaviour*, 12, 436–9.

Uchida, Y. and Kitayama, S. (2009) Happiness and unhappiness in east and west. *Emotion*, 9, 441–56.

Uddin, L.Q. *et al.* (2013) Salience network-based classification and prediction of symptom severity in children with autism. *JAMA Psychiatry*, 70, 869–79.

Udolf, R. (1983) *Forensic Hypnosis: Psychological and legal aspects.* Lexington, MA: Lexington Books.

Ueda, R., Ashida, H., Yanagisawa, K. and Abe, N. (2016) The neural basis of individual differences in mate poaching. *Social Neuroscience*, 1–9.

Ueno, Y. (1993) Cross-cultural study of odor perception in Sherpa and Japanese people. *Chemical Senses*, 18, 352–3.

Uher, R., Brammer, M., Murphy, T., Campbell, I., Ng, V. Williams, S. *et al.* (2003) Recovery and chronicity in anorexia nervosa: brain activity associated with differential outcomes. *Biological Psychiatry*, 54, 934–42.

Ullian, E.M., Sapperstein, S.K., Christopherson, K.S. and Barres, B.A. (2001) Control of synapse number by glia. *Science*, 291, 657–60.

Ullman, M.T. and Pierpont, E.I. (2005) Specific language impairment is not specific to language: The procedural deficit hypothesis. *Cortex*, 41(3), 399–433.

Ullman, S.E. and Knight, R.A. (1993) The efficacy of women's resistance strategies in rape situations. *Psychology of Women Quarterly*, 17(1), 23–38.

Ulusahin, A., Basoglu, M. and Paykel, E.S. (1994) A cross-cultural comparative study of depressive symptoms in British and Turkish clinical samples. *Social Psychiatry and Psychiatric Epidemiology*, 29, 31–9.

Umilta, C., Simion, F. and Valenza, E. (1996) Newborns' preference for faces. *European Psychologist*, 1(3), 200–5.

Ungerleider, L.G. and Mishkin, M. (1982) Two cortical visual systems. In D.J. Ingle, M.A. Goodale and R.J.W. Mansfield (eds) *Analysis of Visual Behavior*. Cambridge, MA: MIT Press.

Unnever, J.D. and Cornell, D.G. (2003) The culture of bullying in middle school. *Journal of School Violence*, 2, 5–27.

Unsworth, N., Redick, T.S., McMillan, B.D., Hambrick, D.Z., Kane, M.J. and Engle, R.W. (2015) Is playing video games related to cognitive abilities? *Psychological Science*, 26(6), 75974.

Uotinen, V. (1998) Age identification: A comparison between Finnish and North-American cultures. *International Journal of Aging and Human Development*, 46(2), 109–25.

Ursu, S. and Carter, C.S. (2005) Outcome representations, counterfactual comparisons and the human orbitofrontal cortex: Implications for neuroimaging studies of decision-making. *Cognitive Brain Research*, 23, 51–60.

US Bureau of Labor Statistics (1998) *National census of fatal occupational injuries, 1997 (USDL 98–336)*. Washington, DC: Department of Labor.

Uskul, A.K., Kitayama, S. and Nisbett, R.E. (2008) Ecocultural basis of cognition: farmers and fishermen are more holistic than herders. *Proceedings of the National Academy of Sciences in the USA*, 105, 8552–6.

Uttal, D.H., Meadow, N.G., Tipton, E., Hand, L.L., Alden, A.R., Warren, C. and Newcombe, N.S. (2013) The malleability of spatial skills: A meta-analysis of training studies. *Psychological Bulletin*, 139(2), 352–402.

Utter, A.A. and Basso, M.A. (2008) The basal ganglia: An overview of circuits and function. *Neuroscience and Biobehavioural Reviews*, 32, 333–42.

Vaananen, A., Buunk, B.P., Kivimaki, M., Pentti, J. and Vahtera, J. (2005) When it is better to give than to receive: Long-term health effects of perceived reciprocity in support exchange. *Journal of Personality and Social Psychology*, 89(2), 176–93.

Vaillancourt, T., McDougall, P. and Hymel, S. (2008) Bullying: Are researchers and children/youth talking about the same thing? *International Journal of Behavioral Development*, 32, 486–95.

Valenza, E., Simion, F., Cassia, V.M. and Umilta, C. (1996) Face preference at birth. *Journal of Experimental Psychology: Human Perception and Performance*, 27(4), 892–903.

Valins, S. and Nisbett, R.E. (1972) Attribution processes in the development and treatment of emotional disorders. In E.E. Jones, D.E. Kanouse, H.H. Kelley, R.E. Nisbett, S. Valins and B. Weiner (eds) *Attribution: Perceiving the causes of behavior*. Morristown, NJ: General Learning Press, pp. 137–50.

Vallar, G. (1998) Spatial hemineglect in humans. *Trends in Cognitive Sciences*, 2(3), 87–97.

van Ballegooijen, W., Cuijpers, P., van Straten, A., Karyotaki, E., Andersson, G., Smit, J.H. and Riper, H. (2014) Adherence to internet-based and face-to-face cognitive behavioural therapy for depression: a meta-analysis. *PLoS ONE*, 9, e100674.

Van Beek, Y., Hopkins, B. and Joeksma, J.B. (1994) Development of communicative behaviours in preterm infants: The effect of birthweight status and gestational age. *Infant Behavior and Development*, 17, 107–18.

Van Bergen, E., de Jong, P.F., Plakas, A., Maassen, B. and van der Leij, A. (2012) Child and parental literacy levels within families with a history of dyslexia. *Journal of Child Psychology and Psychiatry*, 53, 28–36.

Van Bergen, E., de Jong, P.F., Regtvoort, A., Oort, F., van Otterloo, S. and van der Leij, A. (2011) Dutch children at family risk of dyslexia: Precursors, reading development, and parental effects. *Dyslexia*, 17, 2–18.

van Bergen, E., van Zuijen, T., Bishop, D. and de Jong, P.F. (2016) Why are home literacy environment and children's reading skills associated? *Reading Research Quarterly*, 52, 147–60.

Van Bockstaele, B., Verschuere, B., Moens, T., Suchotski, K., Debey, E. and Spruyt, A. (2012) Learning to lie: Effects of practice on the cognitive cost of lying. *Frontiers in Psychology*, 3, 1–7.

Van den Bosch, I., Dalenberg, J.R., Renken, R., van Langeveld, A.W.B, Smeets, P.A.M, Griffioen-Roose, S., . . . and Boesveldt, S. (2014) To like or not to like: neural substrates of subjective flavor preferences. *Behavioural brain research*, 269, 128–37.

Van den Eijnden, R.J.J.M., Meerkerk, G-J., Vermulst, A.A., Spijkerman, R. and Engels, R.C.M.E. (2008) Online communication, compulsive internet use, and psychosocial well-being among adolescents: A longitudinal study. *Developmental Psychology*, 44(3), 655–65.

van den Heuvel, M.P., Stam, C.J., Kahn, R.S. and Pol, H.E.H. (2009) Efficiency of functional brain networks and intellectual performance. *Journal of Neuroscience*, 29(23), 7619–24.

Van der Laan, L.N., de Ridder, D.T.D., Viergever, M.A. and Smeets, P.A.M. (2011) The first taste is always with the eyes: A meta-analysis on the neural correlates of pressing visual food cues. *Neuroimage*, 55, 296–303.

van der Lely, H.K. and Pinker, S. (2014) The biological basis of language: Insight from developmental grammatical impairments. *Trends in Cognitive Sciences*, 18(11), 586–95.

Van der Lely, H.K.J. (2005) Domain-specific cognitive systems: insight from Grammatical-SLI. *TICS*, 9, 53–9.

Van der Lely, H.K.J. and Marshall, C.R. (2010) Assessing component language deficits in the early detection of reading difficulty risk. *Journal of Learning Disability*, 43, 357–68.

Van der Lely, H.K.J. and Pinker, S. (2014) The biological basis of language: insight from developmental grammatical impairments. TICS, 18, 586–95.

Van der Sluis, S., Willemsen, G., de Geus, E.J.C., Boomsma, D.I. and Posthuma, D. (2008) Gene-environment interaction in adults' IQ scores. *Behavior Genetics*, 38, 348–60.

Van der Zwaag, M.D., Janssen, J.H., Nass, C., Westerink, J.H.D.M., Chowdhury, S. and Ward, D de. (2013) Using music to change mood while driving. *Ergonomics*, 56, 1504–14.

van Dijk, T.A. (1987) *Communicating Racism: ethnic prejudice in thought and talk.* Newbury Park, CA: Sage.

Van Drunen, P. (1995) Professional psychology in The Netherlands. In A. Schorr and S. Saari (eds) *Psychology in Europe*. Göttingen: Hogrefe & Huber.

Van Goozen, S.H.M., Cohen-Kettenis, P.T., Gooren, L.J.G., Frijda, N.A. and Van De Poll, N.E. (1995) Gender differences in behaviour: Activating effects of cross-sex hormones. *Psychoneuroendocrinology*, 20, 343–63.

Van Herk, H., Poortinga, Y.H. and Verhallen, T.M.M. (2005) Response styles in rating scales: evidence of method bias in data from six EU countries. *Journal of Cross-Cultural Psychology*, 35(3), 346–60.

Van Heugten, C., Gregorio, G.W. and Wade, D. (2012) Evidence-based cognitive rehabilitation after acquired brain injury: A systematic review of content of treatment. *Neuropsychological Rehabilitation*, 22, 653–73.

van Heugten, C., Wolters Gregório, G. and Wade, D. (2012) Evidence-based cognitive rehabilitation after acquired brain injury: a systematic review of content of treatment. *Neuropsychological Rehabilitation*, 22(5), 653–73.

van Knippenberg, B. and van Knippenberg, D. (2003) Leadership, identity, and influence: Relational concerns in the use of influence tactics. In D. van Knippenberg and M.A. Hogg (eds) *Leadership and Power: Identity processes in groups and organizations*. London: Sage, pp. 123–37.

Van Leeuwen, M., Peper, J.S., van den Berg, S.M., Brouwer, R.M., Hulshoff, Pol, H.E. and Kahn, R.S. (2009) A genetic analysis of brain volumes and IQ in children. *Intelligence*, 37, 181–91.

Van Merriënboer, J.J. (1990) Strategies for programming instruction in high school: Program completion vs. program generation. *Journal of Educational Computing Research*, 6(3), 265–85.

van orden, G.C. (1987) A ROWS is a ROSE: Spelling, sound, and reading. *Memory and Cognition*, 15, 181–98.

van Osch, Y., Blanken, I., Meijs, M.H.J. and van Wolferen, J. (2015) A group's physical attractiveness is greater than the average attractiveness of its members: The group attractiveness effect. *Personality and Social Psychology Bulletin*, 41, 559–74.

Van Petten, C. and Kutas, M. (1990) Interaction between sentence context and word frequency in event-related brain potentials. *Memory and Cognition*, 18, 380–93.

Van Rompay, T.J.L, Vonk, D.J. and Fransen, M.L. (2009) The eye of the camera: Effects of security cameras on prosocial behavior. *Environment and Behavior*, 41, 60–74.

Van Velzen, C.J.M. and Emmelkamp, P.M.G. (1996) The assessment of personality disorders: Implications for cognitive and behavior therapy. *Behaviour Research and Therapy*, 34(8), 655–68.

Van Vugt, F., Treutler, K., Altenmuller, E. and Jabusch, H-C. (2013) The influence of chronotype on making music: circadian fluctuations in pianists' fine motor skills. *Frontiers in Human Neuroscience*, 7(347), 1–9.

vanBaar, A.L., Vermaas, J., Knots, E. and de Kleine, M.J.K. (2009) Functioning at school age of moderately preterm children born at 32 to 36 weeks' gestational age. *Pediatrics*, 124, 251–7.

Vandell, D.L. (2000) Parents, peer groups, and other socializing influences. *Developmental Psychology*, 36, 699–710.

Vandenberghe, R., Duncan, J., Dupont, P., Ward, R (1997) Attention to 1 or 2 features in left or right visual field: A PET study. *Journal of Neuroscience*, 17(10), 3739–50.

Vanderbilt, D. and Augustyn, M. (2010) The effects of bullying. *Paediatrics and Child Health*, 20(7), 315–20.

Vandermosten, M., Hoeft, F. and Norton, E.S. (2016) Integrating MRI brain imaging studies of pre-reading children with current theories of developmental dyslexia: a review of quantitative meta-analysis. *Current Opinion in Behavioural Sciences*, 10, 155–61.

Vandermosten, M., Vanderauwera, J., Theys, C., De Vos, A., Vanvooren, S., Sunaert, G., Wouters, J. and Ghesquiere, P. (2015) A DTI tractography study in pre-readers at risk for dyslexia. *Developmental Cognitive Neuroscience*, 14, 8–15.

Vanderschuren, L.J. and Everitt, B.J. (2004) Drug seeking becomes compulsive after prolonged cocaine self-administration. *Science*, 305, 1017–19.

Vanlancker-Sidtis, D. (2004) When only the right hemisphere is left: Studies in language and communication. *Brain and Language*, 91, 199–211.

Vanneman, R.D. and Pettigrew, T.F. (1972) Race and relative deprivation in the urban United States. *Race*, 13, 461–86.

Vargha-Khadem, F., O'Gorman, A. and Watters, G. (1985) Aphasia and handedness in relation to hemispheric side, age at injury and severity of cerebral lesions during childhood. *Brain*, 108, 677–96.

Varnik, A., Kolves, K. and Wasserman, D. (2005) Suicide among Russians in Estonia: Database study before and after independence. *British Medical Journal*, 330, 176–7.

Varnum, M.E.W., Grossmann, I., Katunar, D., Nisbett, R.E. and Kitayama, S. (2008) Holism in a European cultural context. *Journal of Cognition and Culture*, 8, 321–33.

Varnum, M.E.W., Grossmann, I., Kitayama, S. and Nisbett, R.E. (2010) The origin of cultural differences in cognition: The social orientation hypothesis. *Current Directions in Psychological Science*, 19, 9–13.

Vartanian, L.R., Spanos, S., Herman, C.P. and Polivy, J. (2015) Modeling of food intake: a meta-analytic review. *Social Influence*, 10(3), 119–36.

Vartanian, O., Kwantes, P.J., Mandel, D.R., Bouak, F., Nakashima, A., Smith, I. and Lam, Q. (2013) Right inferior frontal gyrus activation as a neural marker of successful lying. *Frontiers in Human Neuroscience*, 7, 16.

Vase, L., Robinson, M.E., Verne, G.N. and Price, D.D. (2003) The contributions of suggestion, desire, and expectation to placebo effects in irritable bowel syndrome patients: An empirical investigation. *Pain*, 105(1), 17–25.

Vasey, M.W., Vilensky, M.R., Heath, J.H., Harbaugh, C.N., Buffington, A.G. and Fazio, R. (2012) It was as big as my head, I swear! Biased spider size estimation in spider phobia. *Journal of Anxiety Disorders*, 26, 20–4.

Vaughan, E. (1977) Misconceptions about psychology among psychology students. *Teaching of Psychology*, 4, 138–41.

Veijola, J. *et al.* (2014) Longitudinal changes in total brain volume in schizophrenia: Relation to symptom severity, cognition and antipsychotic medication. *PLoS ONE*, 9, e101689.

Venter, A., Lord, C. and Schopler, E. (1992) A follow-up study of high-functioning autistic children. *Journal of Child and Adolescent Psychiatry*, 33, 646–9.

Verhoeven, J.S., Cock, P., Lagae, L. and Sunaert, S. (201) Neuroimaging of autism. *Neuroradiology*, 52, 3–14.

Verma, I.M. (2014) Editorial expression of concern and correction. *PNAS*, 111, 10779.

Vernet, M., Quentin, R., Chanes, L., Mitsumasu, A. and Valero-Cabre, A. (2014) Frontal eye field, where art thou? Anatomy, function, and noninvasive manipulation of frontal regions involved in eye movements and associated cognitive operations. *Frontiers in Integrative Neuroscience*, 8, 1–24.

Vernon, P.E. (1989) The nature–nurture problem in creativity. In J.A. Glover, R.R. Ronning and C.R. Reynolds (eds) *Handbook of Creativity*. New York: Plenum Press.

Vescio, T.K., Gervais, S.J. Snyder, M. and Hoover, A. (2005) Power and the creation of patronizing environments: The stereotype-based behaviours of the powerful and their effects on female performance in masculine domains. *Journal of Personality and Social Psychology*, 88, 658–72.

Vettin, J. and Todt, D. (2004) Laughter in conversation: Features of occurrence and acoustic structure. *Journal of Nonverbal Behavior*, 28(2), 93–115.

Vicari, S., Albertoni, A., Chilosi, A.M., Cipriani, P., Cioni, G. and Bates, E. (2000) Plasticity and reorganization during language development in children with early brain injury. *Cortex*, 36, 31–46.

Vidmar, N., Beale, S.S., Rose, M. and Donnelly, L.F. (1997) Should we rush to reform the criminal jury? Consider conviction rate data. *Judicature*, 80, 286–90.

Vidyasagar, T.R. and Pammer, K. (1999) Impaired visual search in dyslexia relates to the role of the magnocellular pathway in attention. *NeuroReport*, 10, 1283–7.

Vignoles, V.L., Chryssochoou, X. and Breakwell, G.M. (2000) The distinctiveness principle: Identity, meaning, and the bounds of cultural relativity. *Personality and Social Psychology Review*, 4(4), 337–54.

Vijayraghavan, S. *et al.* (2007) Inverted-U dopamine D1 receptor actions on prefrontal neurons engaged in working memory. *Nature Neuroscience*. 10, 376–84.

Vingerhoets, A.J.J.M. and Bylsma, L.M. (2015) The riddle of human emotional crying: A challenge for emotion researchers. *Emotion Review*, 1–11.

Vingerhoets, A.J.J.M. and Scheirs, J. (2000) Sex differences in crying: Empirical findings and possible explanations. *Gender and Emotion: Social Psychological Perspectives*, 2, 143–65.

Viskontas, I.V., Quiroga, R.Q. and Fried, I. (2009) Human medial temporal lobe neurons respond preferentially to personally relevant images. *Proceedings of the National Academy of Sciences*, 106(50), 21329–34.

Visser, P.S. and Krosnick, J.A. (1998) Development of attitude strength over the life cycle: Surge and decline. *Journal of Personality and Social Psychology*, 75, 1389–410.

Vitaliano, P.P., Zhang, J. and Scanlan, J.M. (2003) Is caregiving hazardous to one's physical health? A mata-analysis. *Psychological Bulletin*, 129 (6), 946–72.

Vitevitch, M.S. and Siew, C.S.Q. (2016) Estimating group size from human speech: Three's a conversation, but four's a crowd. *The Quarterly Journal of Experimental Psychology*, 90, 62–74.

Vivar, C. and Van Praag, H. (2013) Functional circuits of new neurons in the dentate gyrus. *Frontiers in Neural Circuits*, 7.

Vlahovic, T. A., Roberts, S. and Dunbar, R. (2012) Effects of duration and laughter on subjective happiness within different modes of communication. *Journal of Computer-Mediated Communication*, 17(4), 436–50.

Voets, N.L., Adcock, J.E., Flitney, D.E., Behrens, T.E.J., Hart, Y., Stacey, R., Carpenter, K. and Matthews, P.M. (2006) Distinct right frontal lobe activation in language processing following left hemisphere injury. *Brain*, 129, 754–66.

Vollenweider, F.X. and Kometer, M. (2010) The neurobiology of psychedelic drugs: implications for the treatment of mood disorders. *Nature Reviews Neuroscience*, 11(9), 642–51.

Vollenweider, F.X. and Kometer, M. (2010) The neurobiology of psychedelic drugs: Implications for the treatment of mood disorders. *Nature Reviews Neuroscience*, 11, 642–51.

Vollmer, C. and Randler, C. (2012) Circadian preferences and personality values: morning types prefer social values, evening types prefer individual values. *Personality and Individual Differences*, 52, 738–43.

Von Cramon, D. and Kerkhoff, G. (1993) On the cerebral organization of elementary visuospatial perception. In B. Gulyas, D. Ottoson and P.E. Roland (eds) *Functional Organisation of the Human Visual Cortex*. Oxford: Pergamon Press.

Von dem Hagen, E.A.H., Nummenmaa, L., Yu, R., Engell, A.D., Ewbank, M.P. and Calder, A.J. (2011) Autism spectrum traits in the typical population predict structure and function in the posterior superior temporal sulcus. *Cerebral Cortex*, 21, 493–500.

Von Glinow, M., Shapiro, D.L. and Brett, J.M. (2004) Can we talk, and should we? Managing emotional conflict in multicultural teams. *Academy of Management Review*, 29, 578–92.

von Stumm, S., Chamorro-Premuzic, T. and Furnham, A. (2009) Decomposing self-estimates of intelligence: Structure and sex differences across 12 nations. *British Journal of Psychology*, 100, 429–42.

Von Wright, J.M., Anderson, K. and Stenman, U. (1975) Generalization of conditioned GSRs in dichotic listening. In P.M.A. Rabbitt and S. Dornic (eds) *Attention and Performance*, Vol. 5. London: Academic Press.

Voracek, M., Rieder, S., Stieger, S. and Swami, V. (2015) What's in a surname? Physique, aptitude, and sports type comparisons between tailors and smiths. *PLoS ONE*, 10, e0131795.

Vorauer, J.D. and Miller, D.T. (1997) Failure to recognize the effect of implicit social influence on the presentation of self. *Journal of Personality and Social Psychology*, 73(2), 281.

Vreeman, R.C. and Carroll, A.E. (2007) A systematic review of school-based interventions to prevent bullying. *Archives of Pediatrics and Adolescent Medicine*, 161, 78–88.

Vrij, A. (2000) *Detecting Lies and Deceit: The psychology of lying and the implications for professional practice*. Chichester: Wiley.

Vrij, A. (2001) Detecting the liars. *The Psychologist*, 14(11), 596–8.

Vrij, A. (2004a) Guidelines to catch a liar. In P-A. Granhag and L. Stromwall (eds) *The Detection of Deception in Forensic Contexts*. Cambridge: Cambridge University Press.

Vrij, A. (2004b) Why professionals fail to catch liars and how they can improve. *Legal and Criminological Psychology*, 9, 159–81.

Vrij, A. and Mann, S. (2001) Who killed my relative? Police officers' ability to detect real-life high stake lies. *Psychology, Crime and Law*, 7, 119–32.

Vul, E., Harris, C., Winkielman, P. and Pashler, H. (2009) Puzzlingly high correlations in fMRI studies of emotion, personality and social cognition. *Perspectives in Psychological Science*, 4, 274–90.

Vuoskoski, J.K. and Eerola, T. (2012) Can sad music really make you sad? Indirect measures of affective states induced by music and autobiographical memories. *Psychology of Aesthetics, Creativity, and the Arts*, 6, 204–13.

Vygotsky, L. (1934/1962) *Thinking and Speaking*. Cambridge, MA: Harvard University Press.

Vygotsky, L. (1976/1933) *Mind and Society: The development of higher mental processes*. Cambridge, MA: Harvard University Press.

Vygotsky, L.S. (1987) Thinking and speech. In R.W. Rieber and A.S. Carton (eds) *The Collected Works of L.S. Vygotsky. Vol. 1: Problems of General Psychology* (N. Minick, trans.) New York: Plenum Press. Original work published in 1934.

W

Waber, R.L., Shiv, B., Carmon, Z. and Ariely, D. (2008) Commercial features of placebo and therapeutic. *JAMA*, 299(9), 1016–7.

Wadden, T.A., Brownell, K.D. and Foster, G.D. (2002) Obesity: Responding to the growing epidemic. *Journal of Consulting and Clinical Psychology*, 70(3), 510–25.

Wade, T.J., Fuller, L., Bresnan, J., Schaefer, S. and Mlynarski, L. (2007) Weight halo effects: individual differences in personality evaluations and perceived life success of men as a function of weight. *Personality and Individual Differences*, 42, 317–24.

Wagenmakers, E.J., Beek, T., Dijkhoff, L., Gronau, Q.F., Acosta, A., Adams Jr, R.B., . . . and Bulnes, L.C. (2016) Registered Replication Report: Strack, Martin and Stepper (1988) *Perspectives on Psychological Science*, 11(6), 917–28.

Wager, T.D., Atlas, L.Y., Lindquist, M.A., Roy, M., Woo, C.W. and Kross, E. (2013) An fMRI-based neurologic signature of physical pain. *New England Journal of Medicine*, 368(15), 1388–97.

Wager, T.D., Rilling, J.K., Smith. E.E., Sokolik, A., Casey, K.L., Davidson, R.J., Kosslyn, S.M., Rose, R.M. and Cohen, J.D. (2004) Placebo-induced changes in fMRI in the anticipation and experience of pain. *Science*, 303 (5661), 1162–7.

Wagner, A., Aizenstein, H., Mazurkewicz, L., Fudge, J., Frank, G.K., Putnam, K., Bailer, U.F., Fischer, L. and Kaye, W.H. (2008) Altered insula response to taste stimuli in individuals recovered from restricting-type anorexia nervosa. *Neuropsychopharmacology*, 33, 513–23.

Wagner, A.R., Siegal, S., Thomas, E. and Ellison, G.D. (1964) Reinforcement history and the extinction of a conditioned salivary response. *Journal of Comparative and Physiological Psychology*, 58, 354–8.

Wagner, U., Galli, L., Schott, B.H., Wold, A., van der Schalk, J., Manstead, A.S.R., Scherer, K. and Walter, H. (2014) Beautiful friendship: Social sharing of emotion improves subjective feelings and activates the neural reward circuitry. *SCAN*, 10, 801–8.

Wagstaff, G.F. (1987) Hypnotic induction, hypnotherapy and the placebo effect. *British Journal of Experimental and Clinical Hypnosis*, 4, 168–70.

Wagstaff, G.F. (1991) Compliance, belief and semantics in hypnosis: A nonstate, sociocognitive perspective. In S.J. Lynn and J.H. Rhue (eds) *Theories of Hypnosis: Current models and perspectives*. New York: Guilford Press.

Wagstaff, G.F. (1993) What expert witnesses can tell courts about hypnosis: A review of the association between hypnosis and the law. *Expert Evidence: The international digest of human behaviour science and law*, 2, 60–70.

Wagstaff, G.F. (1996) Methodological issues in hypnosis. In J. Haworth (ed.) *Psychological Research*. London: Routledge.

Wagstaff, G.F. and Royce, C. (1994) Hypnosis and the treatment of nailbiting: A preliminary trial. *Contemporary Hypnosis*, 11, 9–13.

Wahlheim, C.N., Dunlosky, J. and Jacoby, L.L. (2011) Spacing enhances the learning of natural concepts: An investigation of mechanisms, metacognition, and aging. *Memory and Cognition*, 39, 750–63.

Wakefield, J.C. and First, M.B. (2012) Validity of the bereavement exclusion to major depression: does the empirical evidence support the proposal to eliminate the exclusion in DSM 5? *World Psychiatry*, 11(1), 3–10.

Walker, E. and Lewine, R.J. (1990) Prediction of adult-onset schizophrenia from childhood home movies of the patients. *American Journal of Psychiatry*, 147, 1052–6.

Walker, E., Shapiro, D., Esterberg, M. and Trotman, H. (2010) Introduction to special issue on schizophrenia. *Current Directions in Psychological Science*, 19(4), 1–2.

Walker, I. and Read, J. (2002) The differential effectiveness of psychosocial and biogenetic causal explanations in reducing negative attitudes toward 'mental illness'. *Psychiatry: Interpersonal and Biological Processes*, 65, 313–25.

Walker, M.P. *et al.* (2003) Sleep and the time course of motor skill learning. *Learning and Memory*, 10, 275–84.

Wallach, M. and Kogan, N. (1965) *Modes of Thinking in Young Children*. New York: Holt, Rinehart & Winston.

Wallentin, M. (2009) Putative sex differences in verbal abilities and language cortex: A critical review. *Brain and Language*, 108, 175–83.

Walloe, S., Pakkenberg, B. and Fabricius, K. (2014) Stereological estimation of total cell numbers in the human cerebral and cerebellar cortex. *Frontiers in Human Neuroscience*, 8, 1–8.

Walraven, A., Brand-Gruwel, S. and Boshuizen, H.P. (2008) Information-problem solving: A review of problems students encounter and instructional solutions. *Computers in Human Behavior*, 24(3), 623–48.

Walster, E., Aronson, V., Abrahams, D. and Rottman, L. (1966) Importance of physical attractiveness in dating behavior. *Journal of Personality and Social Psychology*, 4, 508–16.

Walum, H., Waldman, I. and Young, L. (in press) Statistical and methodological considerations for the interpretation of intranasal oxytocin studies. *Biological Psychiatry*, 79, 251–7.

Wang, K., Lu, H., Cheung, E., Neumann, D.L., Shum, D. and Chan, R.C. (2016) 'Female preponderance' of depression in non-clinical populations: A meta-analytic study. *Frontiers in Psychology*, 7, 1398.

Wang, Q. (2004) The emergence of cultural self-construct: Autobiographical memory and self-description in American and Chinese children. *Developmental Psychology*, 40(1), 3–15.

Wang, Q. (2006) Earliest recollections of self and others in European American and Taiwanese young adults. *Psychological Science*, 17, 708–14.

Wang, Q. (2008) Being American, being Asian: The bicultural self and autobiographical memory in Asian Americans. *Cognition*, 107, 743–51.

Wang, Q. and Ross, M. (2005) What we remember and what we tell: The effects of culture and self-priming on memory representations and narratives. *Memory*, 13(6), 594–606.

Wann, D.L. and Dolan, T.J. (1994) Spectators' evaluations of rival and fellow fans. *The Psychological Record*, 44, 351–8.

Wapner, W., Judd, T. and Gardner, H. (1978) Visual agnosia in an artist. *Cortex*, 14, 343–64.

Warr, P. (1990) Job control, job demands and employee well being. *Work and Stress*, 4, 285–94.

Warrington, E.K. (1975) The selective impairment of semantic memory. *Journal of Experimental Psychology*, 27, 635–57.

Warrington, E.K. and James, M. (1967) An experimental investigation of facial recognition in patients with unilateral cerebral lesions. *Cortex*, 3, 317–26.

Warrington, E.K. and McCarthy, R.A. (1987) Categories of knowledge: Further fractionations and an attempted integration. *Brain*, 110, 1273–96.

Warrington, E.K. and Shallice, T. (1980) Word form dyslexia. *Brain*, 103, 99–112.

Warrington, E.K. and Shallice, T. (1984) Category specific semantic impairments. *Brain*, 107, 829–53.

Wason, P. (1968) Reasoning about a rule. *The Quarterly Journal of Experimental Psychology*, 20, 273–81.

Wason, P.C. and Johnson-Laird, P.N. (1972) *Psychology of Reasoning: Structure and content*. Cambridge, MA: Harvard University Press.

Watanabe, K. and Shimojo, S. (2001) When sound affects vision: Effects of auditory grouping on visual motion perception. *Psychological Science*, 12(2), 109–16.

Waters, E., Wippman, J. and Sroufe, L.A. (1979) Attachment, positive affect, and competence in the peer group: Two studies in construct validation. *Child Development*, 50, 821–9.

Watkins, C.E., Campbell, V.L., Nieberding, R. and Hallmark, R. (1995) Contemporary practice of psychological assessment by clinical psychologists. *Professional Psychology: Research and Practice*, 26, 54–60.

Watson, D. (2000) *Mood and Temperament*. New York: Guilford Press.

Watson, J.B. (1913) Psychology as the behaviorist views it. *Psychological Review*, 20, 158–77.

Watson, J.B. (1919) *Psychology from the Standpoint of a Behaviorist.* Philadelphia, PA: Lippincott.

Watson, J.B. (1930) *Behaviorism.* New York: W.W. Norton.

Watson, J.B. and Rayner, R. (1920) Conditioned emotional reactions. *Journal of Experimental Psychology,* 3, 1–14.

Watson, M.W. and Fischer, K.M. (1977) A developmental sequence of agent use in late infancy. *Child Development,* 43, 826–36.

Watson, W.J., Watson, L., Wetzel, W., Bader, E. and Talbot, Y. (1995) Transition to parenthood: What about fathers? *Canadian Family Physician,* 41, 807–12.

Watten, R.G. (1997) Gender and consumption of alcohol: The impact of body composition, sensation seeking and coping styles. *British Journal of Health Psychology,* 2, 15–25.

Waugh, N.C. and Norman, D.A. (1965) Primary memory. *Psychological Review,* 72, 89–104.

Waxman, S.R. and Booth, A.E. (2000) Principles that are invoked in the acquisition of words, but not facts. *Cognition,* 77, B33–B43.

Weaver, C.A. (1993) Do you need a 'flash' to form a flashbulb memory? *Journal of Experimental Psychology: General.* 122, 39–46.

Weaver, I C., Cervoni, N., Champagne, F.A., D'Alessio, A.C., Sharma, S., Seckl, J.R., Dymov, S., Szyf, M. and Meaney, M.J. (2004) Epigenetic programming by maternal behavior. *Nature Neuroscience,* 8, 847–54.

Webb, K. and Davey, G.C.L. (1993) Disgust sensitivity and fear of animals: Effect of exposure to violent or revulsive material. *Anxiety, Stress and Coping,* 5, 329–35.

Wechsler, H. Lee, J.E., Kuo, M., Seibring, M., Nelson, T.F. and Lee, H. (2002) Trends in college binge drinking during a period of increased prevention efforts: Findings from 4 Harvard School of Public Health College alcohol study surveys: 1993–2001. *Journal of American College Health,* 50(5), 203–17.

Weege, B., Lange, B.P. and Fink, B. (2012) Women's visual attention to variation in men's dance quality. *Personality and Individual Differences,* 53, 236–40.

Weeks, S.J. and Hobson, R.P. (1987) The salience of facial expression for autistic children. *Journal of Child Psychology and Psychiatry,* 28, 137–52.

Wegner, D.M. (1994) Ironic process of mental control. *Psychological Review,* 101, 34–52.

Wegner, D.M. and Erber, R. (1992) The hyperaccessibility of suppressed thoughts. *Journal of Personality and Social Psychology,* 38, 719–26.

Wehbe, L., Murphy, B., Talukdar, P., Fyshe, A., Ramdas, A. and Mitchell, T. (2014) Simultaneously uncovering the patterns of brain regions involved in different story reading subprocesses. *PLoS ONE,* 9, e112575.

Wei, S. T., Ou, L. C., Luo, M. R. and Hutchings, J. B. (2012) Optimisation of food expectations using product colour and appearance. *Food Quality and Preference,* 23(1), 49–62.

Weidner, R., Boers, F., Mathiak, K., Dammers, J. and Fink, G.R. (2010) The temporal dynamics of the Muller-Lyer illusion. *Cerebral Cortex,* 20, 1586–95.

Weigel, R.H., Vernon, D.T.A. and Tognacci, L.N. (1974) Specificity of the attitude as a determinant of attitude–behavior congruence. *Journal of Personality and Social Psychology,* 30, 724–8.

Weigelt, S., Koldewyn, K. and Kanwisher, N. (2012) Face identity recognition in autism spectrum disorders: A review of behavioural studies. *Neuroscience and Biobehavioural Reviews,* 36, 1060–84.

Weikart, D.P., Bond, J.T. and McNeil, J.T. (1978) The Ypsilanti Perry Preschool Project: Preschool years and longitudinal results through fourth grade. *Monographs of the High/Scope Educational Research Foundation* (No. 3) Ypsilanti, MI: High/Scope Educational Research Foundation.

Weiler, J.A., Suchan, B. and Daum, I. (2010a) Foreseeing the future: occurrence probability of imagined future events modulates hippocampal activation. *Hippocampus,* 20(6), 685–90.

Weiler, J.A., Suchan, B. and Daum, I. (2010b) When the future becomes the past: Differences in brain activation patterns for episodic memory and episodic future thinking. *Behavioural Brain Research,* 212(2), 196–203.

Weinberger, D.R. (1996) On the plausibility of 'the neurodevelopmental hypothesis' of schizophrenia. *Neuropsychopharmacology,* 14, 1S–11S.

Weinberger, D.R. and Goldberg, T.E. (2014) RDoCs redux. *World Psychiatry,* 13, 36–8.

Weiner, B. (1985) An attributional theory of achievement motivation and emotion. *Psychological Review,* 92, 548–73.

Weiner, B. (2014) The attribution approach to emotion and motivation: History, hypotheses, home runs and headaches/heartaches. *Emotion Review,* 6, 353–61.

Weiner, K.S. (2015) On (ab)normality: Einstein's fusiform gyrus. *Brain and Cognition,* 94, 1–3.

Weiner, M.W., Veitch, D.P., Aisen, P.S., Beckett, L.A., Cairns, N.J., Green, R.C., Harvey, D., Jack, C.R., Jagust, W., Liu, E., Morris, J.C., Petersen, R.C., Saykin, A.J., Schmidt, M.E., Shaw, L., Siuciak, J.A., Soares, H., Toga, A.W. and Trojanowski, J.Q. (2010) The Alzheimer's Disease Neuroimaging Initiative: A review of papers published since its inception. *Alzheimer's and Dementia,* 8, Supplement, A1–A4, S1–S68.

Weinstein, J.J., Chohan, M.O., Slifstein, M., Kegeles, L.S., Moore, H. and Abi-Dargham, A. (2016) Pathway-specific dopamine abnormalities in schizophrenia. *Biological Psychiatry,* 81, 31–42.

Weinstein, N. and Ryan, R.M. (2010) When helping helps: An examination of motivational constructs underlying prosocial behavior and their influence on well-being for the helper and recipient. *Journal of Personality and Social Psychology,* 98, 222–44.

Weinstein, N., Hodgkins, H.S. and Ostvik-White, E. (2011) Humor as aggression: Effects of motivation on hostility expressed in humor appreciation. *Journal of Personality and Social Psychology,* 100, 1043–55.

Weisberg, D., Keil, F., Goldstein, J., Rawson, S. and Gray, J. (2008) The seductive allure of neuroscience explanations. *Journal of Cognitive Neuroscience,* 20, 470–7.

Weisberg, D.S., Keil, F.C., Goodstein, J., Rawson, E. and Gray, J.R. (2008) The seductive allure of neuroscience explanations. *Journal of Cognitive Neuroscience,* 20(3), 470–7.

Weisberg, D.S., Taylor, J.C.V. and Hopkins, E.J. (2015) Deconstructing the seductive allure of neuroscience explanations. *Judgement and Decision Making,* 10, 429–41.

Weisberg, R.W. (1994) Genius and madness? A quasi-experimental test of the hypothesis that manic-depression increases creativity. *Psychological Science,* 5(6), 361–7.

Weiskrantz, L. (1986) *Blindsight: A case study and implications.* Oxford: Oxford University Press.

Weiskrantz, L. (1997) *Consciousness Lost and Found: A neuropsychological exploration.* Oxford: Oxford University Press.

Weiskrantz, L., Cowey, A. and Hodinott-Hill, I. (2002) Prime-sight in a blindsight subject. *Nature Neuroscience,* 5, 101–2.

Weiskrantz, L., Roa, A., Hodinott-Hill, I., Nobre, A.C. and Cowey, A. (2003) Brain potentials associated with conscious after-effects induced by unseen stimuli in a blindsight subject. *Proceedings of the National Academy of Sciences,* 100, 10500–5.

Weisner, T.S. and Gallimore, R. (1977) My brother's keeper: Child and sibling caretaking. *Current Anthropology,* 18, 169–90.

Weisner, T.S. and Wilson-Mitchell, J.E. (1990) Nonconventional family lifestyles and sex typing in six-year-olds. *Child Development,* 61, 1915–33.

Weiss, J.M. (1968) Effects of coping responses on stress. *Journal of Comparative and Physiological Psychology,* 65, 251–60.

Wellcome Trust (2010) *Human Functional Brain Imaging 1990–2009: Portfolio review.* London: Wellcome.

Wellcome Trust Case Control Consortium (2007).

Wellman, H.M., Cross, D. and Watson, J. (2001) Meta-analysis of theory-of-mind development: The truth about false belief. *Child Development,* 72, 655–84.

Wells, A. and Matthews, G. (1994) *Attention and Emotion: A clinical perspective.* Hove: Lawrence Erlbaum Associates.

Wells, C., Morrison, C.M. and Conway, M.A. (2014) Adult recollections of childhood memories: What details can be recalled? *The Quarterly Journal of Experimental Psychology,* 67, 1249–61.

Wells, G.L. and Bradfield, A.L. (1999) Distortions in eyewitnesses' recollections: Can the postidentification-feedback effect be moderated? *Psychological Science,* 10(2), 138–44.

Wells, G.L. and Seelau, E.P. (1995) Eyewitness identification: Psychological research and legal policy on line-ups. *Psychology, Public Policy and Law,* 1(4), 765–91.

Wells, G.L., Small, M., Penrod, S., Malpass, R.S., Fulero, S.M. and Brimacombe C.A.E. (1998) Eyewitness identification procedures: Recommendations for line-ups and photospreads. *Law and Human Behaviour,* 22, 603–48.

Wells, T.T. and Cruess, D.G. (2006) Effects of partial sleep deprivation on food consumption and food choice. *Psychology and Health,* 21(1), 79–86.

Weltzin, T.E., Hsu, L.K.G., Pollice, C. and Kaye, W.H. (1991) Feeding patterns in bulimia nervosa. *Biological Psychiatry,* 30, 1093–110.

Wernicke, K. (1874) *Der Aphasische Symptomenkomplex.* Breslau: Cohn & Weigert.

Wertheimer, M. (1912) Experimentelle Studien über das Sehen von Bewegung. *Zeitschrift der Psychologie,* 61, 161–265.

Wertheimer, M. (1961) Psychomotor co-ordination of auditory–visual space at birth. *Science,* 134, 1692.

Wesnes, K.A., Ward, T., McGinty, A. and Petrini, O. (2000) The memory enhancing effects of Ginkgo biloba/Panax ginseng combination in healthy middle-aged volunteers. *Psychopharmacology,* 152, 353–61.

Wessinger, C.M., Fendrich, R. and Gazzaniga, M.S. (1999) Variability of residual vision in hemianopic subject. *Restorative Neurology and Neuroscience,* 15, 242–53.

Wessinger, C.M., Van Meter, J., Van Lare, J., Pekar, J. and Rauschecker, J.P. (2001) Hierarchical organization of the human auditory cortex revealed by functional magnetic resonance imaging. *Journal of Cognitive Neuroscience,* 13(1), 1–7.

West, R., Beard, E. and Brown, J. (2016) *Trends in electronic cigarette use in England.* UCL: Smoking Toolkit Study.

West, R.L. (1996) An application of prefrontal cortex function theory to cognitive aging. *Psychological Bulletin,* 120, 272–92.

Westen, D. and Morrison, K. (2001) A multi-dimensional meta-analysis of treatments for depression, panic, and Generalized Anxiety Disorder: An empirical examination of the status of empirically supported therapies. *Journal of Consulting and Clinical Psychology,* 69, 875–99.

Westen, D., Lohr, N., Silk, K.R., Gold, L. and Kerber, K. (1990) Object relations and social cognition in borderlines, major depressives, and normals: A Thematic Apperception Test analysis. *Psychological Assessment,* 2, 355–64.

Weston, S.J., Hill, P.L. and Jackson, J.J. (2014) Personality traits predict the onset of disease. *Social Psychological and Personality Science,* 6, 309–17.

Wetter, D.W., Kenford, S.L., Smith, S.S., Fiore, M.C., Jorenby, D.E. and Baker, T.B. (1999) Gender differences in smoking cessation. *Journal of Consulting and Clinical Psychology,* 67(4), 555–62.

Whalley, H.C. et al. (2011) Genetic variation in CNTNAP2 alters brain function during linguistic processing in healthy individuals. *American Journal of Medical Genetics B,* 156, 941–8.

Wheeler, A.L. and Voineskos, A.N. (2014) A review of structural neuroimaging in schizophrenia. *Frontiers in Human Neuroscience,* 8, 653.

Wheeler, M.E. and Fiske, S.T. (2005) Controlling racial prejudice: social-cognitive goals affect amygdala and stereotype activation. *Psychological Science,* 16, 56–63.

Wheeler, R.W., Davidson, R.J. and Tomarken, A.J. (1993) Frontal brain asymmetry and emotional reactivity: A biological substrate of affective style. *Psychophysiology,* 30, 82–9.

Whelan, C.W., Wagstaff, G. and Wheatcroft, J.M. (2014a) High stakes lies: police and non-police accuracy in detecting deception. *Psychology, Crime, and Law,* 21, 127–38.

Whelan, C.W., Wagstaff, G. and Wheatcroft, J.M. (2014b) Subjective cues to deception/honesty in a high stakes situation: An exploratory approach. *The Journal of Psychology,* 1–18

Whisman, M., Goetzinger, J., Cotton, F. and Brinkman, D. (1978) Odorant evaluation: a study of ethanethiol and tetrahydrothiophene as warning agents in propane. *Environmental Science and Technology,* 12, 1285–8.

White, D., Burton, A.M., Jenkins, R. and Kemp, R.I. (2014) Redesigning photo-ID to improve face matching performance. 20, 166.

White, D., Dunn, J.D., Schmid, A.C. and Kemp. R.I. (2015a) Error rates in users of automatic face recognition software. *PLoS ONE,* 10, e0139827.

White, D., Kemp, R.I., Jenkins, R., Matheson, M. and Burton, A.M. (2014) Passport officers' errors in face matching. *PLoS ONE,* 9, e103510.

White, D., Phillips, J., Hahn, C.A., Hill, M. and O'Toole, A.J. (2015b) Perceptual expertise in forensic facial image comparison. *Proceedings of the Royal Society B,* 282, 20151292.

White, G.L. (1980) Physical attractiveness and courtship progress. *Journal of Personality and Social Psychology,* 39, 660–8.

Whitehead, M. (1995) Tackling health inequalities: An agenda for action. In M. Benzenal, K. Judge and M. Whitehead (eds) *Tackling Inequalities in Health: An agenda for action.* London: King's Fund, p. 23.

WHO (2016) http://www.who.int/gho/publications/world_health_statistics/2016/en/

Whorf, B.L. (1956) Science and linguistics. In J.B. Carroll (ed.) *Language, Thought and Reality: Selected Writings of Benjamin Lee Whorf.* Cambridge, MA: MIT Press.

Wichstrom, L. (1999) The emergence of gender difference in depressed mood during adolescence: The role of intensified gender socialization. *Developmental Psychology,* 35(1), 232–45.

Wicker, A.W. (1969) Attitudes versus actions: The relationship of verbal and overt behavioral responses to attitude objects. *Journal of Social Issues,* 25, 41–78.

Wicker, B., Keysers, C., Plailly, J., Royet, J.P., Gallese, V. and Rizzolatti, G. (2003) Both of us disgusted in My insula: the common neural basis of seeing and feeling disgust. *Neuron,* 40(3), 655–64.

Widiger, T.A. and Samuel, D.B. (2005) Diagnostic categories or dimensions? A question for the Diagnostic and Statistical Manual of Mental Disorders, Fifth edn. *Journal of Abnormal Psychology,* 114(5), 494–504.

Widom, C.S. (1978) A methodology for studying non-institutionalized psychopaths. In R.D. Hare and D. Schalling (eds) *Psychopathic Behaviour: Approaches to research.* Chichester: Wiley.

Wiedemann, D., Burt, D.M., Hill, R.A. and Barton, R.A. (2015) Red clothing increases perceived dominance, aggression and anger. *Biology Letters*, 11(5), 20150166.

Wiernega, L.M., Langen, M., Oranje, B. and Dusrton, S. (2014) Unique developmental trajectories of cortical thickness and surface area. *Neuroimage*, 87, 120-6.

Wieselquiest, J., Rusbult, C.E., Foster, C.A. and Agnew, C.R. (1999) Commitment, pro-relationship behavior, and trust in close relationships. *Journal of Personality and Social Psychology*, 77, 942-66.

Wigton, R., Radua, J., Allen, P., Averbeck, B., Meyer-Lindenberg, A., McGuire, P., Shergill, S.S. and Fusar-Poli, P. (2014) Neurophysiological effects of acute oxytocin administration: systematic review and meta-analysis of placebo-controlled imaging studies. *Journal of Psychiatry and Neuroscience*, 40, 1, e1-22.

Wilbanks, W. (1984) *Murder in Miami*. Lanham, MD: University Press of America.

Wilcox, T., Stubbs, J.A., Wheeler, L. and Alexander, G.M. (2013) Infants' scanning of dynamic faces during the first year. *Infant Behaviour and Development*, 36, 513-16.

Wilcoxon, H.C., Dragoin, W.B. and Kral, P.A. (1971) Illness-induced aversions in rat and quail: Relative salience of visual and gustatory cues. *Science*, 171, 826-8.

Wilensky, A.E., Schafe, G.E. and LeDoux, J.E. (1999) The amygdala modulates memory consolidation of fear-motivated inhibitory avoidance learning but not classical fear conditioning. *Journal of Neuroscience*, 20, 7059-66.

Wilhelm, F.H. and Roth, W.T. (1997) Clinical characteristics of flight phobia. *Journal of Anxiety Disorders*, 11, 241-61.

Wilhelm, I., Rose, M., Imhof, K.I., Rasch, B., Buchel, C. and Born, I. (2013) The sleeping child outplays the adult's capacity to convert implicit into explicit knowledge. *Nature Neuroscience*, 16, 391-3.

Wilhite, S.C. (1991) Evidence of a negative environmental reinstatement effect. *British Journal of Psychology*, 82, 325-42.

Wilkes, K.V. (1988) Information, physics, quantum: The search for links. In W. Zurek (ed.) *Complexity, Entropy and the Physics of Information*. Redwood City, CA: Addison-Wesley.

Wilkins, R.W., Hodges, D.A., Laurienti, P.J., Steen, M. and Burdette, J.H. (2014) Network science and the effects of music preferences on functional brain connectivity: From Beethoven to Eminem. *Scientific Reports*, 4, 1-7.

Wilkinson, S. and Kitzinger, C. (2008) Conversation analysis. In C. Willig and W. Stainton-Rogers (eds) *The Sage Handbook of Qualitative Research in Psychology*. London: Sage.

Wilkinson, S.C, Reader, W. and Payne, S.J. (2012) Adaptive browsing: Sensitivity to time pressure and task difficulty. *International Journal of Human-Computer Studies*, 70, 14-25.

Wilkowski, B.M. and Meier, B.P. (2010) Bring it on: Angry facial expressions potentiate approach-motivated motor behavior. *Journal of Personality and Social Psychology*, 98, 201-10.

Will, J.A., Self, P.A. and Datan, N. (1976) Maternal behaviour and perceived sex of infant. *American Journal of Orthopsychiatry*, 46, 135-9.

Willems, R.M., Clevis, K. and Hagoort, P. (2011) Add a picture for suspense: Neural correlates of the interaction between language and visual information in the perception of fear. *Social, Cognitive and Affective Neuroscience*, 6, 404-16.

Willemsen, M.C. and de Zwart, W.M. (1999) The effectiveness of policy and health education strategies for reducing adolescent smoking: A review of the evidence. *Journal of Adolescence*, 22, 587-99.

Williams, J.H. *et al.* (2004) A systematic review of action imitation in autistic spectrum disorder. *Journal of Autism and Developmental Disorders*, 34, 285-99.

Williams, J.M. and Dunlop, L.C. (1999) Pubertal timing and self-reported delinquency among male adolescents. *Journal of Adolescence*, 22, 157-71.

Williams, K.D. (2001) *Ostracism: The power of silence*. New York: Guilford Press.

Williams, K.D. and Sommer, K.L. (1997) Social ostracism by one's co-workers: Does rejection lead to loafing or compensation? *Personality and Social Psychology Bulletin*, 23, 693-706.

Williams, K.D., Harkins, S. and Latané, B. (1981) Identifiability as a deterrent to social loafing: Two cheering experiments. *Journal of Personality and Social Psychology*, 40, 303-11.

Williams, K.D., Harkins, S.G. and Karau, S.J. (2003) Social performance. In M.A. Hogg and J. Cooper (eds) *The Sage Handbook of Social Psychology*. London: Sage.

Williams, K.D., Karau, S.J. and Bourgeois, M. (1993) Working on collective tasks: Social loafing and social compensation. In M.A. Hogg and D. Abrams (eds) *Group Motivation: Social psychological perspectives*. London: Harvester Wheatsheaf, pp. 130-48.

Williams, K.M., Nathanson, C. and Paulhus, D.L. (2010a) Identifying and profiling scholastic cheaters: Their personality, cognitive ability and motivation. *Journal of Experimental Psychology: Applied*, 16, 293-307.

Williams, K.M., Park, J.H. and Wieling, M.B. (2010b) The face reveals athletic flair: Better National Football League quarterbacks are better looking. *Personality and Individual Differences*, 48, 112-16.

Williams, L.E. and Bargh, J.A. (2008a) Keeping one's distance: The influence of spatial distance cues on affect and evaluation. *Psychological Science*, 19(3), 302-8.

Williams, L.E. and Bargh, J.A. (2008b) Experiencing physical warmth promotes interpersonal warmth. *Science*, 24, 606-7.

Williams, W., Blythe, T., White, N., Li, J., Sternberg, R.J. and Gardner, H. (1996) *Practical Intelligence for School Handbook*. New York: HarperCollins.

Willis, F. and Hamm, H. (1980) The use of interpersonal touch in securing compliance. *Journal of Nonverbal Behavior*, 5, 49-55.

Wills, G.I. (2003) Forty lives in the bebop business: Mental health in a group of eminent jazz musicians. *British Journal of Psychiatry*, 183, 255-9.

Wilms, I.L., Petersen, A. and Vangkilde, S. (2013) Intensive video gaming improves encoding speed to visual short-term memory in young male adults. *Acta Psychologica*, 142(1), 108-18.

Wilson, A.E. and Ross, M. (2001) From chump to champ: People's appraisals of their earlier and present selves. *Journal of Personality and Social Psychology*, 80, 572-84.

Wilson, A.J., Andrewes, S.G., Struthers, H., Rowe, V.M., Bogdanovic, R. and Waldie, K.E. (2015) Dyscalculia and dyslexia in adults: Cognitive bases of comorbidity. *Learning and Individuals Differences*, 37, 118-32.

Wilson, B.A. (1991) Long-term prognosis of patients with severe memory disorders. *Neuropsychological Rehabilitation*, 1, 117-34.

Wilson, B.A. (1995) Rehabilitation. In J.G. Beaumont, P.M. Kenealy and M.J.C. Rogers (eds) *Blackwell Dictionary of Neuropsychology*. Oxford: Blackwell.

Wilson, B.A. and Powell, G.E. (1994) Neurological problems: Treatment and rehabilitation. In S.J.E. Lindsey and G.E. Powell (eds) *Handbook of Clinical Adult Psychology*. London: Routledge.

Wilson, B.A., J.C. and Hughes, E. (1997) In A.J. Parkin (ed.) *Case Studies in the Neuropsychology of Memory*. Hove: Psychology Press.

Wilson, C., Nairn, R., Coverdale, J. and Panapa, A. (2000) How mental illness is portrayed in children's television. *British Journal of Psychiatry*, 176, 440-3.

Wilson, C.E., Happe, F., Wheelwright, S.J., Ecker, C., Lombardo, M.V., Johnston, P., Daly, E., Murphy, C.D., Spain, D., Lai, M-C., Chakrabarti, B. and Sauter, D.A., MRC Aims Consortium, Baron-Cohen, S. and Murphy, D.G.M. (2014)

The neuropsychology of male adults with high-functioning autism or Asperger Syndrome. *Autism Research*, 7, 568-81.

Wilson, D.S. (1998) Adaptive individual differences within single populations. *Philosophical Transactions of the Royal Society London B*, 353, 199-205.

Wilson, E.O. (1975) *Sociobiology: The new synthesis*. Cambridge, MA: Harvard University Press.

Wilson, E.O. (2004) *On Human Nature* (2nd edn). Cambridge, MA: Harvard University Press.

Wilson, J.P. and Rule, N.O. (2015) Facial trustworthiness predicts extreme criminal sentencing outcomes. *Psychological Science*, 26, 1325-1.

Wilson, M., Daly, M. and Wright, C. (1993) Uxoricide in Canada: demographic risk patterns. *Canadian Journal of Criminology*, 35, 263-91.

Wilson, M., Johnson, H. and Daly, M. (1995) Lethal and nonlethal violence against wives. *Canadian Journal of Criminology*, 37, 331-61.

Wilson, P. and Provost, S. (2006) Psychology in Australian universities. *International Journal of Psychology*, 41(1), 3-9.

Wilson, P.N., Foreman, N. and Stanton, D. (1999) Improving spatial awareness in physically disabled children using virtual environments. *Engineering Science and Education Journal*, 8(5), 196-200.

Wilson, P.N., Foreman, N. and Tlauka, M. (1996) Transfer of spatial information from a virtual to a real environment in able-bodied adults and disabled children. *Disability and Rehabilitation*, 18, 633-7.

Wilson, R.E., Goslling, S.D. and Graham, L.T. (2012) A review of Facebook research in the social sciences. *Perspectives on Psychological Science*, 7, 203-20.

Wimmer, H. and Perner, J. (1983) Beliefs about beliefs: representation and constraining function of wrong beliefs in young children's understanding of deception. *Cognition*, 13, 103-28.

Winawer, J., Witthoft, N., Frank, M.C., Wu, L., Wade, A.R. and Boroditsky, L. (2007) Russian blues reveal effects of language on color discrimination. *Proceedings of the National Academy of Science*, 104, 7780-5.

Winberg, J. and Porter, R.H. (1998) Olfaction and human neonatal behaviour: Clinical implications. *Acta Paediatrica*, 87, 6-10.

Winch, R. (1958) *Mate Selection: A study of complementary needs*. New York: Harper & Row.

Windholz, G. (1997) Ivan P. Pavlov. *American Psychologist*, 52(9), 941-6.

Winefield, A.H. and Tiggemann, M. (1994) Affective reactions to employment and unemployment as a function of prior expectations and motivation. *Psychological Reports*, 75, 243-7.

Winegard, B.M., Winegard, B. and Geary, D.C. (2013) If you've got it, flaunt it: Humans flaunt attractive partners to enhance their status and desirability. *PLoS ONE*, 8, 1-7.

Wing, R.R. (2002) Behavioural weight control. In T.A. Wadden and A.J. Stunkard (eds) *Handbook of Obesity Treatment*. New York: Guilford Press.

Winograd, E. and Killinger, W.A. (1983) Relating age at encoding in early childhood to adult recall: Development of flashbulb memories. *Journal of Experimental Psychology: General*, 112, 413-22.

Winstock, A.R., Griffiths, P. and Stewart, D. (2001) Drugs and the dance music scene: a survey of current drug use patterns among a sample of dance music enthusiasts in the UK. *Drug and Alcohol Dependence*, 64(1), 9-17.

Wise, R.J.S., Scott, S.K., Blank, C., Mummery, C.J., Murphy, K. and Warburton, E.A. (2001) Separate neural subsystems within 'Wernicke's area'. *Brain*, 124, 83-95.

Wiseman, R. and Watt, C. (2006) Belief in psychic ability and the misattribution hypothesis: A qualitative review. *British Journal of Psychology*, 97, 323-38.

Wiseman, R. and Watt, C. (2015) And now for something completely different: Inattention blindness during a Monty Python's Flying Circus sketch. *i-Perception*, 6, 38-40.

Wissman, K.T., Rawson, K.A and Pyc, M.A. (2012) How and when do students use flashcards? *Memory*, 20, 568-79.

Witelson, S.F., Kigar, D.L. and Harvey, T. (1999) The exceptional brain of Albert Einstein. *The Lancet*, 353, 2149-53.

Witt, J.K. and Sugovic, M. (2013) Spiders appear to move faster than non-threatening objects regardless of one's ability to block them. *Acta Psychologica*, 143, 284-91.

Wittchen, H.U. *et al.* (2011) The size and burden of mental disorders and other disorders of the brain in Europe 2010. *European Neuropsychopharmacology*, 21, 655-79.

Witvliet, C.V., Ludwig, T.E. and Vander Laan, K.L. (2001) Granting forgiveness or harbouring grudges: Implications for emotion, physiology and health. *Psychological Science*, 12(2), 117-23.

Wixted, J.T. and Wells, G.L. (2017) The relationship between eyewitness confidence and identification accuracy: A new synthesis. *Psychological Science in the Public Interest*, 18, 10-65.

Wojcik, S.P., Hovasapian, A., Graham, J., Motyl, M. and Ditto, P.H. (2015) Conservatives report, but liberals display, greater happiness. *Science*, 347(6227), 1243-6.

Wojcik, S.P., Hovasapian, A., Graham, J., Motyl, M. and Ditto, P.H. (2015) Conservatives report, but liberals display, greater happiness. *Science*, 347, 1243-6.

Wolff, P.H. (1969) Crying and vocalization in early infancy. In B.M. Foss (ed.) *Determinants of Infant Behaviour*, Vol. 4. London: Methuen.

Wolpe, J. (1958) *Psychotherapy by Reciprocal Inhibition*. Stanford, CA: Stanford University Press.

Wolpert, L. (1999) *Malignant Sadness: the anatomy of depression*. London: Faber.

Wood, C. and Cowan, N. (1995) The cocktail party phenomenon revisited: How frequent are attention shifts to one's name in an irrelevant auditory channel? *Journal of Experimental Psychology: Learning, Memory and Cognition*, 21, 255-60.

Wood, R.J., Rolls, B.J. and Ramsey, D.L. (1977) Drinking following intracarotid infusions of hypertonic solutions in dogs. *American Journal of Physiology*, 232, R88-R92.

Wood, R.L.I. and Rutterford, N.A. (2004) Relationships between measured cognitive ability and reported psychosocial activity after bilateral frontal lobe injury: An 18-year follow-up. *Neuropsychological Rehabilitation*, 14(3), 329-50.

Wood, W. (2014) Once again, menstrual cycles and mate preferences. *Emotion Review*, 6, 258-60.

Woodall, K.L. and Matthews, K.A. (1993) Changes in and stability of hostile characteristics: Results from a 4-year longitudinal study of children. *Journal of Personality and Social Psychology*, 63, 491-9.

Woodcock, A. and Custovic, A. (1998) ABC of allergies: Avoiding exposure to indoor allergens. *British Medical Journal*, 316, 1075-8.

Woodley, M.A. (2012a) A life history model of the Lynn-Flynn effect. *Personality and Individual Differences*, 53, 152-6.

Woodley, M.A. (2012b) The social and scientific temporal correlates of genotypic intelligence and the Flynn effect. *Intelligence*, 40, 189-204.

Woodman, R.W. and Schoenfeldt, L.F. (1989) Individual differences in creativity: An interactionist perspective. In J.A. Glover, R.R. Ronning and C.R. Reynolds (eds) *Handbook of Creativity*. New York: Plenum Press.

Woodruff-Pak, D.S. (1997) *The Neuropsychology of Aging*. Oxford: Blackwell.

Woods, B.T. (1980) The restricted effects of right-hemisphere lesions after age one: Wechsler test data. *Neuropsychologia*, 18, 65-70.

Woods, R.T. (1994) Problems in the elderly. In S.J.E. Lindsey and G.E. Powell (eds) *Handbook of Clinical Adult Psychology*. London: Routledge.

Woods, S.C. *et al.* (2006) Pancreatic signals controlling food intake: insulin, glucagons and amylin. *Philosophical Transactions of the Royal Society of London B Biological Sciences*, 361, 1219–35.

Woods, S.W., Charney, D.S., Goodman, W.K. and Heninger, G.R. (1988) Carbon dioxide-induced anxiety. *Archives of General Psychiatry*, 45, 43–52.

Woolley, J.D. (1997) Thinking about fantasy: Are children fundamentally different thinkers and believers from adults? *Child Development*, 68(6), 991–1011.

Woolley, K. and Fishbach, A. (2016) A recipe for friendship: Similar food consumption promotes trust and co-operation. *Journal of Consumer Psychology*, in press.

Worchel, F.F., Aaron, L.L. and Yates, D.F. (1990) Gender bias on the Thematic Apperception Test. *Journal of Personality Assessment*, 55, 593–602.

World Health Organization (1983) *Depressive disorders in different cultures: Report of the WHO collaborative study of standardised assessment of depressive disorders*. Geneva: WHO.

World Health Organization (1992) *The ICD-10 Classification of Mental and Behavioural Disorders: Clinical descriptions and diagnostic guidelines.* Geneva: WHO.

World Health Oganization (1998) *Obesity: Preventing and managing the global epidemic*. Geneva: WHO.

World Health Organization (2002a) *The Tobacco Atlas*. http://www.who.it/tobacco/statistics/tobacco_atlas/en/.

World Health Organization (2002b) *The World Health Report 2002: Reducing risks, promoting healthy life.* Geneva: WHO.

World Health Organization (2007) *World Health Statistics 2007*. Geneva: WHO.

World Health Organization (2010) *Mental Health: Strengthening our response.* Geneva: WHO.

Wortman, C.B., Silver, R.C. and Kessler, R.C. (1993) The meaning of loss and adjustment to bereavement. In M.S. Stroebe, W. Stroebe and R.O. Hansson (eds) *Handbook of Bereavement: Theory, research and intervention*. Cambridge: Cambridge University Press.

Wright, B.A., Lombardino, L.J., King, W.M., Puranik, C.S., Leonard, C.M. and Merzenich, M.M. (1997) Deficits in auditory temporal and spectral resolution in language-impaired children. *Nature*, 387, 176–8.

Wright, D.B. (1993) Recall of the Hillsborough disaster over time: Systematic biases of 'flashbulb' memories. *Applied Cognitive Psychology*, 7, 129–38.

Wright, D.B., Gaskell, G.D. and O'Muircheartaigh, C.A. (1998) Flashbulb memory assumptions: Using national surveys to explore cognitive phenomena. *British Journal of Psychology*, 89, 103–22.

Wright, S.C., Aron, A., McLaughlin-Volpe, T. and Ropp, S.A. (1997) The extended contact effect: Knowledge of cross-group friendships and prejudice. *Journal of Personality and Social Psychology*, 73, 73–90.

Wu, M.V. and Hen, R. (2014) Functional dissociation of adult born neurons along the dorsoventral axis of the dentate gyrus. *Hippocampus*, 24(7), 751–61.

Wurtzel, E. (1994) *Prozac Nation*. New York: Houghton Mifflin.

Wycherley, R.J. (1995) Self-evaluation and self-reinforcement in depressed patients. *Clinical Psychology and Psychotherapy*, 2, 98–107.

Wynn, V.E. and Logie, R.H. (1998) The veracity of long-term memory: Did Bartlett get it right? *Applied Cognitive Psychology*, 12, 1–20.

Y

Yabuta, N.H., Sawatari, A. and Callaway, E.M. (2001) Two functional channels from primary visual cortex to dorsal visual cortical areas. *Science*, 292, 297–300.

Yamagata, S., Suzuki, A., Ando, J., One, Y., Kijima, N., Yoshimura, K. *et al.* (2006) Is the genetic structure of human personality universal? A cross-cultural twin study from North American, Europe and Asia. *Journal of Personality and Social Psychology*, 90, 987–98.

Yang, J., Gates, K.M., Molenaar, P. and Li, P. (2015) Neural changes underlying successful second language word learning: An fMRI study. *Journal of Neurolinguistics*, 33, 29–49.

Yang, N.Y.H., Zhou, D., Chung, R.C.K., Li-Ssang, C.W. and Fong, K.N.K. (2013) Rehabilitation interventions for unilateral neglect after stroke: A systematic review from 1997 through 2012. *Frontiers in Human Neuroscience*, 7, 187, 1–11.

Yanovski, S.Z. and Yanovski, J. (2002) Obesity. *New England Journal of Medicine*, 346, 591–602.

Yantis, S. (2008) The neural basis of selective attention. *Current Directions in Psychological Science*, 17, 86–90.

Yao, L. *et al.* (2013) White matter deficits in first episode schizophrenia. *Progress in Neuropsychopharmacology and Biological Psychiatry*, 45, 100–6.

Yao, S., Zhao, W., Cheng, R., Geng, Y., Luo, L. and Kendrick, K.M. (2014) Oxytocin makes females, but not males, less forgiving following betrayal of trust. *International Journal of Neuropsychopharmacology*, 17(11), 1785–92.

Yardley, L., McDermott, L., Pisarski, S., Duchaine, B. and Nakayama, K. (2008) Psychosocial consequences of developmental prosopagnosia: A problem of recognition. *Journal of Psychosomatic Research*, 65, 445–51.

Yeh, M.T., Coccaro, E.F. and Jacobson, K.C. (2010) Multivariate behavior genetic analyses of aggressive behavior subtypes. *Behavioural Genetics*, 40, 603–17.

Yeomans, M.R., Chambers, L., Blumenthal, H. and Blake, A. (2008) The role of expectancy in sensory and hedonic evaluation: The case of smoked salmon ice-cream. *Food Quality and Preference*, 19(6), 565–73.

Yeshurun, Y. and Sobel, N. (2010) An odor is not worth a thousand words: From multidimensional odors to unidimensional odor objects. *Annual Review of Psychology*, 61, 219–41.

Yokoyama, T., Sato, M., Natsui, S., Kuboyama, N., Suzuki, K., Inaba, H. and Shibuya, K. (2017) Effect of gum chewing frequency on oxygenation of the prefrontal cortex. *Perceptual and Motor Skills*, 124, 58–71.

Yong, S., Aguid, F. and Nitsche, M.A. (2015) Transcranial direct current stimulation (tDCS) – Application in neuropsychology. *Neuropsychologia*, 74, 74–95.

Young, A., Stokes, M. and Crowe, M. (1984) Size and strength of the quadriceps muscles of old and young women. *European Journal of Clinical Investigation*, 14, 282–7.

Young, A.H. and Newham, J.I. (2006) Lithium in maintenance therapy for bipolar disorder. *Journal of Psychopharmacology*, 20(2), 17–22.

Young, A.W. and Bruce, V. (2011) Understanding person perception. *British Journal of Psychology*, 102, 959–74.

Young, L.J., Wang, Z. and Insel, T.R. (1998) Neuroendocrine bases of monogamy. *Trends in Neurosciences*, 21(2), 71–5.

Young, M.E., Mizzau, M., Mai, N.T., Sirisegaram, A. and Wilson, M. (2009) Food for thought: What you eat depends on your sex and eating companions. *Appetite*, 53, 268–71.

Young, S.D., Adelstein, B.D. and Ellis, S.R. (2007) Demand characteristics in assessing motion sickness in a virtual environment: Or does taking a motion sickness questionnaire make you sick? *IEEE Transactions on Visualization and Computer Graphics*, 13, 422–8.

Youngstedt, S., O'Connor, P.J. and Dishman, R.K. (1997) The effects of acute exercise on sleep: a quantitative synthesis. *Sleep*, 20, 203–14.

Youngston, R. (1998) *Scientific Blunders*. London: Robinson.

Youniss, J. and Smollar, J. (1985) *Adolescent Relations with Mothers, Fathers, and Friends.* Chicago, IL: University of Chicago Press.

Yousem, D.M., Maldjian, J.A., Siddiqi, F., Hummel, T., Alsop, D.C., Geckle, R.J., Bilker, W.B. and Doty, R.L. (1999) Gender effects on odor-stimulated functional magnetic resonance imaging. *Brain Research*, 818, 480–7.

Yu, D.W. and Shepard, G.H. (1998) Is beauty in the eye of the beholder? *Nature*, 396, 321–2.

Yu, R., Geddes, J.R. and Fazel, S. (2012) Personality disorders, violence and antisocial behaviour: A systematic review and meta-aggression analysis. *Journal of Personality Disorders*, 26, 775–92.

Yufik, T. and Simms, L.J. (2010) A meta-analytic investigation of the structure of posttraumatic stress disorder symptoms. *Journal of Abnormal Psychology*, 119, 764–76.

Yu-Huan, H., Ying-Guan, Q. and Gui-Quing, Z. (1990) Crossed aphasia in Chinese: A clinical survey. *Brain and Language*, 39, 347–56.

Yuill, N. and Oakhill, J.V. (1991) *Children's Problems in Text Comprehension.* Cambridge: Cambridge University Press.

Yuki, M., Maddux, W.W., Brewer, M.B. and Takemura, K. (2005) Cross-cultural differences in relationship – and group-based trust. *Personality and Social Psychology Bulletin*, 31, 48–62.

Yzerbyt, V.Y., Castano, E., Leyens, J-P. and Paladino, M-P. (2000) The primacy of the in-group: The interplay of entitativity and identification. *European Review of Social Psychology*, 11, 257–96.

Yzerbyt, V.Y., Coull, A.I. and Rocher, S. (1999) Fencing off the deviant: The role of cognitive resources in the maintenance of stereotypes. *Journal of Personality and Social Psychology*, 77, 448–62.

Z

Zaccaro, S.J. (1984) Social loafing: The role of task attractiveness. *Personality and Social Psychology Bulletin*, 10, 99–106.

Zadro, L., Williams, K.D. and Richardson, R. (2005) Riding the 'O' train: Comparing the effects of ostracism and verbal dispute on targets and sources. *Group Processes and Intergroup Relations*, 8, 125–43.

Zaehle, T., Sandmann, P., Thorne, J.D., Jancke, L. and Herrmann, C.S. (2011) Transcranial direct current stimulation of the prefrontal cortex modulates working memory performance. *BMC Neuroscience*, 12, 2.

Zahama, M. and Guilleminault, C. (2010) Sleep, noise and health: review. *Noise Health*, 12, 64–9.

Zaimov, K., Kitov, D. and Kolev, N. (1969) Aphasie chez un peintre. *Encephale*, 58, 377–417.

Zajonc, R.B. (1965) Social facilitation. *Science*, 149, 269–74.

Zajonc, R.B. (1968) Attitudinal effects of mere exposure. *Journal of Personality and Social Psychology*, Monograph Supplement, 9, 1–27.

Zajonc, R.B. (1984) On primacy of affect. In K.R. Scherer and P. Ekman (eds) *Approaches to Emotion.* Hillsdale, NJ: Lawrence Erlbaum Associates.

Zajonc, R.B. (1985) Emotion and facial efference: A theory reclaimed. *Science*, 228, 15–21.

Zakowski, S.G., Ramati, A., Morton, C., Johnson, P. and Flanigan, R. (2004) Written emotional disclosure buffers the effects of social constraints on distress among cancer patients. *Health Psychology*, 23(6), 555–63.

Zald, D.H. and Andreotti, C. (2010) Neuropsychological assessment of the orbital and ventromedial prefrontal cortex. *Neuropsychologia*, 48, 3377–91.

Zampini, M., Sanabria, D., Phillips, N. and Spence, C. (2007) The multisensory perception of flavor: Assessing the influence of color cues on flavor discrimination responses. *Food Quality and Preference*, 18(7), 975–84.

Zampini, M., Wantling, E., Phillips, N. and Spence, C. (2008) Multisensory flavor perception: Assessing the influence of fruit acids and color cues on the perception of fruit-flavored beverages. *Food Quality and Preference*, 19(3), 335–43.

Zaragoza, M.S. and Mitchell, K.J. (1996) Repeated suggestion and the creation of false memories. *Psychological Science*, 7, 294–300.

Zatorre, R.J., Fields, R.D. and Johansen-Berg, H. (2012) Plasticity in gray and white: neuroimaging changes in brain structure during learning. *Nature Neuroscience*, 15, 528–36.

Zatorre, R.J., Meyer, E., Gjedde, A. and Evans, A.C. (1996) PET studies of phonetic processing of speech: Review, replication and reanalysis. *Cerebral Cortex*, 6(1), 21–30.

Zattore, R.J., Berlin, P. and Penhune, V.B. (2002) Structure and function of auditory cortex: Music and speech. *Trends in Cognitive Sciences*, 6(1), 37–46.

Zebrowitz, L.A. (1996) Physical appearance as a basis of stereotyping. In C.N. Macrae, C. Stangor and M. Hewstone (eds) *Stereotypes and Stereotyping.* New York: Guilford Press, pp. 79–120.

Zebrowitz, L.A. and Collins, M.A. (1997) Accurate social perception at zero acquaintance: The affordances of a Gibsonian approach. *Personality and Social Psychology Review*, 1, 204–23.

Zeegers, P. (2001) Approaches to learning in science: A longitudinal study. *British Journal of Educational Psychology*, 71, 115–32.

Zeggini, E., Weedon, M N., Lindgren, C.M., Frayling, T.M., Elliott, K.S., Lango, H., . . . and Barrett, J.C. (2007) Wellcome Trust Case Control Consortium (WTCCC), McCarthy MI, Hattersley AT: Replication of genome-wide association signals in UK samples reveals risk loci for type 2 diabetes. *Science*, 316(5829), 1336–41.

Zehnder, F., Martin, M., Altgassen, M. and Clare, L. (2009) Memory training effects in old age as markers of plasticity. *Restorative Neurology and Neuroscience*, 27, 507–20.

Zeidner, M. and Hammer, A.L. (1992) Coping with missile attack: Resources, strategies and outcomes. *Journal of Personality*, 60, 709–46.

Zeier, H., Brauchli, P. and Joller-Jemelka, H.I. (1996) Effects of work demands on immunoglobin A and cortisol in air-traffic controllers. *Biological Psychology*, 42, 413–23.

Zeisel, H. (1971) And then there was none: The diminution of federal jury. *University of Chicago Law Review*, 35, 228–41.

Zeki, S. (1993) *A Vision of the Brain.* Oxford: Blackwell Scientific.

Zeki, S. (1998) Art and the brain. *Daedalus*, 127(2), 71–103.

Zelenski, J.M. and Larsen, R.J. (2000) The distribution of basic emotions in everyday life: A state and trait perspective from experience sampling data. *Journal of Research in Personality*, 34, 178–97.

Zelinski, E.M., Spina, L.M., Yaffe, K., Ruff, R., Kennison, R.F., Mahncke, H.W. and Smith, G.E. (2011) Improvement in memory with plasticity-based adaptive cognitive training. *Journal of the American Geriatric Society*, 59, 258–65.

Zelinsky, W. (1974) Selfward bound? Personal preference patterns and the changing map of American society. *Economic Geography*, 50, 144–79.

Zellner, D.A., McGarry, A., Mattern-McClory, R. and Abreu, D. (2008) Masculinity/femininity of fine fragrances affects color-odor correspondences: A case for cognitions influencing cross-modal correspondences. *Chemical Senses*, 33, 211–22.

Zeng, L.L. *et al.* (2012) Identifying major depression using whole-brain functional connectivity. *Brain*, 135, 1498–1507.

Zhang, H. and Xu, Y. (2006) Teaching of psychology to university students in China. *International Journal of Psychology*, 41(1), 17–23.

Zhao, H. and Seibert, S.E. (2006) The Big Five personality dimensions and entrepreneurial status: A meta-analytical review. *Journal of Applied Psychology*, 91(2), 259–71.

Zhen, Z., Fang, H. and Liu, J. (2013) The hierarchical brain network for face recognition. *PLoS ONE*, 8, e59886.

Zheng, Y., Plomin, R. and von Stumm, S. (2016) Heritability of intraindividual mean and variability of positive and negative affect: Genetic analysis of daily affect ratings over a month. *Psychological Science*, 27, 1611–19.

Zhong, C.B. and Leonardelli, G.J. (2008) Cold and lonely. *Psychological Science*, 19, 838–42.

Zhong, C-B. and DeVoe, S.E. (2010) You are how you eat: Fast food and impatience. *Psychological Science*, 21, 619–22.

Zhong, C-B., Bohns, V.K. and Gino, F. (2010) Good lamps are the best police: Darkness increases dishonesty and self-interested behavior. *Psychological Science*, 21, 311–14.

Zhu, D., Chang, J., Freeman, S., Tan, Z., Xiao, J., Gao, Y. and Kong, J. (2014) Changes of functional connectivity in the left frontoparietal network following aphasic stroke. *Frontiers in Behavioural Neuroscience*, 8, 167.

Zhu, Y., Zhang, L., Fan, J. and Han, S. (2007) Neural basis of cultural influence on self-representation. *Neuroimage*, 34(3), 1310–16.

Ziauddeen, H., Farooqi, I.S. and Fletcher, P.C. (2012) Obesity and the brain: how convincing is the addiction model? *Nature Reviews Neuroscience*, 13, 279–86.

Zijlstra, F.R.H., Roe, A.E., Leonora, A.B. and Krediet, I. (1999) Temporal factors in mental work: Effects of interrupted activities. *Journal of Occupational and Organizational Psychology*, 72, 163–85.

Zilli, I., Giganti, F. and Salzarulo, P. (2007) Yawning in morning and evening types. *Physiology and Behavior*, 91, 218–22.

Zimbardo, P.G. (1970) The human choice: Individuation, reason, and order versus deindividuation, impulse, and chaos. In W.J. Arnold and D. Levine (eds) *Nebraska Symposium on Motivation*. Lincoln, NE: University of Nebraska Press.

Zimring, F. and Hawkins, G. (1997) Lethal violence and the overreach of American imprisonment. *National Institute of Justice Research Report*, 338–58.

Zisook, S., Schuchter, S.R., Irwin, M., Darko, D.F., Sledge, P. and Resovsky, K. (1994) Bereavement, depression and immune function. *Psychiatry Research*, 52, 1–10.

Zola, D. (1984) Redundancy and word perception during reading. *Perception and Psychophysics*, 36, 277–84.

Zorzi, M., Barbiero, C., Facoetti, A., Lonciari, I., Carrozzi, M., Montico, M., Bravar, L., George, F., Pech-Georgel, C. and Ziegler, J.C. (2012) Extra-large letter spacing improves reading in dyslexia. *PNAS*, 109, 11455–9.

Zorzi, M., Houghton, G. and Butterworth, B. (1998) Two routes or one in reading aloud? A connectionist dual-process model. *Journal of Experimental Psychology: Human Perception and Performance*, 24(4), 1131–61.

Zuckerman, M. (1991) *Psychobiology of Personality*. Cambridge: Cambridge University Press.

Zuckerman, M. (1995) Good and bad humors: Biochemical bases of personality and its disorders. *Psychological Science*, 6, 325–32.

Zuckerman, M. (2005) *Psychology of Personality* (2nd edn). Cambridge University Press.

Zuckerman, M., Silberman, J. and Hall, J.A. (2013) The relation between intelligence and religiosity: A meta-analysis and some proposed explanations. *Personality and Social Psychology Review*, 17(4), 325–54.

Zukier, H. and Pepitone, A. (1984) Social roles and strategies in prediction: Some determinants of the use of base-rate information. *Journal of Personality and Social Psychology*, 47, 349–60.

Zwaan, R. A., Pecher, D., Paolacci, G., Bouwmeester, S., Verkoeijen, P., Dijkstra, K., & Zeelenberg, R. (2017). Participant nonnaiveté and the reproducibility of cognitive psychology. *Psychonomic Bulletin & Review*, 1–5.

Zweyer, K., Velker, B. and Ruch, W. (2004) Do cheerfulness, exhilaration, and humor production moderate pain tolerance? A FACS study. *Humor*, 17(1/2), 85–120.

Name Index

Subject Index